Tolley's Value Adde

Tolley's Value Added Tax 2012–13

First Edition

by

Rhianon Davies
BSc (Maths) CTA

and

David Rudling
CTA, AIIT

Consultant Editor: Robert Killington

LexisNexis®

Members of the LexisNexis Group worldwide

United Kingdom	LexisNexis, a Division of Reed Elsevier (UK) Ltd, Halsbury House, 35 Chancery Lane, London, WC2A 1EL, and London House, 20-22 East London Street, Edinburgh EH7 4BQ
Argentina	LexisNexis Argentina, Buenos Aires
Australia	LexisNexis Butterworths, Chatswood, New South Wales
Austria	LexisNexis Verlag ARD Orac GmbH & Co KG, Vienna
Benelux	LexisNexis Benelux, Amsterdam
Canada	LexisNexis Canada, Markham, Ontario
Chile	LexisNexis Chile Ltda, Santiago
China	LexisNexis China, Beijing and Shanghai
France	LexisNexis SA, Paris
Germany	LexisNexis Deutschland GmbH, Munster
Hong Kong	LexisNexis Hong Kong, Hong Kong
India	LexisNexis India, New Delhi
Italy	Giuffrè Editore, Milan
Japan	LexisNexis Japan, Tokyo
Malaysia	Malayan Law Journal Sdn Bhd, Kuala Lumpur
Mexico	LexisNexis Mexico, Mexico
New Zealand	LexisNexis NZ Ltd, Wellington
Poland	Wydawnictwo Prawnicze LexisNexis Sp, Warsaw
Singapore	LexisNexis Singapore, Singapore
South Africa	LexisNexis Butterworths, Durban
USA	LexisNexis, Dayton, Ohio

Published by LexisNexis

A CIP Catalogue record for this book is available from the British Library.

ISBN for this volume: 9780754543633

Printed in the UK by CPI Group (UK) Ltd, Croydon, CR0 4YY

Visit LexisNexis at www.lexisnexis.co.uk

About This Book

Value added tax commenced in the United Kingdom on 1 April 1973. Since that date a mass of legislation, Orders, Regulations, law cases and VAT notices support a system which has become increasingly complex. Tolley's Value Added Tax seeks to aid practitioners and traders by being their first point of reference on this tax.

This edition includes the current law and practice of value added tax up to 31 January 2012. Relevant statutory instruments, tribunal and court cases, VAT Notices, Information Sheets, and HMRC Briefs are also covered.

Chapters in this service are in alphabetical order for ease of reference to a particular subject. Cross-references, an index and a table of statutes provide further ways of quickly finding the matter required.

We relaunched the Tolley Tax Annuals in 2010, aiming to make them more practical and easier to use. This process has continued in 2011–12 with the updating of key points and practical examples.

We hope that the new style continues to meet your requirement for greater accessibility to the changing VAT legislation and the ever increasing demands on you as a practitioner. We would be pleased to receive your feedback on the new style and any suggestions for further improvements. You can do this by e-mailing the Editor, Elaine Pugh at elaine.pugh@lexisnexis.co.uk. Technical queries will be dealt with by the author.

Contributors

Robert Killington

Since 2002 Robert has been the Technical Secretary of the VAT Practitioners Group (VPG) representing the VPG at meetings with HMRC, making submissions to HMRC's many consultations and endeavouring to keep members up to date with changes in UK VAT as editor of the members' newsletter and website. Robert can be found online on LinkedIn, and has his own website and blog.

Contents

Abbreviations and References

All ER	All England Law Reports, (LexisNexis Butterworths, Halsbury House, 35 Chancery Lane, London WC2A 1EL).
Art	Article
C & E	Customs and Excise
CA	Court of Appeal
CCAB	Consultative Committee of Accountancy Bodies
CEMA	Customs and Excise Management Act 1979
Ch D	Chancery Division
CIR	Commissioners of Inland Revenue
Commrs	Commissioners
CS	Court of Session (Scotland)
ECJ	European Court of Justice
EU	European Union
EEC	European Economic Community
ESC	Extra-statutory concession
FA	Finance Act
F(No 2)A	Finance (No 2) Act
HC	High Court
HL	House of Lords
HMRC	Her Majesty's Revenue and Customs
ICTA	Income and Corporation Taxes Act
IMA 1979	Isle of Man Act 1979
ITEPA 2003	Income Tax (Earnings and Pensions) Act 2003
ITTOIA 2005	Income Tax (Trading and Other Income) Act 2005
NI	Northern Ireland
p	Page
QB	Queen's Bench Division
Reg	Regulation

s	Section
Sch	Schedule
Sec	Section
SI	Statutory Instrument
STC	Simon's Tax Cases, (LexisNexis Butterworths, as above).
STI	Simon's Tax Intelligence (LexisNexis Butterworths, as above).
t/a	Trading as
TC	Tax Chamber
TVC	Tolley's VAT Cases
UT	Upper Tribunal
VATA 1994	Value Added Tax Act 1994
VTD	VAT Tribunal decision

Court cases. Citation where appropriate is of Simon's Tax Cases and is preceded by the Court and year of the decision (if different from the citation).

Tribunal cases. Citation is by reference to the number assigned to the decision by the VAT Tribunals Headquarters (e.g. *(VTD 18775)*). In all tribunal cases only the appellant or applicant is named.

Tolley's VAT cases. All case citations include a reference to any summary of that case in *Tolley's VAT Cases 2012* (e.g. (TVC 39.52)). References ending with a letter (e.g. (TVC 39.52A)) are to cases subsequent to the publication of *Tolley's VAT Cases 2012* in a bound book format and are only available in the electronic version of that book.

1

Introduction and General Principles

De Voil Indirect Tax Service. See V1.101.

Introduction

European Union legislation

[1.1] The overriding law on VAT throughout the European Union (EU) is in the EU *Directives*, notably *Directive 2006/112/EC* (formerly the *6th VAT Directive*). The form and method of compliance is left to individual EU countries but, where any of the provisions are mandatory, EU law takes precedence if there are any inconsistencies with national law. See **18 EUROPEAN UNION LEGISLATION** for further details.

UK legislation

[1.2] Value added tax (VAT) was introduced in the UK on 1 April 1973.

VAT was initially introduced into UK legislation by the *Finance Act 1972*. Subsequent amendments to the UK legislation were first consolidated in the *Value Added Tax Act 1983* (*VATA 1983*) and subsequently in the *Value Added Tax Act 1994* (*VATA 1994*). Changes to *VATA 1994* are made by successive *Finance Acts*.

Although *VATA 1994* provides the main framework of the tax, much of the detail is to be found in statutory instruments (SIs), either in the form of *Orders* made by the Treasury or *Regulations* made by HM Revenue and Customs (previously Customs and Excise). SIs both create law in their own right and amend existing law (both SIs and, occasionally, statutes). The principal *Regulations* made by HMRC are the VAT Regulations (*SI 1995/2518*).

Interpretation of the law by HMRC

[1.3] HMRC currently publish in excess of 130 Notices and Leaflets affecting VAT. With certain exceptions (as indicated in the text), these are not part of the law but explain how HMRC interpret the law. They also publish VAT Information Sheets, VAT Notes and Business Briefs.

The fact that HMRC publications largely only interpret the law should be borne in mind where this book indicates a Notice, etc. as source material.

Court and tribunal decisions

[1.4] If a business disagrees with HMRC's interpretation of the law, it has a right of appeal, in certain cases, to a VAT tribunal. In England and Wales, either party can then appeal from that decision to the High Court and, with leave, on to the Court of Appeal and the Supreme Court (formerly the House of Lords). In Scotland, appeals from a tribunal go to the Court of Session and, with leave, directly to the Supreme Court (formerly the House of Lords). A tribunal or Court may also refer a question to the European Court of Justice (ECJ).

Tribunals and even Court decisions relating to VAT do not create law but merely interpret it. They may, however, cause HMRC to change the way that they interpret the law and may lead to amendments being made to the legislation by statute or statutory instrument.

See **5 APPEALS** generally.

General principles of VAT

[1.5] VAT is a tax on consumer expenditure and is collected on business transactions and imports.

The basic principle is to charge VAT at each stage in the supply of goods and services (output tax). If the customer is registered for VAT and uses the supplies for business purposes, he will receive credit for this VAT (input tax). The broad effect is that businesses are not affected and VAT is actually borne by the final consumer.

Scope of VAT

[1.6] A transaction is within the scope of UK VAT if all the following conditions are met.

- *It is a supply of goods or services.* The term 'supply' is not defined in the legislation but is broadly interpreted. See **64.2 SUPPLY: GENERAL** for the meaning of supply and **64.3** and **64.4 SUPPLY: GENERAL** for supplies of goods and services respectively. Certain transactions, although supplies, are regarded as supplies of neither goods nor services and are outside the scope of UK VAT. See **64.5 SUPPLY: GENERAL**.
- *It takes place in the UK.*
- *It is made by a taxable person.* A taxable person is an individual, firm or company, etc. which is registered for VAT or which is required to register for VAT but has failed to do so. See **1.14** below.
- *It is made in the course or furtherance of any business carried on by that person.* See **8.1** to **8.3 BUSINESS** for the interpretation of 'business'.

A transaction which does not meet all of the above conditions is outside the scope of UK VAT.

Place of supply

[1.7] To be within the charge to UK VAT, a supply must be made in the UK. Supplies made outside the UK are outside the scope of UK VAT (although they may be liable to VAT in another country).

Separate rules apply for determining the place of supply of goods and services. See **65.2** and **65.12 SUPPLY: PLACE OF SUPPLY** for the place of supply of goods and services respectively.

> *Example*
>
> John trades as a computer consultant and is not VAT-registered, even though his annual taxable sales exceed the compulsory VAT registration limit.
>
> John is still classed as a 'taxable person' because he should be VAT-registered.

Time of supply (tax point)

[1.8] The time at which a supply of goods is treated as taking place is called the tax point. VAT must normally be accounted for in the VAT period (see **1.19** below) in which the tax point occurs and at the rate of VAT (see **1.12** below) in force at that time. Small businesses can, however, account for VAT on the basis of cash paid and received (see **1.23** below).

Basic tax point

The basic tax point for a supply of goods is the date the goods are removed (i.e. sent to, or taken by, the customer). If the goods are not removed, it is the date they are made available for his use.

The basic tax point for a supply of services is the date the services are performed.

Actual tax points

In the case of both goods and services, where a VAT invoice is raised or payment is made *before* the basic tax point, there is an earlier actual tax point at the time the invoice is issued or payment received, whichever occurs first.

There is also generally an actual tax point where a VAT invoice is issued within 14 days *after* the basic tax point. This overrides the basic tax point but not the actual tax point created by the issue of an invoice or payment before the basic tax point.

There are also special provisions for particular supplies of goods and services.

For further details see **66.1–66.26 SUPPLY: TIME OF SUPPLY**.

Value of supply

[1.9] The value of a supply is the value on which VAT is due. The amount of VAT is then the value multiplied by the VAT rate (see **1.12** below).

The value of a supply normally depends upon what is given in exchange for the supply (i.e. the consideration). If this is wholly in money, the value will be based on that amount. If not, the value is the monetary equivalent of the consideration.

There are special rules relating to discounts offered, transactions between connected persons and values expressed in foreign currencies. Imports (see **1.15** below) and acquisitions from other EU countries (see **1.17** below) also have their own valuation rules.

See **71 VALUATION** for further details.

> *Example*
>
> John is VAT-registered and has sold his business van for £5,000 cash and also received another van from the buyer as part of the deal, which is worth £2,000. The value of John's sale for VAT purposes is £7,000, less the VAT.

Output tax

[1.10] Output tax is the VAT due on taxable supplies and is normally the liability of the person making the supply. In addition to straightforward business transactions, output tax may also be due on business gifts and private use of own goods and services.

A particular supply may be complicated by being a mixed supply where a single inclusive price is charged for a number of separate supplies. Where these supplies are taxable at different rates, a fair and justifiable apportionment of the total price must be made.

See **47 OUTPUT TAX** for further details.

Special schemes for retailers

Traders registered for VAT normally issue an invoice for each sale made in order to have the necessary records to calculate output tax. As this may be difficult or impossible where goods are sold directly to the public, special schemes are available for use by retailers only. See **60 RETAIL SCHEMES** for further details.

Second-hand goods

There are special provisions for second-hand goods. Subject to certain conditions being satisfied, under the Margin Scheme VAT is only chargeable on the amount by which the selling price of a particular item exceeds the price paid when it was obtained. The scheme extends to almost the full range of second-hand goods. There is also a Global Accounting Scheme which is a simplified scheme for VAT on low value, bulk volume second-hand goods. Under this scheme, VAT is accounted for on the difference between the total purchases and sales of eligible goods in each VAT period rather than on an item by item basis. See **61 SECOND-HAND GOODS** for further details.

Flat-rate scheme for small businesses

Small businesses with taxable turnover and total turnover below specified annual limits can opt to join a flat-rate scheme under which they calculate net VAT due by applying a flat-rate percentage to tax-inclusive turnover. The flat-rate percentage varies with the trade sector into which a business falls. See **63.15 SPECIAL SCHEMES.**

Flat-rate scheme for farmers

Farmers who are certified under the scheme do not have to account for VAT on sales of goods and services within designated activities but are not able to recover input tax incurred on purchases. To compensate for this, farmers in the scheme may charge (and retain) a fixed flat-rate addition of 4% on top of the sale price. The customer can recover the addition as if it were VAT. See **63.25** to **63.30 SPECIAL SCHEMES** for further details.

Input tax

[1.11] A taxable person is entitled to reclaim input tax suffered on goods and services supplied to him, imports from outside the EU (see **1.15** below) and acquisition of goods from other EU countries (see **1.16** below) provided that the input tax relates to

- taxable business supplies made by him; or
- supplies made by him which are outside the scope of UK VAT but which would have been taxable if made in the UK; or
- certain supplies by him of exempt insurance and financial services to persons belonging outside the EU.

Taxable supplies are those chargeable at the standard, reduced or zero rate.

VAT cannot be recovered on goods and services which are not used for business purposes (e.g. for private use). Where goods are used partly for business and partly for non-business purposes, the VAT incurred is normally apportioned.

VAT incurred on a number of items is non-deductible. These include motor cars (with certain exceptions), business entertainment, goods sold under one of the second-hand schemes and certain articles installed in buildings by builders.

Where input tax has been claimed but the consideration for the supply is not paid within six months, the input tax must be repaid to HMRC.

Special rules also apply to input tax incurred before registration for VAT and after deregistration.

See **34 INPUT TAX** for further details.

VAT rates

[1.12] There are currently three main rates of VAT, a standard rate of 17.5% (20% from 4 January 2011; 15% from 1 December 2008 to 31 December 2009), a reduced rate of 5% and a zero rate. See **58 REDUCED RATE SUPPLIES** and **74 ZERO-RATED SUPPLIES** (and supporting chapters) for goods and services which are currently zero-rated.

The effect of a supply being zero-rated is as follows.

- The amount of VAT on the supply is nil but it is still a taxable supply.
- As a taxable supply, it must be taken into account in determining whether registration is required (see **1.14** below).
- Input tax may be reclaimed subject to the same rules as for standard-rated supplies.
- Where a supply could be either zero-rated or exempt (see **1.13** below), zero-rating takes priority.

Exempt supplies

[1.13] Certain supplies are exempt from VAT. See **20 EXEMPT SUPPLIES** and supporting chapters. This means that no VAT is chargeable but, unlike zero-rated supplies, related input tax is not recoverable.

Where a person makes both taxable supplies and exempt supplies, he is partially exempt and may or may not be able to recover all his input tax. All input tax directly attributable to taxable supplies can be reclaimed but none of the input tax directly attributable to exempt supplies (subject to a *de minimis* limit). Special rules then apply to work out how much input tax can be reclaimed on general overheads, etc. See **49 PARTIAL EXEMPTION**.

Registration

[1.14] Where a person is in business and making taxable supplies, the value of these supplies is his taxable turnover. If, at the end of any month,

- taxable turnover in the year then ended has exceeded a specified limit, or
- there are reasonable grounds for believing that the value of taxable supplies in the next 30 days will exceed a specified limit,

that person normally becomes a taxable person and must notify HMRC of his liability to register for VAT. There are financial penalties for failing to do so. Where, however, only zero-rated supplies are made, HMRC have a discretion to exempt a person from registration.

Even if taxable turnover is below the specified limit, a person who makes taxable business supplies can request voluntary registration.

A person who is registered for VAT ceases to be liable to be registered and can apply to be deregistered if the VAT-exclusive value of supplies in the next twelve months will not exceed a specified limit.

See **59.1** to **59.10 REGISTRATION** for further details including how to apply for registration and deregistration.

See also

- **8.5 BUSINESS** for anti-avoidance measures to combat business splitting and the conditions for the separation of a previously single business into independent parts for registration purposes;
- **27.1** to **27.5 GROUPS OF COMPANIES** for group registration;
- **48.1** to **48.4 OVERSEAS TRADERS** for registration by overseas traders; and
- **59.37 REGISTRATION** for divisional registration by companies.

Even where there is no liability to register for VAT in respect of UK supplies of goods or services, a liability may arise in respect of

- 'distance selling' to non-taxable persons in the UK by suppliers in other EU countries (see **59.11** to **59.17 REGISTRATION**); or
- acquisitions of goods in the UK from other EU countries (see **59.18** to **59.25 REGISTRATION**).

Imports

[1.15] Unless special relief applies, VAT is charged and payable on the importation of goods into the UK from outside the EU. The rate of VAT is the same as if the goods had been supplied in the UK.

Unless the goods are placed under customs or excise warehousing or certain customs arrangements (e.g. free zones, inward processing relief or Community Transit arrangements) any VAT due must normally either be paid at the time of importation or deferred with any duty if the importer or his agent are approved for deferment. VAT paid on the importation of goods can be claimed as input tax, subject to the normal rules.

See **33 IMPORTS** for further details.

Exports

[1.16] Provided various conditions are met, goods exported outside the EU are zero-rated. See **21 EXPORTS** for further details.

Transactions with other EU countries

[1.17] The concepts of 'imports' and 'exports' of goods apply only to transactions with countries outside the EU. For intra-EU movements of goods, the terms 'acquisitions' and 'supplies' are used. It is not necessary to make an import declaration on an acquisition of goods in the UK from another EU country or to pay VAT at the frontier.

Supplies of goods to a customer registered for VAT in another EU country can be zero-rated provided certain conditions are met. These include obtaining the customer's VAT registration number and showing it on the VAT invoice. The customer then accounts for VAT at the appropriate rate on the goods in the EU country of destination. If the conditions cannot be met, VAT must be charged in the country of origin at the rate applicable to the goods in that country.

VAT must also be charged on supplies of goods to non-registered customers in other EU countries. Where, however, the supplier is also responsible for the delivery of the goods, once the value of such 'distance' sales to any particular EU country exceeds an annual threshold set by that country, the supplier is automatically liable to register for VAT in that other country. VAT on any further sales is then due in the EU country of destination.

Special rules apply to transfers of own goods between EU countries, goods installed or assembled at the customer's premises, new means of transport and goods subject to excise duty purchased by non-taxable persons. There are also special rules for 'triangulation' (i.e. where a chain of supplies of goods involves three parties and, instead of goods physically passing from one party to the next, they are delivered from the first party to the last party in the chain).

See **19 EUROPEAN UNION: SINGLE MARKET** for further details.

Invoices

[1.18] A registered taxable person must issue a VAT invoice where he makes a standard or reduced-rated supply to another taxable person in the UK or a standard, reduced or zero-rated supply to a person in another EU country.

See **39 INVOICES** for further details including the particulars required to be shown on the invoice and special invoices which may be issued by retailers and cash and carry wholesalers.

Returns and payment of VAT

[1.19] Every taxable person must keep a VAT account summarising the output tax and input tax for each VAT period. See **56.12 RECORDS**. A VAT period is normally three months but a one-month period is also allowed, particularly where input tax is likely to exceed output tax on a regular basis.

The information in the VAT account, plus certain statistical information, must then be shown on a VAT return for that period. The return must be sent to HMRC, and any VAT due to HMRC paid, no later than one month after the end of the period. The due date for payment will be extended by seven days where payment is made by credit transfer. Certain large VAT payers must make monthly payments on account.

See **2 ACCOUNTING PERIODS AND RETURNS** and **51.1** to **51.4 PAYMENT OF VAT** for further details.

Annual accounting

[1.20] Smaller businesses with turnover below an annual limit may apply to join the annual accounting scheme. This allows them to complete one VAT return each year. Monthly, or with the agreement of HMRC, quarterly interim payments on account are required based on an estimate of the amount of VAT due. The annual VAT return must be completed and sent to HMRC, with any balancing payment, within two months of the end of the annual VAT accounting period. See **63.9** to **63.14 SPECIAL SCHEMES** for further details.

Records

[1.21] Every taxable person must keep such records as HMRC require. Specifically, these include business and accounting records, the VAT account (see **1.19** above), copies of all VAT invoices and credit notes issued and received, and documentation relating to imports, exports, acquisitions of goods from other EU countries and goods dispatched to other EU countries. All such records must be kept for six years unless HMRC agree to a shorter period.

See **56 RECORDS** for further details.

Bad debts

[1.22] VAT is normally due by reference to the tax point (see **1.8** above). The supplier must therefore account to HMRC for the VAT even if the debt, including the VAT, is not paid. By way of relief, VAT can be reclaimed where a debt has been written off and six months has elapsed from the date of supply and the date payment is due. See **7 BAD DEBT RELIEF**.

The problem of VAT on bad debts can also be removed by using the cash accounting system (see **1.23** below).

> *Example*
>
> A sales invoice raised by a business on 31 January 2010 is due for payment on 31 March 2010. The earliest date that bad debt relief can be claimed in the event of non-payment is 30 September 2010, i.e. after the invoice is at least six months overdue for payment.

Cash accounting

[1.23] Provided turnover is below an annual limit, a taxable person may, subject to conditions, account for and pay VAT on the basis of cash or other consideration paid and received. The main advantages of the scheme are automatic bad debt relief and the deferral of the time for payment of VAT where extended credit is given. See **63.2** to **63.8 SPECIAL SCHEMES** for further details.

Assessments

[1.24] HMRC are given powers to raise an assessment where VAT returns have not been made or it appears to them that returns are incomplete or incorrect. The assessment must normally be made within two years from the end of the return period in question or, if later, within one year of the facts on which the assessment is based coming to their knowledge. An assessment cannot be raised more than three years after the end of the return period except in cases of fraud when the period is extended to 20 years. Where the taxable person has died, an assessment cannot be made more than three years after death or relate to a period more than three years before death.

See **6 ASSESSMENTS** for further details.

Interest and penalties

[1.25] Interest is chargeable in certain circumstances where VAT has been underdeclared or overclaimed. See **51.15 PAYMENT OF VAT**. On the other hand, repayment supplement is due where HMRC do not make a repayment on time and interest can be paid to the taxpayer where VAT has been overpaid or underclaimed as a result of error by HMRC. See **51.17** and **51.18 PAYMENT OF VAT**.

There is an extensive range of criminal and civil penalties including the following.

Offence	*Maximum penalty*
Criminal	
Fraudulent evasion of VAT	Unlimited fine or 7 years imprisonment
Producing false documents	Unlimited fine or 7 years imprisonment
Civil	
Evasion of VAT	Amount of VAT evaded
Misdeclaration or neglect	15% of the VAT which would have been lost
Repeated misdeclarations	15% of the VAT which would have been lost
Failure to register	15% of the VAT which would have been due
Failure to keep records	£500
Default surcharge	15% of the unpaid VAT

See **52 PENALTIES** for further details of these and other penalties. Liability for certain civil penalties can be avoided where there is reasonable excuse for conduct and penalties can be mitigated by HMRC or a VAT tribunal.

Appeals

[1.26] An appeal against a decision of HMRC on certain matters may be made to a tribunal, usually to the First-tier Tribunal at first instance and from there to the Upper Tribunal and continued up, via the Court of Appeal, to the Supreme Court (formerly the House of Lords) under normal procedure. The matters on which an appeal to a tribunal may be made are restricted and certain conditions must be complied with.

See **5 APPEALS** for further details.

Key points

[1.27] Points to consider are as follows.

- Be aware that in relation to VAT issues, EU law will almost invariably take priority over UK VAT law. This situation has been the key factor behind a range of VAT court cases in recent years, whereby UK taxpayers have challenged the compatibility of UK and EU VAT law in certain areas. This state of affairs is likely to continue in the future. HMRC has to apply UK law even where it is out of step with EU VAT law.
- A 'taxable person' is not only a VAT-registered business, but a business (or person) that should have been registered for VAT on the basis that taxable sales (or in some cases, acquisitions of goods from other EU countries) have exceeded the compulsory registration limits at some time in the past. HMRC has the power to backdate a taxpayer's date of VAT registration to the date when he should have been registered for VAT. It is very important that a business (supported by its advisers) carefully monitors its levels of taxable sales to ensure it registers for VAT at the correct time.

- A business will not need to include the value of any 'exempt' or 'outside the scope' sources of income in its calculations to determine whether it should be VAT-registered. Many sales of services to overseas customers (particularly business customers) are outside the scope of UK VAT because the sale is deemed to be taking place in the country where the customer belongs under the place of supply rules, i.e. the sale is not deemed to be taking place in the UK.
- As a general principle, input tax can only be reclaimed on costs relevant to taxable activities. However, there are two important concessions on this rule: a business making supplies to overseas customers that are outside the scope of VAT under the place of supply rules can still claim input tax as long as the service in question would be taxable if supplied to a UK customer (e.g. accountancy services); a business making certain exempt supplies of insurance and financial services can reclaim input tax on related costs as long as the customer receiving the service is based outside the EU.
- Taxable sales are those subject to VAT at either the zero-rate, reduced rate or standard rate of VAT. The zero-rate is still classed as a rate of tax, albeit at 0%. A VAT-registered business making only zero-rated sales will be in a VAT repayment position because it can still claim input tax on all of its costs (subject to normal rules).

2

Accounting Periods and Returns

Cross-references. See **51 PAYMENT OF VAT**; **52 PENALTIES**; **56 RECORDS**; **63.9 SPECIAL SCHEMES** for annual VAT returns.

De Voil Indirect Tax Service. See V5.101–108.

Introduction

[2.1] A taxable person must account for and pay VAT by reference to VAT periods. For this purpose, he must make a return to HMRC, not later than the last day of the month following the end of the return period, showing the amount of VAT payable by or to him and containing full information in respect of other matters specified in the return. [*VATA 1994, s 25(1); SI 1995/2518, Reg 25(1); SI 2000/258, Reg 3*].

Electronic filing

[2.2] A VAT-registered business can use HMRC's eVAT service to submit its returns on-line rather than sending them by post. From 1 April 2010 those with an annual turnover of £100,000 or more (excluding VAT) must file their

VAT returns online. Businesses registering for VAT on or after 1 April 2010 must file their return online whatever their turnover (subject to some minor exceptions). With effect from 1 April 2012, all business (again, subject to some minor exceptions) will be required to file their returns electronically ('removal of turnover test'). A person who is required to make a return electronically only as a result of the removal of the turnover test is only liable to a penalty for returns made for prescribed accounting periods ending on or after 31 March 2013.

Access

In order to get access to the service, a business must:

- *Sign up*. Go to the HMRC website and enter personal details (including setting a password). A User ID will then be displayed for future use.
- *Enrol*. Login with the User ID and password and select 'Enrol for eVAT services'. Then supply the information requested which is available from the certificate of registration and the last VAT return.
- *Activate*. An activation pin will be sent, normally within seven days. To activate the service, go to the Government Gateway at
  www.gateway.gov.uk
  and Login, select the 'Activate' link and enter the activation pin.

A business can then Login to the HMRC website to access its VAT return. Once a business has enrolled for online VAT services, HMRC expect it to continue to use the service and not use paper returns unless it has problems using the site.

Authorisation

When the online application has been successfully completed, the business is authorised to use the service although HMRC reserve the right to deny access to the service where they consider it necessary for the protection of the revenue. Unless permission to use the service has been granted (and not revoked), any return made using the service is treated as not having been made. A person is not treated as being authorised to use the service only because of

- being registered under *SI 1995/2518, Reg 6* in substitution for another person who has been so authorised on the transfer of a business as a going concern (see **59.36 REGISTRATION**); or
- acting in a representative capacity and being required by HMRC under *SI 1995/2518, Reg 30* to comply with the VAT requirements relating to accounting, payment and records (see **15.1** and **15.2 DEATH AND INCAPACITY** and **35.1 INSOLVENCY**).

Sending returns

If transmission of an eVAT return is successful, the business will receive an electronic acknowledgement from HMRC. This is evidence that the business has met its legal responsibility to submit a return. It is therefore recommended that a copy of the acknowledgement is printed and retained in the records. The acknowledgement also shows a unique reference for each return sent which should be quoted in any queries about the return. If an electronic acknowledgement is not received, the business should presume that the return has not been received.

[*SI 1995/2518, Regs 25(4A)–(4M), 25A; SI 2009/2978; SI 2012/33*].

Payment of VAT

A condition of using the eVAT service is that any VAT due on the return is also paid by an approved electronic payment method. [*SI 1995/2518, Reg 40(2A); SI 2000/258*]. See **51.2** PAYMENT OF VAT for methods of paying electronically.

Accounting periods

[2.3] Subject to the exceptions below, returns must be completed for three-monthly periods ending on the dates notified in the certificate of registration (or otherwise). [*SI 1995/2518, Reg 25(1); SI 2000/258, Reg 3*].

In order to spread the flow of returns over the year, taxable persons are allocated to one of the three groups of VAT periods ('VAT periods') as follows.

- Three-month periods ending on 30 June, 30 September, 31 December and 31 March.
- Three-month periods ending on 31 July, 31 October, 31 January and 30 April.
- Three-month periods ending on 31 August, 30 November, 28 February and 31 May.

(VAT Notice 700, para 20.5).

A taxable person who was, or is, required to be registered (but has not done so) will, unless HMRC otherwise allow, be allocated to the first group.

Exceptions

[2.4] The following are exceptions to the above VAT period rules.

Annual returns

See **63.9** SPECIAL SCHEMES.

Monthly returns

HMRC may allow or direct a person to complete returns for periods of one month and to submit these within one month of the period to which they relate. [*SI 1995/2518, Reg 25(1)(a)*]. If repayments are expected to be received (e.g. because most of the outputs are zero-rated) this method of accounting is advantageous. Where monthly VAT returns are prepared and the business changes from receiving repayments to making payment of VAT, it may have to change to three-monthly VAT periods. (VAT Notice 700, para 20.5).

First return period

The first return period commences on the effective date on which the taxable person was, or should have been, registered. [*SI 1995/2518, Reg 25(1)(b); SI 2000/794*].

HMRC variation

HMRC may vary the length of any period or the date on which any return is to be submitted. This applies whether or not the varied period has ended. [*SI 1995/2518, Reg 25(1)(c)*]. There is no appeal against their decision to the VAT tribunal under *VATA 1994, s 83(a)* (*Punchwell Ltd* (VTD 1085) (TVC 59.2); *Selected Growers Ltd* (VTD 10) (TVC 59.1)).

In particular:

- Written application may be made (quoting registration number and dates) to have VAT periods corresponding with the financial year of the business.
- Where there is a new registration either because of a transfer of a going concern or a change in circumstances of a registered business (see **59.36** and **59.7 REGISTRATION** respectively) application can be made to retain the VAT periods of the previous registration.
- Special consideration will also be given, where accounting systems are not based on calendar months, to arrangements for VAT periods to fit in with the particular system. For example, quarterly VAT periods ending within 14 days of the end of the standard period *or* monthly VAT periods ending within seven days of the end of the calendar month (14 days for a four-weekly accounting cycle) are acceptable.
- Any other arrangement will be specially considered.

(VAT Notice 700, para 20.5).

Bankruptcy, etc.

Where control of the assets of any registered person passes to a trustee in bankruptcy, administrative receiver, liquidator or person otherwise acting in a representative capacity, the current VAT period in which the date of the receiving order, appointment of administrative receiver or provisional liquidator or winding up order, etc. (the '*relevant date*') occurs is divided into two periods. The first period ends on the day prior to the relevant date and the appropriate return must be submitted by the last day of the following month. The second period commences on the relevant date and ends (and all subsequent periods end) on the normal last day for the VAT periods. [*SI 1995/2518, Reg 25(3)*].

Final return

Any person who

- ceases to be liable to be registered, or
- ceases to be entitled to be registered under *VATA 1994, Sch 1 para 9* or *VATA 1994, Sch 1 para 10* (see **59.2 REGISTRATION**)

must submit a final return on Form VAT 193 *unless* the registration is allocated to the purchaser on the transfer of a business as a going concern (see **59.36 REGISTRATION**). Unless HMRC allow otherwise, the return must contain full information of the matters specified in the form and a declaration, signed by the taxpayer, that the return is true and complete. The return must be furnished by a person who was or is registered within one month of the effective date for cancellation of registration and by any other person within one month of the date on which he ceases to be liable to be registered. [*SI 1995/2518, Reg 25(4)*].

VAT returns

[2.5] The prescribed forms are

- **Form VAT 193** (or the Welsh version Form VAT 193(W)) in the circumstances under **2.4** above; and
- **Form VAT 100** (or the Welsh version Form VAT 100(W)) for use in all other cases.

Estimated returns

[2.6] Where HMRC are satisfied that a person is not able to account for the exact amount of output tax chargeable or claim the exact amount of input tax to be deducted in any VAT period, that person may estimate a part of his output tax or input tax for that period provided

- the estimate is adjusted and exactly accounted for in the next VAT period; or
- if the exact amount is still not known and HMRC are satisfied that it could not with due diligence be ascertained, the estimate is adjusted in the next but one VAT period.

[*SI 1995/2518, Regs 28, 29(3)*].

Permission for estimated returns must be obtained in advance. If the estimated return is submitted, and the VAT shown paid, by the due date, the taxpayer will not be in default for the purposes of the default surcharge provisions (see **52.21 PENALTIES**). Permission will still be considered after the due date has passed, but it will not affect any default which has already been recorded. (VAT Notice 700, para 21.2).

See **43.10 LOCAL AUTHORITIES AND PUBLIC BODIES** for special estimation schemes for local authorities.

De Voil Indirect Tax Service. See V3.505.

Completion of return Form 100 (or Welsh version VAT 100(W))

[2.7] The completion of return Form 100 requires information to be included in the boxes shown below. [*SI 1995/2518, Reg 39*]. (VAT Notice 700/12/11, paras 3.2–3.10).

- *Box 1* — VAT due in the period on sales and other outputs.
- *Box 2* — VAT due in the period on acquisitions from other EU Member States.
- *Box 3* — Total VAT due.
- *Box 4* — VAT reclaimed in the period on purchases and other inputs (including acquisitions from the EU).
- *Box 5* — Net VAT to be paid to HMRC or reclaimed.
- *Box 6* — Total value of sales and all other outputs excluding any VAT.
- *Box 7* — Total value of purchases and all other inputs excluding any VAT.
- *Box 8* — Total value of all supplies of goods and related costs, excluding any VAT, to other EU Member States.
- *Box 9* — Total value of all acquisitions of goods and related costs, excluding any VAT, from other EU Member States.

Nil returns

If the business has not traded in the period and has no input tax to recover or output tax to declare, a VAT return must still be submitted with all boxes completed as 'None' ('0.00' if the return is sent electronically).

Assessments

When sending in a return after paying an assessment, the VAT return should be completed as usual without adjusting any of the figures to offset what has already been paid by assessment. If the value of Box 5 is more than the assessment, just the extra should be paid. If it is less than the assessment, no payment should be made and HMRC will pay or credit the business with the difference.

(VAT Notice 700/12/11, paras 3.1, 6.5).

Declaration

The return must contain full information in respect of the matters specified in the return and a declaration, signed by the taxpayer, that the return is true and complete. [*SI 1995/2518, Reg 25(1); SI 2000/258, Reg 3*]. This declaration must be unqualified (*DK Wright and Associates Ltd* (VTD 203) (TVC 59.22)).

Disagreeing with HMRC decision

[2.8] Where HMRC have given a decision or ruling concerning a business's VAT liabilities they will normally reject any claim from the business that challenges the decision or ruling. If the claim is formally rejected the business will be invited to apply for a review of the decision. The business has 30 days in which to accept this offer. If the business does not want a review, or if it does not agree with the result of the review, it can appeal to the First-tier Tribunal to decide the matter. If the business appeals, it will preserve its entitlement to a refund, but only if it has made a valid claim, should the HMRC decision be overruled. If however the business decides not to appeal to the tribunal then any future claims will be considered to be new claims, whether made on the same basis or not, and will be subject to the normal time limits.

(VAT Notice 700/45/11, para 8.1).

Incorrect and incomplete returns or failure to make a return

[2.9] Any error in accounting for VAT or in the return generally must be corrected as required by HMRC. [*SI 1995/2518, Reg 35*]. See **56.11 RECORDS**.

The consequences of an incorrect return or failure to make a return are as follows.

- HMRC may assess the amount of VAT due to the best of their judgment (see **6.1 ASSESSMENTS**). HMRC have indicated that incomplete or incorrect returns will be returned for correction. Traders classified as 'payment traders' will be assessed and the notice of assessment will accompany the rejected return with an error-return notice. For traders classified as 'repayment traders' the period will remain open until an acceptable return is received. Repayments will not be made until the error has been corrected.
- A VAT tribunal cannot normally entertain an appeal unless the appellant has paid the VAT due (see **5.4 APPEALS**).
- Criminal or civil penalties may be incurred for failure to comply with the necessary requirements. See **52 PENALTIES** and particularly **52.12** for penalties for misdeclaration or neglect resulting from understatements or overclaims and **52.21** for default surcharge for failure to submit returns on time or pay the VAT due.

Returns by persons selling under a power of sale

[2.10] Where a business is carried on by a taxable person and goods forming part of the business are sold by another person under any power exercisable by him in satisfaction of a debt owed by the taxable person, the goods are deemed to be supplied by the taxable person in the course or furtherance of his business.

Land forming part of the assets of the business is treated as if it were goods and any sale includes a reference to a grant or assignment of any interest in, right over or licence to occupy the land concerned. With effect from 21 March 2007, 'grant' includes surrender.

The auctioneer (on a sale by auction) or the person selling the goods must, *whether or not registered*, within 21 days of the sale, send the VAT and a statement on Form VAT 833 to VAT Central Unit at Southend-on-Sea showing

- his name, address and registration number (if registered);
- the name, address and registration number of the taxable person;
- the date of sale;
- the description and quantity of goods sold at each rate of VAT; and
- the sales proceeds and the VAT charged at each rate.

The auctioneer or person selling the goods must also send a copy of the statement to the taxable person within the same time limit. Both parties must then exclude the VAT chargeable from their normal returns, if any. [*VATA 1994, Sch 4 paras 7, 9, Sch 11 para 2(12); FA 2007, s 99(3); SI 1995/2518, Reg 27*].

The auctioneer, etc. must also issue a VAT invoice but giving the name, address and VAT registration number of the supplier. He need not be registered to issue it and should not ask the supplier for a VAT invoice.

This procedure does not normally apply to liquidators, administrative receivers or trustees in bankruptcy (see **35.1 INSOLVENCY**), who continue to account for VAT in the normal way.

(VAT Notice 700, para 18.4).

De Voil Indirect Tax Service. See V5.142.

EU sales lists

[2.11] Under powers given to them in *VATA 1994, Sch 11 para 2(3)*, HMRC require a business registered for VAT in the UK which

- makes supplies of goods to traders registered for VAT in other EU countries,
- transfers its own goods from the UK to another EU country,
- is the intermediary in triangular transactions between VAT-registered traders in other EU countries, or
- (from 1 January 2010) makes supplies of services subject to the reverse charge in its customer's EU country

to submit statements containing particulars of the transactions involved. Other EU countries have similar requirements. In the UK, these statements are known as EU sales lists (ESLs) but in other EU countries the forms are referred to as 'recapitulative statements' or 'summary statements'. The information provided is used to ensure that VAT has been correctly accounted for.

(VAT Notice 725, paras 17.1–17.3).

Supplies of services subject to reverse charge [*Directive 2008/117/EC*]

From 1 January 2010 EU sales lists are also required for taxable supplies of services to business customers in other EU countries where the customer is required to account for VAT under the reverse charge procedure. *FA 2009, s 78* (inserting *VATA 1994 Sch 11 para 2(3ZA)*) contains enabling legislation. ESLs in respect of services are not required for

- supplies which are exempt from VAT according to the rules in the Member State where the supply takes place;
- business-to-business supplies where the recipient is not VAT registered; and
- business-to-customer supplies. (HMRC Brief 53/08).

Penalties

See **52.24** and **52.25** PENALTIES respectively for inaccuracies in, and failure to submit, ESLs.

De Voil Indirect Tax Service. See V5.271B.

Obtaining forms

[2.12] A business will automatically be sent an ESL (Form VAT 101 or Welsh version VAT 101(W)) by HMRC if at any time it has completed Box 8 of its VAT return (total value of supplies of goods to other EU countries). The form is sent separately from the VAT return.

The form can also be obtained from the VAT Helpline (tel: 0845 010 9000) or can be downloaded from the HMRC website at:

www.hmrc.gov.uk

The following can also be obtained from either of these sources.

- EU Sales List Continuation Sheet (Form 101A or Welsh version Form 101A(W)).
- EU Sales Correction Sheet (Form 101B or Welsh version Form 101B(W)).
- Helpful Hints VAT 101/VAT 101A for the completion of the ESL and Continuation Sheet.
- Helpful Hints VAT 101B for the completion of the ESL Correction Sheet.

(VAT Notice 725, paras 17.5, 17.6).

Return periods and submission dates

From 1 January 2010

[2.13] An ESL may be submitted electronically or via the paper form VAT 101. Frequency of submission depends on whether goods or services are supplied and the quarterly value (excluding VAT) of any goods supplied. However there is no requirement to submit nil ESLs.

If a business	*The business will*
makes supplies of services only,	be required to submit an ESL for each calendar quarter ending 31 March, 30 June, 30 September and 31 December but may choose to submit monthly if preferred.
makes supplies of goods and the value of those supplies has not exceeded £70,000 (excl. VAT) in the current, or four previous quarters, for the period 1 Jan 2010 until 31 Dec 2011, (This threshold reduces to £35,000 from 1 January 2012.)	be required to submit an ESL for each calendar quarter ending 31 March, 30 June, 30 September, and 31 December but may choose to submit monthly if preferred.
makes supplies of goods and the value of those supplies has exceeded £70,000 (excl. VAT) in the current, or four previous quarters, for the period 1 Jan 2010 until 31 Dec 2011, (This threshold reduces to £35,000 from 1 Jan 2012.)	be required to submit ESLs calendar monthly.
makes supplies of goods and services and because the value of the supplies of goods is above the quarterly threshold, the business is required to submit monthly ESLs for goods,	have the choice to either: report both goods and services in each month, (using indicator 3 to identify supplies of services), or report only goods in months 1 and 2, and in month 3 report goods for the month and services for the whole quarter (using indicator 3 to identify supplies of services).
supplies goods or services, makes annual VAT returns and total annual taxable turnover does not exceed £145,000; and annual value of supplies to other member states is not more than £11,000; and the supplies do not include new means of transport (boats, aircraft and motorised land vehicles),	be able to apply to the VAT Helpline for approval to submit an ESL once a year and agree the due date for sending in the annual ESL.
supply goods only (including triangular transactions), have a low level of EU Sales and total taxable turnover does not exceed the VAT registration threshold plus £25,500;	be able to apply to the VAT Helpline for approval to submit a simplified annual ESL and agree the due date for sending in the annual ESL. If approved, the business will be allowed to complete a less detailed ESL, showing only the VAT registration numbers of EU customers. Actual values are not required but a nominal value of £1 for each entry must be entered on the ESL form.

If a business	*The business will*
annual value of supplies to other member states is not more than £11,000; the supplies do not include new means of transport (boats, aircraft and motorized land vehicles),	

The deadlines for submitting an ESL to HMRC, for all frequencies of submissions and for goods and services are: for paper ESLs, within 14 days of the end of the reporting period; and for electronic (online) ESLs, within 21 days of the end of the reporting period.

Before 1 January 2010

Subject to the exceptions below, every business which has, in any calendar quarter, made a supply of, or dispatched, transported or transferred, goods to a person registered in another EU country must submit an ESL within 42 days of the end of the quarter.

HMRC may vary the requirements to prepare ESLs as follows.

Monthly periods

HMRC may allow a business to submit ESLs for monthly periods, in which case the ESL must be submitted within 42 days of the end of the calendar quarter in which the month occurs. Application to prepare monthly ESLs should be made to the National Advice Service.

Persons with low turnover

Where a business satisfies HMRC that

- *either* at the end of any month the value of its taxable supplies in the period of one year then ending is less than the 'relevant figure' *or* at any time there are reasonable grounds for believing that the value of its taxable supplies in the period of one year beginning at that or any later time will not exceed the relevant figure, *and*
- *either* at the end of any month the value of its supplies to persons registered in other EU countries in the period of one year then ending is less than £11,000 *or* at any time there are reasonable grounds for believing that the value of its supplies to such persons in the period of one year beginning at that or any later time will not exceed £11,000, *and*
- it has not supplied a new means of transport (see **19.33 EUROPEAN UNION: SINGLE MARKET**) to any person for the purpose of acquisition by that person in another EU country (in which case a quarterly return for the relevant quarter *must* be prepared)

HMRC may allow the business to submit an annual ESL. If so, full details of values of goods supplied to each EU customer need not be disclosed (see **2.14** below).

An annual ESL must be submitted within 42 days of the end of the year to which it relates.

Relevant figure' is the compulsory VAT registration threshold (see **59.3 REGISTRATION**) plus £25,500.

Businesses preparing annual VAT returns, etc.

Where HMRC have allowed a business to prepare VAT returns for periods longer than three months (i.e. normally annual returns but including any other non-standard return period) and the business satisfies HMRC that

- *either* at the end of any month, the value of its taxable supplies in the period of one year then ending is less than £145,000 *or* at any time there are reasonable grounds for believing that the value of its taxable supplies in the period of one year beginning at that or any later time will not exceed £145,000, *and*
- *either* at the end of any month the value of its supplies to persons registered in other EU countries in the period of one year then ending is less than £11,000 *or* at any time there are reasonable grounds for believing that the value of its supplies to such persons in the period of one year beginning at that or any later time will not exceed £11,000, *and*
- it has not supplied a new means of transport (see **19.33 EUROPEAN UNION: SINGLE MARKET**) to any person for the purpose of acquisition by that person in another EU country (in which case a quarterly return for the relevant quarter *must* be prepared)

HMRC may allow the business to submit an ESL for the same period as its VAT return. The return must be submitted within 42 days of the end of the period for which the VAT return is required. Application to prepare such ESLs should be made to the National Advice Service.

Monthly or quarterly non-standard VAT periods

If a business has agreed non-standard monthly or quarterly VAT return periods, it can apply to the National Advice Service for a similar concession for its ESLs. The requested period must end within 14 days (including weekends) each side of the normal period end for monthly non-standard ESL periods and 20 days (including weekends) for quarterly periods. If agreed, the centrally issued ESLs will still show the standard period dates which should not be altered. ESLs must be submitted within 42 days of the end of the quarter.

Changing VAT periods

It is also possible for a business to change its VAT return period to coincide with the calendar quarterly ESL period. Application should be made to the National Registration Service.

[*SI 1995/2518, Regs 21, 22(1)(2)(6); SI 1996/210; SI 2009/3241, Regs 4–6*]. (VAT Notice 725, paras 17.4, 17.7–17.9).

Information to be disclosed

[2.14] The ESL must contain the following information.

Information	*Description*
Country code	The two letter prefix which identifies the customer's country code (see below).
Customer's VAT registration number	The VAT registration number of the customer in the other Member State.
Total value of supplies in £'s sterling	The total value for the appropriate period of: goods and related services supplied to each customer, leaving the indicator column blank (related services are services which form part of the price of the goods such as freight charges and insurance); triangular transactions, entered on a separate line for each customer and using code '2' in the indicator column, and (from 1 January 2010) supplies of services subject to the reverse charge in the customer's member state, entered on a separate line for each customer and using code '3' in the indicator column. If a supply of services is made to a customer which is not registered for VAT in their Member State because it is below the registration threshold, but which has provided evidence that it is in business (for place of supply purposes), these supplies should not be included on the ESL. For simplified annual ESL £1 must be inserted in the value column for each entry.

Austria	AT
Belgium	BE
Bulgaria	BG
Cyprus	CY
Czech Republic	CZ
Denmark	DK
Estonia	EE
Finland	FI
France	FR
Germany	DE
Greece	EL

Hungary	HU
Ireland	IE
Italy	IT
Latvia	LV
Lithuania	LT
Luxembourg	LU
Malta	MT
Netherlands	NL
Poland	PL
Portugal	PT
Romania	RO
Slovak Republic	SK
Slovenia	SI
Spain	ES
Sweden	SE

[*SI 1995/2518, Reg 21, Reg 22(3)(5); SI 1996/210; SI 2009/3241, Regs 4–6*]. (VAT Notice 725, paras 17.11; Form VAT 101 Notes on Completion).

Method of sending

Electronically

[2.15] An ESL may be submitted electronically using:

- an online form;
- an upload facility for large data (CSV or XML) files;
- UN-EDIFACT (to use this method send an e-mail to: ecu@hmrc.gsi.gov.uk to register); or
- visit the Electronic Data Capture Services section of the HMRC website for the Trade Specification.

The service is free with registration and enrolment via the HMRC website or Government Gateway using PIN and password.

Paper format

ESLs can also be submitted via the paper form VAT 101. A business will automatically be sent an ESL (Form VAT 101) if it puts an entry in Box 8 of its VAT return. The form will be sent to the business separately from its VAT return and should be returned separately. Also copies can be downloaded from the HMRC website, or obtained from the VAT Helpline. If a business has a low level of EU sales it may be eligible to complete a simplified ESL annually. ESL Continuation Sheets (VAT 101A) are available from the HMRC website or via the VAT Helpline.

(VAT Notice 725, paras 17.4, 17.5).

Correction of errors

Errors discovered by the business

[2.16] HMRC must be informed of errors or omissions on an ESL where

- errors exceed £100;
- an incorrect VAT registration number has been quoted; or
- a business has used the wrong transaction type indicator when completing the ESL.

Errors must be disclosed by completion of a Form VAT 101B which can be downloaded from the HMRC website.

Help on the correction of errors is available from the VAT Helpline or by e-mailing:ESL.helpdesk@hmrc.gsi.gov.uk.

Errors discovered by HMRC

The internet service of ESL submission includes front end validation of data so errors will be identified on screen. Where paper ESLs are submitted, HMRC will notify a business of any errors that they identify on Form VAT 104 (EU Sales List Error Report). The form will show the error lines and the reasons for the errors. The errors must be corrected in the spaces provided and the form returned within 21 days of receipt to the address shown.

(VAT Notice 725, paras 17.14, 17.16).

Branch and group registration

[2.17] Written application may be made for

- individual branches of a business,
- individual companies within a group registration, or
- self-accounting branches of a group member

to send in separate ESLs. Each branch or company must then use a separate three-digit identifier when completing its own ESL. Alternatively one ESL can be submitted for the business.

(VAT Notice 725, para 17.17).

Other points

[2.18] *Agents*. An agent may be used to act on the business's behalf, but legal responsibility for the accurate and timely completion and submission of an ESL remains with the business.

Triangular transactions. An ESL must be completed even if the only EU supplies are triangular transactions.

Services. If a business's only EU supplies are services subject to the reverse charge in the customer's Member State, it is still required to submit an ESL.

Zero-rated if supplied within the UK. An ESL must be completed if a business makes supplies of goods to a trader registered for VAT in another Member State, including the transfer of its own goods and goods that would be zero-rated if supplied within the UK.

Deemed supplies. Where a business supplies goods free of charge to a customer in another Member State, it is making a deemed supply of goods and must include it on its ESL. The value to be shown is the cost to the business of the goods. Samples or gifts may be excluded provided it meets certain conditions.

Distance selling. If a business makes supplies of goods to customers who are not VAT-registered in other Member States and it is responsible for delivery of the goods (distance selling) it should not enter these supplies on the ESL.

Temporary movements. A business should not include temporary movements of its own goods to another Member State unless the conditions relating to the transfer change.

Credit notes. The value of the credit note should be deducted from the value of the supplies made to the customer. If the value of credit notes exceeds the value of supplies, the resulting negative figure should be shown using a minus sign.

(VAT Notice 725, paras 17.18–17.25).

Intrastat

[2.19] Intrastat is the name given to the system for collecting statistics on the trade in goods between EU countries. Businesses which are not registered for VAT, and private individuals who move goods within the EU, have no obligations under the Intrastat system.

The statistics are collected from the following two sources.

The VAT return

All VAT-registered businesses must complete Boxes 8 and 9 on the VAT return showing details of goods supplied to ('dispatches') and acquired from ('arrivals') other EU countries.

Supplementary declarations (SDs)

If the annual value of intra-EU trade of a business is below the threshold in the table below, it can be treated as exempt from providing Intrastat information and is not required to prepare SDs. The thresholds separately apply to its

- dispatches of goods to other EU countries; and
- arrivals of goods from other EU countries.

Where the level of its dispatches or arrivals (or both) is above the threshold, the business must prepare SDs.

[*SI 1992/2790, Reg 3; SI 2000/3227; SI 2003/3131; SI 2004/3284; SI 2005/3371; SI 2006/3216; SI 2008/2847; SI 2009/2974*].

Calendar year	*Dispatches*	*Arrivals*
2004–2005	£221,000	£221,000

2006	£225,000	£225,000
2007–2008	£260,000	£260,000
2009	£270,000	£270,000
2010–2012	£250,000	£600,000

Additionally, if a business is not required to provide SDs from the start of a calendar year but the cumulative total of dispatches or arrivals from 1 January in the current calendar year exceeds the threshold for the current year, SDs must be submitted for the rest of the calendar year, commencing with the month in which the threshold is reached. Under these circumstances, the business should inform HMRC in writing at HM Revenue and Customs, Statistics and Analysis of Trade Unit, Intrastat Team, 3rd Floor South East, Alexander House, 21 Victoria Avenue, Southend-on-Sea, Essex SS99 1AA, stating the month the threshold for dispatches or arrivals (or both) was exceeded.

For full details about the preparation of SDs, see HMRC Notice 60.

With effect from 1 April 2008, the data provided on Intrastat declarations is provided for both Intrastat and VAT purposes. [*SI 1995/2518, Regs 23E, 23F; SI 2008/556*]. This does not require any further action on the part of the business concerned but means that the data can be also used, for example, to counter Missing Trader Intra-Community fraud.

Key points

[2.20] Points to consider are as follows.

- For VAT periods beginning on or after 1 April 2012, it is compulsory for a business to submit VAT returns and pay tax by electronic means.
- A business that expects to receive regular repayments of VAT (e.g. a business with wholly or mainly zero-rated sales, such as a farmer or grocer) can benefit from submitting monthly VAT returns. This will improve the cash flow of the business.
- It is sensible for a business to request that its VAT quarters coincide with the end of its financial year. A request can be made to HMRC to change the periods so that they coincide with the financial year. This means that, if HMRC agree to the request, for one period only, a VAT return of one or two months will need to be submitted to bring the periods into line with the requested date.
- A useful concession is that a business can make an advance request to submit its VAT returns based on special accounting periods. For example, some businesses have an accounting period (for management accounts purposes) that ends on the final Friday of the month, which may not be the end of the calendar month for VAT return purposes. However, care is needed to ensure VAT returns are submitted and paid by the due dates that will apply for

the special accounting date. If the business fails to meet the deadline a default surcharge penalty or default surcharge liability notice could be issued by HMRC.

- If a business deregisters for VAT purposes, it will need to complete a final VAT return covering the period from its last VAT return up to the date of deregistration. It is important to remember that the final return will need to ensure output tax is properly accounted for on assets and stock held by the business when it deregisters.
- A business that is unable to submit an accurate VAT return by the due date (e.g. due to the loss of accounting records in a fire or because of computer problems) can request approval from HMRC to submit an estimated return based on its best judgment. Any under or overpayment of tax compared to the actual amount due can then be included on the VAT return for the next period. The method of making the estimate is at the discretion of the business, perhaps based on figures for the same period in the previous year, adjusting for known factors, e.g. in relation to capital expenditure or a change in the mixture of standard and zero-rated sales.
- The completion of the various boxes on VAT returns requires care and attention to ensure correct procedures are adopted. A common error is to include reverse charge transactions (accounting for the suppliers' output tax in the case of most services received from abroad and some mobile phone and computer chip purchases from a UK business) in Box 2 rather than Box 1. The Box 2 entry is only relevant to goods purchased from a VAT registered business based in an EU country outside of the UK, known as 'acquisition tax'.
- The reverse charge entries (Box 1 and Box 4) or acquisition tax entries (Box 2 and Box 4) are not contra entries for the same amount in all cases. If an expense (goods or services) relates to exempt, private or non-business activities, then an input tax block will apply in most cases, i.e. there will be no inclusion of input tax within the Box 4 figure. This is an important point that is often overlooked by advisers.
- A business will sometimes transfer its own goods to a branch based in another EU country. The branch is often VAT-registered in that country. The value of such transfers should be included in both Box 6 (outputs) and Box 8 (sales of goods to VAT-registered customers in other EU countries) of the return.
- Box 8 and Box 9 of the VAT return (sales of goods to and purchases of goods from VAT-registered businesses in other EU countries) only relate to the sale of goods. There should be no inclusion for the value of services bought from or sold to EU customers, e.g. accountancy services, consultancy fees, legal services.

- The EU Sales List (ESL) has been in place for many years to record the details of goods sold to a VAT-registered business in another EU country. From 1 January 2010, that requirement was extended to include sales of services where no VAT charge is made by a UK business under the place of supply rules.
- A business selling goods to VAT-registered customers in other EU countries will automatically be sent an ESL because of the positive entry it would make (if done correctly) in Box 8 of its VAT return. A business selling services where no VAT is charged to an EU customer will not make an entry in Box 8 so is responsible for obtaining an ESL form from HMRC (or completing it online) by the due dates.
- If there are no relevant transactions in an ESL period, no return needs to be completed by the business. There is no requirement to complete a nil return.
- A business selling goods to other EU customers (VAT-registered), with a quarterly value exceeding £35,000 (either in the current quarter or any of the four previous quarters), will need to submit a monthly EU Sales List. Note – prior to 1 January 2012 this threshold was £70,000.
- A business will need to complete Intrastat returns (giving details of its trading in goods with other VAT-registered businesses in the EU) if the value of its acquisitions or dispatches exceeds certain limits on a calendar year basis. Be aware that a big increase in the Intrastat threshold (£270,000 to £600,000) took effect on 1 January 2010 in relation to acquisitions. The threshold for dispatches decreased from £270,000 to £250,000 on the same day.

3

Agents

Cross-references. See **11.9 CATERING** for contract catering.

De Voil Indirect Tax Service. See V3.221.

Introduction

[3.1] There is no definition of 'agent' in the legislation. An agent is someone who acts for, or represents, someone else (the principal) in arranging supplies of goods and services. Supplies arranged by an agent are made by or to the principal represented. The principal cannot avoid any liability to account for VAT on supplies, or to pay VAT on purchases, by using an agent. However, whether or not a person is an agent for another person depends upon the actual arrangement between them and not simply upon the trading titles adopted. For example, 'motor agents and distributors' usually trade as principals and travel agents and employment agencies are not usually agents in all their activities. Solicitors and architects are normally principals but may occasionally arrange supplies as agents for their clients.

An agent/principal relationship exists if both parties agree that it does *and* the agent has agreed with the principal *to act on his behalf* in relation to the particular transaction concerned. The agreement may be written, oral or merely inferred from their general relationship and the way their business is conducted. Whatever form this relationship takes, the following conditions must be satisfied.

- It must always be clearly established between the agent and principal, and acceptable to HMRC, that the agent is arranging transactions for the principal, rather than trading on his own account.
- The agent must never be the owner of the goods or use any of the services bought or sold for the principal.
- The agent must not alter the nature or value of any of the supplies made between the principal and third parties.

(VAT Notice 700, para 22.2).

In *C & E Commrs v Johnson*, QB [1980] STC 624 (TVC 1.1) Woolf J took agency as the 'relationship which exists between two persons, one of whom expressly or impliedly consents that the other should represent him or act on his behalf and the other of whom similarly consents to represent the former or so to act'.

Whether acting as agent or principal — case law

For decisions in specific cases as to whether a person was acting as agent or principal see *JK Hill & Co v C & E Commrs*, QB [1988] STC 424 (TVC 1.6) (sales of craft pottery); *C & E Commrs v Paget and Another*, QB [1989] STC 773 (TVC 1.64), *Flashlight Photography Ltd* (VTD 9088) (TVC 67.53) and *H Tempest Ltd* (VTD 201) (TVC 67.27) (school photographs—see also **16.18 EDUCATION**); *C & E Commrs v Music & Video Exchange Ltd*, QB [1992] STC 220 (TVC 1.7) (second-hand musical equipment); *Bagshawe (JNS) and Walker* (CAE) (VTD 1762) (TVC 1.2) (art dealers); *National Bus Company* (VTD 2530) (TVC 1.38) (refreshments sold by hostesses on buses); *Dr R Nader (t/a Try Us)* (VTD 4927) (TVC 1.4) (meals delivered by taxi); *Prontobikes Ltd* (VTD 13213) (TVC 1.26) (motorcycle courier service); *Cornhill Management Ltd* (VTD 5444) (TVC 1.8) (company investing money deposited by clients); *LS & A International Ltd* (VTD 3717) (TVC 1.14) (purchases of paper); *Jocelyn Feilding Fine Arts Ltd* (VTD 652) (TVC 60.7) (auctioneers); *Leapmagic Ltd* (VTD 6441) (TVC 62.281) (hostesses at night club); and *Ivychain Ltd* (VTD 5627) (TVC 62.315) (service washes at launderette). For a fuller list, see Tolley's VAT Cases.

Agents and VAT

[3.2] An agent will usually be involved in at least two separate supplies at any one time.

- The supply of own services to the principal for which the agent charges a fee or commission.
- The supply made between the principal and the third party.

The VAT liability on the supply of agent's services will not necessarily be the same as the liability of the supply between the principal and the third party.

(VAT Notice 700, paras 22.3, 22.4).

Registration

In determining whether an agent is liable to be registered for VAT, turnover includes the value of services to the principal and the value of any supplies which the agent is treated as making through acting in his own name (see under **3.4** below). (VAT Notice 700, para 22.7).

Agents acting in the name of their principals

[3.3] An agent may only take a minor role in a transaction and simply introduce the principal to potential clients or suppliers. Alternatively, the agent may be more closely involved and receive/deliver goods, make/receive payment and possibly hold stocks of goods on behalf of the principal. However, provided that the invoicing for the supply is between the principal and the customer, the only VAT supply made by the agent is the provision of services to the principal. (VAT Notice 700, para 22.5).

Agents acting in their own name (undisclosed agents)

[3.4] An agent may be empowered by a principal to enter into contracts with a third party on behalf of the principal. In such cases, particularly where the principal wishes to remain unnamed or undisclosed, the agent may receive and issue invoices in his own name for the supplies concerned. In such circumstances, although in commercial terms the transaction remains between the principal and third party, for VAT purposes special rules apply as set out below. (VAT Notice 700, para 22.6).

Goods

Where an agent acts in his own name in relation to a supply and either

- goods are imported from outside the EU by a taxable person who supplies them as agent for a non-taxable person, or
- goods are acquired from another EU country by a non-taxable person and a taxable person acts as agent in relation to the acquisition, and then supplies the goods as agent for that non-taxable person, or
- where neither of the above applies in relation to a supply, goods are supplied through an agent

then the goods *must* be treated, as the case may be, as imported and supplied by the agent, acquired and supplied by the agent or supplied to and by the agent as principal. For these purposes, a person who is not resident in the UK and whose place (or principal place) of business is outside the UK may be treated as being a non-taxable person if as a result he will not be required to be registered under *VATA 1994*.

[*VATA 1994, s 47(1)(2)(2A); FA 1995, s 23*].

Non-EU and intra-EU supplies

In order to put the VAT treatment of UK undisclosed agents on the same footing as that for commissionaires elsewhere in the EU, an undisclosed agent who is involved in non-EU or intra-EU supplies is seen as taking a full part in the underlying supply of any goods. There is no separate supply of the agent's own services to his principal and the commission retained is seen as subsumed in the value of the onward underlying supply. This treatment is for VAT purposes only and has no impact on the legal status of agents or the way in which they are treated for the purposes of other taxes or legislation.

> *Example*
>
> A UK undisclosed agent sells goods to final customer for £100. He retains £20 as commission and pays £80 back to his overseas principal. All figures are net of VAT.
>
> If the goods are imported, the VAT value at importation is arrived at in the normal way. If the goods are acquired from a principal in another EU country, the VAT value at acquisition is £80 based on the value of the invoice raised by the principal to the agent. The agent must account for VAT on the acquisition.
>
> The agent can recover import/acquisition VAT, subject to the normal rules. He then makes an onward supply in his own name to the customer for £100, and accounts for output tax. The commission of £20 is treated as subsumed in the value of the onward supply of the goods and is not treated as a separate supply of own services to the non-UK principal.
>
> Cost incurred in the UK (e.g. warehousing and handling) can be treated as supplied to the agent who can recover the input tax on them (subject to the normal rules).

Domestic supplies

Subject to below, there is an underlying supply between the principal and customer and a separate supply of agent's services to the principal. The agent reclaims input tax and must account for output tax on the supply of the goods but as the nature or value of the supply is unchanged the amount of input and output tax is normally the same. The deemed supplies to and by the agent are simultaneous and he cannot reclaim the input tax on the supply to him in one period but defer the time when he is required to account for output tax to a later period in which he invoices the supply made by him (*Metropolitan Borough of Wirral v C & E Commrs*, QB [1995] STC 597 (TVC 1.73). The VAT liability of the supply of agent's services is not necessarily the same as the liability of the supply of goods.

However, if he wishes, an undisclosed agent may also adopt the VAT treatment set out above for non-EU and intra-EU supplies for his domestic transactions.

Services

Where an agent who acts in his own name arranges a supply of taxable services and both the agent and supplier are registered for VAT, HMRC *may*, if they think fit, treat the supply both as a supply to the agent and by the agent. [*VATA 1994, s 47(3); FA 1995, s 23*]. (VAT Notice 700, para 22.6).

International supplies

In order to put the VAT treatment of UK undisclosed agents on the same footing as that for commissionaires elsewhere in the EU, where an agent is involved in international services the services are treated as supplied to the UK agent as though he was a principal and supplied on by him. The agent's commission is seen as subsumed in the value of the onward supply and he is not regarded as making a separate supply of his own services to the principal. This applies to services being supplied both to and from the UK.

Where the international services are treated as supplied where the supplier belongs, as a UK undisclosed agent is treated as the supplier, the supply takes place in the UK and will be subject to UK VAT. For international services listed in *VATA 1994, Sch 5* which are treated as supplied where the customer belongs (see **65.21 SUPPLY: PLACE OF SUPPLY**), a UK undisclosed agent is treated as receiving the supplies and must therefore account for VAT under the reverse charge. The agent then makes an onward supply in the UK and accounts for output tax in the normal way.

Domestic supplies

Subject to below, there is an underlying supply between the principal and customer and a separate supply of agent's services to the principal. The agent reclaims input tax and must account for output tax on the supply of the main services but as the nature or value of the supply is unchanged the amount of input and output tax is normally the same. The deemed supplies to and by the agent are simultaneous and he cannot reclaim the input tax on the supply to him in one period but defer the time when he is required to account for output tax to a later period in which he invoices the supply made by him (*Metropolitan Borough of Wirral v C & E Commrs*, QB [1995] STC 597 (TVC 1.73)). The VAT liability of the supply of agent's services is not necessarily the same as the liability of the supply of the main services.

However, if he wishes, an undisclosed agent may also adopt the VAT treatment set out above for international supplies of services for his domestic supplies.

Second-hand goods

Where any supplies by an agent acting in his own name are eligible goods under one of the second-hand goods schemes, the agent may be able to include the value of services to the principal (i.e. commission, etc.) in calculating the VAT due. All the conditions of the scheme must be satisfied. See **61 SECOND-HAND GOODS** for full details.

Supplies for travellers

The above arrangements cannot be used for supplies which are for the benefit of travellers (e.g. supplies of accommodation or passenger transport).

(VAT Notice 700, paras 22.6, 24.1, 24.2; Business Brief 9/2000; VAT Information Sheet 3/00).

De Voil Indirect Tax Service. See V3.221, V3.423.

Invoices for supplies made through a selling agent not using a margin scheme

Where an agent is registered for VAT and is acting in his own name

[3.5] The procedure outlined in **3.4** above may be used. Otherwise, if the principal is registered for VAT either the principal must issue a VAT invoice to the agent or the agent can use the self-billing procedure (see **39.6 INVOICES**). The agent must account for output tax on his onward supply to his customer and, if the customer is registered, issue a VAT invoice to him.

Where an agent is acting in the name of his principal

The procedures depend upon whether or not the principal is registered for VAT.

- If the principal is registered for VAT, the principal must issue the invoice made out to the customer. This can be issued direct to the customer or can be passed to the agent for onward transmission. If the agent is VAT registered, he need only account for VAT on services to the principal.
- If the principal is not registered for VAT, no VAT is due on the supply arranged by the agent.

A registered agent must account for output tax on his supply of services to the principal. The agent must also have evidence that he is arranging the supply on behalf of the principal and the supply should be readily distinguishable in his records from supplies on which VAT is charged. The evidence may be a standing agreement between agent and principal or a signed declaration from the principal giving his name and address and confirming that he is not a registered person making a supply in the course of business.

(VAT Notice 700, para 23.1).

Invoices for supplies obtained through a buying agent not using a margin scheme

Where an agent is registered for VAT and is acting in his own name

[3.6] The procedure outlined in **3.4** above may be used. Otherwise, if the supplier is registered for VAT, the supplier must issue a VAT invoice to the agent who may reclaim the VAT as input tax. The agent must account for output tax on his onward supply to the buyer and, if the buyer is registered, issue a VAT invoice to him. The principal (the buyer) should be able to know the price paid by his agent in obtaining the supply.

Where an agent is acting in the name of his principal

The procedures depend upon whether or not the supplier is registered for VAT.

- If the supplier is registered, the supplier should issue the VAT invoice made out to the principal. This can be issued direct to the principal or can be passed to the agent for onward transmission. If the agent is VAT-registered, he need only account for VAT on services to the principal.

- If the supplier is not registered for VAT, no VAT is due on the supply arranged by the agent. A registered agent must account for output tax on his supply of services to the principal.

(VAT Notice 700, para 23.2).

Disbursements

[3.7] Where a supplier incurs incidental costs (e.g. travelling expenses, postage, telephone) in the course of making the supply and charges these items separately on the invoice to the client, such costs must be included in the value when VAT is calculated. See *Rowe & Maw v C & E Commrs*, QB [1975] STC 340 (TVC 62.52) (travelling expenses billed by solicitors to client), *Shuttleworth & Co* (VTD 12805) (TVC 62.340) (bank transfer fees re-charged to client) and *National Transit Insurance Co Ltd v C & E Commrs*, QB 1974, [1975] STC 35 (TVC 1.83) (fee for handling insurance claim). However, where amounts are paid to third parties as agent of a client, such payments may be treated as disbursements if all the following conditions are satisfied.

- The agent acted for his client when paying the third party.
- The client actually received and used the goods or services provided by the third party. This condition usually prevents the agent's own travelling expenses, telephone bills, postage, etc. being treated as disbursements for VAT purposes.
- The client was responsible for paying the third party.
- The client authorised the agent to make the payment on his behalf.
- The client knew that the goods or services would be provided by a third party.
- The agent's outlay must be separately itemised when invoicing the client.
- The agent must recover only the exact amount he paid to the third party.
- The goods or services paid for must be clearly additional to the supplies made to the client.

If a payment qualifies as a disbursement, it can be treated in either of the following ways.

- The disbursement can be passed on to the client as a VAT-inclusive amount (if taxable) and excluded when calculating any VAT due on the main supply to the client. The agent cannot reclaim VAT on the supply (since no goods or services have been supplied to him). Unless the VAT invoice for the disbursement is addressed directly to the client, the client is also prevented from reclaiming input tax as he does not hold a valid invoice. Generally, therefore, it is only advantageous to treat a disbursement in this way if no VAT is chargeable on the supply by the third party or the client is not entitled to reclaim the VAT.

If an agent does treat a payment as a disbursement in this way, he must keep evidence to enable him to show that he was entitled to exclude the payment from the value of his supply to his client. He must also be able to show that he did not reclaim input tax on the supply by the third party.

- The goods or services can be treated as supplied to and by the agent under **3.4** above. The agent can then reclaim the related input tax (subject to the normal rules) and charge VAT on the onward supply if appropriate.

(VAT Notice 700, para 25.1).

Disbursements in particular cases

- *Counsel's fees.* A concessionary treatment has been agreed with HMRC for counsel's fees. The agent (usually a solicitor or accountant) may treat the counsel's advice as supplied directly to the client and the settlement of the fees as a disbursement. Counsel's VAT invoice may be amended by adding the name and address of the client to it and inserting 'per' before the agent's own name and address. The fee note from counsel will then be recognised as a valid VAT invoice in the hands of the client. Where the agent considers that the services of counsel, if supplied directly to the client, would be outside the scope of UK VAT, he may certify the counsel's fee note to this effect and pay the counsel only the net of VAT fee. (Tax Faculty of the ICAEW Guidance Notes 15/94, paras 23–26).
- *Debt collectors.* See **3.16** below.
- *MOT tests.* See **47.8**(13) **OUTPUT TAX**
- *Postal charges.* See **47.8**(19) **OUTPUT TAX.**
- *Search agencies.* See **3.17** below.

VAT representatives and agents for overseas principals

Direction to appoint by HMRC

[3.8] HMRC may direct a person to appoint a VAT representative to act on his behalf for VAT purposes in the UK where that person

(a) is a taxable person or, without being a taxable person, makes taxable supplies or acquires goods in the UK from one or more other EU countries;

(b) is not established, and does not have a 'fixed establishment', in the UK;

(c) is established in a country or territory

- which is neither an EU country nor part of such a country; and
- with which it appears to HMRC that there is no provision for mutual assistance similar in scope to the assistance provided between the UK and other EU countries under *FA 2011, s 87, Sch 25* (recovery of VAT due in other EU countries, see **31.2 HMRC: POWERS**, which replaces *FA 2002, s 134* and *Sch 39* with effect from 1 January 2012), *FA 2003, s 197* (exchange of information between tax authorities of EU countries, see **29.7**

HMRC: ADMINISTRATION) and *Council Regulation (EU)904/2010* (on administrative co-operation and combating fraud in the field of VAT, which recasts and repeals *Council Regulation (EC)1798/2003* with effect from 1 January 2012); and

(d) in the case of an individual, does not have his 'usual place of residence' in the UK.

See **65.14 SUPPLY: PLACE OF SUPPLY** for a consideration of where a business is established, 'fixed establishment' and 'usual place of residence'.

A person is treated as having been directed to appoint a VAT representative if HMRC have served notice of the direction on him or have taken all such other steps as appear to them to be reasonable to bring the direction to his attention.

Voluntary appointment

A person who has not been directed by HMRC to appoint a VAT representative to act on his behalf under the above provisions, but who satisfies the conditions in (*a*), (*b*) and (*d*) above, may with the agreement of HMRC appoint a VAT representative to act on his behalf.

[*VATA 1994, s 48(1)(1A)(1B)(2)(2A)(8); FA 2001, s 100; FA 2003, s 197; SI 2003/3092*].

Effect of appointment

[3.9] Subject to below, any person appointed as a VAT representative

- is entitled to act on his principal's behalf for all purposes relating to VAT;
- must ensure (if necessary by acting on his behalf) that his principal complies with, and discharges, all his obligations and liabilities relating to VAT; and
- is jointly and severally liable with his principal for complying with UK VAT law.

A VAT representative is not, by virtue of the above, guilty of any offence committed by his principal unless he has consented to it or connived in its commission, its commission is attributable to any neglect on his part, or the offence is a contravention by the VAT representative of an obligation which, under those provisions, is imposed on both him and his principal.

[*VATA 1994, s 48(3)(5)*].

Failure to appoint a VAT representative

[3.10] Where a person fails to appoint a VAT representative when directed to do so, HMRC may require him to provide such security, or further security, as they think appropriate for the payment of any VAT which is or may become due from him. A person is treated as having been required to provide security if HMRC have served notice of the requirement on him or have taken all such other steps as appear to them to be reasonable for bringing the requirement to his attention. Where any such security has been required and is not lodged, it can be recovered by distraint on goods (in Scotland through diligence) as if it were VAT due. See **31.4 HMRC: POWERS**. There may also be a liability to a criminal penalty under **52.7 PENALTIES**. [*VATA 1994, s 48(7)(7A)(8), Sch 11 para 5(10); FA 1997, s 53(6); Tribunals, Courts and Enforcement Act 2007, Sch 13 para 118*].

Notification of appointment and changes

[3.11] Any person appointed a VAT representative of another must notify his appointment to HMRC on the appropriate form within 30 days of the appointment first becoming effective. Evidence of the appointment must also be sent. The principal being represented must complete the normal VAT registration forms (Form VAT 1 and, if a partnership, Form VAT 2) and both the principal and tax representative must complete a Form VAT 1TR (or Welsh version Form VAT 1TR(W)) authorising HMRC to accept that the representative is acting on the principal's behalf. HMRC must then register the name of the VAT representative against that of his principal in the register kept for the purposes of *VATA 1994*.

Once appointed, the VAT representative must, within 30 days, notify HMRC in writing of any changes in the name, constitution or ownership of his business or of his ceasing to act as his principal's VAT representative or of any other event which would require a change in the register.

The date of cessation is the earliest of the times when

- HMRC receive notification from the principal of the cessation of the existing tax representative or the appointment of a different tax representative,
- HMRC receive notification of the appointment of a different tax representative or the cessation of the existing tax representative under the above provisions, or
- a tax representative dies, becomes insolvent or becomes incapacitated (which, in the case of a company, includes going into liquidation or receivership or administration)

although if HMRC has received no notification but another person has actually been appointed as VAT representative, HMRC may treat the date of cessation of the existing tax representative as being the date of appointment of that other person.

[*SI 1995/2518, Reg 10; SI 2003/2096, Art 57*].

Records to be kept

[3.12] Although his principal is established abroad, a VAT representative must keep all the **RECORDS (56)** required to be kept under UK law as the principal is making taxable supplies in the UK. The VAT representative must set up and maintain a separate VAT account for each principal represented and keep documents such as VAT invoices to show how the VAT account is built up.

Employment bureaux

[3.13] The bureau will act in one of the following ways.

As a principal

Supplying its own staff to the client. Workers may be employed by the bureau under a contract of service or may be self-employed and engaged by the bureau under a contract for services. In either case, they supply their services to the bureau which makes an onward supply as principal to the client. See, for example, *MG Parkinson* (VTD 6017) (TVC 33.3).

The bureau makes one supply of staff which is normally standard-rated. Output tax is due on the full charge made to the client. Where the client asks the bureau to act on its behalf in paying the travelling and subsistence expenses of candidates attending interviews, the bureau may treat these payments as disbursements for VAT purposes under **3.7** above.

The *Conduct of Employment Agencies and Employment Business Regulations 2003*, made by the Department of Trade and Industry and applying with effect from 6 July 2004, set out new rules governing the conduct of employment businesses and the rights of workers using them. Under normal circumstances *any* temporary workers supplied by an employment bureau will have a contractual relationship with the bureau supplying them (either being an employee of the bureau under a contract of service or self-employed and engaged by the agency under a contract for services) and not the client hiring them. In either case, the bureau will be acting as a principal for VAT purposes and VAT will be due on the full amount received from the client, including salary and associated costs in relation to the temporary worker.

Before 1 April 2009, a staff hire concession (which allows employment bureau hiring out its own staff not to charge VAT on salary costs if the client pays the staff direct, see **44.4 MANAGEMENT SERVICES AND SUPPLIES OF STAFF** applies. (Business Brief 2/04).

As agent for the client

Finding workers who enter into a direct contractual relationship with the client. The bureau must account for VAT on the commission charged to the client. Any payments of a worker's wages by the bureau are made on behalf of the client and may be treated as disbursements by the bureau under **3.7** above.

As agent for the worker

Finding employment openings for the worker who then enters directly into a contractual relationship with his or her new employer.

Output tax is due only on the commission charged to the worker for the bureau's supply of services. Where the worker is not registered for VAT, the bureau must not issue VAT invoices. However, some workers may be registered for VAT and in such cases the bureau may issue VAT invoices on their behalf under the provisions in *VATA 1994, s 47(3)* (see **3.4** above). This applies mainly to fashion models, where social legislation does not prevent the bureau charging a commission to the worker and where earnings are more likely to be high enough to exceed the VAT registration threshold.

As agent for both the employer and the worker

Supplying its agency service to both parties. Once it has brought the parties together, it usually withdraws and the continuing contractual relationship is directly between worker and employer. VAT must be accounted for on the bureau's charges made to both parties, although, where this situation occurs, the bureau normally only charges commission to the employer and the supply to the worker is made for no consideration.

(VAT Notice 700/34/05, para 3.9).

Travel agencies

[3.14] How a travel agency accounts for VAT depends upon its relationship with its customers and will normally be demonstrated by commercial documentary evidence (e.g. agreements or contracts). It may

(a) *act as a principal*, i.e. supply travel packages (including transport or accommodation), part of which is bought in from other businesses although part of which may be supplied in-house from own resources;

(b) *act as an undisclosed agent*, i.e. where the ultimate provider of the goods or services (e.g. the travel or accommodation provider) remains undisclosed to the customer; or

(c) act as an intermediary (agent).

Where (*a*) or (*b*) applies, the travel agency must account for VAT using the **TOUR OPERATORS' MARGIN SCHEME (68)**. The position where (*c*) applies is considered in the rest of this paragraph.

A travel agency is acting as an intermediary (agent) if

- both the travel agency and its principal have agreed that it will act as their intermediary;
- it routinely fully discloses the name of the principal it is acting for (e.g. on all tickets it issues or in its booking terms and conditions); and
- it is not taking any significant commercial risk in relation to the services it is arranging.

(1) Value of supplies

The value of supplies upon which any VAT may be due is the amount of commission due from the principal(s) and fees charged to clients, excluding any VAT itself. It is the travel agency's responsibility to issue invoices for its supplies, although it is common practice in the travel industry for tour operators to use a self-billing system (see **39.6 INVOICES**).

See also (7) and (8) below for supplies by a travel agency to corporate clients.

(2) Place of supply of services

For a detailed consideration of the place of supply of services generally, see **65.12–65.28 SUPPLY: PLACE OF SUPPLY**. If the place of supply of the services is outside the UK, the services are outside the scope of UK VAT, although if the place of supply is in another EU country

- the travel agency may be liable to register and account for VAT in that country; or
- if the principal is registered for VAT in a different EU country to the travel agency, the principal may be responsible for accounting for the VAT under the 'reverse charge' procedure. See **38.4 INTERNATIONAL SERVICES.**

(3) Insurance and financial services

If a travel agency makes arrangements for the supply of insurance or makes a charge for exchanging currency or travellers' cheques, the place of supply of services is

- where the customer belongs if the customer belongs outside the EU; or in another EU country and receives the supply of services for business purposes; and
- where the travel agency belongs in all other cases.

Where the place of supply is in the UK,

- any charges for exchanging currency are exempt under *VATA 1994, Sch 9 Group 5 Item 1* (see **23.8 FINANCIAL SERVICES**); and
- the supply of arranging travel insurance is exempt if supplied
  - (a) in isolation of any travel;
  - (b) in relation to a supply of travel on which no UK VAT is payable; or
  - (c) in relation to a sale of travel services which bears UK VAT provided that the travel agent notifies the traveller, in writing, of the price of the insurance as due under the contract of insurance and any fee related to that insurance charged over and above the premium.

See **36.17 INSURANCE.**

(4) Liability of commission relating to passenger transport services

If a travel agency acts as the *initial* intermediary in arranging zero-rated passenger transport, such as

- scheduled flights,
- journeys from a place within to a place outside the UK and vice versa, and
- most UK transport in vehicles with a carrying capacity of not less than ten people

then its services of arranging the transport are also zero-rated. See below for sub-agents.

See **70.14** to **70.24 TRANSPORT AND FREIGHT** for a more detailed consideration of passenger transport and **70.32 TRANSPORT AND FREIGHT** for services of agents in providing transport generally.

(5) Designated travel services

If a travel agency is acting as an intermediary for a tour operator who is established (or has a fixed establishment) in the UK, then its services are standard-rated.

(6) Sub-agents

If a sub-agent provides services which facilitate the making of supplies (e.g. introduction), the place of supply is where the sub-agent is established. Where this is in the UK, the agent's commission is standard-rated.

If a sub-agent is involved in the making of arrangements for travel services, the place of supply of the services follows the normal rules for supplies by intermediaries. The VAT liability on the supplies for which the sub-agent receives commission follows that of the underlying supply. Where the sub-agent is involved in the provision of zero-rated passenger transport, its commission for those transactions will also be zero-rated. Where it is involved in the provision of a package supplied by a UK tour operator under the tour operators' margin scheme, its commission is standard-rated.

(7) Individual supplies of services to business clients

Where a travel agency

- does not have an agreement or contract with a corporate client to arrange travel services, or
- it sets out what its charges and terms of business will be if the client chooses to use its services,

  it will be making individual supplies of services.

it will be making individual supplies of services.

The value of any individual supply to a corporate client is the amount of the fee charged. Where any of the commission received from the travel provider is offset in calculating the fee, the value of the supply is the net fee charged. VAT must be account for on commission received under the normal rules.

'*Bundled fees*'. Where a travel agent arranges more than one service but only charges one inclusive fee (a 'bundled fee') and the services arranged have different VAT liabilities (e.g. standard-rated hotel accommodation and zero-rated flights), the fee must be apportioned according to the values of the underlying supplies.

> ***Example 1***
>
> A VAT-exclusive fee of £15 is charged to a client for arranging zero-rated air travel of £412.50 and standard-rated EU hotel accommodation of £137.50 (i.e. 75% and 25% of the total cost of £550.00 respectively).
> VAT on the bundled fee is £0.75 (£15 x 25% x 20%).

(8) Continuous supplies of services to business clients

Where a travel agency has a contract or agreement with a corporate client to supply travel services over a period of time and the contract requires the customer to pay from time to time, it is likely that continuous supplies of services are being made. Indicators of a continuous supply are where the travel agency

- carries out periodic reconciliations of fees against services provided (see below);
- is required to have a presence in the client's premises;
- must provide periodic management information to the client under the terms of the contract; or
- is available, and is required to provide a set level of service, during business hours and may have to provide a limited service at other times.

Value and liability of supplies

The value of the travel agent's supplies will depend upon whether the commission received from the travel providers is 'ceded' or 'non-ceded'.

Commission is 'ceded' if, under the terms of the contract with a business client, the legal right to the commission is specifically passed to the client. The definition of ceded commission is not changed if, in practice, the travel agency offsets the amount of the commission against the value of its fees in determining the amount of money to be paid to or by its client.

VAT must be accounted for on commission received under the normal rules. No VAT is due from the business client on the commission passed over. VAT, where appropriate, is due the full value of fees, regardless of whether the travel agency nets it off for cash flow purposes against the commission passed to the client.

Commission is 'non-ceded' if the legal right to it is not passed to the business client by contract. A travel agency may take account of non-ceded commission (e.g. to offset commission received against costs incurred) within a calculation to determine the net amount to be paid by/to the client. This net amount is the value for VAT purposes.

VAT must be accounted for on the commission received under the normal rules. No VAT is due from the business client if the net amount is payable by the travel agency to them. VAT (where appropriate) is due from the travel agency on any net amount of fees charged to the client following the offset of commission.

The travel agency must apportion its fees based on the value of the underlying supplies arranged. (Where foreign exchange is arranged and the travel agency does not know the value of the underlying supply by the financial institution, it can calculate the value as 1% of the total amount exchanged.) It should calculate the percentages of the amount paid by the client according to the different types of underlying supply (excluding any ancillary elements, see (9) below), and apply those percentages to the whole amount charged to the client. Note that the liability of the supply of intermediary services may not be the same as the liability of the underlying supply (e.g. where the client is

VAT-registered in the UK, EU hotel accommodation should be allocated as standard-rated, because the travel agency's supply is standard-rated in the UK, even though the accommodation itself is outside the scope of UK VAT).

Example 2

A travel agent has a contract with a corporate client to provide all its travel needs for a quarterly fee of 5% of the total value of supplies arranged. In the quarter to 31 March 2012 it arranges £50,000 of supplies (excluding ancillary services) which it analyses as £25,000 on zero-rated passenger transport, £15,000 on hotel stays in the UK and the EU, £9,500 on hotel stays outside the EU, and £500 on insurance.

Therefore

50% of its supplies are zero-rated

30% are standard-rated

19% are outside the scope of UK VAT

1% is exempt from VAT

The fee due for the quarter is £2,500 (£50,000 × 5%).

VAT due on the fees is

£2,500 × 30% × 20% = £150.00

The above method has been agreed with relevant trade bodies and is recommended for use by travel agencies. Another method can be used but it should first be submitted in writing to the local VAT Business Advice Centre.

Accounting for VAT

Under the terms of the contract, periodic reconciliations will be made of services against fees. In what follows, '*contract accounting period*' means the time between such reconciliations (generally at least quarterly).

Where interim payments are received, the normal rules for continuous supplies apply, i.e. VAT must be accounted for whenever a VAT invoice is issued or a payment received, whichever is earlier. Therefore, where payments are received within a contract accounting period, the travel agency must account for VAT at the time they are received. The way this is done depends on the type of interim payment received.

- If a payment is received from the customer for every transaction arranged, VAT should be declared on the amount received according to the liability of that individual transaction (e.g. if hotel accommodation within the EU is arranged, VAT should be declared on the full value of the fee).

  At the end of the contract accounting period, the amount of fees payable for the entire period must be totalled (including any final payment due following the reconciliation) and the apportionment calculation carried out as in *Example 2* above. The difference between the total VAT due and that already declared on the individual transaction must be paid to, or reclaimed from, HMRC on the VAT return

covering the end of the contract accounting period (or the date the adjustment is finalised, if later (see below). A final VAT invoice or credit note must be issued to the client as appropriate.
Where a payment in respect of ancillary services (see (9) below) is received during the contract accounting period, an estimate should be made of the VAT due on the payment.

Example 3

Using the figures in *Example 2*, interim fees in the contract accounting period were £1,000 zero-rated (nil VAT), £500 standard-rated (£100.00 VAT) and £25 exempt (nil VAT).

The final payment due is £975 (£2,500 – £1,000 – £500 – £25). VAT due for the period is £150.00 (as in *Example* 2) of which £100.00 has already been accounted for. This leaves a further balance of £50.00 due to HMRC. The invoice for final payment (assuming individual VAT invoices have already been issued for individual transactions) will show net fees of £975, VAT of £50.00 and gross due of £1,025.00.

- Where periodic interim payments are received, VAT should be declared on the amounts received by estimating the amount of the payment that is standard-rated. This can be done by any fair and reasonable method (e.g. estimating the amount of standard-rated sales for the current contract accounting period or using the figures calculated for the last period).
  At the end of the contract accounting period, the same procedure is followed as above.

Example 4

Using the figures in *Example* 2, interim fees in the contract accounting period were £1,700, the vatable proportion of which is estimated at 33%.

The final payment due is £800 (£2,500 – £1,700). VAT due for the period is £150.00 (as in *Example* 2) of which £112.20 (£1,700 x 33% x 20%) has already been accounted for. This leaves a further balance of £37.80 due to HMRC. The invoice for final payment (assuming individual VAT invoices have already been issued for interim payments) will show net fees of £800, VAT of £37.80 and gross due of £837.80.

Where the contract accounting period spans more than one VAT period, it may be necessary to account for VAT on interim payments in an earlier return to that in which the contract period ends. For example, where a contract accounting period is two-monthly (including, say, the two months from 1 June to 31 July) but VAT returns are prepared for calendar quarters, any interim payments received in June must be included on the return to 30 June but the reconciliation carried out at the end of that contract period will be made on the return to 30 September.

The apportionment for a contract accounting period must be carried out within two months of the end of that period. The adjustment must be accounted for on the VAT return during which the apportionment is finalised.

(9) Ancillary supplies to business clients

Ancillary services are those which do not in themselves represent a separate and distinct item purchased from the travel agency by the corporate client but which are provided to improve the core activities. Examples include

- management information;
- re-issuing tickets;
- processing refunds;
- delivering tickets;
- account management; and
- 24 hour helpline.

(VAT Notice 709/6/02; VAT Information Sheet 6/05; HMRC Brief 62/07).

Auctioneers

Agent or principal

[3.15] The main activity of an auctioneer is to act as agent for the vendor of the goods and arrange for a sale to be made to the highest bidder. However, an auctioneer occasionally acts as principal and buys and sells goods in his own right. The key to distinguishing agent and principal activities is that only when title to the goods has passed to the auctioneer does the auctioneer become a principal.

Accounting for VAT

The rules in **3.2–3.7** above apply to auctioneers if they offer goods for sale as agents of the seller. If an auctioneer issues an invoice for goods in his own name, the goods are treated as supplied to the auctioneer by the vendor and by the auctioneer to the buyer. The auctioneer is liable to account for VAT on the supply of the goods (regardless of the VAT status of the vendor) as well as on the commission charged to the seller and, if applicable, on any fee charged to the buyer (the 'buyer's premium'). However, where an auctioneer arranges supplies of second-hand goods, works of art or collectors' items, he may be able to use the special accounting scheme for auctioneers. This scheme allows auctioneers to calculate their VAT on a margin basis. See **61.53 SECOND-HAND GOODS** for further details.

(VAT Notice 700, para 25.2).

See **2.10 ACCOUNTING PERIODS AND RETURNS** where an auctioneer arranges sales of goods in satisfaction of a debt (e.g. under a court order) of a registered person and the goods sold are part of the debtor's business assets. The procedures outlined above for agents must not be followed.

Debt collection agencies

[3.16] The following VAT treatment applies to debt collectors who act as agents.

Court fees

Amounts paid by collectors to solicitors in respect of court fees may be treated as disbursements on behalf of the creditor. Any amount recovered from debtors in respect of such fees and retained by collectors may then be regarded as reimbursement of the amount disbursed and outside the scope of VAT.

Legal fees

Two options are open to collectors in respect of VAT charged by solicitors for their services.

- Collectors may choose not to recover the VAT as input tax and treat the charges as disbursements under **3.7** above. If so, where the agreement with the creditor provides that the collector bears the cost of solicitors' services but may retain, as reimbursement of his costs, any amounts recovered from the debtor in respect of solicitors' scale charges awarded by the court, such amounts may be treated as outside the scope of VAT.
- Collectors may choose to recover the VAT as input tax, subject to the normal rules, but recharge the legal fees, plus VAT, to the creditor under *VATA 1994, s 47(3)* (see **3.4** above). The scale charges retained represent payment of the fees recharged.

If a debt collector considers that he is acting as a principal, any VAT charged to him by a solicitor is recoverable as input tax, subject to the normal rules. However, any amounts recovered by the collector from the debtor in respect of court fees and/or solicitors' scale charges and retained represents consideration for the collector's supply of services to the creditor. Output tax must be accounted for on all such amounts in the normal way. This treatment does not apply if the collector has received an equitable or legal assignment of the debts, whether in whole or in part. Such an assignment is an exempt supply of services to the collector and the collection of the debts is outside the scope of VAT.

(VAT Notice 700, para 25.6).

Search agencies

[3.17] HMRC regard the fiche or document obtained from a source such as Companies House as a piece of information rather than a tangible object. The recharge of a search fee to the customer for the provision of a fiche or document may be treated as a disbursement under **3.7** above provided

- the information is passed on without analysis or comment; or
- the agency carries out a process on the fiche or document (e.g. conversion of a fiche to hard copy or provision of typewritten extracts) but does not use the data to inform an opinion or report.

Where the agency analyses, comments on, or produces a report on a fiche or document, or otherwise uses the information obtained on a search to make a report, the search fee is not a disbursement but a component part of the cost of providing the service to the customer, and is taxable at the standard rate.

(VAT Notice 700, para 25.5).

'Party plan' and 'direct' selling

[3.18] See **71.23 VALUATION** for supplies of goods made to non-taxable persons for retail sale.

See also *Churchway Crafts Ltd (No 1)* (VTD 782) (TVC 1.92) and *(No 2)* (VTD 1186) (TVC 67.39); *C & E Commrs v Pippa-Dee Parties Ltd*, QB [1981] STC 495 (TVC 67.37) and *Younger* (VTD 1173) (TVC 1.93). For a discussion of the nature of the distributor/dealer relationship, see *P & R Potter v C & E Commrs*, CA 1984, [1985] STC 45 (TVC 1.91) where the relationship was found to be that of principal to principal and VAT payable on the recommended retail price. See also *Betterware Products Ltd v C & E Commrs*, QB [1985] STC 648 (TVC 1.96).

For the VAT position of any incentive gifts to encourage individuals to act as agents for mail order concerns, see **47.6 OUTPUT TAX** and *GUS Merchandise Corporation Ltd v C & E Commrs*, CA [1981] STC 569 (TVC 58.1).

Key points

[3.19] Points to consider are as follows.

- The VAT liability of services provided by an agent can be different to the VAT liability of the goods or services being traded. For example, the services of an estate agent selling new residential properties (zero-rated) for a housebuilder will be standard rated.
- Always review correspondence between an agent and a principal to be clear that a genuine agency arrangement is in place. The main condition is normally that the agent will never take ownership of the goods or services being provided and will receive his fee on a commission basis from the principal.
- There may be benefits in an agent registering for VAT on a voluntary basis, i.e. giving scope for input tax recovery on their costs.
- A key issue in deciding whether an agency arrangement is in place is to review contracts and terms of agreement between the various parties. There have been many cases over the years where a business has deemed itself to be acting as an agent arranging supplies for another party but the reality is that it is acting as the principal. A common example is where the proprietor of a hairdressing salon considers that a supply of hairdressing services is taking place between a self-employed stylist and the customer but the reality is that the salon is acting as the principal. The customer perception of what is happening in an arrangement is also a significant factor.

- Be aware of the special rules that exist for transactions involving undisclosed agents – but remember that output tax and input tax on the goods or services in question must be accounted for in the same VAT period. The principle of an undisclosed agency arrangement does not change the underlying nature of a supply, i.e. the agent is not acting as the principal.
- Remember that zero-rated costs cannot be charged as a separate supply to a principal (e.g. as in the case of an estate agent paying a printer to produce colour brochures to help the sale of a property). The charge to the customer is part of the fee for his services as an agent.
- It is possible that agents will pay out costs on behalf of their clients – these costs can avoid a VAT charge if they are genuine disbursements and follow strict rules laid down by HMRC. One of the important rules is that a profit must not be made on the disbursement being recharged to the client.

4

Anti-Avoidance

De Voil Indirect Tax Service. See V3.233, V5.213

Introduction

Direct tax cases

[4.1] The classical interpretation of the constraints upon the Courts in deciding cases involving tax avoidance schemes is summed up in Lord Tomlin's statement in *Duke of Westminster v CIR* HL 1935, 19 TC 490 case that ' . . . every man is entitled if he can to order his affairs so that the tax attaching . . . is less than it otherwise would be.' The judgment was concerned with the tax consequences of a single transaction, but in *W T Ramsay Ltd v CIR, Eilbeck v Rawling* HL 1981, 54 TC 101, and subsequently in *Furniss v Dawson (and related appeals)* [1984] STC 153 (TVC 36.495), the House of Lords set bounds to the ambit within which this principle can be applied in relation to modern sophisticated and increasingly artificial arrangements to avoid tax. In *CIR v McGuckian* HL 1997, 69 TC 1, it was observed that while Lord Tomlin's words in the *Duke of Westminster* case 'still point to a material consideration, namely the general liberty of the citizen to arrange his financial affairs as he thinks fit, they have ceased to be canonical as to the tax consequences of a tax avoidance scheme'. It was further observed that the *Ramsay* principle was 'more natural and less extreme' than the majority decision in *Duke of Westminster*.

Ramsay concerned a complex 'circular' avoidance scheme at the end of which the financial position of the parties was little changed, but it was claimed that a large capital gains tax loss had been created. It was held that where a preconceived series of transactions is entered into to avoid tax, and with the clear intention to proceed through all stages to completion once set in motion, the *Duke of Westminster* principle does not compel a consideration of the individual transactions and of the fiscal consequences of such transactions taken in isolation.

The HL opinions in *Furniss v Dawson* are of outstanding importance, and establish, *inter alia*, that the *Ramsay* principle is not confined to 'circular' devices, and that if a series of transactions is 'preordained', a particular transaction within the series, accepted as genuine, may nevertheless be ignored if it was entered into solely for fiscal reasons and without any commercial purpose other than tax avoidance, even if the series of transactions as a whole has a legitimate commercial purpose.

However, in *Craven v White and related appeals* HL 1988, 62 TC 1 the House of Lords indicated that for the *Ramsay* principle to apply all the transactions in a series have to be pre-ordained with such a degree of certainty that, at the time of the earlier transactions, there is no practical likelihood that the transactions would not take place. It is not sufficient that the ultimate transaction is simply of a kind that was envisaged at the time of the earlier transactions.

In the unanimous decision of the House of Lords in *Ensign Tankers (Leasing) Ltd v Stokes* HL 1992, 64 TC 617, the lead judgment drew a clear distinction between 'tax avoidance' and 'tax mitigation', it being said that the *Duke of Westminster* principle is accurate as far as the latter is concerned but does not apply to the former.

The inheritance tax case *Countess Fitzwilliam and others v CIR (and related appeals)* HL 1993, 67 TC 614 appears to further restrict the application of the *Ramsay* principle, in that the HL found for the taxpayer in a case in which all their Lordships agreed that, once the scheme was embarked upon, there was no real possibility that the later transactions would not be proceeded with. There is, however, some suggestion that a decisive factor was that the first step in the transactions took place before the rest of the scheme had been formulated.

In *MacNiven v Westmoreland Investments Ltd* HL 2001, 73 TC 1 the House of Lords held that the *Ramsay* principle did not apply where a company loaned money to a subsidiary to enable it to pay up outstanding interest and thus crystallise tax losses. Lord Nicholls held that 'the very phrase "the *Ramsay* principle" is potentially misleading. In *Ramsay* the House did not enunciate any new legal principle. What the House did was to highlight that, confronted with new and sophisticated tax avoidance devices, the courts' duty is to determine the legal nature of the transactions in question and then relate them to the fiscal legislation'. Lord Hoffmann held that 'what Lord Wilberforce was doing in the *Ramsay* case was no more . . . than to treat the statutory words "loss" and "disposal" as referring to commercial concepts to which a juristic analysis of the transaction, treating each step as autonomous and independent, might not be determinative'. Lord Hutton held that 'an essential element of a transaction to which the *Ramsay* principle is applicable is that it should be artificial'.

Indirect tax cases

VAT planning does not, in the main, involve complicated schemes designed solely for the purpose of making a VAT liability disappear. Such schemes may give rise to one-off gains (although a significant number have been found by the courts to be ineffective) but in the longer term may simply complicate the administration and collection of the tax. Indeed, it is the creation and aggressive marketing of artificial schemes for avoiding VAT (in a similar way to what happened in the middle 1970s when artificial schemes to avoid direct tax were in vogue) which is leading to increasingly complex anti-avoidance provisions.

Historically, HMRC have sought, largely unsuccessfully, to apply the direct tax principles of *Furniss v Dawson*, *Ramsay*, *Westmoreland* and *McGuckian* above to VAT. Instead, the arguments in the tribunals and courts have revolved mainly around the technical implementation of planning arrangements.

Redefinition of transactions

However, in *Halifax plc v C & E Commrs (and related appeals), ECJ Case C–255/02*, [2006] STC 919 (TVC 22.60) HMRC chose not to argue the technical points, but instead argued that the transactions involved in the planning arrangements should be disregarded on the grounds that they had been entered into solely for a VAT avoidance motive (which the taxpayer accepted as being the case). The Advocate-General expressed the opinion that a person who relies upon the literal meaning of a Community law provision to claim a right that runs counter to its purposes does not deserve to have that right upheld. In such circumstances, the legal provision at issue must be interpreted, contrary to its literal meaning, as actually not conferring the right. Tax law should not become a sort of legal 'wild-west' in which virtually every sort of opportunistic behaviour has to be tolerated so long as it conforms with a strict formalistic interpretation of the relevant tax provisions. The ECJ held that the application of Community law cannot be extended to cover transactions carried out not in the context of normal commercial operations, but solely for the purpose of wrongfully obtaining advantages provided for by Community law. It was for the national court to determine whether action constituting such an abusive practice had taken place. Any transactions involved in an abusive practice must be redefined so as to re-establish the situation that would have prevailed in the absence of the transactions constituting that abusive practice.

In *HMRC v The Atrium Club Ltd*, Ch D [2010] 1493 (TVC 22.73) it was held that the redefinition of transactions under the *Halifax* principles was not designed to create a situation that could be sustained in practice. It was a purely notional device, for the purpose of assessment to tax, that might inevitably involve ignoring the terms of existing contracts.

Prepayment scheme

BUPA Hospitals Ltd v C & E Commrs; Goldsborough Developments Ltd v C & E Commrs, ECJ Case C–419/02, [2006] STC 967 (TVC 22.230) involved a prepayment scheme intended to crystallise an entitlement to input tax before the abolition of zero-rating for drugs and prostheses supplied to hospital in-patients with effect from 1 January 1998. The Advocate-General expressed the opinion that what is now *Directive 2006/112/EC, Art 65* (previously *EC Sixth Directive, Art 10(2)*) referred to situations where a payment was to be made on account before the goods were delivered or the services performed. Properly construed, this required that those goods or services must be specifically identified when the payment on account took place. A payment on account for goods referred to in general terms in a list, from which the buyer could choose in the future one or more items (or none at all) on the basis of an agreement from which the buyer was able to unilaterally resile at any time and recover the unused balance of the prepayment made, did not constitute a payment on account within the meaning of what is now *Directive 2006/112/EC, Art 65* (previously *EC Sixth Directive, Art 10(2)*). The ECJ agreed.

Carousel missing trader fraud

In *Optigen Ltd (and related appeals), ECJ Case C–354/03*, [2006] STC 419 (TVC 22.115) HMRC rejected claims for input tax on the basis that purchases formed part of a 'carousel missing trader fraud', designed to obtain a substantial repayment of sums which had never been paid as output tax. The tribunal dismissed the companies' appeals, observing that 'a circular series of transactions comprising the carousel fraud where the goods enter and leave the UK at the same price certainly does not look like an economic transaction'. On appeal, the Ch D directed that the case should be referred to the ECJ for a ruling on the interpretation of an 'economic activity' in what is now *Directive 2006/112/EC, Art 9* (previously *EC Sixth Directive, Art 4*). The Advocate-General observed that, where an activity falls within the scope of the *Directive*, that does not mean that a country loses its power to take action against it. In fact, what is now *Directive 2006/112/EC, Art 205* (previously *EC Sixth Directive, Art 21*) expressly gives countries the opportunity to introduce joint and several fiscal liability (which the UK has done). But the fact that transactions form part of a circular supply chain in which a trader misappropriates amounts paid to it as VAT, instead of accounting for them to the VAT authorities, does not mean that the transactions cease to constitute an economic activity under what is now *Directive 2006/112/EC, Art 9(1)* (previously *EC Sixth Directive, Art 4(2)*). The ECJ agreed. The principle of fiscal neutrality prevents there being any general distinction between lawful and unlawful transactions. Consequently, the mere fact that conduct amounts to an offence is not sufficient to justify exemption from VAT. Transactions such as those at issue, which are not themselves vitiated by VAT fraud, constitute supplies of goods or services effected by a taxable person acting as such. They are economic activities (if otherwise meeting the criteria), regardless of the intention of another trader involved in the same chain of supply and/or the possible fraudulent nature of another transaction in the chain, of which that taxable person had no knowledge and no means of knowledge. The right of the taxable person to deduct input VAT is not affected.

The ECJ reconfirmed the right of recovery of input tax in such a situation in *Kittel v Belgian State, ECJ Case C–439/04*, [2008] STC 1537 (TVC 22.415). It held that where a recipient of a supply of goods was a taxable person who did not and could not have known that the transaction concerned was connected with a fraud committed by the seller, the right to deduct input tax under what is now *Directive 2006/112/EC* precludes a rule of national law under which the fact that the contract of sale is void (by reason of a civil law provision which renders that contract incurably void as contrary to public policy for unlawful basis of the contract attributable to the seller) means that the taxable person loses the right to deduct the VAT he has paid. It is irrelevant in this respect whether the fact that the contract is void is due to fraudulent evasion of value added tax or to other fraud. By contrast, where it is ascertained, having regard to objective factors, that the supply is to a taxable person who knew or should have known that, by his purchase, he was participating in a transaction connected with fraudulent evasion of VAT, it is for the national court to refuse that taxable person entitlement to the right to deduct.

In *Mobilx Ltd, Calltell Telecom Ltd and Blue Sphere Global Ltd*, CA [2010] STC 1436 (TVC 36.119, 36.105 and 36.87) the Court of Appeal held that in deciding whether a trader ought to have known that he was participating in transactions connected with fraudulent evasion of VAT, the ultimate question was not whether the trader exercised due diligence, but rather whether he should have known that the only reasonable explanation for the circumstances in which his transaction took place was that it was connected to fraudulent evasion of VAT.

Abuse of rights

In *Blackqueen Ltd* (VTD 17680) (TVC 22.65), a scheme was devised (which would no longer be effective following the insertion of *VATA 1994, Sch 3A* by *FA 2000, s 136*) to make use of the provisions of the *EC Eighth Directive* for the refund of VAT to taxable persons not established in EU. The tribunal held that the relevant transactions did not constitute 'supplies' for the purposes of VAT, since 'the series of transactions entered into by the group was wholly alien to the provisions of what is now Directive 2006/112/EC'. Furthermore, the applications had been an 'abuse of rights', applying the decision in *Emsland-Stärke GmbH v Hauptzollamt Hamburg-Jonas, ECJ Case C–110/99*, [2001] All ER (D) 34 (Jan) (TVC 22.59).

The tribunal allowed the companies' appeals in *RBS Property Developments; Royal Bank of Scotland Group plc (No 5)* (VTD 17789) (TVC 22.68). HMRC rejected a claim for input tax by two associated companies (which were not in the same VAT group) on the basis that the transactions were carried out for tax avoidance purposes and, applying *Halifax*, did not constitute supplies for VAT purposes. The tribunal held that although the series of transactions had a substantial element of tax mitigation, they were not *solely* directed to tax avoidance. As there were real and understandable business purposes for structuring the transactions, it could not be said that they were artificial. A taxpayer was entitled to so construct his activities as to obtain favourable tax consequences. The transactions were not an 'abuse of rights' as there was nothing improper, illegal or artificial about the transactions in question so the principles in *Emsland-Stärke GmbH v Hauptzollamt Hamburg-Jonas* above did not apply.

In *HMRC v Weald Leasing Ltd, ECJ Case C–103/09, 22 December 2010 unreported*, (TVC 22.61), W purchased some assets, which it leased to another company (S), which in turn leased them to two companies (CM and CA) which were associated with W but were part of a separate VAT group making exempt supplies of insurance. W reclaimed input tax on the purchase of the assets. HMRC formed the opinion that the transactions were an 'abuse' but the tribunal held that a trader was not precluded from leasing an asset to be used for exempt activities, thus spreading the burden of irrecoverable input tax. The Ch D upheld the tribunal decision. The CA referred the case to the ECJ. The ECJ ruled that a tax advantage accruing from an undertaking's recourse to asset leasing transactions, such as those at issue in the main proceedings, instead of the outright purchase of those assets did not contravene EU law, provided that the contractual terms of those transactions, particularly those concerned with setting the level of rentals, corresponded to arm's length terms; and the involvement of an intermediate third party company in those transactions did not preclude the application of those provisions, which was a matter for the national court to determine. The fact that the undertaking did not engage in leasing transactions in the context of its normal commercial operations was irrelevant in that regard.

See also *Ministero dell'Economia e delle Finanze v Part Service Srl, ECJ Case C–425/06*, [2008] STC 3132 (TVC 22.62) which also concerned leasing transactions. In that case, the ECJ held that there *can* be a finding of an abusive practice when the accrual of a tax advantage constitutes the principal aim of the transaction at issue and that, when a transaction involves the supply of a number of services, the question arises whether it should be considered to be a single transaction or several individual and independent supplies requiring separate assessment. It was for the national court to decide whether the evidence put before it disclosed the characteristics of a single transaction.

In *Newey (t/a Ocean Finance)* [2010] SFTD 836; UKFTT 183 (TC); (TC00487) (TVC 22.74), a financial adviser (N), who was registered for VAT, was the controlling shareholder of a Jersey company (AC), which provided loan broking services in the UK. HMRC assessed N on the basis that he should be treated as supplying the loan broking services, and was liable to a reverse charge on advertising services supplied by another Jersey company (W). The tribunal found that N had established the loan broking operation in Jersey rather than the UK in order to avoid the irrecoverable VAT on advertising costs. However this finding did not entitle HMRC to treat N, rather than AC, as the supplier of the loan broking services or as the recipient of the advertising services. The transactions did not constitute an abuse. It was not permissible simply to compare the current structure with what could have been done or what had been done in the past, and to conclude that, if the current structure is more favourable it is therefore contrary to the purposes of the VAT legislation.

In *RBS Deutschland Holdings GmbH (No 4), ECJ Case C–277/09; 22 December 2010 unreported* (TVC 22.418), a Scottish bank had a German subsidiary company (D), which was registered for UK VAT as a 'non-established taxable person'. D purchased cars in the UK, reclaimed input tax on them, and leased them to UK customers. Although the cars were situated in the UK, D treated their supply under UK VAT law as being a supply of services which took place in Germany, where D had its business establishment. The German authorities did not charge VAT on the basis that the lease of the cars was a supply of goods made in the UK. Consequently D did not account for output tax in either Germany or the UK. In 2003 Customs issued a ruling that D was not entitled to reclaim input tax on its purchase of the cars, on the basis that the fact that no tax was levied takes the rentals out of the VAT system. The tribunal allowed D's appeal, but the CS referred the case to the ECJ. The ECJ ruled that the principle of prohibiting abusive practices did not preclude the right to deduct VAT where a company established in one EU country elected to have its subsidiary, established in another EU country, carry out transactions for the leasing of goods to a third company established in the first EU country, in order to avoid VAT payable on those transactions, the transactions having been categorised in the first EU country as supplies of rental services carried out in the second country, and in that second country as supplies of goods carried out in the first country.

Tackling avoidance schemes

There have been two results of the proliferation of avoidance schemes.

- HMRC have set up special units to monitor tax avoidance and have indicated that they intend to take a much more robust line in dealing with such artificial arrangements.
- The use of certain avoidance schemes and arrangements has to be notified to HMRC (see **4.2** *et seq* below).

Yacht chartering or leasing activities

Following the decisions in *Halifax* and *Part Service Srl* above, HMRC have listed the following features as possibly indicating an abusive structure where pleasure craft are chartered or leased

- the main user of a pleasure craft is the ultimate owner of the chartering or leasing entity;
- the main user of a pleasure craft funded the purchase of the vessel (directly or indirectly);
- the person who funded the purchase of a pleasure craft (directly or indirectly) uses the vessel for prolonged periods in the peak chartering season;
- the chartering of a pleasure craft to third parties would not, alone, be of sufficient continuity and substance to comprise an economic activity;

- the chartering or leasing entity shows significant ongoing losses in its financial statements;
- charter fees or lease instalments due from the main user of a pleasure craft are paper transactions only (e.g. being offset against loans);
- charter fees or lease instalments are below open market value; or
- the terms of a lease differ significantly from normal commercial practice (e.g. the duration of the lease is unusually long). (HMRC Brief 56/09).

Disclosure of VAT avoidance schemes

[4.2] Taxpayers who are party to certain VAT avoidance schemes must disclose their use to HMRC. The requirements apply to schemes used in VAT periods starting on or after 1 August 2004 (including schemes that started before that date). The measures are designed to provide greater information to HMRC about the take-up of avoidance schemes of which they are already aware and early notice of new, potentially damaging, schemes.

There are two categories of schemes that must be notified.

- *Listed schemes*. Certain schemes are 'designated' schemes for these purposes and are named and described in the legislation (by statutory instrument). A business whose annual turnover exceeds £600,000 must notify HMRC if it makes a VAT return or claim (such as a voluntary declaration) which is affected by its use of a listed scheme. See **4.3** to **4.6** below for the detailed provisions. Failure to notify incurs a penalty of 15% of the VAT avoided. See **PENALTIES**.
- *Hallmarked schemes*. Certain features that are regularly associated with avoidance schemes are designated in the law (by statutory instrument). They can relate to the adoption of schemes or be components of them. Hallmarked schemes are those schemes that include at least one of the designated provisions. A business whose annual turnover exceeds £10 million must notify HMRC if it has entered into a scheme for the purposes of securing a tax advantage, the scheme contains one or more of the hallmarks of avoidance, and it makes a return or claim which is affected by the use of the hallmarked scheme. There is also a voluntary facility for anyone, including those who devise and market avoidance schemes, to register hallmarked schemes.
  See **4.7** to **4.11** below for the detailed provisions. Failure to notify incurs a flat-rate penalty of £5,000. See **52.28 PENALTIES**.

[*VATA 1994, s 58A, Sch 11A; FA 2004, s 19, Sch 2; SI 2004/1934*].

Rulings

HMRC are normally prepared to give a ruling on how transactions should be treated for VAT. See **29.5 HMRC: ADMINISTRATION**. However, they will *not* approve tax planning arrangements and will refuse to give rulings where they suspect that the transactions are part of a tax avoidance scheme.

Listed schemes: general

[4.3] The Treasury can designate a scheme for the purposes of these provisions if it appears to them that

- a scheme of a particular description has been, or might be, entered into for the purpose of enabling any person to 'obtain a tax advantage', and
- it is unlikely that persons would enter into a scheme of that description unless the main purpose, or one of the main purposes, of doing so was the obtaining by any person of a tax advantage.

A scheme may be designated even though the Treasury are of the opinion that no scheme of that description could, as a matter of law, result in the obtaining by any person of a tax advantage (i.e. they consider it to be legally ineffective). Each listed scheme must be allocated a reference number.

[*VATA 1994, Sch 11A para 3; FA 2004, Sch 2 para 2*].

Obtaining a tax advantage

A *taxable person* obtains a tax advantage if

- in any VAT period, the excess of output tax accounted for by him over input tax deducted by him is less than it otherwise would be;
- he obtains a VAT credit when he would not otherwise do so, or obtains a larger or earlier VAT credit than would otherwise be the case;
- in a case where he recovers input tax as a recipient of a supply before the supplier accounts for the output tax, the period between the time when the input tax is recovered and the time when the output tax is accounted for is greater than would otherwise be the case; or
- in any VAT period beginning after 31 July 2005, the amount of his non-deductible tax is less than it would otherwise be. Non-deductible tax means input tax for which he is not entitled to credit under *VATA 1994, s 25*, and VAT on any supply of goods or services to him, or on the acquisition or importation of goods by him, which is not input tax and in respect of which he is entitled to a refund from HMRC under any provision of *VATA 1994*

With effect from 1 August 2005, a *non-taxable person* obtains a tax advantage if his 'non-refundable tax' is less than it would otherwise be. '*Non-refundable tax*' means the VAT on any supply of goods or services to him, or on the acquisition or importation of goods by him, other than VAT in respect of which he is entitled to a refund from HMRC under any provision of *VATA 1994*.

[*VATA 1994, Sch 11A paras 2, 2A; FA 2004, Sch 2 para 2; F(No 2)A 2005, Sch 1 paras 3, 4*].

Liability to notify listed schemes

[4.4] A *taxable person* must notify HMRC of the use of a listed scheme when all of the following conditions are met. This applies even if HMRC already know that he is using the scheme.

Condition 1

The total value of his VAT-exclusive taxable supplies and exempt supplies exceeded:

- £600,000 in the year immediately prior to the 'affected VAT return period'; or any of the VAT return periods that are the subject of an 'affected claim'; or
- the 'appropriate proportion' of £600,000 in the VAT return period immediately prior to the affected VAT return period; or any of the VAT return periods that are the subject of an affected claim.

The '*appropriate proportion*' means the proportion which the length of that VAT period bears to twelve months (e.g. one-quarter where quarterly VAT returns are prepared and one-twelfth where monthly VAT returns are prepared).

See Condition 3 below for 'affected VAT return period' and 'affected claim'.

See also **4.12** below for powers given to HMRC to prevent any artificial separation of business activities in an attempt to reduce turnover below the above limits.

Group undertakings

If the taxable person is a 'group undertaking', the conditions must be met by the taxable person *plus* every other group undertaking (i.e. the criteria apply to the whole group). For these purposes, the definitions in *Companies Act 2006, s 1161* apply (so that 'group' does not necessarily mean 'VAT group'). The group will comprise the undertaking in question, together with any undertaking which is

- a parent undertaking or a subsidiary undertaking of that undertaking; or
- a subsidiary undertaking of any parent undertaking of that undertaking.

For the purpose of calculating turnover, intra-corporate group transactions are included but intra-VAT group transactions are ignored. (VAT Notice 700/8/06, para 4.3).

Condition 2

The taxable person is a party to a listed scheme under **4.6** below.

A person is a party to a scheme if he knowingly takes part in it but not if he

- is unwittingly involved in any of the steps of the scheme (i.e. has no knowledge of either the existence of the scheme or the role he plays in it); or
- acts purely in an advisory capacity.

(VAT Notice 700/8/06, para 3.3.1).

Condition 3

One of the following relevant events occurs.

- In a return for a VAT period (the '*affected VAT return period*') beginning after 31 July 2004, the amount of VAT shown as payable by/to the taxable person is less than/greater than it would be but for the use of a listed scheme to which he is party.
- The taxable person makes a claim (the '*affected claim*') for the repayment of output tax or an increase in credit for input tax for any VAT period beginning after 31 July 2004 in respect of which he has previously delivered a return and the amount claimed is greater than it would be but for a listed scheme.
- In a return for a VAT period (the '*affected VAT return period*') beginning after 31 July 2005, the amount of the taxable person's 'non-deductible tax' is less than it would be but for a listed scheme.

'Non-deductible tax' means

- input tax for which he is not entitled to credit under *VATA 1994, s 25*; and
- VAT on any supply of goods or services to him, or on the acquisition or importation of goods by him, which is not input tax and in respect of which he is entitled to a refund from HMRC under any provision of *VATA 1994*.

Condition 4

The taxable person has not on a previous occasion

- notified HMRC as required under these provisions that he is using the scheme; or
- with effect from 1 August 2005, provided HMRC with prescribed information in relation to the scheme under **4.8** below when it was a hallmarked scheme and before it became a listed scheme.

Where a scheme is designed to give an ongoing VAT benefit over time (so that more than one relevant event under (Condition 3 above may occur), a taxable person is only required to notify the scheme once. However, a listed scheme may be used more than once (e.g. listed scheme 1 may be used to remove the VAT cost of refurbishing more than one property). Where this happens, each adoption of the scheme must be notified.

Where a new scheme becomes listed, if a taxable person has previously notified use of the scheme under the rules for hallmarked schemes, he is not required to make a new notification when the scheme becomes listed. But if the scheme is used again, he must notify the new arrangements as above.

(VAT Notice 700/8/06, para 4.4).

[*VATA 1994, Sch 11A paras 6, 7; FA 2004, Sch 2 para 2; F(No 2)A 2005, Sch 1 paras 5, 6; SI 2008/954, Art 20*].

Schemes involving several parties

If a listed scheme involves more than one party, all the parties to that scheme are obliged to notify HMRC if they meet the conditions set out above. However, the parties concerned can make a joint notification. The notification should make it clear that it is a joint notification and who all the parties are that are making the notification. (VAT Notice 700/8/06, para 3.3.4).

Notifying listed schemes to HMRC

Time limit for notification

[4.5] Where a taxable person must notify HMRC of the use of a listed scheme under **4.4** above, he must do so within 30 days from the end of

- the last day for submission of the return for the 'affected VAT return period';
- the date the 'affected claim' is made; or
- where HMRC make a direction under **4.12** below (artificial splitting of business), the last day for submission of the first VAT return made to HMRC following the direction.

See **4.4** above for '*affected VAT return period*' and '*affected claim*'.

[*VATA 1994, Sch 11A para 6; FA 2004, Sch 2 para 2; SI 2004/1929; SI 2005/2009*].

Where a business makes use of electronic means of payment and receives an extension to the due date for submitting returns (see **51.3 PAYMENT OF VAT**), the due date for notifying a scheme is 30 days after the extended due date for submitting the return. (VAT Notice 700/8/06, para 5.1.3).

HMRC will accept early notifications (e.g. before the relevant event has taken place) provided the scheme has been implemented. (VAT Notice 700/8/06, para 5.1.1).

Method of notification

The following provisions relating to notification as set out in VAT Notice 700/8 have the force of law.

HMRC must be notified of the use of a listed scheme either

- by e-mail to: vat.avoidance.disclosures.bst@hmrc.gsi.gov.uk or
- in writing to:

VAT Avoidance Disclosures Unit
Anti-Avoidance Group (Intelligence)
HM Revenue and Customs
1st Floor, 22 Kingsway London WC2B 6NR

Notification sent to any other address (e.g. a local VAT office or the National Advice Service) is not proper notification and may give rise to a penalty.

The notification should be prominently headed

Disclosure of use of listed scheme – Notification under paragraph 6(2) of Schedule 11A to the VAT Act 1994

and give details of

- business name (where notification is by the representative member of a VAT group notifying as a result of a group member being involved in a notifiable scheme, also the name of the member);
- address; and

- VAT registration number.

Otherwise, the only information that is required is the number of the listed scheme (see **4.6** below). [*SI 2004/1929*].

If a taxable person is using more than one scheme at the same time, HMRC must be informed about all of the schemes of each type that are being used and have not been previously reported.

HMRC will acknowledge receipt of notifications received at the above addresses. They will consider what action, if any, to take in respect of the notification and the taxable person will be contacted as necessary.

(VAT Notice 700/8/06, paras 5.2–5.6).

The listed schemes

[4.6] The Treasury have designated the schemes detailed below as listed schemes. The interpretation and examples within boxes are not part of the legislation but taken from VAT Notice 700/8.

A feature of a scheme is regarded as being present where

- it is present as a matter of fact; or
- a taxable person treats it as being present for the purpose of making a VAT return or error correction notification (formerly voluntary disclosure), even if it is not actually present (whether as a matter of law or for any other reason). [*SI 2004/1933, Art 2*].

HMRC give the example of where a feature of a scheme relies on a transaction being a supply for VAT purposes. If, for the purposes of making a return, a taxable person treats the transaction as being such a supply, the feature is regarded as being present (for the purposes of deciding whether disclosure is required), even if the court subsequently decides that there has been no supply as a matter of law. (VAT Notice 700/8/06, para 6.1.1).

(1) First grant of a major interest in a building

Where the relevant VAT period begins after 31 July 2004, any scheme comprising or including the first grant of a major interest in any building of a description falling within *VATA 1994, Sch 8 Group 5 item 1(a)* (see **42.1 LAND AND BUILDINGS: ZERO AND REDUCED RATE SUPPLIES AND DIY HOUSEBUILDERS**) where

- the grant is made to a person 'connected with' the grantor; and
- the grantor, or any body corporate treated as a member of a VAT group (see **27 GROUPS OF COMPANIES**) of which the grantor is a member, attributes to that grant input tax incurred by him
  - (a) in respect of a service charge relating to the building; or
  - (b) in connection with any extension, enlargement, repair, maintenance or refurbishment of the building, other than for remedying defects in the original construction.

A person is '*connected with*' another for the above purposes where

- one of them is an 'undertaking' in relation to which the other is a 'group undertaking', or
- both of them are connected to the same trust

and a person is connected to a trust where

- he is the settlor of the trust, a trustee or beneficiary of it; or
- he holds any shares in a company in accordance with the terms of the trust, or is a person on whose behalf such shares are held.

See **4.4** above for the meaning of '*undertaking*' and '*group undertaking*'.

[*SI 2004/1933, Reg 2, Sch 1; SI 2005/2009*].

This scheme aims to remove the VAT cost of extending, enlarging, repairing, refurbishing or servicing buildings that are zero-rated when sold by developers. Examples of the buildings concerned are houses, student halls of residence and buildings used by charities for non-business activities.

Examples

A housing landlord may seek to use this scheme to recover input tax on the major refurbishment of houses which he had constructed several years earlier. The landlord leases or sells them to a subsidiary in such a way that he attributes to that zero-rated disposal the VAT on the refurbishment (which may be undertaken either before or after the grant). The subsidiary may then simply lease the houses back to the landlord so that he can then let them on again to tenants.

The builder of new halls of residence may try to recover future input tax on repairs and maintenance on the buildings, even though his income from the property at that time will be exempt, by building into the initial zero-rated lease or sale a payment for, and agreement to provide, repairs and maintenance in the future.

(VAT Notice 700/8/06, para 6.2).

(2) Payment handling service

Where the relevant VAT period begins after 31 July 2004, any scheme comprising or including a retail supply of goods or services together with a 'linked supply' to the same customer, where the total consideration for the retail supply and the linked supply is no different, or not significantly different, from what would be payable for the retail sale alone.

'*Linked supply*' means a supply by the retailer or any other person that

- relates to the means of payment used for the retail supply; and
- is a supply of a description falling within *VATA 1994, Sch 9 Group 5* (see **23 FINANCIAL SERVICES**).

[*SI 2004/1933, Sch 1; SI 2005/2009*].

This scheme aims to reduce the VAT due on the advertised price of retail goods or services by transforming an element of the price into an exempt payment handling service (e.g. credit/debit card or cash handling).

> *Example*
>
> When a customer presents his goods at the till and decides to pay by credit or debit card, he may be informed that an element of the price is being paid to a separate company and is in consideration for processing or accepting his card as the means of payment. Agreements signed or agreed by the customer at the point of sale may be alleged to support this. There is no comparable reduction in the value for the goods if he chooses to pay by cash.

(VAT Notice 700/8/06, para 6.3).

(3) Value shifting

Where the relevant VAT period begins after 31 July 2004, any scheme comprising or including a 'retail supply' of goods or services together with a linked supply to the same customer where

- the 'linked supply' is a separate supply under the terms of any agreement made by the customer;
- part of the total consideration for the retail supply and the linked supply is attributed to the linked supply by the terms of any such agreement; and
- the total consideration for the retail supply and the linked supply is no different, or not significantly different, from what it would be for the retail supply alone.

'*Retail supply*' means a supply by retail upon which VAT is charged at standard rate.

'*Linked supply*' means a supply of goods or services made by the retailer or any other person which is zero-rated or exempt.

[*SI 2004/1933, Sch 1; SI 2005/2009*].

This scheme aims to transfer value from standard-rated retail supplies into linked zero-rated or exempt supplies.

> *Example*
>
> *Notification required.* A retail customer making a purchase is offered, at the point of sale, an insurance product with the goods. Rather than paying an additional amount for this cover, the customer is informed that the ticket price has now been apportioned to cover both the goods and the insurance. If the customer then declines the insurance, there is no reduction of the ticket price to reflect this. The overall price paid by the customer remains the same whether he takes the insurance or not.
>
> *Notification is not required.* Notification is not required under this scheme where the linked goods/services are supplied 'free', with no part of the price being attributed to that supply. Notification will also not be required for normal business promotion arrangements. For example, a retailer offers a 'meal deal' where customers can buy a sandwich, a soft drink and packet of crisps for a single price that is lower than the normal combined price of the three items. When apportioning the cost between the zero-rated and standard-rated items the retailer spreads the discount across all the goods supplied. These arrangements

are unlikely to be notifiable as each linked supply would not normally be subject to a separate agreement with the customer and the total amount payable is likely to be significantly different from what it would be for the standard-rated element alone.

(VAT Notice 700/8/06, para 6.4).

(4) Leaseback agreement

Where the relevant VAT period begins after 31 July 2004, any scheme comprising or including the supply of goods, or the leasing or letting on hire of goods ('the relevant supply') by a taxable person to a connected relevant person where

- the taxable person or another taxable person connected with him, including the relevant person, is entitled to credit for all the input tax arising on the purchase of the goods;
- the relevant person uses the goods in the course or furtherance of a business carried on by him, and for the purpose of that business, otherwise than for the purpose of selling or leasing or letting on hire the goods; and
- the relevant person or a person connected with him has directly or indirectly provided funds for meeting more than 90% of the cost of the goods.

'Relevant person' means any person who, in respect of the relevant supply, is not entitled to credit for all the input tax wholly attributable to the supplies he makes.

The provision of funds includes

- the making of a loan of funds; and
- the provision of any consideration for the issue of any shares or other securities issued wholly or partly for raising the funds.

The grant, assignment or surrender of a major interest in land is not a supply of goods for the purposes of this scheme.

See (1) above for the meaning of '*connected persons*'.

[*SI 2004/1933, Sch 1; SI 2005/2009*].

This scheme aims to defer or reduce the VAT cost of acquiring goods by a business that could recover all of the input tax charged to it on those goods if it were directly to buy them itself.

Examples

Notification required. A partly-exempt bank requires new computer equipment. The bank's corporate group purchases the equipment outright but, in order to reduce or remove the VAT effect of the irrecoverable input tax, the group acquires the computers in a subsidiary, which then leases them to the bank. Depending on the values and length of the lease, the intention is to spread the irrecoverable VAT cost, or to avoid a proportion of it altogether.

Notification not required. Notification is not required for leasing arrangements between unconnected parties. For example, an insurance company (A) requires a new computerised telephone system for its call centres. Rather than buy the equipment outright it decides to lease it and contracts with an unconnected commercial leasing business (B) to lease the equipment for a five-year period. As B has no expertise in sourcing the equipment required, it is agreed that A will purchase the equipment from its usual supplier. A then sells the equipment to B who leases it back to A.

(VAT Notice 700/8/06, para 6.5).

(5) Extended approval period

Where the relevant VAT period begins after 31 July 2004, any scheme comprising or including a retail supply of goods whereby

- the goods are sent or taken on approval or sale or return or similar terms;
- payment for the supply is required in full by the retailer before the expiry of any approval, return or similar period; and
- for the purposes of accounting for VAT, the retailer treats the goods as supplied on a date after the date on which payment is received in full.

[*SI 2004/1933, Sch 1; SI 2005/2009*].

This scheme aims to defer accounting for output tax on retail (including mail order) supplies of goods.

Example

A customer orders goods from an internet retailer. The retailer is paid on-line when the order is placed by the customer and delivery follows shortly thereafter. The retailer, either due to various guarantees or specific terms and conditions, seeks to account for VAT on the transaction at a later date, claiming the supply was on 'approval' or 'sale or return', despite the fact that payment has been received, delivery taken place and, in some cases, the goods have been consumed or used by the customer before the retailer regards the goods as having been adopted.

(VAT Notice 700/8/06, para 6.6).

(6) Groups: third party suppliers

Where the relevant VAT period begins after 31 July 2004, any scheme comprising or including supplies made to one or more group members by a 'specified body' in relation to which the 'benefits condition' is not satisfied. See **27.2 GROUPS OF COMPANIES** for whether a body is a '*specified body*' and whether the '*benefits condition*' is satisfied in relation to it.

[*SI 2004/1933, Sch 1; SI 2005/2009*].

This scheme aims to reduce or remove the VAT incurred on bought in taxable services (including outsourced services) by a user that cannot recover all of the input tax charged to it for those services.

> *Example*
>
> A partly exempt insurance company (A) wishes to buy in computer services from a third party company (B) but wants to reduce the irrecoverable VAT cost of doing this. A and B establish another company (C). A controls C by owning 51% of its shares and includes C in its VAT group. B owns the remaining shares, but these shares confer rights to 99% of the dividends declared by C and 99% of the assets on winding up. C holds the contract to provide the computer services required by A from B and employs the staff to provide the service. Besides the dividends, B also receives benefits from C in the form of a management charge for managing C's activity of providing computer services. As a result almost all of the benefits of C's activity accrue to B. Thus, B has access to the profits and benefits of the computing activity, and A hopes to avoid a large VAT cost as there will be no VAT charged within the VAT group.

(VAT Notice 700/8/06, para 6.7).

(7) Exempt education or vocational training by a non-profit making body

Where the relevant VAT period begins after 31 July 2004, any scheme comprising or including the conduct of a 'relevant business' by a 'non-profit making body' where

- it receives a 'relevant supply' from a connected taxable person who is not an 'eligible body'; and
- in any one prescribed accounting period the value of all such relevant supplies is equal to or more than 20% of the cost of making the supplies comprising the relevant business.

'Relevant business' means a business whose activities consist wholly or mainly of the supply of education or vocational training to persons who are not taxable persons.

'Non-profit making body' means a body within *VATA 1994, Sch 9 Group 6 Note 1(e)* (see **16.3**(*e*) **EDUCATION**) which is not otherwise within **16.3**(*a*)–(*f*) **EDUCATION.**

'Relevant supply' means the supply, including the leasing or letting on hire, for use in a relevant business of

- a capital item used in the course or furtherance of the relevant business, and for the purpose of that business, otherwise than solely for the purpose of selling the item;
- staff;
- management services;
- administration services; or
- accountancy services.

'Eligible body' has the meaning in *VATA 1994, Sch 9 Group 6 Note (1)* (see **16.3 EDUCATION**).

'Vocational training' has the meaning in *VATA 1994, Sch 9 Group 6 Note (3)* (see **16.7 EDUCATION**) but does not include vocational training of a description falling within

- *VATA 1994, Sch 9 Group 6 Item 5* (vocational training where the consideration is ultimately a charge to funds provided under *Employment and Training Act 1973, s 2, Employment and Training Act (NI) 1950, s 1A* or *Enterprises and New Towns (Scotland) Act 1990, s 2*); or
- *VATA 1994, Sch 9 Group 6 Item 5A* (vocational training where the consideration is ultimately a charge to funds provided by the Learning and Skills Council for England or the National Council for Education and Training for Wales under *Learning and Skills Act 2000, Parts I* or *II*).

See Scheme 1 above for 'connected persons'.

[*SI 2004/1933, Sch 1; SI 2005/2009*].

This scheme aims to allow a business providing education or training to avoid charging VAT on supplies to customers by arranging for those supplies to be made through a non-profit making body.

Example

A training company which normally trains private individuals and accounts for VAT out of its income, sets up a non-profit making body to provide the training in future, exempt from VAT. However, if the new body really is a non-profit making body, it will not be able to distribute its profits and the shareholders of the existing business will lose out. Various agreements are put in place to act as a mechanism to return those profits to the original training company. For example, the business premises may be leased, the rent for which is set at a rate directly related to the turnover or profit of the non-profit making body.

(VAT Notice 700/8/06, para 6.8).

(8) Taxable education or vocational training by a non-eligible body

Where the relevant VAT period begins after 31 July 2004, any scheme comprising or including the conduct of a 'relevant business' by a non-eligible body connected to an 'eligible body' where

- the non-eligible body benefits or intends to benefit the eligible body by way of gift, dividend or otherwise; or
- the eligible body makes any supply to the non-eligible body which is a relevant supply and, in any one prescribed accounting period, the value of all such relevant supplies is equal to or more than 20% of the cost of making the supplies comprising the relevant business.

'Eligible body' has the meaning in *VATA 1994, Sch 9 Group 6 Note (1)* (see **16.3 EDUCATION**).

'Relevant business' means a business whose activities consist wholly or mainly of the taxable supply of education or vocational training.

'Vocational training' has the meaning in *VATA 1994, Sch 9 Group 6 Note (3)* (see **16.7 EDUCATION**).

'Relevant supply' means the supply, or leasing or letting on hire, for use in a relevant business of

- a capital item used in the course or furtherance of the relevant business, and for the purpose of that business, otherwise than solely for the purpose of selling the item;
- staff;
- management services;
- administration services; or
- accounting services.

See Scheme 1 above for 'connected persons'.

[*SI 2004/1933, Sch 1; SI 2005/2009*].

This scheme aims to enable eligible bodies, that would otherwise make exempt supplies, to make taxable supplies and so avoid incurring irrecoverable input VAT. The typical customers involved would be bodies such as NHS Trusts and Local Authorities, but can also include normal commercial bodies.

Example

A university has a contract to provide training to employees of a NHS Trust. Normally, the training would be exempt from VAT and thus the VAT on costs involved in providing it would not be recoverable. To provide this training, the university needs to build a new facility but wishes to reduce the cost of the irrecoverable VAT on the building. The university establishes a subsidiary which is expressly allowed to distribute its profits, claiming exemption for its training supplies. The subsidiary may have little or no resources and will need to be provided with those resources by the university under various contracts and agreements. The university may also want to access any profits from this activity and may choose to do this by having the subsidiary gift those profits to it under the Gift Aid relief. As a result, the university hopes to transform the training into a fully taxable activity and recover the input tax on the new facility in the subsidiary, together with other taxable costs.

(VAT Notice 700/8/06, para 6.9).

(9) Cross-border face-value vouchers

Where the relevant VAT period begins after 31 July 2005, any scheme comprising or including the supply of a 'relevant service' by a person belonging in the UK (the UK supplier) to a person belonging in an EU country other than the UK (the non-UK recipient) where

- the service is used, or intended to be used, in whole or in part, by the non-UK recipient or any other person belonging in another EU country for the purposes of supplying a relevant service to a person belonging in the UK (the retail supply);
- the recipient of the retail supply uses a 'face-value voucher' issued by a person belonging in a country other than the UK to obtain that supply;
- the person making the retail supply does not account for VAT on that supply in the UK or any other EU country; and
- the UK supplier and the person making the retail supply are connected persons.

'Face-value voucher' means tokens, stamps or vouchers of a description falling within *VATA 1994, Sch 10A para 1(1)* (see **69.11 TRADE PROMOTION SCHEMES**).

'*Relevant service*' means a supply of a description specified in *VATA 1994, Sch 5 paras 7A–7C* (services supplied where received, see **65.22 SUPPLY: PLACE OF SUPPLY**).

References in this scheme to the retail supply do not include any supply of a relevant service made to a taxable person.

[*SI 2004/1933, Sch 1; SI 2005/1724; SI 2005/2009*].

This scheme aims to avoid paying VAT anywhere in the EU on 'relevant services' originating from UK suppliers and provided to UK residents who use face-value vouchers (such as phone cards) to pay for them.

Example

A UK company (C) contracts to supply telecommunication services to a related company (R) in another EU country (say France). A second related French company (I) issues phone cards and sells them to UK retailers. The retailers sell the cards to UK customers who use them to obtain telecommunication services from R. The cards say that, when they are used, R will provide the telecommunication services. R does this by buying in the services under its contract with C. R and I argue that no VAT is due in France or the UK. (Note that only taxable persons in the UK who are party to the scheme, such as U, are required to notify. UK retailers who are not party to the scheme (because they have no knowledge of their involvement in it) and parties who are not taxable persons in the UK are not required to notify.)

(VAT Notice 700/8/06, para 6.10).

(10) Surrender of relevant lease

Where the relevant VAT period begins after 31 July 2005, any scheme comprising or including the 'surrender' by an occupier of a building of a 'relevant lease, tenancy or licence to occupy' where

- the occupier or any person connected to him is a 'relevant person';
- the building is a capital item for the purposes of the capital goods scheme (see **10.2 CAPITAL GOODS SCHEME**);
- before the surrender, the occupier paid 'relevant VAT' and was not entitled to full credit for, or refund of, that VAT under any provision of *VATA 1994* or *Regulations*;
- following the surrender, the occupier continues to occupy at least 80% of the area previously occupied; and
- following the surrender, the occupier pays no relevant VAT or pays less than 50% of the relevant VAT paid before the surrender.

'Surrender' includes any termination by the occupier of the relevant lease, tenancy or licence to occupy where he has entered into any agreement, arrangement or understanding (whether legally binding or not) with the lessor regarding that termination.

'Relevant lease, tenancy or licence to occupy' means any lease of, tenancy of or licence to occupy the building granted or assigned to the occupier where the option to tax has been exercised (and not revoked) in relation to the building.

'Relevant person' means any person who

- is a lessor of the building;
- is an owner of the building for the purposes of the capital goods scheme; and
- has opted to tax the building.

'Relevant VAT' means VAT on rent paid or payable by the occupier in relation to the building.

'Building' includes any part of that building.

[*SI 2004/1933, Sch 1; SI 2005/1724; SI 2005/2009*].

This scheme aims to allow a person to escape, or substantially reduce, the VAT incurred on opted lease rentals whilst remaining in occupation of the building.

> *Example*
>
> Included are arrangements where
>
> - The occupier surrenders or terminates a taxable lease early and, despite the existence of an option to tax, the connected landlord makes a grant of a new lease, or sells the building to the occupier, exempt from VAT by reason of the option to tax disapplication rules.
> - The occupier, who is also a landlord further back in a chain of leases, arranges for all of the leases to be surrendered, leaving the occupier with the building (possibly paying a small amount of taxable ground rent to the ultimate freeholder).

(VAT Notice 700/8/06, para 6.11).

Hallmarked schemes: general

[4.7] In addition to the listed schemes falling within the provisions in **4.3** to **4.6** above, the Treasury can designate certain provisions (including any agreements, transactions, acts or courses of conduct) that it appears to them are, or are likely to be, included in (or associated with) schemes entered into for the purpose of enabling any person to obtain a tax advantage. See **4.3** above for the meaning of '*obtaining a tax advantage*'.

The Treasury can designate a provision even though it considers that the provision is likely to be a feature of schemes that are not tax avoidance schemes.

[*VATA 1994, Sch 11A paras 2, 4, 5; FA 2004, Sch 2 para 2; F(No 2)A 2005, Sch 1 paras 3, 4*].

'**Scheme**' includes any arrangement, transaction or series of transactions. [*VATA 1994, Sch 11A para 1; FA 2004, Sch 2 para 2*].

It is not a scheme *in itself* to

- engage someone to ensure that all the input tax entitlement is claimed,
- utilise an extra-statutory concession or trade facilitation method open to all,
- use the grouping provisions, or
- negotiate a new partial exemption method

even if it involves a hallmark of avoidance. But these features may form part of a scheme.

(VAT Notice 700/8/06, para 7.3).

Liability to notify hallmarked schemes

[4.8] A *taxable person* must notify HMRC of the use of a hallmarked scheme when all of the following conditions are met.

Condition 1

The total value of his VAT-exclusive taxable supplies and exempt supplies exceeded:

- £10 million in the year immediately prior to the 'affected VAT return period', or any of the VAT return periods that are the subject of an 'affected claim'; or
- the 'appropriate proportion' of £10 million in the VAT return period immediately prior to the affected VAT return period, or any of the VAT return periods that are the subject of an affected claim.

The '*appropriate proportion*' means the proportion which the length of that VAT period bears to twelve months (i.e. one-quarter where quarterly VAT returns are prepared and one-twelfth where monthly VAT returns are prepared).

See Condition 4 below for '*affected VAT return period*' and '*affected claim*'.

See also **4.12** below for powers given to HMRC to prevent any artificial separation of business activities in an attempt to reduce turnover below the above limits.

Group undertakings

If the taxable person is a 'group undertaking', the conditions must be met by the taxable person *plus* every other group undertaking (i.e. the criteria apply to the whole group). For these purposes, the definitions in *Companies Act 2006, s 1161* apply (so that 'group' does not necessarily mean 'VAT group'). The group will comprise the undertaking in question, together with any undertaking which is

- a parent undertaking or a subsidiary undertaking of that undertaking; or
- a subsidiary undertaking of any parent undertaking of that undertaking.

For the purpose of calculating turnover, intra-corporate group transactions are included but intra-VAT group transactions are ignored. (VAT Notice 700/8/06, para 7.6).

Condition 2

The taxable person is a party to a scheme that is not a listed scheme (see **4.3** to **4.6** above).

A person is a party to a scheme if he knowingly takes part in it but not if he

- is unwittingly involved in any of the steps of the scheme (i.e. has no knowledge of either the existence of the scheme or the role he plays in it); or
- acts purely in an advisory capacity.

(VAT Notice 700/8/06, para 3.3.1).

Condition 3

The main purpose, or one of the main purposes, of the scheme is to obtain a tax advantage (for any person). See **4.3** above for the meaning of 'obtaining a tax advantage'.

There is no one factor that determines whether the obtaining of a tax advantage is the main, or one of the main, purposes of a scheme. HMRC's view is that all circumstances need to be taken into consideration including

- the overall objectives of the arrangements and transactions (including the objectives of any wider corporate or VAT group to which the parties to the scheme belong and the objectives of any persons or businesses who control the parties); and
- whether the introduction of any unnecessary, complex or costly steps would have taken place were it not for the tax advantage that can be obtained.

In general, it is likely that the main purpose test would be met where, were it not for any VAT advantage arising, either the arrangements would not have been implemented or would have been implemented in a different manner. Similarly, where there are two or more ways of carrying out a genuine commercial objective and the choice is determined on grounds other than the potential VAT saving, it is unlikely the main purpose test would be met, even though a VAT advantage arises when compared to adopting one or more of the alternatives.

(VAT Notice 700/8/06, para 7.4.4).

Condition 4

One of the following relevant events occurs.

- In the return for the '*affected VAT return period*', the amount of VAT shown as payable by/to the taxable person is less than/greater than it would be but for the use of a hallmarked scheme to which he is party.
- The taxable person makes a claim (the '*affected claim*') for the repayment of output tax or an increase in credit for input tax in respect of which he has previously delivered a return and the amount claimed is greater than it would be but for a hallmarked scheme.

- In the return for a VAT period (the '*affected VAT return period*') beginning after 31 July 2005, the amount of the taxable person's 'non-deductible tax' is less than it would be but for a hallmarked scheme.

'*Non-deductible tax*' means

(i) input tax for which he is not entitled to credit under *VATA 1994, s 25*; and
(ii) VAT on any supply of goods or services to him, or on the acquisition or importation of goods by him, which is not input tax and in respect of which he is entitled to a refund from HMRC under any provision of *VATA 1994*.

Condition 5

The scheme contains one or more of the hallmarks of avoidance. See **4.11** below.

Condition 6

The taxable person has not on a previous occasion provided HMRC with prescribed information under these provisions.

A scheme need only be notified once. If a taxable person starts a new scheme that is 'structured in the same way' as a previously notified scheme, he need not notify this new scheme. By 'structured in the same way', HMRC mean that the details of the scheme required to be notified under **4.9** below are the same as a previously notified scheme, even though the parties to the scheme and the hallmarks may be different.

However, if a taxable person starts a new scheme that is structured in a materially different way to a previously notified scheme, he must, subject to the necessary conditions being met, notify use of that scheme, irrespective of whether the hallmarks are the same.

(VAT Notice 700/8/06, para 7.7).

Condition 7

The taxable person has not been provided with a scheme number by someone who has registered the scheme with HMRC.

If someone has already registered the hallmarked scheme being used under the voluntary registration scheme (see **4.10** below) and has advised the taxable person of the scheme reference number allocated to it by HMRC (prefixed by the letters VRS), the taxable person is not required to notify HMRC. (VAT Notice 700/8/06, para 7.8).

[*VATA 1994, Sch 11A paras 6, 7; FA 2004, Sch 2 para 2; F(No 2)A 2005, Sch 1 paras 5, 6; SI 2008/954, Art 20*].

Schemes involving several parties

If a listed scheme involves more than one party, all the parties to that scheme are obliged to notify HMRC if they meet the conditions set out above. However, the parties concerned can make a joint notification. The notification should make it clear that it is a joint notification and who all the parties are that are making the notification. (VAT Notice 700/8/06, para 3.3.4).

Protective notifications

If a taxable person is unsure whether all of the relevant tests for notification are met, he may make a protective notification, explaining which test or tests is causing difficulty and why. (VAT Notice 700/8/06, para 7.2).

Notifying use of hallmarked schemes to HMRC

Time limit for notification

[4.9] Where a taxable person must notify HMRC of the use of a hallmarked scheme under **4.8** above, he must do so within 30 days from the end of

- the last day for submission of the return for the 'affected VAT return period';
- the date the 'affected claim' is made; or
- where HMRC make a direction under **4.12** below (artificial splitting of business), the last day for submission of the first VAT return made to HMRC following the direction.

See **4.8** above for '*affected VAT return period*' and '*affected claim*'.

[*VATA 1994, Sch 11A para 6; FA 2004, Sch 2 para 2; SI 2004/1929; SI 2005/2009*].

HMRC will accept early notifications (e.g. before the relevant event has taken place) provided the scheme has been implemented. (VAT Notice 700/8/06, para 8.1.1).

Method of notification

The following provisions relating to notification as set out in VAT Notice 700/8 have the force of law.

HMRC must be notified of the use of a hallmarked scheme either by e-mail to: vat.avoidance.disclosures.bst@hmrc.gsi.gov.uk or in writing to:

VAT Avoidance Disclosures Unit
Anti-Avoidance Group (Intelligence)
HM Revenue and Customs
1st Floor, 22 Kingsway London WC2B 6NR

Notification sent to any other address (e.g. a local VAT office or the National Advice Service) is not proper notification and may give rise to a penalty.

The notification should be prominently headed

Disclosure of use of hallmarked scheme – Notification under paragraph 6(3) of Schedule 11A to the VAT Act 1994 and give details of

- business name (where notification is by the representative member of a VAT group notifying as a result of a group member being involved in a notifiable scheme, also the name of the member);
- address; and
- VAT registration number.

Information to be notified

All of the following information must be provided to the extent that it is known. Explanations should be given of why any information cannot be provided.

- A statement as to which hallmark or hallmarks listed in **4.11** below are included in or associated with the scheme being notified.
  This need not be a standalone part of the notification and can be included as part of the general explanation of the working of the scheme. If unsure whether a feature is a hallmark, this should be stated. (VAT Notice 700/8/06, para 8.5).
- How the scheme gives rise to a 'tax advantage', including, to the extent that it is material to the tax advantage:
  (a) A description of each arrangement, transaction or series of transactions.
  Sufficient information must be provided to allow HMRC to understand how the tax advantage is obtained. The degree of information to be provided will vary from scheme to scheme but often the inclusion of a summary of the aims of the scheme and a diagrammatic representation of its structure, showing the participants, transaction flows, etc. will be of assistance. Only generic information need be provided, not detail that is specific to the particular circumstances (e.g. a step of the scheme could be described as 'building is leased to Company A' rather than '1 High Street is leased to Bank plc'). Copies of contracts and other documents do not need to be submitted. However, if it is easier to explain the scheme by referring to the specific detail, this may be done and supplementary documentation may be submitted if preferred. (VAT Notice 700/8/06, para 8.4.1).
  (b) The sequence of those arrangements, etc.
  The precise sequence should be made clear. HMRC recommend listing these as 'Step 1', 'Step 2', etc. (VAT Notice 700/8/06, para 8.4.2).
  (c) The timing, or the intervals between, those arrangements, etc.
  Explanation should be given, for example, if transactions are
  (i) due to take place within a short period of time of each other to take advantage of a VAT rule;
  (ii) due to take place over a long period to cause a VAT 'drip feed' effect; or
  (iii) timed to miss or bridge accounting periods.
  (VAT Notice 700/8/06, para 8.4.3).
  (d) The goods or services involved.

- How the involvement of any party to the scheme contributes to the obtaining of the tax advantage.
- Any provision having the force of law in the UK or elsewhere relied upon as giving rise to the tax advantage.

There is no obligation to quantify the amount or expected amount of the tax advantage. (VAT Notice 700/8/06, para 8.4).

See **4.3** above for the meaning of obtaining a '*tax advantage*'. For these purposes, a tax advantage is considered to be obtained (and any arrangement, transaction or series of transactions is considered to take place) provided a taxable person treats it as having been obtained or taken place for the purposes of a VAT return or a claim for repayment of output tax or an increase in credit for input tax.

[*SI 2004/1929*].

Acknowledgement by HMRC

HMRC will acknowledge notifications received at the above addresses. If all the required information is not received, the taxable person will be asked to provide it. If this information is not supplied within the time limit for making a notification (see above), the taxable person will be liable to a penalty. See **52.27 PENALTIES**. (VAT Notice 700/8/06, para 8.9).

Voluntary registration of hallmarked schemes

[4.10] Any person may, at any time, make a voluntary notification to HMRC of the details of a hallmarked scheme (e.g. a business that devises or markets a scheme may wish to do this to relieve its clients of the obligation of having to notify HMRC of the use of the scheme). To do so, the person should notify HMRC, and provide them with the information, as set out in **4.9** above. The notification should make clear that it is a voluntary notification.

HMRC will acknowledge the notification within ten working days of its receipt and normally state the reference number they have allocated to the scheme.

[*VATA 1994, Sch 11A para 9; FA 2004, Sch 2 para 2; SI 2004/1929*].

The hallmarks

[4.11] The Treasury have designated the following as provisions associated with ((1) to (3) below) or included ((4) to (8) below) in schemes.

A provision is treated as fitting a description listed even if it, or any feature of it, is not actually present (whether as a matter of law or for any other reason), provided a taxable person has treated that feature as being present for the purpose of making a VAT return or a claim for the repayment of output tax or an increase in credit for input tax. [*SI 2004/1933, Art 2*].

(1) Confidentiality condition

Where the relevant VAT period begins after 31 July 2004, an agreement preventing or limiting the disclosure of how a scheme gives rise to a tax advantage. [*SI 2004/1933, Sch 2; SI 2005/2009*].

This hallmark is aimed at confidentiality conditions that are intended to protect the competitive advantage of a promoter or creator of the scheme over other promoters and applies where

- a specific condition of confidentiality is imposed; or
- a client specifically undertakes (either in writing or verbally) not to reveal details of how a particular scheme gives rise to a tax advantage.

It is standard practice for advisers to include a 'general confidentiality condition' within their terms of engagement, prohibiting the client from passing on advice to third parties. HMRC do not regard such a clause as being a confidentiality condition if it is simply imposed in relation to all advice, not merely the scheme in question. But HMRC do consider it a hallmark if

- it is introduced specifically to prevent or limit a person from revealing details of how a particular scheme gives rise to a tax advantage; or
- it is specifically drawn to a client's attention by an adviser when introducing a scheme to the client in order to prohibit or limit the client from revealing details of how that particular scheme gives rise to a tax advantage.

(VAT Notice 700/8/06, para 10.2).

(2) The sharing of the tax advantage with another party to the scheme or with the promoter

Where the relevant VAT period begins after 31 July 2004, an agreement that the tax advantage to a person accruing from the operation of the scheme be shared to any extent with another party to it or another person promoting it.

A person is a '*promoter of a scheme*' if, in the course of a trade, profession or business which involves the provision to other persons of services relating to taxation

- he is to any extent responsible for the design of the proposed arrangements; or
- he invites persons to enter into contracts for the implementation of the proposed arrangements.

[*SI 2004/1933, Sch 2; SI 2005/2009*].

(3) Fee payable to a promoter which is in whole or in part contingent on tax savings from the scheme

Where the relevant VAT period begins after 31 July 2004, an agreement that payment to a promoter of the scheme be contingent in whole or in part on the tax advantage accruing from the operation of the scheme.

See (2) above for the meaning of '*promoter of a scheme*'.

[*SI 2004/1933, Sch 2; SI 2005/2009*].

(4) Prepayment between connected parties

Where the relevant VAT period begins after 31 July 2004, a payment for a supply of goods or services between connected persons

(a) before the basic tax point for the supply (see **66.8 SUPPLY: TIME OF SUPPLY** for supplies of goods and **66.18 SUPPLY: TIME OF SUPPLY** for supplies of services) or, where applicable, the special tax point that applies to goods supplied on sale or return (see **66.12 SUPPLY: TIME OF SUPPLY**); or

(b) where the supply is a 'continuous supply' and the payment is before the goods or services are provided.

A supply is a '*continuous supply*' if it is a supply to which any of the following applies:

- *SI 1995/2518, Reg 85* (leases treated as supplies of goods, see **66.13 SUPPLY: TIME OF SUPPLY**).
- *SI 1985/2518, Reg 86* (supplies of water, gas or any form of power, heat, refrigeration or other cooling, or ventilation, see **66.15 SUPPLY: TIME OF SUPPLY**).
- *SI 1985/2518, Reg 90* (continuous supply of services, see **66.19 SUPPLY: TIME OF SUPPLY**).
- *SI 1985/2518, Reg 91* (royalties and similar payments, see **66.20 SUPPLY: TIME OF SUPPLY**).
- *SI 1985/2518, Reg 93* (supplies in the construction industry, see **42.19 LAND AND BUILDINGS: ZERO AND REDUCED RATE SUPPLIES AND DIY HOUSEBUILDERS**).

For the purposes of (*b*) above goods or services are provided at the time when, and to the extent that, the recipient receives the benefit of them.

A person is '*connected with*' another for the above purposes where

- one of them is an 'undertaking' in relation to which the other is a 'group undertaking', or
- both of them are connected to the same trust

and a person is connected to a trust where

- he is the settlor of the trust, a trustee or beneficiary of it; or
- he holds any shares in a company in accordance with the terms of the trust, or is a person on whose behalf such shares are held.

See **4.4** above for the meaning of '*undertaking*' and '*group undertaking*'.

[*SI 2004/1933, Art 2, Sch 2; SI 2005/2009*].

(5) Funding by loan, share subscription or subscription in securities

Where the relevant VAT period begins after 31 July 2004, the funding (in whole or in part) of a supply of goods or services between connected persons by means of a loan between connected persons or the subscription for shares in, or securities issued by, a connected person.

See (1) above for the meaning of '*connected persons*'.

[*SI 2004/1933, Art 2, Sch 2; SI 2005/2009*].

(6) Off-shore loops

Where the relevant VAT period begins after 31 July 2004, a supply of 'relevant services' which is used or intended to be used, in whole or in part, directly or indirectly, in making to a person belonging in the UK, a supply which is zero-rated, exempt or treated as made in another country (and not in the UK) by virtue of *VATA 1994, s 7(10)* (place of supply of services, see **65.15 SUPPLY: PLACE OF SUPPLY**).

'*Relevant services*' are either

- services which are exempt insurance services or exempt financial services (other than the management of an authorised unit trust scheme or an open-ended investment company) and which are
  - (a) supplied to a person who belongs outside the EU; or
  - (b) directly linked to the export of goods to a place outside the EU, insofar as they are supplies falling within *VATA 1994, Sch 9 Group 5 item 2* (the making of any advance or any credit, see **23.11 FINANCIAL SERVICES**); or
  - (c) consist of the provision of intermediary insurance services within *VATA 1994, Sch 9 Group 2 item 4* (see **36.13 INSURANCE**) or intermediary financial services within *VATA 1994, Sch 9 Group 5 item 5* (see **23.25 FINANCIAL SERVICES**) in relation to any transaction within (a) or (b) above; or
- a supply falling within *VATA 1994, Sch 5 paras 1–8* (see **65.22 SUPPLY: PLACE OF SUPPLY**) where the recipient of that supply belongs in a country, other than the Isle of Man, which is not an EU country.

[*SI 2004/1933, Sch 2; SI 2005/2009*].

(7) Property transactions between connected persons

Where the relevant VAT period begins after 31 July 2004, a 'relevant grant' where

- the grantor or grantee of the interest or right is a person who is not entitled to credit for all the input tax wholly attributable to the supplies he makes;
- any work of construction, alteration, demolition, repair, maintenance or civil engineering has been or is to be carried out on the land; and
- the grant is made to a person connected with the grantor.

'*Relevant grant*' means the grant of any interest in or right over land or of any licence to occupy land or, in relation to land in Scotland, any personal right to call for or be granted any such interest or right, other than a grant of a description falling within *VATA 1994, Sch 8 Group 5 Item 1* (first grant of a major interest by a person constructing a building designed for dwelling, or intended for use solely for residential or charitable purposes; or by a person converting a non-residential building to residential use, see **42.1 LAND AND BUILDINGS: ZERO AND REDUCED RATE SUPPLIES AND DIY HOUSEBUILDERS**) or *VATA 1994, Sch 8 Group 6 Item 1* (first grant of a major interest in a protected building by a person reconstructing it, see **42.3 LAND AND BUILDINGS: ZERO AND REDUCED RATE SUPPLIES AND DIY HOUSEBUILDERS**).

'*Grant*' includes an assignment or surrender and the supply made by the person to whom an interest is surrendered when there is a reverse surrender. See (1) above for '*connected persons*'.

[*SI 2004/1933, Art 2, Sch 2; SI 2005/2009*].

(8) Issue of face-value vouchers

Where the relevant VAT period begins after 31 July 2005, the issue of 'face-value vouchers' for consideration except where

- the issuer expects, on reasonable grounds, that at least 75% of the face value of the vouchers will be redeemed within three years of the date on which the vouchers were issued; and
- the vouchers were issued to 'relevant persons'.

A '*relevant person*' is

(a) any person who is not connected with the issuer; or
(b) any body corporate which is a member of the same VAT group as the issuer; and does not intend to supply the vouchers, directly or indirectly, to any person connected with the issuer outside that VAT group.

'*Face-value vouchers*' means tokens, stamps or vouchers of a description falling within *VATA 1994, Sch 10A para 1(1)* (see **69.11 TRADE PROMOTION SCHEMES**).

[*SI 2004/1933, Sch 2; SI 2005/1724; SI 2005/2009*].

The expected redemption rate is measured by reference to the face value of the vouchers taken together. HMRC give the following examples.

- A business issues £1m worth of vouchers and expects £900,000 worth of those vouchers to be redeemed. That is a 90% expected redemption rate (irrespective of whether the expectation is actually met).
- A business issues vouchers that can be partly redeemed and expects 100% of them to be redeemed but on average only 30% of the value to be redeemed. That would be a 30% expected redemption rate (irrespective of whether the expectation is actually met).

(VAT Notice 700/8/06, para 10.9.1).

Power of HMRC to exclude exemption from duty to notify

[4.12] Under normal circumstances, a taxable person does not have to disclose the use of a listed or hallmarked scheme where turnover is below certain limits (see 'Condition 1' in **4.4** and **4.8** above respectively).

The following provisions are, however, designed to prevent the maintenance or creation of any 'artificial' separation of business activities carried on by two or more persons from resulting in any avoidance of the obligations to notify schemes. In determining whether any separation of business activities is '*artificial*', consideration must be given to the extent to which the different persons carrying on those activities are closely bound to one another by financial, economic and organisational links. See **8.7 BUSINESS** for examples illustrating the types of factors indicative of these links.

HMRC may make a direction under which the persons specified therein become treated as a single taxable person carrying on the activities of a business described in the direction with effect from the date of the direction or such later date as is specified. Where this is done, if that single taxable person would not be excluded from notifying a scheme, then the persons named in the direction cannot be excluded.

The direction must be served on each person named in it and remains in force until it is revoked or replaced by a further direction.

Before making a direction naming any person, HMRC must be satisfied that

- he is making or has made taxable or exempt supplies;
- the activities in the course of which he makes those supplies form only part of certain activities, the other activities being carried on concurrently or previously (or both) by one or more other persons; and
- if all the taxable and exempt supplies of the business described in the direction were taken into account, the turnover would exceed the minimum turnover limits.

[*VATA 1994, Sch 11A para 8; FA 2004, Sch 2 para 2*].

Specific anti-avoidance provisions

[4.13] Anti-avoidance legislation is intended to counteract transactions designed to avoid taxation, but *bona fide* transactions may sometimes be caught also. The main provisions relating to VAT are listed below.

Provisions in *VATA 1994*

- Group supplies using an overseas member. [*VATA 1994, s 43(2A)–(2E)*]. See **27.6 GROUPS OF COMPANIES.**
- Groups of companies – eligibility rules. [*VATA 1994, s 43D*]. See **27.2 GROUPS OF COMPANIES.**
- Acquisition of a business as a going concern by a partly-exempt group. [*VATA 1994, s 44*]. See **27.7 GROUPS OF COMPANIES.**
- Missing trader intra-Community fraud. [*VATA 1994, s 55A*]. See **4.14** below.
- Joint and several liability for unpaid VAT. [*VATA 1994, s 77A*]. See **31.3 HMRC: POWERS.**
- Place of supply of services – transitional provisions. [*VATA 1994, s 97A*]. See **65.13 SUPPLY: PLACE OF SUPPLY.**
- Disaggregation of business activities (business splitting). [*VATA 1994, Sch 1 para 1A*]. See **8.5 BUSINESS.**
- Registration by overseas traders in respect of disposals of assets for which a VAT repayment is claimed. [*VATA 1994, Sch 3A*]. See **59.26 REGISTRATION.**
- Telecommunications services. [*VATA 1994, Sch 5 para 7A*]. See **65.22 SUPPLY: PLACE OF SUPPLY.**
- Transactions between connected persons. [*VATA 1994, Sch 6 para 1*]. See **71.19 VALUATION.**

- Demonstration cars. [*VATA 1994, Sch 6 para 1A*]. See **45.7 MOTOR CARS.**
- Direct (party plan) selling. [*VATA 1994, Sch 6 para 2*]. See **71.23 VALUATION.**
- Heated water. [*VATA 1994, Sch 8 Group 2 Item 2(c)*]. See **74.2 ZERO-RATED SUPPLIES.**
- Groups of companies – registration. [*VATA 1994, Sch 9A*]. See **27.5 GROUPS OF COMPANIES.**
- Option to tax land and buildings. [*VATA 1994, Sch 10*]. See **41.12** and **41.17 LAND AND BUILDINGS: EXEMPT SUPPLIES AND OPTION TO TAX.**
- Face value vouchers. [*VATA 1994, Sch 10A*]. See **69.11 TRADE PROMOTION SCHEMES.**
- Power to require security. [*VATA 1994, Sch 11 para 4*]. See **31.1 HMRC: POWERS.**
- Duty to notify certain avoidance schemes. [*VATA 1994, Sch 11A*]. See **4.3** above.

Provisions in the *VAT Regulations 1995*

- Construction industry stage payments. [*SI 1995/2518, Reg 93*]. See **42.19 LAND AND BUILDINGS: ZERO AND REDUCED RATE SUPPLIES AND DIY HOUSEBUILDERS.**
- Assignment of debts. [*SI 1995/2518, Reg 94A*]. See **66.6 SUPPLY: TIME OF SUPPLY.**
- Continuous supplies of services – time of supply. [*SI 1995/2518, Reg 94B*]. See **66.19 SUPPLY: TIME OF SUPPLY.**
- Grants of land – time of supply. [*SI 1995/2518, Reg 94B*]. See **66.13 SUPPLY: TIME OF SUPPLY.**
- Long leases and tenancies – time of supply. [*SI 1995/2518, Reg 94B*]. See **66.13 SUPPLY: TIME OF SUPPLY.**
- Power, heat, water and gas – time of supply. [*SI 1994/2518, Reg 94B*]. See **66.15 SUPPLY: TIME OF SUPPLY.**
- Partial exemption – special method over-ride. [*SI 1995/2518, Regs 102A–102C*]. See **49.10 PARTIAL EXEMPTION.**
- Partial exemption – standard method over-ride. [*SI 1995/2518, Regs 107A–107C*]. See **49.9 PARTIAL EXEMPTION.**
- Attribution of input tax – financial services. [*SI 1995/2518, Reg 103(B)*]. See **49.12 PARTIAL EXEMPTION.**
- Capital goods scheme generally and specifically disposals of capital items during the period of adjustment. [*SI 1995/2518, Regs 112–116*]. See **10 CAPITAL GOODS SCHEME** and specifically **10.7 CAPITAL GOODS SCHEME.**
- Warehoused goods. [*SI 1995/2518, Reg 145K*]. See **72.5 WAREHOUSED GOODS AND FREE ZONES.**
- Bad debt relief – repayment of refund on assigned debts. [*SI 1995/2518, Reg 171*]. See **7.12 BAD DEBT RELIEF.**

Other provisions

- Telecommunications services. [*SI 1992/3121, Art 7*]. See **65.22 SUPPLY: PLACE OF SUPPLY.**

- Margin scheme supplies acquired as part of a TOGC. [*SI 1992/3122, Art 8*]. See **61.4 SECOND-HAND GOODS.**
- Leased cars. [*SI 1992/3222, Art 7*]. See **45.11 MOTOR CARS.**
- Private use of services following a TOGC. [*SI 1993/1507*]. See **47.7 OUTPUT TAX.**
- Land, buildings and civil engineering works used for private purposes – use of *Lennartz* mechanism for recovery of input tax. [*SI 1993/1507*]. See **34.7 INPUT TAX** and **47.7 OUTPUT TAX.**
- Margin scheme supplies acquired as part of a TOGC – motor cars. [*SI 1995/1268, Art 12*]. See **61.4 SECOND-HAND GOODS.**

Reverse charge: missing trader intra-community fraud

[4.14] As a general rule, the taxable person who makes a taxable supply is the person liable to pay the VAT on that supply to the tax authorities. However, to counter missing trader intra-community fraud ('MTIC'), the UK was granted a derogation from *Directive 2006/112/EC, Art 193* allowing it to introduce legislation to make the customer the person liable to register for VAT (if not already registered) and account for and pay the VAT on the supply of specified goods which are commonly used to perpetrate the fraud.

This 'reverse charge' procedure was introduced with effect from 1 June 2007 and applies, with some exclusions, to supplies of mobile phones and computer chips which are made by one VAT-registered business to another and valued at £5,000 and over. VAT-registered businesses which sell such goods will need to consider whether the reverse charge applies to their transactions. Businesses which purchase such goods must consider whether they need to register for VAT (if not already registered) and must account for VAT on those purchases to HMRC.

Full details are given in **4.15** to **4.23** below.

Emissions allowances

Directive 2010/23/EU inserts *art 199a* into *Directive 2006/112/EC* and permits, until 30 June 2015 and for a minimum period of two years, the application of the reverse charge to the trading of greenhouse gas emissions allowances. With effect from 8 April 2010, *VATA 1994 s 55A* (customers to account for tax on supplies of goods of a kind used in missing trader intra-community fraud) was extended to services. From 1 November 2010 the reverse charge applies to emissions allowances supplied in the UK. The zero rate for such supplies has been withdrawn from the same date (see **74.12 ZERO-RATED SUPPLIES**).

[*FA 2010, s 50; SI 2010/2549; SI 2010/2239, Art 6*].

Liability to register for VAT

[4.15] Where

- a taxable (but not a zero-rated) supply of goods or (from 8 April 2010) services ('*the relevant supply*') is made to a person ('*the recipient*'),

- the relevant supply is of specified goods or services falling within **4.16** below but is not an excepted supply within **4.17** below, and
- the total value of the relevant supply (excluding VAT), and of any other supplies to which these provisions apply (excluding VAT) made to the recipient in the month in which the relevant supply is made, exceeds £1,000,

the relevant supply and those other supplies (both excluding VAT) are to be treated for VAT registration purposes as

(a) taxable supplies of the recipient (as well as taxable supplies of the supplier), and
(b) in so far as the recipient is supplied in connection with the carrying on by him of any business, supplies made by him in the course or furtherance of that business,

but only in so far as their total value exceeds £1,000.

Nothing in (*b*) above requires any supply to be disregarded for the purposes of VAT registration on the grounds that it is a supply of capital assets of the recipient's business.

[*VATA 1994, s 55A(1)–(5); FA 2006, s 19(1); FA 2010, s 50*].

The effect of this is that a non-registered business must consider whether the purchase of goods or services, to which the reverse charge would apply if it were registered for VAT, makes it liable to be registered for VAT. This is because such purchases must be included when considering whether the value of its taxable supplies has exceeded the VAT registration threshold. The first £1,000 of such purchases per month is disregarded but any excess does count, along with the other taxable supplies of the business, towards its liability to register for VAT. That value must be included in calculating both the value of taxable supplies in the previous twelve months or less, and in the expected value of taxable supplies in the next 30 days alone, for the purpose of applying these tests for liability to register for VAT.

Specified goods or services

[4.16] Subject to the excepted goods in **4.17** below, goods or services on which customers must account for VAT under the reverse charge are as follows.

Mobile telephones

Mobile telephones, whether or not they have any function in addition to the transmitting and receiving of spoken messages. [*SI 2010/2239, Art 5(a)*].

The definition of a mobile phone takes its everyday meaning in the UK and includes the following.

- Any handsets which have a mobile phone function (i.e. the transmitting and receiving of spoken messages), whether or not they have any other function. It therefore includes other communication devices, such as Blackberrys.

- Mobile phones supplied with accessories (such as a charger, battery, cover or handsfree kit) as a single package.
- Pre-pay (or 'pay as you go') mobile phones, whether or not the selling price includes an element attributable to the cost of future use of the phones.
- Mobile phones locked to a network but not supplied with a contract for airtime.

But the reverse charge does not apply to the following.

- Mobile phones which are supplied with a contract for airtime (see **4.17** below).
- Mobile phone accessories which are supplied separately from a mobile phone.
- Walkie-talkies.
- WiFi phones unless also intended for use with mobile phone networks.
- 3G data cards and WiFi cards.

(VAT Notice 735, para 2.2).

Integrated circuit devices

Integrated circuit devices, such as central processing units and microprocessor units, in a state prior to integration into end-user products. [*SI 2010/2239, Art 5(b)*].

The terminology surrounding computer chips can be confusing. As a guide, all computer chips covered by the reverse charge fall within the tariff commodity code 8542 3190 00. Included are

- small integrated circuits (i.e. Central Processing Units or CPUs);
- discrete integrated circuit devices (i.e. Microprocessors or Microprocessor Units (MPUs) and Microcontrollers or Microcontroller Units (MCUs)); and
- chipsets – the dedicated cluster of integrated circuits which support MPUs.

The reverse charge applies to such items when they are in a state prior to integration into end-user products, or where they are sold separately and not as part of an assembled item (e.g. a motherboard).

Items such as computer servers, laptops or desktop units are excluded from the scope of the reverse charge.

(VAT Notice 735, para 2.3).

Emission allowances

A transfer of

- an allowance within *Art 3* of *Directive 2003/87/EC* (which established the scheme for greenhouse gas emission allowance trading within the European Union);
- an emission reduction unit that can be used by an operator for compliance with that scheme; or

- a certified emission reduction that can be used by an operator for compliance with that scheme. [*SI 2010/2239, Art 6*].

Excepted supplies

[4.17] A supply of any of the following is an excepted supply and the reverse charge does not apply.

- A supply of specified goods within **4.16** above where the VAT-exclusive value of the supply is less than £5,000. This figure is calculated on an invoice basis so where the total value of all the specified goods shown on a particular invoice is £5,000 or more, the reverse charge applies to the total value of the specified goods on that invoice. There is no *de minimis* rule excluding supplies of emissions allowances under £5,000.
- A supply of specified goods within **4.16** above where the goods are also eligible goods under the margin scheme of **SECOND-HAND GOODS (61)** and, in accordance with that scheme, the supplier opts to account for the VAT chargeable on the supply on the profit margin instead of by reference to its value. In such a case, the VAT payable is calculated under the margin scheme rules.
- A supply of a mobile telephone where, at the time a person enters into the agreement to purchase the telephone, he enters into an agreement (including the renewal or extension of an existing agreement) with a provider of a '*public electronic communications service*' (as defined in *Communications Act 2003, s 151*) for the supply, in relation to that telephone, of such a service; and that agreement is not one that requires periodical pre-payments in order to use the service ('Pay as You Go').
- A transfer or disposal of specified goods within **4.16** above which a business gives away for no consideration and that is treated as a supply of goods by virtue of *VATA 1994, Sch 4 para 5(1)* (business gifts). See **47.6 OUTPUT TAX**.

[*SI 2010/2239, Arts 3, 7, 8*]. (HMRC Brief 35/10).

Reverse charge accounting for VAT

[4.18] If

- a taxable person makes a supply of goods or services to a person ('the recipient') at any time,
- the supply is of specified goods or services within **4.16** above and is not an excepted supply within **4.17** above, and
- the recipient is a taxable person at that time and is supplied in connection with the carrying on by him of any business,

it is for the recipient, on the supplier's behalf, to account for and pay VAT on the supply and not for the supplier.

Any provision of *VATA 1994*, any other *Act* and any subordinate legislation that has effect for the purposes of, or in connection with the enforcement of, any obligation to account for and pay VAT applies in relation to any person required under these provisions to account for and pay any VAT as if that VAT were VAT on a supply made by him.

[*VATA 1994, s 55(6)–(8); FA 2006, s 19(1)*].

The reverse charge applies only to supplies of specified goods or services within the UK made by one VAT-registered business to another. The rules and procedures for sales to non-business customers, dispatches of goods or services to persons in another EU country and exports outside the EU are unaffected by the introduction of the reverse charge.

What the supplier must do

[4.19] The supplier must be aware of the following.

(1) Checking that reverse charge applies

Before applying the reverse charge, a supplier must be happy that all the necessary conditions are met. He will have first-hand knowledge as to whether the goods or services being supplied are specified goods or services and any goods are being sold in quantities above the £5,000 threshold. But the goods or services must also be sold to a taxable person for a business purpose, and the supplier must obtain the customers' VAT registration number and carry out reasonable checks to establish the customer's VAT status. If he does not, he may be held liable for incorrect application of the reverse charge (see **4.22** below).

What is reasonable in any case will depend on the business sector involved and the type of relationship the supplier has with the customer. HMRC give the following as indicators in deciding how far a supplier should go before accepting a customer's representations. The list is not exhaustive or definitive.

- Do commercial checks on creditworthiness and customer status, which are good commercial practice for the sector, suggest any reason to doubt the customer's representations?
- Is the VAT registration number genuine and does it belong to the person who is quoting it? Suppliers may use the checking facility provided by the National Advice Service on 0845 010 9000. Large businesses may contact their Client Relationship Manager for advice.
- Is the customer a new customer or a well-established business known to the supplier? In general, there is no need for the supplier to carry out special verification of VAT registration numbers of existing customers with whom they have an established trading relationship.
- Is there any indication in the pattern of orders that the customer is attempting to manipulate the £5,000 threshold?
- Has the supplier any grounds to doubt the *bona fides* of the customer?

There is further advice at **31.3 HMRC: POWERS** relating to the integrity of a supplier and this applies equally to that of a customer under these provisions.

The supplier should keep evidence of the checks that it has performed, so it can be produced to HMRC if subsequently required.

If he cannot satisfy himself of the *bona fides* of his customer or his VAT registration status, the supplier should consider whether to proceed with the transaction. If he does proceed with a reverse charge transaction where there are doubts that the reverse charge applies, the supplier may wish to consider asking the customer for a deposit equivalent to the output tax for which he will become liable if the reverse charge is applied in error. This may be especially helpful if the customer has applied for, but not yet received, a VAT registration number. Any deposit taken in these circumstances can be refunded when evidence of the VAT registration is received.

(VAT Notice 735, paras 4.1–4.3).

(2) Notifying HMRC

On the first occasion on which a business makes a reverse charge supply under these provisions, it must notify HMRC of that fact within 30 days of the day on which the supply is made. It must also give HMRC details of the name and telephone number of a contact.

The notification must be made on-line by using a portal provided by HMRC (although if this is unavailable for any reason, HMRC may allow the notification to be made by e-mail). See under (5) below for further details of the method of notification which is also used for the RCSL system.

HMRC must also be advised of the date on which the business ceases to make reverse charge supplies and, if it subsequently again makes reverse charge supplies, it must notify HMRC of the date and again provide contact details. In each case, notification must be within 30 days of the event.

[*SI 1995/2518, Regs 23A, 23B, 23D; SI 2007/1418, Reg 3; SI 2007/1599*]. (VAT Notice 735, para 14.3).

(3) Invoices

When a supplier makes a sale to which reverse charge accounting applies, he must show all the information normally required to be shown on a VAT invoice but must also annotate the invoice to make it clear that the reverse charge applies and that the customer is required to account for the VAT. The amount of VAT due under the reverse charge rules must be clearly stated on the invoice but should *not* be included in the amount shown as total VAT charged.

The precise wording is not prescribed but a suggested form of wording is

UK customer to pay output tax of £X to HMRC

Alternatively, any of the following would also be acceptable, provided that the amount of VAT is shown elsewhere on the invoice (but not in the box for total output tax charged).

VATA 1994 section 55A applies

Customer to account for the VAT to HMRC

Reverse charge supply – customer to pay the VAT to HMRC

If the seller produces invoices using an IT system, and that system cannot show the amount of VAT to be accounted for under the reverse charge mechanism, then the wording should state that VAT is to be accounted for by the purchaser at 20% (17.5% before 4 January 2011; 15% from December 2008 to

31 December 2009) of the VAT-exclusive selling price for reverse charge goods or services. The customer must be able to identify the reverse charge goods or services, and a legend such as the following may be helpful.

Customer to account to HMRC for the reverse charge output tax on the VAT-exclusive price of items marked reverse charge.

Electronic invoicing

The indication that goods or services are subject to the reverse charge, and that the customer is required to account for output tax on such goods or services, can be provided in the invoice message in coded representation rather than in textual form provided

- both parties to the electronic invoicing exchange agree; and
- its meaning can be demonstrated to an HMRC auditor by both parties to the electronic invoicing exchange.

(VAT Notice 735, paras 5.2, 5.3).

(4) Completion of the VAT return

A supplier who has made a reverse charge supply must include the value of the supply in the total value of sales figure in Box 6 of the VAT return. There is no output tax to include in Box 1 because that is the responsibility of the customer. (VAT Notice 735, para 5.4).

(5) Completion of a Reverse Charge Sales List (RCSL)

A business which starts to make reverse charge supplies within these provisions must notify HMRC (see (2) above). It must then, for any VAT period in which it has made a reverse charge supply of goods (but not emissions allowances), submit an RCSL for that VAT period to HMRC no later than the day by which it is required to make the VAT return. RCSLs may therefore be due monthly, quarterly or annually depending on the length of the VAT return period.

The RCSL must contain the following particulars.

(a) The VAT registration number of the business.

(b) The UK nine-digit VAT registration number of each customer to whom it has made a reverse charge supply. Any 'GB' suffix, branch identifier or EORI number should not be included. If, exceptionally, a business does not know its customer's VAT number at the time it submits a RCSL, it should either
- enter a 'dummy' VAT registration number (e.g. 111 1111 11 or, 222 2222 22), submit with RCSL with value data and subsequently, on receipt of the customer's VAT number, amend the entry (HMRC's preferred option); or
- submit the RCSL excluding that customer and subsequently add the appropriate sales information when the customer's VAT registration number is received.

(c) For each month falling within the VAT period, the total value of the reverse charge supplies made to each customer within (*b*) above. If there are no reverse charge supplies to a customer for one or more months in the VAT period (but not every month), then '0' value for the month(s) must be inserted. Figures should be declared in whole pounds (by either rounding to the nearest pound or truncating the pence). If the total net value is negative the information should be submitted with a leading negative sign.

The RCSL system (including any notifications) is web-based and accessed through the HMRC website at:

www.hmrc.gov.uk

Businesses that do not already use an HRMC on-line service will need to register for the Government Gateway. Guidance on how to register is available at

http://www.gateway.gov.uk/

The RCSL system is menu driven and provides help for each option. All aspects require completion electronically. The information can be entered directly on-line or a comma separated values (csv) file can be uploaded.

Declaration

A RCSL must contain a declaration made by the business that it is true and complete.

Nil returns

If, in any VAT period, no reverse charge supplies are made, a nil declaration is required (unless the business has notified HMRC that it has ceased making reverse charge supplies without intending subsequently to make such supplies). This is done by selecting the 'nil declaration' option on the RCSL home page. There is no facility to submit a nil CSV file.

Correcting errors

If an RCSL has been submitted and a mistake is subsequently discovered, the correct information must be supplied to HMRC by amending the original submission. If the RCSL was submitted by completing the on-line list, it is possible to add, delete or change lines on-line. But if the RSCL was submitted by uploading a csv file, the complete list must be resubmitted with the necessary additions, deletions or changes (i.e. including all the lines that were correct in the original submission).

[*SI 1995/2518, Regs 23A, 23C; SI 2007/1418, Reg 3*]. (VAT Notice 735, paras 14.2, 14.2, 14.4–14.10; HMRC Brief 35/10).

What the customer must do

[4.20] The customer must be aware of the following.

(1) Accounting for the VAT on a reverse charge supply

VAT-registered customers who are not charged VAT because the reverse charge applies must account for the VAT due on the supply. The amount of VAT should be shown on the VAT invoice issued by the supplier (see **4.19**(3) above) and should be accounted for on the VAT return for the period in which the supply is received. The normal tax point rules apply.

The customer can reclaim this VAT as input tax on the same return as it is accounted for, subject to the normal rules, including any partial exemption restriction that may apply.

(VAT Notice 735, para 6.1).

(2) Completion of VAT return

The customer must enter the output tax payable on purchases under the reverse charge in Box 1 but the value of the purchases must not be entered in Box 6. Input tax can be reclaimed, subject to the normal rules, by including it in the total shown in Box 4. The value of the purchases should be entered in Box 7 in the normal way. (VAT Notice 735, para 6.2).

(3) Onward sales of goods or services purchased under the reverse charge system

If the purchaser of reverse charge goods or services sells them on to another VAT-registered business in the UK and that sale also meets the conditions for treatment as a reverse charge supply, then the reverse charge applies to the onward sale. Otherwise, if the goods or services are sold in any other circumstances, then the appropriate normal VAT accounting rules for the transaction in question must be followed. (VAT Notice 735, para 6.3).

Adjustments and corrections

Adjustments in the course of business

[4.21] Adjustments may be required to reverse charge supplies (e.g. because of changes in price after the invoice has been issued or because of returned goods or services).

Where a supplier offers a credit or contingent discount, provided both parties agree, no VAT adjustment need be made by either party (although adjustment will still be required to the RCSL (see **4.19**(5) above). HMRC regard this as the easiest option because of the complexities involved in making adjustments but the following methods are also possible.

- *Return not yet made*. If the supplier or customer identifies a change in the value of reverse charge goods or services before its VAT accounting period is closed, it can simply adjust its primary records of the sale/purchase and make sure the corrected figure feeds through to the VAT account.
- *Return already made and reverse charge applied*. The customer will have to adjust any reverse charge output tax and any input tax to reflect the new values.
- *Return already made and price adjustment brings the supply into the reverse charge*. The supplier will have to credit the output tax accounted for and give back any VAT collected from the customer. The customer will have to correct the value of any input tax taken to reflect the new value and bring the reverse charge output tax to account in the same period.

- *Return already made and price adjustment removes the supply out of the reverse charge.* If both parties agree, the original VAT treatment need not be reversed although an adjustment to the RCSL will still be required (see **4.19**(5) above). If they do not agree, the supplier will need to bring output tax to account and collect the VAT from his customer. The customer will need to reverse the output tax he has entered and correct the input tax entry to reflect the corrected value. In that case, HMRC recommend the whole supply is credited and then re-invoiced with the new VAT treatment.
- *Credit or debit notes issued for supplies made before 1 June 2007.* These are an adjustment to the original supply and cannot therefore bring these supplies into the reverse charge.

Suggested forms of words for credit notes are

UK Customer to account for the output tax adjustment of £X to HMRC

Customer to account to HMRC for the adjustment to reverse charge output tax on the VAT-exclusive price of items marked reverse charge.

Where the output tax liability reverts to the supplier as a result of a decrease in consideration, HMRC recommend the whole supply is credited and then re-invoiced with the new tax treatment. However, if using credit notes is preferred the following would also be acceptable.

Customer to account for output tax adjustment of £X to HMRC, supplier now accounts for £Y output tax to HMRC.

Mistakes

Mistakes made under the reverse charge procedure should be dealt with in a similar manner to other errors involving VAT. See **56.10** and **56.11** RECORDS.

[*SI 1995/2518, Regs 38, 38A; SI 2007/1418, Reg 4*]. (VAT Notice 735, para 7.1, 7.2).

Failure to comply with the reverse charge provisions

Suppliers

[4.22] If the supplier

- applies the reverse charge and has taken sufficient steps to check the *bona fides* of his customer (see **4.19**(1) above) but has been deliberately misled by him, he will not be required to account for output tax on the sale;
- has correctly applied the reverse charge to a sale, he will not be required to account for output tax if the customer fails to do so;
- applies the reverse charge incorrectly, or has not taken sufficient steps to check the *bona fides* of his customer, he will be liable to pay the output tax on the sale; and
- incorrectly charges VAT when the reverse charge should have been applied, the customer will be assessed for the output tax (which will offset any entitlement to input tax recovery) and the supplier will have

to credit his customer with the VAT, returning any money collected as VAT. The supplier will also be subject to the normal error correction procedures. See **56.10** and **56.11 RECORDS**.

Customers

Failure to apply the reverse charge may arise as an oversight or where the customer has been unable to provide the supplier with a VAT registration number because a number is still awaited from HMRC. Where a customer does not account for the reverse charge when they should, HMRC will assess for the output tax due less any input tax the customer may be entitled to.

But failure to notify a supplier that the reverse charge ought to apply may also be an indicator of fraud. This is likely to result in extended verification of any input tax claimed. If a customer takes no action where they are charged VAT and the reverse charge should apply, he may put himself in a position where he could be held to be jointly and severally liable for the VAT or unable to recover the input tax on the supply.

(VAT Notice 735, paras 8.1–8.2).

Treatment in particular cases

[4.23] The treatment in particular cases is as follows.

(1) Other goods or services shown on same invoice as reverse charge goods or services

If supplies of any other goods or services are shown on the same invoice as reverse charge goods or services, the reverse charge does not apply to the other supplies. (VAT Notice 735, para 3.2).

(2) Single supplies including reverse charge good

Where an itemised invoice relates to a single supply (e.g. a computer) which is not subject to the reverse charge, VAT should be charged as normal on the supply, even if certain of the itemised components are reverse charge goods or services. (VAT Notice 735, para 3.2).

(3) Multiple invoices for a single order

Where a business issues several separate invoices in relation to a single order (e.g. a separate invoice for each delivery), and the order value is larger than the invoice value, it is acceptable to apply the reverse charge to all invoices relating to the order provided the order value exceeds the £5,000 threshold and both parties agree. (VAT Notice 735, para 3.2).

(4) Discounts

Where VAT is due on a value reduced by an unconditional discount (e.g. a prompt payment discount), the discounted value should be used to establish the value in applying the £5,000 *de minimis* rule in **4.17** above. But where there are contingent discounts or delayed reductions in price, the full value shown on the invoice must be used. (VAT Notice 735, para 3.2).

(5) Payments on account (POA)

Larger businesses with a net VAT liability of over £2 million per year (increased to £2.3 million, from 1 June 2011 or 1 December 2011 depending on the basic period) are required to make POA of VAT. See **51.4 PAYMENT OF VAT** for full details.

Because some businesses may be required to account for output tax on their purchases of reverse charge goods or services as well as on the onward sale to non-business customers, the reverse charge could have the effect of increasing their net VAT liability (and bringing them within the scope of the POA regime) or increasing their monthly payments if they are already within the regime.

A business which could be affected by this may apply to HMRC to exclude the output tax due under the reverse charge from the calculation to establish whether it is subject to POA or, if already in the regime, the monthly payments it has to make.

Applications for exclusion should be made to: The POA Team, Banking Operations, Queens Dock, Liverpool, L74 4AA.

Some businesses may find that their net liability will decrease with the introduction of the reverse charge. If that is the case, then the normal rules for application to reduce POAs outlined in **51.4 PAYMENT OF VAT** apply.

[*SI 1993/2001, Art 2A; SI 2007/1420, Art 2*]. (VAT Notice 735, para 9).

(6) Bad debts

BAD DEBT RELIEF (7) does not apply with reverse charge supplies as it is the customer who accounts for the VAT. (VAT Notice 735, para 10).

(7) Adjustment of output tax where change in entitlement to input tax after six months

Under *VATA 1994, s 26A*, where the customer has claimed input tax deduction on a supply but has not paid the whole or any part of the consideration for that supply within six months, he must generally repay the appropriate proportion of the input tax originally claimed. See **34.4 INPUT TAX** for full details.

If, as a result of *VATA 1994, s 26A*

- the customer is taken not to have been entitled to any credit for input tax in respect of a supply, and
- the supply is a reverse charge supply,

the customer is entitled to make an adjustment to the amount of VAT which he is required to account for and pay under the reverse charge procedure. The amount of the adjustment is equal to the amount of the credit for the input tax to which the person is taken not to be entitled.

The customer must make a negative entry in the VAT payable portion of his VAT account for the same VAT period as that in which he is required to make an entry in the VAT allowable portion of his VAT return. See **34.4 INPUT TAX**.

[*VATA 2006, s 26AB; FA 2006, s 19(2); SI 1995/2518, Regs 172K, 172L*].

Readjustment of output tax

Where a customer

- has made a negative entry in his VAT account in accordance with the above provisions, and
- in relation to the same supply, he subsequently makes an entry in his VAT account due to the restoration of the entitlement to credit for input tax (see **34.4 INPUT TAX**),

he must make a positive entry in the VAT payable portion of his VAT account for the same VAT period in which he makes that subsequent entry. The amount of the positive entry must be equal to the amount of credit for input tax restored.

The above provisions are not to be regarded as giving rise to any application of error correction notification (formerly voluntary disclosure) requirements (see **56.11 RECORDS**).

[*SI 1995/2518, Regs 172K–172N; SI 2007/1418, Reg 7*].

(8) **Self-billing**

If the reverse charge applies, the customer will be the person issuing the self-billing invoice and accounting for the VAT. He should not charge VAT to the supplier and should indicate on the invoice that he will be accounting for the VAT himself. Suggested forms of words are as follows

We will account for and pay output tax of £X to HMRC

Alternatively, any of the following would also be acceptable, provided that the amount of VAT is shown elsewhere on the invoice (but not in the box for total output tax charged):

VATA 1994, section 55A applies

We will account for the VAT to HMRC

Reverse charge supply – we will pay the VAT to HMRC

A supplier of specified goods (but not emissions allowances) will, however, be required to complete the reverse charge sales list (see **4.19**(5) above).

(VAT Notice 735, para 11).

(9) **Accounting schemes**

- *Flat-rate scheme*. Reverse charge supplies must be excluded from the flat-rate scheme. Any such supplies received and made should be accounted for under the reverse charge provisions. See **63.16 SPECIAL SCHEMES**.
- *Cash accounting scheme*. Reverse charge sales and purchases should be excluded from the scheme and accounted for under the reverse charge provisions. But if a business purchases goods or services to which the

reverse charge applies and sells them on so that it does not (e.g. under the £5,000 *de minimis* limit or because the sale is to a non-business customer), then the onward sale should be dealt with under the cash accounting scheme.

- *Annual accounting scheme*. Use of this scheme is unaffected by the reverse charge and can be used in the normal way with reverse charge supplies being accounted for within the scheme.

(VAT Notice 735, paras 12.1–12.3).

(10) Charities and local authorities

If a charity or local authority purchases goods or services subject to the reverse charge and the goods or services are to be used partly for business purposes and partly for non-business purposes, it should account for output tax under the reverse charge procedure and apply the appropriate restriction to the deduction of the resulting input VAT. (VAT Notice 735, para 13.1).

(11) Health Service and government departments

If a reverse charge supply is made to the NHS or a government department for any element of business purpose, the reverse charge applies as normal. The customer should account for the VAT and restrict the recovery of the input tax as appropriate. (VAT Notice 735, para 13.1).

Key points

[4.24] Points to consider are as follows.

- The ECJ has supported the principle that VAT gains cannot be achieved by a business through what are commonly known as 'abusive practices'. Even though a taxpayer has the right to structure his tax affairs in the most tax efficient manner, any artificial structure intended to produce a tax saving can be disregarded by the courts in most cases and the tax outcome is based on what would have been the result if normal practices had been adopted. In the VAT world, this approach has been particularly relevant in relation to partly-exempt businesses involved in complex property deals with connected parties.
- A taxpayer must disclose certain avoidance schemes to HMRC, known as either 'hallmarked' or 'listed' schemes. See **4.2** above. The key feature of such schemes is that they are intended to produce a VAT saving that is not intended by the legislation.
- The key challenge in deciding whether a hallmarked or listed scheme needs to be notified to HMRC is to consider whether it produces a lower VAT bill than would apply if the scheme was not in place. A lower tax bill either means an increase in input tax or reduction in output tax compared to normal VAT accounting.
- Legitimate VAT planning still has an important part to play in helping to reduce the VAT bills of a business. For example, the creation of a VAT group to avoid VAT being charged on supplies

between group members is an established principle of VAT planning, and a natural outcome of a group registration. VAT savings that can be made by making an option to tax election (input tax recovery) or adopting a VAT scheme (flat-rate scheme or margin scheme) do not create a problem. The key feature of avoidance schemes is that an artificial arrangement is created, solely intended to avoid VAT or tax rather than being inspired by any commercial motive.

- In an attempt to combat carousel fraud, trading in mobile phones and computer chips (value of sales invoice exceeding £5,000) or emissions allowances between VAT-registered businesses in the UK requires the customer to account for output tax in many cases rather than the supplier. The customer fulfils this requirement by making a reverse charge calculation on his own VAT return based on the value of the relevant goods or services bought during the period (output tax accounted for in Box 1 and input tax claimed in Box 4).
- The reverse charge strategy for mobile phones and computer chips avoids the risk of a supplier charging output tax (usually on goods or services acquired VAT free from a supplier in another EU country), being paid this output tax by his customer – but then disappearing before the output tax is declared on a VAT return to HMRC.
- Items such as computer servers, laptops or desktop units are excluded from the reverse charge requirements. In such cases, the supplier will charge output tax to his UK customer in the normal way.
- A sales invoice raised by a supplier where the customer needs to carry out the reverse charge must be clearly noted as such (i.e. along the lines of 'reverse charge supply – customer to pay the VAT to HMRC'). It is useful to specify the actual amount of VAT subject to the reverse charge, particularly if an invoice includes both specified and non-specified goods or services, i.e. where some output tax is charged by the supplier but some needs to be accounted for by the customer.
- A supplier making a sale where the reverse charge applies will only record the value of this sale in Box 6 (outputs) on his VAT return. The Box 1 and Box 4 entries (actual VAT amounts) will be recorded by the customer. The customer will also make an entry in Box 7 (inputs) to reflect the value of the goods or services he is buying (excluding VAT).
- A reverse charge sales list (RCSL) must be submitted to HMRC by the supplier of specified goods (but not emissions allowances) to record the value of sales covered by the reverse charge rules. The return period coincides with the VAT periods of the supplier (i.e. usually the return will be completed quarterly). The return is always submitted online rather than in a paper format.
- In periods where no reverse charge supplies are made, a nil return still needs to be completed. A return must be completed every period unless the trader confirms to HMRC that he has ceased to

trade in specified goods or services (i.e. no qualifying supplies will arise in the future).

5

Appeals

Cross-references. See **6.8 ASSESSMENTS** for correction of assessments on appeal by tribunals; **8.9 BUSINESS** for appeals regarding registration of two or more persons as one taxable person; **27.5 GROUPS OF COMPANIES**; **34.12 INPUT TAX** for appeals in respect of input tax; **52.29 PENALTIES** for mitigation of penalties by a tribunal on appeal.

De Voil Indirect Tax Service. See V5.4.

Introduction

[5.1] Before April 2009 an appeal against a decision of HMRC on certain matters could be made to the VAT and Duties Tribunal. In April 2009 the *Tribunals, Courts and Enforcement Act 2007 (TCEA 2007)*, which received Royal Assent on 19 July 2007, established two new tribunals; the First-tier Tribunal and the Upper Tribunal, each of which are organised into a number of 'chambers'. The functions of most existing tribunals (including the VAT and Duties Tribunal) were transferred to this new tribunal structure.

The five First-tier Tribunal chambers are: Social Entitlement; Health, Education and Social Care; General Regulatory; Taxation; and Land, Property and Housing.

The three Upper Tribunal chambers are: Administrative Appeals; Finance and Tax; and Lands.

On 1 April 2009 VAT and Duties Tribunals were abolished and VAT appeals were transferred to the Tax Chamber in the First-tier Tribunal. There is a right of appeal against decisions of the First-tier Tax Chamber to the Tax and Chancery Chamber (named the Finance and Tax Chamber before 1 September 2009) in the Upper Tribunal. The First-tier Tribunal deals with the majority of appeals, apart from a small number of the most complex appeals that transfer to the Upper Tribunal at first instance. The Upper Tribunal mainly deals with appeals against decisions of the First-tier Tribunal. The Upper Tribunal has limited powers of judicial review. Some appeals are dealt with on paper without the need for HMRC or taxpayers to attend a hearing. In most cases, an appeal can be made against an Upper Tribunal decision to the Court of Appeal.

Constitution

There is a Senior President presiding over the tribunals. Each tribunal consists of its judges and members. Each chamber has a Chamber President. The tribunals work under the supervision of the Administrative Justice and Tribunals Council.

Appeals lodged before 1 April 2009

Where an appeal hearing begins before 1 April 2009 but is not decided until after that date, the proceedings should be continued on and after that date as proceedings under the First-tier Tribunal (or Upper Tribunal, as appropriate). In such cases—

- the tribunal must be comprised for the continuation of that hearing of the person or persons who began it;
- the tribunal may give any direction to ensure that proceedings are dealt with fairly and justly, and may apply any provision, regulating practice or procedure which applied before that date; or disapply any provision of Tribunal Procedure Rules (*SI 2008/2698* and *SI 2009/273*);
- any direction or order which is in force immediately before 1 April 2009 remains in force on and after that date;
- any time period which started before 1 April 2009 and has not expired will continue to apply; and
- an order for costs may only be made if, and to the extent that, an order could have been made prior to 1 April 2009.

Henceforth, the term 'tribunal' refers to the First-tier Tribunal unless otherwise stated.

[*TCEA 2007, ss 3–22, 44; SI 2009/56, Sch 3 para 7; SI 2010/2655*].

Public funding

[5.2] Public funding (formerly legal aid) is not generally available for appeals to tribunals. However, funding may be available for legal advice prior to the tribunal and legal representation at the tribunal where

- the proceedings concern penalties which the courts have declared to be criminal within the terms specified by the European Convention on Human Rights or where an applicant seeks to argue that issue; and
- it is in the interests of justice for an applicant to be legally represented.

In practice, funding is most likely to be available where a penalty, which is substantial either in terms of its amount or its impact, is being contested and where the amount imposed is beyond the assessed liability. The applicant must be financially eligible for funding. Applicants on Income Support and income-based Jobseekers' Allowance are automatically financially eligible. Each application is considered on an individual basis and is subject to the statutory tests of the applicant's means and the merits of the case.

Applications for funding should be made to the Legal Services Commission, 62–68 Hills Road, Cambridge, CB2 1LA via a solicitor or another authorised organisation. Solicitors who carry out public-funded work can be found in the Community Legal Service Directory (available in most local libraries), on the CLS website at www.justask.org.uk or by telephoning the CLS Helpline on 0845 608 1122.

In the case of proceedings before the Upper Tribunal, a party which is granted funding of legal services at any time must as soon as practicable: (a) send a copy of the funding notice, or legal aid certificate as appropriate, to the Upper Tribunal, and (b) notify every other party in writing that funding has been granted. [*SI 2008/2698, Rule 18*].

Appealable matters

[5.3] An appeal to a tribunal against a decision of HMRC may only be made on the following matters.

(1) The registration or cancellation of registration of any person.
(2) The VAT chargeable on the supply of any goods or services, on the acquisition of goods from another EU country or, subject to (ii) below, on the importation of goods from a place outside the EU. A tribunal has no jurisdiction in relation to future supplies (*Allied Windows (S Wales) Ltd v C & E Commrs,* QB April 1973 (unreported) (TVC 2.1); *Odhams Leisure Group Ltd v C & E Commrs,* QB [1992] STC 332 (TVC 2.3, 5.79)).
(3) The amount of any input tax which may be credited to a person.
(4) Any claim for a refund by virtue of regulations made under *VATA 1994, s 13(5)* (acquisitions of goods from another EU country where VAT has also been paid in that other country).
(5) A decision by HMRC under *VATA 1994, s 18A* on the approval of a person as a fiscal warehousekeeper or the withdrawal of such approval or the fiscal warehouse status from any premises. See **72.13 WAREHOUSED GOODS AND FREE ZONES.**
(6) The proportion of input tax allowable under *VATA 1994, s 26.*
(7) A claim by a taxable person under *VATA 1994, s 27* (goods imported for another person for private purposes, see **34.8 INPUT TAX**).

(8) A decision of HMRC refusing or withdrawing authorisation (i) to use the flat-rate scheme for small businesses or (ii) as to the appropriate percentage(s) to be used under the scheme, see **63.15 SPECIAL SCHEMES.**

(9) A decision by HMRC that an election under *SI 1993/2001, Art 12A* (right to elect under the payments on account provisions to pay actual liability for the preceding month rather than the predetermined amount) shall cease to have effect. See **51.4 PAYMENT OF VAT.**

(10) The amount of any refunds under *VATA 1994, s 35* (construction of certain buildings otherwise than in the course of a business by 'do-it-yourself' builders, see **42.24 LAND AND BUILDINGS: ZERO AND REDUCED RATE SUPPLIES AND DIY HOUSEBUILDERS**).

(11) A claim for a refund under *VATA 1994, s 36* or earlier provisions (see **7 BAD DEBT RELIEF**).

(12) A refusal of a repayment under *VATA 1994, s 39* (see **45.12 OVERSEAS TRADERS**).

(13) The amount of any refunds under *VATA 1994, s 40* (supplies of new means of transport to other EU countries by non-taxable persons, see **19.36 EUROPEAN UNION: SINGLE MARKET**).

(14) Any refusal of an application under *VATA 1994, s 43B* (applications re group treatment, see **27.3 GROUPS OF COMPANIES**).

(15) Notice by HMRC under *VATA 1994, s 43C* terminating group membership (see **27.3 GROUPS OF COMPANIES**).

(16) The requirement of any security under *VATA 1994, s 48(7)* or *VATA 1994, Sch 11 para 4(1A)(2)* (for the payment of VAT due or which may become due, see **31.1 HMRC: POWERS**).

(17) Any refusal or cancellation of certification under *VATA 1994, s 54* or any refusal to cancel such certification (flat-rate scheme for farmers, see **63.25 SPECIAL SCHEMES**).

(18) Any liability to a penalty or surcharge under *VATA 1994, ss 59–69B* (see **52.10–52.21** and **52.24–52.27 PENALTIES**). See also **52.30 PENALTIES** for mitigation by the tribunal.

(19) A decision of HMRC under *VATA 1994, s 61* (liability of a director where the conduct of a company gives rise to a penalty for VAT evasion, see **52.9 PENALTIES**).

(20) The making or amount of an assessment under *VATA 1994, s 73(1)(2)* for any period for which the appellant has made a return or under *VATA 1994, s 73(7)(7A)(7B)* or *VATA 1994, s 75* (see **6.1**(*b*)–(*g*) **ASSESSMENTS**).

(21) The amount of any penalty, interest or surcharge specified in an assessment under *VATA 1994, s 76* (see **6.3 ASSESSMENTS**). But without prejudice to the tribunals powers of mitigation (see **52.30 PENALTIES**), the tribunal may only vary the amount assessed insofar as it is necessary to reduce it to the amount which is appropriate under the relevant penalty, etc provision.

(22) The making of an assessment, on the basis set out in *VATA 1994, s 77(4)*, outside the normal time limit where it is believed that VAT may have been lost through fraud, conduct involving dishonesty, failure to notify liability to be registered or unauthorised issue of VAT invoices. See **6.4 ASSESSMENTS.**

(23) Any liability arising under *VATA 1994, s 77A* (joint and several liability for unpaid VAT, see **31.3 HMRC: POWERS**).
(24) Any liability of HMRC to pay interest under *VATA 1994, s 78* or the amount of the interest payable (see **51.17 PAYMENT OF VAT**).
(25) An assessment under *VATA 1994, s 78A* (interest overpayments) or the amount of such an assessment (see **6.5 ASSESSMENTS**).
(26) A claim for the crediting or repayment of overstated or overpaid VAT under *VATA 1994, s 80* (see **51.8 PAYMENT OF VAT**), an assessment under *VATA 1994, s 80(4A)* (repayment to HMRC of overpaid refund, see **6.5 ASSESSMENTS**) or the amount of such an assessment.
(27) An assessment under *VATA 1994, s 80B(1)* or *(1B)* (recovery by HMRC under the unjust enrichment provisions of credits or repayments made to a taxpayer) or the amount of such an assessment (see **6.5 ASSESSMENTS**).
(28) Any direction or supplementary direction under *VATA 1994, Sch 1 para 2* (registration of two or more persons as one taxable person, see **8.5 BUSINESS**).
(29) Any direction under *VATA 1994, Sch 6 para 1, para 1A* or *para 2* or under *VATA 1983, Sch 4 para 2* (VAT on transactions between connected persons and supplies of goods to non-taxable persons for retail sale and, see **71.19**, **71.23**, and **71.30 VALUATION** respectively).
(30) Any direction under *VATA 1994, Sch 7 para 1* (VAT on acquisitions of goods between connected persons to be charged on the open market value, see **71.12 VALUATION**).
(31) Any direction or assessment under *VATA 1994, Sch 9A* (anti-avoidance provisions for groups, see **27.5 GROUPS OF COMPANIES**).
(32) Any refusal to grant any permission under, or otherwise to exercise in favour of a particular person any power conferred by, any provision in *VATA 1994, Sch 10 Pt I* (option to tax, see **41.8 LAND AND BUILDINGS: EXEMPT SUPPLIES AND OPTION TO TAX**).
(33) Any refusal to permit the value of supplies to be determined by a method described in a VAT Notice published under *VATA 1994, Sch 11 para 2(6)* (see **60.1 RETAIL SCHEMES**).
(34) Any refusal of authorisation or termination of authorisation in connection with the scheme under *VATA 1994, Sch 11 para 2(7)* (cash accounting scheme, see **63.2 SPECIAL SCHEMES**).
(35) Any requirement imposed by HMRC in a particular case under *VATA 1994, Sch 11 para 2B(2)(c)* (self-billed invoices, see **39.6 INVOICES**) or *para 3(1)* (production of VAT invoices by computer, see **39.10 INVOICES**).
(36) A direction under *VATA 1994, Sch 11 para 6A* (direction to keep certain records, see **56.1 RECORDS**).
(37) A direction under *VATA 1994, Sch 11A para 8* (power of HMRC to exclude exemption from duty to notify a VAT avoidance scheme in cases of business splitting, see **4.12 ANTI-AVOIDANCE**).
(38) Any liability to a penalty under *VATA 1994, Sch 11A para 10(1)* (penalty for failure to notify use of a notifiable avoidance scheme, see **52.28 PENALTIES**), any assessment of such a penalty under *VATA 1994, Sch 11A para 12(1)* (see **6.3 ASSESSMENTS**) or the amount of such an

assessment. But without prejudice to the tribunals powers of mitigation (see **52.30 PENALTIES**), the tribunal may only vary the amount assessed insofar as it is necessary to reduce it to the amount as correctly calculated under the provisions.

(39) A decision of HMRC about the application of regulations under *FA 2002, s 135* concerning the mandatory electronic filing of returns (see **2.1 ACCOUNTING PERIODS AND RETURNS**). The tribunal may only vary the amount assessed insofar as it is necessary to reduce it to the amount appropriate under the regulations.

(40) A decision of HMRC on a review under *SI 2003/3075, Reg 21* (money laundering regulations).

(41) An information notice under *FA 2008, Sch 36 paras 1, 2* (power of HMRC to obtain information and documents from taxpayer or third party, see **31.6 HMRC: POWERS**).

(42) A penalty imposed under *FA 2008, Sch 36 paras 39–40A* (standard and daily penalties for failure to comply with information notice or deliberate obstruction of HMRC officer in course of an inspection authorised by the tribunal and penalties for inaccurate information and documents, see **52.18 PENALTIES**).

(43) A penalty imposed under *FA 2009, Sch 46 paras 4–9* (failure to comply with duties of senior accounting officers, see **52.29 PENALTIES**).

(44) A notice under *FA 2009, Sch 49 paras 1–3* (power to obtain contact details for debtors, see **31.8 HMRC: POWERS**) or a penalty imposed under *FA 2009, Sch 49 para 5* for failure to comply with such a notice (see **52.19 PENALTIES**).

(45) A data-holder notice (introduced from 1 April 2012) under *FA 2011, Sch 23* (data-gathering powers, see **31.9 HMRC: POWERS**) or a penalty imposed under *FA 2011, Sch 23 paras 30–32* for failure to comply with such a notice or inaccurate data (see **52.20 PENALTIES**).

[*VATA 1994, ss 83, 84(6)(6A)(6B); FA 1996, s 31(3), Sch 3 para 12; FA 1997, s 45(2)(5), s 46(3)(4), s 47(7)(9); FA 1999, Sch 2 para 3; FA 2000, s 137(5); FA 2002, s 23(2); FA 2003, ss 17(6), 18(2); FA 2004, s 22(3), Sch 2 paras 4, 5; F(No 2)A 2005, s 4(5); FA 2006, s 21(4); FA 2007, s 93(8)(9); SI 1997/2542; SI 2001/3641, Reg 17; SI 2003/3075; SI 2008/1146, Art 3; FA 2008, Sch 36 paras 29–33, 47, 48; FA 2009, s 77(4), Sch 46 paras 10, 11, Sch 47 para 18, Sch 49 para 4; FA 2011, Sch 23 paras 28, 29, 36*].

No appeal lies to a tribunal on

(i) any matter which is outside (1) to (44) above (subject to below); or

(ii) any decision which HMRC can be required to review under *FA 1994, s 14* (decisions relating to customs duty or the Community Customs Code or made under *CEMA 1979*) unless no request for a review has been made or the decision relates only to whether or not zero-rating applies to the importation of the goods in question and/or the rate of VAT charged on the goods.

[*VATA 1994, s 84(9)*].

Where an appeal is against a decision of HMRC which depended upon a prior decision taken by them in relation to the appellant, the fact that the prior decision was not within (1) to (44) above (e.g. the exercise of a discretion by

HMRC) does not prevent the tribunal from allowing the appeal on the grounds that it would have allowed an appeal against the prior decision. [*VATA 1994, s 84(10)*]. This follows the decision in *C & E Commrs v JH Corbitt (Numismatists) Ltd, HL* [1980] STC 231 (TVC 60.1).

Extra-statutory concessions

In *RW Shepherd* (VTD 11753) (TVC 25.35), the tribunal held that HMRC were bound to have regard to the terms of their concessions and while the tribunal could not interfere with those terms, it was entitled to consider whether those terms had been complied with. A similar conclusion was reached in *British Teleflower Service Ltd* (VTD 13756) (TVC 40.57). However, it has been held in *Dr BN Purdue* (VTD 13430) (TVC 2.90) and subsequently in *C & E Commrs v Arnold,* QB [1996] STC 1271 (TVC 2.91) that a tribunal has no jurisdiction in relation to non-statutory arrangements or concessions which are a matter for HMRC. In *Arnold*, Hidden J, disapproving of the decision in *British Teleflower Service Ltd*, held that the provisions of *VATA 1994, s 84(10)* (see above) only applied to a case where there were two separate decisions (as had been the case in *JH Corbitt (Numismatists) Ltd*) and did not apply in the present case where there had only been one decision.

The decision in *Arnold* was distinguished in the subsequent case of *R (oao Greenwich Property Ltd) v C & E Commrs,* Ch D [2001] STC 618 (TVC 2.94). The appellant had granted an underlease to a university (of which the appellant was a wholly owned subsidiary) and had treated it as a zero-rated supply. The university had issued a zero-rating certificate to the appellant in reliance on guidelines agreed between HMRC and the Committee of Vice Chancellors and Principals of the Universities of the UK. HMRC ruled that the certificate should not have been issued and raised an assessment to recover input tax. On appeal, the tribunal held that it had no jurisdiction to review the application of a concession. The appellant applied for judicial review. Collins J held that it would be 'unfair and so unlawful for HMRC not to apply the concession . . . provided that the taxpayer had complied with its terms'. HMRC were not entitled to raise the assessment and the appellant was entitled to rely on the concession.

Tribunal's jurisdiction over HMRC actions and decisions

In the case of *Oxfam v HMRC* (Ch) [2010] STC 686 (TVC 11.51), HMRC had decided to amend the terms of an approved method for the apportionment of VAT incurred between business and non-business use. Oxfam sought judicial review of the decision, under the principle of legitimate expectation, as it was unsure as to whether the tribunal had jurisdiction over the matter. The High Court held that a claim based on public law principles and the doctrine of legitimate expectation could properly be raised in an appeal to the tribunal, where that was necessary for it to determine the outcome of an appeal against an HMRC decision whose subject matter fell within one of the headings in *VATA 1994, s 83*.

Conditions for hearing an appeal

[5.4] No appeal will be entertained unless the following conditions are satisfied.

- In the case of an appeal on matters under **5.3**(2), (17), (19), (20), (22), (24) or (37) above,
  - (a) the amount which HMRC have determined to be payable as VAT (or, in the case of **5.3**(24) have notified by assessment) has been paid or deposited with them; or
  - (b) on being satisfied that the appellant would otherwise suffer hardship, HMRC agree, or the tribunal decides, that the appeal be entertained notwithstanding non-payment (see **5.10** below). Note that if the hardship application is granted but, subsequently, the appeal is lost, default interest on the amount of the disputed VAT may be payable. Conversely, if the hardship application is lost but, subsequently, the appeal is won, HMRC are liable to pay interest on any amount of disputed VAT paid or deposited with them which is repayable (see **51.17 PAYMENT OF VAT**).

  The tribunal in *PW Coleman* (VTD 15906, VTD 16178) (TVC 2.23) held that the condition in (a) above was acceptable and did not conflict with what is now *Directive 2006/112/EC* because of the hardship provision under (b) above and because HMRC's decision on that is reviewable by the tribunal.
  [*VATA 1994, s 84(3)(3A); FA 1997, s 45(3)(5); FA 2003, s 18(3); FA 2004, Sch 2 para 5*].
- The appellant has a sufficient interest in maintaining the appeal. (See *Williams and Glyn's Bank Ltd* (VTD 118) (TVC 27.1)). The appellant is not required to be the supplier (*Canterbury Hockey Club; Canterbury Ladies Hockey Club* (VTD 19086) (TVC 2.56)) or a taxable person accountable for the VAT in dispute (e.g. he may be an unregistered recipient of taxable supplies) but where he is the recipient of a supply, he should wherever possible seek the consent of the supplier to the appeal being brought jointly (*Processed Vegetable Growers Association Ltd* (VTD 25) (TVC 2.52) (TVC 62.42)). For other cases where a tribunal allowed an appeal by the recipient of a supply, see *Dr Cameron* (VTD 41) (TVC 33.52); *Gilbourne* (VTD 109) (TVC 2.53); and *Beckley (JR)* (VTD 114) (TVC 2.55).
- In appeals involving group registrations (see **27 GROUPS OF COMPANIES**), only the representative member may appeal.
- Where HMRC have obtained a final judgment against the appellant for VAT on an assessment, the tribunal has no jurisdiction to entertain an appeal unless the applicant first procures the High Court judgment against him to be set aside (*Digwa* (TS) (VTD 612) (TVC 2.194)).

When an appeal is about a penalty, surcharge or an amount of interest, the appellant does not have to pay it before the appeal can be heard.

Categories of appeal

[5.5] There are three different categories of appeal to the tribunal and procedure differs with each.

Default paper cases

These cases are normally disposed of without a hearing.

Basic cases

These cases are normally disposed of after a hearing, with a minimal exchange of documents before the hearing. Most VAT penalty surcharge cases and mitigation appeals are categorised as basic.

Standard cases

These are subject to more detailed case management and are disposed of after a hearing.

Complex cases

A case is allocated or reallocated as a complex case if the tribunal considers that: it will require lengthy or complex evidence or a lengthy hearing; it involves a complex or important principle or issue; or it involves a large financial sum. Complex cases may, with the consent of the parties and the concurrence of the President of the Tax and Chancery Chamber (named the Finance and Tax Chamber before 1 September 2009) of the Upper Tribunal, be transferred to and determined by the Upper Tribunal.

[*SI 2009/273, Rules 23, 28*].

Time limit for appealing

[5.6] Where HMRC are not required or requested to undertake a review, an appeal must be within 30 days of the date of the decision or, where the appellant is not the person to whom the decision was notified, within 30 days of the date when the appellant became aware of the decision. Where the time limit for requesting or requiring a review is extended, the time limit for appeal is similarly extended. Where HMRC are required to undertake a review, an appeal may not be made until the conclusion date (i.e. the date of the document notifying the conclusions of the review), but must be made within 30 days of the conclusion date. Where HMRC do not notify their conclusions within the 45-day time limit, an appeal may be made from the end of that time limit until 30 days after the conclusion date. Where HMRC are requested to carry out a review which is out of time, an appeal may not be made unless HMRC have decided whether or not to undertake a review, and if they decide to undertake a review, not until the conclusion date. An appeal must be made within 30 days of the conclusion date or the date on which HMRC decide not to undertake a review, as applicable.

The tribunal may allow an appeal to be made outside the stipulated time limits. An extension has been allowed where the appellant was mistakenly under the impression that the matter was being handled by his accountants (*Hallam*

(WR) (VTD 683) (TVC 2.176)) and where the appeal was delayed through the illness of a partner (*Hornby (WW & JH)* (VTD 155) (TVC 2.191)). Application was refused, although within the discretion of the tribunal, where to admit it would be to enable the applicant to recover VAT paid voluntarily under a mistake of law (*Kyffin (R)* (VTD 617) (TVC 2.190)). In *WJ Price* (VTD 559) (TVC 2.182) an extension was allowed where, although no real excuse for delay existed, there was evidence that the taxpayer intended to appeal, but this decision was not followed in *Wan & Wan* (VTD 14829) (TVC 2.182) on the grounds that the earlier tribunal's reasoning was inconsistent with subsequent decisions of the Court of Appeal including that in *Norwich & Peterborough Building Society v Steed*, CA [1991] 1 WLR 449; [1991] 2 All ER 880 (TVC 2.182).

[*VATA 1994, s 83G; SI 2009/273, Rule 20*].

Making an appeal

[5.7] An appeal to the tribunal is brought by sending or delivering a notice of appeal to the tribunal (unless it is an appeal under *FA 2008, Sch 36*, in which case the notice of appeal must be given to HMRC), with 'tribunal' here meaning a processing centre established in Birmingham.

A notice of appeal must

- state the name and address of the appellant;
- state the name and address of any representative of the appellant;
- state an address where documents may be sent or delivered to the appellant;
- state details of the disputed decision, the result being sought and the grounds of appeal; and
- have attached a document containing the disputed decision and any statement of reasons for that decision that the appellant has or can reasonably obtain; and
- have attached any request for an extension of time and the reason why the notice of appeal was not provided in time.

When the tribunal receives the notice of appeal it must give notice of the proceedings to the respondent.

[*VATA 1994, s 83G; SI 2009/273, Rule 20*].

Setting aside a decision

[5.8] The tribunal may set aside a decision which disposes of proceedings and re-make the decision if it considers that it is in the interests of justice to do so and at least one of the following conditions is satisfied—

- a document relating to the proceedings was not sent to, or was not received at an appropriate time by, a party or a party's representative;
- a document relating to the proceedings was not sent to the tribunal at an appropriate time;
- there has been some other procedural irregularity in the proceedings; or

- a party, or a party's representative, was not present at a hearing related to the proceedings.

[*SI 2009/273, Rule 38*].

Striking out an appeal

[5.9] Proceedings may or must be struck out as follows—

- where the appellant has failed to comply with a direction that stated that failure to comply would lead to striking out, the proceedings will automatically be struck out;
- where the tribunal does not have jurisdiction in relation to the proceedings and it does not exercise its power under *SI 2009/2763, Rule 5(3)(k)(i)* to transfer the proceedings to another court or tribunal, it must strike out the proceedings;
- where the appellant has failed to comply with a direction that stated that failure to comply could lead to striking out, the tribunal may strike out the proceedings;
- where the appellant has failed to co-operate with the tribunal to such an extent that the tribunal cannot deal with the proceedings fairly and justly, the tribunal may strike out the proceedings;
- where the tribunal considers there is no reasonable prospect of the appellant's case succeeding, it may strike out the proceedings.

The above applies equally to the respondent (i.e. HMRC), except that a reference to the striking out of the proceedings must be read as a reference to the barring of the respondent from taking further part in the proceedings.

[*SI 2009/273, Rule 8*].

Making an application for a direction

[5.10] An application for a direction may be made orally during the course of a tribunal hearing, or by sending or delivering a written application to the tribunal. An application can be made for any of the following purposes —

- the reconsideration by a judge of a decision made by a member of staff delegated to make such a decision under *SI 2009/273, Rule 4(1)*;
- the reinstatement of proceedings struck out under *SI 2009/273, Rule 8(1) or (3)(a)* (failure to comply with a direction stating that such failure could or would lead to striking out);
- a party to be added to the proceedings;
- an order for costs;
- the summoning of a person to attend as witness;
- the reinstatement of a withdrawn case;
- a case to be heard without payment of the amount in dispute (hardship application);
- the reallocation of a case to a different category;
- full written findings and reasons for decision;
- the setting aside of a decision;
- permission to appeal;

- to treat an application as a different type of application.

[*SI 2009/273, Rule 6*].

Withdrawal of an appeal

[5.11] A party to an appeal may withdraw an appeal by giving notice to the tribunal, either orally at a hearing or by notice in writing before the hearing. [*SI 2009/273, Rule 17*].

If an appellant notifies HMRC, whether orally or in writing, that he does not wish to proceed with the appeal, then unless HMRC object in writing to the withdrawal of the appeal within 30 days of notification, the provisions relating to settling appeals by agreement (see **5.13** below) are treated as having effect as if, at the date of the appellant's notification, the appellant and HMRC had come to an agreement, orally or in writing as the case may be, that the decision under appeal should be upheld without variation. [*VATA 1994, s 85(4)*].

Review of decision by HMRC

[5.12] Taxpayers are entitled to request an internal review of appealable VAT decisions. This legal right to a review replaces reconsiderations and mandatory reviews. Reviews are optional and are done by a trained review officer, who has not previously been involved with that decision. HMRC must complete reviews within 45 days (unless another period is agreed with the taxpayer). If taxpayers do not want a review, or they do not agree with the result of the review, they can appeal to the tribunal for a decision.

[*VATA 1994, ss 83A–83G*].

Settling an appeal by agreement

[5.13] Where a person has given notice of appeal and, before the appeal is determined by a tribunal, HMRC and the appellant come to an agreement under which the decision under appeal is to be treated as

- upheld without variation,
- varied in a particular manner, or
- discharged or cancelled,

the agreement is binding as if a tribunal had determined the appeal in accordance with the terms of the agreement (including any terms as to costs). Where the parties have reached such an agreement, a tribunal will not continue the appeal purely in relation to an award of costs (*The Cadogan Club Ltd* (VTD 548) (TVC 2.494)).

The appellant may, however, within 30 days of the agreement, give written notice to HMRC that he desires to repudiate or resile from the agreement.

The agreement need not be in writing but, if it is not, the fact that an agreement was reached and the terms of that agreement must be confirmed in writing by HMRC to the appellant (or *vice versa*). The time of the agreement is then treated as the date of giving that notice of confirmation.

A person may act through an agent in all matters relating to settling appeals by agreement.

[*VATA 1994, s 85(1)–(3)(5)*].

Compounding agreement

Where HMRC and the taxpayer reach a compounding agreement, the dispute between the parties is resolved and any assessments raised effectively treated as discharged. Any outstanding appeal must be treated as having been settled by agreement (*Cummings (C)* (VTD 14870) (TVC 2.206)).

Preparation for the hearing of an appeal

Basic cases

[5.14] There is no requirement for HMRC to send a statement of case to the tribunal. Subject to any direction given by the tribunal, the case proceeds directly to a hearing. However, if HMRC intend to raise new grounds which have not been previously communicated to the appellant, they must notify the appellant of such grounds as soon as reasonably practicable, and in sufficient detail to enable the appellant to respond to such grounds at the hearing.

Default paper cases

HMRC must send or deliver a statement of case to the tribunal and the appellant so that it is received within 42 days after the tribunal sent the notice of the appeal. The statement of case must: state the legislative provision under which the decision under appeal was made; and set out HMRC's position in relation to the case. The statement may also contain a request that the case be dealt with at a hearing or without a hearing. If the statement is made later than the prescribed time limit (or any extension thereto), it must contain a request for an extension of time and the reason why it was not provided on time. The appellant may send or deliver a written reply (with a copy to HMRC) to the Tribunal so that it is received within 30 days after the date on which HMRC sent the statement of case to the appellant. Such a reply may: set out the appellant's response to the statement of case; provide any further relevant information; request that the case be dealt with at a hearing. Where the reply is made after the 30-day period referred to above (or such longer period as the tribunal may allow), it must include a request for an extension of time and the reason why the reply was not provided in time. Following receipt of the appellant's reply (or the expiry of time for its receipt), the tribunal must proceed to determine the case without a hearing, unless it has otherwise directed or a party to the appeal has otherwise requested in writing.

Standard or complex cases

HMRC must send or deliver a statement of case to the tribunal and the appellant so that it is received within 60 days after the tribunal sent the notice of the appeal. Within 42 days of the date on which the statement of case was sent, each party to the appeal must send to the tribunal and each other a list of documents of which the party providing the list has possession, the right to possession, or the right to take copies, and which the party providing the list intends to rely upon or produce in the proceedings. The party providing a list of documents must allow the other party to inspect or take copies of the listed documents (except for any which are privileged). The statement of case must state the legislative provision under which the decision under appeal was made; and set out HMRC's position in relation to the case. The statement may also contain a request that the case be dealt with at a hearing or without a hearing. If the statement is made later than the prescribed time limit (or any extension thereto), it must contain a request for an extension of time and the reason why it was not provided on time.

[*SI 2009/273, Rules 24–27*].

Witnesses

[5.15] On the application of a party to an appeal, or on its own initiative, the tribunal may summons any person to attend as a witness at a hearing; or order any person to answer any question or produce any documents in that person's possession or control which relate to any issue in the proceedings. No person may be compelled to give any evidence or produce any document which he could not be compelled to give or produce on a trial of an action in a court of law in the part of the UK where the proceedings are due to be determined. The person must be given at least 14 days' notice of the hearing, or such shorter period as the tribunal may direct. Provision must be made for payment of relevant expenses. The person may apply to the tribunal for the requirement to be varied or set aside if he did not have an opportunity to object to it before it was made or issued. Such an application must be made as soon as reasonably practicable.

[*SI 2009/273, Rule 16*].

Notice and location of a hearing

[5.16] The tribunal must provide each party with reasonable notice of the time and place of any hearing (including any adjourned or postponed hearing) and any changes thereto. In relation to a hearing to consider the disposal of proceedings, at least 14 days' notice must be given unless the parties agree otherwise, or there are urgent and exceptional circumstances.

[*SI 2009/273, Rule 31*].

Postponement

A tribunal is reluctant to postpone a hearing but if it is essential to do so, the appellant or applicant (or his representative) should contact the tribunal giving reasons for asking for the postponement. An engagement elsewhere is not normally sufficient reason for a postponement and the appellant should be ready to explain why another engagement takes priority. In any event, it should not be assumed that a hearing will be cancelled because a postponement has been requested. The hearing will stand unless the tribunal states otherwise.

Procedure at the hearing

Public or private

[5.17] An appeal is heard in public unless a tribunal directs otherwise. If the hearing is to take place in private the tribunal may determine who is permitted to attend. [*SI 2009/273, Rule 32*].

Representatives

A party may appoint a representative, legal or otherwise, to represent that party in the proceedings. The party must notify the tribunal and the other party of the name and address of its representative (in the case of a legal representative, the representative may carry out the notification). A representative may do anything permitted or required by a party under *SI 2009/273*, a direction or a practice direction, except signing a witness statement. A party may be accompanied by another person at a hearing. With the permission of the tribunal, that person may act as a representative or otherwise assist the party. [*SI 2009/273, Rule 11*].

Failure to appear at a hearing

If a party fails to attend the hearing, the tribunal may proceed to consider the appeal or application in his absence, provided that it is satisfied that that party has been informed of the hearing, or that reasonable steps have been taken to inform him, and that to proceed with the hearing is in the interests of justice. [*SI 2009/273, Rule 33*].

Decision of the tribunal

[5.18] The tribunal may give a decision orally at a hearing. It must, within 28 days or as soon as practicable thereafter, provide each party with a decision notice which states the tribunal's decision and notifies the party of any right of appeal against the decision and the time within which, and the manner in which, the right of appeal may be exercised. Unless each party agrees that it is unnecessary, the decision notice must include a summary of the findings of fact and reasons for the decision; or be accompanied by full written findings of fact and reasons for the decision. If the tribunal provides no such findings and reasons, or summary findings and reasons only, a party to the proceedings may apply in writing for full written findings and reasons, and must do so before making an application for permission to appeal. Such an application must be sent to the tribunal so that it is received within 28 days after the date that the tribunal sent the decision notice. The tribunal must send a full written statement of findings and reasons to each party within 28 days, or a soon as practicable thereafter, of receiving the application. [*SI 2009/273, Rule 35*].

Correction of errors

The tribunal may at any time correct any clerical mistake or other accidental slip or omission in a decision, by: sending notification of the amended decision or direction, or a copy of the amended document, to all parties; and making any necessary amendment to any information published in relation to the decision, direction or document. [*SI 2009/273, Rule 37*].

Review of decision

The First-Tier Tribunal may, on its own initiative or on application by a person who has the right to appeal to the Upper Tribunal, review its decision. It may then: correct accidental errors; amend the reasons given for the decision; or set aside the decision, in which case it must re-decide the matter concerned, or refer the matter to the Upper Tribunal for re-decision. [*TCEA 2007, s 9*].

Costs

[5.19] The costs of and incidental to all proceedings in the First-tier Tribunal, and all proceedings in the Upper Tribunal are at the discretion of the relevant tribunal, which has full power to determine by whom and to what extent the costs are to be paid. However, the First-tier Tribunal may only make an order in respect of costs if: it considers that a party or its representative has acted unreasonably in bringing, defending or conducting the proceedings; or the proceedings have been allocated as a complex case, and the taxpayer has not requested the tribunal in writing, within 28 days of receiving notice that the case had been allocated as complex, to exclude the proceedings from potential liability for costs. The First-tier Tribunal may not make an order for costs against a person without giving that person an opportunity to make representations and, if the person is an individual, considering his financial means. The Upper Tribunal is not so restricted, but it is required to: give a person an opportunity to make representations; and, in judicial review cases, or where the case has been transferred from the First-tier Tribunal, or where a party has acted unreasonably, to consider an individual's financial means.

Application for costs

A person making an application for costs must: send or deliver a written application to the tribunal and to the person against whom it is proposed that the order be made; and send or deliver with the application a schedule of the costs claimed in sufficient detail to allow the tribunal to undertake a summary assessment of such costs. The application may be made at any time during the proceedings but may not be made later than 28 days (in the case of the Upper Tribunal, one month) after the date on which the tribunal sends: a decision notice recording the decision which finally disposes of all issues in the proceedings; or notice of a withdrawal which ends the proceedings.

Award of costs

The amount of costs paid under an order may be ascertained by: summary assessment by the tribunal; agreement of a specified sum between the paying person and the receiving person; or assessment of the whole or a specified part of the costs incurred by the receiving person, if not agreed.

[*TCEA 2007 s 29; SI 2009/273, Rule 10*].

Enforcement of decisions

[5.20] Except in relation to awards made by the Upper Tribunal under its judicial review jurisdiction, a sum payable in pursuance of a decision of the First-tier Tribunal or Upper Tribunal made—

- in England and Wales is recoverable as if it were payable under an order of a county court or the High Court in England and Wales;
- in Scotland may be enforced as if it were an extract registered decree arbitral bearing a warrant for execution issued by the sheriff court of any sheriffdom in Scotland; and
- in Northern Ireland is recoverable as if it were payable under an order of a county court or the High Court in Northern Ireland.

[*TCEA 2007 s 27*].

Further appeal

Appeals from First-tier Tribunal to Upper Tribunal

[5.21] If any party is dissatisfied on a *point of law* with a decision of the First-tier Tribunal, he may appeal to the Upper Tribunal. The decision of the tribunal on a *question of fact* is final. The leading case on the question of the distinction between fact and law is *Edwards v Bairstow & Harrison,* HL 1955, 36 TC 207 (TVC 3.6). The right to appeal does not apply to 'excluded decisions', i.e. a decision by the First-tier Tribunal on review; a decision of the First-tier Tribunal which is set aside on review; or any decision of the First-tier Tribunal which is of a description specified in an order made by the Lord Chancellor.

An appeal may be made only with the permission of the First-tier Tribunal or, if that has been refused or not admitted, permission of the Upper Tribunal. An application to the First-Tier Tribunal must be made in writing and received within 56 days of the latest of the date on which the Tribunal sends to the applicant: full written reasons for the decision; notification of amended reasons for, or correction of, the decision following a review; notification that an application for the decision to be set aside has been unsuccessful. If the First-tier Tribunal grants permission to appeal, the appellant must provide a notice of appeal to the Upper Tribunal so that it is received within one month of the date on which the First-tier Tribunal sent notice of such permission to the appellant. An application to appeal to the Upper Tribunal must be made no later than one month after the date on which the First-tier Tribunal refused the application to appeal.

The Upper Tribunal may set aside the decision of the First-tier Tribunal. If it does so, it must either remit the case to the First-tier Tribunal with directions for its reconsideration, or re-make the decision. Proceedings on appeal to the Upper Tribunal are subject to the *Tribunal Procedure (Upper Tribunal) Rules, SI 2008/2698*, which to a large extent mirror the rules applicable in the First-tier Tribunal.

The Upper Tribunal may, on its own initiative or on application by a person who has the right to appeal to the Upper Tribunal, review a decision made by it. The Upper Tribunal may then: correct accidental errors; amend the reasons given for the decision; or set aside the decision, in which case it must re-decide the matter concerned.

[*TCEA 2007 ss 10–12; SI 2008/2698, Rule 21; SI 2009/273, Rule 39*].

Appeals from a tribunal to the Court of Appeal

There is a right to appeal to the Court of Appeal (Court of Session in Scotland) on any point of law arising from a decision made by the Upper Tribunal. That right may be exercised only with permission given by the Upper Tribunal, or (if the Upper Tribunal has refused permission) by the Court of Appeal. In England, Wales and Northern Ireland, applications for appeal are limited to cases where the Upper Tribunal (or Court of Appeal, as appropriate) considers that the proposed appeal would raise some important point of principle or practice, or there is some other compelling reason for the Court to hear the appeal. The right of appeal does not extend to an 'excluded decision', i.e. a decision of the Upper Tribunal on review; a decision of the Upper Tribunal which is set aside on review; or any decision of the Upper Tribunal which is of a description specified in an order made by the Lord Chancellor. In determining an appeal, the Court of Appeal may set aside the decision of the Upper Tribunal. If it does so, it must either remit the case to the Upper Tribunal or the First-tier Tribunal with directions for its reconsideration, or re-make the decision.

An appeal can be made from the Court of Appeal to the Supreme Court (formerly the House of Lords), with the leave of the Court of Appeal or the Supreme Court.

[*TCEA 2007 ss 13, 14; SI 2008/2834*].

References to the European Court of Justice

[5.22] A tribunal or higher court may refer a question to the ECJ if a decision on that matter is necessary to enable it to give judgment. [*EU Treaty, Art 267*]. Whether or not to refer a question is a matter within the discretion of the tribunal or court and it cannot be compelled to do so. It is not a matter for the parties to the case, although their views are no doubt taken into account. If one of the parties is dissatisfied with a refusal to refer a point to the ECJ, it must appeal under national law and has no right of access to the ECJ direct.

The national court has three options.

- It may decide that a decision on the question is unnecessary and that the case may, for example, be decided on the basis of national law which makes the question of EU law irrelevant.
- It may decide the question of EU law itself. This may be done, for example, where the point has been settled in previous ECJ decisions or where the circumstances of the case make a reference inconvenient.
- It may make a reference to the ECJ.

The courts have applied the following guidelines in exercising their discretion whether or not to make a reference.

- The point must be conclusive since the purpose of a ruling is to enable judgment to be given.
- There must have been no previous ruling which decides or substantially decides the point.

- If the point is reasonably clear and free from doubt it may not be necessary to interpret but simply apply the EU law.
- It is necessary to decide the facts first.
- The question to be referred is a matter of some importance.

The ECJ cannot interpret national law or apply its interpretation of EU law to the facts of the case. Its sole function is to decide what the EU law is, and leave the national courts to implement its ruling.

Key points

[5.23] Points to consider are as follows.

- Since 1 April 2009, most VAT appeals have been heard by the new First-tier Tribunal court, with more complex cases (or appeals against decisions made in the First-tier Tribunal) being heard in the Upper Tribunal.
- As a general principle, any VAT assessment that is being appealed by a taxpayer should be paid before the appeal is heard. However, there is an appeal facility if the payment would cause financial hardship to the business. In reality, HMRC tend to be quite flexible in granting such requests, especially if large amounts of tax are involved. If a taxpayer pays the disputed amount in advance, and is successful with his appeal, then he will be entitled to receive interest on the period between when he paid the tax and when he received his subsequent rebate.
- In relation to appeals against interest, penalties or default surcharges, there is no requirement for the amount to be paid in advance of the appeal hearing.
- Before making an appeal to a tribunal, a taxpayer has the right to request an internal review by a trained review officer in HMRC. The officer is required to carry out and complete his review within 45 days. If a taxpayer does not agree with the outcome of the review (e.g. if a VAT assessment is upheld) then he still has the right to appeal to the First-tier Tribunal. Equally, a taxpayer has the right to immediately appeal to the tribunal if he does not feel there is any benefit in going through the HMRC internal review process.
- The opportunity to be awarded costs is very limited with the new tribunal system. As a general principle, the First-tier Tribunal court will only award costs where it considers that one of the parties (obviously the unsuccessful party) has acted unreasonably in bringing a particular issue to appeal.
- An appeal against a First-tier Tribunal decision can only be made to the Upper Tribunal on a point of law, and not on a question of fact. The next stage of the appeal process after the Upper Tribunal will be the Court of Appeal (Court of Session in Scotland). In some cases, an appeal can then be made to the House of Lords. At various points in the appeal process, a reference can be made to

the ECJ (European Court of Justice) to answer an important matter of uncertainty that affects the case and needs to be clarified. The latter course of action should only be needed on a very infrequent basis.

6

Assessments

Cross-references. See **5 APPEALS; 27.5 GROUPS OF COMPANIES; 51 PAYMENT OF VAT.**

De Voil Indirect Tax Service. See V5.131–140.

Introduction

[6.1] VAT is normally paid (without any assessment being made) on the submission of a return for a VAT period.

However, subject to the time limits in **6.2** below, HMRC are given power to raise assessments where the following circumstances apply.

(a) *Returns have not been made.* Assessments will generally be based on centrally stored data concerning the trader's business and VAT history and will normally be withdrawn if an acceptable return is made and the VAT declared on it paid.

(b) *Documents have not been kept* and facilities have not been afforded to verify returns.

(c) *It appears to HMRC that the returns are incomplete or incorrect.* This will most frequently happen following control visits by HMRC officers.

(d) *Incorrect VAT credits*, i.e. where for any VAT period an amount has been paid or credited to any person as either a repayment or refund of VAT or as being due as a VAT credit and the amount ought not to have been paid or credited. This is further extended to cover an amount which would not have been so paid or credited had the facts been known or been as they later turn out to be (e.g. where bad debt relief has been claimed and subsequently the debt, or part, has been repaid without the VAT element being paid to HMRC). There are conflicting court judgments as to the period HMRC should assess (which is important, particularly in view of the two-year time limit under **6.2** below). HMRC have taken the view that the period to assess is the period for which a return was made that contained the incorrect claim or, following the judgment in *C & E Commrs v The Croydon Hotel & Leisure Co Ltd*, CA [1996] STC 1105 (TVC 3.43), the period in which a voluntary disclosure (now error correction notification) containing the incorrect claim was made. However, the judgment in *C & E Commrs v Laura Ashley Ltd, Ch D 2003*, [2004] STC 635 (TVC 3.44) was that the period to assess should be the period to which the relevant VAT related, i.e. an assessment to recover a repayment or credit wrongly given following a voluntary disclosure of an error in an earlier period should have been made for that earlier period. Finally, in *C & E Commrs v DFS Furniture Co plc*, CA [2004] STC 559 (TVC 3.111) the court took the view, in similar although not identical circumstances, that the period to assess was the period current when the repayment was made.

(e) *Failure to account for goods*, i.e. where goods have, in the course or furtherance of a business, been supplied to a taxable person, acquired or obtained by him from another EU country or imported by him from a place outside the EU and he is unable to prove to HMRC that the goods
- have been, or are available to be, supplied by him;
- have been exported or otherwise removed from the UK without being exported or so removed by way of supply; or
- have been lost or destroyed.

(f) *A fiscal warehousekeeper has failed to pay VAT* required under *VATA 1994, s 18E* on any missing or deficient goods or it appears to HMRC that goods have been removed from a warehouse or fiscal warehouse without payment of the VAT required under *VATA 1994, s 18(4)* or *s 18D*.

(g) *Goods subject to excise duty or new means of transport* have been acquired in the UK from another EU country by a person who at that time was not a taxable person and
(i) no notification of that acquisition has been given to HMRC by the person required to give it;
(ii) HMRC are not satisfied that the particulars in a notification are accurate or complete; or
(iii) there has been a failure to supply HMRC with the information necessary to verify the particulars contained in the notification.

See **19.9** and **19.37 EUROPEAN UNION: SINGLE MARKET** for general provisions relating to such acquisition of dutiable goods and new means of transport respectively.

Any amount assessed and notified under these provisions is deemed to be an amount of VAT due and, if the person fails to pay, enforcement action can be taken to recover the debt.

(h) *VAT has been lost as a result of conduct involving dishonesty* within *VATA 1994, s 60* (see **52.10 PENALTIES**), conduct for which a person has been convicted of fraud, or registration irregularities or unauthorised issue of VAT invoices under *VATA 1994, s 67* (see **52.14 PENALTIES**).

An amount assessed and notified to a person under any of the above provisions is, subject to appeal, deemed to be an amount of VAT due and is recoverable unless the assessment is subsequently withdrawn or reduced.

Where a person is assessed under either of (*a*) to (*c*) *and* (*d*) above for the same VAT period, assessments may be combined and notified to the person in one assessment.

[*VATA 1994, s 73(1)–(4)(7)(7A)(7B)(9), s 75(1)(3); FA 1996, Sch 3 paras 10, 11; FA 2000, s 136(4)*].

HMRC may raise a single or 'global' assessment covering more than one accounting period (*SJ Grange Ltd v C & E Commrs*, CA 1978 [1979] STC 183 (TVC 3.114)). This power may be necessary where it is impossible or impracticable to identify the specific accounting periods for which the VAT claimed is due but is not restricted to such cases. It is a question of fact (important for time limit purposes) whether there is one global assessment or a number of separate assessments notified together. In *Razaq and Bashir (t/a/ Streamline Taxis)* (VTD 17537) (TVC 47.16) HMRC incorrectly issued the registration certificate in the names of Razaq and Shabir and subsequently issued a global assessment covering the period 1 November 1994 to 1 November 1998. The tribunal held that the certificate was invalid. The effect of *SI 1995/2518, Reg 25(1)* was that the partnership was required to be registered and make quarterly returns from 1 November 1984 but since there was no valid certificate of registration, the effect of *VATA 1994, s 73* was that HMRC had to assess accounting period by accounting period and could not make a valid global assessment for the overall period.

The Form on which HMRC notify assessments is clearly intended to be used for either a single or a number of assessments and the fact therefore that demands for multiple accounting periods are included on the same form does not necessarily constitute a single global assessment (*C & E Commrs v Le Rififi Ltd*, CA 1994 [1995] STC 103 (TVC 3.87) not following the earlier decision in *Don Pasquale (a firm) v C & E Commrs*, CA [1990] STC 556 (TVC 2.141)).

The assessment, to be valid, must show the period covered not just the end of that period (*RE Bell* (VTD 761) (TVC 3.136)) although the information need not necessarily be on the assessment itself. See *House (PJ) (t/a P & J Autos) v C & E Commrs*, CA 1995, [1996] STC 154 (TVC 3.127) where the dates covered by the assessment were left blank but the period assessed was indicated by accompanying schedules. A notice of assessment issued 'without prejudice' is not invalid (*McCafferty* (VTD 483) (TVC 3.47)).

Where an assessment has been made as a result of a person's failure to submit a return for a VAT period and, although the VAT assessed has been paid, no proper return has been made for that period, if HMRC find it necessary to raise assessments for later periods due to the failure to submit returns by that person or a representative of his (see **6.9** below) then HMRC may raise the later assessments for amounts greater than that which they would otherwise consider to be appropriate. [*VATA 1994, s 73(8)*].

Subject to the foregoing, assessments under (*a*) to (*c*) and (*e*) to (*g*) above must be made to the best of HMRC's judgment. [*VATA 1994, s 73(1)(7)(7A)(7B), s 75(1); FA 1996, Sch 3 para 10*]. HMRC must exercise their powers honestly and bona fide and there must be material before them on which to make their judgment. Although their decisions must be reasonable and not arbitrary, they are under no obligation to do the work of a taxpayer by carrying out exhaustive investigations but if they do make investigations, they must take into account material disclosed by them (*Van Boeckel v C & E Commrs*, QB 1980, [1981] STC 290 (TVC 3.1)). The function of the tribunal is supervisory. An assessment should only be held to fail the 'best judgment' test if made dishonestly, vindictively or capriciously, where it is a spurious estimate or guess in which all the elements of judgment are missing, or where it is wholly unreasonable. Short of such a finding there is no justification for setting aside an assessment. In the normal case, the important issue is the amount of the assessment (*MH Rahman (t/a Khayam Restaurant) v C & E Commrs*, QB [1998] STC 826 (TVC 3.8) and see also *C & E Commrs v Pegasus Birds Ltd*, CA [2004] STC 1509 (TVC 3.20)) and once the tribunal has accepted that HMRC were entitled to make that assessment, the amount is for the tribunal to decide (*Murat v C & E Commrs*, QB [1998] STC 923 (TVC 3.164)). The function of the tribunal is to decide what information HMRC relied upon to make the assessment and then make a value judgment as to how they arrived at the assessment. It is not a function of the tribunal to engage in a process that looks afresh at all the evidence before it (*Georgiou and another (t/a Mario's Chippery) v C & E Commrs*, CA [1996] STC 463 (TVC 3.6)). See also *Seto v C & E Commrs*, CS 1980, [1981] STC 698 (TVC 3.2). An assessment must be considered as a whole and if it is not made to the best of HMRC's judgment, then it is wholly invalid and void and cannot be corrected by any subsequent amendment to it or treated as partly valid. See *Barber (JH)* (VTD 7727) (TVC 3.37) where an assessment partly covered a period for which a previous assessment had already been raised.

Where an earlier assessment has been held to be defective because it was not made to the best of HMRC's judgment, HMRC are not estopped from issuing a replacement assessment by the principle of '*res judicata*', i.e. that an issue which a court has decided in an action between the parties cannot be questioned in a later action between the same parties (*Bennett v C & E Commrs (No 2)*, Ch D [2001] STC 137 (TVC 2.125) (TVC 34.14)).

Time limits

Provisions applying from 1 April 2009

[6.2] The following time limits for assessments under **6.1** above apply with effect from 1 April 2009.

(a) Under **6.1**(*a*)–(*d*), subject to the provisions relating to death below, an assessment for any VAT period cannot be made after the later of
  (i) two years after the end of the VAT period; or
  (ii) one year after evidence of fact, sufficient in the opinion of HMRC to justify the making of an assessment, comes to their knowledge

  but in any case not more than four years after the end of the VAT period.

In the case of an assessment under **6.1**(*d*) above, the VAT period referred to in (i) above is that in which the repayment or refund of VAT, or the VAT credit, was paid or credited.
See **6.6** below for further assessments.

(b) Under **6.1**(*e*)(*f*), subject to the provisions relating to death below, an assessment cannot be made more than four years after the end of the VAT period or importation or acquisition concerned.

(c) Under **6.1**(*g*), subject to the provisions relating to death below, an assessment cannot be made after the later of
   (i) two years after the time of notification to HMRC of the acquisition of the goods in question; or
   (ii) one year after evidence of fact, sufficient in the opinion of HMRC to justify the making of an assessment, comes to their knowledge

   but in any case not more than four years after the end of the VAT period. See **6.6** below for further assessments.

(d) In the case of an assessment of a person ('P'), or of an amount payable by P,
   (i) involving a loss of VAT brought about deliberately by P (or by another person acting on P's behalf),
   (ii) in which P has participated in a transaction knowing that it was part of arrangements of any kind (whether or not legally enforceable) intended to bring about a loss of VAT,
   (iii) involving a loss of VAT attributable to a failure by P to comply with a 'notification obligation', or
   (iv) involving a loss of VAT attributable to a scheme in respect of which P has failed to comply with an obligation under *VATA 1994, Sch 11A para 6* (see **4 ANTI-AVOIDANCE**)

   subject to the provisions relating to death below, the assessment may be made at any time not more than 20 years after the end of the VAT period or the importation, acquisition or event giving rise to the penalty, as appropriate.

   A loss of VAT brought about deliberately by P or another person includes a loss that arises as a result of a deliberate inaccuracy in a document given to HMRC by that person.

   '*Notification obligation*' means an obligation in connection with registration under *VATA 1994, Sch 1* (registration generally), *VATA 1994, Sch 2* (registration in respect of supplies from other EU countries), *VATA 1994, Sch 3* (registration in respect of acquisitions from other EU countries), *VATA 1994, Sch 3A* (registration in respect of disposals of assets for which a VAT repayment is claimed) and regulations under *VATA 1994, Sch 11 para 2(4)* (certain taxable acquisitions of goods which are subject to excise duty or are new means of transport and are acquired in the UK from another EU country by a non-taxable person).

Death

Where the taxable person has died, any assessment cannot be made more than four years after death.

[*VATA 1994, s 73(6)(6A), s 75(2), s 77(1)(4)(4A)–(4C)(5); FA 1997, s 47(10); FA 2008, s 120, Sch 39 para 34; SI 2009/403*].

Where a single global assessment is made because it is not possible to identify a specific period for which VAT is due, the two-year time limit runs from the end of the *first* VAT period it covers (*International Language Centres Ltd v C & E Commrs*, QB, [1983] STC 394 (TVC 3.41)). Where a global assessment is raised out of time on this basis, it is a nullity *ab initio* even if the taxpayer failed to lodge an appeal against it in due time with a VAT tribunal (*Lord Advocate v Shanks (t/a Shanks & Co)*, CS [1992] STC 928 (TVC 2.196)). See, however, **6.1** above for the different interpretation of what constitutes a global assessment following the decision in *C & E Commrs v Le Rififi Ltd*, CA 1994, [1995] STC 103 (TVC 3.87).

A tribunal considering the possible application of (*a*)(ii) must decide what were the facts which, in the opinion of the officer making the assessment on behalf of HMRC, justified the making of the assessment and then decide when the last of these facts came to the knowledge of the officer. The period of one year then runs from that date (*Heyfordian Travel Ltd* (VTD 774) (TVC 3.115)). Similarly, in *Pegasus Birds Ltd v C & E Commrs*, CA [2000] STC 91 (TVC 3.57) the court observed that provided HMRC acquired the last piece of evidence of sufficient weight to justify an assessment within the one-year time limit, the test in (*a*)(ii) is satisfied. 'Evidence of facts' means what it says; the words do not encompass constructive knowledge (*Spillane v C & E Commrs*, QB 1989, [1990] STC 212 (TVC 3.4)). This was confirmed in *C & E Commrs v Post Office*, QB [1995] STC 749 (TVC 3.55) where it was held that the relevant date was not when any error should have been discovered but when evidence of facts actually came to the knowledge of HMRC. Nothing in the statutory provisions encompasses constructive knowledge. There is no obligation on HMRC to be alert to discover a mistake (*FC Milnes (Bradford) Ltd* (VTD 478) (TVC 3.116)). Following the rule in *C & E Commrs v J H Corbitt (Numismatists) Ltd*, HL [1980] STC 231 (TVC 60.1), the Court is prevented from substituting its opinion for that of HMRC and therefore it can only interfere if there is material to show that an officer's failure to make an earlier assessment was perverse (*Cumbrae Properties (1963) Ltd v C & E Commrs*, QB [1981] STC 799 (TVC 62.24)).

Where returns which are clearly incorrect are in the hands of HMRC, assessments are out of date if made outside the two-year period and no evidence of new facts have come to HMRC's attention to bring the case within (*a*)(ii) above (*Lord (t/a Lords Electrical and Fancy Goods)* (VTD 320) (TVC 3.71)).

The legislation specifies time limits for the 'making' of an assessment rather than the 'notification' of that assessment to the taxpayer. For a consideration of when an assessment is made (as distinct from notified) see *Cheeseman (t/a Well in Tune) v C & E Commrs*, Ch D [2000] STC 1119 (TVC 3.85). However, to avoid any uncertainty, for all assessments issued on or after 1 March 2001, HMRC will apply the time limit rule to the 'notified' date rather than the earlier 'made' date. See **6.7** below.

Provisions applying before 1 April 2009

The time limits for assessments under **6.1** above in respect of any VAT period are as follows.

(a) Under **6.1**(*a*)–(*d*), subject to the provisions relating to death below, an assessment for any VAT period cannot be made after the later of
  (i) two years after the end of the VAT period; or
  (ii) one year after evidence of fact, sufficient in the opinion of HMRC to justify the making of an assessment, comes to their knowledge

  but in any case not more than three years after the end of the VAT period.

  With effect from 19 March 2008, in order to resolve any confusion in the case of an assessment under **6.1**(*d*) above, the VAT period referred to in (i) above is that in which the repayment or refund of VAT, or the VAT credit, was paid or credited.

  See **6.6** below for further assessments.

(b) Under **6.1**(*e*)(*f*), subject to the provisions relating to death below, an assessment cannot be made more than three years after the end of the VAT period or importation or acquisition concerned.

(c) Under **6.1**(*g*), subject to the provisions relating to death below, an assessment cannot be made after the later of
  (i) two years after the time of notification to HMRC of the acquisition of the goods in question; or
  (ii) one year after evidence of fact, sufficient in the opinion of HMRC to justify the making of an assessment, comes to their knowledge

  but in any case not more than three years after the end of the VAT period. See **6.6** below for further assessments.

(d) Under **6.1**(*h*), subject to the provisions relating to death below, an assessment cannot be made more than 20 years after the end of the relevant period or two years after the VAT due for the relevant period has been finally determined.

Death

Where the taxable person has died, any assessment cannot be made more than three years after death. In addition, for assessments under **6.1**(*h*) above, the 20-year time limit above is reduced to three years but any assessment which, from the point of view of time limits, could have been made immediately after death may be made at any time within three years after it.

[*VATA 1994, s 73(6)(6A), s 75(2), s 77(1)(4)(5); FA 1997, s 47(10); FA 2008, s 120*].

De Voil Indirect Tax Service. See V5.136–136A.

Assessments of penalties, interest and surcharges

[6.3] HMRC may assess and notify any amount due by way of

(a) default surcharge under *VATA 1994, ss 59, 59A* (see **52.21** and **52.22** **PENALTIES**),
(b) penalty under *VATA 1994, ss 60–69B* (see **52.10** to **52.17** and **52.24** to **52.27** **PENALTIES**),
(c) interest under *VATA 1994, s 74* (see **51.15** **PAYMENT OF VAT**),
(d) penalty under *VATA 1994, Sch 11A* (see **4.2** **ANTI-AVOIDANCE**),
(e) penalty in connection with the mandatory electronic filing of VAT returns (see **2.1** **ACCOUNTING PERIODS AND RETURNS**), or
(f) penalty under *FA 2008, Sch 36 paras 39–40A* (see **52.18** **PENALTIES**)

except that a penalty under **52.17**(*b*)(vi)–(x) **PENALTIES** can only be assessed if, within the two years preceding the date of the assessment, HMRC have issued a written warning of the consequences of a continuing failure to comply with the relevant requirement.

Unless the assessment is withdrawn or reduced, the amount is recoverable as if it were VAT due (except a penalty under (*f*) which may be enforced as if it were assessed and payable as income tax). The fact that the conduct giving rise to any penalty under (*b*), (*d*) or (*e*) above may have ceased before an assessment is made does not affect the powers of HMRC to make an assessment.

Combining assessments

Where for a particular accounting period a person is assessed for VAT due under **6.1**(*a*)–(*g*) as well as surcharge, penalty or interest under these provisions, HMRC may combine the assessments but the amount of the penalty, interest or surcharge should be shown separately.

Allocation of VAT between periods

Where any penalty, etc. must be calculated by reference to VAT which was paid late or avoided and that VAT cannot be readily attributed to one or more VAT periods, HMRC are empowered to allocate the VAT due to such period or periods as they determine to the best of their judgment.

Penalties, interest accruing on daily basis

Where a penalty or interest accrues on a daily basis, the assessment must specify a date (not later than the date of the notice) to which the penalty or interest is calculated. If the penalty or interest continues to accrue after that date, a further assessment or assessments may be made in respect of amounts so accruing. HMRC, however, may notify the person liable of a period during which he may remedy the failure or default which caused the penalty or pay the amount on which interest was charged. If the person meets this requirement, no further penalty or interest accrues after the date specified in the assessment.

Penalties for tax avoidance

Where HMRC notify a person of a penalty under (*d*) above the assessment must specify the amount of the penalty, the reasons for the imposition of the penalty, how the penalty has been calculated, and any mitigation of the penalty under *VATA 1994, s 70* (see **52.30** **PENALTIES**).

[*VATA 1994, s 76, Sch 11A para 12; FA 1996, s 35(7), Sch 3 para 11; FA 2000, s 137(4); FA 2004, Sch 2; F(No 2)A 2005, Sch 1 para 8; FA 2006, s 21(3); FA 2007, s 93(4)–(7); FA 2008, Sch 36 paras 46, 49; FA 2009, Sch 47 para 20*].

Time limits

[6.4] An assessment for any relevant period under **6.3** above cannot be made after the following times or, where there is an alternative, the *earlier* of such times.

Provisions applying from 1 April 2009

The following time limits apply from 1 April 2009.

(a) In the case of an assessment of a person ('P'), or of an amount payable by P,
   - (i) involving a loss of VAT brought about deliberately by P (or by another person acting on P's behalf),
   - (ii) in which P has participated in a transaction knowing that it was part of arrangements of any kind (whether or not legally enforceable) intended to bring about a loss of VAT,
   - (iii) involving a loss of VAT attributable to a failure by P to comply with a 'notification obligation', or
   - (iv) involving a loss of VAT attributable to a scheme in respect of which P has failed to comply with an obligation *VATA 1994, Sch 11A para 6* (see **4 ANTI-AVOIDANCE**)

   subject to the provisions relating to death below, the assessment may be made at any time not more than 20 years after the end of the VAT period or the importation, acquisition or event giving rise to the penalty, as appropriate.

   A loss of VAT brought about deliberately by P or another person includes a loss that arises as a result of a deliberate inaccuracy in a document given to HMRC by that person.

   '*Notification obligation*' means an obligation in connection with registration under *VATA 1994, Sch 1* (registration generally), *VATA 1994, Sch 2* (registration in respect of supplies from other EU countries), *VATA 1994, Sch 3* (registration in respect of acquisitions from other EU countries), *VATA 1994, Sch 3A* (registration in respect of disposals of assets for which a VAT repayment is claimed) and regulations under *VATA 1994, Sch 11 para 2(4)* (certain taxable acquisitions of goods which are subject to excise duty or are new means of transport and are acquired in the UK from another EU country by a non-taxable person).

(b) For assessments under *VATA 1994, s 59* (default surcharge, see **52.21 PENALTIES**), *VATA 1994, s 63* (misdeclaration, see **52.12 PENALTIES**) or *VATA 1994, s 74* (interest on VAT, see **51.15 PAYMENT OF VAT**)
   - four years after the end of the relevant period; or
   - two years after the VAT due for the relevant period has finally been determined.

(c) For assessments under *VATA 1994, s 62* (incorrect certificates of zero-rating, see **52.23 PENALTIES**), *VATA 1994, s 64* (repeated misdeclaration, see **52.12 PENALTIES**), *VATA 1994, s 68* (breaches of walking possession agreements, see **52.16 PENALTIES**) or *VATA 1994, s 69* (breaches of regulatory provisions, see **52.17 PENALTIES**) four years after the event giving rise to the penalty.

(d) For assessments under *VATA 1994, s 65* (inaccuracies in EU sales statements, see **52.24 PENALTIES**) or *VATA 1994, s 66* (failure to submit EU sales statements, see **52.25 PENALTIES**)
- four years after the event giving rise to the penalty; or
- two years after the time when sufficient facts came to the knowledge of HMRC to indicate that, as the case may be, the statement had a material inaccuracy or there had been a default in the submission of a sales statement.

(e) For assessments under *VATA 1994, s 69A* (breach of record-keeping requirements in relation to transactions in gold, see **52.26 PENALTIES**)
- four years after the transaction giving rise to the penalty; or
- two years after HMRC have evidence of facts '*sufficient in their opinion to justify the making of the assessment*' i.e. facts sufficient both to indicate that there has been a failure to comply with the provisions and to determine the value of the transaction concerned.

(f) For assessments under *VATA 1994, Sch 11A para 12* (failure to notify certain VAT avoidance schemes, see **4.2 ANTI-AVOIDANCE**) two years after the time when sufficient facts come to the knowledge of HMRC to indicate that there has been a failure to comply with those provisions in relation to a notifiable scheme.

Death

Where the taxable person has died, any assessment under (*a*)–(*d*) above cannot be made more than four years after death.

[*VATA 1994, ss 69A(4)(5), 77(1)–(5), Sch 11A para 12(4); FA 1997, s 47(10); FA 1999, s 18; FA 2000, s 137(2); FA 2004, Sch 2; FA 2008, Sch 39 para 34; SI 2009/403*].

The legislation specifies time limits for the 'making' of an assessment rather than the 'notification' of that assessment to the taxpayer. For a consideration of when an assessment is made (as distinct from notified) see *Cheeseman (t/a Well in Tune) v C & E Commrs*, Ch D [2000] STC 1119 (TVC 3.85). However, to avoid any uncertainty, HMRC will apply the time limit rule to the 'notified' date rather than the earlier 'made' date. See **6.7** below.

Provisions applying before 1 April 2009

(a) Where VAT has been lost as a result of conduct falling within *VATA 1994, s 60(1)* (VAT evasion: conduct involving dishonesty, see **52.10 PENALTIES**) or conduct for which a person has been convicted of fraud
- 20 years after the end of the relevant period; or
- two years after the VAT due for the relevant period has been finally determined.

(b) Where VAT has been lost in circumstances giving rise to a penalty under *VATA 1994, s 67* (registration irregularities and unauthorised issue of VAT invoices, see **52.14 PENALTIES**) 20 years after the event giving rise to the penalty.

(c) For assessments under *VATA 1994, s 59* (default surcharge, see **52.21 PENALTIES**), *VATA 1994, s 63* (misdeclaration, see **52.12 PENALTIES**) or *VATA 1994, s 74* (interest on VAT, see **51.15 PAYMENT OF VAT**)
- three years after the end of the relevant period; or
- two years after the VAT due for the relevant period has finally been determined.

(d) For assessments under *VATA 1994, s 62* (incorrect certificates of zero-rating, see **52.23 PENALTIES**), *VATA 1994, s 64* (repeated misdeclaration, see **52.12 PENALTIES**), *VATA 1994, s 68* (breaches of walking possession agreements, see **52.16 PENALTIES**) or *VATA 1994, s 69* (breaches of regulatory provisions, see **52.17 PENALTIES**) three years after the event giving rise to the penalty.

(e) For assessments under *VATA 1994, s 65* (inaccuracies in EU sales statements, see **52.24 PENALTIES**) or *VATA 1994, s 66* (failure to submit EU sales statements, see **52.25 PENALTIES**)
- three years after the event giving rise to the penalty; or
- two years after the time when sufficient facts came to the knowledge of HMRC to indicate that, as the case may be, the statement had a material inaccuracy or there had been a default in the submission of a sales statement.

(f) For assessments under *VATA 1994, s 69A* (breach of record-keeping requirements in relation to transactions in gold, see **52.26 PENALTIES**)
- three years after the transaction giving rise to the penalty; or
- two years after HMRC have evidence of facts '*sufficient in their opinion to justify the making of the assessment*' i.e. facts sufficient both to indicate that there has been a failure to comply with the provisions and to determine the value of the transaction concerned.

(g) For assessments under *VATA 1994, Sch 11A para 12* (failure to notify certain VAT avoidance schemes, see **4.2 ANTI-AVOIDANCE**) two years after the time when sufficient facts come to the knowledge of HMRC to indicate that there has been a failure to comply with those provisions in relation to a notifiable scheme.

Death

Where the taxable person has died, any assessment under (*a*)–(*e*) above cannot be made more than three years after death. In addition, for assessments within (*a*) or (*b*) above, the 20-year time limit is reduced to three years but any assessment which, from the point of view of time limits, could have been made immediately after death may be made at any time within three years after it.

[*VATA 1994, ss 69A(4)(5), 77(1)–(5), Sch 11A para 12(4); FA 1997, s 47(10); FA 1999, s 18; FA 2000, s 137(2); FA 2004, Sch 2*].

Assessments for overpaid interest and repayments

[6.5] HMRC may raise recovery assessments to the best of their judgment in the following circumstances and notify the person accordingly.

(a) Where they have paid interest under *VATA 1994, s 78* (see **51.17 PAYMENT OF VAT**) to any person who was not entitled to it, they may assess the amount paid.

(b) Where they have credited a person with an amount under *VATA 1994, s 80(1)* or *(1A)* (see **51.8**(*a*) and (*b*) **PAYMENT OF VAT**) in excess of the amount for which they were liable at that time, they may assess the excess credited. *For claims made before 26 May 2005*, HMRC may raise recovery assessments where they made a repayment in excess of their repayment liability at that time.

(c) Where any person is liable under *Regulations* made under *VATA 1994, s 80A* to pay to HMRC any VAT previously repaid by HMRC to them on the understanding that it would be reimbursed to customers (see **51.9 PAYMENT OF VAT**), they may assess the amount due.

(d) Where
  (i) they have credited a person with an amount ('the gross credit') under *VATA 1994, s 80(1)* or *(1A)* (see **51.9**(*a*) and (*b*) **PAYMENT OF VAT**),
  (ii) any sums were set against that amount by HMRC, and
  (iii) the amount reimbursed to customers was less than the gross credit,

  they may assess so much of the gross credit as exceeds the amount reimbursed to customers. No liability can arise on the same amount under both (*c*) above and this provision.

Unless the assessment is withdrawn or reduced, the amount is recoverable as if it were VAT due.

Time limits

The time limits for making an assessment under the above provisions are as follows.

- Under (*a*), (*c*) or (*d*) above, an assessment cannot be made more than two years after evidence of facts, sufficient in the opinion of HMRC to justify the making of an assessment, comes to their knowledge.
- Under (*b*) above, *with effect from 19 March 2008*, an assessment cannot be made more than two years after the later of
  (i) the end of the VAT period in which the amount was credited to the person; and
  (ii) the time when evidence of facts, sufficient in the opinion of HMRC to justify the making of the assessment, comes to their knowledge.

  Before 19 March 2008, an assessment could not be made more than two years after (ii) above.

'Evidence of facts' does not include court judgments and their effects. See *C & E Commrs v DFS Furniture Co plc*, CA [2004] STC 559 (TVC 3.111) where an HMRC assessment raised in 2001 to recover VAT relating to periods from

April 1993 to June 1996 was held to be invalid even though it was within two years of the decision by the ECJ in *C & E Commrs v Primback Ltd, ECJ Case C-34/99*, [2001] STC 803 (TVC 22.242) (which overruled the 1996 decision by the CA in that case on the basis of which a repayment had been made to *DFS Furniture*).

Interest

The provisions of *VATA 1994, s 74* (interest payable on VAT, see **51.14 PAYMENT OF VAT**) apply to such an assessment except that in the calculation of the period of interest, interest runs from the date the assessment is notified until the date of payment.

HMRC may assess and notify any amount due by way of interest on a recovery assessment but (without prejudice to the power to make assessments for interest for later periods) the assessment is restricted to interest for a period of no more than two years ending with the time when the assessment to interest is made. The assessment must specify a date (not later than the date of the notice) to which the interest is calculated. If the interest continues to accrue after that date, a further assessment or assessments may be made in respect of the amounts so accruing. HMRC, however, may notify the person liable of a period during which he may pay the underlying assessment and, if the person meets this requirement, no further interest accrues after the date specified in the assessment.

Further assessments

See **6.6**(*b*) below.

Personal representatives

Notification of an assessment to a personal representative, trustee in bankruptcy, interim or permanent trustee, receiver, liquidator or person otherwise acting in a representative capacity is treated as notification to the person on whose behalf he acts.

[*VATA 1994, s 78A, s 80(4A)(4AA)(4C), s 80B; FA 1997, s 45(1)(4), s 46(2)(4), s 47(6)(9); F(No 2)A 2005, ss 3(9), 4(4); FA 2008, s 120*].

Further assessments

[6.6] HMRC may make further assessments in the following circumstances.

(a) Where, after an assessment has been made under **6.1**(*a*)–(*d*) or (*g*) above, further 'evidence of facts', sufficient in the opinion of HMRC to justify the making of an assessment, comes to their knowledge. [*VATA 1994, s 73(6), s 75(2)*]. The further assessment must also be within the time limit (see **6.2** above). Contents of nil returns submitted by a taxpayer do not amount to 'evidence of facts' justifying a further assessment (*Parekh & another v C & E Commrs*, QB [1984] STC 284 (TVC 3.75)). In that case, Woolf J also observed that, where the two-year time limit for an assessment has elapsed. HMRC should only be allowed to make a further assessment in relation to the VAT due based on the evidence which has come to their knowledge since the earlier assessment. Where, however, the two-year period has not elapsed, HMRC are not prevented from withdrawing the earlier assessment and replacing it by another.

(b) If, otherwise than in circumstances falling within (*a*) above, it appears to HMRC that the amount which ought to have been assessed under any of the provisions of **6.1**, **6.3** or **6.5** above exceeds the amount which was so assessed, then a supplementary assessment of the amount of the excess may be made and notified to the person concerned under the same provisions and within the same time limits as the original assessment. [*VATA 1994, s 77(6), s 78A(6); FA 1997, s 45(1)*]. Note that there is no requirement for further evidence as in (*a*) above.

De Voil Indirect Tax Service. See V5.134.

The assessment process

[6.7] Unless there is a danger of losing VAT because of the imminence of a time limit or unless the nature of the irregularity is agreed and already clear, HMRC will normally write to the taxpayer in advance of making an assessment for underdeclared or overclaimed VAT, setting out why they believe an assessment to be necessary and detailing the calculation of arrears. This letter does not constitute the 'making' of an assessment but gives the taxpayer the chance to bring further information to the attention of HMRC and help resolve any misunderstanding or disagreement before the assessment is made. Normally, HMRC give the taxpayer three weeks to reply.

The assessment process itself is made up of three stages.

(a) *The decision to assess.*

(b) *The making of the assessment.* This process includes deciding in principle to assess, the quantification of arrears and any necessary checking of arrears calculations. It ends when the HMRC officer has taken all steps necessary to establish to the best of his judgement that the taxpayer owes a quantified sum for a given reason. That officer, and any checking officer, will sign and date any schedules of calculation. HMRC will normally provide copies of these schedules to the taxpayer to help explain the basis of the assessment.

(c) *The notification of that amount.* HMRC must formally notify the taxpayer by way of assessment of the amount of VAT due [*VATA 1994, s 73(1)*] but there is no express provision as to the manner in which this is to be done. In practice, the taxpayer will be notified in one of two ways.

- Normally, an internal Form VAT 641 is completed, signed and dated. This form is the means of inputting an assessment on to HMRC's computer system which then generates Form VAT 655, the notice of assessment to be issued to the taxpayer. The Form VAT 655 is sent from the central computer centre to the local VAT office where it is checked and then dated and sent to the taxpayer.

- In certain circumstances, for example, where there is some risk of an assessment which has been made in time not being notified to the taxpayer until after the time limit has expired, the assessing officer will send a dated notification of assessment by letter to the taxpayer. The computer generated Form VAT 655 will then normally be issued in due course.

The legislation specifies time limits for the making of an assessment under (*b*) above (see **6.2** and **6.4** above) but there are no time limits rules for notifications under (*c*) above. The date an assessment is made is not normally communicated to the taxpayer. To avoid any uncertainty, where, for example, an assessment is 'made' in time but not notified until after the time limit for assessing has expired, HMRC will always apply the time limit rules to the 'notified date' rather than the earlier 'made date'. The 'notified date' for this purpose is the date on which the assessment is sent by HMRC to the taxpayer. The date will be shown on the letter or other formal notification of the assessment.

(HMRC Notice 915, paras 1.2, 2.1, 4.1–4.4).

Any notice for VAT purposes can be served on a person by sending it by post in a letter addressed to him or his VAT representative (see **3.8 AGENTS**) at the last or usual residence or place of business of that person or representative. [*VATA 1994, s 98*]. See **50.5 PARTNERSHIPS** for the special provisions for serving notice on partners and **6.9** below for service on representatives.

An assessment which is incorrectly notified (e.g. by being sent to the taxpayer's solicitors without authority) is not invalid but simply unenforceable until properly notified to the taxpayer (*Grunwick Processing Laboratories Ltd v C & E Commrs*, CA [1987] STC 357 (TVC 3.61)).

De Voil Indirect Tax Service. See V5.137–V5.139.

Corrections of assessments by tribunals

[6.8] Where on an appeal against a decision within **6.1**(*b*)–(*e*) above it is found that the amount specified in the assessment is less than it ought to have been, the tribunal may give a direction specifying the correct amount. The appellant is deemed to have been notified of the revised amount. [*VATA 1994, s 84(5)*]. A tribunal may exercise its power to increase an assessment in order to correct arithmetical errors or where HMRC have argued at the hearing that the assessment should be increased. A tribunal does not have a free-standing power to increase an assessment entirely of its own initiative. Furthermore, if a tribunal was contemplating increasing an assessment, the appellant should be given a fair opportunity (by adjournment, if necessary) to consider the position (*Elias Gale Racing v C & E Commrs*, QB 1998, [1999] STC 66 (TVC 3.168)).

A tribunal may reduce or discharge an assessment on appeal. See **5 APPEALS**.

Assessments on, and notification to, representatives

[6.9] Where a person required to make a return as a personal representative, trustee in bankruptcy, receiver, liquidator or otherwise in a representative capacity fails to make that return or makes a return which appears to HMRC to be incomplete or incorrect, assessments (including assessments of penalties, interest or surcharges) may be made by HMRC on that person in his representative position and a notification to him is treated as also notifying the person for whom he acts. [*VATA 1994, s 73(5)(10), s 76(10); FA 1997, s 45(6)*].

Similar provisions apply to assessments on, and notifications to, such persons in respect of acquisitions of goods subject to excise duty or new means of transport under **6.1**(*g*) above. [*VATA 1994, s 75(4)*].

Key points

[6.10] Points to consider are as follows.

- If an HMRC officer considers VAT returns to be incomplete or inaccurate, then he has the power to assess tax he considers to be due using his 'best judgment'. A best judgment assessment does not require an analysis of all available records to be made, only those that enable the officer to accurately assess the VAT that he considers to be due from a taxpayer. VAT tribunals in recent years have shown how difficult it is to challenge an officer's conclusions in most cases.
- On 1 April 2009, the three-year period for adjusting VAT errors was increased to four years. However, it was not possible to bring back into time an error that was already out of date on 31 March 2009 under the three-year rule, i.e. errors relating to the period 1 April 2005 to 31 March 2006. Since 1 April 2010, however, a four-year adjustment is fully in place and rolling forward on a time basis.
- Be aware that the four-year assessment period is extended to 20 years if a taxpayer has deliberately understated his VAT liability by fraudulent behaviour.

7

Bad Debt Relief

Cross-references. See **59.36 REGISTRATION** for effect of transfer of registration with a business as a going concern; **60.21 RETAIL SCHEMES** for bad debt relief for mail order businesses.

De Voil Indirect Tax Service. See V5.156.

Introduction

[7.1] Where a business has made supplies of goods or services to customers and has not been paid, it can claim bad debt relief in respect of the unpaid VAT provided certain conditions are met. In particular, relief depends upon the supply being written off as a bad debt in the books of the claimant and a period of six months having elapsed since the date payment became due. See **7.2** below for full details. If, following a claim, the bad debt is paid, any refund received from HMRC must be repaid to them. See **7.12** below. There are also implications for a customer if he does not pay the supplier within six months. See **7.13** below.

Use of credit notes

A business cannot issue a credit note to a customer for unpaid VAT (instead of claiming bad debt relief) simply because he has not paid for a supply. A credit note can only be issued where there is a genuine mistake or overcharge or an agreed reduction in the value of the supply. (VAT Notice 700/18/02, para 5.6). See also *Peter Cripwell & Associates* (VTD 660) (TVC 40.86) and *Temple Gothard & Co* (VTD 702).

Appeals

Where a claim to bad debt relief is refused, an appeal may be made to a VAT tribunal. [*VATA 1994, s 83(h)*]. See **5.3**(11) **APPEALS**.

Conditions for relief

[7.2] A business is entitled, on making a claim, to a refund of VAT where the following conditions are satisfied.

(a) It has supplied goods or services and has 'accounted for and paid' the VAT on the supply.
Relief can be claimed whether the payment due is in money or in goods or services to be provided under a barter arrangement.
For a consideration of the meaning of '*accounted for and paid*' see *Times Right Marketing Ltd (in liquidation)* (VTD 20611) (TVC 4.32). Following that tribunal decision, HMRC now accept that payment is to be taken as made to the extent that output tax is covered by deductible input tax (HMRC Brief 18/09).
Normally, only the actual supplier can claim. There are two exceptions to this rule.
   - *Transfer of VAT registration number*. Where a business (or, with effect from 1 September 2007, part of a business) has been transferred and the transferee takes over the VAT registration of the seller, the transferee acquires the seller's entitlement to any bad debt relief on supplies made by the seller. (VAT Notice 700/18/02, para 5.1).
   - *Gas and electricity suppliers*. By concession, a supplier of gas and/or electricity can obtain relief from VAT on debts owed by a domestic customer where the supplier has accepted the transfer of that customer and his debts from another supply company. See **25.8**(9) **FUEL AND POWER** for full details.

(b) The whole or part of the consideration for the supply has been written off in the accounts as a bad debt. This involves writing the debt off in the day-to-day VAT accounts and transferring it to a separate 'refunds for bad debts account' which must be kept (see **7.4** below).

(c) The debt must be over six months old, i.e. six months must have elapsed from
   - the date of supply; and
   - the time when the consideration became due and payable to (or to the order of) the supplier.

(d) The value of the supply must not exceed its open market value. HMRC interpret this as meaning that the value of the supply must not be more than the customary selling price.

(e) The debt must not have been paid, sold or factored under a valid legal assignment (see **7.11**(2) below).

The normal provisions as to the time of supply of goods or services apply for determining when a supply is treated as taking place for the above purposes. See **66.1** *et seq*. **SUPPLY: TIME OF SUPPLY**.

[VATA 1994, s 36(1)(2)(4)(8); FA 1997, s 39(1); FA 1998, s 23; SI 1995/2518, Regs 6(3), 166A, 172(1)(1A)(2); SI 1996/2960; SI 1997/1086, Regs 3, 12, 14; SI 2002/3027, Reg 3; SI 2007/2085, Reg 4]. (VAT Notice 700/18/02, paras 2.2, 2.6, 2.7).

When to claim relief

[7.3] A claim in respect of a relevant supply cannot be made until six months has elapsed from the later of

- the date on which the consideration (or part) which has been written off as a bad debt became due and payable to, or to the order of, the person who made the relevant supply; and
- the date of supply

but must be made within four years and six months (increased from three years and six months from 1 April 2009) from the later of those dates.

A business entitled to a refund which has not made a claim by the end of that period is regarded as having ceased to be so entitled.

[VATA 1994, s 36(1); SI 1995/2518, Regs 165A, 172(1A); SI 1996/2960; SI 1997/1086, Regs 10, 14; SI 2009/586, Reg 10].

A claim is made on the date that the VAT return including the claim is sent to HMRC. (VAT Notice 700/18/02, para 2.6).

Records required

Evidence required

[7.4] Unless HMRC allow otherwise, before submitting a claim the claimant must hold the following in respect of every relevant supply.

- A copy of any VAT invoice provided or, where there was no obligation to provide a VAT invoice, a document showing the time and nature of the supply, purchaser and consideration.
- Records, or any other document, showing that VAT has been accounted for and paid on the supply and that the consideration has been written off in his accounts as a bad debt.

[SI 1995/2518, Reg 167].

Records required

Any business making a claim for bad debt relief must keep a record of that claim and, unless HMRC allow otherwise, that record must consist of the following information in respect of each claim made.

- In respect of each relevant supply for that claim
  - (a) the amount of the VAT chargeable;
  - (b) the VAT period in which the VAT chargeable was accounted for and paid to HMRC;

(c) the date and number of any invoice issued or, where there is no such invoice, such information as is necessary to identify the time, nature and purchaser; and

(d) any payment received for the supply (including any payment received by the claimant or by a person to whom a right to receive it has been assigned and any payment made by any person by way of consideration for the supply regardless of whether such payment extinguishes the purchaser's debt to the claimant or not).

- The 'outstanding amount' to which the claim relates (see **7.6** below).
- The amount of the claim.
- The VAT period in which the claim was made.
- A copy of any notice to the customer required under **7.2**(*e*) above.

Any records created under these provisions must be kept in a single account to be known as the '*refunds for bad debts account*'.

[*FA 1999, s 15(4); SI 1995/2518, Regs 165, 168; SI 1997/1086, Reg 13; SI 1999/3029*].

Preservation of evidence and documents

Unless HMRC allow otherwise, the claimant must preserve the evidence and records required above for a period of four years from the date of making the claim. He must also produce them, on demand, for inspection by an authorised person and permit that person to remove them at a reasonable time and for a reasonable period. [*SI 1995/2518, Reg 169*]. This requirement does not alter the standard requirement to retain records for six years (see **56.3 RECORDS**).

How to make the claim

[7.5] If all the conditions in **7.2** above are satisfied, a claim may be made for refund of the VAT on the bad debt. The claim is made by including the correct amount of the refund in Box 4 on the VAT return for the VAT period in which entitlement to the claim arises or, subject to **7.3** above, any later return.

Claimants no longer registered

If at the time the claimant becomes entitled to a refund he is no longer required to make returns, he should write to his VAT office giving details of

- former VAT registration number;
- name and address of the debtor(s);
- amount of refund claimed;
- copies of supporting evidence (e.g. invoices);
- proof that the debt has remained unpaid for six months from the date payment became due and payable or, if later, the time of supply; and
- proof that he possesses a separate bad debt ledger.

[*SI 1995/2518, Reg 166; SI 1997/1086, Reg 11*]. (VAT Notice 700/18/02, para 5.3).

Annual returns

By concession, where a business accounts for VAT using annual returns, it can claim bad debt relief on debts over six months old on the same return as that on which VAT on the debt is accounted for. (VAT Notice 700/18/02, para 5.5).

Amount of the claim

[7.6] A business is entitled, on making a claim, to a refund of VAT by reference to 'the outstanding amount'. '*The outstanding amount*' means the consideration for the supply written off in the accounts as a bad debt *less* any part of that consideration 'received' before the time of the claim. '*Received*' means received by the claimant or by a person to whom a right to receive the whole or any part of the consideration written off has been assigned.

Where the whole or any part of the consideration for the supply does not consist of money, the amount in money that is taken to represent any non-monetary part of the consideration is so much of the amount made up of

- the value of the supply, and
- the VAT charged on the supply

as is attributable to the non-monetary consideration in question.

[*VATA 1994, s 36(2)(3)(3A); FA 1998, s 23; FA 1999, s 15*].

Where, under a voluntary arrangement, creditors receive shares in full satisfaction of outstanding debts, there is no longer an '*outstanding amount*' and bad debt relief cannot be claimed (*AEG (UK) Ltd* (VTD 11428) (TVC 4.10)).

The effect of the above is that

- where no payment has been received in respect of a supply or supplies, the claim will be for the amount of VAT accounted for and paid to HMRC; and
- where a part payment has been received in respect of a supply or supplies, a refund can be claimed relating to the amount of VAT that is still outstanding.

Special rules apply to determine the amount of the claim where

- part payments are received relating to more than one supply (see **7.7** below);
- payments are received under hire purchase or conditional or credit sale agreements (see **7.8**(1) below); and
- supplies are made under the margin scheme for second-hand goods or the tour operators' margin scheme (see **7.9** below).

Attributing part payments

[7.7] Subject to **7.8**(1) below, where

- the claimant has made more than one supply (whether taxable or not) to the purchaser, and

- a 'payment' is received in relation to those supplies,

then, unless the purchaser has specified that the payment is for a particular supply and pays for that supply in full, in calculating any VAT due on the outstanding debt the payment is attributed to earliest supplies first. Supplies made on the same day are aggregated and treated as one, the payment being rateably apportioned. [*SI 1995/2518, Reg 170; SI 2002/3027, Reg 4*].

'*Payment*' means any payment or part payment which is made by any person to any person by way of consideration for a supply, regardless of whether such payment extinguishes the purchaser's debt to the claimant or not. [*FA 1999, s 15(4); SI 1995/2518, Reg 165; SI 1999/3029*]. This definition is widely drawn and includes payment in the form of

- any non-monetary payments (e.g. goods or services provided in exchange);
- third party payments received;
- the proceeds from the sale of repossessed goods under finance agreements (see **7.8**(2) below);
- payments received from a guarantor of the customer (see **7.10**(1) below);
- payments made by the *customer's* insurers (but not by the *claimant's* insurers where it has taken out bad debts insurance) (see **7.10**(2) below);
- mutual debts (see **7.10**(3) below); and
- the value of any enforceable security (see **7.10**(5) below).

Example 1

A claimant has made the following supplies to the purchaser.

Date of supply	Supply	VAT-exclusive	VAT	VAT-inclusive
		£	£	£
30.6.11	1	1,000	Zero-rated	1,000
28.7.11	2	1,000	200	1,200
25.8.11	3	2,000	400	2,400
29.9.11	4	350	Exempt	350
27.10.11	5	800	160	960
24.11.11	6	3,000	600	3,600
		£8,150	£1,360	£9,510

A payment of only £3,500 is received. As the payment has not been allocated by the customer, it is allocated to the earliest supplies and treated as relating to supplies 1, 2 and part of 3 as follows.

Supply	VAT-inclusive
	£
1	1,000
2	1,200
3 (part)	1,300
Amount of payment	£3,500

The VAT-inclusive debt outstanding on supply 3 is therefore £1,100 (£2,400 – £1,300) and the VAT outstanding on the supply is £183.33 (£1,100 × 1/6).

The outstanding amount of £6,010 (£9,510 – £3,500) and the bad debt relief that can be claimed is as follows.

Supply	VAT-inclusive	VAT
	£	£
3 (part)	1,100	183.33
4	350	Exempt
5	960	160.00
6	3,600	600.00
	6,010	£913.33

Example 2

The figures are as in *Example 1* above except that supplies 1, 2 and 3 were all made on the same day and are therefore treated as a single supply.

The debt outstanding on supplies 1, 2 and 3 is £1,100 (£4,600 – £3,500) and the proportion of VAT included is

$$\frac{\text{VAT in supplies 1, 2 and 3}}{\text{Total VAT - inclusive value of supplies 1, 2 and 3}} \times \text{debt outstanding}$$

= 600/4,600 × £1,100 = £143.48

The outstanding amount of £6,010 (£9,510 – £3,500) and the bad debt relief that can be claimed is as follows.

Supply	VAT-inclusive	VAT
	£	£
1–3 (part)	1,100	143.48
4	350	Exempt
5	960	160.00
6	3,600	600.00
	£6,010	£903.48

(VAT Notice 700/18/02, paras 3.3, 3.4).

Goods supplied with associated finance

[7.8] When goods are supplied with associated finance the following applies.

(1) Attribution of payments to goods or finance

Bad debt relief is available on supplies of goods made by way of hire purchase or conditional or credit sale agreements where the customer has defaulted. Such supplies have two components, a taxable supply of goods and an exempt supply of associated financial services. The time of supply for goods is typically when they are made available to the customer [*VATA 1994, s 6*] and the time of supply of the financial services is when payment is made. [*SI 1995/2518, Reg 9*]. Therefore, unless the supplier seeks an agreement with HMRC to treat the supply of finance as occurring at the same time as the supply of goods, in applying the part payment rules in **7.6** above, strictly, the supplier should allocate any payments received from their customer first to the supply of the goods and only then to the supply of financial services after the goods element has been 'paid in full'. The provisions detailed below have been implemented in order to avoid this.

In order to avoid this, the following provisions apply where

- the claimant made a supply of goods and, in connection with that supply, a supply of credit,
- those supplies were made under a hire purchase, conditional sale or credit sale agreement, and
- a payment is received in relation to those supplies (other than a payment of an amount upon which interest is not charged, e.g. a deposit).

Supplies before 1 September 2006 (Method A)

The payment is attributed

- as to the supply of credit, by multiplying the payment by the fraction A÷B where
  A = the total of the interest on the credit provided under the agreement (determined as at the date of the making of the agreement); and
  B = is the total amount payable under the agreement, less any amount upon which interest is not charged; and
- as to the balance, to the supply of goods.

Supplies after 31 August 2006 and before 1 September 2007

The payment may be attributed either in accordance with Method A above or Method B below.

Supplies of goods after 31 August 2007 (Method B)

The payment is attributed in respect of payments made on or before termination of the agreement,

- as to the supply of credit, by multiplying the payment by the fraction A÷B where

A= is the total of the interest on the credit provided under the agreement, less any rebate of interest granted, less any interest attributable to any unpaid instalments prior to the termination; and
B= is the total amount payable under the agreement being the total of A plus the 'total for the goods'; and

- as to the balance, to the supply of goods,

'*Total for the goods*' means the amount due for the goods under the agreement, less any reduction as a consequence of termination, less any amount upon which interest is not charged, less any part of the total due for the goods which is unpaid at the time of termination.

The payment is attributed in respect of payments made after termination of the agreement, between the supply of goods and the supply of credit according to the proportion of the balances due at the time the payment is made.

Where an agreement provides for variation of the rate of interest after the date of the making of the agreement then, for the purposes of the above calculation, it is assumed that the rate is not varied.

[*SI 1995/2518, Reg 170A; SI 2002/3027, Reg 5; SI 2007/313, Reg 3*]. (VAT Notice 700/18/02, para 3.5).

The method applying before 1 September 2006 allocated interest equally to instalments over the life of the agreement (the 'straightline' method) although, in practice, many finance companies allocated a greater proportion of interest to the earlier instalments (the 'rule of 78' method). In *Abbey National plc v C & E Commrs*, Ch D 2005 [2006] STC 1 (TVC 4.30) the High Court upheld the decision of the tribunal that the straightline method was the method laid down by the *Regulations* and, unless that method was irrational to the point that no person acting reasonably would use it (which was not the case), it had to be used. The revised method is intended to reflect more accurately commercial practice.

(2) Repossessed goods

Where goods are supplied with finance, if the customer does not make the required payments the seller may have the right to repossess the goods and sell them to recover all or part of the debt due from the customer. The disposal of these second-hand repossessed goods is normally subject to VAT but is outside the scope of VAT provided certain conditions are met. See **23.15 FINANCIAL SERVICES** for full details.

In determining the outstanding amount on which bad debt relief can be claimed

- *if the sale of the repossessed goods is not subject to VAT*, any relief should be based on the amount remaining unpaid, if any, after taking into account payments by the customer and the proceeds from the sale; and
- *if the sale of the repossessed goods is subject to VAT*, only payments by the customer have to be deducted. Where the transaction is the repossession of a car, this only applies if the initial sale was of a new car.

(VAT Notice 700/18/02, para 3.6; Business Brief 19/01; Business Brief 13/02).

Second-hand goods and tour operators' margin scheme

[7.9] Bad debt relief may be claimed in respect of supplies made under the margin schemes for **SECOND-HAND GOODS (61)** or the **TOUR OPERATORS' MARGIN SCHEME (68)** as follows.

- If the debt is equal to or less than the profit margin, bad debt relief may be claimed on the VAT fraction of the debt.
- If the debt is greater than the profit margin, bad debt relief is limited to the VAT fraction of the profit margin (i.e. the amount of VAT which the supplier has paid to HMRC).

Debt for the above purposes means full consideration for the relevant supply *less* any payment received in respect of it. Payment means any payment which is made by any person to any person by way of consideration for a supply, regardless of whether such payment extinguishes the purchaser's debt to the claimant or not. [*FA 1999, s 15(4); SI 1995/2518, Reg 165; SI 1999/3029*].

Example

Second-hand goods purchased for £400 are sold for £500 (i.e. the profit margin is £100). The customer only pays (a) £450 and (b) £350. Bad debt relief is calculated as follows.

(a) The debt is £50 which is less than the profit margin of £100. Bad debt relief can be claimed on
1/6* × £50 = £8.33

(b) The debt is £150 which is greater than the profit margin. Bad debt relief can be claimed on
1/6* × £100 = £16.67

(*3/23 from 1 December 2008 to 31 December 2009, 7/47 from 1 January 2010 to 3 January 2011)

[*SI 1995/2518, Regs 172A, 172B; SI 1997/1086, Reg 15*]. (VAT Notice 700/18/02, paras 5.7, 5.8).

Amount of claim — miscellaneous matters

[7.10] Other matters affecting the amount of the claim are as follows.

(1) Guarantors, etc. of debts

Where a supplier receives payment, in full or in part, from a guarantor or other person (e.g. a director of the debtor company), entitlement to relief is reduced by the amount paid. If full payment is made by the guarantor or third party there is no entitlement to bad debt relief.

(VAT Notice 700/18/02, para 3.10).

(2) Insured debts

Where the claimant has insured its debts, any payment by the insurers does not affect entitlement to relief.

Where the debtor is insured for the costs of the supply (e.g. when a garage repairs a damaged vehicle), for convenience the insurer may pay the supplier direct. If the insured is VAT-registered, the VAT-exclusive amount is usually paid, leaving the customer to pay the VAT element. The supplier can only claim relief on the actual balance written off.

(VAT Notice 700/18/02, paras 3.9, 3.11).

(3) Mutual debts

Where the claimant owes an amount of money to the purchaser which can be set off, the consideration written off in the accounts must be reduced by the amount so owed.

Example

In August 2011 a bad debt arose in respect of a supply for which the claimant charged £720 (£600 + VAT). The claimant also owes £240 (£200 + VAT) to the debtor.

The amount of the debt for relief purposes is £720 – £240 = £480

The amount of the bad debt relief is £480 x 1/6 = £80

[*SI 1995/2518, Reg 172(3)*]. (VAT Notice 700/18/02, para 3.7).

(4) Non-payment of VAT only

If

- a customer refuses to pay the VAT charged on an invoice, or
- the claimant did not charge VAT on a supply but issues a supplementary invoice to recover the VAT and this is not paid,

the claim to relief is limited to the VAT element of the total debt. For example, where a customer was originally charged £100 (which the customer paid) and the claimant then unsuccessfully attempts to recover the £17.50 VAT charge originally omitted, the claimant is only entitled to claim the VAT fraction of £17.50 as bad debt relief.

(VAT Notice 700/18/02, para 3.13).

In *Enderby Transport Ltd* (VTD 1607) (TVC 4.1) the customer paid the full price for the goods (£10,200) but not the VAT (£816). The tribunal held that as the amount of the debt outstanding was £816, the VAT element of this was £106.43 (3/23rds when the standard rate of VAT was 15%) and bad debt relief should be restricted to this amount. In *Palmer (t/a R & K Engineering)* (VTD 11739) (TVC 4.4) the tribunal allowed full bad debt relief where, following registration with retrospective effect, an invoice was raised charging VAT on supplies originally invoiced (and paid) without VAT and the customer went into receivership without paying the VAT. The tribunal did, however, comment that HMRC had been dilatory in dealing with registration and the position might be different where late registration is due to the trader's own default.

(5) Security for debts

Where the claimant holds an enforceable security against the purchaser, the consideration written off must be reduced by the value of the security. [*SI 1995/2518, Reg 172(4)*]. If the claimant holds a security which cannot be enforced, he can write off the full amount of the debt and base his claim to relief on that amount. (VAT Notice 700/18/02, para 3.8).

Treatment of bad debt relief in particular cases

[7.11] The treatment of this relief in particular cases is outlined below.

(1) Cash accounting scheme

Subject to conditions, including an annual turnover limit, a business may account for and pay VAT by reference to the time when the consideration for the supply is received. See **63.2 SPECIAL SCHEMES**. The adoption of such a scheme removes the problem of VAT on bad debts from the supplier.

(2) Factored debts

Where a business factors its debts, bad debt relief is not available where the assignment of the debt is absolute (i.e. where there is no provision for the reassignment of the debt in the contract).

Where there is provision for reassignment, bad debt relief is available, subject to the normal conditions, once the debt has been reassigned to the business. No bad debt relief is available during the period in which the debt remains assigned to the factor.

Any payment from the factor to the business for the purchase of the debts is consideration for an exempt supply of finance and is disregarded for the purposes of bad debt relief.

(VAT Notice 700/18/02, para 3.12).

(3) Group registration

In the case of a group registration (see **27 GROUPS OF COMPANIES**) each member must keep its own separate bad debts record for debts written off. The representative member of the group claims any refund on behalf of each member while they are in the VAT group. Where a member leaves a group, any VAT bad debt relief on supplies made by that company when it was a group member, but which cannot be claimed until after it has left the group, is due to that company (and not the representative member of the group). (VAT Notice 700/18/02, para 5.4). See also *Triad Timber Components Ltd* (VTD 10694) (TVC 4.19) and *Proto Glazing Ltd* (VTD 13410) (TVC 4.20).

(4) Retail schemes

Where a bad debt relief claim is made, any refund must be accounted for outside the retail scheme. If, after claiming a refund, payment is received for the supplies, any repayment of relief to HMRC must also be dealt with outside the scheme.

(5) Reservation of title agreements

Some agreements for the sale of goods include a clause reserving title until the goods have been paid for (known as a *Romalpa* clause). There is no requirement that title to the goods must have passed before a claim for bad debt relief can be made. It is therefore possible to make a claim for supplies of goods on hire purchase and other reservation of title agreements without the requirement formally to give up the rights to title under the agreement.

(VAT Notice 700/18/02, para 5.2).

(6) Sale of property under a power of sale — recovery of VAT on costs incurred by mortgage lenders

Where a property is repossessed by the lender, although the sale of the property is a supply by the borrower, HMRC accept that the lender may be treated as agent of the borrower in relation to certain costs of sale. This applies whether or not the mortgage deed specifies such a relationship. As an agent, the lender may treat these costs incurred as supplies made to him and by him under *VATA 1994, s 47(3)*. Where the proceeds of sale are insufficient to cover all or part of the costs of sale, the lender can therefore recover any unpaid VAT under the bad debt provisions. For these purposes, the order of attribution of the sale proceeds follows the normal rules under the bad debt relief regulations (i.e. allocate to the earliest supply, the mortgage, first) rather than those under *Law of Property Act 1925, s 105* (which requires proceeds to be first allocated to the selling costs). The arrangements apply to VAT on the following costs.

(a) Costs relating directly to the sale of the property which would ordinarily have been incurred by the borrower had he arranged the sale himself (e.g. legal and estate agency fees for professional services connected with the sale).

(b) *Law of Property Act* (LPA) receiver's charges relating specifically to the sale of the property and any costs incurred by the receiver in respect of the sale, but only where the proceeds of sale received by the lender have been reduced by the VAT element of the charges (and not where the LPA receiver recovers the VAT incurred on behalf of a VAT-registered borrower and this is reflected in the proceeds passed to the lender).

(c) Build-out costs (i.e. expenses incurred on completion of a partly-completed building or major refurbishment of the property before sale) but only where
   - the sale of the building by the borrower is the subject of a taxable supply or the transfer of a going concern for VAT purposes; or
   - the property is the subject of a taxable let and output tax on the rents has been accounted for to HMRC.

   The arrangement does not apply if the proceeds of sale or rent received by lenders reflect any input tax on build-out costs recovered by the borrower.

(d) Repair and maintenance expenses.

(e) A lender's own in-house estate agency or solicitor's services to the borrower provided output tax has been accounted for on the supply under normal rules.

The arrangement does not cover any costs incurred in relation to letting (other than those within (*c*) above). Nor does it cover costs incurred on services provided to, and used by, the lender as principal even if charged to the borrower under the mortgage deed (e.g. legal fees associated with taking possession; locksmith's fees for securing the property; and costs incurred in pursuing claims against a valuer for negligence).

(Business Brief 24/94).

Repayment of refund

[7.12] Repayment of any VAT refunded by HMRC under a bad debt claim is required where

(a) a payment for the relevant supply is subsequently received;
(b) a payment is, under **7.7** or **7.8**(1) above, treated as attributed to the relevant supply;
(c) (with effect from 1 March 2007) the consideration for any relevant supply (upon which the claim to refund is based) is reduced after the claim is made; or
(d) the claimant fails to comply with the requirements of **7.4**, **7.7** or **7.8**(1) above.

Under (*a*) and (*b*) above the amount of the repayment is

$$\frac{\text{Amount of payment received or attributed}}{\text{Amount of outstanding consideration}} \times \text{Amount of refund}$$

Under (*c*) above, the amount of the repayment is equal to the negative entry made in the VAT allowable portion of the VAT account as provided for in *SI 1995/2518, Reg 38* (see **39.15 INVOICES**).

Under (*d*) above repayment must be made of the full amount of the refund obtained from HMRC by the claim to which the failure to comply relates.

> *Example*
>
> A business sells goods for £120.00 (£100 plus £20.00 VAT). It receives no payment by the relevant date and claims bad debt relief of £20.00. It subsequently receives £75.00 from the customer for the goods.
>
> The business must repay to HMRC the VAT element of the £75 received, calculated as follows.
>
> £75.00 ÷ £120.00 × £20 = £12.50

The repayment is made by including the appropriate amount in Box 1 on the VAT return for the VAT period in which the payment is received under (*a*) or (*b*) or as designated by HMRC under (*c*). If, at that time, the claimant is no longer required to make returns, the repayment must still be made and the supplier should contact HMRC.

For these purposes, payment does not include a payment received by a person to whom a right to receive it has been assigned. Claimants are not therefore required to repay bad debt relief in respect of payments received by assignees after a refund has been claimed. However, as an anti-avoidance measure, in the case of assignments made after 10 December 2003, this does not apply (and repayment of the VAT refund is still required) where the person to whom the right to receive a payment has been assigned (whether by the claimant or any other person) is connected to the claimant. See **71.19 VALUATION** for connected persons.

[*SI 1995/2518, Reg 171; SI 1999/3029; SI 2002/3027, Reg 6; SI 2003/3220, Regs 22, 23; SI 2007/313, Reg 4*]. (VAT Notice 700/18/02, paras 3.14, 3.15).

Repayment of input tax by purchaser

[7.13] There are general provisions requiring input tax to be repaid where a customer has not paid the supplier within six months of the date of supply or, if later, the date payment is due. These provisions apply whether or not the supplier makes a claim for bad debt relief. See **34.4 INPUT TAX**.

Key points

[7.14] Points to consider are as follows.

- The two main conditions for a supplier to reclaim bad debt relief are that the debt in question must be at least six months overdue for payment, and also be written off for bad debt relief purposes in the business accounts, i.e. by making an entry in the 'refunds for bad accounts' as required by the VAT Regulations 1995. Note – if an invoice is on 60 day payment terms, the earliest point at which bad debt relief can be claimed will be eight months after the invoice date, i.e. when it is six months overdue for payment. There is no requirement for the debt to be written off so that the debtor is no longer pursued for the outstanding amount.
- Bad debt relief claimed on a VAT return is included in the Box 4 (input tax) figure. However, any subsequent payment made by the customer after the debt has been written off (which will create an output tax liability if the goods are standard-rated or reduced-rated) will be included in Box 1 (output tax) on the return.
- A business that is able to use the cash accounting scheme (annual taxable sales less than £1.35m etc.) will automatically benefit from bad debt relief. This is because output tax is not included on a VAT return until payment has been received from a customer. This is different to the usual point at which output tax is declared on a return, i.e. the earlier of invoicing and payment dates. However, be aware that users of the cash accounting scheme cannot claim input tax until payment has been made to a supplier.

- A customer not using the cash accounting scheme will need to adjust any input tax he has claimed on a purchase invoice that is more than six months overdue for payment. The input tax must be credited on the VAT return that is covered by the date when the six-month expiry date takes place. If payment is subsequently made to settle the invoice, then input tax can be reclaimed on the VAT return covered by the payment date.
- A bad debt situation cannot be dealt with by issuing a credit note to cancel the original sales invoice. This is because a credit note can only be issued when either goods have been returned or the original value of the sale has been reduced by, for example, an agreed price reduction for the customer.
- It is possible that a debt will be written off for bad debt relief purposes in a VAT period when the standard rate of VAT is a different percentage to that which applied when the original sales invoice was raised. The key issue as far as bad debt relief is concerned is the output tax charged on the original sales invoice and the rate of VAT that applied at that time.
- In cases where a customer refuses to pay the VAT element of a charge (either on an original invoice or VAT only invoice subsequently raised), then bad debt relief is restricted to the VAT element of the VAT amount. So if an invoice was raised for £100 plus £20.00 VAT, and the customer only paid £100, then bad debt relief would be restricted to £3.33, i.e. £20.00 x 1/6.

8

Business

Cross-reference. See **73.6 WORKS OF ART, ETC.** for sales of antiques, etc. from stately homes.

De Voil Indirect Tax Service. See V2.2.

Introduction

EU legislation

[8.1] *Directive 2006/112/EC* adopts the term 'economic activity' rather than business. See **18.7 EUROPEAN UNION LEGISLATION.** Unless a decision of the ECJ provides otherwise, the meaning of economic activity is not materially different from the meaning of 'business' in the UK legislation.

UK legislation

The proper identification of an activity as a 'business' activity is fundamental to the operation of VAT. Output tax must be charged on any taxable supply of goods or services made in the UK by a taxable person *in the course or furtherance of any business* carried on by him. [*VATA 1994, s 4(1)*]. Similarly, input tax must relate to supplies of goods and services to a taxable person (and, where relevant, acquisitions and importations of goods by him) used or to be used *for the purpose of any business* carried on or to be carried on by him. [*VATA 1994, s 24(1)*].

Despite the importance of the meaning of '*business*', it is not comprehensively defined in UK (or EU) legislation. *VATA 1994, s 94* (as amended) gives the following guidance as to what the term encompasses and excludes. If a particular activity is not covered, then it is necessary to apply the 'business test' developed by the Courts (see **8.2** below).

(a) It includes any trade, profession or vocation.
(b) The following (without prejudice to the generality of anything else in *VATA 1994*) are deemed to be the carrying on of a business.
   - The provision by a club, association or organisation (for a subscription or other consideration) of the facilities or advantages available to its members (but see (*c*) below). See also **14.1 CLUBS AND ASSOCIATIONS.**
   - The admission, for a consideration, of persons to any premises (see *The Eric Taylor Testimonial Match Committee* (VTD 139) (TVC 7.87)).
(c) Where a person accepts any office in the course or furtherance of a trade, profession or vocation, services supplied by him as holder of that office are treated as supplied in the course or furtherance of that trade, profession or vocation. See **8.4** below, **44.8 MANAGEMENT SERVICES AND SUPPLIES OF STAFF** and **50.6 PARTNERSHIPS.**
(d) Anything done in connection with the termination or intended termination of a business is treated as being done in the course or furtherance of that business.
(e) The disposition of a business (or, with effect from 1 September 2007, part of a business) as a going concern, or of the assets or liabilities of the business or part of the business (whether or not in connection with its reorganisation or winding up) is a supply made in the course or furtherance of the business (but see **8.10** below).

The business test

[8.2] When considering whether an activity is to be treated as a business, if it is not one of the deemed businesses under **8.1** above then the 'business test' must be applied. This test is derived from decisions of the VAT tribunals and Courts.

The following principles, as summarised in *C & E Commrs v Lord Fisher*, QB [1981] STC 238 (TVC 7.6) are a guide as to whether an activity is a business although the absence of one common attribute of ordinary businesses (e.g. the pursuit of profit) does not necessarily mean that the activity is not a business and the criteria are not therefore conclusive in every case.

- By providing in *VATA 1994, s 94* (see **8.1** above) that business *includes* any trade, profession or vocation, it is clear that a wide meaning of 'business' is intended.
- In determining whether any particular activity constitutes a business it is necessary to consider the whole of that activity.
- A business activity can generally be identified from the answers to the following criteria (as laid down in *C & E Commrs v Morrison's Academy Boarding Houses Association*, CS 1977, [1978] STC 1 (TVC 7.1)).

(a) Is the activity a 'serious undertaking earnestly pursued' or a 'serious occupation not necessarily confined to commercial or profit making undertakings'?

(b) Is the activity an occupation or function actively pursued with reasonable or recognisable continuity?
A one-off supply or a series of infrequent, unconnected supplies is not normally a business activity in its own right although it is important to consider the nature of the activity. For example, occasional sales by small speculative builders and property developers are business activities.

(c) Does the activity have a certain measure of substance as measured by the quarterly or annual value of taxable supplies made?

(d) Is the activity conducted in a regular manner and on sound and recognised business principles?

(e) Is the activity predominantly concerned with the making of taxable supplies to consumers for a consideration?
This is perhaps the most important point to establish, bearing in mind that 'consideration' need not necessarily be monetary. If a trader is carrying on an activity which does not involve the making of any supplies for a consideration and there is no intention in the future of doing so, then the activity is unlikely to be regarded as business even if all the other criteria are met.
In *C & E Commrs v The Apple and Pear Development Council*, HL [1988] STC 221 (TVC 22.80) the Council's principal activity was to advertise English apples and pears, which activity was financed by a statutory levy on growers. The ECJ ruled that the levy was not consideration because there was no direct link between the payments and the benefits of individual growers on which basis the House of Lords concluded that the activity was not 'business' in the VAT sense. Similarly, a charity raising funds in a 'business-like' manner from its activities was held not to be running a business unless taxable supplies, made for a consideration, formed the basis of the fund raising (*C & E Commrs v Royal Exchange Theatre Trust*, QB [1979] STC 278 (TVC 7.5)).
Where an activity is just beginning and no supplies are being made at the time but there is a clear intention to do so at some time in the future, then the activity may qualify as a business. See *Rompelman v Minister van Financien, ECJ Case 268/83*, [1985] 3 CMLR 202; [1985] ECR 655 (TVC 22.103) and *Merseyside Cablevision Ltd* (VTD 2419) (TVC 36.554).

(f) Are the taxable supplies of a kind which are commonly made by those who seek to profit by them?

(g) If a person is carrying on an activity and it is not clear whether it amounts to a business, it is more likely to be regarded as such if others are carrying on the same type of activity and are clearly doing so on a commercial basis. See *Church of Scientology of California (No 1) v C & E Commrs*, CA 1980, [1981] STC 65

(TVC 7.4) where courses in the study of its beliefs provided by the Church, some of which competed with those offered by trained psychologists and psychiatrists, were found to be business activities.

- Whether the activity is pursued for profit or some other private purpose or motive is not decisive in determining whether the activity is a business.
- If all or a sufficient number of the above criteria are satisfied in sufficient measure to override any contra-indications which might be seen in the facts, then as a matter of law the activity must be held to be a business.

The carrying on, by a regulatory authority, of a statutory licensing activity to protect the public interest is not a business activity even though carried on for a consideration. See *Institute of Chartered Accountants in England and Wales v C & E Commrs*, HL [1999] STC 398 (TVC 62.159) in respect of the Institute's authorisation to issue licences to auditors, insolvency practitioners and persons carrying on investment business.

See the chapter *Business* in *Tolley's VAT Cases* for tribunal and court decisions involving the general meaning of 'business'.

Business and non-business activities

Businesses with more than one activity

[8.3] Where a taxable person undertakes distinct and separate activities, some of these may be business and others non-business. A non-business activity may be a private activity (e.g. a hobby, see below) or, particularly in the grant-funded and voluntary sectors, it might be an activity which forms part of the overall objectives but be non-business for VAT purposes (see, for example, **12.5 CHARITIES** for business and non-business activities of charities). In either case, the business test must be applied to each activity. For cases where the VAT tribunals have been concerned with multiple activities, see *Rainheath Ltd* (VTD 1249) (TVC 7.35) (yacht purchased by a farming business); *DA Walker* (VTD 240) (TVC 7.17) (accountant with furnished letting income); and *RW & AAW Williamson* (VTD 555) (TVC 7.23) (retail partnership also renting out lock-up garages).

Hobbies

Activities of pleasure and social enjoyment, though organised in a business-like way, do not amount to a 'business' if no taxable supplies are made for a consideration (*C & E Commrs v Lord Fisher*, QB [1981] STC 238 (TVC 7.6)).

Traders may sometimes have hobbies that involve the making of taxable supplies (e.g. repairing cars or selling stamps). These supplies are not automatically made in the course or furtherance of business and the business test must be applied. Hobbies which involve a registered trader making minimal supplies are unlikely to be seen as business. However, in some cases, a hobby can involve a trader making substantial supplies and may grow to become a business activity. See, for example, *Haydon-Baillie* (VTD 2072) (TVC 36.550).

Disposal of private assets

This is normally a non-business activity. Where, however, the assets are disposed of through the trader's own business the disposal may occasionally be treated as business. See, for example, *Mittu* (VTD 1275) (TVC 62.76) where a jeweller sold items of jewellery belonging to his wife through the business and paid the proceeds into the business account.

The independent disposal of private assets merely to raise funds for a business is non-business and outside the scope of VAT. See *RWK Stirling* (VTD 1963) (TVC 62.77).

Apportionment of input tax

Where a business incurs VAT on goods and services which it intends to use for both business activities and non-business activities, it is unlikely that it will be able to treat all the VAT as input tax and some form of apportionment will be required. See **34.7 INPUT TAX.**

Particular problem areas

[8.4] Particular problem areas are as follows:

- **Charities.** See **12.4 CHARITIES.**
- **Clubs and associations.** See **14.1 CLUBS AND ASSOCIATIONS.**
- **Education.** See **16.2 EDUCATION.**
- **Local authorities.** See **43.3** and **43.4 LOCAL AUTHORITIES AND PUBLIC BODIES** and for government departments and health authorities see **43.11 LOCAL AUTHORITIES AND PUBLIC BODIES.**
- **Museums and galleries.** Although the main activity of most museums and galleries is the public display of a collection, many have a number of other activities and it is necessary to identify all activities and consider the business/non-business nature of each.
  Admission charges. Where a museum, etc. makes a general admission charge for the public to enter its premises, this constitutes a 'deemed' business activity under *VATA 1994, s 94* (see **8.1**(*b*) above). In general, the full amount of any admission charge is standard-rated. However, admission charges to museums and galleries by certain eligible bodies are exempt and voluntary donations in lieu of admission charges are outside the scope of VAT. See **57.7 RECREATION AND SPORT.**
  A museum or gallery which admits the public free of charge is not carrying on a business activity. Consequently, under the normal rules any VAT it incurs in relation to the provision of free rights of admission cannot be recovered. See, however, **34.13**(21) **INPUT TAX** for a special scheme allowing certain non-charging national museums and galleries to recover related input tax.

- **Office holders.** Under *VATA 1994, s 94(4)* where a person in the course or furtherance of a trade, profession or vocation accepts any office, services supplied by him as the holder of that office are treated as supplied in the course or furtherance of the trade, profession or vocation. See also **44.8 MANAGEMENT SERVICES AND SUPPLIES OF STAFF** for directors or employees or a company, sole traders and partners as office holders.
- **Shooting rights.** See **57.17 RECREATION AND SPORT.**
- **Works of art – disposals from stately homes.** See **73.6 WORKS OF ART, ETC.**

See also HMRC VAT Guidance V1–6.

Disaggregation of business activities

[8.5] For EU legislation, see **18.7 EUROPEAN UNION LEGISLATION.**

The following provisions are designed to prevent the maintenance or creation of any 'artificial' separation of business activities carried on by two or more persons from resulting in the avoidance of VAT. In determining whether any separation of business activities is '*artificial*', consideration must be given to the extent to which the different persons carrying on those activities are closely bound to one another by financial, economic and organisational links.

HMRC may make a direction under which the persons specified therein become treated as a single taxable person carrying on the activities of a business described in the direction. That taxable person is then liable to be registered under *VATA 1994, Sch 1* with effect from the date of the direction or such later day as is specified. The direction must be served on each person named in it.

If, immediately before the direction (or any supplementary direction below) any person named therein is already registered in respect of taxable supplies made by him, he ceases to be liable to be registered from the date of the direction or, if later, the date with effect from which the single taxable person concerned became liable to be registered.

Supplementary directions

HMRC may subsequently make and serve a supplementary direction adding a further person's name to those detailed in the earlier direction where that person appears to HMRC to be making taxable supplies in the course of the activities of the business previously specified. The name is added from the date on which he began making those taxable supplies or, if later, the date with effect from which the single taxable person referred to in the earlier direction became liable to be registered under *VATA 1994, Sch 1*.

[*VATA 1994, Sch 1 para 1A, para 2(1)(3)–(5); FA 1997, s 31(1)(2)(4)*].

De Voil Indirect Tax Service. See V2.190C.

Preconditions for making a direction

[8.6] Before making a direction naming any person HMRC must be satisfied that

- he is making or has made taxable supplies;
- the activities in the course of which he makes or made those supplies form only part of certain activities, the other activities being carried on concurrently or previously (or both) by one or more other persons; and
- if all the taxable supplies of the business described in the direction were taken into account, a person carrying on that business would at the time of the direction be liable to be registered under the normal registration rules.

[*VATA 1994, Sch 1 para 2(2); FA 1997, s 31(2)(4)*].

HMRC's policy

Artificial separation

[8.7] In deciding whether or not to make a direction, HMRC will be concerned with separations which are devices contrived to circumvent the normal VAT registration rules. Whether any particular separation is artificial will, in most cases, depend upon the facts. The following are examples of where HMRC would at least make further enquiries.

- Separate entities supply registered and unregistered customers.
- The same equipment/premises is used by different entities on a regular basis. This may occur, for example, in launderettes, food take-aways or mobile catering equipment.
- Splitting up of what is usually a single supply, e.g. bed and breakfast and the livery trade.
- Artificially separated businesses which maintain the appearance of a single business, e.g. bar sales and catering in a public house (although the relationship between the parties is important here as truly franchised 'shop within a shop' arrangements will not normally be considered artificial).
- One person has a controlling influence in a number of entities which all make the same type of supply in diverse locations.

Financial, economic and organisational links

Again these will depend upon the specific circumstances but the following examples illustrate the types of factors indicative of the necessary links.

Financial links

- Financial support given by one part to another.
- One part would not be financially viable without support from another.
- Common financial interest in the proceeds of the business.

Economic links

- Seeking to realise the same economic objective.

- The activities of one part benefit the other part.
- Supplying the same circle of customers.

Organisational links

- Common management.
- Common employees.
- Common premises.
- Common equipment.

(VAT Notice 700/1/07, paras 13.5, 13.6).

Example

Mr B provides accountancy services from his office in the High Street. Mr C trades from the same premises, offering a service to complete tax returns. Neither of the two businesses is VAT-registered, as they each have sales of £40,000 per annum. The following facts apply to their respective organisations:

- Mr B and Mr C use the same computers to carry out their work – they sit together in an open plan office in the same room;
- they have many common clients, with Mr B doing the accounts work and Mr C the tax returns for these clients;
- Mr B employs a receptionist who also spends a lot of her time working for Mr C;
- Mr C employs a secretary who also spends a lot of her time doing work for Mr B;
- they have a joint advert in the local newspaper – promoting a combined service of 'preparing accounts and completing tax returns'.

This particular arrangement is one where HMRC is likely to decide that there is only one business evident in practice. There are clear financial, economic and organisational links between the two businesses. Equally important, any customer dealing with the business might perceive that there was, in reality, only one business.

Effect of a direction

[8.8] The effects of a direction on the '*constituent members*' (i.e. all those named in the direction and any supplementary direction) are as follows.

(a) The taxable person carrying on the specified business is registrable in such name as the persons named in the direction jointly nominate in writing within 14 days of the direction. Otherwise the taxable person is registrable in such name as may be specified in the direction.
(b) Any supply of goods or services by or to one of the constituent members in the course of the specified business is treated as a supply by or to the taxable person.
(c) Any acquisition of goods from another EU country by one of the constituent members in the course of the specified business is treated as an acquisition by the taxable person.
(d) Each of the constituent members is jointly and severally liable for any VAT due from the taxable person.

(e) Without prejudice to (*d*) above, any failure by a taxable person to comply with any VAT requirement is treated as a failure by each of the constituent members severally.

(f) Subject to (*a*)–(*e*) above, the constituent members are treated as a partnership carrying on the specified business and any question as to the scope of that business at any time is determined accordingly.

HMRC may subsequently give notice that one of the constituent members is no longer to be regarded as such for the purposes of (*d*) or (*e*) above. He then ceases to have any liability for those purposes after a date specified in the notice and, from the same date, ceases to be regarded as a member of the partnership referred to in (*f*) above.

[*VATA 1994, Sch 1 para 2(6)–(8)*].

Appeals

[8.9] An appeal may be made against a direction or supplementary direction but the tribunal cannot allow the appeal unless it considers that HMRC could not reasonably have been satisfied that there were grounds for making that direction or supplementary direction. [*VATA 1994, s 84(7); FA 1997, s 31(3)*].

Cases where HMRC's direction was upheld

See *Chamberlain v C & E Commrs*, QB [1989] STC 505 (TVC 57.35) (associated companies operating launderettes); *Osman v C & E Commrs*, QB [1989] STC 596 (TVC 57.39) (husband and wife acting as tax consultants from the same office); *TSD & Mrs M E Williams* (VTD 2445) (TVC 57.41) (married couple carrying on business as a café and bread shop from the same premises); *MJ & P Summers* (VTD 3498) (TVC 57.45) (health studio operated by married couple and son); *P & RJ Jervis* (VTD 3920) (TVC 57.48) (catering at a public house); *West End Health and Fitness Club* (VTD 4070) (TVC 57.47) (company operating a fitness club and a director and his wife operating a beauty salon in partnership from the same premises); *Old Farm Service Station Ltd & L Williams* (VTD 4261) (TVC 57.52) (company operating a service station and a director's son running a video club at the same premises); *Allerton Motors* (VTD 9427) (TVC 57.58) (car sales and car washing at same premises); *EM, PG & CP Evans* (VTD 10532) (TVC 57.59) (fairground amusement operators); and *A & S Essex (t/a Essex Associates)* (VTD 15072) (TVC 57.60) (married couple providing computer programming services via a partnership and supplying computer hardware via a limited company).

Cases where the appellants were successful

See *D & Mrs LM Horsman* (VTD 5401) (TVC 57.73) (farming and pony trekking carried on by married couple); *P, C & J Allen* (VTD 12209) (TVC 57.76) (where, to avoid inheritance tax, a husband, who ran a bookselling business and three launderettes, took his wife into partnership in the bookselling business, transferred one of the launderettes to her and took his son into partnership in another of the launderettes); *I Reayner, J Colegate & A Reayner* (VTD 15396) (TVC 57.77) (dry-cleaning businesses operated from separate premises by a mother, her son and his common law wife); and *Trippitt (S & AJ)* (VTD 17340) (TVC 57.67) (wife of publican providing bed and breakfast facilities and paying 35% of income to husband).

Transfer of a business as a going concern

[8.10] For EU legislation, see **18.8 EUROPEAN UNION LEGISLATION.**

Normally the sale of the assets of a VAT-registered business are subject to VAT at the appropriate rate. However, where certain conditions are met (see **8.11** below), the transfer of a business as a going concern ('TOGC') involving the sale of a business including assets *must* be treated as 'neither a supply of goods nor a supply of services' and is therefore outside the scope of VAT. VAT must not be charged on the assets transferred (except, in certain circumstances as indicated in **8.12** below, on the land and buildings used in the business).

Typical cases which may be covered by the provisions are where

- the assets of a business are bought by another person and the existing business ceases to trade;
- an existing owner of a business dies or retires and the business assets are taken over by another person;
- part of an existing business is sold to another person; and
- the assets of a business are transferred to a new legal entity (e.g. a sole proprietor may take on a partner, or form a limited company).

There is no TOGC simply because of a change in the constitution of a partnership or the transfer of shares in a limited company from one person to another.

The TOGC rules are compulsory and so it is important to establish from the outset whether a sale is a TOGC or not. If VAT is charged when it should not have been:

- The seller must cancel any VAT invoice issued and provide the new owner with a refund of the VAT charged (normally by issue of a credit note or document giving similar effect).
- If any VAT is incorrectly shown on a VAT invoice which is not cancelled, it is recoverable by HMRC from the seller, see **31.2 HMRC: POWERS.**
- The purchaser will not be able to reclaim this amount as input tax (even if he has paid it to the vendor in good faith) because there was no taxable supply. But it is understood that where HMRC are wholly satisfied that the amount of 'VAT' has been both declared and paid to them by the seller, they may allow the purchaser to recover it as if it were input tax.

(VAT Notice 700/9/08, paras 1.2–1.5, 2.2).

De Voil Indirect Tax Service. See V2.226.

Conditions for transfer not to be a taxable supply

[8.11] Subject to **8.12** below, the supply by a person of the assets of his business to a person to whom he transfers that business (or part thereof) as a going concern is neither a supply of goods nor a supply of services provided all the following conditions are satisfied.

Condition 1

The assets are to be used by the purchaser in carrying on the same kind of business, whether or not as part of an existing business, as that carried on by the seller in relation to the whole or part transferred. [*SI 1995/1268, Art 5(1)*]. If the purchaser is to use the assets to carry on a different kind of business, VAT must be charged in the normal way.

The purchaser does not need to have been pursuing the same type of business as the seller before the assets are transferred to him (*Zita Modes Sàrl v Administration de l'enregistrement et des domaines, ECJ Case C–497/01*, [2005] STC 1059 (TVC 22.167)).

Common areas of difficulty include companies which have more than one trading activity. For example, a brewery is in business selling beers, wines and spirits to the public via their managed house outlets. It is also in business renting properties to tenants (where the tenants are selling to the public). If a brewery was leasing a pub to tenants, and then sold the business to someone who was to run the pub himself, there would not be a TOGC. The brewery had a business of renting the property, the new owner has a business of running a pub.

HMRC accept that there is the same type of business where

- a restaurant or bar is sold but the purchaser is to immediately alter the style of the business (e.g. where a public house is subsequently aimed at different clientele and sells different beer (see *G Draper (Marlow) Ltd* (VTD 2079) (TVC 65.3)) and where an Indian restaurant bcomes an Italian restaurant (see *Tahmassebi (t/a Sale Pepe)* (VTD 13177) (TVC 65.94)); or
- a business is sold to someone who intends to restructure it so that it will not be the same type of business but who continues with the existing business, even if for a very short period of time

but there are different types of business where

- the seller grants franchises to operate trading sites (as opposed to operating the actual trading activity of the business); or
- the purchaser will only use the seller's product to support his existing business and will not be making any supplies of the seller's product to any third parties.

(VAT Notice 700/9/08, paras 7.1–7.3).

There is not necessarily a different kind of business because the seller made supplies to wholesalers and the purchaser sells to retail customers. See, for example, *Village Collection Interiors Ltd* (VTD 6146) (TVC 65.23).

It is implied that the seller had to have been carrying on the business, or part of the business, transferred. See *Kwik Save Group plc* (VTD 12749) (TVC 65.80) where a holding company carrying on the business of food retailers purchased foodstores (not a taxable supply) and then transferred them to a subsidiary which carried on a similar business but without itself in the meantime having traded at those foodstores (a taxable supply).

Condition 2

In a case in which the seller is a taxable person (i.e. registered or liable to be registered for VAT), the purchaser must already be a taxable person or immediately become, as a result of the transfer, a taxable person (or Isle of Man equivalent). [*SI 1995/1268, Art 5(1)*]. In determining whether the purchaser is a taxable person, the turnover of the seller must also be taken into account. See **59.3 REGISTRATION**.

This condition is not met if the purchaser is not registered or required to be registered for VAT, for example, because

- at the date the transfer takes place, the purchaser does not expect the value of his taxable supplies in the next twelve months to be above the deregistration limit (e.g. because he intends to reduce trading by introducing shorter working hours); or
- the seller was registered voluntarily at the date of the transfer so that the purchaser is not required to register because the value of his taxable supplies in the twelve-month period then ended is not above the registration limit.

In such circumstances, unless the purchaser has been accepted for voluntary registration, the TOGC conditions are not met and the sale takes its normal liability. Where only part of the business is being transferred, the purchaser must consider the turnover of that part to determine whether he must be registered.

There can be no TOGC where a VAT-registered farmer transfers his business to a farmer who is certified under the agricultural flat rate scheme as the purchaser is not registered or registerable for VAT.

(VAT Notice 700/9/08, paras 1.3, 2.3.4).

Condition 3

In relation to a part transfer, that part must be capable of separate operation. [*SI 1995/1268, Art 5(1)*]. HMRC take the view that an 'in-house' function is not a business for TOGC condition purposes when it only operates internally and the assets of the part transferred must have been used to make supplies (and not merely used for the overheads of the business). However, it does not matter whether the part will, in fact, be operated separately from any other business the purchaser carries on.

(VAT Notice 700/9/08, para 2.3.7).

Condition 4

The effect of the transfer must be to put the purchaser in possession of a business which can be operated as such. A sale of capital assets is not in itself a TOGC but if the effect is to put the purchaser in possession of a business, then it is a TOGC even if the assets are transferred on different dates. (VAT Notice 700/9/08, para 2.3.1).

Condition 5

The business, or part, transferred must be a 'going concern' at the time of transfer. But it can still be a going concern even though it is unprofitable or is trading under the control of a liquidator, administrative receiver or trustee in bankruptcy. (VAT Notice 700/9/08, para 2.3.1).

See *Baltic Leasing Ltd* (VTD 2088) (TVC 65.17) and *C & E Commrs v Dearwood Ltd*, QB [1986] STC 327 (TVC 65.12).

In *JMA Spijkers v Gevroeders Benedik Abattoir CV, ECJ Case C-24/85*, [1986] 2 CMLR 296 (TVC 22.166) it was held that there could be a TOGC even if there had been a cessation of trading before the date on which the transfer took place provided the wherewithal to carry on the business, such as plant, building and employees, were available and were transferred.

Condition 6

There must not be a series of immediately consecutive transfers of the business. Where A sells its assets to B who immediately sells those assets to C, B has not carried on the business. As a result, B can neither receive nor make an onward supply of the assets under the special provisions. In relation to property transactions, such immediate transfers often occur where A contracts to sell property to B, and B sells on to C with both contracts being completed by a single transfer from A to C. There is an exception to this for the transfer of a property rental business in Scotland where, subject to the provisions relating to land and buildings in **8.13** below, the disposition of the ownership of the property (*dominium utile*) may be seen to be direct from A to C. (VAT Notice 700/9/08, para 2.3.3).

Condition 7

There must be no significant break in the normal trading pattern before or immediately after the transfer. The 'break in trade' should be considered in the context of the type of business concerned. For example, HMRC do not consider that where a seasonal business has closed for the 'off-season' as normal at the time of sale, that there has necessarily been a break in trade. In addition, a short period of closure that does not significantly disrupt the existing trading pattern (e.g. for redecoration) will not prevent the business from being transferred as a going concern. (VAT Notice 700/9/08, para 2.3.6).

Deciding whether transaction amounts to TOGC

In deciding whether a transaction amounts to a TOGC, regard must be had to its substance rather than its form, and consideration must be given to the whole of the circumstances, weighing the factors which point in one direction against those which point in another. In the end, the vital consideration is whether the effect of the transaction was to put the purchaser in possession of a going concern, the activities of which he could carry on without interruption. Many factors may be relevant to this decision, though few will be conclusive in themselves. Thus, if the purchaser carries on the business in the same manner as before, this will point to the existence of a TOGC, but the converse is not necessarily true, because the transfer may be complete even though the purchaser does not choose to avail himself of all the rights which he acquires thereunder. Similarly, an express assignment of goodwill is strong evidence of a transfer of a business, but the absence of such an assignment is not conclusive the other way. The absence of the assignment of premises, stock or outstanding contracts will likewise not be conclusive, if the particular circumstances of the purchaser enable him to carry on substantially the same business as before. (*Kenmir Ltd v Frizzell*, QB [1968] 1 All ER 414) (TVC 65.10).

Relevant cases

For cases held to fall within the special provisions (so that VAT charged was not recoverable by the purchaser) see *E & E Phillips* (VTD 1130) (TVC 65.1), *Advanced Business Technology Ltd* (VTD 1488) (TVC 65.8), and *C & E Commrs v Dearwood Ltd*, QB [1986] STC 327 (TVC 65.12). For cases held not to fall within the special provisions (so that VAT was chargeable by the vendor and recoverable by the purchaser), see *Eric Ladbroke (Holbeach) Ltd* (VTD 1557) (TVC 65.54), *Computech Development Ltd* (VTD 9798) (TVC 65.44) and *E J Caunt (t/a Edward James Confectionery)* (VTD 1561) (TVC 65.39).

> *Example*
>
> Mike owns a computer store in a local town centre, and has decided he wants to retire and live in Spain. He holds a big closing down sale to sell his stock; he then sells the fixtures and fittings to another computer shop in the next street; a property developer buys the freehold of the shop because he wants to convert the property into luxury flats.
>
> There is no transfer of a going concern situation here and the VAT liability of each separate sale must be considered. However, if Mike had sold the business as a whole and the buyer was continuing to trade as a computer shop, this would have been the sale of a going concern, and no VAT would have been charged if the relevant rules had been met.

Land and buildings

[8.12] A TOGC often involves the transfer of land and buildings. In such cases, there are extra rules to determine whether VAT should be charged on the transfer of the land and buildings, even if the rest of the transfer does qualify for TOGC treatment.

A supply of assets as part of the supply of a business is not treated as a TOGC under the rules in **8.11** above to the extent that it consists of

- a grant of land or buildings, the supply of which would be exempt under *VATA 1994, Sch 9 Group 1* but for an option to tax which the *transferor* has made (see **41.8 LAND AND BUILDINGS: EXEMPT SUPPLIES AND OPTION TO TAX**), or
- a grant of the fee simple in new and uncompleted buildings liable to VAT at the standard rate under **41.3**(*a*) **LAND AND BUILDINGS: EXEMPT SUPPLIES AND OPTION TO TAX**

unless the following conditions have been met no later than the '*relevant date*', i.e. the date upon which the grant would have been treated as having been made or, if there is more than one such date, on the earliest of them.

Condition 1

The *transferee* must have opted to tax the land or buildings concerned and must have given written notification of the option to HMRC.

HMRC take this to mean that, for the TOGC provisions to apply, the option must be notified to HMRC in writing no later than the time of the supply. This is normally the date of the transfer but also includes receipt of a deposit which may otherwise have created a tax point. A tax point is not created by the receipt of a deposit by a third party acting as an independent stakeholder (as opposed to an agent of the vendor) until the money is released to the vendor.

Following the decision in *Chalegrove Properties Ltd* (VTD 17151) (TVC 65.89) HMRC accept that, where the written notification of the election is sent to HMRC by mail, the notification must be properly addressed, pre-paid and posted on or before the time of supply. The transferee is advised to retain evidence of posting.

(VAT Notice 700/9/08, para 2.4.1).

See also *Higher Education Statistics Agency Ltd v C & E Commrs*, QB [2000] STC 332 (TVC 65.88).

Condition 2

The transferee must have notified the transferor that his option to tax the land or buildings concerned will not be disapplied. To do this, the transferee must be satisfied that the following scenario does *not* apply to him, namely that:

- the land transferred to him would, in relation to him, become a capital item within the **CAPITAL GOODS SCHEME (10)** (whether the transfer to him were to be treated as neither a supply of goods nor a supply of services under a TOGC, or otherwise); and
- his supplies of that land will, or would fall, to be exempt supplies by virtue of the disapplication of the option to tax under the anti-avoidance rules in *VATA 1994, Sch 10 para 12* (see **41.12 LAND AND BUILDINGS: EXEMPT SUPPLIES AND OPTION TO TAX**).

[*VATA 1994, s 5(3); SI 1995/1268, Art 5(2)(2A)(2B)(3); SI 2004/779; SI 2008/1146, Sch 1 para 15*].

If the seller is transferring land or buildings on which there is no option tax and the supply would not be otherwise standard-rated (i.e. if the supply is zero-rated or exempt) then the purchaser is not required to opt to tax. In these circumstances the transfer of the land or buildings can be included in the TOGC.

The seller is responsible for applying the correct VAT treatment and HMRC may require him to support his decision. If the transaction is to be treated as a TOGC, it is advisable for the seller to

- ask the purchaser for evidence that his option to tax is in place by the relevant date (e.g. a copy of the notification letter); and
- ask for written confirmation the transferee's option to tax will not be disapplied.

(VAT Notice 700/9/08, para 2.4).

Where the above conditions are not met, the transfer of the land and buildings is a supply subject to VAT. However, the supply of other assets may still qualify to be treated as a TOGC.

> *Example*
>
> Mr Smith is selling his restaurant business as a going concern to Mr Jones, and the sale includes fixtures and fittings, goodwill and a freehold property on which an option to tax election has been made.
>
> Before the deal is completed, Mr Jones must opt to tax the property with HMRC and provide evidence of this action to Mr Smith. He must confirm in writing to Mr Smith that the option to tax election will not be disapplied. The whole deal will then qualify as outside the scope of VAT, assuming the other TOGC conditions are met.
>
> However, if Mr Jones fails to make the election, or decides it is not in his best interests to make the election (e.g. he expects to make a big profit on selling the property in a few years time to a buyer that may not be able to recover VAT), then Mr Smith will have to charge VAT on the value of the property only. The fixtures, fittings and goodwill will still be outside the scope of the tax.

Transfer of a property rental business

[8.13] HMRC give the following examples of circumstances concerning the transfer of land and buildings where there may (or may not) be a transfer of a business of property rental as a going concern. In those cases where there has been such a transfer, provided the conditions in **8.12** above relating to land and buildings and the general conditions in **8.11** above are satisfied, the supply of the assets can then be ignored for VAT purposes.

Examples where a property business can be transferred as a going concern

The seller:

- Owns freehold property which is let to a tenant and is sold with the benefit of the existing lease (or where a leasehold interest is owned and assigned with the benefit of a sub-lease), even if the property is only partly tenanted.

- Owns a building where there is a contract to pay rent in the future but where the tenants are enjoying an initial rent-free period, even if the property is sold during the rent-free period.
- Granted a lease in respect of a building but the tenants are not yet in occupation.
- Owns a property and tenants have been found although no lease agreement has been entered into, and the freehold property is transferred to a third party with the benefit of a contractual agreement for a lease but before the lease has been signed.
- Is a property developer selling a site as a package (to a single buyer) which is a mixture of let and unlet, finished or unfinished properties, and the sale of the site would otherwise have been standard-rated, provided the purchaser opts to tax the *whole* site.
- Owns a number of let freehold properties, and sells one of them, the sale of this single let or partly-let property.
- Has a partially-let building, providing that the letting constitutes economic activity.
- Is a member of a VAT group and a tenant who is a member of either the outgoing landlord's VAT group or the purchaser's VAT group is one of a number of tenants of the property. The presence of a tenant or tenants outside the group means that the whole transaction can still be treated as a TOGC.

The purchaser:

- acquires the freehold and leasehold of a property from separate sellers without the interests merging, the lease has not been extinguished and the purchaser continues to exploit the asset by receiving rent from the tenant.

There is not a transfer of a going concern in the following circumstances

The seller:

- Is a property developer and has built a building which
  - (a) he has allowed someone to occupy temporarily (without any right to occupy after the proposed sale); or
  - (b) he is 'actively marketing' in search of a tenant.
- Owns the freehold of a property and grants a lease (even a 999-year lease) or owns a headlease and grants a sub-lease (because there is no transfer of a business, just the creation of a new asset).
- Sells a property where a lease previously granted is surrendered immediately before the sale (because the property rental business ceases when the lease is surrendered).
- Sells a property freehold to an existing tenant who leases the whole premises from the seller (because the tenant cannot carry on the same business of property rental).
- Is a member of a VAT group and sells the property, which is being rented to another member of the group, to a third party.

The purchaser:

- of a property rental business is a member of the same VAT group as the existing tenant.

(VAT Notice 700/9/08, paras 4.3, 6.2, 6.3).

Nominee purchaser

[8.14] Strictly, a transfer of a going concern cannot occur where the transferee is a nominee for a beneficial owner because the beneficial owner will be the person carrying on the business, not the nominee. However, where the legal title in land is to be held by a nominee for a *named* beneficial owner, that beneficial owner (and not the nominee) may optionally, for the purposes of establishing the transfer of a property letting business as a going concern, be considered to be the transferee. The transferor, nominee and beneficial owner must agree to this optional treatment in writing. Examples of where a nominee might hold property for a beneficial owner are where the legal title is held on trust for a partnership, unincorporated association or pension fund.

(VAT Notice 700/9/08, paras 8.1–8.3). Para 8.3 contains an example format that the parties can use to record their agreement.

The option does not need to apply to transactions where the nominee is the transferor of the legal title. In these cases, *VATA 1994, Sch 10 para 40* deems the beneficial owner to be the transferor. See **41.5 LAND AND BUILDINGS: EXEMPT SUPPLIES AND OPTION TO TAX.**

Miscellaneous aspects

Registration by purchaser

[8.15] See **59.3 REGISTRATION** for circumstances where the purchaser is liable to be registered at the time the business is transferred.

Transfer of registration number

See **59.36 REGISTRATION** for an application to transfer the registration number of the seller to the purchaser following a TOGC.

Deregistration by seller

If the seller is not continuing to trade, he must cancel his VAT registration. See **59.10 REGISTRATION.** If when doing so he has any goods on which input tax has been claimed and which are not transferred with the business, he must normally account for VAT on these assets. See **59.33 REGISTRATION.** If any of the assets not transferred are capital items covered by the capital goods scheme and still within its adjustment period, the seller will need to make a final adjustment. See **10.7 CAPITAL GOODS SCHEME.**

Reclaiming input tax incurred before the TOGC

One of the consequences of transferring the registration number of the seller to the purchaser is that any right of the seller to credit for, or repayment of, input tax becomes the right of the purchaser. However, even where the registration number is not transferred, there is nothing to prevent the seller from assigning to the purchaser the benefit of any claim for repayment under *VATA 1994, s 80*. See *HMRC v Midlands Co-Operative Society Ltd (No 2)*, CA [2008] STC 1803 (TVC 65.119) where a co-operative society transferred its business to another society.

For all transfers of rights to make a claim for overpaid tax that take place from 25 June 2008, the current creditor is put in the shoes of the original creditor. The current creditor does not receive any more from HMRC than if the original creditor had made the claim. The amount due from HMRC on a claim on a transferred right is determined by first setting off the amount of the outstanding liabilities of the original creditor and then any liabilities of the current creditor. Also, HMRC can refuse to pay a current creditor's claim where they can establish that payment of the claim to the original creditor would have unjustly enriched that original creditor [*FA 2008 s 133*] (HMRC Brief 31/08).

Flat-rate scheme for small businesses

See **63.23** SPECIAL SCHEMES for the consequences of a business that is using the flat-rate scheme transferring its business as a going concern.

Deduction of related input tax

Although a transfer of a going concern is not a supply for VAT purposes, this does not prevent the deduction of input tax on related expenses (subject to the normal rules). There is, however, a distinction between the extent to which the seller and the purchaser can deduct that input tax.

For the position of the purchaser following the decision in *C & E Commrs v UBAF Bank Ltd*, see **49.12**(5) **PARTIAL EXEMPTION**.

In the case of the seller, since the sale of the business as a going concern is not a supply, the input tax incurred on the costs of selling the business cannot be attributed to a supply by the seller. In *Abbey National plc v C & E Commrs, ECJ Case C–408/98*, [2001] STC 297 (TVC 22.419) the ECJ confirmed that, in such circumstances, the seller's costs form part of his overheads and thus, in principle, have a direct and immediate link with the whole of his economic activity so that he can deduct a proportion of the input tax attributable to taxable supplies under his partial exemption method.

The ECJ also indicated that if the seller's costs have a direct and immediate link with a *clearly defined part* of his economic activities, so that the costs form part of the overheads of that part of the business, and all the transactions relating to that part of the business are subject to VAT, he may deduct all the VAT charged on his costs of acquiring those services.

Following the *Abbey National* decision, HMRC take the view that

- VAT incurred on services that have a direct and immediate link with the transferred part of a business should be treated as an overhead of that part of the business;
- where that part of the business makes only taxable supplies, then the VAT incurred is deductible;
- where that part of the business makes only exempt supplies, then the VAT incurred is not deductible; and

- in instances where both taxable and exempt supplies are made by that part of the business, the VAT incurred is partly deductible by reference to the partial exemption method in place. If the partial exemption method fails to achieve a fair and reasonable result, HMRC may be prepared to approve an alternative method.

(VAT Notice 700/9/08, para 2.6.2).

Retention of records

Business records generally have to be kept for up to six years. *With effect from 1 September 2007*, where a business (or part of a business) is transferred as a going concern,

- in all but a few specified cases where the purchaser retains the seller's VAT number, the seller must keep any of its business records which are required to be kept after the transfer under the six-year rule. But, so far as is necessary for the purposes of complying with the purchaser's duties under *VATA 1994*, the purchaser (P) may require the seller to
  - (a) give P within such time and form as P may reasonably require, such information contained in the records and such copies of documents forming part of the records, as P may reasonably specify; and
  - (b) make the records available for inspection by P at such time and place as P may reasonably require (and permit P to take copies of, or make extracts from them); and
- HMRC may disclose to the purchaser information relating to the business when it was carried out by the seller to enable the purchaser to comply with its duties under *VATA 1994*.

[*VATA 1994, s 49(4)–(6); FA 2007, s 100(6)*].

In relation to TOGCs entered into before 1 September 2007, any records relating to the seller's business, which under the six-year rule are required to be kept for a period after the transfer, must be preserved by the purchaser unless HMRC allow otherwise. [*VATA 1994, s 49(1)(b); FA 2007, s 100(2)*].

Supplies to partly-exempt VAT groups

On certain transfers of businesses to partly-exempt VAT groups, the chargeable assets transferred are treated as being supplied to and by the representative member of the group at the open market value. See **27.7 GROUPS OF COMPANIES.**

Capital goods scheme

Where a business is sold as a going concern and the assets transferred include land or buildings or a civil engineering work worth £250,000 or more and/or computer equipment worth £50,000 or more, the purchaser takes over responsibility for applying the capital goods scheme. See **10.12**(4) **CAPITAL GOODS SCHEME.**

Anti-avoidance — subsequent free supply

Where goods or services are transferred as part of a TOGC and the seller (or any previous owner) has deducted input tax on those goods or services, output tax is chargeable on any subsequent free supply of those goods or services by the purchaser. See **47.6** and **47.7** **OUTPUT TAX**.

Key points

[8.16] Points to consider are as follows.

(a) Business or non-business

- In most cases, it will be clear whether an activity carried out by an individual or other entity is classed as a 'business' (or 'economic activity' to use the phrase adopted in EU VAT law). As a general rule, an intention to make a profit from an activity that is carried out on a regular basis will be classed as a business. As a general principle, the exploitation of land (rental arrangement etc.) is always deemed to be business.
- It is important to be clear about the date when a business actually starts to trade as this can have an impact on a person's date of VAT registration, which is usually based on the value of past taxable sales. If early sales can be legitimately considered to be a 'hobby' rather than a 'business', then this could produce a useful extension to the date when a business needs to first register for VAT on a compulsory basis. The 'business test' guidelines (see **8.2** above) confirm that occasional sales made on an infrequent basis are unlikely to be classed as business related.
- Although an important indicator of 'business', the profit motive is not always the crucial factor. Many business activities are intended to just cover costs and, in some cases, serve as a loss leader for other commercial motives. But an intention to make a profit is usually a key indicator of a business arrangement being in place.
- For a VAT-registered business, it is important to identify which of its activities are classed as business and those (if any) that are deemed to be non-business. Input tax cannot be claimed on costs relevant to non-business activities, and a sensible apportionment method is needed if an expense has both business and non-business use. This issue is particularly important for charities.

(b) Separation of business activities

- The separation of business activities into different legal entities (disaggregation) can be blocked by HMRC if they issue a notice of direction that treats the different entities as a single taxable person. However, they can only issue a direction if they consider that the different entities are closely linked by 'financial, economic and organisational' issues. Note the significance of the word 'and' in the legislation. This means that HMRC must prove all three links (financial, economic and organisational) before a direction can be issued.

- A direction can only be issued by HMRC from a current or future date. However, as a warning, if HMRC can prove that the different entities were never actually separated (no separate accounting records, confusion with banking and invoicing arrangements, no proper system of recharging shared overheads etc.), they may seek to assess tax on a retrospective basis (i.e. on the basis that there has only ever been one business).
- As a general observation, it is harder for two businesses to be separated if family members are involved in both entities. This is because the motives for ensuring overheads are properly recharged are reduced when profits are relevant to a single family. Most VAT tribunal cases lost by taxpayers on this issue involve family members (e.g. husband trading as a publican and VAT registered but wife carrying out catering activity on the same premises and trading below the VAT registration limit).

(c) Transfer of a going concern

- When acting for the buyer of a business, ensure that VAT is not incorrectly charged by the vendor – if a transfer of a going concern arrangement is evident, then HMRC has the power to disallow any input tax claimed by the buyer, even if he holds a proper tax invoice and has paid the VAT to the seller in good faith. The only exception to this approach is if HMRC are wholly satisfied the seller has fully declared and paid output tax on its own VAT return.
- Don't forget that the transfer of a going concern rules are compulsory. There is no possibility of choosing to 'opt out' by, for example, playing safe and charging VAT. The various conditions need to be fully considered to see if a transfer of a business is taking place that is outside the scope of VAT.
- It is also important for buyers to avoid paying VAT if possible because of the cash flow problems of paying the VAT to the seller and then waiting up to three months to reclaim it on a VAT return. It is likely to take longer than three months to recover such VAT as HMRC may choose to carry out a pre-payment credibility check.
- If acting for the seller, remember that the buyer must be VAT-registered or liable to be VAT-registered as a result of the sale – otherwise the transfer of a going concern rules are not met. The buyer must take into account the taxable sales of the previous owner as far as the VAT-registration limits are concerned. This usually produces a requirement for the buyer to become VAT-registered from his first day of trading.

- In most cases, it will be clear if a business is being sold as a going concern, or whether individual assets are being sold. Advisers need to be aware of the key rules to consider in cases that are not clear-cut.
- Be aware that even though the proceeds from a transfer of a going concern sale are outside the scope of VAT, the related input tax on selling costs can still be reclaimed as long as the business has activities that are wholly taxable. If part of the business income is exempt, then a restriction on the input tax claimed will be evident using the normal partial exemption method adopted by the business.
- There are important issues to consider if the sale of a going concern includes a property where the option to tax election has been made by the seller – as explained at **8.12**. The main requirement is that if the seller has made an election, then the buyer must also make an election before the transfer takes place, and have notified this election to HMRC. The decision to opt to tax a property is very important for any business, because once made, it is in place for at least 20 years.
- If a seller has no option to tax election in place on a property, then there is no requirement for the buyer to make an election. This is an important point to avoid an unnecessary election being made by the buyer, which could create future problems if he wants to either rent out or sell the property to a business that cannot fully reclaim input tax (e.g. an exempt or partly exempt business such as an insurance broker).
- A common error in transfer of a going concern situations is where a landlord rents property to a tenant (and the tenant trades in goods or services) and the premises are then sold to the tenant. This is not a transfer of a going concern situation because the activity of the seller (property rental) is not the same as the buyer (selling goods or services).
- A transfer of a going concern situation can also apply if only part of a business is sold, as long as this part is capable of independently carrying on trading in its own right. An example might be a firm of accountants selling its tax department and maintaining its audit and accountancy sections.
- It is possible, where the buyer has no current VAT registration, for the buyer of a business to retain the seller's VAT registration number. This course of action is deprecated because the buyer will then be taking over the liability of any potential underpayments of VAT in the last four years. There are very few advantages in retaining the seller's VAT registration number – possibly only a saving of stationery (showing the VAT number) might be the only benefit.
- It is important that the buyer is aware of any potential issues that apply with the capital goods scheme. The buyer will take over any remaining intervals of the seller, i.e. to produce a ten-year input

tax adjustment in the case of relevant buildings and five years in the case of relevant computer purchases.

9

Business Entertainment

De Voil Indirect Tax Service. See V3.446.

Introduction

[9.1] VAT charged on any goods or services supplied to a taxable person, or on any goods acquired or imported by him, is excluded from any credit where the goods or services in question are used or to be used for the purpose of 'business entertainment' unless (from 1 May 2011) the entertainment is provided for an overseas customer and is of a reasonable kind and on a reasonable scale (see below). [*SI 1992/3222, Art 5(1); SI 2011/1071*].

'*Business entertainment*' means entertainment (including hospitality of any kind) provided by a taxable person in connection with a business carried on by him, but does not include the provision of any such entertainment for either or both

- employees of the taxable person; or
- if the taxable person is a company, its directors or persons engaged in the management of the company

unless the provision of entertainment for such persons is incidental to its provision for others. [*SI 1992/3222, Art 5(3)*].

General scope

[9.2] Following on from the definition in **9.1** above, HMRC regard business entertainment as including

- provision of food and drink;
- provision of accommodation (hotels, etc.);
- provision of theatre and concert tickets;
- entry to sporting events and facilities;

- entry to clubs, nightclubs, etc.; and
- use of capital goods such as yachts and aircraft for the purpose of entertaining.

(VAT Notice 700/65/11, para 2.2).

See *C & E Commrs v Shaklee International and Another*, CA [1981] STC 776 (TVC 8.3) for the provision of food and accommodation for self-employed agents undergoing training; *BMW (GB) Ltd v C & E Commrs*, QB [1997] STC 824 (TVC 8.33) for hospitality provided to dealers and potential customers at 'track days' where vehicles could be test driven; *Medicare Research Ltd* (VTD 1045) (TVC 8.6) for refreshments and hospitality provided at business discussion meetings in the course of making taxable supplies; *Webster Communications International Ltd* (VTD 14753) (TVC 8.38) for meals and refreshments provided at sponsored conferences to delegates nominated by the sponsor and attending free of charge; *Wilsons Transport Ltd* (VTD 1468) (TVC 8.10) for launching parties; *Polash Tandoori Restaurant* (VTD 10903) (TVC 8.21) for free drinks supplied to customers; and *William Matthew Mechanical Services Ltd* (VTD 1210) (TVC 8.8) for subscription for theatre seats used to extend hospitality and entertainment to clients. However, if the entertainment is not given gratuitously but is provided under a contractual obligation, it does not fall within the scope of the provision. See *Celtic Football and Athletic Club Ltd v C & E Commrs*, CS [1983] STC 470 (TVC 8.35) and *C & E Commrs v Kilroy Television Company Ltd*, QB [1997] STC 901 (TVC 8.47).

Employees

[9.3] For business entertainment purposes, HMRC regard '*employee*' as including

- directors or anyone engaged in the management of the business (including partners);
- self-employed persons (subsistence expenses only) treated by the employer in the same way for subsistence purposes as an employee; and
- helpers, stewards and other people essential to the running of sporting or similar events

but not as including pensioners and former employees, job applicants and interviewees, and shareholders (who are not also employees).

(VAT Notice 700/65/11, paras 2.3, 2.4).

Staff entertainment

Following the decision in *Ernst & Young* (VTD 15100) (TVC 8.43) HMRC accept that where an employer provides entertainment for the benefit of its employees (e.g. to reward them for good work or to maintain and improve staff morale), it does so wholly for business purposes. Thus, the VAT incurred on entertainment of employees (e.g. staff parties, team building exercises, staff outings and similar events) is input tax and is not blocked from recovery under the business entertainment rules. There are two exceptions to this general rule.

- Where entertainment is provided only for directors, partners or sole proprietors of a business, the VAT incurred is not input tax as the goods or services are not used for a business purpose. But where directors, etc. attend staff parties together with other employees, HMRC accept that the VAT incurred is input tax and is not blocked from recovery.
- Where employees act as hosts to non-employees, the costs are incurred solely for the purpose of entertaining the non-employees and the input tax is blocked under the business entertainment rules.

(VAT Notice 700/65/11, paras 3.1–3.3).

Subsistence expenses

Where meals etc. are provided away from the place of work on a business trip, the VAT incurred on the employee's meal can be claimed as input tax under the subsistence rules (see **34.13**(26) INPUT TAX). (VAT Notice 700/65/11, para 2.5).

Staff parties with guests, etc.

Where a business entertains both employees and non-employees, it can only recover as input tax the VAT it incurs on entertaining its employees. The portion of the input tax incurred in entertaining others is blocked under the business entertainment rules. (VAT Notice 700/65/11, para 3.4). In *KPMG (No 2)* (VTD 14962) (TVC 8.34) an accountancy firm organised dinner dances for its employees, each of whom was entitled to bring one guest. It was held that the related input tax should be apportioned on the basis that the proportion of the expenditure attributable to the guests constituted business entertainment. The entertainment of the non-employees could not be treated as incidental to the entertainment of the employees (in contrast to the specific provision made in the converse case, see **9.1** above). This decision came after the decision in *Thorn EMI plc v C & E Commrs*, CA [1995] STC 674 (TVC 8.30) (see **9.4** below) that input tax relating to business entertainment can be apportioned. The decision in *KPMG (No 2)* was distinguished in *Ernst & Young* (VTD 15100) (TVC 8.43) where a charge of £15 per head was made for guests. The tribunal held that the crucial characteristic of 'entertainment' in the phrase 'business entertainment' was that it was provided free of charge. Although the £15 charge was considerably less than the cost of the party, it was not so small as to say the meal was provided free of charge.

Apportionment between business entertainment and other use

[9.4] In *Thorn EMI plc v C & E Commrs*, CA [1995] STC 674 (TVC 8.30), HMRC sought to exclude credit for all input tax on hospitality chalets constructed to receive customers at shows although accepting that the chalets were used partly for business purposes. It was held, upholding the decision in the High Court and reversing the decision in *C & E Commrs v Plant Repair & Services (South Wales) Ltd*, QB [1994] STC 232 (TVC 8.39), that HMRC's approach was unreasonable. Applying the general principle in *Directive 2006/112/EC* (previously *EC 6th Directive, Art 17*), apportionment should be allowed. HMRC now accept this. (VAT Notice 700/65/11, para 2.7).

Consumable goods

Some goods may be used for a variety of purposes, e.g. food and drink may be used for trading stock or subsistence meals for employees (VAT fully recoverable) or business entertainment (VAT not recoverable). Where possible, stocks to be used for entertaining should be kept separately. If, however, it has not been decided how the goods will be used at the time of purchase, a record should be kept of goods used for entertainment so the input tax recoverable can be calculated at the end of each VAT period. This record forms part of the VAT records and should be available for inspection by visiting VAT officers.

Capital goods

Where a capital asset, such as a yacht or private aircraft, is used solely for business entertainment, the VAT incurred is not recoverable. If it is used for both business entertainment and other business purposes, the input tax must be apportioned.

Exclusions

[9.5] There are a number of circumstances where business entertaining is apparently provided but the associated input tax may be recovered.

Entertainment of members of clubs, associations, etc.

Without specific charge and which is available to all subscribing members or all such members within a particular category. This is considered to be part of the benefits received in return for payment of the appropriate membership subscription. VAT incurred on the cost of entertainment of non-members cannot be reclaimed as input tax. Non-members include a member's family not specifically covered by membership subscription, members of other clubs, visiting teams, etc.

Free drinks to customers at restaurants, etc.

The amounts paid by customers for meals are considered to be inclusive of any drinks, etc. given 'freely'.

Airlines providing catering and accommodation expenses for passengers who have been delayed

Recovery of input tax is allowed in such circumstances. (VAT Notice 700/65/11, para 2.8).

HMRC used to take the view that where in such circumstances meals were supplied direct from the caterer to the passengers, the VAT was not input tax of the airline even if it paid for all or part of the meal. This view had been supported in *British Airways plc v C & E Commrs (No 2)*, QB [1996] STC 1127 (TVC 36.155) but in *British Airways plc (No 3)*, (VTD 16446) (TVC 36.131) the tribunal declined to follow that decision and allowed the claim for input tax. Applying the *dicta* of Lord Hope in *C & E Commrs v Redrow Group plc*, HL [1999] STC 161 (TVC 36.130) the fact that someone else (in this case, the passenger) also receives a supply as part of the same transaction does not deprive the person who instructs the supply and who pays for it (the airline) of the benefit of the deduction.

HMRC also used to take the view that, even where, exceptionally, such meals were supplied to the airline, the input tax was subject to the business entertainment block (except for meals provided to passengers who were denied boarding due to overbooking as such passengers were legally entitled to compensation from the airline and consequently the meals were not free hospitality). They no longer appear to take this point and allow recovery of input tax where passengers are delayed for other reasons (e.g. bad weather, industrial action, etc.).

As regards accommodation provided to delayed air passengers, there is a long-standing agreement that airlines that book accommodation for their delayed passengers may treat the VAT incurred as deductible input tax. Although the validity of this arrangement is not free from doubt, HMRC have decided not to disturb it pending consideration of the EU Commission's proposals for an input tax restriction upon expenditure on accommodation.

Free wine or beer tasting events

for trade customers or journalists which allow sampling but not drinking, or a free glass of whisky following a tour of the distillery, etc.

Free meals for coach drivers at motorway service stations

at motorway service stations. These are considered to be business gifts on which output tax may be due. See **47.6 OUTPUT TAX** and *C & E Commrs v Westmorland Motorway Services Ltd*, CA [1998] STC 431 (TVC 67.143).

Entertainment provided by local authorities at civic functions

This is not business entertainment because the function is a non-business activity.

Entertainment of a non-personal nature provided freely by stores, etc.

To members of the general public, e.g. hiring circus performers, musicians, or other entertainers to attract custom or advertise a trader's premises. This does not apply to promotional events where customers attend by invitation, e.g. where a motor dealer invites customers to the launch of a new car and incurs VAT on providing them with free hospitality.

This is not business entertainment because the function is a non-business activity.

(HMRC VAT Guidance V1–13, para 16.10).

Amateur sports persons

[9.6] Amateur players are, by definition, not employees and input tax on business entertainment provided for them is therefore blocked. Where the entertainment is provided by a club out of players' subscriptions to it, input tax may be reclaimed under the provisions above for entertainment of members of clubs. Where, however, certain bodies choose, from affiliated clubs, individual amateur sports persons to represent their country or county, the persons selected are not full subscribing members of the representative body and therefore the provisions applying to clubs above cannot apply. By concession HMRC have agreed that input tax necessarily incurred on the provision of accommodation and meals for team members selected by such representative bodies, and committee members of that body, may be deductible as input tax. The concession does not cover alcoholic drinks and tobacco. (VAT Notice 48, ESC 3.10).

Supplies by a taxable person

[9.7] Special provisions as below apply where, as a result of **9.1** above, no input tax on goods or services used for business entertaining has been claimed and the taxable person subsequently supplies the goods or services in question.

Supplies of goods

Following the decision in *EC Commission v Italian Republic, ECJ Case C–45/95*, [1997] STC 1062 (TVC 22.349), where, as a result of **9.1** above, no input tax has been claimed by a taxable person on a supply, acquisition or importation of any *goods*, the disposal of those goods is an exempt supply under *VATA 1994, Sch 9 Group 14*, regardless of whether they are sold at a profit or loss. See **20.4 EXEMPT SUPPLIES.**

It should be noted that the provisions only apply where *no* input tax has been claimed (e.g. where a yacht or private aircraft is used solely for entertaining). Where, however, the asset was used for both entertaining and business purposes, on resale VAT must be accounted for on the full selling price. (VAT Notice 700/65/11, para 2.9).

Supplies of services

Where, as a result of **9.1** above, a taxable person has claimed no input tax on a supply of any services to him, VAT must be charged on a supply by him of those services as if made for a consideration equal to the excess of

(a) the consideration for which the services are supplied by him, over
(b) the consideration for which they were supplied to him.

Where (*b*) is greater than (*a*), the supply is treated as outside the scope of VAT.

[*SI 1992/3222, Art 5(2); SI 1999/2930*].

Overseas customers

[9.8] In the light of recent ECJ judgments, HMRC concluded that the UK's block on the recovery of input tax on the business entertainment of overseas clients is inconsistent with EU law. Consequently the legislation was amended with effect from 1 May 2011, as noted above, to permit input tax recovery in relation to the entertainment of 'overseas customers' if it is of a reasonable kind and on a reasonable scale (see below). [*SI 1992/3222, Art 5(1); SI 2011/1071*]. An overseas customer, in relation to a taxable person, is

(a) any person who is not ordinarily resident nor carrying on a business in the United Kingdom or the Isle of Man and avails himself or herself, or may be expected to avail himself or herself, in the course of a business carried on by that person outside the United Kingdom and the Isle of Man, of any goods or services the supply of which forms part of the taxable person's business; and

(b) any person who is not ordinarily resident in the United Kingdom or the Isle of Man and is acting, in relation to such goods or services, on behalf of an overseas customer as defined in paragraph (*a*) above or on behalf of any government or public authority outside the United Kingdom and the Isle of Man.

In addition to the legislative changes, HMRC will consider claims for previously restricted VAT in respect of the entertainment of overseas customer, as a direct effect of EU law.

Time limit

Claims may be made in respect of input tax on the costs of entertaining overseas business customers, subject to the normal four year cap.

VAT incurred in future tax periods in respect of the entertainment of overseas business customers can be recovered in the usual way.

Evidence required

HMRC expects that, as a minimum, claims are supported by the following evidence.

- Details of the overseas customers.
- The type of expenditure, e.g. meals to support business meetings, etc.
- The amount of VAT claimed.
- Evidence that VAT has been incurred and not previously been deducted.
- If required for historical claims, evidence of the type of business entertainment the business normally excludes from recovery by reference to recently rendered tax periods.

Private use charge

Two cases, *Julius Fillibeck Sohne GmbH & Co KG, ECJ Case C-258/95*, [1998] STC 513 (TVC 22.184) and *Danfoss A/S, ECJ Case C-371/07*, [2009] STC 701 (TVC 22.186), introduce separate tests that should be applied when considering private use of the business expenditure.

In the *Fillibeck Sohne* case an employer provided transport to his staff to get them from their homes to a construction site. As commuting expenditure is private, the ECJ was asked to consider whether having recovered tax on the cost of the transport it was appropriate to apply a charge to reflect the private use by the employees. The ECJ's starting point was that a charge applied in principle, but on the particular facts of the case it was practically impossible for the employees to get to the site on their own, and therefore a private use charge should not be applied. Following that decision, HMRC have stated that the 'necessity test' is whether it is necessary for the taxable person to provide goods or services that are enjoyed privately in order for him to make his taxable supplies.

The *Danfoss* case involved the provision of free meals to both employees and business contacts. In the context of the business having recovered VAT on the meals, the ECJ was asked to consider whether it was appropriate to apply a private use charge. The ECJ concluded that where the meals were provided for a strict business purpose no such charge should arise. In reaching this conclusion they carefully considered the circumstances of the free meals. In particular the lack of choice by the recipient of what, when and where to eat, the relatively basic nature of the fare and crucially the fact that the meals were provided to ensure the smooth running of business meetings. This, according to HMRC, is the 'strict business purpose test'.

Example 1

For a meeting, a business takes an overseas customer to a restaurant. If the meal is reasonable in scale and character the input tax is not restricted. However, gourmet dining and fine wine is not reasonable in scale and character and the VAT incurred should not be recovered. In any event such lavish fare goes beyond the business need of providing basic food and refreshment to facilitate the smooth running of a meeting. Therefore output tax is due where related expenditure has been recovered.

Example 2

At corporate hospitality events, many businesses offer their customers or potential customers general entertainment and hospitality. Examples include: golf days; track days; trips to sporting events; evening meals; or trips to nightclubs. Where the related expenditure is incurred for the purpose of the business, and recovered, an output tax charge will be due. This is because such events are unlikely to have a strict business purpose or be necessary for the business to make its supplies.

(VAT Notice 700/65/11, para 2.6).

Key points

[9.9] Points to consider are as follows.

- Input tax can be reclaimed on the costs of entertaining staff, unless the role of staff members is to act as host at an event for non-employees. This provision is intended to recognise that the entertaining of staff can be a key component of rewarding good work or loyalty, i.e. as a motivational tool. Input tax can therefore be claimed on the costs of office Christmas parties, staff outings and other social events provided to employees.

- A useful concession is that input tax can also be claimed on subsistence expenses for self-employed workers (subcontractors etc.), even though they are not employees. However, a condition of the rules is that they must only be entitled to the same subsistence arrangements as employees.
- Input tax cannot be reclaimed on the costs of entertaining if they are relevant to either a director of a company or business owner (sole trader, partner). The exception to this rule is if the director or owner is attending an event that is open to all staff (annual Christmas party etc.), in which case input tax can be claimed.
- Entertaining is only applicable if it is provided without charge. If a charge is made to attend an event, e.g. a charge for the spouses of employees to attend the firm's Christmas party, then input tax can be reclaimed on the costs and output tax will then be due on the payments received from the individuals in question. This is a useful planning opportunity – the charge to the non-employees does not need to cover the full cost of attending the event, i.e. input tax claimed can exceed output tax declared on the payments received.
- If entertaining is provided as part of a contractual obligation, then the input tax block does not apply. So if an overseas football team needs to be provided with food and accommodation by its UK opponents as a condition of a competition rule, then this is not business entertainment in the traditional sense (the entertainer has no choice) and input tax can therefore be claimed on these expenses.
- Input tax can be claimed on the costs of food and drink provided at 'business meetings' where some of the delegates are non-employees. Input tax deduction on the costs of entertaining overseas customers is permissible – see **9.8** above. HMRC has issued guidance on these points.

10

Capital Goods Scheme

Cross-references. See **37.1** INTERACTION WITH OTHER TAXES for the effect on capital allowances where adjustments are made to input tax deduction under the capital goods scheme.

De Voil Indirect Tax Service. See V3.470–478.

Introduction

[10.1] The capital goods scheme (CGS) applies to certain items of capital expenditure on computer equipment, land and buildings, civil engineering works and refurbishments and fitting-out works which are acquired or brought into use after 31 March 1990 and which are not used wholly for making taxable supplies. It also applies to certain ships and aircraft obtained on or after 1 January 2011. The scheme recognises that such items of capital expenditure can be used by a business over a number of years and that there may be variation over those years in the extent to which the items are used to make taxable supplies. It provides a mechanism whereby the initial input tax claimed can be adjusted over a period of up to ten years.

When a capital item within the scheme (see **10.2** below) is acquired, the normal rules for claiming input tax apply, i.e.

- if it is used wholly in making taxable supplies, input tax is recoverable in full;
- if it is used wholly in making exempt supplies, none of the input tax is recoverable; and
- if it is used for making taxable and exempt supplies, a proportion of the input tax may be claimed under the partial exemption rules.

Where, subsequently, in the adjustment period for that item (see **10.3** below) there is a change in the extent of taxable use, an input tax adjustment has to be made to take account of this. If taxable use increases, a further amount of input tax can be claimed and, if it decreases, some of the input tax already claimed must be repaid.

With effect from 1 January 2011, the CGS also takes into account fluctuations in the extent to which a capital item within the scheme is used for business/non-business purposes. This effectively replaces, for such items, the 'Lennartz' method of adjustment described in **34.7**.

Capital items within the scheme

[10.2] Capital items to which the CGS applies are any items within (*a*)-(*f*) and (i)-(vii) below which the owner (or person who holds an interest) uses in the course or furtherance of a business carried on by him, and for the purpose of that business. The scheme does not apply to assets acquired or expenditure on assets held solely for resale (e.g. stock-in-trade). However, if an asset is used in the business before it is sold, it is no longer treated as an asset held solely for resale and the CGS will apply; conversely if a capital item is acquired for use in the business but is sold before being used, it is no longer treated as a capital item.

All values are VAT-exclusive. Where, prior to 1 January 2011, any capital item is only partly used for business purposes, if all the VAT incurred is treated as input tax and output tax is accounted for on the non-business use (the 'Lennartz approach', see **34.7 INPUT TAX**), the value of the capital item is the full tax-exclusive value of the item. Otherwise, if VAT incurred is apportioned between business and non-business use, the value of the capital item is the VAT-exclusive value of the part attributed to business activities. In respect of capital assets obtained on or after 1 January 2011, non-business use is accounted for under the scheme and hence the value in question is the full tax-exclusive value.

From 1 January 2011

(a) Land, where the owner incurs VAT bearing capital expenditure on its acquisition, the value of which is at least £250,000.

(b) A building or part of a building, where the owner incurs VAT bearing capital expenditure on its acquisition, construction, refurbishment, fitting out, alteration or extension, the value of which is at least £250,000.

(c) Civil engineering work or part of a civil engineering work, where the owner incurs VAT bearing capital expenditure on its acquisition, construction, refurbishment, fitting out, alteration or extension, the value of which is at least £250,000.

(d) A computer or item of computer equipment, where the owner incurs VAT bearing capital expenditure on its acquisition, the value of which is at least £50,000.

(e) An aircraft, where the owner incurs VAT bearing capital expenditure on its acquisition, construction, refurbishment, fitting out, alteration or extension, the value of which is at least £50,000.

(f) A ship, boat or other vessel, where the owner incurs VAT bearing capital expenditure on its acquisition, construction, refurbishment, fitting out, alteration or extension, the value of which is at least £50,000.

Prior to 1 January 2011

(i) A computer, or an item of computer equipment, worth £50,000 or more supplied to, or acquired or imported by, the owner.
Any delivery or installation costs should be included unless invoiced separately. If imported, the value for VAT at importation (including import duty) should be taken.
The scheme applies only to individual computers and items of computer equipment, not to complete networks. *Excluded* are
- computerised equipment, e.g. a computerised telephone exchange or computer-controlled blast furnace; and
- computer software.

> *Example*
> A VAT-registered business buys 60 computers on one purchase invoice costing £1,000 each plus VAT. This expenditure is not relevant to the CGS because each computer is considered as a capital item in its own right, i.e. the relevant figure is £1,000 not £60,000.

(ii) Land, a building or part of a building or a civil engineering work or part of a civil engineering work where the value of the interest supplied to the owner, by a taxable supply other than a zero-rated supply, is £250,000 or more. When determining whether the value of the supply is £250,000 or more
- any part of that value consisting of rent (including charges reserved as rent) is excluded provided that it is neither payable nor paid more than twelve months in advance nor invoiced for a period in excess of twelve months; and
- any associated costs (e.g. legal or estate agency fees) should be excluded.

(iii) A building or part of a building where the owner's interest in, right over or licence to occupy it is treated as self-supplied to him under the provisions in **42.1 LAND AND BUILDINGS: ZERO AND REDUCED RATE SUPPLIES AND DIY HOUSEBUILDERS** (change of use of residential or charitable buildings).
The value of the supply, as determined under the respective provisions, must be £250,000 or more. See also *C & E Commrs v Trustees for R & R Pension Fund* QB, [1996] STC 889 (TVC 6.44).

(iv) A building or part of a building where the owner's interest in, right over or licence to occupy was, on or before 1 March 1997, treated as supplied to him under the developer's self-supply charge and the value of that supply was £250,000 or more.

(v) A building not falling, or capable of falling, within (iii) or (iv) above constructed by the owner and first brought into use by him after 31 March 1990 where the aggregate of

- the value of taxable grants relating to the land on which the building is constructed made to the owner after that date, and
- the value of all the taxable supplies of goods and services, other than any that are zero-rated, made or to be made to him for, or in connection with, the construction of the building after that date

is £250,000 or more.

(vi) A building which the owner alters, or an extension or an annexe which he constructs, where additional floor area is created in the altered building, extension or annexe, of 10% or more of the original floor area before the work was carried out. The value of all taxable supplies of goods and services, other than any that are zero-rated, made or to be made to the owner after 31 March 1990 for, or in connection with, the alteration, etc. must be £250,000 or more.

(vii) A civil engineering work constructed by the owner and first brought into use by him after 2 July 1997 where the aggregate of

- the value of taxable grants relating to the land on which the civil engineering work is constructed made to the owner after that date, and
- the value of all the taxable supplies of goods and services, other than any that are zero-rated, made or to be made to him for, or in connection with, the construction of the civil engineering work after that date

is £250,000 or more.

Civil engineering work should be given its everyday meaning and includes such items as roads, bridges, golf courses, running tracks and installation of pipes for connection to mains services.

(viii) A building which the owner refurbishes or fits out where the value of capital expenditure on the taxable supplies of services and of 'goods affixed' to the building, other than any that are zero-rated, made or to be made to the owner for, or in connection with, the refurbishment or fitting out in question after 2 July 1997 is £250,000 or more.

'*Goods affixed*' should be given its everyday meaning. Usually, this includes items of fixtures and fittings and interior decoration that are not easily portable or easily removed. In general terms, these are items that would be sold with the property. Common inclusions (although the deciding factor will be whether the item becomes part of the fabric of the building) are

- materials to build internal and external walls, roofs and ceilings and floors and hard flooring;
- permanent partitioning;
- windows;
- lifts;

- 'built-in' storage such as cupboards or shelving;
- air conditioning;
- lighting; and
- decorative features.

It excludes items secured to the floor for safety or security reasons. Common exclusions are

- office furniture;
- storage unless 'built in';
- carpets;
- computers and computer equipment; and
- factory and office machinery.

Where it is difficult or costly to identify the value of goods affixed from the value of other goods which do not become affixed to the property, by concession, businesses may include any additional amount of capital expenditure (over and above that incurred on items affixed to the building) incurred in connection with the refurbishment, etc. in the total value of capital expenditure for the purposes of the CGS. The concessionary value must then be used in calculating adjustments to the claimed input tax for the whole of the adjustment period. This applies even if those items not affixed have been disposed of (unless they are disposed of as part of the disposal of the whole interest in the building when a final adjustment must be made in the normal way). Businesses must keep a record of the concessionary value of the capital expenditure, including full details of the supplies on which the value was determined. HMRC may withdraw the concession or restrict its use if it considers that it is being used to avoid VAT.

Phased refurbishments are those undertaken in stages. Whether, for the purposes of the CGS, a phased refurbishment should be treated as a whole or as more than one refurbishment will usually be a matter of fact. Indicators that there is more than one refurbishment might be

- separate contracts for each phase of the work or a contract where each phase is a separate option which can be selected; and
- each phase is completed before work on the next phase starts.

If the refurbishment is of one building only and is only 'phased' because the contractors have to do one floor at a time since the building remains occupied throughout, this would usually indicate there is only one refurbishment.

Example

A company is to undertake a big office refurbishment project costing £300,000 excluding VAT, analysed as follows.

- new windows and air conditioning system £170,000;
- new office furniture £130,000.

The project is outside the CGS because the value of the building related supplies (windows and air-conditioning system) is less than £250,000.

What is capital expenditure?

'Capital expenditure' is normally expenditure capitalised for accounting purposes. HMRC will not normally challenge a business's capitalisation policy for the purposes of the CGS, except in cases of avoidance or abuse. In some cases charities may incur expenditure of a capital nature on land and property which is not capitalised in their accounts (e.g. certain heritage buildings, churches etc.). This is generally because the charity does not have unfettered freedom to exploit or dispose of the land or property concerned. This will not prevent expenditure that is essentially capital in nature from being adjusted under the CGS.

Value of capital item

The value of a capital item is the VAT-exclusive value of the item. Only the value of standard or reduced-rated taxable supplies is considered. Before 1 January 2011, the value of a capital item was determined by reference to the business-related expenditure. With effect from 1 January 2011, the value is determined by reference to total expenditure on an asset. This includes both business and non-business expenditure on an asset.

> *Example*
>
> A business purchases a building for £1 million and incurs £200,000 VAT. The building is to be used for 60% business purposes and 40% non-business purposes (e.g. charitable use). Before 1 January 2011, £600,000 (60% of £1 million) determined the value for CGS purposes. Under the new rules that took effect from 1 January 2011, all of the expenditure on the building (£1 million) is the value for CGS purposes. As the CGS threshold for buildings remains at £250,000, the building is a capital item in both scenarios.

Expenditure incurred before and after 1 January 2011

Where expenditure is incurred on a capital item before and after 1 January 2011, it is necessary to determine the amount of business-related expenditure incurred on the asset up to 31 December 2010 and the total amount of expenditure (business and non-business) incurred on or after 1 January 2011. If the sum of these amounts exceeds the relevant CGS threshold, the asset falls within the CGS.

Adjustable amount of VAT

Prior to 1 January 2011, only VAT on the business-related expenditure on an asset (i.e. input tax) fell within the CGS. With effect from 1 January 2011, all of the VAT on an asset (in this instance input tax and non-business VAT) falls within the CGS.

> *Example*
>
> Following on from the above example; prior to 1 January 2011, input tax of £105,000 (17.5% of £600,000) fell within the CGS. With effect from 1 January 2011, VAT of £175,000 (17.5% of £1 million), or £200,000 (20% of £1 million,

if the expenditure was incurred after the VAT rate increase on 4 January 2011) falls within the CGS.

If expenditure is incurred both before and after 1 January 2011, the VAT on the business-related expenditure incurred up to 31 December 2010 and the total VAT incurred on the asset on or after 1 January 2011 fall within the CGS.

Estimated values

If a business does not know whether a project exceeds the value threshold for the CGS until all invoices have been received it will need to estimate the value of the supplies it has received. This may happen with construction projects and refurbishments where VAT is incurred over a period of time and also with contracts that include a retention clause. A retention clause involves a proportion of the contract price being held back and only paid when the work has been satisfactorily completed. If, when a business starts the CGS, it estimates that the value of relevant supplies will exceed the value threshold, the item will become a capital item. Even if it finds later on that the value does not reach the threshold, the item remains in the scheme and it should continue to make adjustments as necessary. If a business does estimate the value of a capital item it will need to keep all the documents it based its estimation on, such as a contract, as HMRC may ask to see it.

Value of land or buildings acquired

A business should only include the value of the interest in the land and/or building supplied to it, if the supply was taxable and not zero-rated. It should not include any associated costs such as legal or estate agency fees. In calculating the value of the interest, it does not need to include the value of any rent or service charges unless

- it has been paid or is payable more than 12 months in advance; or
- it is invoiced by the supplier for a period of more than 12 months. In that case, it should include the value of rent/service charges when calculating the value of the capital item.

Value of constructed building or civil engineering work

The business should include the total VAT-exclusive cost of any of the following supplies made to it.

- The interest in the land, if the supply to it was taxable (other than zero-rated).
- Taxable (other than zero-rated) goods and services supplied for, or in connection with, the construction of the building or civil engineering work.

All the costs involved in making the building ready should be included, such as

- professional and managerial services including architects, surveyors and site management;
- demolition and site clearance;
- building and civil engineering contractors' services;

- materials used in the construction;
- security;
- equipment hire;
- haulage;
- landscaping; and
- fitting out, including the value of any fixtures.

Alteration, extension or annex

Where the value of the goods and services received is £250,000 or more, the total value of all taxable (other than zero-rated) goods or services supplied to the business for, or in connection with, the alteration, extension or annex should be included in the value of the alteration, extension or annex. All the costs involved in making the building or civil engineering work ready should be included.

Refurbishment or fit out

If a capital item is refurbished or fitted out, the value should only include the value of capital expenditure on the taxable (other than zero-rated) supply of services and of goods affixed to the building or civil engineering work supplied for or in connection with the refurbishment or fit out.

What are 'goods affixed' to building?

These are goods which become part of the fabric of the building. Generally these are items that are sold with the property and are not portable or easily removed. 'Goods affixed' does not include items secured for safety or security reasons or computers or computer equipment. These may be subject to the CGS in their own right. The deciding factor is usually whether the item becomes part of the fabric of the building. Common inclusions are

- materials to build;
- internal and external walls;
- roofs and ceilings;
- floors and hard flooring;
- permanent partitioning;
- windows;
- lifts;
- 'built in' storage such as cupboards or shelving;
- air conditioning;
- lighting; and
- decorative features.

Common exclusions are

- office furniture;
- storage unless it is 'built in';
- carpets;
- computers and computer equipment; and
- factory and office machinery.

For capital items where the capital costs are incurred on or after 1 January 2011 there is no longer a requirement for goods used for a refurbishment to be affixed to a building. For capital items where the capital costs were incurred before 1 January 2011, this treatment is already allowed in relation to the 'goods affixed' condition by concession (ESC 3.22) and is adopted by most businesses.

Refurbishment in phases

If the refurbishment is in phases, the business will need to decide whether the work should be treated as a whole for CGS purposes or whether there is more than one refurbishment. If it thinks that each phase is really a separate refurbishment then they should be treated separately for CGS purposes. Normally there is more than one refurbishment when

- there are separate contracts for each phase of the work; or
- there is a contract where each phase is a separate option which can be selected; and
- each phase of work is completed before work on the next phase starts.

A refurbishment which is only undertaken in phases because the building is occupied and where the contractors work on one floor at a time is normally considered to be only one refurbishment.

Regular refurbishments

Regular refurbishments are sometimes referred to as 'rolling refurbishments'. Problems may occur if successive refurbishments begin before each adjustment period has expired. If this happens the business should either

- treat the original refurbishment as destroyed if there is nothing left of the earlier refurbishment or this earlier work is stripped out or replaced. The effect of this is that no further adjustments would be required to the input tax on the previous refurbishment; or
- continue to make adjustments for the remainder of the adjustment period if elements of the earlier refurbishment are retained.

Value of computers

The value of computers should include any delivery and installation costs, unless these are supplied separately. If a business imports a computer it should use the value for VAT at importation. This will include any import duty payable.

[*SI 1995/2518, Regs 112, 113*]. (VAT Notice 706/2/11, paras 3.1–4.14).

The adjustment period

From 1 January 2011

[10.3] The adjustment period is normally

- ten successive intervals in the case of: land, a (or part of a) building or a (or part of a) civil engineering work;

- five successive intervals in the case of: a computer or item of computer equipment, an aircraft, or a ship, boat or other vessel.

Adjustment period exceeding period of owner's interest

If, at the time of the owner's first use, the number of intervals exceeds the number of complete years that the owner's interest in the capital item has to run by more than one, the number of intervals should be reduced to one more than the number of complete years that the owner's interest has to run, calculated from the date of the owner's first use (but not to less than three intervals). In such a case, the denominator in the fraction for the method of adjustment (see **10.6** below) should be adjusted accordingly.

Ownership before VAT registration

Where a person who registers for VAT already owns the capital item, for the purposes of calculating the period of adjustment

- one complete interval should be deducted for each complete year that has elapsed since the date of that person's first use of the capital item prior to the date of registration; and
- the first interval applicable to the capital item that ends after the date of registration should be treated as a subsequent interval (see **10.5** below).

[*SI 1995/2518, Reg 114; SI 2010/3022, Reg 12*].

Prior to 1 January 2011

The adjustment period is the period of time in which the business must review the extent to which a capital item is used in making taxable supplies. It consists of

- five successive intervals for
  - (i) computers, etc. under **10.2**(i) above, and
  - (ii) land, buildings and civil engineering works under **10.2**(ii) above where the interest has less than ten years to run at the time it is supplied to the owner (e.g. an eight-year lease); and
- ten successive intervals for all other land and buildings not within (ii) above.

[*SI 1995/2518, Reg 114(3); SI 1997/1614, Reg 11*].

First interval

From 1 January 2011

[10.4] Subject to the special case below, the rules relating to the transfer of a business as a going concern (see **10.12**(4) below), and the rules relating to the groups of companies (see **10.12**(5) below), the first interval commences on the day on which the owner first uses the capital item and ends on the day before the start of his next tax year, whether or not this is his first tax year.

[*SI 1995/2518, Reg 114(4); SI 2010/3022, Reg 12*]. (VAT Notice 706/2/11, para 6.4).

Prior to 1 January 2011

Subject to the special case below, the rules relating to the transfer of a business as a going concern (see **10.12**(4) below) and the rules relating the groups of companies (see **10.12**(5) below), the first interval commences, as the case may be,

- where the owner is a registered person when he imports, acquires or is supplied with the item as a capital item (or when he appropriates an item to use as a capital item), the date of importation, acquisition, supply or appropriation,
- where the capital item falls within **10.2**(iii) above, on the date of the self-supply under those provisions,
- where the capital item falls within **10.2**(iv) above, on the later of 1 April 1990 and the day the owner first used the building (or part of the building),
- where the capital item falls within **10.2**(v)–(viii) above, on the date that the owner first uses the building, altered building, extension, annexe, civil engineering work or building which has been refurbished or fitted out

and ends on the day before the start of the owner's tax year following that date, i.e. it normally runs to the following 31 March, 30 April or 31 May depending upon his VAT periods, see **49.13 PARTIAL EXEMPTION**.

'*Use*' includes any use in the business. For buildings, it usually consists of the granting of a lease or physical occupation. 'First use' will be the time that any part of the constructed, altered, extended, refurbished or fitted out building is used.

Where the owner is not registered when he first uses an item as a capital item

- if he subsequently becomes a registered person, the first interval commences on his effective date of registration and ends on the following 31 March, 30 April or 31 May depending upon the VAT period allocated to him; and
- if he is subsequently treated as a member of a group for VAT purposes (see **27 GROUPS OF COMPANIES**), the first interval corresponds with, or is that part still remaining of, the then current tax year of the group.

[*SI 1995/2518, Reg 114(4); SI 1997/1614, Reg 11; SI 2008/1146, Sch 1 para 20*]. (VAT Notice 706/2/11, para 6.4).

Special case — extended first interval

Where

- the extent to which a capital item is used in making taxable supplies does not change between what would otherwise have been the first interval and the first subsequent interval under **10.5** below, and
- the length of the two intervals taken together does not exceed twelve months

the first interval applicable to the capital item ends on what otherwise would have been the end of the first subsequent interval, i.e. the two periods are combined to become the first interval.

[*SI 1995/2518, Reg 114(5B); SI 1997/1614, Reg 11*].

Subsequent intervals

[10.5] Subject to the rules relating to the transfer of a business as a going concern (see **10.12**(4) below) and the rules relating the groups of companies (see **10.12**(5) below), each subsequent interval after the first interval corresponds with a longer period applicable to the owner or, if no longer period applies, a tax year. In either case this will normally run to the following 31 March, 30 April or 31 May depending upon the owner's VAT periods, but see **49.13 PARTIAL EXEMPTION** for exceptions. [*SI 1995/2518, Reg 114(5); SI 1997/1614, Reg 11*].

Method of adjustment

[10.6] Where the extent to which a capital item is used in making taxable supplies in a subsequent interval increases or decreases from the extent to which it was so used (or to be used) at the time the original entitlement to deduction of the input tax was determined under the partial exemption rules, an adjustment is required. This is calculated by the formula

$$\frac{\text{Total input tax on the capital item}}{\text{A}} \times \text{the adjustment \%}$$

where

A = usually 5 or 10 depending on the number of intervals in the period of adjustment (see **10.3** above)

From 1 January 2011, '*total input tax on the capital item*' means

- in relation to any capital item, all VAT incurred by the owner on the capital expenditure on that item, including any non-business VAT; and
- where a person is treated as making a supply to himself under *VATA 1994, Sch 10, para 37(1)*, the VAT charged on that supply.

Prior to 1 January 2011, '*total input tax on the capital item*' means

- for a capital item within **10.2**(i) or (ii) above, VAT charged on the supply, acquisition or importation. Any VAT charged on rent (including charges reserved as rent) is excluded unless it is payable or paid more than twelve months in advance or invoiced for a period in excess of twelve months;
- for a capital item within **10.2**(iii) or **10.2**(iv) above, the VAT charged on the supply which the owner is treated as making to himself; and
- for a capital item under **10.2**(v)–(viii) above, the aggregate of the VAT charged on the supplies described, other than VAT charged on rent (if any)

and includes any VAT treated as input tax under the rules relating to pre-registration or pre-incorporation input tax (see **34.10 INPUT TAX**).

'*The adjustment %*' is the difference (if any), expressed as a percentage, between the extent to which the whole or part of the capital item

- was used or to be used for making taxable supplies at the time the original entitlement to deduction of the input tax was determined under the partial exemption rules (for subsequent intervals beginning before 10 March 1999, to which the whole or part of the capital item was used, or regarded as used, in making taxable supplies in the first interval); and
- is so used, or treated as used as the result of a disposal under **10.7** below, in the subsequent interval in question.

Where the owner of a building within these provisions grants or assigns a tenancy or lease in the whole or part of the building and the premium (or if no premium is payable the first payment of rent) is zero-rated, any subsequent exempt supply arising from the grant (e.g. rent) is disregarded in determining the extent to which the building is used in making taxable supplies.

The percentage is

- 100% where the item is used wholly for making taxable supplies;
- 0% where it is used wholly for making exempt supplies; and
- where it is used for making both taxable and exempt supplies, normally the claimable percentage of residual input tax following the partial exemption annual adjustment for the respective year (see **49.13 PARTIAL EXEMPTION**) (although HMRC may allow, or direct, the use of another method). Where the standard method is used (see **49.4 PARTIAL EXEMPTION**) the same percentage applies to the whole of the residual input tax. If a special method is used (see **49.10 PARTIAL EXEMPTION**) involving different calculations for different parts of the business, the percentage to be used is that which applies to the part of the business in which the capital item is used.

Where different percentages are used for different parts of the business, the percentage to be used is that for the part of the business in which the item is used.

[*SI 1995/2518, Reg 115(1)(2)(5), Reg 116; SI 2008/1146, Sch 1 para 21; SI 2010/3022, Reg 13; SI 2011/254, Reg 5*]. (VAT Notice 706/2/11, para 7.4).

Disposals of capital items during the adjustment period

[10.7] From 1 January 2011, the provisions below also apply to the part disposal of a capital item. Therefore references in this paragraph to the supply of a capital item cover the supply of whole or part of a capital item. [*SI 2010/3022, Reg 13*].

If a capital item is sold without ever having been used, HMRC do not regard it as a capital item for the purposes of the CGS. Otherwise, where, during an interval other than the last interval, the owner of a capital item either

- supplies it, or
- is deemed to supply it on ceasing to be a taxable person (see **59.34 REGISTRATION**), or

- would have been deemed to supply it on ceasing to be a taxable person but for the fact that VAT on the deemed supply would not have been more than the amount specified in **59.34**(*c*) **REGISTRATION** (whether by virtue of its value or because it is zero-rated or exempt),

then

(a) if that supply is a taxable supply, the owner is treated as having used the capital item for each of the remaining *complete* intervals wholly in the making of taxable supplies; and

(b) if that supply is an exempt supply, he is treated as not using the capital item for each of the remaining *complete* intervals in making any taxable supplies.

The effect of this is as follows.

For the interval in which the capital item is sold, the adjustment is calculated (or, if it is the first interval, input tax is reclaimed) in the normal way under **10.6** above *as if the capital item had been in use for the whole of that interval.*

For any remaining complete intervals in the adjustment period, the recovery percentage will be 100% where (*a*) above applies or 0% where (*b*) above applies, but subject to the following two provisos.

Proviso 1 (applicable until 1 January 2011)

The aggregate of the amounts which may be deducted in respect of the remaining complete intervals cannot exceed the output tax chargeable on the supply of the whole or part of the capital item. This 'capping' provision was removed with effect from 1 January 2011, although the 'disposal test' (Proviso 2) remains.

Proviso 2

Unless HMRC allow otherwise (see below), a 'disposal test' applies. Where the total amount of input tax deducted or deductible by the owner of a capital item as a result of

- the input tax initially recovered on the capital item;
- any adjustments already made under the CGS; and
- any final adjustment that is required as a result of the sale of the item

would exceed the output tax chargeable on the supply of the capital item, then the owner must pay to HMRC, or as the case may be may deduct, such an amount as results in the total input tax deducted or deductible being equal to the output tax chargeable on the supply of the whole or part of the capital item.

The 'disposal test' is an anti-avoidance measure to ensure that partly exempt businesses such as banks, insurance companies, educational establishments, sports clubs and providers of private healthcare do not obtain an unjustified tax advantage, for example, by making a substantial exempt supply of a long lease of a property followed immediately by the taxable disposal of the freehold for low consideration. HMRC do not intend that the disposal test should be applied to *bona fide* commercial transactions. Given the policy objective, the disposal test will not be applied

- to sales of computer equipment;
- where the owner disposes of an item at a loss due to the market conditions (such as a general downturn in property prices);
- where the value of the capital item has depreciated (as is normally the case with computers);
- where the value of the capital item is reduced for other legitimate reasons (such as accepting a low price for a quick sale);
- where the amount of output tax on disposal is less than the total input tax only because of a reduction in the VAT rate; and
- where the item is used only for taxable (including zero-rated) purposes throughout the adjustment period (which includes the final disposal).

Where there is no unjustified tax advantage, a business need not apply these provisions and it is not necessary to apply to HMRC for a specific ruling. Where there is an unjustified tax advantage, a business must calculate the net tax advantage (i.e. the overall benefit derived from the avoidance device, normally the amount of input tax that would still be subject to adjustment under the scheme were it not for the sale of the capital item less any output tax due on the sale) and then work out how much of the net tax advantage is unjustified. Normally this could be achieved by using the ratio that the value of the final taxable sale bears to the value of both the exempt supply and the final taxable sale.

Example 1

A partly-exempt business purchases a computer for £100,000 (plus £17,500 VAT at 17.5%). For the first three periods it is used for making taxable and exempt supplies. In the fourth period it is sold for £10,000 plus VAT. The percentages of taxable use are as follows.

Interval 1	48%
Interval 2	51%
Interval 3	43%
Interval 4 (until sale)	45%

Interval 1

Initial input tax claim

£17,500 × 48% = £8,400

Interval 2

Additional input tax claimed

£17,500 ÷ 5 × (51 – 48)% = £105

Interval 3

Input tax repayable

£17,500 ÷ 5 × (48 – 43)% = £175

Interval 4

Input tax repayable

£17,500 ÷ 5 × (48 – 45)% = £105

Interval 5

Additional input tax claimed

£17,500 ÷ 5 × (100 – 48)% = £1,820

but restricted under proviso (1) above to £10,000 × 17.5%* = £1,750

A final adjustment of £1,645 (£1,750 – £105) should be made in respect of interval 4.

*20% from 4 January 2011; 15% from 1 December 2008 to 31 December 2009.

Example 2

A developer, whose tax year ends on 31 March, completes a commercial development on 1 June 1998 at a cost of £25 million plus VAT of £4,375,000. The developer opts to tax the property and leases it for two years to a third party tenant at market value plus VAT. On 1 June 2000 the developer grants a 99 year lease at a premium of £24 million and a peppercorn rent to its wholly-owned subsidiary which is wholly exempt. On 1 May 2001 the developer sells the freehold, subject to the 99 year lease, for £250,000 plus VAT of £43,750 to the wholly owned subsidiary.

Interval 1 (to 31 March 1999). The developer can initially deduct all the VAT incurred on the development because of the option to tax.

Interval 2 (to 31 March 2000). No adjustment is required for interval 2 as the building continues to be let under a taxable lease.

Interval 3 (to 31 March 2001). On the grant of the lease, *VATA 1994, Sch 10 para 2(3AA)* operates so as to disapply the developer's option to tax and the premium is not subject to VAT. An adjustment in respect of 1/10th (£437,500) of the initial input tax incurred is required at the end of interval 3. On the basis of that during that interval the property was used for taxable purposes for two months and exempt purposes of ten months, VAT of £364,583 (305/366 × £437,500) must be paid back to HMRC.

Interval 4 (to 31 March 2002). The sale of the property on 1 May 2001 is compulsorily standard-rated under *VATA 1994, Sch 9 Group 1 Item 1(a)* as it is less than three years old (see **41.3(*a*) LAND AND BUILDINGS: EXEMPT SUPPLIES AND OPTION TO TAX**). Output tax is therefore due of £43,750 (£250,000 × 17.5%). Since the building is only used for exempt purposes up to the sale, an adjustment in respect of the full 1/10th (£437,500) of the initial input tax incurred is required.

Intervals 5–10. Since the output tax on the sale of the freehold is less than the input tax claimed in the adjustment period, the disposal test applies. In this instance there is an unjustified tax advantage because the high value exempt grant in interval 3 enables a low value taxable sale of the freehold. At the same time the taxable sale enables full recovery of input tax in respect of the six remaining intervals 5–10. In principle £3,529,167 would be due as follows

Interval	Input tax claim	Output tax declared	Cumulative difference
	£	£	£
1	4,375,000	–	4,375,000
2	–	–	4,375,000
3	(364,583)		4,010,417
4	(437,500)	(43,750)	3,529,167
5–10			3,529,167

However, the net tax advantage is that the developer is able to secure the amount of input tax that would still be subject to adjustment under the scheme for intervals 5–10 were it not for the sale of the property (6/10ths of £4,375,000 = £2,625,000) by making a taxable supply giving rise to output tax of £43,750. The net tax advantage is therefore £2,581,250.

Some form of fair and reasonable apportionment needs to be applied to work out how much of the net tax advantage is unjustified. This could be achieved by using the ratio that the value of the exempt supply bears to the value of both the exempt supply and the final taxable sale, i.e.

24,000,000 ÷ 24,250,000 × £2,554,639

Thus, in practice the disposal test would be applied, but the amount due to HMRC would be the value of the unjustified tax advantage, i.e. £2,554,639.

[*SI 1995/2518, Reg 115(3)–(3B)*]. (VAT Notice 706/2/11, paras 9.1–9.7, 11.1–11.3; Business Brief 30/97).

Lost, stolen, destroyed or expired assets

[10.8] If, during the adjustment period, a capital item is irretrievably lost or stolen or is totally destroyed, no further adjustment must be made in respect of the remaining *complete* intervals applicable to it. [*SI 1995/2518, Reg 115(4); SI 2010/3022, Reg 13*].

The normal scheme adjustment is made for the interval of loss, etc. as if the capital item had been used for the whole interval.

Where a capital item is lost, stolen or destroyed, any evidence of the loss (e.g. an insurance claim) should be kept for possible inspection by a visiting VAT officer.

See also **10.12**(3) below for 'rolling reburbishments' where the original refurbishments are stripped out and replaced before the end of the adjustment period.

(VAT Notice 706/2/11, para 9.8).

Capital items temporarily not used

[10.9] Once the CGS has started, if a capital item is not used for a period of time (e.g. a computer is overhauled) it is treated as still being used during that period for the same purpose as it was previously used. But if a capital item is never used in the business, HMRC do not regard it as an asset for the purposes of the CGS. (VAT Notice 706/2/11, paras 7.12, 9.7).

VAT returns

[10.10] Where an adjustment is required under **10.6** to **10.9** above, it should be included in the return for the second VAT period following the interval to which the adjustment relates or in which the supply as a result of sale, or deemed supply as a result of deregistration, takes place. This is the period after the one in which the partial exemption annual adjustment is made for the year. The adjustment should be included in Box 4 of the VAT return.

Until 1 January 2011, where an interval has come to an end because

- the owner of the capital item has ceased to be a member of a group (see **10.12**(5) below), or
- the owner (who remains a taxable person) has transferred part of his business as a going concern (see **10.12**(4) below),

the adjustment for that interval must be included in the return for the group or transferor (as the case may be) for the second VAT period after the end of the tax year of the group/transferor in which the interval in question fell.

HMRC may allow any adjustment to be made in a later return but only if it is a return for a VAT period commencing within four years (increased from three years from 1 April 2009) of the end of the period when the adjustment should have been made.

If VAT registration has been cancelled, the adjustment should be entered on the final VAT return for the period ending with the effective date of deregistration.

[*SI 1995/2518, Reg 115(6)–(8); SI 2010/3022, Reg 13(h)*]. (VAT Notice 706/2/11, para 8.1).

> *Example*
>
> Company A is partly exempt and uses the standard method. It also has an annual adjustment calculation to make under the CGS. The company completes VAT returns on a calendar quarter basis.
>
> The company will make annual adjustment calculations up to 31 March year for both partial exemption purposes and for the CGS. It has the choice of including the partial exemption adjustment on its March or June VAT return. However, the CGS adjustment must be declared on the September VAT return each year, i.e. the second return after the end of the tax year.

Records

[10.11] See **56 RECORDS** for general requirements for records. In respect of each capital item, the records kept must enable a business to work out the CGS adjustment for each subsequent interval in the adjustment period and should therefore include

- a description of the capital item;
- its value;
- the amount of input tax incurred on it;
- the amount of input tax reclaimed on it;
- the start and end date of each interval, including the first;
- when adjustments are due; and
- the date and value of disposal if the item is sold before the end of the adjustment period.

Although, by law, records only have to be kept for six years, businesses are advised to keep records of *all* capital items in case a CGS adjustment becomes necessary. It is also important to keep detailed records because if

- the capital item is sold as part of the transfer of a business as a going concern (see **10.12**(4) below), or
- the owner moves in or out of a VAT group (see **10.12**(5) below),

the new owner is responsible for any adjustments for the remainder of the adjustment period.

(VAT Notice 706/2/11, paras 2.1, 2.2).

Treatment in particular cases

[10.12] The treatment in particular cases is outlined below.

(1) Input tax incurred before the first interval

Where a business incurs input tax before the first interval, it must work out the overall initial claimable percentage against which it can measure the percentage of taxable use in subsequent periods. This could be done, for example, by expressing the total input tax recovered as a percentage of the input tax incurred on the capital item.

> *Example*
>
> A partly exempt business constructs a new headquarters building. It incurs £600,000 of input tax on the building in the tax year ending 31 March 2012. Its partial exemption reclaimable percentage for the year as a whole is 75% so it reclaims £450,000. In the following tax year, the year ending 31 March 2013, it incurs another £400,000 of input tax on the building and reclaims £320,000 because its partial exemption reclaimable percentage for the year is 80%. It occupies the building for use in its partly exempt business on 1 September 2012 so the first interval runs from 1 September 2012 to 31 March 2013 (the day before the start of the next tax year, which is 1 April 2013).
>
> The business has therefore incurred some VAT before the first interval and will need to work out an overall average reclaimable percentage to measure against for future subsequent intervals:
>
> Total input tax reclaimed × 100% = Average reclaimable percentage
>
> Total VAT incurred = £770,000
>
> £1,000,000 × 100% = 77%
>
> Therefore, 77% is the "baseline" against which future adjustments are measured.

(VAT Notice 706/2/11, para 7.6).

(2) Input tax incurred after the first interval

Some projects, for example, construction projects and refurbishments where the work is carried out over a period of time, may result in additional input tax being incurred after the first interval. This may also occur where a contract includes a retention clause. Input tax incurred in the second interval does not form part of the CGS adjustment in the second interval but should be adjusted where necessary from the third interval onwards.

(VAT Notice 706/2/11, para 7.7). See VAT Notice 706/2/11, para 7.8 for examples of how to calculate the adjustments due using the 'combined adjustments' and 'parallel adjustments' methods.

(3) Rolling refurbishments

Rolling refurbishments occur where a property is refurbished on a regular basis and some or all of the original refurbishments are replaced. If a second refurbishment is undertaken before the original adjustment period has ended

- where the original refurbishment is completely stripped out or replaced, it should be treated as destroyed (see **10.8** above) and no further adjustments made to the input tax on that refurbishment; or
- where elements of the original refurbishment are retained, adjustments to the original input tax must still be made for the remainder of the adjustment period of that refurbishment.

(VAT Notice 706/2/11, para 4.13).

(4) Transfer of a business as a going concern

Where a business or part of a business is transferred as a going concern (see **8.10 BUSINESS**), any capital items included as part of the transfer are not 'sold' for the purposes of the CGS and therefore **10.7** above does not apply. The responsibility for applying the CGS to any capital item transferred passes to the new owner for any remaining intervals. The timing of intervals depends upon whether the new owner takes over the original owner's VAT registration number.

If the new owner takes over the seller's VAT registration number

The interval during which the business is transferred does not end at the time of the transfer and continues without a break. The seller does not need to make any adjustments for that interval. The interval ends on the last day of the new owner's longer period ending immediately after the transfer (or if no longer period then applies, on the last day of his tax year following the day of transfer). The new owner must make any adjustment for that interval and any remaining intervals in the normal way. Longer periods and tax years both normally run to the following 31 March, 30 April or 31 May depending upon the owner's VAT periods, but see **49.13 PARTIAL EXEMPTION** for exceptions.

If the new owner does not take over the seller's VAT registration number

The interval applying to the capital item ends on the day before the transfer takes place. The seller should make any adjustment for that interval on his VAT return for the second period after the end of his tax year in the normal way or, if he is cancelling his registration, he can make any adjustment on his final return. The new owner is responsible for the next interval which runs from the date of transfer to the anniversary date and any other remaining intervals which run for twelve months from each anniversary date. Subsequent intervals applicable to the transferred item may or may not coincide with the new owner's partial exemption tax year. If they do not, the new owner will need to agree a way of calculating subsequent intervals with HMRC.

As the new owner takes over responsibility for applying the CGS, for each relevant capital item the original owner must supply

- a description of the capital item;
- the date of acquisition and number of remaining intervals in the period of adjustment;
- the total input tax incurred; and
- the percentage of that input tax which was claimed on the item in the first interval.

[*SI 1995/2518, Reg 114(5A)(7); SI 1997/1614, Reg 11*]. (VAT Notice 706/2/11, paras 9.2–9.5).

(5) **VAT groups**

On the first occasion during an adjustment period applicable to a capital item that the owner of the item

- being VAT-registered subsequently becomes a member of a group of companies for VAT purposes (see **27 GROUPS OF COMPANIES**), or
- being a member of a group for VAT purposes ceases to be a member of that group (whether or not it immediately becomes a member of another such group)

the interval then applying ends on the day before the owner becomes a member of the group or the day the owner ceases to be a member of the group (as the case may be). The original owner of the capital item must make any adjustment for this interval. The new owner becomes responsible for subsequent intervals (if any) applicable to the capital item which end on the successive anniversaries of that day (irrespective of whether there are any further movements into or out of VAT groups since this provision only applies on the *first* occasion of joining or leaving a group). The new owner will need to agree a way of calculating adjustments for any such intervals with HMRC in the likely event that these intervals do not coincide with its longer periods.

As the new owner takes over responsibility for applying the CGS, for each relevant capital item the original owner must supply

- a description of the capital item;
- the date of acquisition and number of remaining intervals in the period of adjustment;
- the total input tax incurred; and
- the percentage of that input tax which was claimed on the item in the first interval.

[*SI 1995/2518, Reg 114(5A); SI 1997/1614, Reg 11*]. (VAT Notice 706/2/11, paras 12.1–12.3).

(6) Disposal of property by grant of lease followed by sale of freehold reversion

See *Centralan Property Ltd v C & E Commrs, CJEC Case C–63/04*; [2006] STC 1542 (TVC 22.459).

(7) Residential property – sale by developer of long leasehold interest separately from the freehold interest

The first grant of a major interest (freehold sale or lease exceeding 21 years) in residential property by its developer is zero-rated but all subsequent grants in the property are exempt. When a developer makes a first grant of a major interest in a property he has constructed or converted from non-residential property, any input tax incurred is recoverable in full as being wholly attributed to that taxable first grant.

However, if a developer's first grant of a major interest in the building is a long lease, he is using the building for a business purpose other than solely for the purpose of selling the building and, as a result, the building will be treated as a capital item under the CGS. The input tax incurred on the construction or conversion and wholly attributed to the zero-rated long lease will have to be adjusted through the CGS should a subsequent exempt grant be made of the building. (Where the developer's first grant of a major interest is the sale of the freehold, he is using the building solely for the purpose of selling the building and will not have to treat the building as a capital item.)

HMRC identify three ways a developer might grant all the leases and the reversionary interest in the freehold of a residential property (typically a block of flats).

(a) *All flats sold followed by the freehold*. The sale of each individual flat is zero-rated as first grant of a major interest. Although the developer will hold a capital item, HMRC consider that, when the freehold is sold, this is only exempt to the extent that it relates to those areas of the building that were previously the subject of the zero-rated grants of individual flats. Most of the sale of the freehold is zero-rated as it relates to the common parts that have not been subject to any previous supply. Any CGS adjustment would be negligible and, in this situation, HMRC do not require any adjustment to be made.

(b) *Freehold sold before any flats are sold*. The sale of the freehold is zero-rated and since no leases had been granted, is not a capital item. All input tax incurred on the construction costs is fully deductible.
As the new freeholder, the purchaser normally makes any exempt grants of leases to buyers of flats. Even where the consideration for such sales accrues to the developer (so that VAT law treats the developer as the person supplying the flats), this does not impact on the initial deduction of input tax by the developer. It may, however, have implications for any input tax incurred on selling costs.

(c) *Freehold sold after some flats have been sold*. The flats sold before the freehold has been supplied are each a zero-rated first grant of a major interest. Although the developer holds a capital item, HMRC consider that, when the freehold is sold, this is only exempt to the extent that it relates to those areas of the building that were previously the subject of the zero-rated grants of individual flats. Most of the supply of the freehold is zero-rated relating to the common parts and unsold flats that have not been subject to any previous supply. As in (*a*) above, no CGS adjustments are required.

If, under the agreement for sale, the developer has retained the right to receive the monies from the sale of the remaining unsold flats, the considerations set out in (*b*) above apply.

(Business Brief 23/06).

Key points

[10.13] Points to consider are the following.

- The CGS applies when a building is purchased (plus VAT) costing more than £250,000 (excluding VAT) or if it is refurbished or altered with the cost of the project again exceeding £250,000. However, note that any zero-rated costs are excluded from this figure. The scheme also applies when a building is extended, with additional floor space of 10% or more of the original area being created, again subject to the £250,000 limit. Any expenditure on fixtures and fittings is excluded from the scheme (e.g. carpets and machinery).
- The scheme also applies in relation to computer equipment costing at least £50,000 (excluding VAT). However, it should be noted that this is a per-item basis rather than an amount shown on an invoice from a supplier. So 55 laptops costing £1,000 each, bought at the same time, would be excluded from the scheme because each laptop is a purchase in its own right. The scheme does not apply to computer software, only on expenditure relating to computer hardware and equipment.
- From 1 January 2011 the scheme applies to ships and aircraft costing at least £50,000.
- In the case of scheme adjustments for land and building-related costs, the relevant period is ten years. A period of five years is relevant to computer equipment. The first interval runs from when the item is purchased until the end of the taxpayer's partial exemption year, i.e. 31 March, 30 April or 31 May, depending on when VAT periods end.
- Be aware that adjustments under the scheme will always be nil if an item was initially bought and wholly related to taxable supplies (full input tax recovery) and this situation continued throughout the five or ten-year interval period. The same outcome would result if the item was wholly relevant to exempt supplies (no input tax recovery) when first purchased, and this situation continued throughout the five or ten-year period.
- Adjustments will only affect the amount of tax due if either a change of use occurs within the five or ten-year period (e.g. an asset used for exempt activities becomes used for taxable purposes) or if the item is used for both exempt and taxable purposes where the percentage of input tax recovery changes each year according to the percentage of taxable income for the business as a whole.

- Any adjustments made under the scheme are always made on the second VAT return after the end of the partial exemption year, i.e. the VAT period that includes 30 September. Adjustments (both payments and repayments) are declared in the Box 4 (input tax) figure of the VAT return. The adjustment is a normal accounting adjustment carried out in accordance with the scheme – it is not classed as a VAT error. The timing of the annual adjustment is different to the partial exemption year-end adjustment, which is either declared on the return at the end of the tax year (31 March, 30 April or 31 May) or in the first VAT quarter of the new tax year (i.e. the return which includes 30 June).
- It is important that tax advisers do not see the CGS as a threat, e.g. by recommending to clients that they deliberately try to keep projected capital expenditure below the £50,000 and £250,000 limits. In the case of a partly-exempt business that expects to increase its level of taxable activities in the future, any expenditure on assets relevant to taxable and exempt supplies will actually produce a tax advantage by being within the scheme because the adjustments each year will result in additional input tax claims.
- Remember, the key point of the CGS is 'fairness' – so if the final calculations indicate that a business with 90% exempt income has managed to reclaim 50% of the input tax on a capital item, there is likely to be an error in the computations.
- Although a business is only obliged to keep accounting records for six years, it is important to ensure that records relating to a CGS item are kept for the full ten-year period (if the item relates to property).
- Be aware of the 'disposal test' to ensure there is no unfair input tax recovery on assets that are sold by a partly-exempt business before the end of the adjustment period.
- Remember that the new owner must take over the responsibility for any remaining scheme calculations of the seller in the event of a business sale (transfer of a going concern). It is important that the buyer is given adequate records from the seller to ensure accurate calculations can be carried out.
- If a business deregisters, and there is a deemed or actual supply of a scheme asset at the time of deregistration, then the VAT liability of the final sale will determine the recovery percentage for the remaining intervals. So if an asset is a deemed exempt supply at the date of deregistration, and there are four interval adjustments remaining with the CGS, then the final VAT return will treat all these final intervals as exempt and pay any tax due or repayable on this return.

11

Catering

De Voil Indirect Tax Service. See V4.227.

Introduction

[11.1] A supply of food and drink in the course of catering is standard-rated. [*VATA 1994, Sch 8 Group 1(a)*].

To decide whether any supply is in the course of catering, the following three questions should be considered in turn.

- Is it within the ordinary meaning of catering? See **11.2** and **11.3** below.
- Is it for 'on premises' consumption? See **11.4** below.
- Is it hot take-away food? See **11.5** below.

If the answer to any of these questions is 'yes', the supply is a standard-rated supply of catering (but see **11.3** below for special treatment in certain cases).

(VAT Notice 709/1/11, para 1.3).

In joined German cases *Bog and others, Cases C–497/09, C–499/09, C–501/09 and C–502/09* ([2011] STC 1221 (TVC 22.155)), the ECJ held that

- the supply of food or meals freshly prepared for immediate consumption from snack stalls or mobile snack bars or in cinema foyers is a supply of goods within *Directive 77/388/EEC, Art 5* (now *Directive 2006/112/EC, Art 14*), if a qualitative examination of the entire transaction shows that the elements of supply of services preceding and accompanying the supply of the food are not predominant;
- this is unlike the activities of a party catering service which are supplies of services within *Directive 77/388/EEC, Art 6* (now *Directive 2006/112/EC, Art 24*) except where a party catering service does no more than deliver standard meals without any additional elements of supply of services;

- the term 'foodstuffs' in *Directive 77/388/EEC, Annex H, category 1* (now *Directive 2006/112/EC, Annex III, category 1*) must be interpreted as also covering food and meals which have been prepared for immediate consumption by boiling, roasting, baking or other means.

HMRC consider that the ECJ judgment has no implications for the UK treatment of supplies of hot food and businesses should continue to treat their supplies in accordance with published guidance (HMRC Brief 19/11).

Ordinary meaning of catering

[11.2] Where a supply can be identified as catering in its everyday meaning, it is *per se* standard-rated and it is not necessary to consider the problems relating to premises and hot take-away food in **11.4** and **11.5** below. This point was clarified in *C & E Commrs v Cope, QB* [1981] STC 532 (TVC 29.45).

The word 'catering' is not defined in the legislation but in its ordinary meaning includes the supply of prepared food and drink. It is characterised by a supply involving a significant element of service. Examples of supplies in the course of catering include

- supplies made in restaurants, cafés, canteens and similar establishments (except supplies of cold take-away food);
- third party supplies of catering for events and functions (e.g. wedding receptions, parties or conferences);
- a supply of cooking and/or preparation of food provided to a customer at the customer's home (e.g. for a dinner party); and
- delivery of cooked ready-to-eat food or meals (with or without crockery or cutlery).

Examples of supplies that are *not* in the course of catering include

- retail supplies of cold take-away food;
- retail supplies of groceries; and
- supplies of food that require significant further preparation by the customer (see below).

(VAT Notice 709/1/11, para 2.1).

Catering contracts

Any supply of food and/or drink as part of a contract for catering is standard-rated. (A contract that merely entitles a food retailer to occupy a set of premises from which they make their supplies does not automatically determine that a supply is one of catering; in such cases it is necessary to consider all of the activities being carried out.)

- *Food for customer preparation*. The supply of food which customers must prepare themselves before it can be consumed is not a supply in the course of catering. This applies whether the food is delivered to, or collected by, the customers. For these purposes, 'preparation' includes thawing frozen food, cooking food, reheating food and arranging food on serving plates. See **47.8**(19) OUTPUT TAX for the treatment of any delivery charge.

- *Delivered sandwiches and groceries.* Where sandwiches, or other items of food and drink, are taken to buildings in order to sell them, if the supplier
  - (a) has no contract or agreement to do so, this is not a supply in the course of catering and any item can be zero-rated if eligible (see **24.3–24.13 FOOD**); and
  - (b) is supplying the food under a contract to do so (e.g. to cater for an event), this is a supply in the course of catering and all supplies are standard-rated.

  See **47.8**(19) **OUTPUT TAX** for the treatment of any delivery charge. See also *Zeldaline Ltd* (VTD 4388) (TVC 29.28).
- *Grocery items sold from a catering outlet.* Provided these items are in the same form as when sold by a grocer or supermarket, and are clearly not intended for on-premises consumption, they need not be treated as being made in the course of catering. Examples of items that are clearly not intended for on-premises consumption include: packets of tea; packaged coffee granules, powder, beans etc.; sugar; loaves of bread; and cartons of factory-sealed milk.
- *Packed lunches.* Where packed meals are provided as an incidental to an event or a function (e.g. coach parties or race meetings), HMRC consider the meals are supplied in the course of catering and should be standard-rated.

  Where a hotel or similar establishment supplies a packed meal for which a separate charge is made, then provided the supply is for consumption off the premises, the supply can be zero-rated unless comprising items which are always standard-rated (see **24.3–24.13 FOOD**). (Where the supply by a hotel, etc. consists of accommodation and board, including packed meals, at an inclusive price, this should be treated as a single standard-rated supply.)

(VAT Notice 709/1/11, para 2.2).

Cold take-away buffets

A problem often arises in deciding whether a supply of cold buffet platters, etc. is a standard-rated supply of catering or simply a supply of zero-rated food items. There have been a number of tribunal decisions. In *Out to Lunch (a firm)* (VTD 13031) (TVC 29.7) and *Happy Place Ltd (t/a The Munch Box)* (VTD 17654) (TVC 29.6) it was held that the supply of sandwich platters comprising sandwiches, fruit, cakes, etc. available for take-away or delivery from the shop was not in the course of catering even though described as 'for meetings'. But in *Wendy's Kitchen* (VTD 15531) (TVC 29.12) and *PJ & LJ Lawson (t/a Country Fayre)* (VTD 14903) (TVC 29.9) on the evidence, including advertising material, 'finger buffets' supplied to local offices were held to be supplies in the course of catering. See also *C & E Commrs v Safeway Stores plc, QB 1996,* [1997] STC 163 (TVC 29.5) for 'party trays' of food sold from delicatessen counters.

Vending machines

Vending machine supplies follow the same general principles as food and drink supplied from catering outlets.

- Items that are standard-rated under **24.3–24.13 FOOD** are also standard-rated when supplied from vending machines (e.g. sales of beverages or confectionery).
- Supplies of food and drink from vending machines in canteens and restaurant-type areas are standard-rated as supplies to be consumed on the premises where they have been supplied. HMRC will only allow an apportionment to be made if the food seller can produce evidence to show that a proportion of the items of cold food (that would be eligible for zero-rating) are taken-away from the canteen/restaurant premises (see **11.4** below).
- Supplies from machines sited in thoroughfares and areas not designated for the consumption of food follow the liability of the product sold.

See **11.10** below if the machine is on a university campus and is run by the students' union.

(VAT Notice 709/1/11, para 2.4).

See also **47.8**(34) **OUTPUT TAX** for hiring of vending machines.

Special cases

[11.3] Special treatment is required in certain cases as listed below.

(1) Catering on aircraft, ships, etc.

Where the catering is an adjunct to the supply of the transport and no separate charge is made for it, the consideration for the ticket should not be apportioned. The catering is treated as part of the supply of the passenger transport (*British Airways plc v C & E Commrs, CA* [1990] STC 643 (TVC 66.13)).

Otherwise HMRC treat a separate supply of catering as a supply of *goods* which is

- outside the scope of UK under *VATA 1994, s 7(2)* when supplied on a journey to a country outside the EU; and
- outside the scope under *SI 2004/3148, Art 6* when supplied for consumption on board intra-EU transport.

It should be noted that in *Faaborg-Gelting Linien A/S v Finanzamt Flensburg, ECJ Case C-231/94*, [1996] STC 774 (TVC 22.174), the ECJ held that catering supplied on board a ferry travelling between Denmark and Germany was a supply of *services*, supplied where the supplier had his established place of business under what is now *Directive 2006/112/EC, Art 43* (previously *EC Sixth Directive, Art 9(1)*). However, many EU countries, including the UK, have not implemented this judgment and continue to treat catering as a supply of goods.

(HMRC VAT—Place of Supply—Transport Manual VATPOSTR 2420).

(2) Schools, universities, colleges, etc.

Certain supplies of education, training and research are exempt from VAT. Where an educational institution provides exempt education to its own pupils and students, then the supply of catering they make can also be exempt. See **16.8 EDUCATION**. If the supply of education is non-business, as in the case of a local authority school, the supply of catering will also be non-business, provided it is made at, or below, cost.

Whichever treatment is appropriate, it applies to anything provided by way of catering. This includes food supplied at mealtimes and break times from the refectory, canteen or other similar outlet but not items purchased from a university campus shop, as they are not provided by way of catering.

Food and drink supplied at or below cost from a tuck shop run by the school itself takes on the same liability as the education.

VAT must be accounted for on supplies of catering to staff and visitors (except visiting students).

See **11.10** below for catering provided by a student union on behalf, and with the agreement, of the parent institution.

(VAT Notice 709/1/11, para 2.6).

(3) Catering in hospitals, clinics, nursing homes, etc.

Care provided in a hospital or other statutorily-registered institution is exempt from VAT (see **28.10 HEALTH AND WELFARE**). This exemption includes the supply by such institutions of prepared food and drink directly to their patients in the course of care.

Supplies of catering to other persons such as staff and visitors are not exempt and the hospital, etc. must account for VAT on such sales.

(VAT Notice 709/1/11, para 2.7).

Premises

[11.4] A supply in the course of catering is standard-rated. Specifically included is a supply of

- anything for consumption on the premises in which it is supplied; and
- hot food for consumption off those premises (see **11.5** below).

[*VATA 1994, Sch 8 Group 1 Note 3(a)*].

The wording ensures that all food and drink supplied in premises such as restaurants, cafés and canteens is, as Parliament intended, excluded from zero-rating. But 'premises' can be more than just the outlet where food or drink is sold and problems can arise where a catering outlet is within a larger site, e.g. a shopping centre, stadium or office block.

Following the decision in *HMRC v Compass Contract Services UK Ltd, CA* [2006] STC 1999 (TVC 29.31) HMRC's view is that, whether a catering outlet is within an area to which the public has restricted access (e.g. a sports stadium, amusement park, cinema or secure office block) or unrestricted access (e.g. a shopping mall, hospital or railway station), 'premises' are

- the areas controlled by the retailer; and
- those areas which have been specifically provided for the customer to consume the food purchased.

HMRC give the following as examples of premises.

Outlet	*Extent of premises*
Restaurant (or similar café or canteen-type business)	The whole restaurant area, plus any chairs/tables on the pavement, concourse or similar area adjacent to the main premises
Retail outlet in a shopping centre	The outlet itself and any chairs and tables in designated areas belonging to that outlet or provided for the exclusive use of that outlet
Retailer in a shopping centre with a food court	The retail outlet, plus the chairs and tables within the food court if (i) the retailer contributes to the upkeep, provision and cleaning of those facilities; or (ii) those facilities are in a clearly delineated area for the use of customers to consume their food purchases
Retail outlet in a high street	The outlet itself plus any areas containing chairs and tables outside the establishment provided for use of customers
Retail outlet within an office building	The outlet, plus any area for consumption around or next to the outlet that is a seating area or dining room
Supermarket	Any seating areas within the shop, plus any areas of chairs and tables outside the shop for use of customers
Stall in a sports stadium, amusement park, exhibition, gallery or similar pay-entry venue	The stall itself, plus any facilities provided adjacent to the stall for the use of customers

Premises also include any areas of chairs and tables contained in delineated areas which, although not immediately adjacent to the retailer, are situated within the vicinity of the outlet and designated for the use of the retailers' customers. It does not include genuine areas of chairs and tables for general communal use which are not the responsibility of the caterer/retailer.

Before the decision in *Compass Contract Services UK Ltd* above, HMRC had taken the view that, in restricted access sites, the premises were the whole building or site.

Evidence and apportionment

As a result of the above, subject to considering whether there is a supply of catering *per se* (see **11.2** above), the supply of cold food for consumption away from the premises is zero-rated. Where a retailer makes sales of cold food to be taken away from the premises but also has on-site facilities where such food can be consumed, it will need to apportion sales of cold food between those consumed on the premises (standard-rated) and those taken-away (zero-rated).

If the retailer is unable to ascertain the correct liability at the point of sale, it must retain satisfactory evidence to support a fair and reasonable apportionment.

(VAT Notice 709/1/11, paras 3.1–3.3; Business Brief 12/06).

Hot take-away food

[11.5] Any supply of 'hot food' for consumption off the premises ('*hot take-away food*') on which it is supplied is standard-rated. See **11.4** above for the meaning of 'premises'. (Cold take-away food and drink is zero-rated, provided it is not of a type that is always standard-rated.)

'*Hot food*' means food which, or any part of which,

- has been heated for the purposes of enabling it to be consumed at a temperature above the ambient air temperature; and
- is above that temperature at the time it is provided to the customer (before 1 January 2005, at the time of supply).

[*VATA 1994, Sch 8 Group 1 Note 3(b); SI 2004/3343*].

The change in the legislation with effect from 1 January 2005 removes any doubt that, where payment for hot take-away food is made in advance of the basic tax point when the food leaves the shop (e.g. on ordering), this establishes a time of supply before the food is cooked (when it would not therefore be above the ambient air temperature).

Examples of standard-rated items when sold hot are

- fish/chicken and chips
- chips
- Chinese, Indian, Greek, Italian and similar take-away meals and dishes
- baked potatoes with hot or cold filling
- hot dogs and hamburgers
- pies, sausage rolls, pasties and similar items (but see below if sold 'freshly cooked')
- toasted sandwiches
- cups of tea, coffee, chocolate and other hot drinks
- cups of soup
- roasted chestnuts

Freshly cooked products

Freshly cooked products that are sold for consumption while they are still hot are standard-rated. Some of these products are, however, bought for consumption later, either cold or after re-heating. Examples include pies, pasties, sausage rolls and similar savoury products, cooked chickens or joints of meat, bread products and croissants. The liability of such items depends on the way in which they are sold.

- If they are 'specifically sold for consumption while still hot' (as a result of being freshly baked, cooked or reheated) the supply is standard-rated.

- If they are *either* sold warm simply because they happen to be freshly baked and are not intended to be eaten while hot *or* cold or chilled at the time of purchase, the supply can be zero-rated.

Food is '*specifically sold for consumption whilst still hot*' if the retailer

- has an established hot take-away trade and is selling the food as a part of that trade;
- advertises it as either hot take-away food or in any other way that indicates it is meant to be eaten while still hot; or
- sells it accompanied by napkins, forks, etc. to enable it to be eaten before it cools.

HMRC regard the following as *indicators* of the liability.

- Type of outlet. If advertised as a take-away food outlet, supplies of hot food will be standard-rated.
- What happens to the food between the time it is cooked or heated and the time it is handed to the customer. If efforts are made to keep it hot, this may be an indicator for standard-rating, whereas if it is left to cool naturally for a period of time this may be an indicator for zero-rating.
- Type of packaging used. If food is packaged to retain heat, this would be an indicator for standard-rating. The reverse does not necessarily apply, since food intended for immediate consumption will often be sold in packaging that is not heat retentive.
- Availability of condiments, napkins and utensils. This would be an indicator for standard rating.
- The way in which the food is advertised and promoted, including in-store signage and any wording shown on packaging.
- Food hygiene regulations. In some cases food may be kept hot partly for the purpose of complying with food hygiene regulations. But the requirement to comply with these regulations will often not be an aim in itself for the supplier, but merely a consequence of supplying food for consumption whilst hot or warm. If this is the case, then the supplies will be standard-rated.
- Palatability. If an item is generally accepted to be unpalatable when cold, this would be an indicator for standard-rating. The reverse does not necessarily apply and the fact that an item remains palatable when cold does not preclude the possibility that it has been heated for the purpose of enabling it to be consumed hot.

In *John Pimblett & Sons Ltd v C & E Commrs, CA 1987,* [1988] STC 358 (TVC 29.55) the court held that for supplies of freshly baked pies to be taxed as hot take-away food, it had to be shown that the predominant subjective purpose of the seller in heating the food was to enable it to be consumed while still hot. If the seller's predominant purpose was to assure customers that it had been freshly baked, the food was not standard-rated, even though some customers consumed the food while still hot.

In *The Lewis's Group Ltd* (VTD 4931) (TVC 29.64) it was held that the supply of hot freshly roasted chickens from the food department was not a supply in the course of catering because it was not the supplier's predominant purpose, in heating the chicken, to enable customers to eat it at any particular temperature.

In *Pret A Manger (Europe) Ltd* (VTD 16246) (TVC 29.77) the tribunal rejected the argument that filled croissants were heated to keep them fresh and to prevent them from hardening. On the evidence, it found that the company's predominant purpose in cooking the savoury croissants and presenting them for sale hot was so that they could be consumed at a temperature above the ambient air temperature. However, in *The Great American Bagel Factory Ltd* (VTD 17018) (TVC 29.59) the tribunal accepted that the purpose of toasting bagels was to create a crunchy interior and promote freshness rather than enable them to be consumed hot.

In *Deliverance Ltd v HMRC* [2011] UKUT 58 (TC) (TVC 29.68), D delivered a wide range of foods including crispy duck pancakes, spring rolls, samosas, falafels, sesame prawn toasts and onion bhajis. The First-tier Tribunal upheld HMRC's ruling that these items failed to qualify for zero-rating. However the Upper Tribunal allowed D's appeal, holding that D's purpose in heating the food had been to comply with food hygiene regulations, rather than to enable the food to be consumed at a temperature above the ambient air temperature. Accordingly, the supplies qualified for zero-rating.

Microwave ovens provided for use of customers

If food is sold to be taken away for consumption elsewhere but a microwave oven is made available for customers to heat up the food (either before or after the till point) the supply is one of hot food and must be standard-rated (whether or not a charge is made for the use of the oven).

Hot and cold ingredients supplied as a single item

If an item of hot food, together with an ingredient which is cold, is sold as a single item, the whole supply is standard-rated (see *Marshall (t/a Harry Ramsbottom's)* (VTD 13766) (TVC 29.73)). This includes anything in a bun, bap, baguette or other speciality bread with any hot filling such as a sausage, reheated cheese and ham, pastrami, etc. Examples include hot dogs, hamburgers, bacon sandwiches, chip butties, baked potatoes with a cold filling, hot steak sandwiches and kebabs.

Hot and cold food sold at the same time

Where a mixture of standard-rated and zero-rated items is sold for an inclusive price for consumption off the premises, the VAT value of each item must be worked out in order to calculate how much VAT is due on the standard rated item. This can be done on the basis of cost or market values (see **47.3 OUTPUT TAX**). Examples of mixed supplies include

- burger, chips and a milkshake;
- a cup of tea with a non-chocolate coated biscuit; or

- a meal consisting of hot and cold items or dishes supplied in separate containers.

A supply is normally considered to be a mixed supply if each of the items in the inclusively-priced package can be purchased separately from the menu. This is not the same as a single item of food that happens to have hot and cold ingredients for which one charge is made (see above).

Condiments, etc.

Any minor items for which no charge is made (e.g. salt, pepper, vinegar or mustard) should be ignored. This applies whether or not the customer uses the condiments on the food.
(VAT Notice 709/1/11, paras 4.3–4.9; Business Brief 9/05).

Service charges and tips

[11.6] Service charges are standard-rated. Any tips given freely are outside the scope of VAT. (VAT Notice 700, para 8.14; VAT Notice 709/1/11, para 2.3).

Accounting for VAT

Catering provided by the owner of the catering facilities

[11.7] The owner of catering facilities is acting as principal and must account for VAT on any supplies of catering or hot take-away food. He can reclaim any VAT charged as input tax, subject to the normal rules. (VAT Notice 709/1/11, para 5.1).

Normal method of accounting

If each sale can be recorded as it takes place, the normal method of accounting can be used. This applies whether sales are only standard-rated or a mixture of standard-rated and zero-rated.

Retail scheme calculations

If each sale cannot be recorded as it takes place, then the Point of Sale scheme must normally be used (see **60.14 RETAIL SCHEMES**) unless the catering adaptation described below can be used. (It is not normally possible to use the Apportionment or Direct Calculation schemes. These assume that goods bought at one rate of VAT will be sold at the same rate and food bought at the zero rate often becomes standard-rated when supplied in the course of catering.)

Catering adaptation

A caterer may use a special catering adaptation to account for VAT provided

- he can satisfy HMRC that it is impracticable to keep records to operate the Point of Sale scheme;

- he has reasonable grounds for believing that the VAT-exclusive value of standard-rated and zero-rated catering supplies will not exceed £1 million in the next twelve months; and
- the use of the catering adaptation produces a fair and reasonable result in any period.

If the conditions (which have the force of law) are met, he must notify HMRC that he intends to operate the catering adaptation and may then begin to operate it as soon as acknowledgement of the letter is received.

To calculate output tax for each VAT period

Step 1	Add up daily gross takings	A
Step 2	Calculate the percentage of total supplies of catering made at the standard rate (see below)	B%
Step 3	Apply the percentage at Step 2 to the daily gross takings in Step 1	
Step 4	To calculate output tax, multiply the total at Step 3 by the VAT fraction	

In algebraic form, output tax is

A × (B ÷ 100) × V

See **60.8** and **60.9 RETAIL SCHEMES** for general rules applying to the calculation of daily gross takings. Service charges (but not tips) and the value of any meals or drinks given in exchange for an identifiable benefit to the business (see **11.8** below) should be included. It is not necessary to include the cost of food or drink used for free meals for family and staff but the full cost of any standard-rated items of food taken out of business stock for own or family use should be included (see **11.8** below).

The percentage of total supplies of catering made at the standard rate must be based on a sample of actual sales for a representative period. The period depends on the nature of the business but HMRC must be satisfied that it takes account of hourly, daily and seasonal fluctuations. Details of the sample, including dates and times, must be retained and a new calculation must be carried out in each VAT period.

If the conditions of the adaptation are not complied with, HMRC may assess for any undeclared VAT and/or refuse use of the adaptation for future periods.

(VAT Notice 727, paras 8.3–8.8 which have the force of law).

Example

A fish bar sells both fried fish and chips and wet fish and seafoods. It also has a small restaurant. It is impractical for the owner to keep a record of each sale as it takes place. He can, however, note his zero-rated supplies over the representative period, which are

	£
Receipts from wet fish rounds	724
Shop sales of wet fish and seafoods	285
Sundries (cold leftovers)	28
Total	1,037
Overall gross takings	7,580

At the end of a given quarterly tax period, gross takings total £24,016,28.

Standard-rated percentage is

(7,580 – 1,037) ÷ 7,580 × = 86%

Output tax for the VAT period is

£24,016.28 × 86% × 1/6 = £3,442.33

Other retail supplies

Where other retail non-catering supplies are made, it may be possible to run separate retail schemes for each part of the business provided separate books are kept. See **60.4 RETAIL SCHEMES**.

Free supplies of catering

Catering for employees

[11.8] Where employees are provided with food or drink free of charge (including supplies from vending machines), the consideration for the supply is taken to be nil (and no VAT is chargeable). Where there is any consideration, in cash or otherwise (e.g. deduction from wages) the supply, valued at the amount of the payment or deduction, is standard-rated. [*VATA 1994, Sch 6 para 10(1)(2)*]. HMRC accept that where employees are paid a minimum wage under a *Wages Order* for an industry and that *Order* allows for appropriate reductions to be made for catering and accommodation, these calculations are steps in arriving at the amount of the weekly wage to be paid and are not monetary consideration on which the employer is liable to VAT (*RW & MJ Goodfellow* (VTD 2107) (TVC 62.13) and VAT Notice 709/1/11, para 5.8).

Catering for self and family

Where the proprietor of a restaurant, café or other catering establishment provides meals for himself or his family, these are not regarded as catering and VAT need not be accounted for on them. But VAT must be accounted for on the full cost of any standard-rated items which are taken out of business stock for own or family use. See **24.3–24.13 FOOD** for standard-rated items of food. (VAT Notice 709/1/11, para 5.8).

Catering for customers and friends

Free meals or drink provided for customers or friends are regarded as business entertainment and any input tax incurred in the provision of the meal or the purchase of the drink is non-deductible. See also **9 BUSINESS ENTERTAINMENT**.

Free sweets or drinks provided as part of a meal which a customer pays for (e.g. mints or liqueurs with the bill) can be treated as attributable to the taxable supply of the meal and any input tax recovered.

Where meals or drinks are given in exchange for an identifiable benefit to the business (e.g. coach drivers or group organisers in return for bringing a party to the establishment) any VAT incurred can be deducted but output tax must also be accounted for. Output tax should be calculated on the cost of the goods purchased or, if this cannot be established, on the cost of producing the goods.

(VAT Notice 709/1/11, para 5.7).

Contract catering

[11.9] The following rules apply to contract catering.

(1) Catering provided by a catering contractor acting as principal

A catering contractor running catering facilities on someone else's premises as a principal must account for VAT at the standard rate on the following.

- Any supplies of catering or hot take-away food under the rules explained in **11.1** to **11.5** above. VAT charged on supplies is deductible under the normal rules.
- Sales of other standard-rated food items.
- Any fee to the owner of the catering facility.
- Any subsidy received from the owner of the catering facilities. This subsidy should include payments received to balance a profit and loss account for the catering given to the principal.

VAT must be charged on these supplies even if the owner of the facilities makes exempt supplies (as in **11.3**(2) and (3) above).

(2) Catering provided by a catering contractor acting as agent

Although such a person runs the canteen etc., the food and drink is supplied by the owner of the catering facilities (the principal). The owner must account for VAT on the supplies of catering or hot take-away food (unless they make exempt supplies as in **11.3**(2) and (3) above).
The catering contractor should act as follows.

- *Invoices made out to the principal.* If the contractor buys goods or services for his principal and they are invoiced to the principal, the supplier should send the invoices direct to the principal who can reclaim the VAT subject to the normal rules. The contractor should show a VAT-inclusive amount against the purchase of the item in any profit and loss account for the catering given to the principal (see below).
- *Invoices made out to the contractor.* If the contractor buys goods or services for his principal and they are invoiced to the contractor, the contractor should re-invoice them to his principal and account for VAT on them. If the contractor buys goods or services from unregistered suppliers, the principal must be aware that the contractor will have to charge VAT where appropriate. The contractor can reclaim the VAT on the invoice subject to the normal rules.

Provided the contractor issues a separate VAT invoice for these goods or services when charging them on to the principal, the contractor should merely record the VAT-inclusive amount in any profit and loss account for the catering given to the principal (see below). However, if it is the contractor's normal practice to issue a single document to serve as both the VAT invoice and the profit and loss account, he must clearly show the dual purpose of the document and keep the VAT invoice details separate from the other information.

- *Contractor's fee for services to his principal.* The contractor must account for VAT on the fee charged for running the catering facilities. The canteen owner can reclaim the VAT charged subject to the normal rules.
- *Profit and loss account.* If the contractor provides the canteen owner with a profit and loss account, he must show the VAT-inclusive amounts spent on food and received from supplies of meals. If there is a profit that the agent pays to the canteen owner or a loss reimbursed by the canteen owner to the contractor, these amounts are outside the scope of VAT.

(3) Catering provided by a catering contractor acting as both principal and agent

If a catering contractor supplies food and drink to the owner of the catering facilities and then prepares and serves it to the users of the canteen, etc. on the owner's behalf, the contractor is acting both as a principal in his own right and as an agent of the owner. The contractor must account for VAT on both

- his supplies of prepared food and drink to the owner (reclaiming any VAT invoiced to him subject to the normal rules); and
- his fee for services to the owner of the catering facilities for running the canteen.

Although under these arrangements the contractor runs the canteen, he is supplying the food and drink to the canteen owner and the owner supplies the food and drink to the users of the canteen. The owner must therefore account for VAT on standard-rated supplies of catering and hot take-away food under the rules in **11.1** to **11.5** above, unless the owner makes exempt supplies as in **11.3**(2) and (3) above.

(VAT Notice 709/1/11, paras 5.2–5.4).

Catering provided by student unions

[11.10] Where a student union supplies catering or hot take-away food to students both on behalf, and with the agreement, of the parent institution, as a concession it can treat its supplies in the same way as the parent institution itself. This means that a student union can treat its supplies as exempt when made at universities and other institutions supplying exempt education and outside the scope of VAT when supplied at further education and sixth form colleges.

As a result, most supplies of food and drink made by a student union, where the food is sold for consumption in the course of catering, is exempt. This covers food and drink sold from canteens, refectories and other catering outlets, plus food and drink sold from vending machines situated in canteens and similar areas.

The concession does not cover food and drink sold from campus shops, bars, tuck shops or other similar outlets because they are not considered supplies that are made in the course of catering. In addition, the concession does not cover any other goods or services supplied by the student unions.

(VAT Notice 709/1/11, para 5.5).

Key points

[11.11] Points to consider are as follows.

- A supply of food that requires a significant element of service to prepare it will usually be classed as a supply of catering and therefore be standard-rated. This outcome would include buffets and food provided for wedding receptions, office functions etc. A supply of catering also extends to any supply of hot take-away food or any food that is intended for consumption on the same premises as it is sold. This means that a sandwich served to a customer in a café will be standard-rated but the same item sold to a customer in a carrier bag for him to take away from the premises will be zero-rated.
- If a supply of take-away food requires further preparation to be carried out by the customer, then it will not represent a supply of catering and could be zero-rated if it relates to cold food. For these purposes, 'preparation' includes thawing frozen food, cooking food, reheating food and arranging food on serving plates. In the case of food delivered to a customer's premises (e.g. in a delivery van), the sale will be classed as supply of catering if it is to cater for a specific event or a supply of cold zero-rated food if a delivery is for a specific order of items (e.g. ten cheese sandwiches).
- A useful concession allows a hotel or similar establishment to zero-rate the sale of packed lunches, as long as the items in question are cold food items that qualify for zero-rating. Again, the intention must be for the lunch to be consumed away from the hotel premises, e.g. a guest at a seaside hotel buying a packed lunch to take to the beach with him.
- As a planning point, items sold from a vending machine could qualify for zero-rating if the vendor can show that some or all of the items are consumed away from the site of the machine. So if a vending machine is located in a café, and it is clear that all items will be eaten in the café, then all sales will be standard-rated. However, an apportionment can be made if it can be shown that

a percentage of the purchases are consumed away from the site where the machine is located. This assumes that the items in question are zero-rated as a matter of course (e.g. a sandwich rather than a packet of crisps).

- Care is needed when catering is supplied in conjunction with zero-rated transport. The key factor is to determine whether the catering is an aim in its own right (separate supply that is standard-rated) or is merely intended to enhance the customer's enjoyment of the journey. In the latter case, the entire payment made by the customer will be classed as a supply of zero-rated transport, with no output tax liability on the catering element. A practical example is that a cup of tea and biscuit supplied on a flight would not be considered a supply of catering. But a three course meal and wine on the Orient Express would definitely be classed as a 'mixed' supply. In this situation, the customer expects to receive and enjoy both the zero-rated train journey and the standard-rated catering provided during the trip.
- The scope for zero-rating of cold food for take away purposes was extended when HMRC accepted the principles decided in the case of *HMRC v Compass Contract Services UK Ltd*, CA [2006] STC 1999 (TVC 29.31). Following this case, HMRC changed its view that premises consisted of an entire area of a building or arena to the specific area that was under the control of the caterer. So a caterer selling food at a sports stadium would only need to class any seating area linked to his outlet as 'premises' as opposed to the entire stadium.
- A business that sells both zero-rated and standard-rated items will usually need to adopt a retail scheme to enable it to calculate output tax due on its standard-rated sales. In reality, this will usually be based on a point of sale scheme because of the difficulties in applying apportionment or mark-up schemes to supplies of catering. An important check carried out by HMRC on VAT visits will be to ensure that the caterer does not misdescribe some of his standard-rated sales as being zero-rated. It is suggested that advisers encourage catering clients to retain subsidiary records, such as till rolls and other workings, to support the declared split of sales. It is also important that a business owner ensures that his staff are properly trained in the issues of VAT liability, again to confirm that proper VAT systems are in place.
- There is no output tax liability on tips paid by a customer to a restaurant or similar outlet. However, the payment of the tip must be at the total discretion of the customer. A service charge added to a bill is not classed as a tip if the customer is obliged to make the payment and is therefore standard-rated.
- There is no output tax liability (or input tax disallowance) on free food or drink provided to an employee. However, in the case of own consumption (food or drink enjoyed by the business owner), output tax needs to be accounted for on the cost of any standard-rated items that have been consumed.

- Free food or drink supplied to customers and friends is classed as business entertainment and an input tax block will apply on the items in question.

12

Charities

Cross-references. See **25 FUEL AND POWER** for reduced rate on supplies to charities for non-business use.

De Voil Indirect Tax Service. See V4.146, V4.171, V4.261, V4.262, V4.266, V4.406, V4.409, V4.419.

Introduction

[12.1] The term 'charity' has no precise meaning in law. Under the *Recreational Charities Act 1958, s 1* the provision, in the interest of social welfare, of facilities for recreation or other leisure time occupation, is deemed to be charitable (subject to the principle that, unless the trust is for the relief of poverty (*Dingle v Turner*, HL [1972] 1 All ER 878), a trust or institution to be charitable must be for the public benefit).

In England and Wales, most charities are registered with the Charity Commission under the *Charities Act 1993* (which confirms their charitable status) but certain charities (e.g. universities, churches and other places of worship and certain small charities with annual income below £1,000) are exempt from such registration. Charities exempt from registration, and charities in Northern Ireland, must be approved by HMRC Charities in order to be recognised as such for tax (including VAT) purposes.

From April 2006, responsibility for registration of charities in Scotland rests with the Scottish Charity Regulator. HMRC accept that bodies so registered have charitable status.

Subject to the above, what is a charity rests largely on judicial interpretation. A leading case is *Special Commrs v Pemsel*, HL [1891] 3 TC 53 (TVC 15.82) in which Lord Macnaghten laid down that 'charity' should be given its technical meaning under English law and comprises 'four principal divisions; trusts for the relief of poverty, trusts for the advancement of education, trusts for the advancement of religion and trusts beneficial to the community and not falling under any of the previous heads. The trusts last referred to are not the less charitable . . . because incidentally they affect the rich as well as the poor'. Included are trusts for the relief of sickness and infirmity, nature conservation trusts and trusts for support of the arts.

There is no distinction for VAT purposes between those charities registered with one of the charity regulators and those that are not. However, unregistered charities claiming VAT relief may need to demonstrate that they have 'charitable status'. This may be achieved from their written 'objects' or by the recognition of their charitable status by HMRC. (VAT Notice 701/1/04, para 2.2).

Charities and VAT

[12.2] Since the introduction of VAT, the law has provided a range of special reliefs which cover many supplies to and by charities. Zero-rating applies to some supplies to charities and there are some exemptions, zero-rating and other concessions for business supplies by charities. However, there is no general relief from VAT for goods supplied to charities and in general the normal VAT rules apply to business supplies made by charities.

Under charity law, charities can carry out '*primary purpose trading*', i.e. trading activities in the course of carrying out their primary purpose (e.g. the holding of an art exhibition by a charitable art gallery or museum in return for admission charges).

But charities may also wish to carry out '*non-primary purpose trading*' as a way of raising money (e.g. a charity whose primary purpose is providing education may sell Christmas cards and gifts through a catalogue). Charity law does not permit charities to carry out non-primary purpose trading in their own right on a substantial basis. In order to carry out non-primary purpose trading on a significant scale, charities have to establish 'subsidiary trading companies'. These are trading companies controlled by one or more charities but are not themselves charities. Although profits of these subsidiaries can be passed to the charity free of corporation tax, they are not charities and most of the VAT reliefs available to charities are not available to subsidiary trading companies.

Where a charity and its trading subsidiaries are VAT-registered it may be possible, under certain conditions, for them to register as a VAT group. See **27 GROUPS OF COMPANIES.**

(VAT Notice 701/1/04, para 2.3).

Business activities

It is important not to confuse the term 'trading' as frequently used by a charity to describe its non-charitable commercial fund-raising activities (usually carried out by a trading subsidiary) with 'business' as used for VAT purposes. Although trading activities will invariably be business activities, 'business' for VAT purposes can have a much wider application and include some or all of the charity's primary or charitable activities. See **12.4** and **12.5** below for further consideration of business and non-business activities.

Registration and basic principles

Registration

[12.3] Any business (including a charity or its trading subsidiary) that makes taxable supplies in excess of the VAT registration threshold (see **59.3 REGISTRATION**) must register for VAT. Taxable supplies are business transactions that are liable to VAT at the standard rate, reduced rate or zero rate. See **12.4** below for a consideration of what are business activities generally and **12.5** below for common business and non-business activities of charities.

If a charity's income from taxable supplies is below the VAT registration threshold it can voluntarily register for VAT (see **59.2 REGISTRATION**) but a charity that makes no taxable supplies (either because it has no business activities or because its supplies or income are exempt from VAT) cannot register.

Example

A charity has three sources of income – the annual amounts are as follows:

Mediation services	£50,000
Local authority grant towards costs of child helpline service	£20,000
Donations from members	£15,000

The value of taxable supplies made by the charity is £50,000 in relation to the mediation services. The income from the local authority and members' donations is outside the scope of VAT. The taxable income is therefore below the VAT registration threshold and the charity does not need to register on a compulsory basis.

The next question to consider is whether it may be worthwhile for the charity to register for VAT on a voluntary basis. The answer is probably no, because this will create an output tax liability on the mediation services, which will either create an extra VAT charge to the users of this facility – or reduce the net income of the charity if fees are kept at the same rate. The input tax benefits are unlikely to outweigh the output tax charges.

Charging VAT

Where a VAT-registered charity makes supplies of goods and services in the course of its business activities, the VAT liability of those supplies is, in general, determined in the normal way as for any other business. See, however, **12.6** below for certain supplies by charities which are zero-rated and **12.10** below for certain exempt supplies by charities. Even if VAT-registered, a charity should not charge VAT on any non-business supplies or income.

Reclaiming VAT

The first stage in determining the amount of VAT which a VAT-registered charity can reclaim is to eliminate all the VAT incurred that relates to its non-business activities. It cannot reclaim any VAT it is charged on purchases that *directly* relate to non-business activities. It will also not be able to reclaim a proportion of the VAT on its general expenses (e.g. telephone and electricity) that relate to those non-business activities. See **34.7 INPUT TAX** for various methods which can be used to calculate this proportion.

Once this has been done, the remaining VAT relating to the charity's business activities is input tax.

- It can reclaim all the input tax it has been charged on purchases which *directly* relate to standard-rated, reduced-rated or zero-rated goods or services it supplies.
- It cannot reclaim any of the input tax it has been charged on purchases that relate *directly* to exempt supplies.

It also cannot claim a proportion of input tax on general expenses (after adjustment for non-business activities) that relates to exempt activities unless this amount, together with the input tax relating directly to exempt supplies, is below a *de minimis* limit. See **49.3** to **49.11 PARTIAL EXEMPTION.**

Example

A charity that provides support for homeless people buys some new kitchen equipment that includes VAT. The charity provides free meals to homeless people but is VAT-registered because it also sells meals and snacks as a business activity from the kitchen.

In this situation, a proportion of the input tax must be initially disallowed to reflect the non-business use of the equipment, i.e. to provide free meals to homeless people. This calculation can be based on any method that is fair and reasonable, e.g. time basis, number of meals served, number of business customers compared to non-business customers.

Business and non-business activities

[12.4] An organisation such as a charity that is run on a non-profit-making basis may still be regarded as carrying on a business activity for VAT purposes. This is unaffected by the fact that the activity is performed for the benefit of the community. It is therefore important for a charity to determine whether any particular activity is a 'business' or a 'non-business' activity. This applies both when considering registration (if there is no business activity a charity cannot be registered and therefore cannot recover any input tax) and after registration.

If registered, a charity must account for VAT on taxable supplies it makes by way of business. Income from any non-business activities is not subject to VAT and affects the amount of VAT reclaimable as input tax (see **12.3** above).

'*Business*' has a wide meaning for VAT purposes based upon *Directive 2006/112/EC* (which uses the term 'economic activity' rather than 'business'), UK VAT legislation and decisions by the Courts and VAT Tribunals. See **8.1** to **8.3 BUSINESS** for a fuller consideration of the meaning of 'business' and in particular the business test in **8.2 BUSINESS**.

An activity may still be business if the amount charged does no more than cover the cost to the charity of making the supply or where the charge made is less than cost (but see non-business supplies of welfare services in **12.5** below). If the charity makes no charge at all the activity is unlikely to be considered business.

An area of particular difficulty for charities when considering whether their activities are in the course of business is receipt of grant funding (see **12.5** below).

(VAT Notice 701/1/04, para 4.1).

Common income/activities of charities

[12.5] This paragraph considers the VAT treatment of some of the more common income-producing activities of charities.

(1) Admission to premises

Where a charity admits visitors to places of interest, gardens, exhibitions, entertainment, functions, etc. for a charge, this is a business activity.

Fixed admission charges

A VAT-registered charity must account for VAT on this income at the standard rate unless

- the income is for admittance to a qualifying fund-raising event, in which case it is exempt from VAT (see **12.10** below); or
- the income is covered by the exemption for admission to museums, galleries, art exhibitions, zoos and theatrical, musical or choreographic performances (see **57.7**(3) **RECREATION AND SPORT**).

Donations in lieu of admission

True donations are outside the scope of VAT. If admission to the premises is not dependent on a payment then the monies received are donations but if admission is conditional upon payment, VAT must be accounted for at the standard rate.

A charity which 'suggests' an amount that visitors may wish to contribute, but does not insist on payment of that amount before allowing admission, can treat the amounts received as donations. An admission fee of £20 plus a 'minimum voluntary contribution' of £30 has been held to fail this test, implying that the £30 donation was compulsory (*Glasgow's Miles Better Mid Summer 5th Anniversary Ball* (VTD 4460) (TVC 67.135)).

No charge for admission. If no charge is made for admission, there is no business activity and any monies received can be treated as donations and outside the scope of VAT.

(VAT Notice 701/1/04, para 5.1).

(2) Advertising in brochures, programmes, annual reports, etc.

The sale of such advertising space is a business activity and is normally standard-rated with the following exceptions.

(a) By concession, provided 50% or more of the total number of advertisements in a publication are clearly placed by private individuals, the charity can treat *all* sums received from advertisers as non-business and outside the scope of VAT. A private advertisement must make no reference to a business. An example of a private advertisement is one that says 'Good wishes from John and Susan Smith'; but not one taken out by 'John and Susan Smith, Grocers, 49 High Street'.

(b) The supply of advertising to another charity can be zero-rated (see **12.7**(*f*) below).

(c) The sale of advertising space in brochures or programmes for a fund-raising event is exempt (see **12.10** below) unless overridden by zero-rating under (*b*) above.

(VAT Notice 701/1/04, para 5.2).

(3) Affinity credit cards

A charity may receive payments from a bank, building society or other financial institution in return for the charity endorsing that institution's credit card and recommending its use to the charity's members or supporters. This is a business activity and the payments would normally be treated as standard-rated marketing services provided to the financial institution. However, HMRC recognise that a large element of such payments could be charitable and not payment for services rendered. Provided the charity is not acting as an intermediary between the card provider and the applicant (see below), HMRC allow charities to treat part of these payments as standard-rated and the remainder as outside the scope of VAT. Note that this treatment only applies to income from affinity credit cards and does not extend to any other financial products.

Typically, a card provider will pay a fixed amount to the charity (or its trading subsidiary) on the issue of each new card and a percentage of the turnover (value of purchases) on the card.

To benefit from this treatment there must be two separate agreements.

- One agreement, between the charity (or its trading subsidiary) and the card provider should provide for the supply by the charity (or its trading subsidiary) of the necessary marketing and publicity services, access to membership lists and other promotional activity for the card (marketing services). These supplies are taxable at the standard rate.
- A second and separate agreement between the charity and the card provider should provide for contributions to be made by the card provider in respect of the use only of the charity's name and/or logo. Contributions made under this agreement can be treated as outside the scope.

Part (at least 20%) of the initial payment is then treated as the consideration for the standard-rated business supplies by the charity. The remaining 80% (or less) of the initial payment and all subsequent payments based on turnover are outside the scope of VAT.

Intermediary services

A charity acts as an intermediary in arranging a contract between its members and a credit card provider where it

- stands between the parties to a contract in the performance of a distinct act of negotiation, without having any interest of its own in the terms of the contract;
- brings the two parties to the contract together; and
- undertakes preparatory work, such as completing or assisting with completion of application forms, forwarding forms to the credit card company, and making representations on behalf of either party.

If a charity is providing intermediary services the payment they receive from the credit card provider is exempt from VAT. HMRC do not see clerical tasks (e.g. providing a list of names or access to a database) as intermediary services.

See also *BAA plc v C & E Commrs,* CA 2002, [2003] STC 35 (TVC 27.20); *Institute of Directors v C & E Commrs,* CA 2002, [2003] STC 35 (TVC 27.22). Following these cases, charities should consider whether supplies involving affinity credit cards are exempt although HMRC have confirmed that, if they wish, charities can continue to treat their income as before. (Business Brief 18/03).

(VAT Notice 701/1/04, paras 5.3, 8.1, 8.2).

(4) Charity shops and sales of goods

The sale of donated and bought-in goods by charities and their trading subsidiaries is a business activity.

Donated goods

The sale, hire or export of donated goods by a charity and, in most instances, its trading subsidiary is zero-rated. See **12.6**(*a*) and (*b*) below. This also applies where the goods are sold at a qualifying fund-raising event (see **12.10** below).

Bought-in goods

If a charity buys in goods for resale, it must account for VAT at the standard rate on the sale unless the goods are zero-rated or reduced-rated under the general provisions (e.g. children's clothes, books, etc.). Bought-in goods sold at qualifying fund-raising events are exempt (see **12.10** below).

(VAT Notice 701/1/04, para 5.5).

(5) Catering

Catering is normally a business activity liable to VAT at the standard rate. See **11 CATERING**. But some catering can be exempt from VAT when carried out by a charity, e.g.

- catering supplied as part of welfare services (see (21) below), such as meals for residents of care homes, and supplies of food and drink (but not alcohol) from trolleys, canteens and shops to patients in hospitals or inmates in prisons; and
- catering provided as part of a qualifying fund-raising event (see **12.10** below).

Catering may also be non-business when it forms part of a non-business supply of welfare (see (21) below).

(VAT Notice 701/1/04, para 5.6).

(6) Donations

A donation which

- is freely given; and
- does not entitle the donor to any further benefit

is not consideration for a supply and is outside the scope of VAT. The giving of a low value token as an acknowledgement of the donation is not treated as a supply for a consideration, provided no minimum payment is specified.

(VAT Notice 701/1/04, para 5.9).

Example

A commercial company agrees to give a donation of £1,000 to a VAT-registered charity, in return for which it will be allowed to display its products and circulate leaflets at the AGM of the charity, to be attended by 200 members/supporters.

This payment is not a donation because the company is obtaining a marketing benefit from the arrangement. The charity is providing a service to the company by giving it the right to promote its products. The income is therefore standard-rated.

(7) Dividends and interest

Dividends received on shares, and interest received from banks, building societies and other financial institutions, are outside the scope of VAT and regarded as part of the charity's non-business income.

(8) Education, research and training

See **16 EDUCATION**.

(9) Free export of goods

The export of *any* goods by a charity (i.e. including goods exported free of charge, usually in the form of relief-aid) to a place outside the EU is treated as a business activity. See **12.6**(*b*) below.

(10) Free supplies

A free supply of services is a non-business activity and outside the scope of VAT. This may cover many of the services typically provided by a charity (e.g. first aid at public functions, rescue at sea). If the recipient makes a financial contribution towards the work of the charity this does not turn the activity into a business activity, provided it is freely given.

A free supply of goods is also usually a non-business activity (but see (9) above for the free export of goods).

(11) Fund-raising

Fund-raising covers a wide range of activities which must be judged to be business or non-business under normal rules. Some of the most common methods are:

Donations

These are outside the scope of VAT if freely given. See (6) above.

Qualifying fund-raising events

Subject to conditions and exclusions, the supply of certain goods and services in connection with a qualifying event whose primary purpose is the raising of money is exempt from VAT. See **12.10** below.

Sponsored events in the UK

Many charities organise walks, runs, swims and other similar sponsored events or arrange for teams of representatives to participate in these events in order to raise funds.

If a charity is organising and promoting the event it may be able to take advantage of the fund-raising exemption. See **12.10** below.

Sometimes a charity may organise an exempt fund-raising event in association with a different event which may or may not be an exempt fund-raising event in its own right (e.g. a charity may have a marquee and hold an auction of sporting memorabilia at a national sporting event). The charity can use the fund-raising exemption provided the event it is organising meets the conditions set out in **12.10** below.

There are, however, many events that individuals take part in to raise funds for charity that do not fall within the fund-raising exemption (e.g. a commercially organised sports event such as a marathon). Charities may pay for places within such events and then offer those places to individuals.

Where a charity allows individuals to take part in the event regardless of the amount they raise, and the individuals do not receive any benefits in return, the monies they raise can be treated as a donation and outside the scope of VAT. HMRC do not consider the following to be benefits.

- Provision of free training and health advice.
- A free t-shirt, running vest or similar which clearly portrays the charity that the individual is representing.
- Free massages and support for physical well-being during the event.
- Free pre-event meeting, which may include free professional advice or support, a simple meal, energy drinks and encouragement from the charity and other participants.
- Free post-event meeting, which may include medical treatment or advice, changing facilities, light refreshments and gives the charity the opportunity to thank participants.

If the charity provides free travel or accommodation and other benefits or gifts (e.g. bicycles or watches) the amount raised by the participant is taxable at the standard rate.

If a charity requires individuals to pay a registration fee or insists that they raise a minimum amount of sponsorship before they can take part in the event, this is effectively an entry fee and is taxable at the standard rate. Any payment in excess of the minimum amount can be treated as a donation and outside the scope of VAT.

If a charity asks individuals to 'pledge' or 'commit' to raise a certain amount of sponsorship, but do not insist on any payment before allowing the individual to take part in the event, the total amounts raised can be treated as donations and outside the scope of VAT. A charity can encourage individuals to pass on sponsorship money as they receive it, but cannot insist on receiving a certain amount before allowing the individual to take part.

Some charities offer prizes to top fund-raisers. These are not benefits for VAT purposes and do not affect the VAT treatment of income from participants.

Charity challenge events

Charities (or their trading subsidiaries) frequently organise treks, bike rides and other sponsored events in order to raise funds. These are usually arranged to include travel and accommodation and are often known as 'charity challenge events'.

Fund-raising events that include a package of both travel and accommodation; or bought-in accommodation; or more than two nights' accommodation from a charity's own resources do not qualify for the fund-raising VAT exemption. Charities involved with challenge events need to consider the following issues—

- Is the charity making a supply? If the charity insists that the participant makes a payment before allowing them to take part in the challenge event the charity will be making a supply for VAT purposes. The payment might consist of a registration fee; a deposit; and/or payment of a proportion of the target figure that the participant is aiming to raise through sponsorship. However the amount is calculated, if the charity insist on payment before allowing the participant to take part then the charity is making a supply. That supply may be of a package to the participant (if the charity acted as a principal or undisclosed agent) or of agency services in selling the package/holiday for a specialist company who has put the event together (if the charity acted as an agent).

- Is the charity acting as a disclosed agent, undisclosed agent, or principal? Most charities use the services of a specialist company to organise challenge events, in which case they will normally have a contract setting out exactly who is responsible for what. A charity will be acting as a disclosed agent if both the charity and the specialist company have agreed that the charity will act as the company's agent; and the charity discloses the name of the principal (the specialist company), e.g. in the event terms and conditions and on all tickets issued; and the charity is not taking any significant commercial risk in relation to the event (e.g. the charity does not have any financial liability should something go wrong). If these agency disclosure conditions are not met (in which case the charity is acting as an undisclosed agent), or the charity acts as a principal, buying and selling the entire event or putting together the challenge event itself – buying travel, accommodation, itinerary, professional guides, etc. direct – then the charity must account for VAT using the **TOUR OPERATORS' MARGIN SCHEME (68)** (TOMS).
- What is the correct VAT treatment? If the charity is acting as a disclosed agent, the participant contracts with the specialist company and the charity receives a commission. VAT will be due on the commission that the charity charges as an agent. If the charity is acting as principal or undisclosed agent, under TOMS VAT will be due on the margin between what it has cost (excluding overheads) the charity to provide a place on the event and what the charity insists on receiving as payment before allowing the participant to take part. If the charity is providing up to two nights accommodation from its own resources, and is not providing a package of travel and accommodation, the income from the event will be exempt under the fund-raising exemption.

Sponsorship of a charity

Many charities receive money, goods or services from sponsors.

- If the charity is obliged to provide the sponsor with a significant benefit in return the sponsorship (e.g. free tickets, free advertising space in a charity event programme), this is a business activity and is taxable at the standard rate.
- If the sponsor receives no significant benefits in return for its contribution, the charity may be able to treat the income as non-business. HMRC accept that giving a flag or sticker to a donor, or naming a donor in a list of supporters is insignificant.

See **57.19 RECREATION AND SPORT** for further details.

(VAT Notice 701/1/04, paras 5.9, 10).

Professional fund-raising

Charities frequently engage the services of professional fund-raisers to collect donations from the public. Following the decision in *Church of England Children's Society v R & C Commrs,* Ch D [2005] STC 1644 (TVC 11.45) HMRC accept that such fund-raising activities are 'general overheads' and thus 'cost components' of the charity's economic activities.

- Where funds are raised solely for a restricted charitable purposes involving wholly non-business activities, the VAT incurred on raising those funds is not input tax and not recoverable.
- Where, on the other hand, the funds raised are wholly to support the making of business supplies, all of the VAT incurred can be treated as input tax. It will be recoverable in full (subject to the normal rules) where the business supplies are taxable but not recoverable where they are exempt (subject to the *de minimis* rules).
- Where funds raised support both business and non-business activities, VAT incurred can only be recovered to the extent that it supports taxable business supplies. In practice, this means that the VAT incurred is first subject to a business/non-business apportionment to determine how much of the VAT is input tax and then, if the charity has exempt activities, this input tax is subject to the partial exempt rules.

(Business Brief 19/05).

(12) Grant funding

Charities often receive funding to support their charitable activities. If funding is freely given, with nothing supplied in return, then no VAT is due. The funding is not consideration for any supply and is therefore outside the scope of VAT. But if funding is given in return for goods or services supplied by the charity, such funding is consideration for a supply and VAT may be due on the income if the goods and/or services supplied by the charity in return are taxable at either the standard or reduced rate.

To decide whether funding is consideration for a supply, a charity should consider the following questions.

- Does the donor receive anything in return for the funding? (Certain 'benefits' to the donor, such as copies of reports, are seen as necessary safeguards to ensure the money is spent correctly and that the end product is put to proper use; they can be ignored where they are incidental to the primary purpose of the project and are minimal in relation to the amount of funding.)
- If the donor does not benefit, does a third party benefit instead? And if so, is there a direct link between the money paid by the funder and the supply received by the third party?
- Are any conditions attached to the funding, which go beyond the requirement to account for the funds (commonly referred to as 'good housekeeping')?

If the answer to any of the above questions is 'yes', this is an indication that the funding *may* not be freely given and may be consideration for a supply.

Where a charity is supported by outside the scope funding, this does not determine the nature of any supplies it makes (i.e. it does not follow that outside the scope income means that the charity will only have non-business activities).

(VAT Notice 701/1/04, para 5.10).

> *Example*
>
> A charity is responsible for promoting a music festival on behalf of the local council. It will receive a grant from the council for its efforts. The intention is to encourage more people to attend the event and to co-ordinate ticket sales and other support services. In this situation, the grant is standard-rated, as a supply of services is being performed by the charity that benefits the council. If the supply is standard-rated, this means the charity can claim input tax on its related costs. The local authority is not concerned about the VAT charge because it gets special treatment that allows it to reclaim input tax on its non-business expenditure.
>
> Note – the above circumstances applied in the case of *Bath Festivals Trust Ltd*, (11 September 2008, unreported) (LON/06/511 20840) (TVC 42.19).

(13) Hiring out buildings, including village halls

The hiring out of a building for a fee is normally a business activity. The fees received are exempt from VAT unless the charity has opted to tax the building. If so, the fees received are standard-rated except where the option to tax cannot be applied because the hirer is intending to use it

- as a dwelling (e.g. a residential flat above a charity shop);
- for a relevant charitable purpose (e.g. as a village hall or similarly, or for a non-business purpose); or
- for a relevant residential purpose (e.g. a residential home for children or disabled people, or a hospice),

in which case the fees remain exempt.

See **41.2** LAND AND BUILDINGS: EXEMPT SUPPLIES AND OPTION TO TAX for exempt supplies of land and **41.8** *et seq* LAND AND BUILDINGS: EXEMPT SUPPLIES AND OPTION TO TAX for the option to tax.

Where the hire of the building (or part of a building) is incidental to the provision of facilities (e.g. the hiring of facilities for playing sport), the supply is normally standard-rated. However, where rooms are hired as facilities for playing sport for a period exceeding 24 hours or for a series of ten or more sessions, the supply may be exempt. See **57.7** *et seq* RECREATION AND SPORT.

(14) Bequeathed property

HMRC take the view that land and buildings are not goods which have been donated for sale (see **12.6** below). Additionally, the property in most cases would not have been a business asset of the deceased or the charity.

Any supply of property flowing from a bequest is normally therefore outside the scope of VAT and the charity cannot recover input tax on the expenses of sale. (Business Brief 12/92).

(15) Museums and galleries

Where a charity running a museum or gallery makes a charge for admission, the normal rules in (1) above apply.

Admission to a museum or gallery for no charge is a non-business activity. Normally, this means that no input tax can be reclaimed. See, however, **34.13**(21) INPUT TAX for a special scheme allowing certain non-charging national museums and galleries to recover related input tax.

Other activities (e.g. catering and the sale of books and postcards) must be considered separately.

(16) Membership subscriptions

The provision of membership benefits to members is a business activity and the VAT liability of a membership subscription depends on the benefits being supplied. Normally, this means that the provider must decide whether it is making a single or multiple supply and tax the subscription accordingly. However, as a concession, a charity may, if it wishes, treat a single supplies of membership benefits as a multiple supply. The VAT treatment of each benefit can then be considered separately and the subscription charge apportioned so that, for example, the supply of magazines or handbooks to members can be zero-rated. See **14.2** CLUBS AND ASSOCIATIONS for further details.

(17) Nursery and crèche facilities

In *C & E Commrs v Yarburgh Children's Trust,* Ch D 2001, [2002] STC 207 (TVC 15.91) the charity undertook to provide nursery and crèche facilities for pre-school age children as part of its charitable objectives. It charged fees for its services but these were set at a level designed to ensure that it merely covered its costs. The Court decided that the charity was not making supplies by way of business. Despite that decision, HMRC's position remained that the provision of nursery and crèche facilities in such circumstances was a business activity for VAT purposes. However, in the subsequent case of *C & E Commrs v St Paul's Community Project Ltd,* Ch D 2004, [2005] STC 95 (TVC 15.92) in similar circumstances the Court again decided in favour of the charity. It found that the intrinsic nature of the enterprise was not the carrying on of a business, identifying the distinguishing features as the social concern for the welfare of disadvantaged children, lack of commerciality in setting fees and the overall intention simply to cover costs.

Although HMRC do not agree that these features point to the activities being non-business, considering that the charities are making supplies of services for consideration in much the same way as a commercial nursery, they have decided not to appeal further and now accept that the provision of nursery and crèche facilities by charities, along the same lines as those in the *Yarburgh* and *St Paul's* cases, is not a business activity for VAT purposes. In cases that are not broadly in line with the *Yarburgh* or *St Paul's* cases, HMRC will continue to apply the business test, in order to determine whether the supplies concerned are being made by way of business.

(Business Brief 2/05).

(18) Patron and supporter schemes

Many charities operate patron or supporter schemes offering benefits (e.g. free admission to special exhibitions, the right to receive regular publications, discounts on shop purchases, etc.) in return for a minimum payment. The minimum payment is business income and is standard-rated, although if one of the benefits to patrons or supporters is the right to receive publications, it may be possible to treat part of the payment as zero-rated.

If a patron or supporter pays more than the minimum amount, the excess can be treated as a donation and outside the scope of VAT provided the patron or supporter is aware that scheme benefits are available for a given amount, and that anything in excess of that amount is a voluntary donation. This should be explicit in the patron or supporter scheme literature.

(VAT Notice 701/1/04, para 5.14).

(19) Secondment of staff to other charities

Income received for the supply of staff is a business activity and is normally taxable at the standard rate. However if staff are jointly employed there is no supply of staff for VAT purposes. See **44.6 MANAGEMENT SERVICES AND SUPPLIES OF STAFF**. By concession, where staff are seconded from one charity or non-profit-making 'voluntary organisation' to another, the income from the hire or loan can be treated as non-business and outside the scope of VAT provided

- the employee seconded has been engaged only in the non-business activities of the lending charity/organisation and is being seconded to assist in such activities of the borrowing organisation; and
- the payment for the supply of the employee's services does not exceed 'normal remuneration' (calculated *pro rata* for part-time secondments). '*Normal remuneration*' means the total cost incurred by the lending charity/organisation including salary, NIC, pension costs, etc.

A '*voluntary organisation*' is a body that operates otherwise than for profit, but does not include any public or local authority.

(VAT Notice 701/1/04, para 5.17).

(20) Share dealing

The acquisition or disposal of shares and other securities by a charity is not a business activity. Any VAT incurred in connection with such acquisition or disposal, or the management of the investments, cannot be treated as input tax. See *National Society for the Prevention of Cruelty to Children* (VTD 9325) (TVC 11.49) where the tribunal held that the charity's investment activities, although having a turnover in excess of £7 million, did not amount to a business as the charity was not predominantly concerned with those supplies. See also *The Wellcome Trust Ltd v C & E Commrs, ECJ Case C-155/94*, [1996] STC 945 (TVC 22.111) where the court confirmed that the concept of an economic activity is to be interpreted as not including the purchase and sale of shares and other securities by a trustee in the course of the management of the assets of a charitable trust.

(21) Welfare

The supply of welfare services by a charity are normally business and exempt from VAT. Similar provisions now apply to such supplies made by public bodies and state-regulated private welfare institutions. See **28.12 HEALTH AND WELFARE.**

Non-business welfare services

By concession, charities that provide welfare services at significantly below cost, to 'distressed' persons for the relief of their distress, *may* treat these supplies as non-business and outside the scope of VAT. To qualify:

- The subsidy must be at least 15%.
- The subsidy must be available to all distressed persons, i.e. both to those who can and cannot afford to pay the full rate.
- The services must be provided to the distressed individual (and not, for example, to a local authority).

See **28.12 HEALTH AND WELFARE** for the definition of '*welfare services*'.

'*Distressed*' means suffering pain, grief, anguish, severe poverty, etc.

(VAT Notice 701/1/04, para 5.18).

Zero-rated supplies by charities

[12.6] Certain supplies by charities are zero-rated not because of the charitable status of the supplier but because they are covered by general application. See **74.1 ZERO-RATED SUPPLIES.** In addition, the following zero-rating provisions apply specifically to charities.

(a) Sale of donated goods

Subject to below, zero-rating applies to the sale or letting on hire of any 'goods' donated to

- a charity, or
- a taxable person who is a 'profits-to-charity' person in respect of the goods

where the goods are donated for sale, letting or any combination of these two and export.

'*Goods*' means goods in the normal sense of the word. It does not, in particular, include anything that is not goods, even though *VATA 1994* or any other enactment provides that the supply of it is, or is treated as, a supply of goods. Land, for example, is therefore excluded from zero-rating under these provisions.

Goods are donated for letting only if they are donated for letting, re-letting after the end of any first or subsequent letting *and* sale, export or disposal as waste if not, or when no longer, used for letting.

'*Profits-to-charity*' person. A taxable person is a profits-to-charity person in respect of any goods if

- he has agreed in writing (whether or not by deed) to transfer to a charity his profits from supplies and lettings of the goods; or
- his profits from supplies and lettings of the goods are otherwise payable to a charity.

Zero-rating does not apply

(i) unless the sale or letting takes place as a result of the goods having been made available for purchase or hire (whether in a shop or elsewhere such as a charity auction) to
   - the general public; or
   - two or more persons who are handicapped (i.e. chronically sick or disabled) and/or entitled to receive one or more means-tested benefits (income support, housing benefit, council tax benefit, income-based jobseeker's allowance, any element of child tax credit other than the family element, or working tax credit);

(ii) if the sale or letting takes place as a result of any arrangements (whether legally binding or not) relating to the goods and entered into, before the goods were made available as under (i) above, by
   - each of the parties to the sale or letting; or
   - the donor of the goods and either or both of those parties; or

(iii) to any sale or letting of particular donated goods if the goods, at any time after they are donated but before they are sold, exported or disposed of as waste, are whilst unlet used for any purpose other than being available for purchase, hire or export.

[*VATA 1994, Sch 8 Group 15 Items 1, 1A; Tax Credits Act 2002, Sch 3 para 49; SI 2000/805, Arts 6, 8*].

By concession, zero-rating also applies where the goods, although of a kind made available for purchase by the general public under (i) above, are by reason of their poor quality not fit to be so made available. This concession will benefit many charities, particularly those selling scrap clothing to rag merchants or those who are prevented under safety legislation from selling certain goods to the public (e.g. second-hand electrical goods and toys). (VAT Notice 48, ESC 3.21; Business Brief 13/97).

Where a rescue charity takes steps to return genuinely lost animals to their owners so that those offered for re-homing have been deliberately abandoned, the animals given to the charity by the local authority, police and members of the public have been donated (as well as those directly donated by the original owners) and therefore can be zero-rated when sold by the charity (*Gables Farm Dogs and Cats Home* (VTD 20519) (TVC 11.2)). HMRC have accepted this decision. (HMRC Brief 14/08).

(b) Export of goods

Export of any goods by a charity is zero-rated. [*VATA 1994, Sch 8 Group 15 Item 3*]. Proof of export is required. See **21.24 EXPORTS**.

The export is treated as a supply made by the charity in the UK and in the course or furtherance of a business carried on by the charity. [*VATA 1994, s 30(5); FA 1995, s 28*]. This enables a charity to reclaim any VAT paid on the purchase of the goods and any overheads of exporting them (or to register for VAT in order to do so) where the VAT would not otherwise be deductible (e.g. where the goods are given away overseas as part of a non-business activity such as relief aid).

Zero-rated supplies to or for charities

[12.7] The following supplies to charities are zero-rated.

(a) Talking books for the blind and disabled

The supply to the Royal National Institute for the Blind, the National Listening Library or other similar charity of

- (i) magnetic tape specially adapted for the recording and reproduction of speech for the blind or severely handicapped;
- (ii) apparatus designed or specially adapted for the making on magnetic tape, by way of transfer of recorded speech from another magnetic tape, of a recording as in (vi) below;
- (iii) apparatus designed or specially adapted for transfer to magnetic tapes of a recording made by apparatus within (ii) above;
- (iv) apparatus for rewinding magnetic tape described in (vi) below;
- (v) apparatus designed or specially adapted for the reproduction from recorded magnetic tape of speech for the blind or severely handicapped which is not available for use otherwise than by them;
- (vi) magnetic tape on which has been recorded speech for the blind or severely handicapped, such recording being suitable for reproduction only in the apparatus mentioned in (v) above;
- (vii) apparatus solely for the making on a magnetic tape of a sound recording which is for use by the blind or severely handicapped;
- (viii) parts and accessories (other than a magnetic tape for use with apparatus in (vii) above) for goods comprised in (i) to (vii) above; and
- (ix) the supply of a service of repair or maintenance of any goods within (i) to (viii) above.

Included is the letting on hire of eligible goods under (i) to (vii) above. [*VATA 1994, Sch 8 Group 4 Item 1*].

(b) Wireless sets for the blind

Wireless receiving sets or apparatus solely for the making and reproduction of sound recording on a magnetic tape permanently contained on a cassette. In each case, the goods must be solely for gratuitous loan to the blind. Included is the letting on hire of eligible goods. [*VATA 1994, Sch 8 Group 4 Item 2*].

(c) Aids for disabled persons

Certain goods to be made available to persons with disabilities and services of adapting, repairing and installing goods for such persons. See **28.14** to **28.34** HEALTH AND WELFARE.

(d) Donations of goods

The donation of any 'goods' for sale, export or letting by

- a charity; or
- a taxable person who is a 'profits-to-charity' person in respect of the goods.

'*Goods*' means goods in the normal sense of the word. It does not, in particular, include anything that is not goods, even though *VATA 1994* or any other enactment provides that the supply of it is, or is treated as, a supply of goods. Land, for example, is therefore excluded from zero-rating under these provisions.

Goods are donated for letting only if they are donated for letting, re-letting after the end of any first or subsequent letting *and* sale, export or disposal as waste if not, or when no longer, used for letting.

A taxable person is a '*profits-to-charity*' person in respect of any goods if

- he has agreed in writing (whether or not by deed) to transfer to a charity his profits from supplies and lettings of the goods; or
- his profits from supplies and lettings of the goods are otherwise payable to a charity.

[*VATA 1994, Sch 8 Group 15 Item 2; SI 2000/805, Arts 6, 8*].

(e) Lifeboats

Lifeboats, including repairs and maintenance, spares and accessories, and fuel for use in a lifeboat supplied to a charity providing rescue and assistance at sea. See **70.14 TRANSPORT AND FREIGHT**.

(f) Advertising

Subject to the exclusions below, the supply to a charity of

(i) a right to make known an advertisement by means of any medium of communication with the 'public';
(ii) making known an advertisement by means of such a medium;
(iii) services of design or production of an advertisement that is, or was intended to be, made known by means of such a medium (e.g. the design of a poster or the filming or recording of an advertisement to be broadcast); and
(iv) goods closely related to a supply within (iii) above. This would include
  - a finished article like a film or recorded cassette;
  - an element to be incorporated in the advertisement such as a photograph, picture or a sound track; or
  - all alternative versions of an advertisement produced, to see which works best, even if it is the intention that only one version will be used.

(VAT Notice 701/58/02, para 4.2).

Exclusions

Zero-rating does not apply in the following cases.

- Neither (i) or (ii) above includes a supply where any of the members of the public (whether individuals or other persons) who are reached though the medium are 'selected' by or on behalf of the charity. '*Selected*' includes selection by address (whether postal address or telephone number, e-mail address or other address for electronic communications purposes) or at random.
- Selected people could be individually named people, all those at the same address (e.g. family groups) or everyone in a particular building. Advertisements targeted at general groups (e.g. readers of a trade or religious magazine) are not considered to be selected. Neither are groups in particular parts of the country who are, for example, targeted for a general poster campaign in their area. (VAT Notice 701/58/02, paras 3.2, 3.3).
- Direct mail (by post, fax and e-mail) and telesales are both excluded from zero-rating because they are not a supply of advertising time or space but are marketing and advertising addressed to selected individuals or groups. (Individual elements of a postal package may qualify for zero-rating as **PRINTED MATTER, ETC. (54)** or under the class concession for goods used by charities in connection with collecting monetary donations (see (*g*) below).) (VAT Notice 701/58/02, para 3.4).
- None of (i)–(iv) above include any supply used to create, or contribute to, a website that is the charity's own. For this purpose, a website is the charity's own even though hosted by another person. Zero-rating does not therefore apply to advertising in, on or through a charity's own website whether or not the website is owned, rented or loaned to the charity. (VAT Notice 701/58/02, para 3.7).
- Neither of (iii) or (iv) above include a supply to a charity that is used directly by the charity to design or produce an advertisement.
- Where the supply is not directly to a charity but to one of its trading companies, e.g. a wholly-owned subsidiary.
- Any method of advertising which is not a supply of someone else's advertising time and space or is in the form of general marketing and promotion, including direct mail and telesales (see above); anything on the charity's own website (see above); advertisements where there is no supply of time and space to the charity (e.g. advertisements on a charity's own greetings cards); exhibition stands and space; services of distribution; and commemorative items whether or not they bear the charity's logo (e.g. pens and adult clothing). (VAT Notice 701/58/02, para 3.8).

[*VATA 1994, Sch 8 Group 15 Items 8–8C; SI 2000/805*].

The relief covers all types of advertisement on any subject, including staff recruitment. There is no requirement that they mention the name of the charity or show its logo to obtain relief. The wide relief is allowed in the expectation that charities will only place advertisements which comply with their charitable objects. The relief does not override charity law or the need to comply with the British Codes of Advertising or any other relevant regulations.

Zero-rating applies to advertisements placed in any medium which communicates with the public, including conventional advertising media such as television, cinema, billboards, sides of vehicles, newspapers and printed publications. The important factor is whether the advertisement is placed in someone else's time or space. If space is sold to a charity for advertising on other items, such as beer mats, calendars, till rolls, etc. this will be covered by the zero rate although the sale of the items themselves is not zero-rated (unless qualifying in their own right, e.g. advertising on books or children's clothing).

(VAT Notice 701/58/02, paras 2.3, 3.1).

Services involving advertising agencies

If a charity uses an advertising agency instead of contacting the suppliers of advertising or printing direct, the VAT liability depends on whether the agency is acting as a principal or an agent and normal VAT rules for agent/principal agreements apply. See **3 AGENTS** generally but broadly

- where an advertising agency is the principal, the advertising agency's supply of qualifying advertising time or space (e.g. television broadcasting time) and associated production costs to the charity are zero-rated but supplies to the agency are standard-rated; and
- where an advertising agency acts solely as an agent, the agency fees, charged to the charity, are standard-rated. The supply of the advertising time or space is direct to the charity and eligible for zero-rating under this relief in the normal way.

(VAT Notice 701/58/02, para 4.4).

Pay-per-click advertisements

Pay-per-click (PPC) charity advertising is used by organisations on search engines such as Google to encourage searchers to click on the organisation's link. The organisation pays the search engine provider an agreed amount each time their website is accessed through the sponsored link. HMRC previously took the view that a PPC-sponsored link was not an advertisement itself but simply a means of access to the charity's website. As such, HMRC considered the costs of providing PPC were excluded from zero-rating by *VATA 1994, Sch 8, Group 15, Note 10B*, which excludes zero-rating on the costs of providing a charity's website. Following representations from charities, HMRC have revised their VAT treatment and now accept that PPC-sponsored links appearing on search engine websites are advertisements for the purpose of *Items 8 and 8A*, and qualify for zero-rating when supplied to a charity. It follows that the supply of copyright and design services associated with such sponsored links fall within the zero-rating. However, HMRC still maintain that services supplied by copywriters and designers for the purpose of search engine optimisation (structuring a website so that it contains as many keywords as possible) do not qualify for relief; and nor does the listing of a charity in the results of a search engine ('natural hits').

(HMRC Brief 25/10).

Claiming relief

A supplier is responsible for determining the liability of the supplies he makes and must be sure that all the relevant conditions for relief are met. He must take reasonable steps to check with the charity any condition which he cannot verify for himself. For this reason, it is recommended that a charity gives its supplier a declaration that the specific conditions for the claimed relief are fulfilled. See VAT Notice 701/58/02, Part 10 for a suggested form of declaration. Other types of declaration (whether in paper form, faxed or electronic) that contain sufficient verifiable information to accurately identify the customer are acceptable to HMRC. Declarations are not always required, e.g. when a charity requests repeat orders and the information contained in a declaration for the first order has not changed. If a supplier has taken reasonable steps to check the validity of a declaration but fails to identify an inaccuracy and in good faith makes the supplies concerned at the zero rate, HMRC will not seek to recover the VAT due from the supplier. See HMRC ESC 3.11. (VAT Notice 701/58/02, paras 10.1–10.5).

(g) Goods used by charities in connection with collecting monetary donations

By concession, supplies of the following goods to a charity may be treated as if they were zero-rated.

(i) Lapel stickers or attachments designed to be worn on the lapel, which are of no intrinsic value, low cost to the charity and are given as a token in acknowledgement of a donation.

Included are paper stickers, ribbons, artificial flowers (if used as a symbol of the charity) and metal pins and badges. Large items for decorating buildings, vehicles, monuments, etc. are not eligible for relief even if bigger versions of a lapel badge.

Emblems or badges given in return for any non-specified donation or a suggested donation of up to £1 are considered to be of no intrinsic value or low cost. Lapel attachments which are offered for a fixed price, even if this is less than £1, do no qualify for relief because they are not given away freely. Relief will apply if a charity suggests a donation of £1.

If a charity makes its own lapel attachments, equipment for manufacturing badges is not covered by the concession but where it buys identifiable constituent parts which it will assemble into badges in-house, these come within the concession.

(ii) Component parts of items described in (i) above when supplied for self-assembly.

(iii) Any form of receptacle which
- is manufactured specifically for the purpose of collecting donated money;
- is used solely for collecting money for charity;
- is, or will be, clearly marked as collecting for a named charity; and
- can be secured by lock or tamper evident seal.

Examples of receptacles which might be made to comply with the above requirements are pre-printed card collecting boxes, moulded plastic collecting boxes, and models in any material including hollow plaster, wood, base metal or glass. Boxes may be of types that are hand held, floor standing, wall mounted or for placing on a table-top or shop counter. Boxes of greater value, such as those made of precious metal, are not zero-rated. Boxes where a simple balance mechanism moves money from one level to another or the weight of the coin causes it to roll helter-skelter fashion into the box are included; but more elaborate boxes which have additional purposes (e.g. gaming or quiz machines) or have some form of mechanical entertainment are not covered by the concession.

All boxes must bear the name of the charity, for example, by indelible printing or embossing or having raised letters, or allow for the charity name to be added later.

(iv) Bucket lids, designed to fit buckets and provide a secure seal, for use solely in connection with collecting money for charity.

(v) Pre-printed letters the primary purpose of which is to appeal for money for the charity (not necessarily including the addressees' particulars).

(vi) Envelopes used in conjunction with letters in (v) above for forwarding donations, provided that they are over-printed with an appeal request related to that contained in the letter.

(vii) Outer envelopes used in conjunction with letters in (v) above provided that they are over-printed with an appeal request related to that contained in the letter.

(viii) Pre-printed collecting envelopes appealing for money (of the type used by the welfare charities and which are usually hand delivered to domestic premises).

(ix) Stewardship envelopes used for planned giving which, as a minimum requirement, are pre-printed with the name of the relevant place of worship or other charity.

Plain envelopes bearing only a symbol such as a cross printed on them, and available from retailers as general stationery, do not qualify.

The Commissioners may withdraw or restrict the application of this concession if they have reasonable cause to believe that it is being abused.

(VAT Notice 48, ESC 3.3).

There is a separate concession (the 'package test') for determining the liability of a mixed supply of printed items (e.g. items for a mailshot). That concession has been extended to some of the charity stationery zero-rated under the concession for charities above. See **54.16** **PRINTED MATTER, ETC.**

(VAT Notice 701/58/02, paras 6.2, 6.4, 7.1–7.3, 7.5, 8.1, 8.3, 8.4, Part 12).

Claiming relief

A supplier is responsible for determining the liability of the supplies he makes and must be sure that all the relevant conditions for relief are met. He must take reasonable steps to check with the charity any condition which he cannot verify for himself. For this reason, it is recommended that a charity gives its supplier a declaration that the specific conditions for the claimed relief are fulfilled. See VAT Notice 701/58/02, Part 10 for a suggested form of declaration. Other types of declaration (whether in paper form, faxed or electronic) that contain sufficient verifiable information to accurately identify the customer are acceptable to HMRC. Declarations are not always required, e.g. when a charity requests repeat orders and the information contained in a declaration for the first order has not changed. If a supplier has taken reasonable steps to check the validity of a declaration but fails to identify an inaccuracy and in good faith makes the supplies concerned at the zero rate, HMRC will not seek to recover the VAT due from the supplier. See HMRC ESC 3.11. (VAT Notice 701/58/02, paras 10.1–10.5).

(h) Medicinal products

The supply to a charity

- providing care or medical or surgical treatment for human beings or animals; or
- engaging in medical or veterinary research

of a 'medicinal product' or 'veterinary medicinal product' where the supply is solely for use by the charity in such care, treatment or research.

'*Medicinal product*' means any 'substance' or article (not being an instrument, apparatus or appliance) which is for use wholly or mainly in either or both of the following ways, viz. by being 'administered' to one or more human beings for 'medicinal purposes' or as an 'ingredient' in the preparation of a substance or article to be so administered.

'*Veterinary medicinal product*' means any substance (or combination of substances) (i) presented as having properties for treating or preventing disease in animals; or (ii) that may be used in, or administered to, animals with a view *either* to restoring, correcting or modifying physiological functions by exerting a pharmacological, immunological or metabolic action *or* to making a medical diagnosis.

'*Substance*' means any natural or artificial substance, whether in solid or liquid form or in the form of a vapour or gas.

'*Administer*' means administering whether orally, by injection or by introduction into the body in any other way, or by external application, whether by direct contact with the body or not and includes both administering a substance in its existing state or after it has been dissolved, diluted or mixed with some other substance used as a vehicle. See also *Pasante Healthcare Ltd* (VTD 19724) (TVC 11.30) where the tribunal held that condoms given by a charity to its clients were being 'administered for medicinal purposes' and therefore the supply to the charity could be zero-rated. HMRC have accepted this decision. (Business Brief 16/06).

Use for '*medicinal purpose*' includes use for treating or preventing of disease; diagnosing disease or ascertaining physiological condition; contraception; inducing anaesthesia; or otherwise bringing about some alteration in the physical or physiological state of the patient or animal.

'*Ingredient*', in relation to the manufacture or preparation of a substance, includes anything which is the sole active ingredient of that substance as manufactured or prepared.

[*VATA 1994, Sch 8 Group 15 Item 9; Medicines Act 1968, s 130(2)(9), s 132; SI 2006/2407, Reg 2, Sch 9 para 10*].

(i) Substances for medical or veterinary research

The supply to a charity of a 'substance' directly used for synthesis or testing in the course of medical or veterinary research. See (*h*) above for '*substance*'. [*VATA 1994, Sch 8 Group 15 Item 10*].

(j) Major interests in land and buildings

The grant by a person constructing a building of a major interest in it provided the building is intended solely for use for a relevant residential purpose or use for a relevant charitable purpose. See **42.1 LAND AND BUILDINGS: ZERO AND REDUCED RATE SUPPLIES AND DIY HOUSEBUILDERS.**

(k) Construction services

Supplies to a charity of services in the course of construction of a new building intended solely for use for a relevant residential purpose or use for a relevant charitable purpose. See **42.7 LAND AND BUILDINGS: ZERO AND REDUCED RATE SUPPLIES AND DIY HOUSEBUILDERS.**

Proof of zero-rating

Zero-rating of items under (*a*), (*b*), (*e*), (*h*) and (*j*) above may depend on the *use* rather than the nature of the item. The charity must, therefore, give the supplier a certified declaration that the goods are to be used for the specified purpose. Declaration forms are not supplied by HMRC but examples can be found in VAT Notice 701/6 Supplement. These can be reproduced in any convenient way, e.g. by incorporating them in any order form. It is the supplier's responsibility to take reasonable steps to satisfy himself that the charity is entitled to zero-rating and the declaration is correct. Where, however, despite taking all reasonable steps, nonetheless the supplier fails to identify the inaccuracy and in good faith makes the supplies concerned at the zero rate, HMRC will not seek to recover the VAT due from the supplier. (VAT Notice 48, ESC 3.11).

Importation

Imports by charities of any goods within (*a*), (*b*), (*e*), (*h*) and (*j*) above can be zero-rated under the same conditions as supplies made to them in the UK. The appropriate declaration (see under *Proof of zero-rating* above) must be presented with the customs entry form.

Charity-funded equipment for medical, veterinary uses, etc.

[12.8] The following supplies are zero-rated.

(a) Relevant goods (see (1) below) supplied *for donation* to a nominated eligible body (see (2) below). To qualify for relief
- the funds for the purchase (or the letting or hire) must be provided by a charity or from voluntary contributions (see (3) below); and
- where the *donee* of the goods is not a charity, it must not have contributed, wholly or in part, to the purchase (or hiring) of the goods.

[*VATA 1994, Sch 8 Group 15, Item 4 and Notes (5A), (6) and (9)*]. This *Item* zero-rates qualifying goods and services when they are supplied to any person, body or organisation for donation to an eligible body. (VAT Notice 701/6/03, para 6.1).

(b) Relevant goods (see (1) below) supplied to an eligible body (see (2) below). To qualify for relief
- the eligible body must pay for the relevant goods (or hire them) with funds provided by a charity or from voluntary contributions (see (3) below); and
- where the eligible body is not a charity, it must not have contributed, wholly or in part, to the purchase (or hiring) of the goods.

[*VATA 1994, Sch 8 Group 15, Item 5 and Notes (7) and (9)*].

(c) Relevant goods (see (1) below) supplied (or hired) to an eligible body which is a charitable institution providing care or medical or surgical treatment (see (4) below) for handicapped persons (see (5) below). [*VATA 1994, Sch 8 Group 15, Item 5* and *Note (9)*].

(d) The repair and maintenance of relevant goods (see (1) below) owned by an eligible body (see (2) below), and any goods supplied in connection with the repair and maintenance, provided
- the supply is paid for with funds which have been provided by a charity or from voluntary contributions (see (3) below); and
- where the owner (or hirer) of the goods repaired or maintained is not a charity, it must not have contributed, wholly or in part, to those funds.

[*VATA 1994, Sch 8 Group 15, Items 6, 7 and Note (8)*].

(e) By concession, relevant goods (see (1) below) supplied to a charity
- whose sole purpose and function is to provide a range of care services to meet the personal needs of handicapped people (see (5) below) (e.g. a charity established to: provide care or welfare services to disabled people; lobby on behalf of disabled people; or fund medical research into the causes, prevention or cure of disablement); or
- which provides transport services predominantly to handicapped people.

Zero-rating also applies to the repair and maintenance of those goods and the supply of any further goods in connection with that repair and maintenance.

In theory, any relevant goods can be supplied at the zero rate under this concession. In practice, the type of relevant goods which are most likely to be purchased by these charities are motor vehicles adapted for use by disabled passengers (with space for at least one wheelchair user) or a motor vehicle to transport mainly blind, deaf, mentally impaired or terminally sick persons. Boats that are designed or permanently adapted for use by disabled people are also eligible for zero-rating.

It is the responsibility of the purchasing charity to prove that it is entitled to buy the relevant goods at the zero rate. To avoid charities having to keep detailed records simply to prove eligibility, HMRC will use records and documentation already kept by the charity for non-VAT purposes, for example,

- its charitable aims and objectives;
- its publicity and advertising material;
- any documents issued for the purpose of obtaining funds from a third party such as a local authority;
- evidence of its day-to-day operations; and
- any other relevant evidence.

When a charity claims zero-rating on an adapted motor vehicle (or any other relevant goods), it must issue a certificate to the supplier claiming eligibility for zero-rating and, where required, it must attach documentary evidence (as outlined above) to support the claim. (Some documents, particularly funding documents or aims and objectives, are lengthy. A charity need not provide the whole document, but it should provide the parts which will enable it to make the declaration for relief.) The charity should make up two sets of the documents listed above, one set for itself and one to present to *each* supplier. This means the charity in reality has to search for and collate the information only once. It can then be retained by the charity for any future supplies. A charity need only provide the supporting evidence once to each supplier unless there have been relevant changes to its operation.

(VAT Notice 48, ESC 3.19; VAT Information Sheet 8/98, paras 3.3–3.5; VAT Notice 701/6/03, para 3.4.1). See Annexes B to E of the VAT Information Sheet for examples of documents which might be produced by charities intending to purchase an adapted motor vehicle.

(1) Relevant goods

These comprise the following.

(a) Medical, scientific, computer, video, sterilising, laboratory or refrigeration equipment

For use in

- medical or veterinary research (i.e. original research into disease and injury of human beings or animals);
- medical or veterinary training (i.e. training doctors, nurses, surgeons (including dental and veterinary surgeons) and other professionals involved in medical or veterinary diagnosis or treatment. The overall programme of training must include the physical application by the students of theoretical knowledge so that the teaching of subjects such as biology and zoology, where the trainee has no practical medical or veterinary involvement with patients, is not regarded as training for these purposes); or
- medical or veterinary diagnosis or treatment (i.e. the diagnosis and treatment of a physical or mental abnormality by a medical or paramedical practitioner or a veterinary surgeon).

Included are parts and accessories for use with any such equipment.

[*VATA 1994, Sch 8 Group 15, Note (3)(a)(c)*]. (VAT Notice 701/6/03, para 4.3).

'*Equipment*' means articles designed for a specific purpose. It will usually be durable but certain disposable items (e.g. syringes which are designed to be used once only) may still be equipment. *Not included* are

- bulk materials (e.g. liquids, powders, sheets, pellets, and granules);
- clothing (other than specialist medical equipment such as surgical masks, gowns and gloves); and
- consumables (e.g. chemical reagents, fuel, ink, medicines, oil, paper, and cleaning and sterilising fluids).

(VAT Notice 701/6/03, para 4.2.1).

The equipment only qualifies for relief if purchased 'for use in' medical or veterinary research, etc. Where equipment is to be used partly for a qualifying use and partly for other use, it is only eligible for relief where its main use is a qualifying use. In this context, 'main' means real, substantial and continuing. (VAT Notice 701/6/03, para 4.3).

Medical equipment is equipment that has features or characteristics that identify it as having been designed for a medical (including dental) purpose or function, such as the diagnosis or treatment of patients.

Eligible are anaesthetic apparatus; aprons (lead lined for X-ray protection); bandages; bedpans; highly specialised beds (e.g. net suspension beds, medical water beds); catheters; medical clamps; dental chairs, drills, mirrors and spittoons; drip poles; endoscopes; electro-cardiographs; eye test charts; adjustable examination couches; first aid kits (supplied as pre-packaged units); forceps; surgical gloves; heart pacemakers; hypodermic needles; identification bracelets for patients; kidney bowls; mattresses specially designed for the relief/prevention of pressure sores; medicine measures (graduated); operating lights; patient trolleys and stretchers; specialised physiotherapy equipment (other than gymnasium equipment); orthopaedic pillows specially designed and used for neck or spinal injuries; radiography equipment; renal dialysis units; resuscitation equipment; scalpels; sphygmomanometers; splints; stethoscopes; surgical gloves, gowns and masks; suture needles; swabs; clinical thermometers; tongue depressors; wound dressings; X-ray films and plates; medical X-ray machines and X-ray viewers.

Not eligible are alarm bracelets; aprons (not lead lined); blankets; cotton wool; disinfectants; drugs trolleys; gloves (other than surgical); gymnasium equipment; hearing aids; nurse call systems; occupational therapy materials; overbed tables; pagers; pillows (other than specially designed orthopaedic pillows as above); screens; towels; and uniforms. (VAT Notice 701/6/03, paras 4.2.2, 4.11).

Dental simulation equipment and artificial heads for use in training dentists have both been held to be medical equipment. See *The Anglodent Company* (VTD 16891) (TVC 11.4) and *Medical & Dental Staff Training Ltd* (VTD 17031) (TVC 11.5).

Scientific equipment is equipment designed to perform a scientific function. It includes precision measuring equipment and analytical equipment. Equipment that is not designed to perform a scientific function, but merely works on a scientific principle, is not scientific equipment. *Eligible* are barometers; centrifuges; microscopes; non-clinical thermometers; spectrometers; weighing machines; and non-medical X-ray machines. (VAT Notice 701/6/03, paras 4.2.3, 4.11).

Computer equipment includes computer hardware. Machinery or other equipment, that is either operated by computer or has computerised components, is not computer equipment. *Eligible* are computer keyboards; computer disks, tapes, mouses, printers, screens, and screen filters (as accessories to computer equipment); and computer servers. *Not eligible* is computer stationery. (VAT Notice 701/6/03, paras 4.2.4, 4.11). See (*g*) below for certain computer software.

Video equipment includes video recording and playback equipment. *Eligible* are video cameras, tapes, players and monitors. (VAT Notice 701/6/03, paras 4.2.6, 4.11).

Sterilising equipment includes specialised equipment using steam or other high temperature processes. *Eligible* are autoclaves and bedpan washers with sterilising steam cycles. *Not eligible* are microwave ovens and other cooking appliances even if they can be used to sterilise; and sterilising solutions. (VAT Notice 701/6/03, paras 4.2.7, 4.11).

Laboratory equipment includes equipment designed for use in a laboratory. *Eligible* are Bunsen burners; centrifuges; cryostats; fume cupboards; laboratory benches and glassware; microscopes; microtomes; pipettes; specialised sinks and catchpots; and test tubes. *Not eligible* are ordinary cupboards, lockers, seats and other furniture even if used to equip a laboratory; bulk materials such as liquids, powders, sheets, pellets, granules; general purpose items used to equip a laboratory; consumables such as chemical reagents, medicines, and cleaning and sterilising fluids; and laboratory animals. (VAT Notice 701/6/03, paras 4.2.8, 4.11).

In *Research Establishment* (VTD 19095) (TVC 11.9) a ventilation system was held to qualify as laboratory equipment as it had been specifically designed to control not only temperature and humidity but also pressure, allowing experiments to take place under laboratory conditions controlled to the highest practicable level.

Following the decision in *Supplier Ltd* (VTD 18247) (TVC 11.13) HMRC accept that cage and tray liners and research grade litter, bedding and nesting materials are accessories (see below) when designed for use in or with specialised laboratory caging. (Business Brief 21/03).

Refrigeration equipment includes all cooling and freezing equipment, whether designed for industrial, domestic or any other purpose. *Eligible* are deep freezer and ice-making machines. (VAT Notice 701/6/03, paras 4.2.9, 4.11).

Parts means integral components without which the equipment is incomplete. (VAT Notice 701/6/03, para 4.5.2).

Accessories means optional extras that are not necessary for the equipment to operate in its normal course, but which are used to

- improve the operation of the equipment; or

- enable it to be used, or be used to better effect, in particular circumstances.

This would include, for example, a printer for use with a computer; a specially designed camera for use with a microscope; or a rack for holding test tubes. Not included are items which have independent uses (e.g. televisions); accessories to accessories; and generic bulk substances (e.g. liquids, powders, sheets, pellets and granules).

(VAT Notice 701/6/03, para 4.5.2).

Whether an item is an accessory is to be judged subjectively and the fact that the item can also be used otherwise than with relevant goods does not necessarily mean that it fails to qualify as an accessory. See *Royal Midland Counties Home for Disabled People v C & E Commrs,* Ch D 2001, [2002] STC 395 (TVC 11.12) where a stand-by generator, bought as a precaution against power failure, was held to be an accessory where most of the patients were dependant on electrically-powered medical equipment, even though the generator would also power lights, televisions, etc in the event of a power failure.

Ineligible equipment is equipment purchased or hired for any other use than medical or veterinary research, training, diagnosis or treatment and is not eligible for zero-rating under this provision. This includes equipment for

- general biological studies;
- environmental research;
- research into animal husbandry or food production;
- general administration; or
- domestic or leisure purposes.

Examples of ineligible equipment include air conditioners; security and smoke alarms; still cameras; catering equipment; cleaning equipment; closed circuit television systems; curtains; fuel; lockers; overhead projecting units; stationery; tape recorders; television sets; waste disposal bags, boxes, jars and sacks; and waste disposal machinery.

(VAT Notice 701/6/03, paras 4.3, 4.11).

(b) Ambulances (including parts and accessories) [VATA 1994, Sch 8 Group 15, Note (3)(b)(c)].

An '*ambulance*' is an emergency vehicle used for transporting sick and injured people or animals. It includes specially equipped air ambulances or watercraft. The vehicle must have

- the front and both sides permanently fitted with signs indicating that the vehicle is an ambulance;
- in the case of an ambulance for transporting human patients, adequate door space for the loading of a patient on a stretcher;
- seating at the rear of the driver or pilot for at least one attendant; and
- at least one stretcher that, with handles extended, measures at least 1.95 metres, together with permanent fittings to hold it in position. (This size specification applies only to ambulances that transport human patients. For ambulances that transport animals, any reasonable lifting or carrying equipment is acceptable.)

'*Parts*' are integral components without which the ambulance is incomplete. '*Accessories*' means optional extras that are not necessary for the ambulance to operate but are used to improve the operation or enable the ambulance to be used, or be used to better effect, in particular circumstances.
(VAT Notice 701/6/03, para 4.4).

(c) Goods used by people with disabilities of a kind described in VATA 1994, Sch 8 Group 12 Item 2 [VATA 1994, Sch 8 Group 15, Note (3)(d)].

This covers medical and surgical appliances; certain electrically or mechanically adjustable beds, sanitary devices, chair or stair lifts, hoists and lifters; motor vehicles capable of carrying up to 12 people designed, or substantially and permanently adapted, for the carriage of a person in a wheelchair or on a stretcher; boats designed, or substantially and permanently adapted, for use by a disabled person; and other equipment and appliances designed solely for use by a chronically sick or disabled person. See **28.15–28.24 HEALTH AND WELFARE** for full details.

(d) Motor vehicles adapted for wheelchairs

Motor vehicles (other than vehicles with more than 50 seats) designed or substantially and permanently adapted for the safe carriage of a handicapped person (see (5) below) in a wheelchair provided that

- vehicles with 17 to 26 seats have provision for at least two such persons;
- vehicles with 27 to 36 seats have provision for at least three such persons;
- vehicles with 37 to 46 seats have provision for at least four such persons; and
- vehicles with 47 to 50 seats have provision for at least five such persons.

The vehicle must have either a fitted electrically or hydraulically operated lift or, in the case of a vehicle with less than 17 seats, a fitted ramp to provide access for a passenger in a wheelchair.

[*VATA 1994, Sch 8 Group 15, Note (3)(e)*].

(e) Motor vehicles for the handicapped or terminally sick

Motor vehicles with 7 to 50 seats for use by an eligible body (see (2) below) providing care for blind, deaf, mentally handicapped or terminally sick persons mainly to transport such persons. [*VATA 1994, Sch 8 Group 15, Note (3)(f)*].

(f) Telecommunication, aural, visual, light enhancing or heat detecting equipment

Telecommunication, aural, visual, light enhancing or heat detecting equipment (not being equipment ordinarily supplied for private or recreational use) solely for use for the purpose of rescue or first aid services undertaken by a charitable institution providing such services. [*VATA 1994, Sch 8 Group 15, Note (3)(g)*].

Eligible are image intensifiers, heat seekers and similar specialist equipment used to locate casualties; flares used to illuminate large areas for search purposes; and two-way radios that are pre-calibrated to the emergency frequency. *Not eligible* are general items such as mobile phones and pagers, binoculars, torches, searchlights and loudhailers. (VAT Notice 701/6/03, para 4.8).

Early warning sirens were held to be aural equipment in *Severnside Siren Trust Ltd* (VTD 16640) (TVC 11.14).

(g) Computer software

Computer software when purchased by an eligible body (see (2) below) solely for use in medical research, diagnosis or treatment. [*VATA 1994, Sch 8 Group 15, Note (10)*].

Zero-rating does not apply to computer software or programs that are purchased

- for a purpose other than medical research, diagnosis or treatment; or
- by a person, body or organisation other than an eligible body (even if purchased for *donation* to a nominated eligible body).

(h) Resuscitation training models

By concession, human resuscitation training models (i.e. models which include a head and torso) acquired for use in first-aid training in either 'cardiopulmonary resuscitation' or defibrillation techniques or both, together with parts and accessories for training models used for such purposes. '*Cardiopulmonary resuscitation*' means a combination of expired air ventilation and chest compression. (VAT Notice 748, ESC 3.25). Other resuscitation dummies, including intravenous cannulation models, blood transfusion models and static anatomical models are not within the scope of the concession and therefore not eligible for relief. (Business Brief 10/99).

Installation

If the normal selling price of the relevant goods includes an amount for fixing or connecting to mains services and/or testing the equipment on site, the whole selling price can be included in the relief. Any building work (e.g. removal of walls or reinforcing floors) necessary in order to install large items of equipment is standard-rated even if carried out by the supplier of the equipment. (VAT Notice 701/6/03, para 4.10).

(2) **Eligible body**

Eligible body means any of the following.

- A Strategic Health Authority (previously Health Authority) or Special Health Authority in England.
- A Health Authority, Special Health Authority or Local Health Authority in Wales.
- A Health Board in Scotland.
- A Health and Social Services Board in Northern Ireland.

- A hospital or research institution whose activities are 'not carried on for profit'.
  '*Not carried on for profit*' means that the hospital or research establishment
  - (a) cannot, and does not, distribute any profit achieved; and
  - (b) applies any surplus that arises from supplies of hospital or research services to the furtherance of its objectives.
- A charitable institution providing care or medical or surgical treatment (see (4) below) for handicapped persons which satisfies one of the following conditions.
  - (a) It provides the care or medical or surgical treatment in a relevant establishment (see (6) below), the relevant goods are used in that establishment, and the majority of persons who receive the care or treatment there are handicapped (see (5) below).
    HMRC accept that a charitable institution may still be an eligible body if, for a temporary period, handicapped people form less than 50% of the recipients of care or treatment services provided that, over an extended period, the majority of recipients are handicapped.
  - (b) It provides medical care (see (7) below) to handicapped persons (see (5) below) in their own homes, the relevant goods are medical equipment falling within (1)(*a*) above or are parts or accessories for use in or with such equipment, and the goods are used in, or in connection with, the provision of that care.
- The Common Services Agency for the Scottish Health Service, the Northern Ireland Central Services Agency for Health and Social Services, or the Isle of Man Health Services Board.
- A charitable institution providing rescue or first-aid services. Rescue services do not include the operation of a website to help practitioners involved in paediatric medicine to diagnose potential complications (*Isabel Medical Charity* (VTD 18209) (TVC 11.20)).
- A NHS trust established under *National Health Service and Community Care Act 1990, Part I* or *National Health Service (Scotland) Act 1978*.
- A Primary Care Trust established under *National Health Service Act 1977, s 16A*.

Non-eligible bodies under these provisions include day centres, residential care homes or providers of home care services

- that are not charities; or
- where over an extended period the majority of the recipients of care provided are not chronically sick or disabled people (see (5) below).

Animal charities qualify as eligible bodies if

- they are animal *hospitals* providing 'in-patient' facilities; or
- they provide rescue or first-aid services to animals.

Animal clinics or surgeries are not eligible bodies unless they are part of an animal hospital or are run by a charity that also provides rescue or first-aid services.

[*VATA 1994, Sch 8 Group 15 Items 4, 4A, 5A, 5B; FA 1997, s 34; SI 2000/503; SI 2002/2813*]. (VAT Notice 701/6/03, paras 3.3, 3.4.1, 3.5, 3.6).

(3) Voluntary contributions

Where a person, group or organisation contributes funds to an eligible body, and does not receive anything in return, this is a voluntary contribution or donation. Lottery funding is also regarded as a voluntary contribution for the purposes of this relief. (VAT Notice 701/6/03, para 5.1).

(4) Care or medical or surgical treatment

This includes protection, treatment, supervision, control or guidance that is provided to meet medical, physical, personal or domestic needs of an individual. Care or treatment will usually involve some personal contact between the provider and recipient. Examples include

- helping a person with daily personal needs (e.g. bathing, dressing, feeding or toileting);
- medical or surgical treatment;
- nursing sick or injured patients in a hospital, hospice or nursing home; and
- looking after or supervising vulnerable people.

Not included are catering, laundry and other services that do not require direct contact with the recipient.

(VAT Notice 701/6/03, para 3.4.2).

(5) Handicapped

Handicapped means chronically sick or disabled. [*VATA 1994, Sch 8 Group 15, Note (5)*].

Chronic sickness is a condition regarded as such by the medical profession. Disability is a physical or mental impairment that has a substantial and long-term adverse effect on a person's ability to carry out day-to-day activities. Frail elderly people who are not disabled, or people whose mobility is temporarily impaired by short-term illness or injury are not chronically sick or disabled for the purposes of this VAT relief. (VAT Notice 701/6/03, para 3.4.3).

(6) Relevant establishment

Relevant establishment means either of the following.

- A day centre other than one that exists primarily as a place for activities that are social or recreational or both.
  Examples of day centres which would qualify include charitable physiotherapy centres for disabled children and charitable centres that run daily rehabilitation or training classes for disabled adults.
- An institution which is approved, licensed or registered under the relevant social legislation or which is exempt from any such requirement by that legislation.

Examples include charitable hospices and residential care homes.

[*VATA 1994, Sch 8 Group 15, Note (4B); FA 1997, s 34*]. (VAT Notice 701/6/03, para 3.4.1).

(7) **Medical care**

Medical care includes medical treatment and the sort of care that a nurse might carry out or supervise (e.g. washing or feeding a patient, helping a patient out of bed, and administering drugs). It does not include assistance with general domestic tasks such as cooking, cleaning or shopping.

(VAT Notice 701/6/03, para 3.4.4).

Evidence of eligibility

The supplier is responsible for ensuring that all the conditions for zero-rating are met. As this may not always be evident at the time of supply, HMRC recommend that suppliers obtain a written declaration of eligibility from each customer who claims entitlement to VAT relief. The declaration should

- contain sufficient information to demonstrate that the conditions for the relief are satisfied; and
- be separate, or clearly distinguishable from, any order form or invoice against which the goods or services are supplied (i.e. a customer signing an order should not automatically be signing a declaration of eligibility for VAT relief).

Examples of declarations that might be obtained from a customer are reproduced in a Supplement to VAT Notice 701/7 dated April 1997. Any other declaration form used must require the purchaser to provide the same information.

In addition to a written declaration, suppliers may require evidence that the purchaser is an eligible body. This may include in the case of

- a charitable body, evidence that it is a charity;
- domiciliary care agencies, day centres or other establishments, evidence that care or treatment services are provided mainly to chronically sick or disabled people;
- charitable transport providers, evidence that transport services are provided mainly to disabled people;
- other charities, evidence that its sole purpose is the provision of services for, or on behalf of, chronically sick or disabled people.

Suppliers must retain evidence that any supply was eligible for relief.

The receipt of a declaration and/or other evidence from a customer does not authorise the zero-rating of a supply. A supplier must take reasonable steps to check any apparent inconsistencies and to confirm that any information given by the customer is correct. However, the purchaser has a responsibility to make truthful statements and to provide appropriate documentation to support this. HMRC will not, therefore, seek to recover VAT due from a supplier who has taken reasonable steps to check the validity of a declaration, but has failed to identify an inaccuracy, and, in good faith, has zero-rated a supply.

(VAT Notice 48, ESC 3.11; VAT Notice 701/6/03, paras 8.1–8.4).

Imports

Goods that meet all the conditions for zero-rating when purchased in the UK can be zero-rated on importation. Importers should lodge the relevant declaration of eligibility (see above) with HMRC at the point of importation. Special provisions apply to the importation of computer software. See **33.33 IMPORTS**. (VAT Notice 701/6/03, para 7.1).

Acquisitions from other EU countries

Where a VAT-registered eligible body acquires goods from another EU country, the normal rules for acquisitions apply. If the supply meets all the conditions for relief, no VAT is due. Eligibility declarations do not need to be provided to the overseas supplier but evidence that the supply is correctly zero-rated should be retained.

Where an eligible body is not VAT-registered, any goods acquired from another EU country are subject to VAT at the rate in force in that country. The UK relief for charity-funded equipment does not apply.

(VAT Notice 701/6/03, para 7.2).

Supplies to eligible bodies outside the UK

Apart from the specific UK Health Boards, etc., there is no requirement in the legislation that an eligible body must be within the UK. Therefore

- where a supply is made to an eligible body (i.e. a qualifying hospital, research institution or charitable institution) based in another EU country and that body is not VAT-registered there, this relief can be used to zero-rate the supply provided all the conditions are met; and
- if the customer is VAT-registered in another EU country or is outside the EU, the supply of goods can be zero-rated under the normal rules.

(VAT Notice 701/6/03, para 7.3).

Exempt supplies by charities

[12.9] Certain supplies by charities are exempt from VAT not because of the charitable status of the supplier but because they are covered by general application. See **20 EXEMPT SUPPLIES**. In addition, the exemptions in **12.10** and **12.11** below apply specifically to charities and certain other qualifying bodies.

Fund-raising events by charities and other qualifying bodies

[12.10] Subject to the exclusions below, the supply of goods and services in connection with an 'event' whose primary purpose is the raising of money and which is promoted as such is exempt from VAT where

- the supply of goods and services is by a 'charity' and the event is organised for charitable purposes by one or more charities;

- the supply of goods and services is by a 'qualifying body' and the event is organised exclusively for the body's own benefit; or
- the supply of goods and services is by a charity or a qualifying body and the event is organised, jointly by one or more charities and the qualifying body, exclusively for charitable purposes or that body's own benefit or a combination of those purposes.

[*VATA 1994, Sch 9 Group 12 Items 1 and 2; SI 2000/802*].

Evidence that an event was primarily organised to raise funds includes minutes of meetings, costings and similar documents. In order to show that the event is promoted for fund-raising purposes, the publicity material, ticket, etc should clearly refer to fund-raising such as 'fund-raising for', 'in aid of', 'help us to build' or 'help us to raise money for'. Examples should be retained as evidence. (Leaflet CWL4, para 3.16).

The exemption applies to

- all admission charges;
- the sale of commemorative brochures unless zero-rated under **54.4 PRINTED MATTER, ETC.**;
- the sale of advertising space in those brochures;
- any other items sold by the charity or qualifying body at the event (e.g. T-shirts, non-donated auctioned goods, etc.) unless the items would normally be zero-rated (e.g. children's T-shirts) in which case zero-rating applies; and
- sponsorship payments directly connected with the qualifying event.

The exemption does not apply to commemorative goods and souvenirs sold for a period after the qualifying fund-raising event. For example,

- video and audio recordings of the event, surplus T-shirts, mugs, etc will be standard-rated;
- commemorative programmes and children's T-shirts will remain zero-rated; and
- donated goods for sale may still be sold VAT-free provided the normal conditions are met.

(Leaflet CWL4, paras 4.7, 4.8).

'*Event*' includes an event accessed (wholly or partly) by means of electronic communications including an electronic communications network (such as the internet). [*VATA 1994, Sch 9 Group 12 Note 1; Communications Act 2003, Sch 17 para 129; SI 2000/802*]. HMRC regard an event as an incident with an outcome or a result so that activities of a semi-regular or continuous nature (e.g. the frequent operation of a shop or bar) cannot be an event. The relief is not intended to exempt normal trading activities. Events which may qualify include

- a ball, dinner dance, disco or barn dance;
- a performance (e.g. a concert or stage production);
- the showing of a film;
- a fete, fair or festival;
- a horticultural show;

- an exhibition, including art, history, science, etc.;
- a bazaar, jumble sale, car boot sale or good-as-new sale;
- sporting participation (including spectators) such as a sponsored walk or swim;
- sporting performances;
- games of skill, contests and quizzes;
- participation in an endurance event;
- a fireworks display;
- a dinner, lunch or barbecue; or
- an auction of bought-in goods (auction of donated goods is zero-rated).

(Leaflet CWL4, paras 3.2, 3.3).

'*Charity*' includes a body corporate which is wholly-owned by the charity if

- the body has agreed in writing (whether or not by deed) to transfer its profits from whatever source to a charity; or
- the body's profits from whatever source are otherwise payable to a charity.

[*VATA 1994, Sch 9 Group 12 Note 2; SI 2000/802*].

A '*qualifying body*' is

- a non-profit making body within **14.7**(*a*)–(*f*) **CLUBS AND ASSOCIATIONS**;
- any eligible body as defined in **57.10 RECREATION AND SPORT** whose principal purpose is the provision of facilities for persons to take part in sport and physical recreation; or
- any body which is an eligible body for the purposes of *VATA 1994, Sch 9 Group 13 Item 2* (exempt admission charges to entertainment, cultural activities, etc.) as defined in **57.7 RECREATION AND SPORT**.

[*VATA 1994, Sch 9 Group 12 Note 3; SI 2000/802*].

Exclusions

The following events are excluded from exemption.

(a) *Multiple events of the same kind at the same location.* Exemption does not apply to *any* event where in its financial year a charity or qualifying body organises (whether alone or in association with another charity or qualifying body) more than 15 events of the same kind in the same 'location' (i.e. if a charity or body organises 16 similar events in the same location in its financial year, none of those events are exempt). In determining whether the limit of 15 events has been exceeded, there can be disregarded any event of that kind at that location in a week during which the aggregate gross takings from events involving the charity or body of that kind in that location do not exceed £1,000.
Where a charity's or body's financial year is longer or shorter than a year, the maximum number of events qualifying for exemption is
15 × number of days in financial year ÷ 365
expressed to the nearest whole number.
[*VATA 1994, Sch 9 Group 12 Notes 4–7; SI 2000/802*].

'*Location*'. Similar kinds of events held in different locations qualify for exemption provided all the other conditions are met. For example, 20 balls held by a national charity in the same financial year, each in a different town, would all qualify for relief. In determining whether two events are held at the same location

- where events need to be held on special premises (e.g. a sports ground, swimming pool or theatre), each of these premises is a separate location;
- where an event is held in a complex of cinemas, theatres or concert halls, the location is the specific cinema, etc. in which the fund-raising event takes place; and
- a charity's entire website is regarded as a location for events held over the internet.

These rules are designed to be generous to charities that may hold a number of events of the same type in different locations but in the same town. HMRC will not accept arrangements such as weekly car boot sales, each held in different but adjacent fields, as constituting a separate location without considering whether such an arrangement is potentially distorting competition (see (*c*) below).

In determining the number of events held in any location, where an event such as a concert is repeated over successive evenings, each performance counts as a separate event. A single event which takes place at the same location for more than one day (e.g. a golf tournament) is accepted as one event.

(Leaflet CWL4, paras 3.5, 3.6).

(b) *Events where accommodation also provided.* An event does not qualify for exemption where accommodation in connection with the event is provided, directly or indirectly, by

- any of the charities or the qualifying body organising the event, or
- any charity connected with any charity organising the event

unless the accommodation so provided does not exceed two nights in total (whether or not consecutive) *and* the supply of accommodation does not fall within the **TOUR OPERATORS' MARGIN SCHEME (68)**.

[*VATA 1994, Sch 9 Group 12 Notes 8, 9; SI 2000/802*].

(c) *Distortion of competition.* An event does not qualify for exemption if it is likely to cause distortion of competition and place a commercial enterprise carried on by a taxable person at a disadvantage.

[*VATA 1994, Sch 9 Group 12 Note 11; SI 2000/802*].

Non-qualifying events

Supplies made by a charity or qualifying body at a fund-raising event which does not qualify for exemption are subject to VAT in the normal way. See **12.5**(1) above.

Welfare services

[12.11] The supply by a charity of welfare services, and of goods supplied in connection with those services, is exempt. [*VATA 1994, Sch 9 Group 7, Item 9*].

Identical provisions apply to such supplies made by public bodies, state-regulated private welfare institutions and state-regulated private welfare agencies. See **28.12 HEALTH AND WELFARE** for full details.

See **12.5**(21) above for welfare services supplied consistently below cost.

Reduced rate supplies by charities

[12.12] *With effect from 1 July 2006*, supplies of welfare advice or information by a charity (or a state-regulated private welfare institution or agency) are subject to a reduced rate of VAT of 5%. See **28.35 HEALTH AND WELFARE** for details.

Reduced rate supplies to charities

[12.13] Supplies to charities can be subject to the reduced rate as follows.

(a) **Fuel and power.** Supplies of fuel and power can be subject to the reduced rate in certain circumstances. These include
- use in a dwelling or a building used for a relevant residential purpose; and
- use by a charity otherwise than in the course or furtherance of a business.

See **25 FUEL AND POWER.**

(b) **Energy-saving materials.** The installation of certain energy saving materials in a building used solely for a relevant charitable purpose is liable to VAT at the reduced rate. See **58.2 REDUCED RATE SUPPLIES.**

Relief for importations

[12.14] No VAT is payable on the importation of certain goods by or for charities and other philanthropic organisations. See **33.15**(6) **IMPORTS.**

New building projects on a self-build or self-help basis

[12.15] Refunds of VAT may be available to a charity involved in a self-build project of a building intended solely for use for a relevant charitable purpose. See **42.23 LAND AND BUILDINGS: ZERO AND REDUCED RATE SUPPLIES AND DIY HOUSEBUILDERS.**

Key points

[12.16] Points to consider are as follows.

- It will be clear in most cases whether an organisation is a charity and able to benefit from VAT concessions available to charities. In other cases, it will be necessary to consider the aims and objectives of the organisation and put forward a strong argument to HMRC that charitable status is appropriate.
- In some cases, it may be worthwhile for a charity to register for VAT on a voluntary basis. This would be particularly useful if the charity has a high proportion of zero-rated sales, e.g. sales of donated goods.
- If a charity has to register for VAT on a compulsory basis, remember that it is only the value of taxable supplies that need to be taken into account as far as the registration limit is concerned. Exempt supplies and outside the scope income are excluded from the calculations.
- An important challenge as far as VAT is concerned is to ensure that input tax is only reclaimed by a charity that relates to its taxable supplies. Effective procedures need to be in place to ensure that input tax is not reclaimed on non-business expenditure or expenditure relating to exempt supplies. This includes an apportionment of input tax on general overheads where appropriate.
- A charity can use any method to apportion input tax between business and non-business activities on general overhead items as long as the method gives a fair and reasonable result. Remember that an income-based apportionment may not be the most suitable method if the expenditure in question is not directly linked to income.
- Be aware that many sources of income for a charity can be zero-rated or exempt from VAT. For example, income from a fundraising event will be exempt in most cases – although obviously any input tax relevant to the event will not be reclaimable as it relates to an exempt supply. The rules concerning exemption for fundraising events basically require the event to be publicised as such, either on promotional literature or in committee meeting minutes. There are restrictions on the number of similar events that can be held at the same location in the same financial year (15) but these will not be relevant in most cases. The exemption for fundraising also extends to non-profit making bodies (e.g. members of sporting clubs).
- A donation can be treated as outside the scope of VAT as long as the donor does not receive any benefits for his payment. It is important to ensure that donations are freely given by the donor, for example, the request for a 'minimum donation of £x' in connection with the supply of goods or services would not be classed as a freely given donation.

- Do not assume that all grant income received by a charity is outside the scope of VAT. If grant income is linked to the performance of services by a charity, then it will be standard-rated in most cases, although could be exempt if it relates to welfare services.
- There is a range of concessions available to charities as far as VAT on their expenditure is concerned. For example, a charity placing an advert in a local newspaper for a new member of staff should not pay VAT because the supply is zero-rated as advertising for a charity. Fuel and power supplied to a charity will only charge the reduced rate of VAT (currently 5%) if it is relevant to the non-business activities of the organisation.

13

Clothing and Footwear

De Voil Indirect Tax Service. See V4.287

Introduction

[13.1] Zero-rating applies to

- articles of clothing or footwear designed for young children and not suitable for older children (see **13.2** to **13.7** below); and
- certain supplies of protective boots and helmets (see **13.8** below).

Other supplies of clothing and footwear are standard-rated.

Young children's clothing and footwear

[13.2] Articles designed as clothing (including hats and other headgear) or footwear for young children and not suitable for older persons are zero-rated. [*VATA 1994, Sch 8 Group 16 Item 1 and Note 1*]. Special provisions apply to clothing made wholly or partly of fur (see **13.4** below).

In order to qualify for zero-rating, an article must therefore satisfying all of the following conditions.

- It must be an article of clothing or footwear. See **13.3** below.
- It must not be made of fur (with minor exceptions). See **13.4** below.
- It must be designed for young children. See **13.5** below.
- It must only be suitable for young children. See **13.6** below.

(VAT Notice 714, para 1.3).

What qualifies as clothing and footwear

[13.3] The word 'clothing' must be given its ordinary meaning and whether an item is clothing or not is a question of fact. To have a function as clothing, an item should provide cover for the body (either for decency or protection from the elements). But the purpose for which an item was intended to be used is not conclusive and a garment designed primarily for another purposes (see, for example, safety aids below), but also fulfilling a clothing function, can still qualify for zero-rating (*British Vita Co Ltd* (VTD 322) (TVC 12.4)).

For a consideration of the phrase 'articles designed as clothing' see *C & E Commrs v Ali Baba Tex Ltd,* QB [1992] STC 590 (TVC 12.4).

If an item is not an article of clothing or footwear it is standard-rated.

(1) Clothing in general

As well as all the obvious garments, clothing includes items such as hats, caps, braces, belts, garters and scarves.

Not included are clothing accessories and items of haberdashery sold separately, such as

- items of Guide and Scout uniform comprising belt pouches, pins, woggles and sash pins (see *BG Supplies (Birmingham) Ltd* (VTD 11663) (TVC 12.7));
- fastenings such as buckles, buttons and zips;
- badges, collars, cuffs, patches and other sew-on or iron-on items;
- hand muffs and ear muffs; and
- wristbands for sport, etc. (see *Vidhani Brothers Ltd* (VTD 18997) (TVC 12.6)).

(2) Baby wear

Most items of baby wear (e.g. bonnets, bootees and matinee jackets) can be clearly recognised as clothing, but the following less obvious items are also considered to be articles of clothing.

- Bibs, including plastic bibs with a curved tray at the base.
- Hooded rain covers for pushchairs, provided they are suitable for the baby to wear as a rain cape when out of the pushchair.
- Nappies (and nappy liners), both disposable and re-usable, provided they are held out for sale appropriately.
- Babies' shawls, provided they are designed and held out as such.
- Padded sleeping garments, similar in construction to sleeping bags, but shaped at the neck and armholes or having sleeves and/or legs.
- Towelling bathrobes designed with a hood or sleeves enabling the baby to be wrapped in them as a garment.

The following are *not* considered to be baby clothing and are standard-rated.

- Pram and pushchair covers not designed to serve as rain capes outside the pram or chair.
- Disposable nappy material sold in a continuous role from which individual nappies are cut.

- 'Mother-and-baby' shawls intended to wrap around both mother and child.
- Sleeping bags not designed with neck and arm holes or sleeves and/or legs.

See also *Mothercare Ltd* (VTD 323) (TVC 12.1) and *Little Rock Ltd* (VTD 424) (TVC 12.2).

(3) Footwear

Articles of footwear include

- boots, shoes, sandals and slippers, even if they are designed for special purposes (such as ballet shoes or studded football boots); and
- ice-skating or roller-skating boots, with or without skating blades or rollers attached;

but do not include

- blades or rollers sold on their own, or platform type roller skates for attaching to normal shoes; and
- shoelaces, insoles, heel protectors and stick-on soles sold as separate items.

(4) Headgear

Some articles worn on the head cannot be zero-rated even though they are for young children because they are accessories rather than clothing. HMRC regard this as including all articles that do not cover the whole head, e.g.

- alice bands (see *Cassidy (t/a Balou)* (VTD 5760) (TVC 12.5));
- hair ribbons and slides;
- scrunchies;
- sports and other headbands; and
- sun visors and ear muffs.

Novelty hats, party hats and play hats made out of materials such as paper or plastic are toys rather than clothing and are standard-rated.

(5) Safety aids

Clothing includes items that, although primarily designed as safety aids, have the form and function of clothing (e.g. cyclists' tabards and sailors' lifejackets). Other safety aids which have no clothing functions (e.g. reflective armbands and buoyancy aids) are always standard-rated.

(6) Incomplete articles

An unfinished article may be considered to be clothing if it has been processed to such an extent that it could not reasonably be used for any other purpose (e.g. cut-out parts of a garment or pleated skirt lengths). See *Ali Baba Tex Ltd* above.

(VAT Notice 714, paras 2.1–2.3).

Items made of fur

[13.4] Clothing does not included any articles made wholly or partly of 'fur skin' apart from

- headgear,
- gloves,
- buttons, belts and buckles; and
- any garment merely trimmed with fur skin unless the trimming has an area greater than one-fifth of the area of the outside material or, in the case of a new garment, represents a cost to the manufacturer greater than the cost of the other components.

'*Fur skin*' means any skin with fur, hair or wool attached except

- rabbit skin;
- woolled sheep or lamb skin; and
- the skin, if neither tanned nor dressed, of bovine cattle (including buffalo), equine animals, goats or kids (other than Yemen, Mongolian and Tibetan goats or kids), swine (including peccary), chamois, gazelles, deer or dogs.

[*VATA 1994, Sch 8 Group 16 Notes 2 and 3*].

These provisions are designed to exclude zero-rating for children's clothing made from luxury furs. Subject to satisfying the other tests in **13.2** above, zero-rating can be applied to

- articles made using artificial fur; and
- fur lined boots.

(VAT Notice 714, paras 3.1, 4.4).

Items designed for young children

[13.5] Although sizes and measurements are not referred to in the legislation, it has been agreed with the industry working party that they represent a fair reflection of the interpretation of the law.

(1) Clothing

HMRC in general accept that garments are designed for young children provided they are up to the tabled measurements below. These measurements are based on those for children up to the eve of their 14th birthday (as set out in the relevant British Standard). The garments should be measured on a flat surface, with creases smoothed out, buttons (or equivalent) fastened and any intended overlap in place. Chest measurements should normally be taken 2.5 cms below the base of the armhole and multiplied by two. Similarly, waist measurements should be taken from one side of the fastened waistband to the other and multiplied by two.

Maximum garment sizes	*Boys*		*Girls*	
	Chest	Waist	Chest	Waist
Shirts	104cm	—	105cm	—
Knitwear	104cm	—	105cm	—
Jackets/waistcoats	109cm	—	110cm	—
Top coats/outerwear	114cm	—	115cm	—
Dresses	—	—	98cm	—
Skirts*	—	—	—	71cm
Trousers/shorts*	—	72cm	—	71cm
Underwear/swimwear	88cm	72cm	89cm	71cm
Nightwear	105cm	73cm	106cm	72cm

* Garments with elasticated waistbands should be measured at their full stretch. Those that have no fastening may be zero-rated up to a maximum stretched waist of 85 cms for boys and 90 cms for girls.

Some products are normally judged by different criteria or measurements. The following garments are also accepted as being designed for young children.

Maximum garment sizes — other garments
Lifejackets — Max body weight 52kg
Leotards/body stockings/swimsuits — Shoulder to crotch 70cm
Saris — 442cm × 104cm
Lungis — 156cm × 94cm
Socks (by shoe size) — Boys 6.5; Girls/unisex 5.5
Tights — Waist-crotch-waist measurement 51cm for lightweight and 56cm for heavyweight
Teen bras — Size 34B

Style considerations

In a minority of cases, it may be necessary to consider factors inherent in the garment as making it suitable for older persons. If this applies, a garment within the maximum measurements above could still fail the 'design' test and be standard-rated. See, for example, *Walter Stewart Ltd* (VTD 83) (TVC 12.11) where a leather coat which did not exceed the maximum measurements failed the test because it was a relatively high-cost fashion garment more likely to appeal to adults and because a three-inch bust dart had been inserted.

Larger sizes

If the above measurements are exceeded, HMRC will still accept that garments are designed for young children if *either* of the following conditions can be satisfied.

(a) If it can be shown that
- the garment has been designed for a person under 14,
- it is only suitable for young children (see **13.6** below); and
- the body measurements used are at or below those in the table below.

Body size	*Boys*	*Girls*
Height	163cms	161cms
Chest	84cms	85cms
Waist	70cms	69cms
Hips	85cms	90cms
Arm (shoulder to wrist)	59cms	57cms
Inside leg	77cms	76cms

(b) The clothing is restricted by some other design feature to those under 14. HMRC must be satisfied that the body sizes used are appropriate to the under 14s and the garments produced are only suitable for that age group. They must be given the specifications and reasoning and must have given written agreement before zero-rating can be applied in such cases.

One-size and stretch garments

Zero-rating cannot be applied to articles of clothing which are sold in one size only and that are suitable for both children and adults. Articles that stretch to fit, such as some sportswear, can be zero-rated provided the garment is designed to fit a body size in accordance with the second table above or at its maximum stretch does not exceed the measurements for maximum garment sizes in the first table above. See also *Jeffrey Green & Co Ltd* (VTD 69) (TVC 12.10).

(2) Footwear

HMRC accept that footwear is designed for young children up to the following measurements.

- Boys' shoes — up to and including UK size 6.5 or American size 7 (unless 7.5 is marked as equal to UK 6.5) or Continental size 40
- Girls' court shoes (i.e. low cut shoes without straps or other fastenings) — up to and including UK size 3 or American size 4.5 or Continental size 35.5 (or 35 if no half sizes)
- Other girls' shoes — as for court shoes but where the heel height does not exceed the sole depth by more than 4 cms, up to UK size 5.5 or American size 7 or Continental size 38.5 (38 if no half sizes)

See also *Brays of Glastonbury Ltd* (VTD 650) (TVC 12.13) and *Gura (t/a Vincent Footwear)* (VTD 18416) (TVC 12.14).

Larger sizes

It may still be possible to zero-rate larger sizes if HMRC are satisfied that

- the product has been designed exclusively for children under 14; and
- it is only suitable for young children (see **13.6** below)

but HMRC must be given the specifications and reasoning and must have given written agreement before zero-rating can be applied in such cases.

Unisex footwear

Most lines of footwear are designed for one sex or the other and should be zero-rated according to the rules relating to girls' or boys' footwear as appropriate. True 'unisex' footwear can only be zero-rated up to and including size 5.5 (the maximum size for girls' footwear).

Feet of differing sizes

Where a child has one foot significantly larger than the other, or requires an unusually high heel for one foot, the pair of shoes can be zero-rated if the smaller shoe qualifies for the relief.

(3) Hats and other headgear

Many children's hats fit adults. It is still possible to zero-rate hats (including caps and other items of headgear) which are suitable by design only for young children (e.g. babies' bonnets, school hats) or which are clearly held out for sale for young children.

In *Benrose Ltd (t/a Multi-Stock Ltd)* (VTD 15783) (TVC 12.24) which concerned knitted acrylic hats bearing logos of famous football teams, the tribunal held that, although it was physically possible for an adult to wear the hats, they were too close-fitting for comfortable wear over an extended period. Also, as they were intended as cheap imitations of official football club hats, supporters over 14 would want the official hats. This decision stresses the point that size is not always the crucial test and that design or style must be considered.

HMRC have accepted the following items as falling within the relief.

- Protective helmets (such as those for skateboarding or ice hockey) up to a maximum size of 59 cms as long as they are designed and marketed exclusively for children (**13.6** below).
- Riding hats up to and including size 6.75 (jockey skulls up to size 1) even if they are not held out for sale for children. Sales of larger riding hats specifically for young children can be zero-rated as long as they are fitted, adapted or otherwise appropriate only for young children (e.g. by being less sophisticated in terms of design and appearance) but HMRC's written approval must be received before zero-rating larger sizes.

All cycle helmets are zero-rated irrespective of size or how they are held out for sale (see **13.9** below).

(4) Belts, braces and other items

HMRC accept belts, braces, neckties, gloves, garters, scarves, ruffs, collars and shirt frills as traditional items of clothing and they may be zero-rated irrespective of size as long as they are held out for sale for the under 14s only (see **13.6** below).

(VAT Notice 714, paras 4.1–4.5).

Items suitable only for young children

[13.6] The final test that must be satisfied if an item is to be zero-rated (see **13.2** above) is that it must only be suitable for young children, i.e. not suitable for older persons. This can be met by ensuring that it is 'held out for sale' for young children.

'*Held out for sale*' means the way in which an article is labelled, packaged, displayed, invoiced or advertised. It includes any promotional items and the heading under which an article is listed in a catalogue, web page or price list.

Articles cannot necessarily be zero-rated on sale simply because they were zero-rated when purchased. How they are held out for sale affects their VAT liability. Goods, which may qualify at the design stage, fail the suitability test if they are labeled

- to fit sizes larger than those in **13.5** above;
- as suitable for age '13/14' and above; or
- by the ladies sizing system (8, 10, 12, and so on).

In particular:

- *Manufacturers* must be able to show that items qualify for zero-rating from product specification or other documentation and must identify them appropriately on any labelling and packaging, and in any promotional material and on invoices.
- *Wholesalers and distributors* must clearly identify the article as being only suitable for children on invoices and price lists. If the goods are on display they must clearly be identified and segregated. Any catalogue should identify the articles as being for young children, preferably in a separate children's section and the identical product must not appear in both adults' and children's sections.
- *Retailers* can zero-rate clothing for young children only if it is clear from labels, signs, packaging, advertising, etc. that it is intended for young children and they either
  (i) sell it from a shop, a separate department in a shop, or a separate section of a catalogue which caters exclusively for children; or
  (ii) keep it apart from adult garments by selling it from separate shelves, racks, etc. which are clearly marked up as 'boys', 'girls' or 'children's'.

  The extent to which this is possible will vary depending upon the size and type of retail outlet but any retailer should be able to show that it has as good a system as is practical in the circumstances. The potential purchaser should not be left in any doubt that the retailer is selling items for young children.
- *Mail order and internet suppliers* must clearly identify the goods as being for young children in any price list, page, catalogue or other promotional material, preferably using a discrete children's section. The potential purchaser should be in no doubt that the goods they are looking at are for young children and the identical goods must not appear in both adults' and children's sections.

(VAT Notice 714, paras 5.1–5.6).

Treatment in particular cases

[13.7] Children's clothing and footwear can be zero-rated in particular cases as outlined below.

(1) School uniforms

There is no specific relief for items of school uniform which are subject to the normal rules for children's clothes. But, by concession, if garments are supplied under a specific agreement with a school catering exclusively for pupils under 14 years of age, it is possible to apply the zero rate beyond the garment measurements in **13.5** above provided the garments are

- unique to that school by design, such as a prominent badge or piping in school colours, and
- held out for sale as being for that school only.

Where a school also caters for pupils of 14 and over, the normal rules apply and obtaining a declaration that the relevant garment is intended for a pupil under the age of 14 is not sufficient for zero-rating to apply (*Smart Alec Ltd* (VTD 17832) (TVC 12.20)).

(VAT Notice 714, para 6.1).

(2) Youth organisations

By concession, garments worn only as uniform by members of groups or organisations which cater exclusively for under-14 year olds (e.g. Beavers and Brownies) qualify for zero-rating, irrespective of size, provided they are

- designed exclusively for the organisation;
- worn only by under 14s; and
- clearly identifiable to the organisation.

Zero-rating does not apply to items that may also be worn by older groups such as Scouts.

(VAT Notice 714, para 6.1).

(3) Cloth kits

Packaged kits for making children's clothes can be zero-rated provided

- the clothes themselves would be zero-rated;
- the material is already cut to the pattern or the pattern is indelibly printed on the material; and
- it is clear from the labelling or other promotional material that the made-up garment is only suitable for young children.
  (VAT Notice 714, para 7.1).

(4) Multiple supplies

Where an article consists of both zero-rated clothing and *incidental* standard-rated items at an inclusive price (e.g. a cowboy suit with a toy gun or a policeman's uniform with toy handcuffs), HMRC consider this a single supply of children's clothing and the whole price can be zero-rated.

Where the standard-rated element is not incidental (e.g. a baby's gift set comprising of a bib and feeding cup) there is a multiple supply which must be apportioned between the zero-rated and standard-rated elements. See **47.3 OUTPUT TAX.**

(VAT Notice 714, para 8.1).

(5) Hire or loan of children's clothing and footwear

The hire or loan of any item of children's clothing or footwear is zero-rated if the item would itself be zero-rated. [*VATA 1994, Sch 8 Group 16 Note 5*]. This covers, for example, hire of bridesmaids' and page boys' outfits, fancy dress costumes, and nappy hire services where the nappies are collected for laundering and replaced with fresh ones.

The separate supply of ice-skates, roller skates, ten-pin bowling shoes, etc. is also eligible for zero-rating in accordance with the size criteria for footwear in **13.5** above. But a single price for admission that also includes the loan of footwear is a multiple supply which must be apportioned between the zero-rated and standard-rated elements. See **47.3 OUTPUT TAX.**

(6) Supplies of services

Cut, make and trim

Making up young children's clothing from cloth owned by someone else can be zero-rated. Other processes may also be eligible for zero-rating if, after the work is finished, the processed article clearly becomes a child's garment which itself is normally zero-rated or the processed goods can only be incorporated in such an item. This is because such work is treated as a supply of services and zero-rated under *VATA 1994, s 30(2A)* as the application of a process to another person's goods which produces goods which are themselves zero-rated.

Alteration, repair, embroidery and similar services

These services do not qualify for zero-rating as they are applied to goods that maintain their essential nature. For example, a blazer that has its sleeve length altered, its collar repaired, or a school badge embroidered on its pocket, is not sufficiently changed by that process to produce a new item. However, if the blazer were changed into a waistcoat by the process, the service would have produced a new item and, if this waistcoat meets the criteria for zero-rating, the process would also be zero-rated.

(VAT Notice 714, paras 9.1–9.3).

Protective boots and helmets for industrial use

[13.8] The supply to a person for use otherwise than by employees of his of protective boots and helmets for industrial use is zero-rated. [*VATA 1994, Sch 8 Group 16 Item 2*]. In addition to outright sales, zero-rating also applies to a supply of services where the articles are hired or loaned or where they are put to private use provided that, in each case, the articles are for use otherwise than by the employees of the person to whom the services are supplied. [*VATA 1994, Sch 8 Group 16 Note 5; SI 2000/1517*].

The following conditions apply.

Condition 1

The articles must be protective boots or helmets. The British Standards Institution (BSI) defines a boot as having a minimum leg height of 90mm measured vertically from the insole at the back. The European Standard gives the minimum height of the upper (measured vertically from the insole at the back) of 103mm for a size 36 (UK 3) and below, through to a minimum height of the upper of 121mm for a size 45 (UK 11) and above. (The British Standard specifications will eventually be withdrawn and the definition of a boot will then be based on the European specification. In the meantime, HMRC accept both Standard measurements.)

Protective shoes that fall outside these specifications are not eligible for zero-rating, even if they meet the remaining requirements.

(VAT Notice 701/23/11, para 2.2).

Condition 2

The articles must be for industrial use. HMRC apply the normal day-to-day meaning to the words 'industrial use'. They do not see the phrase as covering, for example, motorcycle boots. (VAT Notice 701/23/11, para 2.6).

Condition 3

The articles concerned must

- be manufactured to standards approved by the British Standards Institution and bear a mark indicating conformity with those standards; or
- be manufactured to standards which satisfy requirements imposed (whether under UK law or that of another EU country) to give effect to *EU Council Directive 89/686/EEC as amended* and bear any mark of conformity required to that effect.

[*VATA 1994, Sch 8 Group 16 Note 4; SI 2000/1517; SI 2001/732*].

Approved markings include the appropriate European Standard (EN) or British Standard (BS) numbers and the EU 'CE' mark (indicating conformity with the EU Directive) and/or the British Standard 'kitemark'. The EN for boots and helmets sourced in other EU countries may be prefixed by another country code such as 'NF' for a French manufactured product or 'DS' for one of Danish manufacture.

VATA 1994, Sch 8 Group 16 lists the current standards to which boots and helmets must conform to qualify for zero-rating. It also indicates that the scope of the zero rate will depend on any future amendments to those standards.

In some instances, particular boots and helmets may have been manufactured to a different specification to those laid down in the harmonised European Standards. These alternative specifications must satisfy the requirements of the Directive and be approved by a 'notified body', which in turn has been approved and appointed by the authorities of an EU country. These boots and helmets will still carry the 'CE' mark, but also the notified body number.

(VAT Notice 701/23/11, paras 2.3–2.5).

Condition 4

The articles must not be supplied to a person for use by his employees. Supplies from a manufacturer to a wholesaler who in turn supplies them to a retailer, and supplies from an employer to an employee, can be zero-rated subject to the above conditions. But otherwise, before zero-rating a supply, the supplier should establish that the customer is not an employer purchasing the boots or helmets for use by employees by asking himself does

- the customer's trading style suggest the customer is an employer;
- the quantity ordered suggest a bulk purchase by an employer for use of employees; and
- the nature of the contract indicate a trade order, e.g. a number of pairs of boots paid for by one customer for delivery to individuals.

(VAT Notice 701/23/11, para 2.7).

Zero-rating covers accessories (e.g. visors and ear protectors) fitted as an integral part of a qualifying helmet but not accessories supplied on their own. (VAT Notice 701/23/11, para 2.8).

Protective helmets

[13.9] The supply of protective helmets for wear by a person driving or riding a motor bicycle or riding a pedal cycle is zero-rated provided the helmets are

- of a type that on 30 June 2000 was prescribed by regulations made under *Road Traffic Act 1988, s 17* (types of helmet recommended as affording protection to persons on or in motor cycles from injury in the event of accident), see the *Motor Cycles (Protective Helmets) Regulations 1988* (*SI 1988/1807*); or
- manufactured to a standard which satisfies requirements imposed (whether under UK law or the law of another EU country) to give effect to *EU Council Directive 89/686/EEC as amended* and bear any mark of conformity required to that effect.

In addition to outright sales, zero-rating also applies to a supply of services where the articles are hired or loaned or where they are put to private use.

[*VATA 1994, Sch 8 Group 16 Item 3, Notes 4A, 5; SI 2000/1517; SI 2001/732*].

Motor cycle helmets

To qualify for zero-rating, motor cycle helmets must comply with the appropriate British Standard (in which case it will be marked with a British Standard 'kitemark') or European Standard (in which case it will be marked with a UN 'E' mark).

Zero-rating covers accessories (e.g. visors, ear protectors or communication systems) fitted as an integral part of a qualifying helmet but not accessories supplied on their own.

(VAT Notice 701/23/11, paras 3.1–3.3).

Pedal cycle helmets

Approved markings include the appropriate European Standard (EN) number and the EU 'CE' mark (indicating conformity with the EU Directive). The EN for helmets sourced in other EU countries may be prefixed by another country code such as 'NF' for a French manufactured product or 'DS' for one of Danish manufacture.

Some cycle helmets may have been manufactured to a different specification to those laid down in the harmonised European Standards. These alternative specifications must satisfy the requirements of the Directive and be approved by a 'notified body', which in turn has been approved and appointed by the authorities of an EU country. These helmets will still carry the 'CE' mark, but also the notified body number.

Zero-rating covers accessories (e.g. visors or ear protectors) fitted as an integral part of a qualifying helmet but not accessories supplied on their own.

(VAT Notice 701/23/11, paras 4.1–4.5).

Key points

[13.10] Points to consider are as follows.

- It is important that garments are designed and held out for sale as being suitable for children in order to be eligible for zero-rating. The general aim of the legislation is that zero-rating can apply to clothes worn by children up to the eve of their 14th birthday. If they are 14 or older, then the clothes they wear become standard-rated. To assist this process, HMRC have produced a list of garment sizes, with separate lists obviously in place for boys and girls. If these sizes are exceeded, then the item becomes standard-rated unless there is some other feature of the garment in place that clearly makes it unsuitable for wear by older children. In such cases, the garment must be within another range of sizes published by HMRC or have some restrictive design feature or size measurement that means it is only suitable for young children. There have been a number of VAT cases lost by taxpayers where garments have been within the stipulated size ranges published by HMRC but have a design feature that makes them only suitable for wear by older children or adults.
- Clothing includes items such as hats, caps, braces, belts, garters and scarves but there is an exclusion for items such as badges, wristbands for sport, ear muffs and zips. In the latter cases, the items are not classed as clothing in the traditional meaning of the word and are therefore standard-rated.

- Many businesses that sell children's clothes will also sell adult clothing, and will often be a retailer as well. This means the business must operate a retail scheme that enables it to accurately calculate the output tax payable on its VAT returns. The ideal scheme will be based on a point of sale till reading because this is the most accurate method. But a scheme based on marking up either the zero-rated or standard-rated purchases, or even based on the proportion of standard-rated purchases and applying this to the total sales made by a business, should also produce a sensible result. However, it is important to be aware of the conditions of the various retail schemes, e.g. the scheme based on the proportion of standard-rated purchases can only be adopted by a business with annual sales of £1m or less.
- The increased use of websites to generate sales of goods and services means that extra care is needed in relation to children's clothing and zero-rating. The website or other medium must make it clear that the item being sold is only suitable for young children and not for older children or adults. A separate section on the website for children's clothing will almost certainly achieve this aim. The prospective buyer must be clear that they are buying children's clothing and the same garment sizes should not therefore appear in the adult section of the website.
- A useful concession means that the hire of children's clothing also qualifies for zero-rating, even though this is effectively a service rather than goods arrangement. This concession could be particularly useful for a business that specialises in wedding outfits (e.g. bridesmaid dresses or page boy outfits).
- Be aware that the zero-rating for protective boots only applies if the items are intended for industrial use. This would exclude, for example, motor bike boots. Another important condition is that zero-rating would not apply if the items are being bought by an employer for his employees. It is up to the supplier to make a reasonable assessment as to whether this might be the case (e.g. a bulk order might suggest an employer is buying the items for his workers).
- The zero-rating for protective helmets is more generous. As well as zero-rating for industrial use (again with the exception concerning employers buying helmets for employees), zero-rating also applies to the sale of motor bike and pedal cycle helmets. The items must meet certain British or European Standard conditions.

14

Clubs and Associations

Cross-references. See **9.6 BUSINESS ENTERTAINMENT** for free entertainment of members; and **16.19 EDUCATION** for the provision of youth club facilities.

De Voil Indirect Tax Service. See V2.112, V4.156.

Introduction

[14.1] Under *Directive 2006/112/EC*, countries must exempt certain activities in the public interest. Those relating to clubs and associations are covered by *Art 132(1)(l)* (see **18.25**(*l*) **EUROPEAN UNION LEGISLATION**). The provisions have been incorporated into UK legislation in two ways.

First, under *VATA 1994, Sch 9 Group 9*, if the organisation is a non-profit making trade union, professional or representative body, supplies to members referable to its aims and available without payment other than a membership subscription are exempt. Exemption also applies to such supplies made by a non-profit making body with objects which are in the public domain and are of a political, religious, patriotic, philosophical or philanthropic nature. [*VATA 1994, s 94(3); FA 1999, s 20; SI 1999/2769*]. See **14.7** below.

Secondly, subject to the above, if a 'club, association or organisation' provides facilities or advantages to its members in return for a 'subscription or other consideration', it is deemed to be carrying on a business activity. [*VATA 1994, s 94(2)(a)*]. Such a body must therefore register for VAT (subject to the registration limit) and account for VAT on its subscription income (but see **14.2** below for apportionment of subscriptions).

Particular types of clubs and associations

The provisions of *VATA 1994, s 94(2)(a)* have been held to be applicable in *C & E Commrs v British Field Sports Society*, CA [1998] STC 315 (TVC 13.10) (campaigning on behalf of stag and deer hunting), *Eastbourne Town Radio*

Cars Association v C & E Commrs, HL [2001] STC 606 (TVC 62.32) (association of taxi-drivers) and *Manor Forstal Residents Society Ltd* (VTD 245) (TVC 13.1) (association of local residents); and not applicable in *New Ash Green Village Association* (VTD 245) (TVC 13.11) (village development association), *Nottingham Fire Service Messing Club* (VTD 348) (TVC 13.12) (canteen at fire station) and *Friends of the Ironbridge Gorge Museum* (VTD 5639) (TVC 13.14) (fund-raising association for a museum).

Subscriptions

Single and multiple supplies

[14.2] The same person may be supplied, at the same time, with a number of different goods or services or both. If the individual components are all liable to VAT at the same rate, VAT can be calculated in the normal way but if they are not, it is necessary to decide whether a single or multiple supply is being made.

- In a single supply where one component of the supply is the principal component to which all the other components are ancillary, integral or incidental, the whole transaction is treated as having the VAT liability of the principal component. See below, however, for a concession in the case of non-profit making bodies.
- In a multiple supply, each component is distinct and independent and takes its own VAT liability.

See **64.6 SUPPLY: GENERAL** for more detailed coverage of single and multiple supplies.

Treatment of subscriptions for VAT purposes

Where members pay a subscription to obtain or gain entitlement to any 'substantive' benefits of membership, VAT due is calculated on the total amount of the subscription. '*Substantive benefits*' include

- magazines, periodicals or handbooks;
- priority booking rights;
- guaranteed seats;
- discounts on admission charges; and
- items with a resale value.

These benefits are considered to be substantive regardless of whether there is any cost to the organisation in supplying them and what that cost might be. Benefits that have a nominal value can be ignored (e.g. simple acknowledgements of support in the form of membership badges, flags or stickers, and listing of names in a programme or on a theatre seat or entrance).

The VAT liability of subscriptions depends on the liability of the membership benefits supplied in return. In most cases clubs supply a package of benefits so that the supply will have more than one component. If there is a multiple supply (see above) and the separate components have different VAT liabilities, the subscription charge must be apportioned.

Subscriptions which are voluntary payments or donations

If the whole of the subscription is an entirely voluntary payment and secures nothing or only nominal benefits in return, it is all a donation and must be treated as being outside the scope of VAT.

Subscriptions which may include a voluntary payment or donation

It is only possible to treat part of a subscription as a voluntary payment or donation if the organisation is a charity or a body which has objects that are both in the public domain and of a philanthropic nature (see **14.7**(*e*) below) and either

- all the substantive benefits (i.e. ignoring any nominal benefits) provided are available to non-members at no charge or more cheaply than the subscription; or
- some or all of the substantive benefits are exclusive to members and the organisation can demonstrate that the amount paid is higher than the amount that the subscriber would normally have to pay for similar goods or services.

If these requirements are met, see below for how to apportion the subscription.

A charity or organisation having objects in the public domain (e.g. philanthropic body), may receive a subscription which includes a donational element.

Exempt subscriptions

The supply of benefits to members by trade unions and political, religious, patriotic, philosophical, philanthropic or civic bodies may qualify for exemption. See **14.8** below. See also **57.10 RECREATION AND SPORT** for certain membership subscriptions of non-profit making bodies providing sport and physical education services.

Additional joining fees

Any additional joining fee of a *general* nature should be treated in the same way as a subscription, applying the same apportionment, if any. Where an additional fee is charged for obtaining a *particular* facility, VAT must be accounted for based on the liability of the particular service or goods provided.

Life membership fees

These must be treated in the same way as annual subscriptions, unless life members are supplied with additional benefits not available to ordinary members.

Charges for being placed on a waiting list for membership

Such a fee is exempt if it is

- deducted from the new member's first subscription or entrance fee and the subscription or fee itself will qualify for exemption; and
- refundable in the event that the candidate fails to become a member for any reason, including voluntary withdrawal.

In all other circumstances, the fee is consideration for the right to be on the waiting list and is standard-rated.

Payment by instalments

Where members can pay annual subscriptions by instalments over the subscription period and the total instalments exceed the single annual payment subscription, the additional amount is exempt from VAT as interest on a grant of credit.

Deferred payments

Where an organisation offers annual membership and allows members to defer subscription payment for an additional charge over and above the subscription, the charge is consideration for the exempt grant of credit.

Apportionment of subscriptions

If the subscription is consideration for a multiple supply (see above) and the separate components have different liabilities, the subscription must be apportioned.

In most cases there is one principal benefit or reason for joining. In these circumstances, the subscription is consideration for a single supply (see above) and its liability is determined by the liability of the main benefit. No apportionment can normally be made. However, by concession, *non-profit making bodies* who charge their members a subscription that entitles them to a package of benefits, may apportion the subscription between the various components as if there had been a multiple supply, even if under the general rules there is a single supply. The concession does not work in reverse, i.e. non-profit making bodies cannot treat their multiple supplies as single supplies. It is up to the organisation to decided whether it wishes to take advantage of the concession. If it does (e.g. because of zero-rated printed matter), it must apportion all types and components of subscriptions – it cannot 'pick and choose'. The concession may not be used to make retrospective adjustments, i.e. it cannot be used to rework previously submitted VAT returns.

The fact that subscriptions are used to purchase zero-rated or exempt supplies from a third party will not, in itself, entitle an organisation to apportion the value of subscriptions.

How to apportion

There are no specific rules for making an apportionment. See **47.3 OUTPUT TAX** for general guidance on apportionment. HMRC generally accept apportionment of the total subscription income to reflect the relative cost of providing the different supplies to members. The calculations for the current financial year can be based on the accounts for the previous financial year, provided this method is adopted consistently. Calculations must be kept for inspection by HMRC. If the organisation wishes to use any other method of apportionment, it should write to HMRC, setting out the proposed method and supporting it with copies of the annual accounts and other relevant documents.

Where a subscription includes a donation (see above), if the organisation calculates the value of any standard-rated, zero-rated and exempt supplies, it can treat the balance of the subscription as a donation and outside the scope of VAT. It should calculate the value of the substantive benefits (i.e. ignoring nominal benefits), using the price at which they are available to non-members or the amount the subscriber would normally have to pay for similar goods or services. The difference between the amount of the subscription and the total value of the benefits is the donation.

(VAT Notice 48, ESC 3.35; HMRC Brief 6/09).

Subscriptions from overseas members

Overseas subscriptions normally follow the same VAT liability as subscriptions paid by UK members but are treated differently where overseas members

- receive different benefits from UK members in return for their subscription to a UK club; or
- receive the same benefits as UK members, but the VAT rules require a different treatment.

In these circumstances, the apportionment of the overseas subscription must be carried out separately.

The different treatment of benefits for overseas members is as follows.

- *Services*. In certain situations, some supplies of services are treated as made where the customer belongs, and therefore fall outside the scope of UK VAT. See **65.21 SUPPLY: PLACE OF SUPPLY**.
- *Goods sent to members outside the EU* are zero-rated as exports.
- *Goods sent to VAT-registered members in other EU countries for use in their business* are zero-rated subject to certain conditions.
- *Goods sent to non VAT-registered members in other EU countries*. VAT is due on the goods in the UK until the value of such supplies exceeds a threshold set by the EU country to which the goods are sent. Once this threshold is exceeded, VAT is due in that EU country and the organisation may need to register for VAT there to fulfil its obligations. See **19.10 EUROPEAN UNION: SINGLE MARKET**.

(VAT Notice 701/5/11, paras 4.2–4.6, 5.1–5.14).

Registration

[14.3] Any club or association with business activities and a turnover from standard-rated, reduced-rated and zero-rated supplies (including subscriptions) above the current registration limits must register for VAT and account for VAT on its taxable supplies. Business activities include

- providing benefits to members in return for membership subscriptions (for members' racing clubs where subscriptions finance the purchase of racehorses, see **63.33 SPECIAL SCHEMES**);
- providing benefits to members in return for a separate charge;

- making supplies to non-members for a charge;
- admission to any premises for a charge; and
- providing catering, social and other facilities to non-members in return for a charge.

(VAT Notice 701/5/11, paras 2.1, 2.2).

For the requirements relating to registration see **59 REGISTRATION**. Even if a club, etc. is not required to register under the general requirements based on taxable supplies in the UK, it may be liable to register for VAT where it makes certain acquisitions of goods from other EU countries in excess of an annual threshold. See **59.18 REGISTRATION.**

A club, etc. may be registered in the name of that club and in determining whether goods and services are supplied to or by it, or whether goods are acquired by it from another EU country, no account is taken of any change in its members. HMRC are empowered to make provisions to determine what persons are responsible for carrying out the requirements of the VAT legislation where a club, etc. is managed by its members or a committee. Under these powers HMRC have regulated that the necessary requirements are the joint and several responsibility of

- every member holding office as president, chairman, treasurer, secretary or any similar office; or in default of any thereof,
- every member holding office as a member of a committee; or in default of any thereof,
- every member.

[*VATA 1994, s 46(2)(3); SI 1995/2518, Reg 8*].

Clubs in sections and multi-tiered bodies

[14.4] There are no set rules for determining whether a section or branch has its own separate legal status, independent of its parent organisation, or whether that section or branch should register separately for VAT purposes. Unless the section or branch concerned can demonstrate that it has both constitutional and financial independence from its parent organisation, its supplies should be included with those of the parent organisation when accounting for VAT.

(VAT Notice 701/5/11, para 2.4).

Common transactions other than subscriptions

[14.5] The following is a list of some of the more common transactions made by clubs and associations.

(1) Admission charges

Admission charges are standard-rated in most cases but admission charges to

- museums, galleries, art exhibitions and zoos; and

- theatrical, musical and choreographic performances of a cultural nature

supplied by public authorities and by certain other eligible bodies may qualify for exemption.

See **57.7 RECREATION AND SPORT.**

(2) Bar sales, catering and teas

Food and drink is always standard-rated if it is supplied in the course of catering. This includes hot take-away food and food and drink supplied for consumption on the premises. See **11 CATERING.** The argument that there is no 'supply' because, in law, drinks obtained by members are not sold to them has been dismissed. (*Carlton Lodge Club v C & E Commrs*, QB [1974] STC 507 (TVC 13.29)).

(3) Bingo

The fees for participation in bingo are exempt from VAT. See **57.3 RECREATION AND SPORT.** Admission charges are standard-rated with an exception for certain one-off fund-raising events (see below).

(4) Competition entry fees

Competition entry fees are normally standard-rated but may be exempt in the case of certain competitions in sport or physical recreation (see **57.6 RECREATION AND SPORT**).

(5) Culture

Admission charges to: museums, galleries, art exhibitions and zoos; and theatrical, musical and choreographic performances of a cultural nature, supplied by public authorities and by certain other eligible bodies may qualify for exemption (see **57.7 RECREATION AND SPORT**).

(6) Discos, dances, socials and similar events

Admission charges are standard-rated (but see below for certain one-off fund-raising events).

VAT must be accounted for on the gross amount of taxable supplies (e.g. admission, catering, etc.) and not on the net amounts after band, floor shows, etc. expenses are paid.

(7) Fixture cards

Fixture cards are standard-rated if any portion for completion occupies more than 25% of total area, otherwise they are generally zero-rated. See also **54.5 PRINTED MATTER, ETC.**

(8) Fund-raising events

Admission charges to qualifying events held by charities for charitable purposes and by non-profit making qualifying bodies exclusively for their own benefit may be exempt. See **12.10 CHARITIES.**

(9) Gaming and amusement machines

All receipts from gaming and amusement machines are standard-rated. See **57.4 RECREATION AND SPORT**.

(10) Gaming club subscriptions

Subscriptions to gaming, bingo, bridge, etc. clubs, in return for which members have the right to place bets or play games of chance for no further payment, are standard-rated. See **57.2 RECREATION AND SPORT**.

(11) Hire of rooms, halls and facilities

The hire of a room or a hall, including the provision of lighting and furniture, is generally exempt from VAT provided that

- the person to whom the room or hall is hired has exclusive occupation of it during the period of hire; and
- the organisation has not opted to tax the building in which the room or hall is situated.

(12) Insurance supplied with goods or other services

Depending on the circumstances, where a charge is made for insurance, that charge could be exempt where it is the member's own risk which is insured (rather than the club's risk). See **36.17 INSURANCE**.

(13) Jumble sales

Unless they qualify as fund-raising events (see above)

- any charge for admission is standard-rated; and
- the goods sold are liable to VAT at the rate applicable to such goods.

(14) Levies

These are normally demanded from existing members when a body requires additional funds. Where a levy is raised and members' benefits remain unaltered, the levy is liable to VAT as if it was an additional subscription. However, if the levy entitles the member to different benefits, VAT must be accounted for, where appropriate, based on the liability of those benefits.

(15) Lotteries

Income from lotteries (including raffles, totes, instant bingo tickets, etc.) is exempt (see **57.5 RECREATION AND SPORT**).

(16) Loans from members

Clubs often raise capital to finance the renewal or development of facilities by means of loans from members.

Compulsory interest-free loans

VAT must be accounted for on the notional interest on the loans. This is determined by establishing the amount of interest free loans and calculating the notional interest using the London Clearing Bank's Base Lending Rate in force either on the first day of the month in which the subscriptions are due to be paid or the first day of the club's financial year if more convenient. VAT liability is calculated by applying the same VAT liability to the notional interest as the subscription and using the appropriate VAT fraction to calculate the VAT due.

Obtaining loans at a significantly lower interest rate than from the bank

If the interest rate charged to members is significantly lower than the bank would have charged, VAT liability is determined by

- calculating the notional interest as for compulsory interest-free loans above;
- deducting the amount of interest actually paid, including any on returned loans, from the notional interest; and
- applying the same VAT liability to the remainder as applies to the subscriptions and using the appropriate VAT fraction to calculate the VAT due.

Additional loan repayments to members who are leaving

Members are often required to lend a specified sum which is only repaid on cessation of membership. It is often also a requirement that the member will find a new member to take over the loan or to make an equivalent loan. On cessation the ex-member receives a sum, frequently based on the rate of inflation. VAT liability is determined by

- calculating the notional interest as for compulsory interest-free loans above;
- deducting the amount of interest actually paid (if any);
- deducting the additional payment; and
- applying the same VAT liability to the remainder as applies to the subscriptions and using the appropriate VAT fraction to calculate the VAT due.

Reducing or waiving a member's subscription in return for an interest-free loan or purchase of a share or debenture

Where this is done, VAT must be accounted for, at the time the subscriptions are due, on the amount of subscription payable by a member who has not made any such payment.

Compulsory loans where members decide unconditionally to waive entitlement to repayment

The loan can be regarded as having been converted into an outside the scope donation and the club will no longer be required to account for VAT from the date of waiver on the notional interest.

See also *Exeter Golf and Country Club Ltd v C & E Commrs*, CA [1981] STC 211 (TVC 13.32) and *Dyrham Park Country Club Ltd* (VTD 700) (TVC 13.31).

(17) Payphone charges

See **47.8**(17) **OUTPUT TAX**.

(18) Prizes

Special rules apply to prizes in betting, gaming and lotteries. See **57.1–57.5 RECREATION AND SPORT**. Otherwise prizes awarded to competitors in sports and games competitions are always treated in the same way, regardless of whether the entry fees for the competition are exempt or taxable.

- Where the prize is goods, VAT must be accounted for based on the cost of the goods unless the cost of the individual prize to the organisation was £50 or less (excluding VAT).
- Where the prize is in the form of services (e.g. a holiday), if input tax has been claimed on the purchase of services given away as prizes, an equal sum of output tax is due at the time the prize is awarded. If no input tax is incurred no output tax is due.
- Cash prizes are outside the scope of VAT. However, it is important to distinguish between prize money and payments made by sponsors to event organisers which are called prize money but are, in fact, payments for taxable supplies.
- A trophy which remains the property of the competition organiser is outside the scope of VAT.

For prize money from horseracing see **63.31 SPECIAL SCHEMES**.

(19) Shares and debentures

These are used by clubs to raise extra finance from members or prospective members. It is necessary to consider:

- Whether or not there is a single supply (and, if so, whether it is of an exempt security or standard-rated subscriptions).
- If there is a mixed supply, can either component be disregarded on minimal grounds.
- Whether the standard-rated benefits are only being granted as an inducement to persuade people to acquire the exempt supply. See *Hinckley Golf Club Ltd* (VTD 9527) (TVC 13.15) where the tribunal held that the offer of free membership to certain shareholders was simply an inducement to invest and the only supply to those shareholders was an exempt supply of shares in consideration for the purchase price of those shares. See also *Rugby Football Union* (VTD 18075) (TVC 27.54) where the whole of the amount paid by the purchasers of 75-year non-interest-bearing debentures was held to relate to the exempt supply of the debentures and no part to the right given to them to purchase tickets for rugby matches at Twickenham for ten years.

Where any part of the consideration for a share or debenture is to be treated as an additional payment for the advantages of membership, it should be treated as a levy or, for non-monetary consideration, as an interest-free loan (see above).

(20) Sponsorship rights

Output tax is due not only on the money received from the sponsor but also on any payments made by the sponsor to third parties. This includes expenses of staging a competition or event and the value of any prizes given under the terms of the sponsorship agreement. See **57.19 RECREATION AND SPORT**.

(21) Sport and physical recreation facilities

Use of such facilities (including billiards, pool and snooker, tennis courts, bowling greens, etc.) are normally exempt when made by an eligible body and standard-rated in other cases. Where a grant of facilities for playing any sport or participation in any physical recreation amounts to a grant of land or property, it may qualify for exemption under the '24 hour' rule or the 'series of lets' provisions. See **57.8–57.14 RECREATION AND SPORT**.

When payments are linked to the operation of lighting e.g. squash courts or snooker tables, the full amount payable by players is standard-rated as the charge is for the right to use the facilities and does not relate to the supply of electricity. See *St Anne's-on-Sea Lawn Tennis Club Ltd* (VTD 434) (TVC 30.4).

(22) Swipe cards, vouchers and other types of payment credits

If an organisation arranges for its members to maintain credit balances in order to make payment for goods and services (e.g. when using the bar facilities), it must consider the following points to determine when it must account for VAT.

- Where a member makes a payment that creates or contributes to a credit balance, (whether as a compulsory or voluntary levy) on either
  (a) the issue, renewal or topping up of a card; or
  (b) the purchase of vouchers
  the organisation need not account for VAT until the credit is used to make taxable purchases, even if the payment is not refundable.
  The payment must not be treated as part of the subscription for VAT purposes.
- Where an unused credit balance is repayable to the member, the credit and refund have no VAT consequences.
- Where unused balances or unredeemed vouchers revert to the organisation, it must account for VAT at the time of reversion as if they were part of the member's subscription.

(23) Tours organised by clubs, etc.

Where a club buys hotel accommodation and travel, for example, from a third party, and sells them on as principal, the club must use the **TOUR OPERATORS' MARGIN SCHEME (68)**.

(VAT Notice 701/5/11, paras 6.1–6.7, 7.1, 8, 9.1–9.4, 10.1–10.3).

Non-business activities

[14.6] A club or association may have non-business activities. These are mainly activities for which no payment is required or, where there is a payment, no benefit is provided in return. Examples include

- free admission to premises for non-members;
- spreading political beliefs or lobbying for a public or charitable good cause (but not lobbying on behalf of members which is a business activity);
- providing free literature to non-members; and
- the receipt of freely given donations, where no benefit is supplied in return (see **14.2** above for more information on subscriptions and donations).

See **8 BUSINESS** generally for what constitutes a business for VAT purposes.

Any VAT incurred on goods or services used wholly for the purpose of a non-business activity is not input tax and cannot be reclaimed.

If goods or services are purchased partly for business and partly for non-business purposes, the VAT incurred must be apportioned to reflect the amount attributable to business activities. Only this amount can be reclaimed. Alternatively, in the case of goods (but not services) purchased partly for business and partly for non-business purposes, the full amount of tax can be reclaimed as input tax provided output tax is accounted for on the non-business use in each VAT period. See **34.7 INPUT TAX** for fuller details.

(VAT Notice 701/5/11, paras 2.3, 3.2).

Trade unions, professional and other public interest bodies

[14.7] The provision of facilities and advantages to members of clubs, associations and other organisations is normally standard-rated (see **14.1** above) but their provision by certain professional, learned or representational associations can be exempt. See **18.25**(*l*) and (*o*) **EUROPEAN UNION LEGISLATION** for the provisions of *Directive 2006/112/EC*.

The eligible organisations are those 'non-profit making' bodies falling into one of the following categories.

(a) Trade unions and other organisations

Trade unions and other organisations whose main objectives are to negotiate the terms and conditions of employment of their members.

'*Trade union*' is an organisation (whether permanent or temporary) which consists wholly or mainly of

- workers of one or more descriptions; or
- constituent or affiliated organisations; or
- representatives of such constituent or affiliated organisations. The principal purposes of the organisation must include the regulation of relations between workers and employers or employers' associations.

[*VATA 1994, Sch 9 Group 9 Item 1(a); Trade Union and Labour (Consolidation) Act 1992, s 1*].

What is now *Directive 2006/112/EC, Art 132(1)(l)* (previously *EC 6th Directive, Art 13(A)(l)*) refers to 'organisations with aims of a . . . trade-union . . . nature'. The ECJ has held this to mean 'an organisation whose main aim is to defend the collective interests of its members—whether they are workers, employers, independent professionals or traders carrying on a particular economic activity—and to represent them vis-à-vis the appropriate third parties, including the public authorities' provided those objects were put into practice. (*Institute of the Motor Industry v C & E Commrs, ECJ Case C–149/97*, [1998] STC 1219 (TVC 22.310)).

(b) Professional associations

Professional associations, membership of which are 'wholly or mainly' restricted to individuals who have or are seeking a qualification appropriate to the practice of the profession concerned. [*VATA 1994, Sch 9 Group 9 Item 1(b)*].

Membership of the association should be obligatory, or at least customary, for those pursuing a career in that profession.

'*Wholly or mainly*' is regarded as 75% or more.

The qualifications held or sought must relate to what is a recognised profession. They should be obligatory or customary to enable the profession to be undertaken and should be awarded by the association of which the holder is a member.

'Profession' is not defined but HMRC regard it as restricted to those occupations which would be generally understood to be professions. Indications which point towards this are

- the status of the occupation and those engaged in it;
- whether or not persons within the occupation require a qualification;
- whether the persons within the occupation are governed by a code of conduct;
- a distinctive and broad base of knowledge from which a person may subsequently diversify into more specialised areas;
- the association's aims and objectives; and
- the actual activities carried out by it.

However, these are not fixed criteria and some occupations which are not currently regarded as professions may acquire that status in the future.

(VAT Notice 701/5/11, paras 11.6, 11.8).

Bookmaking (*The Bookmakers' Protection Association (Southern Area) Ltd* (VTD 849) (TVC 64.13)), driving a taxi-cab (*City Cabs (Edinburgh) Ltd* (VTD 928) (TVC 64.14)) and the practice of reflexology (*The Association of Reflexologists* (VTD 13078) (TVC 64.27)) have been held not to be professions but the teaching of dance has been so held (*Allied Dancing Association Ltd* (VTD 10777) (TVC 64.1)). See also *Institute of Leisure and Amenity*

Management v C & E Commrs, QB [1988] STC 602 (TVC 64.18). For a fuller list of associations which have been held to fall within or, as the case may be, outside these provisions, see the chapter *Trade Unions, Professional and Public Interest Bodies* in *Tolley's VAT Cases*.

(c) Learned societies

Learned societies, i.e. any association, the 'primary purpose' of which is the advancement of a particular 'branch of knowledge' or the fostering of professional expertise, connected with the past or present professions or employments of its members. Membership must be restricted 'wholly or mainly' to individuals whose present or previous professions or employments are directly connected with the purposes of the association. [*VATA 1994, Sch 9 Group 9 Item 1(c)*].

An association can have only one primary purpose (although it does not have to be the sole purpose) which should be clear from

- the objects and objectives set out in the memorandum and articles of association or constitution;
- the powers and actual activities of the association;
- what the association itself and the members consider its primary purpose to be.

The '*branch of knowledge*' must be a recognised branch of science or the arts and should therefore be more academic than practical in content. Normally it would be included in a degree course or equivalent. Knowledge relating to the confined area of a specific job does not constitute a branch of knowledge.

See (*b*) above for a consideration of 'profession'. Professional expertise is construed accordingly.

'*Wholly or mainly*' is regarded as 75% or more.

(VAT Notice 701/5/11, paras 11.11–11.14).

See *Royal Photographic Society* (VTD 647) (TVC 64.12) (where lack of the restriction on membership disqualified the Society from exemption) and *Institute of Leisure and Amenity Management v C & E Commrs*, QB [1988] STC 602 (TVC 64.18).

(d) Representational trade associations

Representational trade associations, i.e. any association, the 'primary purpose' of which is to make representations to the Government on legislation and other public matters which affect the business or professional interests of its members. Membership must be restricted 'wholly or mainly' to individuals or corporate bodies whose business or professional interests are directly connected with its aims. [*VATA 1994, Sch 9 Group 9 Item 1(d)*].

See (*c*) above for the primary purpose test. The representations should be to the UK government.

'*Wholly or mainly*' is regarded as 75% or more.

(VAT Notice 701/5/11, para 11.15).

In *European Tour Operators Association* (TC00965) (TVC 64.8) the tribunal held that, for the purpose of *Item 1(d)*, the reference to 'the Government' should not be construed as being restricted to the UK Government; exemption should include representations to EU institutions in relation to matters that will have effect in the UK.

(e) Bodies of a political, religious, patriotic, philosophical, philanthropic or civic nature

Bodies of a political, religious, patriotic, philosophical, philanthropic or civic nature which have objects in the public domain. [*VATA 1994, Sch 9 Group 9 Item 1(e); FA 1999, s 20; SI 1999/2834*]. These bodies have objects which are directed outside the particular organisation and beyond the members themselves to the general community. Bodies which are not registered charities may qualify. Major political or religious bodies will also often satisfy this requirement because the public will have a general interest in their activities.

There are no legal definitions of the various bodies included but HMRC suggest that the following describes their everyday meaning.

- A political body is one that campaigns for or against legislative and constitutional changes or campaigns in local and central government elections.
- A religious body includes all denominations, creeds, old and new, that command a following.
- A patriotic body does good work for the benefit of a nation state or for those who have served their country and their dependants.
- A philosophical body is one whose primary purpose is the advancement of a particular way of thinking but which is not of a political or religious nature. It is very similar to a learned society as described in (*c*) above in that they are both of an academic nature.
- A philanthropic body does good work for the direct benefit of the general community or a particular section of the community or is designed to promote the wellbeing of mankind.
- A civic body is one which has objects which promote rights and duties of citizens in matters of public interest and public affairs, and whose objects do not solely or mainly benefit its members.

(VAT Notice 701/5/11, paras 12.1, 12.2).

See also *The English-Speaking Union of the Commonwealth* (VTD 1023) (TVC 13.5).

(f) Constituent or affiliated associations

An organisation or association, the membership of which consists wholly or mainly of constituent or affiliated associations which as individual associations would be within (*a*) to (*d*) above. [*VATA 1994, Sch 9 Group 9 Note (3)*].

'Non-profit making'

HMRC consider, when judging whether an organisation is non-profit making, the objects for which an organisation has been established, as distinct from the financial policy being pursued. Although the organisation may generate income surpluses from various activities, they will not refuse recognition as a non-profit making organisation simply because these surpluses subsidise other activities. If a body has a constitution or articles of association that bars it from distributing surpluses of income over expenditure to its members, shareholders or any other party, other than in the event of a liquidation or cessation of activities, HMRC normally accept it as non-profit making for the purposes of this exemption. However, the existence of any provision barring distribution will not necessarily be the sole factor in determining whether an organisation is non-profit making. (VAT Notice 701/5/11, para 11.3).

Fund-raising events

The supply of goods and services by a non-profit making body within (*a*)–(*f*) above in connection with an event whose primary purpose is the raising of money and which is promoted as such is exempt from VAT where

- the event is organised exclusively for its own benefit; or
- the event is organised, jointly by one or more charities and the non-profit making body, exclusively for charitable purposes or that body's own benefit or a combination of those purposes.

See **12.10 CHARITIES** for full details.

Exempt supplies

[14.8] Supplies of services, and related goods, by a non profit-making body within **14.7**(*a*)–(*f*) above to its members are exempt provided

- they are made available without payment (other than a membership subscription); and
- they are referable only to the aims of the organisation.

[*VATA 1994, Sch 9 Group 9 Item 1*].

Exemption does not apply to

(a) supplies that do not relate to the body's aims as set out in its rules, articles of association, constitution, etc. (although see **14.9** below for provision of hospitality to members);
(b) the supply of any right of admission to any premises, event or performance (e.g. for a conference) for which non-members have to pay [*VATA 1994, Sch 9 Group 9 Note (1)*];
(c) any supplies which are not provided automatically as part of the membership benefits and for which an additional sum is charged; and
(d) supplies to non-members.

Supplies within (*a*)–(*d*) above are taxable unless exempt under any other provision. These might include training under *VATA 1994, Sch 9 Group 6* (see **16.7 EDUCATION**), fund-raising events organised by charities and non-profit making bodies under *VATA 1994, 9 Sch Group 12* (see **12.10 CHARITIES**) and sporting events under *VATA 1994, Sch 9 Group 10* (see **57.10 RECREATION AND SPORT**).

Subscriptions with a taxable component

Where a subscription includes a component which is not exempt, the rules in **14.2** above on apportionment of subscriptions should be considered.

Subscriptions which include a right of admission

The right of admission to any premises, event or performance is specifically excluded from the exemption. This means that

- any payments for admission in addition to the subscription are always standard-rated; and
- if an event is subsidised by subscriptions, a component of that subscription is standard-rated and an apportionment may be necessary.

The table below sets out examples of possible methods of charging and the VAT consequences. In each case, it is assumed that the organisation is a qualifying organisation that has satisfied all the other criteria for exemption and the event is referable to the organisation's aims.

Method of charging for admission	*Is the standard-rated right of admission included in the subscription?*
Free admission to members only or member and guest	No
Free admission to members: charge to non-members	Yes
Members only for a charge: event self-financing	No
Members only for a charge: event subsidised by subscriptions	Yes
Members and non-members admitted for a charge but members pay less: event self-financing	No

(VAT Notice 701/5/11, paras 13.1–13.3).

Other supplies

Registration fees

[14.9] In certain professions, persons cannot practice unless they are registered with a statutory body and have paid fees which are prescribed by law. Such registration fees are normally outside the scope of VAT because, in carrying out these statutory functions, the organisation is not supplying a service in the course of its business. Where, however, there is no such statutory requirement, the liability is as follows.

- *Registration in return for a subscription payment.* Where no additional fee is charged and the member is automatically registered on payment of the subscription, the service of registration is standard-rated unless referable to the aims of the association in which case it qualifies for exemption under **14.8** above.
- *Registration for a separate fee.* As the registration is in return for a payment 'other than a membership subscription' it cannot qualify for exemption under **14.8** above and is standard-rated.

If the registration is accompanied by other clearly identifiable supplies of goods or services, the fee must be apportioned accordingly.

Collection charges for union subscriptions

Charges raised by employers for deducting union subscriptions from employees' pay are exempt under *VATA 1994, Sch 9 Group 5*. See **23.9**(3) **FINANCIAL SERVICES.**

Provision of hospitality

Where meals, hotel accommodation, etc. are provided to members without charge, then unless directly connected with the organisation's aims (e.g. at the annual conference), the supply is standard-rated and the subscription must be apportioned. Such hospitality is not business entertainment (because the membership in general is paying for it in the subscription) and input tax incurred can therefore be deducted, subject to the normal rules. The business entertaining provisions do apply to free hospitality to non-members and input tax cannot be deducted.

The provision of hospitality for a charge to members or non-members is standard-rated.

(VAT Notice 701/5/11, paras 13.5–13.7).

Key points

[14.10] Points to consider are as follows.

- A club or association that provides benefits to its members in return for a subscription payment will generally have income that is both taxable and exempt. If it receives donations and grants, it will also have income that is outside the scope of VAT. In deciding whether the club needs to be VAT-registered on a compulsory basis, it is important to only consider taxable sources of income. If the total of these income sources has exceeded the VAT registration limit in the past twelve months, or is expected to exceed the limit in the next 30 days, then it will need to be VAT-registered. The VAT registration limit increased from £70,000 to £73,000 annual taxable sales on 1 April 2011.

- Many clubs and associations have non-business activities. It is important that input tax is initially blocked on any expenditure relating to non-business activities. If an expense is partly for business and partly for non-business purposes, then an apportionment must be made using any method that is fair and reasonable.
- The fact that many clubs and associations have both taxable and exempt income means they are partly exempt as far as VAT is concerned. It is therefore important that input tax is claimed on any expenditure directly relevant to taxable activities, e.g. bar stock for resale but not on any expenditure relevant to exempt activities. In terms of apportioning input tax on general overhead items (known as residual input tax in partial exemption terms), it might be worthwhile considering the benefits of a special method of calculation. A special method must be approved by HMRC and can relate to any method of calculation apart from the standard method based on income.
- Many smaller clubs and associations might be able to achieve full input tax recovery on costs relevant to their exempt activities if they are classed as *de minimis* as far as partial exemption is concerned. Be aware that two new *de minimis* tests were introduced on 1 April 2010, which could mean more clubs and associations qualify as *de minimis* from this date. This could produce a useful windfall of up to £7,500 per annum in some cases.
- A useful concession for non-profit making bodies is that subscription income can be apportioned according to the different VAT rates that apply to specific membership benefits, even if there is one main supply that would normally determine the rate at which VAT is charged on the entire subscription. This concession could be useful to produce zero-rating on the value of any newsletter provided as part of a membership scheme. However, zero-rating of printed matter does not apply to a newsletter sent by electronic means (e.g. by email).
- A donation is only relevant if the person making the donation receives no benefits in return for his donation, i.e. no goods or services are supplied by the club or association receiving the donation. A simple acknowledgement of thanks, for example, in an event programme is not classed as a benefit. However, a marketing opportunity or benefit, such as an advertisement on the association website, would be classed as a benefit.
- The supply of benefits to members by trade unions, professional associations, learned societies, representational trade associations and bodies of a political, religious, patriotic, philosophical or philanthropic nature may qualify for VAT exemption. The same principle applies to membership subscriptions relevant to non-profit making bodies providing sport and physical education services (e.g. a members golf club).
- A challenge for clubs and associations can sometimes occur when it is necessary to decide whether a branch or section of the main association is classed as being independent as far as VAT is

concerned (i.e. no output tax due on its income unless it is separately VAT-registered in its own right), or whether it is part of the association and therefore within the scope of the main VAT registration. The key factor will be the constitution of the branch or section, and establishing whether it has its own financial independence.

- It is sometimes thought (incorrectly) that VAT exemption in relation to fundraising events only applies if the event is being organised by a charity. This is incorrect. The exemption also applies to events organised by non-profit making bodies (e.g. the annual fundraising dinner for a members rugby club).
- The VAT liability of room hire income earned by a club or association can sometimes cause a problem. As a general principle, such income is exempt from VAT if the hirer has exclusive use of the room in question, and assuming there is no option to tax election in place on the building where rental income is being generated. However, room hire income can become standard rated (or a mixed supply situation) if the hirer is mainly paying for other benefits (e.g. catering).

15

Death and Incapacity

Introduction

Assets passing to personal representatives

[15.1] Where the control of a deceased person's assets passes to a personal representative or person otherwise acting in a representative capacity, that person must comply with the VAT requirements relating to accounting, payment and records. However, any requirement to pay VAT is limited to the assets over which he has control in his capacity as personal representative. [*SI 1995/2518, Reg 30*]. HMRC may therefore require the personal representative to account for any outstanding returns or VAT which was due on the date of death.

Carrying on a business

Where a taxable person dies, HMRC may, from the date of death until some other person is registered in respect of the taxable supplies made (or intended to be made) by a business, treat any person carrying on the business as a taxable person. The person carrying on the business must, within 21 days of commencing to do so, inform HMRC in writing of the date of death and the fact that the business is being continued. [*VATA 1994, s 46(4); SI 1995/2518, Reg 9*]. The person carrying on the business is responsible for ensuring that all the VAT obligations are complied with and must account for any VAT due on supplies made by the business whilst he controls the business as if he were the taxable person.

Executor *de son tort*

An executor *de son tort* is a person, neither appointed by the deceased or the court to administer the deceased's property, who nevertheless 'interferes' with the deceased's property, e.g. by carrying on the business activities.

Where an executor has been appointed (whether by the deceased or by the court) and there is also an executor *de son tort* who is running the business on a day-to-day basis, HMRC will regard the executor *de son tort* as both the 'person otherwise acting in a representative capacity' within *SI 1995/2518, Reg 30* and as the 'person carrying on that business' within *SI 1995/2518, Reg 9*. This means that the liability for any debts arising from the business activities of the deceased, whether pre-death or post-death, can be treated as being the liability of the executor *de son tort* and the appointed executor will be ignored as far as the VAT debts of the business are concerned.

(HMRC VAT Guidance V1–28, paras 70.1.6, 70.2.3).

Death of a partner

Under *Partnership Act 1890, s 33(1)*, subject to any agreement between the partners, every partnership is dissolved as regards all the partners by the death of any partner. Until the death is notified to HMRC in writing, the registration and VAT liability of the partnership continues unchanged. See **50.3 PARTNERSHIPS**. On the death of a partner

- where the business of the partnership is to continue only for the purposes of winding up the partnership affairs, HMRC will consider using powers under *SI 1995/2518, Reg 9* rather than require the business to be re-registered for VAT purposes;
- where two or more partners remain after the death and continue to trade
  - (a) if the partnership is registered in the name of the firm, HMRC will simply strike off the name of the deceased partner from the Form VAT 2; and
  - (b) if the partnership is registered in the names of the individual partners, it will amend the trader's name on the register (using Form VAT 12) and strike off the name of the deceased partner from the Form VAT 2; and
- where only one surviving partner remains after the death
  - (a) if he intends to continue trading on his own as a sole proprietor, HMRC will deregister the partnership and register the sole proprietor under a new VAT number (using Form VAT 1). The surviving partner may, however, apply for the transfer of the existing registration under the procedure in **59.36 REGISTRATION**, in which case he must sign the Form VAT 68 both on behalf of the partnership and on his own behalf as a sole proprietor;
  - (b) if he intends to find a replacement for the deceased partner and the new partner takes up his position in the partnership more or less immediately, HMRC will amend the trader's name (if the partnership is registered in the names of the individual partners), and ask the new partner to sign a Form VAT 2; and
  - (c) if he intends to find a replacement for the deceased partner but it appears that there may be some delay before this happens, HMRC will register the remaining partner as a sole proprietor either by de-registering the partnership and registering the sole proprietor or, on request, transferring the existing registration under the procedure in **59.36 REGISTRATION**.

(HMRC VAT Guidance V1–28, para 70.3).

Death of a sole proprietor

Normally, on the death of a sole proprietor, HMRC will seek to re-register the person carrying on the business in his own right, regardless of the official status of that person. This may mean deregistration followed by re-registration or the transfer of registration under the procedure in **59.36 REGISTRATION** (with the executor signing a Form VAT 68 on behalf of the deceased's estate in favour of the person carrying on the business). If the executor or administrator of the estate carries on the business, he will not be registered in his official capacity but as the individual and the 'taxable person' who is carrying on the business.

HMRC will only generally invoke the *SI 1995/2518, Reg 9* procedure above where it is clear that the business will be transferred to the beneficiary or sold on as a going concern within the near future. Once the estate is settled and the business is in the hands of the new owner, HMRC will then register the new taxable person, either by deregistration followed by re-registration or the transfer of registration under the procedure in **59.36 REGISTRATION.**

(HMRC VAT Guidance V1–28, para 70.4.1).

VAT consequences of incapacity

Assets passing to another person

[15.2] here a person becomes 'incapacitated' and control of his assets passes to another person, that person must comply with the VAT requirements relating to accounting, payment and records. However, any requirement to pay VAT is limited to the assets of the incapacitated person over which he has control. [*SI 1995/2518, Reg 30*]. HMRC may therefore require that person to account for any outstanding returns or VAT which was due when incapacity commenced.

HMRC consider a person to be '*incapacitated*' if, as the result of some physical affliction or disability or of some mental disorder, he is, either temporarily or permanently, incapable of controlling and managing his property and business affairs and, consequently, incapable of meeting his obligations under the VAT legislation. They will only treat a person as being mentally incapacitated in those cases where a medical determination has been made that a person has a mental disorder within the meaning of the *Mental Health Act 1983*. The question of whether a physical incapacity constitutes incapacity for these purposes will depend on the facts of the particular case. (HMRC VAT Guidance V1–28, para 70.1.9).

Carrying on a business

Where a taxable person becomes incapacitated (see above), HMRC may, from the date of incapacitation until some other person is registered in respect of the taxable supplies made (or intended to be made) by a business, treat any person carrying on the business as a taxable person. The person carrying on the business must, within 21 days of commencing to do so, inform HMRC in writing of the date of incapacity and the fact that the business is being continued. [*VATA 1994, s 46(4); SI 1995/2518, Reg 9*]. The person carrying on the business is responsible for ensuring that all the VAT obligations are complied with and must account for any VAT due on supplies made by the business whilst he controls the business as if he were the taxable person.

Incapacity of a partner

A partnership is not automatically dissolved in the event that one of the partners becomes incapacitated although a partner may apply to the court for a dissolution of the partnership if he can show that one of the partners is 'lunatic' or 'of permanently unsound mind'. [*Partnership Act 1890, s 35*]. On the incapacity of a partner,

- where the incapacity of a partner is likely to be temporary and there are two or more partners continuing to trade, HMRC will allow the partnership to continue accounting for VAT under its existing registration (in accordance with *VATA 1994, s 45(1)*, see **50.2 PARTNERSHIPS**) and make no amendments to the registration details;
- where a court orders the dissolution of the partnership or the incapacitated partner resigns but, in either case, two or more partners remain and continue to trade
  - (a) if the partnership is registered in the name of the firm, HMRC will simply strike off the name of the incapacitated partner from the Form VAT 2; and
  - (b) if the partnership is registered in the names of the individual partners, it will amend the trader's name on the register (using Form VAT 12) and strike off the name of the incapacitated partner from the Form VAT 2; and
- where a court orders the dissolution of the partnership or the incapacitated partner resigns but, in either case, only one partner remains, HMRC will either
  - (a) deregister the partnership and register the sole proprietor under a new VAT number (using Form VAT 1); or
  - (b) at the request of the remaining partner, transfer the existing registration under the procedure in **59.36 REGISTRATION**, in which case he must sign Form VAT 68 both on behalf of the partnership and on his own behalf as a sole proprietor.

(HMRC VAT Guidance V1–28, para 70.6).

Incapacity of a sole proprietor

On the incapacity of a sole proprietor,

- where there is strong evidence that the incapacity is only likely to be short-term, HMRC may treat the person carrying on the business as the taxable person under *SI 1995/2518, Reg 9* above until the proprietor is capable of taking over the business again. The trader's name on the register will be amended to read 'X carrying on the business of Y';

- where the incapacity is likely to be long-term or permanent and another person carries on the business, HMRC will register that person in his own right as the taxable person; and
- where the incapacity is likely to be long-term or permanent and the business ceases altogether, the business will be deregistered with effect from the date on which trading ceased.

(HMRC VAT Guidance V1–28, para 70.7).

Relief for importations of goods acquired by inheritance

[15.3] Certain persons who have become entitled as legatees to property situated outside the EU may import that property without payment of VAT (and duty). See **33.15**(13) **IMPORTS**.

Relief for importations re war graves, funerals

[15.4] Certain goods can be imported without payment of VAT (and duty). These comprise goods for the upkeep of war graves, memorials, etc.; coffins and urns containing human remains; and flowers, wreaths, etc. with no commercial intent. See **33.15**(12) **IMPORTS**.

American war graves

[15.5] In order to place inland purchases on the same footing as imported goods, VAT is remitted on the supply of goods and services to the American Battle Monuments Commission for the maintenance of the American Military Cemetery and Memorial at Maddingley, Cambridge and Brookwood, Surrey. (VAT Notice 48, ESC 2.5).

Burial and cremation

[15.6] *Directive 2006/112/EC, Art 371* allows EU countries to continue to exempt certain services listed in *Annex X*. These include services supplied by undertakers and cremation services, together with goods related thereto. Under this provision, UK law exempts

- the disposal of the remains of the dead, and
- the making of arrangements for, or in connection with, the disposal of the remains of the dead.

[*VATA 1994, Sch 9 Group 8*].

Certain other services, such as the right to a grave space and the right to place an urn in a niche, are exempt under *VATA 1994, Sch 9 Group 1* (see **15.7** below).

HMRC has always regarded the EU and UK law in *Group 8* as applying only to the *essential* goods and services that an undertaker or crematorium has to supply in order to dispose of the remains of the dead. This follows the opinion of the tribunal in *UFD Ltd* (VTD 1172) (TVC 24.26) which considered that the normal meaning of the words 'disposal of the remains of the dead' were to be construed to mean, and to be confined to, the services supplied by undertakers *as such* and cremation services. This allows undertakers and crematoria to exempt their services of burial (including burial at sea) and cremation, and the arrangements that have to be made to provide those services.

Funerals for pets are standard-rated.

(1) Supplies by undertakers and funeral directors

The table below indicates HMRC's view of the liability of supplies provided by undertakers and funeral directors.

Supply	*VAT liability*
The following goods and services when provided as part of a funeral package that includes the disposal of the remains of the dead • Supply of a coffin • The cover and fittings for a coffin • The casket or urn • Embalming • The digging, preparation and refilling of graves • The transport of the deceased to the burial ground or crematorium • A shroud or robe • Use of a chapel of rest • Provision of bearers • Transport of mourners in own limousines • Bell tolling and music at the funeral service	Exempt
The following services provided the dead body has been released from the mortuary to the bereaved family to arrange the funeral (regardless of whether the service is provided direct to the bereaved or to a third party, such as another undertaker or funeral director) • Embalming • Use of a chapel of rest • Digging, preparation and the refilling of graves • Burial or cremation • The interment of ashes	Exempt
Selling coffins, urns, shrouds or embalming fluid	Standard-rated (unless provided by an undertaker as part of a funeral package – see above)
Flowers, wreaths, announcement cards and other commemorative items	Standard-rated

Supply	*VAT liability*
Newspaper announcements	Standard-rated
Hire of hearse with driver by an undertaker or funeral carriage master	Exempt
Hire of limousine with driver from one undertaker to another for the transport of mourners as part of the funeral	Exempt
Hire of vehicle with driver in other circumstances	Standard-rated
Hire of a hearse or limousine without a driver	Standard-rated
Catering	Standard-rated
Fees payable to Registrars for certified copies of death certificates	Outside the scope of VAT
Fees payable to churches for ministers' services	Outside the scope of VAT
Orders of service for use in funeral commemorative services	Zero-rated as printed matter
Agency services	Standard-rated
Services aimed at checking customer satisfaction	Standard-rated

Packages of mixed supplies

Where exempt supplies and standard-rated supplies are provided as a single price package, a suitable apportionment must be made for VAT purposes. There is no special method of apportionment but the result must be fair and justifiable. See **47.3 OUTPUT TAX** for various methods of apportionment.

Disbursements

Funeral packages frequently contain 'bought in' supplies (e.g. an undertaker may pay a hotel, caterer, newspaper publisher, etc. for goods and services as the agents of his client and recharge the client the exact amount paid out. If the payments meet the relevant conditions set out in **3.7 AGENTS**, they may be treated as disbursements and can be excluded when calculating any VAT due on the main supply.

(VAT Notice 701/32/12, para 3).

(2) Supplies by cemeteries and crematoria

The following supplies are exempt from VAT.

- Burial (including reburial) and cremation
- Interment of ashes
- Digging, preparation and refilling of a grave
- Supplying an urn or casket in connection with a particular funeral
- Brick, block or concrete lining of a grave when constructed as a requirement of the cemetery management (or in the case of a churchyard, the church authorities) where, for example, the soil is unstable
- Any interest in, right over or licence to occupy land within *VATA 1994, Sch 9 Group 1* (see **41.2 LAND AND BUILDINGS: EXEMPT SUPPLIES AND OPTION TO TAX**) including the right to a grave space and the right to place an urn in a niche

- The exhumation of a body that is reburied elsewhere at the behest of the bereaved
- The supply of a cremation certificate (form B, C or F) by a doctor
- The removal of a pacemaker from the deceased prior to cremation

The following supplies are not exempt from VAT and are standard-rated.

- Charges for erecting, working on, or repairing monuments within a cemetery or crematorium, except where the removing or refixing of memorial headstones is necessary to allow further burial
- Any interest in, right over or licence or to occupy land that the business has opted to tax, including the right to any grave space or the right to place an urn in a niche
- Goods and services in connection with the commemoration of dead people
- Exhumation services not connected with reburial to another site

See also **15.7** below.

(VAT Notice 701/32/12, para 5).

Local authorities

In *Rhondda Cynon Taff County Borough Council* (VTD 16496) (TVC 22.146) the tribunal held that the provision and maintenance of *cemeteries* by a local authority was not a business activity for VAT purposes as the activities had been carried out under a special legal regime applicable to public authorities. The tribunal also concluded that, as there are so few privately-owned cemeteries, the non-business ruling would not distort competition. Following this decision, HMRC take the view that:

- The decision only applies to the provision and maintenance of local authority cemeteries. Non-business activities include the grant of a right to an exclusive burial, the right to place and maintain a tombstone, the keeping and storage of the plans and records of burials, general maintenance, and any actions intended to remove dangerous obstructions, e.g. collapsed vaults or broken headstones. Other services offered for which a charge is made (e.g. the provision of books of remembrance and the erection of headstones) remain business activities as the provision of these services is not covered by the special legal regime applicable to cemeteries.
- Although crematoria are governed by special legal provisions similar to those which apply to cemeteries, the higher incidence of privately-owned crematoria means that a distortion of competition would result if local authorities were allowed to treat these activities as non-business.
- Where local authorities operate sites which contain both cemeteries and crematoria and they have exceeded the partial exemption *de minimis* limits, a business/non-business apportionment must be made between the activities.

(3) Memorials and commemoration of the dead

Supplies of goods or services which are concerned with the commemoration, as opposed to the burial or cremation, of the dead are normally standard-rated. These include

- The supply of memorial headstones
- Erecting, repairing or maintaining memorial headstones
- Inscribing services for headstones, plaques or other commemorative items
- Flowers and wreaths
- Planting trees or rosebushes
- Memorial vases and seats
- Plaques including services of fixing them
- Placing 'In Memoriam' announcements in newspapers
- Recording entries in books of remembrance.

The removal, refixing and incidental cleaning of a memorial headstone, when a grave is disturbed to allow for a further burial, is exempt as it forms part of the arrangements made in connection with that burial. But VAT must be charged for adding another inscription to the memorial.

(VAT Notice 701/32/12, para 6).

(4) Transportation of the dead

Within the UK

Where an undertaker or a funeral carriage master transports a dead person	*Tax treatment*
to a burial ground or crematorium as part of a funeral (whether this service is supplied to the bereaved family or to another undertaker)	Exempt
to an undertaker or funeral director who will provide the funeral	Exempt
from a school, university or research institution to a burial ground or crematorium	Exempt
to a public mortuary	Standard-rated

Repatriation packages supplied by undertakers

Where an undertaker or business specialises in repatriation and supplies a repatriation package consisting of goods and services that are normally provided by undertakers, the supply will be exempt from VAT to the extent that it consists of the supply of:

- goods and services such as coffin, embalming, use of chapel of rest (see those exempt in **15.6**(1) above);
- services of obtaining documents and permits necessary to repatriate the deceased; and
- transportation of the deceased to burial ground, crematorium or to another undertaker.

The place of supply is where the customer (that is, the person with whom they contract) belongs if the customer is 'in business' (e.g. an insurance company or undertaker) and receives the services otherwise than wholly for private purposes.

If the customer is a private individual, such as a member of the deceased's family, the place of supply is where the undertaker belongs.

International transportation supplied by airlines and other carriers

If an airline or other general purpose carrier transports a body between the UK and another country, they should apply the same VAT rules as those for transporting goods. A summary is below.

If a body is transported for an insurer, undertaker or other business customer, the place of supply, from 1 January 2010, is where the customer belongs for the purposes of receiving the supply. It does not matter where the dead body is being transported to or from.

A dead person is transported for a business customer, and the customer belongs	*then, the place of supply of services is*	*Tax treatment*
In the UK	UK	supply is zero rated if the dead person is transported from a place within to a place outside the EU (or vice versa). Otherwise, it is standard-rated.
In another EU country	EU country in which the customer belongs	the customer should account for VAT (if applicable) in their Member State under the 'reverse charge'
	outside the EU	the supply is outside the scope of EU VAT

If the transport services are supplied to a non-business/private individual, such as a relative of the deceased, the place of supply is as follows.

A dead person is transported for a private individual	*Tax treatment*
The transportation is from the EU to a third country (or vice versa)	the place of supply is where the transportation is performed in proportion to the distances covered. The supply is zero rated to the extent that it takes place in the UK. The supplier may have to register for VAT in the other EU country.

The transportation begins and ends in the EU	the place of supply is wholly where the transportation begins. If the transportation begins in the UK, the supplier must account for standard-rated VAT in the UK (unless the movement is from, to or between the islands of the Azores or Madeira, in which case it is zero-rated). If the transportation begins in another EU country, the supplier may have to register for VAT there.

If the place of supply is outside the UK then the supply is outside the scope of UK VAT and there is no VAT liability within the UK. However, the supplier will be able to recover any input tax incurred in making the supply, subject to the normal rules. The supplier may have a liability to VAT register in other EU countries where the supplies are made.

When human remains are brought to the UK from overseas, there is no import VAT or acquisition tax due when a coffin containing a dead body or an urn containing ashes is brought into the UK from overseas. The same rules apply to flowers and wreaths accompanying the coffin or urn.

(VAT Notice 701/32/12, para 7).

(5) Prepayments and funeral plans

Many individuals wish to pay for their funeral in advance. As funeral directors cannot legally accept advance payments for a funeral, this can be done by either of the following methods.

A trust-based plan

The individual pays a plan provider, by lump sum or instalments, for an agreed funeral package. On the death of the plan holder, the provider pays the nominated funeral director for the funeral as specified in the plan.

The nature of the supplies by the plan provider depends upon whether it is acting as principal or agent.

- If the plan provider acts as principal (i.e. is contractually responsible for delivering the funeral to the plan holder's estate), the full amount paid by the plan holder into the plan is consideration for the provider's supply of a funeral package. The provider must apportion the payment between exempt and standard-rated elements of the package.
- If the plan provider acts as agent (i.e. the contract for the delivery of the funeral is between the funeral director and the plan holder and the plan provider's role is to facilitate this arrangement), any administration or other fee charged by the plan provider is standard-rated.

The payments which the funeral director receives for providing the funeral are exempt to the extent that the plan covers exempt supplies. If the plan covers any standard-rated supplies, an apportionment must be made.

Any commissions or marketing fees received by funeral directors (or others) for selling trust-based prepayment plans are standard rated.

A whole life insurance policy

The following table covers the VAT liability of payments and supplies made in connection with each.

Supply	*VAT liability*	
	Trust-based plan	*Life insurance plan*
Payment from plan provider to nominated funeral director on death of customer for burial or cremation	Exempt	Exempt
Payment from plan provider to nominated funeral director on death of customer for a funeral package of different liabilities	The funeral director must apportion the payment between the exempt and standard-rated supplies	The funeral director must apportion the payment between the exempt and standard-rated supplies
Deposit or advance payment made by plan provider to nominated funeral director for a funeral package of different liabilities	Generally to be apportioned on same basis as whole package	Generally to be apportioned on same basis as whole package
Payments made by individual to a plan provider	If plan provider is acting as agent — outside the scope of VAT If plan provider is acting as principal — apportioned between the exempt and standard-rated elements of the funeral package	Exempt
Management fee charged by plan provider	If plan provider is acting as agent — standard-rated If plan provider is acting as principal — apportioned between the exempt and standard-rated elements of the funeral package	N/A
Agent's fee for selling a plan (but see *Funeral Planning Services Ltd*) (VTD 19975) (TVC 16.5)	Standard-rated	Exempt
Payment by deceased's estate to nominated funeral director to cover shortfall	Exempt to the extent that it relates to exempt elements of the package	Exempt to the extent that it relates to exempt elements of the package
Charges for cancelling or amending plan	Standard-rated	N/A

(VAT Notice 701/32/12, para 4).

De Voil Indirect Tax Service. See V4.151.

Grants re land

[15.7] The grant or an interest in, right over or licence to occupy land is exempt under *VATA 1994, Sch 9 Group 1*. See **41.2 LAND AND BUILDINGS: EXEMPT SUPPLIES AND OPTION TO TAX.** Services which are exempt under this *Group* do not have to rely on a connection with a particular funeral. Examples include the right to

- a grave space; and
- place an urn in a niche.

(VAT Notice 701/32/12, para 5.1).

The grantor, however, has the option to tax any such supply at the standard rate (see **41.8 LAND AND BUILDINGS: EXEMPT SUPPLIES AND OPTION TO TAX**).

Key points

[15.8] Points to consider are as follows.

- In the event of the death of a sole trader, the person carrying on the business after his death will be treated as a taxable person by HMRC in terms of expecting all VAT responsibilities to be met and tax to be correctly accounted for and declared on VAT returns. The situation is not the same if a member of a partnership dies because continuity will be given by the surviving partners.
- If a partner dies, and two or more partners continue to run the business after his death, there is no need for the partnership to deregister. An amendment to form VAT2 (list of partners) can be made instead. If only one partner survives, then he has the choice of either retaining the same VAT registration number by completing form VAT68 to register as a sole trader, or the partnership can deregister and he can reregister as a sole trader from a current date with a new VAT number.
- In some cases, it is possible that the death of a partner will mean that taxable sales of the business in the next twelve months could be less than the deregistration threshold (annual sales of £70,000 or less with effect from 1 April 2011). In such cases, the opportunity to deregister might be a worthwhile planning opportunity. However, it is important to be aware of the need to account for output tax on most stock and assets held at the time of deregistration.
- The services of funeral directors and undertakers are mainly exempt from VAT if they relate to arrangements for the disposal of the dead. However, some services are not exempt because they do not directly relate to the disposal procedures. For example, services linked to arranging flowers, catering and newspaper announcements are all standard-rated.
- In certain situations, an undertaker or funeral director will arrange for costs to be paid on behalf of his client, which he will include on his final sales invoice. If he is merely acting as an agent

in arranging and paying for these supplies, then they could qualify as a disbursement and be outside the scope of VAT. However, it is important that the rules relating to disbursements are correctly applied to avoid the potential risk that HMRC could deem them to be standard-rated.

- Be aware that the supply of goods or services intended to recognise or commemorate the dead, as opposed to being linked to their burial or cremation, are standard-rated rather than exempt from VAT. An example is the cost of supplying and erecting a memorial headstone.

16

Education

Cross-references. See **18.24 EUROPEAN UNION LEGISLATION** for the provisions of Directive 2006/112/EC; **25.8 FUEL AND POWER** for supplies of fuel and power to charitable schools; **28.12 HEALTH AND WELFARE** for supplies by registered nurseries and playgroups.

De Voil Indirect Tax Service. See V4.141.

Introduction

[16.1] VAT exemption for education, research and training is largely dependent on

- whether the body is in business for VAT purposes (see **16.2** below); and
- if so, whether it is an eligible body (see **16.3** below).

Having established that the activities are business

(a) supplies of education and vocational training by an eligible body are exempt (see **16.4** and **16.7** below respectively);
(b) supplies of research by an eligible body to another eligible body are exempt (see **16.6** below); and
(c) supplies of certain goods and services related to exempt supplies within (*a*) and (*b*) above are also exempt (see **16.8** below).

Where the business is not an eligible body, exemption may also apply, subject to conditions, to

- private tuition (see **16.9** below);
- examination services (see **16.10** below); and
- government approved training schemes (see **16.14** below).

Business

[16.2] For VAT purposes, business has a wide meaning and includes any continuing activity which is mainly concerned with making supplies to other persons for any form of payment or consideration. For a general consideration of the meaning of business, see **8.1** to **8.3 BUSINESS**.

A supply of education takes place for VAT purposes where it is provided by way of business and in return for a consideration. If there is no payment, the education is not a supply and is a non-business activity outside the scope of VAT.

Education is normally funded in one of three ways.

(1) By making a charge

In such cases, there is a business activity whoever pays the charges (e.g. a student, an employer or a local authority) and whether charges raised are sufficient to meet full costs or are subsidised (e.g. by central government grant, bursaries or scholarships).

Establishments which normally provide education in return for fees and are therefore in business include

- independent fee paying schools, including non-maintained special schools;
- universities; and
- institutions teaching English as a foreign language.

(2) By direct funding from local or central government

Education funded in this way is not a business activity and the supply is outside the scope of VAT. This normally applies to

- community schools;
- foundation schools;
- voluntary aided schools, including former special agreement schools;
- voluntary controlled schools;
- community special schools;
- foundation special schools;
- grant maintained (integrated) schools (Northern Ireland);
- self-governing schools (Scotland);
- city technology colleges; and
- free schools; and
- academies.

Where such schools charge for additional tuition (e.g. music or sport instruction), this is a business activity.

(3) By a combination of government grants and charges

In such cases, there is a supply for VAT purposes. The government funding is an outside the scope contribution to a business activity. Institutions which *may* require payment include

- sixth form colleges;
- tertiary colleges; and
- colleges of further education.

These institutions normally provide education for no charge to students who are 19 or under (18 or under in Scotland) at the start of their courses (non-business) but charge for older students and foreign nationals (business). The important factor is always whether they require payment, not the age or identity of the student.

(VAT Notice 701/30/11, paras 2.1–2.5, 3.1–3.2).

Eligible bodies

[16.3] An '*eligible body*' for the purposes of providing exempt education comprises any of the following.

(a) Schools

A school within the meaning of *Education Act 1996*, *Education (Scotland) Act 1980*, *Education and Libraries (Northern Ireland) Order 1986 (SI 1986/594)* or *Education Reform (Northern Ireland) Order 1989 (SI 1989/2406)* which is

(i) provisionally or finally registered (or deemed to be registered) as a school within the meaning of that legislation in a register of independent schools;
(ii) a school in respect of which grants are made by the Secretary of State to the proprietor or managers;
(iii) a community, foundation or voluntary school within the meaning of the *School Standards and Framework Act 1998*, a special school within the meaning of *Education Act 1996, s 337* or a maintained school within the meaning of *Education and Libraries (Northern Ireland) Order 1986*;
(iv) (before 31 December 2004) a public school within the meaning of *Education (Scotland) Act 1980, s 135(1)*;
(v) a self-governing school within the meaning of *Self-Governing Schools (Scotland) Act 1989*; or
(vi) a grant-maintained integrated school within the meaning of *Education Reform (Northern Ireland) Order 1989, Art 65*.

This covers all of the schools listed in **16.2** above. Many of these schools (notably community, foundation and voluntary schools and their counterparts in Scotland and NI) do not generally make a charge for the education they provide and this education is, for the most part, non-business and outside the scope of VAT (see **16.2** above). However, under limited circumstances, they can make a charge (e.g. music or sport tuition or mature students filling sixth form places) and, because they are eligible bodies, such charges are exempt.

Schools not covered by (i)–(vi) above may be covered by the eligible body criteria in (e) below.

(b) Universities

A UK university, and any college, institution, school or hall of such a university. Not included are subsidiary companies that universities and colleges set up to pursue commercial business.

Previously, HMRC treated companies owned or controlled by universities as eligible bodies only where they had been formally approved by the parent university as a college, institution, school or hall of the university. Following the cases of *C & E Commrs v School of Finance and Management (London) Ltd*, Ch D [2001] STC 1690 (TVC 21.11) and *HIBT Ltd* (VTD 19978) (TVC 21.17), HMRC have revised their policy with regard to education supplied by university trading companies. From 11 March 2010, a university owned/controlled company is an eligible body where it provides university level education leading to a qualification awarded by a university or nationally recognised body; and it has close academic links with the parent university, e.g. students on the company's courses are registered/enrolled with the parent university, subject to its rules and regulations and awarded qualifications by it. (VAT Information Sheet 3/10).

A Students Union was held not to be an integral part of the University and therefore not part of an eligible body in *C & E Commrs v University of Leicester Students Union*, CA 2001, [2002] STC 147 (TVC 21.19).

The UK campus of a foreign university is not covered but it is likely to be an eligible body under (e) below.

(c) Further and higher education

An institution

- falling within *Further and Higher Education Act 1992, s 91(3)(a) or (b) or s 91(5)(b) or (c)*;
- which is a designated institution as defined in *Further and Higher Education (Scotland) Act 1992, s 44(2)*;
- managed by a board of management as defined in *Further and Higher Education (Scotland) Act 1992, s 36(1)*; or
- to which grants are paid by the Department of Education for Northern Ireland under *Education and Libraries (Northern Ireland) Order 1986, Art 66(2)*.

This includes all further education colleges or organisations defined or designated as such under the various *Education Acts* (including the Workers' Educational Association (WEA)), together with higher educational institutions defined in the *Education Acts* but not covered by (b) above.

(d) Public bodies

A government department or local authority (or a body which acts for public purposes and not for its own profit and performs functions similar to those of a government department or local authority). Included are executive agencies and Health Authorities.

(e) Charities

A body which

(i) is precluded from distributing and does not distribute any profit it makes; and
(ii) applies any profits made from exempt supplies of education, research or vocational training to the continuance or improvement of such supplies.

Most such bodies will be charities, professional bodies or companies limited by guarantee. However, provided they satisfy the conditions in (i) and (ii) above, ad hoc groups organising specific conferences or training events are eligible. The UK campuses of foreign universities are also eligible bodies but non-profit making organisations that belong overseas do not qualify as eligible.

(f) Teaching English as a foreign language

A body not falling within *(a)*–*(e)* above which provides the teaching of English as a foreign language (see **16.11** below).

[*VATA 1994, Sch 9 Group 6 Note 1; SI 1994/2969; Education Act 1996, Sch 37 Part 1 para 125; School Standards and Framework Act 1998, Sch 30*].

Eligible bodies do not include bodies such as tutorial colleges, computer training organisations, secretarial schools and correspondence colleges which operate with a view to making and distributing a profit.

(VAT Notice 701/30/11, paras 4.1–4.6).

Education

[16.4] The provision of 'education' is exempt

- when provided by an '*eligible body*' (see **16.3** above); or
- to the extent that the consideration payable is ultimately a charge to funds provided by the Learning and Skills Council for England or the National Assembly for Wales under *Learning and Skills Act 2000, Parts I or II*. *Included* is the supply of any goods or services essential to the education provided directly to the person receiving the education by the person providing the education. See, for example, *Creating Careers* (VTD 19509) (TVC 21.29).

[*VATA 1994, Sch 9 Group 6 Items 1(a), 5A; Learning and Skills Act 2000, Sch 9 para 47*].

'*Education*' is not defined in the legislation. HMRC regard education as meaning a course, class or lesson of instruction or study in any subject, regardless of where and when it takes place. Education includes lectures, educational seminars, conferences and symposia, together with sporting and recreational courses. It also includes distance learning (see **16.5** below) and associated materials. Any separate charge for registration is part of the supply of education.

In the sports sector, education includes classes that are led and directed rather than merely supervised. For example

- in a gymnasium, the supply of instruction in the use of equipment and warming-up techniques and the assessment of a person when he or she first enrols is the supply of education; but a charge to use the gym in a separate session where no instruction takes place is a charge for admission; and
- in a swimming pool, if the staff are on hand primarily to coach, any charge is the supply of education; but if staff are on hand primarily to satisfy health and safety and insurance requirements, any charge is for admission.

(VAT Notice 701/30/11, paras 5.1, 5.2).

See **16.10** below for the teaching of English as a foreign language.

Distance learning

[16.5] Distance learning covers home study or correspondence courses from suppliers that range from commercial businesses to colleges of further education and universities and in subjects that range from leisure pursuits to those leading to full academic qualifications.

The VAT liability of the supply depends upon the exact nature of what is being supplied. This may be

- an exempt supply of education by an eligible body;
- a standard-rated supply of education by a business which is not an eligible body;
- a single supply of zero-rated printed matter; or
- a multiple supply of printed matter and education, in which case an apportionment is necessary.

In *The College of Estate Management v C & E Commrs*, HL [2005] STC 1597 (TVC 5.36) the tribunal held that there was single exempt supply of education and the House of Lords upheld this decision stating that it was inappropriate to analyse the transaction in terms of what was a principal and ancillary supply.

See also *The Rapid Results College Ltd* (VTD 48) (TVC 5.2) where fees for correspondence courses were held to be apportionable between the supply of books and tuition but compare *International News Syndicate Ltd* (VTD 14425) (TVC 5.3) where the small element of external tuition was held to be incidental and the whole supply treated as zero-rated. However, these decisions pre-dated the decision in *Card Protection Plan* and must be read in the light of the criteria set out in that case.

Research

[16.6] *Note.* In *EC Commission v Federal Republic of Germany, ECJ Case C–287/00*, [2002] STC 982 (TVC 22.303) the ECJ held that remunerated research activities of State universities were not closely related to university education and did not fall within the scope of the exemption. While such projects might be of assistance to university education, they were not essential to the objective of teaching students to enable them to carry out a profession and many universities achieved that aim without carrying out research projects for consideration. The exemption of research under UK law and the following provisions of this paragraph must be read in the light of that decision.

The provision of research supplied *by* an 'eligible body' *to* an eligible body is exempt. [*VATA 1994, Sch 9 Group 6 Item 1(b)*]. See **16.3** above for '*eligible body*'.

'*Research*' is not defined in the legislation. HMRC regard research as meaning 'original investigation undertaken in order to gain knowledge and understanding'. It is the intention at the beginning of a project that determines whether a supply qualifies as research. If the intention is to advance knowledge and understanding, the supply is one of research. By contrast, merely confirming existing knowledge and understanding is not research. The fact that a project may have a specific commercial application does not necessarily mean that it cannot also be research.

The following are examples of work which HMRC do not regard as being research.

- Consultancy and business efficiency advice.
- Collection and recording statistics, without also collating, analysing or interpreting of them.
- Market research and opinion polling.
- Writing computer programs.
- Routine testing and analysis of materials, components and processes.

But some of these activities do qualify if supplied as an integral part of a research project (e.g. where a specialised software program must be devised before the provider can embark upon the main body of the project).

(VAT Notice 701/30/11, para 5.6).

If either of the parties to a supply of research is not an eligible body (e.g. a commercial organisation) the supply will normally be standard-rated (but see below for supplies to overseas bodies). Note, however, that the recipient of the supply does not have to be involved in the field of education, research or vocational training. If the recipient is a non-profit making body satisfying the criteria in **16.3**(*e*)(i) above, but making no supplies of education, etc., the criteria of **16.3**(*e*)(ii) above have no relevance and it is an eligible body. Supplies of research to that body are exempt. The supplier must determine the status of the customer and, if not satisfied that the customer is an eligible body, must standard-rate the supply.

European Commission Framework 6 and 7 research programmes

If a research provider carried out research under the Framework 6 programme, payments received are consideration for a supply. VAT should not be charged to the Commission as it is recognised as an international organisation by its host country, Belgium, and the supply is therefore exempt under *Directive 2006/112/EC, Art 151(1)(b)*, see **18.31**(*b*) EUROPEAN UNION LEGISLATION. The provider can recover input tax directly attributable to the exempt supply under *Directive 2006/112/EC, Art 169(b)*.

However, funding under the Framework 7 programme is grant income. As such, where VAT is incurred on goods and services purchased purely to support non-business research activities, it is not input tax and cannot be recovered.

(VAT Notice 701/30/11, para 5.8).

Government grant-funded research

Grants provided by central government to fund research (as opposed to research commissioned by the government) are generally paid by the granting body to fulfil the body's statutory and public duties to fund research, not to secure a benefit for it or any third parties. The majority of public-funded research is generally for the public good and the body funding it does not receive any supply of goods or services in return for the funding. In those cases, the grant does not constitute consideration for a supply and is thus outside the scope of VAT.

(VAT Information Sheet 4/08).

Vocational training

[16.7] The provision of 'vocational training' by an 'eligible body' is exempt. [*VATA 1994, Sch 9 Group 6 Item 1(c)*]. See **16.3** above for '*eligible body*'.

'*Vocational training*' means training, re-training or the provision of work experience for

- any trade, profession or employment; or
- any voluntary work connected with education, health, safety or welfare or with the carrying out of activities of a charitable nature.

[*VATA 1994, Sch 9 Group 6 Note 3; SI 1994/2969*].

Vocational training includes courses, conferences, lectures, workshops and seminars designed to prepare those attending for future employment or to add to their knowledge in order to improve their performance in their current work. *Not included* are services such as counselling, business advice and consultancy, which are designed to improve the working practices and efficiency of an organisation as a whole.

Supplies by persons other than eligible bodies

Although falling outside the above provisions, such supplies may be exempt if

- the business contracts or subcontracts to provide vocational training under one of the government's approved vocational training schemes and its services are ultimately funded by the Young People's Learning Agency or the Skills Funding Agency, the National Council for Education and Training for Wales, a Local Enterprise Company or the European Social Fund (under a scheme approved by the Department for Education), see **16.14** below; or
- provided by a sole proprietor or partnership and also qualifying as private tuition within **16.8** below.

(VAT Notice 701/30/11, paras 5.5, 6.1–6.2).

Related goods and services

[16.8] Exemption also applies to the supply of any goods or services (other than examination services within **16.10** below) which are 'closely related' to an exempt supply within **16.4** to **16.7** above (the 'principal supply') provided

- the supply is made *by* or *to* the 'eligible body' making the principal exempt supply;
- the goods or services are for the direct use of the pupil, student or trainee (as the case may be) receiving the principal supply; and
- where the supply is *to* the eligible body making the principal supply, it is made by another eligible body.

[*VATA 1994, Sch 9 Group 6 Item 4*].

See **16.3** above for '*eligible body*'.

Meaning of closely related

'*Closely related*' limits the provisions to goods and services that are necessary for delivering the education to the pupil, student or trainee. An eligible body may treat as closely related any accommodation, catering, transport, school trips and field trips it provides (subject to the rules below for selling goods to pupils).

HMRC give the following examples of goods and services that are not closely related to supplies of education and are taxable, in principle, unless relief is available elsewhere. (This is subject to the overriding principle that supplies of catering by an eligible body to its pupils, students or trainees may be treated as closely related.)

- Supplies to staff (including tutors on summer schools) and to other non-students.
- Sales of goods from school shops, campus shops and student bars.
- Sales from vending machines.
- Sales of goods that are not needed for regular use in class.
- Separately charged laundry and other personal services.
- Sales of school uniforms and sports clothing.
- Admission charges (other than for taking part in sports activities), e.g. admissions to plays, concerts, dances, sporting venues, exhibitions, museums, zoos.
- Administration and management services.
- Commission for allowing sales by outside organisations at an educational establishment.
- Sales by a sole proprietor or partnership in connection with private tuition.

Where closely related supplies are eligible for exemption and zero-rating (e.g. books and other printed matter and transport) either liability may be applied. Supplies of goods and services which are not closely related to education are taxable unless relief is available elsewhere.

Closely related goods and services sold to pupils by an eligible body providing education, etc.

The provisions relating to closely related supplies only apply where the principal supply is an *exempt* supply. They do not apply where the principal supply is outside the scope of VAT as a non-business supply. As a result where education, research or vocational training is supplied by an eligible body

- in the course or furtherance of business (an exempt supply), closely related goods or services sold to pupils are also exempt; and
- for no charge (outside the scope of VAT), closely related goods or services sold to pupils are non-business and outside the scope of VAT provided they are sold at or below cost (otherwise they assume their normal VAT liability).

If the goods and services sold to pupils are not closely related to the education, etc. provided, they are standard-rated unless relief is available elsewhere.

(VAT Notice 701/30/11, paras 8.1–8.7).

Private tuition

[16.9] The supply of private tuition is an exempt supply provided it is

(a) in a subject ordinarily taught in a school or university; and
(b) given by an individual teacher acting independently of an employer.

[*VATA 1994, Sch 9 Group 6 Item 2*].

A reasonable test for 'ordinarily' is whether the subject is taught in a number of schools and/or universities on a regular basis.

Following the tribunal decision in *C & E Clarke; A & H Clarke* (VTD 15201) (TVC 21.40) HMRC accept that private tuition is exempt when supplied by a sole proprietor, a partnership or any member of a partnership. However, because of the wording in (*b*) above, exemption does not extend to instruction delivered by anyone employed (even if the teacher concerned is the sole shareholder of a company) and is restricted to tuition provided by a teacher acting in an individual or personal capacity (see *HMRC v Empowerment Enterprises Ltd*, CS [2006] CSIH 46 (TVC 22.306)). Where a sole proprietor or partnership also employs teachers, supplies can be apportioned between exempt and taxable elements using and fair and reasonable method. If this is impractical, all supplies of tuition can be treated as standard-rated regardless of who actually delivers them. Employing someone in a non-teaching capacity has no effect on the VAT liability of tuition supplied.

Supplies of any goods and services in connection with the supply of tuition

Even if such supplies are closely linked, they are standard-rated unless relief is available elsewhere (e.g. books may be zero-rated).

(VAT Notice 701/30/11, paras 6.1–6.2).

Examination services

[16.10] The provision of 'examination services'

(a) by or to an 'eligible body', or
(b) to a person receiving education or vocational training which is
   - exempt under **16.4**, **16.7** or **16.9** above or **16.14** below, or
   - provided otherwise than in the course or furtherance of a business

is an exempt supply.

'*Examination services*' include

- the setting and marking of examinations;
- the setting of educational or training standards;
- the making of assessments; and
- other services provided with a view to ensuring educational and training standards are maintained.

[*VATA 1994, Sch 9 Group 6 Item 3* and *Note 4; Learning and Skills Act 2000, Sch 9 para 47*].

See **16.3** above for '*eligible body*'.

Examples of activities treated as examination services are services connected with GCSE examinations, etc., National Vocational Qualification (NVQ) assessments, course accreditation services, validation, certification, assessment and registration of candidates. *Not included* are

- services of printers, graphic designers, and typesetters; and
- non-specialist secretarial, advertising or promotional services (unless provided as part of a broader package of predominantly examination services by the same person who provides those services).

Supplies direct to pupils

Included under (*b*) above is the supply of examination services *directly* to

- pupils of independent fee paying schools;
- pupils of community, foundation or voluntary schools;
- students of further education colleges;
- trainees of government approved training schemes; and
- employees receiving in-house training from their employers.

Examination boards normally provide GCSE examinations direct to school pupils. Schools can usually treat as disbursements the payments they receive from and on behalf of pupils for these examinations. See **3.7 AGENTS** for the treatment of disbursements.

School inspections

School inspections are in principle within the scope of exemption for examination services and are therefore exempt if provided by or to an 'eligible body' (see (*a*) above).

(VAT Notice 701/30/11, paras 7.1–7.4).

English as a foreign language (EFL)

[16.11] Exemption applies to tuition in EFL by *any* body (see **16.3**(*f*) above). Where, however, the body does not also qualify as an eligible body under another category within **16.3**(*a*)–(*e*) above, exemption does not extend to any other supplies which the body makes apart from the 'teaching of English as a foreign language'. [*VATA 1994, Sch 9 Group 6 Note 2; SI 1994/2969*].

HMRC interpret this as meaning that exemption does not extend to other education, research or vocational training (e.g. tuition in a language other than English or training in the teaching of EFL) supplied by a commercial provider of EFL who is not within **16.3**(*a*)–(*e*) above.

Following the decision in *Pilgrims Languages Courses Ltd v C & E Commrs*, CA [1999] STC 874 (TVC 21.20) HMRC accept that all elements integral to the supply of any course in the teaching of EFL by a commercial provider are covered by the exemption (e.g. sports, recreational, sightseeing or social activities aimed at promoting fluency in the use of the English language). In addition, any separate supplies of closely related goods and services are also exempt provided they meet the conditions set out in **16.7** above.

Where courses are supplied in modular form, comprising some tuition in EFL plus broader coverage of other subjects, the supply can be apportioned to reflect the exempt element using any fair and reasonable method. If this is inconvenient or impractical, the whole supply can be standard-rated.

(VAT Notice 701/30/11, paras 9.1–9.3).

Education supplied by local authorities

[16.12] Any education or vocational training provided by local authorities for no charge, or which they provide acting as a public authority, is a non-business activity. Local authorities are, however, eligible bodies (see **16.3**(*d*) above) and all other educational or vocational training courses that they provide for any form of charge or payment are generally exempt business supplies, irrespective of any subsidy they may receive. See *City of London Corporation* (VTD 17892) (TVC 22.148) where the tribunal held that, on the facts, the Corporation was not carrying on a business activity in respect of three schools, even though it charged fees to most of the parents. The schools had been established under special legal provisions and the Corporation was required to maintain them.

Most schools in the state sector belong to one of three categories of 'maintained school', namely community, foundation or voluntary. All such schools are maintained by a local authority (LA) and receive funding from it. The governing body of each school acts as agent of the LA for goods and services it pays for either out of the school's delegated budget from the LA or from amounts given to the school from LA central funds for specific purposes. Where the local authority has a statutory duty to defray all expenses of maintaining a school, e.g. community schools, then it can recover VAT incurred on such purchases under *VATA 1994, s 33* (see **43.7 LOCAL**

AUTHORITIES AND PUBLIC BODIES). However, in the case of voluntary aided schools the governing body retains statutory responsibility for certain capital expenditure, including when made from the school's delegated budget. HMRC previously accepted that local authorities could recover the VAT incurred on expenditure which is the responsibility of the governing bodies but which the authority funds. They are now of the opinion that *VATA 1994, s 33* is confined to VAT incurred by local authorities etc. on the goods and services that they purchase, not on the goods and services that another legal entity purchases. Therefore, with effect from 1 September 2009, with respect to projects initiated after that date, VAT may no longer be recovered by local authorities in these circumstances, as the supplies are not made to them (whether or not paid for from the delegated budget). A local authority may, however, continue to recover VAT on expenditure at a voluntary aided school for which the local authority is statutorily responsible, or where the local authority, rather than the governing body, procures a supply of works and pays for that supply from its own funds.

Private funds of LA schools

LA maintained schools can also generate income independently (e.g. through vending machines or charges for the use of the premises outside normal hours). Such 'private fund' income is generally kept in a separate bank account and is not part of the local authority for VAT purposes but a separate entity. The private fund might be held in the name of the governing body, the head teacher (acting as agent of the governing body) or some other entity (e.g. a Parent Teacher Association). Subject to the normal threshold, a school (in the guise of its private fund) must register for VAT separately if it makes taxable supplies that generate income which does not belong to the LA and which it uses purely to augment its own funds.

Input tax recovery on purchases using private funds

If the private fund is separately registered for VAT, it can recover input tax subject to the normal rules and the local authority cannot recover the VAT incurred on any private fund purchases.

Alternatively, where a private fund has obtained income other than via the local authority, it can opt to donate the money to the local authority for them to buy goods and services on the private fund's behalf. The local authority can then recover the VAT incurred provided it

- makes the purchase itself (i.e. places the order, receives the supply and a VAT invoice addressed to it, and makes the payment);
- retains ownership of the purchase and uses it for its own non-business activities; and
- keeps sufficient records of the purchase and the purpose for which it is made.

This donational route is not, however, available in respect of

- certain direct grants from the Department for Education and Skills (DfES) to the governing bodies of foundation schools; and

- income, including direct grants from the DfES, used to fund works which are the responsibility of the governors of a voluntary aided school.

Where the school keeps the income it obtains from letting its premises, the income can be treated in the same way as budget share funds when the school uses it to buy goods and services (i.e. the school is deemed to be acting as agent of the LA in spending the money and the LA is entitled to recover VAT incurred on the purchases).

Sales of 'closely related' supplies made by a local authority to its own pupils and students

Local authorities are 'eligible bodies' so that any education they provide for a charge (e.g. adult education classes) is an exempt business activity. Any closely related goods and services they supply in connection with this education are also exempt (see **16.8** above). However, most of the education that local authorities provide is not for a charge and is therefore a non-business activity and outside the scope of VAT. Because LA maintained schools do not supply education in the course or furtherance of business, it follows that any goods and services they provide to their pupils for a charge in connection with this education are not exempt, even though they might be closely related. As a concession, LA maintained schools can treat the closely related goods and services they supply to pupils as non-business, provided it complies with the following rules which have been agreed with CIPFA.

- The goods and services must be closely linked to the education provided (i.e. for the direct use of the student and necessary for delivering the education to the student).
- The pupil must receive education from the LA in either an LA maintained school or in connection with some other LA run educational activity (e.g. an orchestra).
- The goods and services required must be purchased from the LA.
- Payment for the goods must be made either to the LA or to the school (and, if the latter, it must be paid into official funds).
- Some evidence (e.g. an order form) must be kept to show that the recipient of the goods and services has been receiving education from the LA, and that what has been supplied was essential to that education.
- The price of the goods and services supplied must be at or below cost. 'Cost' means the overhead-inclusive price of supplying the goods or services to the pupil.

Where any goods are leased, the same conditions apply as for sales.

In practice, regardless of the precise nature of the activity, any school trips that a school organises for the benefit of its pupils can be treated as part of its non-business provision of education.

Supplies of food and drink in LA schools

Sales of food and drink by an LA in its maintained schools to its pupils are non-business and therefore outside the scope of VAT if made at or below cost (see above). The 'at or below cost' criterion can be determined in one of two ways.

- A school can look at all the LA catering outlets on its premises (e.g. canteen, refectory, tuck shop, kiosk, trolley, vending machine. etc.). Provided the total sales are at or below cost, the school can treat all its sales of food as non-business. HMRC, exceptionally, allow a school to apply the 'at or below cost' criterion for each catering outlet. Output tax would then only be due in relation to the outlets where cost is exceeded.
- An LA can analyse all its school catering outlets together. This will produce a single set of figures, from which the LA can determine whether catering is provided at or below cost across its whole school portfolio.

This treatment applies only to sales of food and drink by a local authority school to its pupils and from outlets operated by either the local authority itself or the governing body. If the supply of food and drink is by a catering contractor, see **11.9 CATERING.**

If staff and visitors are free to use any of the catering outlets provided by the school, an apportionment by any fair and reasonable means must be applied to determine the level of taxable business sales.

Closely related supplies made by a local authority other than to its own pupils and students

By concession, LA maintained schools may treat as non-business any closely related goods and services they supply direct to the *pupils* of other schools and to the students or trainees of eligible bodies (e.g. FE colleges and universities). They cannot exempt any closely related goods and services they supply to *other eligible bodies* unless they also supply the education or training itself.

Grant assistance for students on training courses

Where a local authority provides a grant to a student attending further education establishments (e.g. to cover tuition, board, and other necessary expenses), regardless of whether the grant is paid to the training establishment or the student, it does not represent payment for any supplies made to the local authority. As the supplies are made to the student and not the local authority, there is no entitlement to input tax recovery by the local authority. This remains the case even where the local authority is billed direct for any of the supplies made.

Community education

Local authorities must ensure that certain forms of community education are available in their area although they are not obliged to supply it themselves. If they choose to do so, they compete with a broad range of education providers offering similar services in different parts of the country. This is a business activity.

School photographs

See **16.18** below.

Fuel and power

See **25.8**(1) **FUEL AND POWER.**

(VAT Notice 701/30/11, paras 10.1–10.9; VAT Notice 749, para 5.8; HMRC VAT Guidance V1–14, para 12.2; Business Brief 14/95; HMRC Brief 53/09).

Education Action Zones ('EAZs')

[16.13] EAZs consist of local clusters of maintained schools working in partnership with the local authorities ('LAs'), local parents, businesses, Training and Enterprise Councils and others. A major aim of the EAZ initiative is to raise education standards in certain deprived areas. Under the scheme, the governing bodies of participating schools can delegate their powers to the Education Action Forum which runs the EAZ. Membership of the Forum is drawn from the above groups. EAZs receive Government funding each year and are expected to raise further funding from the private sector. They are not, however, part of the local authority and are not entitled to make use of the refunds scheme for non-business activities under *VATA 1994, s 33* (see **43.7 LOCAL AUTHORITIES AND PUBLIC BODIES**).

Recovery of VAT by an EAZ

If a statutory EAZ buys goods and services

- using funds delegated to it by an LA via the governors of participating schools, the LA can recover any VAT incurred (as the EAZ is acting as agent to the LA in the purchase);
- using funds that it has obtained from other sources, the LA cannot recover any VAT incurred (as the EAZ is not acting as its agent);
- via the governors of participating schools using funds it has obtained from non-LA sources, the LA cannot recover any VAT incurred (as the governors are not acting as its agent);
- and incurs VAT that the LA cannot recover, the VAT sticks with the EAZ as a real cost (as the EAZ makes no taxable supplies of its own and so is not registrable for VAT); and
- from an LA using funding channelled to it by the LA via the governors of participating schools, the transaction is outside the scope of VAT (as the EAZ is acting as agent of the LA and no supply takes place).

If an LA supplies teaching staff to an EAZ for purposes of instruction, the LA should not charge VAT (as both the LA and the EAZ are eligible bodies and the supply is exempt).

If an EAZ is non-statutory (i.e. one not established under the *School Standards and Framework Act 1998*), then the LA can recover VAT on goods and services supplied to the EAZ (as the EAZ is acting as agent of the LA in the purchase).

(VAT Notice 701/30/11, paras 11.1–11.3).

Government approved vocational training schemes

[16.14] The provision of 'vocational training' is exempt to the extent that the consideration payable is ultimately a charge to funds provided

- pursuant to arrangements made under *Employment and Training Act 1973, s 2, Employment and Training Act (Northern Ireland) 1950, s 1A* or *Enterprises and New Towns (Scotland) Act 1990, s 2*; or
- by the Learning and Skills Council for England or the National Council for Education and training for Wales under *Learning and Skills Act 2000, Parts I or II*.

Included is the supply of any goods or services essential to the vocational training provided directly to the trainee by the person providing the training. [*VATA 1994, Sch 9 Group 6 Item 5 and Note 5; Learning and Skills Act 2000, Sch 9 para 47; SI 1994/2969*].

The provisions exempt the supply of vocational training under government approved vocational training schemes by suppliers who are not 'eligible bodies' within **16.3** above. Supplies of vocation training by eligible bodies are exempt under the wider provisions in **16.7** above, which see for a general consideration of 'vocational training'.

This exemption covers supplies of

- vocational training, including work experience, and
- any goods and services supplied directly to trainees that are essential to the training

to the extent that they are ultimately funded by schemes approved by the Department for Education, the Department for Work and Pensions (through Job Centre Plus), and devolved administrations in Wales, Scotland and Northern Ireland. The schemes are administered and funded by the Young People's Learning Association (YPLA), the Skill Funding Agency (SFA), local authorities in England (working together with the YPLA), the Welsh Assembly, Skills Development Scotland, and the Training and Employment Agency in Northern Ireland. Approved schemes also include schemes that are paid for using funds derived from the European Social Fund, training administered by further education colleges and funded by any of the bodies listed above, training of workplace assessors in connection with NVQs, and training aimed at providing additional skills for use in the workplace.

Exemption does not cover

- counselling and careers guidance services (unless a compulsory part of a vocational training package); or
- accreditation or assessment services (although these might qualify for exemption as examination services (see **16.10** above).

Supplies by training providers

Where a training provider contracts to supply vocational training under one of the government's approved schemes, its supply is exempt to the extent that the consideration payable is ultimately a charge to funds from one of the approved schemes. But the following should be taken into account.

- If the contract allows for a separate supply of management services, these are not covered by the exemption and must be standard-rated.
- If the trainee or an employer pays part of the cost of the training from their own resources, that part of the supply is not covered by the special exemption. The training provider should apportion between the exempt and standard-rated elements (unless it is an eligible body, see **16.3** above).
- Where the training provider's contract is with a further education college, it must find out what proportion of the payment by the college derives from approved funds within these provisions as, similarly, only this proportion qualifies automatically for exemption (unless the training provider is an eligible body). In determining the proportion, the college may opt to apply a global formula rather than perform a separate calculation each time it buys in a supply of vocational training, i.e. it may express its annual funding allocation as a percentage of its total income for the year and apply this percentage to each purchase of vocational training made in the subsequent year in order to arrive at the proportion that qualifies for exemption.

Where a training provider is given a training credit voucher by a trainee to redeem with the local office of the YPLA or SFA, the income received from the voucher is part of the consideration for the exempt supply.

Supplies by subcontractors

Exemption also extends to a subcontractor's supplies to the extent that the training provider pays for the supplies using government funding obtained within these provisions. It may be difficult to establish the extent to which exemption applies. The subcontractor should ask the training provider for, and keep, evidence that all or part of the supplies are ultimately funded under the scheme. The subcontractor can then exempt supplies to the extent of the funding. If not fully funded, HMRC should accept any apportionment which seems reasonable on the available information. Otherwise, unless the subcontractor is an eligible body within **16.3** above, it should account for VAT on its supplies if the training provider does not confirm that the supplies are ultimately funded under an approved scheme.

Any funding received which must be passed on to trainees or students (e.g. statutory living allowances, travel costs and lodging expenses) is outside the scope of VAT and does not form part of the supply of vocational training.

Work placement providers

Where a work placement provider supplies work experience to a trainee who is its own employee, any payments made to the trainee as wages or allowances are outside the scope of VAT. Where it supplies work experience to

- a trainee or employee of another business, or
- a college student under one of the government's approved vocational training schemes,

any charge for the services of the employee by the business, or the trainee by the college, are standard-rated. This is separate from the supply of exempt vocational training by the work provider to the trainee or student.

Unemployed trainees qualify for a statutory living allowance and, in some cases, expenses. If the work provider funds any such allowances or expenses from its own resources, the amount paid is consideration for a standard-rated supply of the trainee's services by the training provider or college. This applies even if no actual payment is made to the training provider or college.

(VAT Notice 701/30/11, paras 13.1–13.5; Business Brief 13/96).

New Deal programme

[16.15] New Deal is a programme designed primarily to help young people aged 18–24 who have been unemployed for six months or more to obtain long-term employment by providing opportunities for education, vocational training and work experience. The intention is to encourage employers to recruit these people, in return for which they are paid a subsidy. The unemployed are given opportunities to study towards accredited qualifications whilst continuing to claim an allowance equivalent to Jobseeker's Allowance. Although aimed primarily at the 18–24 age group (see **16.16** below), there is also provision for the over 25s (see **16.17** below).

(VAT Information Sheet 3/99, paras 1, 3).

Components of New Deal for 18–24 age group

[16.16] For 18–24 year olds the package is made up of the following components.

Gateway

This lasts for a maximum of four months and offers an intensive period of counselling, advice and guidance, including extensive help from the Jobcentre Plus (JP). Other organisations (the 'partners' in the scheme) provide specialist help where needed (e.g. professional careers advice or debt, homelessness or dependency counselling). Where necessary, short courses in basic skills and brief 'tasters' of the various options available are included in order to decide which is best suited to the individual.

VAT liabilities

- Statutory living and travel allowances are outside the scope of VAT when paid by the Department of Work and Pensions/JP to the partners and in turn by the partners on to the unemployed person.
- The provision of careers guidance and other advice by the JP itself is outside the scope of VAT.
- If partners contract with the JP to supply specific services of counselling, careers advice and other forms of guidance, the supply is to the JP and is standard-rated (unless provided as part of a vocational training package, in which case it is exempt).
- Separately identifiable short courses and 'tasters' covered by such contracts qualify as exempt training and work experience under **16.14** above. However, these elements can be treated as standard-rated if it is impractical to separately identify them.

- If partners use the money they have obtained from the JP to buy in supplies of vocational training and work experience, the supplies made to them are exempt under **16.14** above but supplies of careers advice and other guidance are standard-rated (unless provided as part of a vocational training package, in which case it is exempt).

Options

After entering the Gateway, and assuming that they have not already been successful in securing unsubsidised employment, 18–24 year olds are obliged to take up one of five options, all of which include an element of education or vocational training.

(1) Employment option

Under this option, employers receive a subsidy of £60 per week for up to six months in return for offering young people a job with training. Up to £750 is available towards the cost of vocational training. Young people are paid a wage from the employer and have full employee status with normal conditions of employment.

VAT liabilities

- Payments by the JP to employers of £60 per week wage subsidies and lump sum payments towards the cost of vocational training are outside the scope of VAT.
- If employers use this money to buy in vocational training or work experience, the supply to them is exempt under **16.14** above.

(2) Voluntary sector option

This option offers work with training within the voluntary sector for six months. Up to £750 is available towards the cost of training for an approved qualification, in addition to the fee paid to the job provider. Young people on this option receive an allowance equivalent to Jobseeker's Allowance benefit, plus a grant of up to £400 paid in instalments. Voluntary bodies taking part in the scheme are encouraged to take on participants as employees if they prefer and pay them a wage.

VAT liabilities

- Payments by the JP to work placement providers for non-employed trainees are consideration for exempt supplies of work experience and vocational training under **16.14** above.
- If placement providers use this money to buy in vocational training and work experience, the supply made to them is exempt under **16.14** above.
- Any separately identifiable payments for careers guidance, counselling, job search, etc. are consideration for standard-rated supplies by partners to the JP.
- If placement providers employ the participants, the payments they receive from the JP are outside the scope subsidies towards wage costs.
- Living and travel allowances, and grants of up to £400, passed on to the unemployed person, are also outside the scope of VAT.

(3) Environmental task force option

The option offers work with training on an environmental task force for six months. Payments both to providers and trainees are on the same basis as (2) above.

VAT liabilities

As (2) above.

(4) Full-time education and training

This option, aimed primarily at young people without NVQ level 2 qualifications or the equivalent, lasts up to twelve months. The education and training is available through a variety of local sources (e.g. further education colleges and private training providers). Allowances are paid that are equivalent to benefit, and access is provided to a discretionary fund for help with general living expenses.

VAT liabilities

- Supplies of vocational training and work experience are exempt under **16.14** above.
- Living and travel allowances paid by the JP to partners, and by partners on to unemployed persons, are outside the scope of VAT.

(5) Employment option (self-employment)

Participants normally enter the self-employment route after three months in Gateway. At this stage, they benefit from a special package of counselling, advice and support carried out by a training provider, including a basic awareness and information session. A second stage involves a period of one-to-one counselling or, alternatively, a short course spread over four weeks. At the final stage (self-employment proper), participants receive further training and support from a training provider and the opportunity to set up and run a business on a trial basis whilst receiving a training/trading allowance for up to 26 weeks.

VAT liabilities

At the first stage, the JP pays the training provider £25 for each participant who attends an awareness session. This is consideration for a standard-rated supply by the provider to the JP.

At the second stage, the JP pays the training provider £200 for each participant who successfully completes the short course and produces an approved business plan. This is consideration for a supply of vocational training by the provider to the JP which is exempt under **16.14** above. If the provider is paid the £200 for any participant who has successfully produced a business plan without undergoing a training course, payment is consideration for a standard-rated supply of counselling. Sometimes the provider receives an additional sum of £100 for any participant going straight from Gateway into independent self-employment or unsubsidised work with an employer. This payment is further consideration for the standard-rated supply of general Gateway services by the training provider to the JP.

At the final stage, the JP pays the training provider £1,500 for each participant in three stages, the first two of 25% each and the final of 50% when the training provider confirms to the JP that the participant is still in self-employment or in a job with an employer 13 weeks after leaving the option. All payments are consideration for the exempt supply of vocational training by the training provider to the JP. It follows that, where training providers subcontract for any of these final stage services, supplies by the subcontractors to them are also exempt under **16.14** above to the extent that payments are ultimately derived from JP funding.

Living and travelling allowances paid to participants are outside the scope of VAT if separately identifiable.

Follow-through

This is designed to meet the needs of young people who return to unemployment after completing their option. It involves further intensive help from the JP to get them into work.

VAT liabilities

If partners contract with the JP to supply specific services of careers advice, guidance and mentoring (including access to jobclubs), the supply is to the JP and is standard-rated.

The supply of work experience (including trial placements) and key skills training is exempt under **16.14** above.

If partners use money they have obtained from the JP to buy in vocational training or work experience, the supply to them is also exempt under **16.14** above.

Other services are exempt or standard-rated depending on precisely what is offered and the balance between training and guidance elements.

General principles

The above analysis is based on the premise that, under all the possible arrangements between the JP and partners/contractors (see **16.15** above), the JP is the recipient of a supply of services by the partners/contractors. Where this is the case, the following general principles apply.

- That supply is standard-rated counselling, advice and careers guidance unless it consists of vocational training, in which case it is exempt under **16.14** above.
- Where a single supply comprises elements of both vocational training and careers advice, etc. the vocational training element may be exempted where separately identifiable. If this is impractical, the supply is standard-rated. Alternatively, if the supply is predominantly one of vocational training, any standard-rated elements can be disregarded if it is impractical to separately identify them. At the Gateway and Follow-through stages, elements are predominantly standard-rated. At the Options stage, elements are predominantly exempt.

- Consideration for the supply is the total payment made by the JP to the partner less any element that the partner is obliged to pass on to the unemployed by way of living allowances and travel expenses. (This is subject to the proviso that all payments made by the JP in respect of employed trainees can be treated as outside the scope subsidies towards wage costs.)
- If one partner subcontracts work to another, or to an unrelated third party, in return for payment, that payment is consideration for a supply of services.
- Under consortium and joint venture arrangements, no supply is made to a lead partner or administrator when these merely disburse the JP funding to another partner. The supply is by that partner to the JP.
- Any charge made by the lead partner or administrator to other partners in return for disbursing the JP payments is consideration for the standard-rated supply of a management service.

(VAT Information Sheet 3/99, paras 2, 4; HMRC VAT Guidance, V1–7 Chapter 21 paras 17.3, 17.4).

New Deal for job seekers aged 25 and over

Main 25+ scheme

[16.17] Jobseekers aged 25 and over who have been unemployed for two years or more are covered by an Employment Option under which employers are encouraged to offer jobs, for which they receive a subsidy equal to £75 per week for up to six months. These payments from Jobcentre Plus (JP) are outside the scope of VAT, together with any contribution towards the cost of vocational training.

Jobseekers may also take up an Education and Training Option under which they receive, for example, basic literacy and numeracy training at a further education college. Payments to the college by the JP are consideration for exempt supplies of education or training.

25+ pilot New Deal schemes

A number of pilot schemes have been introduced which aim to extend to unemployed persons as a whole, the principles of the New Deal that applies to the young unemployed (see **16.16** above). The broad objective of the scheme is to allow the individual to benefit from a package of advice and counselling, vocational training, work experience and jobsearch activities to enhance prospects of long-term employment. The schemes have the following components.

(a) *Gateway*. This is a period usually lasting a maximum of 13 weeks with a series of advisory interviews with a personal adviser. Contractors must be able to provide access to a formal training needs assessment, together with basic skills and pre-vocational training for those who need it.

(b) *Intense Activity*. For participants not successful in finding a job as a direct result of (*a*) above, an Intensive Activity period (usually lasting for 13 weeks or until the unemployed person leaves

Jobseeker's Allowance) comprises continuing and concentrated job-search. If this still does not result in full-time subsidised or unsubsidised work with an employer, participants are entitled to a tailored package which may include work experience, training, advice on self-employment, and further help with jobsearch. Throughout this period, in addition to their full entitlement to Jobseeker's Allowance, participants also qualify for a top-up grant of up to £200, together with an employer subsidy of £75 per week for six months. Both the grant and subsidy paid to employers are outside the scope of VAT.

(c) *Follow-through*. There is provision in the scheme for assistance in the form of advice and training to be extended into a further period known as Follow-through, where the help can either be provided by the JP itself or by the contractor in conjunction with the JP.

(d) *Follow-up*. For those who find employment, New Deal contractors must be able to offer additional help to both the participant and the employer, aimed at ensuring wherever possible that the individual remains in that employment. This period of sustained assistance in employment is known as Follow-up.

Funding levels

The JP pay contractors an average of £1,300 per participant. This payment by the JP is consideration for the supply of New Deal services by the contractor to the JP, with the liability of the supply depending on exactly what is provided and the extent to which it can be separately identified. In the absence of appropriate evidence to the contrary, the funding from the JP should be treated as consideration for the standard-rated supply of placement services.

(VAT Information Sheet 3/99, para 5; HMRC VAT Guidance V1–7, Chapter 21 para 17.5).

School photographers

[16.18] The photographer may supply the photographs

- direct to the pupils, in which case the school or LA makes a separate supply of the use of premises, facilities and other services to the photographer in return for the commission or discount they receive; or
- to the school or local authority (LA), in which case the school or LA sells the photos on to the pupils.

Sales of photographs by the photographer directly to pupils

The photographer must account for VAT on the final selling price of the photographs to the pupils.

The position of the school depends upon whether it is independent or LA maintained and, if the latter, also upon whether it acts for the LA or for the governing body in supplying the use of its facilities to the photographer, the type of school and whether it is VAT-registered.

In order to decide the correct VAT treatment of the commission or discount, each time a contract is entered into, the photographer must first establish whether the head teacher is acting for the LA or the governors.

In the following examples, the head teacher is employed by the governors of the school and acts as such on their behalf.

- Foundation and voluntary aided schools in England.
- Self-governing schools in Scotland.
- Voluntary maintained, voluntary grammar and grant maintained integrated schools in Northern Ireland.

In these cases the school will have to charge VAT on the supply of the premises and use of facilities to the photographer, if either

- the taxable turnover from the school, including the income that the school receives from the photographer, exceeds the VAT registration threshold; or
- the school has registered voluntarily for VAT.

The consideration for this supply is the commission or the discount that the photographer pays to the school.

Sales of photographs by the photographer to LAs or schools

Where the contractual arrangements provide that the supply of photographs is to the LA, school or other body,

- *if the LA, etc. is registered for VAT*, the photographer must account for VAT on the price actually charged. The LA, etc. can recover the VAT as input tax subject to the normal rules and must account for output tax on the full value of the supply to the pupils.
- *if the LA, etc. is not registered for VAT*, the photographer should contact HMRC and, pending their advice, account for VAT on the amount actually charged to the LA, etc. HMRC may subsequently issue a Notice of Direction under *VATA 1994, Sch 6 para 2* requiring the photographer to account for VAT on the final selling price charged by the unregistered school to the pupils.

(VAT Notice 701/30/11, paras 12.1–12.3).

Youth clubs

[16.19] The provision of 'facilities' is exempt if supplied by

- a 'youth club' or an 'association of youth clubs' to its members; or
- an association of youth clubs to members of a youth club which is a member of that association.

Youth club

A club is a '*youth club*' if

(a) it is established to promote the social, physical, educational or spiritual development of its members;

(b) its members are mainly under 21 years of age;
(c) it is precluded from distributing and does not distribute any profit it makes; and
(d) it applies any profits made from exempt supplies to the continuance or improvement of such supplies (i.e. it must not use any of its income to subsidise any outside activity).

[*VATA 1994, Sch 9 Group 6 Item 6 and Note 6*].

An '*association of youth clubs*' is an organisation, the members of which are youth clubs.

In addition to (*a*)–(*d*) above, HMRC expect a club to meet the following conditions in order to qualify as a youth club.

- It should provide a range of activities. A single activity club (e.g. a swimming club) is not regarded as a youth club even if its members are mainly under 21 years of age.
- It should have its own constitution. HMRC do not regard youth sections of organisations such as sports clubs, cultural societies and environmental groups as youth clubs unless separately constituted. See also *Haggs Castle Golf Club* (VTD 13653) (TVC 21.53).
- It should be able to produce its own accounts.

Exemption

Exemption covers

- in the case of a youth club, any facilities which the club supplies to members in return for their subscriptions or, provided the facilities are directly related to the club's ordinary activities, for an additional payment; and
- in the case of an association of youth clubs, any facilities which the association supplies to
  (i) youth clubs that are members of the association in return for subscriptions, affiliation fees or similar payment; and
  (ii) members of an individual youth club that is part of the association of youth clubs where the facilities are of a type that would be exempt if provided by a youth club.

Not exempt

Not exempt under these provisions are

- supplies to non-members; and
- supplies not commonly provided by a youth club to its members, e.g.
  — sales of foods and drink;
  — overnight accommodation similar to the type provided by a hotel;
  — purely recreational holidays; and
  — fund-raising events where tickets are sold to the public (although certain fund-raising events may be exempt under *VATA 1994, Sch 9 Group 12*, see **12.10 CHARITIES**).

Facilities

HMRC takes '*facilities*' to mean the provision of an amenity or service that enables an activity to be carried out. Facilities therefore include

- a shop (but not selling items from the shop);
- a fitness centre (but not aerobics classes);
- an internet café (but not surfing the web);
- a library (but not the hire of videos and DVDs or use of photocopier); and
- access to student union bar through payments of union subscriptions (but not the purchase of alcohol and food from the bar).

(VAT Notice 701/35/11).

Key points

[16.20] Points to consider are as follows.

- As a general principle, supplies of education are standard-rated if provided by a commercial business (excluding private schools). Exceptions to this statement include private tuition provided by a sole trader or member of a partnership, courses that are funded by the Young Persons Learning Agency (YPLA) or the Skills Funding Agency (SFA) (or similar bodies in Wales, Scotland and Northern Ireland), examination services and courses where English is taught as a foreign language.
- Education provided by schools, colleges and universities is exempt from VAT as these institutions are classed as eligible bodies. However, it is likely that these bodies will have other sources of taxable income so they may need to be VAT-registered. This means they will be partly exempt as an entity (with input tax restrictions) so will need to consider whether a special method might be worthwhile for partial exemption purposes. A special method requires HMRC approval, and is appropriate when the standard method based on income does not produce a fair and reasonable result in terms of input tax recovery.
- A training course provided by a charity or non-profit making body is only exempt if any profit that may be made from the course is reinvested into future courses. This is an important condition of the legislation that is often overlooked.
- Be aware that exemption in relation to training courses and education does not apply if a course or event is provided by a trading subsidiary of a charity. The trading subsidiary company is not a charity in its own right (but a private limited company in most cases) and courses are therefore standard-rated, even though the company probably pays any surplus back to the main charity.
- Any business that teaches English as a foreign language can benefit from VAT exemption on these courses. This exemption is usefully extended to other activities that are intended to improve

the English skills of the students, e.g. sightseeing trips, recreational or sporting activities. However, the exemption would not extend to other courses provided to the students, e.g. computer training for foreign students. The only exception would be if the training business was an eligible body (charity/non-profit making body etc.) able to benefit from VAT exemption through a different section of the legislation.

- The exemption for educational services extends to the supply of goods and services that are closely related to the education in question. For example, exemption also extends to accommodation and catering charges if the nature of a course is residential. However, for such supplies to be exempt, the main supply of the education must be exempt as a starting point.
- A common arrangement in relation to a course that is ultimately funded by the YPLA, SFA or similar body is for part of the course fee to be directly paid by the students or their employees. In such cases, this income is not exempt from VAT unless the training provider is an eligible body. In the situation where a training provider (e.g. commercial company) provides training services to a course provider that receives part funding from the YPLA or SFA or similar body, then an apportionment of the training provider charges must be made between standard rated and exempt supplies. Only the proportion of the training funded by the government approved body can benefit from exemption.
- If a course or training event is provided without charge, then it is classed as a non-business activity and is therefore outside the scope of VAT. There is no scope for input tax recovery on costs related to non-business activities. This would mean, for example, that if a charity used premises partly for business courses (a charge being made to customers) and partly for non-business courses, then an initial amount of input tax should be blocked to recognise the principle of non-business use. Any method can be used that is fair and reasonable, although a time-based apportionment will probably give the fairest result.
- The rules concerning exemption for private tuition are very strict. If a course is provided by an employee of a sole trader or partnership business, then the exemption does not apply. It does not apply to any education provided by a limited company. This is because a director of a limited company is classed as an employee of the business and is therefore not creating a private tuition arrangement.
- The scope of subjects that can benefit from the private tuition exemption is very wide. It generally covers subjects normally taught in a school or university but HMRC accepts that this extends to subjects of a sporting or recreational nature. So piano lessons would be included as an example. The exemption is not affected by whether lessons are given on an individual or group basis by the tutor concerned.

- Distance learning courses will be subject to VAT in most cases if provided by a commercial business. There may be an opportunity to separately sell course material, which will be zero-rated in most cases as a supply of printed material. However, recent tribunal cases have highlighted that it is very difficult to split an inclusive course fee so that some of the fee relates to the course books and is therefore zero-rated. The outcome in most of these tribunal cases has been that the business is providing a single supply of education, standard rated in most cases.
- As a general principle, supplies of research are not exempt from VAT because they are not classed as supplies of education. The exception to this statement is where supplies of research are charged from one eligible body, e.g. a university, to another eligible body, e.g. a charity. In such cases, income received by the body carrying out the research is exempt from VAT.

17

European Union: General

Introduction

[17.1] The European Union was set up by *The First Treaty of Rome* ('*EC Treaty*') with effect from 1 January 1958 and was entered into initially by Belgium, Federal Republic of Germany, France, Italy, Luxembourg and The Netherlands (who were also the initial members of European Coal and Steel Community and European Atomic Energy Community). By *The Treaty of Accession*, the UK, Ireland and Denmark entered with effect from 1 January 1973. The relevant UK legislation is *European Communities Act 1972*. Greece joined with effect from 1 January 1981, Spain and Portugal with effect from 1 January 1986 and Austria, Finland and Sweden with effect from 1 January 1995. Cyprus, Czech Republic, Estonia, Hungary, Latvia, Lithuania, Malta, Poland, Slovak Republic and Slovenia joined with effect from 1 May 2004. Bulgaria and Romania joined with effect from 1 January 2007, raising the total number of EU countries to 27.

The current treaty, *Treaty on the Functioning of the European Union ('EU Treaty')*, is widely drafted and there is an emphasis on provisions for the free movement of persons, goods, services and capital as well as powers for the implementation of common policies in many areas of economic and social life. It provides for a *Council of Ministers* which is composed of representatives of the governments of the member countries and effectively has the power to make decisions.

The *European Commission* is the executive constitution of the EU and also formulates the policy acted upon by the Council.

The *European Parliament* has, primarily, only supervisory and consultative powers.

The *European Court of Justice* is empowered to ensure that in the interpretation and application of the *EU Treaty* the law is observed. In this connection it is the ultimate court of appeal.

The *European Council*, consisting of Heads of State of the member countries, is not recognised as such by the *EU Treaty*, although this body has become an important focus of attention.

Territories of the EU

VAT territory

[17.2] The VAT territory of the EU consists of

- Austria
- Belgium
- Bulgaria (from 1.1.07)
- Cyprus (including the British Sovereign Base Areas of Akrotiri and Dhekelia but excluding the UN buffer zone and the part of Cyprus to the north of the buffer zone where the Republic of Cyprus does not exercise effective control)
- Czech Republic
- Denmark (excluding the Faroe Islands and Greenland)
- Estonia
- Finland (excluding the Aland Islands)
- France (including Monaco but excluding Martinique, French Guiana, Guadeloupe, Reunion and St Pierre and Miquelon)
- Germany (excluding Büsingen and the Isle of Heligoland)
- Greece (excluding Mount Athos (also known as Agion Oros))
- Hungary
- Ireland
- Italy (excluding Campione d'Italia, the Italian waters of Lake Lugano and Livigno)
- Latvia
- Lithuania
- Luxembourg
- Malta
- Netherlands (excluding the Antilles)
- Poland
- Portugal (including the Azores and Madeira)
- Romania (from 1.1.07)
- Slovakia
- Slovenia
- Spain (including the Balearic Islands but excluding the Canary Islands, Ceuta or Melilla)
- Sweden
- United Kingdom (including the Isle of Man but excluding the Channel Islands and Gibraltar)

[*VATA 1994, s 93; SI 1995/2518, Regs 136, 137, 139; SI 2004/1082, Reg 6*].

Other areas *not* within the VAT territory include Leichtenstein, the Vatican City, Andorra and San Marino.

De Voil Indirect Tax Service. See V1.213–218.

Customs territory

[17.3] The customs territory of the EU consists of the VAT territory plus

- Andorra (only Tariff Chapters 25 onwards)
- The Aland Islands
- Channel Islands
- The Canary Islands
- The overseas departments of the French Republic (Guadeloupe, Martinique, Reunion and French Guiana)
- Mount Athos (Agion Poros)

Excise territory

[17.4] The excise territory of the EU consists of the VAT territory plus

- San Marino

Trade statistics territory

[17.5] EU countries and their associated or dependent territories for Intrastat purposes are as follows.

Austria

Belgium

Bulgaria

Cyprus (including the British Sovereign Base Areas but excluding Northern Cyprus (see note below)

Czech Republic

Denmark (excluding the Faroe Islands)

Estonia

Finland (including the Aland Islands)

France (including Monaco but excluding all French Overseas Departments and territories (see note below))

Germany (including Heligoland but excluding Busingen)

Greece (including Mount Athos)

Hungary

Ireland

Italy (excluding Campione d'Italia, San Marino, the Italian Waters of Lake Lugano, The Vatican, and Livigno (see note below))

Latvia

Lithuania

Luxembourg

Malta

Netherlands (excluding all dependent/associated territories)

Poland

Portugal (including the Azores and Madeira)

Romania

Slovakia

Slovenia

Spain (including the Balearic Islands but excluding Ceuta, Melilla, and the Canary Islands (see note below))

Sweden

United Kingdom (including the Channel Islands and the Isle of Man but excluding Gibraltar)

Notes. The French territories of French Guiana, Guadeloupe, Martinique and Reunion are part of the statistical territories of France, and Canary Islands are part of the statistical territory of Spain, and Livigno is part of the statistical territory of Italy. However, as customs documentation (the SAD) is still required for trade with these territories HMRC continue to collect trade statistics from the SAD.

The EU *acquis* (the body of European law) is currently only applicable in the Government Controlled Area of the Republic of Cyprus.

Andorra and Liechtenstein are both outside the customs territory, and therefore the statistical territory, of the EU.

(HMRC Notice 60, para 2.5).

Trade with territories with which the EU has special relations

[17.6] The following rules apply.

- For trade with such territories outside the VAT, customs, excise *and* trade statistics territories, the same procedures apply as before the introduction of the single market. Such territories are treated in the same way as any other non-EU country.
- For trade with the Azores, the Balearic Islands, Madeira and Monaco (which are within the VAT, customs, excise *and* trade statistics territories), the same procedures apply as for trade with other EU countries. This also applies to trade between the Isle of Man and EU countries other than the UK.

- Where goods are imported into the EU from any of the additional territories within the customs territory, there is no liability to customs duty but VAT may be payable. (There are special schemes for goods such as cut flowers which enter the UK from the Channel Islands.) Excise duty may also be payable but not on goods imported from San Marino (which is inside the Excise territory).

Refunds of VAT for EU businesses: overview

[17.7] The electronic cross-border refund system enables a business that incurs VAT on expenditure in a Member State where it is not established and makes no supplies, to recover that VAT directly from that Member State (the Member State of refund). The previous system, known as the 8th VAT Directive refund system, was a lengthy, burdensome, paper-based system. Following agreement between EU Finance Ministers, EU legislation to reform the system was adopted in February 2008, as part of the VAT package of legislation. The electronic system will apply to all claims submitted on or after 1 January 2010. Requests for refunds will continue to be dealt with by the Member State of refund. The amount refundable will also continue to be determined under the deduction rules of the Member State of refund and the relevant repayment will be made directly by that Member State to the business. The system will be an electronic one, with specified timescales and interest payable if these are not met. Any references below to the UK are taken to include the Isle of Man.

General rules

Electronic claims will be completed and submitted via the competent authorities in the Member State in which the claimant is established.

Applicants

The applicant must be a taxable person established in a Member State other than the Member State of refund, or their authorised agent. The applicant must meet the following conditions

- they must not be registered, liable or eligible to be registered in the Member State from which they are claiming the refund;
- they must have no fixed establishment, seat of economic activity, place of business or other residence there; and
- during the refund period they must not have supplied any goods or services in the Member State of refund with the exception of: transport services and services ancillary thereto; and supplies of goods or services where VAT is payable by the person to whom the supply is made.

Checks

Basic registration checks will be carried out by the Member State of establishment before the application is forwarded electronically to the Member State from which the refund is being claimed. The Member State of establishment will not forward the application to the Member State of refund where during the period of refund the applicant

- is not a taxable person for VAT purposes;
- makes only exempt supplies;
- is covered by the exemption for small enterprises; or
- is operating the flat-rate scheme for farmers.

If the Member State of establishment decides not to forward the application it must notify the applicant of this decision.

Applications

A separate application must be completed for each Member State. Applications can be commenced and stored in an incomplete state on the system and may be recalled and finalised to be submitted at a later date.

The refund period must not be more than one calendar year or less than three calendar months unless the period covered represents the remainder of a calendar year (e.g. where interim applications have already been submitted earlier in the year, or if the applicant has recently become VAT registered).

If the refund application relates to a period of less than a calendar year, but not less than three months the minimum amount claimable is ECR 400 or the equivalent in national currency. If the refund application relates to a period of a calendar year or the remainder of a calendar year the minimum amount claimable is ECR 50 or the equivalent in national currency.

Properly completed applications must be submitted to the Member State of establishment at the latest on 30 September of the calendar year following the refund year (extended from 30 September 2010 to 31 March 2011 for VAT incurred in 2009 [*Directive 2010/66/EU*]). If the applicant deregisters for VAT during the refund year they should submit their application as soon as possible following deregistration.

Scope of the application

Supplies of goods or services received with a tax point during the period of the refund application; and goods imported into the Member State of refund during the period of the refund application. In addition, the application may include supplies or imports not included in a previous application as long as they relate to the same calendar year. The application may not include: amounts of VAT that have been incorrectly invoiced; or amounts of VAT that have been invoiced in respect of goods despatched to other member states or exported outside the EU.

Standard fields

The use of the following standard fields of information and expense codes will aid completion and are mandatory:

- Applicants name and full address.
- An address for contact by electronic means (email address).
- A description of the applicant's business activity for which the goods and services are acquired.
- Period dates to which the refund application relates.
- The applicants VAT identification number or tax reference number.

- Bank account details including IBAN and BIC codes.

Standard fields for invoices or importations included in the refund application:

- Name and address of the supplier.
- Except in cases of importation the VAT identification number or tax reference number of the supplier.
- Except in the case of importation, the prefix of the Member State of refund.
- Date and number of the invoice or importation document.
- Taxable amount and amount of VAT expressed in the currency of the Member State of refund.
- The amount of deductible VAT expressed in the currency of the Member State of refund. This is the amount of VAT recoverable taking account of any partial exemption restriction, and any restriction on the recovery of input tax applying in the Member State of refund.
- Where applicable the deductible proportion calculated in accordance with the rules applying in the Member State of establishment.
- Nature of the goods and services acquired, described according to the following expenditure codes.

Expenditure codes:

(1) Fuel.
(2) Hiring of means of transport.
(3) Expenditure relating to means of transport.
(4) Road tolls and road user charge.
(5) Travel expenses, such as taxi fares, public transport fares.
(6) Accommodation.
(7) Food, drink and restaurant services.
(8) Admissions to fairs and exhibitions.
(9) Expenditure on luxuries, amusements and entertainment.
(10) Other.

Members States may require further sub codes to be used in respect of each of the above. If code 10 is used without a sub code, a narrative description of the goods and services must be provided.

Method of payment

The payment will be made in the Member State of refund or, at the applicant's request, in any other Member State. In the latter case, any bank charges for the transfer will be deducted by the Member State of refund from the amount to be paid to the applicant.

Time limits for processing applications

The Member State of refund must notify the applicant of the decision to approve or refuse the application within four months of the date they first received the application. If the Member State of refund requires additional information in order to process the application, it can request this from the applicant, the applicant's tax authority, or a third party before the expiry of the four-month period. The additional information must be provided by the person to whom the request is made within one month of receiving the request.

Once the Member State of refund has received the additional information it has two further months in which to notify its decision. If further additional information is requested by the Member State of refund the final deadline for making a decision can be extended up to a maximum of eight months from the date they received the application. Payment must be made within ten working days following expiry of the appropriate decision deadline.

Incorrect application/payment errors

If an applicant discovers that it has made an error on an application, a corrected application can be submitted. The correction procedures allows existing lines on the application to be amended or deleted (by reducing to 'nil'), but does not allow new lines to be added. The correction procedure can also be used to amend incorrect bank details, email addresses etc. If an application is found to be incorrect any overpayment will be recovered, normally by deducting it from any refund due. All Member States take a very serious view of incorrect applications. Refunds obtained on the basis of any incorrect application can be recovered, penalties and interest may be imposed and further refund applications suspended.

Refused applications

If the Member State of refund refuses an application fully or partly they must also notify the applicant of the reasons for refusal. If this happens the applicant can appeal against the decision using the appeals procedure of that Member State. This means that the normal VAT appeals rules of that Member State on time limits, form of appeal etc., will apply. If the Member State of refund has not notified its decision within the appropriate decision deadline the applicant should consider that the application has been rejected unless any alternative procedures apply in that Member State. The applicant's own VAT authority cannot intervene on its behalf.

Interest

Interest may be payable by the Member State of refund to the applicant if payment is made after the final payment deadline set out above. If applicable it will be paid from the day following that deadline up to the date the refund is actually paid. Interest rates must be the same as those applied to refunds of VAT to taxable persons established in the Member State of refund under the national law of that Member State. If no interest is payable under national law in respect of refunds to established taxable persons, the interest payable will be equal to the interest or equivalent charge which is applied by that Member State in respect of late payments of VAT by taxable persons.

[*SI 1995/2518, Regs 173–173X; SI 2009/3241, Regs 11–18*]. (VAT Notice 723A, paras 2.1–2.21).

Refunds for UK and Isle of Man businesses claiming from other Member States

[17.8] All applications made on or after 1 January 2010 regardless as to whether they cover periods prior to 1 January 2010 must be submitted using the electronic online system. In order to be able to make an electronic application for refund of VAT the applicant first needs to register for VAT Online Services, using details on their VAT 4 Certificate of Registration and last VAT return. An activation PIN number will be mailed to the business address registered with HMRC within set time limits (currently seven to ten days). Once this is received the applicant will have 28 days from the date of the letter to activate the service.

Agents

Agents can register to enable them to make refund applications on behalf of their clients and additional security procedures have been built in to their online application process.

Eligibility

An applicant must be a taxable person registered for VAT in the UK or in the Isle of Man, and must meet the following conditions:

- must not be registered, liable or eligible to be registered in the Member State of refund;
- must not have any fixed establishment, seat of economic activity, place of business or other residence in the Member State of refund;
- during the refund period they must not have supplied any goods or services in the Member State of refund with the exception of: transport services and services ancillary thereto; and any goods or services where VAT is payable by the person to whom the supply is made.

If the applicant is registered as a VAT group, and the group has member companies in the Member State of refund, they may only use the refund scheme to claim VAT incurred by companies who are not established in, and do not make supplies in, the Member State of refund.

Proof of taxable person status

Applications will be subjected to automated registration verifications by HMRC before being forwarded electronically to the Member State from which the refund is being claimed. Certificates of Status (VAT 66) are therefore no longer required for refund applications from other Member States. Applications will only be forwarded to the Member State of refund if these checks are satisfactory. If the checks are not satisfactory the application will be rejected by the electronic portal and they will receive an appropriate error message. Deregistered applicants must submit their applications as soon as possible, and not later than three months from their date of deregistration.

Claims

A separate online application is required for each Member State from which the applicant wishes to claim. In order to start an application they must access the relevant online services section using their unique PID and password and enter their standard data into the required fields, along with invoice or importation details for expenditure they wish to reclaim. Applications can be commenced and saved if incomplete and can be recalled for completion and submission at a later date.

Refund period

The refund period must not be more than one calendar year or less than three calendar months (unless the period covered represents the remainder of a calendar year, for example, where interim applications have already been submitted earlier in the year covering more than nine months, or if they have recently become VAT registered). Generally refund periods do not have to cover strict calendar quarters. For example, they may submit two applications covering five months each, and a final one covering two months. However, some Member States have their own requirements, and details of these can be obtained from the relevant tax authority. Generally refund periods may not overlap. For example, they may not submit an application covering 1 January to 31 March and another for 1 March to 31 May. However they may submit a further application covering the whole refund year after the year end. This enables they to claim for any purchases which they have missed in earlier periods.

Minimum claim

If the refund application relates to a period of less than a calendar year, but not less than three months the minimum amount claimable is ECR 400 or the equivalent in national currency. If the refund application relates to a period of a calendar year or the remainder of a calendar year the minimum amount claimable is ECR 50 or the equivalent in national currency.

Invoices

The following can be included on the application: invoices relating to supplies of goods or services with a tax point during the period of the refund application; and invoices relating to an importation of goods into the Member State of refund during the period of the refund application. Also, invoices or imports not included in a previous application can be claimed as long as they relate to the same calendar year. The application may not include amounts of VAT that have been: incorrectly invoiced; invoiced in respect of goods despatched to another member state or exported outside the EU; or incurred in respect of non business activities.

Member States may require invoices with values of ECR 1,000 or more (ECR 250 or more in the case of fuel), or the equivalent in national currency, to be scanned and submitted electronically with the application. All other invoices should be retained as they may be requested at a later date by the Member State of refund. If there are imported goods, the applicant must have the VAT copy of the import entry or other Customs document showing the amount of VAT paid.

Partial exemption

The applicant must apply the appropriate recovery rate for the goods or services purchased against each invoice or importation on their application, and show the amount of VAT recoverable in the appropriate box. The recovery rate to be applied is the last percentage appropriate to the refund period covering the invoice date. For example, if the claimable percentage for the

March 2010 period is 5% and the application is submitted in April before the annual adjustment is calculated the claim should be restricted to 5%. However if they only make one application at the year end and have already calculated that the annual adjustment covering the March 2010 quarter is 3% then they may only claim 3%. Following the annual adjustment, they will not be required to amend refund applications already submitted. The invoices can only be entered once and the percentage to be used is that covering the invoice date.

Non-business expenses

Expenditure incurred in another Member State that relates to non business activities is not claimable under the refund scheme.

[*SI 1995/2518, Regs 173–173X; SI 2009/3241, Regs 11–18*]. (VAT Notice 723A, paras 3.1–3.22).

Refunds in the UK for EU businesses

[17.9] The applicant must be a taxable person established in a Member State other than the UK and must meet the following conditions:

- must not be registered, liable or eligible to be registered in the UK;
- must not have any place of business in the UK or in the Isle of Man; and
- must not make any supplies in the UK (other than transport services related to the international carriage of goods, or goods and services where VAT is payable by the person to whom the supply is made).

Agents

If the applicant uses an agent to submit the application and/or receive payment of refunds on their behalf, they must submit a letter of authority, in hard copy, to the UK Overseas Repayment Unit (ORU).

Refund period

The refund period must not be more than one calendar year or less than three calendar months (unless it covers the remainder of a calendar year, for example, where applications have already been submitted covering more than nine months). Refund periods do not have to cover strict calendar quarters. For example, they may submit two applications covering five months each, and a final one covering two months. Generally, refund periods may not overlap. For example, they may not submit an application covering 1 January to 31 March, and another for 1 March to 31 May. However, they may submit a further application covering the whole of the refund year after the year end. This enables them to claim for any purchases or imports which they have missed in earlier periods.

Submission

The applicant must submit the application through the electronic facility provided by the tax authority in their Member State, at the latest by 30 September of the year following that in which the VAT was incurred (extended from 30 September 2010 to 31 March 2011 for VAT incurred in 2009 [*Directive 2010/66/EU*]).

Claim limits

There is no maximum limit, but there are minimum limits below which an application cannot be submitted. These are: £295 where the application covers less than a calendar year but not less than three calendar months, and £35 where the application covers a calendar year or the remainder of a calendar year.

Claimable VAT

The applicant can claim VAT on goods and services purchased during the refund period, and VAT on goods imported into the UK during the refund period. They may not claim:

- amounts of VAT that have been incorrectly invoiced, or where VAT has been charged on the despatch of goods to another Member State, or the export of goods outside the EU (they must take this up with the supplier);
- VAT on the purchase of a motor car;
- VAT on goods and services used for business entertainment; or
- VAT on goods and services used for non-business activities.

In addition, where VAT is incurred on charges for hiring or leasing a motor car, only 50% of the total VAT charged may be claimed.

Taxable and exempt supplies

The applicant must apply the appropriate restriction to the VAT reclaimed, following the rules that apply in their own Member State, with any pro-rata adjustments submitted through their tax authority's electronic facility.

Scanned invoices

Scanned copies of all invoices and import documents must be attached where the taxable amount exceeds: £200 in the case of fuel; and £750 in the case of all other goods and services.

[*SI 1995/2518, Regs 173–173X; SI 2009/3241, Regs 11–18*]. (VAT Notice 723A, paras 4.1–4.14).

Key points

[17.10] Points to consider are as follows.

- Be aware that the Isle of Man is part of the UK as far as VAT is concerned whilst the Channel Islands (Jersey and Guernsey) are outside the UK and EU. The latter are classed as outside of the EU for VAT purposes but within the EU for customs purposes.
- 1 January 2010 was an important date for all businesses that pay VAT in other EU countries (other than their own) and wish to reclaim this VAT by making what is known as an 8th Directive claim. A new electronic claims system was introduced on this date to hopefully make the claims process more efficient than the old paper-based system that used to apply. The new system offers increased hope that VAT will be repaid to a claimant within specified time limits by the tax authority of the country where the VAT was paid. The new system introduces an interest payment for taxpayers who do not receive their repayment within the specified time limit.
- New rules on invoicing are to be introduced on 1 January 2013. The aim is to make cross-border transactions easier. HMRC considers that the new EU rules will have little impact on the UK's current rules.

18

European Union Legislation

De Voil Indirect Tax Service. See V1.220–233.

Introduction

[18.1] Statements of the European Council and European Commission are graded under the *EU Treaty* as follows.

- **Regulations** are binding in their entirety and have general effect to all EU countries. They are directly applicable in the legal systems of EU countries.
- **Directives** are binding as to result and their general effect is specific to named EU countries. The form and methods of compliance are left to the addressees.
- **Decisions** are binding in their entirety and are specific to an EU country, commercial enterprise or private individual.
- **Recommendations and Opinions** are not binding and are directed to specific subjects on which the Council's or Commission's advice has been sought.

EU legislation as part of UK legislation

[18.2] EU law is made effective for UK legislation. [*European Communities Act 1972, s 2*]. The effects of EU law as regards UK VAT legislation can be summarised as follows.

Direct effect

Although *EU Treaty, art 288* does not specifically allow for direct effect in an EU country, the Court of Justice has held 'wherever the provisions of a directive appear . . . to be unconditional and sufficiently precise, those provisions may . . . be relied upon as against any national provision which is incompatible with the directive insofar as the provisions define rights which individuals are able to assert against the state' (*Becker v Finanzamt Münster-Innenstadt*, *ECJ Case 8/81*, [1982] ECR 53, [1982] 1 CMLR 499 (TVC 22.352)). See also *Staatssecretaris van Financien v Cooperatieve Vereniging Cooperatieve Aardappelenbewaarplaats GA*, *ECJ Case 154/80*, [1981] ECR 445, [1981] 3 CMLR 337 (TVC 22.78) which case was considered in *UFD Ltd* (VTD 1172) (TVC 24.26) in which it was said 'in all appeals involving issues of liability, the tribunal should consider the relevant provisions of the Council directives to ensure that the provisions of the UK legislation are consistent therewith'. See also *Yoga for Health Foundation v C & E Commrs*, *QB* [1984] STC 630 (TVC 22.283) where exemption from VAT was allowed for certain welfare services although there was no corresponding provision in the UK legislation.

Primacy of EU Directives over national legislation

A national court which is called upon, within the limits of its jurisdiction, to apply provisions of Union law, is under a duty to give full effect to those provisions, if necessary refusing of its own motion to apply any conflicting provision of national legislation, even if adopted subsequently, and it is not necessary for the court to request or await the prior setting aside of such provisions by legislative or other constitutional means (*Amministrazione delle Finanze dello Stato v Simmenthal SpA*, *ECJ Case C–106/77*, [1978] ECR 629, [1978] 3 CMLR 263 (TVC 22.22)).

In *EC Commission v United Kingdom, ECJ Case C–416/85*, [1988] STC 456 (TVC 22.505) the ECJ ruled that the UK had contravened the provisions of what is now *Directive 2006/112/EC* by zero-rating certain supplies of sewerage and water, news services, supplies of fuel and power and the construction of commercial buildings. In the earlier decision *EC Commission v United Kingdom, ECJ Case–353/85*, [1988] STC 251 (TVC 22.271) the ECJ had similarly ruled in relation to the exempting of supplies of spectacles, contact lenses and hearing aids. As a result of each decision, the UK law was amended.

In *Direct Cosmetics v C & E Commrs, ECJ Case 5/84*, [1985] STC 479 (TVC 22.496) it was held that an amendment to UK legislation, which had been previously enacted under the derogation powers in what is now *Directive 2006/112/EC, Art 395* (previously *EC 6th Directive, Art 27*) (see **18.31** below), was itself a 'special measure' requiring derogation to be authorised by the European Commission. As this had not been obtained, the whole provisions failed and could not be relied on against the taxpayer.

Interpretation of UK law

If the domestic VAT legislation of the UK is unclear or ambiguous, tribunals are 'entitled to have regard to the provisions of the [*Directive 2006/112/EC*] in order to assist in resolving any ambiguity in the construction of the provisions under consideration' (*English-Speaking Union of the Commonwealth* (VTD 1023) (TVC 13.5)). If EU law appears unclear it may be interpreted by referring to the legislative history ('*travaux preparatoires*') but such evidence has been held to be admissible only by reference to tests in *Fothergill v Monarch Airlines Ltd*, [1981] AC 251 (*The Open University* (VTD 1196) (TVC 21.3)). This decision is open to doubt. See, for example, *EC Commission v The Kingdom of Belgium ECJ Case 324/82*, [1984] ECR 1861 [1985] 1 CMLR 364 (TVC 22.498) where the Belgium government used minutes of a Council meeting held prior to the adoption of what is now *Directive 2006/112/EC* in evidence.

State liability to pay damages for failure to implement Directive

In an Italian case, the ECJ held that the Italian government was liable to pay compensation to employees of an insolvent company, who had suffered financial loss through Italy's failure to implement a directive guaranteeing such employees their arrears of wages (*Francovich v Italian State, ECJ Case C–6/90*, [1991] 1 ECR 5357; [1993] 2 CMLR 66 (TVC 22.30)). The principles laid down in *Francovich* were applied in two subsequent cases in which national legislation was held to be contrary to EU law. The ECJ ruled that 'the principle that Member States are obliged to make good damage caused to individuals by breaches of Union law attributable to the state is applicable where the national legislature was responsible for the breach in question' (*Brasserie du Pêcheur SA v Federal Republic of Germany*; *R v Secretary of State for Transport (ex p. Factortame Ltd & Others) (No 3), ECJ Cases C–46/93, C–48/93*, [1996] 1 ECR 1029, [1996] 1 CMLR 889; [1996] 2 WLR 506; [1996] AEECR 301 (TVC 22.31)) See also *R v Secretary of State for Employment (ex p. Equal Opportunities Commission), HL* [1994] 1 All ER 910 (TVC 22.36) where

Lord Keith of Kinkel observed that 'if there is any individual who believes that he or she has a good claim to compensation under the *Francovich* principle, it is the Attorney-General who would be defendant in any proceedings directed to enforcing it'.

Judgments in the European Court of Justice also have supremacy over domestic decisions even if the proceedings commenced in another EU country.

De Voil Indirect Tax Service. See V1.235.

VAT harmonisation directives

[18.3] A directive must be read as a whole. The preamble, which sets out the purpose of the legislation, is an essential part of it. Moreover, as distinct from UK law, it is acceptable when determining the purpose of the legislation to consider the discussions, decisions, etc. ('*travaux preparatoires*') which led to the legislation being drafted in its final form.

The principal directives issued by the EU Council on the harmonisation of legislation of EU countries concerning turnover taxes, and which are relevant in the UK, are as follows.

- *1st Directive*. [*67/227/EEC*]. This provided for a common VAT system to be operated by EU countries. It is now incorporated in *Directive 2006/112/EC*.
- *6th Directive*. [*77/388/EEC*]. This was the so-called 'harmonisation directive' and clarified many of the definitions of basic terms used in the legislation of individual EU countries. It is now incorporated in *Directive 2006/112/EC*.
- *7th Directive*. [*94/5/EEC*]. This provides for special arrangements applicable to second-hand goods, works of art, collectors' items and antiques. See **SECOND-HAND GOODS (61)**.
- *8th Directive*. [*79/1072/EEC*]. This provides for the refund of VAT suffered by Union traders in those EU countries where they do not have a business establishment. It was replaced from 1 January 2010 by *Directive 2008/9/EC*. See **18.44** below.
- *10th Directive*. [*84/386/EEC*]. This amends and clarifies the provisions of the *6th Directive* in connection with the hiring out of movable tangible property.
- *13th Directive*. [*86/560/EEC*]. This provides for refund of VAT to taxable persons not established in the EU. See **18.45** below.
- *18th Directive*. [*89/465/EEC*]. This abolishes a number of derogations provided for in what is now *Directive 2006/112/EC*.
- *Directive 2006/112/EC*. This re-casts the provisions of the *1st Directive* and *6th Directive* as amended. See **18.4** *et seq* below.
- *Directive 2008/8/EC*. This amends the place of supply of services rules in *Directive 2006/112/EC* with effect from 1 January 2010 (and subsequent dates). See **18.15** below.

- *Directive 2008/9/EC*. This repealed and replaced the *8th Directive* with effect from 1 January 2010. It introduces an electronic procedure for the claiming of VAT incurred in other EU Member States. It is to be given effect in the UK by amendments to *VATA 1994*, and implementing secondary legislation. See **18.44** below.
- *Directive 2008/117/EC*. This amends *Directive 2006/112/EC* with regard to the submission of EU sales lists (ESLs) (see **18.41**(8) below) and the time of supply of services subject to the reverse charge (see **18.17**(1) below). The amendments have effect from 21 January 2009 and the deadline for implementation is 1 January 2010.
- *Directive 2009/162/EU*. This amends *Directive 2006/112/EC* with regard to supplies of gas, electricity, heat or cooling energy (see **18.8**(iv), **18.12**(4) below), and with regard to immovable property used both for business and non-business purposes (see **18.34** below). Member States must bring into force the necessary implementing laws with effect from 1 January 2011.

A number of subsidiary directives have also been made.

Directive 2006/112/EC

[18.4] Many of the Articles of *Directive 2006/112/EC* are similar to the provisions of the *VATA 1994*. Where they are unconditional and precise (e.g. as evidenced by the use of the word 'must' in the text below) their wording takes preference to that in the *VATA 1994*. Where *Articles* are discretionary (e.g. as evidenced by the use of the words 'countries may' in the text below) the UK may apply the provisions or not as it wishes. However, where they are applied, the provisions once adopted must be applied precisely.

With effect from 1 July 2011 *Council Regulation (EU)282/2011* (which recasts and repeals *Council Regulation (EC)1777/2005*) lays down implementing measures for *Directive 2006/112/EC*, in particular giving guidance on determining the status of the customer, whether he acquires services for business use and where he is located. (EC press release dated 1 July 2011).

Definitive arrangements

The arrangements provided for in **18.5** to **18.43** below for the taxation of trade between EU countries are transitional and due to be replaced by definitive arrangements based in principle on the taxation in the EU country of origin of the supply of goods or services. [*Directive 2006/112/EC, Art 402*]. The possibility of this happening is becoming increasingly unlikely as time passes and the members of the EU increase.

Introduction

[18.5] This Directive establishes the common system of VAT throughout the EU. This entails the application to goods and services of a general tax on consumption, exactly proportional to the price of the goods and services, however many transactions take place in the production and distribution process before the stage at which the tax is charged.

On each transaction, VAT, calculated on the price of the goods or services at the rate applicable to such goods or services, must be chargeable after deduction of the amount of VAT borne directly by the various cost components.

VAT must be applied up to and including the retail trade stage.

[*Directive 2006/112/EC, Art 1*].

Scope

[18.6] Subject to the derogation and exceptions below, the following transactions must be subject to VAT.

(a) The supply of goods for consideration within the territory of an EU country by a taxable person acting as such.

(b) The intra-EU acquisition of goods for consideration within the territory of an EU country by the following persons.

  (i) A taxable person acting as such, or a non-taxable legal person, where the vendor is a taxable person acting as such who is not eligible for the exemption for small enterprises provided for in **18.42**(2) below and who is not covered by *Art 33* or *Art 36* (see **18.12**(*b*) below).

  (ii) In the case of new means of transport (as defined), a taxable person, or a non-taxable legal person, whose other acquisitions are not subject to VAT pursuant to *Art 3* below, or any other non-taxable person.

  (iii) In the case of products subject to excise duty (as defined), where the excise duty on the intra-EU acquisition is chargeable within the territory of the EU country, a taxable person, or a non-taxable legal person, whose other acquisitions are not subject to VAT pursuant to *Art 3* below.

(c) The supply of services for consideration within the territory of an EU country by a taxable person acting as such.

(d) The importation of goods.

[*Directive 2006/112/EC, Art 2*].

Derogation

By way of derogation from (*b*)(i) above, the following transactions must not be subject to VAT.

(i) The intra-EU acquisition of goods by a taxable person or a non-taxable legal person, where the supply of such goods within the territory of the EU country of acquisition would be exempt pursuant to **18.30** below and *Art 151* (see **18.31** below).

(ii) The intra-EU acquisition of goods other than

- those referred to in (i) above,
- the *Exceptions* below, and
- new means of transport or products subject to excise duty,
- by a taxable person
- for the purposes of his agricultural, forestry or fisheries business subject to the common flat-rate scheme for farmers, or

- who carries out only supplies of goods or services in respect of which VAT is not deductible,

or by a non-taxable legal person.

But this only applies if during the previous calendar year and during the current calendar year, the total value of intra-EU acquisitions of goods does not exceed a threshold to be determined by each EU country (which may not be less than 10,000 euro or the equivalent in national currency).

Taxable persons and non-taxable legal persons must be granted the right to opt out of this derogation and to apply the general scheme provided for in (*b*)(i) above.

[*Directive 2006/112/EC, Art 3*].

Exceptions

In addition to the transactions referred to in *Art 3* above, the following transactions must not be subject to VAT.

- The intra-EU acquisition of second-hand goods, works of art, collectors' items or antiques where the vendor is a taxable dealer acting as such and VAT has been applied to the goods in the EU country in which their dispatch or transport began, in accordance with the margin scheme provided for in **18.42**(5) below.
- The intra-EU acquisition of second-hand means of transport where the vendor is a taxable dealer acting as such and VAT has been applied to the means of transport in the EU country in which their dispatch or transport began, in accordance with the transitional arrangements for second-hand means of transport.
- The intra-EU acquisition of second-hand goods, works of art, collectors' items or antiques where the vendor is an organiser of sales by public auction, acting as such, and VAT has been applied to the goods in the EU country in which their dispatch or transport began, in accordance with the special arrangements for sales by public auction.

[*Directive 2006/112/EC, Art 4*].

For consideration

It follows from the above that there is no supply for VAT purposes where there is no consideration. See *Staatssecretaris van Financiën v Cooperatieve Vereniging 'Cooperatieve Aardappelenbewaarplaats GA', ECJ Case 154/80*, [1981] ECR 445, [1981] 3 CMLR 337 (TVC 22.78). Similarly, in *Staatssecretaris van Financiën v Hong Kong Trade Development Council, ECJ Case 89/81*, [1982] ECR 1277, [1983] 1 CMLR 73 (TVC 22.79) the ECJ held that the provision of services for no consideration could not be subject to VAT and, where no other activity was involved, the provider of the services could not be regarded as a taxable person.

In *Apple & Pear Development Council v C & E Commrs, ECJ Case 102/86*, [1988] STC 221 (TVC 22.80) the ECJ held that, for a supply of services to be for consideration within the above provisions, there must be a direct link between the service provided and the consideration received. On the evidence in that case, there was no relationship between the level of the benefits which individual fruit growers obtained from the Council's services and the amount of the mandatory charges which they were obliged to pay. Accordingly, the compulsory annual charges did not constitute 'consideration' and the Council was not making supplies of services for consideration.

In *Tolsma v Inspecteur der Omzetbelasting Leeuwarden, ECJ Case C–16/93*, [1994] STC 509 (TVC 22.84) an individual who played a barrel organ on the public highway and invited donations from the public was held not to be supplying services for a consideration. There was no agreement between the parties and also 'no necessary link between the musical service and the payment to which it gave rise'.

Lawful and unlawful transactions

The principle of fiscal neutrality precludes a generalised differentiation between lawful and unlawful transactions except where, because of the special characteristics of certain products, all competition between a lawful economic sector and an unlawful sector is precluded. Thus the illegal sale of drugs is not a supply for VAT purposes (*Mol v Inspecteur der InVoerrechten Accijinzen, ECJ Case C–269/86*, [1988] ECR 3627, [1989] BVC 205 (TVC 22.81)) but the supply of counterfeit perfume is. See *R v Goodwin and Unstead, ECJ Case C–3/97*, [1998] STC 699 (TVC 22.82). The prohibition on such products stems from the fact that they infringe intellectual property rights and is conditional not absolute (as in the case of drugs and counterfeit money). There is scope for competition between counterfeit perfumes and perfumes which are traded lawfully and although supply of the former is unlawful, such perfume is not liable to seizure in the hands of the final customer. The unlawful operation of a form of roulette was similarly held to be a supply for VAT purposes in *Fischer v Finanzamt Donaueschingen, ECJ Case C–283/95*, [1998] STC 708 (TVC 22.371). However, although the unlawful playing of a game of chance is a supply, it is not taxable where the corresponding activity is exempt when carried on lawfully by a licensed casino.

Taxable person acting as such

In *Finanzamt Ülzen v Armbrecht, ECJ Case C–291/92*, [1995] STC 997 (TVC 22.93), a hotelier sold a guesthouse, part of which had been used for private rather than business purposes. The ECJ ruled that where a taxable person sold property, part of which he had chosen to reserve for private use, the sale of that part was outside the scope of the above provisions. This should be compared to the decision in *Bakcsi v Finanzamt Fürstenfeldbruck, ECJ Case C–415/98*, [2002] STC 802 (TVC 22.94) where a trader purchased a car and used it mainly for business purposes but partly for private purposes. The ECJ held that where a taxable person used a capital item for both business and private purposes, and had incorporated that item wholly into his business assets, the sale of that item was wholly subject to VAT. The ECJ also observed that a taxable person who acquired a capital item for mixed purposes 'may retain it wholly within his private assets and thereby exclude it entirely' from the VAT system.

Taxable persons

[18.7] '*Taxable person*' means any person who independently carries out in any place any economic activity whatever the purpose or result of that activity.

Any activity of producers, traders and persons supplying services, including mining and agricultural activities and activities of professions, must be regarded as an economic activity. Included is the exploitation of tangible and intangible property for the purposes of obtaining income on a continuing basis.

In addition to the persons referred to above, any person who, on an occasional basis, supplies a new means of transport, which is dispatched or transported to the customer by the vendor or the customer, or on behalf of the vendor or the customer, to a destination outside the territory of an EU country but within the territory of the EU, must be regarded as a taxable person.

Economic activity

In *Rompelman v Minister van Financien, ECJ Case 268/83*, [1985] 3 CMLR 202; [1985] ECR 655 (TVC 22.103) the acquisition of a future right of joint ownership in property under construction with a view to letting that property in due course was held to be an economic activity although objective evidence (e.g. proposed contracts, planning permission) that arrangements have been made to begin making taxable supplies should be produced. The first investment expenditure incurred for the purpose of a business can be regarded as an economic activity even if it does not give rise to any taxable transactions. See *Intercommunale voor Zeewaterontzilting (in liquidation) v Belgian State, ECJ Case C–110/94*, [1996] STC 569 (TVC 22.110) where VAT was held to be deductible on a profitability study although, as a result of the study, the company did not move to the operational phase. See also *WM van Tiem v Staatssecretaris van Financien, ECJ Case C–186/89*, [1993] STC 91 (TVC 22.109) and *Finanzamt Goslar v Breitsohl, ECJ Case C–400/98*, [2001] STC 355 (TVC 22.122). In the latter case it was held that the right to deduct the VAT paid on transactions carried out with the view to a realisation of a planned economic activity still existed even where the tax authorities were aware, from the time of the first tax assessment, that the economic activity envisaged, which was to give rise to taxable transactions, would not be taken up (although, in such cases, the input tax recovery might be subject to later adjustment).

The holding of shares does not amount to an economic activity if the shareholder is not involved in the management of the companies whose shares it holds. Neither is it the exploitation of assets for the purposes of obtaining income because any dividend received arises from the ownership of the shares, not from an economic activity (*Polysar Investments Netherlands BV v Inspecteur der Invoerrechten en Accijnzen, Arnhem, ECJ Case C–60/90*, [1993] STC 222 (TVC 22.106)). See also *Harnas & Helm CV v Staatssecretaris van Financien, ECJ Case C–80/95*, [1997] STC 364 (TVC 22.112). The purchase and sale of shares by trustees in the course of the management of a charitable trust does not amount to an economic activity (*The Wellcome Trust Ltd v C & E Commrs, ECJ Case C–155/94*, [1996] STC 945 (TVC 22.111)).

See **8.1 BUSINESS** for the meaning of 'business' under UK legislation.

Independently

The hiring out of intangible property with a view to obtaining income therefrom on a continuing basis is an economic activity even where a person's sole economic activity consists in the letting of such an item to a company or partnership of which he is a member (*Staatssecretaris van Financiën v Heerma, ECJ Case C–23/98*, [2001] STC 1437 (TVC 22.108)).

The use of the word 'independently' excludes employed and other persons from VAT in so far as they are bound to an employer by a contract of employment or by any other legal ties creating the relationship of employer and employee as regards working conditions, remuneration and employer's liability.

Occasional transactions

Countries may also treat as taxable persons anyone who carries out, on an occasional basis, a transaction relating to an economic activity and in particular

- the supply before first occupation of buildings (or part) and the land on which they stand. Countries may apply criteria other than first occupation, e.g. the period elapsing between the date of completion of the building and the date of first supply (not exceeding five years) or the period elapsing between the date of first occupation and the date of subsequent supply (not exceeding two years); and
- the supply of building land.

Single taxable person

Each country may treat different persons established in their territory as a single taxable person where those persons, although legally independent, are closely bound to one another by financial, economic and organisational links. See **8.5 BUSINESS** for UK provisions.

Local authorities, etc.

States, regional and local government authorities and other bodies governed by public law must not be regarded as taxable persons in respect of the activities or transactions in which they engage as public authorities, even where they collect dues, fees, contributions or payments in connection with those activities or transactions. But when they engage in such activities or transactions, they must be regarded as taxable persons in respect of those activities or transactions where their treatment as non-taxable persons would lead to significant distortions of competition.

In any event, bodies governed by public law must be regarded as taxable persons in relation to certain activities, provided they are not carried out on such a small scale as to be negligible. Those activities are telecommunications; the supply of water, gas, electricity and thermal energy; the transport of goods; port and airport services; passenger transport; the supply of new goods manufactured for sale; transactions in respect of agricultural products carried out by agricultural intervention agencies; the organisation of trade fairs and exhibitions; warehousing; the activities of commercial publicity bodies and travel agents; the running of staff shops, cooperatives and industrial canteens and similar institutions; and activities carried out by radio and television bodies of a commercial nature. For a general consideration of these provisions see *Ufficio Distrettuale delle Imposte Dirette di Fiorenzuola d'Arda v Comune di Carpaneto Piacentino* and *Ufficio Provinciale Imposta sul Valore Aggiunto di Piacenza v Comune di Rivergaro and Others, ECJ Case 231/87*, [1991] STC 205 (TVC 22.129).

Countries may also treat certain exempt activities of these bodies as activities they engage in as public authorities. This applies even if the body acted in a similar manner to a private trader (*Finanzamt Augsburg-Stadt v Marktgemeinde Welden, ECJ Case C–247/95*, [1997] STC 531 (TVC 22.133)).

[*Directive 2006/112/EC, Arts 9–13*].

See **43 LOCAL AUTHORITIES AND PUBLIC BODIES** for EU and UK provisions.

Supply of goods

[18.8] Supply of goods means the transfer of the right to dispose of 'tangible property' as owner.

'*Tangible property*' includes electricity, gas, heat, or cooling energy and the like. Countries may consider it to include certain interests in immovable property; rights *in rem* giving the holder a right of user over immovable property (see *WM van Tiem v Staatssecretaris van Financien, ECJ Case C–186/89*, [1993] STC 91 (TVC 22.109)); and shares, etc. giving the holder *de jure* or *de facto* rights of ownership or possession over immovable property.

The following must be treated as supplies of goods.

(a) The transfer, by order made by or in the name of a public authority or in pursuance of the law, of the ownership of property against payment of compensation.
(b) The actual handing over of goods under a contract for the hire of goods for a certain period, or for the sale of goods on deferred terms, where the contract provides that in the normal course of events ownership is to pass at the latest upon payment of the final instalment.
(c) The transfer of goods pursuant to a contract under which commission is payable on purchase or sale.
(d) The application by a taxable person of goods forming part of his business assets for his private use or for that of his staff, or their disposal free of charge or, more generally, their application for purposes other than those of his business, where the VAT on those goods or the component parts thereof was wholly or partly deductible. But the application of goods for business use as samples or as gifts of small value must not be treated as a supply of goods for consideration.
(e) The transfer by a taxable person of goods forming part of his business assets to another EU country. But the dispatch or transport of goods for the purposes of any of the following transactions must not be regarded as a transfer to another EU country.

(i) The supply of the goods by the taxable person within the territory of the EU country in which the dispatch or transport ends, in accordance with the conditions laid down in *Art 33* (see **18.12**(2) below).

(ii) The supply of the goods, for installation or assembly by or on behalf of the supplier, by the taxable person within the territory of the EU country in which dispatch or transport of the goods ends, in accordance with the conditions laid down in *Art 36* (see **18.12**(2) below).

(iii) The supply of the goods by the taxable person on board a ship, an aircraft or a train in the course of a passenger transport operation, in accordance with the conditions laid down in *Art 37* (see **18.12**(3) below).

(iv) The supply of gas through a natural gas system situated within the EU or any network connected to such a system, or the supply of electricity, or the supply of heat or cooling energy through heating or cooling networks, in accordance with the conditions laid down in *Arts 38* and *39* (see **18.12**(4) below).

(v) The supply of the goods by the taxable person within the territory of the EU country, in accordance with the conditions laid down in *Arts 138* (see **18.27**(1) below), *146* or *147* (see **18.29** below), *148* (see **18.30** below), or *151* or *152* (see **18.31** below).

(vi) The supply of a service performed for the taxable person and consisting of work on the goods in question physically carried out within the territory of the EU country in which dispatch or transport of the goods ends, provided that the goods, after being worked upon, are returned to that taxable person in the EU country from which they were initially dispatched or transported.

(vii) The temporary use of the goods within the territory of the EU country in which dispatch or transport of the goods ends, for the purposes of the supply of services by the taxable person established within the EU country in which dispatch or transport of the goods began.

(viii) The temporary use of the goods, for a period not exceeding 24 months, within the territory of another EU country, in which the importation of the same goods from a country outside the EU with a view to their temporary use would be covered by the arrangements for temporary importation with full exemption from import duties.

If one of the conditions governing eligibility under any of the above situations is no longer met, the goods must be regarded as having been transferred to another EU country at the time when that condition ceases to be met.

The following may be treated as supplies of goods.

(i) The handing over of certain works of construction.

(ii) The application by a taxable person for the purposes of his business of goods produced, constructed, extracted, processed, purchased or imported in the course of the business, where the VAT on the goods, had they been acquired from another taxable person would not be wholly deductible.

(iii) The application of goods by a taxable person for the purposes of a non-taxable area of activity, where the VAT on such goods became wholly or partly deductible upon their acquisition or upon their application in accordance with (ii) above.

(iv) With the exception of business transfers below, the retention of goods by a taxable person, or by his successors, when he ceases to carry out a taxable economic activity, where the VAT on such goods became wholly or partly deductible upon their acquisition or upon their application in accordance with (ii) above.

[*Directive 2006/112/EC, Arts 14–18*].

Transfers of businesses, etc.

In the event of a transfer (whether for consideration or not or as a contribution to a company) of a totality of assets or part thereof, an EU country may consider that no supply of goods has taken place and that the person to whom the goods are transferred is to be treated as the successor to the transferor. See **8.10 BUSINESS** for UK provisions. [*Directive 2006/112/EC, Art 19*].

See **64.3 SUPPLY: GENERAL** for the UK provisions.

Intra-EU acquisition of goods

[18.9] '*Intra-EU acquisition of goods*' means the acquisition of the right to dispose as owner of movable tangible property dispatched or transported to the person acquiring the goods, by or on behalf of the vendor or the person acquiring the goods, in an EU country other than that in which dispatch or transport of the goods began.

Non-taxable legal persons

Where goods acquired by a non-taxable legal person are dispatched or transported from a country outside the EU and imported by that non-taxable legal person into an EU country other than the EU country in which dispatch or transport of the goods ends, the goods must be regarded as having been dispatched or transported from the EU country of importation. That EU country must grant the importer liable for payment of VAT a refund of the VAT paid in respect of the importation of the goods, provided that the importer establishes that VAT has been applied to his acquisition in the EU country in which dispatch or transport of the goods ends. [*Directive 2006/112/EC, Art 20*].

Taxable persons

The application by a taxable person, for the purposes of his business, of goods dispatched or transported by or on behalf of that taxable person from another EU country

- within which the goods were produced, extracted, processed, purchased or acquired, or
- into which they were imported by that taxable person for the purposes of his business,

must be treated as an intra-EU acquisition of goods for consideration. [*Directive 2006/112/EC, Art 21*].

Armed forces

The application by the armed forces of a State party to the North Atlantic Treaty, for their use or for the use of the civilian staff accompanying them, of goods which they have not purchased subject to the general rules governing taxation on the domestic market of an EU country must be treated as an intra-EU acquisition of goods for consideration, where the importation of those goods would not be eligible for the exemption provided for in **18.28***(i)* below). [*Directive 2006/112/EC, Art 22*].

Treatment of transactions

EU countries must take the measures necessary to ensure that a transaction which would have been classed as a supply of goods if it had been carried out within their territory by a taxable person acting as such is classed as an intra-EU acquisition of goods. [*Directive 2006/112/EC, Art 23*].

Supply of services

[18.10] '*Supply of services*' means any transaction which does not constitute a supply of goods. This may include

- the assignment of intangible property;
- an obligation to refrain from an act or to tolerate an act or situation; and
- the performance of services in pursuance of an order made by or in the name of a public authority or in pursuance of the law.

The following transactions must be treated as a supply of services for consideration.

(i) The use of goods forming part of the assets of a business for the private use of a taxable person or of his staff or, more generally, for purposes other than those of his business, where the VAT on such goods was wholly or partly deductible.

(ii) The supply of services carried out free of charge by a taxable person for his private use or for that of his staff or, more generally, for purposes other than those of his business.

Countries may derogate from the provisions of (i) and (ii) above provided that this does not lead to distortion of competition. However, this power to derogate from the obligation to charge tax on private use of business assets does not allow them to impose tax where VAT on the original purchase was not wholly or partly deductible (*Kühne v Finanzamt München III*, *ECJ Case 50/88*, [1990] STC 749 (TVC 22.179)).

Where a taxable person acting in his own name but on behalf of another person takes part in the supply of services, he must be deemed to have received and supplied the services himself.

Self-supply of services

To prevent distortion of competition, countries may treat as a supply of services for consideration the supply by a taxable person of a service for the purposes of his business, where the VAT on such a service, were it supplied by another taxable person, would not be wholly deductible.

Transfers of businesses, etc.

Art 19 (see **18.8** above) applies in like manner to the supply of services.

[*Directive 2006/112/EC, Arts 24–29*].

See **64.4 SUPPLY: GENERAL** for the UK provisions.

Importation of goods

[18.11] '*Importation of goods*' means the entry into the EU of goods which are not in free circulation.

In addition, the entry into the EU of goods which are in free circulation, coming from outside the VAT territory of the EU but from a territory forming part of the customs territory of the EU, must be regarded as importation of goods.

[*Directive 2006/112/EC, Art 30*].

Place of supply of goods

[18.12] See *Council Regulation (EU)282/2011, Chapter V section 2* for implementing measures for *Directive 2006/112/EC, Arts 31–39* on place of supply of goods.

The place of supply of goods is deemed to be as follows.

(1) Supply of goods without transport

Where goods are not dispatched or transported, the place of supply is deemed to be the place where the goods are located at the time when the supply takes place. [*Directive 2006/112/EC, Art 31*].

(2) Supply of goods with transport

Where goods are dispatched or transported by the supplier, the customer or a third person, the place of supply is deemed to be the place where the goods are located at the time when dispatch or transport of the goods to the customer begins. But if dispatch or transport of the goods begins outside the VAT territory of the EU, both the place of supply by the importer liable for payment of VAT and the place of any subsequent supply is deemed to be in the EU country of importation of the goods. [*Directive 2006/112/EC, Art 32*].

Derogation

By way of derogation from *Art 32* (but subject to *Art 34* below), the place of supply of goods dispatched or transported by or on behalf of the supplier from an EU country other than that in which dispatch or transport of the goods ends is to be deemed to be the place where the goods are located at the time when dispatch or transport of the goods to the customer ends, where the following conditions are met.

- The supply of goods is carried out for a taxable person, or a non-taxable legal person, whose intra-EU acquisitions of goods are not subject to VAT pursuant to *Art 3* (see **18.6** above) or for any other non-taxable person.
- The goods supplied are neither new means of transport nor goods supplied after assembly or installation, with or without a trial run, by or on behalf of the supplier.

Where the goods supplied are dispatched or transported from outside the VAT territory of the EU and imported by the supplier into an EU country other than that in which dispatch or transport of the goods to the customer ends, they are regarded as having been dispatched or transported from the EU country of importation.

[*Directive 2006/112/EC, Art 33*].

Exception to derogation

Provided the following conditions are met, *Art 33* above does not apply to supplies of goods, all of which are dispatched or transported to the same EU country, where that country is the country in which dispatch or transport of the goods ends.

- The goods supplied are not products subject to excise duty.
- The total value, exclusive of VAT, of such supplies effected under the conditions laid down in *Art 33* within that EU country does not in any one calendar year exceed 100,000 euro (or the equivalent in national currency).
- The total value, exclusive of VAT, of the supplies of goods, other than products subject to excise duty, effected under the conditions laid down in *Art 33* within that EU country did not in the previous calendar year exceed 100,000 euro (or the equivalent in national currency).

EU countries may substitute 35,000 euro for 100,000 euro if the higher threshold might cause serious distortion of competition.

But EU countries within the territory of which the goods are located at the time when their dispatch or transport begins must grant those taxable persons who carry out supplies of goods eligible under this exception the right to opt for the place of supply to be determined in accordance with the derogation under *Art 33*.

[*Directive 2006/112/EC, Art 34*].

Second-hand goods, etc.

Arts 33 and *34* above do not apply to supplies of second-hand goods, works of art, collectors' items or antiques, nor to supplies of second-hand means of transport, subject to VAT in accordance with the relevant special arrangements. [*Directive 2006/112/EC, Art 35*].

Installed or assembled goods

Where goods dispatched or transported by the supplier, by the customer or by a third person are installed or assembled, with or without a trial run, by or on behalf of the supplier, the place of supply is deemed to be the place where the goods are installed or assembled. Where the installation or assembly is carried out in an EU country other than that of the supplier, the EU country within the territory of which the installation or assembly is carried out must take the measures necessary to ensure that there is no double taxation in that country. [*Directive 2006/112/EC, Art 36*].

(3) Supply of goods on board ships, aircraft or trains

Where goods are supplied on board ships, aircraft or trains during the 'section of a passenger transport operation effected within the EU', the place of supply is deemed to be at the point of departure of the passenger transport operation.

'*Section of a passenger transport operation effected within the EU*' means the section of the operation effected, without a stopover outside the EU, between the 'point of departure' and the 'point of arrival' of the passenger transport operation.

'*Point of departure*' of a passenger transport operation means the first scheduled point of passenger embarkation within the EU, where applicable after a stopover outside the EU.

'*Point of arrival*' of a passenger transport operation means the last scheduled point of disembarkation within the EU of passengers who embarked in the EU, where applicable before a stopover outside the EU.

In the case of a return trip, the return leg is regarded as a separate transport operation.

Pending adoption of the proposals of a report to the Council, EU countries may exempt or continue to exempt, with deductibility of the VAT paid at the preceding stage, the supply of goods for consumption on board in respect of which the place of taxation is determined in accordance with the above.

[*Directive 2006/112/EC, Art 37*].

(4) Supply of goods through distribution systems

Supplies to taxable dealers

In the case of the supply of gas through a natural gas system situated within the EU or any network connected to such a system, or of electricity, or of heat or cooling energy through heating or cooling networks to a 'taxable dealer', the place of supply is deemed to be the place where that taxable dealer has established his business or has a fixed establishment for which the goods are supplied (or, in the absence of such a place of business or fixed establishment, the place where he has his permanent address or usually resides).

'*Taxable dealer*' means a taxable person whose principal activity in respect of purchases of gas or electricity, heat or cooling energy is reselling those products and whose own consumption of those products is negligible.

[*Directive 2006/112/EC, Art 38*].

Other supplies

In the case of the supply of gas through a natural gas system situated within the EU or any network connected to such a system, or of electricity, or supply of heat or cooling energy through heating or cooling networks, not covered by *Art 38*, the place of supply is deemed to be the place where the customer effectively uses and consumes the goods.

Where all or part of the gas, electricity or heat or cooling energy is not effectively consumed by the customer, those non-consumed goods are deemed to have been used and consumed at the place where the customer has established his business or has a fixed establishment for which the goods are supplied. In the absence of such a place of business or fixed establishment, the customer is deemed to have used and consumed the goods at the place where he has his permanent address or usually resides.

[*Directive 2006/112/EC, Art 39*].

Place of an intra-EU acquisition of goods

[18.13] See *Council Regulation (EU)282/2011, Chapter V section 3* for implementing measures for *Directive 2006/112/EC, Arts 40–42* on place of intra-EU acquisitions of goods.

Subject to below, the place of the intra-EU acquisition of goods is deemed to be the place where dispatch or transport of the goods to the person acquiring them ends. [*Directive 2006/112/EC, Art 40*].

Without prejudice *Art 40* but subject to *Art 42* below, the place of an intra-EU acquisition of goods referred to in **18.6**(*b*)(i) above is deemed to be within the EU country which issued the VAT identification number under which the person acquiring the goods made the acquisition (unless the person acquiring the goods establishes that VAT has been applied to that acquisition in accordance with *Art 40*).

If VAT is so applied to the acquisition and subsequently applied, under *Art 40*, to the acquisition in the EU country in which dispatch or transport of the goods ends, the taxable amount must be reduced accordingly in the EU country which issued the VAT identification number under which the person acquiring the goods made the acquisition.

[*Directive 2006/112/EC, Art 41*].

The first paragraph of *Art 41* above must not apply (and VAT is deemed to have been applied to the intra-EU acquisition of goods in accordance with *Art 40*) where the following conditions are met.

- The person acquiring the goods establishes that he has made the intra-EU acquisition for the purposes of a subsequent supply, within the territory of the EU country identified in accordance with *Art 40*, for which the person to whom the supply is made has been designated in accordance with *Art 197* (see **18.39**(*e*) below) as liable for payment of VAT.
- The person acquiring the goods has satisfied the obligations laid down in *Art 265* (see **18.41**(8) below) relating to submission of the recapitulative statement.

[*Directive 2006/112/EC, Art 42*].

Place of supply of services before 1 January 2010

General rule

[18.14] Subject to (1)–(5) below, the place of supply of services is deemed to be the place where the supplier has established his business or has a fixed establishment from which the service is supplied or, in the absence of any such place of business or establishment, the place where he has his permanent address or usually resides. [*Directive 2006/112/EC, Art 43*].

For a consideration of 'fixed establishment', see *Berkholz v Finanzamt Hamburg-Mitte-Altstadt, ECJ Case 168/84*, [1985] ECR 2251, [1985] 3 CMLR 667 (TVC 22.198) and *ARO Lease BV v Inspecteur der Belastingdienst Grote Ondernemingen Amsterdam, ECJ Case C–190/95*, [1997] STC 1272 (TVC 22.199).

(1) Supply of services by intermediaries

The place of supply of services by an intermediary acting in the name and on behalf of another person (other than those services referred to in *Arts 50, 54* and *56* below) is the place where the underlying transaction is supplied in accordance with this *Directive*.

But where the customer of the services supplied by the intermediary is identified for VAT purposes in an EU country other than that within the territory of which that transaction is carried out, the place of the supply of services by the intermediary is deemed to be within the territory of the EU country which issued the customer with the VAT identification number under which the service was rendered to him.

[*Directive 2006/112/EC, Art 44*].

(2) Supply of services connected with immovable property

The place of supply of services connected with immovable property, including the services of estate agents and experts, and services for preparing and co-ordinating construction services (e.g. architects and firms providing on-site supervision) is the place where the property is located. This includes services of organising the exchange of timeshare usage rights in holiday accommodation (see *RCI Europe v HMRC, ECJ Case C–37/08* [2009] STC 2407 (TVC 22.207). [*Directive 2006/112/EC, Art 45*].

(3) Supply of transport

The place of supply of transport other than the intra-EU transport of goods is the place where the transport takes place, proportionately in terms of distances covered. [*Directive 2006/112/EC, Art 46*].

The place of supply of 'intra-EU transport of goods' is the 'place of departure' of the transport. But where intra-EU transport of goods is supplied to customers identified for VAT purposes in an EU country other than that of the departure of the transport, the place of supply is deemed to be within the territory of the EU country which issued the customer with the VAT identification number under which the service was rendered to him.

'*Intra-Union transport of goods*' means any transport of goods in respect of which the place of departure and the 'place of arrival' are situated within the territories of two different EU countries.

'*Place of departure*' means the place where transport of the goods actually begins, irrespective of distances covered in order to reach the place where the goods are located.

'*Place of arrival*' means the place where transport of the goods actually ends.

[*Directive 2006/112/EC, Arts 47, 48*].

The transport of goods in respect of which the place of departure and the place of arrival are situated within the territory of the same EU country must be treated as intra-EU transport of goods where such transport is directly linked to transport of goods in respect of which the place of departure and the place of arrival are situated within the territory of two different EU countries. [*Directive 2006/112/EC, Art 49*].

Intermediaries

The place of the supply of services by an intermediary, acting in the name and on behalf of another person, where the intermediary takes part in the intra-EU transport of goods, is the place of departure of the transport. But where the customer of the services supplied by the intermediary is identified for VAT purposes in an EU country other than that of the departure of the transport, the place of the supply of services by the intermediary is deemed to be within the territory of the EU country which issued the customer with the VAT identification number under which the service was rendered to him. [*Directive 2006/112/EC, Art 50*].

Supplies outside territorial waters

EU countries need not apply VAT to that part of the intra-EU transport of goods taking place over waters which do not form part of the territory of the EU. [*Directive 2006/112/EC, Art 51*].

(4) Supply of cultural and similar services, ancillary transport services or services relating to movable tangible property

The place of supply of the following services is the place where the services are physically carried out.

(a) Cultural, artistic, sporting, scientific, educational, entertainment or similar activities, including the activities of the organisers of such activities and, where appropriate, ancillary services. [*Directive 2006/112/EC, Art 52(a)*].

(b) Ancillary transport activities, such as loading, unloading, handling and similar activities. [*Directive 2006/112/EC, Art 52(b)*].

By way of derogation, the place of supply of services involving activities ancillary to the intra-EU transport of goods, supplied to customers identified for VAT purposes in an EU country other than that in the territory of which the activities are physically carried out, is deemed to be within the territory of the EU country which issued the customer with the VAT identification number under which the service was rendered to him. [*Directive 2006/112/EC, Art 53*].

The place of the supply of services by an intermediary, acting in the name and on behalf of another person, where the intermediary takes part in the supply of services consisting in activities ancillary to the intra-EU transport of goods, is the place where the ancillary activities are physically carried out. But where the customer of the services supplied by the intermediary is identified for VAT purposes in an EU country other than that within the territory of which the ancillary activities are physically carried out, the place of supply of services by the intermediary is deemed to be within the territory of the EU country which issued the customer with the VAT identification number under which the service was rendered to him. [*Directive 2006/112/EC, Art 54*].

(c) Valuations of movable tangible property or work on such property. [*Directive 2006/112/EC, Art 52(c)*].

By way of derogation, the place of supply of services involving the valuation of movable tangible property or work on such property, supplied to customers identified for VAT purposes in an EU country other than that in the territory of which the services are physically carried out, is deemed to be within the territory of the EU country which issued the customer with the VAT identification number under which the service was rendered to him. This derogation only applies where the goods are dispatched or transported out of the EU country in which the services were physically carried out. [*Directive 2006/112/EC, Art 55*].

(5) Miscellaneous services

The place of supply of the following services to customers established outside the EU, or to taxable persons established in the EU but not in the same country as the supplier, is the place where the customer has established his business or has a fixed establishment for which the service is supplied or, in the absence of such a place, the place where he has a permanent address or usually resides.

(a) Transfers and assignments of copyrights, patents, licences, trade marks and similar rights.

(b) Advertising services (see *EC Commission v French Republic, ECJ Case C–68/92*, [1997] STC 684 (TVC 22.218)).

(c) Services of consultants, engineers, consultancy bureaux, lawyers, accountants and other similar services, as well as data processing and the provision of information.

(d) Obligations to refrain from pursuing or exercising, in whole or in part, a business activity or a right within this list.

(e) Banking, financial and insurance transactions including reinsurance, with the exception of the hire of safes.

(f) The supply of staff.

(g) The hiring out of movable tangible property, with the exception of all means of transport.

(h) The provision of access to, or transmission or distribution through, a natural gas system situated within the EU or any network connected to such a system, the electricity system or heating or cooling networks, and the provision of other services directly linked thereto.

(i) Telecommunications services.

(j) Radio and television broadcasting services.

(k) Electronically supplied services, such as

- website supply, web-hosting, distance maintenance of programmes and equipment;
- supply of software and updating thereof;
- supply of images, text and information and making available of databases;
- supply of music, films and games, including games of chance and gambling games, and of political, cultural, artistic, sporting, scientific and entertainment broadcasts and events; and
- supply of distance teaching.

Where the supplier of a service and the customer communicate via electronic mail, that does not (of itself) mean that the service supplied is an electronically supplied service for these purposes.

Where these services are supplied

- to non-taxable persons who are established in an EU country, or who have their permanent address or usually reside in an EU country,
- by a taxable person who has established his business outside the EU or has a fixed establishment there from which the service is supplied, or who, in the absence of such a place of business or fixed establishment, has his permanent address or usually resides outside the EU,

  the place of supply is the place where the non-taxable person is established, or where he has his permanent address or usually resides.

(l) The supply of services by intermediaries, acting in the name and on behalf of other persons, where those intermediaries take part in the supply of the services referred to in this list.

[*Directive 2006/112/EC, Arts 56, 57*].

Effective use and enjoyment

To avoid double taxation, non-taxation or distortion of competition, EU countries may, with regard to

- the supply of the services in (*a*)–(*l*) above (other than services in (*l*) where those services are rendered to non-taxable persons), and
- the hiring out of means of transport

consider the place of supply of any or all of those services

(a) if situated within their territory, as being situated outside the EU, if the effective use and enjoyment of the services takes place outside the EU; and

(b) if situated outside the EU, as being situated within their territory, if the effective use and enjoyment of the services takes place within their territory.

EU countries must apply (*b*) above to telecommunications services and radio and television broadcasting services supplied

- to non-taxable persons who are established in an EU country or who have their permanent address or usually reside in an EU country; and
- by a taxable person who has established his business outside the EU or has a fixed establishment there from which the services are supplied, or who, in the absence of such a place of business or fixed establishment, has his permanent address or usually resides outside the EU.

[*Directive 2006/112/EC, Arts 58, 59*].

See **65.13 SUPPLY: PLACE OF SUPPLY** for the UK provisions.

Place of supply of services from 1 January 2010

Taxable person

[18.15] See *Council Regulation (EU)282/2011, Chapter V section 4* for implementing measures for *Directive 2006/112/EC, Arts 43–59* on place of supply of services.

For the purpose of applying the rules concerning the place of supply of services

- a taxable person who also carries out activities or transactions that are not considered to be taxable supplies of goods or services in accordance with *Art 2(1)* shall be regarded as a taxable person in respect of all services rendered to him;
- a non-taxable legal person who is identified for VAT purposes shall be regarded as a taxable person.

[*Directive 2006/112/EC, Art 43*].

General rules

The place of supply of services to a taxable person acting as such shall be the place where that person has established his business. However, if those services are provided to a fixed establishment of the taxable person located in a place other than the place where he has established his business, the place of supply of those services shall be the place where that fixed establishment is located. In the absence of such place of establishment or fixed establishment, the place of supply of services shall be the place where the taxable person who receives such services has his permanent address or usually resides.

The place of supply of services to a non-taxable person shall be the place where the supplier has established his business. However, if those services are provided from a fixed establishment of the supplier located in a place other than the place where he has established his business, the place of supply of those services shall be the place where that fixed establishment is located. In the absence of such place of establishment or fixed establishment, the place of supply of services shall be the place where the supplier has his permanent address or usually resides.

[*Directive 2006/112/EC, Arts 44, 45*].

Supply of services by intermediaries

The place of supply of services rendered to a non-taxable person by an intermediary acting in the name and on behalf of another person shall be the place where the underlying transaction is supplied in accordance with this *Directive*.

[*Directive 2006/112/EC, Art 46*].

Supply of services connected with immovable property

The place of supply of services connected with immovable property, including the services of experts and estate agents, the provision of accommodation in the hotel sector or in sectors with a similar function, such as holiday camps or sites developed for use as camping sites, the granting of rights to use immovable property and services for the preparation and coordination of construction work, such as the services of architects and of firms providing on-site supervision, shall be the place where the immovable property is located.

[*Directive 2006/112/EC, Art 47*].

Supply of transport

The place of supply of passenger transport shall be the place where the transport takes place, proportionate to the distances covered.

The place of supply of the transport of goods, other than the intra-Union transport of goods, to non-taxable persons shall be the place where the transport takes place, proportionate to the distances covered.

The place of supply of the intra-Union transport of goods to non-taxable persons shall be the place of departure.

'Intra-Union transport of goods' shall mean any transport of goods in respect of which the place of departure and the place of arrival are situated within the territories of two different Member States. 'Place of departure' shall mean the place where transport of the goods actually begins, irrespective of distances covered in order to reach the place where the goods are located and 'place of arrival' shall mean the place where transport of the goods actually ends.

Member States need not apply VAT to that part of the intra-Union transport of goods to non-taxable persons taking place over waters which do not form part of the territory of the Union.

[*Directive 2006/112/EC, Arts 48–52*].

Supply of cultural, artistic, sporting, scientific, educational, entertainment and similar services, ancillary transport services and valuations of and work on movable property

From 1 January 2010 to 31 December 2010

The place of supply of services and ancillary services relating to cultural, artistic, sporting, scientific, educational, entertainment or similar activities, such as fairs and exhibitions, including the supply of services of the organisers of such activities, shall be the place where those activities are physically carried out.

The place of supply of the following services to non-taxable persons shall be the place where the services are physically carried out: (a) ancillary transport activities such as loading, unloading, handling and similar activities; (b) valuations of and work on movable tangible property.

From 1 January 2011

The place of supply of services in respect of admission to cultural, artistic, sporting, scientific, educational, entertainment or similar events, such as fairs and exhibitions, and of ancillary services related to the admission, supplied to a taxable person, shall be the place where those events actually take place.

The place of supply of services and ancillary services, relating to cultural, artistic, sporting, scientific, educational, entertainment or similar activities, such as fairs and exhibitions, including the supply of services of the organisers of such activities, supplied to a non-taxable person shall be the place where those activities actually take place.

The place of supply of the following services to a non-taxable person shall be the place where the services are physically carried out: (a) ancillary transport activities such as loading, unloading, handling and similar activities; (b) valuations of and work on movable tangible property.

[*Directive 2006/112/EC, Arts 53, 54*].

Supply of restaurant and catering services

The place of supply of restaurant and catering services other than those physically carried out on board ships, aircraft or trains during the section of a passenger transport operation effected within the Union, shall be the place where the services are physically carried out.

[*Directive 2006/112/EC, Art 55*].

Hiring of means of transport

The place of short-term hiring of a means of transport shall be the place where the means of transport is actually put at the disposal of the customer. For these purposes, 'short-term' shall mean the continuous possession or use of the means of transport throughout a period of not more than 30 days and, in the case of vessels, not more than 90 days.

[*Directive 2006/112/EC, Art 56*].

Supply of restaurant and catering services for consumption on board ships, aircraft or trains

The place of supply of restaurant and catering services which are physically carried out on board ships, aircraft or trains during the section of a passenger transport operation effected within the Union, shall be at the point of departure of the passenger transport operation. For these purposes, 'section of a passenger transport operation effected within the Union' shall mean the section of the operation effected, without a stopover outside the Union, between the point of departure and the point of arrival of the passenger transport operation. 'Point of departure of a passenger transport operation' shall mean the first scheduled point of passenger embarkation within the Union, where applicable after a stopover outside the Union. 'Point of arrival of a passenger transport operation' shall mean the last scheduled point of disembarkation within the Union of passengers who embarked in the Union, where applicable before a stopover outside the Union. In the case of a return trip, the return leg shall be regarded as a separate transport operation.

[*Directive 2006/112/EC, Art 57*].

Supply of electronic services to non-taxable persons

The place of supply of electronically supplied services, in particular those referred to in *Annex II* (i.e. website supply, web-hosting, distance maintenance of programmes and equipment; supply of software and updating thereof; supply of images, text and information and making available of databases; supply of music, films and games, including games of chance and gambling games, and of political, cultural, artistic, sporting, scientific and entertainment broadcasts and events; supply of distance teaching), when supplied to non-taxable persons who are established in a Member State, or who have their permanent address or usually reside in a Member State, by a taxable person who has established his business outside the Union or has a fixed establishment there from which the service is supplied, or who, in the absence of such a place of business or fixed establishment, has his permanent address or usually resides outside the Union, shall be the place where the non-taxable person is established, or where he has his permanent address or usually resides. Where the supplier of a service and the customer communicate via electronic mail, that shall not of itself mean that the service supplied is an electronically supplied service. (These provisions to be substituted by *Directive 2008/8/EC, Art 5(1)* with effect from 1 January 2015.)

[*Directive 2006/112/EC, Art 58*].

Supply of services to non-taxable persons outside the Union

The place of supply of the following services to a non-taxable person who is established or has his permanent address or usually resides outside the Union, shall be the place where that person is established, has his permanent address or usually resides—

(a) transfers and assignments of copyrights, patents, licences, trade marks and similar rights;

(b) advertising services;
(c) the services of consultants, engineers, consultancy firms, lawyers, accountants and other similar services, as well as data processing and the provision of information;
(d) obligations to refrain from pursuing or exercising, in whole or in part, a business activity or a right referred to in this *Article*;
(e) banking, financial and insurance transactions including reinsurance, with the exception of the hire of safes;
(f) the supply of staff;
(g) the hiring out of movable tangible property, with the exception of all means of transport;
(h) the provision of access to, and of transport or transmission through, natural gas and electricity distribution systems and the provision of other services directly linked thereto;
(i) telecommunications services;
(j) radio and television broadcasting services;
(k) electronically supplied services, in particular those referred to in *Annex II* (i.e. website supply, web-hosting, distance maintenance of programmes and equipment; supply of software and updating thereof; supply of images, text and information and making available of databases; supply of music, films and games, including games of chance and gambling games, and of political, cultural, artistic, sporting, scientific and entertainment broadcasts and events; supply of distance teaching).

Where the supplier of a service and the customer communicate via electronic mail, that shall not of itself mean that the service supplied is an electronically supplied service. (Points *(i)*, *(j)*, *(k)* to be substituted by *Directive 2008/8/EC, Art 5(2)* with effect from 1 January 2015.)

[*Directive 2006/112/EC, Art 59*].

Prevention of double taxation or non-taxation

In order to prevent double taxation, non-taxation or distortion of competition, Member States may, with regard to services the place of supply of which is governed by *Arts 44, 45, 56 and 59*

(a) consider the place of supply of any or all of those services, if situated within their territory, as being situated outside the Union if the effective use and enjoyment of the services takes place outside the Union;
(b) consider the place of supply of any or all of those services, if situated outside the Union, as being situated within their territory if the effective use and enjoyment of the services takes place within their territory.

However, this provision shall not apply to the electronically supplied services where those services are rendered to non-taxable persons not established within the Union. (This provision to be substituted by *Directive 2008/8/EC, Art 5(3)* with effect from 1 January 2015.)

Member States shall apply *(b)* above to telecommunications services and radio and television broadcasting services, as referred to in point (j) of *Art 59* above, supplied to non-taxable persons who are established in a Member State, or who have their permanent address or usually reside in a Member State, by a taxable person who has established his business outside the Union or has a fixed establishment there from which the services are supplied, or who, in the absence of such a place of business or fixed establishment, has his permanent address or usually resides outside the Union. (This provision to be repealed by *Directive 2008/8/EC, Art 5(3)* with effect from 1 January 2015.)

[*Directive 2006/112/EC, Arts 59a, 59b*].

See **65.12 SUPPLY: PLACE OF SUPPLY** for the UK provisions.

Place of importation of goods

[18.16] The place of importation of goods is the EU country within whose territory the goods are located when they enter the EU. [*Directive 2006/112/EC, Art 60*].

By way of derogation from *Art 60*, where, on entry into the EU, goods which are not in free circulation are placed under

- one of the arrangements or situations referred to in *Art 156* (see **18.33**(*a*) below),
- temporary importation arrangements with total exemption from import duty, or
- external transit arrangements,

the place of importation of such goods is the EU country within whose territory the goods cease to be covered by those arrangements or situations.

[*Directive 2006/112/EC, Art 61*].

Chargeable event and chargeability of VAT

[18.17] The provisions relating to a chargeable event and the chargeability of VAT are outlined below.

(1) Supply of goods or services

A chargeable event occurs and VAT becomes chargeable when the goods or the services are supplied. [*Directive 2006/112/EC, Art 63*].

Where it gives rise to successive statements of account or successive payments, the supply of goods (other than that consisting in the hire of goods for a certain period or the sale of goods on deferred terms) or the supply of services is regarded as being completed on expiry of the periods to which such statements of account or payments relate. Supplies of services for which VAT is payable by the customer pursuant to *Art 196* (see **18.39**(*e*) below), which are supplied continuously over a period of more than one year and which do not give rise to statements of account or payments during that period shall be regarded as being completed on expiry of each calendar year until such time as the supply of services comes to an end. But EU countries may provide that, in certain other cases, the continuous supply of goods or services over a period of time is to be regarded as being completed at least at intervals of one year. [*Directive 2006/112/EC, Art 64*].

Where a payment is to be made on account before the goods or services are supplied, VAT becomes chargeable on receipt of the payment and on the amount received. [*Directive 2006/112/EC, Art 65*].

Derogation

By way of derogation from *Arts 63–65* above, countries may provide that VAT is to become chargeable, in respect of certain transactions or certain categories of taxable person, either

- no later than the time the invoice is issued;
- no later than the time the payment is received; or
- where an invoice is not issued, or is issued late, within a specified period from the date of the chargeable event.

The derogation shall not, however, apply to supplies of services in respect of which VAT is payable by the customer pursuant to *Art 196* (see **18.39**(*e*) below).

[*Directive 2006/112/EC, Art 66*].

Where, in accordance with the conditions laid down in *Art 138* (see **18.27**(1) below),

- goods dispatched or transported to an EU country other than that in which dispatch or transport of the goods begins are supplied VAT-exempt, or
- goods are transferred VAT-exempt to another EU country by a taxable person for the purposes of his business,

VAT becomes chargeable on the 15th day of the month following that in which the chargeable event occurs. By way of derogation from this, VAT becomes chargeable on issue of the invoice, if that invoice is issued before the 15th day of the month following that in which the chargeable event occurs.

[*Directive 2006/112/EC, Art 67*].

See **66.1 SUPPLY: TIME OF SUPPLY** for the UK provisions.

(2) Intra-EU acquisition of goods

The chargeable event occurs when the intra-EU acquisition of goods is made, i.e. when the supply of similar goods is regarded as being effected within the territory of the relevant EU country. [*Directive 2006/112/EC, Art 68*].

VAT becomes chargeable on the 15th day of the month following that in which the chargeable event occurs. By way of derogation from this, VAT becomes chargeable on issue of the invoice, if that invoice is issued before the 15th day of the month following that in which the chargeable event occurs. [*Directive 2006/112/EC, Art 69*].

See **19.7 EUROPEAN UNION: SINGLE MARKET** for the UK provisions.

(3) Importation of goods

The chargeable event occurs and VAT become chargeable when the goods are imported. [*Directive 2006/112/EC, Art 70*].

Where, on entry into the EU, goods are placed under one of the arrangements or situations referred to in

- *Art 156* (see **18.33**(*a*) below),
- under temporary importation arrangements with total exemption from import duty, or
- under external transit arrangements,

the chargeable event occurs and VAT becomes chargeable only when the goods cease to be covered by those arrangements or situations.

However, where imported goods are subject to customs duties, to agricultural levies or to charges having equivalent effect established under a common policy, the chargeable event occurs and VAT becomes chargeable when the chargeable event in respect of those duties occurs and those duties become chargeable.

Where imported goods are not subject to any duties referred to above, countries must, as regards the chargeable event and the moment when VAT becomes chargeable, apply the provisions in force governing customs duties.

[*Directive 2006/112/EC, Art 71*].

See **33.2 IMPORTS** for the UK provisions.

Taxable amount: open market value

[18.18] For the purposes of this *Directive*, '*open market value*' means the full amount that, in order to obtain the goods or services in question at that time, a customer at the same marketing stage at which the supply of goods or services takes place, would have to pay, under conditions of fair competition, to a supplier at arm's length within the territory of the EU country in which the supply is subject to VAT.

Where no comparable supply of goods or services can be ascertained, '*open market value*' means

- in respect of goods, an amount that is not less than the purchase price of the goods or of similar goods or, in the absence of a purchase price, the cost price, determined at the time of supply; and
- in respect of services, an amount that is not less than the full cost to the taxable person of providing the service.

[*Directive 2006/112/EC, Art 72*].

Taxable amount: supply of goods and services

[18.19] Apart from (*a*)–(*d*) below, the taxable amount in respect of the supply of goods or services includes everything which constitutes consideration obtained (or to be obtained) by the supplier in return for the supply from the customer or a third party, including 'subsidies directly linked to the price' of the supply. [*Directive 2006/112/EC, Art 73*].

'*Subsidies directly linked to the price*' must be interpreted as covering only subsidies which constitute the whole or part of the consideration for a supply of goods or services and which are paid by a third party to the seller or supplier (*Office des Produits Wallons ASBL v Belgium, ECJ Case C–184/00*, [2003] STC 1100 (TVC 22.246)).

But

(a) where a taxable person applies or disposes of goods forming part of his business assets, or where goods are retained by a taxable person, or by his successors, when his taxable economic activity ceases, the taxable amount is the purchase price of the goods or of similar goods or, in the absence of a purchase price, the cost price, determined at the time when the application, disposal or retention takes place [*Directive 2006/112/EC, Art 74*];
(b) in respect of the supply of services where goods forming part of the assets of a business are used for private purposes or services are carried out free of charge, the taxable amount is the full cost to the taxable person of providing the services [*Directive 2006/112/EC, Art 75*];
(c) in respect of the supply of goods consisting in transfer to another EU country, the taxable amount is the purchase price of the goods or of similar goods or, in the absence of a purchase price, the cost price, determined at the time the transfer takes place [*Directive 2006/112/EC, Art 76*]; and
(d) in respect of the self-supply by a taxable person of a service for the purposes of his business, the taxable amount is the open market value of the service supplied [*Directive 2006/112/EC, Art 77*].

The taxable amount includes

- taxes, duties, levies and charges, excluding the VAT itself; and
- incidental expenses, such as commission, packing, transport and insurance costs, charged by the supplier to the customer,

but does not include

(i) price reductions by way of discount for early payment;
(ii) price discounts and rebates granted to the customer and obtained by him at the time of the supply; and
(iii) amounts received by a taxable person from the customer, as repayment of expenditure incurred in the name and on behalf of the customer, and entered in his books in a suspense account. The taxable person must furnish proof of the actual amount of such expenditure and cannot deduct any VAT which may have been charged.

[*Directive 2006/112/EC, Arts 78, 79*].

In order to prevent tax evasion or avoidance, where the consideration

- is lower than the open market value and the recipient of the supply does not have a full right of deduction,
- is lower than the open market value and the supplier does not have a full right of deduction and the supply is subject to an exemption, or
- is higher than the open market value and the supplier does not have a full right of deduction

countries may take measures to ensure that, in respect of the supply of goods or services involving family or other close personal ties, management, ownership, membership, financial or legal ties as defined by the country, the taxable amount is to be the open market value.

[*Directive 2006/112/EC, Art 80*].

Works of art, etc.

Countries which, at 1 January 1993, were not applying a reduced rate may, if they opt under *Art 89* (see **18.21** below) to treat the taxable amount on importation to be equal to a fraction (at least 5%) of the otherwise taxable amount, provide that the taxable amount is also reduced to a fraction (at least 5%) on the supply of works of art. [*Directive 2006/112/EC, Art 81*].

Exempt investment gold

Countries may provide that, in respect of the supply of goods and services, the taxable amount is to include the value of exempt investment gold which has been provided by the customer to be used as a basis for working and which as a result, loses its VAT-exempt investment gold status when such goods and services are supplied. The value to be used is the open market value of the investment gold at the time that those goods and services are supplied. [*Directive 2006/112/EC, Art 82*].

See **71 VALUATION** for the UK provisions.

Taxable amount: intra-EU acquisition of goods

[18.20] In respect of the intra-EU acquisition of goods, the taxable amount is established on the basis of the same factors as are used in **18.18** above to determine the taxable amount for the supply of the same goods within the territory of the EU country concerned. In the case of the transactions to be treated as intra-EU acquisitions of goods referred to in *Arts 21* and 22 (see **18.9** above), the taxable amount is the purchase price of the goods or of similar goods or, in the absence of a purchase price, the cost price, determined at the time of the supply. [*Directive 2006/112/EC, Art 83*].

Countries must take the measures necessary to ensure that the excise duty due from or paid by the person making the intra-EU acquisition of a product subject to excise duty is included in the taxable amount. Where, after the intra-EU acquisition of goods has been made, the person acquiring the goods obtains a refund of the excise duty paid in the EU country in which dispatch or transport of the goods began, the taxable amount must be reduced accordingly in the EU country in the territory of which the acquisition was made. [*Directive 2006/112/EC, Art 84*].

Taxable amount: importation of goods

[18.21] In respect of the importation of goods, the taxable amount is the value for customs purposes, determined in accordance with the Union provisions in force. [*Directive 2006/112/EC, Art 85*].

The taxable amount includes, in so far as they are not already included,

- taxes, duties, levies and other charges due outside the EU country of importation, and those due by reason of importation, excluding the VAT to be levied; and
- incidental expenses, such as commission, packing, transport and insurance costs, incurred up to the 'first place of destination' within the territory of the EU country of importation, as well as those resulting from transport to another place of destination within the EU, if that other place is known when the chargeable event occurs.

'*First place of destination*' means the place mentioned on the consignment note, etc. or, if no such mention is made, the first place of destination is deemed to be the place of the first transfer of cargo in the EU country of importation.

[*Directive 2006/112/EC, Art 86*].

The taxable amount does not include

- price reductions by way of discount for early payment; or
- price discounts and rebates granted to the customer and obtained by him at the time of importation.

[*Directive 2006/112/EC, Art 87*].

Where goods temporarily exported from the EU are reimported after having undergone, outside the EU, repair, processing, adaptation, making up or re-working, countries must take steps to ensure that the tax treatment of the goods for VAT purposes is the same as that which would have been applied had the repair, processing, adaptation, making up or re-working been carried out within their territory. [*Directive 2006/112/EC, Art 88*].

Works of art, etc.

Countries which, at 1 January 1993, were not applying a reduced rate may provide that in respect of the importation of works of art, collectors' items and antiques the taxable amount is to be equal to a fraction (at least 5%) of the otherwise taxable amount. [*Directive 2006/112/EC, Art 89*].

See **71.15 VALUATION** for UK the provisions.

Taxable amount: miscellaneous provisions

[18.22] Miscellaneous provisions are outlined below.

(a) In case of *cancellation, refusal or total or partial non-payment*, or where the price is reduced after the supply takes place, the taxable amount must be reduced accordingly under conditions determined by each EU country although, in the case of total or partial non-payment, countries may derogate from this rule.

(b) Where information for determining the taxable amount is expressed in *foreign currency*,
   - for importations, the exchange rate must be determined in accordance with Union provisions governing the calculation of the value for customs purposes; and

- the exchange rate applicable for transactions other than importations is the latest selling rate recorded, at the time the VAT becomes chargeable, on the most representative exchange market or markets of the EU country concerned.

For certain transactions, countries can use the exchange rate determined in accordance with the Union provisions in force governing the calculation of the value for Customs purposes.

See **71.18 VALUATION** for the UK provisions.

(c) As regards *returnable packing costs*, countries may either
- exclude them from the taxable amount and take the necessary measures to see that this amount is adjusted if the packing is not returned; or
- include them in the taxable amount and take the necessary measures to see that this amount is adjusted where the packaging is returned.

[*Directive 2006/112/EC, Arts 90–92*].

Rates

[18.23] The rate applicable to taxable transactions is that in force at the time of the chargeable event. However, in the following situations, the rate applicable is that in force when VAT becomes chargeable.

- In the cases referred to in *Arts 65* and *66* (see **18.17** above).
- Intra-EU acquisitions of goods.
- In the cases, concerning the importation of goods, referred to in *Art 71* (see **18.17** above).

[*Directive 2006/112/EC, Art 93*].

Intra-EU acquisitions and imports

The rate applicable to the intra-EU acquisition of goods is that applied to the supply of like goods within the territory of the EU country. Subject to the option under *Art 103* of applying a reduced rate to the importation of works of art, etc. (see below) the rate applicable to the importation of goods is that applied to the supply of like goods within the territory of the EU country. [*Directive 2006/112/EC, Art 94*].

Standard rate

Each EU country must fix a standard rate which must be the same for goods and services. [*Directive 2006/112/EC, Art 96*]. Until 31 December 2010, the standard rate may not be less than 15%. [*Directive 2006/112/EC, Art 97*].

Reduced rates

Countries may apply either one or two reduced rates (which cannot be less than 5%). They can only apply to selected categories of goods and services comprising

- foodstuffs;

- supply of water;
- pharmaceutical products, medical equipment and aids for the disabled;
- children's car seats;
- transport of passengers and their accompanying luggage;
- supply of books and other printed matter;
- admission to shows, theatres, circuses, fairs, amusement parks, concerts, museums, zoos, cinemas, exhibitions and similar cultural events and facilities;
- reception of radio and television broadcasting services;
- supply of services by writers, composers and performing artists, or of the royalties due to them;
- housing supplies as part of a social policy;
- supply normally intended for use in agricultural production (excluding capital goods);
- accommodation in hotels and similar establishments, including holiday accommodation and the letting of places on camping or caravan sites;
- admission to sporting events and use of sporting facilities;
- supply of goods and services by organisations recognised as being devoted to social well-being;
- supply by undertakers and cremation services;
- medical and dental care;
- street cleaning, refuse collection and waste treatment;
- supplies of natural gas, electricity or district heating (after consultation of the VAT Committee);
- the importation of works of art, collectors' items and antiques and, provided the reduced rate is applied to such imports, the supply of works of art, etc.
  - (i) by their creator or his successors in title; and
  - (ii) on an occasional basis, by a taxable person other than a taxable dealer, where the works of art have been imported by the taxable person himself, or where they have been supplied to him by their creator or his successors in title, or where they have entitled him to full deduction of VAT.

[*Directive 2006/112/EC, Arts 98, 102, 103, Annex III*].

Labour-intensive services

Until 31 December 2010 at the latest, an EU country can also apply a reduced rate to any two (in exceptional circumstances, three) of the following categories services. The services concerned must be labour-intensive, be provided largely to final consumers, be mainly local and not likely to create distortions of competition. There must be a close link between the lower prices resulting from the rate reduction and the foreseeable increase in demand and employment.

- Minor repairing of bicycles, shoe and leather goods, and clothing and household linen.
- Renovation and repairing of private dwellings (excluding materials which form a significant part of the value of the supply).
- Window cleaning and cleaning in private households.

- Domestic care services (e.g. home help and care of young, elderly, sick or disabled).
- Hairdressing.

[*Directive 2006/112/EC, Arts 106, 107, Annex IV*].

Transitional provisions

During a transitional period until a definite VAT system is decided upon, exemptions with refund of VAT paid at the preceding stage (i.e. zero-rating in the UK) may be maintained provided they were in force on 1 January 1991 and were in accordance with Union law. [*Directive 2006/112/EC, Art 110*].

Exemptions

[18.24] EU countries must exempt certain activities under conditions that they lay down for the purpose of ensuring the correct and straightforward application of those exemptions and of preventing any possible evasion, avoidance or abuse. [*Directive 2006/112/EC, Art 131*]. These are divided into

- exemptions for certain activities in the public interest (see **18.25** below);
- exemption for other activities (see **18.26** below);
- exemptions for intra-EU transactions (see **18.27** below);
- exemptions on importation (see **18.28** below);
- exemptions on exportation (see **18.29** below);
- exemptions related to international transport (see **18.30** below);
- exemptions relating to certain transactions treated as exports (see **18.31** below);
- exemptions for the supply of services by intermediaries (see **18.32** below); and
- exemption for transactions related to international trade (see **18.33** below).

Exemptions for certain activities in the public interest

[18.25] The following activities should be exempt.

(a) The supply by the public postal service of services other than passenger transport and telecommunications services, and the supply of goods incidental thereto. In *R (oao TNT Post UK Ltd) v HMRC, ECJ Case C–357/07* [2009] STC 1438 (TVC 22.272), the ECJ held that 'public postal services' must be interpreted as including operators, whether they are public or private, who undertake to provide, in a member state, all or part of the universal postal service. The exemption only applies to the services that Royal Mail supplies in its capacity as universal service provider (i.e. its services available to the public at the standardised rates). It does not extend to services that the Royal Mail supplies under contracts individually negotiated with customers to meet their specific needs.

(b) Hospital and medical care and closely related activities undertaken by bodies governed by public law or, under social conditions comparable to those applicable to bodies governed by public law, by hospitals, centres for medical treatment or diagnosis and other duly recognised establishments of a similar nature. See *Future Health Technologies Ltd v HMRC, ECJ Case C–86/09* [2010] STC 1836 (TVC 20.65) for the ECJ's interpretation of 'hospital and medical care' and 'closely related activities'.

(c) The provision of medical care in the exercise of the medical or paramedical professions as defined by the country concerned. See *Future Health Technologies Ltd v HMRC, ECJ Case C–86/09* [2010] STC 1836 (TVC 20.65) for the ECJ's interpretation of 'provision of medical care'.

(d) Supplies of human organs, blood and milk.

(e) Services supplied by dental technicians in their professional capacity and dental prostheses supplied by dentists and dental technicians.

(f) Services supplied by independent groups of persons whose activities are exempt from or not subject to VAT, for the purpose of rendering their members the services directly necessary for the exercise of their activity, where these groups merely claim from their members exact reimbursement of their share of joint expenses, provided that such exemption is not likely to produce distortion of competition. This covers services supplied by independent groups to their members even if those services were supplied to only one or several of those members (*Stichting Centraal Begeleidingsorgaan voor de Intercollegiale Toetsing v Staatssecretaris van Financien, ECJ Case C–407/07*, [2009] STC 869 (TVC 22.292)).

(g) The supply of services and of goods closely linked to welfare and social security work, including those supplied by old people's homes, by bodies governed by public law or by other organisations recognised as being devoted to social well-being. The expression 'social welfare' means the well-being (whether in the physical, mental or material sense) of individuals as members of society. The provision of benefits which tends directly to improve the health or conditions of life of individuals comes *prima facie* within the expression 'social welfare' (*Yoga for Health Foundation v C & E Commrs*, QB [1984] STC 630 (TVC 22.293)). 'Spiritual welfare' is also included (*International Bible Students' Association v C & E Commrs*, QB 1987, [1988] STC 412 (TVC 22.294)).

In *Bulthuis-Griffioen v Inspector der Omzetbelasting, ECJ Case C–453/93*, [1995] STC 954 (TVC 22.297) the ECJ held that this exemption was only available to 'bodies governed by public law or other organisations' and did not apply to sole proprietors. This decision was not followed in *J & M Gregg v C & E Commrs, ECJ Case C–216/97*, [1999] STC 934 (TVC 22.298) where the ECJ held that the provisions were sufficiently broad to include natural persons as well.

(h) The supply of services and of goods closely linked to the protection of children and young persons by bodies governed by public law or by other organisations recognised as being devoted to social well-being.

(i) Children's or young people's education, school or university education, vocational training or retraining, including the supply of services and of goods closely related thereto, provided by bodies governed by public law having such as their aim or by other organisations defined by the country concerned as having similar objects. Exemption does not extend to the undertaking by State universities of research projects for consideration as this cannot be regarded as an activity closely related to university education (*EC Commission v Federal Republic of Germany, ECJ Case C–287/00*, [2002] STC 982 (TVC 22.303)).

(j) Tuition given privately by teachers and covering school or university education.

(k) Certain supplies of staff by religious or philosophical institutions for the purposes of (*b*), (*g*), (*h*) or (*i*) above and with a view to spiritual welfare.

(l) The supply of services and goods closely linked thereto for the benefit of their members in return for a subscription fixed in accordance with their rules by non-profit-making organisations with aims of a political, trade union, religious, patriotic, philosophical, philanthropic or civic nature, provided that this exemption is not likely to cause distortion of competition.

(m) Certain services closely linked to sport or physical education supplied by non-profit-making organisations to persons taking part in sport or physical education.

(n) Certain cultural services and goods closely linked thereto supplied by bodies governed by public law or by other cultural bodies recognised by the country concerned. The expression 'other cultural bodies' does not exclude soloists performing individually (*Hoffmann, ECJ Case C–144/00*, [2004] STC 740 (TVC 22.318)).

(o) The supply of services and goods by organisations whose activities are exempt under (*b*), (*g*), (*h*), (*i*), (*l*), (*m*) and (*n*) above in connection with fund-raising events organised exclusively for their own benefit provided that exemption is not likely to cause distortion of competition. Countries may introduce any necessary restrictions in particular as regards the number of events or the amount of receipts which give entitlement to exemption.

(p) The supply of transport services for sick or injured persons in vehicles specially designed for the purpose by duly authorised bodies.

(q) Activities of public radio and television bodies other than those of a commercial nature.

The supply of goods and services under (*b*), (*g*), (*h*), (*i*), (*l*), (*m*) and (*n*) above is not exempt if

- it is not essential to the transaction exempted; or
- its basic purpose is to obtain additional income for the organisation by carrying out transactions which are in direct competition with those of commercial enterprises liable for VAT.

Countries may make the granting to bodies other than those governed by public law of exemption under (*b*), (*g*), (*h*), (*i*), (*l*), (*m*) and (*n*) above subject to one or more of the following conditions.

(i) They do not systematically aim to make profit. Any surplus arising must not be distributed but assigned to the continuance or improvement of the services supplied.

(ii) They must be managed and administered on an essentially voluntary basis by persons who have no direct or indirect interest in the results of the activities concerned. See *C & E Commrs v Zoological Society of London, ECJ Case C–267/00*, [2002] STC 521 (TVC 22.321).
(iii) They charge prices approved by the public authorities or which do not exceed such approved prices or, in respect of those services not subject to approval, prices lower than those charged for similar services by commercial enterprises subject to VAT.
(iv) Exemption of the service concerned must not be likely to create distortions of competition such as to place at a disadvantage commercial enterprises liable to VAT.

[*Directive 2006/112/EC, Arts 132–134*].

Exemption of other activities

[18.26] Countries must exempt the following transactions.

(a) Insurance and reinsurance transactions, including related services performed by insurance brokers and agents.
(b) The granting and the negotiation of credit and the management of credit by the person granting it.
(c) The negotiation of, or any dealings in, credit guarantees or any other security for money and the management of credit guarantees by the person who is granting the credit.
(d) Transactions, including negotiations, concerning deposit and current accounts, payments, transfers, debts, cheques and other negotiable instruments, but excluding debt collecting and factoring.
(e) Transactions, including negotiations, concerning currency, bank notes and coins used as legal tender, with the exception of collectors' items.
(f) Transactions, including negotiations but excluding management and safekeeping, in shares, interests in companies or associations, debentures and other securities, excluding documents establishing title to goods.
(g) Management of special investment funds as defined by countries.
(h) The supply at face value of postage stamps valid for use for postal services within the territory of the country, fiscal stamps and similar stamps.
(i) Betting, lottery and other forms of gambling, subject to conditions and limitations laid down by each country.
(j) The supply of buildings or parts thereof, and of land on which they stand, other than the supply before first occupation.
(k) The supply of land which has not been built on other than building land as defined by each country.
(l) The leasing or letting of immovable property other than
- the provision of accommodation in the hotel or similar sectors, including holiday camps and camping sites;
- the letting of premises and sites for parking vehicles;
- letting of permanently installed equipment and machinery; and
- hire of safes.

The letting of a building constructed from prefabricated components fixed to or in the ground in such a way that they cannot be either dismantled or easily moved constitutes a letting of immovable property, even if the building was to be removed at the end of the lease and reused on another site (*Maierhofer v Finanzamt Augsburg-Land*, *ECJ Case C–315/00*, [2003] STC 564 (TVC 22.337)).

(m) Supplies of goods
- used wholly for an activity exempted by **18.25**(*a*)–(*q*) above, (*a*)–(*l*) above or by an EU country under a derogation if these goods have not given rise to deductibility; or
- on the acquisition or application of which VAT was not deductible.

For a consideration of the scope of (*d*) and (*e*) above see *Sparekassernes Datacenter (SDC) v Skatteministeriet*, *ECJ Case C–2/95*, [1997] STC 932 (TVC 22.357). See also *Paymex Ltd* (TC01210) (TVC 20.81) with regard to the inclusion of insolvency practitioners' services within (*d*). Electronic messaging services do not fall within (*d*) and (*f*) above (see *Nordea Pankki Suomi Oyj v Finland*, *ECJ Case C–350/10*, [2011] STC 1956 (TVC 22.365)).

Countries may allow taxable persons a right of option to tax in cases of

- the financial transactions in (*b*)–(*g*) above;
- the supply of a building or of parts thereof, and of the land on which the building stands, other than the supply before first occupation;
- the supply of land which has not been built on other than the supply of building land; and
- the leasing or letting of immovable property.

[*Directive 2006/112/EC, Arts 135–137*].

Exemption for intra-EU transactions

[18.27] Exemptions for intra-EU transactions are listed below.

(1) Exemptions related to the supply of goods

Countries must exempt the following transactions.

(a) Supplies of goods dispatched or transported to a destination outside their own territory but within the EU, by or on behalf of the vendor or the person acquiring the goods, for another taxable person or a non-taxable legal person acting as such in an EU country other than that in which dispatch or transport of the goods began. This exemption does not apply to
- supplies of goods carried out by taxable persons who are covered for the exemption for small enterprises provided for in *Arts 282–292* (see **18.42**(2) below);
- supplies of goods to taxable persons or non-taxable legal persons whose intra-EU acquisitions of goods are not subject to VAT under *Art 3* (see **18.6** above);

- the supply of goods subject to VAT in accordance with the margin scheme provided for in *Arts 312–325* (see **18.42**(*5*) below) or the special arrangements for sales by public auction; or
- the supply of second-hand means of transport, subject to VAT in accordance with the transitional arrangements for second-hand means of transport.

(b) Supplies of new means of transport, dispatched or transported to the customer at a destination outside their own territory but within the EU, by or on behalf of the vendor or the customer, for taxable persons or non-taxable legal persons whose intra-EU acquisitions of goods are not subject to VAT under *Art 3* (see **18.6** above), or for any other non-taxable person.

(c) Supplies of products subject to excise duty, dispatched or transported to a destination outside their own territory but within the EU, to the customer, by or on behalf of the vendor or the customer, for taxable persons or non-taxable legal persons whose intra-EU acquisitions of goods other than products subject to excise duty are not subject to VAT under *Art 3* (see **18.6** above). This does not, however, apply to

- the supply of products subject to excise duty by taxable persons who are covered by the exemption for small enterprises provided for in *Arts 282–292* (see **18.42**(2) below); or
- the supply of goods subject to VAT in accordance with the margin scheme provided for in *Arts 312–325* (see **18.42**(5) below) or the special arrangements for sales by public auction.

(d) The supply of goods, consisting in a transfer to another EU country, which would have been entitled to exemption under (*a*) to (*c*) above if it had been made on behalf of another taxable person. This does not, however, apply to

- the supply of goods subject to VAT in accordance with the margin scheme provided for in *Arts 312–325* (see **18.42**(5) below) or the special arrangements for sales by public auction; or
- the supply of second-hand means of transport, subject to VAT in accordance with the transitional arrangements for second-hand means of transport.

[*Directive 2006/112/EC, Arts 138, 139*].

(2) Exemptions for intra-Union acquisitions of goods

Countries must exempt the following transactions.

- The intra-EU acquisition of goods the supply of which by taxable persons would in all circumstances be exempt within their respective territory.
- The intra-EU acquisition of goods the importation of which would in all circumstances be exempt under **18.28**(*a*), (*b*), (*c*) or (*e*) to (*m*) below.
- The intra-EU acquisition of goods where, pursuant to *Arts 170 and 171* (see **18.34** below) the person acquiring the goods would in all circumstances be entitled to full reimbursement of the VAT due under **18.6**(*b*) above.

[*Directive 2006/112/EC, Art 140*].

Each EU country must also take specific measures to ensure that VAT is not charged on the intra-EU acquisition of goods within its territory where the following conditions are met.

(a) The acquisition of goods is made by a taxable person (A) who is not established in the EU country concerned but is identified for VAT purposes in another EU country.
(b) The acquisition of goods is made for the purposes of the subsequent supply of those goods, in the EU country concerned, by A.
(c) The goods thus acquired by A are directly dispatched or transported, from an EU country other than that in which he is identified for VAT purposes, to the person for whom he is to carry out the subsequent supply (B).
(d) B is another taxable person, or a non-taxable legal person, who is identified for VAT purposes in the EU country concerned.
(e) B has been designated in accordance with *Art 197* (see **18.39** below) as liable for payment of the VAT due on the supply carried out by A.

[*Directive 2006/112/EC, Art 141*].

(3) Exemptions for certain transport services

Countries must exempt the supply of intra-EU transport of goods to and from the islands making up the autonomous regions of the Azores and Madeira, as well as the supply of transport of goods between those islands.

[*Directive 2006/112/EC, Art 142*].

Exemptions on importation

[18.28] Countries must exempt the following transactions.

(a) The final importation of goods of which the supply by a taxable person would in all circumstances be exempt within their own territory.
(b) The final importation of goods governed by *Council Directives 69/169/EEC, 83/181/EEC* and *2006/79/EC*.
(c) The final importation of goods, in free circulation from third territory forming part of the Union customs territory, which would be entitled to exemption under (*b*) above if they had been imported within the meaning of the first paragraph of *Art 30* (see **18.11** above).
(d) The importation of goods dispatched or transported from a third territory or a third country into an EU country other than that in which the dispatch or transport of the goods ends, where the supply of such goods by the importer designated or recognised as liable for payment of VAT is exempt under *Art 138* (see **18.27**(1) above).
(e) The reimportation, by the person who exported them, of goods in the state in which they were exported, where those goods are exempt from customs duties.
(f) The importation, under diplomatic and consular arrangements, of goods which are exempt from customs duties.

(g) The importation of goods by the European Community, European Atomic Energy Community, the European Central Bank or the European Investment Bank, or by the bodies set up by the Communities to which the Protocol of 8 April 1965 on the privileges and immunities of the European Communities applies, within the limits and under the conditions of that Protocol and the agreements for its implementation or the headquarters agreements, in so far as it does not lead to distortion of competition.
(h) The importation of goods by international bodies (other than those referred to in (*g*)) recognised as such by the public authorities of the host EU country, or by members of such bodies, within the limits and under the conditions laid down by the international conventions establishing the bodies or by headquarters agreements.
(i) The importation of goods, into EU countries party to the North Atlantic Treaty, by the armed forces of other EU countries party to that Treaty for the use of those forces or the civilian staff accompanying them or for supplying their messes or canteens where such forces take part in the common defence effort.
(j) The importation of goods by the armed forces of the UK stationed in the island of Cyprus pursuant to the *Treaty of Establishment concerning the Republic of Cyprus*, dated 16 August 1960, which are for the use of those forces or the civilian staff accompanying them or for supplying their messes or canteens.
(k) The importation into ports, by sea fishing undertakings, of their catches, unprocessed or after undergoing preservation for marketing but before being supplied.
(l) The importation of gold by central banks.
(m) The importation of gas through a natural gas system or any network connected to such a system or fed in from a vessel transporting gas into a natural gas system or any upstream pipeline network, of electricity or of heat or cooling energy through heating or cooling networks.
(n) The supply of services relating to the importation of goods where the value of such services is included in the taxable amount.

[*Directive 2006/112/EC, Arts 143, 144*].

Exemptions on exportation

[18.29] Countries must exempt the following.

(a) The supply of goods dispatched or transported to a destination outside the EU
- by or on behalf of the vendor, or
- by or on behalf of a customer not established in the country (except for goods transported by the customer himself for equipping, fuelling, etc. pleasure boats and private aircraft or any other means of transport for private use). In the case of a supply of goods to be carried in the personal luggage of travellers, this exemption applies on condition that the traveller is not established within the EU; the goods are transported to a destination outside the EU before the end of the third month

following that in which the supply takes place; and the total value of the supply (including VAT) is more than the equivalent of 175 euro in national currency (countries may exempt supplies with lower values).

(b) Goods supplied to approved bodies which export them from the EU as part of their humanitarian, charitable or teaching activities outside the EU.

(c) The supply of services consisting of work on movable property acquired or imported for the purpose of undergoing such work in the EU and dispatched or transported out of the EU by the supplier, by the customer if established outside the country or on behalf of either of them.

(d) The supply of services including transport and ancillary transactions (but excluding the supply of services exempted under **18.25** and **18.26** above) where these are directly linked with the export of goods or the import of goods covered by *Art 61* (see **18.16** above) or *Art 157(1)(a)* (importation of goods intended to be placed under warehousing arrangements other than customs warehousing).

[*Directive 2006/112/EC, Arts 146, 147*].

Exemptions related to international transport

[18.30] Countries must exempt the following transactions.

(a) The supply of goods for the fuelling and provisioning of
- vessels used for navigation at sea and carrying passengers for reward or used for the purposes of commercial, industrial or fishing activities;
- vessels used for rescue or assistance at sea;
- vessels used for inshore fishing (but not ship's provisions); or
- vessels of war leaving the country and bound for foreign ports or anchorages.

(b) The supply, modification, repair, maintenance, chartering and hiring of vessels within (*a*) above or aircraft used by airlines operating for reward chiefly on international routes and the supply, hiring, repair and maintenance of equipment (including fishing equipment) incorporated or used therein.

(c) The supply of goods for the fuelling and provisioning of aircraft within (*b*) above.

(d) The supply of services other than those referred to in (*b*) above to meet the direct needs of sea-going vessels or aircraft referred to in (*b*) above or of their cargoes.

[*Directive 2006/112/EC, Art 148*].

Exemptions relating to certain transactions treated as exports

[18.31] Countries must exempt the following transactions.

(a) The supply of goods or services under diplomatic and consular arrangements.

(b) The supply of goods or services to the European Community, European Atomic Energy Community, the European Central Bank or the European Investment Bank, or by the bodies set up by the Communities to which the Protocol of 8 April 1965 on the privileges and immunities of the European Communities applies, within the limits and under the conditions of that Protocol and the agreements for its implementation or the headquarters agreements, in so far as it does not lead to distortion of competition.
(c) The supply of goods or services to international bodies (other than those referred to in (*b*)) recognised as such by the public authorities of the host EU country, and to members of such bodies, within the limits and under the conditions laid down by the international conventions establishing the bodies or by headquarters agreements.
(d) The supply of goods or services within an EU country which is a party to the North Atlantic Treaty, intended either for the armed forces of other countries party to that Treaty for the use of those forces, or of the civilian staff accompanying them, or for supplying their messes or canteens when such forces take part in the common defence effort.
(e) The supply of goods or services to another EU country, intended for the armed forces of any State which is a party to the North Atlantic Treaty, other than the EU country of destination itself, for the use of those forces, or of the civilian staff accompanying them, or for supplying their messes or canteens when such forces take part in the common defence effort.
(f) The supply of goods or services to the armed forces of the UK stationed in Cyprus pursuant to the *Treaty of Establishment concerning the Republic of Cyprus*, dated 16 August 1960, which are for the use of those forces, or of the civilian staff accompanying them, or for supplying their messes or canteens.
(g) The supply of gold to central banks.

Under (*a*)–(*g*) above, where the goods are not dispatched or transported out of the EU country in which the supply takes place, and in the case of services, the exemption may be granted by means of a refund of the VAT.

[*Directive 2006/112/EC, Arts 151, 152*].

Exemptions for the supply of services by intermediaries

[18.32] Countries must exempt the supply of services by intermediaries, acting in the name and on behalf of another person, where they take part in the transactions referred to in **18.29–18.31** above or transactions carried out outside the EU. This exemption does not apply to travel agents who, in the name and on behalf of travellers, supply services which are carried out in other EU countries. [*Directive 2006/112/EC, Art 153*].

Exemptions for transactions relating to international trade

[18.33] Countries may take special measures designed to exempt all or some of the following transactions, provided that those measures are not aimed at final use or consumption and that the amount of VAT due on cessation of the arrangements or situations corresponds to the amount of tax which would have been due had each of those transactions been taxed within their territory. [*Directive 2006/112/EC, Art 155*].

(a) The supply of goods which are intended to be
  (i) presented to customs and, where applicable, placed in temporary storage;
  (ii) placed in a free zone or in a free warehouse;
  (iii) placed under customs warehousing arrangements or inward processing arrangements;
  (iv) admitted into territorial waters in order to be incorporated into drilling or production platforms, for purposes of the construction, repair, maintenance, alteration or fitting-out of such platforms, or to link such drilling or production platforms to the mainland; or
  (v) admitted into territorial waters for the fuelling and provisioning of drilling or production platforms.

(b) The importation of goods which are intended to be placed under warehousing arrangements other than customs warehousing.

(c) The supply of goods which are intended to be placed under warehousing arrangements other than customs warehousing. But countries may not apply exemption in such a way for goods which are not subject to excise duty where those goods are intended to be supplied at the retail stage unless, by derogation, the goods are intended for
  (i) tax-free shops, for the purposes of the supply of goods to be carried in the personal luggage of travellers taking flights or sea crossings outside the VAT territory of the EU where that supply is exempt under **18.29**(*a*) above;
  (ii) taxable persons, for the purposes of carrying out supplies to travellers on board an aircraft or a ship in the course of a flight or sea crossing where the place of arrival is situated outside the EU; or
  (iii) taxable persons, for the purposes of carrying out supplies which are exempt from VAT under **18.31**(*a*)–(*g*) above.

(d) The supply of services relating to the supply of goods under (*a*) or (*c*) above.

(e) The supply of goods or services carried out in the locations referred to in (*a*) or (*c*) above where one of the situations specified therein still applies within their territory.

(f) The supply of goods (and related services) while they remain covered by arrangements for temporary importation with total exemption from import duty or by external transit arrangements.

(g) The supply of goods imported from a territory within **17.2 EUROPEAN UNION: GENERAL** while they remain covered by the internal Union transit procedure.

Where countries exercise the option to exempt under the above provisions, they must take the measures necessary to ensure that the intra-EU acquisition of goods intended to be placed under one of the arrangements or in one of the situations under (*a*) or (*c*) above is covered by the same provisions as the supply of goods carried out within their country under the same conditions.

If the goods cease to be covered by the arrangements or situations referred to above (thus giving rise to an importation for the purposes of **18.16** above), the EU country of importation must take the measures necessary to prevent double taxation.

[*Directive 2006/112/EC, Arts 156–163*].

Re-exportations

Countries may exempt the following transactions carried out by, or intended for, a taxable person up to an amount equal to the value of the exports carried out by that person during the preceding twelve months.

- Intra-EU acquisitions of goods made by the taxable person, and imports for and supplies of goods to the taxable person, with a view to their exportation from the EU as they are or after processing.
- Supplies of services linked with the export business of the taxable person.

Where countries exercise this option of exemption, they must apply that exemption also to transactions relating to supplies carried out by the taxable person, in accordance with the conditions under **18.27**(1) above, up to an amount equal to the value of the supplies carried out by that person, in accordance with the same conditions, during the preceding twelve months.

[*Directive 2006/112/EC, Art 164*].

Deductions

[18.34] The right of deduction arises at the time the deductible VAT becomes chargeable. [*Directive 2006/112/EC, Art 167*].

To the extent that goods and services are used for the purposes of the taxed transactions of a taxable person, the taxable person is entitled, in the EU country in which he carries out these transactions, to deduct the following from the VAT which he is liable to pay.

(a) VAT due or paid in that EU country in respect of supplies to him of goods or services, carried out or to be carried out by another taxable person.

(b) VAT due in respect of transactions treated as supplies of goods or services under the self-supply rules.

(c) VAT due in respect of intra-EU acquisitions of goods.

(d) VAT due on transactions treated as intra-EU acquisitions in accordance with *Arts 21* and *22* (see **18.9** above).

(e) VAT due or paid in respect of the importation of goods into that EU country.

[*Directive 2006/112/EC, Art 168*].

In the case of immovable property forming part of the business assets of a taxable person and used both for the purposes of the business and for his private use or that of his staff, or, more generally, for purposes other than those of his business, VAT on expenditure related to this property shall be deductible in accordance with the principles set out in *Arts 167, 168, 169* and *173* only up to the proportion of the property's use for business purposes.

By way of derogation from *Art 26* (see **18.10** above), changes in the proportion of use of immovable property are to be taken into account in accordance with the principles provided for in *Arts 184–192* as applied the respective EU country (see **18.38** below).

EU countries may also apply this provision in relation to VAT on expenditure related to other goods forming part of the business assets as they specify.

[*Directive 2006/112/EC, Art 168a*].

The taxable person is also entitled to deduct the VAT referred to in so far as the goods and services are used for the following purposes following.

- Transactions relating to economic activities carried out outside the EU country in which that VAT is due or paid, in respect of which VAT would be deductible if the transactions had been carried out within that EU country.
- Transactions which are exempt under **18.27**(1)(3), **18.28**(*n*), **18.29–18.32**, **18.33** (other than **18.33**(*b*)) above.
- Transactions which are exempt under **18.5**(*a*)–(*f*) above where the customer is established outside the EU or where those transactions relate directly to goods to be exported from the EU.

[*Directive 2006/112/EC, Art 169*].

See **34.1–34.3 INPUT TAX** for the UK provisions.

All taxable persons who are not established in the EU country in which they purchase goods and services or import goods subject to VAT are entitled to obtain a refund of that VAT in so far as the goods and services are used for the purposes of transactions

- within *Art 169* above; or
- for which the VAT is solely payable by the customer in accordance with *Arts 194–197* or *Art 199* (see **18.39** below).

Where the taxable person is established in another EU country, the VAT is refunded under the *8th Directive* (see **18.44** below) and where the taxable person is not established in the EU, the VAT is refunded under the *13th Directive* (see **18.45** below).

[*Directive 2006/112/EC, Arts 170, 171*].

New means of transport

Any person who is regarded as a taxable person by reason of the fact that he supplies, on an occasional basis, a new means of transport is, in the EU country in which the supply takes place, entitled to deduct the VAT included in the purchase price or paid in respect of the importation or the intra-EU acquisition of this means of transport, up to an amount not exceeding the amount of VAT for which he would be liable if the supply were not exempt. A right of deduction arises and may be exercised only at the time of supply of the new means of transport. [*Directive 2006/112/EC, Art 172*].

Proportional deduction

[18.35] Where goods or services are used by a taxable person both for transactions in respect of which VAT is deductible under **18.34** above and for transactions in respect of which VAT is not deductible, only such proportion of the VAT as is attributable to the former transactions is deductible. This is determined by the formula

$$A \div B$$

where

A = the total amount, exclusive of VAT, of turnover per year attributable to transactions in respect of which VAT is deductible; and

B = the total amount, exclusive of VAT, of turnover per year attributable to transactions within A and transactions in respect of which VAT is not deductible.

The proportions must be determined on an annual basis, fixed as a percentage and rounded up to a figure not exceeding the next whole number. The provisional proportion for a year is to be calculated on the basis of the preceding year's transactions. In the absence of any such transactions or where they were insignificant, the deductible proportion is to be estimated provisionally, under the supervision of the tax authorities, by the taxable person on the basis of his own forecasts. Deductions made on the basis of such provisional proportions must be adjusted when the final proportion is fixed during the following year.

By derogation, countries may exclude from the calculation supplies of capital goods, incidental real estate and financial transactions and incidental transactions within **18.26**(*b*)–(*g*) above.

Countries may, however, authorise or compel the taxable person to determine a proportion for each sector of his business and keep separate accounts for each sector or to make deductions on the basis of the use of the goods and services. Countries may also provide that where non-deductible VAT is insignificant it is treated as nil.

[*Directive 2006/112/EC, Arts 173–175*].

See **49 PARTIAL EXEMPTION** for the UK provisions.

Restrictions on the right of deduction

[18.36] The Council must determine the expenditure in respect of which VAT is not deductible. VAT must in no circumstances be deductible in respect of expenditure which is not strictly business expenditure, such as that on luxuries, amusements or entertainment.

Pending the entry into force of these provisions, countries may retain all the exclusions provided for under their national laws at 1 January 1979 (or, in the case of the countries which acceded to the Union after that date, on the date of their accession).

[*Directive 2006/112/EC, Art 176*].

Exercising of the right of deduction

[18.37] In order to exercise the right of deduction, a taxable person must for the purposes of deductions under

(a) **18.34**(*a*) hold a proper invoice;
(b) **18.34**(*b*) comply with the formalities as laid down by each EU country;
(c) **18.34**(*c*) set out in the VAT return all the information needed for the amount of the VAT due on his intra-EU acquisitions of goods to be calculated and hold a proper invoice;
(d) **18.34**(*d*), complete the formalities as laid down by each EU country; and
(e) **18.34**(*e*), hold an import document specifying him as consignee or importer, and stating the amount of VAT due or enabling that amount to be calculated.

When required to pay VAT as a customer where *Arts 194–197* or *Art 199* apply (see **18.39** below), he must comply with the formalities as laid down by each EU country.

[*Directive 2006/112/EC, Art 178*].

The taxable person makes the deduction by subtracting from the total amount of VAT due for a given tax period the total amount of VAT in respect of which, during the same period, the right of deduction has arisen.

Countries may require that taxable persons who carry out occasional transactions exercise their right of deduction only at the time of supply.

[*Directive 2006/112/EC, Art 179*].

Where, for a given tax period, the amount of deductions exceeds the amount of VAT due, countries may, in accordance with conditions which they determine, either make a refund or carry the excess forward to the following period. [*Directive 2006/112/EC, Art 183*].

Adjustment of deductions

[18.38] The initial deduction must be adjusted where it is higher or lower than that to which the taxable person was entitled. [*Directive 2006/112/EC, Art 184*]. Adjustment must, in particular, be made where, after the VAT return is made, some change occurs in the factors used to determine the amount to be deducted (e.g. where purchases are cancelled or price reductions are obtained). [*Directive 2006/112/EC, Art 185*].

Capital goods

In the case of capital goods, adjustments must be spread over five years including that in which the goods were acquired or manufactured. By derogation the period may commence from the time the goods are first used. The annual adjustment must be made only in respect of one-fifth of the VAT charged on the goods and must be made on the basis of the variations in the deduction entitlement in subsequent years in relation to that for the year in which the goods were acquired or manufactured (or, where applicable, used for the first time).

In the case of immovable property, the adjustment period may be extended to up to 20 years.

Where capital goods are supplied during the period of adjustment, they are treated as if they had still been applied to an economic use of the taxable person until the expiry of the period of adjustment. Such economic activity is presumed to be fully taxed in cases where the supply of the goods is taxed and fully exempt where the supply is exempt. The adjustment is made only once for the whole period of adjustment still to be covered.

[*Directive 2006/112/EC, Arts 187, 188*].

See **CAPITAL GOODS SCHEME (10)** for the UK provisions.

Persons liable for payment of VAT

[18.39] The person liable to pay the VAT is as follows.

(a) Any taxable person carrying out a taxable supply of goods or services, except where the VAT is payable by another person in the cases referred to in (*b*)–(*g*) and (*j*) below. [*Directive 2006/112/EC, Art 193*].

(b) Where the taxable supply of goods or services is carried out by a taxable person not established in the EU country in which the VAT is due, that country may provide that the person liable for payment of the VAT is the person for whom the goods or services are supplied. [*Directive 2006/112/EC, Art 194*].

(c) VAT is payable by any person who is identified for VAT purposes in the EU country in which the tax is due and to whom goods are supplied in the circumstances under **18.12**(4) above, if the supplies are carried out by a taxable person not established within that country. [*Directive 2006/112/EC, Art 195*].

(d) VAT is payable by

- any taxable person to whom the services referred to in *Art 56* are supplied, or
- any person identified for VAT purposes in the EU country in which the tax is due to whom the services referred to in *Arts 44, 47, 50, 53, 54* and *55* are supplied,

if the services are supplied by a taxable person not established in that EU country.

See **18.14** above.

In *Kollektivavtalsstiftelsen TRR Trygghetsrådet v Skatteverket, ECJ Case C–291/07*, [2008] All ER (D) 71 (Nov) (TVC 20.36), the ECJ ruled that *Art 56(1)(c)* must be interpreted as meaning that where consultancy services are supplied to the customer by a taxable person established in another EU country, and the customer carries out both an economic activity and an activity which falls outside the scope of the directive, that customer is to be regarded as a taxable person even where the supply is used solely for the purposes of the latter activity.

(e) VAT shall be payable by any taxable person, or non-taxable legal person identified for VAT purposes, to whom the services referred to in *Art 44* (see **18.15** above) are supplied, if the services are supplied by a taxable person not established within the territory of the EU country.

[*Directive 2006/112/EC, Art 196*].

(f) The person to whom the goods are supplied where
- the taxable transaction is a supply of goods carried out in accordance with the conditions in *Art 141* (see **18.27**(2) above);
- the person to whom the goods are supplied is another taxable person, or a non-taxable legal person, identified for VAT purposes in the EU country in which the supply is carried out; and
- the invoice issued by the taxable person not established in the EU country in question conforms to the requirements in *Arts 220–236* (see **18.41**(2)–(4) below).

A country may, however, provide for a derogation from this obligation where the non-established taxable person has appointed a tax representative in that country as the person liable for the tax.
[*Directive 2006/112/EC, Art 197*].

(g) Where specific transactions relating to investment gold between a taxable person who is a member of a regulated gold bullion market and another taxable person who is not a member of that market are taxed under *Art 352* (see **18.42**(6) below), countries must designate the customer as the person liable for payment of VAT.
If the customer is a taxable person required to be identified for VAT purposes in the EU country in which the tax is due solely in respect of the transactions under *Art 352*, the vendor must fulfil the tax obligations on behalf of the customer, in accordance with the law of that country.
Where gold material or semi-manufactured products of a purity of 325 thousandths or greater or investment gold is supplied by a taxable person exercising one of the options under *Arts 348–350* (see **18.42**(6) below), countries may designate the customer as the person liable for payment of VAT.
[*Directive 2006/112/EC, Art 198*].

(h) Countries may provide that the person liable for payment of VAT is the taxable person to whom any of the following supplies are made.
(i) The supply of construction work, including repair, cleaning, maintenance, alteration and demolition services in relation to immovable property, as well as the handing over of construction works regarded as a supply of goods.
(ii) The supply of staff engaged in activities covered by (i) above.
(iii) The supply of immovable property, as referred to in **18.26**(*j*) and (*k*) above, where the supplier has opted for taxation of the supply.
(iv) The supply of used material, used material which cannot be re-used in the same state, scrap, industrial and non-industrial waste, recyclable waste, part processed waste and certain goods and services, as listed in *Directive 2006/112/EC, Annex VI*.
(v) The supply of goods provided as security by one taxable person to another in execution of that security.
(vi) The supply of goods following the cession of a reservation of ownership to an assignee and the exercising of this right by the assignee.

(vii) The supply of immovable property sold by a judgment debtor in a compulsory sale procedure.

[*Directive 2006/112/EC, Art 199*].

(i) VAT is payable by any person making a taxable intra-EU acquisition of goods. [*Directive 2006/112/EC, Art 200*].

(j) On importation, VAT is payable by any person or persons designated or recognised as liable by the EU country of importation. [*Directive 2006/112/EC, Art 201*].

(k) VAT is payable by any person who causes goods to cease to be covered by the arrangements or situations listed in **18.33** above. [*Directive 2006/112/EC, Art 202*].

(l) VAT is payable by any person who enters the VAT on an invoice. [*Directive 2006/112/EC, Art 203*].

(m) Where, under (*a*)–(*e*), (*g*) and (*h*) above, the person liable for payment of VAT is a taxable person who is not established in the EU country in which the VAT is due, countries may allow that person to appoint a tax representative as the person liable for payment of the VAT.

Furthermore, where the taxable transaction is carried out by a taxable person who is not established in the EU country in which the VAT is due and no legal instrument exists with the country in which that taxable person is established or has his seat, relating to mutual assistance similar in scope to that provided for in *Directive 2010/24/EU* (mutual assistance recovery directive, which replaces *Directive 2008/55/EC* with effect from 1 January 2012) and *Council Regulation (EU)904/2010* (on administrative co-operation and combating fraud in the field of VAT, which recasts and repeals *Council Regulation (EC)1798/2003* with effect from 1 January 2012), countries may take measures to provide that the person liable for payment of VAT is to be a tax representative appointed by the non-established taxable person. But countries may not apply this option to a non-established taxable person who has opted for the special scheme for electronically supplied services.

[*Directive 2006/112/EC, Art 204*].

(n) In the situations referred to in (*a*)–(*h*) and (*j*)–(*l*) above, countries may provide that a person other than the person liable for payment of VAT is to be held jointly and severally liable for payment of VAT. [*Directive 2006/112/EC, Art 205*].

Payment arrangements

[18.40] Any taxable person liable for payment of VAT must pay the net amount of the VAT when submitting the VAT return. Countries may, however, set a different date for payment of that amount or may require interim payments to be made. [*Directive 2006/112/EC, Art 206*].

Obligations of taxable persons

[18.41] Taxable persons should be aware of the following obligations.

(1) Identification

Every taxable person must state when his activity as a taxable person commences, changes or ceases. Countries must allow, and may require, the statement to be made by electronic means, in accordance with conditions which they lay down.

Without prejudice to the above, every taxable person or non-taxable legal person who makes intra-EU acquisitions of goods which are not subject to VAT under **18.6**(i) and (ii) above must state that he makes such acquisitions if the conditions, laid down in that provision, for not making such transactions subject to VAT cease to be fulfilled.

[*Directive 2006/112/EC, Art 213*].

(2) Issue of invoices

Every taxable person must ensure that, in respect of the following, an invoice is issued, either by himself or by his customer or, in his name and on his behalf, by a third party.

(i) Supplies of goods or services which he has made to another taxable person or to a non-taxable legal person.
(ii) Supplies of goods as referred to in *Art 33* (see **18.12**(2) above).
(iii) Supplies of goods carried out in accordance with the conditions specified in **18.27**(1) above.
(iv) Any payment on account made to him before one of the supplies of goods referred to in (i)–(iii) above was carried out.
(v) Any payment on account made to him by another taxable person or non-taxable legal person before the provision of services was completed.

[*Directive 2006/112/EC, Art 220*].

EU countries may

- impose on taxable persons an obligation to issue an invoice in respect of supplies of goods or services made in their territory, other than those referred to above;
- release taxable persons from the obligation to issue an invoice in certain cases in respect of supplies of goods or services which they have made in their territory and which are exempt;
- impose time limits on taxable persons for the issue of invoices when supplying goods or services in their territory.

[*Directive 2006/112/EC, Arts 221, 222*].

Self-billing

Invoices may be drawn up by the customer in respect of the supply to him, by a taxable person, of goods or services, if there is a prior agreement between the two parties and provided that a procedure exists for the acceptance of each invoice by the taxable person supplying the goods or services. Tax authorities must determine the terms and conditions of such prior agreements and of the acceptance procedures between the taxable person and the customer. [*Directive 2006/112/EC, Art 224*].

(3) Content of invoices

Without prejudice to the particular provisions laid down in the *Directive*, only the following details are required for VAT purposes on invoices.

- The date of issue.
- A sequential number, based on one or more series, which uniquely identifies the invoice.
- The VAT identification number under which the taxable person supplied the goods or services.
- The customer's VAT identification number under which the customer received a supply of goods or services in respect of which he is liable for payment of VAT, or received a supply of goods as referred to under **18.27**(1) above.
- The full name and address of the taxable person and of the customer.
- The quantity and nature of the goods supplied or the extent and nature of the services rendered.
- The date on which the supply of goods or services was made or completed or the date on which the payment on account was made, in so far as that date can be determined and differs from the date of issue of the invoice.
- The taxable amount per rate or exemption, the unit price exclusive of VAT and any discounts or rebates if they are not included in the unit price.
- The VAT rate applied.
- The VAT amount payable, except where a special arrangement is applied under which, in accordance with the *Directive*, such a detail is excluded.
- In the case of an exemption or where the customer is liable for payment of VAT, reference to the applicable provision of the *Directive*, or to the corresponding national provision, or any other reference indicating that the supply of goods or services is exempt or subject to the reverse charge procedure.
- In the case of the supply of a new means of transport, its identifying characteristics.
- Where the margin scheme for travel agents is applied, reference to *Art 306*, or to the corresponding national provisions, or any other reference indicating that the margin scheme has been applied.
- Where one of the special arrangements applicable to second-hand goods, works of art, collectors' items and antiques is applied, reference to *Art 313*, *326* or *333*, or to the corresponding national provisions, or any other reference indicating that one of those arrangements has been applied.
- Where the person liable for payment of VAT is a tax representative for the purposes of *Art 204*, the VAT identification number of that tax representative, together with his full name and address.

[*Directive 2006/112/EC, Art 226*].

Tax authorities may also require the customer's VAT identification (see (1) above) to be indicated in other cases [*Directive 2006/112/EC, Art 227*] but may allow some of the compulsory details to be omitted. [*Directive*

2006/112/EC, Art 228]. They cannot require invoices to be signed [*Directive 2006/112/EC, Art 229*] but may require invoices in respect of supplies of goods or services in their territory and invoices received by taxable persons established in their territory to be translated into their national languages for control purposes. [*Directive 2006/112/EC, Art 231*].

The amounts which appear on the invoice may be expressed in any currency, provided that the amount of VAT payable is expressed in the national currency of the country in which the supply of goods or services takes place, using the conversion mechanism laid down in **18.22**(*b*) above. [*Directive 2006/112/EC, Art 230*].

(4) Sending invoices by electronic means

Invoices may be sent on paper or, subject to acceptance by the recipient, they may be sent or made available by electronic means. [*Directive 2006/112/EC, Art 232*].

Invoices sent or made available by electronic means must be accepted by tax authorities provided that the authenticity of the origin and the integrity of their content are guaranteed by means of

- an advanced electronic signature; or
- electronic data interchange (EDI) if the agreement relating to the exchange provides for the use of procedures guaranteeing the authenticity of the origin and integrity of the data.

Invoices may, however, be sent or made available by other electronic means, subject to acceptance by the tax authority.

[*Directive 2006/112/EC, Art 233*].

(5) Simplification of invoices

Countries may, in accordance with conditions which they lay down, provide that in the following cases some of the information otherwise required on an invoice need not be entered in respect of supplies of goods or services in their territory.

- Where the amount of the invoice is minor.
- Where commercial or administrative practice in the business sector concerned or the technical conditions under which the invoices are issued make it difficult to comply with all the obligations.

But invoices must, in any event, contain

- the date of issue;
- identification of the taxable person;
- identification of the type of goods or services supplied; and
- the VAT amount payable or the information needed to calculate it,

and the simplified arrangements may not be applied to

- intra-EU acquisitions of goods under **18.9** above;
- supplies of goods under the derogation, or under the provisions relating to the installed or assembled goods, in **18.12**(2) above; or

- transactions within **18.27**(1) or (2) above.

[*Directive 2006/112/EC, Art 238*].

(6) Accounting

Every taxable person must

- keep accounts in sufficient detail for VAT to be applied and its application checked by the tax authorities;
- keep a register of the goods dispatched or transported, by that person or on his behalf, to a destination outside the EU country of departure but within the EU for the purposes of transactions consisting in work on those goods or their temporary use as referred to in **18.8**(*e*)(vi)–(viii) above;
- keep accounts in sufficient detail to enable the identification of goods dispatched to him from another EU country, by or on behalf of a taxable person identified for VAT purposes in that other country, and used for services consisting in valuations of those goods or work on those goods;
- ensure that copies of the invoices issued by himself, or by his customer or, in his name and on his behalf, by a third party, and all the invoices which he has received, are stored and made available to the competent authorities without undue delay whenever they so request; and
- ensure that the authenticity of the origin and the integrity of the content of the invoices stored, as well as their legibility, is guaranteed throughout the storage period (as determined by the tax authorities).

[*Directive 2006/112/EC, Arts 242–247*].

(7) Returns

Every taxable person must submit a return within an interval after the end of the VAT period (not more than two months) to be determined by each EU country. The tax authorities must allow, and may require, the taxable person to make such returns by electronic means. The return must set out

(i) all the information needed to calculate the VAT that has become chargeable and the deduction to be made;

(ii) where appropriate, the total value of transactions relative to the VAT and deductions within (i) above and the value of any exempt transactions;

(iii) the total value, exclusive of VAT, of supplies of goods within **18.27**(1) above on which VAT has become chargeable in the period;

(iv) the total value, exclusive of VAT, of the supplies of goods referred to in *Arts 33* and *36* (see **18.12**(2) above) carried out within the territory of another EU country in respect of which VAT has become chargeable in the return period, where the place where dispatch or transport of the goods began is situated in the EU country in which the return must be submitted;

(v) the total value, exclusive of VAT, of intra-EU acquisitions of goods, or transactions treated as such, made in the EU country in which the return must be submitted and in respect of which VAT has become chargeable during the tax period;

(vi) the total value, exclusive of VAT, of supplies as in (iv) above carried out in the EU country in which the return must be submitted and in respect of which VAT has become chargeable during this tax period, where the place where dispatch or transport of the goods began is situated within the territory of another EU country; and

(vii) the total value, exclusive of VAT, of the supplies of goods carried out in the EU country in which the return must be submitted and in respect of which the taxable person has been designated as liable for payment of VAT and in respect of which VAT has become chargeable during this tax period.

[*Directive 2006/112/EC, Arts 251–253*].

(8) Recapitulative statements

Every taxable person identified for VAT purposes shall submit a recapitulative statement of

- the acquirers identified for VAT purposes to whom he has supplied goods in accordance with the conditions specified in **18.27**(1)(*a*) and (*d*) above; and
- the persons identified for VAT purposes to whom he has supplied goods which were supplied to him by way of intra-EU acquisitions referred to in *Art 42* (see **18.13** above).

The recapitulative statement must be drawn up for each calendar month within a period not exceeding one month. However, countries may allow taxable persons to submit it for each calendar quarter within a time limit not exceeding one month from the end of the quarter, where the total quarterly amount, excluding VAT, of the supplies of goods as referred to in *Art 264(1)(d)* and *Art 265(1)(c)* does not exceed either in respect of the quarter concerned or in respect of any of the previous four quarters the sum of EUR 50,000 or its equivalent in national currency. Until 31 December 2011, countries may set the sum at EUR 100,000 or its equivalent in national currency. In the case of supplies of services as referred to in *Art 264(1)(d)*, countries may allow taxable persons to submit the recapitulative statement for each calendar quarter within a time limit not exceeding one month from the end of the quarter. Countries must allow (and may require) statements to be submitted by electronic means. With approval from the Council, countries may allow

- taxable persons to submit simplified annual statements where their supplies do not exceed specified limits; and
- taxable persons who already prepare annual VAT returns to prepare the recapitulation statements for the same periods where their supplies do not exceed (higher) specified limits.

The statement must set out details of the VAT registration numbers of the taxable person and his customers in other EU countries and the aggregate value of supplies to each of those customers.

[*Directive 2006/112/EC, Arts 262–265, 270, 271*].

See **2.11** ACCOUNTING PERIODS AND RETURNS for the UK provisions.

Special schemes

[18.42] The provisions relating to special schemes are outlined below.

(1) Simplified procedures for charging and collection

Countries which might encounter difficulties in applying the normal VAT arrangements to small enterprises, by reason of the activities or structure of such enterprises, may, subject to such conditions and limits as they may set, apply simplified procedures for charging and collecting VAT provided that they do not lead to a reduction in the VAT. [*Directive 2006/112/EC, Art 281*].

(2) Exemptions and graduated relief

Countries may provide exemption (and graduated tax relief) for the supply of goods and services by small enterprises. [*Directive 2006/112/EC, Art 282*]. Countries which, at 17 May 1977 (when the *EC Sixth Directive* came into force), exempted taxable persons whose annual turnover was equal to or higher than the equivalent in national currency of 5,000 euros at the conversion rate on that date, may raise that ceiling in order to maintain the value of the exemption in real terms. [*Directive 2006/112/EC, Art 286*].

Turnover for these purposes consists of (exclusive of VAT)

- the value of taxable supplies of goods and services; and
- the value of real estate transactions, financial transactions within **18.26**(*b*)–(*g*) above and insurance services, unless those transactions are ancillary transactions

but disposals of the tangible or intangible capital assets of an enterprise are not to be taken into account for the purposes of calculating turnover.

[*Directive 2006/112/EC, Art 288*].

Taxable persons exempt from VAT must not be entitled to deduct VAT in accordance with **18.34** to **18.36** above and may not show the VAT on their invoices. [*Directive 2006/112/EC, Art 289*].

Taxable persons who are entitled to exemption from VAT may opt either for the normal VAT arrangements or for the simplified procedures provided for in *Art 281* above. [*Directive 2006/112/EC, Art 290*].

See **59.2** and **59.3** REGISTRATION for the UK provisions.

(3) Common flat-rate scheme for farmers

Countries may apply such a scheme to farmers where the application of the normal VAT scheme, or the simplified rules for small undertakings above, would give rise to difficulties. [*Directive 2006/112/EC, Art 296*].

See **63.25** SPECIAL SCHEMES for UK provisions.

(4) Special scheme for travel agents

Where a travel agent (including a tour operator) deals with customers in his own name and uses supplies of goods and services provided by other taxable persons in the provision of travel services, transactions made in respect of a journey are treated as a single service supplied by him to the traveller. The single service is taxable in the EU country in which the travel agent has established his business or has a fixed establishment from which he has carried out the supply of services. The taxable amount and the price exclusive of VAT in respect of the single service provided is the travel agent's margin, i.e. the difference between the total amount (exclusive of VAT) to be paid by the traveller and the actual cost to the travel agent of supplies of goods and services provided by other taxable persons where these transactions are for the direct benefit of the traveller.

The above provisions do not apply to travel agents where they act solely as intermediaries and to whom **18.19**(iii) above applies for the purposes of calculating the taxable amount.

[*Directive 2006/112/EC, Arts 306–308*].

See *Independent Coach Travel (Wholesaling) Ltd* (VTD 11037) (TVC 63.3) where the tribunal held that 'customers' should be construed as a reference to 'travellers' and that these provisions only apply to travel agents dealing with travellers and not those who act as wholesalers making supplies to retailers.

If transactions entrusted by the travel agent to other taxable persons are performed by such persons outside the EU, the supply of services carried out by the travel agent is treated as an intermediary activity exempt under **18.32** above. If the transactions are performed both inside and outside the EU, only that part of the travel agent's service relating to transactions outside the EU may be exempted. [*Directive 2006/112/EC, Art 309*].

VAT charged to the travel agent by other taxable persons on the transactions which are referred to in *Art 307* above and which are for the direct benefit of the traveller is not eligible for deduction or refund in the EU. [*Directive 2006/112/EC, Art 310*].

The fact that the travel agent provides accommodation only, and not transport, does not exclude such a service from the ambit of these provisions (*Beheersmaatschappij Van Ginkel Waddinxveen BV and Others v Inspecteur der Omzetbelasting, Utrecht, ECJ Case C–163/91*, [1996] STC 825 (TVC 22.485)).

See **68 TOUR OPERATORS' MARGIN SCHEME** for the UK provisions.

(5) Second-hand goods, works of art, collectors' items and antiques

In respect of the supply of second-hand goods, works of art, collectors' items or antiques (all as defined) carried out by taxable dealers, countries must apply a special scheme for taxing the profit margin made by the taxable dealer where those goods have been supplied to him within the EU by

- a non-taxable person;

- another taxable person, in so far as the supply of goods by that other taxable person is exempt under **18.26**(*m*) above;
- another taxable person, in so far as the supply of goods by that other taxable person is covered by the exemption for small enterprises under (2) above and involves capital goods; and
- another taxable dealer, in so far as VAT has been applied to the supply of goods by that other taxable dealer in accordance with this margin scheme.

The taxable amount is the profit margin (i.e. the difference between the selling price and the buying price) made by the taxable dealer less the amount of VAT relating to the profit margin.

[*Directive 2006/112/EC, Arts 313–315*].

Countries must allow taxable dealers the right to opt to use the scheme for supplies of works of art, collectors' items and antiques which they have imported and works of art supplied to the taxable dealer by their creators (or their successors in title). [*Directive 2006/112/EC, Art 316*].

To simplify the procedure for collecting VAT, countries may provide that, for certain transactions or certain categories of taxable dealer, the taxable amount of supplies of goods subject to the scheme is to be determined for each VAT period as a whole (rather than for each individual transaction). The definitions of 'taxable amount' and 'profit margin' are suitably adjusted. [*Directive 2006/112/EC, Art 318*].

A taxable dealer may apply the normal VAT arrangements to any supply covered by the margin scheme. [*Directive 2006/112/EC, Art 319*].

Where supplies are made under the scheme, any input tax incurred on the purchase of the goods cannot be deducted.

In so far as goods are used for the purpose of supplies carried out by him and subject to the margin scheme, the taxable dealer may not deduct the following from the VAT for which he is liable.

- The VAT due or paid in respect of works of art, collectors' items or antiques which he has imported himself.
- The VAT due or paid in respect of works of art which have been, or are to be, supplied to him by their creator or by the creator's successors in title.
- The VAT due or paid in respect of works of art which have been, or are to be, supplied to him by a taxable person other than a taxable dealer.

[*Directive 2006/112/EC, Art 322*].

The taxable dealer must not enter separately on the invoices which he issues the VAT relating to supplies of goods to which he applies the margin scheme. [*Directive 2006/112/EC, Art 325*].

Sales by public auction. Countries may make special arrangements for taxation of the profit margin made by an organiser of a sale by public auction (an 'auctioneer') in respect of the supply of second-hand goods, works of art, collectors' items or antiques by that auctioneer, acting in his own name and on behalf of the persons referred to below, pursuant to a contract under which commission is payable on the sale of those goods by public auction. [*Directive 2006/112/EC, Art 333*].

Where such special arrangements are adopted, they apply to supplies carried out by an auctioneer, acting in his own name, on behalf of

- a non-taxable person;
- another taxable person, in so far as the supply of goods, carried out by that taxable person in accordance with a contract under which commission is payable on a sale, is exempt under **18.26**(*m*) above;
- another taxable person, in so far as the supply of goods, carried out by that taxable person in accordance with a contract under which commission is payable on a sale, is covered by the exemption for small enterprises provided for in (2) above and involves capital goods; and
- a taxable dealer, in so far as the supply of goods, carried out by that taxable dealer in accordance with a contract under which commission is payable on a sale, is subject to VAT in accordance with the margin scheme.

The supply of goods to a taxable person who is an auctioneer is to be regarded as taking place when the sale of those goods by public auction takes place.

The taxable amount in respect of each supply of goods within these provisions is the total amount invoiced as below to the purchaser by the auctioneer less

- the net amount paid or to be paid by the auctioneer to his principal (i.e. the difference between the auction price of the goods and the amount of the commission obtained or to be obtained by the auctioneer from his principal pursuant to the contract under which commission is payable on the sale); and
- the amount of the VAT payable by the auctioneer in respect of his supply.

An auctioneer using the scheme must indicate in his accounts, in suspense accounts, both the amounts obtained or to be obtained from the purchaser of the goods and the amounts reimbursed or to be reimbursed to the vendor of the goods.

An auctioneer must

- issue to the purchaser an invoice itemising
  (i) the auction price of the goods;
  (ii) taxes, duties, levies and charges; and
  (iii) incidental expenses, such as commission, packing, transport and insurance costs, charged by the organiser to the purchaser of the goods;

  but not indicating any VAT separately; and
- issue a statement to his principal specifying separately the amount of the transaction (i.e. the auction price of the goods less the amount of the commission obtained or to be obtained from the principal). This statement serves as the invoice which the principal, where he is a taxable person, must issue to the auctioneer.

[*Directive 2006/112/EC, Arts 334–340*].

See **61 SECOND-HAND GOODS** for UK provisions.

(6) Special scheme for investment gold

All countries must exempt the supply, intra-EU acquisition and importation of investment gold (as defined), including investment gold represented by certificates for allocated or unallocated gold or traded on gold accounts and including, in particular, gold loans and swaps, involving a right of ownership or claim in respect of investment gold, as well as transactions concerning investment gold involving futures and forward contracts leading to a transfer of right of ownership or claim in respect of investment gold. Countries must also exempt services of agents who act in the name of and on behalf of another person, when they take part in the supply of investment gold for their principal. [*Directive 2006/112/EC, Arts 336, 347*].

Option to tax

Countries must allow taxable persons who produce investment gold, or transform any gold into investment gold, the right to opt for the taxation of supplies of investment gold to another taxable person who would otherwise be exempt under the above provisions. They may also allow taxable persons who, in the course of their economic activity, normally supply gold for industrial purposes, the right to opt for the taxation of supplies of gold bars or wafers to another taxable person. [*Directive 2006/112/EC, Arts 348, 349*].

Where the supplier has exercised a right to opt for taxation, any agent acting for that supplier must be allowed to opt to tax his services. [*Directive 2006/112/EC, Art 350*].

Transactions on the regulated gold bullion market

An EU country may apply VAT to specific transactions relating to investment gold which take place in that country (other than intra-EU supplies or exports)

- between taxable persons who are members of a regulated bullion market; or
- between a member of a regulated bullion market and another taxable person who is not such a member.

[*Directive 2006/112/EC, Art 352*].

Input tax

Where a taxable person's subsequent supply of investment gold is exempt under the above provisions, he is entitled to deduct the VAT due or paid in respect of

- investment gold supplied to him by a person who has exercised the right of option to tax as above or under the procedure for regulated bullion markets as above;
- the supply to him, or intra-EU acquisition or importation by him, of gold other than investment gold which is subsequently transformed by him (or on his behalf) into investment gold; and

- services supplied to him consisting of change of form, weight or purity of gold including investment gold.

Taxable persons who produce investment gold, or transform any gold into investment gold, are entitled to deduct VAT due or paid in respect of supplies, intra-EU acquisitions, importations or services linked to the production or transformation of that gold as if their subsequent supply of the gold exempted under these provisions were taxable.
[*Directive 2006/112/EC, Arts 354, 355*].

See **26 GOLD AND PRECIOUS METALS** for the UK provisions.

(7) Special scheme for non-established taxable persons supplying electronic services to non-taxable persons

EU countries must permit a 'non-established taxable person' (NETP) supplying 'electronic services' to a non-taxable person who is established or has his permanent address or usually resides in an EU country to use a special scheme in accordance with the following provisions. The special scheme must apply to all those supplies within the EU. A '*non-established taxable person*' means a taxable person who has not established his business in the EU, who has no fixed establishment within the EU and who is not otherwise required to be identified for VAT purposes in the EU. '*Electronic services*' mean those referred to in **18.14**(5)(*k*) above. [*Directive 2006/112/EC, Arts 358, 359*].

The NETP must state to the '*EU country of identification*' (i.e. the EU country which he chooses to contact to state when his activity as a taxable person within the EU commences in accordance with these provisions) when his activity as a taxable person commences, ceases or changes to the extent that he no longer qualifies for the special scheme. Such a statement must be made electronically. [*Directive 2006/112/EC, Art 360*].

The information from the NETP to the EU country of identification when his taxable activities commence must contain details of name; postal address; electronic addresses, including websites; national tax number, if any; and a statement that the person is not identified for VAT purposes within the EU. The NETP must notify the EU country of identification of any changes in the information provided. The EU country of identification must allocate to the NETP an individual VAT number and must notify him of the number allocated by electronic means. Based on the information used for this identification, the *EU country of consumption* (i.e. the EU country in which the supply of the electronic services is deemed to take place under *Art 57*, see **18.14**(5) above) may keep its own identification systems. [*Directive 2006/112/EC, Arts 361, 362*].

The EU country of identification must strike the NETP from the identification register if

- he notifies it that he no longer supplies electronic services;
- it otherwise can be assumed that his taxable activities have ended;
- he no longer meets the conditions necessary to use the special scheme; or
- he persistently fails to comply with the rules concerning the special scheme.

[*Directive 2006/112/EC, Art 363*].

The NETP must submit a VAT return by electronic means, whether or not electronic services have been supplied, to the EU country of identification for each VAT return period within 20 days following the end of the period. The VAT return must set out the identification number and, for each EU country of consumption where VAT is due, the total value, less VAT, of supplies of electronic services for the VAT period and total amount of the corresponding VAT. The applicable VAT rates and the total VAT due must also be indicated. The VAT return must be made in euro. EU countries which have not adopted the euro may require the VAT return to be made in their national currencies. If the supplies have been made in other currencies, they must be converted using the exchange rates published by the European Central Bank for the last date of the reporting period or, if there is no publication on that day, on the next day of publication. [*Directive 2006/112/EC, Arts 364–366*].

The NETP must

- pay the VAT when submitting the return to a bank account designated by the EU country of identification [*Directive 2006/112/EC, Art 367*];
- instead of making deductions for input tax under **18.34** above, be granted a refund under the *EC 13th Directive* (see **18.45** below) [*Directive 2006/112/EC, Art 368*]; and
- keep records of the transactions covered by the special scheme in sufficient detail to enable the tax authorities of the EU country of consumption to verify that the VAT return is correct. These records should be made available electronically on request to the EU countries of identification and consumption. They must be maintained for a period of ten years from the end of the year when the transaction was carried out. [*Directive 2006/112/EC, Art 369*].

Derogations

[18.43] The Council may authorise any EU country to introduce special measures for derogation from the provisions of this *Directive* in order to simplify the procedure for collecting VAT (without affecting the overall amount of VAT due at the final consumption stage except to a negligible extent) or to prevent certain types of tax evasion or avoidance. In addition, countries are allowed to retain special measures which were in force on 1 January 1977 provided that they notified the Commission of them before 1 January 1978 (when the *6th Directive* was implemented). [*Directive 2006/112/EC, Arts 394, 395*].

Countries which, at 1 January 1978, taxed the transactions listed in *Directive 2006/112/EC Annex X, Part A* may continue to tax those transactions. Similarly, countries which exempted the transactions listed in *Directive 2006/112/EC Annex X, Part B*, may continue to exempt those transactions in accordance with the conditions applying in the Member State concerned on that date. [*Directive 2006/112/EC, Arts 370, 371*].

The derogations granted to the UK government include the following.

- Special **RETAIL SCHEMES (60)**.

- Exemption from registration where, although taxable supplies exceed the registration limit, all supplies are, or would be, zero-rated if the taxable person was registered. See **59.6 REGISTRATION.**
- Valuation for VAT purposes where certain companies, for example, in the field of cosmetics, sell products to individuals who are outside the tax net for resale to the final customer. See **18.2** above and **71.23 VALUATION.**
- Operation of UK **TERMINAL MARKETS (67).**
- Long stays in hotels. See **32.2 HOTELS AND HOLIDAY ACCOMMODATION.**
- Treatment of goods in warehouse.
- Voluntary accounting scheme for transactions in **GOLD AND PRECIOUS METALS (26).**
- Fuel expenditure for company cars. See **45.16 MOTOR CARS.**
- Cash accounting scheme. See **63.2 SPECIAL SCHEMES.**
- Transfer of assets to a partly exempt group. See **27.7 GROUPS OF COMPANIES.**
- Direction to use open market value for exempt supplies to connected persons (see **71.19 VALUATION**) and acquisitions of goods from connected persons (see **71.12 VALUATION**).
- Taxation of self-supplies of land and buildings to be based on open market value. This derogation has not been introduced.
- Preparation of annual EU sales lists by persons with low turnover and by persons who prepare annual VAT returns. See **2.13 ACCOUNTING PERIODS AND RETURNS.**
- Transport services directly linked to an intra-EU transport of goods. See **70.27 TRANSPORT AND FREIGHT.**
- Restricting to 50% the right of the hirer or lessee to deduct input tax on car hire or leasing transactions where the car is used for private purposes and waiving VAT payable on the private use of the car in question. See **45.11 MOTOR CARS.**
- The place of supply of telecommunications services. See **65.23 SUPPLY: PLACE OF SUPPLY.**

Refunds of VAT to persons established in other EU countries

[18.44] The so-called 'VAT package' came into force on 1 January 2010 and included the replacement of the *EC 8th Directive* (see below) with a scheme providing for the submission and payment of claims electronically. The salient features (taken from *Directive 2008/9/EC*) are as follows.

A claim for VAT incurred in one Member State (the Member State of refund) may be submitted by a person established in another Member State, provided:

- that person is not established, and does not have an establishment, or its domicile or normal place of business, in the Member State of refund;
- that person has not made any supplies of goods or services in the Member State of refund, other than certain zero-rated services relating to transport, and goods or services where the reverse charge applies;

- the VAT claimed meets the normal conditions for its recovery as input tax; and
- the activities of the person give rise to a right to input tax credit in the Member State where it is established. In the case of a partly exempt person, the extent of the claim must be in accordance with the rules applying in the Member State of establishment.

The claimant must submit an electronic refund application to the Member State of refund via an electronic portal set up by the Member State in which it is established. The application is then forwarded to the Member State of refund. The application must contain the information previously required for *EC 8th Directive* claims, with additional codes identifying the type of expenditure. It appears that the submission of invoices will not be a requirement unless the Member State of refund specifically requests and the invoice value exceeds the equivalent of €1000 (€250 for fuel), in which case an electronic copy of the invoice must be submitted.

A claim must be submitted within nine months of the end of calendar year. Any claim must be for a period of at least three months (and must be for at least the equivalent of €400), unless it is a claim for the remainder of the year (in which case the minimum is the equivalent of €50).

The Member State of refund must notify the claimant that the claim has been received. It must notify its decision to approve or refuse the refund within four months of the date of receipt, although this may be extended to a maximum of eight months if the Member State of refund requests further information. If approved, the refund must be made within four months and ten days of the date the claim is received (extended to a maximum of eight months and ten days if the Member State of refund has requested additional information). If refunds are made late, the claimant is entitled to interest.

If a false claim is made, penalties and interest applicable in the Member State of refund may be imposed.

FA 2009, s 77 contains enabling provisions relating to the new claims procedure. See **17.7–17.9 EUROPEAN UNION: GENERAL** for more details.

The *8th Directive*

Before 1 January 2010 the *8th Directive* enabled a taxable person to recover VAT suffered in another EU country provided he was not already registered in that country (in which case that country's domestic VAT legislation would apply).

Subject to the conditions below, an EU country had to refund to 'a taxable person who is not established in that country' (but *is* established in another EU country) any VAT charged in respect of

- services or movable property supplied to him by other taxable persons within that EU country, or
- the importation of goods into that country

to the extent that such goods and services were used for the purposes of

(a) transactions relating to economic activities carried out in another country which would have been deductible if performed within that country;
(b) transactions related to imports and exports and the international goods traffic; and
(c) supplies of services where the VAT on the supply was accounted for solely by the person to whom they were supplied. (These might differ slightly between EU countries but broadly corresponded to those listed in *VATA 1994, Sch 5* (see **65.21 SUPPLY: PLACE OF SUPPLY**).)

[*8th Directive, Art 2*].

The effect of (*a*) above was that a taxable person who carried out taxable and exempt transactions in his own country (and so was partially exempt there) only had a right of partial refund under the *8th Directive* in the other EU country. The refundable amount should be calculated, first, by determining which transactions gave rise to a right of deduction in the country of establishment and, second, by taking account solely of the transactions which would also have given rise to a right of deduction in the EU country of refund if they had been carried out there and of the expenses giving rise to a right to deduction in the later country (*Ministre du Budget and another v Société Monte Dei Paschi Di Siena, ECJ Case C–136/99*, [2001] STC 1029 (TVC 22.532)).

'*A taxable person who is not established in that country*' means a person carrying out an economic activity within *Directive 2006/112/EC, Art 9* who, during the period of the claim,

- has had neither the seat of his economic activity nor a fixed establishment from which business transactions are effected in that country;
- if no such seat or fixed establishment exists, has not had his domicile or normal place of residence in that country, and
- has supplied no goods or services deemed to have been supplied in that country except for *either* transport (and related) services carried out in connection with the international carriage of goods *or* services within (*c*) above.

[*8th Directive, Art 1*].

To qualify for a refund, the taxable person had to

- submit to the competent authority of the relevant country a prescribed application form *completed in block capitals in the language of that country* attaching originals of invoices or import documents (but see *Société Générale des Grandes Sources d'Eaux Minérales Françaises v Bundesamt für Finanzen, ECJ Case C–361/96*, [1998] STC 981 (TVC 22.538) where it was held that a country *could* accept duplicate or photocopied invoices where the originals had been lost through no fault of the taxpayer and there was no risk of a further application for a refund. Moreover, if that country accepted internal claims for input tax in similar circumstances, the principle of non-discrimination in the preamble to the *8th Directive* required it to extend the same possibility to persons established in other EU countries);

- produce a certificate of status (valid for one year) issued by the official authority of the country in which he is registered stating that he is a taxable person (see *Debouche v Inspecteur der Invoerrechten en Accijnzen, ECJ Case C–302/93*, [1996] STC 1406 (TVC 22.537));
- give a written declaration that no goods or services have been supplied in the EU country (except as above); and
- undertake to repay any sum recovered in error.

[*8th Directive, Arts 3, 4*].

VAT was not refundable if it would be disallowed for credit if incurred by a person registered in the EU country. Similarly, exempt supplies of goods were outside the provisions. However, the country could not impose any condition as to recoverability outside the *Directive's* provisions otherwise than to justify an application. [*8th Directive, Arts 5, 6*].

Applications had to relate to invoiced supplies or imports made during a period of not less than three months or not more than one calendar year. Applications could, however, relate to a period of less than three months where the period represents the remainder of a calendar year. An application could relate to invoices, etc. not covered by previous applications although applicable to charges incurred during the calendar year in question, but applications had to otherwise be submitted within six months of the end of the calendar year in which the VAT became chargeable. Provision was made for the exclusion of small claims, the prevention of invoices being used more than once and the return of documents to the claimant within one month. A decision whether or not to grant an application had to be made by the relevant authority within six months of submission. Payment had to be made within the same period either in the relevant country or in the country in which the applicant was registered, in which case any bank charges were borne by the applicant. Refusal to grant an application had to give grounds for the decision and appeals were allowed to be made on the same basis as domestic cases. A competent authority was given powers to reclaim amounts paid under fraudulent applications for a period of two years from the date of the fraudulent application. [*8th Directive, Art 7*].

Refunds of VAT to persons established outside the EU

[18.45] The *13th Directive* requires each EU country to introduce a scheme to enable a taxable person established outside the EU to recover VAT suffered in that country provided he is not already registered there.

The taxable person must not make supplies of goods or services in the particular EU country other than

- supplies of transport (and related) services carried out in connection with the international carriage of goods; or
- services where the VAT on the supply is accounted for solely by the person to whom they are supplied.

Countries may make the refunds conditional upon the granting of comparable advantages regarding turnover tax by the territory where the taxable person is established. [*13th Directive, Arts 1, 2*].

Administrative arrangements and conditions for submitting applications, time limits and periods covered, minimum amounts claimable and methods of repayment are left to the individual countries. Refunds cannot be granted on terms more favourable than those applied to EU taxable persons. Countries may provide for the exclusion of certain expenditure. [*13th Directive, Arts 3, 4*].

See **48.5 OVERSEAS TRADERS** below for the scheme introduced in the UK.

Key points

[18.46] Points to consider are as follows.

- In situations where UK VAT law contradicts the provisions of EU law, the latter must take priority. This outcome has led to many revisions to UK VAT law over the years, to ensure it is compatible with the provisions of EU law.
- The standard rate of VAT adopted by an EU country must be between 15% and 25%. The UK rate is very close to the average EU rate.
- Be aware that the definition of 'taxable person' has a different meaning in UK and EU VAT law. In the case of UK law, a 'taxable person' is someone who is either registered for VAT or should be registered on the basis that his past taxable sales (or expected taxable sales in the future) have exceeded the relevant limits. In the case of EU law, a 'taxable person' is someone who carries out an 'economic activity' (the EU phrase for 'business') anywhere in the world.
- An important outcome of the phrase 'economic activity' is that any income earned on a continuing basis from the exploitation of land and property is within the VAT system. So a sole trader registered for VAT as a car mechanic, for example, cannot disregard the VAT implications of any property income he earns through the same legal entity. As a practical example, this is a relevant factor in relation to the flat-rate scheme (a scheme available to a small business with taxable sales of less than £150,000 per annum excluding VAT) which means that scheme users must include all exempt business income in the tax calculations, i.e. including buy-to-let income from a residential property.
- The UK has acquired a number of derogations from the EU that enable the burden of VAT to be eased in many practical situations. An example of a useful derogation is where a business that has exceeded the relevant VAT registration limits can avoid being VAT-registered if it would submit repayment returns on a regular basis, i.e. because all or most sales are zero-rated. In such cases, the business can agree with HMRC that it does not need to register for VAT.

- A business registered for VAT in one EU country has always had the right, in most cases, to claim VAT paid on expenses incurred in other EU countries (subject to normal rules). This VAT is repaid through a separate claims system, rather than by an inclusion as input tax on the VAT returns of the business in question. On 1 January 2010, the claims procedure was greatly simplified with the introduction of new electronic procedures. The new electronic claims system also introduced revised deadlines for claims to be submitted and repaid (a claim must now be submitted within nine months of the end of a calendar year), with an interest penalty payable by countries who did not meet the relevant repayment deadline.

19

European Union: Single Market

Key points **19.41**

Cross-references. See **2.11 ACCOUNTING PERIODS AND RETURNS** for EU sales statements; **2.19 ACCOUNTING PERIODS AND RETURNS** for Intrastat; **17.2 EUROPEAN UNION: GENERAL** for the VAT territory of the EU; **39.5 INVOICES** for particulars required on VAT invoices issued to persons in other EU countries and **39.13 INVOICES** for the time limit for issuing invoices; **56 RECORDS** generally; **59.11** *et seq* **REGISTRATION** for the liability to register in the UK in respect of distance sales from another EU country; **59.18** *et seq* **REGISTRATION** for the liability to register in the UK in respect of acquisitions from other EU countries; **65.2 SUPPLY: PLACE OF SUPPLY** for the place of supply of goods; **70.26** and **70.31 TRANSPORT AND FREIGHT** for special provisions applying to intra-EU freight transport and handling and storage; **71.11–71.14 VALUATION** for the valuation rules applying to acquisitions from other EU countries; **72 WAREHOUSED GOODS AND FREE ZONES** for movement of goods in warehouse and free zones to and from EU countries.

Introduction

[19.1] The concepts of 'imports' and 'exports' of goods applies only to transactions with countries outside the EU. For intra-EU movements of goods, goods coming into the UK from other EU countries are referred to as 'acquisitions' and goods leaving the UK to go to other EU countries are referred to as 'despatches' or 'removals'.

The rules are complex and were only intended to be transitional until a definitive system for the taxation of trade between EU countries was introduced, based on the principle of taxing goods and services in the EU country of origin. However, there seems little possibility that such a system will be introduced in the near future.

See **17.2 EUROPEAN UNION: GENERAL** for a list of the territories which make up the VAT territories of the EU.

De Voil Indirect Tax Service. See V1.210, V3.361–V3.398, V4.341–V4.361.

Movement of goods between EU countries: general provisions

Transfers of goods to be treated as supplies

[19.2] Unless specifically overridden by other provisions, where goods forming part of the assets of a business are

- removed from any EU country, by or under the directions of the person carrying on the business, and
- so removed in the course or furtherance of the business for the purpose of being taken to another EU country

then whether or not the removal is, or is in connection with, a transaction for a consideration, there is a supply of goods by that person. [*VATA 1994, Sch 4 para 6(1)*]. Specifically excluded is the removal of gas through a natural gas system situated within the territory of an EU country or any network connected to such a system; electricity; or heat or cooling supplied through a network [*SI 2010/2925*]. (Prior to 1 January 2011, the exclusion applied to the removal of gas through the natural gas distribution network or electricity [*SI 2004/3150*].) The supply is treated as taking place in the EU country from which the goods are removed. [*VATA 1994, s 7(7)*].

There is no supply under these provisions where

- the goods are removed from an EU country in the course of their removal from one part of that country to another part of the same country (e.g. goods removed from England to Northern Ireland via Ireland); or
- the goods have been removed from a place outside the EU for entry into the territory of the EU and are removed from an EU country before the time when any EU customs duty on their entry into the EU would be incurred. See **33.18 IMPORTS**.

[*VATA 1994, Sch 4 para 6(2)*].

The effect of these provisions is that, in addition to normal commercial transactions, certain transfers by a business of its own goods to another EU country are also treated as supplies of goods (see **19.25** below).

Charging and accounting for VAT

Subject to special rules in the cases listed below:

- *For transactions between VAT-registered traders*, a supplier in one EU country need not charge VAT on dispatch of goods to a customer in another EU country. Any VAT due is payable on acquisition of the goods by the customer who must account for it on their normal VAT return at the rate in force in the country of destination of the goods.
- *Where the customer in another EU country is a private individual or is not registered for VAT*, VAT is normally charged and accounted for by the supplier in the EU country from which the goods are dispatched.

See **19.3** *et seq* below for acquisitions of goods in the UK from other EU countries and **19.11** *et seq* below for supplies from the UK to other EU countries.

Special rules

Special rules apply to the following.

- The supply of goods subject to excise duty purchased by non-taxable persons. See **19.9** below for acquisitions in the UK and **19.17** below for supplies to other EU countries.
- Distance sales (i.e. sales to non-taxable persons in other EU countries where the supplier is responsible for delivery) above certain limits. See **19.10** below for distance selling to the UK and **19.18** for distance selling from the UK.

- Goods lost or stolen in transit. See **19.19** below.
- Supplies to diplomats, international organisations, NATO forces and other entitled persons and bodies in other EU countries which may in certain circumstances be relieved from VAT. See **19.21**(1) below.
- Freight containers. See **19.21**(2) below.
- Samples. See **19.21**(3) below).
- Triangulation. See **19.22** below.
- Certain transfers of own goods between EU countries, including goods sold on sale or return. See **19.25** and **19.26** below.
- Certain temporary movements of goods. See **19.27** below.
- Goods sent for processing, repair, etc. see **19.28** and **19.29** below.
- The supply of goods to be installed or assembled at a customer's premises in another EU country. See **19.31** below.
- Call-off stock. See **19.32** below
- New means of transport. See **19.33** *et seq* below.
- Acquisitions by non-VAT-registered businesses and non-taxable organisations in excess of an annual threshold. See **59.18 REGISTRATION** for the liability to register for VAT in the UK in respect of acquisitions where there is no liability to be registered in respect of UK supplies.

Returns

In addition to the appropriate entries on the VAT return, a business trading with other EU countries may also have to complete

- an EU sales list (a list of supplies made to VAT-registered traders in other EU countries, see **2.11–2.18 ACCOUNTING PERIODS AND RETURNS**); and
- an Intrastat supplementary declaration (for use, together with VAT returns, in the compilation of statistics on the trade in goods between EU countries, see **2.19 ACCOUNTING PERIODS AND RETURNS**).

De Voil Indirect Tax Service. See V3.213.

Acquisitions of goods in the UK from other EU countries

[19.3] There is an acquisition in the UK for VAT purposes where

- there is an intra-EU movement of goods to the UK;
- the goods are received in the UK by a VAT-registered trader; and
- the supplier is registered for VAT in the EU country of departure.

Under these circumstances, it is not necessary to make an import declaration (with certain exceptions) or pay VAT at the frontier. Instead, the UK VAT-registered trader is required to account for VAT on the goods acquired in the UK. [*VATA 1994, s 1(1)*]. The rate of VAT due is that applicable to the supply of identical goods in the UK. No VAT will therefore be due on the acquisition of goods which are currently zero-rated in the UK. Any VAT due must be accounted for on the VAT return for the period in which the tax point occurs and, subject to the normal rules, may be treated as input tax on the same VAT return.

(VAT Notice 725, paras 7.1, 7.2, 7.4).

These provisions are considered in more detail in **19.4** to **19.10** below.

De Voil Indirect Tax Service. See V3.361–V3.398.

Meaning of 'acquisition of goods from another EU country'

[19.4] An '*acquisition of goods from another EU country*' is any acquisition of goods under a transaction where both of the following conditions are satisfied.

- The transaction is, or is treated for the purposes of *VATA 1994* as, a supply of goods.
- The transaction involves the movement of goods from another EU country.

For these purposes, it is immaterial whether the removal of the goods is undertaken by or on behalf of the supplier, the customer or some other person.

Where the person with the property in the goods does not change in consequence of anything treated as a supply under *VATA 1994*, that supply is to be treated as a transaction under which there is an acquisition of goods by the person making it. (The transfer of a business's own goods to another EU country therefore leads to an acquisition of goods by it in that country. See **19.25** below.)

The Treasury may provide by Order that, in relation to any type of transaction, the acquisition of goods under such a transaction is not to be treated as an acquisition of goods from another EU country. See, for example,

- **26.7 GOLD AND PRECIOUS METALS** for gold supplied to a Central Bank by a supplier in another EU country; and
- **61.7 SECOND-HAND GOODS** for goods bought from a registered business in another EU country where VAT on the supply is accounted for in that EU country by reference to the profit margin.

[*VATA 1994, s 11*].

De Voil Indirect Tax Service. See V3.363.

Scope of VAT on acquisitions

[19.5] Subject to the provisions under *Zero-rating* and *VAT relief* below, VAT is charged in the UK on any acquisition from another EU country where the following conditions are satisfied.

(a) The acquisition is a 'taxable acquisition' and takes place in the UK. See **19.6** below for the place of acquisition.

An acquisition from another EU country is a '*taxable acquisition*' if the goods are

- acquired by
  - (i) a person in the course or furtherance of a business carried on by him, or
  - (ii) by a body corporate, club, association, organisation or other unincorporated body in the course or furtherance of any activities carried on by it otherwise than by way of business,

and the supplier is taxable in another EU country at the time of the relevant transaction and is acting in the course or furtherance of a business carried on by him, or

- a new means of transport (see **19.33** below)

but provided that, in either case, the acquisition is not an '*exempt acquisition*' i.e. an acquisition where the goods are acquired in pursuance of an exempt supply falling within *VATA 1994, Sch 9* (see **20 EXEMPT SUPPLIES**).

(b) The acquisition is not in pursuance of a taxable supply in the UK. See, for example, **19.30** below for installed and assembled goods.

(c) Either
   (i) the person making the acquisition is a '*taxable person*' (i.e. a person who is, or is required to be, registered);
   (ii) the goods are subject to excise duty (see **19.9** below); or
   (iii) the goods are a new means of transport (see **19.33** below).

[*VATA 1994, ss 10, 31(1)*].

See **59.18 REGISTRATION** for the requirement to register by persons within (*a*)(ii) above who make acquisitions above an annual threshold and who would not otherwise be liable for registration in respect of supplies made.

Liability for VAT

The VAT on any acquisition is a liability of the person who acquires the goods and, subject to provisions about accounting and payment, becomes due at the time of acquisition (see **19.7** below). [*VATA 1994, s 1(3)*].

Zero-rating

Where the goods acquired fall within *VATA 1994, Sch 8*, no VAT is chargeable on their acquisition, except as otherwise provided in that *Schedule*. [*VATA 1994, s 30(3)*].

VAT relief

Certain goods imported into the UK from outside the EU are subject to relief from import VAT under *SI 1984/746*. These goods are also subject to relief when coming into the UK from other EU countries

- if supplied by a taxable person in another EU country to a taxable person in the UK; or
- where there is a deemed supply on the transfer of a taxable person's own goods from another EU country to the UK (see **19.25** below).

See **33.15**(1)–(12) **IMPORTS** for details of the qualifying goods.

Samples. See **19.21**(3) below.

[*VATA 1994, s 36A; FA 2002, s 25; SI 2002/1935*].

De Voil Indirect Tax Service. See V3.361–V3.398.

Place of acquisition

[19.6] VAT on an acquisition is due in the country where the acquisition is deemed to take place. Subject to below, the following provisions apply for determining whether goods acquired from another EU country are acquired in the UK.

(a) Goods are treated as acquired in the UK if the transaction involves their removal to the UK and does not involve their removal from the UK (i.e. the transport of the goods ends in the UK). The goods are otherwise, subject to the following provisions, to be treated as acquired outside the UK.

(b) Goods are treated as acquired in the UK where a business uses a UK VAT registration number in order to acquire the goods (whether or not the goods are to be transported to the UK) unless it can establish to HMRC that VAT fell to be paid (and has been paid) in another EU country on the acquisition of those goods there under provisions corresponding to the UK provisions in (*a*) above.

The above is subject to the special provisions applying to

- warehoused goods (see **72.6 WAREHOUSED GOODS AND FREE ZONES**);
- triangulation where three parties are involved in the transaction (see **19.22** below); and
- installed or assembled goods (see **19.30** below).

[*VATA 1994, s 13; FA 1996, Sch 3 para 4*].

In most cases, VAT on an acquisition will only be due under (*a*) above in the country where the goods are received and (*b*) above is a 'fallback' provision that applies where the VAT registration number quoted to the supplier to secure zero-rating has been issued in a different EU country to that in which the goods are received.

Following the ECJ decision in the joined cases of *X, ECJ Case C–536/08* and *Facet Trading BV, ECJ Case C–539/08*, [2010] STC 1701 (TVC 22.411), HMRC have clarified that there is no right to recover the acquisition VAT as input tax where it fell due under the fallback provision. The only basis on which the UK VAT may be adjusted is where it can be demonstrated that acquisition VAT has been accounted for in the EU country of arrival. (HMRC Brief 20/11).

> *Example*
>
> A UK business acquires goods from a supplier in Germany for delivery to the UK and quotes its VAT registration number.
>
> The place of supply is the UK under both (*a*) and (*b*) above.
>
> But if a UK business quotes its UK VAT registration number to a supplier in Germany and the goods are delivered to France, there is an acquisition in France (under French rules similar to (*a*) above) and an acquisition in the UK under (*b*) above. In such circumstances
>
> - the business is liable to account for acquisition VAT in the UK unless it can demonstrate that VAT has already been paid in the EU country to which the goods were sent (France); and

- if it has accounted for acquisition VAT in the UK and is later required to pay VAT on the acquisition in France, it can obtain a refund of the VAT paid in the UK but only where it has not claimed, or not been able to claim, full input tax credit in respect of the acquisition (see **19.8** below).

(VAT Notice 725, paras 7.7–7.9).

De Voil Indirect Tax Service. See V3.376–V3.384.

Time of acquisition

[19.7] Any VAT on an acquisition becomes due in the VAT period in which the tax point (time of acquisition) occurs. Subject to below, the time of acquisition of goods from another EU country (which is the same time as the corresponding supply of goods in the EU country of dispatch, see **19.16** below) is the earlier of

(a) the 15th day of the month following that in which the *first* removal of the goods involved in the transaction forming the basis of the acquisition occurred; and

(b) the date of issue of an invoice in respect of the transaction containing such details as HMRC require. For this purpose, the invoice is one which is issued by the supplier or the customer under the provisions of the law of the EU country from which the goods were despatched and which correspond to the provisions in *SI 1995/2518, Regs 13, 13A, 14* relating to invoices for supplies in the UK. See **39 INVOICES**.

Note that, unlike the rules for supplies in the UK, part or full payment for an intra-EU supply of goods does not create a tax point for the acquisition. However, the receipt of a payment on account does make the supplier liable to raise an invoice which will in turn trigger a tax point under (*b*) above.

HMRC may make Regulations relating to the time at which an acquisition is treated as taking place where the whole or part of any consideration is determined or payable periodically, or from time to time, or at the end of a period. Under these powers, where any water, gas or any form of power, heat, refrigeration or other cooling, or ventilation within **66.15 SUPPLY: TIME OF SUPPLY** is acquired from another EU country on such terms, the goods are treated as separately and successively acquired on each occasion that an invoice is issued under (*b*) above.

See also **72.6 WAREHOUSED GOODS AND FREE ZONES** for special rules for warehoused goods.

[*VATA 1994, s 12; FA 1996, Sch 3 para 3; SI 1995/2518, Regs 83, 87; SI 2003/3220, Regs 12, 14*]. (VAT Notice 725, paras 7.3, 7.5, 7.6).

De Voil Indirect Tax Service. See V3.388.

Recording and accounting for VAT due on acquisitions

[19.8] In addition to the normal VAT records, a UK-registered business which acquires goods from businesses registered for VAT in other EU countries must

(a) keep VAT invoices issued to it and any other documents relating to the goods it acquires from other EU countries;
(b) calculate the VAT due on the acquisition of these goods and enter it on the 'VAT payable' side of its VAT account; and
(c) subject to the normal rules for allowable input tax, deduct the VAT due on the acquisition as input tax on the 'VAT allowable' side of the VAT account.

Where the time of acquisition of any goods from another EU country is determined under **19.7**(*b*) above by reference to the issue of an invoice, VAT must be accounted for and paid in respect of the acquisition only on so much of its value as is shown on the invoice. [*SI 1995/2518, Reg 26*].

The amount of VAT due on an acquisition is the tax value multiplied by the VAT rate. See **71.11–71.14 VALUATION** for the valuation rules applying to acquisitions from other EU countries.

VAT return

VAT due under (*b*) above should be entered in Box 2 of the VAT return for the VAT period in which the time of acquisition occurs (see **19.7** above) and the input tax under (*c*) above in Box 4 on the same return. The value of the acquisition must be included in Boxes 7 and 9.

Supplementary declarations

Details of an acquisition may have to be disclosed on a supplementary declaration as an arrival. See **2.19 ACCOUNTING PERIODS AND RETURNS**.

(VAT Notice 725, paras 7.11, 16.4, 16.6).

Acquisition of goods subject to excise duty

[19.9] All taxable acquisitions (i.e. acquisitions for business purposes and acquisitions for non-business purposes by clubs, associations, etc. from registered businesses in other EU countries, see **19.5** above) of exciseable goods are taxed in the EU country of destination.

Acquisitions by VAT-registered businesses

Where the business that acquires the exciseable goods from a supplier in another EU country is UK VAT-registered, it must account for VAT in the same way as for any other acquisition.

Acquisitions by non-registered persons

Where the person making the taxable acquisition is not registered for UK VAT (because turnover is under the registration limit or because activities are not business activities), VAT cannot be accounted for by means of a VAT return. In order to avoid the need to register all persons making such acquisitions, HMRC are empowered to introduce a special mechanism to collect the VAT due.

Under these provisions, where

(a) a taxable acquisition of goods subject to excise duty takes place in the UK,
(b) the acquisition is not in pursuance of a taxable supply (see below), and
(c) the person acquiring the goods is not a taxable person at the time of the acquisition,

the person acquiring such goods must notify HMRC of the acquisition at the time of the acquisition or the arrival of the goods in the UK, whichever is the later. The notification must be in writing in English and contain the following particulars.

- The name and current address of the person acquiring the goods.
- The time of acquisition.
- The date when the goods arrived in the UK.
- The value of the goods including any excise duty payable.
- The VAT due on the acquisition.

The notification must include a signed declaration that all the information given is true and complete.

The VAT due is payable at the time of notification and, in any event, not later than the last date on which the person is required to make such notification as above. Where the person required to make the notification dies or becomes incapacitated, the liability to notify passes to the personal representative, trustee in bankruptcy, liquidator, etc., as does the liability to pay the VAT (although only to the extent of assets passing to that person).

Note

The effect of (*b*) above is that the provisions are only necessary where the person acquiring the goods arranges for their delivery. If the supplier arranges delivery, the distance selling provisions in **19.10** below apply and the supplier must register for VAT in the UK, whatever his level of sales in this country.

[*VATA 1994, Sch 11 para 2(4)(5); SI 1995/2518, Regs 31(3), 36*].

De Voil Indirect Tax Service. See V5.126.

Distance selling to the UK from other EU countries

[19.10] Distance selling occurs when a taxable supplier in one EU country supplies and delivers goods to a customer in another EU country who is not registered or liable to be registered for VAT. Such customers are known as 'non-taxable persons' and include not only private individuals but public bodies, charities and businesses too small to register for VAT or with activities that are entirely exempt. The most common examples of distance sales are goods supplied by mail order and goods ordered over the internet.

Such distance sales to non-taxable persons in the UK from another EU country are normally subject to VAT in that other country. But once the value of such distance sales to the UK exceeds the UK annual threshold of £70,000

- the supplier is automatically liable to register for VAT in the UK (see **59.11 REGISTRATION**);

- the UK becomes the place of supply (see **65.5 SUPPLY: PLACE OF SUPPLY**); and
- VAT on any further sales is taxed in the UK.

The supplier may, if he wishes, opt to make the UK the place of supply before reaching the annual threshold. See **59.14 REGISTRATION**.

Note that each EU country has the option of applying a distance selling threshold of €35,000 or €100,000 per calendar year (or its own currency equivalent). The UK has adopted a threshold of €100,000 euro, set at £70,000.

Goods subject to excise duty

Distance sales of goods subject to excise duty are not subject to the threshold. An EU supplier must register for VAT immediately it makes any supplies of such goods.

Reporting requirements

The following table summarises the reporting requirements for distance sales to the UK.

Type of supply	*VAT return*	*EU sales list*
Distance sales to UK below UK distance selling threshold	No	No
Distance sales to UK above UK distance selling threshold (or where the seller has voluntarily registered in the UK)	Enter the output tax in Box 1 and the value of the supply in Box 6	No

(VAT Notice 725, paras 6.4, 6.16, 6.17).

Supplies of goods from the UK to other EU countries

[19.11] Supplies of goods to other EU countries can be zero-rated provided the following conditions are satisfied.

(a) The supply involves the removal of the goods from the UK to another EU country.
(b) The goods are acquired by a customer who is registered for VAT in another EU country (not necessarily the same one).
(c) The supplier obtains his customer's VAT registration number and shows this (including the 2-letter country code prefix) on his VAT invoice. See **19.12** below for checking a customer's VAT registration number and **39.1** and **39.5 INVOICES** for the obligation to provide a VAT invoice and the particulars to be included thereon.
(d) The supplier obtains and keeps valid commercial documentary evidence that the goods have been removed from the UK
    - within three months of the time of supply (see **19.16** below) for direct and indirect removals and goods involved in groupage or consolidation prior to removal; and

- within six months of the time of supply for goods involved in processing or incorporation prior to removal.

See **19.13–19.15** below for evidence of removal.

(e) The goods must not be second-hand goods or works of art, etc. which the supplier has opted to tax on the profit margin. See **61.12 SECOND-HAND GOODS.**

[*VATA 1994, s 30(8); SI 1995/2518, Reg 134*]. (VAT Notice 703, para 8.4 and VAT Notice 725, paras 4.3, 4.4 which have the force of law; VAT Information Sheet 2/00).

If all of the above conditions cannot be met, the UK supplier must charge VAT at the same rate applicable to a supply of the goods in the UK. The standard UK time of supply rules will then apply (see **66.8 SUPPLY: TIME OF SUPPLY**). A sale must not be zero-rated, even if the goods are subsequently removed to another EU country, where

- the goods are supplied to a UK VAT-registered customer (unless that customer is also registered for VAT in another EU country in which case the customer must provide his EU VAT registration number and the goods must be removed to another EU country);
- the supplier delivers to, or allows the goods to be collected by, a UK customer at a UK address; or
- the supplier allows the goods to be used in the UK in the period between supply and removal (except where specifically authorised to do so).

(VAT Notice 725, para 4.3).

Supplies of goods

See **64.3 SUPPLY: GENERAL** for a general consideration of what is a supply of goods (as opposed to a supply of services).

Reporting requirements

The following table summarises the reporting requirements for supplies of goods to customers in other EU countries.

Type of supply	*VAT return*	*EU sales list*
Supplies of goods to VAT-registered customers in other EU countries where the zero-rating conditions above are satisfied	Enter the value of the supply in Boxes 6 and 8	Enter the customer's VAT number and the value of the supply
Supplies of goods to customers in other EU countries where the zero-rating conditions above are not satisfied	Enter the VAT due in Box 1 and the value of the supply in Box 6	No

(VAT Notice 725, para 3.7).

Invoicing requirements

See **39.5 INVOICES.**

Failure to receive evidence of removal

Where a supply is initially zero-rated on the assumption that the necessary evidence of removal will be received within the time limit but this is not the case, the supplier must account for VAT on the supply at the standard rate (unless the goods are zero-rated in their own right). VAT records must be amended and VAT accounted for on the taxable proportion of the invoiced amount or consideration received, i.e. 7/47ths of the total for a VAT rate of 17.5% (1/6th of the total for a VAT rate of 20% from 4 January 2011; 3/23rds of the total for a VAT rate of 15% from 1 December 2008 to 31 December 2009). This amount must be entered on the VAT payable side of the VAT account and included in Box 1 of the VAT return for the period in which the time limit expires. If the supplier subsequently receives the evidence of removal of the goods, he can then zero-rate the supply and adjust the VAT account for the period in which the evidence is obtained (provided the goods have not been used in the UK before removal).
(VAT Notice 725, paras 16.10, 16.11).

Effect of failure to comply with conditions

Where the supply of any goods has been zero-rated under the above provisions and either any of the above conditions is not complied with or the goods are found in the UK after the date of alleged removal, the goods are liable to *forfeiture*. Any VAT which would have been due but for zero-rating is payable forthwith by the person to whom the goods were supplied or by any other person in whose possession the goods are found in the UK. HMRC may waive payment of the VAT in whole or in part. [*VATA 1994, s 30(10)*].

See, however, the decision in *Teleos plc & Others v C & E Commrs, ECJ Case C–409/04*, [2008] STC 706 (TVC 22.518). The court confirmed that goods must physically leave the territory of the EU country of supply to qualify for zero-rating. But if the supplier, acting in good faith, has done everything in his power to ensure the proper application of the VAT provisions and presents objective proofs that the goods supplied by him have left that country, the tax authorities cannot hold the supplier to account for the VAT on the goods if it turns out that the proofs relied upon contained false information and the supplier neither knew nor could have known anything of it. Thus the supplier must not be involved in tax evasion and must take every reasonable step to ensure that the transaction did not lead to his participation in VAT evasion.

De Voil Indirect Tax Service. See V4.341–V4.361.

Checking VAT registration numbers

[19.12] HMRC recommend that UK businesses

- write to customers in other EU countries asking for VAT registration numbers which have been allocated for intra-EU trade (to ensure that they do not provide an internal tax or fiscal number used only in their own country); and
- keep a record of these VAT registration numbers and retain the accompanying letters or advices.

Where a business has a doubt as to whether a particular registration number is valid, it should check that it follows the format for the appropriate country and contact the National Advice Service who can validate the VAT number and verify that any name and address is correct.

A business will not be liable to account for VAT where a supply is zero-rated and a customer's VAT number subsequently proves to be invalid but only if

- it has taken all reasonable steps to ensure that its customer is registered for VAT in the EU;
- it has obtained and shown the customer's EU VAT number on its VAT sales invoice; and
- it holds valid documentary evidence that the goods have left the UK.

HMRC do not regard reasonable steps as having been taken if a VAT number is used

- which does not conform to the published format for the customer's country;
- after HMRC advise that it is invalid; or
- which is known not to belong to the customer.

(VAT Notice 725, paras 4.7–4.11).

Evidence of removal of goods

[19.13] A combination of the documents shown below must be used to provide clear evidence that a sale has taken place and that the goods have been removed from the UK.

- Customer's order (including customer's name, VAT number and delivery address for the goods).
- Inter-company correspondence.
- Copy sales invoice (including a description of the goods, an invoice number and customer's EU VAT number etc.).
- Advice note.
- Packing list.
- Commercial transport document(s) from the carrier responsible for removing the goods from the UK.
- Details of insurance or freight charges.
- Bank statements as evidence of payment.
- Receipted copy of the consignment note as evidence of receipt of goods abroad.
- Any other documents relevant to the removal of the goods in question which would normally be obtained in the course of intra-EU business.

Photocopy certificates of shipment or other transport documents are not normally acceptable as evidence of removal unless authenticated with an original stamp and dated by an authorised official of the issuing office.

Documents used as proof of removal must clearly identify the following. (These requirements have the force of law.)

- The supplier.

- The consignor (where different from the supplier).
- The customer.
- The goods.
- An accurate value.
- The mode of transport and route of movement of the goods.
- The EU destination.

Vague descriptions of goods, quantities or values are not acceptable (e.g. 'various electrical goods' must not be used when the correct description is '2000 mobile phones Make ABC and Model Number XYZ2000').

Goods delivered by the supplier

In addition to the examples of acceptable documentary evidence listed above, travel tickets can also be used to demonstrate that an intra-EU journey took place for the purpose of removing the goods from the UK.

(VAT Notice 725, paras 5.1, 5.2, 5.4).

Goods collected in the UK by the customer

[19.14] If a VAT-registered EU customer collects the goods, or arranges for their collection and removal from the UK, it can be difficult for the supplier to obtain adequate proof of removal as the carrier is contracted to the customer. As a result, for this type of transaction the standard of evidence required to substantiate VAT zero-rating is high. The supplier should seek confirmation of how the goods are to be removed from the UK and what evidence of removal will be provided. He should also consider taking a deposit from the customer equal to the amount of VAT, in case satisfactory evidence of removal is not received.

Evidence must show that the goods supplied have left the UK. Copies of transport documents alone are not sufficient and information held must identify the date and route of the movement of goods and the method of transport involved. It should include the following.

- A written order from the customer which shows their name, address and EU VAT number, and the address where the goods are to be delivered.
- Copy sales invoice showing customer's name, EU VAT number, a description of the goods and an invoice number.
- Date of departure of goods from the supplier's premises and from the UK.
- Name and address of the haulier collecting the goods.
- Registration number of the vehicle collecting the goods and the name and signature of the driver.
- Where the goods are to be taken out of the UK by a different haulier or vehicle, the name and address of that haulier, signature for the goods and registration number of the vehicle.
- Route (e.g. Channel Tunnel, port of exit).
- Copy of travel tickets.
- Name of ferry or shipping company and date of sailing or airway number and airport.

The information held should also include (where applicable):

- Trailer number.
- Full container number.
- Name and address for consolidation, groupage, or processing.

(VAT Notice 725, para 5.5).

Other forms of evidence in particular cases

[19.15] See also VAT Notice 725 for acceptable forms of evidence in the following cases.

Removal of goods to the Republic of Ireland across the Irish Land Boundary	Para 5.3
Groupage or consolidation transactions	Para 5.8
Goods sent by post	Para 5.9
Couriers and fast parcel services	Para 5.10

Time of supply

Zero-rated supplies to taxable persons in another EU country

[19.16] Where any supply of goods involves both

- the removal of the goods from the UK, and
- their acquisition in another EU country by a person who is liable for VAT on the acquisition under the provisions of that country corresponding to those in **19.3** above,

the time of supply (tax point) is the earlier of

- the 15th day of the month following that in which the goods are removed (i.e. sent to the customer or, as the case may be, taken away by the customer); and
- the day of the issue of a VAT invoice or other prescribed invoice in respect of the supply.

Unlike a UK domestic supply, the receipt of payment before the issue of an invoice does not create a tax point. However, it does make the supplier liable to issue an invoice for the amount paid (see **39.1 INVOICES**) which in turn will create a tax point in respect of the amount invoiced.

Where a series of invoices are issued relating to the same supply of goods, the three-month time limit for obtaining valid evidence of removal (see **19.11**(*d*) above) begins from the date of the final invoice.

The tax point should be used as the reference date for including these supplies on the VAT return and EU sales list.

Supplies to non-taxable persons in another EU country

These are taxable in the UK and the tax point is determined under the normal rules. See **66.1** *et seq* **SUPPLY: TIME OF SUPPLY**.

[*VATA 1994, s 6(7)(8)*]. (VAT Notice 725, paras 3.4–3.6, 6.2).

Supplies of exciseable goods to other EU countries

Accompanying documents

[19.17] All exciseable goods must travel with an accompanying document which will be either an Administrative Accompanying Document (AAD) or a Simplified Administrative Accompanying Document (SAAD).

- If the goods are moving between warehouses and they are moving under authorised duty suspension arrangements (e.g. from an excise warehouse), the consignor must complete an AAD. There must be a financial guarantee to cover all excise duty liabilities during the movement. The consignee must complete a certificate of receipt for the goods on the reverse of Copy 3 of the AAD and return it to the consignor.
- If the goods are moving between warehouses and UK excise duty has already been paid, they should travel with a SAAD. The customer must also provide evidence that the excise duty has been paid in the EU country of destination or secured to the satisfaction of the VAT authorities there, *before* the supplier despatches the goods.

Excise goods supplied to a VAT-registered customer

Excise goods sold to a VAT-registered customer in another EU country are treated in the same way as any other type of goods.

Excise goods supplied to persons not VAT-registered but not for private purposes

There are special arrangements for supplies of exciseable goods to non-registered persons in other EU countries when the purchases are made for *non-private* purposes. This applies to purchases by businesses which are below the registration threshold in their country or by non-registered legal persons (associations and unincorporated bodies, etc.) whose activities are not business activities for VAT purposes. Such supplies can be zero-rated provided the following conditions are met.

(1) The goods are removed from the UK to a destination in another EU country.

(2) The supply is to a person who is non-taxable in another EU country but the place of supply is not treated as outside the UK under the place of supply rules in **65.6 SUPPLY: PLACE OF SUPPLY**. (This effectively means that the goods must be removed by or on behalf of the customer as if the supplier arranges for delivery of excise goods to a non VAT-registered person in another EU country, he is liable to register in that country under the distance selling arrangements whatever the level of sales.)

(3) Within 15 days of the end of the month in which they are moved, the supplier must obtain (and keep) a receipted copy 3 of the AAD. This must be certified by the consignee or VAT authority in the EU country

of destination. The movement of goods must be completed as soon as possible and the certificate of receipt for the goods must be issued within four months of the time of supply.

(4) The goods are not second-hand goods or works of art, etc. which the supplier has opted to tax on the profit margin. See **61.12 SECOND-HAND GOODS**.

If these conditions are met, the customer is liable for the excise duty and VAT. If duty suspended goods go missing in transit, the person who supplied the movement guarantee is liable for the duty, along with any person who may be jointly and severally liable.

Excise goods supplied for private purposes

Excise goods supplied for private purposes where the supplier arranges delivery to a customer in another EU country are covered by the special VAT arrangements for distance selling (see **19.18** below). The vendor must pay the duty in the EU country of destination at the time the goods are delivered and may therefore have to register for excise purposes with the VAT authorities in that country. In the UK, people receiving goods under distance selling arrangements, must appoint a duty representative to account for UK excise duty, before the goods are dispatched.

[*SI 1995/2518, Reg 135*]. (VAT Notice 725, para 15.4).

De Voil Indirect Tax Service. See V4.352.

Distance selling from the UK to other EU countries

[19.18] Distance selling occurs when a taxable supplier in one EU country supplies and delivers goods to a customer in another EU country who is not registered or liable to be registered for VAT. Such customers are known as 'non-taxable persons' and include not only private individuals but public bodies, charities and businesses too small to register for VAT or with activities that are entirely exempt. The most common examples of distance sales are goods supplied by mail order and goods ordered over the internet.

Distance sales by a UK business to customers in another EU country are subject to UK VAT until

- the value of supplies to any particular EU country exceeds an annual threshold set by that country for distance selling; or
- the UK business exercises the option below.

Then

- the supplier is automatically liable to register for VAT in that country;
- that country becomes the place of supply (see **65.6 SUPPLY: PLACE OF SUPPLY**); and
- VAT on any further sales is taxed in the EU country of destination of the goods.

A UK business that is required to register for VAT in another EU country must notify the tax authority in that country, allowing sufficient time to become registered by the appropriate date in accordance with the rules of that country.

Each EU country sets its own distance selling threshold and has the option of applying a threshold of €35,000 or €100,000 per calendar year (or its own currency equivalent). The latest available thresholds are as follows.

Country	
Austria	€100,000
Belgium	€35,000
Bulgaria	70,000 BGN
Cyprus	€35,000
Czech Republic	1,000,000 CKZ
Denmark	280,000 DKK
Estonia	550,000 EEK
Finland	€35,000
France	€100,000
Germany	€100,000
Greece	€35,000
Hungary	8,800,000 HUF
Ireland	€35,000
Italy	€27,889*
Latvia	24,000 LVL
Lithuania	125,000 LTL
Luxembourg	€100,000
Malta	€35,000
Netherlands	€100,000
Poland	160,000 PLN
Portugal	€35,000
Romania	118,000 RON
Slovakia	1,500,000 SKK
Slovenia	€35,000
Spain	€35,000
Sweden	320,000 SEK
UK	£70,000

* Euro equivalent of the national currency limits set before the introduction of the euro.

Goods subject to excise duty

Distance sales of excise goods to another EU country are always taxed (for excise duty and VAT purposes) in the country of destination *whatever the level of sales* and a UK supplier must register in that country.

New means of transport

See **19.32** below.

Records

A UK business must keep a separate record of its distance sales to each EU country to allow it to determine whether a liability to register for VAT in that country arises.

Tax representatives

If a UK business has to register in another EU country, it may be obliged to appoint someone to act on its behalf there and should contact the relevant VAT authority. Alternatively it may be able to register personally and deal with its VAT obligations itself.

Option to account for VAT in another EU country

A UK business may, if it wishes, opt to make the EU country of destination the place of supply of goods *before* reaching the distance selling threshold as above. If it does so, it must

- notify HMRC (by writing to the written enquiries team or phoning the National Advice Service, see **29.4 HMRC: ADMINISTRATION**) not less than 30 days before the date of the first supply to which the option relates, informing HMRC of the name of the country/countries involved;
- notify the EU country/countries involved, at least 30 days before making the first supply, of its exercise of the option, providing written evidence that it has informed the UK authorities;
- register for VAT in country/countries concerned from the date of the first supply and comply with the VAT rules there; and
- within 30 days of the first supply after the option, provide HMRC with documentary evidence that it has notified the tax authority in the other EU country/countries.

Where a business has exercised such an option, it can be withdrawn (and the place of supply moved back to the UK) by further written notice to HMRC but not earlier than

- 1 January which is, or next follows, the second anniversary of the date of the first supply following the option (i.e. until at least two full *calendar* years have elapsed); and
- 30 days after the receipt by HMRC of notification of withdrawal;

and not later than 30 days before the date of the first supply the business intends to make after the withdrawal.

[*SI 1995/2518, Reg 98*].

VAT groups

UK VAT groups are not recognised outside the UK and each individual group member must monitor the value of its own distance sales to each EU country to determine whether it is liable to register for VAT in that country in its own right. A group member can exercise the option to account for VAT on its distance sales before it reaches an EU country's threshold.

Reporting requirements

The following table summarises the reporting requirements for supplies of goods to customers in other EU countries.

Type of supply	*VAT return*	*EU sales list*
Distance sales from the UK below the distance selling threshold in the EU country of arrival of the goods	Enter the VAT due in Box 1 and the value of the supply in Box 6	No
Distance sales from the UK on or over the distance selling threshold in the EU country of arrival (or where the business has opted to register there before reaching the threshold)	Enter the value of the supply in Boxes 6 and 8	No

(VAT Notice 725, paras 6.4–6.17).

Example

Marie sells handbags to wealthy individuals through her internet site and she is VAT-registered in the UK where she lives. Her sales to Ireland are as follows:

Trading month	**Sales**
October 2011 (first month of trading)	€10,000
November 2011	€10,000
December 2011	€10,000
January 2012	€10,000
February 2012	€10,000
March 2012	€20,000

The distance selling limits are based on calendar years. Marie did not exceed the Irish limit of €35,000 in 2011 (total sales in 2009 were €30,000) so the point at which she has exceeded the limit on a calendar year basis is at the end of March 2012. She will now need to register for VAT in Ireland and charge Irish VAT (rather than UK VAT) on all future sales to non-registered customers in that country. She will then complete an Irish VAT return each quarter and pay VAT to the Irish tax authorities.

Goods lost, destroyed or stolen in transit

[19.19] Whether or not there is a liability to account for VAT on goods lost, destroyed or stolen in transit depends on the circumstances.

- **If lost, etc. before supplied** (e.g. whilst in storage awaiting delivery) no VAT is due.
- **If lost, etc. while being transported in the UK** (by either the supplier or the customer), VAT is due unless the supplier holds evidence of loss, destruction or theft (e.g. an insurance claim or police investigation).

- **If lost, etc. while being transported outside the UK** (by either the supplier or the customer), the goods may continue to be zero-rated provided the supplier has valid proof of removal of the goods from the UK and the VAT registration number of the customer. The customer may still be liable to account for acquisition tax. It should also be noted that there may be additional VAT liabilities if the loss, etc. occurs *en route* through an EU country.

(VAT Notice 725, para 3.8).

Sales at ports/airports and on ships/aircraft

[19.20] There are no VAT and duty-free sales to travellers on 'intra-EU journeys'. See, however, **33.17 IMPORTS** for transitional provisions for certain countries joining the EU from 1 May 2004 and 1 January 2007.

'*Intra-EU journeys*' are those commencing in one EU country and ending in another EU country without calling at any country or territory outside the EU. It is irrelevant whether or not the journey passes through international seas or airspace.

As a result, subject to those transitional arrangements

(a) *sales from a shop at a port or airport situated in the UK* to persons travelling on intra-EU journeys are subject to UK VAT (and duties) at rates applicable to other retail sales in the UK; and

(b) *sales on board a ship or aircraft on an intra-EU journey* are subject to VAT at the rate applicable in the EU country of departure (i.e. the first passenger point of embarkation in the EU) provided
   - the goods are to be taken away at the end of the journey (see below for 'onboard consumption'); and
   - the sales take place either on a wholly intra-EU journey or a leg of a journey from the first point of passenger embarkation of the ship or aircraft in the EU until the final point of passenger disembarkation in the EU.

Examples

(1) Goods sold on a Dover to Calais ferry are subject to UK VAT. On the return Calais-Dover leg they are subject to French VAT.

(2) Goods sold on an aircraft flying from London to Paris and then on to Rome are subject to UK VAT throughout the journey.

(3) Goods sold on a flight from London to New York are outside the scope of UK/EU VAT.

(4) A flight from London to New York makes a stop-over in Paris. If passengers disembark at Paris, the London to Paris leg is an intra-EU journey and UK VAT is due on goods sold during the leg; the Paris to New York leg is an international journey and sales of goods are outside the scope of UK/EU VAT. If passengers do not disembark at Paris, the whole flight is an international journey and sales of goods on board are outside the scope of UK/EU VAT.

(5) A flight from New York to Frankfurt makes a stop-over at London. If passengers embark at London, the London to Frankfurt leg is an intra-EU journey and any goods sold are subject to UK VAT. If there is no passenger embarkation in London, the sale of goods throughout the journey is outside the scope of UK/EU VAT.

(6) A flight from New York to Vienna makes stop-overs at London and Frankfurt with passengers embarking in London. The New York to London leg is an international journey outside the scope of UK/EU VAT. The first place of passenger embarkation in the EU is at London and therefore UK VAT is due on goods sold on board during the entire journey from London to Frankfurt to Vienna. The Frankfurt to Vienna journey is not a separate leg for VAT purposes.

As VAT is due in the EU country of departure, airline and ferry operators may be liable to register for VAT in more than one EU country.

On board consumption

Goods (e.g. foods, drink and tobacco) sold for consumption on

- ships and aircraft are free of VAT and excise duty; and
- trains are free of VAT (but not excise duty).

All sales of these commodities from an on-board bar or restaurant are treated as being for immediate consumption although sales of alcohol and tobacco are subject to certain conditions and restrictions. For example, alcohol must be sold by the glass or, in the case of wine, from opened bottles and there are set maximum quantities for tobacco products on ferries. (As smoking is not permitted in aircraft, no sales of tobacco qualify for consumption on board.)

For VAT purposes, food, confectionery and soft drinks sold anywhere on board a ship or aircraft are treated as goods consumed on board and relieved of VAT, provided it is self-evident that these products are of a type that are more suitable for on-board consumption than gift purchase or home use. Products that, by virtue of their packaging, are clearly not suitable to be treated as consumed on board (e.g. boxes of chocolates or tins of biscuits) are subject to VAT in the normal way, even if actually consumed on board the ship or the aircraft.

Cruises

HMRC accept that food, drink, tobacco and most toiletries sold on an intra-EU cruise ship are normally consumed on board. Sales of these goods continue to be relieved from VAT provided the quantities sold indicate that the passengers are unlikely to take them away at the end of the cruise. Such goods bought with the intention of taking them away at the final port of disembarkation are subject to VAT at the rate applicable in the country of departure (see (*b*) above). Where a cruise which starts and ends in the UK calls at a non-EU country (e.g. Egypt) or a place outside the EU fiscal territory (e.g. the Channel Islands) VAT-free sales to passengers for take-away are allowed provided the passengers have the opportunity to disembark and make purchases in that country or territory. See also *Köhler v Finanzamt Düsseldorf-Nord, ECJ Case C-58/04*, [2006] STC 469 (TVC 22.195) where the court held that stops made by a ship in the port of a country outside the EU during which passengers could leave the ship, even for a short period, were stops within a third territory. As a result, any sales made from a shop on board whilst the ship had stopped at that territory were not taxable in the EU but fell within the tax jurisdiction of that territory.

(VAT Information Sheet: Excise duty and VAT arrangements following the withdrawal of duty free sales of goods to intra-Community travellers; Business Brief 17/04).

Miscellaneous

[19.21] Miscellaneous matters relating to supplies of goods to other EU countries are outlined below.

(1) Arrangements for diplomatic missions, consulates, 'international organisations' and 'NATO visiting forces' in other EU countries

Under international agreements, certain people and bodies hosted by other EU countries may make purchases free of VAT. The host government determines who qualifies and it may impose limitations. If the customer has any doubts regarding these arrangements, it should contact its host VAT authority for advice.

These arrangements apply only to supplies that would otherwise be subject to UK VAT at a positive rate. They do not apply to new means of transport (which may be zero-rated but under the different rules in **19.34** below).

For these purposes:

- '*International organisation*' means an organisation established by a treaty between sovereign governments. An organisation formed by agreement between non-governmental bodies (e.g. limited companies or charities) is not an international organisation for these purposes; nor is a body set up by a single state or government (e.g. a government department). Well-known international organisations include the institutions of the European Union, the United Nations and its various subsidiary organisations, and the North Atlantic Treaty Organisation (NATO).
- '*NATO visiting force*' means an armed force contingent that belongs to a NATO Member State, is stationed in an EU country, and does not belong to the country in which it is stationed.

Zero-rating supplies of goods

A supply qualifies for zero-rating if it satisfies the following conditions:

- The supplier receives a certificate of entitlement (see below).
- The goods must be for
  (a) the 'official use' of an embassy, high commission, consulate, international organisation, NATO visiting force or British armed force contingent based in Cyprus; or
  (b) the personal use of a member of staff of one of these bodies.

'*Official use*' includes goods the body receives for distribution (including sale) to its members and their accompanying dependants.

'*Personal use*' includes distributing goods to their accompanying dependants for no reward.

- The supplier, or a forwarder acting on its behalf, must remove the goods to an official address of the embassy, etc. It may consign goods to the post or to a courier or fast parcel service, including the British Forces Post Office (BFPO). If the customer is a British embassy or high commission in another EU country, the supplier may consign goods to the Foreign and Commonwealth Office for delivery through diplomatic channels.
- The supplier must obtain and keep proof of the removal of the goods from the UK to the customer's address in the host country. Proof of posting is sufficient.
- If the supply is for a contingent of British forces in Cyprus or its staff, or for a NATO visiting force in Germany or its staff, the order must be placed by an Official Procurement Agency for the force, such as the NAAFI or a regimental purchasing officer.

Zero-rating supplies of services

A supply of services qualifies for zero rating if it satisfies the following conditions:

- The supplier receives a certificate of entitlement (see below).
- The supply of services must be made to an international organisation, a NATO visiting force, or a British force in Cyprus, for the official use of the force or organisation.
- The person placing the order must be based in an office of the force or international organisation in an EU country other than the UK.
- A supply of services to British forces must in addition satisfy the following conditions:
  - (a) The service must consist of training, software development, a supply of staff, or goods forwarding.
  - (b) For training, the trainees must all be members of a British contingent based in an EU country other than the UK, or members of British forces Cyprus.
  - (c) For software development, the software must be for the use of the force, and not for use in the UK.
  - (d) For a supply of staff, the staff must work exclusively for the force in the visiting force's host country or in a Sovereign Base Area in Cyprus.
  - (e) If the service is goods forwarding, the goods must all be forwarded to or from the force's premises in the other EU country or in a Sovereign Base Area in Cyprus.

Certificate of entitlement

The supplier must obtain and keep documentation uniquely identifying the supply and claiming entitlement under *Directive 2006/112/EC, Art 151*. This must be either

- a certificate bearing the original signature of the head or acting head of the embassy, etc. with evidence of the qualifying status of the signatory; or
- any other form of certificate specified by their host government.

Exceptionally, in the case of a supply for the British force in Cyprus or its members, or for a visiting force in Germany or its members, the supplier must obtain and keep a certificate from the person placing the order uniquely identifying the supply for which relief is claimed, and claiming entitlement

- for British forces in Cyprus – under *Directive 2006/112/EC, Art 143(i)*; or
- for a visiting force in Germany – under *Directive 2006/112/EC, Art 151*.

EU sales lists

Entries on EU sales lists are not required for these supplies.

Distance sales

In general, transactions zero-rated under these provisions are not regarded as distance sales and do not count towards distance selling thresholds. Exceptionally supplies to Germany, do count towards your distance selling threshold in that country.

(VAT Notice 725, paras 14.1–14.7, 14.9; VAT Notice 48, ESC 2.6).

(2) Freight containers

The removal of a container to another EU country can be zero-rated provided

- the supplier obtains the customer's VAT registration number (with a two digit country code prefix) and shows this on the VAT invoice;
- the container is sent from the UK to a destination in another EU country; and
- within three months of the date of supply, the supplier obtains and keeps valid commercial evidence that the container has been removed from the UK.

See **21.8 EXPORTS** for the definition of a 'container'.

Where the customer collects or arranges collection of the container and its removal from the UK, the supplier should confirm with the customer how the container is to be removed and what evidence of this will be available.

If the customer is not registered for VAT in another EU country, or all the above conditions are not met, the supply is standard-rated.

(VAT Notice 703/1/10, para 4 which has the force of law).

Leasing or hiring of containers

Where a container is leased/hired to a customer in business in another EU country, the supply is treated as made in that other country. No UK VAT is due and the customer will normally have to account for VAT there under the reverse charge procedure. If the customer is a private individual then the place of supply is where the supplier belongs, and the supplier must charge UK VAT.

Incidental charges which under the terms of the lease agreement are charged to the lessee are regarded as part of the consideration for the leasing of the container and have the same VAT liability. Included are repair, delivery, regulator and handling charges, extra rental and any charge for the option to terminate the lease at an earlier date.

(VAT Notice 703/1/10, paras 5.3, 5.5).

Temporary movements of containers

The temporary movement of a container from the UK to another EU country (whether involved in transporting goods or where the container is on lease/hire) is not treated as a removal from the UK with acquisition in the destination country. See **19.27** below. Details of the movement must be entered in a register of temporary movements. See **19.30** below. (VAT Notice 703/1/10, para 6).

(3) Samples

Movements of goods that qualify as samples are disregarded for intra-EU supply and acquisition purposes provided the conditions in **47.8**(26) **OUTPUT TAX** are met.

Reporting requirements

Where qualifying samples are sent to, or received from, another EU country, no entry is required on the VAT return or EU sales list

(VAT Notice 725, para 15.6).

(4) Goods sent for testing

Goods sent to another EU country for testing are disregarded provided

- ownership remains unchanged; and
- the goods are either returned to the country of departure or destroyed.

No entry is required on a VAT return or an EU sales list.

(VAT Notice 725, para 15.7).

(5) Goods removed to customers in other EU countries after processing or incorporation

The following provisions have the force of law.

When a business makes a supply of goods to a VAT-registered customer in another EU country but has to deliver them to a third person in the UK who is also making a taxable supply of goods or services to that customer, the business can zero-rate the supply provided

- it obtains and shows the customer's EU VAT registration number, including the two-letter country prefix code, on its VAT sales invoice;
- the goods are only being delivered and not supplied to the third person in the UK;

- no use is made of the goods other than for processing or incorporation into other goods for removal;
- it obtains and keep valid commercial evidence that the goods have been removed from the UK within the time limits in **19.11** above; and
- its records show
  - (a) the name, address and VAT number of the customer in the EU;
  - (b) the invoice number and date;
  - (c) the description, quantity and value of the goods;
  - (d) the name and address of the third person in the UK to whom the goods were delivered;
  - (e) the date by which the goods must be removed; and
  - (f) proof of removal obtained from the person responsible for transporting the goods out of the UK; and
  - (g) the date the goods were actually removed from the UK.

The records must also be able to show that the goods supplied have been processed or incorporated into the goods removed from the UK.

In cases where the third person is not in the UK but in another EU country, the same conditions generally apply to allow a business to zero-rate its supply.

(VAT Notice 725, para 4.5).

(6) Tools for the manufacture of goods for export

Machine tools are goods used in the manufacture of other goods (e.g. jigs, patterns, templates, dies, moulds, punches and similar tools). The supply of machine tools, that remain in the UK, are normally standard-rated. However, the supply of a tool can be zero-rated if

- the customer specifically asks the supplier to make it, or buy it, for him;
- the supplier uses the machine tool to manufacture goods for the same customer and makes a specific charge to him for the supply of the tool;
- the tool is an integral part of the contract, or series of contracts, to supply goods to a VAT-registered customer in another EU country and title to the tool passes to the customer;
- the supplier obtains and shows the customer's VAT registration number (with its two digit country code prefix) on the VAT sales invoice;
- the manufactured goods are sent or transported out of the UK to a destination in another EU country; and
- the supplier holds commercial documentary evidence that the goods have been removed from the UK.

(VAT Notice 701/22/02, paras 1.2–1.4, 3.1).

Triangulation

[19.22] Triangulation is the term used to describe a chain of intra-EU supplies of goods involving three parties. Instead of the goods physically passing from one party to the other as in a normal two-party transaction, they are delivered directly from the first party to the last party in the chain.

> *Example*
>
> A (the '*intermediary supplier*') receives an order from a customer (C) in another EU country. To fulfil the order, A orders the goods from another supplier (B) (the '*original supplier*') in a third EU country who delivers the goods directly to C. The original supplier B invoices the intermediate supplier A who in turn invoices the customer C.

Normal procedure

Unless the simplified procedure below is adopted, such supplies are treated for VAT purposes as follows.

- The supply by B to A involves the removal of goods from one EU country to another (even though this is not to the country where A is established). B can therefore zero-rate the supply of goods to A, subject to meeting the normal conditions in **19.11** above.
- The supply by A to C does not involve the movement of goods from the country where A belongs. As a result, A is treated as making an acquisition of the goods in the EU country to which the goods are delivered (see **19.6**(*a*) above) and an onward supply of the goods there. A should therefore register for VAT in that country and account for VAT there on its acquisition and onward supply.
- C need do nothing as it is receiving a domestic supply.

A is therefore required to register for VAT in the EU country to which the goods are delivered.

(VAT Notice 725, paras 13.1–13.4).

Simplified procedure

To avoid imposing this burden of registration on A, all EU countries have agreed to a simplified procedure. As a result, businesses registered for VAT in one EU country may no longer be required to register for VAT in another EU country purely because of such triangular transactions. Instead, based on the above example, provided A is not registered or otherwise required to be registered in the country to which the goods are sent, and C is registered there, A can opt to have C account for the VAT due in the country of destination on his behalf. If A does so opt, C *must* account for the VAT on the supply of goods made to him (i.e. the simplification procedure is compulsory if A so opts) and the acquisition of the goods by A is disregarded both in the country where he belongs and the country of destination. B still treats his transaction in the same way as any other intra-EU supply, i.e. he may zero-rate the supply subject to the usual conditions in **19.11** above and should record the supply on an EU sales list in the normal way. (VAT Notice 725, paras 13.5, 13.6).

> *Example*
>
> Jeff is VAT-registered in the UK and has received an order to supply goods to a Spanish customer. However, the Spanish customer is reselling the goods in question to a French customer, and has asked for the goods to be shipped direct to France rather than via Spain. The Spanish and French customers are both registered for VAT in their own countries.
>
> As long as Jeff obtains proof of export that the goods have left the UK, and the VAT number of his Spanish customer, he can zero-rate the supply of goods on his invoice to the Spanish customer.

UK provisions

UK provisions specifically cover the two positions where either the customer C is registered in the UK (see **19.23** below) or the intermediary supplier A is registered in the UK (see **19.24** below).

De Voil Indirect Tax Service. See V3.380.

Simplified procedure: customers registered in UK

[19.23] Where

- the original supplier B (in, say, France) makes a supply of goods to an intermediary supplier A who 'belongs in another EU country' (say Germany),
- that supply involves the removal of the goods from another EU country (Germany) and their removal to the UK but does not involve the removal of goods from the UK,
- both the supply by B, and the removal of the goods to the UK, are for the purposes of making a supply by A to a customer C who is UK VAT-registered,
- neither of those supplies involves the removal of the goods from an EU country in which A is taxable at the time of the removal without also involving the previous removal of the goods to that country, and
- there would be a taxable acquisition by C in the UK if the supply to him involved the removal of goods from another EU country to the UK,

then, provided A complies with requirements laid down by HMRC, the supply by B to A is disregarded for the purposes of *VATA 1994*, and the supply by B to C is treated, other than for the purposes of *VATA 1994, Sch 3* (registration in respect of acquisitions from another EU country), as a taxable acquisition. The taxable acquisition is treated as taking place on the date of the issue of the invoice for the transaction.

A person 'belongs in another EU country' if

- he has no business establishment or other fixed establishment in the UK and does not have his usual place of residence in the UK;
- he is neither registered nor required to be registered under *VATA 1994* (ignoring supplies disregarded under these provisions);
- he does not have, and is not for the time being required to appoint, a VAT representative; and

- he is taxable in another EU country.

[*VATA 1994, s 14(1)(3)(4)(5)*].

Notification

Where an intermediate supplier A wishes to take advantage of the simplified procedure, he must notify HMRC and the customer C in writing of his intention to do so. The notification must include

- his name and address;
- his VAT registration number (including alphabetical code, see **39.5 INVOICES**) used, or to be used, for the purposes of obtaining zero-rating of the supply to him by the original supplier B;
- the date upon which the goods were first delivered (or are intended to be delivered) to the customer; and
- the name, address and VAT registration number of the UK customer to whom the goods are supplied (and who will account for the VAT).

Notification to HMRC must be direct to The Non Established Taxable Persons Unit (NETPU), HM Revenue and Customs, Ruby House, 8 Ruby Place, Aberdeen, AB10 1ZP.

The notification must be made no later than the provision of the first invoice in relation to the supply (see below).

A separate notification must be made for each customer to whom supplies are made under these provisions but, once made in relation to the first supply to any particular customer a notification is deemed to apply to all subsequent supplies to that customer as long as the intermediary supplier A continues to belong in another EU country.

[*SI 1995/2518, Reg 11*].

Invoices

The intermediary supplier A must issue an invoice to the UK customer which must comply with the requirements of the EU country in which he is VAT-registered and, for invoices issued before 1 October 2007, which must be endorsed 'VAT: EU Article 28 Simplification invoice'. The invoice must be issued no later than 15 days after, and must relate to a supply of at least the same extent as would have been required under, the normal time of supply rules if these provisions had not applied. Such an invoice is then treated as if it were an invoice for the purposes of **19.7**(*b*) above. [*SI 1995/2518, Reg 18; SI 2007/2085, Reg 9*].

Recording and accounting for VAT. On receipt of a copy of the supplier's notification to HMRC (see above), the UK customer C must account for the VAT on the goods supplied to him under the simplified procedure as an acquisition. See **19.8** above.

(VAT Notice 725, paras 13.9–13.11).

Simplified procedure: intermediate suppliers registered in UK

[19.24] If the simplified procedure is used in a triangular transaction where the intermediate supplier A in the example above is registered in the UK and the goods are removed to another EU country of destination, the supply of those goods by the original supplier B to A and the supply of those goods by A to the customer C are both disregarded for the purposes of *VATA 1994* but without prejudice to the power of HMRC to require production of records and accounts and furnishing of information. [*VATA 1994, s 14(6)*]. In order to use the simplified procedure, the intermediate supplier A must

- use his UK VAT registration number to allow the original supplier B to zero-rate the supply of the goods in the EU country from which the goods were dispatched;
- issue his customer C with a VAT invoice which must contain all the details normally required for intra-EU supplies (see **39.5 INVOICES**) and, for invoices issued before 1 October 2007, be endorsed 'VAT: EU Article 28 Simplification invoice'. [*SI 1995/2518, Reg 17; SI 2007/2085, Reg 8*];
- not enter details of triangular transactions on his VAT return; and
- on his EU sales lists
  - (a) include the supply, quoting the VAT number of the customer C in the country of destination of the goods;
  - (b) enter the total value of the triangular transactions to each EU customer on a single line separately from the total of other intra-EU supplies to that customer; and
  - (c) identify triangular transactions by inserting the figure '2' in the indicator box.

If an intermediate supplier's intra-EU supplies only involve triangular transactions, he should contact the National Advice Service who will arrange for EU sales lists to be sent to him automatically.

(VAT Notice 725, paras 13.7, 13.8).

Transfer of own goods to another EU country

[19.25] Subject to the exceptions below, and unless specifically overridden by other provisions, the transfer of goods within the same legal entity from one EU country to another (e.g. between branches of the same company) is deemed to be a supply of goods for VAT purposes under the general provisions of *VATA 1994, Sch 4 para 6* (see **19.2** above) and is liable to VAT under the normal arrangements for intra-EU supplies. (Specifically excluded is the removal of gas through a natural gas system situated within the territory of an EU country or any network connected to such a system; electricity; or heat or cooling supplied through a network [*SI 2010/2925*]. Prior to 1 January 2011, the exclusion applied to the removal of gas through the natural gas distribution network or electricity [*SI 2004/3150*].)

As a result, where a UK business transfers its own goods from the UK to another EU country in the course of its business (e.g. to sell them on from that country or to use them there), it must register for VAT in that country in order to

- support zero-rating of the deemed supply when the goods leave the UK (subject to the conditions in **19.11** above); and
- account for acquisition VAT in that country and account for output VAT if there is a subsequent supply of the goods there.

If the UK business does not register in the EU country to which its own goods are transferred, the deemed supply must be treated as a domestic supply. It must account for VAT in the UK on the goods (and cannot recover this as input tax in the other EU country). In *Cudworth* (TC01173) (TVC 23.22), C was a clothing retailer. He sometimes travelled to Germany, where he made sales from trade stands at agricultural shows. He was VAT registered in the UK but not in Germany. The tribunal held that when C travelled with his goods to Germany, there was a deemed supply on the removal of the goods from the UK. He should have accounted for VAT on the cost price when he removed the goods from the UK, not on the sale price when he sold them to German customers.

Similarly, where a business transfers its own goods from another EU country to the UK in the course of its business, if not already registered here it may need to do so in order to account for VAT on the acquisition of the goods in the UK. But see **19.5** above for VAT relief on certain transfers.

Exceptions

The rules relating to transfers of own goods do not apply to

- temporary movements of goods within **19.27** below;
- movements of goods for processing and repair, etc. under **19.28** below; and
- installed and assembled goods under **19.30** below.

Reporting requirements

The following table summarises the reporting requirements for transfers of own goods to other EU countries.

Type of supply	*VAT return*	*EU sales list*
Transfers of own goods from the UK to other EU countries	Enter the value of the goods based on cost in Boxes 6 and 8	Enter value based on cost of the goods
Transfers of own goods from another EU country to the UK	Enter acquisition VAT (for positive-rated goods) in Box 2 and input tax (subject to the normal rules) in Box 4. Enter the value of the goods based on cost in Boxes 7 and 9	No

(VAT Notice 725, paras 9.1–9.9).

Consignment stock

Consignment stocks are goods that a business transfers between EU countries in order to meet future supplies to be made by the business, or on its behalf, in the country of arrival. The important feature is that the movement of the goods occurs *before* a customer has been found for them. It can include goods not meeting the all conditions necessary for treatment as call-off stocks (see **19.32** below).

Consignment stocks are treated as a transfer of own goods for VAT accounting and reporting purposes.

(VAT Notice 725, para 15.3).

Goods sent on sale or return, approval or similar terms

[19.26] Goods sent on sale or return, approval or similar terms are not supplied until

- the customer indicates that he is going to keep them; or
- a time when it is agreed between the parties that the goods are to be automatically treated as accepted (if earlier).

Consequently, when such goods are sent to another EU country, they should be treated as a transfer of own goods.

(a) When a UK business sends goods on such terms to a customer in another EU country
  - it initially makes an acquisition of the goods in that country; and
  - it makes a supply of the goods there if, and when, the goods are eventually adopted by the customer.

  The business may need to register there to account for any VAT due on the acquisition and supply of the goods.

(b) When a business in another EU country sends goods on such terms to a UK customer
  - it initially makes an acquisition of the goods in the UK;
  - it makes a supply of goods in the UK on the earlier of
    (i) the date when the goods are eventually adopted by the customer;
    (ii) twelve months after their time of removal to the UK; or
    (iii) the time of issue a VAT invoice in respect of the goods

    under the normal UK rules for sale or return goods in the UK (see **66.12 SUPPLY: TIME OF SUPPLY**).

  The business will be liable to register for VAT in the UK to account for any VAT due on the acquisition and supply of the goods.

Reporting requirements

The following table summarises the UK reporting requirements for goods sold on sale or return, approval or similar terms.

Type of supply	*VAT return*	*EU sales list*
Goods sent from UK to another EU country	Enter the value based on the cost of the goods in Boxes 6 and 8	Enter value based on cost of the goods
Goods sent to the UK from another EU country	Enter acquisition VAT (for positive-rated goods) in Box 2 and input tax (subject to the normal rules) in Box 4. Enter the value based on the cost of the goods in Boxes 7 and 9	No

(VAT Notice 725, para 15.5).

Temporary movements of goods

[19.27] The following temporary movements of own goods between EU countries are not treated as deemed supplies of goods for VAT purposes under **19.25**. No acquisition VAT is due in the country to which the goods are transferred.

Where

(i) the owner is established in the EU country of dispatch but not that of arrival;
(ii) the goods are removed for the sole purpose of being used by the owner in the course of a supply of services to be made by him;
(iii) at the time of their removal, there is a legally binding obligation to make that supply of services (i.e. a specific contract to fulfil); and
(iv) the owner intends to remove the goods back to the EU country of dispatch upon ceasing to use them in making the supply (and does in fact do so).

This could apply, for example, to tools and equipment taken to another EU country for use there to repair machinery. It also applies to goods that are loaned or leased to someone there.

The removal back to the EU country of dispatch under (iv) is also not treated as a supply for VAT purposes.

Where goods are removed to another EU country for temporary use there and

(i) temporary importation relief would have been given if the goods had been imported from outside the EU; and
(ii) the owner intends to export the goods outside the EU or remove them to an EU country other than the country to which the goods have been removed, in either case not later than two years after the day upon which the goods were removed (and he does in fact do so).

See **33.26 IMPORTS** for goods eligible for temporary import relief.

The export or removal under (ii) is also not treated as a supply for VAT purposes.

If the circumstances of the transfer outlined above change and the movement no longer qualifies for treatment under these temporary movement provisions (e.g. the goods are sold or are to remain in the other EU country for more than two years), the original movement should be treated, belatedly, as a deemed supply and acquisition under **19.25** above. The owner must account for VAT in the VAT period in which the condition is not complied with.

[*SI 1992/3111, Arts 4(f)(g)(h), 5; SI 1995/2518, Reg 42*]. (VAT Notice 725, paras 10.1–10.6).

Although the above transfers are not treated as supplies for VAT purposes, commercial documentary evidence should be held to prove that the goods have left the UK and have later returned. (VAT Notice 725, para 10.7).

Register of temporary movements of goods

See **19.30** below for the requirement to keep such a register.

Reporting requirements

No entries are required on the VAT return or EU sales list when goods are sent from the UK and the conditions above are satisfied.

(VAT Notice 725, para 10.8).

Goods sent for processing, valuation, etc.

[19.28] A supply of goods is not treated as taking place when goods are removed from one EU country to another in the following circumstances.

Where

(i) the owner is registered in the EU country of dispatch but is not registered in the EU country of arrival,

(ii) the goods have been removed for the purpose of delivering them to a person (other than the owner) who is to produce goods by applying a treatment or process to the goods removed; and

(iii) the owner intends that the goods produced will be returned to him by their removal back to the country of dispatch upon completion of the treatment or process.

It is a condition for the dispatch of the goods not to be treated as a supply of goods that the intention of the owner under (iii) above is fulfilled. Where it is not, the original movement of goods must be belatedly treated as a deemed intra-EU supply and acquisition and the owner must account for VAT in the VAT period in which the condition is not complied with.

Where

(i) the goods have been removed for the purpose of delivering them to a person (other than the owner) who is to value or to carry out any work on the goods; and

(ii) the supply made by the person to whom the goods have been delivered is (or will be) a supply of services treated as having been made in the country of arrival.

The return of the goods to the original EU country is also not treated as a supply of goods.

[*SI 1992/3111, Art 4(d)(e)(h)(i), Art 5; SI 1995/2518, Reg 42*].

See **19.30** below for the requirement to keep a register of movement of the goods.

Accounting for VAT on the movements of goods for process, valuation, repair, etc.

[19.29] Special place of supply rules apply to the *services* of work carried out on goods and the valuation of goods where the goods are moved between EU countries. See **65.20 SUPPLY: PLACE OF SUPPLY** for full details.

The VAT treatment of goods that are moved between EU countries in circumstances where some form of service (e.g. processing, repair and valuation) is to be applied to those goods is as follows.

(1) Goods sent from the UK for work to be carried out in another EU country

Provided the conditions in **19.28** above are satisfied, there is no deemed supply of own goods when a UK business sends goods from the UK for work to be carried out in another EU country. The UK owner must

- record the movement of the goods in his register of temporary movements of goods (see **19.30** below);
- hold commercial documentary evidence that the goods have been removed from the UK; and
- account for VAT on each of the supplies of services he has received as a reverse charge.

The movement of goods is not required to be shown on EU sales lists.

Where the conditions are not met (e.g. the goods are not returned to the UK), the normal rules for transfer of own goods to another EU country in **19.25** apply. The UK owner may be liable to register for VAT in the other EU country.

(2) Goods sent to the UK for work to be carried out

Provided the conditions in **19.28** above are satisfied, no entry is required on the VAT return of the UK supplier of services in relation to the goods either when they are received in the UK from the EU customer or subsequently returned to him. But he must

- record the movement of the goods in his register of temporary movements of goods (see **19.30** below); and
- hold commercial documentary evidence that the goods have been removed from the UK.

The movement of goods is not required to be shown on EU sales lists.

Where the conditions are not met (e.g. the goods are not returned to abroad), the normal rules for transfer of own goods to another EU country in **19.30** apply. The owner may be liable to register for VAT in the UK.

(3) Work performed on goods in another EU country before removal to the UK

A UK business may buy goods in another EU country and have work performed on them before they are removed to the UK. In these circumstances, the provisions in **19.28** above do not apply (because the goods are not physically sent to another EU country for processing as they are already there). The UK customer must

- account for acquisition VAT on the supply of the goods in the normal way; and
- account for VAT on the supplies of the services of work performed on the goods under the reverse charge procedure.

(4) Work performed on goods in the UK before removal to another EU country

A customer in another EU country may buy goods from a UK business but have work performed on the goods by another UK business before removing the goods from the UK. The UK business can still zero-rate the supply under **19.11** above provided it meets all the relevant conditions. In particular, it must ensure that the customer provides evidence of removal of the goods from the UK once the work has been completed.

(VAT Notice 725, paras 12.1–12.7).

Register of temporary movement of goods

[19.30] Every taxable person must keep and maintain a register of goods moved to, and goods received from, other EU countries on a temporary basis. The register need not be kept in any particular format but it must be readily available for all goods temporarily moved to and from the UK.

The register *must* include the following information for all goods moved between the UK and other EU countries if they are to be returned within a period of two years after their first removal or receipt. (It would be advisable also to include any goods where the date of return is not certain.)

- The date of removal of goods to another EU country and the date of receipt of those goods when they are returned from that or another EU country.
- The date of receipt of goods from another EU country and the date of removal of those goods when they are returned to that or another EU country.
- A description of the goods sufficient to identify them.
- A description of any process, work or other operation carried out on the goods either in the UK or in another EU country.
- The consideration for the supply of the goods.
- The consideration for the supply of any processing, work or other operation carried out on the goods either in the UK or another EU country.

[*SI 1995/2518, Reg 33*]. (VAT Notice 725, paras 16.7–16.9).

De Voil Indirect Tax Service. See V5.212.

Installed and assembled goods

[19.31] A supply of installed or assembled goods occurs where the supplier of the goods has a contractual obligation to install or assemble them (e.g. a supplier of studio recording equipment could have a contractual obligation to supply the equipment and install it in the customer's studio). (VAT Notice 725, para 11.1).

General rule

Where the supply of goods involves their installation or assembly, they are treated as supplied in the country where they are installed or assembled. [*VATA 1994, s 7(3)*].

Reporting requirements

Unless the simplification procedure below is applied, the reporting requirements for installed or assembled goods are as follows.

- Where a UK business supplies goods which it is to install or assemble in another EU country, its supply takes place in that country and it is liable for any VAT there. The business may need to register there in order to account for the VAT due. For UK VAT purposes, the value of the supply should be included in Box 6 on the VAT return and the value based on the cost of the goods at the time of dispatch should be entered in Box 8. No entries are required on an EU sales list.
- Where a business supplies goods from outside the UK to be installed or assembled here (the goods may be sourced from another EU country or from a third country), the supply is liable to UK VAT and the business may have to register for VAT in the UK. If the business registers, it must include output tax in Box 1 of its VAT return and the value of the supply in Box 6. No entries are required on an EU sales list.

(VAT Notice 725, paras 11.6, 11.11).

Simplification procedure

To avoid imposing the burden of registration in another EU country on the supplier of installed or assembled goods, *some* EU countries have adopted a simplified procedure under which the supplier can opt to have his customer account for the VAT due in the country of installation or assembly. Where the simplification procedure is available, it can be used provided

- the customer is registered for VAT in the EU country of installation or assembly;
- the supplier is not required to be registered in that country for any other reason;
- the supplier is registered for VAT in another EU country; and

- the necessary procedures required by the VAT authorities in the country of installation or assembly are complied with.

If the supplier so opts, the customer *must* account for the VAT (i.e. the simplification procedure is compulsory if the supplier opts).

The operation of this simplified procedure is a matter for each EU country. A business should contact the VAT authority in the EU country where it is proposing to make a supply to find out if they are operating a simplified procedure. In the absence of simplification arrangements, the general rules above apply.

Installation or assembly in the UK

The UK has adopted the simplification procedure. Under those provisions, where

(a) a 'person belonging in another EU country' makes a supply of goods to a UK VAT-registered person and the supply involves their installation or assembly at a place in the UK to which they are removed; and
(b) there would be a taxable acquisition by the UK-registered person if, instead of treating that supply as a taxable supply in the UK (under the general rule above), it was treated as involving the removal of the goods from another EU country to the UK,

then, provided the supplier complies with the requirements laid down by HMRC, the supply is treated, other than for the purposes of *VATA 1994, Sch 3* (registration in respect of acquisitions from another EU country), as a taxable acquisition. The taxable acquisition is treated as taking place on the date of the issue of the invoice for the transaction.

For these purposes, a person is treated as '*belonging in another EU country*' if

- he has no business establishment or other fixed establishment in the UK and does not have his usual place of residence in the UK;
- he is neither registered nor required to be registered under *VATA 1994* (ignoring supplies disregarded under these provisions);
- he does not have, and is not for the time being required to appoint, a VAT representative; and
- he is taxable in another EU country.

[*VATA 1994, s 14(2)–(5)*].

Notification

If the EU supplier wishes to take advantage of the simplification provisions and avoid registering for VAT in the UK, he must notify HMRC of his intention to do so. The notification must include

- his name and address,
- his VAT registration number (including alphabetical code, see **39.5 INVOICES**) by which he is identified for VAT in the EU country in which he belongs,
- the date upon which the installation or assembly of the goods began or will begin, and

- the name, address and VAT registration number of the UK VAT-registered customer

and be sent in writing to The Non-Established Taxable Persons Unit (NETPU), HM Revenue and Customs, Ruby House, 8 Ruby Place, Aberdeen, AB10 1ZP.

The notification must be made no later than the provision of the first invoice in relation to the supply (see below). A separate notification must be made for each customer to whom it is intended to make supplies under the simplification procedure but, once made in relation to the first supply to any registered person, is deemed to apply to all subsequent supplies to that registered person as long as the person making the supply continues to belong in another EU country.

A copy of the notification must be sent to the UK customer to advise him that the simplified arrangements are to be applied and that he will be required to account for the VAT. The copy must be sent no later than the date of issue the first invoice.
[*SI 1995/2518, Reg 12*]. (VAT Notice 725, para 11.8).

Invoices

The EU supplier must issue an invoice to the UK VAT-registered customer which must comply with the requirements of that EU country and, for invoices issued before 1 October 2007, be endorsed 'Section 14(2) VATA invoice'. The invoice must

- be issued no later than 15 days after what would have been the normal time of supply in the UK, and
- relate to a supply of at least the same extent as would have been required under the normal time of supply rules

if these provisions had not applied. The invoice is then treated as if it were an invoice for the purposes of **19.7**(*b*) above. [*SI 1995/2518, Reg 19; SI 2007/2085, Reg 10*].

Reporting requirements

The UK customer must account for VAT on the acquisition. The acquisition VAT should be included in Box 2 of the VAT return. (VAT is not due on goods which are zero-rated in the UK.) The VAT can also be included in Box 4 as input tax on the same return (subject to the normal rules). The value of the must be included in Boxes 7 and 9.

No entry is required on an EU sales list.

(VAT Notice 725, para 11.11).

De Voil Indirect Tax Service. See V3.381.

'Call-off' stocks

[19.32] Call-off stocks are goods transferred by the supplier between EU countries to be held for an individual customer in the country of arrival pending 'call-off' for use by the customer as needed. Until call-off, title and ownership of the goods remains with the supplier. To be treated as call-off stock, the goods must be transferred for a single identified customer either

- for consumption within its business (e.g. as part of a manufacturing process); or
- to make onward supplies to their own customers.

Goods that are transferred to maintain the suppliers own stocks in another EU country, or are available for call-off by more than one customer, must be dealt with as consignment stocks (see **19.25** above).

The goods should normally be stored by the supplier at the customer's premises. But goods delivered to storage facilities operated by the supplier can still be treated as call-off goods provided the above conditions are met and the customer is aware of the details of deliveries into storage. If not, the goods should be treated as consignment stocks (see **19.25** above).

The VAT treatment of call-off stock is as follows.

(a) If a UK business sends goods to another EU country to be held as call-off stock, the normal intra-EU rules apply. The supply is treated as taking place in the UK and can be zero-rated when sent from the UK subject to the normal requirements in **19.11** above.

(b) If a UK business receives call-off stocks in the UK from a supplier in another EU country, the normal intra-EU rules apply and it should account for acquisition VAT in the normal way.

Reporting requirements

The following table summarises the UK reporting requirements for call-off stocks.

Type of supply	*VAT return*	*EU sales list*
Goods supplied to VAT-registered customers in other EU countries	Enter the value based on the cost of the goods in Boxes 6 and 8	Enter value based on cost of the goods
Goods received in the UK from VAT-registered suppliers in other EC	Enter acquisition VAT (for positive-rated goods) in Box 2 and input tax (subject to the normal rules) in Box 4. Enter the value based on the cost of goods in Boxes 7 and 9	No

(VAT Notice 725, para 15.2).

New means of transport

[19.33] The following are regarded as new means of transport (NMT) for the purposes of **19.34–19.38** below, provided that, in each case, it is intended for the transport of persons or goods.

(a) Any ship, including a hovercraft, exceeding 7.5 metres in length (overall) provided that three months or less have elapsed since its first entry into service or, since that time, it has travelled under its own power for 100 hours or less. A ship is treated as having first entered into service
- when it is delivered from its manufacturer to its first purchaser or owner or is first made available to that person (whichever is the earlier); or
- if applicable, when its manufacturer first takes it into use for demonstration purposes.

(b) Any aircraft, the take-off weight of which exceeds 1,550 kilograms, provided that three months or less have elapsed since its first entry into service or, since that time, it has travelled under its own power for 40 hours or less. An aircraft is treated as having first entered into service
- when it is delivered from its manufacturer to its first purchaser or owner or is first made available to that person (whichever is the earlier); or
- if applicable, when its manufacturer first takes it into use for demonstration purposes.

(c) Any motorised land vehicle which
- has an engine with a displacement or a cylinder capacity exceeding 48 cc; or
- is constructed or adapted to be electrically propelled using more than 7.2 kilowatts

provided that six months or less have elapsed since its first entry into service or, since that time, it has travelled under its own power for 6,000 kilometres or less. A motorised land vehicle is treated as having first entered into service

(i) on its first registration for road use in the EU country of its manufacturer or when a liability to register for road use is first incurred there (whichever is the earlier); or

(ii) where (i) does not apply, its removal by its first purchaser or owner, its first delivery or its being made available to its first purchaser (whichever is the earlier); or

(iii) if applicable, when its manufacturer first takes it into use for demonstration purposes.

Where the time of first entry into use under (*a*)–(*c*) above cannot be established to the satisfaction of HMRC, a means of transport is to be treated as having first entered into service on the issue of an invoice relating to its first supply.

[*VATA 1994, s 95; SI 1994/3128; SI 1995/2518, Reg 147*].

De Voil Indirect Tax Service. See V1.294.

Supplies by persons registered in the UK to non-registered persons in other EU countries

[19.34] A non-registered person who buys an NMT in the UK to take to another EU country must pay any taxes due on it in the EU country of destination under the laws of that country. To avoid double taxation, a UK-registered supplier can zero-rate the supply of an NMT to such a person provided the following conditions are met (which have the force of law).

(a) The means of transport qualifies as 'new' under **19.33** above.
(b) The purchaser (or his authorised chauffeur, pilot or skipper) personally takes delivery of the NMT and removes it from the UK to the EU country of destination within two months of the date of supply.
(c) The supplier and the customer make a joint declaration on Form VAT 411.

Form VAT 411 is a declaration by the customer that he will take the NMT to another EU country within two months and pay the VAT there. It is also a declaration by the supplier that he has supplied an NMT to the customer for removal from the UK.

Copies of Form VAT 411 are obtainable from the VAT Helpline (tel: 0845 010 9000). It comprises an original (or top sheet) and three copies. When the form has been fully completed, the supplier must send the original to

HM Revenue and Customs

Central Processing Unit

Postal Depot

Charlton Green

Dover

Kent CT16 1EH

within six weeks of the end of the calendar quarter in which the supply is made.

The first copy of Form VAT 411 should be given to the customer. The second copy is retained by the supplier and, where the NMT is a vehicle, the third copy is used to register it for road use if it is to be driven out of the UK (see below).

Sales subject to a finance agreement

Where a non-registered person funds the purchase of the NMT using a hire purchase or similar agreement, the dealer makes a standard-rated supply to the finance house and the finance house makes a zero-rated supply of the NMT to the non-registered person. The dealer should ensure that the VAT 411 clearly shows that it is the finance house supplying the vehicle and must send the second copy of the Form VAT 411 to the finance house to support the zero-rating of the supply. The other copies of the form should be distributed in the normal manner.

Using a new vehicle on UK roads

Any new vehicle cannot be used on UK roads before its removal to another EU country unless it is licensed, registered and properly insured against third party liability. If the vehicle is not already licensed at the time of purchase, the supplier will obtain the registration number (a special 'VAT-free' series which allows the vehicle to be identified as tax free whilst it remains in the UK prior to removal) by presenting the third copy of the completed Form VAT 411, attached to the application for registration, to one of the following DVLA local offices.

Scotland	
Aberdeen	Greyfriars House, Gallowgate, Aberdeen AB10 1WG Tel: 01224 648216
Dundee	Caledonian House, Greenmarket, Dundee DD1 4QP Tel: 01382 225765
Edinburgh	Department of Transport, Saughton House, Broomhouse Drive, Edinburgh EH11 3XE Tel: 0130 455 7919
Glasgow	46 West Campbell Street, Glasgow, G2 6TT Tel: 0141 226 4161
Inverness	Longman House, 28 Longman Road, Inverness IV1 1SF Tel: 01463 239321/2
North England	
Beverley	Crosskill House, Mill Lane, Beverley HU17 9JB Tel: 01482 887884
Carlisle	Ground Floor, 3 Merchants Drive, Parkhouse CA3 0JW Tel: 01228 539401/2
Chester	Norroy House, Nuns Road, Chester CH1 2ND Tel: 01244 348195
Leeds	Ist Floor, 42 Eastgate, Leeds LS2 7DQ Tel: 0113 244 3035
Manchester	Trafford House, Chester Road, Manchester M32 0SL Tel: 0870 241 2146
Newcastle upon Tyne	Eagle Star House, Regent Farm Road, Newcastle upon Tyne NE3 3QF Tel: 0191 284 1026
Preston	Buckingham House, Glovers Court, Preston PR1 4DQ Tel: 01772 823911
Sheffield	Bank House, 100 Queen Street, Sheffield S1 1JX Tel: 0114 272 236
Stockton	St Marks House, St Marks Court, Thornaby, Stockton on Tees TS17 6QR Tel: 01642 796600
Midlands	
Birmingham	2nd Floor, Edward House, Edward Street, Birmingham B1 2RF Tel: 0121 212 0155

Northampton	Wootton Hall Park, Northampton NN4 0GA Tel: 01604 762131
Nottingham	Block 6, Government Buildings, Chalfont Drive, Nottingham NG8 3RA Tel: 0115 929 9924
Shrewsbury	Whitehall, Monkmoor Road, Shrewsbury SY2 5DR Tel: 01743 366422/350511
Worcester	Clerkenleap Barn, Broomhall, Kempsey WR5 3HR Tel: 01905 821720
Eastern England	
Chelmsford	2nd Floor, Parkway House, 49 Baddow Road, Chelmsford CM2 0XJ Tel: 0870 241 2147
Ipswich	Podium Level, St Clare House, Greyfriars, Ipswich IP1 1UT Tel: 01473 258451
Lincoln	Firth House, Firth Court, Lincoln LN5 7WD Tel: 01522 543681
Luton	2 Dunstable Road, Luton LU1 1EB Tel: 01582 412143
Norwich	11 Prince of Wales Road, Norwich NR1 1UP Tel: 01603 616411
Peterborough	88 Lincoln Road, Peterborough PE1 2ST Tel: 01733 551671
London and Southern England	
Bournemouth	Tregonwell Court, 118 Commercial Road, Bournemouth BH2 5LN Tel: 01202 5585531
Brighton	4th Floor, Mocatta House, Trafalgar Place, Brighton BN1 4UE Tel: 01273 692271
Maidstone	Coronet House, 11 Queen Anne Road, Maidstone ME14 1XB Tel: 01622 675432
Oxford	Ground Floor, 3 Cambridge Terrace, Oxford, OX1 1RW Tel: 01865 724056
Portsmouth	5th Floor, Baltic House, Kensington Crescent, North End, Portsmouth PO2 8AH Tel: 02392 639421
Reading	77–81 Basingstoke Road, Reading RG2 0ER Tel: 0870 241 5161
Sidcup	12–18 Station Road, Sidcup DA15 7EQ Tel: 020 8302 2134
Stanmore	Government Buildings, Canon Park, Honeypot Lane, Stanmore HA7 1BD Tel: 0870 241 1269
Wimbledon	Ground Floor, Connect House, 133–137 Alexandra Road, Wimbledon SW19 7JY Tel: 0870 600 6767

West of England

Bristol	Northleigh House, Lime Kiln Close, Stoke Gifford, Bristol BS34 8SR Tel: 0117 969 2211
Exeter	Hanover House, Manaton Close, Matford Business Park, Marsh Barton Trading Estate, Exeter EX2 8EF Tel: 01392 824330
Truro	Pydar House, Pydar Street, Truro TR1 2TG Tel: 01872 278635

Wales

Bangor	Penrhos Road, Penrhosgarnedd, Bangor LL57 2JF Tel: 01248 351822
Cardiff	Archway House, 77 Ty Glas Avenue, Llanishen CF14 5DX Tel: 0292 075 3355
Swansea	Hoel Pentrefelin, Swansea SA6 7HG Tel: 01792 783900

Northern Ireland

Coleraine	Vehicle Licensing Central Office, County Hall, Castlerock Road, Coleraine, Co. Londonderry BT51 3HS Tel: 01265 44133

Failure to remove the NMT from the UK within the time allowed

If, in exceptional circumstances, the customer is unable to remove the NMT from the UK, he must inform HMRC immediately in writing at HM Revenue and Customs, Personal Transport Unit, PO Box 242, Dover, Kent CT17 9GP. HMRC will then calculate the VAT due and issue a demand for immediate payment. If the NMT is not removed from the UK within the time allowed and HMRC have not been informed, the vehicle may be liable to forfeiture.

Type approval

'*Type approval*' is the official recognition that the vehicle has satisfied certain international safety standards. A vehicle cannot be licensed and registered in the UK unless it is type approved or otherwise exempt. For type approval purposes a motor vehicle is

- a passenger vehicle with four or more wheels, or three wheels if it has a maximum gross weight of more than 1,000 kilograms, intended to carry no more than eight passengers, excluding the driver; or
- a three-wheeled passenger vehicle with a maximum gross weight of under 1,000 kilograms, if it has either a maximum speed of more than 50 kilometres per hour or an engine capacity of more than 50 cubic centimetres; or
- a goods vehicle.

Further information on type approval can be found from The Vehicle Certification Agency, 1 The Eastgate Office Centre, Eastgate Road, Bristol BS5 6XX (Tel: 01272 524125).

NMT vehicles supplied in the UK are exempted from UK-type approval requirements for as long as they are relieved from VAT whilst awaiting removal from the UK. If the vehicle is not removed, and as a consequence becomes liable to UK VAT, the exemption from type approval is withdrawn. The absence of type approval may affect the customer's ability to register the vehicle in the UK for permanent use on UK roads.

[*SI 1995/2518, Regs 22C, 155; SI 2009/3241, Reg 6*]. (VAT Notice 728, paras 6.1–6.7, 8.8, 8.11, 8.12, 9.2, 9.5, 9.7, 9.9, 9.10, 10).

De Voil Indirect Tax Service. See V4.356, V5.272.

Supplies by persons registered in the UK to persons registered in other EU countries

[19.35] A supplier who is registered for VAT in the UK should zero-rate the supply of an NMT to a VAT-registered person from another EU country provided

(a) the means of transport qualifies as 'new' under **19.33** above;
(b) the customer's VAT registration number (with two digit code prefix) is shown on the invoice;
(c) the NMT is dispatched or transported from the UK to another EU country within two months of the date of issue of the invoice for the supply; and
(d) the supplier holds valid commercial documentary evidence that the NMT has been removed from the UK (see **19.13** above).

The customer must account for any VAT due on the acquisition in the EU country of destination under the laws of that country.

Using a new vehicle on UK roads

If any new unregistered vehicle is to be used in the UK before its removal to another EU country, it must be licensed, registered and insured against third-party liabilities before delivery. The supplier and the customer must complete and sign a declaration on Form VAT 411A obtainable from the National Advice Service (tel: 0845 010 9000). This form must be sent or produced to one of the DVLA local offices listed in **19.34** above who will allocate a registration mark in the tax-free series.

If the customer's plans change and he decides to keep the vehicle in the UK permanently, he cannot retain the tax-free registration mark and should contact HMRC at HM Revenue and Customs, Personal Transport Unit, PO Box 242, Dover, Kent CT17 9GP.

Failure to remove the NMT from the UK within the time allowed

If the customer does not remove the NMT from the UK in the time allowed, he will be liable to pay UK VAT.

Type approval

See **19.34** above.

EU sales lists

An entry is required in any EU sales list. See **2.11** *et seq* **ACCOUNTING PERIODS AND RETURNS.**

(VAT Notice 728, paras 8.8. 8.10, 8.14, 9.3–9.5).

Supplies by non-registered persons: recovery of VAT

[19.36] Where a non-taxable person supplies an NMT which involves its removal to another EU country, HMRC must, on a claim, refund to him the VAT which he paid on the supply to him (or acquisition or importation by him, as the case may be) but not exceeding the amount of VAT which would have been payable on the supply by him involving removal if it had been a taxable supply by a taxable person and had not been zero-rated. [*VATA 1994, s 40*].

The claim must be in writing and be made no earlier than one month, and no later than 14 days, before the making of the supply by virtue of which the claim arises. It must include a signed declaration that all the information entered in, or accompanying it, is true and complete and must be sent to HM Revenue and Customs, Personal Transport Unit, PO Box 242, Dover, Kent CT17 9GP. It must contain the following information. (A form for the purpose is reproduced in VAT Notice 728, section 11.)

- The name, current address and telephone number of the claimant.
- The place where the NMT is kept and the times when it may be inspected. (HMRC may need to inspect the NMT before it is sold to confirm its eligibility for refund.)
- The name and address of the person who supplied the NMT to the claimant.
- The price paid by the claimant for the supply of the NMT to him, excluding VAT.
- The amount of any VAT on that supply.
- The amount of any VAT paid by the claimant on the acquisition or importation of the NMT by him.
- The name and address of the proposed purchaser, the EU country to which the NMT is to be removed and the date of the proposed purchase.
- The price to be paid by the proposed purchaser.
- A full description of the NMT (make, model, colour, registration number, engine number and chassis/hull/airframe number) including, in the case of a motorised land vehicle, its mileage since first entry into service and, in the case of a ship or aircraft, its hours of use since that time. See **19.33** above for the time of first entry into service.
- Details (as the case may be) of
  - (i) the ship's length in metres
  - (ii) the aircraft's take-off weight in kilograms; or
  - (iii) the motorised land vehicle's displacement or cylinder capacity in cubic centimetres (if powered by a combustion engine) or maximum power output in kilowatts (if an electrically propelled vehicle).
- The amount of the refund being claimed.

HMRC will advise the claimant if they wish to examine the NMT before it is sold to confirm its eligibility for refund.

Before any refund is received, HMRC will also need to see

- proof of original purchase (normally the invoice or import entry);
- evidence that the VAT has been paid on the original purchase;
- proof of sale (normally the bill of sale and evidence that payment has been received); and
- evidence that the NMT has been removed to another EU country.

[*SI 1995/2518, Regs 146, 149–154*]. (VAT Notice 728, paras 7.1–7.5).

Acquisitions by non-registered persons in the UK from other EU countries

[19.37] An acquisition of an NMT is taxed in the EU country of destination. In order to avoid the need to register persons making such acquisitions in the UK who would not otherwise be liable to be registered, HMRC are empowered to introduce a special mechanism to collect the VAT due. [*VATA 1994, Sch 11 para 2(4)(5)*].

Under these powers, where a non-taxable person makes a taxable acquisition of an NMT in the UK, he must notify HMRC within seven days of its acquisition or its arrival in the UK, whichever is the later.

The notification should be in writing in English on Form VAT 415 which is available from the National Advice Service (tel: 0845 010 9000) and DVLA local offices or it can be downloaded from HMRC website at:

www.hmrc.gov.uk

The completed form should be sent by post to HM Revenue and Customs, Personal Transport Unit, PO Box 242, Dover, Kent CT17 9GP or can be handed to the DVLA local office when the vehicle is licensed and registered. See **19.34** above for a list of DVLA local offices. (Note that the Personal Transport Unit only accepts postal notifications and has no public enquiry counters and if the notification is made via a DVLA local office, it will send the necessary documents to HMRC.)

HMRC will also need to see the final purchase invoice showing the chassis number and price paid and any invoices for accessories purchased with the vehicle. They can process the notification more quickly if it is accompanied by these documents.

Foreign currency conversion

If the invoice for the NMT is in currency other than sterling, the Personal Transport Unit will convert it into sterling using the rate of exchange current at time of acquisition. This will automatically be done using the HMRC period rate of exchange which closely reflects the UK market rate. However, the purchaser may make a specific request in writing at the time of notification to use the actual market rate applicable on the date of acquisition. The rates published in national newspapers will be acceptable as evidence of the rate at the relevant time.

Calculation of VAT due

VAT is calculated on the total amount paid for the NMT, including any extras fitted to it at the time it was supplied, plus any delivery or incidental charges made by the supplier.

Payment of VAT

HMRC will calculate the VAT due and send a written demand which must be paid within 30 days of issue.

Disabled persons

Where the NMT is a vehicle constructed or adapted for a disabled person, see **28.32 HEALTH AND WELFARE.**

Records

The person acquiring the NMT must keep his copy of the purchase invoice, and proof that he has paid the VAT, for six years. If the NMT is sold within this period, these records should be passed on to the new owner so that he can demonstrate its VAT status. [*VATA 1994, Sch 11 para 6(1); SI 1995/2518, Reg 31(3)*].

[*SI 1995/2518, Reg 148*]. (VAT Notice 728, paras 3.1–3.15).

Penalties

The provisions of *VATA 1994, s 67* (failure to notify) are extended to impose a penalty where an unregistered person fails to notify an acquisition of a new means of transport. See **52.14 PENALTIES.**

Acquisitions by persons registered in the UK from other EU countries

[19.38] Where a VAT-registered person in the UK acquires an NMT free of VAT from a registered person in another EU country, he should

- provide the supplier or vendor with his UK VAT registration number to enable them to zero-rate the supply of the vehicle;
- account for the VAT due on his normal VAT return for the period in which he acquires the NMT.

If the NMT is a vehicle, it must be licensed and registered before it is used on public roads. When a person applies to register a vehicle on his own behalf, or on behalf of a customer, the DVLA local office (see **19.34** above) will ask for completion of Form VAT 414 declaring the VAT-free status of the vehicle and the VAT registration number used to make the acquisition into the UK. See also **19.34** above for 'type approval' requirements.

Onward supply

Where a VAT-registered person acquires and makes an onward supply of an NMT, he must still account for acquisition VAT on the vehicle. If it forms part of his stock in trade, he can recover input tax equal to the amount of acquisition VAT declared. Output tax must be charged on the onward supply.

(VAT Notice 728, paras 8.1–8.4).

Sales and purchases of second-hand goods

[19.39] The liability of sales and purchase of second-hand goods within the EU is as follows.

Sale by UK-registered person to a person registered in another EU country

Such a sale under the Margin Scheme is taxable in the UK with no further liability to pay VAT on acquisition in another EU country. If the sale is excluded from the Margin Scheme, it may be zero-rated subject to the normal conditions but the customer must account for VAT on the acquisition and will not be able to include the goods in a margin scheme in his own country.

Sale by UK-registered person to a private individual in another EU country

Such a sale is taxable in the UK. VAT is calculated on the margin for eligible goods sold under one of the schemes for **SECOND-HAND GOODS (61)**.

Acquisition by UK-registered person from a person registered in another EU country

Such an acquisition from a seller who deals with the goods under a margin scheme is subject to VAT in the other EU country with no liability to acquisition VAT on entry into the UK. Eligible goods may be sold under one of the schemes for **SECOND-HAND GOODS (61)** as the invoice will not show VAT as a separate item. If the sale is not dealt with under a margin scheme in the other EU country, it will be zero-rated subject to the normal conditions and the UK buyer must account for any VAT due on the acquisition. The UK buyer cannot deal with the goods under the Margin Scheme.

Acquisition by UK-registered person from a private individual in another EU country

No VAT is due when the goods are brought into the UK and the goods can therefore be sold under one of the special schemes for **SECOND-HAND GOODS (61)**.

Acquisition by a private individual in the UK from a registered person in another EU country

Such an acquisition is subject to VAT in the other EU country.

Goods obtained in the EU by travellers returning to the UK via a non-EU country

[19.40] Where travellers return to the UK through non-EU countries (including the Channel Islands) carrying goods, purchased for their personal use, duty and VAT paid in another EU country, no further duty will be payable in the UK on production, if requested, of evidence of payment of that duty and VAT (e.g. an invoice). (C & E News Release 57/93, 20 August 1993).

Key points

[19.41] Points to consider are as follows.

- An important principle of the EU VAT system is that no VAT is charged on the sale of goods to a VAT-registered business in a different EU country. In such cases, the customer accounts for any tax that is due on its own VAT returns (known as acquisition tax). A business making sales of goods to non-VAT registered customers will charge domestic VAT based on the same rate that would apply if it was supplying goods to a customer in its own country. However, it is important to remember that if the value of such sales exceeds certain limits (known as 'distance selling' limits), then it will need to become VAT-registered in the country of the customer.
- Each EU country has a choice of adopting either a 35,000 or 100,000 Euros annual limit for distance selling (calendar year basis). As a general observation, countries with higher rates of VAT favour the lower level of 35,000 Euros, i.e. to minimise the VAT disadvantage to businesses that are based in their own countries.
- A business in another EU country outside the UK that is selling goods to non-VAT registered customers in the UK will exceed the distance selling limits if sales exceed £70,000 in a calendar year. The exception is if the goods in question are subject to excise duty, in which case a nil threshold applies.
- An important clause in VAT law (and often forgotten) is that if a UK business that is not VAT-registered acquires goods from other EU countries that has exceeded the VAT registration limit on a calendar year basis (or will exceed the VAT registration limit in the next 30 days), then it will need to register for VAT in the UK under what are known as the 'acquisition' rules. This situation means that a business could be VAT-registered on a compulsory basis, even though it makes no taxable supplies in the UK. The aim of the rules is to ensure a business unable to reclaim input tax cannot gain a VAT advantage by buying goods from EU countries where the standard-rate of VAT is lower than in its own country.
- It is often forgotten that an acquisition of goods still takes place if a business transfers its own goods from one EU country to another (e.g. a branch it has in another EU country). In this situation, it is classed as making an acquisition in the country where the goods are received.
- A VAT-registered business acquiring goods from another EU country will account for acquisition tax in Box 2 of its relevant VAT return, based on the value of the goods and its own rate of VAT. This assumes that the goods in question are not zero-rated in

its own country. In most cases, the business will reclaim the same amount of VAT as input tax in Box 4 of the same VAT return. However, such a claim would not be correct if the goods in question either suffered an input tax block, or related to exempt, non-business or private activities. The net value of the acquisition will also be recorded in both Box 7 and Box 9 of the same VAT return.

- If a UK business sells goods to a VAT-registered customer in another EU country (zero-rated) then it must obtain the customer's VAT registration number and show this on its sales invoices. It must also obtain and retain proof that the goods have left the UK. This evidence will be needed in the event of a visit by an HMRC officer to review the records.
- The proof that the goods have left the UK must be obtained within three months of the supply taking place. If this deadline is not met, then output tax should be declared on the supply in question, as if it had taken place in the UK. However, the output tax paid can be subsequently adjusted if evidence is eventually obtained in the future.
- The situation where a supplier obtains proof of goods leaving the UK will not usually be penalised by HMRC if the documentation is subsequently found to be false. However, this statement assumes that the supplier has at all times acted in good faith and has received documentation that appears to give assurance that the goods have left the UK.
- A business selling goods to VAT-registered customers in other EU countries must also take reasonable steps to ensure the customer has provided a genuine VAT registration number. There are a number of ways of checking the validity of a number but the most important check is that a supplier should always be satisfied that he is dealing with a bona fide customer.
- A higher risk situation is where a customer collects the goods from a supplier and is responsible himself for shipping the goods out of the UK, and acquiring the relevant transport documents. In such cases, a sensible strategy would be for the supplier to take a refundable deposit from the customer, equivalent to the amount of VAT on the transaction, on condition that the deposit will be refunded once the supplier has provided adequate proof to confirm the goods have left the UK.
- Triangulation will avoid the need for a business having to register for VAT in a country where goods are delivered from its supplier (based in another EU country other than its own) directly to the country of the customer in a third EU country. For example, a UK business buying goods from a French supplier, for sale to its customer in Germany, and where the goods are delivered directly from France to Germany, would avoid the need to register for VAT in Germany if the procedures relevant to triangulation are

adopted. The end result is that the final German customer will account for acquisition tax on his own VAT return.

20

Exempt Supplies

Introduction

[20.1] A supply of goods or services is an exempt supply if it is of a description for the time being specified as such under various Group headings in *VATA 1994, Sch 9*. [*VATA 1994, s 31(1)*]. A person who makes exempt supplies but no taxable supplies is not a taxable person and cannot be registered. [*VATA 1994, s 3(1), s 4(2)*]. Output tax is not chargeable on exempt supplies or recoverable on related input tax. Where both exempt and taxable supplies are made, the rules as to **PARTIAL EXEMPTION (49)** are applied and only part of the input tax may be reclaimable.

The general categories of exemption are

Group 1	Land (see **41.2 LAND AND BUILDINGS: EXEMPT SUPPLIES AND OPTION TO TAX**)
Group 2	Insurance (see **36 INSURANCE**)
Group 3	Postal services (see **20.2** below)
Group 4	Betting, gaming and lotteries (see **57.2–57.5 RECREATION AND SPORT**)
Group 5	Finance (see **23 FINANCIAL SERVICES**)
Group 6	Education (see **16 EDUCATION**)
Group 7	Health and welfare (see **28.1 HEALTH AND WELFARE; 12.11 CHARITIES; 43.12 LOCAL AUTHORITIES AND PUBLIC BODIES** and **20.3** below)
Group 8	Burial and cremation (see **15.6 DEATH AND INCAPACITY**)
Group 9	Subscriptions to trade unions, professional and other public interest bodies (see **14.7 CLUBS AND ASSOCIATIONS**)
Group 10	Sport, sports competitions and physical education (see **57.6** and **57.10 RECREATION AND SPORT**)
Group 11	Works of art, etc. — certain disposals exempted from capital taxes (see **73.1 WORKS OF ART, ETC.**)
Group 12	Fund-raising events by charities and other qualifying bodies (see **12.10 CHARITIES**)
Group 13	Cultural services, etc. — admission to museums, exhibitions, zoos and performances of a cultural nature supplied by public bodies and eligible bodies (see **57.7 RECREATION AND SPORT**)

Group 14	Supplies of goods where input tax cannot be recovered (see **20.4** below)
Group 15	Investment gold (see **26.2 GOLD AND PRECIOUS METALS**)

[*VATA 1994, Sch 9*].

The descriptions of the Groups above are for ease of reference only and do not affect the interpretation or the description of items within them. [*VATA 1994, s 96(10)*]. The Treasury may vary the Groups (and notes contained therein which form an integral part) by adding, deleting or amending any description of supply for the time being specified. The *Schedule* may also be varied so as to describe a supply of goods by reference to the use which has been made of them or to other matters unrelated to the characteristics of the goods themselves. [*VATA 1994, s 31(2), s 96(9)*].

Where a supply of goods falls within one of the above Groups but is also covered by the provisions relating to **ZERO-RATED SUPPLIES (74)**, the latter take priority. [*VATA 1994, s 30(1)*].

De Voil Indirect Tax Service. See V4.101–V4.103.

Postal services

[20.2] For EU legislation see **18.25**(*a*) and **18.26**(*b*) **EUROPEAN UNION LEGISLATION.**

From 1 January 2011

Under UK legislation, the following are exempt from VAT.

- The supply of public postal services by a universal service provider.
- The supply of goods by a universal service provider which is incidental to the supply of public postal services by that provider.

A '*universal service provider*' (USP) is a person providing a (or part of a) universal postal service in the UK.

'*Public postal services*' are any postal services that a USP is required to provide in the discharge of a specified condition (prior to 1 October 2011, in the discharge of a licence duty). These include postal services allowing a person access to (from 1 October 2011) the USP's postal network and which are required to be provided by a specified condition (prior to 1 October 2011, the USP's postal facilities, where such services are provided pursuant to a licence duty).

However, services are not public postal services if

- the price is not controlled by or under a condition; or
- if any of the other terms on which the services are provided are freely negotiated,

unless a specified condition requires the USP to make the services available to persons generally at the same price or on such terms.

A 'specified condition' means a designated USP condition, a USP access condition or a transitory condition under the *Postal Services Act 2011, Sch 9 para 5*.

[*VATA 1994, Sch 9 Group 3; F(No 3)A 2010, s 22(2); SI 1995/2518, reg 2(1); SI 2011/2085, Sch 1 para 28*].

Prior to 1 January 2011

Under UK legislation, the following are exempt from VAT.

- The conveyance by the Post Office Company (or any of its wholly-owned subsidiaries) of any postal packets i.e. letters, postcards, reply postcards, newspapers, printed packets, sample packets, parcels and every packet or article transmissible by post (but not telegrams).
- The supply by the Post Office Company (or any of its wholly-owned subsidiaries) of any services (except the letting on hire of goods) in connection with the conveyance of postal packets.

[*VATA 1994, Sch 9 Group 3; Postal Services Act 2000, Sch 8 para 22*]. (VAT Notice 48, ESC 3.33).

The cost of postage charged by a supplier in addition to the cost of goods is not within the exemption, see **47.8**(19) **OUTPUT TAX**.

Stamps

Unused current or valid UK and Isle of Man postage stamps are not chargeable with VAT if supplied at or below face value. *First day covers* are taxable at the standard rate on their full value whether supplied by the Post Office Philatelic Bureau or stamp dealers. For stamps generally, see **57.20 RECREATION AND SPORT**.

De Voil Indirect Tax Service. See V4.126.

Religious communities

[20.3] The supply, 'otherwise than for a profit', of goods and services incidental to the provision of 'spiritual welfare' by a religious community (e.g. a nunnery or monastery) is exempt when supplied to a resident member of that community in return for a subscription or other consideration paid as a condition of membership. [*VATA 1994, Sch 9 Group 7 Item 10*].

Otherwise than for a profit'

Following the decision in *C & E Commrs v Bell Concord Educational Trust Ltd*, CA 1988, [1989] STC 264 (TVC 21.9), HMRC accept that supplies are made '*otherwise than for a profit*' if they are made by charities in circumstances where any surpluses are applied solely to the furtherance of the activity which generated the surplus. Where, however, a charity pursues more than one activity, the welfare services will not be supplied otherwise than for a profit if surpluses from welfare services are applied to the maintenance or furtherance of the other activities, even though charitable.

Spiritual welfare

'*Spiritual welfare*' can include

- spiritual counselling to an individual;
- guided exploration of spiritual needs and development; and
- discussion, meditation and prayer or worship sessions

but does not include

- conferences or retreats when the predominant purpose is not spiritual welfare;
- educational courses in theology, or similar subjects, where the predominant purpose is to expand knowledge of spiritual matters rather than to provide spiritual welfare services; or
- meetings to discuss theology or aspects of Church doctrine.

(VAT Notice 701/2/11, para 2.3).

Supplies of goods where input tax cannot be recovered

[20.4] A supply of goods is an exempt supply where each of the following conditions is satisfied.

(a) The person making the supply (the '*relevant supplier*'), or any 'predecessor' of his, has incurred (or will incur) input tax on obtaining
  - the goods supplied; or
  - any other goods used in the process of producing the goods supplied so as to be incorporated in them.

  For this purpose, input tax is deemed to include VAT incurred by the person concerned when he was not a taxable person (i.e. when he was not registered or liable to be registered).

  In the particular case where the supply is the grant of a 'major interest' in land (see **41.1**(9) LAND AND BUILDINGS: EXEMPT SUPPLIES AND OPTION TO TAX), other than one excluded under (*c*) below, the input tax must be incurred on either
  - acquiring a major interest in the land concerned; or
  - goods used in the construction of a building or civil engineering work so as to become part of the land.

(b) All of the input tax referred to in (*a*) above is 'non-deductible input tax'. '*Non-deductible input tax*', subject to below, comprises the following.
  - Input tax on goods used to make exempt supplies. No part of the input tax may be deductible as attributable to supplies giving a right to input tax deduction, whether the right to deduction arises before or after the supply of goods under consideration. However, an input tax entitlement arising only from the operation of the partial exemption *de minimis* rules (see **49.11** PARTIAL EXEMPTION) is ignored.
  - Input tax which is solely excluded from credit under the provisions relating to
    - BUSINESS ENTERTAINMENT (**9**);

        - non-building materials incorporated in a building or its site (see **42.4 LAND AND BUILDINGS: ZERO AND REDUCED RATE SUPPLIES AND DIY HOUSEBUILDERS**); or
        - motor cars (see **45.3 MOTOR CARS**).
    - VAT incurred by the person concerned when he was not a taxable person (i.e. when he was not registered or liable to be registered).

    Specifically excluded from non-deductible input tax is any VAT which has been, or will be, recovered under *VATA 1994, s 33* (see **43.7 LOCAL AUTHORITIES AND PUBLIC BODIES**), *VATA 1994, s 33A* (museums and galleries, see **34.13**(22) **INPUT TAX**), *VATA 1994, s 33B* (academies, see **34.13**(30) **INPUT TAX**), *VATA 1994, s 39* (repayments of VAT to overseas traders, see **48.5 OVERSEAS TRADERS**) or *VATA 1994, s 41* (refunds to government departments, see **43.11 LOCAL AUTHORITIES AND PUBLIC BODIES**). This ensures that exemption under these provisions cannot apply in such cases.

(c) The supply made by the relevant supplier is not a supply which would be exempt under *VATA 1994, Sch 9 Group 1 Item 1* (see **41.2 LAND AND BUILDINGS: EXEMPT SUPPLIES AND OPTION TO TAX**) but for the option to tax having been exercised (see **41.8 LAND AND BUILDINGS: EXEMPT SUPPLIES AND OPTION TO TAX**).

Self-supplies

Input tax arising on any supply, acquisition or importation of goods is disregarded for the purposes of (*a*) and (*b*) above if, after that supply, etc. and before the supply by the relevant supplier, the relevant supplier or any predecessor of his is treated as having self-supplied the goods to himself under any provision of *VATA 1994*. This ensures that, in cases of self-supplies (e.g. the self-supply of a motor car, on which input tax was initially recovered, following a change of use) exemption under these provisions can still apply.

A person (A) is the '*predecessor*' of another (B) if the goods (or anything comprised in the goods)

- are transferred from A to B as part of a transfer of a going concern which was treated as neither a supply of goods nor a supply of services (see **8.10** *et seq.* **BUSINESS**); or
- formed part of the assets of A when it became a member of a VAT group of which B was the representative member;
- formed part of the assets of A, or any other company which was a member of the same VAT group as A, when the representative member of the VAT group changed from A to B; or
- formed part of the assets of B when it ceased to be a member of a VAT group of which A was the representative member.

A person's predecessors include the predecessors of his predecessor through any number of transactions.

[*VATA 1994, Sch 9 Group 14; FA 2001, s 98(9); FA 2011, s 76(4); SI 1999/2833; SI 2008/1146, Sch 1 para 4*].

Examples where the above provisions apply

- Business cars (see **45.3 MOTOR CARS**).
- Goods used for business entertainment (see **9.7 BUSINESS ENTERTAINMENT**).
- Fixtures and fittings incorporated by developers in new homes (see **42.4 LAND AND BUILDINGS: ZERO AND REDUCED RATE SUPPLIES AND DIY HOUSEBUILDERS**).
- Goods used by charities for exempt and non-business activities, provided VAT has been incurred on the goods and has not been recovered.

Examples where the above provisions do not apply

- Goods on which any part of the input tax has been or will be recovered, either on purchase or later as a result of partial exemption or capital goods scheme adjustments.
- Goods eligible for the second-hand margin scheme.
- Goods on which no VAT is incurred.

The resale of services of any type (e.g. copyrights).

Key points

[20.5] Points to consider are as follows.

- Exempt supplies of goods or services are not classed as taxable and therefore input tax cannot be reclaimed on related costs. The value of exempt sales is also ignored when deciding whether a business has exceeded the VAT registration limit and needs to register for VAT on a compulsory basis.
- It is an advantage for sales to either the general public or other exempt businesses to be exempt from VAT because there is no output tax charge to customers that they are unable to recover. In most cases, this situation will outweigh the disadvantages of the input tax relevant to the supply not being reclaimable.
- There are occasions when a standard-rated supply being incorrectly treated as exempt could prove costly for a business. For example, a VAT charge to another registered business would not be a problem if the business could reclaim the charge as input tax. The supplier can then recover related input tax on its own expenses because it has made a taxable supply. It is important to get the VAT liability right on all sources of business income.
- Output tax is not charged on the sale of goods where the original input tax was not reclaimed because it was either non-deductible or relevant to an exempt supply. The sales in these cases are exempt from VAT. A motor car available for private use is an example of an input tax block that means the subsequent sale of the vehicle by the business will be exempt from VAT.

21

Exports

De Voil Indirect Tax Service. See V4.301–339.

Introduction

[21.1] Some general notes are as follows:

Trade with other EU countries

The provisions of this chapter only apply to goods which are exported outside the EU. See **17.2 EUROPEAN UNION: GENERAL** for the VAT territory of the EU. For the provisions relating to supplies of goods from the UK to other EU countries, see **19.11 EUROPEAN UNION: SINGLE MARKET**.

Cyprus

The European Commission has advised that the application of *Directive 2006/112/EC* is to be suspended in those areas of Cyprus in which the Government of the Republic of Cyprus does not exercise control. From 1 May 2004, goods sent to these destinations continue to be eligible for treatment as exports.

The Isle of Man

Although the Isle of Man has its own VAT authority, sales to the Isle of Man are treated as any other sale within the UK and cannot be treated as exports. (VAT Notice 703, para 2.7).

The Channel Islands

The Channel Islands are part of the EU for customs purposes but *outside* the EU for VAT purposes. Supplies of goods sent to the Channel Islands are therefore regarded as exports. (VAT Notice 703, para 2.7).

Conditions for zero-rating

[21.2] To zero-rate supplies for export, an 'exporter' must comply with all the following conditions (which have the force of law). If all the conditions cannot be met, the supply cannot be zero-rated as an export and VAT must be accounted for at the appropriate UK rate.

(a) The exporter must ensure that the goods are exported from the UK within a specified time limit. For 'direct exports' and 'indirect exports' the time limit is three months from the time of supply.
In most cases, the time of supply is the earlier of
- the date on which the goods are sent to the customer or the customer takes them away, and
- the date full payment is received for the goods.

Any deposit or progress payment received is an advance part payment towards the total cost of the supply and has the same VAT liability as the final supply. If the final supply is to be zero-rated as an export, these payments can also be zero-rated. But if the goods are not eventually exported (or the supplier fails to obtain valid evidence of export), he must account for VAT on the total value of the supply, including any deposit or progress payments.
'*Direct exports*' are where the supplier sends the goods to a destination outside the EU and is responsible either for arranging the transport himself or appointing an agent (see below). The goods may be exported in own baggage or transport, by rail, by post or courier service, by a shipping line or airline, or by an agent employed by the supplier (but not by the customer).
'*Indirect exports*' are where the overseas customer or his agent collects, or arranges for the collection of, the goods from the supplier in the UK and then takes them outside the EU.

(b) The exporter must obtain and keep valid commercial evidence or official evidence of export. See **21.25** *et seq* below for acceptable proof of export. The time limit for obtaining this evidence is, for direct exports and indirect exports, three months from the time of supply.

(c) In the case of direct exports, the supplier must not
- deliver or post the goods to a customer's address in the EU (including the UK); or
- allow the goods to be collected by or on behalf of the customer even if it is claimed that they are for subsequent export. See **21.10** below for details of deliveries made to another UK trader for consolidation, processing or incorporation prior to export.

(d) In the case of indirect exports, the supplier must not supply goods to
- a private individual who is resident in the UK; or
- a business registered for VAT in the UK (including an overseas business that has a place of business in the UK from which taxable supplies are made).

(e) The exporter must keep supplementary evidence of the export transaction (see **21.25** *et seq* below).

(f) The exporter must comply with the conditions specified in the legislation and in VAT Notice 703 which for this purpose has the force of law. As to whether the conditions laid down by HMRC are reasonable or complied with, see *Henry Moss of London Ltd and Another v C & E Commrs*, CA 1980, [1981] STC 139 (TVC 25.1).

An '*exporter*' is the person who, for VAT purposes,

- supplies or owns goods and exports or arranges for them to be exported to a destination outside the EU; or
- supplies goods to an 'overseas person', who arranges for the goods to be exported to a destination outside the EU. An '*overseas person*' is either
  (i) a person or company that is not resident or registered for VAT in the UK;
  (ii) a person or company that has no business establishment in the UK from which taxable supplies are made; or
  (iii) an overseas authority.

(VAT Notice 703, paras 2.3, 2.4, 2.10, 2.11, 2.13, 3.3, 3.4, 11.5).

Effect of failure to comply with conditions

Where the supply of any goods has been zero-rated as an export and either

- any of the above conditions (or any other specific conditions relating to a particular type of export) is not complied with, or
- the goods are found in the UK after the date of alleged exportation,

the goods are liable to *forfeiture*. Any VAT which would have been due but for zero-rating is payable forthwith by the person to whom the goods were supplied or by any other person in whose possession the goods are found in the UK. HMRC may waive payment of the VAT in whole or part. [*VATA 1994, s 30(10)*].

Appointment of an agent

A supplier (or for indirect exports a customer) can appoint a freight forwarder, shipping company, airline or other person to handle the export transactions and produce the necessary declarations to customs on their behalf. The agent must be provided with a full description of the goods, including value, quantity and weight, together with export invoices, packing lists and technical details to enable the export declaration and transport documents to be completed accurately. The agent must then

- take reasonable steps to ensure that the goods are as described by the exporter;
- ensure the customs formalities are complied with;
- ensure the goods exported within the time limits;
- keep records of each export transaction; and
- obtain and provide valid evidence of export and send it to the exporter once the goods have been exported.

If the agent fails to fulfil its obligations, the supplier or overseas customer is responsible for accounting for any VAT which becomes chargeable.

(VAT Notice 703, paras 2.5, 2.6).

Categories of zero-rated exports

[21.3] Subject to meeting the general conditions in **21.2** above and any specific conditions in the appropriate paragraph of this chapter, the following categories of exports are zero-rated.

- **Direct exports.** [*VATA 1994, s 30(6)*]. See **21.2**(*a*) above.
- **Stores for ships, aircraft, etc.** [*VATA 1984, s 30(6)*]. See **21.4** below.
- **Certain supplies in connection with the management of defence projects.** [*VATA 1994, Sch 8 Group 13 Item 2*]. See **21.5** below.
- **Tools for the manufacture of goods for export.** [*VATA 1994, Sch 8 Group 13 Item 3*]. See **21.6** below.
- **Goods exported by a charity** (whatever the nature of the goods). [*VATA 1994, Sch 8 Group 15 Item* 3]. See **12.6 CHARITIES.**
- **Exports of freight containers.** [*SI 1995/2518, Reg 128*]. See **21.8** below.
- **Supplies to overseas persons.** [*SI 1995/2518, Reg 129*]. See **21.9** and **21.10** below.
- **Supplies to persons departing from the EU – retail export scheme.** [*SI 1995/2518, Regs 130, 131*]. See **21.12** to **21.16** below.
- **Exports of motor vehicles.** [*SI 1995/2518, Regs 132, 133*]. See **21.17** to **21.19** below.
- **Sailaway boats supplied for export** (prior to 1 January 2012). See **21.20** below.
- **Supplies to the FCO and other government departments.** See **21.21** below.
- **Supplies to regimental shops.** See **21.22** below.
- **Supplies intended for continental shelf installations.** See **21.23** below.

- **Supplies at tax-free shops.** Where goods which are liable to VAT are supplied to persons leaving on flights to destinations outside the EU at tax-free shops approved by HMRC, the supplier may be regarded as the exporter and zero-rate the supply of those goods which are exported. See VAT Notice 48, ESC 9.1.

Stores for use in ships, aircraft or hovercraft

[21.4] Stores are goods for use in a ship, aircraft or hovercraft and include

- fuel;
- goods for running repairs or maintenance (e.g. lubricants, spare and replacement parts);
- goods for general use on board by the crew; and
- goods for sale by retail to persons carried on voyages or flights who intend to use the stores on board only.

A supplier can zero-rate supplies of stores for the fuelling and provisioning of vessels and aircraft provided

- they are for use on a voyage or flight with a non-private purpose and with an eventual destination outside the UK (see below for an extra-statutory concession covering supplies of marine fuel to vessels for voyages in home waters);
- they are shipped from the UK within three months of supply; and
- the conditions outlined in (*b*) below are met.

A VAT-registered shipping line or airline operator can choose either of the following options for supplies made to it.

(a) It can have all supplies, including those intended for stores, delivered to its premises and charged to VAT at the appropriate rate. If so, input tax can be deducted (subject to the normal rules) and the subsequent transfer of the goods from the premises to the ship or aircraft is a non-supply.

(b) It can have supplies of eligible stores made direct to the foreign-going craft. Such supplies can then be zero-rated provided the following conditions are met.

  (i) The person to whom the goods are supplied is the end user (e.g. the master of the vessel).

  (ii) The goods are for use as stores on a voyage or flight which is to be made for a non-private purpose and the person to whom the goods are to be supplied declares this in writing.

  (iii) The stores are to be shipped from the UK within three months of supply.

  (iv) The supplier obtains and keeps a written order or confirmation given by the master or duly authorised agent. This must contain a declaration that the goods are solely for use as stores on a named ship or aircraft that is entitled to duty-free stores for the voyage or flight in question i.e. to an eventual destination outside the UK. Aircraft making through international flights are eligible to receive VAT-free stores even if the aircraft makes one or more stops in the UK in the course of such a flight.

(v) The goods must be sent either direct to the ship or aircraft or through freight forwarders for consolidation and delivery direct to the ship or aircraft or addressed and delivered to the master c/o the shipping company or agent.

(vi) The supplier must obtain and keep a receipt confirming delivery of the goods on board the ship or aircraft signed by the master, commander or other responsible officer of the ship or aircraft. The supplier can accept such a receipt signed by a responsible official of the airline concerned but airlines using this facility must obtain prior written agreement from HMRC. The airline must confirm that the signatory is in a position to provide the receipt based on personal knowledge of flight details and that the airline will maintain documentation enabling HMRC staff to verify entitlement to relief.

(vii) Where supplies are made direct from a warehouse not operated or owned by the supplier to an eligible vessel or aircraft, the supplier must hold a signed and dated certificate of export from the warehousekeeper. The advice note issued by the warehouse-keeper normally serves this purpose.

Where goods are supplied to a shore-side storage tank, the supplier may not zero-rate the supply unless he holds the necessary evidence that his customer is the exporter of the goods.

Goods for sale

These provisions also apply to goods supplied for sale in ships' shops and on board aircraft even though there may be no taxable supply at the time of shipment (e.g. transfer of own goods, supply on sale or return terms). Where goods have been shipped on a foreign-going ship or aircraft, any later sale of the goods is a supply outside the UK and there is no further liability to VAT unless they are re-landed (see below). VAT is charged on goods sold on board a vessel on a coastwise journey or aircraft on an internal flight.

Relanded stores

Stores supplied under the above provisions and re-landed are treated as **IMPORTS (33)**.

Marine fuel

By concession, vessels engaged on commercial voyages within UK territorial waters (or within the limits of a port) may receive certain types of fuel VAT-free. The supplier can zero-rate the supply provided

- a written declaration is obtained from the person to whom the marine fuel is supplied that the goods are for use as stores on a non-private voyage;
- a written order or confirmation is obtained from the master, owner or duly authorised agent of the vessel declaring that the fuel is solely for use on a named ship;
- the fuel is sent direct to the ship or addressed and delivered to the master of a named vessel c/o the shipping agent or line; and

- a receipt confirming delivery of the fuel on board, signed by the master or other responsible officer, is held.

The concession extends only to those supplies of fuel which were zero-rated before 1 July 1990. It does not cover petrol, ultra low sulphur diesel (ULSD) or lubricating oil.

Mess and canteen stores

Goods can be zero-rated where supplied for use as mess and canteen stores on HM ships about to leave for a foreign port or a voyage outside UK territorial waters of more than 15 days' duration. The goods must be ordered for the general use on board by the ship's company. Orders must be certified by the Commanding Officer and goods delivered direct to the ship. A receipt must be obtained and kept.

Duty-free goods supplied on sale or return to messes in HM ships cannot be zero-rated when sent out to the ship. The taxable supply occurs only when the goods are adopted, i.e.

- when the customer pays for the goods or otherwise indicates his wish to keep them; or
- at the end of twelve months or any shorter period agreed for the goods to be bought or returned.

The supplier is responsible for ensuring that the messes inform him promptly of when the adoption of the goods took place. If adoption occurs when the vessel is in UK territorial waters, the supply is taxable; if outside, there is no supply for VAT purposes. Commanders of HM ships will provide suppliers with this information.

[*VATA 1994, s 30(6)*]. (VAT Notice 703, paras 8.2, 10.1–10.7; VAT Notice 48, ESC 9.2).

International collaboration defence arrangements (ICDAs)

[21.5] The supply to, or by, an 'overseas authority', 'overseas body' or 'overseas trader', charged with the management of any defence project which is the subject of an 'international collaboration arrangement' (or under direct contract with any government or government-sponsored international body participating in defence projects under such an arrangement) of goods or services made for the purpose of fulfilling contracts is zero-rated. The zero-rating only applies to a limited number of projects and traders who are concerned with them are notified individually by HMRC.

'*Overseas authority*' means any country other than the UK or any part of, or place in, such a country or the government of such a country, part or place.

'*Overseas body*' means a body established outside the UK.

'*Overseas trader*' means a person who carries on a business and has a principal place of business outside the UK.

An '*international collaboration arrangement*' is any arrangement made between the UK government and the government of one or more other countries (or any government-sponsored international body, e.g. NATO) for collaboration in a joint project of research, development or production. The arrangement must specifically provide for participating governments to relieve the cost of the project from taxation.

[*VATA 1994, Sch 8 Group 13 Item 2*].

Tools for the manufacture of goods for export

[21.6] The supply to an 'overseas authority', 'overseas body' or 'overseas trader' (see **21.5** above) of jigs, patterns, templates, dies, moulds, punches and similar machine tools used in the UK solely for the manufacture of goods for export is zero-rated. The overseas authority, etc must not be

- a taxable person,
- another EU country,
- any part of or place in another EU country,
- the government of any such country, part or place,
- a body established in another EU country, or
- a person who carries on business, or has a place of business, in another EU country,

otherwise the supply is taxable in the normal way.

[*VATA 1994, Sch 8 Group 13 Item 3*].

A machine tool is supplied for these purposes where the customer specifically asks the supplier to make it, or buy it, for him and the supplier

- uses the machine tool to manufacture goods for the same customer; and
- makes a specific charge to the customer for the supply of the tool.

In addition to holding normal commercial proof of export, the supplier must obtain a signed statement (or other similar definite evidence) from the customer that they are neither registered nor required to be registered in the UK and are not an authority, body or trader in another EU country.

(VAT Notice 701/22/02, paras 1.4, 2.1).

Export houses

[21.7] An 'export house' is any person registered for VAT in the UK who, in the course of business in the UK, arranges or finances the export of goods from the UK to a place outside the EU.

Supplies by export houses

Export houses can zero-rate supplies to overseas customers as exports subject to the normal conditions.

Supplies to export houses

Supplies to export houses are treated in the same way as any other supplies made to UK customers.

Freight containers supplied for export

[21.8] Subject to such conditions as HMRC impose, the supply of a 'container' is zero-rated where HMRC are satisfied that it is to be exported.

For these purposes, a '*container*' is defined as an article of transport equipment (lift-van, movable tank or similar structure)

- fully or partially enclosed to constitute a compartment for goods;
- of a permanent character strong enough for repeated use;
- designed to facilitate the carriage of goods, by one or more modes of transport, without intermediate reloading;
- designed for ready handling and to be easy to fill and empty; and
- having an internal volume of one cubic metre or more.

It includes accessories and equipment as appropriate but excludes vehicles, spares for vehicles and packaging.

[*SI 1995/2518, Regs 117(2), 128*].

Although not strictly within the definition, 'flats' or 'Lancashire flats' (i.e. bases with or without head and tail boards which are designed to carry goods and have the floor area of a 20 ft or 40 ft container) are included, as are air transport containers whatever their internal volume. Pallets, road vehicles and trailers including tanks on wheels are not included. (VAT Notice 703/1/10, para 2.2).

Direct export

The supply of a container for direct export may be zero-rated provided the container is actually exported and the normal conditions for export are complied with. (VAT Notice 703/1/10, para 3.1).

Indirect export

The supply of a freight container for indirect export may be zero-rated provided the supplier obtains a written undertaking from the customer that

(a) the container will be exported from the EU;
(b) the container will not be used in the EU except for
   (i) a single domestic journey before export (on which inland freight may be carried) on a reasonably direct route between the point of supply and the place where the container is to be loaded with the export cargo or exported; and
   (ii) international movement of goods (which may include a journey within the UK for the purpose of loading or unloading the goods);
(c) the customer will keep records sufficient to satisfy HMRC that
   (i) the container has not been used in the EU (except as allowed under (*b*) above); and
   (ii) the container has either been exported or has been sold/leased to someone else who has given a similar written undertaking.

(VAT Notice 703/1/10, paras 3.2, 3.3 which have the force of law).

Lease or hire of containers

Where the supplier and the customer both belong in the UK, the supply is treated as made in the UK and VAT must be charged on the supply. However, if the customer is to export the container from the EU, the leasing/hiring may be zero-rated provided the supplier obtains a written undertaking from the customer as for indirect exports above.

Where the supplier belongs in the UK but the customer belongs outside the EU, the supply is treated as being made in the customer's country and no UK VAT is due.

Where the customer belongs in another EU country and is in business in another EU country, the supply is treated as being made in the customer's country, and so the supplier does not charge UK VAT. The customer will normally have to account for VAT under the reverse charge procedure. If the customer is a private individual then the place of supply is where the supplier belongs, and the supplier must charge UK VAT.

Incidental charges which under the terms of the lease agreement are charged to the lessee are regarded as part of the consideration for the leasing of the container and have the same VAT liability. Included are repair, delivery, regulator and handling charges, extra rental and any charge for the option to terminate the lease at an earlier date.

(VAT Notice 703/1/10, paras 5.1–5.5).

Supplies to overseas persons

[21.9] Where HMRC are satisfied that goods intended for export have been supplied to an 'overseas person' who is not a taxable person, the supply is zero-rated. For export of motor vehicles generally, see **21.17** to **21.19** below.

'*Overseas person*' is

- a person not resident in the UK;
- a trader who has no business establishment in the UK from which taxable supplies are made; or
- an overseas authority (i.e. any country other than the UK or any part or place in such a country or the government of any such country, part or place). This includes goods ordered through embassies, High Commissions and purchasing agents of foreign governments in the UK.

[*SI 1995/2518, Regs 117(7), 129; SI 1996/210; SI 2003/1485*].

Supplies to overseas persons generally are indirect exports and must meet the normal conditions for zero-rating of such supplies (see **21.2** above). In addition, in the case of supplies to overseas authorities which are ordered through their embassies, High Commissions or purchasing agents in the UK, HMRC require the following conditions to be satisfied before the supply can be zero-rated.

- The supplier must keep a separate record of each transaction, including evidence that the supply has been to an overseas authority (e.g. the order for the goods, sales invoice made out to the overseas authority, evidence of payment from the overseas authority, etc.).

- The goods must not be used between the time of leaving the supplier's premises and export, either for their normal purpose or for display, exhibition or copying.

(VAT Notice 703, paras 3.4, 4.12).

Supplies to overseas persons for export after consolidation, processing or incorporation

[21.10] Goods supplied for export to an overseas person but delivered to a third person in the UK who is also making a taxable supply to that overseas person are zero-rated provided

(a) the goods are only being delivered and not supplied to the third person in the UK;
(b) no use is made of the goods other than for processing or incorporation into other goods for export;
(c) the goods are exported from the EU within six months of the time of supply and proof of export is obtained within the same time limit;
(d) the supplier's records show the
  - name and address of the overseas person,
  - invoice number and date,
  - description, quantity and value of goods,
  - name and address of the third person in the UK to whom the goods were delivered,
  - date by which the goods must be exported and proof of export obtained, and
  - date of actual exportation.

The records must be able to show that the goods supplied have been processed or incorporated into the goods exported.

In cases where the third party is not the UK but in another EU country, the same conditions will generally apply to allow the supply to be zero-rated.

(VAT Notice 703, paras 3.5, 3.6).

Racehorses

Where a racehorse is supplied to an overseas person but is to remain in the UK for breaking, conditioning, training or covering before export, under an agreement between HMRC, the British Horseracing Board and the Thoroughbred Breeders Association the vendor can ask HMRC to extend the time limit in (*c*) above from six months to twelve months from the date of purchase. The extension is subject to the conditions that

- the horse must not be raced in the UK before export; and
- the relief cannot be transferred to another overseas person.

(VAT Notice 700/57/04).

Multiple transactions leading to a single movement of goods

[21.11] Where a single movement of goods is supported by two or more transactions, only the final transaction can be zero-rated.

(VAT Notice 703, para 4.1).

> *Example*
>
> A (outside the EU) orders goods from B (in the UK). B purchases the goods from C (also in the UK) but instead of taking delivery of the goods, agrees with C that it will send the goods directly to A.
>
> The supply of goods from C to B is a UK supply and VAT must be charged at the appropriate rate. The supply of goods by B to A is zero-rated as an export if the necessary conditions are met.

Retail export scheme

[21.12] The VAT retail export scheme allows

- overseas visitors (see **21.13** Condition 1 below) to receive a refund of VAT paid on goods exported to destinations outside the EU subject to the conditions in **21.13** below being met; and
- retailers to zero-rate goods sold to overseas visitors when they have the necessary evidence of export and have refunded the VAT to the customer.

See **17.2 EUROPEAN UNION: GENERAL** for the VAT territory of the EU.

It is a voluntary scheme and retailers do not have to operate it. Where it is operated, retailers

- need not operate it for all lines of goods; and
- can set a minimum sales value below which they will not operate the scheme.

A simplified Notice aimed specifically at travellers, VAT Notice 704/1 *Tax Free Shopping: VAT Refunds for travellers departing from the European Community (EC)*, highlights the main aspects of the scheme. It is available, in various languages, from the National Advice Service (tele: 0845 010 9000). Copies can be usefully given to customers using the scheme.

(VAT Notice 704, paras 1.5, 2.1, 2.2, 2.7).

Conditions for using the scheme

[21.13] Retailers and refund companies can only operate the scheme when the following conditions (which have the force of law) are met.

Condition 1

The customer must be an 'overseas visitor'. For these purposes, an '*overseas visitor*' is one of the following.

(a) A traveller (including a member of the crew of a ship or aircraft) who is not established in the EU. This means a person

- whose domicile or habitual residence is not situated within the EU. For this purpose, a person's domicile or habitual residence is the place entered as such on their valid passport, identity card or other acceptable document such as a driving licence (which must be produced to the retailer to prove eligibility);
- who intends to leave the UK for a final destination outside the EU, with the goods, by the last day of the third month following that in which the goods were purchased; and
- who exports the goods having produced them, their receipts and the VAT refund document to an HMRC officer at the point of departure from the EU.

Student or migrant workers entering the UK from outside the EU are classed as overseas visitors but to avoid abuse of the system (by reclaiming VAT under the scheme prior to returning home and then bringing the goods back to the UK within a short period of time), with effect from 1 October 2004, such persons additionally

- are only entitled to purchase goods under the scheme during the last four months of their stay in the UK; and
- having left the EU must remain outside the EU for a minimum period of twelve months.

Such a visitor will have been issued with a pre-entry visa and, in the case of work periods of six months or more, a separate work permit document by the UK authorities. The visa is contained in the passport and shows the start and end date for the study or work period authorised. Retailers should ask to see the visa or work permit before selling goods under the scheme.

(b) For the purposes of this scheme only, a traveller established in the EU who

- intends to leave the UK with the goods by the last day of the third month following that in which the goods were purchased for an immediate destination outside the EU;
- remains outside the EU for a period of at least twelve months (which must be proved to the retailer typically by evidence such as an overseas work permit, approved visa application or residency permit); and
- exports the goods having produced them, their receipts and the VAT refund document to an HMRC officer at the point of departure from the EU.

Condition 2

The goods must be eligible to be purchased under the scheme. Any standard-rated and lower-rated goods can be sold under the scheme except for the following.

- New and second-hand motor vehicles for personal export (see **21.17** below).
- Sailaway boats (see **21.20** below).
- Goods over £600 in value (excluding VAT) exported for the customer's business purposes.
- Goods that will be exported as freight or unaccompanied baggage.

- Goods requiring an export licence (apart from antiques). Antiques may be exported only on production of a valid export licence to HMRC at the point of departure from the UK. Further advice can be obtained from
  The Department of Culture, Media and Sport
  2–4 Cockspur Street
  London SW1Y 5DH
  A retailer selling goods treated as antiques should explain this to customers as they will probably need assistance to obtain an export licence.
- Unmounted gemstones.
- Bullion (over 125g, 2.75 troy ounces or 10 Tolas).
- Goods for consumption in the EU. (No certification of export will be given for used consumable items (e.g. perfumes) which are wholly or partly consumed in the EU.)
- Goods purchased by mail order including those purchased over the internet. However, a mail order company or an internet retailer with a retail outlet can use the scheme for goods sold from that outlet provided all the conditions of the scheme are complied with.

The scheme cannot be used for

- zero-rated goods (e.g. books and children's clothing); or
- supplies of services (e.g. hotel accommodation, meals and car hire). This applies even where services are sold with the goods (e.g. labour costs for fitting spare parts to a motor vehicle). Where a vehicle brought into the UK for the use of the overseas visitor requires repairs, the sale of the spare parts only and not the cost of fitting can be included in the scheme. Extended warranty work cannot be zero-rated under the retail export scheme.

Condition 3

The customer must make the purchase in person and complete the form in full at the retailer's premises at the time of sale (although a third party may pay for the goods). It is not possible for a representative to attend in place of the customer at the time of sale.

Condition 4

The goods must be exported from the EU by the last day of the third month following that in which the goods are purchased (e.g. goods bought on 3 February must be exported by 31 May). This time limit cannot be extended. Goods exported after the time limit must not be zero-rated even if the VAT refund document has been stamped in error by a UK or other EU Customs officer.

Condition 5

The customer must send the retailer or refund company evidence of export stamped by HMRC on an official version of Form VAT 407, an approved version of Form VAT 407 or an officially approved invoice. See **21.14** below.

Condition 6

The retailer or refund company must not zero-rate the supply until the VAT has been refunded to the customer (see **21.16** below).

[*SI 1995/2518, Regs 117(7A)–(7D), 131; SI 1995/3147; SI 1999/438, Reg 10; SI 2003/1485*]. (VAT Notice 704, paras 2.3, 2.4, 2.6, 2.8, 2.9, 3.1, 6.5).

Procedure

[21.14] *At the time of sale*, a retailer should:

- Check that the customer is entitled to use the scheme (see **21.13** Condition 1 above).
- Check that the goods are eligible for the scheme (see **21.14** Condition 2 above).
- Check the eligible customer is present to buy the goods (see **21.13** Condition 3 above).
- Check that the customer intends to leave the EU with the goods for a final destination outside the EU by the last day of the third month following that in which the goods were purchased.
- Fill in a VAT refund document (see below). A responsible member of staff should ensure all sections are fully completed, unused lines are ruled through and the customer and retailer declarations are signed at the time of the sale.

  By concession, HMRC allow completion of the refund form on production of receipts for past purchases provided the retailer can satisfy HMRC that it has adequate security procedures in place to prevent abuse of the scheme. This includes
  - stamping till receipts to show that the goods have been purchased under the retail export scheme (e.g. 'VAT Export');
  - a till system allowing the retailer to check that the receipts produced are genuine and can only appear once on a VAT 407 refund document; and
  - a system allowing the retailer to check whether a refund for returned goods has already been made for a receipt produced or a VAT 407 refund document has been issued for goods where a refund for returned goods is sought.
  - Where a retailer cannot show that it has adequate security procedures in place, it must only complete VAT refund documents at the time of the sale.

  Where a retailer does have adequate safeguards in place and a customer asks for a refund document to cover a series of purchases over a period of time, the retailer must include only those goods that will be exported by the last day of the third month following that in which the goods were purchased. The purchase date entered on the refund document must be the date of the earliest purchase.
- Give the customer a copy of VAT Notice 704/1 *VAT refunds for travellers departing from the EU*.
- Agree with the customer how the refund will be made.
- Explain any administrative or handling fees to be deducted from the VAT refund to avoid any subsequent misunderstanding.

- Mark the customer's sales receipt to indicate that the goods have been included on a VAT refund document (e.g. 'VAT Export').
- Explain that no refund will be made on items (e.g. perfume) wholly or partly consumed in the EU.
- Advise the customer that any items not exported from the UK should be clearly deleted from the refund document before it is presented to a UK or EU Customs officer for stamping and that it is an offence to make a false declaration.
- Advise the customer that he must produce the refund document (together with the goods and receipts, if required) to the Customs officer for stamping at the point of departure from the EU and explain that failure to do so will mean that a VAT refund will not be made.
- Advise the customer to allow plenty of time in which to produce the goods and refund form prior to departure. (This is particularly important if they are exporting goods in hold baggage as they may need to allow up to two hours in addition to the advised check in time.)
- Advise the customer to carry items of high value (e.g. jewellery, furs, cameras, watches, silverware, lap top computers and small antiques) in hand baggage.

VAT refund document

The VAT refund document can be either of the following.

(a) Form VAT 407, in which case it can be either
   - Form VAT 407 issued by HMRC and available free of charge from the National Advice Service; or
   - the retailer's or refund company's own version of Form VAT 407 containing the same information as HMRC's version and approved beforehand by HMRC.

   Part A of the form must be completed in full by the customer at the time of sale.

   Part B, which is for completion by the retailer, must include a full and accurate description of the goods quoting identification numbers, serial numbers or other identifying marks (e.g. hallmarks) together with the quantity (and weight in the case of jewellery) of goods sold. Descriptions such as stock numbers, 'See invoice attached', 'Jewellery' or 'Designer goods' are not acceptable. The description must be clear enough to allow the UK or EU Customs officer to readily identify the goods. Any unused lines on the form should be crossed through. Each of the following must be shown.
   - The total amount payable (including VAT) in both words and figures.
   - The VAT included in the price.
   - The amount of any administration fee that will be deducted from the refund.
   - The amount of refund to be paid to the customer.

   Part C is the retailer's declaration. It must show
   - the retailer's full business name, address and VAT number; and
   - the date the goods were sold to the customer;

   and must be signed by a responsible person.

Part D is for official use and will be stamped by the Customs officer at the point of departure from the EU to validate the export. (Whilst desirable, it is not essential the Customs officer signs the form.) Customs officers may refuse to stamp refund forms completed incorrectly or not completed in full. For example, forms showing inadequate descriptions of goods may be rejected.

(b) A sales invoice approved beforehand by HMRC. It must closely follow the design of Form VAT 407.

It must include the data protection statement shown on the face of the form and the information shown on the reverse side of the HMRC version of Form VAT 407. This includes

- the heading 'Retail Export Scheme';
- providing spaces for the retailer's and the customer's declarations as stipulated on the Form VAT 407, including details of the customer's passport/identity number and country of issue, date of arrival in the EU, intended date of departure from the EU; and
- a separate box not less than 5cm by 3.5cm for official stamping by a Customs officer at the customer's point of departure from the EU.

The total amount payable must be shown in words as well as figures. The invoice must also show the amount of any administrative charge and the net refund due to the customer.

(c) In addition, any officially approved invoice must also meet the requirements of invoicing legislation generally. See **39.7 INVOICES** for requirements of a retailer's less detailed invoice where the consideration does not exceed £250 and, where the customer agrees, a modified invoice. Otherwise the invoice must comply with the full requirements of an invoice under **39.4 INVOICES**.

Whilst a single refund document is acceptable, it is recommended that retailers issue separate VAT refund documents (but make only one administrative charge) for customers intending to carry some goods in hand baggage and other goods in hold baggage. This is particularly important for customers leaving on a through (transit) flight via another EU airport because the goods in hold baggage must be declared before check in, whilst the goods in hand baggage must be declared at the final point of departure from the EU.

On completion of the refund document, the customer should be given

- the refund document;
- a reply-paid envelope addressed to the retailer or, as the case may be, the refund company administering the refund (alternatively, the retailer should make it clear that it is the customer's responsibility to provide the envelope and pay the correct postage); and
- a copy of VAT Notice 704/1

and advised to produce the refund document (together with the goods and receipts if required) to the Customs officer at the point of departure from the EU.

Control of blank or partly completed VAT refund documents

Whichever form of refund document is used, retailers must keep stocks of the blank documents secure and not issue blank or partly completed forms to any person outside the business.

Goods returned for refund or exchange

If a customer wishes to return goods that have been sold under the scheme (either for a full refund or for exchange) he must take the receipt and the VAT refund document back to the retailer. The retailer should delete the entry for the returned goods (or cancel the VAT refund document and issue a new one) as appropriate.

Action required by the customer on leaving the UK

If the customer decides to leave any goods bought under the scheme in the EU, he must clearly delete those items from the VAT refund document before presenting it, and the remaining goods, to HMRC for examination and stamping.

Action required for goods which are taken outside the EU depends upon how the customer is leaving the EU.

- If leaving for an immediate destination outside the EU, the VAT refund document must be presented to HMRC at the port/airport of departure from the UK. The goods and receipts must be available for inspection if required. (If leaving by air, goods too large or too heavy to be carried on board an aircraft can be packed in hold baggage but, in this case, the VAT refund document should be presented to HMRC before checking in. But high value items including jewellery, furs, cameras, expensive watches, silverware, laptop computers and small antiques, should be carried in hand baggage.)
- If leaving the EU via another EU country, the goods and the refund form must be presented to the Customs authorities of that country.
- If leaving the EU on a through (transit) flight via another EU airport,
  - (i) goods carried as hand baggage must be produced, with the refund form, to Customs in the last EU airport before leaving the EU; and
  - (ii) goods carried as hold baggage must be produced, with the refund form, to HMRC before checking in baggage.

Where a HMRC officer cannot be located to stamp the refund document (e.g. because there is no 24-hour HMRC presence) there will either be a telephone to speak to HMRC or a clearly marked post box to deposit the refund document and a reply-paid envelope.

There is no facility to have a refund document stamped in the country of destination outside the EU.

If satisfied, HMRC will certify the VAT refund document and return it to the customer. The customer must then (depending on whichever method was agreed with the retailer)

- post the refund document back to the retailer to arrange payment of the refund;

- post the refund document to a VAT refund company to arrange payment of the refund; or
- hand the refund document to a cash refund booth operated by the refund company at the airport of departure from the UK which will arrange immediate payment. (Not all airports or refund companies offer this facility.)

Receipt of evidence by the retailer

On receipt of a refund document stamped by UK or other EU Customs, the retailer or refund company must check that all goods have been exported from the EU by the last day of the third month following that in which the goods were purchased and, if so, make the refund to the customer by the method agreed at the time of sale. If a refund document is sent back unstamped, the retailer cannot zero-rate the supply because export of the goods from the EU has not been certified as required by the scheme.

Loss of VAT refund documents

If a customer loses the refund document *before* leaving the EU, the retailer may provide a duplicate clearly marked as such. When issuing the document, the retailer should

- make sure the original document has not been received and already processed;
- be satisfied that a sale took place by the production of till receipts or other information; and
- advise the customer that, if he subsequently finds the original refund document, it is to be cancelled.

If the customer loses the refund document *after* certification by HMRC, a duplicate may only be issued where a photocopy of the stamped original is produced. The duplicate and photocopy must then be sent to the HMRC officer who stamped the original document for certification of the duplicate. Only then should the refund be made.

(VAT Notice 704, paras 3.1–3.7, 4.1–4.4, 4.7, 4.8, 4.10, 4.11, 6.1, 6.4, 7.5–7.7).

Special arrangements for intra-EU cruises

[21.15] Non-EU passengers on wholly intra-EU cruises may not have access to their luggage and to any purchases made under the retail export scheme from disembarkation until they arrive at their final non-EU destination. They cannot, therefore, produce the goods and VAT refund document to the Customs officer for stamping at their point of final departure from the EU. The special arrangements outlined below apply to wholly intra-EU cruises

- which start in the UK; and
- where the final port of disembarkation is also within the UK.

(a) Individual purchases below £1,000

Cruise operators may produce an omnibus bulk refund document for all eligible goods below £1,000 per item purchased on board by entitled individual passengers. This document must accompany the passengers' luggage to the airport of departure. If satisfied, the Customs officer will stamp the bulk refund form and return it to the cruise operator. On receipt of the certified form, the cruise operator must account for the sales in their VAT records as under **21.16** below.

The format of the bulk refund document must be approved beforehand by HMRC. It must be clearly headed 'Retail Export Scheme' and must only include those goods that

- were sold on board the vessel;
- are supplied to entitled customers (see **21.13** Condition 1 above); and
- are eligible to be supplied under the retail export scheme (see **21.13** Condition 2 above).

It must also give the following details.

- Cruise operator's name, address and VAT registration number.
- Customers' name and usual address.
- Customers' passport number and country of issue.
- A description which clearly identifies the goods and the quantity involved.
- The amount payable per item. (Where this includes VAT, the amount payable inclusive of VAT and the amount of VAT included in the total price should be shown.)

In addition, the refund document must include a retailer declaration as stipulated on Form VAT 407 which must be signed by a responsible ship's officer, and a separate box (at least 5 cm by 3.5 cm) for official certification by Customs.

The cruise operator must account for VAT on any goods on the bulk refund form that are not exported from the EU within the prescribed limits.

(b) Individual purchases over £1,000

The normal VAT 407 form or equivalent (see **21.14** above) must be completed for individual purchases over £1,000 per item. The customer must produce the goods and the form for certification to the Customs officer at the point of final departure from the EU.

(VAT Notice 704, paras 8.1, 8.2).

Accounting for VAT

[21.16] At the point of sale, any standard-rated and lower-rated goods sold under the scheme must be treated as liable to VAT. It is therefore in the interest of the retailer to initially charge VAT to the customer. A sale can only be zero-rated when

- the stamped refund document has been received; and

- the refund of VAT has been made to the customer by the agreed method.

The stamped refund document must be retained together with evidence of the refund made to the customer to support zero-rating.

If the certified VAT refund document is received after VAT has been accounted for, the VAT can be refunded and the sale can be zero-rated by reducing output tax by the relevant amount in Box 1 of the VAT return for the period in which the evidence is received and the refund is made.

Suppliers also using a special retail scheme

See **60.9 RETAIL SCHEMES.**

Retailers not using a retail scheme

Such retailers must keep a record of all sales including VAT under the retail export scheme. When a stamped VAT refund document is received and the VAT has been refunded, the sale can be zero-rated in the records.

Refund companies

Where a retailer contracts with a refund company to administer the refund on its behalf, the refund company normally provides an officially approved VAT refund document of its own design for use by the retailer. In such circumstances, the retailer must still account for the VAT as explained above and must retain the certified VAT refund documents and evidence that the VAT has been refunded in its records to support any zero-rating claimed.

Concession shops

Where a larger store operates concessions for other retailers within its own store:

- If the sale is rung through the main store tills, it is acceptable for the VAT refund document to be issued by the host store (typically at the main customer service desk). The host store is then responsible for complying with the conditions of the scheme and accounting for the VAT.
- If the concession operates its own tills and issues receipts showing its own name and VAT number, any VAT refund documents must be issued by the concession and not the host store. The concession is then responsible for complying with the conditions of the scheme and accounting for the VAT.

Direct reclaim system

This involves two distinct transactions: a retailer sells goods to a refund company who immediately sells them on to an eligible traveller. The accounting procedure is as follows.

- The retailer must invoice the sale to the refund company as this is a business-to-business supply (not a retail sale) and must account for VAT on the supply. It may, however, include the sale in its daily gross takings for retail scheme purposes if it wishes.

- The refund company may use the retailer's invoice to reclaim input tax on the purchase. It must also account for VAT on the sale to the traveller. It may subsequently zero-rate the supply but only where all the conditions of the scheme are met.

Sales under the margin scheme for second-hand goods

The margin scheme for second-hand goods and the retail export scheme can both be used for the same transaction but as the amount of VAT charged cannot be shown separately on a valid invoice under the margin scheme, the VAT refund document should be adapted as follows.

- Head the document 'Second-hand goods – this document is adapted in accordance with Notice 704, para 5.8'.
- Leave the line 'Amount of VAT included in the price' blank.
- Complete the refund due box.

Sales by auctioneers

If an auctioneer sells goods on behalf of a retailer to a person entitled to use the retail export scheme and a VAT refund document is completed, the retailer can zero-rate the sale when the stamped refund document is returned and the refund has been made to the customer. Note, however, that the scheme cannot be used for goods exported as freight.

If the auctioneers are registered for VAT and sell goods in their own name to someone who is entitled to use the scheme then, for VAT purposes, they may be treated as both receiving and making a supply of goods. They can zero-rate the sale provided they hold a certified VAT refund document and have refunded the VAT to the customer.

Administration or handling fees

If an amount is deducted from the VAT refund due to cover administrative or handling expenses, the amount deducted is consideration for the supply of services to the customer in connection with the export of goods to a destination outside the EU, and is zero-rated under *VATA 1994, Sch 8 Group 7 Item 2(a)*.

(VAT Notice 704, paras 5.1–5.10).

Motor vehicles

Direct exports

[21.17] Any motor vehicle, new or second-hand, supplied for direct export may be zero-rated provided it is exported from the EU and the conditions in **21.2**(*a*) above are satisfied. Evidence of exportation must be obtained and retained.

Indirect exports

The supply of a new or second-hand motor vehicle can be zero-rated under the conditions in **21.18** below. A motor vehicle can also be zero-rated under the Personal Export Scheme in **21.19** below.

Vehicles delivered in the UK for subsequent export by or on behalf of the purchaser

[21.18] The supply to an overseas person (see **21.9** above) of any motor vehicle (new or second-hand) can be zero-rated provided

- the supplier keeps supplementary evidence of the export (see **21.26** below);
- the vehicle is exported within three months of the supply; and
- the supplier obtains proof of export within three months of the time of supply.

Vehicles delivered in the UK for temporary use and subsequent export by the purchaser (the 'Personal Export Scheme')

[21.19] The Personal Export Scheme allows new and used motor vehicles (including motor cycles and motor caravans but not pedal cycles and trailer caravans) to be purchased free of VAT provided certain conditions (which have the force of law) are met. It should be noted that

- it is not possible to get a refund of VAT on a motor vehicle purchased VAT-paid even if it is later exported and would have qualified under the scheme; and
- it can be very difficult to import motor vehicles into some countries and it is advisable to check with the relevant Embassy or High Commission in the UK before ordering a vehicle under the scheme.

The conditions are as follows.

(a) The vehicle must be purchased from a VAT-registered business which operates the Personal Export Scheme.

(b) Only the purchaser who applies to use the scheme may take delivery of the vehicle in the UK without the written authority of the Personal Transport Unit (see below for contact details).

(c) The purchaser must intend to leave the EU within
- 15 months or less if an 'overseas visitor'; or
- nine months or less in any other case.

See **17.2 EUROPEAN UNION: GENERAL** for the VAT territory of the EU.

(d) An '*overseas visitor*' for these purposes is a person who has not been in the EU for more than either 365 days in the two years immediately before the date of application or 1,095 days in the six years immediately before that date.

(e) The purchaser must export the vehicle within
- twelve months of the date of delivery if an overseas visitor (see (*c*) above); or
- six months of the date of delivery in any other case.

For new vehicles, the final date for exportation is shown in the registration document. *For second-hand vehicles*, the final date of export is shown on the Form VAT 410 (see below).

(f) The purchaser (whether or not an overseas visitor) must intend to leave and remain outside the EU with the vehicle for a period of at least six months.

(g) The vehicle may be driven in the UK in the period before exportation but only by
- the purchaser or their spouse;
- a chauffeur; or
- provided the purchaser is still in the UK, any other person who has his permission to use it and who intends to leave the EU.

(h) The purchaser must not attempt to dispose of the vehicle in the UK (or elsewhere in the EU) by hire, pledge as security, sale, gift or any other means.

If any of the above conditions are broken, the vehicle is liable to forfeiture and may be seized. VAT is then payable on the value of the vehicle when purchased. Even if the vehicle cannot be exported for unavoidable reasons (e.g. theft or accident write-off) the VAT must still be paid.

(1) Procedure at time of sale

If the supplier is satisfied that the applicant is entitled to use the scheme, he should

- give the applicant a copy of Notice 705 *Buyer's guide to personal exports of motor vehicles to destinations outside the EU* and an application form VAT 410 (both obtainable from the VAT Helpline on 0845 010 9000);
- explain the conditions of the scheme; and
- advise the applicant that it is an offence to give incorrect information on the form and that, if they do so, they may be liable to prosecution.

The applicant must complete the form and sign the declaration. In doing so, the applicant declares that they have received, read and understood Notice 705 and will comply with all the conditions of the scheme.

The form VAT 410 is carbonated and incorporates 4 copies:

Part 1 (blue) – Customs copy

Part 2 (green) – Purchaser's copy

Part 3 (pink) – Supplier's copy

Part 4 (yellow) – DVLA local office copy.

Completed application forms must be serially numbered by the supplier in the top right hand corner. (Each separate franchise at the same location requires a separate series of numbers.) Part 1 must be submitted, at least two weeks before date of delivery of the vehicle, to

HM Revenue and Customs
Personal Transport Unit
Building 22
Priory Court
St Johns Road
Dover
Kent CT17 9SH
Tel: 01304 664171
Fax: 01304 664179

An incomplete or incorrect application form will be returned to the supplier for correction and this may delay the delivery of the vehicle.

(2) Cancellation of order before delivery

If, after the application is approved, the order for the vehicle is cancelled by the applicant before delivery, the supplier must immediately notify the PTU at the above address, quoting

- name of applicant,
- make/model of vehicle;
- serial number of the application; and
- in the case of second-hand vehicles, the vehicle registration number.

(3) Invoicing

The supplier must supply and invoice a VAT-free vehicle direct to the applicant. Factory fitted extras can only be supplied VAT-free if they are included on the initial invoice for the supply of the vehicle at the time of purchase.

(4) Registration and licensing with the Driver and Licensing Agency (DVLA)

New vehicles. To register a new vehicle, the supplier must complete an application form V55 headed prominently in block letters 'PERSONAL EXPORT (VAT FREE) VEHICLE', attach it to the DVLA copy (Part 4) of form VAT 410, and send it to the DVLA local office in either Beverley, Birmingham, Bristol, Chelmsford, Glasgow, Leeds, Luton, Lincoln, Maidstone, Manchester, Northampton, Norwich, Oxford or Stockton (see **19.34** **EUROPEAN UNION: SINGLE MARKET** for addresses).

Second-hand vehicles. As a second-hand vehicle will already have been registered, the supplier must notify the DVLA local office of the change of keeper and apply for a special tax disc. This is done by submitting

- the completed V5 Registration Document,
- form V10 (vehicle licence application form),
- the DVLA copy (Part 4) of form VAT 410, and
- form VX304 if the purchaser is entitled to claim exemption from payment of vehicle excise duty

to the DVLA local office in either Beverley, Birmingham, Bristol, Chelmsford, Glasgow, Leeds, Luton, Lincoln, Maidstone, Manchester, Northampton, Norwich, Oxford or Stockton (see **19.34** **EUROPEAN UNION: SINGLE MARKET** for addresses).

A second-hand vehicle must not be supplied with any pre-existing tax disc. If a disc is already in force, it should be surrendered separately to the DVLA local office for a refund.

(5) Insuring the vehicle

The purchaser should insure the vehicle for its full VAT-inclusive value because

- it must be insured before it is used; and

- if the purchaser is unable to export the vehicle (e.g. because it has been stolen or involved in an accident and written-off), the VAT amount not paid at the time of purchase becomes due.

(6) Delivering the vehicle

Before delivering a new vehicle, the supplier must complete the details required on pages 5 and 8 of the pink registration book, showing the amount of VAT remitted, the date of delivery, and the final date for export (see (*c*) above).

The vehicle must be delivered to the applicant in the UK (see (*b*) above). On delivery, the supplier must obtain a dated certificate of receipt for the vehicle signed by the applicant. This must be kept with the other records.

(7) Urgent delivery procedure

Where an overseas visitor intends to leave the UK within one month of their application to use the scheme, the supplier must complete a Certificate for Urgent Delivery authorised by a sole proprietor, partner, director, company secretary or a duly authorised person at a responsible level. At least three working days before the date of delivery of the vehicle to the applicant, the supplier must then fax to the Personal Transport Unit

- a copy of the Certificate for Urgent Delivery;
- a copy of the VAT 410 form; and
- for new vehicles, the V55 Form.

The original papers should then be posted to the Personal Transport Unit.

This procedure must not be used if the initial application by the customer has been rejected or returned for amendment.

(8) Supplier's records

For a new vehicle, in addition to the normal VAT records and his copy of the form VAT 410, the supplier must keep a separate record of each vehicle supplied under the scheme showing

- date of delivery;
- applicant's name and UK address;
- particulars of the vehicle including type, chassis number and registration number;
- amount of VAT remitted on the delivery price (including any accessories or extras and any delivery charges, less any discount allowed); and
- a certificate of receipt of the vehicle, detailing chassis number and registration number, which must be signed and dated by the applicant.

For a second-hand vehicle, the supplier should already have a record of it in his second-hand stock book under the margin scheme for second-hand goods. When he sells a second-hand vehicle under the Personal Export Scheme, he must close this stock book entry and include a cross-reference to the serial number of the form VAT 410, inserting 'zero-rate' in the VAT rate column of his stock book and 'Nil' in the VAT due column. He must then record the sale separately and include the same details as required for sales of new vehicles above. He can, if he wishes, include his second-hand sales with his records of new vehicle sales (if any).

(9) Use of vehicle before exportation from the EU

The vehicle can be used in the UK before exportation provided it is insured, exported by the final due date (see (*d*) above) and only used by an approved person (see (*f*) above).

It may also be used to make a temporary visit to another EU country. If so, it can be brought back to the UK without any Customs formalities provided it is returned to the UK before the final due date for exportation (see (*d*) above) and the customer still intends to export and depart with the vehicle from the EU by that date. The purchaser is advised to check with the relevant VAT authority of the other EU country to establish whether, because the vehicle has been supplied free of VAT, it is necessary to comply with any Customs requirements on entry into that country.

It is not normally advisable to make a temporary visit to a non-EU country prior to the final date for export (see (*d*) above). When the vehicle is re-imported into either the UK or another EU country, the VAT amount not paid at the time of purchase will become due (unless qualifying for relief under the re-importation rules (see below).

(10) Change of plans by purchaser before exportation from EU

If the purchaser changes his plans before the vehicle is removed from the UK and can no longer comply with the conditions in (*c*) or (*d*) above, he must notify the Personal Transport Unit immediately and pay the full amount of VAT not paid when the vehicle was bought. If the vehicle is in another EU country, the purchaser should contact the fiscal authorities of that country (and pay VAT and any other local taxes due).

(11) Procedure on exportation

For new vehicles, the final date for exportation is shown on the pink registration document. The tear-off section of the document must be completed and returned to the DVLA local office as shown on the document.

For second-hand vehicles, the final date of exportation is shown on the customer's copy (Part 1) of form VAT 410. The customer must complete the relevant section of the V5 registration document and send the entire document to the DVLA local office as shown on the document. The DVLA will issue an export certificate to enable the vehicle to be re-registered in the country of destination. If the purchaser intends to leave the UK within 14 days of acquiring the vehicle, he should tell the dealer before purchase so that the dealer can arrange for the DVLA to issue an export certificate straightaway.

Shipping arrangements must be made in good time to ensure that the vehicle is exported by the final date.

(12) Reimportation

If the vehicle is brought back into the UK after the date shown for export, taxes must be paid on importation unless the person is eligible for relief from VAT and duty (see Customs Notice 3 Bringing your belongings and private motor vehicle to the UK from outside the European Community) in which case no VAT will be charged. Where the purchaser is not eligible for relief,

- if the vehicle is re-imported six months or more after the date for export (or the owner can show that he and the vehicle have remained outside the EU for at least six consecutive months), the VAT payable will be based on the value of the vehicle at the time of re-importation; and
- in all other cases, the VAT payable will be that which was not charged on purchase.

The vehicle must also be registered and licensed on return to the UK unless it is not to be used or kept on the public roads. The owner should contact the nearest DVLA local office and produce proof of payment of, or exemption from, VAT in order to re-license or re-register the vehicle.

If the vehicle is re-imported into another EU country after it was exported from the EU, the owner should contact the VAT authority in that country and pay the VAT (and any other local taxes) due.

[*SI 1995/2518, Regs 117(8), 132, 133; SI 1999/438, Reg 10; SI 2000/258, Reg 6*]. (VAT Notice 707).

Sailaway boats supplied for export

[21.20] From 1 January 2012 the concessionary treatment described below is being withdrawn. However, a business may zero-rate the supply of a boat to a UK resident provided that it meets the conditions for zero-rating a direct export (see **21.2**(*a*) above). (HMRC Brief 38/11).

Prior to 1 January 2012, under the conditions outlined below (which have the force of law) it is possible to zero-rate the supply of a '*sailaway boat*', i.e. a boat to be

- delivered to the purchaser or their authorised skipper within the EU; and
- to be exported under its own power to a destination outside the VAT territory of the EU (see **17.2 EUROPEAN UNION: GENERAL**).

As the supply can only be zero-rated after receipt of evidence that the boat has been exported in the time limit allowed, it is advisable to treat any sale under the scheme as liable to VAT until this evidence is received. It is recommended, therefore, that a deposit is taken equal to the amount of VAT, to be refunded when the required evidence of export is received.

Who is entitled to use the scheme

The scheme can only be used for the private purchase of a boat by

- an overseas visitor who intends to export the boat under its own power to a destination outside the EU within six months of the 'date of delivery'; or
- an UK resident who intends to export the boat under its own power to a destination outside the EU within two months of the date of delivery. The boat must be kept outside the EU for a continuous period of at least twelve months.

The scheme must not be used for commercial purchases.

'*Date of delivery*' is normally the date the boat leaves the manufacturer's or supplier's premises.

The scheme cannot be used

- where the supplier arranges delivery of the boat (either on a trailer or by using a skipper employed by the supplier) to a destination outside the EU (see **21.2**(*a*) above for the conditions for zero-rating direct exports);
- for a boat supplied for private use for removal from the UK to another EU country (see **19.34 EUROPEAN UNION: SINGLE MARKET** for the conditions for zero-rating such a sale); or
- for parts or accessories (which may be supplied under the retail export scheme (see **21.12** above)).

Forms

The supplier needs to prove that the boat has been removed from the EU before zero-rating the sale in his records. The forms needed for this purpose are

- **Form VAT 436** – Notification of VAT-free purchase of a sailaway boat, and customers declaration. This form is in four parts.

Copy 1	copy for certification
Copy 2	Customs copy
Copy 3	customer's copy
Copy 4	supplier's copy

- **Form C88** (Single Administrative Document). This form is in three parts.

Copy 1	Community transit copy where applicable
Copy 2	UK Customs copy
Copy 3	For certification when the boat finally leaves the EU

- **Form C1331** – to advise departure from the UK.

Action required by the supplier

The supplier must

- check that the customer is entitled to use the scheme (see above);
- ensure that the customer intends to export the boat from the EU under its own power within the permitted time limit;
- where the customer is a UK resident, the supplier must have evidence that the customer intends to keep the boat outside the EU for a continuous period of at least twelve months;
- give the customer a copy of VAT Notice 703/2 and an application form VAT 436;

- ensure that the customer knows that he must not dispose, or attempt to dispose, of the boat in the EU by hire, pledge as security (other than as part of the financing arrangement for the purchase of the boat itself), sale, gift or any other means;
- agree how any refund of deposited VAT will be paid;
- ensure that Form VAT 436 is fully completed and, at least two weeks before due delivery of the boat, that Part 2 is submitted to: HMRC, Personal Transport Unit (PTU), Priory Court, St John's Road, Dover, CT17 9SH (Tel: 01304 664171; Fax: 01304 664179). Forms which are incorrect or incomplete will be returned for correction and this may delay the delivery of the boat. If, after the form is processed, the order for the boat is cancelled by the customer before delivery, the supplier must immediately notify the PTU of the customer's name, details of the boat, and the reference number of the form; and
- keep a separate record for the sale.

Export procedure

If the customer is leaving the UK directly for a destination outside the EU, the customer must

- ensure that the boat is exported within time limits;
- complete Form C1331 Notice of Intended Departure;
- make the boat available for inspection by Customs at exportation (where possible this should be arranged in advance);
- take completed Form VAT 436 and Form C1331 to the UK Customs nearest the place of departure. Customs will retain Form C1331, sign and stamp Form VAT 436 to show that the boat has been declared for exportation, and return the Form VAT 436 to the customer; and
- return the certified Form VAT 436 to the supplier.

If the customer is calling into another EU country before finally exporting the boat from the EU, the customer must

- ensure that the boat is exported within time limits;
- take the completed Form C88 (copies 2 and 3) and Form VAT 436 to the UK Customs office nearest the place of departure from the UK. Customs will keep copy 2 of Form C88 and return copy 3 with Form VAT 436 to the customer;
- take copy 3 of Form C88 and VAT 436 to the Customs office at the place of final departure from the EU for certification; and
- return the certified Form C88 and VAT 436 to the supplier.

Accounting arrangements

A separate record must be kept of all boats sold under the scheme. The sales invoice must clearly show that the supply of the boat was made under the sailaway boat scheme.

If evidence of export within time limits is not obtained and held, VAT must be accounted for. Any deposit taken of the VAT due should be brought to account. Where no deposit has been taken, the VAT records must be amended and VAT accounted for on the taxable proportion of the invoiced amount or consideration received (i.e. where the rate of VAT is 17.5%, the VAT element is 7/47; where the rate of VAT is 20% from 4 January 2011, the VAT element is 1/6; where the rate of VAT is 15% from 1 December 2008 to 31 December 2009, the VAT element is 3/23). The amendment should be made in the VAT account and VAT return for the period in which the time limit expires.

If evidence of export within the permitted time limit is subsequently received, the supply can be zero-rated and any deposit refunded. The VAT account can be adjusted for the period in which evidence is received.

Re-importation of VAT-free boats

If a boat that was supplied VAT free at purchase is brought back to the EU, it must be declared to Customs in the EU country of importation. The supplier should ensure that the customer is fully aware of the need to make an import declaration. VAT will be payable unless some other relief is available.

The Channel Islands

The Channel Islands are outside the EU VAT area and therefore qualify as a final destination for boats supplied under the sailaway boat scheme. EU residents who register VAT-free boats in the Channel Islands cannot claim VAT-free temporary importation of such boats into an EU country. VAT is payable on these importations. Private persons resident in the Channel Islands may be entitled to import their own boats temporarily into the VAT territory of the EU for their own personal use for up to 18 months, without payment of import VAT.

(VAT Notice 703/2/11; VAT Notice 48, ESC 8.1).

Supplies to the FCO and other government departments

Foreign and Commonwealth Office (FCO)

[21.21] Goods ordered by British Embassies, High Commissions and diplomats abroad which are delivered to FCO for export via diplomatic channels can be zero-rated provided a certificate of receipt for the goods is obtained from the FCO within three months of the time of supply of the goods. See VAT Notice 703, para 12.1 for an example of the certificate. The certificate may be on a copy of the sales invoice or itemised list and must be retained. To show that the supply was to an overseas person, the supplier must also retain documents (e.g. the order) to identify the destination of the goods.The supply of goods ordered by and delivered to the FCO for general distribution cannot be zero-rated.

Ministry of Defence (MOD)

The MOD is registered for VAT in the UK and all supplies to them or to any military establishment in the UK on their behalf should include VAT at the appropriate rate. Direct exports to overseas military and similar installations may be zero-rated provided the supplier holds valid proof of export.

Other government departments

The supply of goods to other government departments can only be zero-rated if supplied by direct export to a destination outside the EU. Goods for export delivered to government departments in the UK must not be zero-rated even if the goods are ordered for or by an overseas establishment.

(VAT Notice 703, paras 4.9, 4.11 7.11).

Supplies to regimental shops

[21.22] Supplies to regimental shops are normally taxable. However, where the regiment (or equivalent military unit) is about to be posted to a location outside the EU, supplies of goods (except new and second-hand motor vehicles) to a regimental shop can be zero-rated provided the following conditions are satisfied.

- Each written order received from the President of the Regimental Institute (PRI) states that the regiment is about to take up an overseas posting and that the goods ordered will be exported from the EU.
- The goods are delivered to the PRI ready packed for shipment no more than 48 hours before the regiment is due to depart for the overseas posting.
- The goods are exported outside the EU.
- The supplier retains a certificate of receipt signed by the PRI which clearly identifies the goods, gives full shipment details and states the date on which they were exported from the EU.

The PRI will keep a full record of such transactions for reference purposes for a period of not less than six years.

(VAT Notice 703, para 4.10).

Supplies intended for continental shelf installations

[21.23] The following provisions apply to the export of goods to structures such as oil rigs, dwelling units, accommodation platforms and similar oil or gas exploration/exploitation structures. It also applies to mobile floating structures such as drill ships, tankers, jack-up rigs, semi-submersible rigs and Floating Production Storage and Offloading (FPSO) vessels which are often stationed at fixed locations.

Exports to installations outside EU territorial waters

- *Goods supplied and exported by a supplier to an installation which he does not own.* Such supplies are zero-rated as direct exports provided proof of export is obtained within three months of the supply.
- *Goods sent to an installation owned by the supplier or goods sent to replenish own stocks on an installation not owned by the supplier.* This is a transfer of own goods and not a taxable supply (see **21.24** below). Valid proof of export must still be held to demonstrate how the goods have been disposed of.

Goods supplied for sale on installations situated outside UK territorial waters

Such supplies can be zero-rated provided

- a written order for the goods is obtained from a responsible person on the installation to which the goods are to be sent;
- the goods are supplied either direct to the installation or through an agent for consolidation followed by direct delivery to the installation; and
- a receipt for the goods, signed by a responsible person on the installation, is obtained within three months of the time of supply.

(VAT Notice 703, paras 4.7, 4.8).

Goods supplied and delivered within the UK (including territorial waters).

If such goods are

- supplied to an overseas person (see **21.9** above) for export by that person as an indirect export and the necessary conditions in **21.2** above are met, or
- supplied to an overseas person but delivered to a third person in the UK for processing, etc. and subsequent export and the conditions in **21.10** above are met,

the supply can be zero-rated.

Otherwise, VAT must be charged at the appropriate rate.

Exports where there is no taxable supply

[21.24] There is no need to account for VAT in the following circumstances.

- The supply and export of goods which the supplier is to install outside the EU for his customer (as the supply takes place in the country where the goods are installed).
- The temporary export of goods for exhibition or processing.
- The export of goods on sale or return where the goods remain the property of the supplier until they are sold.
- The transfer of own goods to a place outside the EU by a UK business. Any related input tax can be deducted (subject to the normal rules) but the value of any transferred goods should not be included in Box 6 of the VAT return.

The supplier must still hold valid proof of export to demonstrate to HMRC how the goods were disposed of. He must also declare any goods returned to the UK.

(VAT Notice 703, paras 2.14, 2.15).

Proof of export

[21.25] A supplier must ensure that he has proof of export readily available for HMRC. This must be obtained within the appropriate time limit (see **21.2**(*a*) above) and retained for six years.

Proof of export consists of:

- *Official evidence* — this is produced by HMRC (e.g. Goods Departed Messages (GDM) generated by the New Export System (NES)). Alternatively it may be in the form of a Single Administrative Document (SAD) endorsed by HMRC at the point of exit from the EU or confirmation of the electronic discharge of an NCTS movement.
- *Commercial evidence* — e.g. authenticated sea-waybills or air-waybills; PIM/PIEX International consignment notes; master air-waybills or bills of lading; certificates of shipment containing the full details of the consignment and how it left the EU; or International Consignment Note/Lettre de Voiture International (CMR) fully completed by the consignor, the haulier and the receiving consignee, or Freight Transport Association (FTA) own account transport documents fully completed and signed by the receiving customer.

Equal weight is put on official and commercial evidence but both must be supported by supplementary evidence.

Supplementary evidence

A supplier must hold sufficient evidence to prove that a transaction has taken place and that the transaction relates to the goods physically exported. Accounting records are likely to include the following (although it will probably not be necessary to hold all the items listed).

- Customer's order.
- Sales contract.
- Inter-company correspondence.
- Copy of export sales invoice.
- Advice note.
- Consignment note.
- Packing list.
- Insurance and freight charges documentation.
- Evidence of payment.
- Evidence of the receipt of the goods abroad.

Evidence of export

The evidence obtained as proof of export, whether official or commercial, or supporting must clearly identify the following. (These requirements have the force of law.)

- The supplier.
- The consignor (where different from the supplier).
- The customer.
- The goods.

- An accurate value.
- The export destination.
- The mode of transport and route of the export movement.

Vague descriptions of goods, quantities or values are not acceptable (e.g. 'various electrical goods' must not be used when the correct description is '2000 mobile phones make ABC and model number XYZ2000').

Lost or mislaid export evidence

If an exporter has lost or mislaid the official or commercial evidence of export supplied by the ship owner or carrier, duplicate evidence of export may be obtained. The replacement evidence of export must be clearly marked 'DUPLICATE EVIDENCE OF EXPORT' and be authenticated and dated by an official of the issuing company.

Photocopies

Photocopy certificates of shipment are not normally acceptable as evidence of export, nor are photocopy bills of lading, sea waybills or air waybills (unless authenticated by the shipping or air line).

(VAT Notice 703, paras 6.1–6.5, 6.10).

Evidence where the supplier does not arrange shipment

[21.26] If the overseas customer collects or arranges the collection of the goods and their removal from the UK, it can be difficult for the supplier to obtain adequate proof of export as the carrier is contracted to the customer. As a result, for this type of transaction the standard of evidence required to substantiate VAT zero-rating is high. The supplier should seek confirmation of what evidence of export will be provided. He should also consider taking a deposit from the customer equal to the amount of VAT, in case satisfactory evidence of export is not received.

Evidence must show that the goods supplied have left the EU. Copies of transport documents alone are not sufficient and information held must identify the date and route of the movement of goods and the method of transport involved. It should include the following.

- A written order from the customer which shows their name, address and the address where the goods are to be delivered.
- Copy sales invoice showing invoice number, customer's name, and a description of the goods.
- Delivery address for the goods.
- Date of departure of goods from the supplier's premises and from the EU.
- Name and address of the haulier collecting the goods, registration number of the vehicle collecting the goods and the name and signature of the driver.
- Where the goods are to be taken out of the EU by an alternative haulier or vehicle, the name and address of that haulier, the registration number of the vehicle and a signature for the goods.

- Route (e.g. Channel Tunnel, port of exit).
- Copy of travel tickets.
- Name of ferry or shipping company and date of sailing or airway number and airport.

The information held should also include (where applicable):

- Trailer number.
- Full container number.
- Name and address for consolidation, groupage, or processing.

(VAT Notice 703, para 6.6).

Evidence in specific circumstances

[21.27] See VAT Notice 703 as indicated below for specific evidence of export that must be obtained according to the method of export used. In all cases the official or commercial transport evidence obtained must be supported by the supplementary evidence in **21.25** above to show that the transaction has taken place.

Air and sea freight	Para 7.1
Road freight	Para 7.2
Merchandise in Baggage (MIB)	Para 7.3
Groupage or consolidation transactions	Para 7.4
Postal exports	Para 7.5
Exports by courier and fast parcel services	Para 7.6
Exports by rail	Para 7.7
Exports through packers	Para 7.8
Exports from Customs, Excise and/or fiscal warehouses	Para 7.10

Exports through auctioneers

Auctioneers not acting in their own name

[21.28] A supplier who sells goods through auctioneers who

- are not acting in their own name; and
- export the goods

may zero-rate the supply provided a certificate of export is obtained from the auctioneers within three months of the time of supply (see VAT Notice 703, paras 12.2 and 12.3 for the format of the certificates). The auctioneer must hold valid evidence of export for the goods.

Auctioneers acting in their own name

If a supplier sells goods through auctioneers who act in their own name, the goods are treated as being supplied to the auctioneer and must not be zero-rated by the supplier as an export. The auctioneer will be able to zero-rate the onward supply subject to the normal rules.

(VAT Notice 703, para 7.9).

Exports to the Channel Islands

[21.29] Evidence of export for goods sent to the Channel Islands is one of the following (as appropriate).

- Official proof of export produced by NES.
- For goods shipped by air — an authenticated master air-waybill or house air-waybill.
- For goods carried as Merchandise in Baggage — a Customs' certified copy 3 of the SAD (Form C88).
- For goods shipped through a freight forwarder — a certificate of shipment issued by the freight forwarder or an authenticated copy of the Consignment Note and Customs Declarations (CNCD).
- For goods shipped through a fast parcel or courier service — evidence as per VAT Notice 703, para 7.6.
- For goods shipped directly by the south coast ferry companies — an authenticated copy of the CNCD.

(VAT Notice 703, para 7.12).

Exports via EU countries

[21.30] Where goods are exported outside the EU but via other EU countries, official or commercial documentary evidence is required that the goods have left the EU.

Official evidence of export will normally be copy 3 of the export SAD (Form C88) or NES equivalent endorsed at the customs office of exit from the EU. The office of exit will vary depending on the type of transport used and the nature of the supply.

Where goods subject to excise duty are moving under duty suspension arrangements, the customs office of exit from the EU will certify the accompanying document (an 'attestation' in EU terms) and return it to the consignor as evidence of exportation from the EU. The standard time limits for obtaining the evidence of export apply.

(VAT Notice 703, para 7.13).

Records and returns

[21.31] Where goods are exported (or supplied as ships' stores), the normal rules for record keeping still apply (see **56 RECORDS**). In addition, evidence of export must be retained as set out in **21.25** to **21.27** above.

Exports can be zero-rated in the records at the time of supply to the customer. But if the supplier does not ensure the goods have been exported and obtain and hold the required evidence of export within the relevant time limit for the supply, he must account for VAT at the appropriate rate on a supply of the goods in the UK.

VAT must be accounted for on the taxable proportion of the invoiced amount or consideration received (i.e. for a VAT rate of 17.5% the VAT element would be calculated at 7/47; for the VAT rate of 20% from 4 January 2011 the VAT element would be calculated at 1/6; for the VAT rate of 15% from 1 December 2008 to 31 December 2009 the VAT element would be calculated at 3/23). This VAT must be included in Box 1 of the VAT return for the period in which the relevant time limit expires.

If the goods are subsequently exported and/or evidence of export is obtained, the supply can then be zero-rated and the VAT account adjusted for the period in which the evidence is obtained.

Retail schemes

See **60.9 RETAIL SCHEMES** for treatment of exports where a retail scheme is used.

Goods returned damaged

Where export goods are damaged after shipment and relanded in the UK, they must be declared to HMRC. If the supplier, or a member of a salvage association, subsequently sell the goods, the seller must account for VAT at the appropriate UK rate on the sale price.

(VAT Notice 703, paras 11.1–11.4).

Goods accidentally lost, destroyed or stolen before export

[21.32] VAT must be accounted for on goods destined for export outside the EU which have been accidentally lost, destroyed or stolen in the UK as follows.

- Where lost, etc. before being supplied, no VAT is due.
- Where lost, etc. after being supplied for direct export, no VAT is due provided that evidence of loss, destruction or theft is held (e.g. an insurance claim, police investigation etc.).
- Where lost, etc. after being supplied for indirect export, VAT is due at the appropriate rate if the goods have been delivered to or collected by the overseas person, or their agent, in the UK.

(VAT Notice 703, para 2.16).

Key points

[21.33] Points to consider are as follows.

- Remember that an export of goods outside the EU is always zero-rated, irrespective of the status of the customer. However, the priority is to ensure that proper export evidence is held to confirm the goods have left the EU.

- There can only ever be one exporter in a supply of goods arrangement. So if UK business 'A' takes an order from UK business 'B' to supply goods, then this cannot be an export arrangement, even if business 'A' directly ships the goods to a customer outside the EU. It is only business 'B' that can be classed as the exporter, as it is effectively making the sale to the final customer based outside the EU. The sale from business 'A' to 'B' is standard-rated, although business 'B' can reclaim input tax subject to the normal rules.
- The importance of obtaining proper export evidence to support zero-rating cannot be emphasised enough. If HMRC is not satisfied with the export evidence provided, it can treat the goods as being supplied in the UK from a VAT point of view. This could create an output tax charge if the goods in question are standard-rated. Export evidence must be obtained within three months of the export taking place.
- If goods are collected from a UK supplier and taken out of the EU by an overseas customer, it is worthwhile to collect a deposit from the customer equal to the amount of VAT due on the supply. The deposit can then be refunded to the customer when he provides export evidence to confirm the goods have left the EU. This arrangement is known as an 'indirect export' and the standard of export evidence required by HMRC to support zero-rating is very high because it is a higher risk transaction.
- If export evidence is not acquired within three months of the supply, then the exporter must treat the sale as taking place in the UK, i.e. as a standard-rated sale if the goods in question would be standard-rated if sold in the UK. If evidence is subsequently acquired at a future date, then the output tax adjustment can be credited on the VAT return when the evidence was acquired, i.e. so that zero-rating again applies to the sale.
- The retail export scheme can offer commercial benefits to some retailers by giving certain overseas customers the chance to buy goods on a VAT-free basis. The conditions of the scheme must be fully met in order to secure zero-rating. One of the conditions is that the customer buying the goods must take them to a destination outside of the EU before the last day of the third month following his purchase (e.g. goods bought on 3 February must be exported before 31 May).
- A UK trader whose sales are wholly or mainly exports will probably be in a repayment situation as far as VAT is concerned. The cash flow benefits of submitting returns monthly rather than quarterly should therefore be considered.

22

Extra-Statutory Concessions

Extra-statutory concessions

[22.1] *From 21 July 2008*, HMRC have the power to legislate concessions by Treasury Order [*FA 2008, s 160*]. The following is a summary of all VAT concessions in force as published by HMRC in Notice 48 (March 2009).

International field

2.1 **Visiting forces, NATO and US and Canadian government expenditure.** VAT (and duty including all import and excise duties) are remitted or refunded on

(a) goods and services imported by or supplied to visiting forces and their instrumentalities, for the official use of the force, or their instrumentalities;

(b) goods and services imported by or supplied to NATO military headquarters, organisations or agencies, for their official use;

(c) US and Canadian government expenditure on mutual defence or mutual aid contracts; and

(d) temporary importations of equipment required by contractors for fulfilling NATO infrastructure contracts or in connection with the provision and maintenance of US forces defence facilities in the UK.

2.2 **UK-manufactured alcoholic liquor and tobacco products purchased by diplomats.** VAT (and duty) are remitted on alcoholic liquor and tobacco products of UK manufacture imported by, or supplied to, diplomatic representatives of foreign states in the UK who are entitled to similar privileges in respect of imported products of foreign manufacture under *Diplomatic Privileges Act 1964*.

2.3 **United States Air Force.** Relief from VAT (and/or excise duty) is allowed, in accordance with certain conditions agreed with the US Air Force, on

(a) charges for admission to air shows and open days; and

(b) goods sold by US forces organisations during air shows and open days to persons not entitled to receive/consume them unless customs charges have been paid.

2.4 **Gifts by US forces.** VAT (and duty) are remitted on gifts (whether imported or purchased in the UK) from US forces to charitable organisations.

2.5 **American war graves.** See **15.5 DEATH AND INCAPACITY**.

2.6 **Supplies to diplomatic missions, international organisations, NATO forces etc. in other EU countries.** See **19.21 EUROPEAN UNION: SINGLE MARKET**.

2.7 **Aircraft ground and security equipment.** See **33.22 IMPORTS**.

Concessions designed to remove inequities or anomalies in administration

3.1 **Purchases of road fuel.** *VATA 1994, s 56* requires payment of a scale charge if road fuel purchased by a business is used for private journeys. However, where input tax is not claimed on *any* road fuel used by the business, whether for business or private journeys, the VAT scale charge will not apply. See **45.16 MOTOR CARS.**

> *Example*
> A business has two company cars and two vans, all of which are used for business journeys, and the cars have some private use as well. To avoid applying the scale charge payment to the motor cars, the business will need to sacrifice input tax recovery on all road fuel purchases, i.e. including the fuel used for the two vans.

3.2 **Group supplies using an overseas member: anticipation of legislative changes.** A charge to VAT arises where supplies of a type within *VATA 1994, Sch 5* are purchased by an overseas group member and used for making supplies within *Sch 5* to a UK group member. The amount of the VAT charge is calculated by reference to the value of the supply by the overseas member to the UK member but may be reduced to the value of the *Sch 5* services purchased by the overseas member provided certain conditions are met. See **27.6 GROUPS OF COMPANIES.**
This concession cannot be used for tax avoidance purposes.

3.3 **Zero-rating of supplies of certain goods used in connection with collection of monetary donations by charities.** The supply to a charity of certain goods may be treated as if it were a zero-rated supply. See **12.7 CHARITIES.**

3.4 **Misunderstanding by a VAT trader.** Where certain conditions are fulfilled, VAT undercharged by a registered trader as a result of a*bona fide* misunderstanding may be remitted. See **47.1 OUTPUT TAX.**

3.6 **Coin-operated machines.** As an accounting convenience, operators may delay accounting for VAT until the takings are removed from the machine. See **57.4 RECREATION AND SPORT** and **66.25 SUPPLY: TIME OF SUPPLY.**

3.7 **VAT on minor promotional items supplied in linked supply schemes.** These are schemes in which a minor article is linked with a main article and sold at a single price. Provided the cost of the minor article is within certain limits, it can be treated as taxable at the same rate as the main article. See **69.5 TRADE PROMOTION SCHEMES.**

3.8 **Use of margin scheme for vehicle sales when incomplete records have been kept.** Where a dealer has the required information on the purchase or sale of a car but not both, subject to conditions VAT may be accounted for on the purchase price or half the selling price. See **61.35 SECOND-HAND GOODS.**

3.9 **Recoveries of VAT under*VATA 1994, Sch 11 para 5*(VAT charged by unregistered persons).** Where an amount is shown or represented as VAT on an invoice issued by a person who is neither registered nor required to be registered for VAT at the time the invoice is issued, HMRC may require that person to pay an equivalent amount to them. By concession, the person may be permitted to deduct any VAT incurred on supplies to him that were directly attributable to the invoiced supplies. Also by concession, if the recipient of the supplies is a taxable person HMRC may allow the recipient to treat the amount shown or represented as VAT as input tax. See **31.2 HMRC: POWERS.**

3.10 **VAT on necessary meals and accommodation provided by recognised representative sporting bodies to amateur sports persons chosen to represent that**

body in a competition. In such circumstances, the input tax incurred may be deductible as input tax and not treated as business entertainment. See **9.6 BUSINESS ENTERTAINMENT.**

3.11 **Incorrect customer declaration.** Where a customer provides an incorrect declaration claiming eligibility for zero-rating under*VATA 1994* and the supplier, despite having taken all reasonable steps to check the validity of the declaration, fails to identify the inaccuracy and, in good faith, zero-rates the supply, HMRC will not seek to recover the VAT due from the supplier. See **12.7 CHARITIES, 25.2 FUEL AND POWER, 28.33 HEALTH AND WELFARE, 42.22 LAND AND BUILDINGS: ZERO AND REDUCED RATE SUPPLIES AND DIY HOUSE-BUILDERS, 47.1 OUTPUT TAX, 70.14 TRANSPORT AND FREIGHT** and **74.2 ZERO-RATED SUPPLIES.**

3.12 **Buses with special facilities for carrying disabled persons.** Where a vehicle has less than ten seats because it is equipped with facilities for carrying persons in wheelchairs, it can be treated, for VAT purposes, as if it had at least ten seats. See **45.1 MOTOR CARS** and **70.17 TRANSPORT AND FREIGHT.**

3.13 **Repayment of import VAT to shipping agents and freight forwarders.** Under certain conditions, import VAT may be repaid directly to shipping agents and freight forwarders where importers go into insolvency or receivership leaving the agents unable to recover VAT paid on their behalf. See **33.8 IMPORTS.**

3.14 **Zero-rating of certain supplies of free zone goods.** The supply of goods subject to import VAT which are free zone goods in the UK may be zero-rated on condition that there is an agreement between the supplier and the customer that the customer will clear the goods for removal from the zone and will take responsibility for payment of the import VAT. See **72.23 WAREHOUSED GOODS AND FREE ZONES.**

3.15 **Printed matter published in instalments.** Individual component parts of loose-leaf books may be zero-rated. See **54.3 PRINTED MATTER, ETC**

3.16 **Connection to gas and electricity mains supply.** The first time connection to the gas or electricity mains supply of a qualifying building, residential caravan or houseboat may be zero-rated. See **25.7 FUEL AND POWER.** (Withdrawn from 1 January 2012).

3.17 **Zero-rating of supplies of training for foreign governments.** Zero-rating applies to training services supplied to a foreign government in furtherance of its sovereign activities. See **38.6 INTERNATIONAL SERVICES.**

3.18 **Exemption of all domestic service charges.** All mandatory service charges paid by occupants of residential property towards the upkeep of the property and the provision of caretakers are exempt. See **41.4 LAND AND BUILDINGS: EXEMPT SUPPLIES AND OPTION TO TAX.**

3.19 **Supplies of 'relevant goods' to charities.** Zero-rating may be applied to supplies of 'relevant goods' to a charity either whose sole or main purpose is to provide a range of care services to meet the personal needs of handicapped people or which provides transport services predominantly for handicapped people. See **12.8 CHARITIES.**

3.20 **Bad debt relief: disapplication of repayment of input tax: insolvency.** Where certain conditions are met, an insolvency practitioner need not repay input tax under *VATA 1994, s 36(4A)* where, after an insolvency procedure has commenced, the practitioner receives notice of a claim to VAT bad debt relief from a supplier in respect of a pre-insolvency transaction. See **7.13 BAD DEBT RELIEF** and **34.4 INPUT TAX.**

3.21 **Sale of poor quality donated goods.** The supply by a charity of goods which have been donated to it for sale can be zero-rated where the goods, although of a kind normally zero-rated by being made available to the general public for purchase, are by reason of their poor quality not fit to be so made available. See **12.6 CHARITIES.**

3.22 **Valuation of the refurbishment or fitting out of a building for the purposes of the capital goods scheme.** Where it is difficult to identify goods affixed to a building for the purposes of *SI 1995/2518, Reg 113(h)*, subject to conditions, goods which have not been affixed may be included in the value of capital expenditure. See **10.2 CAPITAL GOODS SCHEME.**

3.23 **Supplies by Financial Ombudsman Services Ltd to ombudsman authorities.** Payments of any amount by the

- Office of the Building Societies Ombudsman (OBSO)
- Office of the Banking Ombudsman (OBO)
- Insurance Ombudsman Bureau (IOB)
- Personal Assurance Arbitration Service (PASS)
- PIA Ombudsman Bureau (PIAOB)
- Office of the Investment Ombudsman Bureau (OIOB)
- SFA Complaints Bureau and Arbitration Service (SFACBAS)
- FSA Independent Investigator (FSAII)

to Financial Ombudsman Services Ltd (FOS) for the supply of services by FOS in connection with the ombudsman and complaint handing scheme duties by OBSO, OBO, IOB, PAAS, PIAOB, OIOB, SFACBAS and FSAII (as the case may be) between 1 April 2000 and 1 October 2000 are not treated as consideration for any supply in the course of any business carried on by FOS.

3.24 Charities providing care in an institution and also supplying goods to disabled persons resident in their own and other institutions. Where conditions are met, zero-rating can be applied to supplies by a charity at or below cost of certain goods designed solely for use by a visually handicapped person even though the recipient of the supply is a resident, or is attending the premises of, the charity's own institution. See **28.15 HEALTH AND WELFARE.**

3.25 Resuscitation training models supplied to charities and other eligible bodies for use in first aid training. These can be treated as relevant goods for the purposes of *VATA 1994, Sch 8 Group 15 Note (3)* and their supply zero-rated in certain cases. See **12.8 CHARITIES.**

3.26 Works of art, antiques and collectors' items. Where certain works of art, collector's items and antiques are imported for exhibition with a view to possible sale, any sale of those items by auction when still subject to temporary importation arrangements is treated as neither a supply of goods nor a supply of services. See **73.4 WORKS OF ART, ETC.**

3.27 Use of the auctioneers' scheme for sales of goods at auction on behalf of non-taxable persons. An auctioneer selling, on behalf of a third party vendor who is a non-taxable person, goods which have been grown, made or produced (including bloodstock or livestock reared from birth) by that person, may enter the goods into the auctioneers' scheme provided he holds an appropriate certificate from the vendor. See **61.54 SECOND-HAND GOODS.**

3.28 Supplies by Financial Services Authority to self-regulating organisations. The payment of any amount at any time by

- the Investment Management Regulatory Organisation (IMRO),
- the Personal Investment Authority (PIA) or
- the Securities and Futures Authority (SFA)

to the Financial Services Authority (FSA) for the supply by the FSA in the carrying out of the regulatory functions of IMRO, PIA or SFA (as the case may be) between 1 April 1998 and 1 October 2000, and similar payments by

- the Registrar of Friendly Societies (RFS), and
- the Insurance Directorate of HM Treasury (ID)

(as the case may be) between 1 January 1999 and 1 October 2000 are not treated as consideration for any supply in the course or furtherance of any business carried on by FSA.

3.29 **Charitable buildings.** Where a building is used for business and non-business purposes, business use can be disregarded if less than 10%. See **41.1**(13) **LAND AND BUILDINGS: EXEMPT SUPPLIES AND OPTION TO TAX.**

3.30 **Retail pharmacists.** In applying a retail scheme, certain goods which are standard-rated when dispensed to individuals for personal use whilst an inpatient or resident of, or attending, a hospital or nursing home may be treated as zero-rated. See **60.19 RETAIL SCHEMES.**

3.31 **Supplies by the Financial Services Compensation Scheme Ltd (FSCS) to compensation scheme authorities.** The payment of any amount at any time by the Investors Compensation Scheme (ICS), the Deposit Protection Scheme (DPS), the Building Societies Investor Protection Scheme (BSIPS), the Policy-holders Protection Scheme (PPS), the Friendly Societies Protection Scheme (FSPS), and the Section 43 Scheme (S43S) for the supply of services by FSCS in carrying out the compensatory scheme functions of ICS, DPS, BSIPS, PPS, FSPS, and S43S (as the case may be) between 1 February 2001 and the coming into effect of the *Financial Services and Markets Act 2000* shall not be treated as consideration for any supply in the course of any business carried on by FSCS.

3.32 **Electronic face value vouchers.** Under *VATA 1994, Sch 6 para 5*, where a right to receive goods or services for an amount stated on any token, stamp or voucher is granted for a consideration, the consideration is disregarded except to the extent (if any) that it exceeds that amount. Although before 9 April 2003 the law only had application in relation to face value vouchers, etc which had a physical form, such as paper vouchers, from 8 March 2001 it was extended to face value vouchers, etc in electronic form provided that they operated in the same way as their physical counterparts. See **69.11 TRADE PROMOTION SCHEMES.** *Note.* With effect from 9 April 2003, electronic face value vouchers are covered by legislation.

3.33 **Supplies previously made by the Post Office.** The *Postal Services Act 2000* replaced each reference to 'the Post Office' within VAT legislation with a reference to the Post Office Company. This concession maintains the scope of existing VAT reliefs following a restructuring of the Post Office corporation immediately prior to the transfer of the property, rights and liabilities of the corporation to the Post Office Company.

This concession extends the reference to the 'the Post Office Company' to include a reference to any wholly owned subsidiary of the Post Office Company providing the public postal service, for the purposes of

(a) the VAT exemption provided for postal services in *VATA 1994, Sch 9 Group 3, Items 1 and 2*; and
(b) the zero-rating of transport services provided for in *VATA 1994, Sch 8, Group 8, Item 4(b)*; and
(c) the interpretation of 'datapost packet' provided for in *SI 1995/2518, Reg 2(1)*.

Any reference in this concession to a wholly owned subsidiary shall be construed in accordance with *Companies Act 2006, s 1159 and Sch 6*.

3.34 **VAT reclaimed by museums and galleries covered by *VATA 1994, s 33A*.** Museums and galleries specified in an *Order* made under *VATA 1994, s 33A(9)* are not required to repay input tax, properly recovered at the time, on goods and services used in connection with taxable supplies of admitting the public for payment, solely on account of the move to free admission. See **34.13**(21) **INPUT TAX.**

3.35 **Apportionment of certain membership subscriptions to non-profit making bodies.** Bodies that are non-profit making and supply a mixture of zero-rated, exempt and/or standard-rated benefits to their members in return for their subscriptions may apportion such subscriptions to reflect the value and VAT liability of those individual benefits, without regard to whether there is one principal benefit. See **14.2 CLUBS AND ASSOCIATIONS.Facilitation of exports**

> *Example*
>
> An annual subscription to a charity includes a monthly newsletter being sent in the post to subscribers, giving details about the charity's activities and events. The value of the newsletter within the subscription can be treated as zero-rated, producing either an output tax saving on the subscription if it is standard-rated or increased input tax recovery if it is exempt from VAT.

8.1 **Sailaway boats.** Where a boat is supplied to a UK resident who intends to export it under its own power within two months of delivery and keep the boat outside the VAT territory of the EU for a continuous period of at least twelve months, the supplier may, subject to conditions, zero-rate the supply of the boat. See **21.20 EXPORTS.** (Withdrawn from 1 January 2012.)

Non-commercial transactions

9.1 **VAT on goods supplied at duty-free and tax-free shops.** Where goods liable to VAT are supplied to intending passengers at duty-free and tax-free shops approved by HMRC, the supplier may be regarded as the exporter and zero-rate the supply of those goods which are exported. See **21.3 EXPORTS.**

9.2 **Marine fuel.** Certain supplies of marine fuel may be received free of VAT. See **21.4 EXPORTS.**

9.3 **Personal reliefs for goods permanently imported from third countries.** Property purchased by diplomats, members of certain international organisations and NATO forces which otherwise qualifies for relief on the transfer of normal residence from outside the EU will not be refused relief solely because HMRC cannot satisfy themselves that the goods have borne all duties and taxes normally applicable in their country of origin. See **33.15**(13) **IMPORTS.**

9.4 **Personal reliefs for goods permanently imported from third countries.** Property purchased outside the EU by UK forces which otherwise qualifies for relief on the transfer of normal residence from outside the EU will not be refused relief solely because HMRC cannot satisfy themselves that the goods have borne all duties and taxes normally applicable in their country of origin. See **33.15**(13) **IMPORTS.**

9.5 **Personal reliefs for goods permanently imported from third countries.** Property purchased under a UK export scheme by members of the UK diplomatic service, members of UK forces and members of International Organisations and which otherwise qualifies for relief on the transfer of normal residence from outside the EU will not be refused relief solely because HMRC cannot satisfy themselves that the goods have borne all duties and taxes normally applicable in their country of origin. See **33.15**(13) **IMPORTS.**

9.6 **Personal reliefs for goods permanently imported from third countries.** Personal belongings otherwise qualifying for relief on the transfer of normal residence from outside the EU may still be granted relief from VAT on importation if failing to qualify only because they have not been possessed and used for the specified period. See **33.15**(13) **IMPORTS.**

9.7 **Personal reliefs for goods permanently imported from third countries.** Personal belongings otherwise qualifying for relief on the transfer of normal residence from outside the EU may still be granted relief from VAT on importation if failing to qualify only because the property is declared for relief outside the specific periods. See **33.15**(13) **IMPORTS**.'

De Voil Indirect Tax Service. See V1.239.

Agreements with trade bodies

[22.2] HMRC have entered into a number of agreements with trade bodies which permit their members to use procedures to meet their obligation under VAT law and which take into account their individual circumstances.

The agreements apply only to areas where HMRC can exercise discretion and they convey no direct financial advantage or relief from the legal requirements. Some of the agreements might usefully be applied to other businesses but note that any special method based on these arrangements can only be adopted with the approval of HMRC.

Agreements entered into at the time of publication are as follows. For full details, see VAT Notice 700/57/04.

- London Bullion Market Association (supplies of bullion).
- Brewers' Society (deduction of input tax in respect of brewers' tenanted estate).
- Association of British Factors and Discounters (partial exemption).
- Finance Houses Association Ltd (partial exemption).
- Association of British Insurers (recovery of input tax incurred in the UK in connection with supplies by branches outside the EC).
- Association of Investment Trust Companies (partial exemption).
- British Printing Industries Federation (apportionment of subsidy publishing supplies).
- Marine, aviation and transport insurance underwriters who are members of an (unnamed) trade organisation (claims-related input tax and associated imported services).
- Association of British Insurers, Lloyd's of London, the Institute of London Underwriters and the British Insurance and Investment Association (coding supplies of marine, aviation and transport insurance services).
- National Caravan Council Limited and the British Holiday and Home Park Association Limited (method of valuing removable contents sold with zero-rated caravans).
- Association of Unit Trust and Investment Managers (VAT liability of charges made in connection with personal equity plans).
- British Bankers' Association (VAT liability of electronic banking/cash management services).
- British Vehicle Rental and Leasing Association (car leasing and repairs and maintenance services).
- Society of Motor Manufacturers and Traders (output tax on the self-supply of a motor vehicle).

- Gaming Board for Great Britain and the British Casino Association (competitions in card rooms).
- British Phonographic Industry (VAT liability of promotional items given free of charge).
- Thoroughbred Breeders Association (arrangements under which race-horse owners may register for VAT).
- British Horseracing Board (revised arrangements under which race-horse owners may register for VAT).
- British Horseracing Board and Thoroughbred Breeders Association (racehorses applied permanently to personal or other non-business use).
- British Horseracing Board and Thoroughbred Breeders Association (keeping of stallions at stud).
- British Horseracing Board and Thoroughbred Breeders Association (racehorses and time limits for exportation).
- Agriculture and Horticulture Development Board (VAT treatment of levies collected (invoiced) from 1 April 2008 by the Board from operators of slaughterhouses and exporters of live animals).
- Society of Motor Manufacturers and Traders Ltd (how the one tonne payload test will be applied in practice to double cab pick-ups).
- Society of Motor Manufacturers and Traders Ltd (simplified method by which motor manufacturers, importers and wholesale distributors may calculate the VAT due on the private use of stock in trade cars provided to directors and employees free of charge).
- Retail Motor Industry Federation (simplified method by which retail motor dealers may calculate the VAT due on the private use of demonstrator cars provided to directors and employees free of charge).
- British Vehicle Rental and Leasing Association (simplified method which daily rental companies may use to calculate the VAT due on the incidental private use of their hire fleets).

Key points

[22.3] Points to consider are as follows.

- A business can avoid applying a scale charge payment to account for road fuel used for private motoring in a car if it decides not to reclaim any input tax on road fuel. However, this non-claim would apply to all road fuel purchases made by the business, not just those relevant to motor cars.
- A useful concession for charities and non-profit making bodies in relation to their subscription income is that the usual mixed supply rules can be overridden so that each element of the supply (benefits to members) can be considered in isolation. So if a minor part of the subscription fee gives zero-rated benefits (e.g. a newsletter or book), this part of the supply can be treated as zero-rated, even if it would usually be incidental to the main supply and therefore ignored.

- HMRC have agreed a number of special VAT concessions with various trade bodies and associations in the UK. It is always worth suggesting to clients that they check with their trade association (if applicable) whether any such agreements are in place as they may save time and administration costs in relation to VAT accounting.
- Remember, these are concessions and HMRC is entitled to withdraw them at any time and can do this on a case by case basis.
- HMRC are gradually replacing these concessions with legislation where it is possible to do so. Unfortunately some concessions are being withdrawn.

23

Financial Services

Cross-reference. See **18.26 EUROPEAN UNION LEGISLATION** for the provisions of *Directive 2006/112/EC*.

De Voil Indirect Tax Service. See V4.136, V4.136A–V4.136J.

Introduction

[23.1] Before considering the question of the VAT liability of financial services, there are other relevant related areas of VAT law which affect financial services and which need to be taken into account.

Place of supply of financial services

From 1 January 2010

[23.2] With effect from 1 January 2010, the supply of financial services falls within the general rule for the place of supply of services, unless they are supplied to a recipient who is not a 'relevant business person' (see **65.15 SUPPLY: PLACE OF SUPPLY**), and belongs in a country which is not a Member State (other than the Isle of Man). In such a case, the place of supply is where the recipient belongs.

[*VATA 1994, Sch 4A para 16; FA 2009, Sch 36 para 11*].

Before 1 January 2010

Special place of supply rules apply to services falling within *VATA 1994, Sch 5 paras 1–8*. This includes financial services (*Sch 5 para 5*) and services rendered by one person to another in procuring such services for the other (*Sch 5 para 8*).

The place of supply of such services is treated as being

(a) where the *recipient* belongs if
- he belongs outside the EU; or
- he belongs in an EU country other than that of the supplier and the services are supplied to him for his business purposes; and

(b) where the *supplier* belongs in all other cases, i.e. where the recipient
- belongs in the UK or Isle of Man; or
- belongs in an EU country but not in the same country as the supplier and receives the supply other than for business purposes.

[*VATA 1994, s 7(10)(11); SI 1992/3121, Art 16*].

These provisions are considered in more detail in **65.21** and **65.23 SUPPLY: PLACE OF SUPPLY**. See **65.14 SUPPLY: PLACE OF SUPPLY** for the place of belonging. For the countries making up the EU, see **17.2 EUROPEAN UNION: GENERAL.**

In the case of a UK supplier, supplies within (*a*) above are outside the scope of UK VAT and supplies within (*b*) above are exempt or taxable in the UK (depending on the nature of the supply).

Special 'easement' rule for sales of securities

If a business belonging in the UK sells securities and cannot identify the customer or their place of belonging, it may either

- treat the supply as being in the UK and exempt;
- use the place of belonging of a nominee account for the purchaser to determine the place of supply; or
- use a special rule known as the 'easement' which determines the place of supply by using the following tests in sequential order.
  (1) Where the place of transaction (i.e. the relevant security exchange) is known, a sale transacted

(i) in the UK is treated as made to a person belonging in the UK and exempt;
(ii) in any other EU country is treated as made to a taxable person belonging in that country, and is outside the scope of UK VAT; and
(iii) outside the EU is treated as made to a person belonging outside the EU and is outside the scope of UK VAT.

(2) Where the place of the transaction is not known, then the place of supply is deemed to be a place where the security is listed.

(3) Where the place of transaction is not known and the security is not listed or is listed on both an EU and non-EU exchange, then the place of supply is deemed to be the place where the last known broker in the transaction belongs.

(VAT Notice 701/49/11, para 6.16).

Input tax recovery

[23.3] Subject to the normal rules, input tax may be recovered which relates to

- taxable supplies of financial services (i.e. supplies with a place of supply in the UK other than exempt supplies);
- supplies of financial services with a place of supply outside the UK but which would be taxable supplies if made in the UK;
- supplies of financial services which
  (i) are supplied to a person who belongs outside the EU; or
  (ii) are directly linked to the export of goods to a place outside the EU; or
  (iii) consist of the provision of intermediary services (see **23.25** below) in relation to any transaction within (i) or (ii) above

  provided the supply is exempt or would have been exempt if made in the UK.

[*VATA 1994, s 26(1)(2); SI 1999/3121*].

Reverse charge on financial services from abroad

[23.4] A supply of financial services is treated as made by the recipient if

- (prior to 1 January 2010) the services fall within *VATA 1994 Sch 5*; or (from 1 January 2010) the services are treated as supplied in the UK and (if the services fall within *VATA 1994, Sch 4A Parts 1 and 2*) the recipient is registered for VAT in the UK (see **65.12** *et seq*. SUPPLY: PLACE OF SUPPLY);
- the recipient belongs in the UK;
- (prior to 1 January 2010) receives the services for the purposes of any business carried on by him; or (from 1 January 2010) is a relevant business person (see **65.15** SUPPLY: PLACE OF SUPPLY); and
- the services are supplied by a person who belongs in a country other than the UK.

[*VATA 1994, s 8(1), (2); FA 2009, Sch 36 para 5*].

He must account for output tax, calculated on the full value of the supply received, in Box 1 of its VAT return and, subject to the normal rules, can include the VAT as input tax in Box 4 on the same return.

This 'reverse charge' procedure does not apply to services provided by an overseas head office or branch which is the same legal entity as the business (unless it simply pays for such a service received by the UK business). But it does apply to certain services received within a VAT group, which are bought in by an overseas group member and supplied on either in their own right or as a component in a larger supply, to the UK members of the group. See **27.6 GROUPS OF COMPANIES**.

Outsourcing

[23.5] Financial institutions often buy-in or sub-contract services that once would have been provided in-house. This is sometimes known as 'outsourcing'. It can include such services as data processing, telephone helplines and general administration. Outsourcing is a contentious area because financial institutions seek exemption wherever possible in order to keep overheads down.

The key decision on outsourcing is *Sparekassernes Datacenter (SDC) v Skatteministeriet, ECJ Case C-2/95*, [1997] STC 932 (TVC 22.357). A company (SDC) carried out a variety of operations on behalf of Danish savings banks which each bank would have otherwise had to carry out for itself. These included the execution of transfers of funds by electronic means between the various banks and between those banks and their clients, the provisions of advice on and trade in securities, and the management of deposits, purchase contracts and loans. The ECJ held that exemption is not restricted to transactions effected by financial institutions or any particular type of legal person. Nor does it matter that the supply is carried out wholly or partly by electronic means or manually. It is not necessary for the services to be provided by an institution which has a legal relationship with the end customer and the fact that the services are provided by a third party does not prevent those services from falling within the exemption. Transactions concerning transfers and payments, and services consisting of the management of deposits, purchase contracts and loans included operations carried out by a data-handling centre if those operations were distinct in character and were specific to, and essential for, the exempt transactions. However, services which merely consisted of making information available to banks and other users did not qualify for exemption.

The liability of a supply of outsourced services to a supplier of exempt financial services depends, therefore, on the nature of the services performed, not whether it is supplied to someone who is making exempt supplies. The exact nature of the supply must be determined and, to be exempt, the outsourced service must, when viewed broadly, form a distinct whole fulfilling the essential functions of a supply which itself falls within the exemption for financial services.

If the business providing the outsourced services is acting as an intermediary, see **23.25** below. If it is providing outsourced services to a loan provider, see **23.11** below.

(VAT Notice 701/49/11, para 1.8).

In *CSC Financial Services Ltd v C & E Commrs, ECJ Case C–235/00,* [2002] STC 57 (TVC 22.360) a company supplied services to a group of companies which issued personal equity plans. It dealt with telephone enquiries and with replies to advertisements placed by the group and sent application forms to potential customers and checked completed application forms. The ECJ held that exemption under what is now *Directive 2006/112/EC, Art 135(1)(f)* (previously *EC 6th Directive, Art 13B(d)(5)*) for 'transactions including negotiation' did not extend to services limited to providing information about a financial product and, as the case may be, receiving and processing applications for subscriptions, without issuing them.

Single or multiple supply

[23.6] Certain financial services (e.g. intermediary services and outsourcing) can constitute a number of component services which, if supplied separately, may have different VAT liabilities. In order to establish the correct liability of such packaged services, certain tests must be applied to determine the overall VAT liability. See **64.6 SUPPLY: GENERAL**. (VAT Notice 701/49/11, para 1.7).

Overview of the law on the liability of financial services

EU legislation

[23.7] Certain financial services are exempt from VAT under *Directive 2006/112/EC, Art 135(1)(b)–(g)*. See **18.26**(*b*)–(*g*) **EUROPEAN UNION LEGISLATION.**

UK law

The equivalent UK provisions are in *VATA 1994, Sch 9 Group 5*. This lists a number of *Items* which provide for exemption for the following categories (subject to qualifications and definitions which are dealt with in the appropriate part of the chapter).

(1) The issue, transfer or receipt of, or any dealing with, money, any security for money or any note or order for the payment of money. See **23.8** below.
(2) The making of any advance or the granting of any credit. See **23.11** below.
(3) The management of credit by the person granting it. See **23.11** below.
(4) The provision of the facility of instalment credit finance in a hire purchase, conditional sale or credit sale agreement for which facility a separate charge is made and disclosed to the recipient of the supply of goods. See **23.11** below.

(5) The provision of administrative arrangements and documentation and the transfer of title to the goods in connection with the supply described in Item (3) if the total consideration therefore is specified in the agreement and does not exceed £10. See **23.11** below.

(6) The provision of intermediary services in relation to any transaction comprised in Items (1), (2), (3), (4) or (6) (whether or not any such transaction is finally concluded) by a person acting in an intermediary capacity. See **23.25** below.

(7) The underwriting of an issue within Item (1) or any transaction within Item (6). See **23.23** below.

(8) The issue, transfer or receipt of, or any dealing with, any security or secondary security. See **23.17** below.

(9) (Deleted).

(10) The operation of any current, deposit or savings account. See **23.24** below.

(11) The management of authorised open-ended investment companies, authorised unit trust schemes or certain collective investment schemes. See **23.20** below.

(12) The management of closed-ended collective investment undertakings. See **23.21** below.

Many services which are associated with finance are not covered by the exemption. In addition to services covered in the text generally when dealing with exemptions, see **23.29** below for a list of some of the more common finance-rated supplies which are standard-rated.

Dealings with money and securities for money

[23.8] Exemption applies to the issue, transfer or receipt of, and any dealings with

- money,
- any security for money; or
- any note or order for the payment of money

but excludes the following.

- All services falling within **23.17** below (which are exempt under those provisions).
- Preparatory services carried out separately, before an exempt transaction concerning money (e.g. the preparation and delivery of data such as a wages roll, which is then put into effect by someone else). Preparatory services carried out by an intermediary as part of their overall exempt supply are exempt (see **23.25** below).
- The supply of coins or banknotes (whether legal tender or not) as collectors' pieces, investment articles or items of numismatic interest. Such a supply is normally taxable on the full selling price, whether or not they are sold for more than their face value. Examples include bank notes, proof coins, Maundy money and precious or base metal coins.

See, however, **61.3 SECOND-HAND GOODS** for the use of the second-hand scheme for supplies of collectors' pieces. Sales of some gold coins are exempt as investment gold. See **26 GOLD AND PRECIOUS METALS.**

[*VATA 1994, Sch 9 Group 5 Item 1 and Notes 1, 1A, 2; SI 1999/594*]. (VAT Notice 701/49/11, paras 2.4, 2.6).

Issue

The issue of *money* can only be by a bank or similar financial institution. A coin or banknote can only be issued once (the first time) and this can only be done by a bank with a statutory entitlement to do so (e.g. the Bank of England). The above exemption is normally superseded by *VATA 1994, Sch 8 Group 11 Item 1* which zero-rates the issue by a bank of a note payable to the bearer on demand (see **74.4 ZERO-RATED SUPPLIES**). But see *Royal Bank of Scotland Group plc v C & E Commrs,* CS [2002] STC 575 (TVC 27.4) where the bank was authorised to issue its own bank notes, which it did from automated cash machines. The court held that the 'reciprocity fees' which the bank received from other banks whose customers had used its machines to withdraw cash were not consideration for a zero-rated supply of bank notes but for an exempt supply of the provision of the facilities to obtain money.

Transfer

For the purposes of *Directive 2006/112/EC, Art 135(1)(d)* (previously *EC Sixth Directive, Art 13B(d)(3)*) a 'transfer' has been defined as a 'transaction consisting of the execution of an order for the transfer of a sum of money from one bank account to another. It is characterized in particular by the fact that it involves a change in the legal and financial situation existing between the person giving the order and the recipient and between those parties and their respective banks.' (*Sparekassernes Datacenter v Skatteministeriet, ECJ Case C–2/95* [1997] STC 932 (TVC 22.357)).

In *HMRC v Axa UK plc, ECJ Case C–175/09*, [2010] STC 2825 (TVC 22.362) the ECJ ruled that the exemption provided by *Art 13B(d)(3)* did not cover A's services, which consisted in collecting fees from dental patients by monthly direct debit instalments and passing the fees (less A's remuneration) on to the dentists, sending the dentists statements, contacting patients with regard to non-payment, and other services such as registration and use of a website. Such services fell within the exclusion for 'debt collection and factoring'. Following the ECJ decision, the CA unanimously allowed HMRC's appeal ([2011] EWCA Civ 1607 (TVC 22.362)).

Following the ECJ decision in *Axa*, HMRC stated that 'debt collection' does not apply solely to the service of chasing and recovering overdue payments on behalf of the creditor. All services principally concerned with collecting payments from the person owing them for the benefit of the entity to which those payments are owed (regardless of whether those payments are received before, on or after their due date) fall within the exclusion to the exemption. (HMRC Brief 54/10).

Money

'*Money*' includes currencies other than sterling [*VATA 1994, s 96(1)*] and comprises currency, coins or banknotes, in sterling or any other currency, when supplied as legal tender in a financial transaction. With effect from 1 July 2006, it does not include platinum nobles. (VAT Notice 701/49/11, para 2).

Security for money

A 'security for money' has been defined as a document under seal or under hand at a consideration containing a covenant, promise or undertaking to pay a sum of money (*Dyrham Park Country Club Ltd* (VTD 700) (TVC 13.31)). Examples include bills of exchange, financial guarantees and promissory notes.

For the purposes of *Item 1* above, securities do not include stocks, shares, bonds and other similar securities for which exemption is covered by *VATA 1994, Sch 9 Group 5 Item 6* (see **23.17** below).

(VAT Notice 701/49/11, para 3.1).

Dealing with money

A supply of services involving dealing with money is exempt provided a financial transaction is carried out.

The more obvious dealings with money are the routine financial transactions carried out by banks, building societies, bureaux de change and similar institutions, e.g.

- the acceptance of deposits of money on current account or otherwise;
- money transfer services; and
- exchange of legal tender.

(VAT Notice 701/49/11, para 2.1).

Related transactions

[23.9] Listed below are examples of common transactions connected with supplies within **23.8** above and their VAT liability.

(1) Automatic teller machines (ATMs)

The supply of

- an ATM or the software required to run it (whether or not the consideration is based on the ATM's use), and
- services provided in connection with the routine operation of an ATM (e.g. filling with cash, maintenance and repair)

are taxable supplies.

ATM providers sometimes make charges described as convenience fees, interchange fees or reciprocity fees. These are charges to banks by other banks when those other bank's customers use their ATM facilities. Where the charge is for

- the facility to obtain money,
- the provision of money,
- transaction processing, or
- the operation of accounts

the supply is exempt.

The granting of a right to permanently attach an ATM to the ground, or for its incorporation into the fabric of a building, is an exempt supply unless the grantor has elected to waive exemption.

(VAT Notice 701/49/11, para 2.9).

See also *Royal Bank of Scotland Group plc v C & E Commrs*, CS [2002] STC 575 (TVC 27.4).

In *Concept Direct Ltd* (VTD 19721) (TVC 27.3) a company found suitable sites for ATMs on behalf of a bank and received commission for each site plus a 'swipe fee' of 15p on each occasion the machine was used. The swipe fee (as well as the commission) was held to be standard-rated as the company took no part in the operation of the machine or the issue of money.

(2) Clearing and settlement services

A service supplied by a clearing-house for settling indebtedness between members is an exempt supply. (VAT Notice 709/49/11, para 2.8).

(3) Deductions from pay

Charges made by an employer for deductions from pay of employees for items such as insurance premiums, mortgage repayments or union subscriptions are exempt.

Any charges made for deductions from the pay in compliance with an attachment of earnings order are seen as reimbursement for expenses incurred in carrying out a statutory duty and are outside the scope of VAT.

(VAT Notice 701/49/11, para 2.13).

(4) Derivatives

Derivatives are financial instruments. They are known as 'derivatives' because their price is directly dependant upon the value of the underlying commodity, financial instrument or currency. To establish the VAT liability of the derivative, it is necessary to know what the 'underlying' product is.

(a) Commodity futures, options and other derivatives

A commodity is a raw material such as grain, coffee, metal or oil and is traded on a commodity market. This can be based in the country of the commodity's origin or on a 'terminal market' (a commodity market in a trading centre, such as London). As commodity prices fluctuate widely, commodity exchanges assist in enabling producers and users of the commodity to hedge the price risk with outside speculators and investors.

See **67 TERMINAL MARKETS** for the zero-rating of transactions traded on certain terminal markets by or with a member of that market or by a person acting as an agent or broker between a member of the market and another person.

For transactions not traded on one of those terminal markets:

- Commodity futures and actuals follow the liability of the underlying commodity.
- The premium paid for a commodity option is separate from the price of underlying commodity and is payable whether or not the buyer exercises the option. The payment for the right to buy a commodity, rather than a contract to buy it, is a standard-rated supply of services. If the option is exercised, there will be a separate supply of the commodity itself.

(b) Futures contracts

Financial futures are exempt from VAT and for VAT purposes are divided into two categories, cash settled contracts and non-cash settled contracts. Although both are exempt, which category the supply falls into is important because it may affect whether the supply by an agent or intermediary arranging the transaction is exempt or taxable. See **23.28** below.

(i) *Cash settled contracts* (*Item 1* contracts) are contracts where there are no underlying deliverable securities or contracts. These include short-term interest rate futures, FT-SE 100 futures, other stock index futures and weather derivatives.
The supply of cash settled contracts for a consideration is exempt from VAT. Where a futures contract runs to maturity, there is no further supply for VAT purposes. Cash settlements under these contracts are not consideration for a supply and must be excluded from partial exemption calculations and VAT returns.

(ii) *Non-cash settled contracts* (*Item 6* contracts) i.e. contracts where there are underlying deliverable securities. These include gilts, T-bonds and other securities (not being securities for money).
The supply of a non-cash settled contract is exempt. If a contract runs to maturity there is a separate exempt supply of the underlying security. Transactions on exchanges are treated as being made between either the member and the client or the member and the relevant clearing house. The value of the supply of the securities is the price that was agreed when the contract was made.

(c) Financial futures – exchange trading

- *Fees charged by members*. Members of certain exchanges deal as principals and the 'turn' (or commission) charged by the member to a client for transacting a financial futures contract represents the value of the member's supply. A member may charge for each leg, or for a 'round trip' in a closed-out transaction. The full value of each charge is the measure of the supply for VAT purposes. The 'turn' (or commission) is consideration for an exempt supply of financial futures.
  Where a member acts for another member in executing a transaction, he is a principal and the 'turn' (or commission) charged is exempt. The value of the supply is the amount charged to the member. Clearing fees charged by a clearing member to a non-clearing member are also consideration for an exempt supply.

- *Client-to-member transactions*. There is no supply by a client to a member in a closed-out financial futures transaction.
- *Margin payments*. Margin payments (whether initial or variation) fall outside the scope of VAT.

(d) Financial options

Financial options are exempt from VAT. The sale of an option as a financial instrument is a supply of services separate from the underlying transaction to which the option relates.

There are three main types of financial options contracts.

- *Options based on financial futures contracts*. Options on short-term interest rate futures, index-based futures and cash settled futures are exempt from VAT. (These are options on cash settled contracts under (*b*)(i) above.) There is no further supply when an option is exercised to obtain or supply the underlying futures contracts.
- *Equity options*. These options have equities, rather than financial futures contracts, as the underlying instrument and are exempt from VAT. (These are options on non-cash settled contracts under (*b*)(ii) above.)
- *Index-based options*. Unlike equity options, index-based options do not provide for delivery but are cash settled. This type of option is exempt (as an option on a cash settled contract under (*b*)(i) above).

When a financial option is sold for a premium, a right has been granted. The value of the supply is the premium charged and the supply is exempt.

(e) Trade by locals

Locals are traders registered to members of exchanges who act in an independent capacity to some degree, but in the embodiment of the member to whom the local is registered. Locals can be employees, self-employed or engaged in a joint venture or partnership with a member. The VAT treatment depends on the status of the local.

- Employee locals may manage or trade on an account for their member and will be on the member's payroll. The payments from the member to the local are outside the scope of VAT.
- Self-employed locals may trade on their own account. When the local makes a trade, the member is the principal to the contract. However, when the trade is completed there is another contract between the member and the local, now in the same position for VAT purposes as a third party client, in which both parties are also principals (i.e. there is a back-to-back arrangement). The supply made by the member to the client is an exempt supply of a financial futures contract or, as the case may be, a taxable supply of a commodities contract.
  A self-employed local may also act as the embodiment of the member with which the local is registered. For VAT purposes the local is acting as an agent.

- Where the local and the member are engaged in a joint venture or partnership, every trade executed by the local is a trade of the member to whom the local is registered and the rules regarding transactions by members (see above) apply to this initial transaction.
  The VAT liability of the remuneration received by the local under the joint venture or partnership arrangements depends on the nature of the agreement between the parties.

(f) Trading Over-The-Counter (OTC)

Financial futures and options can be traded OTC. These are non-standard contracts traded off-exchange. Both are exempt from VAT. See **23.28** below acting as an intermediary.

Commodity futures and options can similarly be traded OTC. Both are taxable.

(g) Trading on non-UK exchanges

The value and liability of the supplies made for VAT purposes depends on whether the supplier is a principal or an agent in respect of transactions in commodities contracts or financial futures and options contracts traded on non-UK exchanges. The rules of the overseas exchange and the local legislation could also have a significant effect on how the transaction should be viewed for UK VAT purposes. Each transaction must be examined and the VAT liability determined on its own merits.

(h) Interest rate swaps

For VAT purposes, during the term of the swap, there is a continuous supply of services and, to the extent that any money changes hands, there is an exempt supply under the *VATA, Sch 9 Group 5, item 1.*

(i) Currency swaps

Currency swaps provide both a currency and interest hedge. For VAT purposes no supply takes place in relation to the exchange of principal amounts of underlying loans in currency swaps.

(j) Financial Spread Bets (FSBs)

This involves speculating by placing a bet on an index, eg commodity prices or the FT-SE100 index. In the same way as sports betting, financial spread betting is liable to general betting duty and is exempt from VAT under the *VATA 1994, Sch 9 Group 4*. Duty is calculated by the bookmaker based on the total amount due from customers less any winnings paid out.

(k) Contracts for Differences (CFDs)

Contracts offer speculators the opportunity to buy or sell the performance of a share, equity, etc. without the need to own the underlying asset. A CFD provided for a consideration (turn/commission) is an exempt supply of financial services. The CFD is treated as a cash settled contract for the purposes of defining the VAT liability of an intermediary's supply (see **23.28** below).

(VAT Notice 701/9/11, paras 2.1, 2.2; VAT Notice 701/49/11, paras 8.1–8.11).

(5) Dishonoured cheques or direct debit payments

A bank or a supplier of goods or services may charge a customer because

- it has failed to honour its cheques or direct debit payments; or
- in the case of a supplier, the supplier has borne the cost of bank charges.

Where a bank makes such a charge to its customer, the charge will be a part of the overall service for running the customer's account and exempt from VAT.

Where a supplier makes such a charge to its customer, the charge will be outside the scope of VAT.
(VAT Notice 701/49/11, para 2.11).

(6) Face value vouchers

Face value vouchers that give a right to goods or services are not seen as securities for money. However, at the point the voucher can be exchanged for money, it is a security for money and any consideration for it is exempt. For example, where the voucher is presented to a retailer as payment for goods or services it is not a security for money, but when the retailer presents the voucher to a third party to be exchanged for money, it becomes a security for money at that point. See **69 TRADE PROMOTION SCHEMES**. (VAT Notice 701/49/11, para 3.2).

(7) Foreign exchange transactions

Foreign exchange transactions are normally exempt supplies. Where a person acts as principal, the consideration is any fees or commission charged. Following the decision in *C & E Commrs v First National Bank of Chicago, ECJ Case C–172/96,* [1998] STC 850 (TVC 22.89) HMRC accept that where no specific commission or fee is charged on particular transactions (e.g. where services are paid for by the spread between the bid and offer rates), those transactions are nevertheless supplies for VAT purposes, the consideration being 'the net result of the transactions of the supplier of the service over a given period of time', i.e. the net profit on the transactions. In most cases it will be appropriate to isolate the input tax incurred on foreign exchange transactions and deal with VAT separately within the partial exemption method used.

However, in *Willis Pension Trustees Ltd* (VTD 19183) (TVC 62.196) a company which acted as trustee of the pension fund entered into a number of foreign currency transactions with a number of banks in order to hedge or minimise the pension scheme's exposure to adverse exchange rate fluctuations. The tribunal decided that any 'profit' retained by Willis from the foreign exchange transactions was not consideration for a supply. HMRC accept this decision which will apply to a business entering a foreign exchange transaction in the specific set of circumstances in *Willis*. In such cases, VAT paid on associated costs of foreign exchange transactions relates to the business as a whole. It can be treated as residual input tax under a partial exemption method. HMRC are considering whether the decision has any wider application.

Despite the decision in *Willis*, the ECJ judgment in *First National Bank of Chicago* remains the leading authority on the VAT treatment of forex transactions. In general, forex transactions are supplies for VAT purposes if a spread position is adopted over a period of time when buying and selling currency. This applies whether this is being carried out by a business on its own account (in support of other areas of its business) or to reduce any exposure position in forex that it holds. Such forex transactions include both 'spot' and 'forward' transactions.

HMRC have indicated that in their opinion

- a business simply exchanging one currency for another to realise foreign earnings into sterling, for example, or to acquire currency to settle liabilities incurred outside the UK, or
- a business entering into forward forex deals in order to limit its exposure to forex fluctuations in respect of future obligations

is unlikely to be seen as making supplies for VAT purposes provided such transactions are not part of a wider economic activity being carried out for an identifiable consideration.

But a business with a corporate treasury operation that typically runs a 'forex desk' in a similar manner to any other financial institution or market maker is likely to be taking a spread position and making supplies. HMRC take the view that all their forex transactions (whether spot or forward and whether proprietary or in support of other activities or areas of the business) should be treated as forex supplies.

(VAT Notice 701/49/11, para 2.7; Business Briefs 16/98, 21/05; HMRC Brief 5/07).

(8) Guarantees and surety bonds

The VAT liability of these types of products depends on the precise nature of the arrangements. To qualify for exemption, they must be financial instruments which are securities for money. This means that an exempt guarantee or surety involves a third party providing a guarantee or security for payments to be made under a contract. Exemption does not extend to

- performance guarantees whereby a third party performs a service or makes payment if a contractual party fails to fulfil their obligations (to perform a service or supply/repair goods) under the contract; or
- the supply of warranties or contracts for the supply, repair or maintenance of goods even though they are sometimes referred to as guarantees.

(VAT Notice 701/49/11, para 3.3).

(9) Household bills

Any charge for the acceptance of over-the-counter payments for household bills is an exempt supply. (VAT Notice 701/49/11, para 2.5).

(10) Sorting and counting money

Services of carriage of cash, re-stocking cash machines, sorting and counting money are, when supplied on their own, taxable. This is because the services being applied to the money are the same as that which could be applied to any type of goods. For the exemption to apply the service must deal with money as money and not purely as goods. See *Williams & Glyn's Bank Ltd* (VTD 118) (TVC 27.1) and *Nationwide Anglia Building Society* (VTD 11826) (TVC 27.2).

Services that include an element of making payments or transfers between bank accounts are exempt. Where a supply has a mixture of taxable and exempt elements, its overall character will determine the liability.

(VAT Notice 701/49/11, para 2.2).

(11) Travellers' cheques

The issue or encashment of travellers' cheques is exempt. Unissued or unsigned travellers' cheques are neither securities for money nor notes for the payment of money, and their supply to, or importation by, the issuing bank is taxable on their value as stationery.

(VAT Notice 701/49/11, para 3.4).

Debts and related services

[23.10] Debts and related services are treated as follows:

(1) Sale of debts

Instead of waiting for payment of a debt and carrying the risk of late settlement or default, a business may sell the debt to someone else. The unencumbered sale of a debt for a consideration is exempt under *VATA 1994, Sch 9 Group 5 Item 1* (see **23.8** above). The value of the supply is the gross amount that the purchaser pays for the debt. (VAT Notice 701/49/11, para 5.1).

(2) Factoring and invoice discounting

A client assigns his debts to the factor. The factor opens a client account to which he credits the face value of the debts and debits his charges. These charges may be consideration for a number of standard-rated administrative, clerical and accounting services. The balance, less an agreed retention, is available for the client to draw upon. Depending on the extent to which he does so, the factor debits a further charge, often described as 'discount'.

The factor may operate on a recourse or non-recourse basis.

- In a recourse agreement the factor puts the responsibility for bearing any loss on the client. If the debtor defaults, the factor re-assigns the debt to the client.
- In a non-recourse agreement the factor accepts the risk of default.

The VAT treatment of the various services supplied by a factor to his client are as follows.

Supply	*VAT liability*
Assignment or re-assignment of debt	Not treated as a supply for VAT purposes
Discount or interest charge	Exempt
Administration or service charge (this may cover the provision of a full sales ledger management service, credit advice, debt collection service and the provision of management information)	Standard-rated
Guarantee of payment	Standard-rated
Electronic transfer of funds (if charged for separately)	Exempt supply

Bad debt relief

A factor cannot claim bad debt relief for debts assigned to him by his client. The client cannot claim bad debt relief for a debt assigned to a factor but can do so if the factor re-assigns the debt to him. See **7.1 BAD DEBT RELIEF**.

Cash accounting scheme

See **63.6 SPECIAL SCHEMES** for accounting for VAT where the cash accounting scheme is used.

(VAT Notice 701/49/11, paras 5.2–5.8).

(3) Debt negotiation

In *Debt Management Associates Ltd* (VTD 17880) (TVC 27.30) the tribunal held that a creditor who granted his debtor some indulgence in repayments was granting him credit (even if it was additional credit) and that a company providing the 'debt negotiation services' was providing exempt intermediary services.

Following this tribunal decision, HMRC accept that debt negotiation services involving bringing together the credit provider with the debtor and acting between them in an attempt to mediate a change to the payment terms is an exempt supply. But see (4) and (5) below. (VAT Notice 701/49/11, para 5.9).

'*Debt negotiation services*' may include

- taking details of income and expenditure, along with details of the creditor(s) and the amounts outstanding, and preparing and presenting a payment plan to the creditor;
- agreeing to act on behalf of such a debtor with the creditor in negotiating the payment plan; and
- agreeing to receive payments from the debtor and passing these payments on to the creditors (with or without first taking a fee or commission for doing so).

'*Negotiation*' is taken to refer to the activity of an intermediary providing a distinct act of mediation in order for two parties to enter into a contract, but without the person who is acting as the intermediary having any interest of his own in the terms of the contract. If that person is merely providing a service typically undertaken by a company as part of its contract this is not 'negotiation of debts' and falls within (4) below.

(Business Brief 30/03).

(4) Debt collection

The supplies made by a debt collection agency, or by a business involved in debt collection, are taxable.

Although debt collection services undertaken on behalf of a creditor company may involve some negotiation of the repayment of a debt by the debtor to the creditor this is not an exempt debt negotiation service. For example, if a business

- issues letters to the debtor on behalf of the creditor demanding payment,
- chases the debt in some other form (e.g. contacting the debtor by telephone etc.),
- attempts to locate a debtor on behalf of the creditor, or
- provides accounting services to the creditor (i.e. monitors the debtor's payment account and notifies the creditor of any defaulted payments)

these services are taxable. Any debt negotiation services are ancillary to the principal service of debt collection.

(VAT Notice 701/49/11, para 5.10).

(5) Insolvency practitioner services

Supplies made by insolvency practitioners are taxable. Although these services sometimes require negotiating the suggested repayment terms of a voluntary arrangement between the debtor and the creditors, this service is ancillary to the principal service provided. (VAT Notice 701/49/11, para 5.11).

Provision of credit

[23.11] The following supplies of financial services in the UK are exempt from VAT.

(a) The making of any advance or the granting of any credit. *Included* is the supply of credit by a person, in connection with the supply of goods or services by him, for which a separate charge is made and disclosed to the recipient of the supply of goods or services. [*VATA 1994, Sch 9 Group 5 Item 2 and Note 3*].

Item 2 covers most of the normal types of credit transactions, e.g. loans, overdrafts and other forms of advances. The value of the exempt supply is the gross interest or other sum received.

Interest paid on deposits with a bank or building society is also consideration for the making of an advance – the advance being made by the customer.

(VAT Notice 701/49/11, para 4.1).

(b) The management of credit by the person granting it. [*VATA 1994, Sch 9 Group 5 Item 2A; SI 2003/1569*]. But the provision of credit management by a person who does not grant the credit is taxable.

A supply of third party taxable credit management could typically include the following transactions:

(i) Credit checking (includes debt profiling, assessing credit worthiness, electoral roll checks and obtaining references).

(ii) Valuation of assets such as property, land, vehicles.

(iii) Authorisation services (including those that go beyond just checking the applicant's signature or agreeing credit or payment limits set by the person providing the credit).

(iv) Taking decisions on credit applications on behalf of the credit provider.

(v) Creating and maintaining records on behalf of the credit provider in order to enable them to fulfil legal obligations.

(vi) Monitoring a creditor's payment record or dealing with overdue payments.

(VAT Notice 701/49/11, para 4.10).

(c) The provision of the facility of instalment credit in a hire purchase, conditional sale or credit sale agreement for which a separate charge is made and disclosed to the recipient of the goods. [*VATA 1994, Sch 9 Group 5 Item 3 and Note 3*]. The value of the exempt supply is the interest paid with each repayment. See **23.12** to **23.15** below for hire purchase, conditional sale and credit sale agreements generally.

(d) The provision of administrative arrangements and documentation and the transfer of title to the goods in connection with the supply within (*c*) above if the total consideration is specified in the agreement and does not exceed £10. [*VATA 1994, Sch 9 Group 5 Item 4*]. The value of the exempt supply is the fee for the administrative arrangements, etc.

See, however, *Wagon Finance Ltd* (VTD 16288) (TVC 27.17) where the tribunal held that administrative fees in connection with credit transactions were exempt from VAT irrespective of the £10 limit as the company had provided customers with the facility of instalment credit within (*c*) above. HMRC decided not to appeal against this decision and accept that exemption applies to any connected credit ancillary charge unless the contract explicitly states that the charge relates, wholly or partially, to the supply of goods. Such exempt charges are likely to be shown as administration, documentation or acceptance fees. Fees related to the goods (e.g. option fees or fees for transfer of title) are taxable unless within the £10 limit. (Business Brief 27/99).

Hire purchase, etc.

[23.12] If the possession of goods is transferred under agreements which expressly contemplate that the property also will pass at some time in the future (determined by, or ascertainable from, the agreements but in any case not later than when the goods are fully paid for) a supply of goods takes place. [*VATA 1994, Sch 4 para 1(2)(b)*].

The most common methods of supplying goods with credit are:

(a) **Hire purchase agreements.** Legally, under such agreements goods are hired for periodic payments and the hirer has the option to purchase. However, the VAT supply position is the same as for conditional sale (see below) because it is intended that ownership is to be transferred.
(b) **Conditional sale agreements.** These are agreements for the sale of goods where the price is payable by instalments and the goods remain the property of the seller until the full price is paid or another condition is met by the customer. The full amount of VAT on the goods is normally payable with the first instalment.
(c) **Credit sale agreements.** These are agreements for the sale of goods which immediately become the property of the customer but where the price is payable by instalments.

Supplies not involving finance companies

If an agreement is made to supply goods under (*a*)–(*c*) above without involving a finance company (self-financed credit), any charge for credit disclosed as a separate charge to the customer is exempt. The consideration for the taxable supply of goods is the cash price stated in the agreement, before any deposit is paid.

If the goods are supplied on interest-free credit, allowing the customer to pay for the goods over a set period without charging interest, the supply of the goods is taxed according to their liability. As there is no charge for credit, there is no exempt supply for VAT purposes.

Any connected credit ancillary charges are exempt unless the contract explicitly states that the charge relates, wholly or partially, to the supply of goods. If the supply relates to the credit, normally shown as administration, documentation or acceptance fees, it is exempt. Fees that relate to the goods (e.g. option fees or fees for transfer of title) are not exempt unless the charge for them is £10 or less (see **23.11**(*d*) above).

Finance companies

If the finance company becomes the owner of goods (e.g. when a purchase is financed by a hire-purchase agreement) the supply of goods is by the supplier to the finance company, not the customer, and is taxable. The finance company in turn, makes a supply of goods and a supply of credit. The supply of credit is exempt if the credit charge is disclosed to the customer in writing.

If the finance company does not become owner of the goods (e.g. when a purchase is financed by a loan agreement) the supply of goods is to the customer, not the finance company, even though that company may make the

payment direct to the supplier. The supply is taxable and VAT is due on the selling price to the customer even if a lesser amount is received from the finance company. See *C & E Commrs v Primback Ltd, ECJ Case C–34/99,* [2001] STC 803 (TVC 22.242). The finance company, in a separate transaction, makes a supply of credit facilities to the customer.
(VAT Notice 700, para 8.4).

Time of supply

VAT is due on the full value of the *goods* at the time of supply (see **66.1 SUPPLY: TIME OF SUPPLY**). The tax point for the exempt supply of the *services* is treated as taking place each time a payment is received unless HMRC has approved a written application for an earlier date to be used. (VAT Notice 700, para 15.11). For administrative reasons, application is often made to treat the supply of goods and exempt services as taking place together.

Transfers of agreements

[23.13] Transfers of agreements are treated as follows:

(a) **By the owner.** If the owner of the goods assigns his rights, interests and ownership under a hire-purchase or conditional sale agreement to
- *a bank or finance company* (for example, under a block discounting arrangement) the transfer is outside the scope of VAT. [*SI 1995/1268, Art 5(4)*]; or
- *a dealer* (for example, under a recourse agreement) the transfer is a single supply of goods and is taxable in the normal way.

(b) **By the customer.** If a customer buys goods under a hire purchase or conditional sale agreement and subsequently transfers his rights and obligations to another customer, he is making a standard-rated supply of services to the new customer. There is no supply for VAT purposes from the owner to the new customer. VAT must be accounted for on the open market value of the supply, i.e. the total amount payable by the new customer to the owner to complete the agreement plus any amount he pays to the original customer to secure the transfer. See also *Phillip Drakard Trading Ltd v C & E Commrs,* QB [1992] STC 568 (TVC 62.107).

Repossession of goods

[23.14] Repossession of goods is treated as follows:

- *Hire purchase and conditional sale agreements.* Where goods are supplied under such agreements (including a reservation of title (Romalpa) agreement) title does not pass in the goods until all payments under the agreement have been made. But all VAT due under the agreement on the goods is payable at the outset (see **23.12** above). Where the goods are subsequently repossessed or returned and the agreement ends early, if the agreement includes terms that result in the customer becoming liable to pay nothing more or a lesser amount than the remaining instalments, an adjustment can be made to the VAT accounted for at the outset of the agreement. (There may be circumstances where no VAT was accounted for on the sale of the goods, such as the sale of second-hand goods where no margin is achieved. In such a case there is no VAT adjustment to make.) Where the reduction in price contains elements of capital and interest, any reasonable method for apportioning the value of the reduction may be used. The method of allocation should be consistent and reflect the accounting methods used within the business.

If the customer is VAT-registered, he must be sent a document effecting the adjustment to ensure that he makes a corresponding adjustment to any input tax he may have claimed.

- *Conditional sale agreements*. Under these agreements, title passes at the outset of the agreement and the return of the goods is treated as a supply from the customer to the finance company. The value of the original sale is not affected by the return.

Where goods are repossessed (following default by a customer), the supplier may be entitled to claim bad debt relief on any amount outstanding following the adjustment. See **7.8 BAD DEBT RELIEF**.

(VAT Notice 701/49/11, para 4.3).

Sale of repossessed assets

[23.15] As a result of (*d*) below, sales of most repossessed goods under hire purchase and conditional sale agreements will be supplies for VAT purposes and VAT must be accounted for in the normal way. However, the disposal of

(i) works of art, antiques and collectors' items (see **73.3 WORKS OF ART, ETC.**), and second-hand goods by a person who has repossessed them under the terms of a finance agreement, or

(ii) boats and aircraft by a mortgagee after he has taken possession of them under the terms of a marine or aircraft mortgage,

remain outside the scope of VAT if the following conditions are met.

(a) The goods so disposed are in the same condition at the time of disposal as when they were repossessed or taken into possession. The condition of goods has been changed if any improvements, repairs, replacement parts or the generally making good of any damage has been carried out. The cleaning of goods generally does not affect the condition nor does the inclusion of instruction manuals if they are otherwise missing. (Business Brief 19/01).

(b) For goods other than motor cars,
- if the goods had been supplied in the UK by the person from whom they were obtained, that supply would not have been chargeable with VAT or would have been chargeable on less than full value (e.g. because the defaulting customer had not acquired the goods for business purposes or they were margin scheme supplies);
- if the goods have been imported into the UK, they must have borne VAT which has neither been reclaimed nor refunded; and
- the goods must not have been reimported having previously been exported from the UK free of VAT by reason of zero-rating.

(c) In the case of motor cars, the VAT on any previous supply, acquisition or importation must have been wholly excluded from credit.
(d) In relation to all goods delivered after 31 August 2006 under finance agreements entered into after 12 April 2006, where (i) above applies no adjustment must have taken place, or may later take place, of VAT on the initial supply under the finance agreement as a result of repossession.

[*SI 1992/3122, Arts 2, 4; SI 1995/1268, Arts 2, 4; SI 1995/1269; SI 1995/1385; SI 1995/1667; SI 1999/3118; SI 1999/3120; SI 2001/3649, Art 432; SI 2004/3084; SI 2004/3085; SI 2006/869; SI 2006/874*].

See **36.11 INSURANCE** for insurers taking possession of goods in settlement of claims under insurance policies.

Where the above conditions are not satisfied, VAT is normally chargeable on the full amount realised on the sale (not the original cost of the asset, see *Darlington Finance Ltd* (VTD 1337) (TVC 44.80)). Where, however, the goods in question were second-hand at the time when a finance agreement was entered into, the repossessed goods can be sold under the margin scheme. The purchase price for the purpose of calculating the margin is then the original price paid by the finance company to the dealer.

Following the decision in *C & E Commrs v General Motors Acceptance Corporation (UK) plc,* Ch D [2004] STC 577 (TVC 44.53) HMRC accept that, in the case of a finance company, 'repossessed goods' can mean goods

- voluntarily returned under an HP agreement;
- repossessed under the terms of a finance agreement; or
- returned by a customer under the *Consumer Credit Act* once they have made 50% of the total payments due.

(VAT Notice 718, para 13.8).

De Voil Indirect Tax Service. See V3.117.

Transactions related to the provision of credit

[23.16] Transactions related to the provision of credit are treated as follows:

(1) Check trading companies

Check trading is a means of buying goods on credit whereby a check trading company sells a trading check for a specified amount to a customer who pays for the check on credit terms over a period of time. The customer then uses the check to purchase goods from the participating retailer.

Charges made by check trading companies to participating retailers are treated as exempt. (C & E Press Notice 1045, 21 October 1985).

(2) Credit, debit and charge cards

Any supply by a person carrying on a credit card, charge card or similar card operation is exempt when made in connection with that operation to a person who accepts the card used in the operation when presented to him in payment for goods or services. [*VATA 1994, Sch 9 Group 5 Note (4)*]. The consideration for these supplies usually takes the form of a discount on the amount reimbursed to the retailer, etc. See *C & E Commrs v Diners Club Ltd and Another,* CA [1989] STC 407 (TVC 27.60).

Credit, debit and charge cards include MasterCard, Visa, American Express, Diner's Club, Connect and Switch. Banks and financial services institutions issue these cards under the umbrella of these organisations. In addition, certain companies provide in-house card schemes for retailers or retail outlets.

Accounting for VAT on retail credit, debit and charge card sales

Retailers must account for VAT at the time of supply on the full price charged to the customer for the goods/services supplied. If the retailer charges for accepting payment by one of the above cards, the charge is further consideration for the supply of goods/services. VAT is chargeable at the same rate as the goods or services supplied.

Liability of various associated services

Cardholders can either pay their outstanding balance on the receipt of their statement or pay on an instalment basis, interest being charged on the outstanding amount. The following list of charges are normally consideration for exempt supplies:

- Interest charged on the outstanding balance on a card account.
- Annual membership, joining and subscription charges or charges made by card companies to the cardholder for the issue of the card.
- The charge made to merchants (retailers) by credit card companies. This charge usually takes the form of discounts from the amounts the card companies reimburse the merchant.
- Joining fees charged to merchants by card companies.
- Interchange fees.
- Imprinter/terminal rental charges when provided as an ancillary part of other exempt card services.

The following charges are consideration for taxable supplies:

- Imprinter/terminal rental charges when an optional or additional service by card company to retailer.
- The consideration for a sale of goods (e.g. imprinters/terminals in connection with any card scheme).

(VAT Notice 701/49/11, paras 4.6–4.8).

(3) Deferred payment

The expression 'the granting of credit' in **23.11**(*a*) above is wide enough to encompass credit provided by a supplier of goods in the form of deferment of payment for the goods. The wording does not require exemption to be confined to credit granted by banks and financial institutions (*Muys en De Winters's Bouw-en Aannemingsbedriff BV v Staatssecretaris van Financiën, ECJ Case C–281/91,* [1997] STC 665 (TVC 22.345)).

Where customers are allowed to defer payment but for an extra charge, if the charge relates to

- periods before and up to the time of the supply, it is not a charge for credit but further consideration for the supply of the goods or services; and
- periods beyond the time of supply, such a charge is consideration for an exempt supply of credit.

(VAT Notice 701/49/11, para 4.5).

(4) Discount for prompt payment

Where goods are supplied for a consideration in money and on terms allowing a discount for prompt payment, the consideration is to be taken as reduced 'by the discount', whether or not payment in made in accordance with those terms. [*VATA 1994, Sch 6 para 4*].

In *Saga Holidays Ltd* (VTD 18591) (VTD 67.88) S sold holidays and offered customers discounts for prompt payment. It failed to take account of such discounts and submitted a repayment claim. HMRC agreed to refund the amounts which S had overpaid where customers actually received discounts but rejected the claim where discount had been offered but the customers had not actually taken advantage of it. The tribunal agreed with this treatment, observing that the legislation provided that the consideration should be taken as reduced 'by the discount' and holding that these words could more readily be interpreted as a reference to a discount that has actually come into existence than to one that was available but may never come into existence. Therefore, *Sch 6 para 4(1)* should be construed as meaning that the consideration is only reduced where the discount is achieved.

This does not appear to be the interpretation which HMRC state in their published material. In VAT Notice 700, para 7.3 and VAT Notice 701/49/11, para 4.4 they indicated that the value for VAT is the discounted amount 'whether or not the customer takes up the offer'.

(5) Fuel card schemes

See **45.14 MOTOR CARS.**

(6) Late payment penalties

It is common for hire-purchase companies, credit card companies and similar institutions to impose a penalty for late payment. Where a customer is not explicitly allowed to defer payment and a late payment penalty is imposed because payment is not made by the due date, the penalty is not consideration for a supply and is outside the scope of VAT. (VAT Notice 701/49/11, para 4.4).

(7) Loan arrangements and execution services

In *C & E Commrs v Electronic Data Systems Ltd*, CA [2003] STC 688 (TVC 22.361) a bank (L) arranged for a company (E) to operate a call centre on its behalf. E received and processed loan applications, gathered and verified information about applicants, signed loan agreements on behalf of L, and released L's funds to borrowers. The Court of Appeal held that the supplies qualified for exemption under what is now *Directive 2006/112/EC, Art 135(1)(b)* (previously *EC 6th Directive, Art 13B(d)*). Following that decision, HMRC accept that where a business provides a package of outsourced service to a loan provider, the supply is exempt if

- it consists of services prior to and after the granting of a loan; and
- the business provides, as a central part of the supply, the services of
  - (i) the operation of bank accounts on behalf of the credit provider;
  - (ii) arranging the transfers of funds to the borrower; and
  - (iii) the processing of loan repayments (and any additional charges or fees) by direct debit or cheque.

(VAT Notice 701/49/11, para 4.11).

(8) Pawnbrokers

Redeemed pledges. There is no supply for VAT purposes if a person redeems a pledge within the agreed redemption period.

Unredeemed pledges. The following rules apply. The relevant law is in *Consumer Credit Act 1974, ss 120, 121*.

(a) Loans not exceeding £75 with a six month redemption period

Ownership of the pledge passes to the pawnbroker if the goods are not redeemed within the six months statutory redemption period. A disposal of the goods to a third party after that time is a taxable supply.

Where, however, the goods are restored by the pawnbroker to their original owner within three months following the end of the redemption period, the transaction is treated as a redeemed pledge and there is no supply for VAT purposes. [*SI 1986/896*]. The pawnbroker must record the redemption in his pledge stock records and stamp the 'Credit Agreement and Pawn Receipt' with the date of redemption and keep it for inspection by HMRC. If the pawnbroker and pledgor have agreed to extend the original agreement by one or more further six month periods, the three month 'grace period' starts when the extension expires.

The restoration of an unredeemed pledge more than three months after the redemption period is a taxable supply.

(b) Other loans

For loans over £75 or where the redemption period has been agreed for a period other than six months, ownership of the pledge does not pass to the pawnbroker at the end of the redemption period. The onward supply to a third party is not, therefore, a taxable supply by the pawnbroker. It is, however, a taxable supply by the pledgor if he is a taxable person and the pledge is something he has acquired in the course of his business. The pawnbroker (or auctioneer if the goods are sold by auction) must follow the procedure in **2.10 ACCOUNTING PERIODS AND RETURNS**.

Other charges.

- *Interest payments* received under credit agreements are exempt from VAT.

- *Valuation fees* relating to the pledged goods are regarded as part of the charge for the loan and are exempt.
- *Charges for selling unredeemed pledges*, provision for which is made in the loan contract, are exempt as a further charge for the granting of credit. Included is an element for cleaning and repairing the goods before they are put on display.

Second-hand goods scheme. Pawnbrokers may use the scheme for **SECOND-HAND GOODS (61)** for sales of unredeemed pawns within (*a*) above provided they have taken title to the goods and the normal scheme conditions are met. The purchase price is the amount of the loan plus the initial six months interest payable, less any payment received. The interest relating to the three month period of grace and other items such as cleaning, repair charges, storage and overhead expenses must not be added to the purchase price.

Pawnbrokers may, if they wish, use the credit agreement and pawn receipt as the purchase invoice provided

- the contract number is entered in the stock record and is cross-referred to the agreement; and
- a copy of the interest calculations and total purchase value for margin scheme purposes is attached to the document if it differs from the amount shown.

(VAT Notice 718, paras 18.1–18.4).

Pawnbrokers selling at auction. A pawnbroker may use the auctioneers' scheme for the sale of eligible second-hand goods (see **61.61 SECOND-HAND GOODS**) provided the pawn value is greater than £75 and the pledgor is not VAT-registered. If the pledgor is VAT-registered, VAT must be accounted for on the full selling price. (VAT Notice 718, para 7.10).

Securities

[23.17] The issue, transfer or receipt of, or any dealing with, any security or secondary security in the UK is exempt from VAT. For these purposes, a security or secondary security comprises

- shares, stock, bonds, notes (other than promissory notes), debentures, debenture stock or shares in an oil royalty;
- any document relating to money, in any currency, which has been deposited with the issuer or some other person, being a document which recognises an obligation to pay a stated amount to bearer or to order, with or without interest, and being a document by the delivery of which, with or without endorsement, the right to receive that stated amount, with or without interest, is transferable;
- any bill, note or other obligation of the Treasury or of a Government in any part of the world, being a document by the delivery of which, with or without endorsement, title is transferable, and not being an obligation which is or has been legal tender in any part of the world;

- any letter of allotment or rights, any warrant conferring an option to acquire a security included in these provisions, any renounceable or scrip certificates, rights coupons, coupons representing dividends or interest on such a security, bond mandates or other documents conferring or containing evidence of title to or rights in respect of such a security;
- units or other documents conferring rights under any trust established for the purpose, or having the effect of providing, for persons having funds available for investment, facilities for the participation by them as beneficiaries under the trust, in any profits or income arising from the acquisition, holding, management or disposal of any property whatsoever.

[*VATA 1994, Sch 9 Group 5 Item 6*].

Securities transactions

Despite the wording of the legislation, following the decision of the ECJ in *Kretztechnik AG v Finanzamt Lenz, ECJ Case C–465/03,* [2005] STC 1118 (TVC 22.91) the first issue of securities such as shares, bonds, loan notes, debentures, etc by a company is not a supply for VAT purposes. For further details, including the input tax recovery position, see **49.8**(3) **PARTIAL EXEMPTION.**

Transactions in shares which are already in existence are exempt where they are sold or transferred in the ordinary course of business and the normal partial exemption rules apply.

(VAT Notice 701/49/11, para 6.1).

International transactions

See **23.2** above for the place of supply of services within these provisions, including the special rule for the place of supply of securities sold where the identity of the purchaser is not known. The place of supply affects both the VAT liability of a financial service and whether the supplier can reclaim related input tax. See **23.3** above.

Stock lending

[23.18] Stock lending describes a situation where one person (the 'lender') transfers to a second person (the 'borrower') the legal title, along with all dividends and rights, to securities. The borrower agrees to return to the lender an equivalent number of the same securities at a later date.

For VAT purposes, there is an exempt supply under **23.17** above by the lender to the borrower, the consideration being the fee charged to the borrower. The borrower should not account for the value of securities returned to the lender. Any dividends which the borrower receives whilst the stocks are loaned are not consideration for a supply.

(VAT Notice 701/49/11, para 6.3).

Transactions related to securities

[23.19] Transactions related to securities are treated as follows:

(1) Custody services (before 1 January 2010)

Safe custody services are standard-rated. This includes the provision of the purely physical service of safekeeping (safe deposit facilities) and applies irrespective of where the recipient belongs and irrespective of whether the securities are stored in the UK, at an overseas branch of the business or elsewhere. This is because such services are expressly excluded from services within *VATA 1994, Sch 5 para 5* and therefore the place of supply is, under the general rule, where the supplier belongs.

Where a specific site is hired to a client (rather than the service of secure storage within the supplier's own premises), the supply is in the UK if the site is in the UK, but outside the scope of UK VAT if the site is overseas. There may, however, be a liability to account for VAT in another EU country if the place of supply is elsewhere in the EU.

Global custody services involve a package of services that may include safe custody, collection of dividends/interest on securities held, dealing with scrip/rights issues, and payment against the delivery or receipt of stock. In such a case, the supply of the whole service, including the safe custody element, is exempt.

(VAT Notice 701/49/11, para 6.6).

(2) Dealing systems and data services

The operation of a dealing system which allows

- a user to insert bid and offer quotes for securities,
- another user to insert acceptance, and
- for the system to match buy and sell deals,

is exempt.

Electronic data services which simply provide subscribers with a message facility or an information service (e.g. on share price movements or financial news) are taxable.

(VAT Notice 701/49/11, paras 6.12, 6.13).

(3) Management of special investment funds

EC Directive 2006/112/EC, Art 135(1)(g) exempts 'the management of special investment funds as defined by Member States'. Until 30 September 2008, UK law (*VATA 1994, Sch 9 Group 5 Items 9 and 10*) defined the following funds for the purposes of the exemption: authorised unit trust schemes (AUTS); open-ended investment companies (OEIC); and trust-based schemes (TBS). From 1 October 2008, following a European Court ruling (*Claverhouse, ECJ Case C–363/05*, [2008] STC 1180 (TVC 22.369)) the exemption has been extended so that there is a level VAT playing field for all similar collective investment undertakings which compete in the UK retail market (that is, for investment by the general public) under comparable conditions. This includes closed/open-ended collective investment undertakings which meet the revised definitions regardless of where they are established. TBS are no longer included in the exemption. CIU are in the business of collective investment, that is they pool and invest capital raised from the public and do so for a fee or 'management charge'. It is this management charge that is the subject of the VAT exemption. CIU may be constituted in various legal forms, but common to all of these is that investors hold shares or units in the CIU. See **23.20** and **23.21** below.

(VAT Notice 701/49/11, paras 7.1, 7.2).

(4) Listing fees charged by regulatory bodies

Fees charged by regulatory bodies, such as the Financial Services Authority, for listing companies that wish to float on an exchange are outside the scope of VAT. (VAT Notice 701/49/11, para 6.8).

(5) Nominee services

The services of acting as nominal holder of securities on behalf of the beneficial owner are exempt. (VAT Notice 701/49/11, para 6.5).

(6) Share registration services

Share registration services may include some or all of the following (the list is not exhaustive).

- All aspects of operating company share registers.
- Administration of scrip schemes, share option schemes, profit-sharing schemes and dividend reinvestment plans.
- Arrangements for advertising the closure of a share offer.
- Attending shareholders' meetings and organising polls at such meetings.
- Arranging 'break out' for bulk nominee accounts.
- Capital gains enquiries and other correspondence and enquiries.
- Conversion of loan stock.
- Preparation, designation and despatch of certificates, correction of errors on certificates, and issuing of duplicated documents.
- Administrative services in relation to mergers, placings, rights issues, reorganisations and acquisitions.
- Processing forms of proxy.
- Registration of grants of probate.
- Regular reports on share movements.
- Administrative services in relation to savings plan schemes.

These services are treated as supplied where the business customer belongs under the general rule for the supply of services (see **65.15 SUPPLY: PLACE OF SUPPLY**). They are standard-rated if supplied in the UK unless provided as one element of a single composite supply featuring other services with a different VAT liability, in which case the liability may change. See **64.6 SUPPLY: GENERAL** for single and multiple supplies.

See **23.20** and **23.21** below where share registration services are supplied for an authorised unit trust or an open-ended investment company.

(VAT Notice 701/49/11, para 6.7).

(7) Specialist services

In most cases, the exemption for intermediary services (see **23.25** below) does not cover

- the professional services of accountants and lawyers; and
- services of advice in general (e.g. to investors deciding whether to accept or reject a take-over bid).

Services supplied in connection with share issues, acquisitions or disposals that do not bring together the buyer and seller are also taxable. This includes

- valuation of assets;
- assessing the direct tax liabilities of a holding;
- investment analysis;
- market sector research;
- share consultancy;
- general financial or investment advice;
- accountancy services;
- tax and legal advice; and
- supplying a draft prospectus.

One or more of these services may qualify for exemption if they are provided as part of a complete service and are ancillary to an exempt financial service.

See **23.20** and **23.21** below where such services are provided to either an authorised unit trust or open-ended investment company.

(VAT Notice 701/49/11, para 6.14).

(8) Fees charged by stock exchanges

Basic admission or membership charges are taxable at the standard rate, with the place of supply being where the supplier belongs.

The liability of other charges (e.g. market maker charges, transaction charges and exchange charges) depends on exactly what is being done by the exchange for the charge. If the service is not an intermediary service then the fee will be taxable at the standard rate.

(VAT Notice 701/49/11, para 6.9).

Investment funds

[23.20] Following the decision of the ECJ in *Kretztechnik AG v Finanzamt Lenz, ECJ Case C–465/03*, [2005] STC 1118 (TVC 22.91) the issue of units in an authorised unit trust are not supplies for VAT purposes. (Business Brief 21/05).

A unit trust itself will hold and carry out transactions in securities within **23.17** above. The sale of these underlying securities is an exempt supply by the trust.

Investment management services are normally taxable (see **23.19**(3) above). However, under *EC Directive 2006/112/EC, Art 135(1)(g)* (previously *EC Sixth Directive, Art 13B(d)(6)*) 'the management of special investment funds as defined by Member States' is exempt. The UK has applied this exemption to the management of

- an authorised open-ended investment company;
- an authorised unit trust scheme;
- a Gibraltar collective investment scheme that is not an umbrella scheme, or a sub-fund of any other Gibraltar collective investment scheme;
- an individually recognised overseas scheme that is not an umbrella scheme, or a sub-fund of any other individually recognised overseas scheme;
- a recognised collective investment scheme authorised in a designated country or territory that is not an umbrella scheme, or a sub-fund of any other recognised collective investment scheme authorised in a designated country or territory;
- a recognised collective investment scheme constituted in another EEA state that is not an umbrella scheme, or a sub-fund of any other recognised collective investment scheme constituted in another EEA state; or
- up until 1 October 2008, a trust-based scheme.

'Authorised open-ended investment company' and *'authorised unit trust scheme'* have the meaning given in the *Financial Services and Markets Act 2000, s 237(3)*.

'*Collective investment scheme*' has the meaning given in *FSMA 2000, s 235*.

'*Gibraltar collective investment scheme*' means a collective investment scheme to which *FSMA 2000, s 264* applies pursuant to an order made under *FSMA 2000, s 409(1)(d)*; or a collective investment scheme to which *FSMA 2000* applies pursuant to an order made under *FSMA 2000, s 409(1)(f)*.

'Individually recognised overseas scheme' means a collective investment scheme declared by the Financial Services Authority to be a recognised scheme pursuant to *FSMA 2000, s 272*.

'Recognised collective investment scheme authorised in a designated country or territory' means a collective investment scheme recognised pursuant to *FSMA 2000, s 270*.

'Recognised collective investment scheme constituted in another EEA state' means a collective investment scheme which is recognised pursuant to *FSMA 2000, s 264*.

'Sub-fund' means a separate part of the property of an umbrella scheme that is pooled separately.

'Umbrella scheme' means a collective investment scheme under which the contributions of the participants in the scheme and the profits or income out of which the payments are to be made to them are pooled separately in relation to separate parts of the scheme property.

'*Trust based scheme*' means a scheme the purpose or effect of which is to enable persons taking part in the scheme, by becoming beneficiaries under a trust, to participate in or receive profits or income arising from the acquisition, holding, management or disposal of property of a kind described in *Financial Services and Markets Act 2000, s 239(3)(a)* or sums paid out of such profits or income.

The above provisions do not cover a collective investment scheme, or sub-fund, that is not for the time being marketed in the UK if it has never been marketed in the UK or less than 5% of its shares or units are held by, or on behalf of, investors who are in the UK.

[*VATA 1994, Sch 9 Group 5 Item 9 and Notes 6, 6A; SI 2008/2547*]. (HMRC Brief 35/08 and HMRC Brief 48/08).

Meaning of 'management': the VAT exemption concerns the management charge or fee which is normally deducted from the assets in the CIU periodically. For UK open-ended funds, the manager is required by regulation to be a separate entity. The term 'management' also includes certain activities of administering the CIU as well as investment management of the assets. If a third party is delegated to carry out a package of administrative services which overall has the distinct characteristic of a single supply of fund management services, this too will be exempt. Trustee and depositary services in relation to funds are always taxable.

(VAT Notice 701/49/11, para 7.5).

Management of an unauthorised unit trust is liable to VAT at the standard rate.

Closed-ended collective investment undertakings

[23.21] *EC Directive 2006/11//EC, Art 135(1)(g)* (previously *EC Sixth Directive, Art 13B(d)(6)*) exempts the management of 'special investment funds' as defined by individual EU countries. In *JP Morgan Fleming Claverhouse Investment Trust plc v HMRC (and related appeal), ECJ Case C-363/05*, [2008] STC 1180 (TVC 22.369) the ECJ held that the phrase 'special investment funds' was capable of including closed-ended investment funds such as investment trust companies (ITCs). Although the EU provisions gave EU countries a discretion to determine the special investment funds whose management is exempt from VAT, in exercising that power, countries must have regard to the objectives of the provision and to the principle of fiscal neutrality.

Following the decision in *Morgan Fleming*, the management of 'closed-ended collective investment undertakings' is exempt. 'Closed-ended collective investment undertaking' means an undertaking in relation to which the following conditions are satisfied

- its sole object is the investment of capital, raised from the public, wholly or mainly in securities;
- it manages its assets on the principle of spreading investment risk;

- all of its ordinary shares (of each class if there is more than one) or equivalent units are included in the official list maintained by the Financial Services Authority pursuant to the *Financial Services and Markets Act 2000, s 74(1)*; and
- all of its ordinary shares (of each class if there is more than one) or equivalent units are admitted to trading on a regulated market situated or operating in the UK.

Although the amended law comes into effect on 1 October 2008, it represents the situation as it should have been since 1 January 1990 when the exemption was first introduced. Businesses that have accounted for VAT on fund management services that qualify for exemption under the amended legislation may wish to submit claims to HMRC for output tax over-accounted for, subject to the three-year limitation period and unjust enrichment provisions.

[*VATA 1994, Sch 9 Group 5 Item 10 and Note 6; SI 2008/2547*]. (HMRC Brief 35/08; VAT Notice 701/49/11, para 7.4).

Wrapper products, administrative agreement and wrap accounts

Wrapper products

[23.22] Wrapper products hold investments in a tax-efficient wrapper making them free of income and capital gains tax, and are aimed at trying to stimulate the general public into saving and investing money. Examples of these products (current and historical) include Individual Savings Accounts (ISAs), Child Trust Funds (CTFs), Personal Equity Plans (PEPs) and Self-Invested Person Pensions (SIPPs). See the VAT Finance Manual for more information on these products and the VAT treatment of the associated charges.

Administrative agreement

An agreement was entered into on 1 April 1994 between HMRC and the Investment Management Association (formerly the Association of Unit Trusts and Investment Funds or 'AUTIF') concerning the VAT treatment of PEP managers' charges. This was used in subsequent years as a basis to determine the treatment of charges in respect of other tax-efficient wrapper products. Following discussions with industry representatives, the AUTIF Agreement has now been withdrawn and replaced with the tax treatments outlined in the VAT Finance Manual.

Wrap accounts

A wrap account is an arrangement that holds a range of investments, providing a single point of contact and management for investors and their agents. A wrap manager is usually a separate legal entity within a financial services or insurance group that offers to hold, manage and administer the whole or part of an individual's portfolio. The wrap account itself might typically be an interest-bearing bank account, with a set of sub-accounts, allowing payments to be made and received within broad product silos. The wrap manager nominates a third-party discretionary investment manager and an execution-only broker. The discretionary investment manager generally offers, or is required by the wrap manager to offer, nominee account services. It may also offer custody services, or these may be provided by another entity. The typical charging structures for wrap products are based on transaction charges, calculated by reference to the value of investments within the wrap account (taken as a strong indicator of activity going through the account), including dividends, interest, and principal amounts. Because the nature of the supplies made in connection with a 'wrap' account vary from one product to another, the VAT liability of wrap-related services depends upon whether the supplies in question fall within the VAT exemptions for either principal or intermediary financial services. For further information on wrap accounts and their VAT treatment see the VAT Finance Manual.

(VAT Notice 701/49/11, paras 7.7–7.9).

Underwriting

[23.23] The underwriting of an issue within *VATA 1994, Sch 9 Group 5 Item 1* (see **23.8** above) or any transaction within *VATA 1994, Sch 9 Group 5 Item 6* (see **23.17** above) is exempt. [*VATA 1994, Sch 9 Group 5 Item 5A; SI 1999/594, Art 3*].

A share underwriter guarantees to buy a proportion of any unsold shares when a new issue is offered to the general public, and usually receives either commission or charges a fee. A share underwriter may also underwrite an issue by agreeing to guarantee that buyers will be found. In either case the supply is exempt.

The sale of the securities by the issuer to the underwriter is not a supply for VAT purposes but there is a subsequent exempt supply by the underwriter when those securities are sold.

Where an underwriter's charge for services is adjusted to reflect the entitlement to purchase his allotted securities at a special price, the value of the discount must be regarded as part of the consideration for his exempt supply of underwriting services. However, where an underwriter is obliged to buy further securities which remain unsold and the underwriting agreement allows him to buy these unsold securities at a price lower than the offer price, this reduction is not regarded as consideration for the underwriting service and is outside the scope of VAT.

Sub-underwriters

Exemption also applies to the supply made by a sub-underwriter who agrees to underwrite a proportion of the issue or sale, whether the sub-underwriter's services are supplied to the underwriter or to the issuer.

(VAT Notice 701/49/11, para 6.4).

Banks and building societies

[23.24] The operation of any current, deposit or savings account is exempt. [*VATA 1994, Sch 9 Group 5 Item 8*].

Many of the charges made by banks, building societies or similar organisations are covered by this exemption including

- the issue of certain types of financial certificate (e.g. audit and balance certificates supplied to third parties); and
- the extra cost of special printing or overprinting of cheque books and paying-in books.

(VAT Notice 701/49/11, para 2.10).

Electronic banking and cash management services

Electronic banking services (including account management) are supplied by banks to business and individual customers as an addition, or alternative, to conventional banking services. In the case of business customers, the business uses computer equipment (sometimes leased or purchased from the bank) to obtain

- services which would otherwise have been provided by the bank in the course of its operation of the business's account (e.g. statements of the business's current balance or transfers of funds between accounts); and
- general finance related services (e.g. information about share prices or foreign exchange rates).

To determine the liability of an electronic banking service, it is first necessary to determine whether it is provided as a supply in its own right or as part of a package of services. In principle, services which would have been treated as exempt under *VATA 1994, Sch 9 Group 5* if they had been provided by the bank by conventional means should be treated as exempt when provided within the framework of electronic banking services. Other finance-related services which are not so covered should be treated as standard-rated.

HMRC have indicated the following VAT liabilities.

Supply	*Liability*
Provision of information on share prices, foreign exchange rates, balances on accounts with other financial institutions	Standard-rated
Provision of information on the state of the client's accounts by the bank providing the electronic banking services, bank statements, the transfer of funds and the debiting and crediting of accounts	Exempt
Hire of equipment and related charges, such as training	
(a) if supplied and shown as a separate item on the invoice	Standard-rated

Supply	*Liability*
(b) if not shown as a separate item on the invoice	Dependent on predominant or intended use when absorbed with other charges
Hire of equipment which can be used for other purposes (e.g. where the link gives access to Bloomburg, etc.)	Standard-rated
Sale of equipment	Standard-rated
Service charges/overall service charges	Dependent on predominant use

(VAT Notice 701/49/11, para 2.12).

Intermediary services

[23.25] *Directive 2006/112/EC* exempts the 'negotiation' of many financial services. See **18.26**(*b*)–(*f*) **EUROPEAN UNION LEGISLATION.**

Under UK legislation, the provision of 'intermediary services' in relation to a transaction within

(a) *VATA 1994, Sch 9 Group 5 Item 1* (the issue, transfer or receipt of, and any dealings with money or securities for money, see **23.8** above),
(b) *VATA 1994, Sch 9 Group 5 Item 2* (the making or an advance or the granting of credit, see **23.11**(*a*) above),
(c) *VATA 1994, Sch 9 Group 5 Item 3* (the provision of instalment credit finance by hire purchases, etc, see **23.11**(*c*) above),
(d) *VATA 1994, Sch 9 Group 5 Item 4* (the provision of administrative arrangements, etc. in connection with a supply under *Item 3* where the consideration does not exceed £10, see **23.11**(*d*) above), or
(e) *VATA 1994, Sch 9 Group 5 Item 6* (the issue, transfer or receipt of, or dealings with certain securities and secondary securities, see **23.17** above)

by a person 'acting in an intermediary capacity' is exempt. This applies whether or not any such transaction is finally concluded so that where qualifying intermediary services are performed but the deal falls through and there is no financial transaction, the intermediary service is still exempt.

'*Intermediary services*' for these purposes consist of

- 'bringing together' persons who are or may be seeking to receive financial services and persons providing such services, with a view to the provision of such services; *together with*
- in the case of financial services falling within (*a*)–(*d*) above (but *not* (*e*) above) the performance of 'work preparatory to the conclusion of contracts' for the provision of those financial services

but do not include the supply of any market research, product design, advertising, promotional or similar services or the collection, collation and provision of information in connection with such activities.

A person is '*acting in an intermediary capacity*' where he is acting as an intermediary (or one of the intermediaries) between

- a person providing financial services; and
- a person who is or may be seeking to receive such services.

[*VATA 1994, Sch 9 Group 5 Item 5 and Notes 5, 5A, 5B; SI 1999/594; SI 2003/1569*].

'*Bringing together*'. An intermediary should be independent of the parties entering into a financial services contract and not carrying out sub-contracted services for one of the parties. In *CSC Financial Services Ltd v C & E Commrs, ECJ Case C–235/00,* [2002] STC 57 (TVC 22.360), CSC supplied services to Sun Alliance, which issued personal equity plans. It dealt with telephone enquires, sent application forms to potential customers and checked completed application forms. But the customers had already been approached by Sun Alliance and the parties were not brought together by CSC, who acted not in an intermediary capacity but as a sub-contractor for Sun Alliance in processing applications. The ECJ confirmed that CSC was not an intermediary because it was standing in the shoes of Sun Alliance while taking calls and receiving forms, and also because CSC's activities were clerical activities which would normally have been done by Sun Alliance.

'*Work preparatory to the conclusion of contracts*' refers to work done of a specialised nature. This could include helping to set the terms of the contract or making representations on behalf of a client, but would not include work done of a general nature such as administrative or clerical formalities. (VAT Notice 701/49/11, para 9.3). Note that the legislation provides that, in relation to a transaction falling within (*e*) above, preparatory work is not necessary and exemption can apply to the mere introduction of a person seeking to buy or sell securities to a person effecting transactions in securities.

Intermediary services may contain more than one component. Services which include market research, product design or similar services excluded above may still be exempt provided that this is a minor and ancillary part of the overall intermediary service. (VAT Notice 701/49/11, para 9.13). See also **23.28** below for where financial advisers provide mixed supplies of advice and intermediary services.

International transactions

The VAT liability of transactions with an international element are affected by the place of belonging of the recipient of the services. In addition, where the underlying supply is made to a person belonging outside the EU, this may affect the entitlement to input tax deduction. The following table summarises the liability of intermediary services in the most common transactions.

Underlying supplier belonging in		*Sells to*	*Underlying recipient belonging in*	
	VAT on commission charged to supplier			*VAT on commission charged to recipient*
UK or other EU (private)	E		UK or other EU (private)	E

Underlying supplier belonging in		*Sells to*	*Underlying recipient belonging in*	
	VAT on commission charged to supplier			*VAT on commission charged to recipient*
UK or other EU (private)	E		Other EU (business)	OS
UK or other EU (private)	E(R)		Non-EU	OS(R)
Other EU (business)	OS		UK or other EU (private)	E
Other EU (business)	OS		Other EU (business)	OS
Other EU (business)	OS(R)		Non-EU	OS(R)
Non-EU	OS(R)		UK or other EU (private)	E
Non-EU	OS(R)		Other EU (business)	OS
Non-EU	OS(R)		Non-EU	OS(R)

Key
E = Exempt
E(R) = Exempt but with refund of related input tax
OS = Outside the scope of UK VAT with no refund of related input tax
OS(R) = Outside the scope of UK VAT with refund of related input tax

> *Example*
>
> An intermediary arranges for the sale of shares from a UK customer to a Japanese counterparty. The intermediary's supply is exempt and because the place of supply of the underlying supply is outside the EU, he is entitled to deduct related input tax.

It should be noted that the above table only applies where there is an underlying supply. There is no entitlement to deduct input tax in relation to underlying transactions, such as issues of securities, which are not supplies for VAT purposes. (VAT Notice 701/49/11, para 9.12).

Securities broking services

[23.26] The introductory service of bringing together a person who wishes to buy securities to a person selling securities is exempt if made in the UK, even if the intended securities transaction later falls through (see **23.25**(*e*) above). The exemption covers

- any stock or share broking services (see below); and

- arranging issues or placements of securities whether as offers for sale, rights issues, cash offers, vendor placings or bids with underwritten cash alternatives, including the service of co-ordinating an issue when a number of participants are involved in the share or other placing. But see **23.27** below which covers corporate finance services.

Broking services

Where a broker acts as an 'execution only' broker, buying or selling securities on client's instructions, but does not offer advice on securities, his supply is exempt. Where a broker provides advice and this is incidental to transactions in securities, the supply is exempt.

Where a broker arranging a securities transaction splits the contract note to show as separate items the basic charge for execution services and any compliance or regulatory charges made to cover the cost of meeting regulatory requirements, the additional charges are still part of the consideration for his exempt broking service. This does not, however, apply to any statutory levies (e.g. stamp duty) which are a liability of the client. These are outside the scope of VAT.

(VAT Notice 701/49/11, paras 6.10, 6.11).

Corporate finance services

[23.27] The provision of advisory services (e.g. on raising capital or defending take-over bids) is taxable. Where advice leads to, or is associated with, a transaction in securities by the client, the services may themselves be exempt as a provision of intermediary services for a transaction in securities, but only if the criteria set out in **23.25** above are met.

These principles may be applied to contracts that are aborted, but in some circumstances it may be necessary to apportion the liability of the supplies between taxable advice and exempt intermediary services.

(VAT Notice 701/49/11, para 9.7).

Other intermediary services

[23.28] Other intermediary services are treated as follows:

(1) Affinity credit card schemes

These schemes typically involve a charity or interest group endorsing a credit card and recommending its use to their members, supporters or customers. The charity or interest group receive a commission or similar income, usually linked to the taking out and subsequent usage of the card.

Charities have been granted a special concession which recognises a 'donational' element in the affinity card scheme. See **12.5**(3) CHARITIES.

Non-charity organisations operating affinity credit card schemes are subject to the normal VAT rules. In *BAA plc v C & E Commrs,* CA 2002, [2003] STC 35 (TVC 27.20) a company, in return for a commission, provided a bank with information concerning potential credit card customers. It targeted suitable applicants, issued applications, assisted in the completion of the forms and screened and processed them on return. In *Institute of Directors v C & E Commrs, CA 2002,* [2003] STC 35 (TVC 27.22), which case was heard in the Court of Appeal with *BAA plc*, the IoD similarly provided a list of suitable members, encouraged members to apply, and assisted them with their applications and validated completed forms. The Court of Appeal held that, in both cases, the activities carried out were within the definition of 'negotiation of credit' for the purposes of what is now *Directive 2006/112/EC, Art 135(1)(b)* (previously *EC 6th Directive, Art 13B(d)*) and exempt from VAT in the UK as intermediary services.

As a result of these judgments, HMRC take the view that a body that introduces its members, supporters or customers to a credit card provider and brings the two parties together, carrying out independent negotiation services as a distinct act of mediation, is providing exempt intermediary services.

HMRC view marketing and promotional services supplied in isolation, and the performing of clerical functions (e.g. providing a list of names or access to a database) as standard-rated.

(VAT Notice 701/49/11, para 4.9).

(2) Credit and debit card handling services

In *Bookit Ltd v R & C Commrs,* CA [2006] STC 1367 (TVC 27.23) the company arranged advance bookings for cinema seats by telephone or the internet. It checked seat availability and took details of the customer's card details. It charged an administration fee of 50p per ticket. The Court held that it was making exempt supplies because its services involved transmitting the card information with the necessary security information and the card issuers' authorisation codes to Girobank (i.e. it had the effect that funds were transferred to its account with Girobank).

Following this decision, HMRC accept that if an agent, acting for the supplier of the goods or services, makes a charge to the customer over and above the price of the actual goods or services, for a separately identifiable service of handling payment by credit or debit card, *and that service includes the transfer of funds to its account*, the additional charge is exempt. (Business Brief 18/06).

(3) Derivatives

Services of a person acting as an agent, broker or other intermediary for supplies of *financial* derivatives may be exempt from VAT. The rules are different depending on the type of financial service which is provided.

- Cash settled contracts (see **23.9**(4) above). The supply is exempt if the intermediary
  - acts between a person selling and a person buying a cash settled financial derivative;
  - brings those parties together; and
  - carries out some form of preparatory work to the conclusion of contracts.

- Non-cash settled contracts (see **23.9**(4) above). The supply is exempt if the intermediary
  - acts between a person selling and a person buying non-cash settled financial derivatives; and
  - brings those parties together.

(VAT Notice 701/49/11, para 8.12).

(4) Financial investigations

Financial investigation includes activities such as checking the validity of documents, normally on behalf of a financial institution. These services are taxable. (VAT Notice 701/49/11, para 9.6).

(5) Independent financial advisors (IFAs)

An IFA may

(a) provide advice only (a taxable supply);
(b) act between his customer and the provider of a financial product, in which case his supply is exempt if he meets the criteria in **23.25** above; or
(c) provide a mixture of (*a*) and (*b*).

Where (*c*) above applies, it is necessary to establish which of the two elements of the service predominates.

(a) Where the advice directly results in the customer taking out a financial product and all the criteria for intermediary services in **23.25** above are met, the whole of the service (including the advice element) is exempt. The advice is seen as ancillary to an exempt intermediary service. If any commission is received from the finance product provider, it is consideration for a separate exempt supply by the IFA of intermediary services.
(b) Where the advice far outweighs the work done to arrange a contract (e.g. because a customer has received a general financial review, with advice covering a range of financial issues, but then only buys a minor product requiring minimal intermediary services), those intermediary services are ancillary to the advice, and VAT is due on the whole supply.

(VAT Notice 701/49/11, para 9.9).

IFA networks

IFA firms frequently operate as networks through agreements with persons known as appointed representatives (ARs) for whom the authorised IFA firm takes regulatory responsibility. The arrangements enable the AR to carry out regulated activities without the need to be authorised directly by the Financial Services Authority (FSA).

These network arrangements are permitted under UK legislation and are subject to strict regulatory rules. In particular, the following should apply.

- The network appoints the ARs and trains them to operate in accordance with FSA requirements.

- In all dealings with the client, the ARs make it clear, both orally and on any paperwork, that they are acting on behalf of the network.
- The network has the contractual relationship with the financial product providers and at all times the AR acts on the network's behalf.
- The network maintains a high level of control over the ARs, carrying out regular checks and audits and imposing sanctions where appropriate.
- The network accepts responsibility for the actions of the ARs and handles all customer complaints made against the AR.
- The network holds liability insurance to cover any claims resulting from the activities of the ARs and is legally liable for any sanctions imposed under the *FSMA 2000*.
- All fees or commissions for regulated activities are paid by the clients or product providers to the network and these form part of the income of the network for accounting and direct tax purposes.
- The network pays the ARs for their services and these payments can be adjusted at the discretion of the network should, for example, the AR be found to have failed to conduct the business in accordance with the regulatory requirements.

When networks operate in this way, a 'sub-agency' or 'sub-contract' arrangement in effect exists between the network and the ARs. The network acts as principal, making supplies of financial intermediary services to the financial product providers and supplies of advice and/or financial intermediary services to the clients. The networks effectively sub-contract their functions to the ARs who interact directly with the client and the product providers in the provision of individual supplies on behalf of the network.

The VAT treatment of such arrangements is as follows.

- All payments (whether by fee or commission) received from the product providers or clients for the supplies of financial *intermediary services* provided via the ARs is the network's VAT exempt income and the onward payments made to the ARs is consideration for the AR's VAT exempt intermediary services supplied to the network.
- Fees either paid directly to the network or via the ARs, in respect of *advice only* services supplied via the ARs (which fall outside the exemption for financial intermediary services) is the network's standard rated income. Any onward payments made to the ARs is consideration for the provision of those services by the ARs to the network on which VAT is due if the AR's taxable income is above the VAT registration threshold.
- Any optional services supplied by the network to their ARs for additional consideration (e.g. specific compliance or IT services) are separate supplies and the relevant VAT liability applies.
- Any non-regulated services provided by ARs fall outside the network arrangements altogether and are made directly by the ARs to the client/product provider.

A different VAT treatment applies to supplies made by networks that do not operate in the way outlined above (e.g. firms which on first appearance look like networks but are not authorised entities and are set up to provide marketing and/or compliance support services to directly authorised IFA firms). In the event of any doubt, businesses are advised to contact HMRC.

(VAT Notice 701/49/11, para 9.10).

(6) Soft commissions

Soft commissions are an arrangement by which an intermediary can use his income from the provider to fund (either directly or indirectly) some of his client's costs, in recognition of the amount of business the client will (or has) put his way. Such commissions are outside the scope of VAT as they do not represent consideration for any supply. (VAT Notice 701/49/11, para 9.8).

(7) Individual voluntary arrangements

In *Paymex Ltd* (TC01210) (TVC 20.81) a company provided insolvency practitioners (IPs) to run and maintain individual voluntary arrangements (IVAs) for consumers who had fallen into financial difficulties. The tribunal found that the company was making supplies of financial services concerned with debts, which qualified for exemption under *Directive 2006/112/EC, Art 135(1)(d)*. It held that the services were related to a financial transaction which has as its purpose both a change in the legal and financial situation of the debtor and creditors, and the alteration and/or extinguishment of their respective rights and obligations in relation to those debts.

Following that decision, HMRC have stated that:

- Although the tribunal decision itself applied purely to consumer IVAs, HMRC considers that the terms of the tribunal decision read across to all IVAs. The important point for IPs to consider here is not the specific type of IVA, but rather whether the nature of the services they provide are covered by the terms of the *Paymex Limited* ruling.
- Although HMRC does not consider the terms of the tribunal decision to be restricted to a particular type of IVA, the tribunal decision does not deal with company voluntary arrangements (CVAs) or partnership voluntary arrangements (PVAs). If IPs consider, on the basis of *Paymex Limited*, that they have overpaid VAT arising from their role as supervisors of CVAs or PVAs and seek to reclaim such VAT, these claims will be rejected.

Refund claims are subject to the rules on input tax adjustments, the four-year cap and unjust enrichment.

(HMRC Brief 35/11).

Standard-rated supplies

[23.29] There are various services which, although associated with finance, are not covered by the exemption. These include:

- Bookkeeping services
- Debt collection (see **23.10** above) and credit control
- Depository and trustee services
- Equipment leasing
- Executor and trustee services and the administration of estates
- Investment, finance and taxation advice
- Management consultancy
- Merger and take-over advice
- Portfolio management (see **23.19**(4) above)
- Registrar services (see **23.19**(7) above)
- Safe custody services (see **23.19**(1) above) and safe transportation services
- Service companies' activities, e.g. administration, payment of salaries and wages

(VAT Notice 701/49/11, para 1.6).

Islamic products

[23.30] According to Sharia'a principles the following are prohibited.

- The charging or receipt of interest ('riba').
- Uncertainty or deception (e.g. an ambiguity or lack of clarity in the terms of a contract that can give rise to speculation ('gharar')).
- Gambling or speculation (e.g. any transaction undertaken for purely speculative purposes ('maisir')).
- Unethical investments (e.g. dealing in activities or commodities that include pork, pornography, arms or munitions, conventional financial services, cinema, tobacco, gambling or alcohol).

Because of this, many Muslims have been unable or unwilling to obtain conventional credit finance in order to purchase goods and/or services because those products are prohibited in their faith. In order to be able to provide Sharia'a compliant products, financial institutions and boards of Sharia'a scholars have worked together to create certain products which operate via a trade or rental arrangement as these are allowed under Sharia'a.

See VAT Information Sheet 11/06 for details of the schemes and their VAT treatment.

Key points

[23.31] Points to consider are as follows.

- Many financial services supplied by a business are exempt from VAT. This means that input tax recovery is not possible on related costs under the rules of partial exemption.
- An exception to the input tax block is if the exempt financial service is provided to a customer who belongs outside the EU. In such cases, input tax recovery is allowed.

- A key challenge for any business making supplies of financial services, or related support services, is to be very clear about the exact nature of the service being performed. In the past, many tribunal decisions have confirmed that services being provided are of an 'administrative' nature (and therefore standard-rated) rather than being directly relevant to arranging financial services that are exempt.
- A hire purchase transaction involves a supply of goods because the intention is that the hirer will take ownership of the goods at the end of the agreement. This means that the hirer can claim input tax on the full value of the goods (subject to the normal rules, e.g. not in relation to motor cars available for private use where an input tax block applies) at the time he first acquires the goods in accordance with the agreement. The finance company will account for output tax.
- It is common practice for many retail outlets to charge an additional fee for goods and services, where the customer pays for the goods by credit card, rather than by cheque or cash. In such cases, this is an additional charge for the goods or services in question. It is not relevant to an exempt supply of financial services.
- In situations where a supplier offers settlement or prompt payment discount to a customer, the VAT charge (in the case of standard-rated or reduced-rated supplies) will be based on the discounted price, irrespective of whether the customer takes the discount option.
- The activities of independent financial advisers (IFAs) can be both exempt and standard-rated. Advisory services for a client are standard-rated, but services of arranging a financial product for the client (with a commission earned from either the client or financial institution in question) is exempt from VAT because the IFA is acting as a financial intermediary.

24

Food

Cross-references. See also CATERING **(11)** for supplies in the course of catering and take-away food; **47.8**(16) OUTPUT TAX for packaging of food products.

De Voil Indirect Tax Service. See V4.221; V4.226; V4.228.

Introduction

[24.1] The supply of food (including drink) comprised in the following *General items*, is zero-rated.

(a) Food of a kind used for human consumption (see **24.2** to **24.14** below).
(b) Animal feeding stuffs (see **24.15** and **24.19** below).
(c) Seeds or other means of propagation of plants within (*a*) or (*b*) above (see **24.20** below).

(d) Live animals of a kind generally used as, or yielding or producing, food for human consumption (see **24.21** to **24.23** below).

There are, however, a number of *Excepted items* (which are standard-rated) and *Overriding items* (which are zero-rated because they override the *Excepted items*).

Catering

Specifically excluded from zero-rating is any supply in the course of catering which includes

- any supply of food for consumption on the premises where it is supplied; and
- any supply of hot food for consumption off those premises.

See **11 CATERING** for full details.

[*VATA 1994, Sch 8 Group 1 General Items 1–4*].

Food for human consumption

[24.2] The supply of food of a kind used for human consumption is zero-rated. Food includes drink. [*VATA 1994, Sch 8 Group 1 General Item 1*].

Meaning of '*food*'

The law does not include a definition of 'food' and the word should therefore be given its ordinary and everyday meaning (applying *Brutus v Cozens*, [1972] 2 All ER 1297).

A product is considered to be 'food' if the average person would consider it so. HMRC regard the term as including products eaten as part of a meal or snack. However, many products are sold in a form in which they are not fit to be consumed without some preparation by the user and the words 'of a kind used for' are included to reflect this fact (*C & E Commrs v Macphie & Co (Glenbervie) Ltd*, CS [1992] STC 886 (TVC 29.88)). Products, therefore, like flour which, although not eaten by themselves, are generally recognised as food ingredients are included. 'Food' would not normally include

- medicines and medicated preparations (but see **28.13 HEALTH AND WELFARE** for zero-rating of certain medicines),
- dietary supplements (see **24.11** below), or
- food additives and similar products (see **24.12** below)

which, although edible, are not generally regarded as 'food'.

Palatability and other matters may be taken into account (*Marfleet Refining Co Ltd* (VTD 129) (TVC 29.97)) and also nutritive value (*Soni* (VTD 897) (TVC 29.82)).

Waste and contaminated food products (including used cooking oil) are not allowed zero-rating because, although they could be described as 'food', they are not 'of a kind used for human consumption'. (They may, however, qualify for zero-rating as animal feeding stuffs, see **24.15** below.)

(VAT Notice 701/14/11, para 2.3).

Exceptions

Food of a kind used for human consumption is generally zero-rated under *General Item 1* above. There are, however, a number of categories of *Excepted items* (including ice cream and similar products, confectionery, alcoholic and other beverages, crisps, roasted and salted nuts) which are standard-rated and *Overriding items* (including tea and coffee) which override the *Excepted items* and remain zero-rated.

For a consideration of food for human consumption generally, see **24.3** to **24.14** below.

Catering

For food supplied in the course of catering and take-away food generally, see **CATERING (11)**.

Asian food products and additives

For a useful list of such products and their VAT liabilities, see HMRC VAT Guidance V1–7, Chapter 1 paras 13.1, 13.2.

Basic foodstuffs

[24.3] All supplies of unprocessed foodstuffs such as raw meat and fish, vegetables and fruit, nuts and pulses and fresh culinary herbs are zero-rated provided they are of a quality fit for human consumption. This applies whether the produce is supplied direct to the public or for use as ingredients in the manufacture of processed foods. (If not fit for human consumption, it may still be eligible for zero-rating as animal feeding stuffs, see **24.15** below.)

Meat and poultry

Zero-rating applies whether sold as a complete carcass or butchered and extends to more exotic meats such as ostrich, crocodile, kangaroo, horsemeat, etc. (The rules are different for sale of live animals where zero-rating only applies if the animal is of a species generally used for consumption in the UK so that, for example, the sale of a live horse is standard-rated, see **24.21** below.)

Fish

The same rules apply as for meat above. Provided the species is one generally used for human consumption in the UK, it is zero-rated whether supplied live, whole or filleted.

Vegetables, fruit and culinary herbs

These are zero-rated when sold unprocessed provided they are fit for human consumption (e.g. ornamental cabbages are standard-rated). See **24.20** below for supplies of growing plants and seeds. Zero-rating only applies to culinary herbs not medicinal ones (unless in the form of herbal teas). See **24.12** below for a list of herbs accepted by HMRC as culinary.

Fruit and vegetable pulps are zero-rated but pulps that are to be made into beverages and most juices and juice concentrates are standard-rated as beverages (see **24.8** below).

Cereals

Cereals (wheat, barley, maize, etc.) of a kind fit for human consumption are zero-rated whether supplied as a growing crop, in bulk, or cleaned and packaged for retail sale. (Cereals unfit for human consumption may be eligible for zero-rating as animal feeding stuffs, see **24.15** below.)

See **24.14** below for processing other people's cereal crop.

Nuts and pulses

Raw and unprocessed nuts and pulses fit for human consumption are zero-rated, as are nuts roasted or salted in their shells. This applies whether they are sold in bulk or in small retail packs. Nuts which are shelled and either roasted or salted are standard-rated (see **24.9** below).

Bakery products

Bread and bread products (e.g. rolls, baps, pitta bread) are zero-rated unless supplied as part of a hot take-away meal (e.g. a bun containing a hot hamburger). For hot take-away food, see **11 CATERING**. *Cakes* and *biscuits* (other than chocolate covered biscuits) are normally zero-rated (see **24.6** below) but other confectionery is normally standard-rated (see **24.5** below).

Freshly baked products

Many bakery products (e.g. pies, pasties and other savouries) are baked on the premises and sold while hot. See **11.2 CATERING** for the distinction between freshly baked food (zero-rated) and hot take-away food (standard-rated).

Processed food

Canned and *frozen foods* take the liability of the equivalent unprocessed product. Ice creams, etc. are standard-rated (see **24.4** below).

Ready meals: sales of convenience foods and prepared meals which require further preparation (e.g. reheating) at home are zero-rated; but where premises and/or facilities for eating the food are provided or hot take-away food is supplied, there could be a supply of standard-rated catering. See **11 CATERING**.

Cold sandwiches are zero-rated as prepared food unless they are a supply made in the course of catering. See **11 CATERING**.

(VAT Notice 701/14/11, paras 3.1, 3.3, 3.4).

Ice cream, etc.

[24.4] The supply of ice cream, ice lollies, frozen yoghurt, water ices and similar frozen products, and prepared mixes and powders for making such products, are standard-rated. [*VATA 1994, Sch 8 Group 1 Excepted Item 1*].

Yoghurt unsuitable for immediate consumption when frozen is zero-rated. [*VATA 1994, Sch 8 Group 1 Overriding Item 1*]. The use of the expression 'similar frozen products' assumes that the adjective 'frozen' applies to any of the former, specifically enumerated items. What those items have in common is that they are supplied for consumption at a temperature below the freezing point of water. They do not have in common any particular degree of viscosity or solidity. See *Meschia's Frozen Foods v C & E Commrs*, Ch D 2000, [2001] STC 1 (TVC 29.126) where the court held that frozen yoghurt in the context of *Excepted Item 1* meant yoghurt reduced to a temperature below the freezing point of water.

Standard-rated items include

- sorbets and granitas
- ice cream gateaux and cakes, including arctic rolls
- fruit syrups sold in plastic tubes for home freezing as ice lollies

Zero-rated items include

- products which are supplied frozen but which have to be cooked (e.g. baked alaska) or thawed completely (cream gateaux, mousse) before eating
- desserts which can be eaten either straight from the freezer or left to thaw (unless primarily designed for eating while frozen and made substantially of ice cream or any of the other excepted items)
- toppings, sauces and syrups for serving with ice cream (unless sold on the ice cream)

Wafers, cones, etc. sold complete with ice cream are standard-rated as part of that ice cream. If sold separately, they are treated as biscuits (i.e. zero-rated unless wholly or partly covered in chocolate or a similar product) (see **24.6** below).

(VAT Notice 701/14/11, para 3.5).

Confectionery

[24.5] 'Confectionery' is standard-rated. '*Confectionery*' includes chocolates; sweets; biscuits wholly or partly covered with chocolate or with some product similar in taste and appearance; drained, glacé or crystallised fruits (but not drained cherries or candied peel which are zero-rated); and any item of sweetened prepared food which is normally eaten with the fingers. [*VATA 1994, Sch 8 Group 1 Excepted Item 2; Overriding Items 2 and 3* and *Note (5)*].

In *Popcorn House Ltd*, [1968] 4 All ER 782 (TVC 29.145) (a purchase tax case) 'confectionery' was described as any form of food normally eaten with the fingers and made by a cooking process, other than baking, which contains a substantial amount of sweetening matter.

In *C & E Commrs v Ferrero UK Ltd*, CA [1997] STC 881 (TVC 29.137), the Court confirmed the following principles adopted by the tribunal as the correct approach to take when deciding whether a product is confectionery or a cake or biscuit.

- The words in the law must be given their ordinary meaning.
- What is relevant is the view of the ordinary man in the street.
- VAT treatment of other products is not relevant.
- If a product has characteristics of two categories, it can be placed in the category in which it has sufficient characteristics to qualify.
- Factors that should also taken into account include appearance, size and ingredients, manufacturing process, taste and texture, time and place of eating, and packaging. Marketing may also be of varying degrees of relevance.

Items of sweetened prepared food do not need to have added sweetening if they are inherently sweet, e.g. certain fruit and cereal bar products. Standard-rating applies to products falling within the general definition of confectionery even if intended to meet special nutritional needs (e.g. chocolate for diabetics and slimmers' meal replacements in biscuit form with a chocolate or similar coating).

Standard-rated items include

- chocolates, chocolate bars (including those containing nuts, fruit, toffee, biscuit or any other ingredient), liqueur chocolates
- boiled sweets, lollipops and candyfloss
- fruit pastilles and gums and similar jelly sweets
- turkish delight
- sherbet
- marshmallows, 'snowballs', fondants and similar confectionery
- chewing and bubble gum
- nuts or fruit with a coating, e.g. of chocolate, yoghurt or sugar
- crystallised or sugared ginger (but ginger preserved in syrup, drained ginger or dusted ginger can be zero-rated as long as not held out for sale as confectionery)
- compressed fruit bars and other items or prepared dried fruit confectionary that are sweet to the taste
- bars consisting mainly of sesame seeds and sugar or other sweetening matter (but halva is zero-rated unless coated with chocolate or chocolate substitute or held out for sale as confectionery)
- marrons glacé
- sweetened popcorn (*C & E Commrs v Clark's Cereal Products Ltd*, QB 1965, [1968] 3 All ER 778 (TVC 29.144) – a purchase tax case)
- sweetened dried fruit, e.g. banana chips, pineapple and papaya (unless sold as suitable for confectionery/snacking *and* home cooking (see **24.12** below) when zero-rated irrespective of bag size)
- cereal bars, whether or not coated with chocolate (except for bars qualifying as cakes)
- florentines
- coconut ice

Zero-rated items include

- Angelica, 'glacé' cherries, and cocktail or maraschino cherries
- cakes (see **24.6** below)
- biscuits not covered with chocolate or a similar product (see **24.6** below)

- chocolate spread
- liquid chocolate icing
- toffee apples (*Candy Maid Confections Ltd & Others v C & E Commrs*, Ch D [1968] 3 All ER 773 (TVC 29.128) – a purchase tax case) and other apples on a stick covered with chocolate, nuts, etc.
- traditional Indian and Pakistani delicacies, e.g. barfis, halvas, jelabi, laddoos (but not petha which is crystallised fruit)
- traditional Japanese delicacies
- chocolate cups

See **24.6** below for edible and inedible cake decorations and **24.13** below for mixtures and assortments.

(VAT Notice 701/14/11, paras 3.4, 3.6).

Cakes and biscuits

[24.6] Cakes and biscuits (other than biscuits wholly or partly covered with chocolate or some product similar in taste and appearance) are zero-rated. [*VATA 1994, Sch 8 Group 1 Excepted Item* 2].

Cakes

Cakes include (whether or not they are covered with chocolate)

- sponges and fruitcakes
- meringues
- slab gingerbread (gingerbread men are treated as biscuits)
- flapjacks (but not flapjack-type products containing cereals other than oats, which are confectionery, see **24.5** above. See also *Asda Stores Ltd* (TC00211) (TVC 29.161) in which it was held that, apart from oats, the 'flapjack bars' did not contain the typical ingredients of a flapjack)
- marshmallow teacakes (despite the fact that they comprise a combination of chocolate coated biscuit and marshmallow, both of which are regarded as standard-rated confectionery) but not 'snowballs' which are confectionery, see **24.5** above
- 'crunch cakes' consisting of corn flakes or other breakfast cereal products coated in chocolate or carob and pressed into flat cakes (see *Doves Farm Foods Ltd* (VTD 17805))
- caramel or 'millionaire's' shortcake (*Marks & Spencer plc* (VTD 4510) (TVC 29.134))
- lebkuchen
- jaffa cakes (see *United Biscuits (UK) Ltd* (VTD 6344) (TVC 29.135))

Cakes provided as part of a supply of catering are standard-rated as part of that supply. See **11 CATERING**. However, if a commemorative cake is provided to a caterer or individual, the supply can be zero-rated provided the supplier

- takes no further part in the provision of catering; and
- does not take the cake to the premises to set it up/supervise its disposal.

Cake decorations

Inedible cake decorations are standard-rated where sold on their own. If supplied as part of a cake, an inedible decoration can be zero-rated unless it is clearly a separate item in its own right (e.g. a toy with a child's birthday cake intended to be used after the cake is eaten although, even then, if the linked goods concession can be applied, the supply can be treated as a single supply, see **24.13** below).

Edible cake decorations are zero-rated when sold as part of a cake. They are also zero-rated when sold separately unless standard-rated as confectionery (see **24.5** above) or roasted nuts (see **24.9** below).

Zero-rated cake decorations include

- chocolate couverture
- chocolate chips
- hundreds and thousands, vermicelli and sugar strands
- chocolate leaves, scrolls, etc., jelly shapes, and sugar flowers, leaves, etc. (provided designed specifically for cake decorations)
- royal icing
- toasted coconut and toasted almonds held out specifically for baking use
- cherries used in baking ('glacé')

Standard-rated cake decorations include

- chocolate buttons except packets of mini-chocolate buttons sold for use in baking
- chocolate flakes (except where supplied within the bakery and ice cream industries when they may be zero-rated if sold in packs of 144 or more and clearly labelled 'for use as cake decorations only: not for retail sale')
- any other items sold in the same form as confectionery

Biscuits

Biscuits covered or partly covered in chocolate (or some other product similar in taste and appearance) are standard-rated. Other biscuits are zero-rated.

Standard-rated biscuits include

- chocolate shortbread
- gingerbread men decorated with chocolate (unless only dots for eyes)
- ice cream wafers partly covered in chocolate, e.g. chocolate oysters (but see *Marcantonio Foods Ltd* (VTD 15486) (TVC 29.131) for waffle cones)

Zero-rated biscuits include

- chocolate chip biscuits where the chips are either included in the dough or pressed into the surface before cooking
- bourbon and other biscuits whether the chocolate or similar product only forms a sandwich layer
- biscuits coated with caramel or some other product that does not resemble chocolate in taste and appearance

See also *C & E Commrs v Ferrero UK Ltd*, CA [1997] STC 881 (TVC 29.137).

Mixtures and assortments

See **24.13** below.

(VAT Notice 701/14/11, para 3.4).

Alcoholic drinks

[24.7] Beverages chargeable with any excise duty specifically charged on spirits, beer, wine or made-wine and preparations thereof are standard-rated. [*VATA 1994, Sch 8 Group 1 Excepted Item 3*].

All supplies of drinks containing alcohol are standard-rated, whether sold for consumption on or off the premises. This includes

- beer, cider and perry (including black beer and shandy)
- wine (including made-wine and fermented communion wine)
- spirits and liqueurs

Food products, other than beverages, containing alcohol follow the normal liability rules, e.g. fruit preserved in alcohol is zero-rated as any other preserved fruit and rum babas are zero-rated as cakes. Liqueur chocolates are standard-rated.

(VAT Notice 701/14/11, para 3.7).

Non-alcoholic drinks

[24.8] Supplies of 'beverages' not within **24.7** above (including fruit juices and bottled waters) and syrups, concentrates, essences, powders, crystals or other products for the preparation of beverages are standard-rated, subject to the following overriding exceptions which are zero-rated.

(a) Tea, maté, herbal teas and similar products, and preparations and extractions thereof.
(b) Cocoa, coffee and chicory and other roasted coffee substitutes, and preparations and extractions thereof.
(c) Milk and preparations and extracts thereof.
(d) Preparations and extracts of meat, yeast or eggs.

[*VATA 1994, Sch 8 Group 1 Excepted Item 4, Overriding Items 4–7; FA 1999, s 14*].

In *Dr X Hua* (VTD 13811) (TVC 29.84) the tribunal held that herbal teas sold at a homeopathic clinic were substantially the same as herbal teas sold commercially and can be zero-rated. In *Thorncroft Ltd* (TC01536) (TVC 29.176) it was held that iced tea concentrates were zero-rated as tea was the principal ingredient.

All hot beverages and any drinks, including zero-rated drinks, sold for consumption on the premises, are standard-rated. Cold drinks that are zero-rated in their own right, e.g. milk, and are supplied for off-premises consumption are zero-rated.

'*Beverage*' must be given its ordinary meaning and covers drinks and liquids that are commonly consumed. Liquids that are commonly consumed are those that are characteristically taken to increase bodily liquid levels, to slake thirst and to fortify or give pleasure (*Bioconcepts Ltd* (VTD 11287) (TVC 29.166)). HMRC have accepted this definition.

Following the tribunal decision in *McCormick (UK) plc* (VTD 15202) (TVC 29.173) HMRC accept that mulling spices, whiskey todd mixtures, spiced cider mixtures, etc. are not 'products for the preparation of beverages' and are zero-rated.

Standard-rated beverages include

- carbonated drinks such as lemonade, cola and mixers such as tonic and soda
- fruit cordials and squashes
- mineral, table and spa waters held out for sale as beverages
- alcohol-free beer and wines
- fruit and vegetable juices (but lemon juice for culinary use is not a beverage)
- ginger, glucose, honey, peppermint and barley water drinks
- flavourings for milk shakes (except preparations and extracts of cocoa or coffee, which are zero-rated)
- purgative and laxative 'teas', such as senna, and similar medicinal teas
- soft drinks containing tea as only one of several ingredients, e.g. fruit flavoured 'iced tea', see *Snapple Beverage Corporation* (VTD 13690) (TVC 29.175).

Khat (or Chat) is standard-rated as HMRC do not regard it as a food product. (Business Brief 25/97).

Drinks which are not beverages

Some drinks do not fall within the definition of 'beverage'. Such drinks, and mixes, etc. for making them, can therefore be zero-rated. These include

- plain soya or rice milk (unflavoured and unsweetened)
- coconut milk
- meal replacement drinks for slimmers or invalids
- unfermented fruit juice specifically for sacramental purposes (see **24.11** below)
- angostura bitters

(VAT Notice 701/14/11, para 3.7).

Milk based drinks

In *Rivella (UK) Ltd* (VTD 16382) (TVC 29.178) a canned sparkling drink included 35% lactoserum but on a dry analysis of the ingredients (i.e. excluding water) the lactoserum was over 50% of the contents. The tribunal noted that the relative weight of the four factors considered in the *Snapple* case above (i.e. ingredients, manufacturing process, appearance and taste, and marketing and packaging) would vary on a case by case basis but, in this case, it found that the first two were predominant and decisive, supported by the marketing process which has been successful in linking in the minds of the potential consumers the principal source of the products as extracts of milk. The appearance and taste test had little or no value because the lactoserum did not possess the 'milkiness' of milk or preparations of milk. The tribunal concluded that Rivella was zero-rated.

Fruit-flavoured soya milk was held not to be a beverage and zero-rated in *Alpro Ltd* (VTD 19911) (TVC 29.180).

Savoury snacks

[24.9] The following are standard-rated.

(a) Potato crisps, sticks or puffs and similar products made from potato, potato flour or potato starch when packaged for human consumption without further preparation.
(b) Savoury food products made by swelling cereals or cereal products when packaged for human consumption without further preparation.
(c) Salted or roasted nuts other than nuts in shell.

[*VATA 1994, Sch 8 Group 1 Excepted Item 5*].

Standard-rated products include

- potato crisps, potato sticks, potato puffs, and similar products including those made from a combination of potato starch or flour and cereal flour
- savoury popcorn (but not corn for popping, e.g. 'microwave' popcorn)
- prawn crackers made from cereals (but not unpackaged prawn crackers, e.g. those supplied in unsealed bags as part of a takeaway meal)
- rice cakes (but not unflavoured rice cakes intended for consumption with cheese or other toppings)
- all roasted or salted nuts not zero-rated below

Zero-rated products include

- savoury snacks consisting of sliced and dried or roasted vegetables other than potatoes, e.g. beetroot, carrot etc.
- tortilla chips, corn chips, bagel chips, cocktail cheese savouries and Twiglets
- prawn crackers made from tapioca
- roasted pulses and legumes, e.g. chick peas and lentils
- roasted or salted nuts supplied while still in their shells (such as 'monkey nuts' and pistachios), toasted coconut, toasted almonds and other toasted chopped nuts held out for sale in retail packs specifically for home baking

(VAT Notice 701/14/11, para 3.8).

In *Procter & Gamble UK*, CA [2009] All ER (D) 177 (May) (TVC 29.185) a partnership manufactured a product known as 'Pringles', which contained potato flour, corn flour, wheat starch and rice flour. About 42% of the product consisted of potato, and about 33% was fat. HMRC issued a ruling that they were excluded from zero-rating by *VATA 1994, Sch 8, Group 1, Excepted*

Item No 5. The partnership appealed, contending that the products were not 'potato crisps' or 'similar products'. The Court of Appeal rejected this contention, holding that the Pringles were similar to the potato crisp and made from the potato, and there was no requirement that the products should be made wholly (or substantially wholly) from the potato or potato derivative.

In *United Biscuits (UK) Ltd (No 8)* (TC01515) (TVC 29.186), the tribunal held that the defining essential ingredient of savoury snacks ('Discos' and 'New recipe frisps') made from a blend of wheat and potato was wheat, and therefore the products were not excluded from zero-rating as potato crisps or similar products.

See **24.13** below for mixtures containing standard and zero-rated items (e.g. Bombay mix).

Ingredients for domestic beer and wine making

[24.10] Goods otherwise qualifying as food for human consumption, animal feeding stuffs (see **24.15** below) or seeds (see **24.20** below) but which are canned, bottled, packaged or prepared for use in domestic

- brewing of beer,
- making of cider or perry, or
- production of wine or made-wine

are standard-rated. [*VATA 1994, Sch 8 Group 1 Excepted Item 7*].

Included are

- kits for home-brewing, wine-making, etc.
- retail packs of hopped malt extract, malted barley, roasted barley and hops
- special wine and brewer's yeast
- grape concentrates
- retail packs of foods which are specialised to home wine-making, e.g. dried elderberries or sloes

Any general food product that is held out for sale specifically for home wine making or brewing must also be standard-rated. In this context, goods are held out for sale for home brewing and wine making if

(a) sold in a retail outlet (or department or section of a general outlet) specialising in home brewing and wine making;
(b) labelled, advertised or otherwise displayed as materials for home brewing or wine making; or
(c) provided or packaged with any brewing or wine making recipes or instructions for using them in the making of beer or wine.

(VAT Notice 701/14/11, para 3.7).

Specialised products

[24.11] The liability of such products depends upon whether they fall within the normal meaning of 'food' (see **24.2** above). If they do, then they are treated under the normal rules and are zero-rated unless falling within one of the *Excepted items*.

(a) Food supplements

Dietary supplements of a kind not normally purchased and used as food are standard-rated. This includes

- vitamin and mineral supplements of all kinds
- royal jelly products but not regular products such as honey which have royal jelly added (see *Grosvenor Commodities Ltd* (VTD 7221) (TVC 29.98))
- tablets, pills and capsules containing, for example, wheatgerm, iron, calcium, fibre, yeast, garlic, pollen, propolis, seaweed, evening primrose, guarana or other similar herbal preparations, and powders of these other than garlic and yeast. See *Nature's Balance Ltd* (VTD 12295) (TVC 29.100) and *Hunter Ridgeley Ltd* (VTD 13662) (TVC 29.101) for algae tablets and *National Safety Associates of America (UK) Ltd* (VTD 14241) (TVC 29.102) for fruit and vegetable tablets. See *Durwin Banks (No 1)* (VTD 18904) (TVC 29.98) and *Durwin Banks (No 2)* (VTD 20695) (TVC 29.93) for linseed oil. A high protein powder marketed as a dietary supplement and intended to be mixed with water and drunk was held to qualify as food in *Arthro Vite Ltd* (VTD 14836) (TVC 29.90)
- charcoal biscuits
- cod liver oil and other fish oils held out for sale as dietary supplements (see *Marfleet Refining Co Ltd* (VTD 129) (TVC 29.97))
- elixirs and tonics, including mixtures of cider vinegar and honey sold as a dietary supplement
- malt extract with cod liver oil (but the supply of plain malt extract, with or without added vitamins, is zero-rated unless held out for sale for home brewing, etc.)

(b) Invalid foods

These products, including parenteral products given intravenously, can be zero-rated (subject to the normal rules) provided they are designed to meet the nutritional needs of the consumer and not to provide treatment for any medical condition. See *Ridal* (C149) (TVC 29.92) (a customs duty case) where the tribunal held that NuTriVeneD powder, an anti-oxidant specially formulated for Down's Syndrome sufferers and taken mixed with a fruit puree at each meal, was exempt from customs duty and VAT on importation from the USA as being within the definition of food. Foods intended to build patients up which are sold in liquid form are zero-rated as food since they fall outside the definition of a beverage (see **24.8** above).

(c) Diabetic and hypoallergenic products

Specialised foods designed for diabetics or allergy sufferers are zero-rated (e.g. sugar-free preserves or gluten-free flour and cakes) unless falling within any of the *Excepted items* (e.g. sugar-free confectionery or gluten-free chocolate biscuits) in which case they are standard-rated.

(d) Slimmers' foods

Low calorie foods for slimmers are treated in the same way as their mainstream food equivalent. Slimmers' meal replacement products (including drinks) are zero-rated unless in the form of confectionery (see **24.5** above).

Appetite suppressants in whatever form are not food and must be standard-rated. Genuine slimmers' food products containing appetite suppressants (e.g. soups containing cellulose) can be zero-rated provided the product is obviously food and is meant to take the place of a 'normal' food equivalent in the slimmers' daily food intake.

(e) Sports products

HMRC express the following opinion on the VAT liability of sports products.

- *Sports/energy drinks.* These are standard-rated beverages (see **24.8** above) unless a product meets all the following conditions in which case it is zero-rated. The conditions are
  - (i) it is aimed at supplying energy to enhance performance and/or accelerate recovery after exercise and both the packaging and advertising of the product reflect this;
  - (ii) it is not primarily marketed for consumption as a soft drink;
  - (iii) its primary purpose is the provision of energy or creatine or to build bulk and not rehydration;
  - (iv) it is in the form of powder, syrup, concentrate, essence, crystal or gel or is the equivalent of these with water added; and
  - (v) it has as its main ingredient(s), other than water, *either* carbohydrate (the majority of which is not sugar) *or* creatine *or* protein *or* a mixture of each.

  Drinks that are preparations of milk, meat, yeast or egg are zero-rated in their own right.

  See also *SIS (Science in Sport) Ltd* (VTD 16555) (TVC 29.91) where the tribunal held that zero-rating applied to products consisting primarily of carbohydrate or creatine, in powder form, which were designed to be mixed with water and drunk. They were consumed for nutritional purposes and therefore within the normal meaning of 'food'.
- *Tablets* are standard-rated with the exception of glucose, dextrose and Horlicks tablets which are zero-rated.
- *Creatine.* With the exception of sports/energy drinks (see above), items made up wholly or mainly of creatine are standard-rated. Where it is clear that the main benefit of the product is not the creatine but carbohydrate, protein or fat, then it is treated as a food, and is zero-rated unless falling within one of the excepted items.

- *Cereal/fruit bars.* Standard-rating applies to any product falling within the general definition of confectionery even when that product is intended to meet the special nutritional needs of athletes. See **24.5** above.

In *GlaxoSmithKline Services Unlimited*, UT November 2011, FTC/06/2011 (TVC 29.173) the tribunal held that 'Lucozade Sport', containing carbohydrates and electrolytes, was a beverage and thus excluded from zero-rating, as it was drunk by a significant number of consumers when not engaging in sport or any exercise and was not mainly purchased or consumed on account of its nutritional ingredients.

(f) Food and drink for religious and sacramental use

Religious laws requiring certain foods to be prepared in particular ways (e.g. kosher or halal) does not affect the liability of the final product. However, by concession, zero-rating has been agreed for the following food products which have exclusive sacramental use.

- Communion wafers used in the celebration of the Christian Communion, Mass or Eucharist
- Unfermented communion wine (fermented wine is standard-rated)
- Unfermented grape juice for use at the Jewish seder or kaddish provided it is marked prominently in English 'for sacramental use only'

(VAT Notice 701/14/11, paras 4.1–4.7).

Ingredients and additives

Home cooking

[24.12] Most ingredients used in home cooking and baking (e.g. flour and sugar) are clearly foodstuffs in their own right. As a general principle, products sold for use as an ingredient in home cooking or baking can be zero-rated if

- it has some measurable nutritional content;
- it is used solely or predominantly, in the particular form in which it is supplied, in the manufacture of food; and
- it does not fall within any *Excepted item*.

Pre-mixes: prepared cake, soup, sauce and other mixes sold for making up in the home kitchen are zero-rated except for mixes for ice creams and similar frozen products within **24.4** above.

Cooking oils: maize (corn) oil, rapeseed oil, groundnut (arachis) oil, olive oil (including olive oil BP), almond oil (but not bitter almond oil), sesame seed oil, sunflower seed oil, palm kernel oil, walnut oil, soya oil and blends of any of these oils can be zero-rated provided

- they are of a type suitable for culinary use; and
- they do not contain any substance, such as perfume, that would make them unsuitable for culinary use.

If they meet these conditions, such oils may be zero-rated even if held out for sale for other purposes (e.g. massage or cosmetic oils).

Essential oils are always standard-rated. Waste and used oils for recycling are ineligible for relief as 'food for human consumption' but may be eligible for relief as animal feeding stuffs (see **24.15** below).

Starch and gelatine are zero-rated if edible but standard-rated if inedible or unsuitable for human consumption (e.g. starch for stiffening collars and 'photographic' gelatine).

Salt for culinary use is zero-rated. This includes fine salt (undried vacuum and pure dried vacuum), dendritic salt, and rock and sea salt in retail packs for culinary use (12.5 kilo packs or less). Non-culinary salt is standard-rated. This includes compacted, granular and soiled salt, and salt of any type specifically held out for use in dishwashers or for other non-food use.

Sweeteners: natural products used as sweeteners (e.g. sugar and honey) are food products in their own right and zero-rated. Artificial sweeteners (e.g. saccharin, aspartame and sorbitol) can also be zero-rated.

Sweetened dried fruit sold as suitable for home baking *and* snacking can be zero-rated irrespective of the bag size. If sold purely as confectionery, it is standard-rated under **24.5** above. (Business Brief 18/98).

Herbs: see **24.20** below.

Other flavourings and flavour enhancers: zero-rating applies to

- natural flavouring essences (e.g. vanilla, peppermint and culinary rosewater)
- synthetic flavourings if designed specifically for food use
- flavouring mixes (e.g. dusting powders or blended seasonings) whether made or natural or synthetic components
- mixes for marinating meat, fish or poultry before cooking
- mulling spices, whiskey todd mixtures, spiced cider mixtures, etc. (see *McCormick (UK) plc* (VTD 15202) (TVC 29.174))

Unflavoured brining mixes (wet or dry) and flavour enhancers (e.g. monosodium glutamate) which do not contribute flavour themselves are standard-rated.

Other additives: by concession, zero-rating applies to baking powder, cream of tartar and rennet. Pectin is zero-rated if supplied in retail packs for culinary use.

Bicarbonate of soda is always standard-rated, as are saltpetre and other single chemicals that may be sold for use in the brining or other processing of meats or fish.

(VAT Notice 701/14/11, para 3.2).

Commercial food manufacture

Many substances are used in the preparation of commercially produced foodstuffs which would not be used in the domestic kitchen. The distinction between standard and zero-rated products is largely the distinction between zero-rated ingredients (which are included for their nutritional content and are food products in their own right) and standard-rated additives (which are included for other than strictly nutritional reasons and are not themselves food).

Ingredients

Most ingredients in commercial food production are the same as those used in home cooking and baking and clearly foodstuffs in their own right. As a general principle, any edible product supplied for incorporation as ingredients in foodstuffs be zero-rated if

(a) it has some measurable nutritional content;
(b) it is used solely or predominantly, in the particular form in which it is supplied, in the manufacture of food; and
(c) it is not one of the *excepted items*.

Products which do not meet these criteria are standard-rated as food additives with the exception of flavourings (natural and synthetic) which may be zero-rated provided they meet the criteria in (*b*) and (*c*) above. This includes sausage skins (see *Devro Ltd* (VTD 7570) (TVC 29.89)).

Additives

Products supplied for incorporation in foodstuffs which do not meet the requirements in (*a*)–(*c*) above are treated as additives and standard-rated. They are generally included for commercial reasons (e.g. to prolong shelf life) and do not fall within the everyday meaning of the word 'food' (see **24.2** above). This includes

- preservatives including unflavoured wet and dry brine mixes and cures for curing or salting meats
- anti-oxidants including vitamins A and E
- vitamin supplements (including those required by law to fortify flour before it can be put on the market)
- stabilisers and thickening agents (e.g. agar, carageenan, guar gum, gum arabic, gum tragacanth and xanthan gum, but not corn starch)
- fillers and bulking agents other than flour and starch
- colourants other than naturally-derived colourings which are also culinary spices in their own right (e.g. caramel, cocoa, saffron, turmeric and cochineal)
- flavour enhancers (e.g. monosodium glutamate), ribonucleotides and hydrolysed vegetable protein
- flour improvers and bleaching agents

Some commercial additives are accepted for VAT purposes as food in their own right. These are

- food grade, naturally derived emulsifiers and stabilisers (e.g. lecithin) specifically tailored and mixed for food purposes which are essential to the production of that food and cannot be used for any other purpose
- artificial sweeteners and artificial flavourings

(VAT Notice 701/14/11, paras 5.1–5.3).

Mixed supplies and assortments

[24.13] There is a mixed supply if standard and zero-rated food items, or zero-rated food items and standard-rated non-food items) are supplied together for a single price. Examples of mixed supplies containing foodstuffs include

- food hampers
- special gift or presentation packs containing linked items (e.g. coffee supplied with a mug, tea with a pack of chocolate biscuits)
- linked goods promotions
- food supplied in or with re-usable storage containers

Normally, the total price must be apportioned in order to arrive at the output tax due. See **47.3 OUTPUT TAX** for the general rules on the treatment of mixed supplies and various methods of apportionment.

Linked goods concession

Where, however, a *minor* standard-rated item is supplied with a main zero-rated item, the supply can be treated as a single supply of the main zero-rated item provided the standard-rated item

- is not charged at a separate price;
- costs no more than 20% of the total cost of the supply; and
- costs no more than £1 (excluding VAT).

Once these conditions have been met, the linked goods are treated as a single zero-rated supply throughout the distribution chain. A wholesaler or retailer receiving goods already linked, and who is unsure whether the conditions have been met, should refer to the supplier's supporting documentation and, if still in doubt, check with the supplier.

In *Supercook UK Llp* (TC00332) (TVC 29.87), S sold kits for making 'chocolate-flavoured lollies'. The kits comprised a plastic tray of moulds, lolly sticks, edible icing and chocolate-flavoured edible buttons. HMRC contended that the principal element of each supply was the tray and the sticks, so that the supplies were standard-rated. The tribunal found that since the buttons contained no cocoa they were not 'chocolate'; the lollies were not 'ice lollies'; and the buttons and icing were not 'confectionery'. Accordingly none of the edible components of the supply were excluded from zero-rating. They represented more than 81% of the total cost, whereas the mould and the sticks represented less than 19%. The principal element of each supply was of 'food', and the mould and sticks were ancillary, so that the whole of the consideration qualified for zero-rating.

Mixtures and assortments

Some food contains mixtures which are both zero-rated and standard-rated when supplied separately. Generally, the tax value of each part must be ascertained to calculate VAT due. See **47.3 OUTPUT TAX**. However, the following products, containing only small quantities of standard-rated items, may, by concession, be treated as a single zero-rated supply.

- Assortments of biscuits where the weight of standard-rated chocolate biscuits (see **24.6** above) does not exceed 15% of total net weight.
- Fruit and nut mixes (including Bombay and similar savoury mixes) where the weight of standard-rated items (e.g. sweetened fruit, chocolate pieces or roasted nuts) does not exceed 25% of total net weight.
- Petits fours where the net weight of chocolate biscuits and sweets does not exceed 15% of total net weight (25% where sweets only are included).

The concession only applies to mixtures and assortments supplied in a single pack, not to 'variety' selections of individual packs.

If any of the above assortments fail to meet the conditions, they can still be treated as a single zero-rated supply if they satisfy the linked goods concession above.

(VAT Notice 701/14/11, paras 6.1, 6.2; VAT Notice 48, ESC 3.7).

For mixtures involving food packaging (e.g. containers, storage jars), see **47.8**(16) OUTPUT TAX.

Food processing

[24.14] Any work done on another person's goods is a supply of services. The supply of a treatment or process to another person's goods can be zero-rated, if by doing so, zero-rated goods are produced. [*VATA 1994, s 30(2A); FA 1996, s 29(2)(5)*]. Processing which results in the production of a new zero-rated food product may therefore be zero-rated. Processing which does not result in the production of a new food product, or which results in the production of a standard-rated food product, is a standard-rated supply.

New goods are produced when a process alters the essential characteristics of the goods. This may include size and shape, appearance, composition, use and, specifically for food items, readiness to use or eat. For example, the process of smoking salmon is zero-rated because the new product, the smoked salmon, is a new zero-rated food item. The smoked salmon is immediately edible and thus distinct and different following the process of smoking. The process of smoking cod, on the other hand, is standard-rated as it does not produce a new zero-rated food item (because the smoked cod is not immediately edible) and the essential characteristics have not changed following the smoking.

Zero-rated processes

Meat and fish processing

- butchering carcasses including boning and jointing meat
- brining or curing pork into ham
- processing meat into sausages
- smoking trout and salmon

Fruit and vegetable processing

- drying, cleaning and coating seeds or grain to make it marketable as seed for sowing

- milling grain into flour, meal or semolina
- cooking, canning or otherwise preserving fruit and vegetables
- drying fruit
- roasting and/or grinding coffee beans
- grinding granulated sugar into caster or icing sugar

Other services

- refining crude oil into edible oil
- processing used or contaminated oil into edible oil
- processing of liquid milk into dried milk
- kneading blocks of frozen butter, adding salt and water and packing

Standard-rated processes

Meat and fish processing

- slaughtering animals without further process (see **24.24** below)
- smoking herring to make kippers
- smoking cod and haddock
- shelling shrimps, prawns or other shellfish
- skinning fish

Fruit and vegetable processing

- cleaning and conditioning grain
- drying grain
- harvesting crops
- malting barley
- blending tea
- roasting or salting peanuts or other nuts

Other services

- sorting, grading or packaging any product
- maturing cheese or any other product (effectively a process of storage during which a natural change occurs)
- pasteurisation or sterilisation
- supervision of foodstuffs to ensure that manufactured and prepared foods meet religious dietary regulations

(VAT Notice 701/40/11, paras 1.1–1.4, 2.1, 2.2).

Animal feeding stuffs

[24.15] The supply of 'animal' feeding stuffs is zero-rated. '*Animal*' includes bird, fish, crustacean and mollusc. [*VATA 1994, Sch 8 Group 1 General Item* 2].

Most commodities recognised as animal feeds are zero-rated unless

- sold for non-food purposes (e.g. bedding, packaging, thatching, fertiliser); or
- 'held out for sale' (see **24.1** above) as pet food or food for wild birds (see **24.19** below).

Zero-rated items

Zero-rated items (subject to the above) include the following.

- Cereal and cereal by-products including bran, sharps and similar residues
- Compound feeds consisting of a number of different ingredients (including major minerals, trace elements, vitamins and other additives), mixed and blended in appropriate proportions to provide properly balanced diets for all types of livestock at every stage of growth and development
- Feed blocks
- Fish meal and fish residue meal
- Forage crops
- Ground oyster shell
- Hay and straw unless held out for sale for non-feed purposes (e.g. bedding). In the case of straw holding out for sale for non-food use includes supplies to customers known to be market gardeners or other horticultural concerns and industrial packers or other non-agricultural businesses
- Molasses
- Oils and fats (including tallow) suitable for use in animal feeding stuffs unless *either* they require further processing before becoming suitable for inclusion in animal feeds *or* are held out for sale for non-feed purposes. Waste oil from fish and chip shops, etc. normally requires processing and is therefore standard-rated (a need for sieving, decanting or heating does not disqualify the oil from zero-rating)
- Oilseed residue (except castor oil)
- Peanuts
- Protein concentrates
- Rabbit food
- Specialised diets formulated for laboratory animals
- Specialised diets formulated for racing greyhounds (other than biscuit or meal)
- Straights
- Supplements. Nutritional supplements are zero-rated (whether intended to be added to normal feed or given separately, e.g. in pill or capsule form). Included are grit (soluble and insoluble) for poultry and game; and mineral blocks, mixes and licks. Supplements designed for pet species, and held out for sale for pets, are standard-rated

Standard-rated items

Standard-rated items include the following.

- Additives
- Bait (e.g. lugworms, maggots) except for fish of a kind and quality suitable for human consumption which may be zero-rated. See also *Fluff Ltd (t/a Mag-It) v C & E Commrs*, QB 2000, [2001] STC 674 (TVC 29.108)
- Castor oil seed residue

- Single chemicals and minerals, other than salt (even when fed direct to animals)
- Thatching material (e.g. Norfolk reed, wheat reed or straw reed)
- Urea (unless specifically held out for sale for animal feeding purposes)

(VAT Notice 701/15/11, paras 5.1, 5.3, 5.4, 9.3, 9.5, 9.7, 9.8).

Keep of animals and grazing rights, etc.

Keep of animals

[24.16] The supply of the keep of animals is standard-rated. Even if animal feed is supplied as part of the service of keeping animals, the full consideration for the service provided is standard-rated, i.e. the feed cannot be treated as a separate zero-rated supply.

Grazing rights

The granting of grazing rights (i.e. the right to allow someone else's animal(s) to graze on your land, also known as grass keep letting) is zero-rated as a supply of animal feeding stuffs (i.e. grass). However, if an element of 'care' for the animal(s) is included, then the supply becomes that of the keep of animals and the whole consideration is standard-rated as above. In this context 'care' includes turning the animals out to graze, feeding, mucking out, spreading straw or other bedding, exercising, and taking on behalf of the owner any responsibility for the welfare of the animal(s) beyond a minimal 'seen daily' or 'twice daily' arrangement.

Stabling services

Where a business rents stabling to a horse owner then, provided the owner is allowed exclusive use of the stabling (i.e. is allocated all or an identifiable part of the stabling for the sole use of their horse), there is a supply of a right over land. This is an exempt supply unless the business has exercised the option to tax (see **41.8 LAND AND BUILDINGS: EXEMPT SUPPLIES AND OPTION TO TAX**). Where the business does not make a supply of a right over land, the supply is standard-rated.

Where, in conjunction with a supply of stabling, the owner is also supplied with feed (either as general animal feed or in the form of grazing rights) this can be treated as a separate zero-rated supply of animal feeding stuffs *provided* that there is no element of care. If any elements of care are present, then there is a single supply of the keep of animals, and the whole supply is standard-rated (see above).

Livery services

Livery services are services provided for horses in a stable that go beyond the right to occupy the stable. They may include feeding or turning the animal out to graze; mucking out, spreading straw or other bedding; worming and clipping; grooming and plaiting; or taking on any responsibility for the welfare of the animal, including arranging for veterinary treatment (but not clearly identifiable separate supplies such as vets' services).

The supply of livery services must be standard-rated, including any food provided, unless the stabling is an exempt right over land that the business has not opted to tax.

If the supply of stabling is a right over land and the business has not opted to tax it, the whole livery package is exempt unless it is provided by a special purpose stable. Livery packages provided by special purpose stables (such as race horse trainers, stud farms and stables involved in schooling horses or breaking them in) are standard-rated. (See *Window* (VTD 17186) (TVC 41.15)).

D-I-Y livery is a supply of stabling only (see above).

(VAT Notice 701/15/11, paras 10.1–10.3; Business Brief 21/01).

Products which may be used both as animal feed and for other purposes

[24.17] Many products sold as animal feed ingredients have other uses. In deciding the VAT liability of these products, it is necessary to determine whether the trader is supplying the product as zero-rated animal feed or some other standard-rated supply.

The borderline between feed and medicine

[24.18] Purely medicinal products are not covered by the zero rate even where they are administered in an animal's feed. The VAT liability of feeding stuffs incorporating medicines is determined by the basic nature of the product. A product is zero-rated only if the addition of medicinal substances does not alter the essential nature of the product as a feeding stuff. As a general guideline, a product is standard-rated if it is the subject of a product licence or marketing authorisation issued by the Department for Environment, Food and Rural Affairs.

Probiotics, which act on the digestive system but have no nutritional value in themselves, are always standard-rated.

(VAT Notice 701/15/11, paras 5.2, 9.4).

Pet food

[24.19] The following items are standard-rated.

(a) Pet food which is canned, 'packaged' or 'prepared'. [*VATA 1994, Sch 8 Group 1 Excepted Item 6*]

Meaning of 'pet': there is no definition of 'pet' in *VATA 1994*. In *Popes Lane Pet Food Supplies* (VTD 2186) (TVC 29.189) the tribunal suggested that a pet was 'an animal (tamed if it was originally wild) which is kept primarily as an object of affection [including] an animal kept primarily for ornament.' On this basis, HMRC regard the following animal species as 'pet species' in that the great majority of that species are kept and reared as objects of affection.

- Cage birds.
- Cats.
- Dogs (but see below for working dogs and racing greyhounds).
- Ferrets.
- Goldfish, aquarium fish and pond fish.
- Guinea pigs.
- Hamsters, gerbils, rats and mice (except rats and mice bred specifically for the laboratory).

Other species (including most farm animals) can be as clearly identified as 'non-pets'.

Between these extremes are animals that are not pet species but which may be kept as pets (e.g. chickens, horses and ponies, rabbits, reptiles and sheep). Their food can be zero-rated unless it is packaged or held out for sale in a way that shows it is intended for a pet. Tribunals have also treated dogs as within this category, distinguishing between pet dogs and working dogs (e.g. sheep dogs, police dogs, guard dogs, gun dogs and packs of hounds). See *Popes Lane Pet Food Supplies* above, *LJ & H Norgate (t/a Dog's Dinner)* (VTD 5241) (TVC 29.191) and *Peters & Riddles (t/a Mill Lane Farm Shop)* (VTD 12937) (TVC 29.192). In *Supreme Petfoods Ltd* (TC00896) (TVC 29.195) the tribunal held that ferrets could be classified generally as a pet species, notwithstanding that a minority were kept as working ferrets.

'*Packaged*' means pre-packed for retail sale in a sealed bag, carton or other container of 12.5 kilograms or less. Putting a loose product in a plain paper or polythene bags at the point of sale (whether after purchase by the customer or in anticipation of sales) is not considered packaging. See *B Beresford* (VTD 9673) (TVC 29.194).

'*Prepared*' means having undergone any of the following (or similar) processes.

(1) Products, other than food for working dogs (see below) and food for human consumption, which have undergone any of the following processes are pet food and are standard-rated however they are held out for sale.
   - The addition of colouring, flavouring, preservative or gelling agents (e.g. sodium metabisulphite).
   - The mixing or blending of ingredients to meet specific nutritional requirements of a pet species (e.g. blending a mix of cereal products specifically for hamsters).
   - The cooking of meats or meat products.
   - The mixing or blending of four or more meats, fish or fish and meat products.

(2) Products which have undergone any of the following processes are animal food but are standard-rated only if they are packaged or held out for sale as pet food
   - Mixing or blending of different ingredients (other than those described in (1) above).
   - Washing or polishing.
   - Cooking (except meat or meat products, see (1) above).
   - Mincing, dicing and similar processes (except meat for dogs, see below).

- Inclusion of additives.

Food for working dogs: food claimed as suitable for all breeds is standard-rated. But food which is specially formulated and held out for sale exclusively for

- working sheep dogs of any breed,
- dogs trained and used as gun dogs, or
- racing greyhounds

can be zero-rated unless it is biscuit or meal (see (*c*) below).

*Dead animals: d*ead mice, rats and day old chicks sold for feeding to 'exotic' pets (e.g. reptiles) may be zero-rated unless they are specifically prepared or canned or otherwise packaged as pet food. See **24.21** below for sales of live animals.

(b) Bird food

Packaged foods (not being pet food) for birds other than poultry (see **24.22** below) and game is standard-rated. [*VATA 1994, Sch 8 Group 1 Excepted Item 6*].

Cage birds

Cage birds (e.g. budgerigars, finches, parrots, etc.) are treated as a 'pet species' (see (*a*) above). Food for such birds is therefore treated as pet food. Prepared foods include mixes specifically designed for cage bird species and seeds compressed into blocks, millet sprays or seeds and sunflower seed. Packaged foods include packaged seeds.

Wild bird food

Any food which is both packaged and held out for sale for feeding to wild birds (other than poultry or game) is standard-rated. As well as ordinary retail packages (see above), special packs (e.g. 'bird nets' of food designed for hanging from a tree or bird table) are standard-rated.

Special mixes of foods for wild birds are zero-rated provided they are not packaged for retail sale.

Other birds

Zero-rating can be applied to

- food for game birds;
- pigeon food (unless containing ingredients similar to food for caged birds when standard-rated); and
- pigeon grit.

(c) Biscuits and meal for cats and dogs. [*VATA 1994, Sch 8 Group 1 Excepted Item 6*]

Biscuits and meal for cats and dogs is standard-rated whether or not for pet animals and whether or not sold packaged or loose. HMRC regard the terms 'biscuit' and 'meal' as meaning dry products either

- coarsely ground basic commodities; or
- baked products consisting predominantly of cereal and fat and not providing all the nutrients required by the animal.

(VAT Notice 701/15/11, paras 6.1–6.5, 7.2–7.5, 8.1–8.5, 9.2).

Seeds and plants

[24.20] Plants grown as food for human consumption or animal feeding stuffs are zero-rated under *VATA 1994, Sch 8 Group 1 General Items 1 and 2*. See **24.2** *et seq* and **24.15** *et seq* above. Any crop that generally produces items that are not fed to humans or animals (i.e. for 'industrial' purposes) is always standard-rated.

Seeds or other means of propagation of plants used for human consumption or animal feeding stuffs are also zero-rated. [*VATA 1994, Sch 8 Group 1 General Item 3*].

Examples of zero-rated plants and seeds

- Seeds, seedlings, crowns, spores, tubers and bulbs of edible vegetables and fruit.
- Mushroom spawn.
- Cucumber and tomato 'rootstock'.

Examples of standard-rated plants and seeds

- Plants that are primarily grown for their ornamental effect (e.g. ornamental nursery stock including trees, shrubs, herbaceous plants, alpines and pot plants).
- Seeds, tubers, bulbs, corms, crowns, rhizomes, cuttings, etc. of flowers (but see (5) below for seeds producing edible flowers).
- Cut flowers which are bought for their ornamental effect.
- Plants, seeds and fruit of a kind used for the production of perfumes, pharmaceutical products, insecticides, fungicides and other non-food uses (e.g. evening primrose which is grown for the extraction of its oils and Norfolk reed which is grown for thatching material).
- Any produce which is 'held out for sale' as pet food or packaged as food for birds other than poultry or game (see **24.19** above).
- Any produce which is 'held out for sale' for non-food purposes.
- Rootstock (plants, usually the common thorn, used in the horticultural industry for grafting purposes) irrespective of whether they are used in the growing of zero-rated or standard-rated plants and trees (but not cucumber and tomato rootstocks which are zero-rated).

'*Held out for sale*' means the way a product is labelled, packaged, displayed, invoiced, advertised or promoted and the heading under which the product is listed in any catalogue, web page or price list.

In addition to the general provisions above, HMRC give the following information.

(VAT Notice 701/38/11, paras 2, 3.1, 3.2).

(1) Trees and fruit bearing shrubs

Plants, bushes and trees normally used in this country for the production of edible fruit (including nuts) are zero-rated.

HMRC regard the following as the *definitive* list of fruit-producing plants which may be zero-rated.

Almond (not 'flowering almond')	Apple	Apricot
Blackberry	Blackcurrant	Blueberry
Boysenberry	Bullace	Cherry (not 'flowering cherry')
Citrus trees (not ornamental varieties)	Cobnut	Common quince (not chaenomeles)
Cowberry	Crab (only fruiting varieties)	Cranberry
Damson	Fig	Filbert
Gages	Gooseberry	Grapevines
Hazel	Huckleberry	Loganberry
Medlar	Mulberry	Nectarine
Peach	Pear	Raspberry plum (not 'flowering plum')
Redcurrant	Strawberry	Sweet chestnut
Tayberry	Walnut	Whitecurrant
Wineberry	Worcesterberry	

(VAT Notice 701/38/11, para 3.5).

(2) Oilseed rape

Some varieties of oilseed rape are not suitable for human consumption. The liability of those that are not suitable will depend on the purpose for which they are supplied.

(a) *'OO' type*. Most oilseed rape is of this type and the oilseed yields oil fit for human consumption as well as meal for animals. These 'OO' varieties of oilseed rape, including the actual seeds and edible meal by-products, are zero-rated.

(b) *'HEAR' varieties*. These varieties of oilseed rape give a high erucic acid content in the oil and this is regarded as nutritionally undesirable in food for human consumption. The pressed oil is primarily used as an anti-corrosion agent and lubricant in mineral oil extraction and is standard-rated. The residual meal can be used to feed ruminant livestock and it is zero-rated when supplied for feeding purposes. The actual seeds of the HEAR varieties are used to plant for subsequent crops and as an animal feed and are zero-rated.

(VAT Notice 701/38/11, para 3.3).

(3) Linseed and flax

Varieties of the crop are grown for its seeds and subsequent oil and residual meal, or for its flax fibre. As the predominant use of linseed oil is for industrial purposes (e.g. paint, varnish, linoleum), it is standard-rated. The residual meal is largely used for incorporating into animal feed and can be zero-rated. Zero-rating also applies to the actual seed when used as animal feed or for sowing.

Where flax varieties are grown for the resulting fibre, both the stems (processed into linen) and the left over woody portion (used for making paper) are standard-rated. The small yield of seeds are zero-rated when used as animal feed.

(VAT Notice 701/38/11, para 3.4).

(4) Herbs

Culinary herbs

Plants of species which are generally accepted as reared primarily for culinary use are zero-rated irrespective of how they are held out for sale. These comprise the following.

Angelica	Anise	Anise hyssop
Basil	Borage	Caraway
Cardamom	Cardoon	Celery wild
Celery wild alpine	Chervil	Chicory
Chives	Coriander	Cumin
Curry leaf	Dandelion	Dill
Fennel	Fenugreek	Garlic
Ginger	Good King Henry	Horseradish
Lemon grass	Liquorice	Lovage
Marjoram	Mint	Onion
Orache	Oregano	Parsley
Pennyroyal	Rocket	Rosemary
Saffron	Sage	Salad burnet
Savory	Skirret	Sorrel
Tarragon	Thyme	Watercress

Ornamental herbs sometimes used for culinary purposes. Plants which, although not species supplied predominantly as culinary herbs, do have recognised culinary uses, may be zero-rated provided

- they have been raised according to the conditions required by *Food and Environment Protection Act 1985* (evidence of which may be required);
- they have been held out for sale (see above) as culinary herbs and, where appropriate, displayed apart from ornamentals with other culinary herbs;
- they are supplied in individual pots (not bedding strips) of a size less than two litres; and

- in the case of bay plants, they do not exceed 50cm in height and have not been clipped, shaped or topiarized in such a way as to specialise them as ornamentals.

Provided the above conditions are satisfied, the following herbs can also be zero-rated.

Alecost	Alexanders	Allspice
Asafoetida	Bay	Bergamot
Bistort	Catmint	Chamomile
Comfrey	Clove pink	Clover
Cowslip	Curry plant	Elder
Feverfew	Hop	Hyssop
Juniper	Landcress	Lavender
Lemon balm	Lemon verbena	Marigold, pot
Melilot	Nasturtium, salad	Pelarqonium (scented)
Purslane	Rue	Sweet Cecily
Tansy	Violet (sweet)	Woodruff

Medicinal herbs

Herbs supplied for medical rather than culinary use are not eligible for zero-rating as 'food' and are standard-rated, even if they have been raised under the same conditions as culinary herbs. This includes plants used in the preparation of food supplements (e.g. evening primrose and ginseng).

(VAT Notice 701/38/11, para 4).

(5) Seeds

All seeds that produce food of a kind for human consumption or animal feeding stuffs can be zero-rated. Included are

- vegetable seeds;
- seeds for producing culinary herbs; and
- wheat, barley and other agricultural seeds grown to produce food for human or animal consumption.

But any seed that generally produces items that are not fed to humans or animals is always standard-rated. This applies to

- seeds or bulbs for growing flowers (but see edible flowers below);
- plants and trees mainly for ornamental effect; and
- agricultural crops for industrial/non-feed use.

Seeds producing edible flowers

The seed varieties listed below are zero-rated where it can be demonstrated that they are held out for sale as food of a kind used for human consumption. For these purposes, seeds would be so held out for sale if

- the variety is indicated as edible in a catalogue (or, where no catalogue is produced, in information at the point of display);

- further details of food usage can be supplied on a customer's request; and
- food-based information is available on seed packets (e.g. recipe ideas).

Bergamot Nasturtium Poppy Violets	Clove pink Pelargonium Pot Marigold	Lavender Pink Sunflower

Grass seed

Most grass seed is zero-rated because of the extensive use of grass as animal feed. This includes supplies to and by garden centres, local authorities and grass seed to be grown on set aside land. Pre-germinated grass seed and turf are not used for the propagation of animal feed and are therefore standard-rated. See **24.15** above for supplies of hay and straw and **24.16** above for grazing rights.

Seeds that undergo a treatment or process. See **24.14** above.

Seeds sold with a book. See (7) below.

(VAT Notice 701/38/11, para 5).

(6) Plant-growing kits

Plant-growing kits typically include seeds, growing medium, fertilizer, a container, and an instruction leaflet. Such kits are generally standard-rated but may be zero-rated if the seeds are zero-rated and either

- the standard-rated element (e.g. growing medium, fertiliser and pot) accounts for less than 10% of the total cost; or
- the planting medium, which is impregnated with edible vegetable or fruit seeds, is no more than a means of simplifying the planting of the seeds (e.g. peat cubes of less than 125cc impregnated with seeds, or thin layers of tissue incorporating seeds).

(VAT Notice 701/38/11, para 6.1).

Mushroom growing kits

VAT treatment depends upon the container. If the kit is supplied in a non-reusable container, HMRC take the view that the whole supply can be zero-rated as the container is seen as normal and necessary packaging.

If the kit is supplied in a plastic bucket or similar reusable container, there may be a mixed supply, the spawn and growing medium being zero-rated and the container standard-rated. Each case needs to be judged on its own merits after consideration of general principles in *Card Protection Plan* (see **64.6 SUPPLY: GENERAL**). See also the decisions in *Kimberley-Clark Ltd v C & E Commrs*, Ch D [2004] STC 473 (TVC 12.25) (which related to nappies sold in a plastic reusable box) and *Cheshire Mushroom Farm* (VTD 71) (TVC 29.119) (although the latter case preceded the judgment in *Card Protection Plan*).

(VAT Notice 701/38/11, para 6.2).

Live animals

[24.21] The 'supply' of 'animals' of a kind generally used as, or yielding or producing, food for human consumption is zero-rated. '*Supply*' includes sale, hire or loan and supply of a part interest (a share) as '*animals*' include birds, fish, crustacea and molluscs. [*VATA 1994, Sch 8 Group 1 General Item 4*].

Examples of zero-rated animals are

- meat animals;
- dairy animals;
- poultry (see **24.22** below) including those for egg production;
- honey bees; and
- fish (except ornamental breeds and coarse fish), including those for production of edible roes (see **24.23** below).

Examples of standard-rated animals are

- bumble bees;
- ornamental birds and fish;
- racing pigeons; and
- horses.

The test is whether the animal is of a kind generally used as, or yielding or producing, food for human consumption. Subject to this, the actual use does not matter. For example:

- Kangaroo steak may be sold as food in shops but kangaroos are not animals of a kind generally reared for food in the UK so that live kangaroos are standard-rated.
- Rabbits, other than ornamental breeds, are animals of a kind that is normally used for human food production and are therefore always zero-rated even if kept as pets.
- Sheep kept mainly for their wool, or bulls used for breeding, are zero-rated because they are animals of a kind normally producing food for human consumption.

Animals which are removed from the human food chain because they are no longer fit for human consumption (e.g. because of disease) are standard-rated.

Embryos, eggs and semen for breeding

Embryos of species which are normally used for human food may be zero-rated if they are to be used for breeding. Anything below the embryo stage is standard-rated. Eggs and fish roes which are normally used for food for human consumption and are fit for such use are always zero-rated.

(VAT Notice 701/15/11, paras 2.1–2.8).

Birds

[24.22] Most breeds of chicken are zero-rated, as are game birds and ostriches. Ornamental breeds of birds are standard-rated.

The following breeds of ducks, geese and turkeys are zero-rated.

- Ducks (Aylesbury, Campbell (Khaki Campbell), Indian Runner, Muscovy, Pekin and derivatives and crossbreeds of these).
- Geese (Brecon Buff, Chinese Commercial, Embdem, Roman, Toulouse and derivatives and crossbreeds of these).
- Turkeys (Beltsville White, British White, Broadbreasted White, Bronze (Broadbreasted Bronze), Norfolk Black and derivatives and crossbreeds of these).

(VAT Notice 701/15/11, para 3.1).

Fish

[24.23] The VAT liability of fish is as follows.

- *Freshwater fish*. Eels, salmon and trout and others recognised as food for human consumption are zero-rated. Bream, perch, pike, carp and tench are standard-rated.
- *Shellfish*. Oysters, mussels, whelks, etc. are zero-rated but non-food species are standard-rated.
- *Fish for aquaria* are standard-rated.
- *Fish used as* bait. Fish of a kind used for, and fit for, human consumption are zero-rated. All other supplies are standard-rated.
- *Ornamental fish* are standard-rated. See *JR Chalmers* (VTD 1433) (TVC 29.119) for koi carp.

(VAT Notice 701/15/11, para 3.2).

Abattoirs

Processing generally

[24.24] Any work done on another person's goods is a supply of services. The supply of a treatment or process to another person's goods can be zero-rated, if by doing so, zero-rated goods are produced. [*VATA 1994, s 30(2A); FA 1996, s 29(2)(5)*]. Processing which results in the production of a new zero-rated food product may therefore be zero-rated. Processing which does not result in the production of a new food product, or which results in the production of a standard-rated food product, is a standard-rated supply. New goods are produced when a process alters the essential characteristics of the goods. This may include size and shape, appearance, composition, use and, specifically for food items, readiness to use or eat.

Slaughtering and dressing

The service of slaughtering animals without applying further processes is standard-rated (see *Darlington Borough Council* (VTD 961) (TVC 29.96)). If other processes are applied at the same time to produce new zero-rated goods, for example, dressing the carcass, then the whole supply is zero-rated. Not all services of slaughtering and dressing produce new zero-rated goods. The liability of some of the goods produced by abattoirs is considered below.

Standard-rated goods

Goods produced in abattoirs are standard-rated if

- held out for sale for a non-feeding purpose, e.g. blood for fertiliser (normally recognisable by declaration of nitrogen/phosphoric acid content);
- used for a non-feeding purpose, e.g. hair, hides, horns, hoofs, manure, pelts, skins and wool;
- held out for sale without further process as canned, packaged or prepared pet food (see **24.19** above);
- they have undergone some further preparation beyond mincing and dicing, which would specialise the products to the pet food market (see **24.19** above); or
- used exclusively in the preparation of pharmaceutical products, e.g. gall bags, glands, ovaries, placenta.

Greaves supplied in pieces of a size suitable for feeding to pets are also standard-rated.

Zero-rated goods

Goods produced in abattoirs are zero-rated if

- they are fit for human consumption; or
- they are animal materials, used in the manufacture of food for animals or pets, and
  - (a) the *Animal By Products Order 1992* permits the use of the materials, and
  - (b) the animal materials are used in premises approved by that *Order*.

Examples of zero-rated goods from cattle, sheep, goats and pigs are

- *Organs* including bladders, hearts, kidneys, livers, lungs or lites, manifolds, pancreas glands, rede, stomach, and sweetbreads (pancreas only in cattle);
- *Body parts* including bones, feet, paddywacks, runners (except cattle), tails, udders and weasand; and
- *Fluids and tissue* including blood, dripping, fat (provided it is not attached to specific risk material), and meat.

Other zero-rated parts commonly produced from cattle include melts (from calves under six months), tripe and vells.

Incidental supplies

Where the services of slaughtering and then processing the carcass produce new standard-rated and zero-rated goods (e.g. standard-rated skins and zero-rated foodstuffs)

- if the standard-rated goods are incidental to the main zero-rated supply back to the owner of the animal, the whole supply is zero-rated; and
- if the new standard-rated goods are the main element of the supply to the owner of the animal, and the zero-rated goods are incidental, then the whole supply is standard-rated.

Ancillary services supplied by abattoirs

Supplies of separate ancillary services are normally standard-rated, for example

- cold storage;
- pennage;
- carriage; and
- porterage.

If specific stalls or pens are allocated for the exclusive use of a customer, the supply is exempt from VAT (subject to the option to tax being exercised, see **41.8 LAND AND BUILDINGS: EXEMPT SUPPLIES AND OPTION TO TAX**).

Agriculture and Horticulture Development Board (AHDB)

There is a levy in two parts: on slaughterers and livestock exporters; and on livestock producers. The levy is absorbed and paid to AHDB by the slaughterers/exporters, of which 50% is to be reclaimed statutorily from the producer. The levy is payment for a range of benefits received from AHDB and includes VAT.

A *slaughterer* is charged the whole amount of levy by the AHDB, and then must recharge the producers 50% of the levy. AHDB provides one invoice to the slaughterer confirming the amount of levy and the output and input tax due. The slaughterer can recover the VAT charged on his 50% of the general levy as input tax, subject to the normal rules. As he acts as agent for AHDB in recharging their part of the levy to the producers, he must account for the VAT as follows.

- The input tax he incurred on the rechargeable elements of the levy may be recovered in full.
- He must charge, and account for in the same period, a corresponding amount of output tax to the producers.

A producer can recover the VAT charged to him by the slaughterer as input tax, subject to the normal rules.

An exporter of live animals must follow the above procedures to account for VAT on levies incurred and recharged.

(VAT Notice 700/57/04; VAT Notice 701/40/11; VAT Notice 701/15/11, para 9.1).

Key points

[24.25] Points to consider are as follows.

- A fundamental principle of the rules concerning VAT and food is that a supply of any food intended for consumption on the premises where it is sold is standard-rated. The same outcome applies if food is served hot and is for take-away consumption. There have been a number of tribunal cases over the years that have challenged both the meanings of 'hot' and 'premises' as far as the legislation is concerned.
- A key conclusion in recent years has been that 'premises' only includes an immediate area surrounding an outlet, not the wider area such as entire sports stadium. This outcome gives more scope for zero-rating of cold take away food sold by a business in such cases.
- There are a number of specific items that are excluded from the zero-rating provisions in relation to food. These exceptions include confectionery items, alcoholic drinks, and snacks such as crisps. It is important that any business selling food items is very clear about the items that qualify for zero-rating and, equally importantly, those that are exceptions to the zero-rating provisions and are therefore standard-rated.
- A retail business selling both standard-rated and zero-rated items must have proper accounting procedures in place to ensure the mix of takings is properly identified at the point of sale. The relevant split will need to be accurately recorded in the books and records of the business on a daily basis and output tax must be correctly declared on a VAT return.
- HMRC visiting officers will be keen to ensure that zero-rated sales are not being overstated by, for example, the wrong till button being entered at the point of sale. They are likely to apply an overall mark-up calculation to zero-rated and standard-rated purchases to check that the declared output tax figures are credible.
- HMRC officers will also be keen to ensure that staff involved in selling goods where more than one rate of tax is applicable (e.g. cashiers in a supermarket) are properly trained in till management procedures. This would be particularly relevant if goods do not have a pre-coded bar reader that will automatically determine the rate of VAT at the point of sale.
- Some retail schemes base output tax payments on the ratio of standard-rated and zero-rated purchases made by a business, or by applying a mark-up to either zero-rated or standard-rated purchases. In the case of many businesses selling food, these schemes will not be suitable because of the hot food or consumption on premises provisions. For example, a meat pie would be zero-rated when purchased from a wholesaler but standard-rated

if supplied as either a hot product (take away or on the premises where sold) or a cold product on the premises where it is sold.

25

Fuel and Power

Cross-reference. See **21.4 EXPORTS** for stores for use in ships, aircraft and hovercraft; **66.15 SUPPLY: TIME OF SUPPLY** for the time of supply rules; **74.2 ZERO-RATED SUPPLIES** for supplies of hot water and steam.

De Voil Indirect Tax Service. See V4.406.

Introduction

[25.1] The supply of any form of power, heat, refrigeration or (from 1 January 2011) other cooling, or ventilation is a supply of goods (and not a supply of services). [*VATA 1994, Sch 4 para 33; F(No 3)A 2010, s 20(2)*].

The rates of VAT on supplies of fuel and power are as follows.

4.1.11 onwards	5% for 'qualifying use' 20% for all other supplies
1.9.97–3.1.11	5% for 'qualifying use' 17.5%* for all other supplies
1.4.94–31.8.97	8% for 'qualifying use' 17.5% for all other supplies
1.7.90–31.3.94	Zero-rated for 'qualifying use' 17.5% for all other supplies

*15% from 1 December 2008 to 31 December 2009.

The reduced rates applying from 1 April 1994 also apply to acquisitions from other EU countries and importations from outside the EU.

[*VATA 1994, ss 2(1A)–(1C), 29A(1)(2); FA 1995, s 21; F(No 2)A 1997, s 6; FA 2001, s 99*].

Qualifying use

[25.2] '*Qualifying use*' means domestic use or use by a charity otherwise than in the course or furtherance of a business.

The following *de minimis* supplies are always supplies for domestic use, even when supplied to a business.

(a) A supply of not more than one tonne of coal or coke held out for sale as domestic fuel. The weight limit of one tonne applies to the total delivered weight of all types of such coal or coke supplied at any one time, not to the weight of supplies of individual products (e.g. lignite, anthracite, etc.).
(b) A supply of wood, peat or charcoal not intended for sale by the recipient (regardless of the amount supplied).
(c) A supply to a person at any premises of '*piped gas*' (i.e. gas within **25.4** below, or petroleum gas in a gaseous state, provided through pipes) where the gas (together with any other piped gas provided to him at the premises by the same supplier) was not provided at a rate exceeding 150 therms a month or, if the supplier charges for gas by reference to the number of kilowatt hours supplied, 4397 kilowatt hours a month. (This limit applies whether the bill is based on a meter reading or on an estimate.)
(d) A supply of petroleum gas in a liquid state where the gas is supplied in cylinders the net weight of each of which is less than 50 kilogrammes and either the number of cylinders supplied is 20 or fewer or the gas is not intended for sale by the recipient.
(e) A supply of petroleum gas in a liquid state, otherwise than in cylinders, to a person at any premises at which he is not able to store more than two tonnes of such gas.
(f) A supply of not more than 2,300 litres of fuel oil, gas oil or kerosene. HMRC regard a supply for this purpose as comprising all deliveries to the same customer at the same site on the same day. This is the case even if separate delivery notes or invoices are issued. Deliveries that take place on different days or to different sites are regarded as separate supplies, even if a single invoice is raised for more than one delivery. Supplies of different products (e.g. fuel oil and gas oil) are always regarded as separate supplies. But supplies of different types of the same product (e.g. different grades of kerosene) must not be broken down into each type when considering whether the *de minimis* limit has been exceeded.
(g) A supply of electricity to a person at any premises where the electricity (together with any other electricity provided to him at the premises by the same supplier) was not provided at a rate exceeding 1,000 kilowatt hours a month. (This limit applies whether the bill is based on a meter reading or on an estimate.)

Supplies not within (*a*)–(*g*) above are supplies for domestic use if, and only if, the goods supplied are supplied for use in

(i) a building, or part of a building, which consists of a dwelling or number of dwellings or which is used for a 'relevant residential purpose';

(ii) self-catering holiday accommodation (including any accommodation advertised or held out as such);

(iii) a caravan; or

(iv) a 'houseboat' i.e. a boat or other floating decked structure designed or adapted for use solely as a place of permanent habitation and not having means of, or capable of being readily adapted for, self-propulsion.

Use for a '*relevant residential purpose*' means use as a home or other institution providing residential accommodation either for children or with personal care for persons in need of such care by reason of old age, disablement, past or present dependence on alcohol or drugs or past or present mental disorder; a hospice; residential accommodation for students or school pupils or members of any of the armed forces; a monastery, nunnery or similar establishment; or an institution which is the sole or main residence of at least 90% of its residents. *Excluded* is use as a hospital, a prison or similar institution or an hotel or inn or similar establishment.

[*VATA 1994, Sch 7A Group 1, Notes 3, 5, 6, 7; FA 1995, s 21; FA 2001, Sch 31 para 1*]. (VAT Notice 701/19/10, paras 6.1, 7.1).

The following are treated as a part of the same residential unit.

- Buildings such as garages used with houses.
- Subsidiary buildings situated a short distance away (e.g. a garage in a block located away from the house).
- Corridors, lifts, hallways and stairways in a residential unit.

(VAT Notice 701/19/10, para 3.2).

Part qualifying use

Where a supply of fuel or power is partly for qualifying use and partly not, then provided at least 60% is supplied for qualifying use, the whole supply is to be treated as a supply for qualifying use. In any other case, an apportionment must be made. [*VATA 1994, Sch 7A Group 1, Note 4; FA 2001 Sch 31 para 1*].

Certificates

If in doubt about the liability of the supply under (i)–(iv) above, the supplier should get a certificate from the customer declaring what percentage of the fuel or power supplied for use at each premises is for qualifying use. A certificate is not required if the supply falls within (*a*)–(*g*) above. The following information should be shown on the certificate.

- Supplier's name and address.
- Customer's name, address and, if applicable, VAT registration number.
- Address of the premises to which the supply relates.
- Amount of qualifying use expressed as a percentage of the total use. A precise percentage should always be given. Do not say 'over 60%' or use any similar form of words.
- A declaration given by a responsible officer or official of the customer as to the truth and accuracy of the facts given. This should include

(i) the signature, name, and position of the person giving the declaration;
(ii) the date on which it is made; and
(iii) an endorsement that the customer has read and understood the guidance, and that they know they must notify the supplier if there is a change in the qualifying use.

If any supply is incorrectly charged at the reduced rate, the supplier may have to pay any VAT undercharged unless he holds a valid certificate *and* has good reason to believe that the fuel or power supplied to the customer is for qualifying use. It is the supplier's responsibility to take reasonable steps to satisfy himself that the customer is entitled to be charged at the reduced rate and the declaration is correct. Where, however, despite taking all reasonable steps, the supplier fails to identify the inaccuracy and in good faith makes the supplies concerned at the reduced rate, HMRC will not seek to recover the VAT due from the supplier. (VAT Notice 48, ESC 3.11).

(VAT Notice 701/19/10, para 3.5).

See **52.23 PENALTIES** for the penalty for giving an incorrect certificate.

Solid fuels

[25.3] Supplies of coal, coke and other solid substances are taxable at the reduced rate provided they are held out for sale solely as fuel and are supplied for qualifying use (see **25.2** above). Included are combustible materials put up for sale for kindling fires but not matches. [*VATA 1994, Sch 7A Group 1 Item 1(a) and Note 1; FA 2001, Sch 31 para 1*]. All other supplies of solid fuels are standard-rated.

To be taxable at the reduced rate, the fuel must be offered in a form and at a price that is compatible with it being sold as fuel.

'*Held out for sale*' as fuel means that the supplier advertises and otherwise describes the product at its point of sale as fuel or firewood, and that this is consistent with the packaging and wrapping in which it is supplied.

Reduced-rate supplies

Provided the conditions for qualifying use are met, the reduced rate can be applied to the following solid fuels.

- Coal (including anthracite and lignite)
- Coal dust
- Coal briquettes
- Coke (e.g. Coalite, Thermabrite, Coalite Nuts, Beacon Beans, Sunbrite small nuts, Blazeglow)
- Pulverised coal
- Smokeless fuel
- Wood logs
- Other firewood (including offcuts, chips, shavings, scrap or damaged wood and compresses or agglutinated sawdust)

- Barbecue fuels
- Briquettes of straw and recycled waste or other combustible materials
- Charcoal
- Firelighters
- Peat blocks, sods or briquettes
- Solid methaldehyde (solid meths)

Standard-rated supplies

The following items are always standard-rated.

- Any product not consumed in the lighting process (e.g. pumice blocks, pottery, etc soaked in paraffin, gas pokers, electric hot-air igniters)
- Artists' charcoal
- Binding agents used to convert coal dust or sawdust in blocks
- Coke for use in manufacturing
- 'DIY' offcuts and remnants
- Filtration charcoal or coke
- Forestry thinnings for fencing or staking
- Laboratory charcoal blocks
- Peat for use in horticulture or as cattle litter
- Sawdust, chips or shavings for pet litter
- Standing trees
- Wood for pulping

(VAT Notice 701/19/10, para 7.1).

Barbecue food flavour enhancers (e.g. hickory chips) which are absorbed into the food by burning are not fuel (or food for human consumption) and are standard-rated. (VAT Notes 1992 No 1).

Gases

[25.4] Coal gas, water gas, producer gas and similar gases and petroleum gases, and other gaseous hydrocarbons, whether in a gaseous or liquid state, are taxable at the reduced rate provided they are supplied for qualifying use (see **25.2** above). Excluded is any road fuel gas (within the meaning of the *Hydrocarbon Oil Duties Act 1979*) on which excise duty has been or is chargeable. [*VATA 1994, Sch 7A Group 1 Items 1(b)(c) and Note 1; FA 2001, Sch 31 para 1*].

Reduced rate supplies

Provided the conditions for qualifying use are met, the reduced rate can be applied to liquefied petroleum gas (e.g. propane or butane), acetylene, butylene, methane, natural gas and propylene. Minor impurities in a hydrocarbon gas can be ignored but otherwise any such gas that does not consist entirely of carbon and hydrogen is standard-rated.

Standard-rated supplies

Supplies of all other gases (e.g. carbon dioxide, hydrogen, oxygen, ammonia, chlorine, nitrogen and refrigeration and aerosol gases) are standard-rated although certain gases for medical care (e.g. anaesthetics and oxygen) may be zero-rated under *VATA 1994, Sch 8 Group 12* or exempt under *VATA 1994, Sch 9 Group 7*.

(VAT Notice 701/19/10, paras 4.1, 4.3).

Standing charges

Gas bills include a variable consumption charge and a fixed standing charge. The standing charge represents the upkeep of the pipes required to deliver gas. For VAT purposes it is regarded as part of the charge for a supply of gas even though shown separately on bills. If the supply of gas is for qualifying use (see **25.2** above) the whole bill, including the standing charge, is taxable at the reduced rate.

Where standing charges for gas are made by a third party (e.g. a local authority) rather than the fuel supplier, they do not form part of the supply of gas and are standard-rated, regardless of the customer.

(VAT Notice 701/19/10, para 10.10).

Charges made by fuel and power suppliers

See **25.7** below.

VAT treatment in particular cases

See **25.8** below.

Special rules for place of supply and supplies by persons outside the UK

See **25.9** below.

Gas sold in cylinders and similar containers

Disposable cartridges

When gas is supplied in disposable cartridges at an inclusive price covering both gas and cartridge, the supply is standard-rated throughout the supply chain until the point of final sale. A supply of disposable cartridges at the point of final sale is taxable at the reduced rate.

Charged refillable cylinders

On the first sale of a refillable cylinder containing gas taxable at the reduced rate, the price must be apportioned and VAT accounted for on the standard-rated cylinder which becomes the property of the buyer. (The price of the cylinder should be taken as the difference between the VAT-exclusive price of the filled cylinder and the charge for refilling a customer's own cylinder.)

When a filled container is exchanged for an empty one of the same size owned by the customer, the refill charge is treated as being wholly for the supply of gas and any nominal charge for inspection and maintenance can be ignored.

Rented cylinders

On the first supply of gas in a rented cylinder, VAT must be accounted for at the standard rate on the hire charge. When an empty cylinder is exchanged for a full one of the same size, any refill charge, including any nominal charge for inspection or maintenance, can be taxed at the reduced rate (subject to qualifying use of the gas). Any charge made for a lost or damaged cylinder (such as the loss of a deposit) is outside the scope of VAT. But if a separate charge is made for the retention of a cylinder this is standard-rated.

Bulk storage tanks

Bulk storage tanks installed on customers' premises normally remain the property of the supplier. Charges for gas consumed are at the reduced rate (subject to qualifying use) but any charge specifically for repair, maintenance etc of equipment is standard-rated.

(VAT Notice 701/19/10, paras 4.5–4.8). See *Calor Gas Ltd* (VTD 47) (TVC 30.1).

Gases used as road fuel

Supplies of gases for use as road fuel are standard-rated. VAT is due on the total value including the excise duty chargeable. (VAT Notice 701/19/10, para 4.4).

Oils

[25.5] 'Fuel oil', 'gas oil' and 'kerosene' are taxable at the reduced rate provided they are supplied for qualifying use (see **25.2** above). Excluded is hydrocarbon oil on which a duty of excise has been or is to be charged without relief from, or rebate of, such duty by virtue of the provisions of the *Hydrocarbon Oil Duties Act 1979*. From 1 November 2008 the exclusion does not apply to oil that is kerosene or oil for which a relevant declaration has been made under the *Hydrocarbon Oil Duties Act 1979, s 13AC(3)* (use of rebated kerosene for private pleasure flying) or *s 14E(3)* (use of rebated heavy oil for private pleasure craft). All other supplies of oil are standard-rated.

'*Fuel oil*' means heavy oil containing in solution an amount of asphaltenes of not less than 0.5 per cent or which contains less than 0.5 per cent but not less than 0.1 per cent of asphaltenes and has a closed flash point not exceeding 150°C.

'*Gas oil*' means 'heavy oil' of which not more than 50 per cent by volume distils at a temperature not exceeding 240°C and of which more than 50 per cent by volume distils at a temperature not exceeding 340°C.

'*Kerosene*' means heavy oil of which more than 50 per cent by volume distils at a temperature not exceeding 240°C.

'*Heavy oil*' has the same meaning as in the *Hydrocarbon Oil Duties Act 1979*.

Fuel oil, gas oil and kerosene chargeable with excise duty at a full (unrebated) rate, together with other heavy hydrocarbon oils, light hydrocarbon oils, lubricating oils and lubricants, are standard-rated.

[*VATA 1994, Sch 7A Group 1 Item 1(d) and Notes 1, 2; FA 2001, Sch 31 para 1; SI 2008/2676*].

The effect of the above is that fuel oil, gas oil or kerosene (which includes paraffin) within the above definitions are taxed at the reduced rate provided they are supplied for qualifying use, are not supplied as road fuel and (except fuel for propelling private pleasure craft and for private pleasure flying) are either chargeable with excise duty at a rebated rate or are relieved from excise duty.

Standard-rated supplies

Standard-rated supplies include any heavy oil for use as road fuel; aviation spirit; avgas; creosote; crude oil; derv; kerosene, paint thinners or white spirit; liquid lighter fuel; waste oil; bitumen; black varnish; coal tar; lubricating oils and greases; methylated spirit; other articles which contain hydrocarbon oil but are not themselves wholly hydrocarbon oil; petrol substitutes; and petrol and other light oils (e.g. benzene, toluene and naphtha).

(VAT Notice 701/19/10, paras 6.1, 6.2).

Marine fuel

Supplies of fuel to foreign-going vessels is zero-rated provided certain conditions are met. By concession, commercial vehicles engaged on voyages within UK territorial waters may also receive certain types of fuel VAT-free. See **21.4** **EXPORTS**.

Lifeboats

Fuel supplied to a charity providing rescue at sea is zero-rated where the fuel is for use in a lifeboat. See **70.14** **TRANSPORT AND FREIGHT**.

Electricity, heat and air conditioning

[25.6] Supplies of electricity, heat and air conditioning are taxable at the reduced rate provided they are supplied for qualifying use (see **25.2** above). [*VATA 1994, Sch 7A Group 1 Item 1(e); FA 2001, Sch 31 para 1*]. All other supplies of electricity, etc. are standard-rated.

Electricity supplied by mobile generator

Where electricity is supplied through the use of a mobile generator, the liability of the supply depends upon whether the supplier is supplying the electricity or hiring out the machine.

- If the supplier operates the equipment and charges for power supplied for a qualifying use, the total charge is at the reduced rate.
- If the supplier charges for the hire of the generator to the customer, the supply is standard-rated.

Batteries

Supplies of batteries on hire, recharging of batteries or exchanging charged batteries for discharged ones are standard-rated.

Standing charges

Electricity bills include a variable consumption charge and a fixed standing charge. The standing charge represents the upkeep of the wires required to deliver electricity. For VAT purposes it is regarded as part of the charge for a supply of electricity even though shown separately on bills. If the supply of electricity is for qualifying use (see **25.2** above) the whole bill, including the standing charge, is taxable at the reduced rate.

Where standing charges for electricity are made by a third party (e.g. a local authority) rather than the fuel supplier, they do not form part of the supply of electricity and are standard-rated, regardless of the customer.

(VAT Notice 701/19/10, para 10.10).

Charges made by fuel and power suppliers

See **25.7** below.

VAT treatment in particular cases

See **25.8** below.

Special rules for place of supply and supplies by persons outside the UK

See **25.9** below.

Use of system, transmission and other charges

Where a price includes a charge for electricity and standing and/or other charges, the whole supply is taxed at the reduced rate (even if the supplier has incurred costs in making that supply that were taxed at the standard rate).

If a supplier makes a charge to allow the use of transmission or distribution lines, transformers, meters, or makes other similar supplies of services, without any supply of electricity, such supplies are always standard-rated.

New electricity trading arrangements (NETA)

These arrangements have replaced the pool system. Generators, suppliers, and non-physical traders now negotiate bilateral and multilateral contracts 'over-the-counter'. These contracts are for wholesale supplies of electricity and are standard-rated. The arrangements provide a mechanism for the settlement of imbalances between physical and contractual positions. The following elements arising from the balancing mechanism are standard-rated.

- Balancing mechanism unit cash flow
- Non-delivery charges
- Energy imbalance cash flow
- Residual element cash flow

The information imbalance charges are outside the scope of VAT.

(VAT Notice 701/19/10, paras 5.4–5.7).

Steam and heated water

Supplies of steam and heated water are not eligible for the zero-rating applicable to water (see **74.2 ZERO-RATED SUPPLIES**). Instead they are, for VAT purposes, a form of heat.

Supplies of steam and heated water for qualifying use (see **25.2** above) are taxed at the reduced rate. For these purposes

- water that has been heated as part of a treatment process but is supplied at the temperature at which it was before it was heated (i.e. after it has cooled down) is not heated water;
- water that is hot because it is drawn from a hot spring is not treated as heated water; and
- water that has been deliberately heated by geo-thermal, solar or other natural heat or energy sources is treated as heated.

(VAT Notice 701/19/10, para 8.1).

Ventilation, air-conditioning and refrigeration

Supplies of air-conditioning, refrigeration and quick-freezing for a qualifying use (see **29.2** above) are taxed at the reduced rate. Supplies of ventilation, air-conditioning or refrigeration provided from a central plant are taxable at the reduced rate when supplied for a qualifying use.

Where premises are in multiple occupation, any charges to tenants in addition to the rent which are made in respect of the common parts or areas, are treated as further payment for the right to occupy and have the same liability as the main supply. See **41.4**(6) **LAND AND BUILDINGS: EXEMPT SUPPLIES AND OPTION TO TAX.**

(VAT Notice 701/19/10, para 9).

Charges made by fuel and power suppliers

Reduced rate supplies

[25.7] Any of the charges listed below are treated as part of the payment for a reduced rate supply of fuel and power provided the charges are

(a) made by a person who supplies the fuel and power to the consumer (up to and including the meter),
(b) made to that consumer, and
(c) inseparable from a supply of fuel or power to that consumer

and the supply of fuel and power is for a qualifying purpose;

- Disconnection and re-connection of the supply and special meter readings at the instigation of the supplier

- Installation by a supplier of liquefied petroleum gas of a bulk gas tank regarded as essential to the supply of liquefied petroleum gas
- Installation of check meters
- Installation or replacement of lines and switchgear belonging to the electricity supplier
- Installation tests and re-tests where required by the supplier to protect their equipment
- Maximum demand and minimum guarantee charges
- Removal of damaged coins from meters
- Rental charges for meters, including secondary meters used by landlords to apportion charges between their tenants
- Rental of a bulk gas tank in conjunction with the supply of liquid petroleum gas to that tank
- Repair, maintenance or replacement of equipment and gas pipes or electric cables belonging to the supplier up to and including the consumer's meter. (Where the supplier's conduits are within the fabric of a building, reduced rate supplies by the supplier are limited to work essential for getting at the conduits, and making good. All consequential work is standard-rated. Contractors' supplies to the supplier are standard-rated.)
- Replacing a credit meter with a pre-payment meter under the supplier's Code of Practice, or replacing or re-siting by a supplier of their meter at their instigation
- Replacement of mains fuses and provisions of earthing terminals
- Standing charges (see also **25.4** and **25.6** above).

Any of the above supplies are standard-rated when supplied

- by a contractor other than the supplier of fuel and power (even if a fuel and power supplier instructs a contractor to send a bill direct to a consumer for work that would have been at the reduced rate if invoiced by the supplier); and
- by a subcontractor to a fuel and power supplier.

Standard-rated supplies

The following supplies are always standard-rated.

- Repairs, maintenance and replacement of pipes not belonging to the fuel or power supplier (normally those on the consumer's side of the meter)
- Servicing contracts (other than supplies of insurance)
- Sale of meters to commercial, industrial and domestic consumers for their own use
- Altering coin mechanisms of secondary meters
- Services in connection with tests carried out, for example, at the request of estate agents or prospective purchasers of premises
- Replacement of meters not under the supplier's Code of Practice and re-siting meters at the request of the consumer
- Diverting mains to meet local authority requirements (these supplies are zero-rated when work is carried out in the course of construction of new dwellings)

- Raising or lowering of overhead power lines in connection with the movement of abnormal loads, including escorting the loads (these supplies are zero-rated when work is carried out in the course of construction of new dwellings)
- Supply, repair and maintenance of public lighting circuits to local authorities
- Temporary floodlighting, emergency or decorative lighting
- Charges for playing games such as squash, tennis, billiards and snooker collected by means of a coin-operated lighting meter (i.e. a time switch controlling the availability of light for a fixed period of time (may be exempt in certain circumstances, see **57.10 RECREATION AND SPORT**)
- Blast freezing

Outside the scope supplies

The following charges are outside the scope of VAT.

- Replacement by the gas or electricity supplier of dangerous, obsolete or inefficient appliances or parts, after the meter, under statutory contractual obligation. (This covers only the limited circumstances of work undertaken by gas and electricity utilities to comply with their statutory contractual obligations to supply fuel and power. It does not cover modification works to gas water heater flues in caravans.)
- Charges by a gas or electricity supplier for repairs to its own property following damage.

Zero-rating

Supplies of civil engineering services in the course of construction, alteration or conversion of a building may be zero-rated in certain circumstances. See **42.7** to **42.10 LAND AND BUILDINGS: ZERO RATING AND REDUCED RATE SUPPLIES AND DIY HOUSEBUILDERS**. This includes the first time provision of gas and electricity from the building up to the nearest existing supply.

In addition, by concession, customer contribution to a first time connection to the gas or electricity mains supply which would have been zero-rated before 1 April 1994 may continue to be zero-rated after that date provided it is the connection to the mains of

- a building, or part of a building, which consists of a dwelling or number of dwellings;
- a building, or part of a building, used solely for a 'relevant residential purpose' (see **41.1**(15) **LAND AND BUILDINGS: EXEMPT SUPPLIES AND OPTION TO TAX**);
- a residential caravan (i.e. a caravan on a site in respect of which there is no covenant, statutory planning consent or similar permission precluding occupation throughout the year);
- a houseboat; or
- a building, or part of a building, used by a charity for its non-business activities

and provided that the person receiving the supply does not do so for the purposes of any business carried on by him. (VAT Notice 48, ESC 3.16).

(VAT Notice 701/19/10, paras 2.2–2.4, 2.6).

From 1 January 2012, ESC 3.16 will be withdrawn. From that date, first time connection to electricity or gas will be subject to the reduced rate of VAT if the utility is for domestic or non-business charity use and the connection charge is made by a person who supplies the fuel.

Charges made by caravan site owners and houseboat mooring providers for first time connection to electricity, gas, water and sewerage will be subject to the same VAT liability as the caravan pitch or mooring (standard-rated or exempt, depending on the circumstances) unless the site owner or mooring provider can identify the actual consumption of users (i.e. through metering), in which case, the connection charge will be subject to the same VAT liability as the supply of the utility (reduced-rated for electricity and gas, zero-rated for water and sewerage).

(HMRC Brief 37/11).

VAT treatment in particular cases

[25.8] In particular cases, VAT is treated as follows:

(1) Supplies to schools and other educational institutions

Supplies of fuel and power to educational institutions are taxed at the reduced rate in the following circumstances.

(a) *The institution has charitable status and is receiving the supply for non-business use.* If the charity does not make a charge, its activities are generally non-business. Independent and other schools which are charities but which do charge fees are in business for VAT purposes and supplies of fuel and power to them are generally standard-rated (but see (*b*) below).

(b) *The fuel and power is supplied to separate residential premises for the accommodation of pupils and students.* Where the residential quarters form part of the main building, the supply partly qualifies for the reduced rate and must be apportioned (subject to the 60% rule, see **25.2** above) unless the school, etc. also qualifies under (*a*) above.

(VAT Notice 701/19/10, para 10.1).

(2) Supplies by wholesalers to retailers

Supplies of fuel and power by wholesalers to retailers are standard-rated unless supplied in small *de minimis* amounts (see **25.2** above). This applies even if it is known that the goods will eventually be supplied for qualifying use. (VAT Notice 701/19/10, para 10.2).

(3) Supplies by shops and other retailers

There are no special rules for supplies by retailers. In practice, most supplies of fuel and power by retail (e.g. coal supplied in bags) will be taxed at the reduced rate because the amount supplied will be below the *de minimis* limits for that fuel (see **25.2** above). (VAT Notice 701/19/10, para 10.3).

(4) Supplies to landlords, managing agents, caravan park owners and residents' associations

Such supplies are taxable at the reduced rate provided the fuel or power is used for qualifying purposes. The charge should be apportioned if only part of the premises to which the supply relates is used for qualifying purposes (e.g. on-site accommodation for employees or proprietors). In all other cases supplies of fuel and power to landlords, etc. are standard-rated. (VAT Notice 701/19/10, para 10.4).

(5) Supplies by landlords (other than local authorities)

(a) Heated, air-conditioned or refrigerated accommodation

Where a landlord supplies fuel and power to tenants in the form of heated, air-conditioned or refrigerated accommodation, this will usually be a single supply of accommodation. This accommodation can be used for any purpose (domestic, charitable or business). In practice, heated and air-conditioned accommodation is usually used for residential or office purposes and cold stores are used for storing perishable goods. Storage with no specific right over land is normally standard-rated. If the landlord grants the user of a cold store a right over land, then the supply is exempt (subject to the option to tax, see **41.8** LAND AND BUILDINGS: EXEMPT SUPPLIES AND OPTION TO TAX).

- Where a landlord and tenant contract for a single supply of heated, air-conditioned or cooled accommodation, it is a single supply of accommodation and is taxed as such. If the landlord makes a fixed charge for supplies of gas or electricity or includes an amount in the rent to cover them, the payment is normally treated as part of the rent and liable to VAT at the same rate as the supply of accommodation.
- Where a landlord and tenant contract for two separate supplies, one of heat, air-conditioning or cooling, and the other of accommodation, each supply is dealt with separately. If tenants have coin-operated gas or electricity meters, the money placed in the coin box is payment for a supply of gas or electricity and is taxed at the reduced rate when made for qualifying use. This applies whether the gas or electricity is supplied at cost or with a mark-up. If the landlord rents or owns a secondary credit meter, supplies of gas or electricity are liable to VAT at the reduced rate when made for a qualifying use.

(b) Service charges for common areas

Mandatory charges for fuel and power used in common areas (e.g. corridors and stairwells in blocks of flats) that are included in the service charge made to owners of flats and/or freehold property, form part of the payment for the overall supply. See **41.4**(6) LAND AND BUILDINGS: EXEMPT SUPPLIES AND OPTION TO TAX.

(VAT Notice 701/19/10, paras 10.6, 10.7).

(6) Supplies by local authorities

(a) Domestic tenants – single supplies of heated accommodation

The supply of accommodation by a local authority is a non-business activity for VAT purposes. The VAT liability of any supplies of fuel and power made by local authorities to their domestic tenants as part of the single supply of heated accommodation follows that of the main supply which is one of accommodation. The fuel and power element of the supply is therefore outside the scope of VAT.

(b) Separate supplies of fuel and power

Separate supplies for domestic use is liable to VAT at the reduced rate. Where a local authority continues to supply fuel and power to accommodation it previously owned, it is a business activity and the supply is taxed at the reduced rate if it is for a qualifying use (see **25.2** above).

(c) Mandatory service charges

Mandatory service charges raised by a local authority to leasehold owners are non-business and outside the scope of VAT.

(VAT Notice 701/19/10, paras 10.5, 10.7).

(7) Heating contracts

If a contractor, under a heating contract, supplies both the fuel and the staff required to operate and maintain a customer's heating system, the whole supply is taxable at the reduced rate (subject to qualifying use of the heat). But maintenance or repairs or replacement of the plant alone can only be taxable at the reduced rate if

- covered by an overall contract for the supply of heat; and
- directly related to and essential for maintaining that supply of heat.

Where a contract is for labour only for the operation and routine maintenance of a customer's boiler and distribution system, and the customer obtains fuel from another source, the supply is always standard-rated.

(VAT Notice 701/19/10, para 10.8).

(8) Facilities requiring fuel and power

The use of washing machines, hot showers and all other facilities (including those for playing sport) which depend on temporary power or light and which are charged for by meter, are *not* supplies of fuel and power. They are supplies of the particular facility concerned and liable to VAT at the appropriate rate. (VAT Notice 701/19/10, para 10.9). See *Mander Laundries Ltd* (VTD 31) (TVC 69.1) and *St Anne's-on-Sea Lawn Tennis Club Ltd* (VTD 434) (TVC 30.4).

See also *Showtry Ltd* (VTD 10028) (TVC 30.9) where the supply of fuel for use in hired agricultural machinery was held to be part of a composite standard-rated supply under the hire contract.

(9) Gas and electricity suppliers: bad debt relief on transferred debts

Subject to meeting certain conditions, a business can recover some or all of the VAT it has paid to HMRC on supplies made where a customer has failed to pay. See **7 BAD DEBT RELIEF**. One of the conditions is that the person who makes the supply is the only person entitled to claim relief.

With effect from 2 August 2004, by concession, a supplier of gas and/or electricity can obtain relief from VAT on debts owed by a domestic customer where the supplier has accepted the transfer of that customer and his debt from another supply company. The detailed provisions of the concession are as follows.

Where a contract for the supply of 'gas' or electricity is substituted by a new contract ('novation') as a result of a 'domestic consumer' transferring from one supplier to another, then, by concession, the new supplier may claim bad debt relief on a supply of gas or electricity made by the former supplier to that consumer, provided that

- the whole or any part of the consideration for the supply is outstanding at the time of the novation;
- the whole of the debt is transferred to the new supplier;
- at the time of the novation, the former supplier (if he has not already done so) accounts for VAT on the supply at the appropriate rate or, if he has already received a refund upon a claim for bad debt relief in relation to that supply, repays to HMRC the amount of that refund;
- the claim is not made until six months after payment for the novation and takes account of any payments made by the customer after the date of the novation;
- both the former supplier and the new supplier have evidence of
  - (i) the value of the debt (including the VAT amount) that has been transferred, and
  - (ii) the date of payment for the novation; and
- the new supplier has a copy of the document issued by him to the consumer to recover the debt (not required if a pre-payment meter is in use).

'*Gas*' means gas that is conveyed through pipes to premises by a person authorised to do so under *Gas Act 1986, s 7*.

'*Domestic consumer*' means a person to whom fuel or power is supplied for domestic use (see **25.2** above).

This concession does not apply in circumstances where its application would give rise to tax avoidance.

(Business Brief 20/04).

Special rules for gas, electricity, and heat or cooling supplies

[25.9] There are special rules for supplies of '*relevant goods*', which means

- gas supplied through a natural gas system situated within the territory of an EU country or any network connected to such a system;
- electricity; and
- (from 1 January 2011) heat or cooling supplied through a network.

[*VATA 1994, s 9A; F(No 3)A 2010, s 20(1)*].

Place of supply

The place of supply of relevant goods is determined as follows.

(a) Relevant goods supplied to a 'dealer' are treated as supplied at
- the place where that dealer has established his business or has a fixed establishment to which the relevant goods are supplied, or
- in the absence of such a place of business or fixed establishment, the place where he has his permanent address or usually resides.

'*Dealer*' means a person whose principal activity in respect of receiving supplies of relevant goods is the re-selling of those goods and whose own consumption of those goods is negligible. Re-selling does not include
- re-sale as part of a single composite supply of other goods or services, or
- re-sale as a supply that falls to be disregarded as a supply to another member of the same VAT group where relevant goods are to be effectively used and consumed by a member of the VAT group.

(b) Supplies of relevant goods not falling within (*a*) above are treated as supplied at
(i) the place where the recipient of the supply has effective use and consumption of the goods or
(ii) in relation to any part of the goods not consumed,
- the place where the recipient of the supply has established his business or has a fixed establishment to which the goods are supplied, or
- in the absence of such place of business or fixed establishment, the place where he has his permanent address or usually resides.

For the purposes of (i) above effective use and consumption includes a supply of the goods
- by the recipient as part of a single composite supply of other goods or services; and
- to a member of a VAT group, where the goods are effectively used and consumed by a member of that group.

[*SI 2004/3148, Arts 9–13*].

Reverse charge on supplies by persons outside the UK

The reverse charge procedure applies where a person who is outside the UK supplies 'relevant goods' to a person who is registered under *VATA 1994* for the purposes of any business carried on by the recipient. The recipient is treated as if he had himself supplied the relevant goods in the course or furtherance of his business and as if that supply were a taxable supply. He must therefore account for output tax on the full value of the supply received. He can, however, subject to the normal rules, include the VAT as input tax on the same VAT return. Supplies which are treated as made by the recipient under these rules are not taken into account when calculating any entitlement to input tax under the **PARTIAL EXEMPTION (49)** rules.

[*VATA 1994, s 9A; FA 2004, s 21*].

For these purposes a person is outside the UK if

- he has established his business or has a fixed establishment outside the UK; or
- in the absence of such a place of business or fixed establishment, the place where he has his permanent address or usually resides is outside the UK.

[*SI 2004/3148, Art 14*].

Time of supply

Goods which are treated as supplied by a person under *VATA 1994, s 9A* above are treated as being supplied when the goods are paid for or, if the consideration is not in money, on the last day of the VAT accounting period in which the goods are removed or made available. [*SI 1995/2518, Reg 82A; SI 2004/3140, Reg 4*].

Valuation of supply

Where any goods are treated as made by a UK VAT-registered recipient under *VATA 1994, s 9A* above, the value of the supply is taken to be

- where the consideration for the supply was in money, the amount of that consideration; and
- where the consideration did not consist, or not wholly consist, of money, such amount in money as is the equivalent to that consideration.

[*VATA 1994, Sch 6 para 8; F(No 2)A 2005, s 5*].

Key points

[25.10] Points to consider are as follows.

- The reduced rate of VAT applies to domestic supplies of fuel and power and also supplies to a charity for a building it uses for its non-business purposes. The latter is an example of a useful concession that is available to a charity to save VAT on its costs. In cases where a charity has incorrectly paid standard rate VAT over the last four years, there will be scope to approach the utility supplier and obtain a credit note for overpaid VAT. Any VAT incorrectly paid before this date is out of date under the error correction rules.

- The onus is on the supplier to get the VAT treatment right. This gives some protection to the customer if the reduced rate of VAT has been incorrectly charged on fuel and power supplied to a building.
- A useful concession is that any non-qualifying use of a building is ignored, e.g. a charitable building partly used for business purposes, as long as the qualifying use is at least 60% of total use. If the qualifying use is less than 60%, then an apportionment must be made so that the reduced rate of VAT is only charged on the percentage of qualifying use.

26

Gold and Precious Metals

Cross-reference. See **67 TERMINAL MARKETS** for zero-rating of certain transactions in gold on the London Gold Market.

De Voil Indirect Tax Service. See V4.186, V4.277, V5.143.

Introduction

[26.1] A special scheme applies for investment gold. It puts investment in gold on a similar footing with other financial investments, e.g. shares, by making it exempt from VAT (see **26.2** below). Businesses are generally unable to reclaim input tax directly attributable to an exempt supply. Unlike shares, however, gold may be purchased from a variety of taxable sources before being transformed into investment gold. If the normal rules applied, the input tax incurred on these costs would not be reclaimable and the seller would either have to absorb the VAT cost or pass it on to the investor (which would make investing in the gold less attractive). The scheme for investment gold therefore has three special features.

- Certain persons may opt to tax specified transactions, so enabling them to reclaim all of their input tax (subject to the normal rules). See **26.3** below.
- Taxable persons can reclaim the input tax incurred on purchases of gold and on the costs of transforming any gold into investment gold. See **26.4** below.
- Taxable persons who are producers and transformers of investment gold can reclaim the input tax they incur on certain costs linked to the production or transformation process. See **26.4** below.

The special scheme for investment gold also allows special procedures for transactions on the London Bullion Market. See **67.3 TERMINAL MARKETS**.

Exempt supplies of investment gold

[26.2] The following supplies are exempt.

(a) The supply of 'investment gold'.

(b) The grant, assignment or surrender of any right, interest, or claim in, over or to investment gold if the right, interest or claim is or confers a right to the transfer of possession of investment gold. *Not included* is

- the grant of an option; or
- the assignment or surrender of a right under an option at a time before the option is exercised.

A supply of this description includes supplies of unallocated investment gold (i.e. gold which is an unidentifiable part of a larger stock held by the supplier), loans, swaps, and forward and future contracts concerning investment gold. (VAT Notice 701/21/11, para 2.2).

(c) The supply, by a person acting as an agent for a disclosed principal, of services consisting of

- effecting a supply within (*a*) or (*b*) above that is made by or to his principal; or
- attempting to effect such a supply which is not in fact made.

The effect of this is that if an agent (including an auctioneer) sells and invoices the goods in the name of their principal, the supply of investment gold is made by the principal (and exempt under (*a*) or (*b*) above). The agent supplies only his services which are exempt under this provision. The agent may opt to tax the services if the principal also opts to tax his onward supply (see **26.3**(*c*) below).

Where an agent acts in his own name (i.e. for an undisclosed principal), the goods are treated for VAT purposes as supplies both to and by the agent. See **3.4 AGENTS**. The special scheme for investment gold applies to the agent in the same way as it would apply to a principal and the agent's supply is exempt unless he can opt to tax under **26.3** below. However, when an agent or auctioneer is acting in their own name their supply of services to either the buyer or the seller is taxable.
(VAT Notice 701/21/11, para 7.3 which has the force of law).

Excluded is a supply

- between members of the London Bullion Market Association; or
- by a member of that association to a taxable person who is not a member; or
- by a taxable person who is not a member to a member of that association.

'*Investment gold*' means any of the following.

(i) Gold of a purity not less than 995 thousandths in the form of a bar or wafer of a weight accepted by the bullion markets. See VAT Notice 701/21/11, para 15 for list of the weights in which bars and wafers are commonly traded.

(ii) A gold coin minted after 1800 that
- is of a purity of not less than 900 thousandths;
- is, or has been, legal tender in its country of origin; and
- is of a 'type' that is 'normally sold' at a price that does not exceed 180% of the open market value of the gold contained in the coin.

(iii) A gold coin of a 'description' laid down in VAT Notice 701/21A/11, Section 3 which for these purposes has the force of law. The list, comprising over 500 gold coins from around the world, is produced by the EU Commission and is updated annually. It applies in all EU countries.

All gold coins falling within (ii) or (iii) above that have the same denomination (face value), size and gold fineness constitute a single 'type' or 'description' for the purposes of these provisions. Thus a gold coin type may be a single issue for one year or may have been produced for many years (e.g. a British sovereign). (VAT Notice 701/21A/11, para 2.2).

HMRC regard the price at which a coin is 'normally sold' as the price that can most usually be demanded for that particular type of coin. It does not matter that an individual coin is of special interest to collectors; if the usual value of the coin type does not exceed 180% of the value of the gold contained therein, all coins of that type are exempt. Similarly, if a coin type is usually valued at more than 180% of the gold value (because of interest to collectors), any coin of that type is taxable even if a particular coin is in such poor condition that it is worth less than 180% of its gold value. The normal selling price of coins is affected by the finish. Investment gold coins fall into two broad classes. First, relatively older issues made to circulate as currency and normally worn from circulation. Secondly, generally more recent issues primarily produced as a store of wealth. The second type may have been issued in a number of finishes (e.g. 'brilliant uncirculated' or 'proof') and if the majority of a type of coin are, for example, of brilliant uncirculated quality, then the brilliant uncirculated value normally reflects the normal selling price. If a trader is uncertain whether the normal selling value falls within the 180% criterion, he should contact HMRC. (VAT Notice 701/21A/11, paras 2.4, 2.5).

[*VATA 1994, Sch 9 Group 15; SI 1999/3116, Reg 2*].

Option to tax investment gold

[26.3] The special scheme for investment gold allows some businesses to opt to tax certain otherwise exempt transactions provided they meet conditions laid down by HMRC (which have the force of law).

(a) **Producers and transformers of gold.** Where a taxable person supplies investment gold which he has produced or transformed *to another taxable person* and the supply would otherwise fall within **26.2**(*a*) or (*b*) above, the supplier can elect to waive exemption and opt to tax the supply. The business must notify HMRC if it intends to make use of this provision who will send an acknowledgement. If this is not received within 28 days, it is the responsibility of the business to check that HMRC have received the notification.

(b) **Other taxable persons.** HMRC may permit a taxable person, who in the normal course of his business makes supplies of gold for industrial purposes, to opt to tax the supply of investment gold described in **26.2**(i) above if made to another taxable person. Prior permission must be obtained by writing to HMRC, giving the VAT registration number and confirming that the business normally trades in gold for industrial purposes. If permission is given, HMRC will send a letter of approval within 28 days setting out the conditions of permission. Once authorisation is received, the business may opt to tax supplies of investment gold bars or wafers made to other taxable persons. It cannot opt to tax supplies of investment gold coins or sales to non-taxable persons. HMRC may withdraw authorisation for the protection of the revenue. In such a case, the election ceases to have effect from the date specified in the notification.

(c) **Agents.** Where an agent acts on behalf of a named principal and that principal has made an election under (*a*) or (*b*) above as supplier, then the agent may also opt to tax any supply of services which would otherwise fall to be exempt under **26.2**(*c*) above and which is directly linked to the relevant supply. The agent must notify HMRC that he intends to opt to tax his services. HMRC will send an acknowledgement. If this is not received within 28 days, it is the agent's responsibility to check that HMRC have received the notification.

Any such election made by the supplier or his agent is subject to any conditions laid down by HMRC and

- applies in respect of an individual supply;
- has effect on or after the day from which the election is made;
- is irrevocable.

How to opt

Once the conditions outlined above have been fulfilled, to opt to tax a particular transaction it is simply necessary to include the following statement on the sales invoice.

'We have opted to tax this transaction.'

Special accounting arrangements for opted transactions

By opting to tax a transaction in investment gold, the transaction becomes subject to the special accounting scheme under which the responsibility to account for and pay the output tax falls to the purchaser. See **26.9** below.

Invoicing requirements

A taxable person selling investment gold which he has opted to tax must comply with all the normal invoicing requirements for taxable transactions (see **39 INVOICES**) and the requirements of the special accounting scheme for gold (see **26.9** below).

[*SI 1999/3116, Reg 3*]. (VAT Notice 701/21/11, paras 4.3–4.7 which have the force of law).

Deduction of input tax

[26.4] Where a business opts to tax a particular supply of investment gold (see **26.3** above) it can reclaim all the related input tax as it is making a taxable supply of investment gold. To reclaim all input tax, it must be able to show that none of its input tax relates to any exempt supplies of investment gold.

As a general rule, input tax incurred on goods or services which are used to make exempt supplies cannot be reclaimed. Exceptionally, where a taxable person makes exempt supplies of investment gold within **26.2**(*a*) or (*b*) above

- input tax incurred in any VAT period in respect of such supplies is allowable as being attributable to those supplies to the extent that it is incurred on
  (i) the purchase of investment gold which would have fallen to be exempt within **26.2**(*a*) or (*b*) above but for
    - an option to tax having been exercised under **26.3** above; or
    - the supply having been excluded from exemption because it was between a member of the London Bullion Market Association and a taxable person who was not a member;

  (ii) the acquisition of investment gold from another EU country;
  (iii) a supply to him, or an acquisition or importation by him, of gold other than investment gold which is to be transformed by him (or on his behalf) into investment gold; and
  (iv) services supplied to him comprising a change of form, weight or purity of gold; and
- if he produces investment gold or transforms any gold into investment gold, he is also entitled to credit for input tax incurred on any goods or services supplied to him, or goods acquired or imported by him, to the extent that they are linked to the production or transformation of that gold into investment gold. This includes, for example, in addition to the gold itself
  - tools, tooling and equipment;
  - machinery, plant and fittings;
  - fuel and power;
  - crucibles and furnace linings;
  - buildings and maintenance of buildings;
  - laboratory instruments and equipment; and
  - fume abatement and effluent treatment

  but not, for example, a computer used to record exempt sales because the input tax is not directly linked to the production or transformation process.
  If a building is to be used for the production of investment gold which will be sold exempt from VAT and an area of the building is set aside for the sale of that investment gold, the input tax on the building must be apportioned to reflect the fact that only a part of it is linked to the *production* of the investment gold.

Input tax partly attributable to exempt supplies of investment gold

Where input tax has been incurred on goods or services which are used or to be used in making supplies of investment gold within **26.2**(*a*) or (*b*) above and other supplies, the proportion attributable to the investment gold must first be established (by being expressed as a proportion of the whole use or intended use) and the rules in (*a*) and (*b*) above must then be applied to the proportion attributable to the investment gold.

Examples

(1) A business makes exempt supplies of investment gold but is not a producer or transformer of gold and does not buy in transformation services. It receives a mixed supply, part of which is investment gold that it intends to supply partly as exempt investment gold and partly as other goods or services.
The business can only deduct VAT incurred on the investment gold itself. It must first work out the extent to which the input tax on the mixed supply received is attributable to the various supplies to be made. For the element attributable to the exempt supply of investment gold, it must then work out how much of that input tax relates to the gold itself. It cannot, for example, deduct any input tax incurred on a separate delivery service of that gold.

(2) A business makes exempt supplies of investment gold and is not a producer or transformer of gold. However, it does buy in transformation services.
The business can deduct VAT incurred on the investment gold itself (or other gold) and the VAT incurred on any out-sourced transformation services. If it incurs any input tax which is partly attributable to supplies of exempt investment gold and party attributable to other supplies, it must first work out the extent to which the input tax incurred is attributable to its various supplies. Then, for the element attributable to the exempt supply of investment gold, it must work out the extent to which it relates to the gold itself and to the transformation services.

(3) A business makes exempt supplies of investment gold and is also a producer and/or transformer of gold.
The business can deduct the VAT incurred on any related gold and also any VAT incurred on production and/or transformation costs. If it incurs any input tax which is partly attributable to its supplies of exempt investment gold and partly attributable to other supplies, it must first work out the extent to which that input tax is attributable to its various supplies and then, for the element attributable to the exempt supply of investment gold, it must work out the extent to which it relates only to the gold and production/transformation.

[*SI 1995/2518, Reg 103A; SI 1999/3114*]. (VAT Notice 701/21/11, paras 5.1–5.4).

Accounting and record keeping requirements

[26.5] There are special accounting and record keeping requirements for persons who trade in exempt investment gold. The requirements apply to exempt sales of investment gold where the gold is delivered, or otherwise made available, to the customer. The requirements apply whether or not the supplier is registered or liable to be registered for VAT. [*SI 1995/2518, Regs 31A, 31B; SI 1999/3114*]. (VAT Notice 701/21/11, para 6.1). See **52.26 PENALTIES** for penalties for failure to comply with the record-keeping requirements.

Notification

On the first occasion that a person makes an exempt supply of investment gold which exceeds £5,000 in value, or when the value of his supplies of investment gold to any one customer exceeds £10,000 in any twelve-month period, he must notify HMRC at the following address.

HM Revenue and Customs
Written Enquiries Section
Alexander House
Victoria Avenue
Southend
Essex SS99 1BD

If, at the time of notification, the person is not VAT-registered, he must also provide the following information.

- Name of company, partnership or sole proprietor.
- Company number or details of partners.
- Address(es).
- Telephone number.
- Contact name.
- Accountant name, address and telephone.
- Any associated VAT registration numbers.

HMRC will send an acknowledgement. If this is not received within 28 days, it is the person's responsibility to check that HMRC have received the notification.

It is not necessary to notify HMRC of subsequent supplies.

(VAT Notice 701/21/11, para 3.1 which has the force of law). See VAT Notice 701/21/11, para 3.2 for a standard letter which may be used.

Invoicing requirements

Where an invoice is issued for the sale of exempt investment gold which is over £5,000 or the total value of sales of exempt investment gold to that customer have exceeded £10,000 in the last year, the invoice must contain the following details if appropriate.

(i) A unique identifying number.
(ii) Name and address of seller and name and address of person raising invoice (if different to the seller, e.g. an agent).
(iii) Name and address of the purchaser, delivery address (if different) and unique customer reference (see under *Customer record* below).
(iv) Date of invoice and delivery date.
(v) Type of supply (for example, sale).
(vi) If the seller, agent or the customer is registered for VAT, the VAT registration number of the seller and agent.

(vii) A description of the gold supplied.
(viii) For bars and wafers: the form, weight and purity and any other identifying feature (including any proprietary mark, hallmark and serial number where applicable).
(ix) For investment gold coins: the coin type, country of origin and whether or not the coin is included on the list of gold coins reproduced in VAT Notice 701/21A/11, Section 3.
(x) The number of items.
(xi) The total amount payable.

Where a business sells investment gold on which it has charged VAT (e.g. because it has opted to tax), the invoice must comply with the normal invoicing requirements (see **39 INVOICES**) and the requirements for the special accounting scheme for gold (see **26.9** below).

(VAT Notice 701/21/11, paras 6.2, 6.4 which have the force of law).

Where taxable items (including gold) and exempt investment gold are supplied together, all the items may be included on the same invoice, provided the invoice contains all the appropriate details.

(VAT Notice 701/21/11, para 6.6).

Purchasing investment gold from persons not trading in investment gold

Where a person purchases exempt investment gold from a person who does not trade in investment gold and

- the value of the purchase is more than £5,000, or
- if more than one purchase has been made from the same customer, the total value of purchases from that customer has exceeded £10,000 in the last year,

the purchaser must issue an invoice on behalf of the seller containing all the relevant details specified in (i)–(xi) above.

In addition, the invoice must bear the following declaration which must be signed by the seller.

'I declare that to the best of my knowledge the details shown on this invoice are correct.' (signature and name).

The purchaser must keep and maintain a copy of the invoices so issued with his purchase records.
(VAT Notice 701/21/11, para 6.3 which has the force of law).

Special records

Subject to below, any person (whether or not registered for VAT) who sells exempt investment gold which is delivered or available to be taken away by the customer must keep and maintain a record showing the following information as part of the business records.

(A) Accounting records

Accounting records showing

- invoice number;
- invoice date;
- customer reference number;
- customer's VAT registration number (if applicable);
- description of the gold (form, quantity and purity);
- name and address of the agent (if applicable);
- name and address of the purchaser; and
- transaction value.

(B) Customer record

Customer record identifying customers who purchase exempt investment gold. This record must have a unique reference number and contain details of the purchaser's

- name;
- date of birth;
- current address; and
- telephone number if available.

The seller must take reasonable steps to ensure that the customer has given correct information. In order to do this, the seller must ask for and examine at least one document from each of the following lists.

List 1
Passport
Full driving licence
National Insurance card
Birth certificate
National identity card

List 2
Telephone bill
Other utility bill
Deeds
Tenancy lease
Council tax bill
Hotel key card (for non-UK residents only)

Alternative satisfactory evidence may be agreed with HMRC.

If possible, copies should be kept of the documents seen. The seller should write on each copy 'certified as original document' and must sign and date this declaration. If it is not possible to keep a copy of any document seen, the seller must record, as part of your customer record, sufficient details to enable HMRC to obtain a copy if they so require. As a minimum the seller should record

- the name of the document;
- the reference number; and
- the name and address of the issuing authority.

The seller must insist that the customer produces the original document.

Internet and mail order sales

If investment gold is sold over the internet or by mail order, the seller may as an alternative to the customer record under (B) above keep and maintain the following record.

- If the supply is paid for by credit card and the delivery address is also the card holder's address, a record of the customer's name, the credit card issuer and the card number.
- If the supply is paid for by cheque, a record of the customer's name, the name of the bank and the customer's account number.

Whether payment is by credit card or cheque, the seller must also keep proof of despatch of the investment gold to the customer's address.

Sales to other VAT-registered businesses

If investment gold is sold to another VAT-registered business, the seller may, as an alternative to the customer record under (B) above, ask the customer for their VAT registration number. The seller must, however, check with HMRC that the VAT registration number provided is authentic.

Banks and other financial service businesses

If the seller is a bank or other financial service business which, for the purposes of the *Money Laundering Regulations 1993* (*SI 1993/1933*) is a 'relevant financial business' it may, as an alternative to the customer record set out in (B) above, keep and maintain the records specified in those *Regulations*. Relevant financial businesses to whom this applies must conduct the appropriate identification procedures and keep the required records in the case of all transactions in investment gold where

- the value of a one-off transaction exceeds 15,000 euro, or
- two or more one-off transactions appear linked and their value together exceeds 15,000 euro.

For these purposes, the exchange rate between the euro and the UK £ is the rate published in the Official Journal of the Communities.

(VAT Notice 701/21/11, paras 7.1, 7.2, 7.4, 7.6 which have the force of law).

Additional special record for taxable persons

If the seller is registered for VAT and is

- authorised to opt to tax supplies of investment gold (see **26.3** above), or
- a producer or transformer of investment gold,

he must keep and maintain with his VAT account, in addition to the records set out above, a record of any supply of investment gold made to another taxable person where the seller has delivered or otherwise made the gold available to that person, and on which the seller has *not* opted to tax.

(VAT Notice 701/21/11, para 7.5 which has the force of law).

Records of exports and dispatches

A seller is not required to keep any of the records described above for supplies of investment gold physically exported outside the EU or despatched to a business in another EU country. (VAT Notice 701/21/11, para 7.1). See **26.8** below.

Retention of records

The seller must retain all the documents and records specified above for a minimum of six years from the date of the transaction. In the case of regular customers, he must keep the customer record under (B) above for six years following the most recent supply of investment gold.

Any person who purchases investment gold must keep the purchase invoice for a minimum of six years from the date of the transaction.

(VAT Notice 701/21/11, para 7.7 which has the force of law).

Supplies of gold other than investment gold

Zero-rated supplies of gold involving Central Banks

[26.6] The supply of gold (including gold coins) held in the UK by

- a Central Bank to either another Central Bank or a member of the London Bullion Market, or
- a member of the London Bullion Market to a Central Bank

is zero-rated. Included is the granting of a right to acquire gold and the supply of a part interest in gold. [*VATA 1994, Sch 8 Group 10*].

Other supplies

The VAT liability of a supply of gold which is not

- zero-rated under the above provisions,
- investment gold within the meaning in **26.2** above, or
- eligible for relief under the provisions relating to **TERMINAL MARKETS (67)**

generally falls into one of the following categories.

(a) **'Allocated gold'**. The supply of allocated gold held
  (i) outside the UK is outside the scope of UK VAT; and
  (ii) in the UK is standard-rated (unless zero-rated because the gold is physically exported under the normal rules for the export of goods).

  '*Allocated gold*' is gold set apart and designated as belonging to or reserved for specific persons or purposes. If gold, etc. is delivered, it is of necessity allocated.

(b) **'Unallocated gold' supplied by UK traders.** The supply is
  (i) standard-rated if the customer belongs in the UK;

(ii) outside the scope of UK VAT (but with input tax credit) if made to a customer who belongs outside the EU;
(iii) outside the scope of UK VAT (but with input tax credit) if the customer is a business in another EU country; and
(iv) standard-rated if made to a customer in another EU country not fulfilling the conditions in (iii).

'*Unallocated gold*' is gold or gold coins forming an unidentifiable part of a large stock held by a supplier. The supply of unallocated gold or gold coins is a supply of a service for VAT purposes which is a financial service for the purposes of *VATA 1994, Sch 5* (see **65.22 SUPPLY: PLACE OF SUPPLY**). As a result, under (ii) and (iii) above, the place of supply of services is treated as made where the recipient belongs under *SI 1992/3121, Art 16* but under (i) and (iv) is made where the supplier belongs under the general rule for place of supply of services.

(c) **Unallocated gold—supplies received in the UK from suppliers belonging abroad.** Such a supply of 'unallocated gold' (see (*b*) above) is
- standard-rated as the importation of a financial service if received by a taxable person, the UK customer accounting for the VAT under the reverse charge procedure (see **38.4 INTERNATIONAL SERVICES** and **65.22**(5) **SUPPLY: PLACE OF SUPPLY**); and
- outside the scope of UK VAT if received by a private or non-taxable person.

See **17.2 EUROPEAN UNION: GENERAL** for the VAT territory of the EU.

(VAT Notice 701/21/11, paras 10.2, 16).

Importations and acquisitions of gold

Importations

[26.7] VAT is not chargeable on

- the importation of gold (including gold coin) from outside the EU by a Central Bank [*SI 1992/3124*]; or
- the importation of investment gold (see **26.2** above) from outside the EU [*SI 1999/3115*]. The investment gold must be entered to Customs Procedure Code (CPC) 40 00 73 in order to gain the exemption.

Other importations of gold are chargeable to VAT at the standard rate. But see **73.3 WORKS OF ART, ETC.** for special valuation provisions applying to the importation of gold coins which are collectors' pieces.

Acquisitions

Acquisitions of gold in the UK from another EU country are subject to the normal rules, i.e. the rate of VAT is the same as would be applicable if the gold in question was the subject of a supply in the UK (see **19.3 EUROPEAN UNION: SINGLE MARKET**). The effect of this is that the acquisition of investment gold is exempt from VAT but the acquisition of other gold is standard-rated.

Central banks

Where gold is supplied to a Central Bank by a supplier in another EU country and the transaction involves the removal of the gold from that or some other EU country to the UK, the taking possession of the gold by the Central Bank concerned is not treated as an acquisition of goods from another EU country. [*SI 1992/3132*]. Consequently, VAT does not become chargeable on the receipt of such gold by the Central Bank concerned.

(VAT Notice 701/21/11, paras 8.1, 10.7).

Exports and removals

[26.8] Exports and removals of gold are treated as follows:

- **Investment gold.** The supply of investment gold which is physically exported to a place outside the EU or despatched to a business in another EU country does not attract UK VAT. It is not necessary to keep the special records in **26.5** above but the normal evidence of the export or despatch is required. See **21.25 EXPORTS** and **19.13 EUROPEAN UNION: SINGLE MARKET.**
  EU sales lists/intrastat. There is no need to complete ESLs for exempt sales of investment gold to businesses in other EU countries but any required intratstat declaration must be completed.
  (VAT Notice 701/21/11, paras 8.2, 8.3).
- **Other gold.** The supply of gold, other than investment gold which is physically exported to a place outside the EU or despatched to another business in another EU country is zero-rated with input tax recovery (subject to the normal rules).
  (VAT Notice 701/21/11, para 10.8).

For the liability of sales to overseas customers where the gold is not physically removed from the UK, see **26.6** above.

Special accounting scheme for gold transactions

[26.9] A special accounting scheme for gold must be used for certain transactions between VAT-registered traders. Where it applies, it transfers the responsibility for paying the VAT due to HMRC from the seller to the buyer. The detailed provisions are set out below.

The scheme must be applied in relation to 'supplies of gold', where

(a) the seller and buyer are both registered for VAT or liable to be registered as a consequence of the transaction (see below),
(b) the supply by the seller is by way of business, and
(c) the buyer is making the purchase in connection with any business carried on by him.

In determining liability for registration under (*a*) above for the purposes of *VATA 1994, Sch 1*, a standard-rated supply of gold (but not a zero-rated supply) is treated as a taxable supply by the buyer in the course or furtherance of his business (as well as a taxable supply by the seller). The supply by the purchaser cannot be disregarded on the grounds that it is a supply of capital assets for his business. In such a case, if the purchaser is not entitled to register or is exempted from registration, he must account for output tax on the purchase directly to HMRC.

'*Supplies of gold*' within the scheme are as follows.

(i) Supplies of fine gold of a purity of 995 parts per thousand or greater. *Excluded* are supplies of dental gold, gold slugs and gold targets.

(ii) Supplies of gold grain of any purity.

(iii) Supplies of gold coins of any purity. Gold coins, if they are collectors' items of numismatic interest, may be accounted for under the margin scheme for **SECOND-HAND GOODS (61)**. However, gold coins may not be sold under the margin scheme if they are investment gold coins or if they were purchased under the special accounting scheme.

(iv) Supplies of goods containing gold where the amount paid or payable for the supply (apart from the VAT) does not exceed, or exceeds by no more than a negligible amount, the 'open market value' of the gold contained in the goods. This includes supplies of scrap (including live scrap, i.e. scrapped jewellery, broken jewellery, watch cases, cigarette cases, etc.) and sweepings. The '*open market value*' of the gold is the 'fix price' of the gold at the time of supply. This is the price set twice a day in London by members of the London Bullion Market Association.

(v) The supply of the services of treating or processing goods to make fine gold, gold grain or gold coins.

(vi) The supply of investment gold which would otherwise fall to be exempt under **26.2**(*a*) or (*b*) above but which is standard-rated because the seller has exercised the option to tax under **26.3** above. [*SI 1999/3116, Reg 4*].

(vii) A supply of investment gold by

- a member of the London Bullion Market Association (LBMA) to a taxable person who is not a LBMA member, or
- a taxable person who is not a LBMA member to a LBMA member.

Such a transaction is not zero-rated, is specifically excluded from the exemption applying under **26.2** above and as a result is standard-rated. The special accounting scheme applies to these transactions regardless of whether the supply is classed as a supply of goods or a supply of services.

However, where the non-member who makes or receives the supply is only liable to be registered for VAT under *VATA 1994, Sch 1* or *Sch 3* solely by virtue of that supply or acquisition, the non-member is not required to notify liability for registration and the LBMA member must, on the non-member's behalf, keep a record of the transaction and pay the VAT due to HMRC.

[*SI 1973/173, Arts 5–7; SI 1999/3117*].

Operation of the scheme

If a VAT-registered person supplies goods within (i)–(vii) above, the goods must be sold to another VAT-registered person in order for the scheme to apply. The seller may therefore wish to ask his customer to provide a purchase order detailing the name, address and VAT registration number appropriate to the business.

Under the special scheme, the purchaser of the gold pays the seller the VAT-exclusive price of the gold and must declare the VAT due to HMRC on his VAT return. At the same time the purchaser can deduct, as input VAT, the amount of VAT shown on the seller's invoice (subject to normal rules).

If a VAT-registered person purchases manufactured goods containing gold which are held out for sale as such, and pays over VAT to the seller, the purchaser may be required to prove that the purchase did not fall within the provisions of the special accounting scheme for gold. If he cannot prove this, he may be treated as if he purchased gold and will be required to account for the output tax due under the special accounting scheme.

Issue of VAT invoices

For supplies under the special scheme, the seller must issue a VAT invoice to the buyer showing all the information normally required on a VAT invoice (see **39.4 INVOICES**) and, for investment gold, the information required under **26.5** above. The time of supply is ordinarily the date of delivery of the gold or when the gold is made available for removal by the purchaser. The description of the goods must include the weight and purity of the gold; the number of individual items where possible; and the fix price of the gold on the day of delivery.

The invoice must also include a form of words to the effect that the output tax shown on the invoice is payable to HMRC by the purchaser of the gold. The suggested form of words is:

'£. . . . . output tax on this supply of gold to be accounted for to HM Revenue and Customs by the buyer.'

Completion of the VAT return

Box 1

Include VAT due on any purchases of gold under the special scheme in the period covered by the return. VAT on any sales of gold under the scheme should *not* be shown in this box.

Box 2

Include acquisition VAT on gold acquired from other EU countries.

Box 4

Include the VAT due on purchases of gold under the special scheme (subject to the normal rules).

Box 6

Include the VAT-exclusive value of sales under the special scheme and purchases under the scheme (which are treated as deemed supplies).

Box 7

Include the value of gold purchased under the special scheme.

Sales of gold to non-registered persons

Where gold that falls within the scheme is sold to a person who is not registered or liable to be registered for VAT, the seller should charge and account for VAT in the normal way. The purchaser should pay the full amount due including VAT.

Antique items

Antique items containing gold may fall outside the scheme (because the value of the goods substantially exceeds the open market value of the gold in them or because VAT due on the supply of the item may be treated under the second-hand scheme). However, antique gold coins cannot be sold under the second-hand scheme if they are investment gold or if they were purchased under the special accounting and payment scheme.

Smuggled gold

All smuggled gold is liable to forfeiture even if the gold is found in the hands of an innocent purchaser. It is therefore important that a purchaser of gold looks at the evidence of origin of the gold before agreeing to buy it. See VAT Notice 701/21/11, para 14.1 for guidance for dealers who may be invited to purchase gold so that they can satisfy themselves as to the origin of the gold on offer.

[*VATA 1994, s 55; FA 1996, ss 29(3)(5), 32*]. (VAT Notice 701/21/11, paras 11.1–11.6, 12.14).

De Voil Indirect Tax Service. See V5.143.

Manufactured gold jewellery

[26.10] For a consideration of the basis of the valuation of a supply for VAT purposes where gold jewellery is made for customers wholly or partly by refashioning gold supplied by the customer, see *C & E Commrs v SAI Jewellers*, QB [1996] STC 269 (TVC 67.61).

Other precious metals

[26.11] The provisions in **26.6**(*b*) and (*c*) above relating to supplies of unallocated gold also apply to supplies of unallocated silver, platinum, palladium, rhodium, ruthenium, osmium and iridium. (Business Brief 20/94).

Key points

[26.12] Points to consider are as follows.

- The special VAT scheme for investment gold means that an option to tax can be applied in certain situations, i.e. to ensure input tax recovery on related costs. If a business decides to use this facility, it must notify HMRC within 28 days of the decision being made and note sales invoices with the narrative 'We have opted to tax this transaction.'
- In certain situations, a business that buys gold and converts it into investment gold can also claim input tax on the conversion and buying costs, even though the final sale of the investment gold is exempt from VAT. This is intended to create parity with share investments, because the latter investments do not have associated costs that include VAT.
- In situations where an option to tax applies, the output tax will be accounted for by the buyer of the gold rather than the seller. The buyer will pay the seller the VAT-exclusive value of the gold, and include output tax in Box 1 of his return, usually claiming the same amount as input tax in Box 4.

27

Groups of Companies

Cross-references. See **7.11 BAD DEBT RELIEF**; **19.18 EUROPEAN UNION: SINGLE MARKET** for distance selling from the UK by VAT groups; **41.8 LAND AND BUILDINGS: EXEMPT SUPPLIES AND THE OPTION TO TAX** for the option to tax.

De Voil Indirect Tax Service. See V2.114, V2.190, V2.190B.

Introduction

EU legislation

[27.1] EU legislation allows countries to treat independent legal persons as a single taxable person provided such legal persons are closely bound to one another by financial, economic and organisational links and are established within the confines of the particular country. [*Directive 2006/112/EC, Art 11*].

UK legislation

UK legislation applicable to the registration of groups of companies is considered in **27.2** to **27.4** below. It should be noted that the term 'group' in this context is used for VAT purposes only.

VAT group registration reduces the burden on businesses by allowing two or more associated companies to account for VAT as a single taxable person. It may be administratively convenient where a group accounting function is centralised. Also, because supplies between group members are normally disregarded for VAT purposes, VAT invoices need not be issued for such supplies. On the other hand, because a single VAT return is submitted for the whole group, there may be practical problems in gathering together the information necessary to complete the return on time.

Eligibility for group treatment

[27.2] Two or more 'bodies corporate' (see (1) below) are eligible to be treated as members of a group if

- each of the bodies is 'established' (see (3) below) or has a 'fixed establishment' (see (4) below) in the UK;
- they satisfy the control test, i.e.
  - (a) one of them 'controls' (see (2) below) each of the others,
  - (b) one person (whether a body corporate or an individual) controls all of them, or
  - (c) two or more individuals carrying on a business in partnership control all of them; and
- where applicable, they satisfy the anti-avoidance provisions below.

But a body corporate cannot be treated as a member of more than one group at a time and a body which is a member of one group is not eligible by virtue of the above provisions to be treated as a member of another group.

[*VATA 1994, ss 43A(1), 43D(1)(2); FA 1999, Sch 2 para 2; FA 2004, s 20(2)*].

HMRC have no discretion to accept group registration where these requirements are not met (*E Du Vergier & Co Ltd* (VTD 4) (TVC 32.1)).

Anti-avoidance provisions

Special provisions apply in order to stop abusive arrangements whereby a jointly-owned entity would otherwise be able to join a VAT group, even though it was run by and for the benefit of an external third party which exercised control over it in practice. Additional conditions prevent certain suppliers from being in the same VAT group as their customers where third parties control the suppliers or receive most of the benefits of their activities.

Specifically, a body corporate that is a 'specified body' (see (5) below) is only eligible to be treated as a member of a group if

- it satisfies the control test above; *and*
- it satisfies both the 'benefits condition' (see (6) below) and the 'consolidated accounts condition' (see (7) below).

[*SI 2004/1931, Art* 2].

A specified body which was a member of a VAT group at 1 August 2004 but failed either the benefits condition or consolidated accounts provision at that date is no longer eligible to be a member of a VAT group. It must leave the group from a date agreed with, or determined by, HMRC. (VAT Notice 700/2/11, para 3.2).

Definitions for the above purposes

(1) Body corporate

A body corporate is a form of corporation where a number of persons are united and consolidated together so as to be considered as one person in law. There are several ways in which a body might be incorporated.

- *Companies Act 2006* provides five ways in which a body may be incorporated (public limited companies limited by shares or by guarantee with a share capital; private companies limited by shares; private companies limited by guarantee with a share capital; private companies limited by guarantee; and unlimited companies).
- Bodies may also be incorporated by Act of Parliament, Royal Charter or company law of another country.

(VAT Notice 700/2/11, paras 6.1–6.3).

(2) Control

A body corporate is taken to control another body corporate in two sets of circumstances.

- If it is 'empowered by statute' to control the company's activities. 'Empowered by statute' means empowered by a provision contained in an Act of Parliament (*British Airways Board* (VTD 846) (TVC 32.3)).
- If it is the company's 'holding company' within the meaning of *Companies Act 2006, s 1159 and Sch 6*.

An individual or individuals shall be taken to control a body corporate if he or they, were he or they a company, would be that body's holding company.

[*VATA 1994, s 43A(2)(3); FA 1999, Sch 2 para* 2].

A company is a subsidiary of another company, its 'holding company', if

- that other company holds a majority of the voting rights in it;
- that other company is a member of it and has the right to appoint or remove a majority of its board of directors;
- that other company is a member of it and controls alone, pursuant to an agreement with other shareholders or members, a majority of the voting rights in it; or
- it is a subsidiary of a company which is itself a subsidiary of that other company.

[*CA 2006, s 1159 and Sch* 6].

Example

Holding Co Ltd owns 75% of the shares in Sub Ltd. The latter company owns 100% of the shares in Second Sub Ltd. Holding Co Ltd also has a joint venture arrangement whereby it owns 50% of the shares in Joint Ltd.

To date, each of the companies has been registered for VAT in its own right – but the group finance director now wishes to apply for a group registration to bring all four companies under one VAT umbrella.

There is no problem with Sub Ltd being part of the group registration as it is controlled by Holding Co Ltd because of share capital ownership. Equally, Second Sub Ltd is effectively owned by Holding Co Ltd as well through its relationship with Sub Ltd. However, Joint Ltd cannot be part of the group because it is not controlled by Holding Co Ltd. A separate company has the same level of control over the company (the joint owner) so the control test is not met.

(3) Established

A company is established in the UK if it has its principal place of business or registered office in the UK, which means if

- the central management and control of the company are carried on in the UK; or
- its headquarters or head office are in the UK.

A company will normally be established in only one country.

(VAT Notice 700/2/11, para 6.4).

(4) Fixed establishment

A company has a fixed establishment in the UK for VAT group purposes if it has a real and permanent trading presence in the UK. This would apply, for example, if it has

- a permanent place of business with the necessary human and technical resources to carry on its business activities; or
- a branch or office in the UK with its own staff and equipment.

For VAT group purposes, a company does not have a fixed establishment in the UK purely by virtue of the fact that

- it is incorporated and has its registered office in the UK;
- it has a simple brass plate presence in the UK; or
- it has a UK-based branch.

(VAT Notice 700/2/11, para 6.4).

(5) Specified body

A body corporate or limited liability partnership which is in, or applying to join, a VAT group is a specified body if all of the following conditions are satisfied.

(a) It carries on a relevant business activity (see (6) below). A dormant company cannot therefore be a specified body.

(b) The value of the group's supplies in the year then ending has exceeded £10 million or there are reasonable grounds for believing that it will exceed £10 million in the year then beginning.
Turnover is the value of all supplies made by the VAT group to persons outside the group whether (i.e. it excludes intra-group supplies) whether or not the place of supply is in the UK. This is the same as the definition for Box 6 of the VAT return. The expected turnover for the coming year should be determined on the assumption that the specified body applying to join the group is included in the group. If the body corporate is the sole general partner of a limited partnership, then the limited partnership's turnover is included. (VAT Notice 700/2/11, para 3.3).

(c) At any time when the relevant business activity is being carried on the body corporate concerned is

- not a 'wholly-owned subsidiary' of a person who controls all of the other members of the group (or, where the body corporate is or will be a member of the group, all of the other members apart from himself);
- managed, directly or indirectly, in respect of the business activity concerned, by a third party (see (9) below) in the course or furtherance of a business carried on by him; or
- the sole general partner of a limited partnership.

A body corporate is a 'wholly-owned subsidiary' of a person if it has no members except that other person and that other person's wholly-owned subsidiaries or persons acting on behalf of that other person or his wholly-owned subsidiaries. In determining whether a body corporate is a wholly-owned subsidiary of a person, the membership of

- any employee or director of the body, or
- where the body is a limited liability partnership, any member of the body

is disregarded.

(d) The body corporate is not

- a body corporate that controls all of the members of the VAT group (or, where it is a member of the group, all of the members apart from itself);
- a body corporate whose activities another body corporate is empowered by statute to control;
- a body corporate whose only activity is acting as the trustee of an occupational pension scheme (as defined by *Pension Schemes Act 1993, s 1*) established under a trust; or
- a charity.

[*SI 2004/1931, Arts 3, 7(3)*].

(6) Relevant business activity

A relevant business activity is one where

(a) the business activity involves making one or more supplies of goods or services to one or more members of the VAT group;
(b) those supplies are not 'incidental' to the business activity;
(c) at least one of those supplies is chargeable to VAT at a rate other than the zero rate (or would be if the body corporate was not in the VAT group); and
(d) the representative member is not entitled to credit for the whole of the VAT on supplies falling within (*c*) above as input tax (or would not be able to do so if the body corporate was not in the VAT group).

When applying this criteria to a body corporate which is already a member of the VAT group, it is deemed not to be a member.

[*SI 2004/1931, Art 4*].

'*Incidental*' has its normal meaning. In general, intra-group supplies are incidental to a business activity if:

- they are occasional or minor supplies made in connection with the activity;

- they do not employ a substantial proportion of the resources devoted to the activity; and
- they are not sufficiently separate from the main business activity to constitute a business activity in their own right.

HMRC give the example of occasional intra-group supplies made by a retailer whose business is mainly selling to the public.

(VAT Notice 700/2/11, para 3.4).

(7) Benefits condition

The benefits condition is satisfied unless 50% of the benefits of the relevant business activity (see (6) above) 'accrue', directly or indirectly, to one or more third parties (see (9) below).

The following are benefits of a business activity for these purposes.

(a) Profits (whether or not distributed).
(b) Charges for managing the business activity (including charges for providing staff to manage it).
(c) The amounts, if any, by which any other charges made to the body exceed the open market value of the goods or services concerned.

If there are no such benefits, any business activity is deemed to generate profits of £100.

Benefits that accrue to a person in his capacity as a member of a body corporate which controls all of the other members of the group (or, where the body is or will be a member of the group, all of the other members apart from itself) are not to be regarded as accruing to a third party.

If the specified body is the sole general partner of a limited partnership, then the benefits concerned are those arising from the limited partnership's business activity.

[*SI 2004/1931, Arts 5, 7(1)*].

Benefits do not include

- cost savings made by being a customer of the body corporate (e.g. price reductions, discounts or rebates); and
- under (*b*) above remuneration or bonuses paid to directors or employees of the body.

As regards (*c*) above, HMRC do not expect traders in normal commercial relationships to undertake extra work to verify that transactions are at open market value.

'*Accrue*'. Technically the benefits condition applies at a given time but profits, etc. are normally determined for a period (usually a year). They can be taken to accrue evenly over that period. Profits accrue to the persons who are expected to get the benefit in practice (e.g. side agreements between shareholders or expectations that profits are to be gifted to a particular person should be taken into account). If ownership of a company changes during the year, profits up to the point of change will normally accrue to the former owner (whether or not distributed to him).

(VAT Notice 700/2/11, para 3.5).

(8) Consolidated accounts condition

The consolidated accounts condition is satisfied if

(a) consolidated accounts prepared for the person who controls all of the other members of the group (or, where the person is or will be a member of the group, all of the other members apart from himself) would be required by 'generally accepted accounting practice' to include accounts for the specified body as his subsidiary; and

(b) consolidated accounts prepared for a third party (see (9) below) would not be required by generally accepted accounting practice to include accounts for the specified body as his subsidiary.

Where the specific body is the general partner of a limited liability partnership, then the consolidation condition applies to the limited partnership (e.g. the limited partnership must be consolidated as a subsidiary in the consolidated group accounts).

In applying this test at any particular time

- the reference to consolidated accounts is a reference to consolidated accounts for a period including that time and insofar as they relate to that time;
- any principle of generally accepted accounting practice that permits accounts of a subsidiary undertaking to be excluded from a consolidation as being immaterial are disregarded; and
- the reference to consolidated accounts prepared for a person is a reference to consolidated accounts of a kind that could be prepared for him in accordance with generally accepted accounting practice; and for this purpose it does not matter
  (i) whether accounts are actually prepared for him (whether for a particular period or at all), or
  (ii) in particular, whether he is required to prepare accounts.

  This covers the rare situations where a person controlling a VAT group with a turnover of over £10 million does not have to prepare consolidated accounts (e.g. where the only person controlling the VAT group is an individual or partnership).

'*Generally accepted accounting practice*' means the same as it does for corporation tax purposes. It is normal accounting practice in the UK. It means that the accounts should comply with UK Financial Reporting Standards (FRSs), in particular UK FRS 2 (Subsidiary undertakings), FRS 5 (Reporting the substance of transactions) and FRS 9 (Associates and joint ventures). From 1 January 2005, GAAP also includes consolidated accounts prepared to International Accounting Standards (IASs), e.g. IAS 27 (Consolidated and separate financial statements), IAS 28 (Investment in associates) and IAS 31 (Investment in joint ventures).

If more than one person controls the VAT group (e.g. there is a series of holding companies), condition (a) above only has to be satisfied by one of them.

The consolidated accounts provision has to be applied at a current date for which consolidated accounts will not yet have been prepared. In most cases, whether the condition is satisfied will be obvious from the most recent consolidated accounts unless there has been some significant change in the specified body since then. Where the position is not clear, HMRC will normally accept a professional accountant or auditor's statement that the specified body will be consolidated as a subsidiary in the accounts for the current period. [*SI 2004/1931, Art 6*]. (VAT Notice 700/2/11, para 3.6).

(9) Third party

For the purposes of (5), (7) and (8) above, a third party is any person or partnership except

(a) anyone who controls the body corporate and all of the other members of the group (i.e. the direct holding company and indirect holding companies up to the ultimate holding company);
(b) anyone controlled by a person in (a) above (which therefore includes all fellow subsidiaries);
(c) an individual who is an employee or director of the body corporate; and
(d) where the body corporate is a limited liability partnership, any individual who is a partner in the partnership.

Broadly speaking, therefore, any person outside the corporate group that includes the VAT group is a third party, except individuals working for the body corporate itself.

[*SI 2004/1931, Art 7(3)*]. (VAT Notice 700/2/11, para 3.3).

Transitional provisions at 27 July 1999

A company treated as a member of a VAT group under the eligibility rules applying before 27 July 1999 (see Tolley's VAT 2002 and earlier editions) continues to be treated as a member under the current rules even if no longer eligible (because it is not established or does not have a fixed establishment in the UK) until HMRC give notice terminating its treatment as a member of the group (see **27.3** below).

Divisional registration

Group treatment and divisional registration under **59.37 REGISTRATION** are mutually exclusive. A corporate body which is registered for VAT in the names of its divisions cannot have one of its divisions included in a VAT group. Similarly, a company that is a member of a VAT group will not be allowed to register one of its divisions separately outside the group. (VAT Notice 700/2/11, para 1.13).

Applications re group treatment and termination of membership

Applications

[27.3] An application can be made to HMRC for

(a) two or more eligible bodies corporate (see **27.2** above) to be treated as members of a group;
(b) another eligible body corporate to be treated as a member of an existing group;
(c) a body corporate to cease to be treated as a member of an existing group;
(d) a member to be substituted as the group's representative member (see **27.4** below); or
(e) the bodies corporate forming an existing group no longer to be treated as members of a group.

An application is taken to be granted with effect from the day on which the application is received by HMRC or such earlier or later time as HMRC allow. In practice, a grouping application is given immediate provisional effect from the date it is received (although HMRC then have 90 days in which to make enquiries and refuse it, see below). HMRC aim to respond within 15 working days of receipt to confirm the application has been approved and give the new VAT registration number. They will also confirm that the application has been successful or advise that further enquiries need to be made. HMRC should be contacted immediately if a new VAT registration number has not been received within 15 working days.

[*VATA 1994, s 43B(1)–(4); FA 1999, Sch 2 para 2, para 6(3)(5); FA 2004, s 20(4)*]. (VAT Notice 700/2/11, paras 2.6, 2.7, 2.12).

Making the application. The application must be made using the following forms.

Under (*a*) above	Form VAT 1 signed by the representative member Form VAT 50 (signed by either the applicant company or the person controlling the group) Form VAT 51 for each company applying to join the group (signed by the same person as the Form VAT 50)
Under (*b*) and (*c*) above	Form VAT 50 and a Form VAT 51 for each company joining or leaving the group
Under (*d*) above	Form VAT 56 (and Forms VAT 50 and VAT 51 if the new representative member is not already a member of the group)
Under (*e*) above	Form VAT 50 and a Form VAT 51 for each member of the group to be excluded

The completed application form should be sent to HM Revenue and Customs, Imperial House, 77 Victoria Street, Grimsby DN31 1DB.

Existing VAT registration numbers already held are cancelled in respect of new members forming a group. The group itself is allocated a new registration number (in the name of the representative member) which identifies the group as a taxable person. This number remains unchanged even if the membership is varied or the representative member changes. On the termination of the group treatment, the group registration number is cancelled. Any member still liable to be registered, or wishing to register voluntarily, is allocated a new number.

(VAT Notice 700/2/11, paras 1.8, 2.4, 2.5, 7.3, 7.4).

Retrospective effect

The wording of the legislation permits retrospective group registration but only within the discretion of HMRC and not a tribunal (*C & E Commrs v Save and Prosper Group Ltd,* QB 1978, [1979] STC 205 (TVC 32.4)). HMRC may give retrospective effect to an application to form a new group or amend an existing one by up to 30 days before the date on which the application is received by HMRC or, if later

- the beginning of the current VAT period of an existing group; or
- the beginning of the current VAT period of any of the companies applying to form, join or leave the VAT group.

Applications for retrospective group registration for periods longer than 30 days will only be allowed if

- HMRC lose an application and the applicant can supply details of its original application and attempts to follow it up; or
- if the delay was caused by lack of action on HMRC's part.

(VAT Notice 700/2/11, paras 2.13, 2.14).

Companies already members of another VAT group

Where

- an application is made under (*a*) above and at the time of the application one or more of bodies corporate is already a member of another VAT group, the application has effect but with the exclusion of that body or those bodies;
- an application is made under (*b*) above and the applicant body is already a member of another VAT group, the application has no effect; and
- a body is subject to two applications under (*a*) or (*b*) above that have not been granted or refused, the applications have no effect.

[*VATA 1994, s 43D(3); FA 2004, s 20(2)*].

Refusal of application

HMRC may refuse an application within 90 days of receipt

- under (*a*) above if the bodies corporate are not eligible to be treated as members of a group under the criteria in **27.2** above;
- under (*b*) above if the proposed additional member is not eligible to be treated as a member of the group under the criteria in **27.2** above; or
- under any of (*a*)–(*e*) above if necessary for the protection of the revenue.

[*VATA 1994, s 43B(5)(6); FA 1999, Sch 2 para 2; FA 2004, s 20(4)*].

HMRC have given the following as broad examples of where an application for group treatment may be refused, but the list should not be taken as exhaustive.

- The proposed group members have poor compliance records which might pose a threat to HMRC's ability to collect VAT.

- HMRC have reason to believe that the applicants intend to use the grouping facilities to operate a VAT avoidance scheme.
- Group treatment would create a distortion in the VAT liability of the group's supplies (e.g. where exempt supplies would become taxable with consequent increase in input tax recovery or where entitlement to recover previously irrecoverable input tax is increased).

(Business Brief 31/97).

Where application is refused, it will be treated as if it had never been made in the first place. As a result:

- If any of the proposed members were registered for VAT before applying for group treatment, the previous registration will be reinstated with effect from the date on which it was cancelled.
- If, during the period that a company was provisionally treated as a member of a VAT group, it would have been required to notify its liability to register for VAT, it will have 30 days after the date of the letter of refusal to register.
- If a company was not liable to register at the time it applied for grouping and it would not have become liable during the period when it was provisionally treated as a member of a VAT group, it can apply for voluntary registration after group membership has been annulled.
- If, while the application to join a VAT group was being considered, the group submitted a VAT return which included supplies made and received by any 'group' company, the representative member must correct the error by adjusting the return following HMRC's decision (if below an upper limit) or by submitting an error correction notification (formerly voluntary disclosure).

(VAT Notice 700/2/11, para 2.10).

'Protection of the revenue'

The protection in question may be against any loss of revenue which is not *de minimis* whether or not it follows from the normal operations of grouping. It certainly covers an artificial avoidance scheme but it also covers a straightforward case which would not be characterised as avoidance or abusive. The phrase must be considered in its totality and involves a balancing exercise in which HMRC must weigh the effect of refusal on the applicant (e.g. higher administrative costs) against the loss of revenue likely to result from grouping (*National Westminster Bank plc* (VTD 15514)). HMRC will not normally use their protective powers when they consider that the revenue loss follows from the normal operating of the group, i.e. because VAT is eliminated on supplies between group members. This includes any loss arising from supplies between group members being disregarded where the recipient would not normally be able to deduct that VAT because it makes exempt supplies.

If HMRC have concerns that the revenue loss goes beyond the accepted consequences of VAT grouping, they will ask for

- relevant information about the administrative savings that grouping brings in the particular circumstances, and
- an estimate of the revenue impact of grouping.

They will also normally ask for comment on the impact on the business of any refusal to allow grouping or removal of a company from the VAT group.

HMRC will make a judgement based on the information provided, and any other information that they have. If a business fails to provide the information requested, although HMRC will endeavour to come to a balanced decision based on the information that they have, some factors may not be taken into account and this may affect the outcome of their considerations. Consistent failure to provide information or records reasonably requested in the course of enquiries may be treated as sufficient grounds for exercising the revenue protection powers.

(VAT Notice 700/2/11, paras 4.1–4.4).

Appeals against HMRC's refusal

An appeal may be made against HMRC's refusal of an application under (*a*)–(*e*) above. See **5.3**(13) **APPEALS**. Where the refusal of the application is on the grounds of protection of the revenue, the tribunal's jurisdiction is supervisory in that it cannot allow the appeal unless it considers that HMRC could not reasonably have been satisfied that there were grounds for refusing the application. Any refusal has effect pending the determination of the appeal but, if the appeal is allowed, the refusal is deemed not to have occurred. [*VATA 1994, s 84(4A); FA 1999, Sch 2 para 4*].

Ceasing to satisfy eligibility criteria

If any member of a VAT group ceases to satisfy the criteria for group treatment under **27.2** above (e.g. by ceasing to be a subsidiary or ceasing to be established, or have a fixed establishment, in the UK) HMRC must be notified within 30 days of the change in circumstances. [*SI 1995/2518, Reg 5(2); SI 2000/794*]. This is effectively done in the application to HMRC for the company in question to cease to be a member of the VAT group. The application is taken to be granted with effect from the day on which it is received by HMRC or such earlier or later time as HMRC allow (see above). This means that, if the application is made *after* the company leaves the group, HMRC are not obliged to exclude the company as soon as it ceases to be a member. This was confirmed in *C & E Commrs v Barclays Bank plc*, CA [2001] STC 1558 (TVC 32.15) where HMRC were able to prevent the company leaving the VAT group before the introduction of the anti-avoidance provisions in **27.5** below. HMRC have confirmed that, as this could cause commercial difficulties, in practice their policy will be to agree the date requested by the selling group. They will set a later date only if VAT avoidance is involved or is otherwise likely to arise. (Business Brief 30/02).

Termination of membership by HMRC

Where a body corporate is treated as a member of a group and it appears to HMRC that the body is not, or is no longer, eligible to be so treated under the criteria in **27.2** above, they must give notice to that body terminating its treatment as a member of the group from a date specified in the notice. [*VATA 1994, s 43C(3); FA 1999, Sch 2 para 2; FA 2004, s 20(4)*]. The date specified can be earlier than the date the notice is given but cannot be *earlier* than the date on which, in HMRC's opinion, the body became ineligible to be treated as a member of the group. [*VATA 1994, s 43C(4); FA 1999, Sch 2 para 2*].

HMRC may also give notice to a body terminating its treatment as a member of a group from a specified date if it appears necessary for the 'protection of the revenue' (see above). The date specified can be the date the notice is given or any later date. [*VATA 1994, s 43C(1)(2); FA 1999, Sch 2 para 2*].

Appeals

An appeal may be made against any notice by HMRC terminating membership of a group. See **5.3**(14) **APPEALS**. Where the appeal is against

- notice of termination of membership due to ineligibility and the grounds for the appeal relate (wholly or partly) to the date specified in the notice, or
- notice of termination of membership on the grounds of protection of the revenue,

the tribunal's jurisdiction is supervisory in that it cannot allow the appeal unless it considers that HMRC could not reasonably have been satisfied that date was appropriate or, as the case may be, there were grounds for giving the notice.

In either case, the notice has effect pending the determination of the appeal but, if the appeal is allowed, the notice is deemed never to have had effect.

[*VATA 1994, s 84(4B)–(4D); FA 1999, Sch 2 para 4*].

Consequences of group treatment

[27.4] Group registration is a facilitation method which allows two or more corporate bodies to be treated as a single taxable person. One of the companies applying for group treatment is nominated as the representative member (see **27.3** above) and the registration is then made in the name of that member (VAT Notice 700/2/11, paras 1.3, 1.4).

The consequences of group treatment include the following.

(a) Any business carried on by a member of the group is treated as though carried on by the representative member.

(b) Subject to the anti-avoidance provisions in **27.5** below and the provisions relating to group supplies using an overseas member in **27.6** below, any supply of goods or services by a member of the group to another member of the group is disregarded for VAT purposes. This means that VAT need not be accounted for on these supplies and no VAT invoices must be issued in respect of them.

(c) Any supply not disregarded under (*b*) above which is a supply of goods (including a **SELF-SUPPLY (62)**) or services (including deemed supply) by or to a group member is treated as a supply by or to the representative member.

(d) Any VAT paid or payable by a group member on the acquisition of goods from an EU country or on the importation of goods from outside the EU is treated as paid or payable by the representative member and the goods are treated as having been acquired or imported by the representative member.

(e) Input tax recovery is determined in accordance with the use of the VAT group as a whole of the goods and services received by each individual member.

> *Example*
>
> Group member A buys in computer equipment and leases it to group member B, who uses the equipment to make exempt supplies to third parties outside the group.
>
> The input tax is attributable to exempt supplies and restricted (subject to the normal *de minimis* limits).

Input tax incurred by all the group members can be deducted to the extent that it is attributable to supplies made to persons outside the group which carry the right to deduct input tax.

(f) All members of the group are jointly and severally liable for any VAT due from the representative member. If the representative member is unable to meet a debt of the group, each member will be held liable for the amount of the debt until it is discharged. A former member is also liable for VAT due during its period of membership.

For liability of members when the representative member goes into liquidation, see **35.13 INSOLVENCY**, and where a corporate pension trustee is a member, see **53.3 PENSION SCHEMES**.

(g) Assessments can be validly raised on the representative member where relating to earlier periods when it was not the representative member and even if it was not a member of the group at that time (*Thorn plc* (VTD 15283) (TVC 32.22)). Also, under the anti-avoidance provisions in **27.5** below, current members of a VAT group may be held liable for assessments relating to periods when they were not members of the group.

(h) Most of the **PARTIAL EXEMPTION (49)** rules apply to a VAT group in the same way as they would to a stand-alone business. Therefore

- the *de minimis* limits apply to the group as a whole and not the members individually; and
- any change in the group members may have a significant effect on an agreed special method which may need revising.

Special care should be taken over a prospective member which makes any exempt supplies to ensure that the group as a whole does not suffer the loss of input tax through the partial exemption rules.

See also **27.7** below for special provisions where a partly exempt group acquires a business as a going concern.

(i) The limit for error correction notifications (formerly voluntary disclosures) applies to the group as a whole. See **56.11 RECORDS**. The representative member must be informed of any misdeclarations made by any other members of the group since joining it, and either
  - enter the amount to the group's VAT account; or
  - if necessary, make a single error correction notification (formerly voluntary disclosure) on behalf of the whole group.

(j) The cash accounting limits apply to the group as a whole and not to the members individually. See **63.2** and **63.7 SPECIAL SCHEMES**.

(k) The payment on account limits (see **51.4 PAYMENT OF VAT**) apply to the group as a whole and not to the members individually.

(l) Special provisions also apply under the capital goods scheme when a VAT group is formed or disbanded or there is a change in membership. See **CAPITAL GOODS (10)**.

(m) In *J & W Waste Management Ltd; J & W Plant & Tool Hire Ltd* (VTD 18069) (TVC 32.9) the tribunal held that VAT group membership does not imply abandonment of any right to appeal against demands for VAT. It specifically disapproved of the earlier decision in *Davis Advertising Service Ltd* (VTD 5) (TVC 2.83) that only the representative member has *locus standi* to bring an appeal.

The representative member is therefore responsible for

- accounting for any VAT due on supplies made by the group to third parties outside the group;
- completing a single VAT return and paying/reclaiming VAT on behalf of the whole group.

This is particularly helpful if accounting is centralised but group members will need to make sure that the representative member has all the necessary information to submit a VAT return for the group by the due date.

No taxable supplies outside the VAT group

The fact that no taxable supplies are made outside the VAT group does not prevent a group being formed provided one of the members is making taxable supplies which would make it liable or eligible for registration in its own right. However, as taxable supplies between group members are ignored, a group will not be able to recover any input tax unless it makes

- UK taxable supplies outside the group;
- supplies outside the UK that would be taxable supplies if made in the UK; or
- exempt financial/insurance supplies to customers outside the EU.

See **34.3 INPUT TAX** for fuller details.

> ***Example***
>
> Good Causes Ltd is a registered charity that owns a trading subsidiary called Good Causes Trading Ltd. Neither company is registered for VAT because their supplies are either outside the scope of VAT or exempt from VAT. However, Good Causes Ltd incurs costs on behalf of Good Causes Trading Ltd, and wants to make a management charge of £100,000 per annum for these services.

> The problem with the above situation is that Good Causes Ltd will need to charge output tax on the management services once it has exceeded the VAT registration limit (£73,000 per annum with effect from 1 April 2011) but Good Causes Trading Ltd will not be able to reclaim this VAT as input tax because it is not making any taxable supplies.
>
> However, the two companies could register for VAT as a group registration (the control conditions are met without any problem), which means that supplies of goods and services between group members are made without charging VAT.

'Special status' companies

The VAT liability of certain supplies, acquisitions and importations is dependent on the status of the person by or to whom the supply, etc. is made (e.g. education, water and certain supplies involving charities). In such cases, the VAT liability is decided by looking at the status of the person actually making/receiving the supply, even though for other VAT purposes the representative member is treated as making/receiving the supply.

[*VATA 1994, s 43(1)(1AA)(1AB); FA 1995, s 25; FA 1997, s 40(1)(3); FA 1999, Sch 2 para 1; FA 2004, s 20(4)*]. (VAT Notice 700/2/11, paras 1.5–1.7, 5.1, 5.5, 5.7–5.9, 5.12).

Anti-avoidance provisions

[27.5] HMRC may direct that

- separately registered companies eligible to be treated as members of a VAT group are to be treated as grouped from a specified date;
- a company within a group is removed from that group from a specified date; or
- a supply within a VAT group initially treated as a disregarded supply is to be subjected to VAT.

The provisions are designed for use only against certain categories of avoidance scheme which rely on the existence of the group registration provisions in *VATA 1994, ss 43–43C*. Features common to such avoidance schemes are that input tax deduction is taken against standard-rated supplies, but output tax does not fall on the full value of those supplies because they are treated to some extent as being made between members of the same VAT group and so are disregarded for VAT. The simplest means of bringing the disregard into play is by moving a company into or out of a VAT group at a critical moment. But a similar result could be secured by entering into some other transaction, such as the transfer of assets or the assignment of an agreement to or from a group member.

The detailed provisions are outlined below. HMRC have issued a Statement of Practice (SP) dated June 1996 setting out how they will seek to apply the provisions. Extracts are included in the text where appropriate.

Power to give directions

HMRC may give a direction if certain conditions are met. [*VATA 1994, Sch 9A para 1(1); FA 1996, Sch 1*]. Taken together, the conditions require that a relevant event causes a situation where standard-rated supplies, which have given rise to an input tax credit by any person, are not taxed on their full value, so leading to a tax advantage. The conditions are as follows.

(a) A '*relevant event*' has occurred, ie a company has either
  (i) joined or ceased to be a member of a group, or
  (ii) entered into any 'transaction'

  after that date. [*VATA 1994, Sch 9A para 1(2), para 4(2); FA 1996, Sch 1*].

  The word '*transaction*' is capable of a very wide meaning but, in the context of this provision, the key to its interpretation is that a relevant event occurs when a taxpayer *enters into* a transaction. Generally, HMRC will take this to mean when the taxpayer enters into a contract or other disposition, such as a gift. For example, HMRC will regard entering into a lease or the assignment, variation or surrender of a lease as a transaction which might potentially bring a company within the provisions. The performance of obligations under the lease (e.g. carrying out repairs or paying rent) would not normally be caught unless, exceptionally, such obligation constituted the entering into of a separate contract. (SP, para 3.5).

(b) There has been (or will or may be) a taxable supply on which VAT has been (or will or may be) charged otherwise than by reference to its full value due to the supply in question being disregarded under **27.4**(*b*) above. [*VATA 1994, Sch 9A para 1(3)(a)(9); FA 1996, Sch 1*]. Supplies which, although not disregarded under **27.4**(*b*) above, are less than full value for other reasons are not covered. HMRC could not, for example, compulsorily group the parties to a lease and leaseback agreement under arrangements that had nothing to do with the operation of an intra-group disregard. (SP, para 3.6).

(c) At least part of the supply in (*b*) above is not (or would not be) zero-rated. [*VATA 1994, Sch 9A para 1(3)(b); FA 1996, Sch 1*].

(d) The charging of VAT on the supply in (*b*) above otherwise than by reference to full value gives rise (or would give rise) to a tax advantage because a person has become entitled to
  (i) credit for input tax as attributable to that supply (or part of it); or
  (ii) a repayment of VAT under the provisions in **17.9 EUROPEAN UNION: GENERAL** or **48.5 OVERSEAS TRADERS** (refunds of VAT to persons in business abroad).

  [*VATA 1994, Sch 9A para 1(3)(c)(4)(5); FA 1996, Sch* 1].

  It is not essential that the right to credit or repayment should be that of the supplier of the undercharged supply. The legislation specifically provides that the condition is also fulfilled where the supplier acquires the goods and/or services VAT free under the provisions relating to the transfer of a business as a going concern, and the transferor (or some previous owner) of the business has been entitled to an input tax credit. [*VATA 1994, Sch 9A para 1(6)(7); FA 1996, Sch 1*].

(e) The requirements in (*b*)–(*d*) above would not be fulfilled apart from the occurrence of the relevant event.

(f) Where the relevant event is a transaction within (*a*)(ii) above, the supply on which VAT is undercharged must not be the only supply by reference to which the case falls within (*a*)–(*e*) above.

To pre-empt avoidance of the provisions, in determining whether the input tax credit is used to make an undercharged supply, separate rights to goods or services (including options or priorities in connection with goods or services), and the goods or services themselves are treated as a single supply. [*VATA 1994, Sch 9A para 1(8)(10); FA 1996, Sch 1*].

HMRC must not give a direction if satisfied that the main purpose, or each of the main purposes, of the relevant event was a genuine commercial purpose unconnected with the consequences in (*b*)–(*d*) above. This does not apply where the relevant event is the termination of a body corporate's treatment as a member of a group by HMRC under *VATA 1994, s 43C* (see **27.3** above). [*VATA 1994, Sch 9A para 2; FA 1999, Sch 2 para 5*]. This recognises the fact that, in the vast majority of cases, businesses are moved into and out of groups for reasons which have no avoidance motive whatsoever. However, it is important to realise that where, in addition to acceptable commercial purpose, HMRC also identify other main purposes indicating VAT avoidance, they will seek to use their powers to nullify that advantage. (SP, paras 3.11–3.13, Annexes 1–3).

Form of directions

A direction may take the following forms.

(i) That a supply of goods or services, in whole or part, from one company to another does not fall within **27.4**(*b*) above (where it otherwise would).

(ii) That for such periods as may be described in the directions a company is not to be treated as a member of a group (where it otherwise would). To the extent that the direction applies to VAT periods after the direction is issued, *all* supplies between that company and other group members are treated as taxable supplies. For events prior to the issue of the direction, see under the heading *Assessments* below.

(iii) That for such periods as may be described in the directions, a company is to be treated as a member of a group (where it otherwise would not). Such a direction may also identify the company which is assumed to be the representative member of the group for those periods.

Subject to the time limits below, the periods under (ii) or (iii) above may comprise times before the giving of the direction or times afterwards or both.

Where a direction requires any assumptions to be made, *VATA 1994* has effect from the date of the direction in accordance with those assumptions. (For periods before the date of the direction, the assumptions are given effect by HMRC raising an assessment for unpaid VAT, see below.)

The fact that HMRC have accepted or refused an application for a company to join a group does not prejudice their powers to make a direction to the opposite effect.

[*VATA 1994, Sch 9A para 3(1)–(6)(8); FA 1996, Sch 1; FA 1999, Sch 2 para 5*].

Withdrawal of direction

HMRC may withdraw a direction at any time by notice in writing to the person to whom it was given. [*VATA 1994, Sch 9A para 3(7); FA 1996, Sch 1*].

Time limits

A direction cannot be given more than six years after the later of

- the occurrence of the relevant event; and
- the time when the entitlement to input tax under (*d*)(i) or (*d*)(ii) above arose.

However, where a direction is appropriate, it can require assumptions to be made about transactions made before either of those times without any limit. [*VATA 1994, Sch 9A para 4(1)(3); FA 1996, Sch 1*].

HMRC will not, however, seek application of any direction from a date earlier than that required to nullify the tax advantage derived from the relevant event. Usually, this will be the first day of the VAT period in which the scheme commences or the relevant event occurs (whichever is earlier). (SP, para 3.18).

Method of giving directions

A direction relating to a supply under (i) above may be given to the person who made the supply and a direction relating to a company under (ii) or (iii) above may be given to that company. In either case, the direction may also be given to the representative member of the group. Any direction must be in writing and must specify the relevant event by reference to which it is given. [*VATA 1994, Sch 9A para 5; FA 1996, Sch 1*].

Assessments

Where a direction is given and there is an amount of unpaid VAT for which a 'relevant person' would have been liable based on the assumptions specified in the direction, HMRC may, to the best of their judgment, assess the amount of unpaid VAT as VAT due from a relevant person and notify their assessment to that person. The assessment may be incorporated in the direction. See **6.1 ASSESSMENTS** for interpretation of 'to the best of HMRC's judgment'. Where, however, HMRC are satisfied that the actual revenue loss is less than the unpaid VAT the amount assessed must not exceed the revenue loss (calculated to the best of their judgment). [*VATA 1994, Sch 9A para 6(1)–(5); FA 1996, Sch 1*].

'*Relevant person*' means the person to whom the direction is given, the representative member of the group to which that person was treated as being a member, or any company which, under the direction, is treated as being the representative member of such a group. [*VATA 1994, Sch 9A para 6(11); FA 1996, Sch 1*].

Calculation of VAT charge

- Where a direction is made under (i) above, VAT will become payable according to its value (adjusted as appropriate to take account of any direction issued under *VATA 1994, Sch 6 para 1* — supplies between connected persons, see **71.19 VALUATION**). A credit will be allowed for that part of the VAT which would have been deductible according to the partial exemption method of the VAT group registration.
- Where a direction is made under (ii) above, in relation to events prior to the issue of the direction, only those transactions relevant to the tax advantage will be affected. Input tax that would have been deductible on the basis of the assumptions in the direction can be taken into account in appropriate cases. All other supplies made by the parties involved will be unaffected so there will be no need for any retrospective VAT accounting adjustment in their regard.
- Where a direction is made under (iii) above, the purpose of the direction will normally be to enable HMRC to recoup any excess claim to input tax. In such cases, the amount of VAT to be charged will be the amount of input tax recovered less the amount which would otherwise have been recoverable in accordance with the partial exemption method of the appropriate VAT group registration. A credit will also be allowed in connection with any output tax charged between the parties which would not have been due according to the assumptions specified in the directive.

(SP, paras 3.18, 5.1–5.3).

The amount assessed and notified to a person is, subject to appeal, deemed to be an amount of VAT due and is recoverable, from that person or the representative member of the group, unless the assessment is subsequently withdrawn or reduced. To the extent that more than one person is liable for the same unpaid VAT under any assessment, they are each jointly and severally liable for the full amount. [*VATA 1994, Sch 9A para 6(7)(8); FA 1996, Sch 1*].

Time limit

An assessment under these provisions cannot be made more than one year after the date of the direction or in the case of any direction which has been withdrawn. [*VATA 1994, Sch 9A para 6(6); FA 1996, Sch 1*].

Supplementary assessments

Where it appears to HMRC that the amount which ought to have been assessed exceeds the amount actually assessed, a supplementary assessment of the amount of the excess may be made and notified under the same provisions and within the same time limit as the original assessment. [*VATA 1994, Sch 9A para 6(9); FA 1996, Sch 1*].

Interest payable

The provisions of *VATA 1994, s 74* on interest (see **51.15 PAYMENT OF VAT**) also apply to assessments under the above provisions, except that interest runs from the date on which the assessment is notified rather than the reckonable date.

The period for interest is confined to the two years ending with the time when the assessment to interest is made. [*VATA 1994, Sch 9A para 6(9)(10); FA 1996, Sch 1*].

Appeals against directions by HMRC

An appeal may be made against a direction by HMRC under the above provisions. See **5.3**(30) **APPEALS**. The tribunal must allow the appeal if satisfied that

- the conditions for making the direction were not fulfilled; or
- the main purpose, or each of the main purposes, of the relevant event was a genuine commercial purpose unconnected with the consequences in (*b*) above.

[*VATA 1994, s 84(7A); FA 1996, s 31*].

Following correction of a tax advantage

Following correction of a tax advantage to the satisfaction of HMRC, they will consider any subsequent application to join or leave a group subject to their normal powers of discretion. (SP, para 3.20).

De Voil Indirect Tax Service. See V2.190B.

Group supplies using an overseas member

[27.6] A supply between a member of a VAT group ('*the supplier*') and another member of the group ('*the UK member*') is not disregarded under **27.4**(*b*) above if the following conditions are satisfied.

(a) If there were no group, the supply would be a supply of services: (before 1 January 2010) falling within *VATA 1995, Sch 5*; or (after 1 January 2010) to which *VATA 1994 s 7A(2)(a)* applies, to a person belonging in the UK.

(b) Those services are not within any of the descriptions specified in *VATA 1994, Sch 9* (exempt supplies).

(c) The supplier has been supplied (whether or not by a person belonging in the UK) with any services: (before 1 January 2010) falling within *VATA 1994, Sch 5 paras 1–8* (see **65.22 SUPPLY: PLACE OF SUPPLY**); or (after 1 January 2010) *VATA 1994 s 7A(2)(a)* applied to the supply (see **65.15 SUPPLY: PLACE OF SUPPLY**), which are not within any of the descriptions specified in *VATA 1994, Sch 9* (exempt supplies).

(d) The supplier belonged outside the UK when it was supplied with the services in (*c*) above.

(e) Those services have been used by the supplier for making the onward supply to the UK member.

    The provisions apply even if the bought-in supply only forms a cost component of the onward supply to the UK group member but generally HMRC will treat bought-in supplies as *de minimis* if their value is less than 5% of the value of the onward supply. However, HMRC will not apply this rule rigidly (e.g. where they suspect that supplies or values have been manipulated to meet the 5% test or where, despite the fact that the 5% test is not met, the charge would be insignificant). The extent to which VAT on the charge could be recovered under the group's partial exemption method, along with the amount of the charge in the context of the group's size, will also be considered when deciding whether a potential charge is *de minimis*. (Business Brief 11/97).

Where the condition are met, the following consequences apply.

(1) The supply is treated as a taxable supply in the UK by the representative member to itself.

(2) Except as allowed by HMRC, the deemed supply by the representative member cannot be taken into account when determining its allowable input tax.

(3) The deemed supply is treated as a supply between connected persons for the purposes of any direction by HMRC as to open market value under *VATA 1994, Sch 6 para 1* (see **71.20 VALUATION**).

(4) Subject to (3) above, the deemed supply has the normal value rules for supplies subject to the reverse charge (see **38.4 INTERNATIONAL SERVICES**), i.e. it is calculated on the value of the supply by the overseas member to the UK member. However, by concession, the value may be reduced to the value of the services *purchased* by the overseas group member where
   - (i) evidence of this valuation can be produced in the UK;
   - (ii) those services have not been undervalued; and
   - (iii) the concession is not used for tax avoidance purposes.

   (VAT Notice 48, ESC 3.2).

   Under (i) above, where a service is bought in by an overseas group member for the exclusive use of a UK group member, copies of invoices from the external supplier are acceptable evidence. Alternatively, businesses may be able to agree with their VAT office that different evidence is adequate (e.g. evidence that the overseas group member buys in services and applies a fixed mark-up would normally be satisfactory evidence that the value of the bought-in service was equal to the value of the onward supply less the mark-up). Where services are not bought in for exclusive use or mark-ups vary, a fair and reasonable value must be calculated. HMRC have indicated that, in most cases, the evidence required to support the reduced value consists of a summary statement of the overseas member's costs; an outline of the basis on which the overseas member calculates its charge; and a record of the method for reducing the charge to an amount based on the bought-in supplies. (Business Brief 11/97).

Transfers of going concerns

Where a business or part of a business is transferred as a going concern and is treated as neither a supply of goods nor services under **8.10 BUSINESS** (or would be so treated if made in the UK), if the transferor satisfied conditions (*c*) and (*d*) above before the transfer and the services in question are used by the transferee to make the supply within (*e*) above, the services are deemed to have been supplied to the transferee at a time when the transferee belonged outside the UK (so that the above conditions are deemed to have been met). The conditions are also deemed to be met in cases involving successive business transfers.

[*VATA 1994, s 43(2A)–(2E); FA 1997, s 41; FA 2009, Sch 36 para 7*].

Interim payments

Where interim payments are made in respect of supplies subject to these provisions, VAT must be accounted for on each payment. If the group cannot calculate the reduced value of the charge by the time it has to account for VAT, it should account for VAT from month to month on a best estimate, making an appropriate adjustment at the end of the year.

Misdeclaration penalties

Failure to comply with the provisions may incur a misdeclaration penalty, subject to normal rules. See **52.12 PENALTIES**.

(Business Brief 11/97).

De Voil Indirect Tax Service. See V3.267.

Acquisition of a business as a going concern by a partly exempt VAT group

[27.7] Where a business, or part of a business, carried on by a taxable person is transferred as a going concern to any member of a VAT group and the transfer of any 'chargeable assets' involved is treated as neither a supply of goods nor a supply of services (see **8.10 BUSINESS**), then, subject to below, the chargeable assets are treated (at the time of the transfer) as being supplied to the representative member of the group for the purpose of its business and supplied by that member in the course or furtherance of its business. The supply is at the 'open market value' of the chargeable assets.

Assets are '*chargeable assets*' if their supply in the UK by a taxable person in the course or furtherance of his business would be a taxable supply (and not a zero-rated supply).

'*Open market value*' is the price that would be paid on a sale (on which no VAT was payable) between a buyer and seller who are not in such a relationship as to affect the price.

The above provisions do not apply if

(a) the representative member is entitled to credit for the whole of the input tax on supplies to it and acquisitions and importations by it during the VAT period in which the assets are transferred *and* any longer accounting period over which input tax is attributed under the partial exemption provisions;
(b) HMRC are satisfied that the assets were assets of the taxable person transferring them more than three years before the day on which they are transferred; or

(c) the chargeable assets consist of certain computers, computer equipment, land or buildings covered by the capital goods scheme (see **10.2 CAPITAL GOODS**).

A supply treated as made by the representative member under these provisions is not taken into account when determining the allowance of input tax for the group under the partial exemption provisions.

[*VATA 1994, s 44*].

HMRC may reduce the VAT chargeable under these provisions if they are satisfied that the previous owner did not receive credit for the full amount of input tax arising on the supply to him, or acquisition or importation by him, of the chargeable assets (e.g. because he was partly exempt or the input tax was blocked on the purchase of a car).

If the previous owner is unconnected with the VAT group, the open market value will normally be accepted as the consideration paid for the assets on which VAT is due. If VAT is not due on some of the assets, the consideration must be apportioned fairly between the standard-rated and other assets.

In a case where the seller's partial exemption recovery rate (during the partial exemption tax year in which the assets were purchased) is equal to or less than the purchaser's recovery rate (during the partial exemption tax year in which the assets were acquired), the VAT charge will be reduced to nil, although no VAT will be refunded.

(VAT Notice 700/9/08, paras 5.2–5.4).

De Voil Indirect Tax Service. See V3.246.

Surrender of corporation tax losses

[27.8] Under *CTA 2010, Part 5*, companies within a *corporation tax* group may surrender the benefit of corporation tax losses from one to another under certain circumstances. The company receiving the benefit usually makes a payment for the use of the losses. See *Tolley's Corporation Tax*. Where the two companies involved are also within the same VAT group the surrender has no VAT effect following **27.4** above. Where the two companies are not in the same VAT group HMRC have stated that group relief payments in themselves do not usually give rise to taxable supplies (CCAB Statement TR 344 June 1979). See, however, **44.3 MANAGEMENT SERVICES AND SUPPLIES OF STAFF**.

Holding companies

[27.9] The basic functions of a holding company are to acquire and hold shares in subsidiaries from which it may receive dividends; defend itself and its subsidiaries from takeovers; and make disposals. From time to time it may invest, deposit or lend money, and issue or sell shares. Some of these activities are outside the scope of VAT while others are exempt. A holding company which has no other activities is not eligible to register for VAT and is not able to recover any VAT on its purchases.

Registration

Holding companies are liable to register for VAT where they have taxable trading activities, supply management services to subsidiaries or are included in a VAT group with trading subsidiaries.

In *Cibo Participations SA v Directeur régional des impôts du Nord-Pas-de-Calais, ECJ Case C–16/00,* [2002] STC 460 (TVC 22.113) the ECJ held that the management of subsidiary companies could qualify as an economic activity if it was accompanied by activities such as the performance of administrative, financial, commercial or technical services. See also *Polysar Investments Netherlands BV v Inspecteur der Invoerrechten en Accijnzen, ECJ Case C–60/90,* [1993] STC 222 (TVC 22.106) and *Newmir plc* (VTD 10102) (TVC 7.116).

Input tax deduction

Subject to below, deduction of input tax for holding companies is calculated on the following basis.

- Input tax on supplies to the holding company must be attributed to taxable, exempt or other non-taxable outputs to the greatest possible extent, and the normal rules applied.
- Any residual input tax which cannot be directly attributed will be accepted as a general overhead of the taxable person.
- The amount of the residual input tax which can be recovered will be determined in accordance with the partial exemption rules.

Most costs related to acquisitions and defence against takeovers fall into the 'overhead' category.

However, where a VAT-registered holding company is not

- an active trading company in its own right, or
- grouped with active trading subsidiaries making taxable supplies outside the group, or
- providing genuine management services to separate trading subsidiaries,

it will not be able to recover input tax on costs incurred in acquiring another company, disposing of a subsidiary, restructuring the group or any subsidiary, or holding investments. This is because HMRC do not regard such costs as relating to any taxable supply. This change follows the decision in *Polysar* (see above) which held that the basic activities of a holding company are not business activities and there is no right to deduct the VAT incurred in carrying out such activities.

(C & E News Release 59/93, 10 September 1993).

In *Empresa de Desenvolvimento Mineiro SGPS v Fazenda Publica, ECJ Case C–77/01,* [2005] STC 65 (TVC 22.448) the ECJ held that the simple sale of securities (e.g. holdings in investment funds) did not constitute economic activities and that placement in investment funds did not constitute supplies of services effected for a consideration. As a result, turnover relating to such transactions should be excluded from any partial exemption calculation. However, the annual granting by a holding company of interest-bearing loans to companies in which it had shareholdings and placements by that holding company in bank deposits or in securities (e.g. Treasury notes or certificate of deposit) constituted economic activities carried out by a taxable person acting as such (and were exempt from VAT under what is now *Directive 2006/112/EC, Art 135(1)*). In any partial exemption calculation, such transactions were to be regarded as 'incidental transactions' insofar as they involved 'only very limited use of assets or services subject to VAT' and it was for the national court to establish whether this was the case.

See also *BLP Group plc v C & E Commrs, ECJ Case C–4/94,* [1995] STC 424 (TVC 22.399) where input tax on professional fees incurred in connection with the disposal of shares in a subsidiary company to pay debts was held as being not recoverable as relating to the exempt sale of shares (rather than recoverable as relating to the payment of debts derived from taxable transactions effected by the company).

Dividends and interest

Dividends received by a holding company from subsidiaries where there is no involvement in the management are to be excluded from total income in making any proportionate calculations (*Satam SA v Minister Responsible for the Budget, ECJ Case C-333/91,* [1997] STC 226 (TVC 22.443)). This was confirmed in *Floridienne SA v Belgian State; Berginvest SA v Belgian State, ECJ Case C-142/99,* [2000] STC 1044 (TVC 22.447) where the court also held that interest paid on loans to subsidiaries should be similarly excluded where the relevant loans did not constitute an economic activity of the holding company within what is now *Directive 2006/112/EC, Art 9(1)* (previously *EC Sixth Directive, Art 4(2)*). Whether the loans were within the charge to VAT was for the national courts to decide.

Key points

[27.10] Points to consider are as follows.

- A worthwhile advantage of group registration is that no VAT is charged on supplies of goods or services made between group members. This reduces the risk that supplies between connected companies could forget to take VAT into account where the entities are separately VAT-registered. A common error is for such recharges to be forgotten about when they are made by journal through inter-company accounts, or as a year-end adjustment by accountants. A group arrangement avoids this risk.
- For a group registration to be accepted by HMRC, the control test needs to be fully met. This means that joint venture arrangements (50:50 control between separate parties) will not be eligible for group registration.

- HMRC have the power to allow group registration on a retrospective basis but only in limited circumstances and where the backdating is 30 days or less. It is therefore important that a business identifies the benefits of a group registration in advance, e.g. to avoid a potential VAT liability on charges from a business to a connected party that is input tax blocked because of partial exemption.
- A holding company making management charges to its trading subsidiaries will have to charge VAT on these supplies if it is registered for VAT. This could lead to a source of non-claimable VAT if the recipient makes some exempt supplies. A group registration avoids this problem because no VAT is charged on supplies between entities within the same group.
- However, be aware of the need to consider input tax for the group as a whole and its relationship to supplies made to external customers. If input tax incurred by one group company relates to exempt supplies made by another group company, then the input tax will be classed as relevant to an exempt supply, i.e. partial exemption implications.
- It is important that a holding company registered for VAT is making genuine taxable supplies to its trading subsidiaries, e.g. for management services, consultancy fees, etc. If no taxable supplies are being made, the holding company should not be registered for VAT.
- There is scope for a group registration to be formed even if the only taxable supplies relate to management services between group members. This strategy will avoid output tax being charged on such supplies and therefore prevent non-reclaimable input tax being incurred by the recipient, e.g. in relation to exempt or non-business activities.
- Although HMRC tend to approve a request for group registration within 15 days, it is common practice for them to inform the applicant in writing about their power to make further checks of the application within 90 days of it being approved. In most cases, this statement will not cause a problem as long as the fundamental rules concerning group registration have been properly met and there are no anti-avoidance issues that cause a problem.

28

Health and Welfare

Cross-references. See **12.8** CHARITIES for charity funded equipment for medical and veterinary use; **18.25**(*b*)–(*e*), (*g*), (*h*), (*o*) and (*p*) EUROPEAN UNION LEGISLATION; **33.15**(5) IMPORTS for relief from VAT on the importation of various health-related goods.

De Voil Indirect Tax Service. See V4.146.

Introduction

[28.1] The UK's approach to exemption for health supplies is to link it to statutory registration of the relevant 'health professional'. By '*health professional*', HMRC mean the following professionals when they are enrolled or registered on the appropriate statutory register.

- Medical practitioners (see **28.3** below).
- Optometrists and dispensing opticians (see **28.4** below).
- Professionals registered under the *Health Professions Order 2001* (see **28.5** below).
- Osteopaths (see **28.5** below).
- Chiropractors (see **28.5** below).
- Nurses, midwives and health visitors (see **28.6** below).
- Dentists, dental hygienists, dental therapists, dental nurses, clinical dental technicians, dental technicians, orthodontic therapists (see **28.7** below).
- Pharmacists (see **28.9** below).

This means that therapists such as acupuncturists, psychologists, hypnotherapists and others who do not have statutory registers cannot currently exempt their services. (Psychiatrists are qualified medical practitioners and are exempt under **28.3** above.)

(VAT Notice 701/57/11, paras 2.1, 2.2).

Qualifying services

Historically, the UK's position was that where registered health professionals provided services using their professional training and knowledge, those services (with certain limited and specified exceptions) were exempt from VAT. This was taken to be the correct implementation of what is now *EC Directive 2006/112/EC, Art 132(1)(c)* which provides for the exemption of 'the provision of medical care in the exercise of the medical and paramedical professions as defined by the Member State concerned'. However, in *d'Ambrumenil v C & E Commrs; Dispute Resolution Services Ltd v C & E Commrs, ECJ Case C–307/01,* [2005] STC 650 (TVC 22.282) the ECJ defined the term 'medical care' for the purposes of the *Directive* as services having a therapeutic nature and examinations or other medical interventions of a preventative nature for persons not suffering from any disease or heath disorder. The effect of this is that exemption is limited to those services intended principally to protect (including maintain and restore) the health of individuals. Services not intended principally to do this should be taxable. Liability is therefore dependent on the principal purpose for which the supply is made.

UK legislation was amended with effect from 1 May 2007 to make it clear that services provided by registered health professionals can only qualify for exemption when consisting of medical care. General advice on registration, VAT liability and VAT recovery for those affected by the change is available in VAT Information Sheet 5/07 *Further information for health professionals affected by the changes to the exemption for medical services.*

The concepts of 'hospital and medical care' in *EC Directive 2006/112/EC, Art 132(1)(b)* and 'the provision of medical care' in *Art 132(1)(c)* are both intended to cover services that have as their purpose the diagnosis, treatment and, in so far as possible, cure of diseases or health disorders. See *Future Health Technologies Ltd v HMRC, ECJ Case C–86/09* [2010] STC 1836 (TVC 20.65).

Exemption for services

[28.2] Following the decision in *d'Ambrumenil* (see **28.1** above) HMRC regards services of a health professional as exempt when

(a) the services are within the profession in which he is registered to practise; and
(b) the primary purpose of the services is the protection, maintenance or restoration of the health of the person concerned.

Goods supplied with exempt services

HMRC also regard the exemption as extending to any charge made for bandages, drugs, medicines or prostheses, administered or applied to a patient in the course of exempt medical treatment. Any items that are separable from the treatment (e.g. privately dispensed drugs supplied for self-administration by a patient) are not exempt from VAT, and will normally be standard-rated. The supply of drugs, medicines and other items to patients by a pharmacist or doctor is zero-rated in certain circumstances (see **28.13** below).

Examples of exempt services

Health services provided under General Medical Services, Primary Medical Services, Alternative Provider Medical Services, Primary Care Trust Medical Services, General Dental Services and Personal Dental Services contracts

Sight testing and prescribing by opticians (only in England, Wales and Northern Ireland)

Primary eye examinations and secondary eye examinations (only in Scotland)

Enhanced eye health services

Laser eye surgery

Hearing tests

Treatment provided by osteopaths and chiropractors

Nursing care provided in a patient's own home

Pharmaceutical advice

Certain insurance or education-related services may be exempt regardless of purpose because they qualify under other exemptions (see below).

Examples of standard-rated services

Health services not performed by an appropriately qualified and registered health professional (except when either directly supervised by such a person (see **28.8** below) or provided within a hospital or similar institution (see **28.10** below)

Services not aimed at the prevention, diagnosis, treatment or cure of a disease or health disorder, such as paternity testing and the writing of articles for journals
Services directly supervised by a pharmacist
General administrative services such as countersigning passport applications and providing character references
Supplies of health professional staff, except where they are treated as being exempt from VAT under the nursing agencies' concession

(VAT Notice 701/57/11, paras 2.3, 2.5, 3.1).

Services that can be taxable or exempt

Some services may be taxable or exempt, depending on whether or not the primary purpose falls within (*b*) above. Some of the more common services are considered below. The services will normally be provided by doctors although some may be carried out by other registered health professionals. To avoid duplication, 'doctor' should be taken as including other health professionals where appropriate.

(1) Clinical trials

The supply is only exempt if it involves patient care, e.g. where the doctor is required to monitor a patient involved in the trial for adverse reactions which may be detrimental to his health. If involvement with the patient is restricted to monitoring side-effects for analytical purposes, or if the doctor is providing analytical testing services with no patient contact, the service is standard-rated.

(2) Access to medical records

In certain circumstances individual patients or their representatives are entitled to access to, or copies of, health records (including hand-written clinical notes, copies of letters to and from other health professionals, laboratory reports, X-rays and other imaging records, and printouts from monitoring equipment) or medical reports written about them.

- Under the *Data Protection Act 1998*, where the holder of the records receives a subject access request (SAR), it must provide the information requested but may make a charge for so doing. The maximum amount of the fee is a nominal sum to cover the expense of complying.
- Under the *Access to Medical Reports Act 1988*, a patient is entitled to ask for a copy of any medical reports made by his GP for insurance or employment purposes. Where such a request is made, the GP can charge a reasonable fee to cover costs incurred.
- Under the *Access to Health Records Act 1990* and the *Access to Health Records (Northern Ireland) Order 1993*, any individual's personal representatives, and anyone with a claim arising out of the death, may have access to the health records of the deceased. The record holder may charge a fee.

Where a doctor provides a copy of all or part of a medical record or report under these statutory requirements, that activity is outside the scope of VAT. But where a copy of a health record is provided in other circumstances, there is a standard-rated supply of services.

(3) Certificates and reports

Most supplies of certificates and reports are standard-rated because they enable a third party to make a decision and contain no element of therapeutic care (e.g. they may enable claims to compensation, benefits or registration as a blind or disabled person). But where the principal purpose of a certificate or report is to protect, maintain or restore the health of the individual (e.g. sick notes and certain reports required as part of adoption procedures) then the supply is exempt.

Fitness certificates were one of the supplies considered by the ECJ in the *d'Ambrumenil* case (see **28.1** above). It was held that exemption applied

- where the certificate was intended principally to protect the health of the individual such as the certification
  - (i) of fitness to travel; or
  - (ii) provided to an employer so that the employer recognises that the individual's health places limitations on certain activities (e.g. heavy lifting due to a severe back problem),

but that standard-rating applied

- to giving certificates as to a person's medical condition for purposes such as entitlement to war pension (see also *Unterpertinger v Pensionversicherungsanstalt der Arbeiter, ECJ Case C–212/01*, [2005] STC 678 (TVC 22.281) where the services of a doctor in making an expert report on a person's health in order to support a claim for disability pension was held to be subject to VAT);
- to the preparation of medical reports following examinations concerning
  - (i) issues of liability and the quantification of damages for individuals contemplating personal injury litigation; or
  - (ii) professional medical negligence for individuals contemplating litigation

  or the preparation of reports for these purposes based on medical notes without conducting a medical examination; or
- where certificates are provided as a condition of a person taking up a particular profession or sporting activity.

See also under Occupational health at (12) below.

(4) Psychologists' services

From 1 July 2009 practitioner psychologists became regulated by the Health Professionals Council, meaning that any supplies of medical care they make became exempt from VAT from that date. Practitioner psychologists come under seven domains: clinical, counselling, educational, forensic, health, occupational, and sport/exercise. Psychologists who work purely in academic research and experimental psychology and who do not offer services to the general public are excluded from regulation, meaning that there is no change in the VAT treatment of their services.

'Medical care' means any service relating to the protection, maintenance or restoration of the mental health of the person concerned. Medical care includes services such as counselling, working with children with emotional problems, dealing with criminals' behavioural problems or running stress management courses. It does not include supplies of time management services, which are not related to the mental health of the client.

(5) Cosmetic services

HMRC will generally accept that cosmetic services are exempt where they are undertaken as an element of a health care treatment programme. But where services are undertaken purely for cosmetic reasons, they are standard rated.

(6) Education services

Doctors carry out a wide variety of education-related activities. Before considering whether there is an exempt supply of healthcare, consideration should be given as to whether the services qualify as an exempt supply of education. For example, lectures given as part of a medical training course or as continuing professional development and training sessions to first aiders are exempt as a supply of private tuition where provided by a doctor in either a sole proprietor or partnership capacity. See **16 EDUCATION** generally.

Presentations aimed at promoting health are exempt but presentations given to a non-medical audience on, for example, the latest medical developments are considered to be standard-rated.

(7) Family planning

HMRC accept that services such as counselling, contraception and sterilisation (and reversals) are exempt.

(8) Forensic physicians

Where crime levels do not justify the appointment of a full-time forensic physician employed by the Home Office, and this work is undertaken as and when required by local doctors on a fees basis, HMRC accept that the principal purpose is to provide medical services to those requiring it and that there is a single supply of exempt healthcare. If a statement or report is required at a later stage, this is a separate supply which is standard-rated.

(9) Insurance services

Medicals and reports are requested by insurance companies for a broad range of insurance purposes. Some services, whilst forming a mandatory condition of the policy once accepted, have a therapeutic purpose and HMRC accept that the following medical services commissioned by insurance companies in principle qualify as exempt supplies of health.

- Health screening under private medical insurance policies.
- Medical services where the policy holder under an income/credit protection insurance has fallen ill (as opposed to losing his job) and which are aimed at assisting the individual in returning to a normal life.
- Medicals services provided under a motor insurance policy to assist in enabling an injured motorist to return to full health and/or work. (This does not include medicals undertaken for DVLA purposes to ensure initial or continued fitness to drive which are standard-rated).

- Any other medical service provided in connection with an insurance policy where the principal aim is to assist in restoring the health of the individual.

Where medicals and reports are provided in connection with the bringing together of parties to a contract of insurance, the administration of policies or the handling of insurance claims under such contracts, these services are exempt as insurance-related services. See **36 INSURANCE**.

Medicals and reports provided purely for the purposes of valuing policies for tax reasons (e.g. in relation to inheritance tax) are standard-rated.

(10) Medico-legal work

This includes such work as medicals, reports and expert witness testimony for the judicial system and is considered to be standard-rated, even where the ultimate decision arrived at by the court may concern the well-being of an individual. Medical evidence services that are outsourced administrative services, such as arranging the provision of expert witnesses and obtaining medical reports, are also liable to VAT at the standard rate.

(11) Mental health tribunals

These are panels of registered health professionals who determine whether a person should commence or continue being detained under the *Mental Health Act*. HMRC accept that services provided by way of the preliminary examination, observations and the tribunal sitting are exempt.

(12) Occupational health

Occupational health services are provided by individual doctors and a wide range of organisations with varying legal status. Broadly speaking, services provided in this field fall into the following categories with liability as indicated.

- Pre-employment medicals. These are taxable supplies as they are primarily for the purpose of enabling a prospective employer to take a decision on recruitment. This includes medicals (and reports) for the purpose of determining whether a person is medically fit enough to join a professional register. However, in most cases medicals now only take place once an applicant has been offered a job and a job offer is made conditional on the results of the medical. Again these medicals are taxable because they are primarily done so that the employer can make a decision on recruitment. Sometimes medicals are performed on successful job applicants to help determine the most suitable location for them to work within an organisation. As the medical is done primarily with the health interests of the successful applicants in mind, the employers having already decided to recruit them, such supplies are exempt.
- Post-employment medicals. Where these are to
  - (i) ensure a person is medically well enough to undertake proposed work activities,
  - (ii) assess whether proposed work could adversely affect a person's health and to make recommendations to minimise any risk accordingly, or

(iii) to determine whether early retirement on ill-health grounds is appropriate,

then the supply is exempt. But where the medical is undertaken to determine whether a person can join a pension scheme, the supply is taxable.

- In-service health screening.
- Risk assessments including advice on ergonomic layouts. These identify, quantify and advise on risk in the workplace. Whilst many are undertaken as a result of statutory health and safety requirements, they are generally not undertaken by health professionals in the exercise of their professions. As such, HMRC consider them to be standard-rated whether undertaken by a registered or non-registered health professional.
- Training and advice. This may qualify as an exempt supply of education (see (6) above), but otherwise essentially represents the occupational health provider's role in promoting and advising on health issues for the purposes of maintaining the good health of the company's employees. It is therefore considered to qualify for exemption as medical care.

(13) Rehabilitation services

These services are exempt if their principal purpose is to improve both the physical and psychological health of the individual. Reports commissioned for the purpose of determining what is required to assist rehabilitation and recovery are also exempt. Reports commissioned for the purpose of quantifying the additional costs of disability and hence, the value of any claims for compensation are liable to VAT at the standard rate.

(14) Statutory services

Doctors supply various services under various statutes. Where no fee is charged, there is no consideration and therefore no supply. Where a fee is charged, but the doctor is compelled by statute to provide the service, it will be outside the scope of VAT. In all other circumstances, the doctor will be making a supply by way of business, which may be taxable or exempt depending on the principal purpose of the supply. Examples of the type of services covered by statute include

- Registration of deaths. The medical practitioner attending a person during their last illness prior to death must issue a death certificate. No fee is chargeable.
- Public health legislation. A medical practitioner who becomes aware that a patient is suffering from a notifiable disease or food poisoning must issue a certificate to the local authority. The practitioner is entitled to make a charge for this but the supply is outside the scope of VAT.
- Legislation relating to coroners' services. Coroners can appoint a pathologist to carry out a post mortem if necessary. As the pathologist is compelled to accept this appointment, the charge made for this supply is outside the scope of VAT.

- *Supreme Court Act 1981*. A High Court may call in the aid of a specialist to give evidence of facts. As the specialist is required to attend where called, the charge made for attending (including any re-imbursement of allowances) is outside the scope of VAT.
- *Blood Test (Evidence of Paternity) Regulations*. Doctors are not obliged by statute to provide these services (although fees charged are set by statute). Fees charged are therefore consideration for a supply and are standard-rated.

(15) Witness testimony and allowances

Services of providing

- professional witness evidence (giving evidence of facts acquired as a result of a professional position and not covered by the *Supreme Court Act 1981* under (13) above), and
- expert witness evidence (giving an expert opinion)

for the courts are standard-rated. Allowances paid to doctors to cover their costs whilst appearing in court as professional or expert witnesses (including travelling and accommodation costs and reimbursement of a locum's charges) are regarded as part of the overall payment for the witness's services and are also standard-rated.

Allowances paid to doctors where they are called as an ordinary witness are considered to be outside the scope of VAT as they are called as a member of the public and not in their professional capacity.

(VAT Notice 701/57/11, paras 2.4, 2.6, 4.1–4.14).

Supplies of staff

Generally speaking, apart from the nursing agencies' concession mentioned below, all supplies of health professional staff are taxable for VAT purposes. An agent's commission, fee or any other charge made for arranging and administering the supply is standard-rated. Whether a supplier is acting as an agent or principal is determined by reference to the contractual and other arrangements.

Supplies of registered health professionals (other than nurses) by employment businesses acting as a principal

The *Employment Agencies Act 1973* defines an 'employment business' as a 'business (whether or not carried on with a view to profit and whether or not carried on in conjunction with any other business) of supplying persons in the employment of the person carrying on the business, to act for, and under the control of, other persons in any capacity'. Staff supplied by an employment business may be either employees of that business, or self-employed and engaged by that business. In both cases the workers' services are provided to the employment business, which in turn makes a supply of that worker to the client. If the worker comes under the direction and control of the client, this is a supply of staff. The employment business in these circumstances is acting as the 'principal'. When an employment business supplies registered health professionals (other than staff subject to the nursing agencies' concession below) as a principal to a third party, where the health professional is working under the control and guidance of the third party, it is making a taxable supply of staff to that third party – not an exempt supply of healthcare. It is the third party which is responsible for providing healthcare to the final patient, rather than the business supplying the staff which has no such responsibility. A taxable supply of staff is made even where the employment business is responsible for ensuring that the workers it provides are properly trained and qualified when they work under the control of the third party. However, if the employment business maintains the direction and control of its health professional staff to make a supply of medical care directly to a final consumer, then the employment business is providing medical services rather than merely a supply of staff. In these circumstances, the business is making an exempt supply of health services.

Supplies of self-employed locum GPs

When self-employed locum GPs supply their services to an employment business which makes an onward supply to a third party who is legally responsible for providing health care to the final patient, both the supplies to and from the employment business are taxable. The fact that the locum GPs may be supplied to a prison or other institution where they may not be supervised by any medical staff does not mean that the employment business supplying the locum doctor to the third party is legally responsible for providing healthcare to the final patient.

Supplies of nurses, nursing auxiliaries and care assistants by state-regulated agencies (the nursing agencies' concession)

By an informal extra-statutory concession, nursing agencies (or employment businesses that provide nurses and midwives, as well as other health professionals) may exempt the supply of nursing staff and nursing auxiliaries supplied as a principal to a third party, if the supply is of

- a person registered in the register of qualified nurses and midwives maintained under the *Nursing and Midwifery Order 2001, Art 5* providing medical care to the final patient;
- an unregistered nursing auxiliary who is 'directly supervised' by one of the above; or
- an unregistered nursing auxiliary, whose services are supplied to a hospital (NHS or private), hospice, care home with nursing under *VATA 1994, Sch 9 Group 9 item 4* and form part of the care made to the patient.

A nursing auxiliary (also known as a healthcare assistant) is an individual who is not enrolled on any register of medical or health professionals but whose duties must include the provision of medical, as well as personal, care to patients. The institution to which staff are supplied may be operated by a local authority, NHS body, charity or other organisation operating in the public or private sector. To qualify for the concession, the employment business must be registered with one of the following organisations.

- Scottish Commission for the Regulation of Care
- Care Standards Inspectorate for Wales

- Northern Ireland Health and Personal Social Services Regulation and Improvement Authority
- Care Quality Commission (for supplies before 1 October 2010)

In England, with effect from 1 October 2010 (as a result of changes announced in the *Health and Social Care Act 2008*), the legal requirement for nursing agencies to be registered under the Care Quality Commission ceased and responsibility for quality standards has passed to those organisations that provide the regulated activity. Therefore for supplies on or after 1 October 2010, the concession applies to employment business that would have been required to be registered with the Care Quality Commission before that date.

For the supply of nursing auxiliaries or care assistants to benefit from the concession, they must undertake some direct form of medical care, such as administering drugs or taking blood pressures, for the final patient. The concession does not apply to supplies of general care assistants who are

- only involved in providing personal care such as catering, washing or dressing the patients;
- working in care homes without nursing where they do not require supervision by health professionals to provide their services.

However, where a state-regulated domiciliary care agency supplies the services of its care assistants directly to the final patient, HMRC would see the agency as making an exempt supply of welfare services.

Wording of terms and conditions of agreements

Some employment businesses state in their contract terms that their staff are still working under their control and direction rather than the third party to which their staff are being supplied. If that is the case, the business is not acting as an 'employment business' within the definition of the *Employment Agencies Act 1973*. The VAT liability of a supply is not determined conclusively by the terms of any contract or other documentation alone. If the wording of a contract does not reflect any changes in the way that the business actually operates in practice, the VAT liability of a taxable supply of staff will not change.

Supplies of contracted-out health services

As is clear from above, employment businesses in the health sector make a taxable supply of staff to third parties, such as hospitals or hospices, if the third party is legally responsible for the onward supply of providing care to the final recipient. This is subject to the nursing agencies' concession. The mere fact that an employment business is state-regulated does not mean that its supplies of staff are exempt if they are not covered by the nursing agencies' concession. However, when state-regulated health providers provide health services to the final consumer, these services remain exempt even if they are contracted out and paid for by a hospital or other third party.

(VAT Notice 701/57/11, para 6).

Doctors

[28.3] The supply of services (with effect from 1 May 2007, consisting in the provision of medical care) by a person registered or enrolled on the register of medical practitioners is exempt. [*VATA 1994, Sch 9 Group 7 Item 1(a); SI 2006/1914; SI 2007/206*].

See **28.1** and **28.2** above for an overview of the conditions for exemption and the liability of various services supplied by health professionals and, in particular, doctors.

NHS work

GP practices receive a monthly Statement of Fees of NHS payments due to the practice. All of these payments (other than accounting or timing adjustments) are consideration for the practice's supplies of medical services.

Payments are liable to VAT depending on their principal purpose and according to the principles and guidance outlined in **28.1** and **28.2** above. Thus, payments relating to activities where the principal purpose is the protection, maintenance or restoration of the health of the patient (before 1 May 2007, the care, diagnosis, treatment or assessment of a patient) are payments for exempt supplies. Examples include payments relating to anti-coagulant monitoring, childhood immunisations, flu and pneumococcal vaccinations. However, payments in relation to services such as the completion of forms to enable persons to obtain blue/orange disability badges are liable to VAT at the standard rate.

'General' payments and reimbursements of practice costs (e.g. General Medical Services global sum, Minimum Practice Income Guarantee correction factor, computer costs, notional rent) are also payments directly related to exempt services unless the practice has dispensing activity, in which case they cover taxable and exempt supplies.

(VAT Notice 701/57/11, para 7.1).

Payments for dispensing

GPs can, in certain cases, be authorised to dispense drugs to particular patients. Payments received from the NHS for items dispensed to those patients are zero-rated under *VATA 1994, Sch 8 Group 12 Item 1* (see **28.13** below).

Fees for private dispensing are always standard-rated.

(VAT Notice 701/57/11, para 7.4).

Payments for personally administering drugs

All GPs can administer drugs at the time of treatment (whether or not they are also NHS dispensing GPs). HMRC have always taken the view that drugs and other items (e.g. vaccines, anaesthetics, injections, diagnostic reagents, intra-uterine, contraceptive caps and diaphragms, and pessaries) personally administered ('immediately administered' in Scotland) to the patient by the doctor at the time of treatment are an inseparable part of the exemption for medical care under *VATA 1994, Sch 9 Group 7 Item 1(a)* above. This was confirmed in *C & E Commrs v Dr Beynon & Partners*, HL 2004, [2005] STC 55 (TVC 19.8) (reversing the earlier tribunal decision in *Drs Woodings, Rees, Crossthwaite & Jones* (VTD 16175) (TVC 19.7)). Applying the principles laid down in *Card Protection Plan Ltd v C & E Commrs, ECJ Case C–349/96*, [1999] STC 270 (TVC 22.324), the court held that, where drugs are administered at the time of treatment, there is a single supply of exempt services, the transaction being the patient's visit to the doctors which should not be split into smaller units.

Deputising services to doctors

The provision of a deputy for a person registered in the register of medical practitioners is exempt. [*VATA 1994, Sch 9 Group 7 Item 5; SI 2006/1914*].

Visiting EU practitioners

Included in the exemption under *VATA 1994, Sch 9 Group 7 Item 1(a)* is the supply of services in an urgent case as mentioned in the *Medical Act 1983, s 18(3)* by a person who is not registered in the visiting EU practitioners list in the register of medical practitioners at the time he performs the services but who is entitled to be registered in accordance with that *section*. [*VATA 1994, Sch 9 Group 7 Note 4*].

This covers the situation where a medical practitioner registered in another EU country visits the UK to treat a patient but has not been able to enrol on one of the UK statutory medical registers prior to the visit. In such a case, his services of treating a patient in the UK is exempt provided that he

- is eligible to be included on the statutory register of medical practitioners with limited registration; and
- submits the necessary enrolment documentation to the relevant body as soon as possible after the treatment.

(VAT Notice 701/57/11, para 9.1).

Opticians

Overview

[28.4] The supply of services by a qualified optician is exempt (see below). Exemption can also extend to the services of unqualified staff if they are directly supervised by a qualified optician (see **28.8** below). But the supply of spectacles and contact lenses is standard-rated (see below). As the charge for spectacles or contact lenses normally includes an element for services, an apportionment is required.

Supplies of services

The supply of services (with effect from 1 May 2007, consisting in the provision of medical care) by persons registered in

- either of the registers of ophthalmic opticians or the register of dispensing opticians kept under the *Opticians Act 1989*, or

- either of the lists under *section 9* of that *Act* of bodies corporate carrying on business as ophthalmic opticians or as dispensing opticians

is exempt. [*VATA 1994, Sch 9 Group 7 Item 1(b); SI 2007/206*].

See **32.1** to **32.3** above for an overview of the conditions for exemption and the liability of various services supplied by health professionals in general.

Supplies of spectacles

Supplies of spectacles are standard-rated unless the goods are certain specialised appliances designed solely for use by the handicapped (e.g. artificial eyes and certain low vision aids), in which case they are zero-rated (see **28.21** below). Supplies of ancillary goods (e.g. cases, cleaning solution) are also standard-rated.

In *C & E Commrs v Leightons Ltd*, QB [1995] STC 458 (TVC 33.8), the court held that the price paid for spectacles includes two separate supplies – a standard-rated supply of goods (the spectacles) and an exempt supply of opticians' services. Although this decision pre-dated the criteria for single/multiple supplies set out by the ECJ in *Card Protection Plan Ltd v C & E Commrs, ECJ Case C–349/96*, [1999] STC 270 (TVC 22.324) (see **64.6 SUPPLY: GENERAL**) a tribunal has subsequently accepted that the decision in *Leightons* was correct in law and that payments should be apportioned (*Leightons (No 2); Eye-Tech Opticians (No 3)* (VTD 17498) (TVC 33.9)).

There are no set methods of apportionment of spectacle sales between exempt and standard-rated elements. If practicable, opticians should calculate VAT by separating the standard-rated and exempt elements at the point of sale. If this is not possible, an individual method must be agreed with HMRC which gives a fair and reasonable valuation of VAT payable without placing an undue burden on the optician.

The following is the suggested method of apportionment based on full cost apportionment.

(1) Establish the cost of goods

This is made up of the following.

- Cost of purchase of bought-in frames.
- Cost of purchase of bought-in lenses. (Where, rather than buying in lenses cut to individual patients' prescriptions, a business purchases blank lenses and glazes them in-house, establish the cost of glazing and the directly attributable expenses incurred on consumables. Indirect costs such as depreciation of equipment should not be included.)
- Cost of delivery if the business has frames/lenses delivered from a central point of distribution to a chain of outlets. (The cost must be apportioned where the delivery charge also relates to other goods such as cases, chains, contact lens fluids, etc.)

These costs should include any VAT.

(2) Establish the cost of services

This is made up of the following.

- 'Direct costs' of any ophthalmic optician (OO) relating to spectacle sales. An OO is allowed to carry out sight tests as well as dispense spectacles. Eye tests have always been exempt and opticians need to determine what proportion of the cost of an OO is attributable to the exempt eye test and what proportion is to be attributed to the exempt dispensing service element of spectacle sales. In some practices, the OO may also perform various administrative activities. If the actual costs attributable to each activity are not identifiable, the total costs will need to be apportioned, possibly using the formula

$$\frac{\text{Income from spectacles}}{\text{Income from spectacles} + \text{contact lenses} + \text{sight tests}} \times \text{direct cost of OO}$$

  This formula may not be appropriate for all opticians and alternatives may be agreed with HMRC. For example, if an OO spends half his time providing eye examinations and the other half dispensing, it would be more appropriate simply to use half the costs for the purposes of the apportionment calculation. An optician who considers that factors other than time should be taken into account in the apportionment should identify those factors and submit an appropriate apportionment method for HMRC's approval.

  In general, HMRC are prepared to accept that an element of an OO's time is spent on dispensing activity. The actual level of dispensing activity should be demonstrated and agreed with HMRC.
- 'Direct costs' of any dispensing optician (DO). The direct labour costs to the practice of the time that any DO spends in the dispensing of spectacles must be calculated.
- 'Direct costs' of directly supervised persons. A proportion of the direct labour costs of those unqualified employees providing a dispensing service, and who either work as part of a qualifying body corporate or who are directly supervised by a registered optician (see **28.8** below) may also be included in the calculation. The actual percentage of these costs relating to dispensing duties must be agreed between the trader and HMRC.

'*Direct costs*' should be calculated using conventional accounting procedures. In calculating the direct cost of OOs, DOs and directly supervised persons, the following principal costs should be included (although this is not necessarily an exhaustive list).

- Salary
- Employers' national insurance contributions
- Pension contributions by employer
- Cost of provision of vehicle to OOs and DOs involved in dispensing of spectacles
- Optical training of opticians and supervised persons
- Professional body subscriptions incurred by the practice (only in respect of services received, not goods)
- Professional indemnity costs incurred by the practice
- Recruitment costs

These costs should include any VAT.

(3) Calculation of percentage of income from spectacle sales attributable to taxable supplies

Once the above costs of goods and services have been calculated, it is necessary to establish the average cost of each supply. This is achieved by dividing the costs of the goods and services by the number of spectacles (new and re-glazed) dispensed in the period.

The taxable element of the sale is then calculated using the formula

$$\text{VAT due on sale} = \frac{\text{Cost of goods}}{\text{Cost of goods and services}} \times \text{spectacles income} \times \frac{7}{47}$$

Having established the percentage applicable to taxable sales, this percentage should be used as the basis of the optician's VAT return. As businesses change over time, the percentage should be recalculated whenever a major change takes place in the optician's business, and in any case at three-yearly intervals. HMRC consider a 'major change' as constituting anything which significantly alters the costs of the supplies including

- opening an additional branch or closing an existing one;
- increasing or decreasing the number of OOs, DOs or supervised staff employed;
- restructuring the practice (e.g. where an OO who has previously performed both eye examinations and dispensing services exclusively performs eye examinations); and
- changing from buying in lenses to glazing in-house (or vice versa).

New business

When a new practice opens, it is not possible to immediately perform an accurate apportionment of the charges made for spectacles and dispensing, particularly if the apportionment method is based on costs. New practices should therefore agree a provisional basis of apportionment with HMRC and revise the apportionment in the light of actual costs at the end of the first year's trading.

(VAT Information Sheet 8/99).

Supplementary professions, osteopaths and chiropractors

EU law

[28.5] Under *Directive 2006/112/EC, Art 132(1)(c)*, EU countries must exempt the provision of medical care in the exercise of the paramedical professions as defined by the EU country concerned. See *Solleveld and another v Staatssecretaris van Financiën, ECJ Cases C–443/04 and C–444/04*, [2001] STC 71 (TVC 22.284) for a consideration of how countries must apply their discretion in applying exemption.

UK law

The supply of services (with effect from 1 May 2007, consisting in the provisions of medical care) by persons on the following registers is exempt. See **28.1** and **28.2** above for an overview of the conditions for exemption and the liability of various services supplied by health professionals in general.

- Any register kept under the *Health Professions Order 2001* (*SI 2002/254*). [*VATA 1994, Sch 9 Group 7 Items 1(c); SI 2002/254; SI 2007/206; SI 2009/1182, Sch 2 para 16(d)*]. These professionals are
  arts therapists;
  biomedical scientists;
  chiropodists/podiatrists;
  clinical scientists;
  dieticians;
  hearing aid dispensers;
  occupational therapists;
  operating department practitioners;
  orthoptists;
  paramedics;
  physiotherapists;
  practitioner psychologists (from 1 July 2009);
  prosthetists and orthotists;
  radiographers; and
  speech and language therapists.
  (VAT Notice 701/57/11, para 2.1).
  Any drugs, appliances etc. which are administered by the above practitioners at the time of treatment are considered a minor and inseparable part of their professional service and also exempt.
  Standard-rating applies to
  - supplies of goods which are not minor and inseparable; and
  - supplies by practitioners who are not registered under the *Health Professions Order 2001* (e.g. acupuncturists, psychologists, psychotherapists and psychoanalysts). (Psychiatrists are qualified medical practitioners and are exempt under **28.3** above.)
- The register of osteopaths maintained in accordance with the provisions of the *Osteopaths Act 1993*. [*VATA 1994, Sch 9 Group 7 Items 1(ca); SI 1998/1294; SI 2007/206*].
- The register of chiropractors maintained in accordance with the provisions of the *Chiropractors Act 1994*. [*VATA 1994, Sch 9 Group 7 Items 1(cb); SI 1999/1575; SI 2007/206*].

Nurses, midwives and health visitors

[28.6] The supply of services (with effect from 1 May 2007, consisting in the provision of medical care) by a person registered in the register of qualified nurses, midwives and health visitors kept under *Nurses, Midwives and Health Visitors Act 1997, s 7* is exempt. [*VATA 1994, Sch 9 Group 7 Item 1(d); Nurses, Midwives and Health Visitors Act 1997, Sch 4; SI 2007/206*].

See **28.1** and **28.2** above for an overview of the conditions for exemption and the liability of various services supplied by health professionals in general.

Exemption only applies to the professional services for which the nurse, etc. has been trained. HMRC do not accept that, for example, a nurse can exempt supplies of acupuncture or osteopathy under this provision.

Dentists, etc.

[28.7] The supply of

(a) any services (with effect from 1 May 2007, consisting in the provision of medical care) or dental prostheses by
- a person registered in the dentists' register, or
- a person registered in the dental care professions register established under *Dentists Act 1984, s 36B*, or

(b) any services or dental prostheses by a dental technician

is exempt. [*VATA 1994, Sch 9 Group 7 Items 2, 2A; SI 2005/2011, Sch 6 para 3; SI 2007/206*].

Exemption covers drugs or appliances provided in the course of dental care and treatment but items, other than prostheses, that are separable from dental treatment provided to a patient are normally standard-rated (e.g. toothbrushes, toothpaste and dental floss).

Dental prostheses

These include dentures, artificial teeth, crowns, bridges, palates and other orthodontic appliances.

Advisory services

Services such as advising on clinical governance, poor performance and standards supplied on a *self-employed basis* by dentists to Primary Care Trusts are standard rated. Where such services are provided on an *employee* basis, any income received is outside the scope of VAT.

Cosmetic dentistry services

These must be considered on a case-by-case basis and are exempt only where supplied as an element of oral health treatment by a registered health professional.

(VAT Notice 701/57/11, para 10.1).

Supplies between dentists in the same practice

Where there is more than one dentist within a practice operating from the same premises, there may be payments between the dentists in respect of shared facilities, equipment, prostheses and staff. Such charges are exempt if relating to services or facilities that are predominantly medical in nature and are necessary to allow the recipient to perform dentistry. This exemption does not apply to

- any supplies made by a dentist who has ceased to practise, or by a landlord who is not a dentist;
- supplies of goods (other than dental prostheses) that are held out for sale to patients (e.g. toothpaste and toothbrushes); or
- any sales of dental equipment by a practice owner.

See HMRC VAT Guidance V1-7 Chapter 22, para VATHLT2520 for the four main types of agreements under which dentists may co-operate in a practice (according to model agreements issued by the British Dental Association) and the VAT consequences of each.

(VAT Notice 701/57/11, para 10.2).

Services performed by persons not registered, etc.

[28.8] Health and nursing care services performed by a person not enrolled on a statutory medical register can be exempt in some circumstances but only when provided

- under the direct supervision of certain health professionals (see below); or
- in a hospital or nursing home (see **28.10** below).

(VAT Notice 701/57/11, para 5.2).

Supervised services

Supplies of services made by a person who is not registered or enrolled in any of the registers or rolls specified in **28.3** to **28.6** or **28.7**(*a*) above are exempt where the services are 'wholly performed' or 'directly supervised' by a person who is so registered or enrolled. [*VATA 1994, Sch 9 Group 7 Note 2*].

See **28.1** and **28.2** above for limitations on the services which are exempt.

'Wholly performed'

This covers, for example, the situation where a company (which is not a 'person registered or enrolled') makes the supply but uses the services of its medically qualified staff (e.g. a company employing registered chiropodists).

'Directly supervised'

HMRC require all the following conditions to be satisfied.

(1) The services are supervised by one of the registered health professionals listed in **28.1** above (other than a hearing aid dispenser or pharmacist), and the supervisor is professionally qualified to perform and supervise the service.
(2) The service requires supervision by a registered health professional, and is provided predominantly to meet the medical needs of a client.
(3) The supervisor has a direct relationship with the staff performing the service, and is contractually responsible for supervising their services.
(4) A qualified supervisor is available for the whole time that the care service is provided.

(5) No more than 2000 hours per week of staff time are supervised by a single health professional.
(6) A supervisor has a say in the level of care to be provided to the client, and will usually see the client prior to the commencement of the care service.
(7) The supervisor must be able to demonstrate that he monitors the work of the unregistered staff.

Where the above conditions are not met, the services are standard-rated, even when performed to meet the medical or health care needs of a client.

(VAT Notice 701/57/11, para 5.3).

The above guidelines were considered in detail in *Land (t/a Crown Optical Centre)* (VTD 15547) (TVC 33.6) where the tribunal held that an unqualified dispenser of spectacles, and his unqualified staff, were directly supervised by an ophthalmic medical practitioner who performed eye tests in the shop on five half-days a fortnight. On the evidence, the tribunal held that the supplies were supervised even though there was no explicit contract requiring the supervisor to undertake this task (as required by HMRC, see condition (3)). The tribunal observed that, although a contract may be valuable evidence of responsibility, its absence did not prove that there was no responsibility. On the evidence, supervision was an implicit term of the relationship.

See also *A & S Services* (VTD 16025) (TVC 33.25).

Supervision does not necessarily require the supervisor continually to observe the unqualified person or necessarily be on the same premises provided there is a check as often as the circumstances require and a system for that person to contact the supervisor. Supervision is 'direct' if carried out on a one-to-one basis without an intermediary. (*Elder Home Care Ltd* (VTD 11185) (TVC 33.4)). See also *M G Parkinson* (VTD 6017) (TVC 33.3).

VATA 1994, Sch 9 Group 7 Note 2 above does not exempt services of complementary practitioners, who do not appear on any statutory register, to whom patients are referred by consultants or medical practitioners. Neither the act of referral nor the relationship between the two parties (who are invariably from two distinct areas of medicine/treatment and thus, have different skills) constitute any degree of supervision. This was confirmed in *Pittam* (VTD 13268) (TVC 33.26) which related to patients referred to a chiropractor. (Note that the services of a registered chiropractor are now exempt (see **28.5** above) but the principle involved still applies.)

Pharmacists

[28.9] The supply of any services (but not the letting on hire of goods) by

- a person registered in the register of pharmacists maintained under the *Pharmacy Order 2010, Art 19 (SI 2010/231)* or in the register of pharmaceutical chemists kept under the *Pharmacy (Northern Ireland) Order 1976*, or
- by a person who is not so registered (e.g. a company or partnership) but where the services are performed by a person who is so registered

is exempt. [*VATA 1994, Sch 9 Group 7 Item 3 and Notes 2A and 3*].

See **28.1** and **28.2** above for limitations on the services which are exempt.

Item 3 above exempts professional services for which a pharmacist has been trained and is required to exercise professional judgement.

Community pharmacies

Under a revised contractual framework for community pharmacy services in England and Wales, community pharmacies are obliged to provide patients with certain essential services; they may also provide advanced and enhanced services depending on the terms of their contract. These services have varying VAT liabilities.

Essential services

These comprise:

(a) Dispensing. From 2 December 2009 supplies of qualifying goods prescribed by appropriate practitioners and dispensed by a pharmacist (prior to 2 December 2009 goods prescribed by a doctor or dentist), are zero-rated under *VATA 1994, Sch 8 Group 12, Item 1* (see **28.13** below).

(b) Disposal of unwanted medicines, i.e. taking in unwanted medicines, sorting and storing them until the Primary Care Trust (in Wales, the local Health Board) arranges for them to be collected and destroyed. This supply is standard-rated.

(c) Signposting, i.e. providing patients with information about other, non-pharmaceutical services which might be beneficial to them. The service does not need to be performed by a registered pharmacist and is standard-rated.

(d) Promotion of healthy lifestyles. This comprises
- the provision of information by means of leaflets and poster displays; and
- individually tailored advice given by the pharmacist to patients in certain identified at-risk groups.

As the latter element is the predominant one and is aimed at the maintenance of a person's health, this service is exempt.

(e) Support for self-care, i.e. providing patients with pharmaceutical advice about medicines and other products available over-the-counter. The pharmacist's provision of advice is exempt but any medicines sold over-the-counter are a separate, standard-rated supply.

(f) Support for people with disabilities. This activity is a further aspect of dispensing prescribed medicines and is zero-rated when the medicines themselves are zero-rated. See **28.12** below.

Clinical governance

This is funding to support the professional delivery of NHS pharmacy services and is outside the scope of VAT.

Practice payment

All supplies within (*b*) to (*f*) above and clinical governance are covered by the 'practice payment'. The practice payment is therefore made up of six elements (two standard-rated, two exempt, one zero-rated and one outside the scope) and must be apportioned to reflect the different liabilities. Information on the percentage weighting to be applied to each element is available from the Pharmaceutical Services Negotiating Committee (PSNC).

Advanced services

The 'medicines use review' and 'prescription intervention' are advance services. These involve reviewing a patient's needs for and use of medicines, including whether the patient is experiencing any side effects or other problems. These are exempt services.

Enhanced services

Primary Care Trusts and local Health Boards can also contract with pharmacies to deliver local enhanced services. HMRC advice on the most commonly encountered services is set out below but as enhanced services are tailored to meet local needs and actual contractual terms can be subject to variation, the correct VAT liability will depend upon the particular arrangements, the single/multiple supply rules and the status of the person performing the services.

- Needle and syringe exchange. This service may involve making clean needles and syringes available free of charge to drug users and diabetics; disposing of used needles safely; and providing health education advice and information to service users.
  The free issue of sterile needles and other materials is not subject to VAT.
  Where a registered pharmacist
  (a) assesses the condition of service users and, where appropriate, provides one-to-one health advice or treatment,
  (b) provides one-to-one advice to service users about safe injecting techniques, or
  (c) provides one-to-one advice on dealing with injecting or drug-related infections and illnesses
  the service is an exempt supply. The pharmacist does not need to provide these services to every service user for exemption to apply but HMRC expect the contract to require these services to be provided to service users on request or where considered appropriate by the pharmacist.
  The service will be standard rated where
  (a) the pharmacist is merely issuing new needles and overseeing the surrender of old ones and has no role in assessing the health condition of the service user;
  (b) the service does not require the skills and experience of a pharmacist, and is such that it could be, or is, carried out by a pharmacy assistant or any other member of staff who is not a registered pharmacist; or

(c) the pharmacist's provision of health education or information goes no further than issuing standard leaflets to service users.

- Minor ailment service. Under this service, pharmacies provide support to eligible patients presenting with a minor ailment (e.g. conjunctivitis or diarrhoea). Following assessment, the pharmacist might give advice, supply appropriate over-the-counter medicines or dressings to treat the ailment and/or refer the patient to another health professional. In providing the service the pharmacy works to guidelines set out in a local protocol.
  Where assessment of the patient's condition and the provision of advice and support in managing the ailment are carried out by a pharmacist, this is an exempt service. But any medicines or dressings issued are standard-rated where they constitute separate supplies of goods. Payment for the goods is made by the NHS rather than the patient.
- Patient group directions (PGDs). These directions are drawn up locally and permit pharmacists to issue defined drugs to a class of patients presenting with particular conditions. PGDs do not amount to 'prescriptions' because they are not written in respect of an identified, individual patient. The supply of goods is standard-rated.

The Electronic Prescription Service (EPS)

This enables prescriptions to be sent and received electronically rather than by paper prescriptions. Fees for implementing and operating the system are not consideration for supplies made and are outside the scope of VAT.

Exit payments

During the first year of the framework, any pharmacy dispensing less than 2000 items per month, and which decides to close, receives a one-off payment. This payment is outside the scope of VAT.

(VAT Notice 701/57/11, para 11.8.3).

Hospitals and health institutions

[28.10] Exemption applies to the provision of

- care or medical or surgical treatment, and
- in connection with it, the supply of any goods,

in any hospital or other institution approved, licensed or registered (or exempted from registration) by any Minister or other authority pursuant to a provision of a public general Act of Parliament or the Scottish Parliament (or equivalent NI legislation) other than a provision that is capable of being brought into effect at different times in relation to different local authority areas. [*VATA 1994, Sch 9 Group 7 Item 4 and Note 8*].

Qualifying institutions

Exemption under this provision cover

- hospitals

- hospices and nursing homes which are approved, licensed or registered under the relevant social legislation (or exempted from obtaining such an approval or registration by the relevant legislation).

An institution may be qualifying regardless of whether its activities are carried out on a charitable or commercial basis.

(VAT Notice 701/31/11, paras 2.1, 2.2).

Care and treatment

Examples of medical care or treatment supplied by a qualifying institution include

- performing medical or surgical procedures with the aim of protecting, maintaining or restoring the health of an individual;
- nursing of sick or injured patients in a hospital, hospice or nursing home; and
- meals and accommodation provided to in-patients, residents or other care beneficiaries;

(VAT Notice 701/31/11, para 2.3).

Services supplied by qualifying institutions which are not exempt

Supplies which are not exempt under these provisions include the following.

- Any service that is not provided under the terms of an approval, license, registration or exemption from registration, granted under the appropriate social.
- Any service provided to a person other than an in-patient, resident or other beneficiary of care or treatment. This includes any supply made to visitors. Special rules apply to the supply of meals and accommodation to parents staying with a sick child in hospital (see below).
- Any goods or services that are separable from care or treatment provided within the institution (e.g. charges made for the use of public telephones).

Class 3B and 4 lasers and Intense pulse light source (IPL) machine

Use of such machines is exempt when supplied as part of a treatment programme drawn up by a registered health professional following the diagnosis of a medical condition. But where treatment is carried out for a purely cosmetic reason, this service is standard-rated.

(VAT Notice 701/31/11, paras 2.4, 2.5).

Drugs and other items supplied to patients in a hospital or nursing home

Drugs, medicines, bandages, plasters or ointments provided by a qualifying institution in the course of care or treatment are exempt when provided to

(a) an in-patient;
(b) any person attending the premises of the qualifying institution for care or treatment; or

(c) any other person or establishment where the item is for use by, or in connection with, either of the above.

Supplies of drugs or medicines to any of the above people other than by a qualifying institution are usually standard-rated (even when the items are dispensed on the prescription of a medical practitioner). However, by concession, HMRC allow pharmacists (including in-house or independent pharmacists operating from hospital premises) to zero-rate drugs, medicines and other qualifying goods that are supplied to any person within (*a*) or (*b*) above if all of the following conditions are met.

- The items dispensed are goods designed or adapted for use in connection with medical or surgical treatment.
- The items are dispensed by a pharmacist in the normal way on the prescription of a medical practitioner who is providing primary health care services.
- The items are intended for self-administration by the person named on the prescription.
- The items are supplied separately from, and do not form any part of, any medical services, treatment or care provided in the hospital or nursing home.
- In the case of NHS prescriptions, the pharmacist is acting under the appropriate NHS Pharmaceutical regulations, and is reimbursed for the dispensed items by one of the NHS bodies that pay for community pharmacy services.

The application of this concession must not give rise to any abuse of the VAT system and HMRC may withdraw or restrict the application of the concession if they have reasonable cause to believe that it is being used for VAT avoidance purposes.

(VAT Notice 701/31/11, para 2.8).

Goods supplied as part of a package of care and treatment in a qualifying institution

Most goods supplied by a qualifying institution as part of a package of care or treatment are exempt. Examples include

- incontinence products; drugs and medicines; bandages; plasters and ointments supplied to hospital patients;
- meals and refreshments provided to in-patients, residents or other beneficiaries of care or treatment; and
- accommodation and meals provided to relatives staying with a sick child in hospital (see *Nuffield Nursing Homes Trust* (VTD 3327) (TVC 33.40) where the provision of accommodation and catering to a parent of a child patient was held to be a supply of care to the patient). No other supplies to visitors, relatives or carers qualify for exemption;
- transport provided that forms an integral part of an exempt supply of care or treatment (see also **28.11** below); and
- toiletry products provided to in-patients, residents or other beneficiaries of care or treatment for which no additional charge is made.

Items that are separable from the care and treatment provided by the qualifying institution are not exempt. Examples include cigarettes, use of bedside phones and televisions, toiletries provided to in-patients for an additional charge, newspapers, merchandise such as commemorative T-shirts, and goods provided to any person other than the beneficiary of the medical care or surgical treatment (but see above for accommodation and meals provided to relatives staying with a sick child in hospital). The liability of such goods should be determined in accordance with the normal liability rules.

(VAT Notice 701/31/11, paras 2.6, 2.7, 2.11).

Goods and services supplied on the premises of a qualifying institution

Some qualifying institutions allow outside businesses or practitioners to operate from their premises.

For a supply made by such a business to qualify for exemption, all of the following conditions must be met.

- The goods or services supplied must form part of the medical care or treatment provided within the qualifying institution.
- The goods or services supplied must be of a type commonly provided to beneficiaries of such services.
- The supply must not consist of drugs, medicines, incontinence products, bandages, plasters, ointments or any other items that are integral to the care or treatment provided in the qualifying institution.
- The supply must involve direct contact between the provider and the beneficiary, and must contribute directly to the welfare of the beneficiary.
- The supply must not take place in a qualifying institution for reasons of geographical convenience only. This means that the supply must not be of a type that might equally be provided at a location other than the premises of a qualifying institution.

There are very few supplies made by outside businesses from the premises of a qualifying institution that meet all of the above conditions but examples include

- care supplied by unregistered nursing staff and other carers; and
- treatment supplied by outside contractors providing renal dialysis services in hospitals.

(VAT Notice 701/31/11, para 5.1; VAT Notice 701/57/11, para 4.3).

Other exempt supplies

[28.11] Other exempt supplies are as follows:

(1) Human blood, organs and tissue

The supply of

- human blood,
- products for therapeutic purposes derived from human blood, and

- human (including foetal) organs or tissue for diagnostic or therapeutic purposes or medical research

is exempt. [*VATA 1994, Sch 9 Group 7 Items 6–8*].

The importation of these items is also exempt from VAT. See **33.15**(5) **IMPORTS**.

Recombinant factor VIII (as opposed to plasma-derived human factor VIII) is outside the exemption as it is not derived from human blood. (HC Written Answer, Vol 267 col 837, 30 November 1995; *Baxter Healthcare Ltd* (VTD 14670) (TVC 33.61)).

(2) Transport of sick and injured

The supply of transport services for sick or injured persons in vehicles specially designed for that purpose is exempt. [*VATA 1994, Sch 9 Group 7 Item 11*].

(3) Hire of equipment

The letting on hire of goods in connection with a supply of other services within *VATA 1994, Sch 9 Group 7 Item 1* (see **28.3** to **28.6** above) is exempt. [*VATA 1994, Sch 9 Group 7 Note 1*].

Increasingly, companies are purchasing specialised equipment and offering the use of it to NHS and private hospitals. The effect of *Note 1* above is that

- if goods are let on hire without attendant staff, or the attendant staff are not qualified under *Item 1*, the supply is taxable; and
- if the equipment is supplied as part of a package,
  - (a) where the principal supply is the hire of equipment and the provision of *Item 1* services is subsidiary to that supply, the whole supply is standard-rated; and
  - (b) where the principal supply is the provision of *Item 1* services and the hire of the equipment is subsidiary to that supply, the whole supply is exempt under *Item 1*.

  See *Aslan Imaging Ltd* (VTD 3286) (TVC 33.18) where the tribunal held that the principal supply was the standard-rated hiring of a radiological scanner and the services supplied by the radiographer who accompanied it were subsidiary and *Cleary & Cleary (t/a Mobile X-rays)* (VTD 7305) (TVC 33.1) where the tribunal held that the principal supply was an exempt mobile chest X-ray service and the equipment hiring was secondary.

Welfare services

[28.12] *Directive 2006/112/EC, Art 132(1)(g)* directs countries to exempt 'the supply of services and of goods closely linked to welfare and social security works'. In *Yoga for Health Foundation v C & E Commrs*, QB [1984] STC 630 (TVC 22.293), it was held that the word 'welfare' was not confined to services connected with the relief of poverty or provision of purely material benefits.

Under UK legislation, the supply by a

(a) charity,

(b) 'public body',
(c) 'state-regulated' private welfare institution (e.g. a residential care home), or
(d) from 31 January 2003, 'state-regulated private welfare agency' (and from 31 January 2003 to 9 December 2010, private welfare agency pending registration (VAT Notice 48, ESC 3.37, withdrawn with effect from 9 December 2010))

of 'welfare services', and of goods supplied in connection with those welfare services, is exempt.

The supply of accommodation or catering is excluded unless ancillary to the provision of care, treatment or instruction. The supply of catering to elderly people in sheltered housing accommodation was held to be ancillary in *Viewpoint Housing Association Ltd* (VTD 13148) (TVC 33.63) and the supply of hotel accommodation and catering to cancer patients and their families was held to be ancillary in *Trustees for the Macmillan Cancer Trust* (VTD 15603) (TVC 33.70).

See **12.1 CHARITIES** for bodies qualifying as charities. It should be noted that not all welfare services provided by charities are business. If such services are provided consistently below cost to distressed people for the relief of their distress, they are non-business supplies. See **12.5**(21) **CHARITIES**.

'*Public body*' means

- a government department,
- a local authority, or
- any other body which acts under any enactment or instrument for public purposes and not for its own profit and which performs functions similar to those of a government department or local authority (e.g. most NHS trusts).

'*State-regulated*' means approved, licensed, registered or exempted from registration by any Minister or other authority pursuant to a provision of a public general Act of Parliament or the Scottish Parliament (or equivalent NI legislation) other than a provision that is capable of being brought into effect at different times in relation to different local authority areas.

[*VATA 1994, Sch 9 Group 7 Item 9 and Notes 5, 7 and 8; SI 2002/762; SI 2003/24*].

Supplies by intermediaries

In *Staatssecretaris van Financiën v Stichting Kinderopvang Enschede, ECJ Case C-415/04* [2007] STC 294 (TVC 22.301) the ECJ held exemption could apply under these provisions to services provided by a qualifying body where it was acting as an intermediary between persons seeking, and persons offering, a qualifying welfare service. For exemption to apply

- the qualifying welfare service must be of a nature or quality that recipients cannot be assured of obtaining a service of the same value without the assistance of such an intermediary service; and

- the basic purpose of the intermediary services must not be to obtain additional income for the service provider by carrying out transactions which are in direct competition with those of commercial enterprises liable for VAT.

State-regulated private welfare institution or agency

A state-regulated private welfare institution or agency means an institution or agency that is registered with and/or regulated by

- Care Quality Commission;
- Scottish Commission for the Regulation of Care;
- Care Standards Inspectorate for Wales;
- Northern Ireland Health and Personal Social Services Regulation and Improvement Authority;
- Office for Standards in Education (OFSTED); or
- any other similar regulatory body.

It can include a domiciliary care agency, an independent fostering agency, a voluntary adoption agency, and a nursing agency.

(VAT Notice 701/2/11, para 3.3).

Welfare services

Welfare services mean services directly connected with (1)–(3) below. In the case of services supplied by a state-regulated private welfare institution under (*c*) above, it only includes those services in respect of which the institution is so regulated.

(1) Provision of care, treatment or instruction designed to promote physical or mental welfare of elderly, sick, distressed or disabled. [VATA 1994, Sch 9 Group 7 Note 6(a); SI 2002/762]

In *Watford & District Old People's Housing Association Ltd (t/a Watford Help In The Home Service)* (VTD 15660) (TVC 33.64) the tribunal held that domestic help services such as cleaning, cooking and shopping could constitute 'care' when supplied to people for whom there is either current or imminent substantial risk to the health and welfare of the person, and who are unable to provide even basic self care or who have major difficulty in safely carrying out some key daily living tasks. The tribunal stressed the significance of the high level of recipients' needs which, in that case, had been identified by Social Services assessments.

Following that case, HMRC reviewed their interpretation of 'care'. They regard care or treatment as including 'the protection, control or guidance of an individual, when this is provided to meet medical, physical, personal or domestic needs'. The following are examples of care that is a welfare service when: provided to an elderly, sick, disabled or distressed person; the care is part of a specific individual care plan and the service relates to it; and an assessment of the recipient's health condition and medical needs has been carried out by an appropriately trained person.

- Personal or nursing care (including assistance with bathing, dressing, toileting and other personal hygiene).

- General assistance and support with everyday tasks such as form-filling, letter reading/writing, bill-paying.
- Certain routine domestic tasks (such as housework, simple odd jobs, shopping and collecting a prescription or pension) provided all of the following conditions are met.
  - (a) An assessment of the recipients' health condition, medical needs and ability to perform each task has been carried out by an appropriately trained person (e.g. a medical or health professional or any person with relevant training or experience in social work or social care).
  - (b) This assessment has shown that the recipient is unable to carry out the tasks safely (because performance involves a likelihood of physical harm or injury) or properly or effectively (e.g. an elderly or disabled person who has mobility problems may be unable to shop regularly enough to meet their nutritional needs) or without 'significant' pain or discomfort and that this inability presents a risk to their health or welfare. 'Significant' is used to distinguish between low levels of pain or discomfort (experienced by many people in carrying out routine domestic tasks) and a significant level of pain or discomfort (that restricts ability to carry out such tasks).
  - (c) A record of each assessment is maintained by the supplier of the service.
  - (d) The service provided is a routine domestic task that the majority of the population would expect to carry out for themselves and which is required to keep a household going. This would exclude specialist services (e.g. non-essential gardening, decorating and other house maintenance including re-roofing, plumbing and electrical services).
- Counselling.
- Looking after or supervising vulnerable people.
- Support or instruction designed to develop or sustain a person's capacity to live independently in the community.
- Protection, control, guidance or companionship that is required to meet an individual's personal or domestic needs.
- Residential care, including accommodation, board and other services provided to residents as part of a care package.

(VAT Notice 701/2/11, para 2.1).

(2) The care or protection of children and young persons. [VATA 1994, Sch 9 Group 7 Note 6(b); SI 2002/762]

HMRC regard this as applying to services directly connected with the care and protection of specific children, rather than children in general. Examples include

- care provided in a children's home;
- day care services such as those provided by a nursery, playgroup or after school club (but not activity-based clubs such as dance classes, etc.);
- the placement of children with foster carers by fostering agencies;
- the assessment of families to be included on the risk register;

- the care, support and protection of looked-after children; and
- training and assessment of prospective adopters by an adoption agency.

After school clubs and other providers of *non-residential* care for children, including after-school clubs, are only required to register under the appropriate social legislation if they provide a designated number of hours of care to children under the age of eight. A qualifying institution that

- provides care on a commercial basis to children who are under the age of eight as well as to older children,
- operates identical hours of opening for all age groups, and
- provides activities for over-eights that are comparable with those provided for younger children,

may, if it wishes, treat the care provided to over-eights as VAT exempt (in addition to the care provided to younger children).

Some welfare providers, such as independent fostering agencies, receive fees for services that, although concerned with the overall welfare of one or more child, are not primarily and directly connected with the care or protection of a specific child. HMRC do not usually regard these services as exempt unless they are provided as part of an exempt composite supply of care and protection. Examples include fees received for

- training of carers, or potential carers, where this is not linked to the needs of a specific child;
- assessment of potential foster carers suitability to look after children, where this is not linked to the needs of a specific child;
- play centres and activity-based clubs that provide services such as football and dancing lessons, indoor soft play areas and children's entertainment;
- consultancy or research services; and
- education of children.

See, however, **16 EDUCATION** for exemption for certain education and training services provided by eligible bodies.

(VAT Notice 701/2/11, para 2.2).

(3) Provision of spiritual welfare by religious institution as part of course of instruction or retreat, not being course or retreat designed primarily to provide recreation or a holiday. [VATA 1994, Sch 9 Group 7 Note 6(c); SI 2002/762]

Examples include

- spiritual counselling to an individual;
- guided exploration of spiritual needs and development; and
- discussion, meditation and prayer or worship sessions

but does not include

- conferences or retreats when the predominant purpose is not spiritual welfare;
- educational courses in theology, or similar subjects, where the predominant purpose is to expand knowledge of spiritual matters rather than to provide spiritual welfare services; and

- meetings to discuss theology or aspects of Church doctrine.

(VAT Notice 701/2/11, para 2.3).

Goods provided in connection with welfare services

Goods provided as part of, or in connection with, an exempt supply of welfare services are also exempt. Examples include

- meals and refreshments provided to beneficiaries of welfare services in the course of care or spiritual welfare services for which no additional charge is made;
- bandages, plasters or ointments supplied in the course of a supply of care and treatment in the recipient's home; and
- items provided to children by playgroups or nurseries (e.g. picture books, crayons and toys) when provided in connection with the care.

Any goods that are separable from an exempt welfare service, or are not provided in connection with such a service, are not exempt.

(VAT Notice 701/2/11, para 3.4).

De Voil Indirect Tax Service. See V4.146.

Zero-rated dispensing of drugs, etc.

[28.13] The supply of goods can be zero-rated in the following circumstances.

(1) **Pharmacists**

The supply (including the letting on hire) of any 'qualifying goods' dispensed to an individual for his 'personal use' where the dispensing is by a registered pharmacist (as defined) on the 'prescription' (NHS or private) of, from 2 December 2009, an appropriate practitioner, i.e.

- a registered medical practitioner;
- a person registered in the dentists' register under the *Dentists Act 1984*;
- a community practitioner nurse prescriber;
- a nurse independent prescriber;
- an optometrist independent prescriber;
- a pharmacist independent prescriber; or
- a supplementary prescriber.

Prior to 2 December 2009 the zero-rating applied where the prescription was of a person registered in

- the register of medical practitioners; or
- the dentists' register; and

HMRC also allowed items dispensed against a nurse's prescription to be zero-rated. (VAT Notice 701/57/11, para 3.2).

For these purposes, a person who is not registered in the visiting EU practitioners lists in the register of medical practitioners at the time he performs services in an urgent case (as mentioned in *Medical Act 1983, s 18(3)*) is treated as being so registered where he is entitled to be registered under that section.

[*VATA 1994, Sch 8 Group 12 Item 1 and Notes 2B, 5; SI 1997/2744; SI 2006/1914; SI 2007/289; SI 2009/2972*].

'*Qualifying goods*' means any goods designed or adapted for use in connection with any medical or surgical treatment except hearing aids, dentures, spectacles and contact lenses [*VATA 1994, Sch 8 Group 12 Note 2A*].

'*Personal use*' is not defined but see **28.15** below for a general consideration of the term. Specifically, however, it does not include use by an individual while being provided with medical or surgical treatment, or any form of care, as an in-patient or resident of, or whilst attending, a hospital, nursing home or other institution which is approved, licensed or registered (or exempted by legislation from any requirement to be so approved, etc.). [*VATA 1994, Sch 8 Group 12 Notes 5A, 5I; SI 1997/2744*].

Acquisitions and imports

Goods prescribed as above which are acquired in the UK from another EU country or imported from a place outside the EU are not zero-rated on acquisition or importation. [*VATA 1994, Sch 8 Group 12 Note 1*].

There are a number of NHS payments which relate to the dispensing activity, all of which are zero-rated where the conditions for zero-rating are met. These are

- item fee;
- establishment payment;
- protected payment;
- repeat dispensing annual payment;
- transitional payment; and
- special fees for dispensing controlled or expensive drugs and for measuring and fitting appliances that the pharmacy also customises.

Support for people with disabilities

Pharmacists are required to give support to patients, in response to their assessed need, in order to facilitate their safe self-administration of medicines. This can comprise

- special labelling of containers for use by visually disabled patients;
- removing drugs from blister packs and repackaging them in replacement containers such as multi-compartment boxes; and
- reminder charts.

This activity is an adjunct to the dispensing of prescribed medicines and is zero-rated where the medicines themselves are zero-rated.

(VAT Notice 701/57/11, para 11.4.6).

Drugs administered by nurse at home of patient

In *Healthcare at Home Ltd* (VTD 20379) (TVC 19.6) a company, which had its own pharmacists and whose supply of drugs alone to patients was accepted as being zero-rated, also arranged for nurses to visit patients and administer drugs that had been prescribed for them. HMRC ruled that, the effect of the decisions in *Dr Beynon & Partners* (see **28.3** above) was that the company was making a single exempt supply of medical services. The tribunal, however, held that the supply was zero-rated since, in the present case, the determining characteristic was the requirement for the drug and not the necessity for a nurse (whereas in *Beynon* it was the supply of the doctor's services and not the drugs administered to the patients).

(2) Dispensing doctors

The supply (including the letting on hire) of any 'qualifying goods' where dispensing is in accordance with a requirement or authorisation under NHS regulations, on the 'prescription' (NHS or private) of, from 2 December 2009, an appropriate practitioner, i.e.

- a registered medical practitioner;
- a person registered in the dentists' register under the *Dentists Act 1984*;
- a community practitioner nurse prescriber;
- a nurse independent prescriber;
- an optometrist independent prescriber;
- a pharmacist independent prescriber; or
- a supplementary prescriber.

Prior to 2 December 2009 the zero-rating applied where the prescription was of a person registered in

- the register of medical practitioners; or
- the dentists' register; and

HMRC also allowed items dispensed against a nurse's prescription to be zero-rated. (VAT Notice 701/57/11, para 3.2).

[*VATA 1994, Sch 8 Group 12 Item 1 and Note 5; SI 1995/652; SI 1997/2744; SI 2006/1914; SI 2009/2972*].

Under such regulations dispensing doctors can be required or authorised by the NHS to provide pharmacy services to particular patients. The usual qualification is that the patient lives more than one mile from the nearest pharmacy (although there are others). Dispensing doctors cannot dispense drugs to their other patients and other doctors are not authorised to dispense drugs to any of their patients.

See under (1) above for '*qualifying goods*'.

Acquisitions and imports

Goods dispensed as above which are acquired in the UK from another EU country or imported from a place outside the EU are not zero-rated on acquisition or importation. [*VATA 1994, Sch 8 Group 12 Note 1; SI 1995/652*].

Registration

Following changes in Department of Health funding, with effect from 1 April 2006, dispensing doctors who wish to recover VAT incurred on the drugs they dispense must register for VAT. General advise for doctors seeking to register is available in VAT Information Sheet 3/06 *Dispensing doctors and VAT registration: how and when to register; taxable or exempt supplies; VAT recovery and what records need to be kept* and VAT Information Sheet 12/06 *Further information for dispensing doctors*.

Administration of drugs at the time of treatment

This must be distinguished from the dispensing of drugs and is an exempt supply. See **28.3** above. As a result, zero-rating under *VATA 1994, Sch 8 Group 12 Item 1A* above only applies to dispensing of 'take-away' goods which the patient will self-administer.

Private prescriptions

The dispensing of goods on private prescription (e.g. drugs, vitamin supplements and homeopathic preparations) by a doctor is always standard-rated.

De Voil Indirect Tax Service. See V4.281.

Zero-rated supplies to disabled persons and charities

[28.14] The legislation zero-rates certain supplies of specialised goods and services when needed by '*handicapped*' persons. As the term 'handicapped' is not now in general usage, in line with HMRC's practice, in the following paragraphs the term 'disabled' is used instead.

Meaning of 'disabled'

'*Handicapped*' in the context of zero-rating is defined as 'chronically sick or disabled' [*VATA 1994, Sch 8 Group 12 Note 3*] but there is no further definition of 'chronically sick' and 'disabled' in the legislation.

The Shorter Oxford English dictionary defines 'chronic' as 'lasting a long time, lingering, inveterate' or 'constant, also bad'. The opposite of chronic is 'acute' which is defined as 'coming sharply to a crisis, not chronic'.

HMRC regard a person as 'chronically sick or disabled' if he/she

- has a physical or mental impairment which has a long-term (as opposed to acute or short-term) and substantial adverse effect upon his/her ability to carry out everyday activities,
- has a condition which the medical profession treats as a chronic sickness (e.g. diabetes), or
- is terminally ill

but do *not* regard the term as extending to

- a frail elderly person who is otherwise able-bodied (see also *C & E Commrs v Help the Aged*, QB [1997] STC 406 (TVC 11.17)); or

- any person who is only temporarily disabled or incapacitated (e.g. where suffering from a broken limb).

Tribunals have similarly held that a person is not chronically sick or disabled where suffering from a slipped disc (*Aquakraft Ltd* (VTD 2215) (TVC 19.10)) or neck and back pain *Posturite (UK) Ltd* (VTD 7848) (TVC 19.51)).

See *Tempur Pedic (UK) Ltd* (VTD 13744) (TVC 19.27) for a consideration of the meaning of the words 'chronically sick'.

Despite the tribunal decisions in *The Dyslexia Institute Ltd* (VTD 12654) (TVC 11.22) and *GD Searle & Co Ltd* (VTD 13439) (TVC 19.58), HMRC accept that equipment designed for people suffering from asthma, psoriasis and dyslexia qualifies for zero-rating if they can be regarded as disabled sufferers of the condition.

(VAT Notice 701/7/02, paras 3.2, 4.5.2).

Parents, spouses, etc.

If a parent, spouse or guardian acts on behalf of a disabled person, the supply is treated as being made to that disabled person. (VAT Notice 701/7/02, para 3.2).

Conditions for zero-rating

For zero-rating to apply, it is essential that both

- the goods or services qualify; and
- the recipient qualifies.

The relief is not intended to cover all supplies of goods and services to disabled persons (or charities providing facilities for the disabled), nor does it mean that eligible goods and services can be zero-rated when supplied to people who are not disabled. For example, supplies to a nursing home would not be zero-rated under these provisions even if all the residents were disabled. See *Conroy* (VTD 1916) (TVC 19.95).

The supplier is responsible for correctly accounting for VAT and ensuring that all the conditions for zero-rating are met. Therefore where relief depends on the designer's intention and the supplier has not designed or manufactured the goods himself (e.g. a retailer), he should seek written confirmation from the manufacturer (or importer) that the goods are eligible for VAT relief (see below and also **28.21** below). HMRC will not normally provide binding VAT rulings to a retailer or distributor on the eligibility of specific items for VAT relief. They also recommend that suppliers obtain written declarations from each customer claiming entitlement to VAT relief. See **28.33** below.

(VAT Notice 701/7/02, para 2.3).

De Voil Indirect Tax Service. See V4.281.

Supplies of goods

[28.15] Subject to the exclusions below, zero-rating applies to the supply (including the letting on hire) to

- a disabled person for 'domestic or personal use', or
- a charity for making available, by sale or otherwise, to disabled persons for domestic or personal use

of any of the goods within **28.16** to **28.23** below. [*VATA 1994, Sch 8 Group 12, Item 2* and *Note 5*].

See **28.14** above for the interpretation of 'disabled'.

Domestic or personal use

This phrase is not defined in the legislation (apart from the specific exclusion below). See *Attorney General v Milliwatt Ltd*, KB [1948] All ER 331 (TVC 19.9) where Cassels J stated that domestic in the context of that case (which concerned electric pads and blankets) meant the house or the home.

In *Aquakraft Ltd* (VTD 2215) (TVC 19.10) the tribunal held that 'personal use' meant 'private or exclusive' use. HMRC therefore take the view that the goods must be used specifically by an eligible individual (or series of eligible individuals) so that zero-rating will not apply under these provisions to

- goods and services used for business purposes; or
- supplies made widely available for a whole group of people to use as they wish, even if all such users are disabled (see *Portland College* (VTD 9815) (TVC 19.56)). For example, a stair lift in a charity building for the use or convenience of all disabled persons who might use the building would not qualify for relief. This is because the charity is making the lift available for the general use of all those people who might require it, rather than for the personal use of specified individuals.

(VAT Notice 701/7/02, para 3.5).

Exclusions

Subject to the extra-statutory concession below, zero-rating is restricted in the following circumstances.

(1) '*Domestic or personal use*' does not include any use by the disabled person in question while being provided (whether or not by the person making the supply) with medical or surgical treatment or any form of care
- as an in-patient or resident of a 'relevant institution', or
- whilst attending at the premises of a relevant institution

in respect of

(a) supplies to a disabled person by

(i) a Strategic Health Authority or Special Health Authority in England; a Health Authority, Special Health Authority or Local Health Authority in Wales; a Health Board or Special Health Board in Scotland; a Health and Social Services Board in Northern Ireland; the Common Services Agency for the Scottish Health Service, the Northern Ireland Central Services Agency for Health and Social Services and the Isle of Man Health Services Board; a

National Health Service trust established under the *National Health Service Act 2006*, the *National Health Service (Wales) Act 2006* or the *National Health Service (Scotland) Act 1978*; an NHS Foundation Trust; a Primary Care Trust established under the *National Health Service Act 2006, s 18*; or a Health and Social Services trust established under the *Health and Personal Social Services (Northern Ireland) Order 1991, Art 10*, or

(ii) any person not falling within (i) above who is engaged in the carrying on of any activity in respect of which a relevant institution is required to be approved, licensed or registered or as the case may be, would be so required if not exempt

other than the supply of a wheelchair or invalid carriage or any parts or accessories designed solely for use therein; and

(b) supplies to a disabled person by any other person not within (*a*) above of

- medical or surgical appliances within **28.16** below and parts and accessories designed solely for use with such goods; and
- incontinence products and wound dressings.

Supplies to charities are not affected by this restriction.

(2) Zero-rating does not apply to

(a) a supply made in accordance with an agreement, arrangement or understanding to which any of the persons mentioned in (1)(*a*)(i) or (ii) above is or has been a party otherwise than as the supplier, or

(b) a supply where all or any part of the consideration has been provided (directly or indirectly) by any such person

but in the case of a supply of an invalid wheelchair or invalid carriage to a disabled person only if *either* a person within (1)(*a*)(ii) is involved *or* the *whole* of the consideration has been provided by a person within (1)(*a*)(i) above.

For the purposes of (1) and (2) above, references to an invalid wheelchair and invalid carriage do not include references to any mechanically propelled vehicle intended or adapted for use on roads.

A '*relevant institution*' is any institution (whether a hospital, nursing home or other institution) which provides care or medical or surgical treatment and is *either* approved, licensed or registered *or* specifically exempt from any such requirement.

By concession, the above exclusions do not apply (and a supply of goods can be treated as if it were zero-rated) where

- the goods fall within **28.21** below and are supplied by a charity at or below cost;
- the goods are goods other than spectacles or contact lenses, and are designed solely for use by a visually disabled person;
- the recipient of the supply is a resident, or is attending the premises of, a relevant institution; and

- the charity is not actively engaged in supplying such goods solely to disabled persons who are resident in or attending the premises of a relevant institution operated, managed or controlled by the charity.

(VAT Notice 48, ESC 3.24).

[*VATA 1994, Sch 8 Group 12 Notes 5B–5I; Health and Social Carer (Community Health and Standards) Act 2003, Sch 4 para 96; National Health Service (Consequential Provisions) Act 2006, Sch 1 paras 173, 174; SI 1997/2744; SI 2000/503; SI 2002/2813*].

The effect of the above exclusions is that it prevents institutions such as private hospitals, nursing homes and residential homes from recovering VAT charged on the purchase of supplies for disabled persons which are used in their supply to in-patients and residents. It also prevents them, and the NHS, from making arrangements for third parties to make VAT-free supplies (e.g. incontinence products and wound dressings) on the institution's behalf to patients who live in their own homes and for which the institution pays. Instead, such supplies are supplied by the institution as part of its exempt care. Supplies of incontinence products, etc direct to the disabled person by independent suppliers and for which the disabled person pays are not affected. (VAT Information Sheet 6/97).

Medical and surgical appliances

[28.16] Provided the conditions in **28.15** above are met, zero-rating applies to medical or surgical 'appliances' designed solely for the relief of a 'severe abnormality' or 'severe injury'.

Excluded are hearing aids (unless designed for auditory training of deaf children, see **28.21** below); dentures (but these are usually exempt under **28.7** above); and spectacles and contact lenses (but see **28.21** below for certain low vision aids).

Included are

- clothing (e.g. mastectomy bras and swimwear), footwear and wigs (which are often supplied during illness to mask hair loss); and
- renal haemodialysis units, oxygen concentrators, artificial respirators and other similar apparatus.

[*VATA 1994, Sch 8 Group 12, Item 2(a) and Note 4*].

An '*appliance*' is a device or piece of equipment with a specific function. It can be designed for use outside or inside the body.

The words 'severe abnormality' and 'severe injury' are not defined but among the disabilities falling within this category are amputation, rheumatoid or severe osteo-arthritis, severe disfigurement, congenital deformities, organic nervous diseases, learning disabilities and blindness.

Examples of zero-rated appliances, in addition to those specified in the legislation above, include

- artificial joints;

- artificial limbs;
- heart pacemakers;
- leg braces; and
- neck collars.

Examples of appliances that are not zero-rated, in addition to those specified in the legislation above, include

- plates or pins for use in repairing broken bones, bandages, plasters or other wound dressings as they are not appliances; and
- medical or surgical appliances that are not designed solely for the relief of a severe abnormality or severe injury, particularly those used in cosmetic surgery, such as breast implants.

(VAT Notice 701/7/02, para 4.2).

Adjustable beds

[28.17] Provided the conditions in **28.15** above are met, zero-rating applies to electrically or mechanically adjustable beds designed for invalids. [*VATA 1994, Sch 8 Group 12, Item 2(b)*].

A distinction must be made between a bed and a mattress (*Back In Health Ltd* (VTD 10003) (TVC 19.53)). The same tribunal also considered what makes a bed 'electrically or mechanically adjustable' and held that the key factor was whether it was adjustable for height, drop and angle, so as to enable a person to slide from a wheelchair to a bed at a lower level.

Beds must clearly stand out as being something specialised for the use of invalids. As well as being electrically or mechanically adjustable, they should additionally have specific design features which distinguish them from a standard bed. (VAT Notice 701/7/02, para 4.3).

See also *Niagara Holdings Ltd* (VTD 11400) (TVC 19.14) and *Hulsta Furniture (UK) Ltd* (VTD 16289) (TVC 19.15).

Sanitary devices

[28.18] Provided the conditions in **28.15** above are met, zero-rating applies to

- commode chairs and stools,
- devices incorporating a bidet jet and warm air drier, and
- frames or other devices for sitting over or rising from sanitary appliances.

[*VATA 1994, Sch 8 Group 12, Item 2(c)*].

Chair lifts and stair lifts

[28.19] Provided the conditions in **28.15** above are met, zero-rating applies to chair lifts and stair lifts designed for use in connection with invalid wheelchairs. [*VATA 1994, Sch 8 Group 12, Item 2(d*].

Although the lift must be capable of conveying a wheelchair-bound disabled person up and down stairs or from one level to another, the legislation does not require the disabled person to be seated in the wheelchair when using the lift. (VAT Notice 701/7/02, para 4.3).

See also **28.29** below for zero-rating of ordinary vertical lifts for disabled people who are not wheelchair-bound.

Hoists and lifters

[28.20] Provided the conditions in **28.15** above are met, zero-rating applies to hoists and lifters designed for use by invalids. [*VATA 1994, Sch 8 Group 12, Item 2(e)*].

Equipment designed solely for the disabled

[28.21] Provided the conditions in **28.15** above are met, zero-rating applies to equipment and appliances not falling within **28.16** to **28 20** above but which is 'designed solely for use by a disabled person'. *Specifically included* are invalid wheelchairs and carriages (other than mechanically propelled vehicles intended or adapted for use on roads) and hearing aids designed for the auditory training of deaf children. *Excluded* are other types of hearing aids, dentures (but these are usually exempt under **28.7** above); and spectacles and contact lenses (but see below for certain low vision aids). [*VATA 1994, Sch 8 Group 12, Item 2(g)* and *Notes 4, 5G*].

It is not sufficient that the equipment or appliance is merely intended for use by a disabled person, or is mainly purchased by disabled persons. General purpose equipment (e.g. ordinary or orthopaedic beds, orthopaedic or reclining chairs, etc.) may benefit disabled people but is designed for general use or for use by disabled and able-bodied people alike. Such products are not, therefore, eligible for relief. On the other hand, equipment designed solely for use by disabled people will remain eligible for relief when supplied to a disabled person or charity, even though available to be purchased by able-bodied people. (VAT Notice 701/7/02, para 4.5.1).

'Designed solely for use by a disabled person'

In the opinion of HMRC, this means that the original intention of the designer was to produce equipment or an appliance designed solely to meet the needs of persons with one or more disabilities (see also, for example, *Tempur Pedic (UK) Ltd* (VTD 13744) (TVC 19.27)). The design must succeed in that the product does, in fact, meet the needs of disabled persons. There are a number of conditions which may, but do not invariably, result in disability (e.g. asthma, psoriasis and dyslexia). Equipment which meets the needs of people with such conditions only qualifies for zero-rating if designed solely for the purpose of meeting the needs of *disabled* sufferers of the condition. (VAT Notice 701/7/02, para 4.5.2).

In *The British Disabled Flying Association* (TC01580) (TVC 19.33), the tribunal held that the fact that aircraft had not originally been manufactured for use by disabled people was not conclusive. There was no reason for an item not to be designed solely for use by a disabled person simply because a factory manufactured item, not so designed, had then been subject to modifications to make it so designed. The tribunal concluded that *Item 2(g)* should be construed as referring to the quality of the item as used by the handicapped person, not the quality of that item when it left the factory.

Determination of zero-rating

Only the designer or manufacturer can determine whether the goods qualify for zero-rating. The designer, manufacturer or importer of the goods must retain evidence which demonstrates that the goods in question fulfil the conditions for relief including

- the disability needs to be addressed;
- the product specification for meeting those needs;
- results of tests demonstrating that the product meets the design intention; or
- patents or patent applications.

If necessary, the manufacturer or importer should seek liability rulings from HMRC.

Any other person, who thinks that the equipment or appliances he is selling have been designed solely for use by a disabled person, should seek confirmation from the manufacturer or importer. (Their advertising literature may contain a statement to this effect.) Local Business Advice Centres have been asked to refuse requests for liability rulings from retailers.

(VAT Notice 701/7/02, para 4.5.3).

VAT liability of specific equipment and appliances

The following is a list of equipment and appliances which have been considered (either by HMRC, a tribunal or the courts) for inclusion within *VATA 1994, Sch 8 Group 12, Item 2(g)*.

Air conditioning, etc.

Air-conditioning and similar general purpose equipment does not qualify for relief.

See also *Simmons* (VTD 6622) (TVC 19.49) where two air-conditioning units, purchased by a person suffering from multiple sclerosis, and which helped considerably in coping with the condition, were held to have been designed for general purpose use and not for use by a disabled person. The fact that the design would have been the same whether the equipment was to be used by a disabled person or for the general purposes did not bring the equipment within the scope of Item 2(g). Air-conditioning units could also not be regarded as 'similar apparatus' (see above) and therefore fall within **28.16** above.

An air filtration system installed in the house of a person suffering from multiple allergies was held to qualify for zero-rating in *Symons* (VTD 19174) (TVC 19.31).

Asthma, hay fever and allergy products

Supplies of all vacuum cleaners, air purification products and similar allergy relief products are standard-rated irrespective of to whom they are supplied. (Business Briefs 16/96, 17/96, and 20/97).

See also *GD Searle & Co Ltd* (VTD 13439) (TVC 19.58) which concerned aerosol pesticide sprays, designed to kill dust mites and supplied to pharmacists for sale to asthmatics or sufferers from eczema. The tribunal held that, as not all sufferers from asthma could be described as 'chronically sick or disabled', the sprays were not 'designed solely for use by a handicapped person', and thus failed to qualify for zero-rating.

Carpets

In *The David Lewis Centre*, QB [1995] STC 485 (TVC 19.34) woollen carpets, purchased to protect patients from scorching when falling as a result of an epileptic seizure, were held not to qualify for zero-rating since the carpets were not specifically designed for the use of the disabled.

Similarly, in *Vassall Centre Trust* (VTD 17891) (TVC 19.38) carpets, adapted by having a light coloured strip along both edges up to the doorway or access point to assist the partially sighted in moving about the building, were held not to be designed solely for use by disabled persons.

Computer equipment

Computer systems are increasingly being used to aid disabled people. They are generally made up of both standard-rated, general use items of hardware and software, together with other items designed solely for use by a disabled person and which are therefore eligible for zero-rating. To simplify the application of VAT for such computer systems sold as a complete package, suppliers may use either or both of the following concessions provided

- the computer system is a tool to aid the disabled person to overcome communication problems; and
- the computer system is for the personal or domestic use of a disabled person.

The arrangements apply only to complete packages. Replacement units or upgrading items are subject to VAT at the standard rate unless they are designed solely for use by disabled people.

(a) *Concession 1 – zero-rating of central processor.* A central processor may be zero-rated if
   - it is sold as part of a computer system; and
   - it has software installed which enables a disabled person to use the computer system or other software effectively, or to carry out tasks effectively when otherwise they could not.

   No other general purpose hardware may be zero-rated under this or any other concession.

(b) *Concession 2 – composite rate of VAT for computer systems.* Traders supplying disabled people with complete computer systems that contain significant specialist items for use by disabled customers may use a composite VAT rate for such supplies. This rate is based on supplies of such packages made by that supplier over a recent representative period. In addition to the items of equipment designed solely for the use of a disabled person, the suppliers may include the values of the following elements of the package in the zero-rated portion.
   - The central processor described in (*a*) above; and
   - costs charged to the customer for the installation of the equipment and for the training in its use.

Example

Z Ltd supplies five different qualifying packages of computer equipment in a representative period of three months. In package A, the zero-rated element (central processor, speech synthesiser, Braille embosser, specialist software, installation and training) is £1,500 at sales value and the standard-rated element (printer, keyboard, VDU and standard software) is £500 plus £100.00 VAT. The total cost of the package is £2,100.00 of which £100.00 is VAT. The composite rate is the rate which needs to be applied to the total VAT-exclusive sale value (£2,000) to ensure the correct VAT is declared, ie

100 ÷ 2,000 × 100 = 5% (usually rounded to one decimal place)

The composite rates and value of sales for each of the five packages offered in the representative period are as follows.

Package	Composite rate	Sales value £	VAT £
A	5%	50,000	2,500
B	6%	20,000	1,200
C	3%	10,000	300
D	3.8%	10,000	380
E	4.1%	10,000	410
		£100,000	£4,790

The overall composite rate is

4,790 ÷ 100,000 × 100 = 4.79% (rounded to 4.8%)

Z Ltd can apply a composite rate of 4.8% to all sales of qualifying packages. The overall composite rate should be recalculated every twelve months.

(VAT Notice 701/7/02, paras 4.5, 9.1–9.5).

Golf buggies

In *Foxer Industries* (VTD 13817) (TVC 19.59) single-seat golf buggies, marketed for sale to elderly golfers, were held not to have been designed solely for the use of disabled persons. (In a subsequent appeal (*Foxer Industries* (VTD 14469) (TVC 19.74)) the partnership claimed that work done in adapting a number of buggies for specific customers should be treated as qualifying for zero-rating. The tribunal held that, in one case, the modifications to the basic design were so fundamental that the entire buggy should be treated as zero-rated under *Item 2(g)*. In the other eight cases, an appropriate proportion of the price was treated as zero-rated under **28.25** below.)

See also *C F Leisure Mobility Ltd* (VTD 16790) (TVC 19.59).

Hearing aids and induction loop systems

Most hearing aids are specifically excluded from zero-rating (see above). But certain specialist equipment designed for people with severely defective hearing as the term is generally used, may be zero-rated. These include the following.

- Hearing aids designed for the auditory training of deaf children. [*VATA 1994, Sch 8 Group 12 Note 4*].

- Tinnitus maskers (an earpiece which generates a constant noise to mask the effect of ringing in the ears).
- Induction loop equipment.

(VAT Notice 701/7/02, paras 4.5, 4.6).

Hydrotherapy pools

Following the decisions in *The David Lewis Centre* (VTD 10860) (TVC 19.34) and *Boys' and Girls' Welfare Society* (VTD 15274) (TVC 19.35), although it remains their general policy that swimming pools are not equipment that has been designed solely for the use of disabled persons, HMRC now accept that a hydrotherapy pool qualifies for zero-rating in certain conditions.

Incontinence products

HMRC have always accepted that incontinence products are goods of a kind which qualifying for zero-rating but their supply can only be zero-rated in certain circumstances.

- *Retail sales*. People who are incontinent and live in their own homes are entitled to buy incontinence products at the zero rate. Eligible incontinence products can be zero-rated on the shelf without a written declaration under **28.33** below to the retailer by the customer.
- *Internet and mail order sales* also qualify for zero-rating provided they are made to individuals and not institutions.

Zero-rating does not apply to incontinence products supplied to a disabled person (whether by a Health Authority, hospital or any other person) whilst that person is an in-patient or receiving residential care (see under **28.16** below).

Bulk sales: HMRC will expect retailers, internet and mail order suppliers to have a signed declaration, or other supporting evidence that the supply is to an incontinent individual (and not to an institution such as a nursing home) for customers who buy more than

- 200 disposable pads;
- 50 washable pads;
- 5 collecting devices; or
- 10 pairs of waterproof or leak-proof underwear.

(VAT Notice 701/7/02, para 4.5).

Kitchens

Kitchen furniture fitted into a kitchen during the construction of a new dwelling may be zero-rated under *VATA 1994, Sch 8 Group 5 Item 4* (see **42.16 LAND AND BUILDINGS: ZERO AND REDUCED RATE SUPPLIES AND DIY HOUSEBUILDERS**).

For existing kitchens, equipment designed solely for use by a disabled person, together with the services of installation (see **28.27** below) and the services of adapting goods to suit the condition of a disabled person (see **28.25** below) can also be zero-rated.

See also *Softley Ltd (t/a Softley Kitchens)* (VTD 15034) (TVC 19.26) where it was held that certain items of kitchen equipment could be zero-rated when made to the individual specifications of a disabled person.

Low vision aids and other aids for the blind

Although spectacles and contact lenses are specifically excluded (see above), zero-rating can be applied to other types of low vision aids. This equipment tends to fall into two categories.

- Spectacle-mounted low vision aids which are custom made to the prescription of a qualified optician where the prescription identifies the appliance as a low vision aid.
- Other low vision aids, including technical aids for reading and writing, which are designed exclusively for visually impaired people (e.g. closed circuit video magnification equipment capable of magnifying text and images).

HMRC also list the following as examples of equipment qualifying for relief.

- Braille embossers.
- Whistling cups for blind people.
- White canes for blind people.

(VAT Notice 701/7/02, paras 4.5, 4.7).

Over bed tables

This type of equipment is designed for use by hospital patients in general and not just those who are chronically sick or disabled. They therefore cannot be said to be 'designed solely for use by a handicapped person' and do not qualify for relief. See *Princess Louise Scottish Hospital* (VTD 1412) (TVC 19.39).

Pain relief equipment

Following the tribunal decision in *Neen Design Ltd* (VTD 11782) (TVC 19.11) TENS (Transcutaneous Electrical Nerve Stimulators) machines are taken as designed solely for use by disabled persons (i.e. sufferers of chronic pain) even though frequently used by sufferers of acute (short-term) pain (e.g. sports injuries and labour pains). Neither the latter, nor the fact that the product was subsequently marketed for use by sufferers of chronic *and* acute pain, outweighed the original design intention. As a result, TENS machines can be zero-rated when meeting the conditions in **28.17** above. TENS machines supplied for use by people suffering short-term pain are taxable at the standard rate.

Radiators

In *The David Lewis Centre* (VTD 10860) (TVC 19.34) low surface temperature radiators, designed so that their surface would not burn the skin of a disabled person who fell against them, were held to be zero-rated because the heating system in its entirety had been designed specifically for the charity. HMRC regard this decision as one made on the facts of the case.

In *Boys' and Girls' Welfare Society* (VTD 15274) (TVC 19.89) the tribunal held that low surface temperature radiators did not qualify for zero-rating under *Item 2(g)* since they were not 'designed solely for use by a handicapped person', but that they qualified for zero-rating under **28.28** below where they were installed in bathrooms, washrooms or lavatories.

In *Joulesave EMES Ltd* (VTD 17115) (TVC 19.30) the tribunal held that radiator and pipe covers had been designed solely for use by disabled people and were eligible for zero-rating when meeting the conditions in **28.17** above.

Soft games rooms and observation windows

The design, supply and equipping of soft games rooms, and observation windows, used by disabled persons were held to be standard-rated supplies of construction services in *C & E Commrs v The David Lewis Centre*, QB [1995] STC 485 (TVC 11.7).

Spa baths

In *Aquakraft Ltd* (VTD 2215) (TVC 19.10) the tribunal held that a spa bath supplied to hospitals and nursing homes, even though it had special features such as handrails, provision for the fitting of a hoist and recessed taps for safety, was not subject to relief under *Item 2(g)* because all kinds of hospital patients could be expected to use it.

A spa bath might be eligible for zero-rating under **28.28** below (as a supply of goods in connection with extending or adapting a bathroom in a disabled person's private residence).

Walkways

Walkways do not incorporate any special features that render them 'designed solely for use by a disabled person' and so are not eligible for zero-rating under *Item 2(g)*. See *Portland College* (VTD 9815) (TVC 19.52).

Wheelchairs

Invalid wheelchairs and carriages (other than mechanically propelled vehicles intended or adapted for use on the roads) are specifically included in *VATA 1994, Sch 8 Group 12 Item 2* by *Notes 4(b)* and *5G*.

An '*invalid carriage*' is defined by *The Chronically Sick and Disabled Persons Act 1970, s 20* as a vehicle, whether mechanically propelled or not, constructed or adapted for the carriage of one person, being a person suffering from some physical defect or disability.

Writing boards

Zero-rating does not apply to a general purpose item that is marketed for use by disabled people, even if some changes are made to the design to make it useful for them. An objective test must be applied to see if the item has been designed solely for use by a disabled person. The design intention must be met for zero-rating to be achieved. See *Posturite (UK) Ltd* (VTD 7848) (TVC 19.51).

Parts and accessories

[28.22] Provided the conditions in **28.15** above are met, zero-rating applies to 'parts' and 'accessories' designed solely for use in or with goods described in **28.16** to **28.21** above and **28.24**(*a*) below. [*VATA 1994, Sch 8 Group 12, Item 2(h)*].

'*Parts*' means integral components without which the equipment is incomplete. '*Accessories*' means optional extras which can be used to improve the operation of the equipment, or enable it to be used, or to be used to better effect, in particular circumstances.

Zero-rating does not apply to general use items even if purchased to be used with a zero-rated item. See *Poole Shopmobility* (VTD 16290) (TVC 19.69) (standard batteries) and *Mills* (VTD 1893) (TVC 19.71) (portable generator). If, however, batteries were designed solely to operate within a zero-rated item, they would be eligible for zero-rating. (VAT Notice 701/7/02, para 4.8). See also *The Princess Louise Scottish Hospital* (VTD 1412) (TVC 19.39) where overbeds were held not to qualify as accessories to a zero-rated bed within **28.17** above, even though designed by the same designer, as they could be used on other beds.

Boats

[28.23] Provided the conditions in **28.17** above are met, zero-rating applies to boats designed, or substantially and permanently adapted, for use by disabled persons. [*VATA 1994, Sch 8 Group 12, Item 2(i)*].

To qualify for relief, the boat should include all or most of the following features.

- A ramp for wheelchairs.
- Lifts and level non-cambered surfaces to accommodate wheelchair movements.
- Specialised washing and lavatory facilities accessible to disabled people.
- Specially equipped galley and sleeping areas and steering facilities designed for use by disabled people.
- Handrails.
- Wheelchair clamps.

(VAT Notice 701/7/02, para 4.4).

Prior to 1 January 2012 concessionary treatment allowed zero-rating on the supply of parts and accessories designed solely for use in or with boats designed or adapted for use by disabled persons. The concession was withdrawn from 1 January 2012. However, zero-rating continues to apply to: parts and accessories used in connection with repairs or maintenance to qualifying boats; and parts and accessories that are included as part of the single supply of qualifying boats. (HMRC Brief 42/11).

Motor vehicles

[28.24] Zero-rating applies to the supply of a motor vehicle in the following circumstances.

(a) The supply (including the letting on hire) to
- a disabled person for 'domestic or personal use', or
- a charity for making available, by sale or otherwise, to disabled persons for domestic or personal use

of a motor vehicle designed or substantially and permanently adapted for the carriage of a disabled person in a wheelchair or on a stretcher and of no more than eleven other persons.

See **28.15** above for the interpretation of '*domestic and personal use*'. [*VATA 1994, Sch 8 Group 12, Item 2(f); SI 2001/754*].

(b) The supply (including the letting on hire) of a 'qualifying motor vehicle' to
- a disabled person, who usually uses a wheelchair or is usually carried on a stretcher, for domestic or his personal use; or
- a charity for making available to such a disabled person, by sale or otherwise, for domestic or his personal use.

A '*qualifying motor vehicle*' is a motor vehicle (other than one capable of carrying 12 or more persons including the driver) that
- is designed or substantially and permanently adapted to enable a disabled person, who usually uses a wheelchair or who is usually carried on a stretcher, to enter, and drive or otherwise be carried in, the motor vehicle; or
- by reason of its design, or being substantially or permanently adapted, includes features whose design is such that their sole purpose is to a allow a wheelchair used by a disabled person to be carried in or on the motor vehicle.

[*VATA 1994, Sch 8 Group 12 Item 2A and Notes 5, 5L; SI 2001/754*].

HMRC give the following advice and interpretations on the above.

(1) A wheelchair user can choose to remain in the wheelchair or use any of the seats.

(2) A '*wheelchair*' is a chair for invalids on wheels which is manually or mechanically propelled. A mobility scooter (i.e. a scooter which is mechanically propelled, has a central steering column, has a maximum speed of four miles per hour for pavement use, and is generally only used outside the home) is not a wheelchair for VAT purposes.

(3) A '*wheelchair user*' is anyone who has to use a wheelchair (electrically powered or otherwise) in order to be mobile. A disabled person with a degenerative condition, such as multiple sclerosis, who does not need to use a wheelchair all the time, but only when the condition requires it, also qualifies as a wheelchair user. A person who only occasionally uses a wheelchair (e.g. when visiting a shopping centre or gardens) or temporarily (e.g. because he has a broken leg) is not considered normally to use a wheelchair and is not eligible for the relief.

(4) A '*stretcher user*' for these purposes is anyone who has to use a stretcher in order to be transported.

(5) '*Domestic or personal use*'. To qualify for zero-rating the adapted vehicle must be for the domestic or personal use of the disabled wheelchair/stretcher user. This may also include vehicles that are used by the disabled wheelchair/stretcher user in his work capacity provided this is incidental to the vehicle's main use as a private vehicle.

Zero-rating does not apply to vehicles supplied to businesses regardless of who uses them or how they have been adapted (e.g. it is not possible to zero-rate an adapted vehicle that will be used as a taxi).

(6) *Adapted motor vehicles*. An eligible adapted motor vehicle is one adapted to meet the specific needs of a disabled wheelchair/stretcher user where the adaptation

- allows him to enter and travel in the vehicle whilst seated in the wheelchair or on the stretcher;
- allows him to enter, travel in or leave the vehicle;
- enables him to drive the vehicle; or
- allows a wheelchair to be carried on, or in, the vehicle.

A '*permanent*' adaptation is one that can be used for as long as the disabled person requires it. Generally the adaptation would require welding or bolting to the vehicle.

A '*substantial*' adaptation enables a wheelchair/stretcher user to use a vehicle which he could not use before it was adapted. For example, a spinner device, such as a knob on a steering wheel, may not seem substantial to an able-bodied person but it would be substantial for a disabled wheelchair user who could not otherwise drive the vehicle.

Included are

- a swivel seat;
- a hoist to lift a wheelchair into or onto the vehicle;
- a box for the wheelchair, which is fitted to the top or the back of the vehicle;
- adaptations that enable a wheelchair user to drive the vehicle, such as a push/pull brake and accelerator, hand controls or other aids that operate the primary driving controls; and
- an infra-red control unit that operates the secondary controls.

Not included are

- the fitting of a roof rack or standard roof box,
- the attachment of a trailer to the back of a vehicle, or
- the fitting of automatic transmission

because they are for general use and not specifically designed for disabled people.

Second-hand adapted motor vehicles can be zero-rated if the above conditions are met. (Although second-hand cars are usually sold under the second-hand margin scheme, an eligible vehicle can be sold outside that scheme and invoiced in the normal way.)

A family member can purchase the adapted vehicle provided that it is purchased for the personal use of the disabled wheelchair/stretcher user.

(VAT Notice 701/59/02, paras 2.2–2.5, 2.7, 3.2–3.6, 4.1).

From 1 January 2012 the concessionary arrangement that allowed a motor vehicle supplied to a disabled wheelchair user to be zero-rated if the vehicle was adapted shortly *after* it was supplied to the disabled person has been withdrawn. However, zero-rating continues to apply on motor vehicles that are adapted *before* the supply. (HMRC Brief 41/11).

Motability scheme

See also **28.31** below for zero-rating of motor vehicles under this scheme.

Adaptation of goods

[28.25] Zero-rating applies to the supply

- to a disabled person of services of adapting general purpose goods to suit his or her condition, and
- to a charity of services of adapting general purpose goods to suit the condition of a disabled person to whom the goods are to be made available, by sale or otherwise, by the charity,

and to any goods necessarily supplied in connection with the services of adaptation.

Zero-rating applies only to the adaptation services (and incidental goods). It does not apply to the goods themselves being adapted. Therefore, where the supplier of the services also supplies the goods, and has adapted them prior to the supply of adaptation services, he must apportion the value of the supply between the unadapted standard-rated goods and the zero-rated service of adaptation.

[*VATA 1994, Sch 8 Group 12 Items 3, 4, 6 and Note 8*].

Separate rules apply to the sale of substantially and permanently adapted motor vehicles. See **28.24** above.

Buildings

Apart from the first grant of a major interest in a building which is deemed to be a supply of goods by virtue of the *VATA 1994, Sch 4 para 4*, buildings are not 'goods' and therefore the adaptation of a building to suit the condition of a disabled person does not fall within the above provisions. See *Arthritis Care* (VTD 13974) (TVC 19.63). The only reliefs which apply to adaptations of buildings are those in **28.28** and **28.29** below.

Apportionment

See **47.4 OUTPUT TAX** for various methods of apportionment. It may not be valid to look merely at the price difference between the adapted model and a standard factory model. Any initial research and development costs related to the adaptation should be costed as zero-rated in addition to the basic extra cost passed on to the customer (see *Foxer Industries* (VTD 14469) (TVC 19.74)).

Repair and maintenance

[28.26] Zero-rating applies to the supply to a disabled person or charity of a service of repair or maintenance of

- any goods which were zero-rated on supply under **28.15** to **28.24** above,
- any goods supplied in connection with adaptation services under **28.25** above or repair and maintenance services under these provisions,
- any goods supplied in connection with the installation of a lift under **28.29** below, and
- any alarm call system zero-rated under **28.30** below

together with a supply of any goods in connection with those repair and maintenance services.

[*VATA 1994, Sch 8 Group 12 Items 5 and 6; SI 2001/754*].

See also **28.28** below under the heading *Goods supplied in connection with construction services*.

Installation of goods

[28.27] Zero-rating applies to the supply to a disabled person or to a charity of services necessarily performed in the installation of equipment or appliances (including parts and accessories for them) which are zero-rated under **28.15** to **28.23** above. [*VATA 1994, Sch 8 Group 12 Item 7*].

Examples of services of installation which can be zero-rated under these provisions are

- plumbing in a sanitary appliance;
- wiring up an electrically adjustable bed; and
- installing a chair lift.

(VAT Notice 701/7/02, para 5.1).

Where parts and accessories are used, these are eligible for zero-rating under this provision provided they are part of the single supply of installation services. Parts and accessories supplied separately are eligible for relief under **28.22** above.

Building alterations

[28.28] Zero-rating applies to the following supplies.

(a) The supply to a disabled person of a service of constructing ramps or widening doorways or passages (but not constructing new doorways or passages) for the purposes of facilitating his entry to, or movement within, his private residence. [*VATA 1994, Sch 8 Group 12 Item 8*].
Construction of a ramp includes
  - the raising of a floor level to match that of another existing floor level so as to remove a step or steps;
  - the reduction of the angle of an incline; or
  - the creation of a slope.

  A passage can be outdoors as well as indoors. Widening a passage includes
  - the widening of a room through which a disabled person passes to gain access to another room, e.g. a bedroom which has an en suite facility (see *Cannings-Knight* (VTD 11291) (TVC 19.81)); or
  - the widening of an existing path across a disabled person's garden (but not the construction of a new path).

  (VAT Notice 701/7/02, para 6.2).

(b) The supply to a charity of services within (*a*) above for the purpose of facilitating a disabled person's entry to, or movement within, *any* building (not just a private residence). [*VATA 1994, Sch 8 Group 12 Item 9*].

(c) The supply to a disabled person of a service of providing, extending or adapting a bathroom, 'washroom' or lavatory in that person's private residence where such provision, extension or adaptation is necessary by reason of his condition. [*VATA 1994, Sch 8 Group 12 Item 10*].

(d) The supply to a charity of a service of providing, extending or adapting a bathroom, 'washroom' or lavatory for use by disabled persons
- in a residential home or self-contained living accommodation, in either case provided as a residence (whether on a permanent or temporary basis or both) for handicapped persons (but not including an inn, hotel, boarding house or similar establishment or accommodation in any such type of establishment), or
- in a day-centre where at least 20% of the individuals using the centre are handicapped persons

where such provision, extension or adaptation is necessary by reason of the condition of the disabled persons.
[*VATA 1994, Sch 8 Group 12 Item 11 and Note 5J; SI 2000/805*].
Zero-rating applies even if the residential home, etc. is not managed or used by the charity to which the supply is made. Care, however, should be taken when supplies are made to residential homes as many such homes are not operated by charities, in which case supplies to them do not qualify for zero-rating under these provisions. (VAT Notice 701/7/02, para 6.3).

(e) The supply to a charity of a service of providing, extending or adapting a 'washroom' or lavatory for use by disabled persons in a building (or part of a building) used principally by a charity for charitable purposes (e.g. a church hall, day centre or village hall) where such provision, etc. is necessary to facilitate the use of the washroom or lavatory by disabled persons. [*VATA 1994, Sch 8 Group 12 Item 12*].

(f) The supply of goods in connection with the supply of services within (*a*)–(*e*) above. [*VATA 1994, Sch 8 Group 12 Item 13*].
Building materials and other goods can be zero-rated under this provision when supplied by
- the building contractor in connection with the zero-rated services (see above), or
- a builders merchant, etc. to the disabled person or charity themselves for use by their building contractor (see *Flather* (VTD 11960) (TVC 19.82)) provided the builders merchant is happy that the actual building work will qualify for zero-rating and can demonstrate this subsequently to any visiting HMRC officer

but not when the materials are bought by a disabled person or charity in connection with building works which will be performed free of charge by a friend or relative, or in a do-it-yourself capacity by the disabled person or charity themselves (because there is no subsequent supply of zero-rated construction services to which these materials can be connected).
(VAT Notice 701/7/02, para 6.9).

For the purposes of (*c*)–(*e*) above

- '*washroom*' means a room that contains a lavatory or washbasin (or both) but does not contain a bath or a shower or cooking, sleeping or laundry facilities [*VATA 1994, Sch 8 Group 12 Notes 5K; SI 2000/805*];
- bathroom includes a shower room (VAT Notice 701/7/02, para 6.3); and
- lavatory is a room containing a toilet and possibly, but not always, a washbasin (VAT Notice 701/7/02, para 6.3).

Preparatory work

Preparatory work and necessary restoration work can also be zero-rated provided the supply is made to the disabled person or charity concerned, as the case may be. This would include, e.g.

- when widening a doorway, the removal of bricks and mortar and restoration of the immediate décor; and
- when providing a bathroom, the preparation of footings, including ground levelling, work for the provision of water, gas, electricity and drainage as necessary, and restoration of the immediate décor.

Professional services

Services of an architect, surveyor or any person acting as a consultant or in a supervisory capacity, even when supplied in connection with a supply of qualifying building services, are standard-rated in all circumstances.

Additional construction work in the course of a zero-rated supply

Where economy and feasibility dictate that a bathroom, washroom or lavatory has to be constructed in, or extended into, a space occupied by an existing room (e.g. a bedroom or kitchen), the restoration of that room to its original size can be regarded as part of the work essential to the provision of the bathroom, etc. and can be zero-rated provided the supply is also made to the disabled person. Where, on the other hand, a builder constructs, extends or adapts a bathroom, washroom or lavatory and at the same time constructs additional accommodation (e.g. an adjoining new bedroom/day room), the supply must be apportioned between the zero-rated and standard-rated parts.

(VAT Notice 701/7/02, paras 6.5, 6.7, 6.8).

Lift installation

[28.29] The following supplies are zero-rated.

(a) The supply to a disabled person of services necessarily performed in the installation of a lift for the purpose of facilitating his or her movement between floors within that person's own private residence. [*VATA 1994, Sch 8 Group 12 Item 16*].
This provision overlaps with **28.19** above (zero-rating of chair and stair lifts) but extends relief to lifts which, although not specially designed for use by disabled people, help them to move between floors within their home.

(b) The supply to a charity providing a permanent or temporary residence or day centre for disabled persons of services necessarily performed in the installation of a lift for the purpose of facilitating movement of disabled persons between floors in that building. [*VATA 1994, Sch 8 Group 12 Item 17*].

To qualify as a day centre, the building need not have been set up principally or exclusively for disabled persons but it must be capable of being regarded as a day centre in the ordinary sense of the term. This probably means that the disabled persons receive some form of care. See *Union of Students of the University of Warwick* (VTD 13821) (TVC 19.97) and *Aspex Visual Arts Trust* (VTD 16419) (TVC 19.98) where a lift in a students union building and an art gallery respectively failed to qualify for zero-rating.

Educational institutions. As a consequence of comments made by the High Court in *C & E Commrs v Help the Aged*, QB [1997] STC 406 (TVC 11.17) HMRC initially formed the view that charitable educational institutions (e.g. grant-maintained schools and universities) could be regarded as day centres providing care for disabled people and therefore the installation of lifts in their *non-residential* buildings could be zero-rated under the above provisions (providing all other conditions were met). They subsequently decided that this view was incorrect. As a transitional measure, where a contract for the installation of a lift in a non-residential building was entered into before 31 March 2005, HMRC accept that the supply can be zero-rated providing all other conditions have been met. Where the installation of a lift has been zero-rated under these arrangements, subsequent supplies of repair and maintenance of that lift can also be zero-rated. Where a contract for the installation of a lift in a non-residential building is entered into after that date, the supply of installation services (and any subsequent supplies of repair and maintenance) is standard-rated. This does not apply to lift installations in those buildings where an educational institution provides permanent or temporary residence, which remains zero-rated, provided all other conditions are met. (Business Brief 3/05).

(c) The supply of goods in connection with the supply of services within (*a*) or (*b*) above. [*VATA 1994, Sch 8 Group 12 Item 18*].

Building materials and other goods can be zero-rated under this provision when supplied

- by the building contractor in connection with the zero-rated services (see above), or
- by a builders merchant, etc. to the disabled person or charity themselves for use by their building contractor (see *Flather* (VTD 11960) (TVC 19.82)) provided the builders merchant is happy that the actual building work will qualify for zero-rating and can demonstrate this subsequently to any visiting HMRC officer

but not when the materials are bought by a disabled person or charity in connection with building works which will be performed free of charge by a friend or relative, or in a do-it-yourself capacity by the

disabled person or charity themselves (because there is no subsequent supply of zero-rated construction services to which these materials can be connected).
(VAT Notice 701/7/02, para 6.9).

Preparatory work

Preparatory work and necessary restoration work can also be zero-rated provided the supply is made to the disabled person or charity concerned, as the case may be.

Professional services

HMRC take the view that services of an architect, surveyor or any person acting as a consultant or in a supervisory capacity, even when supplied in connection with a supply of qualifying building services, are standard-rated in all circumstances. See, however, the decision in *Friends of the Elderly* (VTD 20597) (TVC 19.99). The lift manufacturer required the appellant to approve technical designs and insure the installer of the structural capability of the building, etc. which required professional advice. Since the installation of a lift is complicated and potentially dangerous, the tribunal held that there was no reason to suppose that Parliament impliedly intended to exclude architect's services from being zero-rated as 'necessarily performed in the installation of a lift'.

(VAT Notice 701/7/02, paras 6.7, 6.8).

Repair and maintenance of any qualifying goods is zero-rated under **28.26** above.

Alarm call systems

[28.30] The following supplies are zero-rated.

(a) The supply to
- a disabled person for his 'domestic or personal use', or
- a charity for making available to disabled persons, by sale or otherwise, for domestic or their personal use

of an alarm system designed to be capable of operation by a disabled person, and to enable him to alert directly a 'specified person or a control centre'.

(b) The supply of services necessarily performed by a control centre in receiving and responding to calls from an alarm system within (*a*) above.

A '*specified person or control centre*' is a person or centre who or which is appointed to receive directly calls activated by the alarm system; and who or which retains information about the disabled person to assist that person in the event of illness, injury or similar emergency.

[*VATA 1994, Sch 8 Group 12 Items 19, 20* and *Note 9*].

See **28.15** above for HMRC's interpretation of '*domestic or personal use*'.

Not included is the installation of ordinary telephone lines or the supply of ordinary telephones, internal communication systems, and intruder alarm systems which activate bells, lights or sirens.
(VAT Notice 701/7/02, para 7.1).

Repair and maintenance of any qualifying item is zero-rated under **28.26** above.

Motability scheme

[28.31] Zero-rating applies to the letting on hire of *any* motor vehicle (i.e. whether or not specially designed/adapted for a disabled person) to a disabled person in receipt of a disability living allowance by virtue of entitlement to the mobility component or of mobility supplement (as defined) provided

- the lessor's business consists predominantly of the provision of motor vehicles to such persons;
- the vehicle is unused at the commencement of the period of letting;
- the letting is for a period of not less than three years; and
- the consideration for the letting consists wholly or partly of sums paid to the lessor, directly by the Department for Works and Pensions or the Ministry of Defence on behalf of the lessee, in respect of mobility allowance or mobility supplement to which the lessee is entitled.

[*VATA 1994, Sch 8 Group 12 Item 14*].

In practice, only vehicles leased under the Motability scheme meet the above conditions. Further information on the scheme is available from Motability Operations, City Gate House, 22 Southwark Bridge Road, London SE1 9HB (Tel: 0845 456 4566) or from their website at
www.motability.co.uk

Sale of ex-lease vehicles

The sale of the motor vehicle which has been let on hire under the above conditions is also zero-rated provided the sale constitutes the first supply after the period of letting. [*VATA 1994, Sch 8 Group 12 Item 15*]. In practice, Motability only sells the vehicle back to the car dealer from whom it was originally purchased. Following the tribunal decisions in *Peugeot Motor Co plc* (VTD 15314) (TVC 44.68), HMRC accept that the subsequent sale by the dealer of these motor vehicles is within the margin scheme.

See also **28.24** above for letting on hire of other vehicles.

Imports, acquisitions, exports and removals

Imports into the UK

[28.32] Where goods within **28.15** to **28.31** above are imported from outside the EU by

- a disabled person for domestic or his personal use, or

- a charity for making available to disabled persons (by sale or otherwise),

they can be relieved of the VAT due on importation under the same conditions as for zero-rating the supply of such goods in the UK. [*VATA 1994, Sch 8 Group 12 Note 1*].

The disabled person or charity (as the case may be) must make a declaration in the appropriate form (see **28.33** below) and lodge it with the import entry declaration made to HMRC at the port, airport or postal depot of importation.

A supplier importing goods does not qualify for relief in this way. He must pay any VAT due on importation but can reclaim it as input tax, subject to the normal rules.

(VAT Notice 701/7/02, para 8.1).

Acquisitions from other EU countries

VAT-registered traders acquiring goods from other EU countries are not normally required to pay VAT at the place of importation but must account for any VAT due (and, subject to the normal rules, claim it back as input tax) on their next VAT return. A *VAT-registered* charity which acquires qualifying goods within **28.15** to **28.31** above from another EU country for disabled persons can account for VAT at the zero rate on its acquisition of such goods.

Persons who are not registered for VAT (including disabled persons and non-registered charities) do not have this facility.

- If they buy goods in another EU country, they may be required to pay tax on those goods in that EU country at the prevailing rate there. Any tax payable cannot be refunded in the UK by HMRC. Each EU country has its own rules about the extent of VAT relief on goods for disabled persons and the reliefs set out in **28.15** to **28.31** above do not apply to supplies made in other EU countries.
- If they buy goods in another EU country but the supplier arranges delivery, special 'distance selling' rules apply (see **19.10 EUROPEAN UNION: SINGLE MARKET**) and the VAT treatment will depend upon whether the supply is treated as taking place in that other EU country or the UK.

Motor vehicles for disabled wheelchair/stretcher users. If the vehicle acquired qualifies as a new means of transport (see **19.33 EUROPEAN UNION: SINGLE MARKET**), VAT is not due in the country in which the vehicle is purchased, but is due in the UK at the time of acquisition. VAT relief on the acquisition will apply, provided the same conditions are met to enable the supply of the adapted vehicle to a disabled person to be zero-rated (see **28.24** above) if it had been supplied in the UK. If the vehicle does not qualify as a new means of transport, VAT is due at the rate applicable in the EU country where the vehicle is purchased.

(VAT Notice 701/7/02, para 8.2; VAT Notice 701/59/02, para 6.2).

Exports and removals of goods from the UK

Goods or services supplied to disabled people from other countries, who are visiting the UK, can be zero-rated under the conditions set out in **28.15** to **28.31** above. If the goods do not qualify for this VAT relief, it may still be possible to zero-rate the supply, subject to certain conditions, under the retail export scheme (see **21.11 EXPORTS**) which applies to persons resident outside the EU who are exporting the goods to a place outside the EU. VAT must be charged on all other retail sales of standard-rated goods. (VAT Notice 701/7/02, para 8.3).

The eligibility declaration regime (see **28.33** below) applies to these exports and removals in exactly the same way as it does to internal UK sales.

Where the value of a UK supplier's sales to citizens (whether disabled or not) of any single EU country exceeds that country's threshold for distance selling, then

- the other country becomes the place of supply; and
- VAT on any sales to that country becomes due there at the rate applicable in that country.

See **19.18 EUROPEAN UNION: SINGLE MARKET** for further details.

Eligibility declarations by disabled persons and charities

[28.33] HMRC recommend that a supplier obtains a written declaration from each customer claiming entitlement to VAT relief for goods and services under **28.15** to **28.31** above. Such a declaration should contain sufficient information to demonstrate that a customer fulfils all the criteria for eligibility. It should be separate, or clearly distinguishable from, any order form or invoice against which the goods or services are supplied. A customer signing an order should not automatically be signing a declaration of eligibility for VAT relief.

Suggested forms of declaration are reproduced in VAT Notice 701/7. The supplier should keep this declaration for production to any VAT officer.

Electronic declarations (e.g. received over the internet or by fax) are acceptable. Not all electronic declarations will have the means to incorporate a signature. In these circumstances, it is important that the supplier retains evidence of the origin of the document, such as the e-mail message incorporating the sender's address. As with paper declarations, electronic ones should be distinguishable from an order form or invoice.

Where a disabled person is unable to sign a declaration, the signature of a parent, guardian, doctor or another responsible person is acceptable.

A declaration only confirms the customer's status as a person eligible to receive zero-rated goods and services and the use to which he will put them. It does not mean that the goods and services themselves fulfil all the conditions for zero-rating. It is still the supplier's responsibility to take reasonable steps to satisfy himself that the goods or services being supplied qualify for zero-rating, the customer is entitled to zero-rating and the declaration is correct. If he believes an eligibility declaration to be inaccurate or untrue, he must not zero-rate the supply. The supplier should also take care that procedures, forms and literature do not encourage or lead customers to make such a declaration. HMRC will not, however, seek to recover VAT due from a supplier where a customer provided an incorrect declaration and the supplier, having taken all reasonable steps to check the validity of the declaration, fails to identify the inaccuracy and, in good faith, makes the supply at the zero rate. (VAT Notice 48, ESC 3.11).

(VAT Notice 701/7/02, paras 3.7–3.10, 10.1–10.4; VAT Notice 701/59/02, paras 13, 14).

Zero-rated 'talking books' for the blind

[28.34] 'Talking books' for the blind and severely handicapped are zero-rated when supplied to the Royal National Institute for the Blind, the National Listening Library and other similar charities. Included is certain apparatus and tapes designed or specially adapted for such use and non-specialist sound recording equipment. Also zero-rated are wireless receiving sets and non-specialist sound recording equipment supplied to a charity for free loan to the blind. See **12.7**(*a*) and (*b*) **CHARITIES** for full details.

Reduced rate supplies of welfare advice or information

[28.35] *With effect from 1 July 2006*, supplies of 'welfare advice or information' by

- a charity, or
- a 'state-regulated' private welfare institution or agency

are subject to a reduced rate of VAT of 5%.

'*Welfare advice or information*' means advice or information which directly relates to the following.

(a) The physical or mental welfare of elderly, sick, distressed or disabled persons.
Examples include advice on
- caring for people with Alzheimer's disease;
- dealing with domestic violence; and
- home safety for the elderly.

(b) The care or protection of children and young persons.
Examples include advice on
- contraception and sexual health for young people;
- caring for children with special needs or disabilities;
- stranger awareness for children and young people; and
- strategies for dealing with bullying.

'*State-regulated*' has the same meaning as in **28.12** above.

The reduced rate does *not* apply to the following.

- Supplies that would be exempt by virtue of *VATA 1994, Sch 9 Group 6* (education) if they were made by an eligible body within the meaning of that *Group* (see **16 EDUCATION** generally and **16.3** for eligible bodies).
- Supplies of goods, unless the goods are supplied 'wholly or almost wholly' for the purpose of conveying the advice or information.
  HMRC treat '*wholly or almost wholly*' as meaning that at least 90% of the purpose of any goods used must be the conveying of the welfare advice. Subject to this, the inclusion of incidental information (e.g. an appeal for donations or information on the charity's objects) does not affect the reduced rate.
  The reduced rate can, therefore, apply not only to advice given in person but also by means of DVD, audio cassette or CD Rom. Where supplied in the form of a book, leaflet, pamphlet or similar item then the supply is zero-rated if certain conditions are met. See **54 PRINTED MATTER, ETC.**
  Goods that have an independent use and also carry incidental welfare advice (e.g. mugs and T-shirts bearing a slogan) are not covered by the reduced rate.
- Supplies of advice or information provided solely for the benefit of a particular individual or according to his personal circumstances. (This is a supply of welfare services and exempt under **28.12** above.)

Free supplies of welfare advice or information are a non-business activity for VAT purposes.

[*VATA 1994, Sch 7A Group 9; SI 2006/1472*]. (VAT Notice 701/2/11, paras 6.1, 6.3–6.5).

Reduced rate supplies of mobility aids for elderly

[28.36] A reduced rate of VAT of 5% applies to

- the supply of services of installing 'mobility aids', and
- the supply of mobility aids by a person installing them

for use in 'domestic accommodation' by a person who, at the time of the supply, is aged 60 or over.

'*Mobility aids*' for these purposes means

- grab rails;
- ramps;
- stair lifts;
- bath lifts;
- built-in shower seats or showers containing built-in shower seats; and
- walk-in baths fitted with sealable doors.

'*Domestic accommodation*' means a building, or part of a building, that consists of a dwelling or a number of dwellings.

[*VATA 1995, Sch 7A Group 10; SI 2007/1601*].

Key points

[28.37] Points to consider are as follows.

- VAT exemption generally applies to medical services provided by a registered health professional, as long as the services are intend to protect, maintain or restore the health of individuals.
- In certain cases, a supply can be partly exempt and partly taxable – for example, an optician supplying a pair of spectacles is providing standard-rated goods but exempt medical services in making the spectacles suitable for the patient, i.e. dispensing services. A cost-based apportionment method will normally determine how much output tax is payable on a mixed sale.
- Exemption can also apply in relation to services provided by non-registered health professionals, as long as they are being directly supervised by a registered health professional. HMRC impose very strict conditions concerning the supervisory arrangements in order for exemption to apply.
- Welfare services provided by relevant bodies and institutions are also exempt from VAT if intended to help people in need (e.g. elderly, disabled, sick people). The scope of the exemption is very wide and includes, for example, assistance with form filling and general every day needs.
- Zero-rating applies to a wide range of goods and services that are specifically intended for disabled people. The zero-rating does not include everyday items that might make life easier for a disabled person, only those that are specifically designed for their use. Various conditions need to be met by suppliers in order to secure zero-rating.
- The reduced rate of VAT (5%) applies to welfare advice provided by a charity or a state-regulated private welfare institution or agency. The advice must be for the benefit of elderly, sick, distressed or disabled persons, or relevant to the care or protection of children and young persons.

29

HMRC: Administration

De Voil Indirect Tax Service. See V1.262–V1.287A.

Introduction

[29.1] The collection and management of VAT is the responsibility of the Commissioners for Her Majesty's Revenue and Customs ('HMRC') (previously the Commissioners of Customs and Excise). [*VATA 1994, s 96(1), Sch 11 para 1; CRCA 2005, Sch 4 para 56*].

The Central Unit at Alexander House, 21 Victoria Avenue, Southend-on-Sea SS99 1AA (Tel: 01702 348944; Fax: 01702 366687) keeps registration records, despatches return forms and reminders, receives completed forms and VAT payments, and repays VAT.

VAT offices deal with the administration of VAT in their area but not the issue of return forms or the receipt of VAT which is dealt with by VAT Central Unit. All VAT offices are linked to the central VAT computer.

HMRC Charter

[29.2] On 12 November 2009, HMRC launched the Charter below, setting out what individuals, businesses and other groups dealing with HMRC can expect from the department, as well as what it expects from them.

> **A person's rights: what a person can expect from HMRC**
>
> *Respect*: HMRC will treat people with courtesy and consideration; listen to their concerns; answer their questions in a way they can understand; try to understand

their circumstances; make them aware of their rights, including their right to appeal HMRC decisions; and tell them how to exercise their right to appeal.

Help and support to get things right: HMRC will provide information that helps a person understand what they have to do and when they have to do it; provide information that clearly explains the taxes, duties, exemptions, allowances, reliefs and tax credits that HMRC are responsible for; process the information a person gives HMRC as quickly and accurately as they can; and put mistakes right as soon as they can.

Treat people as honest: HMRC will presume a person is telling the truth; accept that they will pay what they owe and only claim what they are entitled to; explain why HMRC need to ask questions and why they have decided to check a person's records; and only question what a person tells them if they have good reason.

Treat people even-handedly: HMRC will act within the law and their published guidance; help people understand their legal rights; explain what a person can do if they disagree with HMRC decisions or want to make a complaint; provide them with information in a way that meets their particular needs; and consider any financial difficulties they may be having.

Be professional and act with integrity: HMRC will act with integrity; make sure that a person is dealt with by people who have the right level of expertise; make decisions in accordance with the law and published guidance and explain them clearly; respond to enquiries and resolve any problems as soon as they can; and let people how appeals, investigations or complaints are progressing.

Tackle people who deliberately break the rules and challenge those who bend the rules: HMRC will identify people who are not paying what they owe or claiming more than they should; recover the money and charge interest and penalties where appropriate; distinguish between legitimately trying to pay the lowest amount and bending the rules through tax avoidance; and use HMRC powers reasonably.

Protect information and respect privacy: HMRC will protect information they obtain, receive or hold about a person; explain why they need information, if asked; only allow HMRC staff to see information when they need it to do their job; give a person the information held about them when asked, as long as the law allows; only share or release information about a person when the law allows and it is necessary; and respect a person's legal rights when they visit premises.

Accept that someone else can represent a person: HMRC will respect a representative's right to act for a person and deal with them appropriately.

Do all they can to keep the cost of dealing with HMRC as low as possible: HMRC will try to make their services straightforward and easy to access; make it as cheap as they can for a person to contact them; explain clearly what they need; do their best to give complete, accurate and consistent advice; and do their best to get things right first time.

A person's obligations: what HMRC can expect from a person

Be honest: HMRC expect people to be truthful, open and act within the law; give accurate information; give all the relevant facts; and tell HMRC as soon as they can if they think they have made a mistake.

Respect HMRC staff: HMRC expect people to be polite; and accept that HMRC will not tolerate rude or abusive behaviour.

Take care to get things right: HMRC expect people to take reasonable care when they complete tax returns and fill out forms; send tax returns and forms on time; make payments on time; respond in good time if HMRC ask them to do something; talk to HMRC if there is anything that they are not sure about or if they are having difficulty meeting obligations; tell HMRC if they have any particular needs so they can be taken into account; tell HMRC about any changes in circumstances that will affect payments or claims; and keep adequate records that support what they tell HMRC and hold them for as long as the law says is necessary.

Publications and interpretation of law

[29.3] HMRC issue

- **Notices** and (formerly) **leaflets**, which are numbered booklets explaining various aspects of VAT. See **30.1 HMRC NOTICES, INFORMATION SHEETS AND FORMS** for those currently in issue. Most of the notices and leaflets are available from the National Advice Service (tel: 0845 010 9000). When requesting a new or revised Notice or an update, it is advisable to quote the issue date or update number to check that the correct copy is received (and not an out-of-date one). It is also advisable to make a note of the date of the request.
- **VAT Notes** to bring to the notice of all registered persons details of information available from VAT offices. They are sent out with VAT return forms.
- **News releases** and **briefs** are issued as informative news items. They are numbered and dated.
- **VAT information sheets** on items of particular interest.

Changes in interpretation of the law

When HMRC advise on the correct interpretation of the law, taxpayers will usually only be required to apply the new interpretation from a current or future date announced by HMRC. If, following HMRC's announcement of its new interpretation of the law, a business nevertheless chooses to correct historical errors, HMRC will accept the corrections providing all of the following conditions are met.

- all past errors are corrected;
- the neutrality of the tax is respected; and
- the business is no better off and the Exchequer no worse off than they would have been if the mistaken interpretation had not been made.

(HMRC Brief 14/11).

Contacting HMRC

National Advice Service

[29.4] The National Advice Service deals with all general telephone enquiries from both businesses and the public on 0845 010 9000. A textphone service, for customers with hearing difficulties, is available on 0845 000 0200 and a Welsh speaking service is available on 0845 010 0300. All services are available from 8.00am to 8.00pm on Mondays to Fridays.

The service is for all general enquiries about HMRC's taxes and duties, including VAT, Excise, Customs, Insurance Premium Tax, Landfill Tax, Aggregates Tax, Air Passenger Duty, Climate Change Levy and Mineral Oils. The service should be used in particular for

- queries on HMRC rules and procedures;
- rates of VAT chargeable on particular goods;
- requests for publications (e.g. forms and notices); and
- requests for duplicate VAT returns.

Where a question cannot be answered, it will be re-routed to the appropriate office or the caller will be given the phone number of the office required.

General written enquiries

The single postal address for VAT general enquiries is HMRC National Advice Service, Written Enquiries Section, Alexander House, Victoria Avenue, Southend, Essex SS99 1BD apart from supplies by or to charities which should be sent to HMRC Charities, St Johns House, Merton Road, Bootle, Merseyside L69 9BB.

E-mail enquiries

The e-mail address for all enquiries relating to VAT is:

Enquiries.estn@hmrc.gsi.gov.uk

Personal visits

The National Advice Service can make appointments for one-to-one consultations on any VAT matter at a mutually convenient venue.

VAT registration, change in registration details and deregistration

General applications for registration should be made directly to HM Revenue & Customs, Deansgate, 62–70 Tettenhall Road, Wolverhampton, WV1 4TZ. Changes and applications for deregistration should be notified to HM Revenue & Customs, Imperial House, 77 Victoria Street, Grimsby DN31 1DB.

All VAT 68 (request to retain VAT registration number of previous owner of business), VAT group applications, annual accounting requests and agricultural flat-rate scheme applications should be made to HM Revenue & Customs, Imperial House, 77 Victoria Street, Grimsby DN31 1DB.

VAT registration of overseas traders with no UK establishment, tax representative or agent

Contact should be made directly with:

Non-Established Taxable Persons Unit, HM Revenue and Customs, Ruby House, 8 Ruby Place, Aberdeen, AB10 1ZP.

Payment problems

Where a business has problems in clearing an existing VAT debt, it should contact the National Advice Service (0845 010 9000) and will be put in touch with the appropriate Regional Debt Management Unit.

National Insolvency Helpdesk

Telephone 0151 703 8450.

Tax advisers

Tax advisers should address written queries about specific client's affairs to the client's VAT office. Factual queries which are not specific to a particular client should be by telephone to the National Telephone Advice Service (see above) or in writing to the tax adviser's own VAT office. Approach should only be made to HMRC Headquarters if enquiries are being made on behalf of an entire industry or if lobbying or otherwise acting as a member of a representative or consultative body concerned with the effect of present or proposed legislation.

HMRC rulings

[29.5] Most VAT enquiries can be dealt with by a telephone call to HMRC National Advice Service or, in the case of more detailed questions, in writing to one of the written enquiries teams. See **29.4** above.

It is also possible to write to HMRC to ask for their view on how a particular transaction that has occurred, or is due to occur shortly, should be treated for VAT purposes. Normally, the supplier should ask for a ruling on the liability to VAT of goods or services and a customer should apply for a ruling on a question of VAT recovery.

Applying for a ruling

When requesting a ruling on VAT, the following information should be provided.

- Business name and VAT registration number. (VAT advisers should give these details for the business on whose behalf they are writing.)
- The full facts and context concerning the transactions or issues in question (see below).
- The intended use of the decision.
- A statement that, to the best of the taxpayer's knowledge and belief, the facts given are correct and that the full facts and relevant information have been disclosed.

Information to be given to HMRC

For a ruling to be binding, HMRC must be given the full facts and context of the transaction or issues in question by the taxpayer and/or his adviser at the time when the ruling is sought. It is the responsibility of the taxpayer/adviser to ensure that this happens. The information required will depend on the circumstances of the individual case but, where there is any doubt about whether particular details are relevant, they should be disclosed. HMRC advise taxpayers/advisers to include the following.

- A clear explanation of the precise point(s) about which they are unclear of the VAT consequences.
- Where a taxpayer has received professional advice in respect of the query being raised, the reason for uncertainty.
- Where possible alternative VAT treatments have been considered, a brief indication of them.
- If the point at issue concerns a transaction which has yet to take place, a copy of the final draft contract, where appropriate, and full details of the other parties involved, to the extent that this is possible. (Where a ruling is sought before contracts are finalised, a ruling may still be given, but will not be binding if a contract is produced later and the facts vary significantly from those disclosed.)
- Copies of all of the relevant documents with the relevant areas clearly highlighted (or otherwise drawn attention to).
- An estimate of the money associated with the decision (e.g. the annual value of sales of an item in respect of which a ruling on the liability to VAT is sought).
- Any transactions (proposed or actual) related to, consequent upon, or forming part of a series with the transaction in respect of which a ruling is sought, whether or not these transactions are certain to take place.

Circumstances where HMRC do not give rulings

HMRC do not give

- general rulings and, unless clearly stated otherwise, will only be bound in respect of the taxpayer who sought the ruling;
- rulings on hypothetical transactions or answer 'what if?' questions;
- tax planning advice and, in particular, they do not 'approve' tax planning arrangements and will refuse to give rulings if they suspect that the transactions are part of a tax avoidance scheme;
- advance rulings on transactions unless reasonably satisfied that the transaction, as described, will take place;
- rulings in response to applications that do not involve genuine points of doubt or difficulty to taxpayers or their professional advisers; and
- rulings where they believe that the point is covered by their Notices or other published guidance (in which case they will refer the applicant to the relevant publications).

Time limit for response

HMRC aim to resolve most enquiries within 15 days but in complex cases they will acknowledge the enquiry and let the applicant know when a full reply can be expected. They will attempt to respond in the timescale that the business circumstances require but sufficient time should be allowed for the query to be properly considered.

Disagreeing with a ruling

A taxpayer or adviser who disagrees with a ruling given by HMRC can ask for the ruling to be reconsidered. There is no general right of appeal to a VAT tribunal against an HMRC ruling although some rulings are appealable matters (e.g. the VAT liability of a particular supply).

Reliance on rulings by others

Normally, only the taxpayer requesting the ruling can rely upon it. This does not, however, apply where

- HMRC agree rulings with trade bodies;
- HMRC' correspondence clearly states otherwise; or
- the ruling is about a particular type of product or activity.

Where a taxpayer wishes to pass on the decision to other businesses or a trade association, this should be made clear in the application so that HMRC can explain how far it has a general application.

Where a taxpayer subsequently wishes to use a ruling given to an associated company carrying on an identical activity or operation, a simplified procedure can be used. The associate can send a copy of the existing ruling to HMRC, and explain either that it operates in precisely the same way or explain how its procedures differ from that of the original company. In some such circumstances, HMRC may need to ask for further information before confirming that the same ruling can be used.

(VAT Notice 700/6/08).

Making complaints about HMRC

[29.6] The following remedies are available to a person who has a complaint against HMRC.

(a) Complaints to HMRC

If a person has a complaint against HMRC, and is unable to resolve it on the spot with the officer concerned, he should contact one of the Regional Complaints Units listed below. Complaints may be made

- by speaking directly to an HMRC officer;
- by phone; or
- in writing, by letter, e-mail, or fax.

It should be made clear that the problem is to be treated as a complaint.

Central	Haven House, 17 Lower Brook Street, Ipswich IP4 1DN (tel 01473 235831; fax 01473 235702; e-mail complaints.cen@hmrc.gov.uk,
London	Dorset House, Stamford Street, London SE1 9PY (tel 020 8929 6731; fax 020 8929 6788; e-mail complain ts.slt@hmrc.gov.uk,
North	Peter Bennett House, Redvers Close, West Park Ring Road, Leeds LS16 6RQ (tel 0113 389 4222; fax 0113 389 4482; e-mail complaints.nth@hmrc.gov.uk,
Northern Ireland	Custom House, Custom House Square, Belfast BT1 3ET (tel 028 9056 2618; fax 028 9056 2970; e-mail complaints.ni@hmrc.gov.uk,
Scotland	44 York Place, Edinburgh EH1 3JW (tel 0131 469 7347; fax 0131 469 7341; e-mail complaints.sco@hm rc.gov.uk,
South	Compass House, Ordnance Survey Site, Romsey Road, Southampton SO16 4HP (tel 023 8079 7013; fax 023 8079 7018; e-mail complaints.sth@hmrc.go v.uk,
Wales	Portcullis House, 21 Cowbridge Road East, Cardiff CF11 9SS (tel 029 2038 6423; fax 029 2038 6440; e-mail complaints.wwb@hmrc.gov.uk,
Investigation/Intelligence	Custom House, Lower Thames Street, London EC3R 6EE (tel 0870 785 7798; fax 0870 785 6549; e-mail complaints.nis@hmrc.gov.uk,

As much background information as possible should be given, e.g. VAT registration number and date of visit or correspondence if appropriate. The appropriate local manager will carry out a thorough investigation of the complaint and will send a full reply, normally within ten working days of receipt. If this is not possible, he will indicate when a full reply will be sent.

If unhappy with the response to the complaint, a person can ask for it to be reconsidered on behalf of the Regional or Business Head. If still not satisfied with the decision reached by HMRC, the independent Adjudicator can be asked to look into the case (see (*b*) below).

Reimbursement of costs

If, as a direct result of mistake or unreasonable delay by HMRC, a person is left out of pocket, HMRC will consider reimbursing reasonable costs. These might include the costs of postage, phone calls, travelling expenses, professional fees or financial charges. HMRC will not compensate for the time spent by the complainant unless he can show lost earnings as a direct result. They may ask for evidence in support of the claim.

Compensation for worry and distress

Mistakes by HMRC can, in some circumstances, cause considerable worry and distress. If so, they may be able to make a payment in addition to any direct costs they reimburse to acknowledge any distress suffered. Similarly, they may also make a payment if they handle a complaint badly or take an unreasonable time to deal with it. HMRC consider each case on its own merits. These payments are not intended to put a value on the distress which might have been suffered and will typically range from £25 to £500.

(HMRC Notice 1000).

(b) Complaint to the independent Adjudicator

The Adjudicator for the Inland Revenue also deals with unresolved complaints about HMRC. The Adjudicator will consider (amongst other things) complaints about delay, rudeness, mistakes, harassment during a VAT investigation, application of extra-statutory concessions, requests for time to pay and refusal of information under the Open Government provisions. The Adjudicator will not examine cases which are appealable to a VAT tribunal nor intervene once a matter is before the criminal courts.

The address of the Adjudicator is

The Adjudicator's Office
8th Floor
Euston Tower
286 Euston Road
London NW1 3US
Tel: 020 7667 1832
Fax: 020 7667 1830
adjudicators@gtnet.gov.uk

(c) Complaint to a Member of Parliament

A person can complain to his local MP. If appropriate, the MP can deal with the complaint

- personally (e.g. by direct correspondence with HMRC or by asking a Parliamentary question); or
- with the person's consent, by forwarding the complaint to the Parliamentary Commissioner for Administration (PCA) normally known as the 'Ombudsman'.

The PCA can only act on written complaints forwarded by an MP alleging maladministration and has no power to enforce a remedy.

The postal address for MPs is (Name of MP), House of Commons, London SW1A 1AA or, as the case may be, The Scottish Parliament, Edinburgh EH99 1SP, The National Assembly for Wales/Cynulliad Cenedlaethol Cymru, Cathays Park, Cardiff CF10 3NQ, or The Northern Ireland Assembly, Parliament Buildings, Belfast BT4 3XX.

(d) Appeal to a VAT tribunal

An appeal to a VAT tribunal can only be made against a decision of HMRC falling within one of the categories in *VATA 1994, s 83* (see **5.3 APPEALS**). Although some of these categories relate to administrative decisions, in general a VAT tribunal does not have supervisory jurisdiction over administrative decisions taken by HMRC. Tribunals do have jurisdiction to hear appeals against decisions which, although not falling within *VATA 1994, s 83*, result in a decision (e.g. an assessment) which does. [*VATA 1994, s 84(10)*].

(e) **Judicial review**

Where a tribunal does not have power to review an administrative decision, a taxpayer can apply to the High Court for a judicial review. Applications are heard by the Queen's Bench Division.

Disclosure of information by HMRC officials

[29.7] Subject to **29.8** below, 'Revenue and Customs officials' may not disclose information which is held by HMRC in connection with a function of it. '*Revenue and Customs officials*' is a reference to any person who is or was

- a Commissioner of HMRC;
- an HMRC officer;
- a person acting on behalf of the Commissioners or an officer; or
- a member of a committee established by the Commissioners.

[*CRCA 2005, s 18(1)(4)*].

Authorised disclosure

[29.8] The general provisions in **29.7** above do not apply, and disclosure of information is allowed, in the following circumstances. But it should be noted that this does not authorise the making of a disclosure which

- contravenes the *Data Protection Act 1998*; or
- is prohibited by *Regulation of Investigatory Powers Act 2000, Part 1*.

[*CRCA 2005, s 22*].

Circumstances where disclosure is permitted

(a) Functions of HMRC

Disclosure of information is permitted where it is made for the purposes of a function of HMRC and does not contravene any restriction imposed by the Commissioners. [*CRCA 2005, s 18(2)(a)*].

(b) Public interest disclosure

Public interest disclosure is permitted where

- it is of a kind listed below or as specified in regulations made by the Treasury, and
- it is made on the instructions of the Commissioners (which may be general or specific) and the Commissioners are satisfied that it is in the public interest.

The listed categories are as follows.

(i) Disclosure made to a person exercising public functions (whether or not within the UK) for the purposes of the prevention or detection of crime, and in order to comply with an obligation of the UK government under an agreement relating to the movement of persons, goods or services.

(ii) Disclosure to a body which has responsibility for the regulation of a profession and which relates to misconduct on the part of a member of the profession relating to a function of HMRC.

(iii) Disclosure to a constable where either the constable is exercising functions which relate to the movement of persons or goods into or out of the UK or the disclosure is made for the purposes of the prevention or detection of crime.

(iv) Disclosure to the National Criminal Intelligence Service for a purpose connected with its functions under *Police Act 1997, s 2(2)* (criminal intelligence).

(v) Disclosure to a person exercising public functions in relation to public safety or public health and for the purposes of those functions.

(vi) Disclosure to the National Policing Improvement Agency for the purpose of enabling information to be entered in a computerised database, and which relates to a person suspected of or arrested for an offence, the results of an investigation, or anything seized.

[*CRCA 2005, ss 18(2)(b), 20*].

(c) Disclosure to a 'prosecuting authority'

Disclosure to a prosecuting authority is permitted if made for the purpose of enabling the authority

- to consider whether to institute criminal proceedings in respect of a matter considered in the course of an investigation conducted by or on behalf of HMRC;
- to give advice in connection with a criminal investigation or criminal proceedings; or
- in the case of the Director of Revenue and Customs Prosecutions, to exercise his function under *Proceeds of Crime Act 2002, Pt 5* or *8*.

'*Prosecuting authority*' means the Director of Revenue and Customs Prosecutions, in Scotland, the Lord Advocate or a procurator fiscal and, in Northern Ireland, the Director of Public Prosecutions for Northern Ireland.

It is an offence to disclose further any information disclosed to a prosecuting authority under these provisions except for a purpose connected with the exercise of the prosecuting authority's functions or with the consent of the Commissioners (which may be general or specific).

[*CRCA 2005, ss 18(2)(b), 21; Proceeds of Crime Act 2007, Sch 8 para 164*].

(d) Civil and criminal proceedings, etc.

Disclosure of information is permitted if made for the purposes of civil proceedings, criminal investigation or criminal proceedings (in each case whether or not within the UK) relating to a matter in respect of which HMRC have functions. [*CRCA 2005, s 18(2)(c)(d)*].

(e) Court orders

Disclosure of information is permitted if made in pursuance of an order of a court. [*CRCA 2005, s 18(2)(e)*].

(f) Her Majesty's Inspectors of Constabulary, etc.

Disclosure of information is permitted if made to Her Majesty's Inspectors of Constabulary, the Scottish inspectors or the Northern Ireland inspectors for the purpose of an inspection by virtue of *CRCA 2005, s 27*. [*CRCA 2005, s 18(2)(f)*].

(g) Independent Police Complaints Commission

Disclosure of information is permitted if made to the Independent Police Complaints Commission, or a person acting on its behalf, for the purpose of the exercise of a function by virtue of *CRCA 2005, s 28*. [*CRCA 2005, s 18(2)(g)*].

(h) With agreement of parties

Disclosure of information is permitted if made with the consent of each person to whom the information relates. [*CRCA 2005, s 18(2)(h)*].

(i) Inland Revenue (before the merger with Customs to form HMRC)

Customs were authorised to disclose information to the Commissioners of Inland Revenue (or an authorised officer of the Commissioners) to assist them in the performance of their duties. Information could also be disclosed for the purposes of any proceedings connected with the duties performed. [*FA 1972, s 127 repealed by CRCA 2005, Sch 4 para 16*]. In practice, exchanges of information took place at local level with particular emphasis on combating large cases of suspected tax evasion. (C & E News Release 12/88, 8 March 1988).

Following the formation of HMRC, information acquired by HMRC in connection with a function may be used by them in connection with any other function (subject to any provision which restricts or prohibits the use of information and which is contained in any *Act* (other than of the Scottish Parliament or NI Assembly) or international or other agreement of which the UK is a party). [*CRCA 2005, s 17(1)(2)*].

(j) Department of Works and Pensions

HMRC may disclose information to the Department for the purposes of preventing, detecting, investigating and prosecuting offences relating to social security and for maintaining and improving the accuracy of social security information. [*Social Security Administration (Fraud) Act 1997, s 1; SI 1997/1577*].

(k) Charity Commission

HMRC may disclose to the Charity Commission the name and address of any institution which they have treated as established for charitable purposes; information on the purposes of an institution (and the trusts under which it is established or regulated) in order to determine whether that institution should be treated as established for charitable purposes; and information about an institution which has been so treated but which HMRC believe has carried on activities which are not charitable or has applied funds for non-charitable purposes. [*Charities Act 1993, s 10*].

(l) Statistics Board or the Department for Business, Enterprise and Regulatory Reform

For statistical purposes, HMRC are authorised to disclose the following to the Statistics Board or the Department for Business, Enterprise and Regulatory Reform: VAT registration numbers allocated to persons and reference numbers for members of a group; the names, trading styles and addresses of persons so registered or of members of groups and status and trade classifications of businesses; and actual or estimated value of supplies. The information disclosed may be further disclosed only to another government department for similar purposes. Otherwise it may only be disclosed with the consent of the registered person or in such a form that individual particulars cannot be identified. [*VATA 1994, s 91; Statistics and Registration Service Act 2007, Sch 2 para 6; SI 1996/273*].

Further, HMRC may disclose to the Statistics Board information relating to the estimated or actual value of business purchases, excluding VAT, contained in a return, and the date on which the return was received. [*SI 2011/2878*].

(m) Isle of Man Customs

Isle of Man Customs may be given information for the purpose of facilitating the proper administration of common duties and the enforcement of prohibitions or restrictions on imports or exports between the IOM and the UK. [*IMA 1979, s 10*].

(n) Tax authorities of other EU countries

No obligation as to secrecy (imposed by statute or otherwise) precludes HMRC from disclosing to the competent authority of another EU country any information required to be so disclosed under *Council Regulation (EC)1798/2003* and *Council Regulation (EU)904/2010* (on administrative co-operation and combating fraud in the field of VAT, which recasts and repeals *Council Regulation (EC)1798/2003* with effect from 1 January 2012). Before disclosing any information, they must be satisfied that the competent authority is bound by, or has undertaken to observe, rules of confidentiality not less strict than in the UK and that it will use the information for tax purposes or to facilitate legal proceedings for failure to observe the tax laws of the receiving country. [*FA 2003, s 197*].

Council Regulations (EC)1798/2003 and (EU)904/2010 lay down the rules and procedures to enable the competent authorities of EU countries to cooperate and exchange with each other any information that may help to effect a correct assessment of VAT, monitor the correct application of VAT, particularly on intra-Community transactions, and combat VAT fraud. In particular, they lay down rules and procedures for EU countries to collect and exchange such information by electronic means. Under the Regulations, information may be exchanged

- on the request of an EU country (which must have exhausted its own usual sources of information); or
- without prior request where
  - taxation is deemed to take place in the EU country of destination and the information provided by the EU country of origin is necessary for the effectiveness of the control system of the country of destination;
  - the EU country has grounds to believe that a breach of VAT legislation has been committed or is likely to have been committed in the other EU country;
  - there is a risk of tax loss in the other EU country,

  either by
  - automatic exchange (i.e. the systematic communication of predefined information); or
  - spontaneous exchange, where information has not been forwarded under the automatic exchange of which the country is aware, and which it considers may be useful to the other EU countries.

(o) Proceeds of crime

Information may be disclosed to the Criminal Assets Bureau in Ireland (the 'CAB') and any other specified body (in the UK or elsewhere) to enable it to exercise any of its functions in connection with the identification of proceeds of crime, the bringing of civil proceedings for enforcement purposes in relation to proceeds of crime or the taking of other action in relation to proceeds of crime. Information so disclosed must not be further disclosed unless relating to the exercise of any of the functions of the CAB or specified public authority in connection with such matters and, even then, only with the consent of the HMRC. [*Serious Crimes Act 2007, s 85*].

Compounded settlements

Although not specifically covered in legislation, HMRC have powers under *CEMA 1979 s 152* to compound any offence (whether or not proceedings have been instituted in respect of it) and compound proceedings, i.e. offer an alleged offender the option of paying a penalty out of court rather than be prosecuted. See **52.2 PENALTIES**. HMRC will disclose details of any settlement reached to

- other Government Departments whose statutory responsibilities are directly affected;
- the courts for sentencing purposes after conviction, in cases where there has been an earlier compounded settlement for a similar matter within the five-year time limit specified for offences by the *Rehabilitation of Offenders Act*;
- employers when it is apparent that
  - (i) the nature of the employment has facilitated the offence; or
  - (ii) where drugs offences or indications of serious alcohol abuse are involved, the nature of the employment or duties requires a high degree of unimpaired judgment or faculties; and

- in response to enquiries from Parliament or the media about cases which have excited public attention, if disclosure is considered to be in the public interest.

In all cases, persons considering an offer to compound for an alleged offence will be warned when the offer is made that details of the settlement may be disclosed in the above circumstances.

(Hansard Vol 151, cols 562, 563, 26 April 1989; HMRC Notice 12, para 1.6).

Wrongful disclosure

[29.9] A person commits an offence if he contravenes the provisions of **29.7** above by disclosing 'revenue and customs information relating to a person' whose identity is specified in the disclosure or can be deduced from it.

'*Revenue and customs information relating to a person*' means information about, acquired as a result of, or held in connection with, the exercise of a function of HMRC in respect of the person; but it does not include information about internal administrative arrangements of HMRC (whether relating to Commissioners, officers or others).

It is a defence for a person charged with an offence under these provisions to prove that he reasonably believed that

- the disclosure was lawful, or
- the information had already and lawfully been made available to the public.

A person guilty of an offence under these provisions is liable, on conviction on indictment, to imprisonment for a term not exceeding two years or to a fine or to both and, on summary conviction, to imprisonment for a term not exceeding twelve months (six months in Scotland and NI) or to a fine not exceeding the 'statutory maximum' or to both. The '*statutory maximum*' is currently £5,000.

[*CRCA 2005, s 19*].

Before the merger of the Inland Revenue and Customs, the offence for wrongful disclosure was contained in *FA 1989, s 182*. The provisions, which also apply to VAT tribunals (and the General and Special Commissioners), have not been repealed and therefore continue to apply to Revenue and Customs officers. Under those provisions, a person who discloses any information which he holds or has held in the exercise of 'tax functions' is guilty of an offence if it is information about any matters relevant, for the purposes of those functions, to VAT in the case of any 'identifiable person'.

'*Tax functions*' means, *inter alia*, functions relating to VAT of HMRC and its officers and persons carrying out the administration work of any VAT tribunal, together with any other person providing, or employed in the provision of, services to any such officer or person.

'*Identifiable person*' means a person whose identity is specified in the disclosure or can be deduced from it.

The provisions do not apply to any disclosure of information with 'lawful authority'; with the consent of any person in whose case the information is about a matter relevant to VAT; or which has been lawfully made available to the public before the disclosure is made. A disclosure of information is made with '*lawful authority*' if, and only if, it is made

- by a Crown servant in accordance with his official duty,
- by any other person for the purposes of the function in the exercise of which he holds the information and without contravening any restriction duly imposed by the '*person responsible*' i.e. the Commissioners,
- to, or in accordance with an authorisation duly given by, the person responsible,
- in pursuance of any enactment or of any order of a court, or
- in connection with the institution of, or otherwise for the purposes of, any proceedings relating to any matter within the general responsibility of HMRC.

It is a defence for a person charged under these provisions to prove that, at the time of the alleged offence, he believed that he had lawful authority to make the disclosure and had no reasonable cause to believe otherwise *or* he believed that the information had previously been lawfully made available to the public and had no reasonable cause to believe otherwise.

A person guilty of an offence under these provisions is liable, on conviction on indictment, to imprisonment for a term not exceeding two years or a fine or both, and on summary conviction, to imprisonment for a term not exceeding six months or a fine not exceeding the statutory maximum or both.

[*FA 1989, s 182; CRCA 2005, Sch 4 para 39*].

Disclosure of information to HMRC

[29.10] The following are authorised to disclose information to HMRC.

Department of Works and Pensions

The Department are authorised to pass information to the Commissioners (or any person by whom services are being provided to the Commissioners) for use in the prevention, detection, investigation or prosecution of offences which it is the function of HMRC to prevent, etc. The information may also be used in connection with the assessment or determination of non-criminal penalties and to check the accuracy of information held by HMRC. [*FA 1997, s 110; Tax Credits Act 2002, Sch 5 para 13; SI 1997/1603*].

Charity Commission

The Charity Commission may disclose to HMRC any information received by them, under or for the purposes of any Act or statutory instrument, where the disclosure is made for any purpose connected with the discharge of their functions and to enable or assist HMRC to discharge any of its functions. Where any information has been disclosed to the Charity Commission under

Charities Act 1993, s 10 (which also applies to other government departments, etc.) subject to any express restriction on the disclosure of the information by the Charity Commission, their power of disclosure to HMRC (and other government departments, etc.) under these provisions is exercisable subject to any such restriction. [*Charities Act 1993, s 10*].

Inland Revenue (before the merger with Customs to form HMRC)

The Inland Revenue were authorised to disclose information to the Commissioners of Customs and Excise (or an authorised officer of the Commissioners) to assist them in the performance of their duties. Information could also be disclosed for the purposes of any proceedings connected with the duties performed. [*FA 1972, s 127 repealed by CRCA 2005, Sch 4 para 16*]. In practice, exchanges of information took place at local level with particular emphasis on combating large cases of suspected tax evasion. (C & E News Release 12/88, 8 March 1988). *Following the formation of HMRC*, information acquired by HMRC in connection with a function may be used by them in connection with any other function (subject to any provision which restricts or prohibits the use of information and which is contained in any Act (other than of the Scottish Parliament or NI Assembly) or international or other agreement of which the UK is a party). [*CRCA 2005, s 17(1)(2)*].

HMRC access to correspondence, etc. between businesses and their tax advisers

Information relating to goods and services, etc.

[29.11] HMRC need access to information relating to goods and services and to their supply, acquisition or importation, to enable them to check the amounts of VAT payable or recoverable by a business and to ensure that liabilities are correctly accounted for. They have statutory powers of access in this respect.

Confidential advice by tax advisers

As part of their services to clients, tax advisers communicate with clients or other tax advisers to give or obtain opinions or advise about client's past and future affairs. Such communications may include notes of meetings and telephone calls, internal memoranda, letters and faxes. HMRC will not normally request a tax adviser or trader to produce such a communication relating to confidential opinions or advice. Auditors' working papers and management letters also fall into this category unless containing information relating to goods and services, etc.

Mixed information

Where a document (e.g. working papers or a management letter) contains both information relating to goods and services (e.g. details about the origins of figures in accounts, returns and other information submitted to HMRC, or the relationship of those figures with the books and records of the business) and confidential advice, HMRC will normally accept an extract from the document. This should be supported by a written statement from the tax adviser or auditor that in his opinion HMRC do not have the power to see the other part or parts of the document.

(VAT Leaflet 700/47/93).

From 1 April 2009, a notice requiring information or documents (see **31.6**) does not require a tax adviser to provide information or documents about tax advice given for a client and does not require a person appointed as an auditor to provide certain information or documents related to that function. This exclusion does not cover explanatory material provided to a client by an accountant in connection with information or documents provided to HMRC.

[*FA 2008, Sch 36 paras 24–26; SI 2009/404*].

Direct correspondence between HMRC and tax advisers

[29.12] HMRC cannot reveal confidential information it holds on individual taxpayers unless statutory provisions allow (see **29.8** above).

As many taxpayers instruct their tax advisers to assist in their VAT affairs, HMRC have produced the following standard wording so that they can disclose confidential information to them. The signed letter should be sent to the appropriate written enquiry office (see **29.4** above).

Example letter from a taxpayer to HMRC authorising disclosure of confidential information to a third party

[Date]

I [name and VAT registration number] authorise HM Revenue and Customs to disclose VAT information held about my business affairs to [name and address of nominee], who is acting on my behalf. This authorisation covers all VAT matters within the responsibility of HM Revenue and Customs and includes approaches which may be made to obtain information from all sections of the department, such as the National Advice Service, Debt Management Units, National Registration Service and Complaints Units. This authority will remain in force until I give you written notice to the contrary.

I do not wish the following information to be disclosed*

I undertake to inform HM Revenue and Customs of any change to the above authorisation.

(Signed)

*To be included if applicable.

Key points

[29.13] Points to consider are as follows.

- The HMRC charter was published in November 2009, and explains what service and behaviour a taxpayer can expect to receive from HMRC and its officers. It also explains what the department expects from a taxpayer in terms of behaviour. The charter could be a useful reference point in the event of a dispute with HMRC or, more likely, where concerns are evident about the standard of service being given in relation to a particular issue.
- As a general principle, a taxpayer who makes every effort to correctly calculate and pay his tax should not have any concerns about his relationship with HMRC. Even in situations where honest errors have been made, the approach of HMRC should be to support rather than penalise a taxpayer. This strategy is consistent with the new penalty regime, introduced on 1 April 2009, where the levels of penalty are based on the behaviour of the taxpayer.
- Be aware of the 'What's New' facility on the HMRC website, which highlights all relevant changes that have been announced or introduced by HMRC. For example, the facility will alert a user to new Business Briefs that have been issued and when relevant HMRC public notices have been reissued.
- A telephone enquiry to the National Advice Service can be worthwhile in many situations, e.g. to clarify a minor point or to obtain VAT forms or contact telephone numbers. However, it is important to recognise that a telephone ruling does not give protection to a VAT-registered business in the same way as a written ruling. If an issue has important outcomes, e.g. whether a major product being sold by a business is exempt or standard-rated, then a written ruling is essential.

  When contacting the National Advice Service remember to ask for the call reference number.
- In the case of written requests to HMRC for a ruling on a particular VAT issue, it is important that full, accurate and complete information is given about the transaction in question. If a key piece of information is omitted or reported incorrectly, then it could invalidate the subsequent ruling given by HMRC.

30

HMRC Notices, Information Sheets and Forms

Notices

[30.1] The following notices relating to VAT have been issued and not withdrawn or superceded at the time of publication.

48	Extra-statutory concessions (2011)
60	Intrastat—general guide (2012)
101	Deferring duty, VAT and other charges (2009)
160	Compliance checks into indirect tax matters (2011)
161	Investigation into traders with suspected serious indirect tax irregularities (2011)
179	Motor and heating fuels – general information and accounting for excise and VAT (2011)
334	Free zones (2011)
700	The VAT guide (2011)
700/1/10	Should I be registered for VAT? plus Supplement to Notices 700/1 and 700/11 (2010)
700/2/11	Group and divisional registration
700/6/09	VAT rulings
700/7/02	Business promotion schemes (with Update 1)
700/8/06	Disclosure of VAT avoidance schemes
700/9/08	Transfer of a business as a going concern
700/11/10	Cancelling your registration plus Supplement to Notices 700/1 and 700/11 (2010)
700/12/11	Filling in your VAT return
700/14/04	Video cassette films: rental and part-exchange
700/15/02	The ins and outs of VAT
700/17/11	Funded pension schemes
700/18/02	Relief from VAT on bad debts (with Update 1)
700/21/07	Keeping records and accounts
700/24/03	Postage and delivery charges

700/25/02	Taxis and hire cars
700/34/05	Staff
700/35/97	Business gifts and samples
700/41/11	Late registration penalty
700/42/11	Misdeclaration penalty and repeated misdeclaration
700/43/10	Default interest
700/44/07	Barristers and advocates
700/45/11	How to correct VAT errors and make adjustments or claims
700/46/11	Agricultural flat rate scheme
700/47/93	Confidentiality in VAT matters (tax adviser) – statement of practice
700/50/11	Default surcharge
700/52/10	Notice of requirement to give security to HMRC
700/56/11	Insolvency
700/57/04	Administrative agreements entered into with trade bodies (with Update 1)
700/58/10	Treatment of VAT repayment returns and VAT repayment supplement
700/60/09	Payments on account
700/62/03	Self-billing
700/63/07	Electronic invoicing
700/64/11	Motoring expenses
700/65/11	Business entertainment
700/67/02	Registration scheme for racehorse owners
701/1/04	Charities (with Updates 1 and 2)
701/2/11	Welfare
701/5/11	Clubs and associations
701/6/03	Charity-funded equipment for medical, veterinary, etc. uses (with Update 1 and Supplement issued in 1997)
701/7/02	VAT reliefs for disabled people
701/8/03	Postage stamps and philatelic supplies
701/9/11	Commodities and terminal markets
701/10/11	Zero-rating of books, etc
701/12/11	Disposal of antiques, works of art etc from historic houses
701/14/11	Food
701/15/11	Animals and animal food
701/16/02	Water and sewerage services (with Update 1)
701/18/11	Women's sanitary protection products
701/19/10	Fuel and power
701/20/04	Caravans and houseboats
701/21/11	Gold
701/21A/11	Investment gold coins
701/22/02	Tools for the manufacture of goods for export
701/23/11	Protective equipment
701/29/11	Betting, gaming and lotteries
701/30/11	Education and vocational training
701/31/11	Health institutions

701/32/12	Burial, cremation and the commemoration of the dead
701/35/11	Youth clubs
701/36/11	Insurance
701/38/11	Seeds and plants
701/40/11	Food processing services
701/41/02	Sponsorship
701/45/11	Sport
701/47/11	Culture
701/48/02	Corporate purchasing cards (with Update 1)
701/49/11	Finance
701/57/11	Health professionals and pharmaceutical products
701/58/02	Charity advertising and goods connected with collecting donations (with Update 1)
701/59/02	Motor vehicles for disabled people
702	Imports (2010)
702/7/10	Import VAT relief for goods supplied onward to another country in the EC
702/8/11	Fiscal warehousing
702/9/05	Imports customs procedures with economic impact and end-use relief and free zones (with Update 1)
702/10/09	VAT: Tax warehousing
703	Exports of goods from the UK (2006 with Update 1)
703/1/10	Supply of freight containers for export or removal from the UK
703/2/11	Sailaway boats supplied for export outside the EC
704	VAT Retail exports (2004 with Update 1)
704/1/12	Tax free shopping in the UK
706	Partial exemption (2011)
706/2/11	Capital goods scheme
707	VAT personal export scheme (2011)
708	Buildings and construction (2011)
708/6/11	Energy-saving materials
709/1/11	Catering and take-away food
709/3/11	Hotels and holiday accommodation
709/5/09	Tour operators margin scheme
709/6/02	Travel agents and tour operators
714	Zero-rating young children's clothing and footwear (2011)
718	Margin scheme and global accounting (2011)
718/1	Margin scheme on second-hand cars and other vehicles (2011)
718/2	Auctioneers' scheme (2011)
723A	Refunds of VAT in the European Community for EC and non-EC businesses (2011)
725	The single market (2010)
726	Joint and several liability for unpaid VAT (2008)
727	Retail schemes (2011)
727/2/11	Bespoke retail schemes
727/3/11	Retail schemes: how to work the point of sale scheme

727/4/11	Retail schemes: how to work the apportionment schemes
727/5/11	Retail schemes: how to work the direct calculation schemes
728	New means of transport (2008)
730	Civil penalty investigations: statement of practice (2004) (superseded by Code of Practice 9 (2005) for investigations commencing after 1 September 2005)
731	Cash accounting (2011)
732	Annual accounting (2010)
733	Flat rate scheme for small businesses (2011)
735	Reverse charge for mobile phones and computer chips (2008)
741A	Place of supply of services (2010)
742	Land and property (2002 with Updates 1 to 3)
742A	Opting to tax land and buildings (2010)
742/3/11	Scottish land law terms
744A	Passenger transport (2009)
744B	Freight transport and associated services (2009)
744C	Ships, aircraft and associated services (2011)
747	VAT notices having the force of law (2003)
749	Local authorities and similar bodies (2002)
915	Assessments and time limits: statement of practice (2002)
920	The single currency (1999)
930	What if I don't pay? (2002)
989	Visits by Customs officers (2002)
998	VAT refund scheme for National museums and galleries (2003 with Updates 1 and 2)
999	Catalogue of publications (2005)
1000	Complaints and putting things right – replaced by factsheet at http://www.hmrc.gov.uk/factsheets/complaints-factsheet.pdf
CWL4	Fund-raising events: exemption for charities and other qualifying bodies (2000) (with Update 1)

VAT information sheets

[30.2] The following information sheets relating to VAT had been issued and not withdrawn or superceded at the time of publication.

3/96	Tour operators' margin scheme: practical implementation of the 'airline charter option' following the changes which came into effect on 1 January 1996
4/96	Tour operators' margin scheme: practical implementation of the 'agency option' following the changes which came into effect on 1 January 1996
1/97	Tour operators' margin scheme: practical implementation of the 'trader to trader (wholesale) option' following the changes which came into effect on 1 January 1996
3/98	Local authorities and NHS joint stores depots

5/98	Local authorities: supplies to new unitary authorities under local government reorganisation (transitional arrangements)
6/98	Local authority pension funds: VAT treatment and administrative concessions
8/98	Charities: supply, repair and maintenance of relevant goods (including adapted motor vehicles) (with correction)
2/99	Local authorities: agreement of section 33 recovery methods
3/99	VAT: New Deal Programme
6/99	Charities: liability of routine domestic tasks
8/99	Opticians: apportionment of charges for supplies of spectacles and dispensing
9/99	Imported works of art, antiques and collectors' pieces: changes to the reduced rate of VAT
12/99	VAT on business cars: changes to take effect on 1 December 1999
2/00	Exports and removals: conditions for zero-rating
3/00	Supplies through undisclosed agents: revised VAT treatment
2/01	Single or multiple supplies — how to decide
4/02	Budget 2002: VAT: partial exemption – standard method over-ride
1/03	Electronically supplied services and broadcasting services: new EU place of supply rules
3/03	Modernisation of face value vouchers
4/03	Electronically supplied services: a guide to interpretation
5/03	Electronically supplied services: evidence of customer location and status
6/03	Tribunal decision on VAT treatment of repossessed and voluntarily returned cars
7/03	Electronically supplied services: special scheme for non-EU businesses
10/03	Electronically supplied services: supplementary information on the special scheme for non-EU businesses
11/03	Electronic point of sale (EPOS) systems
12/03	Face value vouchers
13/03	Electronically supplied services: VAT on e-services special scheme for non-EU businesses – currency exchange rates for the reporting period ending 30 September 2003
14/03	New time of supply rules for on-going supplies
1/04	Electronically supplied services: special scheme for non-EU businesses – currency exchange rates for reporting period ending 31 December 2003
3/04	Electronically supplied services: EU enlargement
4/04	Electronically supplied services: special scheme for non-EU businesses – currency exchange rates for reporting period ending 31 March 2004
5/04	Claims made in the light of GMAC High Court decision: VAT treatment of returned cars and other goods
6/04	Electronically supplied services: special scheme for non-EU businesses – currency exchange rates for reporting period ending 30 June 2004

7/04	Eligibility rules for VAT grouping
8/04	Electronically supplied services: special scheme for non-EU businesses – currency exchange rates for reporting period ending 30 September 2004
11/04	Electronically supplied services: special scheme for non-EU businesses – currency exchange rates for reporting period ending 31 December 2004
1/05	E-supplied services: special scheme for non-EU businesses – exchange rates
2/05	Electronically supplied services: changes to Greece VAT rate
3/05	Electronically supplied services: special scheme for non-EU businesses – currency exchange rates for reporting period ending 30 June 2005
4/05	Electronically supplied services: change to Portugal VAT rate
5/05	Electronically supplied services: special scheme for non-EU businesses – currency exchange rates for reporting period ending 30 September 2005
6/05	British travel agents
8/05	Recovery of VAT by businesses on road fuel purchased by their employees on their behalf
1/06	Electronically supplied services: currency exchange rates – period end 12.05
2/06	Electronically supplied services: special scheme for non-EU businesses – change to Hungary VAT rate
3/06	Dispensing doctors and VAT registration: how and when to register; taxable or exempt supplies; VAT recovery and what records need to be kept
5/06	Supplies of goods under finance agreements
8/06	Electronically supplied services: special scheme for non-EU businesses
9/06	Electronically supplied services: special scheme for non-EU businesses
10/06	Electronically supplied services: special scheme for non-EU businesses
11/06	Guidance on the VAT treatment of certain Islamic products
12/06	Further information for dispensing doctors
1/07	Electronically supplied services: special scheme for non-EU businesses – currency exchange rates for reporting period ending December 2006
2/07	Electronically supplied services: special scheme for non-EU businesses – VAT rates for Bulgaria and Romania
3/07	Electronically supplied services: special scheme for non-EU businesses – changes to Germany VAT rates
4/07	Electronically supplied services: special scheme for non-EU businesses – EU enlargement 1 January 2007
5/07	Further information for health professionals affected by the changes to exemption for medical services announced in HMRC Brief 6/07
6/07	Reverse charge for purchases and sales of mobile phones and computer chips

7/07	Electronically supplied services: special scheme for non-EU businesses – currency rates of exchange for reporting period ending March 2007
8/07	Reverse charge for purchases and sales of mobile phones and computer chips
9/07	Electronically supplied services: special scheme for non-EU businesses – currency exchange rates for reporting period ending June 2007
10/07	Changes to VAT invoicing with effect from 1 October 2007
11/07	Accounting for VAT on standard-rated prescription products
12/07	TOGCs: changes to VAT record-keeping requirements
14/07	HMRC guidance: assets used partly for non-business purposes
15/07	Supply of parts and equipment for qualifying ships and aircraft
1/08	Electronically supplied services: special scheme for non-EU businesses – currency exchange rates for reporting period ending December 2007
2/08	Electronically supplied services: special scheme for non-EU businesses – currency exchange rates for reporting period ending March 2008
4/08	Supplies of government grant funded research
5/08	Electronically supplied services – currency exchange rates to June 2008
6/08	Electronically supplied services: special scheme for non-EU businesses – changes
7/08	Partial exemption – VAT adjustments when house builders let their dwellings before selling them
9/08	Special scheme for non-EU businesses – exchange rates for period ending September 2008
11/08	Electronically supplied services – changes to VAT rates
12/08	Electronically supplied services – special scheme for non-EU businesses and changes to the VAT rate
1/09	Electronically supplied services – special scheme for non-EU businesses – changes
2/09	Special scheme for non-EU businesses – exchange rates for period ending December 2008
3/09	Withdrawal of the VAT staff hire concession on 1 April 2009
4/09	Partial exemption – changes to the standard method
5/09	Special scheme for non-EU businesses – exchange rates for period ending March 2009
7/09	Private use charge for motor manufacturer's company cars, dealer demonstrators and daily rental cars
8/09	Changes to the zero-rate for buildings used for a relevant charitable use
9/09	Special scheme for non-EU businesses – exchange rates for period ending June 2009
10/09	Electronically supplied services – special scheme for non-EU businesses – changes
11/09	Electronically supplied services – special scheme for non-EU businesses – changes

13/09	Electronically supplied services – special scheme for non-EU businesses – changes to VAT rate in Lithuania
14/09	Changes to the operation of the option to tax on supplies of land and buildings
15/09	Special scheme for non-EU businesses – exchange rates for period ending September 2009
16/09	Electronically supplied services – special scheme for non-EU businesses – change to UK VAT rate from 1 January 2010
17/09	Electronically supplied services – special scheme for non-EU businesses changes
1/10	Special scheme for non-EU businesses – exchange rates for period ending December 2009
3/10	VAT status of university trading companies – new guidelines
4/10	Partial exemption – changes to the de minimis rules
5/10	Electronically supplied services – special scheme for non-EU businesses
6/10	Electronically supplied services – special scheme for non-EU businesses
7/10	Land and buildings – minor changes in relation to the option to tax (superseded by 8/10)
8/10	Land and buildings – minor changes in relation to the option to tax (supersedes 7/10)
9/10	Special scheme for non-EU businesses – exchange rates for period ending March 2010
11/10	Electronically supplied services – special scheme for non-EU businesses – Spain
13/10	Calculating qualifying use for a charitable or a communal residential building
14/10	Electronically supplied services – special scheme for non-EU businesses – Finland
15/10	Electronically supplied services – special scheme for non-EU businesses – Greece
16/10	Electronically supplied services – special scheme for non-EU businesses – Romania
17/10	Special scheme for non-EU businesses – exchange rates for period ending June 2010
18/10	Electronically supplied services – special scheme for non-EU businesses – Portugal
19/10	Special scheme for non-EU businesses – exchange rates for period ending September 2010
20/10	Special scheme for non-EU businesses – change to UK VAT rate from 4 January 2011
21/10	Place of supply of natural gas and electricity (also heat and cooling)
22/10	Electronically supplied services – special scheme for non-EU businesses – Poland
23/10	Electronically supplied services – special scheme for non-EU businesses – Portugal
1/11	Electronically supplied services – special scheme for non-EU businesses – Latvia

2/11	Special scheme for non-EU businesses – exchange rates for period ending December 2010
3/11	Electronically supplied services – special scheme for non-EU businesses – Slovakia
4/11	Change in use provisions
5/11	Dispensing doctors (Scotland) and VAT registration
6/11	Implementing the VAT technical directive and changes to the partial exemption and capital goods scheme rules
7/11	Special scheme for non-EU businesses – exchange rates for period ending March 2011
8/11	Motor manufacturer's company cars, dealer demonstrators, daily rental cars
9/11	VAT refund scheme for academies
10/11	Special scheme for non-EU businesses – exchange rates for period ending June 2011
11/11	Special scheme for non-EU businesses – change to the Italian VAT rate from 17 September 2011
12/11	Special scheme for non-EU businesses – exchange rates for period ending September 2011
13/11	Electronically supplies services – special scheme for non-EU businesses – Ireland
1/12	Special scheme for non-EU businesses – exchange rates for period ending December 2011
2/12	Electronically supplies services – special scheme for non-EU businesses – Hungary

HMRC Standard Forms

[30.3] The following is a list of the more common forms issued by HMRC for VAT use and which can be downloaded from the HM Revenue and Customs website (apart from Form VAT 100) at

www.hmrc.gov.uk/home.htm

SIVA 1	Application for simplified VAT accounting (SIVA)
SIVA 2	Deferment schedule — SIVA reduced security
VAT 1	VAT — application for registration (see **59.5 REGISTRATION**)
VAT 1A	Application for registration — distance selling (see **59.13 REGISTRATION**)
VAT 1B	Application for registration — acquisitions (see **59.20 REGISTRATION**)
VAT 1C	VAT registration notification (see **59.28 REGISTRATION**)
VAT 1TR	Appointment of tax representative (see **3.11 AGENTS**)
VAT 2	VAT — partnership details (see **59.5 REGISTRATION**)
VAT 7	Application to cancel your VAT registration (see **59.32 REGISTRATION**)

VAT 50	Application for VAT group treatment (see **27.3 GROUPS OF COMPANIES**)
VAT 51	Application for VAT group treatment — company details (see **27.3 GROUPS OF COMPANIES**)
VAT 56	Application to change the representative member of a VAT group (see **27.3 GROUPS OF COMPANIES**)
VAT 65	Application by a business person established in the Community for refund of VAT
VAT 65A	Application by a business person not established in the Community for refund of VAT (see **48.5 OVERSEAS TRADERS**)
VAT 68	Request for transfer of a registration number (see **59.36 REGISTRATION**)
VAT 98	Flat rate scheme for agriculture — application for certification (see **63.27 SPECIAL SCHEMES**)
VAT 100	VAT return (see **2.7 ACCOUNTING PERIODS AND RETURNS**)
VAT 101	EC sales lists (see **2.12–2.15 ACCOUNTING PERIODS AND RETURNS**)
VAT 101A	EC sales list continuation sheet
VAT 101B	VAT — EC sales list (correction sheet) (see **2.12 ACCOUNTING PERIODS AND RETURNS**)
VAT 126	Claim for refund by local authorities and similar bodies (see **43.9 LOCAL AUTHORITIES AND PUBLIC BODIES**)
VAT 407	VAT retail export scheme (see **21.13 EXPORTS**)
VAT 411	New means of transport — removal from the UK to another member state of the EC (see **19.34 EUROPEAN UNION: SINGLE MARKET**)
VAT 411A	New motorised land vehicle purchase by EC VAT registered enterprises only (see **19.35 EUROPEAN UNION: SINGLE MARKET**)
VAT 414	Motor vehicles brought into the UK from within the EC (see **19.38 EUROPEAN UNION: SINGLE MARKET**)
VAT 415	New means of transport — notification of acquisition (see **19.37 EUROPEAN UNION: SINGLE MARKET**)
VAT 426	Insolvent traders claim for input tax after deregistration (see **35.12 INSOLVENCY**)
VAT 427	Claim for input tax relief from VAT on cancellation of registration (see **34.5 INPUT TAX**)
VAT 431C	VAT refunds for DIY housebuilders — claim form and notes for conversions (see **42.24 LAND AND BUILDINGS: ZERO AND REDUCED RATE SUPPLIES AND DIY HOUSEBUILDERS**)
VAT 431NB	VAT refunds for DIY housebuilders — claim form and notes for new houses (see **42.24 LAND AND BUILDINGS: ZERO AND REDUCED RATE AND DIY HOUSEBUILDERS**)
VAT 484	Change of details — variations
VAT 600 AA	Application to join the annual accounting scheme (see **63.10 SPECIAL SCHEMES**)
VAT 600 AA/FRS	Application to join the annual accounting scheme and the flat rate scheme (see **63.10 SPECIAL SCHEMES**)
VAT 600 FRS	Application to join the flat rate scheme (see **63.18 SPECIAL SCHEMES**)
VAT 622	Standing order/BACS authority

VAT 623	Annual accounting scheme only — instruction to your bank or building society to pay by direct debit
VAT 652	Voluntary disclosure of errors on VAT returns (see **56.11 RECORDS**)
VAT 769	VAT — notification of insolvency details (see **35.2 INSOLVENCY**)
VAT 833	Statement of VAT on goods sold in satisfaction of debt (see **36.12 INSOLVENCY**)
VAT 1614A	Notification of an option to tax land and/or buildings

Key points

[30.4] Points to consider are as follows.

- A useful tip if a public notice is being viewed on the HMRC website is to use the facility at the top of the screen that says 'view change history'. This section will highlight the dates when a notice has been updated and may include the main changes included in the revised notice. As a general principle, it is also important to recognise that information in a public notice is only totally correct at the time that it is published. Subsequent changes may be announced in VAT Information Sheets or Revenue & Customs Briefs.
- Use the 'What's New' section on the HMRC website to keep up to date on VAT developments – supported by other publications either produced by HMRC or within the tax profession. The 'What's New' section is intended to alert a user to any important changes of policy or interpretations of the legislation that are relevant for all taxes, not just VAT. It will also highlight when a new edition of a particular public notice has been issued.
- As well as VAT Information Sheets, a lot of useful information is often provided by HMRC in Revenue and Customs Briefs. The Briefs are issued in numerical order within a calendar year, e.g. 01/10, 02/10, 03/10 etc. It is possible to sort the Briefs on a tax subject basis so that you can see all Briefs issued in the last twelve months that specifically relate to VAT.
- The HMRC search engine continues to improve as a route to finding relevant information on the website. As a general tip, by entering a VAT form number into the search box, the form will immediately be found in PDF format, along with any supporting notes about its completion.

31

HMRC: Powers

Cross-references. See **6.1 ASSESSMENTS** for powers of HMRC to raise assessments and to assess an over-repayment and **6.3 ASSESSMENTS** for assessments of penalties, interest and surcharges; **8.5 BUSINESS** for powers to make a direction treating two or more persons as one taxable person; **29.7 HMRC: ADMINISTRATION** for the power to disclose or exchange information with other authorities and government departments; **27.5 GROUPS OF COMPANIES** for powers re groups; **51.5 PAYMENT OF VAT** for power to withhold a repayment of VAT due where returns are outstanding; **52.2–52.5 PENALTIES** for powers of arrest; **52.30 PENALTIES** for power of mitigation; **56.1 RECORDS** for the power to require records to be kept; and **59.10 REGISTRATION** for powers to enforce compulsory deregistration.

Introduction

[31.1] HMRC have the following powers relating to the production of evidence and the requirement for security.

(a) HMRC can, as a condition of allowing or repaying any input tax to any person, require the production of such evidence relating to VAT as they may specify (before 10 April 2003, require the production of such documents relating to VAT as may have been supplied to that person). [*VATA 1994, Sch 11 para 4(1); FA 2003, s 17(3)*].

(b) If they think it necessary for the protection of the revenue, HMRC can require, as a condition of making any VAT credit, the giving of such security for the amount of the payment as appears appropriate to them. [*VATA 1994, Sch 11 para 4(1A); FA 2003, s 17(3)*].
HMRC may issue a Notice of Requirement under this provision where a business makes a large or unusual VAT claim which they need time to verify. They may also do so in other circumstances (e.g. where a business has been, or is about to be, notified that it may be jointly and severally liable for unpaid VAT, see **31.3** below). The amount of security will be no more than the VAT credit that HMRC are due to make or are considering making. HMRC will usually accept security in the form of: a performance bond from an approved financial institution that is payable on demand; or a joint bank or building society account. A performance bond must be signed and witnessed by an authorised person on behalf of the financial institution and an HMRC officer. If any security required is not provided, any VAT claim covered by the Notice of Requirement will be withheld until it is verified (or until any notices of joint and several liability for unpaid VAT are paid or withdrawn). The security will be returned once the claim is verified (or any notices of joint and several liability for unpaid VAT are paid or withdrawn). If all or part of the repayment claim is disallowed, HMRC may offset the security to recover any credit already paid. They may also offset the security against any unpaid notices of joint and several liability. (VAT Notice 700/52/10, paras 2.1–2.8).

(c) If they think it necessary for the protection of the revenue, HMRC may require a taxable person, as a condition of his supplying (or after 9 April 2003 being supplied with) goods and services under a taxable supply, to give security (or further security) for the payment of any VAT that is or may become due from the taxable person. The security can be of such amount, and must be given in such a manner, as HMRC determine.
[*VATA 1994, s 48(7), Sch 11 para 4(2)(4)(5); FA 2003, s 17(4)*].
This provision allows HMRC to require an amount of security from a business if they consider there is a risk of VAT being unpaid by the business. They may issue a Notice of Requirement if, for example
- a person in his previous or current business has failed to comply with his VAT obligations;
- a business is run by disqualified directors or by undischarged bankrupts;
- a person has previously been prosecuted or penalised for a VAT offence; or
- other persons concerned in the current registration of a business are connected with past failures to pay VAT due.

Where they have strong grounds to suspect that revenue is at risk, HMRC may require security without warning. Factors which may be taken into account in determining the amount of security include
- VAT declared on VAT returns from the current and any previous business;
- VAT declared on VAT returns from businesses of a similar size, with similar customers and in the same trade class; and

- taxable turnover.

HMRC may also add any outstanding VAT from the current registered business. Where quarterly returns are submitted, HMRC will require an amount of security based on the VAT they estimate the business would have to pay over six months (four months if monthly returns are made). There is no rule to prevent security being required in excess of estimated liabilities (*Labelwise Ltd* (VTD 1499) (TVC 14.47)).

HMRC normally accept security by way of

- cash or bankers draft;
- bank or building society guarantee; or
- a joint bank or building society account

but they will only accept a guarantee from a financial institution approved by them.

It is a criminal offence to continue to trade without providing the security. On conviction, a penalty of up to £5,000 may be charged for each taxable supply made without providing the security. If a business does not provide the security, HMRC may prosecute for the whole period of trading from the date the Notice of Requirement was issued. Where the business is a company, both the company and individuals involved may be prosecuted and individuals may be liable for paying any fines and compensation awarded by the court.

HMRC will regularly review the requirement for security and will return it when they consider there is no longer a risk to the collection of VAT. At the very least, they will review the requirement within twelve months of it being provided in the case of monthly returns and two years in the case of quarterly returns.

If the business falls behind with payments of VAT, HMRC may offset the security against the VAT due and may then ask the business to provide a further amount of security.

(VAT Notice 700/52/05, paras 3.1–3.10).

(d) If they think it necessary for the protection of the revenue, HMRC may require a taxable person, as a condition of his supplying or being supplied with goods and services under a taxable supply, to give security (or further security) for the payment of any VAT that is or may become due from any person by or to whom goods or services supplied by or to the taxable person are supplied. The security can be of such amount, and must be given in such a manner, as HMRC determine. [*VATA 1994, s 48(7), Sch 11 para 4(2)–(5); FA 2003, s 17(4)*].

(e) Where a person fails to appoint a VAT representative when required to do so (see **3.8 AGENTS**), HMRC may require him to provide security, or further security, as they think appropriate for the payment of any VAT which is or may become due from him. [*VATA 1994, s 48(7)*].

Reconsiderations and appeals

Where a business has been issued with a Notice of Requirement under (*b*)–(*e*) above, they can ask HMRC to review the requirement or appeal against the decision to a VAT tribunal (see **5.3**(15) **APPEALS**).

Where an appeal is brought against a requirement for security under (*d*) above, the tribunal must allow the appeal unless HMRC satisfy the tribunal that

- there has been an evasion of, or an attempt to evade, VAT in relation to goods or services supplied to or by that person, or
- it is likely, or without the requirement for security it is likely, that VAT in relation to such goods or services will be evaded

and for these purposes evading VAT includes obtaining a VAT credit that is not due or a VAT credit in excess of what is due.

[*VATA 1994, s 84(4E)(4F); FA 2003, s 17(7)*].

Subject to this, when considering HMRC's requirement for security, the tribunal's jurisdiction is appellate rather than merely supervisory. The tribunal should consider whether HMRC acted reasonably and took account of all relevant material, but has no power to substitute its own decision for one reached on an incorrect basis (except that it can dismiss an appeal where it is shown that, even if additional material had been taken into account, the decision would *inevitably* have been the same). The tribunal should consider whether HMRC acted in a way in which no reasonable panel of Commissioners could have acted or whether they took into account some irrelevant matter or disregarded something to which they should have given weight. However, the tribunal cannot exercise a fresh discretion since the protection of the revenue is not a responsibility of the tribunal or of a court (*C & E Commrs v John Dee Ltd*, CA [1995] STC 941 (TVC 14.31)). In that case, the tribunal found that HMRC had failed to enquire into the company's financial status and that, if it had done, the result would not have inevitably been the same.

In *C & E Commrs v Peachtree Enterprises Ltd*, QB [1994] STC 747 (TVC 14.59) Dyson J observed that the tribunal must limit itself to considering facts and matter which existed at the time the challenge to the decision was taken and should not, for example, take into account the fact that the person concerned had subsequently made all returns and paid the VAT due on time.

De Voil Indirect Tax Service. See V5.186, V5.225.

Recovery of VAT

[31.2] Where an invoice shows a supply of goods or services with VAT chargeable on it, the person issuing the invoice is liable for the amount of VAT shown (or the amount of VAT included if not shown separately) whether or not

(a) the invoice has been correctly prepared as required by the legislation (see **39 INVOICES**);
(b) the supply actually takes, or has taken, place;
(c) the amount shown as VAT, or any amount of VAT, is or was chargeable on the supply; or
(d) the person issuing the invoice is a taxable person.

[*VATA 1994, Sch 11 para 5(1)–(3)*].

If any of the conditions in (*b*)–(*d*) above are not met, the sum recoverable is not VAT due under *VATA 1994* but is a debt due to the Crown. The practical effect of this is that normal assessment procedures cannot be used. The recovery of the incorrectly shown VAT is effected by means of a formal demand letter.

Penalties for unauthorised issue of invoices (see **52.14 PENALTIES**) and interest on late paid VAT (see **51.15 PAYMENT OF VAT**) may also be due.

Concessionary reliefs

Where HMRC requires payment under the above provisions because of (*d*) above, the person issuing the invoice has no legal entitlement to treat the VAT incurred on his own related purchases as input tax. Equally, the person receiving the invoice has no legal entitlement to claim the VAT shown on the invoice as representing VAT. However, by concession, HMRC may

- allow the person making such a payment to HMRC to deduct from it the amount of VAT incurred on supplies to him of goods and services directly attributable to any invoiced supply in respect of which payment is required; and
- take no action against a taxable person who has received the supply and, in good faith, treated the amount shown as representing VAT as his input tax.

(VAT Notice 48, ESC 3.9).

Partnerships

See also **50.4 PARTNERSHIPS** for recovery of VAT from individual partners.

VAT due to other EU countries

Where recovery of a debt in any EU country proves unsuccessful, that country can request another EU country to attempt recovery where it appears that the debtor now resides, or has assets, there. The provisions of the Mutual Assistance Recovery Directive (*Directive 2010/24/EU*, which replaces *Directive 2008/55/EC* from 1 January 2012) are enacted in the UK as *FA 2011, s 87, Sch 25* (which replaces *FA 2002, s 134, Sch 39* from 1 January 2012) (and supporting regulations) in relation to the recovery in the UK of amounts in respect of which a request for enforcement has been made by the tax authorities of another EU country. Such proceedings may be taken by, or on behalf of, HMRC to enforce the foreign claim (by way of legal proceedings, distress, diligence or otherwise) as might be taken to enforce a corresponding UK claim.

Unless otherwise permitted, no proceedings can be taken against any person if he shows that proceedings relevant to his liability on the foreign claim are pending, or about to be instituted, in the other EU country concerned but proceedings may be taken in the UK if the proceedings in that other country are not prosecuted or instituted with reasonable expedition. If the person shows that a final decision on the foreign claim has been given in his favour in the other EU country, no proceedings can be taken in the UK under these provisions.

De Voil Indirect Tax Service. See V1.271; V5.171, V5.175.

Joint and several liability for unpaid VAT

[31.3] Where

- a taxable person receives a taxable supply of 'relevant goods and services',
- at the time of the supply he knew, or had 'reasonable grounds to suspect', that some or all of the 'VAT payable' on that supply, or on any previous or subsequent supply of those goods or services, would go unpaid to HMRC, and
- HMRC have served on him a notice of liability under these provisions

that person, and the person otherwise liable for the amount specified in the notice, are jointly and severally liable to HMRC for the 'net VAT unpaid' on those goods or services.

> *Example*
>
> A business buys 100 mobile phones from a supplier who bought them as part of an order for 1000 mobile phones.
>
> It may be held liable, under joint and several liability, for any unpaid VAT on the 100 phones it has bought (but not the remaining 900 phones which its supplier has bought).

Relevant goods and services

The provisions apply to '*relevant goods and services*' which fall within any one or more of the following descriptions.

- Any equipment made or adapted for use as a telephone and any 'other equipment' made or adapted for use in connection with telephones or telecommunication.
- Any equipment made or adapted for use as a computer and any 'other equipment' made or adapted for use in connection with computers or computer systems (including, in particular, with effect from 1 May 2007, positional determination devices for use with satellite navigation systems).
- With effect from 1 May 2007, any other electronic equipment made or adapted for use by individuals for the purposes of leisure, amusement or entertainment and any 'other equipment' made or adapted for use in connection with any such electronic equipment.

'*Other equipment*' includes parts, accessories and, with effect from 1 May 2007, software.

[*VATA 1994, s 77A(1)–(3); FA 2003, s 18; SI 2007/939*].

Parts and accessories include computer chips, telephone chargers, memory cards and games cards but not parts such as screws and wires used in the manufacture of general items when sold separately. (VAT Notice 726, para 1.4).

Reasonable grounds to suspect

Without prejudice to any other way of establishing reasonable grounds for suspicion, a person is presumed to have reasonable grounds for suspecting some or all of any VAT payable has not been paid if the price payable by him for the goods or services in question was less than the

- lowest price that might reasonably be expected to be payable for them on the open market, or
- price payable on any previous supply of those goods.

This presumption is, however, rebuttable on proof that the low price payable for the goods was due to circumstances unconnected with failure to pay VAT.

[*VATA 1994, s 77A(6)–(8); FA 2003, s 18*].

Businesses trading within a market should have a reasonable idea of the market prices for the goods an any given day. If goods are offered for what appears to be bargain prices, a business should find out the reason for the low cost. (VAT Notice 726, para 3.2).

VAT payable

The amount of VAT that is payable in respect of a supply is the lesser of

- the amount chargeable on the supply, and
- the amount shown as due on the supplier's return for the VAT period in question (if he has made one), together with any amount assessed as due from him for that period (subject to any appeal by him). The latter includes any amount assessed by HMRC even where it is not notified to the supplier because it is impracticable to do so.

[*VATA 1994, s 77A(4)(5); FA 2003, s 18*].

Net VAT unpaid

'*Net VAT unpaid*' means the VAT charged on the goods or services in question less any input tax incurred on their purchase by the person who has not paid the VAT. For goods acquired from another EU country, the net VAT unpaid on the first UK supply is the amount of the output tax (acquisition VAT – input tax + output tax). (VAT Notice 726, para 2.2). An amount of VAT counts as unpaid only to the extent that it exceeds the amount of any refund due. [*VATA 1994, s 77A(1); FA 2003, s 18*].

Exceptions

HMRC will not apply these provisions on the supply of specified goods and services where

- VAT goes unpaid as a result of genuine bad debts or genuine business failure;
- goods are bought by a business for its own use, rather than onward sale;
- a business can demonstrate that the low purchase price paid for the goods was due to circumstances unconnected with the failure to pay VAT; or
- a business has genuinely done everything it can to check the integrity of the supply chain and its suppliers and customers, can demonstrate it has done so, has addressed concerns raised through its checks and has no other reason to suspect VAT would go unpaid.

HMRC will use this measure to combat MTIC fraud. As this fraud generally involves the wholesale of the relevant goods and their dispatch from the UK, it is highly unlikely that manufacturers or retail suppliers of the relevant goods will be affected by these provisions.

(VAT Notice 726, paras 2.4, 4.9).

HMRC's application of the provisions

HMRC will send a notification letter to a business if

- the business has bought and/or sold relevant goods or services;
- the transaction took place within a supply chain where VAT was unpaid by another supplier in the chain; and
- they believe they can show that the business knew, or had reasonable grounds to suspect, that VAT would go unpaid.

Before the issue of a notification letter, each case will be independently reviewed and authorised by a central team within HMRC to ensure that the case is an appropriate one for the joint and several liability provisions and that there is sufficient evidence, on balance of probabilities, to show the requisite knowledge or reasonable grounds for suspicion.

A notification letter will be sent to each known business in the chain of supply that HMRC considers may be jointly and severally liable for the unpaid VAT. Each business will have 21 days to demonstrate that it did not know, or have reasonable grounds to suspect, that VAT would go unpaid and, where applicable, that there was a legitimate reason for the low purchase price of the goods. Any factors a business wishes to bring to HMRC's attention will be considered by the officer who issued the letter and then independently reviewed.

If, after a period of 21 days, a business has not responded or HMRC do not accept that the evidence or explanation provided is satisfactory, HMRC will issue the business with a notice of liability for the net tax unpaid. This will demand payment of the amount of VAT for which HMRC consider it is jointly and severally liable.

(VAT Notice 726, paras 4.1–4.3).

Reasonable checks

HMRC advise that it is good commercial practice for a business to carry out checks to establish the credibility and legitimacy of its customers, suppliers and supplies in order to avoid being involved in a supply chain where VAT would go unpaid. They do not expect a business to go beyond what is reasonable but they do expect a business to make a judgement on the integrity of its supply chain and the suppliers, customers and goods within it. Factors which a business may wish to take into account include the nature of the supply, payment arrangements and conditions and details of the movement of goods. (VAT Notice 726, para 4.5).

See VAT Notice 726, para 6.1 for examples of indicators that could alert a business to the risk that VAT might go unpaid and VAT Notice 726, para 6.2 for examples of specific checks which could be made (although the list is not exhaustive).

HMRC also recommend that any paperwork received in addition to invoices (e.g. purchase orders, pro-forma invoices, delivery notes, CMRs (Convention Merchandises Routiers) or airway bills, allocation notifications, and inspection reports, etc.) should be kept as evidence of a transaction's legitimacy. (VAT Notice 726, para 6.2).

If the checks carried out by a business indicate that there may be a fraud, it should consider whether it wishes to continue with the transaction and may also wish to inform HMRC Confidential on 0800 595 000. (VAT Notice 726, para 4.7).

Taking control of goods for unpaid VAT

[31.4] There are special provisions to allow HMRC to enforce the recovery of VAT due but not paid. Different rules and procedures apply in England and Wales, Scotland and Northern Ireland.

England and Wales

With effect from a date to be appointed, if a person does not pay a sum that is payable by that person to HMRC

- under or by virtue of an enactment, or
- under a '*contract settlement*', i.e. an agreement made in connection with any person's liability to make a payment to HMRC under or by virtue of any enactment

HMRC may use the procedure in *Tribunals, Courts and Enforcement Act 2007, Sch 12* (taking control of goods) to recover that sum.

[*FA 2008, ss 127, 139*].

See *Tribunals, Courts and Enforcement Act 2007, Sch 12* and supporting Regulations for full details.

Before the appointed day, the same provisions apply as in Northern Ireland. [*FA 1997, s 51; Tribunals, Courts and Enforcement Act 2007, Sch 13 para 126*].

Northern Ireland

Where, following a written demand, a person neglects or refuses to pay any VAT due (or any amount recoverable as if it were VAT) an HMRC officer may levy distress on that person's goods and chattels. He may also direct, by warrant, any authorised person to levy such distress in which case distress must be levied by or under the direction of, and in the presence of, that authorised person. [*FA 1997, s 51; SI 1997/1431*].

Scotland

From 23 November 2009, if a person does not pay a sum that is payable by that person to HMRC

- under or by virtue of an enactment, or
- under a '*contract settlement*', i.e. an agreement made in connection with any person's liability to make a payment to HMRC under or by virtue of any enactment

an HMRC officer may apply to the sheriff for a summary warrant. The application must be accompanied by a signed certificate which

- states that
  - (a) none of the persons specified in the application has paid the sum payable by that person;
  - (b) the officer has demanded payment from each such person of the sum payable by that person; and
- specifies the sum payable by each person specified in the application.

When granted, a summary warrant authorises the recovery of the sum payable by attachment, money attachment, earnings arrestment, or arrestment and action of furthcoming or sale.

[*FA 2008, ss 128, 139; SI 2009/3024*].

Before 23 November 2009, broadly similar provisions applied. [*FA 1997, s 52, Sch 18; Abolition of Poindings and Warrant Sales Act 2001, s 3 and Sch; Debt Arrangement and Attachment (Scotland) Act 2002, Sch 3 para 26; FA 2008, Sch 43 para 15; SI 1995/2518, Reg 213; SI 1996/2098; SI 1997/1432*].

De Voil Indirect Tax Service. See V5.173, V5.174.

Investigations under Police and Criminal Evidence Act 1984

[31.5] With effect from 1 December 2007, certain provisions of the *Police and Criminal Evidence Act (PACE) 1984* (as modified in some cases) are extended, in England and Wales, to relevant criminal investigations conducted by officers of Revenue and Customs. This does not confer on such officers any power to charge a person with an offence, release a person on bail or detain a person for an offence after he has been charged with it.

Where *PACE 1984* gives a constable power to seize and retain any thing found upon a lawful search of person or premises, an officer of Revenue and Customs has the same power, despite the fact that the thing found is not evidence of an offence which relates to a matter in relation to which HMRC have functions.

The provisions of *PACE 1984* which apply to officers of Revenue and Customs are as follows.

- *s 8* (power of justice of the peace to authorise entry and search of premises)
- *s 9 and Sch 1* (special provisions as to access and special procedure)
- *s 14A* (exception re excluded material and special procedure material)
- *s 14B* (restriction on other powers to apply for production of documents)

- *s 15* (search warrants – safeguards)
- *s 16* (execution of warrants)
- *s 17(1)(b)(2)(4)* (entry for purpose of arrest, etc.)
- *s 18* (entry and search after arrest) (as modified by *SI 2007/3175, Art 8*)
- *s 19* (general power of seizure etc.)
- *s 20* (extension of powers of seizure to computerised information)
- *s 21* (access and copying) (as modified by *SI 2007/3175, Art 5*)
- *s 22(1)–(4)* (retention)
- *s 24(2)* (arrest without warrant: constables) (as modified by *SI 2007/3175, Art 17*)
- *s 28* (information to be given on arrest)
- *s 29* (voluntary attendance at police station, etc.)
- *s 30(1)–(4)(a), (5)–(11)* (arrest elsewhere than at police station)
- *s 31* (arrest for further offence)
- *s 32(1)–(9)* (search upon arrest) (as modified by *SI 2007/3175, Art 5*)
- *s 34(1)–(5)* (limitations on police detention)
- *s 35(1)(2)(3)(4)* (designated police stations) (as modified by *SI 2007/3175, Art 9*)
- *s 36(1)(2)(3)(4)(5)(6)(7)(8)(9)(10)* (custody officers at police stations) (as modified by *SI 2007/3175, Art 10*)
- *s 37* (duties of custody officer before charge)
- *s 39* (responsibilities in relation to persons detained)
- *s 40* (review of police detention)
- *s 41(1)(2)(4)(6)–(9)* (limits on period of detention without charge) (as modified by *SI 2007/3175, Art 11*)
- *s 42(1)(2)(4)–(11)* (authorisation of continued detention)
- *s 43(1)–(12)(14)–(19)* (warrants of further detention)
- *s 44* (extension of warrants of further detention)
- *s 50* (records of detention) (as modified by *SI 2007/3175, Art 12*)
- *s 51(d)* (savings)
- *s 54* (searches of detained persons)
- *s 55* (intimate searches) (as modified by *SI 2007/3175, Arts 5, 13*)
- *s 56(1)–(9)* (right to have someone informed when arrested)
- *s 57* (additional rights of children and young persons)
- *s 58(1)–(11)* (access to legal advice)
- *s 62* (intimate samples)
- *s 63* (other samples)
- *s 64* (except (6B)) (destruction of fingerprints and samples) (as modified by *SI 2007/3175, Art 14*)
- *s 66* (codes of practice)
- *s 67* (codes of practice-supplementary)
- s 77 (confessions by mentally handicapped persons) (as modified by *SI 2007/3175, Art 15*)
- *s 107* (police officers performing duties of higher rank)

Search of persons

Where an officer searches premises under a warrant obtained under *PACE 1984, s 8* or *Sch 1*, he may search any person found on the premises where he has reasonable cause to believe that person to be in possession of material which is likely to be of substantial value to the investigation of the offence. But no person should be searched except by a person of the same sex.

[*FA 2007, ss 82, 84; SI 2007/3175*].

Furnishing of information and production of documents

Provisions applying from 1 April 2009

Notice requiring information or documents

[31.6] An HMRC officer may serve a notice on a taxpayer or a third party requiring the production of information or documents that are reasonably required to check the taxpayer's tax position. The requirement for a notice does not preclude oral requests, but such requests are not enforceable until formalised in a written notice. A third party notice must name the taxpayer to whom it relates unless the tribunal has approved the notice and disapplied this requirement. A third party notice may not be given without the consent of the taxpayer or the tribunal, unless the notice refers only to information or documents that form part of a person's statutory records and relate to the supply of services or supply, acquisition or importation of goods. The HMRC officer must give the relevant taxpayer a copy of the third party notice unless the tribunal disapplies this requirement. If the tribunal has approved the giving of an information notice then the notice must say so, as this affects whether the rules on penalties (see **52.17 PENALTIES**) or the rules on offences (see **52.3 PENALTIES**) apply. Applications to the tribunal for approval of notices are heard without the taxpayer being present.

With the tribunal's approval, an authorised HMRC officer may require a person to provide information or produce a document by a written notice that is reasonably required to check the tax position of a person or class of persons whose identities are not known.

An information notice may specify or describe the information or documents to be produced or provided. The option to 'describe' means that HMRC are not restricted to asking for documents that they can specifically identify.

Where a person is required to provide information or documents it must be done within the period and time and in the means and format specified in the notice. The notice does not need to specify means or form, but it may be necessary, for example where an original is required. A copy of the requested document may be produced unless the notice specified the original document or an HMRC officer subsequently makes a written request for the original document. Where a notice requires production of a document it must be produced at either a mutually agreed place or a place specified by an HMRC officer, but the officer must not specify a place used solely as a dwelling (i.e. a home).

An officer may take copies of, or make extracts from, documents produced. He may remove and retain documents produced where it appears to him to be necessary, but he must provide a receipt or copy where requested.

An information notice only requires a person to produce documents in his possession or power. It does not require the production of information relating to the conduct of a pending tax appeal; journalistic material; personal records, except where they omit personal information; documents that are more than six years old, except with the agreement of an authorised officer. An information notice does not require a person to provide or produce legally privileged information or documents. A dispute as to whether information or a document is subject to legal professional privilege can be referred to the tribunal.

Where a third party notice is given to check the tax position of a group's parent undertaking and any subsidiary undertaking, the notice need only state this and name the parent, not every subsidiary. Only the parent undertaking needs to be sent a copy of the notice. Where a business is carried on in partnership and a third party notice is given for the purpose of checking the tax position of more than one partner, the notice need only state this and give the partnership's registered name, not each partner's name. A copy of the notice need only be given to one of the partners.

[*FA 2008, Sch 36 paras 1–9, 15–23, 34, 35, 37; FA 2009, Sch 47 para 3; SI 2009/404; SI 2009/1916*].

Appeals against information notices

There is no right of appeal against a decision of the tribunal to approve an information notice. Where an information notice was not approved by the tribunal, the taxpayer may appeal to the tribunal against the notice or any requirement therein, except a requirement to provide information or documents forming part of his statutory records. A right of appeal also exists for third party notices and notices requiring information and documents about persons whose identities are not known, but only where it would be unduly onerous to comply with the notice or requirement. Notice of an appeal must be given in writing before the end of the period of 30 days from the date on which the information notice is given. On appeal, the tribunal may confirm, vary or set aside the notice or a requirement therein, and the tribunal's decision is final.

[*FA 2008, Sch 36 paras 29–33; SI 2009/404; FA 2009, Sch 47 para 4*].

De Voil Indirect Tax Service. See V5.234.

Provisions applying before 1 April 2009

Furnishing of information

[31.7] In order to maintain their records, HMRC have powers to make regulations requiring taxable persons to notify them of any changes in personal or business circumstances. In addition, every person

(a) who is concerned (in whatever capacity) in the supply of goods or services in the course or furtherance of a business, or

(b) to whom a supply within (*a*) above is made, or
(c) who is concerned (in whatever capacity) in the acquisition of goods from another EU country, or
(d) who is concerned (in whatever capacity) in the importation of goods from a place outside the EU in the course or furtherance of business

must furnish HMRC, within such time and in such form as they may reasonably require, such information relating to the goods or services or to the supply, acquisition or importation as HMRC may reasonably specify.

A person to whom the right to receive the whole or part of the consideration for a supply of goods or services has been assigned is treated as a person concerned in the supply.

[*VATA 1994, Sch 11 para 7(1)(2)(9); FA 1999, s 15*].

The above does not entitle HMRC to send an officer to put oral questions to a taxable person and demand oral answers on the spot (*C & E Commrs v Harz & Power*, HL 1966 [1967] 1 All ER 177 (TVC 14.86)). See also *EMI Records Ltd v Spillane and Others*, CD [1986] STC 374 (TVC 14.88).

Production of documents

In addition, any person who is connected (in whatever capacity) with the activities in (*a*)–(*d*) above must, upon demand by a person acting under the authority of HMRC (an '*authorised person*') produce for inspection by that person any 'document' relating to the goods or services or to the supply, acquisition or importation. The document must be produced at the principal place of business (or at such other place as may be reasonably required) at such time as may be reasonably required. The authorised person also has power to require the production of the documents concerned from any other person who appears to be in possession of them (but without prejudice to any right of lien). He may take copies or make extracts of any document and may, at a reasonable time and for a reasonable period, remove any document, giving a receipt if requested. Where any document removed is reasonably required for the proper conduct of the business, a copy must be provided free of charge as soon as practicable. If any documents removed are lost or damaged, reasonable compensation must be paid. [*VATA 1994, Sch 11 para 7(2)(3)(5)–(8)*].

'*Document*' means anything in which information of any description is recorded and '*copy*', in relation to a document, means anything onto which information recorded has been copied, by whatever means and whether directly or indirectly. [*VATA 1994, s 96(1); Civil Evidence Act 1995, Sch 1 para 20*]. Any profit and loss account or balance sheet, relating to the business in the course of which the goods or services are supplied or the goods are imported, is included. In the case of an acquisition from another EU country, any profit and loss account or balance sheet relating to any business or other activity of the person by whom the goods are acquired is included. [*VATA 1994, Sch 11 para 7(4)*].

[*FA 2008, Sch 36 para 87; SI 2009/404*].

Power to obtain contact details for debtors

[31.8] From 21 July 2009, where:

- a sum is payable by a person ('the debtor') to HMRC under or by virtue of an enactment or under a contract settlement;
- an HMRC officer reasonably requires contact details for the debtor for the purpose of collecting that sum;
- the officer has reasonable grounds to believe that a person ('the third party') has any such details; and
- the third party is a company, a local authority or a local authority association, or the officer has reasonable grounds to believe that the third party obtained the details in the course of carrying on a business

an HMRC officer may by notice in writing require the third party to provide the details. The notice must name the debtor. These provisions do not apply if the third party is a charity and obtained the details in the course of providing services free of charge, or the third party is not a charity but obtained the details in the course of providing services on behalf of a charity that are free of charge to the recipient of the service.

The third party must provide the details within such period, and at such time, by such means and in such form (if any), as is reasonably specified or described in the notice. The third party may appeal against the notice or any requirement in the notice on the grounds that it would be unduly onerous to comply with the notice or requirement. Notice of an appeal must be given in writing before the end of the period of 30 days from the date on which the notice is given. On appeal, the tribunal may confirm, vary or set aside the notice or a requirement therein, and the tribunal's decision is final.

If the third party fails to comply with the notice, he is liable to a penalty (see **52.19 PENALTIES**).

[*FA 2008, Sch 36, para 32; FA 2009, Sch 49 paras 1–5*].

De Voil Indirect Tax Service. See V5.234.

Data-gathering powers

[31.9] From 1 April 2012 HMRC have information powers for collecting data from certain third parties for use in HMRC's compliance activities. HMRC may by notice in writing require a relevant data-holder to provide relevant data, i.e. data of a kind specified in regulations made by the Treasury. The data may be general or relating to particular persons and matters, and may include personal data.

The powers are additional to and not limited by other HMRC powers to obtain data, but may not be used in place of the power to obtain information under a taxpayer notice (see **31.6** above) to obtain data required to check the relevant data-holder's own tax position, except for the purpose of obtaining data relating to the beneficial ownership of certain payments.

The data-holder notice must specify the data to be provided, which HMRC must have reason to believe could have a bearing on chargeable or other periods ending on or after the first day of the period of four years ending with the day on which the notice is given.

HMRC may ask for the approval of the tribunal before giving a data-holder notice. The decision of the tribunal is final. The tribunal may not approve the giving of the notice unless

- the application for approval is made by, or with the agreement of, an authorised officer;
- the tribunal is satisfied that, in the circumstances, the officer giving the notice is justified in doing so;
- the data-holder has been told that the data are to be required and has been given a reasonable opportunity to make representations to HMRC, unless the tribunal is satisfied that this might prejudice any purpose for which the data are required; and
- the tribunal has been given a summary of any representations made by the data-holder, unless the tribunal is satisfied that this might prejudice any purpose for which the data are required.

An HMRC officer may take copies of, or make extracts from, any document provided pursuant to a data-holder notice.

If an HMRC officer thinks it reasonable to do so, HMRC may retain documents provided pursuant to a data-holder notice for a reasonable period. The retention does not break any lien on the document. The data-holder may request a copy of the document if it is reasonably required. If a document is lost or damaged, HMRC are liable to compensate its owner for replacement or repair costs.

[*FA 2011, s 86, Sch 23, paras 1–7*].

Relevant data-holders

The term 'relevant data-holder' includes many categories of persons involved in the following

- salaries, fees or commission;
- interest paid or credited;
- income or assets belonging to others;
- payments derived from securities;
- grants and subsidies out of public funds;
- licences or approvals;
- rent and other payments arising from land;
- dealing in securities;
- dealing in other property;
- Lloyd's;
- investment plans;
- petroleum activities;
- insurance activities;
- environmental activities;
- settlements; and

- charities.

[*FA 2011, s 86, Sch 23, paras 8–27*].

Appeals

If the tribunal approved the giving of the notice, there is no right of appeal. Otherwise, the data-holder may appeal against a notice, or any requirement in such a notice, on the following grounds

- it its unduly onerous to comply with (unless the data form part of his statutory records);
- he is not a relevant data-holder; or
- the specified data are not relevant data.

Notice of appeal must be given in writing to the HMRC officer who gave the data-holder notice, within 30 days from the date on which the notice was given. The tribunal may confirm, vary or set aside the notice or a requirement in it. The tribunal's decision is final.

[*FA 2011, s 86, Sch 23, paras 28–29*].

De Voil Indirect Tax Service. See V5.234, V5.404.

Power to take samples

[31.10] A person acting under the authority of HMRC may at any time, if he deems necessary on the grounds of fraud or mistake, take samples from the goods in the possession of

- any person who supplies goods or acquires them from another EU country, or
- a fiscal warehousekeeper

in order to determine how the goods, or the materials of which they are made, should be treated for VAT purposes. Any sample may be disposed of and accounted for as HMRC may direct but where it is not returned in a reasonable time (not defined) and in good condition, HMRC must pay compensation of the cost of the sample or any greater amount as they determine. [*VATA 1994, Sch 11 para 8; FA 1996, Sch 3 para 16*].

De Voil Indirect Tax Service. See V5.240.

Opening of gaming machines

[31.11] A person acting under the authority of HMRC may at any reasonable time require a person supplying services by means of gaming machines (or any person acting on his behalf) to open any gaming machine and to carry out any other operation which may be necessary in order to ascertain the value of taxable supplies. [*VATA 1994, Sch 11 para 9*]. See **57.3 RECREATION AND SPORT** for the definition of 'gaming machine'. The provisions do not apply to amusement machines.

De Voil Indirect Tax Service. See V5.238.

Inspection of premises

From 1 April 2009

[31.12] An HMRC officer may enter a person's business premises and inspect the premises, business assets and business documents if the inspection is reasonably required for the purpose of checking that person's tax position. An HMRC officer may also enter premises and inspect the premises, any goods and related documents where he has reason to believe that the premises are used in connection with the supply/acquisition of goods under taxable supplies/acquisitions and the goods or related documents are on the premises, or the premises are used as or in connection with a fiscal warehouse. These powers do not include the power to enter or inspect any part of the premises that is used solely as a dwelling. An inspection may be carried out at a time agreed to by the occupier or, if the occupier has been given at least seven days' notice or the inspection is carried out by or agreed to by an authorised HMRC officer, at any reasonable time. In the latter case, the inspecting officer must provide a notice in writing to the occupier or other person who appears to be in charge, or it must be left in a prominent place on the premises. The notice must state the possible consequences of obstructing the officer (see **52.17 PENALTIES**).

An officer may ask a tribunal to approve an inspection. If the giving of the notice has been approved by the tribunal then the notice must say so, as this is relevant to the rules on offences (see **52.3 PENALTIES**). Applications to the tribunal to approve an inspection of a business are heard without the taxpayer being present. There is no right of appeal against a decision of the tribunal to approve an inspection.

An officer may take copies of, or make extracts from, inspected documents. He may remove and retain inspected documents where it appears to him to be necessary, but he must provide a receipt or copy where requested. An officer may mark business assets to indicate that they have been inspected, and may obtain and record information relating to inspected premises, property, goods, assets and documents. An HMRC officer can only inspect a business document if an information notice at the time of inspection could have required production of the document or part of it.

[*FA 2008, Sch 36 paras 10–17, 28; SI 2009/404; FA 2009, Sch 47 para 8, Sch 48 para 7*].

Before 1 April 2009

A person acting under the authority of HMRC (an '*authorised person*') could at any reasonable time

(a) enter premises used in connection with the carrying on of a business;
(b) enter and inspect any premises and any goods found on them if he has reasonable cause to believe those premises are used as a fiscal warehouse or in connection with

(i) the supply of goods under taxable supplies,
(ii) the acquisition of goods under taxable acquisitions from other EU countries, or
(iii) supplies of investment gold within **26.2**(*a*) or (*b*) **GOLD AND PRECIOUS METALS**

and that goods to be so supplied or acquired are on those premises.

With effect from 19 July 2006, the power to inspect any goods includeed, in particular the power to

- mark the goods, or anything containing the goods, for the purposes of indicating that they have been inspected; and
- record any information (which may be obtained by electronic or any other means, e.g. scanning of barcodes) relating to the goods that have been inspected.

[*VATA 1994, Sch 11 para 10(1)(2)(2A); FA 1996, Sch 3 para 17; FA 2006, s 20; SI 1995/2518, Reg 31C; SI 1999/3114; FA 2008, Sch 36 para 87; SI 2009/404*].

Officers were invariably authorised in writing and instructed to produce the authority on request. Entry was normally by prior appointment, e.g. under (*a*) for an audit visit (see **31.15** below). There was no requirement that the supplier was registered for VAT purposes and the provisions were sufficiently wide to include domestic premises from which a business was conducted. See **52.8 PENALTIES** for obstruction of officers in the performance of their duties.

See also **31.13** below for procedure where documents are removed.

For matters relating to issues of warrants generally, see *CIR and Another v Rossminster Ltd and Others*, HL 1979, 52 TC 106 [1980] STC 42.

De Voil Indirect Tax Service. See V5.231–233.

Order for access to recorded information

[31.13] Subject to below, on application, a justice of the peace (justice in Scotland) may make an order permitting a person acting under the authority of HMRC (an '*authorised person*') to have access to, copy or make extracts from, or remove recorded information reasonably required. Where the recorded information consists of data stored in electronic form, the information must be produced in a visible and legible form (or from which it can be produced in a visible and legible form) and, if required, in a form which can be removed. The justice must be satisfied that there are reasonable grounds for believing that a VAT offence has, is being, or is about to be committed and that the information in the possession of the person named in the order may be required as evidence. The order must be acted upon within seven days of issue (or such longer period as the order specifies). [*VATA 1994, Sch 11 para 11; Criminal Procedure (Consequential Provisions) (Scotland) Act 1995, Sch 4 para 91; Criminal Justice and Police Act 2001, Sch 2 para 13*].

For the conditions for making an order, see *R v Epsom Justices (ex p Bell and Another)*, QB 1988 [1989] STC 169 (TVC 14.97) and *R v City of London Magistrates (ex p Asif and Others)*, QB [1996] STC 611 (TVC 14.98).

Restrictions on use of the above powers

With effect from 1 December 2007, an authorised person can only make an application under the above provisions if he thinks that the material required does not consist of or include 'special procedure material'. If he does, then he must instead make an application under *PACE 1984, Sch 1*. See **31.5** above. '*Special procedure material*' broadly means either of the following.

- Materials in the possession of a person who
  - (a) acquired or created it in the course of any trade, business, profession or other occupation or for the purpose of any paid or unpaid office; and
  - (b) holds it subject to *either* an express or implied undertaking to hold it in confidence *or* a restriction on disclosure or an obligation of secrecy contained in any enactment

  other than
  - items subject to legal privilege;
  - personal records acquired or created as in (a) above and held in confidence; and
  - human tissue or tissue fluid which has been taken for the purposes of diagnosis or medical treatment and which a person holds in confidence.
- Journalistic material other than such material which a person holds in confidence.

[*SI 2007/3175, Art 7*].

Procedure where documents are removed

Where an authorised person removes any documents under **31.12** above or recorded information under the above provisions, he must, on request and within a reasonable time, provide a record of what has been removed. The officer in overall charge of the investigation (i.e. the person whose name is endorsed on the order) must, on request, allow access to such documents etc. and allow them to be copied or photographed unless he has reasonable grounds for believing that to do so would prejudice any investigation or criminal proceedings. Where a person acting on behalf of HMRC has failed to comply with these requirements, an application may be made to a magistrate's court (sheriff in Scotland and court of summary jurisdiction in Northern Ireland) which may order that person to comply.

[*VATA 1994, Sch 11 paras 12, 13*].

De Voil Indirect Tax Service. See V5.236.

Computer records, etc.

With effect from 1 April 2009

[31.14] A person authorised by HMRC may, at any reasonable time, obtain access to, and inspect and check the operation of, any computer (and any associated apparatus or material) used in connection with a document that a person has been, or may be, required to

(i) produce, furnish or deliver (or cause to be produced, etc.) to HMRC; or
(ii) permit HMRC to inspect, to make or take copies of or extracts from, or to remove.

An authorised person may also require the person by whom, or on whose behalf, the computer is used, or any person concerned with the operation of the computer, apparatus or material, to provide the authorised person with such reasonable assistance as may be required for those purposes.

Any enactment which requires a person to comply with (i) or (ii) above has effect as if

- any reference to a document were a reference to anything in which information of any description is recorded; and
- any reference to a copy of a document were a reference to anything onto which information recorded in the document has been copied, by whatever means and whether directly or indirectly.

Any person who obstructs the exercise of a power conferred by the above provisions or who fails to assist an authorised person within a reasonable time is liable to a penalty of £300. *FA 2008, Sch 36 paras 45–49A, 52; SI 2009/404* (assessment of and appeals against penalties) (see **52.18 PENALTIES**) apply to the penalty here as they apply to a penalty under *FA 2008 Sch 36 para 39*.

[*FA 2008, s 114*].

Note that these provisions allow computer records to be copied and removed but the computer itself may not be removed.

Before 1 April 2009

Similar provisions applied except that the penalty was level 4 on the standard scale (currently £2,500).

[*FA 1985, s 10; Civil Evidence Act 1995, Sch 1 para 11*].

De Voil Indirect Tax Service. See V5.237.

Visits by HMRC officers

[31.15] A Revenue and HMRC officer will examine the business records, methods and premises and give guidance. HMRC emphasise that it is the taxpayer's responsibility to account for VAT correctly. It cannot be assumed that this is so simply because a Revenue and HMRC officer does not find any errors. The interval between visits will vary depending on the size and complexity of the business and past compliance. Businesses which send in late or incorrect declarations and payments are visited more often. For a small business, a visit may only take a few hours; for a large or complex business it can last two or more days. A visit will normally take place at the main place of business. If records are kept elsewhere, HMRC should be informed when the appointment is made. The person in charge of VAT affairs should be present. A professional adviser can also be there.

Before the visit

HMRC will

- confirm who they will want to see;
- agree a mutually convenient appointment date and time;
- advise the name and contact number of the officer conducting the visit;
- indicate the records and relevant periods required;
- indicate the likely length of the visit;
- give the business the opportunity to indicate any matters of concern so that the officer can be better prepared; and
- give the business the option to have the above details confirmed in writing.

If it is necessary to postpone a visit, HMRC should be given as much notice as possible.

On occasions, HMRC will call without an appointment. One reason for this may be to see the day-to-day operation of the business. At this time, HMRC will indicate what records are required for inspection.

During a visit

HMRC will

- identify themselves by name on arrival, and if requested, produce an identity card;
- explain the main purpose of the visit;
- discuss the various aspects of the business at the outset so as to keep claims on staff's time to a minimum (although new points may arise as they look at the records);
- examine the records of the business and, where appropriate, inspect the premises and goods thereon;
- where appropriate, take details of supplies made to/by the business to check the correct VAT treatment in the records of the business's suppliers/customers. (Occasionally, this will be the main purpose for the visit but HMRC will explain this at the time they make the appointment.);
- deal with VAT affairs confidentially;
- advise of overpayments as well as underpayments;
- where possible, endeavour to resolve matters during the visit.

At the end of the visit

HMRC will

- review the main work done;
- explain any areas of concern in relation to that work, discuss them and agree any future action that needs to be taken; and
- illustrate as fully as possible the size and the reason for any adjustment to the VAT payable, describe how the adjustment will be made, agree the adjustment whenever possible, and inform the business of how it may seek review or appeal of the decision if it disagrees.

After the visit

HMRC will

- where requested, or where they feel it is necessary, put in writing a summary of the visit, any rulings, agreements or recommendations; and
- where matters are unresolved, give the business a reasonable time within which to provide further information or comment.

(VAT Notice 700, para 2.2; HMRC Notice 989).

De Voil Indirect Tax Service. See V5.221–224.

Estoppel

[31.16] Where, following a visit or otherwise, a Revenue and HMRC officer makes representations which are later shown to be incorrect, a taxpayer may seek to claim that the doctrine of estoppel should be applied. This doctrine prevents a person from acting inconsistently with a representation which he has made to another party, in reliance upon which that other party has acted to his detriment. The representation may be by words, conduct or silence, but it must be a representation of existing fact and not a representation of law or of intention.

In *Société Internationale de Télécommunications Aeronatiques (No 2)* (VTD 17991) (TVC 2.124) a Belgian company (S) operated a telecommunications network for aircraft. In 1973, HMRC issued a ruling that its supplies should be standard-rated but a tribunal allowed an appeal by S that its supplies should be treated as zero-rated (VTD 19) (TVC 66.44). In 1997 HMRC issued a further ruling that the supplies were standard-rated. S appealed contending, amongst other things, that HMRC were bound by the earlier tribunal decision. The tribunal rejected this and held that the 1973 decision did not give rise to any estoppel, observing that the public policy behind the general application of issue estoppel is to ensure the finality of litigation. In taxation cases, however, that aspect of public policy has been overridden by a different element of public policy. Where recurring business transactions, which fall to be assessed period by period, are involved (as is the case of supplies of a VAT-registered trader), administrative flexibility is needed to enable the even-handed management of the revenue. To impose on a trader the unalterable privilege or disadvantage of a particular tax treatment of his supplies as the result of a decision of a tribunal or court might lead to inequity as between him and other traders making similar supplies the liability of which had been determined at a later date. The principle of public policy that applies in that situation is that of ensuring that the tax operates uniformly.

It has been held that there is no question of estoppel against HMRC (*Cupboard Love Ltd* (VTD 267) (TVC 2.110)), the Crown (*T Wood* (VTD 6992) (TVC 2.115)) or the mandatory provisions of a taxing statute (*Medlam* (VTD 545) (TVC 2.112)). More specifically, there is no claim if the element of detriment or prejudice is lacking e.g. where on advice VAT has been incorrectly calculated but the taxpayer has had the benefit of the cash he should have accounted for at the time and there is no evidence that he has charged lower prices because of the advice (*Ribbans* (VTD 346) (TVC 2.111)). It has also been held that an inspection of a trader's records and a general assurance that they are in order is insufficient to form the basis of an estoppel (*GUS Merchandise Corporation Ltd* (VTD 553) (TVC 2.113)).

Scotland

In Scotland, the equivalent of estoppel is a plea of personal bar. It has been held that such a plea, at all events in matters of taxation, does not operate against the Crown, following *Lord Advocate v Meiklam*, (1860) 22 D 1427 (TVC 2.120) and other authorities (*Milne and Mackintosh (t/a Jack and Jill)* (VTD 1063) (TVC 2.121, 2.122)).

HMRC's practice where taxpayer misled by an officer

The HMRC online guidance "When you can rely on advice provided by HMRC" states that where HMRC provide information or advice that is incorrect in law, they are bound by such advice provided that it is clear, unequivocal and explicit and the taxpayer can demonstrate that: he reasonably relied on the advice; where appropriate, he made full disclosure of all the relevant facts; and the application of the statute would result in his financial detriment. Where this is the case, to apply the statute may be so unfair that it could amount to an abuse of power. But, where HMRC have given incorrect information or advice, their primary duty always remains to collect the correct amount of tax as required by the law. Therefore there will be some circumstances where they will not be bound by the advice they have given. Where HMRC provide erroneous advice that is binding on them and subsequently notify the taxpayer that it is incorrect, the established legal position is that the taxpayer will only be required to start accounting for tax on the correct basis from the date of notification. (HMRC Brief 15/09).

De Voil Indirect Tax Service. See V1.286; V1.287.

Evidence by certificate, etc.

[31.17] A certificate of HMRC of any of the following is sufficient evidence of that fact until proved to the contrary.

- A person was, or was not, at any date, registered.
- Any return required has not been made or had not been made at any date.
- Any EU sales list (see **2.11 ACCOUNTING PERIODS AND RETURNS**) has not been submitted or had not been submitted by any given date.
- Notification of liability on an acquisition of exciseable goods or a new means of transport (see **19.9** and **19.37 EUROPEAN UNION: SINGLE MARKET**) has not been given or had not been given by any date.
- A person was or was not, at any date, taxable in another EU country.
- Any VAT payable under the law of another EU country has or has not been paid.

A photograph of any document furnished to HMRC, certified by them, is admissible in any civil or criminal proceeding to the same extent as the document itself.

Any document purporting to be a certificate under the above provisions is deemed to be such a certificate until the contrary is proved.

[*VATA 1994, s 92(5), Sch 11 para 14; FA 2008, Sch 44 para 6*].

Subject to any provision treating a certificate as *conclusive* evidence, a certificate of an HMRC officer that, to the best of that officer's knowledge and belief, any VAT has not been paid is *sufficient* evidence that the sum mentioned in the certificate is unpaid. Any document purporting to be such a certificate is treated as if it were such a certificate until the contrary is proved.

[*CRCA 2005, s 25A; FA 2008, s 138*].

Key points

[31.18] Points to consider are as follows.

- HMRC has the power to request security from a taxpayer when it considers there is a potential risk to the revenue that VAT charged to customers may not be paid and declared when returns are submitted. This decision is usually made when a business is managed or owned by a person or persons who have previously been involved with a business that has failed with a major debt owing to the crown. The HMRC approach is justified by the need to 'protect the revenue'. Experience shows that a VAT tribunal rarely supports a taxpayer who challenges an HMRC request for security. The tribunal's power is limited to deciding whether HMRC has acted reasonably in requesting security from a taxpayer – the tribunal cannot substitute its own decision, even if it feels an alternative measure was more appropriate in the circumstances.
- It is very important that a business checks that its suppliers are correctly charging VAT. A basic principle of VAT law is that a business can only reclaim correctly charged VAT as input tax. This requires the business to ensure that the supplier is registered for VAT (showing VAT registration number on tax invoices etc.) and that the goods or services in question are standard-rated rather than zero-rated or exempt. Although HMRC will not generally hold a customer responsible for any fraudulent actions of the supplier (assuming he was not aware of such intentions), it is important that a business receiving goods or services carries out reasonable checks to ensure a charge of VAT has been correctly made by a bona-fide business.
- It is important that advisers know how MTIC (Missing Trader Intra-Community Fraud) works and the main goods used by the fraudsters. This is not only to ensure they do not act for fraudulent companies but also to advise innocent traders of the potential risks of receiving illegal goods in a supply chain.

- Recent court cases have supported HMRC's strategy of disallowing input tax on the purchase of any fraudulent goods (assuming they are 'relevant goods' as defined in the legislation, i.e. mobile phones etc.) if it can prove that the trader had reason to suspect that the goods were part of an illegal supply chain where output tax was unlikely to be declared by the supplier. The onus is on HMRC to prove that the trader knew or ought to have known that he was dealing in goods where the intention was to fraudulently evade VAT.
- It is important that all traders in 'relevant' high-risk goods take adequate measures to 'ensure the integrity of their supply chain'. HMRC does not provide an exhaustive list of the measures that need to be taken – but it gives very clear guidelines as to the issues that should be considered.
- HMRC officers have the power to demand the production of documents to check a taxpayer's tax position, as long as the demand is given in writing to the taxpayer. Other powers include the right to open gaming machines and the right to take away samples to check the VAT position of the goods in question. An officer also has the right to inspect premises where goods or services are supplied by a business but not in relation to the private dwelling of a taxpayer. Separate provisions also give an officer the power to copy computer records but not to physically remove the computer itself.
- VAT visits are now carried out by HMRC officers largely on the basis of 'risk' factors. A business that is partly exempt, or has transactions where the VAT liability is complex, may expect to receive more regular visits than say a small business using the flat rate scheme. Equally, a business that has submitted a lot of error notifications for large amounts may also receive a visit if it is suspected that accounting controls in the business are not particularly strong. The aim of any VAT-registered business should be to ensure checks and procedures are in place to confirm that figures declared on VAT returns are accurate and complete. This is particularly important now that past errors (underpayments as well as overpayments) can be corrected going back four years rather than three and heavy penalties could be charged if 'careless behaviour' has caused underpayments of VAT.
- A taxpayer can acquire protection regarding the VAT treatment of a transaction if he has received a written ruling from HMRC confirming the procedure to adopt. However, this ruling will only give protection if the taxpayer has fully disclosed all relevant facts and information about the transaction at the time of requesting a decision. The information provided must also be complete and accurate. If a key piece of information is subsequently found to be missing, then HMRC could overrule their written guidance and seek to collect VAT on a retrospective basis. This could apply if,

for example, a product has been incorrectly treated as zero-rated on the basis of incorrect data provided by the taxpayer to HMRC.

32

Hotels and Holiday Accommodation

Cross-reference. See **68 TOUR OPERATORS' MARGIN SCHEME.**

De Voil Indirect Tax Service. See V4.113.

Introduction

Supplies of accommodation

[32.1] The provision in a hotel, inn, boarding house or 'similar establishment' of

(a) sleeping accommodation;
(b) accommodation in rooms which are provided in conjunction therewith (e.g. private bathrooms and sitting-rooms in suites); and
(c) accommodation for the purpose of a supply of catering

is standard-rated.

'*Similar establishment*' includes premises in which there is provided furnished sleeping accommodation (with or without board or facilities for the preparation of food) and which are used by or held out as being suitable for use by visitors or travellers.

[*VATA 1994, Sch 9 Group 1 Item 1(d)*].

Accommodation in motels, guest houses, bed and breakfast establishments, private residential clubs, hostels and serviced flats (other than those for permanent residential use) is included. In most cases such establishments will provide one or more meals, possibly at an inclusive price, but board, or the facilities for the preparation of food, is *not* necessary for an establishment to be regarded as a hotel, etc. (VAT Notice 709/3/11, para 2.1).

See also *International Student House* (VTD 14420) (TVC 41.97) where buildings were not held to be 'similar establishments' and fees for accommodation were held to be exempt because the charity was providing the accommodation to help overseas students and improve international relations. But compare *Acorn Management Services Ltd* (VTD 17338) (VTD 41.98) where accommodation for US students was held to be standard-rated.

In *Namecourt Ltd* (VTD 1560) (TVC 41.100) the tribunal held that *Item 1(d)* above was directed at the sort of establishment which provided accommodation for a transient or floating class of resident. It could be long-term (see also *McGrath v C & E Commrs*, QB [1992] STC 371 (TVC 41.106)) or short-term but it was accommodation which a person would go to with a view to moving on from in due course.

A lodge used to provide supervised residential accommodation for people with mental health problems was held not to be a 'similar establishment' in *Dinaro Ltd (t/a Fairway Lodge)* (VTD 17148) (TVC 41.102).

Accommodation used for catering

Where accommodation is supplied in a hotel, etc. for the purpose of a supply of catering, the supply is standard-rated under (*c*) above whatever the length of the let. Thus, wedding receptions, private parties and other functions held in hotels, etc. are fully taxed. See *Willerby Manor Hotels Ltd* (VTD 16673) (TVC 41.112) where the tribunal held that, following the decision in *Card Protection Plan Ltd v C & E Commrs, ECJ Case C–349/96*, [1999] STC 270 (TVC 22.324), the hire of a function room for an evening reception was a supply ancillary to those of wedding reception facilities and the company had made a composite supply of standard-rated wedding reception facilities, the main ingredient of which was a supply of catering.

(VAT Notice 709/3/11, para 4.1).

Hotel conference/function facilities

Hotels and similar establishments often provide rooms for meetings, conferences and similar functions organised by third parties, making inclusive charges per delegate. Unless the primary purpose for the use of the room is a supply of catering (in which case the supply is always standard-rated) the VAT liability depends on the requirements of individual delegates.

- *Delegates requiring use of the conference room only*. The supply by the hotel is exempt from VAT (unless an option to tax has been made).
- *Delegates requiring use of conference room plus meal(s) ('8 hour conference delegate rate')*. Each element is treated as a separate supply. The conference room element is exempt from VAT (unless an option to tax has been made) but the part of the consideration relating to the provision of food is standard-rated (unless the provision of refreshments is minimal, such as tea and biscuits).
- *Delegates requiring use of conference room plus meals plus overnight sleeping accommodation ('24 hour conference delegate rate')*. With effect from 19 January 2006, HMRC accept that supplies under the 24 hour delegate rate, even where made in return for an inclusive charge,

should be treated as separate supplies. These are taxable supplies, with the exception of the conference/function room hire, which is an exempt supply, unless the hotel has opted to tax its supplies. In cases where a single consideration is paid for supplies having different liabilities, a fair and reasonable apportionment of the consideration must be made.

Where hotels organise and run conferences or similar events themselves and charge for entry to delegates, their supplies are always taxable supplies.

Hotels, etc. are not required to make adjustments in respect of supplies made before 19 January 2006 but they may do so if they wish. All adjustments or claims are subject to the three-year cap and must take into account input tax that has been claimed, but which under the revised interpretation will not relate to taxable supplies. Businesses must be able to produce evidence that they accounted for VAT and must be able to substantiate the amount claimed. Subject to the three-year limitation period, any claim should be for all VAT periods in which the liability error occurred. All or part of a claim may be rejected if repayment would unjustly enrich the claimant.

As a result of the above rules, some hotels will make exempt supplies and the input tax that they incur may be subject to restriction under the partial exemption rules. If hotels prefer, they can continue to treat their supplies as taxable (and be entitled to continue claiming their input tax in full) by opting to tax.

(Business Brief 1/06).

Any goods or services provided such as restaurants, car parking, use of equipment, licensed bars, commissions from taxi firms, or goods or services charged for separately, are standard-rated.

Stays over four weeks

[32.2] For the first four weeks of any stay VAT is due on the full amount payable in the normal way.

Where accommodation within **32.1** above is *provided to an individual* for a period exceeding four weeks, from the 29th day of the stay (or letting) VAT is only due on

(a) meals, drinks and service charges; and
(b) facilities provided apart from the right to occupy the accommodation (i.e. the value of the accommodation is excluded from the VAT calculation).

The value of the facilities subject to VAT under (*b*) above must not be less than 20% of the total amount due for those facilities and the accommodation.

Throughout the period the accommodation must be provided *for the use of the individual* either alone or with one or more other persons who occupy the accommodation with him but not either directly or indirectly at their own expense.

[*VATA 1994, Sch 6 para 9*].

The rule does not apply to bookings by companies where the accommodation is used by a succession of short-term occupants, and each stay is less than 29 days at a time (e.g. it does no apply where airlines make block bookings of hotel accommodation for crew stopovers). However, where the supply is made to someone other than the individual who will be using the accommodation, but the stay by the individual is for more than 28 days, then the rule does apply. This often occurs where the supply of accommodation for homeless people is made to a local authority. In such cases the reduced value applies from the 29th day of each individual's stay. See also *Afro-Caribbean Housing Association Ltd* (VTD 19450) (TVC 67.91).

(VAT Notice 709/3/11, para 3.3).

Example

Weekly terms for accommodation, facilities and meals are £720 (£600 plus £120 VAT) of which £282 (£288 + £48 VAT) represents the charge for meals. For the first 4 weeks, the VAT charge is the full £120 but thereafter a reduced VAT value may be calculated in one of the following ways. The proportion for meals has been taken to be 40% but this will not always be so.

(a) *If charges are expressed in VAT-exclusive terms*

	£	£
Total VAT-exclusive weekly charge	600.00	
VAT-exclusive charge for meals	240.00	48.00
	£360.00	
VAT-exclusive value of facilities (20% minimum)	72.00	14.40
VAT due		£62.40

Weekly terms are therefore £600.00 + £62.40 VAT.

(b) *If charges are expressed in VAT-inclusive terms and the total amount charged to the guest is reduced to take account of the reduced element of VAT*

VAT is as under (*a*) above but the calculation is

	£	£
Total VAT-inclusive charge	720.00	
VAT-inclusive charge for meals	288.00	48.00
VAT-inclusive charge for facilities and accommodation	432.00	
VAT included 1/6 × £423	72.00	
Balance (exclusive of VAT)	£360.00	
VAT-exclusive value of facilities (20% minimum)	72.00	14.40
VAT due		£62.40

The weekly terms are £600 + £62.40 VAT.

(c) *If charges are expressed in VAT-inclusive terms but the total amount charged to the guest is not reduced to take account of the reduced element of VAT*

	£	£
Total VAT inclusive charge	720.00	
VAT-inclusive charge for meals	288.00	48.00
VAT-inclusive charge for facilities and accommodation	432.00	
VAT included 1/26 × £423	16.62	16.62
VAT-exclusive charge for facilities and accommodation	£415.38	
Total VAT		£64.62

The weekly terms are not reduced (i.e. £720 including £64.62 VAT).

* = (20 × facilities element %) ÷ (100 + [20 × facilities element %])

= 1/26 where the facilities element is 20%

Although VAT is only due on the reduced amount, the full VAT-exclusive amount (£600.00 in (*a*) and (*b*) and £655.38 in (*c*)) must be included in Box 6 of the VAT return. This is because the accommodation element of the total charge continues to be the consideration for a standard-rated supply even though the value for the purposes of calculating the VAT becomes nil after the first four weeks.

Breaks in stays

Normally, the reduced value rules above cannot be used unless the guest stays for a continuous period of more than four weeks. For example, stays of three weeks in every month are subject to VAT in full. Similarly, if a guest stays for five weeks, is away for a week and then returns for five weeks, each stay is treated separately and the reduced value basis can only be used for the fifth week of each stay. There are exceptions to this. A guest's departure is not treated as ending a stay if the guest

- is a long-term resident and leaves for an occasional weekend or holiday; or
- is a student who leaves during the vacation but returns to the same accommodation for the next term; or
- pays a retaining fee.

In such cases, the stay is treated as continuous and VAT need only be charged in full for the first four weeks of the overall stay. A guest need not necessarily occupy the same room for his stay to be treated as continuous.

If a retaining fee is paid for a period of absence during the first four weeks of a stay, VAT is due on it at the standard rate. If paid for a period of absence after that period, then the reduced value rules above apply. Provided the fee is no more than the amount treated as payment for accommodation, no VAT is due. Otherwise the fee must be treated as payment for both accommodation and facilities using the rules outlined above.

(VAT Notice 709/3/11, paras 3.3, 7.4).

Accommodation and catering supplied by employers to employees

[32.3] The value of accommodation and catering in a hotel, etc. supplied to its employees is to be taken to be nil unless made for a consideration wholly or partly in money in which case the value is determined without regard to any consideration other than money. [*VATA 1994, Sch 6 para 10(1)(b)*]. Any payments (e.g. in cash or by a deduction from wages not provided for in the contract of employment) are treated as VAT-inclusive. The reduced value provisions in **33.2** above may apply to accommodation. Where employees are paid a minimum wage under a *Wages Order* for an industry and that *Order* allows for appropriate reductions to be made for catering and accommodation, these calculations are steps in arriving at the amount of the weekly wage to be paid and are *not* monetary consideration on which the employer is liable to VAT (*RW & MJ Goodfellow* (VTD 2107) (TVC 62.13)). (VAT Notice 709/3/11, para 4.2).

Deposits, cancellation charges, booking fees and retention fees

[32.4] Most deposits are advance payments on which VAT must be accounted for in the return period in which they are received. If a deposit has to be refunded, any VAT accounted for can be reclaimed.

HMRC state that if a cancellation charge is made when a customer cancels a booking, no VAT is due on the charge (because it is not a payment in respect of a supply). They also indicate that, if the customer has to forfeit a deposit, any VAT accounted for on the deposit can be reclaimed. See also *Société Thermale d'Eugénie-les-Bains v Ministère de l'Économie, des Finances et de l'Industrie, ECJ Case C–277/05* (unreported) (TVC 22.86) where the court held that a deposit in relation to standard-rated hotel services must be regarded, where the purchaser uses a cancellation option available and the deposit is retained by the hotelier, as a fixed cancellation charge paid as compensation for the loss suffered as a result of the client default and which has no direct connection with the supply of any service for a consideration. As such, it is not subject to VAT. The earlier decision in *C & E Commrs v Bass plc*, QB 1992, [1993] STC 42 (TVC 62.93) (where the court held that charges levied on customers who book hotel accommodation but do not take up that accommodation are subject to VAT as making the room available is a supply for VAT purposes) must now be read in the light of the ECJ decision.

If a business arranges or provides a guarantee or insurance against a customer having to pay a cancellation charge, the charge may be exempt if the business has a block insurance policy. See **36.6 INSURANCE**. Also, if the business arranges for insurance to be provided to the customer along with the goods or services supplied and, under the policy, it is the individual customer's risk which is insured, the supply by the business of arranging the insurance may be exempt providing certain disclosure requirements are met. See **36.17 INSURANCE**.

Booking fees charged by a person supplying accommodation are treated as deposits above. Booking fees charged by agents who arrange a supply on behalf of someone else are the consideration for a taxable supply and VAT is due whether or not the accommodation is taken up.

Retention fees paid to reserve accommodation for future use are standard-rated (but see **32.2** above for retention fees paid for a period of absence after the first 28 days).
(VAT Notice 700, para 8.13; VAT Notice 709/3/11, paras 7.1–7.4).

Holiday accommodation, etc. in the UK

[32.5] The grant of any interest in or right over or licence to occupy 'holiday accommodation' is standard-rated. *Included* is

- the grant of an interest in, or in any part of, a building designed as a dwelling or number of dwellings or the site of such a building if
  - (a) the interest granted is such that the grantee is not entitled to reside in the building, or part, throughout the year; or
  - (b) residence there throughout the year, or the use of the building or part as the grantee's principal private residence, is prevented by the terms of a covenant, statutory planning consent or similar permission; and
- any supply made pursuant to a tenancy, lease or licence under which the grantee is or has been permitted to erect and occupy holiday accommodation.

Excluded (and therefore exempt) is the grant of the fee simple, or a tenancy, lease or licence to the extent it is granted for consideration in the form of a premium, in a building or part which is not a 'new building'. A '*new building*' is one completed less than three years before the grant.

'*Holiday accommodation*' includes any accommodation in a building, hut (including a beach hut or chalet), caravan, houseboat or tent which is advertised or held out as holiday accommodation or as suitable for holiday or leisure use, but excludes any accommodation within **32.1** above. Residential accommodation that happens to be situated in a holiday resort is not necessarily holiday accommodation.

See **41.1**(7) **LAND AND BUILDINGS: EXEMPT SUPPLIES AND OPTION TO TAX** for the meaning of '*interest in or right over*' and **41.1**(8) **LAND AND BUILDINGS: EXEMPT SUPPLIES AND OPTION TO TAX** '*licence to occupy*'.

[*VATA 1994, Sch 9 Group 1 Item 1(e), Notes 11–13*].

The effect of the above is that the sale or lease of a house, flat or other accommodation is generally standard-rated as holiday accommodation if the property is new and the purchaser cannot reside there throughout the year or use it as his principal private residence. VAT must be accounted for on the initial charge and on any periodic charges such as ground rent and service or other charges. If the accommodation is no longer new, any payment for the freehold or premium under the lease is exempt but any periodic charges, including rent and service charges, are standard-rated. However, following the tribunal decision in *Ashworth (Mrs B)* (VTD 12924) (TVC 41.127), the sale or lease of a flat or house which can be used as a person's principal private residence but which cannot be occupied throughout the year due to a time-related restriction on occupancy (in *Ashworth* the lessees were unable to occupy the property for the month of February each year) is exempt provided the development on which the property is situated is not a holiday development and is not advertised or held out as such. This also applies to any periodic charges such as rent and service charges.

The provision of a site for holiday accommodation under a tenancy, lease or licence is standard-rated even if the person to whom the site is provided is responsible for erecting the accommodation on it.

(VAT Notice 709/3/11, paras 5.1, 5.3, 5.4).

See *RW and B Sheppard* (VTD 481) (TVC 41.116) for a case concerning short letting of furnished flats treated as holiday accommodation in which the above tests were considered.

Even where a property has been 'held out' as holiday accommodation, where there is no causative nexus between the publication of the advertisement of holiday accommodation and the letting of the whole building for some different purpose, there is no provision of holiday accommodation. See *Cooper and Chapman (Builders) Ltd v C & E Commrs*, QB 1992, [1993] STC 1 (TVC 46.205).

Options to purchase interests or rights

The grant of any right to call for or to be granted an interest or right which would be standard-rated under the provisions above is also standard-rated. *Included* is an equitable right, a right under an option or right of pre-emption and, in relation to Scotland, a personal right. [*VATA 1994, Sch 9 Group 1 Item 1(n)*].

Value for VAT purposes

VAT is payable on the full amount due for the holiday accommodation, including incidental services, irrespective of the length of the stay. (See **32.2** above for long stay arrangements in hotels, etc.) (VAT Notice 709/3/11, para 5.8).

Deposits, cancellation charges and booking fees

See **32.4** above.

Off-season letting

[32.6] Holiday accommodation let during the off-season can be treated as exempt from VAT provided

- it is let to a person as residential accommodation;
- it is let for more than 28 days; and
- holiday trade in the area is clearly seasonal.

A copy of the tenancy agreement or similar evidence should be kept to show that the accommodation was occupied for residential purposes only. In such cases the whole of the let, including the first 28 days, can be treated as an exempt supply.

The holiday season normally lasts from Easter to the end of September, though some areas such as London and Edinburgh are not regarded as having a seasonal holiday trade.

(VAT Notice 709/3/11, para 5.6).

See, however, **41.8 LAND AND BUILDINGS: EXEMPT SUPPLIES AND OPTION TO TAX** for the option to tax such lettings.

Time-share and multi-ownership schemes

[32.7] A supply of holiday accommodation in a house, flat, chalet, etc. under a time-share or multi-ownership scheme is standard-rated if the supply is of 'new' accommodation. The supply of a timeshare, etc. in a property that is not new is exempt to the extent that the grant is made for a consideration in the form of a premium. A property is *'new'* if completed less than three years before the grant. Rent payments made after the initial lump sum, and any annual management fees and service charges, are standard-rated in all cases. (VAT Notice 709/3/11, para 5.7).

See *American Real Estate (Scotland) Ltd* (VTD 947) (TVC 41.118). Time-shares, etc. cannot be zero-rated as tenancies for a term certain exceeding 21 years (or Scottish equivalent) within the definition of 'major interest'. [*VATA 1994, Sch 8 Group 5 Item 1 and Note 13; SI 1995/280*]. See also *Cottage Holiday Associates Ltd v C & E Commrs*, QB 1982, [1983] STC 278 (TVC 15.149) and *Mr & Mrs Cretney* (VTD 1503) (TVC 41.119) where an option to purchase freehold reversion was also offered.

For time-sharing of a yacht based abroad, see *Oathplan Ltd* (VTD 1299) (TVC 41.121).

Construction of holiday accommodation

[32.8] A builder can zero-rate the supply of services in the course of construction of a dwelling even though it will be used to supply holiday accommodation. The word 'dwelling' takes on its normal everyday meaning.

Caravans and camping

[32.9] Holiday accommodation provided in any type of caravan already sited on a pitch is standard-rated. (The provision of *other* accommodation in such a caravan is exempt.)

[*VATA 1994, Sch 8 Group 9 Item 3; Sch 9 Group 1 Item 1(e)*]. (VAT Notice 709/3/11, para 6.2).

Caravan pitches

See **41.3**(*e*) LAND AND BUILDINGS: EXEMPT SUPPLIES AND OPTION TO TAX for caravan pitches.

Camping

The provision of holiday accommodation in a tent is standard-rated. [*VATA 1994, Sch 9 Group 1 Item (e)*]. Any associated facilities are also standard-rated. See **41.3**(*e*) LAND AND BUILDINGS: EXEMPT SUPPLIES AND OPTION TO TAX for tent pitches.

Key points

[32.10] Points to consider are as follows.

- The basic principle that renting land is exempt from VAT (*VATA 1994, Sch 9, Group 1*) is overridden in cases where accommodation is provided in a hotel, inn or similar establishment. In such cases, the supply is standard-rated. It is important to recognise that the accommodation charge is still standard-rated in such cases, even if no catering is provided as part of the deal. So a 'room only' booking in a hotel will be standard-rated in exactly the same way as a 'bed and breakfast' arrangement. It is the nature of the facility that counts, i.e. furnished accommodation usually for short-term occupancy provided by an establishment similar to a hotel.
- There have been a number of VAT tribunal cases over the years regarding the definition of a 'similar establishment' to a hotel. There can be grey areas, but a key indicator has often been the fact that the facility is provided on a furnished basis for the use (generally) of short term visitors who generally move on to alternative accommodation within a short space of time, i.e. holiday makers, tourists, visitors on short term breaks etc.
- In the case of a hotel providing an inclusive package to delegates at a conference or similar event (for example, a 24-hour delegate package to include food, overnight accommodation and the hire of a room), then the element of the charge for room hire is exempt from VAT. This assumes there is no option to tax election in place on the building, in which case this element of the charge will also be standard rated.
- The exempt element of the delegate charge above will produce an output tax saving (very useful if the customer(s) are not VAT-registered or using the venue for private or non-business purposes, e.g. a wedding function) but means that the hotel business is partly exempt. The ideal situation would then be that there is no input tax block through partial exemption rules because of the 'de minimis' limits (see **49.11**). In basic terms, if a partly-exempt business is within the *de minimis* limits, then it obtains full input tax recovery (subject to normal rules), including recovery on those costs relating to its exempt activities.
- An individual staying in a hotel or similar establishment will not be charged VAT on his accommodation charges, once he has stayed in the hotel for four weeks. However, the other services provided by the venue as part of the deal (catering, service charges etc.) are still standard-rated and this element must represent at least 20% of the payment he makes. The facility also extends to bookings made through an organisation (e.g. a charity or housing association), as long as the same person is staying in the hotel room.

- No output tax is payable on free food or accommodation provided by a hotel to its employees – the value of the supply is taken to be nil. However, output tax will be payable on any contribution made by employees towards their food or accommodation, including any deductions made from their wages.
- A deposit received from a customer to secure a hotel booking is classed as an advance payment and therefore creates a tax point for VAT purposes. However, if the customer does not arrive to take up his booking, and sacrifices the deposit, then the output tax accounted for by the hotel can be reclaimed because the payment then represents a cancellation charge. A cancellation charge is outside the scope of VAT because the customer (hotel guest) has received no supply of goods or services in return for his payment.
- Holiday accommodation is always standard-rated – the key issue is how the accommodation is held out for sale and advertised. So accommodation provided in a holiday cottage, holiday flat, caravan or tent at a camp site would always be standard-rated. In the cases of caravan lettings, there is usually an exclusion to prevent twelve-month occupation, i.e. so that the caravan cannot be classed as a residential letting. This is not always the overriding factor in confirming whether an arrangement is classed as holiday accommodation but it is often a key factor.
- Holiday accommodation rented out as residential accommodation during the 'off season' period (usually between October and Easter) can qualify for VAT exemption if certain conditions are met. The accommodation must be intended to serve as the main residence of the tenant for the period of the agreement, and must be for at least 28 days. In such cases, the whole of the letting period can qualify for VAT exemption. There should be evidence of a residential arrangement, i.e. letting agreement, contract with terms etc.
- A useful concession is that building services provided by a builder to construct new holiday accommodation for a developer or landlord can still qualify for zero-rating as work being carried out on a new dwelling (e.g. a block of holiday flats). The zero-rating would extend to any materials provided by the builder as part of his work.

33

Imports

Cross-references. See **26.7 GOLD AND PRECIOUS METALS** for importations of gold; **38.4 INTERNATIONAL SERVICES** for imported services; **52.31–52.34 PENALTIES** for penalties for evasion of, and non-compliance with, import VAT; **71.15 VALUATION** for valuation of imports; **72 WAREHOUSED GOODS AND FREE ZONES**; **73.3**, **73.4** and **73.5 WORKS OF ART, ETC.** for importations and reimportations.

De Voil Indirect Tax Service. See V3.301–358.

Introduction

Trade with other EU countries

[33.1] The provisions of this chapter only apply to importations of goods from outside the EU. See **19.2 EUROPEAN UNION: GENERAL** for the VAT territory of the EU. For the provisions relating to acquisitions of goods from other EU countries, see **19.3 EUROPEAN UNION: SINGLE MARKET**.

Cyprus

The European Commission has advised that the application of *Directive 2006/112/EC* is to be suspended in those areas of Cyprus in which the Government of the Republic of Cyprus does not exercise control. From 1 May 2004, goods from these areas continue to be treated as imports.

The Isle of Man

Although not part of the UK, the Isle of Man is treated as part of the UK for VAT purposes. VAT is chargeable in the Isle of Man under Manx law which generally parallels UK legislation. Goods removed from the Isle of Man to the UK are not normally treated as imports provided any VAT has been accounted for in the Isle of Man or, if the goods were relieved of VAT in the Isle of Man, the conditions of that relief have not been broken. However, where goods are removed from the Isle of Man into the UK and were charged to VAT in the Isle of Man at a different rate to that applicable in the UK (or were relieved from VAT subject to a condition which was not subsequently complied with) the difference in the tax will be charged in the UK. [*SI 1982/1067, Art 3*]. (VAT Notice 702, para 1.7).

The Channel Islands

The Channel Islands are part of the Customs territory of the EU but not part of the VAT territory. Any goods received from the Channel Islands are therefore regarded as imports. (VAT Notice 702, para 1.8).

Economic Operator Registration and Identification (EORI)

All regular importers of goods from outside the EU are given an Economic Operator Registration and Identification (EORI). In the UK this number comprises the letters 'GB' followed by the importer's VAT registration number plus a three-digit suffix. Computer-produced VAT certificates (Form C79) are sent to the importer whose EORI is shown on the import entry. Since Form C79 constitutes evidence of entitlement to input tax, the use of the correct EORI is essential to ensure that the import VAT appears on the correct certificate.

(VAT Notice 702, paras 8.2, 8.7).

The charge to VAT

[33.2] VAT is charged and payable on the importation of goods into the UK (which for VAT purposes includes the territorial sea of the UK i.e. waters within twelve nautical miles of the coastline) as if it were a duty of customs. The rate of VAT is the same as if the goods had been supplied in the UK (whether or not the person importing the goods is registered for VAT). The VAT is chargeable in addition to any customs and/or excise duty or other charges due and is calculated on the value which includes such charges. See **71.15 VALUATION.**

CEMA 1979 and other UK legislation relating to customs or excise duties charged on importation into the UK and any Union legislation relating to customs duties charged on goods entering the EU, apply in modified form so as to relate to VAT on importations.

Goods are treated as imported from a place outside the EU where

- they arrive in the UK directly from outside the EU and are entered for free circulation in the UK (or customs duty otherwise becomes payable on them); or
- they have been placed, in another EU country or in the UK, under one of the customs arrangements listed in **33.24** below and are entered for free circulation in the UK (or customs duty otherwise becomes chargeable on them).

[*VATA 1994, s 1(1)(4), s 2(1), s 15, s 16, s 96(11)*].

Example

Jean is VAT-registered in the UK and has imported 500 special plant pots at a cost of £20 each from a supplier in Hong Kong (outside the EU). The plant pots will attract Customs duty of £10 each when they arrive in the UK.

VAT is charged and payable on the importation of goods into the UK – and the VAT is charged on the value of the goods, including customs duty. The total amount of VAT charged on the importation is £3,000 (500 x £30 x 20%) and Jean can reclaim this amount in Box 4 of her next VAT return. No entry is needed in Box 9 of the return because the purchase is not an acquisition of goods from another EU country.

Time of importation

The time of importation of any goods is

- where brought by sea, when the ship carrying them comes within the limits of a port;
- where brought by air, when the aircraft carrying them lands in the UK or when the goods are unloaded in the UK, whichever is the earlier;
- where brought by land, when the goods are brought across the boundary into Northern Ireland;
- where brought by pipeline, when the goods are brought within the limits of a port or brought across the boundary into Northern Ireland.

[*CEMA 1979, s 5(2)(6)*].

In short, the time of importation for VAT purposes is the moment when customs duty is due on the goods.

Supplies between the time of arrival in the UK and before delivery of import entry

If imported goods are supplied between the time of their arrival in the UK and the time when an import entry is delivered to Customs, the supply can be zero-rated provided, by arrangement, the purchaser is required to make the import entry. [*VATA 1994, Sch 8 Group 13 Item 1*].

Import entry procedure

[33.3] Goods are declared to Customs using the Single Administrative Document (SAD) (Form C88). Import VAT is dealt with in the same way as customs duty.

The import declaration must normally be accompanied by a declaration of value on Form C105, C105A, C105B or C109 as appropriate.

Unless the goods are placed under excise warehousing or one of the customs arrangements listed in **33.24** below, any VAT due must normally either be paid at the time of importation or be deferred with any duty if the importer or his agent are approved for deferment.

Amendment of declarations

Where amendment of a declaration is made after the goods have been released out of official charge and this results in less VAT being payable than was originally declared and paid, the higher amount of VAT can be reclaimed in the normal way. Alternatively, the procedure for reclaiming VAT overpaid in **33.6** below can be used. Where amendment of a declaration results in more VAT being payable, a completed Form C18 must be submitted together with the additional amount of VAT due. The additional payment will appear on the import VAT certificate as evidence for input tax deduction (see **33.11** below).

Postal imports

(1) *Consignments (other than International Datapost/EMS packets) not exceeding £2,000.* A VAT-registered person importing goods for business purposes does not have to pay VAT immediately on importation. Instead, he may account for the VAT due in Box 1 of the VAT return covering the period of importation. Input tax deduction can be claimed on the same return (subject to the normal rules). A customs declaration must accompany the goods showing the consignee's VAT registration number and the nature, quantity and value of the goods. If the VAT number is not clearly shown, VAT may be charged. A cash refund will not be made so the charge label, postal wrapper and any customs declaration attached to the package must be kept to support the claim to input tax. [*SI 1995/2518, Reg 122*].

(2) *International Datapost/EMS packets not exceeding £2,000 in value.* For such imports, the Royal Mail/Parcelforce require payment of the VAT when the package is delivered. The charge label attached must be kept to support any claim to input tax. It is not possible to defer payment of import charges.

(3) *Consignments over £2,000 in value.* For these imports, a declaration on Form C88 (which will be sent to the consignee) must be made and returned to HMRC together with an invoice or other acceptable evidence of value. VAT and other charges due at importation are payable immediately unless the consignee is approved to use the deferment scheme. After payment, HMRC send the consignee a copy of the entry to support any claim to input tax.

Goods imported from outside the EU and destined for another EU country

Where a person receives goods from outside the EU and consigns them to a destination in another EU country, he must normally either

- put the goods in free circulation in the UK, paying any customs duty and/or import VAT due; or
- place the goods under the external Community Transit (T1) arrangements, in which case any duty and/or VAT is payable in the EU country of destination.

See, however, **33.18** below for VAT relief for goods imported and put into free circulation in the UK in the course of a zero-rated supply of those goods to a taxable person in another EU country.

(VAT Notice 702, paras 2.2, 4.1–4.4).

Payment of VAT

[33.4] Payment of VAT on imported goods is due at the time of importation (or removal from warehouse) unless the importer or his agent is approved for deferment. [*CEMA 1979, s 43(1), s 44(1), s 45, s 93(1)(2); VATA 1994, s 38*].

De Voil Indirect Tax Service. See V5.115–122.

Deferment of VAT

[33.5] A business, approved by HMRC and holding a Deferment Approval Number (DAN), can defer paying charges due on importation or removal of goods from a customs or an excise warehouse or from a free zone. An agent (including a warehousekeeper) who enters goods for an importer or owner may also use the scheme.

The charges which can be deferred are:

- *Where payable on imported goods at the time of import or on removal from Customs warehouses or free zones*: import VAT; customs duties; excise duties (including tobacco products duty); levies imposed under the Common Agricultural Policy (CAP) of the EU; positive Monetary Compensatory Amounts under the CAP; anti-dumping or countervailing duties imposed by the EU; compensatory interest on IPR goods diverted to free circulation; temporary import interest on TI goods diverted to free circulation; and interest charged on Customs debts.

- *Where payable on removal from excise warehouse*: VAT and excise duty on the following home-produced or home-manufactured goods, namely spirits and liqueurs (including perfume and composite goods containing excisable spirit); wine and made-wine fortified or rendered sparkling in the warehouse; cider and perry; beer and other alcoholic beverages.
- *Where payable on hydrocarbon oils on removal from warehouse*: Excise duty and VAT.

Deposits for the above charges may also be deferred.

Period of deferment

Except for excise duties, charges deferred during a calendar month ('*the accounting period*') must be paid as a total sum on the 15th of the next month or, if that is not a 'working day', on the next working day *after* it. For excise duty, the accounting period runs from the 15th of one month to the 14th of the next month and payment must be made on the 29th of the latter month (28th February in non-leap years) or, if that is not a working day, on the working day *before* it. '*Working day*' is any day on which the Bank of England in London is open for business.

Payment

Payment must be made by the BACS system of direct debit (although HMRC may require special arrangements if an emergency prevents them collecting that way). No other method of payment is accepted for the deferment scheme. A business wishing to pay by other means must pay each time its goods are cleared.

If a direct debit fails, the business will be expected to settle immediately. Failure to do so may result in the duty deferment facility being stopped or even withdrawn. Other customs facilities that are dependent upon duty deferment may also be affected and interest charges may also arise.

An agent (see below) acting in his own name but on behalf of an importer is jointly and severally liable for any customs debt that may arise.

It is not currently possible to make BACS direct debit payments in euro.

Guarantees

A guarantee on Form C1201 is required from an approved bank, insurance company or building society. The form is obtainable from the Central Deferment Office, (see below under *Approval*) although some guarantors hold their own supplies. The guarantor agrees to cover all amounts deferred up to an overall maximum amount in any calendar month (the '*deferment limit*') which must be enough to cover all deferrable liabilities (but see below for import VAT under SIVA).

If the guarantee level/deferment limit is exceeded in any calendar month, it is not possible to defer any more charges for the remainder of that month (and all further import charges would need to be paid immediately by another payment method until either the guarantee level/deferment limit is increased or a new calendar month begins). The guarantee can be varied by replacement with a bigger (or smaller) amount or by giving a supplementary guarantee to cover extra liabilities in peak periods.

Guarantees can be cancelled by contacting the guarantor or by advising the Central Deferment Office directly in writing. A period of notice of termination of no less than seven days must be given.

Simplified import VAT accounting (SIVA)

From 1 December 2003, a trader who holds a live deferment account (or who intends to apply for one) can apply to reduce the level of financial guarantee required to operate it *for VAT purposes only*. Customs duties and excise duties must still be fully secured. Applicants must satisfy the following criteria.

- VAT-registered for three years or more.
- A good VAT compliance history.
- A good payment history with HMRC.
- Sufficient financial means to meet any amount deferred under SIVA.
- A good HMRC offence record (serious offences will result in automatic expulsion).
- A twelve-month record of international trade operations.
- A good compliance record for international trade.

The SIVA application form (SIVA 1) can be downloaded from HMRC's website:

www.hmrc.gov.uk

Application forms should be completed and returned to SIVA Approvals Team, HMRC, Ruby House, 8 Ruby Place, Aberdeen, AB10 1ZP.

If approval is granted, businesses will then have to arrange any subsequent changes to their guarantee amount with their guarantor and then with HMRC. The deferment account will have two limits.

- A deferment account limit which must be sufficient to cover all deferred charges.
- A deferment guarantee level which must be backed up by a deferment guarantee and sufficient to cover all deferred customs and excise duties.

Approval

Application forms for deferral can be downloaded from HMRC's website (see above) and are also available from HM Revenue and Customs, A&CGs Branch 6, Central Deferment Office, 10th Floor South East, Alexander House, 21 Victoria Avenue, Southend-on-Sea, Essex SS99 1AA (Tel: 01702 367425/29/31/50; Fax: 01702 366091). A set of forms comprises

Form C1200	Application for approval of deferment arrangements
Form C1201	Guarantee for payment of sums due to HMRC
Form C1202	Duty deferment – instruction to bank or building society to pay by direct debit
Form C1207N	Standing authority for agent/freight forwarder to request duty deferment of duty payment against importer's DAN (see below)

If satisfied with the application, guarantee given and payment arrangements, HMRC will issue a Certificate of Approval showing a deferment approval number (DAN). This must be quoted on each request for deferment and in any correspondence with HMRC (including correspondence from the guarantor).

Approval covers the business to the limit of its guarantee (or deferment account limit if SIVA is approved, see above) for deferment of all eligible charges and can be used at any port, airport, warehouse, etc in the UK. Companies which are members of the same group registration for VAT can apply for group approval.

The CDO must be notified immediately if the business

- changes its name, address or VAT registration number;
- ceases to trade (including where the business is carried on by another legal entity); or
- wishes to cancel its duty deferment account.

A new direct debit mandate on Form C1202 must be sent at least ten days before the next payment is due if the bank account is transferred to another bank.

Approval can be revoked at any time for reasonable cause. The direct debit mandate must not be cancelled until all deferred payments have been made.

Procedure

At importation, deferment is requested on the import entry by entering the DAN and the correct payment code in the boxes provided. Charges may be deferred against the importer's DAN or an agent's DAN (see below). Deferment cannot be requested on importations for which no entry is required (unless an entry is made for them) or on postal importations (except those with a value exceeding £2,000 and entered on Form C88A).

On removal from an approved customs and excise warehouse, deferment is requested on the entry or warrant for removal. This also applies under scheduling or other approved simplified arrangements where the entry is presented after the removal of the goods. Charges due on deficiencies in warehouse or in transit cannot be deferred.

On removal from a free zone, deferment is requested on the entry presented when the goods are removed from the zone.

Where, after having allowed deferment, it is found that more or less was payable on the entry, HMRC will normally adjust the deferment account accordingly. Where this is not possible, if more was payable, the balance is payable immediately and if less was payable, the amount overdeclared will be repaid on, or as soon as possible after, the direct debit day on which it is paid. However, repayments of VAT are not normally made to VAT-registered traders who are expected to recover the amount on their next VAT return.

Agents

An agent making an entry can request deferment against his principal's approval number provided he is authorised to do so. This can be done in two ways.

- On Form C1207N, at the time of seeking approval for deferment (see above) or subsequently. This is a standing authority which allows the agent to use his principal's approval number whenever or wherever entering goods on his behalf.
- On Form C1207S which is a 'one-off' authority in respect of a specific consignment or removal of goods. The form is available on the HMRC website (see above). The completed form must be given to the agent to present with the entry.
- In emergencies (e.g. when goods are diverted to another port at short notice) HMRC will accept:
  - (a) A fax on company-headed paper authorising the agent to act. It must be signed by a responsible officer and sent to the agent to present with the entry. The fax should be worded:
    To HM Revenue and Customs at (insert name of port/airport)
    - (1) I am/we are (insert name of business)
    - (2) My/our telephone number is (insert number)
    - (3) I/we hereby authorise (insert name of agent) to use my/our deferment approval number (insert number) when requesting deferment of the charges on the goods imported by me/us on the attached entry.
  - (b) A fax copy of a completed Form C1207S signed by a responsible officer. It must be sent to the agent to present with the entry.
  - (c) A fax copy of a completed form C1207N sent to the Central Deferment Office.
  - (d) An e-mail from the importer, sent to the port of entry, giving specific authority and providing a contact name and telephone number for the importer, along with all other importer and agent's details. Customs at the port of entry should be contacted for the appropriate e-mail address.

If an agent appoints a sub-agent (e.g. because he has no office at a particular port)

- where the sub-agent is shown as declarant on the entry, he can request deferment against his own DAN or the importer's DAN if authorised under the above procedure; and
- where the main agent is shown as the declarant on the entry and the sub-agent signs the declaration as a representative of the main agent, the sub-agent can request deferment against the importer's DAN (if that importer has authorised the main agent) or against the main agent's DAN.

An agent making a bulked entry of goods consigned to several importers may use his own account to defer the charges payable but cannot defer the charges against individual importer's accounts.

Statements

HMRC send out 'periodic deferment statements' at approximately weekly intervals summarising details of deferments at each of their accounting centres and showing the total amount deferred so far in that particular month. Any queries should be taken up immediately with the accounting centre concerned. 'Nil' statements are not normally sent.

Deferment statements cannot be used as evidence for input tax deduction. See **33.11** below for evidence required.

The Duty Deferment Electronic Statements (DDES) service offers a facility to obtain copies of periodic deferment statements electronically via the internet. In order to use DDES a business must register, enrol and activate the service through a central registration process within the Government Gateway. Once registered, DDES can be accessed via the HMRC website and selecting the 'Electronic services' and 'DDES' links. More information on electronic services is provided on the Government Gateway website at

www.governmentgateway.gov.uk

[*SI 1976/1223; SI 1978/1725*]. (Customs Notice 101).

De Voil Indirect Tax Service. See V3.306, V5.117–V5.119.

Reclaiming VAT overpaid

General

[33.6] Import VAT can only be reclaimed as input tax by a VAT-registered importer. However, amounts overpaid as import VAT (e.g. because of misclassification of goods) are generally repayable to the person who paid the amount to HMRC, subject to certain conditions.

Repayments to VAT-registered traders

A VAT-registered trader who has overpaid import VAT can apply for the payment to be adjusted. The importer or his agent must complete Form C285 and the importer must support the request with the signed written declaration:

'I am expecting direct repayment/partial repayment to be made, and no claim to input tax deduction has been or will be made by me on the basis of the document as originally issued.'

If the request is accepted, HMRC will make the repayment. Any such repayment will be processed through the duty adjustment system. VAT repayments are not given special priority, and consideration should therefore be given as to whether the money could be recovered more quickly through the normal input tax deduction system.

A claim for immediate repayment may also be made if VAT has been wrongly charged because an incorrect Deferment Approval Number (DAN) has been quoted or keyed. Any claim should be submitted to the National Repayment Centre, Priory Court, St John's Road, Dover, CT17 9SH.

Repayments to agents

See **33.8** below for the normal rules. However, an agent who has overpaid import VAT (e.g. because goods have been misclassified) may be able to reclaim the amount overpaid if he can provide evidence that he has not been, and will not be, reimbursed by his importer.

(VAT Notice 702, para 2.6).

Goods lost or destroyed before release from official control

[33.7] In such an event, application can be made to HMRC at the place where the import entry was presented for repayment or remission of the VAT due using Form C285 (see above under *Reclaiming VAT overpaid*). (VAT Notice 702, para 2.9).

Repayment of import VAT to shipping and forwarding agents by HMRC if the importer fails to pay them

[33.8] If an importer fails to pay a shipping or forwarding agent any VAT paid by the agent on his behalf, in normal circumstances the agent's only recourse is to the importer. However, by concession, if an importer becomes insolvent without reimbursing the agent for VAT paid or deferred, HMRC will repay the import VAT to the agent provided all the following conditions are satisfied.

(a) Either
- the importer has gone into liquidation; or
- an administrator or administrative receiver has been appointed who certifies that in his opinion the assets of the insolvent importer are insufficient to cover payment of *any* dividend to the unsecured creditors.

(b) The interval between the date of import entry for the goods and the date of insolvency is no more than six months.

(c) The agent entered the goods in accordance with instructions from the importer.

(d) The goods have been re-exported from the UK in the same state as they were imported and, during the time they were in the UK, the goods were under the control of the agent and were not used.

(e) The agent must write to the National Duty Repayment Centre, Priory Court, St John's Road, Dover CT17 9SH enclosing
- evidence that the input tax has been paid to HMRC;
- a certificate from the liquidator, etc. that the VAT has not been, and will not be, reclaimed as input tax;
- confirmation from the liquidator, etc. of (*b*) above;

- a declaration that he will not recover the relevant VAT in whole or in part from the insolvency; and
- evidence to satisfy HMRC of (*c*) above.

(VAT Notice 702, para 2.5; VAT Notice 48, ESC 3.13).

De Voil Indirect Tax Service. See V5.160.

Unregistered persons

[33.9] Where goods are imported for business purposes, the same procedures apply for entry of goods on importation and payment or deferment of VAT as for registered traders except that an unregistered person does not require an import VAT certificate (C79) and is not entitled to claim import VAT and does not therefore receive a copy of the import VAT certificate. He may reclaim VAT paid on imported goods only when VAT was overpaid at importation (by using Form C285) or the goods are not what he ordered or are otherwise not in accordance with contract (see **33.20** below). See also **33.19** below for relief for re-importations by unregistered persons. (VAT Notice 702, para 6.1).

> *Example*
>
> Alan buys and sells toy cars and is not VAT-registered because he trades below the compulsory VAT-registration limits. He buys a shipment of toy cars from Holland (EU) and another one from Australia (non-EU). In the case of the purchase from the Dutch supplier, he will be charged Dutch VAT, based on the rate of VAT that applies in Holland. In the case of the purchase from the Australian supplier, he will not be charged Australian GST (Goods and Service Tax), but will be charged UK VAT and possibly Customs duty at the point the goods enter the UK.

Input tax deduction

[33.10] VAT paid on the importation of goods can be claimed as input tax subject to the normal rules.

Evidence for input tax deduction

[33.11] The normal evidence of the payment of import VAT is the Import VAT Certificate (Form C79) which is issued monthly. This certificate is sent, normally around the 12th day of the following month, to the VAT-registered person whose Economic Operator Registration and Identification (EORI) is shown on the import entry. In the UK the EORI comprises the letters 'GB' followed by the importer's VAT registration number plus a three-digit suffix. The date when the VAT shown on the certificate may be treated as input tax is normally the accounting date alongside each item, not the date when the certificate is issued.

The certificate may be copied for internal purposes and a copy is allowed as an accounting document for input tax deduction provided the original is made available for inspection by the control officer on demand.

If a monthly certificate is lost, replacements can be obtained (for up to six years) from HM Revenue and Customs, VAT Central Unit, Microfilm Section, 8th Floor Alexander House, Victoria Avenue, Southend-on-Sea, SS99 1AU. Applications should be in writing, by faxing the request to fax number 01702 367385 on business headed paper, quoting VAT registration number and the month(s) for which replacement is required.

There are still, however, some types of importation which do not appear on Form C79. The following list summarises the various methods of import procedures and the acceptable evidence of payment.

Import procedure	*Evidence for input tax deduction*
Air/sea imports	
Single Administration Document (SAD) – manually processed	Monthly VAT certificate
SAD – trader input/computer processed	Monthly VAT certificate
SAD – Customs input/computer processed	Monthly VAT certificate
SPIC imports not exceeding £600 Form C1451	Monthly VAT certificate
Bulked entries (SAD)	Customs authenticated invoices
Registered consignees	Customs authenticated invoices
Period entry	Trader produced computer schedule
SAD (simplified)	PE 33 (not authenticated by Customs)
Period entry – Adjustment schedules only	Monthly VAT certificate
Transit Shed Register – imports not exceeding £600 (non-DTI)	Customs authenticated commercial invoice or locally produced forms certified by Customs. The concession allowing use of copies of agents' disbursement invoices in certain circumstances will continue
Postal imports	
Exceeding £2,000 – SAD	Authenticated copy 8 SAD
Not exceeding £2,000 – Customs declaration Form CI or C2/CPU	No input tax evidence issued
Post entry correction	Monthly VAT certificates
Removals from warehouse	
Customs warehouse	Monthly VAT certificates
Excise or HMRC warehouse	Monthly VAT certificates
Hydrocarbon oils	Monthly VAT certificates

(VAT Notice 702, paras 8.1, 8.6, 8.7, 8.12, 8.17, 8.18).

Shipping and forwarding agents

[33.12] Where a shipping or forwarding agent acts for an importer and pays the VAT on his behalf (or defers it under his own deferment guarantee), this is only a commercial arrangement. The agent cannot claim the VAT as input tax as the goods are not imported for the purpose of his business. Only the importer has the legal right to reclaim the VAT paid on the imported goods as input tax, subject to the normal rules. (VAT Notice 702, para 2.4). See, however, **33.8** above for concessional repayment of import VAT to agents in certain cases where the importer fails to pay him.

Goods lost or destroyed after release from official control

[33.13] In such an event, the VAT paid can be deducted as input tax (subject to the normal rules) provided the goods were to be used for business purposes. There is no need to account for output tax unless the goods were supplied to someone else before the loss or destruction. (VAT Notice 702, para 2.9).

Reliefs from charge

[33.14] There are a number of reliefs available as a result of which import VAT is not due on specific goods.

- Aircraft ground and security equipment (see **33.22** below).
- Capital goods and equipment on transfer of activities from abroad (see **33.15**(2) below).
- Certain imports by and for charities (see **33.15**(6) below).
- Decorations and awards (see **33.15**(9) and **33.15**(13) below).
- Electricity and natural gas (see **33.23** below).
- Fuel, animal fodder and feed, and packing necessary during transportation (see **33.15**(11) below).
- Funerals, war graves, etc. (see **33.15**(12) below).
- Goods for examination, analysis or test purposes (see **33.15**(4) below).
- Goods imported for sale to another EU country (see **33.18** below).
- Health, including animals and biological or chemical substances for research, blood and human organs, blood-grouping and tissue-typing re-agents, and equipment for medical research funded by charities and voluntary contributions (see **33.15**(5) below).
- Inherited goods (see **33.15**(13) below).
- Miscellaneous items, including consignments not exceeding £15 in value (low value consignment relief (LVCR)) (see **33.15**(8) below).
- Personal belongings (see **33.15**(13) below).
- Printed matter (see **33.15**(3) and **33.15**(7) below).
- Promotion of trade (see **33.15**(3) below).
- Reimported goods (see **33.19** below).
- Rejected goods (see **33.20** below).
- Small non-commercial consignments (see **33.16** below).
- Temporary importations (see **33.25** below).
- Travellers' allowances (see **33.17** below).
- United Nations visual and auditory materials (see **33.15**(1) below).

- Visiting forces (see **33.21** below).
- Works of art and collectors' pieces. See **33.15**(10), **33.24** and **33.26** below and **73.3** and **73.4** WORKS OF ART, ETC.
- Zero-rated goods under *VATA 1994, Sch 8* (with some exceptions). See **74.1** ZERO-RATED SUPPLIES. [*VATA 1994, s 30(3)*].

Imports relieved under EC Council Directive 83/181/EEC and equivalent UK provisions

[33.15] The following provisions describe goods that can be imported into the UK free of VAT from

- outside the customs territory of the EU (see **17.3** EUROPEAN UNION: GENERAL); and
- the 'special territories' or countries having a customs union with the EU.

The 'special territories' are the Aland Islands, the Canary Islands, the Channel Islands, French Guiana, Guadeloupe, Martinique, Mount Athos and Reunion. These countries or areas are part of the customs territory of the EU but not part of the VAT territory. VAT is therefore due on imports from these territories unless any of the reliefs detailed below are applicable and claimed.

The customs territory of the EU has customs unions with Turkey, San Marino and Andorra. These enable most goods in free circulation to move freely between them without the need to claim duty relief, subject to the production of any necessary preference or Community Transit documentation. (In the case of Andorra, the union only covers goods in Chapters 25–97 of the Tariff.) VAT is still due on imports from Turkey, San Marino and Andorra, however, unless any of the reliefs detailed below are applicable and claimed.

General condition for relief

Where relief is available under any of the provisions listed below by reference to a use or purpose of the goods, the goods must be put to that use or purpose in the UK.

(1) United Nations visual and auditory materials

No VAT is charged on the importation, for whatever purpose, of the following goods produced by the United Nations or by a United Nations organisation.

- Holograms for laser projection.
- Multi-media kits.
- Materials for programmed instructions, including materials in kit form, with the corresponding printed materials.
- Films and film strips of an educational, scientific or cultural character.
- Newsreels (with or without soundtrack) depicting events of current news value (limited to two copies of each for copying) and archival film material (with or without soundtrack) for use with newsreel films.
- Microcards or other information storage media required in computerised information and documentation services of an educational, scientific or cultural character.

- Recordings of an educational, scientific or cultural nature.
- Wall charts, patterns and models of an educational, scientific or cultural character designed solely for demonstration and education purposes.
- Mock-ups or visualisations of abstract concepts such as molecular structures or mathematical formulae.

[*SI 1984/746, Art 4, Sch 1; SI 1987/2108; EC Council Directive 83/181/EEC, Art 79, Annex*].

(2) Capital goods and equipment on transfer of activities from abroad

No VAT is charged on 'capital goods and equipment' imported by a person for the purposes of a business

- he has ceased to carry on *either* outside the customs territory of the EU *or* in the 'special territories' *or* in countries having a customs union with the EU (see above);
- which he notifies HMRC is to be carried on by him in the UK; and
- which is concerned exclusively with making taxable supplies.

For these purposes, a person is not to be treated as intending to carry on a business in the UK if such business is to be merged with, or absorbed by, another business already carried on there, unless a new activity is to be set up.

The goods must

(a) have been used in the business for at least twelve months before it ceased to be carried on abroad;
(b) be imported within twelve months of the business ceasing to be carried on abroad; and
(c) be appropriate both to the nature and size of the business to be carried on in the UK.

HMRC can waive the conditions under *(a)* and *(b)* above in special circumstances (e.g. if political upheaval in the country where the business was located prevented twelve months use or the import within twelve months of cessation). (Customs Notice 343, para 2.4).

'*Capital goods and equipment*' includes livestock where the business transferred is an agricultural holding (but not livestock in the possession of a dealer) but not food for human consumption or animal feeding stuffs, fuel, stocks of raw materials or finished or semi-finished products or any motor vehicle ineligible for deduction of input tax (see **45.3 MOTOR CARS**). Examples of items included are office and shop equipment or machinery, and other tools of trade; means of transport used for the purposes of production or for providing a service; and computer and other technical equipment needed to run the business. (Customs Notice 343, para 2.2).

[*SI 1984/746, Sch 2 Group 1; SI 1992/3120; EC Council Directive 83/181/EEC, Arts 24–28*].

It is not necessary to obtain prior authorisation from the DTI or to present a DTI approval letter to HMRC at the time of import. Instead, HMRC will consider eligibility for relief from duty and VAT at the time the goods are imported and grant relief if appropriate.

(3) Promotion of trade

No VAT is charged on the following imports.

(a) Articles of no intrinsic commercial value sent free of charge by suppliers of goods and services for the sole purpose of advertising.

(b) Samples of negligible value of a kind and in quantities capable of being used solely for soliciting orders for goods of the same kind. Where HMRC require, the goods must be rendered permanently unusable, except as samples, by being torn, perforated, clearly and indelibly marked, or by any other process.
Relief is not available for goods not presented as samples at import but subsequently to be made into samples (e.g. unaltered rolls of fabric imported to be cut up and made into swatch books). (Customs Notice 367, para 2.4).

(c) Printed advertising matter, including catalogues, price lists, directions for use or brochures, which relates to goods for sale or hire by a person established outside the EU or to transport, commercial insurance or banking services offered by a person established outside the EU. The material must clearly display the name of the person established outside the EU by whom the goods or services are offered. Subject to below, relief does not apply to consignments containing two or more copies of different documents or to consignments containing two or more copies of the same document (unless the total gross weight of the consignment does not exceed one kilogram). Any goods which are the subject of grouped consignments from the same consignor to the same consignee are also excluded. These restrictions on relief do not apply in the case of imported printed matter intended for free distribution and relating to either goods for sale or hire.

(d) Goods to be distributed free of charge at an 'event' as small 'representative samples' for use or consumption by the public (excluding fuels, alcoholic beverages and tobacco products).

(e) Goods imported solely for the purpose of being demonstrated at, or used in the demonstration of any machine or apparatus displayed at, an 'event' (excluding fuels, alcoholic beverages and tobacco products).

(f) Paints, varnishes, wallpaper and other low value materials to be used in the fitting out or decoration of a temporary stand at an 'event'.

(g) Catalogues, prospectuses, price lists, advertising posters, calendars, unframed photographs and other printed matter or articles advertising goods displayed at an 'event', supplied without charge for distribution free of charge to the public at such event.

'*Event*' comprises

- any trade, industrial, agricultural or craft exhibition, fair or similar show or display which is not being organised for private purposes in a shop or on business premises with a view to the sale of the goods displayed;
- any exhibition or meeting primarily organised for charitable purposes or to promote *either* friendship between peoples *or* religious knowledge or worship *or* any branch of learning, art, craft, sport or scientific, technical, educational, cultural or trade union activity or tourism;

- any meeting of representatives of international organisations and ceremonies of an official or commemorative character; and
- any representative meeting or ceremony of an official or commemorative character.

'*Representative samples*' means goods which are

- imported free of charge or obtained at such event from goods imported in bulk;
- identifiable as advertising samples of low value;
- not easily marketable and, where appropriate, packaged in quantities which are less than the lowest quantity of the same goods as marketed; and
- intended to be consumed at such event, where the goods comprise foodstuffs or beverages not so packaged.

Relief under (*d*)–(*g*) above only applies where the aggregate value and quantity of the goods is appropriate to the nature of the event, number of visitors and extent of the exhibitor's participation. Where relief is available under (*e*) or (*f*) above in respect of goods for demonstration or use, the goods must be consumed, destroyed or rendered incapable of being used again for the same purpose either in the course of, or as a result of, such demonstration or use.

[*SI 1984/746, Art 6(2), Sch 2 Group 3; SI 1988/2212; SI 1992/3120; EC Council Directive 83/181/EEC, Arts 61–69*].

(4) Goods for examination, analysis or test purposes, etc.

No VAT is charged on goods imported for examination, analysis or testing

- to determine their composition, quality or their technical characteristics;
- to provide information; or
- for industrial or commercial research.

To qualify for relief

- the quantities imported must not exceed the amounts necessary for their purpose;
- the examination, etc. itself must not constitute a sales promotion;
- the examination, etc. must be completed within such time as HMRC require; and
- any goods not completely used up or destroyed in the course of (or as a result of) the examination, etc., and any products resulting from the examination, etc., must be destroyed or rendered commercially worthless or exported (see further below).

[*SI 1984/746, Art 6(3), Sch 2 Group 4; EC Council Directive 83/181/EEC, Arts 70–76*].

Testing must normally be completed by the date stated on the SAD or postal form. If this is not possible, a letter of explanation with a request for an extension of time should be sent, before the stated time is reached, to

National Import Reliefs Unit
HM Revenue and Customs
Custom House
Killyhevlin Industrial Estate
Enniskillen
County Fermanagh, Northern Ireland BT74 4EJ
Tel: 028 6632 2298
Fax: 028 6632 4018

If the goods are transferred, at least 48 hours prior notice must be given to NIRU stating to whom and where the goods are to be transferred.

When testing is completed, NIRU must be informed in writing of

- place of importation or postal depot;
- number and date of the customs entry or postal docket;
- quantity, value and description of the goods and date of receipt;
- details of the tests, including the address(es) where the testing took place and where records are available for inspection;
- the date on which testing was completed; and
- details of any materials remaining and proposals for their disposal.

Any materials remaining (including goods not used, or not completely used up in the test and goods resulting from the test, including waste and scrap) may

- have VAT (and duty) paid on them; or
- with HMRC's permission, be destroyed, free of duty and VAT; or
- with HMRC's permission, be converted into waste or scrap and released on payment of any VAT (and duty) which may be due.

NIRU will consider applications to export goods remaining after the testing is over on satisfactory explanation of why the goods cannot be destroyed or converted into waste or scrap and have to be exported.

(Customs Notice 374, paras 4.2–4.5).

(5) Health

Certain goods can be zero-rated on supply in the UK to disabled persons or to charities for making available to disabled persons. Such goods can also be relieved of any VAT payable on importation. See **28.14** to **28.33 HEALTH AND WELFARE.**

In addition, the following importations are free of VAT.

(a) Animals specially prepared for laboratory use and sent free of charge to a 'relevant establishment'.
'Relevant establishment' means
  - a public establishment, or a department of such, principally engaged in education or scientific research (e.g. a university, NHS or teaching hospital, mobile health laboratory, research laboratory of a government department, or laboratory of a research council); or
  - a private establishment so engaged, which is approved by the Home Office.

A private establishment must apply for a letter from the Home Office confirming that it is a designated establishment under the terms of the *Animals (Scientific Procedures) Act 1986*. (Customs Notice 365, para 2.1). Also see Customs Notice 365 for import prohibitions and restrictions and animal welfare provisions.

[*SI 1984/746, Sch 2 Group 5 item 1; EC Council Directive 83/181/EEC, Art 35*].

(b) Approved biological or chemical substances (see Customs Notice 366, para 4) sent to a 'relevant establishment' (see (*a*) above) from outside the EU.

A private establishment must apply to the National Import Reliefs Unit (at the address under (4) above) for authorisation to claim relief. The application must be made in advance of importation and detail the research project for which the imported substance will be used. If the application is successful, NIRU will issue an approval letter. (Customs Notice 366, para 3.1).

[*SI 1984/746, Sch 2 Group 5 item 3; SI 1992/3120; EC Council Directive 83/181/EEC, Art 35*].

(c) Any of the following goods, namely

- human blood
- products for therapeutic purposes derived from human blood (whole human blood, dried human plasma, human albumin and fixed solutions of human plasmic protein, human immunoglobulin and human fibrinogen);
- human (including foetal) organs or tissue for diagnostic or therapeutic purposes or medical research;
- 'Blood-grouping re-agents' and 'tissue-typing re-agents' imported by 'approved institutions or laboratories' for use exclusively for non-commercial medical or scientific purposes.

Relief also applies to any special packaging essential for transport of the goods and any solvents or accessories necessary for their use.

'*Blood-grouping reagents*' means all re-agents (whether of human, animal, plant or other origin) used for blood-type grouping and for the detection of blood grouping incompatibilities.

'*Tissue-typing reagents*' means all re-agents (whether of human, animal, plant or other origin) used for the determination of human blood types or in determining human tissue types.

'Approved institutions and laboratories' include

- a public establishment or laboratory (e.g. Regional and District Health Authorities, Health Boards in Scotland, Health and Social Service Boards in Northern Ireland, public health laboratories, research laboratories of government departments, research councils and similar bodies, all blood transfusion services, schools of pharmacy and medical schools); and
- a private establishment which has been authorised by the Department of Health to receive such goods VAT (and duty) free.

A private establishment must apply in advance of importation to the Department of Health Public Health Group, PH6.6, Room 631B, Skipton House, 80 London Road, London SE1 6TE (tel: 020 7972 5142) indicating

- the status of the establishment;
- the nature of activities (e.g. medical research); and
- the type of goods to be imported.

If the application is successful, the DoH will issue a letter of authorisation. (Customs Notice 369, para 3.1).
[*SI 1984/746, Sch 2 Group 5 items 4–8; EC Council Directive 83/181/EEC, Arts 36–38*].

(d) Pharmaceutical products by or on behalf of persons or animals for their use while visiting the UK to participate in an international sporting event.
[*SI 1984/746, Sch 2 Group 5 item 9; EC Council Directive 83/181/EEC, Art 39*].

(e) Samples of reference substances approved by the World Health Organisation for the quality control of materials used in the manufacture of medicinal products provided the samples are addressed to consignees authorised to receive them free of VAT.
[*SI 1984/746, Sch 2 Group 5 item 10; SI 1988/2212; EC Council Directive 83/181/EEC, Art 38c*].

(6) Charities, etc.

Certain goods which can be zero-rated on supply to or for charities in the UK can also be relieved of any VAT payable on importation. See **12.7** and **12.8 CHARITIES**.

In addition, no VAT is payable on the importation of the following goods.

(a) Basic necessities (i.e. food, medicines, clothing, blankets, orthopaedic equipment and crutches, required to meet a person's immediate needs) obtained without charge for distribution free of charge to the needy by a 'relevant organisation'. *Excluded* are alcoholic beverages, tobacco products, coffee, tea and motor vehicles other than ambulances.

(b) Goods donated by a person established outside the EU to a 'relevant organisation' for use to raise funds at occasional charity events for the benefit of the needy. There must be no commercial intent on the part of the donor. *Excluded* are alcoholic beverages, etc. as in (*a*) above. HMRC treat an occasional charity event as one held not more than four times a year by any one organisation.

(c) Equipment and office material donated by a person established outside the EU to a 'relevant organisation' for meeting its operating needs and carrying out its charitable aims. There must be no commercial intent on the part of the donor. *Excluded* are alcoholic beverages, etc. as in (*a*) above.

(d) Goods imported by a 'relevant organisation' for distribution or loan, free of charge, to victims of, or for meeting its operating needs in the relief of, a disaster affecting the territory of one or more EU countries. This relief only applies where the EU Commission has made a decision authorising the importation of the goods.

(e) Articles donated to and imported by an approved organisation principally engaged in the education of, or the provision of assistance to, blind or other physically or mentally handicapped persons for loan, hiring out or transfer other than on a profit-making basis (and whether for consideration or free of charge) to such persons and specially designed for their education, employment or social advancement. There must be no commercial intent on the part of the donor.

(f) Spare parts, components or accessories for any article within (*e*) above, including tools for its maintenance, checking, calibration or repair. The goods must be imported with an article within (*e*) above to which they relate or, if imported subsequently, must be identifiable as being intended for such an article.

The above reliefs are conditional on

- any guarantee, declaration, undertaking, document or other details being given to HMRC as required;
- the goods being put to the use or purpose specified; and
- unless specifically allowed above, the goods not being lent, hired out or transferred unless to an organisation which would itself be entitled to the relief if importing the goods on that date. In the latter case, prior notification in writing must be received from HMRC and the goods must be used solely in accordance with the relieving provisions.

Where any condition ceases to be satisfied and written notice of this fact is given to HMRC, VAT becomes payable as if the goods had been imported on that date and VAT is calculated accordingly. The VAT must not, however, exceed the VAT relieved in the first place.

'*Relevant organisation*' means a State organisation or other approved charitable or philanthropic organisation. HMRC have given general approval to the following charitable and philanthropic organisations.

- Organisations registered with the Charity Commissioners or the Office of the Scottish Charities Regulator.
- State organisations which are devoted to welfare.
- Any of the following organisations provided they are non-profit making and their objective is the welfare of the needy, *viz* hospitals; youth organisations; clubs, homes and hostels for the aged; orphanages and children's homes; organisations set up for the relief of distress caused by particular disasters in the EU; and organisations concerned with the relief of distress generally (such as the British Red Cross and the Salvation Army).

[*SI 1984/746, Art 6(1), Art 7, Art 8, Sch 2 Group 6; SI 1992/3120; EC Council Directive 83/181/EEC, Arts 41–55*]. (Customs Notice 317, para 2.1).

(7) ***Printed matter, etc.***

The following printed matter may be imported free of VAT from a country outside the EU.

- Documents sent free of charge to public services in the UK.
- Publications of foreign governments or official international organisations for free distribution.

- Ballot papers for elections organised by bodies outside the EU.
- Specimen signatures and circulars concerning signatures forming part of exchanges of information between banks and public services.
- Official printed matter sent to a Central Bank in the UK.
- Documents from a company incorporated outside the EU to holders of its issued securities.
- Files and other documents for use at international meetings, etc and reports of such gatherings.
- Plans, drawings, traced designs and other documents sent by any person for participating in a competition in the UK or to obtain or fulfil an order executed outside the EU.
- Documents to be used in examinations held in the UK on behalf of institutions established outside the EU.
- Printed forms to be used as official documents in the international movement of vehicles or goods pursuant to international conventions.
- Printed forms, labels, tickets and similar documents sent to travel agents (including airlines, national railway undertakings, ferry operators and similar organisations) in the UK by transport and tourist undertakings outside the EU.
- Used commercial documents.
- Official printed forms from national or international authorities.
- Printed matter conforming to international standards for distribution by an association in the UK and sent by a corresponding association outside the EU.
- Documents (leaflets, brochures, books, magazines, guidebooks, posters (whether or not framed), unframed photographs and photographic enlargements, maps (whether or not illustrated) window transparencies, and illustrated calendars for free distribution to encourage persons to visit foreign countries, in particular to attend cultural, tourist, sporting, religious, trade or professional meetings or events (provided the goods do not contain more than 25% of private commercial advertising)).
- Free distribution copies of hotel lists and yearbooks published by or on behalf of official tourist agencies and timetables for foreign transport services (provided the goods do not contain more than 25% of private commercial advertising).
- Yearbooks, lists of telephone and telex numbers, hotel lists, catalogues for fairs, specimens of craft goods of negligible value and literature on museums, universities, spas or similar establishments, supplied as reference material to accredited representatives or correspondents appointed by official national tourist agencies and not intended for distribution.
- Official publications issued under the authority of the country of exportation, international institutions, regional or local authorities and bodies governed by public law established in the country of exportation (provided VAT or any other tax has been paid on the publication or printed matter in the third country from which it has been exported and the publication, etc. has not benefited from any relief from payment by virtue of exportation).

- Printed matter distributed by officially recognised political organisations, established outside the EU on the occasion of European Parliament or national elections in the country in which the printed matter originates (provided VAT or any other tax has been paid on the publication or printed matter in the third country from which it has been exported and the publication, etc. has not benefited from any relief from payment by virtue of exportation).

[*SI 1984/746, Art 2(5), Sch 2 Group 7; SI 1988/2212; SI 1992/3120; EC Council Directive 83/181/EEC, Arts 78, 79*].

(8) Articles sent for miscellaneous purposes

No VAT is charged on the following imports.

- Materials relating to trademarks, patterns or designs and supporting documents and applications for patents imported for submission to competent bodies to deal with protection of copyright or industrial or commercial patent rights.
- Objects imported for submission as evidence, or for a like purpose, to a court or other official body in the EU.
- Photographs, slides and stereotype mats for photographs sent to press agencies and publishers of newspapers or magazines.
- Recorded media, including punched cards, sound recordings and microfilm, sent free of charge for the transmission of information.
- Goods (other than alcoholic beverages or tobacco products) sent on an occasional basis as a gift of friendship or goodwill between bodies, public authorities or groups carrying on an activity in the public interest. The goods must not be of a commercial character.
- Any consignment of goods (other than alcoholic beverages, tobacco products, perfumes or toilet waters) not exceeding £15 in value (decreased from £18 from 1 November 2011). This relief is called low value consignment relief (LVCR). From 1 April 2012 LVCR does not apply to goods imported to the UK from the Channel Islands.

[*SI 1984/746, Sch 2 Group 8 Items 1–4, 7, 8; FA 2011, s 77; SI 1988/2212; SI 1995/3222; EC Council Directive 83/181/EEC, Arts 22, 57–59, 77, 79*].

(9) Decorations and awards

No VAT is charged on the following imports.

- Any honorary decoration conferred by a government or Head of State outside the EU on a person resident in the UK and imported on his behalf.
- Any cup, medal or similar article of an essentially symbolic nature, intended as a tribute to activities in the arts, sciences, sport or public service, or in recognition of merit at a particular event. It must be donated by an authority or person established outside the EU for the purpose of being presented in the UK or awarded outside the EU to a person resident in the UK and imported on his behalf.

- Awards, trophies and souvenirs of a symbolic nature and of limited value intended for free distribution at business conferences or similar international events to persons normally resident in a country other than the UK.

The awards, etc must not be of a commercial character.

[*SI 1984/746, Sch 2 Group 8 Items 5, 6, 9; SI 1988/2212; SI 1992/3120; EC Council Directive 83/181/EEC, Art 56*].

A person is resident where he spends at least 185 days in a period of twelve months because of personal ties and occupational ties (if any) but if personal ties are in one country and occupational ties in another, HMRC treat a person as resident in the country of his personal ties if

- his stay in the country of his occupational ties is in order to carry out a task of definite duration; or
- he returns regularly to the country of his personal ties.

Not eligible for relief are

- watches, cameras, cars;
- long service awards made to employees by employers or colleagues;
- prizes won in unimportant competitions such as deck games and card games;
- articles purchased with prize money;
- gifts or prizes given in lieu of payment;
- gifts where the donor appears to be motivated largely by commercial considerations;
- any consumables, e.g. alcoholic drinks, tobacco products, foods; and
- souvenirs distributed which are not in keeping with the nature of the event.

VAT relief may be claimed by the recipient or the person who is to present the award, etc. As proof that relief is due, HMRC will normally be satisfied with any certificate or press publicity material relating to the decoration or award, or a letter or statement from the donor or organiser of the event.

(Customs Notice 364, paras 2.1, 2.3–2.5).

(10) Works of art and collectors' pieces for exhibition

Works of art and collectors' pieces imported by approved museums, galleries or other institutions for a purpose other than sale can be imported free of VAT provided the following conditions are met.

- The institution must be approved by the National Import Reliefs Unit. It should apply for approval in writing to NIRU as far in advance of the first anticipated importation as possible. If successful, NIRU will issue a letter of approval against which HMRC will allow relief.
- The exhibits must be of an educational, scientific or cultural character.
- The exhibit must be dispatched directly to the approved establishment and must be used exclusively as exhibits or specimens under its control.
- Records of the imported exhibits must be kept.

- The exhibits must be imported either free of charge, or, if for a consideration, must not be supplied to the importer in the course or furtherance of any business.

The exhibits may be lent, hired out or transferred to other institutions which are approved under this procedure provided prior permission is obtained from NIRU.

[*SI 1984/746, Sch 2 Group 9; EC Council Directive 83/181/EEC 3, Art 79*]. (Customs Notice 361, paras 2.1, 3.1).

See also **73.3** and **73.4 WORKS OF ART, ETC.** for an effective reduced rate of VAT of 5% on the importation of works of art including any antique more than 100 years old.

(11) Fuel, animal fodder and feeding stuffs, and packing for use during transportation

No VAT is charged on the following imports.

- Fuel contained in the standard tanks (as defined) of a motor road vehicle or of a 'special container', for use exclusively by such vehicle or such special container. '*Special container*' means any container fitted with specially designed apparatus for refrigeration, oxygenation, thermal insulation and other systems.
- Fuel, not exceeding ten litres for each vehicle, contained in portable tanks carried by a motor road vehicle, for use exclusively by such vehicle. This does not apply to a special purpose vehicle or one which, by its construction and equipment, is designed for and capable of transporting goods or more than nine persons including the driver.
- Lubricants contained in a motor road vehicle, for use exclusively by such vehicle and necessary for its normal operation during the journey.
- Litter, fodder and feeding stuffs contained in any means of transport carrying animals, for the use of such animals during their journey.
- Disposable packings for the stowage and protection (including heat protection) of goods during their transportation to the UK and where the cost is included in the consideration for the goods transported.

[*SI 1984/746, Sch 2 Group 10; SI 1988/2212, Art 8; EC Council Directive 83/181/EEC 3, Arts 80–86*].

(12) Funerals, war graves, etc.

The following goods are relieved from VAT on importation from a country outside the EU.

- Goods imported by an approved organisation for use in the construction, upkeep or ornamentation of cemeteries, tombs and memorials in the UK which commemorate war victims of other countries.
- Coffins containing human remains and urns containing human ashes, together with accompanying flowers, wreaths or other ornamental objects.
- Flowers, wreaths or other ornamental objects imported without commercial intent by a person resident outside the EU for use at a funeral or to decorate a grave.

[*SI 1984/746, Art 2, Sch 2 Group 11; SI 1992/3120; EC Council Directive 83/181/EEC, Arts 87, 88*].

(13) Personal belongings, etc.

Personal property can be imported without VAT liability in the circumstances set out in (*a*)–(*e*) below. See also **33.19**(1) below for belongings returned to the UK after previously being exported.

In addition to any specific conditions, relief is only due if the following general conditions are met.

- The goods are declared for relief to the proper officer on importation. Where any goods are declared before the date on which a person becomes normally resident in the UK or, if he intends to become so resident on the occasion of his marriage, before such marriage has taken place, relief is subject to such security as HMRC require being furnished.
- Where relief is given otherwise than under (*c*) or (*d*) below, the goods must not, unless indicated otherwise below, be lent, hired-out, given as security or transferred in the UK without authorisation from HMRC within a period of twelve months from the relief being given. Where HMRC do give authorisation, they may discharge the relief and require payment of the VAT at the rate then in force (or, if lower, the rate at the time of importation).
- Any conditions for receiving relief (including the intention of becoming normally resident and the use to which the goods are put) must be complied with. If not, the VAT becomes payable forthwith (unless HMRC see fit to waive payment or part) and the goods are liable to forfeiture.

[*SI 1992/3193, Arts 6–10*].

(a) Relief for persons transferring their normal residence from outside the EU

A person entering the UK is not required to pay VAT (or duty) chargeable on 'property' imported into the UK provided

- he has been 'normally resident' outside the EU for a continuous period of at least twelve months;
- he intends to become normally resident in the UK;
- the property has been in his possession and used by him in the country where he has been normally resident for at least six months before its importation;
- the property is intended for his personal or household use in the UK;
- the property is declared for relief not earlier than six months before the date of becoming normally resident in the UK (or earlier where HMRC are satisfied that a person has given up normal residence outside the EU but is prevented by occupational ties from becoming normally resident in the UK) and not later than twelve months after that date; and
- HMRC are satisfied that the property has borne (and not been exempted from, or had refunded, because of exportation) all duties and taxes normally applicable in its country of origin or exportation.

'*Property*' means any personal property intended for personal use or meeting household needs, including household effects, provisions and pets; riding animals, cycles, motor vehicles, caravans, pleasure boats and private aircraft; but excluding any goods which, by their nature or quantity, indicate they are being imported for a commercial purpose. Specifically excluded are

- alcoholic beverages and tobacco products;
- any motor vehicle designed for or capable of transporting more than nine persons including the driver, or goods;
- any special purpose vehicle or mobile workshop; and
- any articles for use in a trade or profession, other than portable instruments of the applied or liberal arts.

'*Normally resident*'. A person is treated as normally resident in a country where he usually lives

(i) for a period, or aggregate of periods, of at least 185 days in a period of twelve months; and
(ii) because of his 'occupational ties'; and
(iii) because of his 'personal ties'.

Where a person has no occupational ties, he is treated as normally resident in a country on the basis of (i) and (iii) above only, provided his personal ties show close links with that country.

Where a person has occupational ties and personal ties in different countries, he is treated as normally resident in the country where he has personal ties provided

- the stay in the country where he has occupational ties is to carry out a task of a definite duration; or
- he returns regularly to the country with personal ties.

However, a UK citizen with personal ties in the UK but with occupational ties outside the EU may be treated as normally resident in the country of his occupational ties provided that he satisfies the condition in (i) above in the country with occupational ties.

'*Occupational ties*' do not include attendance by a pupil or student at a school, college or university.

'*Personal ties*' mean family or social ties to which a person devotes most of his time not devoted to occupational ties.

[*SI 1992/3193, Arts 2, 3, 11, 12; EC Council Directive 83/181/EEC, Arts 2–10*].

See also *Rigsadvokaten v N C Ryborg*, ECJ [1993] STC 680.

By concession, relief may still be granted where personal belongings fail to qualify only because they have not been possessed and used for the specified period or have been declared for relief outside the specified time limit. In addition, property (including motor vehicles) purchased

- by diplomats, members of certain international organisations and NATO forces,

- by UK forces (or civilian staff accompanying them) outside the EU, and
- under a UK export scheme by members of the UK diplomatic service, members of UK forces and members of certain international organisations

which otherwise qualifies for relief will not be refused relief solely because HMRC cannot satisfy themselves that the goods have borne all duties and taxes normally applicable in their country of origin.

(VAT Notice 48, ESCs 9.3–9.7).

(b) Relief on marriage

A person entering the UK is not required to pay VAT (or duty) on 'property' imported into the UK provided

- he has been 'normally resident' outside the EU for a continuous period of at least 12 months;
- he intends to become normally resident in the UK on the occasion of his marriage; and
- declared for relief not earlier than two months before the date fixed for the marriage (in which case security for the VAT and duty will be required which will be discharged on subsequent submission of the marriage certificate to HMRC) and not later than four months after the marriage.

'*Property*' for these purposes is limited to household effects and trousseaux, other than tobacco products and alcoholic beverages (i.e. it does not extend to motor vehicles and their trailers, caravans, mobile homes, pleasure boats and aircraft although some of these may alternatively qualify for relief under (*a*) above).

In addition, such a person is not required to pay VAT (or duty) on any wedding gift (meaning any property, other than tobacco products or alcoholic beverages, customarily given on the occasion of a marriage) not exceeding £800 in value imported into the UK by him or on his behalf provided the gift is

- given or intended to be given to him on the occasion of his marriage by a person normally resident outside the EU; and
- declared for relief not earlier than two months before the date fixed for the marriage (in which case security for the VAT and duty will be required which will be discharged on subsequent submission of the marriage certificate to HMRC) and not later than four months after the marriage.

See (*a*) above for the definition of '*normally resident*'.

[*SI 1992/3193, Arts 13–15; EC Council Directive 83/181/EEC, Arts 11–15*].

(c) Pupils and students

A person is not required to pay VAT (or duty) in respect of 'scholastic equipment' imported in to the UK provided

- he is a pupil or student normally resident outside the EU who has been accepted to attend a full-time course at a school, college or university in the UK; and

- the equipment belongs to him and is intended for his personal use during the period of his studies.

'*Scholastic equipment*' means household effects representing the normal furnishings for the room of the pupil or student, clothing, uniforms, and articles or instruments normally used by pupils or students for their studies, including calculators and typewriters.

[*SI 1992/3193, Art 16; EC Council Directive 83/181/EEC, Arts 20, 21*].

(d) Honorary decorations, awards and goodwill gifts

No VAT (or duty) is chargeable on the importation into the UK

- by a person normally resident in the UK of any honorary decoration confirmed on him by a government outside the EU or any cup, medal or similar article of an essentially symbolic nature awarded to him outside the EU as a tribute to his activities in the arts, sciences, sport or public service or in recognition of merit at a particular event;
- by a person normally resident in the UK, returning from an official visit outside the EU, of goods not intended for a commercial purpose given to him on his visit by the host authorities; or
- by a person normally resident outside the EU paying an official visit to the UK of goods not intended for a commercial purpose which are in the nature of an occasional gift he intends to offer to the host authorities during his visit.

Imports of tobacco products and alcoholic beverages are excluded.

[*SI 1992/3193, Arts 17–20*].

(e) Personal property acquired by inheritance

A person who is either

- 'normally resident' in the UK or Isle of Man,
- a 'secondary resident' who is not normally resident outside the EU, or
- a body incorporated in the UK or Isle of Man solely concerned with carrying on a non-profit making activity

and who has become entitled as legatee to 'property' situated outside the EU is not liable to pay any VAT (or duty) on importation of the property into the UK provided

- the property is imported not later than two years after the date of entitlement as legatee is finally determined (unless HMRC allow otherwise); and
- the person produces the property to the proper officer for examination and furnishes proof of his entitlement as legatee.

'*Property*' means any personal property intended for personal use or meeting household needs, including household effects, provisions and pets; riding animals, cycles, motor vehicles, caravans, pleasure boats and private aircraft; but excluding any goods which, by their nature or quantity, indicate they are being imported for a commercial purpose. Specifically excluded are

- alcoholic beverages and tobacco products;

- any motor vehicle designed for or capable of transporting more than nine persons, including the driver, or goods;
- any special purpose vehicle or mobile workshop;
- articles (other than portable instruments of the applied or liberal arts) used in the exercise of a trade or profession before his death by the person from whom the legatee has acquired them;
- stocks of raw materials and finished or semi-finished products; and
- livestock and agricultural products exceeding the quantities for normal family requirements.

See (*a*) above for the meaning of '*normally resident*'.

A '*secondary resident*' is a person who, without being normally resident in the UK or Isle of Man, has a home there which he owns or is renting for at least twelve months.

[*Customs and Excise Duties (General Reliefs) Act 1979, s 7; SI 1992/3193, Art 21; EC Council Directive 83/181/EEC, Arts 16–19*].

The following must be provided as proof of inheritance.

- A copy of the will (or other legal documents if the deceased died intestate) proving entitlement to the relief and identifying the goods, certified by the executors of the estate or other persons responsible for winding up the deceased's estate.
- If the goods are not precisely specified in the will, etc. (e.g. where they formed part of the residue) a list of the goods and their approximate value prepared by the executors, etc and confirmation from them that title to the goods passed to the legatee.
- A signed declaration on Form C1421 (claim for relief).

(Customs Notice 368, paras 3.1, 4).

Small non-commercial consignments

[33.16] No VAT is charged on the importation of a small non-commercial consignment, not forming part of a larger consignment, provided

- the consignment is of an occasional nature;
- the value for customs purposes does not exceed £40 (45 euro);
- it is consigned by one private individual to another;
- it is not imported for any consideration in money or money's worth; and
- it is intended solely for personal use of the consignee, or of his family, and not for any commercial purpose.

Any of the following goods included in the consignment must be below the permitted quantities shown. Otherwise no relief is given for any goods of that description in the consignment.

Tobacco	50 cigarettes *or* 25 cigarillos *or* 10 cigars *or* 50g of smoking tobacco

Alcoholic beverages	1 litre of spirits, etc. with an alcoholic strength exceeding 22% by volume *or* 1 litre of spirits, aperitifs, etc. with an alcoholic strength of no more than 22% by volume, fortified wines and sparkling wines *or* 2 litres of still wines
Perfume and toilet water	50g of perfume *or* 250cc/ml of toilet water

This relief does not apply to goods contained in the baggage of, or carried with, a person entering the UK (for which see **33.17** below).

[*SI 1986/939; SI 2010/1185*].

Travellers' allowances

[33.17] A person who has travelled from a country outside the VAT territory of the EU (see **17.2 EUROPEAN UNION: GENERAL**) is relieved from payment of VAT on goods of up to the values listed below which he has obtained outside the VAT territory of the EU (or in a duty free shop in the EU on an outward journey) and which are contained in his personal luggage. The goods must not be imported or used for commercial purposes otherwise they are liable to forfeiture.

Tobacco	200 cigarettes *or* 100 cigarillos *or* 50 cigars *or* 250g of smoking tobacco
Alcoholic beverages	1 litre with an alcoholic strength of more than 22% by volume *or* 2 litres with an alcoholic strength of no more than 22%; 4 litres of still wines; 16 litres of beer
Other goods	£390 (£340 before 1 January 2010) if travel by air or sea; £270 (£240 before 1 January 2010) if travel not by air or sea

No one under the age of 17 is entitled to relief for tobacco or alcoholic beverages. Private pleasure-flying or private pleasure-sea-navigation do not constitute travel by air or sea.

Before 1 December 2008 the threshold for other goods (which included beer) was £145; there were quantitative limits on perfume and toilet water; and the allowance for still wine was 2 litres.

Transitional provisions

Although the following countries are now EU countries, the above provisions continue to apply to the specified items until the dates shown.

Bulgaria	200 cigarettes	31 December 2009
Czech Republic	200 cigarettes	31 December 2007
	50 cigars, 100 cigarillos or 250 grammes of smoking tobacco	31 December 2006

Estonia	200 cigarettes or 250 grammes of smoking tobacco	31 December 2009
Hungary	200 cigarettes	31 December 2008
Latvia	200 cigarettes	31 December 2009
Lithuania	200 cigarettes	31 December 2009
Poland	200 cigarettes	31 December 2008
Romania	200 cigarettes	31 December 2009
Slovakia	200 cigarettes	31 December 2008
Slovenia	200 cigarettes	31 December 2007

[*SI 1994/955; SI 2004/1002; SI 2006/3157; SI 2008/3058; SI 2009/3172*].

Goods imported for sale to another EU country

[33.18] Subject to such conditions as HMRC impose, the VAT charged on the importation of goods from outside the EU is not payable where

- a taxable person imports goods in the course of an onward zero-rated supply of those goods by him to a taxable person in another EU country; and
- HMRC are satisfied that he intends to remove the goods to another EU country and he does in fact so remove the goods within one month of the date of importation (i.e. the date the goods enter free circulation). HMRC may approve a longer period.

HMRC may require the deposit of security up to the amount of the VAT chargeable on the importation.

[*SI 1995/2518, Reg 123*].

In the above circumstances, no import VAT is due in the UK or the EU country of destination but VAT on the supply/acquisition is accounted for by the purchaser in the EU country of destination.

Relief under these provisions cannot be claimed for goods imported for process and supply to a customer in another EU country.

To claim the relief the person must be making a zero-rated supply of the imported goods, not merely acting as freight forwarder/shipper, to a taxable person in another EU country.

Records

As the onward supply is to a consignee in another EU country who will account for tax on the acquisition, the normal procedures must be adopted. In particular a VAT invoice must be issued and details recorded on an EU sales list and, where appropriate, a Supplementary Declaration.
(VAT Notice 702/7/10).

Reimported goods

[33.19] Goods which have previously been exported can be reimported without payment of VAT in the following circumstances.

(1) Returned goods relief

Returned goods relief renders the payment of VAT unnecessary on the importation of goods into the UK that are in the same state as when they were previously exported from the EU by the importer.

In relation to any reimportation of goods occurring after 5 April 2006, the rules for such import VAT relief are aligned with those for returned goods relief from import duty.

Goods which, having been exported from the EU, are reimported and released for free circulation within a period of three years (or such longer period as may be allowed in special circumstances) may be granted relief from VAT provided:

- The goods are reimported by the same person who originally exported them.
- The goods are reimported in the state in which they were exported. This does not apply where they only received
  - (i) treatment necessary to maintain them in good condition or handling which altered their appearance only; or
  - (ii) treatment or handling not falling within (i) above but which proved to be defective or unsuitable for their intended use and *either* the treatment or handling was applied to the goods solely with a view to repairing them or restoring them to good condition *or* their unsuitability for their intended use became apparent only after such treatment or handling had commenced.
- The goods were not exported under the outward processing procedure (unless those goods remain in the state in which they were exported).

Relief is not available if

- the reimporter
  - (i) supplies the goods whilst under the inward processing procedure or in the course of, or after, the relevant exportation;
  - (ii) the place of that supply is outside the UK; and
  - (iii) the goods may be stored or physically used in the UK by or under the direction of that reimporter or the recipient; or
- the goods in question were supplied at any time to any person under *SI 1995/2518, Regs 131–133* (persons departing from the EU, see **21.13** and **21.19 EXPORTS**).

But where, prior to their exportation, the returned goods had been released for free circulation at the reduced or zero-rate of VAT because of their use for a particular purpose, exemption from VAT can be granted only if they are to be reimported for the same purpose. Where the purpose for which the goods in question are to be imported is no longer the same, the amount of VAT chargeable on them is reduced by any amount charged on the goods when they were first released for free circulation. Should this amount exceed that charged on the entry for free circulation of the returned goods, no refund will be granted.

The amount of the relief due is reduced by any '*unpaid VAT*', i.e. any part of the VAT charged and due on

- a supply or acquisition of the goods in another EU country before the reimportation, or
- an importation of the goods from outside the EU before the reimportation,

but repaid, remitted or otherwise not paid. Paid does not mean deducted as input tax.

Returned goods are exempt from VAT even where they represent only a proportion of the goods previously exported from the EU. The same applies where the goods consist of parts or accessories belonging to machines, instruments, apparatus or other products previously exported from EU.

[*SI 1995/2518, Reg 121D; SI 2006/587, Regs 4, 5; EC Council Regulation 2913/92/EEC, Arts 185–187; EC Commission Regulation 2454/93/EEC, Arts 844–856*].

(2) Reimportation after exportation for treatment or process

Subject to any conditions that HMRC may impose, VAT chargeable on the importation of goods which have been temporarily exported outside the EU and are reimported

- after repair, process or adaptation outside the EU, or
- after having been made up or reworked outside the EU

is payable as if such treatment or process had been carried out in the UK, provided HMRC are satisfied that

- at the time of exportation the goods were intended to be reimported after completion of the treatment or process; and
- the ownership in the goods was not transferred to any other person at exportation or at any time the goods were abroad.

[*SI 1995/2518, Reg 126*].

See also Customs Notice 235 *Outward processing relief*.

Repayment or remission of VAT on rejected goods

[33.20] Repayment or remission of VAT on rejected goods is treated as follows:

(1) Goods not in accordance with contract

Repayment or remission of VAT can be claimed on goods imported if the goods

- are rejected because, at the time of declaring them to Customs, they
  - (i) are defective;
  - (ii) do not comply with the terms of the contract under which they were imported; or
  - (iii) were damaged before being cleared by Customs;
- are those declared to Customs;

- have not been used more than was necessary to establish that they were defective or did not comply with contract;
- have not been sold after they have been found to be defective or not to comply with the contract; and
- are disposed of by
  - (i) exportation;
  - (ii) destruction at the expense of the importer;
  - (iii) destruction by order of a public authority; or
  - (iv) placing in a customs warehouse or a free zone (in which case the goods are treated as non-Union goods and can be subsequently re-entered to free circulation or another customs procedure or re-exported).

HMRC must be notified on Form 1179 at least 48 hours before the intended disposal and disposal must take place under Customs control. Any waste or scrap resulting from authorised destruction of the goods is liable to VAT (and duty) unless exported from the EU.

Claims must be made within 12 months of the date Customs charges became due and for an amount exceeding 10 euros.

A fully taxable VAT-registered person importing goods for business purposes should normally be able to deduct the VAT due on importation on his next VAT return. However, a direct repayment can be claimed under the above provisions. If so, he must surrender the import VAT certificate relating to the goods and make a signed declaration that he will not make a corresponding claim for input tax deduction on a VAT return.

A partly exempt person whose method of apportionment does not allow him to recover all the relevant input tax, a non-registered person or a taxable person importing goods for non-business purposes should submit a claim for direct repayment.

See Customs Notice 266 for details of how to make the claim.

(2) Goods in special situations

Repayment or remission of VAT can be claimed on imported goods in a number of special situations provided the goods have not been used or sold after import and the claim (which must be for an amount exceeding 10 euros) is made within twelve months of the date Customs charges became due. Each case will be decided on its merits but examples include where the goods are

- in a means of transport which it is impossible to open on arrival at its destination after the goods have been released for free circulation (provided the goods are immediately re-exported);
- forbidden to be marketed by a judicial body and are re-exported from the EU or destroyed under customs supervision (provided the goods have not been used in the UK);
- entered by a declarant empowered to do so on their own initiative and which, through no fault of the declarant, cannot be delivered to the consignee;

- addressed to the consignee in error, e.g. wrongly labelled, not ordered by the consignee, or received in excess of the quantity ordered (provided the goods are re-exported to the original supplier or to an address specified by them and, in the case of excess goods, the consignee refused the goods immediately the excess was discovered);
- found to be unsuitable because of an obvious error in the consignee's order (e.g. wrong goods received due to quoting an incorrect reference number);
- found not to have complied, at the time of entry into free circulation, with the rules in force concerning their use or marketing and cannot therefore be used as the consignee intended;
- unable to be used because of official measures taken after the date of entry for free circulation (e.g. new safety or hygiene laws);
- delivered to a consignee after a fixed delivery date (e.g. because of shipping delays); and
- found to be unsaleable in the EU and are to be donated to charity, in which case the goods must either be
  - (i) exported and given free of charge to a charity operating outside the EU, provided that the charity is also represented in the EU; or
  - (ii) delivered free of charge to a charity operating in the EU, provided the charity is eligible to import similar goods free of VAT and duty under **33.15**(6) above, **12.7**, **12.8 CHARITIES** or **28.32 HEALTH AND WELFARE**.

(Customs Notice 266, paras 3.1, 3.2).

Visiting forces

[33.21] No VAT is required where

- an 'entitled person' imports any goods, or
- a gift of goods, other than tobacco products or alcoholic beverages, is made to an entitled person by dispatching them to him from outside the EU

subject to the following conditions.

(a) The goods must not be lent, hired-out, given as security or transferred in the UK without the prior authorisation in writing by HMRC. Where HMRC do authorise such disposal, the entitled person must then pay the VAT relieved at the lower of the rate in force at the time of relief and the rate at the time of disposal.

(b) The goods must be used exclusively by the entitled person or a member of his family forming part of his household.

(c) In the case of a motor vehicle,
  - no relief is available if the entitled person has previously been afforded relief in respect of any other motor vehicle unless he has disposed of all such vehicles (or all but one if his spouse or civil partner is present in the UK) and paid any duty or tax required by HMRC as under (*a*) above; and

- the entitled person must deliver, or cause to be delivered, four copies of a completed Form C941, each signed by the entitled person and his commanding officer. One copy is to be delivered to the visiting forces, and three copies to the proper officer.

An '*entitled person*' means a person who is

- a serving member of a visiting force, other than the UK, which is a member of NATO or a person recognised by the Secretary of State as a member of the civilian component of such a force; or
- a person who is a military or civilian member of NATO International Military Headquarters

who is neither a UK national nor a permanent resident of the UK.

Where any conditions are not complied with, the VAT becomes payable forthwith (unless HMRC sanction non-compliance in writing) and the goods are liable to forfeiture. Any VAT due is the liability of the entitled person or any person in possession of the goods at that time.

[*SI 1992/3156; SI 2005/2114; SI 2007/5*].

Aircraft ground and security equipment

[33.22] By concession, no VAT or duty is chargeable on the importation of the following ground and security equipment for aircraft by an airline of another contracting state of the Convention on International Civil Aviation (Chicago Convention).

- All repair, maintenance and servicing equipment; material for airframes, engines and instruments; specialised aircraft repair kits; starter batteries and carts; maintenance platforms and steps; test equipment for aircraft, aircraft engines and aircraft instruments; aircraft engine heaters and coolers; ground radio equipment.
- Passenger-handling equipment: passenger-loading steps; specialised passenger-weighing devices; specialised catering equipment.
- Cargo-loading equipment: vehicles for moving or loading baggage, cargo, equipment and supplies; specialised cargo-loading devices; specialised cargo-weighing devices.
- Component parts for incorporation into ground equipment including the items listed above.
- Security equipment: weapon-detecting devices; explosives-detecting devices; intrusion detecting devices.
- Component parts for incorporation into security equipment.

Claims for relief under this concession should be addressed to the Customs Entry Processing Unit where the goods are to be cleared.

(Customs Notice 48, ESC 2.7).

Gas, electricity, heat and cooling

[33.23] With effect from 1 January 2011, VAT is not payable on the importation of

- gas through a natural gas system or any network connected to such a system, or fed in from a vessel transporting gas into a natural gas system or any upstream pipeline network;
- electricity; or
- heat or cooling supplied through a network.

[*SI 2010/2924*].

Prior to 1 January 2011 VAT was not payable on the importation of

- gas through the natural gas distribution network; or
- electricity.

[*SI 2004/3147*].

Goods imported under Customs suspensive arrangements

[33.24] For import VAT purposes, goods are normally treated as imported when they arrive in the UK and are entered to free circulation (whether by direct import from a place outside the customs territory of the EU or by indirect import on removal to the UK via another EU country).

But for any goods placed under one of the following suspensive arrangements, import VAT (and duty) only become due when the goods are removed to free circulation in the UK.

The suspensive arrangements are:

- Temporary importation with total relief from customs duties (see **33.25–33.29** below).
- IPR suspension (see **33.30–33.32** below).
- Processing under customs control (see **33.33** below).
- External transit (T1) arrangements or internal transit (T2) arrangements. (Although internal transit is not a customs suspensive procedure it is included here as import VAT may become due if the goods are subsequently removed to free circulation.) See **33.34** below.
- Customs warehousing (see **72.2 WAREHOUSED GOODS AND FREE ZONES**).
- Free zones (see **72.21 WAREHOUSED GOODS AND FREE ZONES**).
- Temporary storage. (Although such goods are not strictly under customs arrangements, goods arriving from outside the EU have the status of temporary storage until they are entered and cleared to free circulation or another procedure.)

Suspension of import VAT does *not* apply to goods entered to:

- IPR drawback.
- Temporary importation with partial relief from customs duty.
- End-use relief (other than goods for the continental shelf). See **33.35** below.
- Outward processing relief.

Transfers of goods under suspensive arrangements

Goods can be moved from one suspensive regime to another without payment of import VAT.

Acquisitions of goods held under suspensive arrangements

VAT-registered traders who acquire goods held in one of the suspensive regimes listed above from a taxable person in another EU country must normally account for VAT on the acquisition in accordance with the normal rules, even though the import VAT remains suspended.

Valuation

The valuation rules for imports (see **71.15 VALUATION**) also apply to any of the reliefs mentioned in this notice with the exception of certain goods entered to temporary importation relief (see **33.26** below).

Onward supply relief

Any goods imported under IPR suspension, processing under Customs control, temporary importation, Customs warehousing arrangements or placed in free zones which are imported in the course of an onward supply to a taxable person in another EU country may be put into free circulation in the UK without the payment of import VAT. VAT is accounted for on the supply/acquisition by the purchaser in the EU country of destination.

Any goods imported for processing and supply to a customer in another EU country under IPR suspension or processing under customs control may claim onward supply relief once the imported goods are entered to free circulation in the UK and dispatched to that EU country.

Supplies of goods under suspensive arrangements

Supplies of goods held under suspensive arrangements are chargeable with VAT in the normal way. This is subject to the following special rules.

- *Goods in temporary storage*. Where there is a supply of imported goods between the time of their arrival in the UK and the time when a customs entry is made and the purchaser is required to make the import entry, then the supplier may zero-rate the supply.
- *Goods under temporary import arrangements supplied to persons established outside the EU*. Where goods held under temporary import arrangements are supplied, that supply is treated as neither a supply of goods nor a supply of services provided that
  (i) the goods remain eligible for temporary importation arrangements; and
  (ii) the supply is to a person established outside the EU.
  [*SI 1992/3130*].
- *Second-hand goods and works of art under temporary import arrangements*. Subject to below, where
  (a) second-hand goods are imported with a view to their sale by auction, or

(b) 'works of art' are imported for exhibition with a view to possible sale,

any sale of the second-hand goods (provided it is by auction) or the works of art at a time when the goods are still subject to temporary importation arrangements with total exemption from import duty is treated as neither a supply of goods nor a supply of services and can be disregarded for VAT purposes.

The provision of any services relating to such supplies (e.g. auctioneers' charges) may similarly be disregarded (but must be included in the value for VAT at importation).

'*Works of art*' mean any such items falling within the definition in *VATA 1994, s 21* (see **73.3**(*a*) **WORKS OF ART, ETC.**).

With effect from 1 September 2006, the above treatment does not apply where

- any goods falling within **73.3**(*a*)–(*c*) **WORKS OF ART, ETC**. are sold by auction at a time when they are subject to the temporary importation arrangements; and
- following the sale by auction, arrangements are made by or on behalf of the purchaser which result in the importation of the goods from a place outside the EU.

  Such transactions are treated as supplies of goods in the ordinary way.

  [*SI 1995/958; SI 1999/3119; SI 2006/2187*].

Security

HMRC do not normally require security apart from

- most goods entered to temporary importation (see **33.25** below); and
- transfers of certain goods considered to bear increased risks.

(VAT Notice 702/9/05, paras 2.1, 2.5–2.10).

Relief for temporary importations (TI relief)

[33.25] Persons who temporarily import goods may either

- take advantage of the TI relief provisions, pay no VAT (or duty) at the time of importation but deposit any security required by HMRC for VAT (and duty) which would become due if the conditions for temporary importation are not met; or
- if they are taxable persons importing the goods for business purposes, pay the VAT at the time of temporary importation (or defer it under the provisions relating to deferment of VAT, see **33.5** above) and reclaim the VAT paid as input tax subject to the normal rules. If this is done, there is no limit on the length of time that the goods may be held in the UK before re-exportation (although the relevant controls and time limits for any duty remain).

Subject to meeting certain conditions, it is possible to obtain total relief from import duties and VAT on a range of goods imported from outside the EU if they are intended for re-export within a specified time (usually a maximum of two years). See **33.26** below for eligible goods. In most cases, application for authorisation to use TI relief can be made at the time of importation. There are, however, other types of authorisations available. See Customs Notice 200 for the various types of authorisation and how to apply for them, and the documentary evidence which must be presented to HMRC to use the relief.

For most importations, it is necessary to provide security (either by cash deposit or bank guarantee) equal to the full amount of duty and import VAT potentially due. This may be reclaimed when the goods have been re-exported and satisfactory documentary evidence can be provided. See **33.27** below.

Goods eligible for TI relief

[33.26] The various TI reliefs that provide for total relief from duties and VAT on importation are as listed below. The following general conditions apply.

- Unless otherwise stated, goods imported under TI provisions may remain in the EU for a maximum of two years. Application can be made in writing, before expiry of the original TI period, for a longer period. If TI goods are transferred to another Customs suspensive arrangement (e.g. IPR or customs warehousing) only the remaining balance of the TI period will be available to those goods if they are re-entered to TI at a later date.
- Goods must remain in the same state. Repairs and maintenance, including overhaul and adjustments or measures to preserve the goods or to ensure their compliance with the technical requirements for their use under the arrangements are admissible.

[*EC Commission Regulation No 2454/93, Arts 553, 554*].

(1) Pallets

[*EC Commission Regulation No 2454/93, Art 556*].

(2) Containers

Containers which have been durably marked in an appropriate and clearly visible place with the following information.

- The identity of the owner or operator shown by either full name or an established identification (symbols such as emblems or flags being excluded).
- (With certain exceptions), the identification marks and numbers of the container, given by the owner or operator; its tare weight, including all its permanently fixed equipment.
- Apart from containers used for transport by air, the country to which the container belongs.

Containers may be used once in the UK before being re-exported for transporting goods loaded and intended to be unloaded within the UK where the containers would otherwise have to make an unloaded journey.

[*EC Commission Regulation No 2454/93, Art 557*]. See also Customs Notice 306.

(3) Means of transport

Means of road, rail, air, sea and inland waterway transport where

- they are registered outside the EU in the name of a person established outside the EU (or, if the means of transport are not registered, they are owned by a person established outside the EU);
- they are used by a person established outside the EU; and
- in the case of commercial use and with the exception of means of rail transport, are used exclusively for transport which begins or ends outside the EU except that they may be used in internal traffic where the provisions in force in the field of transport, in particular those concerning admission and operations, so provide.

Where the means of transport referred to above are re-hired by a professional hire service established in the EU to a person established outside the EU, they must be re-exported within eight days of entry into force of the contract.

Persons established in the EU benefit from total relief from VAT and import duties where

- means of rail transport are put at their disposal under an agreement whereby each network may use the rolling stock of the other networks as its own;
- a trailer is coupled to a means of road transport registered in the EU;
- means of transport are used in connection with an emergency situation and their use does not exceed five days; or
- means of transport are used by a professional hire firm for the purpose of re-exportation within a period not exceeding five days.

Natural persons established in the EU benefit from total relief from VAT and import duties

- where they privately use means of transport occasionally, on the instructions of the registration holder, this holder being in the EU at the time of use; and
- for the occasional private use of means of transport, hired under a written contract, to
  - (i) return to their place of residence in the EU, or
  - (ii) leave the EU.

The means of transport must be re-exported or returned to the hire service established in the EU within five days of the entry into force of the contract under (i) above and re-exported within two days of the entry into force of the contract under (b) above.

Total relief from VAT and import duties is also granted where

- means of transport are to be registered under a temporary series in the EU, with a view to re-exportation, either in the name of a person established outside the EU or in the name of a natural person established inside the EU where that person is preparing to transfer normal residence to a place outside the EU (in which case the means of transport must be exported);

- means of transport are used commercially or privately by a natural person established in the EU and employed by the owner of the means of transport established outside the EU or otherwise authorised by the owner. Private use must have been provided for in the contract of employment; and
- (in exceptional cases) means of transport are commercially used for a limited period by persons established in the EU.

Period of discharge. Without prejudice to other special provisions, the periods for discharge are as follows.

- For means of rail transport: twelve months.
- For commercially used means of transport other than rail transport: the time required for carrying out the transport operations.
- For means of road transport privately used by students: the period the student stays in the EU for the sole purpose of pursuing their studies.
- For means of road transport privately used by persons fulfilling assignments of a specified duration: the period this person stays in the EU for the sole purpose of fulfilling their assignment.
- For means of road transport privately used in other cases, including saddle or draught animals and the vehicles drawn by them: six months.
- For privately used means of air transport: six months.
- For privately used means of sea and inland waterway transport: 18 months.

[*EC Commission Regulation No 2454/93, Art 558–562*].

(4) Personal effects and goods for sports purposes

Personal effects and goods for sports purposes imported by a traveller from outside the EU. [*EC Commission Regulation No 2454/93, Art 563*].

Personal effects. TI relief can be claimed for personal effects reasonably required for a journey (e.g. clothing, toiletries, personal jewellery and other articles clearly of a personal nature, including pets). Relief can be claimed for the period of stay in the EU up to a maximum of 24 months. Sporting firearms and ammunition are also eligible for relief but a full TI authorisation is needed and this requires prior approval from HMRC on Form 1331 at least one month before the intended import.

Students coming to stay in the EU for the purpose of full-time study do not need to use the TI procedures for clothing and household linen, items to be used in their studies (e.g. PCs), and household effects for furnishing their student's room.

Private motor vehicles. TI relief can be claimed on a vehicle temporarily imported for private use (including any accompanying spare parts, accessories and equipment) if

- it is registered outside the EU or, if not registered, belongs to the visitor, etc or someone else who has their normal home outside the EU;
- the vehicle is not sold, lent or hired out or otherwise disposed of in the EU; and

- it is re-exported from the EU within six months except that, in the case of a student or someone on an assignment of a specific duration, the vehicle can remain in the EU for the period of studies or until the end of the assignment.

Extending the period of a visit or deciding to live permanently in the EU. The period allowed under TI relief can, in exceptional circumstances, be extended within reasonable limits. Written application, giving reasons for the extension, must be made to National Import Reliefs Unit (NIRU), Custom House, Killyhevlin Industrial Estate, Enniskillen, County Fermanagh, Northern Ireland BT74 4EJ (Tel: 028 6632 2298; Fax: 028 6632 4018) or by e-mail to enquiries.niru.rbs@hmrc.gsi.gov.uk

If a visitor decides to live permanently in the EU, any personal effects and vehicle may qualify for other reliefs in this chapter. The visitor should write to NIRU advising them of the decision and giving details of the personal effects and vehicle.

(Customs Notice 3, paras 4.1, 4.3, 4.6).

Goods for sports purposes include track and field equipment (e.g. hurdles, javelins, discuses, poles, shots, hammers); ball game equipment (e.g. balls of any kind, rackets, mallets, clubs, sticks and the like; nets of any kind, goal posts); winter sports equipment (e.g. skis and sticks, skates, bobsleighs, curling equipment); sports wear, shoes, gloves, headgear, etc. of any kind; water sports equipment (e.g. canoes and kayaks, sail and row boats, sails, oars and paddles, surf boards and sails); motor vehicles and craft (e.g. cars, motor bicycles, motor boats); equipment for miscellaneous events (e.g. sports arms and ammunition, non-motorised bicycles, archer's bows and arrows, fencing equipment, gymnastics equipment, compasses, wrestling mats and tatamis, weight-lifting equipment, riding equipment, sulkies, hang-gliders, delta wings, windsurfers, climbing equipment, music cassettes to accompany the performance; and auxiliary equipment (e.g. measuring and score display equipment, blood and urine test apparatus). (Customs Notice 200, para 4.4).

(5) Welfare materials for seafarers

Where they are

- used on a vessel engaged in international maritime traffic;
- unloaded from such a vessel and temporarily used ashore by the crew; or
- used by the crew of such a vessel in cultural or social establishments managed by non-profit-making organisations or in places of worship where services for seafarers are regularly held.

[*EC Commission Regulation No 2454/93, Art 564*].

Included are reading material (e.g. books of any kind, correspondence courses, newspapers, journals and periodicals, pamphlets on welfare facilities in ports); audio-visual material (e.g. sound and image reproducing instruments, tape-recorders, radio sets, television sets, cinematographic and other projectors, recordings on tapes or discs of language courses, radio programmes, greetings, music and entertainment, films, exposed and developed, film slides, videotapes); sports gear (e.g. sports wear, balls, rackets and nets, deck games, athletic equipment, gymnastic equipment); hobby material (e.g. indoor games, musical instruments, material for amateur dramatics, materials for painting, sculpture, woodwork and metalwork, carpet making, etc.); equipment for religious activities; and parts and accessories for welfare material. (Customs Notice 200, para 4.5).

(6) Disaster relief material

Where it is used in connection with measures taken to counter the effects of disasters or similar situations within the EU and intended for state bodies or bodies approved by the competent authorities. [*EC Commission Regulation No 2454/93, Art 565*].

(7) Medical, surgical and laboratory equipment

Where it is dispatched on loan at the request of a hospital or other medical institution which has urgent need of such equipment to make up for the inadequacy of its own facilities and where it is intended for diagnostic or therapeutic purposes. [*EC Commission Regulation No 2454/93, Art 566*].

(8) Animals owned by a person established outside the EU

[*EC Commission Regulation No 2454/93, Art 567*].

(9) Goods for use in frontier zones

Goods for use in frontier zones, i.e.

- equipment owned by a person established in the frontier zone adjacent to the frontier zone of temporary importation and used by a person established in that adjacent frontier zone, and
- goods used for the building, repair or maintenance of infrastructure in such a frontier zone under the responsibility of public authorities.

[*EC Commission Regulation No 2454/93, Art 567*].

(10) Sound, image or data carrying media

For processing information for the purpose of presentation prior to commercialisation, or free of charge, or for provision with a sound track, dubbing or copying. [*EC Commission Regulation No 2454/93, Art 568*].

(11) Publicity material

[*EC Commission Regulation No 2454/93, Art 568*].

Included is material for display in the offices of the accredited representatives or correspondents appointed by the official national tourist agencies or in other places approved by the customs authorities of the EU country of temporary importation, pictures and drawings, framed photographs and photographic enlargements, art books, paintings, engravings or lithographs, sculptures and tapestries and other similar works of art; materials intended for display in show-cases, stands and similar articles, including electrical and mechanical equipment required for operating such display; a reasonable number of flags; dioramas, scale models, lantern-slides, printing blocks, photographic negatives, specimens, in reasonable numbers, of articles of national handicrafts, local costumes and similar articles of folklore. (Customs Notice 200, para 4.11).

(12) Professional equipment

- owned by a person established outside the EU;
- imported either by a person established outside the EU or by an employee of the owner (the employee may be established in the EU); and
- used by the importer, or under their supervision, except in cases of audiovisual co-productions.

Relief does not apply to equipment to be used for the industrial manufacture or packaging of goods or, except in the case of hand tools, for the exploitation of natural resources, for the construction, repair or maintenance of buildings or for earth moving and like projects.

[*EC Commission Regulation No 2454/93, Art 569*].

Included is

- Equipment for the press.
- Sound broadcasting, television broadcasting and cinematographic equipment and vehicles designed or specially adapted for use with such equipment.
- Other equipment for erection, testing, commissioning, checking, control, maintenance or repair of machinery, plant, means of transport, etc.
- Equipment necessary for: businessmen, business efficiency consultants, productivity experts, accountants and members of similar professions; experts undertaking topographical surveys or geophysical prospecting work; experts combating pollution; doctors, surgeons, veterinary surgeons, midwives and members of similar professions; archaeologists, palaeontologists, geographers, zoologists and other scientists; entertainers, theatre companies and orchestras; lecturers to illustrate their lectures; photography trips; and vehicles designed or specially adapted for these purposes (e.g. mobile inspection units, travelling workshops and travelling laboratories).

(Customs Notice 200, para 4.12).

(13) Educational material and scientific equipment

- owned by a person established outside the EU;
- imported by public or private scientific, teaching or vocational training establishments which are essentially non-profit making and exclusively used in teaching, vocational training or scientific research under their responsibility;
- imported in reasonable numbers, having regard to the purpose of the importation; and

- not used for purely commercial purposes.

[*EC Commission Regulation No 2454/93, Art 570*].

Included is

- sound or image recorders or reproducers;
- sound and image media;
- specialised material (e.g. bibliographic equipment and audio-visual material for libraries, mobile libraries, language laboratories, simultaneous interpretation equipment, programmed teaching machines, mechanical or electronic, material specially designed for the educational or vocational training of handicapped persons);
- other material (e.g. wall charts, models, graphs, maps, plans, photographs and drawings, instruments, apparatus and models designed for demonstration purposes, collections of items with visual or audio educational information, prepared for the teaching of a subject, instruments, apparatus, tools and machine-tools for learning a trade or craft equipment, including specially adapted or designed vehicles for use in relief operations, which is imported for the training of persons involved in relief operations); and
- other goods imported in connection with educational, scientific or cultural activities (e.g. costumes and scenery items sent on loan free of charge to dramatic societies or theatres, music scores sent on loan free of charge to music theatres or orchestras).

(Customs Notice 200, para 4.13).

(14) Packings

Where

- if imported filled, is intended for re-exportation whether empty or filled; and
- if imported empty, is intended for re-exportation filled.

Packings are not to be used in internal traffic, except with a view to the export of goods. In the case of packings imported filled, this condition only applies from the time that they are emptied of their contents.

[*EC Commission Regulation No 2454/93, Art 571*].

(15) Moulds, dies, etc.

Moulds, dies, blocks, drawings, sketches, measuring, checking and testing instruments and other similar articles

- owned by a person established outside the EU, and
- used in manufacturing by a person established in the EU

provided at least 75% of the production resulting from their use is exported.

[*EC Commission Regulation No 2454/93, Art 572(1)*].

(16) Special tools

Special tools and instruments where the goods are

- owned by a person established outside the EU, and

- made available free of charge to a person established in the EU for the manufacture of goods which are to be exported in their entirety.

[*EC Commission Regulation No 2454/93, Art 572(2)*].

(17) Goods for testing, etc.

Relief applies to

(a) goods subjected to tests, experiments or demonstrations;
(b) goods subject to satisfactory acceptance tests that are imported in connection with a sales contract containing the provisions of the satisfactory acceptance tests and subjected to those tests; and
(c) goods used to carry out tests, experiments or demonstrations without financial gain.

The period for re-export of goods under (b) above is six months.

[*EC Commission Regulation No 2454/93, Art 573*].

(18) Samples

Imported in reasonable quantities and solely used for being shown or demonstrated in the EU. [*EC Commission Regulation No 2454/93, Art 574*].

(19) Replacement means of production

Temporarily made available to a customer by a supplier or repairer, pending the delivery or repair of similar goods. The period for re-export is six months. [*EC Commission Regulation No 2454/93, Art 575*].

(20) Goods to be exhibited or used at a public event

Not purely organised for the commercial sale of the goods, or obtained at such events from goods placed under TI arrangements. [*EC Commission Regulation No 2454/93, Art 576(1)*].

(21) Goods for approval

Where they cannot be imported as samples and the consignor wishes to sell the goods and the consignee may decide to purchase them after inspection. The period for re-export is two months. [*EC Commission Regulation No 2454/93, Art 576(2)*].

(22) Works of art, collectors' items and antiques

Imported for the purposes of exhibition, with a view to possible sale. [*EC Commission Regulation No 2454/93, Art 576(3)(a)*].

(23) Second-hand goods

Imported with a view to their sale by auction. [*EC Commission Regulation No 2454/93, Art 576(3)(b)*].

(24) **Spare parts, accessories and equipment**

Used for repair and maintenance, including overhaul, adjustments and preservation of goods entered for the arrangements. [*EC Commission Regulation No 2454/93, Art 577*].

(25) **Miscellaneous goods**

Goods

- not falling within other than those listed in (1)–(24) above, or
- falling within (1)–(24) above but not complying with the relevant conditions

which are imported

- occasionally and for a period not exceeding three months; or
- in particular situations having no economic effect.

[*EC Commission Regulation No 2454/93, Art 578*].

Security and guarantees

[33.27] Security is required on most temporary importations to cover the full amount of charges (including VAT and duty) that could become due if the goods are not ultimately re-exported. Any security required must be provided by a cash deposit or banker's guarantee. Regular importers may be able to lodge a single guarantee which HMRC will adjust accordingly as goods subject to TI relief (or any other procedure requiring a security) are imported. Cash deposits can be taken from a deferment account.

To re-claim any security or guarantee, the importer must show that he has

- re-exported the goods;
- transferred the goods to another authorised trader (evidence will depend upon the method of transfer used and type of authorisation held); or
- diverted the goods to free circulation (attaching a copy of the Customs entry).

For goods imported for a specific purpose, evidence will also be required to show that conditions attached to their import have been met.

(Customs Notice 200, paras 9.1, 9.4, 9.5).

Customs checks and records

[33.28] While goods remain in the EU they are subject to Customs supervision. A record must be kept of

- the declaration entering the goods to TI;
- when, where and how the goods are used;
- how the goods are identified (e.g. manufacturers marks, serial numbers, technical descriptions or illustrations); and
- evidence of disposal.

These records must be kept for four years after disposal of the goods. For the reliefs in **33.26**(5) and (16) above, it is also necessary to keep records of products manufactured using TI goods and evidence that the manufactured products are exported outside the EU.

(Customs Notice 200, para 3.14).

Discharging TI arrangements

[33.29] TI is completed or discharged as follows.

- The goods are exported from the EU (directly or via another EU country).
- The goods are transferred to another Customs suspensive arrangement or to another operator authorised to use one of those procedures.
- The goods are transferred to another EU country to be entered to another Customs suspensive procedure in that country.
- The goods are transferred to another TI authorisation holder in the UK or another EU country.
- The goods are diverted to free circulation in the UK.
- In respect of goods imported to be exhibited or used at a public event not purely organised for commercial sale of the goods, if they are consumed, destroyed or distributed free of charge to the public at the event, provided the quantity of goods corresponds to the nature of the event, the number of visitors and the authorisation holder's participation in the event. (This does not apply to alcoholic beverages, tobacco goods or fuels.)
- In respect of moulds, dies, blocks, drawings, sketches, measures, checking and testing instruments and other similar articles, when they have been used in manufacturing and at least 75% of products resulting from their use are exported. Records that the manufactured products have been exported must be kept.
- In respect of special tools and instruments made available free of charge for the manufacture of goods, when they are re-exported and all products resulting from their use are exported. Records that the manufactured products have been exported must be kept.
- The goods are destroyed under Customs supervision. If goods are found on or after entry, to be defective, contaminated, obsolete or otherwise unusable, they may be destroyed, without payment of the VAT and duty, with prior agreement of HMRC. VAT and duty will be charged if any waste and scrap resulting from destruction has a commercial value.

(Customs Notice 200, paras 7.1, 7.12).

Inward processing relief (IPR)

[33.30] Duty is relieved on imports of non-EU goods which are processed in the EU and re-exported (or transferred to another IPR authorisation holder in the UK or another EU country) provided the trade does not harm the essential interests of EU producers of similar goods. Processing can be anything from re-packing or sorting goods to the most complicated manufacturing.

There are two methods of duty relief.

- **Suspension.** Customs duties are suspended when the goods are first entered to IPR in the EU. Import VAT is not due unless the goods are released to the EU market. See Customs Notice 221, section 21 for the conditions for using suspension.
- **Drawback.** Customs duties and import VAT are paid when the goods are entered to IPR. Duty can only be reclaimed if the goods are exported, transferred to an IPR suspension authorisation holder or disposed of in an approved way. Import VAT can be reclaimed as input tax. See Customs Notice 221, section 20 for the conditions and restrictions for using drawback.

In either case there must be an intention to re-export goods from the EU and an authorisation to enter goods to IPR will be required. Goods must be processed within a certain period and records kept for all operations carried out. Under the suspension method, returns detailing receipts and disposals must be submitted.

(Customs Notice 221, paras 1.3, 1.4, 1.7, 1.8, 1.10).

Records

[33.31] Records must be kept of all goods entered to IPR showing

- details of the quantities of goods entered to IPR. If authorisation restricts the quantity or value of goods on which IPR can be claimed, records must be sufficient to allow this to be monitored;
- what goods are entered, i.e. the commercial or technical description of the goods sufficient to identify them;
- when and where goods were entered to IPR, including transfers received and documents relating to their entry;
- where all goods and compensating products held under the authorisation are held at any time including any movement of goods and compensating products to or between operators specified in the authorisation;
- what processing is carried out on the goods;
- locations where processing takes place;
- how goods entered to IPR are identified in the products produced;
- production data that establishes the rate of yield achieved, i.e. how many products are produced including any secondary compensating products (by-products); and
- when and where goods were exported or disposed of including documents relating to their disposal.

Where computerised records are to be kept, HMRC must be advised when applying for authorisation to ensure that these records meet their requirements.

All records must be kept for four years after disposal of the goods.

(Customs Notice 221, para 3.7).

Discharging IPR

[33.32] Duty and VAT can be reclaimed on drawback goods or IPR liability can be discharged on suspension goods if the goods are disposed of in one of the following ways.

- Export from the EU directly or via another EU country.
- Transfer either to another Customs procedure or to another operator authorised to use one of those procedures.
- Transfer to another EU country to be entered to another Customs procedure in that country.
- Transfer to a Customs approved use such as export shops, armed forces, NAAFI, embassies, ships stores or bunkers or use as commissary stores and use in tray type meals.
- Disposal of aircraft or aircraft parts and using goods in satellite construction.
- Use of aviation fuel for third country or intra-EU flights.
- Export to the Continental Shelf (outside territorial waters).
- Diversion to the EU market with payment of duty, import VAT and compensatory interest (suspension goods).
- Diversion of goods that are eligible for end use relief.
- Destruction of the goods under customs supervision (suspension goods only).

(Customs Notice 221, para 10.1).

Processing under Customs Control (PCC)

[33.33] Generally, imported goods carry higher rates of duty than the raw materials or components from which they are manufactured. But in the instances where this does not apply due to tariff anomalies, without special provisions it would be more economical to import finished products than to import the raw materials and manufacture the products in the EU. The PCC procedure is a trade facilitation measure intended to encourage processing in the EU by allowing certain raw materials or components to be imported under duty suspension arrangements.

After processing the imported goods, the finished products must be declared to free circulation and customs duty and import VAT become due. Customs duty is chargeable at the lower rate that applies to the goods rather than the rate which applied to the raw materials. Import VAT is due on the customs value of the goods declared plus the amount of customs duty payable.

VAT-only PCC

The value of the goods released to free circulation is broadly the import value plus processing costs. Given the increase in value there would be no benefit in VAT-only PCC as the processed goods would be subject to the same rate of VAT as if the processed products had been imported. For this reason, applications to use PCC for VAT-only purposes will not be accepted.

(VAT Notice 702/9/05, paras 8.1–8.3).

External and internal transit

[33.34] Transit is a customs procedure which enables goods to be moved within the customs territory of the EU without the payment of import duties and other charges until they reach their final destination.

The external transit (T1) procedure allows the movement of mainly 'non-Union goods' within the customs territory of the EU without their being subject to import duties and other charges. The external procedure ends (and the obligations of the holder are met) when the goods placed under the procedure and the required documents are produced at the office of destination in accordance with the provisions of the relevant customs procedure.

The internal transit procedure (T2) allows the movement of 'Union goods' from one point to another within the customs territory of the EU to pass through the territory of a country outside the customs territory without any change in their customs status.

'*Non-Union goods*' are goods which are not of EU origin or imported goods which have not been released into free circulation.

'*Union goods*' are goods which are

(a) entirely obtained or produced in the Customs territory of the EU, without the addition of goods from third countries or territories that are not part of the Customs territory of the EU;
(b) imported from countries or territories not forming part of the Customs territory of the EU which have been released for free circulation in an EU country; or
(c) obtained or produced in the Customs territory of the EU either wholly from those under (*b*) or partly from (*a*) and (*b*).

Treatment for import VAT

Any goods placed under external transit have the import VAT (and customs duty) suspended. Import VAT (and customs duty) only become due if the goods are subsequently removed to free circulation in the UK.

Goods placed under internal transit may have the import VAT suspended in particular circumstances (e.g. the 'T2F' procedure for movements to/from 'special territories', i.e. territories which are within the EU for customs purposes but outside it for VAT purposes, see **17.3 EUROPEAN UNION: GENERAL**).

Third country goods subject to VAT only

Any goods imported from outside the EU that are not subject to a positive duty rate may be placed under external transit for import VAT purposes only.

(VAT Notice 702/9/05, paras 10.1–10.7).

End-use relief

[33.35] End-use relief is a trade facilitation regime to assist certain industries and trades within the EU by allowing reduced or nil rates of customs duty on certain goods imported from non-EU countries, provided the goods are put to a prescribed use.

Subject to below, end-use relief does not affect liability to import VAT, which must be paid or accounted for in the normal way, unless one of the reliefs under **33.14** above applies.

Goods for the continental shelf

Imported goods which are intended for

- incorporation in offshore drilling or production platforms/workpoints for the purpose of their construction, repair, maintenance, fitting out or conversion,
- equipping those platforms/workpoints,
- downhole well construction,
- subsequent shipment to a platform/workpoint which are required to be tested before use, or
- training, provided that at the end of the programme, the goods are shipped to a platform/workpoint

are eligible for shipwork end-use relief for the continental shelf.

(VAT Notice 702/9/05, paras 6.1, 6.4).

Importing computer software

[33.36] Imported computer software may be classified as goods and/or services.

Goods

Goods are the tangible carrier medium on which the software resides.

- If the tangible carrier medium is magnetic tape, disk, diskette compact disk (CD) and read only CD videos, the VAT treatment depends on whether, at the time of importation, the items are 'normalised' (off the shelf) or 'specific' (custom made) products as explained below.
- If the information resides on semiconductors, integrated circuits or similar devices or articles incorporating such circuits or devices, VAT must be paid on the whole value of the medium/device, including information residing on it.

Services

Services may comprise the data, program and/or instructions (but not sound, cinematographic or video recordings). The VAT treatment of services received from outside the EU depends on whether they are 'normalised' (off the shelf) or 'specific' (custom made) software as explained below.

The transmission and provision of information by satellite, telephone, telex, facsimile, etc. is treated as a service. See **38.9 INTERNATIONAL SERVICES**.

Normalised

'*Normalised*' comprises mass-produced items which are freely available to all customers and usable by them independently, after installation and limited training, in a standard form to carry out the same applications or functions. They are made up of a coherent set of programs and support material and often include the service of installation, training and maintenance. *Included are* personal and home computer software, game packages, etc. and standard packages adapted at the supplier's instigation to include security or similar devices.

Importations of normalised items are regarded as importations of both goods (made up of the carrier medium, see above) and services (the data and/or the instructions).

- Where the goods and services are not identified separately, the whole importation is treated as an importation of goods.
- Where the goods and services are identified separately, a UK taxable person may pay VAT on importation only on the cost or value of the carrier medium. Normal valuation rules apply (see **71.15 VALUATION**). The supply of services falls within *VATA 1994, Sch 5 para 3* and VAT on these must be accounted for under the 'reverse charge' procedure (see **38.4 INTERNATIONAL SERVICES**).

Specific software

'*Specific*' software products are

- items made to customers' special requirements (either as unique programs or adaptations from standard programs);
- inter-company information data and accounts;
- enhancements and updates of existing specific programs; and
- enhancements and updates of existing normalised programs supplied under contractual obligation to customers who have bought the original program.

The importation of a specific item of software is made up of an importation of goods (the carrier medium, see above) and a supply of services (the data and/or the instructions) but to simplify import procedures, the carrier medium is treated as a supply of services. No import VAT is charged on the carrier medium at importation.

The supply of services falls within *VATA 1994, Sch 5 para 3* and a UK business must account for VAT on the supply under the 'reverse charge' procedure. See **38.4 INTERNATIONAL SERVICES**. No VAT is payable for specific items imported free of charge.

(VAT Notice 702, paras 7.1–7.13).

Key points

[33.37] Points to consider are as follows.

- It is important to recognise that different VAT rules apply depending on whether goods being acquired from overseas are imports (i.e. from a non-EU country) or acquisitions (i.e. from another EU country). Advisers should ensure that relevant clients have procedures in place to deal with the two different situations.
- It should be noted that no VAT is due on imported goods if the item in question would be zero-rated if supplied in the UK. Examples would include books, children's clothing and many food items.
- Ensure that all importers obtain an Economic Operator Registration and Identification (EORI) number so that evidence will be sent by HMRC to support input tax claims (C79 certificate).
- Be aware of the main benefits of holding a deferment account with HMRC to delay paying VAT on imports until the 15th day of the following month. However, it is important to note that periodic deferment statements are not acceptable as evidence for input tax purposes – the C79 certificate is the evidence required to support any input tax claim. The payment method on the 15th day is always through a direct debit arrangement.
- It is worthwhile for importers with (or applying for) a deferment account to utilise the SIVA arrangements. This scheme reduces the level of a bank guarantee required for VAT on imports via a deferment account.
- If a business is not registered for VAT, it is important to regularly review the value of its EU acquisitions to ensure they do not exceed the VAT registration limits during a calendar year on a cumulative basis. If the limits are exceeded, then the business will have to register for VAT.
- Some import transactions will be processed through the deferment account of the import agent. However, this is a commercial arrangement only and there is no entitlement for the import agent to reclaim input tax as he is not buying the goods himself. Only the importer can claim input tax, supported by a C79 document as evidence.

34

Input Tax

Cross-references. See **9 BUSINESS ENTERTAINMENT** for disallowed input tax; **10 CAPITAL GOODS SCHEME; 17.7 EUROPEAN UNION: GENERAL** for recovery of input tax suffered in another EU country; **27.9 GROUPS OF COMPANIES** for recovery of input tax by holding companies; **33 IMPORTS; 42.23 LAND AND BUILDINGS: ZERO AND REDUCED RATE SUPPLIES AND DIY HOUSEBUILDERS** for refund of VAT to do-it-yourself housebuilders; **43.7 LOCAL AUTHORITIES AND PUBLIC BODIES** for refund of input tax for non-business purposes; **45 MOTOR CARS** for disallowed input tax on cars, accessories and petrol, etc.; **49 PARTIAL EXEMPTION** for restriction on recovery of input tax where exempt supplies are made; **53.2 PENSION SCHEMES.**

Introduction

EU legislation

[34.1] See **18.34 EUROPEAN UNION LEGISLATION** for the provisions of *Directive 2006/112/EC.*

UK legislation

Input tax, in relation to a taxable person, comprises VAT

- on goods and services supplied to him;
- on the acquisition of any goods by him from another EU country; and
- paid or payable by him on the importation of goods from outside the EU

provided the goods or services are used, or to be used, for the purpose of business carried on, or to be carried on, by him.

[*VATA 1994, s 24(1)*].

VAT paid does not, however, become input tax simply because it has been incurred. It becomes input tax when it satisfies various criteria in **34.2** below arising out of the above definition and other legal requirements.

Criteria for VAT incurred to be treated as deductible input tax

[34.2] Before any VAT paid can be deducted as input tax, the following criteria must be met.

(a) The recipient of the supply, or the person acquiring or importing the goods, must be a taxable person (i.e. registered or required to be registered under *VATA 1994*) at the time the VAT was incurred. See, however, **34.10** and **34.11** below for pre-registration and post-deregistration VAT.

(b) The VAT must relate to an actual supply, acquisition or importation. Where payments are made in advance but the goods are never physically supplied, input tax cannot be reclaimed as no supply has taken place. See *Weldons (West One) Ltd* (VTD 984) (TVC 36.620), *Theotrue Holdings Ltd* (VTD 1358) (TVC 36.622) and *C & E Commrs v Pennystar Ltd*, QB 1995, [1996] STC 163 (TVC 36.627).

(c) The amount to be claimed is the VAT properly chargeable and not the VAT actually charged where this is different. See *Podium Investments Ltd* (VTD 314) (TVC 36.662) and *Genius Holding BV v Staatssecretaris van Financien, ECJ Case 342/87*, [1991] STC 239 (TVC 22.413). This gives rise to a number of problems.

  (i) If the supplier is not a taxable person but shows VAT on the invoice, the VAT is not input tax and there is no automatic right of deduction. However, by concession, HMRC may allow a claim in these circumstances where they are satisfied that
  - the recipient of the supply is neither involved in nor has close knowledge of the supplier's business;
  - it was reasonable for the recipient to consider that he had been lawfully charged VAT; and
  - the claim is made in respect of goods and services genuinely supplied at the stated value.

  (ii) If the supplier is a taxable person but is not registered for VAT. In *Ellen Garage (Oldham) Ltd* (VTD 12407) (TVC 40.11), a supplier had failed to register for VAT. The tribunal held that any VAT charged was recoverable as input tax (subject to meeting the other conditions for recovery) even though there could be no valid VAT invoice because, *inter alia*, the supplier has no registration number.

In *Ahmed (t/a New Touch)*, LON/04/1840 (VTD 20119) (TVC 40.37) a supplier had previously been registered for VAT but had subsequently been deregistered by HMRC. The tribunal held that VAT was not recoverable on invoices issued after deregistration and the fact that the supplier had remained a 'taxable person' was not conclusive. Disapproving of the decision in *Ellen Garage* above, the tribunal held that HMRC were entitled to require some corroborative documents or other similar evidence of the specific transactions entered into.

The decision in *Ellen Garage* above was also disapproved of in *Hargreaves (UK) plc* (VTD 20382) (TVC 36.661) where a haulage company reclaimed VAT on substantial quantities of 'laundered' rebated fuel which it was illegal to use in road vehicles and where the VAT numbers shown on the invoices belonged to deregistered companies. The tribunal held that a taxable person who knew (or should have known) that by making a purchase he was taking part in a transaction connected with the fraudulent evasion of VAT must be regarded as a participant in that fraud. As a result, it lost the right to deduct the VAT it paid.

(iii) VAT wrongly charged on a supply, etc. which is outside the scope of VAT, exempt or zero-rated is not input tax. See *Da Conti International Ltd* (VTD 6215) (TVC 36.670).

(d) The goods or services on which the VAT was charged must have been supplied to, or acquired or imported by, the person seeking to claim the input tax. See **34.5** below.

(e) The supplies must have been incurred for the purpose of the business. See **34.6** below.

(f) The supplies received must not be subject to input tax restriction either in the form of a Treasury 'blocking order' or otherwise. See **34.8** below.

(g) The supplies must normally be received in the accounting period in which the claim is to be made. See **34.9** below.

(h) The person seeking to claim input tax must hold a valid invoice or other satisfactory documentation. See **56.7 RECORDS**.

See, however, *Croydon Hotel & Leisure Co Ltd* (VTD 14920) (TVC 36.641) where it was held that a person is entitled to reclaim input tax even where a VAT invoice has not been issued, the right to deduct not being limited to cases were output tax has been paid but extending to cases where it is payable. In that case, the tribunal held that a payment of £2 million by the company was VAT-inclusive even though an earlier tribunal (*Holiday Inns (UK) Ltd* (VTD 10609) (TVC 62.142)) had (incorrectly in the second tribunal's opinion) held that in the hands of the recipient the payment did not represent consideration for a taxable supply.

(VAT Notice 48, ESC 3.9).

De Voil Indirect Tax Service. See V3.402.

> *Example*
>
> John is VAT-registered and buys a book that is relevant to his business. He pays £50 plus VAT to the book seller. In this situation, John cannot reclaim input tax on the cost of the book, even if he obtains a VAT invoice from the seller, because it is a zero-rated supply (printed matter). The VAT has been incorrectly charged by the book seller. John should obtain a VAT credit note from the book dealer to correct the position.

Amount of allowable input tax

[34.3] The amount of allowable input tax is so much of the input tax on supplies, acquisitions and importations in the period as is allowable as being attributable to the following supplies made, or to be made, by the taxable person in the course or furtherance of his business.

(a) '*Taxable supplies*', i.e. supplies of goods or services made in the UK other than exempt supplies.

(b) Supplies outside the UK which would be taxable supplies if made in the UK.

(c) Supplies of services which
   - (i) are supplied to a person who belongs outside the EU, or
   - (ii) are directly linked to the export of goods to a place outside the EU, or
   - (iii) consist of the provision of intermediary services in relation to any transaction within (i) or (ii) above

   provided that the supply is exempt (or would have been exempt if made in the UK) by virtue of *VATA 1994, Sch 9 Group 2* (insurance) or *VATA 1994, Sch 9 Group 5 Items 1–8* (finance).

(d) Supplies made either in or outside the UK which fall, or would fall, within *VATA 1994, Sch 9 Group 15 item 1* or *2* (investment gold, see **26.2 GOLD AND PRECIOUS METALS**).

HMRC must make regulations for securing a fair and reasonable attribution of input tax to the supplies within (*a*) to (*c*) above.

[*VATA 1994, ss 4(2), 26; SI 1992/3123; SI 1999/3121*].

See **18.34 EUROPEAN UNION LEGISLATION** for the provisions of *Directive 2006/112/EC*.

The effect of the above is that VAT cannot be reclaimed on goods and services which are not used for business purposes (see **34.6** below) and, where exempt supplies are made, it may not be possible to recover all input tax incurred. See **PARTIAL EXEMPTION (49).**

If input tax can be reclaimed in full, the amount to reclaim is normally that shown on the VAT invoice received from the supplier (but see **34.2**(*c*) above where VAT is incorrectly charged). In the case of a less detailed tax invoice (see **39.7 INVOICES**) which does not show VAT separately, input tax is found by applying the VAT fraction (see **47.2 OUTPUT TAX**) to the total amount charged.

No taxable supplies

Where a person has made no taxable supplies in the period concerned or any previous period, any refunds of input tax are subject to such conditions as HMRC think fit to impose, including conditions as to repayment in specified circumstances. [*VATA 1994, s 25(6)*]. This could arise, for example, where a person has recently registered and is incurring expenditure but has yet to make any supplies. See, however, *D A Rompelman v Minister van Financien, ECJ Case 268/83*, [1985] 3 CMLR 202 (TVC 22.103) for when input tax credit becomes deductible.

De Voil Indirect Tax Service. See V3.418.

> *Example*
>
> ABC Accountants is VAT-registered in the UK. The firm has just completed some accounts for a business in Belgium. The fee from this work is outside the scope of VAT under the place of supply rules (place of supply is Belgium where the customer is based because this is a business to business sale). However, ABC Accountants can still get full input tax recovery on related costs (subject to normal rules) because the service provided would be subject to VAT if supplied to a UK customer.

Repayment of input tax where consideration not paid

[34.4] Where a person has

- claimed deduction of the whole or part of the VAT on the supply as input tax, and
- not paid the whole or any part of the consideration for that supply by the '*relevant date*' i.e. within six months of
  - (i) the date of the supply, or
  - (ii) if later, the date on which the consideration for the supply, or (as the case may be) the unpaid part of it, became payable

then, subject to below, he must make a negative entry in the VAT allowable portion of his VAT account for the VAT period in which the end of the relevant six-month period falls. The amount of this negative entry is calculated by formula

$$I \times \frac{U}{C}$$

where

I = the input tax claimed on the supply

U = relevant six-month period; and

C = the total consideration for the supply.

The above provisions

- do not apply where the cash accounting scheme is used and the operative date for the recovery of input tax is the date of payment (see **63.6 SPECIAL SCHEMES**); and
- are not to be regarded as giving rise to any application of the error correction notification (formerly voluntary disclosure) requirements (see **56.11 RECORDS**).

Example 1

B purchases goods for £1,200 (£1,000.00 plus £200.00 VAT) and reclaims the full amount of VAT. By the relevant date, it has only paid £500.00 (leaving £700 unpaid).

It must make a repayment of input tax to HMRC of

200 × (700 ÷ 1,200) = £116.67

For the purposes of (ii) above, HMRC will accept the date of invoice as the due date for payment. This means that, normally, the date on which input tax becomes repayable is six months after the date of invoice (unless the supplier allows time to pay, for example, 30 or 60 days, in which case repayment of input tax is not required until six months from this later date). The only exception is, on the rare occasions, where the invoice is not issued within 14 days of the date of supply and where the due date for payment falls before the date on which the invoice is issued. In such a case, the input tax will become repayable six months after the date of supply or, if later, the date when the payment was due. (VAT Notice 700/18/02, para 4.3).

Where a customer is in dispute with the supplier, and the supplier agrees to extend the due date for payment of the amount in dispute, repayment is not required until six months after the agreed extended date for payment. (VAT Notice 700/18/02, para 4.4).

Insolvency

By concession, an insolvency practitioner need not repay input tax under the above provisions where the supply was made prior to the insolvency procedure commencing but the requirement to repay input tax occurs after that date provided

- HMRC have been properly notified of the insolvency (see **35.2 INSOLVENCY**); and
- the application of the concession does not give rise to tax avoidance.

The concession applies whether or not the business of the insolvent person is carried on.

The '*insolvency procedures*' to which the concession applies are bankruptcies, compulsory liquidations, creditors' and members' voluntary liquidations, administrative receiverships, administration orders, individual and company voluntary arrangements, Scottish trust deeds, deeds of arrangement, partnership voluntary arrangements and liquidations, partnership administration orders, sequestrations, county court administration orders, schemes of arrangement, and deceased persons' administration orders.

The effective date for the application of the concession is the date of HMRC's claim in the insolvency (i.e. the relevant date of the insolvency and the date of the insolvency meeting if applicable or, in the case of an administration order, the date of that order). The concession only applies to a provisional liquidation if it is followed by a permanent liquidation although, in such a case, the concession takes effect from the date of the provisional liquidation.

If an insolvency arrangement fails, the requirement to account for clawback is reinstated.

(VAT Notice 48, ESC 3.20; VAT Notice 700/18/02, para 4.9).

Restoration of an entitlement to credit for input tax

Where a person

- has made an entry in his VAT account in accordance with the above provisions (*'the input tax repayment'*),
- has made the return for the VAT period concerned, and has paid any VAT payable by him in respect of that period, and
- after the end of the relevant period, has paid the whole or part of the consideration for the supply in relation to which the input tax repayment was made,

then, subject to below, he may make a positive entry in the VAT allowable portion of his VAT account for the VAT period in which payment of the whole or part of the consideration is made. The amount of this positive entry is calculated by the formula

$R \times P \div C$

where

R = the amount of the input tax repayment;

P = the whole or part of the consideration for the supply in relation to which the input tax repayment was ade and which is subsequently paid; and

C = the consideration for the supply which was not paid before the end of the relevant period.

> *Example 2*
>
> The facts are the same as in *Example 1* above. After making the repayment of £116.67 to HMRC, B subsequently makes a further payment of £300.
>
> B can now reclaim VAT from HMRC of
>
> 116.67 × (300 ÷ 700) = £50.00

The above provisions are not to be regarded as giving rise to any application of the error correction notification (formerly voluntary disclosure) requirements (see **56.11 RECORDS**).

Attribution of payments

The rules on the attribution of payments in **7.6** under Method A and in **7.8**(1) **BAD DEBT RELIEF** apply for determining whether anything paid is to be taken as paid by way of consideration for a particular supply.

[*VATA 1994, s 26A; FA 2002, s 22; SI 1995/2518, Regs 172F–172J; SI 2002/3027, Reg 8; SI 2002/3028; SI 2003/532*].

Who can claim input tax

[34.5] Subject to below, for an input tax claim to be valid, the claim must be made by the person to whom the supply was made.

Where a third party pays for goods or services which are supplied to another person, the third party does not have the right to deduct input tax. This applies whether the payment was made due to a legal requirement or is simply a normal commercial practice. Examples of where this is likely to occur include

- payment of legal costs awarded against the unsuccessful party in litigation (see **34.13** below);
- payment of a landlord's costs by a tenant for the drawing up of a lease (see **41.4 LAND AND BUILDINGS: EXEMPT SUPPLIES AND OPTION TO TAX**); and
- payment by a business of the costs of a viability study undertaken by a bank in respect of the business's activities (see **35.10 INSOLVENCY**).

For a consideration of whether a supply has been made to a taxable person, even though it is physically delivered to a third party (e.g. in a tripartite arrangement) see *Leesportfeuille 'Intiem' CV v Staatssecretaris van Financien, ECJ Case 165/86*, [1989] 2 CMLR 856 (TVC 22.402) (petrol supplied to employees) and *C & E Commrs v Redrow Group plc*, HL 1998, [1999] STC 161 (TVC 36.130) (estate agents' fees for sales of existing homes paid for by builder on purchase of one of its new houses). See also the Input Tax chapter in *Tolley's VAT Cases* under the heading *Whether supplies made to the appellant*.

In *HMRC v Loyalty Management UK Ltd*, L operated a points scheme in which a customer, purchasing goods or services from a participating retailer, received points which could be redeemed for 'rewards' from certain suppliers ('redeemers'). The main issue was whether L was entitled to input tax recovery in respect of the cost of the rewards. The Court of Appeal held that the redeemer made a supply of rewards to the customer. But the redeemer also made a supply of redemption services to L, in respect of which L was entitled to input tax credit ([2008] STC 59). The House of Lords referred the case to the ECJ, which ruled that L's payment to the redeemer was third party consideration for a supply by the redeemer to the customer, although payment might also include consideration for a separate supply of services (a question for the national court to decide) [2010] STC 2651 (TVC 22.153).

In *HMRC v Airtours Holiday Transport Ltd*, [2010] UKUT 404 (TCC) (TVC 36.163), a large holiday company suffered financial difficulties. It agreed that a major accountancy firm (P) should liaise on its behalf with its banks, bondholders and other creditors, and prepare a detailed report on its financial status. The holiday company reclaimed input tax in respect of P's supplies. HMRC issued assessments to recover the tax, on the basis that the supplies had actually been made to the holiday company's creditors, rather than to the company itself. The Upper Tribunal upheld the assessments, finding that the company's creditors had first approached P, and contracted for the work and therefore authorised it.

Supplies to employees

HMRC accept that, in certain circumstances, a supply which is *prima facie* to an employee, can be treated as made to the employer provided the employer meets the full cost and the supply is legitimately financed by the employer for the purposes of the business. Examples include

- road fuel (see **45.15 MOTOR CARS**);
- subsistence costs (see **34.13**(21) below); and
- removal expenses arising from company relocations or transfer of staff (see **34.13**(18) below).

See also *Stormseal (UPVC) Window Co Ltd* (VTD 4538) (TVC 62.241) where the tribunal held that the company was also entitled to recover input tax on hotel accommodation in respect of *self-employed* representatives whom the company required to work outside their normal area as the accommodation was made available to them in their capacity as persons engaged on company business.

Example

A business is borrowing some money from a bank to develop its trading activities. A condition of the loan, which is secured against its property, is that the business must pay for a survey fee on the property to ensure adequate security is in place for the bank.

In this situation, the business cannot claim input tax on the survey fee, despite the fact that it has paid the cost, including VAT. The surveyor is working for the bank, not the borrower, so a key condition for input tax recovery is not being met.

Use for business purposes

[34.6] There is no definition of whether goods or services have been supplied for the 'purposes of the business'. Where the connection between the expenditure and the business is not clear, the following tests can be applied.

(a) Determine the intention of the person at the time of incurring the expenditure. This is a subjective test and where there is no obvious association between the business and the expenditure concerned, the court should approach any assertion that it is for the business with circumspection and care (*Ian Flockton Developments Ltd v C & E Commrs*, QB [1987] STC 394 (TVC 36.341)).

(b) Establish whether or not there is a clear connection between the actual or intended use of the goods or services and the activities business. This is an objective test of the use to which the goods or services are put.

Expenditure, even if for the benefit of the business, is not necessarily for the purpose of the business. See, for example, *C & E Commrs v Rosner (t/a London School of International Business)*, QB 1993, [1994] STC 228 (TVC 36.232) and *Wallman Foods Ltd* (VTD 1411) (TVC 36.238) where VAT on legal costs incurred in defending a sole trader/director against criminal charges was held to be non-deductible under this principle. Compare, however, *P & O European Ferries (Dover) Ltd* (VTD 7846) (TVC 36.230) where VAT on legal costs in defending the company and certain of its employees charged with manslaughter following the sinking of a ferry was held to be deductible as it had clearly been incurred for the purpose of the business even though it also had the effect of benefiting individual employees.

Where goods or services supplied are not used for business purposes, any VAT suffered is not input tax and cannot be reclaimed. This includes

- expenditure related to domestic accommodation (see **34.13**(7) below);
- pursuit of personal interests such as sporting and leisure activities (see also **34.13**(20) below);
- expenditure for the benefit of company directors, proprietors, etc.;
- supplies used in connection with a non-business activity (see **34.7** below for apportionment where used for both a business and non-business activity);
- supplies for another person's business; and
- supplies to another person, even if the taxable person pays for them (see **34.5** above).

Tribunal and court decisions

There have been a large number of court and tribunal cases concerned with whether supplies are used for the purpose of the business, in particular in relation to legal costs, premises costs of sole traders and partnerships, sporting activities (horse racing, show jumping, powerboat racing, motor racing and rallying, yachting, etc.) and personalised number plates. See the chapter Input Tax in *Tolley's VAT Cases* under the heading *Whether supplies used for the purposes of the business*.

De Voil Indirect Tax Service. See V3.405A–V3.410.

Goods and services only partly used for business purposes

[34.7] Where a taxable person incurs VAT on goods and services (whether by way of supply to him or, in the case of goods, acquisition or importation by him) that are intended for both business and private/non-business purposes, he has a choice as to how to treat the goods and services for VAT purposes.

- He may treat them as wholly non-business or private. In this case, the VAT incurred is not deductible. But if an asset treated in this way is later sold, no VAT is payable.
- He may treat them as part business, part non-business, in which case the VAT incurred is only deductible to the extent that it relates to the taxable business activities. [*VATA 1994, s 24(5)*]. See (1) below for apportionment for private use and (2) below for apportionment for non-business use.

If an asset treated in this way is later sold, VAT is due on the 'portion' of the asset which was originally treated as a business asset.
From 1 January 2011 a taxable person may use a partial exemption special method to apportion input tax incurred on goods or services which are used/to be used partly for business purposes and partly for other purposes (see **49.10 PARTIAL EXEMPTION**).

- In some cases, he may treat the goods or services as wholly business, under the 'Lennartz' approach (see (3) below), in which case the VAT incurred is treated as input tax and is deductible in full (subject to any partial exemption restriction). But
  - (i) VAT must be accounted for if the goods are used for private or non-business purposes; and
  - (ii) if an asset treated in this way is later sold, VAT is due on the full selling price as it was originally treated as wholly business.

(1) Apportionment for private use

Common examples of goods and services which are part business/part private are telephone, light and heat, repairs and maintenance, etc. where a business is conducted from home or the taxpayer lives above a shop.

Example

VAT of £100 is paid on an item and one quarter of its use is for business purposes.

Input tax is £100 × ¼ = £25

(2) Apportionment for non-business use

Where both business and non-business activities are undertaken (e.g. by a charity) it is unlikely that all the VAT incurred can be treated as input tax. The following procedure should be adopted.

- Identify as far as possible VAT which relates to goods or services obtained solely for the purposes of the business activity. This is input tax and can be recovered subject to the normal rules.
- Identify as far as possible VAT which relates solely to the non-business activity. This is not input tax and cannot be recovered.
- VAT which relates to both business and non-business activities (e.g. VAT incurred on overhead costs) should be apportioned in order to identify the proportion which is input tax.

Methods of apportionment

The VAT legislation does not specify any particular method of apportionment. Any method used must be fair and reasonable taking into account the various activities and the purposes for which the expenditure is incurred. It may be that a single apportionment of all overhead VAT does not achieve a 'fair and reasonable' result and that a range of apportionments for different items of overhead expenditure is required. The following are example methods of how VAT could be apportioned.

(a) *Fixed percentage*. The simplest method is to adopt a fixed percentage figure and apply this to the total non-attributable VAT incurred. This can be an acceptable approach where the balance between business and non-business activities does not fluctuate.

(b) *Income methods*. These are probably the most common methods of apportionment. The apportionment is calculated each quarter by dividing the total of business income by total income.

> *Example*
>
> A taxable person pays £1,000 VAT on purchases which are used for both business and non-business purposes. Income from business activities (taxable and exempt supplies) amounts to £20,000 in the VAT period. Total income from all sources, including business activities, grants and donations, amounts to £50,000. Input tax is calculated as follows.
>
> Proportion of income which is business income =
>
> £20,000 ÷ £50,000 = 40%
>
> VAT to be provisionally treated as input tax = £1,000 × 40% = £400

Income methods, although simple, will not give a fair and reasonable result where

- the balance of business/non-business activities does not reflect the balance of funding (e.g. where the majority of time and resources is devoted to non-business activities but the majority of income arises from business supplies); or
- commercial activities are partially subsidised by the receipt of grants (e.g. where a heavily subsidised transport operator also runs free community projects).

It may be possible to adapt income methods so that distortive income is removed from the calculation or alternatively the calculation is weighted in some way.

(c) *Expenditure-based methods*. These are similar in calculation to the income-based methods except that the ratio of business/non-business expenditure is applied to the unattributable VAT. Such methods are only appropriate if

- the majority of expenditure can be attributed to distinct business/non-business categories; and
- this ratio is a fair reflection of business/non-business activities (e.g. an expenditure-based method would not be appropriate where a charity with overwhelmingly non-business expenditure purchased a computer system principally to make taxable business supplies).

(d) *Time-based methods*. Where detailed records are kept of the amount of time that staff spend on business and non-business activities, these can provide the basis for a method of apportionment if the business/non-business ratio of staff time reflects the extent of business use of non-attributable expenditure. Such methods would not be appropriate where non-business activities are staff intensive but business activities are goods and services intensive.

A time-based method can also be applied by keeping records of the use made of an object (e.g. a yacht or aircraft).

(e) *Transaction-based methods*. A method can be based upon a record of transactions (e.g. paid admissions to a museum or books loaned out for a charge by a library). A common difficulty with such a method is that non-business activities often do not involve recordable transactions. HMRC officers are advised not to automatically dismiss transaction-based methods but to take extra care to ensure that they are founded on a valid indicator of business and non-business activity.

(f) *Area-based methods*. These, for example, involve calculating within a building the extent to which the floor areas are used for business and non-business purposes.

Whatever method of apportionment is used, provisional input tax is reclaimed at the end of each VAT period, subject to the normal rules. At the end of each VAT year, an adjustment is made by applying the same calculation to total figures for the year. Where quarterly returns are made, the VAT year ends on 31 March, 30 April or 31 May depending on the VAT periods allocated. Where monthly returns are made, the VAT year ends on 31 March.

Waiver of apportionment

Where the non-business element is regarded as insignificant, HMRC officers may use their discretion to allow a waiver of apportionment, in which case the business will be advised that the concession applies only for as long as the existing rate of non-business activity prevails.

Change in method of apportionment

If any method used is considered no longer suitable, details of a proposed new method should be submitted to HMRC. A retrospective change will only be agreed if the business can show that

- the former method did not produce a fair and reasonable result; and
- the proposed method does achieve this objective.

See *Victoria & Albert Museum Trustees v C & E Commrs*, QB [1996] STC 1016 (TVC 11.53). Although the income-based method of apportionment outlined in (*b*) above previously used by the Museum was criticised in *Whitechapel Art Gallery v C & E Commrs*, QB [1986] STC 156 (TVC 11.46) on the grounds that grants and donations received should not be included in the calculation, that method was still held to be a fair and reasonable method of apportionment and its adoption, even if disadvantageous, did not constitute an 'error' which could be subsequently corrected.

(3) The Lennartz mechanism

In *Lennartz v Finanzamt Munchen III, ECJ Case C–97/90*, [1995] STC 514 (TVC 22.456), the court ruled that a person who had a genuine intention to use a car partly for business and partly for private purposes had a right to a full and immediate input tax deduction in respect of VAT incurred on the purchase of the car. (Note that, unlike the UK, Germany did not have a specific restriction preventing deduction of VAT in respect of cars purchased for business use. The UK restriction prevents use of Lennartz VAT accounting in respect of cars intended to be used for business and private or non-business purposes, see below.) The Court also ruled that where goods are acquired *solely* for a private or non-business purpose, VAT incurred is not recoverable, even if the goods in question are later put to a deductible business use. This is because the right to deduct VAT arises, and is exercisable, at the time when the VAT is incurred.

It should be noted that:

- The choice to use the 'Lennartz' mechanism must be made at that time the input tax is incurred (i.e. in sufficient time for the VAT to be deducted in the return period in which the VAT was charged). The input tax claim cannot be re-visited at a future date even if business use of the asset subsequently increases. If the choice is not made, the apportionment route must be followed if and when the taxable person seeks to deduct any of the VAT. The taxable person should therefore retain contemporaneous evidence of a decision to treat the goods as wholly a business asset, to support the resulting input tax claim.
- The 'Lennartz' mechanism can be used even if the use to which the goods will be put will be overwhelmingly private, providing there is some genuine business use intended.
- A taxable person cannot use the 'Lennartz' mechanism where the only business use of the asset is exempt.
- Where the 'Lennartz' mechanism is applied, the taxable person is then obliged to account for output tax in respect of any private or non-business use over the economic life of the goods. See **47.7 OUTPUT TAX**. Records must be kept showing how the relevant asset has been used.

Vereniging case

The case of *Vereniging Noordenlijke Land en Tuinbouw Organisatie v Staatssecretaris van Financien, ECJ Case C–515/07*, [2009] STC 935 (TVC 22.187), concerned an association, VNLTO, that promotes the interests of the agricultural sector. Its members, who are traders in that sector, pay a membership subscription to it, the greater part of which goes towards activities designed to promote their general interests. In addition to promoting those interests, VNLTO provides a number of individual services to its members for which it charges a fee. Even though the activities of promoting members' interests are not subject to VAT, the ECJ held that this did not mean they were non-business activities. The ECJ stated that 'business' in the context of 'Lennartz' accounting extends beyond economic activities giving rise to supplies within the scope of VAT. It also includes use for any activity that forms part of the wider purpose of the taxable person's undertaking or enterprise, even those activities that are not economic activities (such as those outside the scope of VAT), and that are not normally regarded as 'business' for UK VAT purposes.

As a result of that decision, HMRC have stated that from 22 January 2010, 'Lennartz' accounting is only available where:

- the goods are used in part for making supplies in the course of an economic activity that give a right to input VAT deduction (broadly, taxable supplies, supplies that would be taxable if made in the UK, or certain financial and insurance supplies to non-EU customers); and
- they are also used in part for the private purposes of the trader or his staff, or, exceptionally, for other uses which are wholly outside the purposes of the taxpayer's enterprise or undertaking.

From that date, where 'Lennartz' accounting is not available, and goods are used (or to be used) for both economic activities and non-economic business activities, subject to the transitional provisions, the VAT incurred must be apportioned between these different activities on the basis of use (or intended use). The VAT attributed to the economic activities is input tax and is recoverable to the extent that the economic activities give rise to supplies with a right to input VAT deduction. The VAT attributed to the non-economic business activities is not input tax and cannot be recovered. (HMRC Brief 2/10).

Goods covered (prior to 1 January 2011)

The 'Lennartz' mechanism is available for the VAT incurred on the purchase of any goods, including computers, motor caravans, yachts, aircraft, etc. It is also available for taxable land and buildings allocated wholly to business purposes, whatever the nature of the taxable person's interest in the land and buildings (short lease, long lease or freehold). It is not available for goods which are subject to input tax restriction or 'block' (e.g. cars, items used for business entertainment, goods on which VAT is charged under a margin scheme or directors' accommodation).

Services covered (prior to 1 January 2011)

HMRC initially took the view that the 'Lennartz' mechanism did not apply to VAT on services so that where there was business and non-business/private use, apportionment was mandatory. However, in *Seeling v Finanzamt Starnberg, ECJ Case C–269/00*, [2003] STC 805 (TVC 22.182) in which a German businessman constructed a house both as his home and for use in his business, the Court held that where a taxable person received supplies of construction services, which resulted in the creation of a new business asset, then the resulting asset could be brought within the 'Lennartz' mechanism.

As a result, where a taxable person incurs VAT on services *that are used to create new goods*, the 'Lennartz' mechanism is available. For example

- the construction of new movable goods (e.g. a yacht);
- the construction of a new building or civil engineering work;
- the construction of an annex to an existing building or the construction of an extension to an existing building (on new land adjoining the existing building and provided it increases the footprint of the existing building by 10%); and
- the reconstruction of an existing building (see *Whitechapel Art Gallery (No 2)* (VTD 20720) (TVC 20.20)). In this case, HMRC's statement that 'Lennartz applies to the acquisition cost of the building but not to costs of improving or refurbishing the building' was rejected by the

tribunal. Nevertheless, it would seem that minor services of repairing, maintaining, refurbishing or renovating existing goods/assets cannot create a new 'Lennartz' asset and cannot be brought within the 'Lennartz' mechanism. Consequently any VAT incurred must be apportioned to reflect actual business use.

The 'Lennartz' mechanism also does not apply to intangible assets (e.g. software licences, intellectual property).

'Construction costs' (prior to 1 January 2011)

To be included in the 'Lennartz' mechanism, costs incurred must relate directly to the 'construction' of the new goods and must be incurred after such time as the taxable person knows for certain that the 'construction' will take place. Not included are any costs incurred on feasibility studies, demolition of pre-existing buildings on site, works which are required as part of the project but which do not form part of the asset, clearance and cleansing of land, financial advice (including costing of the project), obtaining planning permission, and fees charged by consultants such as architects and surveyors that are incurred before the time of a final decision to embark on the construction project.

From 1 January 2011

For VAT incurred on or after 1 January 2011, 'Lennartz' accounting cannot be used for any of the following:

- interest in land;
- building or part of a building;
- civil engineering work or part of such a work;
- goods incorporated or to be incorporated in a building or civil engineering work (whether by being installed as fixtures or fittings or otherwise);
- ship, boat or other vessel; or
- aircraft.

It is replaced by the ability of a taxpayer to adjust for subsequent changes in private use under the capital goods scheme. See **10.1 CAPITAL GOODS SCHEME**.

[*VATA 1994, s 24(5A), Sch 4 para 5(4A); F(No 3)A 2010, Sch 8 paras 1, 3*].

Partial exemption

Taxpayers who use, or intend to use, goods or services to make exempt supplies as well as taxable supplies must also consider the impact of their partial exemption method on any claim:

- Where initial apportionment is used, the apportionment of VAT incurred between business and private/non-business use must be made first. Only then should any apportionment of input tax be made because of the partial exemption rules.
- Where the 'Lennartz' mechanism is used, if the current partial exemption method does not facilitate the 'Lennartz' mechanism, HMRC will consider proposals for a revised partial exemption method. The revised

method must result in a fair and reasonable attribution of input tax to taxable supplies for all the trading activities within the VAT registration. Methods that give a good result for the 'Lennartz' sector but do not achieve a fair and reasonable result overall will not be approved.

(VAT Notice 700, paras 33.1–33.7; Business Brief 15/05; VAT Information Sheet 14/07, paras 2.1–2.8).

De Voil Indirect Tax Service. See V3.408; V3.409.

Non-deductible input tax

[34.8] Input tax cannot usually be reclaimed on the following.

- Goods to be sold under one of the margin schemes for **SECOND-HAND GOODS (61)**.
- Goods or services to be used for the purpose of **BUSINESS ENTERTAINMENT (9)**.
- Motor cars other than taxis unless purchased for one of the qualifying uses (see **45.3 MOTOR CARS**).
- Certain accessories installed in motor cars (see **45.13 MOTOR CARS**).
- Purchases which fall within the **TOUR OPERATORS' MARGIN SCHEME (68)**.
- Certain articles to be installed in new dwellings (see **42.4 LAND AND BUILDINGS: ZERO AND REDUCED RATE SUPPLIES AND DIY HOUSEBUILDERS**).
- Assets acquired under the transfer of a business as a going concern (see **8.10 BUSINESS**).
- Domestic accommodation for its directors or proprietors (see **34.13**(7) below).
- Goods imported by a taxable person where
  - (i) at the time of importation the goods belong wholly or partly to another person, and
  - (ii) the purposes for which they are to be used include private purposes either of himself or of the other person.

  In such a case, the VAT due on import is not available for deduction as input tax, but a separate claim for repayment may be made to HMRC if a double charge to VAT would arise. The repayment of VAT to the taxable person will be made only to the extent necessary to avoid a double charge and HMRC will have regard to the circumstances of the importation and, as far as appears relevant, things done with, or occurring in relation to, the goods at any subsequent time.
  [*VATA 1994, s 27*].

De Voil Indirect Tax Service. See V3.416.

When to claim input tax

[34.9] A '*taxable person*' (i.e. a person who is, or is required to be, registered under *VATA 1994*) is entitled, at the end of each VAT period, to credit for so much of his input tax as is allowable. [*VATA 1994, s 3(1), s 25(2)*].

Input tax should be claimed on the VAT return for the period in which the VAT became chargeable, i.e. the period covering

- for supplies of goods and services, the supplier's tax point;
- for goods acquired from another EU country, the date of acquisition;
- for imported goods, the date of the importation; and
- for goods removed from a customs and/or excise warehouse, the date of removal.

However, the taxpayer cannot make a claim until he holds the evidence that is required to substantiate that claim.

[*SI 1995/2518, Reg 29(1); SI 1997/1086, Reg 4*].

Late claims for input tax

The time limit described below for deducting input tax starts to run from the due date for the return that the business is liable to make after it has both incurred the input tax and received the associated VAT invoice. In practice, most traders will deduct any input tax they are entitled to on the next VAT return after they have received the invoice from their supplier.

If the business had the necessary evidence to enable it to claim the input tax in the VAT accounting period in which it became chargeable, but did not record it in its VAT account, this is an error. It cannot claim it on a later return. It may be required to make a return adjustment or an error correction notification.

(VAT Notice 700/45/11, paras 6.1–6.2).

Time limit for late claims

Subject to below, input tax cannot be claimed more than four years (increased from three years from 1 April 2009) after the date by which the return for the first period in which input tax could be claimed is required to be made. [*SI 1995/2518, Reg 29(1A); SI 1997/1086, Reg 4; SI 2009/586, Reg 3*]. The validity of this time limit was confirmed in *Local Authorities Mutual Investment Trust v C & E Commrs*, Ch D 2003, [2004] STC 246 (TVC 48.5).

With effect from 19 March 2008, the time limit does not apply where

- the claim for deduction of input tax became chargeable in a VAT period ending before 1 May 1997;
- the claimant held the required evidence to support the claim before that date; and
- the claim was made before 1 April 2009.

This change in the legislation follows the decisions in *Marks & Spencer plc v C & E Commrs (No 4), ECJ Case C–62/00*, [2002] STC 1036 (TVC 22.55) that a transitional period should have been specified during which taxpayers were able to make claims under the pre-existing rules and, subsequently, in *Fleming (t/a Bodycraft) v C & E Commrs*, HL [2008] STC 324 (TVC 48.6) and *HMRC v Condé Nast Publications Ltd*, HL [2008] STC 324 (TVC 48.7) that, until an adequate transitional period was specified, the time limit must be disapplied in the case of all input tax claims that had accrued before its introduction. Following these cases, HMRC accepted that the time limit did not apply to input tax in respect of which the entitlement to deduct arose in accounting periods ending before 1 May 1997 and the legislation has been amended to reflect this. Claims for repayment of VAT should be submitted to HM Revenue and Customs, 'Fleming' Claims Team (Leeds), Queens Dock, Liverpool, Merseyside L74 4AA. (HMRC Brief 7/08). See also *HMRC v Scottish Equitable plc*, CS 2 July 2009 unreported (TVC 48.57) in which the Court of Session held that the failure to provide for a transitional period did not render the three-year time limit invalid. Following this decision, HMRC consider that the effect of *FA 2008, s 121* is that all VAT claims are now capped at four years, or back to 1 April 2006, whichever is the shorter. (HMRC Brief 41/09).

Cash accounting

Certain small businesses are allowed to account for VAT on the basis of cash paid and received. See **63.2 SPECIAL SCHEMES.** Where the cash accounting scheme is used, a taxable person must not reclaim input tax until the necessary evidence is received and the supply has been paid for.

Pre-registration VAT

[34.10] Although VAT incurred before registration is not input tax, it can be treated as such subject to certain conditions. The VAT should be claimed on the first VAT return required to be made following registration. HMRC may allow the claim to be made on a later return but cannot allow a claim to be made more than four years (increased from three years from 1 April 2009) after the date the first return was required. Any claim must be supported by invoices and such other evidence as HMRC require.

With effect from 1 January 2011, this provision does not apply to items falling within the Capital Goods Scheme, since the VAT in question may from that date be adjusted under the scheme.

VAT on goods

HMRC may allow a taxable person to treat as input tax any VAT on goods supplied to him before the date on which he was (or was required to be) registered or paid by him on the acquisition or importation of goods before that date provided the following conditions are satisfied.

- The goods are for the purpose of a business which either was carried on or was to be carried on by him at the time of the supply or payment.
- The goods have not been supplied *by* or (unless HMRC otherwise allow) consumed by the taxable person before the date with effect from which he was (or was required to be) registered (see *Schemepanel*

Trading Co Ltd v C & E Commrs, QB [1996] STC 871 (TVC 36.612)). HMRC deem this condition to be satisfied if the goods have been used to make other goods which are still held at that date. (VAT Notice 700, para 11.2).

- The goods must not have been supplied to, or imported or acquired by, the taxable person more than four years (increased from three years from 1 April 2009) before the date with effect from which he was (or was required to be) registered.
- All the normal rules allow the input tax to be reclaimed.
- A stock account is compiled (and preserved for such a period as HMRC require) showing separately quantities purchased, quantities used in the making of other goods, date of purchase and date and manner of subsequent disposals of both such quantities.

VAT on services

HMRC may allow a taxable person to treat as input tax any VAT on services supplied to him before the date on which he was (or was required to be) registered provided the following conditions are satisfied.

- The services are for the purpose of a business which either was carried on or was to be carried on by him at the time of such supply.
- The services have not been supplied *by* the taxable person before the date with effect from which he was (or was required to be) registered.
- The services have not been performed on
  - (i) goods which have been supplied *by* or (unless HMRC otherwise allow) consumed by the taxable person before the date with effect from which he was (or was required to be) registered (e.g. repairs to a machine sold before registration); or
  - (ii) goods which have been supplied to, or imported or acquired by, the taxable person more than four years (increased from three years from 1 April 2009) before that date.
- The services have not been supplied to the taxable person more than six months before the date with effect from which he was, or was required to be, registered. There is no discretion to allow VAT recovery on services received more than six months before registration. The only way that this can be done is by backdating the registration.
- All the normal rules allow the input tax to be reclaimed.
- A list showing the description, date of purchase and date of disposal (if any) of the services is compiled and preserved for such period as HMRC require.

> *Example*
>
> Steve trades as a car mechanic, repairing vehicles for a wide range of customers. He became VAT-registered on 1 June 2010.
>
> Steve uses the services of a sub-contractor to repair a lot of the cars, who is also VAT-registered. However, Steve cannot reclaim input tax on the fees charged by the subcontractor in the six months before he became VAT-registered if the work

on the vehicles in question was completed (and therefore an invoice raised) before Steve became VAT-registered.

VAT on supplies before incorporation

HMRC may allow a body corporate (including a company, charity or association) to treat as input tax any VAT on goods obtained for it before its incorporation, or on the supply of services before that time for its benefit or in connection with its incorporation, provided the following conditions are satisfied.

- The person to whom the supply was made or who paid VAT on the importation or acquisition
  - (i) became a member, officer or employee of the body and was reimbursed (or has received an undertaking to be reimbursed) by the body for the whole amount of the price paid for the goods or services;
  - (ii) was not at the time of supply, acquisition or importation a taxable person; and
  - (iii) imported, acquired or was supplied with the goods or received the services for the purpose of a business to be carried on by the body and has not used them for any purpose other than such business.
- The conditions for recovery of input tax on goods or, as the case may be, services as detailed above are satisfied. In the case of pre-incorporation supplies, the references in those conditions to supplies, etc. of goods and services to and by the taxable person before registration are to be taken as references to such supplies to and by the person who obtained the supplies for the company before registration.

With effect from 1 January 2011, this provision does not apply to items falling within the Capital Goods Scheme, since the VAT in question may from that date be adjusted under the scheme.

[*SI 1995/2518, Reg 111(1)–(4); SI 1997/1086, Reg 7; SI 2009/586, Reg 8; SI 2010/3022, Reg 9*].

Partial exemption

The provisions in *Reg 111* above do not specify how pre-registration VAT of a partly exempt business should be treated. HMRC take the view that it is only allowable to the extent that, at the time the VAT was incurred, the relevant goods and services were used, or to be used, to make taxable supplies, i.e. they apply direct attribution. This approach was upheld by the tribunal in *T Douros (t/a Olympic Financial Services)* (VTD 12454) (TVC 46.222) and *GN Byrd (t/a GN Byrd and Co)* (VTD 12675) (TVC 46.224).

De Voil Indirect Tax Service. See V3.431; V3.432.

Post-deregistration VAT

[34.11] As a general rule, input tax cannot be claimed on supplies received after the date of deregistration. However, on a claim, HMRC may refund to a person any VAT on *services* supplied to him after the date from which he ceased to be (or to be required to be) registered and which relate to taxable supplies of the business carried on by him before deregistration. No such claim can be made more than four years (increased from three years from 1 April 2009) after the date on which the supply of services was made. [*SI 1995/2518, Reg 111(5)–(7); SI 1997/1086, Reg 7; SI 2009/586, Reg 8*].

This covers, for example, solicitors' and accountants' services which cannot be claimed on the final returns as the invoices are not received in time. Claims should be made as soon as possible after cancellation of registration on Form VAT 427. The relevant invoices must be submitted. (VAT Notice 700/11/10, paras 8.2, 8.5).

See also *I/S Fini H v Skatteministeriet, ECJ Case C–32/03*, [2005] STC 903 (TVC 22.105) where the court held that a person who has ceased an economic activity but who continued to pay the rent and charges on premises previously used for that activity was entitled to deduct the VAT on the amounts thus paid. There had to be a direct and immediate link between the payments made and the commercial activity and an absence of any fraudulent or abusive intent.

Insolvencies

For the procedure for claiming post-deregistration input tax in insolvencies, see **35.12** INSOLVENCY.

The provisions of *Reg 111* above do not specify how post-deregistration VAT of a partly-exempt business should be treated. It is suggested that direct attribution should be used and with regard to non-attributable input tax, the recoverable proportion applicable immediately prior to deregistration should be used.

Dissolved and struck-off companies

If a company is dissolved or struck-off the register at Companies House, it ceases to exist. Immediately upon dissolution, all assets of the company are deemed *bona vacantia* and become the property of the Crown. It is therefore very important to ensure that the affairs of the company are settled prior to dissolution as HMRC are unable to repay any VAT to a company if it has been dissolved. (VAT Notice 700/11/10, para 8.6).

De Voil Indirect Tax Service. See V3.431A; V5.165.

Appeals in respect of input tax

[34.12] An appeal may be made to a VAT tribunal in connection with the amount of input tax that may be credited and the proportion of input tax allowable under *VATA 1994, s 26*. See **5.3**(3)(6) APPEALS.

Luxuries, amusements and entertainment

In any appeal relating to input tax where

(a) the appeal relates, in whole or in part, to a determination by HMRC
  - (i) as to the purposes for which any goods or services were, or were to be, used by any person, or
  - (ii) as to whether and to what extent input tax was attributable to matters other than the making of supplies within **34.3**(*a*)–(*c*) above, and

(b) the input tax for which, following the determination, there is no entitlement to credit relates to a supply, acquisition or importation or something in the nature of a luxury, amusement or entertainment,

the tribunal cannot allow the appeal so far as it relates to that determination unless it considers that it was unreasonable to make that determination. In reaching this conclusion, the tribunal may take into consideration information brought to their attention which could not have been made available to HMRC at the time.

[*VATA 1994, s 84(4)(11)*].

The effect of the above provisions is that in cases involving expenditure on luxuries, amusements and entertainment, a tribunal cannot apply a decision of its own to the case but is restricted to considering whether HMRC's decision was reasonable. Even though it might not have arrived at the same decision, the tribunal must uphold HMRC's decision unless it considers that they acted unreasonably.

Treatment of input tax in particular cases

[34.13] In particular cases, input tax is treated as follows:

(1) Accountancy fees

Accountancy fees of a sole trader or a partnership normally relate to a number of services, e.g. general accountancy advice, VAT advice and income tax advice. Although it is arguable that income tax is the responsibility of the sole trader or partner as an individual and is not strictly a business matter, to avoid lengthy disputes, HMRC's policy is that such fees should usually be allowable in full, subject to the normal rules. The only exception to this treatment is where the accountant's fees clearly relate to taxation matters which are not related to the VAT-registered business (e.g. significant costs relating to inheritance tax).

The position is similar in the case of companies paying corporation tax. The exception in this case would cover, for example, advice relating to a director's inheritance tax liabilities.

(HMRC VAT Guidance V1–13, para 13.10).

(2) Bad debt relief

See **7.13 BAD DEBT RELIEF** for repayment of input tax by the purchaser on supplies made before 1 January 2003 where a valid claim for bad debt relief has been made by the supplier.

(3) Barristers in chambers

Barristers may share chambers, office equipment and services, etc. and apportion costs between them on an agreed basis. Invoices for the supply of common goods or services may be made out to the head of chambers, a nominated member or the barristers' clerk (if the clerk is not a registered person). The appropriate payment is then made by each member of the chambers for their share of the expenses.

Three special accounting methods have been agreed. The choice of method is up to the barristers, but whichever method is chosen the conditions relating to it must be complied with.

Method 1

The nominated member to whom invoices are addressed treats the full amount of VAT as input tax. Output tax is accounted for on the shares charged to all the other members of chambers. VAT-registered members are entitled to deduct the VAT charged to them as input tax. By concession, VAT invoices need not be issued by the nominated member. Each member's record must be cross-referenced to

- output tax charged by the nominated member;
- the input tax deducted by other members; and
- the original VAT invoice.

This will help to ensure that no more than the total VAT stated on the invoice is deducted.

The records of all members of chambers must be available during a visit to any one of them.

Method 2

The nominated member to whom invoices are addressed does not charge output tax on the member's contributions. The input tax is apportioned so that registered members may deduct it on the basis of their own contributions. Records must be kept of the apportionment of input tax between the members of chambers. Each member's records should cross-reference the input tax deducted to the VAT invoice to ensure that no more than the total VAT stated on the invoice has been deducted. The records of all members of chambers must be available during a visit to any one of them.

Method 3

The nominated member to whom invoices are addressed deducts the whole amount of input tax but also pays an equal amount into the common fund. This method may only be used when all members of chambers are registered for VAT.

Special rules must be followed by chambers using Method 3 if any of the barristers use the flat-rate scheme. See **63.22**(7) **SPECIAL SCHEMES.**

(VAT Notice 700/44/07, paras 6.3, 6.4).

(4) Capital goods

See **10 CAPITAL GOODS SCHEME** for possible adjustment in subsequent years to the initial input tax recovery on certain items of computer equipment, land and buildings and civil engineering works used for non-taxable purposes.

(5) Churches and cathedrals, etc.

Cathedrals and churches exist primarily for non-business purposes but frequently derive significant income from their status as tourist attractions. Informal agreement has been reached between HMRC and The Churches Main Committee on the recovery of input tax which is not directly attributable to a business or non-business activity, notably repairs and maintenance, etc. to the cathedral or church itself and all associated buildings within its curtilage except domestic accommodation. A *cathedral* is allocated to one of the following bands for rate of recovery of input tax.

- Band A (90%) — to apply where there are significant admission charges to all main areas (e.g. St Paul's Cathedral, Ely Cathedral).
- Band B (65%) — to apply where there is no admission charge into the Cathedral, but there are high numbers of visitors and significant taxable income (e.g. from admission charges to other areas such as crypt, museum, tower, etc.; lettings for concerts, etc.).
- Band C (45%) — to apply where is no admission charge into the Cathedral, insignificant taxable income from admission charges for other areas, but a reasonable number of visitors generating income from other sources (e.g. the book/souvenir shop).
- Band D (25%) — to apply where there are no admission charges or only a few small charges and small numbers of visitors and little taxable income.

Where any exempt supplies are made, a separate partial exemption calculation must be made based on the total of input tax attributable to business activities and the proportion of residual input tax as calculated above.

Churches such as Bath Abbey, Beverley Minster, etc. are considerable tourist attractions and make significant taxable supplies. Where a church is in this position it can be allowed to use the 'Cathedral' banding system above. The vast majority of churches, however, have only minimal business activities, i.e. the sale of books, magazines, postcards, etc. (often on an 'honesty' basis from a table near the church door) and in these cases the normal apportionment provisions should apply.

Domestic accommodation is outside the banding system. HMRC consider input tax recovery to be dependent upon the occupants' terms of employment and duties and whether they are engaged on business or non-business activities. For persons engaged by the Church for religious purposes HMRC consider none of the tax is input tax. For lay persons engaged on some business activities an apportionment of VAT may be agreed. See *The Dean and Chapter of Hereford Cathedral* (VTD 11737) (TVC 36.297), concerning VAT incurred on renovation work to accommodation lived in by vergers. On the facts, the tribunal allowed 50% of the VAT to be treated as input tax although each case will need to be decided on its own merits. (Only 25% of the VAT on refurbishing houses occupied by the Dean and three Canons was allowed in *Dean and Chapter of Bristol Cathedral* (VTD 14591) (TVC 36.552).)

(HMRC VAT Guidance V1–13, paras 11.2–11.7).

Repairs to listed places of worship: a special grant scheme (the 'Listed Place of Worship Grant Scheme') has been introduced for all works of repair and maintenance to listed buildings throughout the UK that are principally used as places of worship. See **42.10 LAND AND BUILDINGS: ZERO AND REDUCED RATE SUPPLIES AND DIY HOUSEBUILDERS.**

(6) Clothing

Subject to the special cases below, the provision of clothing is normally a personal responsibility. VAT on clothing purchased 'to cultivate a professional image' in order to attract business was disallowed in *BJ Brown* (VTD 6552) (TVC 36.186) as was VAT on suits worn while working in *JK Hill and SJ Mansell (t/a JK Hill & Co)*, [1988] STC 424 (TVC 36.187). VAT on a fur coat purchased by an author was held to be partly input tax in *RA Sisson* (VTD 1056) (TVC 36.185) although an appeal in such a case would now be restricted under **34.12** above. The following special cases are recognised.

(a) *Uniforms and protective clothing*. VAT incurred by a business person on uniforms or protective clothing worn by the proprietors or their employees in the performance of their duties is input tax.

(b) *Employees*. Perks are an accepted business expense therefore if employers decide to provide their employees with clothing (not falling within (*a*) above) the VAT incurred is input tax. However, a supply of goods has also taken place and the normal business gifts rules apply. See **47.6 OUTPUT TAX.**

(c) *Barristers*. The wig, gown and bands that a barrister is required to wear in court are considered to be a uniform and the VAT incurred is input tax. It is also a court requirement that barristers wear dark clothing. For example, male barristers may wear striped trousers, a black jacket and a waistcoat with a white wing-collar, and for a female barrister a dark (black, navy or grey) suit and a white blouse. If barristers claim that this clothing would not have been purchased if they did not have to attend court, the VAT may be deducted as input tax. See also *EM Alexander* (VTD 251) (TVC 36.184).

(d) *Entertainers*. The VAT on clothing used solely as stage costumes is input tax. Ordinary clothing worn by an entertainer or TV personality will usually be worn privately as well, in which case HMRC regard the provisions of **34.7** above for part business/private use as applying. See, however, *J Pearce* (VTD 7860) (TVC 36.190) where the tribunal allowed full input tax recovery on clothing such as dress suits worn by a actor where it had not been worn privately. See also *JM Collie* (VTD 6144) (TVC 36.192) where input tax was allowed in full on a wig purchased by a professional musician to maintain his image.

(HMRC VAT Guidance V1–13, para 23.3).

(7) Debt enforcement services provided by Under Sheriffs and Sheriffs' Officers

HMRC are prepared to treat debt enforcement services provided by Under Sheriffs and Sheriffs' Officers in enforcing High Court judgment debts, and those of the County Court transferred to the High Court for enforcement, as supplies by Under Sheriffs to creditors. As a result, where such creditors are registered for VAT, they can recover VAT charged on the services, subject to the normal rules. Where Under Sheriffs and Sheriffs' Officers collect fees for their enforcement services from debtors, they must only issue VAT invoices to creditors. Any documents issued to debtors must make it clear that they are not VAT invoices.

(Business Brief 6/00).

(8) Domestic accommodation

As a general principle, the provision of domestic accommodation is regarded as a personal rather than a business responsibility and in most cases the VAT incurred is not input tax. However, the fact that a business is operated from home does not prevent VAT that is genuinely incurred for business purposes being deducted as input tax.

(a) Sole proprietors and partners. If a sole proprietor or partner carries on a business from home and uses a particular room or area specifically for business (e.g. an office or workshop), VAT incurred on costs which can be identified specifically to that area can be treated wholly as input tax. This would apply mainly to fixtures and fittings and decorating costs. VAT on any items used purely for domestic purposes (e.g. a bedroom suite) is not deductible. Where expenditure relates to both domestic and business use (e.g. fuel and power, security systems and general maintenance), the procedure in **34.7** above should be followed. (HMRC VAT Guidance V1–13, para 14.3). See also under (*d*) below for farmhouses.

(b) Directors. Prior to 1 January 2011, where a company purchases, acquires or imports goods or services which are used or to be used in connection with the provision of domestic accommodation by the company for a 'director' of the company or a person connected with a director of the company, those goods and services are not treated as used or to be used for the company's business and any input tax is not recoverable.

'*Director*' means

- where the company is managed by a board of directors or similar body, a member of that board or body;
- where it is managed by a single director or similar person, that director or person; and

- where it is managed by the members, a member of the company.

A person is connected with a director if that person is the director's wife or husband, or is a relative (or the wife or husband of a relative) of the director or of the director's wife or husband.
[*VATA 1994, s 24(3)(7); F(No 3)A 2010, Sch 8 para 1*].
For apportionment on the purchase of time share accommodation used by the directors for business and domestic purposes, see *Suregrove Ltd* (VTD 10740) (TVC 36.332). See also *Giffenbond Ltd* (VTD 13481) (TVC 36.338) for apportionment where a garage was constructed at a director's home on land transferred to the company.

(c) Employees. Where a business has to provide domestic accommodation to its employees in order to facilitate the running of the business, the expenditure is regarded as having been incurred wholly for a business purpose. The most frequent instances of employers providing accommodation for staff are in the farming and hotel industries where it is essential to have staff available at all times of the day and where there is very little or no suitable accommodation available within reasonable distance of the business premises.
If an employer pays for

- goods which become the property of its employees
- the domestic fuel and power of its employees, or
- the private telephone calls of employees

the VAT incurred is treated as the employer's input tax, but the business must account for output tax as a supply of goods or services as appropriate (see **47.7 OUTPUT TAX**).
(HMRC VAT Guidance V1–13, para 14.4).

(d) Repairs, renovations, etc. to farmhouses. The following guidelines have been agreed with the National Farmers Union as regards input tax claims by sole proprietors and partnerships. Where the occupant of the farmhouse is a director of a limited company, or a person connected with the director of the company, the provisions under (*a*) above apply. The guidelines do not give an automatic entitlement to recover VAT and businesses should continue to consider their own particular circumstances, and use the guidelines to assess the proportion of input tax that is claimable.

- Where VAT is incurred on repairs, maintenance and renovations, 70% of that VAT may be recovered as input tax provided the farm is a normal working farm and the VAT-registered person is actively engaged full-time in running it. Where farming is not a full-time occupation and business for the VAT-registered person (i.e. income is received from either full-time employment or other sources) input tax claimable is likely to be between 10%–30% on the grounds that the dominant purpose is a personal one.
- Where the building work is more associated with an alteration (e.g. building an extension) the amount that may be recovered will depend on the purpose for the construction. If the dominant purpose is a business one then 70% can be claimed. If the

dominant purpose is a personal one HMRC would expect the claim to be 40% or less, and in some cases, depending on the facts, none of the VAT incurred would be recoverable.

(Business Brief 18/96 which also see for retrospective claims).

De Voil Indirect Tax Service. See V3.410.

(9) Employee benefits and perks

(a) General. Businesses commonly provide their employees with certain benefits and rewards. These may take the form of either goods or services. Such benefits are a legitimate business expense and are provided for the purposes of the business (mainly to reward or motivate staff). The VAT incurred on their provision is consequently all input tax and no apportionment under **34.7** above is necessary although a charge to output tax may be necessary under **47.7 OUTPUT TAX**. Even if a charge to output tax is due, HMRC do not generally apply such a charge to benefits or facilities which are provided to all employees. However, 'perks' which are provided to specific individuals within a business should generally be subject to an output tax charge.

(b) Retraining prior to redundancy. VAT incurred on the provision of such programmes is incurred for the purposes of the employer's business and is input tax. It is not HMRC's policy to apply a charge to output tax on the free supply of services to the employees. (HMRC VAT Guidance V1–13, para 5.24.1).

(c) Relocation expenses. See (23) below.

(d) Home computers made available by employers. *With effect from 13 August 2007*, a business is only able to claim full VAT recovery (subject to partial exemption restrictions) without any requirement to account for VAT on private use where the provision of a computer is necessary for the employee to carry out the duties of employment. In such circumstances, HMRC's view is that it is unlikely that any private use will be significant when compared with the business need.

Where a business cannot show that a home computer is necessary in order to carry out the duties of employment, only a proportion of the VAT incurred is recoverable as input tax. HMRC will accept any method of apportioning the VAT incurred as long as the result fairly and reasonably reflects the extent of business use. It may be possible to agree a set percentage with HMRC based on a representative period.

Before 13 August 2007, where computers were not put to any business use, the VAT incurred on the machines was not input tax; but if there was an intention that *some* home business use would occur, then the VAT suffered was input tax and no apportionment was required.

Transitional provisions. Where a business continues to provide a computer under a Home Computer Initiative agreement (the scheme was withdrawn with effect from 6 April 2006), full VAT recovery can continue until the agreement (normally three years) has expired. (HMRC Brief 55/07).

(e) Mobile telephones. See (19) below.

(f) Domestic accommodation. See (8) above.

(g) Sports, canteen and recreational facilities available to staff in general. Where such facilities are provided by a business and are available to all employees, whether or not for a charge, the VAT incurred in the provision of these facilities can be treated as input tax. It is not HMRC's policy to apply a charge to output tax on the free supply of services to the employees.
If a business is unable to provide suitable facilities within its own organisation and chooses to provide membership for their employees at external establishments, input tax can be recovered (and no output tax charge applies) as long as all employees are provided with the facilities. Where such facilities (e.g. membership of a golf or health club, etc.) are provided as a 'perk' to specific employees, there is an onward supply of services under **47.7 OUTPUT TAX.**
(HMRC VAT Guidance V1–13, para 5.24.6).

(10) Entertainment

See **9.1–9.6 BUSINESS ENTERTAINMENT.**

(11) Financial services

See **23.3 FINANCIAL SERVICES** for input tax recovery in respect of financial services.

(12) Holding companies

See **27.9 GROUPS OF COMPANIES.**

(13) Imports

See **34.10–34.13 IMPORTS.**

(14) Insurance

See **36.3 INSURANCE** for input tax recovery in respect of insurance services and **36.10 INSURANCE** for input tax re insurance claims.

(15) Land and buildings

See **42.4 LAND AND BUILDINGS: ZERO AND REDUCED RATE SUPPLIES AND DIY HOUSEBUILDERS** for deduction of input tax by developers; and **42.23 LAND AND BUILDINGS: ZERO AND REDUCED RATE SUPPLIES AND DIY HOUSEBUILDERS** for deduction of input tax by do-it-yourself housebuilders.

(16) Legal costs

For VAT on legal costs to be recoverable as input tax, the legal services should be supplied for the purpose of the business rather than for the trader, directors or employees in a personal capacity.

Criminal cases

VAT on legal costs has been disallowed in *Wallman Foods Ltd* (VTD 1411) (TVC 36.238) (handling stolen property); *Britwood Toys Ltd* (VTD 2263) (TVC 36.239) (successfully defending a charge of corruption in relation to acquisition of stock); *LHA Ltd* (VTD 11911) (TVC 36.241) (personal assault); *C & E Commrs v Rosner (t/a London School of International Business)*, QB 1993, [1994] STC 228 (TVC 36.232) (conspiracy to defraud); and *RN Scott* (VTD 2302) (TVC 36.235) (motoring offences). VAT has been held to be deductible in *P & O European Ferries (Dover) Ltd* (VTD 7846) (TVC 36.230) (employees charged with manslaughter). In *SR Brooks* (VTD 12754) (TVC 36.231) VAT on legal costs of successfully defending charges in connection with evasion of Customs duties on gold transactions was held to be allowable although the tribunal indicated that this might not have been the case if the defendant had been charged with a smuggling offence.

Civil cases

VAT on legal costs has been disallowed in *JG & MV Potton* (VTD 2882) (TVC 36.44) (freeholder's costs paid by lessees in a breach of covenant case); *Ingram (t/a Ingram & Co)* (VTD 4605) (TVC 36.54), *C Mills* (VTD 4864) (TVC 36.205), *B Stone* (VTD 12442) (TVC 36.57) and *K Lister* (VTD 13044) (TVC 36.206) (partnership disputes); *G A Swinbank* (VTD 18192) (TVC 36.217) (defending claim by former wife over assets including business assets); *Brucegate Ltd* (VTD 4903) (TVC 36.51) and *Ash Fibre Processors Ltd* (VTD 12201) (TVC 36.209) (transfer of share capital); *Morgan Automation Ltd* (VTD 5539) (TVC 36.218) (director's dispute with previous company); and *HD Marks* (VTD 11381) (TVC 36.221) and *P Oldfield* (VTD 12233) (TVC 36.222) (action against former employer).

Payment of another party's legal costs

See the note published in the Law Society's Gazette (July 1983).

Debt collection agencies

See **3.16** AGENTS.

(17) Local authorities

See **43.6** LOCAL AUTHORITIES AND PUBLIC BODIES.

(18) Memorial VAT refund scheme

A special refund scheme, administered by the Department for Culture, Media and Sport, refunds the VAT costs incurred on qualifying supplies made after 15 March 2005 on the construction, renovation and maintenance of statues, monuments and similar constructions. The scheme is due to run until 31 March 2011.

(19) Mobile phones provided to employees

HMRC have agreed the following treatment where a business provides its employees with mobile phones.

(a) *Purchase and connection*. If the phones are provided for business use, the business can treat as input tax all VAT incurred on purchasing the phone and on standing charges for keeping it connected to the network (whether or not it allows private use of the phone). See, however, (*e*) below.

(b) *Calls where business use only*. If the business does not allow employees to make private calls, all VAT incurred on calls is input tax. HMRC will accept that this is the case where a business has imposed clear rules prohibiting private use and enforces them. Under such circumstances, a small amount of private use will be treated as insignificant and will not prevent all VAT incurred being treated as input tax.

(c) *Charges by business for private use*. If a business charges its employees for any private calls, it may treat all VAT incurred on calls as input tax but must account for output tax on the amount it charges.

(d) *Free private calls*. If a business allows its employees to make private calls without charge, it must apportion the VAT incurred on the call charges by a method which produces a fair and reasonable result. For example, it could analyse a sample of bills taken over a reasonable period of time and use the ratio for future VAT recovery.

(e) *Fixed monthly charges*. Where the phone package allows the business to make a certain quantity of calls for a fixed monthly payment and there is no separate standing charge, it must apportion the VAT on the total charge for the package. Similarly, where the contract is for the purchase of the phone and the advance purchase of a set amount of call time for a single charge, apportionment applies to the whole charge.

(VAT Notice 700, paras 12A.1–12A.3).

(20) Motor cars and motoring expenses

See in particular **45.3 MOTOR CARS** for purchases of cars, **45.7 MOTOR CARS** for car dealers, **45.11 MOTOR CARS** for leasing or hiring motor cars, **45.12 MOTOR CARS** for repairs and maintenance, **45.13 MOTOR CARS** for accessories and **45.14** and **45.15 MOTOR CARS** for motor fuel.

(21) Museums and galleries

Museums and galleries that offer free admission to the public are not regarded as being engaged in any business in relation to this activity. Ordinarily, it is not possible to recover the VAT incurred on goods and services purchased to support non-business activities and VAT incurred in connection with the free admission of the public would be irrecoverable. However, the Government reimburses this otherwise irrecoverable VAT to certain national museums and galleries under a special VAT refund scheme. The detailed provisions are set out below. (VAT Notice 998, paras 1.1, 1.5).

Where

- VAT is chargeable on the supply of goods or services to, or the acquisition or importation of goods by, a specified 'body',
- the supply, acquisition or importation is attributable to the provision by the body of free rights of admission to a 'relevant museum or gallery', and

- the VAT is not excluded from credit under *VATA 1994, s 25(7)* (see, for example, **9 BUSINESS ENTERTAINMENT** and **45.3 MOTOR CARS**),

HMRC must, on a claim being made in the appropriate form, refund to the body the amount of VAT so chargeable. The claim must be made within the period of four years (increased from three years from 1 April 2009) beginning with the day on which the supply is made or the acquisition or importation takes place (or such shorter period as HMRC determine). [*FA 2008, Sch 39 para 33; SI 2009/403*].

Where the goods or services in question cannot conveniently be distinguished from goods or services supplied to, or acquired or imported by, the body that are not attributable to free admissions, the refund is the amount remaining after deducting from the whole of the VAT to which the claim relates such proportion as HMRC consider to be attributable otherwise than to free admissions.

'Bodies' and their 'relevant museums and galleries'

The Treasury has specified the following bodies and their relevant museums and galleries from 1 April 2001 or such later date as indicated.

Body	*Relevant museums and galleries*	*Date*
British Museum	British Museum, Great Russell Street, London WC1B 3DG	
Imperial War Museum	Imperial War Museum, Lambeth Road, London SE1 6HZ	1.12.01
	IWM North, Trafford Wharf Road, Trafford Park, Manchester M17 ITZ	1.4.02
The National Gallery	The National Gallery, Trafalgar Square, London WC2N 5ND	
National Maritime Museum	National Maritime Museum, Romney Road, London SE10 9NF	1.12.01
National Museums and Galleries on Merseyside	Walker Art Gallery, William Brown Street, Liverpool L3 8EL	1.12.01
	Liverpool World Museum, William Brown Street, Liverpool L3 8EN	1.12.01
	Merseyside Maritime Museum, Albert Dock, Liverpool L3 4AQ	1.12.01
	Museum of Liverpool, Pier Head, Liverpool L3 1PZ	1.12.01
	The Lady Lever Art Gallery, Port Sunlight Village, Bebington, Wirral, Merseyside CH62 5EQ	1.12.01
	Sudley House, Mossley Hill Road, Liverpool L18 8BX	1.12.01
	National Conservation Centre, Whitechapel, Liverpool L1 6HZ	1.12.01
	HM Revenue and Customs National Museum, Merseyside Maritime Museum, Albert Dock, Liverpool L3 4AQ	1.12.01

Body	*Relevant museums and galleries*	*Date*
	International Slavery Museum, Dock Traffic Office, Albert Dock, Liverpool L3 4AX	1.4.06
National Portrait Gallery	National Portrait Gallery, St Martin's Place, London WC2H OHE	
Natural History Museum	Natural History Museum, Cromwell Road, London SW7 5BD	1.12.01
	Natural History Museum Zoological Museum, Akeman Street, Tring, Herts HP23 6AD	1.12.01
Royal Armouries	The Royal Armouries, Armouries Drive, Leeds, West Yorkshire LS10 ILT	1.12.01
	Royal Armouries at Fort Nelson, Fort Nelson, Down End Road, Fareham, Hants PO17 6AD	1.12.01
Science Museum	Science Museum, South Kensington, London SW7 2DD	1.12.01
	National Museum of Photography, Film and Television, Bradford, West Yorkshire BD1 ILQ	
	National Railway Museum, Leeman Road, York YO26 4XJ	1.12.01
	Science Museum, Wroughton Airfield, Swindon Wilts SN4 9NS	
	National Coal Mining Museum for England, Caphouse Colliery, New Road, Overton, Wakefield, West Yorkshire WF4 4RH	1.4.02
	Locomotion, the National Railway Museum at Shildon, Shildon, County Durham DL4 1PQ	10.2.03
Tate Gallery	Tate Britain, Millbank, London SW1P 4RG	
	Tate Modern, Bankside, London SE1 9TG	
	Tate Liverpool, Albert Dock, Liverpool L3 4BB	
Victoria and Albert Museum	Victoria and Albert Museum, Cromwell Road, London SW7 2RL	22.11.01
	Bethnal Green Museum of Childhood, Cambridge Heath Road, London E2 9PA	
	Theatre Museum: National Museum of Performing Arts, Russell Street, Covent Garden, London WC2 7PR	22.11.01
	Wellington Museum, Apsley House, 149 Piccadilly, Hyde Park Corner, London W1J 7NT	22.11.01
The Wallace Collection	The Wallace Collection, Hertford House, Manchester Square, London W1U 3BN	
The Greater Manchester Museum of Science and Industry	Museum of Science and Industry in Manchester, Liverpool Road, Castlefield, Manchester M3 4FP	1.12.01
Sir John Soane's Museum	Sir John Soane's Museum, 13 Lincoln's Inn Fields, London WC2A 3BP	
Museum of London	Museum of London, London Wall, London EC2Y 5NH	1.12.01

Body	*Relevant museums and galleries*	*Date*
	Museum of London Archaeological Service, Mortimer Wheeler House, 46 Eagle Wharf Road, London N1	1.12.02
Geffrye Museum	Geffrye Museum, Kingsland Road, London E2 8EA	
Horniman Museum	Horniman Museum, 100 London Road, Forest Hill, London SE23 3PQ	
British Library[1]	British Library, 96 Euston Road, London NW1 2DB	
The National Army Museum	The National Army Museum, Royal Hospital Road, Chelsea, London SW3 4HT	
The Royal Air Force Museum	The Royal Air Force Museum, Hendon, London NW9 5LL	1.12.01
	The Royal Air Force Museum, Cosford, Shifnal, Shropshire TF11 8UP	24.8.05
National Museums & Galleries of Wales	National Museum & Gallery, Cathays Park, Cardiff CF10 3NP	
	National Museums of Welsh History:	
	Roman Legionary Museum, High Street, Caerleon NP6 1AE	
	Segontium Roman Fort Museum, Beddgelert Road, Caernarfon, Gwynedd LL55 2LN	
	Museum of Welsh Life St Fagans, Cardiff CF5 6XB	
	National Museums of Welsh Industry:	
	Welsh Slate Museum, Llanberis, Gwynedd LL55 4TY	
	Big Pit, National Mining Museum of Wales, Blaenafon Torfaen NP4 9XP	
	Museum of the Welsh Woollen Industry, Drefach Felindre, Llandysul SA44 5UP	
	Collections Centre, Nantgarw, Trefforest Industrial Estate, Pontypridd CF15 7QT	
	National Waterfront Museum Swansea, Museum Square, Maritime Quarter, Victoria Road, Swansea SA1 1SN	18.10.01
	National Museum of Art:	
	Turner House, Plymouth Road, Penarth, South Glamorgan CF64 3DM	
The National Library of Wales[1]	The National Library of Wales, Aberystwyth, Ceredigion SY23 3BU	
National Museums and Galleries of Northern Ireland	Ulster Museum, Botanic Gardens, Belfast BT9 5AB	
	Armagh County Museum, The Mall East, Armagh	
National Museums of Scotland	Royal Scottish Museum, Chambers Street, Edinburgh EH1 1JF	
	Museum of Scotland, Chambers Street, Edinburgh EH1 1JF	

Body	*Relevant museums and galleries*	*Date*
	National War Museum of Scotland, Edinburgh Castle, Edinburgh	
National Galleries of Scotland	National Gallery of Scotland, The Mound, Edinburgh EH2 2EL Scottish National Portrait Gallery, Queen Street, Edinburgh EH2 1JD Scottish National Gallery of Modern Art, Belford Road, Edinburgh EH4 3DR Dean Gallery, Belford Road, Edinburgh EH4 3DR	
National Library of Scotland[1]	George IV Bridge, Edinburgh EH1 1EW 33 Salisbury Place, Edinburgh	
Keele University	Keele University Art Gallery, Keele Arts, Keele University, Staffordshire ST5 5BG	1.8.04
Lancaster University	Peter Scott Gallery, Lancaster University, Lancaster LA1 4YW	1.8.04
	Ruskin Library, Lancaster University, Lancaster LA1 4YH	1.8.04
London Metropolitan University	The Women's Library, London Metropolitan University, Old Castle Street, London E1 7NT	1.8.04
Manchester Metropolitan University	Manchester Metropolitan University Special Collections, Sir Kenneth Green Library, All Saints, Manchester M15 6BH	1.8.04
Middlesex University	Museum of Domestic Design and Architecture, Middlesex University, Cat Hill, Barnet, Hertfordshire EN4 8HT	1.8.04
Queen's University, Belfast	The Naughton Gallery at Queen's and Queen's University Art Collection, Lanyon Building, Queen's University, Belfast BT7 1NN	1.8.04
School of Oriental and African Studies	Percival David Foundation of Chinese Art, 53 Gordon Square, London WC1H 0PD	1.8.04
The Royal Academy of Music	York Gate Collections, Royal Academy of Music, Marylebone Road, London NW1 5HT	1.8.04
The Royal College of Surgeons of England	Hunterian Museum at the Royal College of Surgeons, 35–43 Lincoln's Inn Fields, London WC2A 3PE	1.8.04
University of Aberdeen	Marischal Museum, University of Aberdeen, Marischal College, Broad Street, Aberdeen, Scotland AB10 1YS	1.8.04
	Natural Philosophy Collection, University of Aberdeen, Department of Physics, Fraser Noble Building, King's College, Aberdeen, Scotland AB24 3UE	1.8.04
	Zoology Museum, University of Aberdeen Zoology Building, Tillydrone Avenue, Aberdeen, Scotland AB24 2TZ	1.8.04
University of Birmingham	Barber Institute of Fine Arts, University of Birmingham, Edgbaston, Birmingham B15 2TS	1.8.04

Body	*Relevant museums and galleries*	*Date*
	Lapworth Museum of Geology, University of Birmingham, Edgbaston, Birmingham B15 2TT	1.8.04
University of Bristol	University of Bristol Theatre Collection, Cantocks Close, Bristol BS8 1UP	1.8.04
University of Cambridge	Sedgwick Museum of Earth Sciences, 3 Downing Street, Cambridge CB2 3EQ	1.8.04
	University Museum of Zoology, Cambridge, Downing Street, Cambridge CB2 3EJ	1.8.04
	The Fitzwilliam Museum Cambridge, Trumpington Street, Cambridge CB2 1RB	
University College Chichester	Otter Gallery, University College Chichester, Bishop Otter Campus, College Lane, Chichester, W Sussex PO19 6PE	1.8.04
University of East Anglia	The Sainsbury Centre for Visual Arts, University of East Anglia, Norwich NR4 7TJ	28.10.04
University of Edinburgh	Talbot Rice Gallery, The University of Edinburgh, Old College, South Bridge, Edinburgh EH8 9YL	1.8.04
University of Exeter	The Bill Douglas Centre for the History of Cinema and Popular Culture, The Old Library, Prince of Wales Road, Exeter EX4 4SB	1.8.04
University of Glamorgan	University of Glamorgan Artworks Collection, Oriel y Bont, The University of Glamorgan, Treforest, Pontypridd CF37 1DL	1.8.04
University of Glasgow	Hunterian Museum, Gilbert Scott Building, University of Glasgow, University Avenue, Glasgow G12 8QQ	1.8.04
	Hunterian Art Gallery, 82 Hillhead Street, University of Glasgow, Glasgow G12 8QQ	1.8.04
	Zoology Museum, Graham Kerr Building, University of Glasgow, University Avenue, Glasgow G12 8QQ	1.8.04
University of Hull	University of Hull Art Collection, University of Hull, Hull HU6 7RX	1.8.04
University of Kent	Centre for the Study of Cartoons and Caricature, Templeman Library, University of Kent, Canterbury CT2 7NU	1.8.04
University of Manchester	Labour History Archive and Study Centre, People's History Museum, Head Office, 103 Princess Street, Manchester M1 6DD	1.8.04
	The John Rylands Library, 150 Deansgate, Manchester M3 3EH	1.8.04
	The Manchester Museum, Oxford Road, Manchester M13 9PL	1.8.04
	Whitworth Art Gallery, The University of Manchester, Oxford Road, Manchester M15 6ER	1.8.04
University of Newcastle upon Tyne	Hancock Museum, Barras Bridge, Newcastle upon Tyne NE2 4PT	28.2.05
	Hatton Gallery, University of Newcastle upon Tyne, Newcastle upon Tyne NE1 7RU	1.8.04

Body	*Relevant museums and galleries*	*Date*
	Museum of Antiquities, University of Newcastle upon Tyne, Newcastle upon Tyne NE1 7RU	1.8.04
	Shefton Museum of Greek Art & Archaeology, University of Newcastle upon Tyne, Newcastle upon Tyne NE1 7RU	1.8.04
University of Northumbria at Newcastle	University Gallery and Baring Wing, Northumbria University, Sandyford Road, Newcastle upon Tyne NE1 8ST	1.8.04
University of Oxford	Ashmolean Museum of Art and Archaeology Beaumont Street, Oxford OX1 2PH	1.8.04
	Oxford University Museum of Natural History, Parks Road, Oxford OX1 3PW	1.8.04
	Pitt Rivers Museum, South Parks Road, Oxford OX1 3PP	1.8.04
	Museum of the History of Science, Broad Street, Oxford OX1 3AZ	1.4.07
University of Reading	Cole Museum of Zoology, School of Animal and Microbial Sciences, University of Reading, Whiteknights, Reading RG6 6AJ	1.8.04
	Museum of English Rural Life, University of Reading, Redlands Road, Reading RG1 5EX	1.8.04
	Ure Museum of Greek Archaeology, University of Reading, Room 38, HUMUSS Building, Whiteknights, Reading RG6 6AH	1.8.04
University of Strathclyde	Collins Gallery, University of Strathclyde, 22 Richmond Street, Glasgow G1 1XQ	1.8.04
University of Wales Aberystwyth	Ceramics Gallery, The University of Wales, Buarth Mawr, Aberystwyth, Ceredigion SY23 1NG	1.8.04
	School of Art Gallery and Museum, The University of Wales, Buarth Mawr, Aberystwyth, Ceredigion SY23 1NG	1.8.04
University of Wales Swansea	Egypt Centre, University of Wales Swansea, Singleton Park, Swansea SA2 8PP	1.8.04
People's History Museum	People's History Museum, The Pump House, Bridge Street, Manchester M3 3ER	9.8.05
National Football Museum	National Football Museum, Sir Tom Finney Way, Deepdale, Preston PR1 6PA	1.7.05
University of Liverpool	The Victoria Gallery and Museum, The Foundation Building, 765 Brownlow Hill, Liverpool L69 7ZX	24.10.05

[1] In respect of the historical collections in its galleries, temporary exhibitions and other related public programmes and events.

[*VATA 1994, s 33A; FA 2001, s 98(2); SI 2001/2879; SI 2005/1993; SI 2005/1993; SI 2008/1339*].

Input tax refundable under the scheme

Refunds of VAT can be claimed on goods and services purchased in order to make the principal collections in the museum or gallery available and accessible to the public free of any charges. The museum must place the order, receive the supply, receive a VAT invoice addressed to it, and pay from its own funds (including funds awarded to it, e.g. lottery funds). Provided these conditions are met, VAT incurred can be reclaimed on

- items and collections on display provided they have borne VAT (e.g. buying, acquiring or importing the items and collections);
- goods and services necessary for their upkeep (e.g. cleaning and restoring the displayed items);
- upkeep of the part of the building (including common areas) in which the items are housed (e.g. making secure, cleaning, repairs and maintenance);
- provision of free information in relation to the items on display (e.g. advertising and other promotional material; 'virtual' access to, and information about items via a free website provided it is not a business activity; free lectures);
- building a new wing to house items; and
- costs related to those areas, such as office space, that are not themselves open to the public but which are used for administration purposes in connection with free admissions.

Provided the public has free access to the principal collections on display, it does not matter that the public are occasionally charged to see special exhibitions, etc. However, any VAT incurred in relation to such a special exhibition is subject to the normal rules of input tax deduction.

VAT cannot be reclaimed under the scheme on

- non-business activities other than providing free admission to the public (e.g. grant-funded research); or
- any business activities (e.g. shops, catering outlets, commercial sponsorship (including commercially sponsored websites), or educational courses provided for consideration).

(VAT Notice 998, paras 2.3, 2.5–2.8).

Recovering the VAT

- *VAT-registered museums* should claim a refund in Box 4 of the VAT return (in addition to any input tax incurred in making taxable business supplies). The net value of total purchases should be included in Box 7.
- *Non-VAT-registered museums* must make a claim in writing to Banking/GABS, HM Revenue and Customs, 7th Floor SW, Alexander House, 21 Victoria Avenue, Southend-on-Sea SS99 1AU. Any claim must relate to a period of at least one calendar month or, if it is for less than £100, at least twelve months. The period chosen must end on the last day of a calendar month.

There is no special form to apply for the repayment and a declaration can be made along the following lines

> I am claiming a refund of £ for the period to cover VAT charged on goods and services bought for (name of body) in connection with the provision of free admission to the public.

Signed
For (name of body)
Address
Contact name
Contact telephone number

The basis of calculation should be explained and the museum should keep invoices and other records to support its claims for six years unless HMRC agrees in writing to a shorter period.

(VAT Notice 998, paras 3.2, 3.5, 4.3–4.5).

VAT groups

Bodies within these provisions can group for VAT purposes if they meet the requirements for VAT group treatment in **27.2 GROUPS OF COMPANIES**. (VAT Notice 998, para 1.10).

Extra-statutory concession

A qualifying museum or gallery can recover the VAT attributable to the free right of admission from the date specified in the above list. The scheme is not retrospective and does not, therefore, extend to goods or services acquired before the admission date (and used in connection with the taxable business activity of charging admissions) but subsequently used in connection with the non-business activity of admitting the public free of charge.

By concession, HMRC will apply the following provisions (unless used for VAT avoidance) to ensure that a museum or gallery is not required to repay input tax, properly recovered at the time, solely on account of the move to free admission. The concession takes effect from 1 April 2001 (or such later date specified for the qualifying museum or gallery in the above table), whether or not that date was before the date of publication of the concession.

- A qualifying museum or gallery need not account for output tax on goods and services which, after purchase, are subsequently put to a non-business use. Such transactions, which would otherwise be taxable (see **47.7 OUTPUT TAX**), are treated as neither a supply of goods nor a supply of services, provided the change in use of the goods and services arose solely as a direct result of the body using them for the purpose of offering free rights of admission to their relevant museum or gallery.
- A qualifying museum or gallery need not make adjustments in the case of goods within the **CAPITAL GOODS SCHEME (10)** where input tax has been recovered, insofar as a change in use of a capital item relates to free admission with related refunds under the scheme. Where this applies, the museum, etc. should, in each subsequent interval, adjust the total input tax on the capital item and the extent of its taxable use as follows.

(i) The total input tax on the capital item is deemed to be the proportion that would have been input tax if admissions, which have subsequently become free, had been free at the time the VAT was incurred.

(ii) The extent of taxable use of the capital item, at the time the original entitlement to deduction was determined, is deemed to be the extent of taxable use at that time if admissions which have subsequently become free had been free at that time.

Where free admission is introduced part way through a capital goods scheme interval (e.g. a museum with a VAT year ending 31 March charges for admission until 31 December, then gave free admission from 1 January onwards), the CGS adjustment comprises two calculations. In the example given, three-quarters of the input tax should be adjusted under normal rules and one quarter of the input tax should be adjusted using the concession. Where free admission is phased in, gradual variations can be covered by looking at the year as a whole. Significant variations should be handled with more than one calculation.

(VAT Notice 48, ESC 3.34; VAT Notice 998, paras 5.1–5.3, 6.4, 6.5).

(22) Pension schemes

See **53.2 PENSION SCHEMES** for input tax deductible by employers.

(23) Removal/relocation expenses

Employers may provide assistance to employees or future employees in relocating nearer their new job. Assistance may take many forms, including

- the payment of estate agent's fees,
- payment for a removal firm when moving house,
- the provision of maintenance/gardening for an employee's former property awaiting sale, and
- short-term accommodation in a hotel, etc.

Providing such expenditure is linked to the actual relocation, it can be treated as being the employer's input tax. It is not HMRC's policy to apply a charge to output tax on the free supply of services to the employees.

If, however, the expenditure is not linked specifically to the relocation, but forms part of the ongoing living expenses at the new property, then it is not input tax. For example, the provision of new, bespoke curtains or carpets for a new house is acceptable as it is a normal expense of moving house; but the provision of a new stereo system would not be acceptable as it is an expenditure unrelated to the relocation.

(HMRC VAT Guidance V1–13, para 5.24.2).

(24) Second-hand goods

See **61.2 SECOND-HAND GOODS** for disallowance of input tax on goods sold under the scheme.

(25) Sporting, recreational and sponsorship activities

There can be considerable difficulties in establishing to what extent, if any, there is entitlement to deduct input tax in respect of sporting, recreational and sponsorship activities. HMRC's policy in this area is to ensure that the legitimate costs of a taxable person in promoting his business or providing facilities to his staff are allowed, whilst not providing, in effect, a tax subsidy to persons who control businesses in respect of their own favoured sporting or recreational activities.

(a) Provisions for staff

Where sports and recreational facilities are available to all employees, whether or not for a charge, any VAT incurred can be treated as input tax. This equally applies where smaller businesses are unable to provide suitable facilities within their own organisation and provide membership for their employees at external establishments.

Where such facilities (e.g. membership of a golf or health club, etc.) are provided as a 'perk' to specific employees, the provisions relating to private use of services in **47.7 OUTPUT TAX** may apply.

(b) Provisions for sole proprietors, partners and company directors

Where the sporting or recreational facilities provided (e.g. membership of a golf or country club) are available only to the proprietor, partners, or directors of a company (and the relatives and friends of these persons), it is unlikely that this expenditure can be treated as being for the purpose of the business and the VAT incurred does not therefore qualify as input tax. Even if membership does result in business contacts, following the decision in *C & E Commrs v Rosner (t/a London School of International Business)*, QB 1993, [1994] STC 228 (TVC 36.224), the expenditure is probably not sufficiently connected to the purpose of the business.

(c) Sponsorship, advertising and business promotion

In certain cases, there is undoubtedly widespread exposure gained by the sponsoring business (e.g. 'Dunhill' golf masters, FA Barclays Premiership, etc.) so that no difficulty arises in allowing input tax deduction. In the case of sponsorship of sporting events by smaller businesses, there is, however, more likelihood that the 'sponsorship' is actually conducted for a private purpose (e.g. a trader may 'sponsor' a local amateur football club because of a personal connection with the team).

Similarly, participation in various sporting or recreational events may be claimed to be for business purposes in the form of advertising or promotion.

HMRC approach such cases by applying the 'business purpose' test in **34.6** above. If, at the time the VAT is incurred, the business purpose tests are met, the VAT is input tax. It is irrelevant whether the business's intentions are misconceived or that the envisaged benefits do not materialise, and the fact that the participant enjoys the activity is not sufficient reason in itself to deny input tax.

(HMRC VAT Guidance V1–13, paras 12.1–12.4).

(26) Subsistence expenses

Where an employee is paid a flat rate for subsistence expenses, no VAT can be claimed as input tax. If the business pays the actual cost of the supplies, input tax incurred can be reclaimed as below. If the business pays a proportion of the actual costs, it can reclaim as input tax the VAT fraction (see **47.2 OUTPUT TAX**) of the amount it pays.

Meals

If the business provides canteen facilities, all input tax incurred in providing these facilities can be recovered subject to the normal rules (even on meals for a sole proprietor, partner or director). Any VAT incurred on meals for employees can be treated as input tax. In the case of a sole proprietor, partner or director, the VAT must be incurred on meals taken away from the normal place of work on a business trip.

Hotel accommodation

All VAT incurred on accommodation for employers and employees when away from the normal place of work on business trips can be treated as input tax. See, however, *Co-operative Insurance Society Ltd* (VTD 14862) (TVC 36.17) where input tax was disallowed on hotel accommodation reserved by employees and only deductible if reserved by the company.

(VAT Notice 700, para 12.1).

See also *British Broadcasting Corporation* (VTD 73) (TVC 36.311) and *Ledamaster Ltd* (VTD 344) (TVC 36.312). See **9 BUSINESS ENTERTAINMENT** where accommodation, meals etc. are provided for persons other than employees.

(27) Tour operators' margin scheme

See **68.14 TOUR OPERATORS' MARGIN SCHEME** for disallowance of input tax on goods or services acquired for re-supply as margin scheme supplies.

(28) Transfers of going concerns

See **8.15 BUSINESS** for deduction of related input tax.

(29) Viability studies by accountants

See **35.10 INSOLVENCY**.

(30) Academies

For supplies made, and acquisitions and importations taking place, after 1 April 2011, proprietors of academies may recover the VAT incurred on non-business activities, primarily the provision of free education. Academies are schools in England that enter into academy arrangements with the Secretary of State under the *Academies Act 2010, s 1* or have entered into an agreement with the Secretary of State under the *Education Act 1996, s 482*. Any refund claim must be made before the end of the four-year period beginning on the day the supply is made or the acquisition or importation takes place (or such shorter period as HMRC determine). Where the goods or services cannot be conveniently distinguished from goods or services supplied, acquired or imported for business purposes, the refund is the amount remaining after deducting from the whole of the VAT chargeable such proportion as HMRC consider to be attributable to the carrying on of the business.

[*VATA 1994, s 33B; FA 2011, s 76*].

Key points

[34.14] Points to consider are as follows.

- A number of important conditions must be met before input tax can be claimed on a VAT return. The expense must be relevant to both the business that is registered for VAT and its taxable supplies. So input tax cannot be claimed on a non-business or private expense, or an expense that is relevant to exempt activities.
- It is important that a business does not pay incorrectly charged VAT on the basis that it is VAT-registered and able to reclaim input tax. The regulations are clear that only properly charged VAT can be claimed, so if a supplier incorrectly charges VAT on a zero-rated item (e.g. a book) then the correct route is to get a VAT credit note from the supplier rather than make an incorrect input tax claim. An HMRC officer has the power to disallow any input tax claimed on incorrectly charged VAT.
- A useful concession is that input tax can still be claimed on expenses relevant to supplies of services to non-UK customers that are outside the scope of VAT under the place of supply rules. The requirement here is that the service in question must be taxable (not exempt) if it had been supplied to a UK customer.
- Input tax is usually claimed according to the date of a purchase invoice. An exception to this situation is where a business uses the cash accounting scheme (see **63.1**) where the payment date become the relevant date as far as a claim is concerned. If an invoice (or any part of the invoice) becomes more than six months overdue for payment, then any input tax claimed by the customer must be credited in its VAT account until it is actually paid.
- A general requirement is that input tax can only be claimed by a business if it is receiving a supply and also acquires a purchase invoice that is addressed to the business. An important exception to this rule is where expenses are incurred by employees of a business in relation to, for example, road fuel and hotel bills. Input tax can be claimed in such cases as long as the expense is business related and paid for by the employer. There is not a problem if the employee pays for the expense himself and is then subsequently reimbursed by his employer.

- A key challenge is to consider whether an expense is for the 'benefit' of the business or 'purpose' of the business in deciding whether input tax can be claimed. There are many cases where an expense can be shown to 'benefit' a business, e.g. a sole trader could probably show that membership of his local golf club produces benefits as a source of potential customers. However, it is the 'purpose' of the expense that is relevant and must be linked to the business.
- There is an assumption (incorrect) that if an expense is partly relevant to business and partly relevant to non-business purposes, and the input tax claimed therefore needs to be apportioned, the amount of input tax claimed as business related must be made using an income-based apportionment method. The legislation allows any method to be used as long as it produces a 'fair and reasonable' result. There are many situations where an apportionment based on the ratio of business to total income does not produce a fair result because the expense in question is not determined by income.
- An alternative method to apportioning input tax on some expenses that are partly used for private or non-business purposes is to fully reclaim input tax on the initial purchase and then account for output tax on private/non-business use over the life of the asset. This approach is known as the *Lennartz* mechanism, but its application since 22 January 2010 has been greatly restricted, and was further restricted in 2011 as well. The input tax apportionment method is now the only available option in most cases.
- For a business that has both non-business and exempt supplies, it is important to adopt the correct order in dealing with VAT incurred on expenditure. The first challenge is to eliminate any VAT relevant to private or non-business activities (this VAT is not input tax) and the remaining VAT will then need to take into account the principles of partial exemption. This means that a further VAT loss will be evident if the expense in question is partly or wholly used for exempt purposes.
- The main input tax blocks in the UK (known as non-deductible input tax) apply to business entertainment and motor cars available for private use. However, it should be noted that the input tax block on entertaining does not apply to staff entertaining, and there are certain businesses that can reclaim input tax on motor cars if they are a tool of the trade, i.e. driving school business, taxi or car hire firm.
- A newly VAT-registered business can claim input tax on its first return on stock or assets bought within the four years before it became registered as long as certain conditions are met. The stock and assets in question must still be held by the business at the time of VAT registration and be used for taxable business purposes. There is also scope to claim input tax on certain services bought in the six-month period before VAT registration.

- There is also an opportunity to claim input tax on certain services invoiced to a business after it has deregistered. The VAT that can be claimed will mainly relate to professional services and can be claimed by completing form VAT427. There is no scope to reclaim VAT on goods acquired by a business after it has deregistered.
- Input tax can be claimed on costs incurred by a sole trader or partner who uses part of his house for business purposes and incurs costs, e.g. decorating his office, a proportion of light and heat bills. Input tax can also be claimed on the cost of providing domestic accommodation to employees (but not directors) as long as this is done for business purposes, e.g. the need for a farm or hotel to have an employee living on the premises.
- Be aware that input tax can only be fully claimed on the cost of a computer provided to an employee if it can be shown that the employee needs the computer for the purposes of his job. In cases where a computer is not required, an input tax apportionment will be needed to reflect the split between business and private use.
- A business that allows employees to make private calls on mobile telephone bills it pays must make some input tax adjustment to reflect the private use element. There is no problem with claiming input tax on the line rental or purchase of the phone, as long as the employee has some business use of the telephone. A clear policy of not allowing employees to make private telephone calls on business phones will deal with the input tax problem.

35

Insolvency

Cross-references. See **5.7 APPEALS** by persons becoming insolvent; **6.9 ASSESSMENTS** for assessments on persons representing insolvent persons.

Introduction

[35.1] Insolvency occurs when businesses do not have sufficient assets to cover their debts, or are unable to pay their debts when they become due. HMRC refer to the official receiver, or to the insolvency practitioner appointed over an insolvent business's affairs, as the 'office holder'. Office holders are liable to account for VAT in the normal way following their appointment (see below).

Types of insolvency

There are various types of insolvency procedure into which a VAT-registered business may enter. HMRC group them into formal insolvencies and business rescue procedures. There are also certain receiverships which HMRC do not treat procedurally as insolvencies.

Formal insolvencies

- *Administrative receivership*. An administrative receiver may be appointed to manage the affairs of a company by a secured creditor who holds a debenture agreement containing floating, or fixed and floating, charges over the whole, or substantially the whole, of a company's assets. Upon the appointment of the administrative receiver, the floating charges crystallise. The administrative receiver must treat the business assets covered by the charges in such a way as to recover the money due to the secured creditor. If the administrative receiver deems it to be in the best interests of the secured creditor, the business may continue to trade.

- *Bankruptcy*. A bankrupt is an individual against whom a bankruptcy order has been made by the court. The court can declare a person bankrupt on petition from the individual, one or more creditors, or the supervisor of an individual voluntary arrangement. The order indicates that the person is unable to pay his debts and, subject to certain exceptions, deprives him of his property, which can then be sold in order to pay creditors.

  The bankruptcy process of an individual or partnership (firm) in Scotland is known as sequestration.
- *Creditors' voluntary liquidation*. A creditors' voluntary liquidation usually relates to an insolvent company and is commenced by a resolution of the shareholders. A creditors' meeting is called so that the creditors of the company may, if they wish, appoint another insolvency practitioner in place of the shareholders' appointee.
- *Members' voluntary liquidation*. The directors of a company, or the majority of its directors, make a Declaration of Solvency stating that, in their opinion, the company will be able to settle its debts in full (plus interest) within the period of twelve months from the date of liquidation. The declaration must be made within the five weeks immediately preceding the date of the passing of the resolution for winding up. Liquidation takes place when the resolution is passed.
- *Compulsory winding up*. A compulsory winding up is ordered by the court as the result of the presentation of a petition by the company, its creditors, its directors, one or more of its shareholders, or the Secretary of State.
- *Partnership winding up*. A compulsory winding up is ordered by the court as a result of the presentation of a petition by the members of the partnership or by a creditor.
- *Provisional liquidation*. A provisional liquidator may be appointed by the court after the presentation of a petition for a winding up in order to protect the assets of a company before a winding up order is made. Where a provisional liquidator has been appointed, HMRC do not treat the case as an insolvency until a winding up order is made and a 'permanent' liquidator appointed.

Business rescue procedures

- *Administration*. An administrator may be appointed by a court order following an application by either the company, its directors or one or more of its creditors. In addition, an administrator may be appointed out of court by the company or its directors or the holders of a qualifying floating charge. The administrator's main function is to rescue the company. If this is not possible, the second objective is to achieve a better result for the company's creditors as a whole than would be achieved on a winding up. If that is not possible, the third objective is to do the best for the secured and preferential creditors without unnecessarily harming the interests of the creditors as a whole.

- *Partnership administration.* An administrator is appointed by a court order following an application by the members of the partnership or by a creditor, which is intended to allow
  (a) the partnership, or part of it, to survive in a restructured form;
  (b) the approval of a partnership voluntary arrangement; and
  (c) a better realisation of the partnership's assets than would be obtained from winding up the partnership.
- *County court administration.* The court makes an order for regular payments to be made over a period of time in settlement of debts. The court administers the scheme. The scheme is only available to individuals.
- *Administration of a deceased person's estate.*
- *Deed of arrangement.* This is a method by which an individual can arrange terms with creditors.
- *Scheme of arrangement.* This term is normally used to describe a compromise or arrangement between a company and its creditors or members (or any class of them) which may involve a scheme for the reconstruction of the company.
- *Scottish trust deeds.* A debtor grants a deed in favour of the trustee which transfers their assets to the trustee for the benefit of creditors.
- *Voluntary arrangements.* A voluntary arrangement provides an alternative to bankruptcy or liquidation. The debtor makes proposals through a licensed insolvency practitioner which are presented at a meeting of creditors. Creditors must be given 14 clear days notice of such a meeting. The proposals usually entail delayed and/or reduced payment of debts, and can be advantageous to both the debtor and the creditors. A supervisor is appointed to monitor the scheme for its duration, although the business usually continues to be responsible for its own business activities.
- *Partnership and company voluntary arrangements.* These are similar to *Voluntary arrangements* above but have no moratorium.

Procedures not treated as insolvencies by HMRC

- *Agricultural charge receivership.* A secured creditor can appoint a receiver under the *Agricultural Credits Act 1928* over the assets of a farm estate.
- *Fixed charge receivership.* A receiver, or receiver and manager, is appointed by a secured creditor who holds a fixed charge over specific assets which belong to a business. The assets are used for the benefit of the secured creditor.
- *Law of Property Act receivership.* A lender, such as a bank, can appoint a receiver over a mortgaged property under the *Law of Property Act 1925* to recover money advanced. The receiver usually tries to arrange

for the property to be sold or is responsible for collecting rents for the mortgagee. The business may continue to trade independently of the receiver's appointment.

(VAT Notice 700/56/11, paras 2.1–2.5).

Person carrying on the business

If a taxable person becomes 'bankrupt or incapacitated', HMRC may treat any person carrying on the business as a taxable person from the date of the bankruptcy or incapacity until either some other person is registered in respect of the taxable supplies made (or intended to be made) by that taxable person or the incapacity ceases. Any person carrying on the business must notify HMRC in writing within 21 days of

- the nature of any incapacity and the date on which it began; and
- the date of any bankruptcy order.

The VAT provisions apply to any person treated as carrying on the business as though he were a registered person.

[*VATA 1994, s 46(4); SI 1995/2518, Reg 9; SI 1996/1250, Reg 5*].

See **35.2** and **35.3** below.

Where any person becomes bankrupt or incapacitated and control of his assets passes to another person, that other person must, if HMRC require and so long as he has control, comply with the general accounting, record and payment requirements of VAT. However, any requirement to pay VAT only applies to the extent of the assets of the incapacitated person over which he has control so that he is treated to that extent as if he were the incapacitated person himself. [*SI 1995/2518, Reg 30*].

If no person carries on the business

If no person carries on the business (i.e. taxable supplies cease to be made) the normal procedures for cancellation of registration apply (see **59.33 REGISTRATION**).

Companies in receivership and liquidation

In relation to a company which is a taxable person, the references above to a taxable person becoming 'bankrupt or incapacitated' are to be construed as references to its going into liquidation or receivership or to administration. [*SI 1995/2518, Reg 9; SI 2003/2096, Art 56*].

Notification of insolvency

[35.2] Subject to below, a person appointed

- office holder over the affairs of an insolvent VAT-registered trader, or
- liquidator in a members' voluntary liquidation

must notify HMRC within 21 days of appointment (or, in the case only of an office holder appointed after an official receiver and who has difficulty in obtaining the necessary information, within 21 days of becoming aware of the required information). This must be done on Form VAT 769, supplies of which are available from the National Advice Service (tel: 0845 010 9000).

Form VAT 769 should not be used in the following circumstances and notification should simply be made in writing to the VAT Business Advice Centre which controls the area of the principal place of business of the insolvent business.

- Notification of a proposed creditors meeting for either voluntary arrangements or creditors' voluntary liquidations.
- The appointment of a receiver under *Law of Property Act.*
- The appointment of a receiver or manager under a fixed charge only.
- The appointment of a receiver under the *Agricultural Credits Act 1928* over assets of a farm estate.
- The appointment of a provisional liquidator (as such a person has no status with regard to the trader's VAT registration).
- Notification to appoint a liquidator under *IA 1986, s 98.*

Where a liquidator is appointed after the appointment of an administrative receiver

It is not necessary to complete a second Form VAT 769. HMRC will, however, need extra information (e.g. who is in control of the assets and who will be responsible for completing VAT returns). This information, together with the name, address and date of appointment of the liquidator, should be sent to HM Revenue and Customs, National Insolvency Unit, 3rd Floor N/W, Queens Dock, Liverpool L74 4AA quoting the VAT registration number.

(VAT Notice 700/56/11, paras 3.1, 3.2, 3.6).

Claims by HMRC

[35.3] On notification of an insolvency, HMRC will calculate its claim based on the amount outstanding at the 'relevant date'. A more detailed breakdown of the claim is available on request.

'*Relevant date*' is

- in relation to a company which is being wound up
  - (i) where the company is being wound up by a court and the winding-up order was made immediately upon the discharge of an administration order, the date of the making of the administration order;
  - (ii) in a case not within (i) above where the company is being wound up by the court and had not commenced to be wound up voluntarily before the date of the making of the winding-up order, the date of appointment (or first appointment) of a provisional liquidator or, if no such appointment has been made, the date of the making of the winding-up order; and

(iii) in any other case not within (i) or (ii) above, the date of the passing of the resolution for the winding up of the company;

- in relation to a company in receivership, the date of appointment of the receiver; and
- in relation to a bankrupt
  (i) where at the time the bankruptcy order was made there was an interim receiver of the debtor's estate appointed under *Insolvency Act 1986, s 286*, the date on which the interim receiver was first appointed after the presentation of the bankruptcy petition; and
  (ii) in any other case, the date of making the bankruptcy order.

[*Insolvency Act 1986, Sch 6*] (VAT Notice 700/56/11, paras 2.3, 2.4).

Where the business continues to trade, the office holder has responsibility for the VAT affairs of the business from the relevant date onwards with the exception of bankrupts continuing to trade, voluntary arrangements, deeds and schemes of arrangement, and county court administration orders (see **35.1** above for these terms).

(VAT Notice 700/56/11, paras 4.1, 4.2).

De Voil Indirect Tax Service. See V5.187.

Amount of claim

[35.4] HMRC's claim comprises the following.

- The amount of outstanding VAT at the relevant date.
- The amount of any penalty, default surcharge or default or penalty interest assessed in respect of any period before the relevant date. This is because the penalty, etc. is recoverable 'as if it were' VAT and is not VAT as such.

(VAT Notice 700/56/11, paras 4.1, 4.5).

Assessments

[35.5] Where a return has not been submitted for any VAT period prior to the relevant date, HMRC will raise an assessment and initially base their claim upon the amount so assessed. Where the office holder submits an acceptable VAT return for the period in question, the assessment will be withdrawn.

(VAT Notice 700/56/11, para 4.4).

Set-off of credits

[35.6] As a general rule, under *VATA 1994, s 81(3)(3A)* any amount due from HMRC to any person ('the credit') must be set against any sum due from that person by way of VAT, penalty, interest or surcharge ('the debit') and to the extent of the set-off, the obligations of both HMRC and that person are discharged. See **51.6 PAYMENT OF VAT** for full details.

However, this general rule does not apply where

- an 'insolvency procedure' has been applied to the person entitled to the credit;
- the credit became due after that procedure was so applied; and
- the liability to pay the debit either
  - (a) arose before that procedure was so applied; or
  - (b) (having arisen afterwards) relates to, or to matters occurring in the course of, the carrying on of any business at times before the procedure was so applied.

For these purposes, the time when an '*insolvency procedure*' is to be taken to be applied to any person is when

- a bankruptcy order, winding up order or an award of sequestration is made or an administrator is appointed in relation to that person;
- that person is put into administrative receivership;
- that person, being a corporation, passes a resolution for voluntary winding up;
- any approved voluntary arrangement comes into force in relation to that person;
- a registered deed of arrangement takes effect in relation to that person; or
- that person's estate becomes vested in any other person as that person's trustee under a trust deed.

But references to the application of an insolvency procedure to a person do not include

- the application of an insolvency procedure to a person at a time when another insolvency procedure applies to the person; or
- the application of an insolvency procedure to a person immediately upon another insolvency procedure ceasing to have effect.

[*VATA 1994, s 81(4A)–(4D)(5), Sch 13 para 21; FA 1995, s 27; FA 2008, s 132; SI 1994/1253; SI 2003/2096, Art 26*].

De Voil Indirect Tax Service. See V5.172.

Crown set-off

[35.7] HMRC can offer credits arising from insolvent traders' VAT repayment claims accruing before the relevant date to other government departments. [*IA 1986, s 323; SI 1986/1925, Rule 4.90*]. See also *Re Cushla v C & E Commrs*, Ch D [1979] STC 615 (TVC 37.15) and *Re DH Curtis (Builders) Ltd*, [1978] 2 All ER 183 (TVC 37.16).

HMRC currently only operate the Crown set-off procedure for repayments which exceed £500 and offer credits to the Inland Revenue, the Department of Works and Pensions, the Department of Trade and Industry and the Ministry of Defence. Any VAT repayments due falling below the limit are automatically repaid to the office holder (or to the trader in the case of voluntary arrangements, deeds or schemes of arrangement and County Court administration orders).

Crown set-off takes place after all pre-relevant date returns have been received and/or assessments raised and offset.

If a creditor is secured by a fixed charge on book or other debts of the business, Crown set-off does not apply to any VAT credit due from HMRC. See also **35.10**(3) below.

(VAT Notice 700/56/11, paras 13.1, 13.2).

Dividends

[35.8] If the office holder declares a dividend from an insolvent estate, cheques should be made payable to HM Revenue and Customs and sent to HMRC, Datapost/Team 7, Insolvency Unit, 4th Floor N/W, Alexander House, Southend-on-Sea, Essex, SS99 1AA.

Dividends for businesses subject to

- any form of administration orders, should be sent to HMRC, National Insolvency Unit, 3rd Floor N/W, Queens Dock, Liverpool L74 4AA;
- Scottish trust deeds and deeds or schemes of arrangement, should be sent to HMRC, Portcullis House, 21 India Street, Glasgow, Strathclyde, G24 PHY; and
- voluntary arrangements should be sent to HMRC, Voluntary Arrangement Service, Durrington Bridge House, Barrington Road, Worthing, West Sussex BN12 4SE.

(VAT Notice 700/56/11, paras 8.1, 8.2).

Returns

[35.9] All returns completed by the office holder for pre- and post-insolvency periods must be sent to VAT Central Unit in Southend in the normal way. See **35.16** below for bankrupts continuing to trade.

Pre-insolvency returns

The insolvent business is responsible for submitting pre-insolvency returns. However, the office holder may submit a return for any pre-relevant date period for which the business has not rendered a return. Such a return should be unsigned but carry the legend, 'completed from the books and records of the company/trader'.

The final pre-insolvency return covering the period up to the relevant date is issued automatically to the office holder and is not subject to default surcharge.

Split period return covering the relevant date

Where the relevant date (see **35.3** above) falls within a VAT period, that period is divided into two periods. The first period ends on the day prior to the relevant date. The return for that period is issued directly to the person in charge of the insolvency and must be submitted by the last day of the following month. Default surcharge is not applicable to this return. The second period begins on the relevant date and ends (and all subsequent periods end) on the normal last day for the VAT periods of the insolvent trader. [*SI 1995/2518, Reg 25(3)*].

Post-insolvency returns

Post-insolvency returns are the legal responsibility of the office holder (except for voluntary arrangements, deeds and schemes of arrangement, and county court administration orders, see **35.1** above for these terms). Returns are issued automatically to the office holder. The returns must be submitted, and any VAT paid, by the normal due date (see **51.1 PAYMENT OF VAT**).

Repayments

Repayments due are, subject to below, repaid in the name of the insolvent business, c/o the office holder. The repayment should be made by HMRC within 30 days of receipt of the return but may be delayed by any inaccuracies on the Form VAT 769 or failure to notify HMRC of the appointment of the officeholder.

Repayments for businesses in voluntary arrangements, deeds and schemes of arrangement or county court administration orders (see **35.1** above for these terms) are sent to the address of the registered business unless the trader has given written permission for the payment to be sent to the officeholder.

Repayment supplement is added if the normal conditions are satisfied (see **51.16 PAYMENT OF VAT**).

Penalties, etc.

Penalties, default surcharge and default interest are not normally applied to post-insolvency VAT returns. They are, however, applied in the case of administration orders, partnership administration orders, deceased persons administration orders, deeds and schemes of arrangement, Scottish trust deeds, county court administration orders; and voluntary arrangements (see **35.1** above for these terms). Inaccuracy penalties due under *FA 2007, Sch 24* (see **52.13 PENALTIES**) are applied to both pre- and post-insolvency VAT returns and relevant documents in all cases.

Compliance

HMRC have the right to check the accuracy of all returns submitted and to require that the books and records of the business are made available for inspection. In certain circumstances, where it can be shown that an office holder has consistently not complied with regulations, a report may be made to the appropriate licensing authority.

(VAT Notice 700/56/11, paras 5.1–5.8).

Miscellaneous VAT procedures

[35.10] Some miscellaneous VAT procedures are as follows:

(1) Bad debt relief

Bad debt relief (see **BAD DEBT RELIEF (7)**) can be claimed in insolvencies subject to the normal rules. Claims can be made on the normal VAT return where the VAT registration remains open and on Form VAT 426 where registration has been cancelled. A letter scheduling the claim, together with copies of the relevant invoices, must be submitted to the National Insolvency Unit for approval. (VAT Notice 700/56/11, paras 10.1, 10.2). See also **7.13 BAD DEBT RELIEF** for a concession concerning the repayment of input tax where an insolvency practitioner receives notice of a claim for bad debt relief on a pre-insolvency transaction.

(2) Cash accounting

The cash accounting scheme allows VAT-registered businesses to account for VAT on the basis of payments received and made rather than on VAT invoices issued and received. See **63.2 SPECIAL SCHEMES**. The office holder responsible for the business may use the scheme in the post relevant date period if the insolvent business was eligible to use the scheme pre-insolvency and continues to be eligible to do so. This may be appropriate in cases where trading has continued after the relevant date.

The office holder must also, within two months of the date of insolvency, account for VAT due on all supplies made or received up to the date of the insolvency which have not previously been accounted for. [*SI 1995/2518, Reg 62*]. The VAT due should be entered on to the VAT return for the period immediately preceding the relevant date, and is treated as a liability arising before the insolvency.

(VAT Notice 700/56/11, paras 11.1–11.3).

(3) Charges over book debts

HMRC and Redundancy Payments Service have agreed a joint approach to the question of fixed charges over book debts following the decision of the Privy Council in *Re Brumark Investments Ltd* [2000] 1 BCLC 353 casting new light on the distinction between fixed and floating charges. This will impact on the distribution of book debt proceeds in insolvent cases.

A fixed charge is a form of mortgage debenture on specified property, including uncollected book debts. In insolvency cases, lenders holding a fixed charge are paid ahead of all other creditors, including preferential creditors. The decision in *Brumark* states that a charge that allows the collection and free use of the proceeds of a book debt by the company is not a fixed charge. A fixed charge requires the collected proceeds to be paid into a blocked account (i.e. an account to which the company does not have unfettered access and cannot draw on the proceeds without the specific consent of the chargeholder). It is not enough for a debenture to provide for a blocked account: such an account must actually be operated.

The ruling means that the Crown Departments will monitor the distribution of book debt proceeds in insolvency cases and reserve the right to challenge distributions made to fixed chargeholders if they believe the charge in question was actually a floating charge. In addition, pre-insolvency VAT credits will be paid to companies subject to insolvency procedures in preference to other Crown creditors only in cases where a debenture is provided showing a fixed charge over book debts that HMRC are satisfied is a valid fixed charge.

(Business Brief 5/02).

(4) Credit notes

Where the office holder issues or receives a credit note evidencing a decrease in consideration for supplies made in a pre-insolvency VAT period, the VAT adjustment is related back to the period in which the original supply took place and HMRC's claim in the insolvency will be reduced or increased accordingly. To enable HMRC to make the necessary adjustments to the trader's VAT account, such credit notes should not be declared on a VAT return. Instead, they should be declared to the relevant office, either by letter or by means of an error correction notification (formerly voluntary disclosure), giving details of the VAT element and the date of the original supply.

Note that because of the introduction of the three-year time limit for VAT adjustments, a credit note adjustment cannot take effect if the credit note is issued more than three years after the end of the VAT accounting period in which the original supply took place.

(VAT Notice 700/56/11, paras 12.1–12.3).

(5) Partial exemption

The provisions relating to **PARTIAL EXEMPTION (49)** apply to all VAT-registered businesses including those which are insolvent. The person in charge must comply with these requirements in respect of returns completed for pre- and post-relevant date VAT periods. An insolvent business can apply to change the method of calculating entitlement to input tax recovery if there has been a substantial change in circumstances although such changes cannot be applied retrospectively.

Where a business is already partly exempt, the annual adjustment should be made at the end of the business's partial exemption year. Approval may be sought from HMRC to allow the annual adjustment to be made in the VAT period which ends with the relevant date.

(VAT Notice 700/56/11, paras 15.1, 15.2).

(6) Capital goods scheme (CGS)

If the insolvent business had assets covered by the CGS (see **10.2 CAPITAL GOODS SCHEME**) then those assets pass to the office holder on insolvency. If the use of the assets changes while under the office holder's control then adjustments may arise, which must be declared on returns due from the office holder. The office holder will need to establish the following information

- what assets covered by the CGS are held;
- when they came into use in the business; and
- how much input tax was initially incurred and deducted on them.

Assets still used within the business

Any adjustments are likely to be modest as they will only address the time of use by the office holder and the difference between their use and that originally made by the business prior to insolvency. If the office holder brings the company out of insolvency or sells its assets as a transfer of a business as a going concern (TOGC) (see **8.10 BUSINESS**) then any CGS items will pass on to the new owners at that point.

Assets no longer used within the business but held for eventual sale

If the original use was taxable and the sale will be exempt then there may be substantial adjustments due. As the sale will be made by and under the direction of the office holder adjustments must be declared by them on returns that they submit. If the asset is a building then it may be possible to prevent the sale from being exempt by opting to tax (see **41.8 LAND AND BUILDINGS: EXEMPT SUPPLIES AND OPTION TO TAX**), although this may restrict which buyers may be interested. If the original use of the assets was partly exempt, and if the sale is to be taxable, then adjustments in the office holder's favour may arise. If the business is deregistered without a sale of the asset taking place then an adjustment may arise at that time.

(VAT Notice 700/56/11, para 15.3).

(7) **VAT on insolvency practitioners' fees**

As the practitioner's services do not relate to any specific supply, fees are a general overhead of the business concerned.

Insolvent businesses which continue to trade

- Where the business remains fully taxable it can deduct input tax on the practitioner's fees.
- Where the business remains or becomes partly exempt, deduction of input tax is subject to restriction in accordance with the partial exemption method used.

Insolvent businesses which cease to trade but which remain registered

The principal activity will be the sale of assets. As anything done in connection with the termination or intended termination of a business is done in the course or furtherance of that business, input tax incurred on the practitioner's fees should be considered in the light of the taxable status of the business prior to the insolvency. Where the business was previously fully taxable, the input tax on these fees is fully deductible. Where the business was previously partially exempt, the business should continue to use the method in place in the normal way.

A change of partial exemption method should be requested from HMRC if, in the light of changing circumstances, the method in place no longer produces a fair and reasonable attribution of input tax to taxable supplies.

(VAT Notice 700/56/11, para 15.4).

(8) Distraint/attachment

HMRC may levy distraint (attachment in Scotland). See **31.4** and **31.5 HMRC: POWERS** respectively. In the case of

- a bankruptcy order (or compulsory winding up order), any incomplete distraint action (i.e. the goods distrained upon have not been sold) may be completed by HMRC with the authority of the trustee in bankruptcy, or the trustee may insist on the goods being released to him to sell subject to an undertaking provided by HMRC. If distraint has been completed within the three months immediately preceding the date of a bankruptcy order, the proceeds of the distraint may be surrendered to the trustee in bankruptcy if the trustee is unable to pay the preferential creditors in full from other realisations. The trustee must satisfy HMRC that such a shortfall regarding preferential creditors exists. Where distraint is completed by sale more than three months before the making of the bankruptcy order HMRC are entitled to retain the sale proceeds. In Scotland, attachment will not be taken used against a sequestrated trader for the duration of the sequestration; and
- a creditors' or members' voluntary winding up or an administrative receivership, if distraint has been levied (goods attached) before the appointment of a liquidator or administrative receiver, then the distraint/attachment remains valid and will be maintained and/or completed.

In the case of voluntary arrangements, distraint action will normally be suspended once an interim order has been made, a moratorium granted or proposals for a voluntary arrangement have been received and a creditors meeting arranged unless there are exceptional circumstances which justify not suspending, e.g. evidence of fraud or lack of probity. Where the proposals are rejected at the creditors' meeting HMRC will proceed to complete the distraint by sale. If the proposals are approved HMRC will normally withdraw the distraint, though in exceptional circumstances they may maintain it and include it as security in modified proposals.

In the case of administration orders, once an administrator has been appointed, distraint may not be instituted or continued against the company or the property of the company except either with the consent of the administrator or leave of the court. HMRC will generally try to reach a financial settlement with the administrator without the need to seek court directions.

Any money received by HMRC for the sale of distrained goods will be set against the earliest pre-insolvency liability and HMRC's claim amended accordingly.

Where a floating charge crystallises on the appointment of an administrative receiver or some other event specified in the debenture, the distraint will be maintained and completed if HMRC have already levied on goods which are subject to the floating charge. HMRC may choose to let the administrative receiver sell the goods, subject to an undertaking, and pass the proceeds to HMRC.

(VAT Notice 700/56/11, paras 14.1–14.4).

(9) Retention of records

The liquidator of an insolvent company may destroy the books, papers and records, including the VAT records, one year after the date of dissolution of the company. [*SI 1994/2507, Reg 16*]. By concession, official receivers may also, on request and with HMRC approval, destroy the books and records of a company after six months. Normal rules for retention of records apply to other insolvencies, i.e. records should normally be retained for six years. (VAT Notice 700/56/11, para 19.1).

(10) Viability studies by accountants

Accountants engaged to conduct viability studies are treated as making supplies of their services to the person who has commissioned the work, instructed them and who receives the end product. The effect of this is as follows.

- Where either the company or the bank commission the work, the accountants should issue any invoices to the company or bank (as the case may be). The supply is then received for business purposes and input tax is deductible subject to the normal rules. The fact that the other party, or a third party, receives a copy of the report is not relevant.
- Where the bank receives one report and the company another, the accountant is making two separate supplies and should issue separate invoices to allow recovery of input tax subject to the normal rules.
- Where the company and bank issue joint instructions and receive copies of the same report, the accountant should issue invoices for 50% of the cost to each party.
- Where the company commissions the work but does not receive a copy of the report, the accountant's supply is to the company but is not used for business purposes. Therefore neither the company nor the bank can recover any input tax.

(Business Brief 6/95).

See also *Eagle Trust plc* (VTD 12871) (TVC 36.161).

Deregistration

[35.11] The deregistration process depends on the type of insolvency.

- In a bankruptcy, sequestration, compulsory liquidation, partners' liquidation or creditors' or members' voluntary liquidation, HMRC issue Form VAT 167 (a deregistration questionnaire) to establish the level of stocks and assets on hand. They subsequently issue a warning letter (Form VAT 168) five weeks after Form VAT 167 advising that, unless a reply is received within seven days, deregistration will be automatically effected on the eighth day without notification (but see below for administrative receiverships). If at any time after the issue of Form VAT 167 and within seven days of issue of Form VAT 168, the office holder contacts HMRC to say that deregistration is not appropriate, the deregistration process will be suspended until agreed with HMRC. Once deregistration has been agreed, a final VAT return (Form VAT 193) is issued for completion.

- In an administrative receivership, HMRC issue the initial Form VAT 167 but deregistration is not effected until the office holder confirms that it is appropriate. Once deregistration has been agreed, a final VAT return (Form VAT 193) is issued for completion.
- In voluntary arrangements, deeds and schemes of arrangement, county court administration orders, Scottish trust deeds, administration orders, partnership administration orders, and deceased persons' administration orders, the normal rules for deregistration and submission of VAT returns apply.

(VAT Notice 700/56/11, paras 6.1–6.4).

Post-deregistration

Output tax

[35.12] Any output tax arising after the date of deregistration should be accounted for on Form VAT 833.

- In deeds and schemes of arrangement, county court administration orders, Scottish trust deeds and deceased persons' administration orders (see **35.1** above for these terms), Form VAT 833 can be obtained from the National Advice Service (tel: 0845 010 9000) and submitted to the VAT Central Unit at Southend.
- In all other insolvencies, Form VAT 833 can be requested from the National Insolvency Unit, Liverpool, and must be returned there with full payment of any VAT due.

See **35.15** below for how *Law of Property Act* receivers should account for output tax.

Input tax – Form VAT 426 procedure

A special scheme for claiming post-deregistration input tax on Form VAT 426 can be used by a trustee in bankruptcy, a trustee in sequestration (in Scotland), an official receiver, a liquidator or an administrative receiver. The scheme is *not* available for use by solvent deregistered traders, office holders in business rescue procedures (see **35.1** above) and other incapacitated traders. These categories include supervisors in voluntary arrangements, administrators in administration orders, a trustee appointed under a trust deed (in Scotland), a receiver appointed under the *Law of Property Act 1925*, a receiver appointed in a partnership dispute, a receiver appointed by a court, a receiver appointed under the *Agricultural Credits Act 1928*, an office holder appointed for a scheme of arrangement, an administrator appointed for a deceased persons' administration order, and a liquidator in a members' voluntary liquidation.

Subject to the normal rules, the form can be used to claim VAT on

- services supplied after deregistration but relating to business carried on before deregistration;
- goods and services supplied and invoiced before deregistration that has not already been claimed on a VAT return;
- the services of agents (e.g. solicitors, estate agents, stockbrokers) unless relating to exempt supplies; and
- realisation fees.

The form can also be used to claim bad debt relief. It cannot be used to claim VAT relating to a petitioning creditor's costs.

The completed form should be sent to HMRC, VAT 426 Claims Section, National Insolvency Unit, 3rd Floor N/W, Queens Dock, Liverpool L74 4AA. It is not necessary to send supporting invoices with the claim unless felt necessary to clarify any transaction. The claim should be processed and paid within 30 working days. HMRC select some claims for verification, in which case a VAT officer will make arrangements to visit the office holder within 30 working days of receipt of the claim. Most verification visits will be made after HMRC have authorised the repayment claim. Because of the possibility of verification, all invoices supporting the claim must be retained with the relevant books and records.

Input tax – Form VAT 427 procedure

The normal procedure for reclaiming post-deregistration VAT on Form VAT 427 (see **34.11 INPUT TAX**) should be used where a liquidator has been appointed in

- members' voluntary liquidations and all administration orders (in which case the Form VAT 427 should be sent to HMRC, VAT 427 Claims team, Accounting and Adjustment Unit, Queens Dock, Liverpool, L74 4AA);
- Scottish trust deeds and deeds or schemes of arrangement (in which case the Form VAT 427 should be sent to HMRC, Portcullis House, 21 India Street, Glasgow, Strathclyde G24 PHY); and
- voluntary arrangements (in which case the Form VAT 427 should be sent to HMRC, Voluntary Arrangement Service, Durrington Bridge House, Barrington Road, Worthing, West Sussex BN12 4SE).

(VAT Notice 700/56/11, paras 7.1–7.9).

Groups

[35.13] In a VAT group of companies, the claim for preferential debts extends to a non-representative member because under *VATA 1994, s 43(1)* such a member is jointly and severally liable for VAT due from the representative member (*Re Nadler Enterprises Ltd*, Ch D [1980] STC 457 (TVC 32.10)). See **27 GROUPS OF COMPANIES**.

Where the representative member of a group becomes insolvent, HMRC regard the group treatment as ceasing to have effect from the relevant date. All the members of the group are automatically deregistered and each solvent member which continues to trade is automatically re-registered. Any insolvent member can also apply to be re-registered provided the company continues to trade. Continuation of group treatment may be allowed on request, however, but this will require prompt action to avoid automatic deregistration.

If the representative member of a group remains solvent but another group member becomes insolvent, HMRC will not automatically exclude that member from the group.

Partnerships

[35.14] Where a partnership becomes insolvent, HMRC may pursue any of the partners for any liability due.

If all partners are insolvent

HMRC will lodge one claim with the office holder in the name of the partnership. This claim should stand in the joint estate and separate estates of all the insolvent partners. HMRC should therefore be included in any dividend declared in any of the insolvent estates.

If one or more partners remain solvent

Responsibility for rendering returns and paying VAT remains with the solvent partner(s). HMRC may lodge a claim with the office holder of the estate of the insolvent partner(s) for any debts accrued up to the date of insolvency. An office holder who has VAT to account for on the administration of the insolvent estate must not account for it on a solvent partner's return. HMRC will issue forms to the office holder on request so that the VAT can be accounted for direct to HMRC.

If a partnership is wound up but individual partners remain solvent

The office holder is treated as the taxable person with effect from the date of the winding up and will be responsible for rendering returns and paying any VAT due on returns for the period after the date of winding up. A claim will be lodged with the office holder in the name of the insolvent partnership for any liabilities due to HMRC up to the date of winding up.

Where insolvent partners have different relevant dates

HMRC will lodge individual claims in the individual estates of the partners calculated from their respective relevant dates.

(VAT Notice 700/56/11, paras 16.1–16.5).

Receivers appointed under the Law of Property Act 1925

[35.15] A receiver appointed under the *Law of Property Act* is unlikely to be allowed to register separately for VAT. This is because the receiver is appointed under a legal charge and is deemed to be the agent of the company. The trader/directors retain responsibility for their own VAT registration and all taxable supplies made by either the trader or the receiver must normally be accounted for on the trader's registration. See *Sargent v C & E Commrs*, CA [1995] STC 399 (TVC 37.11) where it was held that 'incapacitated' in *SI 1995/2518, Reg 9* should be construed as 'incapable of carrying on business'. This would only result from administrative receivership, liquidation or administration and not from the partial incapacity resulting from the appointment of a receiver of specific properties.

If a *Law of Property Act* receiver makes continuing supplies such as renting or leasing, then any VAT due should be accounted for through the trader's VAT account and the trader's VAT registration number should be used on any invoices issued. If the VAT-registered person does not agree to this, the receiver may account for output tax separately via a Form VAT 833.

If assets are sold, then the VAT due must be accounted for and paid to HMRC using Form VAT 833 (obtainable from the National Advice Service (tel: 0845 010 9000)). The trader's VAT registration number should be used on sales invoices or quoted on the Form VAT 833.

Law of Property Act receivers cannot make a separate claim for the input tax which should properly be claimed via the trader's VAT return.

(VAT Notice 700/56/11, paras 17.1, 17.2).

Bankrupt continuing to trade

[35.16] Where trading continues after bankruptcy, the bankrupt retains responsibility for the submission of VAT returns and payment of VAT covering post-bankruptcy periods. HMRC will establish the pre-bankruptcy position so that they can lodge a claim with, or make a repayment to, the office holder, or operate Crown set-off (see **35.7** above) as appropriate.

If the office holder has VAT to account for in respect of the period of office, he must not include this VAT on the business's post-bankruptcy returns. HMRC will issue forms on request so that VAT can be accounted for. Completed forms should be returned to the National Insolvency Unit.

(VAT Notice 700/56/11, paras 9.1, 9.2).

Key points

[35.17] Points to consider are as follows.

- A business that is unable to pay its VAT liabilities by the due date should consider contacting HMRC's Business Payment Support Service (BPSS) to negotiate payment of the liability over a longer period of time, perhaps a proposal to make three monthly instalments. However, the BPSS is intended to support a business with temporary cash-flow problems. It is not intended to provide long-term finance (through a deferral arrangement every VAT period) to a business with more fundamental cash problems.

- An example of a situation that would justify seeking assistance from the BPSS is if an important and usually reliable customer did not settle his account on the due date, i.e. leaving the business short of working capital. An important point is to always agree a time to pay arrangement with the BPSS before the tax is due for payment. This approach will avoid a default surcharge penalty or default surcharge liability notice being issued in relation to the VAT return in question.
- In cases where an insolvent business has deregistered, there is a facility for input tax to be claimed after the cancellation of the registration using form VAT426. There are various conditions that need to be met for a claim to be valid, the key one being that the cost must relate to the business that was VAT-registered. The majority of input tax claims made on form VAT426 relate to professional fees.

36

Insurance

De Voil Indirect Tax Service. See V4.121–V4.124.

Introduction

Characteristics of insurance

[36.1] There is no legal definition of insurance. In *Medical Defence Union Ltd v Department of Trade* [1979] 2 All ER 421 the judge held that there must be three specific elements present in any contract of insurance.

- The contract must provide that the insured will become entitled to money or money's worth on the occurrence of some event. The reference to 'money or money's worth' means that a claim can be settled through the provision of a service or replacement goods.
- The event must be one which involves some element of uncertainty. If the element of uncertainty is absent, any 'premiums' paid would more closely resemble contributions to a savings plan. (It could be argued that there is no uncertainty involved with life insurance. However, the timing of claims is the uncertain factor.)
- The insured must have an insurable interest in the subject matter of the contract. This means that if the insured risk occurs, the person who is insured stands to suffer some loss.

Generally, HMRC regard something as insurance for VAT purposes if it is an activity that requires the provider to be authorised as an insurer under the provisions of the *Financial Services and Markets Act 2000 (FSMA)*.

In addition to this, they accept that

- certain funeral plan contracts are insurance (and therefore exempt from VAT) even though they are not regulated as such under the *FSMA* insurance regulatory provisions (see **36.6**(3) below); and
- vehicle breakdown insurance is insurance even though providers are given a specific exclusion under the *FSMA* from the requirement to be authorised (see **36.6**(11) below).

The regulation of insurance

Financial services, including insurance, are regulated in the UK by the *Financial Services and Markets Act 2000.*

The provisions of the *FSMA* make it illegal for UK businesses to effect contracts of insurance without being authorised to do so (with the exception of certain bodies specifically granted exemption from the need for authorisation). The regulation of companies and unincorporated bodies under *FSMA, s 19* is carried out by the Financial Services Authority (FSA).

(VAT Notice 701/36/11, paras 2.2, 2.3).

Place of supply of insurance services

[36.2] Although no VAT is payable on insurance wherever it is supplied, the place of supply is important for VAT purposes because it determines whether or not VAT can be recovered on any costs incurred in making that supply.

From 1 January 2010

With effect from 1 January 2010, the supply of insurance services falls within the general rule for the place of supply of services, unless they are supplied to a recipient who is not a 'relevant business person' (see **65.15 SUPPLY: PLACE OF SUPPLY**), and belongs in a country which is not a Member State (other than the Isle of Man). In such a case, the place of supply is where the recipient belongs.

[*VATA 1994, Sch 4A para 16; FA 2009, Sch 36 para 11*].

Before 1 January 2010

Special place of supply rules apply to services falling within *VATA 1994, Sch 5 paras 1–8*. These include insurance services (*Sch 5 para 5*) and services rendered by one person to another in procuring such services for the other (*Sch 5 para 8*).

The place of supply of such services is treated as being

(a) where the *recipient* belongs if the recipient
  - belongs in a country, other than the Isle of Man, which is not an EU country; or

- belongs in an EU country other than that of the supplier and the insurance services are supplied to the recipient for business purposes; and

(b) where the *supplier* belongs in all other cases, i.e. where the recipient
- belongs in the UK or Isle of Man; or
- belongs in an EU country but not in the same country as the supplier and receives the supply other than for business purposes.

[*VATA 1994, s 7(10)(11); SI 1992/3121, Art 16*].

See **65.14 SUPPLY: PLACE OF SUPPLY** for the place of belonging and **17.2 EUROPEAN UNION: GENERAL** for the countries comprising the EU.

The place of supply rules for insurance above, also apply to reinsurance. Supplies of reinsurance are made to the principal insurer and not to the parties insured under the policy. The VAT treatment of a supply of reinsurance, therefore, is determined by the place of belonging of the insurer to whom the reinsurance is supplied.

Multiple insured parties

Some policies name more than one party as being insured under the contract. The customer's place of belonging in such instances should be determined by reference to the principal insured. Where there is no one principal insured and insured parties are based both inside and outside the EU, the supply of insurance should be treated as being received where the majority of the insured parties belong or, where applicable, where the party belongs that has been most directly involved in entering into the contract and/or stands to be the main beneficiary.

(VAT Notice 701/36/11, paras 6.1, 6.3, 6.4).

Input tax recovery in respect of insurance services

[36.3] Subject to the normal rules, input tax may be recovered which relates to

(a) taxable supplies of insurance services (i.e. supplies with a place of supply in the UK other than exempt supplies);

(b) supplies of insurance services with a place of supply outside the UK which would be taxable if made in the UK; and

(c) supplies of insurance services which
- (i) are supplied to a person who belongs outside the EU; or
- (ii) are directly linked to the export of goods to a place outside the EU; or
- (iii) consist of the provision of intermediary services in relation to any transaction within (i) or (ii) above

where that supply is exempt or would have been exempt if made in the UK.

See **65.14 SUPPLY: PLACE OF SUPPLY** for the place of belonging and **17.2 EUROPEAN COMMUNITY: GENERAL** for the countries comprising the EU.

Apart from the special cases in (*c*) above, input tax which relates to exempt supplies of insurance services cannot be recovered.

[*VATA 1994, s 26(1)(2); SI 1992/3123; SI 1999/3121*].

HMRC regard the entitlement to input tax under (*c*)(ii) above as only applying where

- the goods are being exported by the recipient of the insurance;
- the insurance is directly linked to the specific goods being exported; and
- the insurance covers the risks of the person who owns the goods or is responsible for their export.

(VAT Notice 701/36/11, para 6.6).

Supplies of insurance and reinsurance

[36.4] For EU legislation see **18.26**(*a*) **EUROPEAN UNION LEGISLATION**.

Exemption applies to all insurance and reinsurance transactions [*VATA 1994, Sch 9 Group 2, Item 1; SI 2004/3083*] and no longer depends upon the status of the provider.

This change in the legislation follows the decision in *Card Protection Plan Ltd v C & E Commrs, ECJ Case C–349/96,* [1999] STC 270 (TVC 22.324) where the ECJ held that under EU law the UK could not restrict the scope of exemption for insurance transactions exclusively to supplies by insurers who were permitted by national law to pursue the activity of an insurer. The House of Lords subsequently held that, in the light of the ECJ ruling, the company was making exempt supplies of insurance (HL [2001] STC 174 (TVC 38.44)).

Although this means that insurance supplied by an unauthorised insurer is exempt from VAT, such a business could be liable to prosecution under the *Financial Services and Markets Act 2000* and HMRC may refer cases that come to their attention to the Financial Services Authority. Businesses are therefore advised to clarify their regulatory position with the Financial Services Authority (Authorisation Enquiries Department, 25 The North Colonnade, Canary Wharf, London E14 5HS: tel 020 7676 1000).

As a result of the UK legislation, the place of supply rules in **36.2** above, and the input tax recovery rules in **36.3** above, the VAT position of insurance and reinsurance in the UK can be summarised as follows.

	Insured belonging in			
	UK	*EU (non-business)*	*EU (business)*	*Non-EU*
Insurance directly related to the export of goods to a place outside the EU	E(R)	E(R)	OS(R)	OS(R)

	Insured belonging in			
	UK	*EU (non-business)*	*EU (business)*	*Non-EU*
All other classes of insurance	E	E	OS	OS(R))

Key

E = Exempt (no input tax recovery)

E(R) = Exempt but with refund of related input tax

OS = Outside the scope of UK VAT with no refund of related input tax

OS(R)= Outside the scope of UK VAT with refund of related input tax

(VAT Notice 701/36/11, para 6.6).

In *Winterthur Life UK Ltd* (VTD 14935) (TVC 38.10) the operation of personal pension schemes by a group of companies was held to be an exempt supply of insurance services. On the facts, the services were not simply trust administration but embodied insurance contracts and were 'part and parcel' of the provision of insurance.

Reinsurance

[36.5] Reinsurance contracts are those under which an original insurer is indemnified by a reinsurer for a risk undertaken by the original insurer. (VAT Notice 701/36/11, para 2.2). Unless specifically stated otherwise, references to insurance in this chapter are to be taken to include reinsurance.

Particular supplies of insurance

[36.6] Particular supplies of insurance are as follows:

(1) Block insurance policies

The key characteristics of a block policy are that

- there is a contract between the block policyholder and the insurer which allows the block policyholder to effect insurance cover subject to certain conditions;
- the block policyholder, acting in its own name, procures insurance cover for third parties from the insurer;
- there is a contractual relationship between the block policyholder and third parties under which the insurance is procured; and
- the block policyholder stands in place of the insurer in effecting the supply of insurance to the third parties.

Following the decision in *Card Protection Plan Ltd v C & E Commrs, ECJ Case C–349/96*, [1999] STC 270 (TVC 22.324) HMRC regard supplies made by block policyholders as being insurance transactions for the purposes of the VAT exemption, even though they would not be seen as insurance for regulatory purposes. This means that block policyholders are acting as principals when they are effecting insurance transactions rather than as intermediaries arranging supplies of insurance.

This type of policy is often taken out by a supplier of goods or services to cover a number of small transactions over a set period, e.g.

- a removal company may take out a block policy to provide its customers with insurance against the risk of damage to their belongings during the house move; or
- a pony club may arrange insurance under a block policy to provide its members with cover against the risk of injury or liability for another's injury whilst taking part in equestrian events.

Sometimes a block policy will cover the risks of the block policyholder as well as those of their customers (e.g. the removal company's policy may also cover its own risk of damaging its customers' property).

Block policyholders supply VAT-exempt insurance transactions as principals rather than insurance-related services as intermediaries. As a result, the whole consideration received by a block policyholder (i.e. in respect of own services and the purchase of the insurance cover for customers) is income of the business. This could have implications for the calculation of recoverable input tax under the partial exemption method used.

(VAT Notice 701/36/11, para 2.5).

(2) Supplies by Friendly Societies

Friendly Societies are organisations registered under the *Financial Services and Markets Act 2000*. Their main purpose is to provide insurance against distress in the event of accident, sickness, old age and widowhood. Their insurance capital is provided by subscriptions from members.

Where these subscriptions relate solely to the provision of insurance, they are exempt from VAT. If the subscription also covers other goods and services, the part of the subscription relating to those other supplies is not exempt as insurance but may qualify for VAT relief elsewhere (e.g. under the exemption which covers certain supplies relating to health and welfare).

(VAT Notice 701/36/11, para 3.2).

(3) Funeral plans

Some funeral plans are written under contracts of insurance, so that on death a life insurance policy pays out the cost of the funeral. These types of funeral plan are treated as insurance for VAT purposes, and therefore exempt, even though they are not regulated as such.

Where a funeral plan represents pre-payment for a funeral it will not be exempt as insurance but will probably be eligible for exemption as the provision of a funeral (see **15.6 DEATH AND INCAPACITY**).

Management charges for funeral plans which are not insurance and are not prepayments (for example, where the client's money is placed in a trust to be spent on a funeral on his death) are standard-rated.

(VAT Notice 701/36/11, para 3.5).

(4) Guarantees and warranties

Retailers often sell guarantees and warranties with certain goods, such as domestic electrical equipment and cars.

Under a '*guarantee or warranty arrangement*', the purchase price of the goods includes an amount in consideration of which the manufacturer or retailer undertakes to replace or repair defective goods within a specified period.

Under an '*extended warranty arrangement*' the provider enters into a distinct contract under which it undertakes, for a consideration, to be subject to the same (and possibly some additional) obligations as covered in the original warranty. The provider of an extended warranty could be the retailer or manufacturer of the goods (or possibly a company within the same group as either of them), or be an independent third party company completely unconnected to the original supply of the goods.

Guarantees and warranties that are written under contracts of insurance (that is, those which are recognised as insurance by the Financial Services Authority (FSA)) will, in principle, fall within the VAT exemption for insurance (but see **36.7** below for insurance supplied with other goods and services).

The supply of a non-insurance warranty by a UK business is standard-rated. Guarantees and warranties provided by the manufacturer or retailer of the goods are very unlikely to be seen as insurance by the FSA because

- when provided by the retailer, the guarantee or warranty is seen as an automatic (often statutory) consequence of the contract of sale, not the provision of insurance cover; and
- in the case of the manufacturer's warranty, the risk of product failure lies within the control of the manufacturer and contracts under which the occurrence of an uncertain event lie within the control of either the provider or the recipient are unlikely to be regarded as insurance.

Some extended warranties may not be seen as insurance by the FSA regardless of who provides them (e.g. because the provider undertakes to maintain or repair goods at least partly at the recipient's expense or because the contract contains both insurance and non-insurance elements, such as regular servicing, and on balance the provider's obligation is not seen as being one to insure).

Where a business takes out an insurance policy to protect against the risk of there being a shortfall in the fund used to pay for any repairs covered by a warranty, there is no contract of insurance between the insurer and the customer taking out the warranty. The supply of the insurance and the supply of the warranty are two separate supplies, one exempt and one taxable.

(VAT Notice 701/36/11, para 3.7).

(5) Insurance directly linked to exports of goods outside the EU

There is specific provision for input tax to be recovered if it is incurred in respect of supplies of insurance which are *directly linked* to exports of goods to a place outside the EU. See **36.3**(*c*) above.

(6) Marine Aviation and Transport (MAT) insurance

The classes of risk covered by MAT insurance are

- accident (in connection with MAT risks only);
- railway rolling stock;
- aircraft;
- ships;
- goods in transit;
- aircraft liability; and
- liability of ships

but not

- motor and land vehicles;
- oil and gas rigs permanently fixed to the sea bed;
- specific policies for ships laid-up or aircraft grounded;
- specific policies for ships and aircraft under repair; and
- port and airport owners and operators' liability and manufacturers' liability.

Due to the nature of MAT insurance, HMRC have agreed guidelines with trade representatives for determining and recording where MAT insurance is supplied for VAT purposes. The trade agreement, summarised below, only applies to supplies of MAT insurance, it does not extend to supplies of other types of insurance or to MAT reinsurance.

Coding MAT insurance

There are three codes that should be used to identify the VAT status of supplies of MAT insurance.

X	to indicate that the supply of insurance was not directly related to an export of goods from inside to outside the EU and was made to a customer belonging within the EU and therefore carries with it no entitlement to input tax recovery.
Z	to indicate that the insurance was supplied to a customer belonging outside the EU or directly related to an export of goods from inside to outside the EU and therefore carries with it an entitlement to input tax recovery.
M	only if the insurance does not directly relate to the export of goods from inside to outside the EU and the policy has no clear principal insured and at least one, but not all, of the insured parties belongs outside the EU. The M (mixed) code gives an entitlement to treat 50% of input tax incurred on related goods and services as recoverable and 50% as non-recoverable.

Determining the place of supply for MAT insurance

The following rules should be used to determine whether the X or the Z code is appropriate, based on the location of the insured party/ies.

(a) *Single insured*. The insurer's address shown on the broker's slip (or equivalent document) is to be taken as the place of belonging of the insured. If no address is shown, the address should be determined by asking the broker or other intermediary who arranged the supply.

Where the insured has more than one address, the address on the slip or equivalent document should be used unless it is clear that this is simply an administrative address for payment or other purposes.

(b) *Multiple insureds*. Certain types of insurance (e.g. hull) often have multiple insureds identified on the slip, including the owner, managers, operators, the manning or crew agents, time charterers and mortgagors. Where possible, the principal insured should be identified and their place of belonging used to decide the VAT code as with a single assured under (*a*) above. The principal insured may be the only named insured (as distinct from others shown as additional insured) or may be the first-named on the policy. Where the principal insured cannot be identified, the places of belonging of all the insureds should be ascertained (if practicable) and the business coded according to whether the insured parties are all based in the EU, or all outside the EU or some inside and some outside.

(c) *Unidentified insured(s)*. Where the place(s) of belonging of the insured(s) cannot otherwise be determined, VAT coding should be decided by reference to

- the country of origin of the business;
- the address of the originating broker/cover holder;
- the address of the overseas agent (where applicable) and
- any additional information on the slip.

In the case of conflict between indicators, best judgement should be used.

Where it is not possible to determine whether the X or Z code is appropriate using the above guidelines, then specific transactions may be coded M. The M code should only be used as a last resort where it is not possible to determine the place of belonging of the insured party or where an insurance contract provides cover for insured parties belonging both inside the EU and outside the EU and it is not possible to identify the principal insured party.

(VAT Notice 701/36/11, para 6.7; VAT Notice 700/57/04).

Also see VAT Notice 700/57/04 for details of an arrangement allowed to MAT insurance underwriters who are members of a particular trade association in respect of claims-related input tax and associated imported services.

(7) Supplies by Medical and Welfare funds

Subscriptions to such funds which, although not friendly societies, provide *specified* benefits in the event of illness, accident, etc. are exempt from VAT as insurance.

Where the benefits are *not specified* and the amounts paid out are at the discretion of persons controlling the fund, the subscriptions may qualify as donations and be outside the scope of VAT.

(VAT Notice 701/36/11, para 3.3).

(8) Protection and indemnity (P & I) clubs

A P & I club is normally a mutual association of ship owners established to insure its members and specialising mainly in third party liability cover and insurance of the balance of collision risks not covered by the company or London market. P & I clubs are non-profit making and operate on a system of payments (usually based on the previous year's costs) with supplementary payments (termed 'calls') to settle claims and rebates to balance underwriting years. The club is deemed to be making a supply of insurance, the liabilities of which are determined as in the table in **36.4** above.

(VAT Notice 701/36/11, para 3.4).

(9) Run-off business

Where an insurer has ceased to underwrite insurance (or a particular class) but a liability remains to deal with claims under contracts already underwritten, such contracts are said to be 'running-off'. Any additional premiums receivable under existing contracts follow the liability of the original supply of insurance.

An insurer will often appoint third parties to administer the run-off of contracts on their behalf. Where a third party takes over responsibility for an insurer's run-off business, (including handling and settling claims and dealing with premium adjustments), the services supplied are not exempt as insurance transactions (i.e. as supplies of insurance). This is because the third party does not have a contractual relationship with the insured party and is not taking on the risk attached to the insurance which remains with the original insurer. It is possible, however, that some or all of the run-off services supplied by the third party will qualify for exemption as insurance-related services (see **36.15** below).

(VAT Notice 701/36/11, para 3.8).

(10) Sale of part paid endowment policies

The sale of part-paid endowment policies is not exempt under the insurance exemption because the risk covered by the underlying insurance remains that of the original policyholder. There is, however, a financial transaction taking place and the consideration received is exempt as finance.

(VAT Notice 701/36/11, para 3.9).

(11) Vehicle breakdown services

Subscriptions to motoring organisations usually include an element for assistance in the event of a breakdown provided under a contract of insurance. With this kind of insurance the benefits to the insured party (the member) are given in kind rather than in monetary form (that is, roadside repairs and recovery services).

Where vehicle breakdown insurance is provided as an independent supply, the element of the subscription that is attributable to it will be exempt from VAT. See **36.7** below for information on the VAT treatment of goods and/or services supplied together.

(VAT Notice 701/36/11, para 3.6).

Insurance supplied with other goods or services

[36.7] Where exempt insurance is supplied with goods or services that are liable to VAT, it is necessary to determine the correct VAT treatment of the supplies. See **64.6 SUPPLY: GENERAL** for the tests laid down in *Card Protection Plan Ltd v C & E Commrs, ECJ Case C–349/96,* [1999] STC 270 (TVC 22.324). These involve:

(1) Identifying the essential features of a transaction to determine what the customer is actually receiving (i.e. is the customer receiving two or more supplies each distinct and independent from the other or is the customer receiving one supply made up of a number of component parts).

(2) If (1) above does not identify separate supplies, it is necessary to consider whether any of the parts can properly be regarded as a principal supply to which the other goods or services are ancillary (i.e. they do not constitute an aim in themselves but rather a means of better enjoying the principal supply).

Applying these tests to

- where there are two or more distinct supplies each independent of the other, the part of the consideration received which relates to insurance is exempt from VAT and the rest of the consideration is liable to VAT at the appropriate rate; and
- where there is one principal supply to which the other goods or services are ancillary, the whole transaction will take the VAT treatment of the principal supply. As a result,
  - (i) where the insurance is the principal supply, the whole consideration received for both the insurance and the taxable goods or services is VAT-exempt; and
  - (ii) where the insurance is ancillary to a supply of taxable goods or services, the whole consideration received is liable to VAT at the appropriate rate.

Each case has to be considered on its own merit but factors that could indicate separate rather than composite supplies include

- whether the customers can choose to have the goods or services without the insurance and (where appropriate) vice versa;
- whether both the insurance and the goods or services have their own price and this is reflected in the amount customers pay should they choose to have one without the other (i.e. the overall amount customers pay is reduced by the cost of the insurance should they decide to buy your goods or services without insurance); and
- whether customers are fully aware they are receiving more that one supply, as evidenced by the invoicing and contractual arrangements in place.

(VAT Notice 701/36/11, paras 4.1–4.3).

In *Peugeot Motor Co plc and Another v C & E Commrs*, Ch D [2003] STC 1438 (TVC 38.51), the appellants sold cars to the public (end-users) either through dealers within the same VAT group (direct sales) or through independent franchised dealers or finance houses (indirect sales). In both categories, the appellants used various promotion schemes in which the end-user received motor insurance from an insurance company for no additional payment, the insurance company being paid by the appellants. The court held that the appellants made an insurance-related supply in respect of both direct and indirect sales but that, first, this formed part of a single supply with the motor car and, secondly, the insurance element of the supply was ancillary to the supply of the car. The full price paid for the car by the end-user (in the case of direct sales) or by the independent dealer or finance house (in the case of indirect sales) was taxable at the standard rate.

See also *Ford Motor Co Ltd v HMRC*, CA [2007] EWCA Civ 1730 (TVC 38.29).

Add-on services

[36.8] Add-on services are additional services supplied as part of a package with the main supply of insurance (e.g. helplines). They may be supplied under the contract of insurance itself or under a separate contract. They may also be provided by

- companies (which may or may not be insurers) other than the insurance company or companies underwriting a particular contract of insurance; or
- one or more of the underwriting insurers themselves.

The VAT treatment of these services depends upon the contractual arrangements in place between the parties and the nature of the services being supplied.

Add-on services supplied by third party to insurers

Where the add-on service being supplied to an insurer for incorporation into an insurance contract is

- itself insurance provided by one insurer (the 'add-on insurer') to another insurer (the 'direct insurer') who has a contract with a policyholder, the premium received by the add-on insurer from the direct insurer is exempt from VAT; and
- not insurance, and the service does not fall within another exemption or zero rate, VAT is chargeable on the supply by the third party to the insurer.

Some add-on services may qualify for VAT exemption as insurance-related services.

Add-on services supplied to policyholders

Where the add-on service is insurance, the entire supply is exempt. Each insurer is treated as making an exempt supply, the value of which is the part of the premium they have underwritten.

Where the add-on service is not insurance but is supplied by the insurer under the same contract as the insurance, there may be a liability to VAT on the consideration received by the insurer in respect of the add-on service. This depends on the liability of the add-on service and the nature of the package being supplied by the insurer (see **36.7** above).

Where the add-on service is not insurance and is supplied under a separate contract from that under which the insurance is supplied, there may be a liability to VAT on the consideration received in respect of the add-on service. In this instance, the add-on service is less likely to be ancillary to the supply of insurance and more likely to be a separate supply in its own right, but consideration should still be given to the guidance on single and composite supplies in **36.7** above.

(VAT Notice 701/36/11, para 4.4).

Engineering insurance and inspection services

[36.9] Engineering insurance provides cover for large items of capital plant, machinery or structures on land such as industrial boilers, cranes and lifts. It is intended to protect the insured against the risk of the plant or equipment going wrong.

Insurers providing such insurance may also contract with customers to provide inspection services in connection with the insurance, perhaps to identify ways to reduce cover or prevent the need for a claim. Inspection services supplied on their own are subject to VAT at the standard rate. Therefore, an insurer supplying inspection services with insurance will need to determine the correct VAT treatment for its supplies under the rules in **36.7** above.

(VAT Notice 701/36/11, para 4.5).

Insurance claims

[36.10] Establishing who is receiving supplies made in connection with, or in settlement of, insurance claims is important because this will determine who could have the right to recover any VAT charged on those supplies as input tax.

Supplies made to the insured party

Where supplies of claims-related goods or services are made to the insured party and the claim relates to their VAT-registered business, any VAT incurred on those supplies may be deducted as input tax subject to normal rules. Where the insured party can recover the VAT from HMRC, the insurer need normally only pay the net amount due (less any excess payable by the insured party) under the insurance claim.

Supplies made to the insurer

Where supplies of claims-related goods and services are made to the insurer, the amount of VAT recoverable depends on the insurer's partial exemption method.

Where an insurer incurs costs in respect of an individual claim (e.g. legal costs where the insurer is in dispute with the policyholder), any VAT on those costs is directly attributable to the associated supply of insurance and the recoverability of any VAT charged will depend upon whether or not the relevant supply of insurance gives a right to input tax deduction (see **36.3** above). See also *C & E Commrs v Deutsche Ruck Reinsurance Co Ltd*, QB 1994, [1995] STC 495 (TVC 46.5).

Goods supplied to the insurer for transfer to the insured party

The insurer may choose to recover the VAT charged on the goods as input tax and account for output tax on the cost price when the goods are handed over. Alternatively, the insurer may refrain from claiming the VAT charged and, therefore, not be liable to account for output tax when the goods are transferred to the insured party.

Legal costs

Where an insurer obtains legal services in connection with, for example, policy interpretation or in relation to a dispute with a policyholder, the supply of the legal services is to the insurer. In the case of subrogated claims (i.e. claims where the insurer exercises its right to pursue or defend a claim against a third party in the name of the insured party) supplies of legal services in connection with those claims are made to the insured party and not to the insurer.

Loss adjusters, etc.

Loss adjusters are normally contracted to act on behalf of the insurer and the supply of their services is therefore made to the insurer rather than the insured party. Loss assessors, on the other hand, are normally appointed by, and act in the interest of, the insured party and the supply of their services is therefore made to the insured party rather than to the insurer.

Indemnification by way of replacement goods or services

Where settlement of a claim is made by way of replacement goods or services, the supply position depends upon the terms of the contractual arrangements between the parties concerned. The supply of these replacement goods or services by a third party supplier is normally seen as being made to the insured party, although in some instances, the facts, including the terms of the insurance contract, may mean that the supply is made to the insurer.

Financial indemnification

If an insurer settles an insurance claim by paying money by way of financial indemnification to the insured party, there is no supply for VAT purposes. The money paid by the insurer in settlement of the claim is outside the scope of VAT.

(VAT Notice 701/36/11, paras 5.1–5.5).

Surrender of goods following an insurance claim

[36.11] The disposal of

- works of art, antiques and collectors' items (see **73.3 WORKS OF ART, ETC.**), and
- second-hand goods (i.e. tangible movable property that is suitable for further use either as it is or after repair)

by an insurer who has taken possession of them in settlement of a claim under an insurance policy (e.g. salvaged goods damaged by fire or water or stolen goods recovered after a claim has been paid) is outside the scope of VAT provided the following conditions are met.

- The goods are in the same condition at the time of disposal as when they were taken into the insurer's possession. The condition of goods has been changed if any improvements, repairs, replacement parts or the generally making good of any damage has been carried out. The cleaning of goods generally does not affect the condition nor does the inclusion of instruction manuals if they are otherwise missing. (Business Brief 19/01).
- For goods other than motor cars
  - (a) if the goods had been supplied in the UK by the policyholder, that supply would not have been chargeable with VAT or would have been chargeable on less than full value;
  - (b) if the goods have been imported into the UK, they must have borne VAT which has neither been reclaimed nor refunded; and
  - (c) the goods must not have been reimported having previously been exported from the UK free of VAT by reason of zero-rating.
- In the case of motor cars, the VAT on any previous supply, acquisition or importation must have been wholly excluded from credit.

[*SI 1992/3122, Arts 2, 4; SI 1995/1268, Arts 2, 4; SI 1995/1269; SI 1995/1385; SI 1995/1667; SI 1999/3118; SI 1999/3120; SI 2001/3649, Art 432; SI 2004/3084; SI 2004/3085*].

Where the above conditions are not satisfied, VAT is chargeable on the full amount realised on the sale (not the original cost of the asset, see *Darlington Finance Ltd* (VTD 1337) (TVC 44.80)).

The insurer will therefore need to know the VAT status of the policyholder and be able to cross reference this information to the disposal of each item in order to decide whether VAT must be accounted for.

Motor vehicles received by an insurer as scrap metal are treated as tangible movable property rather than motor cars. Insurers are not required to account for VAT on the disposal of the scrap unless the policyholder would have charged VAT.

(VAT Notice 701/36/11, para 5.6).

Accounting for VAT on insurance transactions

Recovery of input tax

[36.12] See **36.3** above for the rules on input tax recovery. Where input tax is recoverable relating to insurance within **36.3**(*c*)(i) or (ii), HMRC will expect to see appropriate documentation in support of the claim, such as

- policy documents;
- cover notes;
- credit/debit notes;
- broker's slips; and
- any relevant correspondence.

Recovery of input tax incurred on supplies made by overseas branches

UK insurers can recover VAT incurred in the UK in connection with supplies made by overseas branches belonging outside the EU. As insurance companies may have difficulty identifying this input tax, HMRC have agreed with the Association of British Insurers (ABI) methods by which the amount of recoverable input tax can be arrived at. See VAT Notice 700/57/04.

Contact and representative offices of overseas insurers

Such offices are established for public relations purposes generally. They are not permitted to accept insurance business in the UK and do not normally make supplies in the UK.

A contact office can apply for voluntary registration in the UK if it incurs input tax in connection with supplies of insurance made outside the EU by the overseas insurer. Input tax reclaimed should be based on the proportion of supplies made by the overseas supplier as a result of contacts made by the contact office. It can only recover input tax on supplies on which VAT would have been recoverable had they been supplied in the UK.

Where the overseas insurer is unable to provide a breakdown of actual supplies made to policyholders, the notional liability of its supplies can be determined as follows.

- If the head office/branch is in the EU, it is treated as if it makes all supplies within the EU with no entitlement to recovery of related input tax.
- If the head office/branch is outside the EU, it is treated as if it makes all its supplies outside the EU with entitlement to recovery of input tax.
- If some establishments to which the contact office supplies services are inside, and some outside, the EU, the proportion of its input tax which may be reclaimed can be arrived at using the ratio of the number of non-EU establishments to the total number of establishments.

The contact office may apply for an alternative method. The agreement referred to above for recovery of input tax incurred in connection with supplies made by overseas branches also applies to overseas insurers with branches in the UK.

Tax point (time of supply)

Although, as a general rule, supplies of insurance are exempt, the time of supply may be important for partial exemption purposes, e.g. to determine the recoverable proportion of non-attributable output tax where an outputs-based method is used.

The tax points for supplies of insurance covering one-off (short-term) risks are

- basic tax point – this occurs on completion of cover (i.e. when the insurance contract is finalised and signed); and
- actual tax point — this may arise when some or all of the premium is received in advance of the basic tax point.

Renewable policies covering long-term risks will normally represent continuous supplies of services, in which case the only tax point is the date of receipt of the premium.

Value of supplies

The value of supplies of insurance is the total gross premiums due under the contract without deducting any commission due to brokers and agents.

Accounting for VAT on run-off business

Where an insurer has contracts in run-off (see **36.6**(9) above, and uses a partial exemption method based on the ratio of supplies which attract input tax recovery to total supplies, it should exclude return premiums from its calculations for run-off business only. This is to prevent the return premiums that are attributable to earlier VAT years/periods distorting the ratios of the current VAT year/period. Alternatively, to avoid complex calculations it may apply in writing to HMRC to use a method whereby a flat-rate recovery percentage is applied to its gross input tax based on the premium income for the last three years of active underwriting.

Accounting arrangements for the Lloyd's insurance market

HMRC have agreed special VAT accounting arrangements for the Lloyd's insurance market.

- *Syndicates with two or more members*. Where a syndicate has two or more members, it is the syndicate rather than the member that is registered for VAT as the taxable person for all syndicate transactions. Where there is a syndicate registration, a Lloyd's member, whether corporate or natural, can also have its own registration in relation to non-syndicate activities. Syndicate activities cannot, however, be dealt with through that registration.
- *Syndicates with only one member*. Where syndicate has only one member (which in practice only occurs with a corporate member) the syndicate cannot itself be registered. The corporate member must be registered and all syndicate business accounted for under its registration. Where the corporate member is covered by a group VAT registration, the group registration is used.
- *Managing agents*. Managing agents administer syndicates on behalf of members but are not themselves insurers. They may be VAT registered, and their supplies are those of an insurance agent (see **36.13** below). The VAT treatment follows that of the insurance underwritten by the syndicate or syndicates that they manage.

Each Lloyd's syndicate, member or managing agent that registers for VAT and makes taxable and/or specified supplies in addition to exempt supplies, must agree a special partial exemption method with HMRC.

(VAT Notice 701/36/11, paras 7.1–7.7).

Intermediary services

[36.13] Note: In *Staatssecretaris van Financiën v Arthur Andersen & Co, ECJ Case C–472/03*, [2005] STC 508 (TVC 22.327) (a Netherlands case) the ECJ held that what is now *Directive 2006/112/EC, Art 135(1)(a)* (previously *EC Sixth Directive Art 13B(a)*) must be interpreted as meaning that 'back office' activities, consisting in rendering services, for payment, to an insurance company do not constitute the performance of services relating to insurance transactions carried out by an insurance broker or an insurance agent within the meaning of that provision and do not qualify for exemption. The activities carried out by Andersen Consulting Management Consultants (ACMC) included the issuing, management and cancellation of policies, the management of claims and, in most cases, taking decisions that bound the insurer to enter into insurance contracts. To qualify for exemption, ACMC had to qualify as either insurance brokers or insurance agents. The ECJ held that the essential characteristic of insurance brokers was that they had complete freedom as to choice of insurer for their clients and that, although insurance agents were tied to a particular insurer, their essential characteristic was that they introduced prospective customers to that insurer. As ACMC did not qualify on either count, its services were taxable at the standard rate. The ECJ judgment is binding on the UK and the UK VAT exemption for insurance-related services is too wide and must be amended. However, as the VAT treatment of financial services and insurance is to be reviewed by the European Commission, the Government has decided to delay implementation of the ECJ judgment and will monitor the progress of the review in deciding when to make the necessary changes to UK law. Businesses affected may, however, apply the revised VAT liability to their services from a current date or make an adjustment retrospectively. (Business Brief 11/05; Business Brief 23/05).

Subject to the above and the exceptions in **36.14** below, the provision by an insurance broker or an insurance agent of any of the 'services of an insurance intermediary' is exempt from VAT where those services are

- related to an insurance transaction or a reinsurance transaction (before 1 January 2005, related to the provision of exempt insurance or reinsurance within **36.4** above) (whether or not a contract of insurance or reinsurance is finally concluded); and
- provided by the broker or agent in the course of acting in an '*intermediary capacity*' i.e. acting as an intermediary (or one of the intermediaries) between a person providing insurance or reinsurance (before 1 January 2005 a person providing exempt insurance under **36.4** above) and a person who is seeking insurance or reinsurance or is an insured person.

'*Services of an insurance intermediary*' consist of any of the following.

(a) Bringing together, with a view to the insurance or reinsurance of risks, of persons seeking and persons providing insurance and reinsurance

It is sometimes difficult to distinguish between exempt introductory services under this heading and advertising services which are excluded from exemption (see **36.14**(*a*) below). In such cases, HMRC accept that there is a single exempt supply of insurance-related introductory services where

- the intermediary is targeting its own customer base;
- the intermediary is paid per successful take-up of an insurance policy; and
- the product or the insurer is endorsed by the intermediary.

> *Example*
>
> A finance company is an agent for an insurer providing loan protection insurance. It recommends this insurance to all its customers. Those customers that take out a policy when taking out a loan complete a proposal form included with the loan agreement papers and returning this to the finance company. The finance company forwards it to the insurer and receives commission.
>
> There is an argument that the finance company is providing an advertising service. However, as the finance company is targeting its own customers; is recommending the product; and is being paid per successful take up, the commission it receives is treated as consideration for an exempt supply of introductory insurance services.

(VAT Notice 701/36/11, para 8.3).

Note that in *JCM Beheer BV v Staatsseccretaris van Financiën, ECJ Case C–124/07* (April 2008 unreported) (TVC 22.328) the ECJ concluded that the fact that an insurance broker or agent did not have a direct relationship with the parties to the insurance or reinsurance contract in the conclusion of which he had been instrumental (but merely had an indirect relationship through the intermediary of another taxable person who was in a direct relationship and to whom the insurance broker or agent was contractually bound) did not prevent his services from being exempt from VAT.

In *The Governor & Company of the Bank of Ireland* (VTD 20824) (TVC 38.25) a bank formed a subsidiary company to provide insurance products to customers of the Post Office. The bank paid commission to the Post Office for introducing potential customers. The bank was not itself an authorised insurer, and referred the customers to an unrelated company (J), which in turn arranged for a panel of insurers to quote for the customers' business. It was accepted that the services which the bank provided to J qualified for exemption as the services of an insurance intermediary. However, these arrangements did not prove profitable for either the bank or the Post Office, and the bank decided to select a specific insurance company (N) as a 'primary insurer' with the opportunity to undercut any quotes provided by other members of the panel of insurers. N paid commission to the bank. The tribunal decided that the revised arrangements continued to qualify for exemption, holding that N was paying for the continued existence of the whole intermediary structure that was the panel, albeit in a refigured form. The bank was assisting in bringing about a contract of insurance. Its supplies to N were exempt services of an insurance intermediary.

In *InsuranceWide.com Services Ltd and Trader Media Group Ltd*, CA [2010] STC 1572 (TVC 38.23), it was held that certain supplies of insurance introductory services provided via the internet were exempt from VAT. Following that decision, HMRC accepted that insurance introductory services are exempt from VAT where the provider of such services ('the introducer') is doing much more than acting as a 'mere conduit' through which a potential customer is passed to an insurance provider. This can be demonstrated by all of the following four conditions being met.

- The introducer is engaged in the business of putting insurance companies in touch with potential clients or more generally acting as intermediary between the two parties (although this may not necessarily be their principal business activity).
- The introducer provides the means (that is, by way of an internet 'click through' or some other form of introduction) by which a person seeking insurance is introduced to a provider of insurance or to another intermediary in a chain leading to an insurance provider.
- That introduction takes place at the time a customer is seeking to enter into an insurance contract (although in some instances an insurance contract may not actually go on to be finally concluded).
- The introducer also plays a proactive part in putting in place the arrangements under which that introduction is effected. (HMRC Brief 31/10).

(b) Carrying out work preparatory to the conclusion of a contract of insurance or reinsurance

(c) Assistance in the administration and performance of such contracts, including claims handling

Assistance in the administration

HMRC regard assisting in the administration and performance of contracts as covering the services that insurance intermediaries perform in connection with the day-to-day administration of policies, e.g.

- maintaining up-to-date details of policyholders; and
- dealing with requests from policyholders for changes to cover.

UK courts have found that the definition of assisting in the administration and performance of contracts of insurance goes wider than the examples above and include the following.

- Pension review services carried out as a result of the Financial Services Authority inspired review of possible pension mis-selling (see *Century Life plc v C & E Commrs*, CA 2000, [2001] STC 38 (TVC 38.13)). Following that decision, HMRC accept that mis-selling review services carried out on behalf of insurers are exempt when the supplier is required to be involved in the decision-making process (i.e. assessing whether, and how much, loss has occurred and/or the amount and appropriate form of redress) and acts as an insurance intermediary, having contact with insured persons on behalf of insurers.

See also *Winterthur Life UK Ltd (No 3)* (VTD 17572) (TVC 38.14) where a company provided services to another company concerning the management of a self-administered personal pension scheme.

- Certain kinds of helpline services. See *C & V (Advice Line) Services Ltd* (VTD 17310) (TVC 38.17) where a company providing a telephone helpline service to an insurance company's customers was held to be acting as an insurance intermediary so that its supplies qualified for exemption.

  HMRC accept that where telephone helplines provide assistance to insured parties on matters such as variations of contract and the making of claims, these services are directly related to the supply of insurance and, where a third party supplies them to the insurer, their supplies will be exempt. Where such helpline services are only incidental to the supply of insurance (e.g. where a legal helpline gives advice to insured parties on legal matters generally but does not advise on matters specific to the contract of insurance itself, such as scope of cover or claims procedures) the supply to the insurer is taxable.

Claims handling

The term 'claims handling' is used to describe a number of services that may be provided by an intermediary following the making of a claim by a policyholder, including

- checking that documents are correctly completed;
- ensuring that the claim falls within the terms of a policy;
- processing the claim;
- ensuring that insurers are advised of their exposure;
- agreeing the validity and/or quantum of the claim and
- arranging for settlement to be made.

The supply of claims handling may also include a number of elements of an advisory, investigative, or administrative nature that would be subject to VAT if supplied in isolation. Where these elements form a minor and ancillary part of a single composite supply of claims handling, however, the entire supply will be exempt from VAT. See also **36.16** below for the VAT treatment of claims handling services supplied by loss adjusters and other experts in connection with the assessment of a claim.

(VAT Notice 701/36/11, paras 8.4, 8.5, 10.3, 10.4; Business Brief 3/01).

(d) The collection of premiums

An insurance intermediary may collect insurance premiums as part of another supply (e.g. exempt insurance introductory or administration services) but where a separate charge is made for these services, it will be exempt under this heading.

If the premium collection services are not supplied in connection with other insurance intermediary services, they may be liable to VAT (e.g. the services of a debt-collector collecting overdue premiums for an insurer).

Where an employer, who did not arrange the original insurance, allows an insurer to use its payroll system to collect premiums from its employees by deductions from their pay, the consideration received by the employer falls within the exemption for finance rather than insurance.

(VAT Notice 701/36/11, para 8.6).

[*VATA 1994, Sch 9 Group 2 Item 4, Notes (1), (2); FA 1997, s 38; SI 2001/3649, Art 347; SI 2004/3083*].

In *Re Försäkringsaktiebolaget Skandia, ECJ Case C–240/99*, [2001] STC 754 (TVC 22.325) (a Swedish case) an insurance company (S) undertook to run the insurance business of one of its subsidiary companies including the sale of insurance and the settlement of claims. The ECJ held that the undertaking did not qualify as an 'insurance transaction' so that the supply was one of management services on which VAT was chargeable. The decision was reached on the basis that the third party service provider did not have any relationship with the insured. The Court did not examine whether the services could have been exempt 'insurance-related services', because the terms of Skandia's licence under Swedish insurance regulations prevented it from acting as an agent or broker. As a result, the decision is expected to have limited impact in the UK, where services provided to an insurer on an outsourced basis would normally fall within the 'insurance-related services' definition.

Brokers and agents

For VAT purposes, brokers and agents are defined in terms of what they do rather than what they are and, as well as insurance brokers and agents by profession, it can apply to other intermediaries making supplies of 'related services'. (VAT Notice 701/36/11, para 9.1).

Members' agents for Lloyd's underwriters

In *SOC Private Capital Ltd* (VTD 17747) (TVC 38.15) the tribunal held that supplies of insurance were made by underwriting members (rather than the syndicates) and therefore a company acting as a members' agent for Lloyds' underwriters was an insurance agent within *VATA 1994, Sch 9 Group 2 Item 4* above and its supplies qualified for exemption.

Supplies not regarded as services of an insurance intermediary

[36.14] Supplies of the following services are specifically excluded from exemption under **36.17** above.

(a) Market research, product design, advertising, promotional or similar services (or the collection, collation and provision of information for use in connection with such activities).

(b) Valuation or inspection services. See also **36.9** above for inspection services and engineering insurance.

(c) Services by loss adjusters, average adjusters, motor assessors, surveyors or other experts unless
   (i) the services consist of claims handling under a contract of insurance or reinsurance; and
   (ii) the person handling the claim is authorised to act on behalf of the insurer or reinsurer and has written authority to accept or reject the claim, and to settle any amount agreed to be paid.

   See also **36.16** below.

(d) Services supplied in pursuance of a contract of insurance or reinsurance (or any arrangements in connection with such a contract) either instead of any financial indemnity which the insurer is contractually obliged to provide or for the purpose of satisfying any claim under that contract (in whole or part). This applies, for example, where a plumber's services are supplied free of charge to the insured to mend a burst pipe and the insurer meets the plumber's fee. The fee is excluded from exemption. (VAT Notice 701/36/11, para 8.2).

[*VATA 1994, Sch 9 Group 2 Notes (7)–(10); FA 1997, s 38*].

Where one of the above excluded supplies is provided as a minor and ancillary part of a single composite supply of exempt insurance-related services provided in an intermediary capacity, the entire supply is treated as exempt. (VAT Notice 701/36/11, para 8.2). See also **23.30 FINANCIAL SERVICES** for mixed supplies of advice and financial services by a financial adviser. These provisions equally apply to mixed supplies of advice and insurance-related intermediary services.

Particular supplies of insurance-related services

[36.15] See the Note at **36.13** above.

(1) Broker-managed funds offered by life assurance companies

Life assurance backed broker-managed funds are provided under contracts between the life company which operates the fund, the policyholder and the broker who arranges the policy (usually referred to as the 'Broker Fund Adviser'). The Broker Fund Adviser, with authorisation from the policy holder/investor, provides investment advice to the life assurance company, recommending the switching of money invested between the various funds operated by the assurance company or, where permitted, directly into other forms of investment (e.g. shares or gilts).

Commission paid to the Broker Fund Adviser for arranging the life insurance policy is exempt under **36.13** above. Any other fees for services (including investment advisory services and any 'performance fee' based on the increased value of investments) are standard-rated.

(VAT Notice 701/36/11, para 10.7).

(2) Internet services

There are any number of ways in which the internet can be used in connection with insurance and the liability of supplies of internet services to insurers (or possibly to insured or prospective insured parties) needs to be considered on the supplies' own merits using the guidance laid out in **36.13** above. Factors indicating that a supply of Internet services is exempt as a supply of insurance-related services include:

- acting between insurers and insured (or prospective insured) parties;
- requirement for some specific insurance input rather than just pure facilitation; and
- direct connection to contracts of insurance either by bringing them about initially, or administering them, or handling claims made under them.

(VAT Notice 701/36/11, para 10.5).

See also *InsuranceWide.com Services Ltd* and *Trader Media Group Ltd* CA [2010] STC 1572 (TVC 38.23), in which it was held that internet introductory services to insurers or brokers qualified as exempt intermediary services.

(3) Protection and Indemnity (P & I) Club managers and agents

See **36.6**(8) above for what is meant by a P & I Club.

P & I Club managers are required to be separately VAT-registered from the clubs they manage. Services which they carry out include the day-to-day running of the club, employing staff, and assessing the level and weighting of contributions. They may also supply premises and facilities. If P & I Club managers are empowered to accept risks on behalf of the club, HMRC accept that they are intermediaries making supplies of related services that are exempt from VAT when supplied in the UK.

A P & I Club agent acts for a P & I Club manager when the manager has no presence in the UK. They make supplies of management services to the manager that would be taxable if supplied in the UK. These services are usually the kind of intangible services that are supplied where the recipient of the supply belongs. Where these services are supplied to P & I Club managers belonging outside the UK, therefore, they are outside the scope of VAT with input tax recovery. Management services that do not qualify as intangible services, however, will be liable to UK VAT regardless of where the recipient belongs.

(VAT Notice 701/36/11, para 10.2).

(4) Run-off services

See **36.6**(9) above for run-off business generally. An insurer will often appoint a third party to administer the run-off of insurance contracts on its behalf. The sort of services supplied could include

- responsibility for accountancy and legal work in connection with the business in run-off;
- services of handling and settling claims; and

- dealing with additional or return premium adjustments.

A composite supply of such run-off services falls within the VAT exemption as insurance-related services. Separate supplies of administrative services (such as accountancy, supplies of staff and management of invested premiums) do not qualify for exemption and are liable to VAT when supplied in the UK.

(VAT Notice 701/36/11, para 10.6).

(5) Telephone sales services

In *Teletech UK Ltd* (VTD 18080) (TVC 38.16) the company acted on behalf of an insurance company, cold-selling health insurance policies by telephone using contact lists provided by the insurer. The tribunal held that the company's services were exempt on the grounds that it was selling (or trying to sell) insurance policies as agents. The decisive factor was that, where calls led to sales, the company was able to put the insurer on risk and the customer on cover. The Tribunal Chairman also observed that the manner of remuneration, i.e. whether by flat fee (as in this case) or commission, had no bearing on the VAT treatment.

As a result of this decision, HMRC now accept that supplies of telephone sales services to insurers are exempt when the call centre is able to put the insurer 'on risk' and the customer 'on cover' at the point of sale. This applies regardless of whether the call centre provider is remunerated by way of commission or flat-rate fee.

(VAT Notice 701/36/11, para 10.4; Business Brief 7/03).

Loss adjusters and similar 'experts'

[36.16] See the Note at **36.13** above.

Services of loss adjusters, average adjusters, motor assessors, surveyors or 'other experts' (e.g. assessing damage or investigating potential fraud) are normally standard-rated. If they also provide insurance claims handling services, however, their services will be exempt when acting as the agent of the insurer when supplying those services. But services qualify for exemption where all of the following conditions are met.

- The services consist in the handling of a claim under a contract of insurance or reinsurance;
- The person handling the claim is authorised when doing so to act on behalf of the insurer or reinsurer.
- That person holds the insurer's written authority (see below) to determine whether to accept or reject a claim.
- Where the claim is accepted in whole or in part, that person has the insurer's written authority to settle the amount to be paid on the claim.

[*VATA 1994, Sch 9 Group 2 Note (9); FA 1997, s 38*].

'*Other experts*' means anybody who is contracted by insurers to assess or value insurance claims because of their expertise in a particular field and could include

- solicitors assessing loss in personal injury claims cases;
- jewellers valuing items of stolen jewellery; or
- antiques experts assessing damage to antique furniture.

The term 'other expert' does not apply to specialist claims handling organisations. Where an insurer contracts a supply of claims handling services from a business, not because of that business's expertise in a particular field, but because of its expertise in claims handling generally, the services of the business are exempt under **36.13**(c) above and the above provisions do not apply.

Insurer's written authority

If an insurer gives written authority to another person (such as a broker) who in turn issues written authority to a loss adjuster, the loss adjuster's services will still be exempt provided that the original authority from the insurer gave the original recipient power to delegate the authority in this way.

The written authority must allow the loss adjuster, etc. to investigate claims, perform any service necessary for the claim to be settled and agree the amount of a claim or cost of repairs or replacement without reference to the insurer. The authority may also include avoiding or repudiating claims. In all circumstances it must bind the insurance company to pay the amount of a claim or meet the cost of repair or replacement as determined by the loss adjuster.

Claims handling supplied with valuation/assessment services

Where a loss adjuster, etc. supplies exempt claims handling services with taxable claims valuation and/or assessment services, the VAT treatment of the services depends upon whether they are provided as two separate supplies or as one composite supply with the claims handling services ancillary to the taxable services or vice versa. Where taxable valuation and/or assessment services are ancillary to a principal supply of claims handling, the whole supply is exempt from VAT.

(VAT Notice 701/36/11, para 9.3).

Insurance-related services supplied with other goods or services

[36.17] See the Note at **36.13** above.

Insurance is frequently arranged by businesses in connection with other services or goods they are supplying as their main business activity, e.g.

- mechanical breakdown insurance (MBI) with cars and domestic appliances;
- travel insurance with holidays;
- insurance with removal services;
- insurance with rented property; and
- insurance with car hire.

Where this insurance is provided under a block insurance policy with the supplier of the goods or services being the policyholder, the appropriate VAT treatment is given in **36.6**(1) above.

In other instances not involving block policies, there will be a separate supply of exempt insurance by the insurer to the customer buying the goods or services where

- the cover being supplied is genuine insurance which qualifies for exemption under **36.4** above; and
- it is the customer's own risk which is being insured and not the risk of the supplier of the goods or services.

A supplier of the goods or services who arranges cover for customers may be able to treat the insurance premiums received from the customers or onward payment to the insurer as a disbursement. See **36.19** below.

Treatment of arrangement fees and commission charged by suppliers of goods and services

Where

(i) a person supplies goods or services to a customer,
(ii) those goods or services are liable to VAT (and not zero-rated),
(iii) a transaction under which insurance is to be, or may be, arranged for the customer is entered into in connection with that supply,
(iv) insurance-related services are provided by the supplier of the goods or services (or a person 'connected' with that person (see **71.19 VALUATION**) who deals directly with the customer in connection with the insurance), and
(v) the insurance-related services are not claims handling services (which are exempt under **36.13**(c) above without considering these requirements),

any amount charged by the supplier to the customer (e.g. an arrangement fee or commission) in addition to the premium is not exempt under **36.13** above unless

- a document containing details of the amount of the premium, and also any fees charged in addition to the premium, is prepared;
- those matters are disclosed to the customer at or before the time when the insurance transaction is entered into; and
- the supplier complies with any published requirements of HMRC as to the preparation and form of the document, the manner of disclosing those matters to the customer and delivery of a copy of the document to the customer.

If these conditions are not met, there is still no VAT chargeable on the amount collected by the supplier and passed on to the insurer for the supply of insurance. But any fees or commission received by the supplier for arranging the insurance is liable to VAT at the same rate as the goods or services themselves.

HMRC have published specific requirements in the following circumstances (which have the force of law).

(1) *Transactions by telephone or electronic communication.* The disclosure conditions may create a problem in such cases as the customer and supplier are not physically together when the sale takes place. To overcome this, if the insurance-related services are to be exempt, HMRC require a supplier selling taxable goods by such means to
- make full disclosure of the premium at the time of the transaction (e.g. a trader selling holidays over the telephone must orally inform the customer of the amount of the premium and any fee charged over and above the premium in relation to the insurance);
- have in place a system whereby the sales staff must annotate a document (even if this only involves ticking a box) at the time they make the oral or electronic disclosure to customers to indicate that they have done so;
- prepare, and issue to the customer, a document with the information required as above (albeit after the time the insurance transaction has been entered into); and
- retain a copy of these records as they would their normal VAT records.

(2) *Second-hand schemes.* Where a person supplies goods or services under one of the second-hand schemes, the disclosure must be made on the relevant VAT invoice issued by that person.

Subject to these requirements, it was held in *Smith Glaziers (Dunfermline) Ltd v C & E Commrs*, HL [2003] STC 419 (TVC 38.22) that the above provisions are concerned with identifying the information which the document must disclose rather than specifying any particular form. All that is necessary is that the allocation is unequivocally stated in the document, even if this requires some knowledge of arithmetic.

[*VATA 1994, Sch 9 Group 2 Notes (3)–(6); FA 1997, s 38*]. (VAT Notice 701/36/11, paras 11.1–11.3).

Insurance-related services supplied outside the UK

[36.18] See the Note at **36.13** above.

Place of supply

Although no VAT is payable on qualifying insurance-related services regardless of where those services are supplied, the place where insurance-related services are supplied for VAT purposes is important because it helps to determine whether VAT on any costs incurred making that supply can be recovered. See **36.2** above for determining the place of supply of insurance services.

Determining who the customer is for services related to insurance and reinsurance

An insurance intermediary could be supplying insurance-related services to either the insured party (or the party seeking insurance) or to the insurer supplying the insurance. He could also be acting as a sub-agent and be supplying his services to another agent in the chain of supply of the insurance.

It is, therefore, important to determine precisely who the customer is when one or more of the parties in the supply chain belongs outside the UK. This will be clear-cut in some cases (based on the contractual, financial and practical arrangements in place at the time) but in other instances, it is not so easily determined. HMRC will normally see the supply of intermediary services as being made to the insured party unless there are clear indications to the contrary. In the case of reinsurance, unless there are clear indications otherwise, services related to reinsurance are assumed to be made to the ceding insurer.

Input tax recovery

See **36.3** above. The following table summarises the position in relation to supplies of intermediary services by UK businesses.

	VAT treatment where place of supply is		
	UK	*Elsewhere in EU*	*Outside EU*
Services related to insurance directly linked to the export of specific goods from the EU to outside the EU	E(R)	OS(R)	OS(R)
Other insurance-related services when insured party belongs in the UK or elsewhere in the EU	E	OS	OS(R)
Other insurance-related services when the insured party belongs outside the EU	E(R)	OS(R)	OS(R)

Key

E = Exempt (no input tax recovery)

E(R)= Exempt but with refund of related input tax

OS = Outside the scope of UK VAT with no refund of related input tax

OS(R)= Outside the scope of UK VAT with refund of related input tax

(VAT Notice 701/36/11, paras 12.1–12.3).

Claims handling services supplied to non-UK customers

The recipient of claims handling services is usually the insurer and not the insured. In order to determine the liability of claims handling services supplied outside the UK, it is necessary to establish the place of belonging of

- the insurance company;
- the claimant (the insured party); and
- the person providing the claims handling service.

The supply to an insurer of claims handling services that fall within the insurance exemption will be

- exempt if the insurer belongs in the UK;
- outside the scope of VAT with no input tax recovery if the insurer belongs in the EU; and
- outside the scope of VAT with input tax recovery if the insurer belongs outside the EU.

However, where the insurer belongs in the UK or elsewhere in the EU, there is a right of input tax recovery where the insured party belongs outside the EU.

If a supply of claims handling services does not qualify for exemption as an insurance-related service, it is liable to VAT at the standard rate when supplied in the UK and outside the scope with input tax recovery when supplied elsewhere.

(VAT Notice 701/36/11, para 12.4).

Accounting for VAT on insurance-related services

Input tax recovery

[36.19] See **36.3** above for the rules on input tax recovery.

Tax points (time of supply)

The time of supply for insurance-related services follows the normal tax point rules (see **66.18** *et seq.* **SUPPLY: TIME OF SUPPLY**). The actual tax point occurs when a debit note or (where appropriate) VAT invoice is issued to the customer to collect the premium or separate fee (if one is charged) or the date on which payment is received, whichever happens first.

Value of supplies of related services

The value of a supply of insurance-related services is the amount of consideration received in respect of gross commission, flat-rate fee and/or recharge of costs incurred, whichever payment method applies to the particular transaction. In the case of commission, no deduction should be made for any commission payable in turn to other intermediaries employed. It is the gross commission, not the net retained or earned commission, that is the value for VAT purposes.

The amount of any premium collected to be passed back to the insurer in respect of the supply of insurance itself should not be included in the value of the supplies of related services.

Mechanical breakdown insurance (MBI)

There are special rules for determining the value attributable to MBI when it is sold with a used vehicle for a single selling price. See **61.31 SECOND-HAND GOODS**.

Disbursements

If a business makes supplies of goods or services and arranges insurance cover for its customers in connection with those goods or services, any premium collected from the customer to be passed on to the insurer for the supply of insurance may, in certain circumstances, be treated as a disbursement and therefore outside the scope of VAT. This applies only to the amount due from the customer to the insurer. It does not cover any amount retained by the business in respect of commission for insurance-related services or costs incurred in making the supplies (e.g. travel, subsistence and overhead costs passed on).

For the premium due to an insurer to qualify as a disbursement, all of the following conditions must be met.

- The customer must have specifically requested that the insurance cover is obtained on his behalf.
- It must be the customer's own risks which are insured under the policy.
- The supplier must recover only the exact amount of net premium from the customer.
- The amount paid by the customer must be in respect of cover for the customer alone.
- The exact amount of the net premium must be separately itemised on any invoice issued by the supplier to the customer.

Accounting procedures for company groups

Where a holding company arranges insurance cover for the group as a whole, any amount charged to each company for arranging the insurance are exempt as insurance-related services (subject to the conditions **36.17** above if the insurance is supplied with other goods or services). Where the exact insurance premium is charged to an associated or subsidiary company, this may be treated as a disbursement if the conditions under the heading *Disbursements* above are satisfied.

If the companies are all part of the same VAT group (see **27 GROUPS OF COMPANIES**), any charges between the members are not supplies for VAT purposes.

(VAT Notice 701/36/11, paras 13.1–13.5).

Key points

[36.20] Points to consider are as follows.

- As a general principle, supplies of insurance are exempt from VAT. This means that input tax is not recoverable on any costs relevant to the activity. However, it is important that a business involved in insurance still reviews all its sources of income to identify if taxable sales are being made. If the level of taxable sales exceeds the VAT registration limit (taxable sales of £73,000 or more in the last twelve months or £73,000 or more in the next 30 days) then the business will still need to register for VAT.

- An insurance-related business will also need to be aware of the other situations when VAT registration might be necessary, i.e. if the value of acquisitions from other EU countries has exceeded £73,000 on a calendar year basis or will exceed £73,000 in the next 30 days. These rules are intended to prevent a business that is making wholly exempt supplies (and therefore not registered for VAT) from buying goods in an EU country with a lower rate of VAT than its own.
- An important concession for insurance-related services is that if a customer receiving a supply of insurance is based outside the EU (or insurance is being arranged by a business as an intermediary for someone outside the EU), then input tax recovery is still allowed on related costs, even though the supply of insurance would be exempt if supplied to an EU customer. This is a very worthwhile concession, one of the few situations in VAT legislation where input tax recovery is allowed on costs relevant to an exempt supply.
- Care is needed in determining the VAT liability of 'extended warranties' or guarantees provided by a retailer or manufacturer of goods. In most cases, these warranties will not relate to a contract of insurance and therefore payment received from the customer will be standard-rated.
- The exemption for insurance activities also extends to the services of an insurance agent or broker in bringing together an insurer and insured for the purposes of arranging insurance, i.e. acting as an intermediary. Care is needed to ensure the intermediary is actually providing an intermediary service rather than providing, for example, standard-rated advertising or marketing services. The key point with brokers and agents is to look at what they are actually providing as a service, rather than looking at the payment arrangements in relation to a particular deal.
- It is important to recognise that the professional services of loss adjusters, average adjusters, motor assessors, surveyors and solicitors are usually standard-rated. If they also provide insurance claim handling services, their services will be exempt when they are acting as an agent for the insurer in supplying those services.

37

Interaction with Other Taxes

Introduction

[37.1] Direct taxes which are likely to interact with VAT are income tax, corporation tax and capital gains tax. In general such taxes are imposed on profits or gains or some other measure of monies receivable less monies payable. VAT as an indirect tax is charged on the *supply* of goods and services in the course or furtherance of a business [*VATA 1994, s 4*], so it is immaterial for the charging of VAT whether there is any money payment and whether any profit is made on the supply. For information regarding direct taxes see *Tolley's Income Tax*, *Tolley's Corporation Tax* and *Tolley's Capital Gains Tax*.

Business profits

Taxable persons making wholly taxable supplies

[37.2] In general, a taxable person making wholly taxable supplies should treat the receipt for income tax or corporation tax purposes as being exclusive of any VAT charged. Similarly, expenditure for income tax, etc. purposes (including capital items) should be treated as being exclusive of VAT if input VAT is able to be reclaimed on the related supply. If credit for input tax is specifically denied (e.g. most supplies of motor cars and business entertainment) the expenditure inclusive of VAT should be taken into account for income tax purposes. Any allowance made for bad debts for income tax purposes is inclusive of the VAT which has been accounted for on the related supply. (VAT on bad debts may be reclaimed from HMRC in certain circumstances, see **7 BAD DEBT RELIEF**. It follows that if VAT is recoverable from HMRC it cannot be claimed for income tax purposes or alternatively a recovery of VAT should be treated as a taxable income receipt if a VAT-inclusive bad debt has previously been allowed.)

Taxable persons making both exempt and taxable supplies

A taxable person who makes both exempt and taxable supplies should treat income tax receipts as above. However, as under the partial exemption rules such a person will only be able to obtain credit for part of the input VAT applicable to expense etc. payments made, it is necessary to allocate the VAT ultimately suffered to the various expense payments made. Inspectors of taxes are prepared to consider any reasonable arrangements made to carry out this apportionment. Where credit for VAT input is specifically denied, the related expenditure is VAT-inclusive for income tax purposes as explained above.

Non-taxable persons

A person who is *not* a taxable person (e.g. making wholly exempt supplies or below the registration limit) should treat all expenses, etc. as being VAT-inclusive for income tax, etc. purposes (including capital allowances).

(Inland Revenue Statement of Practice SP B1 7 May 1973).

Stock

[37.3] Individuals, partnerships and companies, who are taxable persons for VAT should treat the cost of purchases, and hence the value of stock, as being VAT-exclusive. A taxable person who makes both taxable and exempt supplies is unable to obtain credit for input tax attributable to exempt supplies and accordingly the cost of purchases and value of trading stock should be inclusive of the VAT unable to be credited. (Inland Revenue Statement of Practice SP B2 3 December 1974).

Tax on employment income

[37.4] Returns of expenses incurred by employees, etc. and subsequently reimbursed by the employer (Forms P9D and P11D) should include any amounts of VAT suffered in connection with the expenses, whether or not the employer may subsequently obtain credit for the relevant input tax. Similar observations apply to returns of employee pecuniary liabilities met by the employer and to expenditure incurred by the employer in providing a benefit (including the use of an asset) for an employee. (Inland Revenue Statements of Practice SP A6 29 March 1973 and SP A7 17 July 1974).

Entertainers' expenses

Where agents' fees paid by actors, musicians, etc. are deductible for employment income purposes, any additional VAT payable is also deductible. [*ITEPA 2003, s 352*].

Subcontractors in the construction industry

[37.5] A subcontractor who is a taxable person for VAT should account for VAT on the total consideration which he charges for his services. Where the appropriate valid tax exemption certificate is not held or not presented, the person paying the consideration is obliged to make a deduction at a specified rate from the part of the payment representing labour and profit on materials. VAT and cost of materials are excluded. [*ICTA 1988, s 559(4)*]. (Inland Revenue Pamphlet IR 14/15).

Capital gains tax

[37.6] If VAT is payable in respect of the acquisition of an asset but is available for credit by a taxable person, then the cost of the asset for capital gains tax purposes is the cost exclusive of VAT. Where no VAT credit is available the cost is inclusive of VAT ultimately suffered.

Where an asset is disposed of, any VAT on the supply of the asset is disregarded in computing the disposal consideration for capital gains tax purposes. It appears that a taxable person making both taxable and exempt supplies should treat as part of the capital gains tax cost of an asset the input VAT that was not available for credit in respect of the acquisition (see under **37.2** above). (Inland Revenue Statement of Practice SP D7 7 June 1973).

Capital allowances

[37.7] Where the **CAPITAL GOODS SCHEME (10)** applies adjustments to the original input tax reclaimed may be necessary for a period of up to ten years. Any additional VAT liability under the scheme is to be treated as extra qualifying capital expenditure incurred at the time when the VAT is paid. Similarly, any additional VAT rebate is to be taken into account in the capital allowances computation for the period in which it is repaid by HMRC. Earlier capital allowances computations are not disturbed. [*FA 1991, s 59, Sch 14*].

VAT penalties, surcharge and interest

[37.8] No deduction is allowed in computing any income, profit or loss for tax purposes in respect of

- default surcharge under *VATA 1994, s 59* (see **52.21 PENALTIES**);
- a penalty under *VATA 1994, ss 60–70* (see **52.10–52.17, 52.23–52.26 PENALTIES**); or
- interest under *VATA 1994, s 74* (see **51.15 PAYMENT OF VAT**).

Repayment supplement for VAT under *VATA 1994, s 79* is disregarded for income tax and corporation tax purposes.

[*ICTA 1988, s 827; VATA 1994, Sch 14 para 10; IT(TOI)A 2005, ss 54(1)–(3), 869(3)–(5)*].

Indirect taxes

[37.9] In valuing imported goods for VAT purposes, indirect taxes (e.g. customs duty) levied (whether abroad or in the UK) are specifically taken into account if not already included in a price in money. See **71.15 VALUATION.**

Key points

[37.10] Points to consider are as follows.

- A business that pays VAT on an expense that it cannot reclaim as input tax should follow the accounting treatment for the VAT element as for the rest of the expense. So the VAT element on a capital asset bought by a business where the VAT cannot be reclaimed (e.g. a motor car available for private use where an input tax block applies) will be capitalised to the balance sheet rather than debited as an expense on the profit and loss account. The VAT element of the asset will then qualify for any capital allowances (for direct tax purposes) in the normal way.
- A subcontractor in the building trade who suffers a deduction of income tax at source (construction industry scheme) must still account for VAT on his gross fee where appropriate, i.e. the amount he is entitled to receive before any income tax or other deduction.
- The capital goods scheme requires input tax on certain capital items to be adjusted over a five-year period (in relation to computer hardware expenditure exceeding £50,000 excluding VAT) and ten years in relation to certain property expenditure (exceeding £250,000 excluding VAT). The extra amounts of VAT that are payable or repayable over the life of the capital goods scheme will be adjusted for capital allowance purposes in the year of the relevant VAT adjustment. This means that capital allowance calculations in the year when the asset was originally purchased are not disturbed.
- Amounts paid to HMRC in relation to either penalties, interest or default surcharges cannot be deducted against profits for direct tax purposes. However, a repayment supplement received from HMRC, for example a delay in a repayment due on a VAT return being received also avoids a charge for direct tax purposes.
- There are many occasions when VAT is due on a price that includes other indirect taxes, e.g. the VAT charge for imported goods subject to Customs duty will be based on the price including the Customs duty. In the case of certain property transactions, subject to stamp duty land tax (SDLT), there is an SDLT charge based on the VAT-inclusive cost of the property.

38

International Services

Cross-references. See **36.4** and **36.18** **INSURANCE** for the supply of international insurance services; **40 ISLE OF MAN**; **70 TRANSPORT AND FREIGHT** for certain international movements of passengers and freight.

De Voil Indirect Tax Service. See V4.246.

Introduction

[38.1] Certain services *received by* UK persons from outside the UK are deemed to be *supplied by* those persons who must account for VAT on them if required to be registered. See **38.4** below.

In addition, certain supplies of international services *made by* UK taxable persons are zero-rated or outside the scope of UK VAT. See **38.5** *et seq* below.

Territorial extent of UK

[38.2] The UK consists of Great Britain, Northern Ireland and the territorial sea of the UK (i.e. waters within 12 nautical miles of the coast line). [*VATA 1994, s 96(11)*].

For VAT purposes the Isle of Man is treated as part of the UK and VAT is chargeable there under Manx law which generally parallels UK legislation. See **40 ISLE OF MAN**. *References in this chapter to the UK apply also to the Isle of Man unless otherwise indicated.*

De Voil Indirect Tax Service. See V1.215.

Place of supply of services

[38.3] See **65.12** *et seq* **SUPPLY: PLACE OF SUPPLY** for a detailed consideration of the place of supply of services.

Reverse charge on services received from abroad

[38.4] Normally, the supplier of a service is the person who must account to the tax authorities for any VAT due on the supply. However, in certain situations, the position is reversed and it is the customer who must account for any VAT due. This is known as the '*reverse charge*' procedure.

The reverse charge applies to almost all business to business ('B2B') supplies of services except those of a description in *VATA 1994, Sch 9* (exemptions). It does not apply to land on which the option to tax has been exercised. Under the procedure, the customer credits their VAT account with an amount of output tax, calculated on the full value of the supply they have received, and at the same time debits their VAT account with the input tax to which they are entitled, in accordance with the normal rules. If the customer can attribute the input tax to taxable supplies, and can therefore reclaim it all, the reverse charge has no net cost to them. If they cannot, the effect is to make them pay VAT on the supply at the UK rate. This puts them in the same position as if they had received the supply from a UK supplier rather than from one outside the UK.

Valuation of supplies

The amount payable to the overseas supplier for the services excludes UK VAT. The value of the transaction on which VAT must be accounted under the reverse charge is the total amount paid together with the value of any other form of consideration. This includes any taxes levied abroad.

Time of supply

The time of supply (tax point) for these services depends on whether a single supply of services is made or continuous supplies of services. The time of supply for a single supply of services subject to the reverse charge is the date of completion of the service or, to the extent a payment for the service is made before completion, the date of payment. The time of supply for continuous supplies of services subject to the reverse charge is the end of each periodic billing or payment period (or payment where this is earlier), with a compulsory tax point on 31 December each year in cases where a billing/payment period or payment has not arisen.

UK suppliers

The reverse charge does not apply to supplies of services where both the supplier and the customer belong in the UK. It only applies where services are supplied in the UK by suppliers belonging overseas. Services which, under the place of supply rules, are supplied in another country are outside the scope of UK VAT. Such services can only be subject to tax in that country.

International companies

The reverse charge does not apply to services provided by an overseas establishment to a customer belonging in the UK within the same legal entity as the overseas establishment, since this is not a supply for VAT purposes.

UK VAT incurred by non-UK suppliers

Suppliers who belong outside the UK, and whose customers account for UK VAT by means of the reverse charge, may be able to reclaim VAT incurred in the UK (see Notice 723A *Refunds of VAT in the EC for EC and non-EC businesses*).

B2B general rule services

If the customer belongs in the UK and receives supplies of any B2B general rule services where the supplier belongs outside the UK the reverse charge applies. The reverse charge does not apply to exempt services or zero-rated services. If the customer is not already UK VAT registered and they receive supplies of B2B general rule services which meet these conditions and are treated as supplied where the recipient belongs, the value of those supplies must be added to the value of their own taxable supplies in determining whether they should be registered for UK VAT. Even if they make no taxable supplies themselves they will still be a taxable person if the value of their imported services exceeds the registration limits.

Groups

Where B2B general rule services (except services of a description in *VATA 1994, Sch 9* (exemptions) and land on which the option to tax has been exercised) are purchased by an overseas member of a UK VAT group and provided to a UK member of that VAT group, its representative member is required to account for any UK VAT due under the intra-group reverse charge.

Extension to other services supplied in the UK

The reverse charge also applies to the following services when they are made in the UK:

- services relating to land and property;
- services supplied where performed;
- passenger transport;
- services covered by the additional rules for hired goods (including hired means of transport), telecommunications services, radio and television broadcasting services; and
- services covered by the additional rules for electronically supplied services.

The extension to the reverse charge applies if the customer is UK VAT registered and receives B2B supplies of the above services which are supplied in the UK, where the supplier belongs outside the UK. The customer should give their UK VAT registration number to their supplier as evidence that the supplier is not liable to account for any UK VAT due. If the customer receives supplies for wholly private purposes the reverse charge does not apply; the customer should not give a UK VAT registration number; and the supplier is liable to account for any UK VAT due. If the customer is not UK VAT registered and receives such services supplied in the UK the reverse charge does not apply. Such supplies do not count as their taxable supplies for the purposes of determining whether they are liable to be registered as a taxable person. The supplier is liable to account for any UK VAT due. For a non-UK supplier of these services, where the customer does not give a UK VAT registration number, the supplier is responsible for accounting for any UK VAT due on the supply, and if not already registered in the UK may be liable to register.

[*VATA 1994, s 8(4); SI 1995/2518, Reg 82; SI 2009/3241, Reg 10*]. (VAT Notice 741A, para 18).

De Voil Indirect Tax Service. See V3.231.

VAT liability of international services

[38.5] The liability of a supply of international services depends on the rules for the place of supply of services. These are considered in detail in **65.12** *et seq* **SUPPLY: PLACE OF SUPPLY**. Where the place of supply is deemed to be outside the UK, the services are outside the scope of UK VAT. Where the place of supply is deemed to be in the UK, the services are subject to the normal UK provisions. Apart from the specific categories of zero-rating for international services in **38.6–38.8** below, international services deemed to be supplied in the UK are therefore standard-rated unless they can be treated as **ZERO-RATED SUPPLIES (74)** or **EXEMPT SUPPLIES (20)** under the general rules.

See **34.3 INPUT TAX** for the position regarding the right to deduct input tax in respect of most (but not all) international services deemed to be made outside the UK.

Training supplied to overseas Governments

[38.6] By concession, zero-rating applies to training services (other than exempt training within **16.7 EDUCATION**) supplied in the UK to overseas Governments for the purpose of their sovereign activities (and not their business activities). The supplier must retain a statement in writing from the Government concerned (or its accredited representative) certifying that the trainees are employed in the furtherance of its sovereign activities. *Included* is the training of Government officials, public servants and members of organisations such as the armed forces, police, emergency services and similar bodies answerable to the Government concerned. *Excluded* is training of personnel from Government-owned businesses or sponsored commercial organisations such as state airlines or nationalised industries. Relief does not extend to any associated services supplied *separately* (e.g. accommodation or transport). (VAT Notice 48, ESC 3.17; VAT Notice 741A, para 8.2).

Work on goods obtained, acquired or temporarily imported for that purpose and subsequent export

[38.7] For EU legislation see **18.29**(*c*) **EUROPEAN UNION LEGISLATION.**

Note: The following provisions do *not* apply where the work is carried out for a VAT-registered customer in another EU country, the goods physically leave the EU country where the work has been carried out, and the customer gives a valid VAT registration number. In such a case, the place of supply moves to the country where the customer belongs and the customer must account for VAT under the reverse charge procedure. See **65.20 SUPPLY: PLACE OF SUPPLY**.

The supply of services of work carried out on goods which, for that purpose, have been obtained or acquired in, or imported into, any EU country is zero-rated provided the goods are intended to be (and are) subsequently exported to a place outside the EU. The goods must be exported by (or on behalf of) the supplier or, where the recipient of the services belongs outside the EU, by (or on behalf of) the recipient. *Excluded* are any services of a description falling within *VATA 1994, Sch 9 Group 2* (insurance) or *Group 5* (finance). [*VATA 1994, Sch 8 Group 7 Item 1*].

See **65.14 SUPPLY: PLACE OF SUPPLY** for the concept of belonging. The goods must be exported within a reasonable time after the work on them has been carried out. The goods must not be used in the UK between the time of leaving the supplier's premises and exportation. Normal rules apply for proof of export of the goods (see **21.24 EXPORTS**). If, in anticipation of export, the supply is zero-rated but, in the event, the goods are either used before export or export does not take place, it will be necessary to reconsider both the place of supply of the services and, if it is in the UK, the appropriate VAT rate.

Any goods used in conjunction with the work performed (e.g. spare parts, paint, etc.) should be treated as part of the supply of services.

Included are

- alterations and repairs, calibrations, cleaning, insulating, lacquering, painting, polishing, resetting (jewellery), cutting (of precious stones), sharpening, varnishing and waterproofing;
- the repair of freight containers;
- services directly related to the 'covering' of a mare provided the mare is exported before the birth of the foal;
- the gelding and/or breaking in of a young horse (e.g. training yearling racehorses to the stage where they can be ridden safely in races) but note that actual racing is not accepted as training and if any horse is acquired or temporarily imported with the intention of racing it in the EU before re-export, zero-rating under this provision will not be allowed; and
- the restoration of classic cars.

Not included is

- work which is not physical work carried out on the goods themselves (e.g. mere inspection or testing and analysis);

- repair or other work which becomes necessary after acquisition or importation of goods (e.g. incidental running repairs while the goods are being used); and
- valuation services.

(VAT Notice 741A, para 8.6).

De Voil Indirect Tax Service. See V4.246.

Services of intermediaries

[38.8] There are special place of supply rules for services of intermediaries. See **65.28** SUPPLY: PLACE OF SUPPLY. Where the supply of an intermediary's services is within the scope of UK VAT, it is zero-rated if consisting of the making of arrangements for

- the export of any goods to a place outside the EU;
- a supply of services of the description specified in *VATA 1994, Sch 8 Group 7 Item 1* (see **38.7** above); or
- any supply of services which is made outside the EU.

Excluded are any services of a description falling within *VATA 1994, Sch 9 Group 2* (insurance) or *Group 5* (finance).

[*VATA 1994, Sch 8 Group 7 Item 2*].

The intermediary's services can be supplied to the supplier (in finding a customer) or the customer (in finding a supplier) or even to both.

(VAT Notice 741A, paras 12, 13).

Telecommunication services

[38.9] There are special rules for relevant telecommunications services. See **65.22**(9) SUPPLY: PLACE OF SUPPLY for the definition of telecommunication services.

Place of supply rules and summary of UK VAT position

See **65.21–65.23** SUPPLY: PLACE OF SUPPLY.

Reverse charge on services received from abroad

Where the reverse charge procedure on services received from abroad applies to relevant telecommunication services, the normal value and time of supply rules are applied (see **38.4** above) but only to the extent that the services are not chargeable to VAT in another EU country.

[*SI 1997/1523, Regs 4, 7, 10*].

Continuous supplies of telecommunications services

Special time of supply rules apply to continuous supplies of any services. See **66.19** SUPPLY: TIME OF SUPPLY.

Rights to relevant telecommunications services

The place of supply of a 'right' to services is the same as the place in which the supply of services to which the right relates would be treated as made by the supplier of the right to the recipient in question. A 'right' includes any right, option or priority with respect to the supply of services and the supply of an interest deriving from any right or services.

[*SI 1992/3121, Art 21; SI 1997/1524, Art 5; SI 2006/1683*].

Broadcasting and electronically supplied services

[38.10] The place of supply of radio and TV broadcasting services and electronically supplied services is normally in the country where the customer belongs subject, in certain circumstances, to where the services are effectively used and enjoyed. See **65.21–65.23 SUPPLY: PLACE OF SUPPLY** for further details of the place of supply rules.

For special scheme for non-EU suppliers of electronically supplied services, see **63.34 SPECIAL SCHEMES**.

Key points

[38.11] Points to consider are as follows.

- It is important to be aware of the difference between a service for an overseas customer that is zero-rated, and one that avoids a charge of UK VAT under the place of supply rules. In the latter case, a supply will be outside the scope of UK VAT, rather than zero-rated. A supply can only be zero-rated if it is within *VATA 1994, Sch 8*.
- Important changes took effect on 1 January 2010 in relation to the place of supply rules for services performed for business customers outside the UK (known as B2B sales). In the majority of cases, the place of supply is now where the customer is based and, for EU business customers outside the UK, this means they will account for the VAT on their own return by making a reverse charge calculation.
- In most cases, the reverse charge calculation will produce a nil payment effect because the customer will account for output tax on his return and be entitled to claim the same amount as input tax. Exceptions to this situation would apply if the service in question was used for either non-business or exempt purposes, i.e. where an input tax block is relevant.
- It should be noted that the Isle of Man is deemed to be part of the UK as far as VAT is concerned but that the Channel Islands are excluded.
- Certain services provided by a UK supplier to an overseas customer are zero-rated under *VATA 1994, Sch 8, Group 7*. In such cases, there is no VAT charge on these services, even if the

place of supply is in the UK. Examples of zero-rated supplies include training services provided for an overseas government in connection with its sovereign activities, and work on goods that are intended to be exported (before use) to a country outside the EU.

39

Invoices

Cross-references. See **52.14 PENALTIES** for improper use of invoices; **56.3** and **56.10 RECORDS** for obligations to retain invoices and adjustments of errors in invoices; **63.30 SPECIAL SCHEMES** for invoices raised by flat-rate farmers; **71.24 VALUATION** for discounts on invoices.

De Voil Indirect Tax Service. See V3.511–V3.529.

Introduction

[39.1] With certain exceptions or unless HMRC allow otherwise, a registered person *must* provide the customer with an invoice showing specified particulars including VAT (a '*VAT invoice*') in the following circumstances.

(a) He makes a supply of goods or services in the UK (other than an exempt supply) to a taxable person.

(b) He makes a supply of goods or services to a person in another EU country for the purposes of any business activity carried on by that person. But no invoice is required where the supply is an exempt supply which is made to a person in another EU country which does not require an invoice to be issued for the supply. (Because practice varies widely across the EU, HMRC guidance is that businesses should be guided by their customers as to whether invoices are required for exempt supplies.)

(c) He receives a payment on account from a person in another EU country in respect of a supply he has made or intends to make.

A VAT invoice is important as it is normally essential evidence to support a customer's claim for deduction of input tax. The supplier must keep the copy and the original should be retained by the recipient.

[*VATA 1994, Sch 11 para 2A; FA 2002, s 24; SI 1995/2518, Reg 13(1); SI 2007/2085, Reg 6*].

Exceptions

The above provisions do not apply to the following supplies.

- Zero-rated supplies (other than supplies for acquisition by a person registered in another EU country, see (*b*) above). [*SI 1995/2518, Reg 20(a)*].
- Supplies where the VAT charged is excluded from credit under *VATA 1994, s 25(7)* (e.g. business entertaining and certain motor cars) [*SI 1995/2518, Reg 20(b)*] although a VAT invoice may be issued in such cases.
- Supplies on which VAT is charged but which are not made for a consideration. [*SI 1995/2518, Reg 20(c)*]. This includes gifts and private use of goods. See, however, **39.2** below under the heading *Business gifts* for 'tax certificates' issued in connection with business gifts to support a deduction of input tax.
- Sales of second-hand goods under one of the special schemes. [*SI 1995/2518, Reg 20(d)*]. Invoices for such sales must not show any VAT. See **61.11** and **61.45 SECOND-HAND GOODS** for the special invoices required.
- Supplies that fall within the **TOUR OPERATORS' MARGIN SCHEME (68)**. VAT invoices must not be issued for such supplies.
- Supplies where the customer operates a self-billing arrangement. See **39.6** below.
- Supplies by retailers unless the customer requests a VAT invoice.
- Supplies by one member to another in the same VAT group.
- Transactions between one division and another of a company registered in the names of its divisions. See **59.37 REGISTRATION**.
- Supplies where the taxable person is entitled to issue, and does issue, invoices relating to services performed in fiscal and other warehousing regimes. [*SI 1995/2518, Reg 13(1); SI 1996/1250, Reg 6*]. See **72.19 WAREHOUSED GOODS AND FREE ZONES.**

Continuous supplies of services

In *Europhone International Ltd v Frontier Communications Ltd*, Ch D [2001] STC 1399 (TVC 62.470) F agreed to provide E with telecommunications services. E fell into arrears with its payments. F continued to provide the relevant services but did not issue invoices (which would have obliged it to account for output tax). E went into receivership and the receivers claimed that F was obliged to issue a VAT invoice. The court held that *SI 1995/2518, Reg 13(1)* above imposed a requirement to provide a VAT invoice upon a person who made a taxable supply. The making of the taxable supply must, therefore, precede or be contemporaneous with the arising of the obligation. Under the rules for continuous supplies of services (see **66.19 SUPPLY: TIME OF SUPPLY** for full details), F only made a taxable supply to E when it received payment or it issued a VAT invoice. As there was no question of E making a payment in respect of the services supplied by F, *Reg 13* was ineffective to impose an obligation on F to issue a VAT invoice.

Documents treated as VAT invoices

[39.2] Although not strictly VAT invoices, certain documents listed in (1)–(4) below are treated as VAT invoices either under the legislation or by HMRC.

(1) Self-billing invoices

Self-billing is an arrangement between a supplier and a customer in which the customer prepares the supplier's invoice and forwards it to him, normally with the payment. See **39.6** below.

(2) Sales by auctioneer, bailiff, etc.

Where goods (including land) forming part of the assets of a business carried on by a taxable person are, under any power exercisable by another person, sold by that person in or towards satisfaction of a debt owed by the taxable person, the goods are deemed to be supplied by the taxable person in the course or furtherance of his business.

The particulars of the VAT chargeable on the supply must be provided on a sale by auction by the auctioneer and where the sale is otherwise than by auction by the person selling the goods. The document issued to the buyer is treated as a VAT invoice. [*VATA 1994, Sch 4 paras 7, 9; FA 2007, s 99(3); SI 1995/2518, Reg 13(2)*]. See **2.10 ACCOUNTING PERIODS AND RETURNS.**

(3) Authenticated receipts in the construction industry

See **42.21**(1) **LAND AND BUILDINGS: ZERO AND REDUCED RATE SUPPLIES AND DIY HOUSEBUILDERS.**

(4) Business gifts

Where a business makes a gift of goods on which VAT is due (see **47.6 OUTPUT TAX**), and the recipient uses the goods for business purposes, that person can recover the VAT as input tax (subject to the normal rules). The donor cannot issue a VAT invoice (because there is no consideration) but instead may provide the recipient with a 'tax certificate' which can be used as evidence to support a deduction of input tax. The tax certificate may be on normal invoicing documentation overwritten with the statement:

> **Tax certificate**
>
> No payment is necessary for these goods. Output tax has been accounted for on the supply.

Full details of the goods must be shown on the documentation and the amount of VAT shown must be the amount of output tax accounted for to HMRC.

(VAT Notice 700/35/97, para 1.4).

Not VAT invoices

The following are not to be regarded as VAT invoices (even if showing all the details required of a VAT invoice) provided they are clearly marked 'This is not a VAT invoice'.

- Any consignment note, delivery note or similar document (or any copy thereof) issued by the supplier before the time of supply where
  - (a) goods are removed before it is known whether a supply will take place (e.g. goods on approval or sale or return), or
  - (b) the tax point is treated as taking place at the time an invoice is issued under the 14-day rule (see **66.8 SUPPLY: TIME OF SUPPLY**).
- Any pro-forma invoice used to offer goods or services to a potential customer.

[*SI 1995/2518, Reg 14(3)*]. (VAT Notice 700, para 17.3).

Invoicing requirements and particulars

[39.3] A VAT invoice must contain certain basic information. See **39.4** below. In addition, special rules apply to

- VAT invoices issued to persons in other EU countries (see **39.5** below);
- self-billing invoices (see **39.6** below);
- retailers' invoices (see **39.7** below);
- invoices issued by cash and carry wholesalers (see **39.8** below);
- arrangements for particular businesses (see **39.9** below); and
- electronic invoicing (see **39.10** below);
- invoices using corporate purchasing cards (see **39.11** below).

VAT invoices generally

[39.4] Unless HMRC allow otherwise, a VAT invoice must show the following particulars.

(a) A sequential number based on one or more series which uniquely identifies the document.

The 'invoice number' can be numerical, or it can be a combination of numbers and letters, as long as it forms part of a unique and sequential series. Where there is a break in the series (e.g. where an invoice is cancelled or spoiled and never issued to a customer), this is still acceptable as long as the relevant invoice is retained. (VAT Information Sheet 10/07).

(b) The time of the supply, i.e. tax point.

(c) The date of issue of the document.

(d) The name, address and registration number of the supplier.

(e) The name and address of the person to whom the goods or services are supplied.

(f) A description sufficient to identify the goods or services supplied. See **39.8** below for use of coded descriptions by cash and carry wholesalers. Coded descriptions may also be accepted in other circumstances (e.g. builders' merchants) where businesses whose trade is restricted to a large number of specialised parts or fittings issue illustrated catalogues to customers.

(g) For each description, the quantity of the goods or extent of the services, the rate of VAT and amount payable, excluding VAT, expressed in any currency.

(h) The unit price. This applies to 'countable' goods and services. For services, the countable element might be, for example, an hourly rate or a price paid for standard services. If the supply cannot be broken down into countable elements, the total VAT-exclusive price is the unit price. Additionally, the unit price may not need to be shown at all if it is not normally provided in a particular business sector *and* is not required by the customer. (VAT Notice 700, para 16.3).

(i) The gross amount payable, excluding VAT, expressed in any currency.

(j) The rate of any cash discount offered.

(k) The total amount of VAT chargeable expressed in sterling.

(l) Where the margin scheme for **SECOND-HAND GOODS (61)** or the **TOUR OPERATORS' MARGIN SCHEME (68)** is applied, *either* a reference to the appropriate provision of *EC Council Directive 2006/112/EC* or the corresponding provision of *VATA 1994 or* any indication that the margin scheme has been applied.
The way in which margin scheme treatment is referenced on an invoice is a matter for the business and not HMRC but examples of acceptable indications include
   - This is a second-hand margin scheme supply/This invoice is for a second-hand margin scheme supply.
   - This is a Tour Operators Margin Scheme supply/This supply falls under the Value Added Tax (Tour Operators) Order 1987.

The requirement only applies to TOMS invoices in business to business transactions.
(VAT Information Sheet 10/07).

(m) Where a VAT invoice relates in whole or in part to a supply where the person supplied is liable to pay the VAT, *either* a reference to the appropriate provision of *EC Council Directive 2006/112/EC* or the corresponding provision of *VATA 1994 or* any indication that the supply is one where the customer is liable to pay the VAT.
This covers UK supplies where the customer accounts for the VAT (e.g. under the gold scheme or any reverse charge requirement under the missing trader intra-community rules). The way in which margin scheme treatment is referenced on an invoice is a matter for the business and not HMRC but examples of acceptable indications include
- Reverse charge supply.
- This supply is subject to the reverse charge.

(VAT Information Sheet 10/07).

Exempt or zero-rated supplies

Invoices do not have to be raised for exempt or zero-rated transactions when supplied in the UK. But if such supplies are included on invoices with taxable supplies, the exempt and zero-rated supplies must be totalled separately and the invoice must show clearly that there is no VAT payable on them.

Leasing of motor cars

Where an invoice relates wholly or partly to the letting on hire of a motor car other than for self-drive, the invoice must state whether the car is a qualifying vehicle (see **45.11 MOTOR CARS**).

[*VATA 1994, Sch 11 para 2A; FA 1996, s 38; FA 2002, s 24; SI 1995/2518, Reg 14(1)(4)(6)(8); SI 1995/3147; SI 1996/1250, Reg 7; SI 2003/3220, Reg 7; SI 2007/2085, Reg 7*].

Example of a VAT invoice

ABC plc
26 Green Road, South Croydon, CR2 5ZX
VAT Reg. No. 987 6543 21

Sales invoice No 15,618
AN Other Ltd
9 North Street
London N8 5QQ

Time of supply 31/01/12				Date of Issue 3/02/12
Quantity	Description and price	Amount excluding VAT	VAT rate	VAT
		£	%	£
12	Purple kingsize quilt covers @ £15	180.00		
20	Pillows at £12.50	250.00		
50	Purple pillow cases at £8.50 per pair	212.50		
		642.50	20	128.50
	Delivery (strictly net)	12.00	20	2.40
Terms: Cash discount of 5% if paid within 30 days		654.50		108.92
	VAT	130.90		
	Total	£785.40		

VAT invoices to persons in other EU countries

[39.5] Unless HMRC allow otherwise, where a registered person provides a person in another EU country with

- a VAT invoice or,
- any document that refers to a VAT invoice and is intended to amend it (e.g. a credit note)

it must show the following particulars.

(a) A sequential number based on one or more series which uniquely identifies the document.
The 'invoice number' can be numerical, or it can be a combination of numbers and letters, as long as it forms part of a unique and sequential series. Where there is a break in the series (e.g. where an invoice is cancelled or spoiled and never issued to a customer), this is still acceptable as long as the relevant invoice is retained. (VAT Information Sheet 10/07).

(b) The time of the supply, i.e. tax point.

(c) The date of issue of the document.

(d) The name, address and registration number of the supplier. The letters 'GB' must be shown as a prefix to the registration number.

(e) The name and address of the person to whom the goods or services are supplied.

(f) The registration number, if any, of the recipient of the supply of goods or services containing the alphabetical code of the EU country in which the recipient is registered, namely
Austria—AT
Belgium—BE
Bulgaria—BG
Cyprus—CY
Czech Republic—CZ
Denmark—DK
Estonia—EE
Finland—FI

France—FR
Germany—DE
Greece—EL
Hungary—HU
Ireland—IE
Italy—IT
Latvia—LV
Lithuania—LT
Luxembourg—LU
Malta—MT
Netherlands—NL
Poland—PL
Portugal—PT
Romania—RO
Slovak Republic—SK
Slovenia—SI
Spain—ES
Sweden—SE

Enquiry letters in a number of foreign languages to request the correct VAT registration number from an EU customer are available on the HMRC website.

(g) A description sufficient to identify the goods or services supplied. Where the supply is of a new means of transport (see **23.33 EUROPEAN UNION: SINGLE MARKET**) a description sufficient to identify it as such.

(h) For each description, the quantity of the goods or the extent of the services, and where a positive rate of VAT is chargeable, the rate of VAT and the amount payable, excluding VAT, expressed in sterling.

(i) The unit price.
This applies to 'countable' goods and services. For services, the countable element might be, for example, an hourly rate or a price paid for standard services. If the supply cannot be broken down into countable elements, the total VAT-exclusive price is the unit price. Additionally, the unit price may not need to be shown at all if it is not normally provided in a particular business sector *and* is not required by the customer. (VAT Notice 700, para 16.3).

(j) The gross amount payable, excluding VAT.

(k) The rate of any cash discount offered.

(l) Where the supply of goods is a taxable supply, the total amount of VAT chargeable expressed in sterling.

(m) Where the margin scheme for **SECOND-HAND GOODS (61)** or the **TOUR OPERATORS' MARGIN SCHEME (68)** is applied, *either* a reference to the appropriate provision of *EC Council Directive 2006/112/EC* or the corresponding provision of *VATA 1994* *or* any indication that the margin scheme has been applied.
The way in which margin scheme treatment is referenced on an invoice is a matter for the business and not HMRC but examples of acceptable indications include

- This is a second-hand margin scheme supply/This invoice is for a second-hand margin scheme supply.

- This is a Tour Operators Margin Scheme supply/This supply falls under the Value Added Tax (Tour Operators) Order 1987.

The requirement only applies to TOMS invoices in business to business transactions.
(VAT Information Sheet 10/07).

(n) Where a VAT invoice relates in whole or in part to a supply where the person supplied is liable to pay the VAT, *either* a reference to the appropriate provision of *EC Council Directive 2006/112/EC* or the corresponding provision of *VATA 1994 or* any indication that the supply is one where the customer is liable to pay the VAT.
The way in which margin scheme treatment is referenced on an invoice is a matter for the business and not HMRC but examples of acceptable indications include
- Reverse charge supply/This supply is subject to the reverse charge.
- Subject to reverse charge in the country of receipt/Subject to reverse charge in another member state.
- This is a UK exempt supply which may be chargeable in the country of receipt/This is a UK exempt supply which may be chargeable in another member state.

(VAT Information Sheet 10/07).

(o) Where the supply is an exempt or zero-rated supply, *either* a reference to the appropriate provision of *EC Council Directive 2006/112/EC* or the corresponding provision of *VATA 1994 or* any indication that the supply is exempt or zero-rated as appropriate.
For these purposes, an exempt supply is a supply that, if made in the UK, would be exempt under *VATA 1994, Sch 9*.
The way in which the intra-EU exempt or zero-rated treatment is referenced on an invoice is a matter for the business and not for HMRC, but examples of acceptable indications include
- Exempt supply/Exempt supply for VAT purposes/This is an exempt supply.
- Zero-rated intra-EU supply/This is an intra-Union supply/Intra-Union supply subject to VAT in the country of acquisition.

(VAT Information Sheet 10/07).

[*VATA 1994, Sch 11 para* 2A; *FA 1996, s 38; FA 2002, s 24; SI 1995/2518, Regs 2, 14(2); SI 1996/1250, Reg 7; SI 2003/3220, Reg 8; SI 2004/1082, Reg 3; SI 2007/2085, Reg 7*].

Note that there is no requirement for the gross amount payable (excluding VAT) to be in sterling. Where, therefore, a VAT invoice is issued in respect of a zero-rated supply for acquisition by a customer registered in another EU country and their registration number is quoted on the invoice, the invoice may be in any currency. Where UK VAT is chargeable (e.g. on distance sales) this must always be expressed in sterling.

Example of a VAT invoice

ABC plc
26 Green Road, South Croydon, CR2 5ZX
VAT Reg. No. GB987 6543 21

Sales invoice No 15,618
Eine Andere AG
9 Nord Straße
Berlin
VAT Reg. No. DE 123456789

Time of supply 31/01/12 — Date of Issue 3/02/12

Quantity	Description and price	Amount excluding VAT £	VAT rate %	VAT £
12	Purple kingsize quilt covers @ £15	180.00		
20	Pillows at £12.50	250.00		
50	Purple pillow cases at £8.50 per pair	212.50		
		642.50	0	0
	Delivery	35.00	0	0
Terms: Cash discount of 5% if paid within 30 days		677.50		
	VAT	0.00		
	Total	£677.50		

Self-billing

[39.6] Self-billing is an established practice under which the customer prepares a VAT invoice in the name of, and on behalf of, the supplier and then sends it to the supplier, normally with the payment.

Prior approval from HMRC is no longer required but all businesses wishing to use the scheme need to meet conditions set out in *SI 1995/2518, Reg 13* and VAT Notice 700/62. HMRC may also impose further conditions in particular cases.

The detailed provisions are as follows.

Where a registered person (the '*customer*') provides a document to himself (a '*self-billed invoice*') that purports to be a VAT invoice in respect of a supply of goods or services to him by another registered person (the '*supplier*'), that document is treated as the VAT invoice required to be provided by the supplier provided certain conditions are met.

(a) The self-billed invoice must have been provided under an agreement (a '*self-billing agreement*') entered into between the supplier and the customer.

(b) The self-billed invoice must contain the particulars required under **39.4**(*a*)–(*m*) above or, as the case may be, **39.5**(*a*)–(*o*) above.

(c) The self-billed invoice must relate to a supply or supplies made by a supplier who is a taxable person. If not, any amount claimed as input tax will be disallowed, see *MJ Gleeson plc* (VTD 13332) (TVC 40.57).

(d) The self-billed invoice must be clearly marked
'THE VAT SHOWN IS YOUR OUTPUT TAX DUE TO REVENUE & CUSTOMS'

(e) The customer must keep the names, addresses and VAT registration numbers of all the suppliers who have agreed to self-billing, and be able to produce them for inspection by HMRC if required.

(f) The customer must raise self-billed invoices for all transactions with the supplier during the currency of the agreement.

If all the conditions are not met, any self-billed invoices issued are not proper VAT invoices. As such, they cannot be used as evidence of entitlement to input tax by the customer and the supplier will have to issue his own invoices.

Self-billing agreements

A self-billed invoice can only be issued under an agreement between the customer and supplier (see *(a)* above).

A self-billing agreement must:

- Authorise the customer to produce self-billed invoices in respect of supplies made by the supplier for a specified period ending not later than either
  - (i) the end of a period of twelve months, or
  - (ii) the end of the period of any contract between the customer and the supplier for the supply of the particular goods or services to which the self-billing agreement relates.

  Most self-billing agreements will therefore normally last for twelve months and must then be renewed. However, where the customer has a business contract with its supplier, the self-billing agreement can be incorporated in the contract, in which case the self-billing agreement lasts until the end date of the contract.
- Specify that the supplier will not issue VAT invoices in respect of supplies covered by the agreement.
- Specify that the supplier will accept each self-billed invoice created by the customer in respect of supplies made to him by the supplier.
- Specify that the supplier will notify the customer if he ceases to be a taxable person, changes his registration number or transfers his business as a going concern. (A new agreement must be set up if the supplier changes his VAT registration number or if he transfers his business as a going concern and the new supplier wants to continue operating self-billing.)
- Be in writing (either on paper or in electronic form).
- Be produced to HMRC on request (by the customer or supplier).

It is also helpful for the agreement to make it clear if the customer intends to outsource responsibility for issuing the self-billed invoices to a third party (e.g. an accounting bureau), although it should be noted that in such a case the customer still remains responsible for ensuring that all the conditions of the scheme are met.

An example of a self-billing agreement acceptable to HMRC is reproduced below. It is not necessary to follow the exact wording provided the agreement used contains all the relevant information.

Self-Billing Agreement

This is an agreement to a self-billing procedure between

Customer name	VAT number
Supplier name	VAT number

The self-biller (the customer) agrees:

(a) To issue self-billed invoices for all supplies made to them by the self-billee (the supplier) until. . . . . /. . . . . /. . . . . (insert either an end date for the agreement or the date the contract ends).

(b) To complete self-billed invoices showing the supplier's name, address and VAT registration number, together with all the other details which constitute a full VAT invoice.

(c) To make a new self-billing agreement in the event that their VAT registration number changes.

(d) To inform the supplier if the issue of self-billed invoices will be outsourced to a third party.

The self-billee agrees:

(1) To accept invoices raised by the self-biller on their behalf until . . . . /. . . . . /. . . . . (insert either an end date for the agreement or the date the contract ends).

(2) Not to raise sales invoices for the transactions covered by the agreement.

(3) To notify the customer immediately if they
- change their VAT registration number
- cease to be VAT-registered; or
- sell their business, or part of their business.

Signed by	Signed by
On behalf of	On behalf of
Date	Date

Customers in other countries

Self-billing is not restricted to domestic supplies and self-billing agreements can be made with businesses in other EU countries and in countries outside the EU. However, it should be borne in mind that EU countries set their own conditions for self-billing agreements and any such agreement negotiated must meet the conditions and procedures in place in the EU country in whose territory the goods or services are supplied. Points to bear in mind include:

- Where a customer in another EU country provides a document to himself in respect of a supply to him by a UK-registered person,
  - (i) the document must comply with the conditions set out in (*a*)–(*c*) above and, in the case of an electronic self-billed document, must be one which the UK supplier's accounting system can accept; and
  - (ii) in the case of a supply of goods, the UK supplier must still be able to meet all the conditions in **19.11 EUROPEAN UNION: SINGLE MARKET** in order to have evidence for zero-rating.
- Where a UK customer raises a self-billed invoice on behalf of his supplier in another EU country,
  - (i) that invoice may establish the time of acquisition in the same way as an invoice issued by the supplier (see **19.7 EUROPEAN UNION: SINGLE MARKET**); and
  - (ii) in the case of an electronic self-billed invoice, the supplier may have problems with the format of the invoice if the electronic method used is neither advanced electronic signature nor electronic data interchange (EDI). This is because some tax authorities do not accept all the electronic methods of raising invoices that are permissible in the UK.
- Where a customer outside the EU provides a document to himself in respect of a supply of goods to him by a UK-registered person, the UK supplier must still be able to meet all the requirements for documentary evidence of export (see **21.24 EXPORTS**).
- Where a UK customer raises a self-billed invoice on behalf of a supplier of goods from outside the EU, the customer may need to check what information the supplier will need to be included on the invoice raised on his behalf so that it is acceptable to his own tax authorities as evidence of export.
- For supplies of services to and from all non-UK businesses, the UK customer/supplier must be familiar with the place of supply rules (see **65.12–65.28 SUPPLY: PLACE OF SUPPLY**) and agree the correct VAT treatment of the supply with the other party from the outset.

Tax points for self-billed supplies

See **66.4 SUPPLY: TIME OF SUPPLY**.

Self-billed debit notes

Where a self-billing arrangement is in operation, a customer cannot reduce the value of the supply on a subsequent self-billed invoice. He must issue a debit note showing the amount of the adjustment to the value of the supply.

[*SI 1995/2518, Reg 13(3)(3A)–(3F); SI 2003/3220, Reg 4*]. (VAT Notice 700/62/03, paras 3.1, 3.3, 3.4, 4.1, 4.2, 4.4, 4.6, 7.1–7.4, 8).

Understated VAT

If the self-billed invoice understates the VAT chargeable on the supply, HMRC may, by notice served on the recipient and the supplier, elect that the amount of VAT understated by the document is VAT due from the recipient and not the supplier. [*VATA 1994, s 29*].

Retailers' invoices

[39.7] Where the registered taxable person is a retailer, he is not required to provide a VAT invoice unless a customer requests it. Where an invoice is requested, one of the following options may be available.

(a) **Less detailed VAT invoices.** Provided the consideration does not exceed £250 and provided the supply is not to a person in another EU country, the VAT invoice need only contain particulars of
- the name, address and registration number of the retailer;
- the time of supply;
- a description sufficient to identify the goods or services supplied;
- the total amount payable including VAT; and
- for each rate of VAT chargeable, the gross amount payable including VAT, and the VAT rate applicable.

The effect of the above is that where an EU customer requests an invoice a full VAT invoice must be issued.
The invoice must not contain any reference to any exempt supply. [*SI 1995/2518, Reg 16; SI 2003/3220, Reg 10*].
See below for VAT invoices for petrol and derv.
Where *credit cards* are accepted, the sales voucher given to the cardholder at the time of sale may be adapted to serve as a less detailed VAT invoice by including all the above information. Where an invoice is issued as well as the credit card voucher, only one of the documents must be in the form of a VAT invoice.
To calculate the amount of VAT in a VAT-inclusive price, the VAT fraction 7/47 (1/6 from 4 January 2011; 3/23 from 1 December 2008 to 31 December 2009) must be applied to the total invoice amount.

(b) **Modified VAT invoices.** Provided the customer agrees, an invoice can be issued showing the *VAT-inclusive* value of each standard-rated or reduced rate supply (instead of the VAT-exclusive value — see **39.4**(*g*) above). At the foot of the invoice, there must be shown separately
- the total VAT-inclusive value of standard-rated or reduced rate supplies;
- the total VAT payable on those supplies shown in sterling;
- the total value, excluding VAT, of those supplies;
- the total value of any zero-rated supplies included on the invoice; and
- the total value of any exempt supplies included on the invoice.

In all other respects the invoice should show the details required for a full VAT invoice (see **39.4** above).

Where options (*a*) or (*b*) are not available, a full VAT invoice under **39.4** above must be supplied. (VAT Notice 700, para 16.6).

Petrol and diesel oil (derv)

Where the VAT-inclusive amount is £250 or less, a less detailed VAT invoice may be issued (see *(a)* above). Where the VAT-inclusive amount is more than £250 the particulars required on a full VAT invoice are modified so that the vehicle registration number and not the customer's name and address is shown on the VAT invoice. The type of supply and the number of gallons/litres need not be shown. (VAT Notice 700, para 17.1).

Foreign currency invoices

If a VAT invoice is issued in a foreign currency, all values required to be entered for VAT purposes under *(a)* and *(b)* above must be converted into sterling. See **71.18 VALUATION**.

Cash and carry wholesalers

[39.8] Cash and carry wholesalers may adapt their till rolls to meet the VAT invoice requirements provided all the following conditions are met. If not, HMRC may require normal VAT invoices to be issued.

- A product code is used which identifies the different classes of goods sold. The coding system should be devised by the wholesaler using a number of at least two digits and probably three or more digits where the range of products sold is wide.
- Product code lists are prepared and provided to all VAT-registered customers.
- The till roll must provide all the details required for a full VAT invoice (see **39.4** above).
- Copy till rolls and product code lists must be kept for six years or such shorter period as HMRC may allow.

(VAT Notice 700, para 17.2).

Arrangements for particular businesses

[39.9] The arrangements for particular businesses are listed below.

(a) **Authenticated receipts in the construction industry.** See **42.21**(2) **LAND AND BUILDINGS: ZERO AND REDUCED RATE SUPPLIES AND DIY HOUSE-BUILDERS.**

(b) **Banks.** It has been agreed with the British Bankers' Association that a bank may modify the details required on a full VAT invoice in the following ways.
- The customer's account number may be used instead of the address on VAT invoices for services provided by the bank.
- Identifying numbers may be omitted from such invoices.
- The bank branch or department issuing invoices may use their sorting code number in place of the bank address.

(HMRC VAT Guidance V1–24A, para 16.1.1).

(c) **Cash and carry wholesalers.** See **39.8** above.

(d) **Retailers.** See **39.7** above.

(e) **Solicitors.** For reasons of confidentiality, many solicitors invoice clients with a two-part document, usually consisting of
- a bill section in the upper part showing separate charges for professional services and expenses; and
- a tear-off VAT invoice in the lower part for production to HMRC.

The bill section must not be capable of being mistaken for a VAT invoice. In particular it should not show the supplier's VAT registration number and should preferably contain a statement such as 'This is not a VAT invoice'. If VAT is shown as a separate amount, the rate should not be specified and a clear reference to the accompanying VAT invoice should be made.

The VAT invoice section should contain a description of the supply sufficient to identify it as solicitor's professional services.

(HMRC VAT Guidance V1–24A, para 16.6).

(f) **Stockbrokers.** Contract notes are frequently the only transaction records issued by stockbrokers who adapt them for use as VAT invoices. As contract notes often show only an abbreviated address for the client (or show no address at all), HMRC have agreed with the Stock Exchange Council that computerised unique code reference numbers will be accepted in lieu of addresses on contract notes used as VAT invoices provided
- clients are formally advised of their code reference numbers and asked to retain the advice for production to HMRC when required; and
- the record of code reference numbers is available for similar inspection at the offices of the stockbroker.

HMRC reserve the right to insist on full addresses being shown if considered necessary in any particular case.

(HMRC VAT Guidance V1–24A, para 16.7).

Electronic invoicing

[39.10] '*Electronic invoicing*' is the transmission and storage of invoices, without the delivery of paper documents, by electronic means. Electronic equipment employing wires, radio transmission, optical technologies or other electromagnetic means is used for the processing (including digital compression) and storage of data.

Conditions for electronic transmission of invoices

Where, in respect of a supply of goods of services, a registered business provides a document that purports to be a VAT invoice by electronic transmission, the document can only be treated as a VAT invoice if certain conditions are satisfied.

(a) *Contents of the invoice.* Electronic invoices must contain the same information as paper invoices. See **39.4** and, in respect of invoices to other EU countries, **39.5** above.

Batches of invoices. Where a business provides invoices in batches to the same recipient by electronic transmission, details common to each invoice need only be stated once for each batch file (rather than once per invoice). For example, instead of repeating the full name and address of the customer on every invoice in the batch, a business could include the full information on the batch header and use an abridged or coded version of that information within each individual invoice message.

Credit notes. See **39.15** below for details required on credit notes raised for UK supplies. Where a business provides a person in another EU country with a document which amends a VAT invoice (e.g. a credit note) that document must contain all the information required to be included on an invoice (see **39.5** above).

(b) *Authenticity of the origin and integrity of the invoice data.* Both the supplier and the customer must be able to guarantee the authenticity of the origin and integrity of the contents of the invoice data. All EU countries must allow electronic invoicing using an advance electronic signature or Electronic Data Interchange (see (i) and (ii) below) but they can also accept other means of e-invoicing for supplies in their own country. HMRC accept the following means.

(i) An '*advanced electronic signature*', i.e. an 'electronic signature' which is
- uniquely linked to the 'signatory';
- capable of identifying the signatory;
- created using means that the signatory can maintain under his sole control; and
- linked to the data to which it relates in such a manner that any subsequent change of the data is detectable.

'*Electronic signature*' means data in electronic form which are attached to or logically associated with other electronic data and which serve as a method of authentication.

'*Signatory*' means a person who holds a signature-creation device and acts either on his own behalf or on behalf of the natural or legal person or entity he represents.

An electronic invoicing system that meets these requirements can be used without HMRC authorisation and can be used for both UK domestic electronic invoicing and electronic invoicing to other EU countries.

(ii) '*Electronic data interchange*' ('EDI'), i.e. the computer-to-computer exchange of structured data that permits automatic processing by the recipient. It is traditionally more commonly used for high-volume data transfers between businesses, using agreed standards (e.g. UN/EDIFACT) to structure the data. There should be an interchange agreement between the EDI trading partners making provision for the use of procedures that guarantee the authenticity of the origin and integrity of the data. Examples of such procedures include
- use of secure networks;
- controls over access to networks (e.g. checking 'trading relationships');

- syntax checking of data in accordance with the rules of the transmission standard; and
- summary file control reporting.

An electronic invoicing system that meets these requirements can be used without HMRC authorisation and can be used for both UK domestic electronic invoicing and electronic invoicing to other EU countries.

(iii) *Such other electronic means as may be approved by HMRC where the document relates to supplies of goods or services made in the UK* provided the supplier (or, in the case of self-billed electronic invoices, the customer) is able to

- impose a satisfactory level of control over the authenticity and integrity of the invoice data (e.g. security of networks/communication links, access controls, and message transfer protocols (such as http-s)); and
- meet all the other conditions for electronic invoicing.

Examples of allowable systems are

- Internet-based systems (including EDI via Internet) such as XML/XSL messages transmitted using http; EDI files sent under FTP or as attachments to e-mail; and free format or structured text messages sent by Internet e-mail;
- intermediary service providers; and
- bill presentment where invoices are 'presented' on websites, hosted either by suppliers or their agents, and customers simply access these websites to view their invoices.

Tax authorities in some other EU countries may not accept invoicing where the authenticity of the origin and integrity of the invoice data are guaranteed using these means. If so, potential customers in those countries would not be able to use a supplier's invoices as evidence of a taxable supply to them and may not be willing to do business with that supplier.

Where a business wishes to invoice electronically but its system is not covered by (i) or (ii) above and it is not sure whether its system meets the requirements of (iii) above, it should write to the National Advice Service with, if possible,

- an indication of the standard under which the invoice message has been drafted;
- a formatted 'dump' of an example invoice; and
- an overview of the main system concepts, including control over authenticity and integrity of data.

HMRC will then comment on the acceptability of the invoice message. If it is not acceptable, they will advise on what further information is required and how this may be accommodated.

(c) *Controls over the transmission of invoices*. Businesses must transmit invoices in a secure environment, using industry-accepted security technologies on

- the messages themselves; or

- communication links/networks over which the invoices are transferred.

Examples of these include http-s, SSL, S-MIME and FTP. Other procedural means that offer similar assurances may also be used.

(d) *Protecting the authenticity and integrity of invoices.* Businesses must be able to ensure the authenticity and integrity of their invoice data during the transfer between trading partners. HMRC will not be over-prescriptive in specifying the detailed forms that control may take but a business must be able to demonstrate that it has control over

- completeness and accuracy of the invoice data;
- timeliness of processing;
- prevention of, or detection of, possible corruption of data during transmission;
- prevention of duplication of processing (by the recipient); and
- prevention of the automatic processing, by the recipient, of certain types of invoice on which VAT may not be recoverable (e.g. margin scheme invoices).

A business must also be able to demonstrate that it has a recovery plan in case of a system failure or loss of data and maintain an audit trail between its electronic invoicing system(s) and the internal application system(s) that are used to process the electronic invoices.

Supplies to other EU countries

Where a UK business issues electronic invoices for supplies to other EU countries, it must meet the UK conditions for electronic invoicing. But it should also check whether the customer's system can accept invoices in the format used before mutually agreeing to invoice electronically. The tax authorities of certain other EU countries, although accepting the use of advance electronic signature and EDI, do not accept all the electronic methods of raising invoices that are permissible in the UK.

Supplies to non-EU countries

Electronic transmission of invoices and credit notes to non-EU countries is permitted provided the acceptability of this is confirmed with the tax authorities in the receiving country.

Conditions for electronic storage

A business (whether supplier or customer) must:

- Guarantee the authenticity and integrity of its invoice data during and after application processing (see (*d*) above) and throughout the storage period by electronic or procedural means, and store all the data related to its invoices.
- Store its invoices in a readable format and be able to readily recreate the invoice information as at the time of its original transmission.
- Keep history files so that it can find the appropriate details from any particular time in the past if asked to do so by an HMRC officer.
- Keep copies of all electronic invoices issued or received for six years (although if this causes serious storage problems or undue expense, HMRC may agree to a shorter period for some records).

This also applies to scanned images of paper documents used and stored as electronic records for VAT purposes.

Storage abroad

Electronic invoices can be stored in another EU country provided they can be produced to HMRC when required in a readable form, and within a reasonable period of time, at a mutually agreed place. HMRC recommend that a business maintains on-line access to its records if it stores them outside the UK. Electronic invoices can also be stored outside the EU provided that, additionally, the country where they are stored respects European Data Protection principles regarding the storage of personal data (names, addresses, etc.).

Outsourcing electronic invoices

A business may outsource the physical responsibility for the issuing of its electronic sales invoices to a third party, although all the legal obligations relating to the contents, storage and production of the invoices raised remain with the business.

Inability to meet the e-invoicing conditions

If a business

- is unable to meet all the conditions for transmission and storage of electronic invoicing set out above, it must issue paper invoices;
- has issued and stored invoices electronically, but failed to meet the conditions, it must issue paper invoices until HMRC are satisfied that its system is acceptable; and
- persistently fails to meet the conditions, it may be liable to a penalty.

Use of paper and electronic VAT invoicing at the same time

In normal circumstances, it is only possible for a business to run a dual system (i.e. raising both electronic and paper invoices for the same supplies or with the same trading partners) when running a controlled trial of an electronic invoicing system. Once the trial is over, the business must stop running the dual system and the electronic invoice becomes the legal document for VAT purposes. However, where a business has a specific need to run a dual system, it should contact the National Advice Service who will decide whether an exception can be made.

HMRC access to electronic systems

In order to check electronic systems, HMRC may request access to

- the operations of any computer systems which produce or receive VAT invoices or documents, and to the data stored on them;
- supporting documentation including file structures etc., audit trail, controls, safe keeping, and information on how the accounting system is organised; and
- advice on interrogation facilities available on the system.

HMRC must be able to take copies of information from the system, if required. A business may be able to meet its obligations as regards production of records by giving HMRC

- physical access to systems at its premises;
- indirect access (by providing information on electronic media or possibly via remote access);
- a resident audit programme installed at the request of the visiting HMRC officer; or
- any other reasonable method agreed with HMRC.

See also **31.12 HMRC: POWERS** for powers of HMRC to inspect computers generally.

[*SI 1995/2518, Regs A13, 13A; 14(6); SI 2003/3220, Regs 3, 5, 9*]. (VAT Notice 700/63/07; VAT Information Sheet 16/03, para 5.3).

Corporate purchasing (procurement) cards

[39.11] Such cards are designed to eliminate much of the paperwork in the purchasing process. Where a purchase is made, the supplier normally transmits the invoice information to the appropriate card company or bank (the 'transmission date'). At agreed intervals, the purchaser receives a VAT invoice report from the card company or bank. Some purchasing cards offer two levels of invoice detail, the level of detail received by the cardholder being dependent upon the capability of the supplier's accounting system. *The provisions in both (1) and (2) below have the force of law.*

(1) Line Item Detail (LID) invoices

These provide detailed, itemised information on a line-by-line basis. HMRC have agreed to waive the requirement to show the date of issue of the document under **39.4**(*c*) above. The invoice report issued to the purchaser will show the transmission date for each transaction and is acceptable as evidence for input tax recovery (subject to the normal rules) from that date.

(2) Summary VAT invoices

Where a supplier's system cannot transmit LID invoices, HMRC generally do not require a supplier to issue an invoice to the customer. Instead they accept a Summary VAT invoice report issued by the card company or bank in support of an input tax claim provided no single transaction has a value of more than £5,000 and the report contains the following information.

- Value of the supply.
- VAT amount charged.
- VAT rate.
- Time of supply.
- Description of the goods.
- Supplier's name, address and VAT registration number.
- Customer's name and address.

A supplier must issue a VAT invoice if the value of a 'single transaction' exceeds £5,000 or if specifically requested by the customer. In the latter case, the invoice must be clearly endorsed 'Paid by Purchasing Card – Supplementary VAT invoice'. A '*single transaction*' is the total value of purchases made using a card at any one time, e.g. one 'swipe' of the card.

In all cases, the supplier must continue to generate contemporaneous VAT invoices for output tax accounting purposes for all purchasing card transactions.

(VAT Notice 701/48/02, paras 3.1–3.4).

Rounding of VAT on invoices

Invoice traders

[39.12] By concession, invoice traders (as opposed to retailers) may round *down* the total VAT payable on all goods and services shown on a VAT invoice to a whole penny (i.e. they may ignore any fraction of a penny). The concession is applicable only where the VAT charged to customers and the VAT paid to HMRC is the same.

Calculations of VAT based on lines of goods or services included with other goods or services in the same invoice must either be made by

(a) rounding down to the nearest 0.1p; or
(b) rounding to the nearest 1p or 0.5p.

For example, 86.76p and 86.74p would both be rounded down to 86.7p under (*a*) but rounded up to 87p and down to 86.50p respectively under method (*b*).

Whichever method is used must be adopted consistently. The final amount of VAT payable may be rounded down to the nearest whole penny.

Calculations of VAT based on VAT per unit or per article, e.g. for price lists, must be either

- to four decimal places and then rounded down to three places (e.g. £0.0024 rounded down to £0.002 (0.2p)); or
- to the nearest 1p or 0.5p (but not to 'nil' on any unit or article, i.e. a minimum of 0.5p per article or unit).

Calculation of VAT at retailers

Retailers who do not use a retail scheme but use till technology to identify the VAT due on each transaction and issue an invoice, calculating VAT at line level or invoice level, must not round the VAT figure down. They may, however, round (up and down) each VAT calculation. Retailers using a retail scheme to account for VAT are not affected by these provisions.

(VAT Notice 700, paras 17.5, 17.6).

See also *Fiscale eenheid Koninklijke Ahold NV v Staatssecretaris van Financiën, ECJ Case C-484/06; 24 January 2008 unreported* (TVC 22.562) where the Advocate-General held that the VAT Directives do not regulate in detail the rounding up or down of amounts of VAT. This is therefore a matter for national law although this must comply with all the relevant rules and principles which flow from the Directives. Those rules and principles do not permit retailers to round down the amount of VAT in the VAT-inclusive price of each item sold, in order to determine the amount of output tax which they must declare in their regular returns. For a similar case see *JD Wetherspoon plc v HMRC, ECJ Case C-302/07* [2009] STC 1022 (TVC 22.563).

Time limits for issuing invoices

[39.13] A VAT invoice or a document treated as VAT invoice under **39.2** above must be provided within 30 days after the time when the supply is treated as taking place (see **66.1** *et seq* **SUPPLY: TIME OF SUPPLY**) or within such longer period after that time as HMRC allow in general or special directions. [*VATA 1994, Sch 11 para 2A; FA 2002, s 24; SI 1995/2518, Reg 13(5)*]. Extension of this time limit is permitted *without application* where

- an extension has been allowed for tax point purposes under the 14-day rule (see **66.8** and **66.18 SUPPLY: TIME OF SUPPLY**);
- special accounting arrangements have been approved; or
- where a newly registered business has not been notified of its VAT registration number (in which case the VAT invoice must be issued within 30 days from the date of advice of that number).

In all other cases, application must be made, in writing, to HMRC for an extension of the time limit.

(VAT Notice 700, para 16.2).

Transmission of invoices

[39.14] As an alternative to sending VAT invoices by post, they may be sent to customers by fax or e-mail. The normal rules regarding VAT invoices apply. Invoices received in either of these ways are acceptable as evidence for input tax deduction (subject to the normal rules). However, where transmission is by fax, if the customer has a thermal-paper fax machine, the invoice may not be permanent and the customer may not be able to fulfil the obligation to preserve the invoice for six years. It is suggested that the supplier warns the customer of this possibility, preferably on the VAT invoice itself.

See also **39.10** above for electronic transmission of invoices, including the use of 'outsourcing' for the issue of invoices.

(VAT Notice 700, para 17.8).

Credit and debit notes

[39.15] Where credit or contingent discount (e.g. discount on condition that the customer buys more goods at a later date) is allowed to a customer who can reclaim all the VAT on the supply as input tax, there is no obligation to adjust the original VAT charge provided both parties agree not to do so (although records of outputs and inputs will still need to be adjusted). Otherwise an adjustment should be made to the original VAT charge in the appropriate period. See **56.6 RECORDS**. A credit note should be issued to the customer and a copy retained. Alternatively, if both parties agree, the customer can issue a VAT debit note. A valid debit note places the same legal obligations on both parties as a valid credit note and must fulfil the same conditions.

To be valid for VAT purposes, a credit or debit note must reflect a genuine mistake or overcharge or an agreed reduction in the value of the supply and be issued within one month of this being discovered or agreed. It must give value to the customer, i.e. represent a genuine entitlement or claim on the part of the customer for the amount overcharged to be either refunded or offset against the value of future supplies. It should be headed 'credit note' or 'debit note' as appropriate and show

(a) identifying number and date of issue;
(b) supplier's and customer's name and address;
(c) supplier's registration number;
(d) description identifying goods or services for which credit is given;
(e) quantity and amount credited for each description and reason for credit, e.g. 'returned goods';
(f) total amount credited excluding VAT;
(g) rate and amount of VAT credited;
(h) number and date of the original VAT invoice. If not possible, HMRC will need to be satisfied that VAT has been accounted for on the original supply.

Where a credit note includes credits for zero-rated or exempt supplies, each must be totalled separately and the credit note must show clearly that no credit for VAT has been given for them.

Credit notes issued without VAT adjustment should state 'This is not a credit note for VAT'. It will still be necessary to adjust records of outputs and inputs in order to complete the VAT returns.

Credit notes to persons in other EU countries

A credit note issued to a person in another EU country must contain the same particulars as the VAT invoice(s) that it is intended to amend. See **39.5** above.

Accounting for credit or debit notes

A taxable person who makes a supply and a taxable person who receives the supply must adjust their VAT account where

- there is an increase or decrease in the consideration due on a supply;
- the increase or decrease is evidenced by a debit note, credit note or any other document having the same effect;

- the increase or decrease includes an amount of tax; and
- the increase or decrease occurs after the end of the prescribed accounting period in which the original supply took place.

The person receiving the supply must enter the relevant amount of tax as a positive amount (in the case of an increase) or a negative amount (in the case of a decrease). The entry is made in the tax allowable portion of his VAT account which relates to either

- the prescribed accounting period in which the supply was received (if he is insolvent); or
- the prescribed accounting period in which he gives effect to the increase or decrease in his business accounts (in any other case).

The three-year time limit that applied to the adjustment of VAT accounts as a result of changes in consideration was removed with effect from 1 April 2009.

Bankruptcy, insolvent liquidation and administrative receivership

The tax point for credit or debit notes issued by or on behalf of insolvent traders is the date on which the supply was originally made or received.

Reverse charge supplies

For adjustments relating to supplies where the recipient is liable to account for VAT under the reverse charge procedure for mobile phones and computer chips, see **4.21** ANTI-AVOIDANCE.

Cancelled registrations

The tax point for any credit or debit note issued or received after the date of cancellation of registration is the date of the original supply. If this happens after the final VAT return has been submitted, HMRC should be contacted.

VAT rate

The rate of VAT to be used for a credit or debit note is the one in force at the tax point of the original supply.

Returned or replaced goods

Where such goods are replaced with similar goods, the original VAT charge may stand or be cancelled (by issuing a credit note if a VAT invoice has previously been issued) and VAT charged on the replacement. If the original VAT charge is allowed to stand, VAT need not be accounted for on the replacement goods provided they are supplied free of charge. If supplied at a *lower* price, the VAT charged may be reduced by a credit note. If supplied at a *higher* price, additional VAT must be accounted for.

[*SI 1995/2518, Reg 38; SI 1997/1086, Reg 6; SI 2007/1418; SI 2009/586, Reg 5*]. (VAT Notice 700, paras 18.2, 18.3).

Bad debts

Output tax paid on an invoice which proves to be a bad debt cannot subsequently be reclaimed by issuing a credit note for the unpaid amount. See **7 BAD DEBT RELIEF**.

Correction of VAT invoices following a change in the VAT rate

[39.16] Under *VATA 1994, s 88*, a trader may elect to override certain of the normal tax point rules which determine whether a particular supply is taxable at the old or new rate when there is a change in the rate of VAT or in the descriptions of exempt, zero-rated or reduced-rate supplies. The trader is allowed to account for VAT at the old rates on supplies actually 'made' before the date of change but for which the invoice and payment tax points would have occurred later. See **55.10 RATES OF VAT** for full details.

Where under the above circumstances a VAT invoice is issued before the election, the supplier must within 45 days (before 1 December 2008 the limit was 14 days) provide the customer with a credit note headed 'Credit note – change of VAT rate' showing the information required in **39.15** (*a*)–(*d*), (*g*) and (*h*) above. [*SI 1995/2518, Reg 15; SI 2003/1485; SI 2008/3021*]. See **56.6** and **56.9 RECORDS** for the recording of credit notes.

Supplementary charge

Where a supplementary charge is due under *FA 2009 Sch 3* in respect of a supply (see **55.6 RATES OF VAT**) and a VAT invoice has been issued that does not include the supplementary charge, the supplier must, within 45 days after the date when the supplementary charge becomes due, provide the person to whom the supply is made with an invoice headed "Supplementary charge invoice" and containing the following particulars—

- the identifying number and date of issue of the supplementary charge invoice;
- the amount of the supplementary charge to VAT;
- the name, address and registration number of the supplier;
- the name and address of the person to whom the supply is made; and
- the identifying number and date of issue of the VAT invoice. [*SI 1995/2518, Reg 15A; SI 2009/3241, Reg 3*].

Foreign language invoices

[39.17] Where a person in the UK receives a VAT invoice (or part of a VAT invoice) in a language other than English, HMRC may, by notice in writing, require that person to provide them with an English translation of the invoice within 30 days of the date of the notice. [*SI 1995/2518, Reg 13B; SI 2003/3220, Reg 6*]. This will be done on an exceptional basis and any requests will be targeted at selective invoices only. (VAT Information Sheet 16/03, para 7.1).

Key points

[39.18] Points to consider are as follows.

- There is sometimes confusion about when a business must issue a VAT invoice as a compulsory requirement. In basic terms, an invoice must be issued for any taxable supply to a VAT-registered business in the UK or a VAT-registered business in an EU country outside the UK (excluding a zero-rated sale). However, in the case of zero-rated sales of goods to a VAT-registered business in the EU (outside UK), a tax invoice must still be issued as it will be classed as an 'acquisition' for the business receiving the goods.
- A VAT invoice does not need to be issued (as a compulsory requirement) in relation to an exempt supply or any supply where the input tax is blocked for the customer, e.g. if relevant to motor cars or business entertainment.
- It is important that a VAT invoice is issued to any VAT-registered business in the UK that requests one because this will then serve as input tax evidence for the business in question. In certain circumstances (see below) a less detailed VAT invoice can be issued which is also acceptable as input tax evidence.
- If a sale is made under a margin scheme, e.g. for second-hand car dealers, then an invoice must not be issued that shows an amount of VAT as a separate entry. In the case of a sale under the tour operators margin scheme, a VAT invoice must not be issued.
- It is possible that sales made by a retailer will be subject to an input tax claim by the buyer (e.g. in the situation where stationery or computer-related items are being bought from a retail stationery store). In such cases, the retailer is obliged to issue a VAT invoice, although a less detailed VAT invoice may again be sufficient.
- A convenient and acceptable approach in some commercial situations is for the customer to issue a self-billed invoice to a supplier. This document is a substitute for a VAT invoice, and must contain certain pieces of information as a requirement (e.g. supplier's VAT registration number and a message confirming that output tax needs to be declared by the supplier). Self-billing is particularly relevant in those situations when the price of a transaction is fixed by the customer (e.g. the valuation of measured building work in the case of construction services).
- Self-billing does not require permission from HMRC, but does require conditions imposed by HMRC to be fully met for the arrangement to be valid. A self-billing agreement must be in place and agreed between the customer and supplier.
- Another substitute for a VAT invoice in the construction industry is an authenticated receipt. The document will be issued by the customer but only becomes valid for VAT purposes (input tax claim) if it has been signed (authenticated) by the supplier. The authenticated receipt system can only be adopted if payments for

building services are made on a continuous basis (i.e. it would not be relevant to a single supply of services) and if the customer and supplier both agree to adopt the procedure.

- Visiting officers from HMRC will check arrangements for both self-billing and authenticated receipts are being operated correctly. The onus is on the customer to get the procedures right, otherwise a claim for input tax could be invalidated.
- It is common practice in many professions (e.g. accountancy and legal profession) for VAT invoices to be issued only when payment has been made by a customer in relation to a continuous supply of services. Alternative documents raised in advance of the invoice, e.g. fee note, application for payment, pro-forma invoice or request for payment are not classed as a VAT invoice. This means that no output tax liability has been incurred by the supplier (assuming other relevant conditions are met) and no input tax can be claimed by the customer.
- As a technical point, it is suggested that alternative documents that are not VAT invoices (as listed in previous paragraph) be clearly highlighted along the lines of: 'This document is not a VAT invoice, which will be issued to you when payment has been received.'
- Since 1 October 2007, it has been compulsory for each VAT invoice issued by a business to have a 'unique' identifying number. So a business issuing invoices from a pre-printed pad where numbers 001 to 100 are shown on each pad must take steps to ensure each pad has a unique feature to make the numbers in each series different, e.g. pre-fixed by a letter or extra number. The key point is that no two invoices issued by a business should ever have the same number.
- If a customer is responsible for paying the output tax on a sales invoice (e.g. supply to an overseas business customer in another EU country under the reverse charge rules, or to a UK business because of sales of mobile phones/computer chips with an invoice value exceeding £5,000), then a note needs to be included on the invoice to alert the customer to his responsibilities.
- A retailer can issue a less detailed VAT invoice, as long as the total value of the sale (including VAT) is less than £250. In such cases, the VAT does not need to be separately itemised on the invoice, and the name and address of the customer does not need to be shown. However, the invoice must still show enough detail to enable the customer to know exactly how much VAT he has been charged on the sale (e.g. by recognising any zero-rated elements of the sale) for input tax purposes.
- An EU customer (outside the UK) can request a full VAT invoice rather than a less detailed tax invoice, even if the conditions for a less detailed invoice are met, e.g. value of sale is less than £250.
- Always remember that a credit note can only issued if there is a genuine reduction in the value of the original sale in relation to a supply of goods or services (e.g. due to a pricing error or goods

being returned). A credit note cannot be issued to adjust a bad debt – there are separate accounting procedures for bad debt relief.

- If a credit note is issued, the VAT adjustment will be based on the rate of VAT that applied when the original invoice was raised.

40

Isle of Man

De Voil Indirect Tax Service. See V1.216; V1.217.

Introduction

[40.1] The Isle of Man (IOM) is not part of the UK and the common tax area between the two countries results from an administrative agreement between the UK and the IOM governments contained in the *Customs and Excise Agreement 1979* (as amended). In the UK, the agreement was implemented by the *Isle of Man Act 1979*. *Section 6* of that Act relates to VAT.

VAT is administered and collected in the IOM by the Manx Customs and Excise Service under the *Value Added Tax Act 1996* (of Tynwald).

The spirit of the agreement between the UK and IOM is that IOM legislation parallels UK legislation and procedures, with certain exceptions, but so that VAT is not charged twice on the same transaction. [*IMA 1979, s 6; SI 1982/1067; SI 1982/1068*]. Differences include

- legislation relating to VAT on gaming machines under *VATA 1994, s 23* (see **57.4 RECREATION AND SPORT**) does not have an equivalent in the IOM [*IMA 1979, s 1(d)*];
- legislation relating to refund of VAT on the construction of new homes by do-it-yourself housebuilders under *VATA 1994, s 35* (see **42.23 LAND AND BUILDINGS: ZERO AND REDUCED RATE SUPPLIES AND DIY HOUSEBUILDERS**) does not have an equivalent in the IOM [*SI 1982/1067, Art 9*]; and
- the rate of VAT on accommodation in hotels and similar establishments in the IOM, including the provision of holiday accommodation and the letting of camp sites, is 5%.

Registration

[40.2] Separate VAT registers are maintained in the IOM and the UK. There are special provisions for determining, or enabling HMRC to determine, where a person is to be registered who would otherwise be liable to be registered in both places.

A person who is *liable to be registered* in the UK under *VATA 1994, Sch 1 para 1* (see **59.3 REGISTRATION**) and who

- has 'an establishment' both in the UK and the IOM, or
- does not have an establishment in either country

will be registered in the UK or IOM as HMRC determine; but unless or until they determine that he should be registered in the IOM, he is required to be registered in the UK. HMRC may, however, at any time determine that a person within (*a*) or (*b*) above

- who is registered in the UK, is instead to be registered in the IOM, in which case he ceases to be, or required to be, registered in the UK from such date as they determine (although still remaining liable for payment of VAT on business assets held on the last day of registration, see **59.34 REGISTRATION**); and
- who is registered in the IOM, is instead to be registered in the UK from such date as they determine, in which case any amount of VAT required to be paid in the IOM is deemed to have been an amount of VAT due in the UK.

Where a person is registered, or required to be registered, in the IOM, the provisions of *VATA 1994, Sch 1 para 5* (notification of liability for, and date of registration in, the UK, see **59.4 REGISTRATION**) and *VATA 1994, Sch 1 para 9* (entitlement to be registered, see **59.2 REGISTRATION**) do not apply to that person. HMRC may, however, determine that any person to whom those provisions do apply shall be registered in the IOM.

A person registered in the UK who has no establishment in the IOM, or is the representative member of a VAT group (see **27.2 GROUPS OF COMPANIES**) no member of which has an establishment there, must notify HMRC if such an establishment is subsequently acquired. Such notification may be treated as an event requiring the cancellation of the person's, or that group's, registration.

'*An establishment*' in a country is where there is a place from which a person carries on a business in that country or carries on business through a branch or agent in that country. For this purpose an agent is a person who has the authority or capacity to create legal relations between his principal and a third party. [*SI 1982/1067, Arts 11, 12*].

De Voil Indirect Tax Service. See V2.127; V2.140; V2.156.

Imports, exports and removals

[40.3] Within the common tax area of the UK and the IOM, a registered business accounts for VAT in the country in which it is registered. For example, an IOM business, making taxable supplies in the UK accounts for the VAT in the IOM. If the business imports goods into the common tax area, the import VAT can be paid (or deferred) and reclaimed as input tax in the IOM subject to the normal rules for input tax deduction.

Movements of goods from the UK to the IOM and vice versa are not normally treated as exports or imports provided that, for goods removed from the IOM to the UK

- any VAT due has been accounted for in the IOM, or
- if the goods are relieved of VAT in the IOM, the conditions of that relief have not been broken.

Key points

[40.4] Points to consider are as follows.

- By agreement, the IOM and UK adopt a common VAT system, even though the IOM is not part of the UK. This agreement is important to both avoid tax being charged twice in some cases and also to ensure the overall systems are consistent with each other. There are some minor differences in the rules between the two countries – for example, holiday accommodation in the Isle of Man is taxed at 5% rather than being standard-rated as in the UK.
- Goods that are despatched between the UK and IOM and vice versa are not normally treated as exports or imports provided that, for goods removed from the IOM to the UK, any VAT due has been accounted for in the IOM, or if the goods are relieved of VAT in the IOM, the conditions of that relief have not been broken.

41

Land and Buildings: Exempt Supplies and Option to Tax

Cross-references. See **7.11** BAD DEBT RELIEF for sales of repossessed properties by lenders; CAPITAL GOODS SCHEME (**10**) for the deduction, and adjustment of deduction, of input tax on certain land and buildings by partly exempt businesses; **59.33** REGISTRATION for land and buildings in hand in cancellation of registration; **65.16** SUPPLY: PLACE OF SUPPLY for the place of supply of services relating to land outside the UK and the Isle of Man; **66.13** SUPPLY: TIME OF SUPPLY for the time of supply of land and property.

Definitions, etc.

Definitions and meanings of terms

[41.1] The following general definitions and terms apply for the purposes of this chapter.

(1) 'Approved alteration'

An approved alteration means any of the following.

(a) In the case of a '*protected building*' (see (12) below) which is an ecclesiastical building excluded from the planning consent requirements by *Planning (Listed Buildings and Conservation Areas) Act 1990, s 60*, any works of alteration. A building used or available for use by a minister of religion wholly or mainly as a residence from which to perform the duties of his office is not to be treated as an ecclesiastical building for these purposes. [*VATA 1994, Sch 8 Group 6, Note (6)*].

In England and Wales, the religious denominations which have been granted exclusion are the Church of England, the Church in Wales, the Roman Catholic Church, the Methodist Church, the Baptist Union of Great Britain and the Baptist Union of Wales, and the United Reformed Church.

In Scotland and Northern Ireland, all listed places of worship that are in ecclesiastical use are exempt from listed building controls, although they are still subject to planning controls.

Any alteration, which is not work of repair or maintenance (see below), to the fabric of a listed place of worship that has ecclesiastical exemption is an approved alteration.

(VAT Notice 708, para 9.4).

Alterations to ecclesiastical buildings which require planning consent fall within (*b*) below.

(b) In any other case, works of alteration which cannot be carried out unless authorised under *Planning (Listed Buildings and Conservation Areas) Act 1990, Planning (Listed Buildings and Conservation Areas) (Scotland) Act 1997, Planning (Northern Ireland) Order 1991* or *Ancient Monuments and Archaeological Areas Act 1979* and for which consent has been obtained under the appropriate legislation. [*VATA 1994, Sch 8 Group 6, Note (6)*].

'Crown' and 'Duchy' interest buildings

Listed building consent may not be needed for alterations to buildings on Crown or Duchy land even though it would be needed for similar alterations to listed buildings elsewhere. In such a case, an alteration to the fabric of the building which would otherwise have required consent and which is not work of repair or maintenance (see below) is an approved alteration. [*VATA 1994, Sch 8 Group 6, Note (6)*].

Scheduled monuments

All work affecting scheduled monuments requires scheduled monument consent from the Secretary of State. Approved alterations are those works of alteration for which consent has been obtained. It is possible for a building to be both scheduled and listed. If so, only scheduled monument procedures apply and it should be treated as a scheduled monument for VAT purposes.

Listed building consent

In most cases, an approved alteration falls within (*b*) above and is an alteration for which listed building consent is both needed and has been obtained from the appropriate planning authority (or, in some circumstances, the Secretary of State) prior to the commencement of the work. A supplier will need to find out from his customer (or their architect or surveyor) to what extent the work he is contracted to do has both required and received listed building consent. Listed building consent is not the same as planning permission. In general terms, listed building consent is needed for work on a listed building which would affect its character as a building of special architectural or historic interest. The construction of an extension, or alterations following partial demolition, would certainly require consent but it is difficult to generalise about less radical work, especially as regards internal alterations. It is an offence to carry out work to a listed building without obtaining any required listed building consent. Where this happens, the planning authority cannot issue retrospective listed building consent for the work, although they may permit the unauthorised works to be retained. Such works are *not* then approved alterations (because consent has not been granted at the time the work is carried out) and are standard-rated. Where works to a listed building are carried out without listed building consent being obtained or where work carried out does not comply with a condition in the consent, the local planning authority may issue a 'listed building enforcement notice' for the carrying out of further work. An alteration, which is not work of repair or maintenance (see below), to the fabric of the building under the terms of an enforcement notice is an approved alteration.

(VAT Notice 708, para 9.4).

Alteration or repair and maintenance?

HMRC regard a building as being altered when its fabric, such as its walls, roof, internal surfaces, floors, stairs, windows, doors, plumbing and wiring is changed in a meaningful way. Works of repair or maintenance, or any incidental alteration resulting from works of repair or maintenance, are standard-rated, even if the work has been included in the listed building consent.

See *C & E Commrs v Viva Gas Appliances*, HL [1983] STC 819 (TVC 56.10) where Lord Diplock stated that alteration of a building should be construed as any work on the fabric of the building except that which is so slight or trivial as to attract the application of the *de minimis* rule (although it should be noted that in *The Vicar and Parochial Church Council of St Petroc Minor* (VTD 16450) (TVC 55.53) the tribunal specifically declined to apply this *dicta* on the basis that the context in which 'alteration' was used in that case no longer appears in *VATA 1994*).

Works of repair or maintenance are those tasks designed to minimise, for as long as possible, the need for, and future scale and cost of, further attention to the fabric of the building. Changes to the physical features of the building are not zero-rated alterations if, in the exercise of proper repair and maintenance of the building, they are either

- trifling or insignificant, or
- dictated by the nature and use of modern building materials.

Similarly, if the amount of work or cost is significant, that does not make the work a zero-rated alteration if the inherent character of the work is repair and maintenance.

Examples

Work	*VAT treatment*
Extensions	Alteration
Opening/closing doorways	Alteration

Replacement of rotten wooden windows with UPVC double glazing	Repair or maintenance
Replacement of UPVC double glazing with copies of original wooden windows for aesthetic reasons	Alteration
Installing a window where one did not exist before	Alteration
Re-felt and batten roof	Repair or maintenance
Replacement of a flat roof with a pitched roof	Alteration
Replacement of straw thatch with reeds; and changes to the ridge detail of a thatched roof	Repair or maintenance when carried out as part of the normal renewal programme.
Damp proofing	Repair or maintenance
Making good	Follows the liability of the main work
Re-decorating	Repair or maintenance
Re-pointing	Repair or maintenance
Re-wiring	Repair or maintenance
Extending wiring and plumbing systems	Alteration
Replacing boilers with a larger capacity boiler while extending plumbing systems	Alteration
Flood lighting	Alteration when installed on the building. But neither an alteration nor repair or maintenance (and therefore standard-rated) when installed within the grounds of a building – there is no work to the fabric of the building.

(VAT Notice 708, para 9.3).

Only mains electrical wiring and lighting systems that are either on, or in, the structure of the building itself will be considered to be part of the fabric of the building. Those parts which extend beyond the structure into the grounds (e.g. wiring to floodlights) will not. Electrical appliances which are attached to, and serviced by, the mains supply are not considered to be part of the mains wiring system. (Business Brief 7/2000).

The construction of a building 'separate' from, but in the curtilage (see (3) below) of, a protected building does not constitute an alteration of the protected building and cannot be zero-rated as an approved alteration, even if the work has listed building consent. [*VATA 1994, Sch 8 Group 6 Item 2* and *Notes (6)–(8), (10); SI 1995/283*]. The construction of, and the alteration to, fences, walls, railings and other curtilage structures such as patios and terraces, are therefore standard-rated. Zero-rating may, however, be available under the rules for construction of new buildings (see **42.7 LAND AND BUILDINGS: ZERO AND REDUCED RATE SUPPLIES AND DIY HOUSEBUILDERS**) (i.e. if it is (i) the construction of a completely new self-contained dwelling (including a garage built at the same time for use with it) where there are no restrictions on disposal; or (ii) a completely new self-contained building for use solely for a '*relevant residential purpose*' or a '*relevant charitable purpose*' (see (15) and (13) below respectively)). (VAT Notice 708, para 9.3).

See *C & E Commrs v Arbib*, QB [1995] STC 490 (TVC 55.39) for a consideration of the meaning of 'separate'. In that case, a swimming pool connected to a listed farmhouse by a covered walkway and a brick wall was held not to be a separate building so that the building work on it fell to be zero-rated.

(2) 'Construction of a building'

There is no definition in the legislation of the '*construction of a building*' for zero-rating purposes, other than it does not include

(a) the conversion, reconstruction or alteration of an existing building;
(b) any enlargement of, or extension to, an existing building except to the extent that this creates an additional dwelling or dwellings; or
(c) the construction of an annexe to an existing building unless
  (i) the whole or a part of the annexe is intended solely for use for a '*relevant charitable purpose*' (see (13) below);
  (ii) it is capable of functioning independently from the existing building; and
  (iii) the only access (or main access where more than one) to the annexe is *not* via the existing building and *vice versa*.

The significance of (i) above is that, in conjunction with *VATA 1994, Sch 8 Group 5 Note 10* (which provides for apportionment between zero-rated and standard-rated supplies), zero-rating can be applied to supplies made in connection with a part of an annexe which is to be used *solely* for relevant charitable purposes. Where an annexe, or part of an annexe (including common areas such as entrance lobbies) will be used for a mixture of relevant charitable and other purposes, it (or that part) is not used solely for a relevant charitable purpose and is standard-rated. By concession, minor non-qualifying use can be ignored (see (13) below).

For these purposes, a building only ceases to be an existing building when

- it is demolished completely to ground level; or
- the part remaining above ground level consists of no more than a single façade (double façade where a corner site), the retention of which is a condition or requirement of statutory planning consent or similar permission.

[*VATA 1994, Sch 8 Group 5 Notes (16)–(18); SI 1995/280; SI 2002/1101*].

Examples of the construction of a zero-rated building

HMRC give the following as examples of construction work that can be zero-rated.

- The building is either '*designed as a dwelling*' (see (4) below) or a number of dwellings, intended for use solely for a '*relevant residential purpose*' (see (15) below) or a '*relevant charitable purpose*' (see (13) below) and one of the following scenarios apply.
  (i) It is built from scratch, and, before work starts, any pre-existing building is demolished completely to ground level (cellars, basements and the 'slab' at ground level may be retained).

(ii) The new building makes use of no more than a single facade (or a double facade on a corner site) of a pre-existing building, the pre-existing building is demolished completely (other than the retained facade) before work on the new building is started *and* the facade is retained as a condition or requirement of statutory planning consent or similar permission.

(iii) A new building is constructed against an existing building so that they share a wall but there is no internal access between them.

- An existing building is enlarged or extended and the enlargement or extension creates an additional dwelling or dwellings which is/are wholly within the enlargement or extension. So, for example, a new eligible flat built on top of an existing building can qualify for zero-rating. If the new dwelling is partly or wholly contained within the existing building, the work does not qualify for zero-rating, although it may qualify for reduced-rating as a 'changed number of dwellings conversion' under the provisions in **42.12 LAND AND BUILDINGS: ZERO AND REDUCED RATE SUPPLIES AND DIY HOUSEBUILDERS.**
- *Relevant charitable purpose annexes*. The construction of a building intended for use solely for a '*relevant charitable purpose*' (see (13) below) is zero-rated, with additions to an existing building normally being standard-rated. However, an addition can qualify as the construction of a building (and be zero-rated subject to the normal conditions) when all the following conditions are met.

(i) The construction is an 'annexe', rather than an extension or enlargement. There is no legal definition of '*annexe*'. It can be either a structure attached to an existing building or a structure detached from it. (If detached, it is treated as a separate building for VAT purposes and the following does not apply.) If attached to an existing building, in order to be considered an annexe, a structure must not be attached in such a way so as to be considered an enlargement or extension. An enlargement or extension would involve making the building bigger so as to provide extra space for the activities already carried out in the existing building (e.g. a classroom or a sports hall added to an existing school building or an additional function room, kitchen or toilet block added to an existing village hall). An annexe should provide extra space for activities distinct from, but associated with, the activities carried out in the existing building. The annexe and the existing building should form two separate parts of a single building that operate independently of each other (e.g. a day hospice added to an existing residential hospice, a self-contained suite of rooms added to an existing village hall, a church hall added to an existing church or a nursery added to a school building).

(ii) The whole annexe, or a part of it, is intended for use solely for a relevant charitable purpose. The annexe need not be an annexe to a building used solely for a relevant charitable purpose. What is important is that the annexe itself is intended for use solely for a relevant charitable purpose.

(iii) The whole annexe must be capable of functioning independently from the existing building, even if only part of it is used solely for a relevant charitable purpose. An annexe is capable of functioning independently when the activities in the annexe can be carried on without reliance on the existing building, ignoring the existence of building services (electricity and water supplies, etc.) that are shared with the existing building.

(iv) The annexe and the existing building each has its own independent main access. So, even if the annexe has its own entrance, the main access to the annexe must not be through the existing building and the annexe must not create the main access to the existing building.

The demolition and reconstruction of an annexe to an existing building can be zero-rated subject to the above conditions being met. But the demolition and reconstruction of part of an existing building, such as the wing of a building, or the conversion of an existing building (or part) to an annexe, cannot be the construction of an annexe.

- *Infilling*. The building of a new house within an existing terrace of houses on the site of a house that has been totally demolished ('*infilling*') apart from party walls shared with adjoining houses that are not being re-developed.

  Where neighbouring houses in a terrace are being re-developed, the party wall between those houses will also need to be demolished if the works are to qualify as 'constructing a building' for VAT purposes. A party wall need not separate a building from another building, it can also be the wall of a building on one property and a boundary or garden wall for the adjoining property.
- A garage is built, or a building is converted into a garage; and the construction or conversion takes place at the same time as, and the building is intended to be occupied with, a building 'designed as a dwelling or number of dwellings' (see (4) below).
- A building is built that is one of a number of buildings constructed at the same time on the same site and it is intended to be used together with those other buildings as a unit solely for a 'relevant residential purpose' (see (15) below).

Examples not qualifying as the construction of a zero-rated building

HMRC give the following as examples of construction work that cannot be zero-rated.

- A 'granny' annexe which cannot be used, or disposed of, separately from a main house. This is because the conditions of a building 'designed as a dwelling' (see (4) below) have not been met in full.
- A house that cannot be used, or disposed of, separately from a business premises. This is because the conditions of 'a building designed as a dwelling' have not been met in full.

- A house that incorporates a part or parts of an earlier building on the site, e.g. planning permission has been given to alter and extend an existing dwelling. That dwelling is substantially but not fully demolished in order to comply with the planning permission and a new dwelling constructed, incorporating the parts not demolished.
- A detached, enclosed swimming pool in the grounds of a new house. This is because the building being constructed is not a building 'designed as a dwelling' (see (4) below).
- A detached building in the grounds of an existing care home which extends the facilities of the home, such as an accommodation or administration block or 'extra care' units. This is because the building being constructed will not be used for a 'relevant residential purpose' (see (15) below) in its own right and it was not constructed at the same time as the rest of the home. See also HMRC Brief 66/07.

(VAT Notice 708, para 3.2).

(3) 'Curtilage'

In VAT Notice 708 (August 1997 Edition) HMRC defined curtilage as a reasonable amount of land, surrounding the building, which may include other buildings. What constitutes a reasonable amount of land will depend on the type of building and its setting. Although this definition is not reproduced in the latest edition of VAT Notice 708, there is no reason to suppose that their interpretation of the term has changed.

(4) 'Designed as a dwelling'

There is no definition in the legislation of 'dwelling' but see *Calam Vale* and *Amicus Group* considered in (10) below.

For the purposes of zero-rating, a building is designed as a dwelling or number of dwellings where the following conditions are satisfied in relation to each dwelling.

(a) The dwelling consists of self-contained living accommodation.
(b) There is no provision for direct internal access from the dwelling to any other dwelling or part of a dwelling.
(c) The separate use, letting or disposal of the dwelling is not prohibited by the terms of any covenant, statutory planning consent or similar provision. An occupancy restriction is not a prohibition on separate use or disposal if all it does is restrict the occupancy of a building to a certain type of person, such as persons working in agriculture or forestry, or persons over a specified age. But if the wording of the restriction prevents the building from being used separately from another building or from being sold, or otherwise disposed of, separately from another building then it is a prohibition on separate use or disposal. (VAT Notice 708, para 14.2).
(d) Statutory planning consent has been granted in respect of that dwelling and its construction or conversion has been carried out in accordance with that consent.

[*VATA 1994, Sch 8 Group 5 Note (2); SI 1995/280*].

See *University of Bath* (VTD 14235) (TVC 15.65) (students' accommodation) and *A J White* (VTD 15388) (TVC 65.86) (living accommodation over public houses) where in each case cooking and toilet facilities were shared.

For cases where (*c*) above was in point, see *Sherwin & Green* (VTD 16396) (TVC 15.38), *P Thompson*, (VTD 15834) (TVC 15.44), *PH Wiseman* (VTD 17374) (TVC 15.51) and *JFB & FR Sharples* (VTD 20775) (TVC 15.39) and for a case where (*d*) was in point, see *AI Davison* (VTD 17130) (TVC 15.61).

In *Oldrings Development Kingsclere Ltd* (VTD 17769) (TVC 15.36) a single storey, self-contained building was constructed in the grounds of a large house. It comprised one large room, plus a small room with a WC and washbasin, and had its own central heating system, hot water and electricity supply. The tribunal held that it was 'designed as a dwelling' and qualified for zero-rating, even though it was primarily used as an artist's studio, as it was capable of being used as a studio flat.

HMRC accept that 'extra care accommodation' (i.e. accommodation sold or let with the option to purchase varying degrees of care to suit individual needs as and when they arise) is designed as a dwelling if it meets the standard conditions above. (HMRC Brief 47/11).

(5) 'Grant'

Grant includes assignment or surrender. [*VATA 1994, Sch 8 Group 5 Note 2; SI 1995/280*]. It also includes the supply made by the person to whom an interest is surrendered when there is a reverse surrender (i.e. where the person to whom the interest is surrendered is paid by the person by whom the interest is being surrendered to accept the surrender). [*VATA 1994, Sch 9 Group 1 Notes 1, 1A; SI 1995/282*].

A grant is a sale of a freehold or other interest, or a lease or letting of land. An assignment is the transfer of a lease by the existing tenant to a new tenant. A surrender is the giving up of an 'interest in or right over' land (see (7) below) to the grantor. (VAT Notice 742, para 2.2).

The grant of any interest frequently gives rise to a number of further supplies at later times. For example, a supply is made each time that a payment is received for rent. In such cases, the liability of each subsequent supply is determined at the time when that supply is made rather than by reference to the time of the original grant. [*VATA 1994, s 96(10A); FA 1997, s 35(1); SI 2008/1146, Sch 1 para 3*].

(6) 'In the course of construction'

Services supplied 'in the course of the construction' comprise

(a) work on the building itself prior to its 'completion'; and
(b) any other service closely connected to the construction of the building.

For examples of services included, and not included, see **42.14 LAND AND BUILDINGS: ZERO AND REDUCED RATE SUPPLIES AND DIY HOUSEBUILDERS.**

'*Completion*' of a building takes place when an architect issues a certificate of practical completion in relation to it or it is first fully occupied, whichever happens first. [*VATA 1994, Sch 9 Group 1 Note 2*]. HMRC expand on this by saying that completion takes place at a given moment in time. That point in time is determined by weighing up the relevant factors of the project, such as

- when a Certificate of Completion is issued;
- accordance to approved plans and specifications;
- the scope of the planning consent and variations to it; and
- whether the building is habitable or fit for purpose.

Generally, once a building has been completed, any further work to the building is standard-rated. But see **42.14 LAND AND BUILDINGS: ZERO AND REDUCED RATE SUPPLIES AND DIY HOUSEBUILDERS.**

Examples

- A developer is in the process of constructing a house for sale. The buyer would like to include an attached conservatory and so contracts with a conservatory specialist to supply and install it prior to moving in. The developer refuses the conservatory supplier access to the site until after he has finished his work and the house has been conveyed to the buyer.
  In such circumstances, the supply of the conservatory is not work in the course of the construction of the house but work to an existing building and cannot be zero-rated.
- A developer constructs and sells 'shell' loft apartments for fitting out by the buyer. When the developer sells the lofts, their construction is not 'complete'.
  Future work to fit them out can be zero-rated until such time as they are habitable.
- A non-fee paying school obtains planning permission to construct a building that will be used solely for a relevant charitable purpose. Due to limited funds, the extent of the work is scaled down and a smaller building is constructed instead. Funds are later obtained to extend and enlarge the building to produce a building of the same capacity as originally planned.
  In such circumstances, the building would be 'complete' at the end of the first set of works and the later works are standard-rated.

(VAT Notice 708, para 3.3).

In *C & E Commrs v St Mary's Roman Catholic High School*, QB [1996] STC 1091 (TVC 15.189), work began on the building of a new secondary school in 1979 and the school opened to pupils in 1981, although some of its original buildings were not completed until 1983. Under the original plans, the school was to have been equipped with two playgrounds but these were not completed until 1994. The QB held that, on the evidence, the interval between the completion of the building work on the school and the construction of the playgrounds was far too long to establish the necessary temporal link. Accordingly, the building of the playgrounds failed to qualify for zero-rating.

In *Hoylake Cottage Hospital Charitable Trust* (TC00925) (TVC 15.175) the construction of a nursing home at a charity's premises was completed in 2008. In 2009 HMRC issued a ruling that VAT would be chargeable on the proposed construction of a kitchen and laundry block at the site. The charity appealed, contending that this work should be treated as having taken place in the course of construction of the nursing home. The tribunal allowed the appeal, specifically distinguishing the decision in *St Mary's Roman Catholic High School*, and holding that a period of 18 months between the developments was not an unreasonable delay in the circumstances.

A building has been held to be in the course of construction until the main structure is completed, the windows glazed and all essential services and fittings, such as plumbing and electricity, have been installed. Thereafter the building ceases to be in course of construction and the phase of fitting out and furnishing is ready to begin (*University of Hull* (VTD 180) (TVC 15.187)). See also *JM Associates* (VTD 18624) (TVC 15.188) where the supply and construction of conservatories for newly-built houses was held to be standard-rated as the work of construction only took place after the house was completed.

(7) 'Interest in or right over'

An interest in land can be

- a *legal interest*, i.e. the formal ownership of an interest in or right over land such as a freehold or leasehold interest in it; or
- a *beneficial (or equitable) interest*, i.e. the right to receive the benefit of supplies of it (e.g. the sales proceeds or rental income).

A beneficial interest may be held and transferred separately from the legal interest.

Rights over land include

- *rights of entry* which allow an authorised person or authority to enter land (e.g. they might allow someone to come onto land to perform a specific task);
- *easements* which grant the owner of neighbouring land a right to make their property better or more convenient, such as a right of way or right of light;
- *wayleaves*, i.e. a right of way to transport minerals extracted from land over another's land, or to lay pipes or cables over or under another's land; and
- *profits a prendre*, i.e. rights to take produce from another's land, such as to extract minerals.

(VAT Notice 742, para 2.4).

(8) 'Licence to occupy'

A licence is an authority to do something that would otherwise be a trespass. HMRC regard a licence to occupy land as being created when the following criteria are met.

(a) The licence should be granted in return for a consideration paid by the licensee.

(b) The licence to occupy must be of a specified piece of land, even if the licence allows the licensor to change the exact area occupied (e.g. to move the licensee from the third floor to the fourth floor).
(c) The licence is for occupation of the land by the licensee.
(d) Another person's right to enter the specified land does not impinge upon the occupational rights of the licensee; and either
  (i) the licence allows the licensee to physically enjoy the land for the purposes of the grant (e.g. to hold a party in a hall); or
  (ii) the licence allows the licensee to exploit economically the land for the purposes of its business (e.g. to run a nightclub).

(VAT Notice 742, para 2.5).

See also *Abbotsley Golf and Squash Club Ltd* (VTD 15042) (TVC 41.1596) where, applying dicta of Lord Templeman in *Street v Mountford*, HL [1985] 2 All ER 289 (TVC 41.159), the tribunal held that exclusivity of occupation was an essential condition of a tenancy but not of a licence to occupy.

Examples of licences to occupy land

- The provision of office accommodation (e.g. a specified bay, room or floor together with the rights to use shared areas such as reception, lifts, restaurant, rest rooms, leisure facilities, etc.).
- The provision of a serviced office which includes use of telephones, computer system, photocopier, fax machine, etc.
- Granting a concession to operate a shop within a shop where the concessionaires are granted an area from which to sell their goods or services.
- Granting space to erect advertising hoardings.
- Granting space to place a fixed kiosk on a specific site (e.g. sweet/newspaper kiosks, flower stands at railway stations).
- Hiring out a hall or other accommodation for meetings, parties, etc. including use of a kitchen area, lighting, furniture, etc.
- Granting a catering concession, where the caterer is granted a licence to occupy specific kitchens and restaurant areas, even if the grant includes the use of kitchen or catering equipment.
- Granting traders a pitch in a market or at a car boot sale (even if only for one day, see *Tameside Metropolitan Borough Council* (VTD 733) (TVC 41.5)).

Not included as licences to occupy land (and therefore standard-rated)

- Sharing business premises where more than one business has use of the same parts of the premises without having their own specified areas.
- Providing another person with access to office premises to make use of the facilities (e.g. remote sales staff away from home base having access to telephones, fax machines, etc. at another office).
- Allowing the public to tip rubbish on land.
- Storing someone else's goods in a warehouse without allocating any specified area for them.
- Granting an ambulatory concession (e.g. ice-cream vans on the sea front, hamburger vans at sporting events).

- Allowing the public admission to premises or events (see **57.7 RECREATION AND SPORT** but note that admission to certain one-off fund-raising events by charities may be exempt).
- Any grant of land clearly incidental to the use of the facilities on it, such as hiring out safes to store valuables, the right to use facilities in a hairdressing salon or granting someone the right to place a free-standing or wall-mounted vending or gambling machine on premises.
- As regards hairdressers' chairs in open-plan salons, see *Price (N & J)* (VTD 1443) (TVC 41.77); *Field & Field (t/a Paul Field Hair and Beauty Salon)* (VTD 2047) (TVC 41.78); *Genc* (VTD 2595) (TVC 41.79) and *Winder (t/a Anthony and Patricia)* (VTD 11784) (TVC 41.83) although in other cases the tribunal has held that a licence to occupy land existed (see *Quaife* (VTD 1394) (TVC 41.73) and *Daniels & Daniels (t/a Group Montage)* (VTD 12014) (TVC 41.75)). Subsequent, however, to these decisions, in *Simon Harris Hair Design Ltd* (VTD 13939) (TVC 41.85) the tribunal held that there was a single standard-rated supply by the owner to the stylists even though each stylist had (and was separately charged for) an allocated space within the salon. A licence to occupy that space was economically useless without the right to use other facilities such as junior staff, basins and dryers.

  HMRC's view regarding vending/gambling machines follows the decision in *Sinclair Collis Ltd v C & E Commrs, ECJ Case C–275/01*, [2003] STC 898 (TVC 22.327). Before that decision, they took the view that such a supply was a licence to occupy land and therefore exempt. Standard-rating must be applied to such supplies from 1 January 2004 although site owners could apply the change earlier if they wished (Business Brief 18/2003).

(VAT Notice 742, paras 2.6, 2.7).

See also *Altman Blane & Co* (VTD 12381) (TVC 41.8) where payments for non-exclusive use of a room were held to be exempt.

(9) 'Major interest'

In relation to England, Wales and Northern Ireland, a major interest in relation to land means the 'fee simple' or a tenancy for a term certain exceeding 21 years.

In relation to Scotland, following the abolition of feudal tenure, it will mean the interest of the owner or the lessee's interest under a lease for a period of not less than 20 years. Until the abolition, it is

(a) the estate or interest of the proprietor of the *dominium utile*, or
(b) in the case of land not held under feudal tenure, the estate or interest of the owner, or the lessee's interest under a lease for a period of not less than 20 years.

'Fee simple'

- in relation to England and Wales means the freehold;

- in relation to Scotland means the interest of the owner (and, until the abolition of feudal tenure, the estate or interest of the proprietor of the *dominium utile*); and
- in relation to Northern Ireland, includes the estate of a person who holds land under a fee farm grant.

[*VATA 1994, s 96(1); FA 1998, s 24; Abolition of Feudal Tenure etc (Scotland) Act 2000, Sch 12 para 57*].

(10) 'Non-residential'

A building or part of a building is 'non-residential' if

(a) it is neither
 (i) designed nor adapted for 'use as a dwelling' or number of dwellings (see (4) above); nor
 (ii) designed nor adapted for use for a '*relevant residential purpose*' (see (15) below), or
(b) it is designed or adapted for use within (*a*)(i) or (ii) above but
 (i) where the provision in **42.1**(*c*) **LAND AND BUILDINGS: ZERO AND REDUCED RATE SUPPLIES AND DIY HOUSEBUILDERS** applies (grant of major interest by a developer), it was constructed more than ten years before the grant of the major interest and no part of it has been used as a dwelling or for a relevant residential purpose in the period of ten years immediately preceding the grant;
 (ii) where the provision in **42.9 LAND AND BUILDINGS: ZERO AND REDUCED RATE SUPPLIES AND DIY HOUSEBUILDERS** applies (conversion services supplied to housing associations), it was constructed more than ten years before the commencement of the conversion work, no part of it has been used as a dwelling or for a relevant residential purpose in the period of ten years immediately preceding the commencement of those works, and no part of it is being so used; and
 (iii) where the provision in **42.23**(*a*)(iii) **LAND AND BUILDINGS: ZERO AND REDUCED RATE SUPPLIES AND DIY HOUSEBUILDERS** applies (D-I-Y housebuilders), it was constructed more than ten years before the commencement of the conversion work and no part of it has been used as a dwelling or for a relevant residential purpose in the period of ten years immediately preceding the commencement of those works.

References to a non-residential building or a non-residential part of a building do not include a reference to a garage occupied together with a dwelling. But see the tribunal decision in *Cottam* (VTD 20036) (TVC 15.123) where the tribunal allowed a claim for a refund under *VATA 1994, s 35* in relation to a two-storey outbuilding, the lower floor of which had been used as a garage. [*VATA 1994, Sch 8 Group 5 Notes (7)(7A)(8); SI 1995/280; SI 2001/2305*].

For a building to be have been in '*use as a dwelling*' under (*a*)(i) above, HMRC state that the living accommodation need not have been self-contained or to modern standards. Buildings, therefore, that have been in use as a dwelling include

- public houses and shops where any private living accommodation for the landlord, owner, manager or staff is not self-contained – normally because part of the living accommodation, such as the kitchen, is contained within the commercial areas rather than the private areas;
- bed-sit accommodation; and
- crofts.

As a result, where these types of property are converted into a building '*designed as a dwelling or number of dwellings*' (see (4) above) or intended for use solely for a '*relevant residential purpose*', (see (15) below) then, unless the ten-year rule applies, the sale of, or long lease in, the property cannot be zero-rated under the provision in **42.1**(*c*) **LAND AND BUILDINGS: ZERO AND REDUCED RATE SUPPLIES AND DIY HOUSEBUILDERS** and the supply of conversion services to housing associations cannot be zero-rated under the provisions in **42.9 LAND AND BUILDINGS: ZERO AND REDUCED RATE SUPPLIES AND DIY HOUSEBUILDERS**.

The case law in this area has been confusing. In *Temple House Developments Ltd* (VTD 15583) (TVC 15.113) the tribunal held that living accommodation over a public house did not satisfy the test of 'designed as a dwelling' as the cooking and toilet facilities were shared with the public house below. In particular, it read (*a*)(i) above in terms of the test for dwellings in *VATA 1994, Sch 8 Group 5, Note (2)* which requires that a dwelling consists of self-contained living accommodation (see (4) above). In *Look Ahead Housing Association* (VTD 16816) (TVC 15.204) the tribunal similarly held that bedsits were non-residential. Although it concluded that (*a*) above should *not* be read in terms of *Note (2)*, it followed the tribunal decision in *University of Bath* (VTD 14235) (TVC 15.65). To be a dwelling in the ordinary sense, each of the bedsits would have to have contained within it all the major activities of life, particularly sleeping, cooking and feeding, and toilet facilities. As they had shared bathroom and kitchen facilities, they were not 'dwellings' and qualified as 'non-residential'.

However, in *Calam Vale Ltd* (VTD 16869) (TVC 15.133) the tribunal, although following *Look Ahead Housing Association* in concluding that (*a*) above should *not* be read in terms of *Note (2)*, decided that living accommodation which had shared a kitchen with a downstairs public house was, in common usage of the term, a dwelling because the landlord and his family had lived there. Subsequently, in *Amicus Group Ltd* (VTD 17693) (TVC 15.215) where a housing association converted two properties from bedsits into self-contained flats, the tribunal specifically disapproved of the decision in *Look Ahead Housing Association*. Applying the *dicta* of Lord Irvine in *Uratemp Ventures Ltd v Collins*, HL, [2002] 1 All ER 46 (TVC 15.216) (a non-VAT case) a 'dwelling' should be interpreted as 'a place where one lives, regarding and treating it as a home'. It was no less a person's home because he did not cook there. Therefore, the bedsit accommodation had qualified as 'dwellings' and did not qualify as 'non-residential'. These later cases are more in line with HMRC's views. See also *Agudas Israel Housing Association Ltd* (VTD 18798) (TVC 15.37) where, again applying *Uratemp Ventures* above, the tribunal held that premises with their own front door, en suite bathing facilities and the ability to cook with a microwave cooker and a kettle were self-contained living accommodation.

See also *C & E Commrs v Lady Blom-Cooper*, CA [2003] STC 669 (TVC 15.132) where a claim for refund under the D-I-Y builders scheme was made for work on converting a former public house into a single family dwelling. HMRC rejected the claim on the basis that the first and second floors had previously been used by the publican as residential accommodation, so that it was not a 'non-residential building' as defined above and the work was therefore not a residential conversion as defined by *VATA 1994, s 35(1D)*. The CA upheld HMRC's rejection of the claim, holding that the effect of *VATA 1994, Sch 8, Group 5, Note 9* (conversion of a non-residential part of a building which already contains a residential part is not zero-rated unless the result of the conversion is to create an *additional* dwelling or dwellings) was that no refund was due. *VATA 1994, s 35(4)* plainly required that that same restricted meaning also applied for the purposes of *VATA 1994, s 35(1D)*.

Unoccupied for ten years

It is the responsibility of the developer, contractor or D-I-Y converter (as the case may be) to hold evidence that, on balance, the property has not been lived in for the relevant ten-year period under (*b*) above. Evidence can include electoral roll and council tax data, information from utilities companies, evidence from empty property officers in local authorities, or information from other reliable sources. If a developer, etc. holds a letter from an empty property officer certifying that a property has not been lived in for ten years, no other evidence is needed. If an empty property officer is unsure about when a property was last lived in, he should write with his best estimate and HMRC may then call for other supporting evidence.

When considering when a dwelling was last lived in, any

- illegal occupation by squatters;
- occupation by 'guardians' (i.e. persons installed by the owner to deter squatters and vandals); and
- use that is not residential in nature, such as storage for a business

can be ignored.

If the dwelling has been lived in on an occasional basis (e.g. because it was a second home) in the ten-year period, it does not qualify as 'non-residential'.

(VAT Notice 708, paras 5.3, 6.3).

(11) 'Person constructing a building'

A person is a 'person constructing' a building if, in relation to that building, he is, or has at any point in the past

- acted as a developer (i.e. physically constructed, or commissioned another person to physically construct, the building, in whole or in part, on land that he owns or has an interest in); or
- acted as a contractor or subcontractor (i.e. provided construction services to the developer or another contractor for the construction of the building, sub-contracting work as necessary).

More than one person can enjoy 'person constructing' status but such status is not transferred when the property is transferred. Each person must meet the conditions specified above. For example, where a developer takes over and finishes a partly completed building, both the first and second developer has 'person constructing' status because they have both been involved in physically constructing the building.

VAT groups

Although for VAT purposes, any business carried on by a member of a VAT group is treated as carried on by the representative member, when determining whether a supply can be zero-rated, 'person constructing' status is only considered from the perspective of the group member who, in reality, makes the supply (which may not be the representative member).

> *Examples*
>
> A VAT group includes a holding company as the representative member and a development company as a member. The development company constructs and sells houses to the public.
>
> The development company has 'person constructing' status and so the sales can be zero-rated.
>
> A VAT group includes a development company as representative member and an investment company as a member. The development company constructs a block of flats and sells it to the investment company, which in turn leases the flats to the public on long leases.
>
> The investment company does not have 'person constructing' status. Even though the representative member does, the leases cannot be zero-rated and are exempt.

Beneficial interests

Where the beneficial owner of a property must register for VAT instead of the legal owner (see **41.5** below), the beneficial owner must have 'person constructing' status before the sale or long lease of the property can be zero-rated.

(VAT Notice 708, para 4.5).

In *C & E Commrs v Link Housing Association Ltd*, CS [1992] STC 718 (TVC 15.1), the court held that the phrase 'a person constructing' should be read as meaning 'a person who has constructed' and the original builder is therefore entitled to zero-rate his supply of a dwelling, however long after construction that might be. (In the case of *Link* the houses had been constructed before the introduction of VAT in 1973.) It held that the phrase is purely descriptive and designed only to ensure that it was the person who was constructing or had constructed the building who was entitled to zero-rating. HMRC have taken the narrow view that the decision applies only in relation to input tax on disposal costs. (Business Brief 15/92).

(12) 'Protected building'

A protected building means any building which is

- a listed building (within the meaning of *Planning (Listed Buildings and Conservation Areas) Act 1990* or *Planning (Listed Buildings and Conservation Areas) (Scotland) Act 1997* or *Planning (Northern Ireland) Order 1991*), or
- a scheduled monument (within the meaning of *Ancient Monuments and Archaeological Areas Act 1979* or *Historic Monuments and Archaeological Objects (Northern Ireland) Order 1995*)

and which satisfies one of the following conditions.

(a) It is designed to remain as or become a dwelling or number of dwellings. This condition is satisfied where, in relation to each dwelling
  - the dwelling consists of self-contained living accommodation; and
  - there is no provision for direct internal access from the dwelling to any other dwelling or part of a dwelling; and
  - the separate use or disposal of the dwelling is not prohibited by the terms of any covenant, statutory planning consent or similar provision. An occupancy restriction is not a prohibition on separate use or disposal if all it does is restrict the occupancy of a building to a certain type of person, such as persons working in agriculture or forestry, or persons over a specified age. But if the wording of the restriction prevents the building from being used separately from another building or from being sold, or otherwise disposed of, separately from another building then it is a prohibition on separate use or disposal. (VAT Notice 708, para 14.3).

    In *Lunn* [2009] UKUT 244 (TCC) (TVC 55.12) the Upper Tribunal decided that planning permission specifying that the house 'shall only be used for purposes either incidental or ancillary to the residential use' of the main house did prohibit separate use.

  Included is a garage (occupied together with the dwelling) either constructed at the same time as the building or, where the building has been substantially reconstructed, at the same time as that reconstruction. Following the decision in *Grange Builders (Quainton) Ltd* (VTD 18905) (TVC 55.6) HMRC accept that, provided a garage is in use as a garage before any alteration or reconstruction takes place and continues to be used as one afterwards, it is not necessary for the garage to have been constructed as a garage. It can also have been constructed as something different (e.g. as in this instance, as a barn). (Business Brief 11/05).

(b) It is intended for use solely for a '*relevant residential purpose*' or a '*relevant charitable purpose*' (see (15) and (13) below respectively) after the reconstruction or alteration.

[*VATA 1994, Sch 8 Group 6 Notes (1)* and *(2); SI 1995/283; SI 1995/1625*].

Listed buildings

A listed building is one included in a statutory list of buildings of special architectural or historic interest compiled by the Secretary of State for National Heritage in England and by the Secretaries of State for Scotland,

Wales and Northern Ireland. In England and Wales there are three categories of listed building, Grade I, Grade II*, and Grade II. In Scotland the equivalent categories are Grade A, Grade B and Grade C(S). In Northern Ireland the equivalent categories are Grade A, Grade B+ and Grade B. Unlisted buildings in conservation areas, or buildings included in a local authority's non-statutory list of buildings of local interest, which used to be known as Grade III buildings, are not 'protected' buildings for VAT purposes.

Under *Planning (Listed Buildings and Conservation Areas) Act 1990, s 1(5)*, a listed building also includes

(i) any object or structure fixed to the building; and
(ii) any object or structure within the curtilage of the building which, although not fixed to the building, forms part of the land and has done so since before l July 1948 (the date listed building control began in its present form).

For VAT purposes, any approved alteration carried out to buildings within (ii) above can only be zero-rated if the building being altered falls within (*a*) or (*b*) above. It must therefore either be a qualifying garage (see (*a*) above) or an outbuilding, etc. which is itself designed to remain as or become a dwelling within (*a*) above or is intended solely for relevant residential or charitable purposes under (*b*) above. This view has been upheld in *C & E Commrs v Zielinski Baker & Partners Ltd*, HL [2004] STC 456 (TVC 55.9). In that case, the owners of a protected building arranged for the conversion of an outbuilding into changing rooms and a games room. Both the protected building and the outbuilding had been built in 1830 but the outbuilding, which was accepted as being within the curtilage of the protected building, had only been used for residential purposes for about twelve months in 1945. The court held that the outbuilding was not designed to remain as or become a dwelling house. As it was only the outbuilding, not the house, that was altered and it was the house, not the outbuilding, that had been listed, the outbuilding was not within the definition of a 'protected building' and the work on it failed to qualify for zero-rating.

(VAT Notice 708, para 9.2).

(13) 'Relevant charitable purpose'

This means use by a charity in either or both of the following ways.

(a) *Otherwise than in the course or furtherance of a business.* It is essential that all or part of the building is used for non-business purposes. The term 'business' is a widely drawn concept. See **8 BUSINESS**. See also *Newtownbutler Playgroup Ltd* (VTD 13741) (TVC 15.90).
Activities that do not make a profit, or activities where any profit is only used to further the aims and objectives of the charity, can still be business activities.
Examples of buildings typically seen as non-business
- places of worship;
- offices used by charities for administering non-business activity, such as the collection of donations;

- school buildings where no fee is charged for the provision of education;
- research buildings where the research is grant-funded; and
- scout and guide huts that are used purely for scouting and guiding activities.

Examples of buildings typically seen as being used for business purposes

- buildings used by membership organisations where the organisation charges a membership fee;
- school buildings where a fee is charged for the provision of education; and
- offices used by charities for administering business activities, such as fund-raising events where an entrance fee is charged; and
- village halls and similar buildings (but see (*b*) below).

The construction of a garage, within the curtilage of a church building, for cars used for pastoral work has been held to be for a relevant charitable purpose, any private use being *de minimis* and disregarded (*St Dunstan's Roman Catholic Church Southborough* (VTD 15472) (TVC 15.98)).

Interpretation of 'solely' for relevant charitable purpose from 1 July 2009

In HMRC's view, the term 'solely', as used in the phrase 'solely for a relevant residential or relevant charitable purpose', can incorporate an appropriate *de minimis* margin. In order to avoid unnecessary disputes in marginal cases, HMRC accept that this statutory condition is satisfied if the relevant use of the building is 95% or more.

For the purposes of determining whether a building is eligible for the zero rate or not, any method may be used to calculate the qualifying use of the building, so long as it is fair and reasonable, and prior approval from HMRC for the method is not required. If a building is zero-rated as a result of applying this interpretation, there will be a change of use charge if it ceases to be eligible within ten years of the buildings completion.

Under their revised interpretation, HRMC accept that, where the customer and supplier agree, the option to tax can be excluded on supplies of a building (or part of a building) that is to be used 95% or more for a relevant purpose where

- a building (other than used as an office) will be used by a charity solely for a relevant charitable purpose;
- a grant is made in a building designed solely for a relevant residential purpose;
- a grant in a building is made to a person who intends to use it solely for a relevant residential purpose. (HMRC Brief 33/10).

The concession below has been withdrawn, subject to a twelve-month transitional period starting on 1 July 2009, during which either the concession or the revised interpretation may be applied.

Concession for small business use until 30 June 2010

By concession, and subject to any necessary HMRC approval where a building is used by a charity for business and non-business purposes, business use can be disregarded if

(i) the entire building will be used solely for non-business activity for more than 90% of the total time it is available for use;
(ii) in the case of an identifiable part of a building, that part will be used solely for non-business activity for more than 90% of the total time that part of the building is available for use;
(iii) 90% or more of the floor space of the entire building will be used for non-business activity; or
(iv) 90% or more of the people using the entire building (on a head count basis) will be engaged solely on non-business activity,

and, with effect from 21 March 2007, there is no intention at the time of zero-rating that the building will be used for business or other non-qualifying use in excess of 10% within ten years of zero-rating.

For any one building, only one of the four methods can be used. Once a method is chosen, it cannot be changed, even if circumstances change. Methods (iii) and (iv) can only be applied to the whole building. The concession must be calculated and applied at the time a relevant supply is made and must be applied in a way which ensures a result which is fair and reasonable to both the taxpayer and HMRC.

Permission must be sought from HMRC to use methods (ii)–(iv). Written application should be made to HMRC with

- a full description of how the building (or the part on which zero-rating or reduced-rating is sought) will be used, including the non-qualifying use;
- when applying to use the floor space method, details of the total floor space and qualifying floor space in the building, and supporting plans that clearly identify the qualifying parts;
- when applying to use the head count method, a full list of the normal occupants of the building, a description of their role in the organisation, and confirmation as to whether they take part in the non-qualifying use of the building;
- the representative period over which it is intended to monitor the use of the building (or part); and
- if the building (or part) is also to be occupied by another person, how that person will use their part of the building and copies of any lease arrangements with that person.

HMRC will not approve use of a method that produces an unfair or unreasonable result, uses a combination of methods or is used for tax avoidance purposes. They may also withdraw or restrict the concession once in force if they consider that it is being used to avoid tax.

Change of use following application of concession

If, during the ten years following zero-rating, the qualifying charitable use of a building (or part) falls below the 90% concessionary limit, the charity is potentially liable to a deemed self-supply charge under the provisions in **42.2 LAND AND BUILDINGS: ZERO AND REDUCED RATE SUPPLIES AND DIY HOUSEBUILDERS** on the change of use. *With effect from 21 March 2007*, HMRC will not enforce this charge where there has been change of use that was not anticipated at the time that zero-rating was obtained under the concession. But if it is apparent that, at the time zero-rating was obtained, it was intended that non-qualifying use would exceed 10% within the ten-year adjustment period, HMRC will consider that the original supply should never have been zero-rated in the first place. Any charity that paid a change of use charge in the three years before 21 March 2007 may be entitled to a refund.

(VAT Notice 48, ESC 3.29, withdrawn from 1 April 2010).

(b) *As a village hall or similarly in providing social or recreational facilities for a local community*. In the opinion of HMRC, in order to qualify, the building must have the following characteristics.

- There must be a high degree of local community involvement in the building's operation and activities. See *C & E Commrs v Jubilee Hall Recreation Centre Ltd*, CA 1998, [1999] STC 381 (TVC 55.15) in which a charity used premises to run a sports and fitness centre. The charity contended that work on a substantial refurbishment should be zero-rated on the basis that the building was intended for use solely for a 'relevant charitable purpose'. The CA rejected this contention. On the evidence, the use of the building was not 'similar to the use of a village hall in providing social or recreational facilities for a local community'. The relevant conditions were only satisfied 'where a local community is the final consumer in respect of the supply of the services . . . in the sense that the local community is the user of the services (through a body of trustees or a management committee acting on its behalf) and in which the only economic activity is one in which they participate directly'. *Jubilee Hall* was heard together with *C & E Commrs v St Dunstan's Educational Foundation*, CA 1998, [1999] STC 381 (TVC 15.104) in which a charity arranged for the construction of a sports hall, which was intended to be used by an independent fee-paying school, and to be made available for community use at specified times. The Court similarly held that the building was not intended for use 'in providing . . . recreational facilities for a local community', since the community use was secondary to the use by the school. Insofar as pupils at the school benefited from that facility, they did so not as members of the local community, but as pupils on whose behalf fees were paid to the school. See also *Ormiston Charitable Trust* (VTD 13187) (TVC 15.102).
- There is a wide variety of activities carried on in the building, the majority of which are for social and/or recreational purposes (including sport).

The users of the building need not be confined to the local community but can come from further afield.

Buildings that are seen as being similar to village halls when the characteristics above are present include

- scout or guide huts (where they are not used purely for scouting and guiding activities);
- sports pavilions;
- church halls;
- community centres; and
- community sports centres.

Buildings that are not typically seen as being similar to village halls include

- community swimming pools;
- community theatres (but see *Ledbury Amateur Dramatic Society* (VTD 16845) (TVC 15.87) where a theatre was held to be used similarly to a village hall);
- membership clubs (although community associations charging a notional membership fee can be excluded); or
- community amateur sports clubs.

[*VATA 1994, Sch 8 Group 5 Note 6; SI 1995/280*]. (VAT Notice 708, para 14.7; VAT Information Sheet 8/09).

(14) 'Relevant housing association'

A relevant housing association is

- (from 1 April 2010) a private registered provider of social housing;
- in Wales, a Welsh registered social landlord within the meaning of *Housing Act 1996, Part I*;
- in Scotland, a Scottish registered social landlord within the meaning of *Housing (Scotland) Act 2001 (asp 10)*; or
- in Northern Ireland, a Northern Irish registered housing association within the meaning of *Housing (Northern Ireland) Order 1992 (SI 1992/1725), Part II.*

Until the coming into force of provision defining 'private registered provider of social housing', it means persons listed in the register of providers of social housing maintained under the *Housing and Regeneration Act 2008, Pt 2 Ch 3* who are not local authorities within the meaning of the *Housing Associations Act 1985.*

[*VATA 1994, Sch 8 Group 5 Note (21); SI 1997/50; SI 1997/51; SI 2010/486*].

(15) 'Relevant residential purpose'

Use for a relevant residential purpose means use as

- a home or other institution providing residential accommodation for children;
- a home or other institution providing residential accommodation with personal care for persons in need of such care by reason of old age, disablement, past or present dependence on alcohol or drugs or past or present mental disorder;
- a hospice;
- residential accommodation for students or school pupils;
- residential accommodation for members of any of the armed forces;
- a monastery, nunnery or similar establishment; or
- an institution which is the sole or main residence of at least 90% of its residents.

Excluded is use as a hospital, prison or similar institution or an hotel, inn or similar establishment.

Where a number of buildings are constructed at the same time and on the same site and are intended to be used together as a unit solely for a relevant residential purpose, each of those buildings (to the extent that they would not otherwise be so regarded) are to be treated as intended for use solely for a relevant residential purpose.

[*VATA 1994, Sch 8 Group 5 Notes (4) and (5); SI 1995/280*].

'*Home*' and '*institution*': to determine if a building (or group of buildings) is used as a home or institution, all relevant factors need to be considered including

- the use to which the building is put;
- whether the building is used in conjunction with other buildings nearby;
- whether there is common ownership, financial control, management or administration;
- how the use of the building is promoted in advertising, etc.; and
- how the use of the building is licensed by any controlling authority.

For example, a bedroom block constructed in the grounds of a registered care home cannot be zero-rated as the construction of a building intended for use solely for a relevant residential purpose because it is not, in itself, a home or institution but part of a larger home or institution.

A rehabilitation home for people who have suffered brain injuries has been held to be a 'home or other institution providing residential accommodation' rather than a 'hospital or similar institution' (*General Healthcare Group Ltd* (VTD 17129) (TVC 15.73)).

'*Residential accommodation*' means lodging, sleeping or overnight accommodation and does not suggest the need for such accommodation to be for any fixed or minimum period. See *Urdd Gobaith Cymru* (VTD 14881) (TVC 15.70). For example, accommodation for students attending a residential training course is residential accommodation. A building containing living accommodation is not residential accommodation unless the building contains sleeping accommodation. For example, if the only living accommodation in a building is a dining hall then that is not residential accommodation. But a dining hall constructed at the same time as another building (or buildings) containing sleeping accommodation with the intention that they are to be used together to provide living accommodation, is residential accommodation. If a building contains both bedrooms and a dining hall then both parts are residential accommodation. The dining hall must be used exclusively by those persons using the sleeping accommodation in that building. Use by persons sleeping in other buildings prevents the dining hall from being residential accommodation unless all the buildings involved were constructed together and were intended to be used collectively as living accommodation.

(VAT Notice 708, para 14.6).

De Voil Indirect Tax Service. See V4.232–V4.232H.

Land and property transactions

Exempt supplies

[41.2] See **18.25**(*k*) and (*l*) **EUROPEAN UNION LEGISLATION** for the provisions of *Directive 2006/112/EC.*

The 'grant' of any

- 'interest in or right over' land,
- 'licence to occupy' land, or
- in relation to Scotland, any 'personal right' to call for or be granted any such interest or right (see below)

is, subject to certain exceptions, an exempt supply. [*VATA 1994, Sch 9 Group 1*].

See **41.1**(5) above for the meaning of '*grant*', **41.1**(7) above for '*interest in or right over*' and **41.1**(8) above for '*licence to occupy*'.

'*Land*' includes buildings, civil engineering works, walls, trees, plants and other structures and natural objects in, under or over it as long as they remain attached to it. (VAT Notice 742, para 2.1). Where fixtures are included with a building or land, they are not treated as supplies for VAT purposes and their liability is the same as that for the land or buildings with which they are being supplied. (VAT Notice 742, para 7.9).

A '*personal right*' in Scotland is right enforceable only against a specific person or limited class of persons, e.g. a contractual right. The disadvantage of personal rights is that, if the person against whom the right is enforceable becomes insolvent, the right is likely to be worthless in practice. (VAT Notice 742/3/11).

Under *Directive 2006/112/EC, Art 135(1)(k)* countries must exempt the supply of land which has not been built upon other than '*building land*' i.e. any unimproved or improved land defined as such by the individual country. In *Norbury Developments Ltd v C & E Commrs, ECJ Case C–136/97*, [1999] STC 511 (TVC 22.511) the tribunal held that building land should therefore be taxable rather than exempt unless the exemption was authorised by *Art 28(3)(b)* (which allows countries to continue to exempt certain supplies, including building land, for a transitional period). The tribunal referred the case to the ECJ which held that the UK was entitled to exempt the supply under *Art 28(3)(b)*.

Anti-avoidance provisions

After 8 April 2003, where any grant of a fee simple (freehold) is exempt under the above provisions (and not standard-rated under the provisions in **41.3** below), those standard-rating provisions do not prevent the exemption of a supply arising from the prior exempt grant. This is designed to block avoidance schemes involving the sale of vacant land and the subsequent construction of a commercial building. [*VATA 1994, s 96(10B); FA 2003, s 20*].

Exceptions include

- the first grant of a major interest in a 'qualifying building' i.e.
  (i) a dwelling or building intended for use for a relevant residential or charitable purpose,
  (ii) a dwelling converted from a non-residential building, or
  (iii) a substantially reconstructed protected building
  by the person constructing, converting or, as the case may be, reconstructing it (which is zero-rated, see **42.1** and **42.3 LAND AND BUILDINGS: ZERO AND REDUCED RATE SUPPLIES AND DIY HOUSEBUILDERS**);
- the sale of the freehold interest in a new or uncompleted non-qualifying building or civil engineering work (which is standard-rated, see **41.3**(*a*) below);
- supplies falling within one of the categories in **41.3**(*b*)–(*k*) below which are specifically excluded from exemption and standard-rated;
- any supply which would otherwise be exempt but in respect of which an election to waive exemption ('option to tax') has been exercised (see **41.8** below); and
- certain supplies which form part of the transfer of a business as a going concern (which are outside the scope of VAT, see **8.10 BUSINESS**).

Example

In the case of a building being converted from offices into flats, the subsequent sale of the flats would be zero-rated as the grant of a major interest in a qualifying building. However, the sale of two flats that had been converted from a detached house would be exempt from VAT rather than zero-rated. This is an important distinction in terms of input tax recovery on related costs.

Options to purchase/sell or lease land

A person granted an option to purchase an interest in land and buildings (a 'call option') acquires the right to buy it at a future date for a specified price. That right is an interest in land and therefore the grant of the option is exempt if the purchase of the property would be exempt at the time of the grant. If the purchase would be taxable at that time, the grant of the option is taxable (see **41.3**(*k*) below).

A person granted the right to require someone to purchase his interest in land or buildings at a fixed price at a future date (a 'put' option) does not receive an interest in land and the grant of such an option is generally standard-rated.

(VAT Notice 742, para 7.4).

'Virtual assignments'

In *Abbey National plc v C & E Commrs (and cross-appeal) (No 4)*, CA [2006] STC 1961 (TVC 41.19) a bank outsourced its property holdings, including its lease interests, to an unconnected company (M) for a lump sum. The bank was unable legally to assign some short leases to M as the landlord's permission had not, or could not, be obtained. In the absence of such permission, the bank entered into an agreement whereby it assigned to M the 'economic benefits and burdens' of the leases. The intention was to leave M in the same economic position as though the leases had been legally assigned to it, so that it could then grant purported leases of those properties back to Abbey. The bank remained in occupation of the premises, and paid a fee to M which was similar to the rent which would have been charged under a formal leaseback. This was referred to as a 'virtual assignment'.

HMRC took the view that M was making a standard-rated supply of agency and property management services to the bank. The Court agreed with this view. As M had acquired no right of occupation (and thus could not retransfer such a right), the supply made by M to the bank under the contractual arrangements was not a supply of leasing or letting within the meaning of what is now *Directive 2006/112/EC, Art 135(1)(l)* and thus not exempt from VAT.

A secondary issue in the case (which did not go to the Court of Appeal) was the VAT treatment of those leases that the bank had virtually assigned to M and where the property was occupied by the bank's sub-tenants. The Court held that the agreement between the bank and M incorporated a clear and unambiguous declaration of trust, whereby the rents paid by the sub-tenants accrued in full for the benefit of M. There was a deemed supply under what is now *VATA 1994, Sch 10 para 40* by M to the sub-tenants as the consideration for the sub-leases granted by the bank accrued to M, despite M not having a legal interest in the property. The deemed supply was exempt unless the option to tax had been exercised.

Serviced building plots

With effect from 17 October 2007, following the decision in *D & S Virtue (t/a Lammermuir Game Services)* (VTD 20259) (TVC 41.22), HMRC accept that the supply of a serviced building plot of land (i.e. bare land in respect of which civil engineering works have been carried out to provide access to essential services such as gas, electricity, water, drainage and sewerage) is a single exempt supply of land by the landowner. *Previously*, HMRC had treated the supply of a services building plot by the landowner as a mixed supply of exempt land and standard-rated civil engineering work. (HMRC Brief 64/07).

De Voil Indirect Tax Service. See V4.111; V4.112.

Standard-rated supplies

[41.3] The supplies of within (*a*)–(*k*) below are excluded from the general VAT exemption for land under **41.2** above and are standard-rated.

(a) New and uncompleted non-qualifying buildings and civil engineering works

The 'grant' or assignment of the fee simple (freehold interest) in

- a building which has not been 'completed' and which is not a '*qualifying building*' (i.e. is neither designed as a 'dwelling' or number of dwellings nor intended for use for solely a 'relevant residential purpose' or a 'relevant charitable purpose'),
- a 'new' building which is not to be used as a qualifying building after the grant,

- a civil engineering work which has not been completed, or
- a new civil engineering work

is standard-rated. (Supplies of qualifying buildings are exempt unless zero-rated under the provisions in **42.1** or **42.3** LAND AND BUILDINGS: ZERO AND REDUCED RATE SUPPLIES AND DIY HOUSEBUILDERS.)

A building/civil engineering work is to be taken as '*completed*' when an architect/engineer issues a certificate of practical completion in relation to it or it is fully occupied/used, whichever happens first. It is to be taken as '*new*' if it was completed less than three years before the grant.

See **41.1**(5) above for the meaning of '*grant*', **41.1**(15) above for '*relevant residential purpose*' and **41.1**(13) above for '*relevant charitable purpose*'.

Issue of certificates

A grant or assignment cannot be taken as relating to a building (or part) intended for use solely for a relevant residential or charitable purpose as above unless

- it is made to a person who intends to use the building (or part) for such a purpose; and
- before it is made, that person has given the grantor a certificate stating that the grant relates to such a building.

See **42.22** LAND AND BUILDINGS: ZERO AND REDUCED RATE SUPPLIES AND DIY HOUSEBUILDERS for further details on the issue and form of certificates.

Part-qualifying buildings

Where part of a building is designed as a dwelling or number of dwellings or intended for relevant use as above and part is not (e.g. shop premises with a flat over them) an apportionment is necessary if the grant does not relate exclusively to one part or the other.

[*VATA 1994, Sch 9 Group 1 Item 1(a) and Notes 1 to 6*].

Anti-avoidance provisions

After 8 April 2003:

- Where any grant is standard-rated under these provisions, any subsequent supply arising from that grant is also standard-rated. This is designed to block avoidance schemes that deliberately made the price uncertain in order to take advantage of the provisions of *SI 1995/2518, Reg 84(2)* allowing VAT to be declared when the payment is received rather than at the date of sale. See **66.13** SUPPLY: TIME OF SUPPLY.
- Where any grant of a fee simple (freehold) is exempt under **41.2** above (and not standard-rated under these provisions), these provisions do not prevent the exemption of a supply arising from the prior exempt grant. This is designed to block avoidance schemes involving the sale of vacant land and the subsequent construction of a commercial building.

[*VATA 1994, s 96(10B); FA 2003, s 20*].

Options, etc. to purchase

See (*k*) below.

Supplies of land and civil engineering work

Where the freehold interest in bare land is sold but that land is ancillary to new or part completed civil engineering works (e.g. an airfield or oil refinery) there is a single standard-rated supply.

See **41.2** above for the sale of serviced building plots of land.

(b) Gaming and fishing rights

The 'grant' of any interest, right or licence to take game or fish is standard-rated unless, at the time of the grant, the grantor grants to the grantee the fee simple of the land over which the right to take game or fish is exercisable. Where a grant of an interest in or right over land or a licence to occupy land includes a valuable right to take game or fish, an apportionment must be made to determine the exempt and standard-rated parts. [*VATA 1994, Sch 9 Group 1 Item 1(c)* and *Note 8*]. See **57.15 RECREATION AND SPORT** for further details.

Options, etc. to purchase

See (*k*) below.

(c) Hotel accommodation

The provision in an hotel, inn, boarding house or 'similar establishment' of sleeping accommodation or of accommodation in rooms which are provided in conjunction with sleeping accommodation or for the purposes of a supply of catering is standard-rated. '*Similar establishment*' includes premises in which there is provided furnished sleeping accommodation, whether with or without the provision of board or facilities for the preparation of food, which are used by, or held out as being suitable for use by, visitors or travellers. [*VATA 1994, Sch 9 Group 1 Item 1(d)* and *Note 9*].

Where guests stay for a continuous period of four weeks or more, VAT is chargeable on a reduced value from the 29th day.

See **32.1** to **32.4 HOTELS AND HOLIDAY ACCOMMODATION** for further details.

Options, etc. to purchase

See (*k*) below.

(d) Holiday accommodation

The grant of any interest in or right over or licence to occupy holiday accommodation (including any accommodation in a building, hut, chalet, caravan, houseboat or tent which is advertised or held out as holiday accommodation or as suitable for holiday or leisure use) is standard-rated. *Excluded* is the grant of the fee simple, or a lease, etc. for a premium, in a building which is not a 'new building'. [*VATA 1994, Sch 9 Group 1 Item 1(e)* and *Notes 12* and *13*]. See **32.5** to **32.9 HOTELS AND HOLIDAY ACCOMMODATION** for further details.

Options, etc. to purchase

See (*k*) below.

(e) Caravan and tent pitches and camping facilities

The provision of 'seasonal pitches' for caravans, and the grant or assignment of facilities at caravan parks to persons for whom such pitches are provided, are standard-rated. The provision of pitches for tents or of camping facilities is also standard-rated.

From 1 March 2012 a 'seasonal pitch' is

- a pitch on a holiday site other than an employee pitch; or
- a non-residential pitch on any other site.

'Employee pitch' means a pitch occupied by an employee of the site operator as that person's principal place of residence during the period of occupancy. 'Holiday site' means a site or part of a site which is operated as a holiday or leisure site. 'Non-residential pitch' means a pitch which is provided

- for less than a year; or
- for a year or more and is subject to an occupation restriction,

and which is not intended to be used as the occupant's principal place of residence during the period of occupancy. 'Occupation restriction' means any covenant, statutory planning consent or similar permission, the terms of which prevent the person to whom the pitch is provided from occupying it by living in a caravan at all times throughout the period for which the pitch is provided.

Prior to 1 March 2012 a 'seasonal pitch' is

(i) any pitch which is provided for a period of less than a year; and
(ii) a pitch provided for a year or more but which the person to whom it is provided is prevented by the terms of any covenant, statutory planning consent or similar permission from occupying by living in a caravan at all times throughout the period for which the pitch is provided.

[*VATA 1994, Sch 9 Group 1 Items 1(f)(g)* and *Notes 14, 14A; SI 2012/58*].

In *HMRC v Tallington Lakes Ltd*, Ch D [2007] STI 2018 (TVC 41.134) licence agreements for caravans provided that, in accordance with relevant planning permission, they could not be occupied during February of each year. However, the company had ceased to enforce this restriction. The court held that the effect of the *Town and Country Planning Act 1990, s 171B(3)* was that the local authority had retained the right to enforce the original planning permission which prevented occupation during February. The fact that Tallington had allowed some owners to breach that condition did not prevent the definition of 'seasonal pitch' above from applying. Accordingly, the receipts did not qualify for exemption.

Following the tribunal decision in *Ashworth (Mrs B)* (VTD 12924) (TVC 41.127), HMRC accept that a pitch is only regarded as seasonal under (ii) above if it is on a site, or part of a site, which is advertised or held out for holiday use. (VAT Notice 701/20/04, para 4.1).

The effect of the above is that exemption applies to the provision of pitches at

- permanent residential caravan parks;
- sites for travellers; and
- seasonal sites provided
  - (i) the site is not advertised or held out for holiday use; and
  - (ii) the caravan can be used as a principal private residence. (This applies even if it cannot be occupied throughout the year due to a time-related restriction or occupancy imposed by the site owner.)

(VAT Notice 701/20/04, para 4.1).

The supply of rented accommodation in any caravan or mobile home is exempt unless the accommodation is holiday accommodation which is always standard-rated under (*d*) above.

See also **42.26 LAND AND BUILDINGS: ZERO AND REDUCED RATE SUPPLIES AND DIY HOUSEBUILDERS** for caravans generally.

Options, etc. to purchase

See (*k*) below.

(f) Parking facilities

The grant or assignment of facilities for parking a vehicle is standard-rated. [*VATA 1994, Sch 9 Group 1 Item 1(h)*].

There is normally a standard-rated supply of parking facilities if a specific grant is made and the facilities are designed for, or provided specifically for the purpose of, parking vehicles.

Standard-rated supplies

Standard-rated supplies include the following.

- The letting or licensing of garages (even if used for other purposes, e.g. storage of goods) or designated parking bays or spaces. See *C & E Commrs v Trinity Factoring Services Ltd*, CS [1994] STC 504 (TVC 41.142) where the court held that the lease of a lock-up garage was standard-rated even though the lessor and lessee had agreed in advance that the garage would be used for the storage of goods. *Prima facie* facilities had been granted for parking a vehicle and the terms of the lease did not preclude such usage.
  The letting of a garage or parking space *separately* from the letting of a dwelling is standard-rated. This scenario commonly occurs when a local authority tenant renting a dwelling and garage then decides to purchase the dwelling. The local authority retains the garage and continues to lease it to their former tenant. As the local authority is only supplying a garage, and not domestic accommodation, the supply is standard-rated. See (viii) below for the letting of a garage in conjunction with the letting of a dwelling.
- The provision of rights to park vehicles (and accompanying trailers) in, for example, car parks and commercial garages.

- The letting or licensing of land specifically for the construction of a garage or for use solely for the parking of a vehicle.
- The letting or licensing of a purpose-built car park (e.g. to a car park operator).
- The letting of taxi ranks.
- The provision of storage for bicycles or touring caravans.
- The freehold sale of a 'new' or partly completed garage, car park or car parking facilities other than in conjunction with the sale of a new dwelling. See (*a*) above for the meaning of '*new*'. (The sale of a garage or parking space together with a new dwelling by the person constructing it is normally zero-rated under the provisions in **42.1 LAND AND BUILDINGS: ZERO AND REDUCED RATE SUPPLIES AND DIY HOUSEBUILDERS** unless the dwelling is standard-rated holiday accommodation under (*d*) above.)

Exempt supplies

The following supplies are not regarded by HMRC as supplies of parking facilities and are therefore exempt under the general provisions in **41.2** above (subject to the exercise of an option to tax under **41.8** below).

(i) The letting of land or buildings (other than garages) where the conveyance or contract makes no specific reference to use for parking facilities.

(ii) The letting of land or buildings where any reference to parking a vehicle is incidental to the main use.

(iii) The letting of land or buildings to a motor dealer for storing stock-in-trade.

(iv) The letting of land or buildings to a vehicle transportation firm, a vehicle distributor or a vehicle auctioneer for business use.

(v) The letting of land (including land used at other times as a car park) for purposes such as a market or car boot sale.

(vi) The letting of land for the exhibition of vehicles.

(vii) The letting of land to a travelling fair or circus (and the incidental parking of vehicles).

(viii) The letting of a garage or parking space in conjunction with the *letting* of a dwelling for permanent residential use provided it is reasonably near to the dwelling and the letting is by the same landlord to the same tenant (whether under a single or separate agreement). See also *Skatteministeriet v Henriksen, ECJ Case 173/88*, [1990] STC 768 (TVC 22.332). However, in *Civilscent Ltd* (TC00070) (TVC 41.144) the tribunal held that the grant of parking space leases was a separate economic transaction from the grant of the apartment leases, as at the time of the grant of the apartment lease there was no arrangement or understanding that a grant of a parking space lease would follow, and therefore the leasing of car parking spaces was a separate standard-rated supply. (If a dwelling is owned freehold, the letting of the garage is standard-rated, see above.)

(ix) The freehold sale of garages, car parks or parking facilities which are not 'new'. See (*a*) above for the meaning of '*new*'.

The supply of garage or other parking facilities provided in conjunction with the letting of *commercial* premises is treated as a single supply provided both lettings are by the same landlord to the same tenant and *either* the facilities are on or reasonably near the property *or* the facilities are with a complex. The supply may therefore be exempt or, where the option to tax under **41.8** below has been exercised, standard-rated. In any other circumstances, the provision of parking facilities with commercial property is standard-rated. See also *Skatteministeriet v Henriksen* above.

(VAT Notice 742, paras 4.2–4.5).

Excess charges

Where a car park operator makes an offer of parking under clear terms and conditions, setting punitive fines for their breach, the fines constitute penalties for breaching the contract, rather than additional consideration for using the facilities. Consequently they are outside the scope of VAT. However, where the terms and conditions make it clear that the driver can continue to use the facilities after a set period upon payment of a further amount without being in breach of the contract then the payment is consideration for use of the facilities and subject to VAT.

(HMRC Brief 57/08).

Local authorities

See **43.4 LOCAL AUTHORITIES AND PUBLIC BODIES.**

Caravans and houseboats

See **42.26** and **42.27 LAND AND BUILDINGS: ZERO AND REDUCED RATE SUPPLIES AND DIY HOUSEBUILDERS** for parking facilities for caravans and houseboats.

Options, etc. to purchase

See (*k*) below.

(g) Timber rights

The grant or assignment of any right to fell and remove standing timber is standard-rated. [*VATA 1994, Sch 9 Group 1 Item 1(j)*].

The grant must be separate and specific. If land is sold which happens to contain standing timber which the buyer will be able to fell, the whole supply is exempt with the option to tax under **41.8** below. (VAT Notice 742, para 3.1).

Options, etc. to purchase

See (*k*) below.

(h) Storage, mooring of aircraft, ships, etc.

The grant or assignment of facilities for housing, or storage of, an aircraft or for 'mooring', or storage of, a ship, boat or other vessel is standard-rated. '*Mooring*' includes anchoring or berthing. [*VATA 1994, Sch 9 Group 1 Item 1(k) and Note 15*].

Included is both the letting of water-based mooring berths for pleasure boats and land sites for storage of boats on port land. (*Fonden Marselisborg Lystbådehavn v Skatteministeriet, ECJ Case C-428/02* [2006] STC 1467 (TVC 22.329)).

Even if a person is merely granted permission to lay down his own mooring and owns the ground tackle, the grant is considered to be excluded from exemption and is standard-rated whether or not there is a formal lease or licence. (C & E Press Notice 355, 25 June 1975). See also *J W Fisher* (VTD 179) (TVC 41.149) and *Strand Ship Building Co Ltd* (VTD 1651) (TVC 41.150).

See, however, **70.9 TRANSPORT AND FREIGHT** for facilities zero-rated when supplied in ports or customs airports and **42.27 LAND AND BUILDINGS: ZERO AND REDUCED RATE SUPPLIES AND DIY HOUSEBUILDERS** for exempt mooring of qualifying houseboats.

Options, etc. to purchase

See (*k*) below.

(i) Boxes, seats, etc.

The grant or assignment of any right to occupy a box, seat or other accommodation at a sports ground, theatre, concert hall or other place of entertainment is standard-rated. [*VATA 1994, Sch 9 Group 1 Item 1(l)*]. Included is any kind of accommodation which is intended for use by individuals or groups for viewing a match, race, show or other form of entertainment, regardless of whether the entertainment is actually in progress when the accommodation is used. (VAT Notice 742, para 3.4).

Options, etc. to purchase

See (*k*) below.

(j) Sports facilities

The grant or assignment of facilities for playing any sport or participating in any physical recreation is standard-rated. [*VATA 1994, Sch 9 Group 1 Item 1(m)*].

Exemption is, however, retained where the facilities are to be used for more than 24 hours or, provided certain conditions are met, a series of at least ten shorter periods. See **57.9 RECREATION AND SPORT**. See also **57.10 RECREATION AND SPORT** for certain sporting services provided by non-profit making bodies.

(k) Options, etc. to purchase interests or rights within (*a*) to (*j*) above

The grant of any right, including

- an equitable right,
- a right under an option or right of pre-emption, or
- in relation to land in Scotland, a ‘personal right’,

to call for or to be granted an interest or right which would fall to be standard-rated under (*a*) to (*j*) above is also standard-rated.

A 'personal right' in Scotland is right enforceable only against a specific person or limited class of persons, e.g. a contractual right. The disadvantage of personal rights is that, if the person against whom the right is enforceable becomes insolvent, the right is likely to be worthless in practice. (VAT Notice 742/3/11).

[*VATA 1994, Sch 9 Group 1 Item 1(n)*].

De Voil Indirect Tax Service. See V4.113.

Supplies between landlords and tenants

[41.4] Supplies between landlords and tenants are treated as follows:

(1) Lease payments

Inducements (reverse premiums) by landlords

Following representations from, and detailed discussions with, various bodies, HMRC now accept that lease obligations, to which tenants are normally bound, do not constitute supplies for which inducement payments on entering leases are consideration. As a result, they believe that the majority of such inducements are likely to be outside the scope of VAT, being no more than inducements to tenants to take leases and to observe the obligations in them. There will be a taxable supply only where a payment is linked to benefits a tenant provides outside normal lease terms. This change of policy effectively puts inducement payments on a similar VAT footing to rent free periods (see below) in being mainly outside the scope of VAT and only a taxable consideration where directly linked to a specific benefit supplied by a tenant to a landlord.

Examples of taxable benefits by tenants that may be supplied in return for such inducements are

- carrying out building works to improve the property by undertaking necessary repairs or upgrading the property (undertakings to use improved materials as part of continuous repairs under a tenant repairing lease would not constitute a taxable benefit to the landlord);
- carrying out fitting-out or refurbishment works which the landlord has responsibility for and is paying the tenant to undertake; and
- acting as anchor tenant (publicity indicating that Company X is to take a lease in a development does not, in itself, determine that the company is an anchor tenant).

Past transactions*:* tenants who have wrongly declared output tax on inducements received are not obliged to adjust their VAT position. However, if they choose to, then, subject to the three-year capping provisions,

- where both the tenant and the landlord are registered for VAT, and provided they both agree, the tenant may raise a credit note and both parties would then adjust their VAT account; or
- where the landlord is not registered for VAT, the tenant may make a claim under *VATA 1994, s 80* for overpaid tax (see **51.9 PAYMENT OF VAT**). Any such claim would be also be subject to the unjust enrichment defence.

In all cases where a tenant chooses to correct past transactions, it will be necessary for the tenant to review the attribution of any input tax incurred on costs and rework partial exemption calculations. A VAT-registered landlord will also have to reduce input tax deductions in respect of the inducements which could also require partial exemption calculations to be revised.

(Business Brief 12/05).

Previously, HMRC regarded such an inducement paid by a landlord to a prospective tenant for the latter to enter into a lease as consideration for a standard-rated supply of services by the tenant/assignee following the decision in *Mirror Group plc v C & E Commrs, ECJ Case C–409/98*, [2001] STC 1453 (TVC 22.335).

Inducements (reverse premiums) from old tenant to new tenant

The provisions above do not apply in the situation where a tenant *assigns* his interest in a lease to another tenant and makes an inducement payment for him to take the assignment. In such circumstances, following the decision in *C & E Commrs v Cantor Fitzgerald International, ECJ Case C-108/99*, [2001] STC 1453 (TVC 22.334) any payment made is taxable. But where a tenant pays an inducement to another party to take a sub-lease from him, the provisions outlined in Business Brief 12/05 above will apply as the payment is effectively a landlord inducement.

Grant of a lease

The grant of a lease is, subject to certain exceptions, exempt from VAT. See **41.2** above.

Subsequent supplies under a lease

The granting of a lease usually gives rise to a number of further supplies at later times. For example, a supply is made each time that lease is surrendered or assigned. In such cases, the liability of each subsequent supply is determined at the time when that supply is made rather than by reference to the time of the original grant. [*VATA 1994, s 96(10A); FA 1997, s 35(1); SI 2008/1146, Sch 1 para 3*].

Variations of leases

Sometimes a lease is varied either to alter its terms (e.g. so that it can be used for different purposes), to extend the length of the tenancy or to alter the demised premises (e.g. by renting additional floor space). Under English land law, the effect of such a variation is that the old lease is deemed to be surrendered (see below) and a new lease granted in its place. Where there is no consideration, no supply is seen as taking place. (VAT Notice 742, para 10.5).

Surrender of lease

The grant of an 'interest in or right over' land or a 'licence to occupy' land includes a surrender of that interest, etc. [*VATA 1994, Sch 9 Group 1 and Note (1); SI 1995/282*].

The general provisions relating to grants in **41.2** above therefore also apply to surrenders, i.e. they are exempt subject to certain exceptions. Similarly, the assignment of any interest, etc. back to the lessor or licensor, by the lessee or licensee, is generally exempt. However, a surrender of an interest falling within the exclusions from exemption in **41.3** above remains standard-rated and where a tenant has, prior to the surrender, opted to tax the property in question under **41.8** below, the surrender is covered by the election and therefore taxable. (VAT Notice 742, para 10.3).

Reverse surrenders and assignments

Normally, when a lease is surrendered, consideration is paid by the landlord to the tenant. A '*reverse surrender*' occurs where a tenant surrenders an onerous lease to the landlord before the term of the lease has expired and pays the landlord to accept the surrender.

The grant of an interest in or right over land, or of any licence to occupy land, includes the supply made by the person to whom an interest is surrendered when there is a reverse surrender. [*VATA 1994, Sch 9 Group 1 and Notes (1) and (1A)*]. The general provisions relating to grants in **41.2** above therefore also apply to reverse surrenders, i.e. they are exempt subject to certain exceptions. Where the person making the supply (i.e. the landlord) has opted to tax the property, the supply is standard-rated. (VAT Notice 742, para 10.4).

Dilapidation payments

A lease may provide for the landlord to recover from a tenant, at or near the end of the lease, an amount to cover the cost of restoring the property to its original condition. Such dilapidation payments represent a claim for damages by the landlord against the tenant. The payment is not consideration for a supply for VAT purposes and is outside the scope of VAT. (VAT Notice 742, para 10.10).

Indemnity payments under lease agreements

In general any payment made by a prospective tenant to obtain the grant of a lease or licence, including any disbursement or indemnification of the costs incurred by the landlord, is part of the consideration for that grant.

Many leases provide that an existing tenant reimburses the landlord for legal or other advisory costs incurred by the landlord as a result of the tenant exercising rights already granted under the lease. For example, the tenant may be able to assign the lease, sublet or make alterations provided the tenant first obtains the landlord's consent. Such reimbursements by the tenant to the landlord are consideration for the principal supply of the lease.

If a tenant makes a payment to the landlord to obtain an *additional* right, it is consideration for the variation of the lease (see above).

(VAT Notice 742, para 10.8).

(2) Mesne profits

These are damages for the profits lost by a landlord by reason of wrongful occupation of his property and can only be recovered in respect of continued occupation of property after that right of occupation has expired. As such, an award of mesne profits is not consideration for a supply and is outside the scope of VAT. Where a landlord on the cash accounting system has opted to tax and, in addition to a claim for mesne profits, arrears of rent accrue, payment received following litigation should be treated firstly as relating to rent arrears and only then as relating to mesne profits to the extent that the total received exceeds the outstanding rents. (If the landlord is not on the cash accounting basis, the tax points for the periods in respect of which he is claiming rent arrears will have already been determined under the normal rules.) (Law Society's Gazette, 14 October 1992, p 16).

(3) Rental payments

Rent is the periodic payment made by a tenant to a landlord and is normally the subject of a written agreement. Rent payments can be non-monetary, and can include costs incurred by the landlord under the agreement which are recharged to the tenant. This may include items such as service charges and rates where the landlord is the rateable person.

Rental income is generally exempt from VAT although the landlord may opt to tax rents from non-domestic property (see **41.8** below).

Rent adjustments when buildings are sold or leases assigned

Rent adjustments between landlords on the sale of tenanted property and between tenants on the assignment of a lease are outside the scope of VAT. For VAT purposes the consideration for the sale of the building or the assignment of the lease is the full value of the supply before any rent adjustment is made. (VAT Notice 742, para 10.9).

Recovery of rent from a third party

There are two common ways in which a landlord can recover rent from a third party. Where such payments are received, the landlord should still address any related VAT invoice to the tenant to whom the premises have been leased or let. The supply is still to the tenant, not the third party.

(i) If a tenant sub-lets land or buildings to a third party and the tenant defaults on payment of rent to the landlord, the landlord can issue a notice under the *Law of Distress Amendment Act* and collect the rent arrears from the third party. In turn, the third party can reduce his rent payable to the tenant by the amount he has paid to the landlord. If this happens the supply chain remains the same. There is a supply of the land or building from the landlord to the tenant and from the tenant to the third party. If the landlord has opted to tax, any VAT invoice must be issued to the tenant.

(ii) A surety or guarantor is normally party to any agreement between the landlord and the tenant. If the tenant is unable to meet the agreed periodic rental payments to the landlord, the surety or guarantor will make the payments on the tenant's behalf. There is no supply by the landlord to the surety or guarantor who will not be able to recover any VAT paid.

(VAT Notice 742, para 7.5).

Rent-free periods

The grant by a landlord of a rent-free period is not a supply for VAT purposes except where the rent-free period is given in exchange for something which the tenant agrees to do (e.g. carry out works for the benefit of the landlord). In the latter case, VAT is due on the amount of the rent foregone. (VAT Notice 742, para 4.10). See *Neville Russell* (VTD 2484) (TVC 62.127) where a rent-free period was held not to be consideration for a supply but compensation for the fact that the landlord had failed to finish the fitting out before occupation of the building by the tenant; and *Port Erin Hotels v The Isle of Man Treasury* (VTD 5045) (TVC 62.130) and *Ridgeons Bulk Ltd v C & E Commrs*, QB [1994] STC 427 (TVC 3.179) where waiver of rent was held to be consideration for building work carried out by the tenant and therefore subject to VAT.

Rent paid while premises unoccupied

In *Harper Collins Publishers Ltd* (VTD 12040) (TVC 46.54), the company, following reorganisation, moved out of two floors of its leased business premises but was unable to sublet immediately. The landlords in the meantime exercised the option to tax (see **41.8** below). The tribunal held that, although unoccupied, the two floors were still retained by the company for business purposes, the original purpose in taking the leases not having changed. Input tax suffered on the rents paid could be recovered (in this instance in part only by inclusion in the residual input tax on general overheads under the company's partial exemption computations).

(4) Restricted covenants

Restrictive covenants may be placed on land to control its use. The lifting of such a restricted covenant (e.g. to permit development which was previously forbidden) is exempt from VAT (unless the person receiving the payment has opted to tax). (VAT Notice 742, para 10.6).

(5) Service charges, etc.

The VAT treatment of service charges and other payments relating to premises depends upon the nature of the property and the terms of the arrangements.

General services for tenants of leasehold non-domestic property provided by the landlord

Leases often stipulate that the landlord will provide, and the tenants pay for, the services required for the upkeep of the building as a whole. The lease may provide for an inclusive rental or it may require the tenants to contribute by means of an additional charge to the basic rent, generally referred to as a service or maintenance charge. This service charge assumes the same VAT liability as the premium or rent payable under the lease or licence provided

(a) it is connected with the external fabric or the common parts of the building, etc. as opposed to the demised areas of the property of the individual occupants; and
(b) it is paid for by all the occupants through a common service charge.

The service charge is therefore generally exempt unless the landlord has opted to tax the property (see **41.8** below) or the underlying lease is standard-rated, e.g. holiday or time share accommodation (see **32.5 HOTELS AND HOLIDAY ACCOMMODATION**).

(VAT Notice 742, paras 11.1, 11.2, 11.4).

Specific services for tenants of leasehold non-domestic property provided by the landlord

A payment made by a tenant to the landlord may be

(a) further payment for the main supply of accommodation and therefore exempt or, if the option to tax has been exercised, standard-rated,
(b) for supplies other than accommodation (normally standard-rated), or
(c) disbursements and therefore outside the scope of VAT (see **3.7 AGENTS**).

The following are typical examples.

(i) *Insurance and rates*. If the landlord is the policyholder or rateable person, any payment for insurance or rates from the tenant is part payment for the main supply. If the tenants are the policyholders or rateable persons, any payments on their behalf by the landlord should be treated as disbursements. See also **36.17 INSURANCE** for insurance supplied with other goods and services.
(ii) *Telephones*. If the telephone account is in the name of the landlord, any charge to the tenants (including calls, installation and rental) is standard-rated. If the account is in the name of the tenant but the landlord pays the bill, any recovery from the tenant is a disbursement.
(iii) *Reception and switchboard*. A charge by the landlord under the terms of the lease for use of such facilities which form a common part of the premises is further consideration for the main supply.
(iv) *Office services*. A separate charge for such services (e.g. typing and photocopying) is a separate standard-rated supply. If, however, under the terms of the lease, one inclusive charge is made for office services and accommodation, and the tenant is expected to pay for the services whether used or not, the liability for the services follows that of the main supply.
(v) *Fixtures and fittings*. These are regarded as part of the overall supply of the property and any charges for them are normally included in the rent. Where a separate charge is made by the landlord, the supply is standard-rated.
(vi) *Electricity, light and heat*. If the landlord makes a separate charge for un-metered supplies of gas and electricity used by tenants, it should be treated as further payment for the main supply of accommodation. However, where a landlord operates secondary credit meters, the charges to the tenants for the gas and electricity they use are consideration for separate supplies of fuel and power. These supplies will be standard-rated. See **25.8 FUEL AND POWER** for further details. See, however, *Suffolk Heritage Housing Association Ltd* (VTD 13713) (TVC 30.13) where the tribunal held that the association's long standing practice of recovering heating costs as a separate charge from the rent should be treated as a separate supply for VAT purposes.

(vii) *Management charges*. Charges by landlords for managing a development as a whole and administering the collection of service charges is additional consideration for the main supply.

(viii) *Recreational facilities*. If the charges for the use of recreational facilities are compulsory, irrespective of whether the tenant uses the facilities, then the liability follows the main supply of accommodation.

(VAT Notice 742, para 11.7).

Services for occupants of leasehold non-domestic property provided by third parties

Where a person is responsible for providing services to occupants of property but has no interest in that property (e.g. a managing agent) the supply of services is always standard-rated as they are not part of the supply of the accommodation itself. (VAT Notice 742, para 11.5).

Services supplied to freehold occupants of non-domestic property

Service charges raised where the property has been sold freehold are a separate standard-rated supply as there is no continuing supply of accommodation to the occupant by the provider of the services. (VAT Notice 742, para 11.3).

Shared premises

Where the owner or tenant of premises does not grant other occupants an exempt licence to occupy, any service charge must be standard-rated. This applies even if the owner/tenant is simply passing on appropriate shares of costs (e.g. electricity, gas, telephone and staff wages). The only exception is where a bill is paid which is entirely the liability of another occupant (e.g. a telephone bill or insurance premium in the other occupant's name) which can be treated as a disbursement. (VAT Notice 742, para 11.8).

Service charges on domestic accommodation

Common areas

Service charges relating to the upkeep of common areas of an estate of dwellings, or the common areas of a multi-occupied dwelling, are exempt from VAT so long as they are required to be paid by the leaseholder or tenant to the landlord under the terms of the lease or tenancy agreement. This is because the service charge is treated as ancillary to the main supply of exempt domestic accommodation.

Services provided to freehold owners of dwellings are taxable because there is no supply of domestic accommodation to link those services to. However, by concession, all *mandatory* service charges paid by occupants of dwellings toward the

(a) upkeep of the common areas of a housing estate (e.g. such as paths, driveways and communal gardens),

(b) upkeep of the common areas of a block of flats (e.g. lift maintenance, corridors, stairwells and general lounges),

(c) general maintenance of the exterior of the block of flats or individual dwellings (e.g. painting) if the residents cannot refuse this, and

(d) provision of an estate warden, house manager or caretaker,

can be treated as exempt from VAT. (VAT Notice 48, ESC 3.18).

In *Devine* (VTD 15312) (TVC 41.56) the leaseholders were obliged to keep their properties in good repair with the landlords reserving the right to appoint a factor to ensure this was done. The landlords subsequently appointed a factor and imposed VAT on the service charge. The tribunal held that the charges did not qualify for exemption (because they were not part of the original supply of land) and noted that they did not fall within ESC 3.18 because they were not mandatory in the sense required by the concession, drawing a distinction between the obligations to maintain the property (which were mandatory) and the methods by which the proprietors chose to implement those obligations (which were not).

Electricity, light and heat

If the landlord makes a separate charge for *un-metered* supplies of gas and electricity used by occupants, it should be treated as further payment for the main supply of exempt domestic accommodation. However, if the landlord operates a secondary credit meter, the charges to the occupants for the gas and electricity they use are separate supplies of fuel and power subject to VAT at the reduced rate. See, however, *Suffolk Heritage Housing Association Ltd* (VTD 13713) (TVC 30.13) where the tribunal held that the association's long standing practice of recovering heating costs as a separate charge from the rent should be treated as a separate supply for VAT purposes.

Optional services

Optional services supplied personally to occupants (e.g. shopping, carpet cleaning or painting a private flat) are standard-rated. See *RLRE Tellmer Property sro v Finanční ředitelství v Ústí nad Labem, ECJ Case C–572/07* [2009] STC 2006 (TVC 22.346), in which the tenants were not required to obtain the cleaning of the common parts from their landlord. The court ruled that the letting of immovable property and the cleaning service of the common parts must, in circumstances such as those at issue, be regarded as independent, mutually divisible operations.

Managing agents

A managing agent acting on behalf of a landlord can treat the mandatory service charges to occupants as exempt, providing the agent invoices and collects the service charges directly from the occupants. Any management fee collected from the occupants is standard-rated because it relates to the managing agent's supply to the landlord.

Tenant-controlled management companies

Occupants of an estate may form a tenant-controlled management company which sometimes purchases the freehold of the estate and engages a service provider to maintain the common areas and provide any necessary warden or housekeepers. Providing the company is bound by the terms of the lease to maintain the common areas of the estate (or provide a warden), and the occupants are invoiced by, and pay the service charges directly to, the service provider, the service charges may still be treated as exempt. However, any management fee collected from the occupants is standard-rated because it relates to the service provider's supply to the tenant-controlled management company.

(VAT Notice 742, paras 12.1–12.5).

(6) Statutory compensation

Statutory compensation paid by a landlord to a tenant under the terms of the *Landlord and Tenant Act 1954* or the *Agricultural Tenancies Act 1995* is outside the scope of VAT. This applies even if, for example, an agricultural tenant has issued a 'notice to quit' having decided to retire from farming. Examples of items for which statutory compensation is given on a tenant quitting property are milk quotas left behind, manurial values and standing crops.

Where the landlord and tenant agree that the tenant will leave in return for additional payments, these payments are consideration for the tenant surrendering the lease and are exempt unless the tenant has opted to tax.

(VAT Notice 742, para 10.7).

De Voil Indirect Tax Service. See V4.111.

Joint ownership of land and beneficial interests

Joint owners

[41.5] Where more than one person owns land or buildings or receives the benefit of the consideration from the grant of an interest in land or buildings, (e.g. tenants in common), those persons are treated as a single person. If they are required to register for VAT purposes, they must register as if they were a partnership even if no legal partnership exists. (VAT Notice 742, para 7.2).

Beneficial interests

Where the benefit of the consideration for the grant of an interest in, right over or licence to occupy land accrues to a person (the 'beneficiary') other than the person making the grant, the beneficiary is to be treated for VAT purposes as the person making the grant. So far as any input tax of the person actually making the grant is attributable to the grant, it is to be treated for VAT purposes as input tax of the beneficiary. [*VATA 1994, Sch 10 para 40; SI 2008/1146, Art 2*]. For example, where property is held on bare trusts, although the trustees are the legal owners, if the benefit of the income accruing from the property passes to beneficiaries it is they who are treated as the person making the grant and who may need to register for VAT and, if so, can, subject to the normal rules, claim any input tax arising. (VAT Notice 742, para 7.1).

Benefit accruing to trustees

Where the benefit of the consideration for a grant, etc. accrues directly to trustees, it is the trustees who should, if required, register for VAT. (VAT Notice 742, para 7.1).

Commonhold

[41.6] The *Commonhold and Leasehold Reform Act 2002* recognises a third form of property ownership in addition to freehold and leasehold. This is known as commonhold and is available for residential, commercial or mixed use developments. It confers upon owners ('unit-holders') of parts of a building occupied in common, freehold interests in their respective parts (units) of the property. The freehold interest in the property's communal area and often its structure (the common parts) is owned by a commonhold association whose membership comprises the owners of the units. The commonhold association is responsible for the upkeep of the common parts and provides an estimate of annual expenditure (the commonhold assessment).

A commonhold unit is a freehold in a property that follows the normal VAT accounting rules. Some of the more common situations where a VAT liability may arise are considered below.

(1) Supplies of qualifying buildings (e.g. residential property)

Where the normal conditions for zero-rating are met (see **42.1 LAND AND BUILDINGS: ZERO AND REDUCED RATE SUPPLIES AND DIY HOUSEBUILDERS**), the developer of a '*qualifying building*' (i.e. a building designed as a dwelling or number of dwellings or intended for use solely for a relevant residential or a relevant charitable purpose) can zero-rate

- the first sale of the freehold units in a commonhold to prospective unit-holders; and
- the transfer by operation of law of the freehold of the common parts in the commonhold to the commonhold association, on the registration of the commonhold.

Any subsequent supplies of the units are exempt.

(2) Supplies of non-qualifying buildings (e.g. commercial property)

Such supplies are exempt from VAT unless the supply is either the sale of

- a commonhold unit or freehold of a new building (i.e. one that is less than three years old) or a partly-completed 'non-qualifying' building; or
- a commonhold unit or freehold of a commercial property where the option to tax has been exercised (and not disapplied), see **42.8** *et seq.* below),

in which case it is standard-rated.

(3) Setting up of a commonhold by a developer following construction of a new building

In the case of commercial property, the first supply of each unit is standard-rated provided it is made before the property is three years old or, if not, the developer has opted to tax (subject to the disapplication rules).

In the case of residential property, the supply is zero-rated.

For both residential and commercial property, the freehold interest in the common parts is vested in the commonhold association. Although there is normally no consideration attributed to this disposal, it may be a supply for VAT purposes with a requirement to charge VAT. See **41.7**(4) below.

(4) A number of freeholds are converted into a single commonhold

This may occur where freeholders apply for commonhold status because they have communal facilities (e.g. shared roadways, paths or services, etc.) and may involve some of the existing freeholders giving up title to areas of their land which are to become the common parts. It is likely that any payment made to a former freeholder will be seen as consideration for the surrender of the freehold interest with the VAT liability being

- in the case of commercial property, exempt (standard-rated where the property is less than three years old or an option to tax has been made (and not disapplied)); and
- in the case of residential property, exempt (zero-rated where a major interest has not been previously granted in the property, e.g. because the freeholder was also the person who constructed the building for his own occupation).

(5) A leasehold is converted into commonhold

On registration as commonhold, all pre-existing leases are extinguished.

Where the former leaseholder gains ownership of a commonhold unit in the same property as under the lease, the only supply is that of the freehold. The lease ceases to have legal effect and there is no supply of it for VAT purposes.

However, where the lease is extinguished and the freehold is transferred to some other person, or the freehold units have different boundaries from the previous leasehold premises, for VAT purposes there is a supply of a surrender of an interest in the property by the former leaseholder with the VAT liability being

- in the case of commercial property, exempt (standard-rated if the lessee has opted to tax the supply (subject to the disapplication rules); and
- in the case of residential property, exempt.

Where the leaseholder pays a consideration for the freehold interest in the unit he acquires, the liability for

- commercial property is exempt (unless the property is less than three years old or the option to tax has been exercised), and
- residential property is exempt (unless it is the first supply of a major interest in which case it is zero-rated).

(6) Sale of a commonhold unit by a unit holder

The disposal of a unit in a commercial property is exempt unless the property is less than three years old or an option to tax has been made (and not disapplied) in which case the supply is standard-rated.

The disposal of a unit in a residential property is exempt.

On purchase of a commonhold unit, the purchaser will also acquire membership of the commonhold association and an interest in the common parts. Normally, there will be no consideration attributed to the transfer of interest but it is a supply for VAT purposes and VAT must be charged if the conditions in **41.7**(4) below apply.

(7) The termination of a commonhold

A commonhold can be terminated in the following circumstances.

- *Voluntary winding up*. The commonhold association must specify proposals for the transfer of the commonhold land and explain how the assets of the association are to be distributed. Any payment received by either the commonhold association or by the unit-holders is consideration for a freehold interest and the liability is in accordance with the normal rules as above.
- *Winding up by court*. Where a commonhold association becomes insolvent, a successor commonhold association may be registered as the proprietor of the freehold estate in the common parts. Normally, there will be no consideration attributed to the disposal but it is a supply for VAT purposes and VAT must be charged if the conditions in **41.7**(4) below apply.

(8) Treatment of the commonhold assessment

Charges ('commonhold assessments') will normally be levied by the commonhold association to pay for the upkeep of common parts. These charges are treated in the same way as service charges to a long leaseholder or a non-commonhold freeholder. See **41.4**(5) above.

(VAT Notice 742, paras 13.1–13.8).

Other land transactions

[41.7] Other land transactions are treated as follows:

(1) Compulsory purchase

The disposal of land under a compulsory purchase order is an exempt supply unless standard-rated because it is a new building or civil engineering work within **41.3**(*a*) above, holiday accommodation less than three years old (see **41.3**(*d*) above) or the option to tax has been exercised (see **41.8** below). If the full amount of compensation is not known at what would otherwise be the time of supply under the normal rules, there is a tax point each time any compensation payment is received. (*SI 1995/2518, Reg 84(1)*; VAT Notice 742, para 7.3). See, however, *L Landau* (VTD 13644) (TVC 57.103) where the tribunal chairman gave the opinion that VAT generally became chargeable on the transfer of the right to dispose of the land and the taxable amount included consideration to be obtained later. Where consideration was not quantified, there was no reason why VAT should not be accounted for on an estimated amount.

(2) Dedications of roads and sewers, transactions under planning agreements, etc.

If a developer

(a) dedicates, for no monetary consideration, a new road to a local authority (under *Highways Act 1980* or *Roads (Scotland) Act 1984*) or a new sewer or ancillary works to a sewerage undertaker (under *Water Industries Act 1991* or *Sewerage (Scotland) Act 1968*),

(b) provides goods or services free, or at a purely nominal charge, to a local or other authority (under *Town and Country Planning Acts* or other similar agreements which may loosely be described as 'planning gain agreements'), or

(c) transfers (usually for a nominal consideration) the *basic* amenities of estate roads, footpaths, communal parking and open space of a private housing or industrial estate to a management company which maintains them,

this does not constitute a taxable supply by the developer and no VAT is chargeable.

Included under (*b*) are buildings such as community centres or schools, amenity land or civil engineering works or an agreement to construct something on land already owned by a local authority or third party.

Any input tax incurred on such work is, however, attributable to the supply (or self-supply) of the main development (i.e. houses, shops, community centre, factory units, etc.) and recoverable or not depending upon whether that supply is taxable or exempt.

Any sums of money which have to be paid by the developer to the local authority, etc. (e.g. for the future maintenance of the building or land or as a contribution towards improvement of the infrastructure) are not consideration for a taxable supply to the developer by the local authority, etc.

(3) Agreements with the Highways Agency

When a development is undertaken, there may need to be road improvements. These will normally be undertaken in one of the following ways

Works carried out by the Highways Agency

The Highways Agency will arrange for the works to be carried out and may then, under *Highways Act 1980, s 278*, recover from the developer the costs of certain road improvements. These costs normally include irrecoverable VAT that has been charged to the Highways Agency by a contractor. As there is no supply between the Highways Agency and the developer, merely a reimbursement of VAT-inclusive costs, the developer is not entitled to recover the VAT element as input tax.

Works carried out by the developer

If the developer is permitted by the Highways Agency to carry out the works at his own cost, then there is no supply by the developer of the works to the Highways Agency (because the developer does not receive any consideration for the works from the Highways Agency). However, the developer may recover the input tax as attributable to his own ultimate supply of land and buildings from the development if the development is a taxable supply.

(VAT Notice 742, paras 8.1–8.5).

(4) Free supplies of land and buildings

The normal rules for business gifts and private use of property apply. Where

(a) land or buildings forming part of the assets of a business are transferred or disposed of free of charge, or
(b) such land or buildings are made available for anyone else to use, free of charge or for a private or non-business purpose

the business must account for output tax on such supplies if

- it was charged VAT on the purchase, construction, reconstruction or refurbishment of the land or buildings;
- it treated all that VAT as input tax and did not apportion it between business and non-business use;
- it was eligible to treat all or part of the input tax as deductible; and
- the supply is standard-rated (see below).

Any such transfer or disposal of land or buildings is taxable if it is standard-rated in its own right or the business has opted to tax (and the option is not disapplied). The value is the market value at the time of its disposal.

Making a building available free of charge, or for private or non-business use, is always taxable. The amount of the charge is equal to that part of the input VAT deducted on the building that is fairly attributable to this use. Where no VAT was incurred on the building before 9 April 2003, then this charge only arises if the intended use of the building is changed after incurring the VAT (as a single output tax charge at the time of the change of use). If the free of charge, private or non-business use is intended at the time the VAT is incurred, the business must apportion the VAT incurred at that point and there will be no further charge when the free of charge, private or non-business use actually happens.

(VAT Notice 742, para 7.6).

See **47.6** and **47.7 OUTPUT TAX** for full details.

(5) Mortgages

The mortgaging of a property, as security for borrowing money, is not regarded as a supply of the property for VAT purposes.

Sales of repossessed property

- *Sales under a power of sale.* Where a financial institution or any other lender sells land or buildings under a power of sale in satisfaction of a debt owed to it, there is a supply of the property by the *borrower*. If VAT is due on that supply, the *lender* or other person selling the property is responsible for accounting for that VAT using the procedure set out in **2.10 ACCOUNTING PERIODS AND RETURNS.**

- *Foreclosures*. If, instead of selling property under a power of sale, a lender obtains a Court Order and forecloses on land or buildings belonging to the borrower, there is a supply by the borrower to the lender of the land or building unless it is treated as an asset of a business transferred as a going concern (see **8.10 BUSINESS**). If the land or building is subsequently sold, this is a supply by the lender foreclosing, who may, if he wishes, opt to tax the property.

Renting out of repossessed property

If a lender

- repossesses land or buildings, or
- appoints a *Law of Property Act* receiver without foreclosing

and rents the property out to tenants, the borrower makes a supply to the tenant if the rental income received by the lender is used to reduce the debt owed or to service interest payments due in respect of that debt. If the supply is a standard-rated supply, the lender or LPA receiver should account for VAT using the procedure set out in **2.10 ACCOUNTING PERIODS AND RETURNS**.

(VAT Notice 742, paras 9.1–9.4).

See also **7.11 BAD DEBT RELIEF** for recovery of VAT on costs incurred by mortgage lenders.

(6) Transfer of a business as a going concern

See **8.10 BUSINESS**.

Option to tax: supplies made on or after 1 June 2008

[41.8] The option to tax provisions allow for a person to tax certain supplies of land which would otherwise be exempt. The purpose of the option is to allow the recovery of input tax which would otherwise be lost. For these purposes, '*land*' includes any buildings or structures permanently affixed to it. A business does not need to own the land in order to opt to tax. (VAT Notice 742A, para 1.3).

In relation to supplies made on or after 1 June 2008, the provisions relating to the option to tax in *VATA 1994, Sch 10* have been rewritten (with amendments). In addition, certain provisions in VAT Notice 742A have the force of law as tertiary legislation. The revised rules are considered in **41.9** to **41.21** below.

Transitional provisions

(1) The re-enactment of any provision does not affect the continuity of the law (except where there is a change in the law relating to that provision). Anything done (or having effect as if done) under a superseded provision which was in force or effective immediately before the commencement of the corresponding rewritten provision has effect afterwards as if done under or for the purposes of the rewritten provisions.

(2) Any reference (express or implied) in any enactment, instrument or document to
- a rewritten provision, or
- things done or falling to be done under or for the purposes of a rewritten provision,

is to be read as including, in relation to times, circumstances or purposes in relation to which any corresponding superseded provision had effect, a reference to the superseded provision or (as the case may be) things done or falling to be done under or for the purposes of the superseded provision.

(3) Any reference (express or implied) in any enactment, instrument or document to
- a superseded provision, or
- things done or falling to be done under or for the purposes of a superseded provision,

is to be read as including, in relation to times, circumstances or purposes in relation to which any corresponding rewritten provision has effect, a reference to the rewritten provision or (as the case may be) things done or falling to be done under or for the purposes of the rewritten provision.

An election made before 1 November 1989 continues to have effect from 1 August 1989 (or any later day specified in the election).

(4) An election made before 1 March 1995 and having effect before that day continues to have effect notwithstanding that it has not been notified to HMRC.

(5) The fact that the words 'or of a description specified' in *VATA 1994, Sch 10 para 3(2)* as it stood before rewriting are not rewritten does not affect the continued operation of an option to tax any land which was made before 1 June 2008 and which specified a description of land.

[*SI 2008/1146, Sch* 2].

Effect of the option to tax

[41.9] If

- a person exercises the option to tax any land, and
- a 'grant' is made in relation to the land at any time when the option to tax it has effect,

the grant does not fall within *VATA 1994, Sch 9 Group 1* (exemption for land) if it is made by

- the person exercising that option; or
- where that person is a body corporate, a 'relevant associate' (see **41.10**).

'*Grant*' includes an assignment or surrender and the supply made by the person to whom an interest is surrendered when there is a reverse surrender (i.e. where the person to whom the interest is surrendered is paid by the person by whom the interest is being surrendered to accept the surrender).

[*VATA 1994, Sch 10 paras 2, 33; SI 2008/1146, Art* 2].

Once a business has opted to tax any property, it must charge VAT on *all* future supplies it makes in relation to that property which would otherwise be exempt unless

- the anti-avoidance provisions in **41.12** below prevent the supplies from being taxable even if though the option to tax has been made; or
- the option has been revoked (see **41.16** below).

It is not possible, for example, for a business to opt to tax rents but then not tax a subsequent sale of the property. The option remains effective even if the business ceases to be registered for VAT due to a fall in turnover but subsequently has to register again (VAT Notice 742A, para 12.1).

Only supplies which the business makes are affected. Its option to tax will not affect supplies made by anyone else. For example, if a business is selling an opted building, the purchaser has the choice of whether to opt to tax or not. Similarly, if a tenant of the business is sub-letting, they too have this same choice. For this reason, it is advisable to inform any tenant of the decision to opt at the earliest opportunity so that they may safeguard their right to recover input tax by opting to tax, if they should so wish. (VAT Notice 742A, para 4.4).

Supplies arising from earlier grants

If an option to tax is exercised after the time of a grant relating to land, any supplies arising from the grant which are made after the option takes effect are treated as taxable supplies. [*VATA 1994, Sch 10 para 31; SI 2008/1146, Art 2*].

Effect on existing leases

Unless the lease specifically provides otherwise, the lessor or licensor has a right to add VAT to the rent agreed under the lease following an option to tax. [*VATA 1994, s 89; SI 2008/1146, Sch 1 para 2*]. If an election has been made but, under the terms of the lease, VAT cannot be added, any rent received should be treated as VAT-inclusive and the VAT element calculated by multiplying the rent received by the appropriate VAT fraction.

> *Example*
>
> Company A is the landlord of a commercial building and owns the freehold of the building. It has made an option to tax election with HMRC, and will therefore charge VAT on the rent to its tenant Company B. The latter company sublets part of the premises to Company C but is not obliged to opt to tax its own interest in the building and charge VAT on the rent to Company C just because Company A has made an election. It will make a commercial decision as to whether an election is in its best interests and act accordingly.

Groups of companies

[41.10] An option to tax made by a member of a VAT group is generally binding upon other members of the same VAT group (see **41.9**). A body corporate that is bound by another body corporate's option to tax under these rules is known as a 'relevant associate' of the opter. If a body corporate is a relevant associate, it must normally charge VAT on any supplies it makes of the opted property, even after it has left the VAT group.

Relevant associate

Where a body corporate ('the opter') exercises an option to tax in relation to any building or land, another body corporate is a relevant associate of the opter if

- it was treated as a member of the same group as the opter at the time when the option first had effect;
- it has been treated as a member of the same VAT group as the opter at any later time when the opter had a 'relevant interest' in the building or land; or
- it has been treated as a member of the same VAT group as the opter, or a relevant associate of the opter, at a time when either of them had a relevant interest in the building or land.

A '*relevant interest*' in the building or land means an interest in, right over or licence to occupy the building or land (or any part of it).

Ceasing to be a relevant associate

A body corporate ceases to be a relevant associate of the opter in relation to the building or land in the following circumstances.

(a) The body corporate ceases to be a relevant associate of the opter in relation to the building or land at the time when all of the following conditions are first met.
   - The body corporate has no relevant interest in the building or land.
   - Where the body corporate has disposed of such an interest, it is not the case that a supply for the purposes of the charge to VAT in respect of the disposal is yet to take place, or would be yet to take place if one or more conditions (such as the happening of an event or the doing of an act) were to be met.
   - The body corporate or the opter is no longer a member of the group mentioned above.
   - The body corporate is not connected with any person who has a relevant interest in the building or land where that person is the opter or another relevant associate of the opter. For these purposes, whether a person is connected with another person is determined in accordance with *ICTA 1988, s 839* (see **71.19 VALUATION**). A company is not connected with another company only because both are under the control of the Crown, a Minister of the Crown, a government department, or a Northern Ireland department.

   If these conditions are met, the body corporate automatically ceases to be a relevant associate from the time that all three conditions are met. There is no need to notify HMRC or to seek permission.

(b) If the conditions in (*a*) above are not met, a body corporate also ceases to be a relevant associate of the opter in relation to the building or land at a time when it meets all of the conditions specified below *and* has notified HMRC that it does so on.
The conditions are:
(1) *The grouping condition.* The body corporate has ceased to be treated as a member of the VAT group by virtue of which it became a relevant associate of the opter.
(2) *The 20-year condition.* The body corporate has
- held any 'relevant interest' in the building or land acquired whilst a member of that VAT group for a period of at least 20 years; and
- been treated as a relevant associate of the opter for a period of at least 20 years.

(3) *The capital item condition.* Any land or building that is subject to the option is not, in relation to the body corporate, subject to input tax adjustment as a capital item under the capital goods scheme.
(4) *The valuation condition.* The body corporate, or a person connected with it, has not, within a period of ten years ending on the date that the body corporate ceases to be a relevant associate, made a supply of a relevant interest in the building or land that is subject to the option that
- was for a consideration that was less than the open market value of that supply; or
- arose from a 'relevant grant'.

(5) *The pre-payment condition.* No supply of goods or services has been made for a consideration to the body corporate (or to a person connected with it) which will be wholly or partly attributable to a supply or other use of the land or buildings made by that body (or by a person connected with it) more than twelve months later.

See above for the meaning of '*relevant interest*'. '*Relevant grant*' means a grant that the grantor intends or expects will give rise to a supply for a consideration significantly greater than any consideration for any earlier supply arising from the grant (except as a result of a rent review determined according to normal commercial practice).
Notification must be made on form VAT 1614B and must contain the information requested on that form. The form can be downloaded from www.hmrc.gov.uk
or obtained from the National Advice Service on 0845 010 9000.

(c) If a body corporate does not meet all the conditions in (*a*) or (*b*) above, it may apply for written permission from HMRC to cease to be a relevant associate.
Permission will not be granted unless both conditions 1 and 2 under (*b*) above are met. In deciding whether or not to grant permission, HMRC will give particular consideration to whether or not the applicant or a third party has received a VAT benefit as a result of the applicant's actions.

If HMRC grants permission, the body corporate ceases to be a relevant associate of the opter from the day on which HMRC give their permission or such earlier or later day as is specified in their permission. HMRC may specify an earlier day only if

- the body corporate has previously purported to give a written notification of its ceasing to be a relevant associate of the opter;
- the conditions specified in (*b*) above are not, in the event, met in relation to the body corporate; and
- HMRC consider that the grounds on which those conditions are not so met are insignificant.

The day specified may be the day from which the body corporate would have ceased to be a relevant associate of the opter if those conditions had been so met.

HMRC may specify conditions subject to which their permission is given and, if any of those conditions are broken, they may treat the application as if it had not been made.

Application for permission must be made on form VAT 1614B (obtainable as in (*b*) above).

[*VATA 1994, Sch 10, paras 3, 4, 34; SI 2008/1146, Art 2; SI 2009/1966, Arts 3, 8*]. (VAT Notice 742A, para 6.3).

Exclusions from effect of the option to tax

[41.11] There are some supplies of land and buildings where, even if the business has opted to tax, the option will not apply and the supplies remain exempt from VAT. This may have an impact on how much input tax can be claimed.

(1) Dwellings designed or adapted, and intended for use, as dwelling, etc.

An option to tax has no effect in relation to any grant in relation to a building or part of a building if the building or part of the building is designed or adapted, and is intended, for use

- as a dwelling or number of dwellings; or
- solely for a 'relevant residential purpose' (see **41.1**(15) above) provided the purchaser or tenant has informed the grantor of his intention to use the property for such a purpose and has given him a certificate to that effect.

See **41.1**(4) above for when building is '*designed as a dwelling*'.

[*VATA 1994, Sch 10 paras 5, 33; SI 2008/1146, Art 2*].

Where a building or part of a building is used for both relevant residential purposes and business purposes, the option to tax will not apply to the part used for relevant residential purposes, provided that the different functions are carried out in clearly defined areas. In such circumstances the value of the supply should be fairly apportioned between the exempt and taxable elements. (VAT Notice 742A, para 3.3).

(2) Conversion of buildings for use as dwelling, etc.

An option to tax has no effect in relation to any grant made to a person ('*the recipient*') in relation to a building or part of a building (not designed, adapted or used as a dwelling or part of a dwelling) if the recipient certifies that the building or part of the building is intended for use

(a) as a dwelling or number of dwellings; or
(b) solely for a 'relevant residential purpose' (see **41.1**(15) above).

The recipient must give a certificate on form VAT 1614D to the person making the grant ('*the seller*'), containing the information requested on that form. Copies of the form can be downloaded from

www.hmrc.gov.uk

or obtained from the National Advice Service on 0845 010 9000.

The certificate must normally be given before the price for the grant to the recipient by the seller is legally fixed (e.g. by exchange of contracts, by letters or missives, or by the signing of heads of agreement). The seller may, at his discretion, accept a certificate at a later time, but only in respect of supplies that arise after the certificate is given. For example, where a lease for periodic rental payments has been granted, the seller may only exempt the rental supplies that take place after the certificate is received. The recipient may give the certificate to the seller only if the recipient satisfies one of the following conditions.

- He intends to use the building or part of the building as mentioned in (*a*) or (*b*) above.
- He intends to convert the building or part of the building with a view to its being used as mentioned in (*a*) or (*b*) above.
- He is a '*relevant intermediary*', i.e.
  - he intends to dispose of the whole of the interest in the building or part of the building that is to be supplied to him by the seller to another person (P); and
  - P has already given the recipient a certificate stating that he (P) intends to *either* convert the building for use as in (*a*) or (*b*) above *or* dispose of the interest to another person who intends to convert the building for such use *or* dispose of the interest to another person who, in turn, intends to dispose of it to another person for such use.

For these purposes, a building or part of a building is not to be regarded as intended for use as a dwelling or number of dwellings at any time if there is intended to be a period before that time during which it will not be so used (but disregarding use for incidental or other minor purposes).

Where only part of a building is to be converted or adapted for use as in (*a*) or (*b*) above, the certificate must make it clear that this is the case and must contain a description of the qualifying part. The option to tax will apply to the part of the building that is not intended for qualifying use and the seller must fairly apportion his supply between the exempt and taxable elements.

[*VATA 1994, Sch 10 para 6; SI 2008/1146, Art 2*]. (VAT Notice 742A, para 3.4).

(3) Charities

An option to tax has no effect in relation to any grant made to a person in relation to a building or part of a building intended by the person for use solely for a '*relevant charitable purpose*' (see **41.1**(13) above) but *not* as an office, provided the purchaser or tenant has informed the grantor of his intention to use the property for such a purpose and has given him a certificate to that effect.

[*VATA 1994, Sch 10 para 7; SI 2008/1146, Art 2*].

HMRC do not specify the form of a certificate.

Where a building or part of a building is used for relevant charitable purposes and business or general administration purposes, the option to tax will not apply to the part used for relevant charitable purposes, provided that the different functions are carried out in clearly defined areas. In such circumstances, the value of the supply should be fairly apportioned between the exempt and taxable elements. (VAT Notice 742A, para 3.5).

(4) Residential caravans

An option to tax has no effect in relation to any grant made in relation to a pitch for a residential caravan. A caravan is not a residential caravan if residence in it throughout the year is prevented by the terms of a covenant, statutory planning consent or similar permission. [*VATA 1994, Sch 10 para 8; SI 2008/1146, Art 2*].

(5) Residential houseboats

An option to tax has no effect in relation to any grant made in relation to facilities for the 'mooring' of a residential 'houseboat'.

'*Mooring*' includes anchoring or berthing.

'*Houseboat*' means a boat or other floating, decked structure that is designed or adapted for use solely as a place of permanent habitation and not having the means of, or capable of being readily adapted for, self-propulsion.

A houseboat is not a residential houseboat if residence in it throughout the year is prevented by the terms of a covenant, statutory planning consent or similar permission.

[*VATA 1994, Sch 10 para 9; SI 2008/1146, Art 2*].

(6) Relevant housing associations

An option to tax has no effect in relation to any grant made to a 'relevant housing association' in relation to any land if the association certifies that the land is to be used (after any necessary demolition work) for the 'construction of a building' or buildings intended for use

- as a dwelling or number of dwellings; or
- solely for a 'relevant residential purpose'.

A relevant housing association is

- (from 1 April 2010) a private registered provider of social housing;
- in Wales, a Welsh registered social landlord within the meaning of *Housing Act 1996*;
- in Scotland, a Scottish registered social landlord within the meaning of *Housing (Scotland) Act 2001*; or
- in Northern Ireland, a Northern Irish registered housing association within the meaning of *Housing (Northern Ireland) Order 1992 (SI 1992/1725)*.

Until the coming into force of provision defining 'private registered provider of social housing', it means persons listed in the register of providers of social housing maintained under the *Housing and Regeneration Act 2008, Pt 2 Ch 3* who are not local authorities within the meaning of the *Housing Associations Act 1985*.

See **41.1**(15) above for '*relevant residential purpose*' and **41.1**(2) above for '*construction of a building*'. The construction of a building includes the construction of a garage provided the dwelling and the garage are constructed at the same time and the garage is intended for occupation with the dwelling or one of the dwellings.

The housing association must give a certificate, on form VAT 1614G to the person making the grant ('*the seller*'), containing the information requested on the form. The form can be downloaded from

www.hmrc.gov.uk

or obtained from the National Advice Service on 0845 010 9000.

The certificate must normally be given before the price for the grant to the recipient by the seller is legally fixed (e.g. by exchange of contracts, by letters or missives, or by the signing of heads of agreement). The seller may, at his discretion, accept a certificate at a later time, but only in respect of supplies that arise after the certificate is given. For example, where a lease for periodic rental payments has been granted, the seller may only exempt the rental supplies that take place after the certificate is received.

[*VATA 1994, Sch 10 paras 10, 33; SI 2008/1146, Art 2; SI 2010/485, Art 4*]. (VAT Notice 742A, para 3.6).

The certificate cannot be issued retrospectively (*Langstane Housing Association Ltd* (VTD 19111) (TVC 6.6)).

(7) Grant to individual for construction of dwelling (DIY buildings)

An option to tax has no effect in relation to any grant made to an individual if

- the land is to be used for the 'construction of a building' intended for use by the individual as a dwelling; and
- the construction is not carried out in the course or furtherance of a business carried on by the individual.

See **41.1**(2) above for the meaning of '*construction of a building*'. The construction of a building includes the construction of a garage provided the dwelling and the garage are constructed at the same time and the garage is intended for occupation with the dwelling.

[*VATA 1994, Sch 10 paras 11, 33; SI 2008/1146, Art 2*].

Where a grant within (1) to (7) above gives rise to supplies at different times after the making of the grant (e.g. rent), the liability of each of those supplies is determined at the time when the supply is made rather than by reference to the time of the original grant. [*VATA 1994, s 96(10A); SI 2008/1146, Sch 1 para 3*].

Supplies partially affected by an option

Where a business has opted to tax a property but the option cannot have effect in relation to part of that property (e.g. a shop with a flat to be used as a dwelling over it), the consideration for any supply must be apportioned between the standard-rated element and the exempt or zero-rated part. [*VATA 1994, Sch 8 Group 5 Note 10, Sch 10 para 32; SI 2008/1146, Art 2*]. The business can choose the method of apportionment but it must provide a fair and reasonable result. (VAT Notice 742A, para 3.10).

Anti-avoidance provisions

[41.12] Certain businesses, which are not entitled to recover all of the input tax they incur on the purchase of land or buildings or on major construction projects, enter into arrangements designed to either increase the amount of input tax they can claim or to spread the VAT cost of the purchase or construction over a number of years. To counter this, HMRC have introduced anti-avoidance provisions which are applied each time a grant is made. If the provisions apply, the option to tax will not have effect (it will be 'disapplied') in respect of the supplies that arise from that particular grant. A business that normally receives credit for most of the input tax it incurs is unlikely to be affected by these anti-avoidance measures. (VAT Notice 742A, para 13.1).

A supply is not, as a result of an option to tax, a taxable supply if

- the 'grant' giving rise to the supply was made by a person ('*the grantor*') who was a developer of the land; and
- at the time when the grant was made (or treated for these purposes as having been made), the grantor or a 'development financier' intended or expected that the land
  - (i) would become exempt land whether immediately or eventually and whether or not as a result of the grant; or
  - (ii) would continue, for a period at least, to be exempt land.

Supply by a person other than the grantor

If a supply is made by a person other than the person who made the grant giving rise to it, for the above purposes

- the person making the supply is treated as the person who made the grant giving rise to it; and
- the grant is treated as made at the time when that person made the first supply arising from the grant.

[*VATA 1994, Sch 10 para 12; SI 2008/1146, Art 2*].

The following definitions apply for the above purposes.

(1) Grant

Grant refers to the act that transfers the land or building (e.g. a freehold sale of land or a building, the leasing or licensing of land or a building, or the assignment or surrender of that lease or licence). (VAT Notice 742A, para 13.3).

(2) Grantor

The grantor is the person who sells, leases or lets any of the land or buildings and can be anywhere in the chain of people who have an interest in the land or buildings concerned. For example, where a freeholder sells land to another party who constructs a new commercial building on the land and lets it to another business for occupation for its own use, there are two grantors: the seller of the land and the business which constructs and leases the new commercial building. If the occupying business sub-lets part of the building to another business, there would then be three grantors. The test should be applied to each grant made. (VAT Notice 742A, para 13.3).

(3) Grants made by a developer

A grant made by any person ('the grantor') in relation to any land is made by a developer of the land if the following conditions are met.

(a) The land either
   (i) is a relevant capital item (i.e. the land, or the building or part of a building on the land, is a capital item under the capital goods scheme in relation to the grantor); or
   (ii) was intended or expected to be a relevant capital item (i.e. the grantor, or a 'development financier' intended or expected that the land, or a building or part of a building on or to be constructed on, the land, would become a capital item under the capital goods scheme in relation to the grantor or any 'relevant transferee').

   A person is a '*relevant transferee*' if the person is someone to whom the land, building or part of a building was to be transferred in the course of a supply or in the course of a transfer of a business or part of a business as a going concern.

(b) The grant is made at an eligible time as respects that capital item (i.e. it is made before the end of the period provided for the making of adjustments relating to the deduction of input tax as respects the capital item under the capital goods scheme).

But if

- a person other than the grantor is treated as making the grant of the land (see above), and
- the grant is consequently treated as made at what would otherwise be an ineligible time,

the grant is treated instead as if it were not made at an ineligible time.

[*VATA 1994, Sch 10 para 13; SI 2008/1146, Art 2*].

(4) Development financier

A development financier in relation to the grantor of any land means a person who

- has provided finance for the grantor's development of the land, or
- has entered into any agreement, arrangement or understanding (whether or not legally enforceable) to provide finance for the grantor's development of the land,

with the intention or in the expectation that the land will become 'exempt land' or continue (for a period at least) to be exempt land.

Providing finance for the grantor's development of the land is widely defined. It covers directly or indirectly providing funds *either* for meeting the whole (or any part) of the cost of the grantor's development of the land *or* for discharging (in whole or in part) any liability that has been or may be incurred by any person for or in connection with the raising of funds to meet that cost. It also includes directly or indirectly procuring the provision of such funds by another person for either of those purposes. The ways funds can be provided include

- making a loan of funds that are, or are to be, used for that purpose;
- providing any guarantee or other security in relation to such a loan;
- providing any of the consideration for the issue of any shares or other securities issued wholly or partly for raising those funds;
- providing any consideration for the acquisition by any person of shares or other securities issued wholly or partly for raising those funds; or
- any other transfer of assets or value as a consequence of which any of those funds are made available for that purpose.

For these purposes, references to

(a) the grantor's development of the land are to the acquisition by the grantor of the asset which
  (i) consists in the land or a building or part of a building on the land; and
  (ii) is, or (as the case may be) was intended or expected to be, a relevant capital item under the capital goods scheme in relation to the grantor (within the meaning in (3) above); and
(b) the acquisition of the asset includes
  (i) its construction or reconstruction; and
  (ii) the carrying out in relation to it of any other works by reference to which it is, or was intended or expected to be, a relevant capital item under the capital goods scheme in relation to the grantor (within the meaning in (3) above).

[*VATA 1994, Sch 10 para 14; SI 2008/1146, Art 2*].

(5) Exempt land

Land is exempt land if, at any time before the end of the adjustment period under the capital goods scheme as respects that land

- the land is occupied by
  (i) the grantor,

(ii) a person connected with the grantor,
(iii) a development financier, or
(iv) a person connected with a development financier; and

- that occupation is not wholly (i.e. 100%) or substantially wholly (i.e. at least 80%) for 'eligible purposes'.

From 1 March 2011, where a person is in occupation of the land at any time before the end of the relevant adjustment period, he is treated as not in occupation of the land at that time if

- the building occupation conditions are met at that time; or
- his occupation of the land arises solely by reference to any automatic teller machine of his.

The building occupation conditions are met if

- the grant consists of or includes the grant of a relevant interest in a building; and
- the person (or anyone connected with him if occupation is not wholly, or substantially wholly, for eligible purposes) does not, at the time in question, occupy any part of the land that is not a building, or more than the maximum allowable percentage of any relevant building.

The maximum allowable percentage means

- 2% where the person is (or is connected with) the grantor; and
- 10% where the person is (or is connected with) a development financier (but not also (or connected with) the grantor).

From 1 April 2010 to 28 February 2011, a person is treated as not in occupation of the land at the relevant time if he is within (iii) or (iv) but not within (i) or (ii), and the following building occupation conditions are met

- the grant consists of or includes the grant of a relevant interest in a building; and
- the person (or anyone connected with him) does not, at the time in question, occupy any part of the land that is not a building, or more than 10% of any relevant building.

For these purposes, whether a person is connected with another person is determined in accordance with *ICTA 1988, s 839* (see **71.19 VALUATION**).

[*VATA 1994, Sch 10 paras 15, 15A, 34; SI 2008/1146, Art 2; SI 2010/485, Arts 5, 6; SI 2011/86, Arts 5, 6*]. (VAT Notice 742A, para 13.11).

'Eligible purposes'

Occupation for eligible purposes means one of the following.

- Occupation by a taxable person for the purposes of making supplies which
  (i) are, or are to be, made in the course or furtherance of a business carried on by the person; and
  (ii) are supplies of such a description that the person would be entitled to a credit for any input tax wholly attributable to those supplies.

- Occupation of land by a body within *VATA 1994, s 33* (see **43.2 LOCAL AUTHORITIES AND PUBLIC BODIES**) so far as the occupation is for purposes other than those of a business carried on by the body.
- Occupation of land by a Government department (see **43.11 LOCAL AUTHORITIES AND PUBLIC BODIES**).
- Until 1 March 2011, occupation of land by a person in so far as the occupation arises merely by reference to any automatic teller machine of the person which is fixed to the land.

In determining whether land is held for eligible purposes

- if a person occupying land
  (i) holds the land in order to put it to use for particular purposes, and
  (ii) does not occupy it for any other purpose,
  that person is treated, for so long as the conditions in (i) and (ii) continue to be met, as occupying the land for the purposes for which the person proposes to use it;
- if land is in the occupation of a person ('A') who
  (i) is not a taxable person, but
  (ii) is a person whose supplies are treated for the purposes of *VATA 1994* as made by another person ('B') who is a taxable person,
  the land is treated as if A and B were a single taxable person; and
- a person occupies land whether the person
  (i) occupies it alone or together with one or more other persons; and
  (ii) occupies all of the land or only part of it.

[*VATA 1994, Sch 10 para 16; SI 2008/1146, Art 2; SI 2011/86, Art 7*].

Intentions and expectations

HMRC will consider commercial documents and other evidence such as minutes of meetings, business plans and finance requests to establish the intention and expectation of the businesses that are involved in the particular development. There does not have to be an intention to avoid VAT for a grant to be caught by the anti-avoidance provisions. (VAT Notice 742A, para 13.4).

In occupation of

In *Newnham College in the University of Cambridge* [2008] STC 1225 (TVC 6.10) the House of Lords held that a college was not in occupation of a library as it did not have the right to occupy the library as if it were the owner and to exclude any other person from enjoyment of such a right. HMRC's interpretation is that to be 'in occupation' a person must have actual possession of the land along with a degree of permanence and control. Such a right will normally result from the grant of a legal interest or licence to occupy. Occupation could also, however, be by agreement or de facto and it is therefore necessary to take account of the day-to-day arrangements, particularly where these differ from the contractual terms. An exclusive right of occupation is not a requirement, nor is it necessary for a person to be utilising all of the land for all of the time. A person whose interest in land is subject to an inferior interest, such as to prevent him from having rights of occupation for the time being, is not in occupation until the inferior interest expires. However, the test is forward looking and takes account of the intended or expected occupation of the building at any time during the Capital Goods Scheme (CGS) adjustment period. As a result, a person who has granted an inferior interest but intends during that adjustment period to occupy the land himself would intend to be in occupation and so must consider whether his intended occupation was for eligible purposes. However, a person can ignore the following types of occupation for the purposes of the test: occupation which is purely for the purpose of making his rental supplies under the grant, since those are the very supplies whose liability he is trying to determine by applying the test (e.g. occupation by the grantor between the date of the grant and the start of occupation by the tenant which is for the purpose of undertaking refurbishment or repairs, or occupation by maintenance, security or reception staff (or similar), unless it is for the purpose of providing ongoing services separate from the letting itself); and occupation at a future date, but within the CGS adjustment period, which is solely for the purpose of re-letting the property or making a fresh grant. (HMRC Brief 33/09)

Scope of the option to tax

[41.13] An option to tax has effect in relation to the particular land specified in the option.

If an option to tax is exercised in relation to

- a building or part of a building, the option has effect in relation to the whole of the building and all the land within its curtilage; and
- any land but is not exercised by reference to a building or part of a building, the option is nonetheless taken to have effect in relation to any building which is (or is to be) constructed on the land (as well as in relation to land on which no building is constructed).

For these purposes

- buildings linked internally are treated as a single building unless the internal link is created after the buildings are completed;
- buildings which are linked by a covered walkway (apart from a covered walkway to which the general public has reasonable access) are treated as a single building unless the walkway starts to be constructed after the buildings are completed;
- complexes consisting of a number of units grouped around a fully enclosed concourse are treated as a single building; and
- '*building*' includes an enlarged or extended building, an annexe to a building, and a planned building.

HMRC also make the following comments.

(a) A link does not include a car park (above or below ground), a public thoroughfare or a statutory requirement (e.g. a fire escape).

(b) *Land.*

   - An option to tax covers all the land, and any buildings or civil engineering works which are part of the land.

- It covers only the discrete area of land that is specified and does not affect any adjoining land.

(c) *Buildings*.

- An option to tax covers the whole of the building, and the land under and immediately around that building (e.g. forecourts and yards). If the business's interest in the building is restricted to one floor, the option to tax will still cover the remaining floors of the building.
- If the building stands in a large area of land, how far the option to tax extends over the land depends on how far the services of the building can be utilised. For example, a racecourse grandstand may provide electricity and shelter for stalls, or other facilities, within its peripheral area. An option to tax on the grandstand would extend over the whole area of land that uses the benefits.
- From 1 June 2008, if a building is demolished or destroyed, any option to tax will still apply to the land on which the building stood and to any future buildings that are constructed on the land. However, if a business opted to tax before 1 June 2008 *and* it is clear from the notification that the option was made on the building only, then it can, if it wishes, treat the option as revoked once the building is demolished. There is no need to notify HMRC before revoking but the business should retain evidence in case it is requested in the future.
- From 1 June 2008, if a new building is constructed on land that has been opted, the building will be covered by the option to tax unless the business notifies HMRC that it wishes to exclude the building from the effect of the option (see **41.18**).
- If a business make changes to a building after it has opted to tax, it will need to consider whether the option to tax covers those changes. The most common changes are as follows.
  - (i) *Extensions*. Any option to tax a building will apply to any later extension (whether upwards, downwards or sideways).
  - (ii) *Linked buildings*. If a link is created after buildings are completed, the option to tax will not flow through with the link.
  - (iii) *Forming a complex*. Where a group of units that have been treated as separate buildings for the option to tax are subsequently enclosed, the option to tax will not spread to the un-opted units.

[*VATA 1994, Sch 10 para 18; SI 2008/1146, Art* 2]. (VAT Notice 742A, paras 2.3–2.6).

Day from which the option has effect

[41.14] Subject to

- the requirement to notify HMRC of the option (see **41.15**), and
- the provisions where the application for prior permission is required under **41.19** below,

an option to tax has effect from the start of the day on which it is exercised or the start of any later day specified in the option. But if, when an option to tax is exercised, the person exercising the option intends to revoke it under the cooling-off in **41.18** below, the option is treated as if it had never been exercised.

[*VATA 1994, Sch 10 para 19; SI 2008/1146, Art 2*].

In no circumstances can an option to tax have effect from a date before a business makes the decision to opt. (VAT Notice 742A, para 4.3).

Time of supply (tax point)

The normal tax point rules apply to all supplies of land or buildings. See **66.13 SUPPLY: TIME OF SUPPLY**. In a tenanted building, a tax point might not occur until payment is received. In these circumstances, where a business opts to tax after the rent becomes due but before it is paid, it must account for output tax on the rental receipt. This is the case even if the payment covers a period before the option to tax took effect. (VAT Notice 742A, para 10.3).

Making and notifying the option

[41.15] There are two stages in opting to tax.

- Making the decision to opt which may take place at a board meeting or similar, or less formally. However reached, HMRC recommend that a written record is kept showing clear details of the land or buildings to be covered by the option and the date the decision is made. (Notice 742A, para 4.1).
- Notifying HMRC of the decision. An option to tax has effect only if
  - (i) notification of the option is given to HMRC before the end of the period of 30 days beginning with the day on which the option was exercised (or such longer period as HMRC may in any particular case allow); and
  - (ii) that notification is given together with such information as HMRC may require.

Notification of an option to tax does not need to be given under this provision where the option is treated as exercised in accordance with *VATA 1994, Sch 10 para 29(3)* (requirement for prior permission where previous exempt supply, see **41.19** below).

[*VATA 1994, Sch 10 para 20; SI 2008/1146, Art 2*].

Notification must be in writing and state clearly what land or buildings is covered by the option to tax and the date from which the option has effect. HMRC suggest that Notification Form VAT 1614A is used (obtainable from the National Advice Service). If a business is opting to tax discrete areas of land, HMRC suggests that it sends a map or plan clearly showing the opted land with the notification. Similarly, if opting to tax a building, the full postal address, including post code, should be included.

It is important that an appropriate person signs the notification, and any accompanying list or schedule (see further below).

For businesses already VAT-registered, all notifications of the option to tax should be made by

- post to the Option To Tax National Unit, HM Revenue and Customs, Portcullis House, 21 India Street, Glasgow, G2 4PZ; or
- fax to 0141 555 3367.

Where a business becomes liable to be registered for VAT purposes as a result of the option to tax, the application to register for VAT *and* the notification of the option to tax should be submitted together to the appropriate VAT registration unit.

HMRC will normally acknowledge receipt of notification within 15 working days but this is not necessary for the option to tax to have legal effect and a business should not delay charging VAT just because it has not received acknowledgement.

(VAT Notice 742A, para 4.2).

Belated notification: clarification of HMRC policy

HMRC has discretion to accept notification later than the 30-day period allowed (although they cannot grant retrospective permission). This discretion is designed to cover situations where a business has genuinely made the decision to opt to tax, but has failed to notify it to HMRC in time. Before considering whether to exercise this discretion, HMRC would need to be satisfied that the decision was made on the date stated in the written notification. HMRC will usually accept a belated notification if a business provides evidence (e.g. the minutes of a Board or management meeting, correspondence referring to the decision, etc.). If this is not available, they would normally accept a statement from the responsible person, plus evidence that

- all the relevant facts have been given;
- output tax has been properly charged and accounted for from the date of the supposed election; and
- input tax recovery in respect of the land or building is consistent with the trader having made taxable supplies of it.

Belated notification may also be accepted in other cases depending on the individual circumstances.

On the other hand, HMRC may not accept that a decision to opt was taken, even when the above conditions are met if, for example

- there has been correspondence concerning, or investigation into, the liability of supplies of the property in question since the supposed date of the option, and no mention of the option to tax was made; or
- the business or its representative has previously put forward an alternative explanation for the charging of output tax (e.g. that the supply was not of land and buildings, or was of a sports facility).

HMRC reserves the right to refuse to accept belated notification if to do so would produce an unfair result, or if the exercise of the discretion was sought in connection with a tax avoidance scheme.

(Business Brief 13/05).

Responsibility for opting to tax

The person responsible for making the decision and notifying the option to tax depends on the type of legal entity holding (or intending to hold) the interest in the land or building, and who within that entity has the authority to make decisions concerning VAT. Following the tribunal decision in *Blythe Limited Partnership* (VTD 16011) (TVC 6.13) where written notification of an option made by solicitors acting for the partnership was held to be inaccurate and not binding, HMRC have issued guidance on notifying an option to tax.

In most cases notification will be made by the sole proprietor, one or more partners (or trustees), a director or an authorised administrator. If a business authorises a third party to notify an option on its behalf, HMRC require confirmation that the third party is authorised to do so. They would also like to be notified if the business withdraws that authority. Other more unusual situations are as follows.

- *Beneficial owners*. Where there is a beneficial owner and a legal owner of land or buildings (e.g. a bare trust), for VAT purposes it is the beneficial owner who is making the supply of the land or building and who should opt to tax. Where, however, there are numerous beneficiaries (e.g. unit trusts and pension funds) the person making the supply is the trustee who holds the legal interest and receives the immediate benefit of the consideration.
- *Joint owners* should together notify a single option to tax if they want supplies of the jointly-owned land or building to be standard-rated.
- *Limited partnerships*. The general partner(s) should opt to tax. Where title to the land or building is held jointly in the names of the general partner(s) and the limited partner(s), only the titleholders can make any supplies of that land or building together. That suggests that the limited partner(s) is/are involved in the management and running of the partnership and, as such, HMRC treat them as general partners. If the partnership decides to opt to tax, one or more of the partners should sign the notification.
- *Limited liability partnerships*. A limited liability partnership is a corporate body and is liable to register for VAT, subject to the normal registration rules. If the partnership decides to opt to tax, one or more members must sign the notification.

(VAT Notice 742A, paras 7.1–7.5).

Real estate elections

[41.16] A real estate election ('REE') is a formal decision to opt to tax all future property acquisitions. If a person makes an REE, he is treated (with certain exceptions) as having opted to tax every property in which he subsequently acquires an interest.

Under an REE, each property is treated as separately opted, with effect from the time of acquisition. This means that each option is capable of being separately revoked if the conditions for revocation are met. For example, if a person has made an REE but acquires a property that he does not want to be opted, he may be able to revoke within six months of acquisition under the cooling-off provisions (see **41.17** below) and the option is treated as though it was never made. (VAT Notice 742A, para 14.3).

The detailed provisions are considered below.

(1) Making an REE

A person (E) may make a real estate election (an 'REE') in relation to 'relevant interests' in any building or land which

- E acquires after the election is made; and
- a body corporate acquires after the election is made at a time when the body is a 'relevant group member'.

A '*relevant interest*' in relation to any building or land means any interest in, right over or licence to occupy the building or land (or any part of it) and a '*relevant group member*', in relation to any person making an REE at any time means a body corporate which is treated as a member of the same VAT group as that person at that time.

The time at which a relevant interest in any building or land is acquired is the time at which a supply is treated as taking place for the purposes of the charge to VAT in respect of the acquisition, or if there is more than one such time, the earliest of them.

[*VATA 1994, Sch 10 para 21(1)(12)(13); SI 2008/1146; SI 2009/1966, Art 4*].

Any member of a VAT group can make an REE although HMRC expect that normally this will be done by the VAT group representative member. (VAT Notice 742A, para 14.14).

(2) Consequences of making an REE

If E makes an REE

- E is treated as if E had exercised an option to tax in relation to the building or land in which the relevant interest is acquired;
- that option is treated as if it had been exercised on the day on which the acquisition was made and as if it had effect from the start of that day; and
- the requirement to notify an option under **41.15** above does not apply in relation to that option.

[*VATA 1994, Sch 10 para 21(2); SI 2008/1146*].

(3) Acquisitions excluded from the effects of an REE

An REE will not generate an option to tax for the following types of acquisitions.

- Any acquisition of a property in respect of which the person has already exercised an option to tax: if a person acquires an interest in a property and has (or a body corporate that was in their VAT group at the time, has) previously opted to tax the building or land, under the normal rules, with effect from a date prior to the acquisition date, the REE has no effect in relation to that property.

- Any acquisition of a property in respect of which the person already holds an interest when acquiring another different interest: if the person who acquires an interest after the REE is made already held a different interest in the property before the REE was made and continues to hold that interest when acquiring the further, different interest, the REE will not generate an option to tax. This situation can typically arise where a leasehold interest is held prior to the purchase of the freehold. Alternatively, an interest in part of a building (e.g. one floor) may be held at the time an interest in another part of the same building is acquired.
- Any acquisition of a property for which permission to opt might ordinarily be required: the REE will not generate an option to tax for an acquisition if the person has made exempt supplies of the property within the ten years prior to the date of acquisition.

[*VATA 1994, Sch 10 para 21(3)–(6); SI 2008/1146*]. (VAT Notice 742A, para 14.4).

(4) Automatic revocation where no interest held

Any options to tax exercised by the person (or by a person within their VAT group at the time) before making an REE will generally be revoked automatically when he makes an REE if he does not hold an interest in the opted land or building at that time (and no one within the VAT group holds an interest). Details are in the table below. However, there are exceptions to this rule, which are explained below the table.

If . . .	*and . . .*	*then...*
The person previously opted to tax a building (or part of a building)	he does not have a relevant interest in the building at the time he make an REE	his option is revoked (subject to the exceptions below)
The person previously opted to tax land (without reference to a particular building or buildings)	he does not have a relevant interest in the land at the time he makes an REE	his option is revoked (subject to the exceptions below)
The person previously opted to tax land (without reference to a particular building or buildings)	he only has an interest in part of the land at the time he makes an REE	his option is revoked in relation to the parts of land in which he does not hold a relevant interest (subject to the exceptions below)

Exceptions to automatic revocation?

Automatic revocation of an option will not occur at the time an REE is made in any of the following circumstances. All references to 'relevant time' mean the time the REE is made or, in other words, the time the option would otherwise be revoked:

(a) Where the opter has sold the property on terms that may require the purchaser to make additional payment after the 'relevant time'. Such payments are often referred to as 'overages' and can be contingent on such things as the purchaser obtaining planning permission.

The following two circumstances can only apply if the person who opted to tax ('the opter') is or has been a member of a VAT group.

(b) Where a 'relevant associate' of the opter in relation to the opted property has sold the property on terms that may require the purchaser to make additional payment after the relevant time.

(c) Where before the relevant time a relevant associate of the opter in relation to the property left the opter's VAT group and at the time of leaving any of the following applied:
- the relevant associate had an interest in or licence to occupy the property;
- the relevant associate had, prior to leaving the VAT group, disposed of an interest on terms that might have required the purchaser to make additional payment at a later date; or
- the relevant associate was connected to the opter or another relevant associate of the opter and that person had an interest in or licence to occupy the property.

[*VATA 1994, Sch 10 para 22(2)–(5); SI 2008/1146*]. (VAT Notice 742A, para 14.8).

(5) Conversion of a single option (e.g. a global option) into separate options

An option to tax ('*the original option*') exercised in relation to any land (otherwise than by reference to any building or part of a building) by

- a person (E) who makes an REE, or
- any relevant group member

before the making of the REE may, in certain circumstances, be converted by E into separate options to tax different parcels of land. This choice is only available in relation to land or buildings in which E or any relevant group member has a relevant interest at the time of making the REE. (If there is no relevant interest in the property at that time, the option is revoked, see (4) above.)

Each parcel of land that is to be treated as being separately opted must

- be identified by at least one of the following, namely its postal address, land registry title number, map or plan or other description sufficient to identify it; and
- meet the conditions relating to the scope of an option in **41.13**.

The separate options to tax are treated as if they had been exercised by E (in the case of a VAT group, irrespective of which member of the group made the original option) and as if they had effect from the time from which the original option had effect. But the cooling-off period for revocation of an option (see **41.17** below) does not apply to those separate options to tax.

[*VATA 1994, Sch 10 para 22(6)–(10); SI 2008/1146*]. (VAT Notice 742A, paras 14.8.3).

(6) Notifying a real estate election

A real estate election has effect only if

- notification of the election is given to HMRC before the end of the period of 30 days beginning with the day on which it was made (or such longer period as the HMRC may in any particular case allow);
- the notification is made on form VAT 1614E and contains the information requested on that form. The form can be downloaded from www.hmrc.gov.uk
  or obtained from the National Advice Service on 0845 010 9000.

[*VATA 1994, Sch 10 para 21(7); SI 2008/1146*]. (VAT Notice 742A, para 14.9).

If the person making the REE holds relevant interests in any property other than in dwellings or buildings designed or adapted for use as a dwelling (see **41.1**(4) above), in addition to notifying the REE, he must also provide a list of all properties in which he holds a relevant interest at the time of notifying the REE. This list must be sent to HMRC within the time specified for notifying the REE; otherwise the REE will not be effective. This list must contain the following information in respect of each property (other than dwellings or buildings designed or adapted for use as a dwelling) in which the person holds a relevant interest.

- A description of the land or buildings, identified by reference to postal address, land registry title number, map, plan or other description.
- In the case of land or buildings in respect of which no option to tax made by the maker of a REE has effect, the date of acquisition of a relevant interest in that land or buildings.
- In the case of land or buildings in respect of which an option to tax made by the maker of a REE has effect, the date when the relevant interest in the land or building was first acquired or, if later, the date when the option first had effect.
- Where an option has effect in relation to two or more separately listed parcels of land or buildings, they must be identified as being subject to the same option.

For these purposes, if the person making an REE

- has more than one relevant interest in a parcel of land or a building that were acquired at different times, only the date of acquisition of the most recently acquired relevant interest is to be provided; and
- is required to provide the date when an option first had effect in relation to a parcel of land or a building and that date is unknown, that person should record that fact and enter an approximate date, using best judgement, and provide a written explanation of why that date is considered reasonable.

If an incomplete list, or one which contains incorrect information, is submitted, a revised and current up-dated list should be submitted (to the person's Client Relationship Manager or, if he does not have one, to the Option to Tax Unit in Glasgow) as soon as the error is identified.

(VAT Notice 742A, paras 14.9, 14.11).

(7) Information requirements after a real estate election has been made

HMRC may require a person who has made an REE to give them information specified in a public notice within 30 days (or such longer period as they in any particular case allow).

If a person (P) does not comply with that requirement, HMRC may revoke the election, in which case that revocation has effect in relation to relevant interests in any building or land acquired after the 'notified time' by P or a body corporate which is a relevant group member at the time of acquisition.

The '*notified time*' means the time specified in a notification given by HMRC to P (which may not be before the notification is given).

[*VATA 1994, Sch 10 para 21(8)(9); SI 2008/1146*].

Under these powers, the maker of an REE must provide to HMRC the information detailed below in relation to any land or buildings (other than buildings designed or adapted for use as a dwelling) in which that person or a relevant group member

(i) holds a relevant interest at the time of providing the required information; or
(ii) has ceased to hold a relevant interest since making an REE or, if later, since the last occasion on which the maker of the REE provided such information to HMRC.

In respect of every such property

- the description of the land or buildings identified by reference to its postal address, land registry title number, map, plan or other description;
- in the case of land or buildings in respect of which no option to tax made by the maker of a real estate election or relevant group member has effect, the date of acquisition of the relevant interest in the land or buildings;
- in the case of land or buildings in respect of which an option to tax made by the maker of a real estate election or a relevant group member has effect, the date when the relevant interest in the land or building was acquired or, if later, the date when the option first had effect; and
- where an option has effect in relation to two or more separately listed parcels of land or buildings, they must be identified as being subject to the same option.

In respect of every property in which a relevant interest has been acquired or disposed of by the maker or the REE or a relevant group member since the date of the last such list (if any)

- as appropriate, the date of the maker of the REE or a relevant group member
  (i) acquiring a relevant interest in land or buildings in which that person has no other relevant interest;
  (ii) ceasing to hold a relevant interest in land or buildings without retaining another relevant interest in that property;

  - (iii) opting to tax land or buildings otherwise than by virtue of an REE;
  - (iv) converting a building or buildings into a dwelling or dwellings;
  - (v) excluding a new building from the effect of an option; and
  - (vi) revoking an option to tax in relation to land or buildings;

  identifying the land or building to which each occurrence relates;
- the VAT-exclusive value of the supply of a relevant interest acquired or disposed of by the maker of an REE or relevant group member; and
- the VAT (if any) charged on the supply of a relevant interest by the maker of an REE or, where the supply occurred before its admission to the group, the relevant group member.

For these purposes,

(a) where the maker of an REE or relevant group member has more than one relevant interest in the same land or building that were acquired at different times, only the date of acquisition of the most recently acquired relevant interest is to be provided;

(b) in the case of land or a building in which an interest has been held before the date of an REE, the date of the occurrence of the making of an option to tax by the person making an REE or a relevant group member is the date when that option first has effect; and

(c) the date of the occurrence of the revocation of an option is the date from which the revocation has effect.

The requirement to provide the information set out above does not apply to the revocation of an option to tax by virtue of the 'cooling-off' period or the lapse of six years since having a relevant interest (see **41.17** below).

(VAT Notice 742A, para 14.12).

(8) Revocation of a real estate election

Once made, an REE may not be revoked except by HMRC under their powers in (7) above for failure to provide information. If an REE made by a person (P) is so revoked by HMRC, another REE may be made at any subsequent time by P or any body corporate which is a relevant group member at that subsequent time, but only with the prior written permission of HMRC. [*VATA 1994, Sch 10 para 21(10)(11); SI 2008/1146*]. In such circumstances, (5) above will not apply to the new REE. (VAT Notice 742A, para 14.15).

Revocation of the option to tax

[41.17] Once made, the option to tax can only be revoked

- by the taxpayer in a six-month cooling-off period (see (1) below);
- automatically where no interest has been held in the property for over six years (see (2) below); or
- by the taxpayer where more than 20 years has lapsed since it first had effect (see (3) below).

(1) Revocation of an option to tax during the cooling-off period

An option to tax any land exercised by any person ('*the taxpayer*') may be revoked with effect from the day on which it was exercised if all of the following conditions are satisfied.

(a) The time that has lapsed since the day on which the option had effect is less than six months.

(b) The taxpayer has not used the land since the option had effect (including own occupation). This condition was removed with effect from 1 April 2010. [*SI 2010/485, Art 7*].

(c) No VAT has become chargeable as a result of the option.

(d) Since the option had effect, no grant in relation to the land has been made which is treated as neither a supply of goods nor a supply of services because the supply is a supply of the assets of a business by
  (i) the taxpayer to a person to whom the business (or part of it) is transferred as a going concern; or
  (ii) a person to the taxpayer to whom the business (or part of it) is so transferred.

(e) Notification of the revocation is given to HMRC on form VAT 1614C and contains the information requested on that form. The form can be downloaded from
www.hmrc.gov.uk
or obtained from the National Advice Service on 0845 010 9000.

(f) Any further conditions published by HMRC in a notice are satisfied. HMRC have specified that either prior permission for the revocation must be sought from HMRC, or one of the following conditions must be met
  - neither the opter nor any relevant associate has recovered extra property input tax;
  - by virtue of the revocation, the opter and all relevant associates would be liable to account for all extra property input tax they have recovered; or
  - extra property input tax has been recovered entirely on one capital item and amounts to less than 20% of the total input tax incurred on that item.

The 'cooling-off' period does not apply to new options to tax of a person making an REE that are created following the conversion of an existing option to tax into several separate options to tax at the time an REE is made. See **41.16**(5) above.

[*VATA 1994, Sch 10 para 23; SI 2008/1146, Art 2*]. (VAT Notice 742A, para 8.1).

(2) Revocation of option to tax where no interest has been held for more than six years

Subject to the anti-avoidance provisions below, an option to tax exercised by any person in relation to any building or land is treated as revoked if the person does not have a 'relevant interest in the building or land' throughout any continuous period of six years beginning at any time after the option has effect. The option to tax is then treated as revoked from the end of that period.

'*Relevant interest in the building or land*' means an interest in, right over or licence to occupy the building or land (or any part of it).

[*VATA 1994, Sch 10 para 24; SI 2008/1146, Art 2*].

(3) Revocation of option where more than 20 years have lapsed since option first had effect

An option to tax any land exercised by any person (the taxpayer) may be revoked if the time that has lapsed since the day on which the option had effect is more than 20 years and either of conditions (*a*) or (*b*) below are met.

(a) At the time when the option is to be revoked the conditions specified by HMRC in a public notice are met in relation to the option and notification of the revocation is given to HMRC on form VAT 1614J which contains the information requested on that form. The form can be downloaded from
www.hmrc.gov.uk or obtained from the National Advice Service on 0845 010 9000.
The conditions specified by HMRC are that *either* condition 1 below *or* all of conditions 2 to 5 are met.
 (1) *The relevant interest condition.* The 'taxpayer' or a relevant associate connected to the taxpayer has no 'relevant interest in the building or land' at the time when the option is revoked; and (from 1 April 2010) if either of them has disposed of such an interest, no supply is yet to take place or would be yet to take place if one or more conditions were to be met.
 (2) *The 20-year condition.* The taxpayer or a relevant associate connected to the taxpayer held a relevant interest in the building or land after the time from which the option has effect and more than 20 years before the option is revoked.
 (3) *The capital item condition.* Any land or building that is subject to the option at the time when it is revoked does not fall, in relation to the taxpayer or a relevant associate connected to the taxpayer, for input tax adjustment as a capital item under the capital goods scheme.
 (4) *The valuation condition.* The taxpayer or a relevant associate connected to the taxpayer has made no supply of a relevant interest in the building or land subject to the option in the ten years immediately before revocation of the option that was *either* for a consideration that was less than the open market value of that supply *or* arose from a 'relevant grant'.
 (5) *The pre-payment condition.* No part of a supply of goods or services made for consideration to the taxpayer or a relevant associate connected to the taxpayer before the option is revoked will be attributable to a supply or other use of the land or buildings by the taxpayer more than twelve months after the option is revoked.

'*Taxpayer*' means

(i) a person who exercised the option to tax or who is treated as making that option by virtue of a real estate election (see **41.16** above); and

(ii) in relation to an option to tax treated as exercised by virtue of a real estate election by a body corporate treated as a member of a VAT group other than the person described in (i) above, the body corporate whose relevant interest gave rise to the option to tax.

'*Relevant interest in the building or land*' means an interest in, right over or licence to occupy the building or land (or any part of it).

'*Relevant grant*' means a grant that the taxpayer intends or expects will give rise to a supply made after the option is revoked for a consideration significantly greater than any consideration for any supply arising from the grant before the revocation (except as a result of a rent review determined according to normal commercial practice).

In relation to condition (2) above, it does not matter whether, at the time the option is revoked, the taxpayer continues to hold the relevant interest in the building or land that meets the condition.

(b) If all the conditions in (*a*) above are not met, a taxpayer may still seek permission from HMRC to revoke an option, although they cannot give permission unless condition 2 (the 20-year condition) is met. Application must be made on form VAT 1614J and must contain the information requested on that form. In deciding whether or not to grant permission, HMRC will give particular consideration to whether or not the taxpayer or a third party has received a VAT benefit as a result of his actions.

Once HMRC have granted permission, the revocation will have effect from the day permission is granted, or such earlier or later day or time specified in their permission. They may specify a time by reference to the happening of a particular event or meeting of a condition, e.g. they may specify that revocation will take effect after the sale of a property has been completed. They can only specify an earlier day if the taxpayer has purported to give a notification of the revocation, and HMRC consider that the grounds on which the conditions are not met are insignificant. In granting permission HMRC may specify further conditions subject to which the permission is given. If any of these conditions are subsequently broken, they may treat the revocation as if it had not been made.

[*VATA 1994, Sch 10 para 25; SI 2008/1146, Art 2; SI 2009/1966, Art 5*]. (VAT Notice 742A, para 8.3).

Anti-avoidance provisions

The revocation provisions under (2) above (lapse of six years since having a relevant interest) do not apply if condition A, B or C is met, and the revocation provisions under **41.16**(4) (revocation of existing options to tax on property in which the taxpayer has no relevant interest at the time of making a real estate election) do not apply if condition A or B is met.

Condition A is met if at the relevant time, further supplies will or may arise (for example overages) in relation to the prior disposal of the building or land by the opter or a relevant associate of the opter.

Condition B is met if the opter was a member of a VAT group prior to the relevant time and a relevant associate of the opter in respect of the property had left the VAT group, without at the same time meeting all of the following additional conditions

- at the time the relevant associate left the VAT group they did not hold an interest in the property;
- where an interest had been held by the relevant associate but previously disposed of no further supplies will or may yet arise in relation to that disposal (for example, overages);
- the relevant associate was not connected with any person who has a relevant interest in the property where that person is the opter or another relevant associate of the opter.

Condition C is met if at the relevant time, a relevant associate of the opter is in the same VAT Group as the opter and holds or has held a relevant interest in the property at any time in the previous six years.

[*VATA 1994, Sch 10 para 26; SI 2009/1966, Art 6*]. (VAT Notice 742A, para 8.2).

Exclusion of new building from effect of an option

[41.18] With effect from 1 June 2008, the provisions make it clear that an option to tax land equally applies to a building upon it (either at the time of opting or constructed later) and vice versa. Previously, HMRC had a policy of allowing businesses to opt to tax land and buildings separately. In order to provide business with similar flexibility to earlier provisions, a new building (and the land within its curtilage) may be permanently excluded from the effects of an option to tax at certain points in time as follows.

If

- a person ('the taxpayer') has at any time opted to tax any land,
- at any subsequent time the 'construction of a building' ('the new building') on the land begins (which is taken to be the time when it progresses above the level of the building's foundations), and
- no land within the curtilage of the new building is within the curtilage of an existing building

the taxpayer may exclude the whole of the new building, and all the land within its curtilage, from the effect of the option. Notification of the exclusion must be made on form VAT 1614F and must contain the information requested on that form. The form can be downloaded from

www.hmrc.gov.uk

or obtained from the National Advice Service on 0845 010 9000.

The earliest time that a building can be excluded is when construction begins. Construction of a building begins when it progresses above the level of the building's foundations, which is usually the point at which the first brick is laid.

Exclusion has effect from the earliest of the following times.

- When a grant of an interest in, or in any part of, the new building is first made.
- When the new building, or any part of it, is first used.
- When the new building is completed.

An exclusion is only valid if it is notified to HMRC. Notification must be made after construction has begun and normally within 30 days of the date the exclusion has effect. A longer period may be allowed in exceptional circumstances.

'*Construction of a building*' for these purposes is to be read in accordance with *VATA 1994, Sch 8 Group 5 Notes (16)–(18)* (see **41.1**(2) above but ignoring (a)(ii) and the reference to a building ceasing to be an existing building when the part remaining above ground level consists of no more than a single façade).

If a taxpayer decides to exclude a new building from an option to tax, the effect of that exclusion is permanent (although he may make a fresh option to tax in the future).

[*VATA 1994, Sch 10 paras 27, 33; SI 2008/1146, Art 2*]. (VAT Notice 742A, para 2.7).

Requirement for prior permission to opt to tax where prior exempt grant

[41.19] Where

- a person wants to exercise an option to tax any land with effect from a particular day,
- an exempt supply of the land has been made in the period of ten years before that day

he cannot exercise the option to tax the land unless either of the following applies.

(a) Any of the following conditions for automatic permission specified in VAT Notice 742A, para 5.2 (which have the force of law) are met

(1) It is a mixed-use development and the only exempt supplies have been in relation to the dwellings.

(2) The person does not wish to recover any input tax in relation to the land or building incurred before the option to tax has effect; *and*

- the consideration for exempt supplies has, up to the date when the option to tax is to take effect, been solely by way of rents or service charges and excludes any premiums or payments in respect of occupation after the date on which the option takes effect. Regular rental and/or service charge payments can be ignored for the purposes of this condition. Payments are considered regular where the intervals between them are no more than a year and where each represents a commercial or genuine arms-length value; and

- the only input tax relating to the land or building that the person expects to recover after the option to tax takes effect will be on overheads, such as regular rental payments, service charges, repairs and maintenance costs. If he expects to claim input tax in relation to refurbishment or redevelopment of the building, he will not meet this condition.

In deciding whether this condition is met, a person should disregard

- any VAT refundable to a local authority or similar body under *VATA 1994, s 32(2)(b)* (see **43.8 LOCAL AUTHORITIES AND SIMILAR BODIES**);
- any input tax he can otherwise recover by virtue of the partial exemption *de minimis* rules; and
- any input tax he is entitled to recover on general business overheads not specifically related to the land or building, such as audit fees.

(3) (Until 30 April 2009.) The only input tax the person wishes to recover in relation to the land or building incurred before the option to tax takes effect relates solely to VAT charged by a tenant or tenants upon surrender of a lease; *and*

- the building or relevant part of the building has been unoccupied between the date of the surrender and the date the option to tax is to take effect;
- there will be no further exempt supplies of the land or building; and
- the person does not intend or expect that he will occupy the land or building other than for taxable purposes.

(4) (Replacing (3) above from 1 May 2009.) Automatic permission may be granted where Condition A and, if applicable, Condition B, are satisfied.

Condition A: The person does not intend or expect that any supply which is taxable as a result of the option will: (a) be made to a connected person, unless that person will be entitled to recover at least 80% of the VAT on that supply; or (b) arise from an agreement under which an exempt supply in respect of a right to occupy the property has been or will be made, and that right begins or continues after the effective date of the option. 'Permissible exempt supplies' may be disregarded.

Condition B (this condition only applies where the person has been, or expects to be, entitled to credit for any input tax incurred on capital expenditure on the property by virtue of the option): The person does not intend or expect to use any part of the capital expenditure for the purposes of:

- making exempt supplies which do not confer a right to credit under *VATA 1994 s 26(2)(c)*, unless: (a) all the exempt supplies fall within *VATA 1994 Sch 10 paras 5-11* (compulsory exclusions); or are permissible exempt supplies; or are incidental supplies falling within *VATA 1994 Sch 9 Group 5* (finance); or (b) exempt supplies are made but it is intended or expected that input tax on capital expenditure on the property which is attributed to those exempt supplies will not exceed £5,000; or

(c) the person expects to be entitled to full credit for all input tax incurred on capital expenditure on the property under *VATA 1994 s 33(2)* (statutory bodies: insignificant exempt input tax); or

- for private or non-business purposes, other than those giving right to a refund under *VATA 1994 s 33* (statutory authorities), *s 33A* (museums and galleries) or *s 41(3)* (Government departments).

(5) The exempt supplies have been incidental to the main use of the land or building. For example, where the person has occupied a building for taxable purposes, the following would be seen as incidental to the main use and this condition would be met.

- Allowing an advertising hoarding to be displayed.
- Granting space for the erection of a radio mast.
- Receiving income from an electricity sub-station.

The letting of space to an occupying tenant, however minor, is not incidental.

If any one of the above conditions is met, the person must still notify HMRC of the option on form VAT 1614H which must contain the information requested on the form. The form can be downloaded from

www.hmrc.gov.uk

or obtained from the National Advice Service on 0845 010 9000.

The notification should state that, although the business has made previous exempt supplies of the land or building, it satisfies the conditions for automatic permission.

(b) The person gets the prior permission of HMRC

If a person does not meet any of the conditions for automatic permission in (*a*) above, before he can opt to tax he must obtain written permission from the Option to Tax National Unit, HM Revenue and Customs, Portcullis House, 21 India Street, Glasgow, G2 4PZ. An application for prior permission must be made on form VAT 1614H and contain the information requested on the form.

The taxpayer must also advise HMRC of the date from which it would like the option to have effect (which can be any date on or after he makes the application).

HMRC cannot grant permission to opt to tax unless the taxpayer has provided all the specified information, and any additional information requested. They must refuse their permission if they are not satisfied that there would be a fair and reasonable attribution of relevant input tax. In deciding this, they must have regard to all the circumstances of the case, but in particular to

- the total value of any exempt supply to which any grant in relation to the land gives rise and which is made or to be made before the day from which the person wants the option to have effect;
- the expected total value of any supply to which any grant in relation to the land gives rise that would be taxable (if the option has effect); and
- the total amount of input tax incurred, or likely to be incurred, in relation to the land.

If HMRC are satisfied, permission is granted and the option takes immediate effect from the start of the day on which the application was made or the start of any later day specified in the application. There is no requirement for separate written notification after permission is granted.

HMRC cannot grant retrospective permission. Therefore

- any VAT charged in error is not output tax and, unless it is corrected, HMRC will collect it as a debt due to them; and
- any input tax claimed in error is exempt input tax and is not allowable.

Purported exercise where prior permission not obtained

If an option to tax has been notified to HMRC under **41.15** but should have been subject to their prior permission, HMRC *may* subsequently dispense with the requirement for their prior permission and allow the option to be retained. In such a case, the option is treated as having been validly made and effective from the date it was originally notified. HMRC will generally only exercise this discretion in cases of genuine error, or where tax would otherwise be at risk.

[*VATA 1994, Sch 10 paras 28–30; SI 2008/1146, Art 2*]. (VAT Notice 742A, paras 5.2–5.8; VAT Notice 742A, paras 5.2–5.8).

Input tax

Input tax incurred on or after the date of the option

[41.20] Once the option to tax has been exercised, a business can recover input tax on any related expenditure subject to the normal rules.

- Where taxable supplies of the land or buildings are made, any input tax relating to those supplies can be recovered.
- Where wholly exempt supplies of the land or building are made (because the supplies are not affected by the option to tax, see **41.11** above), any input tax relating to those supplies cannot be recovered.
- Where supplies that are both taxable and exempt are made (e.g. where an opted building is to be used for both commercial and residential purposes), the input tax relating to the taxable supplies can be recovered under the partial exemption rules.

Input tax incurred before the date of the option to tax

This can be recovered in the following circumstances.

- Where the supply of land or buildings is taxable in its own right (e.g. a freehold sale of a commercial building within three years of its completion is always taxable).
- Input tax prior to the making of supplies can be recoverable where there is a clear intention, at the time the costs are incurred, that the supplies of the buildings or land will be taxable. An option to tax is the best evidence of an intention to make taxable supplies for land and property transactions. But where, exceptionally, a business wishes to delay the making of the option until a future date, it may still be able to recover

the input tax relating to supplies which will follow the option if it can produce unequivocal documentary evidence that, at the time it seeks to reclaim the input tax, it intends the supplies to be taxable.

HMRC give the following as examples of the types of documents that may contain evidence of intention.

(i) A signed agreement/contract that specifies that the vendor will opt to tax prior to the sale.

(ii) An investment appraisal or business plan accepted by a bank that confirms that supplies will be treated as taxable.

(iii) Marketing literature that has been distributed to the public and where the scale and type of distribution, together with the nature of the advertisement itself, makes it clear that taxable supplies will be made.

(iv) Instructions or advice from professional advisers that specifies the VAT treatment, together with confirmation of acceptance of the advice by the business.

(v) Any other similar document that shows that the intention is to make taxable supplies.

The list is not intended to be exhaustive and whether a particular document provides the evidence will depend largely upon its content. It is unlikely that any single document alone will provide sufficient evidence and a business is advised to hold a number of separate documents to prove its intention. HMRC will normally consider evidence as satisfactory where it involves third parties and shows a firm commitment to the making of taxable supplies. A document that merely sets out an option or number of options will not be acceptable.

Where input tax relating to future taxable supplies has been recovered, a business should retain any documents used as evidence of intention and make tham available to HMRC on request. If there is any change in the intention to make taxable supplies, a record must be kept of the date of change (together with appropriate evidence) and HMRC must also be informed of the change as soon as possible. Any VAT previously deducted before the intention changed may need to be adjusted and repaid to HMRC.

An option to tax must be made and notified to HMRC prior to any supplies of the land or buildings being made.

- Where, prior to supplies being made, the intention to make exempt supplies changes to an intention to make taxable supplies, a business may be able to recover previously exempt input tax under the 'payback' rule. See **49.14 PARTIAL EXEMPTION**. But where the change of intention is not accompanied by an option to tax, the business will need to retain suitable evidence of its new intention (see (i) to (v) above).
- Where a business made exempt supplies of the land or building before opting to tax and incurred exempt input tax, it may be able to recover this under the permission procedure in **41.20** above.

Pre-registration VAT

A business may become registered for VAT as a result of the option to tax. Special rules apply to all newly registered businesses under which they may be entitled to claim relief for VAT incurred on supplies they obtained before registration. See **34.10** INPUT TAX. The amount claimable is restricted on supplies of services to those received not more than six months before registration. This restriction may lead to inequitable treatment compared with a business carrying out similar activities, but which was already VAT-registered when the tax was incurred. If a business considers that it has suffered because of this, it should write to the Option To Tax National Unit, HM Revenue and Customs, Portcullis House, 21 India Street, Glasgow, G2 4PZ and explain the circumstances.

In all cases, relief for VAT incurred before registration is restricted to VAT which can be directly attributed to a taxable activity. If a business incurred VAT before registration that was attributable both to exempt supplies before registration as well as taxable supplies after registration, the relief will be restricted proportionately.

(VAT Notice 742A, paras 9.1, 9.2, 9.4).

Appeals

[41.21] An appeal may be made against any refusal by HMRC to grant any permission under, or otherwise to exercise in favour of a particular person any power conferred by, any provision in **41.8** to **41.19** above.

Where there is an appeal against such a refusal,

- the tribunal must not allow the appeal unless it considers that HMRC could not reasonably have been satisfied that there were grounds for the refusal; and
- the refusal has effect pending the determination of the appeal.

[*VATA 1994, ss 83(wb), 84(7ZA); SI 2008/1146, Art 3*].

Key points

[41.22] Points to consider are as follows.

- For a builder to zero-rate his services on a listed building, it is important that he confirms that the work qualifies as an approved alteration, i.e. the building falls within one of the definitions in 41.1(1) above and listed building planning consent has been obtained. Fail to meet these conditions and the work will be standard-rated.
- Work that is classed as repair or maintenance on a listed building is always standard-rated.
- It is possible for a building to still be classed as new, and benefit from zero-rated building services in some cases, even if it has not been totally demolished. The retention of a single facade, or

double façade on a corner site, will still enable a building to be classed as new as long as the retention of the facade(s) is a condition of planning consent.

- A new building either designed as a dwelling, or to be used for a relevant charitable or residential purpose, can benefit from zero-rated construction services, as long as the builder holds a certificate from the building user in the case of charitable or residential buildings.
- It is important to recognise that any zero-rating of building work is only possible up to the time when the building is completed, e.g. certificate of completion issued by an architect. Any work carried out after this date tends to be standard-rated, unless it is to correct a defect or problem with the original building work.
- A relevant charitable purpose only applies to a building that is solely used by a charity for non-business purposes (e.g. a place of worship). Any business use, other than a very minor amount, would mean the building would not qualify as being for a relevant charitable purpose.
- The rules concerning the minor business use of a charitable building that can be ignored changed on 1 July 2009, with a transitional period up to 30 June 2010. The business use that can be ignored is now considered to be 5% of total use, compared to 10% with the previous rules.
- There are many exceptions to the general rule that supplies involving land are exempt from VAT. For example, accommodation provided in a hotel or similar establishment is always standard-rated, as is a charge for parking a vehicle on land.
- A service charge from a landlord to a tenant to cover building repairs, window cleaning and other costs etc., will follow the same VAT liability as the main rental payment. So if an option to tax election is in place on the building by the landlord, the service charge and rental payments will both be standard-rated – otherwise, they will both be exempt.
- An option to tax election on a building means that income generated by the building will be standard-rated rather than exempt (with important exceptions for residential parts of the building and building use by a charity for non-business purposes other than as an office). The motive for making an election with HMRC is to enable input tax to be recovered on the related costs of the building.
- There is no such thing as an 'opted building'. Each person with an interest in a property makes his own decision as to whether an election is worthwhile. So a landlord may have opted to tax a property, and will charge VAT on the rent to his tenant, but the tenant might have decided not to make an election, i.e. he will not charge VAT on the rent to a subtenant.
- If a person sells a building on which he has made an option to tax election, and the opted building includes both a residential and non-residential element, then the value of the sale should be

apportioned so that only the non-residential element is standard-rated. The option to tax election does not apply to residential properties.

- A common practical problem with option to tax arrangements is where a business decides to opt to tax a property, but forgets to notify HMRC of the option. In such cases, a belated notification can be made to HMRC, as long as it can be shown that the intention was clearly made (e.g. through a board meeting, correspondence or charging of VAT on rent to a tenant).
- The decision to make an option to tax election should only be made after a great deal of consideration. This is because it cannot be revoked for 20 years (apart from an initial cooling off period in limited circumstances) so has long-term consequences.
- It is important for tenants or buyers of a building to enquire whether the option to tax election could be revoked by a landlord under the 20-year rule. This is particularly important if the buyer or tenant has an input tax restriction (partly exempt etc.) but there are also cash flow and SDLT (stamp duty land tax) advantages in not being charged VAT on the purchase of a building.

42

Land and Buildings: Zero and Reduced Rate Supplies and DIY Housebuilders

Property developers

Zero-rated supplies of qualifying buildings

[42.1] The following supplies are zero-rated.

(a) **New dwellings**

The first 'grant' of a 'major interest' in, or in any part of, a building, dwelling or its site by a 'person constructing a building' 'designed as a dwelling' or number of dwellings unless either

(i) the interest granted is such that the grantee is not entitled to reside in the building, or part, throughout the year (e.g. a time-share); or

(ii) residence there throughout the year or the use of the building or part as the grantee's principal private residence, is prevented by the terms of a covenant, statutory planning consent or similar permission (i.e. accommodation which cannot lawfully be occupied as a permanent residence).

[*VATA 1994, Sch 8 Group 5 Item 1(a)* and *Note (13); SI 1995/280*].

See **41** LAND AND BUILDINGS: EXEMPT SUPPLIES AND OPTION TO TAX at **41.1**(5) for the definition of 'grant', **41.1**(9) for 'major interest', **41.1**(11) for 'person constructing a building' and **41.1**(4) for 'designed as a dwelling'.

First sale or long lease

The above provisions only zero-rate the first sale of, or grant of a long lease in, a building but zero-rating is not affected by

- the length of time between completion of construction and sale of, or grant of a long lease in, the building;
- any sale of, or grant of a long lease in, the building made by other people (even if they also have 'person constructing' status or have made their own zero-rated supply in the building);
- any short leases that may have been made (although this is likely to affect input tax recovery); or
- any sales of, or grant of long leases in, other parts of the building that the same person may have made (e.g. the developer of a block of flats can zero-rate his first long lease in each flat).

A grantor cannot zero-rate any second or subsequent long lease in the building (or the sale of the building after leasing it on a long lease).

If the first grant is a long lease, and the developer is using the building for a business purpose, other than solely for the purpose of selling it, the building may have to be treated as a capital for the purposes of the CAPITAL GOODS SCHEME (10).

Where house builders are unable to sell new dwellings due to the economic climate, they may wish to make, in advance of any short term lets, the first grant of a major interest in completed dwellings to a connected person who is not a member of the builder's VAT group. The connected person would then rent out the properties until such a time as they can be sold. The rentals would be exempt and not give rise to input tax deduction on ongoing costs, including the costs of the eventual sale (e.g. estate agency and legal costs), but deduction of the VAT associated with the original construction would have been secured. HMRC have stated that such arrangements would not been seen as abusive. However, if the VAT deducted goes beyond that which would normally be deducted in relation to the supply of the new dwelling (e.g. VAT on costs such as repairs, maintenance or refurbishment, which is not normally deductible) such arrangements are likely to be challenged by HMRC as abusive.

Land included

In addition to the dwelling, zero-rating also applies to

- the land on which the building stands (the 'foot print');

- a reasonable plot of land surrounding it. This will depend on the size, nature and situation of the building and the nature of the surrounding land; and
- the right to park a vehicle, so long as the parking place is close by and is intended to be used in conjunction with the building or dwelling.

Partly-constructed buildings

Provided the other conditions above are met, zero-rating also applies to the sale of, or grant of a long lease in, land that will form the site of a building provided a building is clearly under construction.

Deposits relating to sales of land

Where development land is sold, in particular to registered social landlords (RSLs), it is common for a deposit to be released to the vendor (thus creating a tax point) at the time of exchange of contracts when construction has not commenced and the land is still bare land. HMRC's view is that where the deposit is released to the vendor and it is clear from the contract or agreement that what will be supplied at completion, or the time of the grant, will be partly completed dwellings (beyond 'golden brick'), the deposit is part payment for the grant/supply that will occur at that time. It follows that the VAT liability of the deposit is determined by the anticipated nature of the supply and that zero-rating will be appropriate if it is intended that the conditions for zero-rating will be satisfied at the time of completion. For example, there must be a clear intention that the vendor will have commenced construction of the dwellings at that time and acquired 'person constructing' status. It is possible that the state of the land at completion will differ from that which was anticipated and where this is the case it will be necessary to revisit the VAT treatment of the deposit. (HMRC Brief 36/09).

Apportionment for part-qualifying buildings

(1) *General*. Where part of a building qualifies for zero-rating under the above provisions and part does not (e.g. shop premises with a flat over them), a grant or supply relating only to the part within these provisions is to be treated as relating to a zero-rated building and, similarly, a grant or supply relating only to the part outside those provisions is not to be so treated. In the case of any other grant or supply, an apportionment must be made to determine the extent to which it is to be so treated. [*VATA 1994, Sch 8 Group 5 Note (10); SI 1995/280*].
Building work that relates to the fabric of the building affecting both qualifying and non-qualifying parts of the building must be apportioned, such as work to
    - roofs,
    - foundations,
    - lifts, and
    - building services that supply the whole building (e.g. wiring and plumbing).

> *Example*
>
> ABC Property Ltd has built a new ground floor shop and first floor flat, which is being sold to DEF Ltd for an inclusive price of £500,000 plus any VAT that is due. The proceeds of the sale need to be apportioned so that VAT is charged on the market value of the shop, which is standard-rated because it is a new commercial building that is less than three years old. The element of the sale relating to the flat is zero-rated as relevant to the first sale of a new dwelling by the person constructing it.

(2) *Communal areas in blocks of flats*. Blocks of flats normally consist of individual dwellings and areas for the use of all residents (e.g. lounge, laundry, refuse area and, occasionally, gym, pool and leisure facilities). The first sale of each flat is zero-rated and the buyer also acquires a right to use the communal areas. Where the communal areas are only used by residents and their guests, HMRC accept that the construction of the whole building is zero-rated. Where the communal areas are partly used by others, then the construction of the communal areas is standard-rated.

(3) *Live-work units*. In a live-work unit (i.e. a property that combines, within a single unit, a dwelling and commercial or industrial working space as a requirement or condition of planning permission), zero-rating is only available to the extent that the unit comprises the dwelling (provided it meets the other conditions for zero-rating above). Dwellings that contain a home office are not live-work units and no apportionment is needed.

Units where the work area is shown as a discrete area of floor space, whether an office or workshop, must be apportioned to reflect the presence of the commercial element. Where planning permission requires that a minimum amount of the unit (e.g. 20%) must be used for commercial or industrial purposes, the remaining amount (i.e. 80%) can be treated as being the dwelling element for VAT purposes.

However, where a unit has neither

- an area that must, as a requirement or condition of planning permission, be used for commercial or industrial purposes, nor
- planning permission requiring a certain percentage of the floor space be used for commercial or industrial purposes;

it may be treated for VAT purposes as if it were entirely a dwelling and no apportionment is required.

Apportionment for mixed sites

Where a person sells, or grants a long lease in, a qualifying dwelling at the same time as a non-qualifying building or land that does not form part of the site (see under *Land included* above), an apportionment must be made between them on a fair and reasonable basis.

Shared ownership schemes

These involve the sharing of equity in a dwelling between, typically, an occupier and a housing association. The occupier purchases a dwelling at a proportion of its value and then pays rent to cover the share in the retained equity. Occupiers have the option of increasing their share of the equity by making additional payments, acquiring a further share related to the current value of the property ('staircasing'). The rent is then reduced accordingly. The initial payment by the occupier for his share of the equity can be zero-rated but the subsequent rental payments and any additional 'staircase' payments are not zero-rated but exempt.

Holiday homes

The restrictions under (i) and (ii) above typically prevent holiday homes from qualifying for zero-rating.

(VAT Notice 708, paras 4.3, 4.4, 4.6, 4.8, 15.1–15.4; HMRC Brief 54/08).

(b) New residential and charitable buildings

The first 'grant' of a 'major interest' in, or in any part of, a building, dwelling or its site by a 'person constructing a building' intended for use solely for a 'relevant residential purpose' or a 'relevant charitable purpose'. [*VATA 1994, Sch 8 Group 5 Item 1(a); SI 1995/280*].

See **41 LAND AND BUILDINGS: EXEMPT SUPPLIES AND OPTION TO TAX** at **41.1**(5) for definition of 'grant', **41.1**(9) for '*major interest*', **41.1**(11) for '*person constructing a building*', **41.1**(15) for '*relevant residential purpose*' and **41.1**(13) for '*relevant charitable purpose*'.

The provisions within (*a*) above under the headings *First sale or long lease*, *Land included*, *Partly constructed buildings*, *Apportionment for part-qualifying buildings* and *Apportionment for mixed sites* also apply for these purposes.

In addition, where the supply is in connection with a building intended for use as

- residential accommodation for students or school pupils, or
- residential accommodation for members of any of the armed forces

the supply can only be zero-rated to the extent that it relates to the residential accommodation. Where the supply is in connection with a building intended for use as a home or other institution, zero-rating or reduced-rating is not restricted to the residential accommodation but can extend to other areas within the building(s) such as administration offices or leisure or educational facilities.

(VAT Notice 708, paras 4.6, 4.8, 15.5).

Issue of certificates

Where all, or any part of, a building is intended for use solely for a relevant residential purpose or relevant charitable purpose, the grant of a major interest cannot be zero-rated under this provision unless, before the grant is made, the grantee has given the grantor a certificate to that effect. See **42.22** below.

(c) Conversion of non-residential buildings

The first 'grant' of a 'major interest' in, or in any part of, a building, dwelling or its site by a 'person converting'

(i) a 'non-residential' building, or
(ii) a non-residential part of a building

into a building 'designed as a dwelling' or number of dwellings or a building intended for use solely for a 'relevant residential purpose' unless either

(A) the interest granted is such that the grantee is not entitled to reside in the building, or part, throughout the year (e.g. a time share); or
(B) residence there throughout the year or the use of the building or part as the grantee's principal private residence, is prevented by the terms of a covenant, statutory planning consent or similar permission (i.e. accommodation which cannot lawfully be occupied as a permanent residence).

Where (ii) applies and the building already contains a residential part, then for zero-rating to apply, the conversion must either be to a building for use for a relevant residential purpose or must create an additional dwelling or dwellings.

[*VATA 1994, Sch 8 Group 5 Item 1(b)* and *Note (9); SI 1995/280*].

See **41 Land and Buildings: Exempt Supplies and Option to Tax** at **41.1**(5) for the definition of '*grant*', **41.1**(9) for '*major interest*', **41.1**(10) for '*non-residential*', **41.1**(4) above for '*designed as a dwelling*', and **41.1**(15) for '*relevant residential purpose*'.

'*Person converting*' a building has the same meaning as 'person constructing' a building in **41.1**(11) above substituting references to converting/conversion for constructing/construction throughout.

Examples of a non-residential conversion include the conversion of

- a commercial building (such as an office, warehouse, shop, etc.),
- an agricultural building (such as a barn), or
- a redundant school or church

into a building designed as a dwelling or number of dwellings.

The provisions within (*a*) above under the headings *First sale or long lease* and *Land included* apply in the same way for these purposes.

Garages

The conversion of a garage, occupied together with a dwelling, into a building designed as a dwelling is not a non-residential conversion. '*Garage*' not only covers buildings designed to store motor vehicles but also buildings such as barns which are used as garages. But if it can be established that the garage was never used to store motor vehicles (or has not been used as a garage for a considerable length of time prior to conversion) its conversion into a building designed as a dwelling can be a non-residential conversion.

Holiday homes

The restrictions under (A) and (B) above typically prevent holiday homes from qualifying for zero-rating.

Amalgamating non-residential parts of a building with other parts

To qualify for zero-rating, the conversion must only use non-residential parts of the building. For example, a two-storey public house containing bar areas downstairs and private living areas upstairs (and so in part being used as a dwelling, although see the case law uncertainty on this point in **41.1**(10) **LAND AND BUILDINGS: EXEMPT SUPPLIES AND OPTION TO TAX**) is converted into two flats, one created out of the bar areas and one out of the private living area. The onward sale or long lease of the former is zero-rated but that of the latter will be exempt. On the other hand, if the conversion uses a mixture of non-residential parts of the building and other parts, such as when the same property is converted

- into a single house, or
- by splitting it vertically into a pair of semi-detached houses, each of which use part of what was the living accommodation,

the onward sale or long lease is not zero-rated and is exempt.

Partly converted buildings

Subject to satisfying the other conditions, zero-rating can be applied to the sale of, or grant of a long lease in, a building where a real and meaningful start on the conversion has been made. This means that the work must have been more than securing or maintaining the existing structure.

Apportionment

(1) *Apportionment for converted parts of buildings.* It is only possible to zero-rate the sale of, or grant of a long lease in, a building (or part of a building) when the new qualifying residential accommodation is created wholly from a non-residential building or part of a building. Where a mixture of qualifying and non-qualifying conversions in a building is carried out, the charge can be apportioned and zero-rating applied to the sale of, or grant of a long lease in, the qualifying parts. For example
   - A shop is converted into a flat and existing flats above the shop, that have been lived in within the last ten years, are refurbished. Zero-rating applies to the sale of, or grant of a long lease in, the converted shop but not the refurbished flats.
   - A two-storey public house containing private living areas and bar areas is converted into a pair of flats. The living areas have been 'used as a dwelling' (although see the case law uncertainty on this point in **41.1**(10) **LAND AND BUILDINGS: EXEMPT SUPPLIES AND OPTION TO TAX**) and so the sale of, or long lease in, those parts cannot be zero-rated. The sale of, or grant of a long lease in, the converted bar areas can be zero-rated provided that the new flat is created solely from the non-residential areas.

(2) *Apportionment for mixed sites.* Where a development site, containing a mixture of buildings that qualify for zero-rating as the conversion of a non-residential building (or part of a building) and other buildings, is sold or long-leased, the supplies must be apportioned on a fair and reasonable basis.

(VAT Notice 708, paras 5.3–5.8).

Issue of certificates

Where all, or any part of, a building is intended for use solely for a relevant residential purpose, the grant of a major interest cannot be zero-rated under these provisions unless, before the grant is made, the grantee has given the grantor a certificate to that effect. See **42.22** below.

Garages

The construction of a building under (*a*) above or the conversion of a non-residential building under (*c*) above includes the construction of, or conversion of a non-residential building to, a garage provided

- the dwelling and the garage are constructed or converted at the same time; and
- the garage is intended for occupation with the dwelling or one of the dwellings.

[*VATA 1994, Sch 8 Group 5 Note (3); SI 1995/280*].

Tenancies and leases

Where the major interest granted under (*a*)–(*c*) above is a tenancy or lease, zero-rating only applies to the premium payable on the grant or, if no premium is payable, the first payment of rent due under the tenancy or lease. [*VATA 1994, Sch 8 Group 5 Note (14); SI 1995/280*]. Ongoing payments, such as further rents, ground rent or service charges cannot be zero-rated.

Change of use of relevant residential or charitable buildings

Where the grant of a major interest in a building is zero-rated under these provisions because the grantee certifies that the building will be used for a relevant residential purpose or a relevant charitable purpose, the grantee will be treated as making a standard-rated supply of the property if, within ten years of its completion, he either sells, lets or uses the building for any other purpose. See **42.2** below for full details.

Groups of companies

In the rare situation when a group member makes more than one grant of a major interest in a building, the first of which is to another group member, HMRC do not consider that first grant to be the 'first grant of a major interest' in the building for the purpose of zero-rating. In effect, this means that the first grant of a major interest to a person outside the group can be zero-rated, regardless of the previous activity within the VAT group, so long as the group member making the grant is a person constructing (or converting) the building and it meets all the other criteria. (Business Brief 11/03).

Joint ownership and beneficial interests

See **41.5 LAND AND BUILDINGS: EXEMPT SUPPLIES AND OPTION TO TAX.**

De Voil Indirect Tax Service. See V4.233; V4.234.

Residential and charitable buildings: change of use

[42.2] A charge to VAT arises where the construction of, or grant of an interest in, a building has been zero-rated on the basis of its intended use (a relevant residential or charitable purpose) and that use changes after the grant has been made. Before 1 March 2011, the charge to tax and the method of calculating it differed depending on whether or not the recipient of the zero-rated supply subsequently granted an interest to a third party. Where a change in use occurred in an unidentifiable part of the premises, the charge arose on the entire premises or part of the premises. For buildings completed on or after 1 March 2011, and whose use changes on or after 1 March 2011, new measures provide for a uniform application of the charge to VAT and a single method for its calculation.

From 1 March 2011

A charge arises on each occasion that there is an increase in the use of the premises for a non-relevant purpose, where a person disposes of the entire interest in the premises (or part of), or the premises (or part of) are used for a non-relevant purpose.

Where use is made of the premises (or part of) for both a relevant and a non-relevant purpose, the proportion of use for a non-relevant purpose is to be calculated in the same proportion as if an identifiable part of the building were used for a non-relevant purpose.

Where a charity is using the relevant premises (or a part of) as a village hall or similarly in providing social or recreational facilities for a local community, the premises are (or the part is) treated as being used for a relevant charitable purpose whether or not the occupier is using them for a relevant charitable purpose.

Where the charge applies, the person's interest, right or licence in the relevant premises held immediately prior to the time when the increase occurs is treated as

- supplied to him for the purposes of a business which he carries on; and
- supplied by him in the course or furtherance of that business

immediately prior to the time of that increase.

The supply is taken to be a taxable supply which is not zero-rated, the value of which is taken to be

- in the case of the first deemed supply, the amount obtained by the formula
  $R2 \times Y \times ((120 - Z) / 120)$; and
- in the case of any subsequent deemed supply, the amount obtained by the formula
  $(R2 - R1) \times Y \times ((120 - Z) / 120)$

Where

R2 is the proportion of the relevant premises disposed of or used for non-relevant purposes in the relevant period.

R1 is the proportion of the relevant premises disposed of or used for non-relevant purposes at an earlier time in the relevant period.

Y is the amount that yields the amount of VAT that would have been chargeable on the relevant supply if it had not been zero-rated (or the aggregate amount of VAT if there was more than one supply).

Z is the number of whole months since the day on which the relevant premises were completed.

'Relevant zero-rated supply' means a grant or other supply relating to a building (or part of) intended for use solely for a relevant residential or charitable purpose and which is zero-rated as a result of *VATA 1994, Sch 8, Group 5*.

'Relevant premises' means the building (or part of) in relation to which a relevant zero-rated supply has been made to the person.

'Relevant period' means ten years beginning with the day on which the relevant premises are completed.

[*VATA 1994, Sch 10, paras 35–37; SI 2011/86, Art 8*].

Example

A charity constructs/acquires a new five-floored building, which it intends to use solely for a non-business purpose. The value of the zero-rated supply is £5 million. After five years, during which the building is used as intended, the charity decides that it will use the top floor for a business purpose. The VAT due on the self-supply is calculated as follows.

Proportion of building affected by change is 1/5 floors, ie 20%.

Number of months remaining in ten-year period that part of the building will not be used as intended is 60/120 months, ie 50%.

Value of self-supply is 20% × £5m × 50% = £500,000.

VAT due on self-supply is £500,000 × 20% = £100,000*.

After a further two years, the charity decides that it will use a further two floors for a business purpose. The VAT due on the self-supply is calculated as follows.

Proportion of building now being used for a non-relevant purpose is 3/5 floors, ie 60%.

Number of months remaining in ten-year period that the further part of the building will not be used as intended is 36/120 months, ie 30%.

Value of self-supply is (60 – 20)% x £5m × 30% = £600,000.

VAT due on the self-supply is £600,000 × 20% = £120,000*.

*This VAT may be recovered to the extent that it relates to a taxable activity in accordance with the normal VAT rules.

Before 1 March 2011

(1) Disposal, part disposal or letting

The following provisions apply if

- one or more 'relevant zero-rated supplies' relating to a building (or part of a building) have been made to a person;

- within the period of ten years beginning with the day on which the building is 'completed', the person grants an 'interest in, right over or licence to occupy'
  - (i) the building or any part of it; or
  - (ii) the building or any part of it including, consisting of or forming part of the part to which the relevant zero-rated supply or supplies related; and
- after the grant
  - (i) the whole or any part of the building or of the part to which the grant relates, or
  - (ii) the whole of the building or of the part to which the grant relates, or any part of it including, consisting of or forming part of the part to which the relevant zero-rated supply or supplies related,

  is not intended for use solely for a 'relevant residential purpose' or a 'relevant charitable purpose'.

In such circumstances, so far as the grant relates to so much of the building as

- by reason of its intended use gave rise to the relevant zero-rated supply or supplies, and
- is not intended for use solely for a relevant residential purpose or a relevant charitable purpose after the grant,

it is taken to be a taxable supply in the course or furtherance of a business which is not zero-rated as a result of *VATA 1994, Sch 8 Group 5*.

A '*relevant zero-rated supply*' means a grant or other supply which relates to a building (or part of a building) intended for use solely for a 'relevant residential purpose' or a 'relevant charitable purpose' and which, as a result of *VATA 1994, Sch 8 Group 5* is zero-rated in whole or in part.

See 41 **LAND AND BUILDINGS: EXEMPT SUPPLIES AND OPTION TO TAX** at **41.1**(6) for when '*completion*' of a building takes place; **41.1**(7)(8) for the meaning of '*interest in, right over or licence to occupy*'; **41.1**(13) for '*relevant charitable purpose*' and **41.1**(15) for '*relevant residential purpose*'.

The VAT due must be accounted for on the VAT return for the VAT period in which the supply is made.

[*VATA 1994, Sch 10 paras 35, 36, 38; SI 2008/1146, Art* 2]. (VAT Notice 708, para 18.2).

(2) Change of use without disposal

The following provisions apply if

- one or more 'relevant zero-rated supplies' (see (1) above) relating to a building (or part of a building) have been made to a person; and
- within the period of 10 years beginning with the day on which the building is completed (see (1) above), the person uses
  - (i) the building or any part of it, or
  - (ii) the building or any part of it including, consisting of or forming part of the part to which the relevant zero-rated supply or supplies related,

for a purpose which is neither a 'relevant residential purpose' nor a 'relevant charitable purpose'.

In such circumstances, the person's 'interest in, right over or licence to occupy' so much of the building as

- by reason of its intended use gave rise to the relevant zero-rated supply or supplies, and
- is used otherwise than for a relevant residential purpose or a relevant charitable purpose,

is treated as supplied *to* the person for the purposes of a business which the person carries on and supplied *by* the person in the course or furtherance of the business when the person first uses it for a purpose which is neither a relevant residential purpose nor a relevant charitable purpose.

The supply is taken to be a taxable supply which is not zero-rated as a result of *VATA 1994, Sch 8 Group 5*. The value of the supply is calculated by the formula

$$A \times (10 - B) \div 10$$

where

A = the amount that yields an amount of VAT chargeable on it equal to the VAT which would have been chargeable on the relevant zero-rated supply (or, if there was more than one supply, the aggregate amount of the VAT which would have been chargeable on the supplies) had so much of the building not been intended for use solely for a relevant residential purpose or a relevant charitable purpose.

B = the number of whole years since the day the building was completed for which the building or part concerned has been used for a relevant residential purpose or a relevant charitable purpose.

See 41 **LAND AND BUILDINGS: EXEMPT SUPPLIES AND OPTION TO TAX** at **41.1**(7)(8) for the meaning of '*interest in, right over or licence to occupy*'; **41.1**(13) for '*relevant charitable purpose*' and **41.1**(15) for '*relevant residential purpose*'.

[*VATA 1994, Sch 10 paras 35, 37; SI 2008/1146, Art 2*].

Example

A charity paid £1 million for a new zero-rated building for its non-business use. After two years and seven months it changes the use of the entire building to business use.

The VAT that would have been payable if the initial supply had been standard-rated is

£1m × 17.5%* = £175,000

The amount due to HMRC is £175,000 × 80% = £140,000.

*20% from 4 January 2011; 15% from 1 December 2008 to 31 December 2009.

The VAT due on the deemed self-supply must be accounted for as output tax on the VAT return for the period in which the use is changed. The VAT can be deducted as input tax on the same return to the extent that it relates to any other taxable supplies made. It may be necessary to make subsequent adjustments to the amount of input tax deducted under the **CAPITAL GOODS SCHEME (10)** where

- the tax charge is £250,000 or more, and
- the building is used to make exempt supplies.

(VAT Notice 708, paras 18.2).

Limitation of above provisions

The affect of the above provisions only applying to zero-rating under *VATA 1994, Sch 8 Group 5* means that the rules only apply where the original grant or supply was

- zero-rated as the construction of a new building;
- zero-rated as the sale of, or long lease in, a new building;
- zero-rated as the sale of, or long lease in, a non-residential building; or
- zero-rated as the conversion of a non-residential building for a relevant housing association,

and the concession for minor non-qualifying use in buildings intended for use solely for a relevant charitable purpose has not been invoked (see **41.1**(13) **LAND AND BUILDINGS: EXEMPT SUPPLIES AND OPTION TO TAX**).

The rules do not apply to the extent that the original grant or supply was

- zero-rated as approved alterations to a protected building;
- zero-rated as the sale or long lease in a substantially reconstructed protected building;
- reduced-rated;
- an interest in a building that was exempt from VAT; or
- more than ten years ago

or where a refund was received under the D-I-Y builders scheme.

VAT registration

The charges and deemed self-supplies described above are included in taxable turnover when deciding whether VAT registration is required.

(VAT Notice 708, paras 18.1, 18.2).

De Voil Indirect Tax Service. See V3.248.

Substantial reconstructions of protected buildings

[42.3] The first 'grant' by a person 'substantially reconstructing' a 'protected building' of a 'major interest' in, or in any part of, the building or its site is zero-rated. [*VATA 1994, Sch 8 Group 6 Item 1; SI 1995/283*].

See **41 LAND AND BUILDINGS: EXEMPT SUPPLIES AND OPTION TO TAX** at **41.1**(5) for the definition of '*grant*', **41.1**(12) for '*protected building*' and **41.1**(9) for '*major interest*'.

The grant of an interest in a building 'designed as a dwelling' (see **41.1**(4) **LAND AND BUILDINGS: EXEMPT SUPPLIES AND OPTION TO TAX**) or number of dwellings (or the site of such a building) is *not* zero-rated under these provisions if either

(i) the interest granted is such that the grantee is not entitled to reside in the building throughout the year (e.g. a time-share); or

(ii) residence there throughout the year, or use of the building as the grantee's principal private residence, is prevented by the terms of a covenant, statutory planning consent or similar permission (i.e. accommodation which cannot lawfully be occupied as a permanent residence).

[*VATA 1994, Sch 8 Group 5 Note (13), Group 6 Note (3); SI 1995/283*].

The restrictions under (i) and (ii) above typically prevent holiday homes from qualifying for zero-rating. (VAT Notice 708, para 10.5).

'Substantially reconstructing'

A protected building is substantially reconstructed when reconstruction takes place that is a major work to its fabric, including the replacement of much of the internal or external structure. (VAT Notice 708, para 10.3). In addition, a protected building is not to be regarded as substantially reconstructed unless one or both of the following conditions are fulfilled when the reconstruction is completed.

- At least 60% of the cost of the reconstruction work would, if supplied by a taxable person, qualify for zero-rating as the supply of services in the course of approved alterations under **42.10** below or building materials and other items to carry out those works under **42.16** or **42.17** below. When determining if at least 60% of the work could be zero-rated as 'approved alterations', all of the work to the building should be considered, even if only part will be used for qualifying purposes. But only those alterations to the qualifying parts can count towards the zero-rated element.
- The reconstructed building incorporates no more of the original building before reconstruction began than the external walls, together with other external features of architectural or historic interest.

[*VATA 1994, Sch 8 Group 6 Note (4); SI 1995/283*].

Tenancies and leases

Where the major interest is a tenancy or lease, zero-rating only applies to the premium payable on the grant or, if no premium is payable, the first payment of rent due under the tenancy or lease. [*VATA 1994, Sch 8 Group 5 Note (14); Group 6 Note (3); SI 1995/283*]. (The effect of this is that zero-rating only covers the sum payable when the lease is granted and subsequent payments such as ground rent or service charges cannot be zero-rated.)

Part-qualifying buildings

(1) *General.* Where part of a protected building qualifies for zero-rating under the above provisions and part does not (e.g. shop premises with a flat over them), a grant or supply relating only to the part within these

provisions is to be treated as relating to a zero-rated building and, similarly, a grant or supply relating only to the part outside those provisions is not to be so treated. In the case of any other grant or supply, an apportionment must be made to determine the extent to which it is to be so treated. [*VATA 1994, Sch 8 Group 6 Note (5); SI 1995/283*].

Building work that relates to the fabric of the building affecting both qualifying and non-qualifying parts of the building must be apportioned, such as work to

- roofs,
- foundations,
- lifts, and
- building services that supply the whole building (e.g. wiring and plumbing).

(2) *Facilities for tenants in blocks of flats.* Work to build facilities shared by the tenants of a block of flats (e.g. a swimming pool, gym or laundry room) is standard-rated.

(3) *Live-work units.* In a live-work unit (i.e. a property that combines, within a single unit, a dwelling and commercial or industrial working space as a requirement or condition of planning permission) zero-rating is only available to the extent that the unit comprises the dwelling (provided it meets the other conditions for zero-rating above). Dwellings that contain a home office are not live-work units and no apportionment is needed.

Units where the work area is shown as a discrete area of floor space, whether an office or workshop, must be apportioned to reflect the presence of the commercial element. Where planning permission requires that a minimum amount of the unit (e.g. 20%) must be used for commercial or industrial purposes, the remaining amount (i.e. 80%) can be treated as being the dwelling element for VAT purposes.

However, where a unit has neither

- an area that must, as a requirement or condition of planning permission, be used for commercial or industrial purposes, nor
- planning permission requiring a certain percentage of the floor space be used for commercial or industrial purposes;

it may be treated for VAT purposes as if it were entirely a dwelling and no apportionment is required.

Apportionment for mixed sites

Where a person sells, or grants a long lease in, a development site containing buildings that qualify for zero-rating as substantially reconstructed protected buildings (or parts of buildings) and other buildings, he must apportion the charge between them on a fair and reasonable basis.

Issue of certificates

Where all or any part of the substantially reconstructed building is intended for use solely for a relevant residential or charitable purpose, the grant of a major interest cannot be zero-rated under these provisions unless, before the grant is made, the grantee has given the grantor a certificate to that effect. See **42.22** below.

'Person substantially reconstructing' status

A person is a 'person substantially reconstructing' a protected building if, in relation to that building, he is, or has at any point in the past

- acted as a developer (i.e. physically substantially reconstructed, or commissioned another person to physically substantially reconstruct, the building that he owns or has an interest in); or
- acted as a contractor or subcontractor (i.e. provided reconstruction services to the developer or another contractor for the substantial reconstruction of the building, sub-contracting work as necessary).

More than one person can enjoy 'person substantially reconstructing' status but such status is not transferred when the property is transferred. Each person must meet the conditions specified above. For example, where a developer takes over and finishes a partly reconstructed building, both the first and second developer has 'person substantially reconstructing' status because they have both been involved in physically reconstructing the building.

VAT groups

Although for VAT purposes, any business carried on by a member of a VAT group is treated as carried on by the representative member, when determining whether a supply can be zero-rated, 'person substantially reconstructing' status is only considered from the perspective of the group member who, in reality, makes the supply (which may not be the representative member). For example

(1) A VAT group includes a holding company as the representative member and a development company as a member.
The development company substantially reconstructs and sells a protected building. It has 'person substantially reconstructing' status and so the sales can be zero-rated.

(2) A VAT group includes a development company as representative member and an investment company as a member. The development company substantially reconstructs a block of flats and sells it to the investment company, who in turn leases the flats to the public on long leases.
The investment company does not have 'person substantially reconstructing' status. Even though the representative member does, the leases cannot be zero-rated and are exempt.

Beneficial interests

Where the beneficial owner of a property must register for VAT instead of the legal owner (see **41.5 LAND AND BUILDINGS: EXEMPT SUPPLIES AND OPTION TO TAX**), the beneficial owner must have 'person substantially reconstructing' status before the sale or long lease of the property can be zero-rated.

First sale or long lease

The above provisions only zero-rate the first sale of, or long lease in, a building (or part of a building) but zero-rating is not affected by

- the length of time between completion of the reconstruction and sale of, or long lease in, the building;
- any sale of, or long lease in, the building made by other people (even if they also have 'person reconstructing' status or have made their own zero-rated supply in the building);
- any short leases that may have been made (although this is likely to affect input tax recovery); or
- any sales of, or long leases in, other parts of the building that the same person may have made (e.g. if the developer of a block of flats can zero-rate his first long lease in each flat).

A grantor cannot zero-rate any second or subsequent long lease in the building (or sell the building after leasing it on a long lease).

Land included

In addition to the protected buildings, zero-rating also applies to

- the land on which the building stands (the 'foot print'); and
- a reasonable plot of land surrounding it. This will depend on the size, nature and situation of the building and the nature of the surrounding land.

Garages

Where a grant of a major interest in a substantially reconstructed dwelling is zero-rated under these provisions, zero-rating extends to a garage constructed, or converted from a non-residential building, provided that

- the dwelling and the garage are constructed or converted at the same time; and
- the garage is intended to be occupied with the dwelling or one of the dwellings.

Extensions

A protected building is not 'substantially reconstructed' where the only major alteration is the addition of an extension. However, as work to extend a protected building could be zero-rated as an 'approved alteration' if supplied by a builder, provided other major works are carried out to reconstruct the building, the construction of the extension can count towards the 60% substantial reconstruction calculations (see above).

Joint owners and beneficial interests

See **41.5 LAND AND BUILDINGS: EXEMPT SUPPLIES AND OPTION TO TAX.**

Exempt supplies

Other supplies of protected buildings not within the above provisions are normally exempt, e.g. where

- the building has not been substantially reconstructed;
- the interest granted is not a major interest;
- a major interest is granted by a person other than someone with 'person substantially reconstructing' status (see above);
- the building is not used as a dwelling or for a qualifying purpose.

See, however, **41.8 LAND AND BUILDINGS: EXEMPT SUPPLIES AND OPTION TO TAX** for the option to tax under certain circumstances.

(VAT Notice 708, paras 10.3, 10.6–10.9).

De Voil Indirect Tax Service. See V4.235.

Deduction of input tax

Speculative and abortive costs

[42.4] Developers must normally attribute input tax to either taxable or exempt supplies, depending on the supplies they intend to make, using the partial exemption rules. However, they may investigate many potential projects and incur costs (e.g. finders' fees in looking for sites, options to purchase lands, oil tests, general feasibility, viability and research studies, consultants and other professional fees, etc.) without knowing what, if any, supplies they will eventually make. Such '*speculative supplies*' may not be followed through, in which case they are '*abortive supplies*'.

- Where a developer has a clear intention of what supplies he intends to make, he must attribute the input tax incurred to the liability of the intended supply. So, for example, if the intention is only to build and sell new houses, input tax on speculative costs is attributable to the intended taxable (zero-rated) supplies. See also *Beaverbank Properties Ltd* (VTD 18099) (TVC 36.550).
- Where a developer has no firm intention of what supplies he will make, VAT incurred on speculative costs is input tax (because investigating potential projects is a business activity) but the input tax is 'residual' for partial exemption purposes.

If potential projects are not followed through and no supplies are actually made, where, up to the time of aborting the project, there is no firm intention regarding the liability of the supplies to be made (and as a result it is not possible to attribute the input tax to the liability of the intended supply), the related input tax should be left as residual.

If, on the other hand, the developer decides to proceed with a project, he will have a clear intention as to what supplies will be made and hence what the VAT liability of those supplies will be. (It is normally at this point that the developer decides whether to opt to tax for land and property supplies.) If the developer has not attributed the input tax previously, he should then adjust the input tax accordingly under the 'payback' and 'clawback' rules (see **49.14** **PARTIAL EXEMPTION**). Input tax on the ongoing costs should be attributed to the expected taxable or exempt supplies.

> *Example*
>
> ABC Property Ltd has paid £20,000 plus VAT to an architect for developing plans in relation to land that the company would like to buy and build new houses on. The project is aborted because the cost of the land is excessive but the architect is still entitled to his fee.
>
> If the company intended to sell the new houses if the project had proceeded, then the input tax on the architect fees can be fully reclaimed because they relate to an abortive taxable supply. If the intention was to rent them out, then the input tax would be blocked as relevant to an abortive exempt supply.

(VAT Notice 742A, para 9.3).

Goods incorporated into the building or its site

Where a taxable person constructing a building or effecting any works to a building, in either case for the purpose of granting a major interest in the building (or any part of it) or its site, incorporates goods other than building materials in any part of the building or its site, input tax on the supply, acquisition or importation of the goods is excluded from credit. [*SI 1992/3222, Art 6; SI 1995/281*].

See **42.16** and **42.17** below for examples of zero-rated building materials and zero-rated electrical goods and **42.18** below for a list of standard-rated goods on which VAT is not recoverable under these provisions.

Input tax on related services of installing the goods can be reclaimed provided the services are separately identified and VAT is correctly charged by the person supplying them.

Goods not incorporated into the building

Input tax can be recovered on goods which are not incorporated into the building or its site (e.g. free-standing items). A separate supply takes place when these goods are sold with the building on which output tax must be accounted for at their normal rate.

Showhouses

VAT cannot be reclaimed on standard-rated goods within **42.18** below incorporated into a showhouse if they are to be included in the sale of the house. No output tax is due when these goods are sold with the house.

Removing and disposing of goods on which input tax has been blocked

Where goods to which 'blocking' applies are removed from a property and sold independently (e.g. where the customer prefers a different model appliance), the developer is blocked from deducting input tax on both the original item and any replacement. The disposal of the original item is exempt from VAT.

(VAT Notice 708, paras 12.1–12.4).

Supplies of goods on which input tax blocked

With effect from 1 March 2000, where, under the above provisions, input tax has been blocked on goods incorporated in a building, any onward supply of those goods is an exempt supply. See **20.4 EXEMPT SUPPLIES.** This includes items incorporated in showhouses where these sales are not treated as part of the supply of the building.

De Voil Indirect Tax Service. See V3.444, V3.461B.

Supplies in the construction industry

Introduction

[42.5] The construction of a new building and work to an existing building is normally standard-rated. There are, however, various exceptions to this.

- Certain supplies of construction services may qualify for zero-rating. See **42.6** below.
- Other construction services may be taxable at the reduced rate of 5%. See **42.11** below.

All work that is not specifically zero-rated or taxable at the reduced rate is standard-rated.

Rate of VAT chargeable

The lowest rate applicable to a supply should be charged. For example, where an approved alteration to an empty listed dwelling qualifies for zero-rating under **42.10** below (as an approved alteration to a protected building) and for reduced-rating under **42.13** below (as an alteration of an empty dwelling), zero-rating should be applied.

Retention payments

The same VAT rate applies to retention payments as applied to previous payments made under the contract.

Subcontractors

Subcontractors are contractors who work for other contractors. In most circumstances they can zero-rate or reduce-rate their suppliers in the same way as a main contractor. But where the work requires a certificate for VAT purposes, a subcontractor must standard-rate his supplies to the main contractor (see **42.7** below for supplies in connection with buildings for relevant residential/charitable purposes and **42.9** below for conversion services supplied to housing associations).

(VAT Notice 708, para 2.1).

> *Example*
>
> Mainwell Housing Association has commissioned a building contractor to construct a new building that will be used as a home for elderly people. This building will qualify as a new relevant residential building, so the Association can benefit from zero-rating on the building work if it issues a certificate to the contractor before the work is started.
>
> However, the services provided by subcontractors working for the main contractor are standard-rated because they will not hold a valid certificate from the Association.

De Voil Indirect Tax Service. See V4.237–V4.242.

Zero-rated supplies

[42.6] Zero-rating applies to the following.

- Services supplied in the course of construction of new qualifying dwellings and certain other residential properties and charitable buildings. See **42.7** below.
- Services supplied in the course of construction of civil engineering work for the development of a new permanent residential caravan park. See **42.8** below.
- Services supplied to housing associations in the course of converting non-residential buildings into residential buildings. See **42.9** below.
- Approved alterations to protected buildings. See **42.10** below.
- Building materials and certain electrical goods incorporated into a building by a builder who is also supplying any of the above zero-rated services. See **42.16** to **42.18** below.
- Certain goods and services supplied to disabled persons. See **28.14** *et seq* **HEALTH AND WELFARE**.
- Until 31 December 2011, the first time connection to the gas or electricity mains of dwellings and certain other residential buildings. See **25.7 FUEL AND POWER**.

Construction services

[42.7] Services supplied 'in the course of construction' of a building

(a) 'designed as a dwelling' or number of dwellings, or
(b) intended for use solely for a 'relevant residential purpose' or 'relevant charitable purpose'

and which relate to the construction, are zero-rated. Specifically excluded (and therefore standard-rated) are

- the separate supply of architectural, surveying, consultancy or supervisory services. See **42.21**(1) below for where a supply of such services takes place under different forms of building contract;
- the hire of goods on their own (e.g. plant and machinery without an operator, scaffolding without erection/dismantling, security fencing and mobile office); and
- the private use of goods.

[*VATA 1994, Sch 8 Group 5 Item 2(a)* and *Note (20); SI 1995/280*]. (VAT Notice 708, para 3.4).

Building materials and certain electrical goods, supplied by the person providing the above services and incorporated into the building in question, are also zero-rated. See **42.16** to **42.18** below.

See **41 LAND AND BUILDINGS: EXEMPT SUPPLIES AND OPTION TO TAX** at **41.1**(6) for the definition of '*in the course of construction*', **41.1**(4) for '*designed as a dwelling*', **41.1**(15) for '*relevant residential purpose*', and **41.1**(13) for '*relevant charitable purpose*'.

With certain exceptions, '*constructing a building*' specifically excludes converting, reconstructing, altering, enlarging and extending an existing building or constructing an annexe to an existing building. See **41.1**(2) **LAND AND BUILDINGS: EXEMPT SUPPLIES AND OPTION TO TAX** for full details.

See **42.14** below for examples of services zero-rated under these provisions and other services not regarded as within these provisions and therefore standard-rated.

Garages

The construction of a building designed as a dwelling or number of dwellings includes the construction of a garage provided that

- the dwelling and the garage are constructed at the same time; and
- the garage is intended to be occupied with the dwelling or one of the dwellings.

[*VATA 1994, Sch 8 Group 5 Note (3); SI 1995/280*].

Civil engineering work on serviced plots

With effect from 17 October 2007, following the decision in *D & S Virtue (t/a Lammermuir Game Services)* (VTD 20259) (TVC 41.22) that a supply of a serviced building plot is a single exempt supply (and not a mixed supply of exempt land and standard-rated civil engineering work), HMRC accept that the supply of civil engineering works *to* a landowner in connection with the supply of a serviced plot of land *by* the landowner is zero-rated where the landowner can demonstrate that the civil engineering services have been made in the course of the construction of qualifying buildings within (*a*) or (*b*) above. For zero-rating to apply, HMRC would normally expect all the following conditions to be met to demonstrate that zero-rating is appropriate.

- The landowner holds sufficient planning consent to demonstrate that the civil engineering works were received in the course of construction of qualifying buildings.

- The civil engineering is closely connected with or facilitates the construction of buildings.
- The construction of the buildings will follow on closely after the completion of the civil engineering works.

The extent to which the above conditions have been met will be a matter of fact and degree. HMRC would need to be satisfied that, at the time the civil engineering is supplied, any potential purchaser of a serviced plot can only construct qualifying buildings on the plot. In addition, it must be clear that the landowner has a firm intention to sell the serviced plots once the civil engineering is complete and that any purchaser is ready to begin actual construction of the buildings as soon as possible.

(HMRC Brief 64/07).

Apportionment for part-qualifying buildings

(1) *General*. Where part of a building qualifies under the above provisions and part does not (e.g. shop premises with a flat over them), a supply of services relating only to the qualifying part of the building is zero-rated and, similarly, a supply of services relating only to the non-qualifying part is standard-rated. In the case of any other supply, an apportionment must be made to determine the extent to which the supply is zero-rated. [*VATA 1994, Sch 8 Group 5 Note (10); SI 1995/280*].

Building work that relates to the fabric of the building affecting both qualifying and non-qualifying parts of the building must be apportioned, such as work to

- roofs,
- foundations,
- lifts, and
- building services that supply the whole building (e.g. wiring and plumbing).

(2) *Communal areas in blocks of flats*. Blocks of flats normally consist of individual dwellings and areas for the use of all residents (e.g. lounge, laundry, refuse area and, occasionally, gym, pool and leisure facilities). The first sale of each flat is zero-rated and the buyer also acquires a right to use the communal areas. Where the communal areas are only used by residents and their guests, HMRC accept that the construction of the whole building is zero-rated. Where the communal areas are partly used by others, then the construction of the communal areas is standard-rated.

(3) *Live-work units*. In a live-work unit (i.e. a property that combines, within a single unit, a dwelling and commercial or industrial working space as a requirement or condition of planning permission) zero-rating is only available to the extent that the unit comprises the dwelling (provided it meets the other conditions for zero-rating above). Dwellings that contain a home office are not live-work units and no apportionment is needed.

Units where the work area is shown as a discrete area of floor space, whether an office or workshop, must be apportioned to reflect the presence of the commercial element. Where planning permission requires that a minimum amount of the unit (e.g. 20%) must be used for commercial or industrial purposes, the remaining amount (i.e. 80%) can be treated as being the dwelling element for VAT purposes. However, where a unit has neither

- an area that must, as a requirement or condition of planning permission, be used for commercial or industrial purposes, nor
- planning permission requiring a certain percentage of the floor space be used for commercial or industrial purposes;

it may be treated for VAT purposes as if it were entirely a dwelling and no apportionment is required.

(4) *Relevant residential purpose buildings*. Where the supply is in connection with a building intended for use as

- residential accommodation for students or school pupils, or
- residential accommodation for members of any of the armed forces

the supply can only be zero-rated to the extent that it relates to the residential accommodation. Where the supply is in connection with a building intended for use as a home or other institution, zero-rating or reduced-rating is not restricted to the residential accommodation but can extend to other areas within the building(s) such as administration offices or leisure or educational facilities.

(VAT Notice 708, paras 3.5, 15.1–15.5).

Apportionment for mixed sites

Where a service falling within the above provisions is supplied in part in relation to the construction of a building and in part for other purposes (e.g. a mixed site development including new dwellings and shops), an apportionment may be made to determine the extent to which the supply is to be treated as falling within the above provisions.

[*VATA 1994, Sch 8 Group 5 Note (11); SI 1995/280*].

Buildings for relevant residential/charitable purposes

The following additional provisions apply where all or part of a building is intended for use solely for a relevant residential or relevant charitable purpose.

- *Issue of certificates.* Where all or part of a building is intended for use solely for a relevant residential or relevant charitable purpose, a supplier of services within these provisions cannot zero-rate the supply until the customer has given him a certificate to that effect. See **42.22** below.
- *Subcontractors' supplies, etc.* No supply of services relating to a building (or part of it) can be taken for the above purposes as relating to a building intended for such use unless it is made to a person who intends to use the building (or part) for such a purpose. [*VATA 1994, Sch 8 Group 5 Note (12); SI 1995/280*]. The main effect of this is that, although the main contractor can zero-rate the construction of such a building, a subcontractor must standard-rate all supplies to the main contractor on such building projects.

Civil engineering work for residential caravan parks

[42.8] Services supplied 'in the course of construction' of any civil engineering work necessary for the development of a permanent park for 'residential caravans', and which relate to the construction, are zero-rated. Specifically excluded (and therefore standard-rated) are

- the separate supply of architectural, surveying, consultancy or supervisory services. See **42.21**(1) below for where a supply of these services takes place under different forms of building contract;
- the hire of goods on their own (e.g. plant and machinery without an operator, scaffolding without erection/dismantling, security fencing and mobile office); and
- the private use of goods.

Building materials, supplied by the person providing the above services and incorporated into the site in question, are also zero-rated. See **42.16** below.

See **41.1**(6) **LAND AND BUILDINGS: EXEMPT SUPPLIES AND OPTION TO TAX** for the meaning of '*in the course of construction*'. The construction of a civil engineering work does not include the conversion, reconstruction, alteration or enlargement of a work.

'Residential caravan'

A caravan is not a residential caravan if residence in it throughout the year is prevented by the terms of a covenant, statutory planning consent or similar permission. The development of a holiday park of fixed caravans, or parks for touring caravans, is, therefore, normally standard-rated. (VAT Notice 708, para 19.2).

[*VATA 1994, Sch 8 Group 5 Item 2(b)* and *Notes (15), (19)* and *(20); SI 1995/280*].

Examples of zero-rated civil engineering work

- Laying new roads, drives, parking bays and paths
- Laying new pitches or bases for the caravans
- Installing water, electricity and gas supplies
- Installing drainage and sewerage

Examples of civil engineering work that is unnecessary (and standard-rated)

- Construction of playgrounds
- Hard landscaping

Examples of work that is not civil engineering work (and standard-rated)

- Indoor swimming pools
- Social centres
- Shops
- Fitness clubs
- A doctor's surgery
- A manager's house (although the work may be zero-rated under **42.7** above)

Alterations to existing works

The reconstruction, alteration or improvement of an existing work (e.g. widening or upgrading an existing road) cannot be zero-rated.

Apportionment

(1) *Zero-rated and standard-rated work*. Where both zero-rated and standard-rated civil engineering work is supplied, an apportionment must be made to reflect the differing liabilities.

(2) *Mixed site developments*. Where a service is supplied in part in relation to necessary civil engineering work and in part for other purposes, an apportionment may be made to determine the extent to which the supply is treated as being zero-rated. If the supplier decides not to make an apportionment, then none of the work can be zero-rated.

(VAT Notice 708, paras 19.1, 19.3–19.5).

Conversion services supplied to housing associations

[42.9] Zero-rating applies to services supplied to a 'relevant housing association' 'in the course of conversion' of

(a) a 'non-residential' building, or
(b) a non-residential part of a building

into a building (or part of a building) which is

(i) 'designed as a dwelling' or number of dwellings, or
(ii) intended solely for use for a 'relevant residential purpose'

and where the services relate to the conversion.

Specifically excluded (and therefore standard-rated) are

- the separate supply of architectural, surveying, consultancy or supervisory services. See **42.21**(1) below for where a supply of such services takes place under different forms of building contract;
- the hire of goods on their own (e.g. plant and machinery without an operator, scaffolding without erection/dismantling, security fencing and mobile office); and
- the private use of goods.

Building materials and certain electrical goods, supplied by the person providing the above services and incorporated into the building in question, are also zero-rated. See **42.16** to **42.18** below.

Where (*b*) above applies and the building already contains a residential part, for zero-rating to apply the conversion must either be to a building for use for a relevant residential purpose or must create an additional dwelling or dwellings.

See **41 LAND AND BUILDINGS: EXEMPT SUPPLIES AND OPTION TO TAX** at **41.1**(14) for the definition of '*relevant housing association*', **41.1**(10) for '*non-residential*', **41.1**(4) for '*designed as a dwelling*', and **41.1**(15) for '*relevant residential purpose*'.

[*VATA 1994, Sch 8 Group 5 Item 3* and *Notes (9), (20)* and *(21); SI 1995/280; SI 1997/50*].

Conversions to garages

The conversion of a non-residential building to a building designed as a dwelling or number of dwellings includes the conversion of a non-residential building to a garage, provided that

- the dwelling and the garage are converted at the same time; and
- the garage is intended to be occupied with the dwelling or one of the dwellings.

[*VATA 1994, Sch 8 Group 5 Note (3); SI 1995/280*].

Examples of a non-residential conversion include the conversion of

- a commercial building (such as an office, warehouse, shop, etc.),
- an agricultural building (such as a barn), or
- a redundant school or church,

into a building designed as a dwelling or number of dwellings.

Conversions of garages

The conversion of a garage, occupied together with a dwelling, into a building designed as a dwelling is not a non-residential conversion. '*Garage*' not only covers buildings designed to store motor vehicles but also buildings such as barns which are used as garages. But if it can be established that the garage was never used to store motor vehicles (or has not been used as a garage for a considerable length of time prior to conversion) its conversion into a building designed as a dwelling can be a non-residential conversion.

See **42.14** below for examples of services zero-rated under these provisions and other services not regarded as within these provisions and therefore standard-rated.

Evidence and certificates

A supplier must hold evidence to show that his customer is a relevant housing association (e.g. a copy of their registration certificate). In addition, a supplier who is converting the building into a building intended for use solely for a relevant residential purpose must also hold a certificate confirming the intended use of the building. See **42.22** below.

Subcontractors

Subcontractors' services are not made directly to a relevant housing association and are, therefore, not zero-rated.

Amalgamating non-residential parts of a building with other parts

To qualify for zero-rating, the conversion must only use non-residential parts of the building. For example, a two-storey public house containing bar areas downstairs and private living areas upstairs (and so in part being used as a dwelling, although see the case law uncertainty on this point in **41.1**(10) **LAND AND BUILDINGS: EXEMPT SUPPLIES AND OPTION TO TAX**) is converted into two flats, one created out of the bar areas and one out of the private living area. The onward sale or long lease of the former is zero-rated but that of the latter will be exempt. On the other hand, if the conversion uses a mixture of non-residential parts of the building and other parts, such as when the same property is converted

- into a single house, or
- by splitting it vertically into a pair of semi-detached houses, each of which use part of what was the living accommodation,

the onward sale or long lease is not zero-rated and is exempt.

Apportionment

(1) *Part qualifying buildings*. Where part of a building qualifies under the above provisions and part does not (e.g. shop premises with a flat over them), a supply of services relating only to the qualifying part of the building is zero-rated and, similarly, a supply of services relating only to the non-qualifying part is standard-rated. In the case of any other supply, an apportionment must be made to determine the extent to which the supply is zero-rated. [*VATA 1994, Sch 8 Group 5 Note (10); SI 1995/280*]. For example, if a shop is converted into a flat and at the same time an existing flat above the shop (that has been lived in within the last ten years) is refurbished, zero-rating applies to the work to convert the shop but not the refurbishment of the flat.

(2) *Mixed sites*. Where a service falling within the above provisions is supplied in part in relation to the conversion of a building and in part for other purposes (e.g. a mixed site development including new dwellings and shops), an apportionment may be made to determine the extent to which the supply is to be treated as falling within the above provisions. [*VATA 1994, Sch 8 Group 5 Note (11); SI 1995/280*]. For example, a road that serves a building being converted and a neighbouring house (e.g. a barn and a farm house) is upgraded as part of the conversion. As the road serves both buildings, the work carried out relates, in part, to the conversion and, in part, for other purposes. The liability of upgrading the road may be apportioned on a fair and reasonable basis. If the supplier decides not to make an apportionment, then none of his work can be zero-rated.

(VAT Notice 708, paras 6.2, 6.3, 6.5, 6.6).

Approved alterations of protected buildings

[42.10] The supply of services in the course of an 'approved alteration' of a 'protected building' is zero-rated. Specifically excluded (and therefore standard-rated) are:

- The separate supply of architectural, surveying, consultancy or supervisory services. See **42.21**(1) below for where a supply of such services takes place under different forms of building contract.

- The hire of goods on their own (e.g. plant and machinery without an operator, scaffolding without erection/dismantling, security fencing and mobile office).
- The private use of goods.

Building materials and certain electrical goods, supplied by the person providing the above services and incorporated into the building in question, are also zero-rated. See **42.16** to **42.18** below.

See **41 Land and buildings: exempt supplies and option to tax** at **41.1**(1) for the definition of '*approved alteration*' and **41.1**(12) for '*protected building*'.

[*VATA 1994, Sch 8 Group 6 Item 2* and *Note (11); SI 1995/283*]. (VAT Notice 708, para 9.6).

Provided the necessary conditions are satisfied, this provision can be used to zero-rate services supplied in carrying out an approved alteration to

- a protected building which is a dwelling, relevant residential building or relevant charitable building; and
- any other protected building in order to convert it into a dwelling, relevant residential building or relevant charitable building.

Services 'in the course of an approved alteration'

A business supplies services in the course of an approved alteration of a protected building when it

(a) physically carries out the approved alteration; or
(b) provides any other service closely connected to the alteration (see **42.14** below).

The effect of (*b*) above is that, even if the work did not require approval, it can still be zero-rated provided it is closely connected to an approved alteration. Examples include

- preparation work for an approved alteration; or
- the carrying out of remedial work resulting from an approved alteration.

(VAT Notice 708, para 9.5).

Issue of certificate by recipient of services

Where all or part of a protected building is intended for use solely for a relevant residential or relevant charitable purpose, a supplier of approved alterations to the building within these provisions cannot zero-rate the supply until the customer has given him a certificate to that effect. See **42.22** below.

Apportionment

(1) *Part qualifying work*. In cases where a service is supplied partly in relation to an approved alteration and partly for other purposes (e.g. repairs and maintenance), an apportionment can be made to determine the part zero-rated. [*VATA 1994, Sch 8 Group 6 Note (9); SI 1995/283*].

(2) *Part qualifying buildings*. Where only part of a building is a protected building, zero-rating can be applied to the work to the qualifying parts. For example, if alterations are carried out to a listed building used by a charity, it may be that only part of the building will be used solely for a relevant charitable purpose. If so, only the approved alterations to that part of the building can be zero-rated.

(3) *Mixed site developments*. Where a service (e.g. carrying out civil engineering work) is supplied in part in relation to an approved alteration and in part for other purposes, a fair and reasonable apportionment may be made to determine the extent to which the supply is treated as falling within these provisions.

If the supplier decides not to make an apportionment, then none of his work can be zero-rated.

(VAT Notice 708, para 9.7).

Repairs to listed places of worship

Unless qualifying as part of an approved alteration under the above provisions, any repair and maintenance work is standard-rated and the UK is not permitted under current EU legislation to tax such supplies at a reduced rate. However, a special non-discretionary grant scheme (the 'Listed Place of Worship Grant Scheme') has been introduced for all works of repair and maintenance to listed buildings throughout the UK that are principally used as places of worship. For eligible work carried out after 31 March 2004, the scheme returns the full amount of VAT paid. Listed places of worship of all religions are eligible and the scheme also applies to places of worship owned or vested in a number of specified organisations which look after redundant churches. Applications are only accepted in arrears. For expenditure incurred after 31 March 2006, the scheme is extended to include professional fees and repairs to certain fixtures and fittings. The scheme is currently due to continue until 31 March 2011 unless a permanent reduced rate in achieved earlier. (The government has made proposals to the European Commission for a reduced rate of 5% for repairs and maintenance to listed places of worship.) Documentation relating to the scheme can be obtained

- via the internet at www.lpwscheme.org.uk;
- by telephoning 0845 601 5945; or
- by writing to Listed Places of Worship Grant Scheme, PO Box 609, Newport NP10 8QD.

Reduced rate supplies

[42.11] VAT is charged at the reduced rate of 5% on

(a) qualifying services supplied in the course of certain residential conversions (see **42.12** below);

(b) qualifying services supplied in the course of renovating and altering certain buildings that have been empty for two or more years (see **42.13** below);

(c) building materials and certain electrical goods incorporated into a building by a builder who is also supplying services within (*a*) or (*b*) above (see **42.16** to **42.18** below);

(d) installation of energy-saving materials and the grant-funded installation of heating equipment or security goods or connection of a gas supply. See **58.2** and **58.3 REDUCED RATE SUPPLIES**; and

(e) installation of mobility aids for the elderly for use in domestic accommodation. See **28.36 HEALTH AND WELFARE.**

Residential conversions

Overview

[42.12] The VAT liability of conversion work generally is summarised in the following table.

Before conversion	*After conversion*		
	Single household dwelling(s)	*Multiple occupancy dwelling(s)*	*Relevant residential purpose building*
Single household dwelling(s)	Normally standard-rated unless the number of dwellings changes when reduced-rated	Reduced-rated	Reduced-rated
Multiple occupancy dwelling(s)	Reduced-rated	Standard-rated	Reduced-rated
Relevant residential purpose building	Reduced-rated	Reduced-rated	Standard-rated
Any building not listed above (e.g. a building which has never been lived in)	Reduced-rated	Reduced-rated	Reduced-rated

Detailed provisions

'Qualifying services' supplied in the course of a 'qualifying conversion' and which are related to the conversion are subject to a reduced rate of VAT of 5%.

Building materials and certain electrical goods, supplied by the person providing the above services and incorporated into the building in question or its immediate site, are also subject to the reduced rate. See **42.16** to **42.18** below.

The reduced rate also applies to the acquisition from another EU country, or the importation from outside the EU, of goods the supply of which would be subject to the reduced rate.

[*VATA 1994, s 29A(1)(2), Sch 7A Group 6 Items 1* and *2; FA 2001, ss 97, 99, Sch 31*].

'Qualifying conversion'

A '*qualifying conversion*' means one of the following three types of conversion provided, in each case, any statutory planning consent needed and any statutory building control approval needed for the conversion has been granted. [*VATA 1994, Sch 7A Group 6 Note (10); FA 2001, Sch 31*].

(1) **Conversions into 'single household dwellings'**, i.e. the conversion of premises consisting of a building or part of a building where
   (i) after the conversion the premises being converted contain a number of single household dwellings that is different from the number (if any) that the premises contain before the conversion, and greater than, or equal to, one; and
   (ii) there is no part of the premises being converted that is a part that, after the conversion, contains the same number of single household dwellings (whether zero, one or two or more) as before the conversion.

   [*VATA 1994, Sch 7A Group 6 Note (3); FA 2001, Sch 31*].
   This covers the following scenarios.

Building before conversion	*Building after conversion*
One single household dwelling	Two or more single house dwellings
A number of single house dwellings	A different number of single house dwellings (more or less)
Non-residential	One or more single house dwellings
One or more houses in multiple occupation	One or more single house dwellings
Relevant residential property	One or more single house dwellings

   The provisions also cover the conversion of a building which may have been lived in but which does not qualify as a single household dwelling (such as a public house with staff accommodation) into one or more single household dwellings. (VAT Notice 708, para 7.3).

(2) **Conversions into 'multiple occupation dwellings'**, i.e. the conversion of premises consisting of a building or part of a building where the following conditions are satisfied.
   (i) Before the conversion the premises being converted do not contain any multiple occupancy dwellings.
   (ii) After the conversion those premises contain only a 'multiple occupancy dwelling' or two or more such dwellings.
   (iii) The use to which those premises are intended to be put after the conversion is not to any extent use for a 'relevant residential purpose'.

   [*VATA 1994, Sch 7A Group 6 Note (5); FA 2001, Sch 31; SI 2002/1100*].

A qualifying conversion includes the conversion into a multiple occupancy dwelling of

- a single household dwelling;
- a building used for a relevant residential purpose, such as a care home; and
- a property that has never been lived in.

It does not include, for example, the creation of additional bedrooms at a dwelling consisting of bed-sits.
(VAT Notice 708, para 7.4).

(3) **Conversions into premises for use for a 'relevant residential purpose'**, i.e. a conversion of premises consisting of one or more buildings or one or more parts of buildings (or any combination of buildings and parts of buildings) where the following conditions are satisfied.

(i) The use to which the premises being converted were last put before the conversion was not to any extent use for a relevant residential purpose and those premises are intended to be used solely for a relevant residential purpose after the conversion.

(ii) Where the relevant residential purpose for which the premises are intended to be used is an 'institutional purpose', the premises being converted must be intended to form, after the conversion, the entirety of an institution used for that purpose.

For such a conversion to be subject to the reduced rate

- it must be made to the person who intends to use the premises being converted for the relevant residential purpose; and
- before it is made, that person must give the supplier a certificate of intended use. See **42.22** below.

[*VATA 1994, Sch 7A Group 6 Notes (7)(8); FA 2001, Sch 31; SI 2002/1100*].

A qualifying conversion includes the conversion of

- a single household dwelling,
- a multiple occupancy dwelling, and
- a property that has never been lived in

into premises that will be used solely for a relevant residential purpose. It does not include

- the remodelling of an existing relevant residential purpose building; or
- any conversion where a new qualifying residential home or institution is not created in its entirety, such as the conversion of outbuildings into additional bedrooms for an existing care home.

'Single household dwelling'

A single household dwelling means a dwelling that

- is designed for occupation by a single household either because
  (i) it was originally designed on construction for occupation for that purpose and has not been subsequently adapted for occupation of any other kind; or
  (ii) it is so designed as a result of adaptation;
- consists of self-contained living accommodation;

- has no provision for direct internal access to any other dwelling or part of a dwelling; and
- is not prohibited from separate use or separate disposal by the terms of any covenant, statutory planning consent or similar provision. An occupancy restriction is not a prohibition on separate use or disposal if all it does is restrict the occupancy of a building to a certain type of person, such as persons working in agriculture or forestry, or persons over a specified age. But if the wording of the restriction prevents the building from being used separately from another building or from being sold, or otherwise disposed of, separately from another building then it is a prohibition on separate use or disposal. (VAT Notice 708, para 14.4).

[*VATA 1994, Sch 7A Group 6 Note (4); FA 2001, Sch 31*].

'Multiple occupancy dwelling'

A multiple occupancy dwelling means a dwelling that

- is designed for occupation by persons not forming a single household either because
  - (i) it was originally designed on construction for occupation for that purpose and has not been subsequently adapted for occupation of any other kind; or
  - (ii) it is so designed as a result of adaptation;
- is not to any extent used for a relevant residential purpose;
- consists of self-contained living accommodation;
- has no provision for direct internal access to any other dwelling or part of a dwelling; and
- is not prohibited from separate use or separate disposal by the terms of any covenant, statutory planning consent or similar provision. An occupancy restriction is not a prohibition on separate use or disposal if all it does is restrict the occupancy of a building to a certain type of person, such as persons working in agriculture or forestry, or persons over a specified age. But if the wording of the restriction prevents the building from being used separately from another building or from being sold, or otherwise disposed of, separately from another building then it is a prohibition on separate use or disposal. (VAT Notice 708, para 14.5).

[*VATA 1994, Sch 7A Group 6 Note (4); FA 2001, Sch 31; SI 2002/1100*].

A multiple occupancy dwelling is normally a dwelling consisting of a number of bed-sits. it does not include

- single household dwellings with accommodation for au pairs, family guests or 'live-in' lodgers; or
- hotels, guest houses, and similar establishments providing accommodation for holiday makers, travellers and similar temporary guests.

(VAT Notice 708, para 14.5).

Use for a relevant residential purpose

'*Use for a relevant residential purpose*' means use as

(a) a home or other institution providing residential accommodation for children;
(b) a home or other institution providing residential accommodation with personal care for persons in need of such care by reason of old age, disablement, past or present dependence on alcohol or drugs or past or present mental disorder;
(c) a hospice;
(d) residential accommodation for students or school pupils;
(e) residential accommodation for members of any of the armed forces;
(f) a monastery, nunnery or similar establishment; or
(g) an institution which is the sole or main residence of at least 90% of its residents.

except use as a hospital, prison or similar institution or an hotel, inn or similar establishment.

Use for an '*institutional purpose*' means a purpose under (*a*)–(*c*), (*f*) or (*g*) above.

[*VATA 1994, Sch 7A Group 6 Notes (6)(7); FA 2001, Sch 31*].

Qualifying services

Qualifying services mean either of the following.

- Carrying out work to the fabric of the building/part of the building being converted (excluding the incorporation, or installation as fittings, in the building/part of any goods that are not building materials).
- Carrying out work within the immediate site of the building in connection with
  - (i) the means of providing water, power, heat or access to the building/part,
  - (ii) the means of providing drainage or security for the building/part, or
  - (iii) the provision of means of waste disposal for the building/part.

[*VATA 1994, Sch 7A Group 6 Note (11); FA 2001, Sch 31*].

This includes all works of repair, maintenance (e.g. decoration) or improvement (e.g. the construction of an extension or the installation of double glazing) to the fabric of the building where the work forms an intrinsic part of changing the number of dwellings.

> *Example 1*
>
> A block of flats consists of four floors, each with four flats. A lift is installed and work is carried out throughout the whole building. On the ground, first and second floors the footprint of each flat is changed to take account of the new lift. This results in the internal configuration of each flat being changed. On the third floor three penthouse flats are created from the original four.
>
> Although the overall number of dwellings in the building has changed (there has been a reduction by one unit) only the work to convert the top floor will be eligible for the reduced rate because it is only in this part of the building that the number of dwellings has changed.

Example 2

The facts are as in *Example 1* except that the reduction in the number of flats on the third floor happens by combining two of the original flats together, the other two being refurbished.

The reduced rate will only apply to the work to merge the two flats together.

Example 3

The facts are as in *Example 1* above except that, as well as the changes to the top floor, the number of flats on the ground floor is changed to five smaller units.

Although the overall number of dwellings in the building has not changed (there are 16 units both before and after the work) as the number of dwellings has changed on both the ground floor and the third floor, the reduced rate can apply to the conversion work done on these floors.

All other services are standard-rated. For example

- the installation of goods that are not building materials, such as carpets and fitted bedroom furniture;
- the hire of goods;
- landscaping; and
- the provision of professional services, such as those provided by architects, surveyors, consultants and supervisors.

(VAT Notice 708, paras 7.3, 7.6).

Part-qualifying services

Where part of a supply of services qualifies under these provisions and part does not, the supply can be apportioned to determine the extent to which the reduced rate can be applied. [*VATA 1994, Sch 7A Group 6 Note (1); FA 2001, Sch 31*].

Garages

A qualifying conversion within (1)–(3) above includes the construction of a garage or the conversion of a 'non-residential' building (or of a non-residential part of a building) that results in a garage provided

- the garage works are carried out at the same time as the conversion; and
- the resulting garage is intended to be occupied
  - (i) where (1) above applies, with a single household dwelling that will after the conversion be contained in the building, or part of a building, being converted;
  - (ii) where (2) above applies, with a multiple occupancy dwelling that will after the conversion be contained in the building, or part of a building, being converted; or
  - (iii) where (3) above applies, with the institution or other accommodation resulting from the conversion.

'*Non-residential*' means neither designed, nor adapted, for use as a dwelling or two or more dwellings, or for a relevant residential purpose.

[*VATA 1994, Sch 7A Group 6 Note (9); FA 2001, Sch 31*].

Provided the above conditions are satisfied, the construction of a drive serving the garage can also be zero-rated. (VAT Notice 708, para 7.6).

Subcontractors

Subcontractors who carry out some or all of the qualifying renovation or conversion work can apply the reduced rate to their services *unless* the work is the conversion into a relevant residential property.

Dwellings adapted for non-residential use and subsequently converted back into a dwelling

If a property was originally a dwelling but then adapted for non-residential use, on conversion back to a dwelling the reduced rate would apply where the whole building had been used for a non-residential purpose as the conversion is of a non-residential building into a single household dwelling. It is the use of the building at the time of conversion that is relevant and not any earlier use.

> *Example 1*
>
> A building originally designed as a dwelling has been adapted for use as a dental surgery. No part of the building after adaptation has been used as living accommodation.
>
> The reduced rate applies to the work of converting the building back into a dwelling as there has been a change in the number of single household dwellings from none to one.
>
> *Example 2*
>
> A building originally designed as a dwelling is adapted for use as a dental surgery on the ground floor with a self-contained flat on the first floor.
>
> The reduced rate does not apply to the conversion of the whole building back into a single dwelling as the building is a single household dwelling before and after conversion.
>
> *Example 3*
>
> A room in a building designed as a single dwelling is used as an office. The rest of the house is used as living accommodation.
>
> The conversion of the room used as an office back into use as part of the existing house does not qualify for the reduced rate as there is single household dwelling before and after conversion. However, if the area used as the office is converted to create a self-contained dwelling, there would be a change in the number of single household dwellings (from one to two) the work would then qualify for the reduced rate.

De Voil Indirect Tax Service. See V4.411.

Residential renovations and alterations

[42.13] VAT is charged at the reduced rate of 5% on the renovation or alteration of a single household dwelling that has not been lived in for two (before 1 January 2008, three) years or more and a building to be used solely for a relevant residential purpose (e.g. a care home) or a multiple occupancy dwelling (e.g. bed-sits), again provided the premises have not been lived in for at least two (before 1 January 2008, three) years. Included are works in connection with garages. The detailed provisions are considered below.

'Qualifying services' supplied in the course of the renovation or alteration (including extension) of 'qualifying residential premises', and which are related to the renovation or alteration, are subject to a reduced rate of VAT of 5% provided the following conditions are satisfied.

- Empty home condition (1) below is satisfied or, if the premises are a 'single household dwelling' either empty home condition (1) or (2) below is satisfied.
- Any statutory planning consent needed for the renovation or alteration has been granted.
- Any statutory building control approval needed for the renovation or alteration has been granted.
- Where the premises in question are a building, or part of a building, which, when it was last lived in, was used for a relevant residential purpose,
  - (i) the building or part must be intended to be used solely for such a purpose after the renovation or alteration, and
  - (ii) before the supply is made, the person to whom it is made must give the supplier a certificate stating that intention. See **42.22** below.

  Where a number of buildings on the same site are renovated or altered at the same time and intended to be used together as a unit solely for a relevant residential purpose, then each of those buildings, to the extent that it would not be so regarded otherwise, is to be treated as intended for use solely for a relevant residential purpose.

Building materials and certain electrical goods, supplied by the person providing the above services and incorporated into the qualifying residential premises in question or their immediate site, are also subject to the reduced rate. See **42.16** to **42.18** below.

The reduced rate also applies to the acquisition from another EU country, or the importation from outside the EU, of goods the supply of which would be subject to the reduced rate.

[*VATA 1994, s 29A(1)(2), Sch 7A Group 7 Items 1*, 2 and *Notes (3)(4)(4A); FA 2001, s 99, Sch 31; SI 2002/1100; SI 2007/3448*].

'*Qualifying residential premises*' means

- a 'single household dwelling',
- a 'multiple occupancy dwelling', or
- a building, or part of a building, which, when it was last lived in, was used for a 'relevant residential purpose'. Where a building, when it was last lived in, formed part of a 'relevant residential unit' then, to the extent that it would not be so regarded otherwise, the building is to be treated as having been used for a relevant residential purpose. For these purposes, a building forms part of a relevant residential unit at any time when

(i) it is one of a number of buildings on the same site, and
(ii) the buildings are used together as a unit for a relevant residential purpose.

The expressions '*multiple occupancy dwelling*', '*single household dwelling*', and '*use for a relevant residential purpose*' have the same meaning as in **42.23** above.

[*VATA 1994, Sch 7A Group 7 Note (2); FA 2001, Sch 31; SI 2002/1100*].

Empty home conditions

The empty home conditions are as follows.

(1) Neither
  (a) the premises concerned, nor
  (b) where those premises are a building, or part of a building, which, when it was last lived in, formed part of a 'relevant residential unit' (see above), any of the other buildings that formed part of the unit,

  have been lived in during the period of two (before 1 January 2008, three) years ending with the commencement of the 'relevant works'.

(2) To cover the situation where a dwelling is occupied whilst the work is being carried on, the reduced rate can also be applied where
  (i) the dwelling was not lived in during a period of at least two (before 1 January 2008, three) years;
  (ii) the person, or one of the persons, whose beginning to live in the dwelling brought that period to an end was a person who (whether alone or jointly with another or others) acquired the dwelling at a time
    - no later than the end of that period, and
    - when the dwelling had been not lived in for at least two (before 1 January 2008, three) years;
  (iii) no works by way of renovation or alteration were carried out to the dwelling during the period of two (before 1 January 2008, three) years ending with the acquisition (although HMRC are prepared to ignore any minor works that were necessary to keep the dwelling dry and secure, see VAT Notice 708, para 8.3);
  (iv) the supply is made to a person who is
    - the person, or one of the persons, whose beginning to live in the property brought to an end the period in (i), and
    - the person, or one of the persons, who acquired the dwelling as mentioned in (ii); and
  (v) the 'relevant works' are carried out during the period of one year beginning with the day of the acquisition.

For the purposes of (1) and (2) above, the '*relevant works*' means

- where the supply is qualifying services within these provisions, the works that constitute the services supplied; and
- where the supply is building materials supplied with those services, the works by which the materials concerned are incorporated in the premises concerned or their immediate site.

References in (2) above to a person acquiring a dwelling are to that person having a major interest in the dwelling granted, or assigned, to him for a consideration.

[*VATA 1994, Sch 7A Group 7 Note (3); FA 2001, Sch 31; SI 2002/1100; SI 2007/3448*].

To reduce-rate his supply, a supplier must hold evidence that, on balance, shows the premises have not been lived in during the two (before 1 January 2008, three) years immediately before his work starts. The evidence can include the electoral roll and council tax data, information from empty property officers in local authorities and other sources of reliable information. If a contractor holds a letter from an empty property officer certifying that a property has not been lived in for two (before 1 January 2008, three) years, or will have been when the work starts, no other evidence is needed. If an empty property officer is unsure about when a property was last lived in, he should write with his best estimate. HMRC may then call for other supporting evidence.

In determining whether a property has been lived in, any

- illegal occupation by squatters,
- occupation by 'guardians' (persons installed by the owner to deter squatters and vandals), and
- non-residential use, such as storage for a business

can be ignored but if the dwelling has been lived in on an occasional basis (e.g. as a second home) in the two (before 1 January 2008, three) years immediately before work starts, the supply cannot be reduced-rated.

(VAT Notice 708, para 8.3).

Qualifying services

Qualifying services means either of the following.

- Carrying out work to the fabric of the premises (excluding the incorporation, or installation as fittings, in the premises of any goods that are not building materials).
- Carrying out work within the immediate site of the premises in connection with
  - (i) the means of providing water, power, heat or access to the premises;
  - (ii) the means of providing drainage or security for the premises; or
  - (iii) the provision of means of waste disposal for the premises.

[*VATA 1994, Sch 7A Group 7 Note (5); FA 2001, Sch 31; SI 2002/1100*].

This includes any work of repair, maintenance (e.g. redecoration) or improvement (e.g. an extension or the installation of double glazing) carried out to the fabric of the premises.

All other services are standard-rated, including

- the installation of goods that are not building materials, such as carpets or fitted bedroom furniture;

- the hire of goods;
- landscaping; and
- the provision of professional services, such as those provided by architects, surveyors, consultants and supervisors.

(VAT Notice 708, para 8.4).

Part-qualifying services

Where part of a supply of services qualifies under these provisions and part does not, the supply can be apportioned to determine the extent to which the reduced rate can be applied. [*VATA 1994, Sch 7A Group 7 Note (1); FA 2001, Sch 31*].

Related garage work

For the above purposes, a renovation or alteration of any premises includes any 'garage works' related to the renovation or alteration. '*Garage works*' means

- the construction of a garage,
- the conversion of a building, or of a part of a building, that results in a garage, or
- the renovation or alteration of a garage

and garage works are related to a renovation or alteration if

- they are carried out at the same time as the renovation or alteration of the premises concerned, and
- the garage is intended to be occupied with the premises.

[*VATA 1994, Sch 7A Group 7 Note (3A); FA 2001, Sch 31; SI 2002/1100*].

Subcontractors

Subcontractors who carry out some or all of the qualifying renovation or conversion work can apply the reduced rate to their services unless the work is the renovation of an empty single household dwelling where the owner is in residence (as only a person making supplies to the occupier can apply the reduced rate, see above).

De Voil Indirect Tax Service. See V4.413.

Construction services — examples

Zero-rated services

[42.14] The services which can be zero-rated under **42.7** to **42.10** above include the following where supplied in the course of construction.

(a) *Work on the building itself* (including applying any usual decorative features) prior to 'completion' of the building (see **41.1**(6) **LAND AND BUILDINGS: EXEMPT SUPPLIES AND OPTION TO TAX**).
'*Snagging*' (or the correction of faults) is often carried out after the building has been completed. The work can be zero-rated if provided by the supplier who carried out the initial building work and the snagging

forms part of that building contract. If, however, the work is carried out as a separate supply (e.g. a builder may be contracted to correct work performed by another person) and it is performed after the building has been completed, then the work is to an existing building and cannot be zero-rated under these provisions.

(b) *Work closely connected to the construction of the building.* Subject to (*c*) below, work is closely connected to the construction of the building when it either

(i) allows the construction of the building to take place, for example

- demolishing existing buildings and structures as part of a single project to construct a new building/buildings in their place (the grant of a right to remove materials is not a supply of demolition services and is standard-rated);
- providing or improving an access point to a building site to allow deliveries to be made;
- carrying out ground works (including the levelling and drainage of land) as part of the process of constructing a new building or buildings in its place;
- providing site clearance or 'builders' clean' services; and
- securing the site; or

(ii) produces works that allow the building to be used, such as works in connection with

- the means of providing water and power to the building (this can extend to the work required to make the connection to the nearest existing supply);
- the means of providing, within the development site, access to the building (e.g. roads, footpaths, parking areas, drives and patios);
- the means of providing security (such as walls, fences and gates – but note that most electrical appliances are always standard-rated, see **42.17** below); or
- the provision of soft landscaping within the site of building (e.g. the application of top-soil, seeding with grass or laying turf); the planting of shrubs, trees and flowers to the extent that it is detailed on a landscaping scheme approved by a planning authority under the terms of a planning consent condition. It does not include work outside the plot (e.g. screening planted along roadside verges) or the replacement of trees and shrubs that die, or become damaged or diseased. See *Rialto Homes plc* (VTD 16340) (TVC 15.257).

The lists are not exhaustive.

(c) *Services carried out before or after the construction of the building.* Services closely connected to the construction of the building, and carried out either before or after the physical construction of the building takes place, may only be zero-rated if it can be shown that there is a close connection between when they are performed and when the physical construction of the building takes place. Where there is a time delay, both the reason for, and the length of, any delay must be considered.

Services described in (*b*) above may be zero-rated (subject to the normal conditions) where, for example

- civil engineering services are supplied to a landowner for the purposes of servicing a building plot and it is clear that the construction of a qualifying building by a developer will take place shortly afterwards;
- soft landscaping work is carried out after the building has been completed because the work has been delayed due to seasonal weather conditions

but are standard-rated where, for example

- site investigation or demolition work is carried out prior to the letting of a building contract;
- the services for a building (water, electricity, etc.) are installed on land which is to be sold as building land and where it is not clear that the construction of a qualifying building will take place shortly afterwards; or
- the work is delayed until after the building is complete owing to an insufficiency of funds.

(d) *Connecting utilities to existing buildings*. The connection of utilities to an existing building is normally standard-rated as work to an existing building. However, as a concession, until 31 December 2011, the first time connection of gas or electricity supplies can sometimes be zero-rated. See **25.7 FUEL AND POWER.**

(VAT Notice 708, para 3.3).

Standard-rated services

[42.15] Examples of work that cannot be zero-rated include

- the provision of on-site catering;
- the cleaning of site offices;
- landscaping, except to the extent zero-rated above;
- the provision of outdoor leisure facilities for a dwelling such as tennis courts and swimming pools (although the provision of a playground at a school would qualify as it is needed for the school to be used);
- works outside the site of the building (other than those zero-rated above), including where that work is carried out under a 'planning gain' agreement with a planning authority; and
- the granting of a right to remove materials.

(VAT Notice 708, para 3.3; Business Brief 7/2000).

Building materials and other goods

[42.16] Subject to the exceptions in **42.18** below, where a person supplies

- zero-rated construction services within **42.7** to **42.10** above, or
- reduced rate construction services within **42.12** or **42.13** above,

building materials, supplied by the person providing those services and incorporated into the building in question or its immediate site, are also zero-rated or, as the case may be, subject to the reduced rate.

'*Building materials*' in relation to a particular building, mean goods 'ordinarily' incorporated or installed as fittings by builders in a building of that description (or its site) but do not include any of the supplies within **42.18**(*a*)–(*c*) below.

[*VATA 1994, Sch 7A Group 6 Note (12), Sch 7A Group 7 Note (6), Sch 8 Group 5 Item 4* and *Notes (22)* and *(23), Sch 8 Group 6 Item 3* and *Note (3); FA 2001, s 97, Sch 31 para 1; SI 1995/280; SI 1995/283*].

The effect of the above is that building materials can be zero-rated or reduced-rated, as the case may be, along with the supply of building services where all of the following conditions are met.

(1) The articles are 'incorporated' in the building or its site

HMRC regard an article as 'incorporated' in a building (or its site) when it is fixed in such a way that its fixing or removal would either

- require the use of tools; or
- result in either the need for remedial work to the fabric of the building (or its site), or substantial damage to the goods themselves.

Examples of articles incorporated in a building (or its site) include

- built-in and fitted furniture (although only built-in or fitted *kitchen* furniture are building materials, see **42.18**(*a*) below);
- built-in, wired-in or plumbed-in appliances such as boilers or wired-in storage heaters (although only certain gas and electrical appliances are building materials, see **42.17** below, and most are normally standard-rated, see **42.18**(*b*) below);
- flooring (although carpets are not building materials, see **42.18**(*c*) below); and
- topsoil, trees, shrubs, turf, grass seed and plants (although trees, shrubs and plants are only 'building materials' in certain circumstances, see **42.14** above).

Examples of goods that are not incorporated in a building (or its site) include

- free-standing appliances that are merely plugged in; and
- free-standing furniture such as sofas, tables and chairs, etc.

(2) The articles are 'ordinarily' incorporated by builders in that type of building

HMRC take the view that an article is '*ordinarily*' incorporated in a building or its site when, in the ordinary course of events, it would normally be incorporated in a building of that generic type, such as a dwelling, church, or school. They do not split generic types of buildings into sub-categories so no distinction is drawn between large detached houses and small terraced houses. HMRC also take the same approach when determining if the goods themselves are the 'norm' for that type of building (e.g. a tap would be regarded as being ordinarily incorporated whether it is chromium or gold-plated). The range of items considered to be ordinarily incorporated is likely to change over time in line with trends and consumer expectations. Goods which need to be installed in defined areas of the country (e.g. sound-proofing near airports) can still qualify (*British Airports Authority (No 5)* (VTD 447) (TVC 15.241)).

Examples of articles ordinarily incorporated in a dwelling include

- Air conditioning
- Bathroom accessories, such as fixed towel rails, toilet roll holders, soap dishes, etc.
- Builders' hardware
- Burglar alarms
- Curtain poles and rails
- Decorating materials
- Doors
- Dust extractors and filters (including built-in vacuum cleaners)
- Fencing permanently erected around the boundary of the dwelling
- Fireplaces and surrounds
- Fire alarms and sprinkler systems
- Fitted furniture (although only kitchen furniture is building materials, see **42.18**(*a*) below)
- Flooring materials (but not carpet or carpeting materials, see **42.18**(*c*) below)
- Gas and electrical appliances when wired-in or plumbed-in (although only certain gas and electrical appliances are building materials, see **42.17** below)
- Guttering
- Heating systems (including radiators and controls, ducted warm-air systems, storage heaters and other wired in heating appliances, gas fires, underfloor heating and solar powered heating)
- Immersion heaters, boilers, hot and cold water tanks
- Kitchen sinks, work surfaces and fitted cupboards
- Letter boxes
- Lifts and hoists
- Light fittings (including chandeliers and outside lights)
- Mirrors
- Plumbing installations, including electric showers and 'in line' water softeners
- Power points (including combination shaver points)
- Sanitary ware
- Saunas
- Shower units
- Smoke detectors
- Solar panels
- Solid fuel cookers and oil-fired boilers

- Swimming pools inside the house, including water heaters and filters but not diving boards and other specialist equipment. Movable tiled floors that can be locked at varying depths are not ordinarily incorporated in a building, see *Rainbow Pools London* (VTD 20800) (TVC 15.240)
- Turf, topsoil, grass seed, plants and trees (although the trees, shrubs and plants are only 'building materials' in certain circumstances, see **42.14** above)
- TV aerials and satellite dishes
- Ventilation equipment (including cooker hoods)
- Warden call systems
- Window frames and glazing
- Wiring (including power circuits and computer, telephone and TV cabling)

Examples of articles ordinarily incorporated in buildings used for a relevant residential purpose include

- Mirrors
- Safes
- External lighting systems

Examples of articles ordinarily incorporated in buildings used for a relevant charitable purpose include

- Blinds and shutters
- External lighting systems
- Mirrors
- Safes

Examples of articles ordinarily incorporated in schools include

- Blackboards/whiteboards fixed to or forming part of the wall
- Gymnasium wall bars
- Notice and display boards
- Mirrors and barres (in ballet schools)

Examples of articles ordinarily incorporated in churches include

- Altars
- Church bells
- Fonts
- Lecterns
- Pipe organs
- Pulpits

(3) Other than kitchen furniture, the articles are not finished or prefabricated furniture, or materials for the construction of fitted furniture.

See **42.18**(*a*) below.

(4) With certain exceptions, the articles are not electrical or gas appliances

See **42.17** and **42.18**(*b*) below.

(5) The articles are not carpets or carpeting material

See **42.18**(*c*) below.

(VAT Notice 708, paras 13.2–13.4, 13.8).

Electrical and gas appliances

[42.17] Most electrical and gas appliances are not building materials for VAT purposes, even if they are required to be incorporated in a building as a requirement of *Building Regulations*. They are, therefore, standard-rated (see **42.18**(*b*) below). The following can, however, be zero-rated when supplied with zero-rated construction services within **42.7** to **42.10** above or charged at the reduced rate when supplied with reduced rate construction services within **42.12** and **42.13** above.

(a) An appliance designed to heat space or water (or both) or designed to provide ventilation, air cooling, air purification or dust extraction.
(b) A door-entry system, waste disposal unit or machine for compacting waste but only if in each case it is intended for use in a building designed as a number of dwellings (e.g. a block of flats).
(c) A burglar alarm, fire alarm or fire safety equipment designed solely for the purpose of enabling aid to be summoned in an emergency.
(d) A lift or hoist.

[*VATA 1994, Sch 7A Group 6 Note (12), Sch 7A Group 7 Note (6), Sch 8 Group 5 Note (22), Group 6 Note (3); FA 2001, s 97, Sch 31 para 1; SI 1995/280; SI 1995/283*].

Cookers which are designed to have the dual purpose of heating the room or the building's water are included under (*a*) above but telephones or electric gates and barriers are not included under (*c*) above. Fixed amplification equipment in churches may also be zero-rated.

Appliances powered by other fuels (e.g. solid fuel or oil-fired cookers) are building materials when they are ordinarily incorporated in the building.

(VAT Notice 708, para 13.6).

In *Leisure Contracts Ltd* (VTD 19392) (TVC 15.239) it was held that electric covers for indoor swimming pools were electrical applicances and therefore standard-rated. However, in the subsequent decision in *Rainbow Pools London Ltd* (VTD 20800) (TVC 15.240) such covers were held to be zero-rated.

Standard-rated goods

[42.18] The following goods are specifically excluded from the definition of building materials and their supply is always standard-rated.

(a) Finished or prefabricated 'furniture' (other than furniture designed to be fitted in kitchens) and materials for the construction of 'fitted furniture' (other than kitchen furniture)

'*Furniture*' is not defined in law and whether an item is furniture is very much a matter of impression (see *C & E Commrs v McLean Homes Midland Ltd*, QB [1993] STC 335 (TVC 15.226)).

HMRC give the following as examples of articles which are *not* furniture and are building materials for VAT purposes. They therefore qualify for zero-rating or reduced-rating, subject to meeting the conditions in **42.16** above.

- Basic storage facilities formed by becoming part of the fabric of the building, such as airing cupboards and under-stair storage cupboards.
- Items that provide storage capacity as an incidental result of their primary function, such as shelves formed as a result of constructing simple box work over pipes, and basin supports which contain a simple cupboard beneath.
- Basic wardrobes installed on their own with *all* the following characteristics.
  - (i) The wardrobe encloses a space bordered by the walls, ceiling and floor. But units whose design includes, for example, an element to bridge over a bed or create a dressing table are furniture and are not building materials.
  - (ii) The side and back use three walls of the room (such as across the end of a wall), or two walls and a stub wall. But wardrobes installed in the corner of a room where one side is a closing end panel are furniture and are not building materials.
  - (iii) On opening the wardrobe the walls of the building can be seen. These would normally be either bare plaster or painted plaster. Wardrobes that contain internal panelling, typically as part of a modular or carcass system, are furniture and are not building materials.
  - (iv) The wardrobe should feature no more than a single shelf running the full length of the wardrobe, a rail for hanging clothes and a closing door or doors. Wardrobes with internal divisions, drawers, shoe racks or other features are furniture and are not building materials.

All other finished or prefabricated furniture, and materials for the construction of fitted furniture, are not building materials for VAT purposes and cannot be zero-rated or reduced-rated as the case may be. These include

- wardrobes (other than the basic wardrobes described above) including basic wardrobes installed as part of a larger installation of furniture in the room;
- elaborate vanity units;
- wall units, such as bathroom cabinets;
- laboratory work benches; and
- pews, choir and clergy stalls.

(b) Electrical or gas appliances

Except for those specifically covered in **42.17** above. Standard-rated items include refrigerators; cookers (including split-level cookers); washing and dish-washing machines; tumble dryers; and waste disposal units and entry phone systems (except in buildings designed as a number of dwellings, e.g. blocks of flats, see **42.17** above).

(c) Carpets or carpeting material

Carpets, carpet tiles and underlay are not building materials for VAT purposes. Other forms of flooring or floor covering, such as linoleum, ceramic tiles, parquet and wooden floor systems are building materials.

> *Example*
>
> Carpet Fitters Ltd have fitted carpets into two ten new dwellings for a property developer. If a single charge is made to the developer for supplying and fitting the carpets, then the fee will be wholly standard-rated. However, if a separate charge is made for the 'fitting' element, this charge can be zero-rated as relevant to building services carried out on a new dwelling. The supply of the carpets (goods only) will then be standard-rated, and an input tax block will apply to the builder.

[*VATA 1994, Sch 7A Group 6 Note (12), Sch 7A Group 7 Note (6), Sch 8 Group 5 Note (22), Group 6 Note (3); FA 2001, s 97, Sch 31 para 1; SI 1995/280; SI 1995/283*]. (VAT Notice 708, paras 13.5, 13.7).

Time of supply

[42.19] The rules applying to the time of supply are outlined below.

(1) Single payment contracts

Single payment contracts are subject to the normal tax point rules (see **66.18 SUPPLY: TIME OF SUPPLY**) including the creation of a basic tax point when the work has been completed. (VAT Notice 708, para 22.1).

Retention payments

Building contracts frequently include retention clauses which allow customers to hold back a proportion of the contract price on completion of the work pending confirmation that the supplier has done the work properly and has rectified any immediate faults that might be found.

There are special tax point rules that apply to retention payments generally *other than those for stage or interim payment contracts under (2) below*. The tax point for the retention element of the contract is the earlier of

- the time when a payment in respect of any part of the retention is received by the supplier; or
- the date that the supplier issues a VAT invoice relating to the retention.

[*SI 1995/2518, Reg 89; SI 1997/2887, Reg 3; SI 2003/3220, Reg 16*]. (VAT Notice 708, para 23.1).

(2) Stage or interim payment contracts

Where services, or services together with goods, are supplied in the course of the construction, alteration, demolition, repair or maintenance of a building or of any civil engineering work under a contract which provides for payment for such supplies to be made periodically or from time to time (often referred to as 'stage' or 'interim' payment contracts), those services (or goods and services) are normally treated as separately and successively supplied at the earliest of the following times.

(a) Each time a payment is received by the supplier.
(b) Each time the supplier issues a VAT invoice.

There is, therefore, no basic tax point when the work is completed unless the contract is covered by the following special anti-avoidance rules that can apply in some cases.

Special anti-avoidance rules

If a VAT invoice is not issued, the tax point (and therefore VAT payment) can be delayed. The special anti-avoidance rule counters the VAT effect of contracts where payment does not become due for many years after the completion of the work. The rules are complex but, briefly, do *not* apply if

- whoever will be occupying the works will be doing so wholly or mainly for eligible purposes;
- the supplier is unconnected with the proposed occupiers *and* can be sure that neither he, nor any of his subcontractors, is receiving any form of finance from the proposed occupiers, nor anyone connected with them. In this connection, finance does not include interim payments for supplies, on which VAT is accounted for.

(VAT Notice 708, para 23.2).

In more detail, where services are 'relevant services' which have not already been treated as supplied under (*a*) or (*b*) above, there is an additional tax point on the day on which the services are performed.

Services are '*relevant services*' if, at the time they are performed, either of the following conditions is satisfied.

(a) The supplier or a 'person responsible for financing the supplier's costs' intends or expects that the land on which the building or civil engineering work in question is situated will be occupied (whether immediately or eventually) or will continue to be occupied (for a period at least) by
  - the supplier,
  - a person responsible for financing the supplier's costs, or
  - a person connected with either such person under *ICTA 1988, s 839* (see **71.19 VALUATION**). A company is not connected with another for these purposes only because both are under the control of the Crown, a Minister of the Crown, a government department or a Northern Ireland department

  other than wholly or mainly (see under the heading *The 80% test* below) for 'eligible purposes'.

  Occupation for '*eligible purposes*' means

- occupation by a taxable person for the purpose of making supplies which are in the course of furtherance of a business and are supplies of such a description that any input tax wholly attributable to those supplies would be input tax for which he would be entitled to credit, or
- occupation by a specified body within *VATA 1994, s 33* (see **43.2 LOCAL AUTHORITIES AND PUBLIC BODIES**) to the extent that the body occupies the land for non-business purposes, or
- occupation by a government department

and for these purposes, where occupation is by a person who is not a taxable person but whose supplies are treated for the purposes of *VATA 1994* as made by another person who is a taxable person, those two persons are to be regarded as a single taxable person.

(b) The supplier has received (and used in making his supply) from a subcontractor any supply of services, or services together with goods, the time of supply of which was determined under these anti-avoidance provisions (or would have been but for the issue by that subcontractor of a VAT invoice other than one which has been paid in full).

Thus a main contractor is affected by the anti-avoidance rules if any of his subcontractors are affected by it. If, for example, a bank gives a loan to a subcontractor specifically to do work on one of its banks, the subcontractor would be affected by the anti-avoidance rule, and so would the contractor. However, HMRC will not be seeking to catch a contractor out on a technicality in this area, and if it does come to their attention that a contractor is inadvertently affected by the rule because of his subcontractors, they will look at his case sympathetically. (VAT Notice 708, para 23.8).

A '*person responsible for financing the supplier's costs*' is a person who has

- provided finance for the supplier's costs; or
- entered into an agreement or understanding (whether or not legally enforceable) to provide finance for the supplier's costs.

Providing funds is widely defined. It includes directly or indirectly providing funds *either* to meet the whole or part of the supplier's costs *or* to discharge the whole or part of any liability incurred in raising funds to meet those costs. It also includes directly or indirectly procuring the provision of funds by another person for either of those purposes. The funds may be provided by way of loan, guarantee or other security, consideration for a share issue used to raise the funds or any other transfer of assets or value as a consequence of which the funds are made available. Providing funds does not include making interim payments for construction work on which VAT is accounted for.

A '*supplier's costs*' are his costs of supplying the services, or services together with goods, and comprise

- amounts payable by the supplier for supplies to him of goods and services used in making his supply; and
- the supplier's staff and other internal costs of making his supply.

[*SI 1995/2518, Reg 93; SI 1997/2887, Reg 5; SI 1999/1374; SI 2009/1967, Reg 5*].

HMRC give the following decision table to show the questions a supplier must ask himself to determine whether the anti-avoidance provisions apply to him.

(1) Do you know who will occupy the works?
If 'yes', go to step 3.
If 'no', go to step 2.

(2) Do any of your subcontractors know who will occupy the works?
If 'yes', go to step 4.
If 'no', you do not have to account for VAT when you complete your work and you can follow the normal rules for stage and interim payment contracts.

(3) Will you, or someone connected with you, occupy the works?
If 'yes', go to step 7.
If 'no', go to step 4.

(4) Will one of your subcontractors, or someone connected with one of your subcontractors, occupy the works?
If 'yes', go to step 7.

(5) If 'no', go to step 5.

(6) Will someone who gave you finance to pay for the costs of your work, or someone connected with your financer, occupy the works?
If 'yes', go to step 7.
If 'no', go to step 6.

(7) Will someone who gave your subcontractor finance to pay the costs of his work, or someone connected with his financer, occupy the works?
If 'yes', go to step 7.
If 'no', you do not have to account for VAT when you complete your work and you can follow the normal rules for stage and interim payment contracts.

(8) Will the occupier be doing so wholly or mainly for eligible purposes?
If 'yes', you do not have to account for VAT when you complete your work and you can follow the normal rules for stage and interim payment contracts.
If 'no', you must account for VAT no later than when you complete your work.

(VAT Notice 708, para 23.3).

'Wholly or mainly' test

HMRC take the view that a building is used 'wholly or mainly' for eligible purposes if the occupier can recover 80% or more of the VAT relating to that building. It does not matter whether their overall ability to recover VAT is greater or less than 80%. Buildings that *are not* normally seen as being 'wholly or mainly for eligible purposes' include those used

- as a bank, or the headquarters of a banking group;
- as an insurance broker's office, or the office of an insurance company;
- as a school, college or university;
- as an office for a charity (but the special anti-avoidance rules do not apply if the work for a charity is zero-rated);
- as a private hospital, or the head office of a private healthcare business; or

- for any purpose if the occupier is not registered for VAT (but the special anti-avoidance rules do not apply if the work is zero-rated, such as constructing a house).

Buildings that *are* normally seen as being 'wholly or mainly for eligible purposes' include those used

- as the head office of a fully taxable business
- for any purpose where the occupier is a government department
- by a local authority for carrying on its statutory functions
- as a retail shop,
- as a wholesale outlet,
- as a factory or workshop,
- as an importer's office or warehouse, or
- as a charity shop

provided that the retailer, etc. is registered for VAT.

(VAT Notice 708, para 23.7).

When services are performed

HMRC treat services as performed when the work is completed. See **41.1**(6) **LAND AND BUILDINGS: EXEMPT SUPPLIES AND OPTION TO TAX** for a general consideration of the meaning of 'completion'. (VAT Notice 708, paras 23.3, 23.9).

Accounting for VAT

Where the anti-avoidance rules apply, VAT must be accounted for on the full value of the contract, less any amounts on which VAT has already become due because a payment has been received or a VAT invoice issued. The full value of the contract includes retentions and disputed amounts.

Where there is a dispute, or where it is not possible to know the exact value of the contract for any other reason, a reasonable estimate of the value must be made. In cases of dispute, a supplier need not account for VAT on the full amount he is claiming from the customer if he feels that he will most likely be forced in the end to settle for a lower amount. He should account for VAT on his best estimate of the amount that will eventually be agreed. (HMRC recommend that the supplier documents the basis of his estimate, so that he can later show that it was reasonable.) Subsequently, when the value of the contract is finalised, the supplier may need to make an adjustment to the VAT paid.

(VAT Notice 708, para 23.10).

Public/Private Partnership (formerly Private Finance Initiative)

If a PPP or PFI arrangement relates to a building that will be occupied exclusively by a government department (including an NHS hospital), the anti-avoidance rules do not apply. However, some PPP and PFI arrangements relate to buildings that will be occupied by private sector businesses as well as government departments. In such cases, the part of the building occupied by the private sector business may be caught by the special anti-avoidance rules.

If so, there is no need to account for VAT on the entire building on completion, only on a proportion of the overall price that fairly reflects the part of the building that will be occupied by private companies. (VAT Notice 708, para 23.7).

(3) Self-billing

Under a self-billing arrangement, the customer makes out VAT invoices on behalf of the VAT-registered supplier (e.g. a main contractor makes out VAT invoices on behalf of its registered subcontractor) and sends a copy of the invoice to the supplier with the payment. See **39.6 INVOICES** for conditions of self-billing and **66.4 SUPPLY: TIME OF SUPPLY** for the time of supply and a notional tax point for input tax deduction purposes.

(4) Goods supplied without services

(5) Materials not supplies in connection with supply of services

Where materials, etc. are not supplied in connection with the supply of services (e.g. a supply by a builders' merchant to a builder), the time of supply is that under the normal rules for supplies of goods. See **66.8 SUPPLY: TIME OF SUPPLY**.

(6) Insolvency

There are no concessions for tax points in the construction industry when a business becomes insolvent. The normal tax point rules as in (1)–(4) above apply equally to transactions before and after the appointment of an insolvency practitioner. (Business Brief 4/96).

Self-supply of construction services

[42.20] Where a person, in the course or furtherance of a business carried on by him, and for the purpose of that business and otherwise than for a consideration, performs any services in connection with

(a) the construction of a building,
(b) the extension or alteration of, or the construction of an annexe to, any building such that additional floor area of not less than 10% of the floor area of the original building is created,
(c) the construction of any civil engineering work, or
(d) the carrying out of any demolition work at the same time as, or in preparation for, any of the services in (*a*) to (*c*) above

those services are treated as both supplied to him for the purpose of that business and supplied by him in the course or furtherance of it (i.e. self-supplied) unless

- the open market value of the services performed is less than £100,000, or
- such services would, if supplied for a consideration in the course or furtherance of a business by a taxable person, be zero-rated.

VAT must be accounted for on the open market value of the services performed (subject to the *de minimis* limit of £100,000) in the VAT return for the period in which the services are performed. This output tax on the self-supply can be recovered as input tax in the same period to the extent that it is attributable to taxable supplies under the normal rules, i.e. to the extent that the building in question is used or to be used for making taxable supplies. Therefore

- where the building or work is occupied or used for a taxable business activity, or is sold or let after the exercise of an option to tax, the self-supply VAT should be fully recoverable;
- where the building or work is used wholly for exempt purposes or let without the option to tax being exercised, the self-supply VAT is not recoverable; and
- where the building or work is used partly for exempt and partly for taxable business purposes, VAT on the self-supply charge is recoverable according to the partial exemption method used.

Where the value of the self-supply exceeds £250,000, adjustments may be required in future years under the **CAPITAL GOODS SCHEME (10)**.

Input tax incurred on goods and services for such building works are treated as relating to the taxable self-supply and can be deducted in full (subject to the normal rules).

In relation to **GROUPS OF COMPANIES (27)**, for these purposes all companies within a VAT group are treated as one person but anything done which would fall to be treated under these provisions as services supplied to and by that person are to be treated as supplied to and by the representative member (see **27.4 GROUPS OF COMPANIES**).

Registration

Where a person not registered for VAT makes a self-supply falling within these provisions, the value of the self-supply will make him liable for registration.

[*SI 1989/472*]. (VAT Notice 708, paras 24.3, 24.4).

De Voil Indirect Tax Service. See V3.244.

Treatment in particular circumstances

[42.21] The treatment of land and buildings in particular circumstances is outlined as follows.

(1) Architects, surveyors, consultants and supervisors

The separate supply of architectural, surveying, consultancy and supervisory services is always standard-rated. However, these services can be procured in a number of ways.

Design and build

The building client engages a contractor to carry out both the design and construction elements of the project. Where it is clear in the contract that any services of architects, surveyors or others acting as a consultant or in a supervisory capacity are no more than cost components of the contractors supply and are not specifically supplied on to the customer, then the whole supply can be treated as being eligible for the zero rate.

Project management

The building client engages a project manager (usually a construction company) to plan, manage and co-ordinate the whole project, including establishing competitive bids for all elements of the work. The successful contractors are employed directly by the building client. Management fees paid by the building client to the project manager are standard-rated.

Management contracting

This system can take various forms but normally the building client first appoints a professional design team and engages a management contractor to advise them. If the project goes ahead, the management contractor acts as the main contractor for the work (engaging 'works contractors' to carry out work to him as necessary). His preliminary advisory services are then treated in the same way as his main construction services. If the project does not go ahead, his preliminary advisory services are standard-rated.

(VAT Notice 708, para 3.4).

(2) Authenticated receipts

The authenticated receipt procedure (not to be confused with self-billing, see **39.6 INVOICES**) allows a supplier to issue an authenticated receipt for payment instead of a normal VAT invoice.

The procedure works by the customer preparing a receipt for a supply received and forwarding it to the supplier with payment. The receipt is only valid for VAT purposes when the supplier has authenticated it. The time limits for the issue of an authenticated receipt is the same as for a VAT invoice (see **39.13 INVOICES**).

The procedure can only be used when all of the following conditions are satisfied.

- The customer and the supplier mutually agree to operate the procedure.
- Services, or services together with goods, are supplied in the course of the construction, alteration, demolition, repair or maintenance of a building or of any civil engineering work.
- The contract provides for payments for such services to be made periodically, or from time to time ('stage' or 'interim payment' contracts). The procedure should not therefore be used for supplies made under single payment contracts.
- The receipt contains all the particulars required on a VAT invoice (see **39.4 INVOICES**).
- No VAT invoice or similar document is issued.

An authenticated receipt is not a VAT invoice and its issue does not create a tax point. The tax point for the supply is therefore solely determined by the receipt of payment by the supplier or, where the special anti-avoidance rules described in **42.19**(2) above apply, the date the work is completed.

An authenticated receipt is, however, acceptable as evidence for input tax purposes. The customer may claim input tax in the VAT period in which the supplier receives the stage payment, without waiting for an authenticated receipt. But he must obtain and keep a copy of the authenticated receipt. Suppliers cannot authenticate a receipt and return it to the customer until they have received the payment.

If a customer experiences difficulty in obtaining an authenticated receipt from a supplier, he should contact HMRC in writing on the third successive occasion that this happens. A claim to input tax may still be allowed if satisfactory alternative evidence is available, or the customer can show that reasonable efforts were made to secure an authenticated receipt and the claim is otherwise correct.

[*SI 1995/2518, Reg 13(4)*]. (VAT Notice 708, para 22.3).

(3) CITB levy

Any agreed deduction in respect of the Construction Industry Training Board levy can be deducted from the gross amount for the purposes of calculating VAT due, and the value of the supply is treated as reduced by any such levy. (VAT Notice 708, para 21.2).

(4) Income tax deductions

Where a contractor is required to make a deduction on account of income tax from a payment to a subcontractor who is not exempt from such deduction, the value of the subcontractor's services for VAT purposes is the gross amount before income tax is deducted. (VAT Notice 708, para 21.1).

(5) Liquidated damages

Liquidated damages are agreed pre-estimated sums to be paid in the event of a breach of contract by one of the parties. The amount is either a set figure or determined by a formula.

- Liquidated damages received are not payment for a supply made and no VAT is due on the amount received.
- Where a person is due to make a payment for liquidated damages and also due to receive from the other party a payment for a supply, he cannot reduce the value of his supply (and therefore cannot reduce the amount of VAT chargeable), even if he sets the amounts off against each other.

(VAT Notice 708, para 21.3).

Certificates

Certificates for relevant residential/charitable purposes

[42.22] Where a zero-rated or reduced-rated supply is made in connection with all or part of a building which is intended for use solely for a '*relevant residential purpose*' or a '*relevant charitable purpose*' (see **41.1**(15) and

41.1(13) **LAND AND BUILDINGS: EXEMPT SUPPLIES AND OPTION TO TAX** respectively), the grant or other supply cannot be taken as relating to the building (or part) intended for such use unless

(a) it is made to the person who intends to use the building (or part) for such purposes (the 'customer'); and
(b) before it is made, the customer has given to the grantor or supplier a certificate, in such form as is prescribed by HMRC, stating that the grant or other supply relates to such a building (or part).

[*VATA 1994, Sch 7A Group 6 Note (8), Group 7 Note (4A), Sch 8 Group 5 Note (12), Group 6 Note (3); SI 1995/280*].

The effect of the above is that, before a developer or builder can zero-rate or reduce-rate certain grants and other supplies, he must obtain a certificate from the customer. A certificate must be used for any of the following supplies.

(1) The first grant of a major interest in a building (or part of a building) for use solely for a relevant residential purpose or a relevant charitable purpose (see **42.1** above).
(2) The first grant of a major interest in a building (or part of a building) for use solely for a relevant residential purpose by the person who has converted it (see **42.11** above).
(3) The first grant of a major interest by a person substantially reconstructing a protected building where the building is to be used solely for a relevant residential purpose or a relevant charitable purpose (see **42.13** above).
(4) The supply of goods and services in the course of construction of a new building intended solely for a relevant residential purpose or a relevant charitable purpose (see **42.17** above).
(5) The supply to a relevant housing association of goods and services in the course of conversion of a non-residential building (or a non-residential part of a building) into a building (or part of a building) intended for use solely for a relevant residential purpose (see **42.9** above).
(6) The supply of goods and services in the course of an approved alteration to a protected building intended solely for use for a relevant residential purpose or a relevant charitable purpose (see **42.10** above).
(7) The supply of qualifying services in the course of a qualifying conversion into premises for use for a relevant residential purpose (see **42.13** above).
(8) The supply of qualifying services in the course of the renovation or alteration of a qualifying residential property last used for a relevant residential purpose (see **42.13** above).

Possession of a valid certificate does not mean that a supplier can automatically zero-rate or reduce-rate his charge. He must still meet all of the conditions for zero-rating or reduced-rating. The supplier must also take all reasonable steps to check the validity of the certificate, including corresponding with his customer to confirm the details of the use of the building. Such correspondence should be retained within his records. Where, however, despite taking all reasonable steps to check the validity of the certificate, a supplier fails to identify the inaccuracy and, in good faith, zero-rates or reduce-rates the supply, HMRC will not seek to recover VAT due from the supplier.

Subcontractors

Subcontractors working for a main contractor should not be issued with a certificate and so should always standard-rate their supplies.

Issue of certificates

The customer issues the certificate. He can either copy the certificate from VAT Notice 708 or create his own certificate provided it contains the same information and declaration. It must be issued before the supplier makes his supply. However, as a concession, HMRC will allow a supplier to adjust his VAT charge on receipt of a belated certificate (subject to the three-year cap) provided that

- the customer can demonstrate to the supplier that, at the time of supply, he intended that the building would be used in the way being certified; and
- all other conditions for zero-rating or reduced-rating are met.

The two available certificates confirm that the customer is eligible to receive either

- zero-rated or reduced-rated building work; or
- a zero-rated sale or long lease.

Penalties for incorrect certificates

See **52.23 PENALTIES**.

Form of certificate

The two certificates prescribed by HMRC (which have the force of law) are as follows.

Certificate for zero-rated and reduced-rated building work
1. Address of the building:
2. Name and address of organisation receiving the building work: VAT Registration number (if registered): Charity registration (if registered):
3. Date of completion (or estimated date of completion) of the work: Value (or estimated value) of the supply: £ Name, address and VAT registration number of building contractor:
4. I have read the relevant parts of Notice 708 *Buildings and construction* and certify that this organisation (in conjunction with any other organisation where applicable) will use the building, or the part of the building, for which zero-rating or reduced rating is being sought solely for (tick box as appropriate):

Certificate for zero-rated and reduced-rated building work

- a relevant charitable purpose, namely by a charity in either or both of the following ways:
  - (a) otherwise than in the course or furtherance of business,☐ or
  - (b) as a village hall or similarly in providing social or recreational facilities for a local community.☐
- a relevant residential purpose, namely as:
  - (a) a home or other institution providing residential accommodation for children,☐
  - (b) a home or other institution providing residential accommodation with personal care for persons in need of personal care by reason of old age, disablement, past or present dependence on alcohol or drugs or past or present mental disorder,☐
  - (c) a hospice,☐
  - (d) residential accommodation for students or school pupils,☐
  - (e) residential accommodation for members of any of the armed forces,☐
  - (f) a monastery, nunnery or similar establishment,☐ or
  - (g) an institution which is the sole or main residence of at least 90 per cent of its residents;☐

  and will not be used as a hospital, prison or similar institution or an hotel, inn or similar establishment.

5. I certify that the information given is complete and accurate and acknowledge that if the building, or the part of the building, for which zero-rated supplies have been obtained, within a period of 10 years from the date of its completion:

- ceases to be used solely for a relevant residential purpose and/or relevant charitable purpose;
- is no longer used to the same extent for a relevant residential purpose and/or relevant charitable purpose decreases; or
- is disposed of,

a taxable supply will have been made, on which this organisation will have to account for VAT at the standard rate.

Name (print):	Position held:
Signed:	Date:

General warning

1. Customs reserves the right to alter the format of the certificate through the publication of a new notice. You must ensure that the certificate used is current at the time of issue.

Warnings for the issuer

2. You may be liable to a penalty if you issue a false certificate.

3. You are responsible for the information provided on the completed certificate.

Warnings for the developer

4. You must take all reasonable steps to check the validity of the declaration given to you on this certificate.

5. You must check that you meet all the conditions for zero-rating or reduced-rating your supply – see Notice 708 *Buildings and construction*.

Certificate for sales and long leases of zero-rated buildings	
1. Address of the building:	
2. Name and address of organisation buying, or entering into a long lease on, the building (or part of the building): VAT Registration number (if registered): Charity registration (if registered):	
3. Date (or estimated date) of purchase or commencement of the lease: Value (or estimated value) of the supply: £ Name, address and VAT registration number of the developer:	
4. I have read the relevant parts of Notice 708 *Buildings and construction* and certify that the building, or the part of the building, for which zero-rating is being sought will be used solely for (tick box as appropriate): • a relevant charitable purpose, namely by a charity in either or both of the following ways: (a) otherwise than in the course or furtherance of business,☐ or (b) as a village hall or similarly in providing social or recreational facilities for a local community.☐ • a relevant residential purpose, namely as: (a) a home or other institution providing residential accommodation for children,☐ (b) a home or other institution providing residential accommodation with personal care for persons in need of personal care by reason of old age, disablement, past or present dependence on alcohol or drugs or past or present mental disorder,☐ (c) a hospice,☐ (d) residential accommodation for students or school pupils,☐ (e) residential accommodation for members of any of the armed forces,☐ (f) a monastery, nunnery or similar establishment,☐ or (g) an institution which is the sole or main residence of at least 90 per cent of its residents;☐ and will not be used as a hospital, prison or similar institution or an hotel, inn or similar establishment.	
5. I certify that the information given is complete and accurate and acknowledge that if the building, or the part of the building, for which zero-rated supplies have been obtained, within a period of 10 years from the date of its completion: • ceases to be used solely for a relevant residential purpose and/or relevant charitable purpose; • is no longer used to the same extent for a relevant residential purpose and/or relevant charitable purpose decreases; or • is disposed of, a taxable supply will have been made, on which this organisation will have to account for VAT at the standard rate. Name (print):	Position held:
Signed:	Date:

Certificate for sales and long leases of zero-rated buildings
General warning
1. Customs reserves the right to alter the format of the certificate through the publication of a new notice. You must ensure that the certificate used is current at the time of issue.
Warnings for the issuer
2. You may be liable to a penalty if you issue a false certificate.
3. You are responsible for the information provided on the completed certificate.
Warnings for the developer
4. You must take all reasonable steps to check the validity of the declaration given to you on this certificate.
5. You must also check that you meet all the conditions for zero-rating your supply—see Notice 708 *Buildings and construction*.

Student accommodation

Provided a new building is clearly intended primarily for use as student accommodation for ten years from the date of its completion, HMRC have agreed that higher education institutions may issue a certificate for the construction or acquisition of such a building as a relevant residential building despite any letting of the accommodation for holiday use or for non-educational conferences, etc. during vacations. (Concordat between HMRC, University Vice-Chancellors and Principals, para 37a). See also *R v C & E Commrs (oao Greenwich Property Ltd)*, Ch D [2001] STC 618 (TVC 2.94). (VAT Notice 48, ESC 3.11; VAT Notice 708, paras 16.1–16.7, 17.1, 17.2).

D-I-Y housebuilders

[42.23] A special VAT Refund Scheme puts D-I-Y builders and converters in a broadly similar position to a developer selling a zero-rated property, by refunding them the VAT on their main construction or conversion costs.

Under the scheme, HMRC must refund any VAT chargeable on the supply, acquisition or importation of any goods used in connection with construction or conversion work where the following conditions are satisfied.

(a) The work must comprise
   - (i) the 'construction of a building' 'designed as a dwelling' or number of dwellings;
   - (ii) the constructing of a building for use solely for a 'relevant residential purpose' or for a 'relevant charitable purpose'; or
   - (iii) a '*residential conversion*', i.e. the conversion of a 'non-residential' building or a non-residential part of a building into *either* a building designed as a dwelling or number of dwellings *or* a building intended solely for a relevant residential purpose *or* anything which would fall into either of those categories if different parts of a building were treated as separate buildings.

(b) The work is carried out lawfully and otherwise than in the course or furtherance of any business.

(c) The goods are building materials which, in the course of the works, are incorporated in the building in question or its site. See **42.16** to **42.18** above for goods which do and do not qualify. Refunds can be claimed on the building materials which would be zero-rated when supplied with the zero-rated work but *not* on those which would be standard-rated.

(d) The claim is made within such time and in such form and manner, contains such information, and is accompanied by such documents as HMRC require. See **42.24** below.

See **41 LAND AND BUILDINGS: EXEMPT SUPPLIES AND OPTION TO TAX** at **41.1**(2) for the definition of '*construction of a building*', **41.1**(4) for '*designed as a dwelling*', **41.1**(15) for '*relevant residential purpose*', **41.1**(13) for '*relevant charitable purpose*' and **41.1**(10) for '*non-residential*'.

Refund also covers VAT chargeable on a supply of any goods under the law of another EU country.

Conversions using contractors, etc.

Where a person carries out a residential conversion and arranges for the work to be done by someone else ('a contractor'), then provided

(i) the person's carrying out of the residential conversion is lawful and otherwise than in the course or furtherance of any business, and

(ii) the contractor is not acting as an architect, surveyor or consultant or in a supervisory capacity,

HMRC must, on a claim, refund any VAT chargeable on any services consisting of work done by the contractor.

Garages

The construction of, or the conversion of a non-residential building to, a building designed as a dwelling or number of dwellings includes the construction of, or conversion to, a garage. The dwelling and the garage must be constructed or converted at the same time and the garage must be intended for occupation with the dwelling or one of the dwellings.

[*VATA 1994, s 35; FA 1995, s 33; FA 1996, s 30; SI 2001/2305*].

Conversion of mixed use buildings

Following the decision in *C & E Commrs v Jacobs*, CA [2005] STC 1518 (TVC 15.120) (in which a former boys school used for residential and non-residential purposes was converted into four dwellings) HMRC accept that the conversion of a building that contains both a residential part and a non-residential part comes within the scope of the Refund Scheme provided the conversion results in an additional dwelling being created. It is not necessary for the additional dwelling to be created exclusively from the non-residential part. However, VAT recovery is restricted to the conversion of the non-residential part. (Business Brief 22/05).

Holiday homes

In *Jennings* [2010] UKFTT 49 (TC) (TC00362) (TVC 15.42) the tribunal decided that *VATA 1994, Sch 8, Group 5, Note 13* (which denies relief if residence throughout the year is not permitted) only applied to cases within *Group 5, Item 1*, i.e. where a building was purchased from a developer. It did not apply to cases within *Group 5, Item 2*, i.e. where a landowner arranged for a contractor to construct a building on his land. Also it should not be treated as applying to cases within *VATA 1994, s 35*, where a landowner purchased materials for the construction of a building. The tribunal observed that if a DIY builder agrees with a contractor for the construction of the entire building, that supply is zero-rated by *Group 5, Items 2 and 4*, both of which are unaffected by *Note 13*. The materials used in the construction are effectively zero-rated.

Following the *Jennings* decision, HMRC have accepted that the DIY house-builders and converters refund scheme applies to the construction of new holiday homes and to the conversion of non-residential buildings into holiday homes. HMRC had previously never applied the scheme to holiday homes since their supply by a developer attracts VAT at the standard rate. However, they have now stated that the relevant legislation does allow the same recovery of VAT on building materials for holiday homes that have been constructed by the individual for a non-business purpose (HMRC Brief 29/10).

De Voil Indirect Tax Service. See V5.164.

Making the claim

[42.24] The following two claim packs, each consisting of a claim form and guidance notes, are available from the HMRC helpline (Tel: 0845 010 9000) or from www.hmrc.gov.uk – VAT 431C 'How to claim a VAT refund for converting an existing building into a dwelling' and VAT 431NB 'How to claim a VAT refund for a new build'.

Conversions

A person is eligible to claim back VAT on building materials and services if they

- are converting a previously non-residential property (e.g. an office, shop, agricultural building or redundant school or church) into a dwelling (not for business purposes but to be used either by them or their relatives as a principal place of residence);
- are converting a previously residential property, that has not been lived in for the last ten years or more into a principal place of residence for either them or their relatives;
- have bought a converted building as a 'shell' from a developer and are fitting it out to completion as a principal place of residence for either them or their relatives; or
- are converting a building into one that is intended solely for a relevant residential purpose so long as it is not for business purposes. A relevant residential purpose means a building that is to be used for communal

residential accommodation such as a children's home, student accommodation, hospice, residential accommodation for members of the armed forces, monastery, nunnery or similar establishment.

New builds

A person is eligible to claim back VAT on building materials if they

- are constructing a new dwelling not for business purposes but to be used either by them or their relatives as a principal place of residence;
- have bought a new building as a 'shell' from a developer and are fitting it out to completion, as a principal place of residence for either them or their relatives; or
- are constructing a new building that is intended for use solely for either a relevant charitable purpose (i.e. intended to be used for non-business purposes such as a place of worship or offices used by charities for administering non-business activity, such as the collection of donations), or a relevant residential purpose (so long as it is not for business purposes). A relevant residential purpose means a building that is to be used for communal residential accommodation such as a children's home, student accommodation, hospice, residential accommodation for members of the armed forces, monastery, nunnery or similar establishment.

Extra work

Once the building has been completed, the following are examples of work that cannot be claimed for – a conservatory, a patio, double-glazed windows, tiling or a garage. Also, a person cannot claim for extra work that is done to a building which has been completed before they purchased it from a builder or developer.

Outbuildings

A claim cannot be made for any work that has been carried out on outbuildings, e.g. rooms above or attached to a detached garage; detached workshops or store rooms; sheds; stables; detached swimming pools; and annexes (such as 'granny' annexes) that cannot be disposed of or used separately from another dwelling because the annexe is not 'designed as a dwelling' in its own right. The only outbuilding that can count as part of the eligible building project is a garage, providing it is constructed or converted at the same time as the eligible building, and it is intended to be used at the same time as that building.

Submission of claims

All claims must be submitted to

HMRC DIY Claims Unit
2 Broadway
Broad Street
Five Ways
Birmingham
West Midlands B15 1BG

Tel: 0121 697 4000
Fax: 0121 697 4002

The following documentation must be sent with the claim forms.

- The planning permission.
- Evidence that the work is completed.
- A full set of building plans.
- The original VAT invoices, bills and credit notes.

Receiving the refund

HMRC aim to acknowledge a claim within five working days, and deal with the claim within six weeks of receipt, unless they need more information. If the claim is successful they will write to the taxpayer to tell them when they can expect to receive the refund.

[*SI 1995/2518, Regs 200, 201, 201A; SI 2009/1967, Regs 7–9*].

Appeals

If a claim for a refund is refused or HMRC disagree with the amount of the refund, an appeal may be made to a VAT tribunal. See **5.3**(*g*) APPEALS.

Caravans and houseboats

Zero-rated supplies

[42.25] Supplies of the following are zero-rated.

(a) **Caravans** exceeding the limits of size currently in force for trailers which may be towed on roads by a motor vehicle having an unladen weight of less than 2,030 kilogrammes. *Excluded* are certain removable contents, see **42.26** below. [*VATA 1994, Sch 8 Group 9 Item 1 and Note (a)*].
At present the limits referred to above are 7 metres long and 2.55 metres (increased from 2.3 metres from 20 April 2010: HMRC Brief 20/10) wide (excluding towing bars and similar apparatus used solely for the purpose of attaching the caravan to a vehicle). Consequently, the supply of a caravan which exceeds either of these dimensions is zero-rated. The supply of any other caravan is standard-rated.
The term 'caravan' is not defined in the VAT legislation. In practice, HMRC follow the definition in *The Caravan Sites and Control of Development Act 1960*, i.e. 'any structure designed or adapted for human habitation that is capable of being moved from one place to another (whether being towed, or by being transported on a motor vehicle so designed or adapted)'. In the case of a twin unit caravan, HMRC follow the definition in *The Caravans Sites Act 1968*, i.e. a structure 'composed of not more than two sections separately constructed and designed to be assembled on site by means of bolts, clamps or other devices'.

HMRC see the term 'caravan' as including mobile homes, residentials, statics, etc.
(VAT Notice 701/20/04, paras 2.1, 2.2).

(b) **Houseboats**, i.e. boats or other floating decked structures designed or adapted for use solely as places of permanent habitation and not having means of, or capable of being readily adapted for, self-propulsion. *Excluded* are certain removable contents. [*VATA 1994, Sch 8 Group 9 Item 2 and Note (a)*].
The term '*self-propulsion*' refers to any vessel that is either
- independently propelled; or
- not independently propelled but could readily be adapted to be capable of self-propulsion (e.g. by installing an engine, propeller or mast).

It is unlikely, therefore, that a vessel such as a barge or a yacht would be regarded as a houseboat.
(VAT Notice 701/20/04, para 7.2).

(c) **Caravans or houseboats** qualifying under (*a*) or (*b*) above which are let or loaned or, if business assets, are put to any private use or are used, or made available to any person for use, for non-business purposes, subject to the overriding exception for accommodation below. [*VATA 1994, Sch 8 Group 9 Item 3*].

The supply of *accommodation* is excluded. [*VATA 1994, Sch 8 Group 9 Note (b)*].

De Voil Indirect Tax Service. See V4.275.

Supplies associated with caravans

[42.26] For a general consideration of the recovery of input tax in relation to caravan parks, see *Stonecliff Caravan Park* (VTD 11097) (TVC 15.153) and *Harpcombe Ltd*, QB [1996] STC 726 (TVC 46.24).

(1) Accommodation

Holiday accommodation

The provision of accommodation in a caravan
- sited on a park advertised or held out for holiday use; and
- let to a person as holiday accommodation

is standard-rated.

Off-season letting

The provision of accommodation in a caravan during the off-season can be treated as exempt provided
- it is let to a person as residential accommodation;
- it is let for more than 28 days; and
- holiday trade in the area is clearly seasonal.

The supplier should keep a copy of his tenancy agreement or similar evidence to show that the caravan was occupied for residential purposes only. In such cases the whole of the let, including the first 28 days, should be treated as an exempt supply.

The holiday season normally lasts from Easter to the end of September although some areas (e.g. London) are not regarded as having a seasonal holiday trade.

Residential accommodation

The provision of accommodation in a caravan is exempt where it is

- on a site designated by the local authority as for permanent residential use; and
- let to a person as residential accommodation.

(VAT Notice 701/20/04, paras 5.1–5.3).

(2) Brick skirting

The provision of brick skirting is generally integral to the agreement to supply a caravan and its liability follows the liability of that supply.

The input tax that is attributable to these supplies should be determined accordingly.

(VAT Notice 701/20/04, para 3.6).

(3) Car parking/garage fees

The supply of a garage or parking space in conjunction with the supply of a permanent residential caravan pitch is exempt providing

- the supplier retains ownership of the land on which the garage or parking space is sited; and
- the garage or parking space is reasonably close to the caravan pitch.

In all other circumstances supplies of garages and parking are standard-rated.

(VAT Notice 701/20/04, para 6.1).

(4) Caravan pitches

See **41.3**(*e*) **LAND AND BUILDINGS: EXEMPT SUPPLIES AND OPTION TO TAX** for the liability of pitch fees and rents received for the granting of the right to caravan owners to keep their caravans on pitches.

Pitch agreements generally impose certain obligations upon site owners such as the construction of pitches, bases and the park infrastructure. Any one-off charge raised which is directly related to these obligations follows the liability of the supply of the pitch.

Reservation fees or premiums charged by a park owner are part of the consideration for the pitch and follow the liability of the pitch fee or rent.

(VAT Notice 701/20/04, paras 4.1, 4.7, 4.8).

(5) Commission received

Park owners' commission on sales of second-hand sited caravans

The 'commission' which a park owner is entitled to receive under the *Mobile Homes Acts* and/or Code of Practice when a caravan owner sells a caravan 'on site' at his park follows the liability of the pitch fee or rent.

Any additional charge to the seller in connection with the sale (e.g. for agency services) is standard-rated.

Charges made to dealers, allowing them to place caravans which have been sold on an owner's site, are standard-rated. Where the charge is passed on to the caravan purchaser it is treated as part of the dealer's costs and forms part of the consideration for the caravan. The VAT treatment will follow the liability of the caravan.

Fees received by park owners from third parties

Any commission from a caravan manufacturer/dealer for the sale of a caravan is standard-rated.

(VAT Notice 701/20/04, paras 3.4, 3.5).

(6) Delivery, unloading and positioning charges

Such charges made by the supplier of the caravan at the same time as that supply, provided they are reasonable, follow the liability of the 'delivered' caravan. This applies whether the supply is made by the manufacturer, dealer or site owner. Any delivery service provided which is unconnected with the supply of the caravan is standard-rated.

(VAT Notice 701/20/04, para 3.3).

(7) Electricity, gas, water and sewerage charges

Connection to mains services

Where a park owner makes a charge to a caravan owners to connect their caravan to the mains services (gas, electricity, water and sewerage) available at their pitch:

- If the charge is for a first and one-off connection fee, it forms part of the consideration for the supply of the caravan and its liability follows that of the caravan. (The connection fee does not include general maintenance or the provision of the infrastructure which supplies the utilities to the pitch itself.)
- In all other cases connection fees are to be treated as standard-rated.

From 1 January 2012 charges made by caravan site owners for first time connection to electricity, gas, water and sewerage will be subject to the same VAT liability as the pitch (generally standard-rated, in the case of holiday/leisure sites; exempt, in the case of residential sites) unless the site owner identifies and charges for the actual consumption of users (i.e. through metering at the pitch), in which case the connection charge will be subject to the same VAT liability as the supply of the utility (reduced-rated for electricity and gas; zero-rated for water and sewerage). (HMRC Brief 37/11).

Electricity and gas

Supplies of electricity and gas to a caravan are liable at the reduced rate provided the users actual consumption can be identified (i.e. it is metered). Otherwise, the liability of the supply follows that of the main supply of the pitch rental.

Where, for touring caravans and motor homes, an optional hook-up charge is made and the caravan owner chooses to have electricity supplied to the pitch, the supply is subject to VAT at the reduced rate. Any non-optional charge forms part of the overall pitch fee which is standard-rated.

Water and sewerage charges

Charges by a park owner to individual caravan owners for these utilities may be zero-rated if they cover supplies received by the park owner which are supplied on to the caravan owners. The supplies received by the park owner must be apportioned on a fair and reasonable basis and consumption by the communal buildings, other common parts of the park and caravans owned by the park owner must be excluded in calculating the zero-rated charges to individual caravan owners. As an apportionment method, it would normally be acceptable to use the rateable value of that part of the site attributable to the individually owned caravans.

Where, for touring caravans and motor homes, an optional hook-up charge is made, the supply is zero-rated. Any non-optional charge forms part of the overall pitch fee which is standard-rated.

(VAT Notice 701/20/04, paras 3.2, 4.2, 4.3).

From 1 January 2012 charges made by caravan site owners for water and sewerage will remain zero-rated if actual consumption can be identified (i.e. through metering at the individual pitch). In other circumstances, charges will follow the VAT liability of the caravan pitch (generally standard-rated, in the case of holiday/leisure sites; exempt, in the case of residential sites). (HMRC Brief 37/11).

(8) Fixtures, fittings and removable contents

Where the supply of a caravan is zero-rated, then zero-rating also applies to those goods which a builder would ordinarily incorporate into a new house (e.g. sinks, baths, WCs, fixed partitions and water heaters). See **42.16** and **42.17** above for further details. Other fixtures and any removable contents supplied with the caravan (e.g. tables, chairs, mattresses, seat cushions, fridges, carpets, washing machines) are standard-rated. The fact that they form a single supply with the zero-rated caravan does not prevent the fixtures from being standard-rated under UK legislation. *Talacre Beach Caravan Sales Ltd v C & E Commrs, ECJ Case C-251/05*, [2006] STC 1671 (TVC 22.507).

If a caravan and its removable contents are advertised at separate prices and the customer is entirely free to purchase the caravan at the lower price without the removable contents, then, provided the breakdown between the two figures is not a sham, the charges for the removable contents may be treated as a separate taxable supply. Otherwise, and in all cases where there is a single consideration, an apportionment is required. Methods for arriving at the value of the removable contents in new and used caravans are described below. These methods do not have to be used but any different method must give a fair and reasonable result.

New caravans

Standard-rated removable contents included in the price of a new caravan can be calculated by reference to the costs incurred.

> *Example*
>
> In November 2011 a caravan is purchased from a manufacturer for resale. Its cost is £20,000 plus £150 VAT giving a total cost of £20,150. It is sold for £30,000 including VAT.
>
> The VAT on sale must be the same proportion of the sale price as it was of the total cost.
>
> VAT due = sale price × VAT on purchase ÷ total cost
>
> = £30,000 × 150 ÷ £20,150 = £223.32

If further removable contents are added to those provided by the manufacturer (or some provided are taken out) before sale, these costs must be added/subtracted as appropriate before making the above calculations.

Used caravans

Standard-rated removable contents included in the price of used caravans can be calculated using either of the following methods. Whichever method is adopted, it must be applied consistently and a supplier must not alternate between methods when calculating the VAT due on each of his supplies.

- *Actual values.* Calculate a precise value for each of the standard-rated removable contents. Adequate documentary evidence must be produced to support each valuation if required.
- *Standard apportionment of values.* This is a standard method of apportionment that has been agreed with the National Caravan Council Ltd and the British Holiday and Home Parks Association Ltd. The value of the standard-rated removable contents is taken as 10% of the VAT-exclusive selling price of the complete caravan. If a caravan is sold at a VAT-inclusive price, the VAT element in that price is 1/6 (7/47 before 4 January 2011; 3/23 from 1 December 2008 to 31 December 2009).

  If the margin scheme for **SECOND-HAND GOODS (61)** is used for sale of the caravan, then the 10% apportionment is applied to the margin rather than the full selling price. The margin is always be VAT-inclusive, so the VAT is calculated as follows:

  Margin on the sale of caravan × 10% × 1/6 (7/47 before 4 January 2011; 3/23 from 1 December 2008 to 31 December 2009).

Other charges included in the selling price

Charges made at the time of supply of the caravan for delivery, unloading and positioning (see (6) above) and for connections to mains services (see (7) above) are regarded as part of a single supply of the caravan, and form part of its price. If any of the above methods of apportionment are used, the calculation should be made on the total of all such amounts. Other charges, such as reservation fees or premiums, pitch fees or commissions should be excluded from the calculations.

(VAT Notice 701/20/04, paras 3.1, 8.1–8.6; VAT Notice 700/57/04).

(9) Insurance

Insurance premiums paid by a park owner to cover general liability or risks are exempt. If the park owner recovers this cost by making a separate charge to caravan owners, the charge is treated as part of the overall consideration for the supply of the pitch and has the same VAT liability as the pitch fee or rent.

Where a park owner is asked by a caravan owner to arrange insurance cover for the caravan owner's risks, any charge made, or any commission earned, for arranging the insurance is exempt provided the caravan owner is the recipient of the supply of insurance made by the insurer.

Any payments received in relation to the renewal of existing insurance policies follow the liability of the original supplies as above.

(VAT Notice 701/20/04, para 4.6).

(10) Local authority charges

For seasonal or holiday parks, the park owner must pay non-domestic rates on the whole site. If the park owner attributes a proportion of the rates to individual caravan owners using the official apportionment made by the local valuation officer (under Regulation 4 notice), any charge is outside the scope of VAT.

Any onward charge of the rates element for the communal buildings, general facilities, etc. or any caravans owned by the site owner, is part of the pitch fee or rental and is standard-rated.

For permanent caravan parks, caravans not owned by the site owner attract non-domestic rates and are subject to council tax for which the resident or owner is liable.

(VAT Notice 701/20/04, para 4.4).

From 1 January 2012 where caravan site owners recharge a proportion of their business rates to individual caravan owners, the recharge will follow the VAT liability of the pitch fee (usually standard-rated in the case of holiday/leisure sites). (HMRC Brief 37/11).

(11) Maintenance of common areas

Any costs relating to the development or maintenance of the common areas of the park (e.g. installation of street lighting, resurfacing of roads, planting of trees and erection of fences) relate exclusively to the supply of the pitches. Recovery of the input tax depends on whether the site is a residential or holiday site.

(VAT Notice 701/20/04, para 6.3).

(12) Miscellaneous charges

Other charges made to individual caravan owners by the park owner are standard-rated. These include:

- Holiday booking services
- Off-season storage and security (on-pitch or off-pitch). Storage of touring caravans is always standard-rated (whether or not a specific area of land is granted to the caravan owner and including contracts where the period of storage is in excess of one year).
- Club membership.
- Repair and maintenance of caravans.
- Drainage of water-systems.

(VAT Notice 701/20/04, paras 6.2, 6.4).

(13) Service charges

Service charges to individual caravan owners for general upkeep and maintenance of the park as a whole (its common areas) follow the liability of the pitch fee or rent. Specific services provided to particular residents are normally standard-rated.

(VAT Notice 701/20/04, para 4.5).

Houseboats

Accommodation; Delivery, unloading and positioning charges; Connection to mains services; and Fixtures, fittings and removable contents

[42.27] The same provisions apply as for caravans in **42.26** above.

Mooring rights

Mooring rights for a houseboat are exempt. See **41.3**(*h*) **LAND AND BUILDINGS: EXEMPT SUPPLIES AND OPTION TO TAX** for moorings generally.

Garages and parking spaces

The supply of a garage or parking space to the owner of a houseboat is exempt provided it is

- supplied by the person who is supplying the mooring; and
- reasonably close to the mooring.

(VAT Notice 701/20/04, paras 7.4–7.8).

Key points

[42.28] Points to consider are as follows.

- The freehold or long leasehold sale of a new dwelling by the person constructing it is zero-rated. This includes the sale of a building that has been converted from a non-residential building, e.g. a barn converted to a bungalow and sold.
- A long leasehold sale means a lease that is greater than 21 years (20 years in Scotland).
- The advantage of a property sale being zero-rated rather than exempt (as in the case of the second and subsequent sales of the dwelling) is that input tax can be reclaimed on the related costs of the project, i.e. building materials, professional fees.
- A planning point, if a builder rents out a new dwelling rather than sells it (rental income is exempt), is to sell the new building to a connected business, and the latter business then generates the rental income. This protects the input tax recovery for the first business, i.e. it has still made the zero-rated sale of a new dwelling, even though to a connected party.
- A property can only be classed as a new dwelling if the conditions of building use (usually linked to planning issues) allow the buyer to use the property as his main residence and live there throughout the year. Restrictions on use mean that zero-rating will not apply (e.g. as in the case of holiday accommodation).
- In cases where a sale includes both a new dwelling and another building, e.g. flat above a shop, then the value of the sale must be apportioned on a fair and reasonable basis so that zero-rating only applies to the new dwelling. Surveyor or estate agent valuations are usually the best methods of determining the split.
- Zero-rating also applies to the first time sale of a new building by a builder if it is to be used as either a 'relevant residential building' (e.g. an elderly persons home, student accommodation) or as a 'relevant charitable building' (e.g. a church). In both cases, the builder must obtain a certificate from the buyer to confirm the use will qualify for zero-rating.
- The services of a builder involved in the construction of a new dwelling are also zero-rated. This applies irrespective of whether the builder is acting as the main contractor or a sub-contractor working for the main contractor.
- In the case of building services carried out on a new relevant residential building or relevant charitable building, zero-rating only applies in relation to the services of the main contractor. He must hold a certificate from the building owner confirming the intended use of the building when it has been completed. The services provided by subcontractors working for the main contractor are always standard-rated.

- Building services that involve converting a non-residential building into a dwelling(s) or relevant residential building (office into elderly persons home) are subject to the reduced rate of VAT. The exception is if the work is being carried out for a housing association, in which case zero-rating can be applied (but only for the main contractor).
- A useful planning point is that zero-rating in the case of building services also applies to materials provided by the builder as part of his work. This is particularly useful if there is no input tax recovery for the building owner on the project in question (e.g. renting out dwellings).
- Building work which is classed as an approved alteration to a protected building is zero-rated, as long as the building in question is either (or will become after the work has been carried out) a dwelling, relevant residential building or relevant charitable building.
- An approved alteration in the case of work on a protected building means that listed building or other planning consent must have been obtained in relation to the work. Work of a repair or maintenance nature is always standard-rated.
- A builder carrying out an approved alteration to either a relevant residential building or relevant charitable building will need a certificate from the building owner to confirm the use or intended use of the building. The certificate should be issued at the beginning of the project.
- Professional services relating to architects, surveyors and managing agents etc. are always standard-rated, irrespective of the work being carried out.
- It is important to identify when the reduced rate of VAT can be applied by builders working on a project. This is particularly important if the landlord cannot reclaim input tax on the project as there is a big difference between the reduced rate of VAT (5%) and the standard rate of VAT.
- The main situations when the 5% rate of VAT applies to building works are as follows: conversion of a non-residential property into a residential property; work on a residential property that has been empty for two or more years; work on a residential property (or properties) where a different number of units is evident after the work has been completed compared to the beginning (e.g. converting a detached house into two flats).
- The reduced rate of VAT also applies to the services of subcontractors, unless it relates to a relevant residential building, when only the main contractor in receipt of a certificate from the building owner can benefit from charging the reduced rate.
- In the case of work carried out on a property that has been empty for two years or more, it is important that the builder obtains and retains evidence of the empty period (e.g. council tax records etc.). This evidence is important to confirm the reduced rate of VAT was correctly charged in the event of an HMRC visit.

- An input tax block applies to certain goods installed in a new dwelling, if the items are not classed as building materials. Carpets, white goods (washing machines, dishwashers etc.) and furniture items are examples of goods where an input tax block is applied. There is no problem with wood flooring or tiling.
- A useful planning point for a builder supplying standard-rated (or reduced rated) services is to raise an application for payment or request for payment in relation to ongoing contracts, rather than a tax invoice. If an invoice is then issued when payment has been received from the customer, this will become the date when VAT is payable on a return.
- Many builders could also benefit from the cash flow advantages of the cash accounting scheme. The scheme is available to any business with annual taxable sales (excluding VAT) of £1.35m or less. The disadvantage of the scheme is that input tax cannot be reclaimed on a supply until payment has been to a supplier.
- The flat-rate scheme can be used by a builder with annual taxable sales of £150,000 or less (excluding VAT). However, the scheme is unlikely to be worthwhile for a builder who has some zero-rated or reduced rated sales because the relevant scheme percentage is applied to these sales as well.
- Private individuals building their own homes (or converting a non-residential property into a new dwelling) can benefit from VAT recovery on material costs through the DIY scheme.
- It is important that any zero-rated or reduced rated building services are correctly identified because HMRC will not refund any incorrectly charged VAT through the DIY scheme.

43

Local Authorities and Public Bodies

Cross-references. See **8.1 BUSINESS** for the meaning of 'business'; **16.12 EDUCATION**; **51.16 PAYMENT OF VAT** for repayment supplement; **52.12 PENALTIES** for serious misdeclaration or neglect resulting in understatements or overclaims; **53 PENSION SCHEMES**.

Introduction

[43.1] For a transaction to be within the scope of VAT, it must, amongst other conditions, be made by a taxable person. Certain 'bodies governed by public law' are given special treatment under EU legislation. They are not treated as being taxable persons when they engage in certain transactions which, if engaged in by other persons, would result in them being considered taxable persons.

Although the term '*bodies governed by public law*' is used in *Directive 2006/112/EC*, the phrase is not used in UK law. In *EC Council Directive 93/36* it is interpreted as any body

- established for the specific purpose of meeting needs in the general interest, not having an industrial or commercial character;
- having legal personality; and
- financed, for the most part, by the State, or regional or local authorities, or other bodies governed by public law, or subject to management supervision by those bodies, or having an administrative, managerial or supervisory board, more than half of whose members are appointed by the State, regional or local authorities or by other bodies governed by public law.

Treatment as non-taxable persons

Specifically, state, regional and local government authorities and other bodies governed by public law are not considered taxable persons in respect of activities or transactions where the following conditions are met. This applies even where they collect dues, fees, contributions or payments in connection with these activities or transactions.

(a) The body is engaged in the activity or transaction 'as a public authority'

There is nothing in EU legislation specifying those activities in which bodies engage as public authorities and it does not follow that just because a body is a public authority that all activities it undertakes are non-taxable activities (or 'non-business' as such activities are more commonly referred to in the UK).

In *Comune di Carpaneto Piacentino and Others v Ufficio Provinciale Imposta sul Valore Aggiunto di Piacenza, ECJ Case C–4/89*, [1990] 3 CMLR 153 (TVC 22.130) the ECJ held that activities pursued as 'public authorities' were those engaged in by bodies governed by public law under the special legal regime applicable to them, but did not include activities pursued by them under the same legal conditions as those applying to private traders.

For example, a body would be acting as a public authority where the law gives it

- the right to make people or organisations pay for a service provided but without giving them any say in what is, or how it is provided; and
- powers to impose penalties where people do not comply.

Following the Court of Session decision in the case of *Edinburgh Telford College v HMRC* [2006] STC 1291 (TVC 22.149), HMRC accept that when considering whether activities are undertaken under a 'special legal regime', it is necessary to consider the wider legal regime governing the management and conduct of an activity, and not to focus solely on the legal regime governing the delivery of a particular service (HMRC Brief 27/08).

In *Norwich City Council* (VTD 11822) (TVC 42.11) it was accepted that the Council was a body governed by public law. The Council granted advertising facilities to commercial sponsors of various campaigns which it organised but did not account for VAT on the sponsorship payments. The tribunal held that although the Council was using the sponsorship payments in support of its statutory functions, the sponsorship deals were not in themselves part of the statutory functions of the Council and were carried out under the same legal provisions as applied to private traders.

In *Arts Council of Great Britain* (VTD 11991) (TVC 7.80) the Council's main activity was the distribution of an annual Parliamentary grant. The tribunal held that this was not an economic activity. Although the Council was not a specified body within *VATA 1994, s 33(3)* (see **43.2** below), it was 'a public body, performing a public function, whose costs were paid out of public funds'.

See also *Royal Academy of Music* (VTD 11871) (TVC 55.15) where the tribunal held that the Academy was not a public authority body and was not governed by public law so that its activities fell outside the scope of what is now *Directive 2006/112/EC, Art 13*.

Following the High Court judgment in *Riverside Housing Association Ltd v HMRC* [2006] STC 2072 (TVC 15.115), HMRC stated that the term 'body governed by public law' was narrow in application, in that a body only satisfies that criterion if it is a public body that forms a part of the UK's public administration, such as a government department, a local authority or a non-departmental public body (HMRC Brief 27/2008).

(b) Treatment as a non-taxable person does not lead to a significant distortion of competition

There is no definition in UK law to quantify the term 'significant' in relation to distortion of competition. In *Comune di Carpaneto Piacentino* above the ECJ considered the matter but did no more than decide that individual EU countries should determine whether distortion of competition was significant and that they were not required to lay down precise quantitative limits. In *HMRC v Isle of Wight Council (No 2), ECJ Case C–288/07* [2008] STC 2964 (TVC 22.138) the ECJ held that significant distortions of competition must be evaluated by reference to the activity in question, without such evaluation relating to any local market in particular. The expression 'would lead to' was to be interpreted as encompassing not only actual competition, but also potential competition, and the word 'significant' was to be understood as meaning that the actual or potential distortions of competition must be more than negligible.

HMRC take the view that significant distortions of competition occurs when non-business treatment

- places private traders at a commercial disadvantage compared to the body; or
- deters private traders from starting up businesses supplying similar goods or services in competition with the body.

Significant distortion can result if a body

- does not charge VAT on a supply, while its competitors making similar supplies have to; or
- recovers the VAT attributable to an exempt supply or a non-business activity, while the VAT incurred by its competitors in making similar supplies effectively sticks with them as a real cost.

See *Metropolitan Borough of Wirral* (VTD 14674) (TVC 22.145) where a district council operated an information service, collecting and distributing information relating to the county in which it was located, in accordance with a statutory requirement. The tribunal held that the work in question could have been undertaken by a private organisation and that to treat the council as a non-taxable person would be unfair on private organisations.

If a body has no local competitor, an activity can be treated as non-business provided no other person could carry out the activity in the same way, and in similar conditions, as the body has to carry it out, and thereby achieving the results as the body has to achieve. HMRC regard this as normally applying where

- the body's clients could not equally well obtain the goods or services from some other supplier;
- the activity is not carried on generally by suppliers outside the public authority sector, unless on such a small scale as to be negligible; and
- non-business treatment would not act as a disincentive to a private trader capable of going into business in direct local competition with the body.

The question of the extent of competition was considered in *The Lord Mayor and Citizens of the City of Westminster* (VTD 3367) (TVC 22.143). The city council managed a hostel providing accommodation to homeless men. The tribunal held that the accommodation provided was of such a type that the council was clearly not supplying services in competition with proprietors of commercial hotels, inns or boarding houses and therefore no distortion of competition arose from the supply being treated as non-business.

In most cases it should be clear whether treating a particular activity as non-business would lead to significant distortion of competition. In cases of doubt, the body should contact HMRC.

Many of the activities which local authorities have a statutory obligation to provide are now subject to contracting out and competitive tendering (e.g. domestic refuse collection). In these cases, whilst the tenderers are in competition to supply the service to the responsible local authority, there is no competition to provide the service to third parties. Such services provided under a statutory obligation to a third party using an outside body acting as agent are non-business provided there is no competition between the local authority and others to supply the services to the third party.

(c) Unless carried out on such a scale as to be negligible, the activity does not relate to

- telecommunications;
- the supply of water, gas, electricity and steam;
- the transport of goods;
- port and airport services;
- passenger transport;
- supply of new goods manufactured for sale;
- the transactions of agricultural intervention agencies in respect of agricultural products carried out pursuant to Regulations on the common organisation of the market in these products;
- the running of trade fairs and exhibitions;
- warehousing;
- the activities of commercial publicity bodies;
- the activities of travel agencies;
- the running of staff shops, co-operatives and industrial canteens and similar institutions; and

- transactions of radio and television bodies of a commercial nature.

[*Directive 2006/112/EC, Art 13(1)*]. (VAT Notice 749, paras 5.4–5.7).

Exempt activities

EU countries *may* consider activities of bodies governed by public law which are exempt under *Directive 2006/112/EC, Arts 132–137* (see **18.25** and **18.26** **EUROPEAN UNION LEGISLATION**) or *Art 371* (see **18.43** **EUROPEAN UNION LEGISLATION**) as activities which they engage in as public authorities. [*Directive 2006/112/EC, Art 13(2)*].

UK provisions

[43.2] UK law does not specifically refer to 'bodies governed by public law' (see **43.1** above). However, it does provide special treatment for 'specified bodies'. The combined effect of the EU and UK provisions is as follows.

(1) All 'bodies governed by public law', which phrase includes but is not restricted to 'specified bodies', can treat certain of their activities as non-taxable activities (or 'non-business' activities as they are more commonly referred to in the UK). See **43.3** below for a consideration of business and non-business activities.
Any such body that is registered, or liable to be registered, for VAT (see **43.5** below) must charge and account for VAT on all its business activities, subject to the normal rules. This applies whether the customer is a private individual, trader, government department or another public body. It must not charge VAT on non-business activities.

(2) As a general rule, it is only possible to recover VAT incurred if registered for VAT and if the VAT can be attributed to taxable business activities. Where VAT relates to non-business or (subject to certain *de minimis* limits) exempt activities, any VAT incurred 'sticks' as a real cost. To minimise this sticking VAT, a special scheme allows 'specified bodies', whether or not registered for VAT, to
   - reclaim the VAT suffered on non-business activities (see **43.7** below); and
   - recover any VAT attributed to exempt business activities where HMRC consider it an insignificant proportion of the total VAT incurred (see **43.8** below).

It should be noted that 'bodies governed by public law' which are not 'specified bodies', although not benefiting from the special scheme under (2) above, are still able to treat certain otherwise taxable business supplies as non-business.

The '*specified bodies*' are as follows.

(a) A '*local authority*', i.e.
   - the council of a county, county borough, district, London borough, parish or group of parishes (or, in Wales, community or group of communities),
   - the Common Council of the City of London,
   - the Council of the Isles of Scilly,

- any joint committee or joint board established by two or more of the foregoing, and
- in relation to Scotland, a regional, islands or district council within the meaning of the *Local Government (Scotland) Act 1973*, any combination and any joint committee or joint board established by two or more of the foregoing, and any joint board to which *section 226* of that *Act* applies.

The following are not considered to be local authorities.

- Joint boards/committees set up by bodies other than local authorities, even where they include local authorities as members or participants, e.g. boards established by order of a Minister of the Crown.
- Bodies which merely receive financial assistance from local authorities.
- Purely advisory committees which do not carry out local authority functions.
- Community Councils in England or Scotland.
- Community Associations.
- Parish meetings.
- Parochial church councils.
- Village hall management committees.
- Charities.

(b) A river purification board established under *Local Government (Scotland) Act 1973, s 135* and a water development board within the meaning of the *Water (Scotland) Act 1980, s 109*.

(c) An internal drainage board.

(d) An integrated transport authority, passenger transport authority or passenger transport executive for the purposes of *Transport Act 1968, Part II*.

(e) A port health authority within the meaning of *Public Health (Control of Disease) Act 1984*, and a port local authority and joint port local authority constituted under *Public Health (Scotland) Act 1897, Part X*.

(f) A police authority.

(g) A development corporation within the *New Towns Act 1981* or the *New Towns (Scotland) Act 1968*; a new town commission within the *New Towns Act (Northern Ireland) 1965* and the Commission for the New Towns.

(h) A general lighthouse authority within the meaning of *Merchant Shipping Act 1995, Part VIII* (except that no VAT refund is made which HMRC consider is attributable to activities other than the provision, maintenance or management of lights or other navigational aids).

(i) The British Broadcasting Corporation.

(j) The appointed news provider referred to in *Communications Act 2003, s 280* (except that no VAT refund is made which HMRC consider is attributable to activities other than the provision of news programmes for broadcasting by holders of regional Channel 3 licences within the meaning of *Broadcasting Act 1990, Part 1*).

(k) Any body specified by an order made by the Treasury. Currently, these comprise

- the Commissions for Local Administration in England, Wales, and Scotland; and the Commission for Local Authority Accounts in Scotland [*SI 1976/2028*];
- the Inner London Education Authority, the Inner London Interim Education Authority; The Northumbria Interim Police Authority; the London Fire and Civil Defence Authority; the London Residuary Body; a metropolitan county Police Authority, Fire and Civil Defence Authority, Passenger Transport Authority or Residuary Body [*SI 1985/1101*];
- a probation committee constituted by the*Powers of Criminal Courts Act 1973, s 47, Sch 3 para 2* (now replaced by local probation boards under *Criminal Justice and Courts Act 2000*); a magistrates' courts committee established under *Justice of the Peace Act 1979, s 19*; and the charter trustees constituted by *Local Government Act 1972, s 246(4)* or *(5)* [*SI 1986/336*];
- authorities established under *Local Government Act 1985, s 10* (waste regulation and disposal authorities) [*SI 1986/532*];
- National Rivers Authority [*SI 1989/1217*];
- the Environment Agency [*SI 1995/1978*];
- a National Park authority (within the meaning of *Environment Act 1995, s 63*) [*SI 1995/2999*];
- a fire authority constituted by a combination scheme made under *Fire Service Act 1947, s 6* [*SI 1995/2999*];
- charter trustees established under *Local Government Act 1992, s 17* or any other statutory instrument made under*Part II* of that Act [*SI 1997/2558*];
- the Broads Authority [*SI 1999/2076*];
- the Greater London Authority [*SI 2000/1046*];
- the London Fire and Emergency Planning Authority [*SI 2000/1515*];
- Transport for London (the body established under *Greater London Act 1999, s 154*) [*SI 2000/1672*];
- the Greater London Magistrates' Courts Authority [*SI 2001/3453*];
- the London Pensions Fund Authority [*SI 2006/1793*];
- a Transport Partnership created by an order made under *Transport (Scotland) Act 2005, s 1(1)* [*SI 2006/1793*];
- the Charter Trustees for the City of Chester, Crewe, the City of Durham, Ellesmere Port and Macclesfield [*SI 2009/1177*]; and
- the Wimbledon and Putney Commons Conservators [*SI 2009/1177*].

[*VATA 1994, ss 33(3)–(5), 96(4); Merchant Shipping Act 1995, Sch 13; Communications Act 2003, Sch 17 para 129; SI 1995/1510, Art 2*]. (VAT Notice 749, paras 2.2, 4.1, 4.2).

Business and non-business activities

[43.3] Because of the special provisions which apply to them, it is important for 'bodies governed by public law' (see **43.1** above), which include the 'specified bodies' listed in UK law (see **43.2** above), to distinguish between their business and non-business activities. The following steps should be considered in reaching a decision.

(a) Is the body making the supply a 'body governed by public law' (see **43.1** above)?
(b) If Yes, go to (*b*).
If No, the activity is business.
(c) Is the body engaged in the activity 'as a public body' (see **43.1**(*a*) above)?
If Yes, go to (*c*).
If No, the activity is business.
(d) Would non-business treatment lead to a significant distortion of competition (see **43.1**(*b*) above)?
If Yes, the activity is business.
If No, go to (*d*).
(e) Is the activity one of those specified in the list in **43.1**(*c*) above?
If Yes, go to (*e*) below.
If No, go to (*f*) below.
(f) Is the activity carried out on a negligible scale?
If Yes, go to (*f*) below.
If No, the activity is business.
(g) Is the body a Government Department or Health Authority (see **43.11** below)?
If Yes, go to (*g*) below.
If No, the activity is non-business.
(h) Is the activity subject to a Treasury direction (see **43.11** below)?
If Yes, the activity is business.
If No, the activity is non-business.

The restriction on non-business treatment for the activities under (*d*) above has little practical effect on most specified bodies as

- they do not generally engage in these activities as 'public authorities' and therefore fail the test under (*b*) above; and
- where the activities are carried out as 'public authorities', they are generally also provided by private bodies and non-business treatment would lead to a significant distortion of competition so that the test under (*c*) above would be failed.

(VAT Notice 749, para 5.1).

De Voil Indirect Tax Service. See V2.108, V2.242.

Common activities of local authorities and police authorities

[43.4] Specified bodies within **43.2** above which are registered for VAT can claim a refund of the VAT they incur on both their business and their non-business activities (see **43.7** below) and do not have to separate the VAT incurred on the two types of activity. It is, however, important to distinguish between business and non-business activities for output tax and partial exemption purposes. It is also important to distinguish between such activities when dealing with non VAT-registered bodies who may incorrectly treat business activities as non-business and consequently not register for VAT at the correct time.

This paragraph considers a number of activities in relation to specified bodies.

(1) Bailiffs

If local authorities are unsuccessful in obtaining payment of council tax from defaulters, they may contract with bailiffs to collect the arrears plus any statutory charges for the enforcement of the debt. Bailiffs supply their services to, and should therefore invoice, the local authority for their statutory charges and any agreed commission based on the amount of the arrears due or collected. VAT is chargeable on the full value of these services and not the lesser amount received from the local authority where payments from debtors are retained and netted-off against the total charge. The local authority can recover the VAT it is charged because it relates to its non-business activity of collecting the council tax. (HMRC VAT Guidance V1–14, para 7.2).

(2) Beach huts

Under *Public Health Act 1936, s 232* local authorities may provide huts or other conveniences for bathing on any land belonging to them or under their control, and may make charges for their use. The law neither requires local authorities to provide beach huts nor states that they must do so in a particular way. Consequently, provision of beach huts by a local authority is a standard-rated business activity. See also *Shearing* (VTD 16723) (TVC 7.26) and *Poole Borough Council* (VTD 7180) (TVC 41.126). (HMRC VAT Guidance V1–14, para 7.3).

(3) Car parking charges

Where a public authority imposes charges (including excess parking charges) for parking at meter bays on the public highway, it does so under statutory powers that nobody other than a public authority can exercise. This activity is non-business.

As regards off-street parking in garages, buildings and open spaces, in *C & E Commrs v Isle of Wight Council*, Ch D 2004 [2005] STC 257 (TVC 22.138) the tribunal held that the Council was not engaged in a business activity when providing off-street parking as the provision of those spaces was subject to the *Road Traffic Regulation Act 1984*. On appeal, the High Court remitted the case to the tribunal to consider the substantive issue of whether treating the council's receipts as non-taxable would lead to 'significant distortions of competition' (which the tribunal had not originally taken into account). The tribunal held that, in this particular case, non-taxation of off-street parking did not significantly distort competition. It also held that, in the case of car parking, competition should be considered in the circumstances prevailing in individual local authorities rather than on a nationwide basis although it did state the view that taxation on the grounds of significant distortion of competition should be applied only in exceptional circumstances. On appeal of this decision, the High Court referred the case to the ECJ for a ruling on the interpretation of 'significant distortions of competition'. ([2007] All ER(D) 208 (Feb)). The ECJ held that significant distortions of competition must be evaluated by reference to the activity in question, without such evaluation relating to any local market in particular. The expression 'would lead to' was to be interpreted as encompassing not only actual competition, but also potential competition, and the word 'significant' was to be understood as meaning that the actual or potential distortions of competition must be more than negligible (*Case C–288/07* [2008] STC 2964). Pending the decision, HMRC will not accept claims for refunds from other local authorities which should continue to account for VAT. (Business Brief 4/06).

HMRC have always accepted that penalty charges imposed by local authorities operating off-street parking under the *Road Traffic Act 1991* are outside the scope of VAT. In *Bristol City Council* (VTD 17665) (TVC 62.214) the tribunal decided that excess charges levied by the Council in its off-street car parks were outside the scope of VAT because they were levied under the *Road Traffic Regulation Act 1984* and were not part of the contract between the driver and the council. In HMRC's view, where a car park operator makes an offer of parking under clear terms and conditions, setting punitive fines for their breach, the fines constitute penalties for breaching the contract, rather than additional consideration for using the facilities. Consequently they are outside the scope of VAT. However, where the terms and conditions make it clear that the driver can continue to use the facilities after a set period upon payment of a further amount without being in breach of the contract then the payment is consideration for use of the facilities and subject to VAT. This applies whether the operator of the car park is a local authority or a commercial enterprise.

(VAT Notice 749, para 5.8; HMRC Brief 57/08).

(4) Care and welfare

Most local authorities are required to provide a wide range of services to people of all ages, ranging from children and young persons to the provision of accommodation and domiciliary care for elderly persons. They may be entitled to make a charge to recover all or part of the costs they incur in providing these services.

- Where an authority is acting under a special legal regime applicable to it and not under the same legal conditions as those that apply to private traders, these activities are non-business.
- Where an authority merely provides residential accommodation, for example, because someone has chosen it in preference to similar facilities available from a charity or commercial provider, if such accommodation is not provided under a statutory function the supply of accommodation by the authority is a business activity. Similarly, the supply of services such as creches and playgroups, and recreational holidays for elderly people not in statutory care is a business activity.

(VAT Notice 749, para 5.8).

(5) Cemeteries and crematoria

The provision and maintenance of cemeteries by a local authority is a non-business activity but the provision of crematoria is primarily a business activity. (VAT Notice 749, para 5.8). See also **15.6 DEATH AND INCAPACITY**.

(6) Coastal defence contributions

Local authorities which border the sea are required to obtain contributions, usually from those who derive most benefit, towards the cost of maintaining coastal defence facilities (e.g. sea walls). HMRC take the view that these contributions are not consideration for a supply of services but outside the scope of VAT. (HMRC VAT Guidance V1–14, para 7.8).

(7) Disposal of goods under special legal provisions

The police have statutory powers to dispose of goods the owners of which cannot be traced (e.g. property handed into police stations and recovered after the detection of a crime, abandoned vehicles, goods found in local authority property, etc.). The statutory powers relate only to the circumstances of acquisition and disposal and not to the supply of the goods. As the goods disposed of are second-hand goods commonly supplied in the private sector, their supply is a business activity. (HMRC VAT Guidance V1–14, para 15.6).

(8) Education

See **16.12 EDUCATION**.

(9) Housing and property improvements

Local authorities have wide statutory obligations and powers in relation to housing.

(a) The provision and operation of social housing

(i) *Bed and breakfast accommodation*. Where, due to a shortage of its homes for letting, a local authority has to place homeless people in bed and breakfast accommodation, it is carrying out a non-business activity. The local authority does not have to account for output tax on any contributions it receives towards the cost of providing such accommodation (e.g. housing benefit paid directly to it by the Department of Work and Pensions).

The supply of the accommodation is to the local authority, not to the homeless, so the reduced VAT rate for long-term residents cannot be applied.

(ii) *Home improvements and tenants contributions*. Most local authorities have a rolling programme to maintain or improve the quality of their housing stock. Where a tenant has no choice in the matter, any permanently increased rent is a charge for the overall supply of the right to occupy the accommodation which is a non-business activity.

Where improvements are carried out only at the tenants request, the local authority may seek a contribution from the tenant towards the costs of the improvement work. These contributions may take the form of a lump sum payment or instalments paid with the rent. Lump sum payments, or instalments paid with the rent but over a limited period only, are generally standard-rated (but see **28.14** *et seq* **HEALTH AND WELFARE** for zero-rating of certain supplies to disabled persons). Any permanently increased rent is a charge for the overall supply of the right to occupy the accommodation which is a non-business activity.

(iii) *Third party management of local authority housing stock*. Many local authorities delegate the management and maintenance of their housing stock to a tenant management company either in the form of a Tenant Management Co-operative (TMC) or a Tenant Management Organisation (TMO).

A TMC enters into a standard agreement with the local authority under which repairs and maintenance are the delegated responsibility of the TMC. It acts as principal in purchasing materials and carrying out the work or engaging contractors to carry it out on its behalf. The TMC receives the supplies of goods or services and receives a management and maintenance allowance from the local authority. The local authority cannot recover input tax on the supplies of goods and services. But, if the TMC is VAT-registered, as the delegated maintenance relates to the non-business activity of providing housing, the local authority can recover any VAT charged to it by the TMC under **43.7** below.

A TMO takes on varying degrees of management responsibility and receives payments from the local authority for a range of services it may undertake. It can also administer and collect rents. Most supplies received by the TMO, whose costs are reimbursed by the local authority, are supplies to an agent acting in its own name. The only supplies a TMO normally makes as principal relate to its management charges to the local authority. If the TMO is VAT-registered, this can be recovered by the local authority under **43.7** below as relating to its non-business activity.

(iv) *Local authority garage rentals*. The letting of garages is normally standard-rated but, subject to certain conditions, where it is let in conjunction with a dwelling it can take on the same liability as the dwelling. See **41.3**(*f*) **LAND AND BUILDINGS: EXEMPT SUPPLIES AND OPTION TO TAX** for further details. As the letting of houses and flats by a local authority is a non-business activity, where it lets garages/parking spaces to a housing tenant and the necessary conditions are met, the supply is non-business.

Under 'right to buy' legislation, council tenants can buy, rather than rent, their homes. Where they have continued to rent a garage, the liability of the garage rental depends on whether the main property has been sold freehold or leasehold. Following a freehold sale, the rental of the garage becomes a taxable supply because the local authority is no longer the landlord for the dwelling. But following a leasehold sale, where the tenant continues to pay ground rent to the local authority, the local authority remains the landlord (albeit only the ground landlord). In these circumstances, where a tenant pays ground rent for both the dwelling and the garage, or pays ground rent for the dwelling and rents the garage, the provision of the parking facility is a non-business activity.

(v) *Repair and maintenance of dwellings.* Any repairs to its housing stock which a local authority is responsible for and which it carries out without charge are considered to be part of the non-business activity of providing public sector housing.
Any charge made to a tenant still in residence is a standard-rated supply of services to the tenant. Any charge for repairs and making good to a tenant who has vacated premises and left them in an unfit condition are regarded as compensation and outside the scope of VAT. Similarly, charges made to third parties to recover the costs of repairing damage to council dwellings are also regarded as compensation.
Any VAT incurred in carrying out repairs to dwellings can be recovered, either as input tax or under the refund scheme in **43.7** below.

(vi) *Refugees.* The provision of housing (and lighting, heating, food, etc.) for refugees by a local authority is a non-business activity.

(b) Property improvements, including grant funding

(i) *Care and Repair scheme.* This is designed to provide help to elderly and disabled homeowners to enable them to improve their property. Any grant from a local authority or the Office of the Deputy Prime Minister is outside the scope of VAT. The scheme is administered by a limited company but is carried out by a care and repair agency which may be a charity or housing association but is usually a local authority. The agency makes all arrangements for the work to be carried out and makes all payments on behalf of the homeowner, charging a percentage of the cost of the building works as its fee.
The services of the agency are a business activity when carried out by a local authority although the supplies are exempt under *VATA 1994, Sch 9 Group 7, Item 9* (see **28.12 HEALTH AND WELFARE**).
As actual contracts for the work are between the homeowner and the building contractor, the local authority cannot recover VAT charged by the builder to the homeowner.

(ii) *Default works.* A local authority may issue an enforcement notice to a person who has failed to maintain their property in a satisfactory state of repair.
Where the recipient of the notice agrees to the work being carried out and arranges for either the local authority or some other contractor to undertake it, the contractor's service are supplies to the recipient of the notice. If the local authority arranges the contractor's supplies on behalf of the recipient, it may treat the supply as being made both to it and by it under *VATA 1994, s 47(3)* (see **3.4 AGENTS**).
Where the recipient of the notice refuses to comply, the local authority may exercise its statutory powers to have the work carried out and recover the cost from the recipient. As only a local authority can issue the default notice and exercise these statutory powers, this is a non-business activity. See also *Glasgow City Council* (VTD 15491) (TVC 42.6) where the tribunal held that works in default and the subsequent recovery of costs under *Housing (Scotland) Act 1987, ss 108, 109* were not supplies for VAT purposes.

When the supply of the work is to the local authority, it can recover the VAT charged by the contractor. If it makes an onward taxable supply of the work in the course or furtherance of business, it can recover the VAT incurred as input tax. If it does not make a taxable supply but imposes the work under its statutory powers, it can recover the VAT under the refund scheme in **43.7** below.

(iii) *Property improvement grants*. For a consideration of grants generally, see **71.9**(2) **VALUATION**. The most important points to consider are to whom is the supply made, who actually owns the grants, and what happens to any contributions made by third parties.

The most common situations are those where a local authority funds part of the cost of a householder's planned improvements work by means of a grant. There are normally two ways in which grant-funded improvements are carried out.

The first method is where the homeowner has arranged directly with a builder to carry out some works and a grant is paid by the local authority for that work to be done. The local authority payment is a third party consideration which does not entitle it to recovery under the scheme in **43.7** below. See *Doncaster Borough Council* (VTD 12458) (TVC 42.2).

The second method is where the homeowner has arranged with the local authority for it to act as his agent in organising the building work. The local authority's contributions are still third party consideration and it is not entitled to recovery under the scheme in **43.7** below. If the local authority charges for its agency services to the homeowner, then that fee is standard-rated. This follows the decision in *Ashfield District Council v C & E Commrs*, Ch D [2001] STC 1706 (TVC 42.3).

(iv) *Group repair schemes and block improvement grants*. Local authorities in England and Wales have powers under *Housing Grants, Construction and Regeneration Act 1996, s 65* to carry out improvements to the exterior of blocks and terraces of private sector housing with the permission of the properties' owners ('group repair schemes'). Normally, the local authority receives a grant from central government and a compulsory contribution from the property owner towards the costs of the work. The contribution by the property owner and any grant received direct from central government are also outside the scope of VAT. However, where the owner asks the local authority to provide additional works for a separate payment, this is a business supply.

The local authority can recover any VAT incurred in carrying out non-business activities under the provisions in **43.7** below but any VAT incurred in making business supplies must be recovered under the normal rules.

(c) Building inspection fees

(i) *Planning, building notice, inspection and reversion fees. In England and Wales*, competition exists across the whole range of building control work and such services provided by local authorities are business. *In Scotland and Northern Ireland*, the supply of building control services is the monopoly of local authorities and classed as non-business for VAT purposes.

Local authorities retain their statutory monopoly over planning applications and reversions and the fees they charge for this work is non-business.

(ii) *Regularisation fees.* Where a local authority issues a regularisation certificate because building work has been carried out without its prior approval, as approved inspectors in the private sector do not have the legal power to carry out this function, this is a non-business activity.

(d) The provision and maintenance of community projects, including village halls

(i) *Village halls owned by the local authority.* Where the local authority uses its own funds to carry out work to the hall, it is not making a supply for VAT purposes. Where it receives funds from another body (e.g. a village hall management committee) the funds are most likely to be consideration for its use of the hall. Alternatively, the funds may be a donation and outside the scope of VAT.

Whether the local authority can recover the VAT incurred on the work depends on the use to which the hall is put. If it is used for the local authority's own non-business activities, the VAT is recoverable under **43.7** below. If it is used to make a business supply (e.g. use in return for a payment), the normal VAT rules will apply. If the local authority uses donated funds to make a purchase it can recover the VAT incurred under **43.7** below provided it makes the purchase itself (i.e. places the order, receives the supply and a VAT invoice addressed to it and makes payment), retains ownership of the purchase and uses it or makes it available for its own non-business purposes, and keeps sufficient records for the purchase (and the purpose for which it is made) to be easily identified.

(ii) *Village halls not owned by the local authority.* If the local authority uses its own funds to carry out work to such a hall, and it then gives this work away to the owners (e.g. a voluntary group), this is not a supply for VAT purposes provided that it receives nothing in return. Any VAT incurred is recoverable under the scheme in **43.7** below. If it does receive something in return (including non-monetary consideration such as use the hall) it is likely to be consideration for the taxable business supply of the works.

If the hall is owned by a voluntary group and they, or a third party, pass funds to the local authority which arranges work to the hall, then these funds are likely to be the consideration for the supply of the work to the voluntary group. The local authority may act as a 'main contractor' (receiving supplies and making an onward business supply to the voluntary group, the consideration for which is the funding received) or may act as the agent of the voluntary group in arranging the work on its behalf.

(e) Shared ownership schemes

Such arrangements usually involve the sharing of equity in a dwelling between an occupier and a housing association. The occupier purchases a dwelling at a proportion of its value and then pays rent to cover the share in the equity retained by the housing association. Under these circumstances, the rent paid by the occupier is consideration for a supply in the course of business by the housing association. Where local authorities enter into similar shared ownership schemes and receive payment of rents, the activity is also business.

(f) Sales and letting of land

Where a local authority sells and lets land and property, it is in direct competition with the private sector. These are normally business transactions. However, by concession, where a local authority provides domestic accommodation to people seeking housing (normally on a list maintained by the authority) or disposes of properties under the 'right to buy' legislation, it is non-business, regardless of the circumstances and whether or not they are acting under any special legal regime applicable to them.

(g) Housing stock transfers

In order to bring their housing stock up to the Government's 'decent homes standard', many local authorities have transferred their stock to registered social landlords (RSLs) once residents have been balloted and agreed to proposals.

The transfer of housing stock is considered to be a non-business activity by the selling local authority (apart from any commercial properties, shops, garages for non-residents and residential or other properties bought for investment purposes, where the normal rules apply).

Housing stock transfers can take one of two forms with differing VAT consequences.

Under the first method, the RSL agrees to purchase the housing stock in its existing condition, and any refurbishment works that may be required is paid for by the purchasing RSL. Any VAT that the purchasing RSL incurs on the refurbishment works cannot be recovered as it is wholly attributable to the letting activities of the RSL. This was confirmed in *South Liverpool Housing Ltd* (VTD 18750) (TVC 42.21).

Under the second method, the RSL agrees to purchase the housing stock, but as a condition of purchase (normally a contractual requirement) requires the local authority to improve the properties. As sometimes thousands of properties are involved, and it would be impractical for the parties to enter into a piecemeal arrangement whereby a housing unit only passed to the RSL once the local authority had upgraded it, normally the house stock passes to the RSL before it has been upgraded, but the local authority enters into a binding obligation to ensure that the necessary works of maintenance are undertaken at its expense. The local authority can recover the VAT incurred on these works under the scheme in **43.7** below (even though most of the work actually takes place after the housing has been transferred) provided the following conditions are satisfied.

- The transfer contract must contain a clear obligation on the part of the local authority to carry out the works (or there must be a suitable addendum or other document detailing this obligation).
- The scope and quantum of the works must have been agreed prior to the transfer, and this information should form part of the contract.
- The scope of the works should only relate to local authority tenants, common areas, and the outside fabric for right-to-buy leaseholders or freeholders.
- The works in question must be supplied to the local authority (i.e. the local authority must have entered into one or more contracts for the works to be done and paid consideration for the works).
- From time to time the local authority will be expected to substantiate any VAT claims by providing a clear audit trail which links the VAT to the works required under the transfer contract.

It does not matter that the parties have agreed for the RSL to undertake the works as building contractor and charge the local authority accordingly. The local authority is not allowed to recover VAT on works that are the responsibility of the RSL after the transfer has taken place (e.g. day-to-day repairs and maintenance).

(VAT Notice 749, para 5.8; HMRC VAT Guidance V1–14, paras 9.1, 11.2–11.5; Business Brief 19/98).

(10) Local authority and NHS joint stores depots

Operation

Some joint store depots are operated by a local authority and others by NHS bodies. The organisation which operates and maintains a depot must charge VAT on the income received as payment for the services it supplies (e.g. salary costs and fuel and power). This charge is often made as a supplement to charge for stock or as a periodic charge. A local authority recipient of these services is able to reclaim this VAT (subject to the normal rules). An NHS body recipient may currently claim it as a refund under the contracted-out service regime.

Stock purchase

Only one participant in a joint stores' arrangement is responsible for accounting for an item of stock within its books. It is this participant that is to incur any VAT charged when the goods are taken into stock. When stock is ordered, arrangements should be made to ensure that the purchase invoice provided by the supplier to the operator is made out to the participant with accounting responsibility for the item in question. However, HMRC are willing to grant prior approval for an alternative to cover the few occasions where this may cause difficulty (e.g. the inability to use bulk purchase facilities). This allows the store operator

(i) to initially purchase the stock;
(ii) to sell on those items for which the other party has accounting responsibility; and

(iii) for the items referred to at (ii) to reclaim the equivalent VAT on the supplier's invoice as input tax, having invoiced the other party and charged VAT as output tax.

VAT reclaims on stock items are available only by a local authority recipient and only when it has accounting responsibility (subject to the normal rules).

Hire of stock

Where the participant with responsibility for accounting for an item of stock within its books 'lends' or hires it to the other (i.e. to cover temporary shortages) VAT should not be levied on any charge made because this is not seen to be a business activity for VAT purposes. Where items are hired in from outside contractors, VAT reclaims are available only to a local authority recipient and only when it has accounting responsibility (subject to the normal rules)

(HMRC VAT Guidance V1–14, para 8.10).

(11) Local authority purchasing consortia

Under *Local Authorities (Goods and Services) Act 1970* a number of authorities may get together to form a joint committee which acts as a central purchasing organisation known as a Local Authority Purchasing Consortia (LAPC).

Following the decision in *Comune di Carpaneto Piacentino and Others v Ufficio Provinciale Imposta sul Valore Aggiunto di Piacenza, ECJ Case C–4/89*, [1990] 3 CMLR 153 (TVC 22.130) HMRC have concluded that LAPCs are not acting under any special legal regime and that their supplies do not fall to be treated as non-taxable under *Directive 2006/112/EC, Art 13*. They are not, therefore, entitled to use the refund scheme under **43.7** below.

(HMRC VAT Guidance V1–14, para 7.28).

(12) Mayoral/chairman's expenses

A mayor or chairman, although elected, is treated in the same way as an employee when carrying out official duties. Any input tax incurred in the course of official duties can be recovered provided

- the local authority accepts responsibility for the actual expenses incurred and enters them in its normal accounts;
- the goods/services are ordered in the name of the authority and invoices are addressed to it, and
- adequate records are kept.

If a car is used to transport the mayor between home and civic events, the related motoring expenses can be recovered if the above conditions are met. If a car is made available for a mayor's private use, VAT recovery on its purchase is blocked.

Input tax cannot be recovered on any flat-rate allowance given in the form of money placed freely at the disposal of the mayor/chairman.

(HMRC VAT Guidance V1–14, para 7.21).

(13) Meals on wheels

Local authorities may use the services of their own staff to provide the meals or may buy them in from outside contractors. Alternatively, they may use the services of voluntary organisations who act as their agent in preparing and/or delivering the meals. The provision of meals to the elderly for a charge is a non-business activity of the local authority if provided as a part of a package of care (see **43.12** below). Otherwise the supply is liable to VAT at the standard rate. Any charge made to the local authority by the voluntary body or other organisation for implementing the service is also taxable, regardless of whether the supply is below cost or whether it includes an incidental element of care provided to the recipient of the meal. However, the local authority can recover the VAT charged under **43.7** below.

Facilities for home cooking

Instead of making arrangements for a daily delivery of meals on wheels, some local authorities make periodic deliveries of frozen meals. To support this activity, they supply cost price mini freezers, microwaves and steamers to the recipients of the food. Equipment sold in this way to facilitate a package of non-business welfare is itself a non-business supply. Any equipment that is sold for a profit, or which does not form part of a package of care, is subject to normal VAT liabilities.

(HMRC VAT Guidance V1–14, para 9.4).

(14) Motor mileage allowances and fuel scale charges

Where a local authority or other 'specified body' within **43.2** above pays its employees mileage allowances to reimburse them for the cost of road fuel incurred on business activities, the body can recover the input tax under the same conditions as apply to other businesses. See **45.15 MOTOR CARS**. By concession, a statutory body can recover the VAT it incurs on mileage allowances paid to all persons engaged on its official activities, including its non-business activities. The concession extends not only to employees but also to councillors, JPs and voluntary workers acting as agents of the authority (e.g. the WRVS delivering meals on wheels). It also covers mileage rates paid to police doctors and to parents taking their children to school where the local authority would otherwise be obliged to provide transport (e.g. in rural areas). HMRC require that

- the individual receiving the mileage allowance is not a taxable person;
- there is a contract (written or oral) between the body and the individual covering the activities in question;
- the individual carries out the activity on a regular basis; and
- the body is obliged to undertake the activity on which the road fuel costs are incurred (or would be if the recipient of the mileage allowance did not do so).

Alternatively, where a specified body provides an employee or other person with road fuel or reimburse them for fuel used, VAT must be accounted for using the scale charges in **45.17 MOTOR CARS** if the car is used for the *business* activities of the body and the latter funds any private motoring.

(HMRC VAT Guidance V1–14, Chapter 2 paras 7.23, 7.30).

(15) Open government

Normally, the provision of information is a standard-rated supply, unless it can be zero-rated as printed matter. But under the *Freedom of Information Act 2000* public authorities (including all local authorities, police authorities and Government departments) must provide certain information if requested. Any charge made is non-business. This non-business treatment also extends to information that they are not obliged to provide (because the cost of provision is too high) but which they choose to provide for a charge.

There is no obligation for authorities to provide information that is available from other sources, even if the enquirer cannot readily access those other sources (e.g. because they do not have internet access). Information provided in these circumstances is a business activity.

(HMRC VAT Guidance V1–14, para 7.27).

(16) Police authorities

(i) *The escort and transportation of prisoners.* Following the increasing tendency for the majority of such services to be supplied by private security firms, this is now regarded as a business activity. In a few instances, there is still a legal requirement for police authorities, or other similar official bodies, to carry out prisoner escort duties. Such services remain non-business activities.

(ii) *Police attendance at sporting events.* Local authorities are required by the *Safety of Sports Grounds Act 1975* to issue safety certificates on such terms and conditions as they consider necessary to designated stadia in their area. Where such a certificate includes conditions which make it obligatory on the holder to request the provision of police officers prior to each event, this creates a statutory monopoly for the police authority and therefore the provision of the police is a non-business activity. If, however, the holder of the certificate is not under an obligation to request the presence of the police but can instead have the event 'policed' by a private sector security firm, there is no statutory monopoly. Provision of police in these circumstances is in competition with the private sector and is a business activity.

Policing outside a stadium is non-business as this is policing in a public place. Policing in off-street shopping centres is commonly a business supply when a charge is made because many of these sites are privately owned, and the police patrol at the request of the centre managers. The supply is standard-rated as private security firms can also provide such a service.

(iii) *Contracted out vehicle removal.* See **47.8**(14) **OUTPUT TAX.**

(HMRC VAT Guidance V1–14, paras 15.7, 15.14).

See also HMRC VAT Guidance V1–14, para 16 for examples of police activities and their VAT liabilities.

(17) Recycling credits

Under *Environmental Protection Act 1990, s 52(1)* waste disposal authorities must pay waste collection authorities when they divert waste from the household waste stream for recycling. Where waste is collected and sent for recycling by third parties (e.g. local scout groups or existing recycling companies) then both disposal and collection authorities have powers, under *Environmental Protection Act 1990, s 52(3)(4)* to pay credits to the third parties.

The payment of these recycling credits is not the consideration for a supply and is therefore outside of the scope of VAT. However, in some cases, although credits may be due to a third party, they may be retained by a local authority as consideration for a supply made to that third party (e.g. the granting of a licence to occupy a site for a bottle bank). In these circumstances, the credits retained by the local authority are not outside the scope of VAT but follow the liability of the supply for which they are being treated as consideration.

(HMRC VAT Guidance V1–14, para 7.29).

(18) Returning officers' and other election expenses

Parliamentary and European elections

Council officers frequently act as returning officers in Parliamentary and European elections. However, they are not acting as an officer of the council but in a different capacity. The Office of the Deputy Prime Minister (ODPM) makes a payment to the local authority for the provision of a returning officer to compensate it for one of its staff being diverted from local authority functions. As a local authority has to provide a returning officer by law, this payment is not subject to VAT. Similarly, where a local authority is required by law to provide polling places (e.g. schools) and other services, any reimbursement by the ODPM is not subject to VAT. The transport of ballot boxes is not done under any statutory obligation and is standard-rated.

Where local authorities have to provide certain facilities by law, any VAT incurred on their provision will be recoverable under **43.7** below. But where the returning officer has bought goods or services from sources other than the local authority, any VAT incurred is not recoverable by the local authority and should be included in any reimbursement received from the ODPM.

The ODPM also provides funding for the purchase of such election requirements as polling booth screens and ballot boxes. Often these will be bought for the returning officer by the local authority. If the items will be used in a local election (see below) as well as other elections, the local authority can recover the VAT in full. If, however, they are bought exclusively for Parliamentary or European elections, the local authority can only recover VAT to the extent that it recharges it to the returning officer as his buying agent. Such VAT recharged to the returning officer should form part of his funding from the ODPM.

Local elections

The local authority is under a statutory obligation to provide the returning officer and it can recover any VAT it incurs in connection with local elections under the refunds scheme in **43.7** below.

(HMRC VAT Guidance V1–14, para 7.12).

(19) Social services activities

See HMRC VAT Guidance V1–14, para 10.3 for a list of the duties and VAT status of various social services activities in relation to children, the elderly, and the disabled.

(20) Sports and leisure

If a local authority charges members of the public for sporting or recreational facilities, it is not acting in its capacity as a public authority and the activity is business.

(i) *Supplies of sporting services*. Most sporting services are exempted from VAT. See **57.10 RECREATION AND SPORT**. However, local authorities are specifically excluded from the exemption and sporting services provided by them remain taxable. If the services include an element of educational training or instruction, they may qualify as exempt supplies of education. See **16.4 EDUCATION**.

(ii) *Operation of leisure centres*. Local authorities may deliver leisure services by means of a
- direct service organisation (DSO) within the local authority's own leisure services department;
- non-profit distributing organisation (NPDO) such as a trust or industrial and provident society, in which the local authority may have a degree of representation; or
- a wholly independent 'for profit' leisure management contractor.

In the case of a DSO, it is the local authority itself that makes all supplies. Otherwise, the various arrangements that flow from the contracting-out process can give rise to a number of potential supplies for VAT purposes. The precise nature of these supplies and the VAT treatment of them is set out in a Memorandum of Understanding jointly agreed by HMRC and the Chartered Institute of Public Finance and Accountancy.

Leisure service membership schemes

Many local authorities offer leisure schemes where a customer can make periodic payments, normally monthly or annually, to receive free or discounted use of the authority's leisure facilities. This scheme membership is a standard-rated charge for the right to use the facilities unless the membership is exclusively for exempt activities when the charge is exempt. If the membership is used for a variety of taxable and exempt activities the charge is not to be apportioned, but is treated as wholly standard-rated. A tax point arises every time that the member pays an instalment of the fee. If the total charge for paying by instalments is greater than that for a one-off fee, then the extra charge is for an exempt supply of finance.

(VAT Notice 749, para 5.8; HMRC VAT Guidance V1–14, paras 13.1–13.3). See HMRC Brief 28/07 for the Memorandum of Understanding referred to above.

(21) Statutory licences, etc.

Public authorities charge for various forms of licensing and approval in a broad range of public activities taking place in their area (e.g. approving premises for civil marriages, registering childminders, issuing fire certificates, and licensing and registering firearms). In doing so, they are empowered to act under special legal provisions that private traders cannot call upon. This is a non-business activity. (VAT Notice 749, para 5.8).

(22) Supplies between local authorities

(i) *Supplies of goods*. Following the decision in *Comune di Carpaneto Piacentino and Others v Ufficio Provinciale Imposta sul Valore Aggiunto di Piacenza, ECJ Case C–4/89*,, [1990] 3 CMLR 153 (TVC 22.130) HMRC have concluded that supplies of goods between local authorities are not made under any special legal regime and that the supplies do not fall to be treated as non-taxable under *Directive 2006/112/EC, Art 13*. They are not, therefore, eligible for the refund scheme under **43.7** below.

(ii) *Supplies of services*. Supplies of services which include a supply of goods should be treated as business and taxable according to the normal rules. Services supplied between local authorities are non-business where they are made under a statutory obligation or where they are not in competition with the private sector. Otherwise supplies of services are business supplies.

(VAT Notice 749, para 5.2; HMRC VAT Guidance V1–14, para 7.32; Business Brief 9/95).

(23) Supplies of staff

Following the decision in *Comune di Carpaneto Piacentino and Others v Ufficio Provinciale Imposta sul Valore Aggiunto di Piacenza, ECJ Case C–4/89*, [1990] 3 CMLR 153 (TVC 22.130), if a specified body within **43.2** above supplies the services of its staff

- under the same legal conditions as those applying to private businesses, it is not acting in its capacity as a public body and the supply is in the course or furtherance of a taxable business activity; and
- under a special legal regime applicable to it, the body is acting in its capacity as a public body. It can treat the supplies of staff it makes as non-business providing that such treatment would not lead to a significant distortion of competition with other bodies. See **43.1**(*b*) above.

Taxable business activities include secondments of staff by

- one police authority to another for purely administrative purposes;
- a police authority to outside organisations to advise, for example, about security matters;

- a local fire service to an outside organisation to advise on fire safety matters;
- a local authority Direct Labour Organisation (DLO) to boost the management team of another DLO; or
- an LEA to an examination board to advise on methods of assessment.

Non-business activities include

- a police authority providing normal policing assistance to another force (e.g. in connection with an ongoing investigation) or seconding officers to the National Crime Squad or the National Criminal Intelligence Service;
- local authority fire brigades seconding experienced serving officers to the Fire Service College to act as instructors in advanced safety and rescue techniques (as no other organisations have the necessary expertise to offer an equivalent service to the college); and
- agreements to release, rather than supply, staff (e.g. where teachers undertake GCE and GCSE exam work or where staff are seconded to other government departments or commercial companies for career development purposes). Where staff are seconded in these circumstances and have two discrete contracts, then the authority is not considered to be making a taxable supply of the services of staff. Any reimbursement of salary is not liable to output tax. However, if the authority makes a charge for administration, this is consideration for the supply of a payroll service, and it must account for output tax on the supply.

(VAT Notice 749, para 5.8; HMRC VAT Guidance V1–14, para 7.33).

(24) Voucher schemes

Local authorities operate a number of different voucher schemes to enable them to fulfil their statutory obligations (e.g. for clothing/school uniform, decorating materials, etc.). The schemes involve the issue of vouchers by the local authority which the holder can exchange for specific goods or services at nominated suppliers. The supplier forwards the redeemed vouchers to the local authority which then refunds the supplier up to the value of the vouchers redeemed.

There are no output tax implications for the authority when the vouchers are issued (providing it receives no consideration). It can only recover input tax on goods/services supplied under the various schemes where the supply is to the local authority which then makes an onward supply to the recipient. These conditions are met if the local authority

- holds a proper VAT invoice addressed to it from the supplier;
- has entered the purchase in its normal accounts; and
- holds the redeemed vouchers submitted to it by the supplier of the goods.

The local authority can only recover input tax on the value of the voucher or, if less, the value of the goods or services supplied.

(HMRC VAT Guidance V1–14, para 7.34).

(25) Weighing instruments

The *evaluation* and *surveillance* of non-automatic weighing instruments, to meet EU requirements, is a service that any trader with the necessary expertise can supply commercially. If a local authority carries it out, the activity is business. On the other hand, where a local authority charges to *verify* such instruments, it does so in its capacity as a public authority, using legal powers that no private contractor is entitled to exercise. Such verification is a non-business activity. (VAT Notice 749, para 5.8).

(26) Youth centres

There are two types of youth centre.

- *A youth centre which is part of the local authority*. HMRC accept that any purchase it makes from its own funds is actually made by the local authority which can reclaim any VAT incurred (subject to the normal rules). If income from taxable activities of the youth centre accrues to the local authority, it must also account for output tax.
- *Youth centres with charitable status*. These are independent of the local authority which is not normally entitled to recover VAT on any of the costs incurred.

However, in some cases, independent youth centres may donate funds to the local authority for a specific purpose. Where this occurs, the local authority is eligible for VAT refund if it

(i) makes the purchase (i.e. places the order, etc.);
(ii) retains ownership;
(iii) uses the items purchased for its own non-business purposes; and
(iv) keeps sufficient records of the purchase and the purpose for which it was made to enable it to be easily identified.

If these conditions are not met, the normal VAT rules apply. The money given represents consideration for a supply by the local authority to the independent youth centre and the local authority must account for VAT.

VAT recovery

Common areas of expenditure incurred by youth centres include the following.

(a) *Utility costs* (e.g. gas and electricity). The VAT incurred is only recoverable by the local authority under **43.7** below if the youth centre is part of the local authority (and not if the centre is independent of the local authority but donates money to it to cover utility costs).
(b) *Repairs and maintenance to buildings*. The treatment is broadly similar to that under (*a*) above. However, if the local authority holds the freehold or lease on the premises and does not charge the independent youth centre for use of the premises, the authority is normally entitled to recover any VAT incurred.
(c) *Minibuses*. Where an individual youth centre purchases a minibus, the VAT treatment is as under (*a*) above. Where the purchase is by a local authority using donated funds, the local authority can recover the VAT if it satisfies (i)–(iv) above. Alternatively, HMRC may accept that the local authority can recover VAT on the purchase if

- use of the minibus is pooled, i.e. it is available for use by more than one youth centre;
- the minibus carries the local authority logo;
- the local authority treats it as part of its assets, covering repair and maintenance costs; and
- the local authority does not charge the centres for use of the minibus.

Where this applies, however, the local authority must account for output tax when the vehicle is sold.

Where an independent youth centre buys a minibus using grants provided by the local authority, the authority cannot recover the VAT.

(d) *Fixtures and fittings*. A local authority can recover VAT it incurs on fixtures and fittings, including sports equipment, at its own youth centres. If it uses donated funds to make the purchase, it can recover VAT if it satisfies (i)–(iv) above. This means that the items must become assets of the local authority and be available for use by other youth centres. A local authority may also recover the VAT it incurs on purchases made from its own funds and then freely given away to independent youth centres.

(e) *Private fund income*. Some local authority youth centres may undertake activities independently of the local authority. Any income arising as a result is 'private fund' income, normally paid to a separate account, and does not form part of local authority funds. The private fund is a separate entity for VAT purposes and the local authority cannot recover the VAT incurred on any of its purchases and need not account for output tax on supplies made by the fund.

Liability of income of local authority youth clubs

Because local authority youth centres are provided under the *Education Act 1996*, and this is a special legal regime, membership fees and subscriptions are non-business. Separately charged for activities and events will also generally be non-business.

- *Social evenings, outings and similar events*. Where such activities are arranged by the youth service for the members of the club, this income is non-business. This does not apply to events organised by other parties (e.g. where the youth service merely arranges for its members to be able to buy discounted tickets from an event organiser which remains a business supply by the event organiser to the individuals who take up the offer). Neither does it apply to events and activities attended by other people unless the numbers of such people are minimal (e.g. family outings where youth club members will not be in the significant majority are not non-business).
- *Coin operated machines*. The provision of games, amusements and entertainment machines form part of the youth service and any income derived from them is non-business.
- *Tuck shops and cafes*. Provided that sales within club premises to club members are made at or below their overhead-inclusive cost, they can be treated as non-business.

(HMRC VAT Guidance V1–14, para 7.36).

(27) Youth offending teams (YOTs)

YOTs are set up by local authorities, in partnership with police authorities, probation committees and health authorities, to establish a local structure of teams and services to deal with young offenders. Each YOT must contain at least a social worker, probation officer, police officer, a person nominated by a health authority in the local authority area, and a person nominated by the local authority's Chief Education Officer. The local authority receives funding from the Home Office for the project and the partners (who may or may not receive Home Office funding) are responsible for their share of staff and any associated costs.

Local authorities and police authorities can recover any costs under the refund scheme in **43.7** below. The only bodies unable to benefit from the refund scheme are health authorities and probation committees, although they are able to recover VAT on certain contracted out services under *VATA 1994, s 41* (see **43.11** below).

Because of the possibility of double claims by different bodies, HMRC suggest that YOT committees should 'appoint' the local authority as the claiming body for the purposes of **43.7** below (although they have no objections to the police being appointed). Any staff provided by the members would be outside the scope of VAT (as they are not being supplied to the local authority but to the scheme) and any funds that may be given would be considered outside the scope contributions.

In certain cases, local authorities may form joint YOTs. In such cases, HMRC recommended that one authority takes the lead for refund purposes, with the other simply making outside the scope contributions.

(HMRC VAT Guidance V1–14, para 7.37).

Registration

Public bodies other than local authorities

[43.5] The normal registration rules apply to public bodies other than local authorities, including those specified bodies listed in **43.2** above, i.e. they are required to be registered only if their taxable supplies exceed the registration limit (see **59.3 REGISTRATION**) but they may apply for voluntary registration under **59.2 REGISTRATION**. Exemption from registration can be sought in cases where the majority of supplies are zero-rated and if registered, they would normally be in a repayment situation. See **59.6 REGISTRATION**.

Local authorities

Every local authority which makes taxable supplies (including zero-rated supplies) in the course or furtherance of its business is required to be registered *whatever the value of its supplies*. [*VATA 1994, s 42*]. Despite this, if a local authority makes only infrequent or minimal taxable supplies, it may not need to register for VAT. Advice should be sought from HMRC.

Group registration

Public bodies cannot normally meet the requirements of joining a VAT group. But HMRC will normally grant a request by a local authority joint committee to account for VAT under the registration of its lead authority or any other member if satisfied that

- it does not want the arrangement merely for tax avoidance purposes; and
- it does not create distortion.

(VAT Notice 749, paras 3.1–3.3).

Acquisitions of goods from other EU countries

Even if a local authority or other statutory body is not required to register under the general requirements based on taxable supplies in the UK, it may be liable to register for VAT where it makes certain acquisitions of goods from other EU countries in excess of an annual threshold. See **59.18 REGISTRATION**.

Reclaiming VAT

[43.6] Where bodies within **43.2** above incur VAT in connection with taxable business activities, they can recover the VAT as input tax subject to the normal rules.

However, many of the activities of such bodies are non-business activities for VAT purposes and outside the scope of VAT. As a general rule, it is only possible to recover any VAT incurred if registered for VAT and if the VAT can be attributed to taxable business activities. Any VAT that relates to non-business or (subject to certain limits) exempt activities is not recoverable. To minimise this 'sticking' VAT for such bodies, a special scheme allows them to

- reclaim the VAT suffered on non-business activities (see **43.7** below); and
- recover any VAT attributed to exempt business activities where HMRC consider it an insignificant proportion of the total VAT incurred (see **43.8** below).

Refund scheme for non-business activities

[43.7] Generally, there is no entitlement to recovery of VAT incurred for the purposes of non-business activities. However, a special refund scheme permits a specified body within **43.2** above to reclaim the VAT chargeable on supplies of goods or services to it, acquisitions of goods by it from other EU countries and imports of goods by it from outside the EU if

- the supply, acquisition or importation is not for the purposes of a business activity carried on by the body concerned; and
- the VAT is not excluded from credit in relation to business activities (see under *Non-recoverable VAT* below).

[*VATA 1994, s 33(1)(6)*].

The scheme applies whether or not the body is registered for VAT or makes taxable supplies but non VAT-registered bodies, who cannot quote a VAT registration number when purchasing from other EU countries, will be charged VAT at source on such purchases. Any VAT charged by other EU countries is not recoverable under the scheme and refunds to non VAT-registered bodies are therefore restricted to VAT incurred on supplies and importations only.

The purpose of the scheme is to prevent VAT being a burden on local authority funding. A body can claim refunds on goods and services supplied, etc. to it for non-business purposes provided the following conditions are met.

- It places the order.
- It receives the supply.
- It receives a VAT invoice addressed to it.
- It makes payment from its own funds.

(VAT Notice 749, para 7.1).

The scheme extends to the following.

(a) Goods and services bought using funds given to a body for specified purposes provided
   (i) the person who gives the money does not do so on condition that the body gives something or does something in return or that other persons benefit as a direct result of the payment;
   (ii) the person who has given the money does not in fact receive anything in return;
   (iii) the body buys the goods or services itself (i.e. places the order, receives the supply and a VAT invoice addressed to it and makes payment);
   (iv) the body remains the owner of the goods or services and uses them, or makes them available, for its own non-business purposes; and
   (v) the body keeps sufficient records for HMRC to identify the goods and services bought and the reason for buying them.

   Supplies which are likely to meet these conditions are funds used by community and foundation schools received from Parent Teacher Associations and school funds but funds used for exterior maintenance and repair at a voluntary aided school received from the governors are unlikely to qualify.
(b) Purchases made from funds of a trust but only if
   - the body acts as sole managing trustee without payment;
   - the activities of the trust relate so closely to the functions of the body that they cannot be easily distinguished; and
   - the claim relates to the non-business activities of the trust.

(VAT Notice 749, paras 7.3–7.5).

Where such non-business supplies, acquisitions or importations cannot be conveniently distinguished from business supplies, etc. the refund is the amount remaining after deducting from the whole of the VAT chargeable such proportion as HMRC consider to be attributable to business purposes. [*VATA 1994, s 33(2)*].

Non-recoverable VAT

VAT which is specifically excluded from credit by the Treasury under *VATA 1994, s 25(7)* in relation to business activities is also excluded from credit by bodies in respect of their non-business activities. See, for example, **9 BUSINESS ENTERTAINMENT** and **45.3 MOTOR CARS**.

Input tax attributable to exempt business activities

[43.8] A specified body within **43.2** above can recover input tax incurred directly attributable to its exempt business activities where HMRC consider it to be an 'insignificant' proportion of the total VAT incurred. [*VATA 1994, s 33(2)(b)*].

Where a special partial exemption method for specified bodies within *Sec 33* is used, '*insignificant*' means

- not more than £625 per month on average (i.e. not more than £7,500 p.a.); or
- less than 5% of the total VAT incurred on all goods and services purchased in a year. This total includes goods and services for business and non-business activities but excludes those on which input tax cannot be reclaimed, see **34.8 INPUT TAX**.

If the input tax attributable to exempt supplies exceeds both of the above limits, then none of it may be recovered.

Where a body chooses not to adopt a special partial exemption method for specified bodies within *Sec 33*, it can use any alternative method of partial exemption calculation (see **49 PARTIAL EXEMPTION**) but in that case the normal *de minimis* limits in **49.7 PARTIAL EXEMPTION** apply.

(VAT Notice 749, paras 8.2–8.4).

See also **53.4 PENSION SCHEMES** for concessional treatment for certain local authority pension funds.

Where any partial exemption method is used, the body must do a calculation at the end of each period, followed by an annual adjustment at the end of each financial year. This adjustment should be included in the VAT return for the next period.

Partial exemption methods

All bodies must have a partial exemption method in place that has been agreed with HMRC and continue using it until it is either withdrawn by HMRC or a new method is agreed. If a body has not agreed a special method with HMRC, it must either use the *special method for specified bodies within Sec 33* outlined below or the standard partial exemption method (see **49.4 PARTIAL EXEMPTION**) but in the latter case it must then separate business and non-business activities.

A body wishing to opt for a special partial exemption method must

- contact HMRC before the start of the financial year in order to obtain advice on using a special method;
- by the start of the financial year, agree with HMRC the broad principles of the method intended to be used;
- by three months before the end of the financial year, complete discussions with HMRC and have the final method agreed in writing; and
- by 31 October following the end of the financial year include all annual calculations on a return and submit it to HMRC.

If a special method has not been agreed before the end of a financial year, it cannot be applied to that year. Under these circumstances

- a body can only begin using a special method from the start of the next tax year; and
- in the meantime, it should use the model special partial exemption method outlined below.

(VAT Notice 749, paras 8.5–8.7).

Special partial exemption method for specified bodies within *Sec 33*

This method, which is based on the budget structure, takes a worst case scenario. It assumes that where a budget heading contains an exempt activity, than all taxable expenditure within that heading is attributable to that exempt activity. If this approach shows that a body's exempt input tax is insignificant, there is no requirement to refine the calculations.

Step 1	*Identifying exempt activities.* List, within committee, all budget headings/cost centres that contain any element of exempt activity.
Step 2	*Identifying taxable expenditure.* Within each budget heading/cost centre identified under Step 1, record all expenditure (net of VAT) for both capital and revenue that would normally carry VAT.
Step 3	*Recharges.* For recharges to budget headings/cost centres that contain any element of exempt activity, record all expenditure that would normally carry VAT.
Step 4	*Calculate the percentage of exempt-related input tax.* Add up the standard-rated expenditure identified in Steps 2 and 3 and calculate the VAT on it by multiplying by 17.5% (20% from 4 January 2011; 15% from 1 December 2008 to 31 December 2009).

If the total at Step 4 is insignificant (see above), no further calculations are required. If it is not, a progressively detailed analysis must be made of the amount of expenditure which is put to exempt use. If, at any stage, a result is achieved showing that the VAT is insignificant, no further action is required. There is no set method of allocation or apportionment. A body may adopt a different method for each particular area or activity based on the information available (e.g. number of staff, amount of income, floor area used, number of sessions, or time, etc.) provided it can demonstrate that any method used is fair and equitable. Where, despite detailed analysis of the amount of expenditure put to exempt use, the VAT identified still exceeds the 'insignificant' limit, none of the VAT relating to exempt supplies is recoverable.

(VAT Notice 749, paras 9.1–9.5).

Capital goods scheme and change of intention

Where a specified body within **43.2** above incurs VAT which it has attributed to an intended activity under the **CAPITAL GOODS SCHEME (10)** but subsequently changes its intention before undertaking that activity, it must review its original attribution and make any appropriate adjustment as follows.

(1) Identify the VAT attributable to the activity for which there has been a change of intention.

(2) If the change of intention is from a taxable or non-business activity to an exempt activity, add the VAT identified to the exempt input tax already identified for the year in which the VAT was originally incurred. If the new total cannot be treated as insignificant (see above), the VAT identified must be repaid to HMRC.

(3) If the change of intention is from an exempt activity to a taxable or non-business activity, the VAT identified should be deducted from the exempt input tax already identified for the year in which the VAT was originally incurred. If the new total can be treated as insignificant, the VAT identified can be reclaimed from HMRC (if it has not already been reclaimed).

It is not necessary to rework the calculation itself in full providing the new amount of exempt input tax can be quantified.

Error in attribution

If there has been an error in attribution, the entire calculation must be reworked for the relevant years.

Capital goods items adjustments

The appropriate adjustment to the amount of VAT reclaimed on the initial acquisition must be carried out in accordance with the normal rules of the capital goods scheme except that

- non-business use should be treated as if it were taxable use; and
- if exempt input tax is insignificant, no adjustment is required.

(VAT Notice 749, paras 10.1–10.5).

Claiming the refund

VAT-registered bodies

[43.9] VAT-registered bodies make the claim by including the amount refundable in Box 4 of the VAT return.

Unregistered bodies

The first claim for a refund made by a non-registered body must be in writing. The claim must relate to a period of at least one month and, if for under £100, must cover a period of at least twelve months. The period chosen should always end on the last day of a calendar month. The claim should be set out as follows.

> Banking/GABS
> HM Revenue and Customs
> 7th Floor SW
> Alexander House
> 21 Victoria Street
> Southend-on-Sea SS99 1AU
>
> I am claiming a refund of £ for the period to to cover VAT charged on goods and services bought for [insert name of body] non-business activities. *The tax claimed includes VAT incurred for exempt business activities which can be reclaimed under Notice 749 *Local authorities and similar bodies*.
>
> Signed
>
> For [insert name of authority]
>
> Address
>
> Contact name
>
> Contact telephone number
>
> * Delete as appropriate

Second and subsequent claims are made on Form VAT 126 which is sent out with each repayment.

Time limits for claims

VAT refund claims under *VATA 1994, s 33* are subject to the three-year time limit.

- For VAT-registered bodies, the time limit is three years after the due date for the return for the VAT period in which the VAT became chargeable.
- For bodies which are not registered for VAT, the time limit is three years after the end of the month in which the body received the supply, acquisition or importation.

(VAT Notice 749, paras 8.8, 12.3–12.5).

Repayment supplement, interest and penalties

- *VAT-registered bodies*. Where the repayment of a claim is delayed, repayment supplement may be due. See **51.16 PAYMENT OF VAT**. Any supplement due is calculated on the full amount of the claim, including both business and non-business activities.

Where any VAT has been overpaid or underclaimed under *VATA 1994, s 78*, statutory interest may be payable. See **51.17 PAYMENT OF VAT**. Any interest or penalties due as a result of errors made on VAT returns or late submission/payment of returns is calculated on the full amount of VAT involved, including VAT attributable to both business and non-business activities.

- *Non-VAT-registered bodies*. Claims by such bodies are subject to neither repayment supplement nor interest/penalties. Statutory interest, may be due in certain circumstances.

De Voil Indirect Tax Service. See V5.162.

Estimated returns by local authorities

[43.10] A local authority, because of the wide range of its activities, is not always able to process all its purchase invoices in time to include them on the appropriate VAT return. It may therefore apply to HMRC for permission to estimate input tax and *VATA 1994, s 33* refunds due.

Government departments

EU law

[43.11] Government departments and health authorities are 'bodies governed by public law' and, as such, are covered by *Directive 2006/112/EC, Art 13* and treated as non-taxable persons when satisfying the conditions in **43.1** above.

UK law

VATA 1994 applies in relation to taxable supplies made by the Crown as it applies to taxable supplies by taxable persons. [*VATA 1994, s 41(1)*].

(a) **Supplies by government departments.** Where a 'Government department' supplies goods or services which do not amount to the carrying on of a business but it appears to the Treasury that similar supplies are, or might be, supplied by taxable persons in the course of furtherance of any business, then the Treasury may direct that the supplies by that department are treated as supplies in the course or furtherance of a business carried on by it.
'*Government department*' includes the Scottish Administration, the Welsh Assembly Government, the National Assembly for Wales Commission, a NI department, a Northern Ireland health and social services body, any body of persons exercising functions on behalf of a Minister of the Crown (including a health service body, a National Health Service trust, an NHS foundation trust, a Primary Care Trust and a Local Health Board) and any part of such a department designated for these purposes by the Treasury.

[*VATA 1994, s 41(2)(6)–(8); Government of Wales Act 1998, Sch 12 para 35; Scotland Act 1998, Sch 8 para 30; Health Act 1999, Sch 8 para 86; National Health Service Reform and Health Care Professions Act 2002, Sch 5 para 40, Health and Social Care (Community Health and Standards) Act 2003, s 33(3); SI 2007/1118*].

The Treasury from time to time issues a direction listing, for each Government department, those supplies which are treated as supplied in the course or furtherance of a business when supplied by that department.

For supplies by government departments of welfare services otherwise than for a profit, see **28.12 HEALTH AND WELFARE**.

(b) **Supplies to government departments.** Where VAT is chargeable on

- the supply of goods or services to a 'Government department' (see above),
- the acquisition of goods by a Government department from another EU country, or
- the importation of any goods by a Government department from outside the EU

and the supply, acquisition or importation is not for the purpose of any business carried on by the department (or any supply treated as such under the above provisions) then, on a claim, the VAT may still be refunded if the Treasury so directs. The claim must be in such form and manner as HMRC determine and any refund is conditional on the department complying with requirements as to the keeping, preservation and production of records relating to the supply.

[*VATA 1994, s 41(3)(4)*].

The Treasury periodically issues a direction with a list of eligible government departments and a list of eligible goods and services on which VAT will be refunded provided the supply of those goods and services is not for the purposes of either any business carried on by the department or any supply by the department treated as a supply in the course or furtherance of a business. In practice, the only activities where such a direction is issued are those services which have been 'contracted out' to private contractors and on which the private contractor then charges VAT. See also Business Brief 18/03 for HMRC's views on the VAT position of two PFI (Private Finance Initiative) arrangements, i.e. 'Composite Trade' ('Contract Debtor') and 'NHS LIFT'.

Registration

Government departments and health authorities are subject to the normal VAT registration requirements. They must notify their liability to registration once their taxable turnover exceeds the registration limits (see **59.3 REGISTRATION**). Alternatively, they may seek voluntary registration if their taxable turnover is below the registration threshold (see **59.2 REGISTRATION**).

Accounting for VAT by government departments to the Consolidated Fund

Where a government department makes taxable supplies of goods or services and its receipts include amounts paid to it in respect of those supplies, the Treasury may allow the department to deduct any or all of the output tax due to HMRC on those supplies from the gross receipts due to the Consolidated Fund. [*FA 1999, s 21*]. In practice, such procedures have generally been adopted since the introduction of VAT.

De Voil Indirect Tax Service. See V2.108, V2.242, V5.161.

Welfare services

[43.12] For EU legislation see **18.25**(g) **EUROPEAN UNION LEGISLATION.**

The supply by a public body of welfare services and of goods supplied in connection therewith is exempt. [*VATA 1994, Sch 9 Group 7 Item 9*].

The identical provisions apply to such supplies made by charities, state-regulated private welfare institutions and state-regulated private welfare agencies. See **28.12 HEALTH AND WELFARE** for full details.

Transport services

The supply of transport services for sick or injured persons in vehicles specially designed for that purpose is exempt. [*VATA 1994, Sch 9 Group 7 Item 11*].

Admission charges

[43.13] Subject to certain restrictions, admission charges by public bodies to

- a museum, gallery, art exhibition or zoo, or
- a theatrical, musical or choreographic performance of a cultural nature

are exempt. See **57.7 RECREATION AND SPORT** for full details.

Key points

[43.14] Points to consider are as follows.

- Local authorities and certain other specified bodies get special VAT treatment through being able to reclaim input tax on their non-business activities and, in some cases, their exempt activities as well. This is an exception to one of the key principles of VAT, i.e. that input tax can only be reclaimed on expenditure that relates to taxable activities.
- The fact that local authorities can reclaim input tax on non-business activities could create an opportunity for VAT to be charged by a supplier to the authority, with the VAT element not causing a problem because of input tax recovery. A common example is where a charity can justify a local authority grant being taxable (as a supply of services) rather than outside the scope of VAT, in order to claim input tax on its related expenses.

An increasing number of charity grants now require a specific delivery of services to be met in order to secure the grant, i.e. creating more grants that could be standard rated rather than outside the scope of VAT.

- Other examples of 'specified bodies' that get input tax recovery on non-business activities include the police authority and BBC. So any supplier working for these bodies does not need to worry about a VAT charge reducing its competitive position.
- The rules about a local authority (or other specified body) claiming input tax on exempt business activities state that this is allowed if the activities in question form an insignificant part of the authority's overall activities. In reality, 'insignificant' means less than 5% of the total VAT incurred on all goods and services purchased in a year. This total includes goods and services for business and non-business activities but excludes those on which input tax cannot be reclaimed. If the input tax attributable to exempt supplies exceeds both of the above limits, then none of it may be recovered.

44

Management Services and Supplies of Staff

Introduction

[44.1] Management services commonly arise where several traders who are separately registered for VAT, but are associated in some way, decide that one of them should purchase overhead items required by the various businesses, pay all the bills, and then recover an agreed proportion of the costs from the other traders participating in the scheme. Such an arrangement is common where the same office facilities and/or staff are shared. The 'management charges' or 'service charges' normally contain elements of staff salaries, office equipment, rent, rates, heating and lighting, stationery, telephone and postage, etc. Although such arrangements are 'domestic' and may not involve any element of profit, there may nevertheless be a taxable supply for VAT purposes, as under *VATA 1994, s 5(2)(b)* anything which is not a supply of goods but is done for a consideration is a supply of services.

However, there is no taxable supply if the persons involved are part of the same legal entity or if facilities are provided between businesses covered by a single VAT registration, e.g. businesses run by the same legal partnership or business included in a VAT group registration (see **27 GROUPS OF COMPANIES**).

See *Smith & Williamson; Smith & Williamson Securities* (VTD 281) (TVC 43.14) and *C & E Commrs v Tilling Management Services Ltd* at **44.3** below. For decisions as to whether such supplies are made in the course or furtherance of a business or are domestic arrangements not in the course of any business, see *Cumbrae Properties (1963) Ltd v C & E Commrs*, QB [1981] STC 799 (TVC 62.24), *Durham Aged Mineworkers' Homes Association v C & E Commrs*, QB [1994] STC 553 (TVC 62.45) and *Processed Vegetable*

Growers Association Ltd (VTD 25) (TVC 62.42). For the position where charges are raised between companies for use of capital, see *Laurence Scott Ltd* (VTD 2004) (TVC 40.93).

Sharing of premises

[44.2] The VAT treatment of any costs recovered relating to premises shared with other persons depends upon the precise terms of the arrangements. See **41.4 LAND AND BUILDINGS: EXEMPT SUPPLIES AND OPTION TO TAX** for a general consideration of service charges and joint occupation of premises.

Management services and group relief

[44.3] HMRC have expressed the following views.

(a) If Company A incurs a tax loss and surrenders it to Company B under *ICTA 1988, s 402* without any payment, HMRC do not see any taxable supply of goods or services for VAT purposes.

(b) If Company A incurs a tax loss and surrenders it to Company B under *ICTA 1988, s 402* with a payment or credit to current account for the surrender of the tax loss, again HMRC do not see any taxable supply of goods or services.

(c) It is possible in cases (*a*) and (*b*) above, that Company A might render management services to Company B without a separate charge being made for those services. The position here depends on whether there is any arrangement linking the provision of management services to, say, the procurement or making of group relief payments. If there is, then HMRC would see a non-monetary consideration for the management services which would have to be valued to determine the amount of VAT due. If there is no such arrangement, then if the management services are provided free of charge there is no taxable supply.

(d) Again, Company A may render management services to Company B and make a charge for those services, at the same time surrendering group relief, with or without payment. In such a case there is clearly a taxable supply of management services, but what has to be determined is whether the money charge is the full consideration for the supply. If there is an arrangement linking the supply of management services to the procurement or making of group relief payments, then once again there would be a non-monetary consideration which would have to be valued. In such circumstances VAT would be due on the full consideration, i.e. on the sum of the monetary and non-monetary considerations. However, if there is no link between the management services and the group relief payments, then VAT will be due only on the charge actually made for the management services.

HMRC have also confirmed that where services are rendered between companies within the same VAT group registration then no liability to VAT arises.

(CCAB Statement TR344 June 1979).

See also *C & E v Tilling Management Services Ltd*, QB 1978, [1979] STC 365 (TVC 43.8).

Supplies of staff

Definition

[44.4] A supply of staff (which includes directors and other office holders) is made for VAT purposes if the use of an individual who is contractually employed by the supplier is provided to another person for consideration. This applies whether the terms of the individual's employment are set out in a formal contract or letter of appointment, or are on a less formal basis. The determining factor is that the staff are not contractually employed by the recipient but come under its direction. Where staff are supplied to another person but continue to operate under the direction of the supplier, this is not a supply of staff, but is a supply of those services. (The distinction is significant where the services may be zero-rated or exempt, or when determining whether or not the supply is made in the UK.)

Liability

A supply of staff is normally regarded as being made in the course or furtherance of a business and VAT must be accounted for at the standard rate. This is subject to the following exceptions.

- Certain supplies of staff are not always made in the course or furtherance of business and thus may be outside the scope of VAT. These include
  - (i) secondments between and by government departments,
  - (ii) secondments between National Health bodies, and
  - (iii) some secondments between local authorities and by local authorities where they have a statutory obligation or monopoly.
- The supply of staff to a person who belongs outside the EU or to a business belonging in another EU country is outside the scope of UK VAT.

Where supplies of staff are received from a person who belongs outside the UK, VAT must be accounted for on those supplies at the standard rate under the 'reverse charge' procedure (see **38.4 INTERNATIONAL SERVICES**).

Value of supply

VAT must be charged on the full amount of the consideration for the supply of staff (whether full-time or part-time). As well as any fee, this includes recovery of staff costs from the recipient (e.g. salary, NICs and pension contributions). Even if the arrangements do not involve the recipient paying these staff costs to the supplier (e.g. because the salary is paid directly to the individual or the NICs directly to the DSS) these amounts are still part of the consideration for the taxable supply of staff. See below for limited concessions in certain cases where the recipient of the staff pays their salaries directly to the employees and/or meets the employer's obligations for PAYE, NICs, pension contributions, etc. Even where a concession applies, VAT must still be accounted for on any payments that the recipient makes direct to the employer.

Similar rules apply to the value of supplies received from outside the UK under the reverse charge procedure.

(VAT Notice 700/34/05, paras 1.1, 2.1–2.3).

(1) Concession for hire of staff by employment businesses

Until 1 April 2009, where an employment business within the meaning of the *Employment Agencies Act 1973* supplies a member of its staff (the employee) to another business which

(a) is responsible for paying the employee's remuneration directly to the employee, and/or
(b) discharges the obligations of the employment business to pay to any third party PAYE, NICs, pension contributions and similar payments relating to the employee,

then, to the extent that any such payments form the consideration (or part) for the supply of the employee to the other business, they are disregarded in determining the value of the supply of the employee. HMRC accept that the condition in (*a*) above is satisfied where the client has a contract with a payroll company (which may be owned by, but be separate from, the employment business).

(2) Concession for secondment of staff by businesses other than employment businesses

Where an employer (other than an employment business within the meaning of the*Employment Agencies Act 1973*) seconds a member of its staff (the employee) to another business which

(a) exercises exclusive control over the allocation and performance of the employee's duties during the period of secondment; and
(b) is responsible for paying the employee's remuneration directly to the employee and/or discharges the employer's obligations to pay to any third party PAYE, NICs, pension contributions and similar payments relating to the employee,

then, to the extent that any payments within (*b*) above form the consideration (or part) for the secondment of the employee to the other business, they are disregarded in determining the value of seconding the employee. For these purposes, an employer is not to be treated as seconding an employee to another business if the placing of the employee with that other business is done with a view to the employer (or any person associated with him) deriving any financial gain from

- the placing of the employee with the other business, or
- any other arrangements or understandings (whether or not contractually binding and whether or not for any consideration) between the employer (or any person associated with him) and the other business (or any person associated with it) with which the employee is placed.

(3) Concession for placement of disabled workers under the Sheltered Placement Scheme (or any similar scheme)

Where the sponsor of a disabled worker places the worker with a host company under the Sheltered Placement Scheme (or any similar scheme) and the host company

- is responsible for paying the worker's remuneration directly to the worker; and/or
- discharges the sponsor's obligations to pay to any third party PAYE, NICs, pension contributions and similar payments relating to the worker,

then, to the extent that any such payments form the consideration (or part) for the placing of the worker with the host company, they are disregarded in determining the value of placing the worker with the host company.

(VAT Notice 700/34/05, para 4; HMRC Budget 2008 technical note; VAT Information Sheet 3/09).

Employment agencies and bureaux

See **3.13 AGENTS.**

Charities

See **12.5**(19) **CHARITIES.**

Temporary suspension of an employment contract

[44.5] Where an employee takes up a temporary post with another employer, there is no supply of staff provided that

(a) the temporary post is organised on the employee's own initiative; and
(b) the second employer issues the employee with a new contract or letter of appointment, temporarily suspending the employee's contract with the first employer.

To avoid doubt, a temporary suspension should normally be supported by evidence that

- there is an agreement with the first employer that the employee is to be transferred for a fixed or open-ended period, often with an entitlement to return;
- there are new conditions of employment with the second employer;
- the second employer has control over the terms and conditions of employment; or
- the second employer fixes the salary.

(VAT Notice 700/34/05, para 3.1).

Joint employment

[44.6] In cases of joint employment, there is no supply of staff for VAT purposes between the joint employers.

Staff are regarded as jointly employed if their contracts of employment or letters of appointment make it clear that they have more than one employer. The contract must specify who the employers are (e.g. 'Company A, Company B and Company C' or 'Company A and its subsidiaries').

Staff are not regarded as jointly employed (and the provisions of **44.4** above apply) if their contract is with a single company or person, even if it

- lays down that the employee's duties include assisting other companies;
- lays down that the employee will work full-time for another company; or
- shows by the job title that the employee works for a group of associated companies (e.g. group accountant).

(VAT Notice 700/34/05, para 3.2).

Paymaster services for associated companies

[44.7] Paymaster services commonly arise in two situations.

- Where staff are jointly employed, one of the joint employers may undertake to pay all salaries, National Insurance and pension contributions which are then recovered from the other employers.
- Where a number of associated companies each employs its own staff, one company may pay all salaries, etc. on behalf of the others, each associate then paying its share of the costs to the paymaster.

In either case, the recovery of monies paid out by the paymaster is not subject to VAT and is treated as a disbursement (see **3.7 AGENTS**).

VAT must be accounted for on any charge made for paymaster services over and above the reimbursement of the costs paid out unless

- the recipient belongs outside the EU or is a business which belongs in another EU country (in which case the supply is outside the scope of UK VAT); or
- the supply is between companies within the same VAT group registration (in which case it is disregarded).

(VAT Notice 700/34/05, para 3.3).

Appointments to directorships and other offices

[44.8] The appointments of an individual as a director or other paid office holder (e.g. secretary, treasurer) can give rise to a VAT liability as a supply of staff in the following circumstances.

(1) Sole proprietors and partnerships providing professional services

A sole proprietor providing professional services (e.g. a solicitor or accountant) or a partner in a firm providing such services who takes up a professional appointment as a director or other office holder must account for VAT on any payment received if

(i) the appointment results from the professional expertise exercised in the business or partnership business,

(ii) the duties as a director or other office holder involve, at least in part, the use of that expertise, and

(iii) in the case of a partnership, the payments received accrue to the partnership and are not retained by the partner personally.

See *Birketts* (VTD 17515) (TVC 62.165) concerning various offices held by partners in the firm. The tribunal held that the tests to be applied were 'did one or more of the solicitors accept the offices in the course of furtherance of their profession' and 'did one or more of the solicitors accept the offices in the course or furtherance of the partnership business'.

See also *Oglethorpe Sturton & Gillibrand* (VTD 17491) (TVC 62.164).

Where, however, under the terms of an appointment as an office holder, the person concerned is treated as an employee, any fees or payments made to the sole proprietor or partner personally are outside the scope of VAT.

(2) Employees and directors

(a) *Request made to a company for the supply of a director.* If a company allows an employee or director to serve as a director of a second company, following an approach from that company, it must account for VAT on any payment it receives for agreeing to the appointment.

(b) *Common directors.* An individual involved in a number of companies may be a director of each. In general, where, for convenience, his total emoluments from all the businesses are paid by one company which recovers appropriate proportions from the others, any services to which the charges relate (e.g. attending meetings or approving expenditure) can only be the director's supplies to the companies of which he is a director. As these services are supplied directly to the relevant businesses by the individual and not across from one company to another, there is no supply from one company to another and no VAT is due on the share of money recovered from each company.

(c) *Voluntary personal appointment of a director.* Where an individual director or employee personally arranges to be appointed to the directorship of a second company and receives payment from that company in return, the first company is not required to account for VAT on any payments to the appointee. The appointment must be a purely personal one and not a means for the first company to deliver its service (e.g. consultancy services).

(d) *Right of a company to appoint a director.* Where a company exercises a legal or contractual right to appoint a director to the board of another company (e.g. a company in which it is investing) and that director does not give expert advice or take an active part in the running of the company, there is no supply for VAT purposes and any remuneration is outside the scope of VAT. Normally, however, in such circumstances the director is appointed because of his specialist knowledge and to give expert advice to the other company. In such a case, any fee charged by the company appointing the director for such advice and for taking an active part in the running of the other company is a supply for which the remuneration is taxable.

(e) *Banks, etc.* Where a bank or similar institution appoints a director to the board of a UK investee company as the condition of a loan, any charges for the director's services are part of the consideration for the loan and treated as an exempt supply. (Hansard 3 February 1993, Cols 185, 186).

(VAT Notice 700/34/05, paras 3.4–3.8).

Key points

[44.9] Points to consider are as follows.

- A problem could occur if a business makes a management charge to an associated business that cannot fully reclaim input tax on its expenses due to partial exemption rules. In such cases, a possible solution to avoid a VAT loss might be to create a group registration. With a group registration, supplies of goods or services between group members are outside the scope of VAT.
- Another possible solution to avoid VAT being added to a supply of management services is where a joint contract of employment is in place for the employees whose salaries are being recharged. In such cases, the charge from one employer to the other is outside the scope of VAT.
- It is important to be clear about whether a supply of employees relates to a supply of 'staff' or a supply of specific services. A supply of staff is usually standard-rated (if provided to a UK customer) but a supply of specific services might be exempt or zero-rated in some cases (e.g. in relation to medical services). The key issue is to identify whether the staff concerned are acting under the instruction of the customer (supply of staff) or the supplier (as an employee/employer arrangement) to perform specific tasks for the customer.
- A supply of staff to an EU business customer or any customer outside the EU (business or non-business) is outside the scope of VAT under the place of supply rules. This would apply if, for example, staff employed by a UK airline were supplied to a Spanish airline company based in Spain, working under the instruction of the Spanish management team. In this situation, the VAT on fees charged by the UK airline will be accounted for by the Spanish airline on its own VAT return using the reverse charge calculation.
- If a UK business buys in staff from an overseas business, it must account for the VAT on its own VAT return by applying the reverse charge calculation. This is because the place of supply for the service is based on the location of the customer, i.e. UK. If the supply in question relates to a UK business that is partly exempt, then the reverse charge calculation will produce an input tax restriction in Box 4 of its VAT return, unless it directly relates to

the taxable activities of the business, i.e. giving full input tax recovery.

45

Motor Cars

Cross-references. See **19.36 EUROPEAN UNION: SINGLE MARKET** for the refund of VAT on the supply of a new motor car by a non-taxable person to another EU country; **19.37 EUROPEAN UNION: SINGLE MARKET** for the acquisition of a new motor car from another EU country by a non-taxable person; **21.17 EXPORTS** for sale of vehicles outside the EU; **33.15**(13) **IMPORTS; 61 SECOND-HAND GOODS** for the second-hand scheme for motor cars and **62 SELF-SUPPLY** for explanation of such deemed supplies.

Introduction

[45.1] For VAT purposes a motor car is any motor vehicle of a kind normally used on public roads which has three or more wheels and either

(a) is constructed or adapted solely or mainly for the carriage of passengers; or
(b) has to the rear of the driver's seat roofed accommodation which is fitted with side windows or which is constructed or adapted for the fitting of side windows.

It does not include the following.

(i) Vehicles capable of accommodating only one person.
(ii) Vehicles capable of carrying twelve or more seated persons and which meet the requirements of *Road Vehicles (Construction of Use) Regulations 1986, Sch 6* (road safety regulations).
(iii) Vehicles of not less than three tonnes unladen weight (as defined in *Road Vehicles (Construction of Use) Regulations 1986*).
(iv) Vehicles constructed to carry a 'payload' of one tonne or more. '*Payload*' is the difference between a vehicle's kerb weight and its maximum gross weight, both terms as defined in *Road Vehicles (Construction of Use) Regulations 1986*. This change means that certain dual purpose vehicles, commonly called twin cab or double cab pick-ups, are no longer cars for VAT purposes. A few double cabs carry a payload of under one tonne. Customs Centre of Operational Expertise for the Motor Trade (COPE) maintains a schedule of double cab pick-up vehicles and their ex-works payloads. Agreement has been reached with the Society of Motor Manufacturers and Traders about the treatment of optional accessories which dealers or others may add to a double cab potentially converting it into a car (by increasing the kerb weight and decreasing the payload). (See HMRC VAT Guidance V1–13, para 25.1 and VAT Notice 700/57/04).
(v) Caravans, ambulances and prison vans.
(vi) Vehicles constructed for a special purpose other than the carriage of persons and having no other accommodation for carrying persons than such as is incidental to that purpose.

[*SI 1992/3122, Art 2; SI 1995/1268, Art 2; SI 1999/2831; SI 1999/2832*].

In a case concerning provisions in *Car Tax Act 1983* similar to *SI 1992/3122, Art 2*, it was held that in (*b*) above 'accommodation' means only accommodation for passengers and, if the space is unsuitable for this purpose, the vehicle is not within the definition even if there are side windows (*R v C & E Commrs (ex p Nissan UK Ltd)* CA [1988] BTC 8003 (TVC 44.40)).

Vehicles regarded as motor cars (subject to (iv) above)

- *Imported versions of saloon cars* even where they are 'normally used on public roads' which are outside the UK (*Withers of Winsford Ltd v C & E Commrs*, QB [1988] STC 431 (TVC 44.3)).
- An *estate car* with the rear seat removed (*County Telecommunications Systems Ltd* (VTD 10224) (TVC 44.8)); used for business purposes by a builder (*Gardner* (MC) (VTD 588) (TVC 44.6)); and licensed as a goods vehicle and used by a garage and grocery store (*Howarth* (VTD 632) (TVC 44.7)).
- A Chevrolet K10 Blazer (*Yarlett* (VTD 1490) (TVC 44.9)).
- A Citroen van modified by fitting windows behind the driver's seat (*Browsers Bookshop* (VTD 2837) (TVC 44.23)).
- A Daihatsu Fourtrak Estate (*Specialised Cars Ltd* (VTD 11123) (TVC 44.25)).

- A Datsun pick-up truck, modified by the addition of a detachable hard top superstructure with two side windows and a hatchback to the rear of the driver's seat but no seating accommodation (*HKS Coachworks Ltd* (VTD 1124) (TVC 44.16) but see *R v C & E Commrs (ex p Nissan UK Ltd)* above).
- A Ford Escort, the rear seats of which could be folded away (*RC Lucia* (VTD 5776) (TVC 44.4)).
- An Isuzu pick-up (*BC Kunz (t/a Wharfdale Finance Co)* (VTD 13514) (TVC 44.29)).
- A Land Rover converted into a 'motor car' by being fitted with a hard top body with side windows and upholstered seats (*Chartcliff Ltd* (VTD 262) (TVC 44.1)); or by being modified by the addition of a metal canopy with side windows (*Wigley* (VTD 7300) (TVC 44.2)).
- A Range Rover even though first registered, and taxed, as a heavy goods vehicle and not used for domestic purposes (*C & E Commrs v Jeynes (t/a Midland International (Hire) Caterers)*, QB 1983, [1984] STC 30 (TVC 44.18)).
- A Suzuki jeep modified by the fitting of a rear seat although it had no rear windows (*S Compton (t/a Stan Compton Electrical Engineers & Contractors)* (VTD 10259) (TVC 44.21)); and a Suzuki Vitara Sport (*W McAdam* (VTD 13286) (TVC 44.27)).
- A Toyota Hiace van fitted with side windows (*Knapp* (VTD 778) (TVC 44.11)); a Toyota Hilux (*Western Waste Management Ltd* (VTD 17428) (TVC 44.15)); a Toyota Previa with the middle and rear rows of seats removed for delivery purposes (*Gorringe Pine* (VTD 14036) (TVC 44.12)); and a Toyota Spacecruiser with the rear seats removed and a hanging rail for transporting clothes installed (*Mr & Mrs M Gohil (t/a Gohil Fashions)* (VTD 15435) (TVC 44.14)).
- A Volkswagen tipping truck with, in addition to the driver's cab with room for one other passenger, a second roofed cab behind the driver's cab with room for three more passengers (*Weatherproof Flat Roofing (Plymouth) Ltd* (VTD 1240) (TVC 44.5)); a Volkswagen pick-up truck with roofed accommodation fitted with side windows to the rear of the driver's seat (*Readings & Headley* (VTD 1535) (TVC 44.10)); and a Volkswagen Caravelle with removable rear seats (*Intercraft UK Romania* (VTD 13707) (TVC 44.32)).

Vehicles not regarded as motor cars

- Ice cream vans, mobile shops and offices, hearses (see also *KP Davies* (VTD 831) (TVC 44.37)) and bullion vans (which are all regarded as falling under (v) above). (VAT Notice 700/64/11, para 2.2).
- Vehicles that can seat fewer than 12 passengers solely because they have been adapted for wheelchair users. [*SI 1992/3222, Art 2(b)(ii)*].
- Motor caravans provided they conform with criteria agreed with the Society of Motor Manufacturers and Traders (SMMT). The agreement specifies that, to be treated as a motor caravan, the vehicle must incorporate a permanently installed sink and cooking facilities; seating arrangements to enable diners to sit at the meal table; at least one bed

with a minimum length of 1.82 metres; and a permanently installed fresh water tank with a minimum capacity of 10 litres. (HMRC VAT Guidance V1–13, para 17.6).

- A pick-up truck with an attached, removable canopy (*K M Batty* (VTD 2199) (TVC 44.38)).
- A Daihatsu Fourtrak Commercial Hard Top with two folding rear seats (*AL Yeoman Ltd* (VTD 4470) (TVC 44.44)).
- A Ford van fitted with wooden benches but no side windows (*Chartcliff Ltd* (VTD 262) (TVC 44.36)); and a Ford Transit van adapted by inserting rear seats of heavy duty plastic but with no rear windows, handrails or seat belts (*Chichester Plant Contractors Ltd* (VTD 6575) (TVC 44.42)).
- A Land Rover with two folding seats in the rear (*Bolinge Hill Farm* (VTD 4217) (TVC 44.43)); a 12-seat Land Rover with the rear bench seats removed (*P Oddonetto* (VTD 5208) (TVC 44.45)); and a Land Rover modified by a half-sized window in the nearside rear panel (*TH Sheppard* (VTD 13815) (TVC 44.46)).
- A Peugeot van modified by adding a window on each side behind the driver's seat for safety reasons (*John Beharrell Ltd* (VTD 6530) (TVC 44.47)).
- A Lamborghini Murcielago two-seater sports car, with suspension programmed solely for track use (*Sixth Gear Experience Ltd* (VTD 20890) (TVC 44.52)).

Car-derived vans

A number of manufacturers' models start life as a motor car but are subsequently altered. On the exterior, these vehicles look like a motor car but their interior has been altered to give the appearance and functionality of a van. The rear seats and seat belts along with their mountings have been completely removed and the rear area of the shell is fitted with a new floor panel to create a load area. In addition, the side windows to the rear of the driver's seat are fitted with immovable opaque panels. HMRC do not view such a car-derived vehicle as a motor car for VAT purposes if:

- The technical criteria specified in HMRC guidance are met by the manufacturer. The criteria relate to how any alterations to the vehicle have been effected.
- The adaptations give the vehicle the functionality of a commercial vehicle. (The removal of a bench seat or similar from what is essentially a two-seater car would not automatically satisfy HMRC's requirements.)
- The space that remains behind the front row of seats is highly unsuitable for carrying passengers.

HMRC, in partnership with the manufacturers, are developing a list of car-derived vans on which VAT can be deducted (subject to the normal rules). In the meantime, if businesses are in any doubt, they should obtain confirmation in writing from the vendor that the vehicle meets the technical criteria.

(Business Brief 16/04).

Combination vans

Whilst these vehicles have the appearance of vans, they are designed to be fitted with or include additional seats behind the front row of seats to enable the carriage of passengers. Such vehicles are motor cars for VAT purposes except in the case of:

- Larger vehicles which have a payload of more than one tonne (see (iv) above).
- Those vehicles where the dedicated load area (i.e. that load area which is completely unaffected by the additional seating) is of a sufficient size compared to the passenger area to make the carriage of goods the predominant use of the vehicle.

Where a business has bought a combination van which does not fall within the above exceptions, it is a motor car under VAT legislation. If it has recovered the VAT incurred on the purchase, it must make an adjustment to correct this overclaim.

(Business Brief 16/04).

See, however, *Vauxhall Motors Ltd* (VTD 19425) (TVC 44.48) where the tribunal held that the Vauxhall Combo Crew van was a commercial vehicle and the fact that it contained three folding rear seats did not take it within the statutory definition of a car.

De Voil Indirect Tax Service. See V1.293.

Transactions involving motor cars

[45.2] The Treasury may, by order, provide that VAT charged on specified supplies, acquisitions and importations is excluded from credit for input tax against output tax. [*VATA 1994, s 25(7)*]. Provisions relating to motor cars have been made under *The Value Added Tax (Cars) Order 1992* (*SI 1992/3122*) and the *Value Added Tax (Input Tax) Order 1992* (*SI 1992/3222*) as amended. With certain exceptions, a taxable person cannot reclaim input tax on the purchase of a car (see **45.3** below) and no VAT is chargeable when the car is sold unless the selling price exceeds the purchase price (see **45.4** below). Certain transactions are not treated as taxable supplies (see **45.5** below) and special rules apply to self-supplies (see **45.6** below). For the position of car dealers see **45.7** below.

The validity of the UK input tax blocking order was upheld in *Royscot Leasing Ltd and others v C & E Commrs, ECJ Case C–305/97*, [1999] STC 998 (TVC 22.424).

Fleet buyer bonuses and dealer demonstration bonuses

A fleet buyer bonus is given by a manufacturer or sole concessionaire to a customer who makes a bulk purchase of vehicles. A dealer demonstrator bonus is a payment made, or credit allowed, by a manufacturer or sole concessionaire to a dealer who agrees to adopt a car as a demonstration vehicle. HMRC now accept that such bonuses are normally to be treated as discounts by the manufacturer or sole concessionaires which reduce the value of their supplies. (Business Brief 16/97).

Fleet leasing bonuses

A fleet leasing bonus is given by a car manufacturer or dealer to a business which has leased a number of vehicles previously sold by the manufacturer or dealer to intermediaries. HMRC now accept that such bonuses are normally to be treated as discounts by the manufacturer or dealer which reduce the value of their supplies (rather than consideration for a supply of services by the customer). (Business Brief 1/98).

Purchase of a car

[45.3] Apart from the special cases listed below, VAT cannot be reclaimed on the purchase (including acquisition or importation) of a motor car as defined in **45.1** above. Purchase means not only outright purchase but also any purchase under a hire purchase agreement or any other agreement whereby property in the car eventually passes e.g. a lease-purchase agreement. See **45.11** below for input tax on cars leased or hired.

VAT on supplies integral with the supply of a motor car is only deductible where input tax on the motor car is deductible. This includes manufacturer's warranty (although VAT on the purchase of an extension of the period of warranty is deductible). It has been held to include manufacturer's delivery charges passed on by dealers to customers. See *Wimpey Construction UK Ltd* (VTD 808) (TVC 44.98) and *C & E Commrs v British Telecommunications plc*, HL [1999] STC 758 (TVC 44.99).

See **45.13** below for fitted optional extras and accessories.

Special cases

VAT may be reclaimed on the purchase, acquisition or importation of a motor car in the following special circumstances.

(a) Exclusive business use

The motor car is a 'qualifying' motor car (see below) supplied to, or acquired or imported by, a taxable person who intends to use the motor car exclusively for business purposes. This condition is *not* satisfied if the taxable person intends to

(i) let it on hire to any person either for no consideration or consideration less than would be payable in an arm's length commercial transaction; or

(ii) make it available, otherwise than by letting on hire, to any person (including, where the taxable person is an individual, himself or, where the taxable person is a partnership, a partner) for private use (whether or not for a consideration).

A car is used exclusively for a business purpose if it is used only for business journeys *and* it is not available for private use. A car is available for private use when there is nothing preventing the owner or employees from using the car for private use. HMRC accept that

- VAT can be recovered on the purchase of a pool car provided it is
  (1) normally kept at the principal place of business;
  (2) not allocated to an individual; and
  (3) not kept at an employee's home;
- cars bought or imported for the purpose of sale and lease back will not be treated as available for private use provided output tax is accounted for on the resale to the leasing company in the same VAT period as input tax is recovered on the purchase; and
- VAT can be recovered on cars bought for in-house leasing provided the amounts charged to the lessee are not less than those for a commercial arm's length letting.

(VAT Notice 700/64/11, paras 3.5–3.9).

In *Upton (t/a Fagomatic) v C & E Commrs*, CA [2002] STC 640 (TVC 44.110) the High Court held that the trader's evidence that he did not need to use a car privately was not conclusive. The only cars which could be held to be used exclusively for business purposes were

- those which were not physically available for private use (e.g. cars used for leasing);
- cars which it would not be realistically possible to put to a private use (e.g. marked police cars and emergency vehicles); and
- cars which were insulated from the possibility of private use through the way in which they were allocated to staff (e.g. business cars held in a pool and not allocated to any individual).

The Court of Appeal upheld this decision. The 'intention to use' is not synonymous with the 'intention to make available'. Where an individual trader acquires a car, the very fact of his deliberate acquisition of the car, whereby he makes himself the owner of the car and controller of it, means that he must intend to make it available to himself for private use, even if he never intends to use it privately.

The decision in *Upton* was approved in *C & E Commrs v Skellett (CH) (t/a Vidcom Computer Services)*, CS 2003, [2004] STC 201 (TVC 44.111). It was held that the effect of (i) and (ii) above was that where a motor vehicle is acquired by a sole trader, the vehicle will have been made available to that person for private use unless effective steps are taken to render the vehicle *incapable* of such use by that person.

However, in *C & E Commrs v Elm Milk Ltd*, CA [2006] STC 792 (TVC 44.138) a claim for input tax recovery was allowed where a company had minuted a resolution that a car was for business use only and that it would be breach of the employee's terms of employment to use it for private use. The legislation did *not* state that, in order to show that there was no intention to make a car available for private use, the taxable person had to show that it was not physically so available. There was no reason, therefore, why a car could not be made unavailable for private use by suitable effective constraints.

The difference between the treatment of a company (which can enter into a binding agreement with its sole director prohibiting him from using a car for private purposes) and a sole trader (who cannot make a binding contract with himself) was confirmed in *HMRC v Shaw*, Ch D 2006, [2007] STC 1525 (TVC 44.116) although Lindsay J observed that it was difficult to imagine that Parliament intended to devise a test which expressly included sole traders and yet was such that it was hard to see how a sole trader could ever pass the test.

(b) Mini-cabs, self-drive hire, driving instruction

The motor car is a 'qualifying' motor car supplied to, or acquired or imported by, a taxable person who intends to use the motor car primarily

- (i) to provide it on hire with the services of a driver for the purposes of carrying passengers;
- (ii) to provide it for 'self-drive hire'; or
- (iii) as a vehicle in which instruction in driving of a motor car is to be given by him.

'*Self-drive hire*' means hire where the hirer is the person normally expected to drive the motor car and the period of hire to each hirer (together with the period of hire of any other motor car expected to be hired to him by the taxable person) will normally be less than both 30 consecutive days and 90 days in any twelve-month period.

(c) Motor dealers and manufacturers

The motor car forms part of the 'stock in trade' of a 'motor manufacturer' or a 'motor dealer'.

'*Stock in trade*' means new or second-hand motor cars (other than second-hand motor cars which are not qualifying motor cars as defined below) which are

- produced by a motor manufacturer for the purpose of resale and intended to be sold by that manufacturer within twelve months of their production, or
- supplied to, or acquired from another EU country or imported by, a motor dealer for the purpose of resale and intended to be sold by that motor dealer within twelve months of their supply, acquisition or importation.

Such motor cars do not cease to be stock in trade where they are temporarily put to a use in the motor manufacturer's or motor dealer's business which involves making them available for private use. Where a car does cease to be stock in trade and no longer qualifies for input tax recovery, a self-supply arises under **45.6** below.

'*Motor manufacturer*' means a person whose business consists (in whole or part) of producing motor cars including producing a motor car by conversion of a vehicle (whether a motor car or not).

'*Motor dealer*' means a person whose business consists (in whole or in part) of obtaining supplies of, or acquiring from another EU country or importing, new or second-hand motor cars for resale with a view to making an overall profit on the sale of them (whether or not a profit is made on each sale).

(d) Motability Scheme

The motor car is unused and is supplied to a taxable person whose only taxable supplies are concerned with the letting of motor cars on hire to another taxable person whose business consists predominantly of making supplies within *VATA 1994, Sch 8 Group 12 Item 14* (see **28.31 HEALTH AND WELFARE**).

'Qualifying' motor cars

A 'qualifying' motor car for the purposes of *(a)*–*(c)* above is generally one which has never been supplied, acquired or imported in circumstances where VAT was wholly excluded from credit as input tax. Under normal circumstances, therefore, a qualifying car will be a new car or a used car where the previous owners were able to recover VAT on their purchase in full (e.g. cars disposed of by a leasing company with a registration letter of 'N' or later are likely to be qualifying cars).

This is subject to two qualifications.

(1) Specifically excluded from qualifying is a motor car which is supplied, etc. to a taxable person on or after 1 August 1995 and which has been supplied on a letting on hire by him before that date. However, HMRC are, by concession, prepared to accept a car as 'qualifying' (despite any prepayment of leasing charges made before 1 August 1995) provided the car is first registered and the lease is first invoiced on or after 1 August 1995; the invoice identifies the car as 'qualifying'; and both the lessor and lessee follow the tax rules applying to qualifying vehicles (which includes applying the 50% block to the lessee's deduction of VAT on the prepayment, see **45.11** below). (Business Brief 21/95).

(2) As a transitional measure, a taxable person may elect to treat a motor car as a qualifying motor car if it was supplied, etc. to him before 1 August 1995 in circumstances where VAT was wholly excluded from credit as input tax; it is first registered on or after 1 August 1995; and it was not supplied on a letting on hire by him before that date. Where such an election is made and the motor car meets all the necessary conditions for 100% input tax relief, input tax may be recovered in the first VAT period commencing on or after 1 August 1995.

[*SI 1992/3222, Art 7; SI 1995/281; SI 1995/1666; SI 1999/2930*].

Fleet buyer bonuses

See **45.2** above.

De Voil Indirect Tax Service. See V3.443.

Disposal of a motor vehicle used in a business

Input tax wholly excluded from credit on the purchase of a car

[45.4] Following the decision in *EC Commission v Italian Republic, ECJ Case C–45/95*, [1997] STC 1062 (TVC 22.349), the onward sale of a motor car on which input tax was blocked on purchase is an exempt supply under

VATA 1994, Sch 9 Group 14, regardless of whether it is sold at a profit or loss. See **20.4 EXEMPT SUPPLIES**. Any directly attributable input tax incurred in making the sale (e.g. auction fees) is exempt input tax and not recoverable. (VAT Notice 700/64/11, para 7.2). In addition, the decision in *Nordania Finans A/S v Skatteministeriet, ECJ Case C–98/07*, [2008] STC 3314 (TVC 22.451) has led HMRC to require that 'Italian Republic' claims (in respect of cars on which output tax was accounted for incorrectly on the profit margin) must be revisited and adjusted to take account of the effect on the partial exemption calculation of including the value of cars in the denominator. See **49.5 PARTIAL EXEMPTION**. (HMRC Brief 43/10).

Input tax deductible on purchase

Where any input tax was deductible on purchase

- *in the case of a motor car*, output tax must be accounted for on the full selling price. A VAT invoice must be issued to a VAT-registered buyer who requests one. Such a car cannot be sold under the margin scheme for **SECOND-HAND GOODS (61)**.
- *in the case of a commercial vehicle*, output tax must be accounted for on the full selling price (even if part of the VAT charged was not recoverable because the business was partly exempt).

(VAT Notice 700/64/11, paras 7.1, 7.4).

VAT not charged on the purchase of a vehicle

Where VAT was not charged on the purchase of a vehicle (e.g. a purchase from a private individual or from a dealer who sold it under the VAT second-hand margin scheme) VAT need not be accounted for on the full selling price. The second-hand margin scheme can be used to account for VAT only on any profit made on the sale. See **61 SECOND-HAND GOODS**. (VAT Notice 700/64/11, para 7.3).

Transactions not treated as taxable supplies

[45.5] The following transactions relating to motor cars have been designated as outside the scope of VAT so as to be neither a supply of goods nor a supply of services.

(a) The disposal of a used motor car by a person who repossessed it under the terms of a 'finance agreement' provided the following conditions are met.

  - The motor car so disposed must be in the same condition at the time of disposal as when it was repossessed or taken into possession. The condition of goods has been changed if any improvements, repairs, replacement parts or the generally making good of any damage has been carried out. The cleaning of goods generally does not affect the condition nor does the inclusion of instruction manuals if they are otherwise missing. (Business Brief 19/01).
  - VAT on any previous supply, acquisition or importation must have been wholly excluded from credit under **45.3** above.

- In relation to all motor cars delivered after 31 August 2006 under finance agreements entered into after 12 April 2006, no adjustment must have taken place, or may later take place, of VAT on the initial supply under the finance agreement as a result of repossession.

'*Finance agreement*' means any agreement for the sale of goods whereby the property in those goods is not to be transferred until the whole of the price has been paid and the seller retains the right to repossess the goods.

(b) The disposal of a used motor car by an 'insurer' who has taken it in settlement of a claim under a policy of insurance where the car is disposed of in the same condition as it was when it was so acquired. This does not apply unless the VAT on any previous supply, acquisition or importation was wholly excluded from credit under **45.3** above.
Before 1 January 2005, '*insurer*' was restricted to either

- a person who has permission under *Financial Services and Markets Act 2000, Part 4* to effect and carry out contracts of insurance against risks arising from loss of or damage to goods; or
- an EEA firm of the kind mentioned in *Financial Services and Markets Act 2000, Sch 3 para 5(d)* which has permission under *para 15* of that *Schedule* to effect and carry out in the UK contracts of insurance against risks arising from loss of or damage to goods.

(c) The disposal of a motor car for no consideration (e.g. scrap). This does not apply unless the VAT on any previous supply, acquisition or importation was wholly excluded from credit under **45.3** above.

(d) Services in connection with a supply of a used motor car provided by an agent acting in his own name to the purchaser of the motor car, the consideration for which is taken into account in calculating the price at which the agent sold the car. See **61.26 SECOND-HAND GOODS**.

(e) Services in connection with the sale of a used motor car provided by an auctioneer acting in his own name to the vendor or purchaser of the motor car, the consideration for which is taken into account in calculating the price at which the agent obtained (or, as the case may be, sold) the car. See **61.53 SECOND-HAND GOODS.**

(f) Where a taxable person has purchased or has let on hire a motor car

(i) the letting on hire of that motor car by the taxable person to any person for no consideration or consideration less than would be payable in an arm's length commercial transaction, or

(ii) the making available of that motor car (otherwise than by letting on hire) by the taxable person to any person for private use (whether or not for a consideration)

provided that VAT on any previous supply, acquisition, importation or letting on hire of the motor car was wholly excluded from credit under **45.3** above or partly excluded from credit under **45.11** below.
Where the taxable person is an individual or partnership, included under (ii) above is the making available of the motor car to the individual himself or a partner.

The effect of this is that most charges to employees for the private use of a car are not taxable. See **45.22** below.

[*VATA 1994, s 5(3); SI 1992/3122, Arts 2, 4; SI 1995/1269; SI 1995/1667; SI 2001/3649, Art 432; SI 2004/3084; SI 2006/874*].

Self-supply

[45.6] Where a person has obtained input tax credit on a motor car, and has put it to a use that would not qualify for such credit, special 'self-supply' provisions require him to account for VAT on the motor car. The detailed provisions are as follows.

A motor car is treated as self-supplied where

(a) it is produced by a taxable person otherwise than by conversion of a vehicle obtained by him,
(b) it is produced by a taxable person by the conversion of another vehicle (whether a motor car or not) and VAT on the supply to, or acquisition or importation by, the taxable person of that vehicle was not wholly excluded from credit, or
(c) it is supplied to, or acquired from another EU country or imported by, a taxable person and input tax on that supply, acquisition or importation was not wholly excluded from credit,

and that motor car has not been supplied by the taxable person in the course or furtherance of any business carried on by him but is used by him such that, had the motor car been supplied to, or acquired or imported by, him at that time, any input tax would have been wholly excluded from credit under **45.3** above.

A motor car is also treated as self-supplied where

(i) it was transferred to a taxable person under a transaction relating to the transfer of a business as a going concern (TOGC) which was treated as neither a supply of goods nor a supply of services (see **8.10** *et seq* **BUSINESS**);
(ii) in the hands of the transferor or any 'predecessor' of his the self-supply provisions applied by virtue of (*a*), (*b*) or (*c*) above; and
(iii) the motor car has not been treated as self-supplied under these provisions by the transferor or any of his predecessors.

For this purpose, a person is the '*predecessor*' of the transferor where the transferor acquired the motor car from him under a TOGC which was treated as neither a supply of goods nor a supply of services; and a transferor's predecessors include the predecessors or his predecessor through any number of transactions.

Where a group registration is in operation, self-supplies by group members are deemed to be made by the representative member.

[*VATA 1994, s 5(5), s 43(2); SI 1992/3122, Arts 5, 7; SI 1995/1269; SI 1995/1667; SI 1999/2832*].

Value of self-supply

If the car is new, the value of the self-supply by a UK manufacturer is the full cost of manufacturing the vehicle including related production overheads. For volume manufacturers, this can be taken to be ²/₃rds of the current retail list price. Non-volume manufacturers may also use this approximation with the agreement of HMRC. For non-manufacturing traders, the self-supply cost should include the purchase price plus any cost of incorporated parts of UK manufacture and delivery charge. Discounts received after the time of supply should be disregarded unless contractually agreed before that time. Where delivery charges cannot be determined, a fixed charge of £50 per vehicle may be used. (VAT Notice 700/57/04).

If the car is used, the value of the self-supply is the current purchase price of a vehicle *identical* in every respect (including age and condition and, where appropriate, any accessories fitted) to the car concerned or, if that is not available, the price for the purchase of a *similar* car. Failing this, it is the current production cost [*VATA 1994, Sch 6 para 6; SI 1992/1867*] or two thirds of the current list price approximation of a new vehicle. (VAT Notice 700/57/04).

Time of self-supply

The time of supply is treated as taking place when the motor car is appropriated to the use giving rise to the self-supply. [*VATA 1994, s 6(11)*].

The tax point can only be decided once the vehicle has been used in the business, e.g. as a demonstration model. The tax point is then the date when, by any positive and recorded action, the car is transferred from new car sales stock. (VAT Notice 700, para 15.2).

See **45.8** below if the vehicle has been converted and then applied for business use.

See also *A & B Motors (Newton-le-Willows) Ltd* (VTD 1024) (TVC 44.56).

De Voil Indirect Tax Service. See V3.242.

Motor dealers

[45.7] The position of motor dealers is outlined below.

(1) Purchase of 'stock in trade' motor cars

A motor dealer can reclaim input tax charged on used and unused cars purchased as stock in trade for resale even where there is temporary private use (see **45.3** above).

(2) Private use of stock in trade cars

Dealers must account for VAT on the private use by employees or similar persons of cars which form part of the stock in trade. They are not obliged to account for VAT on the private use of cars which they have loaned to third parties (e.g. cars loaned to potential customers) for business purposes.

As the normal rules are complex, HMRC's policy is to allow dealers to use the normal method or a simplified method.

(a) The 'normal rules'

Under *VATA 1994, Sch 4 para 5(4)* (see **47.7 OUTPUT TAX**), where a manufacturer or dealer allows a demonstration car to be made available for private use, whether or not for a consideration, this is a deemed supply of services. Where there is no consideration, the value of the deemed supply is the full cost to the manufacturer or dealer. [*VATA 1994, Sch 6 para 7*]. Where there is consideration, subject to the anti-avoidance provisions below, the value of the supply is that consideration.

Anti-avoidance provisions. Under the above rules, where a nominal consideration is charged (say £1 per year) for the use of a motor car, VAT is only due on that nominal amount rather than the full cost of providing the motor car. The following anti-avoidance rules allow HMRC to direct that VAT is accounted for on an open market valuation of supplies of such motor cars to employees.

In relation to any use, or availability of use, of a motor car on or after a date to be appointed, where

- the value of a supply made by a taxable person for a consideration is (apart from these provisions) less than its open market value,
- the taxable person is a 'motor manufacturer' or 'motor dealer',
- the person to whom the supply is made is *either* an employee of the taxable person *or* a person who, under the terms of his employment, provides services to the taxable person *or* a relative (i.e. husband, wife, brother, sister, ancestor or lineal descendant) of such a person,
- the supply is a supply of services by virtue of *VATA 1994, Sch 4 para 5(4)* (see above),
- the supply relates to a motor car (whether or not any particular motor car) that forms part of the 'stock in trade' of the taxable person, and
- the supply does not fall within the general rules for transactions between connected persons in *VATA 1994, Sch 6 para 1* (see **71.19 VALUATION**)

HMRC may direct that the value of the supply (and any further supplies satisfying these conditions) is to be taken to be its open market value. Any such direction must be given by notice in writing to the motor manufacturer or dealer but no direction may be given more than three years after the time of the supply.

See **45.1** above for the definition of '*motor car*' and **45.3**(*c*) above for the definitions of '*motor manufacturer*', '*motor dealer*' and '*stock in trade*'.

[*VATA 1994, Sch 6 para 1A; FA 2004, s 22(2)*].

(b) A standard simplified method

HMRC have agreed a simplified method with both the Retail Motor Industry Federation (RMI) and the Society of Motor Manufacturers and Traders Ltd (SMMT). Dealers who choose to use a simplified method must use it for all their cars that are put to private use.

RMI agreement: for each individual who has used a stock in trade car for private journeys in a VAT period, the trader must identify the list price of the car he has typically used and identify the appropriate price band to determine the VAT payable for private use.

From 1 May 2009 to 31 December 2009

List price inc VAT band range	Average price inc VAT	VAT due on annual return	VAT due on quarterly return	VAT due on monthly return
£	£	£	£	£
0–8,999.99	7,469.99	61.14	15.28	5.09
9,000–11,999.99	10,319.99	80.89	20.22	6.74
12,000–16,999.99	14,619.99	110.68	27.67	9.22
17,000–22,999.99	20,469.99	151.22	37.80	12.60
23,000–34,999.99	31,149.99	225.22	56.31	18.77
35,000–49,999.99	44,499.99	317.73	79.43	26.48
50,000–64,999.99	58,499.99	414.74	103.69	34.56
65,000–79,999.99	71.999.99	508.29	127.07	42.36
80,000 upwards	Individual calculation based on actual cost prices			

Before 1 May 2009

List price inc VAT band range	Average price inc VAT	VAT due on annual return	VAT due on quarterly return	VAT due on monthly return
£	£	£	£	£
0–9,000	7,500	80.00	20.00	6.67
9,001–12,000	10,300	106.00	26.50	8.83
12,001–16,000	14,200	142.00	35.50	11.83
16,001–21,000	18,650	184.00	46.00	15.33
21,001–26,000	23,400	228.00	57.00	19.00
Over 26,000	see below			

Dealers with non-standard VAT periods should apply the appropriate proportion to the annual VAT due amount.

For cars with list prices in excess of £26,000, the annual VAT due is calculated by

(1) applying 25% annual depreciation to the cost price of the car or a locally agreed average;
(2) adding a standard £250 for repairs and maintenance to the depreciation;
(3) applying a 25% private use proportion to depreciation plus repairs and maintenance to arrive at the full cost of providing the car for private use ('the value for private use'); and
(4) applying the current VAT rate to the value for private use.

(5) The resulting figure (rounded down to the nearest pound) is the annual VAT due.

SMMT agreement: for each individual who has used a stock in trade car for private journeys in a VAT period, the trader must identify the list price of the car he has typically used and identify the appropriate price band to determine the VAT payable for private use.

From 1 May 2009 to 31 December 2009

List price inc VAT band range	Average price inc VAT	VAT due on annual return	VAT due on quarterly return	VAT due on monthly return
£	£	£	£	£
0–8,999.99	7,469.99	55.05	13.76	4.59
9,000–11,999.99	10,319.99	72.47	18.12	6.04
12,000–16,999.99	14,619.99	98.76	24.69	8.23
17,000–22,999.99	20,469.99	134.53	33.63	11.21
23,000–34,999.99	31,149.99	199.83	49.96	16.65
35,000–49,999.99	44,499.99	281.45	70.36	23.45
50,000–64,999.99	58,499.99	367.05	91.76	30.59
65,000–79,999.99	71.999.99	449.59	112.40	37.47
80,000 upwards	Individual calculation based on actual cost prices			

Before 1 May 2009

List price inc VAT band range	Average price inc VAT	VAT due on annual return	VAT due on quarterly return	VAT due on monthly return
£	£	£	£	£
0–9,000	7,500	72.00	18.00	6.00
9,001–12,000	10,300	95.00	23.75	7.92
12,001–16,000	14,200	127.00	31.75	10.58
16,001–21,000	18,650	163.00	40.75	13.58
21,001–26,000	23,400	202.00	50.50	16.83
Over 26,000				see below

Dealers with non-standard VAT periods should apply the appropriate proportion to the annual VAT due amount.

For cars with list prices in excess of £26,000, the annual VAT due is calculated as under the RMI agreement above.

(VAT Notice 700/57/04; VAT Information Sheet 7/09).

(3) Disposals of cars on which input tax was recovered

VAT must be charged on the full selling price. See also **45.6** above for self-supply, e.g. where an unused car on which VAT has been reclaimed is transferred from sales stock to use in the business that would not qualify for input tax recovery.

(4) 'Bumping'

A car dealer may accept a second-hand car in part-exchange and then make arrangements with a finance company for the sale of the replacement car to the customer, treating the part-exchange value as the deposit required by the finance company. As the finance company normally requires a minimum deposit, it is common practice to inflate the part-exchange value and the sales price of the replacement car by a similar amount so that the minimum deposit can be met without resort to a cash payment from the customer (a practice known as 'bumping'). In such cases, the car dealer must account for VAT on the inflated price of the car as shown on the HP agreement (*North Anderson Cars Ltd v C & E Commrs*, CS [1999] STC 902 (TVC 44.154)).

(5) Premium, 'nearly new' and 'personal import' cars

Franchised dealers are not permitted by the terms of their franchise to sell a new car to another dealer. Therefore, non-franchised dealers must secure regular supplies by other means, e.g. by employing an agent to purchase a car from a franchised dealer. Similarly, 'personal import' cars are sometimes acquired by VAT-registered dealers from private importers immediately following their importation.

The normal rules for supplying goods through buying agents apply (see **3.6 AGENTS**). Non-franchised dealers are only able to recover input tax on the purchase of a motor car if it is purchased

- directly from a manufacturer or another dealer;
- through an agent acting in the name of the non-franchised dealer; or
- through an 'undisclosed agent' acting in his own name if the agent is registered for VAT and has issued a proper VAT invoice. However, to be registered, such an agent must be in business for VAT purposes and, given the nature of the tests which must be applied to establish this (see **8.2 BUSINESS**), it is unlikely that HMRC will regard the intention to sell a single car as constituting 'business'. Even if registered, an undisclosed agent will suffer a block on input tax recovery on the purchase of a car if it is made available for private use. This may apply if there is a gap between the purchase of the car and the supply to the non-franchised dealer.

(Business Brief 4/98).

(6) Dealer demonstration bonuses

See **45.2** above.

Conversion of a vehicle into a motor car and vice versa

Conversion of a commercial vehicle into a car

[45.8] A commercial vehicle can be converted into a car for VAT purposes. Where VAT is recovered on the purchase of the vehicle, output tax must be accounted for when the conversion is completed. The value for VAT purposes is the value of the vehicle at the time the conversion is completed, including the cost of the conversion. VAT incurred on any parts bought for the conversion are recoverable.

Examples of the conversion of a vehicle into a motor car are:

- The fitting of a side window or windows into a van to the rear of the driver's seat.
- The fitting of a rear seat or seats to a van, even without the insertion of side windows.
- The removal of seats from a twelve-seater vehicle.

(VAT Notice 700/64/11, para 2.4).

See, however, *Bolinge Hill Farm* (VTD 4217) (TVC 44.43); *P Oddonetto* (VTD 5208) (TVC 44.45); *John Beharrell Ltd* (VTD 6530) (TVC 44.47) and *Chichester Plant Contractors Ltd* (VTD 6575) (TVC 44.42).

Conversion of a car into a commercial vehicle

This can be done, for example, by removing rear seats and windows or by adding additional seats so that the vehicle can legally seat twelve or more people. VAT can only be recovered on the car if it was bought specifically for this conversion and not used as a car. (VAT Notice 700/64/11, para 2.5).

Car kits

[45.9] Where a car is made from a kit or separately purchased parts, any VAT charged as input tax may be reclaimed subject to the normal rules. If the finished car is used in the business for a purpose that would not qualify for input tax recovery, VAT must be accounted for under the self-supply rules (see **45.6** above). The tax value must be based on the VAT-exclusive cost of the parts and the cost of construction. The VAT cannot be reclaimed. If the finished car is sold, VAT must be accounted for on the full selling price in the normal way. (VAT Notice 700/64/11, para 2.6).

Motor expenses

[45.10] Provided the vehicle is used in the business, VAT on leasing or hiring a vehicle, road fuel (whether bought by the business or reimbursed to employees) and repair and maintenance charges can be treated as input tax. This applies even if the vehicle is used partly for private motoring. Private usage may, however, create a liability to output tax.

The provisions are considered in more detail in **45.11** to **45.22** below. For these purposes it is important to understand the difference between 'business' and 'private' motoring.

A '*business*' journey is one made by an employer or employee for the purpose of the business.

A '*private*' journey is any journey not for the purpose of the business.

Travel between a person's home and normal workplace is private motoring. Travel from home to any other place for business purposes is a business journey.

Leasing or hiring a motor car

[45.11] The following provisions apply to motor cars that are hired or leased for business purposes. The provisions do not apply to hire purchase or lease-purchase agreements, for which see **45.3** above.

If a motor car as defined in **45.1** above is leased or hired, only 50% of the input VAT on the rental charges is available for the credit except in the following circumstances when 100% relief is available.

(a) The motor car is a 'qualifying' motor car let on hire to a taxable person who intends to use the motor car exclusively for business purposes. This condition is *not* satisfied if the taxable person intends to
- let it on hire to any person either for no consideration or consideration less than would be payable in an arm's length commercial transaction; or
- make it available, otherwise than by letting on hire, to any person (including, where the taxable person is an individual, himself or, where the taxable person is a partnership, a partner) for private use (whether or not for a consideration).

(b) The motor car is a 'qualifying' motor car let on hire to a taxable person who intends to use the motor car primarily
- to provide it on hire with the services of a driver for the purposes of carrying passengers;
- to provide it for 'self-drive hire'; or
- as a vehicle in which instruction in driving of a motor car is to be given by him.

'*Self-drive hire*' means hire where the hirer is the person normally expected to drive the motor car and the period of hire to each hirer (together with the period of hire of any other motor car expected to be hired to him by the taxable person) will normally be less than both 30 consecutive days and 90 days in any twelve-month period.

(c) The motor car is not a 'qualifying' motor car. However, following the decision in *C & E Commrs v BRS Automotive Ltd*, CA [1998] STC 1210 (TVC 44.104) (where a tax avoidance scheme was used to exploit the change to the VAT treatment of business cars which took effect from 1 August 1995) this does not apply to leasing charges after 12 November 1998 to a lessee if the only reason that the motor car is not a qualifying motor car is that it was let on hire to that same lessee before 1 August 1995. For further details of the effect of the anti-avoidance provisions, see Business Brief 25/98.

(d) The motor car is unused and is let on hire to a taxable person whose business consists predominantly of making supplies within *VATA 1994, Sch 8 Group 12 Item 14* (see **28.31 HEALTH AND WELFARE**) by a taxable person whose only taxable supplies are concerned with the letting on hire of motor cars to such taxable persons.

See **45.3** above for the definition of a '*qualifying*' motor car.
[*SI 1992/3222, Art 7; SI 1995/281; SI 1995/1666; SI 1998/2767*].

Identifying qualifying cars on leasing invoices

HMRC have agreed with a main leasing trade organisation a recommended form of invoice for leasing companies to adopt for lettings. The invoice must clearly identify whether or not the car is a qualifying car (a legal requirement, see **39.4 INVOICES**) and, if it is, the amount of VAT which is potentially subject to the 50% input tax restriction (depending upon the customer's use). Where the leasing company has not indicated whether the car is a qualifying car or not, the lessee can assume that a car with an 'M' registration or earlier prefix is non-qualifying and recover VAT in full subject to the normal rules. A car with an 'N' or later registration prefix should normally be treated as a qualifying car and the 50% restriction applied (unless the usage qualifies for 100% deduction under (*a*) or (*b*) above). Full input tax relief may, however, be claimed on rental charges on 'N' registration cars if the hirer incurred any VAT on rental on it before 1 August 1995.

The requirement to identify whether or not a car is a qualifying car does not apply to self-drive hire cars (see below). Unless there is evidence to the contrary, any self-drive hire car should be treated as a qualifying car if it has a 'K' registration or later prefix.

Charges subject to the 50% restriction

There are frequently two distinct elements of the rental: basic rental for the provision of the car (including depreciation, funding cost, VED and a proportion of overheads/profit) and an optional additional charge (covering repairs, maintenance and roadside assistance and a proportion of overheads/profit). The optional charges are also subject to the 50% restriction unless they are separately described in the contract hire agreement and periodic invoices and are genuinely optional, in which case they are recoverable in full subject to the normal rules. VAT on an excess mileage charge should similarly be separated into two distinct elements on a basis identical to the split of the rental. For full details, see the agreement between the British Vehicle Rental and Leasing Association and HMRC reproduced in VAT Notice 700/57/04.

Rental rebates

Where a lessor sells a car at the end of a lease and uses the proceeds to rebate the monthly rental payments made to the lessee, a lessee who incurred a 50% input tax restriction on the rental charges on the car need only adjust for 50% of the VAT on the credit note issued by the lessor for rebate of rentals.

Early lease termination

Where a lessee terminates the lease early, the leasing company may choose to either

- treat both the termination payment and any associated rebate of rental as taxable; or
- treat both as outside the scope of VAT.

If the leasing company chooses to tax, it will normally offset the termination payment against the rebate.

- Where the termination payment exceeds the rebate, any VAT is not subject to the 50% restriction.
- Where the rebate exceeds the termination payment, the leasing company must issue a VAT credit note for the balance. A lessee who incurred a 50% input tax restriction on the rental charges need only adjust for 50% of the VAT credit in the VAT account.

Self-drive hire (daily rental)

The 50% restriction applies to self-drive hire as well as leasing on a longer-term basis. If the car is hired simply to replace an off-the-road ordinary company car, the 50% block applies from the first day of hire. By concession, HMRC accept that in other cases (e.g. where the business does not have a company car) the 50% block does not apply if a car is hired for not more than 10 days to use specifically for business purposes.

Interaction with other apportionments

Where the 50% input tax restriction applies and there are both business and non-business activities and/or exempt supplies, the order for carrying out the various apportionments is

- VAT incurred between business and non-business activities (see **34.7 INPUT TAX**)
- 50% input tax restriction on the VAT amount which relates to business activities
- any necessary **PARTIAL EXEMPTION (49)** calculation.

(VAT Notice 700/64/11, paras 4.4–4.10; VAT Information Sheet 12/95; Business Brief 15/95).

VAT due by daily rental companies on incidental private use of their hire fleet

Under the normal rules, where assets are used for private purposes a supply of services takes place. Where the services are provided for no consideration, the value of those services is the cost to the employer of providing those services. The calculation of this value would involve, in each VAT period, reference to

- the depreciation of the capital cost of the car;
- the value (excluding VAT) of repairs, maintenance and other running costs (excluding road fuel) on which VAT had been recovered; and

- the actual proportion of business and private use.

As these calculations might be complex, HMRC and the British Vehicle Rental and Leasing Association have agreed that daily rental companies may choose to apply a simplified method of establishing the output tax due. Daily rental companies who choose to use the simplified method must do so for all their daily rental cars which are put to private use. Daily rental companies who choose not to adopt the simplified method must either apply the normal rules or apply to HMRC to use an individual simplified method. For each VAT period, the daily rental company must calculate output VAT on the private use of the daily rental cars as follows.

- Identify staff that use a daily rental car for private journeys in the period.
- For each person, identify the list price (or before 1 May 2009 the cc band) of car they have typically used in the period.
- For each person, identify the appropriate price band to determine the VAT payable for private use.

From 1 May 2009 to 31 December 2009

List price inc VAT band range	Average price inc VAT	VAT due on annual return	VAT due on quarterly return	VAT due on monthly return
£	£	£	£	£
0–8,999.99	7,469.99	36.29	9.07	3.02
9,000–11,999.99	10,319.99	46.56	11.64	3.88
12,000–16,999.99	14,619.99	62.05	15.51	5.17
17,000–22,999.99	20,469.99	83.13	20.78	6.93
23,000–34,999.99	31,149.99	121.62	30.40	10.13
35,000–49,999.99	44,499.99	169.72	42.43	14.14
50,000–64,999.99	58,499.99	220.17	55.04	18.35
65,000–79,999.99	71.999.99	268.81	67.20	22.40
80,000 upwards	Individual calculation based on actual cost prices			

Before 1 May 2009

Engine size cc	VAT due on annual return	VAT due on quarterly return	VAT due on monthly return
Up to 1200	51.06	12.76	4.25
Up to 1400	61.69	15.42	5.14
Up to 1800	75.95	18.98	6.32
Over 1800	91.19	22.80	7.60

Daily rental companies with non-standard VAT periods should apply the appropriate proportion to the annual amount.

(VAT Notice 700/57/04; VAT Information Sheet 7/09).

Fleet leasing bonuses

See **45.2** above. Receipt of such a bonus reduces the VAT recoverable by the customer (if any) on the lease payments. For example, where 50% of the VAT incurred on lease payments can be recovered, VAT due on the bonus payment is

1/6* × 50% × gross bonus payment

(*7/47 before 4 January 2011; 3/23 from 1 December 2008 to 31 December 2009)

(Business Brief 1/98).

Repairs and maintenance

[45.12] If a vehicle is used for business purposes, VAT on repairs and maintenance can be treated as input tax provided the work done is paid for by the business. This applies even if the vehicle is used for private motoring and even if no VAT is reclaimed on any road fuel in order to avoid use of the scale charges, see **45.16** below. VAT on repairs, etc. relating to a vehicle used solely for private motoring by a sole proprietor or partner cannot be treated as input tax. (VAT Notice 700/64/11, para 5.1).

Accessories

[45.13] Where a car is purchased on which input tax is blocked, VAT charged on accessories fitted to a car when purchased cannot be reclaimed even if optional and separately itemised on the sales invoice. See *Turmeau* (VTD 1135) (TVC 44.100).

VAT on accessories subsequently purchased can only be treated as input tax if

- the vehicle is owned by the business or used in the business but not owned by it (e.g. an employee's or director's own car); and
- the accessory has a business use.

(VAT Notice 700/64/11, paras 5.2, 5.3).

Input tax on personalised number plates has been disallowed in a considerable number of cases including *Ava Knit Ltd* (VTD 1461) (TVC 36.477) and *E N Jones* (VTD 5023) (TVC 36.487) but allowed in *MW Alexander* (VTD 7208) (TVC 36.468); *Sunner & Sons* (VTD 8857) (TVC 36.471) and *Hamlet's (Radio & TV) Ltd* (VTD 12716) (TVC 36.472). See *Tolley's VAT Cases.*

Fuel bought by the business

[45.14] Where a business pays for road fuel, if the fuel is used for business motoring only, subject to the normal rules it can claim all of the VAT because 100% is used for business purposes. Where the fuel purchased is used both for business and private motoring, the business has three options.

(a) In the case of motor cars, it can claim all VAT charged and apply the fuel scale charge (see **45.16** below).

(b) It can use detailed mileage records to separate business mileage from private mileage. This avoids using the scale charge. Records must be kept of total mileage, split between business and private mileage, and total fuel costs.

> *Example*
>
> Total business mileage is 4,290 of which 3,165 relates to business mileage. The total cost of fuel is £250.
>
> The cost of the business mileage is
>
> £250 × 3,165 ÷ 4,290 = £184.44
>
> Input tax is £184.44 × 1/6* = £30.74
>
> (*7/47 before 4 January 2011; 3/23 from 1 December 2008 to 31 December 2009.)

(c) It can neither claim input tax on any road fuel purchased nor apply the scale charge (see **45.16** below).

(VAT Notice 700/64/11, paras 8.1–8.5).

Non-business activities

VAT on non-business journeys (e.g. journeys in connection with charitable activities of charities) is not reclaimable. Where fuel is used for both business and non-business activities, the total cost should be apportioned.

Fuel card schemes

Fuel cards allow companies who own fleets of vehicles to purchase fuel, and other motor-related goods and services, from garages by means of a card. The schemes are designed contractually to provide that, where a card is used to buy fuel, the fuel is supplied from the garage to the card company and then by the card company to the cardholders. (With a normal credit card transaction, the garage supplies goods and services direct to the cardholders, the credit card being used simply as a means of payment.) Whether the schemes work depends upon the precise terms of the contractual arrangements between the parties.

See *Harpur Group Ltd* (VTD 12001) (TVC 27.36) where five different schemes were considered.

See also *Auto Lease Holland BV v Bundesamt fur Finanzen, CJEC Case C–185/01*, [2005] STC 598 (TVC 22.152) where a Netherlands company (H) leased a number of motor vehicles and gave the lessees the use of a credit card to purchase fuel. It contended that it should be treated as having received the fuel from the retail companies and as having made an onward supply to the lessees. The Court held that, in the circumstances of the case, the lessor of a vehicle did not make any supply of fuel to the lessee even if the vehicle was filled up in the name and at the expense of that lessor.

Fuel bought by employees

[45.15] Where

- road fuel is supplied to an employer in circumstances where it is delivered to and paid for by an employee, acting in the employer's name and on its behalf, for use by the employee either in whole or in part for the purposes of the employer's business, and
- the employer has agreed to reimburse (and does so reimburse) the employee for the cost of the road fuel so used in one of the ways specified below,

the employer can deduct input tax on the road fuel in question, quantified by reference to the amount it pays to the employee as reimbursement. The employer must hold a VAT invoice which contains the details prescribed under

(i) **39.4** INVOICES (VAT invoices generally),
(ii) **39.5** INVOICES (VAT invoices to persons in another EU country), or
(iii) **39.7**(*a*) INVOICES (retailers' less detailed invoices)

as applicable. Where required by those provisions, the prescribed invoice must be made out to the employer as the recipient of the supply. (Note. In the vast majority of cases, the invoice will fall under (iii) where there is no requirement for the name of the recipient of the supply to appear on the invoice.)

The specified ways are

(a) *where all the road fuel is used for the purposes of the employer's business*, by payment of the actual cost of the road fuel; and
(b) *where only part of the road fuel is used for the purposes of the employer's business*, by payment of either
  (i) an amount which represents the actual cost of the road fuel so used determined by the total distances travelled by the relevant vehicle and the cylinder capacity of that vehicle; or
  (ii) the actual cost of the road fuel in circumstances where the employer accounts for output tax on any private use using the scale charge (see **45.16** and **45.17** below).

'*Use for the purposes of the employer's business*' means use for the purposes by the employer in making onward taxable supplies.

[*SI 2005/3290*].

The only practical change to the previous system is that an invoice must be retained in support of a claim for VAT recovery. In the vast majority of cases, this will be a retailer's less detailed VAT invoice.

Mileage allowances

Where employees are paid mileage allowances, input tax is calculated by multiplying the fuel element of the mileage allowance by the VAT fraction. The allowance paid to employees must be based upon mileage actually done. (VAT Notice 700/64/11, para 8.7).

Records of mileage

Where employees are paid a mileage allowance, HMRC require the business to keep a record for each employee showing

- mileage travelled;
- whether journeys are both business and private;
- the cylinder capacity of the vehicle;
- the rate of the mileage allowance; and
- the amount of input tax claimed.

(VAT Notice 700/64/11, para 8.8).

Advisory fuel rates

For income tax purposes, HMRC publish advisory fuel rates for company cars based on the engine capacity of the car and the type of fuel used. HMRC will also accept these figures for VAT purposes as the basis for reimbursing an employee for fuel bought for business purposes, although the employer must retain receipts in line with the current legislation.

The rates applying are as follows.

1.12.11–				
Engine size		*Fuel cost per mile*		
Petrol/LPG	*Diesel*	*Petrol*	*Diesel*	*LPG*
Up to 1,400cc	Up to 1,600cc	15p	12p	10p
1,401–2,000cc	1,601–2,000cc	18p	15p	12p
Over 2,000cc	Over 2,000cc	26p	18p	18p

1.9.11–30.11.11				
Engine size		*Fuel cost per mile*		
Petrol/LPG	*Diesel*	*Petrol*	*Diesel*	*LPG*
Up to 1,400cc	Up to 1,600cc	15p	12p	11p
1,401–2,000cc	1,601–2,000cc	18p	15p	12p
Over 2,000cc	Over 2,000cc	26p	18p	18p

1.6.11–31.8.11				
Engine size		*Fuel cost per mile*		
Petrol/LPG	*Diesel*	*Petrol*	*Diesel*	*LPG*
Up to 1,400cc	Up to 1,600cc	15p	11p	12p
1,401–2,000cc	1,601–2,000cc	18p	13p	15p
Over 2,000cc	Over 2,000cc	26p	18p	18p

1.3.11–31.5.11			
Engine size	*Fuel cost per mile*		
	Petrol	*Diesel*	*LPG*
Up to 1,400cc	14p	13p	10p
1,401–2,000cc	16p	13p	12p
Over 2,000cc	23p	16p	17p

1.12.10–28.2.11			
Engine size	*Fuel cost per mile*		
	Petrol	*Diesel*	*LPG*
Up to 1,400cc	13p	12p	9p
1,401–2,000cc	15p	12p	10p
Over 2,000cc	21p	15p	15p

HMRC also accept rates set by recognised motoring agencies (e.g. RAC, AA).

De Voil Indirect Tax Service. See V3.436.

Fuel for private use

[45.16] Where in any VAT period a taxable person supplies 'fuel for private use' to an individual, VAT must be accounted for using the scale charges in **45.17** below which represent the VAT-inclusive value of the fuel in respect of any one vehicle.

'*Fuel for private use*' is fuel which is (or has previously been) supplied to, acquired from another EU country by, imported from outside the EU by, or manufactured by, a taxable person in the course of his business and which is

- provided or to be provided by the taxable person to an individual by reason of his employment or office for private use in his 'own vehicle' or a vehicle allocated to him;
- where the taxable person is an individual, appropriated or to be appropriated by him for private use in his own vehicle; or
- where the taxable person is a partnership, provided or to be provided to any of the individual partners for private use in his own vehicle.

Fuel is not regarded as provided to any person for his private use if it is supplied at a price not less than that at which it was supplied to or imported by the taxable person, or in the case of manufactured fuel, at a price not less than the aggregate of costs of raw materials and of manufacturing together with any excise duty thereon. See below for the VAT treatment where fuel is charged at such a price.

'*Business travel*' is that which an individual is necessarily obliged to do in the performance of the duties of his employment, the partnership, or in the case of the taxable person himself, his business.

'*Own vehicle*' includes any vehicle of which for the time being the individual has the use (other than a vehicle 'allocated to' him).

'*Vehicle*' means any mechanically propelled road vehicle other than a motor cycle or an invalid carriage. HMRC have, however, confirmed that the scale rate charges will apply only to cars.

A vehicle is at any time '*allocated to*' an individual if at that time it is made available (without any transfer of property in it) either to the individual himself or to any other person, and is so made available by reason of the individual's employment and for private use. However, a vehicle is not regarded as allocated to an individual by reason of his employment if, in any VAT period, it is a pooled car i.e.

- it was made available to, and actually used by, more than one of the employees or one or more (of the) employers and, in the case of each of them, it was made available to him by reason of his employment but was not in the period ordinarily used by any one of them to the exclusion of the others;
- in the case of each of the employees, any private use of the vehicle made by him was merely incidental to his other use of it in that period; and
- it was not normally kept overnight on or in the vicinity of any residential premises where any of the employees was residing, except while being kept overnight on premises occupied by the person making the vehicle available to them.

The provision of fuel is treated as a supply in the course or furtherance of a business by the taxable person at the time when fuel for private use is put into the fuel tank of the individual's own vehicle or a vehicle allocated to him. An appropriation by a taxable person to his own private use is treated as a supply to himself in his private capacity. A provision of fuel by a member of a group within *VATA 1994, s 43* (see **27 GROUPS OF COMPANIES**) is treated as provision by the representative member.

Input tax

VAT on the supply, acquisition or importation of fuel for private use is to be treated as input tax subject to the normal rules notwithstanding that the fuel is not used or to be used for business purposes.

Changing vehicles

Where an individual is supplied with fuel for private use for one vehicle in respect of part of a VAT period and another vehicle for another part of the same period, then, provided that at the end of the period one of the vehicles neither belongs to him nor is allocated to him, supplies made to the individual are treated as made in respect of one vehicle only. Where each vehicle falls within the same category in the above tables, the table is applied as if fuel had been supplied for one vehicle only throughout the period. Otherwise the figures are rateably apportioned depending on the period for which fuel for private use was supplied for each vehicle.

[*VATA 1994, ss 56, 57*].

Records

Where the scale charge is used, records must be kept showing

(1) the number of cars for which free or below cost fuel is supplied;
(2) the CO2 band for each car;
(3) the cylinder capacity of each car if the car is too old to have a CO2 emissions figure; and
(4) if a vehicle is changed, the date of the change.

(VAT Notice 700/64/11, para 9.6).

Concession not to pay scale charges

If fuel is supplied for private motoring free or for less than the amount paid for it, the only way to avoid accounting for VAT using the scale charge is by not reclaiming input tax on *any* fuel purchased whether used for business or private motoring in cars or commercial vehicles. (VAT Notice 748, ESC 3.1). If this method is adopted, HMRC must be advised before the start of the period in which it is to take effect and they will then treat the decision as remaining in force until told otherwise.

Partly exempt traders

Where a partly exempt business uses a vehicle for both private and business purposes, the input tax incurred on the petrol for private use is fully recoverable and that on business motoring is recoverable to the extent the vehicle is used to make taxable supplies. To do this, business and private fuel costs must be separated. Where a partly exempt business is unable to separate business and private motoring, all input tax on fuel (including that for private motoring) must be apportioned in the partial exemption calculations. To compensate for this, the scale charge for private motoring may be reduced to equal the percentage of input tax recovered under the partial exemption method. For example, if only 80% of the input tax is recovered, only 80% of the appropriate scale charge is to be paid. Where an annual adjustment is carried out, the scale charge must also be adjusted. (HMRC VAT Guidance V1–15, para PE4450).

Accounting for VAT

The VAT due per the scale charge table in **45.17** below should be included in the total output tax figure on the return. The net amount (i.e. the scale charge for the fuel less the VAT due) should be included in the total value of outputs on the return.

> ***Example***
>
> L Ltd provides its employees with cars and pays all day-to-day running expenses, including the cost of any petrol used for private motoring. Each employee submits a monthly return showing opening and closing mileage, together with fuel and servicing receipts for the period.
>
> T, the sales director, has a car with CO2 emission of 220 g/km and puts in a monthly claim for February 2010. He supports this with petrol bills totalling £176.49 and a service invoice for £282.00 (£240.00 plus VAT £42.00). The company prepares monthly VAT returns.
>
> The company should code the expenses claim as follows.

Debit		£
Servicing		240.00
Fuel £176.49 × 40/47	150.20	
Scale charge — see 45.17 below	19.96	
		170.16
Input VAT — on service	42.00	
— on petrol £176.49 × 7/47	26.29	
		68.29
		£478.45
Credit		
Expenses reimbursed to T		
£176.49 + £282.00		458.49
Output VAT		19.96
		£478.45

De Voil Indirect Tax Service. See V3.266, V3.435.

Fuel for private use — scale charges

[45.17] The UK is authorised, under *Council Decision 659/2006/EC*, to fix flat-rate scale charges in relation to expenditure on fuel used for private purposes based on the CO2 emissions level of the vehicle. This change aligns the basis of the VAT private use charge with that operated for direct tax purposes.

Determination of CO_2 emissions figure

(a) If a CO_2 emissions figure is specified in relation to a vehicle in an EU certificate of conformity or a UK approval certificate, the vehicle's CO_2 emissions figure for the purposes of the scale charge is determined as follows.

- (i) If only one figure is specified in the certificate, that figure is the vehicle's CO_2 emissions figure for those purposes.
- (ii) If more than one figure is specified in the certificate, the figure specified as the CO_2 (combined) emissions figure is the vehicle's CO_2 emissions figure for those purposes.
- (iii) If separate CO_2 emissions figures are specified for different fuels, the lowest figure specified or, in a case within (ii) above, the lowest CO2 emissions (combined) figure specified is the vehicle's CO2 emissions figure for those purposes.
- (iv) If the vehicle's CO_2 emissions figure (determined in accordance with (i)–(iii) above is not a multiple of five, it is rounded down to the nearest multiple of five for those purposes.

(b) If no EU certificate of conformity or UK approval certificate is issued in relation to a vehicle or no emissions figure is specified in relation to it in any such certificate, the vehicle's CO_2 emissions figure for the purposes of the scale charge is

- (i) 140 if its cylinder capacity is 1,400cc or less;

(ii) 175 if its cylinder capacity exceeds 1,400cc but does not exceed 2,000cc; and

(iii) 225 (decreased from 230 from 1.5.11) or more if its cylinder capacity exceeds 2,000cc.

[*VATA 1994, s 57(3)(4A)–(4G)(9)(10); F(No 2)A 2005, s 2; SI 2007/966; SI 2011/898*].

VAT periods beginning on or after 1.5.11

[45.18]

	Annual VAT returns		Quarterly VAT returns		Monthly VAT Returns	
CO_2 emissions, g/km	Scale charge	VAT due at 20%*	Scale charge	VAT due at 20%*	Scale charge	VAT due at 20%*
	£	£	£	£	£	£
120 or less	630	105	157	26.17	52	8.67
125	945	157.5	236	39.33	78	13
130	1,010	168.33	252	42	84	14
135	1,070	178.33	268	44.67	89	14.83
140	1,135	189.17	283	47.17	94	15.67
145	1,200	200	299	49.83	99	16.5
150	1,260	210	315	52.5	105	17.5
155	1,325	220.83	331	55.17	110	18.33
160	1,385	230.83	346	57.67	115	19.17
165	1,450	241.67	362	60.33	120	20
170	1,515	252.5	378	63	126	21
175	1,575	262.5	394	65.67	131	21.83
180	1,640	273.33	409	68.17	136	22.67
185	1,705	284.17	425	70.83	141	23.5
190	1,765	294.17	441	73.5	147	24.5
195	1,830	305	457	76.17	152	25.33
200	1,890	315	472	78.67	157	26.17
205	1,955	325.83	488	81.33	162	27
210	2,020	336.67	504	84	168	28
215	2,080	346.67	520	86.67	173	28.83
220	2,145	357.5	536	89.33	178	29.67
225 or more	2,205	367.5	551	91.83	183	30.5

[*SI 2011/898*].

VAT periods beginning on or after 1.5.10 and before 1.5.11

[45.19]

	Annual VAT returns			Quarterly VAT returns			Monthly VAT Returns		
CO_2 emissions, g/km	Scale charge	VAT due at 17.5%	VAT due at 20%*	Scale charge	VAT due at 17.5%	VAT due at 20%*	Scale charge	VAT due at 17.5%	VAT due at 20%*
	£	£	£	£	£	£	£	£	£
120 or less	570	84.89	95	141	21	23.5	47	7	7.83
125	850	126.60	141.67	212	31.57	35.33	70	10.43	11.67
130	850	126.60	141.67	212	31.57	35.33	70	10.43	11.67
135	910	135.53	151.67	227	33.81	37.83	75	11.17	12.5
140	965	143.72	160.83	241	35.89	40.17	80	11.91	13.33
145	1,020	151.91	170	255	37.98	42.5	85	12.66	14.17
150	1,080	160.85	180	269	40.06	44.83	89	13.26	14.83
155	1,135	169.04	189.17	283	42.15	47.17	94	14	15.67
160	1,190	177.23	198.33	297	44.23	49.5	99	14.74	16.5
165	1,250	186.17	208.33	312	46.47	52	104	15.49	17.33
170	1,305	194.36	217.5	326	48.55	54.33	108	16.09	18
175	1,360	202.55	226.67	340	50.64	56.67	113	16.83	18.83
180	1,420	211.49	236.67	354	52.72	59	118	17.57	19.67
185	1,475	219.68	245.83	368	54.81	61.33	122	18.17	20.33
190	1,530	227.87	255	383	57.04	63.83	127	18.91	21.17
195	1,590	236.81	265	397	59.13	66.17	132	19.66	22
200	1,645	245	274.17	411	61.21	68.5	137	20.40	22.83
205	1,705	253.94	284.17	425	63.30	70.83	141	21	23.5
210	1,760	262.13	293.33	439	65.38	73.17	146	21.74	24.33
215	1,815	270.32	302.5	454	67.62	75.67	151	22.49	25.17
220	1,875	279.26	312.5	468	69.70	78	156	23.23	26
225	1,930	287.45	321.67	482	71.79	80.33	160	23.83	26.67
230 or more	1,985	295.64	330.83	496	73.87	82.67	165	24.57	27.5

*From 4 January 2011 the standard rate of VAT is increased to 20%.

[*SI 2010/919*].

VAT periods beginning on or after 14.5.09 and before 1.5.10

[45.20]

	Annual VAT returns			Quarterly VAT returns			Monthly VAT Returns		
CO_2 emissions, g/km	Scale charge	VAT due at 17.5%	VAT due at 15%*	Scale charge	VAT due at 17.5%	VAT due at 15%*	Scale charge	VAT due at 17.5%	VAT due at 15%*
	£	£	£	£	£	£	£	£	£
120 or less	505	75.21	65.87	126	18.77	16.43	42	6.26	5.48
125	755	112.45	98.48	189	28.15	24.65	63	9.38	8.22
130	755	112.45	98.48	189	28.15	24.65	63	9.38	8.22
135	755	112.45	98.48	189	28.15	24.65	63	9.38	8.22
140	805	119.89	105.00	201	29.94	26.22	67	9.98	8.74
145	855	127.34	111.52	214	31.87	27.91	71	10.57	9.78
150	905	134.79	118.04	226	33.66	29.48	75	11.17	10.33
155	960	142.98	125.22	239	35.60	31.17	79	11.77	10.30
160	1,010	150.43	131.74	251	37.38	32.74	83	12.36	10.83
165	1,060	157.87	138.26	264	39.32	34.43	88	13.11	11.48
170	1,110	165.32	144.78	276	41.11	36.00	92	13.70	12.00
175	1,160	172.77	151.30	289	43.04	37.70	96	14.30	12.52
180	1,210	180.21	157.83	302	44.98	39.39	100	14.89	13.04
185	1,260	187.66	164.35	314	46.77	40.96	104	15.49	13.57
190	1,310	195.11	170.87	327	48.70	42.65	109	16.23	14.22
195	1,360	202.55	177.39	339	50.49	44.22	113	16.83	14.74
200	1,410	210.00	183.91	352	52.43	45.91	117	17.43	15.26
205	1,465	218.19	191.09	365	54.36	47.61	121	18.02	15.78
210	1,515	225.64	197.61	378	56.30	49.30	126	18.77	16.43
215	1,565	233.08	204.13	390	58.09	50.87	130	19.36	16.96
220	1,615	240.53	210.65	403	60.02	52.57	134	19.96	17.48
225	1,665	247.98	217.17	416	61.96	54.26	138	20.55	18.00
230	1,715	255.43	223.70	428	63.74	55.83	142	21.15	18.52
235 or more	1,765	262.87	230.22	441	65.68	57.52	147	21.89	19.17

*From 1 December 2008 to 31 December 2009 the standard rate of VAT is reduced to 15%.

[*SI 2009/1030*].

VAT periods beginning on or after 1.5.08 and before 1.5.09

[45.21]

	Annual VAT returns			Quarterly VAT returns			Monthly VAT Returns		
CO_2 emissions, g/km	Scale charge	VAT due at 17.5%	VAT due at 15%*	Scale charge	VAT due at 17.5%	VAT due at 15%*	Scale charge	VAT due at 17.5%	VAT due at 15%*
	£	£	£	£	£	£	£	£	£
120 or less	555	82.66	72.39	138	20.55	18.00	46	6.85	6.00
125	830	123.62	108.26	207	30.83	27.00	69	10.28	9.00
130	830	123.62	108.26	207	30.83	27.00	69	10.28	9.00
135	830	123.62	108.26	207	30.83	27.00	69	10.28	9.00
140	885	131.81	115.43	221	32.91	28.83	73	10.87	9.52
145	940	140.00	122.61	234	34.85	30.52	78	11.62	10.17
150	995	148.19	129.78	248	36.94	32.35	82	12.21	10.70
155	1,050	156.38	136.96	262	39.02	34.17	87	12.96	11.35
160	1,105	164.57	144.13	276	41.11	36.00	92	13.70	12.00
165	1,160	172.77	151.30	290	43.19	37.83	96	14.30	12.52
170	1,215	180.96	158.48	303	45.13	39.52	101	15.04	13.17
175	1,270	189.15	165.65	317	47.21	41.35	105	15.64	13.70
180	1,325	197.34	172.83	331	49.30	43.17	110	16.38	14.35
185	1,380	205.53	180.00	345	51.38	45.00	115	17.13	15.00
190	1,435	213.72	187.17	359	53.47	46.83	119	17.72	15.52
195	1,490	221.91	194.35	373	55.55	48.65	124	18.47	16.17
200	1,545	230.11	201.52	386	57.49	50.35	128	19.06	16.70
205	1,605	239.04	209.35	400	59.57	52.17	133	19.81	17.35
210	1,660	247.23	216.52	414	61.66	54.00	138	20.55	18.00
215	1,715	255.43	223.70	428	63.74	55.83	142	21.15	18.52
220	1,770	263.62	230.87	442	65.83	57.65	147	21.89	19.17
225	1,825	271.81	238.04	455	67.77	59.35	151	22.49	19.70
230	1,880	280.00	245.22	469	69.85	61.17	156	23.23	20.35
235 or more	1,935	288.19	252.39	483	71.94	63.00	161	23.98	21.00

*From 1 December 2008 to 31 December 2009 the standard rate of VAT is reduced to 15%.

[*SI 2008/722*].

Private use of cars or other vehicles and charges to employees

[45.22] If a business has recovered 100% of the VAT on a car or other vehicle and then puts it to private use, it may have to account for VAT but no VAT is due if the car was

- subject to a 50% input tax block; or
- bought under the second-hand margin scheme.

If the employee pays nothing for the use of the vehicle, VAT must be accounted for on the cost of making the car available for private use. This cost will usually included depreciation, repairs and other running costs (but not any VAT the business has recovered as input tax). See **45.7** above for simplified schemes for calculating the VAT due on free private use of stock in trade cars.

If the employee pays a charge for the private use of the car or other vehicle, the business must account for VAT on these charges.

(VAT Notice 700/64/11, paras 6.1–6.6).

Salary sacrifice

Where an employer gives an employee a choice between

(a) a particular rate of wages, salary or emoluments, or
(b) in the alternative a lower rate of wages, etc. and, in addition, the right to the private use of a motor car provided by the employer,

and the employee chooses (*b*) above, then the provision to the employee of the right to use the motor car privately is not liable to VAT to the extent that the consideration is the difference between the wages, etc. available to him under (*a*) and (*b*) above. [*SI 1992/630*].

However, the case of *Astra Zeneca UK Ltd v HMRC, ECJ Case C–40/09*, [2010] STC 2298 (TVC 22.92), has had a significant impact on HMRC's future policy regarding salary sacrifice. In that case, a pharmaceutical company gave its employees face-value vouchers as part of their remuneration. HMRC ruled that this was a supply of services for consideration, which was subject to VAT. The company appealed, contending that it was not making any supply of services but that it should be allowed an input tax deduction on the costs of purchasing and providing the vouchers. The tribunal referred the case to the ECJ. The Court ruled that the provision of a retail voucher by a company, which acquired that voucher at a price including VAT, to its employees in exchange for their giving up part of their cash remuneration constituted a supply of services effected for consideration.

From 1 January 2012, HMRC have announced that salary sacrifice will be regarded as the consideration for a supply of goods/services. Where that supply is taxable, VAT will be due. In most cases the value of the benefit for VAT purposes will be the same as the amount of salary deducted or the amount foregone. Where this is less than the true value (e.g. where employers supply the benefits at below what it cost to buy them in), the value should be based on the cost to the employer. (HMRC Brief 28/11). For salary sacrifice agreements that were signed or otherwise agreed before 28 July 2011 and which extend beyond 31 December 2011, HMRC will allow the amounts of salary foregone to continue to be VAT free until the agreement ceases or comes up for renewal, or there is any other significant review or renegotiation. (HMRC Brief 36/11).

Trading down

Where a business allows employees to trade down to a cheaper model with a smaller salary sacrificed, HMRC accept that no VAT is due and the above provisions can be applied.

Trading up

Where a business allows employees to trade up to a more expensive model than they are entitled to, and a charge is made for the use of the car, the charge made is consideration for a supply.

Sacrificing benefits

There is a general move in industry towards providing a package of benefits for staff as part of the remuneration package (e.g. enhanced termination arrangements, longer holidays, payment of non-pensionable allowances, and private health insurance). Rather than simply sacrificing salary, employees may also effectively sacrifice other routine benefits and entitlements. However, as long as no specific charge is made for the use of the car, HMRC do not regard the sacrificing of routine benefits rather than salary as consideration for a supply.

(Business Brief 9/92).

Second-hand scheme for motor cars

[45.23] In general, VAT is charged on the full value of any goods, including second-hand motor cars, sold by a taxable person. The Treasury may, however, by order, provide for a taxable person to opt to charge VAT on the profit margin (instead of full value). [*VATA 1994, ss 32, 50A: FA 1995, s 24*]. An order under these provisions has been made by *SI 1995/1268* which covers all second-hand goods. The effect of the provisions is that, provided all the conditions are met, the margin scheme may be used to account for VAT only on the amount by which the selling price exceeds the purchase price. The gross margin includes the VAT to be accounted for.

For full details of the margin scheme, see **61 SECOND-HAND GOODS**.

Key points

[45.24] Points to consider are as follows.

- A basic principle of VAT law is that input tax cannot be reclaimed on the purchase of a motor car that is available for private use. There must be some physical restriction in place to prevent private use, e.g. in relation to insurance. The question about a vehicle being available for private use is a different question as to whether a vehicle is used 100% of the time for business purposes.

- The input tax restriction above does not apply to a car bought for use by a taxi firm, driving school or car hire business, where the vehicle becomes a tool of trading directly linked to the business. In such cases, there is no problem with claiming input tax on the cost of the vehicle, and the same opportunity is also available to a vehicle used as a genuine pool car arrangement.
- If an input tax block applied on the purchase of a vehicle, then no output tax is due on the subsequent resale of the vehicle in the future. The sale in this situation is exempt from VAT, irrespective of whether the car might be sold at a profit (unlikely anyway because of depreciation).
- If input tax has been reclaimed on the purchase of a car, then output tax must be declared on the full value of any future resale of the vehicle by the business that has claimed input tax.
- It is common practice for many car dealers to sell a new vehicle to a customer, the sale being partly funded by the dealer taking the customer's old vehicle as a part-exchange arrangement. In such cases, there are two transactions taking place. Output tax is due on the full selling price of the new vehicle, even though the net cash payment from the customer will obviously be much lower, i.e. to reflect the part-exchange value.
- An alternative method of a business acquiring a vehicle is through a lease hire arrangement. In these situations, the intention is for the business to use the vehicle for an agreed period (often three years), in return for a monthly hire payment that includes VAT. In this situation, the hirer is able to reclaim 50% input tax on the monthly hire payment, subject to normal rules, unless the use is by a business above (taxi-firm, car hire business etc.) in which case 100% input tax recovery is allowed.
- An important concession is that HMRC allows full input tax recovery on the repair costs of a vehicle (subject to normal rules, e.g. vehicle not used for exempt activities), as long as the vehicle has some business use. It is accepted that the vehicle must be in a good state of repair in order to carry out business journeys. This opportunity to claim input tax also extends to the private vehicles of employees, as long as the repair cost is paid by the business and the vehicle has some business use.
- Input tax can be fully reclaimed on road fuel purchased for a business car, or private car used for business purposes, as long as output tax is accounted for on private use based on a scale charge system. The only alternatives to adopting the scale charge are for input tax to be apportioned on a mileage basis between business and non-business/private use or for no input tax at all to be reclaimed on road fuel.

- The opportunity to avoid a scale charge payment by not claiming input tax on road fuel bought by the business applies to all road fuel purchases, not just fuel bought in relation to motor cars. This requirement could work against a business that buys road fuel that is used for commercial vehicles, e.g. vans or lorries.
- Input tax can be claimed by a business on the fuel element of any mileage allowance paid to an employee. HMRC assist this process by producing fuel advisory rates normally on a twice-yearly basis, which are accurate in most cases. A condition of claiming input tax in such cases is that the employee should include tax invoices with his mileage claim, ensuring that the VAT on the invoices is equal to or greater than the VAT being claimed on the mileage rate.
- The fuel scale charges are based on CO2 emissions. The rates are usually revised by HMRC on an annual basis in May. The amounts of output tax payable will also change, as a matter of course, when there is a change in the standard rate of VAT. So new scale charge payments applied from 4 January 2011 when the standard rate of VAT increased to 20%.

46

Northern Ireland

[46.1] The provisions of the *VATA 1994* apply to Northern Ireland [*VATA 1994, s 101(3)*] but not the Republic of Ireland.

Refund of VAT to Government of Northern Ireland

HMRC must refund to the NI Government any VAT charged on

- the supply of goods or services to that Government,
- the acquisition of goods by that Government from another EU country, or
- the importation of any goods by that Government from a place outside the EU

after deducting an amount (agreed between HMRC and the Department of Finance and Personnel for NI) attributable to supplies, acquisitions and importations for the purposes of a business carried on by that Government.

[*VATA 1994, s 99*].

See also **43.11 LOCAL AUTHORITIES AND PUBLIC BODIES** for supplies by 'government departments', including those in NI.

Key points

[46.2] Points to consider are as follows.

- The standard rate of VAT is higher in the Republic of Ireland compared to Northern Ireland. This means there may be an incentive for Republic of Ireland shoppers and some businesses not able to reclaim VAT to buy goods and services in Northern Ireland.
- A potential planning point could allow a small business registered for VAT in Northern Ireland to use the flat-rate scheme to calculate its VAT payments due to HMRC each quarter, but then also benefit from VAT recovery on some expenses bought in the Republic of Ireland, i.e. VAT reclaim is made by making an overseas VAT claim to the Republic of Ireland under the 8th Directive system. This approach has been adopted by some transport-related businesses registered for VAT in Northern Ireland that buy road fuel in the Republic of Ireland. A flat-rate scheme user cannot reclaim input tax on expenses paid in its own country, unless it relates to capital expenditure goods costing more than £2,000 including VAT.

47

Output Tax

Cross-references. See **2.10 ACCOUNTING PERIODS AND RETURNS** for goods sold in satisfaction of a debt by a person selling under a power of sale; **7 BAD DEBT RELIEF**; **20 EXEMPT SUPPLIES**; **23.12 FINANCIAL SERVICES** for output tax under hire purchase, conditional sale and credit sale agreements; **55.7–55.21 RATES OF VAT** for changes in the rate of tax; **59.34 REGISTRATION** for output tax on the deemed supply of business assets when a trader is deregistered; **60 RETAIL SCHEMES** for special schemes for retailers; **61 SECOND-HAND GOODS** for special schemes in operation for such goods; **62.2 SELF-SUPPLY** for output tax on stationery produced and used by partly exempt traders; **71.24 VALUATION** for calculation of output tax where discounts are allowed; **74 ZERO-RATED SUPPLIES.**

De Voil Indirect Tax Service. See V3.5.

Introduction

[47.1] Output tax in relation to a 'taxable person' means VAT on

- supplies which he makes; and
- acquisitions of goods by him from another EU country (including VAT which is also counted as input tax under **34.1 INPUT TAX**).

A '*taxable person*' is a person who is, or is required to be, registered under *VATA 1994*.

[*VATA 1994, s 3(1), s 24(2)*].

Output tax on supplies

A taxable person must charge VAT on any taxable supply of goods or services made in the UK in the course or furtherance of any business carried on by him.

A '*taxable supply*' is a supply of goods or services made in the UK other than an exempt supply. [*VATA 1994, s 4*]. See **8.1 BUSINESS** for the meaning of 'business'. For VAT purposes the UK includes the territorial sea of the UK (i.e. waters within twelve nautical miles of the coast-line).

The output tax is normally the liability of the person making the supply. [*VATA 1994, s 1(2)*]. As a general rule, the determination of the liability of VAT is the responsibility of the supplier. In certain special cases, a supply can be zero-rated where a customer gives the supplier a declaration claiming eligibility for such treatment. Under these circumstances, if the supplier, despite having taken all reasonable steps to check the validity of the declaration, fails to identify any inaccuracy and, in good faith, makes the supply at the zero rate, HMRC will not seek to recover the VAT due from the supplier. (VAT Notice 48, ESC 3.11).

The VAT becomes due at the time of supply [*VATA 1994, s 1(2)*] but in practice is accounted for and paid by reference to tax returns completed for VAT accounting periods. See **2 ACCOUNTING PERIODS AND RETURNS** and **51 PAYMENT OF VAT.**

Certain small businesses are allowed to account for VAT on the basis of cash received and/or by means of only one VAT return a year. See **63 SPECIAL SCHEMES.**

Output tax on acquisitions

See **19.3 EUROPEAN UNION: SINGLE MARKET** for tax on acquisitions from other EU countries.

Rates of output tax

There are currently three main rates of output tax, standard rate (17.5% reduced to 15% from 1 December 2008 to 31 December 2009; increased to 20% from 4 January 2011), reduced rate (5%) and zero rate (nil). See **74 ZERO-RATED SUPPLIES** for the effects of zero-rating and the categories of goods and services to which it applies. See **58 REDUCED RATE SUPPLIES** for a 5% reduced rate applying to a limited number of supplies.

Misunderstanding

Prior to 1 January 2012 VAT undercharged by a registered trader on account of a *bona fide* misunderstanding may be remitted provided all the following conditions are fulfilled.

(a) There is no reason to believe that the VAT has been knowingly evaded.
(b) There is no evidence of negligence.
(c) The misunderstanding does not concern an aspect of VAT clearly covered in general guidance published by HMRC or in specific instructions to the trader concerned.
(d) The VAT due was not charged, could not now reasonably be expected to be charged to customers, and will not be charged.

Where at the time the misunderstanding comes to light there are unfulfilled firm orders from customers, for which the price quoted has been based mistakenly on the assumption that no VAT, or less VAT than properly due, would be chargeable, VAT undercharged may be remitted in respect of such orders provided the conditions above are met. This concessionary treatment has been withdrawn with effect from 1 January 2012. (VAT Notice 48, ESC 3.4).

VAT fraction

[47.2] Normally, VAT is calculated at the appropriate percentage of a price which has first been decided without VAT and the VAT invoice shows these separate amounts. Sometimes, however, VAT has to be calculated from a price in which it is already included (e.g. in a less detailed tax invoice). To do this, the VAT fraction is required.

$$\text{VAT fraction} = \frac{\text{rate of VAT}}{100 + \text{rate of VAT}}$$

Rate of VAT	*VAT fraction*
Standard rate from 4.1.11 20%	1/6
Standard rate 17.5%	7/47
Standard rate from 1.12.08 to 31.12.09 15%	3/23
Reduced rate 5%	1/21

> *Example*
>
> In June 2010 M refills his car with petrol and receives a less detailed invoice totalling £36.78.
>
> The VAT included is £36.78 × 7/47 = £5.48

Apportionment of monetary consideration

[47.3] A single monetary consideration may be the payment for two or more supplies of different liabilities. In such a situation, the business must allocate a fair proportion of the total payment to each of the supplies. [*VATA 1994, s 19(4)*]. The legislation prescribes no set method by which this is to be achieved. The commonest methods are based upon the costs incurred in making the supplies or the normal selling prices of the supplies. Various methods of apportionment are considered in **47.4** below.

Apportionment is only necessary where the price charged is the only consideration for the supplies. If the consideration is not wholly in money, VAT must be accounted for as explained in **71.5 VALUATION**.

However, before an apportionment calculation is carried out, the following questions should be considered in order to determine whether an apportionment is appropriate and, if it is, what supplies it relates to.

(a) **Is there more than one supply?** It is important to distinguish between a single (composite) supply and a multiple (mixed) supply. In a single supply (e.g. air travel and catering during the flight), there is only one overall type of supply and one VAT liability with no scope for apportionment. In a multiple supply, a single inclusive price is charged for a number of separate supplies of goods or services each with their own VAT liability. See **64.6 SUPPLY: GENERAL** for further details.

(b) **Is there a single consideration?** Apportionment can only be applied to a single consideration that is given in return for more than one supply. If each supply has its own consideration, then there is no power under the *VATA 1994* to reapportion the value between them, although it is possible that the arrangement can be challenged if it is purely a 'sham'. See, for example, *Charlesworth (t/a Centurions)* (VTD 9015) (TVC 38.36) regarding the apportionment of profits between a second-hand car and an additional charge for a warranty.

In practice it is not always simple to distinguish between a payment that is a single consideration and a payment that is made up of several considerations that appear to be one because they are made simultaneously. There is no definitive test as to whether there are one or more considerations in any given case but it is likely that the customer has to know the charge for each particular supply before it can be accepted that there is more than one consideration. See *Thorn EMI plc; Granada plc* (VTD 9782) (TVC 38.8).

(c) **What are the liabilities of the supplies in question?** All the supplies to which a consideration relates must be identified and their respective liabilities established. Where all supplies are liable to VAT at the same rate, output tax due is calculated in the normal way and no apportionment is necessary. Otherwise the tax value of each supply must be calculated in order to arrive at the total output tax due.

Example 1

John takes a flight from London to Edinburgh (supply of zero-rated air travel). During the journey, he receives a cup of tea and a biscuit (supply of standard-rated catering).

In this case, the purpose of John's expenditure is to benefit from the air travel. The cup of tea and biscuit serves no other purpose than to make the flying experience more comfortable for him, i.e. it is incidental to the main supply. The whole of the payment made by John will be zero-rated as far as VAT is concerned.

Example 2

John and Jean have booked a day trip on the Orient Express. As well as the comfortable rail journey, their trip also includes a five-course meal with wine and champagne. The rail journey is zero-rated for VAT – catering supplies are standard-rated.

Imagine the likely response of John and Jean if they boarded the train and were suddenly told that the five-course meal was not available and they were only going to benefit from the train journey. They would almost certainly complain to the rail company and demand a refund of part of their fee. In other words, they expect to receive two very distinct benefits – the rail journey and the meal.

The five-course meal is an aim in itself, and cannot be dismissed as incidental to the rail travel. The rail company must account for output tax on the value of the catering supply – the rail travel can be zero-rated.

Example 3

Steve has decided to go and watch a football match at the ground of Hale Town. Hale Town is VAT-registered and charges Steve £10 for admission and, as a special offer just for today's match, his admission fee includes two hamburgers and a portion of chips.

In this situation, the supplies involved (admission fee to watch a football match and supply of catering when inside the ground) are both standard-rated. No VAT problem here – output tax of £1.49 is due on the full price (£10 × 7/47 – assuming a VAT rate of 17.5%).

Methods of apportionment

[47.4] Although *VATA 1994, s 19(4)* provides for apportionment of consideration, it does not stipulate how this has to be done, simply that the values attributed to the various supplies are 'properly attributable', i.e. on a fair and reasonable basis. There are two basic apportionment methods that, with appropriate adaptations, can be used in most circumstances. One of these uses the costs attributable to the different supplies being made, the other is based upon the normal selling prices. However, a business is not obliged to use these methods and can propose any method of apportionment. HMRC have no power to insist that any particular method must be used unless a business refuses to make an apportionment calculation or declines to change a method that produces an unfair result.

Cost-based method of apportionment where costs of all supplies can be identified

Example 1: Apportionment based on cost of both supplies: VAT-inclusive price

In November 2008 a VAT-inclusive price of £140 is charged for a supply of zero-rated goods which cost £23 and standard-rated goods which cost £40 (excluding VAT).

Proportion of the total cost represented by standard-rated goods =	
(40 + VAT) ÷ ([40 + VAT] + 23) = 47/70	
VAT-inclusive price of standard-rated goods = 47/70 × £140 =	£94
VAT included = £94 × VAT fraction = £94 × 7/47 =	£14
Tax value of zero-rated supply = £140 – £94 =	£46
Total price is therefore apportioned	
Value of standard-rated supply	80
VAT on standard-rated supply	14
Value of zero-rated supply	46
	£140

Example 2: Apportionment based on cost of both supplies: VAT-exclusive price

In November 2008 a VAT-exclusive price of £126 is charged for a supply of zero-rated goods which cost £23 and standard-rated goods which cost £40 (excluding VAT).

Proportion of the total cost represented by standard-rated goods = 40/63

VAT-exclusive value of standard-rated goods = 40/63 × £126 =	£80
VAT on standard-rated goods = £80 × 17.5% =	£14
Tax value of zero-rated supplies = £126 – £80 =	£46

Total price is therefore	
Value of standard-rated supply	80
Value of zero-rated supply	46
	126
VAT on £80 at 17.5%	14
	£140

Costs-based method of apportionment where the costs of only one supply can be identified

Difficulties are more likely to be met where it is only possible to directly attribute costs to one of the supplies involved. This is particularly the case if the supply to which a direct attribution of costs is not possible is a significant element of the outputs. Two methods of apportionment have been approved by VAT tribunals in such cases.

In *IC Thomas* (VTD 1862) (TVC 67.118) admission to a greyhound stadium (standard-rated) included the provision of a programme (zero-rated) and it was not possible to directly attribute any costs to the supply of admission. The tribunal approved an apportionment which applied a 'mark-up' to the costs that could be directly attributed, deducted this figure from the total selling price and treated the remainder as the value of the other supply. If appropriate, the figures derived from a sampling exercise in this way can be expressed as a percentage and applied to total relevant income over a period. (Note that, following the decision in *Card Protection Plan v C & E Commrs, ECJ Case C–349/96*, [1999] STC 270 (TVC 22.324) HMRC now expect that, in the majority of cases such as this, there is a single supply of standard-rated admission, the programme being an ancillary item.)

In *BH Bright* (VTD 4577) (TVC 67.119) which was concerned with membership fees of a dating agency, the approved method of apportionment similarly applied a 'mark-up' to the costs that could be directly attributed (annual cost of zero-rated literature). It then calculated the uplifted figure as a percentage of the total costs for the year, arriving at a proportion of costs attributable to zero-rated supplies and, by deduction, the proportion attributable to standard-rated supplies. The latter proportion was then applied to subscription income for the year to arrive at the consideration for standard-rated supplies and consequently the output tax due.

Arguments that standard-rated items are supplied at cost and all profits are derived from exempt or zero-rated supplies are likely to be rejected. See *Waterhouse Coaches Ltd* (VTD 1417) (TVC 67.116) and *Tynewydd Labour Working Men's Club and Institute Ltd v C & E Commrs*, QB [1979] STC 570 (TVC 24.11).

Example 3: Apportionment based on the cost of one supply only

In November 2008 a VAT-inclusive price of £142 is charged for a supply of zero-rated goods which cost £26 and standard-rated services, the cost of which cannot be identified. A fair and reasonable uplift on the zero-rated goods, consistent with actual profit margins of the business, is 50%.

Value of zero-rated supplies = £26 + 50% =	£39.00
VAT-inclusive price of standard-rated goods = £142 – £39 =	£103.00
VAT on standard-rated goods = £103 × 7/47 =	£15.34
The total price is therefore apportioned	
Value of zero-rated supply	39.00
Value of standard-rated supply	87.66
	126.66
VAT on £87.66 at 17.5%	15.34
	£142.00

Example 4: Apportionment based on the cost of one supply only—annual calculation using the method approved in Thomas

Assume that the figures in Example 3 above are representative of similar transactions and the total VAT-inclusive income from such transactions in the year is £25,000.

Zero-rated percentage = 39/142 × 100 =	27.465%
Value of zero-rated supplies in year = £25,000 × 27.465%	£6,866
Consideration for standard-rated supplies in year =	
£25,000 – £6,866 =	£18,134
Output tax due = £18,134 × 7/47 =	£2,700.81

Example 5: Apportionment based on the cost of one supply only—annual calculation using the method approved in Bright

In November 2008 VAT-inclusive subscription income of £400,000 is received in a year in respect of supplies of zero-rated literature with direct costs of £42,000 and standard-rated services, the direct cost of which cannot be identified. The total costs of the business (excluding depreciation) amount to £250,000 in the year. A fair and reasonable uplift to the direct costs of the zero-rated literature to allow for indirect costs is 100%.

Direct cost of zero-rated supplies	42,000
Uplift of 100%	42,000
Full cost of providing zero-rated supplies	£84,000
Proportion of costs attributable to zero-rated supplies =	
84,000/250,000 × 100 =	33.6%
Proportion of costs attributable to standard-rated supplies =	66.4%
Consideration for standard-rated supplies =	
£400,000 × 66.4% =	£265,600.00
Output tax = £265,600.00 × 7/47 =	£39,557.45

Apportionment based upon normal selling prices (market values)

This method is based on the prices the particular business normally charges for supplies, when made for separate considerations, and uses these amounts to apportion a single consideration given in return for comparable supplies.

Example 6: Apportionment based on normal selling-prices: VAT-inclusive price

In November 2008 a VAT-inclusive price of £200 is charged for a zero-rated supply (which would separately be charged at £50) and a standard-rated supply (which would separately be charged at £200 including VAT).

Proportion of the total normal price represented by standard-rated goods =	
200 ÷ (200 + 50) = 4/5	
VAT-inclusive price of standard-rated goods = 4/5 × £200 =	£160.00
VAT included = £160 × VAT fraction = £160 × 7/47 =	£23.83
Tax value of zero-rated supply = £200 – £160	£40.00
The total price is therefore apportioned	
Value of standard-rated supply (£160 – £23.83)	136.17
VAT on standard-rated supply	23.83
VAT on zero-rated supply	40.00
	£200.00

(VAT Notice 700, paras 8.1, 32.1, 32.2; HMRC VAT Guidance V1–12, para 3.11).

Retrospective apportionment

[47.5] Whether HMRC will allow a business to apply an apportionment retrospectively depends on the circumstances of the individual case. Set out below are the situations in which a request for retrospective apportionment is most likely to arise and how HMRC consider they should be treated.

(1) **No apportionment operated in the past and all supplies wholly standard-rated: business unaware that apportionment was available.** The business can make an apportionment in respect of the past for clearly identifiable zero-rated or exempt supplies that have been made. Overpaid VAT can be claimed under *VATA 1994, s 80* for up to three years. See **51.7 PAYMENT OF VAT**.

(2) **No apportionment operated in the past and all supplies wholly standard-rated: business aware that apportionment was available but chose not to apply it.** The business is still entitled to perform an apportionment retrospectively at a later date, even if HMRC have specifically advised of the possibility and the business has chosen not to act on that advice.

(3) **Apportionment operated correctly in the past but business requests retrospective use of a different method.** This is the most problematic scenario. The only requirement under *VATA 1994, s 19(4)* is that an apportionment must achieve a 'proper attribution' of values. The end result must therefore be fair and supportable. However, in many cases, it is possible to apply one of several apportionment methods to a given mixture of supplies, each of which is likely to produce a different attribution of values without any one method being right or wrong. In such cases, therefore, HMRC will expect the business to provide convincing evidence that the previous method was unfair or, at the very least, that the end result achieved by the proposed new method produces a substantially more accurate attribution of values than the old method. Whatever the position, the proposed new method can be allowed from a current date.

(4) **Apportionment operated correctly in the past but discovery of an error not directly connected to the method of apportionment leads to the business requesting retrospective use of a different method.** This might arise, for example, where a supply that should have been exempt was incorrectly treated as standard-rated and, as a result, the business proposes a different apportionment method when the error is discovered. VAT liability for the past periods could be recalculated either by applying the old method to the corrected liabilities or using a new method. HMRC's treatment is as for (3) above.

(5) **Acceptable method of apportionment operated in the past but applied incorrectly: business requests retrospective use of a different method.** In such a case (e.g. where costs have been attributed to zero-rated supplies that were properly attributable to standard-rated supplies), HMRC would normally expect a recalculation for the past periods to be performed using the old method with the correct operation. Any new method would only be accepted from a current date unless the business can demonstrate that the old method, when operated correctly, produced an unfair result or was significantly inaccurate compared to the new one.

(6) **Past agreed apportionment method inherently defective: business requests retrospective use of a different method.** In this case, there has not been a 'proper attribution' of values as required by *VATA 1994, s 19(4)* and retrospection should be allowed in this situation if the proposed new method is acceptable to HMRC.

If HMRC consider that a business has been applying a method of apportionment that has not resulted in a 'proper attribution' of values, then

- if the business has correctly adopted one of the suggested apportionment methods in VAT Notice 700, Part 32 (see *Examples 1, 2, 3* and *6* in **47.4** above) but HMRC subsequently consider that the end result is not fair, it will normally only seek change from a current date; and
- if the operation of the chosen method was flawed (e.g. the business was attributing costs to zero-rated supplies that were properly attributable to standard-rated supplies), then HMRC may issue an assessment in respect of the past period.

(HMRC VAT Guidance V1–12, para 3.14).

Business gifts

[47.6] For VAT purposes, an article is a gift where the donor is not obliged to give it and the recipient is not obliged to do or give anything in return. (VAT Notice 700, para 8.9). Business gifts cover a wide range of items including

- brochures, posters and advertising matter;
- 'executive presents';
- long service awards (see *RHM Bakeries (Northern) Ltd v C & E Commrs*, QB 1978, [1979] STC 72 (TVC 62.9));
- retirement gifts;
- goods supplied to employees under attendance or safety at work schemes;
- items distributed to trade customers;
- prizes dispensed from amusement and gaming machines (see **57.4 RECREATION AND SPORT**); and
- prizes of goods in betting and gaming and free lotteries (see **57.2 RECREATION AND SPORT**).

(VAT Notice 700/35/97, para 1.1).

Gifts of goods

A gift of business assets (including land) is a supply of goods [*VATA 1994, Sch 4 paras 5(1), 9; FA 2007, s 99(3)*] and is taxable as such subject to certain exceptions and special rules, including the following.

(a) There is no supply (and no VAT liability arises) unless the donor (or any of his 'predecessors') has or will become entitled to
  - (i) credit for the whole or any part of the input tax on the supply, acquisition or importation of the goods or of anything comprised in them; or
  - (ii) a refund of VAT on the supply or importation of those goods (or anything comprised in them) under the rules for refunds of VAT to persons established in other EU countries (see **17.9 EUROPEAN UNION GENERAL**) or the *EC 13th Directive* (refunds of VAT to persons established outside the EU, see **48.5 OVERSEAS TRADERS**).

For this purpose, a person is the '*predecessor*' of the donor where the donor acquired the goods from him under a transaction relating to the transfer of a business as a going concern which was treated as neither a supply of goods nor a supply or services (see **8.10** *et seq* **BUSINESS**). The donor's predecessors include the predecessors of his predecessor through any number of transactions. The effect of this is that, for no VAT liability to arise, no entitlement to input tax on the goods must have arisen through any number of such going concern transactions. [*VATA 1994, Sch 4 para 5(5)(5A); FA 1998, s 21; FA 2000, s 136(9)*].

The wording in (i) above is derived from *Directive 2006/112/EC, Art 16*. This was considered in *Finanzamt Burgdorf v Fischer, ECJ Case C–322/99*, [2001] STC 1356 (TVC 22.160) where a car dealer who had not reclaimed input tax on the initial purchase of a vintage car subsequently did so on substantial repairs to it. On ceasing to trade he retained the car as a private asset. The ECJ held that the effect of *Art 16* was that VAT was payable on 'component parts' in respect of which input tax had been deducted (but not on the whole value of the car, since input tax had not been reclaimable on its initial purchase). The taxable amount for this purpose should be determined by reference to the price, at the time of the allocation, of the goods incorporated in the vehicle which constitute component parts of the goods allocated. Furthermore, where input tax had been reclaimed but there was no output tax liability under *Art 16* (e.g. on extensive bodywork repairs which did not involve the addition of component parts), the input tax deducted had to be adjusted under *Directive 2006/112/EC, Arts 184, 185* where the value of the work in question had not been entirely consumed in the context of the business activity of the taxable person before the vehicle was allocated to his private assets.

(b) There is no supply (and no VAT liability arises) on a gift of goods made in the course or furtherance of a business where 'the cost to the donor of acquiring or producing the goods', together with the cost of any other such business gifts made to the same person in 'the same year', was not more than £50. '*The same year*' means any period of twelve months that includes the day on which the gift is made.

In *EMI Group plc v HMRC, ECJ Case C–581/08, 30 September 2010 unreported*, the Court held that *Directive 77/388/EEC, Art 5(6)* (now *Directive 2006/112/EC, Art 16*) did not preclude national legislation that fixed a monetary ceiling for gifts made to the same person within a set period, but it did preclude a presumption that gifts to different individuals having the same employer were to be treated as gifts to 'the same person'.

In determining the '*cost to the donor of acquiring or producing the goods*', where the donor acquired the goods under a transaction relating to the transfer of a business as a going concern which was treated as neither a supply of goods nor a supply or services (see **8.10** *et seq* **BUSINESS**), the donor and his 'predecessors' are treated as if they were the same person. For this purpose, a '*predecessor*' is the transferor under such a transaction and a person's predecessors include the predecessors of his predecessor through any number of transactions. The effect of this is that the cost of the goods gifted remains unchanged by the transfer of a business as a going concern through any number of such transfers.

[*VATA 1994, Sch 4 para 5(2)(2A); FA 1996, s 33; FA 1998, s 21; FA 2003, s 21; SI 2001/735*].

(c) Samples (see **47.8**(26) below).

(d) No VAT is due on free meals or drinks to employees by way of catering (see **11.8 CATERING**) or the provision of accommodation for employees in a hotel, etc. (see **32.3 HOTELS AND HOLIDAY ACCOMMODATION**). [*VATA 1994, Sch 6 para 10*].

(e) No further VAT may be due where additional goods or services are offered with normal taxable supplies as part of a business promotion (see **69 TRADE PROMOTION SCHEMES**).

(f) Prizes donated for competitions in newspapers and magazines (for which special rules apply, see **57.19 RECREATION AND SPORT**).

(g) Free fuel to employees for private use (for which special rules apply, see **45.16 MOTOR CARS**).

(h) Free meals or drinks to non-employees is not normally a supply and no VAT is due (but see **9 BUSINESS ENTERTAINMENT** for non-deductible input tax).

(i) A gift of goods for sale, export or letting by a charity (or a taxable person who is a profits-to-charity person) is zero-rated. See **12.7 CHARITIES.**

(j) Where a business consists of promoting a sporting, entertainment or similar activity and

- the business does no more than organise an event at which trophies are given away,
- there is no other associated competition/event, and
- a charge is made for admission to see the presentation

part of the admission charge is regarded as being payment for the trophies and no further VAT is due on the 'gift' of the trophies. (VAT Notice 700/35/97, para 1.1).

Input tax on goods purchased for business gifts is deductible. If the recipient of the goods also uses them for business purposes, that person can recover any VAT charged on the gift as input tax (subject to the normal rules). The donor cannot issue a VAT invoice (because there is no consideration) but see **39.2 INVOICES** for the form of a VAT certificate which can be issued instead.

Value of the supply

Where a gift of goods is a taxable supply, the value of the goods on which VAT must be accounted for is the price the person would have to pay (excluding VAT), at the time of the supply, to purchase goods *identical* in every respect (including age and condition) to the goods concerned. Where that value cannot be ascertained, the price for the purchase of goods *similar* to, and of the same age and condition as, the goods concerned must be used. If that value is also not possible to ascertain, the cost of producing the goods concerned at that time is to be used. [*VATA 1994, Sch 6 para 6*].

A gift of services

Where the recipient is not required to do or give anything in return is generally not a taxable supply. See, however, **47.7** below where bought-in services are used by any person outside the business free of charge.

Inducements, etc.

Goods or services supplied on condition that a purchase is made or some action is performed of benefit are not true gifts but constitute supplies in return for non-monetary consideration. This includes articles supplied under 'self-introduction' or 'introduce-a-friend' schemes by retail mail order companies where the introducer has a contractual right to receive the chosen articles. See **71.5 VALUATION** and *GUS Merchandise Corporation Ltd v C & E Commrs*, CA [1981] STC 569 (TVC 58.1) and *Empire Stores Ltd v C & E Commrs, ECJ Case C–33/93*, [1994] STC 623 (TVC 22.234). See also *C & E Commrs v Westmorland Motorway Services Ltd*, CA [1998] STC 431 (TVC 67.143) where free meals given to coach drivers as an inducement to stop at a motorway service station were held to be valued at the normal retail price of the meals.

Private or non-business use

[47.7] Private or non-business use is treated as follows:

(1) Goods

Special rules apply to private use of road fuel and motor cars. See **45.16** and **45.22 MOTOR CARS** respectively.

Otherwise, where, by or under the direction of a person carrying on a business, goods held or used for the purpose of the business are

- put to any private use, or
- used, or made available to any person for use, for any non-business purpose

a supply of services is treated as taking place (whether or not there is any consideration for the supply). [*VATA 1994, Sch 4 para 5(4)*].

From 1 January 2011 this provision does not apply to any

- interest in land;
- building or part of a building;
- civil engineering work or part of such a work;
- goods incorporated or to be incorporated in a building or civil engineering work (whether by being installed as fixtures or fittings or otherwise);
- ship, boat or other vessel, or
- aircraft.

[*VATA 1994, Sch 4 para 5(4A); F(No 3)A 2010, Sch 8 para 3*].

There is no supply (and no VAT liability arises) where

- no consideration is received; and
- the person carrying on the business (or any of his 'predecessors') has not or will not become entitled to credit for *any* of the input tax on the supply, acquisition or importation of the goods.

For this purpose, a person is a '*predecessor*' of the person carrying on the business where the later acquired the goods from the predecessor under a transaction relating to the transfer of a business as a going concern (TOGC) which was treated as neither a supply of goods nor a supply or services (see **8.10** *et seq* **BUSINESS**). A person's predecessors include the predecessors of his predecessor through any number of transactions. The effect of this is that, for no VAT liability to arise, no entitlement to input tax on the goods must have arisen through any number of such TOGCs.

[*VATA 1994, Sch 4 para 5(5)(5A), para 9; FA 1995, s 33(3); FA 1988, s 21; FA 2000, s 136(9); FA 2007, s 99(3)*].

The provisions set out below determine the value of the supply and therefore the VAT due. They apply in cases where the 'Lennartz' mechanism has been used for the initial recovery of input tax on the purchase of the goods. See **34.7 INPUT TAX.**

Value of supply where consideration is given: the value of the supply will normally be the consideration actually given although HMRC may direct the value to be the open market value in the case of transactions between connected parties. See **71.10 VALUATION**. See also **71.5 VALUATION** where any of the consideration is non-monetary.

Value of the supply where no consideration is given: except in the cases covered by **71.27 VALUATION** (supplies of accommodation and catering by employers to employees) output tax is due on the 'full cost' of the goods to the person making the relevant supply (or any of his predecessors) who was entitled to credit for the input tax. [*VATA 1994, Sch 6 para 7; FA 1997, s 33(3); FA 2007, s 99(4)(5); SI 1995/2518, Reg 116B; SI 2007/3099*].

'*Full cost*' is determined by reference to taxable VAT-bearing costs of the goods/asset, excluding the VAT itself. If any of the costs of purchase, acquisition or construction are either exempt or zero-rated they should not be included in the 'full cost' of the goods (see *Finanzamt München III v Mohsche, ECJ Case C–193/91*, [1997] STC 195 (TVC 22.181)). All VAT-bearing costs of obtaining the asset are included, even if there are elements that do not depreciate (e.g. the value of bare land). See *J & S Wollny v Finanzamt Landshut, CJEC Case C–72/05* [2008] STC 1618 (TVC 22.249).

The cost of obtaining the goods or asset is then spread over a period called the 'economic life'. The cost attributed to a particular VAT return period is then multiplied by the percentage of private/non-business use in that period to give the 'full cost' of the deemed supplies of making the goods or asset available for private/non-business use in that VAT return period.

After the end of the economic life, the deemed supplies cease as no charge can arise if, at the time when the goods are made available, they have no economic life. [*SI 1995/1268, Art 10A; SI 2007/2923*]. This provision applies with effect from 1 November 2007 but was previously applied by HMRC practice.

(VAT Information Sheet 14/07, paras 2.9.1, 2.9.2).

The provisions are considered in more detail below.

(a) Economic life of goods

With effect from 1 November 2007, goods held or used for the purposes of a business have an economic life beginning on the day when they are first used for any purpose after they have been supplied to, or acquired or imported by, a person (or any of his predecessors) and lasting for a period of

- 120 months in the case of land, a building or part of a building, and
- 60 months for all other goods

unless the economic life of the interest of a person (or any of his predecessors), in land and/or buildings begins at a time when that interest has less than 120 months to run. In such a case, the economic life is limited to the number of months remaining before expiry of that interest (and the value of B in the formula in (*b*) below and D in the formula in (*d*) below are reduced accordingly). This would apply where, for example, a taxable person acquires a short lease with five years left to run.

See also (*c*) and (*d*) below.

[*SI 1995/2518, Regs 116C, 116D; SI 2007/3099*]. (VAT Information Sheet 14/07, paras 2.9.2, 2.9.3).

Where a taxable person has acquired the goods from a predecessor as part of a TOGC, the 'full cost' is based on the taxable asset cost incurred by their predecessor and the economic life starts on the predecessor's first use. The taxable person will therefore need to confirm this cost and date with the predecessor if there is a possibility of private/non-business use of the asset. (VAT Information Sheet 14/07, para 2.9.4).

Before 1 November 2007 there were no statutory periods, but HMRC guidance said that the calculation for private/non-business use of land or buildings should be made over 20 years and the calculation for other goods should be made over five years.

(b) Value of the deemed supply

Subject to below and (*c*) and (*d*) below, the value of the deemed supply is the amount determined using the formula

$$(A \div B) \times (C \times U\%)$$

where

A = the number of months in the VAT period during which the deemed supply occurs and which fall within the economic life of the goods concerned;

B = the number of months of the economic life of the goods concerned or, in the case of an economic life beginning on 1 November 2007 by virtue of (*d*) below, what would have been its duration if it had been determined according to (*a*) above or (*c*) below as appropriate;

C = the full cost of the goods excluding any increase resulting from a supply of goods or services giving rise to a new economic life; and

U% = the extent, expressed as a percentage, to which the goods are put to any private/non-business use as compared with the total use made of the goods during the part of the VAT period occurring within the economic life of the goods.

If A or B is not a whole number of months, it must be computed to two decimal places. For example, the period from 8 February 2008 to 31 March 2008 is one month (March) and 22/29 of another month (February), i.e. 1.76 months to two decimal places.

There is no prescribed method for determining the non-business use percentage of the goods although the method must arrive at a fair and reasonable figure and must reflect the actual use of the goods. For example, in respect of a piece of machinery the appropriate measure may be by reference to hours of usage of the machinery while in respect of a building the appropriate measure may be by reference to the floor area occupied for private/non-business activities.

It should be noted that U% is based on use of the goods so where, for example, in a 90-day VAT return period a yacht is used 10 days for private purposes, 10 days for business purposes and is unused for 70 days, U% is 50% (10/20) and not 11.11% (10/90).

[*SI 1995/2518, Reg 116E; SI 2007/3099*]. (VAT Information Sheet 14/07, para 2.10.1).

Non-use of goods in a VAT period: where a VAT period in which a deemed supply occurs immediately follows a VAT period during which the goods in question were not used (or made available for use) for *any* purpose (i.e. there was no business or non-business/private use), A in the formula above must (without prejudice to any other element of the formula) comprise the total number of months falling within the economic life concerned covered by

- the VAT period in which the deemed supply occurs; and
- all preceding VAT periods which began after the end of the VAT period during which the goods were last used (or made available for use) for any purpose before the VAT period in which the deemed supply occurs.

This situation is particularly common with yachts (which are removed from the water during winter) and buildings (which may close for refurbishment)

[*SI 1995/2518, Reg 116F; SI 2007/3099*]. (VAT Information Sheet 14/07, para 2.10.2).

Example 1

A taxable person buys a yacht for £1,000,000 plus £175,000 VAT at the start of his three-month VAT return period ending 31 January 2008. He decides to make the yacht wholly a business asset and recovers all of the VAT incurred as input tax. Private usage of the yacht in the VAT period to 31 January 2008 is 50%.

The 'economic life' of a yacht is 60 months and the 'full cost' is £1,000,000. Applying the formula above, the net value of the deemed supply is

3/60 × (£1,000,000 × 50%) = £25,000

The output tax due is £25,000 × 17.5% × £4,375

Assuming that the private use percentage and the VAT rate do not change, the output tax due over the yacht's economic life will be

£4,375 × 20 VAT return periods = £87,500

which is 50% of the total VAT incurred on purchase.

Example 2

The facts are the same as in *Example 1*. The yacht is unused (for business or non-business/private purposes) throughout the VAT return period ended 30 April 2008 so that no output tax is due. In the VAT return period ended 31 July 2008, the yacht is again used and private usage is 50%.

The 'economic life' of a yacht is 60 months and the 'full cost' of the asset is £1,000,000 (as before). Applying the formula above, A must be taken to be 6 months (to include the previous VAT period when the yacht was unused) and the net value of the deemed supply is

6/60 × (£1,000,000 × 50%) = £50,000

The output tax due is £50,000 × 17.5% = £8,750

(c) Subsequent increase in 'full cost' of goods

Where

- a supply of goods or services is made to a person (or any of his predecessors) in respect of any goods held or used for the purposes of a business (whether or not the goods have an economic life in relation to that person at that time),
- VAT is chargeable on that supply which is eligible (in whole or part) for input tax credit, and
- by virtue of that supply, the 'full cost' of the goods is greater than their full cost immediately before that supply,

without prejudice to any other economic life having effect in relation to those goods, a new economic life must be treated as commencing in respect of them in accordance with (*a*) above as if they had been supplied, acquired or imported at the time when the supply of goods or services is made.

The calculation of the value of a deemed supply made during a new economic life in accordance with the formula in (*b*) above is varied so that

(i) C is the increase in the full cost of the goods resulting from the supply of the goods or services giving rise to the new economic life; and
(ii) U% is the extent, expressed as a percentage, to which the goods are put to any private/non-business use as compared with the total use made of the goods during the part of the VAT period occurring during the new economic life of the goods.

Where a deemed supply occurs in relation to goods that have two or more economic lives at the time when the private/non-business use takes place, the value of that supply is such amount as represents the total of the amounts calculated in respect of those economic lives.

[*SI 1995/2518, Regs 116G–116I; SI 2007/3099*].

This situation will arise where a taxable person already has an existing asset (e.g. land or a building) which has commenced or completed its 'economic life'. The first use of a new building on the land, or an extension or annex to the building is treated as the commencement of a new 'economic life'. Although under UK law there is only one asset (the land), the asset is treated as having two economic lives (which may overlap), each with its own related costs (e.g. the cost of the land and the cost of the building where a building is constructed on previously used land). The deemed supply value calculation for a VAT return period is done separately for each economic life that is running in the period and the results added together. (VAT Information Sheet 14/07, para 2.9.5).

(d) Transitional provisions

The legislation applying with effect from 1 November 2007 contains specific provisions to assist with the transition from an existing 'Lennartz' calculation. The change principally affects existing calculations for land and buildings (where the 'economic life' of an asset has now normally been set at ten years whereas a period of 20 years was used before that date) although it may apply to other goods where the taxable person has used a different 'economic life' from the five years required by the new legislation. The transitional provisions should have no effect if the asset is not land or buildings and before 1 November 2007 the taxable person was already using a five-year basis for calculating 'Lennartz' charges.

- *Where assets have been used only for business purposes before 1 November 2007*, the duration of the part of their economic life or lives falling after that date will be the remainder of the period of 120 or 60 months as appropriate which commenced on the first use of the goods.
- *Where assets have been used for private/non-business purposes before 1 November 2007*, the legislation treats the economic life or lives as commencing on that day (not upon the first use of the goods) and lasting for a period determined in accordance with a formula (see below). The formula takes into account the amount of VAT paid under the old system in respect of private/non-business use before 1 November 2007.

The detailed provisions are as follows.

Where an economic life

- would otherwise be treated as commencing before 1 November 2007, and
- relates to goods that, before that date, have been put to any private/non-business use by the person who holds or uses the goods concerned for the purposes of his business on 1 November 2007 (or any of his predecessors)

that economic life is treated as commencing on 1 November 2007 and lasting for the period of time determined using the formula

$$D \times (E - F) \div E$$

where

D = the number of months which would have been the economic life of the goods concerned if no 'Lennartz' accounting had occurred before 1 November 2007 (i.e. as calculated under (*a*) or (*c*) above as the case may be)

E = the 'full cost' of the goods represented by C in the formula in (*b*) above (as varied where appropriate in relation to a new economic life by (*c*) above)

F = the value determined using the formula

$$(G \times 100) \div (X\% \times 100)$$

where

G = the total value of deemed supplies of the goods on which VAT has been or will be accounted for in respect of such deemed supplies arising from the goods being put to any private/non-business use before 1 November 2007 (whether or not such supplies are treated as made before or after that day)

X% = the extent, expressed as a percentage, to which the goods have been put to any private/non-business use during the period from what would have been the start of its economic life up to 1 November 2007 as compared with the total use made of the goods in that period.

[*SI 1995/2518, Regs 116J–116M; SI 2007/3099*]. (VAT Information Sheet 14/07, paras 2.9.2, 2.12).

For worked examples of the transitional provisions, see VAT Information Sheet 14/07, para 2.12.

(e) Withdrawal from 'Lennartz' mechanism

Where a person has claimed deduction of input tax on goods which was incurred within the period of two years ending on 21 March 2007, he could withdraw that claim (in whole or part) as if it were made in error (but not so as to render himself liable to any penalty or payment of interest in respect of that claim). The following conditions had to be met.

- The goods must not have been used for any purpose before the claim is withdrawn.
- He must have intended or expected that the goods would be put to private/non-business purposes during their economic life.
- The withdrawal had to be in respect of (i) all of the input tax claimed on the goods; or (ii) that part of the input tax claimed on the goods which was referable to his intended use of those goods for purposes other than business purposes.
- The withdrawal had to be made in accordance with *SI 1995/2518, Reg 35* (whatever the amount of the claim that was withdrawn) before 1 February 2008.

[*SI 1995/2518, Reg 116N; SI 2007/3099*].

(f) Cessation of provisions

The charging provisions cease to apply in the following circumstances.

- At the end of the asset's economic life or lives.
- On sale of the asset. On sale, the asset ceases to be an asset of the business and therefore the charging provisions cease to apply. Where appropriate, VAT is chargeable on the disposal proceeds.
- On disposal of the asset for no consideration or on taking the asset into wholly private/non-business use. As with a sale, the asset ceases to be an asset of the business and the charging provisions cease to apply. In this case, there may be a deemed supply of the asset under *VATA 1994, Sch 4 para 5(1)*. See **47.6** above.
- On deregistration. In this case there may be a deemed supply of the asset under *VATA 1994, Sch 4 para 8*. See **59.34 REGISTRATION**.

A new economic life will start upon the first use by a new owner after the purchase if he also applies the 'Lennartz' mechanism to the goods.

(VAT Information Sheet 14/07, paras 2.9.3, 2.14).

(g) Partly-exempt businesses

Partly-exempt businesses may adopt 'Lennartz' treatment for their assets in the same way as other businesses. Where an asset will be used partly for taxable purposes and partly for exempt purposes, the input tax on it will be 'residual' for partial exemption purposes and its deductibility will depend on the terms of the partial exemption method.

The private/non-business use provisions above do not affect a taxable person's existing partial exemption method. If this leads to an unfair deduction of input tax on the 'Lennartz' asset then a new partial exemption method will be needed. HMRC will agree a new method in these circumstances provided it gives a fair and reasonable result for the business overall. HMRC will not allow the 'Lennartz' asset to be separated out as a sector for more accurate deduction while the overall result remains unfair. If the existing partial exemption method gives an unfairly large recovery of VAT on the asset, then the partial exemption method override provisions may apply or HMRC may direct a new, fairer method.

(VAT Information Sheet 14/07, para 2.11 which also see for worked examples).

See **66.23 SUPPLY: TIME OF SUPPLY** for the time of supply of the private use of goods.

(2) Services

Where a person carrying on a business puts services which have been supplied to him to any private or non-business use, he is treated as having supplied those services in the course or furtherance of the business. Private use includes use outside the business by any person and own personal use where a business is carried on by an individual.

Exceptions

The provisions do not apply, however,

- where the services are used, or made available for use, for a consideration;

- where no input tax has been deducted or will become deductible on the supply to him;
- where any part of the input tax on the supply to him was not counted as input tax because of an apportionment under *VATA 1994, s 24(5),* see **34.7** INPUT TAX (i.e. the provisions do not apply where an apportionment has been made between business and non-business use at the time of supply);
- where the services supplied consist of
  - (i) the provision in the course of catering of food or beverages to employees; or
  - (ii) the provision of accommodation for employees in a hotel, inn, boarding house or similar establishment; or
- where the services supplied consist of the letting on hire of a motor car and 50% of the input tax has already been excluded from credit (see **45.11** MOTOR CARS).

Value of supply

The value of the supply is that part of the value of the supply of services to him as fairly and reasonably represents the cost to him of providing the services. The total VAT charged (cumulative where the services are supplied on more than one occasion) cannot exceed the amount of input tax which has been deducted or will become deductible.

Anti-avoidance re business transfers

Where the transfer of the assets of a business as a going concern is treated as neither a supply of goods nor a supply of services (see **8.10** *et seq* BUSINESS) the liability of the transferee to tax under these provisions is determined as if the transferor and the transferee were the same person. Where the business has been transferred VAT-free as a going concern more than once, the transferee is treated as if he and all the previous transferors were the same person.

[*SI 1993/1507; SI 1995/1668; SI 1998/762*].

The above provisions relating to private use of services are concerned with major changes of use which continue over time or are permanent. Minor or occasional private or non-business use will be treated as *de minimis* and will not give rise to a liability to VAT. The type of services affected include computer software, building construction and refurbishment, particularly to domestic premises, and sporting rights.

Calculating the VAT due

There are no set rules for calculating the VAT due. If use of services permanently changes from business to non-business use, the accounting convention normally adopted for depreciating business assets may be used to calculate the VAT due, i.e. the value on which VAT is due is

$$\text{Cost of services} \times \frac{\text{Projected period of non-business use}}{\text{Period over which comparable assets are depreciated}}$$

Alternatively, any other fair and reasonable basis can be used. VAT should not be accounted for beyond the point at which

- the asset is fully depreciated, or
- the accumulated VAT accounted for equals the amount of input tax on the service which has proved to be not attributable to business use,

whichever is the earlier.

(Business Brief 17/94).

De Voil Indirect Tax Service. See V3.212; V3.216, V3.405A–V3.409.

Treatment of output tax in particular cases

[47.8] In particular cases, output tax is treated as follows:

(1) Accommodation

See **32.1–32.4 HOTELS AND HOLIDAY ACCOMMODATION** for supplies of accommodation in hotels, boarding houses, etc. and **32.5–32.9 HOTELS AND HOLIDAY ACCOMMODATION** for the provision of holiday accommodation in the UK, including time share, caravans and camping.

(2) Adoption services

Charities

Services provided by a charitable adoption agency in connection with domestic adoptions are exempt from VAT where the supply is made 'otherwise than for profit' (see **12.11 CHARITIES**). This includes the provision of pre-adoption training, advice and guidance; the assessment of prospective adopters; as well as the actual placement of a child.

Any charge made by a charitable adoption agency for a home study assessment in connection with an inter-country adoption application is also exempt from VAT, provided that the assessment is supplied on an 'otherwise than for profit' basis. Previously, these assessments had been subject to VAT at the standard rate.

Local authorities

Services provided by a local authority in connection with adoption are non-business activities. They are not subject to VAT when carried out as part of the local authority's statutory responsibility.

Other suppliers

All supplies in connection with any adoption that are not made by a charity on an 'otherwise than for profit' basis or by a local authority are standard-rated.

(Business Brief 21/01).

(3) Agricultural grant schemes

VAT is not to be applied to payments under the following grant schemes.

DEFRA

Farm Woodland Scheme
Set Aside Scheme
Agricultural Act 1986, s 18 (Environmentally Sensitive Areas)
Outgoers under the *Milk (Cessation of Production) Act 1985*

Department of the Environment

Nature Conservancy Council management agreements
Countryside Premium Scheme for Set Aside Land
Countryside Commission Community Forests Scheme

Forestry Commission
Woodland Grant Scheme
Farm Woodland Scheme

(C & E Press Release 58/89, 9 August 1989).

EU grants

Grants paid by the Intervention Board to processors of dried animal fodder are within the scope of VAT although, to the extent that supplies of animal fodder are zero-rated, no VAT is due. Processors who supply dried fodder must include the value of grants received in the total value of sales in Box 6 of the VAT return. Where the grant relates to fodder for the processors' own use, there is no VAT supply and grants should continue to be treated as outside the scope of VAT.

Other EU grants are generally outside the scope of VAT.

(Business Brief 28/99).

(4) Change in rate of VAT

See **55.10** *et seq* **RATES OF VAT** for the effects on the calculation of output tax where there is a change in either the rate of VAT or the VAT liability of a particular supply.

(5) Compensation payments

Compensation payments for damage or loss are normally outside the scope of VAT as they are not consideration for a supply. This is because the payments are made either as a result of a Court Order or through an agreement between the two parties involved to compensate one party for suffering some inconvenience, loss or damage.

Early termination of contracts

Two conflicting tribunal decisions on exactly the same facts show the difficulties in determining the VAT position of payments arising out of early contract termination. In *Holiday Inns (UK) Ltd* (VTD 10609) (TVC 62.142) a company (C) owned a hotel which was managed by another company (H) under a management agreement. As the agreement did not allow for early termination, the parties entered into a separate termination agreement under which C paid H £2m as compensation. C wished to reduce the cost of the settlement by treating part of the payment as VAT (which it recovered as input tax) on the basis the H had made a supply of granting C the right to terminate. The tribunal held that, although drawn up years apart, the termination agreement constituted a part of the original management agreement, effectively inserting a termination clause into the latter. As this meant C already had the right to terminate, it could not have purchased the right from H and therefore there had been no supply for VAT purposes.

As a result of this decision, HMRC sought to obtain repayment of the input tax that C had claimed and C appealed (*Croydon Hotel & Leisure Company Ltd* (VTD 14920) (TVC 36.638)). The tribunal, with the same facts as the earlier hearing, held that the termination agreement and £2m payment did represent a supply for VAT purposes, following the ECJ's subsequent decision in *Lubbock Fine & Co, ECJ Case C–63/92*, [1994] STC 101 (TVC 22.323).

In *Lloyds Bank plc* (VTD 14181) (TVC 62.143) the bank decided to vacate a property it leased. The lease did not provide for early cancellation. Lloyds and its landlord therefore agreed a variation to the lease, setting out terms for early termination and the bank paid £597,220 as compensation. Because the parties effected the early termination on the same day as agreeing the variation, the tribunal held that there had been a supply by the landlord of granting and exercising an option to terminate the lease in return for a payment by Lloyds and its vacating the premises.

Liquidated damages

Agreements that allow for early termination usually include related clauses that provide a formula for payment of compensation in the event of such termination. These amounts are generally to compensate for loss of earnings and are often referred to as liquidated damages. They are not consideration for supplies and are outside the scope of VAT.

Leases for goods

Lease agreements for movable goods frequently include clauses that allow lessees to terminate early on payment of liquidated damages. Such sums are not liable to VAT. However, an agreement with the leasing industry allows lessors to treat lease terminations generally as taxable supplies if they wish (although they cannot be required to do so).

Breach of contract

Leases and other agreements may terminate early if a particular event occurs (e.g. the customer breaches the terms or the lessee calls in receivers). The contract deems that such events cancel its terms or effectively allow the lessor to terminate as though there had been a breach. Again, any moneys deemed to be due as a result are damages and outside the scope of VAT. See *Financial & General Print Ltd* (VTD 13795) (TVC 36.640).

Settlement of disputes

Where disputes involve an argument over price or poor standard of workmanship, any settlement paid by the customer is consideration for the goods or services previously supplied and the value of the supply is the agreed amount of settlement (either following a Court Order or an out of court agreement). If an 'interest' payment is also due under the settlement, this is not consideration for any supply and is a form of damages to compensate the supplier for being paid late.

See *Whites Metal Co* (VTD 2400) (TVC 36.637), *Cooper Chasney Ltd* (VTD 4898) (TVC 62.137) and *Hurley Robinson Partnership* (VTD 750) (TVC 62.135).

Land and property payments

See **41.4 LAND AND BUILDINGS: EXEMPT SUPPLIES AND OPTION TO TAX** for dilapidation payments and statutory compensation from landlords to tenants.

Manufacturers' and retailers' warranties

See **71.9 VALUATION.**

Surrender of firearms

Compensation payments made by the Home Office to VAT-registered firearms dealers required to surrender certain calibre handguns are taxable supplies where the surrendered firearms were business stock. The compensation payments therefore include a VAT element. Under powers contained in *SI 1995/2518, Reg 25(5)*, HMRC are prepared to allow any VAT due to be accounted for on the VAT return for the period in which the payment of compensation is received. (Business Brief 27/97). See also *Parker Hale Ltd v C & E Commrs*, QB [2000] STC 388 (TVC 62.145).

Compensation payments generally

For cases concerning whether compensation was in respect of a taxable supply or outside the scope of VAT, see *F Penny (t/a FMS Management Services)* (VTD 10398) (TVC 62.141) (compensation payment for loss of consultancy); *Galaxy Equipment (Europe) Ltd* (VTD 11415) (TVC 40.55) (compensation for faulty goods); and *Hometex Trading Ltd* (VTD 13012) (TVC 36.638) (compensation payments made by order of court). Compensation under *EC Council Regulation 1336/86* for discontinuing milk production is not subject to VAT (*Mohr v Finanzamt Bad Segeberg, ECJ Case C–215/94*, [1996] STC 328 (TVC 22.172)).

See also **71.9**(1) **VALUATION** for fines and penalty charges.

> *Example 1*
>
> Garage Doors Ltd supplied a customer with a garage door for £1,000 plus VAT that had a loose nut in it. As a consequence, the garage door collapsed on the customer's head when she was opening it – she had to have hospital treatment for cuts and bruises. Garage Doors Ltd pays her £500 compensation. However, the company cannot reduce its output tax figure because the payment to the injured customer is compensation for her inconvenience and suffering – it is not linked to the taxable supply of goods. The payment is outside the scope of VAT.

Example 2

Garage Doors Ltd supplies another customer with a red painted door for £1,000 plus VAT. However, after two weeks the customer notices that the paint is peeling from the door and she demands compensation for the poor quality of the product. Garage Doors Ltd pays her £500 compensation and reduces its output tax by £74.46 (i.e. £500 × 7/47 with a VAT rate of 17.5%).

In this case, the output tax adjustment is correct because the payment directly relates to the goods supplied. In effect, the customer is receiving a reduction in the original price because the goods are sub-standard – there is no compensation for damage or injury suffered.

(6) Energy-saving materials and grant-funded installation of heating equipment or security goods, etc.

Supplies of certain energy-saving materials and other qualifying goods and their installation are subject to VAT at the reduced rate of 5%. See **58.2** and **58.3 REDUCED RATE SUPPLIES**.

(7) Exempt supplies

Output tax is not chargeable on exempt supplies. See **20 EXEMPT SUPPLIES** for a list of the categories of exemption and cross-references to supporting chapters.

(8) Gifts

See **47.6** above.

(9) Goods obtained by fraud

Where the agreement for the supply of goods has been rescinded, no supply has taken place and the supplier can adjust the output tax he has paid provided he gets authorisation before doing so. Adjustment is specifically to the VAT account and credit notes should not be issued. In order to get authorisation, the trader must apply to HMRC enclosing evidence of fraud and a copy of the invoice. The evidence required by HMRC is

- evidence that the trader has been victim of the fraud proved in the courts or, where the person who committed the fraud goes missing, confirmation from the police that they are satisfied that a fraud has actually taken place;
- evidence that the trader has made a statement to the police for use in the prosecution; and
- a verifiable description of the goods involved.

Suitable evidence might take the form of police letters and press reports describing the injured party and the goods.

If the person who committed the fraud is convicted, any part payment made in the course of the fraud (e.g. by paying some cash and the balance by fraudulent cheque) cannot be the consideration for a supply and is outside the scope of the tax. If the person who committed the fraud is ordered to make restitution, that is compensation and outside the scope of the VAT.

If payment is made after conviction and output tax has been adjusted, there is a new contract or agreement and any supply would be considered on its own merits.

Where rescission of the supply is blocked because

- the supplier affirms the agreement by pursuing the person who committed the fraud for payment rather than the return of goods,
- the supplier unduly delays in rescinding the contract after discovering the fraud, or
- the goods have been supplied on to a third party,

by concession, the supplier is allowed to recover the VAT declared if the fraud is reported to the police and HMRC are satisfied that the business has been defrauded.

(HMRC VAT Guidance V1–3, paras 21.4, 21.5).

See also *Harry B Litherland & Co Ltd* (VTD 701) (TVC 62.167).

De Voil Indirect Tax Service. See V5.158.

(10) Lost, stolen or destroyed goods

HMRC may require a taxable person from time to time to account for goods supplied to, or acquired or imported by, him in the course or furtherance of his business (including any goods transferred from another EU country). If such goods have been lost or destroyed, HMRC may assess him on the VAT which would have been chargeable in respect of the supply of the goods if he is unable to prove such loss or destruction. [*VATA 1994, s 73(7)*].

Where, therefore, a taxable person can prove that his goods have been lost, stolen or destroyed, output tax is only chargeable if the goods have been supplied. Where goods are *lost, etc. in transit* to the customer, then

- if, under the contract, the customer is responsible for any loss before delivery, output tax is due; and
- if, under the contract, the supplier is responsible for any such loss, output tax is due where a VAT invoice has been issued. If a VAT invoice has not been issued, no output tax is due because there has not been a supply.

See also **19.19 EUROPEAN UNION: SINGLE MARKET** for goods lost, etc. in transit to other EU countries.

(VAT Notice 700, para 8.10).

(11) Management services

See **44.1–44.3 MANAGEMENT SERVICES AND SUPPLIES OF STAFF.**

(12) Milk quotas

The VAT liability of the supply or transfer of a milk quota to another farmer depends upon whether it is supplied with or without land.

- Where the supply or transfer of a milk quota is linked with the supply of land under one agreement, there is a single supply and VAT liability follows that of the land. This applies whether the land is sold freehold or leasehold and even if separate identifiable sums are shown on the invoice and paid for the land and quota.
- The supply or transfer of a milk quota without land is a standard-rated supply of services.
- Where a milk quota is transferred with a grazing licence, there are two separate supplies, a zero-rated supply of animal feeding stuffs through the grazing licence and a standard-rated supply of the milk quota.

(Business Brief 17/94).

See (3) above for surrender of a milk quota in return for a DEFRA grant.

(13) Motor cars

See **45.4 MOTOR CARS** for disposal of a motor car used in a business and **45.16 MOTOR CARS** for VAT on fuel supplied for private use.

(14) Motor vehicles — statutory fees, etc.

MoT tests

The charge for an MoT test provided direct by an approved garage to its customers is outside the scope of VAT, provided it does not exceed the statutory maximum. Any discount given by an approved garage to an unapproved garage is treated as a normal trade discount and not seen as consideration for a taxable supply by the unapproved garage.

HMRC take the view that where an unapproved garage shows the exact amount charged by an approved garage separately on the invoice to its customer, and meets the other conditions for disbursements in VAT Notice 700, para 25.1 (see **3.7 AGENTS**), it may treat this element as a disbursement and also outside the scope of VAT. Any amount charged over and above the amount charged by the approved garage is consideration for its own service of arranging the test on behalf of its customer and is taxable at the standard rate. If the unapproved garage chooses not to treat the amount charged by the approved garage as a disbursement, or otherwise does not satisfy all the conditions for disbursements (e.g. by not showing the exact amount charged by the approved garage separately), HMRC take the view that it must account for VAT on the full invoiced amount. The view was followed in *Ward (t/a Acorn Garage)* (VTD 15875) (TVC 44.162) and a number of subsequent tribunal decisions but was not followed in *Duncan (t/a G Duncan Motor Services)* (VTD 20100) (44.165). In that case, the tribunal held that this approach did not pay sufficient regard to the legal monopoly of approved testing stations in relation to the conduct of MoT tests. It held that, even if not disclosed separately, the amount paid to the approved garage should not be treated as part of the overall supply of the unapproved garage. The decision in *Duncan* was approved of in *Jamieson (t/a Martin Jamieson Motor Repairs)* (VTD 20269) (TVC 44.166).

(VAT Notice 700, para 25.4; Business Brief 21/96).

Driving tests

Fees charged by the Department of Transport (and training bodies appointed by them) for Part 1 of the *motorcycle* driving test are liable to VAT at the standard rate. The Department of Transport supplies Part 2 of that test and *other motor vehicle* driving tests as part of its statutory obligation and the fees involved are outside the scope of VAT. (C & E Press Notice 909, 27 April 1984).

Removal/recovery services

Statutory fees for removal and storage of vehicles are outside the scope of VAT when levied by the police on the motorist or owner of the vehicle. If the police contract out this service, such fees collected by the contractor on behalf of the police are not consideration for any supply by the contractor to the motorist and are also outside the scope of VAT. Where, however, in such circumstances the contractor retains some or all of the amounts collected, the retained amount represents consideration for the supply of services from the contractor to the police authority and is liable to VAT at the standard rate. (Business Brief 9/99).

Vehicle clamping and towaway fees

Where landowners use parking enforcement contractors to enforce parking restrictions on their premises, fees payable to the contractor, as agent for the landowner, are outside the scope of VAT, being damages or compensation for the trespass suffered by the landowner. Where, however, under the terms of the agreement with the landowner, the contractor retains some or all of the amount collected, the retained amount represents consideration for the supply of services by the contractor to the landowner and is liable to VAT at the standard rate. VAT is also due on any management charge to the landowner. (Business Brief 7/00).

(15) Non-existent goods

A supply of goods is made only when they are passed to someone. Therefore, where goods do not exist and do not later come into existence, no supply can occur, no output tax is chargeable and no input tax is claimable. See also *P Howard* (VTD 1106) (TVC 36.630), *Theotrue Holdings Ltd* (VTD 1358) (TVC 36.613) and *MS Munn* (VTD 3296) (TVC 36.622).

(16) Packaging

General. Normal and necessary packaging, including ordinary tins, bottles and jars, is treated as part of the goods which it contains so that if the goods are zero-rated, zero-rating also applies to the packaging. However,

- where the packaging is more than normal or necessary, there may be a multiple supply. The consideration must then be apportioned if the goods are not standard-rated and VAT is due on the packaging (see **47.3** above). This could apply to storage containers and other types of packaging which could be sold separately;

- where an additional charge is made with a supply of goods for their container to ensure that it is safely returned and the additional charge is to be refunded on its safe return, this additional charge is not subject to VAT; and
- where an additional charge is raised to cover the loan, hire or use of a container, then the charge is standard-rated.

(VAT Notice 700, para 8.2).

Food packaging. Where the purpose of the packaging is simply to contain, protect and promote the food it contains, HMRC consider it as part of the supply of the food inside, rather than a supply in its own right, and it takes the same liability as its contents. This is so even if the packaging is more than the minimum strictly necessary. This follows the decision in *C & E Commrs v United Biscuits (UK) Ltd t/a Simmers*, CS [1992] STC 325 (TVC 29.85) where it was held that decorative biscuit tins amounting to 55% of the total production cost (as opposed to 28% for ordinary cardboard packaging) were normal packaging for biscuits. The court held that the tin was integral to the biscuits, not merely in the sense that it was the container in which they were packaged, but further in that it prolonged their shelf-life and kept the biscuits in better condition once consumption had begun.

Where packaging is clearly designed to be 'extra' to the food, there is a multiple supply of food and packaging and normally the total price must be apportioned in order to arrive at the output tax due (see **47.3** above). Subject to the linked goods concession below, this applies to the following types of containers.

- Any container specifically advertised or held out for sale as having a value in its own right (e.g. by advertising the product as 'with a free storage tin').
- Any container with a clear and obviously intended after-use (e.g. tumblers containing coffee, honey or preserves in ceramic serving bowls).
- Storage jars obviously intended for use in storing future supplies of the product.
- Biscuit tins containing built-in hydroscopic crystals.
- Tea caddies (but not simple tins bearing the supplier's name and details of the weight and variety of tea where it is the supplier's practice to sell tea in this way).
- Ceramic pâté pots and other ceramic containers which are clearly suitable for future decorative use. See, however, *Paterson Arran Ltd* (VTD 15041) (TVC 29.86) where, following *United Biscuits Ltd* above, zero-rating was applied to the sale of quality biscuits in a ceramic jar aimed at the Christmas market, even though the jar represented 70% of the total cost.
- Hampers and picnic baskets (other than simple cardboard cartons).

Outer cases and boxes, etc. and seasonal packaging (although frequently more elaborate than supplied during the rest of the year) are not normally considered separate supplies unless falling within one of the above categories.

Linked goods concession

Where, however, standard-rated packaging is supplied with zero-rated food, the supply can be treated as a single supply of zero-rated food provided the packaging

- is not charged at a separate price;
- costs no more than 20% of the total cost of the supply; and
- costs no more than £1 (excluding VAT).

(VAT Notice 701/14/11, para 6.1).

(17) Payphones

Telephones

Where a payphone is rented from British Telecom or another supplier, the person renting the machine makes the supplies to the users and VAT is due on these supplies. Output tax is calculated by applying the VAT fraction to the money removed.

With some installations it is possible to switch from payphone mode to domestic mode and make calls without inserting money. If the domestic mode is used to make non-business calls, all VAT charged by British Telecom cannot be treated as input tax.

Phonecards

See **60.9**(3) RETAIL SCHEMES.

(VAT Notice 700, para 8.12).

(18) Personal service companies

A service company could be set up to provide the services of a single worker to a client in circumstances where, without the service company, the worker would be an employee of the client. The use of a service company in this way allows the client to make payments to the company, rather than the individual, without deducting PAYE or NICs. The worker could then take the money from the service company in the form of dividends rather than salary, again avoiding NICs. In order to counter such avoidance, under IR35 rules, HMRC can treat the payments made by the service company to the worker as chargeable to income tax on employment and subject to NICs. This 'IR35' status in respect of income ascribed to the worker does not affect the VAT position on supplies by the service company to the client. This is because the company, not the worker, contracts to provide the services to the client and it is, subject to registration requirements, liable to account for VAT on these supplies.

(19) Postage and delivery charges

A supply of goods may involve delivery to the customer. The way any delivery charge is treated for VAT purposes depends on the circumstances in which the goods are supplied.

- Where goods are delivered to a customer with no additional charge. If delivery is free, or the cost is built into the normal price, VAT is accounted for on the goods in the normal way based on the liability of the goods themselves. This applies whether or not delivery is required under the contract.
- Where delivery is required under the sales contract and a charge is made. If, under the terms of the contract, the seller has to deliver the goods to a place specified by the customer (e.g. the address of the customer, his friends or relatives or his own customers), the seller is making a single supply of delivered goods for which the VAT liability is based on the liability of the goods being delivered. The position is not affected by whether the charge made for delivery is separately itemised or invoiced to the customer. For example, any element of the price attributed to the doorstep delivery of milk and newspapers will also be zero-rated. On the other hand, any element attributed to the delivery of standard-rated mail order goods will be standard-rated.
  See also *C & E Commrs v Plantiflor Ltd*, HL [2002] STC 1132 (TVC 24.2).
- Where delivery is not required under the contract or someone else's goods are delivered. Delivery services are normally treated as a separate supply of services where
  (i) goods are supplied under a contract that does not require delivery but where, nevertheless, the seller agrees to deliver the goods and make a separate charge; or
  (ii) a business provides a service of delivering somebody else's goods (see also below for direct mailing services).

  In such cases, the liability of the delivery charge is not affected by the liability of the goods being delivered and there is a separate supply of delivery services which is normally standard-rated (although special rules apply if the delivery forms part of the movement of goods to or from a place outside the UK, see **70.25 TRANSPORT AND FREIGHT**). For example, the charge for the distribution of a publisher's zero-rated newspapers is a standard-rated supplies of services. Similarly, where the seller arranges for goods to be delivered by post, the supply of delivery services is taxable even though the charges are identical to the exempt supply to him by the Post Office.

Direct mailing services. Where a supplier provides the service of posting client's mail (e.g. publicity or advertising material or promotional goods), the supplier may treat the charges by the Royal Mail (which for these purposes includes other operators licensed by Postcomm) as a disbursement for VAT purposes provided

(a) the general conditions for treatment as a disbursement are satisfied (see **3.7 AGENTS**);
(b) the client specifies who to send the mail to or has access to the mailing list before the mail is sent out;
(c) the supplier's responsibility for the mail ceases when it is accepted for safe delivery by Royal Mail; and

(d) the supplier passes on any Royal Mail discount or rebate to the client in full or, if the supplier obtains any discount or rebate from posting various clients' mail at the same time, it is apportioned fairly between them.

If conditions (*a*)–(*d*) are not met, the full amount of postal charges must be included in the value of the direct mailing service. This is normally standard-rated if the mail is sent to addresses in the UK. Special rules, however, apply if the delivery is, or forms part of, the movement of goods to or from a place outside the UK, see **70.25 TRANSPORT AND FREIGHT**.

Freepost

Freepost is an arrangement whereby the recipient (i.e. the advertiser) of a returned mailshot pays the postage costs on behalf of the sender (e.g. a member of the public). Commonly a PO box number will also be used. The supply by Royal Mail of the Freepost and PO Box licences, plus any handling service for which an additional fee is charged, is made to the licence holder. This may be the recipient (advertiser) or an agent handling the mail on the recipient's behalf. However, the supply of postage is made to the sender of the mail, although the recipient (advertiser) or the agent meets the cost. This means that where an agent is employed to handle the Freepost

- any recovery of the postage costs by the agent from the recipient (advertiser) is not liable to VAT; and
- where the licence is taken out by the agent in the name of the recipient (advertiser), the costs may be disbursed to the recipient, subject to the normal rules referred to above.

Retail schemes. For supplies of *delivered goods*,

- under the Point of Sale scheme, include the full amount charged in daily gross takings;
- under Apportionment Scheme 1, include the full amount charged in daily gross takings and do not adjust the record of purchases; and
- under Apportionment Scheme 2 and the Direct Calculation schemes, include the full amount charged in daily gross takings and also allow for the delivery charge element in the calculation of expected selling prices.

If delivery services are provided for an extra charge,

- under the Point of Sale scheme and the Apportionment schemes, account for VAT due on the delivery services outside the scheme used; and
- under the Direct Calculation schemes,
  - (i) where minority goods are zero-rated, include delivery charges in daily gross takings; and
  - (ii) where minority goods are standard-rated, the delivery charges will not be included in the expected selling prices calculation and can be added back as part of the standard-rated sales figure. Otherwise, account for VAT due on delivery services outside the scheme.

Packing services

A separate supply of packing services will normally be standard-rated. Special rules, however, apply if the delivery forms part of the movement of goods to or from a place outside the UK, see **70.25 TRANSPORT AND FREIGHT**.

(VAT Notice 700, para 8.3; VAT Notice 700/24/03; VAT Notice 727/3/11, para 6.10; VAT Notice 727/4/11, para 7.11; VAT Notice 727/5/11, para 6.10).

(20) Postage stamps and philatelic supplies

See **57.20 RECREATION AND SPORT**.

(21) Private or non-business use of goods

See **47.7** above.

(22) Promotion schemes

See **69 TRADE PROMOTION SCHEMES**.

(23) Reduced rate supplies

VAT is chargeable on certain supplies at a reduced rate (currently 5%). See **58 REDUCED RATE SUPPLIES**.

(24) Payments to a retail consortium

Retailers may join together to form a purchasing consortium for the purposes of negotiating lower prices for the goods they purchase. Any payments made by a manufacturer or supplier to the consortium are regarded as the consideration for a taxable supply of services by the consortium of introducing the manufacturer/supplier to a larger customer base. The purchasing consortium must account for VAT at the standard rate on all such receipts. See *Landmark Cash and Carry Group Ltd* (VTD 883) (TVC 62.181). (Business Brief 12/93).

(25) Royalty and licence fees

Where a customer is recharged with payments made for royalty or licence fees incurred in making the supply to him, these charges are not disbursements for VAT purposes. The recharge is part of the consideration for the supply to the customer and VAT must be accounted for on the full value including the recharge. (VAT Notes (No 2) 1985/86).

(26) Samples

From 19 July 2011, the provision to a person, otherwise than for a consideration, of a sample of goods is not a taxable supply [*VATA 1994, Sch 4 para 5(2); FA 2011, s 74*]. The measures are being amended to remove the restriction that only one sample of each product supplied to another person can be disregarded.

Prior to 19 July 2011, a gift to any person of a sample of any goods is not a taxable supply except that, where a number of identical samples (or samples not differing in any material respect) are given to the same person (whether on one or different occasions), only one of those samples is deemed not to be a supply. [*VATA 1994, Sch 4 para 5(2)(3)*].

In *EMI Group plc v HMRC, ECJ Case C–581/08, 30 September 2010 unreported*, the Court held that a 'sample' within *Directive 77/388/EEC, Art 5(6)* (now *Directive 2006/112/EC, Art 16*) was a specimen of a product that was intended to promote the sales of that product, and that allowed the characteristics and qualities of the product to be assessed without resulting in final consumption (other than where final consumption was inherent). National legislation could not limit, in a general way, the term 'sample' to specimens presented in a form that was not available for sale, or to the first of a series of identical specimens given to the same recipient.

Samples for testing

No VAT is due on samples given free of charge to someone for testing. The limit of one sample per person (see above) may be exceeded if it can be shown that the items are given for quality assurance testing either on behalf of the supplier or a potential customer.

Samples given to the general public via an intermediary

For example, samples supplied by a manufacturer to a retailer for giving away as samples to the retailer's customers. No VAT is due provided the following conditions are met.

- Neither the supplier nor the intermediary charge for the goods.
- The samples are supplied for genuine business purposes and are given as an illustrative example of the product.
- The samples remain the property of the supplier until they are given to the final customer.
- Any samples not used are returned to the supplier or destroyed.

Sale of samples

If a person sells goods given to him as samples, VAT is due on the sale.

(VAT Notice 700/35/97, paras 3.1–3.4).

(27) School photographers

See **16.18 EDUCATION**.

(28) Second-hand goods

See **61 SECOND-HAND GOODS**.

(29) Solicitors

Oath fees

Under *Solicitors Act 1974, s 81* every solicitor holding a practising certificate may exercise the powers of a commissioner for oaths. Oath fees are regarded as deriving from the personal qualification of a solicitor, such that the solicitor who administers oaths receives the fees in a personal capacity. Whether or not VAT is due will depend upon the circumstances of the individual solicitor concerned.

(a) *Sole practitioners and partners.* Fees received in respect of oaths administered by a solicitor in sole practice or a partner in a firm of solicitors are regarded as consideration for services supplied in the course of the business. If the practice/partnership is registered for VAT, VAT is due. Fees received in a VAT period should be treated as VAT-inclusive.

(b) *Assistant solicitors.* VAT treatment depends upon whether or not the assistant solicitor accounts to the firm for oath fees received.
- Where fees are accounted for to the firm, they are part of the firm's business receipts and VAT must be accounted for as under (*a*) above.
- Where the firm allows the assistant solicitor to retain fees personally, the fees will not be subject to VAT unless the assistant solicitor is individually registered for VAT by virtue of other activities (or required to be registered taking into account the level of oath fees received).

(c) *Solicitors employed otherwise than in practice or retired solicitors.* Any fees received will not be subject to VAT unless the individual is registered for VAT by virtue of other activities (or required to be registered taking into account the level of oath fees received).

(Law Society's Gazette, 8 June 1994).

(30) Sponsorship income

See **57.19 RECREATION AND SPORT.**

(31) Sport and physical recreation facilities

See **57.8 RECREATION AND SPORT.**

(32) Supplies of staff

See **44.4–44.8 MANAGEMENT SERVICES AND SUPPLIES OF STAFF.**

(33) Toll charges

In *EC Commission v UK, ECJ Case C–359/97*, [2000] STC 777 (TVC 22.134) the court ruled that, in certain circumstances, central and local government bodies act as public authorities when they operate tolled bridges, tunnels and roads. Tolls in this category are outside the scope of VAT. This applies to

- Cleddau Bridge

- Dartford Crossing
- Erskine Bridge
- Forth Road Bridge
- Humber Bridge
- Itchen Bridge
- Mersey Tunnel
- Tamar Bridge
- Tay Bridge
- Tyne Tunnel

But the court held that, in any other circumstances, a toll charge is consideration for a standard-rated supply. The decision was implemented in the UK with effect from 1 February 2003. As a result, from that date:

- Tolls payable to private sector operators for use of roads, road bridges and road tunnels are subject to VAT. As this becomes a business activity, toll operators affected can recover input tax on many of their costs. Arrangements have been put in place by the Department of Transport and the Scottish Executive to manage the impact of these changes.
- VAT-registered businesses can recover the VAT charged on tolls if they are entitled to do so under the normal rules. It is not necessary to obtain a VAT invoice to support a claim for input tax on a toll paid at a toll booth for a single or return journey costing up to £25. Otherwise a VAT invoice or other proof of payment must be obtained as appropriate. Businesses are advised to enquire about the VAT status of toll charges when they pay them.

(Business Brief 3/03).

(34) Vending machines

Where customers are provided with 'free' use of vending or similar machines then, provided the customer pays the same price for the products dispensed (coffee, tea, etc.) as other customers who simply buy the product, no VAT is due on the hire of the machines. If, however, a higher amount is charged, VAT must be accounted for at the standard rate on the price difference. (VAT Notice 700/7/02, para 6.9). For supplies in the course of catering, see **11.2 CATERING**.

(35) Video/DVD films and games

Rental of a video/DVD, where the customer must normally return it by a given date and the film/game remains the property of the supplier, is a supply of services. The value for VAT purposes is the amount paid for the use of the film/game over the rental period.

In a part-exchange transaction, the customer's film/game is accepted as payment (or part payment) for another film/game which then becomes the customer's property. Part-exchange is a supply of goods the value of which is the amount the customer would have had to pay for the film/game if there were no part-exchange. See *C & E Commrs v Bugeja*, CA [2001] STC 1568 (TVC 67.76). In that case, a trader (B) sold videos for, say, £20 but where a customer offered a video previously purchased from B in part-exchange, B only charged the customer £10 for the new video. The Court of Appeal held that the consideration for such a sale was £20 (rejecting both the contention of the appellant that he should only be required to account for output tax on the £10 cash payment and the High Court decision (QB 1999, [2000] STC 1) that consideration for the sale was the £10 paid in cash plus the value of the second-hand video which, on the evidence, could not be more than £2 to £3).

Output tax using one of the special **RETAIL SCHEMES (60).**

Rental: all rental payments and membership fees (see below) can be included in gross takings under

- the Point of Sale scheme; and
- Direct Calculation Schemes 1 and 2 (provided the minority goods under the scheme are zero-rated or taxable at the reduced rate).

Under any other scheme, such receipts must be excluded from gross takings and dealt with outside the scheme. The value of any videos/DVDs bought for rental must also be excluded from the scheme calculations.

Part-exchange: whichever scheme is used, the full normal retail selling price, including VAT, must be included in gross takings without deduction for the value of films/games taken in part-exchange. Where videos/DVDs taken in part-exchange are subsequently resold, it may be possible to use the margin scheme for **SECOND-HAND GOODS (61)**. If not, they can be included in the retail scheme calculations.

Other charges

Membership fees are taxable on the full amount charged even if refunded when the customer gives up membership.

Deposits: a refundable deposit for the safe return of a rental film/game is not taxable even if retained because the film/game is lost or damaged.
Overdue films/games: a charge for an overdue film/game is further payment for the use of the film/game and liable to VAT.

(VAT Notice 700/14/04).

(36) Zero-rated supplies

Output tax is not chargeable on zero-rated supplies. See **74 ZERO-RATED SUPPLIES** for a list of the categories of zero-rating and cross-references to supporting chapters.

Key points

[47.9] Points to consider are as follows.

- Output tax is still being charged on a zero-rated supply but at a rate of 0%. This is important to recognise because it means that full input tax recovery is allowed on the related costs of the activity (subject to normal rules). Input tax cannot be reclaimed on costs that are relevant to exempt activities.

- The standard rate of VAT in the UK increased from 17.5% to 20% on 4 January 2011. The VAT fraction used to work out the VAT element within an inclusive price changed from 7/47 to 1/6 for supplies made from 4 January 2011 onwards.
- The reduced rate of VAT remains unchanged at 5%. The relevant fraction used to work out the VAT element within a price that includes 5% VAT is 1/21.
- When assessing whether a single or multiple supply situation exists, it is necessary to consider whether each supply constitutes an aim in itself, or whether the secondary supply is incidental to the main supply. In the latter situation, the output tax payable will wholly depend on the liability of the main supply. Remember that an analysis of mixed supply situations is only relevant if the goods or services in question attract VAT at different rates.
- Be aware of the two different methods of apportionment in mixed supply situations (i.e. cost-based and revenue-based calculations) and identify if one of the methods gives a fairer result.
- Any errors of principle in apportioning output tax on mixed supplies can be adjusted by going back four years and correcting the error. If the amount of tax involved is less than £10,000 (or 1% of the Box 6 figure on the relevant VAT return up to a maximum of £50,000), this can be done by adjusting the next VAT return, otherwise, a separate disclosure must be made to HMRC.
- It is unlikely to be acceptable for a taxpayer to readjust his method of output tax apportionment on a historic basis, unless the method adopted was totally unfair. HMRC will be rightly suspicious about recalculations that are made just to try and get a better result in terms of output tax paid in the past.
- Recent court cases relevant to mixed supply issues have emphasised the importance of looking at the situation from the perspective of the customer rather than the supplier. In other words, consider whether the customer considers that he is only paying for one main benefit (single supply outcome) or a range of benefits subject to different rates of VAT (multiple supply).
- Output tax is not due on a business gift that costs less than £50 to the donor. This assumes that the total cost of all goods donated to the recipient in any previous twelve-month period is also less than £50. Other situations where no output tax is due include free food and drink provided to employees and also to customers (although an input tax block would need to be considered in the latter case under the business entertainment rules).
- It is important to be clear about whether any donation made by a person or business (e.g. to a charity) is a genuine donation, i.e. the donor is not entitled to receive any goods or services from the recipient as a result of making his donation. If obligations were evident (a small acknowledgement of thanks in a publication would not be classed as a benefit to the donor) then the VAT

liability of the benefits provided to the donor need to be considered. If these benefits are standard-rated, e.g. sponsorship benefit, then output tax will need to be declared on the payment in question.

- When dealing with compensation payments to customers, output tax can be reduced on a payment if it relates to a specific problem with goods supplied, e.g. compensation to reflect the poor quality of a product. However, general compensation payments for injury or inconvenience to the customer will be outside the scope of VAT.
- A business should ensure that it keeps full details of any goods that have been lost, stolen or destroyed, e.g. police reference numbers, documents relating to insurance claims. This could avoid problems on HMRC visits if an officer tries to assess output tax on goods he cannot trace.

48

Overseas Traders

Cross-references. See **3.8 AGENTS** for tax representatives and agents employed by overseas traders; **38 INTERNATIONAL SERVICES** for services generally made to or by overseas traders.

Introduction

[48.1] An '*overseas trader*' (also referred to as a '*non-established taxable person*') is any person who

- is not normally resident in the UK;
- does not have a 'business establishment' in the UK; and
- if a company, is not incorporated in the UK.

A '*business establishment*' is usually premises from which trading activities directly related to the business are carried out. Where a business provides book-keeping, accountancy or invoicing services at its premises for an overseas trader who does not actually make supplies in the UK, HMRC do not consider the premises to be a business establishment.

An overseas business which has a business establishment in the UK is not an overseas trader and must be registered for VAT in the UK at the address of its principal UK place of business. It must keep its VAT records and accounts at this address which must be available for HMRC to inspect. Someone responsible for VAT affairs should be available at the address. If that person is an employee, he must have written authority to act on behalf of the business A suggested form of words for this authority is at **48.3** below under the appointment of an agent. A separate authority will not be required if

- the name of the person concerned has been notified to the Registrar of Companies under the *Companies Act 2006, Part 34* as a UK resident authorised to accept service of process on behalf of the company; or
- for a partnership the person concerned is a partner, resident in the UK.

(VAT Notice 700/1/07, paras 8.1, 8.2, 9.3).

Registration of overseas traders

[48.2] An overseas trader *must* register for VAT in the UK if

- he makes taxable supplies of goods and services in the UK in the course of furtherance of his business (see **47.1 OUTPUT TAX**) and the total value of those supplies exceeds the VAT registration threshold (see **59.3 REGISTRATION**);
- the business is registered for VAT in another EU country, he sells and delivers goods in the UK to customers who are not VAT-registered ('distance sales') and the value of those distance sales exceeds the relevant threshold (see **59.12 REGISTRATION**);
- he acquires goods in the UK directly from a VAT-registered supplier in another EU country (see **19.3 EUROPEAN UNION: SINGLE MARKET**) and the total value of the acquisitions exceeds the acquisitions threshold (see **59.19 REGISTRATION**); or
- he makes a claim under the *EC 8th Directive* or *EC 13th Directive* and subsequently supplies, or intends to supply, the relevant goods in the UK (see **59.27 REGISTRATION**).

For VAT purposes, the UK includes the territorial sea of the UK (i.e. waters within twelve nautical miles of the coastline).

There is no need to register if the only UK supplies are supplies of services on which the customer is liable to account for any VAT due under the 'reverse charge' procedure. See **38.4 INTERNATIONAL SERVICES.**

An overseas trader *may* also be registered if

- he has started in business but is not yet making taxable supplies, provided he can show the intention of making taxable supplies in the future as part of his business; or
- his turnover is below the threshold, provided he can prove to HMRC that he is carrying on a business for VAT purposes and making taxable supplies.

See **59.2 REGISTRATION.**

Consequences of registration

An overseas trader who is registered or required to be registered for VAT in the UK must account for VAT in respect of those supplies and acquisitions taking place in the UK. He is also liable to VAT on importations of any goods into the UK (see **33 IMPORTS**) and on the acquisition in the UK of exciseable goods or of new means of transport from another EU country whether or not he is required to be registered (see **19.9** and **19.37 EUROPEAN UNION: SINGLE MARKET** respectively).

[*VATA 1994, ss 1, 3, 4, 10, 96(11)*]. (VAT Notice 700/1/07, para 8.3).

See **65.2 SUPPLY: PLACE OF SUPPLY** for the place of supply of goods and **65.12 SUPPLY: PLACE OF SUPPLY** for the place of supply of services.

Registration options available

[48.3] An overseas trader who is required or entitled to be registered in the UK can normally choose between three registration options.

(1) He may appoint a VAT representative who will be jointly and severally liable for any VAT debts. The overseas trader must still complete a VAT registration form. In addition to this, both the overseas trader and the VAT representative must complete a Form VAT 1TR. See **3.8 AGENTS** for further details on VAT representatives. It is understood that, in practice, very few businesses are prepared to provide the services of a VAT representative because they are unwilling to become liable for any VAT debts of the overseas trader.

(2) He may appoint an agent to deal with the VAT affairs. The agent cannot be held responsible to HMRC for any VAT debts and HMRC reserve the right not to deal with any particular agent. (In some cases, HMRC could insist that a tax representative is appointed although this cannot now be done where the overseas trader is based in a country where certain mutual assistance arrangements exist.) The overseas trader must still complete a VAT registration form. In addition, HMRC will need a letter of authority. A suggested letter of authority approved by HMRC is:

    (Insert principal's name) of (insert principal's address) hereby appoints (insert name of UK agent or employee) of (insert address of UK agent or employee) to act as agent for the purpose of dealing with all their legal obligations in respect of Value Added Tax.

    This letter authorises the above-named agent to sign VAT return forms 100 and any other document needed for the purpose of enabling the agent or employee to comply with the VAT obligations of the principal.

    Signed (insert principal's signature)

    Date (insert date)

(3) He may deal with all the VAT obligations (including registration, returns and record-keeping) personally. To register, the overseas trader should contact the Aberdeen VAT office at Ruby House, 8 Ruby Place, Aberdeen, AB10 1ZP (Tel: 01224 404807/818).

The appropriate VAT registration application form is

- Form VAT 1 if in respect of taxable supplies;
- Form VAT 1A if in respect of distance sales; or
- Form VAT 1B if in respect of acquisitions.

(VAT Notice 700/1/07, paras 10.1–10.6).

Alternatives to registration

Accounting for VAT through customers

[48.4] *VATA 1994, s 14* implements the VAT simplification procedures for triangular trade between EU countries and the UK. The provisions allow UK customers to be designated as liable to account for the VAT that would otherwise be due to be accounted for by intermediate suppliers in other EU countries. See **19.22 EUROPEAN UNION: SINGLE MARKET** for fuller details.

Import agents

An overseas trader not registered for VAT in the UK who

- imports goods for onward supply in the UK, and
- does not supply any other goods or services within the UK to a total value exceeding the current registration limit,

can arrange for a UK-resident agent registered for VAT to import and supply the goods on his behalf. The agent is treated as importing and supplying the goods as principal. He must make any necessary Customs entries as the importer, pay or defer the VAT and take delivery of the goods. He can reclaim any import VAT as input tax (subject to the normal rules) but must issue proper VAT invoices for the supplies of the goods and charge and account for VAT on the onward sale in the normal way. See **3.4 AGENTS** for the treatment of commission. (VAT Notice 702, para 2.7).

Applications to the UK for refunds of VAT by persons established outside the EU

[48.5] When a trader registered for business purposes in a country outside the EU buys goods or services in the UK, he may have to pay UK VAT. If goods are bought for export, there is usually no problem as the supply will be zero-rated. But if the goods or services bought in the UK are also used here (e.g. at a trade fair), the trader cannot treat the VAT incurred as input tax because he is not registered here.

To avoid this, the *EC 13th Directive* has set up a scheme which allows overseas traders, subject to conditions being met, to reclaim VAT charged on imports into the UK or purchases of goods and services used in the UK. See **18.45 EUROPEAN UNION LEGISLATION** for a summary of the provisions of the *EC 13th Directive*. The provisions have been implemented in the UK as set out below.

Persons to whom the provisions apply

The provisions apply to any trader carrying on a business established in a '*third country*' (i.e. a country outside the EU) provided that in the period of claim

(a) he was not registered or liable to be registered for VAT in the UK;
(b) he was not established in any EU country;
(c) he made no supplies of goods and services in the UK other than
  (i) transport of freight outside the UK or to or from a place outside the UK (and ancillary services);
  (ii) services where the VAT on the supply is payable solely by the person to whom they are supplied under the reverse charge provisions (see **38.4 INTERNATIONAL SERVICES**); or
  (iii) goods where the VAT on the supply is payable solely by the person to whom they are supplied; and

(d) where the trader is established in a third country having a comparable system of turnover taxes, unless HMRC allow otherwise, that country provides reciprocal arrangements for refunds to be made to taxable persons established in the UK.

For these purposes a person is treated as established in a country if

- he has a business establishment there; or
- he has no business establishment (there or elsewhere) but his permanent address or usual place of residence is there. The usual place of residence of a company is where it is legally constituted.

A person carrying on business through a branch or agency in any country is treated as having a business establishment there.

Refundable/non-refundable VAT

A person to whom the provisions apply is entitled to be repaid VAT charged on

- goods imported by him into the UK in respect of which no other relief is available; and
- supplies made to him in the UK if that VAT would be input tax of his were he a taxable person in the UK.

Refunds cannot be claimed on VAT incurred on

- non-business supplies (if a supply covers both business and non-business use, VAT can be reclaimed on the business element of the supply);
- any supply or importation which the trader has used, or intends to use, for the purpose of any supply by him in the UK;
- any supply or importation which has been exported, or is intended for exportation, from the UK by or on behalf of the trader;
- a supply or importation where input tax recovery is restricted in the UK (e.g. most motor cars, business entertainment and second-hand goods for which no VAT invoice is issued, see **34.8 INPUT TAX**);
- VAT charged on a supply to a travel agent, tour operators, etc. which is for the direct benefit of a traveller other than the travel agent or his employee; and
- in relation to VAT charged after 2 December 2004, VAT on a supply used (or to be used) in making supplies of insurance and financial services within **34.3**(*c*) **INPUT TAX**.

Method of claiming

Claim forms (VAT 65A) are obtainable from

HM Revenue and Customs
VAT Overseas Repayments Unit
Foyle House
PO Box 34
Dungreggan Road
Londonderry BT48 7AE

Northern Ireland
Tel: +44 (0) 2871 305100
Fax: +44 (0) 2871 305101
enq.oru.ni@hmrc.gsi.gov.uk

Forms must be completed in English, using block capitals, and must be sent to the above address, together with proof of the VAT paid and, if appropriate, a certificate of status.

Proof of VAT paid

A claim form must be supported by correctly completed invoices, vouchers or receipts from suppliers showing

- supplier's name, address and VAT registration number;
- the date of supply;
- details of goods or services supplied;
- the cost of the goods or services (including VAT); and
- the rate of VAT

and additionally if the value of the supply is over £100 (including VAT)

- an identifying number;
- the claimant's name and address; and
- the amount of VAT charged.

If the goods have been imported, the VAT copy of the import entry or other Customs document showing the amount of VAT paid is also required.

Only originals of documents are acceptable. HMRC will refuse to accept any supporting documentation if it already bears an official stamp indicating that it has been furnished in support of an earlier claim.

Certificate of status

When making the first claim in the UK, a trader must also include a certificate from the official authority in his own country showing that he is registered for business purposes there. When applying for the certificate, it is important to make sure that it shows all the information that the UK authorities will need to process the claim (e.g. if the invoices are made out in a company's trading name, the certificate must show this, as well as the name under which it is registered).

The certificate must be an original (not a photocopy) and contain

- the name, address and official stamp of the authorising body;
- the claimant's name and address;
- the nature of the claimant's business; and
- the claimant's business registration number.

Each certificate is valid for twelve months from its date of issue and will cover any claims made during that year. Once the certificate has expired, the trader must send a new one with his next claim.

Time limit

The claim must be made not later than six months after the end of the 'prescribed year' in which the VAT is incurred. The '*prescribed year*' is the year ended 30 June.

Period of claim

Any claim must be for a period of not less than three months (unless less than three months of the prescribed year remains) and not more than one year. Items missed on earlier claims can be included as long as they related to VAT charged in the year of the claim.

Minimum claim

If the claim is for less than one year, it must be for at least £130 (unless it is for the final part of the prescribed year). No claim can be for less than £16.

Repayment

The refund will be made within six months of receiving a satisfactory claim. Payments can be made by any of the following methods.

- Directly to the claimant's own bank through SWIFT (Society for Worldwide Inter-Bank Financial Telecommunications). The claimant must provide full bank account details (bank name, address and identification code; account name and number; and currency of account) and a copy of a bank credit slip with the claim form.
- To any UK bank.
- By payable order in sterling directly to the claimant or an appointed agent.

Where any repayment is made to a claimant in the country in which he is established, HMRC may reduce the repayment by the amount of any bank charges or costs incurred.

Use of agents

An overseas trader can prepare and send in his own claim or have this done by an agent. Any agent will need either a Power of Attorney or letter of authority before HMRC will accept that he is acting for, and can receive money on behalf of, the trader.

The following is an example of the format of a letter of authority acceptable to HMRC.

I [name and address of claimant] hereby appoint [name and address of agent] to act on my behalf in connection with any claim I make to Her Britannic Majesty's Commissioners of Revenue and Customs under the Value Added Tax Regulations 1995 as from time to time amended or replaced. Any repayment of VAT to which I am entitled pursuant to any such claim made on my behalf by my above named agent shall be paid to [name and address of payee].

Date Signed [by the claimant]

Appeals

An appeal may be made to an independent VAT tribunal against a refusal by HMRC to allow all or part of a repayment. A Notice of Appeal must be served at the VAT tribunal within 30 days of the date of the letter notifying the refusal. Alternatively, the applicant may first ask HMRC to reconsider their decision and extend the time for service of a Notice of Appeal. If HMRC allow an extension but do not change their decision, the applicant then has a further 21 days from the date of the letter upholding the decision to serve a Notice of Appeal.

Isle of Man

For VAT purposes, the Isle of Man is treated as part of the UK. VAT is chargeable in the Isle of Man under Manx legislation, which is broadly similar to UK legislation. The above scheme applies equally to refunds of VAT incurred in the Isle of Man and any references above to the UK are to be taken to include the Isle of Man.

[*VATA 1994, s 39; SI 1995/2518, Regs 185–197; SI 2004/3140, Reg 15*]. (VAT Notice 723A, paras 5.2, 5.5, 5.6, 6.1–6.8).

Insurance and financial transactions

The European Commission (EC) formally requested the UK to amend its legislation relating to the *EC 13th Directive* on insurance or financial transactions. Under UK law a taxable person established outside the EU is denied the right to recover VAT paid or due in the UK on goods or services in so far as they are used for the purpose of insurance or financial transactions supplied to customers established outside the EU. By contrast, a taxable person established in the EU (in the UK or otherwise) is entitled to recover VAT in such cases.

The UK did not take any action to amend its legislation, and so the EC referred the matter to the ECJ. The Advocate General (AG) found in favour of the UK, on the ground that the UK was entitled to rely on *EC 13th Directive, Art 2(1)*, which does not mention the possibility of obtaining a refund in the case of financial and insurance transactions. The Court could not read into *Art 2(1)* the provisions of *Directive 2006/112/EC, Art 169(c)* (which allows for the recovery of VAT incurred in making non-EU supplies of insurance and finance). See *EC Commission v UK (No 7), ECJ Case C–582/08* [2010] STC 2364 (TVC 22.546).

Retail export scheme

A VAT retail export scheme allows non-EU visitors a refund of VAT on certain goods that they buy in the EU. See **21.12 EXPORTS**.

Special scheme for electronically supplied services

There is a special scheme for overseas businesses which provide electronically supplied services to non-business customers in the EU. See **63.34 SPECIAL SCHEMES**. The special scheme provides only for payment of the VAT due on sales to EU customers without any deductions of EU VAT incurred on purchases. However, a business in the scheme can reclaim VAT charged on

- goods it imports into the UK; and
- supplies it makes in the UK

in connection with making qualifying supplies while it is a participant in the special scheme. The provisions outlined above apply with the omission of conditions (*c*) and (*d*) above.

[*VATA 1994, Sch 3B para 22; FA 2003, Sch 2 para 4*].

De Voil Indirect Tax Service. See V5.152.

Key points

[48.6] Points to consider are as follows.

- A common situation where an overseas business will need to register for VAT in the UK is when the 'distance selling' limits are exceeded. This occurs when a business based in another EU country has sold goods into the UK exceeding £70,000 on a calendar year basis but only to customers who are not VAT-registered. If a customer is VAT-registered in the UK, then the VAT is dealt with by the customer (acquisition tax) on his own VAT return.
- If an overseas business based in another EU country sells services into the UK, e.g. accountancy services there is no need to register for VAT in the UK. This assumes that the business in question does not have a fixed or business establishment in the UK, i.e. premises from which it trades. In the cases of B2B (business to business) sales, the customer in the UK will account for VAT by doing a reverse charge calculation.
- There are no distance selling rules for services as there are for goods. So as an example, a Dutch accountancy firm completing private tax returns for UK individuals (B2C – business to consumer sale) will charge Dutch VAT on the services provided, without any need to become VAT-registered in the UK. This again assumes that the Dutch firm does not have an establishment in the UK, i.e. it trades from an office in Holland.
- There is no problem with an overseas business registering for VAT in the UK on either a voluntary basis (taxable sales below the compulsory VAT registration limit) or intending trader basis (intention to make taxable sales at a future date). Many businesses will favour this option to ensure VAT paid on expenditure in the UK can be easily reclaimed as input tax on a UK VAT return.
- A UK business acting for an overseas trader in relation to VAT matters (e.g. a firm of accountants based in the UK) should avoid the option of becoming the VAT representative of the business in question. In such cases, the VAT representative is jointly responsible for the VAT debts of the overseas business.

- A more sensible option to avoid any problems is for an overseas business to appoint a UK agent to deal with its UK VAT affairs. A letter of authority (signed by a director or business owner) must be given to HMRC to confirm the agent's involvement. The main advantage is that the agent cannot be held responsible for the debts of the overseas trader.
- An overseas business can handle its own VAT affairs i.e. without the involvement of a UK agent. In such cases, it will deal with HMRC's office in Aberdeen (see **48.3**).
- It is possible for an overseas business based outside the EU that is not VAT-registered in the UK (or making supplies in the UK) to reclaim VAT paid in the UK through the EU 13th Directive system. This system allows a business based outside the EU to reclaim UK VAT, usually as long as there is a reciprocal arrangement in place that allows a UK business to reclaim indirect taxes paid in that country. Example – a reciprocal arrangement is in place with Australia that allows a UK business to reclaim Australian GST.
- 13th Directive claims made by a non-EU business are dealt with by HMRC's office in Londonderry (see **48.5**). The claimant cannot reclaim tax on any expenses that are input tax blocked to a UK business, e.g. business entertainment costs, motor cars etc. or any expenses relevant to an exempt supply. The claim is made on form VAT65A and must be completed in English. The claimant must also provide evidence (certificate of status) to confirm his business registration in his own country.
- An overseas business making a 13th Directive claim must comply with a very strict time deadline. Claims for the twelve-month period ending 30 June must be submitted by the following 31 December. HMRC will then pay the claim (assuming it is correct) within six months of receipt.
- An overseas business may have to register in the UK under proposed new rules even though its taxable turnover is below the current registration limit for UK businesses. This follows the ruling of the ECJ in the case of *Schmelz (C-97/09)*, [2011] STC 88 (TVC 20.126).

49

Partial Exemption

Cross-references. See **10 CAPITAL GOODS SCHEME** for deduction, and adjustment of deduction, of input tax on capital items by partly exempt businesses; **27.9 GROUPS OF COMPANIES** for input tax incurred by holding companies; **18.34**, **18.35 EUROPEAN UNION LEGISLATION**; **20 EXEMPT SUPPLIES**.

De Voil Indirect Tax Service. See V3.461–467.

Introduction

[49.1] A registered business which makes both taxable and exempt supplies cannot charge VAT on the exempt supplies and equally cannot normally reclaim the VAT incurred on the purchases used to make those supplies. Where input tax cannot be claimed because it relates to an exempt supply, it is known as *exempt input tax* and the registered business is known as *partly exempt*. See **20 EXEMPT SUPPLIES** and supporting chapters for details of goods and services the supplies of which are exempt.

A partly exempt business will normally have to use an approved partial exemption method (see **49.3–49.10** below) to work out how much of its input tax can be reclaimed. This would usually be the standard method (see **49.4–49.8** below) unless it feels that this would not give a fair or reasonable result, in which case it can apply to HMRC for a special method (see **49.10** below). All methods should provide for direct attribution and apportionment of the input tax incurred. Direct attribution involves identifying VAT on goods and services which are used exclusively to make taxable supplies or exempt supplies: the former is deductible, the latter is not. Apportionment is required for the remaining input tax (e.g. on overheads) which cannot be directly attributed.

Where a partly exempt business prepares VAT returns and deducts input tax on a quarterly or monthly basis, the input tax deduction is provisional. The business also has a longer period at the end of which it is required to review the extent of its allowable input tax and revise its deduction accordingly. In general, the longer period ends on the last day of the quarter ending March, April or May and the adjustment is known as the annual adjustment. Newly registered traders have a longer period known as a registration period. See **49.13** below.

Even if a partial exemption method has to be used, the *de minimis* limits in **49.11** below may allow all input tax to be recovered (subject to the normal rules).

Where a business has deducted VAT based on its intention to use the relevant goods and services to make taxable supplies and at any time within six years, not having made the intended supply, it changes its mind and uses, or forms the intention to use, the goods and services to make an exempt supply, it must adjust its original claim. Conversely, rules permit a claim where VAT was restricted because the business's original intention was to make exempt supplies but in the event a taxable supply is either subsequently intended or made. See **49.14** below.

Capital goods scheme

The capital goods scheme covers input tax incurred in respect of land and property or computers above certain values. Under the scheme, the owner of the capital item must review the extent to which the item is used to make taxable supplies over a period of time (five or ten years) and make an adjustment where appropriate. See **10 CAPITAL GOODS SCHEME**.

General provisions relating to allowable input tax

[49.2] The amount of allowable input tax for which a taxable person is entitled to credit at the end of any period is so much of the input tax on supplies, acquisitions and importations in the period as is allowable as being attributable to the following supplies made, or to be made, by the taxable person in the course or furtherance of his business.

(a) '*Taxable supplies*', i.e. supplies of goods and services made in the UK other than exempt supplies.

(b) Supplies outside the UK which would be taxable supplies if made in the UK.

(c) Supplies of services which
  (i) are supplied to a person who belongs outside the EU, or
  (ii) are directly linked to the export of goods to a place outside the EU, or
  (iii) consist of the provision of intermediary services in relation to any transaction within (i) or (ii) above

  provided that the supply is exempt (or would have been exempt if made in the UK) by virtue of *VATA 1994, Sch 9 Group* 2 (insurance) or *VATA 1994, Sch 9 Group 5 Items 1–8* (finance).

(d) Supplies made either in or outside the UK which fall, or would fall, within *VATA 1994, Sch 9 Group 15 Item 1 or 2* (investment gold, see **26.2 GOLD AND PRECIOUS METALS**).

HMRC must make regulations for securing a fair and reasonable attribution of input tax to the supplies within (*a*) to (*c*) above.

[*VATA 1994, ss 4(2), 26; SI 1992/3123; SI 1999/3121*].

Regulations made are considered in **49.3** to **49.14** below. In those paragraphs:

(1) '*Exempt input tax*' means input tax incurred by a taxable person on
- goods or services supplied to, or goods imported or acquired by, him insofar as they are used by him, or a 'successor' of his, in making exempt supplies, or
- supplies outside the UK which would be exempt if made in the UK,

other than input tax which is allowable under
- (with effect from 1 April 2007) *SI 1995/2518, Reg 102* (special methods, see **49.10** below);
- *SI 1995/2518, Reg 103* (attribution of input tax to foreign and specified supplies, see **49.12**(1) below);
- *SI 1995/2518, Reg 103A* (input tax attributable to exempt supplies of investment gold, see **26.4 GOLD AND PRECIOUS METALS**); or
- *SI 1995/2518, Reg 103B* (incidental financial services, see **49.12**(2) below).

See **49.9** below for the meaning of '*successor*'.

(2) Nothing is to be construed as allowing a taxable person to deduct the whole or any part of the VAT on the importation or acquisition by him of goods or the supply to him of goods or services where those goods or services are not used or to be used by him in making supplies in the course or furtherance of a business carried on by him.

[*SI 1995/2518, Regs 99(1)(a), 100; SI 1999/3114; SI 2004/3140, Reg 9; SI 2007/768, Reg 6*].

Calculation of reclaimable input tax

[49.3] If a business is not fully taxable, subject to the *de minimis* limit in **49.11** below, it cannot recover all its input tax. It is therefore necessary to determine how much of the input tax incurred can be reclaimed. This must be done in accordance with the following rules.

(a) Identify goods imported or acquired by, and goods or services supplied to, the business in the VAT period which are used
- *exclusively* in making taxable supplies; and
- *exclusively* in making exempt supplies.

This process is known as *direct attribution*.

(b) Input tax is reclaimable on such of those goods and services as are used, or are to be used, *exclusively* in making taxable supplies or other supplies which carry the right to deduct.

(c) No part of the input tax can be reclaimed on such of those goods or services as are used, or are to be used, in making exempt supplies or other supplies in respect of which input tax is non-deductible.

[*SI 1995/2518, Reg 101(2)*].

In most partly-exempt businesses, however, there will still be further input tax which cannot be directly attributed under (*a*)–(*c*) above because it relates to

- goods and services used, or intended to be used, for making both taxable and exempt supplies; or
- general overheads of the business (e.g. accountancy costs, telephone bills).

Input tax on these costs which cannot be directly attributed is normally referred to as 'non-attributable' or 'residual' input tax. A partial exemption method must then be used to apportion this residual input tax to determine how much of it is reclaimable. A business should normally use the standard method in **49.4–49.8** below to calculate provisionally how much residual input tax can be reclaimed but in certain circumstances it may be possible to apply a special method, subject to prior approval of HMRC. See **49.10** below.

Unless the *de minimis* limit in **49.11** below applies (in which case all input tax is recoverable subject to the normal rules), the total VAT reclaimable in the VAT period is then the directly attributable input tax under (*b*) above plus the reclaimable portion of residual input tax. The provisional amount reclaimed in the VAT period may then need to be adjusted at the end of a 'longer period', normally twelve months. See **49.13** below.

Both the provisional attribution and the annual adjustment must be made on the basis of facts as they existed at the time when the input tax was incurred, not on the changed facts as they existed at the time the claim was made. See *C & E Commrs v University of Wales College Cardiff*, QB [1995] STC 611 (TVC 46.215) where apportionment was based on income received in the relevant periods rather than subsequent use.

The standard method

[49.4] Under the standard method (use of which does not require HMRC approval), the percentage of residual input tax (see **49.3** above) which can be reclaimed is calculated on the basis of use.

De Voil Indirect Tax Service. See V3.461–V3.461C.

Values-based calculation

[49.5] This can be calculated as follows.

Claimable %

$$= \frac{\text{Value of taxable supplies in the period (excluding VAT)}}{\text{Value of all supplies in the period (excluding VAT)}} \times 100$$

If the resulting percentage is not a whole number, it should be rounded *up* to the next whole number except that, for VAT periods beginning on or after 1 April 2005, where the residual input tax to which the fraction is applied is £400,000 per month on average or greater, it should be rounded up to two decimal places.

In making the calculation, the value of all the following supplies must be excluded.

(a) Any sum receivable in respect of a supply of capital goods used for the purposes of the business. There is no statutory definition of capital goods but the term is wider than simply goods within the **CAPITAL GOODS SCHEME (10)**. In *C & E Commrs v JDL Ltd*, Ch D 2001, [2002] STC 1 (TVC 46.98) motor cars were held to be capital goods as they were of substantial durability and value as compared to other articles used in the management and day-to-day running of the business. In *Nordania Finans A/S and anor v Skatteministeriet, ECJ Case C–98/07*, [2008] STC 3314 (TVC 22.451), the ECJ ruled that where goods (in this case, cars) were leased and subsequently sold on the termination of the leasing contracts, those goods were not to be regarded as capital goods. In HMRC's view, the decision in *Nordania* overturns the decision in *JDL Ltd*. Businesses which have submitted a claim for repayment of VAT as a result of the *Italian Republic* case (*Case C–45/95* – sales of cars where the input tax on purchase has been blocked are exempt) will be required to review their claims to take account of the *Nordania* decision. This means that the value of cars owned and used in the business and on which a repayment claim has been made (mainly demonstrator cars) will have to be included in the denominator of the partial exemption calculation, which will have the effect of reducing the amount of residual input tax which is recoverable. (HMRC Brief 43/10).

(b) Any sum receivable in respect of any of the following descriptions of supplies made where such supplies are incidental to one or more of the business activities.
   - Any supply of a description falling within *VATA 1994, Sch 9 Group 5* (exempt supplies of finance).
   - With effect from 1 April 2007, any other financial transaction.
   - With effect from 1 April 2007, any *'real estate transaction'* including any grant, assignment (including any transfer, disposition or sale), surrender or reverse surrender of any interest in, right over or licence to occupy land.

   In *C H Beazer (Holdings) plc* (VTD 3283) (TVC 46.99) the tribunal considered incidental to mean 'occurring or liable to occur in fortuitous or subordinate conjunction with'.

(c) That part of the value of any supply of goods on which output tax is not chargeable by virtue of a Treasury order under *VATA 1994, s 25(7)* unless the business has imported, acquired or been supplied with the goods for the purpose of selling them.

(d) The value of any supply which, under or by virtue of any provision of *VATA 1994*, the business makes to itself.

(e) With effect from 1 April 2009, supplies within *VATA 1994, Sch 9 Group 5 Items 1 or 6* (dealings with money or securities) or supplies made from an establishment outside the UK.

[*SI 1995/2518, Reg 101; SI 2004/3140, Reg 10; SI 2005/762; SI 2007/768, Reg 7; SI 2009/820, Reg 4*].

(f) The value of transactions that are not supplies for VAT purposes, such as the transfer of a business as a going concern and the issue by a company of new shares in the company to raise capital, along with the value of EU acquisitions.

(VAT Notice 706, para 4.8).

Annual adjustments

The claimable proportion of residual input tax for a tax period as calculated is only provisional and subject to adjustment at the end of the 'longer period'. See **49.13** below.

Use-based calculation

[49.6] For tax years commencing on or after 1 April 2009, a new partly exempt business has the option of recovering input tax on the basis of use in the following situations.

- *During its registration period.* This is the period running from the date a business is first registered for VAT to the day before the start of its first tax year (normally 31 March, 30 April or 31 May depending on the periods covered by the VAT returns).
- *During its first tax year (normally the first period of twelve months commencing on 1 April, 1 May or 1 June following the end of the registration period)*, provided it did not incur input tax relating to exempt supplies during its registration period.
- *During any tax year*, provided it did not incur input tax relating to exempt supplies in its previous tax year.

A recovery on the basis of use means that input tax is attributed in accordance with the use or intended use of input tax bearing costs in making taxable supplies. A business is required to examine its main categories of expenditure and determine the extent to which they relate to taxable supplies. Most businesses that embark upon a new activity will have carefully considered how costs will be used, in accordance with cost accounting principles, when preparing its business plan. Provided this is logical, objective and transparent it will invariably form an ideal basis for a fair recovery of input tax.

Where a business calculates its recovery of input tax on the basis of use, it is also required to calculate its annual adjustment on the basis of use. Also, where a business does not recover input tax on the basis of use but would nevertheless have been entitled to do so, it may still calculate a use-based annual adjustment.

Example

A business is registered for VAT on 15 July 2009 and its first year begins on 1 April 2010. Its registration period is therefore 15 July 2009 to 31 March 2010. To secure funding it drew up a three-year business plan which projects taxable and total income as follows.

Year ending	Estimated value of taxable supplies (a)	Estimated value of total supplies (b)	Recovery percentage = (a) × 100/(b)
31 March 2010	4,000	20,000	20%
31 March 2011	70,000	100,000	70%
31 March 2012	150,000	200,000	75%
Total	224,000	320,000	70%

It incurs total residual input tax on start-up costs of £50,000 during the registration period.

The business is satisfied that overall it uses the start-up costs in proportion to the value of taxable and exempt supplies that it makes and intends to make over the three-year period. However, if it operated the normal standard method calculation using the values of supplies made during the registration period, it would only be able to recover 20% of its input tax (£10,000) which does not reflect its intended use of costs.

The new rules allow the business to recover the input tax on costs incurred in each VAT return within the registration period in accordance with the principle of use. Therefore, the business can select its own calculation for recovering the input tax provided it is fair and reasonable. In this case, as the business intends the start-up costs to be used in proportion to the values of supplies made over the three-year period, it can provisionally recover a total of 70% of the residual input tax (£35,000) in the VAT returns that fall within the registration period. It would also be required to perform its first annual adjustment on the basis of use to finalise the calculation. However, this will only affect its input tax recovery if its use or intended use of costs have changed by that time. For simplicity, if we assume that in this example there are no significant changes, the finalised amount of recoverable input tax would be £35,000 and so the annual adjustment would be nil.

For its first tax year that runs from 1 April 2010 to 31 March 2011, the business reverts to the normal values-based calculation. Change 1 means that the business can provisionally recover its input tax during its first year by reference to the recovery percentage determined for the registration period (70% in this example), although this would be finalised by way of an annual adjustment at year-end on the basis of values.

The business is therefore able to recover its input tax on the basis of use for almost two years, after which it reverts to the normal values-based calculation. It is only if the business anticipates that a values-based calculation would be unsuitable that it would need to consider applying for a special method.

[*SI 1995/2518, Reg 101; SI 2009/820, Reg 4*]. (VAT Information Sheet 4/09, para 4).

De Voil Indirect Tax Service. See V3.461A, V3.461B, V3.462.

Use of previous year's recovery percentage

[49.7] For tax years commencing on or after 1 April 2009, a business may use its previous year's recovery percentage to determine the provisional recovery of residual input tax in each VAT return, which is then finalised as normal by way of an annual adjustment. The finalised annual recovery percentage is then used as the provisional recovery percentage for the next year, and so on. A business may continue to operate the old rules and calculate separate recovery percentages for each of its VAT returns. A business must consistently apply either the new rules or the old rules in any given tax year.

> *Example*
>
> ABC Ltd uses the standard method and reclaimed 75% of its residual input tax in the year to 31 March 2010. It will reclaim the same percentage of residual input tax in relation to VAT returns submitted during the year ending 31 March 2011. It will then calculate its annual adjustment for the year and reclaim additional input tax if the percentage of taxable income exceeded 75%, i.e. the provisional recovery rate was too low. It will repay tax to HMRC if the percentage of taxable income was less than 75%, i.e. the provisional recovery rate was too high. The percentage of taxable income for year ended 31 March 2011 will then form the basis of quarterly calculations during year ended 31 March 2012.

[*SI 1995/2518, Reg 101; SI 2009/820, Reg 4*]. (VAT Information Sheet 4/09, para 2).

Scope of the standard method

[49.8] From 1 April 2009 the scope of the standard method has been widened with regard to supplies of services to customers outside the UK; certain financial supplies such as shares and bonds; and supplies made from establishments located outside the UK.

Under the old rules, the standard method only dealt with the recovery of input tax relating to taxable supplies made in the UK. Businesses that made overseas supplies that carried the right of recovery (foreign and specified supplies) were required to carry out an additional calculation (known as a *Reg 103* calculation, see **49.12** below) to determine the recoverable input tax on these supplies on the basis of use. Alternatively, following changes introduced on 1 April 2007 they could seek approval of a combined special method that catered for these types of supply.

From 1 April 2009 the scope of the standard method has been widened so that it now deals with input tax on all supplies unless it is dealt with separately under *SI 1995/2518, Reg 103A* (investment gold).

Supplies described in *VATA 1994, Sch 9 Group 5 Items 1 and 6* (mainly supplies of financial instruments such as shares and bonds) and supplies made from overseas establishments are catered for by the standard method but are excluded from the values-based calculation, irrespective of their place of supply. Instead, input tax relating to these supplies is ring-fenced and recovered on the basis of use.

All remaining input tax is recovered by reference to the values-based calculation (unless a new partly exempt business opts to recover on the basis of use in accordance with *VATA 1994, s 4*).

(VAT Information Sheet 4/09, para 5).

Example

In its tax year beginning on 1 April 2011, X Ltd makes the following supplies.

	Total (excl VAT)	Standard-rated (excl VAT)	Exempt
	£	£	£
First quarter	442,004	392,286	49,718
Second quarter	310,929	266,712	44,217
Third quarter	505,867	493,614	12,253
Fourth quarter	897,135	876,387	20,748
	£2,155,935	£2,028,999	£126,936

Input tax for the year is analysed as follows

	Attributable to taxable supplies	Attributable to exempt supplies	Remaining input tax	Total input tax
	£	£	£	£
First quarter	36,409	4,847	11,751	53,007
Second quarter	20,245	311	5,212	25,768
Third quarter	34,698	1,195	10,963	46,856
Fourth quarter	69,707	5,975	9,357	85,039
	£161,059	£12,328	£37,283	£210,670

First quarter

	£	£
Input tax attributable to taxable supplies	36,409	
Proportion of residual input tax deductible = 392,286/442,004 = 88.75%		
£11,751 × 89% =	10,458	
		46,867

Second quarter

Input tax attributable to taxable supplies	20,245	
Proportion of residual input tax deductible = 266,712/310,929 = 85.78%		
£5,212 × 86% =	4,482	
	£24,727	
The value of exempt input tax is £1,041 (311 + [5,212 – 4,482]). As this is not more than £625 per month on average and is less than 50% of all input tax in the quarter, all input tax in the quarter is recoverable.		
Deductible input tax		25,768

Third quarter

Input tax attributable to taxable supplies	34,698	
Proportion of residual input tax deductible = 493,614/505,867 = 97.58%		
£10,963 × 98% =	10,744	
	£45,442	
The value of exempt input tax is £1,414 (1,195 + [10,963 – 10,744]). As this is not more than £625 per month on average and is less than 50% of all input tax in the quarter, all input tax in the quarter is recoverable.		
Deductible input tax		46,856

Fourth quarter

Input tax attributable to taxable supplies	69,707	
Proportion of residual input tax deductible = 876,387/897,135 = 97.69%		
£9,357 × 98% =	9,170	
		78,877
		£198,368

For the annual adjustment required, see Example 1 in **49.13** below.

De Voil Indirect Tax Service. See V3.461A, V3.461B, V3.462.

Standard method over-ride

[49.9] The standard method is a simple way of calculating how residual input tax can be attributed to taxable supplies and deducted. In the vast majority of cases, it provides for a fair and reasonable apportionment. But a number of larger businesses have aggressively exploited the standard method to deduct large amounts of input tax on purchases used to make exempt supplies. Also, in a few other cases not involving abuse, businesses have been able to either deduct large amounts of input tax on purchases used in making exempt supplies or unable to deduct input tax on purchases used to make taxable supplies. The over-ride provisions below were introduced with effect from

18 April 2002 to address these difficulties. They apply to VAT incurred on or after that date. Except in cases of deliberate abuse, HMRC believe that the provisions will rarely apply. In any case, the provisions do not apply to businesses using a special method.

The over-ride can apply in the two situations in (*a*) and (*b*) below. Normally, it applies, if at all, under (*b*) at the end of a tax year and any over-ride adjustment is made and accounted for in the same period as the annual adjustment (or longer period adjustment). However, where a business does not carry out an annual adjustment (because it first becomes partly exempt in the last period of a tax year) any over-ride adjustment must be accounted for under (*a*) on the next VAT return.

(a) Where

- for a VAT period, a taxable person has used the standard method to attribute a proportion of the residual input tax to taxable supplies using the formula in **49.5** above,
- that VAT period does not form part of a longer period (see **49.13** below),
- the attribution differs substantially from one which represents the extent to which the goods or services are used by him, or are to be used by him, or a 'successor' of his, in making taxable supplies, and
- residual input tax incurred in the VAT period is more than £50,000 p.a. (£25,000 p.a. for group undertakings (as defined in *Companies Act 2006, s 1161*) which are not members of the same VAT group), adjusted *pro rata* for the length of the VAT period in question,

the taxable person must calculate the difference and account for it on the return for the VAT period next following the VAT period in question (unless HMRC allow otherwise). If his registration has been cancelled at or before the end of that VAT period, he must account for any adjustment on his final return.

[*SI 1995/2518, Regs 107A, 107E; SI 2002/1074; SI 2008/954, Art 45*].

(b) Where

- a taxable person has determined for a longer period (see **49.13** below) the input tax attributable to that period under the standard method,
- the attribution differs substantially from one which represents the extent to which the goods or services are used by him, or are to be used by him, or a 'successor' of his, in making taxable supplies, and
- residual input tax incurred in the longer period is more than £50,000 p.a. (£25,000 p.a. for group undertakings (as defined in *Companies Act 2006, s 1161(5)*) which are not members of the same VAT group), adjusted *pro rata* for a period which is not twelve months,

the taxable person must calculate the difference and, in addition to any amount required to be included as over-deducted or under-deducted in respect of the normal annual adjustment, account for the amount so

calculated on the return for the VAT period next following the longer period (unless HMRC allow otherwise). If his registration has been cancelled at or before the end of that VAT period, he must account for any adjustment on his final return.
[*SI 1995/2518, Regs 107B, 107E; SI 2002/1074*].

For the above purposes, a difference is substantial if it exceeds

- £50,000; or
- 50% of the residual input tax incurred in the VAT period or longer period, as the case may be, and £25,000.

A person is the '*successor*' of another if he is a person to whom that other person has transferred assets of his business by means of a transfer as a going concern which is treated as neither a supply of goods nor a supply of services (see **8.10** *et seq* **BUSINESS**). Successor in this context includes a reference to a successor's successor through any number of transfers.

[*SI 1995/2518, Regs 107C, 107D; SI 2002/1074*].

The over-ride only applies where the standard method produces a result that does not fairly reflect the extent to which purchases are used, or to be used, to make taxable supplies. The over-ride may apply when

- costs are incurred in one year that will not result in supplies until a later year;
- high value transactions are undertaken that do not consume inputs to an extent significantly greater than transactions of a lower value;
- there are different business units that make different supplies and use costs in different ways; or
- costs are incurred relating to an intended supply that never comes about.

Calculating the extent of use

The over-ride incorporates the concept of 'fair and reasonable' even though the regulations do not say so explicitly. All UK partial exemption is based on *VATA 1994, s 26*, which requires that regulations exist to provide a fair and reasonable deduction of input tax. Any calculation is acceptable if it produces a fair and reasonable attribution of input tax according to the use, or intended use, of purchases in making taxable supplies. The easiest way to prepare a fair and reasonable calculation is to consider why the standard method breaks down and to correct for it. Provided residual costs (those relating to both taxable and exempt supplies) are used in proportion to the values of taxable and exempt supplies made in the period in which they are incurred, the standard method will give a deduction that reflects use. Any costs that are not used in proportion to the values of supplies made can be dealt with separately from the standard method calculation.

The existing *de minimis* provisions (see **49.11** below) continue to apply. If, after an over-ride adjustment, the input tax attributed to exempt supplies is within the current *de minimis* limits, then all input tax for that period can be deducted.

Capital goods scheme

If a business incurs input tax on an item subject to the **CAPITAL GOODS SCHEME (10)** within a period covered by the over-ride, it must include that input tax when considering whether the over-ride applies and, if so, consider the use or intended use of the capital item in determining if there is a substantial difference.

Capital goods scheme adjustments must not be counted as input tax when determining whether the over-ride applies. However, where the over-ride does apply to a tax year or longer period that is also a subsequent CGS interval, the CGS adjustment will be affected if the standard method is used as the basis of adjustment for the scheme.

(VAT Notice 706, paras 5.3, 5.5, 5.7, 5.8, 5.11). See also VAT Information Sheet 4/02 for examples of how HMRC see the over-ride provisions applying in practice.

De Voil Indirect Tax Service. See V3.461A.

Special methods

[49.10] HMRC may approve or direct the use of another method other than the standard method in **49.4–49.8** above. But this is subject to the following.

- In calculating the proportion of any input tax on goods or services used (or to be used) by a taxable person in making both taxable and exempt supplies which is to be treated as attributable to taxable supplies, the value of any supply of a description within **49.5**(*a*)–(*d*) above (whether made within or outside the UK) must be excluded (i.e. those supplies which must be excluded from the standard method of calculation must also be excluded from any special method). This applies despite any provision in the method approved which purports to have contrary effect.
- The requirement for a declaration by the taxable person (see below).
- *SI 1995/2518, Reg 103* (attribution of input tax to foreign and specified supplies, see **49.12**(1) below).
- *SI 1995/2518, Reg 103A* (input tax attributable to exempt supplies of investment gold, see **26.4 GOLD AND PRECIOUS METALS**).
- *SI 1995/2518, Reg 103B* (incidental financial services, see **49.12**(2) below).

Application and approval

A taxable person may apply to HMRC to use a special method if it considers that the standard method does not provide a fair and reasonable result. HMRC require precise details of how the proposed method will work in practice and are prepared to discuss proposals before a formal application is submitted. HMRC will normally approve a special method provided it is fair and reasonable.

A method approved or directed under these provisions must be in writing and must identify the supplies in respect of which it attributes input tax by reference to the relevant categories in **49.2**(*a*)–(*d*) above.

A method may attribute input tax which would otherwise fall to be attributed under *SI 1995/2518, Reg 103* (attribution of input tax to foreign and specified supplies, see **49.12**(1) below) but where it attributes any such input tax, it must attribute it all.

Example

John has two activities – both generating equal levels of income (i.e. 50% taxable and 50% exempt). The main expenditure of the business on which input tax is incurred is linked to its property. The taxable activity is the organisation of fitness classes which takes up 80% of the premises; the exempt activity is the sale of insurance which takes up 20% of the premises.

Most of the input tax for this particular business relates to the property from which it trades – and 80% of this property is used for taxable activities. But in reality only 50% of the input tax will be recovered on property costs using the standard method of calculation based on income.

In this particular situation, the business would be best advised to submit a special method declaration to HMRC to apply for a special method of calculation based on floor area.

Declaration by the business

HMRC will not approve the use of a special method under these provisions unless the taxable person has made a declaration to the effect that, to the best of his knowledge and belief, the method fairly and reasonably represents the extent to which goods or services are used (or are to be used) by it in making taxable supplies. A declaration is required each time a new method is approved and must relate (i.e. it cannot be restricted to parts of the method or to parts of the business). The declaration must be in writing and be signed by the taxable person or by a person authorised to sign it on his behalf. It must include a statement that the person signing it has taken reasonable steps to ensure that he is in possession of all relevant information.

If HMRC think that a declaration made is incorrect in that it is not fair and reasonable and the person signing the declaration knew (or ought reasonably to have known) this at the time when the declaration was made, they may serve a notice on the taxable person to that effect. The notice must set out their reasons and state the effect of the notice. But HMRC cannot serve such a notice unless they are satisfied that the overall result of the application of the method is an over-deduction of input tax by the taxable person.

Where such a notice is served by HMRC, then in relation to

- VAT periods commencing on or after the effective date of the method, and
- longer periods (see **49.13** below) to the extent of that part of the longer period falls on or after the effective date of the method (except that no adjustment is required in relation to any part of any VAT period)

the taxable person must calculate the difference between

(a) the amount of deductible VAT using the special method, and

(b) the amount of deductible VAT calculated in accordance with the principle of use

and account for the difference on the return for that VAT period or on the return on which that longer period adjustment is required to be made (although HMRC may allow another return to be used for this purpose). This process must continue unless or until the method is terminated (see below).

In relation to any past VAT periods, HMRC may assess the amount of VAT due to the best of their judgement and notify it to the taxable person unless they allow him to account for the difference in such manner and within such time as they may require.

The service of a notice on a taxable person under these provisions is without prejudice to HMRC's powers to serve a notice on him under *SI 1995/2518, Reg 102A* (see below under *Special method over-ride*) and any notice served under these provisions takes priority in relation to the periods which it covers.

The following can be used as a template for the declaration

Partial Exemption — Special Method Declaration Name of Business: Address: VAT Registration Number: This Declaration is in accordance with paragraphs (9) and (10) of regulation 102 of the VAT Regulations 1995. As the taxable person (i.e. where the signatory is a sole proprietor)/the person authorised by the taxable person to sign this declaration on its behalf (delete as appropriate), I hereby declare that to the best of my knowledge and belief, the proposed special method [state precisely where the method is set out] fairly and reasonably represents the extent to which goods or services are used or to be used in making taxable supplies. I also confirm that I have taken reasonable steps to ensure that I am in possession of all relevant information before making this declaration. Name (print): Position (print): Date: Signed:

For further guidance generally on declarations, including HMRC's interpretation of terms in the legislation such as 'fair and reasonable', 'ought reasonably to have known' and 'reasonable steps', see the web version of HMRC Brief 23/07.

'Gaps' in special methods

A special method has a 'gap' if it fails to specify how to deal with an amount of residual input tax. This may arise because the method is poorly drawn up or the circumstances of the taxable person have changed after the method has been approved. Where a taxable person using a special method which has been approved or directed by HMRC incurs input tax

- the attribution of which to taxable supplies is not prescribed in whole or in part by that special method, and
- which does not fall to be attributed to taxable or other supplies under **49.12**(1) or (2) below or **26.4 GOLD AND PRECIOUS METALS**

the input tax is to be attributed to taxable supplies to the extent that the goods or services are used in making taxable supplies, expressed as a proportion of the whole use or intended use. Where the treatment of input tax is only partly covered by the method (i.e. part of the input tax falls into the gap), only that part of the input tax not covered by the method falls within these provisions.

These provisions do not mean that gaps in methods are acceptable. They simply set out how to cope with any gaps that arise. Once a gap has arisen, HMRC will expect that, in due course, the taxable person will make suitable proposals for a new or revised method that takes the gaps into account.

[*SI 1995/2518, Reg 102; SI 2004/3140, Reg 11; SI 2005/762; SI 2007/768, Reg 8*]. (VAT Notice 706, paras 6.9, 6.11; HMRC Brief 23/07).

Possible methods

A special method can be any method agreed by HMRC and devised to suit the needs of the particular business. It can contain any calculations or stages that are needed to ensure it is fair and reasonable. All special methods should reflect all business activities, provide for direct attribution of input tax to taxable supplies and exempt supplies, identify residual input tax, calculate the elements of residual input tax that relate to taxable supplies and to exempt supplies, and allow the business to determine the total input tax that it can recover.

Common methods include those based on the following.

- *Outputs-based apportionment*, i.e. apportioning between supplies in the same ratio as the value of taxable supplies bears to the value of all supplies.
- *Transaction-based apportionment*, i.e. apportioning between supplies in the same ratio as the number of taxable transactions made bears to all transactions made.
- *Staff time and headcount apportionment.* Staff time apportionment is where the apportionment is made in the same ratio as the staff time spent making taxable supplies bears to all staff time.
  A headcount method has a similar effect to the using of staff time except that it can be used by a business that does not keep time sheets.
- *Input tax and inputs-based apportionment.* These are calculations where the apportionment is made in the same ratio as the input tax directly attributable to taxable supplies bears to all directly attributable input tax.
- *Floor space apportionment.* This is apportionment in the same ratio as the floor space occupied by income-generating staff involved exclusively in making taxable supplies bears to the total floor space of income-generating staff. Floor-area based special methods are likely to be acceptable when
  (i) most of the business's VAT-bearing costs relate to its premises; and

(ii) most of the floor-area of those premises is used for either wholly taxable or wholly exempt activities, with only minor areas relating to both.

Methods based on floor area are, therefore, seldom fair and reasonable for retailers and unlikely to be accepted by HMRC. See *Optika Ltd* (VTD 18627) (TVC 46.137), *Vision Express (UK) Ltd* [2009] All ER (D) 146 (Dec) (TVC 46.131) and Business Brief 34/04. See also *London Clubs Management Ltd* [2011] EWCA Civ 1323 (TVC 46.136).

- Costs allocations.
- Management accounts.

A special method may also be based on separate calculations for different sectors of the business or, in the case of a group registration, different businesses or groups of businesses within the VAT group.

The percentage recovery rate produced by a special method should be calculated to two decimal places. The only exception to this is a special method based on a single outputs calculation and agreed with HMRC before 1 April 2005, in which case the recovery rate can be rounded up to the next whole number percentage (because the method closely resembles the standard method which allowed rounding up). But for all new special methods approved or directed on or after 1 April 2005 (and when any pre-existing special method is reviewed or updated), HMRC will only allow rounding to two or more decimal places. (Business Brief 7/05). In *Royal Bank of Scotland Group plc v HMRC (No 6), Case C–488/07*, [2009] STC 461 (TVC 22.445), the court ruled that member states are not obliged to apply the rule for rounding up to the next whole number where the proportion of input tax deductible is calculated in accordance with a special method.

Annual adjustments

The claimable proportion of residual input tax for a tax period as calculated is only provisional and subject to adjustment at the end of the 'longer period'. See **49.13** below.

Changes in circumstances

HMRC should be informed of any change in the business, or in group membership if in a VAT group, which has a substantial effect on the amount of input tax claimable. The special method will then be reviewed by HMRC and if no longer suitable, a direction to stop using the method will be issued. The taxable person must then either use the standard method or propose an alternative special method. But see also under the heading *Special method over-ride* below.

(VAT Notice 706, paras 6.1–6.8).

Agreements with trade bodies

HMRC have agreed special methods with the Association of British Factors and Discounters, the Finance Houses Association Ltd, the Association of British Insurers and the Association of Investment Trust Companies. See VAT Notice 700/57/04 for full details.

Higher education institutions

A framework has been prepared providing guidance on formulating special methods for higher education institutions, in particular, how to determine a fair 'value' for supplies of grant-supported education, when to add 'sectors' to a partial exemption method and how to identify and deal with 'distorting supplies'. The framework is not mandatory but is strongly recommended. It has been prepared in conjunction with the British Universities Finance Directors' Group and the university funding councils via the Higher Education Funding Council for England. See *Framework for HEI partial exemption special methods* (October 2007) for full details which is available on the HMRC website.

See Business Brief 11/06 as to how variable tuition fees, introduced from 1 August 2006, may effect the partial exemption methods of higher education institutions.

See HMRC Brief 34/08 for retrospective claims for input tax by institutions that operated a partial exemption method agreed under the Committee of Vice Chancellors and Principals (CVCP) guidelines, which were withdrawn from 1 September 1997.

Outside the scope supplies

In *C & E Commrs v Liverpool Institute for Performing Arts*, HL [2001] STC 891 (TVC 46.174), the court confirmed HMRC' view that two separate regimes exist for determining the amount of VAT that a business can deduct: *SI 1995/2518, Reg 101* (the standard method, see **49.4–49.8** above) which determines the deduction of VAT relating to supplies made within the UK; and *SI 1995/2518, Reg 103(1)* which determines the deduction of VAT relating to '*foreign supplies*' and '*specified exempt supplies*' made outside the UK (see **49.12**(1) below). Where a business uses a special method instead of the standard method, if that method has been approved by HMRC and already deals with foreign supplies and specified exempt supplies, no further action is needed following the House of Lords' decision. Where a special method does not deal with these supplies, then the business must deal with them under the provisions in **49.12**(1) below before applying the special method. (Business Brief 12/01).

Example

The facts are the same as in the example in **49.8** above except that HMRC allow X Ltd to use a special method and calculate the proportion of residual input tax attributable to taxable supplies by the formula

$$\text{Residual input tax} \times \frac{\text{Input tax attributable to taxable supplies}}{\text{Total input tax}}$$

	£	£
First quarter		
Input tax attributable to taxable supplies	36,409	
Proportion of residual input tax deductible =		
£11,751 × 36,409/53,007 =	8,071	
		44,480
Second quarter		
Input tax attributable to taxable supplies	20,245	
Proportion of residual input tax deductible =		
£5,212 × 20,245/25,768 =	4,095	
	£24,340	
The value of exempt input tax is £1,428 (311 + [5,212 – 4,095]). As this is not more than £625 per month on average and is less than 50% of all input tax in the quarter, all input tax in the quarter is recoverable.		
Deductible input tax		25,768
Third quarter		
Input tax attributable to taxable supplies	34,698	
Proportion of residual input tax deductible =		
£10,963 × 34,698/46,856 =	8,118	
		42,816
Fourth quarter		
Input tax attributable to taxable supplies	69,707	
Proportion of residual input tax deductible =		
£9,357 × 69,707/85,039 =	7,670	
		77,377
		£190,441

For the annual adjustment required at the end of the tax year, see Example 2 in **49.13** below.

Non-business activities

Where a business also carries on non-business activities, it must normally first determine the proportion of VAT incurred relating to those activities and disregard any such VAT before applying the rules in this chapter. Alternatively, it can, in limited circumstances from 1 January 2011, apply the *Lennartz* mechanism to certain supplies. It then treats the supplies as business supplies for input tax purposes but must account for output tax on subsequent non-business use. See **34.7 INPUT TAX** for the calculation of VAT of non-business activities and the *Lennartz* mechanism.

From 1 January 2011

Special methods may also be used to apportion input tax incurred on goods or services which are used/to be used partly for business purposes and partly for other purposes.

The combined method is available if a business needs to carry out only business/non-business (BNB) calculations (excluding apportionments involving private use) or if you need to carry out BNB (excluding apportionments involving private use) and partial exemption calculations. Therefore, it will mainly benefit charities and educational bodies. The combined method does not cater for private use apportionments, which continue to be calculated on a fair and reasonable basis.

The combined method must cover all the business's VAT apportionments apart from those involving private use and certain partial exemption calculations that are always determined on the basis of use.

HMRC will not approve separate BNB and partial exemption methods if the business is partly exempt. In these circumstances, where approval of a method for BNB calculations is sought, it must also cover partial exemption calculations (excluding the aforementioned apportionments). This is to save the cost of seeking approval of two separate methods and also helps to make sure there is a fair recovery of VAT overall as the calculations can be considered in their entirety.

HMRC will approve a single BNB method, provided that the business has not incurred any VAT on costs that relate to exempt supplies (exempt input tax) in its current tax year or immediately preceding tax year (or registration period), that is the business is 'fully taxable'. If the business becomes partly exempt a special method over-ride notice (see below) will automatically apply to the method that requires apportionments covered by the combined method to be recovered on a fair and reasonable basis from the date exempt input tax is first incurred.

The *de minimis* rules, simplified tests and annual test do not apply (see **49.11** below).

[*SI 1995/2518, Reg 102ZA; SI 2010/3022, Reg 6*]. (VAT Notice 706, paras 7.1–7.8).

Special method over-ride

Particularly when business circumstances change, a special method agreed with HMRC might no longer produce a fair and reasonable result and a new method must be found. As this can take time, and because a new method cannot normally be backdated, HMRC or the business can suffer as a result. Special rules allow either HMRC or the business concerned to introduce an over-ride with immediate effect and correct the unfair method to ensure that VAT deducted reflects the principle of use (i.e. that it fairly and reasonably reflects the extent that costs and purchases are used or will be used in making taxable supplies). This will continue until a replacement method is implemented. It is, however, only a temporary measure and HMRC expect its use to be rare. The detailed provisions are as follows.

Notwithstanding HMRC's powers to serve a notice under *SI 1985/2518, Reg 102* above, where that person is using a special method which does not fairly and reasonably represent the extent to which goods or services are used by him (or are to be used by him) in making taxable supplies

- HMRC may serve a notice on him to that effect, setting out their reasons in support of that notification and stating the effect of the notice, and
- subject to any such notice, the taxable person may serve a notice on HMRC to that effect, setting out his reasons in support of that notification.

Where such a notice is served by HMRC (or served by the taxable person and approved by HMRC), then in relation to

- VAT periods commencing on or after the date of the notice (or such later date as may be specified in the notice), and
- longer periods (see **49.13** below) to the extent of that part of the longer period falls on or after the date of the notice (or such later date as may be specified in the notice)

the taxable person must calculate the difference between

(a) the amount of deductible VAT using the current special scheme, and
(b) the amount of deductible VAT calculated in accordance with the principle of use

and account for the difference on the return for that VAT period or on the return on which that longer period adjustment is required to be made. HMRC may allow another return to be used for this purpose.

This procedure then continues until HMRC either approve or direct the termination of the special method currently being adopted.

[*SI 1995/2518, Regs 102A–102C; SI 2003/3220, Reg 21; SI 2007/768, Reg 9*].

HMRC will only serve or approve a notice where

- they have clear evidence that the current special method does not fairly and reasonably reflect the business's use of purchases in making taxable supplies; and
- they are satisfied that preparing a replacement method will not conclude quickly and the direction of a special method is not appropriate.

Serving and approving a notice

A notice must specify that it is a special method over-ride notice and state the date from which it takes effect. It must also give the reasons why the current special method does not produce a fair result.

When HMRC approve a notice served by a business, they will do so in writing as soon as possible, ideally within 30 days of receipt.

Complying with a notice

In most cases the reasons given by HMRC or the business in the notice will provide a basis for determining the notice correction. However, a business must still consider its whole method and determine whether there are any other aspects that would otherwise give an unfair result. The notice correction must therefore ensure that each time a VAT return is prepared, the amount of VAT deducted fairly and reasonably reflects the extent that costs and purchases are used (or will be used) in making taxable supplies (the principle of use). If a business does not make corrections to the amount of VAT deducted, and HMRC conclude that a notice correction should have been made, they will make the correction by way of VAT assessment.

(VAT Notice 706, paras 8.1–8.7).

De Voil Indirect Tax Service. See V3.462.

De minimis limit

Normal *de minimis* rules

[49.11] Subject to special provisions below, where 'relevant input tax'

- in any VAT period, or
- in any longer period, see **49.13** below (taken together, where appropriate, with the amount of any adjustment under **49.9**(*b*) above)

is not more than

(a) £625 per month 'on average', and
(b) one half of all input tax for the period concerned,

all such input tax in that period is treated as attributable to taxable supplies.

When applying these provisions to a longer period,

- any treatment of relevant input tax as attributable to taxable supplies in any VAT period is disregarded, and
- no account is to be taken of any amount or amounts which may be deductible or payable under the CAPITAL GOODS SCHEME **(10)**.

'*Relevant input tax*' is input tax attributed to exempt supplies or to supplies outside the UK which would be exempt if made in the UK (not being supplies falling within **49.2** (*c*) above) under

- the standard method (see **49.4–49.8** above),
- a special method (see **49.10** above),
- the rules for foreign and specified supplies (see **49.12**(1) below),
- the rules for incidental financial supplies (see **49.12**(2) below),
- the rules for attribution to exempt supplies of investment gold, see **26.4** GOLD AND PRECIOUS METALS), and
- where appropriate, the annual adjustment (see **49.13** below).

[*SI 1995/2518, Reg 106; SI 2002/1074, Reg 4; SI 2004/3140, Reg 12*].

'*On average*' means the average over the relevant VAT period or, as the case may be, longer period. For group registrations, the rules apply to the group as a whole.

(VAT Notice 706, paras 11.2, 11.3).

Simplified tests

For VAT periods commencing on or after 1 April 2010, simplified tests have been introduced to save some businesses the need to carry out a full partial exemption calculation to confirm their *de minimis* status. If, in a VAT period, a business passes Test one or Test two (set out below) it may treat itself as *de minimis* and provisionally recover input tax relating to exempt supplies. The business is still required to review its *de minimis* status at year-end as before and account for any under/over recovery of input tax as part of its annual adjustment (see **49.13** below).

Test one: total input tax incurred is no more than £625 per month on average and the value of exempt supplies is no more than 50% of the value of all supplies.

Test two: total input tax incurred less input tax directly attributable to taxable supplies is no more than £625 per month on average and the value of exempt supplies is no more than 50% of the value of all supplies.

'Total input tax' excludes blocked input tax (such as VAT on the cost of business entertainment) which is irrecoverable. 'The value of all supplies' includes taxable supplies made in the UK, supplies made outside the UK which confer the right of recovery (known as '*Reg 103* supplies') and exempt supplies. 'Input tax directly attributable to taxable supplies' is input tax on costs that are used or to be used exclusively in making taxable supplies, e.g. input tax on the cost of goods for resale.

Example 1

A business has a VAT period running from 1 April to 30 June 2010. During that period it incurs total input tax of £1,800 which it uses making taxable supplies of £30,000 and exempt supplies of £20,000. For the quarter ending June 2010, the business incurs total input tax of no more than £1,875 (£625 x 3 months) and the value of its exempt supplies is no more than 50% of its total supplies (20,000/50,000 × 100 = 40%). Therefore, the business is *de minimis* for this period as it passes Test one and can provisionally recover £1,800 input tax on its VAT return without the need to carry out a full partial exemption calculation. This will be subject to review at year-end.

Example 2

A business has a partial exemption year running from 1 May 2010 to 30 April 2011. During that period it incurs total input tax of £30,000, of which £25,000 is on goods for resale which are directly attributable to taxable supplies. It makes taxable supplies of £75,000 and exempt supplies of £60,000. Its total input tax less input tax directly attributable to taxable supplies is £5,000 (30,000 – 25,000) which is less than £7,500 (£625 x 12), and the value of its exempt supplies is no more than 50% of its total supplies (60,000/135,000 × 100 = 44%). Therefore, the business has finalised its *de minimis* status for the year and is entitled to recover £30,000. There is no need for any further partial exemption calculation for that year.

The new tests supplement the original test. A business is *de minimis* if it passes Test one, Test two or the original test, and if it passes any one test there is no need for it to consider the other two. Even if a business fails Test one and Test two, the information gathered is still required to carry out a full partial exemption calculation for the original test.

At the end of the partial exemption year, the *de minimis* test must be applied to the year as a whole. If Test one is passed for the year, all of input tax relating to exempt supplies can be recovered and there is no need to carry out any further partial exemption calculations. When applying Test two, the business first needs to review how much of the input tax incurred over the year is directly attributable to taxable supplies. Then, if Test two is passed for the year, all input tax relating to exempt supplies can be recovered and there is no need to carry out any further partial exemption calculations. If the business fails Test one and Test two for the year, then it needs to carry out a full partial exemption calculation for the year to determine whether it passes the original *de minimis* test and account for any under/over recovery of input tax as part of its annual adjustment in the normal way.

Annual test

For partial exemption years commencing on or after 1 April 2010, an annual test has been introduced to give most businesses the option of applying the *de minimis* test once a year, instead of four or five times a year. It allows a business that was *de minimis* in its previous partial exemption year to treat itself as *de minimis* in its current partial exemption year. This means it can provisionally recover input tax relating to exempt supplies in each VAT period, saving the need for partial exemption calculations. The business must still review its *de minimis* status at year-end and if it fails the *de minimis* test for the year it must repay the input tax relating to exempt supplies that it provisionally recovered in-year. However, there is no need to carry out in-year partial exemption calculations.

> *Example 3*
>
> A business was *de minimis* in its partial exemption year ending 31 March 2010. It has the option of applying the annual test and treating itself as *de minimis* during the year ending 31 March 2011. This means that it can provisionally recover input tax relating to exempt supplies in each VAT period during that year without the need to carry out a partial exemption calculation. The business is then required to review its *de minimis* status at year-end and, if it fails the *de minimis* test for the year, repay the input tax it has incurred during the year that relates to exempt supplies.

There are three conditions on using the annual test. The business must

- pass the *de minimis* test for its previous partial exemption year;
- consistently apply the annual test throughout any given partial exemption year; and
- have reasonable grounds for not expecting to incur more than £1million input tax in its current partial exemption year.

If any of these conditions are not met then the business is required to apply the *de minimis* test in each VAT period, which remains the default position.

[*SI 1995/2518 Regs 105A and 106ZA; SI 2010/559 Regs 2, 6–8*]. (VAT Information Sheet 4/10).

Special provisions where the standard method over-ride applies

Where, taken together with the amount of any over-ride adjustment under **49.9**(*a*) above, input tax attributed to exempt supplies or to supplies outside the UK which would be exempt if made in the UK (not being supplies falling within **49.2**(*c*) above) under

- the standard method (see **49.4–49.8** above),
- the rules for foreign and specified supplies (see **49.12**(1) below),
- the rules for incidental financial supplies (see **49.12**(2) below), and
- the rules for attribution to exempt supplies of investment gold, see **26.4 GOLD AND PRECIOUS METALS**),

is not more than

(a) £625 per month 'on average', and
(b) one half of all input tax for the period concerned,

all such input tax in that period is treated as attributable to taxable supplies.

Where this applies to a taxable person, he must calculate the difference between

- the total amount of input tax for that VAT period, and
- the amount of input tax deducted in that VAT period, taken together with the amount of any adjustment under **49.9**(*a*) above

and include this difference as an under-deduction in the return for the first VAT period next following that in which the substantial difference arose under the provisions in **49.9**(*a*) above (unless HMRC allow otherwise). If his registration has been cancelled by then, the adjustment must be made on his final VAT return.

Where, on the other hand, a taxable person has treated input tax as attributable to taxable supplies under the normal *de minimis* rules but is not entitled to do so because of the special provisions above, he must include the amount so treated as an over-deduction in the return for the first VAT period next following that in which the substantial difference arose under the provisions in **49.9**(*a*) (unless HMRC allow otherwise). If his registration has been cancelled by then, the adjustment must be made on his final VAT return.

[*SI 1995/2518, Reg 106A; SI 2002/1074, Reg 4; SI 2004/3140, Reg 13*].

De Voil Indirect Tax Service. See V3.465.

Attribution of input tax

Direct and immediate link

[49.12] In determining whether a particular cost or purchase has been used to make a specific taxable supply, it is necessary to establish a 'direct and immediate link' between the cost and the supply. Only where a direct and immediate link exists is there a right to deduct VAT incurred on that input. A direct and immediate link will exist if the cost incurred directly forms a component of the price of a supply or supplies being made. If a cost or purchase wholly forms a component of the price of an exempt supply or supplies, the input tax cannot be recovered.

General overheads of a business do not have a direct and immediate link with any specific supplies made by that business. But because they are set against income in calculating overall net profit or loss, they do have a direct and immediate link to the business as a whole. This gives them a direct and immediate link to all of the businesses supplies and means that the input tax incurred on them will always be residual.

In *C & E Commrs v Midland Bank plc, ECJ Case C–98/98*, [2000] STC 501 (TVC 22.400) the ECJ confirmed the need for a 'direct and immediate link'. The full amount of input tax cannot be deducted where the supply in question is used, not for the purpose of carrying out a deductible transaction, but in the context of activities which are no more than the consequence of making such a transaction, unless the taxpayer can show, by means of objective evidence, that the expenditure involved was part of the various cost components of the output transaction.

The national court should apply this 'direct and immediate link' test to the facts of each particular case. The point in question in the *Midland Bank* case was whether VAT on legal costs incurred defending a claim alleging negligent misrepresentation was wholly attributable to the zero-rated supplies made to the client or whether it should be apportioned between taxable and exempt supplies.

In *C & E Commrs v Southern Primary Housing Ltd*, CA 2003, [2004] STC 209 (TVC 46.26) a company purchased some land and paid VAT on the price (because the vendor had elected to waive exemption in respect of the land). It then sold the land to a housing association, under a contract whereby it agreed to build flats on the land for the association. The company considered that the VAT incurred on the purchase of the land was partly attributable to taxable supplies of building work. The Court of Appeal held that the input tax on the cost of buying the land was not a 'cost component' of the contract for the development of the land. There was nothing about the development contract as such which made the land purchase and sale essential. If the housing association had already owned the land or had bought it from some third party, the inputs of the development contract would have been just the costs of carrying it out. The fact that there were commercially linked land transactions did not mean that those transactions were directly linked to the costs of the development contract.

In *HMRC v BAA Ltd*, UT 22 June 2011 (TVC 32.30), a company arranged for the incorporation of a new company (AD) with the aim of making a takeover bid for another company (B), which operated several British airports. After the takeover, AD joined B's VAT group. The representative member of the group claimed a deduction for input tax that AD had incurred in relation to the takeover. The Upper Tribunal held that there was no direct and immediate link between the supplies made to AD, on which the relevant VAT was incurred, and any onward taxable supplies made by or attributed to AD. Accordingly the input tax was not deductible.

> *Example*
>
> A theatre buys the services of a production company to put on a show. There is a direct and immediate link between the costs of the production company and the ticket sales for the shows. If the production company also provides information for the published programme (for the shows) as part of its service, this will then create a direct and immediate link with the programme sales as well. If the ticket sales are exempt from VAT, and the programme sales are taxable (zero-rated), this would mean the input tax on the costs relevant to the production company would be residual rather than exempt.

Ultimate purpose of transactions

It is not possible to deduct input tax used for making an exempt supply even if the ultimate purpose of the transaction is the carrying out of a taxable transaction (*BLP Group plc v C & E Commrs, ECJ Case C–4/94*, [1995] STC 424 (TVC 22.399)). In that case, the company incurred input tax on professional fees in connection with the disposal of shares in a subsidiary company in order to pay debts. The court held that the input tax was not recoverable as it related to the exempt sales of shares, even though the ultimate purpose of this exempt supply was to enable the business to continue to make taxable supplies.

Attribution of input tax in particular cases is considered below.

(1) Foreign and specified supplies

Other than where it falls to be attributed under a method approved or directed by HMRC under *SI 1995/2518, Reg 102* (see **49.10** above) or from 1 April 2009, under the standard method in *SI 1995/2518, Reg 101* (see **49.4–49.8** above), where input tax is incurred by a business in any VAT period on goods or services which are used (or to be used) in whole or part in making

- '*foreign supplies*', i.e. supplies outside the UK which would be taxable supplies if made in the UK; or
- '*specified exempt supplies*', i.e. supplies of services which
  - (i) are supplied to a person who belongs outside the EU, or
  - (ii) are directly linked to the export of goods to a place outside the EU, or
  - (iii) consist of the provision of intermediary services in relation to any transaction within (i) or (ii) above

  and where the supply would have been exempt if made in the UK under *VATA 1994, Sch 9 Group 2* (insurance) or *VATA 1994, Sch 9 Group 5 items 1–8* (finance)

the input tax must be attributed to taxable supplies to the extent that the goods or services are so used (or to be used). The attribution must be expressed as a proportion of the whole use (or intended use). It is up to the business to decide how this can be achieved.

[*SI 1995/2518, Reg 103(1); SI 2007/768, Reg 10; SI 2009/820, Reg 6*].

(2) Services and related goods used partly to make incidental financial supplies

Where, and from 1 April 2009, other than where it falls to be attributed under the standard method in *SI 1995/2518, Reg 101* (see **49.4–49.8** above),

- a business incurs input tax in any VAT period on supplies to it of any of the services listed below and of any related goods,
- those services and related goods are used or to be used by the business in making both
  - (i) a '*relevant supply*' (i.e. a supply of financial services within *VATA 1994, Sch 9 Group 5 Items 1* or *6* (see **23.8** and **23.17 FINANCIAL SERVICES**) or a supply of the same description which is made in another EU country); *and*
  - (ii) any other supply, and
- the relevant supply is incidental to one or more of its business activities,

that input tax must be attributed to taxable supplies (including supplies falling within (1) above) to the extent that the services or related goods are so used (or to be used). The attribution must be expressed as a proportion of the whole use (or intended use). This applies despite any provision of any input tax attribution method that the business is required or allowed to use which purports to have the contrary effect.

The services in question are those supplied by

- accountants;
- advertising agencies;
- bodies which provide listing and registration services;
- financial advisers;
- lawyers;
- marketing consultants;
- persons who prepare and design documentation; and
- any person or body which provides similar services to those listed above.

[*SI 1995/2518, Reg 103B; SI 2004/3140, Reg 8; SI 2009/820, Reg 7*].

Incidental supplies are those which are subordinate to the main activities of the business. They tend to consume little by way of general overheads but may incur significant direct costs. Incidental financial supplies will usually be issues of new shares, bonds and similar securities and sales of existing shares in subsidiaries where these are made on an occasional basis and do not represent a business activity.

General business overheads (e.g. a company's annual audit) are not covered and, if the company is otherwise partly exempt, fall to be dealt with under the normal partial exemption method.

The effect of the above provisions is that input tax incurred on the services listed above must be divided into four categories:

- Input tax used to make financial services within the EU (non-recoverable).

- Input tax used to make financial supplies to individuals and businesses outside the EU (recoverable).
- Input tax used to make taxable supplies (recoverable).
- Input tax used to make other exempt transactions (non-recoverable).

HMRC will accept any calculation to determine extent of use if it provides a fair and reasonable attribution of input tax according to use (or intended use) of the relevant costs. For example, where professional services are incurred in connection with a share issue and shares are issued to subscribers in the UK and Japan, apportionment could be based on the number of subscribers, the number of shares issued or the value of the shares issued, provided the method used gives a fair and reasonable result.

(VAT Information Sheet 9/04).

(3) Share issues, etc.

In *Kretztechnik AG v Finanzamt Linz, ECJ Case C–465/03*, [2005] STC 1118 (TVC 22.91), an Austrian company issued shares and reclaimed input tax on the related costs. The tax authority rejected the claim (on the grounds that the issue of shares was an exempt supply) but the ECJ held that the issue of shares by a public limited company is not a supply within what is now *Directive 2006/112/EC, Art 2(1)(a)* and that input tax on services acquired for the purposes of such a share issue may be deducted to the extent that the company charges VAT on its output transactions.

HMRC accept that this decision applies to companies making first issues of shares in circumstances that are the same as those in *Kretztechnik*. Therefore, companies with wholly taxable outputs are entitled to recover all of the relevant input tax, while those with both exempt and taxable outputs can recover a proportion in accordance with their partial exemption method. Claims for input tax in respect of past share issues can be made subject to the three-year 'capping' rules.

After taking legal advice, HMRC have issued the following guidance on the VAT position of share transactions where the circumstances differ from those in *Kretztechnik*.

(a) *Transactions involving issues of other types of shares*. The *Kretztechnik* principles are applicable to share issues such as preference shares, special rights issues, bonus issues and issues of scrip dividends. All such share issues are to be regarded as non-supplies for VAT purposes.

(b) *Transactions involving issues by different types of companies*. Kretztechnik was a public limited company but, provided that the issuer's motivation is (like Kretztechnik's) the raising of capital, issues of shares by other types of companies (e.g. private companies) are non-supplies for VAT purposes.

(c) *Transactions involving the issue of financial instruments or securities other than shares*. The issue of other types of security (e.g. bonds, debentures or loan notes) should also be treated as non-supplies when the purpose of the issue is to raise capital for the issuer's business.

Similarly, the issue of shares or units in collective investment funds (e.g. open-ended investment companies and authorised unit trusts) are not supplies for VAT purposes.

(d) *Shares and other securities issued in other situations*. An issue of shares or other securities that takes place in the context of wider arrangements (e.g. as part of a company takeover or restructuring through merger or demerger) should still be regarded as a non-supply for VAT purposes.

Claims for input tax in respect of past issues of shares and other securities can be made subject to the three-year 'capping' rule.

Although any of the above transactions which are not supplies no longer have a corresponding VAT liability (e.g. exemption), intermediary and underwriting services in relation to such transactions remain exempt.

(Business Briefs 12/05, 21/05, 22/05). See Business Briefs 21/05 and 22/05 for input tax on issues of shares made outside the EU, and input tax incurred by intermediaries in share issues, following the *Kretztechnik* case.

Before the decision in *Kretztechnik*, HMRC's view, based on the decision in *Trinity Mirror plc v C & E Commrs*, CA [2001] STC 192 (TVC 27.51), was that where a company issued its own shares, input tax incurred exclusively on related costs was deductible according to the liability of the issue. If the issue was wholly exempt, the input tax was not recoverable (subject to the *de minimis* limit). If all the shares were sold to persons outside the EU, the input tax was claimable in full. But where some only of the shares were sold to persons outside the EU, a proportion of the input tax on the share costs was claimable. This could normally be calculated most accurately by using the ratio of the number of shares sold outside the EU to the total number of shares sold. But if this method did not provide a fair and reasonable result, an alternative calculation could be used.

(4) Costs of Stock Exchange listing

A Stock Exchange listing that takes place *without* an issue of shares is not a supply for VAT purposes. Related costs are treated as general overheads of the business. VAT on overhead costs is residual input tax and may be deducted in part according to the partial exemption method in place.

Where a Stock Exchange listing takes place in conjunction with a share issue, costs incurred on the listing are normally treated as wholly related to a share issue and dealt with as under (2) above. This is because, at the time of the listing or afterwards, there is an intention to issue shares to raise capital. This is established HMRC policy and was supported by the tribunal decision in *Actinic plc* (VTD 18044) (TVC 27.52). However, in *Halladale Group plc* (VTD 18218) (TVC 46.44) the tribunal held that an AIM listing was, in part, for general business purposes and was not an essential element of the issue of shares, so that the expenditure had a dual purpose.

Following the decision in *Halladale*, HMRC accept that, on some occasions, costs in connection with Stock Exchange listings can be treated as residual if the number of shares issued is small and this is not done in order to raise capital (although some capital may be raised as a result). For example,

- a business applying for existing shares to be issued on the London Stock Exchange is required to issue additional shares merely to comply with Stock Exchange rules; or
- a close company applying for listing on the Alternative Investment Market issues further shares in order to create a market price for its existing shares.

HMRC will consider each case on its facts but state that it is likely the costs will be considered general overheads if, for example,

- the number of shares issued is small compared to the number listed; and
- the capital raised by the issue is minor compared with the costs incurred.

Supplies of services related to the issue *and* listing must not be artificially aggregated or split to distort VAT deduction. Where a contract for professional services comprises a number of different supplies, each supply must be considered in its own right when determining whether the VAT relates to the share issue or is residual. This was confirmed in *Actinic plc* above.

(Business Brief 30/03).

(5) Self-supplies

Where under or by virtue of any provision of *VATA 1994* a person makes a supply to himself, the input tax on that supply must not be allowable as attributable to that supply. [*SI 1995/2518, Reg 104*].

(6) Acquiring a business as a going concern

Following the decision in *C & E Commrs v UBAF Bank Ltd*, CA [1996] STC 372 (TVC 46.7), HMRC have confirmed that where a business acquires assets by way of the transfer of a going concern, and the assets are used exclusively to make taxable supplies, the VAT incurred on the cost of acquiring those assets should be attributed to those taxable supplies and can be recovered in full. Conversely, if the assets of the acquired business are to be used exclusively to make exempt supplies, none of the input tax on the cost of acquiring those assets can be recovered. However, if the assets are to be used in making both taxable and exempt supplies, any input tax incurred is non-attributable and must be apportioned in accordance with the agreed VAT partial exemption method. In *UBAF Bank Ltd* the court held that input tax on professional fees incurred in connection with the acquisition of shares was on supplies wholly used, or to be used, by the bank in making taxable supplies of equipment leasing and recoverable in full. Before that decision, HMRC had treated such costs as general business overhead costs. (VAT Notice 700/9/08, para 2.6.1).

See, however, the decision in *RAP Group v C & E Commrs*, Ch D [2000] STC 980 (TVC 46.42) which also related to professional services incurred in connection with the acquisition of the issued share capital of another company. The court held that the important question was whether the services were used for an exempt transaction (the issue of shares in RAP) in which case the input tax was not allowable or whether they were used for that and some other taxable supply (in which case apportionment would apply). The tribunal had applied the 'direct and immediate link' test in *Midland Bank plc* above and, on the facts, held that no such link existed between the professional services supplied and the taxable supplies to be made by acquired company. As a result, the VAT on the professional services must relate to the exempt issue of shares and was not recoverable. As this was a question of fact, the court would not disturb the decision (although it did allow the appeal in part on the grounds that the legal services provided related to more general matters than the issue of the shares so that the tribunal should have allowed apportionment).

De Voil Indirect Tax Service. See V3.464.

Annual adjustments

[49.13] The deductions of input tax for each VAT period are provisional whether the standard or a special method is adopted. This is because the amount deductible in some such periods may be unfairly affected, e.g. by seasonal variations. It is normally necessary, therefore, to recalculate the amount of input tax reclaimable over a 'longer period'. If a special method is used, the letter of approval will state whether an annual adjustment is required.

Where a business incurs exempt input tax during any 'tax year', its '*longer period*' corresponds with that tax year unless it did not incur exempt input tax during its immediately preceding tax year or 'registration period' in which case its longer period begins on the first day of the first VAT period in which it incurs exempt input tax and ends on the last day of that tax year. Where, however, the only exempt input tax of the business is incurred in the last VAT period of its tax year, no longer accounting period is applied in respect of that tax year.

There are also rules to deal with special circumstances where the longer period is not a period of twelve months.

- *Newly-registered businesses*. Where a business incurs exempt input tax during its registration period, its longer period begins on the first day on which it incurs exempt input tax and ends on the day before the commencement of its first tax year.
- *Belated registration*. Where a business is registered retrospectively, its first VAT return may cover a period longer than a tax year. In such a case, the period must be broken down and a longer period adjustment made in respect of the registration period and each subsequent tax year.
- *Deregistration*. In the case of a business ceasing to be taxable during a longer period, that period ends on the day it ceases to be taxable.

'*Tax year*' is the twelve months ending on 31 March, 30 April or 31 May according to the VAT periods allocated. HMRC may approve or direct that a tax year be for a period other than twelve months.

The '*registration period*' of a taxable person means the period commencing on his effective date of registration and ending on the day before the commencement of his first tax year.

[*SI 1995/2518, Reg 99; SI 2000/794*]. (VAT Notice 706, paras 12.3, 12.7–12.9).

Calculation of annual adjustments

Unless HMRC dispense with the requirements, a taxable person must calculate the reclaimable proportion of any residual input tax not directly attributed on the same basis as in each of the VAT periods but using the figures for the longer period.

Any difference between the amount of reclaimable input tax recalculated at the end of the longer period and the total amount provisionally deducted during the VAT periods is an over or under declaration of VAT and must be entered on the VAT return for the first VAT period after the end of the longer period (unless HMRC allow otherwise) or, for tax years ending on or after 30 April 2009, there is the option of accounting for the annual adjustment in the last VAT return of the longer period. Where registration has been cancelled, the annual adjustment should be entered on the VAT return for the final period ending on the effective date of registration.

If the recalculation shows that the exempt input tax is below the *de minimis* limits in **49.11** above, any input tax not already reclaimed is an under deduction of VAT and should be entered on the next VAT return.

Annual adjustments which have been correctly carried out are not errors and do not have to be disclosed under the error correction notification (formerly voluntary disclosure) procedure (see **56.11 RECORDS**). Where, however, an error is made in the partial exemption calculation for a VAT period (e.g. input tax is incorrectly treated as exempt when the goods or services were used to make taxable supplies) this should not be 'corrected' by the annual adjustment but should be notified separately under the error correction notification (formerly voluntary disclosure) procedure.

[*SI 1995/2518, Reg 107; SI 1999/599; SI 2002/1074; SI 2009/820, Reg 8*]. (VAT Notice 706, paras 12.4, 12.6; VAT Information Sheet 4/09, para 3).

Example 1

At the end of the tax year, X Ltd in the example in **49.8** above must carry out the following annual adjustment.

	£
Input tax attributable to taxable supplies	161,059
Proportion of residual input tax deductible =	
2,028,999/2,155,935 = 94.11%	
£37,283 × 95% =	35,419
Deductible input tax for year	196,478
Deducted over the four quarters	198,368
Under declaration to be paid to HMRC	£1,890

Example 2

At the end of the tax year, X Ltd in the example in **49.10** above must carry out the following annual adjustment.

	£
Input tax attributable to taxable supplies	161,059
Proportion of residual input tax deductible =	
£37,283 × 161,059/210,670 =	28,503
Deductible input tax for year	189,562
Deducted over the four quarters	190,441
Under declaration to be paid to HMRC	£879

De Voil Indirect Tax Service. See V3.466.

Adjustments for change in use of goods and services

[49.14] Attribution of input tax should be initially carried out on the basis of the use made, or intended to be made, of the goods or services (see **49.3** above). However, there may be occasions when the intended or actual use of those goods or services changes. Where a business either

- changes its intention before using the goods or services, or
- actually uses the goods or services for a different purpose,

the following 'clawback' or 'payback' provisions apply.

(a) 'Clawback' provisions

Clawback provisions apply where a taxable person has deducted an amount of input tax which has been attributed to taxable supplies because he intended to use the goods or services in making either

(i) 'taxable supplies', or
(ii) both taxable and 'exempt supplies',

and during a period of six years commencing on the first day of the VAT period in which the attribution was determined and before that intention is fulfilled, he uses or forms an intention to use the goods or services in making exempt supplies (or where (i) above applies, in making both taxable and exempt supplies).

Subject to below, under such circumstances, unless HMRC allow otherwise, the taxable person must account for an amount equal to the input tax which has ceased to be attributable to taxable supplies in accordance with the method he was required to use when the input tax was first attributed. This should be done on the return for the VAT period in which the use occurs or the revised intention is formed. (VAT Notice 706, paras 13.7, 13.8).

In *Belgium v Ghent Coal Terminal NV, ECJ Case C–37/95*, [1998] STC 260 (TVC 22.406), a company purchased some land, had work carried out on it and reclaimed the input tax on these supplies. Subsequently the local council required the company to exchange the land before it had been used for any taxable purpose. The ECJ held that the right to deduction was exercisable immediately the inputs were incurred and, once it had arisen, remained acquired even if, by reason of circumstances beyond its control, the taxable person never used the goods or services in question for the purposes of taxable transactions. This would not apply in cases of fraud or abuse and such a supply might give rise to a subsequent adjustment under the **CAPITAL GOODS SCHEME (10)**.

(b) Clawback provisions: interim use differing from original intention

In *C & E Commrs v Briararch Ltd; C & E Commrs v Curtis Henderson Ltd*, QB [1992] STC 732 (TVC 46.212) the court held that apportionment of input tax applied under this provision where a property is, or is intended to be, the subject of sequential supplies at different VAT liabilities. In the cases involved, the companies had reclaimed input tax in full on the basis that the properties concerned would be the subject of taxable supplies but, when the building work was completed, they were obliged to obtain temporary rental income on short leases which was an exempt supply. In circumstances such as these, where goods or services are put to an interim use different to that originally intended, provided the original intention is still retained, the input tax must be apportioned on a fair and reasonable basis. In *Briararch Ltd* the company let the property on a four-year exempt lease whilst still intending to make a taxable supply of a 25-year lease. The court held that 25/29 of the input tax related to the intended taxable supply and that the clawback provisions applied to 4/29 of the original claim.

See also *Cooper and Chapman (Builders) Ltd v C & E Commrs*, QB 1992 [1993] STC 1 (TVC 46.205) where a building was converted into flats with the intention that they would all be let as holiday accommodation (standard-rated) but, after some flats had been so let, the company granted a one-year lease of the whole building (an exempt supply).

HMRC have set out their policy where house builders decide to temporarily let their dwellings before selling them, and so become partly exempt. For many house builders the amount of exempt input tax related to their temporary lets is small (*de minimis*) and as a result they can continue to recover all of their input tax; but they must check to avoid VAT mistakes. Exceptionally, HMRC will allow a builder that does not currently operate a partial exemption method, to adopt instead a 'simple check for de minimis'. This simple check is based on the expected time period he will let his building as a proportion of the economic life of that building, which for VAT purposes is ten years. His exempt input tax is determined by applying the proportion to his total input tax. Provided his exempt input tax does not exceed £625 per month on average (up to £7,500 per year), and is not more than half of his total input tax, then his exempt input tax is *de minimis* and he can recover it in full. If a house builder who was previously fully taxable continues to incur exempt input tax in future then he will need to apply a partial exemption method to determine if he remains *de minimis*. He can either apply the standard method or he can seek HMRC approval to apply a special method.

A house builder makes a clawback adjustment as soon as his actual or intended use of a property differs from his original plans against which input tax was recovered. A clawback adjustment is a one-off event and a house builder would only make a second adjustment if the building was never let. There is no need to amend the adjustment if the actual period of letting proved to be longer or shorter than anticipated. A clawback adjustment must be based on the house builders' realistic expectation, judged at the time his original plans were set aside. HMRC may ask for evidence to show that the adjustment calculation is reasonable.

The house builder calculates his clawback adjustment by comparing the amount of input tax deducted with the amount of input tax he would have deducted had he held his changed intention all along. His clawback adjustment is simply the difference between the two input tax amounts. The builder calculates the amount of input tax he would have deducted by applying his partial exemption method at the time the costs were incurred. If a house builder was not already operating a partial exemption method then he must apply the standard method unless he obtains HMRC approval to apply a special method instead. A house builder that does not currently operate a partial exemption method, can exceptionally if he prefers, base his clawback adjustment on an alternative calculation (without first adopting a partial exemption method and without prior approval from HMRC) so long as that calculation is fair. HMRC can allow this under their care and management powers. HMRC will accept any clawback calculation provided it fairly reflects the use of costs in making taxable supplies. A calculation based on the values of supplies is normally fair and straightforward provided it is based on reasonable estimates and valuations. The formula: input tax incurred x (estimated eventual sale value/estimated eventual sale value plus estimated short let premiums and rents) would give the amount of recoverable input tax.

Example

A house builder expects to sell two houses for £500,000 each. The input tax recovered during the tax year was £50,000. After the end of the tax year the decision is taken to rent them for a period of three years generating estimated rental income of £200,000. The house builder makes no other supplies.

£50,000 input tax incurred × £1,000,000/£1,200,000 = £41,667 recoverable input tax

£50,000 input tax previously recovered – £41,666 = £8,334 to be repaid to HMRC

No adjustment should be made for potential bad debts during the letting period. If it is not possible to fairly estimate the values then a different calculation may be needed. Apportionments based on the expected time period of the rental or short-term lease are not recommended except as a quick *de minimis* check. The alternative calculations cannot be used if a partial exemption method was already in place. But, if an existing partial exemption method becomes unfair because of the short-term lets, then HMRC may exceptionally allow an alternative method to be agreed and backdated.

A house builder that expects to continue to incur exempt input tax in his current or future VAT periods would need to adopt a partial exemption method. If he is not already partly exempt, then he must either apply the standard method or seek HMRC approval to apply a special method.

(VAT Information Sheet 7/08).

(c) 'Payback' provisions

Payback provisions apply where a taxable person has incurred input tax which has not been attributed to taxable supplies because he intended to use the goods or services in making either

(i) 'exempt supplies', or
(ii) both 'taxable' and exempt supplies

and during a period of six years commencing on the first day of the VAT period in which the attribution was determined and before that intention is fulfilled, he uses or forms an intention to use the goods or services in making taxable supplies (or where (i) above applies, in making both taxable and exempt supplies).

Subject to below, under such circumstances, HMRC must, on application by the taxable person in such form as HMRC require, repay to him an amount equal to the input tax which has become attributable to taxable supplies in accordance with the method he was required to use when the input tax was first attributed.

In practice, the taxable person should write to HMRC and, when they have confirmed the amount to be repaid, enter the amount due in the VAT account as an underclaim and include it in the next VAT return. (VAT Notice 706, paras 13.9, 13.10).

In *Royal & Sun Alliance Insurance Group plc v C & E Commrs*, HL [2003] STC 832 (TVC 46.216) a company decided that certain properties were no longer needed for its exempt insurance business. It decided to sublet the properties and opted to tax them. It initially treated the input tax incurred on rents and service charges during the periods the properties were vacant prior to the exercise of the option as attributable to exempt supplies. Subsequently, it claimed a repayment of this input tax. The HL (by a 3 to 2 majority, reversing the decisions of the Ch D and CA and restoring the decision of the tribunal) held that to come within the payback provisions, the company must first have had an intention to use the inputs in supplying exempt sub-leases and then used them, or formed the intention to use them, in supplying taxable sub-leases. As the company had not opted to tax at the relevant time, it did not satisfy the second condition and the payback provisions could not apply.

In *Community Housing Association Ltd*, Ch D [2009] STC 1324 (TVC 46.219) CHA was a housing association providing mainly exempt rental housing. It incurred input tax related to the construction of new dwellings for use in its business. It subsequently changed its operation by inserting a new subsidiary between itself and its suppliers. After having raised invoices to the subsidiary for the value of work undertaken on uncompleted projects prior to this change, CHA lodged a 'payback' claim. CHA argued that input tax on costs for part completed projects incurred prior to the change were not used as originally intended and were now attributable to a taxable supply from CHA to the new subsidiary. The High Court allowed the payback claim, finding as fact that CHA made supplies to its subsidiary and that the supplies transferred useful material and rights arising from the old supplies received by CHA.

Supplies outside the UK

Where (*a*) or (*b*) above applies, subject to the provisions relating to foreign supplies in **49.12**(1) above and incidental financial supplies in **49.12**(2) above, if

- the use to which the goods or services are put (or to which they are intended to be put) includes the making of supplies outside the UK, and
- at the time when the taxable person was first required to attribute the input tax he was not required to use a method approved or directed under **49.10** above (or he was required to use such a method but that method did not expressly provide for the attribution of input tax attributable to supplies outside the UK)

then the relevant amount under (*a*) or (*b*) above is to be calculated by reference to the extent to which the goods or services concerned are used (or intended to be used) in making taxable supplies, expressed as a proportion of the whole use (or intended use).

Exempt supplies

'*Exempt supplies*' includes supplies outside the UK which would be exempt supplies if made in the UK (other than those supplies falling within **49.2**(*c*) above). It also includes supplies of investment gold but only to the extent that there is, or would be, no credit for input tax on goods and services under *SI 1995/2518, Reg 103A* (see **26.4 GOLD AND PRECIOUS METALS**).

Taxable supplies

'*Taxable supplies*' includes supplies within **49.2**(*b*) or (*c*) above. It also includes supplies of investment gold but only to the extent that there is, or would be, credit for input tax on goods and services under *SI 1995/2518, Reg 103A* (see **26.4 GOLD AND PRECIOUS METALS**).

[*SI 1995/2518, Regs 108–110; SI 1999/3114; SI 2004/3140, Reg 14*].

De Voil Indirect Tax Service. See V3.467.

Treatment in special circumstances

[49.15] In special circumstances, treatment is as follows:

(1) Abortive supplies

There may be occasions where a business incurs VAT in connection with intended supplies that are never actually made.

- If the goods or services are used to make an alternative supply of a different liability, then the adjustment provisions in **49.14** above apply.
- If the initial intention is frustrated and the goods or services are not used to make any supply (e.g. architect's fees on an aborted building project), following the decision of the ECJ in *Belgium v Ghent Coal Terminal NV*, *ECJ Case C–37/95*, [1998] STC 260 (TVC 22.406), no adjustment to the initial claim of input tax is required. Previously, HMRC' policy was to treat such abortive supplies as part of the general overhead costs of the business so that the input tax formed part of the residual input tax to be apportioned under the partial exemption method used. (VAT Notice 706, para 13.14).

See also **42.4 LAND AND BUILDINGS: ZERO AND REDUCED RATE SUPPLIES AND DIY HOUSEBUILDERS** for abortive supplies by speculative developers.

(2) Holding companies

See **27.9 GROUPS OF COMPANIES.**

(3) Professional fees on share acquisitions

In *Southampton Leisure Holdings plc* (VTD 17716) (TVC 46.43) the tribunal held that whilst certain professional services connected with the acquisition of share capital in a company (e.g. public relations) had been exclusively used in making an exempt transaction (the share issue), other professional services had been used partly for the exempt transaction and partly for the general purposes of the business, so that the relevant input tax fell to be treated as residual input tax.

Following the tribunal's decision, HMRC now accept that any taxed supplies of professional services, which include, in the circumstances of a merger and acquisition or management buy-out,

- acting as financial adviser,
- the drafting of service contracts for the directors,
- the due diligence review of the target company's affairs,
- the investigation of title and/or the valuation of that company's property; and
- coordinating the transaction

has to some extent a direct and immediate link with the whole of the taxpayer's business. The VAT incurred is residual input tax and is attributable to taxable supplies by reference to the partial exemption method used. However, where a taxed supply of professional services is partly used in making an issue of shares to a person belonging outside the EU, then the deductible proportion of tax is to be determined on a 'use' basis under *SI 1995/2518, Reg 103B* (see **49.12**(2) above).

HMRC take the view that the decision has no application where shares are issued for subscription (e.g. an initial public offer or rights issue). In these instances, the taxed professional services relating to the offer are used exclusively for the purposes of the exempt supply of an issue of shares. But

HMRC do accept that any services providing general advice on the means of raising capital (provided it is just that) is part of the business' overheads and that the VAT incurred on any such services should be treated as residual input tax.

HMRC will, subject to the normal capping rules, accept claims for overpaid tax.

(Business Brief 23/02).

(4) Share issues

See **49.12**(3) above.

(5) Transfers of going concerns (TOGCs)

See **49.12**(4) above for the position of the transferee and **8.15 BUSINESS** for the position of the transferor.

See also **31.7 GROUPS OF COMPANIES** for acquisitions of TOGCs by partly-exempt groups.

(6) Costs of settling insurance claims

See **37.10 INSURANCE**.

(7) Petrol scale charges

See **45.16 MOTOR CARS**.

(8) VAT recovery on hire purchase transactions

In most hire purchase transactions, the goods are resold at cost without any margin to cover overhead costs. As there is no margin on the hire purchase goods, the cost of the overheads will normally be built into the price of the exempt supply of credit. In such a situation, HMRC's view is that the overheads are purely cost components of the exempt supply. Otherwise the business would continually enjoy net VAT refunds despite making no zero-rated or reduced rate supplies and charging a total consideration under the hire purchase agreement that fully recovers its costs and an element of profit.

Where overheads are used to make both hire purchase transactions and other supplies on which VAT is charged (e.g. taxable purchase option fees or sales of repossessed goods), then some VAT on overhead costs is recoverable. In such cases, the partial exemption method should reflect the extent to which the overhead costs are a cost component of the prices of the supplies in question.

HMRC expect their above policy to be applied by all businesses that make supplies under hire purchase agreements to consumers. It does not apply to those who only arrange such supplies and receive a commission.

(HMRC Brief 31/07).

(9) Reverse charge on services from abroad

VAT must be accounted for on certain services received from abroad. See **38.4 INTERNATIONAL SERVICES**. The VAT can also be treated as input tax. However, for partial exemption purposes these services are not regarded as supplies and input tax on these imported services can only be claimed in full if the services are used wholly for the making of taxable supplies. If used partly for taxable supplies, the input tax must be included in the non-attributable input tax and apportioned according to the partial exemption method used.

The value of imported services must be excluded from the calculation to apportion residual input tax where either the standard method under **49.4–49.8** above is used or a special method under **49.10** above is used which is based on output values.

Exempt input tax on imported services should be included with other exempt input tax when applying the *de minimis* rules in **49.11** above.

(VAT Notice 706, para 12.8).

(10) Including non-business use within clawback/payback

Before 1 January 2011 only VAT on business-related expenditure (input tax) potentially qualified for adjustment under the clawback/payback rules (see **49.14** above). With effect from 1 January 2011 the clawback/payback rules have been extended to allow for adjustments to non-business (including private) use, unless the option to hold an asset, or part of an asset, wholly outside the business is adopted. VAT which is initially allocated entirely for non-business purposes is not eligible for adjustment.

> *Example*
>
> A charity incurs expenditure of £10,000 and related VAT of £2,000 on goods that it intends using 50% for non-business purposes and 50% for exempt supplies. Its initial entitlement to VAT recovery is therefore nil. 18 months later, before the expenditure has been used for any activities (business or non-business), it changes its intention and decides to put the expenditure entirely to taxable use. It is therefore entitled to a payback of £2,000 which it can claim in the normal way.
>
> Under the old rules (applicable to VAT incurred before 1 January 2011), the VAT initially allocated to non-business activities would not have been subject to adjustment and so the business would only have been entitled to a payback adjustment of £1,000.

(VAT Notice 706, paras 13.16–13.17).

(11) Divisional registration

A corporate body may apply to be registered in the names of its separate divisions. See **59.37 REGISTRATION**. HMRC will not allow divisional registration if the exempt input tax of the body as a whole exceeds the *de minimis* limit in **49.11** above. If, at any time, a body corporate registered in divisions exceeds the *de minimis* limit, it should advise its local VAT Business Centre immediately and a decision will be made as to whether the divisional registration should be allowed to continue. If the divisional registration is cancelled for the corporate body as a whole, then, if it is still liable to be registered, the single VAT registration must cover all the taxable business activities of the body corporate as a whole. (VAT Notice 706, para 15.3).

(12) Group registration

The normal rules for group registration apply (see **27 GROUPS OF COMPANIES**) and input tax must be attributed by 'looking through' intra-group transactions to the supplies made outside the group.

A VAT group can only have one partial exemption method as there is only one taxable person and the *de minimis* limit must also be applied to the group as a whole. However, in deciding whether a VAT group can treat property or financial transactions as incidental for the purposes of the standard method calculation (see **49.5** above) the business activities carried on by the members of a VAT group are considered separately.

(VAT Notice 706, para 15.1).

(13) Local authorities

See **43.8 LOCAL AUTHORITIES AND PUBLIC BODIES**.

(14) Land and property

See **42.4 LAND AND BUILDINGS: ZERO AND REDUCED RATE SUPPLIES AND DIY HOUSEBUILDERS** for input tax and speculative builders.

(15) Higher education institutions

See **49.10** above.

See Business Brief 11/06 for the effect on partial exemption methods of higher education institutions following the introduction of variable tuition fees from 1 August 2006.

(16) Bookmakers – specialist TV services and equipment

Betting shops frequently incur VAT on Satellite Information System (SIS) services and equipment on which they can screen live coverage of horse and dog racing, real time odds, results information and commentary and opinion from pundits.

Historically, HMRC's view was that this information related directly to the over the counter exempt betting activity of bookmakers and the related input tax was not recoverable. But following the tribunal decisions in *Town and County Factors* (VTD 19616) (TVC 46.90) and *Cheshire Racing* (VTD 20283) (TVC 46.91) HMRC now accept that input tax on SIS services is residual as there is a direct and immediate link between the content of the SIS broadcast and gaming machine income. This applies even when the bookmaker adds no additional information to SIS.

(HRMC Brief 1/08).

The Tribunal in *Town and Country Factors* also found that VAT relating to Sky Sports was residual as the costs related to all of the activities of the betting shop even though the broadcasts did not carry adverts for the bookmaker's taxable services.

(Business Brief 17/06).

(17) VAT on insolvency practitioners' fees

See **35.11 INSOLVENCY.**

(18) Theatre production costs

In *Garsington Opera Ltd* (TC00045) (TVC 46.88), G incurred input tax on the costs of putting together its own 'in-house' operatic performances. HMRC maintained that the input tax was irrecoverable because while putting on operas was the core of G's business, the production costs were directly and immediately linked only to exempt admissions. G argued that the input tax was partly deductible (residual) because the production costs had a direct and immediate link not only to exempt admissions, but also to taxable supplies such as corporate sponsorship, touring (supplies of the production to an outside concert hall), programmes, CDs, intellectual property rights and the occasional supplies of production props and equipment. The tribunal found for G having identified a direct and immediate link between the production costs and both the exempt admission and the taxable supplies in issue. HMRC have not appealed this decision and have instead revised their policy on when theatres supplying exempt admission can treat input tax incurred on production costs as residual. Production costs only become partly deductible (residual) if there is a firm intention to make taxable as well as exempt supplies when the costs are incurred. Examples of when production costs relate to taxable supplies include if a theatre has contracted to or intends to

- secure sponsorship – the sponsorship must relate to an event or a clearly defined run of events over a clearly defined time. Putting on the shows must be a condition of the sponsorship so that production costs become cost components of the sponsorship income. The intention may be evidenced by way of clear financial commitment;
- tour the production – once again the intention may be evidenced by way of clear financial commitment;
- record the show for later sale on CD or other media.

Production costs remain residual if an intention to make taxable supplies is frustrated (e.g. a tour is cancelled). The intention to make taxable supplies must be a genuine intention. Furthermore, residual status is not secured if the link to taxable supplies is indirect.

In the case of *Mayflower Theatre Trust Ltd v HMRC*, CA [2007] STC 880 (TVC 46.87), a direct and immediate link to programme sales was found in relation to 'bought in' shows. This was because copyright information necessary for the programmes was obtained as part of the single supply of production services received from the touring company thus creating the direct and immediate link. If an individual actor or designer provides copyright information to a theatre/opera putting together a show 'in house' as part of a single supply of their services this cost will also be residual. However it will not make other costs incurred residual. The *Mayflower* decision also made clear that securing general corporate sponsorship does not make production costs residual even if the sponsorship package includes the provision of seats at performances. Likewise, catering supplies which arise as a consequence of admission do not make production costs residual.

Most theatres use the partial exemption standard method to apportion residual input tax between taxable and exempt supplies. If the standard method results in an over (or under) recovery of input tax which is classed as 'substantial' then the recovery must be re-calculated in accordance with the 'actual use' of the costs in question, under the standard method override (SMO) (see **49.9** above). A 'use-based' calculation is any calculation that fairly reflects how costs are used in making supplies, such as

Recoverable input tax on production costs = A ÷ (A + B) × C
where
A = value of supplies (such as sponsorship or touring) with a direct and immediate link from the production costs of any show

B = value of box office sales

C = residual input tax incurred on production costs
Theatres operating the standard method where the SMO is likely to be triggered on a regular basis may wish to seek approval for a special method. (HMRC Brief 65/09).

Records and accounts

[49.16] See **56 RECORDS** for records and accounts which every registered person is required by law to keep. In addition, for partial exemption purposes records must also enable a business to work out the amount of input tax it can recover in each VAT period and in each VAT year. Any other records that are used in calculating its recoverable input tax must also be kept.
(VAT Notice 706, para 2.6).

Key points

[49.17] Points to consider are as follows.

General points

- The main principle of partial exemption is that input tax can only be reclaimed on expenses relevant to taxable supplies, i.e. not in relation to any exempt activities. It is important to recognise that this is a different issue to input tax restrictions relevant to business and non-business activities. Any input tax relevant to non-business activities must initially be blocked before partial exemption issues are considered.

- An accurate partial exemption calculation can only be made if an accountant (or relevant staff) clearly identifies whether an expense should be coded as taxable, exempt or residual as far as input tax recovery is concerned. A major invoice incorrectly coded as residual instead of taxable (or exempt instead of residual or taxable) could cost a business a lot of money.
- A change of intended use of an item or actual use being different to intended use means that input tax originally claimed on goods or services could be affected by the 'clawback' or 'payback' provisions. In the case of a 'clawback' situation, extra VAT will be payable to HMRC – the opposite applies in a 'payback' situation, with a rebate being due. A change in intended use does not means that input tax claims (or non-claims) on previous VAT returns were incorrect, but that an adjustment is needed on a current VAT return to reflect the change in intended use.
- Be aware of the need to make an annual adjustment for all partial exemption calculations – and the fact that a business has the choice of including the adjustment payment or repayment on the VAT return at the end of the tax year in question (31 March, 30 April or 31 May, depending on VAT periods) or the return for the following quarter.
- Always check to see if a client is *de minimis* as far as partial exemption is concerned and the fact that two additional *de minimis* tests were introduced on 1 April 2010. In such cases, all input tax can be reclaimed if one of the three tests creates a *de minimis* outcome. However, it is the annual position that matters, any quarterly calculations being made on a provisional basis.
- An 'annual test' was introduced on 1 April 2010, which means that a business that was *de minimis* in its previous tax year can reclaim all input tax on its VAT returns for the next tax year, subject to an annual adjustment calculation at the end of that year. This new measure could simplify accounting for a partly exempt business because it avoids having to make quarterly partial exemption calculations.
- A partly-exempt business that buys in services from abroad (with no VAT charged by the overseas business under the place of supply rules) will suffer an input tax restriction if the expense relates to its exempt activities. This is because the reverse charge calculation (value of service multiplied by UK rate of VAT) will produce a VAT return entry to pay output tax (Box 1) but an input tax restriction in Box 4. It is important that a partly exempt business recognises the importance of this adjustment, and is able to identify all payments to overseas suppliers when it completes its accounts or VAT returns.

Standard method

- Most businesses use the standard method of calculation as far as partial exemption is concerned. However, be aware that a special method of calculation can be applied for (as long as HMRC approval is obtained) if the standard method does not give a fair and reasonable result. The starting point in deciding whether a special method is worthwhile is to consider why the standard method breaks down, i.e. why it produces an unfair result in terms of input tax recovery.

- The standard method calculation should exclude capital assets sold by a business and also incidental sources of income, e.g. bank interest received.
- The denominator part of the fraction in the standard method is described as the 'value of all supplies'. It is important to remember that this figure does not include income that is outside the scope of VAT, e.g. many grants or donations received by charities. The inclusion of income that is outside the scope of VAT will lead to an underclaim of residual input tax by the business.
- Optional procedures were introduced on 1 April 2009 that could benefit many partly exempt businesses using the standard method by giving the opportunity to use an in-year recovery rate in relation to residual input tax (based on the overall recovery rate for the previous partial exemption year). However, the business must still do a final annual adjustment calculation at the end of the tax year and pay (or reclaim) any tax due compared to the provisional claims during the year.
- A separate measure effective from 1 April 2009 could also improve input tax recovery when exempt input tax is first incurred by a business by allowing a use rather than income based method of calculation (i.e. residual input tax recovery based on use rather than income as per standard method). The 'use' basis can be based on any method (possibly projected income split over a longer period of time) as long as it is fair and reasonable.
- Compulsory rules were introduced on 1 April 2009 that effect standard method users supplying services to customers outside the UK, certain financial supplies and supplies from establishments located outside the UK. It is important advisers consider these changes for any clients involved in such activities. The basic outcome is that the income and costs from certain foreign supplies is included within the standard method calculation, rather than requiring a separate input tax adjustment based on use.

Special methods

- It is important to regularly review the position of all partly exempt businesses and identify whether to apply to HMRC for a special method. These applications are appropriate when it is considered that the standard method does not give a fair and reasonable recovery of residual input tax.
- In many cases, the standard method gives a perfectly fair result – and overall is easy to calculate. However, it is important to be aware of alternative methods of calculation, particularly those based on inputs, square footage or staff numbers.

- The key principle of any partial exemption calculation is to ensure methods proposed are fair and reasonable. HMRC introduced regulations on 1 April 2007 that require a taxpayer to make a 'fair and reasonable' declaration at the time he submits the application. HMRC has the power to recover tax on a historic basis if this declaration is incorrect.
- Any change in circumstance for a business that could affect the fair and reasonable result of its special method calculations should be immediately notified to HMRC. A revised special method or adoption of the standard method may then be appropriate.
- Remember that it is only appropriate to spend time and effort proposing a special method if a business has a significant amount of residual input tax. If most (or all) input tax can be directly attributed to taxable or exempt supplies, there are negligible benefits to be gained by adopting a special method of calculation.

The key principle of any partial exemption calculation is to ensure methods proposed are fair and reasonable. HMRC introduced regulations on 1 April 2007 that require a taxpayer to make a fair and reasonable declaration at the time he submits the application. HMRC has the power to recover tax on a historic basis if the declaration is incorrect.

Any change in circumstances for a business that could affect the fair and reasonable results of its special method calculations should be immediately notified to HMRC. A revised special method or adoption of the standard method may then be appropriate.

Remember that it is only appropriate to spend time and effort producing a special method if a business has a significant amount of residual input tax. If most (or all) input tax can be directly attributed to taxable or exempt supplies, there are negligible benefits to be gained by adopting a special method of calculation.

50

Partnerships

Cross-references. See **8.5 BUSINESS** for deemed partnerships.

De Voil Indirect Tax Service. See **V2.110**.

Introduction

English law

[50.1] A partnership, or firm, is not a legal entity but is defined as 'the relation which subsists between persons carrying on business in common with a view to profit'. [*Partnership Act 1890, s 1(1)*].

Scottish law

A partnership is a legal person distinct from the partners who compose it.

Despite this, in general VAT legislation applies similarly under English and Scottish law so that the partnership itself is treated as a taxable person.

Case law

See also *Leighton-Jones and Craig (t/a Saddletramps)* (VTD 597) (TVC 47.17) approving *dicta* in *Weiner v Harris* [1910] 1 KB 285.

For alleged husband and wife partnerships see *Cooper* (VTD 1218), *Jackson (RD & Mrs SL)* (VTD 1959) (TVC 47.43) and *Britton* (VJ) (VTD 2173) (TVC 47.46) and for an alleged partnership with infant children see *Bridgeman* (VTD 1206) (TVC 47.52).

For whether joint venture agreements amount to a partnership, see *Strathearn Gordon Associates Ltd* (VTD 1884) (TVC 47.54), *Keydon Estates Ltd* (VTD 4471) (TVC 47.55) and *Fivegrange Ltd* (VTD 5338) (TVC 47.56).

Salaried partners

Whether a salaried partner is a full partner or an employee depends upon the facts of the particular case.

- A salaried partner should be treated as an employee (and not included in the registration of the firm) if, despite being held out as a partner, he is paid either by a fixed salary or a share of the profits but is denied the rights and duties normally accorded to a full partner, i.e. the obligation to contribute capital and to share losses and the right to fully participate in the management of the firm.
- If a person who is called a salaried partner enjoys a share of the profits and an interest in the partnership capital, he should be treated as a full partner and included in the registration of the firm.

If a salaried partner is included as a partner on the VAT registration forms, in the absence of any evidence to the contrary, HMRC take him to be a full partner on the basis that he is holding himself out as such (see **50.4** below).

(HMRC VAT Guidance V1–28, para 3.4.10).

Limited partnerships

Under the *Limited Partnership Act 1907*, a limited partnership is a partnership which consists of

- one or more partners called 'general partners' who are liable for all debts and obligations of the firm, and
- one or more persons called 'limited partners' who cannot take part in the management of the partnership business and do not have power to bind it. If a limited partner should take part in the management of the partnership business, he is liable for all the debts, etc. incurred while he so took part as if he were a general partner.

A limited partnership must be registered as such with the Registrar of Companies, otherwise all the partners are treated as general partners.

Registration

[50.2] VAT registration of persons carrying on business in partnership, or carrying on in partnership any other activities in the course or furtherance of which they acquire goods from another EU country, may be in the name of the firm. In such a case, no account is to be taken of any change in the partnership in determining for the purposes of*VATA 1994* whether goods or services are supplied to or by such persons or are acquired by such persons from another EU country. [*VATA 1994, s 45(1)*].

An application to be registered (Form VAT 1) for a partnership must also be accompanied by Form VAT 2. [*SI 1995/2518, Reg 5(1); SI 2000/794*]. Form VAT 1 must be signed by one of the partners and Form VAT 2 should normally be signed by all the partners.

England and Wales

Where separate businesses are carried on by the same individuals in partnership only one registration applies (*C & E Commrs v Glassborow and Another*, QB [1974] STC 142 (TVC 57.1)).

Scotland

Because a partnership is a legal person, each separate business carried on by the same partners may have a separate registration. For example, if A and B have six retail outlets and treat them as six different partnerships, each can be registered individually even though A and B are the only partners in each partnership. In practice, HMRC are only likely to allow separate registration where it can be shown that there is a separate partnership agreement for each of the businesses.

Limited partnerships

Limited partnerships are registered in the names of the general partners and those treated as general partners (see **50.1** above). The normal procedures for the registration of partnerships is followed except

- where there is only one general partner, the registration will be raised in the name of that sole general partner;
- where a sole general partner is already registered for VAT, the business activities of the limited partnership should be accounted for under the existing registration;
- where two or more persons are registered for VAT as a partnership and those same persons are all the general partners in a limited partnership, the business activities of the limited partnership should be accounted for under the existing registration of the partnership;
- where the general partner is an incorporated company and a member of a VAT group, the business activities of the limited partnership are part of that group and must be accounted for under the existing group registration;
- where two individuals carry on two businesses in partnership, each being a general partner in one business and a limited partner in the other, separate registration applies (*Saunders and Sorrell* (VTD 913) (TVC 47.15)); and
- as a limited partnership cannot own land and property, where property is held jointly in the names of all the general and limited partners, it may be necessary to register all those partners as a normal partnership, separately from any existing registration the limited partnership may have. A Form VAT 2 must be signed by all the general and limited partners.

Ceasing to be a partner

[50.3] Without prejudice to *Partnership Act 1890, s 36*, a person who has ceased to be a partner continues to be regarded as a partner for VAT purposes (in particular for the purposes of any VAT liability) until the date on which the change is notified to HMRC. [*VATA 1994, s 45(2)*]. (*Partnership Act 1890,* *s 36* provides, *inter alia*, that a person who deals with a firm after a change in its constitution is entitled to treat all apparent members of the old firm as still being members of the firm until he has notice of the change.)

Where a person ceases to be a partner in a VAT period, (or is treated as doing so under *VATA 1994, s 45(2)* above) any notice, whether of assessment or otherwise, which is served on the partnership and relates to that period or an earlier period during the whole or part of which he was a partner is treated as served on him. [*VATA 1994, s 45(2)(3)*].

Liability for VAT

[50.4] Subject to below

- **in England and Wales,**
  - (a) all the partners in a firm are liable jointly for all the debts and jointly and severally for the obligations of the firm which arise while they are members of that firm; and
  - (b) after death, a partner's estate is severally liable for such debts so far as they remain unsatisfied but subject to the prior payment of his separate debts; and
- **in Scotland**, because a partnership is a legal person distinct from the persons of whom it is composed, it is the partnership which is liable for debts. The partners themselves only become liable for any debts if the partnership has insufficient assets to meet those debts. Where the partners do become liable, they are liable jointly and severally.

Where a person is a partner during part only of a VAT period his liability for VAT on the supply of goods or services during that period, or on the acquisition during that period of any goods from another EU country, is limited to such proportion of the firm's liability as may be just. [*VATA 1994, s 45(5)*].

However,

- a partner's liability does not end automatically on leaving a partnership (see **50.3** above); and
- limited partners (see **50.1** above) are not liable for any debts or obligations of the limited partnership over and above the capital which they contributed.

Holding out

Anyone who by spoken word, writing or conduct represents himself, or allows himself to be represented, as a partner in a particular firm, is liable as a partner to anyone who has on the faith of any such representation 'given credit' to the firm. [*Partnership Act 1890, s 14*]. This is known as 'holding out'. As a result

- anyone who holds himself out as a partner in a firm will be liable for the debts and obligations of the partnership as if he were a partner; and
- where two or more persons hold themselves out as a partnership in an application for registration, HMRC will treat those persons as partners (with joint liability for all debts).

Notices to and by partnerships

Notices to partnerships

[50.5] Any notice (whether an assessment or otherwise) addressed to the partnership by the name in which it is registered and validly served under *VATA 1994* will be regarded as served on the partnership (including any former partners as in **50.3** above). This is without prejudice to *Partnership Act 1890, s 16* which provides that notice to any partner who habitually acts in the partnership business operates as notice to the firm generally, except in cases of fraud involving that particular partner. [*VATA 1994, s 45(4)*].

Notices by partnerships

Where any notice is required to be given for VAT purposes, it is the joint and several liability of all the partners to give it, but it is sufficient if it is given by one partner. *In Scotland*, any authorised person, whether a partner or not, may give the required notice as specified by *Partnership Act 1890, s 6*. [*VATA 1994, Sch 11 para 7; SI 1995/2518, Reg 7*]. Notice of appeal may be made in the partnership name (see **5.7 APPEALS**).

Partners holding office

[50.6] Where a person (including partners of a firm), in the course or furtherance of a trade, profession or vocation, accepts any office, services supplied by him as the holder of that office are treated as supplied in the course or furtherance of the trade etc. [*VATA 1994, s 94(4)*]. This point will obviously be of importance if the recipient of a supply suffers restriction of input tax or, as regards the supplier, the consideration for the supply was fixed with no contemplation that VAT was applicable. See *Lean & Rose* (VTD 54) (TVC 62.360) where, on the facts, a solicitor who was a partner in a private practice was held to have a personal contract as a part-time salaried solicitor of a borough council and, accordingly, was not making taxable supplies.

See also **44.8 MANAGEMENT SERVICES AND SUPPLIES OF STAFF.**

Contributions to partnerships

[50.7] In *KapHag Renditefonds v Finanzamt Charlottenburg, ECJ Case C–442/01*, [2005] STC 1500 (TVC 22.90) a German partnership admitted a new partner, who made a payment of 38 million marks to the partnership. The partnership reclaimed input tax on legal fees relating to this. The tax authority rejected the claim on the basis that the fees related to an exempt supply of services. The partnership appealed and the case was referred to the ECJ, which ruled that no supply was being made under what is now *Directive 2006/112/EC, Art 2(1)(a)* by either the individual partners or the partnership to the incoming partner in return for the capital contribution.

Although in the *KapHag* case the incoming partner was contributing cash in return for admission into the partnership, contributions are frequently made in the form of other assets. The ECJ decision tacitly accepted the Advocate-General's Opinion that the same principles would apply whether the contribution consisted of cash or other assets. Whatever the nature of the assets comprising the contribution, there is no reciprocal supply from the partnership. However, where the assets are not cash, the making of the partnership contribution may have other VAT consequences.

Following the ECJ decision, HMRC have issued the following guidance on the implications of the decision.

(1) Contribution to partnership comprising services

This could be, for example, a trademark or trading logo or the use of an asset the ownership of which is retained by the incoming partner. A supply can arise under *VATA 1994, Sch 4 para 5(4)* in certain circumstances where a taxable person applies business goods to private use or makes them available for purposes other than those of his business. Similarly, *SI 1993/1507* provides that a supply arises where a taxable person applies bought-in services to private or non-business use for no consideration where he has been entitled to input tax credit. See **47.7 OUTPUT TAX** for fuller details.

Where either of the above circumstances apply, a VAT-registered incoming partner must account for VAT on the supply of services that he is regarded as making in the disposal of the services from his existing business. The partnership may be able to recover this as its input tax where the contributed services are to be used for its business (see (5) below).

(2) Contribution to partnership comprising goods other than land

If a partnership contribution comprises goods other than land that the transferor held as assets, then a deemed supply arises under *VATA 1994, Sch 4 para 5(1)*. See **47.6 OUTPUT TAX**. Where such a deemed supply arises, the incoming partner must account for VAT. The partnership may be able to recover this as its input tax where the contributed assets are to be used for its business (see (5) below).

(3) Contribution to partnership comprising land or interests in land

The VAT treatment of land or interests in land depends upon whether the incoming partner, or his predecessor, was entitled to deduct input tax in relation to the contributed property. For example, if he had opted to tax the property, or it was taxable as new freehold commercial property, there may be a deemed supply as described at (2) above. The incoming partner must then account for VAT on this supply. As with other contributed goods, the partnership may be entitled to recover this as input tax where the property is to be used for the partnership's business (see (5) below).

(4) Transfers of going concerns

It is possible that assets transferred by way of a partnership contribution could qualify to be treated as a transfer of a going concern. If so, no VAT is due from the transferor. See **8.10 BUSINESS**.

(5) Recovery by the partnership of output tax accounted for by an incoming partner on his contribution as its input tax

If an incoming partner contributes goods and/or services (on which VAT is due as described above) and the partnership uses them for its business purposes, the partnership can recover the VAT as input tax subject to the normal rules. The incoming partner cannot issue a VAT invoice, but in order to provide the partnership with acceptable evidence to support a claim for recovery of input tax, he may use his normal invoicing documentation overwritten with the following statement.

'Certificate for VAT on partnership contribution

No payment is necessary for these goods/services. Output tax has been accounted for on the supply.'

The incoming partner must show full details of the goods and/or services on the documentation and the amount of VAT shown must be the amount of output tax accounted for to HMRC.

(6) Capital goods scheme consequences

Where the capital contribution is in the form of an interest in land or a computer, it may be an existing capital item of the incoming partner under the capital goods scheme. If the transfer to the partnership constitutes a supply which is a disposal of an existing capital goods scheme item, a disposal adjustment may be due. If the transfer also constitutes a TOGC, then this ends the current interval for the incoming partner and the partnership becomes responsible for making adjustments for any remaining intervals. See **10 CAPITAL GOODS SCHEME** for full details of the scheme.

(7) Transfer of assets out of a partnership

KapHag was only concerned with assets moving into a partnership in the form of a partnership contribution. It did not cover the reverse situation, where partnership assets are paid out to an outgoing partner or otherwise disposed of by the partnership for no consideration. Where a transfer of assets out of a partnership for no consideration occurs, one of the following sets of circumstances applies.

(a) If the incoming partner accounted for output tax when he contributed the assets to the partnership and the partnership was entitled to recover all or part of this as its input tax, there is a subsequent supply by the partnership when the same assets are transferred out (unless the transfer out satisfies the TOGC rules).

(b) If no output tax was accounted for when the assets were contributed to the partnership because they constituted a TOGC, the transfer out of the same assets is a deemed supply upon which the partnership must account for VAT (unless the transfer out satisfies the TOGC rules).

(c) If the partnership is transferring out more assets than those originally contributed to it, although the original contribution to the partnership may not have been a TOGC, the subsequent transfer out may satisfy the TOGC rules. If so, no VAT is due from the partnership.

(d) If the original contribution to the partnership was a TOGC but the partnership is transferring out less of the assets than were originally contributed, then unless the assets being transferred out still meet the TOGC rules in their own right, there may be a deemed supply upon which the partnership must account for VAT.

(Business Brief 21/04).

Disposal of a share in a partnership

[50.8] *KapHag* (see **50.7** above) established that a partnership or the existing partners make no supply when a new partner is admitted in return for making a capital contribution. This paragraph considers whether the disposal by a partner of his share in the partnership is a supply for VAT purposes. It should be noted that this 'share' is distinct from the assets that were contributed by the partner on joining the partnership. As a result, even if the selling price of the share is determined by the value of those assets, they are not the subject of the later sale which has its own liability for VAT purposes.

Although the ECJ has not considered the disposal of shares in a partnership, it has considered transactions involving shares in companies. These cases have established that the mere acquisition and holding of shares in a company is not to be regarded as an economic activity, although transactions in shares or interests in companies and associations may constitute economic activity in three situations.

- Where the transactions constitute the direct, permanent and necessary extension of an economic activity.
- Where the transactions are effected in order to secure a direct or indirect involvement in the management of a company in which the holding is acquired.
- Where the transactions are effected as part of a commercial share-dealing activity.

HMRC considers that the same principles apply to transactions involving partnership shares and give the following as common examples.

Circumstances in which the disposal of a partnership share will not constitute a supply

- *The share is disposed of for no consideration.* A share in a partnership comprises services rather than goods. When services are transferred, assigned or otherwise disposed of for no consideration, they do not constitute any supply for VAT purposes.
- *The share being sold was acquired simply as an investment.* Where a partner has acquired his share merely to secure a share in any future profits and has had no involvement in running the partnership, the subsequent sale or assignment of that share for consideration will not constitute a supply for VAT purposes.

Circumstances in which the disposal of a partnership share will constitute a supply

- *Where the partnership share was acquired and disposed of as a direct extension of the partner's economic activities.* Where a partner is a taxable person in his own right, the partnership share may have been acquired in the course or furtherance of his own economic activities. If so, the subsequent transfer or assignment of that share for a consideration will also be an economic activity (e.g. a partner may have a business asset for sale and, rather than selling it directly, may have contributed the asset into a partnership and sold the resultant partnership share instead).
- *Where the partnership share was acquired in order to obtain an active role in the business of the partnership.* Where a partner is a taxable person in his own right and had acquired the partnership share in order to actively participate in, or control, the business of the partnership, then the sale of that share can be economic activity on the part of the partner. The sale of the share will constitute a supply for VAT purposes.
- *Where the partnership share was acquired as part of a commercial partnership share-dealing activity.* A partner who is a taxable person may have a business of dealing in partnership shares. This will be an economic activity on the part of the partner. Sales or assignments of the partnership shares that were acquired in the course of this activity and that are sold for a consideration constitute supplies for VAT purposes.

Where the disposal of a partnership share is a supply, the supply is exempt as the supply of a financial service.

VAT on associated purchases

Where the disposal of a partnership share is not a supply, the VAT incurred in connection with the disposal is normally not input tax. Where the disposal is a supply, the related VAT is input tax, but, subject to the *de minimis* provisions, recovery is normally fully restricted under the partial exemption rules.

(Business Brief 30/04).

Limited liability partnerships

[50.9] An LLP has a legal status distinct from its members and can enter into contracts in its own right. Individual members of the LLP are protected from debts or liabilities arising from negligence and wrongful acts or misconduct of another member, employee or agent of the LLP.

An LLP is a corporate body and it, rather than the members, is the legal entity for VAT purposes so that the LLP itself becomes liable for VAT registration (subject to the normal registration rules).

Where an existing partnership changes to an LLP

As the legal entity has changed from that of a partnership to a corporate body, the LLP may have to apply for VAT registration (subject to the normal rules). The normal rules for the transfer of a business as a going concern will apply (see **8.10 BUSINESS**). If the general partnership ceases to exist, it may be possible for the VAT number to be transferred to the LLP (see **59.36 REGISTRATION**).

VAT groups

An LLP can join a VAT group provided it meets the control conditions in *VATA 1994, s 43A* (see **27.2 GROUPS OF COMPANIES**). Where the control conditions are satisfied, a VAT group could be formed by, for example

- an LLP with a number of subsidiary companies; or
- two or more eligible companies and an LLP in which those companies are controlling partners.

(Business Brief 3/01).

Key points

[50.10] Points to consider are as follows.

- A partnership is a different legal entity to a sole trader, so this means that supplies are treated independently as far as VAT is concerned. So a plumber who is VAT-registered as a sole trader will not include any income on his VAT return (or claim input tax on expenses) if he has a separate business with his wife as a partnership. This separation of business activities into different legal entities can, if done correctly, produce a VAT planning opportunity by avoiding the need for one (or possibly both) of the businesses to be VAT-registered, i.e. on the basis of turnover levels. However, this strategy must be carefully planned to avoid any problems with the business splitting legislation.
- A limited liability partnership (LLP) is a separate legal entity to a partnership. In the case of an LLP, it is the corporate body itself that is VAT-registered and liable for any VAT debts. If a business transfers from a general partnership to an LLP, this is a transfer of a going concern situation (TOGC), with the usual TOGC rules taking effect.
- The addition of a new partner to the partnership or retirement of an existing partner does not create the need to deregister for VAT purposes. The VAT 2 (list of partners) form can be amended to reflect the change.

51

Payment of VAT

Cross-references. See **2.20 ACCOUNTING PERIODS AND RETURNS** for payments by persons selling under a power of sale; **5.4 APPEALS** for payment of VAT as a condition of appeal; **6.1 ASSESSMENTS** for repayments of VAT made in error; **31.1–31.5 HMRC: POWERS** for power to require security or production of evidence before making repayments, power to recover VAT and power to distraint for payment and diligence (Scotland); **33 IMPORTS** for VAT payable on importation; and **35.3 INSOLVENCY** for priority of payment in insolvency.

Introduction

[51.1] Subject to the provisions in **51.3** and **51.4** below, VAT due for a VAT period is payable to the Controller at VAT Central Unit, Southend-on-Sea not later than the last day on which the return for that period must be submitted i.e.

- for Form VAT 100 (the normal return) not later than one month after the end of the VAT period; and
- for Form VAT 193 (final return) not later than one month after the effective date for cancellation of registration (or, in the case of a taxable person not registered, one month after the date when liability to be registered ceases).

[*SI 1995/2518, Reg 25(1)(4), Reg 40(2); SI 1996/1250, Reg 9; SI 2000/258, Reg 3*].

Where the amount of VAT due to HMRC is under £1, no payment need be made. [*VATA 1994, Sch 11 para 2(13)*]. Such amount should not be carried forward to the next return. (VAT Notice 700, para 21.5).

De Voil Indirect Tax Service. See V5.108A–V5.109B.

Method of payment

[51.2] VAT can currently be paid by the following methods

- direct debit for returns submitted online, unless the business makes payments on account and submits quarterly returns;
- bank or building society services to pay by internet, telephone banking or Bankers Automated Clearing Systems (BACS) Direct Credit;
- debit or credit card over the internet using the BillPay service (but not American Express or Diners Club cards);
- Clearing House Automated Payments System (CHAPS) transfer;
- Bank Giro using paying slips ordered from HMRC;
- standing order for the annual accounting and payment on account schemes; or
- post by cheque made payable to 'HM Revenue & Customs only' followed by the VAT reference number.

Electronic returns

Where a return is made using HMRC's eVAT return service (see **2.1 ACCOUNTING PERIODS AND RETURNS**) it is a condition of the scheme that any relevant payment must be made solely by electronic means acceptable to HMRC for that purpose. [*SI 1995/2518, Reg 40(2A); SI 2000/258*]. HMRC accept payment by BACS, CHAPS or Bank Giro Credit transfer (see above).

As payments have to be made electronically, the provisions for extending the due date of payment in **51.3** below apply.

Payments in euros

UK businesses can pay VAT (and other duties) in euros, although banks are not making BACS euro direct debit available. All declarations must continue to be made in sterling. Exchange rates are likely to fluctuate between the time payment is initiated and the time the payment is cleared. Businesses will be credited with the sterling value received by HMRC and any over/under payments will be dealt with using existing debt management practices. Costs incurred by HMRC in converting euro payments into sterling will not be passed on to businesses and will be borne by HMRC. (Business Brief 1/99).

Non-payment

If the taxpayer is unable to pay all the VAT due, he should still send in the VAT return by the due date and write to HMRC explaining why he cannot pay. HMRC may be able to help businesses experiencing short-term difficulty by agreeing a brief period in which to pay a VAT debt. Post-dated cheques should *not* be sent. If sent and dated after the due date for payment, the taxpayer will automatically be in default under **52.21 PENALTIES** below. Where a compromise solution cannot be agreed or no response is received to a request for payment, HMRC may take action to recover the VAT due. This may include the issue of a distress warrant (diligence warrant in Scotland) under which assets may be removed and sold (see **31.4 HMRC: POWERS**) or requesting the court to make a bankruptcy or winding up order (see **35 INSOLVENCY**). (VAT Notice 930).

Cheques

Due to the cost involved, HMRC do not re-present cheques to banks which have previously been returned unpaid through lack of funds. The onus is on the taxpayer to cancel and replace any such cheques. (VAT Notes No 4 1996).

From 1 April 2010 all cheque payments sent by post are treated as being received by HMRC on the date when cleared funds reach their bank account, not the date when they receive the cheque. [*SI 1995/2518, Reg 40(2B); SI 2009/2978, Reg 5*].

> *Example*
>
> John is VAT-registered and able to submit his returns and pay tax due in a paper format because his annual sales are less than £100,000, and he was also VAT-registered before 1 April 2010, i.e. he does not have to file returns and pay tax online.
>
> He is about to send his June 2010 return and cheque to HMRC. He must do this so that the payment clears HMRC's bank account by the end of July (when return is due), otherwise the payment will be late and he will possibly incur either a default surcharge or default surcharge liability notice (depending on whether he has been late with any other returns and payments in the last twelve months).

(HMRC Brief 14/10).

Mandatory electronic payment

HMRC have powers to require all payments of VAT to be made by electronic means. [*FA 2003, s 204; FA 2007, s 94*].

Fee for specified methods of payment

Since HMRC expect to pay a fee in connection with amounts paid by credit card, a person who makes a payment by credit card over the phone must pay a fee of 1.25% of the payment (increased from 0.91% from 14 December 2009). Payment by credit card over the internet incurs a fee equal to 1.4% of the payment (increased from 1.25% from 1 April 2011). [*FA 2008, s 136; SI 2009/3073; SI 2011/711*].

Extending the due date

[51.3] A business which makes use of electronic means of payment (BACS direct credit, bank giro credit transfer or CHAPS but not payments via Girobank) will automatically receive a seven-day extension for the submission and payment of VAT returns. Payments must be in HMRC's bank account on or before the 7th calendar day from the standard due date. If the 7th day falls on a weekend, the payment must be received by the previous Friday. If the 7th day falls on a bank holiday, payment must be received by the last working day beforehand (but see *Avonwave Ltd (t/a Gatewood Joinery)* (VTD 17509) (TVC 18.529)). A business is free to change the method of payment on a return-by-return basis (unless submitting electronic returns) without notifying HMRC but if it changes back to payment by cheque for any return, the seven-day extension does not apply to that return.

The concession cannot be used

- by businesses required to make payments on account unless it makes monthly returns (see **51.4** below);
- by businesses using the annual accounting scheme; or
- to make VAT payments other than VAT return payments (e.g. assessments).

(VAT Notice 700, para 21.3)

Note that 'nil' or 'claim' returns do not receive the seven-day extension even if the business would normally submit payment returns and pay the VAT by electronic means.

In *Wood Auto Supplies Ltd* (VTD 17356) (TVC 18.522) the company consistently initiated payment on the penultimate day of the seven-day extension. HMRC imposed a default surcharge when two consecutive payments were not received until the eighth day but the tribunal held that since the company's account had been debited within the seven-day period it had a reasonable excuse for believing that it had made the payments within the extended time limit.

Payments on account

[51.4] The Treasury may, if they consider it is desirable to do so in the interests of national economy, provide by SI that certain taxable persons must make payments on account of their VAT liability for a VAT period. [*VATA 1994, s 28; FA 1996, s 34; FA 1997, s 43*]. Under these provisions, every VAT-registered business with an annual VAT liability of more than £2 million (increased to £2.3 million, from 1 June 2011 or 1 December 2011 depending on the basic period) is required to be in the Payments on Account (POA) regime. Once in the regime each business must make interim payments at the end of the second and third months of each VAT quarter as POAs of the quarterly VAT liability. A balancing payment for the quarter is then made with the VAT return. All POAs and balancing payments must be made by electronic transfer. The detailed provisions of the POA scheme are set out below.

Basic period

POAs are required to be made, in respect of each VAT period exceeding one month beginning after 31 March each year, by

(a) a taxable person whose total VAT liability for the VAT periods ending within the year that ended on the last day of his VAT period ending before the previous 1 December (i.e. normally the year ending the previous 30 September, 31 October or 30 November) exceeded £2 million (increased to £2.3 million from 1 December 2011); and

(b) a taxable person who does not fall within (*a*) above, but whose total VAT liability for the VAT periods ending within the year that ended on the last day of his VAT period ending after the previous 30 November exceeded £2 million (increased to £2.3 million from 1 June 2011).

The period of one year referred to under (*a*) or (*b*) above is known as the '*basic period*'.

VAT liability is calculated by adding together the VAT due to be declared on returns (including assessments or error correction notifications (formerly voluntary disclosures)) and, if applicable, the VAT due on imports and goods ex warehouse. If liability exceeds the threshold, HMRC will notify the business that it is in the scheme.

[*SI 1993/2001, Arts 5, 6; SI 2011/21, Art 2(b), (c)*].

Timing of payments

POAs must be sent so as to clear HMRC's account not later than the last working day of the second and third months of every VAT quarterly period (with the exception of the first period in the scheme when only one payment is required at the end of the third month). Quarterly balancing payments must also be cleared by the last working day of the month following the return period. Where non-standard period end dates have been agreed with HMRC, payments must be cleared to HMRC's account by the due date for those returns (or the last working date before the due date if that date is not a working date).

Set POAs

Unless one of the alternatives below is used, set POAs must be made.

The initial level of POAs are determined by the VAT liability in the period in which the threshold was exceeded under (*a*) or (*b*) above. The amount of each POA is one twenty-fourth of the total amount of VAT (excluding VAT on imports from outside the EU and goods ex warehouse) for that period. If the business has been in operation for less than twelve months, the payments will be calculated on a proportionate basis.

HMRC must notify the business of the amounts it is required to pay and how these amounts have been calculated.

From the beginning of the next annual cycle for POAs, the amount of the POAs is one twenty-fourth of the total amount of VAT (excluding VAT on imports from outside the EU and goods ex warehouse) which the business was liable to pay in its reference year determined as follows.

VAT return periods: quarters ending	*Reference year*	*Annual cycle begins*
31 Mar, 30 Jun, 30 Sept, 31 Dec	Y/ended 30 Sept	1 Apr
30 Apr, 31 July, 31 Oct, 31 Jan	Y/ended 31 Oct	1 May
31 May, 31 Aug, 30 Nov, 28/29 Feb	Y/ended 30 Nov	1 June

Alternatives to set POAs

The following alternatives are available to set POAs.

- *Monthly VAT returns*. A business can contact HMRC and change to monthly VAT returns. It will be expected to continue making such returns for a reasonable period, normally at least twelve months. If monthly returns are prepared and payment made by electronic means (see below) or credit transfer, a further seven days beyond the due date may be allowed to render returns and make payments. This is the only circumstance in which a business liable to be in the POA scheme may be granted such an extension.
- *Payments based on actual liabilities*. A business may elect to pay its actual VAT liability for the preceding month instead of the set POAs but without rendering a monthly VAT return. Such an election must be made in writing to HMRC stating the date on which it is to take effect (which must not be less than 30 days after the date of notification). Such an election then continues to have effect until a date notified in writing to HMRC. An election cannot be withdrawn earlier than the first anniversary of the date on which it took effect and, where an election is withdrawn, a further election cannot be made within twelve months of the date of withdrawal. HMRC may at any time give written notice that an election is to cease with effect from a specified date where they are not satisfied that the correct amounts are being paid. An appeal may be made against any such notice.

  Payments based on actual liabilities may be beneficial where there are seasonal variations in the VAT liability. However, where the business is in credit in any month, no immediate repayment is made. Neither can a credit in respect of the first month of an accounting period be netted off against a liability for the second month to reduce the POA for that month. The business must wait to bring the credit forward to the VAT return as normal. Where immediate repayments are required, the business should consider changing to monthly returns.

Method of payment

Payment must be made by electronic transfer direct to HMRC's account. The VAT registration number should be quoted as a reference when making payments. Acceptable methods of payment are

- Clearing House Automated Payment System (CHAPS);
- Bankers Automated Clearing System (BACS);

- bank giro credit using official HMRC bank giro slips (available by contacting ASD 2C, Alexander House, 21 Victoria Avenue, Southend on Sea, Essex, SS99 1AA; tel: 01702 366376 or the National Advice Centre; tel: 0845 000 0200);
- (exceptionally) bank giro credit using non-official slips; and
- standing order.

In all cases the business must make the necessary arrangements to ensure the payment is received on time. The seven days period of grace allowed for payment by electronic means (see **51.3** above) does *not* apply to payments under the POA scheme. Whichever payment method is used, the same method must also be used to make any balancing payments due in respect of VAT returns.

Failure to pay

Where a business fails to make a POA by the due date, the payment is recoverable as if it were VAT due. The business is also liable to the default surcharge. See **52.21 PENALTIES**.

Completion of VAT return

VAT returns should be completed and submitted in the normal way. The figures must not be adjusted to take account of POAs made. The amount to be paid is the net liability shown on the return less any payments on account already made in respect of that period.

Overpayments

Where the payments made on account for a VAT period exceed the total due in that period, the excess must be repaid by HMRC (if not liable to set-off under *VATA 1994, s 81*, see **51.6** below). If the return is a repayment return, the repayment will be made in the normal way and the POAs made in the quarter will also be repaid.

Removal from scheme

Where VAT liability in a reference year (see above) falls below £2 million, a business will be removed from the POA scheme six months later. HMRC will notify the business of its withdrawal from the scheme and the effective date of withdrawal.

If the total VAT liability in any completed year ending after a reference year is less than £1.6 million (increased to £1.8 million from 1 June 2011), written application may be made to cease making POAs to HMRC at Large Payers Unit, 3rd Floor North, Queen's Dock, Liverpool L74 4AA. The requirement to make such payments then ceases with effect from the date of written approval by HMRC.

[*SI 1993/2001, Art 7; SI 2011/21, Art 2(d)*]. (VAT Notice 700/60/09, para 3.4).

Reduction in payments on account

If

- the total VAT liability (excluding VAT on imports from outside the EU and goods ex warehouse) in any completed year ending after the year on which current payments are based is less than 80% of the liability for that year, or
- HMRC are satisfied that the total VAT liability (excluding VAT on imports from outside the EU and goods ex warehouse) in any year which has commenced but not yet ended will be less than 80% of that liability

written application can be made to HMRC at the Large Payers Unit (see above) to have the POAs reduce to reflect the current liability. Further payments on account will then be based on one twenty-fourth of the reduced amount with effect from the date of written approval by HMRC.

Increase in payments on account

HMRC may increase the POAs due where the total VAT liability (excluding VAT on imports from outside the EU and goods ex warehouse) in any year ending after the year on which current POAs are based exceeds by 20% or more the total liability for that year. Where they do so, further payments on account will be based on one twenty-fourth of the increased amount. There are similar provisions as above to reduce the payments on account where VAT liability in any subsequent year falls below 80% of the increased amount.

Businesses carried on in divisions

Where a company is registered for VAT in the names of divisions, each division is regarded as a separate business for the POA scheme, i.e. the £2 million (increased to £2.3 million, from 1 June 2011 or 1 December 2011 depending on the basic period) test is applied to each division (and not the company as a whole). Any overpayment by a division is not liable to set-off against a liability of the company or another division.

[*SI 1993/2001, Art 16(1); SI 2011/21, Art 2(e)*].

Groups of companies

The POA scheme applies to a VAT group as if all the companies in the group were one taxable person. The representative member is responsible for the POA but, in default, all members are jointly and severally liable.

Deregistration

A business should continue to make POAs until such time as deregistration is confirmed in writing in order to avoid the risk of incurring default surcharge. However, as an alternative to POAs, a business can opt to pay the actual monthly amount due. (VAT Notice 700/11/10, para 6.11).

[*SI 1993/2001; SI 1995/2518, Regs 40A, 44–48*]. (VAT Notice 700/60/09).

Reverse charge for purchases and sales of mobile phones and computer chips

As an anti-avoidance measure, in certain circumstances the customer, rather than the supplier, must account for VAT on transactions involving sales of mobiles phones and computer chips. See **4.14** to **4.23 ANTI-AVOIDANCE** for full details. Some businesses may be required to account for output tax on their purchases under this reverse charge procedure as well as on the onward sale to non-business customers. This could have the effect of increasing their net VAT liability (and bringing them within the scope of the POA regime) or increasing their monthly payments if they are already within the regime.

A business which could be affected by this may apply to HMRC to exclude the output tax due under the reverse charge from the calculation to establish whether it is subject to POA or, if already in the regime, the monthly payments it has to make.

Applications for exclusion should be made to: The POA Team, Banking Operations, Queens Dock, Liverpool, L74 4AA.

Some businesses may find that their net liability will decrease with the introduction of the reverse charge. If that is the case, the normal rules for reduction in POAs (see above) apply.

[*SI 1993/2001, Art 2A; SI 2007/1420, Art 2*]. (VAT Notice 735, para 9).

De Voil Indirect Tax Service. See V5.110.

Repayment of VAT

[51.5] If, at the end of a VAT accounting period, allowable credits exceed any output tax due, HMRC automatically make the appropriate repayment unless the amount of VAT due from HMRC is under £1, in which case no repayment is made. If, however, the business has failed to submit any return for an earlier period, HMRC may withhold payment until it has complied with those requirements. [*VATA 1994, s 25(3)(5), Sch 11 para 2(13)*]. See also the right of set-off under **51.6** below.

Method of repayment

HMRC make repayments by the Bankers Automated Clearing System (BACS). In order to receive repayment by this method, the National Registration Service must be advised of the bank account details in writing. (This is a requirement on the application for VAT registration.) In exceptional circumstances when bank account details are not known, HMRC may make repayment by payable order. (VAT Notice 700, para 21.4).

Right of set-off

[51.6] The right of set-off is as follows:

(1) Set-off for VAT purposes

Subject to special provisions for insolvent traders (see **35.7 INSOLVENCY**) where

(a) any amount is due from HMRC to any person under *VATA 1994*; and
(b) that person is liable to pay any sum by way of VAT, penalty, interest or surcharge,

the amount in (*a*) can be set against the sum in (*b*) and, to the extent of the set-off, the obligations of HMRC and the person concerned are discharged. Any interest payable by HMRC to a person on a sum due to him under or by virtue of any provision of *VATA 1994* is treated (except for the purposes of determining entitlement to, or the amount of, that interest) as an amount due by way of credit under *VATA 1994, s 25(3)* and can therefore be taken into account under (*a*) above.

[*VATA 1994, s 81(1)–(3)*].

The effect of the above provisions is to permit both HMRC and the person concerned to adopt commercial practice and strike a balance between all types of debits and credits within the taxpayer's account.

The set-off provisions and VAT refund claims

Where

- HMRC are liable to pay or repay any amount to a person because of a mistake previously made about the VAT due, and
- because of the mistake, a liability of that person to pay a sum by way of VAT, penalties, interest or surcharges was not assessed,

the normal time limits for enabling recovery (e.g. by assessment) are disregarded in determining the amount under (*b*) above to set off against the amount under (*a*) above. [*VATA 1994, s 81(3A); FA 1997, s 48*].

Effectively, this means that where a taxpayer has overpaid VAT (e.g. because exempt supplies have been treated as taxable) and seeks a refund, any refund can take into account input tax which the taxpayer should not have recovered even if HMRC are out-of-time to issue an assessment for that input tax (e.g. because of lengthy litigation).

(2) General set-off provisions in England, Wales and Northern Ireland

Under common law, or by request, HMRC may set off repayments payable to taxpayers against debts they owe to HMRC.

With effect from 21 July 2008, subject to

- the specific set-off requirements for VAT under (1) above (which take preference), and
- the restrictions below in relation to post-insolvency credits,

HMRC are empowered to make set-offs, at their discretion, across the different taxes, duties, etc that they administer.

Under these provisions, where there is both a 'credit' and a 'debit' in relation to a person, HMRC may set the credit against the debit and, to the extent of that set-off, the obligations of HMRC and the person concerned are discharged.

'*Credit*', in relation to a person, means

- a sum that is payable by HMRC to the person under or by virtue of an enactment; or
- a sum that was paid in connection with any liability (including any purported or anticipated liability) of that person to make a payment to HMRC
  (i) under or by virtue of an enactment, or
  (ii) under a contract settlement

that may be repaid to the person by HMRC.

'*Debit*', in relation to a person, means a sum that is payable by the person to HMRC under or by virtue of an enactment or under a contract settlement.

Contract settlements are contractual agreements made in connection with a person's liability, usually as a result of an enquiry covering a number of years.

[*FA 2008, s 130*].

Post-insolvency credits

Where an insolvency procedure has been applied to a person and there is a 'post-insolvency credit' in relation to that person, HMRC may not use the above powers to set that post-insolvency credit against a 'pre-insolvency debit' in relation to the person.

'*Post-insolvency credit*' means a credit that

- became due after the insolvency procedure was applied to the person; and
- relates to, or to matters occurring at, times after it was so applied.

'*Pre-insolvency debit*' means a debit that

- arose before the insolvency procedure was applied to the person; or
- arose after that procedure was so applied but relates to, or to matters occurring at, times before it was so applied.

For these purposes, an '*insolvency procedure*' is to be taken to be applied to any person when

- a bankruptcy order or winding up order is made or an administrator is appointed in relation to that person;
- that person is put into administrative receivership;
- if that person is a corporation, that person passes a resolution for voluntary winding up;
- any approved voluntary arrangement comes into force in relation to that person; or
- a registered deed of arrangement takes effect in relation to that person.

But references to the application of an insolvency procedure to a person do not include

- the application of an insolvency procedure to a person at a time when another insolvency procedure applies to the person; or

- the application of an insolvency procedure to a person immediately upon another insolvency procedure ceasing to have effect.

[*FA 2008, s 131*].

Claims for VAT credits and refunds

[51.7] A business may be entitled to a credit for, or refund of, VAT for a number of reasons, e.g.

- output tax may have been incorrectly charged because of a mathematical error, a misunderstanding of the law (e.g. charging VAT on a zero-rated supply) or because HMRC incorrectly instructed the business to charge VAT;
- input tax may have been underclaimed in earlier periods; or
- bad debt relief may be available to recover output tax previously paid.

VATA 1994, s 80 contains special provisions covering some, but not all, of the situations where credit or refund is due. Certain conditions must be satisfied. In particular, any credit must not unjustly enrich the claimant and the claim must be made within a set time limit. These provisions are considered in **51.9–51.11** below.

Where *VATA 1994, s 80* does not apply, there can be no defence of unjust enrichment by HMRC and the method of, and time limit for, claiming is different. These provisions are considered in **51.12** below.

See also **51.13** below for a summary of the various scenarios and particular problem areas in relation to claims generally.

Transfer of claim

[51.8] In *HMRC v Midlands Co-Operative Society Ltd (No 2)*, CA [2008] STC 1803 (TVC 65.119), in which a co-operative society transferred its business to another society, the Court of Appeal held that the transferee was entitled to claim for repayment of VAT overpaid by the transferor prior to the transfer.

For all transfers of rights to make a claim for overpaid tax that take place from 25 June 2008, the current creditor is put in the shoes of the original creditor. The current creditor does not receive any more from HMRC than if the original creditor had made the claim. The amount due from HMRC on a claim on a transferred right is determined by first setting off the amount of the outstanding liabilities of the original creditor and then any liabilities of the current creditor. Also, HMRC can refuse to pay a current creditor's claim where they can establish that payment of the claim to the original creditor would have unjustly enriched that original creditor.

[*FA 2008, s 133*]. (HMRC Brief 31/08).

Credit for, or repayment of, overstated or overpaid VAT

[51.9] In relation to claims made after 25 May 2005 (whenever the event occurred in respect to which the claim is made),

(a) where a person
- has accounted to HMRC for VAT for a VAT period (whenever ended), and
- in doing so, has brought into account as output tax an amount that was not output tax due,

HMRC are liable to credit the person with that amount;

(b) where HMRC
- have assessed a person to VAT for a VAT period (whenever ended), and
- in doing so, have brought into account as output tax an amount that was not output tax due,

they are liable to credit the person with that amount; and

(c) where a person has for a VAT period (whenever ended) paid to HMRC an amount by way of VAT that was not VAT due to them, otherwise than as a result of
- an amount that was not output tax due being brought into account as output tax (which is covered by (*a*) above), or
- an amount of input tax allowable not being brought into account

HMRC are liable to repay to that person the amount so paid. This would cover the situation, for example, where a tax liability has been paid twice.

[*VATA 1994, s 80(1)(1A)(1B); F(No 2)A 2005, s 3(2)*].

HMRC are only liable to credit or repay an amount under these provisions if the following conditions are satisfied.

(1) *A valid claim is made*. To be valid,
- a claim must be in writing, state the amount of the claim, and explain the method used to calculate it; and
- the claimant must possess sufficient documentary evidence to substantiate the claim.

[*VATA 1994, s 80(2)(6); SI 1995/2518, Reg 37; F(No 2) A 2005, s 3(3)*].

In theory, this means that any claims not complying with these provisions can be rejected. However, in practice, many claims are not submitted strictly in accordance with these provisions and HMRC accept claims via the 'error correction notification (formerly voluntary disclosure)' route (see **56.11 RECORDS**). However, if a claim is submitted primarily to recover a sum within these provisions, it should be noted that the time limits under **51.11** below apply rather than those under the error correction notification (formerly voluntary disclosure) provisions (see **51.12** below). (HMRC VAT Guidance V1–33, para 2.5).

The only party entitled to submit a claim is the person who actually accounted for the VAT to HMRC. There is no mechanism that allows the recipient of a supply to submit refund claims. See *Aberdeen Estates Ltd* (VTD 13622) (TVC 48.18).

(2) *Unjust enrichment*. In relation to any claim under (*a*) or (*b*) above, the crediting of any amount to the claimant must not unjustly enrich it. [*VATA 1994, s 80(3); F(No 2)A 2005, s 3(5)*]. See **51.10** below for further detail on what is meant by unjust enrichment and for arrangements for reimbursing customers where a claimant accepts that, by receiving a credit, it would be unjustly enriched.

(3) *Time limit*. The claim must be made within the appropriate time limit (see **51.11** below).

Where, as a result of a claim under (*a*) or (*b*) above, HMRC accept that credit is due, they are only liable to pay (or repay) the amount due net of any VAT liabilities of the person concerned. [*VATA 1994, s 80(2A); F(No 2)A 2005, s 3(4)*].

Assessment of excess credits

See **6.5 ASSESSMENTS** for HMRC's power to make a recovery assessment when a person has been overcredited following a claim under (*a*) or (*b*) above.

Unjust enrichment

[51.10] A basic principle under EU law is that when taxes/duties have been paid contrary to EU law they should be refunded. However, it has been accepted by the ECJ that money need not be refunded if the claimant would be unjustly enriched (see *Société Comateb & others v Directeur Général des Douanes et droits indirects, ECJ Case C–192/95*, [1997] STC 1006 (TVC 22.559)).

HMRC take the term 'unjust enrichment' to apply where, by meeting a claimant's VAT claim, the claimant would be put in a better economic position than if it had not mistakenly accounted for the VAT, i.e. it would receive a 'windfall' profit.

HMRC can only successfully invoke the defence of unjust enrichment if they can show that someone other than the claimant effectively bore the burden of the VAT, i.e. that the claimant passed the VAT claimed on to its customers. (Note that it is for HMRC to prove this and not for the claimant to show that it would not be unjustly enriched if the claim were to be paid.) If HMRC can successfully show this, it is then for the claimant to produce evidence that it suffered loss or damage. If it can, the claim will be paid in part or total depending on the extent of that loss or damage. Such loss or damage cannot exceed the amount claimed, even where the actual loss and damage suffered does. [*VATA 1994, s 80(3A)–(3C); FA 1997, s 46(1)(4); F(No 2)A 2005, s 3(6)(7)*].

It cannot be assumed that any VAT charged has been passed on to customers because VAT is meant to be a tax borne by the final consumer or because it is shown on an invoice. The claimant may have absorbed the VAT by accepting a reduced margin. See HMRC VAT Guidance V1–33, para 4.4 for factors taken into account by HMRC officers in deciding whether VAT has been passed on to customers.

Arrangements for reimbursing customers

Where a claimant accepts that, by receiving a credit for (for claims made before 1 September 2005, receiving a refund of) overpaid VAT, it would be unjustly enriched, HMRC will only make the reimbursement if, on or before the time of making the claim, the claimant signs a written undertaking confirming the following.

(a) At the date of the undertaking he is able to identify the names and addresses of the customers he has reimbursed or intends to reimburse.

(b) The reimbursements will be completed by no later than 90 days after the crediting of the amount (for claims made before 1 September 2005, after the repayment) by HMRC.

(c) No deduction will be made from the 'relevant amount' by way of fee or charge (however expressed or effected). If an administration fee is charged, HMRC can recover this amount by assessment (see below).

(d) Reimbursement will be made only in cash or by cheque.

(e) Any part of the relevant amount credited to the claimant that is not reimbursed by the time limit in (*b*) above will be notified by the claimant to HMRC; and any part of the relevant amount paid (or repaid) to the claimant that is not reimbursed by the time limit in (*b*) above will be repaid by the claimant to HMRC.

(f) Any interest paid by HMRC on the relevant amount paid or repaid by them will be treated by the claimant in the same way as the relevant amount falls to be treated under (*b*) and (*c*). (The provisions do not specify how the interest is to be apportioned where some customers paid earlier than others.)

(g) The claimant will keep records of
- the names and addresses of those customers whom he has reimbursed or intends to reimburse;
- the total amount reimbursed to each such customer;
- the total amount of interest included in each total amount reimbursed to each customer; and
- the date that each reimbursement is made.

(h) The records in (*g*) above will be produced to HMRC on receipt of written notice to that effect from an HMRC officer. The notice must state the place and time at which the records are to be produced and may be given before or after HMRC have credited (for claims made before 1 September 2005, paid) the relevant amount to the claimant.

See VAT Notice 700/45/11, para 10 for the format of the undertaking.

The '*relevant amount*' means that part (which may be the whole) of the claim which the claimant has reimbursed or intends to reimburse to customers.

The claimant must

- give any notification to HMRC required under (*e*) above, and
- without prior demand, make any repayments due to HMRC under (*e*) or (*f*) above

within 14 days of the end of the 90-day period referred to in (*b*) above. Where it is not possible to make some of the refunds within this limit (e.g. because customers have moved) HMRC may agree to an extension but not an open-ended one.

[*VATA 1994, s 80A; FA 1997, s 46(2); SI 1995/2518, Regs 43A–43H; SI 1998/59; SI 1999/438; SI 2005/2231, Regs 1–9*].

Where HMRC accept that a claimant has not been unjustly enriched, the reimbursement arrangements above do not apply and no undertaking will be required. (Business Brief 4/98). The arrangements do apply to partial reimbursements. For example, if a business submits a claim for £50,000 and it is agreed that £30,000 should be passed on to customers but the remaining £20,000 can be retained, the £30,000 is subject to the scheme.

To ensure that the terms of reimbursement agreements are complied with, HMRC have powers to assess businesses which fail to reimburse their customers in the manner agreed. See **6.5 ASSESSMENTS**.

Time limit for claims

[51.11] HMRC are not liable to credit an amount to a claimant under **51.9**(*a*) or (*b*) above or repay an amount to a claimant under **51.9**(*c*) above if the claim is made more than four years (increased from three years from 1 April 2009) after the 'relevant date'. (But see below for accounting periods ending before 4 December 1996.) [*FA 2008, Sch 39 para 36; SI 2009/403*].

The 'relevant date' is

(a) in the case of a claim under **51.9**(*a*) above, the end of the VAT period there mentioned (unless (*b*) below applies);
(b) in the case of a claim under **51.9**(*a*) above in respect of an 'erroneous voluntary disclosure', the end of the VAT period in which the voluntary disclosure (now known as error correction notification) was made;
(c) in the case of a claim under **51.9**(*b*) above in respect of an assessment issued on the basis of an 'erroneous voluntary disclosure', the end of the VAT period in which the disclosure was made;
(d) in the case of a claim under **51.9**(*b*) above in any other case, the end of the VAT period in which the assessment was made; and
(e) in the case of a claim under **51.9**(*c*) above, the date on which the payment was made.

Where a claimant has ceased to be registered for VAT, any reference in (*b*) to (*d*) above to a VAT period includes a reference to a period that would have been a VAT period had the person continued to be registered.

For the above purposes, an '*erroneous voluntary disclosure*' occurs where

- a person discloses to HMRC that he has not brought into account for a VAT period (whenever ended) an amount of output tax due for the period;
- the disclosure is made in a later VAT period (whenever ended); and
- some or all of the amount is not output tax due.

[*VATA 1994, s 80(4)(4ZA)(4ZB); F(No 2)A 2005, s 3(8)*].

When is a claim made?

Generally, HMRC accept that a claim takes effect from the date on the claim, rather than the date it is received. But if it arrived (say) two weeks after it is dated, they are more likely to use the post mark as the date of the claim.

Protective claims

Legally there is no such thing as a 'protective' claim. However, HMRC accept that, with a three-year time limit for making claims, it is important for businesses to protect their positions when submitting claims subject to litigation. HMRC will hold the claim on file and reconsider it in light of any judgment that subsequently supports the validity of the claim. In the event that the judgment does go in the taxpayer's favour, the date on which the 'protective claim' was originally submitted will be treated as the effective date for the purposes of applying the time limit. If the claim is rejected, the taxpayer will have 21 days to appeal to a VAT tribunal.

HMRC will not follow this course of action in all cases. For example, they will reject speculative claims submitted on the basis that future litigation of benefit to their claim may be undertaken by an unconnected party, i.e. for a claim to be valid either the claimant must be prepared to defend the basis of the claim before a tribunal or there must already be on-going litigation.

(HMRC VAT Guidance V1–33, para 2.7).

Example

A VAT tribunal decision has ruled in favour of a taxpayer that input tax can be claimed on a particular expense, previously considered to be non-deductible. However, HMRC intend to appeal the outcome to higher courts, which may take a number of years. In such cases, it would be sensible for taxpayers affected by the decision to make a protective input tax claim in advance, so that any VAT rebate in the future will be based on the time the protective claim was made (in relation to the four-year limit) rather than when the final decision is made.

Accidental overpayment

The time limit applies even in cases where VAT is accidentally paid in error. In *R (oao British Telecommunications plc) v HMRC*, QB [2005] STC 1148 (TVC 48.52) BT, because of an error in its accounting software, made overpayments of VAT totalling over £40m between 1993 and 2003. HMRC agreed to repay some £16m but refused to repay the balance on the grounds that the claim had been made outside the statutory time limit. The court held that HMRC were entitled to make concessional repayments of VAT overpaid outside the time limit but were not obliged to do so since this would erase the statutory time limits for claims for repayment of erroneous overpayments. (Note that HMRC have now withdrawn the concession for exception to the time limit in the case of simple duplication of output tax.)

VAT periods ending before 4 December 1996

With effect from 19 March 2008, the above requirement that a claim must be made within three years of the relevant date does not apply to a claim in respect of an amount brought in account, or paid, for a VAT period ending before 4 December 1996 provided the claim is made before 1 April 2009. [*FA 2008, s 121*]. This follows the decisions in *Fleming (t/a Bodycraft) v C & E Commrs*, HL [2008] STC 324 (TVC 48.6) and *HMRC v Condé Nast Publications Ltd*, HL [2008] STC 324 (TVC 48.7). In those cases, the HL held that the three-year time limit did not apply for input tax claims in respect of which entitlement to deduct arose in accounting periods ending before 1 May 1997. HMRC, however, consider that the terms of the judgment also apply to claims to recover VAT overpaid or overdeclared in accounting periods ending before 4 December 1996 and the legislation has been amended to reflect this. Claims can be submitted to HM Revenue and Customs, 'Fleming' Claims Team (Leeds), Queens Dock, Liverpool, Merseyside L74 4AA. (HMRC Brief 7/08). See also *HMRC v Scottish Equitable plc*, CS 2 July 2009 unreported (TVC 48.57) in which the Court of Session held that the failure to provide for a transitional period did not render the three-year time limit invalid. Following this decision, HMRC consider that the effect of *FA 2008, s 121* is that all VAT claims are now capped at four years, or back to 1 April 2006, whichever is the shorter. (HMRC Brief 41/09).

Claims for refunds not falling within VATA 1994, s 80

[51.12] The provisions of *VATA 1994, s 80* described in **51.9** to **51.11** above do not cover all situations where VAT has been overpaid. Where those provisions do not apply, refund claims must be made under one of the following procedures and within the time limits as indicated in the text.

- Late claims for input tax under *SI 1995/2518, Reg 29* (see **34.9 INPUT TAX**).
- Error correction notification (formerly voluntary disclosure) under *SI 1995/2518, Regs 34, 35* (see **56.11 RECORDS**).
- Adjustments to take account of increases and decreases in consideration (e.g. following the issue of a credit/debit note) under *SI 1995/2518, Reg 38* (see **39.15 INVOICES**).
- Pre-registration expenses and post-deregistration expenses under *SI 1995/2518, Reg 111* (see **34.10 INPUT TAX** and **34.11 INPUT TAX** respectively).
- Adjustments under the capital goods scheme under *SI 1995/2518, Reg 115* (see **10.10 CAPITAL GOODS SCHEME**).
- Claims for bad debt relief under *SI 1985/2818, Reg 165A* (see **7.3 BAD DEBT RELIEF**).

There is no four-year limit (increased from three years from 1 April 2009) in the following instances.

- Claims or adjustments which cover VAT appearing on both sides of a VAT return and which therefore cancel each other out (e.g. those in respect of acquisition VAT or the reverse charge).
- Correction of tax point errors.

- (Before 1 July 2005) simple duplications of output tax.
- Returns following *compulsory* backdated registration for VAT. Where a business is registered for VAT with retrospective effect, it can claim input tax on its first return even if the VAT was incurred more than three years previously.
- Claims by DIY housebuilders.
- Penalties paid which are subsequently shown not to be due.
- Where VAT invoices are received from suppliers for supplies made more than four years (increased from three years from 1 April 2009) previously. This most commonly arises in two situations.
  (a) Late registration cases where a trader's registration is backdated more than four years (increased from three years from 1 April 2009) and he issues VAT invoices in the hope that past customers will pay the VAT element of the supplies.
  (b) Where a trader has mistakenly zero-rated a standard-rated supply and as a consequence HMRC have issued an assessment.

  In such cases, although strictly the time limit for late claims for input tax under *SI 1995/2518, Reg 29* applies, by concession, HMRC will treat the four-year time limit (increased from three years from 1 April 2009) as running from the date of receipt of the VAT invoice. They will allow input tax to be recovered by the trader's customers, subject to the normal rules, if satisfied that the trader has paid the VAT due to HMRC and the customer has paid the VAT invoice.

  The concession does not apply where a standard-rated supply was made but the customer did not receive a VAT invoice or mislaid it, and therefore failed to recover input tax. In such cases, HMRC take the view that the customer could have asked them to exercise their discretion and allow alternative evidence to recover the input tax.

(C & E News Release No 10 (Budget), 26 November 1996; Business Brief 9/97; HMRC VAT Guidance V1–33, para 7.1.5). [*FA 2008, Sch 39 para 36; SI 2009/4003*].

> *Example*
>
> John was late registering for VAT – he should have been VAT registered on 1 July 2004. His total sales to Jeff for the period covered by his first VAT return (July 2004 to March 2010) were £20,000, all subject to VAT at the standard rate. Even though some of these sales were made more than four years ago (outside of error adjustment period), John can still issue a VAT only invoice to Jeff, charging VAT on £20,000, and Jeff will pay this VAT to John and be able to reclaim input tax based on the date of the VAT only invoice. This means John is not out of pocket by having to account for output tax on the sales in question.

Summary: scenarios and particular problem areas

[51.13] In summary, there are four different scenarios for claims against HMRC.

- A claim for underclaimed input tax comes under *SI 1995/2518, Reg 29* (see **34.9 INPUT TAX**) whether it

(a) reduces the amount payable to HMRC in respect of an earlier payment return;
(b) increases the amount to which the taxpayer is entitled on an earlier repayment return; or
(c) exceeds the amount paid with an earlier return and turns it from a payment to a repayment return.

- A claim for overdeclared output tax in respect of an earlier payment return (reducing the amount payable to HMRC) comes under *VATA 1994, s 80* (see **51.9** above).
- A claim for overdeclared output tax in respect of an earlier repayment return (increasing the amount to which the taxpayer is entitled)
  (a) for claims made after 25 May 2005 comes under *VATA 1994, s 80* (see **51.9** above); and
  (b) for earlier claims came under *SI 1995/2518, Regs 34, 35* (see **56.11 RECORDS**).
- A claim for overdeclared output tax in respect of an earlier payment return where the amount claimed exceeds the amount paid with the earlier return (and turns it from a payment to a repayment return)
  (a) for claims made after 25 May 2005 comes under *VATA 1994, s 80* (see **51.9** above); and
  (b) for earlier claims, the amount of the claim that was equal to the amount paid with the return came within the scope of *VATA 1994, s 80* (see **51.9** above) and the remainder came under *SI 1995/2518, Regs 34, 35* (see **56.11 RECORDS**).

Particular problem areas

(1) Partial exemption

See **49.11**(10) **PARTIAL EXEMPTION.**

(2) Single long period returns and belated notifications of registration

Single long period returns tend to arise when a business has failed to register for VAT. Since no VAT has been accounted for or paid to HMRC, *VATA 1994, s 80* cannot apply.

- Where a business decides to voluntarily register, HMRC limits retrospective registration to a date no earlier than three years before the date of application (see **59.2 REGISTRATION**). See **34.10 INPUT TAX** for the time limit on claiming pre-registration input tax on goods and services.
- Where a business has failed to register and its registration is compulsorily backdated, the three-year capping rule does not apply and input tax should be recovered and output tax accounted for the full period (up to 20 years).

(HMRC VAT Guidance V1–33, para 6.2.3).

(3) Annual accounting

It is possible for a business using the annual accounting scheme to recover overpaid VAT for more than four years as it is not until the annual return is submitted and 'paid' that the time limit provisions can be applied.

> *Example*
> A business has an annual accounting period from 1 April 2005 to 31 March 2006. It made nine interim payments from July 2005 to March 2006 and submitted the annual return on 31 May 2006. The business has until 30 May 2009 to submit a refund claim for the period 1 April 2005 to 31 March 2006, i.e. 4 years 2 months after the start of the period.

(HMRC VAT Guidance V1–33, para 6.2.4).

(4) Payments on account (POA)

Payments on account made under *VATA 1994, s 28* (see **51.4** above) should be treated for the purposes of the three-year time limit as if they were paid on the due date for the relevant VAT return provided they are actually paid by the due date for that return. Normally, therefore, HMRC will treat a business in the POA scheme which makes

- its two monthly payments on account as required at the end of months 2 and 3 of the VAT period, and
- its correct balancing payment with the return on or before the due date,

as having paid the full VAT return liability on due date.

(HMRC VAT Guidance V1–33, para 6.2.5).

Interest, etc.

Amounts due to HMRC

[51.14] Where a business fails to submit a return and/or pay the VAT shown by the due date, it may be liable to penalty under the default surcharge provisions. See **52.21 PENALTIES**. In addition, where HMRC raise an assessment for VAT undeclared or overclaimed, they may charge interest. See **51.15** below.

Amounts due from HMRC

A business is entitled to repayment supplement where HMRC do not make any repayment due within a specified time. See **51.16** below. In other cases where, due to an error by HMRC, a business overpays output tax or underclaims input tax, HMRC must pay interest to the date of repayment. See **51.17** below.

Interest payable to HMRC (default interest)

Circumstances in which interest may be charged

[51.15] A taxable person may be charged interest in the following circumstances.

(a) Where HMRC raise an assessment for a VAT period to recover any VAT which has been underdeclared or overclaimed on a VAT return.

(b) Where HMRC raise an assessment for a VAT period in respect of which an earlier assessment has already been notified (i.e. where HMRC issue an assessment following the failure to submit a VAT return but a further assessment is necessary as the original assessment is later found to be too low).

(c) Where HMRC raise an assessment relating to a VAT period which exceeds three months and begins on the date with effect from which the person concerned was, or was required to be, registered.

(d) Where HMRC raise an assessment relating to a VAT period at the beginning of which the person concerned was, but should no longer have been, exempted from registration under *VATA 1994, Sch 1 para 14(1)* (see **59.6 REGISTRATION**), *VATA 1994, Sch 3 para 8* (see **59.22 REGISTRATION**) or *VATA 1994, Sch 3A para 7* (see **59.29 REGISTRATION**).

(e) Where, before an assessment is made under *(a)*–*(d)* above, the VAT due or other amount concerned is paid (so that no assessment is necessary).

[*VATA 1994, s 74(1)(2)*].

In general, however, HMRC only charge interest where they consider it represents '*commercial restitution*', i.e. compensation for the loss of use of any underdeclared or overclaimed VAT. They normally only charge interest if they have been deprived of this VAT for a period of time. They would not, for example, generally charge interest if an amount of VAT is underdeclared which would have been immediately reclaimable as input tax by a third party.

(VAT Notice 700/43/10, paras 2.1–2.2).

Circumstances in which interest need not be applied, or an amount chargeable to interest be reduced

If a business makes an error correction which it thinks should not attract interest, in part or in full, it should provide HMRC with as much detail as possible about the error, on a separate sheet if necessary, to enable them to make a decision about whether or not interest should be charged as commercial restitution. Similarly, the business should ensure that when HMRC find underdeclared or overclaimed VAT the officer assessing the VAT is made aware of any facts that might have a bearing on an interest charge. Generally, overclaims of input tax occur where

- evidence of entitlement is not held;
- claims are made too early;
- errors are made within the accounting system;
- claims are made on a non-deductible charge.

Where input tax is claimed by the wrong company, for example, an associated company, interest will only be charged if the other company could not immediately take full credit for that tax. Any differences in tax period groups between the business and its customer or supplier will normally be ignored when considering the need for commercial restitution.

(VAT Notice 700/43/10, para 2.3).

Circumstances in which interest will not be charged

For return net VAT errors discovered during accounting periods starting on or after 1 July 2008, whether or not the error discovered relates to a VAT return submitted prior to this date, and subject to the three-year time limit for correcting errors, these can be adjusted subject to the time limits specified within Notice 700/45 'How to correct VAT errors and make adjustments or claims'. HMRC's previous policy to not charge interest on the notification of errors on VAT returns with a net value limit of up to £2,000 has now been withdrawn. As a consequence, all error notifications (formerly known as voluntary disclosures) requiring an assessment may be subject to a default interest charge. This is regardless of the amount involved. However, net VAT errors below the limit described in the notice may continue to be corrected on a VAT return without incurring a charge to interest. In addition, interest will not be charged on the following.

- VAT declared on returns but unpaid.
- Assessments raised because a VAT return has not been rendered on time (but see (*b*) above for follow-up assessments).
- Penalties and interest.
- Amendments made to VAT returns before they are fully processed.

(VAT Notice 700/43/10, para 2.4).

From 21 July 2008, no interest is charged where HMRC agree to defer payment because of the effects of disaster designated by the Treasury as having national significance. This provision may have retrospective effect; thus the floods in the UK in June and July 2007 caused by weather conditions are a disaster that qualifies for the relief.

[*FA 2008, s 135; SI 2008/1936*].

Calculation of interest

Interest runs on the amount assessed or paid from the 'reckonable date' (even if not a business day) until the date of payment. In practice, however, interest runs to the date shown on the Notice of Assessment (Form VAT 655) or a Notification of errors in returns form. If any interest-bearing VAT shown on the Notice is not paid within 30 days, a further liability to interest arises. Interest will continue to be charged on a monthly basis and notified on Form VAT 658 or VAT 659 until all the interest-bearing VAT charged on the original assessment or error correction notification (formerly voluntary disclosure) is paid. However, interest is limited to a maximum of three years prior to the date of calculation shown on the Notice of Assessment or Notification of errors in returns form. In practice, interest will be charged where appropriate on the net amount of underdeclarations liable to interest, less any overdeclarations, for each VAT period.

The '*reckonable date*' is the latest date on which a return is required for the VAT period to which the amount assessed or paid relates (i.e. one month after the end of the period) except that

- where the amount assessed or paid is an incorrect repayment of VAT or a payment in respect of excess credits, the reckonable date is the seventh day after HMRC authorised the repayment; and

- where an assessment is made under *VATA 1994, s 73(7)* in respect of goods which cannot be accounted for (see **6.1**(*e*) **ASSESSMENTS**), the sum assessed is to be taken to relate to the period for which the assessment was made.

[*VATA 1994, ss 74(1)–(3)(5), 76(1)(7)(8), Sch 13 para 18*]. (VAT Notice 700/43/10, paras 2.5, 2.6, 2.8).

Invoices issued by unauthorised persons

Where an 'unauthorised person' issues an invoice showing an amount as being or including VAT, interest runs on the appropriate amount from the date of the invoice to the date of payment.

'*Unauthorised person*' means anyone other than

- a person registered for VAT; or
- a body corporate within a group registration; or
- a person treated as carrying on the business of a taxable person who has died or become bankrupt or incapacitated; or
- a person selling business assets of a taxable person towards satisfaction of a debt owed by that taxable person (e.g. sale of assets seized by a bailiff); or
- a person acting on behalf of the Crown.

[*VATA 1994, s 74(4)*].

Appeals, etc.

If a taxpayer disagrees with the imposition of interest or with the amount of interest charged, he may ask HMRC to reconsider the matter. This will be done by an officer not involved in the original decision.

If still not satisfied with the amount of the interest charged, the taxpayer may appeal to a VAT tribunal (see **5.3**(20) **APPEALS**). There is no right of appeal against the rate of, or liability to, interest. A tribunal can only vary the amount of interest assessed insofar as it is necessary to reduce it to an amount which is appropriate under the above provisions. [*VATA 1994, s 84(6)*].

Harmonisation of interest rates

From such a day as the Treasury may by order appoint, legislation is being introduced with the aim of harmonising the interest regime on overpayments and late payments across the range of taxes administered by HMRC. Interest is payable on any amount that is payable by a person to HMRC under or by virtue of an enactment. It is not, however, payable on itself (i.e. it applies on a simple, rather than compound, basis). It is to be paid without any deduction of income tax. Interest is payable from the 'late payment interest start date', i.e. the date on which the amount becomes due and payable, until the date on which the payment or repayment is made. However, the late payment interest start date is varied in the following circumstances.

- Where the amount due arises from an amendment or a correction to an assessment, the late interest payment start date in respect of that amount is the date which it would have been had the original assessment been correct and the amount due and payable accordingly.

- Where the amount relates to VAT due in a period during which a person should have been, but was not, registered, the late interest payment start date is the date which it would have been had the person been registered at the correct time.
- Where the amount due arises as a result of an amount described as VAT being shown on an invoice issued by an unauthorised person, the late interest payment start date in respect of that amount is the date of the invoice.

[*FA 2009, ss 101, 103, Sch 53 paras 3, 10, 11*].

De Voil Indirect Tax Service. See V5.361–365.

Repayment supplement

[51.16] Where

- a person is entitled to a repayment of VAT credits under *VATA 1994, s 25(3)*,
- a registered statutory body is entitled to a refund under *VATA 1994, s 33* (see **43.7 LOCAL AUTHORITIES AND PUBLIC BODIES**),
- a registered body is entitled to a refund under *VATA 1994, s 33A* (museums and galleries, see **34.13**(21) **INPUT TAX**), or
- from 1 April 2011, the registered proprietor of an academy is entitled to a refund under *VATA 1994, s 33B* (see **34.13**(30) **INPUT TAX**)

the payment due is increased by a supplement of 5% of that amount or £50, whichever is the greater, provided

(a) the return or claim is received by HMRC not later than the last day on which it is required to be made;
(b) HMRC do not issue a written instruction directing the making of the payment or refund due within the 'relevant period'; and
(c) the amount shown as due on the return or claim does not exceed the amount in fact due by more than 5% of that amount or £250, whichever is the greater.

The '*relevant period*' is the period of 30 days beginning with

- the date of receipt of the return or claim by HMRC; or
- the day after the last day of the VAT period to which the return or claim relates, if later.

Any supplement paid is treated (except for the purposes of determining the amount of the supplement) as an amount due by way of credit under *VATA 1994, s 25(3)* or an amount due by way of refund under *VATA 1994, ss 33, 33A or 33B* or as the case may be. Where the repayment, therefore, is not due in whole or in part and is recoverable by assessment, interest may be due on the repayment supplement as well as the VAT. See **51.15** above.

In calculating the period of 30 days referred to above, periods relating to the following are left out of account.

- The raising and answering of any reasonable inquiry relating to the return or claim in question. This period begins with the date on which HMRC first consider it necessary to make such an inquiry and ends with the date on which HMRC either satisfy themselves that they have received a complete answer to their inquiry or determine not to make the inquiry or, if they have already made it, not to pursue it further.

- The correction by HMRC of any errors or omissions in the return or claim. The period begins on the date when the error or omission first came to their notice and ends on the date when it is corrected by them.
- In a case where a person is entitled to a repayment of VAT credits, the continuing failure to submit returns in respect of an earlier VAT period. The period is determined in accordance with a certificate of HMRC issued to that effect under *VATA 1994, Sch 11 para 14(1)(b)*.
- In a case where a person is entitled to a repayment of VAT credits, failure to produce documents or give security as a condition of repayment of VAT under *VATA 1994, Sch 11 para 4(1)*. The period begins on the date of the service of the written notice of HMRC requiring the production of documents or giving of security and ends on the date when they received the required documents or the required security.

[*VATA 1994, s 79; FA 1999, s 19; FA 2001, s 98(4)–(7); FA 2011, s 76(2); SI 1995/2518, Regs 198, 199*].

For a general consideration of how VAT repayment claims are received and internally processed by HMRC and the their code of practice for dealing with repayment returns, see VAT Notice 700/58/10 *Treatment of VAT repayment returns and VAT repayment supplement*.

Repayment supplement will not be paid on

- refunds paid to EU traders;
- refunds to do-it-yourself housebuilders;
- claims relating to services received after deregistration;
- amounts notified by HMRC as overdeclared (including those resulting from error correction notifications (formerly voluntary disclosures) made in writing to HMRC); or
- claims for interest as a result of official error.

(VAT Notice 700, para 21.6).

De Voil Indirect Tax Service. See V5.191; V5.192.

Interest payable by HMRC in cases of official error

[51.17] Where, due to an error by HMRC, a person has

(a) accounted to HMRC for output tax which was not due to them and, as a result, they are liable to pay (or repay) an amount to him, or

(b) failed to claim credit for input tax to which he was entitled and which HMRC are in consequence liable to pay to him, or

(c) otherwise than under (*a*) or (*b*) paid to HMRC any VAT not due (e.g. import VAT) and which they are in consequence liable to repay, or

(d) suffered delay in receiving payment of an amount due from HMRC in connection with VAT (including, for example, a refund under the DIY builder's scheme or under (*a*) to (*c*) above but excluding any interest due under this provision), then, if they would not otherwise be liable to do so, HMRC must pay interest to him for the 'applicable period'. On 7 January 2009 legislation came into force to enable HMRC to change faster its rates of interest following a movement in market rates. Rates change 13 working days after the meeting of the Monetary Policy Committee of the Bank of England. Previously it took around a month to change the rates.

[*SI 2008/3234*].

Although not specified in the legislation, in *National Council of YMCAs Inc* (VTD 10537) (TVC 48.140), it was held that interest should be calculated on a simple rather than compound basis. However in *Sempra Metals Ltd (formerly Metallgesellschaft Ltd) v IR Commrs* [2007] STC 1559 (TVC 2.520), which related to advance corporation tax, it was held that where money has been wrongly exacted and overpaid, the payer was entitled to a remedy for the loss of use of that money. Such a remedy required the payment of interest at a commercial rate and the interest should be compounded. Following that decision, a test case (*FJ Chalke Ltd v HMRC* [2009] STC 2027 (TVC 48.146)) was brought under the VAT interest cars group litigation. The High Court held that while *VATA 1994 s 78* provided for the payment of simple interest and excluded any other remedy as a matter of domestic law, it was overridden by the principle of effectiveness where an overpayment was caused by breach of directly effective provisions of EU law. The requirement that compound interest should be paid was a requirement of EU law. However, the High Court and the Court of Appeal ([2010] EWCA Civ 313), held that the claims for the recovery of such interest were out of time under the *Limitation Act 1980, s 32(1)(c)*. See also *John Wilkins (Motor Engineers) Ltd v HMRC* [2011] EWCA Civ 429 (TVC 2.520).

The case of *Littlewoods Retail Ltd v HMRC* [2010] STC 2072 was referred to the European Court of Justice, effectively asking whether domestic legislation providing only for simple interest is compatible with EU law, and if not, whether the remedy should take the form of the payment of compound interest, or some other form. The Advocate-General has expressed the Opinion 'that a taxable person who has overpaid VAT which was collected by the Member State contrary to the requirements of EU VAT legislation has a right to reimbursement of the VAT collected in breach of EU law and a right to payment of interest on the principal sum to be reimbursed. The question whether the interest on the principal sum to be reimbursed is to be paid on the basis of a system of 'simple interest' or a system of 'compound interest' concerns the detailed rules governing the interest claim stemming from EU law, which are to be determined by the Member States in accordance with the principles of effectiveness and equivalence. If the referring court should conclude that the detailed rules governing payment of interest on VAT collected in breach of EU law at issue in the main proceedings are less favourable than the detailed rules governing similar domestic interest claims and that there is therefore a breach of the principle of equivalence, it is obliged to interpret and apply the national rules in such a way that interest is paid on the VAT collected in breach of EU law in accordance with the more favourable rules which apply to similar domestic claims.' (*Littlewoods Retail Ltd v HMRC (and related applications) (No 2), ECJ Case C-591/10, 12 January 2012, unreported*) (TVC 22.563A).

These provisions do not require HMRC to pay interest on any amount on which repayment supplement is due under **51.16** above (see *THI Leisure Two Partnership* (VTD 16876) (TVC 48.90)), or on the amount of that repayment supplement. Additionally, where a claim for any payment or repayment has to be made, interest is only due on the amount of the claim which HMRC are required to satisfy or have satisfied (i.e. interest is limited to the period for which VAT is refundable under *VATA 1994, s 80*).

Claims

Interest is only due if a claim is made in writing for that purpose. Any claim must be made within four years (increased from three years from 1 April 2009) after the end of the applicable period to which it relates. [*FA 2008, Sch 39 para 35; SI 2009/403*].

Period of interest

The '*applicable period*' is the period beginning with the date that HMRC

- under (*a*) or (*b*) above received payment, or as the case may be authorised a repayment or set off, for the return period to which the output tax or input tax related;
- under (*c*) above, received the payment; or
- under (*d*) above, might reasonably have been expected to authorise the payment or set-off in question

and ending with the date on which HMRC authorised payment of the amount on which the interest is payable. References to HMRC 'authorising' a payment of any amount include references to their discharging liability to pay that amount by way of set-off against VAT due to them. Broadly, statutory interest is therefore payable on the net amount repayable by HMRC at any particular time.

In calculating the applicable period, any period by which HMRC's authorisation of the payment of interest is delayed by the claimant's conduct is left out of account. This includes, in particular, any period referable to the following.

- Unreasonable delay in making the claim for interest or the claim for payment or repayment of the amount on which interest is claimed.
- A failure by the claimant or his representative to provide HMRC with all the information they require to determine the amount of the payment or repayment due and the interest thereon (whether at or before the time of making the claim or subsequently in response to a request by HMRC). For these purposes, there is to be taken as referable to a person's failure to provide information in response to a request by HMRC any period beginning with the date on which HMRC reasonably require the person to provide it and ending with the earliest date they could reasonably conclude that the information required has been supplied or is no longer necessary.
- The making of a claim (as part of or in association with the claim for payment or repayment or interest) to anything to which the claimant was not entitled.

Appeals

An appeal may be made to a VAT tribunal against a decision of HMRC not to pay interest under these provisions (see **5.3 APPEALS**).

[*VATA 1994, s 78; FA 1996, s 197; FA 1997, s 44; F(No 2)A 2005, s 4(2)*].

A claim for interest was upheld where HMRC incorrectly advised that input tax had to be apportioned because some of the company's income was outside the scope of VAT. This ruling (although pre-dating it) was inconsistent with the decision in *Lennartz v Finanzamt Munchen III* (see **34.7 INPUT TAX**) and led to the company failing to claim credit for input tax to which it was entitled (*North East Media Development Trust Ltd* (VTD 13104) (TVC 48.124)). Following the decision, the company claimed interest on the whole of the input tax which HMRC had wrongly refused to repay. However, the tribunal upheld HMRC's contention that interest should be computed upon an amount equal to the net overpayment of VAT (*North East Media Development Trust Ltd* (VTD 13425) (TVC 48.142)).

A claim for interest was also upheld where the organisation contended that a HMRC leaflet had not been updated and that it had been misled by a VAT officer (*Wydale Hall* (VTD 14273) (TVC 48.137)).

Assessment of overpaid interest

See **6.5 ASSESSMENTS** for HMRC's power to assess for interest that has been overpaid to a claimant under the above provisions.

Harmonisation of interest rates

From a date to be appointed, legislation is being introduced with the aim of harmonising the interest regime on overpayments and late payments across the range of taxes administered by HMRC. Interest is payable on any amount (other than certain amounts which have no relevance to VAT) that is payable (including by set-off) by HMRC to any person under or by virtue of an enactment, and on a 'relevant amount' paid by a person to HMRC that is repaid (including by set-off) by HMRC to that person or another person. Interest is not, however, payable on an amount payable in consequence of an order or judgment of a court having power to allow interest on the amount. Nor is it payable on itself (i.e. it applies on a simple, rather than compound, basis). Interest is payable from the 'repayment interest start date' until the date on which the payment or repayment is made (or set off). Where the amount in question has been paid to HMRC the repayment interest start date is the later of:

- the date on which the amount was so paid; and
- (where applicable) the date on which an amount, paid in connection with a liability to make payment to HMRC which is to be repaid, became due and payable to HMRC.

Where the amount in question has not been paid to HMRC and is payable by virtue of the filing of a return or the making of a claim, the repayment interest start date is the later of:

- the date (if any) on which the return was required to be filed or the claim was required to be made; and
- the date on which the return was in fact filed or the claim was in fact made.

[*FA 2009, ss 102, 103, Sch 54 paras 2–5*].

De Voil Indirect Tax Service. See V5.196.

Key points

[51.18] Points to consider are as follows.

- Be aware that for VAT periods ending March 2010 or later, the payment due on the return (in relation to paper returns) must be made so that it clears HMRC's bank account by the due date of the return, rather than just be received by this date. This means a business will need to submit the return and payment an extra three working days before the due date to meet this requirement.
- A condition of online filing of VAT returns is that any tax due must also be paid by electronic means. The easiest option is to pay by direct debit because the tax is then taken automatically from a taxpayer's bank account, without any instruction being needed for the bank.
- If a business cannot pay the VAT it owes on a return, it should still submit the return and then seek to negotiate a time-to-pay agreement with HMRC's BPSS (Business Payment Support Service).
- If an agreement is reached with the BPSS before the tax is legally due for payment, this will avoid a default surcharge or liability notice being incurred (this statement is correct at time of publication but current HMRC policy must be checked).
- A benefit of electronic filing and payment of tax is that an extra seven calendar days are given to pay the tax due. If the seventh day falls on a weekend, then payment must be received in HMRC's bank account by the end of the previous working day.
- If a business that files its VAT returns online chooses the direct debit payment option, it will receive an additional three working days (in addition to the seven calendar days) before payment is taken from its account. If two weekend days are included within the three extra days, this extends to five calendar days, i.e. by the 12th day of the following month.
- A business with an annual VAT liability of £2m or more must make payments on account (POAs) to effectively pay VAT to HMRC on a monthly rather than quarterly basis. These payments must be made by electronic means.
- If a business has incorrectly accounted for output tax on zero-rated or exempt sales (or possibly charged standard-rated VAT on a reduced rated supply), then it will need to consider whether any such VAT needs to be repaid to the customer (when reclaimed

from HMRC) rather than retained in the business as a cash windfall. This challenge is known as 'unjust enrichment' and means that a business cannot profit out of making VAT errors.

- The key challenge for a business in an 'unjust enrichment' situation is to be able to show that it absorbed the incorrect VAT charge within its selling price, rather than added VAT on a cost-plus basis.
- If a business has to repay VAT to its customers under the unjust enrichment rules, it cannot deduct an administration fee for the time spent co-ordinating claims. The entire VAT amount must be passed back to customers.
- Interest charged by HMRC when they raise an assessment for underpaid tax in a previous period is not classed as a penalty. It is classed as commercial restitution to recognise the fact that the money should have been in HMRC's bank account (rather than the taxpayer's account) in an earlier period.
- A business can adjust past VAT errors on the next VAT return it submits, as long as the net value of the error (or errors) is less than £10,000 or less than £50,000 and 1% of the Box 6 outputs figure for the return where the correction is being made.
- It is important to identify when errors can be included on a VAT return because this adjustment will automatically avoid any default interest being charged. Any tax underpayment separately notified to HMRC (i.e. on form VAT652) will be subject to default interest in most cases.

52

Penalties

De Voil Indirect Tax Service. See V5.3.

Criminal offences and penalties

[52.1] Criminal proceedings may be brought under the offences in **52.2** to **52.8** below. Most VAT defaults are, however, dealt with by civil penalties and only serious cases of fraudulent VAT evasion are investigated as criminal matters. The proceedings may only be instituted by HMRC or a law officer of the Crown.

Except as otherwise provided,

- proceedings for an indictable offence must be commenced within 20 years of the date when the offence was committed; and
- proceedings for a summary offence must be commenced within three years of that date but, subject to that, may be commenced at any time within six months from the date on which sufficient evidence to warrant the proceedings came to the knowledge of the prosecuting authority. For these purposes, a certificate of the prosecuting authority as to the date on which the evidence came to its knowledge is conclusive evidence of the fact.

There are further detailed provisions relating to service of process, place of trial, non-payment of penalties, application of penalties, proof of certain documents and other procedural matters. [*CEMA 1979, ss 145–151, 153–155; VATA 1994, s 72(12)*].

False statements

False statements to the prejudice of the Crown and public revenue are indictable as a criminal offence (*R v Hudson*, CCA 1956, 36 TC 561). False statements may also involve liability to imprisonment for up to two years, under the *Perjury Act 1911, s 5*, for 'knowingly and wilfully' making materially false statements, etc. for VAT purposes.

De Voil Indirect Tax Service. See V5.301–318.

Fraudulent evasion of VAT

[52.2] A person who is knowingly concerned in, or in taking steps with a view to, the fraudulent 'evasion of VAT' by him or any other person, is liable

- on summary conviction, to a penalty of the 'statutory maximum' or three times the 'amount of VAT', whichever is the greater, *or* imprisonment for a term not exceeding six months *or* to both; or
- on conviction on indictment, to a penalty of any amount *or* to imprisonment for a term not exceeding seven years *or* to both.

'*Evasion of VAT*' includes obtaining

(i) a payment of a VAT credit;
(ii) a refund under *VATA 1994, s 35* (do-it-yourself housebuilders), *VATA 1994, s 36* or *VATA 1983, s 22* (bad debts) or *VATA 1994, s 40* (new means of transport supplied to another EU country by a non-taxable person);

(iii) a refund under regulations made by virtue of *VATA 1994, s 13(5)* (VAT paid in the UK on an acquisition from another EU country where VAT has already been paid in that other country); or
(iv) a repayment under *VATA 1994, s 39* (repayment of VAT to those in business overseas).

'*Amount of VAT*' in relation to a payment within (i) above is the aggregate of the amount (if any) falsely claimed as input tax and the amount (if any) by which output tax was falsely understated. In relation to a refund or repayment within (ii) to (iv) above, it is the amount falsely claimed.

[*VATA 1994, s 72(1)(2)*].

'*Statutory maximum*' is currently £5,000.

Nothing in the above denies the right for an assessment to be made in respect of the VAT actually evaded.

'*Evasion*' includes deliberate non-payment of VAT and it is not necessary to show any permanent intention to deprive (*R v Dealy, CA Criminal Division 1994*, [1995] STC 217 (TVC 49.10)).

'*Taking of steps*' to evade VAT need not necessarily be confined to the taking of positive steps (*R v McCarthy*, CA Criminal Division [1981] STC 298 (TVC 49.1)).

The existence of the above provisions does not rule out the possibility of conviction under the common law offence of cheating the public revenue. This offence is preserved by the *Theft Act 1968, s 32(1)* and can include any form of fraudulent conduct which results in diverting money from the public revenue and in depriving the public revenue of money to which it is entitled. In practice, the common law charge is reserved for serious cases and the penalties, including imprisonment, are unlimited. No positive act of deception is required. An omission to do an act is sufficient. See *R v Mavji*, CA [1986] STC 508 (TVC 49.25) and *R v Redford*, CA [1988] STC 845 (TVC 49.26).

Where appropriate, HMRC's policy is to deal with fraud under the civil provisions (see **52.10** below) which are more cost-effective. Criminal investigation will be reserved for cases where HMRC needs to send a strong deterrent message or where the conduct involved is such that only a criminal sanction is appropriate. Examples of the kind of circumstances in which HMRC will generally consider commencing criminal, rather than civil, investigations are

- in cases of organised criminal gangs attacking the tax system or systematic frauds where losses represent a serious threat to the tax base, including conspiracy;
- where an individual holds a position of trust or responsibility;
- where materially false statements are made or materially false documents are provided in the course of a civil investigation;
- where, pursuing an avoidance scheme, reliance is placed on a false or altered document or such reliance or material facts are misrepresented to enhance the credibility of a scheme;
- where deliberate concealment, deception, conspiracy or corruption is suspected;

- in cases involving the use of false or forged documents;
- in cases involving importation or exportation breaching prohibitions and restrictions;
- in cases involving money laundering with particular focus on advisors, accountants, solicitors and others acting in a 'professional' capacity who provide the means to put tainted money out of reach of law enforcement;
- where the perpetrator has committed previous offences or there is a repeated course of unlawful conduct or previous civil action;
- in cases involving theft, or the misuse or unlawful destruction of HMRC documents;
- where there is evidence of assault on, threats to, or the impersonation of HMRC officials; and
- where there is a link to suspected wider criminality, whether domestic or international, involving offences not under the administration of HMRC.

When considering whether a case should be investigated under the civil procedures or be the subject of a criminal investigation, one factor will be whether the taxpayer has made a complete and unprompted disclosure of the offences committed.

However, there are certain fiscal offences where HMRC will not usually adopt the civil procedure. Examples of these are:

- VAT missing trader Intra-Community (MTIC) fraud;
- VAT 'bogus' registration repayment fraud; and
- organised tax credit fraud.

(HMRC criminal investigation policy statement).

Compounding

Under *CEMA 1979, s 152*, HMRC may accept a financial settlement (a '*compound settlement*') in lieu of criminal proceedings. This saves time and money for both the taxpayer and HMRC by avoiding the need for legal proceedings. HMRC do not offer a compound settlement in all cases and will normally prosecute where a HMRC officer has been assaulted or obstructed or the taxpayer is subject to a suspended prison sentence, on parole, an undischarged bankrupt (in liquidation if a limited company), a persistent offender or is being investigated for other related offences (whether by HMRC, the police or other government departments).

Each case is considered on its merits but HMRC will take into account the seriousness of the offence; the penalty that a court might impose; the nature and value of the goods and the amount of tax/duty involved; the costs of investigating the offence; any aggravating circumstances; and the ability of the taxpayer to pay.

HMRC may disclose details of a compound settlement to the courts (if prosecuted for a similar offence in the next five years); an employer; other government departments whose statutory responsibilities are directly affected by the actions involved; and Parliament or the media (if in the public interest).

(HMRC Notice 12).

De Voil Indirect Tax Service. See V5.311.

Offences relating to documents and statements

False documents and statements

[52.3] Any person who

(a) produces, furnishes, sends or otherwise makes use of, for the purposes of VAT, any document which is false in a material particular with the intent to deceive or secure that a machine will respond to the document as if it were a true document; or
(b) causes a document to be produced, etc. as in (*a*) above; or
(c) makes any statement in furnishing information for the purposes of VAT which he knows to be false in a material particular *or* who recklessly makes a statement which is false in a material particular,

is liable

- on summary conviction, to a penalty of the 'statutory maximum' (see **52.2** above) *or* to imprisonment for a term not exceeding six months *or* to both. Where the document referred to is a return *or* a refund or repayment under **52.2**(ii)–(iv) above *or* the information under (*c*) above is contained in or relevant to such a document, an alternative penalty of three times the amount falsely claimed is, if greater, substituted for the statutory maximum; or
- on conviction on indictment, to a penalty of any amount *or* to imprisonment for a term not exceeding seven years *or* to both.

[*VATA 1994, s 72(3)–(7)*].

Concealing documents following information notice

[52.4] From 1 April 2009, a person who conceals, destroys or otherwise disposes of a document covered by an information notice (see **31.6 HMRC: POWERS**) which has been approved by the First-tier Tribunal is guilty of an offence. A person is also guilty of an offence if they conceal, etc. a document after an HMRC officer has informed them in writing that that document is likely to be the subject of an information notice and the officer intends to seek the First-tier Tribunal's approval to the giving of the notice. Punishment for the offence is a fine or imprisonment or both, depending on the nature of the conviction.

[*FA 2008, Sch 36 paras 53–55; SI 2009/404*].

De Voil Indirect Tax Service. See V5.312; V5.313.

Conduct which must have involved an offence

[52.5] Where a person's conduct during any specified period must have involved the commission by him of one or more offences under **52.2** or **52.3–52.4** above, then, whether or not the particulars of the offence are known, he is guilty of an offence and liable

- on summary conviction, to a penalty of the greater of the 'statutory maximum' (see **52.2** above) and three times the amount of any VAT that was, or was intended to be, evaded by his conduct *or* to imprisonment for a term not exceeding six months *or* to both; or
- on conviction on indictment, to a penalty of any amount *or* to imprisonment for a term not exceeding seven years *or* to both.

See **52.2** above for 'evasion of VAT'.

[*VATA 1994, s 72(8)*].

De Voil Indirect Tax Service. See V5.314.

Knowledge that evasion intended

[52.6] A person who acquires possession of, or deals with, any goods or accepts the supply of services, having reason to believe that VAT on the supply, acquisition or importation has been or will be evaded, is liable to a penalty on summary conviction of the greater of level 5 on the 'standard scale' or three times the amount of the VAT evaded. [*VATA 1994, s 72(10)*].

'*Standard scale*' can be altered by statutory instrument and level 5 is currently £5,000.

De Voil Indirect Tax Service. See V5.316.

Failure to provide security

[52.7] A person who supplies, or after 9 April 2003 is supplied with, goods or services in contravention of a requirement to give security under *VATA 1994, Sch 11 para 4(2)* (see **31.1**(*c*) **HMRC: POWERS**) is liable to a penalty of level 5 on the standard scale (see **52.6** above). [*VATA 1994, s 72(11); FA 2003, s 17(5)*].

De Voil Indirect Tax Service. See V5.317.

Obstruction of officers

[52.8] A person commits an offence if, without reasonable excuse, he obstructs an HMRC officer or a person acting on behalf of or assisting an HMRC officer. Any person found guilty of such an offence is liable, on summary conviction, to imprisonment for up to 51 weeks or a fine up to level three on the 'standard scale' or both. The standard scale can be altered by statutory instrument and level 3 is currently £1,000. [*CRCA 2005, s 31*].

Before the merger of the Inland Revenue and Customs, any person who obstructed, hindered, molested, or assaulted a Customs officer or did anything which was likely to impede any search or production of evidence was liable, on summary conviction, to a penalty of £2,500 or imprisonment for a term not exceeding three months or to both, or, on conviction on indictment, to a penalty of any amount or to imprisonment for a term not exceeding two years or to both. [*CEMA 1979, s 16 repealed by CRCA 2005, Sch 4 para 21*].

Civil penalties

[52.9] In addition to the criminal penalties under **52.1** to **52.8** above, there are also civil penalties and surcharges. These are detailed in **52.10** to **52.29** below.

Reasonable excuse for conduct

No penalty or surcharge arises under **52.12** to **52.21** and **52.23** to **52.28** below if the person concerned can satisfy HMRC, or on appeal a tribunal, that there is a reasonable excuse for his conduct. Although 'reasonable excuse' is not defined (and, therefore, to be determined by HMRC or a tribunal) the following are not to be taken as a reasonable excuse.

- An insufficiency of funds to pay any VAT due.
- Where reliance is placed on 'any other person' to perform any task, the fact of that reliance or any other dilatoriness or inaccuracy on the part of the person relied upon. See *C & E Commrs v Harris and Another*, QB [1989] STC 907 (TVC 51.88). '*Any other person*' is not restricted to outside advisers and includes a company's accountant (*Profile Security Services Ltd v C & E Commrs*, QB [1996] STC 808 (TVC 18.589)).

[*VATA 1994, s 71(1)*].

It is necessary to distinguish between the reason and the excuse. Although insufficiency of funds by itself is not a reasonable excuse, where the shortfall is totally unforeseen and not due to the normal hazards of trade (e.g. the dishonesty of a former employee) the defence of reasonable excuse may possibly be invoked (*C & E Commrs v Salevon Ltd*, QB [1989] STC 907 (TVC 18.312)). See also *C & E Commrs v Steptoe*, CA [1992] STC 757 (TVC 18.330) where it was held that there was reasonable excuse where the taxpayer was unable to pay the VAT due because the customer for whom he worked almost exclusively was persistently late in paying invoices. The correct test is whether, given the exercise of reasonable foresight, due diligence and a proper regard for the fact that the VAT will become due on a particular date, the lack of funds which led to the default was reasonably avoidable.

HMRC have indicated the following *guidelines* on the interpretation of 'reasonable excuse' although any decision will be judged by HMRC or a VAT tribunal on the circumstances of the individual case.

(a) **Reasonable excuse for late registration**

- *Compassionate circumstances* where an individual is totally responsible for running a small business and he, or a member of his immediate family, was seriously ill or recovering from such an illness at the time notification was required.
- *Doubt about liabilities of supplies* where there is written evidence of an enquiry to HMRC about the liability of supplies and liability has remained in doubt.
- *Uncertainty about employment status* where there are genuine doubts as to whether a person is employed or self-employed or where correspondence with HMRC can be produced about these doubts.

(VAT Notice 700/41/11, para 4.1).

(b) **Reasonable excuse for not sending in return or paying VAT on time**
- *Computer breakdown* where the essential records are held on computer and it breaks down either just before or during the preparation of the return. Reasonable steps to correct the fault must be taken.
- *Illness* of the person normally responsible for preparing the return provided it can be shown that no-one else was capable of completing the return. If the illness is prolonged, reasonable steps to get someone else to complete the return must be taken.
- *Loss of key personnel* responsible for preparing the return at short notice where there is no-one else to complete it on time.
- *Unexpected cash crisis* where funds are unavailable to pay VAT because of the sudden reduction or withdrawal of overdraft facilities, sudden non-payment by a normally reliable customer, insolvency of a large customer, fraud, burglary or act of God such as fire.
- *Loss of records.* The excuse only applies if records for the current VAT period are stolen or destroyed. If records relating to a future VAT return are lost, HMRC must be notified immediately. If the records are elsewhere (e.g. with accountants or the Revenue) it is the taxpayer's responsibility to get them, or copies of them, back.

HMRC will take into account whether the circumstances could have been foreseen and, if so, what steps were taken to make alternative arrangements; whether HMRC was contacted for help or advice; whether sufficient priority was given to completing the VAT return; and whether a reasonable estimate of the VAT was paid by the due date.

(VAT Notice 700/50/11, paras 6.2, 6.3).

There have been numerous tribunal decisions as to whether, on the facts of a particular case, there is a reasonable excuse against the assessment of a penalty. For a summary of these see the chapters **DEFAULT SURCHARGE, PENALTIES: FAILURE TO NOTIFY, ETC., PENALTIES: MISDECLARATION** and **PENALTIES: REGULATORY PROVISIONS** in *Tolley's VAT Cases*.

Example

John is VAT-registered and has submitted two VAT returns late:

- The first return was late because on the day before the return was due, the business computer system crashed and an engineer had to collect the computer and take it away for five days.
- The next return was late because John's bookkeeper was on holiday for a week and was therefore not available during the last week of the month when the figures needed to be calculated and the return submitted to HMRC.

The computer crash would almost certainly be classed as a reasonable excuse if John could confirm the problem he encountered to HMRC with an engineer's report, invoice for subsequent repair cost etc. The bookkeeper's holiday would definitely not be a reasonable excuse because alternative arrangements should have been made.

> In the case of the computer breakdown, John could have liaised with HMRC about estimating the VAT figures for the period in question, and then declaring an exact figure on the return for the following period.

Mitigation

See **52.30** below.

Right of set-off

See **51.6 PAYMENT OF VAT.**

De Voil Indirect Tax Service. See V5.335.

VAT evasion

[52.10] **Note:** Where conduct involving dishonesty relates to an inaccuracy in a document or a failure to notify HMRC of an underassessment, the provisions in *VATA 1994, ss 60, 61* below are being phased and out replaced by new provisions in *FA 2007, s 97, Sch 24*. See **52.13** below for the replacement provisions although it should be noted that no person is liable for a penalty under those provisions in respect of a VAT period for which a return is required to be made before 1 April 2009. [*SI 2008/568*].

Conduct involving dishonesty

Subject to the note above, cases of VAT evasion are normally dealt with under the following civil provisions but, for aggravated or serious offences, the matter may be investigated for criminal proceedings. See **52.2** above for criminal proceedings and an indication of where cases are likely to be dealt with as such.

Where

(a) for the purpose of 'evading VAT', a person does any act or omits to take any action; and
(b) his conduct involves dishonesty (whether or not it is such as to give rise to criminal liability),

he is liable to a penalty equal to 'the amount of the VAT evaded' (or sought to be evaded). However, where he is convicted of a criminal offence by reason of conduct within (*a*) and (*b*) above, he is not also liable to a penalty under these provisions.

'*Evading VAT*' includes dishonestly obtaining a VAT credit; a refund under *VATA 1994, s 35* (do-it-yourself builders), *VATA 1994, s 36* or *VATA 1983, s 22* (bad debts) or *VATA 1994, s 40* (new means of transport supplied to another EU country by a non-taxable person); a refund under regulations made by virtue of *VATA 1994, s 13(5)* (VAT paid in the UK on an acquisition from another EU country where VAT has already been paid in that other country on the acquisition); and a repayment under *VATA 1994, s 39* (repayment of VAT to those in business overseas).

'*The amount of VAT evaded*' is the amount falsely claimed by way of credit for input tax (including any amount claimed as a deduction from VAT due) or the amount by which output tax is falsely understated *or* the amount falsely claimed by way of refund or repayment.

In any criminal proceedings against the person concerned in respect of any offence in connection with VAT or in any proceedings against him for recovery of any sum due, statements made or documents produced on his behalf are not inadmissible on the grounds that he was (or may have been) induced to make or produce them after it had been brought to his attention that

(i) HMRC might assess a civil penalty rather than bring criminal proceedings against him if he made a full confession of any dishonest conduct and gave full facilities for investigation; or
(ii) the penalties might be mitigated.

[*VATA 1994, ss 60, 71(2)*].

For a consideration of the test of 'dishonesty' see *dicta* of Lord Lane in *R v Ghosh*, CA [1982] 2 All ER 689 (TVC 50.29). It is dishonest if a company officer signs a return containing a mis-statement and he has no honest belief in the truth of the statement he has made, and in particular if he makes the statement recklessly, not caring whether it is true or false. See *Adam Geoffrey & Co (Management) Ltd* (VTD 16074) (TVC 3.103) where the accountant had not declared a sale of a property on a company's return and the controlling director had signed the return without checking its contents and ensuring that they were complete and correct.

The penalty can be applied in cases of non-registration and is not restricted to cases where there has been a fraudulent understatement of output tax or overstatement of input tax (*CS Stevenson v C & E Commrs*, CA [1996] STC 1096 (TVC 50.1)).

Liability of directors, etc.

Where the conduct of a body corporate gives rise to a penalty under the above provisions and it appears to HMRC that that conduct, in whole or part, is attributable to the dishonesty of a person who is (or at the material time was) a director or 'managing officer' (the named officer) of the body corporate, HMRC may serve a notice on the named officer proposing to recover all or part of the penalty from him. The portion specified is then assessable and recoverable as if the named officer were personally liable to that part of the penalty. The body corporate is then only assessed on the balance, if any, and is discharged from liability on the amount assessed on the named officer.

The body corporate may appeal against HMRC's decision as to its liability to the penalty and against the amount of the full penalty as if it were specified in an assessment. The named officer may appeal against the decision that the conduct of the body corporate is, in whole or part, attributable to his dishonesty and against the portion of the penalty which HMRC propose to recover from him. Otherwise, there are no grounds for appeal.

'*Managing officer*' means any manager, secretary or other similar officer of the body corporate and any person purporting to act in any such capacity or as a director. Where the affairs of a body corporate are managed by its members, the provisions apply in relation to the conduct of a member in connection with his functions of management as if he were a director of the body corporate.

[*VATA 1994, s 61*].

The notification of liability to a director, etc must show both the amount of the basic penalty and the portion of it which HMRC propose to recover from that director (*MK & ME Nazif* (VTD 13616) (TVC 50.5)). See *C & E Commrs v Bassimeh*, CA 1996, [1997] STC 33 (TVC 50.3) for apportionment of penalties where there is more than one culpable director.

Standard of proof

In a civil action, the plaintiff has to establish its case on the 'balance of probabilities' whereas in a criminal action the standard of proof required by the prosecution is 'beyond reasonable doubt'. In *First Indian Cavalry Club Ltd v C & E Commrs*, CS 1997, [1998] STC 293 (TVC 50.70) it was held that Parliament had clearly intended the standard of proof for penalties under *VATA 1994, s 60* to be the normal civil standard of the balance of probabilities. See now, however, *C & E Commrs v Han & Yau (and related appeals)*, CA [2001] STC 1188 (TVC 34.5). The tribunal applied the guidelines in *Engel v Netherlands*, ECHR 1980, 1 EHRR 647, namely that in deciding whether a penalty was civil or criminal, the criteria to be considered were the classification of the proceedings in domestic law, the nature of the offence, and the severity of the penalty which may be imposed. On this basis, the tribunal held that the penalties were 'criminal charges' within *European Convention of Human Rights, Art 6*. The Court of Appeal, by a majority, upheld this decision but made it clear that not all civil penalties would be so categorised. The effect of this decision is that statements made with a view to reducing the civil penalty under any 'offence' under *VATA 1994, s 60* may not be admissible because the makers of such statements were induced to do so by statements from HMRC that co-operation would reduce the penalty imposed. However, the Court of Appeal indicated that, if matters were made clear to the taxpayer at the time when the nature and effect of the inducement procedure were also made clear to him, it is difficult to see that there would be any breach of *Article 6*. Even if the *Police and Criminal Evidence Act* were applicable, it was most unlikely that a court or tribunal would rule inadmissible any statements made or documents produced as a result.

See also *Georgiou and another (t/a Mario's Chippery) v UK*, [2001] STC 80 (TVC 34.1).

Civil investigation into cases of suspected fraud

[52.11] HMRC use Code of Practice 9 (COP9) (2012) to investigate suspected serious fraud where, for policy operational reasons, they consider it inappropriate to start a criminal investigation. Where COP9 is employed, the investigation will cover all taxes (direct and indirect). Because the cost to the taxpayer and time involved make it impractical to use this procedure for lower value cases, especially when those cases only involve a single tax, there is an alternative procedure (from 1 September 2007) for compliance checks into indirect tax matters outside of Code of Practice 9 (2012). The two procedures are outlined below.

(1) Code of Practice 9 (2012)

The HMRC Investigation of Fraud Statement

- HMRC reserve complete discretion to pursue a criminal investigation with a view to prosecution where they consider it necessary and appropriate.
- In cases where a criminal investigation is not commenced, HMRC may decide to investigate using the COP9 investigation of fraud procedure.
- Under the investigation of fraud procedure, the recipient of COP9 is given the opportunity to make a complete and accurate disclosure of all irregularities in his tax affairs.
- Where the recipient fails to make a full disclosure of the tax frauds he has committed, HMRC reserve the right to commence a criminal investigation with a view to prosecution.
- In the course of the COP9 investigation, if the recipient makes materially false or misleading statements, or provides materially false documents HMRC reserve the right to commence a criminal investigation into that conduct as a separate criminal offence.

HMRC issues the COP9 in selected cases where they suspect tax fraud. In many cases they carry out criminal investigations of suspected fraud, with a view to prosecution. But under the Code, they offer the taxpayer instead the chance to make a full disclosure under a contractual arrangement, called a Contractual Disclosure Facility (CDF). The taxpayer has 60 days to respond. If the taxpayer makes a full disclosure of all tax frauds and irregularities, HMRC will not pursue a criminal investigation with a view to prosecution.

HMRC expect the taxpayer to stop any fraud immediately. A specially trained authorised officer will handle the COP9 investigation into the taxpayer's tax affairs and the taxpayer will be given a named contact. If the taxpayer co-operates fully with the investigation, he will achieve a greater reduction in any penalty found to be due, and he may be able to avoid other civil sanctions such as insolvency and, in some cases, the publication of his name and details. The taxpayer must read the Code of Practice carefully and discuss it with his tax adviser, if he has one. He must keep all existing records, including any computer records, during the investigation whether or not he is required to do so by law. HMRC may ask to see his business and private financial records. This Code applies to all tax frauds that the taxpayer have been involved in.

Suspicion of fraud

Where HMRC has information that gives them reason to suspect that the taxpayer has committed tax fraud, they will not usually tell him what their suspicions are: it is for the taxpayer to decide to make a disclosure. HMRC will keep an open mind to the possibility that there may be an innocent explanation for the suspected fraud, and will treat the taxpayer fairly and politely, and in accordance with the law. They will investigate the suspected tax fraud, with or without the taxpayer's co-operation. If the taxpayer does not co-operate HMRC may

- commence their own investigation which may ultimately be a criminal investigation
- obtain information about the taxpayer's financial and business affairs from third parties
- take formal action including raising assessments for the tax and interest HMRC consider is due
- charge significantly higher penalties
- commence legal proceedings to secure some or all of the taxpayer's assets
- require a financial security against certain unpaid taxes and duties.

Appointing an agent or adviser

The taxpayer is strongly advised to seek independent professional advice. If he already has an appointed adviser he should contact them immediately. However, many people find it helpful to appoint a specialist adviser who is familiar with the Code, in addition to their regular adviser. If the taxpayer wants HMRC to deal directly with his adviser on all matters covered by the Code, he must make sure he has given HMRC full authority to do so. The taxpayer must give his adviser all the facts because the taxpayer is personally responsible for his tax affairs and the accuracy of the information supplied to HMRC. HMRC expect high standards from the taxpayer's appointed representative. While HMRC will normally deal with them directly, if there are any delays or problems HMRC will contact the taxpayer. Any costs that the taxpayer incurs in connection with HMRC's enquiries cannot be claimed as an expense against tax.

Contractual disclosure facility (CDF)

The CDF offers the taxpayer the chance to disclose any tax fraud he has been involved in. This offer expires 60 days after the taxpayer receives HMRC's letter making the offer. In exchange for the taxpayer's undertaking, HMRC agree that they will not pursue a criminal investigation into the tax frauds the taxpayer discloses. The taxpayer undertakes to make a full disclosure of all his tax irregularities under the terms of the CDF. To comply with the taxpayer's undertaking, he needs to complete the two disclosure stages

- a valid outline disclosure of the tax frauds ('outline disclosure')
- a certified statement that the taxpayer has made a full, complete and accurate disclosure of all tax irregularities together with certified statements of his assets and liabilities, and of all bank accounts and credit cards he has operated ('formal disclosure').

This is the only way that the taxpayer can be certain that HMRC will not carry out a criminal investigation into the tax frauds HMRC suspect.

The CDF is only suitable for the taxpayer if he

- has committed tax fraud
- wishes to fully disclose the tax frauds that he has committed
- will work with HMRC to put his tax affairs in order (including paying any tax, interest and penalty due), and
- stops any continuing fraud immediately.

The CDF is not appropriate for people who want to disclose only careless errors, mistakes, or avoidance arrangements.

Effect of entering into a contract

To comply with his undertaking, the taxpayer will be admitting that tax has been lost due to his deliberate actions. This means HMRC may be able to seek recovery of evaded tax, interest and associated penalties for as far back as 20 years. Full co-operation with the enquiries will ensure the penalties are closer to the minimum penalty levels.

Outline disclosure

The taxpayer must make a valid outline disclosure within 60 days of the date he receives HMRC's offer (this is the same date as the time given for the taxpayer to decide whether to accept the offer). The disclosure should include the following.

- Description of the fraud, giving enough information to identify the fraudulent conduct including—what the taxpayer did; how he did it; the involvement of other people and entities; how he benefited from the conduct. This must be done for each separate tax fraud committed at any time.
- Entities involved.
- Period of fraud.
- Other information, e.g. an indication of the amounts understated and the tax involved; or a description of what records used to disguise what the taxpayer was doing.

Formal disclosure

Where the fraud is self-contained and easily quantified, there may be little further work for the taxpayer to do following his outline disclosure. He will need to agree what he owes, arrange payment and certify that he has disclosed all irregularities. This is the taxpayer's formal disclosure. In most cases, much more work will be necessary before the taxpayer will be in a position to make his formal disclosure. HMRC will expect him to prepare a disclosure report, as this is the best way to ensure that this work is done properly. A typical disclosure report will normally contain

- a brief business history
- a description of all tax irregularities (including any innocent or careless errors) and how any fraud was carried out
- quantification of all the irregularities
- information to show how you quantified the irregularities and ensured that nothing had been missed.
- summaries of tax and/or duties, interest and penalties due

- a reconciliation of his irregularities figure with the summary of tax and/or duties
- a certified statement of his worldwide assets and liabilities
- certificates of bank accounts and credit cards operated.

Making the taxpayer's formal disclosure does not signify the end of the investigation, but it does mean he has complied with his CDF undertaking.

Denial route

If the taxpayer does not believe that he has been involved in tax fraud he can sign and return the CDF denial letter, within the same 60-day period. By engaging and co-operating fully with HMRC from the start the taxpayer will increase the possibility that HMRC can resolve the enquiry quickly and HMRC may not need to use their formal powers and procedures. Where HMRC verify and accept his denial, they will issue confirmation that they no longer suspect the taxpayer of tax fraud. The taxpayer should only choose the denial route if he genuinely believes that he has not committed any tax fraud. If he signs the denial letter, HMRC can commence a criminal investigation into the tax frauds they suspect at any time. When HMRC receive a denial letter in response to their offer, the taxpayer's case may be referred to a criminal investigation team. HMRC are not obliged to tell the taxpayer if they start a criminal investigation. The denial letter may also be used in court or tribunal proceedings as evidence. If HMRC decide to proceed with a civil investigation in response to the taxpayer's denial they reserve the right to escalate the case to a criminal investigation at a later date if they consider it appropriate. Denying tax fraud that the taxpayer is later found to have been involved in may result in a criminal investigation with a view to prosecution, or significantly higher civil financial penalties, and the potential publication of the taxpayer's details.

Non-co-operation route

If HMRC have not heard from the taxpayer 60 days after he receives their offer then he is deemed to have chosen not to co-operate. HMRC will begin a criminal or a civil investigation into the tax fraud they suspect the taxpayer has committed. If they begin a civil investigation and uncover further evidence of tax fraud, the civil investigator may pass the new evidence to the criminal investigation team for review, and the taxpayer's affairs may end up being the subject of a criminal investigation. HMRC may use statutory information powers if necessary, and may approach third parties for information. If irregularities are discovered HMRC will take formal action including the issue of assessments and will pursue collection of any unpaid taxes and interest. The taxpayer will also have lost his opportunity to earn maximum reduction of any penalty that is due.

(Code of Practice 9 (2012), ss 1, 2, 4, 6).

(2) Compliance checks into indirect tax matters outside (1) above

This procedure is designed to be used in lower value cases where there is evidence of dishonest conduct or deliberate behaviour.

The taxpayer will normally be asked to attend a meeting with HMRC. A professional adviser may also attend. At the meeting, HMRC will state

- that the check is not being conducted with a view to prosecution in relation to the matters that are the subject of their check; and
- the matters that are the subject of the check. This means the behaviour(s) and period(s) under enquiry, rather than the specific information that they hold which has given rise to their suspicion of dishonesty or deliberate behaviour.

The taxpayer will have an opportunity to disclose any irregularities or matters in relation to his tax affairs. If he wishes to disclose details in areas that are not the subject of the current enquiry, HMRC may not be able to deal with these as part of the ongoing enquiry but will consider these to determine how they should be treated. Any irregularities outside of the matters being checked may be investigated with a view to prosecution (if appropriate).

It may be necessary to make further checks. If this happens, HMRC will explain the compliance checks process and the steps that need to be taken to establish the relevant facts. HMRC may consider it necessary to use their statutory information powers, including contacting third parties.

The taxpayer will be invited to make payments on account towards any VAT arrears, both at the initial meeting and throughout the check. If, as a result of the check, HMRC believe that the VAT arrears are due to conduct involving dishonesty or deliberate behaviour, they will consider the imposition of a penalty.

Penalties

If the taxpayer decides to co-operate with the compliance check, he should be truthful, as he could face prosecution if he makes a statement to HMRC that he knows is false. If he chooses to co-operate and disclose details of his true liability then he can significantly reduce the amount of any penalties due. At the end of the check HMRC will take into account the extent of his co-operation.

If the taxpayer disagrees with HMRC's decision to charge a penalty or the amount of the penalty, he can have his case reviewed by an officer not previously involved, or have his case heard by an independent tax tribunal. If he opts to have his case reviewed he will still be able to appeal to the tribunal if he disagrees with the outcome. If he wants a review he should write to HMRC within 30 days of the date the penalty notice was sent to him, giving reasons why he disagrees with HMRC's decision.

Costs

The taxpayer has to pay for any costs that he incurs in dealing with the enquiry, including the fees of any professional adviser.

(HMRC Notice 160).

Missing trader intra-Community (MTIC) fraud

HMRC Notice 161 gives an explanation of what happens during a civil investigation where HMRC suspect there are serious VAT irregularities due to dishonest conduct, and knowing involvement in transactions that form part of an MTIC fraud.

De Voil Indirect Tax Service. See V5.341–V5.345.

Misdeclaration

[52.12] **Note:** the provisions below are being phased out and replaced by new provisions in *FA 2007, s 97, Sch 24*. See **52.13** below for the replacement provisions although it should be noted that no person is liable for a penalty under those provisions in respect of a VAT period for which a return is required to be made before 1 April 2009. [*SI 2008/568*].

Misdeclaration or neglect resulting in VAT loss

Subject to below, a person is liable to a penalty where

(a) a return is made understating liability to VAT or overstating entitlement to a repayment of VAT credits, or
(b) an assessment is made understating liability to VAT and, within 30 days from the date of the assessment, the taxpayer has not taken all such steps as are reasonable to draw the understatement to the attention of HMRC

and the 'VAT which would have been lost' for the period concerned if the inaccuracy had not been discovered equals or exceeds the lesser of

- where (*a*) above applies, £1 million and 30% of the 'gross amount of VAT'; and
- where (*b*) above applies, £1 million and 30% of the 'true amount of VAT for the period'.

The penalty is 15% of the VAT which would have been lost.

Where supplementary assessments are raised, any penalty is calculated at the percentage rate in force at the time of the original assessment. A penalty is assessed on the date of the decision to make the assessment and the calculation of the amount due, not the date of the notice of assessment if different (*Dart* (VTD 9066) (TVC 3.69)).

'*VAT which would have been lost*' is the amount of the understatement of liability or, as the case may be, overstatement of entitlement to repayment for the VAT period in question.

'*Gross amount of VAT*' is the total of the amount of input tax and output tax which should have been stated in the return for that period. Input tax for this purpose includes any refunds or repayments due in the period which may be aggregated with input tax on the return.

'*True amount of VAT*' means the VAT due from the person concerned or, as the case may be, the amount of the payment to which he is entitled in the period.

For the purposes of ascertaining the '*VAT which would have been lost*', the '*gross amount of VAT*' and the '*true amount of VAT*' where any under or over statement is correspondingly adjusted in a subsequent return, each of those returns is assumed to be a correct statement (so far as not inaccurate in any other respect) for the VAT period to which it relates.

A person is not liable to a penalty under these provisions

(A) if he is convicted of a criminal offence or assessed to a penalty under **52.10** above by reason of conduct within (*a*) or (*b*) above; or
(B) where he satisfies HMRC, or on appeal a tribunal, that there is 'reasonable excuse' for the conduct (see **52.9** above); or
(C) if, at a time when he had no reason to believe that HMRC were enquiring into his affairs, he furnished them with full information with respect to the inaccuracy concerned.
Additionally, HMRC have indicated that such a penalty *will not normally be imposed*
(D) if the penalty amount would be less than £300;
(E) during a 'period of grace' from the end of the VAT period in which the misdeclaration is made to the date for furnishing the VAT return for the following accounting period;
(F) when a misdeclaration has been corrected by a compensating misdeclaration in respect of the same transaction for the following accounting period with no overall loss of VAT; or
(G) where the misdeclaration has been disclosed
   - *before HMRC begin to make enquiries* (i.e. normally when an appointment is made to visit and inspect the records); or
   - *after a visit has been arranged* (unless HMRC believe that the errors were discovered earlier and only disclosed because of the proposed visit); or
   - *during or after a visit* (unless they believe the disclosure was prompted by an enquiry into the trader's affairs).

In such cases, the disclosure will be treated as an error correction notification (formerly voluntary disclosure), see **56.11 RECORDS**.

See **52.30** below for mitigation of penalties.

Local authorities and similar bodies

The provisions above and in (2) below apply to **LOCAL AUTHORITIES AND PUBLIC BODIES (43)** as if

- any reference to VAT credit included a reference to a refund under *VATA 1994, s 33*; and
- any reference to a credit for input tax to include a reference to VAT chargeable on supplies, acquisitions or importations which were not for the purpose of any business carried on by the body.

Museums and galleries

The provisions above apply to museums and galleries to which *VATA 1994, s 33A* applies (see **35.13**(21) **INPUT TAX**) as if

- any reference to VAT credit included a reference to a refund under those provisions; and
- any reference to a credit for input tax included a reference to VAT chargeable on supplies, acquisitions or importations which were attributable to the provision by the body of free rights to admission to a relevant museum or gallery.

[*VATA 1994, ss 63, 71(2), Sch 13 para 15; FA 2001, s 98(3)*]. See also VAT Notice 700/42/11.

(2) Repeated misdeclarations

A person is liable to a repeated misdeclaration penalty where the following circumstances apply.

(i) He makes a 'material inaccuracy' in respect of any VAT period. Subject to below, a 'material inaccuracy' arises where a return is made which understates liability to VAT or overstates entitlement to a repayment of VAT credits and the 'VAT which would have been lost' for that period if the inaccuracy had not been discovered equals or exceeds whichever is the lesser of £500,000 and 10% of the 'gross amount of VAT' for that period. See (1) above for the meaning of 'VAT which would have been lost' and 'gross amount of VAT'.

(ii) HMRC serve a penalty liability notice on the person concerned before the end of the five consecutive VAT periods beginning with the period in respect of which there was the material inaccuracy.

(iii) The penalty liability notice specifies a penalty period of eight consecutive VAT periods beginning with the period in which the date of the notice falls.

(iv) He makes at least two further material inaccuracies in VAT periods within the penalty period.

No liability arises in respect of the first further material inaccuracy under (iv) above but for the second and any subsequent material inaccuracy the person concerned is liable to a penalty of 15% of the VAT which would have been lost for that VAT period if the inaccuracy had not been discovered.

HMRC have indicated that a penalty will not normally be imposed if either the penalty amount would be less than £30 or the circumstances in (1)(E)–(G) above apply.

An inaccuracy is not regarded as material in the following circumstances.

(a) The person concerned satisfies HMRC, or on appeal a tribunal, that there is a reasonable excuse for the inaccuracy (see **52.9** above).

(b) At a time when he had no reason to believe that HMRC were enquiring into his affairs, he furnished them with full information with respect to the inaccuracy.

(c) By reason of conduct falling within (i) above, the person is convicted of an offence or assessed to a penalty under **52.10** above or (1) above in respect of that inaccuracy. This, however, does not prevent an inaccuracy resulting in the assessment of a penalty under (1) above from being regarded as
   - a material inaccuracy in respect of which HMRC may serve a penalty liability notice under (ii) above; or
   - the first further material inaccuracy under (iv) above.

Where under (*a*)–(*c*) above an inaccuracy is not regarded as material for the purposes of serving a penalty liability notice, any such notice served in respect of that inaccuracy is deemed not to have been served.

[*VATA 1994, s 64, Sch 13 para 16; FA 1996, s 36*].

See also **52.30** below for mitigation of penalties.

De Voil Indirect Tax Service. See V5.343; V5.343A; V5.344.

Penalties for errors

[52.13] *FA 2007, s 97* and *Sch 24* create a single framework for penalties to be imposed on taxpayers who make errors in documents that they send to HMRC or who fail to take reasonable steps to report errors in assessments made by HMRC. The provisions apply to VAT, income tax, capital gains tax, corporation tax, pay as you earn, national insurance contributions and deductions under the construction industry scheme (although only those provisions relevant to VAT are considered below).

Commencement dates

The provisions come into force on

- 1 April 2008, in relation to documents within (1) below relating to VAT periods commencing on or 1 April 2008;
- 1 April 2008 in relation to assessments falling within (2) below for VAT periods commencing on or after 1 April 2008;
- 1 July 2008 in relation to documents within (1) below relating to claims under the *EC Thirteenth Directive* (arrangements for the refund of VAT to persons not established in the EU, see **18.45 EUROPEAN UNION LEGISLATION** and **48.5 OVERSEAS TRADERS**) for years commencing on or after 1 July 2008;
- 1 January 2009 in relation to documents within (1) below relating to claims under the *EC Eighth Directive* (arrangements for the refund of VAT to taxable persons established in other EU countries, see **18.44 EUROPEAN UNION LEGISLATION** and **17.9 EUROPEAN UNION: GENERAL**) for years commencing on or after 1 January 2009;
- 1 April 2009 in relation to documents relating to all other claims for repayments of VAT made on or after 1 April 2009 which are not related to a VAT period; and
- in any other case, 1 April 2009 in relation to documents given where a person's liability to pay VAT arises on or after that date.

But no person is liable to a penalty under these provisions in respect of any VAT period for which a return is required to be made before 1 April 2009.

When the provisions are fully in force, they will replace those in

- *VATA 1994, ss 60, 61* (VAT evasion, see **52.10** above) where the conduct involving dishonesty relates to an inaccuracy in a document or a failure to notify an underassessment; and
- *VATA 1994, ss 63, 64* (misdeclaration, see **52.12** above).

[*SI 2008/568*].

(1) Penalty for error in taxpayer's document

A penalty is payable by a person (P) where he gives HMRC (whether by post, fax, email, telephone or otherwise)

- a VAT return,
- a return, statement or declaration in connection with a claim, or
- any document which is likely to be relied upon by HMRC to determine, without further inquiry, a question about
  - (i) P's liability to VAT,
  - (ii) payments by P by way of or in connection with VAT,
  - (iii) any other payment by P (including penalties), or
  - (iv) repayments, or any other kind of payment or credit, to P

and Conditions 1 and 2 below are both satisfied.

(a) Condition 1

Condition 1 is that the document contains an inaccuracy which amounts to, or leads to

(i) an understatement of a liability to VAT (which includes an overstatement of P's entitlement to a VAT credit);
(ii) a false or inflated statement of a loss; or
(iii) a false or inflated claim to repayment of VAT (or allowance for credit).

(b) Condition 2

Condition 2 is that the inaccuracy was 'careless' or 'deliberate' on P's part.

An inaccuracy is

(i) '*careless*' if it is due to failure by P (or his agent, see (7) below) to take reasonable care;
(ii) '*deliberate but not concealed*' if the inaccuracy is deliberate on P's part but P does not make arrangements to conceal it; and
(iii) '*deliberate and concealed*' if the inaccuracy is deliberate on P's part and P makes arrangements to conceal it (e.g. by submitting false evidence in support of an inaccurate figure).

An inaccuracy in a document given by P (or his agent, see (7) below) to HMRC, which was neither careless nor deliberate when the document was given, is to be treated as careless if P discovered the inaccuracy at some later time and did not take reasonable steps to inform HMRC.

Where a document contains more than one inaccuracy, a penalty is payable for each inaccuracy.

Standard amount of penalty
The penalty payable is

- for careless action (or omission), 30% of the 'potential lost revenue';
- for deliberate but not concealed action (or omission), 70% of the potential lost revenue; and
- for deliberate and concealed action (or omission), 100% of the potential lost revenue.

See (4) below for the meaning of '*potential lost revenue*'. See also (5) below for reductions for disclosure, etc. and (6) below for suspension of all or part of a penalty.

Interaction with other penalties and late payment surcharges

The amount of a penalty for which P is liable in respect of a document relating to a VAT period must be reduced by the amount of any other penalty incurred by P, or any surcharge for late payment of VAT imposed on P, if the amount of the penalty or surcharge is determined by reference to the same VAT liability. Additionally, where penalties are imposed under this provision and (2) below in respect of the same inaccuracy, the aggregate of the amounts of the penalties must not exceed 100% of the potential lost revenue.

> *Example*
>
> Jane is VAT-registered and incorrectly claimed input tax on a rail fare on her June 2009 VAT return. Although the return in question is within the new penalty regime, this error would not be classed as a careless error so would not be subject to any penalty if identified by HMRC on a routine VAT visit.

(2) Penalty for error in taxpayer's document attributable to another person

A penalty is payable by a person (T) where

- another person (P) gives HMRC a document of a kind listed in (1) above;
- the document contains a 'relevant inaccuracy'; and
- the inaccuracy was attributable to T supplying false information to P (whether directly or indirectly), or to T deliberately withholding information from P, with the intention of the document containing the inaccuracy.

A '*relevant inaccuracy*' is an inaccuracy which amounts to, or leads to anything within (1)(*a*)(i)–(iii) above.

T is liable to a penalty whether or not P is liable to a penalty under (1) above in respect of the same inaccuracy (but see below for the maximum combined penalty).

Standard amount of the penalty

The penalty payable is 100% of the 'potential lost revenue'.

See (4) below for the meaning of '*potential lost revenue*'. See also (5) below for reductions for disclosure, etc. and (6) below for suspension of all or part of a penalty.

Interaction with other penalties

Where penalties are imposed under this provision and (1) above in respect of the same inaccuracy, the aggregate of the amounts of the penalties must not exceed 100% of the potential lost revenue.

(3) Penalty where under-assessment by HMRC

A penalty is payable by a person (P) where

- an assessment issued to P by HMRC understates P's liability to VAT; and
- P has failed to take reasonable steps to notify HMRC, within the period of 30 days beginning with the date of the assessment, that it is an under-assessment.

'Assessment' includes determination and accordingly references to an 'under-assessment' include an under-determination.

In deciding what steps (if any) were reasonable HMRC must consider

- whether P knew, or should have known, about the under-assessment; and
- what steps would have been reasonable to take to notify HMRC.

Standard amount of penalty

The penalty payable is 30% of the 'potential lost revenue'. See (4) below for the meaning of '*potential lost revenue*' and (5) below for reductions for disclosure, etc.

Interaction with other penalties and late payment surcharges

The amount of a penalty for which P is liable in respect of a document relating to a VAT period must be reduced by the amount of any other penalty incurred by P, or any surcharge for late payment of VAT imposed on P, if the amount of the penalty or surcharge is determined by reference to the same VAT liability.

(4) Potential lost revenue

Normal rule

The '*potential lost revenue*' in respect of an inaccuracy in a document (including any inaccuracy attributable to a supply of false information or withholding of information) or a failure to notify an under-assessment is the additional amount due or payable in respect of VAT as a result of correcting the inaccuracy or assessment. The additional amount due or payable includes a reference to

- an amount payable to HMRC having been erroneously paid by way of repayment of VAT (or allowance of credit); and
- an amount which would have been repayable by HMRC had the inaccuracy or assessment not been corrected.

Multiple errors

Where P is liable to a penalty under (1) above in respect of more than one inaccuracy, and the calculation of 'potential lost revenue' under the normal rule in respect of each inaccuracy depends on the order in which they are corrected

- careless inaccuracies are to be taken to be corrected before deliberate inaccuracies; and

- deliberate but not concealed inaccuracies are to be taken to be corrected before deliberate and concealed inaccuracies.

In calculating potential lost revenue where P is liable to a penalty under (1) above in respect of one or more 'understatements' in one or more documents relating to a VAT period, account is to be taken of any overstatement in any document given by P which relates to the same VAT period. For this purpose, '*understatement*' means an inaccuracy that satisfies Condition 1 at (1)(*a*) above and '*overstatement*' means an inaccuracy that does not satisfy that condition. Overstatements must be set against understatements in the following order.

- Understatements in respect of which P is not liable to a penalty.
- Careless understatements.
- Deliberate but not concealed understatements.
- Deliberate and concealed understatements.

In calculating (for the purposes of a penalty under (1) above) potential lost revenue in respect of a document given by or on behalf of P, no account must be taken of the fact that a potential loss of revenue from P is, or may be, balanced by a potential over-payment by another person (except to the extent that an enactment requires or permits a person's VAT liability to be adjusted by reference to P's).

Delayed VAT

Where an inaccuracy resulted in an amount of VAT being declared later than it should have been (the '*delayed tax*'), the potential lost revenue is

- 5% of the delayed VAT for each year of the delay; or
- a percentage of the delayed VAT, for each separate period of delay of less than a year, equating to 5% per year.

If a return contains an inaccuracy that relates to a timing error which is automatically reversed in a subsequent tax period, the penalty is not calculated on the full amount of tax underpaid in the first period, but on a reduced amount to take account of the timing error. HMRC's previous approach was that in order for the penalty to be calculated in this way, the business must have submitted both the return containing the initial inaccuracy and the return containing the automatic reversal of the inaccuracy in a later period. This meant that in some cases HMRC charged a penalty on the full amount because they acted to correct the inaccuracy on the first return before the second return could be submitted, thereby preventing the inaccuracy from being reversed. HMRC have changed their approach for cases where HMRC intervened to correct the inaccuracy before the second return was received, preventing the inaccuracy from being reversed. Where HMRC are satisfied that, but for their intervention, the inaccuracy would have been automatically corrected in a subsequent return, businesses will receive the reduced penalty based on the rules for delayed tax. (HMRC Brief 15/11).

(5) Reductions in penalties

Reduction for disclosure

There are provisions for the reduction of penalties under (1)–(3) above where a person discloses an inaccuracy, a supply of false information or withholding of information, or a failure to disclose an under-assessment.

Where a person is liable to a penalty, HMRC *must* reduce the penalty to reflect the 'quality' of the disclosure as follows.

- Where a person who would otherwise be liable to a 30% penalty has made an 'unprompted disclosure' — to any percentage (which may be 0%).
- Where a person who would otherwise be liable to a 30% penalty has made a 'prompted disclosure' — to a percentage, not below 15%.
- Where a person who would otherwise be liable to a 70% penalty has made an unprompted disclosure — to a percentage not below 20%.
- Where a person who would otherwise be liable to a 70% penalty has made a prompted disclosure — to a percentage not below 35%.
- Where a person who would otherwise be liable to a 100% penalty has made an unprompted disclosure — to a percentage not below 30%.
- Where a person who would otherwise be liable to a 100% penalty has made a prompted disclosure — to a percentage not below 50%.

For these purposes, '*quality*' includes timing, nature and extent.

A person discloses an inaccuracy, a supply of false information or withholding of information, or a failure to disclose an under-assessment by

- telling HMRC about it;
- giving HMRC reasonable help in quantifying the inaccuracy, etc. or under-assessment; and
- allowing HMRC access to records for the purpose of ensuring that the inaccuracy, etc. or under-assessment is fully corrected.

A disclosure is '*unprompted*' if made at a time when the person making it has no reason to believe that HMRC have discovered (or are about to discover) the inaccuracy, etc. or under-assessment. Otherwise, it is '*prompted*'.

Special reduction

If HMRC think it right because of special circumstances, they may reduce a penalty under (1)–(3) above. However, 'special circumstances' do *not* include either the ability to pay or the fact that a potential loss of revenue from one taxpayer is balanced by a potential over-payment by another.

Reducing a penalty includes staying a penalty or agreeing a compromise in relation to proceedings for a penalty.

(6) Procedure

Assessments

Where a person becomes liable for a penalty under (1)–(3) above, HMRC must assess the penalty, notify the person and state in the notice a VAT period in respect of which the penalty is assessed. Such a penalty must be paid before the end of the period of 30 days beginning with the day on which notification of the penalty is issued.

Any assessment is to be treated for procedural purposes in the same way as an assessment to VAT (except as expressly provided otherwise in these provisions), may be enforced as if it were an assessment to VAT, and may be combined with an assessment to VAT.

The assessment of a penalty under (1) or (2) above must be made before the end of the period of 12 months beginning with the end of the 'appeal period' for the assessment to VAT correcting the inaccuracy (or, where there is no assessment to the VAT concerned, 12 months from the date on which the inaccuracy is corrected).

The assessment of a penalty under (3) above must be made before the end of the period of 12 months beginning with the end of the appeal period for the assessment of VAT correcting the understatement (or, where there is no assessment to the VAT concerned, 12 months from the date on which the understatement is corrected).

The '*appeal period*' is the period during which an appeal could be brought or an appeal that has been brought has not been determined or withdrawn.

HMRC may make a supplementary assessment in respect of a penalty if an earlier assessment underestimated the potential lost revenue but any such assessment must still be within the time limits as above.

Suspension

HMRC may suspend all or part of a penalty for a careless inaccuracy under (1) above by notice in writing to P. The notice must specify

- what part of the penalty is to be suspended;
- a period of suspension (not exceeding two years); and
- conditions of suspension to be complied with by P (e.g. action to be taken and a period in which it must be taken).

HMRC can only do this if compliance with a condition of suspension would help P to avoid becoming liable to further penalties under (1) above for careless inaccuracy (and so ensure that documents are accurate in future).

On the expiry of the period of suspension, if P satisfies HMRC that the conditions of suspension have been complied with, the suspended penalty is cancelled. If P cannot satisfy HMRC, the suspended penalty becomes payable.

If, during the period of suspension of a penalty, P becomes liable for another penalty under (1) above, the suspended penalty becomes payable.

Appeals

A person may appeal against a decision of HMRC on the following grounds.

- That a penalty is payable by the person. The tribunal may affirm or cancel HMRC's decision.
- As to the amount of a penalty payable. The tribunal may affirm HMRC's decision or substitute another decision that HMRC had power to make.
- That HMRC did not suspend a penalty. The tribunal may order HMRC to suspend the penalty only if it thinks that HMRC's decision not to suspend was 'flawed'. If the tribunal orders HMRC to suspend the penalty, the person may subsequently appeal against a provision of the notice of suspension and the tribunal may order HMRC to amend the notice.
- Setting conditions of suspension of a penalty. The tribunal may affirm or vary the conditions of suspension, but it may only vary them if it thinks that HMRC's decision in respect of the conditions was flawed.

'*Flawed*' means flawed when considered in the light of the principles applicable in proceedings for judicial review.

P does not need to pay the penalty before an appeal in order for the appeal to be heard.

(7) Agency

Subject to below, P is liable

- under (1) above where someone acting on P's behalf gives HMRC a document which contains a careless inaccuracy; and
- under (3) above where someone acting on his behalf in relation to VAT fails to take reasonable steps to notify HMRC of an under-assessment within the 30-day period (in which case, in deciding what steps were reasonably, HMRC must also take into account whether the agent knew, or ought to have known about the under-assessment).

Despite the above, P is not liable to a penalty under (1) or (3) above in respect of anything done or omitted by his agent where he satisfies HMRC that he (P) took reasonable care to avoid inaccuracy (in relation to (1) above) or unreasonable failure (in relation to (3) above).

(8) Liability of officers of companies in the case of deliberate inaccuracy by them

Where a penalty under (1) above is payable by a company for a deliberate inaccuracy which was attributable to an officer of the company the officer is liable to pay such portion of the penalty (which may be 100%) as they may specify by written notice to the officer.

This does not allow HMRC to recover more than 100% of a penalty.

The officer must pay the specified portion before the end of the period of 30 days from the day on which the notice is given.

For these purposes, '*officer*'

- in relation to a body corporate other than a limited liability partnership means a director (including a shadow director within the meaning of *CA 2006, s 251*), a manager and a secretary;

- in relation to a limited liability partnership means a member; and
- in any other case, means a director, manager, secretary or any other person managing or purporting to manage any of the company's affairs.

'Company' means any body corporate or unincorporated association, but does not include a partnership, a local authority or a local authority association.

(9) Double jeopardy

A person is not liable to a penalty under (1)–(3) above in respect of an inaccuracy or failure in respect of which the person has been convicted of an offence.

[*FA 2007, s 97, Sch 24; FA 2008, Sch 40; FA 2009, Sch 57 paras 2, 6, 7*].

'Reasonable care'

Each person has a responsibility to take reasonable care but what is necessary to meet that responsibility depends upon that person's ability and circumstances. For example, HMRC would not expect the same level of knowledge or expertise from a self-employed and unrepresented individual as from a multi-national company. They would also expect a higher degree of care to be taken over large and complex matters than simple straightforward ones. (HMRC Brief 19/08).

Failure to notify and unauthorised issue of invoices: provisions applying from 1 April 2010

[52.14] In relation to obligations arising after 1 April 2010, *FA 2008, s 123, Sch 41* creates a single legal framework for penalising failure to comply with a notification obligation. The provisions apply to VAT, income tax, capital gains tax, corporation tax, insurance premium tax, environmental taxes and excise duties (although only the provisions relevant to VAT are considered below). The provisions also provide for penalties for issue of a VAT invoice by an unauthorised person with a penalty calculated in the same way as failure to notify.

(1) Penalty for failure to notify

A penalty is payable by a person (P) where P fails to comply with any of the following obligations (a '*relevant obligation*').

(a) *VATA 1994, Sch 1 para 5* (obligation to notify liability for registration on the basis of supplies in the previous year under **59.3**(*a*) **REGISTRATION**) or *VATA 1994, Sch 1 para 6* (obligation to notify liability for registration on the basis of supplies in the next 30 days under **59.3**(*b*) **REGISTRATION**),

(b) *VATA 1994, Sch 1 para 7* (obligation to notify liability for registration on the transfer of a going concern under **59.3**(*c*) **REGISTRATION**),

(c) *VATA 1994, Sch 1 para 14(2)(3)* (obligation to notify change in nature of suppliers, etc. by a person exempted from registration, see **59.6 REGISTRATION**),

(d) *VATA 1994, Sch 2 para 3* (obligation to notify liability for registration in respect of supplies from other EU countries, see **59.13 REGISTRATION**),
(e) *VATA 1994, Sch 3 para 3* (obligation to notify liability for registration in respect of acquisitions from other EU countries, see **59.20 REGISTRATION**),
(f) *VATA 1994, Sch 3 para 8(2)* (obligation to notify change in nature of acquisitions by a person exempt from registration in respect of acquisitions from other EU countries, see **59.22 REGISTRATION**),
(g) *VATA 1994, Sch 3A paras 3, 4* (obligation to notify liability for registration by overseas traders in respect of disposal of assets for which a VAT repayment claimed, see **59.28 REGISTRATION**),
(h) *VATA 1994, Sch 3A para 7(2)(3)* (obligation to notify relevant change in supplies by an overseas trader exempt from registration in respect of disposal of assets for which a VAT repayment claimed, see **59.29 REGISTRATION**), or
(i) regulations under *VATA 1994, Sch 11 para 2(4)* (obligation to give notification of acquisition of excise duty goods or new means of transport from another EU country, see **19.9** and **19.37 EUROPEAN UNION: SINGLE MARKET** respectively).

(2) Issue of invoice showing VAT by unauthorised person

A penalty is payable by a person (P) where P is an 'unauthorised person' and issues an invoice showing an amount as being VAT (or as including an amount attributable to VAT).

An '*unauthorised person*' means anyone other than

- a person registered for VAT;
- a body corporate within a group registration;
- a person treated as carrying on the business of a taxable person who has died or become bankrupt or incapacitated;
- a person selling business assets of a taxable person towards satisfaction of a debt owed by that taxable person (e.g. sale of assets seized by a bailiff); or
- a person acting on behalf of the Crown (which is treated as including a reference to the National Assembly for Wales Commission).

The provisions apply in relation to an invoice showing a fixed flat rate addition under the special scheme for farmers which

- fails to comply with the requirements of the scheme, or
- is issued by a person who is not at the time authorised to use the scheme

as if the person issuing the invoice were an unauthorised person and the flat rate addition was an amount attributable to VAT.

(3) Standard amount of penalty

The penalty payable is

- for a 'deliberate and concealed' act or failure, 100% of the 'potential lost revenue' (see (4) below); and

- for a 'deliberate but not concealed' act or failure, 70% of the potential lost revenue; and
- for any other case, 30% of the potential lost revenue.

For these purposes,

- a failure by P to comply with a relevant obligation under (1) above is
  - (i) '*deliberate and concealed*' if the failure is deliberate and P makes arrangements to conceal the situation giving rise to the obligation; and
  - (ii) '*deliberate but not concealed*' if the failure is deliberate but P does not make arrangements to conceal the situation giving rise to the obligation; and
- the unauthorised issue of an invoice by P under (2) above is
  - (i) '*deliberate and concealed*' if it is done deliberately and P makes arrangements to conceal it; and
  - (ii) '*deliberate but not concealed*' if it is done deliberately but P does not make arrangements to conceal it.

But see (5) below for reductions in penalties and (6) below for 'reasonable excuse'.

Interaction with other penalties and late payment surcharges

The amount of a penalty for which P is liable under (1) or (2) above must be reduced by the amount of any other penalty incurred by P, or any surcharge for late payment of VAT imposed on P, if the amount of the penalty or surcharge is determined by reference to the same VAT liability.

(4) Potential lost revenue

The '*potential lost revenue*' is determined as follows.

(a) In respect of a failure to comply with a relevant obligation under (1)(*a*)–(*h*), the amount of the VAT (if any) for which P is, or but for any exemption from registration would be, liable for the 'relevant period'. The '*relevant period*' is in relation to a failure to comply with
  - (i) (1)(*a*), (*b*), (*d*), (*e*) or (*g*), the period beginning on the date of the change or alteration concerned and ending on the date on which HMRC received notification of, or otherwise became fully aware of, that change or alteration; and
  - (ii) (1)(*c*), (*f*) or (*h*), the period beginning on the date with effect from which P is required in accordance with that provision to be registered and ending on the date on which HMRC received notification of, or otherwise became fully aware of, P's liability to be registered.

  But the amount is reduced
  - if it includes VAT on an acquisition of goods from another EU country, by the amount of any VAT which HMRC are satisfied has been paid on the supply in pursuance of which the goods were acquired under the law of that EU country; and

- if it includes VAT chargeable on a supply by virtue of *VATA 1994, s 7(4)* (see **65.5 SUPPLY: PLACE OF SUPPLY**), by the amount of any VAT which HMRC are satisfied has been paid on that supply under the law of another EU country.

(b) In any case where the failure is a failure to comply with (1)(*i*) above, the VAT on the acquisition to which the failure relates.

(c) In the case of the unauthorised issue of an invoice showing VAT under (2) above, the amount shown on the invoice as VAT or the amount to be taken as representing VAT.

In calculating potential lost revenue in respect of a 'relevant act or failure' on the part of P, no account must be taken of the fact that a potential loss of revenue from P is, or may be, balanced by a potential over-payment by another person (except to the extent that an enactment requires or permits a person's VAT liability to be adjusted by reference to P's).

A '*relevant act or failure*' means a failure to comply with a relevant obligation under (1) above or the unauthorised issue of an invoice showing VAT under (2) above.

(5) Reductions in penalties

Reduction for disclosure

There are provisions for the reduction of penalties under (1) and (2) above where P discloses a '*relevant act or failure*' (i.e. a failure to comply with a relevant obligation under (1) above or the unauthorised issue of an invoice showing VAT under (2) above).

Where a person is liable to a penalty, HMRC *must* reduce the penalty to reflect the 'quality' of the disclosure as follows.

- Where a person who would otherwise be liable to a 100% penalty has made an unprompted disclosure — to a percentage not below 30%.
- Where a person who would otherwise be liable to a 100% penalty has made a prompted disclosure — to a percentage not below 50%.
- Where a person who would otherwise be liable to a 70% penalty has made an unprompted disclosure — to a percentage not below 20%.
- Where a person who would otherwise be liable to a 70% penalty has made a prompted disclosure — to a percentage not below 35%.
- Where a person who would otherwise be liable to a 30% penalty has made an 'unprompted disclosure'
  - (i) if the penalty is under (1) above and HMRC become aware of the failure less than twelve months after the time when VAT first becomes unpaid by reason of the failure — to any percentage (which may be 0%); and
  - (ii) in any other case — to a percentage not below 10%.
- Where a person who would otherwise be liable to a 30% penalty has made a 'prompted disclosure'
  - (i) if the penalty is under (1) above and HMRC become aware of the failure less than twelve months after the time when VAT first becomes unpaid by reason of the failure — to any percentage not below 10%; and

(ii) in any other case — to a percentage not below 20%.

For these purposes, '*quality*' includes timing, nature and extent.

P discloses a relevant act or failure by

- telling HMRC about it;
- giving HMRC reasonable help in quantifying the VAT unpaid by reason of it; and
- allowing HMRC access to records for the purpose of checking how much VAT is so unpaid.

A disclosure is '*unprompted*' if made at a time when the person making it has no reason to believe that HMRC have discovered (or are about to discover) the relevant act or failure. Otherwise, it is '*prompted*'.

Special reduction

If HMRC think it right because of special circumstances, they may reduce a penalty under (1) and (2) above. However, 'special circumstances' do *not* include either the ability to pay or the fact that a potential loss of revenue from one taxpayer is balanced by a potential over-payment by another.

Reducing a penalty includes staying a penalty or agreeing a compromise in relation to proceedings for a penalty.

(6) Procedure

Assessments

Where P becomes liable for a penalty under (1) or (2) above, HMRC must assess the penalty, notify P and state in the notice the VAT period in respect of which the penalty is assessed. Such a penalty must be paid before the end of the period of 30 days beginning with the day on which notification of the penalty is issued.

Any assessment is to be treated for procedural purposes in the same way as an assessment to VAT (except as expressly provided otherwise in these provisions), may be enforced as if it were an assessment to VAT, and may be combined with an assessment to VAT.

The assessment of a penalty under (1) or (2) above must be made before the end of the period of 12 months beginning with the end of the 'appeal period' for the assessment to VAT unpaid by reason of the relevant act or failure in respect of which the penalty is imposed (or, if there is no such assessment, 12 months from the date on which the amount of VAT unpaid by reason of the relevant act or failure is ascertained).

The '*appeal period*' is the period during which an appeal could be brought or an appeal that has been brought has not been determined or withdrawn.

HMRC may make a supplementary assessment in respect of a penalty if an earlier assessment operated by reference to an underestimate of potential lost revenue but any such assessment must still be within the time limits as above.

Appeals

P may appeal against a decision of HMRC on the following grounds.

- That a penalty is payable by P. The tribunal may affirm or cancel HMRC's decision.
- As to the amount of the penalty payable by P. The tribunal may affirm HMRC's decision or substitute another decision that HMRC had power to make.

If the tribunal substitutes its decision for HMRC's, the tribunal may rely on the provisions in (5) above under the heading *Special reduction* to the same extent as HMRC (which may mean applying the same percentage reduction as HMRC to a different starting point) or to a different extent (but only if the tribunal thinks that HMRC's decision in respect of the application of those provisions was 'flawed').

'*Flawed*' means flawed when considered in the light of the principles applicable in proceedings for judicial review.

P does not need to pay the penalty before an appeal in order for the appeal to be heard.

Reasonable excuse

Liability to a penalty under (1) or (2) above does not arise in relation to an act or failure which is not deliberate if P satisfies HMRC or (on appeal) the tribunal that there is a reasonable excuse for the act or failure. But for these purposes,

- an insufficiency of funds is not a reasonable excuse unless attributable to events outside P's control;
- where P relies on any other person to do anything, that is not a reasonable excuse unless P took reasonable care to avoid the relevant act or failure; and
- where P *had* a reasonable excuse for the relevant act or failure but the excuse has ceased, P is to be treated as having continued to have the excuse if the relevant act or failure is remedied without unreasonable delay after the excuse ceased.

(7) Agency

Subject to below

- under (1) above, the reference to a failure by P includes a failure by a person who acts on P's behalf; and
- under (2) above the reference to P's unauthorised issue of an invoice showing VAT includes the unauthorised issue by a person who acts on P's behalf.

But P is not liable to a penalty in respect of any failure or action by P's agent where P satisfies HMRC or (on appeal) the tribunal that P took reasonable care to avoid the failure or action.

(8) Liability of officers of companies in the case of deliberate act or failure

Where a penalty under (1) or (2) above is payable by a company for a deliberate act or failure which was attributable to an officer of the company the officer is liable to pay such portion of the penalty (which may be 100%) as they may specify by written notice to the officer.

This does not allow HMRC to recover more than 100% of a penalty.

The officer must pay the specified portion before the end of the period of 30 days from the day on which the notice was given.

For these purposes, '*officer*'

- in relation to a body corporate other than a limited liability partnership means a director (including a shadow director within the meaning of *CA 2006, s 251*), a manager and a secretary;
- in relation to a limited liability partnership means a member; and
- in any other case, means a director, manager, secretary or any other person managing or purporting to manage any of the company's affairs.

'*Company*' means any body corporate or unincorporated association, but does not include a partnership, a local authority or a local authority association.

(9) Double jeopardy

P is not liable to a penalty under (1) or (2) above in respect of a failure or action in respect of which P has been convicted of an offence.

[*FA 2008, Sch 41; SI 2009/511; FA 2009, Sch 57 paras 11, 12*].

Failure to notify and unauthorised issue of invoices: provisions applying before 1 April 2010

[52.15] Note: the provisions in this paragraph apply before 1 April 2010. They will then be replaced by the provisions in **52.14** above.

Failure to notify

Where a person fails to comply with

(a) *VATA 1994, Sch 1 para 5* (duty to notify liability for registration on the basis of supplies in the previous year under **59.3**(*a*) **REGISTRATION**) or *VATA 1994, Sch 1 para 6* (duty to notify liability for registration on the basis of supplies in the next 30 days under **59.3**(*b*) **REGISTRATION**),

(b) *VATA 1994, Sch 1 para 7* (duty to notify liability for registration on the transfer of a going concern under **59.3**(*c*) **REGISTRATION**),

(c) *VATA 1994, Sch 1 para 14(2)(3)* (change in nature of suppliers, etc by a person exempted from registration, see **59.6 REGISTRATION**),

(d) *VATA 1994, Sch 2 para 3* (duty to notify liability for registration in respect of supplies from other EU countries, see **59.13 REGISTRATION**),

(e) *VATA 1994, Sch 3 para 3* (duty to notify liability for registration in respect of acquisitions from other EU countries, see **59.20 REGISTRATION**),

(f) *VATA 1994, Sch 3 para 8(2)* (duty to notify change in nature of supplies by a person exempt from registration in respect of acquisitions from other EU countries, see **59.22 REGISTRATION**),

(g) *VATA 1994, Sch 3A paras 3, 4* (duty to notify liability for registration by overseas traders in respect of disposal of assets for which a VAT repayment claimed, see **59.28 REGISTRATION**),

(h) *VATA 1994, Sch 3A para 7(2)(3)* (duty to notify change in nature of supplies by an overseas trader exempt from registration in respect of disposal of assets for which a VAT repayment claimed, see **59.29 REGISTRATION**), or

(i) regulations under *VATA 1994, Sch 11 para 2(4)* (notification of acquisition of excise duty goods or new means of transport, see **19.9** and **19.37 EUROPEAN UNION: SINGLE MARKET** respectively)

he is, subject to below, liable to a penalty of the greater of £50 and

- 5% of the 'relevant VAT' where HMRC are notified or become aware of the failure no more than nine months late (three months late where (*j*) above applies);
- 10% of the relevant VAT where notification, etc. is over nine months late but not more than 18 months late (over three months but no more than six months where (*j*) above applies); and
- 15% of the relevant VAT in any other case.

Where supplementary assessments are raised, any penalty is calculated at the percentage rate in force at the time of the original assessment (if different).

'*Relevant VAT*' is

(i) subject to below, where (*a*), (*d*), (*e*) or (*g*) above applies, the VAT for which the person would be liable for the period beginning on the date he was required to be registered and ending on the date on which HMRC received notification, or otherwise became fully aware, of his liability to be registered;

(ii) subject to below, where (*b*) above applies, the VAT for which the person would be liable for the period beginning on the date he was required to be registered (or, if later 1 January 1996) and ending on the date on which HMRC received notification, or otherwise became fully aware, of his liability to be registered;

(iii) where (*c*), (*f*) or (*h*) above applies, the VAT for which the person would be liable for the period beginning on the date on which the change in the nature of the supplies, etc. occurred and ending on the date on which HMRC received notification, or otherwise became fully aware, of that change; and

(iv) where (*j*) above applies, the VAT on the acquisition to which the failure relates.

Where the relevant VAT under (i) or (ii) above includes VAT on the acquisition of goods from another EU country and HMRC are satisfied that VAT has been paid under the law of another EU country on the supply in question (either to a supplier or directly to the fiscal authority), an allowance is to be made for the VAT so paid (not exceeding the amount of the VAT due).

A person is not liable to a penalty under these provisions where by reason of conduct falling within (*a*)–(*j*) above, he is convicted of an offence or assessed to a penalty under **52.10** above. Conduct falling within the provisions does not give rise to a penalty if the person concerned satisfies HMRC, or on appeal a tribunal, that there is a 'reasonable excuse' for his conduct. See **52.9** above for '*reasonable excuse*'. See also **52.30** for mitigation.

Unauthorised issue of invoices

Where an 'unauthorised person' issues one or more invoices showing an amount as being, or including, VAT he is, subject to below, liable to a penalty of the greater of £50 and a percentage of the 'relevant VAT' as follows.

Penalty assessed	% of relevant VAT
Before 1.1.95	30%
1.1.95 onwards	15%

Where supplementary assessments are raised, any penalty is calculated at the percentage rate in force at the time of the original assessment.

'*Relevant VAT*' is the amount which is, or is the aggregate of, the amounts which are

- shown on the invoice or invoices as VAT; or
- to be taken as representing VAT.

'*Unauthorised person*' means anyone other than

- a person registered for VAT; or
- a body corporate within a group registration; or
- a person treated as carrying on the business of a taxable person who has died or become bankrupt or incapacitated; or
- a person selling business assets of a taxable person towards satisfaction of a debt owed by that taxable person (e.g. sale of assets seized by a bailiff); or
- a person acting on behalf of the Crown (which is treated as including a reference to the National Assembly for Wales Commission).

It includes any person who issues an invoice showing a fixed flat rate compensation percentage under the special scheme for farmers when not authorised to do so (see **63.25 SPECIAL SCHEMES**).

A person is not liable to a penalty under these provisions where by reason of his conduct, he is convicted of an offence or assessed to a penalty under **52.10** above. Conduct falling within the provisions does not give rise to a penalty if the person concerned satisfies HMRC, or on appeal a tribunal, that there is a 'reasonable excuse' for his conduct. See **52.9** above for '*reasonable excuse*'. See also **52.30** below for mitigation.

[*VATA 1994, s 67; FA 1995, s 32; FA 1996, s 37; FA 2000, s 136(2); SI 2007/1118*].

De Voil Indirect Tax Service. See V5.347–350.

Breaches of walking possession agreements

Northern Ireland

[52.16] The following provisions apply where distress is authorised to be levied on the goods and chattels of a person in default who has refused or neglected to pay any VAT due (or any amount recoverable as if it were VAT due) and the person levying the distress and the person in default have entered into a 'walking possession agreement'. See **31.4 HMRC: POWERS** for levying of distress.

If the person in default breaches the undertakings contained in that agreement, he is liable to a penalty equal to half of the VAT due or amount recoverable unless he satisfies HMRC, or on appeal a tribunal, that there is a 'reasonable excuse' for the breach in question. See **52.9** above for '*reasonable excuse*'.

'*Walking possession agreement*' is an agreement under which the property distrained is allowed to remain in the possession of the person in default and its sale delayed in return for

- an acknowledgement that the property is under distraint, and
- an undertaking not to remove or allow removal of the property from the premises named in the agreement without the consent of HMRC and subject to such conditions as they impose.

[*VATA 1994, s 68; FA 1997, s 53(7)*].

England and Wales

Before a date to be appointed, the provisions above relating to walking possession agreements in Northern Ireland also apply in England and Wales.

[*Tribunals, Courts and Enforcement Act 2007, Sch 13 para 120*].

De Voil Indirect Tax Service. See V5.351.

Breaches of regulatory provisions

[52.17] Penalties are payable under the circumstances in (*a*) and (*b*) below but if the person in default is, by reason of his conduct within those circumstances, convicted of an offence or assessed for a penalty under **52.10** or **52.12** above or a surcharge under **52.21** or **52.22** below, he is not also liable to a penalty under these provisions. Additionally, no liability to a penalty arises under the following provisions if the person concerned satisfies HMRC, or on appeal a tribunal, that there is a 'reasonable excuse' for the failure. See **52.9** above for '*reasonable excuse*'.

(a) If any person fails to comply with a requirement to preserve records under *VATA 1994, Sch 11 para 6(3)* (see **56.3 RECORDS**) he is liable to a penalty of £500.

(b) A person is liable to a penalty where he fails to comply with any requirement imposed under
   (i) *VATA 1994, Sch 1 para 11* or *12* (notification of end of liability or entitlement to be registered, see **59.9 REGISTRATION**);

(ii) *VATA 1994, Sch 2 para 5* (notification of matters affecting the continuation of registration in respect of supplies from other EU countries, see **59.16 REGISTRATION**);

(iii) *VATA 1994, Sch 3 para 5* (notification of matters affecting the continuation of registration in respect of acquisitions from other EU countries, see **59.24 REGISTRATION**);

(iv) *VATA 1994, Sch 3A para 5* (notification of matters affecting the continuation of registration by overseas traders in respect of disposals of assets for which a VAT repayment is claimed, see **59.31 REGISTRATION**);

(v) any regulations made under *VATA 1994, s 48* requiring a VAT representative, for the purposes of registration, to notify HMRC that his appointment has taken effect or ceased to have effect, see **3.11 AGENTS;**

(vi) *VATA 1994, Sch 11 para 6(1)* (duty to keep records, see **56.1 RECORDS**);

(vii) *FA 2008, Sch 36 paras 39–52* (failure to comply with an information notice, deliberate obstruction of an officer in the course of an inspection or inaccurate information and documents, see **52.18** below). From 6 April 2009 these provisions replaced *VATA 1994, Sch 11 para 7* (furnishing of information and production of documents, see **31.6 HMRC: POWERS**);

(viii) any regulations or rules made under that *Act* (other than procedural rules for tribunals);

(ix) any Treasury order made under that *Act*;

(x) any regulations made under the *European Communities Act 1972* and relating to VAT; or

(xi) *VATA 1994, s 18A* (conditions imposed by HMRC in connection with fiscal warehousing, see **72.12 WAREHOUSED GOODS AND FREE ZONES**).

No penalty can be assessed under (vi) to (x) above unless, within the two years preceding the assessment, HMRC have issued a written warning of the consequences of a continuing failure to comply with the requirements.

The daily rate of penalty is £5 if there has been no previous occasion in the two-year period preceding the beginning of the failure in question on which the person concerned has failed to comply with that requirement. If there has been one such occasion in that period, the daily rate is £10 and in any other case, the daily rate is £15. The maximum penalty payable is 100 days at the appropriate rate and the minimum penalty is £50.

Where a person's failure to comply with any VAT regulation consists of not paying VAT or failing to make a return in the required time, for the daily penalties above, there is substituted, if greater, a daily penalty of 1/6th, 1/3rd or ½ of one per cent of the 'VAT due' in respect of that period. '*VAT due*' is, if a return has been furnished, the amount shown on the return; otherwise, it is the amount assessed by HMRC.

For the purposes of calculating the penalty

- a failure is disregarded if, as a result, the person becomes liable to a surcharge under **52.21** or **52.22** below;

- a continuing failure is regarded as one occasion of failure occurring on the date on which it began;
- if the same omission gives rise to a failure to comply with more than one such requirement, it is regarded as the occasion of only one failure;
- if the failure is to comply with the requirements concerning furnishing of returns or payment of VAT, a previous failure to comply with either requirement is regarded as a failure to comply with the requirement in question; and
- any earlier failure is disregarded where HMRC, or on appeal a tribunal, have been satisfied that there is a 'reasonable excuse' for the failure. See **52.9** above for '*reasonable excuse*'.

Where HMRC issue a notice of assessment specifying a date (not later than the date of the notice) to which the penalty is calculated, if the person liable pays the penalty within the period notified by HMRC in the assessment, then the penalty is treated as paid on the specified date (and no further penalty accrues after that date). If the penalty is not paid within the notified period, a further assessment may be made to recover additional penalties.

The Treasury may, by statutory instrument, adjust any of the monetary sums above but not so as to apply to a failure which began before the date on which the order comes into force.

[*VATA 1994, s 69, s 76(2)(7)(8); FA 1996, s 35(6), Sch 3 para 9; FA 2000, s 136(3)*].

De Voil Indirect Tax Service. See V5.352–354.

Failure to comply with information notice, deliberate obstruction during inspection or inaccurate information

Standard and daily penalties

[52.18] From 1 April 2009, a person who fails to comply with an information notice (see **31.6 HMRC: POWERS**) or deliberately obstructs an officer during an inspection authorised by the tribunal (see **31.10 HMRC: POWERS**) is liable to a penalty of £300 ('standard penalty'). Failing to comply includes concealment or destruction of documents. If the failure or obstruction continues after the penalty is imposed, the person is liable to further penalties not exceeding £60 for each day ('daily penalty') on which the failure or obstruction continues. From 21 July 2009, a person is liable to a penalty not exceeding £3,000 if, in complying with an information notice, they provide inaccurate information or produce a document that contains an inaccuracy and either: the inaccuracy is careless (i.e. due to a failure by the person to take reasonable care) or deliberate; or the person subsequently discovers the inaccuracy but fails to take reasonable steps to notify HMRC. Where the information or document contains more than one inaccuracy, a penalty is payable in respect of each inaccuracy.

A person must not conceal, destroy or dispose of any document that is the subject of an information notice unless—

- the information has previously been produced and the taxpayer has not been told that he should continue to make it available; and
- in the case of a copy document, six months has elapsed since the copy was originally provided.

A person must not conceal a document if an HMRC officer has told him that it is *likely to be* the subject of an information notice. This prohibition does not apply for longer than six months after the person was informed or notice was given. A failure to do anything required within a limited period of time does not give rise to a standard or daily penalty if the person did it within an extended time limit allowed by an HMRC officer. A standard or daily penalty does not arise if the person satisfies HMRC (or the tribunal on appeal) that he has a reasonable excuse and, if relevant, the failure is remedied without unreasonable delay after the excuse has ceased.

Assessment

Where a person becomes liable for a penalty HMRC may assess the penalty and notify the person within 12 months of the 'relevant date'. In the case of an appealable information notice, '*the relevant date*' means the later of

- the end of the period in which notice of an appeal could have been given, and
- if notice of an appeal is given, the date on which the appeal is determined or withdrawn.

In any other case, '*the relevant date*' means the date on which the person became liable to the penalty.

Appeal

A person may appeal against the imposition of a penalty or the amount of a penalty. Notice of an appeal must be given in writing to HMRC within 30 days, stating the grounds of appeal. On appeal, the tribunal may confirm or cancel the decision to impose a penalty, and may confirm or substitute the amount of a penalty.

A penalty must be paid before the end of the period of 30 days from the date of the notification or 30 days from the finalisation of an appeal. A penalty may be enforced as if it were assessed and payable as income tax.

Additional tax-related penalty

Where the behaviour causing a standard penalty continues and an officer believes that a significant amount of tax is at stake through the failure to comply, the officer may apply to the Upper Tribunal (see **5.1 APPEALS**) for an additional penalty within twelve months of the relevant date. 'Relevant date' means the date the person became liable to the penalty, or in cases involving an appealable information notice (from 19 July 2011), the latest of

- the date the person became liable to the penalty;
- the end of the period in which notice of appeal could have been given; and
- if notice of appeal is given, the date on which the appeal is determined or withdrawn [*FA 2011, Sch 24 para 5*].

The Upper Tribunal decides the amount of the penalty, and in doing so must have regard to the amount of tax likely to be involved. HMRC must notify a person who becomes liable to such a penalty. This tax-related penalty is in addition to the standard and daily penalties, and no account shall be taken of it in applying the rules on interaction with other penalties [*FA 2007 Sch 24 para 12(2); FA 2008 Sch 41 para 15(1)*] (see **52.13, 52.14** above). The tax-related penalty must be paid within 30 days of notification and may be enforced as if it were assessed as income tax.

Increased daily default penalty

From 1 April 2012 HMRC may apply to the tribunal for an alternative increased daily penalty of up to £1,000 per day if the notice is still not complied with within 30 days of a daily penalty being notified.

[*FA 2008, Sch 36 paras 39–52; SI 2009/404; FA 2009, Sch 47 paras 15–20; FA 2011, Sch 24 para 4*].

Failure to comply with notice requiring contact details for debtor

[52.19] If a third party fails to comply with a notice requiring contact details for a debtor (see **31.8 HMRC: POWERS**), the third party is liable to a penalty of £300.

A failure to comply within a limited period of time does not give rise to a penalty if the person did it within an extended time limit allowed by an HMRC officer. A penalty does not arise if the person satisfies HMRC (or the tribunal on appeal) that he has a reasonable excuse and, if relevant, the failure is remedied without unreasonable delay after the excuse has ceased.

Where a person becomes liable for a penalty HMRC may assess the penalty and notify the person within twelve months of the 'relevant date', i.e. the later of: the end of the period in which notice of an appeal could have been given; and, if notice of an appeal is given, the date on which the appeal is determined or withdrawn.

A person may appeal against the imposition of a penalty or the amount of a penalty. Notice of an appeal must be given in writing to HMRC within 30 days, stating the grounds of appeal. On appeal, the tribunal may confirm or cancel the decision to impose a penalty, and may confirm or substitute the amount of a penalty.

A penalty must be paid before the end of the period of 30 days from the date of the notification or 30 days from the finalisation of an appeal. A penalty may be enforced as if it were assessed and payable as income tax.

The double jeopardy rule states that a person is not liable to a penalty under these provisions in respect of any matter for which he has been convicted of an offence.

[*FA 2008, Sch 36 paras 44–49, 52; FA 2009, Sch 49 para 5*].

Failure to comply with data-holder notice or inaccurate data

Failure to comply

[52.20] If a data-holder fails to comply with a data-holder notice (introduced from 1 April 2012, see **31.9 HMRC: POWERS**), he is liable to an initial fixed penalty of £300. Failing to comply includes disposing of a document that is required by a notice or that the data-holder has been told will be required.

The data-holder is liable to a daily penalty of up to £60 for a failure that continues after the award of an initial penalty. No late-filing penalty arises if the notice was complied with within further time allowed by HMRC. No late-filing penalty arises if the data-holder satisfies HMRC or the tribunal that there is a reasonable excuse for the failure.

Inaccurate information or documents

The data-holder is liable to a penalty of up to £3,000 for deliberately or carelessly providing inaccurate information or documents. The penalty applies if the data-holder submits information or a document knowing about an inaccuracy attributable to another person and fails to tell HMRC at the time. It also applies in cases where an inaccuracy comes to light later and the data-holder does not then take reasonable steps to tell HMRC.

Assessment

If HMRC assess any of the above penalties they must notify the data-holder. An assessment of a penalty for failure to comply must be made within 12 months of the latest of

- the date on which he became liable to the penalty;
- the end of the period in which notice of an appeal against the notice could have been given; and
- if notice of such an appeal is given, the date on which the appeal is determined or withdrawn.

An assessment of a penalty for inaccurate data must be made within the period of

- 12 months from the date on which the inaccuracy first came to HMRC's attention; and
- six years from the date on which the data-holder became liable to the penalty.

Appeal

A data-holder may appeal against HMRC's decision to impose any of the above penalties or against the penalty amount. Written notice of an appeal must be given to HMRC within 30 days from the date notification of assessment was given. It must state the grounds of appeal. The tribunal may confirm or cancel the decision to impose the penalty, or confirm or substitute the penalty amount.

Increased daily default penalty

HMRC may apply to the tribunal for an alternative increased daily penalty of up to £1,000 if the notice is still not complied with within 30 days of a daily penalty being notified to the data-holder.

Enforcement

Any of the above penalties are payable within 30 days of the date that they are notified or, if appealed, the date on which the appeal is determined or withdrawn. Penalties are treated like income tax for enforcement purposes.

[*FA 2011, Sch 23 paras 30–40*].

Default surcharge

[52.21] Unless the provisions in **52.22** below apply, if, by the last day on which a taxable person is required to 'furnish' a return for a VAT period, HMRC have not 'received' that return (or have received the return but not the amount of VAT shown on the return as payable) the taxable person is in default for the purposes of these provisions. See below for the interpretation of '*furnish*' and '*received*'.

Subject to below, a taxable person is liable to a surcharge under these provisions where

(a) he is in default in respect of a VAT period;
(b) HMRC serve on him either
  - a *surcharge liability notice* specifying a surcharge period from the date of the notice to the first anniversary of the last day of the VAT period under (*a*) above; or
  - where that last day occurs during an existing surcharge period, a *surcharge liability notice extension* extending the existing surcharge period to the first anniversary of the last day of the VAT period under (*a*) above;

(c) he is again in default in respect of another VAT period which ends within the surcharge period specified in (or extended by) that notice; and
(d) he has 'outstanding VAT' for the VAT period in (*c*). (There is, therefore, no *liability* to surcharge if a nil or repayment return is submitted late or the VAT due is paid on time but the return is submitted late. HMRC will, however, record the default and issue a surcharge liability extension notice.)

The surcharge is the greater of £30 and the 'specified percentage' of his outstanding VAT for the VAT period under (*d*) above.

The 'specified percentage' is determined by reference to the number of VAT periods in respect of which he is in default in the surcharge period and for which he has outstanding VAT.

	Specified percentage
In relation to the first such period	2%
In relation to the second such period	5%
In relation to the third such period	10%
In relation to each such period after the third	15%

A person has '*outstanding VAT*' for a VAT period if some or all of the VAT due for that period has not been paid by the last day on which he is required to make a return for that period.

Where a liability to surcharge is established, HMRC will not issue a surcharge assessment at the 2% or 5% rates for an amount of less than £400. In these circumstances a default will be recorded, a surcharge liability extension notice will be issued, and the rate of surcharge will increase if there are any further defaults in the surcharge period. (VAT Notice 700, para 21.2).

Example

ABC Ltd is in the default surcharge system and liable to a 2% penalty if it defaults in the December 2011 period. It submits the return on time, but instead of paying the full amount of tax of £25,000, can only make a part-payment of £5,000.

If the part-payment is increased by £1 to £5,001, a default surcharge will be avoided for the period if the part-payment is made on time. This is because the surcharge based on unpaid tax is £399.98 (£25,000 – £5,001 x 2%), which is less than the £400 *de minimis* level for the 2% and 5% rates.

Not treated as in default

A person is not liable to a surcharge and not to be treated as having been in default in respect of the VAT period in question if he satisfies HMRC, or on appeal a tribunal, that in the case of a default which is 'material to the surcharge' either of the following applies.

(i) The return or, as the case may be, the VAT shown on it, was despatched at such time and in such manner that it was reasonable to expect that it would be received by HMRC within the appropriate time limit. The despatch of a cheque within reasonable time cannot be equated with the despatch of the VAT where the cheque proves to be worthless (*C & E Commrs v Palco Industry Co Ltd*, QB [1990] STC 594 (TVC 18.414)). See also below under the heading *Meaning of 'furnish' and 'received'*.

(ii) There is a 'reasonable excuse' for the return or VAT not having been despatched. See **52.9** above for '*reasonable excuse*'.

A default is '*material to the surcharge*' if it is *either* the default which gave rise to the surcharge *or* is a default taken into account in the service of the surcharge liability notice upon which the surcharge depends and the person concerned has not been previously liable to a surcharge in respect of a VAT period ending within the surcharge period specified in, or extended by, the notice.

Where a person is treated as not having been in default under (i) or (ii) above, any surcharge liability notice the service of which depended on that default is deemed not to have been served.

A default is also to be left out of account for the above purposes if the conduct giving rise to the default falls within **52.17**(*b*) above and the person is assessed to a penalty under those provisions.

[*VATA 1994, s 59, Sch 13 para 14; FA 1996, s 35(4)*].

From 21 July 2008, no liability to a surcharge arises where HMRC agree to defer payment because of the effects of disaster designated by the Treasury as having national significance. This provision may have retrospective effect; thus the floods in the UK in June and July 2007 caused by weather conditions are a disaster that qualifies for the relief.

[*FA 2008, s 135; SI 2008/1936*].

Surcharge liability notices

For non-receipt of a surcharge liability notice, see *C & E Commrs v Medway Draughting & Technical Services Ltd; C & E Commrs v Adplates Offset Ltd*, QB [1989] STC 346 (TVC 18.1). Where a surcharge liability notice has not been received, subsequent extension notices are not effective as valid surcharge liability notices as they only specify the end of the surcharge period and not the date on which it began; any surcharge assessments must therefore be discharged (*Dow Engineering* (VTD 5771) (TVC 18.12)). A surcharge liability notice which incorrectly stated that a return had not been received (when it had been received late) has been held to be invalid (*Coleman Machines Ltd* (VTD 3196) (TVC 18.7)).

Appeals

A person who thinks he has grounds for appeal against a default surcharge should write to HMRC within 30 days of the date of issue of the *surcharge liability notice extension* and ask them to reconsider the case. They will either confirm the original decision and give 21 days in which to lodge an appeal with a VAT tribunal or send a revised decision and give 30 days in which to lodge such an appeal. Alternatively a person can appeal directly to a VAT tribunal without contacting HMRC in which case he must do so within 30 days of the issue of the *surcharge liability notice extension*. A VAT tribunal cannot hear an appeal until a surcharge liability notice extension has been issued (see *Expert Systems Design Ltd* (VTD 7974) (TVC 2.43)). At this stage an appeal can be made against any or all of the defaults which led to the person becoming liable to the surcharge. This is the only time that the VAT tribunal can be asked to hear an appeal against these defaults. If the person later becomes liable to a further surcharge because he has defaulted again, he will be outside the time limit for appealing against the earlier defaults. It is not necessary to pay the surcharge before appealing to a VAT tribunal but all outstanding returns and VAT must be paid.

Meaning of 'furnish' and 'received'

'Furnish' means putting the return into the possession of HMRC. The current VAT return states 'You could be liable to a financial penalty if your completed return and all the VAT payable are not received by the due date'. Given this, and the use of the word 'received', a clear distinction should be drawn for those purposes between 'received' and 'despatched'. 'Received' should be taken to mean actual receipt by HMRC. From 1 April 2010 all cheque payments sent by post are treated as being received by HMRC on the date when cleared funds reach their bank account, not the date when they receive the cheque. [*SI 1995/2518, Reg 40(2B); SI 2009/2978, Reg 5*].

HMRC have indicated that a return will be accepted as posted on time if posted at least one working day before the due date (assuming it has been sent in the official envelope or by first class post). At the same time they also indicated that where the due date falls on a weekend or bank holiday, the return and the VAT due will be accepted as received in time if received on the next following working day (but see below for electronic payments). (STI 1991, p 389 quoting from The Tax Journal, 21 March 1991, p 2). Despite this apparent assurance, tribunals have continued to uphold default surcharge assessments where returns have been posted one day before the due date. In *La Reine (Limoges Porcelain) Ltd* (VTD 10468) (TVC 18.45) the tribunal held that a return due on a Sunday and posted at 7 pm on the previous Friday had not been posted early enough that it was reasonable to expect that it would be received by HMRC on or before the Sunday. This decision was not followed, and was implicitly disapproved of, in *Halstead Motor Company* (VTD 13373) (TVC 18.47). In that case the tribunal held that, by posting a return before the last collection on Friday, the company had dispatched the return in a manner such that it was reasonable to expect that it would be delivered on Saturday and be received by HMRC within the appropriate time limit. Treatment otherwise by HMRC would be inconsistent with their statement reproduced at STI 1991, p 389.

A business which uses electronic means of payment will automatically receive a seven-day extension for the submission of the return and the payment of VAT due. In this connection, HMRC expect payments to be in their bank account on or before the 7th calendar day so that if the 7th day falls on a weekend or bank holiday, payment must be in their bank account by the last working day beforehand (see **51.3 PAYMENT OF VAT**). Thus, where, say, the 7th day is a Saturday, payment of the VAT on the previous Friday by bank giro credit would not be sufficient (although, following the decision in *Halstead* above, posting the return on the Friday presumably would be sufficient).

Agreement for deferred payment

On 24 November 2008, HMRC introduced a Business Support Service designed to meet the needs of businesses affected by the downturn in the economy. The service will review the circumstances of such businesses and discuss temporary options tailored to their needs, such as arranging for them to make payments over an extended period. Where an agreement for deferred payment is made on or after 24 November 2008, a person is not liable to a default surcharge if:

- he fails to pay an amount of VAT by the due date;
- before the date on which the failure gives rise to a surcharge, he makes a request to an HMRC officer to defer payment; and
- an HMRC officer agrees, whether before or after the date on which the liability to a surcharge arises, that payment may be deferred.

If the person breaks such an agreement, by failing to pay the tax at the end of the deferral period, or by failing to meet a condition set out in the agreement, the surcharge is effectively reinstated with effect from the date of notice served by HMRC as a result of the breakage of the agreement. [*FA 2009, s 108*].

Penalties for failure to submit return/pay tax

The penalty regime introduced by *FA 2009, Sch 55* (late filing of returns) and *Sch 56* (late payment of tax) will be extended to cover VAT. The regime will treat late payment of VAT and late submission of returns separately. Taxpayers will have a right of appeal against penalties, and no penalties will be chargeable if the taxpayer has a reasonable excuse for their failure. The new rules will be brought into force by Treasury Order, from a date to be announced. The key elements of the new penalty regime will be as follows.

Penalties for late filing returns (quarterly)

- A £100 penalty immediately after the due date for filing (whether or not the tax has been paid);
- The failure also starts a penalty period, which is set for a year;
- If there are further failures within the penalty period, then the fixed penalty escalates by £100 for each of those subsequent failures, up to a maximum of £400 per failure. The penalty period is also extended to the first anniversary of the latest failure;
- If any of the failures are prolonged, then additional penalties of 5% of the tax on the relevant return (or £300, whichever is the greater) are charged at six and twelve months from the date of the failure; and
- If, by failing to make the return, the taxpayer is deliberately withholding information to prevent HMRC from correctly assessing the liability to tax, then penalties of up to 100% of the tax on the return may be chargeable.

Penalties for late filing returns (monthly)

- This is a very similar structure to the quarterly model above, except that the fixed penalties are £100 for the first six failures, and then £200 for any subsequent failures.

Penalties for late payments (quarterly)

- Where a taxpayer first pays late, although there is no penalty, it does start a penalty period, which is set for a period of a year;
- Any further failures within that period will attract a penalty of 2% of the unpaid tax, as well as extending the penalty period to the first anniversary of the latest failure;
- A third failure within the period will attract a penalty of 3%, with further failures attracting a maximum of 4%; and

- If any of the failures are prolonged, then additional penalties of 5% of the unpaid tax are charged at six and twelve months from the date of the failure.

Penalties for late payment (monthly)

- This is a very similar structure to the quarterly model above, except that, after the first failure, the tax-geared penalties are 1% for the next three failures, 2% of the following three failures, etc. up to a maximum of 4% per failure.

There will also be special provisions to deal with circumstances where taxpayers may change from a monthly to a quarterly return, or where annual or occasional obligations may arise.

[*F(No 3)A 2010, Schs 10, 11*].

De Voil Indirect Tax Service. See V5.371–383.

Default surcharge: payments on account

[52.22] A taxable person is in default in respect of any VAT period for which he is required to make payments on account (see **51.4 PAYMENT OF VAT**) if

(i) HMRC have not received in full any payment on account by the due date; or
(ii) he would be in default in respect of that period under **52.21** above (but for the fact that periods in respect of which payments on account are required are specifically excluded from those provisions).

Subject to below, a taxable person is liable to a surcharge under these provisions where

(a) he is in default in respect of a VAT period;
(b) HMRC serve on him either
   - a *surcharge liability notice* specifying a surcharge period from the date of the notice to the first anniversary of the last day of the VAT period under (*a*) above; or
   - where that last day occurs during an existing surcharge period, a *surcharge liability notice extension* extending the existing surcharge period to the first anniversary of the last day of the VAT period under (*a*) above;
(c) he is again in default in respect of another VAT period which ends within the surcharge period specified in (or extended by) that notice; and
(d) the 'aggregate value of defaults' for that VAT period is more than nil. The '*aggregate value of defaults*' is the total value of
   - any payment or payments on account (or part payment or payments) not received by HMRC by the due date for such payments; and
   - any outstanding VAT due for the period not paid by the last day on which he is required to make a return for that period (less the amount of unpaid payments on account).

The surcharge is the greater of £30 and the 'specified percentage' of the aggregate value of defaults for the VAT period under (*d*) above.

The '*specified percentage*' is determined by reference to the number of VAT periods in respect of which he is in default in the surcharge period and for which the value of his defaults is more than nil.

	Specified percentage
In relation to the first such period	2%
In relation to the second such period	5%
In relation to the third such period	10%
In relation to each such period after the third	15%

Not treated as in default

A person is not liable to a surcharge and not to be treated as having been in default in respect of the VAT period in question if he satisfies HMRC, or on appeal a tribunal, that in the case of a default which is 'material to the surcharge' either of the following applies.

(A) The payment on account (where (i) above applies) or the return or VAT shown on it (where (ii) above applies) was despatched at such time and in such manner that it was reasonable to expect that it would be received by HMRC by the due date.
A payment on account is not to be taken as received by the due date unless, by the last day for payment, all the transactions can be completed that need to be completed before the whole of the payment becomes available to HMRC.
The despatch of a cheque within reasonable time cannot be equated with the despatch of the VAT where the cheque proves to be worthless (*C & E Commrs v Palco Industry Co Ltd*, QB [1990] STC 594 (TVC 18.414)). See also **52.21** above under the heading *Meaning of 'furnish' and 'received'*.

(B) There is a 'reasonable excuse' for the payment on account (where (i) above applies) or the return or VAT (where (ii) above applies) not having been despatched. See **52.9** above for '*reasonable excuse*'.

A default is '*material to the surcharge*' if it is either the default which gave rise to the surcharge or is a default taken into account in the service of the surcharge liability notice upon which the surcharge depends and the person concerned has not been previously liable to a surcharge in respect of a VAT period ending within the surcharge period specified in, or extended by, the notice.

Where a person is treated as not having been in default under (A) or (B) above, any surcharge liability notice the service of which depended on that default is deemed not to have been served.

A default is also to be left out of account for the above purposes if the conduct giving rise to the default falls within **52.17**(*b*) above and the person is assessed to a penalty under those provisions.

[*VATA 1994, s 59A; FA 1996, s 35(2)*].

See *VATA 1994, s 59B* for deeming provisions where a VAT period in respect of which payments on account are required ends within a surcharge period begun or extended by the service of a surcharge liability notice under **52.21** above; and a VAT period for which payments on account are not required ends within a surcharge period begun or extended by the service of a surcharge liability notice under the above provisions.

See also **52.21** above under the headings *Surcharge liability notices*, *Appeals* and *Agreement for deferred payment*, which provisions also apply to default surcharges in relation to payments on account.

De Voil Indirect Tax Service. See V5.371–V5.383.

Incorrect certificates as to zero-rating, etc.

[52.23] Subject to below, where

(a) a customer gives to a supplier a certificate
- that the supply or supplies made or to be made fall wholly or partly within *VATA 1994, Sch 8 Group 5* or *6* or *VATA 1994, Sch 9 Group 1* (see **42.22 LAND AND BUILDINGS: ZERO AND REDUCED RATE SUPPLIES AND DIY HOUSEBUILDERS**), or
- in connection with fiscal warehousing as required by *VATA 1994, s 18B* or *s 18C* (see **72.15** and **72.19 WAREHOUSED GOODS AND FREE ZONES**), or
- that the supply or supplies made or to be made are reduced rate supplies falling wholly or partly within any of the Groups of *VATA 1994, Sch 7A* (see **58.1 REDUCED RATE SUPPLIES**), or

(b) a person acquiring goods from another EU country prepares a certificate for the purposes of *VATA 1994, s 18B* (see **72.15 WAREHOUSED GOODS AND FREE ZONES**),

and the certificate is incorrect, the person giving or preparing the certificate is liable to a penalty. The amount of the penalty is, where (*a*) above applies, the difference between the VAT which should have been charged and the VAT actually charged and, where (*b*) above applies, the VAT actually chargeable on the acquisition.

A person is not liable to a penalty under these provisions if

(i) he satisfies HMRC or, on appeal, a VAT tribunal, that there is a reasonable excuse for his having given or prepared the certificate; or

(ii) by reason of his having given or prepared it, he is convicted of an offence.

[*VATA 1994, s 62; FA 1996, Sch 3 para 8; FA 1999, s 17; FA 2001, Sch 31 para 3*].

De Voil Indirect Tax Service. See V5.340.

Inaccuracies in EU sales lists (ESLs)

[52.24] Where

(a) a person has submitted an ESL (see **2.21 ACCOUNTING PERIODS AND RETURNS**) containing a 'material inaccuracy' to HMRC;
(b) within six months of discovering that inaccuracy, HMRC have issued him with a written warning identifying the statement and stating that future inaccuracies might result in the service of a notice under these provisions;
(c) the person submits a second ESL containing a material inaccuracy to HMRC and the 'submission date' is within the period of two years beginning with the day after the warning was issued;
(d) HMRC have, within six months of discovering the second inaccuracy served on him a notice identifying the ESL and stating that future inaccuracies will attract a penalty under these provisions; and
(e) the person submits yet another ESL containing a material inaccuracy to HMRC the submission date of which is not more than two years after
 - the service of the notice under (*d*) above; or
 - the date on which any previous ESL attracting a penalty was submitted,

that person is liable to a penalty of £100 in respect of the statement under (*e*) above.

An ESL contains a '*material inaccuracy*' if, having regard to the matters to be included, the inclusion or omission of any information is misleading in any material respect.

'*Submission date*' means the last date for submission of the ESL or the day on which it was actually submitted, whichever is the earlier.

An inaccuracy is not regarded as material for these purposes if

(i) the person submitting the ESL satisfies HMRC, or on appeal a VAT tribunal, that there is a 'reasonable excuse' for the inaccuracy (see **52.9** above);
(ii) at a time when he had no reason to believe that HMRC were enquiring into his affairs, he furnished them with full information with respect to the inaccuracy; or
(iii) he is convicted of an offence by reason of the submission of the ESL containing the material inaccuracy.

Where the only ESL identified in a warning under (*b*) above or a notice under (*d*) above is one which is regarded as containing no material inaccuracies (whether by virtue of (i) to (iii) above or otherwise) that warning or notice is deemed not to have been issued or served.

[*VATA 1994, s 65*].

De Voil Indirect Tax Service. See V5.346.

Failure to submit EU sales lists (ESLs)

[52.25] If by the last day on which a person is required to submit an ESL (see **2.21 ACCOUNTING PERIODS AND RETURNS**) for any period, HMRC has not received the statement, that person is regarded for the purposes of these provisions as being in default in relation to that statement until such time as it is delivered.

Where any person is in default in respect of any ESL, HMRC may serve a notice on him stating that he is in default but that no action will be taken if the default is remedied within 14 days of the notice, otherwise he will become liable to a penalty as calculated below. The notice may also state that the person will become liable, without further notice, to penalties if he commits any more defaults before a period of twelve months has elapsed without his being in default.

Where such a notice is served, the person will become liable

(a) in respect of the ESL to which the notice relates to a penalty of the greater of £50 *or* £5 for each day the default continues after the 14-day period (up to a maximum of 100 days); and

(b) in respect of any other ESL in relation to which he is in default, the last day for submission of which is after the service and before the expiry of the notice, to a penalty of the greater of £50 *or*, as the case may be, £5, £10 or £15 for each day the default continues up to a maximum of 100 days. The daily fine is £5, £10 or £15 depending upon whether the ESL in question is the first, second, or third or subsequent ESL (including, where applicable, the ESL within (*a*) above) in respect of which the person has become liable to a penalty while the notice is in force.

For the purposes of (*b*) above, the notice continues in force for twelve months from the date of service but, where at any time in that twelve-month period the person defaults in submitting an ESL other than one in relation to which he was in default when the notice was served, the notice continues until a period of twelve months has elapsed without that person becoming liable to a penalty under these provisions in respect of any ESL.

Not treated as in default

A person is not treated as being in default in relation to an ESL under these provisions if he satisfies HMRC, or on appeal a tribunal, that

- the ESL has been submitted at such time and in such manner that it was reasonable to expect that it would be received by HMRC within the appropriate time limit; or
- there is a 'reasonable excuse' for the ESL not having been dispatched (see **52.9** above).

In such a case, he is not liable to a penalty in respect of that ESL and any notice served on him exclusively in relation to the failure to submit that ESL has no effect for the purposes of these provisions.

[*VATA 1994, s 66*].

De Voil Indirect Tax Service. See V5.355.

Breach of record-keeping requirements, etc. in relation to transactions in gold

[52.26] A person who fails to comply with the accounting and record-keeping requirements relating to investment gold in *SI 1995/2518, Regs 31A, 31B* and VAT Notice 701/21 (see **26.5 GOLD AND PRECIOUS METALS**) is liable to a penalty not exceeding 17.5% of the value of the transaction to which the failure relates. HMRC must determine the value of any transaction to the best of their judgement and notify the person liable.

A person is not liable to a penalty under these provisions

- if he is convicted of a criminal offence or assessed to a penalty under **52.10** above by reason of conduct which would otherwise give rise to a penalty under these provisions; or
- where he satisfies HMRC or, on appeal, a tribunal that there is 'reasonable excuse' for the failure (see **52.9** above).

See also **52.30** below for mitigation of penalties.

Where a person is liable for a penalty under these provisions, the provisions under **52.14** above do not apply.

[*VATA 1994, s 69A(1)–(3)(6)(7); FA 2000, s 137(2)*].

Breach of record-keeping requirements imposed by directions

[52.27] *With effect from 19 July 2006*, a person who fails to comply with a requirement to keep specified records imposed by directions under *VATA 1994, Sch 11 para 6A* (see **56.1 RECORDS**) is liable to a penalty equal to £200 multiplied by the number of days on which the failure continues (up to a maximum of 30 days). Any person who fails to comply with a requirement to preserve records imposed under those provisions is liable to a penalty of £500.

A person is not liable to a penalty under these provisions if he

- satisfies HMRC or, on appeal, a tribunal that there is a 'reasonable excuse' (see **52.9** above) for the failure; or
- is assessed to a penalty under **52.10** above or convicted of a criminal offence (whether under *VATA 1994* or otherwise), by reason of conduct which would otherwise give rise to a penalty under these provisions.

[*VATA 1994, s 69B; FA 2006, s 21(2)*].

Failure to notify use of certain avoidance schemes

[52.28] Subject to below, a person who fails to comply with the provisions of *VATA 1994, Sch 11A para 6* (duty to notify HMRC of certain avoidance schemes, see **4.5** and **4.9 ANTI-AVOIDANCE**) is liable to a penalty of

(a) £5,000 for failing to disclose a hallmarked scheme; or
(b) 15% of the 'VAT saving' for failing to disclose a listed scheme.

For the purposes of (*b*) above, the '*VAT saving*' is

(i) where a return gives rise to a requirement to notify, the difference between

- the amount of VAT shown on the returns submitted for the VAT periods beginning with that in respect of which the duty to notify first arose and ending with that in which the taxable person duly notified HMRC or, if earlier, the VAT period immediately preceding the notification by HMRC of the penalty assessment; and
- the amount of VAT which, but for the scheme, would have been shown on those returns;

(ii) where a repayment claim for earlier VAT periods in respect of which returns have been submitted gives rise to a requirement to notify, the difference between the amount claimed and the amount which, but for the scheme, would have been claimed; or

(iii) where an amount of non-deductible tax gives rise to the requirement to notify, the excess amount claimed (to the extent that it is not included in the tax saving under (i) or (ii) above).

A person is not liable to a penalty under these provisions

- if he satisfies HMRC or, on appeal, a tribunal that there is a 'reasonable excuse' (see **52.9** above) for the failure to notify; or
- where, by reason of the failure to notify, he is convicted of a criminal offence (whether under *VATA 1994* or otherwise) or assessed to a penalty under *VATA 1994, s 60* (VAT evasion: conduct involving dishonesty, see **52.10** above).

See also **52.30** below for mitigation.

[*VATA 1994, Sch 11A paras 10, 11; FA 2004, Sch 2 para 2; F(No 2)A 2005, Sch 1 para 7*].

Failure to comply with duties of senior accounting officers

[52.29] With effect for financial years beginning on or after 21 July 2009, if a senior accounting officer of a qualifying company fails to comply with his main duty with regard to accountancy arrangements (see **56.14 RECORDS**), he is liable to a penalty of £5,000. A person is not liable to more than one such penalty in respect of the same company and the same financial year. If a senior accounting officer fails to provide a certificate or provides a certificate that contains a careless or deliberate inaccuracy, he is liable to penalty of £5,000. An inaccuracy is careless if it is due to a failure by the senior accounting officer to take reasonable care. An inaccuracy that was neither careless nor deliberate when the certificate was given is to be treated as careless if the senior accounting officer discovered it some time later and did not take reasonable steps to inform HMRC. A qualifying company is liable to a penalty of £5,000 if, for a financial year, HMRC are not notified of the name of its senior accounting officer. Liability to a penalty for any or the above failures to comply does not arise if the senior accounting officer or qualifying company satisfies HMRC or (on appeal) the tribunal that there is a reasonable excuse for the failure. Where a senior accounting officer or a qualifying company becomes liable for a penalty HMRC may assess the penalty. If they do so, they must notify the officer or company liable for the penalty. An assessment may not be made more than six months after the failure or inaccuracy first comes to the attention of an HMRC officer, or more than six years after the end of the period for filing the company's accounts for the financial year. A person may appeal against a decision of HMRC that a penalty is payable by that person. Notice of an appeal must be given in writing, before the end of the period of 30 days beginning with the date on which the notification was issued, stating the grounds of appeal. On an appeal that is notified to the tribunal, the tribunal may confirm or cancel the decision. A penalty must be paid within 30 days of the date of notification of the assessment, or, if a notice of appeal is given, within 30 days of the date on which the appeal is determined or withdrawn. The penalty is enforceable as if it were income tax.

[*FA 2009, Sch 46 paras 4–11*].

Mitigation of civil penalties

Mitigation by HMRC

[52.30] In relation to penalties assessed under **52.10** to **52.14**, **52.24** and **52.28** above, HMRC may reduce the penalty to such amount (including nil) as they think proper but, in doing so, must not take into account

- insufficiency of funds available to any person to pay VAT due or the penalty;
- the fact that there has been no significant loss of VAT; or
- the fact that the person liable to the penalty or a person acting on his behalf has acted in good faith.

HMRC have no powers to mitigate a penalty under **52.16** to **52.25** above.

HMRC may consider the possibility of mitigation where a trader does not have a reasonable excuse for non-compliance (see **52.9** above).

In deciding how much mitigation to allow, HMRC officers have discretion but each mitigating factor has a suggested range expressed as a percentage (see the mitigation framework table below). If more than one factor applies, then they can be aggregated. It may be necessary to reduce the amount of mitigation to take account of negative factors (e.g. obstructive or unco-operative behaviour). Although the law allows HMRC to reduce a penalty to nil, 100% mitigation is rare.

Mitigation framework table

(1) How the infringement occurred	*Maximum of 50%*
Compassionate grounds (where the circumstances are insufficient to warrant a reasonable excuse), e.g.	20%–50%
— unforeseen serious illness of the person responsible for completing the VAT returns (including third party such as professional adviser); and	
— death of a close relative of the person responsible for completing the VAT returns.	

Mitigation framework table

(1) How the infringement occurred	*Maximum of 50%*
Other unforeseen and relevant events (which are considered not to provide a reasonable excuse in their own right) supported by evidence, e.g.	10%–50%
— computer or software errors;	
— flood, fire or other damage to premises;	
— theft or break in;	
— pressure of work, i.e. exceptional and significant increase in workloads not in keeping with normal work fluctuations;	
— staff problems, i.e. where the person responsible for completing the VAT return leaves at short notice; and	
— clerical errors particularly in complex circumstances where management controls are in place but have failed to spot the error.	
Complexity of liability in relation to the size of the business and frequency of transaction.	10%–50%
(2) *Degree of co-operation in disclosing and quantifying arrears (belated notification)*	Maximum of 50%
An error correction notification (formerly voluntary disclosure) of a belated notification of a liability to be registered, or the acquisition of a new means of transport,	
— accompanied by full quantification of the arrears	Up to 50%
— not accompanied by quantification of the arrears.	Up to 25%
Full quantification of arrears within X number of days of identification of the belated notification of a liability to be registered, or the acquisition of a new means of transport.	Up to 25%
(3) *Degree of co-operation in identifying and quantifying the error (misdeclarations)*	Maximum of 50%
Full co-operation and quantification.	Up to 50%
Partial co-operation and quantification.	Up to 25%
Alleged full quantification that later turns out to be partial but where the reason was unintentional.	Up to 10%
Supplying information promptly and answering questions accurately to allow officers to quantify the underdeclaration.	Up to 10%
Other actions which result in a saving of HMRC's time and resources.	Up to 10%
(4) *Other factors*	Maximum of 50%
Published guidance is unclear or not up-to-date.	Up to 40%
Evidence of efforts made to seek advice.	Up to 10%
Evidence of steps taken to correct systems in order to prevent similar errors in future.	5%–25%
Compliance history of trader over the last three registered years has been good	Up to 25%

(HMRC VAT Guidance V1–27, section 15 paras 4.3, 4.4, 5.1).

See **52.10** above for HMRC's policy with regard to mitigation of VAT evasion penalties.

Mitigation by a tribunal

An appeal may be made to a tribunal against any liability to a penalty or surcharge under **52.10** to **52.26** above or the amount of any such penalty or surcharge in an assessment. See **5.3**(17)(20) **APPEALS**. The tribunal has similar powers of mitigation as HMRC above. In addition, where a penalty has been mitigated by HMRC, a VAT tribunal may, on an appeal relating to the penalty, cancel the reduction in whole or in part.

Subject to the above, a tribunal may not vary the amount assessed by way of penalty or surcharge other than to reduce it to the amount which is appropriate under the relevant provisions.

[*VATA 1994, ss 70, 84(6); FA 2000, s 137(3); FA 2004, Sch 2 para 3*].

De Voil Indirect Tax Service. See V5.334, V5.341.

Publishing details of deliberate tax defaulters

[52.31] With effect from 1 April 2010, HMRC may publish information about any person if, following an HMRC investigation, one or more 'relevant tax penalties' is found to have been incurred by the person, and the related potential lost revenue exceeds £25,000. A relevant tax penalty is:

- a penalty under *FA 2007, Sch 24 para 1* (inaccuracy in taxpayer's document) in respect of a deliberate inaccuracy on the part of the person;
- a penalty under *FA 2007, Sch 24 para 1A* (deliberate supply of false information or deliberate withholding of information by another person);
- a penalty under *FA 2008, Sch 41 para 1* (failure to notify) in respect of a deliberate failure on the part of the person; or
- a penalty under *FA 2008, Sch 41 para* 2 (unauthorised VAT invoice) in respect of deliberate action by the person.

The information may be published in any manner that HMRC considers appropriate. Before publication, HMRC must inform the person of their intention, and afford the person reasonable opportunity to make representations. The following information may be published:

- the person's name (including any trading name, previous name or pseudonym);
- the person's address (or registered office);
- the nature of any business carried on by the person;
- the amount of the penalty or penalties and the potential lost revenue in relation to the penalty (or the aggregate of the potential lost revenue in relation to each of the penalties);
- the periods or times to which the inaccuracy, failure or action giving rise to the penalty (or any of the penalties) relates; and

- any such other information as HMRC consider it appropriate to publish in order to make clear the person's identity.

No information may be published:

- before the day when the penalty becomes final (or the latest day when any of the penalties becomes final);
- for the first time after the end of the period of one year beginning with that day (or that latest day);
- after the end of the period of one year beginning with the day on which it is first published (published information may not continue to be published after this date);
- if the amount of the penalty is reduced under *FA 2007, Sch 24 para 10(3) or (5)*, or *FA 2008, Sch 41 para 13(1) or (3)* (maximum mitigation for unprompted disclosure); or
- if the amount of the penalty is reduced under *FA 2007, Sch 24 para 10(4) or (6)*, or *FA 2008, Sch 41 para 13(2) or (4)* (maximum mitigation for prompted disclosure), and the mitigation is attributable to a disclosure made at such time as HMRC, having regard to the circumstances, consider it inappropriate to publish the information.

[*FA 2009, s 94; SI 2010/574*].

Import VAT: evasion and non-compliance

[52.32] With effect from 27 November 2003, penalties are imposed where a person engages in any conduct

- for the purpose of evading import VAT (see **52.33** below); or
- by which he contravenes a duty, obligation, requirement or condition imposed by or under relevant rules relating to import VAT (see **52.34** below).

The penalties also apply to customs duty, Union export duty, Union import duty and customs duty of a preferential tariff country, but these provisions are outside the scope of this book.
[*FA 2003, s 24; SI 2003/2985*].

Penalty for evasion

[52.33] Where

- a person engages in any conduct for the purpose of 'evading import VAT', and
- his conduct involves dishonesty (whether or not such as to give rise to any criminal liability),

he is liable to a penalty equal to 'the amount import VAT evaded' (or sought to be evaded). However, where by reason of such conduct he is

- convicted of a criminal offence,
- given (and has not had withdrawn) a demand notice in respect of a penalty to which he is liable under **52.34** below, or

- liable to a penalty imposed upon him under any other provision of the law relating to import VAT

that conduct does not also give rise to a liability to a penalty under these provisions.

'*Evading import VAT*' includes wrongly obtaining or securing

(i) any repayment, relief or exemption from, or any allowance against, import VAT, or
(ii) any deferral or other postponement of his liability to pay any import VAT.

It also includes evading the cancellation of any entitlement to, or the withdrawal of, any such repayment, relief, exemption or allowance.

'*The amount of import VAT evaded*' is, as the case may be, the amount of

- the repayment;
- the relief, exemption or allowance; or
- the payment which, or the liability to make which, is deferred or otherwise postponed.

[*FA 2003, s 25*].

Liability of officers of a body corporate

Where the conduct of a body corporate gives rise to a penalty under the above provisions and it appears to HMRC that that conduct, in whole or in part, is attributable to the dishonesty of a person who is (or at the material time was) a director or 'managing officer' (the 'relevant officer') of the body corporate, HMRC may give a notice to the body corporate (or its representative) and to the relevant officer (or his representative) stating

- the full amount of the penalty; and
- that they propose to recover a specified portion (which may be the whole) of that penalty from the relevant officer.

The relevant officer is then treated as if he were personally liable under the above provisions to a penalty corresponding to that specified portion. The body corporate is then only liable to the balance (if any) of the full penalty and is discharged from liability on the amount recoverable from the relevant officer.

'*Managing officer*' means a manager, secretary or other similar officer of the body corporate, and any person purporting to act in any such capacity or as a director. Where the affairs of a body corporate are managed by its members, the provisions apply in relation to the conduct of a member in connection with his functions of management as if he were a director of the body corporate.

[*FA 2003, s 28*].

Reduction of the amount of a penalty

Where a person is liable to a penalty under the above provisions

- HMRC or, on appeal, a tribunal may reduce the penalty to such amount (including nil) as they think proper; and
- HMRC (on a review) or a tribunal (on an appeal) may cancel the whole or any part of the reduction previously made by HMRC

but in doing so neither HMRC or the tribunal must take into account

- insufficiency of the funds available to any person to pay the import VAT or the penalty;
- the fact that there has been no significant loss of import VAT; or
- the fact that the person liable to the penalty, or a person acting on his behalf, has acted in good faith.

[*FA 2003, s 29*].

Penalty for contravention of relevant rules

[52.34] The Treasury may make an order to the effect that a person is liable to a penalty of up to £2,500 if he engages in any conduct by which he contravenes a duty, obligation, requirement or condition relating to import VAT imposed by or under any of the following.

- *CEMA 1979* any other Act or any statutory instrument.
- Union customs rules (as laid down in *EC Council Regulation 2913/92/EEC* of 12 October 1992 and including provisions adopted at Union level or nationally to implement them).
- Any directly applicable EU legislation.
- Any relevant international agreements having effect as part of the law of any part of the UK by virtue of any Act or statutory instrument or any directly applicable EU legislation.

Exceptions

A person is not liable to a penalty under these provisions in the following circumstances.

(a) If he satisfies HMRC, or on appeal a tribunal, that there is a reasonable excuse for his conduct. Although 'reasonable excuse' is not defined (and therefore to be determined by HMRC or a tribunal) the following are not to be taken as a reasonable excuse.
   - An insufficiency of funds available to any person for paying any import VAT or any penalty due.
   - That reliance was placed by any person on another to perform any task.
   - That the contravention is attributable, in whole or in part, to the conduct of a person on whom reliance to perform any task was so placed.

(b) If, by reason of conduct relating to import VAT, that person is
   - prosecuted for an offence;
   - given (and has not had withdrawn) a demand notice in respect of a penalty to which he is liable under **52.33** above;
   - liable to a penalty imposed upon him under any other provision of the law relating to import VAT; or

- liable to a penalty under **52.12** to **52.17** or **52.23** to **52.26** above (or would be so liable except that, by reason of his conduct, he is convicted of an offence or liable to a different penalty under those provisions).

[*FA 2003, ss 26, 27*].

Reduction of the amount of a penalty

The same provisions apply as under **52.33** above. [*FA 2003, s 29*].

Administration, etc. of the penalties

Demand notices

[52.35] Where a person is liable to a penalty under **52.33** or **52.34** above, HMRC may give him (or his representative) a notice in writing demanding payment of the penalty due. Any amount so demanded is recoverable as if it were due from him (or the representative) as an amount of customs duty but subject to

- any appeal to a tribunal (see below);
- the demand being subsequently withdrawn; or
- the amount of the penalty being reduced.

Time limits

A demand notice cannot be given

- in the case of a penalty under **52.33** above,
  - (i) more than 20 years after the conduct giving rise to the penalty ceased;
  - (ii) more than two years after evidence of facts, sufficient in the opinion of HMRC to justify the giving of the demand notice, comes to their knowledge; or
  - (iii) where a deceased person was liable to such a penalty before his death, more than three years after his death; and
- in the case of a penalty under **52.34** above
  - (i) more than three years after the conduct giving rise to the penalty ceased; or
  - (ii) more than two years after evidence of facts, sufficient in the opinion of HMRC to justify the giving of the demand notice, comes to their knowledge.

Consequences of issue on criminal proceedings

Once a demand notice is given for payment of a penalty under **52.34** above in respect of any conduct of a person, no proceedings may be brought against that person for any offence constituted by that conduct (whether or not the demand notice is subsequently withdrawn).

[*FA 2003, ss 30–32*].

Review by HMRC

HMRC can be asked to review their decision in the following circumstances.

(a) Where HMRC give a person (or his representative) a notice informing him that, in their opinion, he is liable to a penalty under **52.34** above but that they do not propose to give a demand notice, the person (or his representative) may give written notice to HMRC requiring them to review their decision that liability to a penalty exists.

(b) Except where (*c*) below applies, where HMRC give a demand notice to a person (or his representative), the person (or his representative) may by written notice require HMRC to review their decision
- that the person is liable to a penalty under **52.33** or **52.34** above; or
- as to the amount of the penalty.

(c) In the case of a penalty under **52.33** above where HMRC give a demand notice to a body corporate and an officer
  (i) the officer (or his representative) may by written notice require HMRC to review their decision
  - that the conduct of the body corporate is, in whole or in part, attributable to the relevant officer's dishonesty, or
  - as to the portion of the full penalty which HMRC are seeking to recover from the officer (or his representative); and

  (ii) the body corporate (or its representative) may by written notice require HMRC to review their decision
  - that the body corporate is liable to a penalty; or
  - as to amount of the full penalty as if it were the amount specified in the demand notice.

Time limit

HMRC need not review any decision under the above provisions unless the required notice is given to them within 45 days of the date which they gave the relevant notice under (*a*)–(*c*) above. But this does not prevent HMRC from agreeing to review a decision in a case where the notice required is not given within the permitted period.

Right to further review

A person can only give notice under the above provisions requiring a decision to be reviewed a second or subsequent time

- on the grounds that HMRC did not, on any previous review, have the opportunity to consider any particular facts or matters; and
- provided he does not, on the further review, require HMRC to consider any facts or matters which were considered on a previous review of the decision (unless they are relevant to any issue to which the facts or matters not previously considered relate).

Powers of HMRC on a review

Where HMRC are required to review a decision or agree to do so outside the time limit, they may

- confirm the decision; or
- withdraw or vary the decision, in which case they may also take such further steps (if any) in consequence of the withdrawal or variation as they consider appropriate.

If HMRC do not give notice of their determination on the review within 45 days beginning with the day on which the review

- is required by the person (or his representative), or
- is agreed to by HMRC,

they are to be taken as having confirmed the decision.

[*FA 2003, ss 33–35*].

Appeals

An appeal can be made to a tribunal against any decision by HMRC on a review (including a case where they fail to review their decision within 45 days and it is assumed that their original decision is confirmed). The appellant must be

- the person who required the review in question;
- where the person who required that review did so as representative of another person, that other person, or
- a representative of a person falling within either of the previous two categories.

The tribunal may quash or vary a decision and may substitute its own decision for any decision so quashed.

The burden of proof as to whether a liability arises under **52.33** or **52.34** above lies with HMRC but it is for the appellant to show that the grounds on which any such appeal is brought have been established.

The provisions of *VATA 1994, s 85* (settling an appeal by agreement) and *VATA 1994, s 87* (enforcement of decisions) also apply for these purposes with the appropriate modifications. See **5.13** and **5.21 APPEALS**. Any costs awarded against an appellant on an appeal are recoverable as if they were an amount of customs duty which the appellant is required to pay.

[*FA 2003, ss 36, 37*].

Admissibility of certain statements and documents in criminal proceedings

Statements made or documents produced by, or on behalf of, a person are not inadmissible in

- any criminal proceedings against that person in respect of any offence in connection with import VAT, or
- any proceedings against that person for the recovery of any sum due from him in connection with import VAT

by reason only that any of the following matters have been drawn to his attention and that he was, or may have been, induced as a result to make the statements or produce the documents.

- HMRC have power, in relation to import VAT, to issue a demand notice by way of a civil evasion penalty rather than begin criminal proceedings.
- HMRC's practice is to take into account, in deciding whether or not to issue a demand notice, that a person has made a full confession of any dishonest conduct and has fully co-operated in an investigation.
- HMRC or, on appeal, a tribunal have power to reduce an evasion penalty and that, in deciding the extent of such a reduction, HMRC or a tribunal will have regard to the extent of the person's co-operation during the investigation.

[*FA 2003, s 38*].

Service of notices

Any notice to be given to any person for the above purposes or for the purposes of **52.33** or **52.34** above may be given by sending it by post in a letter addressed to that person (or his representative) at the last or usual residence or place of business of that person (or representative). [*FA 2003, s 39*].

Representatives

Representative, in relation to any person, means

- his personal representative
- his trustee in bankruptcy or interim or permanent trustee, and
- any receiver or liquidator appointed in relation to that person or any or his property,

together with any other person acting in a representative capacity in relation to that person.

[*FA 2003, s 24*].

Key points

[52.36] Points to consider are as follows.

- A business can avoid a penalty for late submission of VAT returns and payment of tax due etc. if it can show to HMRC that it had a reasonable excuse for its failure to comply with the regulations.
- Although the term 'reasonable excuse' is not defined in the legislation, a shortage of funds to pay tax or reliance on another person to perform a task are specifically excluded from acceptable excuses in most cases. Ill health and computer failure are more relevant reasons.
- A new penalty regime took effect in relation to VAT for returns due for submission on or after 1 April 2009. The level of penalty charged by HMRC from this date is based on the behaviour of the taxpayer that led to the error in question.

- If an error is classed as 'careless', it could be subject to a maximum penalty of 30% of the tax due. However, this penalty can be reduced to zero in most cases if full disclosure is made to HMRC as soon as the error is discovered.
- An error on a past VAT return that is careless can still be corrected on the next VAT return if the net amount of tax is below the error notification limit of £10,000 (or 1% of turnover up to £50,000). The disclosure made by the taxpayer to HMRC would then be in the form of a letter, i.e. to give full details of the error(s) in question.
- The end result of a careless error that is fully disclosed to HMRC will be a reduction in most cases from a potential penalty of 30% of the tax amount to zero. This is an important part of the new system, namely that HMRC want to encourage taxpayers to adjust and disclosure any errors they identify.
- A complete disclosure is made to HMRC by 'telling' them about an error, 'giving' them full details about how the error arose and 'allowing' them full access to the records.
- If a disclosure to HMRC is 'prompted', e.g. if a taxpayer had reason to believe that HMRC were going to review the records so decided to make a disclosure in advance, then the penalty reduction will be lower than for an 'unprompted' disclosure, i.e. where no such knowledge existed.
- HMRC also has the power to suspend a penalty for up to two years, on condition that a taxpayer carries out certain actions to avoid the risk of similar errors occurring again in the future.
- With effect from 1 April 2010, the penalty regime based on behaviour was extended to situations involving late registration for VAT. However, the new regime only applies when the effective date of registration should have been on 1 April 2010 or later.
- The penalty regime based on behaviour now includes the 'unauthorised issue of tax invoices' with effect from 1 April 2010, i.e. mainly relating to the situation where an unregistered business charges VAT on a sale to a customer.
- The default surcharge system is intended to penalise a business that submits its VAT returns or pays the tax on those returns after the due date. If a VAT return is a nil return or repayment return, then a default will be recorded but there will be no actual surcharge imposed by HMRC.
- Be aware that a paper return with cheque payment must now be submitted to HMRC so that the cheque has cleared HMRC's bank account by the due date of the return. This means an extra three working days must be allowed for the clearance procedure.
- The maximum default surcharge that can be imposed by HMRC equates to 15% of the outstanding tax due on the payment date.
- A business must submit returns and pay tax on time for a complete twelve-month period in order to come out of the default surcharge system. This means it can then incur one default, with

only a surcharge liability notice being issued for this period as opposed to an actual surcharge penalty.

53

Pension Schemes

Introduction

[53.1] A funded pension scheme is a pension scheme in which the employers' and employees' contributions are vested in separate trustees, who may be individuals or corporate bodies. The pension scheme is normally separate and distinct from the employer's business. The VAT provisions in **53.2** and **53.3** below apply to such schemes but not to

(a) schemes where the employer makes provision for the payment of pensions by a segregated reserve fund in the balance sheet, represented by specific assets;
(b) unfunded pension schemes where the employer does not set aside funds for this purpose; or
(c) insurance-based schemes where retirement benefits are secured through insurance policies.

The normal VAT rules apply to schemes within *(a)*–*(c)* above.

(VAT Notice 700/17/11, paras 1.2, 1.4).

Employers

Input tax deductible

[53.2] The *management* of a pension fund for own employees (but not normally the business activities of the pension fund) is part of an employer's business. A VAT-registered employer can therefore deduct input tax incurred in setting up the fund and on its day-to-day management. This applies even where the responsibility for the general management of the scheme rests with the trustees or the trustees pay for the services provided. HMRC give the following examples of expenses on which input tax may be reclaimed.

- Making of arrangements for setting up the pension fund
- Management of the scheme (i.e. collection of contributions and payment of pensions)
- Advice on a review of the scheme and implementing any changes

- Accountancy and audit services relating to the management of the scheme (e.g. preparation of annual accounts)
- Actuarial valuations of the assets of the fund
- Actuarial advice in connection with the fund's administration
- Providing general statistics in connection with the performance of the fund's investments, properties, etc.
- Legal instructions and general legal advice including drafting of Trust deeds insofar as they relate to the management of the scheme

To claim input tax, the employer must hold a VAT invoice made out in his name. Where the supplies are paid for by the trustees on behalf of the employer, the employer should arrange for the invoice to be issued in his name.

Input tax not deductible

Except where the employer is the sole trustee of his pension scheme (see below), the pension fund itself is not part of the employer's business activities. Any VAT incurred on supplies relating to the *investment* activities carried on by the trustees (e.g. making investments, acquiring property and collecting rents) is not input tax of the employer even if he pays for such expenses. HMRC give the following examples of services on which employers cannot claim input tax.

- Advice in connection with making investments
- Brokerage charges
- Rent and service charge collection for property holdings
- Producing records and accounts in connection with property purchases, lettings and disposals, investments, etc.
- Trustees' services (i.e. services of a professional trustee in managing the assets of the fund)
- Legal fees paid on behalf of representative beneficiaries in connection with changes in pension fund arrangements
- Custodian charges

For cases concerning the recoverability of input tax by employers, see *Linotype & Machinery Ltd* (VTD 594) (TVC 54.2), *Manchester Ship Canal Co v C & E Commrs*, QB [1982] STC 351 (TVC 54.6) and *Ultimate Advisory Services Ltd* (VTD 9523) (TVC 41.46).

Management of the pension scheme

(a) *Services performed by the employer*. Where an employer uses own staff to manage the pension fund and these services are provided free of charge, there is no supply for VAT purposes. See *National Coal Board v C & E Commrs*, QB [1982] STC 863 (TVC 54.11). The employer's entitlement to claim input tax on office overhead expenses is not affected.
If an employer is reimbursed by the trustees (or specifically charges them) for costs incurred in managing the pension scheme and the services fall within those on which input tax is deductible (see above), there is no need to account for output tax on the supply to the trustees.

However, if such arrangements apply to services for investment advice or other services connected with the pension fund's own business activities, the employer is making a taxable supply to the trustees and must account for output tax.

(b) *Services performed by third parties.* Where a third party (e.g. a fund manager, property manager or professional trustee) is used to manage a pension scheme and their charges cover both general management services to the employer (input tax deductible) and investment services to the trustees (input tax non-deductible) the input tax must be apportioned.

Normally, this apportionment is made by the supplier. Where the supplier only issues one invoice for a composite supply, HMRC generally accept that the employer can treat 30% of the VAT charged as his input tax, with the remaining 70% being proper to the fund (the '30/70 split'). If the employer does not consider that 30% is a fair proportion of the costs attributed to management services they should provide evidence to HMRC in support of this view.

Pensions provided for employees of more than one company

Where a pension fund covers pension arrangements for employees of several companies which are not in the same VAT group registration, each employer may treat as input tax only that proportion of VAT incurred on the management of the fund that is attributable to his own employees. Where the person supplying the management services to the fund issues a single invoice, one of the participating employers (or, in the case of entirely separate employers, the trustees) may act in the capacity of paymaster and claim all the VAT incurred for the eligible services, issuing a VAT invoice to each of the other employers for their share of the costs and VAT thereon. The other employers can then treat that VAT as their input tax.

Cessation of business by employer

If an employer ceases business, the trustees of any continuing pension scheme who are VAT-registered may treat VAT incurred on services connected with the management of the scheme as their input tax (subject to the normal rules). If this situation arises, the trustees should inform HMRC.

(VAT Notice 700/17/11, paras 2.1–2.9; Business Brief 19/05).

Trustees

[53.3] Where the trustees of a pension fund make taxable supplies, they may be required to register for VAT. See **59 REGISTRATION** for details. If registered, the trustees can treat VAT on goods and services used for the purposes of their business activities as input tax. However, except where the employer has ceased to be in business (see **53.2** above) VAT on supplies for the purposes of the management of the pension scheme is not input tax since these supplies are regarded as the responsibility of the employer. Recovery of input tax may also be restricted under the **PARTIAL EXEMPTION (49)** rules.

Corporate trustee in a VAT group registration

Where the sole trustee of a pension fund is a corporate body, it may be possible for that trustee to form part of a VAT group registration with the employer. See **27.2** and **27.3 GROUPS OF COMPANIES** for eligibility and application for group treatment. If a corporate trustee becomes such a member, any business supplies made by the trustee, including dealing in the assets of the fund, are treated as being made by the representative member. Tax incurred on supplies to the trustee can be treated as received by the representative member.

Where the fund provides pensions for employees of companies outside the VAT group registration, any VAT incurred in respect of the *management* of the scheme for those companies is not for the purposes of the representative member's business and not allowable. VAT must therefore be apportioned between that attributable to employees within the VAT group (allowable) and outside the group (non-allowable). Alternatively, the representative member may elect to use the paymaster arrangements. See **53.2** above under *Pensions provided for employees of more than one company*.

VAT incurred by group members is recoverable by the representative member to the extent that it is attributable to supplies made to persons outside the group which carry the right to deduct input tax. Any non-business and exempt supplies made by the employer or trustee must be taken into account when considering VAT recovery. See *BOC International Ltd* (VTD 1248) (TVC 54.7).

All members of a group registration are jointly and severally liable for VAT due from the representative member and in the event of that member being unable to meet the VAT debt of the group, as a general rule each member will be liable for the amount of the debt arising during the period that it was a member of the group. However, where corporate trustees are included in a group registration, HMRC have been advised that this liability does not extend to the assets of any trust (e.g. a pension fund) of which the corporate trustee is the trustee, except to the extent that the group VAT debt is attributable in whole or part to the administration of the trust.

Fund managers, property managers, professional trustees, etc.

Fund managers, property managers, professional trustees, etc. may provide

- supplies to the employer in connection with the management of the scheme; and
- supplies to the trustees in connection with their business activities.

It is important to distinguish between the various kinds of services supplied so that separate VAT invoices can be issued to the employer and the trustees for input tax recovery purposes. If services cannot be segregated, HMRC are prepared to allow the total value of services to be divided in the ratio of 30% to the employer and 70% to the trustees. Any other apportionment will only be agreed to by HMRC if detailed information in support of the split is provided.

(VAT Notice 700/17/11, paras 3.1–3.3, 4.1–4.3).

Key points

[53.4] Points to consider are as follows.

- An employer can claim input tax on the costs of managing a pension fund, as a normal cost of its business. The rules of partial exemption would apply, however, so if the employer's business is partly exempt, then some of the input tax would be blocked.
- Input tax cannot be claimed on the costs of investment activities (e.g. broker fees) even where these costs are paid for by the employer.
- It is possible that a pension fund might need to become VAT-registered itself if, for example, it owns commercial property with option to tax issues to consider. The VAT procedures in such cases are the same as for any other commercial business.

54

Printed Matter, etc.

Cross-references. See **33.15**(7) **IMPORTS** for certain printed matter which may be imported free of VAT from a country outside the EU.

De Voil Indirect Tax Service. See V4.273.

Introduction

[54.1] To determine the liability for any supply involving printed or similar matter, it is helpful to consider the following questions.

(a) Is a complete item of printed or similar matter being supplied?
(b) Is the printed matter being supplied in its own right?

If satisfied that the answers to both of these questions are 'yes', then see **54.2** to **54.13** below for categories of printed matter which can be zero-rated. Other items are normally standard-rated (see **54.14** below).

If the answer to (*a*) is 'no' (or if unsure), consider **54.19** below for guidance on the processes leading to the production of printed matter.

If the answer to (*b*) is 'no' (or if unsure), see **54.15** to **54.18** below for printed matter supplied with other services and goods.

Zero-rated printed matter

[54.2] Supplies of the following are zero-rated.

- Books and booklets (see **54.3** below).
- Brochures and pamphlets (see **54.4** below).
- Leaflets (see **54.5** below).
- Newspapers (see **54.6** below).
- Journals and periodicals (see **54.7** below).
- Children's picture books and painting books (see **54.8** below).
- Music (printed, duplicated or manuscript) (see **54.9** below).
- Maps, charts and topographical plans (see **54.10** below).
- Covers, cases and other articles supplied with any of the above items and not separately accounted for (see **54.11** below).

Included is the letting on hire or loan of, or the supply of a part interest in, any of the above items. See **54.12** below.

Not included are plans or drawings for industrial, architectural, engineering, commercial or similar purposes.

Not included, from 19 July 2011, is a supply of goods connected with a supply of services made by a different supplier. The two supplies are connected if, had they been made by a single supplier, they would have been treated as a single standard-rated, reduced-rated or exempt supply of services. For HMRC's interpretation of this provision see 'VAT zero rating: splitting of supplies–comments on draft legislation' on the HMRC website. [*FA 2011, s 75*].

[*VATA 1994, Sch 8 Group 3*].

The legislation does not define any of the above items. HMRC treat the words in *Group 3* as being used in their ordinary, everyday sense. This means they are restricted to goods produced on paper and similar materials such as card (but see **54.4** below). Most items qualifying for the zero-rating will be products of the printing industry (including items printed in Braille), but goods which are photocopied, typed or hand-written may, in some cases, also qualify.

Goods containing text in other formats (e.g. audio or video cassettes or CD Rom) are standard-rated. This includes the storage and distribution of text by fax, e-mail, microfiche, or any similar process. Transcripts or print-outs made of such information are zero-rated if they are supplied in the form of books, booklets, brochures, pamphlets or leaflets within *Group 3*.

Examples of common zero-rated items

The following is a list of items which HMRC commonly regard as qualifying for zero-rating. A list of items they would normally treat as standard-rated is reproduced at **54.14** below. However, liability of any specific item should not be determined from these lists only and reference should be made to the appropriate paragraph of the text.

- Accounts (fully printed)
- Advertising leaflets
- Agendas (fully printed)

- Almanacs
- Amendments (loose leaf)
- Annuals
- Antique books and maps
- Articles of association (complete in booklet form)
- Astronomical charts
- Atlases
- Autograph books (completed)
- Bibliographies
- Bills of quantity (completed)
- Booklets
- Books
- Brochures
- Bulletins
- Catalogues
- Charts (geographical or topographical)
- Circulars
- Colouring books (children's)
- Comics
- Company accounts and reports
- Crossword books
- Diaries (completed)
- Dictionaries
- Directories (completed)
- Election addresses
- Encyclopaedias
- Football programmes
- Geological maps
- Handbills
- Holiday and tourist guides
- Hydrographical charts
- Hymn books
- Instruction manuals
- Journals
- Leaflets
- Magazines
- Mail order catalogues
- Manuals
- Maps
- Memorandum of association (complete in booklet form)
- Missals
- Monographs
- Music
- Music scores
- Newspapers
- Orders of service
- Painting books (children's)
- Pamphlets
- Periodicals
- Picture books

- Poster magazines (see **54.7** below)
- Prayer books
- Price lists (fully printed leaflets or brochures)
- Programmes
- Rag books (children's)
- Recipe books
- Road maps
- Scrap books (completed)
- Ships' logs (completed)
- Sports programmes
- Staff journals
- Text books
- Theses
- Timetables (in book or leaflet form)
- Topographical plans
- Tracts
- Trade catalogues
- Trade directories
- Travel brochures

(VAT Notice 701/10/11, paras 2, 8).

Books and booklets

[54.3] The supply of books and booklets is zero-rated. [*VATA 1994, Sch 8 Group 3 Item 1*].

A book or booklet normally consists of text or illustrations, bound in a cover stiffer than its pages. It may be printed in any language or characters (e.g. Braille or shorthand), photocopied, typed or hand-written. Zero-rated items include:

- Literary works.
- Reference books.
- Directories and catalogues.
- Antique books.
- Collections of letters or documents permanently bound in covers.
- Loose-leaf books, manuals or instructions, whether complete with their binder or not.
- Amendments to zero-rated loose-leaf books, even if issued separately.
- School work books and other educational texts in question and answer format (because the spaces provided for the insertion of answers are incidental to the essential character of the book or booklet).
- Exam papers in question and answer format provided they qualify as books or booklets (or as brochures, pamphlets or leaflets under **54.4** or **54.5** below).
- Photobooks, produced by processing digital photographs, where they satisfy the characteristics for the appearance of a book or booklet, see *Harrier Llc* (TC01562) (TVC 5.24).

Supplies of the following are standard-rated.

- Parts of books, unbound pages and separate illustrations.

- Books of plans or drawings for industrial, architectural, engineering, commercial or similar purposes (which are specifically excluded from zero-rating by *VATA 1994, Sch 8 Group 3, Note (a)*).
- Picture card and stamp albums, unless they contain a substantial amount of reading matter which is complete in itself, and no more than 25% of the album is set aside for the mounting of cards and stamps.
- Completed stamp albums.
- Products that are essentially stationery items (e.g. diaries and address books). Completed diaries can be zero-rated. This view was upheld in *C & E Commrs v Colour Offset Ltd*, QB 1994, [1995] STC 85 (TVC 5.44) which confirmed that 'book' should be given its ordinary meaning ie as having the minimum characteristics of something to be read or looked at. A filled-in diary of historic or literary interest might be a book but a blank diary was not a book in the ordinary sense. Neither was an address book simply because its name included the word 'book'. Compare, however, *Scholastic Publications Ltd* (VTD 14213) (TVC 5.13) where a children's publication containing a year planner and address section was held to be zero-rated as the remaining pages (more than 50% overall) were quizzes and jokes 'designed to be read as entertainment'.

Books published in instalments

In continuity or part-work publishing, a product is supplied in parts over varying periods but builds up into a greater whole (i.e. a loose-leaf book). The parts may be issued *either* in magazine format with the pages stapled together *or* as a collection of loose pages, possibly wrapped in clear plastic or lightly gummed together, which are often not consecutive but designed to be separated and placed in the appropriate section of a binder. Unless a loose-leaf, when viewed independently, is a book at the time of supply, it is not strictly entitled to zero-rating. By concession, if at that time an instalment is part of a larger finite work which itself would fall to be zero-rated as a book, then the individual component parts may also be zero-rated where they are supplied either direct by the publisher or through a distribution chain to the final consumer. (VAT Notice 48, ESC 3.15).

Card-based publications

By way of further concession, card-based boxed publications, even though not bound or held together other than in or by their container, are treated for VAT purposes as a book provided they have all the other characteristics of a book. (VAT Notice 48, ESC 3.15).

(VAT Notice 701/10/11, paras 3.1, 4.4).

Brochures and pamphlets

[54.4] The supply of brochures and pamphlets is zero-rated. [*VATA 1994, Sch 8 Group 3 Item 1*].

'Brochure' and 'pamphlet' are not defined in law and whether a particular product qualifies as such is a matter of fact and impression. HMRC usually require the item to have the following physical characteristics.

- A brochure usually consists of several sheets of reading matter fastened or folded together (although not necessarily bound in a cover). It usually contains advertising material in the form of text or illustrations.
- A pamphlet is similar but usually comprises material of a political, social or intellectual nature.

See also the definition given by the chairman in *Schusman* (VTD 11835) (TVC 5.61).

Single sheet and 'wallet' type brochures

A brochure designed with a flap may be zero-rated provided it

- conveys information;
- contains a substantial amount of text, with some indication of contents or the issuing organisation;
- is not primarily designed to hold other items; and
- is supplied complete.

Items with areas for completion

An item which might otherwise be considered to be a brochure or pamphlet may not be zero-rated if it is primarily intended for completion or detachment. This distinguishes a brochure or pamphlet from a standard-rated form. HMRC accept that items are not primarily intended for completion or detachment if 25% or less of their total area consists of

- areas which are blank and available for completion; or
- parts to be detached and returned.

Where there is both an area for completion and a part to be detached and returned, then the two together must not exceed 25% of the total area of the publication. However, there is no basis in law for this and the '25% test' is no more than a rule of thumb.

Whatever the area for completion, a publication which is designed to be returned whole after completion is always standard-rated.

See also *Full Force Marketing Ltd; Framesouth Ltd* (VTD 15270) (TVC 5.89) where the sale of an A4 document incorporating a 'discount card' entitling the holder to obtain free meals was essentially a supply of standard-rated services rather than a zero-rated brochure.

(VAT Notice 701/10/11, paras 3.2, 3.4).

Leaflets

[54.5] The supply of leaflets is zero-rated. [*VATA 1994, Sch 8 Group 3 Item 1*].

There is no definition of a 'leaflet' and whether a particular item is a leaflet is a matter of fact and impression.

HMRC normally look for certain physical characteristics if an item is to qualify as a leaflet.

(a) It should be printed on limp paper. In *Panini Publishing Ltd* (VTD 3876) (TVC 5.79) the tribunal held that a leaflet must be limp and generally, if not inevitably, on unlaminated paper. However, in *Multiform Printing Ltd* (VTD 13931) (TVC 5.57) it was held that there is no need for a leaflet to be flimsy. HMRC do not therefore regard items printed on stiff paper as automatically excluded from the definition of leaflets. However, they do regard the use of stiff paper and card as an indicator that an item has a function which *would* exclude it.

(b) It should be designed to be held in the hand for reading by individuals rather than for hanging up or general display. See *Arbroath Herald Ltd* (VTD 182) (TVC 5.72) (car stickers), *Pace Group (Communications) Ltd* (VTD 510) (TVC 5.75) (window banners and door stickers); and *Cronsvale Ltd* (VTD 1552) (TVC 5.56) (advertisements for public meetings).

(c) It should consist of a single sheet of paper not greater than A4 size (although larger publications up to A2 size can be zero-rated provided they are printed on both sides, folded down to A4 or smaller, and meet the other conditions). See *Cronsvale Ltd* above where the tribunal held a leaflet to mean a small-sized leaf of paper or a sheet folded into leaves (but not stitched) and containing printed matter, chiefly for gratuitous distribution.

(d) It should be complete in itself (and not part of a larger work). See *Odhams Leisure Group Ltd v C & E Commrs*, QB [1992] STC 332 (TVC 5.81).

(e) It should be supplied in sufficient quantity (at least 50 copies) to permit general distribution.

(f) It should convey information by means of text.

(g) It should either be ephemeral or designed to accompany some other product or service (e.g. an instruction leaflet).

Examples of items that HMRC would not regard as being leaflets would be those designed

- as a calendar;
- to obtain admission to premises;
- to obtain a discount on goods or services; or
- as reference material.

HMRC also consider that items printed on laminated paper are designed to be kept and therefore are not leaflets. On the other hand, orders of service are not normally designed to be kept and may be zero-rated.

Items with areas for completion

See under **54.4** above which also applies to leaflets.

Letters

Individual manuscript or typed letters are standard-rated, as are collections of such letters if unbound or loosely bound. Permanently bound collections of letters are zero-rated.

The supply of a 'stock' or basic letter with the individual name or address of the recipient added (by whatever means) is standard-rated. Uncompleted 'stock' or basic letters may qualify as leaflets if the portion for completion consists of no more than the recipient's name and address, a reference number and a signature.

(VAT Notice 701/10/11, paras 3.3, 3.4, 4.3).

Newspapers

[54.6] The supply of newspapers is zero-rated. [*VATA 1994, Sch 8 Group 3 Item 2*].

There is no definition of a 'newspaper' and whether a particular item is a newspaper is a matter of fact and impression. HMRC require a newspaper to satisfy the following conditions.

- It should usually consist of several large sheets folded rather than bound together.
- It must be published at regular intervals (usually daily but at least weekly) in a continuous series under the same title. Each issue should usually be dated and/or serially numbered.
- It must contain a substantial amount of news about current events of local, national or international interest. It may also carry 'non-news' articles (e.g. readers letters, the weather forecast, crosswords and features on fashion, gardening etc.) but these should be an incidental feature.

For a general consideration of the requirements of a newspaper, see *Evans and Marland Ltd (t/a Greyform Publications)* (VTD 3158) (TVC 5.94).

Delivery and handling charges

Charges for delivered newspapers are normally zero-rated (see **47.8**(19) **OUTPUT TAX**).

(VAT Notice 701/10/11, para 3.5).

Journals and periodicals

[54.7] The supply of journals and periodicals is zero-rated. [*VATA 1994, Sch 8 Group 3 Item 2*].

There is no definition of a 'journal' or 'periodical' and whether a particular item qualifies is a matter of fact and impression. HMRC usually require an item to satisfy the following conditions.

- It should either be in newspaper format or a paper-bound publication.
- It must be published in a series at regular intervals (more frequently than once a year).
- It may contain information of a specialised nature (e.g. legal, medical, financial, commercial, fashion or sporting) or be of more general interest. It is normally a mix of articles and stories but may also consist

mainly of illustrations or advertising matter. However, publications which serve primarily to promote own products or services do not qualify as periodicals (although they may qualify as brochures, see **54.4** above). See *Snushall Dalby & Robinson v C & E Commrs*, QB [1982] STC 537 (TVC 5.93) where the tribunal held that a monthly property guide, consisting almost entirely of advertisements for houses but with one or two articles on the housing market, could not be regarded as a journal as it contained no news and could not be regarded as a periodical as it was not sold to the public.

HMRC used to take the view that an item had to convey information by way of text to qualify as a journal or periodical. They have now withdrawn this view following the decision in *EMAP Consumer Magazines Ltd* (VTD 13322) (TVC 5.95) where a magazine consisting mainly of posters was held to be a periodical even though some could not be viewed without removing the staples. The tribunal chairman held that the word 'periodical' should be given its ordinary natural meaning and a publication consisting mainly of pictorial matter is capable of being a periodical.

(VAT Notice 701/10/11, para 3.6).

Children's picture books and painting books

[54.8] The supply of children's picture books and painting books is zero-rated. [*VATA 1994, Sch 8 Group 3 Item 3*]. This provision does not cover books for older children where the text is the main component, even if supported by pictures. Such books should be considered for zero-rating under **54.3** above.

Children's picture books

These are zero-rated whether printed on paper, plastic or textiles (e.g. children's rag books) unless the article is essentially a toy. Examples of articles which are standard-rated as toys include:

- Books consisting wholly or mainly of pictures or models for cutting out. HMRC suggest that such books with at least 25% text (other than assembly instructions) related to the material for cutting out can be zero-rated. However, there is no basis in law for this and the '25% test' is no more than a rule of thumb. See also *Scholastic Publications Ltd* (VTD 14213) (TVC 5.13) and *The Book People Ltd* (VTD 18240) (TVC 5.12).
- Books where the 'pages' are boards for games.

For a general consideration of children's reading books and picture books, see *W F Graham (Northampton) Ltd* (VTD 908) (TVC 5.11).

Children's painting books

Children's painting books which are zero-rated include:

- Children's painting books and drawing books with sample pictures for copying, or outlines of pictures for colouring, painting or drawing.

- Similar books with 'invisible' outlines to colour which can be made visible by rubbing with a pencil or applying water with a paint brush.
- Painting books in which the small amounts of water colour required for colouring are contained in the book (e.g. in the form of a palette).
- Activity books which combine pages of colouring with pages of puzzles, quizzes and the like.

(VAT Notice 701/10/11, paras 3.7, 3.8).

Music

[54.9] The supply of music (printed, duplicated or manuscript) is zero-rated. [*VATA 1994, Sch 8 Group 3 Item 4*].

Any complete music which is presented on paper is zero-rated whether

- instrumental or vocal;
- printed or hand-written;
- bound or on loose sheets;
- illustrated or not; or
- in any system of notation, including numerical symbols or Braille.

Not included are

- music rolls;
- blank manuscript paper; and
- a piece of music commissioned from a composer.

See also *Flip Cards (Marine) Ltd* (VTD 14483) (TVC 5.109) where 'music' was defined as 'the written or printed score or set of parts of a musical composition' and held not to include cards containing questions and answers about music.

(VAT Notice 701/10/11, para 3.9).

Maps, charts and topographical plans

[54.10] The supply of maps, charts and topographical plans is zero-rated. [*VATA 1994, Sch 8 Group 3 Item 5*].

Physical characteristics

To qualify for zero-rating as a map, chart or topographical plan, HMRC require the map, etc to be printed on paper or other material (e.g. cloth) and in the form of a single or folded sheets or a collection of such sheets bound together in book form (e.g. an atlas).

In *Brooks Histograph Ltd* (VTD 1570) (TVC 5.110) the tribunal held that the word 'chart' must be construed in the context in which it appears. Since it appears between the words 'maps' and 'topographical plans' it refers to an area of land, sea or the skies and not to an historical chart.

HMRC regard the following as standard-rated.

- Plans or drawings for industrial, architectural, engineering, commercial or similar purposes (which are excluded from zero-rating by *VATA 1994, Sch 8 Group 3, Note (a)*).
- Framed maps which are primarily decorative items.
- Posters.
- Pictorial wall charts.
- Aerial photographs.
- Globes, three dimensional models and similar articles.
- Decorative maps printed or woven into textile items (e.g. scarves, handkerchiefs, tea-towels, tapestries, rugs).

(VAT Notice 701/10/11, para 3.10).

Incidental items supplied with zero-rated printed matter and binders

[54.11] Covers, cases and other articles supplied with items within **54.3** to **54.10** above, and not separately accounted for, are zero-rated. [*VATA 1994, Sch 8 Group 3 Item 6*].

Minor accessories (e.g. dust covers, clasps, book marks and presentation cases) supplied with any zero-rated item are usually regarded as forming part of the zero-rated item (but see **54.15** below).

Most folders and wallets are standard-rated but if they convey information themselves they may qualify as brochures (see **54.4** above).

Binders

For the treatment of loose-leaf binders, see **54.3** above. All other binders or files for general or office use are standard-rated. This includes binders for part works, journals and periodicals (whether specifically titled or not).

Small order surcharges

A surcharge imposed for handling a small order is treated as part of the price of the goods and is zero-rated if the goods are zero-rated.

(VAT Notice 701/10/11, paras 5.1, 5.2, 5.5).

Loans, hire and shares

[54.12] The transfer of any undivided share in, or the possession of, any item zero-rated under **54.3** to **54.11** above is zero-rated. [*VATA 1994, Sch 8 Group 3 Note (b)*].

This provision allows zero-rating to apply to

(a) the lending or hiring out of any item, or
(b) the sale of a share or part interest in any item

which is zero-rated under **54.3** to **54.11** above.

Libraries which charge for the loan of books therefore make zero-rated supplies. This also applies to reference libraries which charge for the use of their books on their own premises.

(VAT Notice 701/10/11, para 5.3).

Supplies of printed advertising to charities

[54.13] Zero-rating applies to supplies of all charity advertisements in all media, i.e. there ceases to be any restriction on either the type of media or the purpose of the advertising. [*VATA 1994, Sch 8 Group 15 Items 8–8C; SI 2000/805*]. These more general provisions are considered in **12.7 CHARITIES**.

Standard-rated printed matter

Examples of common standard-rated items

[54.14] The following is a list of items which HMRC commonly regard as being standard-rated. A list of items they would normally treat as zero-rated is reproduced at **54.2** above. However, it should not be assumed that any item is zero-rated simply because it is not included in the list below and the liability of any specific item should be determined by reference to the appropriate paragraph of the text.

- Acceptance cards
- Account books
- Address books
- Albums
- Amendment slips
- Announcement cards
- Appointment cards
- Autograph albums (uncompleted)
- Badges
- Bags (paper)
- Ballot papers
- Bankers' drafts
- Billheads
- Bills of lading
- Bills of quantity (blank)
- Binders (but see **54.3** above)
- Bingo cards
- Biorhythm charts
- Blotters
- Book covers
- Book marks
- Book tokens
- Bookmakers' tickets
- Business cards
- Calendars
- Certificates
- Cheques and cheque books
- Cigarette cards
- Cloakroom tickets
- Colour cards

- Compliment slips
- Copy books
- Correspondence cards
- Coupon books
- Coupons
- Credit cards
- Delivery notes
- Diaries (unused)
- Dividend warrants
- Dressmaking patterns
- Engineers' plans
- Envelopes
- Exercise books
- Fashion drawings
- Flash cards
- Folders
- Football pool coupons
- Form letters (but see **54.5** above)
- Forms
- Framed decorative maps
- Games
- Globes
- Graph paper
- Greetings cards
- Index cards
- Inlay cards for cassettes, CDs or videos
- Insurance cover notes
- Invitation cards
- Invoices
- Labels
- Letter headings
- Letters (handwritten)
- Log books (blank)
- Lottery tickets and cards
- Manuscript paper
- Manuscripts
- Medical records
- Membership cards
- Memo pads
- Menu cards
- Microfiche
- Microfilm
- Microform copies
- Music rolls
- Note books, pads and paper
- Order books and forms
- Paper (unprinted)
- Parts of books (see **54.3** above)
- Pattern cards
- Photograph albums

- Photographs
- Plans (but see **54.10** above)
- Playing cards
- Poll cards
- Pools coupons
- Postcards (whether completed or not)
- Posters
- Price cards and tags
- Printed pictures
- Questionnaires
- Receipt books and forms
- Record books and labels
- Record books
- Record labels
- Record sleeves
- Registers
- Rent books
- Reply-paid coupons and envelopes
- Reproductions of paintings
- Score cards
- Scrap books (blank)
- Scrolls (hand-written)
- Seals
- Shade cards (unless containing substantial printed text)
- Share certificates
- Stamp albums (whether completed or not)
- Stationery
- Stationery books
- Stickers
- Swatch books
- Swatch cards
- Sweepstake tickets
- Tags
- Temperature charts
- Tickets
- Time cards and sheets
- Tokens (but see book tokens below)
- Toys
- Transcripts
- Transfers
- Transparencies
- Visiting cards
- Vouchers
- Wall charts
- Waste paper
- Wills
- Winding cards
- Wrapping paper
- Wreath cards

Posters

Sheets intended for public display are standard-rated but see **54.7** above for 'poster-magazines'.

Stationery

Stationery items (e.g. account books and exercise books) are standard-rated. Some items which are standard-rated stationery when new and unused can be zero-rated if sold after they have been completed, provided that they then have the physical characteristics of a book or other zero-rated item (e.g. completed diaries or ships' logs but not completed stamp albums).

Letters

Individual manuscript or typed letters are standard-rated as are collections of such letters which are unbound or loosely bound. Permanently bound collections are zero-rated. See **54.5** above for printed stocks of standard letters.

Photocopies

Photocopies of zero-rated items are always standard-rated unless the copies can be properly described as books, booklets, brochures, pamphlets, leaflets, etc. and meet all the criteria for zero-rating such items. A bundle of photocopies does not constitute a book unless it includes copies of all the pages of the book and is in permanent binding. Photocopies of parts of books, extracts from periodicals, etc. cannot be zero-rated unless complete in themselves and having the characteristics of zero-rated items. Where a business provides 'instant' photocopying or duplicating services and cannot determine the VAT liability of the copies supplied, it should charge VAT at the standard rate.

Book tokens

Printing of book tokens is standard-rated. On the sale of a book token to the general public

- for its face value or less, no VAT is due; and
- for more than its face value, VAT is due on the difference between the selling price and its face value.

Any separate charge for a greetings card is standard-rated.

(VAT Notice 701/10/11, paras 4.1–4.3, 4.5, 5.4, 8).

Single and multiple supplies

[54.15] Goods which would normally be zero-rated or standard-rated as printed matter may be supplied in conjunction with other goods and/or services. A single inclusive price may, or may not, be charged. If the individual elements are all liable to VAT at the same rate, VAT due can be calculated in the normal way. But if the individual supplies are not liable to VAT at the same rate, the criteria set out by the ECJ in *Card Protection Plan Ltd v C & E Commrs, ECJ Case C–349/96*, [1999] STC 270 (TVC 22.324) must be used to determine whether there is a single or multiple supply.

(a) A single supply occurs where one element of the supply is the principal element to which all the other elements are ancillary, integral or incidental. An ancillary element does not constitute, for the customer, an aim in itself, but is a means of better enjoying the principal goods or services supplied. Integral elements are elements that are essential and necessary to the main supply. An incidental element is something that naturally accompanies the main supply (e.g. packaging).
HMRC regard the following as indicators of a single supply (although accepting that they are not conclusive).
   - Single price.
   - Advertised as a package.
   - Components not available separately.
   - Goods physically packaged together.

   The customer is likely to regard what he is getting as a single supply and not as a package.

(b) A multiple supply occurs where more than one element is distinct and independent. HMRC regard the following as indicators that more than one supply is taking place (although again they are not conclusive).
   - Separate pricing/invoicing.
   - Items available separately.
   - Time differential between parts of the supply.
   - Elements of the supply are not inter-dependent/connected.

   HMRC indicate that common examples of multiple supplies are books issued with films or tapes and children's colouring books issued with felt-tip pens. This is on the basis that the items supplied can clearly be used independently of each other. But see *International Masters Publishers Ltd v HMRC (No 2)*, CA 2006 [2007] STC 153 (TVC 5.40) where the company supplied CDs of music by classic composers, including a booklet on the composer. The court held that there was a single standard-rated supply. The CDs were the principal supply and the booklets were ancillary.
   A particular problem area is children's activity packs which may contain zero-rated books or booklets and standard-rated items such as jigsaw puzzles or toys. The supplier must determine whether the omission of any one component part would diminish the pack as a whole. Overall guidelines are not possible and each pack must be judged on its own merits.

There are three possible liability outcomes where zero-rated printed matter is supplied with other standard-rated items.

- The standard-rated item may be ancillary to, or an integral part of, the supply of zero-rated printed matter, in which case there is a single zero-rated supply.

- The zero-rated printed matter may be ancillary to, or an integral part of, the supply of the standard-rated item (e.g. an instruction booklet provided with a new washing machine), in which case there is a single standard-rated supply.
- There may be a multiple supply where two or more items are distinct and independent. If the items are sold for a single price and are liable to different rates of VAT, the supplier must apportion the price.

(VAT Notice 701/10/11, paras 6.2–6.4).

There is more detailed coverage of single and multiple supplies in **64.6 SUPPLY: GENERAL.**

However, there are two exceptions to the normal rules for

- packages consisting entirely of items printed on paper or card (see **54.16** below); and
- certain cover mounted items on magazines (see **54.18** below).

> *Example*
>
> A CD of classical music is sold to customers in a retail store. The CD also contains a separate leaflet that explains the background to the music and the composers who wrote it. In this situation, the customer is only seeking to buy the CD to listen to the music, which is standard-rated. The zero-rated leaflet is only intended to enhance his enjoyment of the music, i.e. is not a separate supply in its own right. The entire payment made by customers is standard-rated.

Packages of zero-rated and standard-rated printed matter

[54.16] Where a business makes a multiple supply of a 'package' consisting *entirely* of standard-rated and zero-rated printed matter, it can account for VAT by apportionment between the standard-rated and zero-rated elements. Alternatively, by concession, it can apply the package test so that

- if the package contains more zero-rated than standard-rated items, the package as a whole can be zero-rated;
- if there are more standard-rated items, the package as a whole is standard-rated; and
- where there are equal numbers of zero-rated and standard-rated items, the liability of the package is decided by the costs of the goods. If the zero-rated elements of the package cost more, the whole package is zero-rated and vice versa. In the unlikely event that the standard and zero-rated elements cost exactly the same amount, apportionment should be applied.

For these purpose, a '*package*' is a collection of items printed on paper or card usually enclosed in some sort of wrapper. The articles must physically form a package and have a common link in that they are intended to be used together. Examples include

- packages contained in an outer polythene or paper envelope (e.g. a package sent to a shareholder which includes company reports, circulars, a proxy voting form and a reply-paid envelope);

- cardboard folders with pockets into which are inserted a variety of forms, leaflets, etc.; and
- advertising packages often from financial institutions.

The outer envelope in which the package items are enclosed is *not* taken into account when counting the number of standard/zero-rated items but a reply-paid envelope counts as a standard-rated item.

If any item in the package is not printed on paper or card the package test cannot be applied.
(VAT Notice 701/10/11, para 6.5).

The package test for charities

By concession, supplies of certain goods to a charity for use in connection with collecting monetary donations can be treated as if they were zero-rated. See **12.7**(*g*) **CHARITIES**. *From 1 August 2003*, where a package of printed matter is supplied to a charity some items connected with collecting monetary donations can be treated as zero-rated for the purposes of the package test provided they meet the criteria set out in **12.7**(*g*) **CHARITIES**.

Item	*Treatment for the package test*
Letter appealing for donations	Zero-rated
Printed envelopes for use with appeal letters	Zero-rated
Money collecting envelopes	Zero-rated
Stickers	Standard-rated
Money collecting boxes made of card	Zero-rated
Any item not made of paper or card	Package test cannot be used

(VAT Notice 701/10/11, para 6.6).

Printed matter supplied with other services

[54.17] The following are common situations where printed matter is supplied with other services.

(1) Services of an original or specialist nature

The supply of services such as original writing or composition or those involving a specialism are standard-rated. Any goods supplied with those services are incidental products and must be standard-rated even if they would be zero-rated printed matter. Examples include

- the manuscript of a book supplied by an author;
- a piece of music commissioned from a composer;
- a report commissioned from a consultant;
- a translation;
- a shorthand transcription; and
- a typing service.

Extra copies of such items may be zero-rated provided they are

- in a format which qualifies for zero-rating; and
- supplied at a price which covers only the cost of producing the extra copies and a reasonable mark-up.

(VAT Notice 701/10/11, para 7.2).

(2) Printed matter used to supply discount facilities

See *Status Cards Ltd* (VTD 128) (TVC 5.9), *Graham Leisure Ltd* (VTD 1304) (TVC 5.31) and *Interleisure Club Ltd* (VTD 7458) (TVC 5.32).

(3) Printed matter supplied with correspondence courses

Correspondence courses often involve a mixture of tuition in class and home study through course manuals or booklets. The liability of the supply will depend upon what exactly is being supplied. This may be a single supply of education by an eligible body (exempt) or a non-eligible body (standard-rated), a single supply of printed matter (zero-rated) or a multiple supply of education and printed matter (in which case apportionment is required). See **47.3 OUTPUT TAX** for methods of apportionment.

The criteria set out by the ECJ in *Card Protection Plan Ltd v C & E Commrs, ECJ Case C–349/96*, [1999] STC 270 (TVC 22.324) must be used to determine whether there is a single or multiple supply. Where it is established that there is a single supply, consideration must be given as to whether either of the two elements, education and printed matter, is the principal supply with the other being ancillary. If so, the whole supply takes on the liability of the principal supply. College fees were held not to be divisible into study materials (otherwise zero-rated) and educational services (exempt) in *R & C Commrs v The College of Estate Management*, HL [2005] STC 1597 (TVC 5.34). The Court held that there was a single exempt supply of education and that it was inappropriate to analyse the transaction in terms of what was a principal and ancillary supply. In relation to fees for correspondence course and residential courses generally, earlier tribunal decisions had sometimes reached this decision (see *EW (Computer Training) Ltd* (VTD 5453) (TVC 5.35) and *International News Syndicate Ltd* (VTD 14425) (TVC 5.3)) but had also allowed apportionment (see *The Rapid Results College Ltd* (VTD 48) (TVC 5.2) and *Force One Training Ltd* (VTD 13619) (TVC 5.7)). These earlier decisions, however, pre-dated the decision in *Card Protection Plan* and should now be read in the light of the criteria set out in that case and the decision in *College of Estate Management* above.

(4) Printed matter with 'weight loss' programmes

In *HMRC v Weight Watchers (UK) Ltd, CA* [2008] STC 2313 (TVC 5.91) customers attended weekly meetings and were also given an initial handbook, monthly magazines and weekly leaflets. In 2004 Customs issued a ruling that the company was making multiple supplies and that part of the consideration could be attributed to zero-rated supplies of printed material. In 2005 they withdrew this ruling and ruled that the company was making a single supply of a weight-loss programme, so that it was required to account for VAT on the whole of its takings. The CA upheld Customs' ruling, holding that the company was making a single supply and that none of the consideration qualified for zero-rating.

(5) Printed matter supplied in return for a subscription

For *membership subscriptions*, see also **14.2 CLUBS AND ASSOCIATIONS.**

Magazine subscriptions: where magazines are supplied on an annual subscription basis, the whole supply may be zero-rated provided only the magazine is being supplied. However, where the subscription confers other rights (e.g. the right to buy goods at discounted rates or the right to participate in selling schemes and thereby earn commission) the subscription may need to be apportioned to reflect the zero-rated element relating to the magazine.

(6) Programmes supplied as part of an admission fee

It is common practice for admission to events to include the provision of a programme. Following the judgment of the ECJ in *Card Protection Plan Ltd v C & E Commrs, ECJ Case C–349/96*, [1999] STC 270 (TVC 22.324) in the majority of such cases there is a single supply of admission, the programme being an ancillary item.

(7) Subsidy or vanity publishing

An author who is unable to have a work published through the usual means may sometimes pay for it to be published. This is known as either 'subsidy' publishing or 'vanity' publishing.

Where the publisher, in return for a payment from the author, produces a quantity of books which are *all* delivered to the author, the payment by the author to the publisher is a consideration for a supply of books and is zero-rated.

But where the publisher retains the bulk of the print run, selling the books in the normal manner and paying the author a royalty on copies sold, payment by the author to the publisher is partly the consideration for the zero-rated supply of books to the author and partly consideration for standard-rated publishing services. The following simplified method of calculation of the zero-rated and standard-rated supplies has been agreed between HMRC and the British Printing Industries Federation.

Step A	Calculate non-variable costs of initial print run.
Step B	Calculate variable costs of initial print run.
Step C	Divide total at Step B by number of copies in initial print run and multiply by number of copies issued to author.
Step D	Add totals at Step A and Step C to calculate cost of the zero-rated element of the supply.
Step E	Add the costs of initial print run and run-on charges to establish full cost of supply.
Step F	Divide total at Step D by total at Step E to calculate zero-rated percentage of cost of supply.

Step G	Apply percentage in Step F to the net sales charge to establish the zero-rated element of the supply made.

A business which does not wish to calculate an apportionment for each individual supply may calculate an apportionment on the basis of an average resulting from the application of the above to a number of representative supplies made. The method is subject to review by HMRC to ensure it produces a fair result and should also be regularly reviewed by the business to take account of changing circumstances.

(VAT Notice 700/57/02; VAT Notice 701/10/11, para 5.7).

(8) Printed matter supplied with company formation services

HMRC's view is that, following the judgment in *Card Protection Plan*, where there is a single advertised price for a company formation package that includes some printed matter (e.g. a number of copies of the memorandum and articles of association), there is a single standard-rated supply of company formation services. This supply is the principal supply to which the supply of printed matter is ancillary. See also *Company Registrations Online Ltd* (VTD 19461) (TVC 5.41). Where additional copies of documentation are offered as an option for additional payment, there may be either a single supply or multiple supplies depending upon the facts.

Businesses providing company formation services must review their VAT treatment of these supplies, ensure that any necessary changes are implemented, and account for underpaid output tax.

(Business Brief 1/06).

Printed matter supplied with other goods

[54.18] See **54.16** above for supplies of zero-rated and standard-rated printed matter.

Cover-mounted items

Where a cover-mounted item (e.g. a sachet of perfume or a CD) is linked to a magazine, it can, by concession, be zero-rated if the following conditions are met.

- No separate charge is made for it.
- The issue is sold at the same price as other issues without a cover-mounted item.
- The cost of the item included with any individual issue does not exceed either £1 (excluding VAT) or 20% of the total cost of the combined supply (excluding VAT).

Magazines often pass through a number of traders before they are retailed to the end-customer. In determining whether the concession can apply, it is necessary to identify the first trader in the chain responsible for linking the items and then apply the above conditions to that trader. If, at the point of linkage, the supply satisfies the terms of the concession, it becomes a single zero-rated supply and continues as such throughout the chain. If the supply does not satisfy the terms of the concession, the normal rules must be considered to determine whether it is a single or multiple supply.

(VAT Notice 701/10/11, para 6.7; VAT Notice 48, ESC 3.7).

See also *Keesing (UK) Ltd* (VTD 16840) (TVC 5.103) where the company's magazine was distributed by another company which paid Keesing 55% of the cover price of the magazine. The tribunal held that 'total cost' for the purposes of the concession was the 55% which Keesing received, rather than the full cover price, and on that basis the conditions of the concession were not satisfied.

Production of zero-rated goods

[54.19] Supplies of certain services involve the production of goods that are zero-rated under *VATA 1994, Sch 8 Group 3*. A business supplying such services must consider whether its supply falls into either of the following categories.

(a) **Services of an original or specialist nature.** See **54.17**(1) above.

(b) **Services of the production of new zero-rated goods** (which will be more likely if the business is in the printing industry). Such services are zero-rated where those goods are themselves zero-rated.

- *Preparatory or post-production work.* Where a business supplies items that qualify for zero-rating, it can zero-rate any preparatory or post-production work (other than alterations) that it performs in conjunction with them. This applies whether or not it itemises the various processes on the VAT invoice and charges for them separately, and even if it has employed sub-contractors. See *AP Carpenter* (VTD 15253) (TVC 5.62) (whether a graphic designer was responsible for the production of a brochure).
- *Sub-contract work.* A sub-contractor can only zero-rate work if he produces new zero-rated goods. If not, his supply cannot be zero-rated even if he knows that the final product will be zero-rated. For example, a business providing typesetting only must standard-rate its supply but if it also binds pages together to make a book (with a cover) it is producing a zero-rated item and can zero-rate its supply.
- *Work on other people's goods.* Where a treatment or process is applied to someone else's goods which produces new goods, the liability of the service follows that of the goods produced. For example, binding loose papers into a book is zero-rated but re-covering or otherwise repairing an old book is standard-rated.

  Any other work on other people's goods is standard-rated (e.g. post-production alterations).

(VAT Notice 701/10/11, paras 7.1–7.3).

Incomplete publications

Component parts of books, journals (e.g. covers, unbound pages, illustrations) in the course of production are standard-rated as they have not been assembled into completed books (*Butler & Tanner Ltd* (VTD 68) (TVC 5.28)). (VAT Notice 701/10/11, para 4.4).

Key points

[54.20] Points to consider are as follows.

- An item can only be zero-rated as printed matter if it is in a paper format, i.e. it represents a supply of goods. For example, a newsletter supplied to a customer by electronic means (e.g. emailed to the customer in pdf format) is always classed as a supply of services and therefore standard-rated (assuming sale is to a UK customer).
- A supply of printed matter or text is also standard-rated if supplied as a CD rom or audio cassette etc. This is because text supplied in these formats cannot be read.
- As a general principle, items of printed matter where the main intention is for the document to be written in rather than read are standard-rated, e.g. address book, diary, accounts book to record income and expenditure.
- It is important that a business buying items of printed matter (e.g. annual reports produced by a printer and bought by a charity to circulate to its members) identifies when zero-rating can apply. This is particularly relevant if the business is not VAT-registered or partly exempt, where VAT becomes a cost component. However, as a general principle of VAT, input tax cannot be reclaimed on any supply where VAT has been incorrectly charged in the first place.
- A supply of photocopying services is generally standard-rated, so there is scope for a business to reclaim input tax on such costs, assuming a tax invoice (or less detailed tax invoice) is obtained from the supplier as evidence of VAT being paid.

55

Rates of VAT

Cross-references. See **18.23 EUROPEAN UNION LEGISLATION** for rates allowed under *Directive 2006/112/EC*; **66.1–66.26 SUPPLY: TIME OF SUPPLY** for the rules relating to the tax point of supply.

De Voil Indirect Tax Service. See V1.111–V1.131.

Introduction

[55.1] VAT is levied on the supply of goods and services, the acquisition of goods from another EU country and the importation of goods from a place outside the EU. The Treasury may, by Order, vary the standard rate of VAT for the time being in force by a percentage of the current rate not exceeding 25% but any Order ceases to have effect one year from the date on which it takes effect unless continued by a further Order. This method was used to reduce the standard rate of VAT from 17.5% to 15% for a temporary period (1 December

2008 to 31 December 2009). Since the period in question exceeds twelve months, legislation was included in *FA 2009* to extend the period of reduction for an additional month.

[*VATA 1994, s 2; FA 2001, Sch 31 para 2; SI 2008/3020; FA 2009, s 9(1)*].

Rates

[55.2] Apart from certain **EXEMPT SUPPLIES (20)** and **ZERO-RATED SUPPLIES (74)** on which no VAT is chargeable, there are currently two rates of VAT.

Standard rate		
4.1.11–	20%	[*F(No 2)A 2010, s 3*]
1.1.10–3.1.11	17.5%	[*SI 2008/3020; FA 2009, s 9(1)*]
1.12.08–31.12.09	15%	[*SI 2008/3020; FA 2009, s 9(1)*]
1.4.91–30.11.08	17.5%	[*FA 1991, s 13*]
Reduced rate		
1.9.97–	5%	[*F(No 2)A 1997, s 6*]
1.4.94–31.8.97	8%	[*FA 1995, s 21*]
1.9.97–	5%	[*F(No 2)A 1997, s 6*]
1.4.94–31.8.97	8%	[*FA 1995, s 21*]

See **58 REDUCED RATE SUPPLIES** for the supplies subject to the reduced rate.

Sales spanning 1 December 2008 or 1 January 2010

Businesses that operated beyond midnight on 31 December 2009

[55.3] Special arrangements were set up to help businesses account for the change in the VAT standard rate, if they operated beyond midnight on 31 December 2009 and were: a pub, club, restaurant or similar establishment; a retail shop; or a provider of telecommunications. HMRC allowed them to account for VAT at 15% on takings received up to the earlier of: the end of trading of the 31 December 2009 session; or 6am on the morning of 1 January 2010.

(HMRC Brief 68/09).

Sales spanning 1 January 2010

[55.4] There are special rules for sales which span 1 January 2010. If goods or services are provided before 1 January 2010 and a VAT invoice raised after that date, the business can choose to account for VAT at 15%.

Services started before 1 January 2010 but finished afterwards

If a business started work on a job before 1 January 2010 but finished afterwards, it may account for the work done up to 31 December 2009 at 15% and the remainder at 17.5%. The business must be able to demonstrate that the apportionment is fair.

> *Example*
>
> Mike the decorator carried out a job for a customer which he started on 6 December 2009 and finished on 12 January 2010. He raised an invoice to the customer at the end of the job. No advance payments were made by the customer before this date.
>
> Mike can either charge 17.5% VAT on the entire job, based on the invoice date, or he could apportion the charge between 15% and 17.5% VAT, based on the value of work carried out before and after 1 January. An apportionment based on the number of days work carried out is probably the most suitable method.
>
> A key consideration for Mike will probably be whether his customer can reclaim input tax on the work in question – if he can, it would be easier to just charge 17.5% VAT based on the invoice date rather than spend time calculating a split.

Continuous supplies of services

If a business provides a continuous supply of services, such as leasing of photocopiers, it should account for the VAT due whenever it issues a VAT invoice or receives payment, whichever is the earlier. It must charge 17.5% on invoices issued and payments received on or after 1 January 2010. It may charge 15% on the services provided in the period up to 31 December 2009 and 17.5% on the remainder. The business must be able to demonstrate that the apportionment is fair.

(HMRC Guidance dated 31 December 2010).

Sales spanning 1 December 2008

[55.5] The correct standard rate to be applied to sales that span 1 December 2008 is detailed below.

Supply of goods or individual services

Earlier of payment made or invoice issued before 1.12.08—17.5% but can choose to charge 15% if the goods are to be delivered or services completed on or after 1.12.08.

Earlier of payment made or invoice issued on or after 1.12.08—15%, but should charge 17.5% if goods have been delivered or services completed before 1.12.08 and the invoice was issued more than 14 days* after the goods were delivered or services completed; or the invoice is for a payment received before 1.12.08 (although can choose to charge 15% if the goods are to be delivered or services completed on or after 1.12.08).

*For extensions to the 14-day rule see **66.8, 66.18 SUPPLY: TIME OF SUPPLY**.

Supply of continuous or construction services

Earlier of payment made or invoice issued before 1.12.08—17.5% but can choose to charge 15% for that part of the supply of continuous services made or that part of the construction work performed (covered by the payment or invoice) on or after 1.12.08.

Earlier of payment made or invoice issued on or after 1.12.08—15%.

(HMRC Guidance Note dated 1 December 2008).

Supplementary charge

[55.6] Where the VAT rate is due to increase, some businesses may attempt to create a tax point (e.g. by the issue of a tax invoice or the making of a payment) before the date of the change in respect of supplies which are effectively to be consumed after that date. Consequently, in respect of the reversion of the standard rate to 17.5% from 1 January 2010, anti-forestalling legislation introduced a supplementary VAT charge of 2.5% on supplies of goods/services and grants of rights, subject to the standard rate, which took place on or after 25 November 2008 in the circumstances set out below, where the customer was not entitled to recover all of the VAT on the supply.

In respect of the increase in the standard rate to 20% from 4 January 2011, anti-forestalling legislation introduces a supplementary VAT charge of 2.5% on supplies of goods/services and grants of rights, subject to the standard rate, which take place on or after 22 June 2010 in the circumstances set out below, where the customer is not entitled to recover all of the VAT on the supply.

Supply spanning the date of the VAT change

The first circumstance arises where a supply of goods or services spans the date of the VAT rate change and the supplier raises a VAT invoice or receives payment (or both) prior to the VAT rate change and the basic time of supply takes place on or after the date of the change. The supplementary charge will apply where at least one of the following relevant conditions is met:

- condition A – the supplier and the customer are connected with each other at any time during the period from the date of the supply to the date of the VAT change;
- condition B – the relevant consideration for the supply and any related supply of goods or services amounts to more than £100,000;
- condition C – the supplier or a person connected with him finances a prepayment by the customer; or
- condition D – the supplier raises a VAT invoice where payment is not due until at least six months from the date of the invoice (applies to the issue of a VAT invoice only).

Example (in respect of the increase in the rate of VAT to 17.5% from 1 January 2010)

Bob intends to spend £100,000 plus VAT on the gardens at his mansion at the beginning of the summer in May 2010. He cannot reclaim this VAT because it is a private expense so asks his gardening contractor to raise an advance invoice on 31 December 2009 (creating an actual tax point before the VAT rate increases the next day), charging VAT of £15,000 instead of £17,500 (a saving of £2,500). Bob does not intend to pay the bill until 31 May 2010 when the work is completed and this payment date is confirmed on the sales invoice. Does this arrangement create a VAT problem?

Bob cannot claim input tax so the anti-forestalling legislation needs to be considered. There are four conditions to consider as far as the anti-forestalling legislation is concerned. However, the deal is compliant on all four of them:

- Bob and his gardener are not connected parties (husband, wife, common control of companies etc.).
- The gardening contractor is not funding the purchase (by lending money to his customer who then makes payment etc.).
- Payment is due within six months of the invoice date (31 May 2009 is five months after the invoice date).
- The pre-invoiced amount does not exceed £100,000 excluding VAT.

Note – the 15% VAT charge would have been invalid if any of the four conditions above had failed. A supplementary VAT charge of 2.5% would then have been due on 1 January 2010 when we are at a 17.5% rate of VAT.

The disadvantage is that the gardening contractor will need to include output tax on the VAT return covered by his invoice date, unless he is on the cash accounting scheme in which case he will pay output tax for the VAT period when he receives his money.

Grant of right spanning the date of the VAT change

The second circumstance arises where a supply of the grant of a right to receive goods or services at a discount or free of charge is made before the date of the VAT rate change but the basic time of supply of some or all of the goods or services takes place on or after that date. A right for this purpose includes an option or an interest deriving from a right (or option). The supplementary charge will apply where at least one of the following relevant conditions is met:

- condition A – the grantor and the customer are connected with each other at any time during the period from the date of the supply to the date of the VAT change;
- condition B – the relevant consideration for the grant of the right and any related supply of goods or services amounts to more than £100,000; or
- condition C – the supplier or a person connected with him finances the customer's payment for the grant of the right.

Exceptions

Where a supply consists of the lease, hire or rent of any asset, a supplementary charge will not apply if the VAT invoice or payment covers a period of up to one year and this accords with normal commercial practice. Also, the supplementary charge will not apply if a supply meets condition B in both cases above and it is made in accordance with normal commercial practice.

Also, a supplementary charge shall not be due where the only relevant condition met is condition D (see above); the VAT invoice relates to a supply of goods made under a hire-purchase, conditional sale or credit sale agreement; forms part of that agreement; is issued in accordance with normal commercial practice; and the basic time of supply of the goods is intended and expected to be within six months of the date of the invoice.

Listed supplies

With regard to 'listed supplies' that are supplies of goods or services where payment is made periodically or from time to time and are treated as having taken place by virtue of either the issue of a VAT invoice by the supplier or receipt of payment, the basic time of supply occurs at the end of the period for which a VAT invoice is raised or payment is received. However, where a supplier has raised a VAT invoice or received payment in respect of a listed supply which is still continuing and issues an invoice for a 'billing period' that ends before the end of the period covered by the VAT invoice or payment, the end of the billing period becomes the basic time of supply for that part of the supply. In such cases, the consideration for the listed supply must be apportioned between the periods on a just and reasonable basis. Where a listed supply arises in relation to a premium for the grant of a tenancy or a lease, the basic time of supply is the date of the grant. A 'listed supply' means: a supply of services; a supply arising from the grant of a major interest in land; a supply of water other than distilled water, deionised water or water of similar purity or bottled water; a supply of coal gas, water gas, producer gases or similar gases or petroleum gases or other gaseous hydrocarbons in a gaseous state; a supply of power, heat, refrigeration or ventilation; or a supply of goods together with services in the course of the construction, alteration, demolition, repair or maintenance of a building or civil engineering work.

[*FA 2009, Sch 3; F(No 2)A 2010, Sch 2; SI 2009/3127*].

Change in VAT rates

[55.7] The provisions in **55.8** to **55.21** below apply when there is a change in the VAT rate (i.e. the standard rate is changed or a new rate is introduced) or where there is a change in the VAT liability of particular supplies (e.g. a supply previously standard-rated becomes zero-rated through a change in the law or its interpretation). Any such change is effective from a specific date and VAT is due at the new rate on supplies made on or after that date. The date on which supplies of goods and services are treated as taking place for the purposes of charging VAT is governed by the tax point rules (see **66.1–66.26 SUPPLY: TIME OF SUPPLY**). Normally no change of rate can apply to any supply with a tax point before the effective date of change (but see **55.10** below and the special rules for warehoused goods in **55.21** below). See **60.7 RETAIL SCHEMES** for the effects of a change in VAT rates or VAT liabilities where one or more of the special retail schemes are in operation but see also **55.10** below. (VAT Notice 700, paras 30.2–30.4).

VAT returns

[55.8] VAT must be accounted for in the period in which the normal tax point occurs. This applies even if one the special rules in this chapter is adopted for deciding the rate of VAT to charge. Amounts shown on the return should not be split between the old and new rates. (VAT Notice 700, para 30.7).

Reclaiming input tax

[55.9] Input tax following a change in VAT rate or VAT liability must be reclaimed at the rate charged by the supplier. Where the amount of VAT is not separately shown (e.g. on a less detailed VAT invoice — see **39.7 INVOICES**), VAT is calculated by applying the VAT fraction which was appropriate at the tax point (see **66.1–66.26 SUPPLY: TIME OF SUPPLY**). See also **55.13** below for continuous supplies of services invoiced ahead of the supply. (VAT Notice 700, para 30.6).

Output tax – general principles

[55.10] When there is a change in the VAT rate or a VAT liability, VAT is chargeable according to the normal tax point rules (see **66.1–66.26 SUPPLY: TIME OF SUPPLY**) unless the taxpayer elects for the special change of rate provisions below. It is not possible to avoid the consequences of an announced increase in VAT by preparing invoices which, although agreed by the customer, are not issued (i.e. physically sent or given to him) before the date of change. See *C & E Commrs v Woolfold Motor Co Ltd*, QB [1983] STC 715 (TVC 62.411). In any case, an invoice issued for a zero-rated supply does not create a tax point.

Special change of rate provisions.

(a) On an election, *the rate at which VAT is chargeable on a supply, or any question whether the supply is zero-rated or exempt or a reduced rate supply*, is determined by the *basic tax point* only i.e. the date on which goods are removed or made available or on which services are performed. Election may be made for all affected supplies or only some of them but an election may not be made where VAT invoices are issued under a self-billing arrangement (see **39.6 INVOICES**) or when goods are sold from the assets of a business in satisfaction of a debt. [*VATA 1994, s 88(2)(6); FA 2001, Sch 31 para 4; FA 2002, s 24*]. The effect of the election is that, where the VAT rate increases, VAT may be charged at the old rate on goods removed or services performed before the date of change even though the tax point would normally be established by the issue of a VAT invoice after the change. Similarly, where the VAT rate

goes down, VAT may be charged at the new rate on goods removed or services performed after the date of change, even though payment has been received or a VAT invoice issued before that date.
(VAT Notice 700, para 30.8).

(b) On an election, *the rate at which VAT is chargeable on an acquisition of goods from another EU country, or any question as to whether it is zero-rated or exempt or a reduced rate acquisition*, is determined by reference to the time of the first removal of the goods involved in the transaction (or, in the case of goods on sale or return, such later time when it becomes certain that they have been acquired). [*VATA 1994, s 88(4)(7); FA 2001, Sch 31 para 4*].

Credit notes

[55.11] Where an invoice has already been issued showing VAT at the old rate, it must be corrected with a credit note issued within 14 days of the change. See **39.16 INVOICES** for details. (VAT Notice 700, para 30.8).

Supplies of services

[55.12] Output tax may be charged at the old rate on the part completed before the date of a change in the VAT rate and at the new rate on the part completed on or after that date provided the supply can be apportioned on a basis of measurable work or in accordance with a supplier's normal costing or pricing system. Where VAT is reduced in this way and a VAT invoice was issued or payment was received before the date of VAT change, a credit note must be provided (see **55.11** above). (VAT Notice 700, para 30.9).

Continuous supplies of goods and services

[55.13] Where there is a continuous supply of goods or services (including hire, lease and rental of goods) VAT is normally chargeable at the rate applying at each tax point. See **66.19 SUPPLY: TIME OF SUPPLY** for services and **66.15 SUPPLY: TIME OF SUPPLY** for a continuous supply of goods in the form of water, gas and electricity. Any VAT invoice issued up to one year ahead, giving the amounts and dates when payments are due, is invalid in respect of payments due after the change (and not received before it). [*SI 1995/2518, Reg 90(3)*]. A new invoice, referring to and cancelling the superseded part of the original invoice, must be issued. The customer cannot use the original invoice to support a claim for input tax after the change and must make the necessary adjustments on receipt of the new invoice.

Where a continuous supply spans a change in the VAT rate, VAT may be accounted for at the *old* rate on that part of the supply made before the change even though the normal tax point would occur after the change (e.g. where a payment is received in arrears of the supply). Conversely, VAT may be accounted for at the *new* rate on that part of the supply made after the change even though the normal tax point occurred before the change (e.g. where a payment is received in advance of the supply). In each case, VAT should be accounted for on the basis of the value of goods actually supplied or services actually performed before or after the change as appropriate. Where VAT liability is reduced on a supply for which a VAT invoice has been issued at a higher rate, a credit note must be issued (see **55.11** above). (VAT Notice 700, para 30.10).

Facilities provided by clubs, associations, etc.

[55.14] Clubs, associations, etc. supplying facilities in return for a member's subscription must normally account for VAT at the rate applying when the subscription is received or a VAT invoice is issued, whichever happens first. Where payment is made by instalments or separate invoices are issued, the procedure for continuous supply of services should be followed (see **55.13** above). (VAT Notice 700, para 30.11).

Hire purchase, conditional and credit sales

[55.15] Under any of these agreements, there is a single supply of goods and the normal tax point is the earliest of

(a) the date of removal of the goods;
(b) the date of issue of the agreement (provided the agreement is in the form of a VAT invoice); and
(c) the date of the issue of a separate VAT invoice.

See **66.11 SUPPLY: TIME OF SUPPLY**.

The signing of an agreement, or its date, does not constitute a tax point. Where there is a change in the VAT rate, the tax point will be whichever of (*a*) to (*c*) above results in the lower rate of VAT being charged. (VAT Notice 700, para 30.12).

Deposits and payments in advance of the basic tax point

[55.16] Where full or part payment is made, or a VAT invoice issued, before the basic tax point (see above), VAT will normally be due on the amount paid or invoiced at the rate in force at that date. Where full payment is made in advance but the money is loaned back to the customer on the understanding that it will be repaid as the work proceeds, the transaction has been held to be genuine and not to fall foul of the decision in *W T Ramsay Ltd v IRC* even if the scheme is designed purely to save VAT. A similar decision has been reached where monies are paid into deposit accounts of the builders but only released against architects' certificates (*C & E Commrs v Faith Construction Ltd and related appeals*, CA [1989] STC 539 (TVC 62.423)). If there is a change in the VAT rate before the supply is actually made, VAT may be charged at the rate applicable when the supply is made and a credit note issued (see above) to amend the VAT invoice. These provisions do not apply to deposits taken as security (e.g. to ensure safe return of goods hired out) which are refundable or subject to forfeiture *or* if the deposit does not relate to a particular supply or contract (e.g. money paid into a client's account). (VAT Notice 700, para 30.13).

Credit and contingent discounts

[55.17] Where a credit note (not arising from the change in rate) is issued to adjust an original invoice, VAT should be credited at the rate in force at the tax point of the original supply. Where contingent discount is allowed and the original VAT charge is adjusted, VAT should be credited at the rate in force at the time of each supply qualifying for the discount. (VAT Notice 700, para 30.14).

Price escalation clauses and other adjustments

[55.18] Where an additional payment is required after a change in the VAT rate and after the tax point for the original supply determined under the normal rules, VAT is chargeable on the further payment at the old rate. Where VAT was not determined under the normal rules on the original supply, the tax point for the additional payment is the earlier of the date of receipt of a further payment or the issue of a VAT invoice and VAT is chargeable at the rate then in force. (VAT Notice 700, para 30.15).

Existing contracts

[55.19] Where, after the making of a contract for the supply of goods or services and before those goods or services are supplied, there is a change in the VAT charged, then, unless the contract provides otherwise, the consideration for the supply is increased or decreased by an amount equal to the change. These provisions apply in relation to a tenancy or lease as they apply in relation to a contract.

A landlord is able to add VAT to the rent where

- he makes an election to charge VAT on rents at the standard rate under the option to tax provisions (see **41.8 LAND AND BUILDINGS: EXEMPT SUPPLIES AND OPTION TO TAX**); or
- there is an increase in the rate of VAT

unless the terms of the lease specifically prevent him from passing on VAT to his tenants.

[*VATA 1994, s 89; SI 2008/1146, Sch 1 para* 2].

HMRC do not advise on contracts. (VAT Notice 700, para 30.16).

Second-hand goods

[55.20] VAT chargeable on the sale of a second-hand article under the Margin Scheme for **SECOND-HAND GOODS (61)** is calculated by applying the appropriate VAT fraction at the tax point to the VAT-inclusive amount. The tax point is the earlier of the date of removal of the goods and the receipt of payment. If there is a change in the VAT rate before the goods are removed, VAT may be accounted for at the rate in force when the goods are removed even if payment has already been received. (*Note*. A VAT invoice must not be issued for goods supplied under a second-hand scheme). (VAT Notice 700, para 30.17).

Warehoused goods

Imported goods

[55.21] When imported goods are removed from bonded warehouse for home use, the rate of VAT chargeable is that in force at the time of removal.

Home-produced goods

For home-produced goods subject to excise duty which have been supplied while in warehouse, the rate of VAT chargeable is that in force when the excise duty is paid. For goods relieved of excise duty, the rate of VAT chargeable is that applicable at the time of their removal from warehouse.

(VAT Notice 700, para 30.18).

Key points

[55.22] Points to consider are as follows.

- Be aware of the opportunities to raise invoices or receive payments before a VAT rate increase that will enable some customers to benefit from a lower charge of VAT. However, this will not be worthwhile if customers can claim input tax on the expense anyway.
- The anti-forestalling legislation is designed to prevent an artificial manipulation of the tax point rules to create a lower VAT charge. However, it will only apply in limited circumstances – mainly if the transaction is more than £100,000 and the customer cannot reclaim all of the VAT as input tax.
- The anti-forestalling legislation should not apply if the value of a transaction exceeds £100,000 but is made within the normal commercial practices of the supplier in question. This is particularly relevant for those businesses that either rent out property or are involved with the leasing of assets.
- It may be worthwhile for a business to buy its motor cars before a VAT rate increase. Input tax on motor cars is generally non-deductible if the car is available for private use.
- VAT rate increases lead to extra overheads for many businesses that are not able to fully reclaim input tax (e.g. exempt or partly exempt businesses). One potential planning opportunity is to approach landlords that charge VAT on renting premises to a business, to see if the landlord can revoke his option to tax election on the property in question. This would be possible if 20 years or more have passed since the landlord first made his option to tax election with HMRC. This means that future rental charges would again be exempt from VAT rather than standard-rated.
- A credit note issued to amend a sales invoice must always be issued at the same rate of VAT as the original invoice.

56

Records

Cross-references. See **31.6 HMRC: POWERS** for the production of documents; **39 INVOICES** for details to be recorded on sales invoices; **63.5 SPECIAL SCHEMES** for records under the cash accounting scheme; **63.21 SPECIAL SCHEMES** for records under the flat-rate scheme for small businesses; **63.29** and **63.30 SPECIAL SCHEMES** for records and invoices under the flat-rate scheme for farmers.

Introduction

General requirements

[56.1] Every taxable person must keep such records as HMRC may require. [*VATA 1994, Sch 11 para 6(1)*].

Specifically, every taxable person must, for the purposes of accounting for VAT, keep the following records.

- His business and accounting records.
- His VAT account.
- Copies of all VAT invoices issued by him.
- VAT invoices received by him.
- Certificates issued under provisions relating to fiscal or other warehouse regimes.
- Documentation received by him relating to acquisitions of any goods from other EU countries.

- Copy documentation issued by him, and documentation received by him, relating to the transfer, dispatch or transportation of goods by him to other EU countries.
- Documentation relating to importations and exportations by him.
- All credit notes, debit notes and other documents which evidence an increase or decrease in consideration that are received, and copies of all such documents that are issued by him.
- A copy of any self-billing agreement to which he is a party (see **39.6 INVOICES**).
- Where he is a customer, party to a self-billing agreement, the name, address and VAT registration number of each supplier with whom he has entered into a self-billing agreement (see **39.6 INVOICES**).

[*SI 1995/2518, Reg 31(1); SI 1996/1250, Reg 8; SI 2003/3220, Reg 11*].

Additionally, HMRC may supplement the above provisions by a Notice published by them for that purpose. [*SI 1995/2518, Reg 31(2)*]. These requirements, which are contained in VAT Notice 700, Section 19, are considered below in this chapter. They supplement the statutory requirements and *have legal force*.

Business records include, in addition to specific items listed above, orders and delivery notes, relevant business correspondence, purchases and sales books, cash books and other account books, records of daily takings such as till rolls, annual accounts, including trading and profit and loss accounts and bank statements and paying-in slips.

Unless the business mainly involves the supply of goods and services direct to the public and less detailed VAT invoices are issued (see **39.7 INVOICES**), all VAT invoices must also be retained. *Cash and carry wholesalers* must keep all till rolls and product code lists.

Records must be kept of all taxable goods and services received or supplied in the course of business (standard and zero-rated), together with any exempt supplies, gifts or loans of goods, taxable self-supplies and any goods acquired or produced in the course of business which are put to private or other non-business use.

All records must be kept up to date and be in sufficient detail to allow calculation of VAT. They do not have to be kept in any set way but must be in a form which will enable HMRC officers to check easily the figures on the VAT return. Records must be readily available to HMRC officers on request. If a taxable person has more than one place of business, a list of all branches must be kept at the principal place of business.

(VAT Notice 700, paras 19.2, 19.4).

Special records

In addition to the above general requirements, special records are necessary where the taxable person is operating the cash accounting scheme (see **63.5 SPECIAL SCHEMES**), the flat-rate scheme for farmers (see **63.29 SPECIAL SCHEMES**), one of the **RETAIL SCHEMES (60)** or one of the schemes for

SECOND-HAND GOODS (61). These requirements are dealt with in the appropriate chapter. See also **19.30 EUROPEAN UNION: SINGLE MARKET** for the requirement to keep a register of temporary movement of goods to and from other EU countries.

Direction to keep records where belief VAT might not be paid

With effect from 19 July 2006, where HMRC have reasonable grounds for believing that certain records might assist in them identifying taxable supplies on which the VAT chargeable might not be paid, they may direct any taxable person named in the direction to keep such records as they specify in the direction in relation to such goods as they so specify (in addition to any records under the general requirements above). In this connection

- the direction may require the records to be compiled by reference to VAT invoices or any other matter; and
- the taxable supplies in question may be supplies made by the person named in the direction or any other person.

The direction must be given by notice in writing to the person named in it and must warn that person of the penalty for failure to comply (see **52.28 PENALTIES**). It remains in force until it is revoked or replaced by a further direction.

HMRC may require any records kept under these provisions to be preserved for a period not exceeding six years and the provision in **56.4** below as to the form in which records may be preserved also apply for these purposes.

Appeals

An appeal may be made against a direction but the tribunal cannot allow the appeal unless it considers that HMRC could not reasonably have been satisfied that there were grounds for making the direction. The direction has effect pending the determination of the appeal.

[*VATA 1994, s 84(7B); Sch 11 para 6A; FA 2006, s 21(5)(6); FA 2008, Sch 37 para 6*].

De Voil Indirect Tax Service. See V5.201.

Records by non-taxable persons

[56.2] Non-taxable persons are generally outside the scope of VAT and are not therefore required to keep any records for VAT purposes. However, any person who, at a time when he is not a taxable person, acquires in the UK from another EU country any goods which are subject to excise duty or which consist of a new means of transport must keep such records of the acquisition as HMRC specify in any Notice published by them. [*SI 1995/2518, Reg 31(3)*]. See **19.9** and **19.37 EUROPEAN UNION: SINGLE MARKET**.

Preservation of records

[56.3] Every taxable person must keep such records as are required for a period not exceeding six years as specified in writing by HMRC (and different periods may be specified for different cases). [*VATA 1994, Sch 11 para 6(3); FA 2008, Sch 37 para 5*]. If this causes storage problems or involves undue expense, HMRC should be consulted. They will be able to advise whether some records can be retained for a shorter period. Agreement of HMRC must be obtained before any business records are destroyed within six years. (VAT Notice 700, para 19.2).

HMRC are unlikely to agree to a shorter retention period than

- one year for copies of orders, delivery notes, dispatch notes, goods returned notes, invoices for expenses incurred by employees, production records, stock records (except those for second-hand schemes), job cards, appointment books, diaries, and business letters;
- three years for import, export and delivery from warehouse documents, day books, ledgers, cash books, and second-hand scheme stock books;
- four years for purchase invoices, copy sales invoices, credit notes, debit notes, authenticated receipts, daily gross takings records, records related to retail scheme calculations, and catering estimates; and
- five years for bank statements and paying in books, management accounts, and annual accounts.

Any records containing the VAT account must always be kept for the full six years.

(HMRC VAT Guidance V1–24A, para 3.4.1).

De Voil Indirect Tax Service. See V5.202.

Forms in which records may be preserved

[56.4] The duty to preserve records may be discharged by

- preserving them; or
- preserving the information contained in them

in any form and by any means subject to any conditions or exceptions specified in writing by HMRC.

[*VATA 1994, Sch 11 para 6(4); FA 2008, Sch 37 para 5*].

In addition to the preservation of the full original records, HMRC have approved the use of the following.

- **Microfilm and microfiche** provided that the copies can readily be produced and that there are adequate facilities for HMRC to view when required. Clearance must be obtained in advance from HMRC before any transfer to microfilm or microfiche. HMRC may require the old and new systems to be operated side by side for a limited time.
- **Computer records** provided the storage media e.g. magnetic tape, disc, etc. can readily be converted into a legible form on request by HMRC. Where records are kept on a computer, HMRC can have access to it and

can check its operation and the information stored. They can also ask for help from anyone concerned with the operation of the computer or its software. See **31.11 HMRC: POWERS**. Where the records are kept by a computer bureau, the taxable person is responsible for arranging for the bureau to make the records available to HMRC when required. Normally this will be at the principal place of business. Where a taxable person decides to use a computer or the services of a bureau for VAT accounting after registration, HMRC should be notified (at the systems design stage or earlier for in-house computers).

(VAT Notice 700, para 19.2).

De Voil Indirect Tax Service. See V5.206; V5.207.

Records of output tax

[56.5] Note: the following does not apply to supplies dealt with under one of the special schemes for retailers. For records required in these cases, see **60 RETAIL SCHEMES.**

Records must be kept of all supplies made in the course of business including goods sent out on sale or return, approval or similar terms. Information recorded must contain all the information required on VAT invoices. See **39.3 INVOICES.** Where fully detailed invoices are issued and filed so as to be readily available, the record required is a summary (in the same order as copy invoices) enabling separate totals to be produced for each VAT period of

(a) the amount of VAT chargeable on supplies and acquisitions. The VAT on adjustment for credits allowed (see **56.6** below) should be deducted from the amount of VAT payable in the VAT account (see **56.12** below);
(b) the VAT-exclusive value of standard-rated and zero-rated supplies and acquisitions;
(c) the value of any exempt supplies and acquisitions; and
(d) the amount of VAT due on goods imported by post (other than Datapost) with a value not exceeding £2,000 (see **33.3 IMPORTS**) and on certain services received from abroad (see **38.4 INTERNATIONAL SERVICES**). These amounts should also be carried to the VAT payable portion of the VAT account (see **56.12** below).

Under (*b*) and (*c*) above, no deduction should be made for *cash* discounts allowed but any credits allowed (see **56.6** below) should be deducted.

Goods given away or put to private or other non-business use

If acquired or produced in the course of business, VAT is due and a record must be kept showing date of transaction, description and quantity of the goods, VAT-exclusive cost and rate and amount of VAT chargeable. See **47.6** and **47.7 OUTPUT TAX** for the value of the supply.

Self-supplies

See **45.6 MOTOR CARS** for motor cars used by motor manufacturers or dealers who have produced or acquired them in the course of business. Records must show the tax point, value on which VAT is chargeable and the rate and amount of VAT. See **62.2 SELF-SUPPLY** for records to be kept by a partly exempt trader who self-supplies certain printed matter.

(VAT Notice 700, para 19.5).

Records of credits allowed to customers

[56.6] Note: where a **RETAIL SCHEME (60)** is used, the following only applies where the credit involves a VAT invoice.

Records must be kept of all credits allowed for taxable (including zero-rated) and exempt supplies and acquisitions. A record of a credit relating to

- **a VAT invoice** must contain the information required on VAT invoices (see **39.3 INVOICES**) or indicate (e.g. by cross-reference to filed copies of credit notes) where the details can be found; and
- **zero-rated or exempt supplies** must show the date and amount of the credit and indicate whether an export is a zero-rated supply in the UK or an exempt supply.

For VAT purposes, where filed copies of credit notes are complete and accessible no separate record need be kept.

(VAT Notice 700, para 19.6).

Records of input tax

[56.7] For EU legislation, see **18.37 EUROPEAN UNION LEGISLATION.**

Under UK legislation, records must be kept of all standard-rated, reduced-rated and zero-rated supplies received for business purposes. They must be kept in such a way that, given the invoice date and the supplier's name, they can be easily produced to HMRC.

At the time of claiming input tax deduction, one of the items listed in (*a*)–(*d*) below (as appropriate) must normally be held to support a claim to input tax. HMRC *may*, however, direct that a claimant can hold or provide other evidence of the VAT charged. Such a direction may be made generally or in relation to particular cases or classes of cases.

(a) A supplier's invoice

Subject to below, where the supply is from another UK VAT-registered business, the claimant must hold a 'valid VAT invoice' or a document treated as such (see **39.2 INVOICES**). See also **63.30 SPECIAL SCHEMES** for invoices from flat-rate farmers. An invoice marked 'pro forma' or 'this is not a VAT invoice' is not acceptable for the purposes of reclaiming VAT.

Exceptions

No VAT invoice is required where total expenditure for each taxable supply is £25 or less (including VAT) and relates to

- telephone calls from public or private telephones;
- purchases through coin-operated machines;
- car park charges (on-street parking meters are not subject to VAT); or
- a single or return standard-rated toll charge (see **47.8**(33) **OUTPUT TAX**) paid at the tollbooth. But a VAT invoice is required, irrespective of the price of each individual toll, if
  - (i) a book of toll tickets is purchased; or
  - (ii) a tolled road, bridge or crossing is used under an arrangement where either payment is made in advance (e.g. where an electronic tag is used) or an invoice is raised in arrears (e.g. an account customer).

A '*valid VAT invoice*' is one that meets the full requirements in **39.4**(*a*)–(*m*) **INVOICES** or, as the case may be, the reduced requirements in **39.7** to **39.9** **INVOICES**.

An '*invalid VAT invoice*' is one that does not meet those full requirements. Even if an invoice contains all the information required, it is still invalid if, for example, it relates to a business other than the one making the supply or the details shown relate to a company in liquidation. Some invalidities may be easy to detect (e.g. whether the goods or services are correctly described) but it may be more difficult to detect a false name, address or VAT number. HMRC have established a team who can confirm that any given VAT registration details are current, valid and match information held by them (tel: 01737 734 516/577/612/761) but this cannot be viewed as authorisation of a transaction with that VAT registration by the supplier in question. The claimant should be able to demonstrate that the person shown as making the supply is the same person who actually made the supply.

A claimant holding an invalid VAT invoice should, wherever possible, ask the supplier to issue a valid VAT invoice. HMRC expect that only a very small number of businesses will be unable to obtain a valid VAT invoice in this way.

Where a valid VAT invoice cannot be obtained, HMRC may apply their discretion and still allow recovery.

(i) For supplies of goods comprising
- computers and any other equipment, including parts, accessories and software, made or adapted for use in connection with computers or computer systems,
- telephones and any other equipment, including parts and accessories, made or adapted for use in connection with telephones or telecommunications,
- alcoholic liquors liable to excise duty which are defined by *Alcoholic Liquor Duties Act 1979, s 1* or in any regulations made under that *Act* (e.g. spirits, wines and fortified wines, made-wines, beer, cider and perry), and
- oils that are held out for sale as road fuel

claimants will need to be able to answer satisfactorily *all or nearly all* of questions (1)–(6) below (plus any additional questions HMRC ask in individual circumstances, in particular questions to test whether they took reasonable care in respect of transactions to ensure that their supplier and the supply were 'bona fide').

(ii) For supplies of goods not falling within (i) above, claimants will need to be able to answer satisfactorily *most* of questions (1)–(6) below. In most cases, this will be little more than providing alternative evidence to show that the supply of goods or services has been made. (This has always been HMRC's policy.)

The questions to determine whether there is a right to deduct in the absence of a valid VAT invoice are as follows.

(1) Does the claimant have alternative documentary evidence other than an invoice (e.g. a supplier's statement)?
(2) Does the claimant have evidence of receipt of a taxable supply on which VAT has been charged?
(3) Does the claimant have evidence of payment?
(4) Does the claimant have evidence of how the goods/services have been consumed within the business or their onward supply?
(5) How did the claimant know that the supplier existed?
(6) How was the claimant's relationship with the supplier established? For example:
   - How was contact made?
   - Does the claimant know where the supplier operates from (and has he been there)?
   - How does the claimant contact the supplier?
   - How does the claimant know the supplier can supply the goods or services?
   - If goods, how does the claimant know the goods are not stolen?
   - How can faulty supplies be returned?

Incomplete invoices

Normally the invoice or other document should contain the full particulars required for a valid VAT invoice (see above). However, HMRC may accept as satisfactory evidence an invoice complete except for

- an identifying number;
- the customer's name and address; and
- the tax point (provided there is a date which can be taken to be the tax point)

provided the supplies in question are clearly for business purposes.

Originals normally required

VAT invoices held to substantiate claims to input tax should be originals. Copies are not normally accepted.

Where, however, the accounting arrangements require the original VAT invoice to be sent to a destination within the business which is different from the registered address for VAT (e.g. a branch), HMRC may accept a photocopy of the original as evidence in support of input tax claims provided

- each photocopy is certified by a responsible officer as being a true copy of the original; and
- the original invoice is produced for inspection by HMRC on formal request.

All requirements of a VAT invoice apply to the photocopy. HMRC will notify the business in writing of the conditions and the business must give a written acceptance.

Invoices sent by fax or e-mail

HMRC now accept that, as an alternative to sending VAT invoices by post, they may be sent to customers by fax or e-mail. See **39.14 INVOICES**. If the invoice is received via fax and the recipient has a thermal-paper fax machine, the invoice may not be permanent and the recipient may not be able to fulfil the obligation to preserve the invoice for six years.

Cash and carry wholesalers' invoices

If the invoice is only in the form of a till roll with goods represented by product code numbers, an up-to-date copy of the wholesaler's product code list must be kept with the till rolls.

Invoices in name of employees

Certain invoices made out in the name of employees can be accepted as evidence for input tax purposes. See **34.5 INPUT TAX**.

Court and tribunal decisions

A claim for input tax has been allowed where invoices were destroyed accidentally (*JJ Newman* (VTD 781, VTD 903) (TVC 40.62)) and where invoices were lost on a change of residence but had previously been checked by the firm's accountants (*Read and Smith* (VTD 1188) (TVC 40.64)). See *Chavda (t/a Hare Wines)* (VTD 9895) (TVC 40.10) where the tribunal held that HMRC had not acted reasonably by refusing to exercise their discretion to accept other documentary evidence (delivery notes) of the input tax incurred by the appellant. However, in the vast majority of tribunal and court decisions, claims for input tax without supporting invoices have been rejected and it has been ruled that countries have the power to require production of original invoices (*Reisdorf v Finanzamt Köln-West*, ECJ [1997] STC 180 (TVC 22.472)). Where HMRC refuse to use their discretion to allow credit, tribunals only have a supervisory jurisdiction, the burden of proof being on the appellant to show that HMRC acted unreasonably. See *Kohanzad v C & E Commrs*, QB [1994] STC 967 (TVC 40.73) and the Invoices and Credit Notes chapter in *Tolley's VAT Cases*.

(b) Evidence of VAT on goods imported or removed from bonded warehouse

On importation of goods, the claimant must hold a document showing him as importer, consignee or owner and showing an amount of VAT charged on the goods and authenticated or issued by the proper officer. For goods which have been removed from warehouse, the claimant must hold a document authenticated or issued by the proper officer showing the claimant's particulars and the amount of the VAT charged on the goods. See **33.11 IMPORTS** for the official evidence (or other acceptable evidence) required which serves the same purpose as a VAT invoice from a registered UK supplier.

(c) Evidence of VAT on goods acquired from another EU country

On the acquisition of goods from another EU country, the claimant must hold a document required to be issued by the authority in that other country showing the claimant's VAT registration number (including the prefix 'GB'), the registration number of the supplier (including alphabetical code), the consideration for the supply exclusive of VAT, the date of issue of the document and a description of the goods supplied sufficient to identify them. Where the goods are a new means of transport (see **19.33 EUROPEAN UNION: SINGLE MARKET**) the description must be sufficient to identify the acquisition as a new means of transport.

(d) Evidence of services received from abroad

Where any of the services listed in *VATA 1994, Sch 5* are received from abroad (see **38.4 INTERNATIONAL SERVICES**) the relevant invoice from the person supplying the services should be held.

[*SI 1995/2518, Reg 29(2); SI 2003/1114*]. (VAT Notice 700, para 19.7; HMRC VAT Guidance V1–13, paras 8.7, 8.8; HMRC Statement of Practice *VAT strategy: input tax deduction without a valid invoice*).

Non-deductible items

VAT is not reclaimable on certain supplies received for the business e.g. motor cars and entertainment expenses (see **34.8 INPUT TAX** for details). However, a record must be kept of such supplies received even though the VAT charged is not to be included in the total carried to the VAT account.

De Voil Indirect Tax Service. See V3.415; V3.421; V3.425–427.

Form of records

[56.8] Where fully detailed invoices are received and filed so as to be readily available, the record required is a summary (in the same order as the invoices are filed) enabling a separate total to be produced for each VAT period of

(a) the amount of VAT charged on goods and services received including any VAT paid at import or on removal from bonded warehouse. Where adjustment is required for credit received from suppliers in the period (see **56.9** below) this should be deducted;

(b) the amount of VAT due on any goods imported by post (other than Datapost) with a value of £2,000 or less and on certain services received from abroad (see **38.4 INTERNATIONAL SERVICES**);

(c) the VAT-exclusive value of all supplies received, including all such goods and services within (*b*) above.

Subject to the normal rules, the total amount of deductible input tax ((*a*) plus (*b*)) should be carried to the VAT allowable portion of the VAT account (see **56.12** below).

Under (*c*) above no deduction for *cash* discounts should be made but all credits received from suppliers should be deducted.

An add-list is an acceptable summary if it shows VAT and values separately itemised in the order in which the VAT invoices are batched or filed. Alternatively, **cashbook accounting for inputs** may be used where it is the normal accounting practice to claim input tax when suppliers are paid. In practice, the cash book payments record is adapted to serve as a record of inputs. On a change in basis of accounting to this method, VAT already claimed on a previous return should be excluded. See also **63.2 SPECIAL SCHEMES.**

Note: if any of the **RETAIL SCHEMES (60)** is used, the cash book can also be used to work out the value of goods received for resale provided amounts owed to suppliers at the beginning of the period are subtracted and amounts owed at the end of the period are added.

(VAT Notice 700, para 19.8).

Records of credits received from suppliers

[56.9] Records must be kept of all credits received for taxable (including zero-rated) inputs. A record of a credit relating to

- **a VAT invoice** must contain the information listed in **39.3** *et seq.* **INVOICES**, or indicate (e.g. by cross-reference to filed credit notes) where the details can be found; and
- **zero-rated supplies** need only indicate the date and amount of the credit.

For VAT purposes, where filed credit notes are complete and easily accessible, no separate record need be kept.

VAT adjustments

Where a credit is received relating to deductible input tax (see **39.15 INVOICES**) and a VAT adjustment has to be made, records of supplies received and input tax must be adjusted. Whatever method is used to do this, the nature of the adjustment and reason for it must be clear from the accounts and supporting documents. At the end of each VAT period the deductible input tax entered in the VAT account and the VAT return entries must be the net amount, i.e. after deducting any VAT credits received in the period. If VAT credits received from suppliers exceed VAT charged on purchases in any VAT period, a minus figure (shown in brackets) should be entered in the input tax box on the VAT return. Where debit notes are issued to suppliers from whom credit is due and the commercial records are then adjusted, the VAT record may also be adjusted at that time. If later credit notes are received from suppliers, any errors should be corrected but the debit and credit notes should not be both used as accounting documents.

Provided both parties to the transaction agree, the *original* VAT charged need not be adjusted on a debit note issued by a fully taxable person.

(VAT Notice 700, para 19.8).

Adjustments where wrong amount of VAT shown on VAT invoices

[56.10] Note: this paragraph does *not* apply where there has been a change in the consideration for the supply, i.e. if the price has changed and consequently the amount of VAT. In these circumstances, see **39.15 INVOICES** for the provisions relating to credit and debit notes.

This paragraph explains how to correct an error if the wrong amount of VAT was shown on an invoice, e.g. where

- an arithmetical mistake is made in calculating the VAT value and/or the VAT element of the supply; or
- VAT is charged on a supply where no VAT was due.

Unless both the supplier and customer agree to adjust their VAT accounts (see below):

(a) *If the VAT shown on the invoice is too high,*
   - the supplier must account for the higher amount in his records, unless he corrects the error with the customer by issuing a credit note; and
   - the customer must go back to the supplier for a replacement invoice reducing the amount of VAT charged.

(b) *If the VAT shown on the invoice is too low,*
   - the supplier must account for the amount which should have charged, whether or not he corrects the error with the customer (e.g. by issuing a supplementary invoice); and
   - the customer must go back to the supplier for a replacement invoice increasing the amount of VAT charged.

   Where the supplier is unwilling or unable to recover the whole of the balance due from the customer, a VAT adjustment, calculated from the total VAT-inclusive amount actually charged, should be made.

Example

	£
Value of goods on VAT invoice	500.00
VAT due = £500 × 17.5%* = £87.50 but incorrectly stated as	55.00
Invoiced amount	£555.00
Adjusted VAT due	
£555 × 7/47** (VAT fraction)	82.66
Deduct VAT charged	55.00
Balance payable	£27.66

*20% from 4 January 2011; 15% from 1 December 2008 to 31 December 2009

**1/6 from 4 January 2011; 3/23 from 1 December 2008 to 31 December 2009

(VAT Notice 700, para 19.10; VAT Notice 700/45/11, paras 3.1–3.3).

De Voil Indirect Tax Service. See V3.518; V3.519.

Correction of errors on a return already submitted

[56.11] There are two methods for correcting errors on a return already submitted.

Method 1

This method may be used to adjust the VAT account (see **56.12** below) and include the value of that adjustment on the current VAT return providing

- the net value of errors found on previous returns does not exceed £10,000; or
- the net value of errors found on previous returns is between £10,000 and £50,000 but does not exceed 1% of the box 6 (net outputs) VAT return declaration due for the return period in which the errors are discovered.

To work out the net value of VAT errors on previous returns, the business should work out

- the total amount due to HMRC, if any; and
- the total amount due to the business, if any.

If the difference between the two figures is greater than £10,000 and exceeds 1% of the box 6 (net outputs) VAT return declaration due for the current return period during which the error is discovered, then Method 2 must be used. Method 2 must always be used if the net errors exceed £50,000 or if the errors made on previous returns were made deliberately.

Correcting errors using this method is not a disclosure for the purposes of the penalties for error regime described below. If the business considers that the error was a result of careless conduct, maximum reduction of the penalty will not be granted unless HMRC is notified separately in writing, by letter and/or completion of form VAT 652, of the error and the grounds for seeking a reduction to the penalty.

Example

Alan is VAT-registered and has discovered two VAT errors made in the period ended 31 March 2011:

- input tax incorrectly claimed on the purchase of a motor car available for private use £12,000;
- arithmetical error in output tax calculations – £3,000 overpaid.

The net value of the errors made by Alan (£12,000 – £3,000 = £9,000) is less than £10,000 so they can be recorded in his VAT account for the current VAT period and declared on the next VAT return he submits.

Method 2 (error correction notification)

This method must be used if

- the net value of errors found on previous returns is between £10,000 and £50,000 and exceeds 1% of the box 6 (net outputs) VAT return declaration due for the current return period during which the error was discovered; or
- the net value of errors found on previous returns is greater than £50,000; or
- the errors on previous returns were made deliberately.

This method may be used for errors within the limits shown under Method 1 above, instead of a Method 1 error correction. If this method is used, adjustment must not be made for the same errors on a later VAT return.

When notifying HMRC of an error correction the business should use VAT 652, or should write to the appropriate office providing full details of the errors including

- how each error arose;
- the VAT accounting period in which it occurred;
- if it was an input tax or output error;
- the VAT underdeclared or overdeclared in each VAT period;
- how the VAT underdeclared or overdeclared was calculated;
- whether any of the errors resulted in the business paying HMRC an amount that wasn't due (in which case see **51.9 PAYMENT OF VAT**); and
- the total amount to be adjusted.

(VAT Notice 700/45/11, paras 4.3, 4.4).

Notice of error correction by HMRC and payment

Once an error correction notification has been processed, HMRC will send the business, normally within 21 days, a Notice of Error Correction (confirming the amount of the error correction and any interest calculated on it) and a Statement of Account (showing the current balance payable to or repayable by HMRC). Where, however, the correction generated a repayment which is subject to the unjust enrichment provisions (see **51.10 PAYMENT OF VAT**) the business will be notified by letter and will not receive these documents.

Where payment is due to HMRC, full payment should be sent to The Controller, HMRC, VAT Central Unit, Alexander House, 21 Victoria Avenue, Southend-on-Sea, SS99 1AA. Further interest may be charged if the amount due is not paid in full within 30 days from the calculation date shown on the Notice of Error Correction. Payment can be made by any of the methods outlined in **51.2 PAYMENT OF VAT**. Where repayment is due from HMRC, they will use it to reduce any outstanding balance due to them (if any) and repay the remainder either by BACS or payable order.

(VAT Notice 700/45/11, paras 7.2–7.4).

Time limit for correcting errors

A business cannot adjust its VAT return, or make an error correction notification, for any errors that arose in accounting periods that are outside the time limits below, unless the errors are tax point errors, that is, where the business has declared an amount of VAT on the return that immediately precedes or follows the return for which the amount was due.

The time limit for adjusting returns and correcting errors, including making claims, was increased with effect from 1 April 2009 from three years to four. However, in order to ensure that accounting periods that were out-of-time on 31 March 2009 are not brought back in-time by the change, transitional arrangements have been put in place. The transitional arrangements provide that no adjustment or error correction notification made between 1 April 2009 and 31 March 2010 can be made for any accounting period ending before 1 April 2006.

(VAT Notice 700/45/11, para 4.6).

Penalties for error regime

Errors or inaccuracies relating to return periods beginning on or after 1 April 2008, where the due date for the return is on or after 1 April 2009, are liable to a penalty if they are careless or deliberate. If a person discovers a non-careless error, HMRC expect that they will take steps to correct it, otherwise the inaccuracy will be treated as careless and a penalty will be due.

Careless or deliberate inaccuracies relating to returns commencing on or after 1 April 2008 with a due date on or after 1 April 2009, that are being corrected using Method 1 or 2, are subject to the new penalty regime.

Where careless or deliberate behaviour results in an incorrect error correction notification being made under Method 2 the business will be subject to a penalty if it is correcting errors made on returns commencing on or after 1 April 2008 with a due date on or after 1 April 2009. This applies regardless of whether the original errors were made despite taking reasonable care or not.

In order for HMRC to consider any reduction to a penalty, the business should tell them if it has made a careless error or deliberate inaccuracy regardless of its size or value. Although HMRC also require separate disclosure for the purpose of reducing any penalty, careless errors may be adjusted on the next VAT return subject to the limits described above.

Correction of deliberate inaccuracies must, however, always be notified to HMRC using form VAT 652, providing a description of the inaccuracy, the full amount of the inaccuracy and explaining how and why the inaccuracy arose.

If the business has adjusted a careless error/inaccuracy on its return that is within the limits described above it may still write to HMRC asking them to consider any reduction to a penalty. The letter should contain the same information that is required on form VAT 652, but it is important to also tell HMRC that the adjustment has been made on the return. The majority of such errors will not be careless or deliberate, so no penalty will be due. When considering whether an error was careless, HMRC will seek to establish whether the business has taken the care and attention that could be expected from a reasonable person taking reasonable care in similar circumstances.

(VAT Notice 700/45/11, para 4.1).

Discovery of errors by HMRC

For accounting periods after the introduction of the penalties for errors regime

If HMRC find underdeclarations of VAT on the VAT returns of a business, they will assess for the tax due and may charge interest. The business may also be liable to a penalty.

For accounting periods prior to the introduction of the penalties for errors regime

If HMRC find underdeclarations of VAT on the returns of a business, they will assess for the tax due and may charge interest. The business may also face a misdeclaration penalty (see **52.12 PENALTIES**). To avoid a penalty, the business must disclose full details of the mistakes before HMRC begin to make enquiries into its VAT affairs. Enquiries normally begin when HMRC make an appointment to inspect records. But they accept disclosures for penalty purposes after this point, unless they have reason to believe that

- the business discovered the errors earlier and disclosed them only because it had been told that a visit was to be made; or
- disclosure during or after a visit was prompted by HMRC enquiries into the affairs of the business.

In addition, deliberate failure to correct an underdeclaration of VAT may give rise to a civil penalty for dishonest evasion (see **52.10 PENALTIES**) or criminal prosecution (see **52.2 PENALTIES**).

(VAT Notice 700/45/11, para 4.8).

Adjustments that are not errors

Provided they are accurate and made at the right time, adjustments that are required to be made as part of the normal operation of VAT accounting are not errors. These accounting adjustments include

- retail scheme annual adjustments or other adjustments required when ceasing to use a particular retail scheme;
- adjustments under the **CAPITAL GOODS SCHEME (10)**;
- use of an approved estimation procedure;
- partial exemption annual adjustments (see **49.9 PARTIAL EXEMPTION**);
- partial exemption clawback and payback adjustments (see **49.14 PARTIAL EXEMPTION**);
- exports and intra-European Union supplies of goods (see **21.28 EXPORTS** and **19.11 EUROPEAN UNION: SINGLE MARKET**);
- issuing or receiving credit and debit notes (see **39.15 INVOICES**);
- claims for **BAD DEBT RELIEF (7)**; and
- pre-registration and post deregistration expenses.

If the original accounting adjustment was incorrect, or made at the wrong time, error corrections should be made in the normal way.

(VAT Notice 700/45/11, para 4.10).

Example

Sue is VAT-registered and is partly exempt, using the standard method of calculation. She has just carried out her annual adjustment calculation for the partial exemption year ended 30 April 2010, and calculated that £12,000 is owed to HMRC. This is not a VAT error, as long as the quarterly partial exemption calculations were carried out correctly. The amount of £12,000 can either be included as an adjustment on Sue's April 2010 VAT return or, more favourable to her, on the July 2010 return.

This is because the adjustment period for annual adjustment calculations is either the VAT return at the end of the tax year (March, April or May, depending on VAT periods) or the following return (June, July or August), the period chosen being at the discretion of the taxpayer.

Best time to correct errors

As soon as a business finds an error, it should record it in its VAT records for correction or it could become liable to a penalty. It may be useful to keep a separate record of

- the date the error was discovered;
- the period in which the error occurred;
- any related documentation; and
- whether the error was output or input tax related.

Normally, it would be best to wait until the end of the current accounting period before deciding whether Method 1 or Method 2 applies. However, if an individual error is so large that the 1% box 6 test or £50,000 limit will inevitably be breached, an error correction report should be made to HMRC using Method 2 immediately.

(VAT Notice 700/45/11, para 4.12).

[*SI 1995/2518, Regs 34, 35; SI 1997/1086, Reg 5; SI 2008/1482, Reg 2*].

De Voil Indirect Tax Service. See V3.419; V3.506; V5.144.

VAT account

[56.12] Every taxable person must keep and maintain an account to be known as the VAT account. It must be divided into separate parts relating to the VAT periods of the taxable person and each part must be divided into two portions known as 'the VAT payable portion' and 'the VAT allowable portion'.

VAT payable portion

The VAT payable portion comprises the following.

- Output tax due from the taxable person for that VAT period.
- Output tax due on acquisitions from other EU countries by the taxable person for that VAT period.
- Tax which the taxable person is required to account for and pay on behalf of the supplier under the reverse charge provisions for mobile phones and computer chips. See **4.14 ANTI-AVOIDANCE.**
- Corrections and adjustments to the VAT payable portion of a previous return which may be corrected on the current return (see **56.11** above) and adjustments where a supply becomes, or ceases to become, subject to the reverse charge provisions for mobile phones and computer chips (see **4.21 ANTI-AVOIDANCE**).
- Subject to the time limit below, a positive/negative entry where there is an increase/decrease in the taxable consideration due on a supply *made* in a previous accounting period. The entry must be made in the return for the period in which the adjustment is given effect in the business accounts (unless the taxable person is insolvent in which case the entry must be made in the return for the period in which the supply was made).

  No adjustment must be made where that increase/decrease occurs more than three years after the end of the VAT period in which the original supply took place. The three-year time limit was upheld in *Valley Chemical Co Ltd* (VTD 17989) (TVC 59.29) but in *General Motors Acceptance Corporation (UK) plc* (VTD 17990) (TVC 44.53) the tribunal held that this requirement infringed a person's basic right to be taxed on the consideration received and was incompatible with what is now *Directive 2006/112/EC, Art 90* (see **18.22**(*a*) **EUROPEAN UNION LEGISLATION**). The time limit should not prevent adjustments before the first opportunity to make it arose. HMRC have accepted this. (VAT Information Sheet 6/03).

  It is essential that a credit note or debit note is prepared to support the adjustment (see **39.15 INVOICES**). It is not possible to adjust the consideration on the original invoice without such a document (*British Telecommunications plc* (VTD 14669) (TVC 40.116)).

- Adjustments to the amount of VAT payable by the taxable person for that VAT period which are required, or allowed, by or under any VAT *Regulations*.

VAT allowable portion

The **VAT allowable portion** comprises the following.

- Input tax allowable to the taxable person for that VAT period.
- Input tax allowable in respect of acquisitions from other EU countries by the taxable person for that VAT period.
- Corrections of the VAT allowable portion of a previous return which may be corrected on the current return (see **56.11** above).
- Subject to the time limit below, a positive/negative entry where there is an increase/decrease in the taxable consideration due on a supply *received* in a previous accounting period. The entry must be made in the return for the period in which the adjustment is given effect in the business accounts (unless the taxable person is insolvent in which case the entry must be made in the return for the period in which the supply was received).
  No adjustment must be made where that increase/decrease occurs more than three years after the end of the VAT period in which the original supply took place.
  It is essential that a credit note or debit note is prepared to support the adjustment (see **39.15 INVOICES**).
- Adjustments to the amount of input tax allowable to the taxable person for that VAT period which are required, or allowed, by or under any VAT *Regulations*.

[*SI 1995/2518, Regs 32, 38; SI 1997/1086, Reg 6; SI 2007/1418, Reg 4*].

De Voil Indirect Tax Service. See V5.211.

Audit of VAT records

[56.13] Where a business is subject to an independent audit, the audit will normally cover the VAT account and other records relating to VAT. However, as an auditor's responsibilities normally arise under statute, this does not mean that the auditor must make a specific reference to the VAT records in his report. (VAT Notice 700, para 19.2).

De Voil Indirect Tax Service. See V5.203.

Duties of senior accounting officers

Main duty

[56.14] With effect for financial years beginning on or after 21 July 2009, the senior accounting officer of a qualifying company must take reasonable steps to ensure that the company establishes and maintains appropriate tax accounting arrangements. He must, in particular, take reasonable steps to: monitor the accounting arrangements of the company; and identify any respects in which those arrangements are not appropriate tax accounting arrangements.

Certificates

The senior accounting officer must provide HMRC with a certificate for each financial year of the company. The certificate must: state whether the company had appropriate tax accounting arrangements throughout the financial year; and if it did not, give an explanation of the respects in which the accounting arrangements were not appropriate tax accounting arrangements. The certificate must be provided: by such means and in such form as is reasonably specified by an HMRC officer; and not later than the end of the period for filing the company's accounts for the financial year (or such later time as an HMRC officer may have allowed). A certificate may relate to more than one qualifying company.

Notifying HMRC of senior accounting officer's name

For each financial year a qualifying company must ensure that HMRC are notified of the name of each person who was its senior accounting officer at any time during the year. The notification must be given: by such means and in such form as is reasonably specified by an HMRC officer; and not later than the end of the period for filing the company's accounts for the financial year (or such later time as an HMRC officer may have allowed for providing the certificate for the financial year). A notification may relate to more than one qualifying company.

Penalties

A senior accounting officer may incur a penalty for: failing to comply with his main duty; failing to provide a certificate; or providing a certificate that contains a careless or deliberate inaccuracy. A company may incur a penalty for failing to notify HMRC of the name of its senior accounting officer (see **52.29 PENALTIES**).

[*FA 2009, Sch 46*].

De Voil Indirect Tax Service. See V5.214.

Key points

[56.15] Points to consider are follows.

- Every VAT-registered business must keep a VAT account, which clearly shows the source and calculation of all figures entered on each VAT return, including any adjustments for VAT errors made in past periods and now being corrected.
- A business must retain its records for a minimum period of six years. It may be possible to agree a shorter retention period with HMRC in certain cases.

- For input tax purposes, a valid VAT invoice issued by a supplier must be retained as evidence. In the absence of an invoice, HMRC will usually accept alternative evidence that confirms a valid charge of VAT has been made, and the identity of the goods or services that have been purchased.
- In situations where a supplier charges the wrong amount of VAT on an invoice, the customer can only reclaim input tax based on the amount that should have been charged if the amount is too high, or the actual amount charged if it is too low.
- A supplier charging the wrong amount of VAT on an invoice must account for output tax based on the amount shown on the invoice if it is too high. If the VAT amount is too low, then output tax should be based on the amount that should have been charged.
- A business can adjust a current VAT return to correct errors made on previous returns if the net value of all errors discovered is either less than £10,000 or less than £50,000 and 1% of the Box 6 outputs figure on the return where the error is to be corrected. Don't forget that errors only need to be corrected for the last four years – errors beyond this period are out of date and cannot be adjusted.
- If an error (or 'net' errors) exceeds the above limits, it will need to be notified to HMRC, either in writing or on form VAT652. It is important to give full details about thc crrors in question and the VAT periods to which they relate.
- Interest on underpayments notified to HMRC will be subject to interest in most cases. It is important that the circumstances of an underpayment are clearly explained, as interest might not be applicable, e.g. if input tax incorrectly claimed would have been claimed by another business.
- There is an important difference between VAT errors and VAT adjustments. For example, the annual adjustments for partial exemption and the capital goods scheme are not VAT errors, they are normal adjustments that are included on the return where the adjustment must be made according to the scheme rules.

57

Recreation and Sport

Cross-references. See **18.25**(*m*) and (*o*) **EUROPEAN UNION LEGISLATION** for exemption of certain sporting services supplied by non-profit-making organisations; **34.13**(25) **INPUT TAX** for entitlement to deduct input tax in respect of sporting, recreational and sponsorship activities.

Introduction

[57.1] Most supplies of recreation and sport services are standard rated if supplied within the UK. The principal exceptions are—

- betting and gaming, where some but not all activities are exempt (see **57.2** below);
- lotteries, where the granting of a right to take part in a lottery is exempt (see **57.5** below); and
- cultural and sporting activities for which there is a specific exemption when carried on by certain bodies (see **57.6–57.14** below).

Betting and gaming

[57.2] For EU legislation, see **18.26**(*i*) **EUROPEAN UNION LEGISLATION.**

Under UK legislation, the provisions of any facilities for

- the placing of bets, or
- the playing of any games of chance for a prize

is exempt. '*Prize*' does not include the opportunity to play the game again.

There are, however, four important exceptions which are standard-rated.

(1) Admission to any premises where betting and gaming takes place.

(2) *From 1 September 2007 to 26 April 2009*, the granting of a right to play a game of chance (see below) for a prize unless the playing of the game fell into one of the following categories in which case it remained exempt.

(a) Remote gaming for the purposes of remote gaming duty.

(b) Prize gaming under a permit or at any qualifying centre or fair. In Great Britain, this meant the playing of a game where the provision of facilities for its playing fell within *Gambling Act 2005, ss 289, 290* or *292*. In Northern Ireland, it meant the playing of a game to which *Betting, Gaming, Lotteries and Amusements (Northern Ireland) Order 1985, Art 154* applied and which took place in accordance with the requirements of that Article.

(c) Non-commercial gaming.
In Great Britain, this meant the playing of a game in respect of which the conditions in *Gambling Act 2005, ss 299* or *300* were complied with. In Northern Ireland, it meant the playing of a game to which *Betting, Gaming, Lotteries and Amusements (Northern Ireland) Order 1985, Arts 126* or *153* applied and which took place in accordance with the requirements of that Article.

(d) Equal chance gaming at a qualifying club or institute.
In Great Britain, this meant the playing of a game where the provision of facilities for its playing fell within *Gambling Act 2005, s 269*. In Northern Ireland, it meant the playing of a game to which *Betting, Gaming, Lotteries and Amusements (Northern Ireland) Order 1985, Art 128* applied.

(e) Gaming for small prizes in a bingo hall.
In Great Britain, this meant the playing of a game where the provision of facilities for its playing fell within *Gambling Act 2005, s 291* or the playing at any 'licensed premises' of bingo in respect of which

(i) the amount charged for any one chance to win one or more prizes in a particular game did not exceed 50 pence;

(ii) the aggregate amount charged for participating in a particular game did not exceed £500;

(iii) no money prize for which a game was played exceeded £50; and

(iv) the aggregate amount or value of the prizes for which a game was played did not exceed £500.

'*Licensed premises*' meant premises in respect of which a bingo premises licence (within the meaning of *Gambling Act 2005, Part 8*) had effect.

In Northern Ireland, it meant the playing of a game to which *Betting, Gaming, Lotteries and Amusements (Northern Ireland) Order 1985, Art 77(1)* applied.

From 27 April 2009, all participation fees for playing bingo and other games of chance for a prize are exempt.

Before 1 September 2007, standard-rating applied to charges levied under *Gaming Act 1968, s 14* or the *Betting, Gaming, Lotteries and Amusements (Northern Ireland) Order 1985*.

(3) Club subscriptions (including those to gaming, bingo and bridge clubs, etc.).

(4) The provision of anything which is a gaming machine for the purposes of *VATA 1994, s 23* (see **57.4** below).

[*VATA 1994, Sch 9 Group 4 Item 1 and Notes (1)–(11); SI 2007/2163; FA 2009, s 113*].

Game of chance

'*Game of chance*' includes a game that

- involves both an element of chance and an element of skill;
- involves an element of chance that can be eliminated by superlative skill; and
- is presented as involving an element of chance;

but does not include a sport.

A person plays a game of chance if he participates in a game of chance whether or not

- there are other participants in the game; and
- a computer generates images or data taken to represent the actions of other participants in the game.

[*VATA 1994, Sch 9 Group 4 Notes (2)(3); SI 2006/2685*].

Value of the exempt supply

The value of the exempt output is the full amount of stakes or takings less only any money paid out as winnings or, if prizes are goods, their cost (including VAT) to the supplier. Betting or gaming duty is not deductible. (VAT Notice 701/29/11, para 2.3).

Stake money

Stake money (i.e. the amount paid by each player which they risk in the game and is returned in winning to the winning player) is outside the scope of VAT. (VAT Notice 701/29/11, para 3.2).

Composite charges

Composite charges covering admission charges, stake money and payments for the provision of facilities for placing bets must be apportioned.

Casino card room games

In addition to their conventional games of chance against the house, casinos may hold competitions or tournaments in card room games, such as backgammon or poker. The whole of the participation fee which may be described as 'table money', 'session charge' or 'competition fee' is often put towards the prizes and sometimes the casino puts in an extra sum to make the prizes more attractive. If a business holds such competitions, the entry fee is exempt from VAT even though they may make no contribution to the business's profits.

Entry stakes to card room competitions which are conducted strictly in accordance with guidelines agreed between the British Casino Association and HMRC are outside the scope of VAT. (VAT Notice 701/29/11, para 2.4).

Agent's services

Services of pools agents, concessionaires and collectors are covered by the exemption for betting and gaming and therefore no VAT is payable on their commission charges. The services of bookmakers' agents are exempt, and so are the services of bookmakers themselves when they act as agents in accepting bets for other bookmakers or for the Tote. (VAT Notice 701/29/11, para 2.5).

Use of call centres for telephone betting

In *United Utilities plc v C & E Commrs, ECJ Case C–89/05;* [2006] STC 1423 (TVC 22.374) the court held that supplies by a company providing call centre services relating to the receipt of telephone bets on behalf of Littlewoods did not qualify for exemption as the provision of betting.

Prizes

The following treatment applies.

- Prizes of cash are outside the scope of VAT.
- Prizes of goods in free lotteries and in sports competitions should be treated as business gifts and VAT is only due if the tax exclusive cost of the prize is over £50. Input tax will then be deductible in the normal manner. However if a business purchases a car to be given away as a prize, it may only reclaim the input tax if it does not make the car available for private use before it is given away. If the business does reclaim the VAT on the purchase it must declare output tax on the tax exclusive cost of the car when it is given away. Any input tax claimed will still be subject to the partial exemption rules.
- Prizes awarded from a machine itself (e.g. a crane grab machine) may be treated as business gifts for VAT purposes.
- Prizes of goods and services in exempt betting and gaming should be treated as part of the exempt supply and no output tax is due on such prizes. Any VAT incurred in purchasing the prizes is exempt input tax which is not deductible, subject to the partial exemption rules.
- Where prizes of goods or services are given in taxable competitions, no further tax is due.

- Prizes of services awarded in free lotteries or as bonus prizes in sports competitions, are outside the scope of VAT. However, where the prize is of a holiday or tickets to sporting or other events, input tax is not deductible by virtue of the business entertainment rules. Should a business provide any other services as prizes, input tax may not be deductible.
- If a business supplies prize goods in exchange for machine tokens with a recognised cash value, it must account for VAT on the goods as if it had supplied them by normal retail sale. The value of the supply is the normal retail selling price of the goods or, if the business does not sell such goods to the general public, the equivalent cash value of the tokens it has accepted in exchange for them. The business can reclaim as input tax the VAT incurred on the purchase of the prize goods in the normal way.

(VAT Notice 701/29/11, para 13).

De Voil Indirect Tax Service. See V4.131.

Bingo

From 27 April 2009

[57.3] Participation and session charges are made for the right to take part in a game or series of games of bingo. From 27 April 2009 all bingo participation fees and session charges became exempt from VAT.

A bingo machine is designed or adapted to provide an electronic or video version of a game of bingo. The takings from the machine for the games are exempt.

[*FA 2009, s 113*]. (VAT Notice 701/29/11, para 8).

Prior to 26 April 2009

Participation and session charges were standard-rated unless falling into one of the following categories, in which case they were exempt.

(a) Remote bingo

This included bingo played by the use of the internet, telephone, television or radio.

(b) Bingo played under a permit or at any qualifying centre or fair

(i) In Great Britain, bingo played under *Gambling Act 2005, ss 289, 290* or *292* was exempt provided that
- the maximum individual participation fee was 50p;
- the total amount of participation fees did not exceed £500 per game;
- cash prizes did not exceed a maximum of £50 for bingo played in an adult gaming centre or £35 in all other cases; and
- the total value of prizes did not exceed £500 per game.

(ii) In Northern Ireland, bingo played under *Betting, Gaming, Lotteries and Amusements (Northern Ireland) Order 1985, Art 154* was exempt provided that
- the maximum individual participation fee was 30p;
- total participation fees paid in any one game did not exceed £30; and
- the maximum cash prize was 30p.

(c) Non-commercial bingo

(i) In Great Britain, bingo played for fund-raising purposes under *Gambling Act 2005, s 299* was exempt where the prize money was not determined by reference to the number of people playing the game or the amount raised by the game. There were no limits on stakes or prizes to qualify for exemption.
Bingo played for fund-raising purposes under *Gambling Act 2005, s 300* was exempt provided that
- only one payment of an entrance fee or stake of no more than £8 was made by each player; and
- the total value of prizes did not exceed £600 for a one day event or £900 for events covering more than one day.

(ii) In Northern Ireland, bingo played for fund-raising purposes under *Betting, Gaming, Lotteries and Amusements (Northern Ireland) Order 1985, Art 126* was exempt provided that
- only one payment of entrance fee or stake of not more than £4 was made by each player; and
- the total value of prizes did not exceed £400 for a one day event or £700 for events covering more than one day.

Bingo played under *Gaming, Lotteries and Amusements (Northern Ireland) Order 1985, Art 153* was exempt without limit on stakes or prizes.

(d) Bingo played at a qualifying club or institute

(i) In Great Britain, bingo played in members' or commercial clubs and miners' welfare institutes under *Gambling Act 2005, s 300* was exempt subject to a maximum participation fee of £1 a day or £3 for a commercial club that holds a club machine permit.

(ii) In Northern Ireland, bingo played under *Gaming, Lotteries and Amusements (Northern Ireland) Order 1985, Art 128* was exempt subject to a maximum participation fee of 60p on any one day.

(e) Bingo for small prizes at licensed bingo halls

(i) In Great Britain, bingo played under *Gambling Act 2005, s 291* where the prize money was not determined by the number of people playing the game or the amount raised by the game and other bingo played for small prizes at bingo premises licensed *Gambling Act 2005, Part 8* was exempt provided that
- the maximum individual participation fee was 50p;
- the total amount of participation fees did not exceed £500 per game;

- cash prizes did not exceed a maximum of money exceeding £50 (£35 where children under 18 were admitted to the premises and the bingo was played under *Gambling Act 2005, s 291*);
- the total value of prizes did not exceed £500 per game.

(ii) In Northern Ireland, bingo played under *Gaming, Lotteries and Amusements (Northern Ireland) Order 1985, Art 77* was exempt provided

- the participation fee for anyone to participate once in a game did not exceed 50p;
- the aggregate total of participation fees paid to participate in any one game did not exceed £120;
- the maximum cash prize was £25; and
- the aggregate amount or value of the prizes (both cash and non-cash) in any game did not exceed £120.

Gaming and amusement machines

[57.4] The provision of a 'gaming machine' is specifically excluded from the general exemption from VAT applying to betting and the playing of games of chance (see **57.2** above). The takings from gaming machines (and 'amusement machines' generally) are therefore standard-rated. Note that the provisions of *VATA 1994, s 23* below do not apply to the Isle of Man. [*IMA 1979, s 1(d)*]. Where gaming machine takings would also qualify for exemption by satisfying the requirements for being a lottery under **57.5** below, it has been held that to exempt the supply would defeat the legislative intent (*McCann (t/a Ulster Video Amusements)* (VTD 2401) (TVC 24.18)).

In *Rank Group plc* Ch D [2009] All ER (D) 65 (Jun) (TVC 24.19) the tribunal decided that Rank's takings from gaming machines should be treated as exempt before 6 December 2005, when UK law was changed to make all gaming machine takings taxable. It said that *VATA 1994, Sch 9, Group 4, Note 3* (as originally enacted) and HMRC practice infringed the principal of fiscal neutrality as there were comparator machines which, before 6 December 2005, were exempt as a matter of law and there were comparators which HMRC treated as exempt in practice. The Ch D upheld that decision, holding that there was no discernible justification for the differing tax treatment. The ECJ ruled that similar supplies from the point of view of the consumer should be taxed in the same way and it was not necessary to consider whether the supplies were in competition with each other ('competition test'). When determining whether there had been a breach of fiscal neutrality the actual tax treatment should be based on the legal position rather than any practice that may have been followed (*Case C–259/10, C–260/10;* [2012] STC 23 (TVC 22.375)).

Definition of a gaming machine

With effect from 6 December 2005, 'gaming machine' means a machine which is 'designed or adapted' for use by individuals to 'gamble' (whether or not it can also be used for other purposes). But a machine is not a gaming machine to the extent that it is designed or adapted

- for use to bet on future real events (see *Gambling Act 2005, s 353(1)* for the definition of '*real*');
- for the playing of any version of the game of bingo (irrespective of by what name it is described) if bingo duty is charged under *Betting and Gaming Duties Act 1981, s 17* on the playing of that bingo (or would be charged but for *Betting and Gaming Duties Act 1981, Sch 3 paras 1–5*), or
- for the playing of a real (see above) 'game of chance' if the playing of the game is dutiable gaming for the purposes of *FA 1997, s 10* (or would be dutiable gaming but for *FA 1997, s 10(3)(4)*).

For these purposes, a machine is any apparatus which uses or applies mechanical power or electrical power (or both) and a reference to a machine being

- '*designed or adapted*' for a purpose includes a reference to a machine to which anything has been done as a result of which it can reasonably be expected to be used for that purpose, and
- '*adapted*' includes a reference to computer software being installed on it.

'*Gambling*', with effect from 1 November 2006, means playing a 'game of chance' for a 'prize' and betting. '*Game of chance*' includes a game that

- involves both an element of chance and an element of skill;
- involves an element of chance that can be eliminated by superlative skill; and
- is presented as involving an element of chance,

but does not include a sport. A person plays a game of chance if he participates in a game of chance whether or not

- there are other participants in the game; and
- a computer generates images or data taken to represent the actions of other participants in the game.

'*Prize*', in relation to a machine, does not include the opportunity to play the machine again.

HMRC Brief 70/09 states that 'electronic lottery terminals' are (taxable) gaming machines for the purposes of VAT, rather than (exempt) lottery ticket dispensers or vending machines.

In *Oasis Technologies (UK) Ltd* (TC00581) (TVC 24.23), the tribunal held that the Oasis electronic lottery ticket vending machine (ELTVM) was a gaming machine. However, it also granted the right to participate in a lottery and the takings from the machine were exempt from VAT (see **57.5** below).

[*VATA 1994, s 23(4)–(6); FA 2006, s 16; SI 2006/2686*].

Pinball machines

Before 6 December 2005, takings from pinball machines were standard-rated as the machines fell within the definition of gaming machines. From 6 December 2005 to 31 October 2006, pinball machines were excluded from the definition of gaming machines (because they did not offer prizes) but takings qualified for exemption under **57.2** above as the provision of facilities for playing a game of chance. This was not intentional and, from 1 November 2006, standard-rating is restored as only a game of chance played for a prize qualifies for exemption. Businesses that incorrectly accounted for VAT from 6 December 2005 to 31 October 2006 may claim a repayment of the output subject to certain conditions. See Business Brief 16/06 for details.

Meaning of an amusement machine

An '*amusement machine*' can be either of the following.

- A machine on which there is no prize in any circumstances.
- A 'skill with prizes' machine, i.e. a machine where the prize depends on the skill or knowledge of the player and is not dependent on chance (e.g. a general knowledge quiz).

Other examples of amusement machines are pinball machines, video games (but not games that involve gambling, such as video poker machines) and juke boxes.

(VAT Notice 701/29/11, para 9.2).

Place of supply

Supplies of services consisting of enabling the public to use gaming machines in amusement arcades are regarded as entertainment or similar activities within what is now *Directive 2006/112/EC, Art 52(a)*, so that the place of supply is where the services are physically carried out (*RAL (Channel Islands) Ltd v C & E Commrs (and related appeals), ECJ Case C–452/03*, [2005] STC 1025 (TVC 22.205)). The equivalent UK provisions are in *SI 1992/3121, Art 15* (see **65.18 SUPPLY: PLACE OF SUPPLY**).

Hiring of machines

Hire charges, whether for a fixed rental or a share of the profits, are standard-rated. (VAT Notice 701/29/11, para 10.2).

Site rentals

Charges for siting machines are standard-rated. (VAT Notice 701/29/11, para 10.2). This follows the decision in *Sinclair Collis Ltd v C & E Commrs, ECJ Case C–275/01*, [2003] STC 898 (TVC 22.340) where the court held that the grant by the owner of premises to the owner of a cigarette vending machine

- of the right to install the machine and to operate and maintain it on the premises
- in a place nominated by the owner of the premises
- in return for a percentage of the gross profits on the sales of cigarettes
- but with no rights of possession or control being granted to the machine owner other than those expressly set out in the agreement between the parties

did not amount to the letting of immovable property and was therefore standard-rated. Before the decision in *Sinclair Collis*, HMRC took the view that such rentals were exempt under *VATA 1994, Sch 9 Group 1* as a supply of a licence to occupy land (see **41.2 LAND AND BUILDINGS: EXEMPT SUPPLIES AND OPTION TO TAX**) although the supplier could opt to tax the supply (see **41.8 LAND AND BUILDINGS: EXEMPT SUPPLIES AND OPTION TO TAX**). Standard-rating must in all cases be applied to such supplies from 1 January 2004 although site owners could apply the change earlier if they wished. (Business Brief 18/03).

Accounting for VAT on machine takings

VAT on the takings must be accounted for by the person who supplies the use of the machine to the public. This is normally the person who exercises day-to-day control over the operation of the machine and is entitled to the takings.

(a) *In respect of gaming machines*, this is
- for commercial gaming premises licensed under the *Gambling Act 2005, ss 65 and 150*, the holder of the licence or that person's employee;
- for clubs or miners' institutes with a club machine permit under the *Gambling Act 2005, s 273*, any officer or member of the club, or any person employed by them;
- for travelling pleasure fairs, the showman who owns or operates the fair;
- for public houses, the person named on the permit issued under *Gambling Act 2005, s 283*; and
- for an unlicensed gaming machine, normally the person who controls its operation, but the supply will depend on the particular arrangements in each case. See also *R v Ryan & Others*, CA [1994] STC 446 (TVC 49.29) where, in a criminal prosecution, the machine owners were held to be liable to account for VAT on the unlawful operation of unlawful credit gaming machines.

(b) *In respect of amusement machines*, this is
- the site operator (if the machine is purchased, hired or rented by the occupier of the premises on which it is sited); or
- the owner of the machine (where the owner pays a rent to the occupier of the premises on which the machine is sited).

If the machine is operated on a profit-sharing basis, the supplier of its use to the public is the person who controls its operation.

(VAT Notice 701/29/11, para 11.1).

Examples of supplies between machine owners and site occupiers	
	Supply/accounting for VAT
Gaming/amusement machine supplied to a brewery with a managed pub	Machine owner makes a standard-rated supply of hire of the machine to the brewery and accounts for VAT on the hire charge

	Brewery makes a standard-rated supply of use of the machine to the public and accounts for VAT on the machine takings
Gaming/amusement machine is supplied to the tenant of a brewery-owned pub	Machine owner makes a standard-rated supply of hire of the machine to the tenant and accounts for VAT on the hire charge Tenant makes a standard-rated supply of use of the machine to the public and accounts for VAT on the machine takings Brewery makes a standard-rated supply of a licence to trade to the tenant to site the machine on its premises and accounts for VAT on the charge for siting the machine
Owner of a gaming/amusement machine pays rent (e.g. a fixed sum or share of the profits) to a brewery with a managed or tenanted pub	The brewery makes a standard-rated supply of a licence to trade to the machine owner in allowing the machine to be sited on its premises and accounts for VAT on the charge for siting the machine The machine owner makes a standard-rated supply of the use of the machine to the public and accounts for VAT on the machine takings

(VAT Notice 701/29/11, paras 12.1–12.3).

Calculation of VAT due

The tax point for supplies made from coin-operated machines is the date the machine is used. However, as an administrative convenience, operators may delay accounting for VAT until the takings are removed from the machine. (VAT Notice 48, ESC 3.6). For all other purposes, the normal tax point rules apply. Therefore, in the event of a theft of takings from a machine, VAT must still be accounted for in full on any supplies that have been made from the machine. (VAT Notice 701/29/11, para 11.7).

Taxable take of a gaming machine

Whenever cash or tokens are removed from the machine, the 'taxable take' must be calculated and recorded. '*Taxable take*' is the amount paid by persons to gamble less the amount (if any) received by persons gambling successfully (other than the person making the supply and persons acting on his behalf). [*VATA 1994, s 23(1)(2); FA 2006, s 16)*]. Included is any money in the 'tubes' in excess of the float. Any foreign coins, fakes or facsimiles inserted may be disregarded. In practice, when the machine is opened, the float should be restored to its original level with cash and tokens taken from the machine. The balance of coins and tokens remaining in the machine is then the taxable take upon which VAT is due. VAT is calculated by applying the VAT fraction 7/47

(1/6 from 4 January 2011; 3/23 from 1 December 2008 to 31 December 2009) to this amount. No deduction must be made for hire or rental charges to the machine owner; any share of profits or other charge due to another person; any payments made out of the takings such as those under maintenance contracts; or gaming machine licence duty. See also *HJ Glawe Spiel und Unterhaltungsgeräte Aufstellungsgesellschaft mbH & Co KG v Finanzamt Hamburg-Barmbek-Uhlenhorst, ECJ Case C–38/93,* [1994] STC 543 (TVC 22.239) where it was held that the taxable amount did not include the prescribed proportion of the coins inserted which had, by statute, to be paid out as winnings.

Usually the taxable take should be calculated for each individual machine. However, in the case of an amusement arcade with large numbers of machines, HMRC may give approval to the calculation on a site-wide basis.

(VAT Notice 701/29/11, paras 11.2, 11.4)

See also *Feehan v C & E Commrs,* QB 1994, [1995] STC 75 (TVC 24.20). The wording of the legislation contemplates payment for gambling by insertion of a token 'into the machine' but there is no such restriction on the receipt of winning being 'from a machine'. In that case, the court therefore upheld the tribunal's decision that the value of the supply was the net amount of receipts after deducting winnings paid to gamblers by the publican.

Tokens

The insertion of a token into a machine should be treated as the payment of an amount equal to that for which the token can be obtained. [*VATA 1994, s 23(3); FA 2006, s 16*].

Replayable tokens

The receipt of a replayable token (i.e. one which can be used for gambling) by a person gambling successfully is treated as the receipt of an amount equal to its cash value. [*VATA 1994, s 23(3); FA 2006, s 16*]. This value can be established by reference to the charge for gambling on the machine. For example, if a machine can be operated by the insertion of 20p cash or a token to obtain a single game, then that token would have a value of 20p. Where a machine has a facility for the site occupier or machine owner to return tokens through the 'no play' token return slot, any tokens inserted in this fashion are outside the scope of VAT and can be omitted from the total when the taxable take is calculated.

(VAT Notice 701/29/11, para 11.3).

Non-replayable tokens

These are tokens that are awarded by machines but which cannot be used to gamble on them. Their treatment for VAT purposes depends upon whether or not they have a recognised cash value.

- Where non-replayable tokens have a recognised cash value (i.e. they can be exchanged for cash or goods that the business also sells) they should be treated in the same way as replayable tokens. [*VATA 1994, s 23(3); FA 2006, s 16*].

- Where non-replayable tokens have no recognised cash value (i.e. they are only exchangeable for goods not sold by the business) the full amount of cash removed from the machine (after any necessary adjustment to the cash float) must be recorded. No deduction should be made from machine takings for tokens awarded by the machine, tokens used to restore the machine's float or prizes given in exchange for the tokens.

(VAT Notice 701/29/11, para 11.3).

Retail schemes

Treatment of gaming and amusement machine takings depends on the scheme used.

- Under the Point of Sale scheme, taxable take of the machine should be added to standard-rated daily gross takings on the day the cash and/or tokens are removed.
- Under an apportionment scheme, takings should be excluded from daily gross takings and VAT calculated outside the scheme as explained above.
- Under a direct calculation scheme,
  (i) where minority goods are zero-rated or reduced rate goods, taxable take of the machine should be added to daily gross takings on the day the cash and/or tokens are removed; and
  (ii) where minority goods are standard-rated or reduced-rated, takings should be excluded from daily gross takings and VAT calculated outside the scheme as explained above.

  (VAT Notice 701/29/11, para 11.5).

Amusement machine licence duty

This is outside the scope of VAT if either the licence is obtained by the occupier of the premises where the machine is sited or the machine owner obtains the licence on behalf of the site occupier and itemises its cost separately on the invoice for the machine. However, if the gaming machine supplier charges for the supply of a licensed machine, the cost of obtaining the licence is part of a single supply of a gaming machine, and the whole amount is standard-rated. (VAT Notice 701/29/11, para 11.7).

For details of amusement machine licence duty, see Customs Notice 454.

De Voil Indirect Tax Service. See V4.131.

> *Example*
>
> The fruit machine at the White Horse pub is used by customers who put £1,000 a week of cash into the machine. The machine pays out 60% of the takings as winnings i.e. £600. Output tax is due on the actual cash emptied from the machine by the publican, i.e. based on £400 per week (assuming an equal cash float is maintained).

Lotteries

[57.5] For EU legislation, See **18.26**(*i*) **EUROPEAN UNION LEGISLATION**.

Under UK legislation, the granting of a right to take part in a lottery is exempt. [*VATA 1994, Sch 9 Group 4 Item 2*]. Exemption essentially covers the sale of the lottery tickets to the public as these acknowledge that a right to participate has been granted to the participants. If the lottery is free to enter, there is no exempt supply (but see below for prizes given in free lotteries).

The value of the exempt supply is the gross proceeds from ticket sales *less* the cash prizes given or the cost (inclusive of VAT) of the goods given as prizes.

There is no statutory definition of 'lottery'. In *Readers Digest Association Ltd v Williams,* [1976] 1 WLR 1109 it was defined as 'the distribution of prizes by chance where the persons taking part in the operation, or a substantial number of them, make a payment or consideration in return for obtaining their chance of a prize'. This includes the playing of on-line interactive lottery games. If any merit or skill plays a part in determining the outcome, the event is not a lottery but a competition.
(VAT Notice 701/29/11, paras 4.1–4.3).

Types of lawful lotteries

The promotion of lotteries is only lawful in the specified circumstances set out in the *Gambling Act 2005*. In addition to the National Lottery, there are other kinds of public lottery which fall under the regulatory powers of the Gambling Commission and local authorities, as follows.

- Large society lotteries defined by the *Gambling Act 2005*.
- Local authority lotteries operated by local authorities to support any purpose for which they have power to incur expenditure.
- Small society lotteries which are exempt from holding an operating licence, but must be registered with their local authority.

These lotteries can only be run in support of good causes, such as charity fundraising and cannot be run for commercial purposes. However, there are also three other categories of lottery permitted under the *Gambling Act*, which do not require operating licences or registration with any statutory body, and do not need to be in support of a good cause. These are

- incidental non-commercial lotteries, held at non-commercial events, where all money raised at the event goes entirely to purposes that are not for private or commercial gain;
- private society, work or residents' lotteries, where tickets can only be sold to society members, workers at or residents of a premises;
- customer lotteries, run by occupiers of business premises selling tickets only to customers on the premises itself.

If the society sets up a separate development association or other organisation to promote its lottery, it will be that association or organisation which is making the exempt supply. The net proceeds of the lottery paid by the development association to the society are outside the scope of VAT and any expense relating to the lottery, where these are deductible, cannot be reclaimed by the society as its input tax.

The National Lottery is regulated by the National Lottery Commission and is the only lottery of its kind that may legally be run in the UK.

Local authorities are allowed to promote lotteries under the *Gambling Act*. When a local authority promotes or organises a lottery this is treated the same way as those run by societies.

(VAT Notice 701/29/11, paras 4.4–4.7).

Lottery duty

Most lotteries falling within (*a*) or (*b*) above (but not the National Lottery under (*c*) above) are exempt from lottery duty. See Customs Notice 458 *Lottery duty* for further information.

(VAT Notice 701/29/11, para 4.8).

Lottery management companies

An external lottery manager (ELM) is a person or body who makes arrangements for a lottery on behalf of a society or local authority. These arrangements may include such things as arranging for tickets to be printed, organising publicity, arranging for the sale of tickets by agents and the paying out of prizes. An ELM will not be a member, officer or employee of the society or authority, and will normally be required to obtain a lottery manager's operating licence from the Gambling Commission in order to carry on lottery management activities.

The supply of lottery management services is standard-rated and VAT must be accounted for on

- any fee or commission paid by the lottery promoter, *plus*
- any additional amounts retained from gross ticket sales to cover the cost of running the lottery, *plus*
- any commission received and retained by selling agents used by the lottery management company

less the amount paid out in cash prizes by the management company (or the VAT-inclusive cost of goods given as prizes).

However, if a lottery management company also sells tickets itself using its own outlets and employees (rather than merely arranging for their sale by independent sellers), it can exempt this direct selling service like any other ticket seller (see below). If the company does not specify a separate charge for its own selling service, it must apportion its global charge to the promoter between exempt and standard-rated supplies. The exempt element must be shown separately on the VAT invoice. See **47.3 OUTPUT TAX** for apportionment of consideration.

(VAT Notice 701/29/11, paras 5.1–5.2).

Lottery ticket sales

The service of selling lottery tickets is an exempt supply. Where a retailer sells lottery tickets as an agent (for either a lottery management company or promoter) the commission received is a consideration for the exempt service of selling lottery tickets to the public.

The principal must account for the value of ticket sales to the public. This is usually the lottery promoter but where tickets are sold to a retailer who sells them on to the public at a higher price, the retailer becomes the principal. The purchase of the tickets by the retailer from the promoter is exempt, as is the money retained from sales of the tickets by the retailer.

Use of a retail scheme

Where a retailer selling lottery tickets uses one of the retail schemes to account for VAT, the proceeds from the exempt sale of tickets should be excluded from the scheme calculations. If the proceeds are included in the daily gross takings, the retailer should reduce the daily gross takings by the value of the tickets sold when calculating the daily gross takings for the retail scheme calculation.

(VAT Notice 701/29/11, paras 6.1–6.4).

Electronic lottery ticket vending machines

In *Oasis Technologies (UK) Ltd* (TC00581) (TVC 24.23), the tribunal held that the Oasis electronic lottery ticket vending machine (ELTVM) was a gaming machine within *VATA 1994, Sch 9, Group 4, Note 1(d)* (see **57.4** above). However, the machine also granted the right to participate in a lottery and the takings from the machine were exempt from VAT. Following that decision, HMRC stated that VAT exemption applies to such an ELTVM where

- the machine provides a game of chance;
- the tickets are randomly distributed;
- the player, operator or manufacturer cannot influence the order in which a ticket is revealed;
- the lottery result cannot be determined or influenced by means of the machine; and
- where groups of tickets have been pre-loaded into a machine, the machine may randomly select a new group when the current one is completed.

(HMRC Brief 1/11).

De Voil Indirect Tax Service. See V4.131.

Sports and physical recreation competitions

[57.6] For EU Legislation, See **18.25**(*m*) EUROPEAN UNION LEGISLATION.

Entry fees

An entry fee for the right to enter a 'competition' is normally standard-rated. However, the grant of a right to enter a competition in 'sport or physical recreation' is exempt in the following circumstances.

(a) Where the entry fee is money which is allocated *wholly* towards the provision of a prize or prizes awarded in that competition. [*VATA 1994, Sch 9 Group 10 Item 1; SI 1999/1994*].

(b) Where the grant is made by an 'eligible body' established for the purposes of sport or physical recreation. [*VATA 1994, Sch 9 Group 10 Item 2; SI 1999/1994*]. See **57.10** below for the definitions of '*eligible body*'. Exemption does not, however, apply to competitions organised by local authorities because providing such competitions is not the sole basis of their existence and they are therefore not *established* for that purpose.

HMRC define '*competition*' as meaning 'a structured and organised contest, tournament or race where prizes or titles are awarded'. This definition was supported by the tribunal in *Wimborne Rugby Football Club* (VTD 4547) (TVC 24.31).

'*Sports or physical recreation*' is not defined in the legislation but includes all the activities listed in **57.12** below. Physical recreation activities such as greyhound/pigeon racing, clay pigeon shooting and darts are also included. *Not included* are activities such as chess, card games, dominoes, and spot the ball and other newspaper competitions. Where animals are involved, it is important to distinguish between animal shows (which are outside the exemption) and activities which qualify as sport or physical recreation, such as a competition where the animals are assessed wholly or partially upon their sporting abilities, e.g. jumping and racing. Where an entry fee covers both (e.g. pony shows involving examining the animals and jumping classes) the fee can be apportioned.

Value of the exempt supply

This is normally the full amount of entry fees (without deduction for amounts returned as prizes). However, it is only the supply of the right to enter the competition that is exempt. Where the 'entry fee' includes elements that are standard or zero-rated supplies, it is necessary to decide whether a single or multiple supply is being made. See **64.6 SUPPLY: GENERAL.**

Prizes

The VAT position of prizes awarded to competitors is the same whether the entry fees are exempt or standard-rated.

- *Prizes in the form of goods* (e.g. sports equipment, trophies that are owned permanently by the winner). These are treated as business gifts. No VAT is due on individual prizes costing £50 or less. Where the goods cost more than that amount, VAT must be accounted for on the cost of the goods (and input tax incurred on the purchase can be deducted). See **47.6 OUTPUT TAX.**
- *Prizes in the form of services* (e.g. holidays). Where input tax has been claimed on the purchase of the services given away as prizes, an equal sum of output tax is due at the time the prize is awarded. If no input tax is incurred, no output tax is due.
- *Prizes in the form of cash*. Cash prizes for being successful in a particular competition are outside the scope of VAT. However, prize money must be distinguished from guaranteed prize money and appearance money (see below).

- *Loans of challenge cups, shields and other perpetual trophies* which remain the property of the organisation or club mounting the competition is a supply of services but, because there is no consideration, the supply is outside the scope of VAT. The outright gift of cups, etc. is generally a prize in the form of goods (see above). See also, however, *C & E Commrs v Professional Footballers' Association (Enterprises) Ltd*, HL [1993] STC 86 (TVC 67.11) where it was held that the consideration for trophies presented at a dinner were included in the price of the tickets on which the company had accounted for VAT.

Guaranteed payments and appearance money

Where competitors are paid by the promoter or organiser to take part in an event, the payment is the consideration for the standard-rated supply of the individual's services. Where individuals are guaranteed a participation payment or they negotiate individually a guaranteed amount (even if this depends on the degree of success), such payments must be treated as appearance money.

Input tax

The entitlement to deduct input tax on purchases in connection with the running of competitions is subject to the normal rules, including those for partial exemption. See *Manx International Rally Ltd v Isle of Man Treasury* (VTD 6711) (TVC 46.73) where the company received income from sponsorship (standard-rated) as well as entries fees (exempt). The tribunal held that the rally was the subject of a supply to the sponsors as well as the competitors and the appropriate proportion of the input tax was therefore deductible. HMRC believe that this decision was unique to the facts and does not set a precedent in similar cases.

(VAT Notice 701/5/11, paras 9.1–9.3; VAT Notice 701/45/11, paras 6.1–6.6).

Admission charges to entertainment, cultural activities, sport, etc.

[57.7] The VAT liability of admission charges depends upon the nature of the event and the person promoting the event.

(1) Standard-rated admission charges

Unless falling within (2)–(6) below, the full amount of any admission charges are normally standard-rated. *Included* are admissions to cinemas, theatres, swimming pools, amusement arcades and fun fairs, dances, sports events, museums and galleries, parks and gardens, historic houses, areas of the countryside for general recreational purposes, zoos and safari parks, and air shows.

(2) Exempt admission charges by public bodies

Admission charges by a 'public body' to

(a) a 'museum, gallery, art exhibition or zoo', or

(b) a 'theatrical, musical or choreographic performance of a cultural nature'

are exempt unless this would be likely to create 'distortions of competition' such as to place a commercial enterprise carried on by a taxable business at a disadvantage.

The performance under (*b*) above must be provided exclusively by one or more public bodies, one or more eligible bodies (see (3) below) or any combination of public bodies and eligible bodies. Exemption does not apply where, for example, a local authority acts as ticket broker for a commercial promoter or has a profit/income sharing arrangement with that promoter for a qualifying performance. (VAT Notice 701/47/11, para 3.2).

A '*public body*' means

- a local authority;
- a government department within the meaning of *VATA 1994, s 41(6)* (see **43.11 LOCAL AUTHORITIES AND PUBLIC BODIES**); or
- a non-departmental public body which is listed in the 1995 edition of the publication prepared by the Office of Public Service and known as 'Public Bodies'. (Copies of this document may be obtained from HMSO Publication Centre, PO Box 276, London, SW8 5DT.)

[*VATA 1994, Sch 9 Group 13, Item 1, Notes (1)(3)(4); SI 1996/1256*].

What is a '*museum, gallery, art exhibition or zoo*' has to be judged by reference to the normal everyday meaning of the words, taking into account indicative evidence such as the nature of the collections, objects, artefacts, site and exhibits on show. However, for the avoidance of doubt, a botanical garden does not qualify for exemption.

Similarly, whether an event is a '*theatrical, musical or choreographic performance of a cultural nature*' must be judged on the individual merits of the event. However, HMRC will generally accept a live performance of any form of stage play, dance or music as cultural for the purposes of this exemption.

(VAT Notice 701/47/11, paras 2.3, 2.4)

'Distortions of competition'

A public body must take steps to notify all identifiable commercial suppliers of similar facilities or performances (e.g. a local authority should identify any such supplier within its geographical area of authority from its business rating, planning, taxation and other records). But it only needs to look at (*a*) and (*b*) above in isolation (e.g. if it wishes to exempt admission charges to a museum, it must demonstrate that it would not disadvantage commercial museums, galleries, art exhibitions and zoos within its geographical area, but would not have to take account of commercial theatrical, musical and choreographical performances).

Notice must be in writing but can be by individual letter or public notice in the local press for its geographical area. The notice must specify a date by which objections to exemption must be lodged. If no objections are received, the body can then start to exempt supplies but must retain copies of relevant correspondence and advertisements for future examination. If any objection is received, HMRC should be asked for a ruling (see **29.5 HMRC: ADMINISTRATION**) and in the meantime supplies should not be exempt. Once exemption is in place, it is not necessary to check on competition for each performance under (*b*) above or to make periodic checks for a new commercial supplier. It is for that supplier to approach HMRC.

Even if a public body is unable to identify any commercial supplier of similar services, it is HMRC's policy to allow the body to tax admissions of a qualifying nature if it wishes although this policy remains subject to review.

(VAT Notice 701/47/11, paras 3.3–3.10).

(3) Exempt admission charges by eligible bodies

Admission charges by an 'eligible body' to

(a) a 'museum, gallery, art exhibition or zoo', or
(b) a 'theatrical, musical or choreographic performance of a cultural nature'

are exempt. [*VATA 1994, Sch 9 Group 13, Item 2; SI 1996/1256*].

See (2) above for HMRC's interpretation of '*museum, gallery, art exhibition or zoo*' and '*theatrical, musical or choreographic performance of a cultural nature*'.

An '*eligible body*' means any body (other than a public body, see (2) above) which satisfies the following conditions.

(i) It is precluded from distributing, and does not distribute, any profit it makes. [*VATA 1994, Sch 9 Group 13 Note (2); SI 1996/1256*].
HMRC will normally accept a body as having satisfied this condition if
- its constitution or articles of association preclude it from distributing surpluses of income over expenditure to its members, shareholders, parent or associated companies, or any other party (other than in the event of a liquidation or cessation of activities), and
- it does not, as a matter of fact, distribute any profit.

For these purposes, distribution of profit does not include grants or donations made by charities in pursuit of their wider charitable objectives. (VAT Notice 701/47/11, para 4.5).

(ii) It applies any profits made from admission charges exempt under this provision to the continuance or improvement of the facilities made available by means of the supplies. [*VATA 1994, Sch 9 Group 13 Note (2); SI 1996/1256*]. HMRC regard this as being satisfied if the body applies profits in the making of related cultural supplies (e.g. research or conservation projects). But if profits are applied to any other activities of the body, the body is not eligible for exemption. (VAT Notice 701/47/11, paras 4.3, 4.5).

(iii) It is managed and administered on a 'voluntary' basis by persons who have no 'direct or indirect financial interest' in its activities. [*VATA 1994, Sch 9 Group 13 Note (2); SI 1996/1256*].

Managed and administered on voluntary basis

In *Glastonbury Abbey* (VTD 14579) (TVC 16.1) the tribunal disagreed with HMRC's earlier view and stated that the UK law should read 'managed and administered on an *essentially* voluntary basis' as set out in what is now *Directive 2006/112/EC, Art 133(b)* (see **18.25**(ii) **EUROPEAN COMMUNITY LEGISLATION**). Subsequently, in *C & E Commrs v The Zoological Society of London, CJEC Case C–267/00,* [2002] STC 521 (TVC 22.321) the Court held that the aim of the condition in *Art 133(b)* was to reserve the VAT exemption for bodies with no commercial purpose by requiring that the persons who participate in the management and administration of such bodies have 'no financial interest of their own in their results, by means of remuneration, distribution of profits or any other financial interest'. Therefore, the condition refers only to

- members of that body who are designated to direct it at the highest level; and
- other persons who, without being so designated, in fact direct inasmuch as they take the decisions of last resort concerning the policy of the body, especially in the financial area, and carry out the higher supervisory tasks.

HMRC have accepted this decision and also that '*voluntary*' in UK law means 'essentially voluntary'.

Persons who are remunerated for carrying out purely executory tasks (i.e. those who implement, rather than take high level decisions) will not cause the cultural body to fail this condition.

HMRC regard a person as having a '*direct or indirect financial interest*' in the activities of a body if he receives or has a right to remuneration, takes up an 'as of rights' provision, is in any other way rewarded directly or indirectly by the body, or has any other financial interest in the body.

However, following the decision in *Bournemouth Symphony Orchestra v C & E Commrs,* CA 2006, [2007] STC 198 (TVC 16.7) HMRC take the view that any 'direct or indirect financial interest' only affects entitlement to exemption if it is actual, not potential. A person who is managing and administering the cultural body on a voluntary basis can be seen to have an actual financial interest in its activities only when

- he receives any payments for services supplied to the cultural body above the market rate, paid as routine overheads, or receives any payments which are profit-related (whether below, at or above market rates); and
- there is a link between the payments and his participation in the direction of the cultural body's activities.

For these purposes, remuneration means a commercial rate of pay or profit-related payment. Token payments or payments to reimburse out-of-pocket expenses do not disqualify a body from exemption provided all other conditions are met.

There is no financial interest where the only potential is for a financial loss (e.g. where a risk is underwritten or guaranteed so that the guarantor only stands to lose money and not gain money as a result).

If a person has a right to remuneration but formally opts not to take it, then this 'right' will not disqualify the body from exemption until the person starts exercising his right.

Similarly, payments to individuals for services of managing and administering the body are not financial interests if

- they are allowed by the constitution;
- the recipient is excluded from any decision-making regarding the award of any contract to themselves;
- the payments are not above market rates; and
- the payments are not linked to profits.

An 'as of rights' provision gives a trustee the right to charge and be paid reasonable remuneration for (typically) professional services within the scope of the authority. The right does not depend on the charity or its trustees entering into a contract with the trustee affected. Such provisions are often not exercised for long periods or are used intermittently. The presence of such a clause in itself (i.e. where it has not been exercised) will therefore not disqualify a body from exemption. It is only as and when remuneration is paid under this clause that the potential arises for it to cause disqualification from exemption. However, this will depend on the frequency, number and size of any payments made (see below).

In *Bournemouth Symphony Orchestra* (see above) the court held that the managing director's remuneration of £80,000 p.a. and his participation in the highest decision-making processes of the orchestra made it impossible to say that the management and administration was conducted on an essentially voluntary basis.

In determining whether a body is '*essentially voluntary*'

- the fact that remunerated staff take part occasionally or peripherally in the adoption of the decision of last resort will not, in itself, disqualify a body from exemption;
- if any person identified as managing and administering the body at the highest level receives remuneration, then the body will not qualify for exemption; and
- in the case of 'as of rights' provisions (see above), the issue is one of degree, i.e. the frequency, number and size of any payments made. Each case will depend on its own facts and HMRC recommend that if a body considers that its continued eligibility for exemption turns on payments made under an 'as of rights' provision, it should seek a ruling from its local VAT Office.

(VAT Notice 701/47/11, paras 4.7–4.12).

In *Keele University Students Union* (TC00082) (TVC 16.9) the tribunal held that a university students' union was not managed on an essentially voluntary basis because it was managed by sabbatical officers who were entitled to bursaries which in effect were annual salaries. The bursaries, although below the market rate for jobs of equivalent responsibilities, were significantly more than a nominal rate.

(4) Fund-raising events

Certain admission charges are exempt under more general provisions applying to fund-raising events by charities and other qualifying bodies (including eligible bodies within (3) above). See **12.10** **CHARITIES** for full details.

(5) Donations in lieu of admission

True donations are outside the scope of VAT. Where there is no admission charge and the public are asked for a donation instead, then this money is outside the scope of VAT. However, to qualify as a donation the payment must be entirely voluntary and secure nothing in return for the donor, and the actual amount to be given must be entirely at the donor's discretion. It must also be clear to the donor that admission can be gained whether a payment is made or not. If the person has to pay, or is made to think they have to pay, to get in then it is not a true donation but a standard-rated admission charge (unless otherwise exempt).

For donations in addition to charging admission at charitable functions, see **12.5**(1) **CHARITIES**.

> *Example*
>
> Hale Football Club has decided to allow free admission to all supporters for its next home game, as long as they give a minimum donation of £10 towards the club's ground improvements fund.
>
> In this situation, the £10 payment is not a donation because the donor does not have any choice with the arrangement. If he wants to watch the game, he must pay at least £10, so the charge is standard-rated in the normal way. Any additional amount in excess of £10 paid by a supporter would, however, qualify as a donation.

(6) Admission by programme only

It is common practice for admission to events to include the provision of a programme. Following the decision by the ECJ in *Card Protection Plan Ltd v C & E Commrs, ECJ Case C–349/96,* [1999] STC 270 (TVC 22.324) HMRC now accept that in the majority of cases there is a single supply of admission, the programme being an ancillary item. In any case, a programme does not qualify for zero-rating if it is no more than an elaborate ticket which has to be bought to get into the event, etc. Payment for such a programme is the consideration for admission even if payment cannot be legally enforced.

Boxes, seats, etc.

See **41.3**(i) **LAND AND BUILDINGS: EXEMPT SUPPLIES AND OPTION TO TAX.**

Recovery of input tax

Admission for a charge is always a business activity for VAT purposes and related input tax incurred will normally be deductible unless the admission charges are exempt (see above) in which case the partial exemption rules may apply.

If the public is admitted free of charge to any premises there is no business activity and VAT incurred is not input tax. If the premises are also used for business purposes, input tax may be apportioned, see **34.7 INPUT TAX**.

Sport and physical recreation facilities

[57.8] Subject to the exemptions in **57.9** and **57.10–57.14** below, the granting of facilities for playing any sport or participating in any physical recreation is standard-rated. The grant of any right to call for or be granted facilities which would be standard-rated under this provision is also standard-rated. Included is an equitable right, a right under an option or right to pre-emption and, in relation to Scotland, a personal right.

[*VATA 1994, Sch 9 Group 1 Item 1(m)(n)*].

Standard-rating has been applied to the supply of a football ground for international matches, the presence of ticket-paying spectators not preventing the facilities granted being those for playing sport rather than a licence to occupy land (*Queens Park Football Club Ltd* (VTD 2776) (TVC 41.156)). HMRC accept that this decision applies to supplies by other sporting stadia, both indoors and outdoors. (C & E News Release 72/88, 20 September 1988). Standard-rating has also been applied to the use of a practice range at a golf club (*L H Johnson* (VTD 14955) (TVC 41.158)).

Leisure trusts providing all-inclusive membership schemes

For community leisure centres that are run by non-profit making trusts, in most cases a typical customer who purchases an all-inclusive package will have access to a range of facilities at the leisure centre. VAT liability depends on the nature of the supply which has to be decided at the time the all-inclusive fee is paid. Where the supply is a single supply that would be artificial to split, there can only be one overarching liability. In most cases, the typical consumer who purchases an all-inclusive package will have access to a range of facilities at the leisure centre. Usually most of these facilities would, if supplied individually, be exempt as services closely linked with and essential to sport or physical education in which the individual is taking part (e.g. use of swimming pools, courts, pitches showers, changing rooms, etc). Therefore, in cases where the predominant reason for purchasing an all-inclusive package is to use the range of available sports facilities, the single supply is exempt (see **57.10** below). If the predominant reason a typical consumer purchases an all-inclusive package is to make use of standard-rated facilities (e.g. use of a sauna) the single supply is standard-rated.

(VAT Notice 701/45/11, para 3.5).

Letting of facilities

[57.9] The letting of facilities designed or adapted for playing any sport or taking part in physical recreation is normally standard-rated. However, the letting of such facilities may be exempt if the letting is for over 24 hours or there is a series of lettings to the same person over a period of time. Exemption will also apply if certain general purpose facilities are hired for sporting use or if sports facilities are hired out for non-sporting purposes. See below for further details.

24-hour rule

Where the facilities are provided for a continuous period of use exceeding 24 hours, the grant is exempt. The person to whom the facilities are let must have exclusive control of them throughout the period of letting.

Series of lets

Also exempt is the granting of such facilities for a series of ten or more periods (whether or not exceeding 24 hours) to a school, club, association or an organisation representing affiliated clubs or constituent associations where

(i) each period is in respect of the same activity carried on at the same place;
(ii) the interval between each period is not less than one day and not more than fourteen days;
(iii) consideration is payable by reference to the whole series and is evidenced by written agreement; and
(iv) the grantee has exclusive use of the facilities.

[*VATA 1994, Sch 9 Group 1 Note 16*].

Under (i) above, a different pitch, court or lane at the same sports ground or premises would count as the same place.

Under (ii) above the duration of the sessions may be varied but there is no exception for intervals greater than 14 days through the closure of the facility for any reason.

Under (iii) above, there must be evidence that payment is to be made in full, whether or not the right to use the facility for any specific session is actually exercised. Provision for a refund given by the provider in the event of the unforeseen non-availability of their facility would not affect this condition.

Premises are sports facilities if they are designed or adapted for playing any sport or taking part in any physical recreation (e.g. swimming pools, football pitches, dance studios and skating rinks). Each court or pitch (or lane in the case of bowling alley, curling rink or swimming pool) is a separate sports facility.

(VAT Notice 742, paras 5.1–5.4).

Option to tax

A supplier may be able to choose to standard-rate some of the above supplies which would otherwise be exempt. See **41.8 LAND AND BUILDINGS: EXEMPT SUPPLIES AND OPTION TO TAX.**

Example

Hale Football Club agrees to hire its football pitch to another local club on a Tuesday night for ten weeks from October to mid-December in order that the other club can have training sessions. The agreement gives the other team the right to cancel a night's booking and get a refund of money, as long as they given at least 24 hours notice.

In this situation, the VAT exemption would not apply – the exemption is only unaffected if an 'unforeseen' circumstance arises (e.g. bad weather or pitch damage). The right to cancel for any reason means the regular letting arrangement is not achieved.

Sporting services provided by eligible/non-profit making bodies

[57.10] VAT exemption applies to the supply of services closely linked with and essential to sport or physical recreation supplied to individuals taking part in the activity where the supplies are made by

- an 'eligible body' having a membership scheme to those of its members who are granted membership for a period of three months or more (see **57.11** below); and
- an 'eligible body' which does not run a membership scheme (e.g. a charity).

Specifically excluded are

- the supply of any services of residential accommodation, catering or transport;
- supplies by local authorities;
- supplies by government departments within the meaning of *VATA 1994, s 41(6)* (see **43.11 LOCAL AUTHORITIES AND PUBLIC BODIES**); and
- supplies by non-departmental public bodies (such as Sports Councils) which are listed in the 1993 edition of the publication prepared by the Office of Public Service and Science and known as Public Bodies.

Eligible body

Subject to the specific exclusions above, an eligible body means a non-profit making body which

- cannot distribute any profit it makes otherwise than to another non-profit making body or its own members on winding up or dissolution;
- (except on winding up or dissolution) applies any profits it makes from supplies exempted by these provisions *either* to maintain or improve the facilities made available in connection with those supplies *or* for the purposes of a non-profit making body; and
- is not subject to 'commercial influence'.

To decide whether a body is non-profit making, it is necessary to look at its constitution, its activities and its use of funds to determine whether it was established with a purpose, intention or motive which excluded profit making. A non-distribution clause in the constitution of an organisation does not, in itself, answer this question.

If the organisation is a company limited by shares, HMRC have accepted that

(a) the non-distribution condition will be satisfied by the passing of a resolution to
- delete, if appropriate *Table A, Arts 102–108* (dividend arrangements) and *Art 110* (capitalisation of profits); and
- adopt a new Article preventing distributions by way of dividend, bonus and any other means; and

(b) adoption of *Art 117* on winding up fulfills the winding-up criterion.

(VAT Notice 701/45/11, paras 4.2, 4.3).

Following the decisions in *Messenger Leisure Developments Ltd v R & C Commrs*, CA [2005] STC 1078 (TVC 24.40) HMRC take the view that any company which is precluded from distributing profit, but whose function is nevertheless to create VAT exemption in the context of a wider commercial undertaking, is not a non-profit making body for VAT purposes. It follows that such a company is not entitled to claim the VAT exemption which is directed at such bodies. (Business Brief 22/05).

'Commercial influence'

A body is considered to be subject to commercial influence in relation to any supply which would otherwise be exempt under these provisions (the '*sports supply*') if (and only if), there is a time in 'the relevant period' when

- a person 'associated with the body' made a 'relevant supply' to it; or
- a person 'associated with the body' received an emolument from it determined at least in part by reference to the body's profits or gross income; or
- an arrangement existed for a relevant supply to be made or emolument to be received after the end of the relevant period.

The following definitions apply for the purposes of 'commercial influence'.

(1) '*The relevant period*' for a sports supply is the three years before the sports supply.

(2) Subject to below, a person is '*associated with the body*' at the time, as the case may be, of the relevant supply, receipt of emolument or arrangement, if at any time in the relevant period the person concerned was an 'officer' or 'shadow officer' of the body or an 'intermediary for supplies' to that body or was connected to any such person. '*Officer*' includes director of a body corporate and any committee member or trustee concerned in the general control and management of the administration of the body. '*Shadow officer*' means a person in accordance with whose directions the members or officers of the body are accustomed to act. An '*intermediary for supplies*' is anyone who acts between the body and an officer in making the relevant supply. A

person is treated as connected with another under the provisions of *ICTA 1988, s 839* (see **71.19 VALUATION**). A person is *not* treated as associated with the body at the time of the relevant supply, etc. if the only times when that person, or the person connected with him, was an officer or shadow officer of the body occurred before 1 January 2000 *unless* that body would be treated as subject to commercial influence as a result of an agreement entered into after 13 January 1999 and before 1 January 2000.

(3) '*Emoluments*' include all salaries, fees, wages, perquisites and profits calculated or varied wholly or partly by reference to

- the profits from some or all of the activities of the body paying the emolument; or
- the level of that body's gross income from some or all of its activities.

Perquisites ('perks') are allowances paid, or goods and services provided, over and above a settled wage.

Payment of honoraria to a club secretary or treasurer will not disqualify a club from exemption, unless the amount is calculated by reference to profits or gross income.

(VAT Notice 701/45/11, paras 5.5, 5.7).

(4) A '*relevant supply*' is, subject to below,

(a) the grant of any interest in, right over or licence to occupy land (or, in the case of land in Scotland, any personal right to call for or be granted any such interest or right) which at any time in the relevant period was or was expected to become 'sports land';

(b) a supply arising from a grant falling within (*a*) above made after 31 March 1996 (e.g. rent payable for the use of sports land under a lease);

(c) the supply of any services of managing or administering of any facilities provided by the body; and

(d) the supply of any goods or services for a consideration in excess of what would have been agreed between parties entering into a commercial transaction at arm's length.

Where a club uses a committee member's firm to perform routine bookkeeping, accounting or legal services, HMRC do not treat supplies of such services as management and administration within (*c*) above and this will not therefore disqualify the club from exemption. (VAT Notice 701/45/11, para 5.7).

Included is any such supply between VAT group members which would otherwise be disregarded but specifically excluded is any such supply which is

- by a person to a body whose principal purpose at the time of the sports supply is to provide sports and physical recreation facilities for use by the employees of that person;
- by a charity or local authority;
- a gift of sports land or of the use of sports land;
- sports land supplied for a nominal amount; or
- the use of sports land supplied for a nominal amount provided the original grant of land was also for a nominal amount.

In normal circumstances, HMRC will treat any payment below £1,000 as nominal and will give consideration to claims for higher amounts to be so treated. Bodies wishing to be sure that HMRC will treat a payment as nominal before exempting supplies are advised to write to HMRC setting out the full facts. (VAT Notice 701/45/11, para 5.4).

(5) '*Sports land*' is land used, or held to be used, by the body for or in connection with sport and/or physical recreation.

[*VATA 1994, Sch 9 Group 10 Item 3 and Notes 1–17; SI 1999/1994*].

Individuals qualifying as members of a membership body

[57.11] Where a body has a membership scheme, exemption applies to services supplied to a *playing* 'individual' granted membership for a period of three months or more (including life membership). Where an individual becomes a member less than three months before the end of the club's subscription period and pays less than three months' subscription, the subscription can still be exempt provided the grant of membership is for not less than three months.

It is usually clear from the literature, rules, regulations and constitution of the body whether it is operating a membership scheme, e.g. by references to

- arrangements for application for membership;
- membership categories and subscriptions;
- benefits available to members (including voting rights at AGMs);
- conduct of members; and
- members' involvement in running the club.

For the purposes of this exemption, an '*individual*' is a person who actually takes part in the sporting or physical education activity and this includes

- family groups; and
- informal groups, where one individual makes a booking on behalf of a group of users of the sporting facilities.

Supplies to individuals do not include supplies

- by a club to one of its sections where the individual section has a separate and independent constitution, e.g. the squash section of a multiple-sports club; or
- to travel agents or tour operators, which have agreements with a sports club to supply use of sporting facilities to individuals, groups or corporate bodies. This includes, for example, supplies to individuals who are identified through having booked through a travel agent.

(VAT Notice 701/45/11, para 3.4).

'Privilege cards', issued in conjunction with a monthly or three-monthly season ticket and entitling cardholders to free admission to a sports centre run by an eligible body, do not make the holders 'members' thereby resulting in the standard-rating of facilities used by other 'non-members' (*Basingstoke and District Sports Trust Ltd* (VTD 13347) (TVC 24.32)).

Following this decision, HMRC issued the following clarification.

(i) Where a body does not operate a full membership scheme (e.g. where members do not have voting rights or any form of control over the management of the centre), sporting and physical education services provided are exempt from VAT subject to the normal conditions. This applies irrespective of whether users are called 'members' for the purpose of obtaining discount on use of the facilities.

(ii) Where a body operates a full membership scheme but limits its application to selected activities or locations, exemption of qualifying services is limited to supplies to members even if other activities are not within the membership scheme. For example, where a body provides a swimming pool and squash courts and the membership scheme is only for squash players, supplies to all users of the pool, other than squash members, is standard-rated even though there is no membership scheme for the swimming pool.

(Business Brief 3/96).

Non-members

In *Bridport & West Dorset Golf Club Ltd* (TC01214) (TVC 20.74), for many years a company operating a golf club accounted for VAT on 'green fees' from non-members, in accordance with HMRC's interpretation of the law and with the tribunal decision in *Keswick Golf Club* (VTD 15493) (TVC 20.74). However, in 2009 it submitted a repayment claim on the grounds that it should have treated its green fees as exempt under *Directive 2006/112/EC, Art 132(1)(m)*. The tribunal allowed the company's appeal against HMRC's rejection of the claim. The tribunal declined to follow its own previous decision in *Keswick Golf Club*, and held that the exclusion of supplies to non-members from the scope of the exemption in *VATA 1994, Sch 9, Group 10, Item 3* was not capable of properly achieving the objective of *Directive 2006/112/EC, Art 133(d)* and therefore did not correctly implement its terms.

HMRC have sought permission to appeal to the Upper Tribunal. The First-tier Tribunal decision is only binding on the parties to the decision and HMRC do not propose to pay other claims in the wake of the decision. If any golf clubs decide to exempt their green fees on the basis of the tribunal decision, HMRC will assess the underdeclared tax and enforce the assessments. Penalties may also be applicable. (HMRC Brief 30/11).

Sports qualifying for exemption

[57.12] The following sports, etc. qualify for exemption.

Aikido	American football	Angling
Archery	Arm wrestling	Association football
Athletics	Badminton	Ballooning
Baseball	Basketball	Baton twirling
Biathlon	Bicycle polo	Billiards
Bobsleigh	Boccia	Bowls
Boxing	Camogie	Canoeing

Caving	Chinese martial arts	Cricket
Croquet	Crossbow	Curling
Cycling	Dragon boat racing	Equestrian
Exercise and fitness	Fencing	Field sports
Fives	Flying*	Gaelic football
Gliding	Golf	Gymnastics
Handball	Hang/paragliding	Highland games
Hockey	Horse racing	Hovering
Hurling	Ice hockey	Ice skating
Jet skiing	Ju jitsu	Judo
Kabaddi	Karate	Kendo
Korfball	Lacrosse	Lawn tennis
Life saving	Luge	Modern pentathlon
Motor cycling	Motor sports	Mountaineering
Movement and dance	Netball	Octopush
Orienteering	Parachuting	Petanque
Polo	Pony Trekking	Pool
Quoits	Racketball	Rackets
Racquetball	Rambling	Real tennis
Roller hockey	Roller skating	Rounders
Rowing	Rugby league	Rugby union
Sailing/yachting	Sand and land yacht-ing	Shinty
Shooting	Skateboarding	Skiing
Skipping	Snooker	Snowboarding
Softball	Sombo wrestling	Squash
Stoolball	Street hockey	Sub-aqua
Surf life saving	Surfing	Swimming
Table tennis	Taekwondo	Tang soo do
Tchoukball	Tenpin bowling**	Trampolining
Triathlon	Tug of war	Unihoc
Volleyball	Water skiing	Weightlifting
Wrestling	Yoga	

* Includes those model flying activities, success in which is dependent on physical skill or fitness.

** Includes skittles.

Application may be made to HMRC to include other activities. HMRC will then consult with the Department of Culture, Media and Sport and other representative bodies and give a decision in writing. If exemption is refused, an appeal can be made to a VAT tribunal.

(VAT Notice 701/45/11, para 3.2).

Pigeon racing does not qualify for exemption (*Royal Pigeon Racing Association* (VTD 14006) (TVC 24.50)).

Services qualifying for exemption

[57.13] Services qualifying for exemption where supplied by a membership body to its qualifying members or, where applicable, by a non-membership body (e.g. a sports centre) to individuals include the following.

- Use of changing rooms, showers and playing equipment, trolley and locker hire and storage of equipment essential to sport.
- Provision of playing area (e.g. court, pitch or green fees).
- Use of multi-sport playing facilities.
- Refereeing, umpiring and judging services. Supplies by a self-employed referee registered for VAT are not exempt from VAT because he is not an eligible body.
- Coaching, training and physical education services. Sports coaching by professionals is not within the exemption as it is not supplied by an eligible body (although it may qualify for the exemption for education, see **16.9 EDUCATION**).
- Membership subscriptions covering active participation in sport (including life subscriptions entitling the member to playing services for life where the annual subscription is exempt).

  Clubs and associations often supply a number of different benefits in return for their subscriptions and must decide whether their subscriptions are consideration for a single supply or a multiple supply. If there is one principal benefit or reason for joining, with other benefits supplied being less important, the subscription is consideration for a single supply and its liability is determined by the liability of the main benefit. There is an exception, however, for non-profit making bodies which supply a mixture of benefits with different VAT liabilities. As a concession, these bodies *may* apportion their subscriptions to reflect the value and VAT liability of each individual benefit, even if they are consideration for a single supply. If the subscription is consideration for a multiple supply and the separate elements have different liabilities, the subscription must be apportioned. See **14.2 CLUBS AND ASSOCIATIONS** for further details.
- Joining fees where the benefits supplied in return are the same as for the subscription and the subscription is itself exempt. If the joining fee entitles the member to different benefits, VAT must be accounted for, where appropriate, on the liability of those benefits.
- Fees for remaining on the waiting list for membership but only if
  - (i) they are deducted from the new member's first subscription or entrance fee and this itself qualifies for exemption; and
  - (ii) they are refundable in the event that the candidate fails to become a member for any reason including voluntary withdrawal.

  Otherwise the fee is standard-rated.
- Match fees for the use of playing facilities/pitch hire. Match fees also covering the cost of catering and transport may need to be apportioned.
- Mooring, hangarage, use of workshops (excluding use of parts or services of an engineer).

Services not qualifying for exemption include

- sporting services supplied to
  - (i) members' guests (irrespective of who pays the guests' fees);
  - (ii) temporary members (those granted membership for less than three months); and
  - (iii) visitors from other members' clubs and societies;
- social or non-playing membership subscriptions;
- admission charges for spectators;
- use of residential accommodation;
- use of transport;
- catering, bars, gaming machines and social functions; and
- parking.

(VAT Notice 701/45/11, paras 3.3–3.5).

See *Royal Thames Yacht Club* (VTD 14046) (TVC 24.40) where the subscriptions of ordinary members were apportioned between exempt sporting facilities and standard-rated clubhouse facilities which were capable of being enjoyed to the exclusion of the sporting facilities.

Affiliation fees to sports governing bodies

[57.14] From 1 September 2010 a non-profit-making sports governing body can exempt its affiliation fees only where the fees are for services closely linked and essential to sport, are supplied by non-profit-making organisations, and the true beneficiaries are individuals taking part in sport. Supplies to commercial organisations should be treated as taxable since the true beneficiary of the service is unlikely to be individual taking part in the sport.

Where the conditions of ESC 3.35 (apportionment of membership subscriptions to certain non-profit-making bodies) are met, governing bodies may continue to take advantage of the option to apportion their affiliation fees between the rates of VAT applicable to the individual elements. However, where the principal benefit is of priority purchase rights for tickets of admission to international matches or tournaments, the fee is standard-rated. (VAT Notice 701/45/11, para 3.6).

HMRC previously restricted the exemption to fees calculated on a per person basis (provided the services were closely linked to sport). Affiliation fees calculated by other methods, e.g. on the basis of the club size or the number of teams fielded, were standard rated. However, in the case of *HMRC v Canterbury Hockey Club (and related appeal), ECJ Case C-253/07 16 October 2008 unreported*, (TVC 22.316), the ECJ found that the exemption applies more widely. It ruled that in the context of 'persons taking part in sport' (see *EC Sixth Directive Art 13A1(m)*) (now *Directive 2006/112/EC, Art 132(1)(m)*), the exemption includes services supplied to corporate persons and to unincorporated associations, provided that the supplies are closely linked and essential to sport, that they are supplied by non-profit making organisations and the true beneficiaries are individuals taking part in sport.

Treatment as disbursements

A club can treat the onward charge of the affiliation fees charged by a governing body to its members or customers as disbursements for VAT purposes (and outside the scope of VAT) provided

- the affiliation fee charged by the governing body qualifies for exemption;
- the principal beneficiary of the services supplied by the governing body is the individual sports person;
- the club itemises the fee separately from its subscription or charge to the individual member or customer on the VAT invoice; and
- the amount charged by the club to the individual member or customer does not exceed the fee charged by the governing body.

(VAT Notice 701/45/11, para 3.6).

Sporting rights

[57.15] The grant of any interest, right or licence to take game or fish is standard-rated subject to the exceptions in **57.16** to **57.18** below where sporting rights and land are sold or leased together. The grant of any right to call for or be granted an interest or right which would be standard-rated under this provision is also standard-rated. Included is an equitable right, a right under an option or right to pre-emption and, in relation to Scotland, a personal right. [*VATA 1994, Sch 9 Group 1 Item 1(c)(n)*].

De Voil Indirect Tax Service. See V4.113.

Sporting rights and land

[57.16] Where, at the time of the grant of the rights

- the grantor grants the grantee the fee simple (broadly freehold in England and Wales and *dominium directum* or *dominium utile* in Scotland) of the land over which the right to take game or fish is exercisable, or
- the sporting rights are leased together with that land and the sporting rights represent no more than 10% of the value of the whole supply,

the total consideration is taken to be for the supply of the land alone and is exempt (unless the grantor has opted to tax the supply, see **41.8 LAND AND BUILDINGS: EXEMPT SUPPLIES AND OPTION TO TAX**, in which case the whole of the supply is standard-rated).

Where the sporting rights are leased with the land and represent more than 10% of the value of the whole supply, an apportionment must be made between the standard-rated rights and the exempt supply of land (unless the option to tax has been exercised).

[*VATA 1994, Sch 9 Group 1 Item 1(c)*]. (VAT Notice 742, para 6.2).

Shooting rights only

[57.17] Standard-rating applies to a grant over land owned by the grantor or over which he has the shooting rights. The provisions cover both freehold sales of rights and leasing or letting for any length of time.

Shooting in hand

If a landowner keeps control of the shooting over his land and makes all the arrangements to stock the land with game ('shooting in hand') and invites others to join him in shooting, there is no business activity (and no input tax can therefore be recovered) if the individuals are asked to contribute towards the costs of maintaining the shoot provided

(a) only friends and relatives are permitted to shoot;
(b) the availability of the shoot is not advertised to the public;
(c) the shooting accounts show an annual loss equivalent to, at least, the usual contribution made a 'gun' over a year; and
(d) the loss is borne by the landowner personally rather than by the estate or farm business.

Syndicates

A group of individuals set up solely to share the expenses of a shoot is not normally in business and therefore not regarded as making supplies to the individual members. However, if the syndicate regularly supplies shooting facilities to non-members, or makes taxable supplies of other goods or services, it is regarded as being in business and all its activities, including the supply of shooting facilities to its members, are business activities.

If a landowner or tenant grants shooting rights for less than their normal value to a syndicate of whom he is a member, he must account for VAT on the open market value of those rights. If he supplies other goods or services (e.g. the services of a gamekeeper or beater), VAT should be charged in the normal way.

(VAT Notice 742, para 6.3).

See also *C & E Commrs v Lord Fisher*, QB [1981] STC 238 (TVC 7.6) where, on the facts, shooting was not held to constitute a business. In *Williams* (VTD 14240) (TVC 62.151) a farmer was treated as carrying on a business for VAT purposes even though HMRC treated the shooting as 'hobby farming' giving rise to neither a profit or a loss. In *Harrison* (TC01205) (TVC 7.114) HMRC decided that H, a member of a farming partnership, was making supplies of shooting rights in the course or furtherance of a business. H contended that he was merely supplying administrative services to a shooting syndicate, which was organised for the enjoyment of its members, rather than with a view to a profit. The tribunal allowed H's appeal, distinguishing *Williams*, where the syndicate had been organised by the landowner.

Fishing only

[57.18] Standard-rating applies to the grant of rights to take fish either from the grantor's own waters or from waters over which he has fishing rights. The provisions apply to both freehold sales of the rights and letting or leasing for any length of time.

Still-water fisheries

Any charges made to fishermen are standard-rated even if both fishing rights and fish are supplied. However, if the grantor allows a person freely to choose whether to take away fish caught or to throw them back, and makes a separate charge solely for those fish taken away, that charge is accepted to be the consideration for the zero-rated supply of fish (provided they are of a species generally used as food in the UK).

Lakes

Where a lake that is empty of fish is let to a person who will stock it with fish, there is an exempt supply of land (subject to the option to tax) rather than a standard-rated right to take those fish.

(VAT Notice 742, para 6.4).

Sponsorship income

Sponsorship

[57.19] Sponsorship is a common feature of artistic, sporting, educational and charitable activities. However, it is not restricted to these areas and it can involve payment in the form of goods and services as well as money. The payments may also be described as something else, for example, as a donation.

A person who receives sponsorship, or some other form of support, will normally be making taxable supplies if, in return, he is obliged to provide the sponsor with a significant benefit. This might include

- naming an event after the sponsor;
- displaying the sponsor's company logo or trading name;
- participating in the sponsor's promotional or advertising activities;
- allowing the sponsor to use the name or logo of the person being sponsored;
- giving free or reduced price tickets;
- allowing access to special events such as premieres or gala evenings;
- providing entertainment or hospitality facilities; or
- giving the sponsor exclusive or priority booking rights.

This list is not exhaustive and there are many other situations in which a sponsor may be receiving tangible benefits. What matters is that the agreement or understanding with the sponsor requires the person being sponsored to do something in return.

In *C & E Commrs v Tron Theatre Ltd,* CS 1993, [1994] STC 177 (TVC 67.103) sponsors were entitled, amongst other things, to priority bookings. It was held that the theatre would not have provided the goods and services it did for less than the consideration which the sponsors paid. As a result, the whole of the sponsorship received was consideration in money and subject to VAT.

Donations

Financial or other support might also be received in the form of donations or gifts. Where the sponsor's support is freely given and secures nothing in return, the recipient does not make a taxable supply and the sponsorship (whether in the form of money, goods or services) can be treated as a donation outside the scope of VAT. A taxable supply is not created where the sponsor provides an insignificant benefit such as a minor acknowledgement of the source of the support. Examples of this can include any of the following.

- Giving a flag or sticker.
- Naming the donor in a list of supporters in a programme or on a notice.
- Naming a building or university chair after the donor.
- Putting the donor's name on the back of a seat in a theatre.

In *C & E Commrs v EMAP MacLaren Ltd,* QB [1997] STC 490 (TVC 67.105) a company published a scientific periodical and organised cash awards to scientists. The costs of the awards was met by sponsors who received publicity in the periodical and tickets to attend the annual award. It was held that the sponsorship payments were not consideration obtained in return for the supply of benefits to sponsors.

Mixed sponsorship and donation

Provided it is entirely separate from the sponsorship agreement, a person is not required to account for VAT on any donation or gift (of the kind described above) received from a sponsor in addition to the sponsorship. However, it must be clear that any benefits the sponsor receives are not conditional on the making of the donation or gift.

Provision of goods and/or services by the sponsor rather than money. In such a case, if the sponsor provides

- goods and/or services to somebody who, in return, is making a taxable supply, he is making a taxable supply of those goods and/or services;
- goods to somebody as a gift or donation, he may be liable to account for VAT under the business gift rules (see **47.6 OUTPUT TAX**); and
- services to somebody as a gift or donation, no VAT is due.

Accounting for VAT

VAT must normally be accounted for on everything received under the sponsorship agreement. A VAT invoice must be issued to any VAT-registered sponsor. The sponsor can then reclaim the VAT as input tax subject to the normal rules. Where the amount of the sponsorship is agreed without reference to VAT, it must be treated as VAT-inclusive. A sponsor who provides sponsorship in the form of taxable supplies of goods and/or services is also required to issue a VAT invoice.

Where a charity makes supplies to sponsors as part of a fund-raising event, the supplies may be exempt. See **12.10 CHARITIES**.

Where supplies of advertising services and publicity are made to overseas sponsors, the services may be outside the scope of UK VAT. See **65.21 SUPPLY: PLACE OF SUPPLY**.

(VAT Notice 701/41/02, paras 1.2, 2.1–2.4, 3.1, 3.4).

See *Bird Racing (Management) Ltd* (VTD 11630) (TVC 7.97) where a company incorporated with the aim of attracting sponsorship for a motor racing driver was held, on the facts, to be predominantly concerned with the making of taxable supplies to sponsors for a consideration and therefore carrying on a business and entitled to be registered for VAT.

Example

Smithem Golf Club receives a donation of £1,000 from a golf equipment wholesaler, in return for which it is agreed that a representative of the wholesaler can attend the club's AGM and give a presentation to the members about how good the equipment is and the discounts that are available to those connected with the club.

In this situation, the payment is being made in return for a supply of services, i.e. the right to attend the AGM of the club and promote sales of golf equipment. The payment is not a genuine donation and the £1,000 payment is standard-rated.

Postage stamps and philatelic supplies

Stamps valid for postage in the UK

[57.20] 'Valid postage stamps' are the payment for a postal service that is exempt from VAT.

No VAT is chargeable on the sale of UK or Isle of Man stamps which are valid postage stamps and which are sold at or below face value. If such stamps are sold above face value, VAT must be accounted for at the standard rate on the amount by which the price exceeds that value.

'*Valid postage stamps*' are unused postage stamps of the present monarch's reign on which the value is

- £1 or a multiple of £1;
- in decimal currency, or
- designated for 1st or 2nd class postage.

All other stamps

Sales of other stamps, including

- all used stamps,
- all foreign stamps (even if valid for postage abroad), and
- UK and Isle of Man stamps of earlier reigns or which have a value expressed in pre-decimal currency

are standard-rated. It may be possible to treat such stamps as collector's items so that VAT can be accounted for on the difference between the purchase and selling price under the margin scheme for **SECOND-HAND GOODS (61)**. If the conditions of the scheme are not met, VAT is due on the full selling price.

Combinations of valid and other stamps

Where philatelic items are sold which consist of, or contain, valid postage stamps (see above), VAT must be accounted for on the full amount charged less the face value of the valid stamps.

First day covers

A first day cover is an envelope bearing postage stamps with a postmark of the first day of their issue.

- If an envelope with unfranked stamps (whether the stamps are fixed to the envelope or not) is sold for customers to post themselves, the face value of the unused stamps can be disregarded and VAT accounted for on the rest of the charge only.
- If an envelope with the new stamps is posted to the customer on the first day of issue, VAT must be accounted for at the standard rate on the full selling price of the first day cover (without deduction for the face value of the stamps).
- First day covers sold after the first day of issue are standard-rated. However, it may be possible to treat them as collector's items so that VAT can be accounted for on the difference between the purchase and selling price under the margin scheme for **SECOND-HAND GOODS (61)**.

Stamped stationery

Stamped stationery which is unused and valid for postage in the UK or Isle of Man is standard-rated on the amount charged less the face value of the stamps. This applies whether the stamps are printed on the stationery or are ordinary postage stamps that have been stuck on.

Imported collector's items

Some items of philatelic interest are eligible for a reduced valuation at importation which gives an effective VAT rate of 5%. See **73.3 WORKS OF ART, ETC.**

Postage and packing

If delivery is included in the contract with the customer, there is a single supply of delivered goods (in the case of philatelic supplies) or services (in the case of valid postage stamps). The liability of the delivery or postage and packing charge follows that of the items being delivered, i.e. standard-rated in the case of philatelic supplies or exempt in the case of valid postage stamps. For postage charges generally, see **47.8**(19) **OUTPUT TAX.**

(VAT Notice 701/8/03).

Key points

[57.21] Points to consider are as follows.

- Betting and gaming supplies are generally exempt from VAT. An important exception is that income earned by a business from gaming machines is standard-rated.
- The tax point for gaming machine income is the time when the customer plays the machine. However, by concession, the tax point can be delayed until the point when the machine is actually emptied by the owner. The exception to this rule is when there is a change in the rate of VAT, when takings up to the date of the rate change must be accounted for at the old rate.
- Output tax is due on takings from a gaming machine, net of any cash prizes paid out to the winners.
- Sporting activities and competitions organised by many 'eligible' bodies are exempt from VAT. An 'eligible body' is basically an organisation that is non-profit making and cannot distribute profits to other individuals or entities.
- As a useful planning point, the VAT exemption in relation to charity fundraising events also applies to events organised by non-profit making sports bodies (e.g. a members' golf club). The related costs of such events will be subject to an input tax block under the partial exemption rules, unless the entity in question qualifies as being 'de minimis' in relation to partial exemption.
- An important change of policy by HMRC means they now accept that an inclusive membership fee paid by an individual to a sports centre (organised by a 'non-profit' making body) will be exempt from VAT if the main benefits enjoyed by the customer relate to the use of sporting facilities. The previous policy was that if the user could enjoy any non-sporting facilities, e.g. a sauna, then the entire payment would be standard-rated.
- There have been many VAT tribunal cases in recent years where VAT exemption has been denied to a sporting entity because it is either not classed as 'non-profit' making or because it is subject to commercial influence. The entity must be a genuine non-profit making body in order to qualify for exemption.
- Exemption for sporting membership fees paid to a non-profit making body also extends to joining fees as well. This is particularly relevant to golf clubs.
- Membership of a non-profit making sports club for non-sporting purposes is standard-rated, e.g. social membership (right to use bar and enjoy social facilities etc.) of a club is standard-rated.
- Sponsorship income received by a sporting club or organisation is usually standard-rated. However, if a payment can be classed as a genuine donation (donor receives no significant benefits for his payment), it will be outside the scope of VAT.

58

Reduced Rate Supplies

Introduction

[58.1] VAT is levied on the supply of goods and services, the acquisition of goods from another EU country and the importation of goods from a place outside the EU. The standard rate of VAT is 17.5% (20% from 4 January 2011; 15% from 1 December 2008 to 31 December 2009) but VAT charged on certain supplies of goods and services is chargeable at a reduced rate of 5%. The reduced rate also applies to the acquisition from another EU country, or the importation from outside the EU, of goods the supply of which would be subject to the reduced rate. [*VATA 1994, ss 2(1A)–(1C), 29A(1)(2); FA 1995, s 21; F(No 2)A 1997, s 6; FA 2001, s 99*].

The categories of goods and services to which the reduced rate applies as specified in *VATA 1994, Sch 7A* are as follows.

Group 1	Supplies of domestic fuel or power (see **25 FUEL AND POWER**)
Group 2	Installation of energy-saving materials (see **58.2** below)
Group 3	Grant-funded installation of heating equipment or security goods or connection of gas supply (see **58.3** below)
Group 4	Women's sanitary products (see **58.4** below)
Group 5	Children's car seats (see **58.5** below)
Group 6	Residential conversions (see **42.12 LAND AND BUILDINGS: ZERO AND REDUCED RATE SUPPLIES AND DIY HOUSEBUILDERS**)
Group 7	Residential renovations and alterations (see **42.13 LAND AND BUILDINGS: ZERO AND REDUCED RATE SUPPLIES AND DIY HOUSEBUILDERS**)
Group 8	Contraceptive products (see **58.6** below)
Group 9	Welfare advice or information (see **28.35 HEALTH AND WELFARE**)
Group 10	Installation of mobility aids for the elderly (**28.36 HEALTH AND WELFARE**)

Group 11	Smoking cessation products (see **58.7** below).

The Treasury may vary the Groups (and notes contained therein which form an integral part) by adding, deleting or varying any description of supply for the time being specified. The *Schedule* may also be varied so as to describe a supply of goods or services by reference to matters unrelated to the characteristics of the goods or services themselves including, in the case of a supply of goods, the use that has been made of those goods. [*VATA 1994, ss 2(1A)–(1C), 29A(3)(4), s 96(9); FA 2001, s 99, Sch 31 para 5*].

Installation of energy-saving materials

[58.2] The supplies listed below are subject to a reduced rate of VAT. It should be noted that

- the reduced rate only applies to supplies made by installers of energy-saving materials and does not apply to purchases of energy-saving materials by businesses or to purchases for DIY use;
- relief does not apply to the installation of double glazing and similar products (e.g. low-emissivity glass) or the supply of energy-efficient domestic appliances; and
- energy-saving materials which are incorporated by a builder in a new dwelling are zero-rated (see **42.16 LAND AND BUILDINGS: ZERO AND REDUCED RATE SUPPLIES AND DIY HOUSEBUILDERS**).

The following supplies are subject to a reduced rate of VAT of 5%.

(a) Supplies of services of 'installing' 'energy-saving materials' in 'residential accommodation' or in a building intended for 'use solely for a relevant charitable purpose'.
(b) Supplies of 'energy-saving materials' by a person who installs those materials in 'residential accommodation' or in a building intended for 'use solely for a relevant charitable purpose'.

'*Energy-saving materials*' means any of the following.

(i) Insulation for walls, floors, ceilings, roofs or lofts or for water tanks, pipes or other plumbing fittings. '*Insulation*' means materials designed and installed because of their insulating. *Not included* are essentially decorative products or treatments (e.g. curtains and carpets).
(ii) Draught stripping for windows and doors. These are strips fixed around interior and exterior doors, windows and loft hatches.
(iii) Central heating system controls (including thermostatic radiator valves) and hot water system controls. *Included* are manual or electronic timers, thermostats, and mechanical or electronic valves.
(iv) Solar panels. *Included* are all systems installed in, or on the site of, a building which are
    - solar collectors such as evacuated tube or flat plate systems, together with associated pipework and equipment (e.g. circulation systems, pump, storage cylinder, control panel and heat exchanger); or

- photovoltaic (PV) panels with cabling, control panel and AC/DC inverter.

(v) Wind turbines (including mounting poles, electrical cables, battery banks and voltage controllers).

(vi) Water turbines (including electrical cables, battery banks and voltage controllers).

(vii) Ground source heat pumps (from 1 June 2004).

(viii) Air source heat pumps (from 7 April 2005).

(ix) Micro combined heat and power units (from 7 April 2005).

(x) Boilers designed to be fuelled solely by wood, straw or similar vegetal matter (from 1 January 2006). *Included* is a hopper where integral to the installation. *Not included* is the installation of 'multi-fuel' or 'dual-fuel' boilers.

'*Residential accommodation*' means

- a building, or part of a building, that consists of a dwelling or a number of dwellings (owner-occupied homes, homes rented from private landlords, local authorities and housing associations);
- a building, or part of a building, used for a '*relevant residential purpose*' (see **41.1**(15) **LAND AND BUILDINGS: EXEMPT SUPPLIES AND OPTION TO TAX**);
- a caravan used as a place of permanent habitation (i.e. a residential caravan sited at a permanent caravan park and exceeding the limits of size currently in force for trailers which may be towed on roads, see **42.26 LAND AND BUILDINGS: ZERO AND REDUCED RATE SUPPLIES AND DIY HOUSEBUILDERS**); or
- a houseboat (i.e. a boat designed or adapted for permanent habitation and having no means of self-propulsion *or* a boat used as a person's sole or main residence such as a canal boat on which the owner pays Council Tax or domestic rates).

'*Use for a relevant charitable purpose*' means use by a charity in either or both of the following ways, namely

- otherwise than in the course or furtherance of a business; or
- as a village hall or similarly in providing social or recreational facilities for a local community.

For further interpretation of these uses, see **41.1**(13) **LAND AND BUILDINGS: EXEMPT SUPPLIES AND OPTION TO TAX.**

[*VATA 1994, Sch 7A Group 2; FA 2000, s 135, Sch 35; FA 2001, Sch 31 para 1; SI 1998/1375; SI 2004/777; SI 2005/726; SI 2005/3329*]. (VAT Notice 708/6/11, paras 2.6–2.11, 2.15, 2.18).

'Installing'

The reduced rate is only available where the goods and materials are provided *and* installed by a VAT-registered business. The supply of energy saving-materials without installing them is standard-rated. Installation means putting in place energy-saving materials. This involves some process by which the materials are permanently fixed in place, although loft insulation may simply need to be unrolled and positioned in place to be installed.

Energy-saving materials installed with other works

The installation of just energy-saving materials with ancillary supplies is reduced-rated. An ancillary supply is a supply of goods or services that is a better means of enjoying the principal supply, e.g. installing loft insulation but having to cut a new loft hatch in the ceiling and making good to access the loft. The cutting of the loft hatch and making good is, in itself, a simple construction supply, but as the services have been carried out solely in support of the loft insulation, they become ancillary. However, if an existing roof is replaced with a new insulated one, the insulation clearly is a better way of enjoying the new roof and so the insulation is ancillary to the new roof. As the roof is standard-rated, this applies to the whole job including the insulation.

Sometimes when individual goods and services are provided together, there is not a single dominant supply and so the individual goods and services supplied together have equal importance, often taking the form of something else, e.g. a central heating system may consist of a conventional boiler, radiators, copper pipe, radiator values, heating controls etc. While some components may be reduced-rated if supplied on their own, here they form part of a single supply of a central heating system which is standard-rated (unless grant-funded (see **58.3** below)).

Where more than one job is undertaken at the same premises, the VAT liability depends upon the circumstances, e.g. if, as part of a contract to build an extension, thermostatic valves are fitted to all the radiators in the house, then this is a single standard-rated supply of construction services. However, if there is a contract to build an extension and some time after the work has commenced, the homeowner separately asks for the installation of thermostatic valves, this is then a separate supply and reduced-rated.

(VAT Notice 708/6/11, paras 2.2, 2.3).

De Voil Indirect Tax Service. See V4.409.

Grant-funded installation of heating equipment or security goods or connection of a gas supply

[58.3] The following supplies are subject to a reduced rate of VAT of 5%.

(a) Supplies to a 'qualifying person' of

- services of 'installing' 'heating appliances' in the qualifying person's sole or main residence, and
- 'heating appliances' by the person installing those appliances in the qualifying person's sole or main residence

to the extent that the consideration for the supply is, or is to be, funded by a grant made under a 'relevant scheme'.

'*Heating appliances*' means any of the following.

- Gas-fired room heaters that are fitted with thermostatic controls
- Electric storage heaters
- Closed solid fuel fire cassettes
- Electric dual immersion water heaters with factory-insulated hot water tanks

- Gas-fired boilers
- Oil-fired boilers
- Radiators

(b) Supplies to a 'qualifying person' of

- services of connecting, or reconnecting, a mains gas supply to the qualifying person's sole or main residence, and
- goods by the person connecting, or reconnecting, that gas supply where the installation of those goods is necessary for the connection, or reconnection, of the gas supply

to the extent that the consideration for the supply is, or is to be, funded by a grant made under a 'relevant scheme'.

(c) Supplies to a 'qualifying person' of

- services of 'installing', maintaining or repairing a central heating system (including a system which generates electricity) in the qualifying person's sole or main residence, and
- goods by the person installing, maintaining or repairing that central heating system where installation of those goods is necessary for the installation, maintenance or repair of the central heating system

to the extent that the consideration for the supply is, or is to be, funded by a grant made under a 'relevant scheme'.

Included are

- installation of a boiler, radiators, pipework and controls forming a central heating system;
- micro combined heat and power systems (which are heating systems that also generate electricity); and
- the repair/replacement of a boiler, radiators, pipework and controls forming a central heating system (whether or not the system was originally installed under a relevant grant-funded scheme).

(d) Supplies consisting in the leasing of goods that form the whole or part of a central heating system (including a system which generates electricity) installed in the sole or main residence of a 'qualifying person' to the extent that the consideration for the supply is, or is to be, funded by a grant made under a 'relevant scheme'.

Under this type of arrangement, the installer installs the central heating system as usual but then sells the equipment to a leasing company (standard-rated) which makes an annual 'lease' charge to the householder which is paid for by grant-funding (reduced-rated).

(e) Supplies of goods that form the whole or part of a central heating system (including a system which generates electricity) installed in the sole or main residence of a 'qualifying person' where, immediately before being supplied, the goods were leased under arrangements such that the consideration for the leasing of the goods was, in whole or in part, funded by a grant made under a 'relevant scheme'.

Supplies only fall within this provision to the extent that the consideration for the supply of goods is either

- funded by a grant made under a relevant scheme; or

- a payment becoming due only by reason of the termination (whether by the passage of time or otherwise) of the leasing of the goods in question. This covers the termination fee paid if the householder sells his home before the end of the lease term and the end of the lease payment.

(f) Supplies to a 'qualifying person' of
- services of installing, maintaining or repairing a 'renewable source heating system' in the qualifying person's sole or main residence, and
- goods by the person installing, maintaining or repairing that renewable source heating system where the goods are necessary for the installation, maintenance or repair of the system

to the extent that the consideration for the supply is, or is to be, funded by a grant made under a 'relevant scheme'.

A '*renewable source heating system*' means a space or water heating system which uses energy from renewable sources (including solar, wind and hydroelectric power) or near renewable resources (including ground and air heat).

A '*qualifying person*' is a person who, at the time of the supply, is aged 60 or over or is in receipt of one or more of the following benefits.

- Child tax credit (other than the family element)
- Council tax benefit
- Disability living allowance
- Working tax credit
- Housing benefit
- Income support
- An income-based jobseeker's allowance
- Industrial injuries disablement pension payable at the increased rate to include constant attendance allowance
- War disablement pension payable at the increased rate to include constant attendance allowance or mobility supplement

Where there are qualifying and non-qualifying persons living in the same dwelling, relief applies if the supply is to a qualifying person. In practice, for a supply to be to a qualifying person, that person must be responsible for ordering the work to be done.

A '*relevant scheme*' is a scheme which

- has as one of its objects the funding of the installation of energy-saving materials in the homes of qualifying persons; and
- disburses grants (directly or indirectly) in whole or part out of funds made available to it for that objective by the Secretary of State, the Scottish Ministers, the National Assembly for Wales, a Minister or a Northern Ireland Department, the EU, a local authority or under an arrangement approved by the Gas and Electricity Markets Authority or the Director General of Electricity Supply for Northern Ireland.

[*VATA 1994, Sch 7A Group 3; FA 2000, s 135, Sch 35; FA 2001, Sch 31 para 1; Tax Credits Act 2002, Sch 3 para 48; SI 1998/1375; SI 2002/1100*]. (VAT Notice 708/6/11, paras 3.2–3.8).

'Installing'

The reduced rate is only available where the goods and materials are provided *and* installed by a VAT-registered business. The supply of goods and materials without installing them is standard-rated. Installation means putting in place the goods in question. This involves some process by which the materials are permanently fixed in place.

For energy-saving materials installed with other works, see **58.2** above.

(VAT Notice 708/6/11, paras 2.2, 2.3).

Apportionment where grants received

Where a grant is made to fund supplies within (*a*) to (*g*) above (relevant supplies) and other supplies (non-relevant supplies), the charge must be apportioned. The proportion of the grant attributed to the relevant supplies is

$$G \times A \div B$$

where

G = the full grant received
A = the consideration reasonably attributable to the relevant supplies (excluding VAT)
B = the total consideration for relevant and non-relevant supplies (excluding VAT)

[*VATA 1994, Sch 7A Group 3, Note 3; FA 2001, Sch 31 para 1; SI 1998/1375; SI 2002/1100*].

Example 1: Full grant received covering all work

A builder installs relevant supplies to a value of £300 and carries out other building work to a value of £700 (both excluding VAT) for C in his main residence. A grant is received to cover the full cost of work.

	£	£
Value of relevant supplies	300.00	
VAT thereon (5%)	15.00	
		315.00
Value of non-relevant supplies	700.00	
VAT thereon (17.5%*)	122.50	
		822.50
Total cost covered by grant		£1,137.50

*20% from 4 January 2011; 15% from 1 December 2008 to 31 December 2009

Example 2: Partial grant received which the grant-awarding body allocates to the installation of relevant supplies

The facts are as in *Example 1* above except that C receives a grant of £200 towards the installation of the relevant supplies and pays for the rest of the work himself.

	£	£
Value of relevant supplies which are grant-funded	200.00	
VAT thereon (5%)	10.00	
		210.00
Value of other supplies	800.00	
VAT thereon (17.5%*)	140.00	
		940.00
Total cost including VAT		1,150.00
Grant received		200.00
Contribution from C		£950.00

*20% from 4 January 2011; 15% from 1 December 2008 to 31 December 2009

Example 3: Partial grant received which the grant-awarding body does not allocate

The facts are as in *Example 1* above except that C receives a grant of £200 towards the total cost and pays for the rest of the work himself.

Proportion of total grant allocated to relevant supplies

£200 × 300/1000 = £60

	£	£
Value of relevant supplies which are grant-funded	60.00	
VAT thereon (5%)	3.00	
		63.00
Value of other supplies	940.00	
VAT thereon (17.5%*)	164.50	
		1,104.00
Total cost including VAT		1,167.50
Grant received		200.00
Contribution from C		£967.50

*20% from 4 January 2011; 15% from 1 December 2008 to 31 December 2009

De Voil Indirect Tax Service. See V4.407; V4.408; V4.416.

Women's sanitary products

[58.4] Supplies of 'women's sanitary products' are subject to a reduced rate of VAT of 5%.

'*Women's sanitary products*' means any of the following.

- Products that are designed, and marketed, as being solely for use for absorbing, or otherwise collecting, lochia (discharge from the womb after childbirth) or menstrual flow. *Excluded* are protective briefs or any other form of clothing.

- This includes sanitary towels, sanitary pads, tampons, keepers and maternity pads.
- Panty liners, other than panty liners that are designed as being primarily for use as incontinence products.
  Panty liners designed for sanitary protection, but marketed as also suitable for protection against light incontinence or light feminine discharges, are eligible for supply at the reduced rate. Panty liners designed primarily as incontinence products are not eligible for the reduced rate, but may qualify for a separate VAT relief (see below).
- Sanitary belts (for use with looped towels or pads).

The reduced rate does not apply to

- complementary products such as feminine wipes and sprays;
- incontinence products (which are specifically excluded because zero-rating may be available for such products bought by incontinent people living in their own homes, see **28.21 HEALTH AND WELFARE**);
- clothing or sanitary accessories (e.g. disposable or protective pants or briefs that either hold sanitary protection in place or protect the wearer from leakage). Certain items of children's clothing may be zero-rated under a separate relief, see **13 CLOTHING AND FOOTWEAR**; and
- dual-purpose products designed to protect against both menstrual flow and incontinence.

[*VATA 1994, Sch 7A Group 4; FA 2001, Sch 31 para 1; SI 2000/2954*]. (VAT Notice 701/18/11, paras 2.1–2.5).

De Voil Indirect Tax Service. See V4.417.

Children's car seats

[58.5] The supply, acquisition or importation of 'children's car seats' is subject to VAT at the reduced rate of 5%.

A '*children's car seat*' is any of the following.

(a) A '*safety seat*', ie a seat
- designed to be sat in by a child in a road vehicle;
- designed so that, when in use in a road vehicle, it can be restrained in one or more of the following ways
  - (i) by a seat belt fitted in the vehicle, or
  - (ii) by belts, or anchorages, that form part of the seat being attached to the vehicle, or
  - (iii) by a related base unit, and
- incorporating an integral harness, or integral impact shield, for restraining a child seated in it.

(b) A '*related base unit for a safety seat*', i.e. a base unit that is designed solely for the purpose of attaching a safety seat securely in a road vehicle by means of anchorages that form part of the base unit and which, when in use in a road vehicle, can be restrained in one or more of the following ways
- by a seat belt fitted in the vehicle, or

- by permanent anchorage points in the vehicle, or
- by belts attached to permanent anchorage points in the vehicle.

The reduced rate applies to both ISOFIX (International Standards Organisation Fix) and non-ISOFIX bases.

(c) A children's travel system comprising a combination of a safety seat (see (*a*) above) and a '*related wheeled framework*'. For these purposes a wheeled framework is 'related' to a safety seat if the framework and the seat are each designed so that

- when the seat is not in use in a road vehicle it can be attached to the framework, and
- when the seat is so attached, the combination of the seat and the framework can be used as a child's pushchair.

(d) A '*booster seat*', i.e. a seat designed

- to be sat in by a child in a road vehicle, and
- so that, when in use in a road vehicle, it and a child seated in it can be restrained by a seat belt fitted in the vehicle.

(e) A '*booster cushion*', i.e. a cushion designed

- to be sat on by a child in a road vehicle, and
- so that a child seated on it can be restrained by a seat belt fitted in the vehicle.

For the above purposes, a '*child*' means a person aged under 14 years.

[*VATA 1994, ss 2(1A)–(1C), 29A, Sch 7A Group 5; FA 2001, s 96, Sch 31 para 1; SI 2009/1359*].

Reduced-rating is not tied to any manufacturing standards but children's car seats approved to the latest European Standard will be marked with a UN 'E' mark.

The reduced rate also applies to protective travel systems such as 'lie flat' car seat products that allow babies to safely lie flat while travelling in a car and are secured using a three-point safety harness. These products can also be used with compatible pushchairs to form a pram system.

Children's travel systems

There are currently two types of travel system.

- A safety seat within (*a*) above and a pram/pushchair that can be fitted together and where both of the elements can be used independently of each other.

  In such a case, the safety seat is reduced-rated and the pram/pushchair element is standard-rated.
- A safety seat within (*a*) above, a related wheeled framework as in (*c*) above and a pram/pushchair seat. Any combination of the three elements may be supplied together but either the safety seat or the pram/pushchair seat can be attached to the framework for use as a pram. The framework is only of use when one of the other two elements is attached.

  In such a case

  (i) when supplied separately, a safety seat is reduced-rated, a wheeled framework is standard-rated and a pram seat is standard-rated;

(ii) the supply of just a safety seat and a wheeled framework is wholly reduced-rated;
(iii) the supply of just a pram seat and a wheeled framework is wholly standard-rated; and
(iv) when all three elements are supplied together, the pram seat is standard-rated and the other two elements are reduced-rated.

Cars supplied with a fitted children's car seat

Where a car is supplied with a fitted children's car seat, whether as an integral part or as an optional extra, the supply is wholly standard-rated.

(VAT Notice 701/23/11, paras 5.1–5.5).

De Voil Indirect Tax Service. See V4.418.

Contraceptive products

[58.6] With effect from 1 July 2006, supplies of 'contraceptive products', other than 'relevant exempt supplies', are subject to a reduced rate of VAT of 5%.

'*Contraceptive product*' means any product designed for the purposes of human contraception, but does not include any product designed for the purpose of monitoring fertility.

'*Relevant exempt supplies*' means supplies which fall within *VATA 1994, Sch 9 Group 7 item 4* (exempt supplies of goods in any hospital etc., in connection with medical or surgical treatment, etc.). See **28.10 HEALTH AND WELFARE**.

[*VATA 1994, Sch 7A Group 8; SI 2006/1472*].

The reduced rate applies to sales of contraceptive products by retailers, vending machines or via the internet, regardless of whether purchased by an individual or organisation such as a sexual health charity or the NHS. In addition to the exclusion for relevant exempt supplies above,

- contraceptives obtained on the prescription of a medical practitioner remain zero-rated (see **28.13 HEALTH AND WELFARE**); and
- contraceptives that are fitted, injected or implanted by a health professional still form part of an exempt supply of medical care (see **28.2 HEALTH AND WELFARE**).

(Business Brief 7/06).

Smoking cessation products

[58.7] In relation to supplies made after 30 June 2007, supplies of pharmaceutical products designed to help people to stop smoking tobacco are taxable at the reduced rate of 5%. [*VATA 1994, Sch 7A Group 11; SI 2007/1601; SI 2008/1410*].

Smoking cessation products dispensed by a pharmacist on prescription by a medical practitioner are zero-rated and unaffected by this provision. The 5% reduced rate applies to all other supplies of pharmaceutical smoking cessation products by retailers including supplies made over the internet. This includes all non-prescribed sales of patches, gums, inhalators and other pharmaceutical products held out for sale for the primary purpose of helping people to quit smoking. (HMRC Budget Notice BN77 (2008)).

Key points

[58.8] Points to consider are as follows.

- It is important to identify when the reduced rate of VAT applies on a supply because many such sales (particularly relating to building services on residential property) will be made to non-VAT registered customers unable to claim input tax. So a VAT charge of 17.5% or 20% instead of 5% will produce a higher selling price for the customer and loss of competitiveness for the supplier.
- Even if a business is able to reclaim input tax, it is important that the reduced rate of VAT is charged where appropriate. This is because HMRC has the power to disallow any input tax claimed where a supplier has charged the wrong rate of VAT. So input tax claimed based on a 20% charge of VAT will be reduced to a 5% claim if the reduced rate should have been charged.
- Many builders adopt an approach of 'play safe' and charge standard rate VAT on a job. This approach is deprecated because it is important that the correct rate of VAT is charged on all supplies of goods and services.
- The reduced rate of VAT applies to building work carried out on a residential property that has been empty (unlived in) for at least two years. The builder should acquire and retain evidence from the landlord concerning the empty letting period.
- The reduced rate of VAT also applies to building work that produces a change in the number of residential units before and after the work has been carried out. Remember that this rule also applies where a reduced number of units is evident e.g. converting two flats into a single house.
- The reduced rate of VAT also applies to building work that converts a non-residential property into a residential property, e.g. barn converted to bungalow, offices into flats.
- An important point in relation to the building work considered above is that the reduced rate of VAT will also apply to any building materials supplied by the builder as part of his work.

59

Registration

Cross-references. See **8.5 BUSINESS** for anti-avoidance measures to combat business splitting and the conditions for the separation of a previously single business into independent parts for registration purposes; **8.10 BUSINESS** for sale or transfer of a business as a going concern; **12.3 CHARITIES** for registration by charities; **14.3–14.4 CLUBS AND ASSOCIATIONS** for registration by clubs, etc.: **27 GROUPS OF COMPANIES** for group registration; **34.10 INPUT TAX** for VAT paid on goods and services obtained before registration; **35 INSOLVENCY** for the effect of individuals becoming bankrupt or companies entering receivership or liquidation; **40 ISLE OF MAN**; **43.5 LOCAL AUTHORITIES AND PUBLIC BODIES**; **48.1–48.4 OVERSEAS TRADERS**; **50.2 PARTNERSHIPS** for partnership registration; **53.3 PENSION SCHEMES**; **63.34 SPECIAL SCHEMES** for registration of non-EU suppliers of electronically supplied services.

De Voil Indirect Tax Service. See V2.1.

Introduction

[59.1] A 'person' who is in business and either makes or intends to make 'taxable supplies' of goods or services in the course or furtherance of that business may be liable or entitled to register for VAT. '*Person*' includes a body of persons corporate or unincorporate. [*Interpretation Act 1978, Sch 1*].

It is the 'person' who is required to register, not the business or businesses carried on. Thus, where a person is operating more than one business, even though they are dissimilar, *all* the person's business activities must be covered by one registration (*C & E Commrs v Glassborow and Another QB,* [1974] STC 142 (TVC 57.1)). This applies even if one or more of the businesses would be under the registration limit if carried out alone.

Taxable supplies are the supplies of goods or services made in the UK other than **EXEMPT SUPPLIES (20)**. [*VATA 1994, s 4(2)*].

De Voil Indirect Tax Service. See V2.101–103.

Entitlement to be registered

Persons making or intending to make taxable supplies

[59.2] Where a person who is not registered or liable to be registered in the UK satisfies HMRC that he

(i) makes taxable supplies; or
(ii) is carrying on a business and intends to make such supplies in the course or furtherance of that business,

HMRC must, if he so requests, register him from the day on which the request is made or from such earlier date as may be agreed between the person and HMRC. [*VATA 1994, Sch 1 para 9*]. See **8.1 BUSINESS** for the test of whether an activity is to be treated as a business.

Retrospective registration

The provisions allow a person to negotiate registration from a date prior to the date of application provided this is done at the time of initial application and not subsequently after registration. See also *C & E Commrs v Eastwood Care Homes (Ilkeston) Ltd and Others, CA* [2001] STC 1629 (TVC 32.7).

From 1 April 2009 a business can apply for voluntary registration to be backdated up to four years. However, this does not apply retrospectively, and until 31 March 2010 any request for backdated registration is limited to 1 April 2006. Prior to 1 April 2009 requests for registration could be backdated up to three years from the date of application. (VAT Notice 700/1/10, para 2.10).

'Intending traders'

The provisions under (ii) above allow registration for a person who is carrying on a business, is not yet making taxable supplies at the time of applying but who intends to do so in the future. Intending traders normally seek registration from a current date in order to reclaim input tax incurred in the setting up and development of the business. In some cases the amounts involved may be substantial and cover long periods. HMRC must therefore be satisfied that there is a firm intention to make taxable supplies before allowing registration as an intending trader.

> *Example*
>
> Jane and John (in partnership) have bought an old commercial building and been charged VAT on the purchase of the freehold. Their intention is to refurbish the building and trade as a restaurant. The refurbishment programme will take twelve months before trading can start.
>
> They can apply to register for VAT as an intending trader from the date they bought the building in order to reclaim input tax on both the cost of the building and the ongoing refurbishment costs. They will need to provide documents to HMRC to confirm their trading intentions (e.g. planning permission papers, business plans, trading forecasts etc.).

Persons only making exempt or certain outside the scope supplies

Where a person who is not registered or liable to be registered in the UK satisfies HMRC that

(a) he has a 'business establishment' (including a branch or agency) in the UK or his 'usual place or residence' is in the UK,

(b) he does not make or intend to make taxable supplies in the UK, and

(c) he either

 (i) makes supplies

  - outside the UK which would be taxable supplies if made in the UK, or
  - falling within **34.3**(*c*) **INPUT TAX** (mainly exempt financial services), or

 (ii) he is carrying on a business and intends to make such supplies in the course or furtherance of that business,

HMRC must, on request, register that person from the day on which the request is made or from such earlier date as is mutually agreed.

The '*usual place of residence*' of a company means the place where it is legally constituted.

[*VATA 1994, Sch 1 para 10; FA 1997, s 32*].

For these purposes a '*business establishment*' includes the registered office of an overseas company. Where a business provides accountancy services at its premises for a non-established taxable person who does not make supplies in the UK, HMRC do not consider these premises to be a business establishment.

An overseas business has a branch in the UK if it maintains a permanent office at which staff are employed. It has an agency in the UK if it has a permanent UK agent which enters into contracts for the purchase of goods and services or for the import of goods in its name on a regular basis. An agent who merely acts as an intermediary in bringing together customer and supplier but is not directly involved in the supply chain does not constitute an agency.

(HMRC VAT Guidance V1–28, para 7.7.2).

These provisions allow a UK business to register where it does not make taxable supplies in the UK but makes supplies within (*c*)(i) above. It also means that an overseas business with a business establishment, but no taxable supplies, in the UK can register in the UK and, because of (*b*) above, can recover input tax on taxable supplies it receives from UK VAT-registered businesses or on goods it imports into the UK (subject to the normal rules). See **34.3**(*b*) **INPUT TAX**. An overseas business with no business establishment, and no taxable supplies, in the UK can only recover UK VAT under the *EC 8th Directive* (if established in another EU country, see **18.44 EUROPEAN UNION LEGISLATION**) or the *EC 13th Directive* (if in business outside the EU, see **18.45 EUROPEAN UNION LEGISLATION**).

De Voil Indirect Tax Service. See V2.120; V2.121; V2.144; V2.146.

Example

Consultants Ltd trades from offices in the UK (it has no presence in any other country) but all of its customers are business customers based in either Sweden (EU) or Australia (non-EU). The company's consultancy income is outside the scope of UK VAT (place of supply being in the customer's country) but it can still register for VAT in the UK and claim input tax on its UK overheads. The reason is because consultancy services would be taxable (subject to standard-rated VAT) if supplied to a UK customer.

Any foreign VAT that the company pays in Sweden must be reclaimed through the 8th Directive system (overseas repayments in EU), and a 13th Directive claim would be appropriate to claim GST (Goods and Services Tax) paid in Australia.

Compulsory registration

[59.3] Subject to the exception below, a person who makes taxable supplies but is not registered under *VATA 1994* becomes liable to be registered under these provisions as follows.

(a) At the end of any month if the value of his taxable supplies in the period of one year then ending has exceeded the limit in Table A below. (If taxable supplies have been made for a period of less than twelve months, the value of all taxable supplies to the end of the month in question must be compared to the limit in Table A below, see *Mr & Mrs Norton* (VTD 151) (TVC 57.13).)

(b) At any time, if there are reasonable grounds for believing that the value of his taxable supplies in the period of 30 days then beginning will exceed the limit in Table A below.

(c) Where a business (or, with effect from 1 September 2007, part of a business) carried on by a taxable person is transferred to another person as a going concern and the transferee is not registered under *VATA 1994* at the time of the transfer, the transferee becomes liable to be registered under these provisions at that time if
   (i) the value of his taxable supplies in the period of one year ending at the time of the transfer has exceeded the limit in Table A below; or
   (ii) there are reasonable grounds for believing that the value of his taxable supplies in the period of 30 days beginning at the time of the transfer will exceed the limit in Table A below.

   For these purposes, the transferee is treated as having carried on the business (or part) before as well as after the transfer, i.e. under (i) above the transferor's taxable supplies in the one year to the date of transfer must also be taken into account.

Table A	
Effective date	*Limit*
1.4.11–	£73,000
1.4.10–31.3–11	£70,000
1.5.09–31.3.10	£68,000
1.4.08–30.4.09	£67,000
1.4.07–31.3.08	£64,000
1.4.06–31.3.07	£61,000
1.4.05–31.3.06	£60,000
1.4.04–31.3.05	£58,000

[*VATA 1994, s 49(1)(a), Sch 1 para 1(1)(2); FA 2007, s 100(2)(8); SI 2011/897*].

A person is treated as having become liable to be registered at any time when he would have become so liable under the above provisions but for any existing registration which is subsequently cancelled under **59.10**(3), **59.17**(*b*), **59.25**(*c*) or **59.32**(*b*) below. [*VATA 1994, Sch 1 para 1(5); FA 2000, s 132(6)*].

Exception

A person does not become liable to be registered under (*a*) or (*c*)(i) above if HMRC are satisfied that the value of his taxable supplies in the period of one year beginning at the time at which he would become liable to be registered will not exceed the limit in Table B below.

Table B	
Effective date	*Limit*
1.4.11–	£71,000
1.4.10–31.3.11	£68,000
1.5.09–31.3.10	£66,000
1.4.08–30.4.09	£65,000
1.4.07–31.3.08	£62,000
1.4.06–31.3.07	£59,000
1.4.05–31.3.06	£58,000
1.4.04–31.3.05	£56,000

[*VATA 1994, s 49(1)(a), Sch 1 para 1(3); FA 2007, s 100(2); SI 2011/897*].

This gives HMRC discretion to allow requests for retrospective exception. Exception is generally granted on the basis of the value of taxable supplies made and future anticipated supplies, at the time when the application is made. It should, however, be noted that, if HMRC grant exception, taxable supplies must still be monitored on a monthly basis in order to determine whether a further liability to registration arises. If, for example, a person is granted exception but one month later the value of his supplies render him liable to registration under (*a*) above, then he must either register for VAT or again satisfy HMRC that his expected turnover for the forthcoming twelve months will not exceed the limit in Table B above.

See, however, *dicta* of Lord Granchester in *WF Shephard* (VTD 2232) (TVC 51.56). Where a trader has not applied to HMRC at the right time to consider the relevant circumstances, this exception can only be relied upon by a trader if he establishes that, at the right time, HMRC could not reasonably have come to any conclusion other than that taxable supplies in the year would not exceed the relevant amount. These *dicta* were followed in *RJ & J Nash* (VTD 14944) (TVC 57.24) where, although it was accepted that turnover had fallen below the registration limit following a transfer of a going concern, there were no grounds on which HMRC could have been expected, at the date of the transfer, to have believed that this would be the case. See also *Gray (t/a William Gray and Son) v C & E Commrs,* Ch D [2000] STC 880 (TVC 57.28).

Taxable supplies

A taxable supply is a supply of goods or services made in the UK other than an exempt supply. [*VATA 1994, s 4(2)*]. In determining whether the registration limits in Tables A and B above have been exceeded, it is therefore necessary to take into account the VAT-exclusive value of all standard and zero-rated supplies of goods and services, including

- the value of 'reverse charge' services received from abroad (see **38.4 INTERNATIONAL SERVICES**); and
- the value of any **SELF-SUPPLIES (62)**.

The following special rules, however, apply.

- *Capital assets*. Supplies of goods or services that are capital assets of the business in the course or furtherance of which they are supplied are to be disregarded. Specifically, however, any standard-rated supply of an interest in, right over, or licence to occupy land is not to be regarded as a capital asset and does form part of the person's taxable supplies for registration purposes. [*VATA 1994, Sch 1 para 1(7)(8)*].
Capital assets may be tangible or intangible and include premises, plant, machinery, office machinery, computers, office furniture, used company cars, patent rights which have been exploited and which are sold outright, and goodwill. Capital goods have been defined as 'goods used for the purposes of some business activity and distinguishable by their durable nature and their value and such that the acquisition costs are not normally treated as current expenditure but written off over several years' (*Verbond van Nederlandse Ondernemingen v Inspecteur der Invoerrechten en Accijnzen, ECJ Case 51/76*, [1977] 1 CMLR 413 (TVC 22.432)). In *The Trustees of the Mellerstain Trust* (VTD 4256) (TVC 7.106) the tribunal followed this definition and held that paintings sold from an historic house open to the public were capital assets which had been used to make taxable supplies, and as such did not render the trust liable to register for VAT.
- *Distance sales*. Supplies can be disregarded if they are only taxable supplies in the UK because an overseas business makes distance sales to non-taxable persons in the UK and is required to register under *VATA 1994, Sch 2* (see **59.11** *et seq* below). [*VATA 1994, Sch 1 para 1(7)*].
- *Previous registration*. For the purposes of (*a*) and (*c*)(i) above, supplies made at a time when the person was previously registered under *VATA 1994* can be disregarded if his registration was cancelled otherwise than under **59.10**(3), **59.17**(*b*), **59.25**(*c*) or **59.32**(*b*) below and HMRC are satisfied that before his registration was cancelled he had given them all the information they needed in order to determine whether to cancel his registration. [*VATA 1994, Sch 1 para 1(4); FA 2000, s 136(6)*].
- *Fiscal warehousing*. Supplies to which *VATA 1994, s 18B(4)* (last acquisition or supply before removal from fiscal warehousing) applies and supplies treated as made under *VATA 1994, s 18C(3)* (self-supply of services on removal of goods from warehousing) can be disregarded. See **72.17** and **72.20 WAREHOUSED GOODS AND FREE ZONES** respectively. [*VATA 1994, Sch 1 para 1(9); FA 1996, Sch 3 para 13*].
- *Margin schemes*. Under the schemes for **SECOND-HAND GOODS (61)**, the taxable supplies are the full selling prices of the goods. Under the **TOUR OPERATORS' MARGIN SCHEME (68)**, taxable supplies are the total margin (i.e. difference between buying prices and the selling prices) on margin scheme supplies plus the full value of any other taxable supplies (including all in-house supplies).
- *Supplies of long-term accommodation*. The value of certain supplies of long-term accommodation can be excluded when calculating taxable turnover. See **32.2 HOTELS AND HOLIDAY ACCOMMODATION.**

De Voil Indirect Tax Service. See V2.135–137.

Notification and date of registration

[59.4] Where a person becomes liable to be registered by virtue of

(a) **59.3**(*a*) above, he must notify HMRC of the liability within 30 days of the end of the relevant month. HMRC must then register him (whether or not he so notifies them) with effect from the end of the month following the relevant month or from such earlier date as is mutually agreed;

> *Example*
>
> On 22 May, W determines that his supplies in the past twelve months have exceeded the registration threshold.
>
> W becomes liable to be registered on 31 May. He must notify HMRC of his liability to be registered by 30 June. Unless mutually agreed otherwise, HMRC will register him with effect from 1 July.

(b) **59.3**(*b*) above, he must notify HMRC of the liability before the end of the period by reference to which the liability arises. HMRC must then register him (whether or not he so notifies them) with effect from the beginning of that period;

> *Example*
>
> On 20 January, Y expects that his supplies in the next 30 days will exceed the registration threshold.
>
> Y becomes liable to be registered on 20 January. He must notify HMRC of his liability to be registered by 20 February. HMRC will register him with effect from 20 January.

(c) **59.3**(*c*) above, he must notify HMRC of the liability within 30 days of the time when the business is transferred. HMRC must then register any such person (whether or not he so notifies them) with effect from the time when the business is transferred; and

(d) **59.3**(*a*) above *and* **59.3**(*b*) or **59.3**(*c*) above at the same time, HMRC must register him under (*b*) or (*c*) above, as the case may be, rather than under (*a*) above.

[*VATA 1994, Sch 1 paras 5–8*].

Failure to notify

Failure to notify a liability to register may incur a penalty. See **52.14 PENALTIES**. Late notification of a liability to register will result in the backdating of the registration, HMRC having no discretion in the matter (*SJ Whitehead* (VTD 202) (TVC 57.83)) and VAT must be accounted for from the correct date whether or not it has been charged (*JR Atkinson* (VTD 309) (TVC 57.84)).

De Voil Indirect Tax Service. See V2.126; V2.128.

Application for registration

[59.5] Application for registration under **59.2** and **59.3** above must be made in such form and containing such particulars as HMRC may by regulation prescribe. Application must currently be made on Form VAT 1 (or Welsh version Form VAT 1(W)) and must include a signed declaration that all information entered in it, or accompanying it, is true and complete. A partnership applying for registration must also complete Form VAT 2 (or Welsh version Form VAT 2(W)). [*VATA 1994, Sch 1 para 17; SI 1995/2518, Reg 5(1); SI 2000/794*]. See also **50.2 PARTNERSHIPS**.

When submitting the above VAT application form, details to support an application for VAT periods to correspond with the financial year of the business (see **2.4 ACCOUNTING PERIODS AND RETURNS**) should be sent if appropriate.

The completed application forms, with any extra information requested by HMRC, should be sent to HM Revenue & Customs, Registration and Deregistration Unit, Deansgate, 62–70 Tettenhall Road, Wolverhampton, WV1 4TZ. When HMRC have checked the details on the application form, they send a certificate of registration (Form VAT 4) showing the effective date of registration, the registration number, the date on which the first VAT period ends and the length of future VAT periods (i.e. three-monthly or monthly). If a reply is not received from HMRC within 15 working days of submitting Form VAT 1, it is advisable to contact them to make sure that the application was received. (VAT Notice 700/1/10, para 3.5).

HMRC may amend a certificate of registration issued with the wrong date and issue assessments for any earlier periods then coming within the scope of VAT (*Maidstone Sailing Club (DG Oliver)* (VTD 511) (TVC 57.93)). The certificate is no more than a notification of the registration date and number. Other matters shown on the certificate, including the dates on which returns are to be made, are entered as matters of administrative convenience and therefore are not appealable matters within *VATA 1994, s 83(a)* (*Punchwell Ltd* (VTD 1085) (TVC 59.2)). Further, the allocation of registration numbers is within the administrative discretion of HMRC (see *L Reich & Sons Ltd* (VTD 97) (TVC 57.216) where HMRC refused to reallocate the registration number of a company to a newly formed subsidiary which took over the trade previously carried on by the parent company).

A business must start keeping records and charging VAT to its customers from the date from which it knows it has to be registered. It can increase prices to include VAT due but, until it has received a registration number, it must not show VAT as a separate item on any invoice issued. It should explain to any VAT-registered customers that it will be sending them VAT invoices at a later date. Once the business has its registration number, it should send the necessary invoices showing VAT within 30 days.

Where a business has asked for voluntary registration (see **59.2** above), it should start keeping records and charging VAT from the date it is registered, i.e. normally the date requested on the application form.

(VAT Notice 700/1/10, para 4.1).

Electronic application

A business not yet registered for VAT can use HMRC's eVAT service to register instead of completing the paper version of Form VAT 1. An agent, authorised by the business, may also fill out the online form on its behalf. The business must first be authorised to use the eVAT service. This can be done via Online services on the HMRC website.

At the end of the application process, a business will receive an online acknowledgment and a unique reference number. The date and time shown on this will be the time the notification was made for legal purposes. It is therefore recommended that a copy of the acknowledgement is taken for record purposes. If an electronic acknowledgment is not received, it should be presumed that the request has not been received by HMRC.

All electronic applications are processed in strict date order. HMRC aim to process an application within 15 working days of receiving the online application although it may take longer if additional information is requested. For security reasons, VAT registration numbers are only notified in writing and by post to the address confirmed as the principal place of business. If a VAT registration number has not been received within 15 working days, the business should contact the National Advice Service on 0845 010 9000 and quote the acknowledgment reference number. Similarly, the National Advice Service should be contacted if an error is discovered in the original application or the business wishes to cancel the application.

[*SI 1995/2518, Reg 5(4)–(14); SI 2004/1675*].

Exemption from registration

[59.6] Where a person who makes or intends to make taxable supplies satisfies HMRC that 'any such supply' is zero-rated (or would be so if he were a taxable person) they may, if he so requests and they think fit, grant exemption from registration under the above provisions. On a material change in the nature of the supplies made, the person exempted must notify HMRC of the change within 30 days of the end of the day on which it occurred or, if no particular day is so identifiable, within 30 days of the end of the particular quarter in which it occurred. On a material alteration in any quarter in the proportion of taxable supplies of such a person that are zero-rated, he must notify HMRC of the alteration within 30 days of the end of that quarter. Exemption applies until it appears to HMRC that the request should no longer be acted upon or the request is withdrawn by the trader. [*VATA 1994, Sch 1 para 14*].

'*Any such supply*' has its ordinary meaning and HMRC therefore have discretion in applying the provisions where not all of the supplies are zero-rated (*Fong* (VTD 590) (TVC 57.167)). HMRC may therefore exempt a person from registration if only a small proportion of his taxable supplies is standard-rated provided that, if registered, input tax would normally exceed output tax.

If application for exemption is refused, registration for VAT applies from the date the business would otherwise have been liable and VAT will have to be accounted for from that date. Any application for exemption should therefore be submitted as early as possible to enable HMRC to reach a decision in good time.

(VAT Notice 700/1/10, para 2.13).

A material alteration affecting exemption from registration would arise where, if the person was registered, output tax would exceed input tax in any twelve-month period. (VAT Notice 700, para 26.12).

Exemption saves a person the trouble and expense of having to keep proper records and accounts for VAT purposes and rendering returns but it does mean that input tax paid on purchases of goods or services for the business is not reclaimable.

De Voil Indirect Tax Service. See V2.147.

Example

Marion rents a small unit in a shopping centre selling fruit (zero-rated). Her sales for the twelve months ending 31 March 2010 were £75,000, exceeding the VAT limit for the first time. Her main costs in the business are rent (exempt from VAT), the wages of two employees (outside the scope) and the fruit she buys for resale (zero-rated). Her accountant is not VAT-registered and has offered to complete VAT returns for her at a cost of £300 per year.

In reality, the main overheads and costs of the business do not attract any VAT, so Marion will have negligible input tax to reclaim if she became VAT-registered. It would be very unlikely if the total amount of input tax she could reclaim exceeded the accountancy fee of £300 to complete her returns. Her best option is to apply to HMRC to receive exemption from registration on the basis that she makes zero-rated sales and would therefore always be a repayment trader.

Changes in circumstances

[59.7] Except where other time limits are specified, a registered person must notify HMRC, within 30 days and with full written particulars of any change in the name, constitution or ownership of the business or any other event which may necessitate the variation of the register or cancellation of registration. [*SI 1995/2518, Reg 5(2); SI 2000/794*].

Details of the changes should be notified to Grimsby National Registration Service, HM Revenue & Customs, Imperial House, 77 Victoria Street, Grimsby, DN31 1DB. Registration number and date of change should be given in any correspondence.

Electronic notification

A business can also use HMRC's eVAT service to notify changes in registration details. The business must first be authorised to use the service. This can be done via Online services on the HMRC website. This method of notification can only be used to make changes to an existing and continuing registration.

Changes involving deregistration (see below) or transfer of a registration number to a new business must continue to be made by post, as must the appointment of, or changes to, an appointed VAT representative.

Following notification, the business will receive an online acknowledgment and a unique reference number. The date and time shown on this will be the time the notification was made for legal purposes. It is therefore recommended that a copy of the acknowledgement is taken for record purposes. If an electronic acknowledgment is not received, it should be presumed that the request has not been received by HMRC.

[*SI 1995/2558, Reg 5(4)(11); SI 2004/1675*].

Changes not involving deregistration

Registration details must be amended for changes in any of the following.

- The names of the proprietors of, or partners in, the business.
- The name, business name or trading style of the business.
- The name of an incorporated company.
- The composition of a partnership where one or more of the former partners remains in the partnership.
- The name and/or address of the UK agent for VAT purposes appointed by an overseas company or resident.
- The address of the principal place of business.
- The registered office of an incorporated company.
- The main business activity.
- A limited company is re-registered as an unlimited company, or vice versa.
- A private company is re-registered as a public limited company, or vice versa.
- Bank or National Giro account number or bank sorting code. If the annual accounting scheme is used, the registered person must notify the bank and VAT Central Unit Annual Accounting Section immediately.
- Certain changes affecting group treatment. See **27.3 GROUPS OF COMPANIES.**

Changes involving deregistration

The following changes will require deregistration.

- Sale of the business.
- Death, insolvency or incapacity of a taxable person. See **15.1 DEATH AND INCAPACITY** and **35.1 INSOLVENCY**.
- Conversion of a business into an incorporated company.
- Conversion of an incorporated company into a partnership or a sole proprietorship.
- A sole proprietor takes one or more persons into partnership.
- A partnership ceases to exist but one of the former partners becomes the sole proprietor of the business.
- Changes in the name or status of an unincorporated company.
- The transfer of business from one incorporated company to another.
- The business ceases to supply taxable goods or services.

- There is a complete change in the composition of a partnership at any one time.
- The business is otherwise disposed of.

(VAT Notice 700, para 26.3; HMRC VAT Guidance V1–28, paras 12.7, 12.8).

Cessation of liability to be registered

[59.8] A person who has become liable to be registered under **59.3** above only ceases to be liable to be registered in the following circumstances.

- At any time if HMRC are satisfied that
  (i) he has ceased to make taxable supplies; or
  (ii) he is not at that time a person in relation to whom any of the conditions in **59.3**(*a*)–(*c*) above is satisfied.
- If HMRC are satisfied that the value of his taxable supplies in the period of one year then beginning will not exceed the following specified limits.

Effective date	*Limit*
1 April 2011	£71,000
1 April 2010	£68,000
1 May 2009	£66,000
1 April 2008	£65,000
1 April 2007	£62,000
1 April 2006	£59,000
1 April 2005	£58,000
1 April 2004	£56,000

- However, that person does not cease to be liable to be registered under these provisions if HMRC are satisfied that the reason the value of his taxable supplies will not exceed the above limit is that in the period in question he will cease making taxable supplies or will suspend making them for a period of 30 days or more.
  Taxable supplies in determining the value of a person's supplies for the above purposes, supplies of goods or services that are 'capital assets' of the business in the course or furtherance of which they are supplied are disregarded. However, this is not to include the taxable supply of an interest in, right over or licence to occupy any land which is not zero-rated. See **59.3** above for the definition of '*capital assets*'.
  Any supplies which are taxable supplies only because an overseas trader making distance sales in the UK is required to register under *VATA 1994, Sch 2* (see **59.11** *et seq* below) can also be disregarded in determining the value of his supplies for the above purposes.
  Taxable supplies for the above purposes are determined on the basis that no VAT is chargeable on the supply (i.e. VAT-exclusive).

[*VATA 1994, Sch 1 paras 3, 4, 15, 16; SI 2011/897*].

Notification of end of liability or entitlement to registration

[59.9] A person

- voluntarily registered under *VATA 1994, Sch 1 para 9* (persons making or intending to make taxable supplies, see **59.2** above) or compulsorily registered under **59.3** above who ceases to make or have the intention of making taxable supplies, or
- voluntarily registered under *VATA 1994, Sch 1 para 10* (persons only making exempt or certain outside the scope supplies, see **59.2** above) who ceases to satisfy either of the conditions in **59.2**(*b*) or (*c*) above

must notify HMRC of that fact within 30 days of the date on which he does so unless he would, when he so ceases, be otherwise liable or entitled to be registered under **59.11** *et seq* or **59.18** *et seq* below. [*VATA 1994, Sch 1 paras 11, 12*]. The notification must be in writing and state the date on which the registered person ceased to make or have the intention of making taxable supplies. [*SI 1995/2518, Reg 5(3); SI 2000/794*]. Notification should be sent to Grimsby National Registration Service, HM Revenue & Customs, Imperial House, 77 Victoria Street, Grimsby, DN31 1DB. See **52.17 PENALTIES** for failure to notify within 30 days.

Cancellation of registration

[59.10] In the situations outlined in (*a*) and (*b*) below, the registration of a business making taxable supplies must or, as the case may be, can be cancelled. However, it should be remembered that where a business also makes

- distance sales from another EU country (see **59.11** below),
- acquisitions of goods from another EU country (see **59.18** below), and
- in the case of an overseas trader, disposals of assets for which a VAT repayment is claimed (see **59.26** below)

it cannot apply to deregister until it has either ceased to be liable to be registered for all those supplies/acquisitions.

The provisions are also subject to *VATA 1994, Sch 3B para 18* (cancellation of registration under these provisions where a non-EU business intends to apply for registration under the special scheme for electronically supplied services in the EU, see **63.39 SPECIAL SCHEMES**).

(a) A business *must* cancel its registration if any of the following occur.
   (i) It ceases to make taxable supplies (see **59.9** above).
   (ii) It sells its business (unless the new owner wishes to retain the VAT registration number, see **59.36** below).
   (iii) Its legal status changes (e.g. a sole proprietor takes in one or more partners, a partnership is dissolved and the business run by a sole proprietor, a company is incorporated to take over the business previously carried on by a sole proprietor or partnership, or a company is wound up and replaced by a sole proprietor or partnership). In such a case, the business will normally cancel its existing registration (by completing Form VAT 7) and apply for a new registration number by completing

an application Form VAT 1. It may, however, ask to retain its previous registration number, in which case it must complete an application form as well as Form VAT 68. If the new legal entity is a partnership, it must also complete Form VAT 2.

(iv) It is the representative member of a VAT group (see **27 GROUPS OF COMPANIES**) and wishes to disband the group. In such circumstances, the registered person ceases to exist and the business will therefore need to cancel its registration. If any member of the disbanded group is continuing to trade, it must determine whether it will need to be registered in its own right. Where a member of a VAT group other than the representative member leaves the group, there is no need to cancel its registration unless the group only consists of the representative member and that one other member.

(v) It wishes to join a VAT group. Its existing registration must be cancelled as it is not possible to have two active registrations. Similarly, on the creation of a VAT group, the VAT registrations of any founder members must be cancelled.

(vi) It wishes to join the agricultural flat-rate scheme (see **63.25 SPECIAL SCHEMES**).

(vii) It was allowed registration on the basis that it intended to make taxable supplies and no longer intends to do so (see **59.9** above).

(viii) It was allowed registration on the basis that it made, or intended to make, supplies outside the UK which would have been taxable supplies if made in the UK and it has stopped making, or intending to make, those supplies.

(ix) It was allowed registration on the basis that it made, or intended to make, supplies of warehoused goods which were permitted to be disregarded for VAT and it has stopped making, or intending to make, those supplies.

(b) A business *may* ask for voluntary deregistration if any of the following occur.

(i) It satisfies HMRC that its taxable turnover in the next twelve months will not exceed the deregistration limit.

(ii) It closes down part of its business and satisfies HMRC that its taxable turnover for the remainder will not exceed the deregistration limit.

(iii) Its turnover exceeds the registration limits but it satisfies the conditions for exemption under **59.6** above.

(VAT Notice 700, para 26.2; VAT Notice 700/11/10, paras 1.2, 1.4–1.8, 2.1, 2.2).

Date of deregistration

(1) Where a registered person satisfies HMRC he is no longer liable to be registered, HMRC must cancel his registration with effect from the day on which the request is made from such later date as is mutually agreed (provided they are satisfied that he would not be required to be registered on that date).

(2) Where HMRC are satisfied that a registered person has ceased to be 'registrable', they may cancel his registration with effect from the day on which he so ceased or from such later date as is mutually agreed (provided they are satisfied that he would not be required to be, or entitled to be, registered on that date).

(3) Where HMRC are satisfied that on the day on which a registered person was registered he was not registrable, they may cancel his registration with effect from that day.

'*Registrable*' means liable to be registered or entitled to be registered.

[*VATA 1994, Sch 1 paras 13, 18; FA 2003, Sch 2 para 3*].

Under (1) and (2) above, there is no provision to allow deregistration from an earlier date (see *S Moloney* (VTD 14873) (TVC 57.127)) but, on application, HMRC may agree to defer deregistration by up to six months if considered necessary for either

- the disposal of capital assets for which VAT invoices may need to be issued, or
- to allow input tax to be reclaimed on VAT invoices for supplies attributable to the business but which are not received until after the business has ceased to be a taxable person.

(HMRC VAT Guidance V1–28, para 13.13).

De Voil Indirect Tax Service. See V2.151–153.

Registration in respect of supplies from another EU country ('distance selling')

[59.11] Additional registration requirements may apply in respect of 'distance selling'. This occurs when a supplier in one EU country supplies goods, and is responsible for their delivery, to any person in another EU country who is not registered for VAT. This may include supplies not only to private individuals but to public bodies, charities and businesses too small to register or with activities that are entirely exempt. The most obvious example of this type of supply is mail order. VAT on sales to non-VAT registered customers in another EU country are in principle charged and accounted for by the supplier in the country from which the goods are dispatched. However, once the value of distance sales to any particular EU country has exceeded an annual threshold, further sales are subject to VAT in the EU country of destination and the supplier is liable to register for VAT in that country or appoint a VAT representative (see **3.8 AGENTS**) who will be responsible for accounting for VAT there on his behalf.

The provisions outlined in **59.12** to **59.17** below relate to the registration of suppliers from other EC countries not already registered for VAT in the UK.

For registration by UK suppliers in other EU countries see **19.18 EUROPEAN UNION: SINGLE MARKET**.

De Voil Indirect Tax Service. See V2.171–177.

Liability to be registered

[59.12] A 'person' who is not registered under *VATA 1994*, and is not liable to be registered under **59.3** above, becomes liable to be registered under these provisions on any day if, in the period beginning with 1 January in that year, he has made 'relevant supplies' whose value exceeds £73,000.

In addition, a person who is not registered or liable to be registered as above becomes liable to be registered under these provisions (whatever the value of supplies) in the following circumstances.

(a) He has exercised an option, under the laws of another EU country where he is taxable, to treat relevant supplies made by him as taking place outside that country and
- the supplies to which the option relates involve the removal of the goods from that country;
- if the option had not been exercised, under the law of that country the supplies would have been treated as taking place in that country; and
- he makes any relevant supply in the UK at a time when the option is in force.

(b) He makes a supply of goods subject to duty of excise where
- the supply involves the removal of the goods to the UK by, or under the directions of, the person making the supply;
- the supply is a transaction under which goods are acquired in the UK from another EU country by a person who is not a taxable person;
- the supply is made in the course or furtherance of a business carried on by the supplier and is not treated as a supply only by virtue of *VATA 1994, Sch 4 para 5(1)* or *(6)* (transfers of goods forming part of the assets of the business).

'*Person*' includes a sole proprietor, partnership, limited company, club, association or charity. It is the person who is required to register, not the business or businesses carried on. The registration covers all the businesses of the registered person in the UK.

A supply of goods is a '*relevant supply*' where

(i) the supply involves the removal of the goods to the UK by, or under the directions of, the person making the supply;
(ii) the supply does not involve the installation or assembly of goods at a place in the UK;
(iii) the supply is a transaction under which goods are acquired in the UK from another EU country by a person who is not a taxable person; and
(iv) the supply is made in the course or furtherance of a business carried on by the supplier and is not
- an exempt supply;
- a supply of goods subject to a duty of excise;
- a new means of transport (see **19.33 EUROPEAN UNION: SINGLE MARKET**); or

- treated as a supply only by virtue of *VATA 1994, Sch 4 para 5(1)* or *(6)* (transfers of goods forming part of the assets of the business).

A person is treated as having become liable to be registered under the above provisions at any time when he would have become so liable but for any registration which is subsequently cancelled under **59.10**(3) above or **59.17**(*b*), **59.25**(*c*) or **59.32**(*b*) below.

In determining the value of relevant supplies for the above purposes, any part of the consideration representing a VAT liability of the supplier under the law of another EU country is disregarded. Also disregarded are supplies to which *VATA 1994, s 18B(4)* (last acquisition or supply of goods before removal from fiscal warehousing) applies. See **72.17 WAREHOUSED GOODS AND FREE ZONES.**

[*VATA 1994, Sch 2 paras 1, 10; FA 1996, Sch 3 para 14; FA 2000, s 136(6)*].

Persons already registered in the UK

If a person making relevant supplies of distance sales is already registered for VAT in the UK under **59.3** above in respect of taxable supplies or **59.19** below in respect of relevant acquisitions, he does not need also to register under these provisions but must account for VAT in the UK on distance sales even where the threshold above is not reached. (VAT Notice 700/1/10, para 5.4).

Notification of liability and registration

[59.13] A person who becomes liable to registration under **59.12** above must notify HMRC of the fact within 30 days after that day.

HMRC must then register him (whether or not he so notifies them) with effect from the day on which the liability to register arose or from such earlier time as is agreed between them.

[*VATA 1994, Sch 2 paras 3, 9*].

Notification must be in such form and contain such particulars as HMRC prescribe. Application must currently be made on Form VAT 1A (or Welsh version Form VAT1A(W)) which include a signed declaration that all the information entered on the form, and accompanying it, is correct and complete. Where the person being registered is a partnership, Form VAT 2 must also be completed. [*SI 1995/2518, Reg 5(1); SI 2000/794*].

Request to be registered

[59.14] A person who is not liable to be registered under *VATA 1994* and is not already so registered may request to be registered under these provisions. Provided he can satisfy HMRC that he intends

(a) to exercise an option referred to in **59.12**(*a*) above and, from a specified date, to make relevant supplies to which the option relates, or
(b) from a specified date to make relevant supplies in relation to any such option which has already been exercised, or

(c) from a specified date to make supplies satisfying the conditions in **59.12**(*b*) above,

HMRC may then, subject to such conditions as they think fit, register him from such date as is agreed between them. Any person who decides to opt to tax under this provision before reaching the threshold must notify HMRC at least 30 days before the date of the first supply to which the option is intended to apply. Application should be made using Form VAT 1A (and also Form VAT 1TR if a VAT representative is being appointed). Written evidence should be enclosed showing that firm arrangements have been made to make distance sales.

Where a person who requests registration under the above provisions is also entitled to be registered under **59.2** above, he must be registered under those provisions.

[*VATA 1994, Sch 2 para 4*].

Cessation of liability

[59.15] A person who has become liable to be registered under **59.12** above ceases to be liable if at any time

(a) his relevant supplies in the year ended 31 December last before that time did not exceed £73,000 and did not include any dutiable supply falling within **59.12** above;
(b) HMRC are satisfied that the value of his relevant supplies in the year immediately following that year will not exceed £73,000 and will not include any such dutiable supply; and
(c) no such option as is mentioned in **59.12**(*a*) above is in force in relation to him.

[*VATA 1994, Sch 2 para 2*].

Notification of matters affecting registration

[59.16] A person must notify the following matters to HMRC in writing within 30 days.

(a) Where he is registered under these provisions and 'ceases to be registrable under *VATA 1994*'. Notification must state the date on which he ceased to be registrable.
(b) Where he is registered under **59.14** above, the exercise of any option or, as the case may be, the first occasion after registration when he makes a supply.
(c) Where he has exercised an option under **59.12**(*a*) above, and the option ceases to have effect (as a consequence of its revocation or otherwise) in relation to any relevant supplies by him.

A person '*ceases to be registrable under VATA 1994*' where

- he ceases to be a person who would be liable or entitled to be registered under that *Act* if his registration were disregarded; or

- he has been registered under **59.14** above and ceases to have any intention to exercise an option or make supplies as there mentioned.

Notification must be in such form and contain such particulars as HMRC prescribe.

[*VATA 1994, Sch 2 paras 5, 9; SI 1995/2518, Reg 5(3); SI 2000/794*].

Changes in circumstances

A person registered under these provisions must notify HMRC, within 30 days and with full written particulars, of any change in the name, constitution or ownership of the business or any other event which may necessitate the variation of the register or cancellation of registration. [*SI 1995/2518, Reg 5(2); SI 2000/794*].

Cancellation of registration

[59.17] Subject to below, the registration of a person registered under these provisions must, or as the case may be, can be cancelled in the following circumstances.

(a) Where a person registered under these provisions satisfies HMRC that he is not liable to be so registered, they *must*, on request, cancel his registration with effect from the day on which the request is made or such later date as is mutually agreed. HMRC must be satisfied that, at the date of the proposed cancellation, the person would not be liable to be registered under any other provision of *VATA 1994*.

(b) Where HMRC are satisfied that, on the day on which a person was registered under these provisions, he was not liable to be registered (or, where he was registered under **59.14** above, did not have the intention by reference to which he was registered), they may cancel his registration with effect from that day.

(c) Where HMRC are satisfied that a person who has been registered under **59.14** above and is not for the time being liable to be registered under **59.12** above
   (i) has not, by the date specified in his request to be registered, carried out the intentions by reference to which he was registered; or
   (ii) has contravened any condition of his registration,

   they may cancel his registration from the date so specified or, as the case may be, the date of the contravention (or such later date as may be agreed between them). HMRC must be satisfied that, at the date of the proposed cancellation, the person would not be liable or entitled to be registered under any other provision of *VATA 1994*.

The registration of a person who has exercised an option with **59.12**(*a*) above cannot be cancelled unless it has been in force for two complete calendar years.

[*VATA 1994, Sch 2 paras 6, 7*].

Registration in respect of acquisitions of goods from other EU countries

[59.18] VAT on goods purchased from other EU countries is no longer paid when the goods enter the UK. Instead,

- for most transactions between registered persons, VAT becomes due on the acquisition of the goods by the customer and is accounted for on the normal VAT return; and
- where a person is not registered for VAT in the UK, any goods purchased from a registered supplier in another EU country bear VAT at origin.

To prevent a business distorting trade by buying goods in another EU country at a lower rate of VAT than in the UK, additional registration requirements apply in respect of certain acquisitions from other EU countries by persons who acquire goods in excess of an annual threshold but who are not registered, or required to be registered, under the provisions in **59.1** *et seq* or **59.11** *et seq* above. The provisions will only apply in restricted circumstances. Most businesses acquiring goods above the annual threshold value are likely to be making UK taxable supplies above the compulsory registration threshold in **59.3** above and will be liable to register under those provisions. The provisions will apply, for example, to a business making only exempt supplies in the UK and which acquires the goods for use in its business rather than for resale.

De Voil Indirect Tax Service. See V2.181–188.

Liability to be registered

[59.19] A 'person' who is not registered under *VATA 1994*, and is not liable to be registered under **59.3** or **59.12** above, becomes liable to be registered under these provisions if

(a) at the end of any month, in the period beginning with 1 January in that year, he has made 'relevant acquisitions' whose value exceeds, or

(b) there are reasonable grounds for believing that the value of his relevant acquisitions in the period of 30 days then beginning will exceed,

the following limits.

Effective date	*Limit*
1.4.11–	£73,000
1.4.10–31.3.11	£70,000
1.5.09–31.3.10	£68,000
1.4.08–30.4.09	£67,000
1.4.07–31.3.08	£64,000
1.4.06–31.3.07	£61,000
1.4.05–31.3.06	£60,000
1.4.04–31.3.05	£58,000

'*Person*' includes a sole proprietor, partnership, limited company, club, association or charity. It is the person who is required to register, not the business or businesses carried on. The registration covers all the businesses of the registered person in the UK.

For a transaction to be an acquisition it must, under *VATA 1994, s 11*,

- be a supply of goods (including anything treated for the purposes of *VATA 1994* as a supply of goods); and
- involve the removal of the goods from another EU country.

For the purposes of determining a person's entitlement or requirement to be registered under these provisions, however, only certain acquisitions are taken into account. These are called '*relevant acquisitions*' which are acquisitions which meet all of the following conditions.

- The goods are acquired in the course or furtherance of
  - (i) a business carried on by any person; or
  - (ii) any activities carried on otherwise than by way of business by any body corporate or by any club, association, organisation or other unincorporated body.
- The person who carries on that business or, as the case may be, those activities acquires the goods.
- The supplier is taxable in another EU country at the time of the transaction and the transaction is in the course or furtherance of his business.
- The goods are not acquired in pursuance of an exempt supply.
- The goods are not subject to excise duty (see **19.9 EUROPEAN UNION: SINGLE MARKET**).
- The goods do not consist of a new means of transport (see **19.37 EUROPEAN UNION: SINGLE MARKET**).
- The acquisition is treated as taking place in the UK.

An acquisition is not, however, a relevant acquisition where, although the goods are transported to the UK, they are deemed to be supplied in the UK (e.g. installed goods).

A person is treated as having become liable to be registered under the above provisions at any time when he would have become so liable but for any registration which is subsequently cancelled under **59.10**(3) or **59.17**(*b*) above or **59.25**(*c*) or **59.32**(*b*) below.

In determining the value of relevant acquisitions for the above purposes, any part of the consideration representing a VAT liability of the supplier under the law of another EU country is disregarded. Also disregarded are supplies to which *VATA 1994, s 18B(4)* (last acquisition or supply of goods before removal from fiscal warehousing) applies. See **72.17 WAREHOUSED GOODS AND FREE ZONES**.

[*VATA 1994, s 31(1), Sch 3 paras 1, 10, 11; FA 1996, Sch 3 para 15; SI 2011/897*].

Notification of liability and registration

[59.20] A person who becomes liable to registration under **59.19** above must notify HMRC of that fact as follows.

(a) Where **59.19**(*a*) above applies, within 30 days of the end of the relevant month.
HMRC must then register him (whether or not he so notifies them) with effect from the end of the month following the relevant month or from such earlier date as is agreed between them.

> *Example*
>
> On 22 May, W who is not registered for VAT, calculates that, since the previous 1 January, he has made relevant acquisitions exceeding the registration threshold.
>
> W becomes liable to register on 31 May. He must notify HMRC of his liability to register in respect of acquisitions by 30 June. Unless mutually agreed otherwise, HMRC will register him with effect from 1 July.

(b) Where **59.19**(*b*) above applies, before the end of the period by reference to which the liability arises.
HMRC must then register him (whether or not he so notifies them) with effect from the beginning of that period.

> *Example*
>
> On 22 May, W who is not registered for VAT, estimates that the value of his relevant acquisitions in the next 30 days will exceed the registration threshold.
>
> W becomes liable to register on 22 May. He must notify HMRC of his liability to register in respect of acquisitions by 20 June. HMRC will register him with effect from 22 May.

[*VATA 1994, Sch 3 paras 3, 10*].

Notification must be in such form and contain such particulars as HMRC prescribe. Application must currently be made on Form VAT 1B (or Welsh version Form VAT 1B(W)) which includes a signed declaration that all the information entered on the form, and accompanying it, is correct and complete. Where the person being registered is a partnership, Form VAT 2 must also be completed. [*SI 1995/2518, Reg 5(1); SI 2000/794*]. Completed application forms, with any extra information requested by HMRC, should be sent to HM Revenue & Customs, Registration and Deregistration Unit, Deansgate, 62–70 Tettenhall Road, Wolverhampton, WV1 4TZ. Once registered, in addition to accounting for VAT on acquisitions, VAT must be accounted for on any taxable supplies made.

Entitlement to be registered

[59.21] Where a person who is not liable to be registered under *VATA 1994* and is not already so registered satisfies HMRC that

(a) he makes relevant acquisitions, or
(b) he intends to make relevant acquisitions from a specified date,

HMRC must, if he so requests, register him from the day on which the request is made or such earlier date as is mutually agreed. Any person who decides to register voluntarily under this provision before reaching the threshold must notify HMRC at least 30 days before the date from which registration is to be effective. Application should be made on Form VAT 1B and where (*b*) above applies evidence should be enclosed showing that firm arrangements have been made to make acquisitions.

Where a person who requests registration under the above provisions is also entitled to be registered under **59.2** above, he must be registered under those provisions.

[*VATA 1994, Sch 3 para 4*].

Exemption from registration

[59.22] Where a person who makes or intends to make relevant acquisitions satisfies HMRC that any such acquisitions would be zero-rated if they were taxable supplies by a taxable person, HMRC may, if the person so requests and they think fit, grant exemption from registration under these provisions (although Form VAT 1B must still be completed).

Where a person exempted under these provisions makes a relevant acquisition which would not be zero-rated if it were a taxable supply by a taxable person, he must notify HMRC within 30 days of the date of acquisition.

The exemption remains in force until it appears to HMRC that the request should no longer be acted upon or until it is withdrawn.

[*VATA 1994, Sch 3 para 8*].

Cessation of liability to be registered

[59.23] A person who has become liable to be registered under **59.19** above ceases to be liable if at any time

(a) his relevant acquisitions in the year ended 31 December last before that time did not exceed, and
(b) HMRC are satisfied that the value of his relevant acquisitions in the year immediately following that year will not exceed

the following limits.

Effective date	*Limit*
1.4.11–	£73,000
1.4.10–31.3.11	£70,000
1.5.09–31.3.10	£68,000
1.4.08–30.4.09	£67,000
1.4.07–31.3.08	£64,000
1.4.06–31.3.07	£61,000
1.4.05–31.3.06	£60,000
1.4.04–31.3.05	£58,000

However, that person does not cease to be liable to be registered under these provisions at any time if there are reasonable grounds for believing that the value of his relevant acquisitions in the period of 30 days then beginning will exceed that limit.

[*VATA 1994, Sch 3 para 2; SI 2011/897*].

Notification of matters affecting registration

[59.24] A person must notify the following matters to HMRC in writing within 30 days.

(a) Where he is registered under these provisions and 'ceases to be registrable under *VATA 1994*'. Notification must state the date on which he ceased to be registrable.
(b) Where he is registered under **59.21**(*b*) above, the first occasion after registration when he makes a relevant acquisition.

A person '*ceases to be registrable under VATA 1994*' where

- he ceases to be a person who would be liable or entitled to be registered under that *Act* if his registration were disregarded; or
- he has been registered under **59.21**(*b*) above and ceases to have any intention of making relevant acquisitions.

[*VATA 1994, Sch 3 paras 5, 10; SI 1995/2518, Reg 5(3); SI 2000/794*].

Notification must be sent to Grimsby National Registration Service, HM Revenue & Customs, Imperial House, 77 Victoria Street, Grimsby, DN31 1DB.

Changes in circumstances

A person registered under these provisions must notify HMRC, within 30 days and with full written particulars, of any change in the name, constitution or ownership of the business or any other event which may necessitate the variation of the register or cancellation of registration. [*SI 1995/2518, Reg 5(2); SI 2000/794*]. Notification must be sent to Grimsby National Registration Service, HM Revenue & Customs, Imperial House, 77 Victoria Street, Grimsby, DN31 1DB.

Cancellation of registration

[59.25] The registration of a person registered under these provisions must, or as the case may be, can be cancelled in the following circumstances.

(a) Subject to below, where a person registered under these provisions satisfies HMRC that he is not liable to be so registered, they *must*, on request, cancel his registration with effect from the day on which the request is made or such later date as is mutually agreed. HMRC must be satisfied that, at the date of the proposed cancellation, the person would not be liable to be registered under any other provision of *VATA 1994*.

(b) Subject to below, where HMRC are satisfied that a person registered under these provisions has, since his registration, ceased to be 'registrable' under these provisions, they may cancel his registration with effect from the day on which he so ceased or such later day as is mutually agreed. HMRC must also be satisfied that, at the date of the proposed cancellation, the person would not be liable or entitled to be registered under any other provision of *VATA 1994*.

(c) Where HMRC are satisfied that, on the day on which a person was registered under these provisions
   (i) he was not registrable under these provisions, or
   (ii) where he was registered under **59.21**(*b*) above, he did not have the intention by reference to which he was registered,

   they may cancel his registration with effect from that day.

(d) Where HMRC are satisfied that a person who has been registered under **59.21**(*b*) above and is not for the time being liable to be registered under **59.19** above
   (i) has not, by the date specified in his request to be registered, begun to make relevant supplies, or
   (ii) has contravened any condition of his registration,

   they may cancel his registration from the date so specified or, as the case may be, the date of the contravention (or such later date as may be mutually agreed). HMRC must also be satisfied that, at the date of the proposed cancellation, the person would not be liable or entitled to be registered under any other provision of *VATA 1994*.

A person is '*registrable*' under these provisions at any time when he is liable to be registered under these provisions or makes relevant acquisitions.

The registration of a person

- who is registered under **59.21** above, or
- who would not be liable or entitled to be registered under any provision of *VATA 1994* except **59.21** above if he were not registered,

cannot be cancelled under (*a*) or (*b*) above unless it has been in force for two complete calendar years.

[*VATA 1994, Sch 3 paras 6, 7*].

Registration by overseas traders in respect of disposals of assets for which a VAT repayment is claimed

[59.26] The provisions detailed in **59.27** to **59.32** below require overseas traders (also referred to as non-established taxable persons) to be registered for VAT in the UK if they make claims under the *EC 8th Directive* or *EC 13th Directive* and subsequently supply, or intend to supply, the relevant goods in the UK. The provisions apply regardless of the value of the relevant supplies, i.e. there is no registration threshold. Once registered for VAT, the business must account for VAT on all its taxable supplies and can recover input tax in the normal way. The business will no longer be entitled to claim refunds under the *EC 8th Directive* or *EC 13th Directive*.

De Voil Indirect Tax Service. See V2.189–V2.189D.

Liability to be registered

[59.27] A person who is not registered under *VATA 1994* and is not liable to be registered under **59.3**, **59.12** or **59.19** above becomes liable to be registered under these provisions at any time if

(a) he makes 'relevant supplies'; or
(b) there are reasonable grounds for believing that he will make relevant supplies within the period of 30 days then beginning.

Relevant supplies

A supply is a '*relevant supply*' where

- the supply is a taxable supply;
- the goods are assets of the business in the course or furtherance of which they are supplied; and
- the person by whom they are supplied, or a 'predecessor' of his, has received or claimed, or is intending to claim, a VAT repayment on the supply to him, or the importation by him, of the goods (or of anything comprised in them) under the rules for refunds of VAT to persons established in other EU countries (see **17.9 EUROPEAN UNION GENERAL**) or the *EC 13th Directive* (refunds of VAT to persons established outside the EU (**48.5 OVERSEAS TRADERS**)).

For these purposes, a '*predecessor*' is someone who has transferred the goods in question to the registrable person under the provisions allowing relief from VAT on the transfer of a business, or part of a business, as a going concern (see **8.10 BUSINESS**). A person's predecessors include the predecessors of his predecessor through any number of transactions.

A person is treated as having become liable to be registered under these provisions at any time when he would have become so liable but for any registration which is subsequently cancelled under **59.10**(3), **59.17**(*b*) or **59.25**(*c*) above or **59.32**(*b*) below.

[*VATA 1994, Sch 3A paras 1, 9; FA 2000, s 136(8)(10), Sch 36*].

Notification of liability and registration

[59.28] A person who becomes liable to registration under **59.27** above must notify HMRC of that fact as follows.

(a) Where **59.27**(*a*) above applies, within 30 days of the date on which liability arises. HMRC must then register that person (whether or not he so notifies them) with effect from the beginning of the day on which liability arises.
(b) Where **59.27**(*b*) above applies, before the end of the period by reference to which the liability arises. HMRC must then register that person (whether or not he so notifies them) with effect from the beginning of that period.

[*VATA 1994, Sch 3A paras 3, 4; FA 2000, Sch 36*].

Notification must be in such form and contain such particulars as HMRC prescribe. Application must currently be made on Form VAT1C which includes a signed declaration that the information entered on the form and contained in any accompanying document is true and complete. [*SI 1995/2518, Reg 5(1); SI 2000/794*]. The form is available from the Non-Established Taxable Persons Unit (NETPU), HM Revenue and Customs, Customs House, 28 Guild Street, Aberdeen AB11 6GY (Tel: 01224 844844). Where the person being registered is a partnership, Form VAT 2 must also be completed.

Businesses may appoint a tax representative to act on their behalf (see **48.3 OVERSEAS TRADERS**).

Exemption from registration

[59.29] Where a person who makes or intends to make relevant supplies satisfies HMRC that any such supply would be zero-rated if he were a taxable person, HMRC may, if the person so requests and they think fit, grant exemption from registration under these provisions. Application should be made to Non-Established Taxable Persons Unit (NETPU), HM Revenue and Customs, Customs House, 28 Guild Street, Aberdeen AB11 6GY giving full details. A completed Form VAT1C should also be forwarded.

On a material change in the nature of the supplies made, the person exempted must notify HMRC within 30 days of the date on which the change occurred or, if no particular date is so identifiable, within 30 days of the end of the quarter in which it occurred. On a material alteration in any quarter in the proportion of relevant supplies of such a person that are zero-rated, he must notify HMRC of the alteration within 30 days of the end of the quarter.

Exemption applies until the date it appears to HMRC that the request should no longer be acted upon or until the date the request is withdrawn. HMRC must then register the person with effect from that date.

[*VATA 1994, Sch 3A para 7; FA 2000, Sch 36*].

Cessation of liability to be registered

[59.30] A person who has become liable to be registered under **59.27** above ceases to be liable to be registered if at any time HMRC are satisfied that he has ceased to make relevant supplies. [*VATA 1994, Sch 3A para 2; FA 2000, Sch 36*].

Notification of matters affecting registration

Change in circumstances

[59.31] A person registered under these provisions must notify HMRC, within 30 days and with full written particulars, of any change in the name, constitution or ownership of the business or any other event which may necessitate the variation of the register or cancellation of registration. [*SI 1995/2518, Reg 5(2); SI 2000/794*].

End of liability to be registered

A person registered under these provisions who ceases to make, or have the intention of making, relevant supplies must notify HMRC of that fact within 30 days of the day on which he does so. Notification is not required if the person would, when he so ceases, be liable or entitled to be registered under any other provision of *VATA 1994*. [*VATA 1994, Sch 3A para 5; FA 2000, Sch 36*]. The notification must be in writing and must state the date on which the registered person ceased to make, or have the intention of making, relevant supplies. [*SI 1995/2518, Reg 5(3); SI 2000/794*].

Cancellation of registration

[59.32] The registration of a person under these provisions may be cancelled in the following circumstances.

(a) Where HMRC are satisfied that a registered person has ceased to be liable to be registered under these provisions, they may cancel his registration with effect from the day on which he so ceased or such later date as is mutually agreed. However, HMRC must not cancel a person's registration with effect from any time unless they are satisfied that the person would not be liable or entitled to be registered under any other provision of *VATA 1994*.

(b) Where HMRC are satisfied that on the day on which a registered person was registered he was not registrable, they may cancel his registration with effect from that day.

[*VATA 1994, Sch 3A para 6; FA 2000, Sch 36*].

An application to have registration cancelled should be made on Form VAT 7 (or Welsh version Form 7(W)) obtainable from NETPU at the address in **59.28** above.

Consequences of deregistration

Notice of cancellation and final return

[59.33] When the date of cancellation of registration has been arranged, either a formal notice of cancellation (Form VAT 35) or a formal notice of exemption from registration (Form VAT 8) is sent. Unless the registration number has been re-allocated to a person who is taking over the business as a going concern (see **8.10 BUSINESS**), a final return Form VAT 193 or VAT 197 (Welsh version) is issued. See **2.3–2.5 ACCOUNTING PERIODS AND RETURNS.** (VAT Notice 700/11/10, paras 7.1, 7.2).

VAT invoices

VAT invoices must not normally be issued or VAT charged as from the date of cancellation (although where a deregistered person has undercharged VAT on a supply made before deregistration, HMRC may agree to a VAT invoice being raised to the customer concerned so that the trader does not have to account for any additional VAT due from his own resources). The previous VAT registration number must not be shown on any invoices issued. HMRC should be consulted before using an existing stock of invoices and crossing out the registration number. If a self-billing arrangement (see **39.6 INVOICES**) or the authenticated receipt procedure for the construction industry (see **42.21**(2) **LAND AND BUILDINGS: ZERO AND REDUCED RATE SUPPLIES AND DIY HOUSEBUILDERS**) are in operation customers must be notified immediately of the deregistration and informed that VAT must not be charged. (VAT Notice 700/11/10, para 7.3).

Input tax

Input tax cannot be claimed on purchases made from the date of deregistration except for VAT on the supply of certain services after deregistration made for the purposes of the business carried on before that time. See **34.11 INPUT TAX.**

Partial exemption

Where partial exemption applies to the business, a final adjustment in accordance with the normal partial exemption method must be made on the final return. The period for the final adjustment normally runs from the beginning of the tax year to the date of registration. However, where no exempt input tax was incurred in the previous tax year or, as the case may be, the registration period (see **49.13 PARTIAL EXEMPTION** for definitions) the period for final adjustment runs from the first day of the VAT period in the final tax year in which exempt input tax is incurred and ends on the date of deregistration. (VAT Notice 700/11/10, para 6.8).

Capital goods scheme

A final adjustment may be required in respect of items still within the adjustment period. See **10.7 CAPITAL GOODS SCHEME.**

Records

All VAT records including a list of all business assets on hand, together with their values, should be kept *whether or not they are liable to VAT*. See also **56.1 RECORDS** for preservation of records generally.

Payment of VAT on business assets

[59.34] VAT must be accounted for on the final return of any 'goods' forming part of the business assets which are on hand at the close of business or on the last day of registration as if they were supplied in the course or furtherance of the business unless

(a) the business is transferred as a going concern to another taxable person (see **8.10 BUSINESS**);
(b) the taxable person has died, become bankrupt or incapacitated and the business is carried on by another person who under *VATA 1994, s 46(4)* is treated as a taxable person (see **15.1 DEATH AND INCAPACITY** and **35.1 INSOLVENCY**); or
(c) the VAT on the deemed supply would not be more than £1,000.

'*Goods*' for these purposes means tangible goods (e.g. unsold stock, plant, furniture, commercial vehicles, computer, etc.) but intangible goods such as patents, copyrights and goodwill can be disregarded. (VAT Notice 700/11/10, para 6.1). It includes goods purchased where title has not yet passed to the business but where input tax on the purchase has been allowed (e.g. goods on hire purchase or lease purchase and goods subject to reservation of title). Land forming part of the business assets is treated as if it were goods.

The provisions do not apply to any goods where the taxable person can show to the satisfaction of HMRC that

(i) no credit for input tax has been allowed to him in respect of the supply of goods, their acquisition from another EU country or their importation from a place outside the EU; *and*
(ii) the goods did not become his as part of the assets of a business (or, with effect from 1 September 2007, part of a business) transferred as a going concern from another taxable person (see **8.10 BUSINESS**); *and*
(iii) he has not obtained rebate of purchase tax or revenue duty under *FA 1973, s 4* which was allowed when VAT was introduced.

The provisions also do not apply where a person ceased to be a taxable person in consequence of being certified to join the flat-rate scheme for farmers (see **63.25 SPECIAL SCHEMES**).

[*VATA 1994, Sch 4 paras 8, 9; FA 2007, ss 99(3), 100(9); SI 2000/266*].

The taxable person should exclude items on which he could not reclaim VAT when he bought them. These may be

- goods bought from unregistered businesses;
- cars (except private taxis, self-drive hire cars and driving school cars on which input tax has been claimed);
- goods bought under a VAT second-hand scheme;

- goods used wholly for business entertainment;
- goods which have been directly attributed to an exempt business activity (unless some input tax relating to these goods was reclaimable through the partial exemption rules);
- land or buildings which were obtained VAT free even though he may be using them to make standard-rated supplies (such as holiday accommodation or because he has opted to tax the property);
- goods not bought for business purposes; or
- goods bought before VAT was introduced on 1 April 1973, which were not relieved of Purchase Tax or Revenue Duty.

If the taxable person has opted to tax land or buildings he may be required to account for VAT at the time of deregistration.

If the opted land or property is sold, then VAT may be due on the sale price, subject to transfer of a going concern criteria.

If the land or property is retained and input tax was claimed at the time of the purchase, then a deemed supply must be made at the time of deregistration, for example, VAT will need to be accounted for on the current market value of the land or property.

If no input tax was claimed at the time of the purchase, and the land or property is retained, then VAT will only become due on any subsequent sale of the land or property during the life of the option.

(VAT Notice 700/11/10, paras 6.2, 6.3).

Value of the supply

The value of the goods on which VAT must be accounted for is the price the person would have to pay (excluding VAT), at the time of the supply, to purchase goods *identical* in every respect (including age and condition) to the goods concerned. Where that value cannot be ascertained, the price for the purchase of goods *similar* to, and of the same age and condition as, the goods concerned must be used. If that value is also not possible to ascertain, the cost of producing the goods concerned at that time is to be used. [*VATA 1994, Sch 6 para* 6].

De Voil Indirect Tax Service. See V3.261.

Example

Mike runs a shop that sells confectionery, tobacco and newspapers. His taxable turnover for the twelve months to 31 March 2010 was £53,000 and his expected taxable sales for the next twelve months are expected to be £55,000. He has decided to deregister from VAT.

The cost value of Mike's stock at 31 March 2010 was £20,000 (cost price excluding VAT) – of which newspapers were £4,000. He also has a car that he bought twelve months ago for £10,000 plus VAT and a computer that he bought from a friend (not VAT-registered) for £1,000.

It is clear that the value of stock and assets on hand exceeds £5,000 – so Mike has an output tax liability to declare on his final VAT return. However, the first concession is that he can ignore the computer because it was bought from an unregistered person. In the case of the car, Mike would not have reclaimed input tax on the initial purchase (non-deductible input tax) so the onward supply is exempt under *VATA 1994, Sch 9, Group 14*. The newspapers are zero-rated so they can also be excluded. Output tax is therefore due on the remaining stock, i.e. £16,000 multiplied by standard rate of VAT.

Retail schemes

[59.35] Whichever retail scheme is used, the provisions under **59.34** above apply. See also **60.6 RETAIL SCHEMES** for rules to be followed when ceasing to use a retail scheme.

Transfer of registration

[59.36] Where a business (or, with effect from 1 September 2007, part of a business) is transferred as a going concern (see **8.10 BUSINESS**) then provided

(a) the transferor's registration under *VATA 1994, Sch 1* has not already been cancelled; and
(b) on the transfer of the business (or part) the registration of the transferor is to be cancelled *and* the transferee either becomes liable or entitled to be registered under that *Schedule*,

HMRC may, under powers given to them in *VATA 1994, s 49*, cancel the transferor's registration and, from the date of the transfer, register the transferee with the registration number previously allocated to the transferor. An application must be made on Form VAT 68 (or Welsh version Form VAT 68(W)) by, or on behalf of, both parties and sent to HM Revenue and Customs, Imperial House, 77 Victoria Street, Grimsby, DN31 1DB. The application constitutes notice by the transferor of end of liability or entitlement to registration (see **59.9** above) but must be submitted within 30 days of the transfer to avoid any penalty for late notification. [*SI 1995/2518, Reg 6(1)(2); SI 2007/2085, Reg 3*].

Consequences of transfer of registration number

Where a registration number has been re-allocated as above then both the previous and new owners must agree to the following consequences.

- Any liability of the transferor at the transfer date to submit a return or to account for or pay VAT becomes the liability of the transferee (see *WH & AJ Ponsonby v C & E Commrs*, QB 1987, [1988] STC 28 (TVC 65.108) and *Bjellica (t/a Eddy's Domestic Appliance) v C & E Commrs*, CA [1995] STC 329 (TVC 57.89) where the previous owner should have registered twelve years before he actually did and the firm to which he transferred the business was held liable for the VAT).

- Any right of the transferor, whether or not existing at the date of the transfer, to credit for or to repayment of input tax becomes the right of the transferee (e.g. VAT recoverable on any services supplied to the previous owner for his business before the transfer but which are invoiced afterwards).
- Any right of either the transferor, whether or not existing at the date of transfer, or the transferee to payment by HMRC for recoverable input tax under *VATA 1994, s 25(3)* is satisfied by payment to either of them.
- Any right of the transferor, whether or not existing at the date of the transfer, to a claim for bad debt relief becomes the right of the transferee but, equally, any liability of the transferor to make repayments of input tax where bad debt relief has been claimed and the transferor was the debtor also becomes the liability of the transferee.
- Any records relating to the business which, by virtue of Regulations or a direction made by HMRC, must be preserved for any period after the transfer, must be preserved by the transferee (unless HMRC, at the request of the transferor, otherwise direct).
- Where the transferee of a business (or part) has been registered with the registration number of the transferor during a VAT period subsequent to that in which the transfer took place but with effect from the date of the transfer, any return made, VAT accounted for or paid or right to credit for input tax claimed, is treated as having been done by the transferee (whether in fact done by, or in the name of, the transferee or transferor).

[*SI 1995/2518, Reg 6(3)(4); SI 1997/1086, Reg 3; SI 2007/2085, Reg 4*].

Additional conditions to be met

Apart from the conditions specified in the *Regulations* as detailed above, HMRC require the following conditions to be met before allowing the reallocation of a VAT registration number.

- No VAT group registration must be involved.
- Where the transferor was a company, it must not have been dissolved before the VAT 68 is signed.
- The transferor must not be the subject of a direction in respect of disaggregation of business activities (see **8.5 BUSINESS**).
- Any centrally raised assessment notified to the transferor covering periods after the date of transfer must be paid.
- Any default surcharge incurred by the transferor for periods prior to the date of transfer must have been paid with no indication of an appeal.
- No civil penalty has been or is to be imposed on the transferor under *VATA 1994, s 60* (VAT evasion, see **52.10 PENALTIES**), *VATA 1994, s 68* (breach of walking possession agreements, see **52.16 PENALTIES**) or *VATA 1994, s 69* (breaches of regulatory provisions, see **52.17 PENALTIES**). In the case of a *VATA 1994, s 67* penalty (failure to notify and unauthorised issue of invoices, see **52.14 PENALTIES**), reallocation may be allowed if the penalty has been paid.

(HMRC VAT Guidance V1–28, para 10.6.7).

Accounting schemes

If the transferor had any special arrangements (e.g. annual accounting, use of a retail or flat-rate scheme), these cease from the date of transfer and a fresh application must be made by the transferee.

Preservation of records

It is the responsibility of the transferor to preserve the pre-transfer records of the business. HMRC may, at the request of the transferor, direct otherwise. The transferor must make documents, information and records available to the transferee to the extent necessary for him to meet its VAT obligations. HMRC may disclose to the transferee any information relating to the business while it was operated by the transferor to enable the transferee to meet its VAT obligations.

[*VATA 1994, s 49(2A); SI 1995/2518, reg 6(3)(f)*]. (VAT Information Sheet 12/07).

De Voil Indirect Tax Service. See V2.131.

Divisional registration

[59.37] A 'body corporate' carrying on its 'business' in several divisions may, if it requests and HMRC see fit, register in the names of those divisions. For these purposes, 'business' includes any other activities in the course or furtherance of which the body corporate acquires goods from another EU country. [*VATA 1994, s 46(1)(6)*]. See **27.2 GROUPS OF COMPANIES** for the meaning of '*body corporate*'.

Divisional registration is a facility which allows a corporate body carrying on business through a number of self-accounting units to register each of those units or divisions separately for VAT. Each division is given a separate VAT registration number and makes its own VAT return. However, the corporate body is still a single taxable person and it remains liable for the VAT debts of all the divisions.

Conditions for divisional registration

HMRC will only approve divisional registration if all the following conditions are satisfied.

(a) It is satisfied that there would be real difficulties in submitting a single VAT return for the corporate body as a whole within 30 days of the end of the VAT period.

(b) All the divisions must be registered, even those whose turnover is under the registration limit (see **59.3** above).

(c) All divisions must be independent units with their own accounting systems and must be
   - operating from different geographical locations;
   - supplying different commodities; or
   - carrying out different functions (e.g. manufacture, wholesale, retail, export, etc.).

(d) The corporate body as a whole must be, or be treated as being, fully taxable (i.e. where any exempt supplies are made, input tax attributable to those exempt supplies must be less than the *de minimis* limits in **49.11 PARTIAL EXEMPTION**. The *de minimis* limits apply to the whole corporate body and not to each division).

(e) All divisions must complete VAT returns for the same VAT periods. These will normally be allocated by HMRC although an application for non-standard VAT periods can be made. Where the corporate body as a whole expects to receive regular repayments of VAT, monthly returns may be allowed but, in such a case, all of the divisions must make monthly returns.

If, once registered in divisions, a body corporate no longer satisfies any of the above conditions, it must notify HMRC in writing within 30 days. HMRC will then decide whether to allow the divisional registration to continue.

Applications

Applications must be made by letter and sent to the National Registration Service (see **59.38** below) explaining why it is difficult to submit a single VAT return for the whole body corporate. A Form VAT 1 must be completed for each division with the name of the body corporate entered in Box 1 and the name of the division followed by the name of the corporate body in Box 2 (e.g. Textile division of ABC Ltd). Copies of incorporation certificates and charters and copies of any Acts of Parliament under which the body was incorporated (other than the *Companies Acts*) or any other proof of incorporation should also be included.

Effective date of commencement

Approval of an application for divisional registration normally takes effect from a current date unless there are exceptional circumstances.

Adding and removing divisions

Applications to add any new divisions should be made following the same procedure as above. Where an existing division is sold off or closed down, the National Registration Service must be advised in writing and that division will then be removed from the divisional registration of the corporate body.

Overseas bodies

A corporate body constituted outside the UK may apply for divisional registration provided it has at least two self-accounting units in the UK and it can comply with the above conditions. One of the UK divisions is deemed to cover the activities of those divisions or sites which are outside the UK so that, if any of those overseas divisions, etc. starts to make taxable supplies in the UK, VAT is accounted for on those supplies by the UK-based division covering for them.

VAT groups

Divisional registration and group treatment under **27.1 GROUPS OF COMPANIES** are mutually exclusive. Where a company which is a member of a VAT group wishes to register some of its divisions separately, it must first apply to leave the VAT group. Conversely, a corporate body with divisional registration which wishes to form or join a VAT group must first apply to cancel the registration of all of its divisions.

Accounting for VAT

VAT invoices must not be issued for transactions made between divisions of the same corporate body. These are not considered to be supplies for VAT purposes.

(VAT Notice 700/2/11, paras 1.10–1.13, 8.3–8.13).

De Voil Indirect Tax Service. See V2.190A.

Key points

[59.38] Points to consider are as follows.

Registration

- A new or existing business will need to monitor the level of its taxable sales at the end of each calendar month to identify if it has exceeded the £73,000 limit. It is not acceptable to wait until the end of the first twelve months of trading and then apply the relevant test. Remember, however, that it is only taxable sales that count, not exempt or non-business sales.
- A second test is that a business must also register for VAT if it expects the value of its taxable sales in the next 30 days to exceed £73,000. In such cases, it should become VAT-registered at the beginning of the 30-day period.
- A business is liable to account for VAT from the date it should be registered under the compulsory rules explained above. If sales invoices are issued before a VAT number has been received from HMRC (but the date of registration has passed), the business should still charge VAT but not show it as a separate entry on the invoice.
- When a business has received its belated VAT registration number from HMRC, it needs to issue tax invoices to customers, giving them suitable evidence to support their input tax claims.
- A transferee taking over a business as a going concern must take the taxable turnover of the previous owners into account when deciding if it needs to be VAT-registered from its first day of trading.
- A business trading in second-hand goods must base the value of its taxable turnover on the full value of the sale, rather than just the margin that would be used under a second-hand VAT scheme.

- To make accounting simpler, it is worthwhile for a business to seek VAT periods at the time of registration that coincide with its financial year, e.g. a business with 31 March year end should request calendar VAT periods.
- Ensure that a newly registered business has identified opportunities to reclaim input tax on any relevant expenditure incurred before its date of registration. However, expenditure on goods must have been incurred within the four-year period before the registration date; a six-month time limit is imposed for services.
- It may be in the best interest of many businesses to register for VAT on a voluntary basis – particularly if they are making mainly zero-rated supplies or mainly working for other VAT-registered businesses. Advisers need to regularly review the activities of all non-registered clients to see if they could benefit from voluntary registration.
- VAT registration as an intending trader means a business can reclaim input tax on its costs and capital expenditure, before it starts to trade. It is important to satisfy HMRC that there is a genuine intention to trade in the future, even though this might be many months or possible years in the future.
- A concession allows a business that has no taxable supplies in the UK to still register for VAT and claim input tax if its income is outside the scope of VAT under the place of supply rules. The key point is that the service must either be taxable if it was provided to a UK customer or relate to certain exempt financial services provided for non-EU customers.
- If HMRC backdates a registration, make sure the officer's calculations and procedures for calculating the actual date are correct. Remember that if any arrears of VAT are established through the backdating of the registration, there is likely to be scope to reduce self-assessment tax liabilities because of reduced profits.
- A potential planning opportunity could make it worthwhile for a business to register for VAT on a voluntary basis in order that it can make tax savings by using the flat-rate scheme.
- In some cases, a non-VAT registered business in the UK (e.g. a business that makes wholly exempt supplies) may be required to register if it makes acquisitions of goods from suppliers in other EU countries or buys services where the place of supply is in the UK. The intention of such requirements is to create a level playing field as far as VAT is concerned.

Deregistration

- Any request for deregistration based on future turnover cannot be made because of a decision to suspend trading for 30 days or more.

- A business that is in a repayment situation but has taxable supplies exceeding the VAT limits can still apply for deregistration. This decision would be made if the business is unlikely to lose much input tax by deregistering, and wants to save the administrative burden of being registered.
- Remember that a deregistered business can claim input tax on certain relevant expenses after it has been deregistered. This can be done by using Form VAT 427 – but any claim must be supported by original tax invoices.
- Be aware of the opportunity for the same VAT number to be retained by the new owners in situations where the business has been transferred as a going concern. However, there are potential risks for the new owner of the business, who is effectively taking over the possible VAT debts of the previous owner.
- There is no output tax liability on the value of stocks and assets held at the time of deregistration if the amount of VAT involved is less than £1,000. There are also other concessions to reduce the potential output tax charge, e.g. no output tax due on zero-rated or exempt goods; output tax calculations are based on the present condition of the goods, i.e. taking damage and depreciation into account.
- If a business owns land and property at the time of deregistration, then it is important to be clear about the output tax rules that apply in relation to the option to tax and potential problems with the capital goods scheme.

60

Retail Schemes

Cross-references. See **11.7 CATERING** for accounting for supplies of catering when take-away food is also sold; **47.8**(35) **OUTPUT TAX** for video cassettes; **56 RECORDS; 63.13 SPECIAL SCHEMES** for the annual accounting scheme; and **69 TRADE PROMOTION SCHEMES** where such schemes are operated under a retail scheme.

De Voil Indirect Tax Service. See V3.551–V3.576.

Introduction

[60.1] VAT retail schemes were introduced at the start of VAT in 1973 because it was recognised that many businesses dealing directly with the public (primarily shopkeepers) and making supplies at different rates of VAT would be unable to keep records of every sale in order to calculate the VAT due in the normal way. The retail schemes are therefore methods for arriving at the value of taxable retail supplies and determining what proportion of those sales are taxable at different rates of VAT.

HMRC's powers

Under *VATA 1994, Sch 11 para 2(6)* and *SI 1995 No 2518, Regs 67, 68*, HMRC are empowered to permit the value of supplies by a retailer which are taxable at other than the zero rate to be determined by a method

- described in a notice published by them, or
- agreed with the retailer.

They may refuse to permit a retailer to use a particular scheme in the following circumstances.

(a) If the use of any particular scheme does not produce a fair and reasonable valuation during any period.
(b) It is necessary to do so for the protection of the revenue.
(c) The retailer could reasonably be expected to account for VAT in the normal way.
Since the introduction of VAT, there has been a revolution in information technology available to, and used by, retailers (e.g. use of bar codes and sophisticated till technology). HMRC consider that these changes mean that the original need for retail schemes, which only provide an approximation of the VAT due, is greatly diminished. They are, therefore, examining every retailer's need to continue using a retail scheme and will only permit the use of a scheme where the retailer cannot reasonably be expected to account for VAT in the normal way, i.e. by identifying each individual supply, its value and the rate of VAT. (VAT Information Sheet 7/96).

Retail and non-retail sales

Where both retail and non-retail sales are made, a retail scheme can only be used for the retail sales and VAT on the non-retail sales must be accounted for outside the scheme in the normal way. (VAT Notice 727, paras 2.1, 2.2 which have the force of law). See *The Oxford, Swindon and Gloucester Co-operative Society v C & E Commrs*, QB [1995] STC 583 (TVC 58.9).

Sales to other VAT-registered businesses

These must normally not be included in a retail scheme. However, by exception, *occasional* cash sales (e.g. a garage supplying petrol to a VAT-registered customer or a retail DIY store supplying building materials to a VAT-registered builder) may be included within a retail scheme. (VAT Notice 727, para 2.4 which has the force of law).

Flat-rate scheme for small businesses

No retailer may use a retail scheme at the same time as the flat-rate scheme for small businesses (see **63.15 SPECIAL SCHEMES**). [*SI 1995/2518, Reg 69A; SI 2002/1142*].

Summary of schemes

[60.2] A retail business with an annual VAT-exclusive turnover over £130 million and which needs to use a retail scheme is only eligible to do so if it agrees a bespoke scheme with HMRC. See **60.13** below.

Apart from such bespoke schemes, there are five published standard schemes.

(a) **Point of Sale scheme.** VAT due is calculated by identifying the correct VAT liability of supplies at the time of sale, e.g. by using electronic tills. See **60.14** below.

(b) **Apportionment Scheme 1.** This is the simpler apportionment scheme designed for smaller businesses with an annual VAT-exclusive turnover not exceeding £1 million. Each VAT period, the retailer must work out the value of purchases for resale at different rates of VAT and apply the proportions of those purchase values to sales. For example, if 82% of the value of goods purchased for retail sale are standard-rated, it is assumed that 82% of takings are from standard-rated sales. Once a year, a similar calculation is made based on purchases for the year and any over or under payment adjusted. See **60.15** below.

(c) **Apportionment Scheme 2.** Under this scheme, a retailer must calculate the expected selling prices (ESPs) of standard-rated and reduced rate goods received for retail sale. He must then work out the ratio of these to the expected selling prices of all goods received for retail sale and apply this ratio to takings. For example, if 82% of the ESPs of goods received for retail sale are standard-rated and 18% are zero-rated, then 82% of takings are treated as standard-rated and 18% zero-rated. See **60.16** below.

(d) **Direct Calculation Scheme 1.** This is available to businesses with an annual VAT-exclusive turnover not exceeding £1 million. To work the scheme, a retailer must calculate expected selling prices (ESPs) of goods for retail sale at one or more rates of VAT so that the proportion of takings on which VAT is due can be calculated. ESPs are, as a general rule, calculated for minority goods, i.e. those goods at the rate of VAT which forms the smallest proportion of retail supplies. For example, if 82% of sales are standard-rated and 18% are zero-rated, the minority goods are zero-rated. Expected selling prices of the zero-rated goods received, made or grown for retail sale are calculated and deducted from takings to arrive at a figure for standard-rated takings. However, a retailer may mark up the majority goods if this would be a simpler option. See **60.17** below.

(e) **Direct Calculation Scheme 2.** This scheme works in exactly the same way as Direct Calculation Scheme 1 but requires an annual stock-take adjustment. See **60.18** below.

(VAT Notice 727, paras 3.4–3.13).

Adaptations to the standard schemes

HMRC may approve an adaptation of any of the above standard schemes.

See under the details of the various schemes for adaptations allowed by HMRC.

Choosing a scheme

[60.3] A retailer can chose to use any of the published schemes provided

- he meets the conditions for use of the scheme in question; and
- HMRC have not refused to let him use the scheme (see **60.1** above).

The following general comparisons can be made of the different schemes.

Point of Sale scheme

- Only available scheme if all supplies are standard-rated or all supplies are taxable at the reduced rate. (VAT Notice 727, para 3.4 which has the force of law).
- Turnover limit of £130 million.
- Can be used for services, catering supplies, self-made and self-grown goods.
- Does not involve stock-taking or working out expected selling prices.
- No annual adjustment required.
- The scheme is potentially both the simplest and most accurate but electronic tills are expensive and staff must be able to operate the system correctly at all times.

Apportionment Scheme 1

- Cannot be used for services, catering supplies, self-made or self-grown goods.
- Turnover limit of £1 million.
- Does not involve stock-taking or working out expected selling prices.
- Annual adjustment required.
- The scheme is relatively simple. However, if on average a higher mark-up is achieved for zero-rated goods than standard-rated or reduced rate goods, more VAT could be payable under this scheme than another available alternative scheme.

Apportionment Scheme 2

- Cannot be used for services or catering supplies but can be used for self-made or self-grown goods.
- Turnover limit of £130 million.
- Stock-taking required at the start of using the scheme, but not thereafter.
- Expected selling prices must be worked out.
- No annual adjustment required but a rolling calculation used.
- The scheme can be complex to operate but if worked properly it will provide a more accurate valuation of supplies over a period of time.

Direct Calculation Scheme 1

- Services can only be included if they are liable at a different rate from the minority goods.
- Cannot be used for catering supplies but can be used for self-made or self-grown goods.

- Turnover limit of £1 million.
- Expected selling prices must be worked out. The scheme can produce inaccuracies if expected selling prices are not calculated accurately. In addition, where expected selling prices are set for standard-rated goods and stock of these goods has a slow turnover, the scheme may not be the most appropriate as VAT is paid in the period in which the goods are received and not necessarily when they are sold.
- Does not involve stock-taking.
- No annual adjustment required.
- The scheme can be relatively simple where goods are sold at two rates of VAT and there is a small proportion of supplies at one of those rates.
- The scheme can be complex to work where goods are sold at three rates of VAT although it may be possible to account for a small number of goods at a third rate outside the scheme.

Direct Calculation Scheme 2

- Services can only be included if they are liable at a different rate from the minority goods.
- Cannot be used for catering supplies but can be used for self-made or self-grown goods.
- Turnover limit of £130 million.
- Expected selling prices must be worked out. The scheme can produce inaccuracies if expected selling prices are not calculated accurately. In addition, where expected selling prices are set for standard-rated goods and stock of these goods has a slow turnover, the scheme may not be the most appropriate as VAT is paid in the period in which the goods are received and not necessarily when they are sold.
- Stock-taking required at the start of using the scheme and annually thereafter.
- Annual adjustment required.

(VAT Notice 727, paras 3.4–3.13, 11).

Mixture of schemes and separate accounting by different parts of the business

[60.4] A retailer cannot use more than one scheme at any one time except as indicated in any notice published by HMRC or as specifically allowed by them. [*SI 1995 No 2518, Reg 69*]. Currently HMRC allow the following mixtures of schemes. (Note that it is always possible to use the normal method of accounting with any scheme or any allowable mixture of schemes.)

Mixtures of schemes

It may be necessary to use different schemes in different parts of the business. Provided the retailer is eligible to use the relevant schemes, the Point of Sale scheme can be mixed with either Direct Calculation Scheme 1 or 2 or

Apportionment Scheme 1 or 2. It is also possible to use any individual scheme, or any acceptable mixture of schemes, with normal accounting. It is not possible to mix

- Apportionment Scheme 1 and 2;
- Direct Calculation Scheme 1 and 2; or
- Apportionment Scheme 1 or 2 with Direct Calculation Scheme 1 or 2.

(VAT Notice 727, para 4.1 which has the force of law).

Using the same scheme in different parts of a business

The same scheme can be used separately at a number of distinct business locations. If so, under any scheme other than the Point of Sale scheme, it may be necessary to make adjustments to account for transfers between the different parts of the business. Details of such adjustments must be agreed with HMRC. (VAT Notice 727, para 4.1 which has the force of law).

Changing schemes

Compulsory change of scheme

[60.5] A retailer must cease to use a particular scheme if he becomes ineligible to use it. From the start of the next VAT accounting period, he must then change to another scheme (or a mixture of schemes if permitted, see **60.4** above) or to the normal method of accounting.

Voluntary change of scheme

Unless HMRC allow otherwise, a retailer using a retail scheme must, so long as he remains a taxable person, continue to use that scheme for a period of not less than one year from its adoption and any change from one scheme to another must be made at the end of a complete year reckoned from the beginning of the VAT period in which he first adopted the scheme. This does not apply where a retailer ceases to use a retail scheme and joins the flat-rate scheme for small businesses (see **63.15 SPECIAL SCHEMES**). [*SI 1995/2518, Reg 71; SI 2002/1142*]. If, for exceptional reasons, a change is required at any other time, written agreement from HMRC is required.

Where the annual accounting scheme is used, a retail scheme can only be changed at the end of the annual accounting year.

Retrospective changes

Retrospective changes to a retail scheme are not normally allowed. See *Summerfield* (VTD 108) (TVC 58.13) and *RJ Vulgar* (VTD 304) (TVC 58.14) where HMRC's decision not to exercise discretion to allow retrospective changes in the scheme was upheld by the tribunal. In *A & C Wadlewski* (VTD 13340) (TVC 58.24) the tribunal held that HMRC's refusal was unreasonable because of the high proportion of additional VAT payable but this decision was not followed in *L & J Lewis* (VTD 14085) (TVC 58.20) or *L & P Fryer* (VTD 14265) (TVC 58.21).

HMRC may, in exceptional cases, allow retrospective change, e.g. where

- the business has been misdirected (by omission or commission) by a HMRC officer; or
- the business can clearly demonstrate that the scheme which it is proposed to use retrospectively would produce a more accurate liability *and* the difference in VAT due is a very high proportion of the business's profit. In *Wadlewski* above, the tribunal allowed retrospection where the difference in liability amounted to 40% of the business's profit.

Application should be made in writing to HMRC giving as much detail as possible. The maximum period of recalculation is three years. The retailer must have been eligible to use the new scheme during the full period of recalculation.

(VAT Notice 727, paras 4.2, 4.3; VAT Notice 727/3/11, paras 2.5, 2.6; VAT Notice 727/4/11, paras 2.5, 2.6; VAT Notice 727/5/11, paras 2.5, 2.6).

Ceasing to use a scheme

[60.6] A retailer must notify HMRC before ceasing to account for VAT under a retail scheme. He may then be required to pay VAT on such proportion as HMRC consider fair and reasonable of any sums due to him at the end of the VAT period in which he last used the scheme. [*SI 1995 No 2518, Reg 72*].

See under the individual scheme rules for adjustments which may be necessary on ceasing to use a particular scheme. Apart from these special rules, HMRC may require additional adjustments where unusual patterns of trade prevent the chosen scheme from producing a fair and reasonable result.

The following points should also be noted.

- Only goods sold by retail can be included in the retail scheme. If a retailer ceases to use a scheme because he sells all or part of his business as a going concern, the value of stock transferred must be excluded from the retail scheme.
- On ceasing to trade, VAT may become due on the value of stocks and assets. See **59.34 REGISTRATION**.

(VAT Notice 727, paras 6.1, 6.2 which have the force of law).

Change in VAT rate and VAT liabilities

[60.7] A change in the VAT rate means that a rate of VAT has been changed or a new rate has been introduced. A change in VAT liability occurs when a supply which is either exempt or zero-rated becomes taxable at a positive rate or vice versa. Either change may affect the particular scheme used and a retailer must then take the necessary steps relating to his chosen scheme as directed in VAT Notices or as agreed with HMRC. [*SI 1995 No 2518, Reg 75*].

If the change of rate falls halfway through a VAT period, the retailer must make two calculations: one using the old VAT rate and one using the new rate. This will reflect supplies made before and after the rate change. These amounts must then be added together to give the VAT liability for the period.
(VAT Notice 727, paras 7.1–7.5).

Effect on gross takings

Any change in the rate of VAT or liability is effective from a specified date. VAT is due at the new rate on all amounts charged for supplies made on or after the date of change, except that the special provisions in **55.7** *et seq.* RATES OF VAT can be applied to individual transactions provided they are dealt with outside the retail scheme.

Gross takings

[60.8] All retail schemes work by applying the appropriate VAT fraction(s) to positive-rated daily gross takings in order to establish the amount of VAT due. It is therefore necessary to keep a record of daily gross takings. This term can be misleading because, for retail scheme purposes, daily gross takings is not simply a record of payments received or cash in hand on any particular day but is a record of supplies made that day. The record of daily gross takings can be a listing made from copies of sales vouchers but will normally be a till roll.

Inclusions in daily gross takings

The following must be included in daily gross takings, *the provisions having the force of law.*

- All payments as they are received from cash customers. This includes payment by notes and coins, cheques, debit or credit card vouchers, Switch, Delta or similar electronic transactions, and electronic cash.
- The full value, including VAT, of credit sales (excluding any disclosed exempt charge for credit) on the day the supply is made.
- The value of any goods taken out of the business for own use. See also **60.9**(25) below.
- The cash value of any payment in kind for retail sales.
- The face value of gift, book and record vouchers, etc. taken in place of cash (but see also **69.12** TRADE PROMOTION SCHEMES where the business supplies the voucher at a discount).
- Any other payments for retail sales.

But where turnover is less than £1 million and customers do not pay for goods when received (e.g. milkmen, newsagents) it may be possible to agree an adaptation to eliminate opening and closing debtors in the scheme calculation (see **60.9**(10) below).

Adjustments to daily gross takings

There are a number of required and allowable adjustments to be made to arrive at the final daily gross takings figure for retail scheme purposes. These are to reflect the fact that daily gross takings should, as far as possible, reflect the supplies made by the retailer and the consideration received for those supplies. Thus, where goods are stolen from a retailer, there has been no supply: no VAT is due and nothing should be included in daily gross takings. Where cash is stolen, there has been a supply on which VAT remains due: the value of the supply should be reflected in daily gross takings.

Daily gross takings may be reduced for the following.

- Receipts recorded for exempt supplies.
- Receipts for goods or services which are to be accounted for outside the scheme.
- Refunds given to customers in respect of taxable supplies to cover accidental overcharges or where goods are unsuitable or faulty.
- Instalments in respect of credit sales.
- Void transactions (where an incorrect transaction has not been voided at the time of the error).
- Illegible credit card transactions (where a customer's account details are not legible on the credit card voucher and therefore cannot be presented at the bank).
- Unsigned or dishonoured cheques from cash customers (but not from credit customers).
- Counterfeit notes.
- Where a cheque guarantee card is incorrectly accepted as a credit card.
- Acceptance of out-of-date coupons which have previously been included in daily gross takings but which are not honoured by the promoters.
- Supervisor's float discrepancies.
- Till breakdowns (where incorrect till readings are recorded due to mechanical faults, e.g. till programming error, false reading and till reset by an engineer).
- Use of training tills (where the till used by staff for training has been returned to the sales floor without the zeroing of figures).
- Customer overspends using Shopacheck.
- Inadvertent acceptance of foreign currency where discovered at a later time (e.g. when cashing up) unless reimbursed by the bank.

A record of any adjustments to the daily gross taking should always be kept.

If any adjustment is made for which a payment is subsequently received, the amount received must be included in daily gross takings.

See also **60.9** below generally for special transactions which may require adjustments to be made to figures for daily gross takings.

(VAT Notice 727, para 4.4; VAT Notice 727/3/11, paras 5.1–5.5; VAT Notice 727/4/11, paras 6.1–6.5; VAT Notice 727/5/11, paras 5.1–5.5, all of which have the force of law).

See HMRC VAT Guidance V1–23, Chapter 10 para 5.3 for till shortages and excesses (unders and overs).

Example

Mike is the owner of a retail business. The cash in the till (adjusting for float) at the end of the day's trading is £350. However, he is unsure about how to deal with the following issues as far as VAT is concerned:

- A member of staff stole £50 of cash from the till – she has now been sacked.
- The window cleaner was paid £20 cash from the till for cleaning the shop windows.
- Mike took goods for personal use with a retail price of £12 and cost price of £6.

The basic definition of VAT is that it is a tax on the 'supply of goods or services'. This means the £70 cash removed from the till (illegally in the case of the staff member) relates to sales that have already taken place. The amount of £70 should therefore be included in the takings figure.

Sales to the business owner also need to be included because a supply of goods has again taken place (even though no money has been exchanged). However, the good news for Mike is that he only needs to account for output tax on the cost price of the goods, i.e. £6.

The total daily gross takings figure for VAT purposes is therefore £426 (£350 + £50 + £20 + £6).

De Voil Indirect Tax Service. See V3.556–558.

Special transactions

[60.9] The following is a list of the more common transactions which might have to be taken into account in using a retail scheme and/or calculating gross takings.

(1) Acquisitions from other EU countries

Suppliers from elsewhere in the EU do not charge VAT on their sales and the retailer must account for VAT at the rate applicable to the goods in the UK. See **19.3** *et seq*. **EUROPEAN UNION: SINGLE MARKET** for further details.

For retail scheme purposes, references to zero-rated goods apply only to goods which are zero-rated in the UK. Goods which are zero-rated on acquisition from other EU countries, but standard-rated in the UK, must be treated as standard-rated goods in the retail scheme calculations.

See (22) below for goods imported from outside the EU.

(2) Amusement and gaming machine takings

See **57.4 RECREATION AND SPORT**.

(3) BT phonecards

See **69.11** and **69.12 TRADE PROMOTION SCHEMES**.

(4) Business entertainment/gifts

If goods are purchased specifically to be consumed in the course of business entertainment or to supply as gifts,

- under the Point of Sale scheme, any VAT due must be accounted for by adding the value of the goods to daily gross takings at the relevant time; and
- under the Apportionment Schemes 1 and 2 and Direct Calculation Schemes 1 and 2, any VAT due on the supply must be accounted for outside the scheme.

See **47.6 OUTPUT TAX** for VAT due on gifts.

If goods from normal stock are used for business entertainment or supplied as gifts,

- under the Point of Sale scheme, any VAT due must be accounted for by adding the value of the goods to daily gross takings at the relevant time;
- under Apportionment Scheme 1, the full value of the goods should be included in daily gross takings;
- under Apportionment Scheme 2, the full value of the goods should be included in daily gross takings and the necessary adjustment should be made to expected selling prices;
- under Direct Calculation Schemes 1 and 2, VAT can be accounted for under the scheme as follows:
  - (i) if the goods are standard-rated or reduced rate goods and the minority goods are zero-rated, by adding the value of the supply to daily gross takings; and
  - (ii) if the minority goods are standard-rated or reduced rate goods, no addition to the daily gross takings is necessary but the expected selling prices must be adjusted to reflect the value to be accounted for.

(5) Business overheads

Any purchases of goods and services which are not for resale should be excluded from the scheme calculations.

(6) Business promotion schemes

See **69 TRADE PROMOTION SCHEMES.**

(7) Cash discounts

If goods are offered on cash discount or early settlement terms, the discounted value should be included in daily gross takings at the time of supply.

(8) Catering supplies

Apportionment Schemes 1 and 2 and Direct Calculation Schemes 1 and 2 all assume that goods bought at one rate of VAT will be sold at the same rate. Food bought at the zero rate often becomes standard-rated when supplied in the course of catering and therefore the Point of Sale scheme must normally be used for such supplies. See, however, **11.7 CATERING** for a catering adaptation which may be used.

(9) Credit card transactions

Retailers are allowed to charge different prices to customers using a credit card. The different prices charged may either take the form of discounts to cash customers (see (7) above) or a surcharge being made to those paying by credit card.

- If the charge for payment by credit card is made by the supplier of the goods/services being bought, HMRC regard this as a further payment for the purchase, VAT being payable at the same rate as on the goods/services.
- If the charge is made by an agent acting for the supplier of the goods/services (e.g. a travel agent acting on behalf of a tour operator) HMRC consider that the charge is for a separate supply of exempt services (i.e. accepting payment in the form of a credit card).

> *Example*
>
> A suit bought from a men's clothes shop costs £400. If the customer pays by credit card, the store makes an additional charge of £10. In this situation, the cost of the suit is £410 and the entire payment is standard-rated.

Card-handling fees

Many high street retailers have operated a scheme whereby, when customers pay for goods by credit or debit card, small print on the receipt asks them to agree to pay a 'card-handling fee' (typically 2.5%), even though the price is exactly the same as it would be for a cash sale. The fee is then claimed as an exempt supply so that VAT is only paid on 97.5% of the price of the goods. In *Debenhams Retail plc v C & E Commrs*, CA [2005] STC 1155 (TVC 27.11) the tribunal held that this treatment was incorrect and that the whole amount paid was consideration for a taxable supply of goods. The High Court disagreed with this but the Court of Appeal upheld the tribunal decision. There was a single contract under which Debenhams was the supplier to its card-using customers of goods or services for a consideration consisting of the whole 100% payable by such customers on any such transaction.

(10) Credit transactions

The full value of the goods must be included in daily gross takings at the time of supply. Do not wait until payment is received and do not include instalments as they are received. Additional rules apply depending upon the way credit sales are financed.

(a) Where *credit for customers is arranged through a finance house, etc.* which takes ownership of the goods, the transaction should be treated as a cash sale to the finance house and the full amount payable by the customer should by included in daily gross takings at the time of supply.

In *C & E Commrs v Primback Ltd, ECJ Case C–34/99*, [2001] STC 803 (TVC 22.242) Primback sold furniture on interest free credit. Credit was provided by a separate finance company introduced to the customer by Primback. The finance company did not charge interest and title in the goods passed directly from Primback to the customer. The customer then paid the full price of the goods in instalments to the finance company. The finance company did not pay Primback the full price charged to the customer but a net amount after retaining a 'discount' equivalent to the amount that the finance company would have charged the customer for a loan at a commercial rate. At issue was whether VAT was due on the full amount paid by the customer, or on the lower amount received by Primback. The ECJ held that where a retailer sells goods in return for payment of the advertised price which he invoices to the purchaser and which does not vary according to whether the customer pays in cash or by way of credit, the taxable amount is the full amount payable by the purchaser.

(b) *Where credit transactions are financed from own resources*, any separate credit charge (additional to the cash price) is exempt from VAT provided that it is disclosed to the customer (see **27.11** FINANCIAL SERVICES). If so, it should be excluded from daily gross takings.

Adaptations for newsagents/small retailers

In principle, the above requirements apply to all businesses. However, HMRC recognise that this may cause administrative difficulties for small businesses with turnover of less than £1 million where customers do not pay for goods when they receive them (e.g. milkmen and newsagents). In such cases, retailers can take account of opening and closing debtors for a VAT period in their scheme calculations. (VAT Notice 727, para 4.5).

(11) Delivery charges

See **47.8**(19) OUTPUT TAX.

(12) Deposits

Deposits which are advance payments must be included in daily gross takings. Other deposits (e.g. those taken as security for the safe return of goods hired out) must be excluded (regardless of whether the deposit is eventually refunded or forfeited for loss or damage).

(13) Dishonoured cheques and counterfeit bank notes

Unsigned or dishonoured cheques from cash customers (but not credit customers) and counterfeit notes received may be deducted from daily gross takings.

(14) Disposal of business assets

VAT must be accounted for outside the retail scheme.

(15) Exempt supplies

These must always be dealt with outside the scheme, whichever scheme is used.

(16) Exports (to countries outside the EU)

Retail exports

Where goods are supplied for retail export under the retail export scheme, including supplies to entitled EU residents and ships' crews going abroad (see **21.12** to **21.16 EXPORTS**) the supplies must be allowed for in the scheme calculations as follows.

(a) Under the Point of Sale scheme, Apportionment Schemes 1 and 2 and, if the minority goods are zero-rated, Direct Calculation Schemes 1 and 2, follow the normal scheme rules but
   (i) include all takings, including VAT, for goods sold for retail export in daily gross takings. (Do not deduct the refunds which are expected to be made to the customer.);
   (ii) at the end of each period, add up the takings for standard-rated goods actually exported. (This is the total of amounts shown on the officially certified forms returned during the period.);
   (iii) calculate notional VAT on the takings at (ii) above, using the VAT fraction that applied at the time the sale was included in gross takings; and
   (iv) subtract the notional VAT at (iii) from the scheme output tax.

(b) Under Direct Calculation Schemes 1 and 2 where the minority goods are standard-rated, follow the normal scheme rules but at the end of each VAT period
   (i) add up the original expected selling prices, including VAT, of the standard-rated goods which have actually been exported. (These will be the goods shown on the officially certified forms returned during the period.);
   (ii) calculate notional VAT on the total at (i) above using the VAT fraction that applied when the amounts were included in the scheme calculations; and
   (iii) subtract the notional VAT at (ii) from the scheme output tax.

Direct and indirect exports

Where goods are directly exported or supplied in the UK to an overseas trader for subsequent export,

- under the Point of Sale scheme, the supplies must be dealt with outside the scheme;
- under Apportionment Schemes 1 and 2 and, if the minority goods are zero-rated, Direct Calculation Schemes 1 and 2, the procedure is similar to that for retail exports in (*a*) above except that the calculations relate to goods sent for export and the comments in brackets do not apply. If proof of export is not received within three months of the date of supply, the notional VAT calculated under (*a*)(iii) above must be included as an addition on the VAT payable side of the VAT account for the current VAT period; and
- under Direct Calculation Schemes 1 and 2 where the minority goods are standard-rated, the procedure is similar to that for retail exports in (*b*) above except that the calculations relate to goods sent for export and the comment in brackets does not apply. If proof of export is not

received within three months of the date of supply, the notional VAT calculated under (*b*)(ii) above must be included as an addition on the VAT payable side of the VAT account for the current VAT period.

See (29) below for retail sales to persons from other EU countries.

(17) Foreign currency transactions

Many retailers accept foreign currency in order to encourage spending by tourists to the UK. No reduction to the daily gross takings can be made for commission payable to the bank, etc. for converting the currency. The total sterling equivalent of the value charged on the day the supply is made must be included in the daily gross takings (see **71.18 VALUATION**). Note that this is not necessarily the same as the sterling sale price of the goods and depends on the exchange rate applicable at the time of supply.

If the retailer also charges the customer a 'premium' for accepting payment in foreign currency, this is additional consideration for the supply of goods (or services) and must be included in the daily gross takings.

See **60.8** above for inadvertent acceptance of foreign currency.

(18) Gift, book, and record vouchers

See **69.11** and **69.12 TRADE PROMOTION SCHEMES.**

(19) Goods bought at one rate and sold at another

For some goods, the rate of VAT depends upon how they are held out for sale, e.g. meat held out for sale for human consumption is zero-rated but the same meat held out for sale for pet food is standard-rated.

For the provisions applying to chemists, see **60.19** below and for a special scheme for take-away food, see **11.7 CATERING.**

All other goods bought at one rate and sold at another must be treated as follows.

Point of Sale scheme

No action is required because takings are separated into each rate of VAT at the point of sale.

Apportionment Schemes 1 and 2 and Direct Calculation Schemes 1 and 2

- Where separate stocks are kept of goods that are held out for sale at the different VAT rates, on receipt such goods must be entered in the records of goods for resale at the VAT rate that will apply when they are sold.
- Where common stocks are kept of those goods that are drawn on to sell at different VAT rates, such goods must initially be entered in the scheme records at cost or expected selling price (depending on the scheme used) at the rate of VAT that applied when the goods were received. But when the goods are put up or held out for sale at the other VAT rate, it is necessary to deduct the appropriate amounts from the

scheme records at the VAT rate that applied when the goods were received and enter the corresponding amounts in the scheme records at the VAT rate that applies when the goods are sold.

(20) Goods bought from unregistered suppliers

Where goods for retail sale are bought from unregistered suppliers,

- under Apportionment Schemes 1 and 2, such goods must be included in the retail scheme calculation at the appropriate rate; and
- under Direct Calculation Schemes 1 and 2, only such goods which are taxable at the minority rate must be included in expected selling price calculations.

(21) Goods sold on sale or return or similar terms

A separate record must be kept of goods supplied on a sale or return basis. Such goods should only be included in daily gross takings when the customer adopts the goods. See (12) above if the customer pays a deposit.

(22) Imports (from countries outside the EU)

The normal scheme rules apply, as for other purchases, under all schemes.

See (1) above for goods acquired from other EU countries.

(23) Part-exchange

Where goods or services are accepted in part-exchange, the full retail selling price, including VAT, of the goods supplied must be included in daily gross takings.

Where any goods taken in part-exchange are subsequently resold, it may be possible to sell them under the margin scheme for **SECOND-HAND GOODS (61)**. If not, they can be included in the retail scheme calculations.

(24) Phonecards

See **69.11** and **69.12 TRADE PROMOTION SCHEMES.**

(25) Private or personal use of goods

VAT is normally due on any goods purchased for resale that are taken out of the business for personal or private use. See **47.7 OUTPUT TAX.**

- Under the Point of Sale scheme, the value of any positive-rated goods taken for private or personal use must be included in daily gross takings.
- Under Apportionment Scheme 1, the value of such goods must be included in daily gross takings.
- Under Apportionment Scheme 2, the value of such goods must be included in daily gross takings and the necessary adjustments must be made to expected selling prices.
- Under the Direct Calculation Schemes 1 and 2,

(i) if the minority goods are zero-rated, the value of any positive-rated goods taken for private or personal use must be included in daily gross takings; and

(ii) if minority goods are standard-rated or reduced rate goods, the value of any positive-rated goods taken for private or personal use should be added to expected selling prices and daily gross takings.

(26) Recall of goods by manufacturers

If a manufacturer recalls contaminated or otherwise faulty goods,

- under Apportionment Scheme 1, purchase records must be adjusted;
- under Apportionment Scheme 2 and Direct Calculation Schemes 1 and 2, expected selling price records must be adjusted.

(27) Refunds to customers

Amounts refunded or credited to customers can be deducted from daily gross takings to a maximum of the amount originally charged.

(28) Rented payphones

If a payphone is rented from British Telecom or another supplier, the retailer makes a supply of services to the user of the telephone. VAT is due on the money removed from the payphone which should be dealt with as follows.

- Under the Point of Sale scheme, include the money in standard-rated daily gross takings.
- Under Apportionment Schemes 1 and 2, deal with the supply outside the scheme.
- Under Direct Calculation schemes 1 and 2
  (i) where minority goods are zero-rated or reduced rate goods, include the money in daily gross takings; and
  (ii) where the minority goods are standard-rated, deal with the supply outside the scheme.

See also **47.8**(17) **OUTPUT TAX.**

(29) Retail sales to persons from other EU countries

Any retail sale made in the UK to a person from another EU country should be accounted for as a normal domestic retail sale. Special arrangements apply to distance selling, i.e. where goods are sold to persons in other EU countries who are not registered for VAT and the supplier is responsible for delivery to the customer. See **19.20 EUROPEAN UNION: SINGLE MARKET**.

See (16) above for exports to countries outside the EU.

(30) Road fuel

If road fuel is used for private motoring, VAT due must be accounted for outside the scheme. See **45.16 MOTOR CARS.**

(31) Sale of discount vouchers (or discount cards)

The VAT consequences of selling vouchers or cards entitling the holder to discounts on purchases depend upon where the vouchers or cards can be used.

(a) If vouchers or cards can only be used for purchases from the retailer selling them, he should include the payment received in daily gross takings. Under the Point of Sale scheme, if, for example, the card can only be used for purchases of zero-rated goods, the amount charged for the card should be added to zero-rated takings.

(b) If vouchers or cards can be used at several traders, this is a standard-rated supply of services. See *C & E Commrs v Granton Marketing Ltd; C & E Commrs v Wentwalk Ltd*, CA [1996] STC 1049 (TVC 67.166).
   - Under the Point of Sale scheme, payments received should be added to standard-rated daily gross takings.
   - Under Apportionment Schemes 1 and 2 and Direct Calculation Schemes 1 and 2, payments received must be dealt with outside the scheme used.

(32) Sale or assignment of debts

Where debts due from customers are sold or assigned, no further action is required as the correct amount will have already been included in daily gross takings at the time of supply.

(33) Saving stamps, travel cards and pools coupons

If a retailer

- buys and sells travel cards and/or savings stamps for gas, electricity, television licences, etc., or
- receives commission from distributing and collecting pools coupons

these must be dealt with outside the retail scheme and not be included in daily gross takings. This follows the decision in *TE, M & IJ Parr* (VTD 1967) (TVC 58.6).

(34) Second-hand goods

VAT on second-hand goods sold, may be accounted for

- within the retail scheme in the same way as new goods; or
- under the margin scheme for **SECOND-HAND GOODS (61)**.

(35) Theft, shrinkage, leakage and stock losses

Where there are unexplained accounting discrepancies between stock and sales, to the extent that this is attributable to unrecorded sales, such as theft (see below), shrinkage, etc., the value must be added back to the records of daily gross takings. Where possible, these adjustments should be allocated to the specific VAT period in which they took place. Otherwise such stock losses should be apportioned across relevant VAT periods on a fair and reasonable basis. Unless there is evidence of the liability of the unaccounted supplies, adjustments must be made in line with the usual proportion of standard against zero-rated supplies. Depending upon the scheme used, it may also be necessary to consider whether the shrinkage for which the daily gross takings has been adjusted requires further adjustment to expected selling prices.

See, however, *British American Tobacco International Ltd and Another v Belgian State, ECJ Case C–435/03*, [2006] STC 158 (TVC 22.88) where a quantity of cigarettes was stolen from a warehouse. The court held that the theft of goods did not constitute a supply of goods for consideration within the meaning of what is now *Directive 2006/112/EC, Art 12(a)* and therefore could not be subject to VAT as such.

(VAT Notice 727/3/11, paras 6.1–6.31; VAT Notice 727/4/11, paras 7.1–7.34; VAT Notice 727/5/11, paras 6.1–6.33, all of which have the force of law).

Expected selling prices ('ESPS')

[60.10] Under certain of the retail schemes, a retailer must

- calculate ESPs; and
- make adjustments to those ESPs to reflect factors which prevent him from achieving them.

ESPs are used to calculate the expected value of retail sales at different rates. The way ESPs are calculated has, therefore, a direct effect on the VAT paid and must be done as accurately as possible. For this reason, calculations should never include

- goods sold by wholesale;
- goods bought for private use; or
- disposals of stocks resulting from a sale of all or part of the business.

(VAT Notice 727/4/11, para 5.3; VAT Notice 727/5/11, para 4.3, which have the force of law).

Calculating ESPs

[60.11] ESPs can be calculated in any way which produces a fair and reasonable result. The same method must always be used (but see below for mixtures) and, whatever method is used, the adjustments described below must also be made. The most common methods of calculation are as follows.

(a) *Mark up each line of goods* (the most accurate).
(b) *Mark up classes of goods* (e.g. vegetables or confectionery). This method can only be used if
  - it is not possible to mark up each line (as in (*a*) above);
  - the variation in mark up within the group is no more than 10% (20% under the old scheme calculations);
  - the mark up is reviewed each quarter; and
  - the class of goods has a commercial basis and is not constructed artificially.

(c) *Use recommended retail prices*. This method can only be used if
  - recommended retail prices can be recorded on receipt of the goods; and

- purchases invoices or other supplier documentation (i) shows the VAT-inclusive recommended retail price of each separate line of goods; (ii) distinguishes standard-rated, reduced rate and zero-rated items; and (iii) totals goods at each rate of VAT.

(VAT Notice 727/4/11, para 5.3; VAT Notice 727/5/11, para 4.3, which have the force of law).

Example

In a particular class of zero-rated goods, a retailer purchases the following lines at the actual mark-ups shown.

Line of goods	Purchase price £	Actual mark-up	Expected selling price £
A	150	7%	160.50
B	70	5%	73.50
C	50	16%	58.00
D	30	19%	35.70
E	70	10%	77.00
F	30	6%	31.80
	£400		£436.50

Using the actual mark-up for each line of goods, expected selling prices are £436.50.

If, however, it was not possible to break down the total purchase price of £400 between the various lines, the average mark-up basis could be used.

Average mark-up = (7 + 5 + 16 + 19 + 10 + 6) ÷ 6 = 10.5%

Expected selling prices are £442 (£400 × 1.105).

Adjustment to ESPs

[60.12] As ESPs will rarely be fully achieved, adjustments must be made at the end of each VAT period to take account of factors which affect the selling price. These include (i.e. the list is not exhaustive)

- price changes (increases and decreases), e.g. sell by date reductions;
- special offers and promotion schemes;
- wastage;
- freezer breakdowns;
- breakages;
- shrinkage (i.e. pilferage and loss of stock); and
- bad debts that have been written off in the period.

How such adjustments are made is up to the individual retailer but a consistent method must be used (both within each period and from one period to the next). Records of adjustments and working papers must be kept with the retail scheme calculations.

If it proves difficult to make such adjustments, it may be more appropriate to use another scheme. Alternatively, HMRC may agree to a method of sampling where reductions cannot be established accurately or the omission of certain adjustments where the effect does not distort the retail scheme.

(VAT Notice 727/4/11, para 5.3; VAT Notice 727/5/11, para 4.3, which have the force of law).

Bespoke retail schemes

[60.13] If VAT-exclusive taxable retail supplies in the previous 12 months have exceeded £130 million, a business cannot continue to use a published retail scheme (VAT Notice 727, para 5.1, which has the force of law) and must then do one of the following.

(a) **Account for VAT in the normal way.** A business must do this if it does not wish to use a bespoke scheme or cannot agree such a scheme with HMRC. As the business will be trading by way of retail, it will not be required to issue a VAT invoice to unregistered customers. But it will need to identify the VAT-exclusive value and the amount of VAT for each sale and be able to produce periodic totals of those amounts.

(b) **Agree a bespoke scheme with HMRC.** A bespoke scheme may be based on one of the published schemes but will be tailored to meet the individual needs of the business. HMRC recognise that some large retailers could have difficulty in accounting for VAT in the normal way and will therefore only withhold agreement to a proposed scheme in the following circumstances.

- It does not produce a fair and reasonable result. This is judged on the ability of the scheme to approximate the amount of output tax which would be due under normal accounting. The reasonableness of a scheme is judged by the simplicity with which it can be used by the retailer and checked by HMRC. A scheme which does not reflect commercial reality or which unnecessarily complicates either the retailer's accounting or HMRC's ability to audit the VAT declarations is unlikely to be reasonable. In a large and complex business, there may be a number of different methods of calculating the VAT due, several of which could be regarded as fair and reasonable. But where two methods produce different amounts of VAT, it will often be possible to identify which of them is closer to normal accounting. In these circumstances, for the protection of the revenue, HMRC may refuse, or withdraw its agreement to, the use of a method which is, in principle, fair and reasonable.
- Refusal to use the scheme is necessary for the protection of the revenue.
- The business could reasonably be expected to account for VAT normally.

Using a bespoke scheme

A bespoke scheme must be used from the VAT period following that in which the £130 million threshold is exceeded. A scheme should therefore be agreed in good time because, once that threshold is exceeded, the only alternative is to account for VAT in the normal way. In some circumstances, the start date of a bespoke scheme can be backdated but only with the agreement of both parties.

A bespoke scheme cannot be used for:

- *Sales to other VAT-registered businesses*. The only exception is occasional cash sales in the same form as are made to customers who are not VAT-registered (e.g. a garage supplying petrol to a VAT-registered customer or a retail DIY store supplying building materials to a VAT-registered builder).
- *Non-retail sales*. VAT on these must be accounted for using the normal method of accounting.
- *Internet sales*. HMRC take the view that where a business makes retail sales in the UK via the internet, it will usually have sufficient records of the sales to allow it to account for the VAT in the normal way. But if they are satisfied that a business cannot do this, HMRC may agree that the sales can be included in a bespoke scheme.

Key elements of a bespoke scheme

A bespoke scheme will usually be based on a published scheme (or a mixture of published schemes) but it can be based on any method which meets the tests listed in (*b*) above. HMRC are unlikely to agree a bespoke scheme based on, or including, published schemes with a threshold cap of £1 million (i.e. currently Apportionment Scheme 1 or Direct Calculation Scheme 1).

A bespoke scheme will be agreed in writing and include the following provisions.

- The start date, review date, and end date of the agreement. The agreement must specify how output tax will be calculated in any period between the date at which the business became ineligible to use a published scheme and the date of the agreement.
- Details of which supplies will be accounted for within the scheme and which, if any, will be accounted for in the normal way.
- Full details of the method of determining daily gross takings including use of tills, till breakdowns, deliveries direct to customers, other currencies accepted, concessions and roundings. Also details of how adjustments will be made for special transactions (see **60.9** above), etc. See VAT Notice 727/2/11, paras 6.1, 6.2 for further details and examples but even these checklists are only a guide and all special transactions should also be covered.
- Full details of the method of valuing taxable retail sales.
  - (i) Under a bespoke scheme based on the Point of Sale scheme, the agreement should cover mixed rate products, non-Electronic Point of Sale (EPOS) departments, private use of purchases, product VAT coding, refunds, remote tills, staff discounts, till

breakdowns, unscanned products, VAT code errors, and VAT coding. It relation to vouchers and special offers, it should also cover discount vouchers, multi-saves, out-of-date manufacturers' vouchers, own product vouchers, retailer vouchers within *VATA 1994, Sch 10A* (face-value vouchers/credit vouchers and other vouchers), and special offer prices/price reductions. See VAT Notice 727/2/11, paras 7.1, 7.2 for further details but the list is not exhaustive.

(ii) Under a bespoke scheme based on expected selling prices (ESPs), the agreement should cover the basis of setting and adjusting ESPs, direct deliveries to customers, mixed rate products, the point of receipt of goods into the scheme, product VAT coding, the level of calculation (business, store, department), treatment of services, VAT code errors, VAT coding, and trading patterns (period of calculation, stock adjustments, rolling periods, exclusion of distortive factors). See VAT Notice 727/2/11, paras 8.1–8.3 for further details but the list is not exhaustive.

- Name, status and signature of an HMRC officer and an authorised signatory of the retailer.

Changes to scheme

An agreed bespoke scheme is based on full disclosure of the current business structure and trading patterns at that time. If these change to such an extent that the agreed method ceases to produce a fair and reasonable result, HMRC must be informed immediately.

A bespoke scheme can normally be changed at any time if the retailer and HMRC agree. HMRC would not normally expect any changes to take place from a date earlier than the date that the change or a review was requested. However, retrospective changes may be appropriate where there is a fundamental flaw in the scheme.

Withdrawal of the scheme

HMRC may withdraw their agreement and refuse the use of a previously agreed scheme if it ceases to meet any of the conditions in (*b*) above. They may do so, for example, if they conclude that it was not based on a full disclosure of business circumstances or another method of calculation would produce a more fair and reasonable result. If they do this, they will inform the retailer of the aspects of the current agreement that are unacceptable. If the retailer still wishes to use a bespoke scheme, it must then send new proposals for consideration.

(VAT Notice 727/2/11).

Point of Sale Scheme

[60.14] The Point of Sale scheme can be used if

- taxable turnover does not exceed £130 million (if so a bespoke scheme must be agreed, see **60.13** above); and

- either
  - (i) all supplies are made at one positive rate (i.e. all at the reduced rate or all standard-rated) — if so the Point of Sale scheme is the *only* retail scheme which can be used; or
  - (ii) supplies are made at two or more rates and the correct liability of supplies can be identified at the time of sale. This, increasingly, means an electronic point of sale system (EPOS) utilising bar-code scanners to identify the items being sold and calculate the appropriate VAT amounts. HMRC have produced detailed notes on *VAT guidance for EPOS*. See VAT Information Sheet 11/03. Alternatively, separate tills can be used for different rates.

How to calculate output tax

For each VAT period (quarterly or monthly)

Step 1	Add up daily gross takings from standard-rated supplies =	A
Step 2	Add up daily gross takings from reduced rate supplies =	B
Step 3	To calculate output tax, add the total at Step 1 multiplied by the VAT fraction for standard-rated goods to the total at Step 2 multiplied by the VAT fraction for reduced rate goods	

In algebraic form output tax is

Sales from 4.1.11 (VAT at 20% on standard rate goods and 5% on reduced rate goods)

(A × 1/6) + (B × 1/21)

Sales from 1.1.10 to 3.1.11 (VAT at 17.5% on standard rate goods and 5% on reduced rate goods)

(A × 7/47) + (B × 1/21)

Sales from 1.12.08 to 31.12.09 (VAT at 15% on standard rate goods and 5% on reduced rate goods)

(A × 3/23) + (B × 1/21)

Sales from 31.8.97 to 30.11.08 (VAT at 17.5% on standard rate goods and 5% on reduced rate goods)

(A × 7/47) + (B × 1/21)

Gross takings

See **60.8** and **60.9** above for gross takings together with adjustments and special transactions which have to be taken into account.

Records

In addition to the normal records required, a record of daily gross takings must be kept.

Annual accounting scheme

If this scheme is also used, see **63.13 SPECIAL SCHEMES.**

Change in VAT rate

See **60.7** above.

Cancellation of registration

VAT is due on business assets, including stock in hand. See **59.34** and **59.35 REGISTRATION.**

(VAT Notice 727/3/11, paras 3.2, 3.4, 4.2 which have the force of law).

Adaptations

Retailers who wish to treat minor levels of zero-rated or reduced rate sales as standard-rated may do so. The advantages of such treatment (mainly simplification of VAT records and accounting) must be compared with the disadvantage of paying VAT which is not being charged to customers. (HMRC VAT Guidance V1–23, Chapter 10 para 7.4).

> *Example*
>
> N Ltd is a garden centre selling plants and gardening equipment. It also sells gardening books and magazines and barbecue supplies. Due to the product mix, the company splits takings at the time of sale using multi-button tills. At the end of its VAT period in 2007, standard-rated takings totalled £125,639.34, zero-rated sales of books, etc. totalled £1,549.28 and reduced rate sales of barbecue fuels totalled £194.32.
>
> Output tax for the period is
>
> (£125,639.34 × 7/47) + (£194.32 × 1/21) = £18,721.49

Apportionment Scheme 1

[60.15] In order to use the scheme

- supplies must be made at two different rates of VAT;
- total VAT-exclusive retail sales must be less than £1 million per year. The limit applies to the whole business, e.g. the scheme cannot be applied to one shop if total turnover of two or more shops owned exceeds the limit; and
- any supplies of services, grown or self-made goods or supplies of catering must be dealt with outside the scheme.

How to calculate output tax

For each VAT period (whether quarterly or monthly)

Step 1	Add up daily gross takings =	A

Step 2	Add up the cost, including VAT, of all goods received for resale at the standard rate =	B
Step 3	Add up the cost, including VAT, of all goods received for resale at the reduced rate =	C
Step 4	Add up the cost, including VAT, of all goods received for resale at standard, reduced and zero rates =	D
Step 5	Calculate the proportion of daily gross takings from sales at the standard rate by dividing the total at Step 2 by the total at Step 4 and multiplying by the total in Step 1	
Step 6	Calculate the proportion of daily gross takings from sales at the reduced rate by dividing the total at Step 3 by the total at Step 4 and multiplying by the total in Step 1	
Step 7	To calculate output tax, add the total at Step 5 multiplied by the VAT fraction for standard-rated goods to the total at Step 6 multiplied by the VAT fraction for reduced rate goods	

In algebraic form output tax is

Sales from 4.1.11 (VAT at 20% on standard rate goods and 5% on reduced rate goods)

$(B \div D \times A \times 1/6) + (C \div D \times A \times 1/21)$

Sales from 1.1.10 to 3.1.11 (VAT at 17.5% on standard rate goods and 5% on reduced rate goods)

$(B \div D \times A \times 7/47) + (C \div D \times A \times 1/21)$

Sales from 1.12.08 to 31.12.09 (VAT at 15% on standard rate goods and 5% on reduced rate goods)

$(B \div D \times A \times 3/23) + (C \div D \times A \times 1/21)$

Sales from 31.8.97 to 30.11.08 (VAT at 17.5% on standard rate goods and 5% on reduced rate goods)

$(B \div D \times A \times 7/47) + (C \div D \times A \times 1/21)$

Annual adjustment

An annual adjustment has to be made to cover any under or overpayment of VAT. The adjustment must be made on

- 31 March — for retailers with three-monthly VAT periods ending on 30 June, 30 September, 31 December and 31 March and all retailers with monthly VAT periods;
- 30 April — for retailers with three-monthly VAT periods ending on 31 July, 31 October, 31 January and 30 April; and
- 31 May — for retailers with three-monthly VAT periods ending on 31 August, 30 November, 28/29 February and 31 May.

If, at the first appropriate date for the annual adjustment, the scheme has been operated for one VAT period or less, no adjustment is required until the following year. The first adjustment must include all VAT periods from first use of the scheme. For all later adjustments, only VAT periods since the previous adjustment are included. The adjustment is calculated as follows.

Step A	Calculate the VAT due by following the procedure as in Steps 1 to 7 above but using takings and cost figures for the period since the last adjustments (or, as the case may be, from the start of using the scheme) =	D
Step B	Add together the output tax already accounted for under the scheme in the year =	E

If D is less than E, too much VAT has been paid and the difference should be included in the VAT deductible side of the VAT return for the period covering the adjustment. If D is greater than E, too little VAT has been paid and the difference must be included in the VAT payable side of the VAT return for that period.

Gross takings

See **60.8** and **60.9** above for gross takings together with adjustments and special transactions which must be taken into account.

Imports and acquisitions

The cost of goods received for resale under Steps 2 to 4 above include

- any imports from outside the EU at the full price paid (including customs duty and VAT), and
- any goods acquired from another EU country at the full price paid (including excise duty and with the addition of VAT at the appropriate UK rate).

Opening stock

Goods in stock when the scheme is started are not normally treated as goods received in the period. However, if there are any stock items which are to be sold but not replenished, these may be included in the calculations unless already allowed for in a previous scheme.

Records

In addition to the normal records required, records must be kept of daily gross takings.

Annual accounting scheme

If this scheme is also used, see **63.13 SPECIAL SCHEMES**.

Ceasing to use the scheme

The annual adjustment as explained above must be carried out for the period from the last adjustment to the date of ceasing to use the scheme. This applies even if leaving the scheme before the anniversary of starting to use the scheme.

Cancellation of registration

VAT is due on business assets, including stock in hand. See **59.34** and **59.35 REGISTRATION.**

(VAT Notice 727/4/11, paras 3.3, 3.5, 3.6, 4.2, 4.3 which have the force of law).

Adaptations

HMRC may allow an adaptation to bring the annual adjustment in line with the financial year end. They will, however, consider the effect on the first such annual adjustment and authorise a period longer than twelve months where necessary to ensure any distortions are avoided. (HMRC VAT Guidance V1–23, Chapter 10 para 7.5.1).

Example

B Ltd has figures for the four quarterly periods in 2007 as follows.

	Cost of standard-rated goods for resale (incl VAT)	Cost of reduced rate goods for resale (incl VAT)	Total cost of goods for resale (incl VAT)	Gross takings
	£	£	£	£
First quarter	9,429	78	15,701	21,714.55
Second quarter	10,418	124	17,840	24,316.51
Third quarter	9,972	312	15,919	21,899.29
Fourth quarter	7,076	25	11,293	16,149.61
	£36,895	£539	£60,753	£84,079.96

First quarter

Standard-rated sales are

9,429 ÷ 15,701 × £21,714.55 = £13,040.35

Reduced rate sales are

78 ÷ 15,701 × £21,714.55 = £107.87

Output tax = (£13,040.35 × 7/47) + (£107.87 × 1/21) =	1,947.32
By similar calculations output tax in the remaining quarters is	
Second quarter	2,122.96
Third quarter	2,063.57
Fourth quarter	1,508.80
	£7,642.65

Annual adjustment

Standard-rated sales for the year are

36,895 ÷ 60,753 × £84,079.96 = £51,061.35

Reduced rate sales for the year are

539 ÷ 60,753 × £84,079.96 = £745.96

Output tax = (£51,061.35 × 7/47) + (£745.96 × 1/21) = £7,640.40

£2.25 must be included in the VAT deductible side of the VAT return.

Apportionment Scheme 2

[60.16] In order to use the scheme

- taxable turnover must be less than £130 million (if above a bespoke scheme must be used, see **60.13** above);
- supplies must be made at two different rates of VAT;
- it must be possible to calculate expected selling prices of goods in stock when the scheme is started; and
- any supplies of services or catering must be dealt with outside the scheme.

How to calculate output tax

For the first three quarterly VAT periods or the first eleven monthly VAT periods

Step 1	Calculate the expected selling price, including VAT, of standard-rated goods for retail sale in stock at the commencement of using the scheme =	A
Step 2	Calculate the expected selling price, including VAT, of reduced rate goods in stock for retail sale at the commencement of using the scheme =	B
Step 3	Calculate the expected selling price, including VAT, of *all* goods in stock for retail sale at the commencement of using the scheme =	C
Step 4	Add up daily gross takings for the VAT period =	D
Step 5	Add up expected selling prices, including VAT, of standard-rated goods (i) received, made or grown for retail sale since starting to use the scheme; and (ii) acquired from other EU countries since starting to use the scheme =	E
Step 6	Add the total in Step 5 to the total in Step 1	
Step 7	Add up expected selling prices, including VAT, of reduced rate goods (i) received, made or grown for retail sale since starting to use the scheme; and (ii) acquired from other EU countries since starting to use the scheme =	F
Step 8	Add the total in Step 7 to the total in Step 2	
Step 9	Add up expected selling prices, including VAT, of *all* goods (standard-rated, reduced rate and zero-rated) (i) received, made or grown for retail sale since starting to use the scheme; and (ii) acquired from other EU countries since starting to use the scheme =	G
Step 10	Add the total in Step 9 to the total in Step 3	
Step 11	Calculate the proportion of gross takings from sales at the standard rate by dividing the total at Step 6 by the total at Step 10 and multiplying by the total at Step 4	

Step 12	Calculate the proportion of gross takings from sales at the reduced rate by dividing the total at Step 8 by the total at Step 10 and multiplying by the total at Step 4
Step 13	To calculate output tax, add the total at Step 11 multiplied by the VAT fraction for standard-rated goods to the total at Step 12 multiplied by the VAT fraction for reduced rate goods

In algebraic form, output tax is

Sales from 4.1.11 (VAT at 10% on standard rate goods and 5% on reduced rate goods)

$$[(A + E) \div (C + G) \times D \times 1/6] + [(B + F) \div (C + G) \times D \times 1/21]$$

Sales from 1.1.10 to 3.1.11 (VAT at 17.5% on standard rate goods and 5% on reduced rate goods)

$$[(A + E) \div (C + G) \times D \times 7/47] + [(B + F) \div (C + G) \times D \times 1/21]$$

Sales from 1.12.08 to 31.12.09 (VAT at 15% on standard rate goods and 5% on reduced rate goods)

$$[(A + E) \div (C + G) \times D \times 3/23] + [(B + F) \div (C + G) \times D \times 1/21]$$

Sales from 31.8.97 to 30.11.08 (VAT at 17.5% on standard rate goods and 5% on reduced rate goods)

$$[(A + E) \div (C + G) \times D \times 7/47] + [(B + F) \div (C + G) \times D \times 1/21]$$

For the fourth and all later quarterly VAT periods or the twelfth and all later monthly VAT periods

Step A	Add up daily gross takings for the VAT period =	H
Step B	Add up expected selling prices, including VAT, of standard-rated goods (i) received, made or grown for retail sale; and (ii) acquired from other EU countries In the current VAT period and the previous three quarterly (or eleven monthly) VAT periods =	J
Step C	Add up expected selling prices, including VAT, of reduced rate goods (i) received, made or grown for retail sale; and (ii) acquired from other EU countries In the current VAT period and the previous three quarterly (or eleven monthly) VAT periods =	K
Step D	Add up expected selling prices, including VAT, of *all* goods (standard-rated, reduced rate and zero-rated) (i) received, made or grown for retail sale; and (ii) acquired from other EU countries In the current VAT period and the previous three quarterly (or eleven monthly) VAT periods =	L

Step E	Calculate the proportion of gross takings from sales at the standard rate by dividing the total at Step B by the total at Step D and multiplying by the total in Step A
Step F	Calculate the proportion of gross takings from sales at the reduced rate by dividing the total at Step C by the total at Step D and multiplying by the total at Step A
Step G	To calculate output tax, add the total at Step E multiplied by the VAT fraction for standard-rated goods to the total at Step F multiplied by the VAT fraction for reduced rate goods

In algebraic form output tax is

Sales from 4.1.11 (VAT at 20% on standard rate goods and 5% on reduced rate goods)

$(J \div L \times H \times 1/6) + (K \div L \times H \times 1/21)$

Sales from 1.1.10 to 3.1.11 (VAT at 17.5% on standard rate goods and 5% on reduced rate goods)

$(J \div L \times H \times 7/47) + (K \div L \times H \times 1/21)$

Sales from 1.12.08 to 31.12.09 (VAT at 15% on standard rate goods and 5% on reduced rate goods)

$(J \div L \times H \times 3/23) + (K \div L \times H \times 1/21)$

Sales from 31.8.97 to 30.11.08 (VAT at 17.5% on standard rate goods and 5% on reduced rate goods)

$(J \div L \times H \times 7/47) + (K \div L \times H \times 1/21)$

Opening stock

If it is not possible to perform a physical stocktake on the date of starting to use the scheme, the ESP values of goods received for resale in the previous three months may be used.

Gross takings

See **60.8** and **60.9** above for gross takings together with adjustments and special transactions which must be taken into account.

Expected selling prices

See **60.10** to **60.12** above for calculation of expected selling prices.

Records

In addition to the normal records required, records must be kept of daily gross takings and expected selling prices.

Annual accounting scheme

If this scheme is also used, see **63.13 SPECIAL SCHEMES.**

Ceasing to use the scheme

No adjustment is normally necessary unless ceasing to use the scheme in part only of the business. In such a case, the rolling calculation for that part still using the scheme must not include stock and expected selling prices of the part no longer using the scheme.

Cancellation of registration

VAT is due on business assets, including stock in hand. See **59.34** and **59.35** **REGISTRATION**.

(VAT Notice 727/4/11, paras 3.3, 3.5, 3.6, 5.2, 5.4 which have the force of law).

Adaptations

(1) *Opening stock*. If it is not possible to perform a physical stocktake on the date of starting to use the scheme, the expected selling price values of goods received for resale in the previous three months may be used. Alternatively, where even this is impossible or impractical, HMRC may also approve

- updating the most recent stocktake to take account of goods received for retail sale and supplied since the stocktaking took place;
- allowing a stocktaking to be carried out during the first period of use of the scheme and adjusting this to take account of goods received for retail sale and supplied from the start of using the scheme to the date of the stocktaking; or
- use of stock records produced by management accounts where these are used consistently and considered by the retailer to be of such accuracy that they are relied upon for commercial stock management and statutory accounts.

(2) *Using periodic stock adjustments rather than a rolling calculation.* HMRC may accept an adaptation using quarterly stock adjustments. They may also accept an adaptation using an annual stock adjustment in which case HMRC will also consider bringing the annual adjustment in line with the financial year end.

(3) *Adjusting historical purchase data to reflect changes in the mix of goods.* Where a retailer's mix of goods to be sold under the scheme has changed from the first period under the rolling calculation, HMRC may approve an adaptation under which

- where VAT on supplies made by a particular department or for a specific class of goods is no longer to be accounted for under this rolling calculation scheme (e.g. because a different scheme is to be used), the historic purchase/expected selling price data is excluded from the calculation; and
- similarly when new departments/classes of goods are brought into the scheme, the historic purchase/expected selling price data is also included in the rolling calculation.

(HMRC VAT Guidance V1–23, Chapter 10 para 7.5.2).

Example

Z Ltd owns a store and can analyse all purchases of stock for resale. In 2007 it decides to use Apportionment Scheme 2 and calculates that the expected selling price, including VAT, of stock for retail sale at the commencement of using the scheme is £818,703, of which £331,379 represents standard-rated lines. Trading figures for the first four quarters under the scheme are

	ESP of standard-rated goods received for resale (incl VAT)	Total ESP of goods received for resale (incl VAT)	Gross takings
	£	£	£
First quarter	393,741	1,009,199	835,265
Second quarter	400,829	891,685	829,524
Third quarter	314,227	905,859	1,018,784
Fourth quarter	493,207	1,235,087	1,486,381

Output tax is calculated as follows

First quarter		
Opening stock	331,379	818,703
First quarter	393,741	1,009,199
	£725,120	£1,827,902

Standard-rated sales = 725,120 ÷ 1,827,902 × £835,265 = £331,345

Output tax = £331,345 × 7/47 £49,349.25

Second quarter		
Opening stock	331,379	818,703
First quarter	393,741	1,009,199
Second quarter	400,829	891,685
	£1,125,949	£2,719,587

Standard-rated sales = 1,125,949 ÷ 2,719,587 × £829,524 = £343,435

Output tax = £343,435 × 7/47 = £51,149.89

Third quarter		
Opening stock	331,379	818,703
First quarter	393,741	1,009,199
Second quarter	400,829	891,685
Third quarter	314,227	905,859
	£1,440,176	£3,625,446

Standard-rated sales = 1,440,176 ÷ 3,625,446 × £1,018,784 = £404,702

Output tax = £404,702 × 7/47 £60,274.76

Fourth quarter		
First quarter	393,741	1,009,199
Second quarter	400,829	891,685
Third quarter	314,227	905,859
Fourth quarter	493,207	1,235,087
	£1,602,004	£4,041,830

Standard-rated sales = 1,602,004 ÷ 4,041,830 × £1,486,381 = £589,136

Output tax = £589,136 × 7/47 = £87,743.66

Direct calculation scheme 1

[60.17] In order to use the scheme

- total VAT-exclusive retail sales must be less than £1 million per year. The limit applies to the whole business, e.g. the scheme cannot be applied to one shop if total turnover of two or more shops owned exceeds the limit;
- any supplies of services with the same VAT liability as the minority goods must be dealt with outside the scheme; and
- any supplies of catering must be dealt with outside the scheme.

The scheme works by calculating expected selling prices (ESPs) of goods for retail sale. ESPs are normally only calculated for minority goods, i.e. those goods at the rate of VAT which

- where goods are supplied at two rates of VAT, forms the smallest proportion of retail supplies; or
- where goods are supplied at three rates of VAT, forms the two smaller proportions of retail supplies.

See, however, under the heading *Adaptations* below.

How to calculate output tax

For each VAT period (quarterly or monthly)

Where the minority goods are zero-rated and/or reduced rate goods (ie main goods are standard-rated).

Step 1	Add up daily gross takings =	A
Step 2	Add up ESPs of zero-rated goods received, made or grown for retail sale =	B
Step 3	Add up ESPs of reduced rate goods received, made or grown for retail sale =	C

Step 4	Calculate the standard-rated element of takings by deducting the totals at Step 2 and Step 3 from the total at Step 1
Step 5	To calculate output tax, add the total in Step 4 multiplied by the VAT fraction for standard-rated goods to the total in Step 3 multiplied by the VAT fraction for reduced rate goods

In algebraic form, output tax is

Sales from 4.1.11 (VAT at 20% on standard rate goods and 5% on reduced rate goods)

((A – B – C) × 1/6) + (C × 1/21)

Sales from 1.1.10 to 3.1.11 (VAT at 17.5% on standard rate goods and 5% on reduced rate goods)

((A – B – C) × 7/47) + (C × 1/21)

Sales from 1.12.08 to 31.12.09 (VAT at 15% on standard rate goods and 5% on reduced rate goods)

((A – B – C) × 3/23) + (C × 1/21)

Sales from 31.8.97 to 30.11.08 (VAT at 17.5% on standard rate goods and 5% on reduced rate goods)

((A – B – C) × 7/47) + (C × 1/21)

Where the minority goods are standard-rated and/or reduced rate goods (i.e. main goods are zero-rated).

Step 1	Add up daily gross takings. (Although this figure is not used in the calculation, it is still a requirement of operating the scheme and is also used in completing the VAT return.)	
Step 2	Add up ESPs of standard-rated goods received, made or grown for retail sale =	D
Step 3	Add up ESPs of reduced rate goods received, made or grown for retail sale =	E
Step 4	To calculate output tax, add the total in Step 2 multiplied by the VAT fraction for standard-rated goods to the total in Step 3 multiplied by the VAT fraction for reduced rate goods	

In algebraic form, output tax is

Sales from 4.1.11 (VAT at 20% on standard rate goods and 5% on reduced rate goods)

(D × 1/6) + (E × 1/21)

Sales from 1.1.10 to 3.1.11 (VAT at 17.5% on standard rate goods and 5% on reduced rate goods)

(D × 7/47) + (E × 1/21)

Sales from 1.12.08 to 31.12.09 (VAT at 15% on standard rate goods and 5% on reduced rate goods)

(D × 3/23) + (E × 1/21)

Sales from 31.8.97 to 30.11.08 (VAT at 17.5% on standard rate goods and 5% on reduced rate goods)

(D × 7/47) + (E × 1/21)

Gross takings

See **60.8** and **60.9** above for gross takings together with adjustments and special transactions which must be taken into account.

Expected selling prices

See **60.10** to **60.12** above for calculation of expected selling prices.

Opening stock

Goods in stock when the scheme is started are not normally treated as goods received in the period. However, if there are any stock items which are to be sold but not replenished, these may be included in the calculations unless already allowed for in a previous scheme.

Records

In addition to the normal records required, records must be kept of daily gross takings and expected selling prices.

Annual accounting scheme

If this scheme is also used, see **63.13 SPECIAL SCHEMES.**

Cancellation of registration

VAT is due on business assets, including stock in hand. See **59.34** and **59.35 REGISTRATION.**

(VAT Notice 727/5/11, paras 3.1, 3.6, 3.7, 4.2, 4.4 which have the force of law).

Adaptations

If marking up the 'majority' rather than the 'minority' goods would be more straightforward, retailers may do so. For example, newsagents may find it easier to set estimated selling prices for their majority sales of newspapers and magazines as there are likely to be fewer purchase records than for minority standard-rated sales of tobacco, confectionery, etc. (HMRC VAT Guidance V1–23, Chapter 10 para 7.6.3).

> *Example*
>
> K runs a typical corner shop selling newspapers and magazines (zero-rated), confectionery and tobacco (standard-rated), a limited range of food items (zero-rated) and barbecue fuels (reduced rate goods). At the end of a VAT period

in 2007, gross takings are £18,714.55. The expected selling prices of purchases in the period are £11,236.19 for standard-rated goods, £8,154.27 for zero-rated goods and £157.93 for reduced rate goods.

The minority goods are zero-rated and reduced rate goods. Output tax is calculated as follows.

	£	£
Gross takings		18,714.55
Expected selling prices of zero-rated goods	8,154.27	
Expected selling prices of reduced rate goods	157.93	
		8,312.20
Standard-rated element of takings		£10,402.35
Output tax = (£10,402.35 × 7/47) + (£157.93 × 1/21) =		£1,556.81

Direct calculation scheme 2

[60.18] In order to use the scheme

- taxable turnover must be less than £130 million (if above a bespoke scheme must be used, see **60.13** above);
- it must be possible to calculate expected selling prices of minority goods in stock when the scheme is started and annually thereafter;
- any supplies of services with the same VAT liability as the minority goods must be dealt with outside the scheme; and
- any supplies of catering must be dealt with outside the scheme.

The scheme works by calculating expected selling prices (ESPs) of goods for retail sale. ESPs are only calculated for '*minority goods*', i.e. those goods at the rate of VAT which

- where goods are supplied at two rates of VAT, forms the smallest proportion of retail supplies; or
- where goods are supplied at three rates of VAT, forms the two smaller proportions of retail supplies.

How to calculate output tax

For each VAT period, the same rules apply as for Direct Calculation Scheme 1, see **60.17** above.

Annual adjustment

This scheme is based on retail trade over a full year which runs from the beginning of the first VAT period in which the scheme was used. An annual adjustment is required after making the output tax calculation for the fourth quarter (twelfth month) and any difference is accounted for on the return for that period. The adjustment must take into account any disposals since the last adjustment which were not by way of retail sale. This is done by excluding, from the figures used in the calculation, the value of any goods which were previously part of the scheme calculation (or included in the opening stock figure) but have not been sold by way of retail sale. The adjustment is also required if part of the business leaves the scheme.

Where the minority goods are zero-rated and/or reduced rate goods (i.e. main goods are standard-rated)

Step 1	Add up daily gross takings for the year =	A
Step 2	For zero-rated goods for retail sale calculate: ESPs of such goods in stock at the beginning of the year *Plus* ESPs of such goods received, made or grown for retail in the year *Less* ESPs of such goods in stock at the end of the year =	B
Step 3	For reduced rate goods for retail sale calculate: ESPs of such goods in stock at the beginning of the year *Plus* ESPs of such goods received, made or grown for retail in the year *Less* ESPs of such goods in stock at the end of the year =	C
Step 4	Calculate the standard-rated element of takings for the year by deducting the totals at Step 2 and Step 3 from the total at Step 1	
Step 5	To calculate output tax, add the total in Step 4 multiplied by the VAT fraction for standard-rated goods to the total in Step 3 multiplied by the VAT fraction for reduced rate goods	

In algebraic form, output tax is

Sales from 4.1.11 (VAT at 20% on standard rate goods and 5% on reduced rate goods)

((A – B – C) × 1/6) + (C × 1/21)

Sales from 1.1.10 to 3.1.11 (VAT at 17.5% on standard rate goods and 5% on reduced rate goods)

((A – B – C) × 7/47) + (C × 1/21)

Sales from 1.12.08 to 31.12.09 (VAT at 15% on standard rate goods and 5% on reduced rate goods)

((A – B – C) × 3/23) + (C × 1/21)

Sales from 31.8.97 to 30.11.08 (VAT at 17.5% on standard rate goods and 5% on reduced rate goods)

((A – B – C) × 7/47) + (C × 1/21)

This gives the correct total for output tax due for the year. If the total is less than that calculated under the scheme in the four quarters (twelve months), the difference should be included in the VAT deductible side of the VAT account for the fourth quarter (twelfth month). Similarly, if the total is more, the difference should be included in the VAT payable side of the VAT account for that period.

Where the minority goods are standard-rated and/or reduced rate goods (i.e. main goods are zero-rated)

Step 1	For standard-rated goods for retail sale calculate: ESPs of such goods in stock at the beginning of the year *plus* ESPs of such goods received, made or grown for retail in the year *less* ESPs of such goods in stock at the end of the year =	D
Step 2	For reduced rate goods for retail sale calculate: ESPs of such goods in stock at the beginning of the year *plus* ESPs of such goods received, made or grown for retail in the year *less* ESPs of such goods in stock at the end of the year =	E
Step 3	To calculate output tax, add the total at Step 1 multiplied by the VAT fraction for standard-rated goods to the total at Step 2 multiplied by the VAT fraction for reduced rate goods	

In algebraic form, output tax is

Sales after 4.1.11 (VAT at 20% on standard rate goods and 5% on reduced rate goods)

(D × 1/6) + (E × 1/21)

Sales from 1.1.10 to 3.1.11 (VAT at 17.5% on standard rate goods and 5% on reduced rate goods)

(D × 7/47) + (E × 1/21)

Sales from 1.12.08 to 31.12.09 (VAT at 15% on standard rate goods and 5% on reduced rate goods)

(D × 3/23) + (E × 1/21)

Sales from 31.8.97 to 30.11.08 (VAT at 17.5% on standard rate goods and 5% on reduced rate goods)

(D × 7/47) + (E × 1/21)

This gives the correct total for output tax due for the year. If the total is less than that calculated under the scheme in the four quarters (twelve months), the difference should be included in the VAT deductible side of the VAT account for the fourth quarter (twelfth month). Similarly, if the total is more, the difference should be included in the VAT payable side of the VAT account for that period.

Gross takings

See **60.8** and **60.9** above for gross takings together with adjustments and special transactions which must be taken into account.

Expected selling prices

See **60.10** to **60.12** above for calculation of expected selling prices.

Opening stock

Goods in stock when the scheme is started are not normally treated as goods received in the period. However, if there are any stock items which are to be sold but not replenished, these may be included in the calculations unless already allowed for in a previous scheme.

Records

In addition to the normal records required, records must be kept of daily gross takings and expected selling prices.

Annual accounting scheme

If this scheme is also used, see **63.13 SPECIAL SCHEMES**.

Ceasing to use the scheme

The annual adjustment as explained above must be carried out for the period from the last adjustment to the date of ceasing to use the scheme. This applies even if leaving the scheme before the anniversary of starting to use the scheme. An adjustment must also be made if part of the business ceases to use the scheme.

Cancellation of registration

VAT is due on business assets, including stock in hand. See **59.34** and **59.35 REGISTRATION**.

(VAT Notice 727/5/11, paras 3.1, 3.4, 3.6, 3.7, 4.2, 4.4, 4.5 which have the force of law).

Adaptations

(1) *Using expected selling prices of non-minority goods*. An adaptation which uses estimated selling prices for goods which do *not* form the minority sales will be considered where it is not only simpler for the retailer but also easier for HMRC to audit (e.g. a newsagent whose major portion of sales is newspapers and magazines).

(2) *Valuing stock*. If a physical stocktake at the start of the scheme year is impossible or impractical, HMRC may also approve
- updating the most recent stocktake to take account of goods received for retail sale and supplied since the stocktaking took place;

- allowing a stocktaking to be carried out during the first period of use of the scheme and adjusting this to take account of goods received for retail sale and supplied from the start of using the scheme to the date of the stocktaking; or
- use of stock records produced by management accounts where these are used consistently and considered by the retailer to be of such accuracy that they are relied upon for commercial stock management and statutory accounts.

(3) *Annual adjustment*. HMRC may allow an adaptation to bring the annual adjustment in line with the financial year end. They will, however, consider the effect on the first such annual adjustment and authorise a period longer than twelve months where necessary to ensure any distortions are avoided.

(HMRC VAT Guidance V1–23, Chapter 10 paras 7.6.2, 7.6.3).

Example

In 2007 K decides to use Direct Calculation Scheme 2. When he starts to use the scheme, his opening stock, valued at expected selling prices, is

	£
Standard-rated goods	3,145.91
Zero-rated goods	2,250.34
Reduced rate goods	142.51

For the first four quarters, his relevant details are

	ESP of standard-rated goods purchased	ESP of zero-rated goods purchased	ESP of reduced rate goods purchased	Gross takings
	£	£	£	£
First quarter	11,236.19	8,154.27	157.93	18,714.55
Second quarter	9,075.02	11,667.67	259.32	20,726.40
Third quarter	9,872.90	10,124.75	137.54	20,855.88
Fourth quarter	11,431.39	11,008.62	21.43	22,649.04
	£41,615.50	£40,955.31	£576.22	£82,945.87

At the end of the fourth quarter, his closing stock, valued at expected selling prices, is

	£
Standard-rated goods	4,217.22
Zero-rated goods	3,151.44
Reduced rate goods	119.19

First quarter

The minority goods are zero-rated and reduced rate goods. Output tax is calculated as follows.

	£	£
Gross takings		18,714.55
ESP of zero-rated goods	8,154.27	
ESP of reduced rate goods	157.93	
		8,312.20
Standard-rated element of takings		£10,402.35
Output tax = (£10,402.35 × 7/47) + (£157.93 × 1/21) =		£1,556.81

Second quarter

The minority goods are standard-rated and reduced rate goods. Output tax is calculated as follows.

(£9,075.02 × 7/47) + (£259.32 × 1/21) =	£1,363.95

Third quarter

The minority goods are standard-rated and reduced rate goods. Output tax is calculated as follows.

(£9,872.90 × 7/47) + (£137.54 × 1/21) =	£1,476.98

Fourth quarter

The minority goods are zero-rated and reduced rate goods. Output tax is calculated as follows.

	£	£
Gross takings		22,649.04
ESP of zero-rated goods	11,008.62	
ESP of reduced rate goods	21.43	
		11,030.05
Standard-rated element of takings		£11,618.99
Output tax = (£11,618.99 × 7/47) + (£21.43 × 1/21) =		£1,731.51

The annual adjustment is as follows

The minority goods are zero-rated and reduced rate goods. Output tax is calculated as follows

	£	£
Gross takings		82,945.87
Less zero-rated goods		
opening stock:	2,250.34	
ESP of goods purchased	40,955.31	
	43,205.65	
closing stock	3,151.44	
		40,054.21
		42,891.66
Less reduced rate goods		
opening stock:	142.51	
ESP of goods purchased	576.22	
	718.73	
closing stock	119.19	
		599.54
Standard-rated element of takings		£42,292.12
Output tax = (£42,292.12 × 7/47) + (£599.54 × 1/21) =		6,327.38
Output tax already calculated		
£1,556.81 + £1,363.95 + £1,476.98 + £1,731.51		6,129.25
Additional VAT payable with return for fourth quarter		£198.13

Retail chemists

[60.19] Many of the goods that a retail chemist buys at the standard rate may subsequently be either sold over the counter (at the standard rate) or dispensed on prescription (normally at the zero rate but at the standard rate where dispensed for a patient being cared for in a nursing home or hospital, see **28.13 HEALTH AND WELFARE**). There is thus no direct relationship between the proportions of goods bought and sold at the different rates of VAT.

HMRC give the following guidance on how the standard schemes need to be adjusted to take account of this fact.

Point of Sale scheme

Under this scheme the correct rate of VAT is identified at the time of supply and no adjustment is therefore necessary. (VAT Notice 727, para 9.3).

Apportionment Scheme 1 and Direct Calculation Schemes 1 and 2

The following adjustments are required at the end of each VAT period.

Step 1	Calculate output tax under the normal scheme rules — daily gross takings to include the total amount from prescription charges and NHS cheque (less the value of any exempt supplies such as rota payments) =	A
Step 2	Add up payments *received* in the period for all *Group 12* goods, even if not supplied in the period. (Any exempt or standard-rated supplies in the NHS cheque must be excluded.) =	B
Step 3	Estimate the value of goods included in Step 2 that were zero-rated on receipt. (This must be based on a sample of actual purchases for a representative period, taking account of seasonal fluctuations, etc. A new estimation must be made each VAT period.) =	C
Step 4	Subtract the total at Step 3 from the total at Step 2	
Step 5	Work out the VAT included in Step 1 from *Group 12* goods by multiplying the total at Step 4 by the VAT fraction	
Step 6	Calculate output tax by deducting the total at Step 5 from the total at Step 1	

In algebraic form, output tax is

A – ((B – C) × 7/47*)

(*1/6 from 4 January 2011; 3/23 from 1 December 2008 to 31 December 2009)

Where a Direct Calculation scheme is used, a retail chemist must normally calculate expected selling prices for minority goods (see **60.17** and **60.18** above). If the minority goods are standard-rated when sold but the minority of purchases are zero-rated, the chemist may calculate expected selling prices on the basis of the zero-rated goods received for resale.

Apportionment Scheme 2

The retail chemist adjustment cannot be made with this scheme.

(VAT Notice 727, paras 9.4, 9.5 which have the force of law).

By concession, where

- goods supplied are dispensed to an individual for his/her personal use whilst an inpatient or resident, or whilst attending, a hospital or nursing home,
- the goods are ordered and dispensed in accordance with NHS regulations, and
- the person dispensing the goods is paid for doing so by the Prescription Pricing Authority, the Prescription Information and Pricing Services Division of the Welsh Health Common Services Authority, the Pharmacy Practice Division of the Common Services Agency, or the Central Services Agency,

for the purposes of the retail scheme calculations, the supply may be treated as if it were a zero-rated supply. (VAT Notice 48, ESC 3.30).

Retail florists

[60.20] The following provisions apply to florists and other retailers who are members of organisations such as Interflora, Teleflorist and Flowergram which facilitate the purchase and delivery of flowers. The provisions have the force of law under *SI 1995/2518, Reg 67*.

The adjustments to be made depend upon the retail scheme used and whether the florist is the '*sending member*' (i.e. the member receiving payment direct from the customer) or the '*executing member*' (i.e. the member delivering the flowers and receiving payment from the organisation).

The documentation received from the agency may show output tax payable to HMRC. This is 'self-billed' output tax as the agency issues the invoice for supplies made by the florist. The florist should check the agency documentation and, if correct, add the self-billed output tax to any VAT calculated in accordance with its own retail scheme.

Point of Sale scheme

- *Sending member*. No adjustment is required by a sending member. Payments received should be included in daily gross takings at the time of the order.
- *Executing member*. Do not include payments received from the agency in daily gross takings and account for any VAT due outside the retail scheme.

Apportionment schemes

- *Sending member*. Identify from agency documentation the value of supplies made as a sending member and account for any VAT due outside the retail scheme. Do not include payments for those supplies in daily gross takings under the retail scheme calculations.
- *Executing member*. Do not include payments received from the agency in daily gross takings and account for any VAT due outside the retail scheme on the basis of agency documentation.

  If Apportionment Scheme 1 is used, exclude the value of flowers sent as an executing member from purchase records.

  If Apportionment Scheme 2 is used, adjust expected selling prices for the value of flowers sent as an executing member and accounted for outside the retail scheme.

Direct calculation schemes

- *Sending member*. Identify from agency documentation the value of supplies made as a sending member and account for any VAT due outside the retail scheme. Do not include payments for those supplies in daily gross takings under the retail scheme calculations.

- *Executing member*. Do not include payments received from the agency in daily gross takings and account for any VAT due outside the retail scheme on the basis of agency documentation. Adjust expected selling prices for the value of flowers sent as an executing member and accounted for outside the retail scheme.

(VAT Notice 727, paras 10.1–10.4).

Special arrangements for other retailers

[60.21] See HMRC VAT Guidance V1–23, Chapter 10 for special arrangements for other professions and trades, including

- caterers (para 9.1) (see also **11.7 CATERING**);
- concessions/shops within shops (para 9.3);
- hampers, e.g. Christmas clubs (para 9.6);
- petrol stations (para 9.8);
- sub-post offices (para 9.9);
- Women's Royal Voluntary Service (WRVS) hospital units (para 9.11); and
- mail order businesses (para 10.1).

Key points

[60.22] Points to consider are as follows.

- A retailer with annual VAT-exclusive turnover exceeding £130m must agree a bespoke retail scheme with HMRC. Other retailers can use one of five different schemes allowed by HMRC, assuming they meet the conditions of the scheme in question.
- A business may need to justify to HMRC why it cannot adopt a Point of Sale retail scheme by, for example, using a multi-buttoned till. The Point of Sale scheme should give the most reliable output tax calculation because the VAT liability is based on actual sales made by the business.
- An annual adjustment is needed with Apportionment Scheme 1 and Direct Calculation Scheme 2. The annual adjustment plays an important part in eliminating the unfair results sometimes produced by quarterly calculations.
- Each retail scheme has potential benefits as well as potential problems for users. For example, a Point of Sale method using a multi-button till will only be accurate if the staff operating the till know how to determine the VAT position for each sale. Proper staff training is an important issue.
- Apportionment Scheme 1 avoids the need to identify the VAT liability at the point of sale. However, it is only available to a business with annual VAT exclusive sales of less than £1m.

- Apportionment scheme 1 can produce a higher than usual VAT bill for a business that has a higher mark-up on zero-rated goods. A business where the zero-rated mark-up is considerably higher than on standard-rated goods should consider using an alternative scheme.
- Apportionment Scheme 2 calculates output tax using expected selling prices – so will deal with the problem mentioned above with Apportionment Scheme 1, i.e. where there is a higher mark-up made by the business on its zero-rated goods.
- Direct Calculation Scheme 2 could benefit a business that has slow moving stock of minority standard-rated items. This is because the scheme makes an annual adjustment for stock so that output tax is not actually paid until the goods are sold. Direct Calculation Scheme 1 produces an output tax liability in the period that the goods are purchased.
- It is important to remember that most retail schemes need to exclude the value of services provided by a business – or non-retail sales. These supplies should be accounted for outside of the scheme.
- Remember that some smaller retailers could benefit from using the flat-rate scheme if their annual taxable sales are less than £150,000 excluding VAT. The scheme produces winners and losers in terms of VAT payments.
- A retailer must use his chosen scheme for at least a year before he can make a change to another scheme. An exception is if he ceases to use the scheme because he wants to adopt the flat-rate scheme instead.
- In cases where an additional charge is made by a retailer to customers who make payment by credit card (compared to cash or cheque), the additional fee relates to a further payment for the goods or services in question and is not a 'finance charge' that is exempt from VAT.
- A retail business should retain records and evidence (if possible) of any goods that have not been sold (e.g. stolen goods, damaged goods, obsolete stock). This could be important to justify a lower than expected mark-up to HMRC in the event of a VAT visit.
- It is also necessary to take into account the value of goods that have been purchased but not sold if a retail scheme is used that is based on ESPs (expected selling prices).
- If a retail business deregisters, it is important to remember that output tax is due on any closing stock (standard-rated or reduced rated items, not zero-rated items) or assets held at the time of deregistration. There is a *de minimis* figure i.e. no output tax is due on the final return submitted by the business if the total VAT payment involved is less than £1,000.

61

Second-Hand Goods

Cross-references. See **7.9 BAD DEBT RELIEF; 23.16**(8) **FINANCIAL SERVICES** for sales by pawnbrokers; **33.24 IMPORTS** for the sale of temporarily imported second-hand goods by auction; **36.17 INSURANCE** for insurance supplied in a package with second-hand goods; **55.20 RATES OF VAT** for the effect of a change in the rate of VAT between payment and removal of goods.

De Voil Indirect Tax Service. See V3.531–538.

Introduction

[61.1] In general, VAT is charged on the full value of any goods, including second-hand goods, sold by a business. The Treasury may, however, by statutory instrument, provide for a business to opt to charge VAT on the profit margin (instead of their value) on supplies of

- works of art, antiques or collectors' items;
- motor vehicles;
- second-hand goods; and
- goods through a person who acts as an agent, but in his own name, in relation to the supply.

The purpose of this is to avoid double taxation on goods which have previously borne VAT when sold as new. [*VATA 1994, s 50A; FA 1995, s 24*].

The Margin Scheme covers virtually all second-hand goods. See **61.2** to **61.38** below for details. A similar scheme is available throughout the EU and goods sold under the scheme anywhere in the EU are taxable in the country of origin rather than that of destination. They are not therefore subject to the normal distance selling rules and are not subject to acquisition VAT when taken into another EU country.

There is also a Global Accounting Scheme in the UK because of the low value, bulk volume goods some dealers handle and the impracticality of keeping detailed records of purchases and sales. Under the scheme, VAT is accounted for on the difference between the total purchases and sales of eligible goods in each VAT period rather than on an item by item basis. See **61.39** to **61.52** below for full details.

The margin scheme

[61.2] VAT is normally due on the full value of goods sold. The margin scheme allows a VAT-registered person who meets all the conditions in **61.4** below to calculate VAT on the 'profit margin' i.e. the difference (or margin) between the price at which the goods were obtained and their selling price. If no profit is made (because the purchase price exceeds the selling price) then no VAT is payable. [*VATA 1994, s 50A(4); FA 1995, s 24*]. The seller's margin is not revealed to the buyer.

The scheme is not compulsory and goods eligible for the scheme can still be sold outside the scheme in the normal way, even if bought under the scheme. In that case, there is no input tax to deduct on the purchase and VAT must be charged on the full selling price. Similarly, if an eligible item is sold but all the conditions of the scheme cannot be met (e.g. record-keeping, invoicing and accounting requirements) the margin scheme cannot be used and the sale must be dealt with outside the scheme in the normal way, accounting for VAT on the full selling price.

Although VAT is charged on the profit margin only, taxable turnover for registration purposes includes the total VAT-exclusive value of any goods sold under the scheme.

(VAT Notice 718, paras 2.1, 2.5, 2.10).

Disallowance of input tax

Any input tax charged on the supply to, or acquisition or importation by, a business of eligible goods is excluded from credit where

(a) VAT on the supply was chargeable on the profit margin under the UK margin scheme or corresponding provision of the law of another EU country;
(b) in the case of a motor car, VAT was charged on the margin on a supply before 1 March 2000 because of an earlier input tax restriction; or
(c) the goods are
  (i) a work of art, antique or collectors' item within **61.3**(*b*)–(*d*) below and the business imported the goods itself, or
  (ii) a work of art within **61.3**(*b*) below and were supplied to the business by, or acquired from another EU country by the business from, its creator or his successor in title

  and the business has opted to account for VAT chargeable on its supplies of such goods on the profit margin and not elected to account for VAT by reference to value.

[*SI 1992/3222, Art 4; SI 1995/1267; SI 1995/1666; SI 1999/2930; SI 1999/3118*].

> *Example*
>
> Jim's Motors purchases a second-hand car from a member of the public for £2,000. An amount of £500 plus VAT is paid to a local repair firm to re-spray the car, and then £100 plus VAT is paid to a valet company to clean the interior. The car is then sold to another member of the public for £3,000.
>
> Jim's Motors must keep proper records concerning the buying and selling of this vehicle, to meet the conditions of the margin scheme (see below).
>
> The input tax on the repair/valeting charges can be reclaimed in the normal way.
>
> The margin made on the sale is £1,000 (i.e. £3,000 less £2,000) and this margin is treated as VAT inclusive. An output tax liability of £148.93 must be declared on the relevant return, i.e. £1,000 × 7/47 (assuming a VAT rate of 17.5%).

Eligible goods

[61.3] The following goods are eligible for the margin scheme.

(a) **Second-hand goods** i.e. tangible movable property that is suitable for further use (as it is or after repair) other than
   (i) the items within (*b*)–(*d*) below;
   (ii) precious metals (which includes any goods containing precious metals where the consideration for the supply (excluding VAT) does not exceed the open market value of the metal contained in the goods); and
   (iii) precious stones of any age which are not mounted, set or strung. For this purpose, precious stones are diamonds, rubies, sapphires and emeralds.

(b) **Works of art** falling within the definition in *VATA 1994, s 21* (see **73.3**(*a*) **WORKS OF ART, ETC.**).

(c) **Collectors' items**, i.e. any collection or collector's piece falling within the definition in *VATA 1994, s 25(5)* (see **73.3**(*c*) **WORKS OF ART, ETC.**) but, with effect from 1 January 2000, excluding investment gold coins, i.e.
   - any gold coin minted after 1800 with a purity value of 900 thousandths or more which is, or has been, legal tender in its country of origin and which is of a type normally sold at a price which does not exceed 180% of the open market value of the gold contained in the coin; and
   - any other gold coin specified in VAT Notice 701/21A/11, Section 3.

   Where gold coins falling within the definition of investment gold coins have been mistakenly included as purchases in the margin scheme records, the records should be adjusted and the entry closed and noted accordingly. (VAT Notice 701/21A/11, para 2.6).

(d) **Antiques** i.e. objects not falling within (*b*) or (*c*) above which are more than 100 years old.

[*SI 1992/3222, Art 2; SI 1995/1268, Art 2; SI 1999/3118; SI 1999/3120; SI 2001/3649, Art 500*].

Conditions of the scheme

[61.4] A business may opt to use the margin scheme and account for VAT on the profit margin on any eligible goods within **61.3** above provided the following conditions are met.

(a) It took possession of the goods by any of the following means.
   (i) On a supply on which no VAT was chargeable. This includes purchases from private individuals and unregistered businesses but also includes a zero-rated supply (*Peugeot Motor Co plc* (VTD 15314) (TVC 44.68)).
   (ii) On a supply on which VAT was chargeable on the profit margin under the UK margin scheme or under the corresponding provisions in the Isle of Man or another EU country.
   (iii) Under a transaction treated as neither a supply of goods nor a supply of services (other than a transaction within (iv) below).
   (iv) Under a transaction treated as neither a supply of goods nor a supply of services where the transaction in question was

(1) the transfer of assets of a business as a going concern (see **8.10 BUSINESS**), or

(2) on or after 1 July 2002, the assignment of the rights in hire purchase or conditional sales agreements to a bank or other financial institution

and the business has a 'relevant predecessor'. For this purpose, a '*relevant predecessor*' is the person from whom the business took possession of the motor car or goods and who himself took possession of the motor car or goods in circumstances that qualified for use of the margin scheme (otherwise than under (1) or (2) above). Where the motor car or goods have been the subject of a succession of two or more transactions within (1) or (2) above (or both), culminating in the transaction in question, the relevant predecessor is the first person in the chain who took possession of the motor car or goods in circumstances that qualified for use of the margin scheme.

(v) If the goods are a work of art, on a supply, or acquisition from another EU country, from the creator or his successor in title (whether or not the purchase invoice shows VAT separately). See **61.38** below.

(vi) If the goods are a work of art, collectors' item or antique, by importing the goods himself. *With effect from 1 September 2006*, this includes, if the taxable person is an auctioneer, the auctioneer having placed them under customs procedures for temporary importation with total relief from import duties. See **61.38** below.

(vii) If the goods are a motor car, on a supply received before 1 March 2000 on which VAT was charged on the margin because of an earlier input tax restriction.

Any item which was purchased on a VAT invoice on which input tax is recoverable is not eligible to be sold under the scheme.

(b) The supply by the business is not a letting on hire.

(c) The goods are not sold by the business on a VAT invoice or similar document showing an amount as being VAT or as being attributable to VAT.

(d) If the supply is of an airgun, the business is registered for the purposes of the *Firearms Act 1968*.

(e) If the supply by the business is the sale of repossessed assets within **23.15 FINANCIAL SERVICES** but the supply does not satisfy the conditions for treatment as outside the scope of VAT as there stated.

(f) If the supply by the business is a motor car which the business produced itself, the car must have previously been supplied by the business in the course or furtherance of its business or treated as self-supplied under **45.6 MOTOR CARS.**

(g) The business keeps such records and accounts as HMRC specify.

[*SI 1992/3122, Art 8(1)–(3)(8)(9); SI 1995/1268, Art 12(1)–(4)(8)(10)(11); SI 1995/1269; SI 1997/1615; SI 1997/1616; SI 1999/2832; SI 2002/1502; SI 2002/1503; SI 2006/2187*].

Reclaiming VAT on expenses

[61.5] Subject to the normal rules, a taxable person may reclaim VAT charged on business overheads, repairs, parts and accessories, etc. but must not add these costs to the purchase price of the goods sold under the scheme.

> *Example*
>
> Sue is an antique dealer and registered for VAT. She uses the margin scheme for all of her sales. She has bought an expensive painting for £2,000, which she can resell for £5,000 once she has spent £1,000 plus VAT on restoration costs. In this situation, input tax can be separately claimed on the restoration costs. The output tax due under the margin scheme will be based on £3,000, i.e. £5,000 selling price less buying price of £2,000.

(VAT Notice 718, para 2.11).

Purchases

[61.6] The following provisions have the force of law.

Private person or unregistered dealer not providing invoice

On a purchase from a private person or an unregistered dealer who does not provide an invoice, the buyer must check that the goods are eligible for the scheme and, if so, make out a purchase invoice showing

- seller's name and address;
- own name and address;
- stock book number;
- invoice number;
- date of transaction;
- description of the goods including any unique identification (e.g. registration number, make/model, hallmark, type, class, chassis number, etc.); and
- total price (no other costs may be added to this amount).

Unregistered dealer providing invoice

On purchase from an unregistered dealer who provides an invoice, the buyer must ensure that the invoice contains all the necessary details as above.

VAT-registered dealer

On purchase from another VAT-registered dealer, that dealer will make out the invoice which must include a declaration that 'Input tax deduction has not been and will not be claimed in respect of the goods on this invoice'. See **61.11** below.

Stock book

Details of the purchase must be entered in the stock book (see **61.23** below). (VAT Notice 718, paras 4.1, 5.3).

Invoices in foreign currency

If an invoice is in a foreign currency, it must be converted into sterling using one of the methods in **71.18 VALUATION** or, in the case of acquisitions from another EU country, **71.14 VALUATION**. Where a number of items are bought for an inclusive price which are not to be sold as one lot, the price must be converted into sterling and then apportioned between the various items. The sterling amounts on an item by item basis must be entered in the stock records. (VAT Notice 718, para 5.7).

Acquisitions from other EU countries

[61.7] The margin scheme is available throughout the EU. Eligible goods sold under the scheme in any EU country are taxable in the country of origin rather than of destination and are not subject to the normal distance selling rules.

- *Goods purchased from a private individual in another EU country*. No VAT is due when the goods are brought into the UK and the goods can therefore be sold under the margin scheme or global accounting scheme.
- *Goods purchased from a registered business in another EU country under the margin scheme or global accounting scheme*. Goods purchased from a dealer in another EU country can only be sold under the scheme if the goods are supplied by that dealer under a margin scheme.

(VAT Notice 718, paras 7.1, 7.6).

New means of transport are always liable to VAT on the EU country of destination. See **19.33 EUROPEAN UNION: SINGLE MARKET**. This means that any new means of transport acquired from another EU country is not eligible for the margin scheme. (VAT Notice 718, para 7.5).

Imports from outside the EU

[61.8] VAT is normally due on importation of second-hand goods and the margin scheme cannot be used to sell the goods. On sale, VAT must be charged on the full selling price, the VAT paid at importation being deductible subject to the normal rules. This general rule is subject to the following exceptions.

- Certain works of art, antiques, collections and collectors' pieces are entitled to a reduced valuation at importation (see **73.3 WORKS OF ART, ETC.**). Where any of the works of art, etc. listed there are imported, the purchaser may either use the margin scheme or import and resell the goods under the normal VAT rules. See **61.38** below.
- Second-hand cars. See **61.29** below.

(VAT Notice 718, para 8.1).

Bulk purchases

[61.9] Where a number of eligible goods are bought at an inclusive price with the intention of reselling them separately, the price paid must be apportioned. There is no set way of doing this but the method used must be fair and reasonable and the price allocated to each must be as accurate as possible. The separate figures must be shown in the stock book (see **61.23** below). (VAT Notice 718, para 4.1).

Alternatively, the global accounting scheme may be used for low-value bulk purchases. See **61.39** to **61.52** below.

Purchases of repossessed goods

[61.10] Sales of eligible goods by an insurance company which has taken possession of them in settlement of an insurance claim or by a finance company which has repossessed them are outside the scope of VAT provided certain conditions are met. See **23.15 FINANCIAL SERVICES**. As no VAT is charged on the supply of the goods, they can be purchased for sale under the margin scheme provided the necessary scheme conditions in **61.4** are satisfied. (VAT Notice 718, para 13.9).

Sales

[61.11] Note: the following provisions have the force of law.

On the sale of eligible goods, the seller must check that the rules in **61.6** above were applied on purchase and, if so, make out a sales invoice showing

- own name and address and VAT registration number;
- buyer's name and address;
- stock book number;
- invoice number;
- date of sale;
- particulars of the goods including any unique reference number (e.g. registration number, make/model, hallmark, type, class, chassis number, etc.);
- total price, including VAT. Where more than one item is sold on the same invoice, a separate price must be shown for each item; and
- any of the following: margin scheme – second-hand goods; margin scheme – works of art; or margin scheme – collector's items and antiques.

The invoice must not show VAT as a separate item.

If any insurance product is being sold with the goods, the full price of this must be disclosed separately on the invoice, plus any fees charged for the product outside the contract of insurance. See **36.17 INSURANCE**.

The seller must then give the invoice to his customer, keep a copy for his own records and enter details of the sale in the stock book (see **61.23** below).

(VAT Notice 718, paras 4.2, 5.3).

Invoices in foreign currency

If an invoice is issued in a foreign currency, it must also show the sterling equivalent of the value of the goods. Normally, where a number of items are sold on the same invoice, the foreign currency and sterling price must be shown for each item and the sterling amounts entered in the stock records. If, however, the sales invoice is for one lot of goods which were also bought as one lot, it is only necessary to show a total foreign currency and sterling value for that lot. The foreign currency value must be converted into sterling using one of the methods in **71.18 VALUATION**. (VAT Notice 718, para 5.7).

Sales to other EU countries

[61.12] The margin scheme is available throughout the EU. Eligible goods sold under the scheme in any EU country are taxable in the country of origin rather than of destination and are not subject to the normal distance selling rules.

- *Sales by UK dealers to dealers in other EU countries.* Sales made under the margin scheme are taxable in the same way as sales within the UK and the normal margin scheme sales invoice must be issued. There is no requirement to obtain the dealer's registration number. No further VAT is due from the buyer when the goods are taken into the other EU country. Alternatively, the goods can be sold outside the margin scheme in which case the sale can be zero-rated subject to the normal conditions for supplies of goods to VAT-registered customers in other EU countries (see **19.11 EUROPEAN UNION: SINGLE MARKET**). The buyer must then account for VAT in his own country and cannot sell the goods under the margin scheme.
- *Sales by UK dealers to private individuals in other EU countries.* Such sales are taxable in the UK on the margin.

(VAT Notice 718, para 7.3).

New means of transport are always liable to VAT in the EU country of destination. See **19.31 EUROPEAN UNION: SINGLE MARKET**. This means that any new means of transport sold to another EU country is not eligible for the margin scheme. (VAT Notice 718, para 7.5).

Exports outside the EU

[61.13] Where eligible goods are sold for direct export, the sale is zero-rated provided appropriate evidence of exportation is held. See **21.25 EXPORTS**. The retail export scheme can also be used to zero-rate the indirect export of certain second-hand goods. See **21.16 EXPORTS**. 'Nil' should be entered in the VAT due column of the stock book.

However, it is not normally possible to zero-rate an export of eligible goods if the goods are sold through an auctioneer or dealer who acts as an agent in his own name. This is because, under the special rules for agents who act in their own name, the sale of the goods must be treated as a supply to the agent and a supply by the agent. Thus, the sale by the dealer has to be treated as a supply to the agent, rather than as a supply to the final purchaser, and cannot be treated as a zero-rated export unless the agent is located outside the EU.

(VAT Notice 718, para 8.2).

Where a vehicle is supplied to an overseas person for export, the transaction may be zero-rated provided the vehicle is only used in the UK for the trip to the place of departure from the EU. See **21.18 EXPORTS**.

The Personal Export Scheme can also be used to zero-rate sales of second-hand cars exported outside the EU. See **21.19 EXPORTS**.

See also **21.20 EXPORTS** for special provisions relating to sailaway boats prior to 1 January 2012.

Transfers of own goods to another EU country

[61.14] The transfer of goods within the same legal entity from one EU country to another is deemed to be a supply for VAT purposes. See **19.25 EUROPEAN UNION: SINGLE MARKET**. Where goods are transferred under the margin scheme from the UK to another EU country (e.g. for sale, or use in the business, in that country) there is no liability to UK VAT on the goods provided that they are transferred from the UK at the price for which they were obtained. There should be no liability to account for acquisition VAT in the other EU country. (VAT Notice 718, para 7.4).

Part exchange

[61.15] If a dealer sells eligible goods and takes other goods in part exchange, his selling price includes the amount allowed for the other goods as well as the amount received in cash from the buyer.

Example

A car is sold for £2,000 cash plus a car for which £1,000 is allowed in part exchange.

A selling price of £3,000 must be entered in the stock book. As the article taken in exchange is an eligible article which is to be resold under the scheme, the rules in **61.6** above must be followed. The amount allowed in part exchange (£1,000) is the purchase price. The purchase must also be recorded in the stock book (see **61.23** below).

A dealer must obtain a purchase invoice for part-exchanged goods bought from another VAT-registered dealer. However, if he buys from a private person or an unregistered dealer, he may include details of part-exchange items on his sales invoice provided all the requirements of **61.6** above are met.

(VAT Notice 718, para 13.6).

In *Lex Services plc v C & E Commrs*, HL 2003, [2004] STC 73 (TVC 44.85) the company accepted second-hand cars in part exchange. The documentation showed a vehicle price (say £20,000) and an agreed price for the part exchange car (say £2,000) which was used to arrive at the amount actually payable by the customer (£18,000). In most cases, however, in order to secure the sale the part exchange price was higher than the 'trade value' for the car (say £1,500). The relevant transaction could be cancelled by the customer within 30 days and the documentation stipulated that if the part exchange car had previously been sold, the customer was only entitled to a refund of the lower 'trade value' which was also disclosed in the documentation. The Court held that the taxable amount for VAT purposes was the cash received (£18,000) plus the value of the non-monetary consideration agreed with the customer (£2,000).

Lex Services above was, however, distinguished in *Hartwell plc v C & E Commrs*, CA [2003] STC 396 (TVC 44.86) where the company issued 'purchase plus vouchers' to customers in order to encourage sales without having to overvalue the part-exchanged car. Where, for example, the price of the replacement vehicle was £20,000 but the correct 'trade-value' of the used car was £1,500, if the customer was unwilling to pay £18,500 the company might issue a purchase plus voucher for £500. The court held that the consideration the dealer received for the supply of the £500 voucher was the agreement of the purchaser to the sale and that its non-monetary value was nil. The voucher did not form part of the consideration for the part-exchanged car. The taxable amount for VAT purposes was the cash received (£18,000) plus the trade in value of the used car (£1,500).

Hire purchase sales

[61.16] Note: The following provisions have the force of law.

Eligible goods sold under a hire purchase agreement are sold to the finance company which in turn sells them to the customer. The sale should be treated as a cash sale and the cash price of the goods (as shown on the HP agreement) should be entered in the stock book as the selling price. No VAT is charged on the finance charges if itemised separately. In some circumstances the dealer may issue his own sales invoice to the customer. He must attach a copy of the completed HP agreement to the customer's sales invoice or include a cross-reference to the agreement in his sales records. If the HP agreement is held by the finance company and the dealer does not receive a copy for his records, he should keep a copy of the agreed quotation or agreed proposal documents in his sales records, together with the name of the finance company, date and reference number of the final agreement.

A copy of the HP agreement can be treated as the sales invoice provided

- it shows all the identifying details required; and
- the cash price is shown as the gross price payable i.e. the amount borrowed plus cash paid, plus any amount allowed for part exchange (see **61.15** above).

VAT must not be shown separately on the HP agreement or any invoice.

(VAT Notice 718, para 13.5).

See **23.15 FINANCIAL SERVICES** for the sale of repossessed goods.

Gifts

[61.17] If a taxable person sells an article received as a gift, he must charge VAT on its full selling price and not use the margin scheme.

No VAT is chargeable on eligible goods which could have been sold under the scheme but which are given away but full details of the person to whom the goods are given must be included in the stock book.

(VAT Notice 718, para 13.3).

Private sales

[61.18] The private sale of goods which are not assets of the business is usually outside the scope of VAT.

Where a sole proprietor transfers eligible goods from a private holding to the business, VAT may be accounted for under the margin scheme provided evidence can be produced of the purchase price when originally bought for private use. If not, VAT must be accounted for on the full selling price.

(VAT Notice 718, para 13.4).

Sales from historic houses

[61.19] If owners of historic houses admit members of the public for a charge, any works of art, etc. owned and displayed to the public are treated as business assets and their disposal is normally subject to VAT. There is, however, special VAT relief in certain cases. See **73.6 WORKS OF ART, ETC.**

See also **73.1 WORKS OF ART, ETC.** for exemption from VAT on certain disposals to approved bodies, and property accepted in satisfaction of inheritance tax.

Shares in eligible goods

[61.20] If a share in an eligible article held in stock is sold, no output tax is due on the sale of the share and a VAT invoice must not be issued to the purchaser.

When an item in which other people own shares is sold under the margin scheme, the full amount of VAT due must be accounted for (not just VAT on the taxable person's share of the proceeds). The purchase price is the full purchase price (not just the taxable person's share) and statements must be issued to the other shareholders showing their share of the sale proceeds, excluding VAT. See also **61.21** below.

(VAT Notice 718, para 12.2).

Joint purchases and sales

[61.21] The following procedure (which has the force of law) should be used where dealers jointly buy an eligible article for resale.

(a) **On purchase**, one of the joint buyers (JB1) must keep the purchase invoice with the details set out under **61.6** above and must invoice the other joint buyer(s) for the agreed contribution towards the cost, excluding VAT. Each invoice must be endorsed 'This payment is your contribution towards the purchase of the above article. I shall be accounting for the full amount of VAT due under the scheme when it is sold.' Copies of the invoice(s) must be retained.
JB1 must record the full purchase details in his stock book, together with details of the sales invoices to the other joint buyer(s).

(b) **On resale by the original buyer**, JB1 must issue (and keep a copy of) a sales invoice showing all the details in **61.11** above and enter the sales and accounting details in his stock book. The selling price is the full joint selling price (not just JB1's share of the proceeds).
JB1 must then issue a statement to the other joint buyer(s) showing their share of the proceeds of sale, excluding VAT. The statement must be endorsed 'This payment is your share of the proceeds of sale of [insert details]. I am accounting for the full amount of VAT due on the sale under the scheme.'

(c) **On resale by another joint buyer** (JB2), he must obtain the original purchase invoice from JB1, issue (and keep a copy of) a sales invoice showing all the details in **61.11** above and complete his stock book treating the purchase and sale as being made entirely by him. The purchase price is the full joint purchase price and the selling price is the full joint selling price.
JB2 must then issue a statement to the other joint buyer(s) as in (*b*) above.
JB1, the original buyer, must close the entry in his stock book stating that VAT has been accounted for by JB2 and cross-refer to the statement received from JB2.

(VAT Notice 718, paras 12.1–12.6).

Records and accounts

[61.22] The following requirements as to records and accounts have the force of law. [*SI 1992/3122, Art 8(1); SI 1995/1268, Art 12(1); SI 1995/1269*]. They are in addition to the records generally required of all taxable persons. See **56 RECORDS.**

A business selling goods under the scheme must keep the purchase invoice (see **61.6** above) and a copy of the sales invoice (see **61.11** above), together with a stock book or similar records (see **61.23** below). All records must be kept for six years but if stock includes goods obtained more than six years previously, evidence must also be retained to show eligibility to use the margin scheme at the time of sale. Failure to comply with any of the requirements renders the business liable for VAT on the full value of its sales. (VAT Notice 718, paras 5.1, 5.5). See *C & E Commrs v JH Corbitt (Numismatists) Ltd*, HL [1980] STC 231 (TVC 60.1). The requirements as to the records to be kept do not impose an obligation on the business to verify the identity of purchasers (*Bord* (VTD 9824) (TVC 60.5)).

See, however, **61.39** *et seq* below for a simplified method of operating the margin scheme (global accounting).

Occasional sales

If a trader is not in the business of selling second-hand goods, etc. but occasionally sells eligible goods in the course of his business, he need not comply with the full record-keeping requirements provided he meets the other conditions of the scheme and holds evidence of both the purchase and selling price. (VAT Notice 718, para 13.7).

Motor cars

There is an alternative special method of calculating VAT for second-hand cars where the dealer has the required information on the purchase or sale of the car but not both. See **61.35** below.

Horses and ponies

Special records are required. See **61.37** below.

Stock book

[61.23] A stock book or similar record must be kept with separate headings for each of the following.

Purchase details
Stock number in numerical sequence
Date of purchase
Purchase invoice number
Name of seller
Any unique identification number (e.g. car registration)
Description of the goods (e.g. type, make or model)

Sales details
Date of sale
Sales invoice number
Name of buyer

Accounting details
Purchase price
Selling price or other method of disposal
Margin on sale
VAT due

The purchase price must be the price on the invoice which has been agreed between the buyer and seller and must not be altered. Separate entries must be made where purchases bought in bulk are to be sold separately (see **61.9** above).

Other information can also be included but the above details must always be shown and the stock book must be kept up-to-date.

(VAT Notice 718, paras 5.2, 6.1).

Goods on sale or return

If stock includes goods supplied to the dealer on a sale or return basis, the stock book (or a separate record) must include the following details of the goods.

Date of transfer of the goods
Description of goods including any unique identification number (e.g. car registration)
Name and address of dealer/person transferring the goods
Date of sale or return

Similarly, if any goods are removed from stock on a sale or return basis to another dealer's premises, stock records should be noted with the date and details of the dealer to whom the goods have been transferred.

If a dealer sells goods on behalf of a third party, and issues an invoice for those goods in his own name, he is acting as an agent for VAT purposes (see **61.26** below).

(VAT Notice 718, para 5.6 which has the force of law).

Calculation of VAT

[61.24] If eligible goods are sold for the same as, or less than, the price paid, no VAT is due. The loss cannot be set against profit made on other transactions.

If eligible goods are sold for more than the price paid, VAT is chargeable on the profit margin i.e. the amount by which the consideration for the goods are sold exceeds the purchase price. The profit margin is regarded as being VAT-inclusive i.e. the VAT included is

VAT-inclusive margin × VAT fraction 7/47 (1/6 from 4 January 2011; 3/23 from 1 December 2008 to 31 December 2009)

Profit margin

The following rules apply for the purpose of determining the profit margin.

(a) The price at which the goods were obtained is calculated
  - (i) where the business took possession of the goods by a supply, in the same way as the consideration for the supply would normally be calculated (see **71.2** *et seq* **VALUATION**);
  - (ii) where the business is a sole proprietor and the goods were supplied to him in a private capacity, in the same way as the consideration for the supply to him as a private individual would be calculated;
  - (iii) where the goods are a work of art which was acquired by the business from the creator or his successor in title in another EU country, in the same way as the value of the acquisition would be calculated for VAT purposes (see **71.11 VALUATION**) plus the VAT chargeable on the acquisition;
  - (iv) where the goods are a work of art, antique or collectors' item which the business has imported itself (which includes, with effect from 1 September 2006, if the business is that of an auctioneer, the auctioneer having placed them under customs procedures for temporary importation with total relief from import duties), in the same way as the value would be calculated for the purposes of importation (see **71.15 VALUATION**) plus any VAT chargeable on their importation; and
  - (v) where the business took possession of the motor car or goods under a transaction treated as neither a supply or goods nor a supply of services (other than a transaction within (vi) below), the price it paid by virtue of that transaction; and
  - (vi) where the business took possession of the motor car or goods under a transaction treated as neither a supply or goods nor a supply of services as the result of
    - (1) the transfer of assets of a business as a going concern (see **8.10 BUSINESS**), or
    - (2) on or after 1 July 2002 in the case of a bank or other financial institution, the assignment of the rights in hire purchase or conditional sale agreements

and the business has a 'relevant predecessor', the price at which its relevant predecessor in title obtained the motor car or goods. For this purpose, a '*relevant predecessor*' is the person from whom the business took possession of the motor car or goods and who himself took possession of the motor car or goods in circumstances that qualified for use of the margin scheme (see **61.4** above). Where the motor car or goods have been the subject of a succession of two or more transactions within (1) or (2) above (or both), culminating in the transaction in question, the relevant predecessor is the first person in the chain who took possession of the motor car or goods in circumstances that qualified for use of the margin scheme.

Where the above provisions apply, the business will always require the original purchase invoice to calculate the margin on the goods.

(b) The price at which the goods are sold is calculated in the same way as the consideration for the supply would be calculated for VAT purposes. It includes everything received for the goods whether from the buyer or a third party. It also includes incidental expenses directly linked to the sale. Optional extras charged to the buyer and disbursements do *not* form part of the selling price and should be accounted for separately outside the margin scheme. The consideration may not be wholly in money and the normal rules about value apply. See **71.2** *et seq* VALUATION.

[*SI 1992/3122, Art 8(5)(8)(9); SI 1995/1268, Art 12(5)(10)(11); SI 1995/1269; SI 1998/759; SI 1998/760; SI 2002/1502; SI 2002/1503*]. (VAT Notice 718, para 3.1).

The margin cannot be reduced by deducting expenses e.g. repairs, spares, overheads, cleaning, etc. (VAT Notice 718, para 3.2).

Motor cars

There is an alternative special method of calculating VAT for second-hand cars where the dealer has the required information on the purchase or sale of the car but not both. See **61.35** below.

Completion of VAT return

[61.25] See **2.7** *et seq* ACCOUNTING PERIODS AND RETURNS for notes on the completion of Form VAT 100. The following special rules apply to eligible goods bought and sold under the margin scheme.

Box 1	Include the output tax on all eligible goods sold in the period covered by the return.
Box 6	Include the full selling price of all eligible goods sold during the period, less any VAT.
Box 7	Include the purchase price (inclusive of VAT) of eligible goods bought in the period.

There is no requirement to include margin scheme purchases and sales in Boxes 8 and 9.

(VAT Notice 718, para 5.4).

Agents

[61.26] Dealers frequently sell goods for or on behalf of other dealers or private sellers. The arrangements may include retaining a percentage of the selling price or making a separate charge to the owner. In either case, the seller is acting as the agent of the dealer or individual who owns the goods and the parties must follow the rules set out below.

If different parties own shares in the goods or if different parties have bought goods jointly for resale, see **61.21** above.

An agent who acts in his own name and uses the margin scheme in relation to a supply of goods must, for VAT purposes, treat the supply as a supply to him and a supply by him. See **3.4 AGENTS**. When goods are sold by an agent, the margin scheme treatment will depend on the way the agent has opted to account for his commission. The following paragraphs outline the margin scheme consequences of each option.

(a) **How the owner or principal calculates his margin**. If the agent sells eligible goods on the owner's behalf in his own name, the owner can still account for his sale under the margin scheme. The owner's purchase price is calculated in the normal way (see **61.24** above) but his selling price depends on the way the agent has accounted for his sale and is equivalent to the agent's purchase price.

(b) **How the agent calculates his margin.** An agent selling eligible goods has two options.

- *Option 1*. If the agent invoices his charges to the seller or principal separately, those charges are subject to VAT and his margin for VAT is calculated as follows.
  Purchase price = The gross amount realised by the agent before any deductions are made.
  Selling price = The total price for the goods including any incidental expenses and commission charged to the buyer. (Other optional charges not directly linked to the goods such as packing, transport and insurance costs should be charged outside the margin scheme under the normal VAT rules.)
  Margin = The difference between the purchase price and the selling price.
- *Option* 2. If the agent includes his charges to the seller in his sale of the goods, his margin for VAT is calculated as follows.
  Purchase price = The gross amount realised by the agent less commission charged to the seller (and not including any charges made to the buyer).

Selling price = The total price for the goods including any incidental expenses and commission charged to the buyer. (Other optional charges not directly linked to the goods such as packing, transport and insurance costs should be charged outside the margin scheme under the normal VAT rules.)
Margin = The difference between the purchase price and the selling price.
This method mirrors the method used by auctioneers to calculate their purchase and selling prices under the auctioneers' scheme (see **61.59** below).

An agent selling goods under the margin scheme who issues an invoice in his own name must keep the records described in **61.22** above.

[*SI 1992/3122, Art 8(6); SI 1995/1268, Art 12(6); SI 1995/1269*]. (VAT Notice 718, paras 17.1–17.7).

Second-hand cars

Margin scheme

[61.27] The normal rules and conditions of the margin scheme apply to second-hand motor cars but there are also further specific provisions which apply as outlined in **61.28** to **61.35** below. These provisions have the force of law.

Motor cars are defined in **45.1 MOTOR CARS**. Only second-hand cars can be sold under the margin scheme. To be eligible, the car must have been driven on the road for business or pleasure purposes. Neither the registration of the car for road use nor the delivery mileage incurred transporting a vehicle to a dealer turn a car into a used car for the purposes of the margin scheme. See also *Lincoln Street Motors (Birmingham) Ltd* (VTD 1100) (TVC 44.66).

The margin scheme cannot be used for any vehicle on which input tax was reclaimed on purchase. See **45.4 MOTOR CARS** for sales of such cars.

(VAT Notice 718/1, para 2.3).

Purchases from other EU countries

[61.28] Where a second-hand car is bought from a private individual, or from a registered dealer using the margin scheme, in another EU country, no VAT is due when the car is brought into the UK and the margin scheme can be used for the onward sale.

Where a second-hand car is bought outside the margin scheme from a registered dealer in another EU country, acquisition VAT is due when the car is brought into the UK and the car is not eligible for the margin scheme.

The margin scheme cannot be used for any vehicle qualifying as a new means of transport (see **19.33 EUROPEAN UNION: SINGLE MARKET**).

(VAT Notice 718/1, para 2.4).

Imports from outside the EU

[61.29] VAT is due at the standard rate on the importation of a second-hand car unless it meets the criteria for returned goods relief (see **33.19 IMPORTS**) or it can be classified as a collector's piece. An imported car is not eligible for sale under the margin scheme unless it qualifies as a collectors' piece or antique. See **45.4 MOTOR CARS** for the VAT provisions applying on sale.

Personal imports

If a dealer buys a car from an unconnected person who has personally imported it, the car may be sold under the margin scheme. Where, however, the car is imported by an employee, agent or other person connected with the trader for sale in the dealer's business, the margin scheme cannot be used for the subsequent sale.

(VAT Notice 718/1, para 2.4).

VED and MOTs

Unexpired VED

[61.30] Where a car is purchased with an unexpired VED which is surrendered. A refund of VED is treated as being outside the scope of VAT. The price of the car should not be adjusted to reflect the refund.

Valid VED

Where a car is sold with a valid VED or a VED is offered with the car as part of the agreed sale price, there is a single supply and the selling price entered in the stock book must include the value of the VED.

Separate VED

Where a VED is obtained after the negotiation for the sale of a car, the VED may be treated as a separate supply provided the conditions for treatment as a disbursement are met. See **3.7 AGENTS**. If those conditions cannot be met, the car and the VED are treated as a single supply and VAT must be accounted for on the margin of the total value.

MOT

Where a car is sold with an MOT, this is a single supply and the full selling price, without deduction of any value for the MOT, must be recorded in the stock book and used to calculate the margin.

(VAT Notice 718/1, paras 10.2, 10.3).

Mechanical breakdown insurance and warranties

[61.31] A '*warranty*' is an undertaking or guarantee by a dealer that, if a vehicle proves to be faulty within a specified time limit or mileage, the dealer will bear the cost of repair or replacement parts.

'*Mechanical breakdown insurance*' (MBI) is a contract of insurance, between an insurer (usually someone other than the dealer) and a purchaser, providing cover against the risk of the vehicle proving faulty within a specified time limit or mileage.

(a) *Free warranties or MBI*. The selling price of the car includes the cost of providing the warranty or MBI. The price of the car on the invoice must be entered in the stock book. Any mention of the warranty or MBI on the invoice must show that no separate charge is being made.

(b) *Warranties or MBI for which a separate charge is made*. The VAT treatment depends on whether the risk covered is the dealer's or the customer's.

(i) If a dealer arranges MBI for his customer, the supply is exempt provided

- it is supplied under a contract between an insurer and the customer;
- it is the customer's risks which are insured;
- the customer is entirely free to purchase the item at the price advertised without the MBI; and
- the dealer discloses to the customer the premium and any other amount (fees or commission) being charged.

This is because there are separate supplies of the item and the MBI, each with its own consideration. The following rules must be observed.

- If the dealer subsequently negotiates with the customer a reduced price for the item (including the MBI), the price originally advertised for the MBI must be treated as the value of the exempt supply of the MBI.
- If negotiations with the customer result in the supply of an upgraded MBI, the dealer may use the separately advertised price of the upgraded MBI as the value of the exempt supply of the MBI.
- If the dealer advertises the item and the MBI at a single price (ie does not disclose to the customer the amount they are paying for the MBI) any fee or commission income the dealer would receive in relation to this insurance is standard-rated. The net value of the insurance paid to, and retained by, the insurer remains exempt.

If the insurance contract is between the dealer and the insurer and only the dealer's risk of having to repair defective items is covered, then the charge shown on the dealer's invoice for insurance is standard-rated.

(ii) If a dealer provides a warranty, the charge shown on the invoice is standard-rated.

(c) *Other situations*. The supply of a warranty or MBI under any other type of scheme is standard-rated. This applies, for example, to 'stop loss' arrangements under which the dealer or insurance broker sets up a fund into which amounts charged to customers for warranties or MBI are paid and from which repair claims are met. Insurance cover is then obtained from a permitted insurer against any deficiency in the fund.

Any standard-rated commission or fees under (*b*) above or, if not charged separately, standard-rated warranty charges under (*c*) above must be deducted from the vehicle's selling price before the gross margin is calculated.

(VAT Notice 718/1, paras 9.1–9.6).

Demonstration cars

[61.32] VAT may be reclaimed on the purchase, acquisition or importation of any motor car which forms part of the stock in trade of a motor dealer. See **45.3 MOTOR CARS** for full details. As a result, such cars are no longer eligible for the margin scheme and, on disposal, output tax must be accounted for on the full selling price in the normal way. See **45.4 MOTOR CARS**.

Rebuilt motor cars

[61.33] If a motor car is rebuilt from one or more used cars and the Driver and Vehicle Licensing Authority (DVLA) do not require it to be re-registered, it can be sold under the margin scheme. The purchase price to be entered in the stock book is the price paid for the car for which the registration number is carried forward. If, however, the DVLA give the car a new registration number, the scheme cannot be used and VAT must be accounted for on the full selling price. (VAT Notice 718/1, para 10.6).

Auctions

[61.34] See **61.53** *et seq* below for the general provisions relating to auctions.

Calculation of VAT due

[61.35] *Where all required records are held*, the normal rules in **61.24** above apply. Otherwise the sale must be dealt with outside the scheme, accounting for VAT on the full selling price.

Until 1 April 2010, where records in respect of either the purchase or the sale were available (but not both), and where the dealer satisfied HMRC that the mark-up achieved on the supply did not exceed 100%, HMRC allowed VAT to be accounted for on either

- the price paid for the car (where the necessary purchase records had been kept); or
- half the selling price (where the necessary sales records had been kept).

(VAT Notice 718/1, para 5.1; VAT Notice 48, ESC 3.8, withdrawn from 1 April 2010).

Second-hand motor-cycles

[61.36] Road fund licences, mechanical breakdown insurance and warranties and rebuilt motor-cycles: the provisions applying to motor cars apply equally to motor-cycles. See **61.30**, **61.31** and **61.33** above respectively.

Second-hand horses and ponies

[61.37] The general rules and conditions of the margin scheme also apply to the sale of second-hand horses and ponies. This has been confirmed in *Förvaltnings AB Stenholmen v Riksskatteverket, ECJ Case C–320/02*, [2004] STC 1041 (TVC 22.494). The following rules relate specifically to second-hand horses and ponies and have the force of law.

Horses which the trader has bred and is selling for the first time are not second-hand.

A trader using the margin scheme for horses or ponies may either

- keep the normal records and accounts; or
- keep alternative records based on special three-part forms supplied by The British Equestrian Trade Association.

Each of these options is explained below.

Normal records and accounts

If a dealer decides to keep normal margin scheme records, his stock book must include sufficient details to identify the horse or pony including colour, sex, type (e.g. chestnut, cob, gelding), age (if known), height, stable name (if known), and distinctive markings. (These requirements have the force of law.)

On purchase, the normal conditions in **61.6** above must be complied with. If the purchase is from another VAT-registered dealer who uses the special three-part form (see below), the other dealer will hand over Part C of that form. This can be used as the purchase invoice and appropriate details entered in the stock book.

On purchase at auction, the dealer must comply with the conditions **61.60** below. If the horse or pony is being sold at auction by another VAT-registered dealer who uses the three-part form, the auctioneer will hand over Part C of that form. This can be used as the purchase invoice and appropriate details entered in the stock book.

On sale, the normal conditions in **61.11** above must be complied with. On sale at auction the dealer must comply with the conditions set out in **61.61** below.

(VAT Notice 718, paras 16.1–16.7).

Alternative records and accounts

To sell horses and ponies under the margin scheme, as an alternative to the normal records special three-part forms (produced in numbered sets) with a VAT summary sheet at the back may be used. These are sold by

The British Equestrian Trade Association,
East Wing,
Stockeld Park,
Wetherby,
West Yorkshire LS22 4AW

The three parts of the form are

Part A	Seller's stock record
Part B	Seller's copy sales invoice
Part C	Customer's purchase invoice

These forms are the basis of stock and sales records. No other records are required to operate the scheme. It is not necessary to keep a stock book or invoices. A separate form must be properly completed for each horse, etc. or VAT becomes due on the full selling price i.e. the records are mandatory.

(a) *Purchase of a horse or pony from a private person.* After ensuring that the horse or pony is eligible for the margin scheme, the 'description' and 'written description' sections of Parts A, B and C must be completed in accordance with the standard laid down by the Royal College of Veterinary Surgeons in their booklet 'Colour and Markings of Horses' (obtainable from the Royal College of Veterinary Surgeons, 32 Belgrave Square, London SW1). If the animal is not registered with a recognised Breed Society, Stud Book or Register, then unless the purchase price is less than £500, the buyer and a vet must sign Parts A, B and C to certify that the animal is the one described on the form. If the animal is registered, the signatures are not necessary. The buyer must then give the form a stock number in numerical sequence and complete the Purchase Record section on the reverse of Part A. The buyer must retain all parts of the form which will be needed on a subsequent sale.

(b) *Purchase of a horse or pony from someone selling under the scheme.* Similar rules apply as in (*a*) above but the seller must give the buyer Part C of the form to be kept with the partially completed form. The seller does not have to sign the declaration on the reverse of Part A. If the animal is unregistered and has a purchase price of more than £500, the Part C from the seller should have already been signed by a vet confirming the description. The details of the vet's name, practice, etc. can be copied by the buyer on to his form. There is no need for a vet to sign.

(c) *Sale of a horse or pony.* Check that the correct procedure was followed under (*a*) or (*b*) above on purchase. If not, the margin scheme cannot be used. If the correct procedure was followed, on sale the sales record sections on the reverse of Parts A, B and C must be completed. The seller then retains Parts A and B and gives Part C to the buyer.
The VAT record on the reverse of Part A must be completed.

(d) *Purchases at auction.* The normal rules for purchases under (*a*) or (*b*) above apply. If the animal is being sold under the margin scheme, the auctioneer will pass the seller's completed Part C to the buyer. The buyer must keep this with his own partially completed form. If the animal is being sold by a private person, the buyer must get the auctioneer to complete details of his name, address and Lot number on the reverse of Part A of his form.

(e) *Sales at auction.* The auctioneer must be told that the animal is being sold under the margin scheme and be given Parts B and C of the seller's form which must already be completed as regards his purchase. After the sale, the auctioneer must complete the sales details on the reverse of Parts B and C, adding his name and address. He then returns Part C to the buyer and Part B to the seller. The seller must then complete the sales and VAT record on the reverse of Part A.

(VAT Notice 718, paras 16.1–16.7).

Imported works of art, antiques and collectors' pieces and works of art obtained from the creators or their heirs

[61.38] A business which

(a) imports works of art, collectors' items or antiques within **73.3**(*a*)–(*c*) **WORKS OF ART, ETC.** or
(b) obtains works of art (by supply in the UK or acquisition from another EU country) from the creators or their heirs,

may opt to use the margin scheme or the auctioneers' scheme (see **61.53** *et seq* below) whether or not VAT has been charged on the supply, acquisition or importation. Alternatively, VAT can be accounted for under the normal rules.

Conditions for opting

The conditions for using the margin scheme or the auctioneers' scheme are as follows.

- HMRC must be notified in writing that the option is to be taken up, specifying the date from which it will apply.
- The option must be exercised for a period of at least two years. Thereafter, it will continue to apply until HMRC are advised in writing as to when it is to cease.
- If the option is used, it must be applied to *all* transactions within (*a*) and (*b*) above, not just in respect of certain transactions or certain categories of goods.
- If, having exercised the option, the business subsequently decides to sell any goods covered by the option outside a scheme, it is not entitled to recover any input tax on those goods until the period in which VAT is accounted for on their sale. VAT must be accounted for on the full selling price at the standard rate (unless the goods are exported and qualify for zero-rating under the normal VAT rules for export).

If the option has been exercised,

- for imports within (*a*) it covers imports at the effective 5% rate (see **73.3 WORKS OF ART, ETC.**). Under the margin scheme, the purchase price to be entered in the records is the value for VAT at import, plus the import VAT. For the auctioneers' scheme, the purchase price is calculated according to the normal rules for that scheme. Under both schemes, VAT is calculated on the margin at 17.5% (20% from 4 January 2011; 15% from 1 December 2008 to 31 December 2009) and the import VAT cannot be reclaimed as input tax; and
- for works of art obtained under (*b*) above, any VAT charged when the items are obtained cannot be reclaimed as input tax. The purchase price to be entered in the records is the total price paid inclusive of any VAT.

For acquisitions, acquisition VAT should be accounted for in Box 2 of the VAT return. The corresponding amount should not be recovered in Box 4 but added to the net purchase price for margin scheme purposes. Under the auctioneers' scheme, the purchase price is calculated according to the normal rules for that scheme. If the vendor is VAT-registered, this amount will also be their VAT-inclusive selling price. As the vendor cannot use the margin scheme, any self-billed invoice issued to the vendor must show VAT separately.

Global accounting scheme

A business opting to use the margin scheme may also use the global accounting scheme subject to the normal rules of that scheme (see **61.39** *et seq* below). Eligible taxed goods must not be entered into the global accounting scheme until documentation is received which would have allowed input tax or import/acquisition VAT to be reclaimed if the option had not been used.

(VAT Notice 718, paras 10.1–10.2).

Global accounting scheme

[61.39] The global accounting scheme is a simplified variation of the normal margin scheme, particularly beneficial for accounting for VAT on low value, bulk volume, margin scheme goods where it may be impractical to keep detailed records required under the normal scheme. Dealers using the global accounting scheme account for VAT on the difference between the total purchases and total sales of eligible goods in each VAT period (rather than on an item by item basis). The scheme automatically allows for a loss on one transaction to be set against the profit from others.

The provisions of the scheme as set out in **61.40–61.52** below have the force of law.

De Voil Indirect Tax Service. See V3.535.

Eligible goods

[61.40] The global accounting scheme can be used for any of the eligible goods within **61.3** above other than

(a) motor vehicles including motor-cycles (except those broken up for scrap, see below);
(b) aircraft;
(c) boats and outboard motors;
(d) caravans and motor caravans;
(e) horses and ponies.

[*SI 1995/1268, Art 13*].

Dealers in goods within (*a*)–(*e*) above are able to keep records on an item by item basis and can therefore use the normal margin scheme of accounting. (In any case, the cost of the majority of such goods purchased are likely to exceed £500 and would therefore be excluded from the global accounting scheme, see **61.41** below.)

Sales of scrap

Motor vehicles cannot normally be sold under the global accounting scheme. However, provided the vehicle is otherwise eligible for the margin scheme, it may be included in the global accounting scheme when broken up and sold as scrap. The normal commercial documents must be kept to show that the vehicle no longer exists in order to demonstrate that it is eligible for global accounting.

Where a motor vehicle has already been entered into a stock book under the margin scheme, the entry should be closed and the details transferred to the global accounting scheme purchase records.

If a dealer purchases a scrap motor vehicle for more than £500, he can still use the global accounting scheme for disposal of the components. But any individual component valued at over £500 must be excluded from the scheme.

(VAT Notice 718, para 14.9).

Conditions for using the scheme

[61.41] A person who is registered for VAT may use the scheme provided the following conditions are met.

(a) The goods were not purchased on an invoice on which VAT was shown separately.

(b) Every individual item for which the scheme is used must have been obtained for a price of £500 or less. See **61.24** above for the calculation of price. See **61.44** below for bulk purchases and collections.

(c) The goods are not sold on a VAT invoice or similar document showing an amount as being VAT or as being attributable to VAT.

(d) Such records and accounts are kept as specified by HMRC.

[*SI 1995/1268, Art 13*]. (VAT Notice 718, para 14.4).

Imported works of art, etc.

See **61.38** above for circumstances where imported works of art and works of art obtained from their creators or heirs can be included in the scheme despite the fact that VAT has been charged on their supply, acquisition or importation. These provisions apply also to the global accounting scheme.

Reclaiming VAT on expenses

[61.42] Subject to the normal rules, a taxable person may reclaim any VAT he is charged on business overheads, restoration, repairs, spares, etc. but must not add these costs to the purchase price of the goods for the purposes of the scheme. (VAT Notice 718, para 15.10 which has the force of law).

Purchases

Private person or unregistered dealer not providing invoice

[61.43] On a purchase from a private person or an unregistered dealer who does not provide an invoice, the buyer must check that the goods are eligible for the global accounting scheme and, if so, make out a purchase invoice showing

- own name and address;
- seller's name and address;
- invoice number;
- date of transaction;
- description of the goods sufficient to enable HMRC to verify that the goods are eligible for the global accounting scheme (e.g. 'four tables and ten chairs' is acceptable but 'assorted goods' is not);
- total price (VAT must not be shown separately); and
- an endorsement stating 'Global accounting invoice'.

Unregistered dealer providing invoice

On purchase from an unregistered dealer who provides an invoice, the buyer must ensure that the invoice contains all the necessary details as above.

VAT-registered dealer

On purchase from a VAT-registered dealer, that dealer should make out the invoice with details as above and certify that it is not a VAT invoice.

Purchase record summary

Details of the purchase must be entered in the purchase record or summary (see **61.49** below).

(VAT Notice 718, paras 15.2, 15.3 which have the force of law).

Invoices in foreign currency

If an invoice is in a foreign currency, it must be converted into sterling using one of the methods in **71.18 VALUATION** or, in the case of acquisitions from another EU country, **71.14 VALUATION**. Where an invoice includes individual items with a purchase price over £500 which are not eligible for the global accounting scheme, the foreign currency value must be converted into sterling and then apportioned to exclude these items. The remaining purchase amount in sterling must be entered in the purchase records. (VAT Notice 718, para 15.11 which has the force of law).

Bulk purchases and collections

Bulk purchases

[61.44] The scheme may be used for bulk purchases with a combined price in excess of £500 but if any individual item included has a purchase price of more than £500, it must be deducted from the total purchase price and excluded from the scheme. There is no set way to apportion total price between individual items but HMRC must be satisfied that it is fair and reasonable. Any item costing over £500 can then be sold under either the margin scheme (if eligible) or the normal VAT rules.

Collections

Collections (e.g. of stamps) purchased can be split and sold separately or formed into other collections for sale provided all items are eligible for the global accounting scheme. Two or more items purchased separately can also be combined to produce one item for resale (e.g. by using one item as a spare part for another).

But if an eligible item is purchased for £500 or more, and the item is made up of several components valued at less than £500, the global accounting scheme cannot be used if the item is sold in the same state as it was purchased.

> *Example*
>
> A tea set, including many pieces each valued at less than £500, is purchased for £750.
>
> If the item is bought and sold as a 'tea set', there is only one item and the global accounting scheme cannot be used.

(VAT Notice 718, para 14.10).

Sales

[61.45] On the sale of eligible goods, the dealer must check that the rules in **61.43** above where applied on purchase.

Sales to other dealers

For sales to other dealers, a dealer must issue (and keep a copy of) a sales invoice showing

- own name and address and VAT registration number;
- buyer's name and address;
- invoice number;
- date of sale;
- description of the goods sufficient to enable HMRC to verify that the goods are eligible for the global accounting scheme (e.g. 'four tables and ten chairs' is acceptable but 'assorted goods' is not);
- total price including VAT (but which must not be shown separately); and
- an endorsement stating 'Global accounting invoice'.

If a dealer sells an item for more than £500 but does not wish to disclose to the purchaser that he bought it under the global accounting scheme, instead of the endorsement above he may choose to use the following declaration on his sales invoice: 'Input tax deduction has not been and will not be claimed by me in respect of the goods sold on this invoice'.

Other sales

All other sales should be recorded in the normal way (e.g. by using a cash register).

Details of the daily gross takings and/or totals of copy invoices must be entered in the sales record or summary (see **61.49** below). It is therefore essential to be able to distinguish between sales under the global accounting scheme and other types of transactions at the point of sale.

(VAT Notice 718, paras 15.4, 15.5 which have the force of law).

Invoices in foreign currency

If a global accounting scheme invoice is issued in a foreign currency, it must also show the sterling equivalent of the total value of the goods. Even if more than one item is sold on the invoice, only the total foreign currency and sterling price needs to be shown and the sterling amount should be entered in the sales records. The foreign currency value must be converted into sterling using one of the methods in **71.18 VALUATION**. (VAT Notice 718, para 15.11 which has the force of law).

Transactions with overseas persons

[61.46] The same provisions apply as for the margin scheme provided the goods in question are also eligible for the global accounting scheme.

- **Acquisitions from other EU countries**. See **61.7** above ignoring the reference to motor cars.
- **Imports from outside the EU**. See **61.8** above ignoring the references to motor cars.
- **Sales to other EU countries**. See **61.12** above.
- **Exports outside the EU**. See **61.13** above ignoring the references to motor cars and boats.

Records and accounts

[61.47] Global accounting scheme records do not have to be kept in any set way but must be complete, up-to-date and clearly distinguishable from any other records. Records must be kept of purchases and sales (see **61.49** below) and workings used to calculate the VAT due. All scheme records must be preserved for six years.

The global accounting scheme records are in addition to those generally required of all taxable persons. See **RECORDS (56)**.

Failure to comply with any of the requirements as to records renders the taxable person liable for VAT on the full value of his sales.

(VAT Notice 718, paras 14, 15.1).

Stock

Stock on hand when starting global accounting scheme

[61.48] Any such eligible stock can be treated in either of the following ways.

- Taken into the scheme and included in the calculations for the first accounting period. Some form of stock take or valuation will be required. Where possible, stock should be identified separately and its purchase price established from invoices. Where stock cannot be related to original purchase invoices, the purchase value must be determined in some other way. There is no set way of doing this but HMRC must be satisfied that the method used is fair and reasonable. Any documents used to establish the stock valuation must be kept for six years.
- Not taken into the scheme. If the goods are then sold under the global accounting scheme, there is no 'purchase credit' to set against the sale and VAT will be accounted for on the full selling price rather than the profit margin.

Stock already included under margin scheme

Eligible stock already included in stock records under the margin scheme can either be sold under the margin scheme or transferred to the global accounting scheme. In the latter case, the stock must be deleted from the margin scheme stock book and cross-referred to and included in the global accounting scheme records.

(VAT Notice 718, paras 14.6, 14.7).

Purchases and sales summaries

[61.49] Summary records must be kept of purchases and sales for each accounting period. These do not have to be kept in any particular way but they must include the following details taken from any purchases invoices and any sales invoices issued.

- Invoice number.
- Date of purchase/sale.
- Description of goods sufficient to enable HMRC to verify that the goods are eligible for the global accounting scheme.
- Total price.

At the end of the VAT period, the totals of purchases and sales are used to calculate the VAT due.

(VAT Notice 718, para 15.6 which has the force of law).

Calculation of VAT due

[61.50] VAT is chargeable on the 'total profit margin' on goods supplied during a VAT period. '*Total profit margin*' is the amount (if any) by which the total sales exceed total purchases in the VAT period. See **61.24**(*a*) and (*b*) above for the rules for determining the price at which goods are purchased and sold.

The excess is the VAT-inclusive margin i.e. the VAT included is

VAT-inclusive margin × VAT fraction 7/47 (1/6 from 4 January 2011; 3/23 from 1 December 2008 to 31 December 2009)

Negative margin

If there is a negative margin (because total purchases exceed total sales), no VAT is due and the negative margin is carried forward to the following VAT period for inclusion in the calculation of the total purchases of that period. A negative margin cannot be set off against other VAT due in the same VAT period on transactions outside the global accounting scheme.

Copies of all calculations must be kept as part of the records.

[*SI 1995/1268, Art 13; SI 1999/3120*]. (VAT Notice 718, para 14.8).

> *Example*
>
> A dealer starts to use the global accounting scheme and values his opening stock on hand at £10,000. In the first VAT period, his total purchases from his purchase summary are £2,000 and his sales from his sales summary are £8,000.
>
> The margin for the first VAT period is £8,000 – (£10,000 + £2,000) = (£4,000)
>
> There is a negative margin and no VAT is due. The negative margin is carried forward to the next period in which purchases are £1,000 and sales are £7,000.
>
> The margin for the second VAT period is £7,000 – (£4,000 + £1,000) = £2,000
>
> VAT due = £2,000 × 7/47* = £297.87
>
> (*3/23 from 1 December 2008 to 31 December 2009)

If any of the goods sold in the period were obtained following the transfer of a business as a going concern, see **61.24** above.

Adjustments

Removing goods from the scheme

[61.51] Where purchases are initially included in the global accounting scheme purchase records but it is subsequently decided to sell the goods outside the scheme (e.g. because they are zero-rated on sale for export outside the EU) or the goods cease to be eligible (e.g. investment gold coins purchased before 1 January 2000) the scheme records must be adjusted. In the period in which the goods are removed from the scheme, the purchase value of those goods must be deducted from the global accounting scheme purchase records. There is no set way to apportion values to individual items but it must be fair and reasonable and it must be possible to demonstrate to HMRC how the value was determined.

Goods stolen or destroyed

Any loss of goods by breakage, theft or destruction must be adjusted by the deduction of their purchase price in the global accounting scheme purchase records.

Ceasing to use the global accounting scheme

If a dealer ceases to use the global accounting scheme for any reason, he must make an adjustment to take account of purchases for which he has taken credit but which have not been sold under the scheme.

- If deregistering, in the final period of using the scheme, the dealer must add the purchase value of his closing stock to his sales figure for that period.
- If transferring goods as part of a transfer of a going concern (TOGC), the dealer should add the purchase value of goods included in the scheme to sales figure for the period in which the TOGC takes place. This adjustment is separate from the actual TOGC which is not subject to VAT.

In either case, no adjustment is required if the total VAT due on stock on hand is £1,000 or less.

(VAT Notice 718, paras 15.7–15.9 which have the force of law).

Completion of VAT return

[61.52] See **2.7** *et seq* **ACCOUNTING PERIODS AND RETURNS** for notes on the completion of Form VAT 100. The following special rules apply to eligible goods bought and sold under the global accounting scheme.

Box 1	Where there is a positive margin, include the output tax calculated by reference to the difference between total purchases and total sales of eligible goods in the period covered by the return.
Box 6	Include the full selling price of all eligible goods sold under the scheme during the period, less any VAT included in that price.
Box 7	Include the purchase price (inclusive of VAT) of eligible goods bought in the period.

Any negative margins should not be included on the VAT return.

The auctioneers' scheme

[61.53] If an auctioneer sells eligible goods (see **61.3** above) and invoices in his own name he may either

- account for VAT under the auctioneers' scheme; or
- apply the rules for invoicing as an agent (see **61.26** above).

The auctioneers' scheme is a variation of the margin scheme. It allows auctioneers to account for VAT on a margin, the calculation of which involves

- adding to the hammer price the cost of the auctioneer's services charged to the buyer; and
- deducting from the hammer price the cost of the auctioneer's services charged to the seller.

The detailed provisions of the scheme are set out in **61.54** to **61.61** below and have the force of law. It is therefore important to check with the seller before the sale whether the goods are eligible for inclusion in the auctioneers' scheme.

The auctioneers' scheme and its conditions are for the purposes of calculating VAT liability and do not affect the legal status of agents or the contractual relationships between auctioneers, vendors and buyers.

(VAT Notice 718/2, paras 2.1, 2.3).

Tax point

Where goods are treated as supplied both to and by the auctioneer, there is a common tax point for both supplies which will normally be the earlier of

- the handing over of the goods by the auctioneer to the buyer; or
- the receipt of payment by the auctioneer.

Sales under the auctioneers' scheme to other EU countries

These are treated in the same way as sales within the UK. The sales are liable to VAT in the UK and no further VAT is due in the country of destination.

(VAT Notice 718/2, paras 3.3, 3.5).

De Voil Indirect Tax Service. See V3.533.

Conditions of the scheme

[61.54] The auctioneer's scheme can be used for sales of the following goods.

(a) Eligible goods (see **61.3** above) provided the following conditions are met.

  (i) The seller is

  - not registered for VAT;
  - a VAT-registered person supplying goods under the margin scheme (see **61.2** to **61.38** above) or the global accounting scheme (see **61.39** to **61.52** above);
  - an insurance company selling eligible goods which they have acquired as a result of an insurance claim provided that the goods are sold at auction in the same state; or
  - a finance company selling eligible goods which they have repossessed provided that they are sold at auction in the same state.

  (VAT Notice 718/2, para 2.4).

  (ii) The auctioneer complies with the invoicing requirements in **61.57** below. It is not necessary to maintain a stock book in strict accordance with the margin scheme if sufficient alternative records are retained to provide the same information (e.g. entry forms, sales catalogues, copies of lots and sales of the day and copies of sales and purchases invoices).
  (VAT Notice 718/2, para 4.2 which has the force of law).

(b) By extra-statutory concession, all goods grown, made or produced (including bloodstock or livestock reared from birth) by unregistered (non-taxable) persons.

As a condition of the relief, the auctioneer must obtain a signed certificate from the vendor including the vendor's full name and address, a description of the goods and the date of sale, a declaration that the vendor is not registered nor required to be registered for VAT, the signature of vendor and date, and the signature of auctioneer and date. The completed certificate must be retained with the relevant records for VAT purposes. An example of an acceptable certificate is set out below.

AUCTIONEERS' SCHEME FOR SECOND-HAND GOODS, WORKS OF ART, ANTIQUES AND COLLECTORS' ITEMS

Extra-statutory Concession 3.27

Vendor's Certificate for goods grown, made or produced and sold at auction on behalf of non-taxable persons

I (full name)

of (address)

declare that I am not registered or required to be registered for VAT and that the goods detailed below are to be sold at auction on my behalf by (auctioneer's name)

(Description of goods)

Date of sale (to be completed by auctioneer)

Signature of vendor

Signature of auctioneer

Date

The auctioneer may, with the agreement of HMRC, incorporate the certificate into his existing sales entry.

(VAT Notice 48, ESC 3.27; VAT Notice 718/2, paras 5.1, 5.3).

Charges to be included/excluded under the scheme

[61.55] Any commission or other charges made by the auctioneer to the vendor or buyer which are dependent on the sale of the goods must be included in the auctioneers' scheme calculation as set out in **61.59** below. Treatment of other charges are as follows.

- **Incidental expenses.** Any incidental expenses (e.g. packing, transport and insurance) incurred and charged onward to the buyer must be included in the scheme calculations unless they are a separate supply in their own right.
- **Disbursements for VAT purposes.** Any costs passed on to the client which meet all the conditions regarding disbursements under **3.7 AGENTS** can be excluded from the auctioneers' scheme.
- **Exempt supplies.** Any services supplied to the buyer or vendor which are exempt (e.g. making arrangements for the provision of insurance by a permitted insurer provided the disclosure requirements are complied with, see **36.13 INSURANCE**) should be excluded from the scheme calculations.
- **Services to an overseas vendor.** See **65.12** to **65.28 SUPPLY: PLACE OF SUPPLY** for the rules relating to the place of supply of services. Where the place of supply is in the UK, any services to an overseas vendor must be included in the auctioneers' scheme calculations. Where, however, the supply is treated as taking place outside the UK (e.g. supplies of certain services where the recipient belongs outside the EU or is in

business in another EU country, see **65.21 SUPPLY: PLACE OF SUPPLY**) the supply is outside the scope of UK VAT and should be excluded from the auctioneers' scheme calculations.

- **Other charges.** Charges for other supplies which are optional and not directly related to the hammer price should be excluded from the auctioneers' scheme calculations.

(VAT Notice 718/2, para 3.2).

Zero-rated sales

[61.56] Where the auctioneers' scheme is used for the sale of zero-rated goods (e.g. exports), the auctioneers' margin is also zero-rated. Any charges made outside the scheme are liable to VAT in the normal way. The normal conditions for zero-rating apply. See **21.2 EXPORTS**. (VAT Notice 718/2, paras 3.4, 3.6, 7.8).

Invoicing

[61.57] Auctioneers using the scheme must not itemise VAT separately on any statement or invoice issued to the vendor or buyer except where goods or services are provided in addition to, but separately from, the purchase or sale. Such non-scheme items should be invoiced under the normal VAT rules.

Purchase invoices

The auctioneer should issue to the seller of the goods an invoice or statement satisfying the conditions of a purchase invoice under **61.6** above and also showing

- the hammer price of the goods;
- any commission charges to the seller; and
- the net amount due to the seller.

The net amount due to the seller is the auctioneer's purchase price. If the seller is a VAT-registered dealer using the margin scheme, the net amount due is also his selling price. The auctioneer should therefore allocate any charges included under the auctioneers' scheme against each lot.

Sales invoices

The auctioneer should issue to the buyer of the goods an invoice or statement satisfying the conditions in **61.11** above (including the certificate regarding input tax deduction) and also showing

- the hammer price of the goods;
- any other charges for services made (e.g. buyer's premium); and
- the amount due from the buyer.

The amount due from the buyer is the auctioneer's selling price. If the buyer is a VAT-registered dealer using the margin scheme, the amount due is also his buying price. The auctioneer should therefore allocate any charges included under the auctioneers' scheme against each lot.

(VAT Notice 718/2, para 4.3 which has the force of law).

Invoices in foreign currency

Invoices issued in foreign currency under the auctioneers' scheme must show the sterling equivalent of each element of the invoice (e.g. hammer price of the goods and the amount of commission or other charges due) and not just the total value of supplies made. The foreign currency value must be converted into sterling using one of the methods in **71.18 VALUATION**.

Scheme and non-scheme supplies

If both scheme and non-scheme supplies are made to the same customer, either separate invoices can be issued (advisable) or all supplies can be included on the same invoice. In the latter case, the invoice must clearly distinguish between the two types of supply and comply with all the relevant provisions for both. In the case of a sales invoice, it must also show clearly the amount of the selling price which will form the basis of the purchase price for the buyer's margin scheme or global accounting scheme records.

Re-invoicing

If goods have been sold under the auctioneers' scheme but the buyer subsequently decides that he wishes to treat the transaction outside the scheme (paying VAT separately on the hammer price and the other charges), the auctioneer may re-invoice for the transaction under the normal VAT rules provided

(a) the auctioneer can comply with all the relevant VAT regulations of the substitute transaction;
(b) at the time of the amendment, the auctioneer and buyer hold all the original evidence relating to the transaction;
(c) the auctioneer cancels the first entry in his records and cross-refers to the amended transaction; and
(d) any substitute document (e.g. a VAT invoice) issued to the buyer clearly refers to the original transaction and states that it is cancelled and that the buyer should amend his VAT records accordingly.

Re-invoicing cannot be undertaken more than three years after the due date of the VAT return on which the original supply was accounted for. This is because input tax cannot be claimed under the three-year cap rules.

(VAT Notice 718/2, paras 4.4–4.6).

Imported works of art, antiques and collectors' pieces and works of art obtained from the creators or their heirs

[61.58] Goods which have been obtained with VAT charged on their full value are normally ineligible for the auctioneers' scheme. However, auctioneers acting in their own names may opt to use the auctioneers' scheme to deal with

(a) works of art, antiques and collectors' pieces which they have imported themselves (as principals on behalf of a third party) for onward sale in their own names; and

(b) works of art obtained (i.e. supplied in the UK or acquired from another EU country) from creators or their heirs for onward sale in their own names.

In either case, the auctioneers' scheme may be used despite VAT having already been charged on the importation, acquisition or supply of the goods. The conditions for exercising the option are as follows.

- HMRC must be notified in writing that the option is to be taken up, specifying the date from which it will apply.
- The option must be exercised for a period of at least two years. Thereafter it will continue to apply until HMRC are advised in writing as to when it will cease.
- If the option is used, it must be applied to all transactions within (*a*) and (*b*) above, not just in respect of certain transactions or certain categories of goods.
- If, having exercised the option, the auctioneer decides to sell outside the scheme any goods covered by the option (e.g. he exports the goods), he is not entitled to recover any input tax on those goods until the period in which VAT is accounted for on their sale.

If the option is not used, VAT must be accounted for in accordance with the general rules for auctioneers.

Purchase price

If the option to use the auctioneers' scheme has been exercised, the purchase price is calculated as follows.

(i) *Imported works of art, antiques and collectors' items*. The option applies to imports at a reduced rate of 5%. The auctioneer must not reclaim the import VAT as input tax. His purchase price for the auctioneers' scheme is the hammer price less any commission charges made to the seller. The import VAT incurred must not be included in the auctioneers' scheme calculations although the auctioneer may wish to recoup this amount separately from the seller.

(ii) *Works of art obtained from the creator or his heirs*. The auctioneer must not reclaim any VAT charged by the supplier and must calculate his purchase price in accordance with **61.59** below. Because the creator or heir will have to account for output tax on the full hammer price they may ask the auctioneer to sell the item under the normal margin scheme option. In such cases, any invoice issued for charges for services must show VAT at the standard rate separately. This will enable the supplier to reclaim the input tax on those charges. The auctioneer's purchase price under the normal margin scheme option is the hammer price only.

Buyer's premium

Works of art, antiques and collectors' items are often entered to a Temporary Importation (TI) regime in order to be sold at auction. Following the sale, the goods are then either exported from the EU or finally imported.

If imported, the goods qualify for the 5% reduced rate of import VAT which must be accounted for on the appropriate customs import declaration. But, with effect from 1 September 2006, the commission charged by the auctioneer, known as the buyer's premium, does not qualify for the 5% reduced rate. VAT must be accounted for on the buyer's premium at the standard rate.

If the goods are exported from TI to a place outside the EU, VAT is chargeable on the buyer's premium at the zero rate.

(VAT Notice 718, paras 10.1–10.2).

Calculation of VAT

[61.59] The purchase price, selling price, margin and VAT due are calculated from the successful bid price (hammer price) and commission and other charges.

'*Purchase price*' is the hammer price less commission payable to the auctioneer under his contract with the seller for the sale of the goods (see **61.55** above).

'*Selling price*' is the hammer price plus the consideration for any supply of services by the auctioneer to the purchaser (e.g. buyer's premium) in connection with the sale of the goods (see **61.55** above).

The margin is the difference between the purchase price and the selling price. The margin is regarded as being VAT-inclusive i.e. the VAT included is

VAT-inclusive margin × VAT fraction 7/47 (1/6 from 4 January 2011; 3/23 from 1 December 2008 to 31 December 2009)

> *Example*
>
> Goods are sold at auction for £1,000 (the hammer price). Commission is charged to the seller at 10% net of VAT and a buyer's premium is charged of 15% net of VAT.
>
> | | |
> |---|---|
> | Commission = (£1,000 × 10%) + 17.5%* VAT = | £117.50 |
> | Purchase price = £1,000 – £117.50 = | £882.50 |
> | Buyer's premium = (£1,000 × 15%) + 17.5%* VAT = | £176.25 |
> | Selling price = £1,000 + £176.25 = | £1,176.25 |
> | Margin = £1,176.25 – £882.50 = | £293.75 |
> | Output tax = £293.75 × 7/47* = | £43.75 |
>
> *20% from 4 January 2011; 15% from 1 December 2008 to 31 December 2009
>
> **1/6 from 4 January 2011; 3/23 from 1 December 2008 to 31 December 2009

[*SI 1992/3122, Art 8(7); SI 1995/1268, Art 12(7); SI 1995/1269; SI 2001/3753; SI 2001/3754*]. (VAT Notice 718/2, paras 3.1, 8.3).

Dealers buying at auction

[61.60] Where a taxable dealer buys goods at an auction and wishes to use either the margin scheme or the global accounting scheme for the onward sale of the goods, he should

- check that the goods will be eligible for onward sale under the chosen scheme (usually clear from the auctioneer's sales catalogue). If VAT is charged separately on the hammer price, the goods will not qualify for either scheme; and
- follow the record-keeping requirements under the chosen scheme.

The dealer's purchase price is the hammer price of the goods plus charges for services (which must not show VAT separately) and should be clearly identified on the sales invoice issued by the auctioneer. The invoice should itemise, for each lot, the hammer price of the goods and any charges for services (for example, buyer's premium). The total of these amounts (i.e. the amount due from the dealer to the auctioneer) is the purchase price for the purpose of the margin scheme or global accounting scheme and is the amount that the dealer must show in his stock book. Any other charges for services on which VAT is shown separately must not be included as part of the purchase price.

In some cases a dealer may receive a single invoice from the auctioneer, showing the hammer price of the goods and charges for inclusion in the scheme calculations as well as charges on which VAT is shown separately. To avoid confusion, the dealer may wish to ask the auctioneer to provide him with a separate invoice for these charges. In either case, the dealer can reclaim the VAT shown under the normal rules but must make sure that he does not add the value of these charges to his purchase price for the purposes of the margin scheme.

(VAT Notice 718/2, paras 3.1, 3.2, 4.4).

Dealers selling at auction under the margin scheme or global accounting scheme

[61.61] A taxable dealer selling at auction must tell the auctioneer before the sale is due to take place exactly how he wishes to treat the sale, i.e. under the auctioneers' scheme, margin scheme or global accounting scheme. If the auctioneer uses the auctioneers' scheme he issues an invoice/statement which includes

- the hammer price of the goods;
- his commission charges; and
- the net amount payable to the dealer.

None of these amounts should show VAT separately. Any other charges for services should be invoiced separately with VAT, if applicable, shown on the full amount of each charge.

Alternatively, the dealer can ask the auctioneer to sell the goods under the normal margin scheme. In these circumstances, the auctioneer issues an invoice/statement which only includes the hammer price of the goods. VAT must not be shown separately on this amount. His commission charges and any other charges for his services must be invoiced separately with VAT, if applicable, shown on the full amount of each charge. The dealer can reclaim the VAT on such charges under the normal rules.

Selling price of eligible goods sold at auction

A dealer's selling price for the purpose of the margin scheme should be clearly identifiable on the invoice/statement issued by the auctioneer.

- If the auctioneer has supplied the goods under the auctioneers' scheme, the hammer price of the goods and commission charges will not show VAT separately. The dealer's selling price is the net amount, i.e. the hammer price less the commission charge. If the auctioneer makes other charges, these should be invoiced separately and, if applicable, VAT charged under the normal rules. The dealer must not include these charges as part of his selling price but will be able to reclaim the VAT charged, subject to the normal rules.
- If, in agreement with the auctioneer, the dealer arranges for the goods to be sold by the auctioneer under the normal margin scheme as it applies to agents, the dealer's selling price is the hammer price. Any other charges that the auctioneer makes should be invoiced or itemised separately and, if applicable, VAT charged under the normal rules.

(VAT Notice 718/2, paras 3.1, 3.2).

Key points

[61.62] Points to consider are as follows.

- Margin schemes are very worthwhile for those businesses that deal in second-hand goods. However, it is important to ensure the record keeping requirements of HMRC are fully met, otherwise it could base output tax on the full selling price of an item rather than the profit margin. The record-keeping requirements have the force of law.
- An example of an important record-keeping requirement is that a full purchase invoice must be produced for items bought from members of the public.
- When a VAT-registered trader sells goods under the margin scheme, the sales invoice must be certified with the statement: 'this is a second hand margin scheme supply' (or similar wording).
- An important record with the margin scheme is the stock book maintained by the business, which should be accurate and complete. Items should be fully described, i.e. including any specific descriptions or registration numbers.
- Input tax can be claimed on expenditure incurred by a business improving or repairing a margin item (subject to normal rules). The cost of the repair should not be deducted against the margin on which output tax is due under the scheme.
- An item that is bought by a business and is eligible for use within a margin scheme can still be sold under normal VAT rules, i.e. output tax charged on full selling price. This could be a useful planning point if the customer can claim input tax.

- As far as VAT registration limits are concerned, the relevant taxable sales figure is the full selling price, not the profit margin. An exception to this statement relates to margin sales under TOMS (tour operators' margin scheme).
- A margin item sold to a customer outside the EU can be zero-rated as an export (or possibly retail export). It is important that export evidence is acquired and retained to confirm the goods have left the EU, i.e. shipping documents, insurance documents, commercial documents etc.
- There is no 'loss relief' with a margin scheme (apart from the global accounting scheme). This means that a loss made on one item cannot be offset against a profit made on another item.
- A business selling high quantities of small value items could benefit from using the global accounting scheme – the main benefits of which relate to the reduced record-keeping requirements (compared to the main margin scheme) and the automatic loss relief available on items sold at a loss.
- A business using global accounting can carry forward a loss made in one VAT period (where total purchases exceed total sales), so that the loss can be added to purchases in the next period, i.e. to reduce the profit margin in that period.

62

Self-Supply

Cross-references. See **42.2 LAND AND BUILDINGS: ZERO AND REDUCED RATE SUPPLIES AND DIY HOUSEBUILDERS** for change of use of residential and charitable buildings; **42.20 LAND AND BUILDINGS: ZERO AND REDUCED RATE SUPPLIES AND DIY HOUSEBUILDERS** for self-supply of certain construction services; **45.6 MOTOR CARS** for self-supply of motor cars; **66.14 SUPPLY: TIME OF SUPPLY** for the time of self-supply.

De Voil Indirect Tax Service. See V3.241.

Introduction

[62.1] The Treasury may, by order, provide that where specified goods are taken possession of or produced by a person (not necessarily a *taxable* person) in the course or furtherance of a business carried on by him *and*

(a) are neither supplied to another person nor incorporated in other goods produced in the course or furtherance of that business; *but*

(b) are used by him for the purpose of a business carried on by him,

the goods are treated for VAT purposes as being both supplied to him for the purpose of that business and supplied by him in the course or furtherance of it. [*VATA 1994, s 5(5)(7)*].

Such a power is aimed to prevent an advantage being gained by a person who produces for himself goods on which, if supplied externally, either input tax would be specifically denied, or on which input tax would be denied or restricted because of exempt output supplies being made by the person concerned. Specific orders have been made as regards motor cars (see **45.6 MOTOR CARS**) and stationery (see **62.2** below).

Similar powers to the above as regards goods are also applied to services. [*VATA 1994, s 5(6)*]. See **42.20 LAND AND BUILDINGS: ZERO AND REDUCED RATE SUPPLIES AND DIY HOUSEBUILDERS** for self-supply of certain construction services.

Example

John owns a partly-exempt business, and uses his own employees to carry out alterations on his own trading premises. In the absence of the self-supply rules, he could avoid charging VAT on this supply. However, the self-supply rules treat this as a supply both to and by John and he must therefore:

- account for output tax on the value of the supply; and
- reclaim input tax on the value of the supply in accordance with his existing partial exemption method.

The outcome in the above example is a net payment of VAT by John (i.e. on the basis that the premises in question have some exempt use, and an input tax block therefore applies).

Key points

[62.2] Points to consider are as follows.

- The purpose of the self-supply rules is to ensure that a partly-exempt business cannot obtain a VAT advantage by producing goods or self-supplying services for use in their business, which would otherwise have carried irrecoverable input VAT.
- A business that is not partly-exempt may still face a VAT bill with the self-supply rules if the goods or services in question are non-deductible for input tax purposes, e.g. in relation to a motor car available for private use.

63

Special Schemes

Introduction

[63.1] The following special schemes are available to VAT-registered businesses.

- **Flat-rate scheme for small businesses.** Subject to conditions, including an annual turnover limit, small businesses can opt to join a flat-rate scheme under which they calculate net VAT due by applying a flat-rate percentage to VAT-inclusive turnover. The flat-rate percentage varies with the trade sector into which the business falls. See **63.15** to **63.24** below.
- **Cash accounting scheme.** Subject to conditions, including an annual turnover limit, this scheme can be used by any business. See **63.2** to **63.8** below.
- **Annual accounting scheme.** Subject to meeting certain conditions, including an annual turnover limit, a business can apply to HMRC to prepare an annual VAT return and make payments on account during the year. See **63.9** to **63.14** below.
- **Retail schemes.** There are a number of different retail schemes designed to suit different types of retail business. See **60 RETAIL SCHEMES.**
- **Second-hand schemes.** In general, VAT is charged on the full value of any goods, including second-hand goods, sold by a business. However, provided certain conditions are met, VAT can be charged on the profit margin (instead of value) on supplies of second-hand goods; works of art, antiques and collectors' items; and goods sold through an agent acting in his own name in relation to the supply. See **61 SECOND-HAND GOODS** for details.
- **Tour operators' margin scheme.** All UK businesses that buy travel, hotel and holiday services, etc. from third parties and resell these supplies as principals *must* use a special scheme under which VAT has to be accounted for on the difference between the VAT-inclusive purchase price and selling price. See **68 TOUR OPERATORS' MARGIN SCHEME.**
- **Flat-rate scheme for farmers.** A flat-rate scheme is available to farmers as an option to registering for VAT. Once in the scheme, VAT is not accounted for on sales of goods and services within certain designated activities and input tax is not recoverable on purchases. To compensate for this the farmer charges, and retains, a fixed flat-rate addition on sales, within those activities, to VAT-registered persons. See **63.25** to **63.30** below.
- **Racehorse owners.** A special arrangement has been made between HMRC and the thoroughbred horseracing and breeding industry. See **63.31** to **63.33** below.

Cash accounting scheme

[63.2] A business may, subject to conditions, account for and pay VAT on the basis of cash or other consideration paid and received. The conditions are as laid down in *Regulations* and as described in VAT Notice 731 *which in certain circumstances has the force of law* (see VAT Notice 747). HMRC may vary the terms of the scheme by publishing a fresh Notice or a Notice which amends an existing Notice, but without prejudicing the right of a person to withdraw from the scheme. [*VATA 1994, s 25(1), Sch 11 para 2(7); SI 1995/2518, Regs 57, 59; SI 1997/1614, Reg 4*].

The main advantages of the scheme are automatic bad debt relief and the deferral of the time for payment of VAT where extended credit is given. The scheme will probably not be beneficial for net repayment businesses or where most sales are paid promptly or for cash. (VAT Notice 731, para 1.3).

The cash accounting scheme cannot be used at the same time as the flat-rate scheme for small businesses (see **63.15** below). [*SI 1995/2518, Reg 57A; SI 2002/1142*].

De Voil Indirect Tax Service. See V2.199.

Joining the scheme

[63.3] A business is eligible to start using the scheme if it meets the following conditions:

- it expects the value of its taxable supplies in the next year will be £1,350,000 (£660,000 before 1 April 2007) or less;
- it has no VAT returns outstanding;
- it has not been convicted of a VAT offence in the last year;
- it has not accepted an offer to compound proceedings in connection with a VAT offence in the last year;
- it has not been assessed to a penalty for VAT evasion involving dishonest conduct in the last year;
- it does not owe HMRC any money or if it does, it has made arrangements with them to clear the total amount of outstanding VAT payments (including surcharges and/or penalties);
- HMRC have not written to it withdrawing use of the scheme during the last year;
- HMRC have not written to it and denied it access to the scheme; and
- it complies with the conditions set out in Notice 731.

A business cannot begin to operate the scheme if HMRC consider that, for the protection of the revenue, it should not be able to do so. In such circumstances, the business may ask HMRC to reconsider the decision if it can provide further relevant information or if there are facts which it thinks have not been taken fully into account. If still not satisfied, an appeal may be made to a VAT tribunal. See **5 APPEALS.**

The scheme cannot be applied retrospectively to the business.

[*SI 1995/2518, Reg 58(1)(4); SI 1997/1614, Reg 3; SI 2001/677; SI 2004/767, Reg 7; SI 2007/768, Reg 3*]. (VAT Notice 731, para 2.1 which has the force of law).

VAT group treatment

The turnover limit for the cash accounting scheme applies to the VAT group as a whole. Also, HMRC do not allow one or more companies in a VAT group to operate cash accounting while other members use the normal invoice-based requirements. The following action is therefore required when a new member enters a VAT group.

- The new member must deregister (whether or not using the cash accounting scheme).
- If the existing group is not using the cash accounting scheme but the new member is, the new member must return to the normal method of accounting and account for outstanding VAT whilst using the scheme on its final VAT return.
- If the existing group is using the cash accounting scheme, and the turnover of the enlarged group remains within the tolerance for use of the scheme in **63.7** below, the new member must use the cash accounting scheme from the date of joining the group. (If the new member makes or receives payments, after joining the group, for sales or purchases made whilst separately registered, the associated VAT must be accounted for on its final return and should be excluded from the group's VAT account.)
- If the existing group is using the cash accounting scheme, but the new member pushes the group turnover over the scheme limits, the whole group must leave the scheme at the end of the VAT period in which the new member joins the group.

Supplies to be dealt with inside and outside the scheme

[63.4] Subject to the following exceptions, where the cash accounting scheme is used, it must be used for the whole of the VAT registered business.

Exceptions

The following transactions must be dealt with outside the cash accounting scheme under the normal VAT rules.

- Goods bought or sold under hire purchase, lease purchase, conditional sale or credit sale agreements.
- Goods imported from outside the EU, acquired from another EU country, or removed from a Customs warehouse or free zone. The scheme can be used to account for VAT on the onward supply of these goods in the UK.
- Supplies where a VAT invoice is issued and full payment of the amount shown on the invoice is not due within six months from the date of issue of the invoice.
- Supplies in respect of which a VAT invoice is issued in advance of the delivery or making available of the goods or the performance of the services, as the case may be. This does not apply where goods have been delivered or made available in part (or, as the case may be, services have been performed in part) and the VAT invoice in question relates solely to that part.

- Reverse charge supplies of mobile phones or computer chips under which the recipient has to account for and pay the VAT. See **4.14 ANTI-AVOIDANCE.**

[*SI 1995/2518, Regs 58(2)(3); SI 1997/1614, Reg 3; SI 2007/1418, Reg 6*]. (VAT Notice 731, paras 2.7, 5.5 which have the force of law).

Records

[63.5] The normal requirements regarding copies of VAT invoices and evidence of input tax apply. The following additional records must also be kept.

(a) **Receipted invoices.**
- If payment is made in money (i.e. banknotes or coin) to another VAT-registered business, the copy of the purchase invoice must be receipted and dated (the other business *must* on request provide such an invoice). [*SI 1995/2518, Reg 65(3)*].
- If payment is received in money (i.e. banknotes or coin), a receipted and dated VAT invoice must be issued, if requested, and a copy retained for six years or such lesser period as HMRC allow. [*SI 1995/2518, Reg 65(3)*]. (VAT Notice 731, para 4.1).

(b) **Payment record.** To use the cash accounting scheme, payments made/received must be clearly cross-referenced to the corresponding purchase/sales invoice and to normal commercial evidence such as bank statements, cheque stubs, paying-in slips. This can be done by keeping a cash book summarising all payments made and received with a separate column for VAT. (VAT Notice 731, para 4.3 which has the force of law).

See also **63.6** below for records required for specific transactions.

Accounting for VAT

Output tax

[63.6] Output tax must be accounted for in the return for the VAT period in which payment or other consideration is received. [*SI 1995/2518, Regs 57, 65*]. For this purpose payment by

- *cash* (i.e. coins and notes) is received on the date the money is received;
- *cheque* is received on the date the cheque is received or, if later, the date on the cheque. If the cheque is not honoured, no VAT is due and an adjustment or a refund claim can be made if VAT has already been accounted for;
- *credit or debit card* is received on the date the sales voucher is made out (*not* the date when payment is received from the card company). If the payment is not honoured, no VAT is due and an adjustment or a refund claim can be made if VAT has already been accounted for; and
- *giros, standing orders and direct debits* are received on the day the bank account is credited.

Where an existing VAT-registered business starts to use the scheme, it should separate in its records any payments received for transactions already accounted for under the normal method of accounting. Such payments should be excluded from the scheme records.

(VAT Notice 731, paras 3.1, 4.4 which have the force of law).

Deposits

VAT on deposits must normally be accounted for when received unless the deposit is not payment for supplies (eg deposits taken as security which are either returned or forfeited) in which case there is no requirement to account for VAT. (VAT Notice 731, para 5.1).

Payments received net of deductions

Where a net payment is received after deduction of commission/expenses, VAT should be accounted for on the full value before such deduction. Examples include

- commission deducted by a customer;
- commission or payment for expenses deducted by a factor or agent collecting monies on behalf of the business;
- commission or payment for expenses deducted by an auctioneer selling goods on behalf of the business; and
- deductions made by an employer/contractor who has deducted income tax.

(VAT Notice 731, para 5.8 which has the force of law).

Payments received in foreign currency

Where a business issues an invoice in a foreign currency (including euros), it must also show the amount of VAT due in sterling. Therefore

- if the invoice is paid in full in the foreign currency, there is no need to convert the foreign currency payment and output tax is the sterling amount of VAT due as shown on the invoice; and
- if the invoice is paid in part in the foreign currency, output tax should be determined by calculating the proportion of the total amount due in the foreign currency which has been paid and applying that proportion to the sterling amount of VAT due as shown on the invoice.

Where a business issues an invoice in sterling but is paid in a foreign currency,

- if the invoice is paid in full, the output tax is the amount of VAT due as shown on the invoice; and
- if the invoice is paid in part, the foreign currency payment must be converted into sterling at the rate appropriate at the time of supply (not the time of payment). Output tax should then be determined by calculating the proportion of the total sterling amount due that the sterling equivalent of the payment represents and applying that proportion to the VAT due as shown on the invoice. See **71.18 VALUATION** for methods of converting foreign exchange.

(VAT Notice 731, paras 5.10, 5.11).

Factored debts

Where debts are sold or formally assigned to a factor, output tax must be accounted for on the amount that the factor collects from the customer (not any reduced value for which they are assigned) in the period in which the factor collects payment from the customer. For recourse agreements, if the factor is unable to collect all (or part) of the debt, then that amount must be accounted for under the normal rules. For non-recourse agreements, output tax must be accounted for on the uncollected element of the debt in the period in which any advance made against that debt is written off by the factor. However, if the factor re-assigns all or part of the debt back to the business under a recourse clause, it may claim **BAD DEBT RELIEF (7)** on any unpaid element subject to the normal bad debt rules.

Where a business merely uses a factor or invoice discounter as a debt collector and retains legal title to the debt, it must account for output tax in the VAT period in which the customer pays the debt collector. VAT is due on the amount received by the debt collector from the customer (not any lesser amount after commission, etc. received by the business).

(VAT Notice 731, paras 5.2, 5.3 which have the force of law).

Exports and supplies to other EU countries

The cash accounting scheme can be used to account for VAT which becomes due on goods exported or supplied to another EU country because satisfactory evidence of export/supply has not been received within the time limit allowed for zero-rating. VAT must be accounted for when the time limit expires on all payments already received. If further payments are received, VAT must be accounted for on such payments at the time of receipt. If evidence of export is received after any VAT has been accounted for, the VAT can be adjusted in the VAT period in which the evidence is obtained. (VAT Notice 731, para 5.6).

Input tax

Input tax can be reclaimed in the return for the VAT period in which payment is made or other consideration is given or in a later period as may be agreed with HMRC. [*SI 1995/2518, Regs 57, 65*]. For this purpose payment by

- *cash* (i.e. coins and notes) is made on the date the money is paid (although a receipted VAT invoice must be held before reclaiming VAT on purchases made in this way, see **63.5** above);
- *cheque* is made on the date the cheque is sent to the supplier or, if later, the date on the cheque. If the cheque is not honoured, no VAT is reclaimable and an adjustment or error correction notification (formerly voluntary disclosure) must be made if VAT has already been claimed;
- *credit or debit card* is made when the supplier makes out the sales voucher (*not* the date when payment is made to the card company); and
- *giros, standing orders and direct debits* are made on the day the bank account is debited.

(VAT Notice 731, para 4.5 which has the force of law).

Using the scheme from the date of registration

Newly registered businesses may reclaim VAT on certain goods and services obtained prior to registration. See **34.10 INPUT TAX**. When the cash accounting scheme is used from the date of registration, VAT on such purchases should be reclaimed on the first VAT return if paid pre-registration or otherwise in the VAT period of payment.

Existing businesses starting to use the scheme

Where an existing VAT-registered business starts to use the scheme, it should separate in its records any payments made for transactions already dealt with under the normal method of accounting. Such payments should be excluded from the scheme records.

(VAT Notice 731, paras 3.1, 3.2).

Deposits

If advance payment is made by way of deposit, VAT can be reclaimed when the payment is made unless the deposit is not payment for supplies (e.g. deposits given as security which are either returned or forfeited) in which case there is no entitlement to deduct VAT. (VAT Notice 731, para 5.1).

Allocation of part payments

Where a payment is made or received which is part payment of one or more invoices (which may include both standard and zero-rated supplies), the payment must be allocated to the invoices in date order (earliest first). Where VAT is not identified separately on the part payment, the payment must be treated as VAT-inclusive. In cases where the payment relates to an invoice for supplies at different rates of VAT, the part payment must be apportioned between the different rates and the amounts on which VAT is due at the standard rate or reduced rate treated as VAT-inclusive.

Example

A payment of £2,500 is made against the following two invoices.

Invoice A (dated 1/5/04)	
Standard-rated goods	1,000
VAT	175
	£1,175
Invoice B (dated 26/5/04)	
Standard-rated goods	2,000
Zero-rated goods	1,000
VAT	350
	£3,350

The payment of £2,500 is allocated as follows.

(1) Allocate £1,175 against Invoice A (the earlier invoice) i.e. to include VAT of £175.00

(2) The balance of the payment £1,325 (£2,500 – £1,175) should be allocated against Invoice B. The proportion of the payment relating to VAT is 1,325 ÷ 3,350 × £350 = £138.43

Total amount of VAT to be accounted for on the payment of £2,500 is £313.43 (£175.00 + £138.43). The remaining VAT of £211.57 (£350.00 – £138.43) should be accounted for when any further payment is made.

(VAT Notice 731, paras 5.7, 8.2).

Payments in kind

Where payment is partly or fully in kind (e.g. a part exchange or barter transaction) VAT must be accounted for on the full value of the supply. This is usually the price, excluding VAT, which would have been paid for the supply if money were the only consideration. See **71.5–71.7 VALUATION** for further details. VAT must be accounted for on the 'payment' on the date the business receives/supplies the goods or services agreed in lieu of money. (VAT Notice 731, para 5.9).

See also *A-Z Electrical* (VTD 10718) (TVC 10.12) where a business using the cash accounting scheme received shares in a company in lieu of the money owed to it for supplies of goods. The tribunal held that the business should be taken to have received cash in satisfaction of the debt owed to it, and to have paid the same amount of cash for the shares. The deemed payment for the supplies was liable to VAT.

Partial exemption

A business which makes both taxable and exempt supplies may not be able to reclaim all its input tax. See **49 PARTIAL EXEMPTION**. A partly-exempt business which uses the cash accounting scheme must base its partial exemption calculations on payments made and received rather than purchases and sales. (VAT Notice 731, para 4.6).

Completion of VAT returns

The amounts of VAT due and VAT deductible are based on payments received and made, not on invoices issued. Similarly, the boxes for values of outputs and inputs must be completed on the basis of payments received and made (exclusive of VAT). Where supplies are made to other EU countries, the amount to be put in Box 8 is the total VAT-exclusive value of all supplies of goods and services made and *not* the total of payments received. (VAT Notice 731, para 4.7).

Leaving the scheme

[63.7] The following rules apply.

(a) **Turnover exceeding the limit.** Unless HMRC allow or direct otherwise, a business must withdraw from the cash accounting scheme at the end of a VAT period (and use the normal method of accounting for subsequent periods) if the value of its taxable supplies in the year then ending has exceeded £1.6 million (£825,000 before 1 April 2007). [*SI 1995/2518, Reg 60(1)(3); SI 1997/1614, Reg 5; SI 2001/677; SI 2004/767, Reg 8; SI 2007/768, Reg 4*]. For the purposes of this calculation, disposals of stocks and capital assets must be included. (VAT Notice 731, para 2.5).

Exceptionally, HMRC may allow a business to remain in the scheme where it can demonstrate that

- this limit was exceeded because of a large 'one-off' increase in sales which has not occurred before and is not expected to recur (e.g. the sale of a capital asset);
- the sale arose from a genuine commercial activity; and
- there are reasonable grounds for believing that turnover in the next twelve months will be below £1.35 million (£660,000 before 1 April 2007).

Application must be made to HMRC in writing and will be confirmed by them in writing.

(VAT Notice 731, para 2.6).

(b) **Voluntary withdrawal.** A business may withdraw from the scheme at the end of a VAT period. [*SI 1995/2518, Reg 60(2); SI 1997/1614, Reg 5*].

(c) **Expulsion from the scheme.** A business is not entitled to continue to operate the scheme in the following circumstances.

- It cannot comply with the record-keeping requirements in **63.5** above.
- It has, while operating the scheme,
  - (i) been convicted of an offence in connection with VAT;
  - (ii) accepted an offer to compound proceedings in connection with a VAT offence;
  - (iii) been assessed to a penalty under *VATA 1994, s 60* (VAT evasion involving dishonesty);
  - (iv) failed to leave the scheme although its taxable supplies exceed the £1.6 million limit; or
  - (v) HMRC consider it necessary for the protection of the revenue.

[*SI 1995/2518, Reg 64(1); SI 1997/1614, Reg 9*]. (VAT Notice 731, para 2.6).

Appeals

An appeal may be made against any denial of access to or withdrawal of use of the cash accounting scheme. See **5.3 APPEALS**. If the appeal is against a decision by HMRC to deny access to use the scheme, withdraw use of the scheme for the protection of the revenue or not to allow continued use of the scheme for exceeding the tolerance, the business must cease to use the scheme until the appeal is resolved. For other appeals, HMRC will normally allow continued use of the scheme, pending outcome of the appeal, unless it considers that an appeal facilitates manipulation of the scheme. (VAT Notice 731, paras 6.8, 6.9).

Subsequent accounting for VAT

Unless the transitional arrangements below can be applied, a business which ceases to operate the cash accounting scheme because of *(a)*–*(c)* above must, on the return for the VAT period in which it ceased to operate the scheme, account for

- all VAT that it would have been required to pay to HMRC during the time the scheme was operated if it had not been operating the scheme, minus
- all VAT accounted for and paid to HMRC in accordance with the scheme, subject to any adjustment for credit for input tax.

Transitional arrangements

Where a business ceases to operate the cash accounting scheme because of *(a)* or *(b)* above, then provided the value of its taxable supplies in the three months ending at the end of the VAT period in which it ceased to operate the scheme has not exceeded £1.35 million (£660,000 before 1 April 2007), it may apply transitional arrangements. This means that the business can continue to operate the scheme in respect of its 'scheme supplies' for six months after the end of the VAT period in which it ceased to operate the scheme. '*Scheme supplies*' means supplies made and received while the business operated the scheme that were not excluded from the scheme under **63.4** above and did not fall to be included in the flat-rate scheme for small businesses (see **63.15** below).

Where a business chooses to apply the transitional arrangements, it must, on the return for the first VAT period that ends six months or more after the end of the VAT period in which it ceased to operate the scheme, account for

- all VAT that it would have been required to pay to HMRC during the time the scheme was operated if it had not then been operating the scheme, minus
- all VAT accounted for and paid to HMRC in accordance with the scheme (including any VAT accounted for and paid because it applied transitional arrangements), subject to any adjustment for credit for input tax.

[SI 1995/2518, Regs 61, 64(2); SI 1997/1614, Reg 9; SI 2004/767, Reg 9; SI 2007/768, Reg 5].

There is no need to apply to or notify HMRC if the transitional arrangements are used. During the six-month period it will be necessary to keep normal cash accounting records for payments and receipts for supplies which took place while the scheme was in use and separate records under the normal VAT accounting requirements for new supplies made and received. (VAT Notice 731, paras 6.4, 6.5).

Bad debt relief

If a business stops using cash accounting, it has to account for VAT on supplies it has made and received even if they have not been paid for. If the business has not received any payment then it may be able to claim **BAD DEBT RELIEF (7)**. The key conditions are

- that it is at least six months from the date on which the debt became due and payable or the supply was made, whichever is later;
- the business can provide evidence that the bad debt has been written off in its 'refunds for bad debts' account; and
- for supplies made prior to 1 January 2003, where the customer is registered for VAT, the business has notified the customer of the claim for bad debt relief.

Where the business has opted to use the transitional arrangements, bad debt relief can be claimed in the VAT period which ends at the end of the six months. [*SI 1995/2518, Reg 64A; SI 2004/767, Reg 10*]. (VAT Notice 731, para 6.6).

Cessation of business

[63.8] Where a business operating the cash accounting scheme ceases trading or ceases to be registered, it must, within two months or such longer period as HMRC allow, account for and pay VAT due on all supplies made and received up to the date of cessation which has not otherwise been accounted for, subject to any adjustment for credit for input tax. [*SI 1995/2518, Reg 63(1); SI 1997/1614, Reg 8*].

In practice, where a business ceases trading, HMRC allow the business to continue to use the cash accounting scheme while any remaining stocks and assets are disposed of. Once VAT registration is cancelled, however, the final VAT return must be submitted within two months of deregistration. This applies even if the business has still not been paid for all its supplies, although where any of this relates to bad debts, the concessionary relief in **63.7** above may be applied. (VAT Notice 731, paras 6.10, 6.12).

Insolvency

Where a business operating the cash accounting scheme becomes insolvent, it must, within two months of the date of insolvency, account for VAT due on all supplies made and received up to the date of insolvency which has not otherwise been accounted for, subject to any credit for input tax. [*SI 1995/2518, Reg 62; SI 1997/1614, Reg 7*]. Where trading continues after the date of insolvency, the officeholder responsible for the business may continue to use the cash accounting scheme subject to the normal rules of the scheme. If the officeholder does continue to use the scheme, he must, from the date of insolvency, separate in the business records any payments the business makes or receives for transactions already accounted for on the pre-insolvency VAT return. (VAT Notice 731, para 6.11 which has the force of law).

Transfer of a business as a going concern

Where a business or part of a business operating the cash accounting scheme is transferred as a going concern

- if the transferee does not take over the registration number of the business, the transferor must, within two months or such longer period as HMRC allow, account for and pay VAT due on all supplies made and received which has not otherwise been accounted for, subject to any adjustment for credit for input tax; and
- if the transferee takes over the VAT registration number of the business, the transferor must advise the transferee that the scheme is being used. The transferee must continue to account for and pay VAT as if it were a business operating the scheme on supplies made and received by the transferor before the date of the transfer. The transferee can leave the scheme subject to the normal rules in **63.7** above.

[*SI 1995/2518, Reg 63(2)(3); SI 1997/1614, Reg 8*].

Annual accounting scheme

[63.9] The annual accounting scheme allows businesses to complete one VAT return each year, making interim payments on account (see **63.12** below). The annual VAT return must be completed and sent to HMRC, with any balancing payment, within two months of the end of the annual VAT accounting period.

The main advantages of the scheme are:

- Smoothing out cash flow by paying a set amount each month or quarter.
- Ability to make additional payments as and when they can be afforded.
- Only having to complete one VAT return each year, instead of the normal four.
- Two months to complete and send in the annual VAT return and any balancing payment, instead of the normal one month.
- Being able to align the VAT year with the end of the business tax year and so simplify end of year routines.
- Where the business uses a retail scheme, in most cases the scheme calculations which apply to each quarter are performed once a year. The only exception to this is where the Direct Calculation Scheme 2 is used, in which case calculations under the retail scheme rules follow the rules for the annual adjustment under that scheme (see **60.18 RETAIL SCHEMES**).
- Where the business is partly exempt, the date it makes its partial exemption calculation must coincide with the end of its annual accounting period. This means that it does not have to make partial exemption calculations quarterly and simply make the calculation using the figures for the whole of the annual accounting period. (Where the first accounting period is for a part year, the business must do its partial exemption calculation only at the end of that period.)

(VAT Notice 732, paras 1.5, 7.2, 7.3).

De Voil Indirect Tax Service. See V2.199A.

Admission to the scheme

Conditions for admission

[63.10] A business is eligible to apply to join the scheme if it meets all the following conditions.

(a) There are reasonable grounds for believing that the value of its taxable supplies (excluding VAT) in the period of twelve months beginning at the date of application will not exceed £1,350,000. For this purpose, all standard, reduced and zero-rated supplies should be included except supplies of capital assets previously used in the business. Exempt supplies should be excluded. (VAT Notice 732, para 2.2).
HMRC will not penalise a business for wrongly estimating that the value of its VAT turnover will exceed the upper limit provided it can show that there were reasonable grounds for the estimate. If the estimate had no reasonable basis and a business is above the threshold for the scheme, HMRC will immediately remove the business from the scheme. It is sensible, therefore, to keep a record of how the estimate was made. If a business realises during the year that its turnover has gone or will go over the threshold for leaving the scheme (see **63.14** below), it must notify HMRC immediately and they will remove the business from the scheme. (VAT Notice 732, para 2.5).

(b) Registration is not in the name of a group (see **27 GROUPS OF COMPANIES**) or a division (see **59.37 REGISTRATION**).

(c) The business has not ceased to operate the scheme for any reason under **63.14** below in the twelve months preceding the date of application.

HMRC may refuse to permit a business to use the scheme where they consider it necessary to do so for the protection of the revenue.

[*SI 1995/2518, Reg 52; SI 1996/542; SI 2001/677; SI 2002/1142, Reg 6; SI 2003/1069, Reg 3; SI 2004/767, Reg 4; SI 2006/587, Reg 2*].

A business will not be allowed to join the scheme if it is insolvent or has a rising VAT debt. Entry will not necessarily be refused if there is a small debt provided the business agrees arrangements to clear the outstanding debt with HMRC. (VAT Notice 732, para 2.6).

Application procedure

Application to use the scheme must be made on Form VAT 600 (AA) (where application is to join the annual accounting scheme alone) or Form VAT 600 (AA and FRS) (where application is to join the annual accounting scheme and the flat-rate scheme for small businesses at the same time). Both forms are reproduced in VAT Notice 732 or can be printed from the internet version at www.hmrc.gov.uk

Welsh versions are available (Form VAT 600 AA(W), VAT 600 FRS(W) and VAT 600 AA/FRS(W)). The completed form must be sent to the Annual Accounting Registration Unit, National Registration Service, Imperial House, 77 Victoria Street, Grimsby, North East Lincolnshire, DN31 1DB. Notes on the completion of the form are in VAT Notice 732, para 8.5.

HMRC will notify the business in writing if the application is accepted. The letter will also advise

- the amount and timing of the interim payments to be made by electronic means;
- the method of electronic payment chosen; and
- the due date for the annual return and balancing payment.

(VAT Notice 732, para 8.4).

Annual accounting year and transitional accounting period

A business applying to join the scheme must indicate on the application form the month to the end of which it wishes its annual accounting year to run (normally the end of its financial accounting year). It must match the partial exemption year end (if applicable). If accepted, the first accounting period under the scheme (the '*transitional accounting period*') will normally run from the first day of the accounting period in which the application is made until the chosen year end. Subsequent periods of twelve months are then '*annual accounting years*'. However, HMRC cannot normally issue a VAT return for a period longer than twelve months (the exception being where a business is applying to use the annual accounting scheme from its effective date of registration, when a period of twelve months and 30 days is possible) and do not issue returns for periods of less than three months under the scheme. As a result, there may be instances when a business will receive more than one short period VAT return before a full twelve-month return.

[*SI 1995/2518, Reg 49; SI 1996/542*]. (HMRC VAT Guidance V1–23, Chapter 1 para 3.2).

The annual accounting year can be changed after joining the scheme (e.g. to tie in with a change in financial year end) but this may result in the business being issued with one or two short period returns during the transition because no accounting period can be longer than twelve months. (VAT Notice 732, para 3.5).

Conditions for using the scheme

[63.11] To remain within the scheme, a business must comply with the following conditions.

(a) Make any interim payments on account required by the notified due date. See **63.12** below.

(b) Submit a VAT return, together with any balancing payment of VAT due to HMRC declared on that return
  - in respect of a transitional accounting period of four months or more or an annual accounting year (see **63.10** above) by the end of the second month following that period or year; and
  - in respect of a transitional accounting period of less than four months by the end of the first month following that period.

  [*SI 1995/2518, Reg 50(2)(b), Reg 51(a)(iii)(b); SI 1996/542*].

Notifying changes in business circumstances

If there are, or are expected to be, significant changes that will affect the amount of VAT paid, the business must contact the Annual Accounting Registration Unit (see **63.10** above) immediately. Significant changes include realising that

- the value of taxable supplies will rise above the turnover limit for leaving the scheme (see **63.14** below) for the current year (e.g. due to new contracts, buying another business etc.); or
- VAT payable will, or has, increased by 10% since the last time instalments were calculated.

(VAT Notice 732, para 4.7)

Payments on account

[63.12] A business authorised to use the annual accounting scheme must make interim payments on account as follows.

(1) *Transitional periods* (see **63.10** above).
- (a) Where the transitional accounting period is four months or more and the business and HMRC agree to such a payment pattern,
  - (i) in the case of a business registered for at least twelve months immediately preceding the start of its transitional period, 25% of the total VAT due for those twelve months on the last 'working day' of the 4th, and where the period has such months, 7th and 10th months of the transitional accounting period; and
  - (ii) in any other case, 25% of the total amount of VAT that HMRC are satisfied the business will be liable to pay in respect of the next twelve months, again on the last 'working day' of the 4th, and where the period has such months, 7th and 10th months of the transitional accounting period.
- (b) Where the transitional accounting period is four months or more but the business and HMRC do not agree to quarterly payments as under (*a*) above,
  - (i) in the case of a business registered for at least twelve months immediately preceding the start of the transitional accounting period, 10% of the total VAT due for those twelve months in equal monthly instalments on the last 'working day' of the fourth and each successive month of the transitional accounting period; and
  - (ii) in any other case, 10% of the total amount of VAT that HMRC are satisfied the business will be liable to pay in respect of the next twelve months in equal monthly instalments on the last 'working day' of the fourth and each successive month of the transitional accounting period.
- (c) Where the transitional accounting period is less than four months, no interim payments are required.

(2) *Subsequent annual accounting periods.*

(a) Where the business and HMRC agree to such a payment pattern,

(i) in the case of a business registered for at least twelve months immediately preceding the start of the current accounting year, 25% of the total VAT due for those twelve months on the last 'working day' of the 4th, 7th and 10th months of the annual accounting year; and

(ii) in any other case, 25% of the total amount of VAT that HMRC are satisfied the business will be liable to pay in respect of the next twelve months.

(b) Otherwise, where (*a*) does not apply,

(i) in the case of a business registered for at least twelve months immediately preceding the start of the current accounting year, 10% of the total VAT due for those twelve months in nine equal monthly instalments starting on the last 'working day' of the fourth month of its annual accounting year; and

(ii) in any other case, 10% of the total amount of VAT that HMRC are satisfied the business will be liable to pay in respect of the next twelve months.

The normal method of payment will therefore be by monthly payments under (1)(*b*) or (2)(*b*) above unless the business indicates that it wishes to make quarterly payments under (1)(*a*) or (2)(*a*) above on its application form. If a business does not do so, but subsequently wishes to change from monthly to quarterly payments, it should write to the Annual Accounting Registration Unit (see **63.10** above) although HMRC will normally expect a business to stay on the same payment pattern for at least one year. (VAT Notice 732, paras 4.2–4.4).

'*Working day*' means any day of the week other than Saturday, Sunday, a bank holiday or a public holiday.

[*SI 1995/2518, Reg 49, Reg 50(2)(3), Reg 51; SI 1996/542; SI 2002/1142, Regs 3–5*].

Revision of payments on account

If a business expects its liability to increase or decrease significantly, it should contact the Annual Accounting Registration Unit with information on how it calculates revised interim payments. If they agree, HMRC will notify the new instalment amounts. (VAT Notice 732, para 4.6).

Additional voluntary payments

These can be made at any time. Payments must be made by electronic means (see below) and in multiples of £5. (VAT Notice 732, para 4.8).

Method of payment

All interim payments, whether monthly or quarterly, must be made by electronic means (direct debit, standing order, bank giro credit, Bankers Automated Clearing Service (BACS) or the Clearing House Automated Payment System (CHAPS)). (VAT Notice 732, para 5.2).

Missing a payment

HMRC will send a reminder if an interim payment on account is not received. Payment will have to be made by BACS or CHAPS. (VAT Notice 732, para 5.4).

Accounting for VAT

[63.13] The annual return is completed in the same way as a normal VAT return (including the availability of sending the return electronically) and must be completed and sent to HMRC within two months of the end of the annual VAT accounting period. It is important that the figure for the value of outputs in Box 6 is accurate as this will be used as a basis for allowing continued use of the scheme.

The figure shown in Box 5 of the return is the amount of VAT due for the year. This figure will be calculated automatically if the return is being completed online. The amount payable with the VAT return is the figure in Box 5 less the total of interim payments made for the annual period. If the total amount paid by interim payments is more than the net VAT payable, HMRC will refund the difference.

Returns may be submitted online, after registration and enrolment via the HMRC website. If the return is submitted online, payment of any VAT due must also be paid by electronic means.

Any balance due at the end of the year can be paid by direct debit, BACS, CHAPS, Bank Giro or debit/credit card. Where paper VAT returns are used, payment can also be made by cheque. It should be noted that the additional time for sending or paying VAT returns electronically is not available where the annual accounting scheme is used (because an extra month is already allowed for doing this).

(VAT Notice 732, paras 6.2–6.4).

Use of the annual accounting scheme and the flat-rate scheme for small businesses

The annual accounting scheme can be used together with the flat-rate scheme (see **63.15** *et seq.*) below by simply following the rules of the flat-rate scheme for calculating VAT liability but instead of doing this four times a year, doing it just once when the annual accounting return is due.

If a business makes a joint application to use both schemes, use will normally start together from the beginning of the period in which the annual accounting scheme applies although the application form does allow a business to request different start dates. In the latter case, two calculations are required when completing the annual accounting return.

- A calculation for the period when the business was not in the flat-rate scheme, using normal VAT accounting rules.
- A calculation for the period when the business was in the flat-rate scheme using the rules for calculating liability under the flat-rate scheme.

The total liability for the return period will be the sum of those two calculations.

Where a business already using the annual accounting scheme applies to join the flat-rate scheme in the middle of its annual accounting period, it will have to do two calculations when completing its return as explained above. To avoid two calculations, it is best to apply to use the flat-rate scheme at the beginning of an annual accounting period. If the business does not wish to wait to the end of its annual accounting year, it can change its existing annual accounting year end to an earlier date and start both schemes together. This will result in amendments to the annual accounting periods and payments to accommodate these changes.

If a business becomes ineligible for one scheme, it will normally continue in the other scheme unless it requests removal. If a business leaves the flat-rate scheme in the middle of an accounting period, it must do the two calculations as described above when completing its next VAT return.

(VAT Notice 732, paras 9.2, 9.8–9.11).

Leaving the scheme

[63.14] Provided the business is still authorised to use the scheme, it must continue to use it in the next annual accounting year. [*SI 1995/2518, Reg 53(1); SI 1996/542*].

A business ceases to be authorised to use the annual accounting scheme in the following circumstances.

(a) **Turnover exceeding the limit.**
- After the end of any transitional accounting period (see **63.10** above) if the value of taxable supplies in that period has exceeded £1,600,000.
- After the end of any annual accounting year if the value of taxable supplies in that year has exceeded £1,600,000.

(b) **Expulsion by HMRC.** HMRC *may* terminate an authorisation to use the scheme from any date where
- a false statement has been made by or on behalf of the business in relation to the application to use the scheme;
- a business fails to make any VAT return under the scheme by the due date;
- a business fails to make any payment due under the scheme;
- a business notifies HMRC that it has reason to believe that the value of taxable supplies in the current transitional accounting period (see **63.10** above) or annual accounting year will exceed £1,600,000 (which it must do in writing within 30 days);
- there is reason to believe that the value of taxable supplies made by a business using the scheme will exceed £1,600,000 in the current transitional accounting period (see **63.10** above) or annual accounting year;
- it is necessary to do so for the protection of the revenue; or

- a business using the scheme has not paid over to HMRC all VAT shown as due on any return made before authorisation and all VAT shown as due on any assessment made (including interest and penalties). See, however, **63.10** above for HMRC policy where there is a small amount of VAT outstanding at the time of application to join the scheme.

(c) **Cessation of business.** Where a business authorised to use the scheme
- becomes insolvent and ceases to trade (other than for the purposes of disposing of stocks and assets),
- ceases business or ceases to be registered, or
- if a person, dies or becomes bankrupt or incapacitated

authorisation to use the scheme terminates on the date on which any such event occurs.

(d) **Voluntary withdrawal.** A business authorised to use the scheme may cease to operate it of its own volition at any time by writing to HM Revenue & Customs, Annual Accounting Registration Unit, National Registration Service, Imperial House, 77 Victoria Street, Grimsby, North East Lincolnshire, DN31 1DB. Authorisation to use the scheme terminates from the date HMRC are notified in writing.

[*SI 1995/2518, Regs 53(2), 54, 55(1); SI 1996/542; SI 2001/677; SI 2003/1069, Reg 4; SI 2004/767, Reg 5; SI 2006/587, Reg 3*].

Consequences of leaving the scheme

Where a business leaves the annual accounting scheme, a final return under the scheme must be made and any outstanding VAT must normally be paid within two months of the date on which its authorisation is terminated. From the day following termination, the business must account for and pay VAT in the normal way and cannot rejoin the scheme for twelve months.
[*SI 1995/2518, Reg 55(2); SI 1996/542*].

Flat-rate scheme for small businesses

[63.15] HMRC may make *Regulations* setting up a scheme which allows eligible businesses to calculate their VAT due as a percentage of total turnover. Some of the conditions of the scheme can also be published (and amended) in a VAT Notice *which to this extent has the force of law*. [*VATA 1994, s 26B; FA 2002, s 23; SI 1995/2518, Reg 55T; SI 2002/1142*].

Under these provisions, a flat-rate scheme is available for small businesses with VAT-exclusive annual taxable turnover of up to £150,000 and (until 1 April 2009) VAT-inclusive annual total turnover (including the value of exempt and non-taxable income) of up to £187,500.

The aim of the flat-rate scheme is to simplify the way VAT is recorded and accounted for on sales and purchases. The key points of the scheme are:

- There is no need to record the VAT on individual sales and purchases in order to calculate the VAT due to HMRC.

- Instead, a business simply records all its business supplies, including exempt supplies, and applies a flat-rate percentage (dependent upon the trade sector into which the business falls) to the VAT-inclusive total in each VAT period. The result is the VAT payable to HMRC.
- A business does not recover input tax or VAT on imports or acquisitions. This is because the flat rates are calculated to represent the net VAT that needs to be paid to HMRC, i.e. an allowance for input tax is built into the flat rates. There are, however, special rules for input tax recovery on high value capital goods.

Full details of the scheme are given in **63.16** to **63.24** below.

Deciding whether to use the scheme

All businesses using the scheme benefit from simpler bookkeeping. There is no need to check the deductibility of VAT on purchases (and even their liability to VAT). If the scheme is used together with the annual accounting scheme (see **63.9** above) it can make a significant difference to the cost of complying with VAT requirements. But:

- Any individual business may pay more or less VAT than it would under the normal VAT rules. This is because the flat rates are averages, and one flat rate applies to all businesses in a particular sector.
- Businesses that usually receive repayments from HMRC should not join the scheme.
- As exempt and zero-rated supplies are included in flat-rate turnover, businesses may pay more VAT by using the scheme if these supplies are a larger proportion of business turnover than the average for its trade sector.
- Businesses with VAT-registered customers must still issue VAT invoices (showing VAT calculated in the normal way).
- Businesses that buy and sell goods from outside the UK can find the scheme more complex.

(VAT Notice 733, paras 2.1–2.3).

De Voil Indirect Tax Service. See V2.199B–V2.199D.

How the scheme works

Output tax

[63.16] For any VAT period, the output tax due from a flat-rate trader in respect of his 'relevant supplies' (see below) is deemed to be the appropriate 'flat-rate percentage' of his 'relevant turnover' for that period. [*SI 1995/2518, Reg 55D; SI 2002/1142; SI 2003/1069, Reg 5; SI 2003/3220, Reg 18*].

See **63.19** below for the '*flat-rate percentage*' and **63.20** below for calculating '*relevant turnover*'.

> ***Example***
>
> A motor repair business has a VAT-inclusive turnover of £20,000 for a VAT period.

Its appropriate flat-rate percentage is 8.5% for 2011, and VAT due for the period is
£20,000 – 8.5% = £1,700

Input tax

A flat-rate trader does not normally make a separate claim for input tax or for VAT on imports or acquisitions as the flat-rate percentage includes an allowance for input tax. There are, however, two exceptions to this.

(a) *Capital items costing over £2,000.* See **63.22** below.
(b) *Stocks and assets on hand at registration.* A business can recover VAT incurred before registration subject to certain conditions. See **34.10 INPUT TAX.** These provisions also apply where the first VAT period for which a business is authorised to account for and pay VAT in accordance with the flat-rate scheme is the first VAT period for which it is registered (or required to be registered).
Where the above applies, the whole of the input tax on the goods or services concerned is regarded as used, or to be used, by the taxable person exclusively in making taxable supplies.
[*SI 1995/2518, Reg 55F; SI 2002/1142*].
The claim should be made on the first VAT return following registration. Where such a claim is made, any subsequent disposal of capital assets has to be accounted for in the normal way, i.e. by adding any VAT due on the disposal to the VAT calculated under the flat-rate scheme. See (4) below. (VAT Notice 733, para 7.6).

Relevant supplies and purchases

The following provisions apply in determining whether a purchase or supply is a relevant purchase or supply for the purposes of the flat-rate scheme.

(1) Subject to (3), (5) and (6) below, any supply of goods or services to, or acquisition of importation of goods by, a flat-rate trader is a relevant purchase of his.
(2) Subject to (3)–(6) below, any supply made by a person when he is not a flat-rate trader is not a relevant supply of his.
(3) Subject to (4) and (6) below, where
- a supply is made to, or made by, a person at a time when he is not a flat-rate trader, and
- the operative date for VAT accounting purposes is, by virtue of the cash accounting scheme, a date when he is a flat-rate trader,

that supply is a relevant supply or a relevant purchase, as the case may be, if otherwise it would not be by virtue of (2) above.
(4) Where a person
- is entitled to any credit for input tax in respect of the supply to, or acquisition or importation by, him of capital expenditure goods,
- claims any such credit, and
- makes a supply of those capital expenditure goods,

that supply is not a relevant supply, if otherwise it would be.

(5) Where by virtue of any provision of, or made under, *VATA 1994* a supply is *treated as made* by a flat-rate trader, whether to himself or otherwise, that supply is neither a relevant supply nor a relevant purchase of his.

(6) Where a reverse charge supply under the provisions relating to mobile phones and computer chips (see **4.14 ANTI-AVOIDANCE**) is made to or by a flat-rate trader, the supply is neither a relevant supply nor a relevant purchase.

[*SI 1995/2518, Reg 55C; SI 2002/1142; SI 2007/1418, Reg 5*].

Issuing VAT invoices

The normal rules apply to issuing VAT invoices, i.e. a flat-rate trader must still issue a VAT invoice to any customer who is registered for VAT and the customer can treat the invoice as a normal VAT invoice. VAT must be shown on the sales invoice using the normal rate for the supply (standard, reduced, zero rate or exempt) and *not* the flat-rate percentage assigned to the business. This is because the flat-rate scheme affects the way VAT is calculated but does not change the VAT rate applicable to supplies. When calculating VAT at the end of the VAT period, a flat-rate trader must add up the VAT-inclusive total of all his supplies (whether or not a VAT invoice has been issued) and apply the flat rate percentage to this total.

(VAT Notice 733, paras 7.3, 7.4).

Using the scheme in conjunction with other schemes

The flat-rate scheme can be used in conjunction with the *annual accounting scheme*. The use of both schemes can help reduce the cost of complying with VAT.

The flat-rate scheme *cannot* be used in conjunction with the following schemes.

- *Cash accounting*. Although the cash accounting scheme and the flat-rate scheme cannot be used together, the flat-rate scheme has its own cash-based method that is very similar to the cash accounting scheme. See **63.20** below.
- *Retail schemes*. Although a retail scheme and the flat-rate scheme cannot be used together, the flat-rate scheme has its own retail-based method which is very similar to the ordinary retail schemes. See **63.20** below.
  Where a business wishes to leave a retail scheme to join the flat-rate scheme, it should follow the rules about ceasing to use that retail scheme. See **60 RETAIL SCHEMES** under the appropriate scheme.
- *Margin scheme for second-hand goods*. Where a business sells a significant proportion of second-hand goods using a margin scheme or the auctioneers' scheme, the flat-rate scheme is of limited value to the business. This is because the flat-rate scheme calculates VAT on the total received from sales rather than on the margin.

(VAT Notice 733, para 2.7).

Eligibility and conditions

[63.17] HMRC may authorise a business to account for and pay VAT under the flat-rate scheme with effect from the beginning of its next VAT period after the date on which it notifies HMRC of its wish to use the scheme (or such earlier or later date as may be agreed between them). In practice, although starting to use the scheme from the beginning of a VAT period is simplest, HMRC may agree to any start date other than 29 February. The date with effect from which the business is so authorised is its '*start date*'.

HMRC may refuse to so authorise a business if they consider it is necessary for the protection of the revenue.

[*SI 1995/2518, Reg 55B(1)–(3); SI 2002/1142; SI 2003/3220, Reg 17*].

A business is eligible to account for VAT in accordance with the flat-rate scheme at any time (including with effect from its date of registration) if it satisfies the following conditions.

(a) There are reasonable grounds for believing that
  (i) the value of its taxable supplies (excluding VAT) in the period of one year then beginning will not exceed £150,000; and
  (ii) (until 1 April 2009) the total value of its income (including VAT) in the period of one year then beginning will not exceed £187,500 [*SI 2009/586, Reg 6*].

  In determining the value of taxable supplies or income for these purposes
  - any supply of goods or services that are capital assets of the business in the course or furtherance of which they are supplied, and
  - any supply of services treated as made by the recipient by virtue of *VATA 1994, s 8* (reverse charge on supplies from abroad)

  are disregarded.

  Included in (i) above is the value of standard rate, zero rate and reduced rate supplies; turnover from the sale of second-hand goods sold outside the margin scheme; and any sales of gold covered by the special scheme in **26.9 GOLD AND PRECIOUS METALS**.

  Included in (ii) above, in addition to the total value of supplies within (i) above, was the value of any exempt supplies and any other income received or receivable by the business. This included any 'non-business' income (e.g. income arising from charitable or educational activities).

  Future turnover can be forecast in any reasonable way (e.g. turnover in the last twelve months adjusted for any expected changes). HMRC will not penalise a business if the forecast turns out to be too low provided there were reasonable grounds for the forecast. It is sensible, therefore, to keep a record of how the calculation was made. If HMRC judge that the estimate of turnover had no reasonable basis, a business may be excluded from the scheme immediately or even from the date its ineligible use began.

  (VAT Notice 733, paras 3.2–3.5).

Once in the scheme, a business can remain in it provided total turnover (including VAT) did not exceed £230,000 in the previous year (calculated on the anniversary of joining the scheme) and provided there are not grounds for believing turnover will rise above £230,000 in the next 30 days alone. See **63.23** below for further details.

(b) The business
- is not a tour operator;
- is not required to carry out adjustments in relation to a capital item under the **CAPITAL GOODS SCHEME (10)**; or
- does not intend to opt to account for the VAT chargeable on a supply made by it under a margin scheme (see **61 SECOND-HAND GOODS**).

(c) The business has not, in the period of one year preceding that time
- been convicted of any offence in connection with VAT,
- made any payment to compound proceedings in respect of VAT under *CEMA 1979, s 152*,
- been assessed to a penalty for VAT evasion under *VATA 1994, s 60* (see **52.10 PENALTIES**), or
- ceased to operate the flat-rate scheme.

(d) The business is not and, unless HMRC are satisfied that use of the flat-rate scheme poses no risk to the revenue, has not been within the past 24 months
- eligible to be registered for VAT in the name of a group under *VATA 1994, s 43A* (see **27.2 GROUPS OF COMPANIES**),
- registered for VAT in the name of a division under *VATA 1994, s 46(1)* (see **59.37 REGISTRATION**), or
- 'associated with' another person.

Note that it is eligibility to be in a VAT group which is the key test, not whether the business is actually in one.

A person is '*associated with*' another person at any time if that other person makes supplies in the course or furtherance of a business carried on by him, and
- the business of one is under the dominant influence of the other, or
- the persons are closely bound to one another by financial, economic and organisational links.

HMRC treat this as applying where one business has the right to give directions to another or, in practice, a business habitually complies with the directions of another. The test here is a test of the commercial reality rather than of the legal form. A close connection with another business is not necessarily the same as being associated. For example, a business is not associated with its customers just because it supplies them with the goods they request in the form they request them. Similarly, a husband and wife who are each separately VAT-registered in different types of business are not associated even if they share premises (provided this is charged at a market rate). (VAT Notice 733, paras 3.8, 3.9).

[*SI 1995/2518, Regs 55A, 55L; SI 2002/1142; SI 2003/1069, Reg 7*].

Application to use the scheme

[63.18] Application to use the flat-rate scheme can be made in any of the following ways.

- **By post.** Application should be made on Form VAT 600 (FRS). The form can either be removed from the paper version of VAT Notice 733 or downloaded from the web version available at: www.hmrc.gov.uk.
  Postal applications should be sent to

  HM Revenue & Customs
  Imperial House
  77 Victoria Street
  Grimsby DN31 1DB
  If registering for VAT at the same time, Form VAT 600 (FRS) can be enclosed with the Form VAT 1 Application for Registration.
- **By e-mail.** The scheme application form can be downloaded from HMRC's website, completed on a computer and sent to frsapplications@hmrc.gov.uk
  Any queries or correspondence should be sent to the National Advice Service not this e-mail address.
- **By phone.** The National Advice Service can take application details over the phone on 0845 010 9000. If an accountant or other representative applies to use the scheme by phone on behalf of a business, HMRC will send a copy of the application form completed by them to the business for its records. If there are any errors on it, HMRC should be contacted immediately.

Guidance on completing the form is given in VAT Notice 733, para 5.3.

Application can be made at the time of registration for VAT or any later time. If application is made at the time of registration, a business can begin to use the scheme from the date of registration. (See **63.19** below for a 1% reduction in flat-rate percentage for all businesses in the first year of VAT registration.) If a business is already registered when it applies, it is best to apply as early in a VAT period as possible as authorisation to use the flat-rate scheme normally takes effect from the beginning of the VAT period after HMRC have processed the application.

HMRC will notify the business either that its application has been accepted and the date from which it can operate the flat-rate scheme, or the reason why it has not allowed it.

(VAT Notice 733, paras 5.1, 5.2, 5.5; VAT Information Sheet 17/03, para 5.1).

See **63.13** above for joint application to join the flat-rate scheme and the annual accounting scheme.

Flat-rate percentage

[63.19] Flat-rate percentage is treated as follows:

(1) Appropriate flat-rate percentage

The appropriate percentage to be applied by a flat-rate trader for any VAT period (or part period) is determined in accordance with the following rules and, where appropriate, (2) and (3) below.

(a) For any VAT period beginning with a 'relevant date', the appropriate percentage is that specified in the Table below for the category of business that he is expected, at the relevant date, on reasonable grounds, to carry on in that period.

(b) For any VAT period current at his 'start date' but not beginning with his start date, the appropriate percentage is that specified in the Table below for the category of business that he is expected, at his start date, on reasonable grounds, to carry on in the remainder of the period.

(c) For any VAT period not falling within (*a*) or (*b*) above, the appropriate percentage is that applicable to his relevant turnover at the end of the previous VAT period.

'*Relevant date*' in relation to a flat-rate trader, means any of the following.

- His '*start date*' (i.e. the date from which he is authorised to use the scheme).
- The first day of the VAT period current at any anniversary of his start date.
- Any day on which he first carries on a new business activity.
- Any day on which he no longer carries on an existing business activity.
- Any day with effect from which the Table below is amended in relation to him.
- Where (2) below applies
  (i) the day that his 'newly registered period' (see (2) below) begins, and
  (ii) the first anniversary of his EDR (see (2) below).

But where a relevant date (other than the start date) occurs on a day other than the first day of a VAT period, the following rules apply for the remainder of that VAT period.

(A) For the 'remaining portion', the appropriate percentage is that specified in the Table below for the category of business that he is expected, at the relevant date, on reasonable grounds, to carry on in that period.
'*Remaining portion*' means that part of the VAT period in which the relevant date occurs starting with the relevant date, and ending on the last day of that prescribed accounting period.
The appropriate percentage is applied to relevant turnover in the remaining portion described.

(B) If the rules set out in (A) above apply and then another relevant date occurs in the same VAT period, then the existing remaining portion ends on the day before the latest relevant date, another remaining portion begins on the latest relevant date, and the rules in (A) above are applied again in respect of the latest remaining portion.

[*SI 1995/2518, Regs 55A, 55H; SI 2003/3220, Regs 18, 19*].

(2) Reduced appropriate percentage for newly registered period

Special provisions apply where the date from which a flat-rate trader is authorised to use the scheme (his '*start date*') falls within one year of the date with effect from which he is registered for VAT (his '*EDR*').

In such a case, at any relevant date (see (1) above) falling within his 'newly registered period', the Table below is to be read as if each percentage were reduced by 1% unless HMRC receive notification of, or otherwise become fully aware of, his liability to be registered more than one year after his EDR.

A flat-rate trader's '*newly registered period*' is the period beginning with the later of

- his start date, and
- the day HMRC received notification of, or otherwise became fully aware of, his liability to be registered for VAT

and ending on the day before the first anniversary of his EDR.

The effect of this is that if a business notifies its VAT liability on time and asks to use the scheme from the date of registration, the discounted rates last for one year. But if it registers for VAT late or does not immediately join the scheme, the period will be shortened.

[*SI 1995/2518, Regs 55A, 55JB; SI 2003/3220, Regs 18, 19*].

(3) More than one category of business

Where, at a relevant date (see (1) above), a flat-rate trader was expected, on reasonable grounds, to carry on business in more than one category of business in the period concerned, he is regarded as being expected to carry on that category of business which is expected to be his main business activity in that period, determined by reference to turnover expected to be generated by each business activity concerned.

[*SI 1995/2518, Regs 55A, 55K; SI 2003/3220, Regs 18, 19*].

This means that if a business includes supplies in two or more sectors, it must apply the percentage appropriate to its main business activity as measured by turnover. It should not split its turnover or apply more than one percentage.

> ***Example***
>
> A taxi business expects to have a turnover of £40,000 in the next year but also does car repairs which are expected to generate a turnover of £15,000.
>
> It must apply the flat-rate percentage for a taxi business (9% for 2010) to the total VAT-inclusive turnover for both parts of the business. If this total was £55,000, the business would pay £4,950 in that year.

(VAT Notice 733, para 4.6).

(4) Changes in the balance between two parts of a business

If the balance between activities changes but the business still carries on the same activities, it must carry on using the percentage that was appropriate at the start of the year until the anniversary of joining the scheme. At the start of the VAT period which includes that anniversary, the business should review the balance between the parts of the business and, if this has changed (or is expected to change in the year ahead), it can change categories to that for the larger portion of the business (or expected business). If this also involves a change in the appropriate percentage, the new percentage should be used from the start of the VAT period in which the anniversary date falls (not just from the anniversary to the end of the period). (VAT Notice 733, para 4.7).

(5) Notification of changes to HMRC

- Where at the first day of the VAT period current at any anniversary of his start date (see (1) above) the appropriate percentage to be applied by a flat-rate trader under (1)(*a*) above for the VAT period just beginning differs from that applicable to his relevant turnover at the end of the previous VAT period, he must notify HMRC of that fact within 30 days of the first day of the VAT period current at the anniversary of his start date.
- Where a flat-rate trader begins to carry on a new business activity or ceases to carry on an existing business activity, he must notify HMRC of that fact, the date of change, and the appropriate percentage to be applied to the period immediately before that relevant date and immediately after it. Notification must be within 30 days of the date of change.

[*SI 1995/2518, Reg 55N(1)(2)(4); SI 2003/3220*].

(6) Choice of category of business

It is for the business to choose its appropriate category of business from the table below. In choosing the category, the words should be given their ordinary meanings. The National Advice Service can help where there is doubt.

See also HMRC VAT Guidance V1–23, FRS 7200 (List of trades and the sectors to which HMRC consider they belong) and FRS 7300 (List of sectors and the trades that HMRC consider fit within each) for how HMRC have interpreted the various categories.

Once HMRC have approved a business to join the scheme, they will not change the category of business chosen in retrospect provided the choice was reasonable and records have been kept why it was chosen.

(VAT Notice 733, paras 4.1, 4.2).

Category of business	*Appropriate % from 4.1.11*	*Appropriate % from 1.1.10 to 3.1.11*	*Appropriate % from 1.12.08 to 31.12.09*	*Appropriate % before 1.12.08*
Accountancy or book-keeping	14.5	13	11.5	13
Advertising	11	10	8.5	9.5
Agricultural services	11	10	7	7.5

Category of business	*Appropriate % from 4.1.11*	*Appropriate % from 1.1.10 to 3.1.11*	*Appropriate % from 1.12.08 to 31.12.09*	*Appropriate % before 1.12.08*
Any other activity not listed elsewhere	12	10.5	9	10
Architects	N/A	N/A	N/A	12.5
Architect, civil and structural engineer or surveyor	14.5	13	11	N/A
Boarding or care of animals	12	10.5	9.5	10.5
Business services that are not listed elsewhere	12	10.5	9.5	11
Catering services, including restaurants and takeaways	12.5	11	10.5	12
Civil and structural engineers and surveyors	N/A	N/A	N/A	12.5
Computer and IT consultancy or data processing	14.5	13	11.5	13
Computer repair services	10.5	9.5	10.5	11
Dealing in waste or scrap	10.5	9.5	8.5	9.5
Entertainment (excluding film, radio, television or video production, see below) or journalism	12.5	11	9.5	11
Estate agency or property management services	12	10.5	9.5	11
Farming or agriculture that is not listed elsewhere	6.5	6	5.5	6
Film, radio, television or video production	13	11.5	9.5	10.5
Financial services	13.5	12	10.5	11.5
Forestry or fishing	10.5	9.5	8	9

Category of business	*Appropriate % from 4.1.11*	*Appropriate % from 1.1.10 to 3.1.11*	*Appropriate % from 1.12.08 to 31.12.09*	*Appropriate % before 1.12.08*
General building or construction services (note 1)	9.5	8.5	7.5	8.5
Hairdressing or other beauty treatment services	13	11.5	10.5	12
Hiring or renting goods	9.5	8.5	7.5	8.5
Hotel or accommodation	10.5	9.5	8.5	9.5
Investigation or security	12	10.5	9	10
Labour-only building or construction services (note 1)	14.5	13	11.5	13.5
Laundry or dry-cleaning services	12	10.5	9.5	11
Lawyer or legal services	14.5	13	12	13
Library, archive, museum or other cultural activities	9.5	8.5	7.5	7.5
Management consultancy	14	12.5	11	12.5
Manufacturing fabricated metal products	10.5	9.5	8.5	10
Manufacturing food	9	8	7	7.5
Manufacturing that is not listed elsewhere	9.5	8.5	7.5	8.5
Manufacturing yarn, textiles or clothing	9	8	7.5	8.5
Membership organisations	8	7	5.5	5.5
Mining or quarrying	10	9	8	9
Packaging	9	8	7.5	8.5
Photography	11	10	8.5	9.5
Post offices	5	4.5	2	2
Printing	8.5	7.5	6.5	7.5
Publishing	11	10	8.5	9.5

Category of business	*Appropriate % from 4.1.11*	*Appropriate % from 1.1.10 to 3.1.11*	*Appropriate % from 1.12.08 to 31.12.09*	*Appropriate % before 1.12.08*
Pubs	6.5	6	5.5	5.5
Real estate activities not listed elsewhere	14	12.5	11	12
Repairing personal or household goods	10	9	7.5	8.5
Repairing vehicles	8.5	7.5	6.5	7.5
Retailing food, confectionery, tobacco, newspapers or children's clothing	4	3.5	2	2
Retailing pharmaceuticals, medical goods, cosmetics or toiletries	8	7	6	7
Retailing that is not listed elsewhere	7.5	6.5	5.5	6
Retailing vehicles or fuel	6.5	6	5.5	7
Secretarial services	13	11.5	9.5	11
Social work	11	10	8	8.5
Sport or recreation	8.5	7.5	6	7
Transport or storage, including courier, freight, removals and taxis	10	9	8	9
Travel agency	10.5	9.5	8	9
Veterinary medicine	11	10	8	9.5
Wholesaling agricultural products	8	7	5.5	6
Wholesaling food	7.5	6.5	5	5.5
Wholesaling that is not listed elsewhere	8.5	7.5	6	7

Notes

(1) 'Labour-only building or construction services' means building or construction services where the value of materials supplied is less than 10% of relevant turnover from such services; any other building or construction services are 'general building or construction services'.

[*SI 1995/2518, Reg 55K; SI 2004/767; SI 2008/3021; SI 2009/3241; SI 2010/2940*].

Calculating turnover

[63.20] It is important to determine correctly the turnover to which the flat-rate percentage is to be applied. If items that are not part of turnover are included, too much VAT will be paid and if items are omitted, too little VAT will be paid and the business could have to pay a penalty and interest.

Flat-rate turnover includes all the supplies made by the business, including VAT. This means

- the *VAT-inclusive* sales and takings for standard-rated, zero-rated and reduced rate supplies;
- the value of exempt supplies;
- supplies of capital expenditure goods, unless they are supplies on which VAT has to be calculated outside the flat-rate scheme in accordance with **63.22** below; and
- the value of despatches to other EU countries if the business is making intra-EU supplies.

Income which can be excluded includes

- private income (e.g. dividends);
- bank interest;
- proceeds from the sale of goods owned by the trader but which have not been used in the business;
- any sales of gold for which the special accounting scheme applies (see **26.9 GOLD AND PRECIOUS METALS**);
- non-business income and any supplies outside the scope of VAT; and
- sales of capital expenditure goods on which the business has claimed input tax (see **63.22** below).

(VAT Notice 733, paras 6.2, 6.3).

Methods of calculating turnover

There are three ways of calculating turnover. Whichever method is used, it should normally be used for at least 12 months.

(1) The basic turnover method

Under this method, the flat-rate percentage is applied to the VAT-inclusive total of supplies that have their time of supply (tax point) in the VAT period in question. Time of supply is worked out using the normal rules. See **66.1** to **66.26 SUPPLY: TIME OF SUPPLY**. This method is principally for businesses that deal mainly with other VAT-registered businesses. (VAT Notice 733, para 8.1).

(2) The cash-based turnover method

Under this method, the business applies the flat-rate percentage to the supplies for which it has been paid in the VAT period in question. This method can be helpful if the business gives extended credit or customers pay late.

If the cash accounting system was being used immediately before the flat-rate scheme, the business should carry on as before. There is no need to calculate and pay the VAT still owed when changing schemes. It includes any payments received whilst using the flat-rate scheme in the total to which it applies the flat-rate percentage.

Time of payment

The following rules have the force of law for determining the time of payment.

- *Cash* (coins or notes). Payment is received on the date the money is received.
- *Cheques*. Payment by cheque is received on the date the cheque is received or, if later, the date on the cheque. If the cheque is not honoured, no VAT is due and an adjustment can be made if VAT has already been accounted for.
- *Credit or debit cards*. Payment is received on the date the sales voucher is made out (*not* the date when payment is received from the card provider).
- *Giro, standing orders and direct debits*. Payment is received on the date the bank account is credited.

Change of VAT rate or insolvency

In these special circumstances, the basic turnover method tax point must be used to determine the treatment of the supplies.

(VAT Notice 733, paras 9.1–9.3).

Payments received net of deductions

Where a net payment is received, the full value must be included before such deductions (and including VAT) in the scheme turnover. This will usually be the value shown on the sales invoice. Examples of payments that may be received net of deductions are

- payments where commission has been deducted by the customer;
- payments where commission or payment for expenses has been deducted by a factor or agent collecting money on behalf of the business;
- payments where commission or payment for expenses has been deducted by an auctioneer selling goods on behalf of the business; and
- payments made by an employer/contractor who has deducted income tax.

(VAT Notice 733, para 9.4 which has the force of law).

Payments in kind (e.g. barter and part exchange)

Where a business is paid fully or partly in kind, it must include the value, including VAT, in its flat-rate turnover each time it makes or receives a 'payment'. Such a payment is received on the date the business receives the goods or services agreed in lieu of money. It must account for VAT on the full value of the supply, i.e. the price, including VAT, which a customer would have to pay for the supply if they had paid for it with money only.

(VAT Notice 733, para 9.5 which has the force of law).

Ceasing to use the cash-based method

If at any time a business ceases to use the cash-based accounting method, it must account for VAT on all the supplies made while it was using the method and for which payment has not been received. The supplies must be included in the scheme turnover in the return for the VAT period in which the business ceases to use the cash-based method. The only exception to this is if it ceases to use the flat-rate scheme but immediately starts to use the cash accounting scheme. It may be possible to balance this adjustment with a claim for relief for stocks on hand (see **63.23** below), or a claim in respect of bad debts (see **63.22** below).

(VAT Notice 733, para 9.6 which has the force of law).

(3) The retailer's turnover method

This is essentially the same as a retail scheme and is best if the business is a retailer selling goods to the public. The method is based on 'daily takings'. The business must record payments from customers as they are received and total the takings daily. Flat-rate turnover is the daily gross takings plus any other items of income the business receives, including that from outside the retail environment. At the end of a VAT period, the flat-rate percentage is applied to the flat-rate turnover for that period.

See **60.8 RETAIL SCHEMES** for items to be included in daily takings, adjustments which can be made and the treatment of till shortages and excesses. These provisions also apply to the retailer's turnover method, as do the other adjustments to daily takings for special transactions listed in **60.9 RETAIL SCHEMES.**

Special rules for florists

Special rules apply to members of organisations such as Interflora, Teleflorist or Flowergram.

- A member that receives payment direct from a customer is the 'sending member' and must include the amount the customer pays in its daily gross takings.
- A member that delivers flowers ordered by customers at another florist is the 'executing member' and must add the order value and the VAT shown, from the monthly agency self-billed invoice, to its flat-rate turnover. This is the gross figure.
- When orders taken by one member are delivered by other florists, the invoice from the agency shows the value of these orders as a purchase figure plus VAT. The figures shown may be net or gross depending on which agency is used. The input tax is always shown but this amount cannot be reclaimed under the flat-rate scheme.

(VAT Notice 733, paras 10.1–10.7 which have the force of law).

[*SI 1995/2518, Reg 55G; SI 2002/1142*].

Accounts and records

Invoices

[63.21] VAT invoices must still be issued to VAT-registered customers, charging VAT using the normal rate for the supply (standard rate, reduced rate or zero rate) and *not* the flat-rate percentage. Customers treat these as normal VAT invoices. (VAT Notice 733, paras 7.3, 7.4).

VAT account

A VAT account must still be kept (even if the only VAT to be accounted for is that calculated under the flat-rate scheme). In some cases, however, a business may have VAT to account for outside the flat-rate scheme (e.g. the single purchases or disposals of capital expenditure goods of more than £2,000 in value). This should be entered in the VAT account in the normal way in addition to the flat-rate VAT. (VAT Notice 733, para 7.1).

Records

A record of flat-rate calculations must be kept showing

- flat-rate turnover for the VAT period;
- flat-rate percentage(s) used; and
- the VAT calculated as due.

This record must be kept with the VAT account.

(VAT Notice 733, para 7.2 which has the force of law).

Completing VAT returns

Because a business using the flat-rate scheme is calculating net VAT without reference to output tax and input tax, the rules for completing the VAT return are different. If the value for any box is none, write none in the box. Do not leave any box blank.

Box 1	Include the VAT due under the flat-rate scheme. There may be other output tax to include in this box such as sales of capital expenditure goods on which the business has claimed input tax separately while using the flat-rate scheme. See **63.22** below.
Box 2	Account for VAT on any goods bought from other EU countries at the normal rate of VAT (and not at the flat-rate).
Box 3	Insert sum of boxes 1 and 2 in the normal way.
Box 4	This will normally be none. There may be a claim if
	(i) a single purchase of capital expenditure goods of more than £2,000 in value (including VAT) is made (see **63.22** below);
	(ii) VAT can be recovered on stocks and assets on hand at registration (see **63.16** above); or
	(iii) a claim for bad debt relief is being made (see **63.22** below).

	As with goods and services bought from UK suppliers, VAT must not normally be claim on any acquisitions of goods and related services from other EU countries. But VAT can normally be claimed for any single purchase of capital expenditure goods of £2,000 or more in value (including VAT). See **63.22** below.
Box 5	Insert the difference between Box 3 and Box 4 in the normal way.
Box 6	Enter the value of turnover to which the flat-rate scheme percentage was applied, including VAT. Also include the VAT-exclusive value of any supplies accounted for outside the flat-rate scheme (e.g. supplies of capital expenditure goods).
Box 7	(i) a single purchase of capital expenditure goods costing more than £2,000 (including VAT) is made and input tax us claimed in Box 4; or
	(ii) goods have been acquired from other EU countries, in which case include the VAT-exclusive value in this Box.
Boxes 8 and 9	Complete as normal.

(VAT Notice 733, para 7.5).

Interaction of VAT and direct taxes

HMRC give the following guidance on the direct tax requirements for businesses using the flat-rate scheme.

- *No additional analysis of VAT is required to prepare accounts that are satisfactory for direct tax purposes.* The main bookkeeping advantage of the flat-rate scheme is that each purchase need not be analysed into gross, VAT and net figures when entered into the books of the business. This would be undone if, at the end of each year, these figures still had to be extracted for the preparation of annual accounts acceptable for income tax or corporation tax purposes. HMRC have confirmed that, for businesses that are using the flat-rate scheme, it is expected that accounts will be prepared using gross receipts less the flat-rate VAT percentage for turnover and that expenses will include the irrecoverable input VAT. This is similar in form to accounts prepared by non-VAT-registered businesses who cannot recover VAT they are charged.
- *The standard of records for direct tax purposes is the same as that for VAT.* A key benefit of the flat-rate scheme is that it removes the need to check the deductibility of VAT on purchases and even their liability to VAT. For both VAT and direct taxes, there is still a requirement to keep a record of sales and purchases. But for businesses using the flat-rate scheme, that record does not have to analyse gross, VAT and net separately. HMRC is not prescriptive about the way in which records are kept. For the simplest business, the records may be as little as a file of invoices issued and received in date order with a summary of totals although most businesses will do more than the minimum. In any case, the requirements of HMRC are that the records (whether VAT-exclusive or VAT-inclusive) are orderly and easy to follow.

- *VAT 'profits'*. There is no requirement to keep a separate account of the 'VAT profit' or 'VAT loss' arising from use of the scheme. By its very nature, a scheme based on flat rates for trade sectors leads to almost all businesses that use it paying a different amount of VAT from that they would pay if they were still using the normal system. Those who pay less VAT will have increased profits that are, in principle, taxable. Those who pay more VAT will have increased costs that, in principle, will reduce direct tax on profits.

Treatment in special circumstances

[63.22] In particular circumstances the flat-rate is treated as follows:

(1) Acquisitions of goods from, and sales of goods to, other EU countries

- If a business sells goods to other EU countries, the income must be included in its flat-rate turnover. This means that, if the business has a higher proportion of such sales than others in its trade sector, it may find that operating the scheme puts it a disadvantage compared to competitors.
- If a business buys goods from other EU countries, it must account for VAT on these acquisitions in Box 2 of its VAT return. Acquisition VAT is payable at the standard rate of VAT and not at the flat rate.

(VAT Notice 733, para 6.4).

(2) Supplies of services to and from abroad

- If a business supplies services which, under the place of supply rules, are treated as supplied outside the UK, these supplies should be left out of the flat-rate turnover.
- *VATA 1994, s 8* (reverse charge on supplies of services from abroad) does not apply to any relevant supply or relevant purchase of a flat-rate trader. [*SI 1995/2518, Reg 55U; SI 2002/1142*]. No adjustment should therefore be made to the flat-rate turnover for services purchased from outside the UK to which the reverse charge applies. See **38.4 INTERNATIONAL SERVICES**.

(VAT Notice 733, para 6.4).

(3) Exempt supplies

If a business is eligible for the flat-rate scheme, it is treated as fully taxable and does not have to make partial exemption calculations. It must, however, include its exempt income in its flat-rate turnover.

(VAT Notice 733, para 6.4).

(4) Motoring expenses

A business using the flat-rate scheme does not have to pay any road fuel scale charges as it does not reclaim input tax on its use of road fuel. (VAT Notice 733, para 6.4).

(5) Second-hand goods

A business can, if it wishes, include sales of second-hand goods in its flat-rate turnover but will pay more VAT on these sales than if it uses the margin scheme for second-hand goods. It is, however, the simplest option where a business makes only occasional sales of second-hand goods and it is not possible to use the flat-rate scheme and the margin scheme at the same time. (VAT Notice 733, para 6.4).

(6) Disbursements by a business acting as an agent

If a business

- pays amounts to third parties as the agent for its client, and
- debits its client with the precise amount paid out

it may be able to treat the payments as disbursements. See **3.7 AGENTS** for further details about disbursements. Where such disbursements are made, the money received for them is not part of the flat-rate turnover of the business.

(VAT Notice 733, para 6.4).

(7) Bad debt relief

BAD DEBT RELIEF (7) arises if a business accounts for and pays output tax on supplies for which it is subsequently not paid. The rules in that chapter apply to the flat-rate scheme as explained below.

If using the basic or retailer's turnover methods (see **63.20** above) a business can claim relief on eligible supplies at the standard rate of VAT rather than the flat rate.

If using the cash turnover method, a business may be eligible for bad debt relief if it has

- not been paid by its customer and it has been six months since the supply was made;
- it has not accounted for and paid VAT on the supply; and
- it has written off the debt in its accounts.

Where all these conditions are met, a business can claim the difference between the VAT charged to the customer and the amount it would have declared to HMRC had it been paid. [*SI 1995/2518, Reg 55V; SI 2002/1142*].

> *Example*
>
> In November 2008 C Ltd makes a supply under the flat-rate scheme of £1,000 plus VAT of £175. It uses the cash turnover method to calculate its relevant turnover. The invoice is not paid and C writes off the amount as a bad debt in its accounts after six months. Its flat-rate percentage is 10%.

	£
VAT on the unpaid supply	175.00
Deduct	
VAT which would have been paid under the flat-rate scheme if the customer had paid (£1,175 x 10%)	117.50
Special allowance under the flat-rate scheme.	£57.50

£57.50 should be added to the VAT deductible portion of the VAT account and included in the next VAT return

(VAT Notice 733, paras 14.1, 14.2).

(8) Capital expenditure goods

Capital goods are those goods which are bought to be used in the business but are not used up by it (other than by normal wear and tear over a number of years). Examples include a van (but not the fuel), a computer (but not the printer paper) and a machine.

'*Capital expenditure goods*' under the flat-rate scheme means capital goods that would fall within the above definition, but specifically excluding any goods bought

- for the purpose of resale or incorporation into goods supplied by the business;
- for consumption by the business within one year;
- to generate income by being leased, let or hired.

It also excludes assets covered by the **CAPITAL GOODS SCHEME (10)** as, if a business buys or intends to buy such assets, it is ineligible to use the flat-rate scheme.

Nothing in these provisions allows a business to claim credit for input tax where it would not otherwise be allowed to do so by any *order* made under *VATA 1994, s 25(7)* (e.g. on the purchase of a motor car).

VAT on purchases of capital expenditure goods

- VAT can be reclaimed on the single purchase of capital expenditure goods where the amount of the purchase, including VAT, is £2,000 or more. The normal VAT rules apply to determine whether any particular supply is one, or more than one, purchase.
  Any input tax should be claimed in Box 4 of the VAT return on the VAT return in the normal way.
- Otherwise, input tax on the purchase of capital expenditure goods is treated like any other purchase under the flat-rate scheme and no separate claim for input tax can be made.

Examples

A computer package (computer, printer, camera, scanner, speakers, etc.) bought as one package is one purchase of capital expenditure goods. If the package costs £2,000 or more (including VAT) input tax can be claimed.

Items of kitchen equipment (e.g. pizza oven, a fridge and a dishwasher) bought for a restaurant from one supplier at the same time count as one purchase of capital expenditure goods. If they are bought from three different suppliers, or at three different times, they count as three separate purchases and each must be £2,000 or more (including VAT) to qualify for input tax recovery.

Apportionment for private use

To help simplify the flat-rate scheme, where VAT on capital expenditure goods is reclaimable, the intended use of those items is treated as wholly for taxable supplies. Input tax need not be apportioned to cover any planned private or exempt use of the goods and there is no payment of output tax under the flat-rate scheme.

Disposals

The treatment of the sale of capital expenditure goods under the flat-rate scheme depends on how they were treated when acquired.

- Where input tax has been recovered on the purchase either
  - (i) before joining the flat-rate scheme, or
  - (ii) whilst the scheme is in operation, on capital expenditure goods costing £2,000 or more (including VAT)

  output tax must be accounted for on the sale at the standard rate (not at the flat rate) in the normal way. The income will not form part of the flat-rate turnover.
- Where no separate claim for input tax was made, VAT-inclusive income received from the disposal is included in the flat-rate turnover.

Goods or services

The normal rules apply for determining whether there is a supply of goods or a supply of services. For example, where a van is leased or hired by a business, this is a supply of services. But where it is bought on hire purchase, there is a supply of capital expenditure goods and input tax can be reclaimed if it costs £2,000 or more (including VAT).

[*SI 1995/2518, Regs 55A, 55E; SI 2002/1142*]. (VAT Notice 733, paras 15.1–15.9).

(9) Barristers

Barristers whose chambers use any of the three methods of accounting for common expenses (see **34.13**(3) **INPUT TAX**) may use the scheme.

Chambers using Method 3 must follow the rules below if they have any members using the flat-rate scheme and must ensure that input tax claims are apportioned and only relate to those barristers who are not on the scheme.

Example

A chambers has ten barristers, two of whom use the flat-rate scheme. The common fund has paid £11,750.00, including VAT of £1,750.00, on goods purchased. 30% of the input tax relates to the two barristers using the flat-rate scheme.

> If none of the barristers were using the scheme, input tax of £1,750.00 could have been claimed. But as two of them use the flat-rate scheme, input tax must be apportioned and a claim made, through the nominated member, for 70% (i.e. £1,225.00) of the VAT paid on the goods. This is the input tax relating to the eight barristers not using the scheme.

Chambers using the adaptation of Method 3 explained above, must ensure that barristers do not claim input tax while they use the scheme. To do this, they must monitor the input tax claimed for common expenses and have records that include

- the value of the original VAT invoice;
- the amount and percentage of input tax claimed back by the nominated member for each VAT invoice;
- how the input tax is apportioned to the individual barristers; and
- how the input tax reclaimed is calculated for each VAT invoice.

The records of all members of chambers using the flat-rate scheme must be made available during a visit to the chambers by an officer from HMRC.

(VAT Notice 733, paras 13.1, 13.2).

Leaving the scheme

[63.23] A business using the flat-rate scheme must continue to account for VAT under the scheme until its '*end date*', i.e. the date with effect from which it ceases to be authorised to use the scheme under the provisions below.

Voluntary withdrawal

A business can leave the scheme voluntarily at any time (although HMRC normally expect most businesses to leave at the end of a VAT period). HMRC will confirm the date of leaving the scheme in writing. (VAT Notice 733, para 12.1).

Ceasing to be eligible

A business ceases to be eligible to use the flat-rate scheme in the following circumstances and must withdraw from the date indicated.

(a) At any anniversary of its start date (i.e. the date from which it was authorised to use the scheme) if the total value of its income in the period of one year then *ending* is more than £230,000 unless HMRC are satisfied that the total value of its income in the period of one year then *beginning* will not exceed £191,500.
The above figures include the VAT-inclusive income of all taxable and exempt supplies, *excluding* supplies of capital assets. See **63.20** above for further details of what is included and excluded.
If, at the anniversary date, the turnover of a business has gone above £230,000, it may be able to remain in the scheme with the agreement of HMRC. It must apply in writing to HMRC, National Advice Service, Written Enquiries Section, Alexander House, Victoria Avenue, Southend On Sea, Essex SS99 1BD and be able to demonstrate that

- its VAT-inclusive turnover in the coming year will fall below £191,500;
- the increase was the result of unexpected business activity which has not occurred before and is not expected to recur; and
- the increase arose from a genuine commercial activity.

If, however, the increase occurred in such a way that the business must leave the scheme under (*b*) below, it cannot remain in the scheme even if these conditions are met.
(VAT Notice 733, para 11.2).
Where a business ceases to be eligible under these provisions, it must withdraw from the scheme

(i) in the case of a business using the annual accounting scheme, from the end of the annual VAT period in which the relevant anniversary occurred or the end of the month following the month in which the anniversary occurred, whichever is the earlier, or
(ii) in all other cases, the end of the VAT period in which the relevant anniversary occurred.

> *Example*
> A business starts to use annual accounting and the flat-rate scheme on 1 May 2010. Its annual accounting year runs from 1 May to 30 April. It carries out the turnover test for the flat-rate scheme on 1 May 2011 and has exceeded the income limit.
> The business must leave the flat-rate scheme on the earlier of the end of its current annual VAT accounting period (30 April 2012) and the end of the month following the month in which the anniversary falls (30 June 2011), i.e. 30 June 2011.

(b) There are reasonable grounds to believe that the total value of its income in the period of 30 days then beginning will exceed £230,000. The business must withdraw from the scheme from the beginning of the period of 30 days in question.
The above figures include the VAT-inclusive income of all taxable and exempt supplies, *excluding* supplies of capital assets. See **63.20** above for further details of what is included and excluded.
(c) It becomes a tour operator and must account for VAT under the **TOUR OPERATORS' MARGIN SCHEME (68)**, in which case it must withdraw from that date.
(d) It intends to acquire, construct or otherwise obtain a capital item within the **CAPITAL GOODS SCHEME (10)**, in which case it must withdraw from that date.
(e) It opts to account for VAT on a supply on the profit margin under the second-hand goods scheme or the auctioneers' scheme (see **61 SECOND-HAND GOODS**), in which case it must withdraw from the beginning of the VAT period for which it makes the election.
(f) It becomes
(i) eligible to be registered for VAT in the name of a group under *VATA 1994, s 43A* (see **27.2 GROUPS OF COMPANIES**),

(ii) registered for VAT in the name of a division under *VATA 1994, s 46(1)* (see **59.37 REGISTRATION**); or

(iii) 'associated with' another person.

In either case, the business must withdraw from the scheme from the date the event occurred. Note that it is eligibility to be in a VAT group which is the key test, not whether the business is actually in one.

A person is '*associated with*' another person at any time if that other person makes supplies in the course or furtherance of a business carried on by him, and

- the business of one is under the dominant influence of the other, or
- the persons are closely bound to one another by financial, economic and organisational links.

HMRC treat this as applying where one business has the right to give directions to another or, in practice, a business habitually complies with the directions of another. The test here is a test of the commercial reality rather than of the legal form. A close connection with another business is not necessarily the same as being associated. For example, a business is not associated with its customers just because it supplies them with the goods they request in the form they request them. Similarly, a husband and wife who are each separately VAT-registered in different types of business are not associated even if they share premises (provided this is charged at a market rate). (VAT Notice 733, paras 3.9, 3.10).

(g) Its authorisation to use the scheme is terminated by HMRC because

- they consider it necessary to do so for the protection of the revenue, or
- a false statement was made by, or on behalf of, the business in relation to its application for authorisation

in which case the business must withdraw from the scheme from the date of issue of a notice of termination by HMRC or such earlier or later date as may be directed in the notification.

Notifying HMRC

Where any of (*a*)–(*f*) above apply, the business must notify HMRC in writing of that fact within 30 days.

Consequences of leaving the scheme

A business leaving the scheme can rejoin at a later date but will not be eligible to rejoin for a period of twelve months after leaving the scheme.

The transition from the scheme back to the normal VAT rules is usually simple although there are some circumstances where adjustments must be made to make the VAT returns accurate.

(1) Ceasing to use the flat-rate scheme in the middle of a VAT period

A business which leaves the flat-rate scheme in the middle of a VAT period must do two calculations when completing its next VAT return, one for the part period when it was in the flat-rate scheme using the scheme rules and the other for the part period after leaving the scheme using the normal VAT rules. VAT liability for the return period is the sum of those two calculations. (VAT Notice 733, para 12.7).

(2) Cash-based method used under the flat-rate scheme

Where the cash-based method is used under the flat-rate scheme and the business does *not* move immediately to the cash accounting scheme, it must account for VAT on all the supplies it made while using the flat-rate scheme for which payment has not been received. The supplies should be included in the scheme turnover in the return for the period in which the business ceases to use the cash-based method. (VAT Notice 733, para 12.7).

(3) Adjustments in respect of stock on hand at withdrawal from the flat-rate scheme

Where

- a business remains registered for VAT after leaving the flat-rate scheme,
- at the date it ceases to be authorised to use the scheme, it has stock on hand in respect of which it is not entitled to credit for input tax, and
- the value of that stock on hand exceeds the value of its stock on hand in respect of which it was entitled to credit for input tax when it started to use the scheme

the business is entitled to credit for input tax in respect of its stock on hand calculated as follows.

Step 1	Establish the VAT-exclusive value of stock on hand and on which input tax had been recovered before joining the flat-rate scheme. (If previously using the cash accounting scheme, this will be based on stock for which the business had paid.) — say	£10,000
Step 2	Establish the VAT-exclusive value of stock on hand and on which the business will be unable to recover input tax after it ceases to use the flat-rate scheme — say	£20,000
Step 3	Subtract the figure at Step 1 from the total at Step 2. (If the figure at Step 1 is larger than the figure at Step 2, no adjustment can be made.)	£10,000
Step 4	Multiply the result of Step 3 by the standard rate of VAT = £10,000 × 17.5% (20% from 4 January 2011; 15% from 1 December 2008 to 31 December 2009)	£1,750
Claim the VAT calculated at Step 4 in the VAT recoverable portion of the VAT account in the first return made after leaving the flat-rate scheme.		

There is no need to do a formal stock take for the purpose of the calculation, but figures must be reasonable and a record should be kept of how stock was valued in case HMRC query the figures.

(4) Self-supply of capital expenditure goods on withdrawal from the flat-rate scheme

Where

- a business remains registered for VAT after leaving the flat-rate scheme,
- for any VAT period for which it used the scheme it was entitled to, and claimed, credit for input tax in respect of any capital expenditure goods, and
- it did not, whilst using the scheme, make a supply of those goods,

then, on the day after it ceases to use the scheme, those goods are treated as being both supplied to the business and supplied by the business in the course or furtherance of its business.

The value of the supply is calculated as for a supply for no consideration. See **71.22 VALUATION.**

[*SI 1995/2518, Regs 55B(4), 55M, 55N(3)(4), 55P–55S; SI 2002/1142; SI 2003/1069, Reg 7*].

Appeals

[63.24] If a business disagrees with a decision of HMRC

- refusing authorisation to use the scheme,
- withdrawing authorisation to use the scheme, or
- as to the appropriate flat-rate percentage(s) that applies to the business,

it may appeal to a VAT tribunal.

Where an appeal is brought against such a decision or, to the extent that it is based on such a decision, against an assessment, the tribunal must not allow the appeal unless it considers that HMRC could not reasonably have been satisfied that there were grounds for the decision.

[*VATA 1994, ss 83(fza), 84(4ZA); FA 2002, s 23(2)(3)*].

Flat-rate scheme for farmers

[63.25] The flat-rate scheme is an alternative to VAT registration for farmers. Farmers already registered for VAT may either remain registered or de-register and join the flat-rate scheme (provided the value of their non-farming activities is not above the VAT registration threshold, see below). Farmers whose turnover is below the registration limit may also use the scheme if they would otherwise qualify for voluntary registration.

A farmer has to apply to HMRC to join the scheme. HMRC may then certify him for the purposes of these provisions where satisfied that

- he is carrying on a business involving one or more designated activities (see **63.26** below); and
- he has complied with the necessary conditions for admission to the scheme (see **63.27** below).

[*VATA 1994, s 54*].

Certification

If the application is accepted, the farmer is issued with a certificate (showing a unique reference number) which is proof that he qualifies for the scheme. If application is refused, an appeal may be made to a VAT tribunal.

Where a person is so certified, goods and services supplied as part of those designated activities are disregarded in determining whether he is, has become or has ceased to become liable or entitled to be registered for VAT under *VATA 1994, Sch 1*.

[*SI 1995/2518, Reg 203*].

Flat-rate addition instead of VAT

Farmers who are certified under the flat-rate scheme do not account for VAT, or submit returns, on sales of goods and services within the designated activities to other VAT-registered customers. This means that they cannot reclaim the related input tax.

To compensate for this, on sales of designated goods and services to VAT-registered persons, farmers *may* charge a fixed flat-rate addition of 4% on top of the sales price. This applies even if some of the goods would otherwise be zero-rated. The farmer retains this addition and the registered person is able to recover it as if it were VAT (subject to the normal rules). [*VATA 1994, s 54(3)(4); SI 1992/3221; SI 1995/2518, Reg 209*].

The flat-rate addition must not be charged on supplies of goods and services which are not designated (e.g. sales of machinery) or on supplies to non-registered persons (e.g. the public or other flat-rate farmers).

Sales through farmers' groups and co-operatives

Where a farmer sells produce in this way, the goods are combined with the produce of other farmers and the buyer has no way of knowing whether any of his suppliers are flat-rate farmers. In such cases, the buyer should pay the farmer's group only the price agreed for the produce *without the flat-rate addition*. The group should pay the flat-rate addition to those farmers who have a certificate when the proceeds of sale are shared out. The farmer's group can reclaim this addition on its own VAT return as though it were input tax.

Auctioneers' sales

- *If the auctioneer is using the auctioneers' scheme or the margin scheme and acting in his own name*, he is regarded as a principal for VAT purposes, buying and selling the goods. In such a case, a flat-rate farmer can charge the flat-rate addition to the auctioneer who can reclaim it on his VAT return. The sale by the auctioneer is subject to the normal VAT rules.
- *If the auctioneer is not using either of those schemes and not acting in his own name*, he is not regarded as purchasing and selling the goods for VAT purposes. In such a case, the flat-rate farmer cannot charge the flat-rate addition to the auctioneer but can charge it to the eventual buyer of the goods if the buyer is VAT-registered.

Sales to other EU countries

A flat-rate farmer can charge the flat-rate addition on designated sales to VAT-registered persons in other EU countries (even though no VAT would have been due on the sale). The customer in the other country can reclaim the flat-rate addition charged provided he receives a flat-rate invoice.

Buying from other EU countries

Where a VAT-registered person in the UK acquires goods or services from a farmer in another EU country who charges the flat-rate addition, this can be reclaimed but from the VAT authority in the supplier's country (and not from HMRC). HMRC can give details of the procedure to be followed.

If a flat-rate farmer acquires goods from another EU country in excess of an annual threshold, he may have to register for VAT and lose the flat-rate status. See **59.18 REGISTRATION**.

Sales made outside the EU

A flat-rate farmer can charge the addition on designated goods and services to purchasers outside the EU provided the goods are used for the business purposes of the purchaser.

Other farming income

Where a farmer leases or lets some of the material assets of his farming business on a long-term basis but continues to farm under the flat-rate scheme in respect of the continued farming activity, the income from such a lease and/or letting cannot be treated as taxable under the scheme and must be taxed in the normal way (*Finanzamt Rendsburg v Harbs, ECJ Case C–321/02* [2006] STC 340 (TVC 22.483)).

Non-farming activities

If the taxable turnover of non-farming activities (e.g. bed and breakfast) is less than the VAT registration threshold, a farmer can still be a flat-rate farmer. He must not charge VAT or the flat-rate addition on the non-farming activities.

If his turnover of non-farming activities is above the VAT threshold, a farmer must remain registered for VAT (or, if already in the flat-rate scheme, have his certificate cancelled and register for VAT). The farmer will not be eligible to join the flat-rate scheme unless

- the non-farming activities are zero-rated, in which case the farmer may ask for exemption from registration (see **59.6 REGISTRATION**) and join the scheme; or
- the non-farming business is run as a separate business by a different legal entity (e.g. a farmer could run his farming activities as a sole proprietor and a bed and breakfast business in partnership with another person).

(VAT Notice 700/46/11, paras 4.1–4.4, 5.2, 6.1–6.3, 8.1, 8.2).

Deregistration

Farmers who deregister to join the flat-rate scheme do not have to account for VAT on their stocks and assets on hand, even where they have claimed input tax when purchasing them. [*VATA 1994, Sch 4 para 8(3)*].

De Voil Indirect Tax Service. See V2.191–198.

Designated activities

[63.26] For the purposes of the scheme, a farmer is someone who engages in any of the following activities.

(a) **Crop production** comprising any of the following.
- General agriculture including viticulture
- Growing of fruit, vegetables, flowers and ornamental plants (in the open and under glass)
- Production of mushrooms, spices, seeds and propagating materials
- Nursery production i.e. the rearing of young plants for sale

A marketing co-operative or a business selling peat or top soil is not eligible to join the scheme.

(b) **Stock farming** comprising any of the following.
- General stock farming
- Poultry and rabbit farming
- Bee-keeping and silkworm farming
- Snail farming

The following activities do not qualify.
- Raising budgerigars and other birds in aviaries purely as pets.
- Raising butterflies and any other animals or birds raised for similar purposes, for example, cats and dogs (except sheepdogs).
- Most other activities involving animals (e.g. pony trekking, riding lessons, hunting).
- Training animals as a specialist activity.
- Training horses bred for racing and any specialist training of horses for show-jumping or eventing.
- Training pigeons for racing (however, the breeding, rearing and care of pigeons would fall within the scheme).

(c) **Forestry**. This covers growing, felling and general husbandry of trees in a forest, wood or copse. Included is the conversion of felled timber into sawlogs, industrial small diameter roundwood, pitprops, cordwood, fencing material and firewood. Any activity involving any process beyond that stage is excluded.

(d) **Fisheries** comprising fresh-water fishing; fish farming; breeding of mussels, oysters and other molluscs and crustaceans; and frog farming.

(e) **Processing** by a farmer of products derived from his own activities within *(a)*–*(d)* above using only such means as are normally employed in the course of such activities.

(f) **Supplies of agricultural services**, by a person who also carries out one or more other designated activities falling within *(a)*–*(e)* above, comprising

- field work, reaping and mowing, threshing, bailing, collecting, harvesting, sowing and planting;
- packing and preparation of agricultural products for market (including drying, cleaning, grinding, disinfecting and ensilaging);
- storage of agricultural products;
- stock minding, rearing and fattening;
- hiring out of equipment for use in any designated activity;
- technical assistance in relation to any designated activity;
- destruction of weeds and pests, dusting and spraying of crops and land;
- operation of irrigation and drainage equipment; and
- lopping, tree felling and other forestry services.

Services concerned with the sale or leasing of milk quotas (whether or not they are sold with the land) are not a designated activity.

A person cannot join the scheme if

- his primary activity is to buy and sell animals (e.g. a dealer or trainer); or
- he is engaged in an activity once removed from farming (e.g. processing farm produce).

[*SI 1992/3220*]. (VAT Notice 700/46/11, paras 1.4, 3.1–3.4).

Admission to the scheme and changes in circumstances

[63.27] HMRC must certify a person for the purposes of the flat-rate scheme if the following conditions are satisfied.

(a) He satisfies HMRC that he is carrying on one or more designated activities within **63.26** above.

(b) If he is currently registered for VAT, that registration is cancelled. See **63.25** above for the position where non-farming activities are also carried on.

(c) He has not, in the three years before the date of application for certification,
- been convicted of any offences in connection with VAT;
- accepted an offer to compound proceedings in connection with a VAT offence; or
- been assessed to a penalty for VAT evasion involving dishonest conduct (see **52.10 PENALTIES**).

(d) He makes an application for certification on the correct form (Form VAT 98). The completed form should be sent to HM Revenue and Customs, Imperial House, 77 Victoria Street, Grimsby, DN31 1DB.

(e) He satisfies HMRC that, in the year following the date of his certification, the amounts of the flat-rate additions which he charges will not exceed the amount of input tax to which he would otherwise be entitled to credit by £3,000 or more. This will always be satisfied where the estimated value of agricultural supplies (shown in Box 4 of Form VAT 98) is £75,000 or less.

[*SI 1995/2518, Reg 204*].

Date of admission

The certificate issued by HMRC is effective from the date on which application is received by HMRC or, if the applicant so requests, from a date 30 days or less after that date. Alternatively, it may be such earlier date as HMRC agree to. No certificate can, however, be effective before any existing VAT registration is cancelled. [*SI 1995/2518, Reg 205*].

Further certification

Where a person who has been certified under the scheme, and is no longer so certified, makes a further application, he cannot be certified for a period of three years from the date of cancellation of the previous certificate except as follows.

(i) Where he has not been registered, or required to be registered, for VAT at any time since the cancellation of his previous certificate, HMRC may certify him from the date of his further application.
(ii) Where he has been registered for VAT during that time but no VAT was due on his business assets on hand at the date of deregistration because the VAT would not have been more than £1,000 (see **59.34 REGISTRATION**), HMRC may certify him on a date after the expiry of one year from the date of cancellation of his previous certificate.

[*SI 1995/2518, Reg 208*].

Changes in circumstances

The certificate issued by HMRC shows the full name of the business if the owner is a sole proprietor or company and the address of the business. In the case of a partnership, it shows the trading name of the partnership or, if it does not have one, the names of at least two partners (although, in such a case, the certificate still covers all the partners listed in the application form). HMRC must be informed of any change of name or address, any changes in the members of a partnership and if a sole proprietor takes a partner. HMRC will then reissue the certificate with the same number. In all other cases where the legal entity changes, the existing certificate must be cancelled and the new entity must apply for a new certificate. (VAT Notice 700/46/11, paras 2.3, 9.1).

Cancellation of certificates

[63.28] HMRC may or, as the case may be, must cancel a person's certificate in any of the following circumstances and from the date stated.

(a) Where a statement false in a material particular was made by him or on his behalf in connection with his application. Cancellation is from the date HMRC discover that such a statement has been made.

(b) He has been convicted of, or has accepted an offer to compound proceedings in connection with, a VAT offence or has been assessed to a VAT penalty. Cancellation is from the date of conviction, date of payment of the sum to compound proceedings or 30 days after the date the assessment is notified.

(c) He ceases to be involved in designated activities. Cancellation is from the date of cessation.

(d) He dies or becomes bankrupt or incapacitated. Cancellation is from the date of death, etc. HMRC may, however, in such cases, until such time as some other person is certified in respect of those activities, treat as a certified person any person carrying on those designated activities. That person must inform HMRC in writing within 30 days of the fact that he is carrying on the activities and the date of death, bankruptcy or incapacity.
Where the certified person is a company, the reference to bankruptcy is to be construed as a reference to liquidation, receivership or administration as the case may be.

(e) He is liable to be registered for VAT. Cancellation is from the effective date of registration.

(f) He makes an application in writing for cancellation. Cancellation is from a date not less than one year after the effective date of his certificate or such earlier date as HMRC agree to.

(g) He makes an application in writing for voluntary VAT registration (which application is deemed to be an application for cancellation of his certificate). Cancellation is from a date not less than one year after the effective date of his certificate or such earlier date as HMRC agree to.

(h) HMRC consider it is necessary to do so for the protection of the revenue (e.g. because the farmer is found to be recovering substantially more as a flat-rate farmer than he would if registered for VAT in the normal way). Cancellation is from the date on which HMRC consider a risk to the revenue arises.

(i) HMRC are not satisfied that any of the grounds for cancellation of a certificate within *(a)*–*(g)* above do not apply. Cancellation is from the date in *(a)*–*(g)* as appropriate.

[*SI 1995/2518, Regs 206, 207; SI 2003/2096, Art 59*].

A flat-rate farmer who leaves the scheme to register for VAT is not entitled to claim relief for any VAT incurred on purchases whilst he was a member of the scheme. (HMRC VAT Guidance V1–23, Chapter 2 para 4.5).

Records

[63.29] Every certified person must comply with such requirements relating to keeping, preserving and producing records as HMRC notify to him. In particular, every certified person must

(a) keep and preserve business and accounting records and copies of all invoices showing flat-rate additions (see **63.30** below) for six years (or such lesser period as HMRC allow); and

(b) upon demand by a person acting under the authority of HMRC (an '*authorised person*') produce, or cause to be produced, for inspection by that person any document within (*a*) above. The document must be produced at the principal place of business (or at such other place as may be reasonably required) at such time as may reasonably be required. The authorised person may take copies or make extracts of any document and may, at a reasonable time and for a reasonable period, remove any document. Where any document removed is reasonably required for the proper conduct of the business, a copy must be provided free of charge as soon as practicable. If any documents removed are lost or damaged, reasonable compensation must be paid.

[*SI 1995/2518, Regs 210, 211*].

Invoices

[63.30] In order that a registered person in receipt of a supply of designated goods and services may treat the flat-rate addition as if it were input tax for VAT purposes, the farmer must issue an invoice containing the following particulars.

- An identifying invoice number.
- His name, address and certificate number.
- The name and address of the person to whom the goods or services are supplied.
- The time of the supply.
- A description of the goods or services supplied.
- The consideration of the supply excluding the flat-rate addition.
- An amount entitled 'Flat-rate Addition' or 'FRA'.

[*SI 1995/2518, Reg 209*].

See **52.14 PENALTIES** for the penalty for unauthorised issue of flat-rate farming invoices.

VAT registration scheme for racehorse owners

[63.31] The VAT registration scheme (the 'scheme') for racehorse owners was introduced with the agreement of the thoroughbred horseracing and breeding industry. Subject to conditions, owners are accepted as carrying on a business and can register for VAT.

Conditions for registration

An owner of racehorses can apply for VAT registration under the Scheme if registered as an owner at Weatherbys and either

(a) the horses are covered by a sponsorship agreement registered at Weatherbys or by a trainer's sponsorship agreement registered at Weatherbys; or

(b) the owner can show that he has received business income from horseracing activities (e.g. appearance money or sponsored number cloths) and will continue to do so.

Normal procedure applies on application for registration (see **59.5 REGISTRATION**) with the additional requirement that Form D1 (owners not in partnership) or D2 (partnerships), certified as correct by Weatherbys, must be sent to HMRC with the VAT registration form(s). Forms D1 and D2 are obtained from, and must be sent for certification to, VAT Declarations, Weatherbys, Sanders Road, Wellingborough, Northants, NN8 4BX.

If registration is approved, HMRC will issue a VAT registration number and inform the owner of his effective date of registration (normally the date the completed D form was received at Weatherbys).

Only the registered owner of a racehorse at Weatherbys may register for VAT under the Scheme. The registered owner can be a sole proprietor, partnership or limited company. Where a part share only in a racehorse is owned, the part owner can register in his own name if owning at least 50% of the horse. Otherwise, he must register in partnership with the other joint owners.

Owners already VAT-registered outside the Scheme

Where an owner is already registered for VAT under the normal VAT registration rules for business activities connected with bloodstock, and his racehorse owning activities form part of that business, e.g. if he is

- a breeder who races colts, fillies or home bred geldings with the intention of enhancing the value of their breeding stock,
- a trainer who owns and retains horses to attract owners or buyers and to provide rides for apprentices, provided the number of horses is not disproportionate to the main activity of training, or
- a dealer who purchases and sells racehorses commercially, and who races the horses held as trading stock, provided those racehorses are available for sale,

the owner does not need to register under the Scheme.

Where the owner is registered for VAT for a business activity unconnected with bloodstock or his ownership of racehorses is not regarded as part of his normal bloodstock-related business, HMRC will normally only accept that a racehorse forms part of his existing business if he can show the horse was purchased for business purposes (e.g. it advertises the business). But provided all the conditions of the Scheme are met, any horses owned which are not part of the owner's normal business may still be treated as part of the owner's VAT registration.

Sponsorship

After registration:

(i) If sponsorship is lost, the owner can only remain registered if actively seeking new sponsorship. Although there is no time limit set for an owner to sign up to a new agreement, as a rule of thumb HMRC expect it to be no longer than six months after the expiry of the old agreement. If longer, HMRC will ask the owner to confirm, in writing, the steps being taken to obtain sponsorship. If not satisfied with the explanation, HMRC will consider whether the registration should be cancelled and any input tax implications.

(ii) Any horses owned which are not covered by a sponsorship agreement can still be treated as part of the Scheme but only if the owner can show that he is actively seeking sponsorship for them.

(VAT Notice 700/67/02, paras 1.2, 2.1–2.3, 3.1–3.3; VAT Notice 700/57/04).

Input tax

VAT incurred on the purchase, training, upkeep, etc. of a racehorse put to training (including any period when it is unable to run due to injury provided there is an expectation it will run in the future) is recoverable as input tax. All other amounts of VAT incurred by an owner in pursuit of horseracing activities can be deducted subject to the normal rules.

Output tax

Sponsorship income

Sponsorship income is a standard-rated supply. The normal rules for sponsorship apply. A taxable supply takes place where the owner supplies clearly identifiable benefits to their sponsor (e.g. advertises the sponsors name or products on their colours or reflects the sponsor in the name of the racehorse).

Prize money and appearance money

Both are treated as a standard-rated taxable supplies. These payments are distributed by Weatherbys, and are shown on monthly statements ('transaction analysis summaries') which are sent to all owners. (The statements also show certain expenditure, for example, jockeys' services, on which input tax can be reclaimed.)

Gifts, etc.

VAT is due on racehorses given away or put to non-business use, based on what the horse would cost at the time of its disposal, taking into account its fitness/health, etc. at that time. See, however, VAT Notice 700/57/02 for an agreement between HMRC, the British Horseracing Board and the Thoroughbred Breeders Association on racehorses applied permanently to personal or non-business use.

Margin scheme

Where no VAT was charged on the purchase, the margin scheme for second-hand goods can be used and VAT accounted for on the profit margin. See **61 SECOND-HAND GOODS** generally and, in particular, **61.37** for special provisions applying to horses.

(VAT Notice 700/67/02, paras 5.2, 5.4–5.6).

De Voil Indirect Tax Service. See V2.118.

Special arrangements for point-to-point horses

[63.32] An owner of a 'qualifying horse' (i.e. a horse with a sponsorship agreement which is entered in a hunter chase) can register for VAT under the scheme for the hunter chasing season only (January to June). Registration procedure is as in **63.31** above. If already registered for VAT (under these arrangements, under the scheme or because of other business activities) there is no requirements to apply for separate registration but Form D1 or D2 as appropriate must still be completed. After the end of the hunter chasing season, VAT registration can be retained provided

- the owner can show the intention to enter the horse in hunter chases in the following season; and
- the existing sponsorship agreement is to continue or the owner intends to obtain sponsorship before the horse competes in the first race in the new season.

If these conditions cannot be met, either registration will be cancelled or, if it is continuing for other reasons, no further input tax can be recovered in respect of the horse.

(VAT Notice 700/67/02, paras 6.1–6.4).

Input tax

Input tax cannot be recovered VAT until the horse becomes a qualifying horse. Once it does, 50% of any VAT charged on its purchase can be recovered provided it was incurred no more than three years before the date of registration. (The 50% restriction is a rule of thumb apportionment which recognises that the horse is used partly for business and partly for private purposes.)

With effect from the date of registration, VAT can be recovered on

- the training, keep and other costs of a qualifying horse (temporary periods of absences due to illness or injury can be ignored); and
- the purchase or construction of fixed assets used solely for a qualifying horse. Where, for example, a stable block or horse transporter is used for both qualifying and non-qualifying horses, the VAT must be apportioned to reflect the dual usage.

It is also possible to recover

- 50% of VAT charged on training, keep and other costs of a qualifying horse in the six months prior to registration, or the date a qualifying horse runs in a hunter chase; and
- other VAT charged before registration subject to the normal requirements in **34.10 INPUT TAX**.

Output tax

In addition to the information on output tax in **63.31** above, the following rules also apply to qualifying point-to-point horses.

VAT must be charged on the sale of a qualifying horse if the owner bred the horse and recovered VAT on the breeding cost. (No VAT is due on the sale of a non-qualifying horse if no VAT has been recovered in respect of it.) If a horse ceases to be a qualifying horse (e.g. because it is put to a permanent non-business use), VAT must be accounted for on 50% of the open market value.

(VAT Notice 700/67/02, paras 6.5, 6.6).

VAT treatment of racing clubs, etc.

[63.33] Racing clubs may take a number of forms.

(a) **Limited companies selling shares.** A limited company sells its shares (an exempt supply) and uses the funds to buy racehorses in the company name. Profits may be distributed to shareholders as dividends.
Unless the company has other business activities involving the making of taxable supplies, it can only register for VAT if it meets the conditions of the Scheme in **63.31** above. Any benefits available to shareholders (e.g. visits to trainers, free entry to racecourses, etc.) are disregarded for VAT purposes.

(b) **Racing partnerships selling shares.** A limited company or partnership sets up a racing partnership offering for sale a specific number of shares in the venture. Proceeds from prize money, sale of racehorses, etc. are distributed to the owners on termination of the partnership.
The sale of shares is outside the scope of VAT. Any benefits the owners of the shares receive (e.g. visits to trainers, free entry to racecourses, etc.) are disregarded for VAT purposes. Unless the partnership has other business activities involving the making of taxable supplies, it can only register for VAT if it meets the conditions of the scheme in **63.31** above.

(c) **Members racing club raising subscriptions.** A limited company, partnership or sole proprietor calling itself a 'racing club' (or having the characteristics of a club) invites persons to become members on payment of subscriptions. The subscriptions are used to buy racehorses, etc. and at the end of the year surplus income is distributed to members.
- *If members receive benefits* (e.g. newsletters, visits to trainers, tipping service), the club is carrying on a business. [*VATA 1994, s 94(2)*]. See **14.1 CLUBS AND ASSOCIATIONS**. The subscription income is liable to VAT and the club must register for VAT if above the registration threshold (or otherwise may apply for voluntary registration). The scheme under **63.31** above does not apply.
- *If members receive no benefits*, the club is not in business and the subscriptions are outside the scope of VAT. The club can only register for VAT if it meets the conditions of the scheme in **63.31** above.

(VAT Notice 700/67/02, paras 7.1–7.4).

Special scheme for non-EU suppliers of electronically supplied services

[63.34] With effect from 1 July 2003, the place of supply of electronically supplied services is normally in the country where the customer belongs subject, in certain circumstances, to where the services are effectively used and enjoyed. For further details of the place of supply rules, see **65.21–65.23** SUPPLY: PLACE OF SUPPLY. One effect of this would mean that a non-EU business would be required, under the normal rules, to register separately and account for VAT in each EU country in which it provided electronically supplied services to private individuals and non-business organisations.

To avoid this, a special scheme offers eligible non-EU businesses the *option* of registering electronically in a single EU country of their choice and accounting for VAT on their sales of these services to all such EU consumers. This is done on a single quarterly electronic VAT declaration which provides details of VAT due in each EU country. The declaration is submitted with payment to the tax administration in the EU country of registration which then distributes the VAT to the countries where the services are consumed.

Example

A USA business, with customers in the UK, Italy and Spain, registers for the special scheme in the UK. It charges UK VAT to its UK customers, Italian VAT to its Italian customers and Spanish VAT to its Spanish customers. The business enters the VAT for each country on the appropriate line of the electronic declaration. It sends the declaration electronically with payment to HMRC who retain the UK VAT and pass on the Italian VAT to the Italian authorities and the Spanish VAT to the Spanish authorities.

Any non-EU business which uses the scheme must comply with its conditions, including electronically registering (see **63.36** below) and accounting for and paying the VAT due at the correct time (see **63.37** below). There are no penalties under the scheme but if a business persistently fails to comply with the conditions, its registration may be cancelled. In that event, it must register under the normal rules applying in the various EU countries where its customers belong and could then be subject to any penalties which those countries apply. Similarly, if a non-EU business supplies electronic services to UK consumers and fails to register for VAT (either under the scheme or under the normal rules), it may be compulsorily registered in the UK under the normal rules and may incur a late registration penalty.

This scheme does not apply to non-EU businesses supplying broadcasting or other services. If a non-EU business chooses not to register under the special scheme, or is not eligible for it, it must register under the normal rules which apply in the relevant EU country.

(VAT Information Sheet 1/03, para 9.1; VAT Information Sheet 7/03, paras 1.1, 1.3; VAT Information Sheet 10/03, para 2.1).

For full details of the scheme, see **63.35–63.39** below.

Businesses eligible to join the scheme

[63.35] A business can be registered under the special scheme in the UK if it satisfies the following conditions.

(a) It makes, or intends to make, 'qualifying supplies' in the course of a business.

(b) It has neither a business establishment nor a fixed establishment in the UK or in another EU country in relation to *any* supply of goods or services. See **65.14 SUPPLY: PLACE OF SUPPLY** for the interpretation of 'business establishment' and 'fixed establishment'.

(c) It is not
- registered under *VATA 1994*,
- identified for the purposes of VAT in accordance with the law of another EU country, or
- registered under an *Act of Tynwald* for the purposes of any tax imposed by or under an *Act of Tynwald* which corresponds to VAT.

(d) It is not required to be registered or identified as mentioned in (*c*) above (or if it is required to be so registered or identified, this is solely by virtue of the fact that it makes or intends to make qualifying supplies).

(e) It is not identified under any provision of the law of another EU country which implements the scheme (i.e. it has not registered under a similar special scheme in another EU country).

'*Qualifying supply*' means a supply of electronically supplied services (within the meaning of *VATA 1994, Sch 5 para 7C*, see **65.22**(11) **SUPPLY: PLACE OF SUPPLY**) to a person who

- belongs in the UK or another EU country, and
- receives those services otherwise than for the purposes of a business carried on by him.

[*VATA 1994, Sch 3B paras 2, 3; FA 2003, Sch 2 para 4*].

Provided the above conditions are met, a non-EU business can use the special scheme if it makes supplies to business customers as well as non-business customers. In such a case, it is not required to charge and account for VAT on electronically supplied services supplied to EU businesses (including non-business organisations, such as a government department, receiving supplies for business purposes) because the EU customer accounts for any VAT due under the reverse charge mechanism. See **65.23 SUPPLY: PLACE OF SUPPLY**. (VAT Information Sheet 7/03, para 2.3).

Registration

[63.36] Where a business satisfies HMRC that it meets the conditions in **63.35** above, on request HMRC *must* register the business under these provisions. The only exception to this is that HMRC is not required to, but *may*, register a business under these provisions where it is a '*persistent defaulter*' (i.e. where a previous registration under these provisions has been cancelled for persistent failure to comply with the rules of the scheme (see below) or it has been excluded under the scheme in another EU country for the same reason).

Any registration request must contain the following particulars.

(a) The name of the business making the request.
(b) Its postal address and electronic addresses (including any websites).
(c) Where it has been allocated a number by the tax authorities in the country in which it belongs, that number.
(d) The date on which it began, or intends to begin, making 'qualifying supplies' (see **63.35** above).
(e) A statement that it is not
   (i) registered under *VATA 1994*;
   (ii) identified for the purposes of VAT in accordance with the law of another EU country, or
   (iii) registered under an *Act of Tynwald* for the purposes of any tax imposed by or under an *Act of Tynwald* which corresponds to VAT.

The registration request must be made by such electronic means, and in such manner, as HMRC direct.

[*VATA 1994, Sch 3B paras 4, 9; FA 2003, Sch 2 para 4*].

Businesses can register at the dedicated website https://secure.hmrc.gov.uk/ecom/voes. This is a secure site which automatically guides the applicant through an electronic registration process, including selecting a user name and password for identification purposes when completing and submitting declarations electronically.

HMRC also ask for a contact name and telephone number.

(VAT Information Sheet 7/03, paras 3.2, 3.3).

Effective date of registration

Registration takes effect from the date on which the registration request is made (or such earlier or later date as is agreed with HMRC) but in any case not before 1 July 2003. [*VATA 1994, Sch 3B para 5; FA 2003, Sch 2 para 4*].

Registration number

HMRC must allocate a registration number to each business registered under these provisions and notify the number to the business electronically. [*VATA 1994, Sch 3B para 6; FA 2003, Sch 2 para 4*]. HMRC will normally send the number by e-mail within five working days of receiving the completed electronic registration request. Registration numbers have their own unique format beginning with the prefix 'EU', followed by a nine digit number. (VAT Information Sheet 7/03, para 3.4).

Businesses already registered for VAT in the EU under the normal rules

Where a business is registered for VAT in any EU country under the normal rules, it is not eligible for the special scheme and must account for VAT on any electronically supplied services to EU consumers under those normal rules. However, from 1 July 2003, a business may switch from registration under the normal rules and apply for registration in the UK under the special scheme if, for example,

- it ceases to make supplies of goods or services to EU consumers other than electronically supplied services, or
- it initially makes supplies of electronically supplied services to consumers in a single EU country but subsequently expands its market to consumers in other EU countries

provided it cancels its VAT registration under the normal rules in the EU country concerned. (VAT Information Sheet 7/03, paras 3.6, 3.9).

Changes in business circumstances

A business which has made a registration request must notify HMRC if subsequently

- there is a change in any of the particulars contained in its request under (*a*)–(*d*) above;
- it ceases to make, or to have the intention of making, qualifying supplies; or
- it ceases to satisfy any of the conditions in **63.35**(*b*)–(*e*) above.

The notification must be given, using the dedicated website above, within 30 days of the date of the change of particulars or of the cessation.

[*VATA 1994, Sch 3B para 7; FA 2003, Sch 2 para 4*]. (VAT Information Sheet 7/03, para 3.7).

Cancellation of registration

HMRC must cancel the registration of a business in the following circumstances.

- The business notifies HMRC that it has ceased to make, or to have the intention of making, 'qualifying supplies' (see **63.35** above). Cancellation then takes effect from the date on which the notification is received or such earlier or later date as is agreed with HMRC.
- HMRC otherwise determine that the business has ceased to make, or to have the intention of making, qualifying supplies. Cancellation then takes effect from the date on which the determination is made or such earlier or later date HMRC may direct.
- The business notifies HMRC that it has ceased to satisfy any of the conditions in **63.35**(*b*)–(*e*) above. Cancellation then takes effect from the date on which the notification is received or such earlier or later date as is agreed with HMRC.
- HMRC otherwise determine that the business has ceased to satisfy any of the conditions in **63.35**(*b*)–(*e*) above. Cancellation then takes effect from the date on which the determination is made or such earlier or later date HMRC may direct.
- HMRC determine that the business has persistently failed to comply with its obligations under these provisions. Cancellation then takes effect from the date on which the determination is made or such earlier or later date HMRC may direct.

[*VATA 1994, Sch 3B para 8; FA 2003, Sch 2 para 4*].

Accounting and records

Liability for VAT

[63.37] The amount of VAT which a business is liable to pay under the special scheme on any 'qualifying supply' (see **63.35** above) is calculated as follows.

(a) If the qualifying supply is treated as made in the UK, the amount of VAT that would have been charged on the supply if the business had been registered under *VATA 1994* when it made the supply; and any amount so calculated is regarded as VAT charged in accordance with *VATA 1994*.

(b) If the qualifying supply is treated as made in another EU country, the amount of VAT that would have been charged on the supply in accordance with the law of that EU country if the business had been identified for the purposes of VAT in that country when it made the supply; and any amount so calculated in relation to another EU country is regarded for the purposes of *VATA 1994* as VAT charged in accordance with the law of that EU country.

[*VATA 1994, Sch 3B para 10; FA 2003, Sch 2 para 4*].

Obligation to submit special accounting returns

A business must submit to VAT Central Unit a special accounting return for each 'reporting period' for which it is registered under the special scheme. A '*reporting period*' is each calendar quarter for the whole or part of which the business is registered under the scheme.

The special accounting return must set out the following in sterling.

- The registration number of the business.
- For each EU country in which the business is treated as having made qualifying supplies in the reporting period:
  - (i) the total value of those qualifying supplies in sterling (excluding the VAT which it is liable to pay by virtue of these provisions);
  - (ii) the rate of VAT applicable to those supplies by virtue of (*a*) or (*b*) above, and
  - (iii) the total amount of VAT payable under these provisions in respect of those supplies.
- The total amount of VAT which the business is liable to pay under these provisions in respect of all qualifying supplies treated as made by it in all EU countries in the reporting period.

Any conversion from one currency into another for these purposes must be made using the exchange rates published by the European Central Bank for the last day of the reporting period to which the special accounting return relates (or, if no such rate is published for that day, for the next day for which such a rate is published). To avoid the need for businesses to calculate a conversion from the currency of sale into Euros and then from Euros into sterling, HMRC have published the exchange rates for the following leading currencies direct into sterling.

Country/ currency	*Units of currency to £*				
	31.3.07	30.6.07	30.9.07	31.12.07	31.3.08
EU	1.4791	1.4801	1.4340	1.3490	1.2677
Australia/dollar	2.4214	2.3472	2.2976	2.2492	2.1824
Canada/dollar	2.2865	2.2105	2.0280	1.9580	2.0371
Costa Rica/colon	1011.72	1,024.19	1,030.35	1,061.68	974.004
Hong Kong/dollar	15.4507	15.7206	15.8566	15.4770	15.4606
India/rupee	86.527	80.6759	81.4322	80.9557	78.0219
Japan/yen	232.7318	246.6662	236.2659	221.0117	199.7338
Russia/ rouble	51.3859	51.0114	51.1585	50.1317	48.2321
Singapore/ dollar	3.0013	3.0673	3.0194	2.8511	2.7386
Switzerland/ franc	2.3999	2.4406	2.3809	2.2297	1.9951
USA/dollar	1.9769	2.0111	2.0409	1.9814	1.9853

(VAT Information Sheets 7/07, 9/07, 13/07, 1/08, 2/08).

Alternatively, the conversion can be calculated using the exchange rates shown at the ECB's website at:

www.ecb.int

The special accounting return must be submitted to HMRC by electronic means within 20 days after the last day of the reporting period to which it relates.

[*VATA 1994, Sch 3B paras 11, 12; FA 2003, Sch 2 para 4*]. (VAT Information Sheet 10/03, paras 3.1, 3.2).

Returns must be completed by logging on to the dedicated website

https://secure.hmrc.gov.uk/ecom/voes

and using the VAT identification number, user name and password of the business to ensure security. A return is required even if there are no qualifying supplies in the quarter.

HMRC send an on-line acknowledgment confirming that they have received the return. This acknowledgment also provides a unique reference number for each return submitted. This number should be referred to if it is necessary to contact HMRC with a query about the return. If this confirmation is not received *immediately*, the Customer Services Team should be contacted by e-mail at

voes@hmrc.gsi.gov.uk.

(VAT Information Sheet 7/03, paras 4.1, 4.6).

Payment of VAT

At the same time as submitting the special accounting return, a business must pay to HMRC, in sterling, the total amount of VAT as shown due by the return. [*VATA 1994, Sch 3B para 13; FA 2003, Sch 2 para 4*].

VAT on purchases

The special scheme provides only for payment of the VAT due on sales to EU customers, without any deductions of EU VAT incurred on purchases. However, a business may be able to reclaim VAT it has paid on goods and services used for the purpose of its taxable activities falling within the scheme, from the EU country where that VAT was paid, under the *EC 13th Directive*. See **18.44 EUROPEAN UNION LEGISLATION** for the provisions of the *Directive* and **48.5 OVERSEAS TRADERS** for applications to the UK for refunds.

Obligations to keep and produce records

A business registered under the special scheme in the UK must keep records of its transactions in qualifying supplies (see **63.35** above) in sufficient detail to enable the tax authorities in the EU countries in which those supplies are treated as made to determine whether any special accounting return is correct. These records include normal commercial data held for each transaction (e.g. transaction number, date, type (credit or debit), customer name and location, currency and values including VAT).

Any records required to be kept must, on request, be made available electronically to HMRC and the tax authorities of any EU country where the qualifying supplies were treated as made. HMRC also may request records of a business where its qualifying supplies are treated as made in the UK but it is registered under the scheme in another EU country

The records must be kept for ten years beginning with the 1st January following the date on which the transaction was entered into.

[*VATA 1994, Sch 3B paras 14, 15; FA 2003, Sch 2 para 4*]. (VAT Information Sheet 7/03, para 4.8).

Invoices

There are no special rules for issuing VAT invoices under the special scheme and consequently the normal rules apply. In the UK, a business is not required to issue VAT invoices for such supplies because its customers are not in business and cannot deduct VAT on their purchases. (VAT Information Sheet 7/03, para 4.10).

Errors in special scheme returns

Errors discovered by HMRC

[63.38] If HMRC consider that a business which is, or has been, registered under the special scheme (whether in the UK or another EU country) has submitted a scheme return which understates or overstates liability to UK VAT, they may give the business a notice

- identifying the return in which they consider that the under/overstatement was made; and
- specifying the amount by which they consider that the liability to VAT has been under/overstated.

In the case of an understatement, HMRC will request the business to pay the amount understated to HMRC within 30 days of the date of the notice. There are no penalties for underdeclaring the amount of VAT due under the special scheme. However, failure to declare the full amount may make the business ineligible to use the scheme (see **63.36** above under *Cancellation of registration*).

In the case of an overstatement, HMRC must pay the business the amount specified in the notice. They will normally do this within 30 days.

Time limit

No notice under these provisions may be given more than three years after the end of the period for which the scheme return in question was made.

[*VATA 1994, Sch 3B para 16; FA 2003, Sch 2 para 4*]. (VAT Information Sheet 10/03, paras 5.2, 5.3).

Errors discovered by the non-EU supplier

If a non-EU supplier submits a declaration but subsequently discovers that it has made an error (e.g. entering French VAT in the line for Spain or underdeclaring UK VAT), it should contact HMRC at

voes@hmrc.gsi.gov.uk

quoting the reference number for the return in question and advising the correct amount(s) due for the EU country or countries concerned. There is no need to submit a supplementary declaration.

Where, as a result of the error, additional VAT is due, HMRC will either request that the payment is sent to them or advise that the EC country or countries concerned will contact the business to explain how it should pay the VAT due.

(VAT Information Sheet 10/03, para 4.2).

Business customers initially failing to provide VAT registration numbers

The special scheme is intended for supplies to consumers who cannot recover VAT. A business customer who fails to provide a valid VAT registration number at the time of the transaction must be charged VAT and cannot deduct that VAT as input tax. However, if it subsequently produces a valid VAT registration number and requests a credit, the non-EU supplier can refund the VAT to the business customer. (VAT Information Sheet 10/03, para 4.1).

Miscellaneous matters

[63.39] Some miscellaneous matters are treated as follows:

(1) Appeals

An appeal can be made to a UK VAT tribunal with respect to any of the following.

- The registration or cancellation of the registration of any business under the special scheme.
- A decision of HMRC to give a notice of understatement of UK VAT liability under **63.38** above.
- The amount specified in any such notice or in a notice of overstatement of UK VAT liability under **63.38** above.
- [*VATA 1994, Sch 3B para 20; FA 2003, Sch 2 para 4*].

UK VAT tribunals cannot deal with VAT matters which fall within the jurisdiction of other EU countries. If a non-EU business using the special scheme disagrees with a decision taken by another EU country about any aspect of the scheme (e.g. the amount of VAT owed to it), the matter should be raised with the VAT authorities in that country.

(2) Deregistration

Where a business which is registered under *VATA 1994 Sch 1* (registration in respect of UK supplies, see **59.1–59.10 REGISTRATION**) satisfies HMRC that it intends to apply for

- registration under the special scheme in the UK, or
- identification under any provision of the law of another EU country which implements similar provisions,

they may, if the business so requests, cancel its registration under *VATA 1994 Sch 1* with effect from the day on which the request is made or from such later date as may be agreed between it and HMRC.

[*VATA 1994, Sch 3B para 18; FA 2003, Sch 2 para 4*].

(3) EU enlargement

10 countries (i.e. Cyprus, Czech Republic, Estonia, Hungary, Latvia, Lithuania, Malta, Poland, Slovak Republic, and Slovenia) joined the EU with effect from 1 May 2004 and two further countries (Bulgaria and Romania) joined with effect from 1 January 2007. As a result, non-EU businesses

- not already registered for the special scheme will have a greater choice of EU countries to select from in order to register under the scheme;
- registered under the special scheme but established within any of those countries are excluded from continuing to use the scheme; and
- registered under the special scheme but not established within any of those countries must extend the charging of VAT on their e-services to all non-business users who reside within those countries.

(4) Exempt supplies

Most electronically supplied services within the EU are subject to VAT. However, certain EU countries apply an exemption to some electronically supplied services (e.g. gambling). If a non-EU supplier thinks that its services may qualify for an exemption, it should check with the country or countries concerned. However, unless its services are exempt from VAT in all EU countries where its customers belong, it will still be required to register and account for VAT in the EU either under the normal rules or under the special scheme. (VAT Information Sheet 10/03, para 2.3).

(5) Registration under VATA 1994

Notwithstanding any provision in *VATA 1994* to the contrary, a business in the special scheme is not required to be registered under *VATA 1994* by virtue of making qualifying supplies under the special scheme. [*VATA 1994, Sch 3B para 17; FA 2003, Sch 2 para 4*].

(6) VAT representatives

VATA 1994, s 48(1) (VAT representatives, see **3.8 AGENTS**) does not permit HMRC to direct a business in the special scheme to appoint a VAT representative. [*VATA 1994, Sch 3B para 19; FA 2003, Sch 2 para 4*].

However, although an agent, even an authorised one, cannot register for the special scheme on behalf of a non-EU supplier, the supplier can register itself and authorise an agent to submit declarations and, if necessary, make payments on its behalf under the scheme. But it should be noted that rules regarding agents vary between EU countries and such authorisation may render the agent jointly and severally liable for VAT in some countries. (VAT Information Sheet 10/03, para 2.3).

Key points

[63.40] Points to consider are as follows.

Cash accounting scheme

- The cash accounting scheme can be used by a business with annual turnover of £1.35m per year (taxable sales excluding VAT) or less. The business should also have a good VAT compliance record with HMRC.
- The main outcome of the cash accounting scheme is that output tax is not due on a VAT return until payment has been received from a customer. Input tax cannot be reclaimed until payment has been made to a supplier.
- The cash flow benefits and automatic bad debt relief given by the scheme could be particularly useful for a business that has standard-rated sales and gives extended credit terms to customers, or which has customers that are slow payers.
- The cash accounting scheme is not suitable for taxpayers supplying mainly zero-rated items, or for a business where customers pay in advance or as soon as sales invoices are raised.

- A business should regularly review whether the cash accounting scheme continues to be of benefit. A change in the mixture of standard/zero-rated sales could mean it is more beneficial for a business to account for VAT under normal accounting rules.
- A business that exceeds the exit level of £1.6m per annum in taxable sales can still remain in the scheme if it can prove to HMRC that the increase in sales for the year in question was due to a one-off sale and that it expects taxable supplies in the next twelve months to be less than £1.35m.

Annual accounting scheme

- The annual accounting scheme means that a business only completes one VAT return a year instead of four or twelve. A business can only join the scheme if it expects that its annual taxable sales in the next twelve months will be less than £1.35m (excluding VAT).
- A business in the annual accounting scheme must make payments on account during the course of the year either on a monthly basis in months 4 to 12, or on a quarterly basis at the end of months 4, 7 and 10. A balancing payment is then due when the annual VAT return is submitted at the end of the year
- The payments on account are based on the previous year's VAT liability. These payments could be too high for a business that is not trading as well in the current year as it did in the previous year.
- It should be noted that payments on account that are either too high or too low can be adjusted during the year by writing to the local VAT Business Advice Centre and requesting revised payment terms.
- It is unlikely that the annual accounting scheme will benefit repayment traders because they will have to wait until the end of the accounting year to receive any repayment due.
- Be aware of the potential advantages of the scheme that may appeal to certain traders – particularly the time-saving benefits of completing only one return each year. The scheme may also appeal to partly-exempt taxpayers who will only need to make one partial exemption calculation per year (the annual accounting period must coincide with the partial exemption tax year, i.e. 31 March, 30 April or 31 May).

Flat-rate scheme

- The flat-rate scheme allows a business buying capital goods costing more than £2,000 including VAT to reclaim input tax on the purchase of the assets. There may be opportunities for a business to buy a slightly more expensive asset (e.g. upgraded computer) to exceed the £2,000 limit to benefit from the VAT saving.

- An input tax claim does not apply in relation to building projects costing more than £2,000 including VAT, e.g. an office extension, because the supplies in such cases are of 'building services' rather than 'capital goods'.
- Be aware of the main disadvantage of the flat-rate scheme – namely that the flat-rate percentage needs to be applied to zero-rated and exempt sales. This could make the scheme very unattractive to taxpayers who have an unpredictable level of zero-rated sales, such as builders.
- Exempt income also includes buy-to-let income, the sale of certain property and other capital assets and, according to HMRC, interest received on a business bank account.
- The flat-rate scheme offers potential savings of tax to certain users. As with any scheme based on averages, there will always be winners and losers.
- Even if a business has exceeded the turnover limit where it must leave the scheme (£230,000 per year on the anniversary of when it joined the scheme), there may be scope to remain within the scheme if HMRC is satisfied that the total taxable income in the next twelve months will be less than £191,500 – again within the scheme limits.
- A chosen flat-rate category must be reviewed on an annual basis to ensure it is still valid. This is particularly important for a business with two or more activities because the flat rate is based on the activity with the greater (greatest) percentage of turnover.
- Remember that a business can benefit from an extra 1% discount on the relevant flat rate % in its first year of VAT registration. This could produce a considerable saving of tax in a twelve-month period.
- Be aware of the impact of revised flat-rate percentages following the VAT rate increase that will take place on 4 January 2011, and the potential for a business to retrospectively withdraw from the scheme if it discovers (belatedly) that its new rate has produced an increased tax bill that makes the scheme unattractive to use.

Other schemes

- A flat-rate scheme is available to farmers as an alternative to VAT registration. The basic principle is that they make an additional charge of 4% on sales of specified goods and services (including zero-rated sales) to customers, and retain this money as an alternative to reclaiming input tax.
- A customer can reclaim the 4% charge made by the farmer as if it were VAT, i.e. within box 4 of his relevant VAT return.
- A non-EU business making electronic supplies of services to private and non-business EU customers must either register for VAT in each EU country with which it trades (subject to turnover limits) or register in one country and complete an electronic return each quarter to declare VAT charged to each different country.

- A business registered for the special scheme will charge the rate of VAT that applies in each different EU country, even though it is registered in only one country. This is to ensure a business cannot gain a competitive advantage by registering in an EU country with the lowest rate of VAT.

64

Supply: General

Introduction

[64.1] A transaction is within the scope of UK VAT if the following four conditions are satisfied.

- It is a supply of goods or services.
- It takes place in the UK.
- It is made by a taxable person.
- It is made in the course or furtherance of any business carried on by that person.

[*VATA 1994, s 4(1)*].

The first three conditions are considered in this chapter.

Supplies for VAT purposes

Even before deciding whether goods or services are being supplied, it is necessary to determine whether a transaction is in fact a supply for VAT purposes by considering the following questions.

(a) Is there any consideration?

Under both EU and UK law, a supply takes place for VAT purposes when something is provided or done for a consideration. [*VATA 1994, s 5(2)*].

Consideration for VAT purposes has a wide meaning and covers anything which might be done, given or made in exchange for something else. It does not refer only to money. See **71.3** *et seq* VALUATION for further coverage of consideration.

(b) If there is no consideration, is the transaction one which is deemed to be a supply for VAT purposes?

Even if there is no consideration, certain transactions made for no consideration (i.e. free) are deemed to be supplies of goods or services for VAT purposes. These are the

- permanent transfer/disposal of business assets, see **47.6 OUTPUT TAX**;
- temporary use of business assets for non-business purposes, see **47.7 OUTPUT TAX**;
- retention of certain business assets on deregistration, see **59.34 REGISTRATION**;
- self-supply of goods or services, see **62 SELF-SUPPLY**; and
- private or other non-business use of services supplied to the business, see **47.7 OUTPUT TAX**.

(c) Does the transaction fail to be a supply or is it a supply which is disregarded for VAT purposes?

A transaction is not a supply for VAT purposes if

- there is no consideration for the supply and it is not a deemed supply under (*b*) above;
- the transaction is within the same legal entity;
- there is a specific exclusion in VAT legislation, i.e.
  - (i) a business gift costing the donor £50 or less, see **47.6 OUTPUT TAX**;
  - (ii) samples, see **47.8**(26) **OUTPUT TAX**; or
  - (iii) the transaction is deemed to be 'neither a supply of goods nor services', see **64.5** below.

Supplies of goods and services

Once it has been established that a transaction is a supply, it is then necessary to determine whether it is a supply of goods (see **64.3** below) or a supply of services (see **64.4** below). Certain transactions, although supplies, are regarded as supplies of neither goods nor services and are outside the scope of VAT (see **64.5** below).

The distinction as to whether a supply is one of goods or services is important as different rules apply to the place and time of supply. Also the treatment of the international supply of goods and services is different.

Meaning of supply

[64.2] The legislation does not define the term 'supply'. Subject to express provisions to the contrary, supply includes all forms of supply, but not anything done otherwise than for consideration. Anything which is not a supply of goods but is done for a consideration (including, if so done, the granting, assignment or surrender of any right) is a supply of services. [*VATA 1994, s 5(2)*].

In *C & E Commrs v Oliver*, QB 1979, [1980] STC 73 (TVC 62.168), it was held that supply of goods has a wide interpretation. It is the passing of possession in goods pursuant to an agreement whereunder the supplier agrees to part and the recipient agrees to take possession. By 'possession' is meant in this context control over the goods, in the sense of having immediate facility for their use. This may or may not involve the physical removal of the goods. See also *Carlton Lodge Club v C & E Commrs*, QB [1974] STC 507 (TVC 13.29).

In *Tolsma v Inspecteur der Omzetbelasting Leeuwarden, ECJ Case C–16/93*, [1994] STC 509 (TVC 22.84) an individual who played a barrel organ on the public highway, and invited donations from the public, was held not to be supplying services for a consideration. There was no agreement between the parties and also 'no necessary link between the musical service and the payment to which it gave rise'.

Illegal supplies

The principle of fiscal neutrality requires that all supplies of goods for a consideration are subject to VAT unless the goods are subject to a total prohibition on circulation because they are intrinsically harmful or because all competition between a lawful economic sector and an unlawful sector is precluded. In *Witzemann v Hauptzollamt Munchen-Mitte, ECJ Case C–343/89*, [1993] STC 108 (TVC 22.101), the Advocate-General stated that 'illegality manifests itself in many forms and there are many products that either cannot be lawfully traded or trade in which is subject to certain restrictions: drugs, counterfeit money, weapons, pornography, the pelts of certain animals, stolen goods and so forth. Not every transaction tainted with illegality will be exempt from taxation. A line must be drawn between, on the one hand, transactions that lie so clearly outside the sphere of legitimate economic activity that, instead of being taxed, they can only be the subject of criminal prosecution and, on the other hand, transactions which, though unlawful, must none the less be taxed, if only for the sake of ensuring, in the name of fiscal neutrality, that the criminal is not treated more favourably than the legitimate trader'.

Thus, the illegal sale of drugs is not a supply for VAT purposes (*Mol v Inspecteur der Invoerrechten Accijnzen, ECJ Case 269/86*, [1989] 3 CMLR 729 (TVC 22.81)) but the supply of counterfeit perfume is. See *R v Goodwin and Unstead*, CA [1997] STC 22, ECJ [1998] STC 699 (TVC 22.82). The prohibition on such products stems from the fact that they infringe intellectual property rights and is conditional not absolute (as in the case of drugs and counterfeit money). There is scope for competition between counterfeit perfumes and perfumes which are traded lawfully and although supply of the former is unlawful, such perfume is not liable to seizure in the hands of the final customer. The unlawful operation of a form of roulette was similarly held to be a supply for VAT purposes in *Fischer v Finanzamt Donaueschingen, ECJ Case C–283/95*, [1998] STC 708 (TVC 22.371). However, although the unlawful playing of a game of chance is a supply, it is not taxable where the corresponding activity is exempt when carried on lawfully by a licensed casino.

In *Staatssecretaris van Financien v Coffeeshop 'Siberie vof, ECJ Case C–158/98*, [1999] STC 742 (TVC 22.83) income from renting tables for the sale of cannabis was held to be within the scope of VAT and similarly in *C & E Commrs v R & J Polok*, Ch D [2002] STC 361 (TVC 62.279) income from the running of an escort agency was held to be potentially taxable (as indeed was the income of the escorts themselves).

De Voil Indirect Tax Service. See V3.102–104.

Supplies of goods

[64.3] For EU legislation, see **18.8 EUROPEAN UNION LEGISLATION.**

Under UK legislation, the Treasury may, by Order, deem any transaction to be a supply of services and not a supply of goods (or vice versa). [*VATA 1994, s 5(3)*]. Subject to this, the following supplies are to be treated as supplies of goods.

(a) Any transfer of the whole property in goods. [*VATA 1994, Sch 4 para 1(1)*].

This usually means transfer of both title to the goods and possession of, or control over, the goods. If possession is transferred but title is retained (e.g. where goods are let out on hire) this is a supply of services (see **64.4** below). However, if possession is transferred in circumstances where title would normally pass but does not because the holder of the goods did not have good title (e.g. the sale of stolen goods) this is a supply of goods as if title had passed. See *C & E Commrs v Oliver*, QB 1979, [1980] STC 73 (TVC 62.168).

The transfer of an undivided share of property is a supply of services (see **64.4** below). For the distinction, see *Sir John Astor* (VTD 1030) (TVC 62.361).

(b) The transfer of possession of goods under an agreement for the sale of the goods

or under agreements which expressly contemplate that the property also will pass at some time in the future (determined by, or ascertainable from, the agreements but in any case not later than when the goods are fully paid for). [*VATA 1994, Sch 4 para 1(2)*]. Where the conditions for future transfer are not satisfied, the supply is a supply of services (see **64.4** below).

Supplies under hire purchase contracts, conditional sale agreements and reservation of title agreements are thus supplies of goods. The simple hire or lease of goods, on the other hand, does not envisage the future transfer of title and is a supply of services. However, there a many other types of agreement where the distinction is not clear cut. In cases of doubt it is necessary to look at both the written agreement and the intention of any overall scheme operated. *Directive 2006/112/EC, Art 14(2)(b)* provides that there is a supply of goods where 'in the normal course of events' ownership will pass at the latest upon payment of the final instalment.

(c) The supply of any form of power, heat, refrigeration or (from 1 January 2011) other cooling, or ventilation. [*VATA 1994, Sch 4 para 3; F(No 3) Act 2010, s 20(2)*].

(d) The grant, assignment or surrender of a 'major interest' in land. [*VATA 1994, Sch 4 para 4*]

See **41.1**(9) **LAND AND BUILDINGS: EXEMPT SUPPLIES AND OPTION TO TAX** for the definition of '*major interest*'.

(e) Disposal of business assets

There is a supply of goods where goods forming part of the assets of a business are transferred or disposed of, by or under the directions of the person carrying on the business, so as no longer to form part of those assets (whether or not for consideration). [*VATA 1994, Sch 4 para 5(1)*]. This includes

- the sale of assets (e.g. fixed assets);
- assets permanently taken into private use; and
- assets given away.

Business gifts and industrial samples are excluded provided certain conditions are met. [*VATA 1994, Sch 4 para 5(2)(3); FA 1996, s 33; FA 1998, s 21*]. See **47.6 OUTPUT TAX** for business gifts, **47.7 OUTPUT TAX** for private use of business assets and **47.8**(26) **OUTPUT TAX** for samples.

Land

Where the business assets include land,

- the grant or assignment of a major interest in the land, or
- the grant or assignment of any interest in, right over or licence to occupy the land concerned otherwise than for a consideration

is a supply of goods. Any other supply of the land is a supply of services. With effect from 21 March 2007, 'grant' includes surrender.

[*VATA 1994, Sch 4 para 9; FA 2007, s 99(3)*].

(f) Transfers of own goods between EU countries

There is a supply of goods where, in a case not falling within (*e*) above, goods forming part of the assets of any business are removed in the course of that business from one EU country by or under the directions of the person carrying on the business and taken to another EU country. This applies whether or not the removal is, or is connected with, a transaction for a consideration. [*VATA 1994, Sch 4 para 6*]. There are, however, a number of exceptions and special rules. See **19.25 EUROPEAN UNION: SINGLE MARKET** for full details.

(g) Sales in satisfaction of a debt

Where in the case of a business carried on by a taxable person, goods forming part of the assets of the business are, under any power exercisable by another person, sold by the other person in or towards satisfaction of a debt owed by the taxable person, they are deemed to be supplied by the taxable person in the course or furtherance of his business. [*VATA 1994, Sch 4 para 7*]. Land forming part of the assets of the business is treated as if it were goods and any sale includes a reference to a grant or assignment of any interest in, right over or licence to occupy the land concerned. [*VATA 1994, Sch 4 para 9*].

See **2.10 ACCOUNTING PERIODS AND RETURNS** for the statement to be furnished to HMRC by the person exercising the power.

(h) Deemed supplies on ceasing to be a taxable person

Where a person ceases to be a taxable person, any goods then forming part of the assets of a business carried on by him are (subject to certain exceptions) deemed to be supplied by him in the course of furtherance of his business immediately before he ceases to be a taxable person. [*VATA 1994, Sch 4 para 8*]. See **59.34 REGISTRATION** for further details.

(i) Self-supplies

Where specific goods taken possession of or produced by a person in the course or furtherance of his business are neither supplied to another person nor incorporated in other goods produced in the course or furtherance of that business but are used by him for the purpose of the business, the Treasury have power, by Order, to provide that the goods are deemed to be supplied *to* him for the purpose of the business and *by* him in the course or furtherance of it. [*VATA 1994, s 5(5), s 6(11)*]. Orders have been made in respect of printed matter (see **62.2 SELF-SUPPLY**) motor cars (see **45.6 MOTOR CARS**) and certain construction services (see **42.20 LAND AND BUILDINGS: ZERO AND REDUCED RATE SUPPLIES AND DIY HOUSEBUILDERS**).

(j) Water

The supply of water insofar as it is not otherwise a supply of goods is to be treated as a supply of goods (and not services). [*SI 1989/1114*].

Returned goods and repossessions

If goods supplied are later returned to the supplier for any reason, the VAT treatment of the act of returning the goods depends on whether title to the goods has passed or not.

- *If goods are returned because they are faulty or not in accordance with the sales contract*, the original transaction may be voided. The transfer of title is cancelled and neither the original sale of the unsatisfactory goods nor their return is a supply. If the goods are replaced without further charge, this is strictly speaking a new supply although it is common practice for the original invoice to remain unaltered.
  If the unsatisfactory goods are repaired or improved for the customer and this work is performed in order to meet the original contract, the work is part of that original supply.
- *If goods are returned where title has passed* and the transfer is not cancelled as above, title passes back to the supplier and a second supply is made.

- *If an agreement within (b) above is terminated prematurely and the goods are repossessed*, such a later event cannot change the nature of a transaction. The agreement was a supply of goods for VAT purposes at the outset and this does not change. However, the repossession of the goods is neither a supply of goods (as title has not yet passed) nor a supply of services (as there is no consideration).

De Voil Indirect Tax Service. See V3.112.

Supplies of services

[64.4] For EU legislation, see **18.4 EUROPEAN UNION LEGISLATION.**

Under UK legislation, anything which is not a supply of goods but is done for a consideration (including, if so done, the granting, assignment or surrender of any right) is a supply of services. The Treasury may, however, by Order, deem any transaction to be treated as a supply of goods and not a supply of services (or vice versa). [*VATA 1994, s 5(2)(b)(3)*]. Subject to this, the following supplies are to be treated as supplies of services.

(a) The transfer of any undivided share of the property in goods. [*VATA 1994, Sch 4 para 1(1)*]

This refers to goods that can be owned equally by more than one person and where the title to the goods is shared. If all the shares in goods are simultaneously sold to one person, there is a supply of goods. But if only one of the part shares is sold, title to the goods does not pass to the new owner of the part-share and this supply is not of goods but of services. The most common example of an undivided share in property is a part-share ('nomination') in a racehorse.

Unallocated goods are goods which remain an unidentifiable part of a larger stock of goods held by a supplier as opposed to 'allocated' goods which are set apart and earmarked as belonging to, or reserved for, a specific customer. Where goods are sold but are never allocated, title in the goods does not pass so the supply is one of services and not of goods.

Fiscal warehousing

As an exception to this general rule, the transfer of any undivided share of property in eligible goods where the supply is relieved from VAT under the fiscal warehousing regime is treated as a supply of goods and not a supply of services. See **72.15** and **72.16 WAREHOUSED GOODS AND FREE ZONES.**

(b) The transfer of possession of goods

The transfer of possession of goods where the conditions in **64.3**(*b*) above are not satisfied. [*VATA 1994, Sch 4 para 1(1)*]. Included is the hire, lease, rental or loan of goods.

(c) Work done on another person's goods

Any work done on another person's goods is a supply of services. Where the work produces goods, the services can be zero-rated if the goods produced are zero-rated goods. See **74.1 ZERO-RATED SUPPLIES**.

(d) Non-business use of goods and services

Where, by or under the direction of a person carrying on a business, goods held or used for the purposes of the business are put to private or non-business use, whether or not for a consideration, that is a supply of services. [*VATA 1994, Sch 4 para 5(4)*]. Similarly, where a person carrying on a business puts services supplied to the business to any private or non-business use for no consideration, that is a supply of services. [*SI 1993/1507*].

See **47.7 OUTPUT TAX** for further details.

(e) Exchange units

The exchange of a reconditioned article for an unserviceable article of a similar kind by a person who regularly offers, in the course or furtherance of his business, to provide a reconditioning facility by that means. [*SI 1995/1268, Art 6*]. VAT must be accounted for on the full amount charged for the exchange unit. If the charge to the customer is reduced by giving a refund when the unserviceable article is handed in, the procedure in **39.15 INVOICES** should be adopted.

If the exchange is not part of the person's normal business practice (e.g. where, on a 'one-off' basis, a serviceable article is exchanged for an unserviceable one) or if goods are exchanged for other goods at a reduced price in any other circumstances, the transaction is a supply of goods and should be treated as a part-exchange. (VAT Notice 700, para 8.6).

(f) Services received from abroad

Where a person who belongs abroad supplies certain services to a person who belongs in the UK for the purposes of any business carried on by him and the place of supply of those services is in the UK, the same consequences apply as if the taxable person had himself supplied the services in the UK in the course or furtherance of his business and that supply were a taxable supply. See **38.4 INTERNATIONAL SERVICES**.

De Voil Indirect Tax Service. See V3.113.

Supplies of neither goods nor services

[64.5] The following transactions are treated as neither a supply of goods nor a supply of services.

(a) Transfer of a business as a going concern

The supply by a person of the assets of his business to another person to whom he transfers his business (or part thereof) as a going concern (provided certain conditions are satisfied). See **8.10** ***et seq*** **BUSINESS**.

(b) The assignment of rights under a HP or conditional sales agreement

The assignment of rights under a HP or conditional sales agreement, and the goods comprised therein, by the owner to a bank or other financial institution. See **23.13 FINANCIAL SERVICES**.

(c) Repossession of goods

The sale of certain goods by a person, including a finance company, who has repossessed them under the terms of a finance agreement or by an insured in settlement of a claim under an insurance policy (provided certain conditions are met). See **23.15 FINANCIAL SERVICES**.

(d) Groups of companies

Where a group registration is in force, most supplies of goods or services by a member of the group to another member of the group are disregarded for VAT purposes. See **27.4 GROUPS OF COMPANIES**.

(e) Supplies of dutiable goods in warehouse

Where imported goods subject to duty are supplied while warehoused in bond, the supply is disregarded for VAT purposes if the goods are supplied before payment of the duty to which they are subject. See **72.4 WAREHOUSED GOODS AND FREE ZONES**.

(f) Motor cars

In addition to the sale of motor cars within (*c*) above,

- the disposal of a motor car for no consideration (e.g. as scrap) where, on any previous supply or importation, input tax on the motor car in question has been excluded from credit; and
- the letting on hire of a motor vehicle for less than full consideration or the making available of a motor car (otherwise than by letting) to any person for private use.

See **45.5 MOTOR CARS**.

(g) Companies organised in divisions

Transactions between divisions of the same corporate body are not supplies for VAT purposes. See **59.37 REGISTRATION**.

(h) Supplies by pawnbrokers

The supply by a taxable person of goods the property in which passed to him as pawnee by virtue of *Consumer Credit Act 1974, s 120(1)(a)* where the supply is to a person who was the pawnor of those goods and the supply is made not later than three months after the taxable person acquired the property in the goods. [*SI 1986/896*]. See **23.16**(8) **FINANCIAL SERVICES** for supplies generally by pawnbrokers.

(i) Temporary importations

Sales of temporarily imported goods provided the goods remain eligible for temporary importation arrangements and the supply is to a person established outside the EU. [*SI 1992/3130*].

(j) Second-hand goods and works of art imported for sale by auction

See **33.24 IMPORTS** for the treatment of second-hand goods and works of art imported for sale by auction.

(k) Second-hand goods scheme

The removal of goods to the UK under a supply to a person in the UK made by a person in another EU country who accounts for VAT there on the profit margin under the laws of that country similar to the margin scheme in the UK. [*SI 1995/1268, Art 8*]. No VAT is chargeable on such a supply in the UK and the goods may be sold under the margin scheme. See **61.7 SECOND-HAND GOODS**.

(l) Agents acting in their own name in relation to second-hand goods

Services provided by an agent acting in his own name to the purchaser of second-hand goods where the consideration for the services is taken into account in calculating the price at which the agent obtained the goods. [*SI 1995/1268, Art 9*]. See **61.26 SECOND-HAND GOODS**.

(m) Auctioneers in relation to second-hand goods

Services provided by an auctioneer acting in his own name to the vendor or purchaser of second-hand goods where the consideration for the services is taken into account in calculating the price at which the auctioneer obtained, or as the case may be, sold the goods. [*SI 1995/1268, Art 10*]. See **61.59 SECOND-HAND GOODS**.

De Voil Indirect Tax Service. See V3.114.

Single and multiple supplies

[64.6] There have always been problems in determining the correct VAT liability of transactions consisting of separately identifiable goods or services. This is particularly relevant where, if supplied on their own, some elements would be taxable and others would qualify for relief from VAT. For example, there may be a combination of two or more goods (e.g. zero-rated food in luxury standard-rated packaging), two or more services (e.g. standard-rated car hire with exempt insurance) or goods and services (e.g. standard-rated tuition with zero-rated books). The question is: should the different elements be treated separately for VAT purposes or are they properly part of a single overall supply?

For such transactions, it is therefore necessary to distinguish between

- a 'single' (or 'composite') supply, i.e. where there is one overall type of supply (either goods or services) and one VAT liability; and

- a 'multiple' (or 'mixed') supply, i.e. where the two or more components are separate supplies, each of which is either a supply of goods or services and each of which has its own VAT liability.

Neither UK nor EU VAT legislation provides rules to determine this. Over the years, tribunal and court decisions (or a HMRC ruling, trade agreement or statement of practice based on that litigation) have produced general guidelines on how to approach the problem but these have not provided any certainty on the issue.

More substantial guidance on the proper test for deciding if transactions constitute one or more supplies was given by the ECJ in *Card Protection Plan Ltd v C & E Commrs, ECJ Case C–349/96*, [1999] STC 270 (TVC 22.324). The court stated that, although it is not possible to give exhaustive guidance on the approach in all cases, the following general criteria should be used.

(a) Following the earlier judgment in *Faaborg-Gelting Linien A/S v Finanzamt Flensburg, ECJ Case C–231/94*, [1996] STC 774 (TVC 22.174) where a transaction comprises a bundle of features and acts, regard must first be had to all the circumstances in which the transaction takes place. The essential features of the transaction must be ascertained in order to determine whether the taxable person is supplying the customer, being a typical consumer, with several distinct principal supplies or with a single supply, taking into account that
    (i) it follows from *Directive 2006/112/EC, Art 2(1)(a)* that a supply must normally be regarded as distinct and independent (i.e. it should amount to more than merely a component of the overall supply); and
    (ii) a supply which comprises a single supply from an economic point of view should not be artificially split (so as not to distort the functioning of the VAT system).

> ***Example***
>
> Where a garage services a customer's car, although there are different elements that go to make up a typical service, these cannot be said to be distinct or independent in the context of the overall service required by the customer. Any attempt to describe them as separate supplies would clearly be artificial.

(b) Where (*a*) above does distinguish separate supplies, it is necessary to consider whether each supply can be properly regarded as a principal supply or whether some of them are merely ancillary to the principal supply. There is a single supply, in particular, in cases where one or more elements are to be regarded as constituting the principal supply, whilst one or more elements are to be regarded, by contrast, as ancillary and which share the tax treatment of the principal supply. A supply must be regarded as ancillary to a principal supply if it does not constitute for customers an aim in itself, but a means of better enjoying the principal supply (see *TP Madgett & RM Baldwin (t/a Howden Court Hotel) v C & E Commrs, ECJ Cases C–308/96 and C–94/97*, [1998] STC 1189 (TVC 22.487)).

The fact that a single price is charged is not decisive. Admittedly, if what is provided to customers consists of several elements for a single price, the single price may suggest that there is a single supply. However, notwithstanding the single price, if circumstances indicate that the customers intended to purchase two distinct supplies, then it is necessary to identify the part of the single price that relates to each supply. The simplest possible method of calculation or assessment should be used for this.

Example

Catering is commonly provided together with the transport of passengers.

- In the case of in-flight catering provided to airline passengers, this is not something that the customer specifically seeks to obtain. He assumes the flight will include a meal as this is a normal feature of airline transport. The meal is provided for customers to better enjoy the transport service and, for a typical customer, is not an aim in itself. Therefore, the meal (standard-rated if supplied alone) is not liable to VAT in these circumstances because it is ancillary to the supply of zero-rated transport services. See *British Airways plc v C & E Commrs*, CA [1990] STC 643 (TVC 66.13).
- On the other hand, where a customer books a river cruise that includes a substantial meal, the catering is more than simply an adjunct to the cruise. It is something a typical customer would regard as an end in itself. In these circumstances there are two principal supplies, comprising zero-rated transport and standard-rated catering.

HMRC accept that if a distinct service element represents 50% or more of the price of a bundle of goods and services, this will be a strong indicator that this service is not ancillary to a principal supply of any other goods or services in that bundle and that the consideration may need to be apportioned accordingly. (Business Brief 3/02).

Types of transactions that may be affected

The following list is not exhaustive but illustrates some of the areas where the issue of single and multiple supplies can have an impact.

- Delivered goods (see **47.8**(19) **OUTPUT TAX**).
- Dispensed spectacles (see **28.4 HEALTH AND WELFARE**) and dispensed hearing aids (see **28.5 HEALTH AND WELFARE**).
- Membership of clubs and associations (see **14.2 CLUBS AND ASSOCIATIONS**).
- Cover-mounted goods supplied with magazines (see **54.8 PRINTED MATTER, ETC.**).
- Admissions to sporting events, etc. by programme (see **57.7 RECREATION AND SPORT**).
- Books, etc. supplied with correspondence courses (see **54.17 PRINTED MATTER, ETC.**).

- Airport parking services that include transport.
- Printed matter supplied with advertising services.
- Transport and catering (see **72.18** and **72.22** TRANSPORT AND FREIGHT).
- Installed goods.
- Programme listing magazines and broadcasting services.
- Linked promotional goods.

HMRC consider that the tests laid down in *Card Protection Plan* above will be appropriate in the great majority of cases. Businesses making supplies of the kind listed above must review their VAT treatment of those supplies against the revised criteria.

Single supply

Where this is established, no apportionment must be made and the supply as a whole must be considered to determine the VAT liability, if any.

Since the ECJ decision in *Card Protection Plan* above, single supplies have been held to include the following.

- The purchase of a car and its associated delivery charges (*C & E Commrs v British Telecommunications plc*, HL [1999] STC 758 (TVC 44.99)).
- The purchase of a car and free insurance (*Peugeot Motor Co plc and Another v C & E Commrs*, Ch D [2003] STC 1438 (TVC 38.51)).
- Broadcasting services and a magazine providing details of programmes (*British Sky Broadcasting Group plc* (VTD 16220) (TVC 5.97) but see *Telewest Communications* below).
- Hospitality packages offered by a football club including meals, drinks and a match programme (*Manchester United plc* (VTD 17234) (TVC 5.77)).
- Children's activity programmes where the enrolment fee includes a T-shirt, accident insurance, a magazine for parents, a DVD, a member's handbook and gymbag (*Tumble Tots (UK) Ltd v HMRC*, Ch D [2007] STC 1171 (TVC 12.26)).
- Weight loss programmes comprising weekly meetings as well as handbooks, magazines and leaflets (*HMRC v Weight Watchers UK Ltd*, CA [2008] STC 2313 (TVC 5.91)), or comprising weekly meetings, dietary packs and support services (*HMRC v David Baxendale Ltd*, CA [2009] EWCA Civ 831 (TVC 62.553)).

Earlier decisions held the following supplies to be single supplies (although these must be read in light of the tests in *Card Protection Plan*).

- Services of a launderette (which cannot be treated as separate supplies of water, heat, use of machine, etc., only the single supply of washing or drying clothes) (*Mander Laundries Ltd* (VTD 31) (TVC 69.1)).
- Services of a stud farm providing the supply of the keep of a mare with everything that is involved in maintaining her in reasonable condition and safety (a single standard-rated supply so that the supply of animal feeding stuffs included cannot be zero-rated) (*C & E Commrs v DD Scott*, QB 1977, [1978] STC 191 (TVC 29.111)).

Two-part tariff

This occurs where there are two or more payments involving apparently different transactions at different times but which amount to the purchase of a single supply. This concept was introduced in *British Railways Board v C & E Commrs*, CA [1977] STC 221 (TVC 66.12) where there were two payments, one for a student card allowing students to buy cut-price travel tickets, and the other which the student made when obtaining the actual ticket. The court held that the two payments were both for the supply of discounted travel paid at different stages, rather than for two separate supplies (of the right to a discount and then discounted travel).

Multiple supply

In a multiple supply, even though the supplies are often paid for together, the individual components are not integral to each other and are separate supplies.

Since the ECJ decision in *Card Protection Plan* above, multiple supplies have been held to include the following.

- Promotional/advertising services and printed brochures (*Appleby Bowers v C & E Commrs*, Ch D 2000, [2001] STC 185 (TVC 5.64)).
- Day excursions on a luxury train which included the provisions of meals (*Sea Containers Services Ltd v C & E Commrs*, QB 1999, [2000] STC 82 (TVC 66.26)).
- A monthly magazine providing details of programmes and broadcasting services where each supply was provided by a different company (*Telewest Communications plc v C & E Commrs; Telewest Communications (Publications) Ltd v C & E Commrs*, CA [2005] STC 481) (TVC 62.371), the court ruling that the two supplies could not be treated as a single supply merely because the customer could not enter into one transaction without the other and because there was no authority that the principles propounded in *Card Protection Plan* above could apply where there was more than one supplier.
- Ski passes including the right to transport on a funicular railway (*Cairngorm Mountain* (VTD 17679) (TVC 66.27)).
- The supply of medical services (consultation and diagnosis) by a doctor and any related supply of the provision and administration of drugs (*Dr Beynon & Partners v C & E Commrs*, HL 2004, [2005] STC 55 (TVC 19.8)).

Earlier decisions held the following supplies to be multiple supplies (although these must be read in light of the tests in *Card Protection Plan*).

- Annual subscriptions to the AA (apportionable between the benefits – a magazine, booklet, maps and information, pick-up services, repairs, etc. – to which members are entitled (*C & E Commrs v The Automobile Assn*, QB [1974] STC 192 (TVC 13.17)). Membership bodies frequently treat the supply of benefits to members as multiple supplies. However, the ECJ tests in *Card Protection Plan* may mean that the supply of benefits by a number of membership bodies should be treated as a single supply of the principal benefit. In the case of non-profit making membership bodies, HMRC are considering the introduction of an extra-statutory concession whereby such bodies which supply a mixture of zero-rated, exempt and/or standard-rated benefits to members in return for their subscriptions may continue to apportion the subscriptions.

- Children's colouring books issued with felt tip pens, where the pens are not restricted in use to the book they are sold with.
- A book with an accompanying audio or video tape, each of which may be used independently of the book, and which require particular equipment for their use.
- Consideration under contracts providing for both the hire of a television set from a rental company and the insurance of the set by an insurance company within the same VAT group (*Thorn EMI plc; Granada plc* (VTD 9782) (TVC 38.8)).

Where all the supplies are liable to VAT at the same rate, there is no problem and output tax due is calculated in the normal way. Where, however, there is a mixture of zero-rated, standard-rated and/or exempt supplies, the value of each supply for VAT purposes must be calculated in order to arrive at the total output tax due. Any calculation of the apportionment of the total price must be fair and justifiable. See **47.3 OUTPUT TAX** for apportionment of consideration.

De Voil Indirect Tax Service. See **V3.105–V3.107.**

(Business Brief 2/01; VAT Information Sheet 2/01).

Supplies by 'taxable persons'

[64.7] For EU legislation, see **18.7 EUROPEAN UNION LEGISLATION.**

Under UK legislation, one of the four basic conditions to be satisfied for a transaction to be within the scope of UK VAT (see **64.1** above) is that it is made by a taxable person. Under *VATA 1994, s 1(2)*, VAT on any supply of goods or services is a liability of the person making the supply and under *VATA 1994, s 3(1)* a person is a taxable person while he is, or is required to be, registered for VAT purposes. It follows from this that, to decide whether a transaction meets the condition of being made by a taxable person, it is necessary to establish two facts.

(a) Whether a person is required to be registered

This is usually dependent upon the level of taxable turnover; although there are special provisions covering voluntary registration, registration of intending traders and group registration. All these considerations are dealt with in the chapter **REGISTRATION (59).**

However, another consideration which can determine whether a person is required to be registered is employment status. Under *Directive 2006/112/EC, Art 9(1)* a taxable person means any person who *independently* carries out certain specified activities. The use of the word 'independently' specifically excludes employed and other persons from the scope of VAT in so far as they are bound to an employer by a contract of employment or by any other legal ties creating the relationship of employer and employee as regards working conditions, remuneration and the employer's liability.

Unless there are clear reasons to do otherwise, HMRC policy is normally to follow the employment status for income tax purposes, i.e. they accept that a person paying income tax under the trading income provisions is self-employed and a person paying under the employment income provisions is an employee (and therefore outside the scope of VAT). Note, however, that where a person (e.g. an accountant or solicitor) in the course or furtherance of a trade profession or vocation, accepts any office, services supplied as the holder of that office are treated as supplied in the course or furtherance of the trade, etc. [*VATA 1994, s 94(4)*].

(b) Who is the person making the supply and thus liable for the VAT on that transaction

This will, in the vast majority of cases, be self-evident but the position may require careful consideration when involving **AGENTS (3)** or **PARTNERSHIPS (50)**. See also **11.9 CATERING, 16.18 EDUCATION** for school photographers, **70.24 TRANSPORT AND FREIGHT** for taxis and hire cars and HMRC VAT Guidance V1–5, Chapter 3 generally.

Key points

[64.8] Points to consider are as follows.

- A supply of goods is taking place with a hire purchase contract, even though ownership of the goods does not usually pass to the hirer until the end of the agreement. So a business buying assets on hire purchase will usually pay the VAT element of the goods at the beginning of the agreement and be able to reclaim this amount as input tax, subject to normal rules.
- In the case of assets or goods that are leased, VAT is usually charged on each of the monthly hire payments because the ownership of the goods is retained by the leasing company, and they are normally returned to the company at the end of the agreement.
- In situations where a business is transferred to a new owner as a going concern (TOGC), then the proceeds of the sale are outside the scope of VAT as long as certain important conditions are met. This is because a TOGC arrangement is classed as neither a supply of goods nor services.
- In certain situations, a customer will acquire two or more benefits (goods or services) when he pays for a supply. If each benefit has a value in its own right, then the VAT payable will need to be apportioned if they are subject to different rates of VAT. If the secondary supply is incidental to the main supply, then the VAT liability is wholly based on that of the main supply.

- If goods are never actually in the UK, they cannot be within the scope of UK VAT. So a UK business selling goods that started in Australia and are shipped directly to a customer in America is making sales that are outside the scope of UK VAT.

65

Supply: Place of Supply

Introduction

[65.1] Having determined that a supply of goods or services has taken place, the second condition to be satisfied if the transaction is to fall within the scope of UK VAT is that the supply takes place within the UK (see **64.1 SUPPLY: GENERAL**). The place of supply rules are different for goods and for services. See **SUPPLY: GENERAL** at **64.3–64.5** for a consideration of what constitutes a supply of goods and a supply of services (or neither).

For EU law, see **18.12 EUROPEAN UNION LEGISLATION** for the place of supply of goods and **18.14 EUROPEAN UNION LEGISLATION** for the place of supply of services.

UK law relating to the place of supply is contained in *VATA 1994, ss 7, 9*. The Treasury are empowered to vary the normal rules by statutory instrument [*VATA 1994, s 7(11)*] and to date three main Orders have been made.

- *VAT (Tour Operators) Order 1987 (SI 1987/1806)* which relates to supplies of designated travel services by tour operators and other persons who buy in and resell travel facilities (see **68.5 TOUR OPERATORS' MARGIN SCHEME**);
- *VAT (Place of Supply of Services) Order 1992 (SI 1992/3121)* which has a general impact on the place of supply of services (see **65.12** *et seq* below); and
- *VAT (Place of Supply of Goods) Order 2004 (SI 2004/3148)* which relates to supplies of goods on board ships, aircraft and trains involved in intra-EU transport (see **65.10** below).

Registration of UK suppliers in other EU countries

Where the place of supply of goods or services is outside the UK, there is no UK VAT liability. However, a UK supplier who makes supplies in another EU country may be liable to register there, subject to the registration rules applicable in that country. If they do not have an establishment there, they may have to appoint a local tax representative to account for VAT on their behalf. UK suppliers must make their own enquiries about registration in other EU countries with the authorities of the country concerned: HMRC cannot advise on the rules applicable in other countries.

Registration of traders who have no place of business in the UK

Similarly, a trader belonging outside the UK with no place of business here may be liable to UK VAT registration where the place of supply of those goods or services is in the UK. See **48 OVERSEAS TRADERS** for further details.

Territory of the UK and EU

The UK comprises Great Britain, Northern Ireland and the waters within twelve nautical miles of their coastlines. For VAT purposes it includes the Isle of Man but not the Channel Islands or Gibraltar. See **17.2 EUROPEAN UNION: GENERAL** for the VAT territory of the EU.

Place of supply of goods

[65.2] Subject to certain simplification procedures (see **65.11** below) and special provisions relating to warehoused goods (see **72.2** to **72.11 WAREHOUSED GOODS AND FREE ZONES**), the provisions relating to the place of supply of goods are to be found in *VATA 1994, s 7* (see **65.3–65.9** below) and *The VAT (Place of Supply of Goods) Order 2004, SI 2004/3148* (see **65.10** below). It should be noted that *Sec 7* has a hierarchical structure. The place of supply of any goods may be determined by working through the rules in **65.3–65.8** below in order until one applicable to the particular supply in question is reached. [*VATA 1994, s 7(1); FA 1996, Sch 3 para 2*].

De Voil Indirect Tax Service. See V3.171–V3.178.

Goods which do not leave or enter the UK

[65.3] Where the supply of any goods does not involve their removal from or to the UK, they are treated as supplied

- in the UK if they are in the UK; and
- otherwise as supplied outside the UK.

[*VATA 1994, s 7(2)*].

The first situation covers the vast majority of transactions subject to VAT. The second situation includes sales on the high seas where the goods do not come to the UK and supplies sourced from outside the UK and delivered to a country other than the UK. In these cases it is important to disregard extraneous facts such as where the order was placed, the invoice route or how and where payment was made.

Installed or assembled goods

[65.4] Goods whose place of supply is not determined under **65.3** above are treated as supplied

- in the UK where their supply involves their installation or assembly at a place in the UK to which they are removed; and
- outside the UK where their supply involves their installation or assembly at a place outside the UK to which they are removed.

[*VATA 1994, s 7(3)*].

By concession, where a *one-off* supply of installed or assembled goods would be treated as made in the UK, it is treated as made outside the UK if

- the supplier is not registered for VAT in the UK;
- no further UK business is anticipated;
- the goods are imported from outside the EU; and
- the customer acts as importer and shows the full value of the goods, including installation and assembly costs on the import entry.

(Business Brief 1/98).

See **65.11** below for details of a simplified procedure which eligible EU traders can use to avoid the need to register for VAT in the UK.

Distance sales to the UK

[65.5] Goods whose place of supply is not determined under **65.3** or **65.4** above are treated as supplied in the UK where

(a) the supply involves the removal of the goods to the UK by or under the direction of the supplier;

(b) the supply is a transaction under which the goods are acquired in the UK from another EU country by a person who is not registered or required to be registered under *VATA 1994*;

(c) the supplier is, or is liable to be, registered under *VATA 1994, Sch 2* by virtue of his distance sales in the UK, see **59.11 REGISTRATION** (or would be so liable if he were not registrable under *VATA 1994, Sch 1* in respect of UK supplies, see **59.1 REGISTRATION**); and

(d) the supply is neither
- a supply of goods consisting of a new means of transport (see **19.31 EUROPEAN UNION: SINGLE MARKET**); nor
- anything which is treated as a supply by virtue only of *VATA 1994, Sch 4 para 5(1)* (disposal of business assets, see **64.3**(*e*) **SUPPLY: GENERAL** or *VATA 1994, Sch 4 para 6* (transfer of own goods between EU countries, see **19.25 EUROPEAN UNION: SINGLE MARKET**).

[*VATA 1994, s 7(4)*].

Distance sales from the UK

[65.6] Goods whose place of supply is not determined under **65.3–65.5** above and which do not consist of a new means of transport (see **19.33 EUROPEAN UNION: SINGLE MARKET**) are treated as supplied outside the UK where

(a) the supply involves the removal of the goods to another EU country by or under the direction of the supplier;

(b) the person who makes the supply is taxable in another EU country; and

(c) the provisions of the law of that other EU country corresponding to the provisions under **65.5**(*c*) above make the supplier liable to be registered and account for VAT in that country.

This does not, however, apply where the liability under (*c*) above depends on the exercise by any person of an option in the UK corresponding to such an option made by an overseas trader under **59.12**(*a*) **REGISTRATION** unless that person has given (and not withdrawn) a notification to HMRC that his supplies are to be treated as taking place outside the UK.

[*VATA 1994, s 7(5)*].

Imported goods

[65.7] Goods whose place of supply is not determined under **65.3–65.6** above are treated as supplied in the UK where

(a) their supply involves their being imported from a place outside the EU; and

(b) the supplier is the person by whom, or under whose direction, they are so imported.

[*VATA 1994, s 7(6)*].

The place of supply of imported goods is therefore determined by reference to the importer.

- Where the supplier imports the goods, the place of supply is the UK (under the above rules).
- Where the customer imports the goods, the place of supply is outside the UK (under **65.8**(*b*) below).

Other goods which leave or enter the UK

[65.8] Goods whose place of supply is not determined under **65.3–65.7** above but whose supply involves their removal to or from the UK are treated

(a) as supplied in the UK where their supply involves their removal from the UK without also involving their previous removal to the UK; and
(b) as supplied outside the UK in any other case.

[*VATA 1994, s 7(7)*].

These provisions cover

- under (*a*) above,
  (i) the removal of goods from the UK to another EU country (other than distance sales within **65.6** above); and
  (ii) the export of goods from the UK; and
- under (*b*) above,
  (i) the removal of goods to the UK from another EU country (other than distance sales within **65.5** above); and
  (ii) the importation of goods from outside the EU where the UK customer is the person responsible for the importation (see **65.7** above).

Goods temporarily leaving the UK in the course of a removal to another place in the UK

[65.9] For the purposes of **65.3–65.8** above, where, in the course of their removal from a place in the UK to another place in the UK, goods leave and re-enter the UK, the removal is not treated as a removal from or to the UK. [*VATA 1994, s 7(8)*]. This would occur, for example, where goods moved from Northern Ireland to England passed through Ireland.

Goods supplied on board intra-EU transport

[65.10] Except for goods supplied as part of a 'pleasure cruise', goods which are supplied on board a ship, aircraft or train in the course of 'community transport' are treated as supplied at the 'point of departure' except that goods supplied for consumption on board are treated as supplied outside the EU.

'*Pleasure cruise*' includes a cruise wholly or partly for the purposes of education or training.

'*Community transport*' means transportation of passengers between a point of departure and a point of arrival in the course of which there is a stop in an EU country other than that of the point of departure and there is no stop in a country which is not an EU country.

[*SI 2004/3148, Arts 4–8; SI 2009/215*].

See also *Peninsular and Oriental Steam Navigation Co v C & E Commrs*, QB [2000] STC 488 (TVC 62.479).

Simplification procedures

[65.11] The following measures can, in certain circumstances, be used to avoid unnecessary UK VAT registration in the UK.

- **Import agents acting for an overseas supplier.** Where an overseas trader imports goods into the UK for onward sale and is not otherwise liable to register for VAT in the UK, he may, as an alternative to registration, appoint a UK VAT-registered agent to act on his behalf. See **48.4 OVERSEAS TRADERS** for further details.
- **Installed or assembled goods.** To avoid an overseas person making a supply of installed or assembled goods in the UK having to register for UK VAT, the UK customer can, provided certain conditions are satisfied, account for the VAT as acquisition VAT. See **19.31 EUROPEAN UNION: SINGLE MARKET.**
- Triangular EU trade. See **19.22 EUROPEAN UNION: SINGLE MARKET.**

Place of supply of services from 1 January 2010

Significance of place of supply

[65.12] For VAT purposes, the place where a supply is deemed to be made is called the *place of supply*. This is the only place where the supply can be liable to VAT. Thus, where the place of supply of any services is in an EU country, that supply is liable to VAT (if any) in that country and in no other country. If that country is not the UK, the supply is outside the scope of UK VAT. Where the place of supply of any services is outside the EU, that supply is not liable to VAT in any EU country (although local taxes may apply). The significance for a UK business is as follows.

- **If a UK business supplies services and the place of supply is the UK,** subject to the VAT registration limits the supply is standard-rated, zero-rated or exempt (as the case may be) and any VAT due must be accounted for to HMRC. This applies regardless of where the customer belongs.
- **If a UK business supplies services and the place of supply is in another EU country,** subject to the registration limits in that country either the UK supplier or the customer is liable to account for any VAT due to the VAT authorities in that country.

(VAT Notice 741A, paras 2.1, 2.2).

Changes to the place of supply of services rules were introduced in order to implement the first phases of changes in the VAT Place of Supply of Services Directive (*EC Directive 2008/08/EC*) into UK law. These changes were agreed as part of the VAT Package of legislation adopted in February 2008. From

1 January 2010 the new general rule for the place of supply of services taxes business to business supplies of services at the place where the customer is established, and no longer at the place where the supplier is established. For business to consumer supplies of services, the general rule for the place of supply continues to be the place where the supplier is established. There are exceptions to the general rule for certain services, with a view to achieving taxation in the place of consumption. In the main these changes were implemented on 1 January 2010, with further changes being introduced from 1 January 2011, 1 January 2013 and 1 January 2015.

Example

The services provided by a vet fall under the general rule as far as the place of supply procedures are concerned. So a UK vet providing services to a French farmer (B2B sale) would have charged UK VAT on his services before 1 January 2010 (place of supply is UK), but no VAT from this date because place of supply is now France, i.e. where the farmer is based. It is irrelevant whether the vet carries out his work in the UK or France.

Cultural, artistic, sporting, scientific, educational, entertainment services

Supplies to both business and non-business customers of cultural, artistic, sporting, scientific, educational, entertainment and similar services, as well as valuation and work on goods, were taxed where the service was performed. No change has been made to the taxation of these supplies when made to non-business customers. For supplies to business customers: from 1 January 2010 valuation and work on goods are taxed where the customer is established under the new general place of supply rule; and from 1 January 2011 most supplies of cultural, artistic, sporting, scientific, educational, entertainment and similar services will be taxed where the customer is established, under the new general place of supply rule. However, supplies of admission to cultural, artistic, sporting, scientific, educational and entertainment events will remain taxable where the event takes place.

Land

Land-related services are currently deemed to be supplied where the land is situated. This has remained unchanged.

Example

An architect based in the UK, and registered for VAT in the UK, has agreed to carry out some work for a Spanish customer in relation to a property she owns in France. The place of supply is France (where the building is based), and the architect may need to become VAT-registered in France (depending on VAT registration thresholds in France) and charge French VAT to the Spanish client. This rule is intended to create a level playing field throughout the EU, i.e. to prevent a customer using the services of an architect in a country with a lower rate of VAT.

Hire of means of transport

Previously there was a single treatment for the place of supply of hire of means of transport for supplies to business and non-business customers. This was where the supplier is established (general rule). From 1 January 2010, there is a distinction between short-time hire (no more than 30 days or 90 days for vessels) and long-term hire. For short-term hire, the place of supply is where the vehicle is put at the disposal of the customer. For long-term hire, the place of supply falls under the new general rule. However, from 1 January 2013, the place of supply of long-term hire to non-business customers will be where the customer is established (except for long-term hire of pleasure boats to non-business customers which will be treated as supplied where the boat is actually put at the customer's disposal if the supplier has an establishment there).

Restaurants and catering

There was no exception for restaurant and catering services. From 1 January 2010 these services will be treated as supplied where they are physically performed. For restaurant and catering services carried out on board ships, aircraft or trains as part of transport in the EU, the place of supply will be the place of departure. This mirrors existing rules for goods sold for consumption on board.

Intermediary services

Under the previous rules the place of supply of intermediary services was in the same place as the service being arranged. This was subject to a simplification measure for supplies to business customers registered for VAT in another EU Member State. From 1 January 2010 the services provided by intermediaries to business customers falls under the general rule. Supplies to non-business customers will be unchanged.

Transport of goods

The place of supply of the transport of goods is where the transport takes place, except for intra-Community transport which is supplied in the place of departure. This rule remains the same for supplies to non-business customers. Supplies to business customers fall under the new general rule from 1 January 2010.

Intangible services

The place of supply of certain intangible services, e.g. legal advice, continues to be where the customer belongs when provided to non-business customers outside the EU.

Ancillary transport services

Ancillary transport services (such as loading, unloading or handling services) are deemed to be supplied where they are physically carried out. From 1 January 2010 these services fall under the general rule when supplied to business customers. Supplies of these services to non-business customers continue to be taxed where performed.

Passenger transport

The place of supply of passenger transport services, the use and enjoyment provisions and electronically supplied services (for non-business customers) remain unchanged.

For cross-border supplies, in most cases, the business customer must account for the VAT using the reverse charge procedure (and recover the tax subject to the normal rules) as happened pre-1 January 2010 for a wide range of non-general rule services.

Right to a service

The place of supply of a right to services is the same as the place in which the supply of the services to which the right relates would be treated as made if made by the supplier of the right to the recipient of the right. The expression 'right to services' in this context includes a reference to any right, option or priority with respect to the supply of services and to the supply of an interest deriving from any right to services.
[*VATA 1994, s 7A, Sch 4A; FA 2009, Sch 36*].

Place of supply of services before 1 January 2010

Place of supply rules

[65.13] The rules in **65.15–65.28** below must be used to determine the place of supply of services. The general rule is that services are made where the supplier belongs (see **65.15** below) but this is subject to a number of special rules for

- services relating to land (see **65.16** below);
- certain services which are supplied where physically carried out (see **65.17–65.20** below);
- services falling within *VATA 1994, Sch 5 paras 1–8* (see **65.21–65.23** below);
- transport services (see **65.26** below);
- the hiring of means of transport (see **65.27** below); and
- certain services of intermediaries (see **65.28** below).

In addition to these rules, special place of supply rules apply

- where travel, hotel, holiday and certain other supplies of a kind enjoyed by travellers are bought in from third parties and resold as principal under the tour operators' margin scheme (see **68.5 TOUR OPERATORS' MARGIN SCHEME**); and
- in relation to sales of securities, and brokers' services in connection therewith, where the identity of the purchaser (and hence the place of belonging) is not known (see **23.2 FINANCIAL SERVICES**).

Rights to services

With effect from 1 August 2006, the place of supply of a 'right' to services is the same as the place in which the supply of services to which the right relates would be treated as made by the supplier of the right to the recipient in question. *Before 1 August 2006*, the place of supply of a 'right' to services was the same as the place of supply of the services to which the right related (whether or not the right was exercised). The change of wording was made to clarify its ambiguity and help combat avoidance involving phone card vouchers (which are defined in law as a 'right to receive services').

A '*right to services*' includes any right, option or priority with respect to the supply of services and the supply of an interest deriving from any right to services.

[*SI 1992/3121, Art 21; SI 1997/1524, Art 5; SI 2006/1683*].

Anti-avoidance provisions

Where any statutory instrument made after 16 March 1998 changes the place of supply of any services to the UK with effect from a specified commencement date,

- invoices and other documents issued before the commencement date are disregarded in determining the time of supply of any services which, by virtue of the statutory instrument, would be treated as supplied in the UK if their time of supply occurred on or after the commencement date;
- any payment received by the supplier before the commencement date which relates to services performed on or after the commencement date is treated as if it were received on the commencement date;
- any payment received by the supplier on or after the commencement date which relates to services performed before the commencement date is treated as if it were received before that date; and
- a payment in respect of any services is to be taken as relating to the period of time during which those services are performed. Where a payment is received in respect of a period spanning the commencement date, an apportionment must be made on a just and reasonable basis and the payment is taken as relating to a time before that date to the extent that it is attributable to services performed before that date. The remainder of the payment (if any) is taken as relating to times on or after the commencement date.

[*VATA 1994, s 97A; FA 1998, s 22*].

Input tax recovery

Input tax attributable to certain supplies of services may be recoverable even though, under the place of supply rules, the supply is deemed to take place outside the UK and is outside the scope of UK VAT. See **34.3 INPUT TAX**.

De Voil Indirect Tax Service. See V3.181–V3.197.

Place of belonging

From 1 January 2010

[65.14] A relevant business person 'belongs' in the relevant country. A 'relevant country' means:

- the country in which the person has a business establishment, or some other fixed establishment (if it has none in any other country);
- if the person has a business establishment, or some other fixed establishment or establishments, in more than one country, the country of the relevant establishment (i.e. the establishment most directly concerned with the supply); and
- otherwise, the country of the person's usual place of residence (in the case of a body corporate, where it is legally constituted).

A person who is not a relevant business person 'belongs' in the country of his usual place of residence. The 'belonging' definition applies equally to the recipient of a supply, where relevant.

[*VATA 1994, s 9; FA 2009, Sch 36 para 6*].

Business establishment

Business establishment is not defined in the legislation but is taken by HMRC to mean the principal place of business. It is usually the head office, headquarters or 'seat' from which the business is run. There can only be one such place and it may take the form of an office, showroom or factory.

Examples

- A business has its headquarters in the UK and branches in France, Italy and Germany. Its business establishment is in the UK.
- A company is incorporated in the UK but trades entirely from its head office in Bermuda. Its business establishment is in Bermuda.

(VAT Notice 741A, para 3.3).

Fixed establishment

Fixed establishment is not defined in the legislation but is taken by HMRC to mean an establishment (other than the business establishment) which has both the technical and human resources necessary for providing and receiving services on a permanent basis. A business may therefore have several fixed establishments, including a branch of the business or an agency. A temporary presence of human and technical resources does not create a fixed establishment in the UK.

Examples

- An overseas business sets up a branch comprising staff and offices in the UK to provide services. The UK branch is a fixed establishment.

- A company with a business establishment overseas owns a property in the UK which it leases to tenants. The property does not in itself create a fixed establishment. However, if the company has UK offices and staff or appoints a UK agency to carry on its business by managing the property, this creates a fixed establishment in the UK.
- An overseas business contracts with UK customers to provide services. It has no human or technical resources in the UK and therefore sets up a UK subsidiary to act in its name to provide those services. The overseas business has a fixed establishment in the UK created by the agency of the subsidiary.
- A company is incorporated in the UK but trades entirely overseas from its head office in the USA, which is its business establishment. The UK registered office is a fixed establishment. See *Binder Hamlyn* (VTD 1439) (TVC 62.480).
- A UK company acts as the operating member of a consortium for offshore exploitation of oil or gas using a fixed production platform. The rig is a fixed establishment of the operating member.

(VAT Notice 741A, para 3.4).

Usual place of residence

A *body corporate* has its usual place of residence where it is legally constituted. [*VATA 1994, s 9(5)(b)*]. The usual place of residence of an *individual* is not defined in the legislation. HMRC interpret the phrase according to the ordinary usage of the words, i.e. normally the country where the individual has set up home with his/her family and is in full-time employment. An individual is not resident in a country if only visiting as a tourist.

Persons who are present in the UK but have not been granted a right or permission to remain here (e.g. asylum seekers and those entering without permission) should be treated as belonging in their country of origin.

Examples

- A person lives in the UK, but commutes to France daily for work. He belongs in the UK.
- Overseas forces personnel on a tour of duty in the UK live in rented accommodation with their families. They have homes overseas to which they periodically return on leave. They belong in the UK throughout their tour of duty. See *USAA Ltd* (VTD 10369) (TVC 62.499).

(VAT Notice 741A, para 3.5).

See also *Razzak & Mishari* (VTD 15240) (TVC 62.503) where the tribunal, distinguishing *USAA Ltd* above, held that an Indian woman, who came to the UK in 1992 and remained here until October 1996 during the course of legal proceedings against a former employer, had her usual place of residence in India throughout that period.

More than one establishment

For the purposes of (*c*) above, where the supplier/recipient has establishments in more than one country, the supplies made from/received at each establishment must be considered separately. For each supply of services, the establishment which is actually providing/receiving the services is normally the one most directly connected with the supply but all facts should be considered including

- for suppliers, from which establishment the services are actually provided;
- for recipients, at which establishment the services are actually consumed, effectively used or enjoyed;
- which establishment appears on the contracts, correspondence and invoices;
- where directors or others who entered into the contract are permanently based; and
- at which establishment decisions are taken and controls are exercised over the performance of the contract.

However, where an establishment is actually providing/receiving the supply of services, it is normally that establishment which is most directly connected with the supply, even if the contractual position is different.

Examples

- A company whose business establishment is in France contracts with a UK bank to provide French speaking staff for the bank's international desk in London. The French supplier has a fixed establishment in the UK created by a branch, which provides staff to other customers. The French establishment deals directly with the bank without any involvement by the UK branch. The staff are supplied from the French establishment.
- An overseas business establishment contracts with private customers in the UK to provide information. The services are provided and invoiced by its UK branch. Customers' day-to-day contact is with the UK branch and they pay the UK branch. The services are actually supplied from the UK branch which is a fixed establishment.
- A UK supplier contracts to supply advertising services. Its customer has its business establishment in Austria and a fixed establishment in the UK created by its branch. Although day-to-day contact is between the supplier and the UK branch, the Austrian establishment takes all artistic and other decisions about the advertising. The supplies are received at the overseas establishment.
- A UK accountant supplies accountancy services to a UK incorporated company which has its business establishment abroad. However, the services are received in connection with the company's UK tax obligations and therefore the UK fixed establishment, created by the registered office, receives the supply.
- A customer which has its business establishment in the UK and a fixed establishment in the USA, created by its branch. The supplier is contracted by the UK establishment to provide staff to the USA branch. The supplier invoices the UK establishment and is paid by them. The services are most

directly used by the USA branch and therefore are received at the overseas establishment.

(VAT Notice 741A, para 3.6).

VAT groups

A VAT group is treated as a single entity. This also applies when applying the 'place of belonging' rules (*Shamrock Leasing Ltd* (VTD 15719) (TVC 62.505)). As a result, a group has establishments wherever any member of the group has establishments.

Other case law

In *Faaborg-Gelting Linien A/S v Finanzamt Flensburg, ECJ Case C–231/94*, [1996] STC 774 (TVC 22.174) the court held that where, under what is now *Directive 2006/112/EC, Art 43*, a supply could be treated as taking place at the supplier's business establishment or at another fixed establishment from which the services are supplied, then the primary point of reference had to be the former unless that did not lead to a rational result or created a conflict with another EU country. In any case, services cannot be deemed to be supplied at a fixed establishment other than the place where the supplier has established his business unless that fixed establishment is of a certain minimum size and both the human and technical resources necessary for the provision of the particular services are permanently present (*Berkholz v Finanzamt Hamburg-Mitte-Altstadt, ECJ Case C–168/84*, [1985] 3 CMLR 667 (TVC 22.198)). See also *ARO Lease BV v Inspecteur der Belastingdienst Grote Ondernemingen Amsterdam, ECJ Case C–190/95*, [1997] STC 1272 (TVC 22.199).

Securities

See **23.2 FINANCIAL SERVICES** for a special rule applying where a UK supplier cannot determine the place of belonging of a purchaser of securities.

Before 1 January 2010

Services which fall under the general place of supply rule (see **65.15** below) are supplied where the supplier belongs and services falling within *VATA 1994, Sch 5 paras 1–8* (see **65.21** below) are, in certain cases, supplied where the recipient belongs. It is therefore necessary to have rules defining the place of belonging of both the supplier and the recipient of a service.

General rule

From 1 January 2010

[65.15] The place of supply of services is:

- where the supply is to a relevant business person, where the recipient belongs; and
- where the supply is not to a relevant business person, where the supplier belongs.

The supply of a right to services is treated in the same way as the underlying service. A 'relevant business person', in relation to a supply of services, means:

- a taxable person within the meaning of *EC Directive 2006/112/EC, art 9*;
- a person registered under *VATA 1994*, or equivalent legislation in another Member State; or
- a person registered under an Act of Tynwald (Isle of Man) for the purposes of any tax imposed by or under and Act of Tynwald which corresponds to VAT,

where those services are received by the person otherwise than wholly for private purposes.

[VATA 1994, s 7A; FA 2009, Sch 36 para 4]. (VAT Notice 741A paras 5.2, 5.3).

Before 1 January 2010

Subject to the special rules in **65.16–65.28** below, a supply of services is treated as made

- in the UK if the supplier belongs in the UK; and
- in another country (and not the UK) if the supplier belongs in that other country.

[*VATA 1994, s 7(10)(11)*].

See **65.14** above for the place of belonging of the supplier.

The general rule will therefore only apply if a supply of services does not fall under any of the special rules in **65.16–65.28** below. Before determining that a supply falls under the general rule, the exact nature of the services must be identified and considered against those special rules.

Examples of services supplied where the supplier belongs

- Services described as management services where the actual services are not of a type covered by the special rules in **65.16–65.28** below (see, for example, **65.21** below in particular for consultancy, accountancy, legal and financial services).
- Clerical or secretarial services or the provision of office facilities (but not the office accommodation itself).
- Archiving services involving the maintenance of documents and records.
- Veterinary services. See Business Brief 12/98.
- Services forming part of organising a funeral, where a single supply of a funeral is to be made.
- *VATA 1994, Sch 5 paras 1–8* services when supplied to customers belonging in the same country as the supplier, or to non-business customers belonging in a country different to the supplier's (see **65.22** below).
- Letting on hire of a means of transport under certain circumstances (see **65.27** below).

(VAT Notice 741, para 5.3).

De Voil Indirect Tax Service. See V3.183.

Services relating to land

From 1 January 2010

[65.16] With effect from 1 January 2010, a supply of services in connection with land is made where the land is situated if the supply consists of one of the following descriptions

- the grant, assignment or surrender of any interest in or right over land;
- the grant, assignment or surrender of a personal right to call for or be granted any interest in or right over land;
- the grant, assignment or surrender of a licence to occupy land or any other contractual right exercisable over or in relation to land (including the provision of holiday accommodation, seasonal pitches for caravans and facilities at caravan parks for persons for whom such pitches are provided and pitches for tents and camping facilities);
- the provision in an hotel, inn, boarding house or similar establishment of sleeping accommodation or of accommodation in rooms which are provided in conjunction with sleeping accommodation or for the purpose of a supply of catering;
- any works of construction, demolition, conversion, reconstruction, alteration, enlargement, repair or maintenance of a building or civil engineering work; and
- services such as are supplied by estate agents, auctioneers, architects, surveyors, engineers and others involved in matters relating to land.

[*VATA 1994, Sch 4A para 1(2); FA 2009, Sch 36 para 11*].

'*Land*' includes all forms of land and property (growing crops, buildings, walls, fences, civil engineering works and other structures fixed permanently to the land or sea bed) and plant, machinery or equipment which is an installation or edifice in its own right (e.g. a refinery or fixed oil/gas production platform). Machinery installed in buildings other than as a fixture is normally not regarded as land but as goods. (VAT Notice 741A, para 6.3).

The services must relate *directly* to specific sites of land. It does not apply if there is only an indirect connection with land, or if the land-related service is only an incidental part of a more comprehensive service.

Examples of services relating to land

- The supply of hotel accommodation.
- The provision of a site for a stand at an exhibition where the exhibitor obtains the right to a defined area of the exhibition hall. (If a supply of exhibition stand space is made with the specific location of the stand allocated on arrival, this would fall to be taxed where the exhibition takes place, see **65.19** below.)
- The supply of plant or machinery, together with an operator, for work on a construction site.
- The management, conveyancing, survey or valuation of property by a solicitor, surveyor or loss adjustor.

- Services connected with oil/gas/mineral exploration or exploitation relating to specific sites of land or the seabed (see **65.18** and **65.21** below where services do not relate to specific sites).
- The surveying (such as seismic, geological or geomagnetic) of land or seabed, including associated data processing services to collate the required information.
- Legal services such as conveyancing or dealing with applications for planning permission.
- Packages of property management services which may include rent collection, arranging repairs and the maintenance of financial accounts.

Examples of services which are not land-related

Work falling within **65.20** below

- Repair and maintenance of machinery which is not installed as a fixture.

Work falling within **65.21** below

- The hiring out of civil engineering plant on its own.
- The secondment of staff to a building site.
- The legal administration of a deceased person's estate which happens to include property.
- Advice or information relating to land prices or property markets as they do not relate to specific sites.
- Insurance of property.
- Feasibility studies assessing the potential of particular businesses or business potential in a geographic area (i.e. which do not relate to a specific property or site).
- Provision of a recording studio where technicians are included as part of the supply (which are engineering services).
- Services of an accountant in simply calculating a tax return from figures provided by a client, even when those figures relate to rental income.

(VAT Notice 741A, paras 6.4, 6.5).

UK customers receiving services relating to UK land

If a UK VAT-registered recipient of these services receives them for business purposes they may be required to account for the reverse charge if the supplier belongs outside the UK.

Non-UK suppliers of services relating to UK land

Where a supplier does not belong in the UK and the customer is not registered for UK VAT, the supplier is responsible for accounting for any UK VAT due on the supply.

Non-UK land

A supplier of services relating to land in another EU country may be liable to register for VAT in that country.

(VAT Notice 741A, paras 6.6–6.8).

Before 1 January 2010

The following supplies of services are treated as made where the 'land' in connection with which the supply is made is situated.

(a) The grant, assignment or surrender of
- an interest in or right over land;
- a personal right to call for or be granted such an interest or right; or
- a licence to occupy land or any other contractual right exercisable over or in relation to land.

(b) Any works of construction, demolition, conversion, reconstruction, alteration, enlargement, repair or maintenance of a building or civil engineering work.

(c) Services such as are supplied by estate agents, auctioneers, architects, surveyors, engineers and others involved in matters relating to land.

[*SI 1992/3121, Art 5*].

De Voil Indirect Tax Service. See V3.188.

Services supplied where performed

From 1 January 2010

[65.17] The changes to the place of supply rules for services supplied 'where performed' are being introduced in two phases. The table below sets out the changes for business to business (B2B) and business to customer (B2C) supplies.

Service description	*Place of supply from 1 January 2010*	*Place of supply from 1 January 2011*
Services of work on, or valuation of moveable goods; and ancillary transport services.	B2B supplies are subject to the B2B general rule. B2C supplies are made where the services are physically performed.	
Services relating to cultural, artistic, sporting, scientific, educational, entertainment or similar activities (including fairs and exhibitions); and ancillary services relating to such activities, including services of organisers of such activities.	B2B and B2C supplies are made where the services are physically carried out.	B2B supplies are subject to the B2B general rule and the place of supply is where the customer belongs. B2C supplies are made where the activities actually take place.

Service description	*Place of supply from 1 January 2010*	*Place of supply from 1 January 2011*
B2B supplies of services in respect of admission to cultural, artistic, sporting, scientific, educational, entertainment or similar events (including fairs and exhibitions); and B2B supplies of ancillary services relating to admission to such events.	Supplied where services physically carried out.	The place of supply is where the events actually take place.

Examples of services supplied where performed

- *Services of sportspersons appearing in exhibition matches, races or other forms of competition.* However, where sponsorship or prize money is received, it must be determined whether or not these moneys are received as consideration for a supply. If they are consideration for a supply, the nature of the supply must be determined.
- *Provision of race prepared cars.* Such packages include the hire of the car and support services to ensure optimum maintenance and operation of the car throughout a series of races.
- *Scientific services of technicians carrying out tests or experiments in order to obtain data.* The final compilation of record of results, carried out in the UK, will not make the supply liable to UK VAT provided the services were otherwise performed outside the UK.
- Services of an actor or singer, whether or not in front of a live audience.
- Services relating to conferences or meetings.
- Services of an oral interpreter at an event, such as a meeting.
- The right to participate in an exhibition or the provision of an undefined site for a stand at an exhibition.
- Services relating to a specific exhibition. This includes carpenters and electricians erecting and fitting out stands at exhibition venues.
- Educational and training services. Such services may be exempt when made in the UK.

Examples of services that are not supplied where performed

- Services of sportspersons receiving sponsorship money as consideration for product endorsement or publicity appearances. These are advertising services rather than participation in a sporting event.
- Written translation services or interpreters' services which do not take place at an event. These are consultancy services.
- The hire of goods without any additional services, even if the customer uses those goods at an exhibition or concert.
- The provision of a defined site for a stand at an exhibition, which is land-related.
- Scientific services which include a recommendation or conclusion. These are services of consultancy or provision of information, or if connected with oil/gas/mineral exploration or exploitation of specific sites of land or the seabed, they are land-related.

- Veterinary services. These are general rule services.

(VAT Notice 741A, para 8.1).

Before 1 January 2010

A supply of the following services is treated as made where the services are physically carried out (irrespective of where the customer belongs).

(a) Cultural, artistic, sporting, scientific, educational or entertainment services and any services ancillary to (including organising) any such services. See **65.18** below.
(b) Services relating to exhibitions, conferences or meetings and any services ancillary to (including organising) any such services. See **65.19** below.
(c) Valuation of, or work carried out on, any goods. See **65.20** below.
(d) Ancillary transport services. See **65.26** below.

Tour operators

Where supplies of services within *(a)*–*(d)* above (particularly educational services and services connected with conferences and meetings) involve the onward supply as principal of bought-in supplies of accommodation, travel, etc., the provisions of the **TOUR OPERATORS' MARGIN SCHEME (68)** may apply.

Overseas suppliers of services physically carried out in the UK

Where a supplier of services within *(a)*–*(d)* above belongs overseas

- if the recipient of the services is a UK VAT-registered person, the reverse charge procedure applies and the recipient is liable to account for the VAT (see **38.4 INTERNATIONAL SERVICES**); and
- if the recipient of the services is not registered for UK VAT, the overseas supplier must account for any UK VAT and is liable to be registered (subject to the registration threshold).

(VAT Notice 741, paras 7.7, 7.8).

UK suppliers of services physically carried out overseas

If the services within *(a)*–*(d)* above are physically carried out in another EU country (even if the customer belongs in the UK), the supplier may be liable to register in that country. See **65.1** above. If the services are physically carried out outside the EU, the supply is outside the scope of UK and EU VAT (although it may be subject to the equivalent local indirect taxes).

De Voil Indirect Tax Service. See V3.192.

Cultural, artistic, sporting, scientific, educational or entertainment services

From 1 January 2010

[65.18] From 1 January 2010 to 31 December 2010 the place of supply of services relating to cultural, artistic, sporting, scientific, educational, entertainment or similar activities is where the services are physically carried out.

From 1 January 2011

For business customers, the place of supply in respect of the following services is where the events actually take place: services in respect of admission to cultural, artistic, sporting, scientific, educational, entertainment or similar events (including fairs and exhibitions), and ancillary services relating to admission to such events.

For non-business customers, the place of supply of the following services is where the activities concerned actually take place: services relating to cultural, artistic, sporting, scientific, educational, entertainment or similar activities (including fairs and exhibitions), and ancillary services relating to such activities, including services of organisers of such activities.

[*VATA 1994, Sch 4A paras 4, 9A, 14A; FA 2009, Sch 36 paras 11, 15, 16*].

> *Example*
>
> A tax lecturer who is VAT-registered in the UK delivers a lecture for delegates in Jersey but raises a sales invoice to a training company based in the UK (her customer). Until 31 December 2010, the service will avoid a UK charge of VAT because the place of supply is in Jersey where she is performing her service. The place of supply from 1 January 2011 will produce a UK VAT charge on the same scenario because the place of supply for B2B sales is now based on the location of the customer, i.e. UK.
>
> In effect, the new rules will produce a domestic VAT charge in this particular case where none existed before 1 January 2011.

Before 1 January 2010

Supplies of cultural, artistic, sporting, scientific, educational or entertainment services and any services ancillary to (including organising) any such services are treated as made where the services are physically carried out (irrespective of where the customer belongs). [*SI 1992/3121, Art 15(a)(c)*]. Note that the place of supply of ancillary services is where the services are themselves performed which may be different from where the main services are performed.

(VAT Notice 741, paras 7.1, 7.4).

For a more detailed consideration of the place of supply of services provided within the entertainment industry, see the guidance notes agreed between HMRC and B.E.C.T.U. reproduced in HMRC VAT—Place of Supply—Services Manual VATPOSS 13100.

Accounting for VAT

See **65.17** above for accounting for VAT where overseas suppliers supply these services within the UK and UK suppliers supply these services abroad.

Services relating to exhibitions, conferences or meetings before 1 January 2010

[65.19] Supplies of services relating to exhibitions, conferences and meetings and any services ancillary to (including organising) any such services are treated as made where the services are physically carried out (irrespective of where the customer belongs). [*SI 1992/3121, Art 15(b)(c)*]. Note that the place of supply of ancillary services is where the services are themselves performed which may be different from where the main services are performed.

Examples of services included

- The right to participate in an exhibition or the provision of an undefined site for a stand at an exhibition. The provision of a defined site for a stand at an exhibition falls within **65.16** above.
- Services of tradesmen such as carpenters and electricians erecting and fitting out stands at exhibition venues for organisers or exhibitors.

Example of services not included

- The hiring of equipment for use at a concert without the services of technicians or operators (which falls within **65.21** below).

(VAT Notice 741, paras 7.1, 7.3, 7.4).

Accounting for VAT

See **65.17** above for accounting for VAT where overseas suppliers supply these services within the UK and UK suppliers supply these services abroad.

Valuation of, or work carried out on, any goods

From 1 January 2010

[65.20] For business customers the place of supply of services consisting of the valuation of, or carrying out of work on, goods falls under the general rule (see **65.15** above). For other customers, the place of supply of such services is where the services are physically performed.

[*FA 2009, Sch 36 para 14*].

Work carried out on 'goods' is essentially any physical service carried out on another person's goods. It includes

- processing, manufacturing or assembling;
- repairs, cleaning or restoration;
- alterations, calibrations, insulating, lacquering, painting, polishing, resetting (of jewellery), sharpening, varnishing, waterproofing, etc.; and
- nominations to stallions/covering (i.e. attempting to secure the pregnancy of mares).

'*Goods*' for this purpose include all forms of movable tangible property, covering both finished commodities and raw materials but does not include immovable property such as permanently installed goods and fixtures (for which see **65.16** above).

Examples of services included

- Services of a subcontractor installing machinery supplied by another person.
- Simple valuation of goods by loss adjusters, average adjusters, motor assessors, surveyors and other experts in connection with an insurance proposal or claim. The final compilation of a related report in a different country from the goods will not change the place of supply from the country where valuation work is performed. Where, however, valuation forms only a part of a supply of professional services, there is a supply of consultancy services within **65.21** below.

Examples of services not included

- Work which is not mainly physical work performed on the goods themselves, e.g. mere inspection is not 'work on goods' although it can be 'valuation' if that is the purpose of the inspection.
- Valuation of, or work carried out on, land or property (which falls within **65.16** above).
- (VAT Notice 741A, para 8.5).

Before 1 January 2010

Subject to the exception below, services consisting of the valuation of, or work carried out on, any goods are treated as made where the services are physically carried out. [*SI 1992/3121, Art 15(d); SI 1995/3038; SI 1996/2992*]. See **65.17** above for accounting for VAT where overseas suppliers supply these services within the UK and UK suppliers supply these services abroad.

Exception

Where

(a) the services are supplied to a customer registered for VAT in an EU country other than the EU country in which the services are physically carried out,
(b) the customer gives a valid VAT registration number to the supplier, and
(c) the goods are dispatched or transported out of the EU country where the services were physically carried out (but see below for repairs to containers)

the place of supply is the EU country where the customer is registered. If the customer is registered in the same EU country as the supplier, the supplier must account for any VAT due. Otherwise, the customer must account for the VAT due.

[*SI 1992/3121, Art 14; SI 1995/3038; SI 1996/2992*].

Services falling within VATA 1994, Sch 5 paras 1–8 before 1 January 2010

[65.21] The place of supply of any services falling within *VATA 1994, Sch 5 paras 1–8* (see **65.22** below) is treated as taking place

(a) where the recipient belongs if

(i) the recipient belongs in a country outside the EU and the Isle of Man;

(ii) the recipient belongs in an EU country other than that of the supplier and the services are supplied to him for his business purposes; or

(iii) with effect from 1 July 2003 in the case of electronically supplied services falling within **65.22**(11) below, the recipient belongs in an EU country, he receives the services in a non-business or private capacity, and the services are received from a person who belongs outside the EU and the Isle of Man.

(b) in all other cases, where the supplier belongs under the general rule in **65.15** above, i.e. if

(i) the recipient belongs in the same EU country as the supplier;

(ii) (unless (*a*)(iii) above applies) the recipient belongs in an EU country other than that of the supplier but receives the supplies in a non-business or private capacity;

(iii) the recipient is a government body, municipal authority or similar body of another EU country (unless the services are specifically required for use in a business activity); or

(iv) the supplier is unable to determine where the recipient belongs.

[*SI 1992/3121, Arts 16, 16A; SI 1995/3038; SI 2003/862, Art 3*]. (VAT Notice 741, para 12.6).

See **65.14** above for the place of belonging of a recipient and **65.23** below for additional rules relating to telecommunications services, radio or television broadcasting services, electronically supplied services and the letting on hire of goods other than means of transport. See also **23.2 FINANCIAL SERVICES** for special rules applying where a UK supplier cannot determine the place of belonging of a purchaser of securities.

Accounting for VAT

- Where a UK supplier supplies services to a recipient within (*a*)(i) above, the supply is outside the scope of UK (and EU) VAT (subject to **65.23** below).
- Where a UK supplier supplies services to a recipient within (*a*)(ii) above, the place of supply is the EU country of the recipient (subject to **65.23** below). The UK supplier does not need to account for VAT in that country and the customer must do so under the reverse charge procedure.
- Where a UK-registered person *receives* services within these provisions for the purposes of business from an overseas supplier, the place of supply is the UK (subject to **65.23** below) and the reverse charge procedure applies. The UK recipient is liable to account for the VAT. See **38.4 INTERNATIONAL SERVICES.**

Evidence required

(i) General

A UK supplier who treats services within *VATA 1994, Sch 5 paras 1–8* as supplied where the recipient belongs must hold commercial evidence that

- the services are received and used outside the UK, and,
- where *(a)*(ii) above applies, the customer is in business in another EU country.

A VAT registration number is the best evidence of this and should always be requested but alternative acceptable evidence includes a certificate from the relevant fiscal authorities, business letterheads and other commercial documents indicating the nature of the customer's business activities. Where VAT numbers are available, they should be recorded on the invoice relating to the supply. Enquiry letters in a number of foreign languages to request the correct VAT registration number from an EU customer are available on the HMRC website.

Some customers may be VAT-registered but have non-business as well as business activities (e.g. government departments, municipal authorities). In such circumstances the supplier must be satisfied that the services supplied are being used for the purpose of its business activities before treating the supply as taking place where the recipient belongs. In *Diversified Agency Services Ltd v C & E Commrs*, QB 1995, [1996] STC 398 (TVC 62.495), advertising services were supplied to the Spanish Tourist Board in Spain in its capacity as a state authority and not as a commercial public body. As there was no evidence to show that the Board was treated as liable to VAT in Spain in respect of the advertising services under the reverse charge mechanism, the services were standard-rated in the UK. The Court confirmed that the burden of proof was on the company to show that the supply was outside the scope of UK VAT.

If the supplier cannot determine where his customer belongs, or cannot obtain evidence that his services are outside the scope of UK VAT, he should normally charge his customer VAT.

(ii) Electronically supplied services

With effect from 1 July 2003, suppliers of electronically supplied services need to verify each of the following to determine whether the supplies are subject to VAT and, if so, in which EU country.

- *Business status*. For business-to-business supplies within the EU, the evidence required at the time of the transaction would normally be the customer's VAT registration number and country identification code prefix. The number must conform to the format for the registered person's EU country.
  - VAT numbers should be checked where
  - a relationship has not been established with a business customer and the VAT involved exceeds £500 on a single transaction or £500 on cumulative transactions with a single customer in a VAT quarter; or

— a business has any reason to believe that a VAT number quoted by a customer is false or is being used incorrectly.

Where a business customer is known, it is not necessary routinely to check a VAT number quoted provided that it conforms to the correct country format.

Businesses that supply downloaded music, games, films, etc. of a kind normally made to a private consumer should challenge any VAT number quoted in what is clearly a supply to a private consumer.

Where a customer claims to be in business but not to be VAT-registered, alternative evidence should be obtained in the form of other reasonable commercial evidence or records (e.g. contracts, business letterheads, a commercial website address, publicity material, certificates from fiscal authorities, etc.) A digital certificate from a reputable organisation can also be used for this purpose.

The VAT Information Exchange System (VIES) can be used to verify VAT registration numbers in EU countries. It can be accessed at http://europa.eu.int/comm/taxation_customs/vies/en/vieshome.htm

Businesses may also contact the National Advice Service which can verify names and addresses as well as dates of registration and deregistration where appropriate. This advice can also be found at http://163.171.52.105:8016/site/eu-vat-check.htm

If the above checks fail to confirm that the customer is in business or if there remains any doubt about the use of a VAT registration number, VAT should be charged as appropriate on all supplies to that customer (including supplies that have already been made). Any VAT that has been charged in error may be credited under the normal rules.

- *Verification of location.* Self-declaration by the customer combined with a reasonable level of verification is acceptable. Where one or other of the following practices is followed, customer self-declaration will be acceptable (without prior approval from HMRC) provided alternative evidence is sought if the test proves unsuccessful.

  — Using a customer's postal address provided it has been used to send goods, catalogues, samples, CD ROMs, invoices, correspondence, etc. and the correspondence has not been returned undelivered.

  — Accepting payment by credit/debit card and comparing the customer's home address with the billing address.

  — Accepting payment by credit/debit card and, using proprietary software, comparing the customer's country of residence with the location of the issuing bank.

  — Using geo-location or proprietary software to verify where a customer belongs.

  — Using systems that are configured to identify where the service is used and enjoyed (e.g. telecommunication suppliers). HMRC will accept the arrangement as a proxy for identifying the country where the customer belongs.

(VAT Notice 741, para 12.5; VAT Information Sheet 1/03, para 6.3; VAT Information Sheet 5/03).

Misrepresentation of status by recipient

HMRC have indicated that, where the customer wrongly represents his status, they will not hold the supplier responsible for failing to charge the correct amount of VAT provided they are satisfied that the supplier acted in good faith and made the normal and prudent checks and enquiries about the status of the customer and of any documentation of certification provided by him. (Tax Faculty of the ICAEW Guidance Notes 15/94, para 46).

De Voil Indirect Tax Service. See V3.193.

Provisions of VATA 1994, Sch 5 paras 1–8 before 1 January 2010

[65.22] The provisions of *VATA 1994, Sch 5 paras 1-8* are as follows:

(1) Transfers and assignments of copyright, patents, licences, trademarks and similar rights. [*VATA 1994, Sch 5 para 1*]

'Similar rights' are intellectual property rights which are capable of being legally enforced. Payments for these intellectual rights (often known as 'royalties') can be made on a regular and continuing basis or take the form of a single, one-off fee. Services which do not involve intellectual property are not covered even though they may be described as a right or licence.

Examples of services included

- The assignment by a body established in a third country of television broadcasting rights in respect of football matches when supplied to taxable persons established in an EU country.
- The assignment of rights by a performer for his/her performance to be exploited on record, film, television, etc.
- The granting of a licence to use computer software.
- The granting of a right to carry on a particular business activity within a defined territory (such as within some franchise agreements).
- The transfer of permission to use a logo.
- The granting of a right by a photographer for one of his photographs to be published in a magazine article.
- The assignment of rights in a cinematographic film to a distribution company.

Examples of services not included

- The supply of individual shares in goods (e.g. an animal or yacht) even though certain rights may be included in the supply.
- The supply of a right to obtain reduced rates for admission to conferences and meetings and similar discounts on facilities available to members of clubs, associations or societies in return for a subscription.
- A supply which is simply described as 'goodwill'. However, goodwill may be used to describe part of another supply of services, such as assigning a trademark, providing information or refraining from competition. Therefore the nature of what is actually being provided should be identified.
- The supply of the right to occupy land or property including hotel accommodation (which is a supply of services relating to land).

- The granting of a right to a future supply of a service. The place of supply of that right will be the same place as the underlying supply to which the right relates, even if the right is never exercised.

(VAT Notice 741, para 13.3).

(2) Advertising services. [*VATA 1994, Sch 5 para 2*]

This covers all services of publicising another person's name or products with a view to encouraging their sale. It includes supplies of advertising services in the established media, e.g. radio or television advertising time; of the right to place an advertisement on a hoarding; or of advertising space in any publication. It also covers promotional methods such as an entry in a telephone enquiry directory or advertising space in any electronic location.

Everything provided as part of an advertising campaign is included, even if elements of the campaign would have fallen under other place of supply rules had they been supplied in isolation.

Examples of services included

- An advertising performance or product endorsement by a personality supplied directly to the person whose products are advertised.
- The display of a sponsor's name, or product, by a sponsored person or team in return for 'sponsorship' payments (see **57.19 RECREATION AND SPORT**). See also *John Village Automotive Ltd* (VTD 15540) (TVC 62.527).
- Supplies of services that are the 'means of advertising', i.e. services used in connection with specific advertising, promotion or sponsorship. For example, the supply of a master advertising film, tape, record, poster, picture or photograph, or an advertisement printing block (from which copies are made).
- The devising and undertaking of a promotional campaign by an advertising agency to launch a client's new product, even where this includes trade events or demonstrations for the public in general.
- Website advertising.

Examples of services not included

- The provision of space or stands at a trade fair or exhibition (for the place of supply of which see **65.16** and **65.19** above).
- Organising a cocktail party for an advertising company where the event is part of a promotional campaign for the advertising company's own client.

(VAT Notice 741, para 13.4).

(3) Services of consultants, engineers, consultancy bureaux, lawyers, accountants and other similar services; data processing and provision of information (but excluding from this head any services relating to land). [*VATA 1994, Sch 5 para 3*]

Services of consultants and consultancy bureaux

Included are

- research and development;
- market research;
- written translation services or interpreters' services which do not take place at an event (e.g. interpreting services for a telephone conference). For oral interpreting at an event, see **65.18** above;
- testing and analysis of goods (e.g. drugs, chemicals and domestic electrical appliances). The essential nature of such services is analysis by experts who use the results of the testing to reach a professional conclusion, such as whether goods meet specified standards;
- writing scientific reports;
- production of customised ('bespoke' or 'specific') computer software as well as the services of adapting existing packages (some off-the-shelf software packages are treated as supplies of goods); and
- software maintenance; involving upgrades, advice and resolving any problems. The place of performance is not relevant as solutions may be provided by telephone conversations, remote links or attending a mainframe site. However, a contract for simply maintaining computer hardware relates to work on goods (and the place of supply is covered by **65.20** above).

Not included are

- services relating to specific land or property (the place of supply of which is determined under **65.16** above);
- supplies described as management services, unless they can be shown to be essentially of consultancy services although such services may fall elsewhere within *VATA 1994, Sch 5 para 3* (see, for example, *Vision Express Ltd* (VTD 16848) (TVC 39.7));
- clerical or secretarial services, the provision of office facilities and archiving services;
- services provided by a consultant which are outside the supplier's habitual area of expertise (e.g. gardening carried out by a financial adviser); and
- arbitration services (see *Von Hoffmann v Finanzamt Trier, ECJ Case C–145/96*, [1997] STC 1321 (TVC 22.223) where the court held that the services of a German professor acting as arbitrator for the International Chamber of Commerce based in France were not within the equivalent provisions of what is now *Directive 2006/112/EC, Art 56(1)*).

(VAT Notice 741, para 13.5).

Services of engineers

The services must be of a type expected of an expert or professional. Included are

- the provision of intellectual engineering advice or design. This includes overseeing the resultant physical work, provided that any such supervision is merely to ensure that the design or other advice is properly implemented; and

- services of engineers/technicians within the entertainment industry. This covers editors and sound engineers producing an edit master from which copies can be made (films, videos, compact discs or audio tapes) as well as those who exercise a degree of artistic control or influence over material.

Not included are

- services of surveyors and consultants consisting primarily of work such as design, surveying, site supervision or valuation where these directly relate to land or property (for the place of supply of which see **65.16** above); and
- services carried out by an engineer which consist wholly or mainly of physical work on goods, including installation of goods (for the place of supply of which see **65.20** above).

(VAT Notice 741, para 13.5).

Services of lawyers and accountants

Included are

- legal and accountancy services in the general administration or winding up of a deceased's estate even if that estate includes land or property; and
- services described as management services, the essential nature of which comprise accountancy or legal services.

Not included are

- services consisting primarily of work which directly relates to land or property such as property management, conveyancing, or obtaining planning consent (for the place of supply of which see **65.16** above);
- a claim of ownership over a particular piece of land or property; and
- clerical or secretarial services which include the keeping of financial records.

(VAT Notice 741, para 13.5).

Other similar services

Included are

- services of loss adjusters and assessors in assessing the validity of claims (except where these relate to land). Such services may include examination of goods to establish a value for damage or deterioration as well as negotiating a settlement amount;
- services of surveyors providing opinions which do not relate to specific sites;
- architects' services where there is no specific site of land;
- services of fiscal agents in completing VAT returns and documentation for overseas businesses (provided that the customer does not belong in the UK for the purposes of receiving these services);
- design services;
- services of specialists or technicians which are essentially creative or artistic in nature;

- services of film directors or producers, where their services are not of rights within (1) above; and
- services described as management services which comprise the exercise of corporate or strategic guidance over the running of another (usually associated) company.

Not included are

- services provided by architects and surveyors which directly relate to land or property, including surveying, site supervision, conveyancing, valuation and obtaining planning consent (for the place of supply of which see **65.16** above); and
- loss adjusting services in relation to claims on land or property (for the place of supply of which see **65.16** above) and services provided by a loss adjuster which are simply the valuation of goods (for the place of supply of which see **65.20** above).

(VAT Notice 741, para 13.5).

Data processing

Data processing is the application of programmed instructions on existing data which results in the production of required information. Not included are

- services which simply include an element of data processing;
- processing data from seismic surveys where the computer analysis relates to a specified area of land or seabed (for the place of supply of which see **65.16** above); and
- simple re-formatting where there is no change to the meaning of the content.

(VAT Notice 741, para 13.5).

Provision of information

The provision of information covers the supplying of knowledge of any type and in any form. Information includes facts, data, figures and other material. Included are

- tourist information;
- weather forecasts;
- information supplied by a private enquiry agent;
- telephone helpdesk services (such as for computer software);
- satellite navigational and locational services; and
- provision of on-line information.

Not included as the provision of information are

- the delivery or transmission of another person's information by whatever means; and
- information relating to specific land or property (for the place of supply of which see **65.16** above).

(VAT Notice 741, para 13.5).

(4) Acceptance of any obligation to refrain from pursuing or exercising, in whole or part, any business activity or any such rights as are referred to in (1) above. [*VATA 1994, Sch 5 para 4*]

Examples of services included

- The vendor of a business accepting an undertaking not to compete with the purchaser.
- Agreement by the owner of a trademark to refrain from using it.

(VAT Notice 741, para 13.6).

(5) Banking, financial and insurance services (including reinsurance, but not including the provision of safe deposit facilities). [*VATA 1994, Sch 5 para 5*].

Examples of services included

- Granting of mortgages and loans; selling debts.
- The storage of gold bullion or gold coins by a bank or a dealer in gold who is a subsidiary of a bank.
- The sale of securities as principal.
- The sale of unallocated precious metals (gold, silver, platinum, palladium, rhodium, ruthenium, osmium and iridium) or unallocated precious metal coins.
- Debt collection services.
- Portfolio management services.
- The supply of financial futures and financial options.
- Trustees services.
- Commodity brokers' services of arranging transactions in futures and options.

Examples of services not included

- Services of physical safe custody.
- Rent collection services (for the place of supply of which see **65.16** above).

(VAT Notice 741, para 13.7).

(6) The provision of access to, and of transport or transmission through, natural gas and electricity distribution systems and the provision of other directly linked services. [*VATA 1994, Sch 5 para 5A; SI 2004/3149*]

These services allow access to and use of the distribution networks. The distribution systems are the transmission networks of pipelines, cables and interconnectors, which enable the national and international transport of gas and electricity to be carried out. Also included are 'directly linked' services which, although not directly involving use of the systems, are clearly an adjunct to such usage.

Examples of services included

- Use of the gas National Transmission System.
- Use of the National Grid.

- Provision of data on network usage.
- Storage of gas within the natural gas distribution system.
- Services involving injection of gas into the system.

Examples of services not included

- Balancing and imbalance charges.
- Contract termination payments.
- Fees/subscriptions for membership of regulatory or trade bodies.
- Brokerage fees.

(VAT Notice 741, para 13.8).

(7) **The supply of staff.** [*VATA 1994, Sch 5 para 6*]

A supply of staff is the placing of personnel under the general control and guidance of another party as if they become employees of that other party. A clear distinction must be drawn between a supply of staff and a supply of other services by using staff.

Examples of services included

- The secondment, transfer or placement of a typist with a customer where the typist comes under their general control and direction as an employee is the supply of staff.
- The supply, secondment, loan, hire, lease or transfer as principals of personnel for a consideration by bodies such as employment or recruitment businesses or bureaux.
- The transfer for a fee by a sports club of a professional sportsman who has a contract of service with the club, e.g. a professional footballer.

Examples of services not included

- The supply by a freelance or other person of a specific service or services under a contract for services.
- Supplies by employment or recruitment businesses or agencies of making arrangements for the supply of staff between other parties (which fall within (12) below).
- Where a company that employs typists uses them to supply typing services under a specific assignment, the service is not a supply of staff but of typing services.

(VAT Notice 741, para 13.9).

See also *American Institute of Foreign Study (UK) Ltd* (VTD 13886) (TVC 62.541) where the services of travel couriers provided to associated companies were held to be supplies of staff rather than the supply of courier services.

(8) **The letting on hire of goods other than means of transport.** [*VATA 1994, Sch 5 para 7*]

Goods include all forms of movable property or equipment but not land and property or equipment and machinery installed as a fixture.

Examples of services included

- The hire of mobile telephone handsets (but see (9) below if the supply is of telecommunications services).
- The hire of freight containers (but see **21.7 EXPORTS** for special rules for container exports).
- The hire of computer and office equipment.
- The hire of exhibition stand furniture and equipment without any other services.

Examples of services not included

- The hire of exhibition stand space (for the place of supply of which see **65.16** and **65.19** above).
- The hire of a means of transport (for the place of supply of which see **65.16** above and **65.27** below).
- Supplies which include the services of an operator or technician (the place of supply of which depends on the nature of the services provided).

(VAT Notice 741, para 13.10).

Mobile cranes are not means of transport (*BPH Equipment Ltd* (VTD 13914) (TVC 62.543)).

(9) Telecommunications services

I.e. services relating to the transmission, emission or reception of signals, writing, images and sounds or information of any nature by wire, radio, optical or other electromagnetic systems, including

- the related transfer or assignment of the right to use capacity for such transmission, emission or reception, and
- in relation to any services performed after 30 June 2003, the provision of access to global information networks.

[*VATA 1994, Sch 5 para 7A; SI 1997/1523, Reg 3; SI 2003/863, Art 2*].

The definition covers the sending or receiving of material by electronic or similar communications systems. This may be via cable, fibre optics, radio waves, microwaves, satellite or copper wire. It covers telephony (systems for the transmission of speech and other sound) and telegraphy (systems involving any process that provides reproduction at a distance of written, printed or pictorial matter) as well as the right to use such facilities.

Examples of services included

- telephone calls, calls delivered by cellular phones, paging, the transmission element of Electronic Data Interchange, teleconferencing and call-back services;
- switching, completion of another provider's calls, the provision of leased lines and circuits or global networks;
- telex, facsimile, multi-messaging;
- e-mail;
- basic access to the internet and World Wide Web, the provision of e-mail addresses and chatline facilities (even if related software, some information and customer support facilities are included). If a package

of Internet services is supplied where the emphasis is on content rather than communication, the supply is not of pure telecommunications services and the place of supply of the package depends on the nature of the services provided. Where services are supplied separately or services are simply delivered to a customer by electronic transmission, the place of supply depends on the nature of the services provided;

- transmission or delivery of another person's material by electronic means; and
- satellite transmission services, covering transponder rental/hire and both space segments and earth segments, which includes uplinks and downlinks via land earth stations, coastal stations, outside broadcasting units or similar.

Examples of services not included

- the supply of the 'content' of a transmission, treatment of which depends on the nature of the actual services, For example, if A contracts with B to provide general advisory services and delivers the information by fax, A is providing advisory services within *VATA 1994, Sch 5 para 3* (see (3) above) not the transmission of a fax. The transmission of the fax is a supply of services within *VATA 1994, Sch 5 para 7A* above to A by a third party;
- supplies of information ordered and delivered through the Internet;
- travel information accessed by telephone;
- granting copyright to use transmitted material;
- processing of data; and
- broadcasting to subscribers.

(VAT Notice 741, para 13.11).

(10) Radio and television broadcasting services. [*VATA 1994, Sch 5 para 7B; SI 2003/863, Reg 2*]

Included is broadcasting by audio and video signals, regardless of the means used (landline, line of sight or satellite link). An example of a service covered is a subscription for satellite or cable television.

Not included is the service of transmitting another person's material by electronic means.

(VAT Notice 741, para 13.12).

(11) Electronically supplied services. [*VATA 1994, Sch 5 para 7C; SI 2003/863, Reg 2*]

An 'electronically supplied service' is one that is

- delivered over the Internet or an electronic network (in other words is reliant on the Internet or similar network for its provision); and
- where the nature of the particular service means it is heavily dependent on information technology for its supply. In other words the service is essentially automated, involving minimal human intervention and in the absence of information technology does not have viability.

In general the use of the Internet or other electronic networks by parties to communicate with respect to transactions or to facilitate trading does not, any more than the use of a telephone or fax, affect the VAT treatment. For example, where parties simply use the Internet to convey information in the course of a business transaction (e.g. email), this does not change the nature of that transaction. This differs from a supply that is completely dependent on the Internet in order to be carried out (e.g. searching and retrieving information from a database with no human intervention).

Examples of services included

- Website supply or web hosting services.
- Distance maintenance of programmes and equipment.
- Supplies of software and updating thereof.
- Supplies of images, text and information and making available of databases.
- Supply of music, films and games, including games of chance and gambling games and of political, cultural, artistic, sporting, scientific and entertainment broadcasts and events.
- Supply of distance teaching.
- Downloaded services.
- Web-based broadcasting that is only provided over the Internet or similar electronic network and is not simultaneously broadcast over a traditional radio or television network.

Examples of services not included

- Supplies of goods, where the order and processing is done electronically.
- Supplies of CD-Roms, games on a CD-Rom, floppy disks and similar tangible media.
- Supplies of printed matter, such as books, newsletters, newspapers or journals.
- Supplies of CDs, audio cassettes, videos cassettes, DVDs.
- Services of lawyers and financial consultants and so on, who advise clients through email.
- Teaching services, where the course content is delivered by a teacher over the Internet or an electronic network (in other words, via a remote link).
- Offline physical repair services of computer equipment.
- Offline data warehousing services.
- Advertising services, in particular as in newspapers, on posters and on television.
- Telephone helpdesk services.
- Teaching services purely involving correspondence courses, such as postal courses.
- Conventional auctioneers' services reliant on direct human intervention, irrespective of how bids are made.
- Telephone services with a video component, otherwise known as videophone services.
- Internet and worldwide web access services.
- Telephone services provided through the Internet.

Downloaded publications

All supplies of downloaded publications are regarded as supplies of services and not goods, and therefore the zero-rating of supplies of printed matter does not apply.

(VAT Notice 741, para 13.13).

(12) The services rendered by one person to another in procuring for the other any of the services mentioned in (1)–(11) above. [*VATA 1994, Sch 5 para 8; SI 1997/1523, Reg 3; SI 2003/863, Reg 2*]

Examples of services included

- Stockbroking services.
- Insurance broking services.
- Services of patent, copyright and similar agents.
- Services of advertising agents.

Examples of services not included

- Making arrangements for supplies other than those covered in (1)–(11) above.
- Services of only facilitating a supply within (1)–(11) above, such as simple introduction.

(VAT Notice 741, para 13.14).

Letting on hire of goods (other than means of transport) and telecommunications, broadcasting and electronically supplied services before 1 January 2010

[65.23] In relation to

- the letting on hire of goods (other than means of transport) within **65.22**(8) above,
- telecommunication services within **65.22**(9) above,
- radio and television broadcasting services within **65.22**(10) above, and
- electronically supplied services within **65.22**(11) above when received by a person for the purposes of a business carried on by him

the following rules apply *in addition* to those in **65.21** above.

(a) Where the supply would, under **65.21**(*a*) or (*b*) above, be treated as supplied in the UK, it is not to be so treated to the extent that the 'effective use and enjoyment' takes place outside the EU.

(b) Where the supply would, under **65.21**(*a*) or (*b*) above, be treated as supplied outside the EU, it is to be treated as supplied in the UK to the extent that the effective use and enjoyment of the services takes place in the UK.

[*SI 1992/3121, Arts 17, 18; SI 1998/763; SI 2003/862, Art 5*].

'*Effective use and enjoyment*' takes place where a recipient actually consumes the relevant services or uses the goods. In practice, this will be where the services are physically used or the goods are physically located, irrespective of contract, payment or beneficial interest. Where services are only partly liable to UK VAT because of the use and enjoyment provisions, there is no prescribed method of determining the extent to which services are used in the UK. Any method may be adopted which produces a fair and reasonable reflection of services. Evidence of how apportionment has been made should be retained.

Examples

(1) A Canadian company hires out recording equipment to a UK private individual who uses the equipment in his UK home. The place of supply is the UK. This is because the goods are used in the UK and the place of supply would otherwise have been outside the EU under **65.21**(*b*)(ii) above.

(2) An Australian tourist hires a video camera from a UK provider during a visit to the UK. The place of supply is the UK. This is because the goods are used in the UK and the place of supply would otherwise have been outside the EU under **65.21**(*b*)(ii) above.

(3) A UK golf shop hires out a set of golf clubs to a UK customer for use on a holiday in the USA. The place of supply is outside the EU if the customer is able to demonstrate that the golf clubs are used only in the USA. This is because the goods are used outside the EU and the place of supply would otherwise have been the UK under **65.21**(*b*)(i) above.

(4) A business traveller makes a reservation at a Hong Kong hotel from his London office using a toll-free number. The telecommunications services are supplied to, and used by, the Hong Kong hotel. The place of supply is outside the EU because the services are not effectively used and enjoyed in the UK.

(5) A UK business purchases digitised software from an Irish supplier for use only in its branch in the Channel Islands. Although the supply is received in the UK where the business belongs, it is used outside the EU and is outside the scope of UK (and EU) VAT.

(6) A UK business purchases downloaded information from another UK business for use both in its UK headquarters and its Canadian branch. Although the supply is received in the UK, to the extent it is used in Canada, it is outside the scope of UK VAT. UK VAT is due only to the extent of use by the UK headquarters.

(VAT Notice 741, paras 14.4, 14.6, 14.7, 15.6).

Summary of liabilities

The following tables summarise the UK VAT position for services subject to the use and enjoyment provisions. Each row must be read in its entirety to arrive at the correct position.

(1) *Letting on hire of goods (other than means of transport), telecommunications services and broadcasting services*

	UK VAT position (subject to use and enjoyment provisions)	*Impact of use and enjoyment provisions*
Supplier belongs in the UK Customer belongs		
— in the UK	Services are supplied in the UK and the supplier accounts for UK VAT[1]	Services used and enjoyed outside the EU are outside the scope of UK (and EU) VAT
— in another EU country and receives services for business purposes	Services are supplied in the other EU country and are outside the scope of UK VAT	Do not apply — outside UK jurisdiction
— in another EU country and receives the services for non-business purposes	Services are supplied in the UK and the supplier accounts for UK VAT [1]	Services used and enjoyed outside the EU are outside the scope of UK (and EU) VAT
— outside the EU	Services are supplied outside the EU and are outside the scope of UK (and EU) VAT	Services used and enjoyed in the UK are supplied in the UK and the supplier accounts for UK VAT[1, 2, 3]
Supplier belongs in another EU country Customer belongs		
— in the UK and receives the services for business purposes	Services are supplied in the UK and the customer accounts for UK VAT by applying the reverse charge[1]	Services used and enjoyed outside the EU are outside the scope of UK (and EU) VAT
— in the UK and receives the services for non-business purposes	Services are supplied in the supplier's country and are outside the scope of UK VAT4	Do not apply — outside UK jurisdiction
— in another EU country	Services are supplied in another EU country and are outside the scope of UK VAT	Do not apply — outside UK jurisdiction
— outside the EU	Services are supplied outside the EU and are outside the scope of UK (and EU) VAT	Services used and enjoyed in the UK are supplied in the UK and the supplier accounts for UK VAT[1] unless the customer provides a UK registration number and accounts for UK VAT by applying the reverse charge[2, 3]
Supplier belongs outside the EU Customer belongs		

	UK VAT position (subject to use and enjoyment provisions)	*Impact of use and enjoyment provisions*
— in the UK and receives the services for business purposes	Services are supplied in the UK and the customer accounts for UK VAT by applying the reverse charge[1]	Services used and enjoyed outside the EU are outside the scope of UK (and EU) VAT
— in the UK and receives the services for non-business purposes	Services are supplied in the supplier's country and are outside the scope of UK (and EU) VAT — use and enjoyment provisions are likely to apply	Services used and enjoyed in the UK are supplied in the UK and the supplier accounts for UK VAT[1]
— in another EU country and receives the services for business purposes	Services are supplied in the other EU country and are outside the scope of UK VAT	Do not apply — outside UK jurisdiction
— in another EU country and receives the services for non-business purposes	Services are supplied in the supplier's country and are outside the scope of UK (and EU) VAT	Services used and enjoyed in the UK are supplied in the UK and the supplier accounts for UK VAT[1]
— outside the EU	Services are supplied outside the EU and are outside the scope of UK (and EU) VAT	Services used and enjoyed in the UK are supplied in the UK and the supplier accounts for UK VAT[1] unless the customer provides a UK VAT registration number and accounts for UK VAT by applying the reverse charge[2, 3]

(2) *Electronically supplied services*

	UK VAT position (subject to use and enjoyment provisions)	*Impact of use and enjoyment provision*
Supplier belongs in the UK		
Customer belongs		
— in the UK and receives the services for business purposes	Services are supplied in the UK and the supplier accounts for UK VAT[1]	Services used and enjoyed outside the EU are outside the scope of UK (and EU) VAT
— in the UK and receives the services for non-business purposes	Services are supplied in the UK and the supplier accounts for UK VAT[1]	Do not apply to non-business services[6]
— in another EU country and receives the services for business purposes	Services are supplied in the other EU country and are outside the scope of UK VAT	Do not apply — outside UK jurisdiction

	UK VAT position (subject to use and enjoyment provisions)	*Impact of use and enjoyment provision*
— in another EU country and receives the services for non-business purposes	Services are supplied in the UK and the supplier accounts for UK VAT[1]	Do not apply to non-business services
— outside the EU and receives the services for business purposes	Services are supplied outside the EU and are outside the scope of UK (and EU) VAT	Services used and enjoyed in the UK are supplied in the UK and the supplier accounts for UK VAT[1, 3]
— outside the EU and receives the services for non-business purposes	Services are supplied outside the EU and are outside the scope of UK (and EU) VAT	Do not apply to non-business services[6]
Supplier belongs in another EU country Customer belongs		
— in the UK and receives the services for business purposes	Services are supplied in the UK and the customer accounts for UK VAT by applying the reverse charge[1]	Services used and enjoyed outside the EU are outside the scope of UK VAT
— in the UK and receives the services for non-business purposes	Services are supplied in the supplier's country and are outside the scope of UK VAT. Supplier accounts for any VAT due	Do not apply to non-business services
— in another EU country	Services are supplied in another EU country and are outside the scope of UK VAT	Do not apply — outside UK jurisdiction
— outside the EU and receives the services for business purposes	Services are supplied outside the EU and are outside the scope of UK (and EU) VAT	Services used and enjoyed in the UK are supplied in the UK and the supplier accounts for UK VAT[1] unless the customer provides a UK VAT registration number and accounts for UK VAT by applying the reverse charge[3]
— outside the EU and receives the services for non-business purposes	Services are supplied outside the EU and are outside the scope of UK (and EU) VAT	Do not apply to non-business services
Supplier belongs outside the EU Customer belongs		

	UK VAT position (subject to use and enjoyment provisions)	*Impact of use and enjoyment provision*
— in the UK and receives the services for business purposes	Services are supplied in the UK and the customer accounts for UK VAT due by applying the reverse charge[1]	Services used and enjoyed outside the EU are outside the scope of UK (and EU) VAT
— in the UK and receives the services for non-business purposes	Services are supplied in the UK and the supplier should account for any UK VAT due[5]	Do not apply to non-business services
— in another EU country	Services are supplied in another EU country and are outside the scope of UK VAT	Do not apply — outside UK jurisdiction
— outside the EU and receives the services for business purposes	Services are supplied outside the EU and are outside the scope of UK (and EU) VAT	Services used and enjoyed in the UK are supplied in the UK and the supplier accounts for UK VAT[1] unless the customer provides a UK VAT registration number and accounts for UK VAT by applying the reverse charge[3]
— outside the EU and receives the services for non-business purposes	Services are supplied outside the EU and are outside the scope of UK (and EU) VAT	Do not apply to non-business services

Notes

(1) Subject to registration threshold.

(2) Any telecommunications services used in the UK by customers belonging outside the EU are supplied in the UK. Such services are therefore subject to UK VAT when used in the UK by non-EU visitors (e.g. public pay-phones, fax shop services and calls made from hotel rooms). As an administrative measure, the elements of telecommunications services used in the UK may be ignored if

- simply an incidental part of an established telephone contract or account held by a customer who belongs outside the EU;
- used by a temporary non-EU visitor; and
- HMRC are satisfied that these conditions are not being abused.

(3) Services used in other EU countries are outside the scope of UK VAT but may be within the scope of VAT of the country where used.

(4) Services may be outside the scope of the supplier's EU country if used outside the EU.

(5) Suppliers may opt to use the special scheme for non-EU businesses. See **63.34 SPECIAL SCHEMES**.

(6) *Simplification for businesses supplying telecommunication or broadcasting services as well as electronically supplied services.* HMRC recognise that, in certain situations, the place of supply would be the same whether the rules for telecommunications and broadcasting services, or those for electronically supplied services, were applied. This is because most non-business customers use and enjoy services in the same country in which they belong. Therefore where
- a UK business supplies electronically supplied services;
- its services are supplied to private individuals or non-business organisations; and
- its existing accounting systems are set up to tax supplies where they are effectively used and enjoyed

it can, exceptionally, opt to apply the use and enjoyment rules to its supplies of electronically supplied services. This is a simplification measure which prevents the need for businesses to adjust their systems. However, HMRC will not allow this simplification to be used in any case where they consider it leads to abuse.

(VAT Notice 741, paras 20.1–20.4, 21.1–21.4).

See **38.9 INTERNATIONAL SERVICES** for further coverage of telecommunications services and **38.10 INTERNATIONAL SERVICES** for further coverage of broadcasting and electronically supplied services.

Intangible services from 1 January 2010

[65.24] With effect from 1 January 2010, the supply of intangible services listed below falls within the general rule for the place of supply of services (see **65.15** above), unless they are supplied to a recipient who is not a relevant business person and belongs in a country which is not a Member State (other than the Isle of Man). In such a case, the place of supply is where the recipient belongs. The services in question are:

- transfers and assignments of copyright, patents, licences, trademarks and similar rights, and the acceptance of any obligation to refrain from pursuing or exercising (in whole or in part) any business activity or any such rights;
- advertising services;
- services of consultants, engineers, consultancy bureaux, lawyers, accountants, and similar services, data processing and provision of information, other than any services relating to land;
- banking, financial and insurance services (including reinsurance), other than the provision of safe deposit facilities;
- the provision of access to, or transmission or distribution through a natural gas system situated within the territory of an EU country or any network connected to such a system, or an electricity system, or a network through which heat or cooling is supplied, and the provision of other directly linked services;
- the supply of staff;
- (subject to use and enjoyment provisions) the letting on hire of goods other than means of transport;

- (subject to use and enjoyment provisions) telecommunication services, i.e. services relating to the transmission, emission or reception of signals, writing, images and sounds or information of any nature by wire, radio, optical or other electromagnetic systems, including the related transfer or assignment of the right to use capacity for such transmission, emission or reception; and the provision of access to global information networks;
- (subject to use and enjoyment provisions) radio and television broadcasting services; and
- (subject to use and enjoyment provisions, where supplied to a relevant business person) electronically supplied services, e.g. website supply, web-hosting and distance maintenance of programmes and equipment; the supply of software and the updating of software; the supply of images, text and information, and the making available of databases; the supply of music, films and games (including games of chance and gambling games); the supply of political, cultural, artistic, sporting, scientific, educational or entertainment broadcasts (including broadcasts of events); and the supply of distance teaching. (But where the supplier of a service and the supplier's customer communicate via electronic mail, this does not of itself mean that the service provided is an electronically supplied service for these purposes.)

A further special rule applies to electronically supplied services provided by a person who belongs in a third country to someone who is not a relevant business person and who belongs in a Member State. In such cases the place of supply is where the recipient belongs.

Use and enjoyment provisions

The place of supply rule described above is modified in respect of certain supplies, namely hiring of goods, telecoms and broadcasting services, and electronically supplied services ('relevant services'). Where a supply of relevant services would otherwise be regarded as made in the UK but the effective use and enjoyment of those services is in a third country (i.e. a country which is not a Member State), the supply is to be treated as taking place in that country to the extent that it is so used and enjoyed. Where a supply of relevant services would otherwise be regarded as made in a third country (i.e. a country which is not a Member State) but the effective use and enjoyment of those services is in the UK, the supply is to be treated as taking place in the UK to the extent that it is so used and enjoyed.

[*VATA 1994, Sch 4A paras 7–9, 15, 16; FA 2009, Sch 36 para 11; SI 2010/3017, Arts 1, 2*]. (VAT Notice 741A, paras 15.1–15.13).

Restaurant and catering services from 1 January 2010

[65.25] With effect from 1 January 2010, the provision of restaurant and catering services, other than those supplied in the course of intra-EU passenger transport is made in the country in which the services are physically carried out. The provision of catering or restaurant services on board a ship, aircraft or train in connection with the transportation of passengers during an intra–EU passenger transport operation is made in the country in which the relevant point of departure is located. A return passenger transport operation (i.e. a journey which takes place in more than one country, but ends in the country in which it began) comprises two passenger transport operations; the outward leg and the return leg. The return leg commences with the last stop at a place where there has been no previous stop, and ends where the outward leg began.

[*VATA 1994, Sch 4A paras 5, 6; FA 2009, Sch 36 para 11*].

Transport services

From 1 January 2010

Passenger transport

[65.26] The transportation of passengers (and any accompanying luggage or motor vehicles) is made in the country in which the transportation takes place, having regard (where more than one country is involved) to the proportion of distances covered in each country. Transportation which takes place partly outside the territorial jurisdiction of a country is to be treated as taking place wholly in the country if

- it takes place in the course of a journey between two points in the country (whether or not as part of a longer journey involving travel to or from another country); and
- the means of transport used does not (except in an emergency or involuntarily) stop, put in or land in another country in the course of the journey between those two points.

A pleasure cruise (including a cruise wholly or partly for education or training) is regarded as the transportation of passengers. Consequently services provided as part of such a cruise are treated as supplied in the same place as the transportation of the passengers).

Transportation of goods

The place of supply of the transportation of goods for business customers falls under the general rule, i.e. where the customer belongs (see **65.15** above). However, HMRC have become aware that this change in law has produced an unintended anomaly in the treatment of supplies wholly enjoyed outside the EU, which may also be taxed locally in the place of performance. Therefore, from 15 March 2010, where a supply of freight transport (or services closely associated with freight transport) would be treated as supplied in the UK, it will not be so treated if the use and enjoyment of the services is outside the EU. This administrative easement is being introduced as a temporary measure to allow time for consideration of a more permanent legislative solution. (HMRC Brief 13/10).

For non-business customers, the place of supply is in the country in which the transportation takes place, in proportion to the distances covered (where more than one country is involved). Transportation which takes place partly outside the territorial jurisdiction of a country is to be treated as taking place wholly in the country if

- it takes place in the course of a journey between two points in the country (whether or not as part of a longer journey involving travel to or from another country); and
- the means of transport used does not (except in an emergency or involuntarily) stop, put in or land in another country in the course of the journey between those two points.

Intra-EU transport of goods

The place of supply of the transportation of goods for business customers falls under the general rule (see **65.15** above). For other customers, the place of supply is in the country in which the transportation begins.

Ancillary transport services

The place of supply of ancillary transport services for business customers falls under the general rule (see **65.15** above). For other customers, the place of supply is where the services are physically performed.

If the type of supply is	*the place of supply will be*
B2C domestic freight transport (which takes place wholly within one country);	where the transport takes place.
B2C international freight transport (between the EU and non-EU countries, or wholly outside the EU);	where the transport takes place.
B2C intra-EU freight transport (from one Member State to another);	the Member State in which the transportation begins.
B2C ancillary transport services relating to domestic, international freight transport or intra-EU freight transport;	where the services are physically performed.
making arrangements for or facilitation of B2C domestic or international freight transport;	where the transport takes place.
making arrangements for or facilitation of B2C intra-EU freight transport;	the Member State in which the transportation begins.
making arrangements for or facilitation of related B2C ancillary services;	where the ancillary services are physically performed.

Ship and aircraft charter party contracts

If the supplier supplies the ship or aircraft with crew under a formal written charter party contract, the place of supply is subject to the general rule. B2B supplies are made where the customer belongs. B2C supplies are made where the supplier belongs. But if they supply a ship or aircraft without crew under a written charter party agreement, the supply is the hire of a means of transport. If they supply a ship or aircraft with crew but without a written charter party contract, or of part of the seating capacity in a ship or aircraft, the place of supply of such transport-related services depends on the nature of the services supplied.

[*VATA 1994, Sch 4A paras 2, 11–13; FA 2009, Sch 36 para 11*]. (VAT Notice 741A, paras 10.1, 10.2, 11.1, 11.2).

Before 1 January 2010

Passenger transport services

Services consisting of the transport of passengers (including any accompanying luggage and/or motor vehicle) are treated as supplied in the country in which the transportation takes place (and only to the extent that it takes place in that country). [*SI 1992/3121, Arts 6, 8*]. *For sea and air passenger transport*, provided the means of transport used does not put in or land in another country on the way, any transportation as part of a journey between two points in the same country is treated as taking place wholly inside that country even where it takes place partly outside its territorial jurisdiction. This applies even if the journey is part of a longer journey involving travel to or from another country. [*SI 1992/3121, Art 7*].

Pleasure cruises

Any goods or services provided as part of a pleasure cruise are treated as supplied in the same place as the transportation of the passengers, and for this purpose a pleasure cruise is treated as a supply of passenger transport. [*SI 1992/3121, Art 8*].

See **70.16 TRANSPORT AND FREIGHT** for further details and **70.15–70.24 TRANSPORT AND FREIGHT** for passenger transport generally.

Overseas suppliers of passenger transport services in the UK

Where a supplier of such services belongs overseas

- if the recipient of the services is a UK VAT-registered person, the reverse charge procedure applies and the recipient is liable to account for the VAT (see **38.4 INTERNATIONAL SERVICES**); and
- if the recipient of the services is not registered for UK VAT, the overseas supplier must account for any UK VAT and is liable to be registered (subject to the registration threshold).

UK suppliers of passenger transport overseas

If a UK supplier supplies passenger transport in another EU country, he may be liable to register in that country. See **65.1** above. If the services are physically carried out outside the EU, the supply is outside the scope of UK and EU VAT.

Freight transport and related services

Subject to special rules for intra-EU transport of goods below,

- freight transport services are treated as supplied in the country where the transportation takes place (and only to the extent that it takes place in that country); and
- ancillary freight transport services (loading, unloading, handling and similar activities) are treated as made where those services are physically performed.

For sea and air freight transport, provided the means of transport used does not put in or land in another country on the way, any transportation as part of a journey between two points in the same country is treated as taking place wholly inside that country even where it takes place partly outside its territorial jurisdiction. This applies even if the journey is part of a longer journey involving travel to or from another country.

[*SI 1992/3121, Arts 2, 6, 7, 9*].

For intra-EU freight transport and related services, there are special rules,

(a) Intra-EU freight transport is treated as supplied in the EU country where the transportation begins.
(b) Ancillary freight transport services are treated as made where they are physically performed.
(c) Intermediary services of arranging intra-EU freight transport (or any activity intended to facilitate the making of such a supply) are treated as supplied where the transportation begins.
(d) Intermediary services of arranging ancillary freight transport services in connection with intra-EU freight transport (or any activity intended to facilitate the making of such a supply) are treated as supplied in the same EU country where the ancillary transport services are physically performed.

However, where

- a service within (*a*)–(*d*) above is supplied to a customer registered for VAT in an EU country other than the EU country in which the supply would otherwise be treated as taking place, and
- the customer gives a valid VAT registration number to the supplier,

the place of supply is the EU country of the customer. Where the supplier and customer belong in different EU countries, the customer must account for VAT under the reverse charge procedure.

'*Intra-EU freight transport*' means transport which begins in one EU country and ends in another EU country.

[*SI 1992/3121, Arts 2, 10–12, 14*].

See **70.25–70.31 TRANSPORT AND FREIGHT** for further details of freight transport services, ancillary freight transport services and services of intermediaries.

De Voil Indirect Tax Service. See V3.190.

Hire of means of transport

From 1 January 2010

[65.27] The general rule (see **65.15** above) applies to the hire of means of transport other than short-term hire. 'Short-term' means a continuous period of hire not exceeding 90 days (in the case of a vessel) or 30 days (in all other cases). In the case of short-term hire, the place of supply is where the means of transport is actually put at the disposal of the person by whom it is hired. However, this is subject to 'use and enjoyment' provisions, so that

- where the place of supply would otherwise be the UK but the effective use and enjoyment of the means of transport would be in a third country (i.e. a country which is not a Member State), the supply is to be treated as taking place in that country to the extent that it is so used and enjoyed; and
- where the place of supply would otherwise be in a third country but the effective use and enjoyment of the means of transport is in the UK, the supply is to be treated as taking place in the UK to the extent that it is so used and enjoyed.

Table for short-term or long-term hire of means of transport:

When . . .	*if...*
two or more separate contracts for the hire of the same means of transport follow each other with two days or less between them, the term of the first contract needs to be considered in order to decide whether the second term is short-term or long-term.	the two contracts together exceed 30 days (or 90 days for vessels) then the second and subsequent consecutive contracts are treated as long-term hires. If the first contract is genuinely of a short-term hire it will remain so.
there is a second separate contract for short-term hire between the same two parties.	that second separate hire contract relates to a different means of transport or the terms of the hire differ significantly, the contracts will need to be considered separately.
a short-term hire contract is extended.	that extension means that it exceeds the 30 or 90-day period the place of supply is determined by the long-term hire rule, unless it can be satisfactorily demonstrated that the circumstances leading to the events were outside the control of the parties involved.

From 1 January 2013

From 1 January 2013, the place of supply rules in respect of the long-term hire of means of transport are amended (the rules for short-term hire are unaffected). From that date, the place of supply of the long-term hire of a means of transport to a person who is not a relevant business person is in the country where the recipient belongs. However, the long-term hire of a pleasure boat which is put at the disposal of the recipient at the supplier's business establishment, or some other fixed establishment of the supplier, is treated as supplied in the country where the boat is actually put at the disposal of the recipient. This rule is subject to 'use and enjoyment' provisions, so that

- where the place of supply would otherwise be the UK but the effective use and enjoyment of the means of transport would be in a third country (i.e. a country which is not a Member State), the supply is to be treated as taking place in that country to the extent that it is so used and enjoyed; and

- where the place of supply would otherwise be in a third country but the effective use and enjoyment of the means of transport is in the UK, the supply is to be treated as taking place in the UK to the extent that it is so used and enjoyed.

'*Means of transport*' includes ships, boats, yachts, hovercraft, barges or dracones (bulk liquid barges), aircraft, cars, trucks, lorries, motorcycles, cycles, touring caravans and trailers, trailers and semi-trailers, and railway wagons. It does not include freight containers, static caravans, and racing cars where the provision of the car forms part of a supply of sporting services. Mobile cranes are not means of transport (*BPH Equipment Ltd* (VTD 13914) (TVC 62.543)). Provided the goods hired are a means of transport, their actual use is not important (e.g. the provisions apply to the lease of a train to a transport museum or a yacht for use in racing).

'Effective use and enjoyment'

HMRC do not specifically give their interpretation of 'effective use and enjoyment' in the context of the hire of means of transport. See, however, **65.23** above for their interpretation of the phrase in the context of hire of other goods.

[*VATA 1994, Sch 4A paras 3, 13A; FA 2009, Sch 36 paras 11, 17*]. (VAT Notice 741A, paras 7.1, 7.2).

Before 1 January 2010

The place of supply of the letting on hire of any 'means of transport' is where the supplier belongs under the general rule in **65.15** above *except that*

(a) where the supplier belongs in the UK, to the extent that the 'effective use and enjoyment' of the letting on hire takes place outside the EU, the place of supply is outside the UK (and the EU); and

(b) where the supplier belongs outside the EU, to the extent that the effective use and enjoyment of the letting on hire takes place in the UK, the place of supply is in the UK.

[*SI 1992/3121, Arts 17, 18; SI 1997/1524, Arts 3, 4; SI 1998/763*].

Hire of means of transport in the UK from a supplier outside the EU

Where a UK-registered customer hires a means of transport in the circumstances under (*b*) above and the place of supply is in the UK, the reverse charge procedure applies. The UK recipient is required to account for the VAT. See **38.4 INTERNATIONAL SERVICES**. Where the UK customer is not registered for VAT, the overseas supplier must account for any UK VAT and is liable to be registered (subject to the registration threshold).

(VAT Notice 741, paras 13.13, 13.14).

De Voil Indirect Tax Service. See V3.194.

Services of intermediaries

From 1 January 2010

[65.28] Most business to business intermediary services (i.e. the making of arrangements for a supply by or to another person or of any other activity intended to facilitate the making of such a supply) fall under the general rule and are supplied where the customer belongs. However, when supplied to a person who is not a relevant business person, the place of supply is where the underlying service is made. The place of supply of goods is generally where the goods are located when they are supplied, but there are special rules for the following:

- the place of supply of goods imported by **the supplier** is the Member State of importation;
- the place of supply of goods imported by **the customer** is outside the EU;
- the place of supply of installed or assembled goods is where they are installed or assembled.

Intermediary services supplied in the UK

Where the place of supply of an intermediary's arranging service is the UK, but the place of supply of the service being arranged is outside the EU, the intermediary's supply in the UK can be zero-rated. This does not include banking, financial and insurance services which are exempt in the UK.

[*VATA 1994, Sch 4A para 10; FA 2009, Sch 36 para 11*]. (VAT Notice 741A, paras 12.2, 12.5, 12.6).

Before 1 January 2010

Special place of supply rules apply to

- services of estate agents in arranging supplies of land or property (see **65.16** above);
- making arrangements for a supply of intra-EU freight transport or related ancillary services (see **65.26** above); and
- making arrangements for services within *VATA 1994, Sch 5 para 1–8* which are covered by the provisions in **65.21** above.

Subject to the above, the place of supply of the making of arrangements for a supply by or to another person of any goods or services (or of any other activity intended to facilitate the making of such a supply) is the same place where the supply which is being arranged is deemed to take place, *except that* where the intermediary services are supplied to a customer

- registered for VAT in an EU country other than the EU country in which the services would otherwise be treated as supplied, and
- who has given a valid VAT registration number to the supplier

the services are treated as supplied in the EU country where the customer is registered.

[*SI 1992/3121, Arts 13, 14*].

The normal rules must be followed to determine the place of supply of the supply of goods or services which is being arranged. See **65.1** *et seq* above for the place of supply of goods and **65.12** *et seq* above for the place of supply of services.

Accounting for VAT on intermediary services

Whether the supplier of the intermediary services or his customer has to account for VAT, if any, depends upon whether, and if so where, the customer is registered for VAT.

- Where a UK supplier arranges a supply which is made outside the EU, the supply is outside the scope of UK VAT and any other EU VAT. However, the supplier will still be able to recover any input tax incurred in making the supply.
- Where a UK supplier arranges a supply which is made within the EU to a customer who does not give a valid EU VAT number, the supplier is responsible for accounting for the VAT in the EU country where the supply is made. If not already registered there, the supplier may be required to register to account for the VAT.
- Where a UK supplier arranges a supply which is made within the EU to a customer registered for VAT in the UK for the purposes of receiving the supply, the place of supply is the UK. The supplier must charge and account for VAT to HMRC in the normal way. The reverse charge procedure cannot be applied.
- Where a UK supplier arranges a supply which is made within the EU to a customer registered for VAT in another EU country for the purposes of receiving the supply, the place of supply is the customer's country and the customer must account for VAT there under the reverse charge procedure. The customer must provide the supplier with a valid VAT registration number under which the service is received and which the supplier must quote on his VAT invoice.
- Since the place of supply is outside the UK, the supply is outside the scope of UK VAT and the supplier need not charge UK VAT. However, he will still be able to recover any input tax incurred in making the supply.

Intermediary services received by UK customers from overseas suppliers

Where a supplier of intermediary services belongs overseas

- if the recipient of the services is a UK VAT-registered person, the place of supply is the UK and the reverse charge procedure applies with the recipient liable to account for the VAT (see **38.4 INTERNATIONAL SERVICES**); and
- if the UK customer is not registered for UK VAT and the supply is treated as made in the UK, the overseas supplier must account for any UK VAT and is liable to be registered (subject to the registration threshold).

(VAT Notice 741, paras 11.6, 11.7, 11.12, 11.13).

De Voil Indirect Tax Service. See V3.195.

Key points

[65.29] Points to consider are as follows.

- The place of supply rules were significantly changed on 1 January 2010. From this date, the basic rule as far as B2B (business to business) sales are concerned is that the location of the customer determines the place of supply, i.e. no VAT is charged if the customer is based outside the UK. However, there are exceptions to the basic rule.
- An exception to the basic rule is that certain services are still taxed based on where the work is physically carried out – in relation to cultural, artistic, sporting, scientific, educational, entertainment and similar services. The same principle also applies to services involving conferences, exhibitions and meetings.
- However, the rules in the previous paragraph changed on 1 January 2011 (in relation to B2B sales) because the place of supply became where the customer is based in most cases.
- An exception to the place of supply being where the customer is located from 1 January 2011 (in the cases of the 'where performed' services) is in relation to an admission charge to events. The place of supply will be where the event takes place for both B2B and B2C sales.
- The place of supply for land-related services is where the land is based. This applies to direct construction services, e.g. a bricklayer or plumber as well as professional services such as an architect or surveyor.
- An important change introduced on 1 January 2010 is that a VAT-registered business in the UK selling services to business customers outside the UK but within the EU (B2B) will need to complete an EU Sales List (ESL) if the sale does not produce a UK VAT charge.
- The ESL must be completed on a quarterly basis for a business selling services. The deadline is 14 days after the end of the quarter for a paper return and 21 days if it is submitted online.
- In relation to sales made to a UK customer that relate to the hiring of goods (other than transport) telecom, broadcasting or electronic services, the place of supply will be outside the scope of UK VAT if the service is effectively 'used and enjoyed' outside the EU.

66

Supply: Time of Supply

Introduction

[66.1] For EU legislation, see **18.17 EUROPEAN UNION LEGISLATION.**

VAT becomes due on a supply of goods or services at the time of supply. [*VATA 1994, s 1(2)*]. It is therefore necessary to have 'time of supply' rules to determine when a supply is to be treated as taking place for VAT purposes. The resultant time is often referred to as the *tax point* (although this is not a term that is used in the legislation).

VAT must normally be accounted for on the return for the period in which the tax point occurs and at the rate of VAT in force at that time. The normal tax point rules relating to the supply of goods and services are covered in **66.8** and

66.18 below respectively. HMRC have powers, at the request of a taxable person, to alter the time at which his supplies are to be treated as taking place. [*VATA 1994, s 6(10)*]. These are known as accommodation tax points. See **66.7** below.

In addition, HMRC may make regulations with respect to the time at which a supply is to be treated as taking place where

(a) it is a supply of goods or services for a consideration the whole or part of which is determined or payable periodically, or from time to time, or at the end of any period;
(b) it is a supply of goods for a consideration the whole or part of which is determined at the time when the goods are appropriated for any purpose;
(c) there is a supply to which *VATA 1994, s 55* applies (special scheme for gold); or
(d) there is a supply of services under *VATA 1994, Sch 4 para 5(4)* (non-business use of goods) or under a Treasury Order under *VATA 1994, s 5(4)*.

[*VATA 1994, s 6(14)*].

See **66.9–66.17** below for special provisions relating to goods and **66.19–66.26** below for special provisions relating to services.

Although the principal purpose of the time of supply rules is to fix the time for accounting for VAT, the rules have other uses including

- calculating turnover for VAT registration purposes;
- establishing the period to which supplies (including exempt supplies) are to be allocated for partial exemption purposes, and
- establishing when input tax may be deducted.

Exempt supplies

The time of supply for any exempt supply is determined using the normal tax point rules (see **66.8–66.26** below as appropriate) but, as an invoice issued in respect of an exempt supply is not a VAT invoice (see **66.3** below) references to the issue of a VAT invoice have no effect. Thus, for example, in the case of a single supply of exempt services, the time of supply will normally be the earlier of receipt of payment or performance of the service.

Zero-rated supplies

The time of supply for any zero-rated supply is determined using the normal tax point rules (see **66.8–66.26** below as appropriate) but, subject to the special rules for the supply of zero-rated goods in the UK for acquisition by a registered trader in another EU country (see **19.16 EUROPEAN UNION: SINGLE MARKET**), as an invoice issued in respect of a zero-rated supply is not a VAT invoice (see **66.3** below) references to the issue of a VAT invoice has no effect. Thus, for example, the tax point for a zero-rated supply of goods will normally be the earlier of receipt of payment or the removal/making available of those goods.

Change of rate

Where there is a change in the VAT rate or a VAT liability, VAT is chargeable according to the normal tax point rules (see **66.8–66.26** below as appropriate) unless the taxpayer elects for the special change of rate provisions to apply. See **55.10 RATES OF VAT**. For the anti-forestalling legislation that introduced the supplementary VAT charge see **55.4 RATES OF VAT**.

De Voil Indirect Tax Service. See V3.131–143.

Identifying the correct tax point

[66.2] The following is a step-by-step guide to determine the correct tax point.

(1) Does the supply fall within the scope of an accommodation tax point granted to the person making the supply?	See **66.7**
(2) Is the supply covered by an extra-statutory class concession, e.g. coins operated machines?	See **66.25**
(3) If the supply is a supply of goods	
— is it the permanent diversion of goods to private or non-business use?	See **66.9**
— is it an intra-EU supply of goods eligible for zero-rating?	See **66.10**
— is it on a 'sale or return basis' or 'on approval' terms?	See **66.12**
— does it involve land in that it is either (i) in connection with a compulsory purchase where the price has not been agreed; or (ii) a further 'contingency' payment in respect of an earlier supply of the freehold; or (iii) in connection with leasehold land treated as a supply of goods	See **66.13**
— is it the self-supply of goods?	See **66.14**
— does it involve water, gas or any form of power, heat, refrigeration or other cooling, or ventilation?	See **66.15**
— does it involve the supplier's goods being held by the buyer pending agreement of the price?	See **66.16**
— does it come within the special scheme for gold?	See **66.17**
(4) If the supply is a supply of services	
— is it a continuous supply of services?	See **66.19**
— does it give rise to the payment of royalties?	See **66.20**
— does it involve construction services under a contract that provides for stage payments?	See **66.21**
— does it involve 'reverse charge' services?	See **66.22**
— does it involve the temporary use of business goods for private or non-business purposes?	See **66.23**
— does it involve the free supply of services?	See **66.24**
— does it consist of professional services made by a barrister or advocate?	See **66.26**

(5) Does the contract provide for a retention payment?	See **66.6**
(6) Has an 'actual' tax point been created because	
— the supplier received a payment or issued a VAT invoice in respect of the supply before the 'basic' tax point?	See **66.8**(*b*)(i) for goods and **66.18**(*b*)(i) for services
— the supplier has issued a VAT invoice within 14 days after the 'basic' tax point and has not previously elected to forgo the 14-day rule?	See **66.8**(*b*)(ii) for goods and **66.18**(*b*)(ii) for services
— the supplier has been granted an extension of the 14-day rule and has issued a VAT invoice within that time?	See **66.8**(*b*)(ii) for goods and **66.18**(*b*)(ii) for services
(7) Where none of (1)–(6) above apply, the basic tax point applies	See **66.8**(*a*) for goods and **66.18**(*a*) for services

VAT invoices and the creation of tax points

[66.3] A VAT invoice can create an actual tax point under the normal rules both before and after the basic tax point occurs (see **66.8** and **66.18** below for goods and services respectively) and most of the special time of supply regulations also provide for the issue of a VAT invoice to create a tax point. In addition, in certain instances 'period' VAT invoices issued covering payments due over a period of up to one year may create tax points.

In order to establish the creation of a tax point, the following conditions must be satisfied.

(a) The invoice must be a proper VAT invoice which complies with the necessary requirements. See **39.3** *et seq* **INVOICES**. If the invoice does not conform to the requirements, it is not a VAT invoice and cannot create a tax point. See *ABB Power Ltd* (VTD 9373) (TVC 62.414) and *SR Finch* (VTD 10948) (TVC 62.415). This also means that, as a VAT invoice cannot be issued
- in respect of a zero-rated supply (except for intra-EU supplies of goods, see **66.10** below), or
- in respect of an exempt supply, or
- by a non-registered person

invoices issued in such circumstances are disregarded for time of supply purposes.

(b) The VAT invoice must be issued. In *C & E Commrs v Woolfold Motor Co Ltd*, QB [1983] STC 715 (TVC 62.411) it was held that the issue of a VAT invoice required the provision to the customer of that invoice, i.e. the customer must physically receive it. It is not sufficient for it to simply have been prepared in order to create a tax point.

Where an invoice has in fact been issued,

- it is the date of physical issue that determines the tax point. In the case of invoices issued by electronic data interchange (EDI), an invoice is issued when the data is transmitted (provided the recipient is able to receive the data); and
- where a tax point is established, it is not invalidated because the recipient has never 'processed' the invoice, e.g. by disputing it (*Hurley Robinson Partnership* (VTD 750) (TVC 62.135)).

Where the issue of an invoice does create a tax point so that a supply is treated as taking place, it only does so to the extent covered by the invoice. [*SI 1995/2518, Reg 94*]. The issue of an invoice covering part only of a larger supply does not therefore create a tax point for the whole supply.

Period VAT invoices

Special time of supply rules apply to

- leasehold property (see **66.13** below),
- certain supplies of water, fuel and power (see **66.15** below), and
- continuous supplies of services (see **66.19** below)

where the supplier makes use of 'period' VAT invoices. This facility recognises that, without such arrangements, suppliers might otherwise have to issue a large volume of repetitive VAT invoices to the same customer, e.g. leased equipment subject to monthly rental payments. By adopting the period VAT invoicing arrangements, provided the invoice contains the required details in respect of two or more instalments due, the supplier can issue a single document showing all the payments due over a period of up to one year. The tax point then becomes the earlier of the receipt of the payment or the time when the payment falls due.

(HMRC VAT—Time of Supply Manual VATTOS 5210–5220).

Self-billing

[66.4] Under an approved self-billing arrangement it is the customer who prepares the VAT invoice. See **39.6 INVOICES** for further details. For time of supply purposes, not all self-billed VAT invoices can create a tax point as the law refers consistently to an invoice that has been issued by the supplier or in similar terms. A tax point is not normally created, therefore, where the invoice is issued by the customer as in the case of a self-billing arrangement. The one exception to this are self-billed invoices that fall within the scope of the 14-day rule where specific provision is included for self-billed invoices to be treated as if they were issued by the supplier (see **66.8** and **66.18** below for supplies of goods and services respectively). Therefore, a self-billed invoice issued within 14 days of the basic tax point has the same potential to create the tax point for the supply as if it had been issued by the supplier.

In all other circumstances (e.g. where an invoice is issued in advance of the basic tax point or is in respect of a supply covered by one of the special time of supply regulations) a tax point cannot be created by the issue of a self-billed VAT invoice.

Special arrangements for input tax deduction purposes

Because of the above, HMRC have agreed special arrangements that provide the issuer of the self-billed invoice with a notional tax point *for input tax deduction purposes only*. Under this procedure,

- the person issuing the self-billed invoice must
  (a) show, on the original invoice, the date of despatch (but this must not be referred to as the tax point), and
  (b) retain a copy and show on it the day following the date of issue as the notional tax point for input tax purposes; and
- the person receiving the invoice must, *on receipt of the invoice and payment*, add the date of receipt. This becomes the tax point for output tax purposes.

(HMRC VAT—Time of Supply Manual VATTOS 5225, 9130).

Credit notes

[66.5] The time of supply rules do not apply in any way to the issue of credit notes. Similarly, the issue of a credit note has no direct effect on a tax point once it has been established, i.e. it does not cancel or expunge an existing tax point. It normally simply permits the issuer to adjust the VAT previously accounted for in response to an earlier tax point. (HMRC VAT—Time of Supply Manual VATTOS 5230).

Example

Ten computers are sold to a customer and a sales invoice is raised at the time the goods are sold, One of the computers is subsequently returned by the customer two weeks later because it is faulty. In this situation, the original invoice remains unaffected, but a credit note will be issued by the supplier (based on the date the goods are returned) to reduce the output tax originally charged by the supplier. The exception to this situation is if both the supplier and customer are VAT-registered, in which case the credit note does not need to adjust the original charge of VAT.

Receipt of payment and the creation of tax points

[66.6] The receipt of a payment can create an actual tax point before the basic tax point occurs (see **66.8** and **66.18** below for goods and services respectively) and most of the special time of supply regulations also provide for the receipt of a payment to create a tax point. Where the receipt of a payment does create a tax point so that a supply is treated as taking place, it only does so to the extent covered by the payment. [*SI 1995/2518, Reg 94*]. The receipt of a payment covering part only of a larger supply does not therefore create a tax point for the whole supply.

Deposits

Deposits are frequently required either as an indication of good faith on the part of the customer or to put the supplier in funds to cover costs, etc. Depending on the contract, the deposit may be refundable in the event of the contract subsequently being cancelled or may be liable, either wholly or in part, to forfeiture.

Apart from security deposits (see below) a pre-payment or deposit intended by the payer and recipient to eventually form part of the consideration for an identifiable supply normally creates a tax point when received. See, for example, *JD Fox Ltd* (VTD 1012) (TVC 62.440) (deposits for furniture), *Bethway & Moss Ltd* (VTD 2667) (TVC 62.444) (deposits for fitted kitchens) and *C & E Commrs v Richmond Theatre Management Ltd*, QB [1995] STC 257 (TVC 62.434) (advance payments of theatre tickets). This applies even if the deposit is refundable. See, for example, *C & E Commrs v Moonraker's Guest House Ltd*, QB [1992] STC 544 (TVC 62.443) (deposits for holiday accommodation) and *Clowance plc* (VTD 2541) (TVC 62.432) (advance payments for time-share accommodation). For an exception to this general rule where deposits were not held to create tax points, see *Nigel Mansell Sports Co Ltd* (VTD 6116) (TVC 62.452) (initial deposit from prospective customer in order to be placed on the waiting list for a sports car and paid before a firm order was placed for the car) although the facts in this case were unusual.

Security deposits

Deposits taken as security to ensure safe return of goods hired out, and which are refunded when the goods are safely returned or forfeited to compensate for loss or damage, do not normally create a tax point. A payment tax point can be created if, for example, hire charges are later offset against the refund of an amount originally received as a security deposit but only where this happens before the basic tax point, i.e. completion of the hire period.

(HMRC VAT—Time of Supply Manual VATTOS 5120–5135).

Third parties acting as stakeholders

Where a third party acts as a stakeholder (as opposed to an agent of the vendor) and receives a deposit in connection with a supply of property, a time of supply is not created until the money is released to the vendor. (VAT Notice 700, para 14.2). See *Double Shield Window Co Ltd* (VTD 1771) (TVC 62.421).

Payment by cheque

Under banking law, payment can only be said to have occurred when the cheque has been presented and met by the drawer's bank. In the normal course of events it takes five working days for a cheque to complete the clearance cycle. It is common banking practice for a cheque to be credited to the payee's bank account on the date it is paid in and, therefore, unless the cheque was the subject of special clearance procedures, payment for VAT purposes will not strictly occur until the fifth working day following the date of presentation. However, where a trader's normal commercial practice is to use the date a cheque is received as the date of payment for accounting purposes, and provided the cheque is subsequently presented and cleared without undue delay, that date may be used as the payment date for VAT time of supply purposes. In the event of the cheque not being honoured, however, no payment will have occurred and any VAT accounted for on this basis may be adjusted accordingly. Where presentation of a cheque is delayed for any reason, the date of clearance is to be regarded as the date of payment. (HMRC VAT—Time of Supply Manual VATTOS 5145).

Payment by credit card, charge card, etc.

Payment is not strictly received until the sum involved is paid over to the supplier by the card company. However, a trader may be permitted to treat the date of acceptance of the card as the payment tax point where this conforms with normal commercial accounting practice of the business and provided there is no unreasonable delay in processing the transaction. HMRC do not allow this in cases where the card company withholds payment pending satisfactory delivery of goods (which can occur with mail order transactions). (HMRC VAT—Time of Supply Manual VATTOS 5150).

Payment by bank transfer

Whether by standing order, direct debit, home banking facilities or other forms of electronic transfer, the time of payment for VAT purposes occurs when the amount in question is actually transferred into the recipient's bank account. (HMRC VAT—Time of Supply Manual VATTOS 5155).

Payment by set-off

A payment tax point can be created by a book entry or an adjustment to the accounting records (e.g. supplies between group companies may be recorded by offsetting sales and purchases ledger accounts or making entries in the inter-company current accounts). The time of payment is the date on which the appropriate entries are made in the accounting records (*Pentex Oil Ltd* (VTD 7989, VTD 7991) (TVC 43.2)). In order for there to be a payment tax point by book entry, the debt must actually have been settled or expunged. Entries that simply reflect or acknowledge an outstanding debt should not be regarded as evidence of payment for tax point purposes.

Where the value of a continuous supply of services is not agreed until the annual accounts of the business are drawn up, the date the accounts are approved may be taken to represent a payment tax point where they demonstrate that the supplies have been paid for by way of adjustment to each company's accounts.

(HMRC VAT—Time of Supply Manual VATTOS 5160).

Retention payments

Some contracts for the supply of goods or services provide for the retention of part of the consideration pending full and satisfactory performance of the contract (or of any part of it) by the supplier. This is a common feature of construction contracts and contracts for the supply and installation of plant and machinery.

Without special provisions, under the normal rules, the VAT on the retained element of the contract price would fall due at the basic tax point (see **66.8** and **66.18** below for goods and services respectively). However, in these circumstances the tax point for the retentions is delayed until either a VAT invoice is issued, or a payment is received, in respect of the retentions (whichever is the earlier). This only applies to the retained element of the contract price and the rest of the supply is subject to the normal tax point rules. In any case, the provisions do not apply to

- a supply of goods for acquisition by a taxable person in another EU country; and
- construction services under contracts providing for stage or interim payments (see **42.19 LAND AND BUILDINGS: ZERO AND REDUCED RATE SUPPLIES AND DIY HOUSEBUILDERS**).

[*SI 1995/2518, Reg 89; SI 1997/2887, Reg 5; SI 2003/3220, Reg 16*].

Assignment of debts

A receipt of a payment, however expressed, includes a reference to receipt by a person to whom the right to receive it has been assigned. [*SI 1995/2518, Reg 94A; SI 1999/599*]. Where, therefore, a business assigns any of its debts, it must account for VAT on payments received by the person to whom the debts are assigned as if those payments were received by the business itself (rather than accounting for VAT when payments are received from the assignee). See **66.7** below for an accommodation tax point if this causes any problems.

Accommodation tax points

[66.7] HMRC may, at the request of a taxable person, alter the time at which supplies are to be treated as made by him by either advancing or delaying the tax point. [*VATA 1994, s 6(10)*]. These are often referred to as accommodation tax points, the most common of which are considered below.

Monthly invoicing

Many traders invoice for their supplies periodically, typically issuing a single invoice to each customer detailing the supplies made during the preceding monthly or four/five week commercial accounting period. Provided this represents the trader's normal commercial accounting practice, HMRC, on written application, may grant an accommodation tax point without the trader being required to demonstrate that the normal tax point rules cannot be complied with. Applications should state whether the accommodation tax point is to be linked to the last day of the period covered by the invoice or the date of issue of the invoice. In the latter case, this will not normally be permitted to exceed 14 days from the end of the commercial accounting period. (HMRC VAT—Time of Supply Manual VATTOS 6200).

Exempt supplies of credit

Supplies of goods on credit can involve both a taxable supply of goods and an exempt supply of credit. There is also an exempt supply of credit when a loan is made for interest or for some other form of consideration. In either case, particularly with agreements subject to fixed rates of interest, traders can have difficulty in identifying the proportion of the periodical repayment attributable to the supply of credit and the element in respect of either the goods or repayment of the capital amount in the case of a loan of money.

Application may be made to HMRC to use a single accommodation tax point for the supply of the credit provided the time nominated as the tax point is earlier than would otherwise be the case under the normal rules. For example, for supplies of credit in conjunction with a supply of goods, the accommodation tax point might be linked to the tax point for the supply of the goods. For a loan of money, a convenient tax point might be the date of the agreement or any other date before receipt of the first instalment.

Applications should be in writing and signed by a person eligible to sign the trader's VAT returns. In the case of group registrations, the application must be made by the representative member. Other forms of application may be accepted provided they contain the following information.

- The identity of the supplier.
- Details sufficient to identify precisely which supplies are intended to be covered by the direction.
- The event to be treated as the tax point for the supply.

Applications involving different tax points for different categories of exempt supplies of credit are acceptable provided they can be identified without difficulty.

(HMRC VAT—Time of Supply Manual VATTOS 6300).

Corporate purchasing (procurement) cards

Such cards are intended to be used as a method of payment by corporate customers with high levels of low value expenditure (e.g. stationery, spare parts and other expenditure delegated to individual staff members). They are designed to eliminate much of the paperwork in the purchasing process. The practical arrangements are similar to the use of credit cards and charge cards. Under normal circumstances, suppliers do not issue invoices to card-holders, invoicing being carried out on the supplier's behalf by the card company or bank using transaction information transmitted through the purchasing card system. A difficulty arises with such cards as the supplier is unaware of the date on which the card company or bank actually issues the invoice to the purchaser.

Application may be made to HMRC by the supplier for an accommodation tax point. This allows the tax point for all purchase card transactions to be the time at which the supplier keys the transaction details into the purchasing card system (the 'transmission date') provided all transactions are keyed into the system no later than the basic tax point (the date the goods are sent to, or taken away by, the customer). Card issuers have made it a condition of membership that potential suppliers will apply to use the accommodation tax point. (VAT Notice 701/48/02, paras 1.2, 2.1–2.4; HMRC VAT—Time of Supply Manual VATTOS 6410).

Ministry of Defence contractors

There can be considerable delays in agreeing contract prices in the case of supplies made by defence industry contractors to the Ministry of Defence. Where one of the centrally agreed extensions to the 14-day rule is inadequate (see **66.8** and **66.18** below for supplies of goods and services respectively) application may be made for an accommodation tax point if the difficulties are wholly as a result of delays on the part of the MoD.

Applications should be in writing and signed by a person eligible to sign the trader's VAT returns. In the case of group registrations, the application must be made by the representative member. If HMRC agree, in cases where the consideration under an MoD contract is ascertained or ascertainable at or before the time when the goods are removed or the services performed, the supply in question is treated as taking place on the date a VAT invoice is issued or a payment is received, to the extent covered by the invoice or payment, but in any case not later than six years after the goods are removed or the services performed.

(HMRC VAT—Time of Supply Manual VATTOS 6520).

Assigned debts

Where a business assigns any of its debts, it must account for VAT on payments received by the assignee as if those payments were received by the business itself (rather than accounting for VAT when payments are received from the assignee). See **66.6** above. Where the assignee notifies the business of amounts received from the latter's customers, the business should have no difficulty in complying with the normal payment tax point rules. Alternatively, a tax point may have already been created prior to assignment of the debt by the issue of a VAT invoice. However, HMRC recognise that occasions may arise where the assignor may not receive details of any subsequent payments and will therefore be unaware when a payment tax point has occurred. A business affected in this way can, if it wishes, apply to HMRC to bring forward the time of supply to the time of assignment, although this will mean that any VAT outstanding on the amount assigned must be accounted for at that time. (HMRC VAT—Time of Supply Manual VATTOS 6600).

'En primeur' wine

'En primeur' wine is wine that is offered for sale, whilst still lying in the producer's cellars abroad, for delivery in the UK by the wine merchant at some time in the future. Trade practice is normally to require the customer to pay the net price of the wine when submitting an order. Further charges, based on the duty and VAT payable, together with the costs of transportation, etc. become due from the customer at the time of delivery.

At the time the net price is paid, it is not certain that the wine will ever actually be removed to the UK. Even if it is, the wine may be sold by the customer, before taking delivery, while it is still subject to a warehousing regime in the UK. As a result, it has been agreed that if VAT does become due, the supply may be accounted for at the time the customer is invoiced for the VAT and other charges where, in accordance with trade practice, this takes place immediately prior to delivery in the UK.

(HMRC VAT—Time of Supply Manual VATTOS 8600).

Services received by members of the Institute of London Underwriters

All claims on members of the Institute of London Underwriters (ILU) are processed centrally by the ILU. When a claim has been finalised the ILU issues a 'claim closing slip' to the underwriters advising them of their share of the liability arising from the claim and including details of services received from abroad in respect of the claim which have already been paid for on the underwriters behalf. This can be the first notification the underwriter receives in respect of the claim.

As an accommodation tax point, all supplies relating to the provision of marine and aviation insurance which are received by member companies of the ILU from abroad and which are treated as being made by them in the UK by virtue of the reverse charge procedure may be treated as taking place at the end of the day on which the claims closing advice for the related insurance claim is issued by the ILU.

(HMRC VAT—Time of Supply Manual VATTOS 9450).

Standard-rated prescription goods

Businesses that are not retail pharmacists may experience difficulties in accounting for VAT at the correct time on prescription goods liable to VAT at the standard rate (e.g. stoma and continence care products). This is because, each month a supplier is unaware of the value of supplies made against prescriptions (and consequently the VAT due on those products) until PPA Form FP47(A) is received from the Prescription Pricing Authority.

Businesses in this position may apply to HMRC for approval to use the date of receipt of the FP47(A) notification as their tax point. The application should be sent to HMRC, National Advice Service, Written Enquiries Section, Alexander House, Victoria Avenue, Southend, Essex SS99 1B and should be in the following form.

'We request that supplies by [insert company/business name] of NHS prescription goods which are subject to Prescription Pricing Authority remuneration procedures be treated as taking place at the end of the period during which these procedures are undertaken for the goods in question. The end of each such period to be established by the date we receive the relevant form FP47(A) or equivalent documentation. We confirm that the supplies in question are made other than by way of a retail pharmacy.

We further request that on the issue of such a direction, any existing direction will cease to have effect insofar as it might apply to the above mentioned supplies.

[Signed]

[Status of signatory]'

(VAT Information Sheet 11/07).

Time of supply of goods

[66.8] Subject to

- any accommodation tax points agreed under **66.7** above,
- the special cases in **66.9** to **66.17** below,
- any extra-statutory class concession,
- the provisions relating to warehoused goods (see **70 WAREHOUSED GOODS AND FREE ZONES**), and
- the provisions relating to gas and electricity supplies from persons outside the UK (see **25.9 FUEL AND POWER**),

a supply of goods is treated as taking place at the basic or actual tax point.

(a) Basic tax point

The basic tax point is determined as follows.

(i) *If the goods are to be removed*, the basic tax point occurs at the time of removal.
This normally occurs when the goods are delivered by, or on behalf of, the supplier or collected by, or on behalf of, the customer. Where there is more than one supply but only one movement of the goods (e.g. where the goods are supplied via a third party such as a finance company), it is necessary to determine to which of the supplies the removal relates (the remaining supply/supplies falling within (ii) below).
Where a single supply of goods involves delivery/collection over a period of time, provided there is genuinely a single supply (and not a succession of separate supplies) the basic tax point will not occur until the time of removal of the final consignment (although actual tax points under (*b*) below may have been created before that time).

(ii) *If the goods are not to be removed* at the time when they are made available to the customer.
The words 'if the goods are not to be removed' must be viewed in the context of the supply itself and not the nature of the goods involved. The 'made available' basic tax point is therefore not restricted to goods that are incapable of ever being moved. Examples include
   - the supply of fully-assembled and installed goods on site (delivery of the components being merely a preliminary step to enable the supplier to supply what is required under the terms of the contract); and
   - in the normal case of the supply of goods via a third party finance company where the finance company does not take physical delivery of the goods, the supply of the goods to the finance company by the trader.

(b) Actual tax points

(i) *Advance payment or invoicing*. If, before the basic tax point, the supplier issues a VAT invoice or receives payment in respect of the supply, there is a tax point at the time the invoice is issued or payment is received, whichever occurs first, to the extent covered by the invoice or payment. (There will thus always be a further tax point where the amount invoiced or paid is less than the full value of the supply.)

(ii) *The 14-day rule*. If the supplier issues a VAT invoice (or a taxable person issues a document to himself under the self-billing arrangements, see **39.6 INVOICES**) within 14 days *after* the basic tax point, then, unless he has notified HMRC in writing that he does not wish the rule to be applied, the tax point is the date the invoice is issued. This rule does not, however, override (*b*)(i) above.

Example

What is the tax point in the following situations?

Situation 1

Goods removed – 1 April 2010

Payment received – 15 March 2010

Answer – 15 March 2010 – with receipt of advance payment before supply has taken place.

Situation 2

Goods removed – 1 April 2010

Tax invoice raised – 17 April 2010

Payment received – 1 May 2010

Answer – 1 April 2010 – invoice raised more than 14 days after supply has taken place, so tax point becomes date when goods were supplied, i.e. the basic tax point. This assumes the business does not have an agreement with HMRC that allows an extension of the 14-day rule.

Situation 3

Goods removed – 1 May 2010

Tax invoice raised – 1 April 2010

Payment received – 1 June 2010

Answer – 1 April 2010 – raising an invoice or receiving payment in advance of a supply both create actual tax points – the key date is the one that happened first.

Situation 4

Goods removed – 1 June 2010

Tax invoice raised – 10 June 2010

Payment received – 6 June 2010

Answer – 10 June 2010 – an invoice has been raised within 14 days of the supply taking place. The payment of 6 June 2010 would have created an earlier tax point if it had been received in advance of the goods being supplied but not after the supply has taken place.

Extending the 14-day rule under (b)(ii) above

HMRC may, at the request of the taxable person, extend the 14-day rule in respect of all or part of his supplies.

The following extensions to the 14-day rule have been centrally agreed.

(1) *Members of The British Electrical and Allied Manufacturers Association, The Scientific Instruments Manufacturers Association and The Electronic Engineering Association*. If the consideration for a supply of goods made by member companies under a Government contract is not ascertained or ascertainable at or before the time when the goods are removed, the supply may be treated as taking place at the time when the member issues a VAT invoice, provided it is issued within one year of the date of removal of the goods.

(2) *Government contracts*. Where a taxable person supplies goods for an agreed price under a Government contract and the supplier's invoicing is delayed due to Government procedures (e.g. the use of Ministry of Defence Form 640), the supply may be treated as taking place at the time a VAT invoice is issued, provided it is issued within four months of the date of removal of the goods.

(3) *Local authorities*. Where a local authority supplies taxable goods in the course of business activities, the supply may be treated as taking place at the time a VAT invoice is issued, provided it is issued within two months of the date of removal of the goods.

(4) *Scrap metal*. As the consideration for a supply of 'material on valuation' in the scrap metal trade is not ascertained or ascertainable at or before the time when the goods are removed, the supply may be treated as taking place at the time a VAT invoice is issued, provided it is issued within three months of removal of the goods.

(5) *The Society of British Aerospace Companies Ltd* (SBAC). If the consideration for a supply of goods made by member companies of SBAC is not ascertained or ascertainable at or before the time when the goods are removed (because the price is subject to negotiation and agreement after the work has been completed), the supply may be treated as taking place at the time a VAT invoice is issued, provided it is issued within six months of the date of removal of the goods (one year in the case of a Government contract).

(6) *Supplies made between 18 and 30 November 2008*. In order to allow businesses additional time to amend their accounting systems following the temporary reduction in the standard rate from 1 December 2008 to 31 December 2009, the 14-day limit was extended to 30 days where the goods to be invoiced were provided between 18 and 30 November 2008 inclusive.

[*VATA 1994, s 6(1)(2)(4)–(6)(9)(10); FA 1996, Sch 3 para 1*]. (VAT Notice 700, para 14.2; HMRC VAT—Time of Supply Manual VATTOS 5245; HMRC Guidance Note dated 1 December 2008).

Disposal of business assets

[66.9] Where there is a supply of goods on the transfer or disposal of business assets under *VATA 1994, Sch 4 para 5(1)* (see **64.3**(*e*) **SUPPLY: GENERAL**), the supply is treated as taking place when the goods are transferred or disposed of. [*VATA 1994, s 6(12)*]. This includes goods transferred for no consideration (i.e. goods taken out of the business permanently for non-business use). See also **47.7 OUTPUT TAX**.

Intra-EU supplies of goods

[66.10] Supplies to VAT registered persons in other EU countries. Where a supply of goods involves

- the removal of the goods from the UK, and
- their acquisition in another EU country by a person who is liable for VAT on their acquisition under the provisions of that country corresponding to those in **19.3 EUROPEAN UNION: SINGLE MARKET**,

the time of supply is the earlier of the 15th day of the month following that in which the goods are removed or the date of the issue of a VAT invoice (or other prescribed invoice) in respect of the supply.

[*VATA 1994, s 6(7)(8)*].

Supplies to non-VAT registered persons in other EU countries

Such supplies are subject to UK VAT and the tax point is determined under the normal rules in **66.8** above.

Acquisitions of goods by taxable persons in the UK from another EU country

The time of supply (mirroring those above for supplies from the UK to registered persons) is the earlier of the 15th day of the month following that in which the first removal of the goods occurred and the date of the issue of an invoice by the supplier or, with effect from 1 January 2004, the customer under the provisions of the law in the supplier's country corresponding to those relating the VAT invoices for UK supplies. [*VATA 1994, s 12; FA 1996, Sch 3 para 3; SI 1995/2518, Reg 83; SI 2003/3220, Reg 12*].

Hire purchase, credit sales and conditional sales

The supply of the goods

[66.11] If the credit is 'self-financed', there is one supply of the goods by the trader direct to the customer. If a third party finance company is involved, there will normally be two supplies (by the trader to the finance company and by the finance company to the customer). However, this should not automatically be assumed. For example, there is unlikely to be a supply of the goods to the finance company where the finance consists of an unsecured loan.

Supplies of goods on hire purchase, credit sales and conditional sales are treated in the same way as an outright sale where title passes at the outset.

- *The basic tax point* for the supply to the customer is, in most cases, the date of delivery or collection of the goods. Where there are two supplies (see above) this is the supply by the finance company. The basic tax point for the supply by the trader to the finance company normally occurs at the time the goods are made available to the finance company. Unless the agreement indicates otherwise, this may be taken to be the time when the finance agreement comes into force, possibly at the time when the last party signs up to it.
- *A VAT invoice* issued to the customer (whether it is a conventional VAT invoice or the finance agreement adapted for the purpose) creates a tax point for the supply if it is issued in advance of, or within 14 days after, the basic tax point.
- *A deposit* paid before an agreement has come into force, or before the goods have been removed, or a VAT invoice has been issued, also normally creates a tax point.

The supply of the credit element

The tax point for the separate supply of credit is the date of payment of the interest. Where the instalments include an element attributable to the charge for credit this will mean that a tax point occurs each time that a payment is received. See, however, **66.7** above for an accommodation tax point in these circumstances.

(HMRC VAT—Time of Supply Manual VATTOS 9250).

Goods supplied on sale or return and goods on approval

[66.12] The following rules apply to sale or return agreements, i.e. where goods are supplied on terms whereby the customer has a right to return the goods at any point up until the time they are adopted but, in the meantime, ownership of the goods remains with the supplier. Retail supplies on these terms are generally referred to as being 'on approval'.

If goods are sent or taken on approval or sale or return (or similar terms) so that they are removed before it is known whether a supply will take place, the basic tax point is the time when it becomes certain that the supply has taken place ('adoption') or, if sooner, twelve months after the removal. If, however, before this time a supplier issues a VAT invoice in respect of the supply, the tax point for the amount invoiced is the date the invoice is issued. [*VATA 1994, s 6(2)(c)(4)*].

Retail sales by mail order

In *Littlewoods Organisation plc* (VTD 14977) (TVC 62.393) the company sold goods by mail order and a dispute arose with HMRC as to the time of supply of sales when the standard rate of VAT increased from 15% to 17.5%. The tribunal held that supplies were within *VATA 1994, s 6(2)(a)* and were supplied at the time of removal, ruling that *VATA 1994, s 6(2)(c)* above applied to transactions where there was no contract of sale unless and until the person concerned adopted or was deemed to have adopted the transaction, whereas *VATA 1994, s 6(2)(a)* applied to transactions where there was a contract of sale but the buyer had the right to rescind the contract if he wished.

Land and property

[66.13] Land and property are treated as follows:

(1) Freehold land

The supply of freehold land is a supply of goods [*VATA 1994, Sch 4 para 4*] and the normal time of supply rules apply (see **66.8** above) subject to the rules below where the total purchase price cannot be determined at the time of the transfer.

Basic tax point

As land is incapable of removal, the basic tax point is when the land is made available to the purchaser, i.e. the date of the freehold conveyance (in Scotland, the time of delivery of the disposition which is known as the settlement date). If a prospective purchaser is allowed to enter the property in advance of completion (e.g. to carry out preliminary works or testing on the site), this does not advance the basic tax point for the sale of the freehold. See *Cumbernauld Development Corporation v C & E Commrs*, CS [2002] STC 226 (TVC 62.391) where an exchange of land in Scotland between the Corporation and a local golf club was held to take place 'at the time of the exchange of dispositions' and not at the earlier time when the land had been made available to the club.

Actual tax points

The basic tax point is subject to the creation of an actual tax point by the issue of a VAT invoice in advance of, or within 14 days after, the basic tax point or the receipt of a payment in advance of the basic tax point.

It is common for a contract for the sale of the freehold interest in land to require the payment of a deposit by the purchaser at the time contracts are exchanged. If this is payable either direct to the vendor or to a solicitor acting as the vendor's agent, the deposit creates a tax point to the extent of the amount received. If, on the other hand, the deposit is received by a third party (which can be the vendor's solicitor) acting in the capacity of a stakeholder holding the money on behalf of both parties pending satisfactory performance of the contract, the payment does not create a tax point until it is released by the stakeholder to the vendor.

(HMRC VAT—Time of Supply Manual VATTOS 9360–9365).

(2) Freehold property — total purchase price not determinable at the time of supply

Where the freehold in land or a building is sold, any VAT due must generally be accounted for under the above rules. Sometimes, however, the full value of the supply is not known at this time. This would apply, for example, where the vendor is entitled to receive a further payment in the event of the purchaser later obtaining planning permission, or the final consideration is dependent on any profit from future development of the land. In these cases, a special rule allows VAT to be accounted for when the undetermined part of the consideration is received, thus avoiding the need to estimate the final value of the supply at the time of the sale.

Subject to the anti-avoidance rules below, where the total consideration cannot be determined at the time the grantor grants or assigns the freehold interest in any land, the land is treated as separately and successively supplied

- in respect of that part of the consideration which was determinable at the time of the grant or assignment, under the normal tax point rules as described above and in **66.8** above; and
- in respect of any part of the consideration not so determinable, at the earlier of the times whenever any such part is received by the grantor or the grantor issues a VAT invoice in respect of it.

[*SI 1995/2518, Reg 84(2); SI 2002/2918; SI 2003/3220, Reg 13*].

Anti-avoidance rules applying to grants or assignments made after 9 April 2003

The special rule above does not apply in relation to a grant or assignment falling within *VATA 1994, Sch 9 Group 1 Item 1(a)* (sale of new and uncompleted non-qualifying buildings and civil engineering works, see **41.3 LAND AND BUILDINGS: EXEMPT SUPPLIES AND OPTION TO TAX**) where any of the specified persons listed below intend or expect to occupy the land on a date within ten years of the building or civil engineering work on the land being 'completed', without being in occupation of it wholly or substantially wholly (for supplies before 1 June 2008 wholly or mainly) for 'eligible purposes'.

The specified persons are

(a) the grantor;

(b) any person who, with the intention or in the expectation that occupation of the land on a date within ten years of completion of the building or civil engineering work would not be wholly or substantially wholly (for supplies before 1 June 2008 wholly or mainly) for eligible purposes

  (i) 'provides finance' for the 'grantor's development of the land', or

  (ii) has entered into any agreement, arrangement or understanding (whether or not legally enforceable) to provide finance for the grantor's development of the land; and

(c) any person who is connected with any person falling within (*a*) or (*b*) above under *ICTA 1988, s 839*, see **71.19 VALUATION.** A company is not connected with another for these purposes just because both are under the control of the Crown, Minister of the Crown, a government department or a Northern Ireland department.

For these purposes:

(i) '*Completed*' in relation to a building/civil engineering work is when an architect/engineer issues a certificate of practical completion in relation to it or it is fully occupied/used, whichever happens first.

(ii) '*Occupation for eligible purposes*' means one of the following.

- Occupation by a taxable person for the purpose of making supplies which are in the course or furtherance of a business carried on by him and of such a description that he is entitled to credit for any wholly attributable input tax.
- Occupation by a specified body within *VATA 1994, s 33* (see **43.2 LOCAL AUTHORITIES AND PUBLIC BODIES**) to the extent that the body occupies the land other than for business purposes of the body.
- Occupation by a government department.
- For supplies made on or after 1 June 2008, occupation of land by a person in so far as the occupation arises merely by reference to any automatic teller machine of the person which is fixed to the land.

For these purposes,

- for supplies made on or after 1 June 2008, if a person occupying land (i) holds the land in order to put it to use for particular purposes; and (ii) does not occupy it for any other purpose; the person is treated, for so long as these two conditions continue to be met, as occupying the land for the purposes for which the person proposes to use it;
- where occupation is by a person who is not a taxable person but whose supplies are treated for the purposes of *VATA 1994* as made by another person who is a taxable person, those two persons are to be regarded as a single taxable person; and
- a person is taken to be in occupation of any land whether he occupies it alone or together with one or more other persons and whether he occupies all of that land or only part of it.

(iii) '*Providing finance*' is widely defined. It includes directly or indirectly providing funds *either* to meet the whole (or part) of the cost of the grantor's development of the land *or* to discharge the whole (or part) of any liability incurred in raising funds to meet that cost. It also includes directly or indirectly procuring the provision of funds by another person for either of those purposes. The funds may be provided by way of loan, guarantee or other security, consideration for a share issue used to raise the funds or any other transfer of assets or value as a consequence of which the funds are made available.

(iv) '*The grantor's development of the land*' means any acquisition by the grantor of an interest in the land, building or civil engineering work and includes the construction of the building or civil engineering work.

[*SI 1995/2518, Reg 84(3)–(5); SI 2003/1069, Reg 9; SI 2008/1146, Sch 1 para 17; SI 2009/1967, Reg 3*].

See **41.1**(13) **LAND AND BUILDINGS: EXEMPT SUPPLIES AND OPTION TO TAX** for the meaning of '*relevant charitable purpose*' and **41.1**(15) **LAND AND BUILDINGS: EXEMPT SUPPLIES AND OPTION TO TAX** for the meaning of '*relevant residential purpose*'.

[*SI 1995/2518, Reg 84(3)–(9) as inserted by SI 2002/2918 and replaced by SI 2003/1069, Reg 9*].

(3) Long leases and tenancies

Treatment as supply of goods

The supply of a lease or tenancy exceeding 21 years (or Scottish equivalent) is regarded as a major interest in land and is treated as a supply of goods. [*VATA 1994, Sch 4 para 4*].

General time of supply provisions

Subject to the rules below on *advance invoicing* and *anti-avoidance provisions*, if under the grant of such a lease or tenancy the whole or part of the consideration for the grant is payable periodically or from time to time, the goods are treated as separately and successively supplied each time that

- a part of the consideration is received by the supplier; or
- the supplier issues a VAT invoice relating to the grant,

whichever is the earlier. This applies to rent, ground rent and any premium received.

[*SI 1995/2518, Reg 85(1)*].

Advance invoicing

Where, at or about the beginning of any period not exceeding one year, the supplier issues a VAT invoice which, in addition to the normal requirements for a VAT invoice, shows

(a) the dates on which any parts of the consideration are to become due for payment in the period;
(b) the amount payable (excluding VAT) on each such date; and
(c) the rate of VAT in force at the time of issue of the VAT invoice and the amount of VAT chargeable in accordance with that rate on each payment,

the goods are to be treated as separately and successively supplied each time that a payment in respect of the tenancy or lease becomes due or is received, whichever is the earlier. If there is a change in the rate of VAT before any of the due dates for payment under (*a*) above, the invoice ceases to be treated as a VAT invoice in respect of any supplies for which payment is due after the change (and not received before the change).

[*SI 1995/2518, Reg 85(2)(3)*].

Anti-avoidance provisions

The above continuous supply provisions have enabled some suppliers to delay (sometimes indefinitely) the time at which they accounted for VAT. The following anti-avoidance provisions are designed to prevent this by imposing periodic tax points (usually based on twelve-month periods) on specified supplies between connected persons where VAT has not already been accounted for under the above provisions. The provisions apply to supplies of goods, the benefit of which is received after 1 October 2003.

In relation to supplies of goods where

(1) *either* the supplier and the recipient are '*connected persons*' (see **71.19 VALUATION**) *or* both are members of a 'group undertaking' (see *Companies Act 2006, s 1161*) but are not members of the same VAT group (see **27 GROUPS OF COMPANIES**),
(2) the supply is taxable at a positive rate (i.e. the standard or reduced rate), and
(3) the supplier cannot show that the recipient is able to recover *all* the VAT on the supply

then, subject to below, to the extent that the goods in question have been 'provided' and have not already been treated as supplied under any other provisions, they are treated as separately and successively supplied

(i) in the case of supplies the provision of which commenced on or before 1 October 2003, at the end of twelve-month period after that date;
(ii) in the case of supplies the provision of which commenced after 1 October 2003, at the end of the twelve-month period after the supplies commenced; or
(iii) such earlier date falling within the period specified in (i) or (ii) above notified by the supplier to HMRC in writing and agreed by them

and thereafter at the end of each subsequent twelve-month period. For these purposes, goods are provided at the time when, and to the extent that, the recipient receives the benefit of them.

But where the supplier, within six months after the time applicable under (i)–(iii) above, either

- issues a VAT invoice in respect of it, or
- receives a payment in respect of it,

to the extent that the supply has not already been treated as taking place at some other time under any other provisions, the supply is treated as taking place at the time the invoice is issued or the payment is received. Where the supplier intends to issue a VAT invoice, or payment is due, within the six month's period, he should wait for either of those events before accounting for VAT. However, if, for whatever reason, neither of those events has materialised at the end of the six months, the tax point reverts to the annual tax point date as above. (VAT Information Sheet 14/03, para 4.5).

A supplier can exercise a number of options in relation to the provisions by writing to one of HMRC's written enquiry teams (see **29.4 HMRC: ADMINISTRATION**).

- He can request to vary the six-month period if there are genuine commercial reasons for doing so. Full details of why the variation is required should be given. Such a change is subject to approval by HMRC and a supplier should not therefore start using a revised date until it is formally approved.
- He can elect not to be bound by the six-month rule at any time, in which case thereafter he must account for VAT as required at each annual tax point as described above.
- He can, after the start of any annual period established as above, select an earlier alternative period end date in relation to some or all of his supplies. Provided this is approved by HMRC, the date selected

establishes the end of the supplier's current and subsequent twelve-month periods. Written notice should advise HMRC of the alternative date to be adopted and *either* state that this date is to apply to all supplies to which the rules might apply *or* nominate different dates for different categories of supply. In the latter case, supplies must be identified in sufficient detail so as to be distinguishable from one another.

(VAT Information Sheet 14/03, paras 4.3, 4.5).

Where the leasing depends upon one or more other leases (the superior lease or leases), the reference to a supplier in (1) above includes a reference to any lessor of a superior lease.

Where these anti-avoidance provisions apply, the normal time of supply rules for continuous supplies detailed above do not apply to the extent that supplies have been treated as having taken place under the anti-avoidance rules.

[*SI 1995/2518, Reg 94B; SI 2003/2318, Reg 3; SI 2008/954, Art 44; SI 2008/1146, Sch 1 para 18*].

(4) Short-term leases

Supplies of leases not qualifying as long-term leases above are supplies of services and are normally treated as continuous supplies of services within **66.19** below.

(5) Compulsory purchase

In most cases of compulsory purchase, the transfer does not take place until the price has been agreed and the normal time of supply rules apply (see **66.8** above and **66.18** below for supplies of goods and services respectively). However, where, by or under any enactment, an interest in or right over land is compulsorily purchased and the person from whom the land is purchased does not know the amount of the payment he is to receive at the normal time for the supply, a supply is treated as taking place each time he receives any payment for the purchase. [*SI 1995/2518, Reg 84(1)*].

Taxable self-supplies

[66.14] Where goods are treated as self-supplied by an order made under *VATA 1994, s 5(5)*, the supply is treated as taking place when they are appropriated to the use giving rise to the self-supply. [*VATA 1994, s 6(11)*].

Orders under *VATA 1994, s 5(5)* have been made in respect of motor cars (see **45.6 MOTOR CARS**) and stationery (see **62.2 SELF-SUPPLY**).

Supplies of water, gas or any form of power, heat, refrigeration or other cooling, or ventilation

Treatment as supplies of goods

[66.15] The supply of any form of power, heat, refrigeration or (from 1 January 2011) other cooling, or ventilation is a supply of goods. [*VATA 1994, Sch 4 para 3; F(No 3)A 2010, s 20(2)*].

General time of supply provisions

Subject to the following provisions in this paragraph, a supply of

(a) water (other than distilled or deionised water or water of a similar purity and water comprised in any of the excepted items set out in *VATA 1994, Sch 8 Group 1*, see **24.8 FOOD**),
(b) coal gas, water gas, producer gases or similar gases,
(c) petroleum gases, or other gaseous hydrocarbons, in a gaseous state, or
(d) any form of power, heat, refrigeration or other cooling, or ventilation,

is treated as taking place whenever a payment in respect of the supply is received or a VAT invoice is issued by the supplier, whichever is the earlier.

[*SI 1995/2518, Reg 86(1); SI 2010/3022, Reg 3*].

Supplies to other EU countries

Supplies within (*a*)–(*d*) above made to a taxable person in another EU country are treated as taking place on the day of the issue of the VAT invoice in respect of the supply. [*SI 1995/2518, Reg 86(5)*].

Continuous supplies

Subject to the anti-avoidance provisions below, where the whole or part of the consideration for

- a supply under (*a*)–(*c*) above, or
- a supply of power in the form of electricity

is determined or payable periodically or from time to time, the goods are treated as separately and successively supplied each time that a part of the consideration is received or the supplier issues a VAT invoice relating to the supply, whichever is the earlier.

Where such separate and successive supplies are made under an agreement which provides for successive payments and the supplier, at or about the beginning of any period not exceeding one year, issues a VAT invoice which, in addition to the normal requirements for a VAT invoice, shows

- the dates on which payments under the agreement are to become due for payment in the period,
- the amount payable (excluding VAT) on each such date; and
- the rate of VAT in force at the time of issue of the VAT invoice and the amount of VAT chargeable in accordance with that rate on each payment,

the goods are treated as separately and successively supplied each time that a payment in respect of the supply becomes due or is received, whichever is the earlier. If there is a change in the rate of VAT before any of the due dates for payment, the invoice ceases to be treated as a VAT invoice in respect of any supplies for which payments are due after the change (and not received before the change).

[*SI 1995/2518, Reg 86(2)–(4)*].

Anti-avoidance provisions

The above continuous supply provisions have enabled some suppliers to delay (sometimes indefinitely) the time at which they accounted for VAT. The following anti-avoidance provisions are designed to prevent this by imposing periodic tax points (usually based on twelve-month periods) on specified supplies between connected persons where VAT has not already been accounted for under the above provisions. The provisions apply to supplies of goods, the benefit of which is received after 1 October 2003.

In relation to supplies of goods within (*a*)–(*d*) above, where

- *either* the supplier and the recipient are '*connected persons*' (see **71.19 VALUATION**) *or* both are members of a 'group undertaking' (see *Companies Act 2006, s 1161*) but are not members of the same VAT group (see **27 GROUPS OF COMPANIES**),
- the supply is taxable at a positive rate (i.e. the standard or reduced rate), and
- the supplier cannot show that the recipient is able to recover *all* the VAT on the supply

then, subject to below, to the extent that the goods in question have been 'provided' and have not already been treated as supplied under any other provisions, they are treated as separately and successively supplied

(i) in the case of supplies the provision of which commenced on or before 1 October 2003, at the end of twelve-month period after that date;
(ii) in the case of supplies the provision of which commenced after 1 October 2003, at the end of the twelve-month period after the supplies commenced; or
(iii) such earlier date falling within the period specified in (i) or (ii) above notified by the supplier to HMRC in writing and agreed by them

and thereafter at the end of each subsequent twelve-month period. For these purposes, goods are provided at the time when, and to the extent that, the recipient receives the benefit of them.

But where the supplier, within six months after the time applicable under (i)–(iii) above, either

- issues a VAT invoice in respect of it, or
- receives a payment in respect of it,

to the extent that the supply has not already been treated as taking place at some other time under any other provisions, the supply is treated as taking place at the time the invoice is issued or the payment is received. Where the supplier intends to issue a VAT invoice, or payment is due, within the six-month's period, he should wait for either of those events before accounting for VAT. However, if, for whatever reason, neither of those events has materialised at the end of the six months, the tax point reverts to the annual tax point date as above. (VAT Information Sheet 14/03, para 4.5).

A supplier can exercise a number of options in relation to the provisions by writing to one of HMRC's written enquiry teams (see **29.4 HMRC: ADMINISTRATION**).

- He can request to vary the six-month period if there are genuine commercial reasons for doing so. Full details of why the variation is required should be given. Such a change is subject to approval by HMRC and a supplier should not therefore start using a revised date until it is formally approved.
- He can elect not to be bound by the six-month rule at any time, in which case thereafter he must account for VAT as required at each annual tax point as described above.
- He can, after the start of any annual period established as above, select an earlier alternative period end date in relation to some or all of his supplies. Provided this is approved by HMRC, the date selected establishes the end of the supplier's current and subsequent twelve-month periods. Written notice should advise HMRC of the alternative date to be adopted and *either* state that this date is to apply to all supplies to which the rules might apply *or* nominate different dates for different categories of supply. In the latter case, supplies must be identified in sufficient detail so as to be distinguishable from one another.

Where these anti-avoidance provisions apply, the normal time of supply rules for continuous supplies detailed above do not apply to the extent that supplies have been treated as having taken place under the anti-avoidance rules.

[*SI 1995/2518, Reg 94B; SI 2003/2318, Reg 3; SI 2008/954, Art 44; SI 2008/1146, Sch 1 para 18*]. (VAT Information Sheet 14/03, paras 4.3, 4.5).

Supplier's goods in possession of buyer

[66.16] Subject to below, where goods are supplied under an agreement where

- the supplier retains the property in the goods until all or part are appropriated under the agreement by the buyer, and
- the whole or part of the consideration is determined at that time,

the tax point is the earliest of

(a) the date of such appropriation by the buyer;
(b) the date when a VAT invoice is issued by the supplier; or
(c) the date when a payment is received by the supplier.

If, within 14 days after the appropriation under (*a*) above, the supplier issues a VAT invoice in respect of goods appropriated or, with effect from 1 January 2004, a self-billed invoice is issued by the customer (see **39.6 INVOICES**), then, unless he has notified HMRC in writing that he does not wish the 14-day rule to apply, the tax point is the time that invoice is issued. This does not, however, override (*b*) or (*c*) above if earlier.

The above provisions do not apply to

- goods on sale or return (for which see **66.12** above); or
- supplier's goods in the possession of the buyer where the goods are supplied to somebody liable to account for acquisition VAT on the supply in another EU country.

[*SI 1995/2518, Reg 88*].

Gold

[66.17] *VATA 1994, s 55* provides a special accounting and payment system for supplies of gold. *VATA 1994, s 55(4)* disapplies all tax point rules apart from the basic tax point in **66.8** above and the sale or return provisions in **66.12** above. This means that the tax point for supplies covered by the scheme will normally be the date of removal of the goods. See **26.9 GOLD AND PRECIOUS METALS** for further details of the scheme.

Time of supply of services

[66.18] Subject to

- any accommodation tax points agreed under **66.7** above,
- any extra-statutory class concession, and
- the special cases in **66.19** to **66.26** below,

a supply of services is treated as taking place at the basic or actual tax point.

(a) Basic tax point

The basic tax point for services is the time when the services are performed. This is normally taken as the date when all the work except any outstanding invoicing has been completed.

(b) Actual tax points

(i) *Advance payment or invoicing*. If, before the basic tax point, the supplier issues a VAT invoice or receives payment in respect of the supply, there is tax point at the time the invoice is issued or payment is received, whichever occurs first, to the extent covered by the invoice or payment. (There will thus always be a further tax point where the amount invoiced or paid is less than the full value of the supply.)

(ii) *The 14-day rule*. If the supplier issues a VAT invoice (or a taxable person issues a document to himself under the self-billing arrangements, see **39.6 INVOICES**) within 14 days *after* the basic tax point, then, unless he has notified HMRC in writing that he does not wish the rule to be applied, the tax point is the date the invoice is issued. This rule does not, however, override (*b*)(i) above.

Extending the 14-day rule under (b)(ii) above

HMRC may, at the request of the taxable person, extend the 14-day rule in respect of all or part of his supplies.

The following extensions to the 14-day rule have been centrally agreed.

(1) *Members of The British Electrical and Allied Manufacturers Association, The Scientific Instruments Manufacturers Association and The Electronic Engineering Association*. If the consideration for a supply of services made by member companies under a Government contract is not ascertained or ascertainable at or before the time when the services are performed, the supply may be treated as taking place at the time when the member issues a VAT invoice, provided it is issued within one year of the date of performance of the services.

(2) *Government contracts*. Where a taxable person supplies services for an agreed price under a Government contract and the supplier's invoicing is delayed due to Government procedures (e.g. the use of Ministry of Defence Form 640) the supply may be treated as taking place at the time a VAT invoice is issued, provided it is issued within four months of the date of performance of the services.

(3) *Local authorities*. Where a local authority supplies taxable services in the course of business activities, the supply may be treated as taking place at the time a VAT invoice is issued, provided it is issued within two months of the date of performance of the services.

(4) *Patent agents*. If the consideration for a supply of services by a patent agent is not ascertained or ascertainable at or before the time when the services are performed, the supply may be treated as taking place at the time a VAT invoice is issued, provided it is issued within three months of the date of performance of the service.

(5) *The Society of British Aerospace Companies Ltd* (SBAC). If the consideration for a supply of services made by member companies of SBAC is not ascertained or ascertainable at or before the time when the services are performed (because the price is subject to negotiation and agreement after the work has been completed), the supply may be treated as taking place at the time a VAT invoice is issued, provided it is issued within six months of the date of performance of the services (one year in the case of a Government contract).

(6) *Solicitors*. If the consideration for a supply of services by a solicitor is not ascertained or ascertainable at or before the time when the services are performed, the supply may be treated as taking place at the time a VAT invoice is issued, provided that it is issued within three months of the date of performance of the services.

(7) *Supplies made between 18 and 30 November 2008*. In order to allow businesses additional time to amend their accounting systems following the temporary reduction in the standard rate from 1 December 2008 to 31 December 2009, the 14-day limit was extended to 30 days where the services to be invoiced were provided between 18 and 30 November 2008 inclusive.

[*VATA 1994, s 6(3)–(6)(10), Sch 11 para 2B(4); FA 2002, s 24*]. (VAT Notice 700, para 14.2; HMRC VAT—Time of Supply Manual VATTOS 5245; HMRC Guidance Note dated 1 December 2008).

Continuous supplies of services

Normal rules

[66.19] Subject to

- the provisions below on *advance invoicing* and *anti-avoidance provisions*, and
- special provisions applying in the construction industry (see **66.21** below)

where services are supplied for any period for a consideration the whole or part of which is determined or payable periodically or from time to time, the services are treated as separately and successively supplied each time payment is received or a VAT invoice relating to the supply is issued by the supplier, whichever is the earlier. [*SI 1995/2518, Reg 90(1); SI 1997/2887, Reg 2*].

In *B J Rice & Associates v C & E Commrs*, CA [1996] STC 581 (TVC 62.456) professional services were supplied and invoiced before registration but not paid for until after registration. The tribunal and High Court both held that, as an invoice raised before registration could not be a VAT invoice, the time of supply could only be the date payment was received and therefore VAT was due on the supply. The Court of Appeal, by a majority decision, reversed this decision holding that the provisions as to time of supply determine when, but not whether, VAT is to be charged. Liability is determined under *VATA 1994, s 4* which, *inter alia*, provides that VAT is charged where the supply is made by a taxable person. In this case, the supply was made at a time when the appellant was not a taxable person. See also *C & E Commrs v British Telecommunications plc*, CA [1996] STC 818 (TVC 62.457) for a consideration of the time of supply where customers unintentionally make overpayments. For a payment to represent consideration for a supply of services, there must be a direct link with the service provided. The inadvertent overpayment of a current debt is not a payment on account of a future liability and the recipient is under an immediate obligation to repay it.

Advance invoicing

Where separate and successive supplies of services are made under an agreement which provides for successive payments and, at or about the beginning of any period not exceeding one year, the supplier issues a VAT invoice which, in addition to the normal requirements for a VAT invoice shows

(a) the dates on which payments under the agreement are to become due in the period;
(b) the amount payable (excluding VAT) on each such date; and
(c) the rate of VAT in force at the time of issue of the VAT invoice and the amount of VAT chargeable in accordance with that rate on each payment,

services are to be treated as separately and successively supplied each time that a payment in respect of them becomes due or is received, whichever is the earlier. If there is a change in the rate of VAT before any of the due dates for payment under (*a*) above, the invoice ceases to be treated as a VAT invoice in respect of any supplies for which payment is due after the change.

[*SI 1995/2518, Reg 90(2)(3)*].

The customer must not reclaim, as input tax, any VAT shown on the VAT invoice until the date on which the payment is due or until payment has been received by the supplier, whichever happens first. (VAT Notice 700, para 14.3). See also *The Simkins Partnership* (VTD 9705) (TVC 52.96).

Anti-avoidance provisions

The above continuous supply provisions have enabled some suppliers to delay (sometimes indefinitely) the time at which they accounted for VAT. The following anti-avoidance provisions are designed to prevent this by imposing periodic tax points (usually based on twelve-month periods) on specified supplies between connected persons where VAT has not already been accounted for under the above provisions. The provisions apply to supplies of services, the benefit of which is received after 1 October 2003.

In relation to supplies of continuous supplies of services where

(1) *either* the supplier and the recipient are '*connected persons*' (see **71.19 VALUATION**) *or* both are members of a 'group undertaking' (see *Companies Act 2006, s 1161*) but are not members of the same VAT group (see **27 GROUPS OF COMPANIES**),
(2) the supply is taxable at a positive rate (i.e. the standard or reduced rate), and
(3) the supplier cannot show that the recipient is able to recover *all* the VAT on the supply

then, subject to below, to the extent that the services in question have been 'provided' and have not already been treated as supplied under any other provisions, they are treated as separately and successively supplied

(i) in the case of supplies the provision of which commenced on or before 1 October 2003, at the end of twelve-month period after that date;
(ii) in the case of supplies the provision of which commenced after 1 October 2003, at the end of the twelve-month period after the supplies commenced; or
(iii) such earlier date falling within the period specified in (i) or (ii) above notified by the supplier to HMRC in writing and agreed by them

and thereafter at the end of each subsequent twelve-month period. For these purposes, services are provided at the time when, and to the extent that, the recipient receives the benefit of them.

But where the supplier, within six months after the time applicable under (i)–(iii) above, either

- issues a VAT invoice in respect of it, or

- receives a payment in respect of it,

to the extent that the supply has not already been treated as taking place at some other time under any other provisions, the supply is treated as taking place at the time the invoice is issued or the payment is received. Where the supplier intends to issue a VAT invoice, or payment is due, within the six-month's period, he should wait for either of those events before accounting for VAT. However, if, for whatever reason, neither of those events has materialised at the end of the six months, the tax point reverts to the annual tax point date as above. (VAT Information Sheet 14/03, para 4.5).

A supplier can exercise a number of options in relation to the provisions by writing to one of HMRC's written enquiry teams (see **29.4 HMRC: ADMINISTRATION**).

- He can request to vary the six-month period if there are genuine commercial reasons for doing so. Full details of why the variation is required should be given. Such a change is subject to approval by HMRC and a supplier should not therefore start using a revised date until it is formally approved.
- He can elect not to be bound by the six-month rule at any time, in which case thereafter he must account for VAT as required at each annual tax point as described above.
- He can, after the start of any annual period established as above, select an earlier alternative period end date in relation to some or all of his supplies. Provided this is approved by HMRC, the date selected establishes the end of the supplier's current and subsequent twelve-month periods. Written notice should advise HMRC of the alternative date to be adopted and *either* state that this date is to apply to all supplies to which the rules might apply *or* nominate different dates for different categories of supply. In the latter case, supplies must be identified in sufficient detail so as to be distinguishable from one another.

(VAT Information Sheet 14/03, paras 4.3, 4.5).

Where the supply in question is one of letting, hiring or rental of assets however described, and that letting, etc depends upon one or more other leases of those assets (the superior lease or leases), the reference to a supplier in (1) above includes a reference to any lessor of a superior lease.

Where these anti-avoidance provisions apply, the normal time of supply rules for continuous supplies detailed above do not apply to the extent that supplies have been treated as having taken place under the anti-avoidance rules.

[*SI 1995/2518, Reg 94B; SI 2003/2318, Reg 3; SI 2008/954, Art 44; SI 2008/1146, Sch 1 para 18*].

Royalties and similar payments

[66.20] The granting, assignment or surrender of the whole or part of any right is a supply of services. This can take various forms.

Licences

A licence is a supply of rights that specifically permits the licensee to do something in connection with a copyright or patent held by the licensor. It is may be issued for a set period (with or without option to renew) or for the life of the copyright or patent.

Where a licence is issued for a single payment, the supply is a single supply of services and the basic tax point occurs when the licence is granted. Where the licence agreement provides for payments to be made periodically, or from time to time, the service may be treated as a continuous supply within **66.19** above, VAT becoming due every time a payment is received or a VAT invoice is issued by the licensor, whichever is the earlier.

(HMRC VAT—Time of Supply Manual VATTOS 9500).

Permanent assignments

Alternatively, a supply can take the form of a permanent, outright assignment or surrender of the rights. This is normally a single supply of services to which the normal tax point rules apply. The basic tax point occurs at the time the rights are assigned.

Special provisions, however, apply if the contract provides for the assignor to receive periodic payments of royalties, repeat fees, etc. where some or all of the consideration is dependent on future events (e.g. the level of subsequent sales or repeat broadcasts).

Where the whole amount of the consideration for the supply of services was not ascertainable at the time when the services were performed and subsequently the use of the benefit of those services by a person other than the supplier gives rise to any payment of consideration for that supply which is

- in whole or in part determined or payable periodically or from time to time or at the end of any period,
- additional to the amount, if any, already payable for the supply, and
- not a payment to which the rules relating to continuous supplies of services under **66.19** above apply,

a further supply is treated as taking place each time a payment in respect of the use of the benefit of those services is received, or a VAT invoice is issued, by the supplier, whichever is the earlier.

[*SI 1995/2518, Reg 91*]. (HMRC VAT—Time of Supply Manual VATTOS 9500).

Supplies in the construction industry

[66.21] The tax point for supplies in the construction industry depend upon the terms of payment under the contract for the supply.

(a) Where the contract provides for periodic payments to the supplier (often referred to as stage payments or interim payments) a tax point arises at the earliest of the following dates.

(i) The date a payment is received from the supplier.
(ii) The date the supplier issues a VAT invoice.
(iii) For construction services where, broadly, the building in question is occupied by a person who cannot recover VAT and the construction contractor is connected with the occupier or has been financed by the occupier to carry out the construction work, the day on which the services are performed.

[*SI 1995/2518, Reg 93; SI 1997/2887, Reg 5; SI 1999/1374*].

(b) Single payment contracts (even if payment of part of the price is to be delayed under a retention clause) are subject to the normal tax point rules (see **66.18** above).

See **42.19 LAND AND BUILDINGS: ZERO AND REDUCED RATE SUPPLIES AND DIY HOUSEBUILDERS** for fuller details.

Retention payments

Where a contract within (*b*) above includes a retention clause, the tax point of the retained element is the earlier of the time when a payment is received in respect of the retention and the date the supplier issues an invoice relating to it. See **66.6** above and **42.19 LAND AND BUILDINGS: ZERO AND REDUCED RATE SUPPLIES AND DIY HOUSEBUILDERS** for further details.

Services from outside the UK

[66.22] Before 1 January 2010 services which were treated as made by a person under *VATA 1994, s 8(1)* (reverse charge on services received from abroad, see **38.4 INTERNATIONAL SERVICES**) were treated as being supplied when the supplies were paid for or, if the consideration was not in money, on the last day of the VAT period in which the services were performed.

From 1 January 2010 *Directive 2008/117/EC* changed the time of supply of such services so that it is the earlier of when the service is completed or when payment is made. For continuous supplies of services, the time of supply will be linked to the end of each billing or payment period, but where no invoice or other accounting document is issued or payment made during the year, the time of supply will be the end of each calendar year. (HMRC Brief 2/09).

[*SI 1995/2518, Reg 82; SI 2009/3241, Reg 10*].

See **66.7** above for an accommodation tax point for members of the Institute of London Underwriters.

Goods used for private or non-business use

[66.23] Where business assets are put to any private use or are used (or made available to any person for use) for non-business purposes, a supply of services is treated as taking place under *VATA 1994, Sch 4 para 5(4)* (see **47.7 OUTPUT TAX**). The tax point for this supply of services is when the goods are appropriated to that private or non-business use [*VATA 1994, s 6(13)*]. If the services are supplied for any period, the tax point is the last day of the supplier's VAT period (or of each such VAT period) in which the goods are made available or used. [*SI 1995/2518, Reg 81(1)*].

Free supplies of services

[66.24] Where services specified in any Order made by the Treasury under *VATA 1994, s 5(4)* are supplied for any period, they are to be treated as supplied on the last day of the supplier's VAT period, or of each such VAT period, in which the services are performed. [*SI 1995/2518, Reg 81(2)*].

The only order made under these provision is the *VAT (Supply of Service) Order 1993 (SI 1993/1507)*. This covers certain services, originally acquired for business purposes, which are subsequently put to private or non-business use. See **47.7 OUTPUT TAX.**

Supplies through coin-operated machines

[66.25] Under the normal time of supply rules, the tax point for supplies made via coin-operated machines (e.g. vending machines, amusement machines and gaming machines) is the time the machine is used (or, more strictly, the time money is inserted). However, as an accounting convenience, operators may delay accounting for VAT until the takings are removed from a machine. (VAT Notice 48, ESC 3.6).

For all other purposes, the normal tax point rules apply. Therefore in the event of

- a theft of takings from a machine, VAT must still be accounted for in full on any supplies that have been made from the machine (see *Townville (Wheldale) Miners Sports and Recreation Club and Institute* (VTD 719) (TVC 62.374) where coins fraudulently extracted were subject to VAT); and
- a change in the rate of VAT, operators must revert to the normal tax point rules for the purposes of determining the VAT rates to be applied where takings removed from machines cover supplies made both before and after the rate changed (see *Glasgow Vending Services* (VTD 943) (TVC 62.383)).

Barristers and solicitors

[66.26] Barristers and solicitors are treated as follows:

(1) **Barristers**

Services supplied by a barrister (in Scotland, an advocate), acting in that capacity, are treated as taking place at whichever is the earliest of the following times.

(a) When the fee in respect of those services is received.
(b) When the barrister issues a VAT invoice in respect of them.
(c) The day when the barrister ceases to practise as such.

[*SI 1995/2518, Reg 92*].

These special rules were introduced because a barrister cannot sue for unpaid fees and frequently can have to wait a considerable period of time before outstanding fees are received from instructing solicitors. For most supplies by practising barristers, the tax point will be the receipt of payment under (*a*) above as the fee notes issued to solicitors normally do not become VAT invoices until they are receipted and returned to the solicitor following payment.

These rules make VAT chargeable on all outstanding fees at the time of ceasing to practice. See below, however, for a special scheme allowing a barrister to defer payment of VAT on such fees until payment is received or a VAT invoice issued in respect of them.

Ceasing to practice

Action required depends upon whether the barrister makes other taxable supplies.

- *A barrister who makes no other taxable supplies* must deregister and notify HMRC within 30 days of ceasing to practice. This should be done on Form VAT 7. If the barrister has outstanding professional fees, he should send a letter with the deregistration application stating whether he intends to pay the VAT due on outstanding fees immediately or wishes to defer payment (see below). If deferral is approved, the barrister must still pay VAT due on fees already received, or shown on VAT invoices raised, up to the date of deregistration.
- *A barrister who continues to make other taxable supplies but can show that their value will not exceed the deregistration limit in the next twelve months* (see **59.8 REGISTRATION**) may ask HMRC to cancel his registration by completing Form VAT 7. HMRC will then send a final VAT return on which the barrister must include VAT on all professional fees received, and other supplies made, between the end of the last full VAT period and the date of cancellation of registration. If he wishes to defer payment of VAT on outstanding fees (see below), he must apply to HMRC.
- *A barrister who continues to make other taxable supplies and to be registered* must include, in his VAT return for the period in which he ceased to practice, VAT on all fees received, and other supplies made, during the period. If he wishes to defer payment of VAT on outstanding fees (see below), he must apply to HMRC. VAT on other taxable supplies must be accounted for on subsequent VAT returns in the normal way and is not affected by the special procedure. VAT on professional fees outstanding at the time of ceasing to practise should be excluded from subsequent VAT returns and paid separately with Form VAT 812 (see below).

A barrister may continue to issue VAT invoices for fees which are outstanding after registration has been cancelled but

- the services must have been supplied before the date registration is cancelled;
- the tax point to be shown on the invoice is the date of ceasing to practice; and
- the rate of VAT charged must be the rate in force at that time (and not any different rate applying at the time the invoice is raised).

Deferring payment of VAT on fees outstanding on ceasing to practice

HMRC send a Form VAT 811 to a barrister who asks for deferment. On the form the barrister must list every standard-rated fee which is outstanding (or give an estimate), together with the name of the relevant case, the professional client and the date of the first fee note. The completed form should be sent to VAT Central Unit, GABS, 7th Floor SW, Alexander House, Victoria Avenue, Southend-on-Sea, SS99 1AU. A certified copy of the completed form will be returned when deferment is approved.

A copy of Form VAT 812 is then sent quarterly on which the barrister must declare VAT due on any fees received, or for which a VAT invoice has been issued, during the period specified on the form. The name of the relevant case must be shown together with enough details to cross-reference the fee to the completed Form VAT 811. Form VAT 812 must also show fees for any services which were expected to be zero-rated when the Form VAT 811 was completed but which turn out to be standard-rated.

After the first year, HMRC offer the option of completing Form VAT 812 on a six-monthly basis.

When all outstanding fees have been received and the VAT due paid, the barrister must make a declaration of final payment on Form VAT 812 (with an explanation for any items shown on Form VAT 811 on which VAT has not been paid, eg because the fee has not been collected). Records must be kept for inspection for one year after the declaration of final payment.

Practising barristers who die

The deceased barrister's clerk should notify HMRC as soon as possible and the personal representatives should, within ten days of the grant of probate or order for administration, inform HMRC whether they wish to pay VAT on the barrister's outstanding professional fees straight away or to defer payment. If they choose to defer payment, the personal representatives must use the special deferment scheme outlined above. The personal representatives must give an address to which further communications should be sent and sign an adapted VAT deferment application form.

Barristers who are partly exempt for VAT purposes

Where a barrister has made exempt supplies since the beginning of the VAT year in which he ceased to practise and applies for deferment of VAT on outstanding fees, it may be necessary in due course to make a special adjustment of the input tax reclaimed. Advice should be obtained from HMRC.

(VAT Notice 700/44/07).

De Voil Indirect Tax Service. See V5.145.

(2) Solicitors

There are no special tax point rules for supplies made by a solicitor and, with the exception of the centrally agreed extension to the 14-day rule (see below), they are subject to the normal time of supply rules that apply to services.

Basic tax point

Most supplies by a solicitor are single supplies, even though the supply may involve work undertaken over an extended period of time (e.g. litigation). The basic tax point occurs when the services have been fully completed.

Where a solicitor makes supplies on a regular basis to an individual client, in most cases this represents a series of separate supplies, each of which is subject to its own basic tax point. If the solicitor bills the client periodically for all work performed or completed during the period, the basic tax point rule should be complied with for each of the separate supplies. Only in exceptional circumstances will this kind of relationship represent a continuous supply of services (e.g. where a solicitor is retained as the permanent legal adviser or to act as the client's legal office). However, some legal work is inherently continuous in nature (e.g. the supply of the services of a solicitor acting as a trustee) and such supplies normally fall within the time of supply rules for continuous supplies (see **66.19** above).

Client accounts, etc.

The receipt of a payment into a client's account does not represent receipt of payment for VAT purposes, which only occurs when money is transferred from the client's account to the general office account. This does not, however, apply to the receipt of standard monthly payments for Legal Aid contracting work (see below).

Disbursements

A tax point is not created by the receipt of payments from clients in respect of expenses such as stamp duty and Land Registry fees that are accepted as disbursements for VAT purposes (see **3.7 AGENTS**).

Standard monthly payments for Legal Aid contracting work

Solicitors undertaking work under what is known as the contracting arrangements receive a standard monthly payment (SMP) based on the anticipated level of this work over the forthcoming year. As individual cases are completed the fees, disbursements and VAT are 'billed' and allocated by the solicitor to the SMPs. This means that, depending on the progress of individual cases, the total amounts received from the Legal Services Commission may, at any given time, exceed the value of cases completed or there may be a shortfall.

HMRC have agreed with the Law Society that the normal tax point rules will apply to Legal Aid contracting work. As a result, unless the cash accounting scheme is used, VAT on completed cases must be accounted for at the basic tax point (the date when the supply of services is completed). VAT is due on the SMP received to the extent that it represents advance payment for cases that have not yet started or cases that have started but have not yet been completed.

In the following examples, it is assumed that the solicitor has only one case involving SMPs. In practice, an SMP will generally be for more than one client and the work undertaken for those clients is likely to be at various stages of completion. The SMPs will probably cover a combination of work not yet started, work started but not completed and work completed. However, the VAT rules used should be applied whatever the case.

Example 1

A solicitor receives an SMP of £1,175 per month on the first of each month and prepares VAT returns for calendar quarters. A case commences on 1 January and is completed on 15 March. The total fees and disbursements liable to VAT amount to £3,750 plus £656.25 VAT.

At the end of the March VAT quarter, the following tax points will have occurred with VAT to be accounted for on the return as follows.

	£
1 January	175.00
1 February	175.00
1 March	175.00
15 March	131.25
Total	£656.25

VAT due at the time of the next SMP received on 1 April will be £43.75 as £131.25 has already been accounted for on the previous return.

Example 2

A solicitor receives an SMP of £1,175 per month on the first of each month and prepares VAT returns for calendar quarters. A case commences on 1 January and is completed on 15 April. The total fees and disbursements liable to VAT amount to £1,500 plus £262.50 VAT.

At the end of the March VAT quarter, the following tax points will have occurred with VAT to be accounted for on the return as follows:

	£
1 January	175.00
1 February	175.00
1 March	175.00
Total	£525.00

When the case is completed on 15 April, the VAT due on the supply of £262.50 has already been accounted for in full against SMPs received during the previous quarter.

If a solicitor is required to repay some, or all, of an SMP to the Legal Services Commission (e.g. because of a fall in the amount of work undertaken), then the amount refunded ceases to be consideration for a supply. Any VAT previously accounted for on the amount to be refunded may be adjusted accordingly at that time.

HMRC take the view that the VAT treatment of SMPs is the same whether they are paid into the office account or a client account (i.e. they make a distinction between SMPs and payments received from privately paying clients).

Adjustments to solicitor's fees

In certain circumstances, a solicitor's fees can be subject to third party scrutiny and adjustment before acceptance. The circumstances in which this can occur, and the tax point consequences, are as follows.

- *Contentious work (non-Legal Aid)*. If the losing party to a legal action is ordered to pay costs, the solicitor for the successful party prepares a bill which is then either agreed with the solicitor for the loser or referred to the Court for scrutiny under the taxation procedures. In such cases, settling of the costs is part of the solicitor's overall supply to the client. A basic tax point does not, therefore, occur until either the costs have been agreed between the solicitors or the taxation procedure is complete.
- *Non-contentious work (non-Legal Aid)*. A client may ask the Law Society to scrutinise a solicitor's bill to ensure that it is fair and reasonable. The Law Society can then reduce the amount payable by the client. This procedure does not form part of the supply by the solicitor to the client and the basic tax point still occurs when all the work, except the invoicing, is completed. However, if this means that VAT is accounted for in advance of a reduction to the bill, the solicitor may subsequently adjust the amount accounted for (subject to the normal rules regarding credits).
- *Legal Aid (excluding contract work above)*. Although relatively few bills submitted by a solicitor to the Legal Aid authorities are approved unamended, the solicitor's services are supplied to the client named in the Legal Aid Order and any action by the solicitor in connection with submitting and agreeing the amount of the bill does not form part of the supply to the client. The basic tax point occurs when all the work, except the invoicing, has been completed. Apart from the centrally negotiated extension to the 14-day rule (see below) there are no special tax point rules that apply in these circumstances. VAT must be accounted for on the basis of the normal tax point rules and adjusted later in the event of any subsequent reduction in the fee.

Extension of the '14-day' rule

Where the consideration for a supply of services by a solicitor is not ascertained or ascertainable at or before the time when the services are performed, the supply may be treated as taking place at the time when the solicitor issues an invoice in respect of the supply *provided* that the VAT invoice is issued not later than three months after the date of performance of the services. It should be noted that failure to issue a VAT invoice within the three months means that the tax point reverts to the basic tax point (and is not the end of the three-month period). This is particularly important in the case of Legal Aid work. The Legal Aid authorities are not a taxable person and therefore do not require a VAT invoice. Nevertheless, the solicitor must still issue a VAT invoice if the three-month extension is to apply.

(HMRC VAT—Time of Supply Manual VATTOS 8500–8570).

Key points

[66.27] Points to consider are as follows.

- The 'time of supply' (tax point) regulations for cross-border services changed on 1 January 2010. The key date in relation to most services is when it has been completed (usually the invoice date) rather than when payment has been receive from the customer. This is relevant for both ESL entries (for a business selling services) and reverse charge procedures for a business buying services.
- An understanding of the tax point (time of supply) regulations is important to ensure that output tax is charged to a customer at the correct time, and included on the right VAT return.
- As an example, a VAT invoice should be raised within 14 days of a supply of goods or services taking place, in which case the invoice date becomes the tax point (actual tax point). The tax point for invoices raised more than 14 days after a supply of goods or services will revert to the earlier date of when the goods or services in question were supplied (basic tax point).
- The receipt of money or raising an invoice in advance of a supply being made will create a tax point and output tax liability (assuming the goods or services in question are standard-rated or reduced-rated).
- The sale of land and property is classed as a supply of goods, and the normal tax point rules are followed if the supply involves VAT (e.g. the sale of a property with an option to tax election in place).
- A deposit paid by a person or business buying land before the completion of the deal will create a tax point if the money is made available to either the vendor or his agent. Output tax will therefore be due on the deposit based on the payment date if the supply is standard-rated.
- In relation to a continuous supply of services, a tax point is created when either an invoice is raised or payment received, whichever happens first. A request for payment or fee note document does not create a tax point.
- In certain cases, it is common for an annual tax invoice to be raised, showing tax points that coincide with monthly payments to be made by the customer. Output tax is then accounted for by the supplier according to each payment date, and input tax will be reclaimed by the supplier on the same date (assuming it can be reclaimed under the normal rules of VAT).
- If the rate of VAT changes after an annual VAT invoice has been raised, and the rate change is effective from a date within the year in question, then the annual invoice will become invalid from this date, and a revised invoice will need to be issued by the supplier

showing the new rate of VAT. The customer cannot reclaim input tax until this procedure has been carried out.

67

Terminal Markets

Cross-reference. See **26 GOLD AND PRECIOUS METALS.**

Introduction

[67.1] The Treasury have been given wide powers to make provisions for the VAT treatment of dealings on terminal markets and transactions of people ordinarily engaged in such dealings. These include the right to

(a) zero-rate or exempt the supply of any goods or services;
(b) register any bodies representing persons ordinarily engaged in dealings on a terminal market;
(c) disregard such dealings *by* persons represented under (*b*) above in determining liability to **REGISTRATION (59)** for VAT purposes;
(d) disregard such dealings *between* persons represented under (*b*) above for all purposes; and
(e) refund input tax attributable to such dealings on a terminal market.

Different regulations may be made for different terminal markets.

[*VATA 1994, s 50*].

Qualifying markets and market members

[67.2] Regulations have been made under *SI 1973/173 (as amended)* for the zero-rating of certain supplies of goods and services in the course of dealings on specified terminal markets. To qualify, transactions must involve a member of the market which includes any person ordinarily engaged in dealings on the market. The following is a list of terminal markets included in the *Order* together with persons regarded by HMRC as ordinarily engaged in dealing on the markets.

Market	*Persons regarded as market members*
London Metal Exchange	Members entitled to deal in the 'ring' of the London Metal Exchange.

Market	*Persons regarded as market members*
London Rubber Market	For actuals transactions — Class P (producer members), Class A (selling agent and importer members), Class B (broker members) and Class C (dealer members) of the Rubber Trade Association of London. For futures transactions on the London Rubber Terminal Market — floor and associate members of the London Rubber Terminal Market Association.
London Cocoa Terminal Market, London Coffee Terminal Market, London Meat Futures Market, International Petroleum Exchange of London, London Potato Futures Market, London Soya Bean Meal Futures Market, London Sugar Terminal Market, London Vegetable Oil Terminal Market, London Wool Terminal Market	Full and associate members of these markets, provided the sale is registered with the International Commodities Clearing House Ltd or its successor
London Grain Futures Market	Provided the sale is registered in the Clearing House of the Grain and Feed Trade Association Ltd
Liverpool Barley Futures Market	Provided the sale is registered in the Clearing House of the Liverpool Corn Trade Association
London Platinum and Palladium Market	Provided the transaction is only between any full or associate members of the respective market
London Bullion Market	A person is regarded as being a member of this market only if they are a member of the London Bullion Market Association

[*SI 1973/173, Art 2; SI 1975/385; SI 1980/304; SI 1981/338; SI 1981/955; SI 1984/202; SI 1985/1046; SI 1987/806; SI 1997/1836; SI 1999/3117*]. (VAT Notice 701/9/11, para 4).

Zero-rated transactions

[67.3] The transactions which are zero-rated are as follows.

(a) Actual transactions

A sale *by and to* a market member of any goods (other than investment gold) ordinarily dealt with on the market which results in the goods being delivered. In addition, if the market is the

- London Metal Exchange, the sale must be between members entitled to deal in the 'ring';

- London Cocoa Terminal Market, London Coffee Terminal Market, London Meat Futures Market, International Petroleum Exchange of London, London Potato Futures Market, London Soya Bean Meal Futures Market, London Sugar Terminal Market, London Vegetable Oil Terminal Market, or the London Wool Terminal Market, the sale must be registered with the International Commodities Clearing House Ltd;
- London Grain Futures Market, the sale must be registered in the Clearing House of the Grain and Feed Trade Association Ltd; and
- Liverpool Barley Futures Market, the sale must be registered at the Clearing House of the Liverpool Corn Trade Association Ltd.

(b) Futures transactions

A sale *by or to* a market member of any goods (other than investment gold) ordinarily dealt with on the market where, as a result of other dealings on the market, the sale does not lead to a delivery of the goods by the seller to the buyer.

'*Delivery*' is not defined but is regarded by HMRC as taking place when instructions are given for the goods to be physically removed from the warehouse, vault etc. If a futures transaction leads to a delivery of the goods, VAT must be accounted for on the basis of the original contract price.

Transactions between non-members

Any supply of goods between parties who are not listed in **67.2** above under a futures contract, even if it does not lead to physical delivery of the goods, is not zero-rated under these provisions. It will be subject to the normal VAT rules of the main supply (e.g. a futures contract for the supply of potatoes will be zero-rated as potatoes are zero-rated). (VAT Notice 701/9/11, para 3.3).

(c) The grant of an option

The grant *by or to* a market member of a right to acquire any goods (other than investment gold) ordinarily dealt with on the market where either

- the right is exercisable at a date later than that on which it is granted; or
- the sale resulting from the exercise of the right would be a sale falling within (*a*) or (*b*) above.

When an option is exercised, the resulting transaction should be considered under (*a*) or (*b*) above.

(d) Investment gold

A supply of 'investment gold' between members of the London Bullion Market Association. See **26.2 GOLD AND PRECIOUS METALS** for the definition of '*investment gold*'.

A supply of investment gold by

- a member of the London Bullion Market Association to a taxable person who is not a member, or

- such a person to a member

is not zero-rated and is also excluded from the exemption applying to certain transactions in investment gold (see **26.2 GOLD AND PRECIOUS METALS**). As a result, such a supply is standard-rated.

[*SI 1973/173, Arts 3, 4; SI 1975/385; SI 1981/338; SI 1984/202; SI 1999/3117*]. (VAT Notice 701/9/11, para 3.2).

De Voil Indirect Tax Service. See V4.208.

Brokers' or agents' services

[67.4] Supplies of such services by market makers to their principals are zero-rated where the underlying transaction

(a) is zero-rated under **67.3**(*a*)–(*d*) above; or
(b) involves the supply of investment gold by
  - a member of the London Bullion Market Association to a taxable person who is not a member, or
  - such a person to a member.

[*SI 1973/173, Art 3; SI 1999/3117*].

Brokers' services provided by a non-member are not zero-rated even if in relation to a supply of goods zero-rated under the above provisions or under *VATA 1994, Sch 8 Group 1* (relief for food). Where a person introduces business to a broker and receives from that broker a fee or share of the latter's commission or brokerage, that fee, etc. is the consideration for a standard-rated supply of services, unless the person meets the conditions for zero-rating brokers' or agents' services above.

International services

In the opinion of HMRC, brokers' services of arranging transactions in futures and options are financial services within *VATA 1994, Sch 5 para 5*. See, however, *Gardner Lohman Ltd* (VTD 1081) (TVC 62.538) where the tribunal held that the grant of a purchase option to acquire cadmium through the London Metal Exchange was not a financial service within *Sch 5 para 5*. Subject to this, the supply of services within *Sch 5 para 5* is outside the scope of UK VAT where the recipient either belongs in another EU country and uses the supply for business purposes or belongs outside the EU. [*SI 1992/3121, Art 16; SI 1995/3038*].

(VAT Notice 701/9/11, paras 3.3, 3.4).

Accounting

Zero-rated supplies

[67.5] Where a person (whether a market member or not) supplies goods or services zero-rated under the provisions in **67.3**(*a*)–(*d*) above, he is not required to record such transactions for VAT purposes. If he does wish to include such items in a VAT return (e.g. to increase the proportion of input tax recoverable where exempt supplies are also made), he must record *all* of them. [*SI 1995/2518, Reg 33A; SI 1999/3114*]. (VAT Notice 701/9/11, para 3.5).

Standard-rated supplies of investment gold

Certain supplies of investment gold involving members of the London Bullion Market Association are standard-rated (see **67.3**(*d*) above). The provisions of *VATA 1994, s 55(1)–(4)* normally apply to such supplies and the customer must account for VAT on the supply. However, where the non-member who makes or receives the supply is only liable to be registered for VAT under *VATA 1994, Sch 1* or *Sch 3* solely by virtue of that supply or acquisition, the non-member is not required to notify liability for registration and the London Bullion Market Association member must, on the non-member's behalf, keep a record of the transaction and pay the VAT due to HMRC. [*SI 1973/173, Arts 5–7; SI 1999/3117*]. See **26.8 GOLD AND PRECIOUS METALS** for fuller details. The non-member is not required to keep VAT records or submit EU sales statements. [*SI 1995/2518, Reg 33B; SI 1999/3114*].

Agents' services

Where a supply of agents' services is not zero-rated under **67.4** above, VAT must be accounted for on the full amount of commission or brokerage charged before deduction of any part paid to third parties. (VAT Notice 701/9/11, para 3.5).

68

Tour Operators' Margin Scheme

Cross-references. See **32 HOTELS AND HOLIDAY ACCOMMODATION; 70 TRANSPORT AND FREIGHT.**

De Voil Indirect Tax Service. See V3.591–V3.596.

Introduction

[68.1] For EU legislation, see **18.42 EUROPEAN UNION LEGISLATION.**

Under UK legislation, the tour operators' margin scheme ('TOMS') is a special scheme for businesses that buy in and re-sell travel, accommodation and certain other services as principals or undisclosed agents (i.e. that act in their own name). In many cases, it enables VAT to be accounted for on travel supplies without businesses having to register and account for VAT in every EU country in which the services and goods are enjoyed. It does, however, apply to travel services enjoyed within the UK, within the EU but outside the UK, and wholly outside the EU.

Under the scheme:

- VAT cannot be reclaimed on margin scheme supplies bought in for resale (see **68.14** below). VAT on overheads outside the TOMS can be reclaimed in the normal way.
- A UK-based tour operator need only account for VAT on the margin, i.e. the difference between the amount received from customers (including any amounts paid on behalf of customers by third parties) and the amount paid to suppliers. See **68.17** *et seq* below for calculations of margins and output tax.
- There are special rules for determining the place, liability and time of margin scheme supplies (see **68.5** to **68.7** below).
- VAT invoices cannot be issued for margin scheme supplies (see **68.8** below).
- In-house supplies supplied on their own are not subject to the TOMS and are taxed under the normal VAT rules. But a mixture of in-house supplies and bought-in margin scheme supplies must all be accounted for within the TOMS, using the cost-based method or market value method. See **68.10** below.

(VAT Notice 709/5/09, paras 2.1, 2.5, 2.6, 2.13).

The relevant law is in *VATA 1994, s 53* and the *Value Added Tax (Tour Operators) Order 1987 (SI 1987/1806)* as amended. The law gives HMRC certain powers in relation to the scheme, including specifying what goods and services are covered [*SI 1987/1806, Art 3(4)*] and how to work out the value of the supplies [*SI 1987/1806, Art 7*]. To that extent, the provisions in **68.19–68.24** below and certain other provisions as indicated in the text have the force of law.

Who must use the TOMS?

[68.2] The TOMS does not only apply to 'traditional' tour operators. It applies to anyone who is making the type of supplies detailed in **68.3** below, even if this is not their main business activity. For example, it must be used by

- hoteliers who buy in coach passenger transport to collect their guests at the start and end of their stay;
- coach operators who buy in hotel accommodation in order to put together a package; and

- companies that arrange conferences, including providing hotel accommodation for delegates.

(VAT Notice 709/5/09, para 2.2).

The ECJ have confirmed that to make the application of the TOMS depend upon whether a trader was formally classified as a travel agent or tour operator would create distortion of competition. Ancillary travel services which constitute 'a small proportion of the package price compared to accommodation' would not lead to a hotelier falling within the provisions but where, in return for a package price, a hotelier habitually offers his customers travel to the hotel from distant pick-up points in addition to accommodation, such services cannot be treated as purely ancillary. See *TP Madgett & RM Baldwin (t/a Howden Court Hotel) v C & E Commrs, ECJ Cases C–308/96 and C–94/97*, [1998] STC 1189 (TVC 22.487).

Supplies covered by the TOMS

[68.3] Subject to the exclusions in **68.9** below, the TOMS must be used by a person acting as a principal or undisclosed agent for

- 'margin scheme supplies'; and
- 'margin scheme packages' i.e. single transactions which include one or more margin scheme supplies possibly with other types of supplies (e.g. in-house supplies, see **68.10** below).

(VAT Notice 709/5/09, paras 2.3, 2.11).

'*Margin scheme supplies*' are those supplies which are

- bought in for the purpose of the business, and
- supplied for the benefit of a 'traveller' without material alteration or further processing

by a tour operator in an EU country in which he has established his business or has a fixed establishment.

[*SI 1987/1806, Art 3(1)*].

A '*traveller*' is a person, including a business or local authority, who receives supplies of transport and/or accommodation, other than for the purpose of re-supply.

Examples

If meeting the above conditions, the following are always treated as margin scheme supplies.

- Accommodation
- Passenger transport
- Hire of means of transport
- Use of special lounges at airports
- Trips or excursions
- Services of tour guides

Other supplies meeting the above conditions may be treated as margin scheme supplies but only if provided as part of a package with one or more of the supplies listed above. These include

- Catering
- Theatre tickets
- Sports facilities

(VAT Notice 709/5/09, paras 2.9, 2.10).

In a Dutch case, the ECJ ruled that what is now *Directive 2006/112/EC, Arts 306–310* applies to cases where only accommodation is provided, and is not restricted to cases where transport is also provided (*Beheersmaatschappij Van Ginkel Waddinxveen BV & Others v Inspecteur de Omzetbelasting Utrecht, ECJ Case C–163/91*, [1996] STC 825 (TVC 22.485)). A similar decision was reached in *Hotels Abroad Ltd* (VTD 13026) (TVC 63.6). See also *Aer Lingus plc* (VTD 8893) (TVC 63.2) (where vouchers for accommodation or car hire provided to executive class passengers were held not integral or incidental to the supply of air transport and therefore fell within the margin scheme) and *Virgin Atlantic Airways Ltd* (VTD 11096) (TVC 63.7) (where chauffeur-driven car services provided to certain passengers on international flights were held to fall outside the scheme).

In *Finanzamt Heidelberg v IST Internationale Sprach- und Studienreisen GmbH, ECJ Case C-200/04*, [2006] STC 52 (TVC 22.489) the ECJ held that what is now *Directive 2006/112/EC, Arts 306–310* applied to a trader who offered services involving the organisation of language and study trips abroad and which, in consideration of the payment of an all-inclusive sum, provided in its own name to its customers a stay abroad of three to ten months and which bought in services from other taxable persons for that purpose.

Nature of the supply

[68.4] The sale of a package of margin scheme supplies is treated as a single supply for VAT purposes. [*SI 1987/1806, Reg 3(2)*]. The nature of the services is that of putting together the package or organising the travel services. For example, if hotel accommodation and transport is bought in to provide a tour, the single supply of a tour is made, rather than two separate supplies of transport and accommodation. (VAT Notice 709/5/09, para 4.5).

Place of supply

[68.5] The application of the normal place of supply rules are varied so that margin scheme supplies are treated as supplied

- in the EU country in which the tour operator has established his business, or
- if the supply was made from a fixed establishment, in the EU country in which the fixed establishment is situated.

[*SI 1987/1806, Art 5; SI 1992/3125*].

The effect of this is as follows

(a) Where the supplier is established in the UK only, the place of supply is the UK.

(b) Where the supplier has an establishment in more than one country
- if the establishment from which the supplies are made is in the UK, the place of supply is the UK;
- if the establishment from which the supplies are made is in another EU country, the supply is outside the scope of UK VAT (but within the scope in that other EU country); and
- if the establishment from which the supplies are made is outside the EU, the supplies are not margin scheme supplies and the TOMS does not apply. The normal VAT place of supply rules apply. See **65.13 SUPPLY: PLACE OF SUPPLY**. [*SI 1987/1806, Art 3*].

(VAT Notice 709/5/09, para 4.6).

See **65.14 SUPPLY: PLACE OF SUPPLY** for a consideration of the terms 'business establishment' and 'fixed establishment'. See also *C & E Commrs v DFDS A/S, ECJ Case C–260/95*, [1997] STC 384 (TVC 22.492) where a UK subsidiary acted as agent for a Danish company and received commission on package tours sold on its behalf. On the facts, the subsidiary was held to be a fixed establishment.

Where margin scheme supplies are made from an establishment in another EU country, it may be necessary to register for VAT there.

Liability of TOMS supplies

[68.6] Where margin scheme supplies are made in the UK (see **68.5** above) the whole of the margin is

- standard-rated when the supplies and enjoyed in the EU (see **17.2 EUROPEAN UNION: GENERAL** for the VAT territory of the EU); and
- zero-rated when enjoyed outside the EU.

The liability of in-house supplies (see **68.10** below) is not affected by their inclusion in a margin scheme package.

Transport enjoyed inside and outside the EU. HMRC have given the following guidance.

(a) *Journeys without stops*. Where the journey begins or ends outside the EU, it may be treated as wholly enjoyed outside the EU. Temporary stops for 'comfort' or refuelling are not regarded as stops provided passengers cannot break their journey. Return legs should be treated in the same way as outbound journeys unless there is a material difference between the two legs (e.g. a stop).

(b) *Journeys with stops*.

(i) *General.* Where a journey involves travel both inside and outside the EU and a stop takes place in the EU, a fair and reasonable apportionment must be made between the EU and non-EU elements. This could be on the basis of EU/non-EU mileage or the number of nights spent inside/outside the EU.

(ii) *Cruises.* Apportionment on the basis of days in/out of the EU according to the itinerary is acceptable. For this purpose, the days on which the vessel leaves a non-EU port until it arrives at an EU port are regarded as outside the EU and the days on which it leaves an EU port until it reaches a non-EU port are regarded as inside the EU.

(iii) *Connected flights.* A second and/or subsequent flight is not regarded as a separate journey provided that the connection is made, in the case of an international connecting flight, within 24 hours of the scheduled arrival of the first flight and, in the case of a domestic connecting flight, within six hours of that time.

[*VATA 1994, Sch 8 Group 8, Item 12*]. (VAT Notice 709/5/09, paras 4.10–4.13).

Time of supply

[68.7] The normal time of supply rules do not apply to TOMS supplies. Instead, one of the two methods below must be used to work out the tax point for margin scheme supplies and any in-house supplies (see **68.10** below) sold within a margin scheme package. Whichever method is chosen, it must be applied to all such supplies. Written permission from HMRC is needed to change methods but HMRC will only allow a change in exceptional circumstances and not normally during a financial year.

The two methods for working out tax points are as follows.

(a) The earlier of
- the date of departure of the traveller; and
- the first date on which the traveller occupies any accommodation.

(b) The earlier of
- the date of departure of the traveller;
- the first date on which the traveller occupies any accommodation; and
- the date of receipt of any payment by the tour operator (or a travel agent on its behalf) which
  - (i) is a single payment covering the whole selling price; or
  - (ii) exceeds 20% of the selling price; or
  - (iii) exceeds 20% of the selling price where added to payments received to date on which VAT has not already been accounted for.

Cash accounting scheme

In view of the special tax point rules above, the cash accounting scheme cannot be used for margin scheme supplies or for in-house supplies and agency supplies sold as part of a margin scheme package.

[*SI 1987/1806, Art 4*]. (VAT Notice 709/5/09, paras 4.14–4.16).

VAT invoices

[68.8] VAT invoices cannot be raised for supplies accounted for under the TOMS. This is because, at the time of supply, the true amount of VAT due is not known and can only be determined when the year-end calculation is carried out (see **68.19–68.22** below). The absence of a VAT invoice does not usually matter unless the customer is entitled to claim the VAT. In such a case, it may be possible to exclude the supply from the TOMS (see **68.9** below).

With effect from 1 October 2007 changes were made to the VAT invoicing regulations. These only affect TOMS supplies made to business customers. From that date, when a TOMS supply is sold to a business for use in its business (e.g. travel supplies used by its employees) the invoice has to include a reference to indicate that the TOMS has been applied. It is suggested that the reference either refers to the relevant EU Directive or the relevant UK legislation.

(VAT Notice 709/5/09, para 4.20).

Supplies outside the TOMS

[68.9] The following supplies should be dealt with outside the UK TOMS.

- Margin scheme supplies which are not made in the UK. See **68.3** above for the place of supply provisions. Note that where the place of supply is another EU country, there may be a liability to register for VAT and apply the equivalent TOMS in that country.
- Supplies which have been arranged as a disclosed agent or intermediary provided any commission received is readily identifiable. See **68.12** below.
- In-house supplies (see **68.10** below) and agency supplies (see **68.12** below) which are not packaged/supplied without margin scheme supplies.
- Supplies to business customers for subsequent resale (subject to an election, prior to 1 January 2010, to account for VAT under the TOMS) and, prior to 1 January 2010, supplies to business customers for their own consumption where an election to exclude such supplies from the TOMS has been made. See **68.11** below.
- Prior to 1 January 2010, educational school trips supplied to local authority which are to be enjoyed in the UK. See **68.13** below.

(VAT Notice 709/5/09, para 2.4).

Incidental supplies

The TOMS need not be used if

- no supplies of accommodation or passenger transport are bought in for resale; and
- other supplies which would normally be margin scheme supplies are bought in for resale but there are reasonable grounds for believing that the turnover from such supplies in the one year then beginning will not exceed 1% of all the supplies made in that year.

An example of such supplies might be where a hotelier buys in car hire for re-supply to hotel guests. Provided the 1% test is satisfied, a hotelier buying occasional car hire for guests would be outside the TOMS but occasional taxi trips for guests would not (because the re-supply of taxi trips is considered to be passenger transport).

[*SI 1987/1806, Art 14*]. (VAT Notice 709/5/09, para 3.6).

In-house supplies

[68.10] In-house supplies are supplies which are not margin scheme supplies (see **68.3** above) or agency supplies (see **68.12** below). They therefore comprise supplies which are either

- made from own resources; or
- result from purchases which the business has materially altered or further processed so that what is supplied is substantially different from what was purchased.

Where in-house supplies are sold *without* margin scheme supplies, VAT must be accounted for outside the TOMS in the normal way.

Where in-house supplies are sold *with* margin scheme supplies as part of a package, the margin scheme calculations must be used to work out the value of all parts of the package. See **68.19** to **68.23** below.

Place of supply

The place of supply of in-house supplies, whether or not they are part of a margin scheme package, is determined using the normal VAT rules. The place of supply will therefore depend upon the nature of the services provided. See **65.12** *et seq* SUPPLY: PLACE OF SUPPLY. For example, passenger transport is supplied where it takes place (see **65.26**), hotel accommodation is supplied where the accommodation is situated (see **65.16**) and live entertainment is supplied where it is physically performed (see **65.18**). As a result, if the place of supply is in another EU country, it may be necessary to register and account for VAT in that country.

Examples of in-house supplies

HMRC give the following examples.

(a) *Coach/train transport* where a tour operator owns or hires a coach/train and supplies a driver, fuel, repairs, etc.

(b) *Air transport*. Any supplies of air transport by a business using aircraft owned by itself or a member of the same VAT group. In addition, under a special scheme the supply of a charter flight by a tour operator to a customer may be treated as an in-house supply (thus retaining the zero-rating for the provision of transport) provided the tour operator meets the following conditions.

- It charters the whole aircraft and not just a block of seats.
- It enters into a contract with the airline for the provision of the aircraft and crew for an entire season (e.g. slot 1 every Wednesday from May to October). A season is defined as either a summer season (May to October), a winter sun season (November to April) or a winter sport season (December to April).
- It puts its own catering facilities on board or buys them in from a separate source. This could be a separate catering company (including one set up by the charter airline) or a specialist catering broker.
- It buys in transfer journeys from a separate source.

For further details of the scheme, including implementation and accounting implications, see VAT Information Sheet 3/96 produced in co-operation with ABTA.

(c) *Cruises* where a tour operator

- charters a vessel from another owner including deck/engine crew but employs or engages own 'hotel'/domestic/catering staff; or
- charters a vessel from another owner for a period of two years or more whether only with deck/engine crew or with both deck/engine crew and 'hotel'/domestic/catering staff. The vessel need not necessarily be in service throughout the period but the owner must not have the right to use the vessel to make supplies to other customers during the period.

(d) *Accommodation* where a tour operator

- owns the hotel, etc.;
- hires, leases or rents accommodation under an agreement whereby it takes responsibility for the upkeep of the property and is required to undertake any maintenance to the fabric of the building (i.e. not just general cleaning, changing bed linen, etc.);
- rents space at a camp-site, installs its own tents or caravans, and sells accommodation in them (but not where accommodation in tents/caravans is bought in from a third party who provides both the site and tents/accommodation or where space at a camp-site is bought in and sold to customers who provide their own tents/caravans — both of which are margin scheme supplies); or
- buys in accommodation and provides catering staff from a separate source (e.g. a ski chalet with a chalet-maid).

(e) *Tuition* where a tour operator organises training or tuition courses by putting together a number of elements such as teachers, classrooms, lecture theatres, projectors and other teaching aids, lighting, heating, etc. If a tour operator simply buys in a place on a course from a third party who has organised the course and sells this on as part of a package with transport and/or accommodation, the supply is a margin scheme supply.

(f) *Conferences* where the organiser hires a room and provides necessary equipment (e.g. microphones, projectors, hand-outs), reception staff, etc. Any refreshments served at such a conference form part of the in-house supply of an organised conference, even if purchased from an outside caterer.
Where overnight accommodation and/or passenger transport for delegates is also supplied, this is not part of an in-house organised conference and if these supplies are bought in and re-supplied without material alteration, they must be accounted for under the TOMS (but see **68.11** below where they are re-supplied to business customers). Other supplies (e.g. restaurant meals outside conference hours, theatre tickets) are also margin scheme supplies if supplied as part of a package with overnight accommodation/passenger transport.

(g) *Organised shoots* (including clay pigeons) where a number of elements (e.g. the right to use the land, host services, beaters, clays, etc.) are brought together.
If a shoot is organised as above, but a package is created that includes one or more margin scheme supplies (e.g. passenger transport or accommodation) the supply of the shooting event only is an in-house supply and the passenger transport and/or accommodation are margin scheme supplies.
If a business simply buys in and sells on the right to participate in a shoot organised by someone else, this is a normal (non-TOMS) supply (unless provided in a package with one or more margin scheme supplies).
In some circumstances, shoots are not organised in the course or furtherance of a business and are therefore outside the scope of VAT. See **57.16 RECREATION AND SPORT**.

(VAT Notice 709/5/09, paras 2.12, 4.7, 7.1–7.3, 7.6, 7.9, 7.11–7.14).

Supplies to business customers

[68.11] Whether supplies to business customers should be accounted for under the TOMS depends upon whether those supplies are for subsequent resale or for consumption by the business.

Supplies to business customers for subsequent resale (wholesale supplies)

These supplies are outside the scope of the TOMS and should be accounted for under the normal VAT rules.This allows a tour operator to set up an associated transport broking company to buy in transport from transport providers and sell it on to the tour operator outside the TOMS. This supply to the tour operator is zero-rated or outside the scope of UK VAT depending on the circumstances. See **70.15 TRANSPORT AND FREIGHT**. The transport company cannot be in the same VAT group as the tour operator. For further details of the scheme, including implementation and accounting implications, see VAT Information Sheet 1/97 produced in co-operation with ABTA.

Prior to 1 January 2010

Prior to 1 January 2010, a concession allowed a tour operator to request permission from HMRC to treat wholesale supplies as margin scheme supplies. Permission was granted provided that

- the tour operator accounted for all its wholesale supplies under the TOMS; and
- HMRC were satisfied that the tour operator could account for VAT properly and that its own officers could readily check the accuracy of the VAT returns.

Such treatment meant that business customers could not reclaim any VAT on margin scheme supplies received. Also, other EU countries might not recognise the concession and might require the tour operator to register and account for VAT there.

Supplies to business customers for their own consumption

Supplies made to a business customer for use by that customer for the purposes of its business (e.g. for business travel) fall within the TOMS where they meet the definition of margin scheme supplies.

This means that hotel booking agents who receive invoices in their own name for hotel accommodation and recover the VAT charged must account for VAT on their onward supplies under the TOMS and, in turn, their business customers incur sticking tax. However, HMRC have stated that it is entirely open to hotel booking agents to act in a disclosed capacity, with the hotels supplying accommodation direct to their business clients, rather than buy in and supply the accommodation themselves. HMRC have agreed the following arrangements where agents operate in this way.

- Invoices from hotels should be addressed c/o the hotel booking agent for payment (to indicate that the invoice has been issued to the hotel booking agent in its capacity as an agent).
- The booking field on the hotel invoice should identify the hotel guest, their employer and should ideally carry a unique reference number (until hotels can address their invoices directly to their business customers, it may be necessary for hotel booking agents to enter an employer identification number on the invoice).
- The hotel booking agent should arrange for payment of the invoice(s) but not recover the input tax thereon.
- The hotel booking agent should send the customer a payment request/statement of the expenditure incurred by the hotel booking agent on its behalf, separately identifying the value of its supplies, VAT, etc.
- The payment request/statement should say something along the lines of 'The VAT shown is your input tax which can be reclaimed subject to the normal rules'.
- The customer should use the payment request/statement as a basis for their input tax reclaim.

- The hotel booking agent should retain the original hotel invoices and these should be made available if evidence of entitlement is required by VAT staff.
- The hotel booking agent should send a VAT invoice for its own services, plus the VAT (this may be consolidated with the statement of hotel charges, or it can be a separate document).
- The hotel booking agent should charge its client the exact amount charged by the billback supplier, as a disbursement.

Prior to 1 January 2010

Prior to 1 January 2010, a concession allowed supplies made to a business customer for use by that customer for the purposes of its business to be excluded from the TOMS and treated under normal VAT rules. In the case of supplies enjoyed in the UK, this enabled the tour operator, with the permission of HMRC, to issue VAT invoices to business customers. In the case of any supplies enjoyed in another EU country, it was a condition that VAT on those supplies had been paid to the VAT authority in that country and evidence of this was available for HMRC.

[*SI 1987/1806, Art 3(3); SI 2009/3166, Art 3*]. (VAT Notice 709/5/09, paras 3.1–3.3; HMRC Brief 21/10).

Supplies by agents

[68.12] The TOMS does not cover:

(a) Supplies made by an agent or intermediary not packaged/supplied with margin scheme goods.

(b) Supplies made by a business acting as a disclosed agent in the making of margin scheme supplies (i.e. it names the provider of the margin scheme supplies). The commission and all monies for the supply arranged must be excluded from the TOMS.

But where a business acting as an agent must use the TOMS because it makes margin scheme supplies in its own name *and* it receives variable commission (or commission which is otherwise not readily identifiable) as a disclosed agent, it must include its agency income and directly-related costs in its TOMS calculations.

(VAT Notice 709/5/09, paras 2.4, 2.14, 6.6).

For the liability of arranging travel and other facilities as an agent or intermediary, see **3.14 AGENTS**.

As a result of (*b*) above, a tour operator can use the 'agency option' scheme by entering into an agency arrangement, normally with a transport provider. Provided the conditions of the scheme are met, the supply of transport services is directly from the transport provider to the final customer. As the supply is not made by the tour operator, the transport services are not margin scheme supplies and fall outside the TOMS. Thus, whether supplied singly or as part of a package, the transport element and the tour operator's services of arranging the transport, are free of UK VAT (being either zero-rated or outside the scope).

Similar agency arrangements can be set up for the provision of accommodation and catering. However, as such supplies are subject to VAT at the standard rate, the related commission will normally be standard-rated and there will be no benefit in entering into these arrangements. Additionally, in respect of accommodation, if the accommodation is in another EU country and the commission is charged to a non-VAT registered person, this could give rise to a liability for the tour operator to be VAT-registered in that country. For these reasons, it is unlikely that the 'agency option' scheme should be adopted for such supplies.

See **68.33** below for the accounting implications of using the 'agency option' scheme. For details of how to implement the scheme, see VAT Information Sheet 4/96 produced in co-operation with ABTA.

Supplies to local authorities and public bodies

[68.13] Note: the provisions of this paragraph have the force of law.

Local authority schools

The provision of an educational school trip by a local authority school to its pupils is a non-business activity for VAT purposes. The local authority is entitled to a refund of any VAT incurred under *VATA 1994, s 33* (see **43.7 LOCAL AUTHORITIES AND PUBLIC BODIES**). Northern Ireland Education Boards are entitled to refunds on such supplies under *VATA 1994, s 99* (see **46.1 NORTHERN IRELAND**).

Prior to 1 January 2010

Prior to 1 January 2010, a business supplying trips to such bodies which were to be enjoyed in the UK could exclude the supply from the TOMS. This meant that VAT invoices could be issued to the local authority or Education Board which could recover the VAT.Colleges, universities, non-LEA schools and local authority-run youth clubs were not entitled to such refunds and therefore the exclusion from the TOMS did not apply to any supplies made to them. However, supplies to such bodies might be outside of the TOMS if they, in turn, re-supplied the services provided in a business capacity (see **68.11** above).

(VAT Notice 709/5/09, paras 3.4).

Input tax

[68.14] Input tax cannot be reclaimed on goods or services acquired for re-supply as margin scheme supplies. [*SI 1987/1806, Art 12*]. This applies both to VAT incurred in the UK and in other EU countries.

Input tax can be reclaimed, outside the TOMS and subject to the normal rules, on

- overheads; and
- purchases relating to in-house supplies.

VAT incurred in another EU country on overheads and purchases relating to in-house supplies can be reclaimed from the tax authorities in that country under the procedure in **17.7** and **17.8 EUROPEAN UNION: GENERAL**. Note, however, that where supplies are made in that other EU country, it may be necessary to register for VAT there. If so, this refund procedure may not be appropriate.

(VAT Notice 709/5/09, paras 4.3, 4.4).

Registration and deregistration

[68.15] For VAT registration and deregistration purposes, turnover is

- the total margin on taxable (including zero-rated) margin scheme supplies;
- the full value of taxable (including zero-rated) in-house supplies;
- the full value of taxable agency commission; plus
- the full value of any other taxable (including zero-rated) supplies made in the UK.

(VAT Notice 709/5/09, para 4.1).

VAT group treatment

[68.16] A business making margin scheme supplies cannot belong to a VAT group (see **27 GROUPS OF COMPANIES**) if any other member of the proposed or existing group

- has an overseas establishment; and
- makes supplies outside the UK which would be taxable (including zero-rated) supplies if made in the UK; and
- supplies goods or services which will become, or are intended to become, margin scheme supplies (i.e. which are for resale, whether or not by the other member concerned).

[*SI 1987/1806, Art 13*]. (VAT Notice 709/5/09, para 4.2).

Calculation of margins and output tax

[68.17] Special calculations as laid down by HMRC are required under the TOMS to ensure that sales include only the margin for margin scheme supplies but the full value of any in-house supplies made. The purpose of the calculations are therefore to

- work out the total margin received;
- apportion the total margin between different types of supplies (i.e. margin scheme supplies (see **68.3** above), in-house supplies (see **68.10** above) and agency supplies (see **68.12** above));
- apportion the total margin between supplies with different VAT liabilities (e.g. standard-rated, zero-rated or exempt);

- work out the output tax due on margin scheme supplies and packages; and
- work out net values for supplies with different VAT liabilities.

[*SI 1987/1806, Art 7*]. (VAT Notice 709/5/09, paras 5.1, 5.12).

As precise figures are not usually known at the time of preparing the VAT returns, the TOMS requires VAT to be accounted for each quarter (or month if monthly returns are made) using *provisional* figures. The final margins and output tax are based on an annual calculation and adjustment at the end of the '*financial year*', i.e. the year for which financial accounts are made up. This final calculation determines the output tax due for the preceding financial year and provides the percentage to calculate provisional output tax in the subsequent financial year. See **68.19** to **68.24** below for the methods of calculation which *must* be used.

Starting to use the scheme

[68.18] Where a business is newly registered or an existing business starts to use the TOMS for the first time, it must calculate a provisional percentage to use during the first financial year under the scheme. Depending upon the circumstances, this may be based upon

- previous trading figures;
- projected costings and margins; or
- actual monthly/quarterly figures during the first year.

Whichever method is used, the first year-end calculation (see **68.19** below) will correct any under or over payment of VAT arising in the year.

(VAT Notice 709/5/09, para 5.13).

End of year calculation (annual adjustment)

[68.19] *From 1 January 2010*, there are two TOMS accounting methods, the market value calculation and the cost-based calculation (previously calculations were based on cost). In principle, the market value method should be used where a market value can be established for a package. However, if the supplier is satisfied that the cost-based method is an accurate reflection of the structure of any package, that is, the same percentage mark-up is achieved on all components, they may use the cost-based method.

Market value calculation

Where the market value calculation is used, it is necessary to follow through to the cost-based calculation, as it is possible that packages could consist of in-house supplies with both a market value and without a market value. Many parts of the market value calculation are common to the cost-based method. The market value calculation works on the basis of extracting from a package a selling value for the bought-in designated travel services. This is done by deducting the market value of in-house supplies from the full package price, leaving the selling value of the bought-in designated travel services on which a margin is then calculated.

Cost-based calculation

The formula for this calculation covers every type of supply which might be accountable for via the TOMS. The apportionment of the total margin calculated is based on the **direct** costs of supplies, that is, not indirect/overhead costs. It works on the principle that the same percentage margin is achieved on all the elements of the packages.

The year-end calculation must be done immediately after the financial year-end and any output tax adjustment entered on the VAT return for the first VAT period ending after financial year-end. The supplier must not wait for the production of audited accounts before doing the year-end calculation/adjustment. If the audit identifies errors in the calculation after submission of the relevant VAT return, the calculation must be reworked and the normal procedure for correction of errors followed.

Market value calculation

[68.20] This calculation must only be used if the business has packages or parts of packages being apportioned by the market value of the in-house element of the package. On completion of all the steps M1-M5 the business must then follow the steps in the cost-based calculation, taking forward the figures from this calculation as instructed.

Step	
	Calculate the value of sales of margin scheme packages
M1	Total the VAT-inclusive selling prices of all designated travel services and margin scheme packages supplied during the financial year including any that are not 'market value' packages.
	Working out the market value
M2	Total the VAT inclusive market value of the standard-rated in-house supplies at M1: carry forward this figure to step 21.
M3	Total the VAT inclusive market value of the zero-rated and outside the scope in-house travel services at M1: carry forward this figure to step 26.
M4	Total the VAT inclusive market value of the in-house supplies at step M2 + step M3.
	Working out selling value of designated travel services and non-market value in-house supplies
M5	Deduct the total at step M4 from the total at step M1: carry forward this figure to step 1.

Cost-based calculation

[68.21] This calculation applies to packages being apportioned by reference to the costs of the in-house element of the package, and imports the figures calculated by the market value method where it is used for all or some of the travel packages. Do not include values already entered above unless explicitly instructed.

Step	
	Working out the total sales of margin scheme packages
1	Bring forward the total calculated at step M5. If the market value calculation is not used then enter the VAT-inclusive selling prices of designated travel services and margin scheme packages supplied during the financial year.
	Working out the purchase prices of margin scheme supplies
2	Total the VAT-inclusive purchase prices of the standard-rated designated travel services included in the total at step 1.
3	Total the VAT-inclusive purchase prices of the non-standard-rated designated travel services (supplies enjoyed outside the EU) included in the total at step 1.
	Working out the direct costs of in-house supplies. Steps 4 to 7 can be ignored where a market value is applied to all in-house supplies under the market value calculation.
4	Total the VAT-exclusive direct costs of the standard-rated in-house supplies included in step 1. Add a percentage of that amount equivalent to the standard rate of VAT.
5	Total the VAT-exclusive direct costs of the zero-rated in-house supplies included in step 1.
6	Total the VAT-inclusive direct costs of the exempt in-house supplies included in step 1. Deduct any input tax that recoverable on these costs.
7	Total the direct costs of the in-house supplies included in step 1 that are supplied outside the UK, exclusive of any VAT incurred on these costs that are recoverable. Add to the total an uplift equivalent to the percentage VAT rate applicable to such supplies if VAT has been accounted for on these supplies to the VAT authorities in another Member State.
	Working out the costs of agency supplies
8	Total the VAT-inclusive amounts paid to principals in respect of the agency supplies included in step 1 for which the consideration received is standard-rated.
9	Total the VAT-inclusive amounts paid to principals in respect of the agency supplies included in step 1 for which the consideration received is not standard-rated.
	Working out the total margin
10	Add the totals of costs at steps 2 to 9 inclusive.
11	Calculate the total margin for all the supplies included in step 1 by deducting the total at step 10 from the total at step 1.
	Apportioning the margin
12	Calculate the margin for the standard-rated designated travel services by applying the following formula: total at step 2/total at step 10 x total at step 11.
13	Calculate the margin for the zero-rated designated travel services by applying the following formula: total at step 3/total at step 10 x total at step 11.
	Steps 14 to 17 can be ignored where a market value is applied to all in-house supplies under the market value calculation
14	Calculate the margin for the standard-rated in-house supplies by applying the following formula: total at step 4/total at step 10 x total at step 11.

15	Calculate the margin for the zero-rated in-house supplies by applying the following formula: total at step 5/total at step 10 x total at step 11.
16	Calculate the margin for the exempt in-house supplies by applying the following formula: total at step 6/total at step 10 x total at step 11.
17	Calculate the margin for the in-house supplies made outside the UK by applying the following formula: total at step 7/total at step 10 x total at step 11.
18	Calculate the consideration for the standard-rated agency supplies by applying the following formula: total at step 8/total at step 10 x total at step 11.
19	Calculate the consideration for the non-standard-rated agency supplies by applying the following formula: total at step 9/total at step 10 x total at step 11.
	Working out output tax
20	Calculate the output VAT due on the designated travel services by applying the following formula: total at step 12 x the VAT fraction.
21	Calculate the output VAT due on the standard-rated in-house supplies by applying the following formula: (total at step 4 + total at step 14 + total calculated at step M2) x the VAT fraction.
22	Calculate the output VAT due on the standard-rated agency supplies by applying the following formula: total at step 18 x the VAT fraction.
	Working out sales values
23	Calculate the VAT-exclusive value of the standard-rated designated travel services by deducting the total at step 20 from the total at step 12.
24	Note the value of the zero-rated designated travel services at step 13.
25	Calculate the VAT-exclusive value of standard-rated in-house supplies by applying the following formula: (total at step 4 + total at step 14 + total calculated at step M2) – total at step 21.
26	Calculate the value of the zero-rated supplies made within the scheme by applying the following formula: (total at step 5 + total at step 15 + total calculated at step M3).
27	Calculate the value of exempt in-house supplies made by applying the following formula: total at step 6 + total at step 16.
28	Calculate the value of in-house supplies which are supplied outside the UK by applying the following formula: total at step 7 + total at step 17.
29	Calculate the total VAT exclusive value of the supplies: total of steps 23 to 28. Include this total in box 6 of the VAT return.
	Working out the annual adjustment
30	Calculate the total output VAT due on designated travel services and margin scheme packages by adding the totals at steps 20 to 22 inclusive.
31	Total the provisional output VAT which has been accounted for during the financial year on the supplies included in the total at step 1.
32	Deduct the total at step 31 from the total at step 30. Include the resulting total in box 1 of the VAT return, either as a payable amount where the amount is positive or as a deductible amount where the amount is negative.

(VAT Notice 709/5/09, paras 5.2–5.4, 5.7, 5.8, 8, 9).

Simplified calculation

[68.22] If all component supplies of all margin scheme packages are liable to VAT at the standard rate, the simplified method set out below must be used. It achieves the same results as the full calculation but avoids the need to work out costs of in-house supplies (if included in packages).

Step	
1	Total the VAT-inclusive selling prices of designated travel services and margin scheme packages supplied during the financial year.
2	Total the VAT-inclusive purchase prices of the designated travel services included in the total at step 1.
3	Calculate the VAT-inclusive amount of the supplies included in step 1 by deducting the total at step 2 from the total at step 1.
4	Calculate the total output VAT due on designated travel services and margin scheme packages by applying the following formula: total at step 3 x the VAT fraction.
5	Calculate the VAT-exclusive value of designated travel services and margin scheme packages by deducting the total at step 4 from the total at step 3.
6	Total the provisional output VAT which has been accounted for during the financial year on the supplies included in the total at step 1
7	Deduct the total at step 6 from the total at step 4. Include the resulting total in box 1 of the VAT return, either as a payable amount where the amount is positive or as a deductible amount where the amount is negative.

(VAT Notice 709/5/09, paras 5.5, 5.7, 5.8, 11).

Provisional percentages for the next financial year

[68.23] When the procedure in **68.19** or **68.22** above has been completed, provisional percentages can be obtained for use in completing VAT returns for the next financial year. Revised provisional figures must be calculated each year.

Where the method in **68.19** is used:

	Working out the provisional percentage
A	Calculate the VAT-inclusive amount of standard-rated supplies of designated travel services and margin scheme packages for the preceding financial year by adding the totals from steps 4, 12, 14 and 18 in **68.21**, together with the total M2 in **68.20**.
B	Calculate the VAT-inclusive standard-rated percentage of the total selling price of all designated travel services and margin scheme packages for the preceding tax year by applying one of following formulae: If market value has been used to value in-house supplies: total at step A/total at step M1 x 100. If market value has not been used to value in-house supplies: total at step A/total at step 1 x 100.
	Working out the VAT return figures

C	Total the VAT-inclusive selling prices of the designated travel services and margin scheme packages supplied during the prescribed accounting period.
D	Calculate the provisional VAT-inclusive amount of standard-rated supplies of designated travel services and margin scheme packages made during the prescribed accounting period by applying the following formula: total at step C x percentage at step B.
E	Calculate the provisional amount of output VAT due for the prescribed accounting period by applying the following formula: total at step D x the VAT fraction.

Where the simplified method in **68.22** has been used:

Step	
A	Calculate the VAT-inclusive standard-rated percentage of the total selling price of all designated travel services and margin scheme packages for the preceding tax year by applying the following formula: total at step 3 in **68.22**/total at step 1 in **68.22** x 100.
B	Total the VAT-inclusive selling prices of all of designated travel services and margin scheme packages supplied during the prescribed accounting period.
C	Calculate the provisional VAT-inclusive amount of standard-rated supplies of designated travel services and margin scheme packages made during the prescribed accounting period by applying the following formula: total at step B x percentage at step A.
D	Calculate the provisional amount of output VAT due for the prescribed accounting period by applying the following formula: total at step C x the VAT fraction.
E	Calculate the provisional VAT-exclusive value of all of designated travel services and margin scheme packages made during the prescribed accounting period by deducting the total at step D from the total at step C.

(VAT Notice 709/5/09, paras 5.9, 10, 12).

Separate calculation for non-EU supplies

[68.24] Note: the provisions of this paragraph have the force of law.

Where a business makes supplies (including packages) which are enjoyed outside the EU, it may elect to do separate year-end and provisional calculations for those supplies. If it so elects, it must include in the non-EU calculation all supplies which are enjoyed wholly outside the EU. But where any packages are enjoyed partly within the EU and partly outside the EU, the entire package must be included in the calculation for EU-only supplies, the related direct costs being included in the standard-rated or zero-rated steps within the EU-only calculation depending on where the supplies are enjoyed.

A business can only change to separate calculations (or revert to a single calculation) at the start of its financial year (i.e. no later than the due date of its first VAT return for that financial year). Permission must be requested from the local VAT Business Advice Centre, in writing, and in advance of the financial year in question. Permission will not be granted retrospectively. This policy was confirmed as having the force of law in *C & E Commrs v Simply Travel Ltd*, Ch D 2001, [2002] STC 194 (TVC 63.24).

Permission to switch to separate calculations will only be granted if HMRC are satisfied that the records of the business for direct costs and sales are adequate to calculate accurate, but separate, sets of margins.

(VAT Notice 709/5/09, paras 5.9, 5.10, 13).

Records

[68.25] If the market value calculation is made, a business must keep records of the market value for each in-house supply (where used), and it must be able to show how the figure was calculated and why it is the market value.

Whether the full or simplified calculation is made, a business must keep records of

- the total selling price for margin scheme supplies and/or packages; and
- separate records of the direct costs for margin scheme supplies and the different types of supplies within margin scheme packages, i.e.
  - (i) standard-rated and zero-rated margin scheme supplies;
  - (ii) standard-rated, zero-rated, exempt and outside the scope in-house supplies; and
  - (iii) standard-rated, zero-rated, exempt and outside the scope agency supplies for which its commission is not readily identifiable.

(VAT Notice 709/5/09, para 5.6).

Working out the selling prices

[68.26] The first step in the end of year calculation is to add up the selling prices of supplies with tax points during the financial year.

Include:

- The total VAT-inclusive selling price of all margin scheme supplies, including any charges made for credit card payments (see **68.3** above).
- The total VAT-inclusive selling price of any in-house supplies (see **68.10** above) supplied together with margin scheme supplies.
- Any Air Passenger Duty payable by the customer.
- Any surcharges made.
- Monies received from customers who fail to turn up.
- Where sales are made through agents, 'the total amount to be paid by the traveller' (even if a travel agent deducts commission and only passes over the balance).

  Where a travel agent sells a package for less than the tour operator's advertised brochure price but funds the discount itself (so that the tour operator receives the full price of the holiday but, in effect, part from the traveller and part from the travel agent), the ECJ have held that '*the total amount to be paid by the traveller*' includes the additional amount that the agent, acting as an intermediary, has to pay the tour operator in addition to the actual price paid by the traveller (*C & E Commrs v First Choice Holidays plc, ECJ Case C–149/01*, [2003] STC 934 (TVC 22.493)).

- Amounts received relating to any supplies, packaged with margin scheme supplies, which the business arranges as an agent and where its commission is not readily identifiable (see **68.33** below).

Reduce sales by:

- Any refunds made to customers for unsatisfactory service.

Do not include:

- Packages of supplies which do not include any margin scheme supplies (on which VAT must be accounted for under the normal rules).
- Forfeited deposits and cancellation fees received from customers who cancel bookings.
- Amounts collected by the business as agent if its commission is readily identifiable.
- Any discount the business agrees with its customer.

(VAT Notice 709/5/09, para 6.1).

Market value or purchase price of margin scheme supplies

Market value

[68.27] The market value method is used to apportion the selling price of a package in order to determine the selling price of the in-house supplies. There is no set way to calculate a market value for in-house supplies but there are some general principles that must be considered:

- The market value must reflect the reality of the business, use of third party comparators must truly reflect the business model.
- Market values may be averaged across a range of packages but must be properly weighted and reviewed regularly.
- The calculation of the market value must accommodate child and other discounted packages.
- Full details must be kept of the business model used to calculate the market value for verification by HMRC.

Purchase price

The total VAT-inclusive purchase prices of goods and services bought in for resale as margin scheme supplies must be added up. Only those purchases which relate to the financial year being calculated must be included.

The cost must

- take into account any discounts or price reductions received from suppliers (even if received at a later date);
- include any Air Passenger Duty payable;
- not include the cost of any supplies which do not include any margin scheme supplies; and

- not include indirect costs (see **68.31** below).

(VAT Notice 709/5/09, paras 6.2, 6.3).

Connected persons

Where goods or services are supplied to the tour operator by a connected person (see **71.19 VALUATION**) and the value of the supply would otherwise be greater than its open market value, HMRC may direct that the value of the supply is deemed to be its open market value for the purposes of calculating the value of margin scheme supplies. The direction must be in writing to the tour operator acquiring the supply within three years of the time of supply. It may also specify that the open market value rule is to apply to subsequent supplies acquired from the same connected person. [*SI 1987/1806, Art 8*].

Direct costs of in-house supplies

[68.28] It is not necessary to work out the costs of in-house supplies if all supplies included in margin scheme packages are liable to VAT at the same rate. In such a case the simplified calculation under **68.22** above must be used. Otherwise, the annual calculation under **68.19** above must include the direct costs incurred in making in-house supplies which are supplied with margin scheme supplies as part of a package.

The following are examples (not exhaustive) of costs which may be included.

Direct costs of supplying in-house passenger transport

[68.29] The direct costs of supplying in-house passenger transport are listed below.

General

- Depreciation on vehicles, aircraft, vessels (which the business or a member of its VAT group owns) calculated on the same basis as its audited accounts
- Rental or leasing of vehicles, aircraft or vessels (see **68.31** below as regards HP, leasing and finance charges)
- Crew/drivers costs (including employer's NIC)
- Subsistence paid to crew/drivers
- Fuel
- Insurance
- Repair and maintenance of vehicles, aircraft or vessels

Road or rail transport

- Garaging and parking
- Bridge and road tolls
- Ferry costs
- Road fund licences

Air transport

- Air Passenger Duty (APD)
- Landing fees

Cruises

- Berthing fees

Chartering an aircraft (see 68.10 above)

- Charter fee
- Catering charges
- Transfer journeys

Chartering a vessel (see 68.10 above)

- Charter fee
- 'Hotel'/domestic/catering staff

Only in-house passenger transport supplied with margin scheme supplies can be included in the TOMS calculation. If in-house transport is also used to supply passenger transport outside the TOMS (e.g. coach hire), the direct cost must be apportioned to take account of this, normally

- for road or rail transport, on a mileage basis;
- for air transport, based on hours flown; and
- for sea transport, on the basis of days used on types of supply.

If a business wishes to adopt any other basis for apportionment, it should submit its proposed method in writing to its local VAT Business Advice Centre in advance of when its year-end calculation/adjustment is due.

Direct costs of standard-rated hotel accommodation

[68.30] The direct costs of standard-rated hotel accommodation are listed below.

- Depreciation of buildings, fixtures and fittings (which the business or a member of its VAT group owns) calculated on the same basis as its audited accounts
- Catering purchases
- Heating and lighting
- Rates
- Building insurance
- Rental of equipment and furniture
- Repairs, maintenance and cleaning for which the business is liable
- Staff costs (including wages and employer's NI contributions)

Only costs relating to in-house accommodation supplied with margin scheme supplies can be included in the TOMS calculation. If premises are also used to provide accommodation outside the TOMS, the annual direct costs must be apportioned to take account of this, normally on the basis of number of guests/days booked for each type of supply.

If certain parts of the premises are not used specifically to provide accommodation (e.g. administrative offices, public bars, owner's private accommodation, etc.) costs relating to the entire premises (e.g. rates, insurance, light and heat) must be apportioned on the basis of floor area. Any other bases of apportionment must be agreed in writing with the local VAT Business Advice Centre in advance of when the year-end calculation/adjustment is due.

See also *The Devonshire Hotel (Torquay) Ltd* (VTD 14448) (TVC 63.13).

Sales of assets for which depreciation has been entered as an in-house cost

Where this occurs, an appropriate adjustment must be made to in-house costs in the year-end TOMS calculation for the year in which the sale takes place.

This adjustment is

- a reduction to the relevant in-house costs in respect of any profit made on disposal, or
- an increase to the relevant in-house costs in respect of a loss made on disposal

based on book values in the accounts.

(VAT Notice 709/5/09, paras 6.5, 7.4, 7.5, 7.7, 7.8, 7.10).

Indirect costs

[68.31] Indirect costs must not be included in any of the calculations. Examples of indirect costs include

- brochures
- advertising
- inspection trips made to research resorts, facilities, etc.
- office expenses (telephone, IT equipment, office stationery, rent, etc.)
- accountancy, legal and similar professional services
- hiring and employing representatives at airports and resorts (see **68.35** below)
- financial services including bank, credit card transation fees and foreign exchange charges
- HP, leasing and finance charges for the purchase of assets (including those used for making in-house supplies)
- market research
- commission paid to agents.

(VAT Notice 709/5/09, para 6.4).

Foreign currency purchases

[68.32] Note: the provisions of this paragraph have the force of law.

If any supplies bought for resale as TOMS supplies are billed in foreign currency, these should be converted into sterling at either

(i) the rate of exchange published in the Financial Times using the Federation of Tour Operators' base rate current at the time the supplies are costed by the person from whom the business has acquired the goods or services;
(ii) the commercial rate of exchange current at the time that the supplies in the brochure were costed;
(iii) the rate published in the Financial Times on the date that the business pays for the supplies;
(iv) the rate of exchange which was applicable to the purchase by the business of the foreign currency used to pay for the supplies; or
(v) the period rate of exchange published by HMRC for customs purposes in force at the time the business pays for the supplies.

Documentary evidence relating to the purchase must be kept to show which of the rates have been used. If method (i) or (ii) is used, the rate must be published in any brochure or leaflet in which the supplies are held out for sale.

Once a method has been chosen, HMRC may allow a different method but only from the start of a financial year and if written notification is given to them no later than the due date for rendering the first VAT return for that financial year.

(VAT Notice 709/5/09, paras 6.6, 13(TL2)).

Commission received for agency supplies arranged as part of a margin scheme package

[68.33] Where any commission received for agency supplies made by the business is readily identifiable, exclude from the TOMS calculation

- the commission received; and
- all monies paid for the supply arranged.

Where any commission is received which is not readily identifiable, include in the TOMS calculation

- the gross amount paid by the traveller; and
- the net amount paid to the principal.

(VAT Notice 709/5/09, para 6.7).

Hotel and travel insurance

[68.34] The way hotel or travel insurance is treated for VAT purposes depends upon the precise contractual arrangements and whether it is the tour operator or the traveller who is the insured person.

(a) Where *the insurance policy issued by the permitted insurer makes the traveller the insured person* (the normal case), there is a supply of insurance from the permitted insurer to the traveller. If the tour operator arranges for the insurance to be supplied by a named company to the traveller under such an arrangement, it is acting as an agent.

- Where the commission received is readily identifiable, the full amount paid by the traveller for the insurance and the net premium passed on to the insurance company must be excluded from the TOMS calculations.
- Where the commission received is not readily identifiable, values relating to the insurance must be included in the TOMS calculation (see **68.33** above).
- Where the insurance is offered 'free' as part of a package, the full amount paid by the traveller for the package must be included in the TOMS calculation. Any costs incurred in relation to such insurance must not be included in the TOMS calculation.

(b) Where *the tour operator enters into an agreement with a permitted insurer under which the tour operator is the insured person*, the insurer agrees to reimburse the tour operator in respect of any claims by travellers for delay compensation, medical costs, etc. This is an indirect cost and therefore outside the TOMS. If the tour operator passes on a charge for the insurance (including any Insurance Premium Tax) to the traveller, this should be included in the selling prices in the TOMS calculation.

(VAT Notice 709/5/09, para 6.8).

Representatives and guides

[68.35] The services of representatives at airports and resorts are not normally supplies in their own right and are therefore not regarded as in-house supplies. The costs incurred in providing these services should be treated as indirect costs for the purposes of the TOMS.

The specialist services of a guide, however, are often supplies in their own right. If the supply is made in-house, the place of supply and the liability depends on the exact nature of the service. See **68.10** above.

(VAT Notice 709/5/09, para 6.10).

Unforeseen costs

[68.36] Where it is necessary to buy in accommodation, transport, meals, etc. as a result of delays, breakdowns or other unforeseen circumstances, these costs should usually be treated as margin scheme supplies unless the cost of the additional items is

- ultimately met by someone else (e.g. an airline from whom air transport is bought in has agreed to meet any additional costs arising through flight delays) in which case the costs should be ignored in the TOMS calculation; or
- a direct cost of in-house supplies.

(VAT Notice 709/5/09, para 6.11).

Bad debt relief

[68.37] See **7 BAD DEBT RELIEF** generally for the rules for claiming bad debt relief and in particular paragraph 7.9 under which bad debt relief is restricted to a maximum of the VAT fraction of the profit margin.

The amount of VAT bad debt relief claimable is calculated by the formula

$$B \times s\,\% \times 7/47^{*}$$

where

B = the amount of the bad debt

s = the provisional percentage as calculated under **68.23** above for the financial year in which the supply is made

(*1/6 from 4.1.11; 3/23 from 1.12.08 to 31.12.09)

(VAT Notice 709/5/09, para 6.9).

Key points

[68.38] Points to consider are as follows.

- An important advantage of the TOMS is that it avoids the need for many businesses selling travel services having to register for VAT in different EU countries. The scheme applies in relation to travel services enjoyed within the UK, EU and outside the EU.
- The main principle of the scheme is that output tax is only payable within the scheme based on the margin, i.e. difference between the buying and selling prices of travel services. Input tax cannot be reclaimed on any margin supplies but can be reclaimed on general overhead items.
- TOMS applies to any business that is involved in buying and selling travel services, e.g. a company that organises conferences that include hotel accommodation, rather than only to tour operators and travel agents. This is important to ensure competition is fair between different business entities involved in such supplies.
- Businesses that occasionally organise conferences, e.g. for members, can avoid being caught in the TOMS by taking care in how it organises and manages the supply of accommodation at the venue or in nearby hotels. It is important to take great care when doing this to achieve the best outcome.
- As far as VAT registration is concerned, the relevant figure for determining whether the turnover limits have been exceeded is the margin within a TOMS sale. This is different to the rules for a second-hand car dealer using a margin scheme where the key figure is the full value of the sale.

- The margin calculations for TOMS supplies can be very complex and require great attention to detail. New calculation procedures were also introduced on 1 January 2010.

69

Trade Promotion Schemes

Introduction

[69.1] A large number of trade promotion schemes exist where goods or services are given as rewards to retail customers (the public) or trade customers.

These include

- schemes where goods are linked in a promotion (see **69.4** to **69.7** below);
- schemes where vouchers, coupons, etc. are issued and later redeemed for cash (e.g. money-off coupons) or goods or services with or without further consideration (see **69.8** to **69.14** below);
- manufacturers' promotion schemes aimed at either the trade (see **69.15** below) or the public (see **69.16** below); and
- retail discount schemes (see **69.17** below).

The VAT consequences in many cases depend upon whether there has been a gift of goods or services and whether any non-monetary consideration has been given. These points are considered in **69.2** and **69.3** below.

Gifts

Free gifts of goods for no consideration

[69.2] Where a business gives away goods, on which it is entitled to credit for input tax, without any monetary or non-monetary consideration (see **69.3** below), the VAT rules on gifts apply. If the cost of the goods, together with the cost of any other business gifts made to the same person in the same year, is £50 or less, no VAT is due. Otherwise, output tax must be accounted for on the price the person would have to pay (excluding VAT) at the time of supply, to purchase goods identical to the goods concerned, i.e. normally their cost value. See **47.6 OUTPUT TAX** for further details.

Free provision of own services

Free provision of own services (e.g. free beauty treatment) is generally not a taxable supply. There is no restriction on input tax recovery and no output tax is due. However, if the supply makes use of goods (e.g. cosmetics) which cost more than £50, output tax may be due as above.

Free provision of bought-in services

Free provision of bought-in services (e.g. beauty treatment provided by another business) will give rise to a VAT liability under *SI 1993/1507*. See **47.7 OUTPUT TAX**. If, however, services are merely paid for by the business but supplied directly by a third party to the customer, the business makes no supply for VAT purposes but cannot deduct any VAT charged by the provider of the services (although it may be claimable by the customer).

Goods lent or hired to customer

If goods are lent or hired to a customer, there is a supply of services and, where no consideration is given, output tax is due on the cost of providing the services. Over a period of time, this is the amount of depreciation of the goods (plus any other costs related to the goods) multiplied by the proportion which the use outside the business forms to the total use. See **47.7 OUTPUT TAX** for further details. Some free loans may, however, be outside the scope of VAT, see **69.17** below.

Free discounts on goods or services

If a business gives a discount freely on goods or services, it need only charge VAT on the discounted amount.

Free gifts of vouchers or coupons

See **69.11** below.

(VAT Notice 700/7/02, paras 2.1–2.4).

Non-monetary consideration

[69.3] The VAT treatment of discounts and reward goods/services depends upon whether any consideration is given by the recipient.

Where payment is totally in money, that is the consideration. However, it is also possible to have non-monetary consideration where the customer agrees to do something (or not to do it) in return for a supply of goods or services. Where *any* non-monetary consideration is given, however small, VAT is due on that consideration. The value of the consideration is taken to be such amount in money as, with the addition of the VAT, is equivalent to the consideration, ie normally the price, excluding VAT, which the customer would have to pay to buy the goods or services. [*VATA 1994, s 19(3)*].

An example of non-monetary consideration is where a business offers incentive goods to its customer, either free or at a lower price, on condition that the customer provides it with a service in return. In agreeing to provide this service the customer is providing non-monetary consideration, the value of which is equivalent to the price, or reduction in price, of the goods. In *Empire Stores Ltd v C & E Commrs, ECJ Case C–33/93*, [1994] STC 623 (TVC 22.234) a company sold goods by mail order and offered new customers, and existing customers who introduced new customers, certain goods free of charge as inducements. The ECJ ruled that the goods in question were supplied to the customers in consideration for a service, namely the introduction of a new customer, and not in return for the purchase by the new customer of goods from the catalogue. The value of the goods was the amount that the company was prepared to spend to get the introduction, i.e. the cost of the articles to the company.

HMRC, however, accept that certain acts, including the following, are insignificant for these purposes and do not constitute non-monetary consideration.

(a) Having to buy one article either to get
- another article free at the same time; or
- a discount voucher redeemable against a further purchase; or
- a lottery ticket, etc. (see **69.18** below).

(b) Employees having to exceed certain sales levels or sell most articles in a month, or other such schemes (see **69.19** below).
(c) The act of using an in-house credit card (see **69.18** below).
(d) Entering a free prize draw.
(e) Having to complete a slogan or give a recipe, etc. on entry to a competition.
(f) A gift to an existing customer for their buying more than a certain amount.

In circumstances such as these, the normal rules for gifts set out in **69.2** above apply.

(VAT Notice 700/7/02, paras 3.1–3.3).

Goods linked in a promotion

[69.4] Goods (or goods and services) are sometimes offered together in one promotion for a single price (e.g. coffee and chocolate biscuits or a washing machine and iron). Alternatively, a number of articles may be sold in a multibuy offer, e.g.

- 'buy 1 get 1 free';
- 'buy three for the price of two'; or
- 'buy a sofa and get a free foot stool'.

This is a multiple supply and the amount paid covers all the goods or services offered.

If the items offered are subject to VAT at different rates, apportionment will normally be required. See **47.3 OUTPUT TAX**. However, for certain small items linked with a major item which is liable to VAT at a different rate, the linked supplies concession in **69.7** below may apply.

(VAT Notice 700/7/02, para 4.1).

If the offer is made to other VAT-registered traders, see also the dealer loader scheme under **69.15** below.

Linked goods schemes

[69.5] Theses are promotion schemes where a minor article is linked (not necessarily physically) with a main article (either goods or services) and sold with it at a single price. An example would be an empty plastic storage jar attached to a box of cereals. Where the articles are liable to VAT at the same rate, no problem arises but where they are liable at different rates, the price should normally be apportioned (see **47.3 OUTPUT TAX**). However, by concession, VAT can be accounted for on the minor article at the same rate as the main article (so that the selling price need not be apportioned) provided the following conditions are satisfied.

(a) The minor article is not charged to the customer at a separate price.
(b) The minor article costs no more than
  - (i) 20% of the total cost (excluding VAT) of the combined supply; and
  - (ii) £1 (excluding VAT) if included with goods intended for retail sale or £5 (excluding VAT) otherwise.

Where the conditions are met, the articles need not be detailed separately on the invoice.

In all other circumstances where a VAT invoice has to be issued, details of the minor article must be shown separately.

See also **24.13 FOOD** for mixtures and assortments of food and **54.18 PRINTED MATTER, ETC.** for promotional items in magazines.

(VAT Notice 700/7/02, para 4.2; VAT Notice 48, ESC 3.7).

> *Example*
>
> A musical CD is sold by a retail store. The CD includes a well written leaflet that gives historical information about the composer and his work. Although the leaflet is zero-rated as a supply of printed matter, it is incidental to the main supply of the standard-rated CD and output tax is therefore due on the full selling price of the goods.

Accounting for linked supplies under retail schemes

[69.6] VAT must be accounted for as follows.

(a) *Point of Sale scheme and Direct Calculation Schemes 1 and 2*. Treatment depends upon whether the two articles are liable to VAT at the same rate or different rates.

- (i) If both articles are liable at the same rate of VAT, there are no additional rules to follow.
- (ii) If the articles are liable at different rates of VAT, subject to the linked supplies concession in **69.5** above, the selling price must be apportioned either on the basis in **47.3 OUTPUT TAX** or, where the goods have been linked by the manufacturer, in accordance with the information shown on the supplier's invoice.

  Where apportionment is required, the amount allocated to reduced rate or zero-rated goods must be separated from standard-rated takings before carrying out the scheme calculation.

(b) *Apportionment Schemes 1 and 2*. Any contribution from the supplier or sponsor must be included in daily gross takings.

Under Apportionment Scheme 1, no adjustment to purchases is required.

Under Apportionment Scheme 2, expected selling prices (ESPs) must also be adjusted as follows.

- No adjustment is required for a full contribution. Where only partial contribution is received, ESPs for the appropriate goods must be adjusted to the extent of the amount not supported by the supplier or sponsor. Where no contribution is received, an appropriate adjustment must be made to the ESPs of the promotion goods.
- If the promotion goods are liable to VAT at different rates, the ESPs must be apportioned either on the basis in **47.3 OUTPUT TAX** or, where the goods have been linked by the manufacturer, in accordance with the information shown on the supplier's invoice.

  Where the linked supplies concession under **69.5** above is used, the record of purchases or ESPs of the promotion goods must be adjusted as appropriate.

(c) *Contributions from manufacturers or joint promoters*. Whichever scheme is used, strictly speaking, where the retailer receives a contribution from a manufacturer or joint sponsor representing partial payment for goods supplied to a customer, the retailer should account for this in the period the goods are supplied. However, by concession, the retailer may account for such contributions in the period they are received. If the manufacturer or joint sponsor makes any payment (e.g. towards advertising) this must be treated as consideration for a separate supply of services and dealt with outside the retail scheme.

(d) *Correcting ESPs*. Under Direct Calculation Schemes 1 and 2,

- if a contribution is received from a manufacturer or joint promoter for the class of goods which the retailer has marked up in the retail scheme, no ESP adjustment should be made if the supplier or sponsor makes a full contribution. If a partial contribution is received, ESPs for the appropriate goods should be adjusted to the extent of the amount *not* supported by the sponsor or manufacturer.

- Where no contribution is received from the manufacturer or sponsor, an appropriate adjustment must be made to the ESPs of the promotion goods.

(VAT Notice 727/3/11, para 7.6; VAT Notice 727/4/11, para 8.5; VAT Notice 727/5/11, para 7.5, all of which have the force of law).

Multisave promotions where the manufacturer subsidises the promotion

[69.7] In some multisave promotions of the 'buy 2, get a third free' type, manufacturers make payments to retailers towards the costs of the promotions. In such cases, following the ECJ decision in *Elida Gibbs Ltd v C & E Commrs, ECJ Case C–317/94*, [1996] STC 1387 (TVC 22.235), manufacturers can reduce their output tax by the amount paid to the retailer to support the promotion where it relates to products liable to VAT at the standard rate. The payments received by the retailer are further consideration for the supply to the customer upon which VAT is due and the amounts received should be included within retail scheme takings figures.

In *Elida Gibbs* the company manufactured toiletries and sold the products to both retailers and wholesalers. To promote retail sales, it

- issued money-off coupons which customers could present to a retailer in part payment for Elida Gibbs products and for which retailers sought reimbursement direct from the company; and
- printed cashback coupons directly onto the packaging of its products which, subject to meeting conditions, entitled any consumer to a cash refund direct from Elida Gibbs.

The company claimed a repayment of output tax which it had previously accounted for contending that the reimbursement of money-off coupons to retailers and the cashback payments to consumers constituted a retrospective discount which reduced the consideration for its supplies. The ECJ agreed, holding that the discounts allowed by the manufacturer were deductible but credit notes should not be issued to customers. This left the VAT position of wholesalers and retailers unchanged and maintained the balance of VAT due from them. Retailers should account for output tax on payments received from manufacturers as well as money paid by customers. This decision was subsequently applied in *EC Commission v Federal Republic of Germany, ECJ Case C–427/98*, [2003] STC 301 (TVC 22.237). See also *Yorkshire Co-Operatives Ltd v C & E Commrs, ECJ Case C–398/99*, [2003] STC 234 (TVC 22.244). However, if a VAT-registered customer requests a VAT invoice in respect of purchases made using money-off vouchers, this should be based only on the amount paid by the customer. This achieves fiscal neutrality as required by the judgment.

There may be cases where the manufacturer pays the retailer for providing a service, for example, in undertaking to advertise the promotion and/or products. In such cases, the retailer must charge the manufacturer VAT at the standard rate which is the input tax for the manufacturer subject to the normal rules.

(VAT Notice 700/7/02, para 4.3).

Coupons, vouchers, trading stamps, etc.

[69.8] The provisions in **69.9** to **69.14** below explain the VAT treatment of coupons generally. Particular care must be taken when dealing with 'face value vouchers' and manufacturers' promotions as considered in **69.15** and **69.16** below.

Money-off coupons

[69.9] Money-off coupons are coupons used to offer to the public a reduction in the price of a future purchase. They can be issued in a variety of ways, for example

- given on the purchase of a particular item;
- given on the purchase of goods to a specified value;
- sent by mailshot or electronic means; or
- published as cut-out coupons in newspapers.

They may be issued by retailers under their own schemes or by manufacturers. In either case, it does not matter whether the coupon is attached to a product or not.

Issue of money-off coupons

In most cases, money-off coupons are regarded as issued for no payment (consideration). Even if the issue is dependent upon the purchase of goods, provided the goods are sold at their normal price, no VAT is due on their issue.

Sale of money-off coupons

Where, however, discount coupons or vouchers (or a discount card) entitling the holder to discounts on purchases are *sold*, the VAT consequences depend upon how and where the coupons, etc. can be used.

- Where the coupons, etc. are sold by a retailer using a retail scheme and discounts are only available from that retailer, proceeds must be included in gross takings. Unless the coupons are for a specific line of product, the VAT liability of which can be determined when the coupons are issued, retailers using the point of sale scheme may not be able, when the discount coupons are sold, to determine the liability of the goods or services against which the coupons will be redeemed. Such retailers should agree a method of how to account for VAT on such sales with HMRC, possibly on the basis of the average split of zero-rated and standard-rated sales.

- Where the coupons, etc. sold can be used at several traders, this is a standard-rated supply of services. See *C & E Commrs v Granton Marketing Ltd; C & E Commrs v Wentwalk Ltd*, CA [1996] STC 1049 (TVC 67.166) where cards which entitled the holder to a complimentary meal and wine at certain restaurants were held not to be vouchers and their supply to be standard-rated.
  If a retail scheme is used,
  - under the Point of Sale Scheme, payments received should be added to standard-rated daily gross takings; and
  - under Apportionment Schemes 1 and 2 and Direct Calculation Schemes 1 and 2 payments received should be dealt with outside the scheme used.

Redemption of money-off coupons

Where a business uses a retail scheme, it should only include in its daily gross takings

- any additional payment received when the customer redeems the coupon; and
- any further payment which is due from any other source (e.g. from the manufacturer).

Where no retail scheme is in operation, VAT is due on the money received from the customer and the manufacturer (if any) under the normal time of supply rules.

See *Boots Co plc v C & E Commrs, ECJ Case 126/88*, [1990] STC 387 (TVC 22.251) confirming that money-off coupons are not to be treated as consideration when used to buy other goods but are simply evidence of entitlement to discount.

Handling charges

Any further handling or service charge made to a manufacturer for handling coupons is exempt from VAT.
(VAT Notice 700/7/02, paras 5.2–5.5).

Vouchers, stamps and points schemes

[69.10] Where vouchers, stamps or points can be redeemed for goods ('reward goods') or occasionally services without further payment, the redemption goods and services must be treated as supplied for no consideration. See **69.2** above. (VAT Notice 700/7/02, para 5.6). This follows the decision in *Kuwait Petroleum (GB) Ltd v C & E Commrs, ECJ Case C–48/97*, [1999] STC 488 (TVC 22.158). In that case, the company ran a promotion scheme under which customers were offered vouchers with purchases of fuel. Whether or not customers accepted the vouchers, the price of fuel was the same. The vouchers could be redeemed for goods ('reward goods') or occasionally services without further payment. The ECJ held that the amounts paid by customers were entirely attributable to their original purchases and no part of the payments could be attributed to the supply of reward goods. The reward goods should therefore be treated as gifts and taxed accordingly. This was subsequently confirmed in the UK courts in *Kuwait Petroleum (GB) Ltd v C & E Commrs*, Ch D [2001] STC 62 (TVC 22.159).

In *HMRC v Loyalty Management UK Ltd*, L operated a points scheme in which a customer, purchasing goods or services from a participating retailer, received points which could be redeemed for 'rewards' from certain suppliers ('redeemers'). The main issue was whether L was entitled to input tax recovery in respect of the cost of the rewards. The Court of Appeal held that the redeemer made a supply of rewards to the customer. But the redeemer also made a supply of redemption services to L, in respect of which L was entitled to input tax credit ([2008] STC 59). The House of Lords referred the case to the ECJ, which ruled that L's payment to the redeemer was third party consideration for a supply by the redeemer to the customer, although payment might also include consideration for a separate supply of services (a question for the national court to decide) (*ECJ Case C–53/09*, [2010] STC 2651 (TVC 22.153)).

See **69.19** below where vouchers are used as rewards for employees.

Issue of face value vouchers

[69.11] A '*face value voucher*' means a token, stamp or voucher (whether in physical or electronic form) that represents a right to receive goods or services to the value of an amount stated on it or recorded in it and '*face value*' means the amount stated on such a voucher. [*VATA 1994, Sch 10A para 1; FA 2003, Sch 1 para* 2]. Examples include gift vouchers, telephone cards, book tokens, electronic top-up cards and postage stamps. In *Leisure Pass Group Ltd (No 2)* (VTD 20910) (TVC 67.170), the tribunal decided that the inclusion of a set daily maximum value shown on the face of leisure passes meant that the passes qualified as face-value vouchers.

(1) Face value vouchers issued free

Where a business issues face value vouchers entirely without payment (either monetary or non-monetary, see **69.3** above) which are to be redeemed by the business, no VAT is due at the time of issue. (VAT Notice 700/7/02, para 5.8).

(2) Face value vouchers issued for a payment on or after 9 April 2003

The *issue* of a face value voucher, or any subsequent supply of it, is a supply of services for the purposes of *VATA 1994*. [*VATA 1994, Sch 10A para 2; FA 2003, Sch 1 para* 2]. For the avoidance of doubt, HMRC regard 'issued' as meaning that the voucher has been given or acquired a value, is capable of being used because it carries a right to receive goods or services and has been issued to a third party in return for payment. (VAT Information Sheet 12/03, para 4). This allows the *sale* of the voucher to be equated to the underlying supply so that, if it is known that the voucher has been redeemed for, say, zero-rated goods or services, then an intermediate supplier in the supply chain can make an adjustment to reflect the liability of the final supply (see below).

The legislation recognises four categories of face value vouchers.

(a) 'Credit vouchers'

I.e. face value vouchers issued by a person who

- is not a person from whom goods or services may be obtained by the use of the voucher, and
- undertakes to give complete or partial reimbursement to any such person from whom goods or services are so obtained.

Credit vouchers are typically, therefore, gift vouchers that are administered by trade bodies or associations or that can be redeemed at a number of different retailers.

The consideration for *any* supply of a credit voucher (including by any intermediate supplier) is disregarded for VAT purposes unless

(i) the consideration exceeds the face value of the voucher (in which case the VAT is due on the excess); or

(ii) any of the persons from whom goods or services are obtained by the use of the voucher fails to account for any of the VAT due on the supply of those goods or services to the person using the voucher to obtain them.

The tax loss provisions under (ii) above allow HMRC to collect any VAT due from the person who first sold the voucher (i.e. the issuer) in the event that the redeemer of the voucher fails to account for any VAT due. HMRC have undertaken only to enforce these provisions in the event of a deliberate attempt to avoid paying any VAT due. In cases of genuine error or insolvency, HMRC will not require the issuer to account for the VAT due and will seek to collect it from the redeemer (provided that the issuer has passed the funds to the redeemer).

[*VATA 1994, Sch 10A para 3; FA 2003, Sch 1 para 2; FA 2006, s 22*]. (VAT Information Sheet 12/03, para 6).

(b) 'Retailer vouchers'

I.e. face value vouchers issued by a person

- from whom goods or services may be obtained by the use of the voucher, and
- who, if there are other persons from whom goods or services may be obtained by the use of the voucher, undertakes to give complete or partial reimbursement to those from whom goods or services are so obtained.

Typical examples of retail vouchers are gift vouchers issued and redeemed by a high street retailer.

The consideration for the *issue* of a retailer voucher is disregarded for VAT purposes unless

(i) the consideration exceeds the face value of the voucher (in which case the VAT is due on the excess); or

(ii) the voucher is used to obtain goods or services from a person other than the issuer and that person fails to account for any of the VAT due on the supply of those goods or services to the person using the voucher to obtain them.

Any supply of a retailer voucher, subsequent to the first supply by the issuer, is treated in the same way as the supply of a voucher under (*d*) below.

Where a retailer voucher can be used to obtain goods or services from a third party, it is the responsibility of that third party to account for VAT in respect of those goods or services. The provisions in (ii) above allow HMRC to collect any VAT due from the person who first sold the voucher (i.e. the issuer) in the event that the redeemer of the voucher fails to account for any VAT due. HMRC have undertaken only to enforce these provisions in the event of a deliberate attempt to avoid paying any VAT due. In cases of genuine error or insolvency, HMRC will not require the issuer to account for the VAT due and will seek to collect it from the redeemer (provided that the issuer has passed the funds to the redeemer).

[*VATA 1994, Sch 10A para 4; FA 2003, Sch 1 para 2*]. (VAT Information Sheet 12/03, para 7).

(c) Postage stamps

The consideration for the supply of a postage stamp is disregarded for VAT purposes unless the consideration exceeds the face value of the stamp (in which case the VAT is due on the excess). [*VATA 1994, Sch 10A para 5; FA 2003, Sch 1 para 2*].

Postage stamps are redeemed for an exempt supply of postal services. These provision means that they can pass from the issuer through any intermediate suppliers and on to the final customer without VAT being charged. (VAT Information Sheet 12/03, para 13).

(d) Other kinds of face value voucher

A supply of a face value voucher that does not fall within (*a*)–(*c*) above (a supply by an intermediate supplier) is, subject to below, standard-rated.

An example falling within this category would be where a high street retailer sells gift vouchers to an intermediate supplier. The onward sale of the vouchers by the intermediate supplier is subject to VAT.

VAT need not be charged at the standard rate where one of the following applies.

- Where the voucher is one that can *only* be used to obtain goods or services in one particular non-standard rate category (i.e. reduced-rated, zero-rated or exempt and other non-taxable supplies), the supply of the voucher falls in that category. This has the effect of ensuring that such a voucher can pass through the supply chain at that non-standard rate. In practice, examples of this type of voucher are likely to be limited as vouchers that can be redeemed against non-standard-rated goods and services can often also be redeemed against standard-rated goods or services.
- Where the voucher *is* used to obtain goods or services all of which fall in one particular non-standard rate category (i.e. reduced-rated, zero-rated or exempt and other non-taxable supplies), the supply of the voucher falls in that category. This has the effect of allowing intermediate suppliers in the supply chain to make an adjustment to reflect the liability of the final supply (see below).

- Where the voucher is used to obtain goods or services in a number of different rate categories (i.e. any combination of standard-rated, reduced-rated, zero-rated or exempt and other non-taxable supplies), the supply of the voucher falls within those different categories and the value of each supply must be determined on a just and reasonable basis. This has the effect of allowing intermediate suppliers in the supply chain to make an adjustment to reflect the liability of the final supplies, to be apportioned between the different rate categories.

[*VATA 1994, Sch 10A para 6; FA 2003, Sch 1 para 2*].

Vouchers supplied free with other goods or services

Where

- a face-value voucher (other than a postage stamp) and other goods or services are supplied to the same person in a composite transaction, and
- the total consideration for the supplies is no different, or not significantly different, from what it would be if the voucher were not supplied,

the supply of the voucher is treated as being made for no consideration. This is an anti-avoidance provision to prevent businesses from artificially reducing the consideration for goods or services by issuing a face value voucher which is unlikely to be redeemed.

> *Examples*
>
> An hotel issues a voucher to a customer when the customer settles his bill for staying. The customer does not have the option of a price reduction in lieu of the voucher and very few customers ever redeem their vouchers.
>
> A retailer gives customers a face value voucher on every purchase made over a certain amount. Customers do not have the option of a price reduction in lieu of the voucher and the voucher has a number of restrictions which are likely to limit the number of customers who eventually redeem the voucher.
>
> A retailer sells a mobile phone boxed with a telephone card. The telephone card is a face value voucher. The customer does not have the option of refusing the telephone card for a reduction in the price of the phone.

[*VATA 1994, Sch 10A para 7; FA 2003, Sch 1 para 2*]. (VAT Information Sheet 12/03, para 12).

Input tax recovery by intermediate suppliers

Intermediate suppliers are entitled to recover input tax, subject to the normal requirements. The liability of their sale of face value vouchers is deemed to equate to the underlying supply of goods or services (see above). If it is known that the vouchers have been redeemed for zero-rated, reduced-rated or exempt and other non-taxable goods or services, then the intermediate supplier can make an adjustment to both the output tax and the input tax to reflect the liability of the final supply. Adjustments can be based on retail scheme percentages or other global calculations, rather than tracking individual face value vouchers. Where intermediate suppliers know *in advance* that vouchers can be redeemed for zero-rated, reduced-rated or exempt and other non-taxable goods or services, they may use a percentage split from the outset and avoid the need to make later adjustments.

Where an intermediate supplier is purchasing face value vouchers from the issuer who takes on the obligation to accept them, and is not required to account for VAT until the voucher is redeemed, the intermediate supplier may treat the amount of VAT that will be due on the supply as input tax at the time the purchase is made.

Information regarding any split in liability can only be provided by the issuer who redeems the vouchers. In order to avoid the need to track individual vouchers, redeemers can base adjustment figures on retail scheme percentages or other global calculations, providing the result is fair and reasonable. If the redeemer chooses to make this information available to intermediate suppliers, they may include the percentage split on any VAT invoice they issue to an intermediate supplier. This split should be quoted on any further VAT invoices issued by intermediate suppliers in the supply chain.

(VAT Information Sheet 3/03, para 12; VAT Information Sheet 12/03, para 10).

Invoicing

Issuers of face value vouchers, which are not credit vouchers (see (*a*) above), who redeem them for goods or services must issue a full VAT invoice if the vouchers are sold to a VAT-registered intermediate supplier. As the issuer who redeems the voucher does not need to account for VAT until the voucher is redeemed, HMRC suggest that the invoice is annotated with the words: 'The issuer of the voucher will account for output tax under the face value voucher provisions in Schedule 10A VAT Act 1994'.

Intermediate suppliers of face value vouchers, which are not credit vouchers (see (*a*) above), must account for VAT on the sale of the vouchers at the time the vouchers are sold. They must issue a full VAT invoice to any further intermediate supplier in the supply chain. They can reclaim input tax on the purchase of the vouchers (see above) and the evidence for this is the VAT invoice received from their supplier.

(VAT Information Sheet 12/03, para 10).

Treatment of sales of face value vouchers by an intermediate supplier using a retail scheme

Whether an intermediate supplier under (*d*) above can include sales of face value vouchers within its retail scheme depends on the retail scheme used.

- Under the Point of Sale scheme, sales of face value vouchers should be included in daily gross takings at the appropriate rate of VAT.
- Under an apportionment scheme, output tax on the sale of vouchers should be accounted for outside the retail scheme.
- Under a direct calculation scheme, intermediate suppliers may be able to include the sale of vouchers depending on the minority goods they mark up and the rate of VAT due when the vouchers are redeemed. See **60.17** and **60.18 RETAIL SCHEMES**.

- Intermediate suppliers using a bespoke scheme must agree with HMRC a fair and reasonable method for accounting for output tax on the sale of face value vouchers.

(VAT Information Sheet 12/03, para 11).

Top-up cards with no face value

Top-up vouchers and cards (e.g. telephone cards which allow the customer to add credit to their account) share many similarities to face value vouchers and are now treated in the same manner as face value vouchers. Therefore, issuers of top-up cards who redeem them for goods or services can account for VAT when the top-up is redeemed against goods or services. (VAT Information Sheet 3/03, para 10). See Business Brief 29/03 for HMRC's view of the VAT treatment of phone cards supplied to a UK distributor by an issuer in another EU country. This view has subsequently been supported by the Court of Appeal in *R (oao IDT Card Services Ireland Ltd) v HMRC*, CA [2006] STC 1252 (TVC 67.172).

Face value vouchers given away for no consideration

Where face value vouchers are purchased by businesses in order to be given away for no consideration, (e.g. to employees as 'perks' or under a promotions scheme), the VAT incurred is claimable as input tax (subject to the normal rules). However, output tax is due under *SI 1993/1507* at the time the vouchers are given away (see **47.7 OUTPUT TAX**). The sum due as output tax will be equal to the sum treated as input tax. (VAT Information Sheet 12/03, para 14).

Redemption of face value vouchers

[69.12] See **69.11** above for the definition of a '*face value voucher*'.

(1) Face value vouchers issued free

Where the vouchers are redeemed for goods or services

- without any payment, the VAT must be accounted for on the gift of goods or services as in **69.2** above; and
- with a payment or non-monetary consideration, VAT must be accounted for on the total amount received, including the value of any non-monetary consideration (see **69.3** above).

(VAT Notice 700/7/02, para 5.8).

(2) Face value vouchers issued for a payment

On redemption of the face value voucher for goods or services, its face value is the consideration for payment and the value for VAT purpose.

However, where the business has evidence to prove that a particular voucher was originally sold at below face value, the discounted amount can be used. This follows the decision in *Argos Distributors Ltd v C & E Commrs, ECJ Case C–288/94*, [1996] STC 1359 (TVC 22.236). Argos operated a voucher scheme. The vouchers had a face value printed on them and customers could use the voucher to obtain goods up to the face value in Argos's showrooms. Argos also sold the vouchers either at face value or at a discounted price to other traders who could either distribute them freely to members of staff or resell them to the public at up to face value. The ECJ held that what is now *Directive 2006/112/EC, Art 73* was to be taken to mean that, where all or part of the consideration for a supply was represented by a face value voucher, the taxable amount attributable to the voucher is the money obtained by the supplier of the goods from the sale of the voucher (and not its face value). The court, however, stressed that the supplier was responsible for establishing the actual sale price of the voucher at the time of its redemption. HMRC accept that on redemption of vouchers by a VAT-registered customer, Argos and businesses operating similar schemes, can account for VAT on their discounted price provided, at the time of redemption, it can

- identify the price at which vouchers were sold; and
- issue accurate VAT invoices showing the VAT due on the discounted amount.

If a business cannot meet the above conditions on redemption of vouchers by VAT-registered businesses, VAT must be accounted for on the full face value of the vouchers.

(VAT Notice 700/7/02, para 5.7).

Treatment of coupons and vouchers under retail schemes

[69.13] The VAT treatment under a retail scheme depends upon whether the promotion is funded solely by the retailer or by (or together with) a third party such as the manufacturer.

Discount vouchers

Where discount vouchers are taken as part payment, only the money received from the customer should be included in daily gross takings. If the retailer subsequently receives further payment for the voucher from another source, this payment must be included in daily gross takings. Strictly speaking, the retailer should account for this further payment in the period the goods are supplied. However, by concession, the retailer may account for such contributions in the period they are received.

Any charges by the retailer to the manufacturer for handling the vouchers is payment for an exempt supply and must be excluded from daily gross takings.

Vouchers—general

The following provisions apply to vouchers issued with no value/amounts and which are redeemable for whole items.

- *Vouchers issued by the retailer to customers making a specific purchase or purchases.* No VAT is due upon issue and no further VAT is due when the voucher is used by the customer to obtain the reward goods. Under Apportionment Scheme 2 and Direct Calculation Schemes 1 and 2, records of expected selling prices must be adjusted for the reward goods.

- *Vouchers issued freely by the retailer*. No VAT is due upon issue. When redeemed for goods, the rules in **69.2** above apply. See **60.9**(4) **RETAIL SCHEMES** for the scheme adjustments where goods from normal stock are supplied as gifts.
- *Vouchers issued by another person (e.g. a manufacturer) but redeemed by the retailer.* These are likely to be subject to the terms and conditions of that person's promotion. For example, if the retailer is given certain stocks to give away on behalf of that person, these stocks must not be included in the retail scheme calculations.

See **60.9**(31) **RETAIL SCHEMES** for sale of discount vouchers.

If such vouchers are redeemed for cash, the cash payment is outside the scope of VAT and daily gross takings must not be altered for the cash paid.

(VAT Notice 727/3/11, paras 7.1–7.5; VAT Notice 727/4/11, paras 8.1–8.4; VAT Notice 727/5/11, paras 7.1–7.4, all of which have the force of law).

Businesses selling vouchers

[69.14] A business that sells vouchers to other businesses and can never receive the final benefit shown on the voucher is viewed for VAT purposes as selling a promotion scheme rather than selling vouchers. This sale is a supply of services liable to VAT at the standard rate.

All sales of holiday vouchers by a promoter (or other companies specialising in such schemes) are liable to VAT at the standard rate. The VAT charged is input tax for the purchaser subject to the normal rules. If vouchers bear a face value, the sale of these will also normally be taxable as the value shown is effectively only the value of a discount allowable, since the purchaser cannot receive goods or services without making a further payment. Also, the sale of booklets containing vouchers that can be exchanged for discounted accommodation in selected hotels in the UK is a single supply liable to VAT at the standard rate. The booklets in which such vouchers are usually issued are incidental to the supply of vouchers and not viewed as a zero-rated booklet for VAT purposes.

(VAT Notice 700/7/02, para 5.9).

Manufacturers' promotion schemes aimed at the trade

Vouchers and dealer loader schemes

[69.15] Manufacturers often run promotions to encourage greater purchases of their 'premium' goods, i.e. those goods normally sold in day-to-day trading. Common promotions may be of three different types.

(a) **The issue of vouchers, or a 'proof of purchase'** with the sale of the premium trade goods which can be redeemed later for further goods. Under this type of promotion, the redemption goods are provided for no consideration and must be treated as gifts as in **69.2** above.

(b) **Dealer loader schemes.** These are schemes where rewards are offered on condition that a single trade order of a specified size is made. In such cases, HMRC accept in principle that the manufacturer, in costing the promotion, would have allowed for the cost of the redemption goods within the normal selling price of those 'premium' goods. No further VAT is due on the reward goods.

(c) **Trade orders made over a period of time.** Where rewards are offered on condition that trade orders are placed over a set period of time to a given level, the rewards are being provided for no consideration. If the rewards are goods which cost the manufacturer more than £50 or form part of a series or succession to the same customer, VAT is due on a cost value. Otherwise, no VAT is due. However, as a concession, HMRC will accept that these rewards may be treated as part of a multiple supply if

- the rewards are of a kind to be used in the recipient's business;
- the rewards are not intended for the personal use of the person receiving them; and
- the rewards appear on the final qualifying invoice, i.e. at the point at which the customer qualifies for the reward.

The same rules also apply where the manufacturer supplies the reward goods, but premium supplies may have gone via a wholesaler, for example

- the manufacturer supplies the reward direct to the customer;
- the wholesaler supplies the reward on behalf of the manufacturer from their own stock where the manufacturer either reimburses the wholesaler or replaces stock; or
- the wholesaler supplies the reward from stock provided for this purpose by the manufacturer.

(VAT Notice 700/7/02, para 6.1).

Retrospective discounts

Where a discount is given on condition that the customer reaches a target purchase level within a set time, the normal procedure would be to issue a credit note for the amount of the discount if the target is achieved. See **39.15 INVOICES**.

If, on the other hand, the customer is given goods to the value of the discount earned, the discount has been used to pay for the additional goods supplied. Normally, to avoid accounting for further VAT, a credit note would have to be issued to reflect the reduced value of the qualifying supplies and an invoice raised for the reward goods showing an equal amount of VAT. Instead, provided

- all the goods are liable to VAT at the same rate,
- the reward goods are supplied to the same person and for business purposes,
- no VAT credit note is issued, and
- records are kept to satisfy HMRC of a proper audit trail,

a 'no charge' invoice can be issued without VAT for the additional goods as this achieves the same result.

(VAT Notice 700/7/02, para 6.6).

Goods or 'points' given by manufacturers to customers' employees

Goods given free of charge by a manufacturer to customers' employees as a reward for promoting or selling goods are free supplies for no consideration. Similar VAT treatment applies where customers' employees accumulate voucher 'points' for selling a manufacturer's goods and the points are redeemable for goods. See **69.2** above. Any VAT incurred by the manufacturer on the goods is deductible (subject to the normal rules). (VAT Notice 700/7/02, paras 6.7, 6.8).

'Free' hire schemes for vending machines

See **47.8**(34) **OUTPUT TAX**.

Manufacturers' promotion schemes aimed at the public

Goods given away through a retailer

[69.16] Where

- the public buy from a retailer and send a proof of purchase to the manufacturer to receive further goods (from the manufacturer), or coupons are included by the manufacturer inside the product or as part of the packaging and the coupons are collected and redeemed later for goods, or
- retailers of a manufacturer's products act as its agents in giving reward goods to those customers making qualifying purchases and where the manufacturer has provided the reward goods to the retailer (for no consideration) specifically for this purpose,

the manufacturer is providing the redemption/reward goods for no consideration and must account for VAT as in **69.2** above.

(VAT Notice 700/7/02, para 7.1).

Manufacturers issuing money-off coupons to the public

If a manufacturer issues a money-off coupon which is redeemable

- by the customer with the retailer at the amount stated on the coupon,
- at the manufacturer's expense,
- as part of a sales promotion where the coupon is to be accepted by the retailer in part payment for a specified item of goods,
- where the manufacturer has sold the specified item to the retailer at the original price, and
- where the retailer takes the coupon from the customer on sale of the specified item, presents it to the manufacturer and is paid the stated amount,

the manufacturer can reduce his taxable amount by the value of the voucher which is actually refunded. This does not alter the amount shown on the invoice originally issued. The retailer's position on receipt of money is covered in **69.9** above.

(VAT Notice 700/7/02, para 7.2).

'Points schemes'

Some businesses run promotion schemes that involve issuing points that they will subsequently redeem for goods or services. They may allow other businesses to participate in their scheme by allowing them to issue redeeming businesses' points. If the redeeming businesses make a charge to the participant businesses, HMRC consider this to be payment for the right to participate in the redeeming business's promotions scheme. This is subject to VAT at the standard rate.

See **69.11** above for where points are exchanged for face value vouchers.

If a points scheme allows customers to donate points to schools or other institutions which can redeem the points with the manufacturer for goods (e.g. computer equipment) the manufacturer should account for the VAT as in **69.2** above.

(VAT Notice 700/7/02, para 7.3).

Goods given as prizes for competitions

If a manufacturer provides products as prizes for competitions, (e.g. in magazines, etc), any benefit received in exchange for the goods (e.g. a free advertisement in the magazine), is likely to constitute a barter transaction (see **69.3** above). The VAT due on the supply of the manufacturer's product is the same as it would be on the normal selling price of the product if there were no barter. However, if the prize provided is not something that the manufacturer ordinarily makes or sells, its value will be the actual cost incurred in providing the item. The magazine publisher would also then be making a supply of services to the manufacturer upon which VAT should be charged.

Where there is no exchange of benefits, there is no barter and VAT is due on a cost value subject to the normal business gift rules in **69.2** above.

(VAT Notice 700/7/02, para 7.4).

Cashback schemes

These are normally manufacturers' schemes aimed at the public but where goods are supplied through wholesalers and/or retailers. The cashback is a refund of money from the manufacturer directly to the final consumer if the consumer sends a proof of purchase, etc. to the manufacturer. In these circumstances, the manufacturer can reduce his 'taxable amount', provided it has charged and accounted for UK VAT on the original supply to the wholesaler or retailer. This does not affect the value of its original supply to the wholesaler/retailer. No credit notes are to be issued and the wholesaler/retailer's input tax is unaffected. There is simply a reduction of output tax to be reflected in the manufacturers' VAT account. Where a VAT-registered trader receives a cashback, this reduces the taxable value of its purchase and it must reduce its input tax accordingly. (VAT Notice 700/7/02, para 7.5).

Cross-border cashbacks

Where cashbacks are paid between businesses in different EU countries, no VAT adjustments should be made. This means in practice that where a UK manufacturer pays a cashback to a recipient in another EU country, the manufacturer cannot reduce his output tax and where a UK recipient receives a cashback from a manufacturer in another EU country, no input tax deduction is required by the recipient.

Change of liability in the supply chain

Where the VAT liability of the goods changes in the supply chain (e.g. where a charity buys certain goods zero-rated from the wholesaler which were standard-rated for VAT when supplied by the manufacturer), manufacturers cannot reduce their output tax in relation to the cashback paid to the charity. Where the cashback relates to goods that were supplied VAT-free to a business receiving the cashback, no adjustments should be made.

(HMRC Brief 8/07).

Newspaper promotions

If a manufacturer runs a promotion with a newspaper company whereby vouchers are printed in the newspaper along with the promotion of its product, and the public have to collect the vouchers in order to get reward goods or services, the goods/services are liable to VAT and the manufacturer should account for the VAT as in **69.2** above. If the vouchers offer a discount, the normal rules on redeeming vouchers in **69.9** above must be applied. (VAT Notice 700/7/02, para 7.6).

Goods given to publishers for use as magazine inserts

There are various VAT implications depending upon the exact nature of the particular circumstances.

- Where the goods are supplied to the publishers for a monetary consideration, VAT must be charged. When the goods are sold by the retailer with the magazine, there is normally a multiple supply which may have to be apportioned. See **47.3 OUTPUT TAX**.
- Where the goods are supplied to the publisher for no consideration (monetary or otherwise) VAT is due as under **69.2** above.
- Where the goods are supplied to the publisher without monetary consideration but under a barter arrangement whereby non-monetary consideration is received (e.g. an advertising benefit), VAT is normally due on the value of the goods (see **69.3** above). Where the goods are not normally made or sold by the manufacturer, the value will be the cost incurred in acquiring them. However, where any non-monetary consideration is minimal, it may be ignored and VAT is then due on cost as above.

- Where the goods are not supplied to the publisher but both the publisher and newsagent act purely as agent for the manufacturer in distributing products (e.g. free goods for the retail customer), there is no supply of the free goods to the publisher and the free supply is therefore by the manufacturer to the public. In these circumstances, the business gift rules in **69.2** above apply. See also **47.8**(26) **OUTPUT TAX** for free samples.

(VAT Notice 700/7/02, para 7.7).

Retail discount schemes

[69.17] Discounts are normally treated as reductions in the consideration given so that VAT is due on the discounted price actually paid. See **71.24 VALUATION** for a general consideration of discounts. The following are examples of schemes which generally fall to be treated in this way.

- **Deferred discount scheme.** This entitles a shareholder to a discount off the purchase price of goods. The discount is not deducted from the customer's payment but accumulated and paid out annually. Until the discount is paid to the customer it is to be treated as consideration for the goods supplied.
- **Special events.** In-store credit card holders are invited to preview sales and allowed special discounts, no payment usually being made by the credit company to the retailer. Alternatively, other selected groups may be offered discounts, again with no consideration being received from any other source.
- **'We will pay your VAT'.**
- **Graded promotions.** Graded discount vouchers are given which offer a percentage reduction which increases with the value of the purchases made.

(VAT Notice 700/7/02, paras 8.2, 8.4–8.6).

'Store card' discount schemes

A customer spends a minimum amount on any one purchase using a store card. This entitles the customer to a set amount of credit to be applied to their credit card account. There is no reimbursement by the retailer to the credit card company and the credit card company and retailer may, or may not, be in the same VAT group. If

- the retailer and credit card company are within the same VAT group, the group should only account for VAT on the discounted amount; and
- the retailer and credit card company are not in the same VAT group, the goods are sold by the retailer at their full value and VAT is due on this amount.

(VAT Notice 700/7/02, para 8.1).

Lottery promotion (scratch cards)

Customers who purchase certain items (at normal price) are given a scratch card (for no extra charge) on which certain symbols can be scratched off revealing the details of a prize. Alternatively, there may be no purchasing requirement.

- Where the prize is a free gift of goods, these are supplies for no consideration and the rules set out in **69.2** above apply.
- Where the prize is discount vouchers for use against future purchases, these are normally evidence of entitlement to a discount and, on redemption, the rules set out in **69.9** above apply.
- Where the prize is gift vouchers, the voucher has not been issued for a consideration and on redemption the rules in **69.11** above apply.

(VAT Notice 700/7/02, para 8.3).

Minimum or false value trade-ins

These are promotions in which the customer is allowed either a minimum or a pre-determined (fixed) value for goods taken in part exchange, regardless of the condition of the exchange article (e.g. £50 for a customer's old cooker when buying a new model). The selling price of the goods should be treated as the full amount chargeable before any deductions for part exchange allowances. The purchase price of the goods taken in part exchange is the full amount allowed to the customer and it is this figure that should be used as the purchase price of the goods if sold under the second-hand scheme.

Where, however, it is clear that there is no barter and the promotion is purely for promotional purposes (e.g. '£1 off a tin of paint if you bring in an old tin') this can be treated as a discount.

(VAT Notice 700/7/02, para 8.7).

Employee awards

[69.18] If an employer wishes to reward employees exceeding sales levels, etc by giving gifts of goods or services (e.g. free theatre tickets, restaurant meals or hotel accommodation), HMRC do not regard the services provided by the employees in return as non-monetary consideration (see **69.3** above). Input tax is deductible subject to the normal rules and output tax may be due under the rules for gifts in **69.2** above.

If the reward for the employee extends to non-employees (e.g. a spouse) the rules for the employee are as above but input tax in respect of non-employees may be blocked under the **BUSINESS ENTERTAINMENT (9)** provisions.

(VAT Notice 700/7/02, para 2.5).

Key points

[69.19] Points to consider are as follows.

- No output tax is due on a business gift if the value of the gift (usually the cost) is less than £50. The £50 limit is relevant to the total value of all gifts given to the same customer in a calendar year.
- If the value of a gift (or succession of gifts to the same person in a year) exceeds £50, then output tax is due according to the price that the recipient would have to pay for the gift, i.e. usually the cost price.
- In situations where a customer can reclaim input tax on the gift he has received, the donor can issue a tax certificate (not an invoice) to certify that output tax has been declared on the gift. This will be adequate evidence for the recipient to reclaim input tax (subject to normal rules).
- There is no output tax liability on a free supply of services, e.g. an accountancy business doing a tax return for a charity without making a charge.
- The output tax rules concerning money off coupons, discount vouchers and gift schemes can get complicated. It is important that the VAT issues are fully considered at the planning stage of any scheme that is introduced.
- Discounts given to a customer, for example, prompt payment or bulk buying mean that output tax is due on the discounted price that is charged. In the case of a discount for prompt payment, the VAT charged on a sales invoice should be based on the discounted amount, irrespective of whether the customer takes the discount option.

70

Transport and Freight

Cross-references. See **19.33 EUROPEAN UNION: SINGLE MARKET** for new means of transport; **21.7 EXPORTS** for the supply or hiring of freight containers; **45 MOTOR CARS.**

De Voil Indirect Tax Service. See V4.251.

Introduction

[70.1] The VAT treatment of transport falls into the following five main categories of supplies:

- ships (see **70.2** below);
- aircraft (see **70.3** below);
- lifeboats (see **70.14** below);
- passenger transport (see **70.15** below); and
- freight transport services (see **70.25** below).

[*VATA 1994, Sch 8 Group 8*].

Zero-rated supplies of ships

[70.2] The supply of any 'qualifying ship' is zero-rated. A '*qualifying ship*' is any ship which is

(a) of a gross tonnage of not less than 15 tons; and
(b) neither designed nor adapted for use for recreation or pleasure.

[*VATA 1994, Sch 8 Group 8 Item 1 and Note A1; SI 1995/3039*].

'*Ship*' includes a submarine, hovercraft (see below), light vessel, fire float, dredger, barge or lighter, a mobile floating dock or crane and an offshore oil or gas installation used in the underwater exploitation or exploration of oil and gas resources, which is designed to be moved from place to place. *Not included* are

- fixed oil and gas installations (even though they might be transported to a site as a floating structure); and
- vessels which are permanently moored (e.g. as attractions) *and* not readily capable of navigation.

The supply of a partially completed ship is standard-rated. A ship is considered complete when it is seaworthy or fit to navigate the waterways for which it is designed (*QED Marine* (VTD 17336) (TVC 66.9)). However, supplies of parts and equipment (including part-assembled ships, e.g. fuselage, wings or hull) in the course of construction of a qualifying ship may be zero-rated (see **70.4** below).

(VAT Notice 744C, paras 2.2, 4.5, 7.2).

Recreation and pleasure

As a result of (*b*) above, zero-rating cannot apply to a ship or boat *designed or adapted* for use for recreation or pleasure, i.e. it must be designed for commercial purposes. Features that indicate a commercial design include a cargo hold, commercial fishing equipment or the ability to convey large numbers of passengers.

Motor cruisers, powerboats and yachts

These are designed or adapted for use for recreation or pleasure. As a result, they cannot be zero-rated as qualifying ships even if satisfying (*a*) above or supplied for business use (e.g. sail training). See also *Callison* (VTD 810) (TVC 66.1) and *obiter dicta* in *Hamann v Finanzamt Hamburg-Eimsbuttel, ECJ Case C–51/88*, [1991] STC 193 (TVC 22.202).

Cruise ships

Cruise ships can be zero-rated as qualifying ships provided

- they have a gross tonnage of not less than 15 tons;
- they are unsuitable for private use; and
- they are supplied for use in the business of providing recreation or pleasure cruises for fee-paying passengers.

Residential accommodation

Houseboats without engines may be eligible for zero-rating under a specific relief (see **42.25 LAND AND BUILDINGS: ZERO AND REDUCED RATE SUPPLIES AND DIY HOUSEBUILDERS**). Otherwise, the intended use of a vessel does not affect qualifying ship status. The only factors to be considered are the gross tonnage, the design of the ship and any subsequent adaptations. If a ship is designed or adapted with the ability to be used for recreation or pleasure (e.g. cruising on rivers or canals), rather than predominantly as permanent residential accommodation, it is not a qualifying ship. In *DG Everett; The London Tideway Harbour Co Ltd* (VTD 11736) (TVC 66.3), barges with engines which were used as living accommodation were held to be zero-rated provided they satisfied the conditions in (*a*) above. The barges had not been originally designed for recreation or pleasure. It stretched the ordinary meaning of those words to say that it included a home or place of permanent habitation. The decision was not followed in *Grieve* (VTD 20149) (TVC 66.4) but was applied in *HMRC v Stone*, Ch D [2008] STC 2501 (TVC 66.5). Following the decision in *Stone*, HMRC have changed their policy on the liability of vessels used as residential accommodation (excluding houseboats). They have decided to treat Dutch barges and similar vessels that are designed and supplied for use as the permanent residence of the customer as qualifying ships and eligible for zero-rating. As vessels of less than 15 gross tons can never be zero-rated regardless of their design, the majority of narrow boats designed for permanent residential use will not meet this requirement and their supply will continue to be standard-rated. As a result of this policy change some supplies of goods and services to the owners of such vessels may also be zero-rated by suppliers. These include the following, but do not extend to domestic equipment and fittings: repairs and maintenance of the vessel itself; modification or conversion of the vessel itself provided that it remains a qualifying ship after modification or conversion; and parts and equipment ordinarily installed or incorporated in the propulsion, navigation, communications or structure of a ship. (HMRC Brief 38/09).

Gross tonnage

The gross tonnage of a ship is as ascertained under the *Merchant Shipping Acts*. In the case of an unregistered ship where the gross tonnage of a ship has not been so calculated, for VAT purposes only, the gross tonnage is determines using the formula:

For vessels 24 metres or greater in length:

L × B × D × 0.235

For vessels less than 24 metres in length:

L × B × D × 0.16

where:

L = Length in metres measured from the foreside of the foremost fixed permanent structure to the afterside of the aftermost permanent structure (excluding appendages that do not contribute to the volume of the vessel)

B = Beam-breadth of vessel in metres at the widest part to the outside of the outer planking (excluding the thickness of any moulding or rubbing strake which may be fitted)

D = Depth in metres measured vertically from the midpoint overall. For this purposes, the upper calculation point is

- for a decked vessel, the underside of the deck on the middle line, or (if there is no deck on the middle line) the underside of the deck at the side of the vessel; and
- for an open-decked vessel, the top of the upper strake or gunwale; and

the lower calculation point is

- for a wooden vessel, the upper side of the plank at the side of the keel;
- for a metal vessel, the top of the plating at the side of the keelson; and
- for a moulded vessel (e.g. one made of glass-reinforced plastic), the inside of the hull. Where no keel member is fitted and the keel is of open trough construction, the calculation point is the top of the keel filling, if fitted, or the level at which the inside breadth of the trough is 10 cms (whichever gives the greater depth).

Hovercraft

Hovercraft are not subject to the gross tonnage criteria and are therefore regarded as qualifying ships (unless designed or adapted for use for recreation or pleasure).

Multi-hull vessels

Each hull must be measured separately for overall length, beam and depth and the vessel as a whole must be measured.

Narrowboats

The measurement must be taken from the underside of the deck at the side of the vessel, rather than from the roof of the cabin.

Breaks in deck line

A break is a raised portion of the deck that extends from one side of the ship to the other. Cabins, wheelhouses, hatches and erections above the deck are not breaks. If the ship does have a break, the mean length, breadth and depth should be multiplied together with a factor of 0.35. This resultant figure should then be added to the gross tonnage when calculated using the formula above.

(VAT Notice 744C, paras 2.4–2.12).

Zero-rated supplies of aircraft

[70.3] The supply of any 'qualifying aircraft' is zero-rated.

From 1 January 2011

A 'qualifying aircraft' is any aircraft which—

- is used by an airline operating for reward chiefly on international routes; or
- is used by a State institution and meets the condition that
  - (a) the aircraft is of a weight of not less than 8,000 kilograms; and
  - (b) is neither designed nor adapted for use for recreation or pleasure.

'*Airline*' means an undertaking which provides services for the carriage by air of passengers or cargo (or both).

'*State institution*' has the same meaning as in *Directive 2006/112/EC, Annex X, Part B*.

[*VATA 1994, Sch 8 Group 8 Item 2 and Notes A1–A3; F(No 3)A s 21*].

The definition of qualifying aircraft was amended because the UK had been applying a different criteria to those specified in *Directive 2006/112/EC, Art 148*, which exempts certain supplies of goods and services related to aircraft. The essential condition for those exemptions is that the aircraft must be 'used by an airline operating for reward chiefly on international routes'. In *Cimber Air A/S Skatteministeriet, Case C-382/02*, [2005] STC 547 (TVC 22.393), the ECJ ruled that those exemptions apply even for an aircraft operating on domestic routes, as long as it is used by such an airline. (EU Press Release IR/09/1016 dated 25 June 2009).

'*Aircraft*' includes aeroplanes (civil and military), helicopters and airships but does not include space craft and satellites.

'*Weight*' is the authorised maximum take-off weight specified in the certificate of airworthiness or, for military aircraft, shown in the documents issued by the Ministry of Defence.

Prior to 1 January 2011

A '*qualifying aircraft*' is any aircraft which is

(a) of a weight of not less than 8,000 kilogrammes; and

(b) neither designed nor adapted for use for recreation or pleasure.

[*VATA 1994, Sch 8 Group 8 Item 2 and Note A1*].

'*Aircraft*' includes aeroplanes (civil and military), helicopters and airships but does not include space craft and satellites.

'*Weight*' is the authorised maximum take-off weight specified in the certificate of airworthiness or, for military aircraft, shown in the documents issued by the Ministry of Defence.

(VAT Notice 744C, paras 3.2–3.5).

Ships and aircraft — other zero-rated supplies

[70.4] In addition to the supply of certain ships or aircraft (see **70.2** and **70.3** above) various other supplies and services in connection with such craft may also be zero-rated.

Parts and equipment

Zero-rating applies to

(a) the supply of parts and equipment, of a kind ordinarily installed or incorporated in, and to be installed or incorporated in, the propulsion, navigation or communication systems or general structure of a qualifying ship (see **70.2** above) or a qualifying aircraft (see **70.3** above); and

(b) the supply of life jackets, life rafts, smoke hoods and similar safety equipment for use in a qualifying ship or aircraft.

The letting on hire of goods within (*a*) or (*b*) above is also zero-rated.

Any supply of parts and equipment to a Government department is excluded from zero-rating unless *either* the supply is in the course or furtherance of a business carried on by the department *or* the parts and equipment are to be installed or incorporated in ships or aircraft used for the purpose of providing rescue or assistance at sea.

[*VATA 1994, Sch 8 Group 8 Items 2A, 2B and Notes A1, 2 and 2A; SI 1995/3039*].

Technically, in the light of the decision in *QED Marine* (VTD 17336) (TVC 66.9) that a ship does not become a qualifying ship until it becomes seaworthy, parts supplied up to that time should be standard-rated. However, HMRC consider that zero-rating for the supply of parts and equipment falling within (*a*) above should apply to both existing qualifying ships/aircraft and those under construction that will qualify when they become seaworthy/airworthy. HMRC expect businesses to have contractual or other evidence that the completed ship or aircraft will be qualifying, otherwise all supplies of parts and equipment must be standard-rated.

HMRC also consider that a qualifying ship/aircraft that temporarily loses its seaworthy/airworthy status can continue to be classed as a qualifying ship/aircraft, provided there is clear and evidenced intention to return the ship/aircraft to a seaworthy/airworthy condition.

(VAT Information Sheet 15/07).

Parts and equipment *include*

- Anchors
- Catering and laundering equipment (industrial)
- Communications equipment used for the operation of the ship or aircraft
- Cranes
- 'Expendable' parts and 'rotable' components used by the aircraft industry
- Fishing nets and equipment
- Laundering equipment (industrial)
- Lifeboats (and equipment used therein) and life rafts
- Nuts, bolts, hoses, oil seals and rivets (referred to as 'consumables' by the aircraft industry)
- Propellers and rudders
- Pumps
- Radar and navigation equipment
- Safety equipment (e.g. escape chutes, life jackets, smoke hoods, oxygen masks and winches)
- Sanitary fixtures

Parts and equipment *exclude*

- Aircraft ground equipment
- Binoculars
- Bulk materials (e.g. adhesives, chemicals, fabrics, inhibitors, metals, oils, paints, solvents and thinners)
- Catering and laundering equipment (domestic)
- Crockery and cutlery
- Diving equipment
- Flight simulators or their parts
- Furniture (unfixed) and soft furnishings
- Missiles, shells, etc.
- Raw materials (e.g. fibre board, plastics, specialist metals)
- Ship's stores
- Telephones and televisions
- Tooling and equipment used for manufacturing parts or equipment
- Tools
- Underwater cameras
- Video tapes, video games and similar entertainment equipment

Evidence for zero-rating

Normal commercial documentation is sufficient provided the supplier is satisfied that the parts, etc. qualify for zero-rating. If uncertain (e.g. because the parts could be used on a qualifying or non-qualifying ship or because the customer is a government department) the supplier should obtain an undertaking from the customer that the parts etc. qualify. See Notice 744C, para 13 for a suggested format. Where the customer is unable or unwilling to give an undertaking, the supply should be standard-rated.

(VAT Notice 744C, paras 7.4–7.7).

Government departments

The exclusion from zero-rating for supplies to Government departments (see above) only applies to the supply of parts and equipment, i.e. goods. Supplies of services (e.g. repair and maintenance, modification or conversion) can still be zero-rated. It is therefore necessary to distinguish between the two types of supply. If a contract involves both goods and services, a supplier must determine whether there is a single supply of goods (standard-rated) or services (zero-rated) or whether there is a multiple supply, in which case the VAT treatment for each of the supplies must be determined. Where contracts are complex, the supplier should contact the National Advice Service or their Client Relationship Manager with the full details of the supplies involved, together with the contractual detail. HMRC are also happy to provide VAT advice to the Ministry of Defence and suppliers at the pre-contract stage. (VAT Information Sheet 15/07).

Repairs and maintenance

[70.5] The repair or maintenance of a qualifying ship (see **70.2** above) or a qualifying aircraft (see **70.3** above) is zero-rated. [*VATA 1994, Sch 8 Group 8 Items 1, 2; SI 1995/3039*].

Maintenance includes testing of parts and components, cleaning, fumigation and ship's laundry (provided the articles are not personal to the crew or passengers). Parts, components and materials provided by the supplier of the repairs and maintenance are regarded as part of the zero-rated work.

Repairs and maintenance of parts and equipment can also be zero-rated provided

(a) in the case of a ship
- the repair is carried out on board; or
- the part or component is removed for repair and is replaced in the same ship; and

(b) in the case of an aircraft
- the repair is carried out on board; or
- the part or component is removed for repair and is replaced in the same aircraft; or
- following the repair or maintenance, the parts are returned to be held in stock for future use as spares in qualifying aircraft; or
- if they are unserviceable parts and equipment, they are exchanged for identical parts which have themselves been reconditioned, repaired or maintained.

Subcontracted services supplied in respect of repair and maintenance of a qualifying ship or aircraft can similarly be zero-rated. The subcontractor is advised to obtain evidence to substantiate zero-rating from the main contractor.

(VAT Notice 744C, paras 6.2, 6.5–6.7).

Modifications and conversions

[70.6] The modification or conversion of any qualifying ship (see **70.2** above) or qualifying aircraft (see **70.3** above) is zero-rated provided that, when so modified or converted, it will remain a qualifying ship or aircraft. [*VATA 1994, Sch 8 Group 8 Items 1 and 2; SI 1995/3039*]. Included are structural alterations and rebuilding or lengthening.

Sub-contracted services supplied in respect of modification or conversion of a qualifying ship or aircraft can similarly be zero-rated. The subcontractor is advised to obtain evidence to substantiate zero-rating from the main contractor.

(VAT Notice 744C, paras 6.3, 6.7).

Ship design services supplied in the UK are zero-rated as integral to the supply, modification or conversion of a qualifying ship only where a supplier specifically contracts with a customer to design *and* supply, modify or convert a qualifying ship. In other circumstances, design services are standard-rated. (Business Brief 5/99).

Air navigation services

[70.7] The supply of 'air navigation services' are zero-rated when

- provided for qualifying aircraft (see **70.3** above); or
- supplied to a person who receives the supply for the purposes of a business carried on by him and who belongs outside the UK (whether or not provided for qualifying aircraft).

'*Air navigation services*' have the same meaning as in *Civil Aviation Act 1982, s 105(1)*, i.e. they include information, directions and other facilities furnished, issued or provided in connection with the navigation or movement of aircraft, and include the control of movement of vehicles in any part of an aerodrome used for the movement of aircraft.

[*VATA 1994, Sch 8 Group 8 Items 6A, 11(b), Notes 6A and 7; SI 1995/653; SI 1995/3039*].

Air navigation services are largely provided by the Civil Aviation Authority which has been granted taxable status for its supply of these services. (Business Brief 20/94).

Charter services and letting on hire

[70.8] The supply of services under the charter of a qualifying ship (see **70.2** above) or a qualifying aircraft (see **70.3** above) is zero-rated unless those services consist wholly of any one or more of

- the transport of passengers,
- accommodation,
- entertainment, or
- education,

being services wholly performed in the UK. [*VATA 1994, Sch 8 Group 8 Items 1, 2 and Note 1; SI 1995/3039*].

The correct VAT treatment of supplies of ships and aircraft under charter can cause difficulties. The term 'charter' is used to describe several different types of supply (including freight or passenger transport) and is also used in slightly different ways in respect of ships and aircraft. Also, there is a complex interaction between the rules on both place of supply and liability, of charter, hire, passenger transport and freight transport services. See HMRC VAT Guidance V1–7, Chapter 8 para 11.6 for more detailed information.

Boats for disabled persons

[70.9] Boats which are designed or substantially and permanently adapted for the use of disabled persons may be zero-rated in certain circumstances. See **28.23 HEALTH AND WELFARE.**

Handling services

[70.10] Any services provided for the handling of ships or aircraft in a 'port', 'customs and excise airport' or outside the UK are zero-rated when

- provided for qualifying ships (see **70.2** above) or qualifying aircraft (see **70.3** above); or
- supplied to a person who receives the supply for the purposes of a business carried on by him and who belongs outside the UK (whether or not provided for qualifying ships and aircraft).

The letting on hire of goods is specifically excluded.

'*Port*' means any port appointed for customs purposes and includes all seaports in the UK. At a seaport the port limits include all territorial waters but do not normally extend inland beyond the waterway of the port.

'*Customs and excise airport*' means an airport designated for the landing or departure of aircraft for the purposes of the *Customs and Excise Acts* by an Order in Council made pursuant to *Civil Aviation Act 1982, s 60*. The limit of such an airport is normally the boundary of the airport itself. The designated Customs airports are Aberdeen, Belfast International (Aldergrove), Biggin Hill, Birmingham, Blackpool, Bournemouth, Bristol, Cambridge, Cardiff, Coventry, East Midlands, Edinburgh, Exeter, Farnborough, Filton, Glasgow, Humberside, Leeds/Bradford, Liverpool, London City, London Gatwick, London Heathrow, London Luton, London Stanstead, Lydd, Manchester, Manston, Newcastle, Norwich, Plymouth, Prestwick, Sheffield City, Shoreham, Southampton, Southend, Sumburgh and Teeside.

[*VATA 1994, Sch 8 Group 8 Items 6(a), 11(b), Notes 5–7; SI 1995 No 3039*]. (VAT Notice 744B, para 8.8).

Ship handling

This includes port and harbour dues, dock and berth charges, conservancy charges (including the provision of local lights, buoys and beacons), graving dock charges, mooring charges, demurrage (where this is a charge for failure to load or discharge a ship within specified time), security and fire services, supply of crew members and the day-to-day management of a ship.

Aircraft handling

This includes aircraft landing, parking or housing fees, aircraft compass swinging fees, apron services, airport navigation service charges, security and fire services and the supply of crew members.

(VAT Notice 744C, para 8.3).

Surveys and classification services

[70.11] Any service supplied for, or in connection with, the surveying of any ship or aircraft or the classification of any ship or aircraft for the purposes of any register is zero-rated when

- provided in connection with any qualifying ship (see **70.2** above) or qualifying aircraft (see **70.3** above); or
- supplied to a person who receives the supply for the purposes of a business carried on by him and who belongs outside the UK (whether or not provided for qualifying ships and aircraft).

[*VATA 1994, Sch 8 Group 8 Items 9, 11(b) and Note 7; SI 1995/3039*].

There must be a physical inspection of the ship/aircraft to qualify for zero-rating.

Included are classification services performed for Lloyd's and other registers and survey services for aircraft in relation to the certificate of airworthiness. *Not included* are tonnage measurements or surveys of ships for registration or other purposes required by statute to be carried out by the Department of Transport (which are outside the scope of VAT) or services of arranging for the registering of ships for the purposes of the *Merchant Shipping Acts* (which are standard-rated).

(VAT Notice 744C, para 9.6).

Salvage and towage services

[70.12] Salvage and towage services supplied for shipping are zero-rated whatever the type of ship. [*VATA 1994, Sch 8 Group 8 Item 8*]. Shipping in this context includes inland waterway vessels and all floating objects. Zero-rating also covers dock gates, pier and bridge sections and buoys. It does not cover any subsequent repair work carried out (for which see **70.5** above). (VAT Notice 744C, para 9.4).

Pilotage

[70.13] Pilotage services are zero-rated. [*VATA 1994, Sch 8 Group 8 Item 7*]. This applies to all shipping and is not just confined to qualifying ships. (VAT Notice 744C, para 9.3).

Lifeboats and slipways

[70.14] The following supplies are zero-rated.

(a) The supply to, and repair or maintenance for, a charity providing rescue or assistance at sea of
- any 'lifeboat';
- carriage equipment designed solely for the launching and recovery of lifeboats;
- tractors for the sole use of the launching and recovery of lifeboats; and
- winches and hauling equipment for the sole use of the recovery of lifeboats.

(b) The construction, modification, repair or maintenance for a charity providing rescue or assistance at sea of slipways used solely for the launching and recovery of lifeboats.

(c) The supply of spare parts or accessories to a charity providing rescue or assistance at sea for use in or with goods under (*a*) above or slipways within (*b*) above.

(d) The supply to a charity providing rescue or assistance at sea of equipment that is to be installed, incorporated or used in a lifeboat and is of a kind ordinarily installed, incorporated or used in a lifeboat.

(e) With effect from 1 August 2006, the supply of fuel to a charity providing rescue or assistance at sea where the fuel is for use in a lifeboat.

Included is the letting on hire of qualifying goods.

'*Lifeboat*' means any vessel (whatever the tonnage) used or to be used solely for rescue or assistance at sea.

To qualify for zero-rating the recipient of the supply must, before the supply is made, give the supplier a certificate stating the name and address of the recipient and that the supply is of a description specified in *VATA 1994, Sch 8 Group 8 Item 3*. The supplier must take all reasonable steps to check the validity of the certificate and should consult HMRC if in doubt. Where, however, despite taking such steps, nonetheless the supplier fails to identify an incorrect certificate and in good faith makes the supplies concerned at the zero rate, HMRC will not seek to recover the VAT due from the supplier. (VAT Notice 48, ESC 3.11).

[*VATA 1994, Sch 8 Group 8 Item 3 and Notes 2, 3 and 4; SI 1995/3039; SI 2002/456; SI 2006/1750*].

Passenger transport

[70.15] De Voil Indirect Tax Service. See V3.189, V4.251.

Passenger transport services are supplied when a vehicle, ship or aircraft is provided, *together with* a driver or crew, for the carriage of passengers. Incidental services may also be included. Where a vehicle, ship or aircraft is supplied *without* a driver or crew, this is not a supply of passenger transport services, but a means of transport.

To determine the correct VAT treatment of supplies of passenger transport it is necessary to

- decide whether the supply takes place in the UK (see **70.16** below); and if so
- consider whether the supply is zero-rated (see **70.17** below) or standard-rated (see **70.19** below).

Certain supplies of passenger transport cause particular problems because they can be zero-rated or standard-rated depending upon the precise nature of the services offered. See **70.20** below for transport of vehicles on ships, **70.21** below for cruises and **70.22** below for airline passengers' perks.

See **70.24** below for taxis and hire cars.

Bought-in supplies, packages and inclusive tours

Where passenger transport is bought in and re-supplied, either on its own or as part of a package or inclusive tour, VAT must normally be accounted for under the tour operators' margin scheme. Any other travel, hotel and holiday facilities which have been bought in and re-supplied must also be accounted for using the margin scheme. An 'in-house' supply of passenger transport (e.g. the provision of a driver plus vehicle for passenger transport) does not fall within the scheme and is dealt with in the normal way *unless* it is provided together with other travel and hotel facilities which have been bought in and re-supplied, in which case the 'in-house' transport must be included in the scheme calculation. See **68 TOUR OPERATORS' MARGIN SCHEME** for further details.

Place of supply

[70.16] Services consisting of the transportation of passengers are treated as supplied in the country where the transportation takes place to the extent that it takes place in that country. [*SI 1992/3121, Art 6*]. As a result, subject to the special rules below, if it takes place

- inside the UK, the supplies are all within the scope of UK VAT;
- outside the UK the supplies are outside the scope of UK VAT (see below);
- both inside and outside the UK, the element that takes place within the UK is within the scope of UK VAT and the element that takes place outside the UK is outside the scope of UK VAT.

In cases where cross-frontier transport is provided on an all-inclusive basis, the total consideration must be allocated on a pro-rata basis having regard to the distance covered (rather than the time spent) in each EU country (*Reisebüro Binder GmbH v Finanzamt Stuttgart-Körperschaften, ECJ Case C–116/96*, [1998] STC 604 (TVC 22.212)).

Sea and air passenger transport

Provided the means of transport used does not put in or land in another country on the way, any transportation as part of a journey between two points in the same country is treated as taking place wholly inside that country even where it takes place partly outside its territorial jurisdiction. This applies even if the journey is part of a longer journey involving travel to or from another country. [*SI 1992/3121, Art 7*].

> *Example*
>
> A ferry transports passengers from Liverpool to Dublin via the Isle of Man.
>
> The first leg (Liverpool to the Isle of Man) is treated as taking place in the UK but the remaining part of the journey (Isle of Man to Dublin) takes place outside UK territorial waters and is outside the scope of UK VAT.

Pleasure cruises

Any goods or services provided as part of a pleasure cruise are treated as supplied in the same place as the transportation of the passengers and for this purpose a pleasure cruise is treated as a supply of passenger transport. [*SI 1992/3121, Art 8*]. The place of supply of a cruise follows the general rule above i.e. it is supplied in the country in which it takes place to the extent that it takes place in that country.

Luggage and/or accompanying motor vehicles

The transportation of any luggage or motor vehicle (car, motorcycle, caravan, trailer or small commercial vehicle) accompanying in either case a passenger is treated as supplied in the same place as the passenger transport [*SI 1992/3121, Art 8*] and as a single supply with it. The transportation of an *unaccompanied* vehicle is treated as a supply of freight transport (see **70.25** below).

Passenger transport supplied outside the UK

If the supply takes place:

- In another EU country, the supplier may have to register for VAT in that country and account for VAT at the relevant rate applying there. If the supplier does not have an establishment there, he may need to appoint a local tax representative to account for the VAT there on his behalf.
- In a country outside the EU, the supplier may be liable to account for any tax in that country that is applicable on passenger transport services.
- In international airspace or waters, the supplier may not have to account for any tax on that part of the supply in any country.

Passenger transport supplied in the UK by persons belong outside the UK

Where a business belonging outside the UK is not registered for UK VAT and supplies passenger transport in the UK,

- if its customer is registered for UK VAT, the customer can account for VAT on its supplies under the reverse charge procedure (see **38.4 INTERNATIONAL SERVICES**); and
- if its customer is not registered for UK VAT, it is liable to account for the VAT in the UK and must register for VAT in the UK where its supplies exceed the registration threshold (see **59.3 REGISTRATION**).

(VAT Notice 744A, paras 3.1–3.4).

Services supplied on board passenger transport

Where such services are separate supplies in their own right (i.e. are not part of a single supply of transport) the following place of supply rules apply.

- *Catering*. In *Faaborg-Gelting Linien A/S v Finanzamt Flensburg, ECJ Case C–231/94*, [1996] STC 774 (TVC 22.174), the ECJ held that catering supplied on board a ferry travelling between Denmark and Germany was a supply of *services*, supplied where the supplier had his established place of business under what is now *Directive 2006/112/EC, Art 43*. However, many EU countries, including the UK, have *not* implemented this judgment. HMRC treat catering as a supply of *goods* which is outside the scope of UK VAT when supplied for consumption on board intra-EU transport under *SI 2004/3148, Art 6*. It is also treated as outside the scope of UK VAT when supplied on other international passenger transport under *VATA 1994, s 7(2)*.
- *Gaming machines*. In *Berkholz v Finanzamt Hamburg-Mitte-Altstadt, ECJ Case C–168/84*, [1985] 3 CMLR 667 (TVC 22.394) the ECJ held that the provision of the service of playing on gaming machines is supplied where the supplier is established. Again, this decision has not been implemented in the UK and some other EU countries. The current position is that where a trader operates amusement or gaming machines on a passenger ship which is leaving the UK for a foreign destination (a foreign-going vessel) the supply of services is regarded as being made outside the UK, and therefore outside the scope of UK VAT. Any use of the facilities in UK territorial waters is effectively ignored provided the vessel has cleared to go foreign. Where the machines are operated on vessels which are not foreign-going, i.e. for coastwise journeys within the UK, the supply is made within the UK and is liable to VAT at the standard rate.

(HMRC VAT—Place of Supply—Transport Manual VATPOSTR 2420).

Zero-rating

[70.17] Subject to the standard-rated supplies in **70.19** below, the supply of passenger transport in the UK is zero-rated if falling within any of the following categories.

(a) In any vehicle, ship or aircraft designed or adapted to carry not less than ten passengers. [*VATA 1994, Sch 8 Group 8 Item 4(a)*]

See *Cirdan Sailing Trust v C & E Commrs, Ch D 2005*, [2006] STC 185 (TVC 66.19) for a consideration of how to apply the test of passenger carrying capacity.

For the purposes of determining the carrying capacity, the driver and crew should be treated as passengers. See also *G L Ashton (t/a Country Hotel Narrowboats)* (VTD 14197) (TVC 66.18).

Included (subject to the seating rule) are

- pleasure cruises;
- cliff lifts;
- excursions by coach and train (including steam railways);
- horse-drawn buses;
- mystery coach trips and boat trips;
- sight-seeing tours;
- the transport element of 'park-and-ride' schemes designed to reduce traffic congestion in city centres; and
- the transport of parachutists or divers, provided it is only transportation that is provided.

If the carrying capacity of the vehicle, ship or aircraft is less than ten passengers, the transport is standard-rated unless it can be zero-rated under (*b*)–(*d*) below or the special rule for disabled passengers applies (see below).

(VAT Notice 744A, paras 4.1, 4.2).

Disabled passengers

Zero-rating specifically includes the transport of passengers in a vehicle

- which is designed, or substantially and permanently adapted, for the safe carriage of a person in a wheelchair (or two or more such persons), and
- which, if it were not so designed or adapted, would be capable of carrying no less than ten passengers.

Note that, where the conditions are met, zero-rating applies whether or not the transport service is provided, in a particular case, for disabled persons.

[*VATA 1994, Sch 8 Group 8 Note (4D); SI 2001/753*].

Miniature and narrow-gauge railways

See *Metroland Ltd* (VTD 14550) (TVC 66.35) and *Narogauge Ltd* (VTD 14680) (TVC 66.22).

Narrowboats

In determining whether a narrowboat is designed to carry ten or more passengers, it is the space on each boat, rather than just the number of berths, which determines the carrying capacity (*GL Ashton (t/a Country Hotel Narrowboats)* (VTD 14197) (TVC 66.18)).

Cabin lifts

Each cabin in a cabin lift to a scenic headland has been held to be a separate vehicle and the transport of passengers standard-rated if the individual cabins are designed to hold less than ten people (*Llandudno Cabinlift Co Ltd* (VTD 1) (TVC 66.30)).

(b) From 1 January 2011, by providers of universal postal services. [*VATA 1994, Sch 8 Group 8 Item 4(b); F(No 3)A, s 22(1)*]. **Prior to 1 January 2011, by the Post Office Company (or any of its wholly-owned subsidiaries).** [*VATA 1994, Sch 8 Group 8 Item 4(b); Postal Services Act 2000, Sch 8 para 22*] **(VAT Notice 48, ESC 3.33)**

This applies irrespective of the type of vehicle or its carrying capacity. (VAT Notice 744A, para 7.1).

(c) On any scheduled flight. [*VATA 1994, Sch 8 Group 8 Item 4(c)*]

This applies irrespective of the carrying capacity of the aircraft. A scheduled flight is one that is run either according to a published timetable or so regularly or frequently as to constitute a recognisable systematic series of flights. (VAT Notice 744A, paras 5.1, 5.2).

(d) From a place within to a place outside the UK (or vice versa) to the extent that those services are supplied within the UK. [*VATA 1994, Sch 8 Group 8 Item 4(d)*]

This applies irrespective of the carrying capacity of the vehicle, ship or aircraft. Zero-rating applies to single and return journeys and journeys to or from an oil rig situated outside UK territorial waters. (VAT Notice 744A, para 3.2).

Driver or crew

To qualify for zero-rating as passenger transport, the vehicle, ship or aircraft must be supplied with a driver or crew. Otherwise it is the vehicle, etc. which is being supplied rather than passenger transport.

Incidental supplies

[70.18] Incidental supplies are provided as part of a single transport service. Where a fare is zero-rated, then whether or not a separate charge is made, zero-rating also applies to

- accompanied domestic pets;
- accompanied luggage, including cycles and prams and excess luggage;
- accompanied vehicles and trailers (including Motorail);
- airport passenger charges and passenger load supplements;
- duplicate season tickets;
- pullman supplements;
- seat reservations;
- sleeping berths and cabins on ships (if provided in the course of ordinary transport, but see **70.22** below for cruises); and

(VAT Notice 744A, paras 9.2, 9.3).

Catering on aircraft

Catering on aircraft is an adjunct to the supply of transport and, where no separate charge is made, the consideration for the ticket need not be apportioned (*British Airways v C & E Commrs*, CA [1990] STC 643 (TVC 66.13)).

Payment for an identity card

Payment for an identity card enabling the holder to travel at reduced price has been held to be consideration for the provision of rail transport (*British Railways Board (No 2) v C & E Commrs*, CA [1977] STC 221 (TVC 66.12)).

Standard-rated supplies

[70.19] The following are specifically excluded from zero-rating and become standard-rated.

(a) Passenger transport in places of entertainment or interest

The transport of passengers in any vehicle to, from or within

(i) a place of entertainment, recreation or amusement, or
(ii) a place of cultural, scientific, historical or similar interest

by the person who supplies a right of admission to, or use of facilities at, such a place or by a person connected with him under the provisions of *ICTA 1988, s 839* (see **71.19 VALUATION**) is standard-rated. [*VATA 1994, Sch 8 Group 8 Notes (4A)(4B); SI 1994/3014*]. Such transport services are standard-rated whether included in an overall admission price or made for a separate charge.

Places affected include

- fairgrounds;
- museums;
- piers;
- safari parks;
- stately homes;
- theme parks;
- water parks; and
- zoos.

However, places where the public enjoy totally free access are not affected (e.g. national parks, seaside resorts, historic towns and villages, geographical areas such as the Norfolk Broads, or canals and lakes).

The provisions do not apply to transport to, from or within a place of entertainment or cultural interest when provided *independently* from an operator of such a place. Such services remains zero-rated subject to the normal conditions. Examples include

- a trip by coach or rail to a football ground;
- a coach excursion to a theme park;
- ferries, canal boat trips and other round trips or excursions by boats, without other facilities, on the open sea or other waterways to which the public have free access.

(VAT Notice 744A, paras 8.1, 8.2, 8.5).

(b) Transport in connection with airport car parks

The transport of passengers in any 'motor vehicle' between a car park (or land adjacent) and an airport passenger terminal (or land adjacent) by the person who supplies the parking facilities in that car park or by a person connected with him under the provisions of *ICTA 1988, s 839* (see **71.19 VALUATION**) is standard-rated. '*Motor vehicle*' means any mechanically propelled vehicle intended or adapted for use on the roads. See *Purple Parking Ltd* (TC00118) (TVC 66.39), in which the tribunal held that the companies were making single supplies of parking facilities and the supplies of transport were incidental. [*VATA 1994, Sch 8 Group 8 Notes (4A)–(4C); SI 1994/3014*].

(c) Pleasure flights

The transport of passengers in an aircraft is standard-rated where the flight is advertised or held out to be for the purpose of

(i) providing entertainment, recreation or amusement, or
(ii) the experience of flying or the experience of flying in that particular aircraft

and not primarily for the purpose of transporting passengers from one place to another. [*VATA 1994, Sch 8 Group 8 Notes (4A)(4B); SI 1994/3014*].

Such flights are standard-rated even if they take off from one airport and land at another.

Standard-rated flights include

- hot air balloon rides;
- airship rides;
- 'fear of flying' flights; and
- Concorde 'flights to nowhere' and similar pleasure flights where the aircraft returns to the airport of departure or another UK airport without landing in another country.

(VAT Notice 744A, para 8.4).

Supplies not regarded as passenger transport

The following are standard-rated because they are not regarded as the transport of passengers.

- Donkey rides and similar rides.
- Novelty rides on miniature and model railways, ghost trains, roundabouts, dippers, other fairground equipment and similar attractions (see *C & E Commrs v Blackpool Pleasure Beach Co*, QB [1974] STC 138 (TVC 66.34)).
- The supply of any vehicle with or without a crew for a non-passenger service (e.g. to make a film or carry goods).

(VAT Notice 744A, para 2.2).

Ancillary supplies

[70.20] Ancillary supplies, as opposed to incidental supplies (see **70.18** above) are not part of a single supply of passenger transport services but are supplied separately. The following supplies which are often provided in connection with passenger transport are standard-rated.

- Meals, snacks, sandwiches, drinks, etc. provided in the course of catering *and supplied separately*.

- Car parking (but see **70.23** below when supplied as an airline passenger perk).
- Cycle storage.
- Left luggage and lost property.
- Platform tickets.
- Transportation of unaccompanied luggage, vehicles and trailers.

(VAT Notice 744A, para 9.4).

Club membership

Club membership, entitling economy class passengers to certain facilities normally available only to first class passengers, is not an advance payment for supplies forming an integral part of passenger transport (*El Al Israel Airlines Ltd* (VTD 12750) (TVC 66.38)).

Transport of vehicles on ships, trains etc.

[70.21] The transport or ferry of vehicles on a ship, train or other form of transport may, depending on the circumstances, be a supply of passenger transport or freight transport. HMRC's treatment is as follows.

Passenger transport

- Vehicles with passengers, e.g. coach or bus, whether or not charged at the private car rate.
- Vehicles with drivers or passengers charged under the private car rate, including motorcycles, cars, caravans and trailers.
- Small commercial vehicles charged under the private car rate whether carrying passengers or freight.

Freight transport

- Vehicles unaccompanied or without passengers.

(VAT Notice 744A, paras 2.3, 2.4).

Cruises and other trips

Cruises

[70.22] This paragraph applies where a cruise operator provides cruises from own resources. It applies to all cruise operators whether supplying international and coastal holiday cruises or cruises on rivers and canals or other inland waterways, including disco, dinner, wedding reception and similar entertainment cruises. In all cases, the vessels must be designed or adapted to carry ten or more passengers, including crew, otherwise any supplies in the UK will be automatically standard-rated. However, the provisions do not affect cruises bought in and re-supplied under the **TOUR OPERATORS' MARGIN SCHEME (68)**.

HMRC regard a business as providing a cruise from its own resources where it

- uses its own ship;
- charters a vessel from the owner for a period of two year or more whether only with deck/engine crew or with deck/engine crew and 'hotel'/domestic/catering crew. The vessel need not necessarily be in service continuously throughout the period but the owner must not have the right to use the vessel to make supplies to other customers during the period; or
- takes a vessel including deck/engine crew but employs or engages its own 'hotel'/domestic/catering staff.

A pleasure cruise is treated as a single supply of passenger transport *for the purposes of determining the place of supply*. Once the place of supply has been established under the general rules for passenger transport in **70.16** above, for UK VAT liability purposes a cruise may be a single or multiple supply depending on the facts of the cruise.

In *C & E Commrs v The Peninsular & Oriental Steam Navigation Co*, QB [1996] STC 698 (TVC 66.20) a cruise sold at an inclusive price covering transport, accommodation, catering, entertainment, etc. was held to be a single supply which was zero-rated as a supply of passenger transport, the terms 'pleasure cruise' and 'passenger transport' not being necessarily mutually exclusive. The decision in that case was, however, distinguished in *Virgin Atlantic Airways Ltd* (VTD 13840) (TVC 66.23) where a company operated a river boat which it hired out with optional catering and entertainment. Invoices normally included separate charges for the different services provided. The tribunal held that the company made separate supplies of transport (the hire charge), catering and entertainment and that the supplies of transport were zero-rated.

Following the decisions in *P & O* and *Virgin Atlantic*, HMRC indicated that the guidelines set out below were the main criteria they considered relevant in deciding liability. Since their issue, the ECJ in *Card Protection Plan Ltd v C & E Commrs, ECJ Case C–349/96*, [1999] STC 270 (TVC 22.324) (see **64.6 SUPPLY: GENERAL**) have set out general criteria for deciding whether a supply should be treated as a single or multiple supply and HMRC now require these to be applied in all cases. The following guidelines must therefore be read in the light of the general criteria.

Single zero-rated supply of passenger transport

- The essential nature of the supply is passenger transport and the normal conditions for the relief are met;
- all elements of the cruise are integral and it would be neither practicable nor realistic to separate them; and
- the cruise is held out for sale at a single price with no specific charges or discounts for particular services taken or not taken up.

Multiple supplies

- Different elements of the cruise are the subject of separate negotiation and customer choice;
- there are separately identifiable obligations on the supplier, and separate charges;

- separate supplies are not integral to the main supply and could be omitted; and
- it must be practicable, reasonable and realistic to separate the elements of the cruise.

Where separate supplies of any of the individual elements of a cruise are made, these should be taxed according to their respective liabilities (e.g. a separate element of catering is standard-rated when supplied in the UK).

Example

A rail journey on the Orient Express, to also include a five-course meal with wine, is classed as a multiple supply because the customer expects to receive two very distinct benefits, i.e. a zero-rated train journey and standard-rated food and drink. A ticket price that includes both services for a single price will need to be apportioned so that output tax is paid on the value of the food and drink.

Services of intermediaries

The services of an intermediary making arrangements for the supply of a single zero-rated cruise is zero-rated to the extent that the supply takes place in the UK (see **70.32** below). Where the cruise is treated as a multiple supply, a reasonable apportionment will be accepted.
(VAT Notice 744A, paras 10.2–10.6).

Other trips

The liability of railway and other trips provided with facilities such as catering or entertainment should be determined using the principles outlined above.

In *Sea Containers Services Ltd v C & E Commrs*, QB 1999, [2000] STC 82 (TVC 66.26) a company operated a luxury train on which passengers were supplied with catering. HMRC accepted that, where the train was used for transport to Continental destinations such as Venice, there was a single supply of zero-rated transport. Where, however, the train was used for UK charters, the court confirmed, distinguishing *The Peninsular & Oriental Steam Navigation Co* above, that the company was making separate supplies of transport and catering in the following circumstances.

- Where the whole train plus crew was chartered (whether catering was separately negotiated or included in a single price).
- Where round trips were sold to individual passengers which included high quality catering.
- Where a stopping trip was sold to an individual passenger who alighted before the return journey, again including catering.

HMRC consider that this decision confirms their current policy. (Business Brief 10/99).

See also *A & J Hughes (t/a Pennine Boat Trips of Skipton)* (VTD 15680) (TVC 66.21) where the tribunal held that canal boat trips providing food for parties of 30 or more people were single supplies of zero-rated transport. HMRC consider that this case is confined to the facts and will not accept claims for refunds of VAT on the basis of this decision. (Business Brief 5/99).

Depending on the circumstances 'wine and dine', 'steam and cuisine', disco cruises, dinner cruises, wedding reception cruises and other similar journeys may be standard-rated, zero-rated; or treated as mixed supplies. (VAT Notice 744A, para 9.8).

Airline passenger perks

[70.23] In *Virgin Atlantic Airways Ltd v C & E Commrs; Canadian Airlines International Ltd v C & E Commrs*, QB [1995] STC 341 (TVC 63.7, TVC 66.14) chauffeur-driven limousine services to and from the airport, where the passenger paid one indivisible and irreducible sum for these services and the flight, were held to be part of the zero-rated supply of passenger transport. Following this decision, HMRC have agreed with the airline industry that this treatment would be extended to cover other 'passenger perks'.

To be eligible the perks must

(i) be included in the flight ticket price for the class of travel concerned, with no discount if not taken up;
(ii) form an integral part of an international flight;
(iii) not be gifts of goods (except where currently permitted, e.g. in-flight catering, toiletries); and
(iv) be restricted to one perk per customer (although the customer may be offered a number of options).

The following perks are treated as an integral part of an international flight.

- Limousine transport to and from the airport.
- Up to two days car hire for a one way ticket (four days for a return ticket).
- Car parking at the airport.
- Hotel or similar accommodation provided that it is for no more than one night's stay with breakfast and there is a direct connection with the zero-rated travel (e.g. where it is necessary to catch a connecting flight or it is required for the night prior to take-off or the night after landing).

Not included are

- restaurant meals;
- theatre trips and other entertainment provided during a trip or holiday; and
- hotel accommodation and car hire other than as specified above.

New options will not be automatically disallowed but individual prior approval must be obtained from HMRC to ensure that the services are incidental to and directly connected with the air travel.

The provision of allowable perks will not, in itself, render the airline liable to use the **TOUR OPERATORS' MARGIN SCHEME (68)** although the provision of non-allowable perks may well do so.

(VAT Notice 744A, paras 9.6, 9.7).

Taxis and hire cars

VAT liability of fares

[70.24] Zero-rating of domestic passenger transport does not apply if the vehicle is designed to carry less than ten passengers. Taxi and hire car fares are, therefore, standard-rated and if the business provider is registrable for VAT, it must charge VAT to its customers. Extra charges for baggage, waiting time, etc. are also standard-rated as are referral fees from other taxi businesses. Tips and gratuities given voluntarily are not payments for supplies and are outside the scope of VAT. VAT due is calculated by multiplying the fares, including extras, by the VAT fraction. See **47.2 OUTPUT TAX**.

Invoices

Registered persons must issue VAT invoices to any customer who asks for one. See **39 INVOICES**.

Types of business and VAT consequences

(a) Independent self-employed drivers

If a driver has purchased or rented his own vehicle and operates it on a self-employed basis, he will normally be in business on his own account and will be making taxable supplies in the form of

- transport supplied direct to his own passengers; and/or
- services to another taxi business where he supplies them under a contract for services.

Where the driver supplies transport to his own passengers, he may use the agency services of a taxi business (see (*b*)(iii) below) or a taxi association (see below) to obtain customers. If, however, he drives for a taxi or private hire business as its employee (see (*b*)(i) below), he is not considered to be in business for VAT purposes.

A self-employed driver must register for VAT if making taxable supplies where the full amount he is paid for those supplies exceeds the VAT registration threshold. To calculate this, any amounts, such as vehicle and radio rentals or agency charges, deducted by a taxi firm must be added back to the amounts actually received.

(b) Businesses which engage drivers

This includes all types of business, whether sole proprietorship, partnership or limited company. There are three common scenarios for who is supplying the taxi and hire car services to the customers.

(i) *Drivers are employees of a cab business*. Where a cab business employs staff to drive its taxis or hire cars, the business makes the supplies to the customers and must account for output tax on
   - the full amount payable by customers before deducting any payments made to drivers;
   - any fares the sole proprietor, director or partner, as the case may be, receives if he drives for the firm;

- the full fares payable by passengers even if the work is sub-contracted to an independent business or owner driver; and
- any referral fee received from other taxi businesses.

The drivers are not considered to be in business for VAT purposes. Any money retained by the drivers is outside the scope of VAT as remuneration for their services as employees.

(ii) *Drivers are self-employed and provide their services to a cab business.* The cab business will usually own the vehicles and bear expenses relating to them. Typically, there are more drivers than vehicles and the firm has to exercise control over the drivers to ensure that it is adequately covered at all times. The cab business is buying in the services of drivers and selling the taxi transport on to the final customer as principal. The cab firm must account for output tax as in (i) above. Monies retained by the drivers are consideration for a supply of services by themselves to the cab business under a contract for services (see (*a*) above).

(iii) *Drivers are self-employed and provide their services directly to the customers.* The drivers will usually own their own vehicles and bear expenses relating to them. The cab business or taxi association acts as agent for the drivers, usually providing them with services such as radio hire, booking and support services in return for a commission or fee. This is a standard-rated supply of services by the business or association to the drivers. The business or association must register for VAT if the total of all such charges and any other supplies it makes exceeds the VAT registration limit. Individual drivers need only account for output tax if their supplies exceeds the VAT registration limits (see (*a*) above).

For cases where self-employed drivers were held to supply their services to the cab firm under (*b*)(ii) above, see *Hamiltax* (VTD 8948) (TVC 62.233) and *Knowles (t/a Rainbow Taxis)* (VTD 13913) (TVC 62.234). For cases where the final supply to the customer was held to be by the drivers under (*b*)(iii) above, see *Triumph and Albany Car Service* (VTD 977, VTD 1004) (TVC 62.240) and *Carless v C & E Commrs*, QB [1993] STC 632 (TVC 62.245).

Fees paid to controllers

In *Home Or Away Ltd* (VTD 18195) (TVC 62.250) a company engaged staff (which it treated as self-employed) to act as controllers. Drivers paid 10% of their fares directly to the controllers as fees. The tribunal held that, on the evidence, although the fees were paid directly to the controllers as a matter of convenience, they were paid for a supply by the company of the services of the controllers to the drivers.

Account work

Most taxi and hire car businesses engage in cash work (where customers pay cash to the driver upon completion of the journey) and account work (where regular customers, usually businesses, are allowed to settle their bills periodically). In most cases there will be no difference between the operation of the two types of business, i.e. both will fall within the same category under (*b*)(i)–(iii) above and VAT must be accounted for as indicated under the relevant category. Where both cash and account work falls within (*b*)(iii) above, invoices raised by the business to account customers should itemise separately

- fares collected on behalf of drivers (with the addition of VAT if the *driver* is registered); and
- any administration or similar charge by the business (with the addition of VAT if the *business* is registered).

However, there may be a genuine difference between the treatment of cash and account work with the business acting as agent for cash work under (*b*)(iii) above but principal for account work under (*b*)(ii) above. If such arrangements are adopted, the business must satisfy HMRC that

- the arrangements are reflected in the written terms agreed with the drivers; and
- there is a genuine difference in the operation of the cash and account sides of the business.

If a business operates as an agent for cash work and a principal for account work, it must still account for VAT at the standard rate on the full charge to the drivers for the rental of vehicles, radios or other services supplied to them. This applies even if the charge is

- offset when calculating the rate due to the drivers for account work they perform; or
- deducted before paying them for account journeys.

See *RJ and CA Blanks* (VTD 14099) (TVC 67.121).

The basis of payment (e.g. where drivers are paid a fixed hourly rate for account work but their payment for cash work is directly related to takings) could be one indication of a contractual distinction between cash and account work. See *Triumph and Albany Car Service* and *Carless* above for cases where the cash and account customers were held not to be distinguishable; and *Camberwell Cars Ltd* (VTD 10178) (TVC 62.249) and *A Hussain (t/a Crossleys Private Hire Cars)* (VTD 16194) (TVC 62.242) where the tribunal held there was a real distinction between cash and account work. See also *Macey & Atkins (t/a Sandwich Cars)* (VTD 20257) (TVC 62.241) where the tribunal held that, in the case of account work undertaken for the county council, there was a formal agreement which was only consistent with the firm (and not the individual drivers) acting as principal.

Valuation of services supplied to drivers

In *A2B Radio Cars* (VTD 15145) (TVC 67.122) a partnership which operated a minicab business using self-employed drivers had a number of accounts customers. The partnership paid the drivers 90% of the amounts which it charged the accounts customers, less a deduction which it described as a 'contract levy'. The partnership's other source of income was payments made by the drivers for the hire of radios. HMRC issued an assessment on the basis that the 'contract levy' represented consideration paid by the drivers for a supply of services by the partnership. The partnership appealed, contending that the 'contract levy' was not consideration for a supply, but was simply an amount taken into account in determining the amount payable to the drivers for the services which they provided. The tribunal accepted this contention and allowed the appeal, holding that the consideration for the partnership's services consisted of the amounts paid by the drivers for the hire of radios. There were no grounds for treating the 'contract levy' as additional consideration. On the evidence, the 'contract levy' was simply 'an attempt at creating fairness between drivers who may do more or less contract work' and its true nature was an adjustment to the 90% paid to drivers for client work.

The *A2B Radio Cars* decision was not followed, and was implicitly disapproved, in the subsequent case of *Camberwell Cars Ltd* (No 2) (VTD 17376) (TVC 67.124). However, *A2B Radio Cars* was followed in *Parker Car Services* (TC00528) (TVC 67.125).

Taxi associations

Some independent and self-employed taxi drivers form taxi associations to provide services to the individual driver members. These services can include

- operation of a booking office and radio link;
- hire of radios; and
- provision of rest facilities.

Supplies to members are always standard-rated whether they pay for them by periodic subscription or by deduction/offset from fares collected on the members' behalf. Taxi associations must be registered for VAT if the total of all such charges, together with the total charges for any other supplies they make, exceed the VAT registration threshold. Additional supplies can include an administration fee for services supplied to customers (e.g. providing a breakdown or analysis of journeys made).

Purchases of motor vehicles

VAT can be reclaimed on the purchase of a motor car if

- it is a qualifying motor car; and
- it is intended primarily to be used for letting on hire with a driver for the purpose of carrying passengers.

A qualifying motor car is generally either a new car or a used car where all previous owners were able to reclaim input on their purchases. See **45.3 MOTOR CARS** for further details.

Fuel

Input tax is reclaimable on fuel bought for use in taxis or hire-cars by the proprietor and, for the time being at least, employees of a business. However, if the business funds private motoring, a scale charge is payable.

See **45.10–45.22 MOTOR CARS** for motor expenses generally including fuel and private motoring.

Sales of taxis and hire cars

If a taxi or hire car is sold on which input tax has been previously reclaimed, VAT must be accounted for on the full selling price. If no input tax has been previously reclaimed (e.g. because it was purchased under the second-hand scheme or from a private individual) it may be sold under the second-hand margin scheme provided the conditions for the scheme can be met. VAT need then only be accounted for on the excess, if any, of the sales proceeds over cost. See **61 SECOND-HAND GOODS**.

Where a vehicle is sold with a local authority hackney carriage licence plate, there is a single supply of goods (i.e. a licensed taxi). The full selling price is the total amount charged for the vehicle and licence plate. Licence fees paid to a local authority to operate a taxi cab are treated as separate supplies of services and cannot be included in the purchase price of a vehicle when working out the VAT due on sale under the second-hand margin scheme.

Where a taxi or hire car is exchanged or traded on the purchase of a replacement vehicle, VAT must be accounted for in the same way as if it had been sold at a price equal to the exchange or trade-in allowance received.

Sale of business as going concern

If a taxi or car hire business is sold as a going concern and certain conditions are met, there is no taxable supply for VAT purposes and no VAT liability on the assets sold, including any taxis or hire cars included in the price. See **8.10 BUSINESS**. To be treated as such a sale, the transaction must include more than just the sale of a vehicle (e.g. the rights to a radio network, goodwill, lists of customers).

(VAT Notice 700/25/02).

Freight transport services

[70.25] Freight for these purposes includes

- goods/cargo;
- mail;
- documents;
- unaccompanied vehicles; and
- vehicles transported on ships which are charged at a 'driver accompanied' rate.

To determine the correct VAT treatment of supplies of freight transport or related services, it is necessary to determine

- from 1 January 2010, the status of the customer, i.e. whether the customer is in business or not (prior to 1 January 2010, the nature of the supply, i.e. whether it was domestic, intra-EU or international);
- whether the supply, or any part of it, takes place in the UK;
- who should account for any VAT due; and
- for UK supplies, whether the supplies are zero-rated or standard-rated.

(VAT Notice 744B, paras 1.2, 1.3).

Place of supply

Customer 'in business'

[70.26] Freight transportation and related services fall under the general rule when supplied to customers 'in business'. From 1 January 2010 the general rule is that the place of supply of services to a person who is in business is the place where the customer belongs for the purposes of receiving your supply. It does not matter where the goods being transported move from or to, or where any related service physically takes place.

However, HMRC have become aware that this change in law has produced an unintended anomaly in the treatment of supplies wholly enjoyed outside the EU, which may also be taxed locally in the place of performance. Therefore, from 15 March 2010, where a supply of freight transport (or services closely associated with freight transport) would be treated as supplied in the UK, it will not be so treated if the use and enjoyment of the services is outside the EU. This administrative easement is being introduced as a temporary measure to allow time for consideration of a more permanent legislative solution. (HMRC Brief 13/10).

Example

UK Haulage is VAT-registered in the UK and is transporting some food in India for a UK-based charity as part of an emergency aid programme. The place of supply rules since 1 January 2010 make this transport charge subject to UK VAT because the customer (the charity) is based in the UK and has some business supplies (and is VAT-registered).

The VAT charge causes a problem for the charity because the expense relates to a non-business project, i.e. input tax cannot be claimed, even though it is VAT-registered. The concession in HMRC Brief 13/10 deals with this problem by changing the place of supply to India, i.e. where the transportation takes place. The supply is then outside the scope of UK VAT.

Customer not 'in business'

Freight transportation and related services when supplied to customers who are not 'in business' is largely unchanged from before 1 January 2010. That is, the place of supply of freight transportation

- from the EU to a third country takes place where the transportation is performed in proportion to the distances covered;
- intra-EU transportation takes place wholly where the transportation begins, and
- the place of supply of related services takes place where physically performed.

Intra-EU transportation that transits non-Member State

Transportation between EU Member States that involves transiting a non-EU Member State (for example Sweden to UK via Norway) is to be treated as intra-EU transportation.

Sub-contractors

For a subcontractor supplying freight transportation or related services to a main contractor, the place of supply is determined by the status of the immediate customer and not that of the ultimate customer of the main contractor.

(VAT Notice 744B, paras 3.1–3.4).

VAT liability

Place of supply is the UK

[70.27] If the place of supply of freight transportation or related services is the UK then the supply will be standard rated, except where:

- the supply is of transportation or related services connected with an import or export from the EU; or
- the actual movement of goods is from, to, or between the islands of The Azores or Madeira or the related service is physically performed on these islands; or
- the supply is of handling or storage of ship or aircraft cargo (in certain places),

when the liability will be zero-rated.

Place of supply is outside the UK

If the place of supply is outside the UK then the supply is outside the scope of UK VAT and there is no VAT liability within the UK. However, input tax incurred in making the supply is recoverable, subject to the normal rules.

Accounting for VAT

The procedure for accounting for VAT and who accounts for it will depend on the circumstances of the transaction.

- If the supplier is located in the same Member State as the place of supply he charges and accounts for the VAT due as a domestic supply.
- If the place of supply moves to an EU Member State because that is where a customer who is in-business is located then the customer must account for the VAT as a reverse charge.
- If the place of supply moves to where the transport of the goods for a person not in-business begins then the supplier may have to register for VAT in the Member State of supply.
- If the place of supply is outside the EU then the supply is outside the scope of VAT in any Member State.

(VAT Notice 744B, paras 4.1-4.3).

Import/export and non-EU freight transport

[70.28] Import/export and non-EU freight transport means the transport of goods between the EU and non-EU countries, or wholly outside the EU. The place of supply of import/export and non-EU freight transport follows the rules set out in **70.26** above. Where the place of supply is the UK the law zero-rates:

- the supply of transportation of goods from a place within to a place outside the EU and vice versa;
- the transport, handling and storage of goods, when they are supplied in connection with a journey from the place of importation to their destination either within the UK or within another Member State (to the extent that those services are supplied in the UK); and
- the transport, handling and storage of goods, when they are supplied in connection with a journey from their origin either within the UK or within another Member State to the place of export (to the extent that those services are supplied in the UK).

'*Destination*' is the furthest specified place in the UK or other member state to which the goods are consigned at the time of importation. It is the place stated on the consignment note or any other document by means of which the goods are imported (the delivery terms). When that place is unknown, the destination is the place of importation. 'Origin' is the place from within the UK or other member state from which the goods are first consigned for export. When that place is unknown, the origin is the place of exportation.

If a supplier provides services that form part of an import or export movement they should hold satisfactory evidence that they are providing a service connected with a specific import or export of goods in the form of commercial documentation. Main forms of documentary evidence include: contracts or agreements, consignment notes, bills of landing, certificates of shipment, air/seaway bills, Customs declaration forms C88 (SAD). Additionally, a combination or all of the following may provide suitable evidence: inter-company correspondence, the customer's order documentation, payment details, sales invoices, advice notes.

The following services when connected with imports are not zero-rated:

- services, which are unconnected with a movement of goods from a place outside the EU to a place within the EU or vice versa;
- the transport of goods after their arrival at the destination. For example, the transport after arrival at a warehouse (the destination they were consigned to), where the customer is known but the further destination elsewhere in the UK is not known. When the goods are at some later date called off for consignment to (say) a branch, the transport and any related services cannot be zero-rated;
- services connected with goods which have not specifically been consigned for export at the time of transportation;
- the handling of goods after they have been unloaded at the destination;
- the storage of goods at the destination, unless the storage meets the conditions in **70.31**.

(VAT Notice 744B, paras 5.1–5.4, 5.7, 5.8).

Related transport services

[70.29] Related transport services include the following services when they relate to the transport of goods:

- loading, unloading or reloading;
- stowing;
- opening for inspection;
- cargo security services;
- preparing or amending bills of lading, air or sea-waybills and certificates of shipment;
- packing necessary for transportation; or
- storage.

The place of supply of related transport services follows the rules set out in **70.26**. The procedures for accounting for VAT are set out in **70.27**.

(VAT Notice 744B, paras 6.1-6.3).

The Azores and Madeira

[70.30] When Portugal joined the EU on 1 January 1993, the European Commission decided that freight transport services to and from the Azores and Madeira should be treated differently from supplies of intra-EU freight transport. The place of supply of intra-EU freight transport to the Azores and Madeira is the same as the place of supply for intra-EU freight transport, see **70.26**. Intra-EU freight transport to the Azores and Madeira is zero-rated to the extent that the transport services are treated as supplied in the UK. Transport related services and intermediary services supplied in connection to freight transport to the Azores and Madeira are zero-rated to the extent they are treated as supplied in the UK.

(VAT Notice 744B, paras 7.1-7.5).

Handling and storage services for ship and aircraft cargo

[70.31] Examples of handling and storage services: cargo security services; container handling for which a box charge is made; demurrage; loading stores and discharging empties; loading, unloading, reloading, stowing, securing and shifting cargo; preparing or amending bills of lading, air / or sea-waybills and certificates of shipment; preparing or amending customs entries; presenting goods for customs examination; sorting, opening for inspection, repairing and making good, weighing and taring, taping and sealing, erasing and re-marking, labelling and re-numbering, tallying, checking, sampling, measuring or gauging of goods; stevedoring and porterage; survey of cargo (including damaged cargo); or the movement of goods to or from a ship by lighter.

The handling and storage of ship and aircraft cargo may be zero-rated provided the service is physically performed in the UK: in a port; on land adjacent to a port; in a customs and excise airport; or in a transit shed. However, the grant of a licence to occupy land to store goods in a specific area, as distinct from the service of storing them, may be exempt from VAT.

Handling services relating to goods that have been imported from or are to be exported to, a place outside the EU **may** qualify for zero-rating if the goods concerned have been imported from, or are to be exported to, a place outside the EU, see **70.28**. The letting on hire of any goods including cranes or other lifting equipment is not zero-rated, even though the hire takes place in a port or airport.

(VAT Notice 744B, paras 8.1-8.7).

Intermediary services

[70.32] The place of supply of intermediary services follows the rules set out in **70.26** as they relate to the customer, 'the principal'. For the initial intermediary who is involved in the making of arrangements of the services and the place of supply of their services is the UK, the liability of their supply will be zero-rated when they make arrangements for: the supply of space in a qualifying ship or aircraft, or the supply of handling, storage or transportation of goods imported to or exported from the EU, or the supply of handling or storage services. In all other cases the liability of the supply will be standard-rated.

(VAT Notice 744B, paras 9.2, 9.3).

Key points

[70.33] Points to consider are as follows.

- The supply of passenger transport in a vehicle, ship or aircraft that is capable of carrying at least ten passengers is zero-rated. The zero-rating therefore applies to travel by bus, coach, aeroplane, boat, train or ship.
- A key feature of the supply is that the transport must be provided with a driver to qualify for zero-rating. If there is no driver provided, then the supply is usually standard-rated as the hire of a vehicle.
- The zero-rating only applies to passenger transport where the intention is to get the passenger from 'A' to 'B'. So zero-rating would not apply to a fairground ride, donkey ride or hot-air balloon trip, even if the ride is capable of carrying ten or more passengers. The supply in this case is for pleasure transport rather than passenger transport.
- The zero-rating of the above forms of passenger transport means there is no input tax to reclaim on costs incurred by a business on bus fares, train fares, air fares etc.
- Transport in a taxi is standard-rated because the vehicle carries less than ten passengers. However, be aware that many taxi drivers trade as self-employed drivers, rather than being part of a bigger business, and are usually trading below the VAT registration limits. So there is no input tax to claim on the cost of a business journey in these circumstances.

- A taxi driver or business that is VAT-registered does not need to account for output tax on tips received from customers. Tips are outside the scope of VAT because they are separate to the taxi fares.
- The VAT position of taxi drivers needs to be treated with care to be clear whether supplies to passengers are being made by the driver in business on his own account, or by a separate taxi business that either employs the driver or pays him for his time (e.g. on an hourly basis). Many VAT tribunal cases have considered this issue, with a lot of cases being won by HMRC, producing an unexpected output tax liability to the main taxi business.
- A VAT-registered taxi business can reclaim input tax on the purchase of a new motor car to be used as a taxi. However, output tax must be charged on the full selling price if it is resold in the future.
- Since 1 January 2010, the place of supply for freight transport services is where the customer is based if the customer is in business. The journey route is irrelevant. This is a change from the previous rules before this date when the journey route was the key factor.
- Be aware of a concession in HMRC Brief 13/10, which means the place of supply for freight transport services carried out in a non-EU country (or countries) for a UK customer will be temporarily based on where the transportation takes place, i.e. overriding the general rule (from 1 January) that the place of supply is where the customer is based for business to business (B2B) sales.

71

Valuation

Cross-references. See **5 APPEALS** for appeals regarding valuation; **47.4 OUTPUT TAX** for the valuation of multiply supplies; **60.8**, **60.9 RETAIL SCHEMES** for valuation of gross takings of retailers; **64 SUPPLY: GENERAL** for coverage of supplies generally; **65 SUPPLY: PLACE OF SUPPLY** for place of supply; **66 SUPPLY: TIME OF SUPPLY** for time of supply; and **69 TRADE PROMOTION SCHEMES** for valuation of supplies made by the promoter.

De Voil Indirect Tax Service. See V3.151–166.

Introduction

[71.1] For EU legislation, see **18.18–18.22 EUROPEAN UNION LEGISLATION.**

Under UK legislation, VAT is charged on

- the supply of goods and services in the UK;
- the acquisition of goods in the UK from another EU country; and
- the importation of goods from outside the EU.

[*VATA 1994, s 1(1)*].

Supplies of goods or services are usually made in return for money, i.e. for a consideration wholly in money. In such cases, the value for VAT purposes is normally, under the general rule in *VATA 1994, s 19(2)*, the price paid or payable excluding the VAT itself. See **71.3** below. The rest of this chapter deals with situations where this simple rule cannot be applied, for example

- where a single consideration is payment for supplies with different liabilities so that an apportionment is necessary (see **71.4** below);
- where the consideration is wholly or at least partly not in money (see **71.5–71.7** below); and
- where circumstances exist requiring special valuation rules to be applied which take precedence over the general rules (see **71.10–71.30** below). This includes special valuation provisions for acquisitions from other EU countries (see **71.11–71.14** below) and imports from outside the EU (see **71.15** below).

In all cases, the application of the correct valuation rule depends upon correctly identifying the consideration given for the supply. For the meaning of 'consideration' see **71.8** below.

General valuation rules

[71.2] The general rules for determining the value of a supply of goods or services are to be found in

- *VATA 1994, s 19(2)* where the consideration for the supply is wholly in money (see **71.3** below); and
- *VATA 1994, s 19(3)* where the consideration is not wholly in money (see **71.5–71.7** below).

These general rules are, however, subject to any special valuation rules made by or under *VATA 1994*. [*VATA 1994, s 19(1)*]. These special rules are considered in **71.10–71.30** below.

Consideration wholly in money

[71.3] If a supply is for a consideration in 'money', subject to the special valuation rules in **71.10–71.30** below, its value for VAT purposes is such amount as, with the addition of the VAT chargeable, is equal to the consideration. [*VATA 1994, s 19(2)*].

'*Money*' includes currencies other than sterling. [*VATA 1994, s 96(1)*]. See **71.14** and **71.18** below where acquisitions from other EU countries and supplies respectively are in foreign currency.

The value for VAT purposes is therefore that part of the payment which, when added to the VAT itself, gives a total equalling the payment. The VAT element of a VAT-inclusive consideration is determined by multiplying that consideration by the VAT fraction (see **47.2 OUTPUT TAX**).

> *Example*
>
> In November 2008 goods subject to standard-rated VAT are sold for a cash payment of £96.
>
> The VAT element is 7/47 × £96 = £14.30
>
> The value for VAT purposes is £81.70 (£96.00 – £14.30) and the consideration is £96.

Whether contract price inclusive or exclusive of VAT

Whether a price quoted is inclusive or exclusive of VAT must turn on the terms of the particular contract.

- Where a contract specifically states that a price is *VAT-inclusive*, the supplier must calculate the VAT element as in the above example.
- Where it specifically states that the price is *VAT-exclusive*, it is commonly understood that the purchaser must pay the VAT in addition to the quoted price. See *Hostgilt Ltd v Megahart Ltd*, Ch D 1998, [1999] STC 141 (TVC 67.5) and *Wynn Realisations Ltd (in administration) v Vogue Holdings Inc*, CA [1999] STC 524 (TVC 67.6).
- Where the terms of the contract do not make it clear that a payment of the VAT is required in addition to the contract price, the supplier may be left to account for the VAT out of what he receives. See *Lancaster v Bird*, CA 19 November 1998 unreported (TVC 67.4) which was concerned, *inter alia,* with whether VAT could be charged in addition to the cash price quoted for building a stable block. It was held that, although there may well be a custom in the construction industry that prices are quoted exclusive of VAT, there was no evidence in the particular case that, on a contract between a small builder seeking payment in cash and a part-time farmer, it was an implied custom that VAT would be paid on top of the cash payments.

VAT on other taxes

Under *Directive 2006/112/EC, Art 78(a)* the taxable amount (equivalent to value in UK legislation) expressly includes taxes, duties, levies and charges, excluding the VAT itself. Although *VATA 1994, s 19(2)* does not expressly stipulate that other taxes are included in the value for VAT purposes, any such taxes levied on a supply form part of the purchase price and are therefore included in that part of the consideration upon which the VAT must be calculated. This does mean in certain circumstances, eg spirits and tobacco, that VAT is payable on other taxes.

Adequacy or otherwise of monetary consideration

There is no valuation provision by which an inflated payment in money can be reduced for VAT purposes. Where an artificially reduced payment in money is charged, the transaction can be treated as having a higher value for VAT purposes but only where

- it is between connected persons (see **71.19** below); or
- it relates to supplies of goods made to non-taxable persons for retail sale ('direct selling') (see **71.23** below).

However, in cases where apparently insufficient monetary payment appears to have been made, it may well be that the recipient of the supply has also provided additional consideration in a non-monetary form. This non-monetary consideration must also be valued (see **71.5** below).

Apportionment of monetary consideration

[71.4] Where a supply of any goods or services is not the only matter to which a consideration in money relates, the supply is deemed to be for such part of the consideration as is properly attributable to it. [*VATA 1994, s 19(4)*].

Sometimes a single monetary consideration may be the payment for two or more supplies of different liabilities. In such a situation, the above provision requires the trader to allocate a fair proportion of the total payment to each of the supplies. It does not, however, stipulate how that apportionment should be made. A trader can use, and HMRC can accept, any method provided that it achieves a fair result and can be supported by a valid calculation.

For further coverage of apportionment of consideration, see **47.3 OUTPUT TAX.**

Consideration not wholly in money

[71.5] If a supply is for a consideration not consisting, or not wholly consisting, of money, subject to the special valuation rules in **71.10–71.30** below, its value is to be taken to be such amount in money as, with addition of the VAT chargeable, is equivalent to the consideration. [*VATA 1994, s 19(3)*]. In other words, it is necessary to

- determine the amount that would have been given in money for the supply if goods or services had not instead been used for all or part of the payment; and then
- multiply that amount by the VAT fraction (see **47.2 OUTPUT TAX**) to establish how much VAT is due.

Distinguishing between non-monetary consideration and no consideration

Non-monetary consideration exists when a supply is made in return for payment in the form of goods or services. Where there is only non-monetary consideration, a barter transaction takes place (see **71.7** below). In some cases there may be both a monetary consideration and a non-monetary consideration.

When goods or services are provided for no payment in any form (monetary or non-monetary), there has been no consideration. It is then only necessary to value such a provision of goods or services where *VATA 1994* deems a taxable supply to have taken place. The commonest cases are

- private or non-business use of business assets for no consideration (see **71.20** below);
- private or non-business use of services supplied to the business (see **71.21** below);
- supplies of business goods/assets for no consideration (see **71.22** below); and
- deemed supplies of business goods/assets on hand at the time of deregistration (see **71.22** below).

Establishing the monetary equivalent of non-monetary consideration

Key principles in determining the monetary equivalent of non-monetary consideration have been established by the European Court in *Naturally Yours Cosmetics Ltd v C & E Commrs (No 2), ECJ Case 230/87*, [1988] STC 879 (TVC 22.233) and *Empire Stores Ltd v C & E Commrs, ECJ Case C–33/93*, [1994] STC 623 (TVC 22.234).

In *Naturally Yours Cosmetics Ltd* a company sold cosmetics at wholesale prices to beauty consultants who then resold them, at retail prices recommended by the company, at parties which the consultants had encouraged hostesses to arrange. As a reward, a consultant gave the hostess a pot of cream which had been purchased from the company for £1.50 instead of the usual wholesale price of £10.14. The ECJ held that VAT was due on £10.14. The consultants were providing the company with a service (arranging for the hostess to hold the party) in addition to the cash paid. The value of the service was £10.14 less the £1.50 payment. The fact that the price was reduced only if the party actually took place, showed that the parties *subjectively* assigned to the service provided a value corresponding to that price reduction.

The general rule deriving from the decision in *Naturally Yours Cosmetics Ltd* is that non-monetary consideration has the value of the alternative monetary payment that would normally have been given for the supply. Because this must be arrived at subjectively, it is necessary to determine what the particular recipient would have paid the particular supplier for the particular supply had the payment been in money.

In circumstances similar to *Naturally Yours Cosmetics Ltd*, the alternative monetary consideration is not difficult to establish because the normal price chargeable is self-evident from the contractual arrangement between the parties to the transaction. Alternatively, the monetary equivalent may be set out in a catalogue or price-list which shows what the recipient of the supply would have to pay when he provides no non-monetary consideration (e.g. where persons providing selling or introductory services to a mail-order trader are entitled to receive catalogue goods free or for a reduced cash payment).

However, this rule cannot be followed in case where the goods supplied in return for such services are not otherwise sold to the provider of the services. In *Empire Stores Ltd*, a company sold goods via mail order catalogues. New customers (under a 'self-introduction scheme') and existing customers (under an 'introduce-a-friend scheme') were entitled to select an item from a list (e.g. kettle, toaster or iron) free of charge once they (or, as the case may be, their friend) had been approved as a customer and placed an order for goods from the catalogues. The 'reward goods' in question were not advertised for sale in the catalogues. The ECJ held that the introductory service provided by the customer was non-monetary consideration because there was a direct link between its provision and the supply of the reward good. (The link was direct because, in the absence of the service, no reward good would be supplied.) The value of the goods had to be determined subjectively. Where the value was not a sum of money agreed between the parties (as in *Naturally Yours Cosmetics Ltd* above), in order to be subjective, it must be the value which the recipient of the services attributes to the services which he is seeking to obtain. This must correspond to the amount which he is prepared to spend for that purpose. Where, as in *Empire Stores Ltd*, the supply of goods is involved, the value can only be the price which the supplier has paid for those goods.

See also *C & E Commrs v Pippa-Dee Parties Ltd*, QB [1981] STC 495 (TVC 67.37) and *Rosgill Group Ltd v C & E Commrs*, CA [1997] STC 811 (TVC 67.38) where goods were sold under the 'party plan' system but the provider of the services could choose between taking a 'cash commission' or selecting catalogue goods at a lower price. In *Rosgill Group Ltd* a company sold clothing and other goods. Self-employed 'organisers' displayed and sold the products at parties held in the homes of hostesses. In return for permitting a party to be held in her home, a hostess was entitled to take a cash payment or obtain goods from Rosgill's catalogues at a reduced price. The amounts of cash and price reduction were not equal. In the sample transaction considered by the tribunal, the hostess had the option of £2.89 in cash or purchasing goods for £20.76 that would have cost £27.99 if she had paid the listed retail price, i.e. a reduction of £7.23. It was held that the value of the consideration for the supply of the goods was the usual retail price, i.e. a monetary consideration of £20.76 plus a non-monetary consideration of £7.23, being the subjective value of the services supplied by the hostess. It was clear from the contractual terms of the transaction that, if the hostess had not provided the services, she would have had to pay the normal retail price for the goods. The fact that the hostess could have opted to take cash instead, did not prevent the usual non-monetary consideration valuation rules applying in those cases where the price reduction was selected rather than the cash option.

Barter transactions

[71.6] A barter transaction is one in which no monetary payment is made. It may involve goods or services (or a mixture of both) being supplied in return for a supply of goods or services (or a mixture of both) from the other party. Each trader's supply constitutes the consideration he is providing in return for the supply from the other party. An example of a common barter transaction is where a publisher runs a competition in which prizes have been 'donated' but where the publisher is contractually bound to provide advertising to the donor of the prize in return.

In *Riverside Sports & Leisure Ltd* (VTD 20848) (TVC 67.146) a school granted a lease over some sports fields to a partnership which operated a commercial sports centre. Under the agreement, the school received a peppercorn rent and became entitled to use the facilities in the sports centre at certain defined times. The partnership subsequently transferred its business to a company (R), and also assigned R the benefit of the lease. The tribunal decided that the transaction was a barter transaction and that the user rights were granted as the consideration for the lease.

Example

John is VAT-registered as a window cleaner. He agrees to clean the windows for his local football club free of charge, with the condition agreed that he is given a free advert in the match day programme for the club's next home game. The value of the advert if John had paid for it is £75 (the football club is not VAT-registered). Output tax is therefore payable by John based on the valuation of £75 (£75 x 7/47 with a VAT rate of 17.5%) i.e. because he has received consideration for his services, albeit on a non-monetary basis.

Part-exchange

[71.7] Under a part-exchange transaction, goods are supplied in return for money and other goods.

General rule

Applying the principles in *Naturally Yours Cosmetics Ltd* (see **71.5** above), the general rule is that the goods taken in part-exchange are equal in value to the amount by which the price at which the goods would otherwise have been supplied has been reduced in the particular case. The value of the main supply is therefore the VAT-exclusive amount that would have been charged if no goods had been taken in part-exchange.

Example 1

A sells goods to the majority of his customers for a retail price of £100. To customers in the same line of business he offers the same goods at £95. B is a 'normal customer' and he brings in a part-exchange item which A values at £10. C is a 'trade customer' and he also brings in a part-exchange item which A values at £10.

The total value of the supply to B is £100 (monetary consideration of £90 plus non-monetary consideration of £10, i.e. the amount by which the goods have been reduced for him (£100 – £90)). Similarly, the total value of the supply to C is £95 (£85 plus £10 (£95 – £85)).

See, however, *C & E Commrs v Ping (Europe) Ltd*, CA [2002] STC 1186 (TVC 67.78). In that case, a company (P) sold golf clubs, some of which did not comply with the Rules of Golf and so could not be used for golf competitions. P offered to supply a new club for £22 to anyone surrendering one of the 'illegal' clubs in part-exchange. The new clubs had a normal wholesale price of £49.99 and a normal retail price of £72. HMRC argued that the 'illegal' clubs had a part-exchange value of £27.99, so that P had to account for VAT on the normal wholesale price of £49.99. The tribunal held (and the Ch D and CA unanimously agreed) that the 'illegal' clubs had no value so that output tax was only due on the consideration of £22 which P actually received. The scrap value of the old clubs could be ignored and the value of the non-monetary consideration involved was nil.

Exceptions to the general rule

There are situations in which a number of the general rules above do not apply.

(a) Allowances for traded-in goods

Where, as a sales promotion offer, a dealer offers a fixed allowance for traded-in goods, irrespective of their true value, such an allowance can be treated as a discount rather than a part-exchange in the following circumstances.

(i) If a fixed allowance is offered
- irrespective of the nature of the item traded-in;
- for any item of a particular class without regard to make, age, model or condition; or
- for an item of a particular class or make irrespective of age, model or condition provided that no attempt is made to value the traded-in goods and there is no reason for the goods to be accepted other than for trade promotion (which would not apply where prior arrangements have been made for the traded-in goods to be reconditioned or sold).

(ii) If a manufacturer or distributor advertises nationally or regionally a trade-in allowance on an 'at least' basis (e.g. an allowance of 'at least' £5) which would fall within (i) above if it had simply been a fixed allowance. Retailers can offer more than one minimum allowance but only to promote sales, it must not be because they value the traded-in goods at a higher level. There must be no references to the age or condition of the traded-in items.

Where (i) or (ii) above applies, the value of the supply is only the amount of actual money received.

(b) Bumping

It is common practice in the motor trade to manipulate the value of part exchange vehicles to satisfy the minimum deposit requirements of a finance company. This is referred to as 'bumping'. See **45.7 MOTOR CARS**.

(c) Payments made by suppliers to retailers under money-off coupon schemes or cash-back schemes

Following the decision in *Elida Gibbs Ltd v C & E Commrs, ECJ Case C–317/94*, [1996] STC 1387 (TVC 22.235), where payments have been made by manufacturers or distributors as a result of operating a money-off coupon or cash back scheme, those payments reduce their output tax. The manufacturer or dealer must demonstrate that the payments have been made to the retailers and consumers in the transaction chain and that the payments relate directly to successfully redeemed coupons following a retail sale of the goods. See **69.16 TRADE PROMOTION SCHEMES.**

(HMRC VAT Guidance V1–12, paras 4.11.1–4.11.3).

Meaning of consideration

[71.8] Consideration is not defined either in *Directive 2006/112/EC* or *VATA 1994*. The word was defined in the *EC 2nd Directive, Annex A, para 13* as meaning 'everything received in return for the supply of goods or the provision of services, including incidental expenses (packing, transport, insurance, etc.) that is to say not only the cash amounts charged, but also, for example, the value of goods received in exchange or, in the case of goods or services supplied by order of a public authority, the amount of compensation received.' Even though this *Directive* no longer exists, the definition is still sometimes used in cases brought before the ECJ.

The phrase 'in return for' the supply is interpreted to mean that there must be a direct link between the supply and the consideration. See *Staatssecretaris van Financiën v Cooperatieve Vereniging Cooperatieve Aardappelenbewaarplaats GA, ECJ Case 154/80*, [1981] 3 CMLR 337 (TVC 22.78), and *C & E Commrs v The Apple and Pear Development Council, ECJ Case 102/86*, [1988] STC 221 (TVC 22.80).

De Voil Indirect Tax Service. See V3.103.

Payments which may not be consideration

[71.9] Some payments are not consideration because they do not fulfil the conditions in **71.8** above, i.e. there is no direct link between the payment and the supply or there is no supply of goods or services in return for the payment. This paragraph covers areas requiring special attention.

(1) Fines and penalty charges

A true fine or penalty does not form part of the consideration for a supply and is outside the scope of VAT. This includes money levied to penalise an unlawful act (e.g. parking on yellow lines).

However, a payment may be described as a fine or penalty where it is in essence a further payment for a fulfilment of terms and conditions (i.e. part of the consideration for the supply). In such cases, the payments follow the same liability as the supply.

Examples

- *Video hire fines*. Any fine by a video hire shop is an additional taxable supply for the extended use of a video. See *Leigh (t/a Moor Lane Video)* (VTD 5098) (TVC 67.137).
- *Car park charges*. Any additional charge made by a car park for a driver overstaying the allotted time is not regarded as a penalty, but as an extra taxable charge for an extended stay in the car park. But see **43.4**(3) **LOCAL**

> **AUTHORITIES AND PUBLIC BODIES** for penalties imposed by local authorities.

(2) Grants and donations

If freely given with no expectation of anything in return, grants and donations are not consideration for any supply and are outside the scope of VAT. They should not be confused with sponsorship which normally involves the sponsor receiving clearly identifiable benefits in return. See **57.19 RECREATION AND SPORT**.

Donated services

The provision of donated services for no consideration is not a supply for VAT purposes. If the provider of the services asks for a donation to be made to a charity rather than payment for his usual fee (e.g. as in Will Aid), such payments can be disregarded for VAT purposes as long as it is clear to customer that the services can be obtained without the customer being obliged to pay anything. It must be left entirely up to the customer's discretion whether he wishes to pay anything to the charity. The fact that the provider may recommend an amount equivalent to the fee be paid to the charity does not, in itself, alter the donation status of the payments.

Local authority, central government and EU grants

The essential point to decide is whether the public authority or EU has derived any direct benefit (see **71.8** above). For cases relating to local authority grants, see *Trustees of the Bowthorpe Community Trust* (VTD 12978) (TVC 42.18), *Hillingdon Legal Resource Centre Ltd* (VTD 5210) (TVC 11.47) and *Wolverhampton Citizens Advice Bureau* (VTD 16411) (TVC 11.48). For case relating to EU grants, see *Mohr v Finanzamt Bad Segeberg, ECJ Case C–215/94*, [1996] STC 328 (TVC 22.163) and *Landboden-Agrardienste GmbH & Co KG v Finanzamt Calau, ECJ Case C–384/95*, [1998] STC 171 (TVC 22.172).

(3) Deposits including returnable containers

Most deposit payments represent consideration. The amount paid over is intended to be offset against the purchase price once the supply has been made. Where a deposit is returned (e.g. if a contract is cancelled), it ceases to be consideration for a supply unless part of the supply has already been made, in which case the deposit is regarded as being consideration for that part of the supply and VAT must be accounted for accordingly. In the case where a contract is cancelled and nothing is supplied, the deposit is not consideration even if it is not returned.

Forfeit deposits

Forfeit deposits are in general not consideration for any supplies because they constitute a payment for compensation for breach of contract. See **32.4 HOTELS AND HOLIDAY ACCOMMODATION**.

Security deposits

A deposit taken as security (e.g. against the safe return of goods on hire or loan) is not consideration for a supply. In the event of the deposit being forfeited, either wholly or in part, through the customer failing to fulfil his contractual obligations, the amount retained by the supplier does not represent additional consideration for the original supply or consideration for an additional supply of goods or services.

Returnable containers

Where a charge is added to a supply of goods for the container until it is returned (e.g. the keg with beer), it is necessary to establish why the charge has been raised. If it has been raised to ensure the safe return of the container and the charge is to be refunded on its return, it can be treated in the same way as a security deposit (see above). If, however, the charge has been raised to cover the loan, hire or use of the container, then the charge represents consideration for a supply of services, even if it is refundable when the container is returned.

See also **66.6 SUPPLY: TIME OF SUPPLY**.

(4) Management charges and directors services

See **44 MANAGEMENT SERVICES AND SUPPLIES OF STAFF**.

(5) Gratuities, tips and service charges

If these are genuinely freely given, they are outside the scope of VAT as they are not consideration for VAT purposes. Where, however, the element of choice has been removed, the payment is part of the consideration for a supply.

Service charges in restaurants are part of the consideration for the underlying supply of the meals if customers are required to pay them. This applies even if they are passed on in full as bonuses to the staff (*Potters Lodge Restaurant Ltd* (VTD 905) (TVC 67.128)). If customers have a genuine option as to whether to pay the service charges, HMRC accept that they are not consideration even if the amounts appear on the invoices (*NDP Co Ltd* (VTD 2653) (TVC 67.103)).

(6) Disbursements

See **3.7 AGENTS**.

(7) Salary sacrifice

'Salary sacrifice' describes an arrangement where an employee opts to forgo some of their remuneration in return for receiving goods/services. Prior to 1 January 2012, HMRC did not regard the proportion of renumeration forgone as consideration for a supply of the benefits received. However, from that date, following the ECJ decision in *Astra Zeneca UK Ltd v HMRC, ECJ Case C–40/09*, [2010] STC 2298 (TVC 22.92), HMRC have announced that salary sacrifice will be regarded as the consideration for a supply of goods/services. Where that supply is taxable, VAT will be due. In most cases the value of the benefit for VAT purposes will be the same as the amount of salary deducted or the amount foregone. Where this is less than the true value (e.g. where employers supply the benefits at below what it cost to buy them in), the value should be based on the cost to the employer. The effect of the ECJ judgment in particular circumstances is as follows.

- *Cycle to work scheme* — where employers purchase bicycles and safety equipment and provide them to employees under a salary sacrifice arrangement, employers must account for output tax based on the value of the salary foregone by the employee in exchange for the hire or loan of a bicycle. Employers can continue to recover VAT on the purchase of the bicycle and associated equipment. VAT remains due when a bicycle is disposed of and its value should normally be based on the price of an identical or similar item, taking into account the age and condition, etc. The table used to value bicycles for direct tax purposes may be used.
- *Face value vouchers* — input tax is recoverable but output tax must be declared. Childcare vouchers are not directly affected by the judgment as they are not subject to VAT. However, VAT on administrative fees from employers' voucher providers are directly attributable to the exempt supply of vouchers under the partial exemption rules with the result that the VAT incurred may be irrecoverable.
- *Food and catering provided by employers* — where employees pay for meals, etc. under a salary sacrifice arrangement, employers must account for VAT on the value of the supplies unless those supplies are zero-rated. Subject to the normal rules, the employer can recover the VAT incurred on related purchases.
- *Motor cars* — the input tax block on cars means that employers do not account for output tax when cars are made available to employees. Where VAT recovery is restricted and output VAT is not due the judgment has no direct impact. Where an employer suffers no input tax restriction, output tax remains due. (HMRC Brief 28/11).

For salary sacrifice agreements that were signed or otherwise agreed before 28 July 2011 and which extend beyond 31 December 2011, HMRC will allow the amounts of salary foregone to continue to be VAT free until the agreement ceases or comes up for renewal, or there is any other significant review or renegotiation. (HMRC Brief 36/11).

(8) *Ex gratia* payments

An *ex gratia* payment by a customer to cover unexpected costs is outside the scope of VAT provided

- the amount is clearly additional to the price for the supply;
- the customer has no obligation to make the payment; and
- the customer would still receive the supply if the *ex gratia* payment were not made.

(9) Subject access fees

Individuals are entitled, by law, to request access ('subject access') to personal data held about them from any data user. Under *Data Protection Act 1984, s 21(2)* the data user may charge for providing such information. This subject access fee is merely a nominal sum to cover the expenses of complying with the statute and is not consideration as there is no supply for VAT purposes.

(10) Manufacturers' warranties

A manufacturer's warranty covers the reliability of goods after sale. Where the manufacturer carries out a repair under this warranty, there is no supply at that time by the manufacturer (even if new parts are supplied) because the original goods were costed to allow for such repairs.

However, if a dealer or other third party carries out the repair on behalf of the manufacturer, there is a supply by him to the manufacturer and his charge for that supply is consideration.

(11) Retailers' warranties

Certain retailers (e.g. jewellers) offer customers an 'insurance' or indemnity which provides for free repair or replacement if the goods sold are lost or damaged within a certain period. The retailer may cover its liability either by obtaining insurance cover or by including the cost in the overall price. In such cases, neither a repair free-of-charge by the retailer nor the free replacement of the lost or damaged goods is a taxable supply, as the original charge covered the costs involved.

(12) Compensation payments

Compensation payments for damage or loss are outside the scope of VAT as they are not consideration for a supply. This is because the payments are made either as a result of a Court Order or through an agreement between the two parties involved to compensate one party for suffering some inconvenience, loss or damage. See **47.8**(5) **OUTPUT TAX** for further details.

(13) Payments relating to land

See **41.4 LAND AND BUILDINGS: EXEMPT SUPPLIES AND OPTION TO TAX.**

(14) Overpayments

Where, due to a mistake by the customer, a supplier receives payment twice for the same invoice, the value of the supply is not affected. The value remains the original price billed and cannot be doubled simply because of the overpayment. The overpayment is outside the scope of VAT unless, and until, it is used to pay or part-pay a future invoice of the supplier in which case it becomes consideration.

Special valuation rules

[71.10] The general rules for determining the value of a supply of goods or services under **71.2** *et seq*. above are subject to any special valuation rules made by or under *VATA 1994*. In case of any conflict, the order of precedence of the special valuation rules is as follows.

(a) **Provisions other than those contained in *VATA 1994, Sch 6*.** These principally comprise the following.
- *VATA 1994, s 20, Sch 7* — acquisitions from other EU countries (see **71.11–71.14** below)
- *VATA 1994, s 21* — imports (see **71.15** below)
- *VATA 1994, s 23* — gaming machine takings (see **71.29** below)
- *SI 1993/1507* — non-business use of services supplied to a business (see **71.21** below)

(b) **Provisions in *VATA 1994, Sch 6*.** These comprise
- *Sch 6 para 1* — transactions between connected persons (see **71.19** below)
- *Sch 6 para 1A* — use of stock in trade cars of motor manufacturers and motor dealers for less than market value (see **71.30** below)
- *Sch 6 para 2* — supplies of goods to non-taxable persons for retail sale ('direct selling') (see **71.23** below)
- *Sch 6 para 3* — imports and warehoused goods subject to excise duty (see **71.15** and **71.16** below)
- *Sch 6 para 4* — discounts (see **71.24** below)
- *Sch 6 para 5* — tokens, stamps and vouchers (see **71.25** below)
- *Sch 6 para 6* — supplies of goods for no consideration (see **71.22** below)
- *Sch 6 para 7* — non-business use of business assets (see **71.20** below)
- *Sch 6 para 8* — reverse charge services from abroad (see **71.17** below)
- *Sch 6 para 9* — long-term accommodation at reduced rates (see **71.26** below)
- *Sch 6 para 10* — supplies of catering and accommodation by employers to employees (see **71.27** below)
- *Sch 6 para 11* — supplies in foreign currencies (see **71.18** below)
- *Sch 6 para 12* — money consideration for a supply paid by a third party (see **71.28** below)

[*VATA 1994, s 19(1)*].

Acquisitions from other EU countries

[71.11] The value of any acquisition of goods from another EU country is to be taken to be the value of the transaction in which the goods are acquired as follows.

- Where the goods are acquired from another EU country by means of a taxable supply (e.g. goods installed or assembled in the UK, see **19.33 EUROPEAN UNION: SINGLE MARKET**) the value of that transaction is determined under the general valuation rules (see **71.2** above).
- Where the goods are acquired from another EU country otherwise than in pursuance of a taxable supply, subject to **71.12–71.14** below,
  (i) if the transaction is for a consideration in money, its value is to be taken to be such amount as is equal to the consideration; and
  (ii) if the transaction is for a consideration not consisting, or not wholly consisting, of money, its value is to be taken to be such amount in money as is equivalent to the consideration.

  Note that under (i) above the value is an amount equal to the consideration whereas under the general rule in **71.3** above the value is an amount which, with the addition of the VAT chargeable, is equivalent to the consideration.

[*VATA 1994, s 20(1)–(4); FA 1996, Sch 3 para 6*].

Consideration is any form of payment in money or in kind. It includes any payment made by the customer to cover the supplier's costs in making the supply (e.g. packing, transport or insurance) for which the supplier is responsible under the contract.

The tax value of an acquisition is established as follows.

- Where the consideration is wholly in money, the tax value is the amount paid.
- Where the consideration is non-monetary (e.g. the supply is made in return for payment in goods or services) or is monetary and non-monetary, the tax value is the monetary equivalent of the consideration calculated by reference to the price, excluding VAT, which would have had to have been paid if the consideration were monetary.
- Where the consideration involves a discounted amount and the discounted amount is paid, the tax value is based on the discounted amount.
- Where the consideration includes the offer of a conditional discount which is dependent upon some future event (e.g. on condition that more goods are bought from the supplier or a payment is made within a specified period of time), the tax value is based on the full amount paid. But if the discount is later earned, the tax value is reduced and the amount of tax accounted for can be adjusted (although this should only be done where the business has not claimed, or has been unable to claim, full input tax credit for that acquisition).
- Where there is no consideration (e.g. a transfer of own goods where goods are supplied without charge), the tax value is what it would cost the business, or the person transferring the goods to the business, to purchase the goods in question at the time of the acquisition.

(VAT Notice 725, paras 8.3, 8.4).

Consideration attributable to both an acquisition and other matters

Where the transaction in pursuance of which the goods are acquired from another EU country is not the only matter to which a consideration in money relates, the transaction is deemed to be for such part of the consideration as is properly attributable to it. [*VATA 1994, s 20(5)*].

Goods subject to duty

Where goods acquired in the UK from another EU country are charged in connection with their removal to the UK with a duty of excise (or any Union customs duty or EU agricultural levy having effect for transitional provisions in connection with the accession of any state to the EU), then the value of the acquisition for VAT purposes is its value apart from this provision plus the amount (if not already included) of the excise duty, Union customs duty or agricultural levy which has been or is to be paid in respect of the goods. This does not apply to any transaction relating to warehoused goods treated as taking place before the duty point (see **72.4 WAREHOUSED GOODS AND FREE ZONES**).

[*VATA 1994, Sch 7 para 2; SI 1995/2518, Regs 96, 97*].

De Voil Indirect Tax Service. See V3.390.

Transactions between connected persons

[71.12] Where in the case of any acquisition of goods from another EU country

(a) the value of the transaction is for a consideration in money which is less than its open market value, and
(b) the supplier and the person who acquires the goods are 'connected', and
(c) that person is not entitled under *VATA 1994, ss 25, 26* to credit for all the VAT on the acquisition,

HMRC may direct that the value of the transaction is to be taken to be its 'open market value'.

'*Open market value*' is the amount which would be taken as its value assuming the transaction was for such consideration in money as would be payable by a person standing in no such relationship with any person as would affect the consideration.

A direction is given by notice in writing to the person by whom the acquisition is made within a three year period from the time of the acquisition (or, in certain cases where that person is not a taxable person and the consideration is payable periodically, from the first relevant event for the purposes of taxing the acquisition). The direction may be varied or withdrawn by a further direction given by notice in writing. The direction may also include a direction that the value of any transaction made after the date of notice and to which the above conditions apply is to be taken to be its open market value. An appeal may be made against a direction (see **5.3**(28) **APPEALS**).

See **71.19** below for the meaning of '*connected persons*'.

[*VATA 1994, Sch 7 paras 1, 5*].

De Voil Indirect Tax Service. See V3.391.

Transfers and disposals of business assets

[71.13] Where goods are acquired from another EU country under a transaction treated as a supply of goods under **64.3**(*e*)(*f*) **SUPPLY: GENERAL**, the value of the relevant transaction, in a case where there is no consideration, is to be taken to be

(a) such consideration in money as would be payable by the supplier if he were, at the time of the acquisition, to purchase goods *identical* in every respect (including age and condition) to the goods concerned; or
(b) where the value in (*a*) cannot be ascertained, such consideration in money as would be payable to purchase goods *similar* to, and of the same age and condition as, the goods concerned; or
(c) where the value cannot be ascertained under (*a*) or (*b*), the cost of producing the goods concerned if they were produced at that time.

Any VAT included in the purchase price or production cost is to be deducted in arriving at the value to be taxed.

[*VATA 1994, Sch 7 para 3*].

Currencies other than sterling

[71.14] Where goods are acquired from another EU country and any sum relevant for determining the value of the transaction is expressed in a currency other than sterling, then unless one of the alternatives in (*a*)–(*b*) below is adopted, that sum is to be converted into sterling at the market selling rate for that currency at the time of acquisition. The rates published in national newspapers are acceptable as evidence of the rates at the relevant time. The following alternatives are, however, allowed.

(a) A business may use the period rate of exchange published by HMRC for customs purposes. Details of particular period rates are available from the National Advice Service (0845 010 9000). This alternative can be adopted in respect of all acquisitions or in respect of all acquisitions of a particular class or description. If the latter, that class or description should be noted in the business record at the time of adoption. There is no need to notify HMRC in advance if this alternative is to be adopted but, once it has been, a business cannot then change it without first obtaining the agreement of the National Advice Service.
(b) A business can apply in writing to the National Advice Service to use a rate, or a method of determining a rate, which it uses for commercial purposes. In considering whether to allow the application, the National Advice Service will take into account whether the proposed rate or method is determined by reference to the UK currency market, whether it is objectively verifiable, and the frequency with which the applicant proposes to update it. Forward rates or methods deriving from forward rates are not acceptable.

Whatever rate or method is adopted, the appropriate rate for any supply is the one current at the time of supply.

[*VATA 1994, Sch 7 para 4*]. (VAT Notice 725, para 8.5 which has the force of law).

De Voil Indirect Tax Service. See V3.393.

Importation of goods

[71.15] The value of goods imported from a place outside the EU is, subject to below, to be determined according to the rules for Union customs duties (whether or not the goods in question are subject to such duties). These rules are set out in *Council Regulation 2913/92* and *Commission Regulation 2454/93*. See also Customs Notice 252 *Valuation of imported goods for customs purposes, VAT and trade statistics*.

The following are included in the value (so far as not already included under the above rules).

(a) All taxes, duties and other charges levied outside or, by reason of importation, within the UK (but excluding VAT).

(b) All incidental expenses such as commission, packing, transport and insurance costs, up to the 'first destination' of the goods in the UK. '*First destination*' means the place mentioned on the consignment note or other importation document or, in the absence of such documentation, the place of the first transfer of cargo in the UK.

(c) If at the time of importation of the goods a further destination for the goods is known, and that destination is within the UK or another EU country, all such incidental expenses resulting from the transport of the goods to that other destination.

Subject to *(a)*–*(c)* above, where the consideration is wholly or partly in money and on terms allowing a discount for prompt payment (but not payment of the price by instalments), the value of the goods is reduced by the discount if payment is made in accordance with those terms so that the discount is allowed.

[*VATA 1994, s 21(1)(2)(3); FA 1995, s 22; FA 1996, s 27; FA 2006, s 18*].

Works of art, antiques and collectors' pieces

Special valuation provisions apply for these items which have the effect of subjecting them to VAT at an effective reduced rate of 5%. See **73.3 WORKS OF ART, ETC.** for full details.

Incidental expenses

In addition to the examples given above, 'incidental expenses' also covers items such as customs clearance charges, quay rent, entry fees, demurrage, handling, loading and storage costs. Costs which are taxable under the reverse charge procedure (see **38.4 INTERNATIONAL SERVICES**), e.g. royalties and licence fees, should not be included in the value for import VAT.

HMRC give three methods which may be used to calculate the 'incidental expenses' element of the import VAT value. Individual importers or agents may use whichever method best suits their particular circumstances.

(1) *Method 1*. This method requires the actual costs to be declared at the time the goods are imported. In cases where the costs are later found to be incorrect (e.g. if additional storage costs are incurred) the amount(s) paid will need to be adjusted after importation.

(2) *Method 2*. The agreed rates given below may be used to estimate the incidental expenses to be included in the import VAT value. The rates are intended only for international movements of goods which terminate in the UK and represent average costs of handling, storage, customs declarations and transport to destination. Values for other consignments, including those for delivery in other EU countries, must be based on Methods 1 or 3. Where Method 2 is used, post-importation adjustments are not required. Additionally, where it is found that the amount of import VAT based on actual costs exceeds the amount declared on the basis of Method 2 rates, HMRC will not seek to collect the arrears of import VAT unless the importer concerned is not registered for VAT or, if registered, is restricted in the amount of import VAT that can be claimed as input tax.

    The agreed rates are

    (i) *Airfreight*: 40p per chargeable kilo or a minimum amount of £100 to be added to the value at the time of importation, whichever is the greater.

    (ii) *Surface freight groupage/consolidation consignments by trailer, rail wagon or container*. delivery and handling combination of £90 per gross weight tonne plus a flat 'other ancillaries' rate of £80 per consignment, minimum £170, to be added to the value at the time of importation.

    (iii) *Surface freight full load consignments by trailer, rail wagon or container*. £550 per full load consignment to be added to the value at the time of importation.

(3) *Method 3*. In cases where Methods 1 and 2 are considered inappropriate or impractical to use, individual agreements may be negotiated with the Entry Processing Unit or with the importers local Excise and Inland Customs office. Once a Method 3 rate is used, post-importation adjustments are not required.

(VAT Notice 702, para 3.1).

Value declaration

If goods are liable to *ad valorem* customs duty (i.e. a duty chargeable on the basis of value), a declaration on Form C105 (Valuation Declaration) or Form C109 (General Valuation Statement), made for duty purposes, will also generally be acceptable for VAT. However, the declaration will only provide information which helps determine the customs value of the goods, and it should not be regarded as establishing their full value for VAT purposes (see above).

Where goods are not liable to ad valorem duty but are liable to VAT at the standard rate, a valuation declaration for VAT is needed only if the value exceeds £4,000 and

- the importer is not registered for VAT; or

- the importer is registered for VAT but either the goods are for non-business purposes or input tax deduction would not be allowed (e.g. on motor cars); or
- the value of the goods is not being determined under Method 1 (see HMRC Notice 252, Section 3).

Whether or not a valuation declaration is required for the goods, evidence of value must be produced. Acceptable evidence is a copy of the seller's invoice or other document against which payment will be made. This will include telex or similar messages used instead of invoices.

(VAT Notice 702, para 3.3).

De Voil Indirect Tax Service. See V3.321–V3.329.

Excise duty

Where any goods whose supply involves their removal to the UK are charged in connection with their removal with a duty of excise or car tax (or any Union customs duty or EU agricultural levy having effect for transitional provisions in connection with the accession of any state to the EU), then the value of the supply for VAT purposes is its value apart from this provision plus the amount (so far as not already included) of any duty which has been or is to be paid in respect of the goods. [*VATA 1994, Sch 6 para 3*].

Warehoused goods

[71.16] Where the time of supply of any dutiable goods (or goods comprising a mixture of dutiable goods and other goods) is determined under *VATA 1994, s 18(4)* (goods within the warehouse regime) to be at or after the duty point, then the value of the supply for VAT purposes is its value apart from this provision plus the amount (so far as not already included) of any duty which has been or is to be paid in respect of the goods. [*VATA 1994, Sch 6 para 3*].

See **72.8 WAREHOUSED GOODS AND FREE ZONES** for the provisions of *VATA 1994, s 18(4)* and the definitions of '*dutiable goods*' and '*duty point*'.

Reverse charge services received from abroad

[71.17] Where any supply of services is treated under the reverse charge provisions as made by the recipient of the services (rather than the supplier), the value of the supply is

- if the consideration for the services was a consideration in money, such amount as is equal to that consideration; and
- if the consideration did not, or did not wholly, consist of money, such amount in money as is equivalent to that consideration.

[*VATA 1994, Sch 6 para 8*].

It should be noted that under these provisions, value is derived from the consideration upon a VAT-exclusive basis. It is an amount equal to the consideration rather than, as under the general rule in **71.3** above, an amount which, when VAT is added, equals the consideration.

See **38.4** INTERNATIONAL SERVICES for situations where the reverse charge applies in the UK.

Supplies in foreign currency

[71.18] For EU legislation, see **18.22**(*b*) EUROPEAN UNION LEGISLATION.

Under UK legislation, where there is a supply of goods or services and any sum relevant for determining the value is expressed in a currency other than sterling, subject to below, that sum is to be converted into sterling at the market selling rate for that currency at the time of supply. The rates published in national newspapers are acceptable as evidence of the rates at the relevant time. The following options are, however, allowed.

- Where HMRC have published a notice specifying rates of exchange, or methods of determining rates of exchange, a person may opt to use a rate so specified or determined. This alternative may be adopted for all supplies or for all supplies of a particular class or description. If adopted only for a particular class, that class and the time of adoption should be noted in the records. There is no need to notify HMRC in advance that this alternative has been adopted but, once it has, it cannot be changed without first obtaining the agreement of HMRC.
- HMRC may allow a person to apply to them to use a different rate of exchange for the valuation of all or some of his supplies. Application should be made to HMRC in writing. In considering whether to allow the application, HMRC will take into account whether the proposed rate or method is determined by reference to the UK currency market, whether it is objectively verifiable and the frequency with which it is proposed to update it.

[*VATA 1994, Sch 6 para 11*]. (VAT Notice 700, para 7.7 which has the force of law).

De Voil Indirect Tax Service. See V3.164.

Transactions between connected persons

[71.19] Where all the following conditions are satisfied, then unless the supply falls within **71.27** below (supplies of accommodation and catering by employers to employees), HMRC *may* direct that the value of the supply is to be taken to be its 'open market value'.

(a) The value of a supply made by a taxable person for a consideration in money would otherwise be less than its open market value. A direction *cannot* therefore be made if
    - part of the consideration is non-monetary (in which case the rules in **71.5** above must be followed); or
    - the consideration is greater than the open market value (i.e. a direction cannot be issued to reduce an over-inflated consideration).

(b) The person making the supply and the person to whom it is made are 'connected' (see below).

(c) If the supply is a taxable supply, the recipient is not entitled under *VATA 1994, ss 25, 26* to credit for all of the VAT on the supply. In practice, this means that, where the supply is a taxable supply, a direction can only be issued if the recipient is not registered for VAT or is wholly or partly exempt for VAT purposes.

The provisions are specifically intended to counter tax avoidance. If a supply between connected persons is made below open market value for a legitimate reason that can be substantiated, and which is unconnected with avoidance, HMRC have a discretion not to issue a notice.

'*Open market value*' is the amount which would be taken as its value under (*a*) above assuming the supply were for such consideration in money as would be payable by a person standing in no such relationship with any person as would affect that consideration.

A direction is given by notice in writing to the person making the supply within a three year period from the time of the supply and may be varied or withdrawn by a further notice in writing. The notice may *also* include a direction that the value of any future supply satisfying the above conditions is to be taken to be its open market value (although a notice cannot cover future supplies only). An appeal may be made against a direction (see **5.3**(28) **APPEALS**).

[*VATA 1994, s 19(5), Sch 6 para 1(1)–(3)(5), para 13*].

> *Example*
>
> ABC Ltd is VAT-registered and buys a new commercial property for £200,000 plus VAT. It sells the property to its associated company, DEF Ltd, for £50 plus VAT, DEF Ltd will use the property for its trading activity as an insurance broker, i.e. an exempt activity where input tax claims are blocked.
>
> HMRC will issue a direction in this situation to rule that the value of the supply from ABC Ltd to DEF Ltd be based on its open market value of £200,000 plus VAT. The input tax block to DEF Ltd will then be £40,000 (assuming a VAT rate of 20%), exactly the same as if it had bought the property from the original owner.

Connected persons

Persons are treated as 'connected' with another under the provisions of *ICTA 1988, s 839*. [*VATA 1994, Sch 6 para 1(4)*]. These are as follows.

(i) **An individual** is connected with his spouse, any 'relative' of himself or of his spouse, and with the spouse of any such relative. It appears that a widow or widower is no longer a spouse (*Vestey's Exors and Vestey v CIR*, HL 1949, 31 TC 1). Spouses divorced by decree nisi remain connected persons until the divorce is made absolute (*Aspden v Hildesley*, Ch D 1981, [1982] STC 206).

(ii) **A trustee of a settlement**, in his capacity as such, is connected with
- the settlor (if an individual);
- any person connected with that settlor; and
- a 'body corporate connected with the settlement'.

(iii) **Partners** are connected with each other and with each other's spouses and 'relatives' except in connection with acquisitions and disposals of partnership assets made pursuant to *bona fide* commercial arrangements.

(iv) **A 'company'** is connected with another company if
- the same person 'controls' both;
- one is controlled by a person who has control of the other in conjunction with persons connected with him;
- a person controls one company and persons connected with him control the other;
- the same group of persons controls both; or
- the companies are controlled by separate groups which can be regarded as the same by interchanging connected persons.

(v) **A company** is connected with another person who (either alone or with persons connected with him) has control of it.

(vi) **Persons acting together to secure or exercise control of a company** are treated in relation to that company as connected with each other and with any other person acting on the direction of any of them to secure or exercise such control. For the meaning of 'acting together to secure or exercise control' see *Steele v EVC International NV (formerly European Vinyls Corp (Holdings) BV)*, CA 1996, 69 TC 88. Control may be 'exercised' passively. (See *Floor v Davis*, HL 1979, 52 TC 609).

'*Company*' includes any body corporate, unincorporated association or unit trust scheme. It does not include a partnership.

'*Control*' is as defined in *ICTA 1988, s 416*. See *Tolley's Corporation Tax* for full coverage of this definition.

'*Relative*' means brother, sister, ancestor or lineal descendant.

'*Settlement*' includes any disposition, trust, covenant, agreement, arrangement or transfer of assets. [*ICTA 1988, s 660G(1); FA 1995, Sch 17 para 1*].

'*A body corporate connected with the settlement*' is a 'close company' (or one which would be close if resident in the UK) the 'participators' in which include the trustees of the settlement, or a company of which such a close company, etc. has 'control'. '*Close company*' for this purpose is as defined by *ICTA 1988, s 414*, '*participator*' is as defined by *ICTA 1988, s 417* and 'control' in this case, is as defined by *ICTA 1988, s 840*. See *Tolley's Corporation Tax* for full coverage of these definitions.

'*Settlor*' is any person by whom the settlement was made or who has directly or indirectly (or by a reciprocal arrangement) provided, or undertaken to provide, funds for the settlement. [*ICTA 1988, s 660G(1)(2); FA 1995, Sch 17 para 1*].

De Voil Indirect Tax Service. See V1.296; V3.161; V3.162.

Non-business use of business assets

[71.20] Where there is a free supply of services by virtue of *VATA 1994, Sch 4 para 5(4)* (business goods put to a private or non-business use), then, unless **71.27** below applies (supplies of accommodation and catering by employers to employees), the value of the supply is taken to be the full cost to the taxable person of providing the services.

See **47.7 OUTPUT TAX** for further details.

Non-business use of services supplied to a business

[71.21] Where a person carrying on a business puts services supplied to him to any private or non-business use, he is treated as having supplied those services in the course or furtherance of the business. The value of the supply is that part of the value of the supply of the services to him as reasonably represents the cost to him of providing the services. Where the services are put to a private or non-business use on more than one occasion, the total VAT liability under these provisions cannot exceed the input tax claimed when the services were obtained. [*SI 1993/1507*].

See **47.7 OUTPUT TAX** for further details.

Supplies of goods for no consideration

[71.22] Where there is a supply of goods by virtue of

- a Treasury order under *VATA 1994, s 5(5)* (self-supply of goods, see **45.6 MOTOR CARS** for self-supply of a motor car and **62.2 SELF-SUPPLY** for self-supply of stationery),
- *VATA 1994, Sch 4 para 5(1)* (gifts of business assets, see **47.6 OUTPUT TAX**),
- *VATA 1996, Sch 4 para 6* (removal of business assets from one EU country to another, see **19.2 EUROPEAN UNION: SINGLE MARKET**), or
- *VATA 1994, Sch 4 para 8* (deemed supply on deregistration and termination of business, see **59.34 REGISTRATION**),

then, unless **71.27** below applies (supplies of accommodation and catering by employers to employees), the value of the supply is

(a) such consideration in money (excluding any VAT) as would be payable by the person making the supply if he were, at the time of the supply, to purchase goods *identical* in every respect (including age and condition) to the goods concerned;

(b) where the value cannot be determined as under (*a*) above, such consideration in money (excluding any VAT) as would be payable by that person if he were, at that time, to purchase goods *similar* to, and of the same age and condition as, the goods concerned; and

(c) where the value cannot be determined as under (*a*) or (*b*) above, the cost of producing the goods concerned if they were produced at that time.

[*VATA 1994, Sch 6 para 6*].

Note that what is relevant is what the goods would have cost to purchase or produce at the time of their disposal and not the actual historic cost to the business. Where disposal is close to the date the goods were obtained, the value may have remained unchanged. In most cases, however, depreciation or appreciation over the intervening period must be taken into account.

Supplies of goods made to non-taxable persons for retail sale ('direct selling')

[71.23] In circumstances where

- the whole or part of a business carried on by a taxable person consists in supplying to a number of persons goods to be sold, whether by them or others, by retail, and
- those persons are not taxable persons,

HMRC may direct that the value of any such supply is to be taken as its open market value. The direction is given by notice in writing to the taxable person and is effective from the date of the giving of notice or a later date as specified in the notice and may be varied or withdrawn by a further direction given by notice in writing. An appeal may be made against a direction (see **5 APPEALS**).

[*VATA 1994, Sch 6 paras 2, 13*].

HMRC has authority to issue such a direction in respect of direct selling cases because derogations have been obtained under *Directive 2006/112/EC, Art 395* (see **18.43 EUROPEAN UNION LEGISLATION**). See also *Direct Cosmetics Ltd v C & E Commrs, ECJ Case 5/84*, [1985] STC 479 (TVC 22.480) (and the subsequent appeal by *Direct Cosmetics* and *Laughton Photographs Ltd v C & E Commrs, ECJ Case 138/86*, [1988] STC 540 (TVC 22.481)) and *Gold Star Publications Ltd v C & E Commrs*, QB [1992] STC 365 (TVC 67.30). A direction has been held to be invalid where there was no effective means of determining the open market value of the goods sold by retail. See *Beckbell Ltd* (VTD 9847) (TVC 67.34) where the company did not fix a recommended retail price for goods by salesmen and frequently charged its salesmen different prices for identical goods. See, however, the subsequent decision of the House of Lords in *Fine Art Developments plc* below.

In *Fine Art Developments plc v C & E Commrs*, HL 1995, [1996] STC 246 (TVC 67.33), catalogues containing descriptions and pictures of goods for sale were sent to 'agents'. Some goods were retained by the agents for their own use and some were sold on at less than the catalogue price, although the majority were sold by the agents at the full catalogue price. The company argued that the direction issued under *VATA 1994, Sch 6 para 2* was invalid. It argued that it was not supplying goods to be sold by retail because at the time it made the supply to the agents, it did not know what the agents would be doing with the goods, and that even if the direction was not invalid for that reason, it was otherwise invalid because it was impossible to comply with its terms, i.e. to determine to which goods it was to apply. The House of Lords rejected these arguments and held that the direction was valid. As VAT was a self-assessed tax, it was the duty of the company to modify its order form so as to identify the goods earmarked for onward sale. Where the company was unable to show what the actual sale price for any item was, it was open to HMRC to take the catalogue price as being the true open market value.

De Voil Indirect Tax Service. See V3.161; V3.163.

Discounts

Prompt payment discounts

[71.24] Where goods or services are supplied for a consideration in money and on terms allowing a discount for prompt payment, in valuing the supply the consideration is taken as reduced by the discount, whether or not payment is made in accordance with those terms. However, this treatment does not apply where the terms include any provision for payment by 'instalments'. [*VATA 1994, Sch 6 para 4*].

In *Saga Holidays Ltd* (VTD 18591) (VTD 67.88) S sold holidays and offered customers discounts for prompt payment. It failed to take account of such discounts and submitted a repayment claim. HMRC agreed to refund the amounts which S had overpaid where customers actually received discounts but rejected the claim where discount had been offered but the customers had not actually taken advantage of it. The tribunal agreed with this treatment, observing that the legislation provided that the consideration should be taken as reduced 'by the discount' and holding that these words could more readily be interpreted as a reference to a discount that has actually come into existence than to one that was available but may never come into existence. Therefore, *Sch 6 para 4(1)* should be construed as meaning that the consideration is only reduced where the discount is achieved.

This does not appear to be the interpretation which HMRC state in their published material. In VAT Notice 700, para 7.3 they indicated that the value for VAT is the discounted amount 'whether of not the customer takes up the offer'.

See also *Gold Star Publications Ltd v C & E Commrs*, QB [1992] STC 365 (TVC 67.31) (whether what was described as a discount for prompt payment was in fact such a discount or a commission given to demonstrators).

> *Example*
>
> John sells goods to Sue for £1,000 plus VAT. He offers her a discount of 5% on the price of the goods if she pays the invoice within 14 days. The VAT charge on the invoice will be based on a value of £950 (i.e. £1,000 less 5%), irrespective of whether Sue takes advantage of the discount within the following 14 days.

Unconditional discounts

These are given similar treatment as prompt payment discounts above (e.g. because of the volume of supplies being made or the size and status of a customer).

Contingent discounts

Where a contingent discount is offered on condition that something happens later (e.g. on condition that the customer buys further goods) the discount must initially be ignored and VAT is due on the full amount. If the customer later earns the discount, the tax value is then reduced and the VAT due can be adjusted by issuing a credit note.

Discounts allowed with part-exchange goods

See **71.7** above.

(VAT Notice 700, para 7.3).

'Dividend'

'Dividend' paid to members in respect of their purchases of items from the society have been held to be discount in *Co-operative Retail Services Ltd* (VTD 7527) (TVC 22.252).

Tokens, stamps and vouchers

[71.25] *In respect of tokens, stamps and vouchers issued before 9 April 2003*, where a right to receive goods or services for an amount stated on any token, etc. was granted for a consideration, the consideration was disregarded for the purposes of *VATA 1994* except to the extent (if any) that it exceeded that amount. [*VATA 1994, Sch 6 para 5*].

In respect of tokens, stamps and vouchers issued on or after 9 April 2003, the above provisions are repealed and replaced by special provisions relating to face-value vouchers in *VATA 1994, Sch 10A*.

See **69 TRADE PROMOTION SCHEMES** for the treatment of coupons, vouchers and business promotion schemes generally.

Long-term accommodation at a reduced rate

[71.26] Where accommodation in a hotel, inn, boarding house or similar establishment is

- provided to an individual for a period exceeding four weeks, and
- throughout that period the accommodation is provided for the use of the individual either alone or together with one or more persons who occupy the accommodation with him otherwise than at their own expense,

after the initial four weeks the value of the supply is reduced to that part attributable to facilities other than the right to occupy the accommodation (subject to a minimum of 20%). [*VATA 1994, Sch 6 para 9*].

See **32.2 HOTELS AND HOLIDAY ACCOMMODATION** for further details.

Supplies of catering and accommodation by employers to employees

[71.27] Where an employer makes a supply of goods or services to his employees consisting of

- food or beverages supplied in the course of catering, or
- accommodation in a hotel, inn, boarding house or similar establishment,

the value of that supply is to be taken to be the monetary consideration, if any, paid by the employee (i.e. the consideration is nil where there is no consideration or any consideration other than money).

[*VATA 1994, Sch 6 para 10*].

See **11.8 CATERING** and **32.3 HOTELS AND HOLIDAY ACCOMMODATION** for further details.

See also *Hotel Scandic Gasaback AB v Riksskatteverket, ECJ Case C–412/03*, [2005] STC 1311 (TVC 22.185).

Money consideration for a supply paid by a third party

[71.28] HMRC have power to make regulations so as to require that, in prescribed circumstances, there is to be taken into account as constituting part of the monetary consideration for the purposes of **71.3** above (where it would not otherwise be so taken into account) money paid in respect of the supply by persons other than those to whom the supply is made. [*VATA 1994, Sch 6 para 12*]. No regulations have been made under these provisions.

Gaming machine takings

[71.29] Whenever cash or tokens are removed from a gaming machine, the 'taxable take' is the amount paid by persons to play the game less the amount (if any) received by persons playing successfully. There are also rules for valuing tokens depending upon whether they are replayable tokens or non-replayable tokens. [*VATA 1994, s 23(1)–(3)*].

See **57.4 RECREATION AND SPORT** for further details.

Use of stock in trade cars for less than market value

[71.30] Where a motor manufacturer or a motor dealer allows an employee or his relative to use a stock in trade motor car for a consideration which is less than its open market value, HMRC may direct that the value of the supply is to be taken as the open market value.

[*VATA 1994, Sch 6 para 1A; FA 2004, s 22(2)*].

See **45.7 MOTOR CARS** for full details.

Key points

[71.31] Points to consider are as follows.

- Customers will usually pay for goods or services with money, making it easy to identify (in most cases) the value of a supply for VAT purposes. However, payment in non-monetary consideration is also relevant as far as a VAT charge is concerned (e.g. barter arrangement, part exchange etc.).
- It is important that a supplier and customer are clear whether a contract or deal to supply goods or services is based on prices that include or exclude VAT. A supplier should ensure the answer to this question is clearly established and communicated to the customer before a sale takes place.
- VAT is due on the full value of standard-rated goods or services supplied to a customer, including any other taxes that are levied for customs or excise duties. In the case of alcoholic drinks, this means that VAT is effectively being charged on other taxes.
- The valuation of a non-monetary consideration can present a challenge to a business. The key approach is to convert the non-monetary payment into an amount of money based on what amount would have been paid by the customer if payment was made wholly in money.
- In the case of a part exchange transaction, very common for certain types of business (e.g. a car dealer) there are two sales taking place, and each sale is valued according to its market price, i.e. the two transactions are not 'netted off' as far as output tax is concerned.
- No output tax is due on a free supply of services, e.g. a free advert placed in a publication such as a newspaper. However, there must not be any hidden benefits for the supplier that could represent non-monetary consideration.
- Many grants received by charities and similar bodies are outside the scope of VAT. This is because no specific goods or services are being supplied in return for the grant payment. However, some grants are linked to a supply of services, which means the grant income could be standard rated in many situations.
- In certain situations, a grant being standard-rated rather than outside the scope of VAT could benefit the grant recipient because it means input tax can be claimed on the related costs of the project. The VAT charge to the grant provider might not be a problem in many cases if he can reclaim input tax (as is the case with most local authorities).
- A service charge made by a restaurant, usually based on a percentage of the customer's bill, is standard-rated. However, discretionary payments such as tips are outside the scope of VAT.
- If a prompt payment discount is offered to a customer, the amount of VAT charged on the sales invoice will be based on the discounted price, irrespective of whether the customer takes

advantage of the discount opportunity. For a sale to a connected party, and where the connected party cannot fully reclaim input tax, HMRC may direct that the value of the supply be taken as the open market value if it is made below this figure. This situation will be particularly relevant if the recipient of the supply is either not VAT-registered or unable to reclaim input tax under partial exemption rules.

72

Warehoused Goods and Free Zones

De Voil Indirect Tax Service. See V3.331; V3.332; V3.383; V3.384; V5.141, V5.141A.

Introduction

[72.1] This chapter considers the VAT treatment of goods entering, supplied within and removed from warehouses and free zones, together with the treatment of supplies of services associated with those goods.

Warehouses

[72.2] Customs warehousing permits the payment of VAT (and duties) to be suspended or delayed for goods which are stored in authorised premises.

A '*warehouse*' for these purposes means any warehouse where goods may be stored in any EU country without payment of any one or more of the following.

(a) Union customs duty.
(b) Any agricultural levy of the EU.
(c) VAT on the importation of the goods into any EU country.
(d) Any duty of excise or any duty which is equivalent in another EU country to a duty of excise.

[*VATA 1994, s 18(6)*].

In the UK, a warehouse may be a

- customs warehouse, i.e. premises or an inventory system authorised by Customs for the storage of non-union goods under duty and import VAT suspension;
- tax warehouse, i.e. an authorised place where goods subject to excise duty are produced, processed, held, received or despatched under duty suspension arrangements by an authorised warehousekeeper in the course of his business. Included are excise warehouses, registered premises, distilleries and refineries; or
- fiscal warehouse, i.e. a regime where specified EU goods in free circulation can be traded VAT-free, subject to certain conditions. Fiscal warehouses are dealt with separately under **72.12** *et seq* below.

Goods eligible for warehousing in the UK

The following goods are eligible for warehousing in the UK.

Customs warehouses	*Third country goods of any kind except excise goods whether subject to a positive rate of duty or not*
Tax warehouses (including both manufacturing premises and storage premises)	Third country goods on which customs duty has been paid Union goods UK goods comprising mineral (hydrocarbon) oils, alcohol and alcoholic beverages, manufactured tobacco

(VAT Notice 702/9/05, para 4.3).

Goods entering warehouses

[72.3] No import VAT is due when goods are placed in a customs warehouse. Import VAT will only become due when the goods are removed from the warehouse to free circulation. It is normally payable, together with any customs or excise duty suspended, by the person removing the goods.

Goods which, on arrival in the UK, are placed in a customs warehouse are not deemed to be imported for VAT purposes until such time as they are removed into free circulation in the UK.

The following goods can be stored in a customs warehouse.

- Non-Union goods liable to customs duties and/or VAT (whether or not eligible for preference) and/or excise duties.
- Non-Union goods for which necessary supporting documents (such as DTI licence) are not available at the time of import.
- Non-Union goods imported to another suspensive regime (such as IPR (inward processing relief) or TI (temporary importation)) warehoused for export from the EU.
- Non-Union PCC (processing under customs control) products.
- Non-Union goods that are not subject to a positive rate of customs duty in the tariff, but are liable to import VAT.
- Union produced goods or non-Union goods released to free circulation, eligible for CAP (common agricultural policy) refunds on export. These goods should be warehoused in a specially approved warehouse under the CAP pre-financing arrangements.
- Non-Union goods in free circulation that are subject to a claim under the rejected imports arrangements.

'*Non-Union goods*' are goods which are not of EU origin or imported goods which have not been released into free circulation.

'*Union goods*' are goods which are

(a) entirely obtained or produced in the Customs territory of the EU, without the addition of goods from third countries or territories that are not part of the Customs territory of the EU;
(b) imported from countries or territories not forming part of the Customs territory of the EU which have been released for free circulation in an EU country; or
(c) obtained or produced in the Customs territory of the EU either wholly from those under (*b*) or partly from (*a*) and (*b*).

(VAT Notice 702/9/05, paras 4.1, 4.2).

Supplies within warehouses

[72.4] Supplies of imported goods in warehouse are normally disregarded for VAT purposes as they are treated as taking place outside the UK (see **72.5** below). On removal to home use, the goods may be subject to import VAT.

Within tax warehouses supplies of dutiable goods, whether home produced or acquired from another EU country, are disregarded for VAT purposes but only if a subsequent supply takes place whilst they are still warehoused. See **72.6** and **72.7** below. (If this condition is not met, any VAT due on the sale is to be accounted for when the goods are removed to home use, see **72.8** below.)

Similarly, certain services connected with warehoused goods are relieved when originally supplied (through the mechanism of zero-rating), but may be taxed at the standard rate when the goods to which they relate are removed from the regime. See **72.19** below.

Imported goods

[72.5] Subject to the exceptions below, where

(a) any goods have been removed from a place outside the EU and have entered the EU,
(b) the 'material time' for any supply of those goods or acquisition of those goods from another EU country is while they are subject to a warehousing regime and before the 'duty point', and
(c) such goods are not mixed with any 'dutiable goods' which were
- produced or manufactured in the UK (in which case **72.7** below applies), or
- acquired from another EU country (in which case **72.6** below applies),

then the supply or acquisition referred to in (*b*) above is treated as taking place outside the UK and is disregarded for UK VAT purposes.

The '*material time*' for a supply or acquisition is the time of removal of the goods or, in the case of a supply, if the goods are not removed, at the time they are made available to the person to whom they are supplied.

'*Dutiable goods*' means any goods which are subject to a duty of excise (or any Union customs duty or EU agricultural levy having effect for transitional purposes in connection with the accession of any country to the EU).

'*Duty point*' means the time any excise duty becomes payable or, if the goods are not subject to excise duty, the time when any Union customs debt in respect of duty on the entry of the goods into the EU would be incurred.

[*VATA 1994, s 18(1)(6)(7)*].

The effect of the above provisions is that VAT must not be charged, and a VAT invoice showing VAT must not be issued, in respect of any supplies of imported goods made within a warehousing regime.

Exceptions

As an anti-avoidance measure, the above provisions do not apply where

- there is a supply of goods that would otherwise be treated under the above provisions as taking place outside the UK;
- the whole or part of the business carried on by the supplier of those goods consists in supplying to a number of persons goods to be sold, by them or others, by retail;
- that supplier is a taxable person (or would be a taxable person but for the above provisions); and
- that supply is to a person who is not a taxable person, and is a supply of goods to that person by retail or to be sold, by that person, by retail.

[*VATA 1994, s 18(1A); SI 1995/2518, Reg 145K; SI 2005/2231, Reg 10*].

One of the key assumptions of the provisions of *VATA 1994, s 18(1)* is that the amount of VAT due once the goods leave the warehouse should correspond to the amount of the VAT that would have been due had the transaction not been VAT-free. The anti-avoidance provisions are designed to enforce this. The vast majority of transactions in customs warehouses will not be affected and continue to benefit from relief.

Acquisitions from other EU countries

[72.6] Where

- any 'dutiable goods' are acquired from another EU country, or
- a person makes a supply of dutiable goods which were acquired from another EU country (or a mixture of such goods and other goods)

and the 'material time' for the acquisition or supply is while the goods are subject to a warehousing regime and before the 'duty point', then where the material time for any subsequent supply of those goods is also while the goods are subject to the warehousing regime and before the duty point, the acquisition or supply is treated as taking place outside the UK (and is disregarded for UK VAT purposes).

The '*material time*' for a supply or acquisition is the time of removal of the goods or, in the case of a supply, if the goods are not removed, at the time they are made available to the person to whom they are supplied.

'*Dutiable goods*' means any goods which are subject to a duty of excise (or, any Union customs duty or EU agricultural levy having effect for transitional purposes in connection with the accession of any country to the EU).

'*Duty point*' means the time any excise duty becomes payable or, if the goods are not subject to excise duty, the time when any Union customs debt in respect of duty on the entry of the goods into the EU would be incurred.

[*VATA 1994, s 18(2)(3)(6)(7)*].

The effect of this is that any supply of such goods is disregarded for VAT purposes if the supply is followed by another supply of the goods while they are still warehoused. No VAT should be charged on such disregarded supplies.

Goods produced or manufactured in the UK subject to excise duty

[72.7] Where a person makes a supply of any 'dutiable goods' which were produced or manufactured in the UK (or a mixture of such goods and other goods) and the 'material time' for the supply is while the goods are subject to a warehousing regime and before the 'duty point', then where the material time for any subsequent supply of those goods is also while the goods are subject to the warehousing regime and before the duty point, the earlier supply is treated as taking place outside the UK (and is disregarded for UK VAT purposes).

The '*material time*' for a supply is the time of removal of the goods or, if the goods are not removed, at the time they are made available to the person to whom they are supplied.

'*Dutiable goods*' means any goods which are subject to a duty of excise.

'*Duty point*' means the time any excise duty becomes payable.

[*VATA 1994, s 18(2)(3)(6)(7); FA 1995, s 29*].

The effect of this is that any supply of such goods is disregarded for VAT purposes if the supply is followed by another supply of the goods while they are still warehoused. No VAT should be charged on such disregarded supplies.

Removal of goods from warehouses

[72.8] VAT becomes due when goods are removed from a warehouse to free circulation and is normally payable by the person who removes the goods. The VAT due may be on the importation, acquisition or supply of the goods.

Imported goods

When imported goods are removed from a customs warehouse to free circulation in the UK, an entry must be completed at the time of removal. Any import VAT/customs duty must be paid or deferred by completing a C88 (SAD) unless the goods

- have also been warehoused for excise duty in a customs warehouse, in which case excise duty may be suspended if the goods are now to be placed in tax warehouse;
- qualify for relief from import VAT;
- are removed to another EU country and onward supply relief is claimed; or
- the goods are ex IPR drawback and import VAT has already been paid.

(VAT Notice 702/9/05, para 4.4).

Acquisitions from other EU countries

Where

- either
  - (i) 'dutiable goods' are acquired from another EU country, or
  - (ii) a person makes a supply of dutiable goods which were acquired from another EU country (or a mixture of such goods and other goods),
- the 'material time' for the acquisition or supply is while the goods are subject to a warehousing regime and before the 'duty point', and
- there is no subsequent acquisition or supply of those goods whilst subject to the warehouse regime and before the duty point

the acquisition or supply is treated as taking place at the earlier of the time the goods are removed from the warehouse regime and the duty point.

The '*material time*' for a supply or acquisition is the time of removal of the goods or, in the case of a supply, if the goods are not removed, at the time they are made available to the person to whom they are supplied.

'*Dutiable goods*' means any goods which are subject to a duty of excise (or any Union customs duty or EU agricultural levy having effect for transitional purposes in connection with the accession of any country to the EU).

'*Duty point*' means the time any excise duty becomes payable or, if the goods are not subject to excise duty, the time when any Union customs debt in respect of duty on the entry of the goods into the EU would be incurred.

[*VATA 1994, s 18(2)–(4)(6)(7)*].

The effect of this is that VAT due on the last supply of the goods within the tax warehouse must be accounted for and paid (or deferred) when the goods pass the duty point or are removed for home use. A removal declaration must also be completed. Where no supply takes place, the acquisition VAT must be accounted for on the VAT return for the period covering the date of removal. This VAT can be recovered as input tax on the same return, subject to the normal rules.

Goods produced or manufactured in the UK subject to excise duty

Where

- a person makes a supply of any 'dutiable goods' which were produced or manufactured in the UK (or a mixture of such goods and other goods),
- the 'material time' for the supply is while the goods are subject to a warehousing regime and before the 'duty point', and
- there is no subsequent supply of those goods whilst subject to the warehousing regime and before the duty point,

the supply is treated as taking place at the earlier of the time the goods are removed from the warehouse regime and the duty point.

The '*material time*' for a supply is the time of removal of the goods or, if the goods are not removed, at the time they are made available to the person to whom they are supplied.

'*Dutiable goods*' means any goods which are subject to a duty of excise.

'*Duty point*' means the time any excise duty becomes payable.

[*VATA 1994, s 18(2)(3)(6)(7); FA 1995, s 29*].

The effect of this is that the person removing the UK-produced goods from the warehouse to home use must complete a removal declaration at the time the goods are removed and pay any duty and VAT due. The value for VAT purposes includes any customs and/or excise duty payable.

Goods removed from warehouse to a place outside the UK

Subject to the normal rules, any supply of goods from a warehouse for export outside the EU or for supply to a taxable person in another EU country may be zero-rated. Goods removed directly to a customs warehouse in another EU country under the customs warehouse transfer arrangements can be disregarded for UK VAT purposes. However, in both cases any such supplies must be entered on an EU sales list covering the time of removal and in Box 8 of the VAT return. (VAT Notice 702/9/05, para 4.6).

Transfers from customs warehouses to another customs suspensive procedure

Where goods are transferred to another customs suspensive procedure, the import VAT and customs duty remain suspended under the new procedure. (VAT Notice 702/9/05, para 4.9).

Evidence for input tax deduction

[72.9] The normal evidence of VAT paid on imported goods is the certificate Form C79. The certificate is sent to the VAT-registered person whose Economic Operator Registration and Identification (EORI) is shown in Box 8 of the import entry. In the UK the EORI comprises the letters 'GB' followed by the importer's VAT registration number plus a three-digit suffix. Certificates cover accounting transactions made in each calendar month. (VAT Notice 702/9/05, para 2.12).

Deficiency of warehoused goods

[72.10] Any deficiencies of warehoused goods are deemed to be removed from the customs warehousing regime. Where deficiencies of imported goods are charged with duty, import VAT not already paid on the imported goods also becomes due. Similarly, any acquisition VAT on goods from another EU country which has not been accounted for is also payable. In any case, the VAT may be deducted as input tax, subject to the normal rules. (VAT Notice 702/9/05, para 4.13).

Summary tables

[72.11]

Receipt of goods into a UK customs warehouse and their removal to free circulation in the UK		
	Duty	*VAT*
1. Non-Union goods received direct from a third country and placed in a customs warehouse	*Customs duty*: Suspended on entry into customs warehouse and to be paid on removal *Excise duty*: Duty not due and suspended whilst in warehouse	*Import VAT*: Suspended on entry into customs warehouse and to be paid on removal
2. Non-Union goods received direct from a third country or via another EU country on which there is a nil rate of customs duty —VAT-only customs warehousing	*Customs duty*: N/A *Excise duty*: Duty not due and suspended whilst in warehouse	*Import VAT*: Suspended on entry into customs warehouse and to be paid on removal. Any VAT due in respect of zero-rated services should be paid on removal
3. Non-Union goods received from a third country via another EU country	*Customs duty*: As 1. above *Excise duty*: As 1. above	*Import VAT*: As 1. above *Acquisition VAT*: If the goods are the subject of an acquisition on arrival in the warehouse, VAT must be accounted for on the acquirer's return for the period in which the acquisition tax point falls
4. Goods imported from special territories	*Customs duty*: N/A *Excise duty*: As 1. above	*Import VAT*: As 2. above

Receipt of goods into a UK customs warehouse and their removal other than to free circulation in the UK		
	Duty	*VAT*
1. Non-Union goods for direct export to a country outside the EU	*Customs duty*: Not paid *Excise duty*: Not paid	*Import VAT*: N/A *Supply VAT*: Supplies of goods removed from the UK may be zero-rated as exports (subject to the normal rules)
2. Non-Union goods for indirect export to a country outside the EU	*Customs duty*: Not paid. Goods must move under CPEI arrangements or transit. *Excise duty*: Not paid	*Import VAT*: Any VAT which would be due on removal to UK free circulation is not payable *Supply VAT*: As 1. above
3. Goods transferred to another EU country under a duty suspensive regime	*Customs duty*: As 2. above *Excise duty*: Not paid	*Import VAT*: Any VAT which would be due on removal to UK free circulation is not payable. Otherwise outward movements of goods may be zero-rated (subject to the normal conditions for intra-EU trade) *Supply VAT*: Supplies direct to a customs warehouse in another EU country are outside the scope of UK VAT
4. Non-Union goods moved to another EU country on which customs duty is paid on removal	*Customs duty*: Paid on removal from customs warehouse	*Import VAT*: VAT is payable but may be relieved if the goods are removed in the course of an onward zero-rated supply
5. Non-Union goods transferred to IPR suspension in the UK from a customs warehouse	*Customs duty*: Continues to be suspended and is paid on final removal from IPR if IPR is not discharged *Excise duty*: Continues to be suspended and is paid if IPR is not discharged	*Import VAT*: Any import VAT due is to be paid with the customs duty *Supply VAT*: Supplies of goods under IPR are subject to domestic VAT rules
6. Non-Union goods transferred to IPR drawback in the UK from a customs warehouse	*Customs duty*: To be paid on removal from warehouse *Excise duty*: To be paid on removal from warehouse	*Import VAT*: To be with customs duty on removal *Supply VAT*: As 5. above

(VAT Notice 702/9/03, paras 15.3, 15.4).

Fiscal warehousing

[72.12] The *EC 2nd VAT Simplification Directive* enables countries to introduce a warehousing regime to operate alongside both customs warehouses and excise warehouses. In the UK, this regime is known as fiscal warehousing.

Under the fiscal warehousing regime, certain eligible goods (see **72.14** below) can be placed in a notified warehouse and can then be traded VAT-free whilst subject to the regime. Supplies of goods within a fiscal warehouse and supplies of goods intended to be placed in the regime are, subject to conditions, relieved from VAT. See **72.15** and **72.16** below. The goods may be liable to VAT on removal from the regime. See **72.17** below. Certain services supplied within a fiscal warehousing regime are also VAT-free, the VAT being accounted for when the goods are removed. See **72.19** and **72.20** below.

Dealers in fiscally warehoused goods are not required to be VAT-registered if the value of any other supplies that they make outside of the regime is below the VAT registration threshold.

Retail sales are not allowed under the conditions of a fiscal warehousing regime. [*VATA 1994, s 18A(3); FA 1996, Sch 3 para 5*].

Authorisation for fiscal warehousing

[72.13] HMRC can, on written application, approve any registered person (including any company in a group registration) as a fiscal warehousekeeper, the approval being subject to such conditions as HMRC impose. [*VATA 1994, s 18A(1)(4)(7)(9); FA 1996, Sch 3 para 5; SI 2007/2194, Sch 4 para 85*]. See VAT Notice 702/8/11, para 6 for a specimen application.

The authorisation procedure is stringent so that HMRC can rely on the operators' control procedures and records. All the following basic criteria for authorisation must be met.

- The applicant must be VAT-registered in the UK.
- All business revenue records must be of a high standard (e.g. VAT returns and payments must be up-to-date).
- If already authorised to operate any UK duty suspensive regime, the applicant must have a satisfactory proven records of operation.
- The applicant must be able to comply with the conditions of authorisation and with such regulations as may be laid down for the operation of the regime.
- The administration and organisation of the business must be sound and strictly managed.
- The applicant must provide a list of the addresses of all storage sites which will form part of the fiscal warehouse and any other premises where records will be held. Retail premises cannot be used as fiscal warehouse premises. All notified premises must meet the requirements of health and safety legislation (including any third party premises intended to be used).

- Accounts and stock control records must be capable of meeting the requirements in **72.18** below. In particular, they must be able to distinguish between fiscally warehoused goods and other stocks and be able to identify the location and quantity of any given item held within the fiscal warehousing regime at any stage.

Cancelling or revoking an authorisation

A warehousekeeper wishing to cancel authorisation must give advance notice to HMRC in writing, stating the date by which all goods will cease to be traded and removed from the warehousing arrangements. VAT must be accounted for on all such removals in accordance with **72.20** below.

HMRC can revoke authorisation at any time for any reasonable cause. Except in very exceptional circumstances, they will notify the warehousekeeper in advance of any intended revocation, and the warehousekeeper will have a right to appeal. Where HMRC withdraw authorisation, any goods held in the regime will be treated as though they had been removed by the proprietor at the time of withdrawal and VAT will be due in accordance with **72.20** below.

(VAT Notice 702/8/11, paras 2.7, 2.11).

Qualifying conditions for goods

[72.14] To be eligible for the fiscal warehousing regime,

(a) the goods must be '*eligible goods*' for fiscal warehousing purposes, i.e.
- aluminium, copper, iridium, lead, nickel, palladium, platinum, rhodium, silver, tin, and zinc;
- chemicals in bulk;
- cereals;
- coffee (not roasted), tea, and cocoa beans (whole or broken, raw or roasted);
- grains and seeds (including soya beans);
- mineral oils (including propane and butane and crude petroleum oils);
- nuts;
- oil seeds and oleaginous fruit;
- olives;
- potatoes;
- raw sugar;
- rubber, in primary forms or in plates, sheets or strip;
- vegetable oils and fats and their fractions (whether or not refined, but not chemically modified); and
- wool;

(b) the goods must be in free circulation within the EU (i.e. all duties, taxes and levies must have been either paid or deferred, including customs duty, import VAT, excise duty and any CAP charges due on the goods);

(c) any import VAT payable in respect of the goods must have been accounted for; and

(d) the goods must have been entered in the fiscal warehousing records.

Non-eligible goods may be stored in a place which is a fiscal warehouse but cannot be subject to a fiscal warehousing regime or benefit from the conditions of fiscal warehousing.

[*VATA 1994, s 18B(6), Sch 5A; FA 1996, Sch 3 paras 5, 18*]. (VAT Notice 702/8/11, para 2.4).

Goods entering a fiscal warehouse

[72.15] The following transactions are relieved from VAT (by being treated as taking place outside the UK) if any subsequent supply of the goods in question is made while they are subject to the fiscal warehouse regime.

(a) An acquisition of eligible goods from another EU country where, after the acquisition, but before the next supply (if any), the acquirer places the goods in a fiscal warehousing regime. The acquirer must, not later than the time of acquisition, prepare and keep a certificate stating that he intends to enter the goods into the fiscal warehousing regime.

(b) A supply of eligible goods (other than a retail transaction) where after supply in question but before the next supply, if any, the buyer places the goods in a fiscal warehousing regime. The buyer must give his supplier, not later than the time of supply, a certificate stating that he intends to enter the goods into the fiscal warehousing regime.

[*VATA 1994, s 18B(1)–(3); FA 1996, Sch 3 para 5*].

A supply falling within (*a*) or (*b*) above is treated as a supply of goods (and not a supply of services), even if it is the transfer of an undivided share in the goods, i.e. an unidentified part of a larger stock of eligible goods. [*SI 1996/1255*]. (Normally, such a transfer of an undivided share would be treated for VAT purposes as a supply of services, see **64.4**(*a*) **SUPPLY: GENERAL**.)

Certificates

The certificate required under (*a*) or (*b*) above should be in the following form.

I (full name)
(status in company)
Of (name and address of company)
declare that (name of company) intends to enter to the fiscal warehousing regime at the fiscal warehouse shown below on (insert date) or within (insert number) days commencing today, the goods indicated below:

- name and address of fiscal warehouse
- authorisation number of the fiscal warehousekeeper
- description of goods
- quantity of goods

* I certify that the supply of goods is eligible to be relieved from VAT under VATA 1994, sections 18B(2)(d)/18B(3) (purchases)

* I certify that the acquisition is eligible to be relieved from VAT under VATA 1994, sections 18B(1)(d)/18B(3) (acquisitions).

* Delete as appropriate

(signature)
(date)

Where a taxable person prepares a certificate under (*a*) above or receives one under (*b*) above, he must retain it with his VAT records. Where a non-taxable person prepares a certificate under (*a*) above, he must keep it for six years and produce it to an HMRC officer on request.

[*SI 1995/2518, Reg 31(1), Reg 145B, Sch 1; SI 1996/1250, Regs 8, 13*].

Supplies within fiscal warehouses

[72.16] The following transactions are relieved from VAT (by being treated as taking place outside the UK and therefore outside the scope of UK VAT) if any subsequent supply of the goods in question is made while they are subject to the fiscal warehouse regime.

(a) An acquisition of eligible goods from another EU country where the acquisition takes place while the goods are within a fiscal warehousing regime. The acquirer must, not later than the time of acquisition, prepare and keep a certificate stating that the goods are subject to a fiscal warehousing regime. See **72.15** above for the form of the certificate.

(b) A supply of eligible goods (other than a retail transaction) where the supply takes place while the goods are within a fiscal warehousing regime.

[*VATA 1994, s 18B(1)–(3); FA 1996, Sch 3 para 5*].

The effect of the above is that goods acquired or supplied after being entered to the fiscal warehousing regime are treated as though they are outside the UK and not subject to the normal supply rules *unless* the supply in question is the final supply whilst the goods are warehoused.

A supply falling within (*a*) or (*b*) above is treated as a supply of goods (and not a supply of services), even if it is the transfer of an undivided share in the goods, i.e. an unidentified part of a larger stock of eligible goods. [*SI 1996/1255*]. (Normally, such a transfer of an undivided share would be treated for VAT purposes as a supply of services, see **64.4**(*a*) **SUPPLY: GENERAL**.)

Registration

If transactions falling within (*a*) or (*b*) above are a trader's only UK business activities, he will not be required to register for VAT although he may apply for voluntary registration if he wishes. Liability to register for other business activities is not affected by either the value of supplies made in a fiscal warehouse or the value of deemed supplies of relieved services accounted for by the remover of the goods (see **72.20** below). [*VATA 1994, Sch 1 para 1(9); FA 1996, Sch 3 para 13*]. (VAT Notice 702/8/11, para 2.18).

Removal of goods from fiscal warehousing

[72.17] Subject to the exceptions below, a charge to VAT arises when eligible goods are removed from the fiscal warehouse regime.

- Where the goods were not subject to a supply whilst warehoused, the value on removal is the value at entry into the regime (plus the value of any relieved services performed whilst the goods were fiscally warehoused).
- Where the goods have been supplied whilst warehoused, the value on removal is the amount which would have been due on the last supply within the warehouse. VAT will also be due on any of the relieved supplies of services relating to the goods which have been carried out after that final supply. See **72.20** below.

The VAT due on removal is the liability of the person who causes the goods to cease to be covered by the fiscal warehousing regime and is chargeable and payable at the time of removal. A VAT-registered trader should account for the VAT on the return covering the date of removal. Where the goods are removed by a non-registered trader, Form VAT 150 *Advice of removals from fiscal warehouse by persons unregistered for VAT* must be completed and any VAT due paid in cash or by cheque.

[*VATA 1994, s 18B(4)(5), s 18D; FA 1996, Sch 3 para 5*]. (VAT Notice 702/8/11, para 2.19).

Deemed removals

Where

(a) as a result of an operation on eligible goods in the fiscal warehousing regime, they cease to be eligible goods, or
(b) any person ceases to be a fiscal warehousekeeper or any premises cease to have fiscal warehouse status,

the relevant goods are treated as if they had been removed from the fiscal warehousing regime at that time by the proprietor of the goods.

[*VATA 1994, s 18F(5)(6); FA 1996, Sch 3 para 5*].

VAT is not due on the following removals of goods

- Removals to home use of
  (i) zero-rated goods that have not been subject to relieved supplies of services whilst warehoused; and
  (ii) own goods (either self-produced or purchased VAT paid) which the owner entered to the fiscal warehouse and that have neither been sold nor subject to relieved supplies of services whilst warehoused.
- Goods exported outside the EU. Normal conditions for zero-rating exports apply. (Any associated relieved supplies of services are also not taxable. See **72.20** below.)

- Goods removed in the course of an intra-EU supply. Normal supply/acquisition and Intrastat rules apply for VAT-registered traders. (Any associated relieved supplies of services are also not taxable. See **72.20** below.)
- Transfers to another UK fiscal warehouse.
- Transfers to a corresponding regime to fiscal warehousing in another EU country.
- Temporary removals for repair, processing, treatment or other operations. Authorisation must be sought from HMRC.
- VAT-free sampling. Small quantities of commodities of a negligible commercial value can be removed for this purpose under a simplified removal scheme. The amount and approximate value of the commodity to be removed must be detailed in the authorisation given by HMRC. Such removals must be notified to the warehousekeeper, who is responsible for ensuring that they meet the prescribed conditions.

[*SI 1995/2518, Reg 145H(2); SI 1996/1250, Reg 13*]. (VAT Notice 702/8/11, para 2.20).

Duties and responsibilities of a fiscal warehousekeeper

[72.18] A fiscal warehousekeeper must record all receipts into the warehouse and keep a detailed fiscal warehousing record of stock. There are detailed provisions for recording and control over removals of goods and the transfer of goods to other UK fiscal warehouses or similar regimes in other EU countries. Records must be capable of ready use by an HMRC officer and must be readily reproducible for use off the premises. All records must be kept for six years following the transfer or removal of the goods.

[*SI 1995/2518, Regs 145E–145I, Sch 1A; SI 1996/1250, Reg 13*].

The procedures are stringent so that HMRC can rely on the warehousekeeper's controls and records. Where goods are found to be missing or deficient, a warehousekeeper may be personally liable for the VAT which would have been chargeable on their supply. [*VATA 1994, s 18E; FA 1996, Sch 3 para 5*].

See also VAT Notice 702/8/11, para 2.22.

Supplies of associated warehouse and fiscal warehouse services

[72.19] Certain services associated with goods held in customs, tax and fiscal warehouses can be treated as zero-rated at the time they are supplied provided the supplier and recipient comply with certain requirements. VAT may become due on these services when the goods concerned are subsequently removed from the regime to home use (see **72.20** below).

Conditions for zero-rating

The following conditions must be satisfied for zero-rating to apply.

(a) The taxable person makes a supply of '*specified services*'. These are

(i) Services of keeping the goods in question by an occupier of a warehouse or a fiscal warehousekeeper.

(ii) For goods subject to a warehousing regime, services of carrying out on the goods operations which are permitted under EU customs provisions or warehousing regulations.

(iii) For goods subject to a fiscal warehousing regime, services of carrying out any non-prohibited physical operations on the goods. Zero-rating applies to supplies of the usual forms of handling that are available to goods in a customs warehouse. These are listed in VAT Notice 702/8/11, para 4.1 (simple operations to ensure the preservation of the commodities in good condition during storage), para 4.2 (operations improving the presentation or marketability of the commodities), and para 4.3 (operations preparing the commodities for distribution or resale). Services which cannot be zero-rated are brokerage, agents fees and transport between warehouses.

(b) The services are wholly performed on, or in relation to, goods while subject to the warehousing regime (see **72.2–72.11** above) or the fiscal warehousing regime (see **72.12–72.18** above).

(c) (Except where the services are the supply by an occupier of a warehouse or a fiscal warehousekeeper of warehousing or fiscally warehousing the goods), the person to whom the supply is made (normally the owner of the goods) must give the supplier a certificate, in such form as HMRC specify, that the services are so performed.

To have the services zero-rated, the owner of the goods should give the supplier a certificate before the services are supplied. An example of a certificate is set out below. The owner can create his own version but all the information shown in the example must be provided.

I (full name)

(status in company)

of (name and address of company)

declare that the goods shown below are subject to a fiscal or other warehousing regime at the place indicated below:

- description of goods
- quantity of goods
- warehouse stock number
- name and address of fiscal or other warehouse
- authorisation number of the relevant warehousekeeper/warehouse

and that the following services are to be performed on the goods in the fiscal or other warehouse:

(insert details of services)

I certify that the supply of services is eligible to be zero-rated for VAT purposes under section 18C(1) of the VAT Act 1994.

(signature)
(date)

If the supplier receives such a certificate, he should issue a VAT invoice as normal but VAT should be shown as zero-rated 'in accordance with Section 18C(1) VAT Act 1994' and no VAT should be charged. If the supplier does not receive a such a certificate, he should charge VAT at the standard rate.

Both owner of the goods and the supplier of the services should retain a copy of the certificate in their records to support zero-rating.

As indicated above, a certificate is not required to zero-rate warehouse-keepers storage charges. The invoice issued by the warehouse keeper to enable zero-rating should include the words 'in accordance with Section 18C(1) VAT Act 1994' and no VAT should be charged. If the owner of the goods would prefer VAT to be charged, he should notify the warehousekeeper in writing.

(d) The supply of services would, apart from these provisions, be taxable and not zero-rated. (Services which are exempt when supplied outside the warehouse will therefore remain exempt.)

(e) The supplier of the services must, within 30 days of the services being performed, give the recipient a VAT invoice with the following particulars (unless HMRC allow otherwise).

- An identifying number.
- The material time of the supply of the services in question.
- The date of the issue of the invoice.
- The name, address and registration number of the supplier.
- The name and an address of the person to whom the services are supplied.
- A description sufficient to identify the nature of the services supplied.
- The extent of the services and the amount payable, excluding VAT, expressed in sterling.
- The rate of any cash discount offered.
- The rate of VAT as zero per cent.
- A declaration that in respect of the supply of services in question, the requirements of *VATA 1994, s 18C(1)* (see above) will be or have been satisfied.

[*VATA 1994, s 18C(1)(4); FA 1996, Sch 3 para 5; SI 1995/2518, Regs 145C, 145D; SI 1996/1250*]. (VAT Notice 702/9/05, paras 4.10–4.12, 14).

De Voil Indirect Tax Service. See V3.515A, V5.141, V5.141A.

Subsequent taxation of previously zero-rated services

[72.20] Subject to the exceptions below, services which, at the time of supply, are zero-rated under **72.19** above are subsequently taxed at the time the goods are removed from the warehousing or fiscal warehousing regime or, if earlier, at the duty point. At that time, a taxable (and not zero-rated) supply of services, identical to the zero-rated supply of services, is treated as being made both to the recipient of the zero-rated supply of services and by him in the course or furtherance of his business. The value of the supply is the same as for the zero-rated supply of services. VAT is chargeable on the supply even if the person treated as making it is not a taxable person. [*VATA 1994, s 18C(2)(3); FA 1996, Sch 3 para 5; SI 1996/1249*].

Exceptions

The self-supply charge does not apply in the following circumstances.

- Where the services create new goods.
  If the services or processes applied to existing goods change their nature to the extent that a new product is considered to have been created (e.g. refining crude oil into petrol), the new product is then treated as having been produced in the UK. If the original product was either imported, acquired or supplied before processing, any VAT that would have been due on it is extinguished. No VAT is due in respect of the services because the goods upon which the process has been carried out have ceased to exist and cannot therefore be removed from the warehouse. VAT will only be due if the new goods are subsequently supplied or have further services carried out on them that do not create a new UK product (e.g. secondary packaging).
- Where the goods are supplied (whilst still warehoused) after the services were provided (in which case VAT is only due on any services provided after the last supply in the warehouse).
- Where the goods are exported under duty suspension arrangements directly from the warehouse to a country outside the EU.
- Where the goods are sent under duty suspension arrangements to a customs or tax warehouse in another EU country.

Free zones

[72.21] A free zone is a designated area in which non-Union goods are treated as if they are outside the customs territory of the EU and can be stored without payment of import duties and import VAT. HMRC may make regulations covering the control and operation of such zones and the movement of goods into and out of them and the charging of duty. [*FA 1984, s 8, Sch 4; SI 1984/1177*]. Free zones are currently operating at Liverpool, Prestwick, Southampton, Tilbury and Port of Sheerness.

Goods entering free zones

Import VAT

[72.22] Import VAT (and customs duty) is suspended on non-Union goods entering the UK from places outside the EU and placed in a free zone. But unlike customs warehousing, goods can be released to free circulation in the free zone by paying the customs duties without the import VAT having to be accounted for at the same time. The import VAT is only payable when the goods finally leave the free zone to free circulation or are used or consumed in the free zone.

Acquisitions from other EU countries

The acquisition of Union or non-Union goods from a registered trader in another EU country where the goods are put into a free zone is treated in the same way as the acquisition of goods in the rest of the UK, i.e. VAT must be accounted for on the acquirer's VAT return for the period covering the time of acquisition (see **19.3** *et seq*. **EUROPEAN UNION: SINGLE MARKET**). The value for VAT must include any duty paid.

(VAT Notice 702/9/05, para 5.1).

Supplies within free zones

[72.23] Supplies of goods (and services) within a free zone are normally treated as UK supplies and are subject to the normal domestic VAT rules. However, by concession, the supply of free zone goods which were originally imported in the UK may be zero-rated if the supplier and customer agree that the customer will clear the goods for removal from the free zone to home use and will take responsibility for the import VAT. For the purposes of this concession, removal to home use includes authorised use or consumption within the zone. (VAT Notice 48, ESC 3.14). This concession has two main benefits.

- The customer purchasing the goods would otherwise have to pay, at virtually the same time, both the VAT due on the supply (to the supplier) and the VAT due on importation (to HMRC) on the removal of the goods from the free zone (see **72.24** below).
- It enables overseas traders who supply their imports in UK free zones and properly use the concession, to apply for exemption from registration in the UK.

The same goods can be the subject of a zero-rated supply only once under the concession. Supplies of free zone goods which do not meet the conditions of the concession must be treated in the same way as supplies of goods made outside free zones.

(VAT Notice 702/9/05, paras 5.1, 5.2).

See also **72.24** below for goods supplied within a free zone for onward export to a destination outside the EU.

Supplies to non-registered persons

The above concession cannot be used where the customer is unregistered for VAT and not liable to be registered. But where a supply of goods is made within a free zone to a non-registered person, the amount of import VAT payable by him when he enters the goods to free circulation is reduced by the VAT already paid on the supply. He must produce evidence that the VAT was paid on the supply (e.g. an invoice showing the tax paid and identifying the goods). [*SI 1984/1177, Reg 27*]. (VAT Notice 702/9/05, para 5.3).

Removal of goods from free zones

Goods removed to free circulation

[72.24] Goods used or consumed within a free zone are considered to have been removed from the free zone and must therefore be entered to free circulation. If the goods removed are

- 'non-Union goods' from a third country, import VAT (and customs duty) is due on removal from the free zone to free circulation;
- non-Union goods acquired from another EU country (including those from another duty suspensive regime),
  - (i) import VAT is due on removal from the free zone to free circulation; and
  - (ii) if the goods are the subject of an acquisition on arrival in the free zone, VAT must be accounted for on the acquirer's VAT return for the period in which the acquisition tax point falls;
- 'Union goods' acquired from another EU country, acquisition VAT must be accounted for on the acquirer's VAT return for the period in which the acquisition tax point falls; and
- duty and VAT paid in the UK, or were domestically produced goods placed in the free zone and subsequently removed, the normal UK VAT supply rules apply.

Goods removed other than to free circulation

- If the goods are exported direct to a destination outside the EU, the supply can be zero-rated subject to the normal export rules (see **21.1 EXPORTS**). Where the goods have not been entered to free circulation before being sold for export, it is not necessary to pay import VAT that may otherwise have been due on the goods.
  If goods are supplied to a customer in a free zone for onward export to a destination outside the EU, the supply may be zero-rated as an export provided the supplier holds acceptable evidence of export.
- If the goods are removed direct to another EU country, where the goods are non-Union goods which are not put into free circulation in the UK
  - (i) import VAT is not due in the UK and will be paid with the customs duty in the EU country where that duty is paid;
  - (ii) if the goods are sold to a customer registered for VAT in another EU country, the supply can be zero-rated subject to the normal conditions for zero-rating an intra-EU supply (see **19.11 EUROPEAN UNION: SINGLE MARKET**); and
  - (iii) if the goods are sold to a customer not registered for VAT, and the goods are not for onward export from the EU, the supply of the goods is liable to VAT in the UK; and

(VAT Notice 702/9/05, paras 5.4, 5.5).

See **72.3** above for the meaning of 'Union *goods*' and '*non-Union goods*'.

Transfers to customs suspensive procedures

Where goods are removed from a free zone for entry to another customs suspensive procedure, the import VAT (and customs duty) remain suspended under the new procedure. (VAT Notice 702/9/05, para 5.6).

Destruction of goods in free zone

HMRC must be informed of any intention to destroy free zone goods. Their supervision of destruction is not compulsory but adequate records must be maintained showing all destructions and their dates. Free zone goods may be destroyed without payment of import VAT in circumstances and subject to conditions as HMRC determine. If any scrap or waste resulting from the destruction has a commercial value and is put on the market, VAT (and customs duty) is payable. (VAT Notice 702/9/05, para 5.6).

Deficiency of free zone goods

[72.25] Any deficiencies of imported goods are charged with duty and any import VAT not already paid. Similarly, any acquisition VAT on goods from another EU country which has not been accounted for should be accounted for when deficiencies occur. Deficiencies of home produced goods are not charged with VAT unless the goods have been supplied in the free zone before the loss occurred. In all cases, the VAT may be deducted as input tax, subject to the normal rules. (VAT Notice 702/9/05, para 5.9).

Summary tables

[72.26]

Receipt of goods into a UK free zone and their removal to free circulation in the UK		
	Customs duty	*VAT*
1. Non-Union goods received direct from a third country	Suspended on entry to free zone. To be paid when the goods are removed from the zone to free circulation *or* are consumed or used within the free zone *or* are entered to tariff quota or preference	*Import VAT*: Suspended on entry to free zone. To be paid on removal from the zone to free circulation in the UK *Supply VAT*: VAT is due on supplies of goods in the free zone according to the normal domestic VAT rules unless the supply qualifies for zero-rating under the ESC in **72.23** above
2. Non-Union goods received from a third country via another EU country including those from another duty suspensive regime such as customs warehousing	As 1. above	*Import VAT*: As 1. above *Acquisition VAT*. If the goods are the subject of an acquisition on arrival in the free zone, VAT is to be accounted for on the acquirer's VAT return for the period in which the acquisition tax point falls *Supply VAT*. As 1. above

Receipt of goods into a UK free zone and their removal to free circulation in the UK		
	Customs duty	*VAT*
3. Union goods acquired direct from another EU country	N/A	*Import VAT*: N/A *Acquisition VAT*: VAT is to be accounted for on the acquirer's VAT return for the period in which the acquisition tax point falls *Supply VAT*. As 1. above
Union goods acquired from the UK	N/A	*Import VAT*: N/A *Acquisition VAT*: N/A *Supply VAT*. As 1. above
Non-Union goods entered to free zone for VAT only purposes	N/A	*Import VAT*: Suspended on entry to free zone. To be paid when the goods are removed from the zone to free circulation *Acquisition VAT*: N/A *Supply VAT*. As 1. above

Receipt of goods into a UK free zone and their removal other than to free circulation in the UK		
	Customs duty	*VAT*
1. Non-Union goods exported direct to a country outside the EU	Not paid	*Import VAT*: Not paid *Supply VAT*: VAT is due on supplies of goods in the free zone according to the normal domestic VAT rules unless the supply qualifies for zero-rating under the ESC in **72.23** above. The supply for export may also be zero-rated subject to the normal rules
2. Union goods exported direct to a country outside the EU	N/A	*Import VAT*: N/A *Supply VAT*: As 1. above
3. Non-Union goods removed direct to another EU country and which are not put into free circulation in the UK	Not paid in the UK. The goods must transit under a duty suspensive regime, or transit	*Import VAT*: Not paid in the UK. It will be paid with the customs duty in the EU country where the goods are released to free circulation and the duty is paid *Supply VAT*: VAT is due on supplies of goods in the free zone according to the normal domestic VAT rules unless the supply qualifies for zero-rating under the ESC in **72.23** above. If the goods are sold to a VAT-registered customer in another EU country, the supply may be zero-rated subject to the normal intra-EU rules

Receipt of goods into a UK free zone and their removal other than to free circulation in the UK		
	Customs duty	*VAT*
4. Non-Union goods removed directly to another EU country and which are put into free circulation on removal from the free zone	Paid in the UK on removal from the free zone	*Import VAT*: If customs duty is paid in the UK in the course of an onward supply to an EU recipient who will account for VAT on their acquisition, total relief from import VAT can apply. If not, then VAT is paid with the customs duty *Supply VAT*: As 3. above

(VAT Notice 702/9/05, paras 15.1, 15.2).

Key points

[72.27] Points to consider are as follows.

- The advantage of goods being stored in a warehouse (authorised premises) is that the payment of VAT and duties can be delayed. Tax is only due when the goods are removed from the warehouse into free circulation in the UK.
- Goods supplied in a warehouse are normally disregarded for VAT purposes because the supply is treated as taking place outside the UK. It is when the goods are removed to home use that they may be subject to import VAT.
- A VAT invoice should not be issued for any supplies of warehoused goods unless they are removed to home use.
- The evidence of input tax deduction for any trader importing goods into the UK is the C79 document. No alternative evidence is acceptable. It is important that the details of the importer are correctly declared on the relevant import entry documents so that the C79 document is sent to the correct business.
- A VAT-registered business with a good compliance history can apply to HMRC to use the fiscal warehousing regime, i.e. so that goods within the warehouse are not subject to VAT or duty.

73

Works of Art, etc.

Introduction

[73.1] The disposal of a business asset is exempt from VAT in the following circumstances.

- The disposal is of 'qualifying property' by 'private treaty sale', or disposal otherwise than by sale, to an 'approved body' if estate duty, capital transfer tax, inheritance tax or capital gains tax would not thereby become chargeable.
  A '*private treaty sale*' is a privately arranged sale to one of the approved bodies which are allowed to buy objects by private treaty in accordance with the relevant legislative provisions.
  '*Approved bodies*' are listed in *IHTA 1984, Sch 3* and include The National Gallery, The British Museum and other similar national institutions, museums and art galleries maintained by local authorities or universities in the UK, The National Trust, etc.
- 'Qualifying property' is accepted in lieu of inheritance tax, capital transfer tax or estate duty. Acceptance in lieu allows a person who is liable to pay such taxes to settle part, or all, of the debt by disposing of a work of art or other object to the Board of Inland Revenue.

'*Qualifying property*' is detailed in *IHTA 1984, s 31* and includes pictures, prints, books, manuscripts, works of art, scientific objects, or collections or any of these items, which are pre-eminent for their national, scientific, historic or artistic interest. For further information about the capital tax provisions see *Tolley's Inheritance Tax*.

To support any claim to VAT exemption, a letter should be obtained from the Capital Taxes Office confirming that the private treaty sale, disposal otherwise than by sale, or acceptance in lieu, is exempt from capital taxes.

Value of the supply

This depends upon the reason for the exemption.

- In the case of a private treaty sale, the value of the exempt supply is the amount received for the object.
- In a disposal otherwise than by sale, the normal rules for supplies for no consideration apply. See **71.22 VALUATION**.
- If an object is accepted in lieu, the value of the exempt supply is the amount of inheritance tax, capital transfer tax or estate duty actually satisfied.

[*VATA 1994, Sch 9 Group 11; IHTA 1984, Sch 8 para 24; FA 1985, Sch 26 para 14*]. (VAT Notice 701/12/11, paras 3.1–3.6).

The VAT exemption applies only to disposals under the limited circumstances set out above. Other sales of works of art, etc. by a registered person in the course or furtherance of his business remain subject to VAT. See **73.6** below for sales from historic houses.

Second-hand goods

[73.2] Special schemes may be operated by dealers registered for VAT, or by any other taxable persons, who acquire eligible goods and sell them in the course of business. See **61 SECOND-HAND GOODS** generally and in particular **61.3** for eligible works of art, etc. under the schemes.

> *Example*
> Local Art Dealers buy an item from a private individual that is eligible for a margin scheme for £2,000. It is sold for £3,000. The basic principle of a margin scheme for second-hand goods is that output tax is due on the profit margin, i.e. £1,000, rather than the full selling price.

Imports — reduced rate of VAT

Goods imported from outside the EU

[73.3] The value of any of the goods listed in (*a*)–(*c*) below is to be taken as 28.58% of what would otherwise be their value for VAT purposes unless

(a) the whole of the VAT chargeable is relieved from VAT on importation; or

(b) they were exported from the UK during the period of 12 months ending with the date of their importation. However, this is an anti-avoidance provision and is only to be applied where conditions have been artificially created in order to obtain the advantage of the reduced rate of VAT on importation. In practice, qualifying goods are sent frequently outside the UK for legitimate commercial reasons (e.g. for exhibition prior to auction in the UK, or on a sale or return basis and returned unsold) and return within twelve months. The provision does not operate in such situations. (Business Brief 3/2000) [*SI 2009/730, Art 17*].

The effect of this is that the goods are charged to VAT on importation at an effective reduced rate of 5% (25% of 20% from 4 January 2011; 28.58% of 17.5% from 1 January 2010 to 3 January 2011 and before 1 December 2008; 33.34% of 15% from 1 December 2008 to 31 December 2009).

(a) Any '*work of art*' defined as follows.
- Any mounted or unmounted painting, drawing, collage, decorative plaque or similar picture that was executed by hand. *Excluded* is any technical drawing, map or plan, any picture comprised in a manufactured article that has been hand-decorated, and anything in the nature of scenery (including a backcloth).
- Any original engraving, lithograph or other print which was produced from one or more plates executed by hand without using any mechanical or photomechanical process. The engraving, etc. must either be the only one produced from the plate or plates or must be comprised in a limited edition.
- Any original sculpture or statuary in any material.
- Any sculpture cast, produced by or under the supervision of the individual who made the mould (or became entitled to it by succession on death of that individual), which is either the only cast produced from the mould or is comprised in a limited edition. For this purpose, an edition is limited if the number produced from the same mould does not exceed eight or, where the cast was made before 1 January 1989, such greater number as HMRC allow in exceptional circumstances.
- Any tapestry or other hanging made by hand from an original design which is either the only one made from the design or is comprised in a limited edition not exceeding eight.
- Any ceramic executed by an individual and signed by him.
- Any enamel on copper, executed by hand and signed by the person who executed it or by someone on behalf of the studio where it was executed, which is either the only one made from the design in question or comprised in a limited edition. For this purpose, an edition is limited if the number produced from the same design does not exceed eight and each item in the edition is numbered and signed. *Excluded* from this category are articles of jewellery and articles or a kind produced by goldsmiths or silversmiths.
- Any mounted or unmounted photograph, printed by or under the supervision of the photographer and signed by him, which is either the only print made from the exposure in question or comprised in a limited edition. For this purpose an edition is limited if the number produced from the same exposure does not exceed 30 and each print in the edition is numbered and signed.

(b) Any antique not falling within (*a*) above or (*c*) below that is more than 100 years old.

(c) Any collection or collector's piece that is of zoological, botanical, mineralogical, anatomical, historical, archaeological, palaeontological, ethnographic, numismatic or philatelic interest. A collector's piece is of philatelic interest if it is
- a postage stamp or revenue stamp, a postmark, a first-day cover or an item of pre-stamped stationery; and
- it is franked or (if unfranked) it is not legal tender and is not intended for use as such. Stamps which are currently valid in the UK are those in decimal currency or currently valid for 1st or 2nd class postage *or* with a value of £1 (or multiple thereof) of the present monarch's reign. (VAT Notice 718, paras 20.1, 20.2).

The value of goods imported from a place outside the EU is to be determined according to the rules for Union customs duties (whether or not the goods in question are subject to such duties). These rules are set out in *Council Regulation 2913/92* and *Commission Regulation 2454/93*. See also Customs Notice 252 *Valuation of imported goods for customs purposes, VAT and trade statistics*.

The following are included in the value (so far as not already included under the above rules).

(a) All taxes, duties and other charges levied outside or, by reason of importation, within the UK (but excluding VAT).

(b) All incidental expenses such as commission, packing, transport and insurance costs, up to the 'first destination' of the goods in the UK. '*First destination*' means the place mentioned on the consignment note or other importation document or, in the absence of such documentation, the place of the first transfer of cargo in the UK.

(c) If at the time of importation of the goods a further destination for the goods is known, and that destination is within the UK or another EU country, all such incidental expenses resulting from the transport of the goods to that other destination.

With effect from 1 September 2006, where

- any goods within (*a*)–(*c*) above are sold at auction at a time when they are subject to a temporary importation regime (within *Council Regulation 2913/92, Arts 137–147*), and
- arrangements made, by or on behalf of the purchaser of the goods, following the sale by auction result in the final importation of the goods from a place outside the EU,

the value of the goods, in relation to the final importation, does not include any commission or premium payable to the auctioneer in connection with the sale of the goods. This change in the legislation follows the decision in *EC Commission v United Kingdom (No 5), ECJ Case C–305/03*, [2007] STC 1211 (TVC 22.98) where the court held that the UK was incorrect in including commissions in the value of the goods finally imported as, by doing so, the commissions were taxed at the reduced rate, rather than the standard rate of VAT.

Subject to (*a*)–(*c*) above, where the consideration is wholly or partly in money and on terms allowing a discount for prompt payment (but not payment of the price by instalments), the value of the goods is reduced by the discount if payment is made in accordance with those terms so that the discount is allowed.

[*VATA 1994, s 21; FA 1995, s 22; FA 1996, s 27; FA 1999, s 12; FA 2006, s 18; F(No 2)A 2010, s 3(2)*].

Importation formalities

See Customs Notice 362 for details of how the goods can be imported.

De Voil Indirect Tax Service. See V1.298, V3.325.

Imported goods sold by auction

[73.4] Subject to below, where 'works of art' are imported from outside the EU for exhibition with a view to possible sale, any sale by auction at a time when the goods are still subject to temporary importation arrangements with total exemption from import duty (see **33.24 IMPORTS**) is treated as neither a supply of goods nor a supply of services. The provision of any services relating to the transfer of ownership is similarly treated.

'*Works of art*' mean any such items falling within the definition in *VATA 1994, s 21* (see **73.3**(*a*) above).

With effect from 1 September 2006, the above treatment does not apply where the works of art are sold by auction at a time when they are subject to the temporary importation arrangements and, following the sale by auction, arrangements are made by or on behalf of the purchaser which result in the importation of the goods from a place outside the EU. Such transactions are treated as supplies of goods in the ordinary way.

[*SI 1995/958; SI 1999/3119; SI 2006/2187*].

By concession, the above treatment is extended to all works of art, collectors' items and antiques falling within *Directive 2006/112/EC, Annex IX* (which broadly corresponds to **73.3**(*a*)–(*c*) above). (VAT Notice 48, ESC 3.26).

Museum and gallery exhibits imported

[73.5] Certain works of art imported for a purpose other than sale by approved museums, galleries or other institutions are free of VAT. See **33.15**(10) **IMPORTS**.

Assets of historic houses

Sale of assets

[73.6] Assets sold from a house used as a private residence are not normally business assets and sales of these assets are outside the scope of VAT. This also applies to house clearance sales. But if charges are made for admission to the house, the house is being used for business purposes and where the owner is registered for VAT, there is a presumption that any assets (furniture, antiques, works of art, etc.) on public display are business assets for VAT purposes. As such, they are within the scope of VAT when disposed of. The disposal is normally standard-rated but see **73.1** above for certain supplies which are exempt.

To avoid having an asset treated as a business asset, an owner has two options.

- *Treat an asset as a private asset when it is acquired.* If assets are acquired for both business and private purposes (e.g. furnishings of a historic house in which he lives), the owner can choose to keep them as private assets. If so, input tax on their purchase is not deductible and VAT on their disposal is not accountable. To treat assets in this way, the owner should contact HMRC and provide them with the relevant information.
- *Reallocate an existing asset as a private asset.* The owner must be able to show that the asset is no longer used for any business purpose (e.g. by moving it to another part of the house used for private purposes only). He must contact HMRC at the time he decides to withdraw the asset from the business and advise them of the details.
  If the owner was entitled to any deduction of input tax on purchase of the asset, he must pay VAT when reallocating it as a private asset. The normal rules for the supply of assets for no consideration apply. See **71.22 VALUATION**. If the asset was not chargeable with VAT when acquired (e.g. an inherited asset) no VAT is due on the reallocation.
  When a reallocated asset is subsequently sold the sale is of a private asset and not liable to VAT.
  Where a reallocated business assets consists partly of an item not chargeable with VAT when acquired and partly on asset on which VAT has been recovered (e.g. an inherited painting for which a new frame has been purchased), at the time of reallocation VAT would only payable on the frame.

Input tax

Where an owner purchases an asset wholly for taxable business purposes, he can normally deduct the VAT. If it is purchased

- partly for business and partly for non-business purposes, he may apportion the VAT, enabling him to recover as input tax the proportion relating to business use;
- partly for business and partly for private purposes, he may choose to apportion the VAT, or alternatively treat all the VAT as input tax but then account for VAT as output tax in each accounting period on the private use of the goods;
- partly for business, partly for non-business and partly for private purposes, he may choose to either apportion the VAT so that he only recovers as input tax the proportion relating to business use, or alternatively apportion the VAT so that he only recovers the proportion relating to business and private use, but then he must account for VAT as output tax in each accounting period on the private use of the goods.

See **34.7 INPUT TAX** for further details.

No VAT is recoverable on the purchase of an asset treated as a private asset.

Repair and maintenance

Input tax can be reclaimed on repair and maintenance of an asset treated as a business asset. If a private asset is used for both business and other purposes, input tax can be reclaimed on repair or maintenance services, subject to the normal rules. Any claim must be in proportion to the extent the asset is used for business purposes. The recovery of input tax on such services does not make the future disposal of the asset itself liable to VAT.

(VAT Notice 701/12/11, paras 1.2, 1.3, 1.5, 2.1–2.5, 4.1–4.3).

Key points

[73.7] Points to consider are as follows.

- A 5% reduced rate of VAT applies to the importation of a work of art, antique item over 100 years old or any collection or collector's piece that is of zoological, botanical, mineralogical, anatomical, historical, archaeological, palaeontological, ethnographic, numismatic or philatelic interest.
- The valuation for import purposes includes any duties, taxes, incidental expenses and other related costs.
- Special VAT rules can be applied in relation to the purchase and sale of assets included within historical homes where admissions fees are charged. In certain situations, the proceeds can be exempt or outside the scope of VAT.

74

Zero-Rated Supplies

De Voil Indirect Tax Service. See V4.201; V4.202.

Introduction

[74.1] Where a taxable person supplies goods or services and the supply is zero-rated, then, *whether or not VAT would otherwise be chargeable on the supply*, no VAT is charged but the supply in all other respects is treated as a taxable supply (except that an invoice for a zero-rated supply does not constitute a VAT invoice). [*VATA 1994, s 30(1)*]. The effects of this are as follows.

- The amount of VAT on zero-rated supplies is nil but they are still taxable supplies.
- As taxable supplies, they must be taken into consideration in determining whether registration is required.
- Input tax may be reclaimed in the same way as for standard-rated supplies.
- Where a supply could be either zero-rated or exempt, zero-rating takes priority.

Zero-rating applies to a supply of goods or services and, except as otherwise provided, the acquisition of goods from another EU country or the importation of goods from a place outside the EU, falling within one of the following categories specified in *VATA 1994, Sch 8*.

Group 1	**FOOD (24)**
Group 2	Water and sewerage services (see **74.2** and **74.3** below).
Group 3	Books, etc. (see **54.2–54.12 PRINTED MATTER, ETC.**).
Group 4	Talking books for the blind and handicapped and wireless sets for the blind (see **12.7 CHARITIES**).
Group 5	Construction of buildings, etc. (see **42.1, 42.7–42.9** and **42.16–42.18 LAND AND BUILDINGS: ZERO AND REDUCED RATE SUPPLIES AND DIY HOUSEBUILDERS**).
Group 6	Protected buildings (see **42.3** and **42.10 LAND AND BUILDINGS: ZERO AND REDUCED RATE SUPPLIES AND DIY HOUSEBUILDERS**).
Group 7	International services (see **38.7** and **38.8 INTERNATIONAL SERVICES**).
Group 8	Transport (see **70 TRANSPORT AND FREIGHT**).
Group 9	Caravans and houseboats (see **42.25–42.27 LAND AND BUILDINGS: ZERO AND REDUCED RATE SUPPLIES AND DIY HOUSEBUILDERS**).
Group 10	**GOLD AND PRECIOUS METALS (26).**
Group 11	Bank notes (see **74.4** below).
Group 12	Dispensing of drugs, reliefs for people with disabilities, etc. (see **28.13** to **28.33 HEALTH AND WELFARE**).
Group 13	Imports, exports, etc. (see **33 IMPORTS** and **21.2 EXPORTS**).
Group 14	Tax-free shops before 1 July 1999 (see **19.20 EUROPEAN UNION: SINGLE MARKET**).
Group 15	Charities, etc. (see **12.6** and **12.7 CHARITIES**).
Group 16	**CLOTHING AND FOOTWEAR (13).**
Group 17	Emissions allowances (omitted from 1 November 2010) (see **74.14** below).

The items within the *Groups* are to be interpreted in accordance with the notes contained and the powers given to the Treasury to vary the *Groups* including powers to add to, delete or vary the notes. The descriptions of *Groups* (i.e. the headings shown above) are for ease of reference only and do not affect the interpretation of the description of items in the *Group*.

[*VATA 1994, s 30(2)–(4), s 96(9)(10)*].

Acquisitions of goods

In addition to the zero-rating for exports under *Group 13*, zero-rating also applies where goods are removed from the UK and acquired in another EU country by a person taxable in that country and liable for VAT on the acquisition under the law of that country. See **19.11 EUROPEAN UNION: SINGLE MARKET**.

Work on another person's goods which produces goods

A supply of services which consists of applying a treatment or process to another person's goods is zero-rated if by doing so goods are produced and either

- those goods fall within one of the zero-rating *Groups* above; or
- a supply of those goods by the person applying the treatment to that other person would be zero-rated.

[*VATA 1994, s 30(2A); FA 1996, s 29(2)(5)*].

Water

[74.2] The supply of water insofar as it is not otherwise a supply of goods is to be treated as a supply of goods (and not services). [*SI 1989/1114*].

The supply of water is zero-rated [*VATA 1994, Sch 8 Group 2 Item 2*] unless falling within one of the following categories.

(a) Relevant industrial activity

The supply of water used in connection with the carrying on, in the course of a business, of a '*relevant industrial activity*' is standard-rated.

'*Relevant industrial activity*' means any activity described in any of Divisions 1 to 5 of the 1980 edition of the publication prepared by the Central Statistical Office and known as the Standard Industrial Classification. The activities within Divisions 1 to 5 are:

(1) Energy and water supply industries.
(2) Extraction of minerals and ores other than fuels; manufacture of metals, mineral products and chemicals.
(3) Metal goods, engineering and vehicle industries.
(4) Other manufacturing industries.
(5) Construction.

Mixed use

Where water supplied to a customer is used for both relevant industrial activities within 1 to 5 above and other purposes, the liability of the supply depends upon the *predominant* activity of the 'customer'. Any reasonable basis may be used to determine the predominant activity (e.g. turnover, number of employees). Where water is supplied to a customer who has both domestic (or other non-business) and relevant industrial use, the predominant activity of that person for these purposes is the use to which most of the water is put. Once the supplier has established the predominant activity of a customer, any water supplied must be taxed accordingly without apportionment, i.e. the supply is wholly standard-rated or zero-rated. For example, water (for drinking, washing, toilets, etc.) supplied to an office of a manufacturing company whose predominant activity falls within 1 to 5 above is standard-rated as it is used in connection with that industrial activity.

The only exception to this is where a relevant industrial customer has two or more business activities, one of which is both non-industrial and exempt for UK VAT purposes. If that exempt activity is not the predominant activity, the water supplied to the exempt business activity can be zero-rated provided

- the supply can be separately identified; and
- a separate invoice is raised.

The '*customer*' for these purposes is the person to whom the water supplier addresses the invoice, whatever the corporate structure of the business to which the customer belongs and whether or not the customer is part of, or the representative member of, a VAT group.

Determining the liability of a supply

The supplier is responsible for deciding whether the customer is an industrial customer. If in doubt, an acceptable way to make sure that the liability of the supply is correct is to obtain a written declaration from the customer confirming that its activities are outside 1 to 5 above. The supplier must take all reasonable steps to check the validity of the declaration and should consult HMRC if in doubt. Where, however, despite taking such steps, nonetheless the supplier fails to identify an incorrect declaration and in good faith makes the supplies concerned at the zero rate, HMRC will not seek to recover the VAT due from the supplier. (VAT Notice 48, ESC 3.11).

[*VATA 1994, Sch 8 Group 2 Item 2; SI 1996/1661*]. (VAT Notice 701/16/02, paras 2.2, 2.5–2.7).

(b) Distilled water

The supply of distilled water, deionized water or water of similar purity is standard-rated. [*VATA 1994, Sch 8 Group 2 Item 2(a); SI 1996/1661*].

(c) Beverages

The supply of water comprised in any of the excepted items in *VATA 1994, Sch 8 Group 1* (see **24.8 FOOD**) is standard-rated. [*VATA 1994, Sch 8 Group 2 Item 2(b); SI 1996/1661*]. This includes mineral, table and spa waters in bottles or similar containers held out for sale as beverages.

(d) Heated water

Water which has been heated so that it is supplied at a temperature higher than that at which it was before it was heated. [*VATA 1994, Sch 8 Group 2 Item 2(c); SI 1996/1661*]. Such a supply is not taxed as a supply of water but as a supply of heat and is therefore standard-rated unless supplied for domestic purposes or charity non-business use, in which case it is subject to VAT at the reduced rate. See **25.6 FUEL AND POWER**.

For these purposes

- steam is treated as heated water;
- naturally occurring hot water (e.g. from hot springs) is not treated as heated water; and
- water deliberately heated by geo-thermal energy, solar or other similar methods is treated as heated water.

(VAT Notice 701/16/02, paras 4.1–4.4).

Examples of zero-rated supplies to non-industrial customers

- Ice
- Sterile water (except where additives alter the nature of the product)

- The provision of water against payment of an unmeasured charge, standing charge or other availability charge
- Charges for the abstraction of water by licence
- Specific charges for the supply of water for hosepipes, swimming pools and garden ponds, sprinklers and sprinkler licence fees
- Disconnection and reconnection charges arising as the result of non-payment of bills
- Opening and closing of stopcocks at the request of the water supplier
- Ordinary water, of a kind usually supplied by water mains, supplied in bottles as a drought alleviation or other emergency measure

(VAT Notice 701/16/02, para 2.4).

Other water-related supplies

The following water-related supplies commonly made by water providers are all standard-rated.

- Fluoridation charges
- Pressure testing of fire sprinkler systems
- Installation and repair of fire hydrants
- Temporary or permanent disconnection of, or reconnection of, a water supply at the customer's request
- Testing private pipework at the customer's request
- The opening and closing of a stopcock at the customer's request
- Rewashering ball valves and taps
- Hire of stand-pipes and water bowsers (irrespective of the liability of the water supplied)
- First time connection of an existing building, or a building converted from a non-residential to residential use, to the water or sewerage mains

(VAT Notice 701/16/02, para 5.1).

Civil engineering

Civil engineering work is normally standard-rated but works in the course of

- constructing a new dwelling, residential building or certain buildings used by charities,
- carrying out an approved alteration of a listed dwelling, residential building or certain listed buildings used by charities,
- converting a building into a dwelling or residential building,
- renovating or altering an empty dwelling; and
- developing a residential caravan park

can qualify for zero-rating or reduced-rating. See **42 LAND AND BUILDINGS: ZERO AND REDUCED RATE SUPPLIES AND DIY HOUSEBUILDERS** for further details.

Infrastructure charges

The *Water Act 1989* allows a water company to make 'infrastructure charges' which are intended to contribute to the costs that have been, or will be, incurred on providing the means of supplying water and sewerage services (e.g. sewers, water mains, etc.), and are standard rated. However, for new eligible dwellings or new buildings to be used solely for a relevant residential or charitable purpose, works in connection with the means of providing water are zero-rated. For residential conversions and the renovation or alteration of empty residential premises, works in connection with the means of providing water or drainage qualify for the reduced rate.

(VAT Notice 701/16/02, paras 5.2, 5.3; VAT Notice 708, paras 3.1.1, 3.3.4(b), 7.6, 8.4).

Water meters

The following supplies are always standard-rated.

- The supply of a water meter without installation
- Meter survey fees
- Meter-testing fees at the request of the customer
- Special meter-reading charges at the request of a customer
- Separate charges for maintenance of meters

The supply *and* installation of a water meter is normally standard-rated. But, as for civil engineering work above, it may be zero-rated or reduced-rated. See **42 LAND AND BUILDINGS: ZERO AND REDUCED RATE SUPPLIES AND DIY HOUSE-BUILDERS.**

(VAT Notice 701/16/02, para 5.4).

Water, supplied as part of an overall service

Water supplied as part of an overall service, e.g. in a launderette, is not a separate supply and is standard-rated (*Mander Laundries Ltd* (VTD 31) (TVC 69.1)).

De Voil Indirect Tax Service. See V4.271.

Sewerage services

Zero-rated supplies

[74.3] The following supplies are zero-rated.

(a) *Services of reception, disposal or treatment of foul water or sewage in bulk*. [*VATA 1994, Sch 8 Group 2 Item 1(a)*].
Included is the provision of such sewerage services against payment of an unmeasured charge, a standing charge or other availability charge, or a specific charge (e.g. by reference to quantity and/or nature of the effluent). (VAT Notice 701/16/02, para 3.1).

(b) *Services of emptying of cesspools, septic tanks or similar receptacles*. Zero-rating does not apply if the cesspools, etc. are used in connection with the carrying on in the course of a business of a 'relevant industrial activity'.
'*Relevant industrial activity*' means any activity described in any of Divisions 1 to 5 of the 1980 edition of the publication prepared by the Central Statistical Office and known as the Standard Industrial Classification.

[*VATA 1994, Sch 8 Group 2 Item 1(b)*].

The activities within Divisions 1 to 5 are as follows.

(1) Energy and water supply industries.

(2) Extraction of minerals and ores other than fuels; manufacture of metals, mineral products and chemicals.

(3) Metal goods, engineering and vehicle industries.

(4) Other manufacturing industries.

(5) Construction.

Standard-rated supplies

Standard-rating applies to

- the cleaning, maintenance, unblocking, etc. of sewers and drains;
- the emptying of cesspools, septic tanks or similar receptacles for industrial users (see (*b*) above); and
- the removal, treatment and disposal of industrial, farm, hospital, domestic or other waste *other than* foul water or sewerage.

(VAT Notice 701/16/02, para 3.1).

Connected civil engineering work

Similar provisions apply as for water under **74.2** above.

De Voil Indirect Tax Service. See V4.271.

Bank notes

[74.4] The issue by a bank of a note payable to bearer on demand is zero-rated. [*VATA 1994, Sch 8 Group 11*]. This applies to the Bank of England, Scottish and Northern Irish bank notes. *Issue* includes reissue.

De Voil Indirect Tax Service. See V4.279.

Visiting forces

[74.5] Provided conditions are satisfied, a UK VAT-registered business can supply certain goods and services free of VAT to:

- NATO visiting forces in the UK (see **74.6** and **74.7** below). '*Visiting forces*' are defined as a body, contingent or attachment of the armed forces of a sovereign state stationed in another sovereign state on the invitation of the host state's Government, or a member of such a body. For these purposes, this term includes civilian staff accompanying the force.
- The NATO International Military Headquarters at Northwood and High Wycombe (see **74.8** below).
- The American Battle Monuments Commission in respect of supplies of goods and services for the maintenance of the US military cemeteries at Brookwood and Madingley (see **74.9** below).

The provisions do not apply to supplies to British forces based in the UK or visiting forces from non-NATO countries.

Relief is normally achieved by treating the supply as zero-rated (so that no VAT is charged but any related input tax can be recovered).

Under these provisions, the goods and services can also be supplied free of customs duty, excise duty, landfill tax and climate change levy. Relief is also available from CAP levies and air passenger duty.

Restrictions after supply

Goods which have been sold free of VAT (or any other duty) to a UK-based visiting force or a member of their personnel may not be sold on, given or otherwise disposed of to a person who does not enjoy the same privileges unless the VAT (or other duty) which has been relieved is paid to HMRC.

The supplier can cancel a sale and take the goods back provided he keeps a full and accurate record of the transaction.

(Customs Notice 431, paras 1.5, 2.1–2.3).

Supplies to other EU countries. See **19.21 EUROPEAN UNION: SINGLE MARKET.**

Supplies to US visiting forces

Goods and services for official use

[74.6] A UK-registered business can supply most goods and services free of VAT (and certain goods free of duty) for the official use of US visiting forces provided at least one of the following conditions apply.

(a) *It has a written contract or purchase order from an authorised US visiting forces contracting officer.* The contract or purchase order must have an *original* signature of an authorised contracting officer of the US forces (i.e. it must not be a photocopy or be approved by a rubber stamp) and must include the following statement:
'The goods and/or services listed are to be delivered at a price exclusive of VAT under arrangements agreed between the appropriate US authorities and HM Revenue and Customs (Reference PRIV 46/7). I hereby certify that these goods and/or services are being purchased for United States official purposes only.'
If the contract is for hotel accommodation:
   - The relieved supply must only be for overnight accommodation, inclusive or exclusive of breakfast. Other food or drinks and other services cannot be relieved of VAT.
   - The contract must include a reference to the category of personnel covered, for example Temporary Duty ('TDY') personnel.
   - Every time accommodation is supplied under the contract, the force member must provide a purchase order from the base authority booking the accommodation.

(b) *Payment is made with a Government-Wide Purchase Card (GPC).* This is a VISA card with a special prefix: 4716. The buyer must give the supplier a letter from the contracting office that issued the GPC, stating that the goods or services are being bought for the official use of the US government.
The supplier must keep the credit card slip and letter as evidence that it has treated the supply as zero-rated.

(c) *Payment is made with a Procurement (PRO) card.* This is a Mastercard with a special prefix: 5405. The buyer must give the supplier a letter from the General Manager of the Army and Air Force Exchange Service (AAFES) stating that the goods or services are being bought for the official use of the US government. An example of this letter is shown in Customs Notice 431, section 11.
The supplier must keep the credit card slip and letter as evidence that it has treated the supply as zero-rated.

(d) *It is supplying goods from a Customs or excise warehouse.* See **74.11** below.

(e) *The goods have been imported and processed under the Inward Processing Relief.* See **33.30 IMPORTS**.

Goods or services supplied to members of US forces based in the UK

The following can be supplied VAT free.

- A motor vehicle (see **74.10** below).
- Goods in a Customs warehouse (see **74.11** below).
- Other goods or services costing at least £100 (including VAT) for personal use by members of US forces or their family under the US 'VAT-free purchase scheme'. The supply must not include any supply of land nor any supply of a motor vehicle (for which see **74.10** below).
  The supplier must first provide the buyer with a written quote stating the price of the goods or services (excluding VAT). The quote, and any invoice, must be addressed to a named member of the US visiting forces. The buyer must then give the supplier a US government cheque in pounds sterling and two copies of a US Forces VAT-Free Purchase Certificate (reproduced in Customs Notice 431, section 13) which has been signed by an authorised signatory of the US visiting forces. The supplier must sign one copy of the certificate and return it to the buyer and keep the second copy of the certificate in his VAT records as evidence to support the VAT-free supply.
  This is a voluntary scheme. If a supplier does not wish to participate, it must charge and account for VAT in the usual way.
- Goods from a concession shop on a US base. If a UK-registered business is authorised to operate a US Army and Air Force Exchange Services (AAFES) concession shop on a US base, it must keep a 'Concessionaire's Daily Sales Report'. listing each purchase and include the following statement:

  (a) I certify that this is a true and complete summary of sales made to entitled personnel for . . . . (date) for and on behalf of . . . . (name of concessionaire)

. . . .(Concession manager)

(b) The price to be paid for the goods and/or services liable to VAT covered by this summary shall be exclusive of VAT in accordance with the arrangements agreed between the appropriate US authorities and HM Revenue and Customs (ref: PRIV 46/7).

. . . . (Exchange manager)

The concession manager must complete and sign the certificate and produce two copies of the report to the AAFES authorities. Their US base exchange manager must sign one copy and return it to the concession manager who must keep the certified copy of the report as evidence to support the tax-free supply of goods.

(Customs Notice 432, paras 3.1–3.4, 3.8–3.10)

See **74.5** above for restrictions on disposal after supply.

Supplies to NATO visiting forces (other than US)

[74.7] These provisions relate to NATO visiting forces from Belgium, Canada, the Czech Republic, Denmark, France, Germany, Greece, Hungary, Iceland, Italy, Luxembourg, the Netherlands, Norway, Poland, Portugal, Spain and Turkey.

Goods and services for official use

NATO visiting forces are entitled to VAT (and duty) relief on most goods and services supplied to them for official purposes. In most cases they obtain relief by claiming a VAT (or duty) refund from HMRC by presenting evidence of payment of VAT (and/or duty).

If a UK VAT-registered business is asked to make a supply of goods and services to these visiting forces, it should make the supply inclusive of VAT (and duty) and provide them with evidence that the VAT and duty has been paid by means of a

- VAT invoice for purchases totalling £100 or more; or
- less detailed VAT invoice (see **39.7 INVOICES**) for purchases of less than £100.

See **74.11** below for goods in an excise or Customs warehouse.

Goods or services supplied to members of visiting forces based in the UK

Members of visiting forces can obtain the following free of VAT.

- A motor vehicle (see **74.10** below).
- Consumer durable goods (e.g. domestic electrical equipment, furnishings, similar household effects, items of jewellery and clothing) and road fuel.

  The refund is obtainable from HMRC. If a UK VAT-registered business is asked to make a supply of such goods to a member of a NATO visiting force, it should make the supply inclusive of VAT and provide the customer with evidence that the VAT has been paid by means of a

- VAT invoice for purchases totalling £100 or more; or
- less detailed VAT invoice (see **39.7 INVOICES**) for purchases of less than £100.

- Goods in a Customs warehouse (see **74.11** below).

(Customs Notice 431, paras 4.1–4.3).

See **74.5** above for restrictions on disposal after supply.

Supplies to NATO International Military Headquarters (IMHQ)

[74.8] IMHQ are HQ organisations and outstations set up by NATO as part of its military structure. Currently, there are two NATO IMHQ in the UK: HQ CinCEASTLANT in Northwood and No 9 Combined Air Operations Centre at RAF High Wycombe.

Goods and services for official use

A UK-registered business can supply goods and services VAT (and duty) free to a NATO IMHQ for its official use provided it has an official contract or purchase order from the IMHQ authority. The contract or purchase order must

- be with a specific and named NATO IMHQ;
- be approved by an authorised signatory of the HQ; and
- have an *original* signature of an authorised signatory of the HQ (ie it must not be a photocopy or be approved by a rubber stamp) and must include the following statement:

> I hereby certify that the goods and services listed are being purchased for official use by the North Atlantic Treaty Organisation and should be supplied free of VAT in accordance with the agreement with HM Revenue and Customs Reference PRIV 59/16.

Any faxed order must be confirmed in writing.

The business should obtain an official receipt on completion of the supply and retain this with the contract or purchase order in its VAT records as supporting evidence for the VAT free supply.

Goods or services supplied to a member of a NATO IMHQ for personal use

US members of a NATO IMHQ can be treated in the same way as members of the US visiting forces (see **74.6** above) and other members of a NATO IMHQ can be treated in the same way as members of other NATO visiting forces (see **74.7** above).

(Customs Notice 431, paras 5.1, 5.2).

See **74.5** above for restrictions on disposal after supply.

Supplies to the American Battle Monuments Commission

[74.9] A UK-registered business can supply any goods or services free of VAT to the American Military Cemetery and Memorial at Madingley, Cambridge or Brookwood, Surrey provided the following conditions are met.

- The goods or services must be solely used for the maintenance of those cemeteries.
- The supplier must have an official written order or contract from the American Battle Monuments Commission in Paris or from the American Military Cemetery and Memorial in Cambridge.
- The order or contract must
  (i) be signed by an official of one of those organisations; and
  (ii) certify that the goods and/or services are supplied for the maintenance of US military cemeteries in the UK.
- When the supply is complete, the supplier must obtain (and keep in his VAT records) an official receipt or a stamped certificate to show that the goods or services have been received in accordance with the terms of the contract or order.

(Customs Notice 431, paras 6.1, 6.2).

See **74.5** above for restrictions on disposal after supply.

Supplies of motor vehicles to NATO visiting force

[74.10] A UK-registered business can supply a motor vehicle VAT-free to

- any NATO visiting force in the UK for its official use; or
- a member of any NATO visiting force for their personal use or for the use of their family. At any one time, a member is allowed to own one motor vehicle free of VAT plus a second if his or her spouse is present in the UK. No relief is available to anyone who is a UK national or who is permanently resident in the UK.

A VAT-free supply can be made in either of the following circumstances.

(a) On removal from a Customs warehouse (see **74.11** below).

(b) If the vehicle was manufactured in the EU or EFTA or if the supply is for the official use of US visiting forces.
The customer must demonstrate entitlement to receive a tax-free vehicle by
  - if the vehicle is for the official use of US visiting forces, following the procedures described in **74.6**(*a*)–(*c*) above; and
  - in all other cases, providing a properly completed and authorised Form 941 (if the supply is from a Customs warehouse) or Form 941A (if not). Where the customer is from the US forces, the Pass and Registration Section of the force must have authorised the form. In other cases, the visiting force or NATO IMHQ must authorise the form. The completed form must also have been authorised by HMRC.
  If the supplier is also registering the vehicle on behalf of his customer, he should ask the customer for a further copy of the form to send to the Vehicle Registration Office.

The supplier must keep the completed form with his records to prove entitlement to the tax relief.

Second-hand scheme

A business cannot supply NATO visiting forces with VAT-free goods under the margin scheme for **SECOND-HAND GOODS (61)**. If a dealer has a second-hand vehicle in his margin scheme records and wishes to treat a sale as a zero-rated supply to a member of a visiting force, he must clearly record in his second-hand stock book that the vehicle has been supplied free of VAT to a member of a visiting force outside the margin scheme. He must then obtain and keep in his records a completed and authorised Form 941A.

(Customs Notice 431, paras 7.1–7.5).

See **74.5** above for restrictions on disposal after supply.

Supplies of alcoholic drinks and tobacco products from a UK excise or Customs warehouse

Excise warehouses

[74.11] A business operating an approved excise warehouse in the UK can supply alcoholic drinks and tobacco products free of VAT (and excise duty) to a UK-based NATO visiting force (see **74.6** and **74.7** above) or NATO IMHQ (see **74.8** above) provided the following conditions are met.

- The visiting force authority must complete and present a Form C185 including full details of all the goods required by the members of the force. The form must be signed by an authorised signatory of the visiting force and must be kept with the other warehouse records.
- The warehouse operator must follow the procedures laid down in Customs Notice 197 *Excise goods: holding and movement*.

Customs warehousing

A business operating a Customs warehouse can release goods free of VAT (and duty) provided the following conditions are met.

- Where a UK-based visiting force or IMHQ removes goods for official use, it must make a Customs declaration on Form C88, using Customs Procedure Code (CPC) 40 71 20. Where a member of UK-based visiting force or IMHQ removes goods for personal use, the member must also make a Customs declaration on Form C88 but using Customs Procedure Code (CPC) 40 71 35. In either case, Box 8 of the form must show the name and EORI (Economic Operator Registration and Identification) of the visiting force or IMHQ.
- In the case of goods for personal use, the operator must also receive a completed Form C2 or (for US forces only) DD1434.
- In the case of a motor vehicle, the additional requirements in **74.10** above must be met.

(Customs Notice 431, paras 8.1, 8.2).

See **74.5** above for restrictions on disposal after supply.

Emissions allowances

Background

[74.12] Emissions allowances or 'carbon credits' are issued by governments under various schemes designed to cut carbon emissions by businesses. Within the European Economic Area, Member States issue operators in the EU scheme with EU Allowances (EUA) – carbon credits – and further credits are auctioned by some governments (including the UK). The EUAs can be traded and there is also a secondary market in which anybody can trade, e.g. to speculate on the price of the credits. Operators (or 'polluters') must ensure they have sufficient credits to cover their actual emissions at the end of April each year when these credits are 'retired'. The opportunity for Missing Trader Intra-Community (MTIC) fraud arises where standard-rated goods or services can effectively be traded VAT free between EU Member States. Previously, most emissions allowances were standard-rated in UK to UK transactions and VAT free when purchased from outside the UK by a UK-based company. It was this VAT-free source that provided the opportunity to perpetrate MTIC fraud. It occurred where the UK company purchasing the emissions allowances from overseas sold them to another UK company, charged VAT but then failed to pay it over to HMRC and disappeared. The ability to trade freely in emissions allowances is an important feature of the EU Emissions Trading Scheme. However, the existence of a strong secondary cross-border market in emissions allowances generates very high volume, value and speed of trade. This, combined with the fact that EUAs are only surrendered once a year, provides fraudsters with multiple opportunities to steal VAT following cross-border acquisitions.

From 1 November 2010

Directive 2010/23/EU inserts *Art 199a* into *Directive 2006/112/EC* and permits, until 30 June 2015 and for a minimum period of two years, the application of the reverse charge to the trading of greenhouse gas emissions allowances. From 8 April 2010, *VATA 1994, s 55A* (customers to account for tax on supplies of goods of a kind used in missing trader intra-community fraud) was extended to services. With effect from 1 November 2010 the reverse charge applies to emissions allowances supplied in the UK (see **4.14**, **4.16 ANTI-AVOIDANCE**). From the same date, the zero rate for such supplies was withdrawn. These changes do not affect the application of the Terminal Markets Order 1973, under which certain trades carried out on specific exchanges are treated as zero-rated.

[*FA 2010, s 50; SI 2010/2549; SI 2010/2239, Art 6*]. (HMRC Brief 35/10).

Before 1 November 2010

From 31 July 2009 to 1 November 2010 the supply of emissions allowances was zero-rated. An emissions allowance meant

- a Union tradeable emissions allowance;

- a unit issued pursuant to the Kyoto Protocol; or
- any option relating to any such allowance or unit.

The UK introduced the zero-rating in response to the escalating threat of VAT fraud in connection with trading of emissions allowances (often called 'carbon credits').

[*SI 2009/2093*].

De Voil Indirect Tax Service. See V4.288.

Non-compliance carbon credits

[74.13] Carbon credits fall into two categories:

- compliance market credits, which derive from the Kyoto Protocol and the EU Emissions Trading System ('EUETS'); and
- non-compliance credits, of which the most common example is the Verified Emission Reduction (VER).

Compliance market credits

Compliance market credits are capable of consumption of the type envisaged by the VAT system, and are therefore subject to VAT. The motive of an individual paying for a credit does not matter, nor does it matter what is done with it. Thus if a private individual buys a compliance market credit, the supply of the credit to the individual is still taxable (even though the individual is not subject to any regime) because the credit is capable of consumption.

Verified Emission Reductions

A Verified Emission Reduction (VER) is essentially a promise that carbon has been or may be reduced somewhere in the world. No particular service is rendered which can be identified as a cost component of the business. VERs are not capable of consumption of the type envisaged by the VAT system, and are therefore outside the scope of VAT.

(HMRC Brief 28/10).

Carbon offsetting services

[74.14] 'Carbon offset providers' offer advice and/or the facility to reduce an individual's 'carbon footprint'. The VAT treatment of any individual transaction depends on the particular arrangements.

In many situations, when a member of the public makes a payment to a carbon offset provider, there is no supply for VAT purposes. This is because there is no identifiable, direct benefit being received by the member of the public in return for their money. Examples would be where a carbon offset provider makes a commitment that funds paid across by members of the public will be used to fund overseas projects, wind farms, development of environmentally friendly energy generation projects etc. without making any supply of direct benefit to the person making the payment. In such scenarios, the payment by the member of the public is outside the scope of VAT.

A common arrangement is where an airline offers its passengers the facility to offset the carbon emissions generated by their flights, perhaps via a third party carbon offset provider. Generally the passenger pays across an amount, calculated to be the cost of offsetting the resulting emissions, but receives no identifiable, direct benefit in return. There are a number of possible variants, including:

- the passenger has no choice, being obliged to pay the offsetting charge – the airline is making a single zero-rated supply of transport services;
- the offsetting facility is optional, but a separate administration charge is made to the customer for providing the service – the administration charge is standard-rated, but the amount paid to offset provision is outside the scope of VAT;
- the offsetting service is optional, there is no administrative charge, and the entire payment goes to offset provision – the payment is outside the scope of VAT.

In other situations, a carbon offset provider might make taxable supplies of carbon credits (supplies of compliance market credits are currently zero-rated), or of the purchase and 'retirement' of compliance market credits (standard-rated), or of general advice on how an individual or a business can improve its energy efficiency (standard-rated).

(HMRC Brief 28/10).

Key points

[74.15] Points to consider are as follows.

- Remember that VAT is still being charged on a zero-rated sale albeit at a rate of 0%. This is an important fact because it means that input tax can be reclaimed on related costs.
- A business making wholly or mainly zero-rated supplies will almost certainly benefit from registering for VAT on a voluntary basis if its taxable turnover is less than the compulsory registration limits. This is because it will be in a VAT repayment situation, i.e. receiving regular rebates from HMRC.
- If a business makes both standard-rated and zero-rated sales, it is imperative that systems and procedures are in place to correctly record the correct amount of output tax on each sale. This is particularly important now the standard rate of VAT is 20% because the differential between the two rates is so wide.
- VAT incorrectly charged to a customer on a zero-rated item will produce reduced profits for the customer if he makes some exempt supplies or if he is not VAT-registered. A review of possible items of expenditure where a supplier has incorrectly charged VAT (e.g. in relation to printed matter) could be worthwhile.

- It is unlikely that a business making zero-rated sales will benefit from using the cash accounting scheme or annual accounting scheme. However, there may be occasions when the flat-rate scheme could be worthwhile if the percentage of zero-rated sales for a business is quite low.
- If VAT has been incorrectly charged on a zero-rated supply, then the issue of unjust enrichment needs to be fully considered before trying to obtain a VAT windfall from HMRC. No business is able to make a financial gain from making VAT errors.
- There is scope for a business that makes wholly or mainly zero-rated sales (net repayment situation) to be exempted from being VAT-registered if it has exceeded the compulsory registration limits. HMRC agreement is needed.
- Although a UK business acquiring zero-rated goods from a VAT registered business in another EU country has no acquisition tax to account for on its VAT return, an entry in Box 9 of the return (value of goods bought from other EU countries) is still needed.
- No VAT is payable to HMRC if zero-rated goods are imported into the UK from outside the EU. However, it is possible that customs duties might still be payable on the goods in question.

75 Table of Cases

A

B

C

E

F

G

H

I

J

K

L

M

N

O

P

Q

R

S

T

U

V

W

X

Y

Z

76 Table of Statutes

References are only included where the provisions are covered in the text. Casual references to *Acts* are not included.

77 Table of Statutory Instruments

References are only included where the provisions are covered in the text. Casual references to *Statutory Instruments* are not included.

78 Table of European Union Legislation

79 Index

This index is referenced to the chapter and paragraph number.

C

D

F

H

I

M

N

P